THE Hockey Encyclopedia

THE Hockey Encyclopedia

THE COMPLETE RECORD OF PROFESSIONAL ICE HOCKEY

Stan Fischler and Shirley Walton Fischler

Bob Duff, Research Editor

MACMILLAN PUBLISHING COMPANY

NEW YORK

Production and Design Staff

Jackie Dickens
Casey Kwang-Chong Lee
Jeffrey Neuman
Fred C. Richardson
Larry Eugene Rolly
Nancy Kirsh Sugihara

Macmillan Publishing Company
866 Third Avenue, New York, N.Y. 10022
Collier Macmillan Canada, Inc.

Library of Congress Cataloging in Publication Data

Fischler, Stan.
The hockey encyclopedia.

1. Hockey—Records. 2. Hockey—Dictionaries.
I. Fischler, Shirley. II. Title.
GV847.5.F57 1983 796.96′2′0922 83-16224
ISBN 0-02-538400-7

10 9 8 7 6 5 4 3 2 1

Printed in the United States of America

The authors wish to dedicate this book to its incomparable research editor, Bob Duff, without whom we could not have produced this volume.

Contents

THE Hockey Encyclopedia

Introduction

History of the Game

While historians may debate whether Alexander Cartwright or Abner Doubleday is the father of the diamond game, it is impossible to list with any certainty the man or men responsible for the invention of ice hockey. Archaeological digs have uncovered Athenian friezes that depict athletes hitting a ball with a stick in what would appear to be a distant relative of hockey. However, one would have to use a broad and loose interpretation to find a link between the Athenian game and hockey as we know it. Among other things, the Greeks did not play their game on ice and used a ball instead of a puck.

Another distant relative of hockey is discerned in 16th-century Europe where a form of field hockey was played. In this version of the game dozens of people played for the honor of a village. It has been suggested that the crass nickname for hockey, *shinny,* might have developed in that period because players were regularly hitting their opponents in the shins with their sticks.

The derivation of the name *hockey* also has been a subject for debate and again nobody can say with precision how it came about. One theory has it that the hockey stick's curve suggests a shepherd's crook, and the French term for that is *hoquet*; hence hockey.

The first indisputable evidence of ice hockey's origins dates back to the 19th century, when both the British and Dutch were known to employ primitive skates for playing games on ice. A more refined skate appeared in the 1860s; it essentially consisted of a metal blade strapped onto the shoes. This skate proved to be most effective, and ice skating became a popular pastime in Northern European countries.

The introduction of a crude form of hockey in North America occurred midway through the 19th century as more and more English soldiers were dispatched to the British colony in Canada. As the Dominion expanded and the number of British troops grew, the visitors spent more of their leisure time skating on Canada's frozen rivers and lakes. Some of them made makeshift sticks out of tree branches and developed a form of field hockey on ice. There were, of course, no rules or regulations and what passed for ice hockey was a game played by as few as two or as many as sixteen per team.

The exact site of the first formal game of ice hockey has remained a subject of lively debate, with no definitive resolution in sight. Three Canadian cities — Halifax, Kingston, and Montreal — have laid claim to being the birthplace of the sport. A case can be made for each, and so the argument has raged more than a century after the first matches were played.

Kingston, Ontario, one of Canada's first cities, is belived to have been the site of primitive forms of hockey as far back as 1830. A three-man historical research team has produced evidence suggesting that the first official hockey team consisted of an Imperial Army unit called Her Majesty's Royal Canadian Rifles stationed in Kingston. They played their games on the frozen harbor ice adjacent to the Tete du Pont barracks. Historians in Halifax, Nova Scotia, have produced evidence of their own to back their claims. Montreal's claim on hockey's origins is ironically linked with that of Halifax. The Montrealers note that the first "authentic" game of hockey was a match between two teams of McGill University students who played their match on the Montreal campus. The student who organized the game, J.G.A. Creighton, was a native of Halifax and, ostensibly, was introducing a pastime that already had been played in his home town.

A major effort to once and for all determine hockey's birthplace was made in the mid-1940s when sites were being considered for a Hockey Hall of Fame. It was decided that the Hall of Fame should be located in the city that had the best credentials as the original home of the game. The Canadian Amateur Hockey Association established a committee to research the project. For better or worse, the evidence presented regarding the matches played by Her Majesty's Royal Canadian Rifles seemed most persuasive and Kingston won the designation. (Financial problems prevented actual construction of the Hall of Fame in Kingston. The Hockey Hall of Fame was eventually built on the grounds of the Canadian National Exhibition in Toronto.)

Whatever the merits of Kingston's claim as hockey's birthplace, the city can boast that it had the first official hockey league, a four-club unit including the Kingston Hockey Club, Kingston Athletics, Royal Military College, and Queen's University. The first championship game was played in 1885, with Queen's University defeating the Kingston Athletics, 3–1. The game was played on an open-air ice sheet with a foot-high plank around it to keep the puck from flying into the snowbanks. Goalposts were anchored to the ice in whichever manner the players thought most effective at the time. Neither goal cages nor nets existed at the time. Without the benefit of skates, the goal judge stood at his frigid position behind the goaltender. He held a flag in his hand and raised it to signal a goal if the puck went between the posts and below their tops.

In its first formal stage, hockey had few rules. The original game called for nine men on each side, although the number of players permitted in play at one time varied from community to community. Not until the mid-1880s did more specific rules emerge. A committee of hockey officials gathered in Montreal and hammered out a set of regulations that, among other things, provided for seven-man teams. This included a goalkeeper, two defensemen, three forwards, and a rover who alternated between offense and defense as the situation demanded.

Not surprisingly the early games of organized hockey were virtually bereft of strategy, let alone technique. Nobody had mastered the art of lifting the puck, which meant that the goaltenders had no need to wear protective gear over their legs. Curiously, the first attempts at propelling the puck in the air came as a result of backhand shots rather than the seemingly more natural forehand.

As the backhand lift shot was perfected, goalies began suffering bruises about the ankles, shins, and knees, and it became imperative either to ban the use of a lift shot or produce more adequate protection. A Kingston player who also dabbled at cricket realized that the leg pads worn by wicket-keepers would dull the blows of a puck hitting the leg. In time, all goalkeepers began wearing the cricketeer's equipment and it became *de rigueur.*

With the birth of the first official league in Kingston came the game's first governing body, the Amateur Hockey Association of Canada (AHA). The group, now known as the Canadian Amateur Hockey Association (CAHA), is still operating today. Supervision of the early matches was casual, as were the game's accoutrements. The evolution of equipment had just begun, and various aspects of the rink, including the standard net, had not yet made their appearance. The net, in fact, was developed as an afterthought when a player had a brainstorm during a harborside stroll. He noticed some commercial fishermen fixing their nets and realized he had stumbled upon the answer to lost pucks. He purchased some netting, brought it back to the rink and attached it to a pair of poles: thus the first hockey net.

Enthusiasm for hockey grew simultaneously with the westward growth of Canada. The bitter winters on the western prairie provided excellent ice conditions and the ideal milieu for matches. What was missing was a symbol — preferably a trophy — for which the growing number of players could compete. The solution was provided by a man whose interest in hockey was tangential at best:

Frederick Arthur, Lord Stanley of Preston, an Englishman who was governor general of Canada.

Lord Stanley's son, Arthur, was a hockey buff who became enveloped in the grassroots growth of hockey enthusiasm in Canada. He joined Ottawa publisher P.D. Ross and Lord Kilcoursie, an aide to the Stanleys, in convincing his father to produce a cup that would be awarded annually to the best amateur team in Canada; there were no professional clubs at the time. In 1893 Lord Stanley purchased a silver mug that then was valued at $48.67, and he determined that it should be given to the winner of an annual playoff. The first champion, the Montreal Amateur Athletic Association, never won the Stanley Cup again, although innumerable teams from Montreal have had their names inscribed on the mug since.

Most significant about the Stanley Cup was its symbolic role. Few organized sports in North America had a prize quite like it. There was no equivalent trophy for baseball, soccer, or football, and the lure of the Stanley Cup seemed to infuse hockey with the esteem that had been lacking: the largest crowd ever turned out in 1894 at the Victoria rink in Montreal for a match between Montreal and Ottawa.

While hockey was becoming a prime sporting attraction in Canada, it remained virtually unknown in the United States. New Haven and Baltimore became the first American hotbeds as Canadian students attending Yale and Johns Hopkins began to teach their fellow student the new game. By 1893 hockey was being played in both places, with more cities to follow, thanks to the invention of the artificial-ice-making machine. Artificial ice rinks appeared in several American cities before the turn of the century, much before similar rinks appeared in Canada. Washington, D.C., Pittsburgh, Chicago, Philadelphia, and New York all became seats of hockey interest in the late 19th century.

Prior to the 20th century, professionalism was unknown to hockey. The Canadians followed the British tradition of amateurism, although players were known to occasionally accept some payment under the table. Americans were less concerned with concealing their zeal for the dollar: the first professional hockey league was created in the United States by a dentist named J.L. Gibson. Gibson's organization, the International Pro Hockey League, was centered in the copper mining town of Houghton, Michigan. He imported the best Canadian talent available and paid his stars the then unheard-of sum of $500 a game. The league, which debuted in 1904, eventually welcomed a Canadian team from Sault Ste. Marie, Ontario, giving Canada its first bona fide professional hockey club. It was then that the ice game's original crop of superstars was developed. Fred "Cyclone" Taylor, Edouard "Newsy" Lalonde, and Hod Stuart aroused hockey audiences as no other players before them. Taylor was regarded as the most proficient and exciting player of his time — and he knew it. He commanded the highest salaries and proved to be the first significant gate attraction on both sides of the border. At the end of the Canadian hockey season, Taylor orchestrated barnstorming tours to New York and other American cities. Whenever Taylor played the promoters were assured of a capacity crowd. If he could not make the trip, the game, in many cases, simply would be cancelled.

Despite the appearance of professionals in the early 1900s, the all-amateur Stanley Cup remained the supreme goal of all hockey teams and challengers rose up in the most remote outposts. In Dawson City, the center of the Yukon's Klondike mining region, a team was assembled to challenge for the 1905 Stanley Cup. The problem was distance. The Dawson City Klondikers were situated in a remote section of Canada's northwest while the Stanley Cup tournament would be played in the east, at Ottawa, some 3,300 miles away.

To cover the length of Canada the Klondikers literally had to employ dog sled, bicycle, stage-coach, boat, and train. They left Dawson City on December 19, 1904, some of them running behind dog teams at the start, and covered 46 miles on the first day. Their first major terminal was Skagway, on the southern coast of Alaska and the only exit from the Yukon to traditional ports. At times during their mush from Dawson City to Skagway the temperature dipped to 20 degrees below zero Fahrenheit and the players began suffering severe foot problems.

From Skagway the Klondikers obtained passage on a scow, the S.S. *Dolphin*, bound for Seattle, where they got a train to Vancouver. After a stopover in British Columbia the players climbed aboard a transcontinental train that took them to Ottawa. The entire trip consumed 23 days and left the Dawson City skaters with only one day of respite before their scheduled match with the mighty Ottawa Silver Seven club, which had won the Stanley Cup in the two previous seasons.

The romance of the Klondike challengers proved to be a smashing gate attraction and, once again, the Stanley Cup round invigorated all of Canada's sporting public. The dazzle of the pre-game hoopla, alas, did not extend to the game itself. Weary from their expedition and artistically outclassed, the Klondike club lost the opening game of the two-game series 9–2, and the second match 23–2. Frank McGee of Ottawa scored 14 times, setting a record for goals in one game that has never been equalled.

Star-laden teams such as the Ottawa Silver Seven offered great temptations to Canadian sports promoters. There were sizeable profits to be made from turning *la creme de la creme* of the amateurs into full-fledged professionals and marketing a Canadian professional league. The first such organization in the Dominion was the Ontario Professional League, which was organized in 1908. The play-for-pay hockey explosion was about to begin. In British Columbia the brothers Frank and Lester Patrick founded the Pacific Coast Hockey League, anchored in the cities of Vancouver and Victoria. What set the Patricks' organization apart from the others was their talent for innovation and the fact that they introduced the first artificial ice rinks in Canada.

It was the Patricks who first numbered their hockey players, a practice later adopted by all major sports. The brothers added the penalty shot to their league's rules, and they wrote another rule calling for the deferred-penalty system whereby there could not be fewer than four men including the goaltender on the ice for one team at any time. In addition, Frank and Lester were the first to sanction forward passing and legalize puck-kicking on certain portions of the ice. They invented the assist to complement the goal in scoring statistics and made it legal for the goalkeepers to fall to the ice to make a save. The only area where the Patricks resisted change was in the rule stipulating the number of players per team: the eastern leagues abolished the position of rover and opted for the six-man game; the Patricks retained the rover and the seven-man style.

The Patricks' venture into professional hockey was a success, much to the dismay of the eastern puck barons. More than 3,000 fans turned out for the opening game of the Pacific Coast Hockey League in Victoria on January 2, 1912. The immense Vancouver arena welcomed more than 10,000 fans three nights later and the war between east and west was now on in earnest. The battle was fought behind closed doors where teams from rival leagues tried to outbid one another for star players, and fighting on the ice started in 1912 when the PCHL champions played their eastern counterparts for the Stanley Cup.

While the Patricks were still drawing the blueprints for the Pacific Coast League, the eastern version of the professional game was developing out of a series of squabbles between various arena owners. The major league of that time was the Eastern Canada Hockey Association, which, in 1909, appeared to be on solid footing although it changed its name to the Canadian Hockey Association for political purposes. But that same year another league, the National Hockey Association of Canada, was formed. The NHA would ultimately prove the more durable of the two.

Meanwhile, competition for the Stanley Cup had become increasingly intense as the PCHL teams proved at least the equal of their eastern rivals. What disturbed the easterners even more was the addition of an American team, Seattle, to the Pacific group. In 1917, for the first time since the

Stanley Cup was put up for challenge, an American team was eligible to win Canada's premier sporting trophy. The uproar this caused was so great that the Seattle team refused to take on the Montreal Canadiens in the 1917 Cup finals unless it received assurances from the NHA that the Cup would indeed be delivered south of the border if they won. An affirmative reply was received and the playoffs went on. This proved to be a hockey milestone because the Seattle Metropolitans won the tourney, and the Stanley Cup for the first time was the possession of an American team.

That same year another landmark event took place, this one in a Montreal hotel room where the National Hockey Association gave way to the National Hockey League. Tarnished by petty feuding, NHA moguls believed that a new image was needed for their organization although the teams would remain the same. At a meeting on November 26, 1917 at Montreal's Windsor Hotel, the move that would forever alter the course of professional hockey was made: the NHA was disbanded and the National Hockey League was born. Two teams from Montreal (the Canadiens and the Wanderers), one from Toronto, and one from Ottawa would form the nucleus of the new league.

The success of the "new" venture was predicated on selling tickets, which, in turn, hinged on the magnetism of the players. In one sense the maiden season was difficult for the NHL because it took place while World War I raged in Europe and innumerable Canadian hockey players were serving in His Majesty's armed forces. There were, however, enough aces in the NHL to at least maintain interest. One of them, Joe Malone of the Canadiens, blossomed into a full-fledged superstar every bit as bright as Wayne Gretzky is today. During the 1917–18 season, Malone scored 44 goals in 20 games for the Canadiens.

At the start of the 1920s professional hockey was flourishing in two spheres: the Patricks' Pacific Coast group and the eastern NHL. Together they presented an ironic contrast. The Patrick brothers, whose insights were unmatched, had erected handsome, modern arenas, but the population base in which their teams played was too small to regularly fill the seats. The NHL teams were located in Canada's largest cities, but their rinks were woefully inadequate. The NHL's Montreal Wanderers had to withdraw from the league when their arena burned down less than two years after it joined the NHL. What the NHL needed was Patrick-style buildings, and what the Patricks required was cities the size of Montreal and Toronto.

By the early 1920s the Patricks began to feel the financial pinch. A franchise in Portland, Oregon — the second American city to have a professional team in the Northwest — came and went, and the Patricks concluded that their dream of a western hockey empire would soon vanish. Before it did, a Western Canada Hockey League, embracing Calgary, Saskatoon, Edmonton, and Regina, was organized and made a playoff arrangement with the Patricks' league. When Seattle's franchise folded in 1923 the Patricks merged their remaining teams with the Western League but made only a brief go of it. The problem was money. Although western cities had a large number of high quality players, they could not afford to match the salaries being paid by the NHL, especially since the easterners were now also ready to make the great leap into the United States. With the big bankrolls, the NHL teams from the new, wealthy American cities would soon be able to put the westerners out of business.

Rather than permit their western league to be raided without compensation, the Patricks devised an orderly transition in which players — in some cases entire teams — were sold to the budding American NHL franchises. The first city in the eastern United States to ice a professional hockey year was Boston, where grocery magnate Charles Adams launched the Bruins in 1924. This marked the first step in the slow but relentless shift in the balance of power from Canada to the United States. Simultaneous with the acceptance of the Bruins, the NHL governors welcomed the Montreal Maroons, a decision that magnified another curious aspect of hockey: the sharp split along ethnic lines. Prior to the Maroons' arrival, the Montreal representative, *Les Canadiens*, was comprised almost entirely of French-Canadian players and was regarded by fans as the hockey symbol of French Canada. Dubbed "The Flying Frenchmen", *Les Canadiens (Club de Hockey Canadien)* had virtually no appeal to English-Canadian fans in the province of Quebec. It was to satisfy the latter bloc of potential spectators that the Maroons were organized. This club, bereft of French-Canadian players or executives, was specifically designed to appeal to English speakers, and it did, thereby creating an intense intra-city rivalry with the Canadiens.

Another intra–city competition soon developed in New York where the Americans, accepted into the NHL in 1925, and the Rangers, who entered a year later, produced some of the most engaging hockey games ever seen in the league. The beachhead established by the American entries was widened with the addition of Pittsburgh (1925), Detroit (1926), Chicago (1926), Philadelphia (1931), and St. Louis (1934). The franchises in Pittsburgh, Philadelphia, and St. Louis had little staying power. The same was true in Canada where the Ottawa entry dropped out in 1931, returned a year later, then folded in 1934 and moved to St. Louis.

The six teams to survive over the long haul were the Toronto Maple Leafs, Montreal Canadiens, Boston Bruins, Detroit Red Wings, New York Rangers, and Chicago Black Hawks. The Maroons, a team that seemed an ideal counterpoint for the Canadiens in hockey-mad Montreal, could not weather the Great Depression and went out of business for good in 1938. The Americans, the club that planted the seeds of hockey enthusiasm in New York 17 years earlier, suspended operations in 1942. The circumstances surrounding the Americans' demise were different from those involving the Maroons: manpower losses because of World War II decimated the Americans' lineup. The club's operator, Mervyn (Red) Dutton, planned to revive the team at war's end and place them in a new arena he planned to have built in Brooklyn. He had received assurances from the NHL governors that they would support such a move, but when the war ended they reneged on their promise and the Americans remained a memory.

For its first 26 years the NHL was governed by a former journalist named Frank Calder. It was generally acknowledged that Calder was acting at the behest of his employers, who were the six NHL club owners who ruled the presidency. When Calder died in 1943 he was succeeded by Red Dutton, who agreed to take the post until the war ended and a suitable replacement could be found. As promised, Dutton stepped aside in 1946 to make way for the attorney Clarence Sutherland Campbell, a former NHL referee and Rhodes scholar.

The most critical years of the league's development were those following its expansion into the United States in the 1920s. There was no assurance at the time that fans in New York, Boston, Detroit, or Chicago would be willing to support hockey on a long-term basis. Some skeptics feared that once the game's novelty wore off it would be discarded by the American sporting public. This proved not to be the case.

It was the NHL's good fortune to have assets in vital places on the ice and in the front office. Thanks to the infusion of talent from the western teams, the Rangers, Black Hawks, and Bruins were vigorously competitive from the very outset. The Rangers, for example, boasted a forward line of center Frank Boucher, right wing Bill Cook, and left wing Bun Cook, which to this day is regarded as one of the best offensive units of all time. All three arrived in New York as a unit for the 1926–27 season, the Rangers' first. Other teams benefited similarly. The Bruins obtained an indefatigable defenseman named Eddie Shore whose ability and vigor were such that he became one of the most popular players in all of Boston sports. Visiting teams were loaded with gifted players as well. The Montreal Canadiens' fleet scorer, Howie Morenz, was hockey's answer to Babe Ruth and Jack Dempsey: a drawing card without peer. Colorful characters like Ivan "Ching" Johnson, Albert "Battleship" Leduc, Johnny "Black Cat" Gagnon and Lionel "Big Train" Conacher added further spice to the spectacle.

Most of the managerial personnel was of an equally high caliber. In New York, which was considered pivotal to the league's success, the Rangers were led by Lester Patrick, who had come east when his league folded. Patrick was an astute appraiser of talent as well as a superb promoter, and the Rangers won two Stanley Cup championships in their first seven years. The Bruins' leader, Art Ross, was no less effective, and in Detroit, Jack Adams put the Red Wings on the right track in the early 1930s and they rarely deviated from it. The Black Hawks, who were bedeviled by eccentric ownership in Chicago, had more difficulty producing a winner, yet hockey interest in Illinois remained strong from the very start.

The growing hockey business was predicated on large crowds which, in turn, necessitated adequate arenas. The golden age of rink construction in the 1920s coincided with the burgeoning of the National Hockey League. The Montreal Forum was the first of the massive NHL structures to install artificial ice. The first NHL game was played there on November 29, 1924 when the Canadiens defeated the Toronto St. Patricks, 7–1. In short order Madison Square Garden, Boston Garden, Olympia Stadium in Detroit, and Chicago Stadium were erected. Chicago Stadium, which hosted its first hockey game on December 16, 1929, was the largest, with a seating capacity in excess of 16,000. Toronto remained without a big league style arena until November 12, 1931 when Maple Leaf Gardens opened its doors. The Forum, Chicago Stadium, Maple Leaf Gardens, and Boston Garden are still in use today. Madison Square Garden was replaced by a new structure of the same name, but at a different location. Detroit's Olympia Stadium lasted until 1979, when the Red Wings moved into the Joe Louis Arena.

Unlike baseball, which witnessed the growth of the New York Yankees dynasty during the 1920s, major league hockey saw almost continuous change at the top of the standings. In the decade from 1926 through 1936 eight different teams won the Stanley Cup. In that span only one team, the Canadiens, won championships back to back, accomplishing that feat in 1930 and 1931 with a club spearheaded by Howie Morenz, Aurel Joliat, and Johnny Gagnon.

Throughout the 1920s and into the early 1930s the rosters of big league clubs were kept small. An Eddie Shore would think nothing of playing most if not all of a 60-minute game. Teams retained one top line that was given the most ice time and only occasionally replaced with backup units. As a result, each club developed one formidable offensive unit that generally remained together throughout a season, if not longer. The Rangers' Cook brothers and Boucher became legendary, as did Morenz, Joliat, and Gagnon. In the early 1930s, the Toronto Maple Leafs produced an awesome unit, "The Kid Line," comprised of Joe Primeau at center, Harvey "Busher" Jackson on left wing, and Charlie Conacher on right wing.

The art of goaltending kept pace with the increase in firepower. The first goaltending immortal was Georges Vezina, who starred for the Canadiens in the early 1920s and was dubbed "The Chicoutimi Cucumber" because the native of Chicoutimi, Quebec was so cool under fire. He was followed by other excellent practitioners of the netminding art, including George Hainsworth, Lorne Chabot, Chuck Gardiner, Alex Connell, and Roy "Shrimp" Worters, to name just a few.

Defensemen were not overlooked, either. Shore, because of his flamboyant rushes as much as his crunching bodychecks, emerged as the best-known of the blueliners, but he was in good company among such notables as Ching Johnson, Red Dutton, Clarence "Hap" Day, Red Horner, Frank "King" Clancy and Clarence "Taffy" Abel.

Bodychecking, particularly by defensemen, had been developed into a high art form. Yet no matter how rough the game might have been played, the team rosters were liberally sprinkled with men of small stature. Lightweight skaters such as Clancy, Boucher, Joliat, and Morenz were always able to hold their own, or surpass, the larger players.

Throughout the first 15 years of the NHL's life the league depended on the Dominion of Canada for its talent supply. With precious few exceptions, every player to graduate to the majors learned his hockey in Canada. However, in the early 1930s, Frederic McLaughlin, owner of the Chicago Black Hawks, decided that he would explore the possibilities of hiring American-born players. He embarked on a vigorous campaign to sign gifted hockey players from Minnesota and other states with naturally cold climates. Although McLaughlin was unable to fulfill his dream of an all-American team, he did manage to sign several talented Minnesota-born players as well as an American coach, Bill Stewart. With Stewart at the helm, the Black Hawks won the Stanley Cup in 1938, the second of only three Cups for Chicago.

McLaughlin's success with Americans spurred other clubs to look more closely at the U.S.-bred hockey players. The Bruins did so and in the late 1930s came up with Frank Brimsek, a goaltender from Eveleth, Minnesota. At the time the Boston club already was blessed with the very proficient and popular Cecil "Tiny" Thompson in goal, and there appeared to be no need to replace him. But Brimsek could not be overlooked. The Bruins traded Thompson to the Detroit Red Wings and promoted Brimsek to the varsity. The Minnesotan became so good so fast that he was nicknamed "Mister Zero" as he led the Bruins to the 1939 Stanley Cup championship, their first such triumph in a decade. The Black Hawks also had a superb American goalie in Mike Karakas, who soon was followed by another U.S. native, Sam LoPresti. America's contribution to the hockey supply was growing but would be temporarily stalled by World War II.

The first major threat to the NHL's continued existence occurred in the early 1940s shortly after the United States entered the war. Players from every team in the league began to enlist in the Canadian and American armed forces. The Bruins, who had won the Cup in 1941 largely through the efforts of Brimsek and the "Kraut Line" of Milt Schmidt, Bobby Bauer, and Woody Dumart, lost them all to the war effort. Similarly, the Rangers, who had finished in first place in 1942, saw such aces as Art Coulter, Muzz Patrick, Bryan Hextall, Jim Henry, and Alex Shibicky all enter the service before the start of the 1942–43 season.

So desperate was the manpower situation that president Frank Calder convened the club owners and proposed that the league shut down for the duration of the war. However, wartime leaders of the Canadian government encouraged the NHL to continue on the grounds that hockey provided healthy entertainment and was a positive force in keeping morale high during the war effort. With that support, the league pressed on and sought talent wherever possible.

Many teams whose rosters had been ruined by enlistments found it almost impossible to secure replacements. When the Rangers opened training camp in Winnipeg during the fall of 1942 they did not have a single goaltender on the team. Manager Lester Patrick ordered his scouts to scour the Dominion for a goalie, any goalie, and eventually they came up with Steve Buzinski, who had been playing a low grade of amateur hockey in Swift Current, Saskatchewan. Buzinski became the Rangers' first-string goalie by default.

No team escaped the inroads made by the war. In Toronto, the Maple Leafs were equally hard-pressed to find goaltending assistance, and they eventually settled for Frank McCool, an athlete who was confounded by a severe case of ulcers. McCool's ailment was so severe that he was obliged to drink a quart of milk before taking the ice. During the 1945 Stanley Cup finals McCool posted three consecutive shutouts against the Detroit Red Wings — he actually accumulated a Cup–record 193 minutes without being scored upon — and helped the Maple Leafs to the 1945 championship.

Despite the fact that all teams were obliged to hire players who were either too young or too old, the NHL survived the war years far better than the governors had originally anticipated. Even dreadful teams like the Rangers played to capacity crowds; better clubs like the Black Hawks set new attendance records.

If for no other reason, the war years were memorable for the arrival of Maurice Richard as a member of the Montreal Canadiens. A French-Canadian right wing who played with unmatched intensity, Richard blossomed into the most electrifying scorer of all time. His specialty was taking a pass at the enemy blue line and then barreling by sheer force into scoring position where he would release a backhand shot of unusual power and accuracy. Richard's accomplishments were numerous but the first and most striking of his records came in the 1944–45 season when he totaled 50 goals in 50 games, breaking Joe Malone's record of 44 goals in a season. In no time at all Richard had become hockey's premier gate attraction. Not since the days of Howie Morenz had the NHL displayed such a galvanic talent. Along with linemates Hector "Toe" Blake and Elmer Lach, Richard rounded out Montreal's "Punch Line", one of the best attacking trios of all time.

With war's end, stars who had enlisted in the armed forces mustered out of uniform and returned to their teams. In some cases, that of the Kraut Line in Boston for example, the players were able to pick up where they left off and enjoyed many more successful seasons. The Rangers, who lost more quality players to the service than any other NHL team, were less fortunate. Many of the pre-war reliables such as Mac Colville, Alex Shibicky, and Muzz Patrick returned too rusty to regain their previous skills and quickly retired. Some, like Art Coulter, retired without ever stepping onto the ice again. Others returned but were a mere shadow of their former selves. Frankie Brimsek was the most striking case. He rejoined the Bruins, but never again performed as he had before joining the Coast Guard. He was eventually traded to the Chicago Black Hawks and then retired.

The return of peacetime hockey left the NHL with an egregious imbalance of power. At the top were the Canadiens, Maple Leafs, and Red Wings, with the Bruins trailing not far behind. Far to the rear were the Rangers and Black Hawks, and their repeated failures were damaging to the league. In Chicago, the problem was weak management, a situation that would not improve for many years. The Rangers' problem was their inability to replace the players they lost. It wasn't until the 1949–50 season that the Rangers became a competitive playoff team. Since the NHL permitted four of the six teams to qualify for the Stanley Cup round, it was virtually taken for granted in the mid-1940s that the Rangers and the Black Hawks would bring up the rear.

The biggest surprise of the late 1940s was the development of the Toronto Maple Leafs, the league's first legitimate dynasty. Underdogs in the 1947 playoff against Montreal, the Leafs won the Cup with a blend of brash youngsters — Howie Meeker, Ted Kennedy, Vic Lynn, Bill Ezinicki, Jim Thomson, Gus Mortson, and Bill Barilko — and accomplished veterans, among them Syl Apps, Turk Broda, and Wally Stanowski. Early the following year the Maple Leafs and Black Hawks completed an astonishing trade: Toronto sent an entire line comprised of Gaye Stewart, Gus Bodnar, and Bud Poile to the Hawks along with the defense tandem of Bob Goldham and Ernie Dickens, all in exchange for center Max Bentley, one of the most creative and fleet centers in the league, who was deemed necessary for the Leafs' bid for supremacy. Bentley paid immediate dividends and, with Apps and Kennedy, gave the Torontonians what was arguably the best trio of centers any team has ever had. The Maple Leafs won a second Stanley Cup in 1948 and an unprecedented third straight in 1949. They won again in 1951, giving them four Cups in five years.

Crowds continued to be substantial through the end of the 1940s, but the NHL resisted expansion. A Cleveland group led by James Hendy, a former hockey publicist, almost received approval, but they were rejected at the last minute by the Board of Governors.

The advent of television in the early 1950s caused problems for some of the American cities. Both the Black Hawks and Bruins suffered a severe dip in the gate and, for a time, there were fears that one or both franchises might fold. The Bruins righted themselves on their own, while the Black Hawks required help from the league. Despite some hesitation on the part of some owners, the NHL unofficially approved a "help the poor" move in which the weak teams received some form of assistance. This policy eventually led to approval of an annual player draft but at the outset simply meant a rich team aiding one of the poorer clubs. In reality, the only tangible evidence was a gesture on the part of the Montreal Canadiens, who sold gifted forward Ed Litzenberger to the lowly Black Hawks for a nominal fee. Litzenberger in a few years would be a cornerstone of the Hawks' renaissance. The Canadiens could afford such benevolence because they enjoyed a privilege unique in sports: the Montreal club was given exclusive rights to sign any French-speaking player before any other club. Since Quebec is one of the richest producers of talent, this gave *Les Canadiens* an advantage they utilized for many years until it was abrogated by the arrival of the draft.

By the late 1950s both the Black Hawks and Bruins were once again enjoying the prosperity shared by the other four clubs, and dozens of new stars appeared on the scene. Maurice Richard was still a dominant scorer, but his luster was dimmed slightly by the arrival of another player with more diverse talents and enormous physical strength: right wing Gordie Howe of the Detroit Red Wings. Key man on the "Production Line" with Ted Lindsay and Sid Abel, Howe was nearly killed as a result of a collision with Ted Kennedy of Toronto during a Stanley Cup playoff game in 1950. Physicians doubted he would survive, let alone play hockey again, but he showed up at the Red Wings' training camp in excellent shape the following September. He then set a tone for the years to come by leading the NHL in goals, assists, and points. The only ambidextrous player in the league, Howe was on his way to becoming the game's greatest star, bar none.

With farm teams in Edmonton, Indianapolis, and Omaha dispatching young stars to Detroit, the Wings succeeded the Leafs as the dominant team in the early 1950s. Terry Sawchuk starred in goal for them with Red Kelly, Marcel Pronovost, and Bob Goldham shoring up the defense. When the aging Abel left the club, the Production Line kept right on rolling with the addition of Alex "Fats" Delvecchio at center. Their quality of talent notwithstanding, Detroit never enjoyed a dynasty in the Toronto mold because of its inability to dominate in the playoffs. Although the Red Wings succeeded the Leafs as Cup champions in 1952, they were eliminated from the playoffs a year later in the first round and were never able to string three consecutive Stanley Cups together as had Toronto.

Playing in the shadows of the Red Wings and Maple Leafs through the late 1940s and early 1950s, the Montreal Canadiens, under the orchestration of Frank Selke, Sr., organized an especially productive farm system which delivered Dickie Moore, Bernie "Boom Boom" Geoffrion, Jacques Plante, Doug Harvey, and Henri Richard. Beginning with the 1955–56 season the Canadiens won five straight Stanley Cups, a mark no other team has matched.

Maurice Richard and Gordie Howe remained the two most dominant figures in the game through the 1950s despite their conspicuously contrasting personalities. His inner fire always boiling, Richard contained his anger until unduly fouled by an enemy. He would then explode with a fury unmatched in the NHL. The laconic Howe was more overtly aggressive and kept his foes on the defensive by using his devastating elbows.

The explosion of Richard's temper ignited what was the most fearsome riot in hockey's often turbulent history. Late in the 1954–55 season Richard was fouled by Boston Bruins defenseman Hal Laycoe. Richard retaliated, and then was separated from Laycoe by Cliff Thompson, a former Bruin who was now an NHL linesman. Objecting to the manner in which Thompson was handling him, Richard struck back at the official, hitting him over the head with his stick, and a further brawl ensued. The incident inspired an investigation by NHL President Clarence Campbell, who had previously penalized Richard for other outbursts. This time, however, Richard was the league's leading scorer and, with only a week remaining in the regular season, seemed certain to win the first point-scoring championship in a career fast approaching its twilight.

After a hearing in his Montreal office, Campbell suspended Richard for the remaining week of the season and the entire playoffs. Throughout the province of Quebec, Campbell's ruling was considered grossly unfair, and shortly after it was announced, protests erupted in Montreal. Since Richard was regarded as the hero of French-Canada and Campbell symbolized the aristocratic English-Canadian establishment, many followers of *Les Canadiens* interpreted the decision as an ethnic slap at French Canada. Their anger came to a head on the night of March 17th when the Detroit Red Wings played the Canadiens at Montreal's Forum. Several fans attempted to assault the beleaguered Campbell, who attended the game with his secretary, while another fan threw a tear gas cannister that exploded in the crowd. Choked by the fumes, fans stormed the exits and emptied out onto Ste. Catherine Street, Montreal's main thoroughfare. Within minutes, gangs of hoodlums began setting fire to newsstands, smashing store windows, and looting. The carnage extended for several blocks in the business district, resulting in millions of dollars of damage. Campbell and his secretary escaped from the Forum through a back exit.

Ironically, the riot and its aftermath appeared to have a beneficial effect on the Canadiens in the years to come. Richard's suspension held; he lost the scoring championship and Montreal lost both its bid for first place and the Stanley Cup. The Canadiens' manager, Frank Selke, Sr., blamed his coach, Dick Irvin, for failing to calm Richard. Irvin was released and became coach of the Black Hawks. He was replaced by Richard's former left wing, Toe Blake, who tried a different approach with the sharpshooter, a temperate one that worked well. From 1955 until his retirement after the 1960 Stanley Cup victory, Richard maintained decorum and the Canadiens responded with the best hockey the league had ever seen.

The Black Hawks, who had been in the doldrums ever since Max Bentley was dealt to Toronto, came alive in the 1960s when Bobby Hull, Stan Mikita, Elmer Vasko, and Pierre Pilote graduated from junior amateur hockey to the NHL. With Hull, "The Golden Jet," and Mikita leading the way, Chicago enjoyed its best era, topped by a Stanley Cup championship in 1961. In addition, the Black Hawks introduced new dimensions to both offense and defense. Hull improved on a technique originally introduced by Bernie Geoffrion of Montreal and Andy Bathgate of the Rangers. Instead of propelling the puck with a wrist shot during which the disk remained in contact with the stick, Bathgate and Geoffrion delivered their shot by drawing back their sticks in the manner of a golfer, and then striking it in the follow–through. It was called a slapshot and it proved to be much faster than the traditional wrist drive. But no one shot the puck as hard as Hull, who further traumatized goalies by producing a slight curve in the blade of his stick, which caused the puck to move like a very fast knuckleball. At the same time, the Hawks' goalie Glenn Hall introduced a revolutionary technique for stopping shots. Hall would drop to the ice by fanning his legs out in an inverted "V" formation. It enabled him to effectively cover the net area, then snap back into a standing position in a split second.

More than anyone, Hull popularized the slapshot to a point where it grievously affected offensive strategy. The pre-slapshot plan of attack called for players to pass the puck or carry it to the enemy blue line, where they had the option of stickhandling it into the zone or firing it into the corners where a teammate would attempt to retrieve it. The wrist shot made it impossible to fire the puck effectively from any distance farther from the goal than the blue line. The excitement and effectiveness of Hull's slapshot inspired more and more players to try the weapon, and as their numbers increased more shots were being taken from *outside* the blue line, and fewer players were stickhandling the puck into the offensive zone. Stickhandling and passing became lost arts, and the era of the big shot was ushered in, much to the dismay of the goaltenders.

Unlike the temperamental Richard and the subtle Howe, Hull was a natural superstar with flowing blond locks and a flamboyant style that gave him a visual appeal heretofore missing from the major personalities in the sport. Hull's arrival also coincided with the NHL's first major venture in U.S. network television. By the mid-1960s major league hockey was enjoying a success that was the envy of other leading sports. Teams in every city were playing to more than 90 percent of capacity, and interest continued to grow. Yet, despite this obvious appeal and the fact that other sports like baseball, football, and basketball had expanded on a continent-wide basis, hockey remained buried in a six-team cocoon.

Finally, in 1967 the NHL responded to the clamor for more teams by adding franchises in Los Angeles, Oakland, Minnesota, Philadelphia, Pittsburgh, and St. Louis. Reaction to the new teams was lukewarm in the six cities, but, with the exception of Oakland, grew warmer with time. Within three years Minnesota, Philadelphia, and St. Louis were doing exceptionally well, Pittsburgh and Los Angeles were drawing adequate crowds, and only Oakland was struggling.

The league was pleased enough by the new franchises' drawing power that it expanded again in 1970, taking Buffalo and Vancouver into the fold. Two years later, Atlanta and Long Island (the New York Islanders) fattened the NHL to 16 teams. This period of rapid expansion, from 1967 to 1972, coincided with the rise of hockey's newest superstar, Bobby Orr of the Bruins. Like Hull, Orr helped revolutionize playing technique. Although technically a defenseman, Orr would continually make daring forays into the opponents' territory, triggering the era of the rushing defenseman. Soon, defensemen on all teams would follow suit, and pure defensive play became all but extinct.

Apart from his impact on the game, Orr exerted a significant influence off the ice as well in the sphere of hockey economics. With the backing of Toronto attorney R. Alan Eagleson, Orr became the first major player to be officially represented in contract negotiations by an agent. At first the Bruins' owners fought the idea of even speaking with an agent, but Orr ultimately won out and almost overnight dozens of players sought representation. Shortly thereafter, with Eagleson at the head, the NHL Players' Association was organized over the objections of the owners.

Hockey's popularity in the new expansion cities promised a bonanza in the 1970s. Soon other entrepreneurs sought to exploit the golden egg, and a rival professional league, the World Hockey Association, was hatched in 1972. To give itself credibility, the WHA raided the existing NHL teams and signed such stars as Bobby Hull, Gerry Cheevers, J.C. Tremblay, and Derek Sanderson. A ruthless bidding war was on and, surprisingly, the WHA survived and in some places thrived. When it opened a team in Houston, former NHL immortal Gordie Howe was lured out of retirement to fulfill a dream of playing on a team with his two sons, Mark and Marty. The resulting publicity was another major coup for the league.

The war with the NHL was bleeding both leagues white, but attempts to work out a merger were resisted by NHL hardliners. Each time the NHL believed that the WHA was doomed to die it managed to find another life. At one time or another it had franchises in Edmonton, Winnipeg, Quebec City, Hartford, Vancouver, Calgary, Toronto, Birmingham, Ottawa, New York, Cherry Hill (New Jersey), Philadelphia, Baltimore, Cleveland, Detroit, Chicago, Indianapolis, Cincinnati, Denver, Phoenix, San Diego, Los Angeles, and Miami (which never actually iced a team). For a more detailed look at the checkered history of the WHA, see the section introducing the WHA's statistics year by year in The Teams and their Players.

Meanwhile, the NHL was having problems of its own. In 1974 it expanded to 18 teams with the admission of Kansas City and Washington, D.C., but the Oakland franchise (also known as the California Seals and California Golden Seals at various times) went bankrupt and was operated for several years by the NHL itself. In 1976 the Seals were transferred to Cleveland to become the Barons, while the Kansas City Scouts were moved to Denver to become the Colorado Rockies.

Worse still, the mid-1970s saw the inartistic spectacle of hockey's goon era, which was largely triggered by the ascent of the Philadelphia Flyers. Knowingly promoting the bloodier aspects of the game, Flyers officials sought and obtained so many bruising players that they became known as "The Broad Street Bullies." Their foremost warrior was a two-fisted left wing, Dave "The Hammer"

Schultz, who broke several records for penalty minutes in a season and often overshadowed the efforts of his more talented, though rarely less pugnacious, teammates. The Flyers not only fought well, they played hard and well, winning the Stanley Cup in 1974 and 1975, the first expansion team to gain such honors. This success inspired other NHL and WHA clubs to seek Schultzian types, and pro hockey became all too synonymous with brawling.

The Flyers' influence, however, was considerably mitigated by the second Canadiens dynasty. This Montreal club, coached by Scotty Bowman, won four consecutive Stanley Cups from 1976 through 1979. Bowman's Canadiens featured such deft skaters as Yvan "The Roadrunner" Cournoyer, Jacques Lemaire, Guy Lafleur, and Steve Shutt. The defensive nucleus included Serge Savard, Guy Lapointe, and Larry Robinson fronting for the scholarly Ken Dryden in goal.

When damaged knees forced Bobby Orr into premature retirement, Lafleur succeeded him as hockey's primary gate attraction. As was the case with so many of the Flying Frenchmen before him, Lafleur's hallmark was speed combined with a powerful shot. Lafleur was one of the few remaining players who did not wear a helmet, and his blond hair flowed in the breeze he created while speeding down the ice. This image appealed greatly to fans who were losing a certain rapport with players wearing the helmets which, while safer, detracted from some performers' personal appeal. Most players had turned to wearing helmets by the late 1970s, and all goalies were wearing some version of the face mask originally popularized by Jacques Plante.

In 1977 Clarence Campbell retired as NHL president and was succeeded by John A. Ziegler, Jr., the first American to head the league. The young, progressive Ziegler went about the business of developing a merger agreement with the WHA. While he was doing so, the Cleveland club, which had been moved from Oakland, suffered irreversible financial losses and was itself merged with the Minnesota North Stars in 1978, leaving the NHL with 17 teams. But with the opening of the 1979–80 season, the NHL grew to a record 21 teams when Hartford, Quebec, Winnipeg, and Edmonton were absorbed into the NHL as the WHA ceased operations.

The seven-year war left the NHL in a state of exhaustion, but it was soon revitalized by the infusion of exciting talent from the WHA, most importantly a lanky, teenaged center on the Edmonton Oilers named Wayne Gretzky. As a WHA player, Gretzky had been mocked by NHL rivals as a youth incapable of creating any impact in the NHL because of his fragile physique and lack of professional experience. But in his rookie NHL season Gretzky led the league in scoring as well as assists, won the Hart Trophy as the most valuable player and the Lady Byng Trophy for gentlemanly play and effectiveness. The following season he set league records for assists and points in a regular season, but that was only a prelude to his incredible 1981–82 season, when he rewrote the record books by scoring an astonishing 92 goals in 80 games, adding 120 assists for a total of 212 points, each an all-time record.

The emergence of Gretzky and others like him helped stem the accent on brawn as the pendulum once again swung back to skilled players. This trend was further accelerated by the success of the Soviet national teams in their matches against North America's best, and the triumph of the 1980 American Olympic team, which won a gold medal by employing skillful passing plays rather than applied violence.

The start of the 1980s marked the end of the Canadiens championship era and the beginning of another dynasty: the New York Islanders. Although the club was less than a decade old, it captured the Stanley Cup in 1980 and repeated its triumph in each of the next three seasons under the leadership of coach Al Arbour and general manager Bill Torrey. Sprinkled with superstars like Mike Bossy, Bryan Trottier, Denis Potvin, and goaltender Billy Smith, the Islanders became known as a team that could vary its style to play rough like the Flyers, quick like the Canadiens, or plodding like the Vancouver Canucks. They defeated the Flyers in the 1980 finals, the speedy Minnesota

North Stars in 1981, the rugged Canucks in 1982, and the explosive Edmonton Oilers in 1983. Most of all, the Islanders emphasized defense and unselfish team play. Their defense corps was so effective in their sweep of Edmonton that they kept the incomparable Gretzky from scoring a single goal.

It was also significant that the Islanders won their championships with a mixture of American-born players and Europeans as well as Canadians. Stefan Persson, Tomas Jonsson, and Anders Kallur symbolized the increasing reliance on top Swedish players throughout the league, while Langevin and Morrow demonstrated that more and more Americans were proving to be first-rate major leaguers. In 1983 two of the first three players selected in the junior draft were American born. These players, Brian Lawton and Pat Lafontaine, followed in the footsteps of Bobby Carpenter, Phil Housley, and other Americans who were becoming a force in the NHL.

When the NHL merged with the WHA it had hoped that its economic ills were over, but that was not the case. The Colorado Rockies were unable to attract enough fans in Denver, and the franchise was moved to East Rutherford, New Jersey in 1982 where it became the New Jersey Devils, playing in the new Brendan Byrne-Meadowlands Arena.

Another problem surfaced in 1983 when the Ralston-Purina Company, owners of the St. Louis Blues, announced that it would sell the franchise to a Canadian group and that the team would be relocated to Saskatoon, Saskatchewan. The NHL governors opposed the move, and the league was sued by Ralston-Purina, whereupon the NHL filed a countersuit. The legal wrangling continues, but a suitable buyer was found who kept the club in St. Louis.

Despite these difficulties, the prevailing feeling was that professional hockey had overcome the major threats to its success and would thrive through the end of the 20th century. This feeling was rooted in the discernible decrease in violence, the new emphasis on more sophisticated play resulting in more attractive attacking patterns, and an attentiveness on the part of NHL officials toward making their game even better, indicated by their willingness in 1983–84 to add an overtime period to regular-season games to break ties. This was also aided by the emphatic European influence and the growth of hockey at many major American universities.

The remaining unfulfilled goal was a true world championship between the North American professional titleholder — the Stanley Cup winner — and the European champion. Attempts toward arranging such a tournament were made in the early 1980s, but a playoff that would be mutually agreeable to the NHL leaders and those of the top European hockey nations — the Soviet Union, Sweden, Czechoslovakia, and Finland — could not be developed. All agree, however, that its resolution will be a high priority in the years to come. Ice hockey, now a truly international game, keeps coming closer to selecting and honoring one team as the greatest in the world.

The History of the Rules

Because of the unstructured nature of hockey in the last decade of the 19th and the early part of the 20th centuries, rules of the game developed in a slow and often painful manner. The modern face-off, for example, evolved through trial and error: before it was invented, the referee started play by arranging the puck between two players' sticks. He would then take each stick blade in hand and place them against the puck as done in lacrosse. He would then carefully retreat and shout "Play!" This caused many bruised shins for referees who failed to escape the swinging sticks of overanxious players. Fred C. Waghorne, a hockey official at the turn of the century, decided he had been battered enough and, standing out of harm's way, simply tossed the puck between the opposing players; thus the face-off was born.

The earliest organized games were divided into two 30-minute periods. At the time the seven-man game, with teams consisting of a goaltender, two defensemen, three forwards, and a rover, was played on both sides of the U.S.-Canada border, but in 1911 the National Hockey Association eliminated the rover, and the game became a six-man affair. The Pacific Coast Hockey League retained the seven-man rule. When the champions of east and west met for the Stanley Cup, games alternated between the six- and seven-man styles.

Until 1918 forward passing was not permitted anywhere on the ice. In 1918–19 the complexion of the game was drastically altered in several ways: blue lines were introduced, thereby dividing the ice into two defensive zones and a center neutral zone; and forward passing was legalized, but only in the center zone. Players were also allowed to kick the puck for the first time, and points were awarded to individuals for assists as well as goals.

Beginning in 1920–21 goaltenders were permitted to pass the puck forward in the defensive zone. At this stage, most games followed a distinct pattern: one team would take control of the puck and launch an attack, and if it failed, the other club would counterattack. It was a game of end-to-end rushes until one team scored. Defensemen almost never rushed the puck; they were needed at the blue line to blunt the other team's rushes.

Teams were sometimes compelled to play with fewer than three skaters on the ice because of penalties, but a rule change in 1925 created the delayed penalty when there were already two men in the penalty box. Thereafter, no team could have fewer than three skaters at a time.

A desire for more exciting offensive play led the governors to extend forward passing into the defending zones as well as the center area. Goaltenders' pads, which had ranged as large as a foot across, were now limited to ten inches in width. Both rules were implemented in 1927, along with a 53-inch limitation on the length of sticks.

A year later the forward passing rule was extended slightly; now a pass into the attacking zone was permitted if the pass receiver was in the neutral zone when the pass was made, but forward passing was forbidden inside the attacking zone itself. Still tinkering with the the passing arrangements, in 1929 they eased the regulations so that forward passing was permitted within all three zones, but not across the blue lines. But by the 1930–31 season the rules were amended once again; now forward passing was acceptable across the blue lines and in all zones, but the offsides rule made it illegal to precede the puck into the attacking zone.

In 1934 the penalty shot was introduced. As it was first employed the shooter fired the puck from a line 28 feet from the net. Four years later the rule was amended to allow a player to stickhandle the puck right up to the goalie before shooting.

Prior to 1937, teams could relieve pressure in their defending zone by simply shooting the puck down the ice. That changed in the 1937–38 campaign when icing the puck was penalized with a face-off in the offender's end of the rink.

In the more than two decades of the NHL's existence, the speed of the game gradually and significantly increased. The ice, which was flooded prior to a game, was not cared for until the game ended. This made for extremely choppy ice conditions by the third period; matters would get even worse during overtime, and many games were called with the score still tied due to the poor ice conditions. To produce smoother playing areas, the league ruled in 1940 that the rinks had to be flooded between periods.

Since 1917, regular-season ties were played off in an overtime period. However, the onset of World War II caused a severe strain on Canadian and American railroads, and the NHL believed it would be difficult for teams to catch trains after a game if the match went overtime. On November 21, 1942, overtime was erased from regular-season play, not to be reintroduced for 41 years.

The accent on attack reached a crescendo in the mid-1940s. Many teams were able to force play into the enemy zone for long periods of time, and it was felt that a rule should be added to permit the embattled defenders to break out of the trap. New York Rangers coach Frank Boucher, a member of the rules committee, suggested that a red line be painted at center ice, and that passes from the defending zone be permitted all the way up to the center line, allowing the breakout play. In 1943 this rule was adopted, and the change is often considered to be the line of demarcation of the modern game of hockey.

The NHL had experimented with various combinations of officials over the years, and in 1945 settled on the system employing one referee and two linesmen. At first the linesmen were officials who lived in the cities in which they officiated. This practice of having "home" linesmen was eliminated in 1946, and linesmen, like the referees, became neutral officials who worked in all arenas.

For the greater protection of the goaltenders, who were being abused more and more in their three-by-seven-foot crease, the area was extended by a foot in each direction in 1951. That same year the face-off circle was changed from a 10-foot radius to a 15-foot radius.

The mighty Montreal Canadiens of the late 1950s inspired a rule change because of their potent power play. Heretofore, a team was permitted a power play for the full two minutes of their opponent's penalty. The Canadiens often scored two and sometimes three goals in that time, turning close games into routs. To limit the Canadiens' ability to pull ahead so easily, the NHL ruled in 1956 that a player serving a minor penalty should be permitted to return to the ice when a goal was scored by the opposing team.

Excessive violence at the start of the 1970s led to several rules changes to cut down on the brawling, with extra players piling into battles that began with just two skaters. To eliminate the "third man" from the fight, an automatic game misconduct was assessed for a player joining a fight, beginning in the 1971–72 season. However, the NHL was still plagued with goons who would deliberately set upon better players to incite a retaliatory foul and coincidental penalties. To halt this trend, the NHL introduced new rules in 1976 to penalize the aggressor rather than the target in such bouts. Furthermore, the president of the league was given discretionary power to provide supplementary discipline, and many suspensions followed.

Awards and Achievements

The Stanley Cup

One of the most venerable and treasured trophies in North American sport, the Stanley Cup is awarded annually to the winner of the National Hockey League's playoffs. The Stanley Cup champion has been traditionally considered the world professional hockey titlist, but in recent years the ascent of the Soviet Union as a major hockey power has called this designation into question.

Some believe that the Stanley Cup may one day become the prize for a world challenge tournament. If it does become such, it will be returning to its donor's original intention. Frederick Arthur, Lord Stanley of Preston and son of the Earl of Derby, bought the original Stanley Cup in 1893 to be presented to the amateur hockey champions of Canada. Soon after the turn of the century, professional hockey grew in North America, and in 1910 Canada's National Hockey Association took possession of the prize.

Until 1926, several leagues were eligible to compete for the Cup, with clubs representing the Pacific Coast Hockey League making a strong showing against representatives of the eastern National Hockey League. The demise of the PCHL left the Cup securely in the hands of the NHL beginning with the 1926–27 season.

The Cup itself has led a checkered and often undignified existence. One group of celebrants once punted it into Ottawa's Rideau Canal. A Montreal championship team posed for a photograph with it, but left it behind in the studio, where a cleaning lady mistook it for a vase and planted flowers in it. And once it was left standing by the side of a Montreal street when a group of players stopped to fix a flat tire and forgot to put the Cup back in their car.

Relatively small when it was struck in 1893, the Cup has grown considerably over the years. Additional layers of silver have been added to accomodate the names of every player who has played on every Cup–winning team. It is estimated that the engraving costs alone since 1913 have exceeded $10,000.

1892–93	Montreal A.A.A.
1893–94	Montreal A.A.A.
1894–95	Montreal Victorias
1895–96	Winnipeg Victorias (February)
1895–96	Montreal Victorias (December, 1896)
1896–97	Montreal Victorias
1897–98	Montreal Victorias
1898–99	Montreal Shamrocks
1899–1900	Montreal Shamrocks
1900–01	Winnipeg Victorias
1901–02	Montreal A.A.A.
1902–03	Ottawa Silver Seven
1903–04	Ottawa Silver Seven
1904–05	Ottawa Silver Seven
1905–06	Montreal Wanderers
1906–07	Kenora Thistles (January)
1906–07	Montreal Wanderers (March)
1907–08	Montreal Wanderers
1908–09	Ottawa Senators
1909–10	Montreal Wanderers
1910–11	Ottawa Senators
1911–12	Quebec Bulldogs
1912–13	Quebec Bulldogs Victoria defeated Quebec in challenge series but was not recognized officially.
1913–14	Toronto Blueshirts
1914–15	Vancouver Millionaires
1915–16	Montreal Canadiens
1916–17	Seattle Metropolitans
1917–18	Toronto Arenas
1918–19	No decision. Series between Montreal and Seattle called because of flu epidemic while tied at 2 wins apiece.
1919–20	Ottawa Senators
1920–21	Ottawa Senators
1921–22	Toronto St. Patricks
1922–23	Ottawa Senators
1923–24	Montreal Canadiens
1924–25	Victoria Cougars
1925–26	Montreal Maroons
1926–27	Ottawa Senators
1927–28	New York Rangers

1928–29 Boston Bruins
1929–30 Montreal Canadiens
1930–31 Montreal Canadiens
1931–32 Toronto Maple Leafs
1932–33 New York Rangers
1933–34 Chicago Black Hawks
1934–35 Montreal Maroons
1935–36 Detroit Red Wings
1936–37 Detroit Red Wings
1937–38 Chicago Black Hawks
1938–39 Boston Bruins
1939–40 New York Rangers
1940–41 Boston Bruins
1941–42 Toronto Maple Leafs
1942–43 Detroit Red Wings
1943–44 Montreal Canadiens
1944–45 Toronto Maple Leafs
1945–46 Montreal Canadiens
1946–47 Toronto Maple Leafs
1947–48 Toronto Maple Leafs
1948–49 Toronto Maple Leafs
1949–50 Detroit Red Wings
1950–51 Toronto Maple Leafs
1951–52 Detroit Red Wings
1952–53 Montreal Canadiens
1953–54 Detroit Red Wings
1954–55 Detroit Red Wings
1955–56 Montreal Canadiens
1956–57 Montreal Canadiens
1957–58 Montreal Canadiens
1958–59 Montreal Canadiens
1959–60 Montreal Canadiens
1960–61 Chicago Black Hawks
1961–62 Toronto Maple Leafs
1962–63 Toronto Maple Leafs
1963–64 Toronto Maple Leafs
1964–65 Montreal Canadiens
1965–66 Montreal Canadiens
1966–67 Toronto Maple Leafs
1967–68 Montreal Canadiens
1968–69 Montreal Canadiens
1969–70 Boston Bruins
1970–71 Montreal Canadiens
1971–72 Boston Bruins
1972–73 Montreal Canadiens
1973–74 Philadelphia Flyers
1974–75 Philadelphia Flyers
1975–76 Montreal Canadiens
1976–77 Montreal Canadiens
1977–78 Montreal Canadiens
1978–79 Montreal Canadiens
1979–80 New York Islanders
1980–81 New York Islanders
1981–82 New York Islanders
1982–83 New York Islanders

Hart Memorial Trophy

Of all the individual awards presented annually by the NHL, the Hart Memorial Trophy for the most valuable player in the league is the most prized. Dr. David A. Hart, father of Cecil Hart, the former manager–coach of the Montreal Canadiens, presented the original trophy to the NHL in 1923. When the original Hart Trophy was retired to the Hockey Hall of Fame, it was replaced by the Hart Memorial Trophy, donated by the NHL itself, in the 1960s.

Under the present system, the winner is determined by a vote of the members of the Professional Hockey Writers' Association in each NHL city at the mid-point and conclusion of the season. Only one player, Wayne Gretzky of the Edmonton Oilers, has ever won the trophy in four consecutive seasons. To date, Gretzky has won the trophy in each of his four seasons in the NHL.

1923–24 Frank Nighbor, Ottawa
1924–25 Billy Burch, Hamilton
1925–26 Nels Stewart, Mont. Maroons
1926–27 Herb Gardiner, Mont. Canadiens
1927–28 Howie Morenz, Mont. Canadiens
1928–29 Roy Worters, N.Y. Americans
1929–30 Nels Stewart, Mont. Maroons
1930–31 Howie Morenz, Mont. Canadiens
1931–32 Howie Morenz, Mont. Canadiens
1932–33 Eddie Shore, Boston
1933–34 Aurel Joliat, Mont. Canadiens
1934–35 Eddie Shore, Boston
1935–36 Eddie Shore, Boston
1936–37 Babe Siebert, Mont. Canadiens
1937–38 Eddie Shore, Boston
1938–39 Toe Blake, Mont. Canadiens
1939–40 Ebbie Goodfellow, Detroit
1940–41 Bill Cowley, Boston
1941–42 Tom Anderson, N.Y. Americans
1942–43 Bill Cowley, Boston
1943–44 Walter Pratt, Toronto
1944–45 Elmer Lach, Mont. Canadiens
1945–46 Max Bentley, Chicago
1946–47 Maurice Richard, Mont. Canadiens
1947–48 Herb O'Connor, N.Y. Rangers
1948–49 Sid Abel, Detroit
1949–50 Chuck Rayner, N.Y. Rangers
1950–51 Milt Schmidt, Boston
1951–52 Gordie Howe, Detroit
1952–53 Gordie Howe, Detroit
1953–54 Al Rollins, Chicago
1954–55 Ted Kennedy, Toronto
1955–56 Jean Beliveau, Mont. Canadiens
1956–57 Gordie Howe, Detroit
1957–58 Gordie Howe, Detroit
1958–59 Andy Bathgate, N.Y. Rangers
1959–60 Gordie Howe, Detroit
1960–61 Bernie Geoffrion, Mont. Canadiens
1961–62 Jacques Plante, Mont. Canadiens
1962–63 Gordie Howe, Detroit
1963–64 Jean Beliveau, Mont. Canadiens
1964–65 Bobby Hull, Chicago

1965–66	Bobby Hull, Chicago
1966–67	Stan Mikita, Chicago
1967–68	Stan Mikita, Chicago
1968–69	Phil Esposito, Boston
1969–70	Bobby Orr, Boston
1970–71	Bobby Orr, Boston
1971–72	Bobby Orr, Boston
1972–73	Bobby Clarke, Philadelphia
1973–74	Phil Esposito, Boston
1974–75	Bobby Clarke, Philadelphia
1975–76	Bobby Clarke, Philadelphia
1976–77	Guy Lafleur, Mont. Canadiens
1977–78	Guy Lafleur, Mont. Canadiens
1978–79	Bryan Trottier, N.Y. Islanders
1979–80	Wayne Gretzky, Edmonton
1980–81	Wayne Gretzky, Edmonton
1981–82	Wayne Gretzky, Edmonton
1982–83	Wayne Gretzky, Edmonton

Art Ross Trophy

For most of the NHL's existence no tangible recognition was provided to the player who led the league in points scored during the regular season. That was remedied in 1947 when Arthur Howie Ross presented a trophy bearing his name to the league. This was the same Art Ross who had designed the modern puck and the nets used today. The irascible Ross himself was never known as an extraordinary scorer, but rather as one of hockey's most significant innovators and creative coaches and general managers during his tenure with the Boston Bruins.

If two or more players are tied for first in points scored, the trophy is awarded to the player who has scored the most goals. If there is still a tie, it goes to the player who played in the fewest games. If the tie remains unbroken at this stage, the trophy goes to the player who scored his first goal at the earliest point of the season.

1917–18	Joe Malone, Mont. Canadiens
1918–19	Newsy Lalonde, Mont. Canadiens
1919–20	Joe Malone, Quebec
1920–21	Newsy Lalonde, Mont. Canadiens
1921–22	Punch Broadbent, Ottawa
1922–23	Babe Dye, Toronto
1923–24	Cy Denneny, Ottawa
1924–25	Babe Dye, Toronto
1925–26	Nels Stewart, Mont. Maroons
1926–27	Bill Cook, N.Y. Rangers
1927–28	Howie Morenz, Mont. Canadiens
1928–29	Ace Bailey, Toronto
1929–30	Cooney Weiland, Boston
1930–31	Howie Morenz, Mont. Canadiens
1931–32	Busher Jackson, Toronto
1932–33	Bill Cook, N.Y. Rangers
1933–34	Charlie Conacher, Toronto
1934–35	Charlie Conacher, Toronto
1935–36	Sweeney Schriner, N.Y. Americans
1936–37	Sweeney Schriner, N.Y. Americans
1937–38	Gordie Drillon, Toronto
1938–39	Toe Blake, Mont. Canadiens
1939–40	Milt Schmidt, Boston
1940–41	Bill Cowley, Boston
1941–42	Bryan Hextall, N.Y. Rangers
1942–43	Doug Bentley, Chicago
1943–44	Herbet Cain, Mont. Canadiens
1944–45	Elmer Lach, Mont. Canadiens
1945–46	Max Bentley, Chicago
1946–47	Max Bentley, Chicago
1947–48	Elmer Lach, Mont. Canadiens
1948–49	Roy Conacher, Chicago
1949–50	Ted Lindsay, Detroit
1950–51	Gordie Howe, Detroit
1951–52	Gordie Howe, Detroit
1952–53	Gordie Howe, Detroit
1953–54	Gordie Howe, Detroit
1954–55	Bernie Geoffrion, Mont. Canadiens
1955–56	Jean Beliveau, Mont. Canadiens
1956–57	Gordie Howe, Detroit
1957–58	Dickie Moore, Mont. Canadiens
1958–59	Dickie Moore, Mont. Canadiens
1959–60	Bobby Hull, Chicago
1960–61	Bernie Geoffrion, Mont. Canadiens
1961–62	Bobby Hull, Chicago
1962–63	Gordie Howe, Detroit
1963–64	Stan Mikita, Chicago
1964–65	Stan Mikita, Chicago
1965–66	Bobby Hull, Chicago
1966–67	Stan Mikita, Chicago
1967–68	Stan Mikita, Chicago
1968–69	Phil Esposito, Boston
1969–70	Bobby Orr, Boston
1970–71	Phil Esposito, Boston
1971–72	Phil Esposito, Boston
1972–73	Phil Esposito, Boston
1973–74	Phil Esposito, Boston
1974–75	Bobby Orr, Boston
1975–76	Guy Lafleur, Mont. Canadiens
1976–77	Guy Lafleur, Mont. Canadiens
1977–78	Guy Lafleur, Mont. Canadiens
1978–79	Bryan Trottier, N.Y. Islanders
1979–80	Marcel Dionne, Los Angeles
1980–81	Wayne Gretzky, Edmonton
1981–82	Wayne Gretzky, Edmonton
1982–83	Wayne Gretzky, Edmonton

Lady Byng Memorial Trophy

One of professional hockey's ironies is that this most physical and occasionally brutal of big–league sports offers a good conduct award named after a gentle woman. But each season the player combining high skills with gentlemanly play, generally measured by a low penalty–minute total, receives the trophy donated by Lady Byng, the wife of Canada's Governor–General (Baron Byng of Vimy) in 1925.

After Frank Boucher of the New York Rangers ran off a remarkable streak of seven Lady Byng Trophies in eight seasons, he was given the trophy to keep, and Lady Byng had another one struck in 1936. Lady Byng died in 1949, and the NHL had a new trophy made, renaming it the Lady Byng Memorial Trophy.

The trophy–winner is selected in a vote conducted by the Professional Hockey Writers' Association. The award has taken on a distinct front–line orientation; though many defensemen have been deserving of it, only two have ever won it: Bill Quackenbush of the Detroit Red Wings and Red Kelly of the Red Wings and the Toronto Maple Leafs.

1924–25	Frank Nighbor, Ottawa
1925–26	Frank Nighbor, Ottawa
1926–27	Billy Burch, N.Y. Americans
1927–28	Frank Boucher, N.Y. Rangers
1928–29	Frank Boucher, N.Y. Rangers
1929–30	Frank Boucher, N.Y. Rangers
1930–31	Frank Boucher, N.Y. Rangers
1931–32	Joe Primeau, Toronto
1932–33	Frank Boucher, N.Y. Rangers
1933–34	Frank Boucher, N.Y. Rangers
1934–35	Frank Boucher, N.Y. Rangers
1935–36	Doc Romnes, Chicago
1936–37	Marty Barry, Detroit
1937–38	Gordie Drillon, Toronto
1938–39	Clint Smith, N.Y. Rangers
1939–40	Bobby Bauer, Boston
1940–41	Bobby Bauer, Boston
1941–42	Syl Apps, Toronto
1942–43	Max Bentley, Chicago
1943–44	Clint Smith, Chicago
1944–45	Bill Mosienko, Chicago
1945–46	Toe Blake, Mont. Canadiens
1946–47	Bobby Bauer, Boston
1947–48	Herb O'Connor, N.Y. Rangers
1948–49	Bill Quackenbush, Detroit
1949–50	Edgar Laprade, N.Y. Rangers
1950–51	Red Kelly, Detroit
1951–52	Sid Smith, Toronto
1952–53	Red Kelly, Detroit
1953–54	Red Kelly, Detroit
1954–55	Sid Smith, Toronto
1955–56	Earl Reibel, Detroit
1956–57	Andy Hebenton, N.Y. Rangers
1957–58	Camille Henry, N.Y. Rangers
1958–59	Alex Delvecchio, Detroit
1959–60	Don McKenney, Boston
1960–61	Red Kelly, Toronto
1961–62	Dave Keon, Toronto
1962–63	Dave Keon, Toronto
1963–64	Kenny Wharram, Chicago
1964–65	Bobby Hull, Chicago
1965–66	Alex Delvecchio, Detroit
1966–67	Stan Mikita, Chicago
1967–68	Stan Mikita, Chicago
1968–69	Alex Delvecchio, Detroit
1969–70	Phil Goyette, St. Louis
1970–71	John Bucyk, Boston
1971–72	Jean Ratelle, N.Y. Rangers
1972–73	Gil Perreault, Buffalo
1973–74	John Bucyk, Boston
1974–75	Marcel Dionne, Detroit
1975–76	Jean Ratelle, N.Y. Rangers, Boston
1976–77	Marcel Dionne, Los Angeles
1977–78	Butch Goring, Los Angeles
1978–79	Bob MacMillan, Atlanta
1979–80	Wayne Gretzky, Edmonton
1980–81	Rick Kehoe, Pittsburgh
1981–82	Rick Middleton, Boston
1982–83	Mike Bossy, N.Y. Islanders

The Vezina Trophy

Georges Vezina, nicknamed "The Chicoutimi Cucumber", was the best goaltender of the early 1920s. A member of the Stanley Cup–winning Montreal Canadiens, Vezina died of tuberculosis during the 1925–26 season while still in the prime of his playing career. The following season, Montreal sportsmen Joe Cattarinich, Louis Letourneau, and Leo Dandurand presented the Vezina Trophy to the NHL. At first the prize was given to the goaltender or goaltenders on the team allowing the fewest goals during the regular season. However, in 1981 the system was changed, and the Vezina is now awarded to the goalie deemed best by a vote of the NHL general managers. The distinction formerly saluted by the Vezina Trophy is now recognized with the William M. Jennings Trophy.

1926–27	George Hainsworth, Mont. Canadiens
1927–28	George Hainsworth, Mont. Canadiens
1928–29	George Hainsworth, Mont. Canadiens
1929–30	Tiny Thompson, Boston
1930–31	Roy Worters, N.Y. Americans
1931–32	Charlie Gardiner, Chicago
1932–33	Tiny Thompson, Boston
1933–34	Charlie Gardiner, Chicago
1934–35	Lorne Chabot, Chicago
1935–36	Tiny Thompson, Boston
1936–37	Normie Smith, Detroit
1937–38	Tiny Thompson, Boston
1938–39	Frank Brimsek, Boston
1939–40	Davie Kerr, N.Y. Rangers
1940–41	Turk Broda, Toronto
1941–42	Frankie Brimsek, Boston
1942–43	Johnny Mowers, Detroit
1943–44	Bill Durnan, Mont. Canadiens
1944–45	Bill Durnan, Mont. Canadiens
1945–46	Bill Durnan, Mont. Canadiens
1946–47	Bill Durnan, Mont. Canadiens
1947–48	Turk Broda, Toronto
1948–49	Bill Durnan, Mont. Canadiens
1949–50	Bill Durnan, Mont. Canadiens
1950–51	Al Rollins, Toronto
1951–52	Terry Sawchuk, Detroit
1952–53	Terry Sawchuk, Detroit
1953–54	Harry Lumley, Toronto
1954–55	Terry Sawchuk, Detroit
1955–56	Jacques Plante, Mont. Canadiens
1956–57	Jacques Plante, Mont. Canadiens
1957–58	Jacques Plante, Mont. Canadiens
1958–59	Jacques Plante, Mont. Canadiens
1959–60	Jacques Plante, Mont. Canadiens
1960–61	Johnny Bower, Toronto
1961–62	Jacques Plante, Mont. Canadiens
1962–63	Glenn Hall, Chicago
1963–64	Charlie Hodge, Mont. Canadiens
1964–65	Terry Sawchuk and Johnny Bower, Toronto
1965–66	Gump Worsley and Charlie Hodge, Mont. Canadiens
1966–67	Glenn Hall and Denis Dejordy, Chicago
1967–68	Gump Worsley and Rogie Vachon, Mont. Canadiens
1968–69	Jacques Plante and Glenn Hall, St. Louis
1969–70	Tony Esposito, Chicago
1970–71	Ed Giacomin and Gilles Villemure, N.Y. Rangers
1971–72	Tony Esposito and Gary Smith, Chicago
1972–73	Ken Dryden, Mont. Canadiens
1973–74	Bernie Parent, Philadelphia
	Tony Esposito, Chicago
1974–75	Bernie Parent, Philadelphia
1975–76	Ken Dryden, Mont. Canadiens
1976–77	Ken Dryden and Bunny Larocque, Mont. Canadiens
1977–78	Ken Dryden and Bunny Larocque, Mont. Canadiens
1978–79	Ken Dryden and Bunny Larocque, Mont. Canadiens
1979–80	Bob Sauve and Don Edwards, Buffalo
1980–81	Richard Sevigny, Denis Herron, and Bunny Larocque, Mont. Canadiens
1981–82	Billy Smith, N.Y. Islanders
1982–83	Pete Peeters, Boston

William M. Jennings Trophy

In its quest for an ever–increasing awards list, the NHL governors created the William M. Jennings Trophy in 1981 to honor the goalie or goalies who had previously been awarded the Vezina Trophy — those who allowed the fewest goals during the regular season. To qualify for the Jennings Trophy, a goaltender must have played at least 25 games in goal for the team allowing the fewest goals.

Unlike the Vezina Trophy, which is named for a former goalie, the Jennings Trophy bears the name of a man who never played in the NHL. William (Bill) Jennings was a Manhattan lawyer who became president of the New York Rangers in the early 1960s. Against the opposition of the league's old guard, Jennings led the successful battle for expansion from six teams to 12 in 1967, and spearheaded further expansion through the 1970s.

1981–82 Denis Herron and Rick Wamsley, Mont. Canadiens
1982–83 Billy Smith and Rollie Melanson, N.Y. Islanders

James Norris Memorial Trophy

The Norris Trophy is awarded annually to the defenseman judged to be the best in the NHL by a vote of the Professional Hockey Writers' Association.

Among hockey purists, the Norris Trophy has become an object of some controversy. More often than not of late it has been given to the defenseman who scores the most points. This would not have met with the approval of its namesake, James Norris, owner of the Detroit Red Wings for many years both before and after World War II. Norris's clubs featured such rock–ribbed defensemen as Black Jack Stewart, Jimmy Orlando, and Leo Reise, Jr. When the trophy was originally donated to the NHL by Norris's four children, defensive defense play was still highly prized. But the advent of Bobby Orr's attacking style in the late 1960s altered the mode of backline play. With Orr winning the trophy eight years in a row, it became standard to honor the defensemen who created goals rather than those who prevented them. An indication that this trend may have crested came with the selection of Rod Langway of the Washington Capitals, a defenseman who pays diligent attention to his duties in his own end of the ice, in 1983.

1953–54 Red Kelly, Detroit
1954–55 Doug Harvey, Mont. Canadiens
1955–56 Doug Harvey, Mont. Canadiens
1956–57 Doug Harvey, Mont. Canadiens
1957–58 Doug Harvey, Mont. Canadiens
1958–59 Tom Johnson, Mont. Canadiens
1959–60 Doug Harvey, Mont. Canadiens
1960–61 Doug Harvey, Mont. Canadiens
1961–62 Doug Harvey, Mont. Canadiens
1962–63 Pierre Pilote, Chicago
1963–64 Pierre Pilote, Chicago
1964–65 Pierre Pilote, Chicago
1965–66 Jacques Laperriere, Mont. Canadiens
1966–67 Harry Howell, N.Y. Rangers
1967–68 Bobby Orr, Boston
1968–69 Bobby Orr, Boston
1969–70 Bobby Orr, Boston
1970–71 Bobby Orr, Boston
1971–72 Bobby Orr, Boston
1972–73 Bobby Orr, Boston
1973–74 Bobby Orr, Boston
1974–75 Bobby Orr, Boston
1975–76 Denis Potvin, N.Y. Islanders
1976–77 Larry Robinson, Mont. Canadiens
1977–78 Denis Potvin, N.Y. Islanders
1978–79 Denis Potvin, N.Y. Islanders
1979–80 Larry Robinson, Mont. Canadiens
1980–81 Randy Carlyle, Pittsburgh
1981–82 Doug Wilson, Chicago
1982–83 Rod Langway, Washington

Calder Memorial Trophy

Frank Calder, a former newspaperman, was the president of the NHL at the time of its founding in 1917, and he remained its chief executive until his death in 1943. During the 1936–37 season, he decided that the foremost rookie of each campaign should receive a trophy, purchased by Calder, recognizing him as the rookie of the year. After Calder's death, the NHL renamed the trophy the Calder Memorial Trophy.

Members of the Professional Hockey Writers' Association vote for the winner. To be eligible, a player cannot have played more than 25 games in any single preceding season, nor in six or more games in each of any two preceding seasons in any major professional league.

1932–33 Carl Voss, Detroit
1933–34 Russ Blinco, Mont. Maroons
1934–35 Sweeney Schriner, N.Y. Americans
1935–36 Mike Karakas, Chicago
1936–37 Syl Apps, Toronto
1937–38 Cully Dahlstrom, Chicago
1938–39 Frankie Brimsek, Boston
1939–40 Kilby MacDonald, N.Y. Rangers
1940–41 John Quilty, Mont. Canadiens
1941–42 Grant Warwick, N.Y. Rangers
1942–43 Gaye Stewart, Toronto
1943–44 Gus Bodnar, Toronto
1944–45 Frank McCool, Toronto
1945–46 Edgar Laprade, N.Y. Rangers
1946–47 Howie Meeker, Toronto
1947–48 Jim McFadden, Detroit
1948–49 Penny Lund, N.Y. Rangers
1949–50 Jack Gelineau, Boston
1950–51 Terry Sawchuk, Detroit
1951–52 Bernie Geoffrion, Mont. Canadiens
1952–53 Gump Worsley, N.Y. Rangers
1953–54 Camille Henry, N.Y. Rangers
1954–55 Ed Litzenberger, Chicago
1955–56 Glenn Hall, Detroit
1956–57 Larry Regan, Boston
1957–58 Frank Mahovlich, Toronto
1958–59 Ralph Backstrom, Mont. Canadiens
1959–60 Billy Hay, Chicago
1960–61 Dave Keon, Toronto
1961–62 Bobby Rousseau, Mont. Canadiens
1962–63 Kent Douglas, Toronto
1963–64 Jacques Laperriere, Mont. Canadiens
1964–65 Roger Crozier, Detroit
1965–66 Brit Selby, Toronto
1966–67 Bobby Orr, Boston
1967–68 Derek Sanderson, Boston
1968–69 Danny Grant, Minnesota
1969–70 Tony Esposito, Chicago
1970–71 Gil Perreault, Buffalo
1971–72 Ken Dryden, Mont. Canadiens
1972–73 Steve Vickers, N.Y. Rangers
1973–74 Denis Potvin, N.Y. Islanders
1974–75 Eric Vail, Atlanta
1975–76 Bryan Trottier, N.Y. Islanders
1976–77 Willi Plett, Atlanta
1977–78 Mike Bossy, N.Y. Islanders
1978–79 Bobby Smith, Minnesota
1979–80 Ray Bourque, Boston
1980–81 Peter Stastny, Quebec
1981–82 Dale Hawerchuk, Winnipeg
1982–83 Steve Larmer, Chicago

Conn Smythe Trophy

Despite its relatively brief history, the Conn Smythe Trophy has become one of the NHL's most well-publicized awards. The trophy was presented to the league by Maple Leaf Gardens in 1964 to honor the prime mover behind the building of that arena. Conn Smythe was also one of the original organizers of the New York Rangers, and developed the Toronto Maple Leafs into one of hockey's great franchises as a coach, manager, and president of the club.

The Conn Smythe Trophy honors the most valuable player in the Stanley Cup playoffs. The winner is selected by the Professional Hockey Writers' Association at the conclusion of the final game of the Cup finals.

1964–65 Jean Beliveau, Mont. Canadiens
1965–66 Roger Crozier, Detroit
1966–67 Dave Keon, Toronto
1967–68 Glenn Hall, St. Louis
1968–69 Serge Savard, Mont. Canadiens
1969–70 Bobby Orr, Boston
1970–71 Ken Dryden, Mont. Canadiens
1971–72 Bobby Orr, Boston
1972–73 Yvan Cournoyer, Mont. Canadiens
1973–74 Bernie Parent, Philadelphia
1974–75 Bernie Parent, Philadelphia
1975–76 Reggie Leach, Philadelphia
1976–77 Guy Lafleur, Mont. Canadiens
1977–78 Larry Robinson, Mont. Canadiens
1978–79 Bob Gainey, Mont. Canadiens
1979–80 Bryan Trottier, N.Y. Islanders
1980–81 Butch Goring, N.Y. Islanders
1981–82 Mike Bossy, N.Y. Islanders
1982–83 Bill Smith, N.Y. Islanders

Frank J. Selke Trophy

One of the more recent — and certainly among the more esoteric — NHL awards is the Frank J. Selke Trophy, awarded to the best defensive forward in the league. The trophy was purchased by the league's Board of Governors to honor Frank Selke, Sr., builder of the Montreal Canadiens dynasty of the late 1950s. Ironically, that club, nicknamed The Flying Frenchmen, was known primarily for its powerful offense. Nevertheless, the league decided that the unsung heroes of the front line deserved recognition, and thus the Selke Trophy was created in 1977.

The temptation at first was to rename it the Bob Gainey Trophy; the Montreal forward captured it each of the first four seasons it was presented. In recent years, however, the Professional Hockey Writers' Association, electors for the trophy, have managed to find other worthy candidates.

1977–78 Bob Gainey, Mont. Canadiens
1978–79 Bob Gainey, Mont. Canadiens
1979–80 Bob Gainey, Mont. Canadiens
1980–81 Bob Gainey, Mont. Canadiens
1981–82 Steve Kasper, Boston
1982–83 Bobby Clarke, Philadelphia

Bill Masterton Memorial Trophy

Bill Masterton was virtually unknown until his tragic death following an injury sustained during a hockey game in 1968. Masterton, then a member of the Minnesota North Stars, was a hardworking journeyman who displayed his dedication to the game with unswerving perseverence. In the wake of his death, the National Hockey League Writers' Association — now the Professional Hockey Writers' Association — donated the award to recognize the qualities of sportsmanship and hard work demonstrated by Masterton. Like so many awards, the Masterton Trophy has been been generally won by forwards; since its inception, only one defenseman — Serge Savard — and one goalie — Chico Resch — have won it.

1967–68 Claude Provost, Mont. Canadiens
1968–69 Ted Hampson, Oakland
1969–70 Pit Martin, Chicago
1970–71 Jean Ratelle, N.Y. Rangers
1971–72 Bobby Clarke, Philadelphia
1972–73 Lowell MacDonald, Pittsburgh
1973–74 Henri Richard, Mont. Canadiens
1974–75 Don Luce, Buffalo
1975–76 Rod Gilbert, N.Y. Rangers
1976–77 Ed Westfall, N.Y. Islanders
1977–78 Butch Goring, Los Angeles
1978–79 Serge Savard, Mont. Canadiens
1979–80 Al MacAdam, Minnesota
1980–81 Blake Dunlop, St. Louis
1981–82 Chico Resch, Colorado
1982–83 Lanny McDonald, Calgary

Jack Adams Award

Though the Jack Adams Award has only been in existence for a few years, it has already earned a reputation as a powerful jinx. The award, which honors the coach of the year as selected by the NHL Broadcasters' Association, is viewed by its recipients with a mixture of pride and trepidation. Several winners, among them Don Cherry, Bobby Kromm, Pat Quinn, and Red Berenson, lost their jobs not long after they were presented with it.

Named for Detroit Red Wings general manager Jack Adams, who rarely fired coaches himself, the award came into being in 1974, when it was presented to the league by the Broadcasters' Association.

1973–74 Fred Shero, Philadelphia
1974–75 Bob Pulford, Los Angeles
1975–76 Don Cherry, Boston
1976–77 Scotty Bowman, Mont. Canadiens
1977–78 Bobby Kromm, Detroit
1978–79 Al Arbour, N.Y. Islanders
1979–80 Pat Quinn, Philadelphia
1980–81 Red Berenson, St. Louis
1981–82 Tom Watt, Winnipeg
1982–83 Orval Tessier, Chicago

Lester Patrick Trophy

A Canadian by birth, Lester Patrick was at the forefront of hockey's development in New York during the NHL's first great expansion in the 1920s. Patrick was a great innovator, and one of the finest teachers the game has ever known. As general manager and coach of the New York Rangers he guided the club to playoff berths in 15 of the team's first 16 years in the league. "The Silver Fox", as he was known, became synonymous with hockey leadership in the United States.

The New York Rangers donated the Lester Patrick Trophy to the NHL in 1966. It is presented for outstanding service to hockey in the United States. Its winner is selected by a blue–ribbon panel including members of the electronic and print media, the NHL president, and a member of the league's Board of Governors.

1966	Jack Adams
1967	Gordie Howe
	Charles F. Adams
	James Norris, Sr.
1968	Gen. John R. Kilpatrick
	Walter A. Brown
	Thomas F. Lockhart
1969	Bobby Hull
	Edward J. Jeremiah
1970	Eddie Shore
	James C.V. Hendy
1971	William M. Jennings
	John B. Sollenberger
	Terry Sawchuk
1972	Clarence Campbell
	John Kelly
	Cooney Weiland
	James D. Norris
1973	Walter L. Bush, Jr.
1974	Alex Delvecchio
	Murray Murdoch
	Weston W. Adams, Sr.
	Charles L. Crovat
1975	Donald M. Clark
	Bill Chadwick
	Thomas N. Ivan
1976	Stan Mikita
	George A. Leader
	Bruce A. Norris
1977	Johnny Bucyk
	Murray Armstrong
	John Mariucci
1978	Phil Esposito
	Tom Fitzgerald
	William T. Tutt
	William W. Wirtz
1979	Bobby Orr
1980	Bobby Clarke
	Edward M. Snider
	Fred Shero
	The 1980 U.S. Olympic Hockey Team
1981	Charles M. Schultz
1982	Emile Francis
1983	Bill Torrey

The Emery Edge (Plus–Minus) Award

In an unusual move for the NHL, the league collaborated with an air freight company to create a new individual award for the 1982–83 season, The Emery Edge, honoring the player with the highest plus–minus rating. The first winner was Edmonton defenseman Charlie Huddy, who finished the season with a plus–62 mark, two better than his teammate Wayne Gretzky. Another Edmonton Oiler, Paul Coffey, finished third.

The winners receive a trophy produced by Tiffany and Company and a check for $2,000. In addition, each of the 21 club leaders received a trophy, and a total of $10,000 is annually distributed to charities on their behalf. Only time will tell if this award will go the way of the Avco World Cup, presented to the WHA's champions.

1982–83 Charlie Huddy, Edmonton

The NHL All–Star Team

At the end of each season since 1930–31, first– and second–team all–stars have been selected. The voting is currently conducted by members of the Professional Hockey Writers' Association in the leagues' cities.

1930–31

First Team		Second Team
Charlie Gardiner, Chicago	Goal	Tiny Thompson, Boston
Eddie Shore, Boston	Defense	Sylvio Mantha, Mont. Canadiens
King Clancy, Toronto	Defense	Ching Johnson, N.Y. Rangers
Aurel Joliet, Mont. Canadiens	Left Wing	Bun Cook, N.Y. Rangers
Howie Morenz, Mont. Canadiens	Center	Frank Boucher, N.Y. Rangers
Bill Cook, N.Y. Rangers	Right Wing	Dit Clapper, Boston
Lester Patrick, N.Y. Rangers	Coach	Dick Irvin, Chicago

1931–32

First Team		Second Team
Charlie Gardiner, Chicago	Goal	Roy Worters, N.Y. Americans
Eddie Shore, Boston	Defense	Sylvio Mantha, Mont. Canadiens
Ching Johnson, N.Y. Rangers	Defense	King Clancy, Toronto
Busher Jackson, Toronto	Left Wing	Aurel Joliat, Mont. Canadiens
Howie Morenz, Mont. Canadiens	Center	Hooley Smith, Mont. Maroons
Bill Cook, N.Y. Rangers	Right Wing	Charlie Conacher, Toronto
Lester Patrick, N.Y. Rangers	Coach	Dick Irvin, Toronto

1932–33

First Team		Second Team
John Roach, Detroit	Goal	Charlie Gardiner, Chicago
Eddie Shore, Boston	Defense	King Clancy, Toronto
Ching Johnson, N.Y. Rangers	Defense	Lionel Conacher, Mont. Maroons
Baldy Northcott, Mont. Maroons	Left Wing	Busher Jackson, Toronto
Frank Boucher, N.Y. Rangers	Center	Howie Morenz, Mont. Canadiens
Bill Cook, N.Y. Rangers	Right Wing	Charlie Conacher, Toronto
Lester Patrick, N.Y. Rangers	Coach	Dick Irvin, Toronto

1933–34

First Team		Second Team
Charlie Gardiner, Chicago	Goal	Roy Worters, N.Y. Americans
King Clancy, Toronto	Defense	Eddie Shore, Boston
Lionel Conacher, Chicago	Defense	Ching Johnson, N.Y. Rangers
Busher Jackson, Toronto	Left Wing	Aurel Joliat, Mont. Canadiens
Frank Boucher, N.Y. Rangers	Center	Joe Primeau, Toronto
Charlie Conacher, Toronto	Right Wing	Bill Cook, N.Y. Rangers
Lester Patrick, N.Y. Rangers	Coach	Dick Irvin, Toronto

1934–35

First Team		Second Team
Lorne Chabot, Chicago	Goal	Tiny Thompson, Boston
Eddie Shore, Boston	Defense	Cy Wentworth, Mont. Maroons
Earl Seibert, N.Y. Rangers	Defense	Art Coulter, Chicago
Busher Jackson, Toronto	Left Wing	Aurel Joliat, Mont. Canadiens
Frank Boucher, N.Y. Rangers	Center	Cooney Weiland, Detroit
Charlie Conacher, Toronto	Right Wing	Dit Clapper, Boston
Lester Patrick, N.Y. Rangers	Coach	Dick Irvin, Toronto

1935–36

First Team		Second Team
Tiny Thompson, Boston	Goal	Wilf Cude, Mont. Canadiens
Eddie Shore, Boston	Defense	Earl Seibert, Chicago
Babe Siebert, Boston	Defense	Ebbie Goodfellow, Detroit
Sweeney Schriner, N.Y. Americans	Left Wing	Paul Thompson, Chicago
Hooley Smith, Mont. Maroons	Center	Bill Thoms, Toronto
Charlie Conacher, Toronto	Right Wing	Cecil Dillon, N.Y. Rangers
Lester Patrick, N.Y. Rangers	Coach	T.P. Gorman, Mont. Maroons

1936–37

Norm Smith, Detroit	Goal	Wilf Cude, Mont. Canadiens
Babe Siebert, Mont. Canadiens	Defense	Earl Seibert, Chicago
Ebbie Goodfellow, Detroit	Defense	Lionel Conacher, Mont. Maroons
Busher Jackson, Toronto	Left Wing	Sweeney Schriner, N.Y. Americans
Marty Barry, Detroit	Center	Art Chapman, N.Y. Americans
Larry Aurie, Detroit	Right Wing	Cecil Dillon, N.Y. Rangers
Jack Adams, Detroit	Coach	Cecil Hart, Mont. Canadiens

1937–38

Tiny Thompson, Boston	Goal	Dave Kerr, N.Y. Rangers
Eddie Shore, Boston	Defense	Art Coulter, N.Y. Rangers
Babe Siebert, Mont. Canadiens	Defense	Earl Seibert, Chicago
Paul Thompson, Chicago	Left Wing	Toe Blake, Mont. Canadiens
Bill Cowley, Boston	Center	Syl Apps, Toronto
Cecil Dillon, N.Y. Rangers	Right Wing (tie)	
Gord Drillon, Toronto		
Lester Patrick, N.Y. Rangers	Coach	Art Ross, Boston

1938–39

Frankie Brimsek, Boston	Goal	Earl Robertson, N.Y. Americans
Eddie Shore, Boston	Defense	Earl Seibert, Chicago
Dit Clapper, Boston	Defense	Art Coulter, N.Y. Rangers
Toe Blake, Mont. Canadiens	Left Wing	John Gottselig, Chicago
Syl Apps, Toronto	Center	Neil Colville, N.Y. Rangers
Gordie Drillon, Toronto	Right Wing	Bobby Bauer, Boston
Art Ross, Boston	Coach	Red Dutton, N.Y. Americans

1939–40

Dave Kerr, N.Y. Rangers	Goal	Frankie Brimsek, Boston
Dit Clapper, Boston	Defense	Art Coulter, N.Y. Rangers
Ebbie Goodfellow, Detroit	Defense	Earl Seibert, Chicago
Toe Blake, Mont. Canadiens	Left Wing	Woody Dumart, Boston
Milt Schmidt, Boston	Center	Neil Colville, N.Y. Rangers
Bryan Hextall, N.Y. Rangers	Right Wing	Bobby Bauer, Boston
Paul Thompson, Chicago	Coach	Frank Boucher, N.Y. Rangers

1940–41

Turk Broda, Toronto	Goal	Frankie Brimsek, Boston
Dit Clapper, Boston	Defense	Earl Seibert, Chicago
Wally Stanowski, Toronto	Defense	Ott Heller, N.Y. Rangers
Sweeney Schriner, Toronto	Left Wing	Woody Dumart, Boston
Bill Cowley, Boston	Center	Syl Apps, Toronto
Bryan Hextall, N.Y. Rangers	Right Wing	Bobby Bauer, Boston
Cooney Weiland, Boston	Coach	Dick Irvin, Mont. Canadiens

1941–42

Frankie Brimsek, Boston	Goal	Turk Broda, Toronto
Earl Seibert, Chicago	Defense	Pat Egan, N.Y. Americans
Tommy Anderson, N.Y. Americans	Defense	Bucko McDonald, Toronto
Lynn Patrick, N.Y. Rangers	Left Wing	Sid Abel, Detroit
Syl Apps, Toronto	Center	Phil Watson, N.Y. Rangers
Bryan Hextall, N.Y. Rangers	Right Wing	Gordie Drillon, Toronto
Frank Boucher, N.Y. Rangers	Coach	Paul Thompson, Chicago

1942–43

Johnny Mowers, Detroit	Goal	Frankie Brimsek, Boston
Earl Seibert, Chicago	Defense	Jack Crawford, Boston
Jack Stewart, Detroit	Defense	Flash Hollett, Boston
Doug Bentley, Chicago	Left Wing	Lynn Patrick, N.Y. Rangers
Bill Cowley, Boston	Center	Syl Apps, Toronto
Lorne Carr, Toronto	Right Wing	Bryan Hextall, N.Y. Rangers
Jack Adams, Detroit	Coach	Art Ross, Boston

1943–44

Bill Durnan, Mont. Canadiens	Goal	Paul Bibeault, Toronto
Earl Seibert, Chicago	Defense	Emile Bouchard, Mont. Canadiens
Babe Pratt, Toronto	Defense	Dit Clapper, Boston
Doug Bentley, Chicago	Left Wing	Herb Cain, Boston
Bill Cowley, Boston	Center	Elmer Lach, Mont. Canadiens
Lorne Carr, Toronto	Right Wing	Maurice Richard, Mont. Canadiens
Dick Irvin, Mont. Canadiens	Coach	Hap Day, Toronto

1944–45

Bill Durnan, Mont. Canadiens	Goal	Mike Karakas, Chicago
Emile Bouchard, Mont. Canadiens	Defense	Glen Harmon, Mont. Canadiens
Bill Hollett, Detroit	Defense	Babe Pratt, Toronto
Toe Blake, Mont. Canadiens	Left Wing	Syd Howe, Detroit
Elmer Lach, Mont. Canadiens	Center	Bill Cowley, Boston
Maurice Richard, Mont. Canadiens	Right Wing	Bill Mosienko, Chicago
Dick Irvin, Mont. Canadiens	Coach	Jack Adams, Detroit

1945–46

Bill Durnan, Mont. Canadiens	Goal	Frankie Brimsek, Boston
Jack Crawford, Boston	Defense	Kenny Reardon, Mont. Canadiens
Butch Bouchard, Mont. Canadiens	Defense	Jack Stewart, Detroit
Gaye Stewart, Toronto	Left Wing	Toe Blake, Mont. Canadiens
Max Bentley, Chicago	Center	Elmer Lach, Mont. Canadiens
Maurice Richard, Mont. Canadiens	Right Wing	Bill Mosienko, Chicago
Dick Irvin, Mont. Canadiens	Coach	John Gottselig, Chicago

1946–47

Bill Durnan, Mont. Canadiens	Goal	Frankie Brimsek, Boston
Kenny Reardon, Mont. Canadiens	Defense	Jack Stewart, Detroit
Emile Bouchard, Mont. Canadiens	Defense	Bill Quackenbush, Detroit
Doug Bentley, Chicago	Left Wing	Woody Dumart, Boston
Milt Schmidt, Boston	Center	Max Bentley, Chicago
Maurice Richard, Mont. Canadiens	Right Wing	Bobby Bauer, Boston

1947–48

Turk Broda, Toronto	Goal	Frankie Brimsek, Boston
Bill Quackenbush, Detroit	Defense	Kenny Reardon, Mont. Canadiens
Jack Stewart, Detroit	Defense	Neil Colville, N.Y. Rangers
Ted Lindsay, Detroit	Left Wing	Gaye Stewart, Chicago
Elmer Lach, Mont. Canadiens	Center	Buddy O'Connor, N.Y. Rangers
Maurice Richard, Mont. Canadiens	Right Wing	Bud Poile, Chicago

1948–49

Bill Durnan, Mont. Canadiens	Goal	Chuck Rayner, N.Y. Rangers
Bill Quackenbush, Detroit	Defense	Glen Harmon, Mont. Canadiens
Jack Stewart, Detroit	Defense	Kenny Reardon, Mont. Canadiens
Roy Conacher, Chicago	Left Wing	Ted Lindsay, Detroit
Sid Abel, Detroit	Center	Doug Bentley, Chicago
Maurice Richard, Mont. Canadiens	Right Wing	Gordie Howe, Detroit

1949–50

Bill Durnan, Mont. Canadiens	Goal	Chuck Rayner, N.Y. Rangers
Gus Mortson, Toronto	Defense	Leo Reise, Detroit
Kenny Reardon, Mont. Canadiens	Defense	Red Kelly, Detroit
Ted Lindsay, Detroit	Left Wing	Tony Leswick, N.Y. Rangers
Sid Abel, Detroit	Center	Ted Kennedy, Toronto
Maurice Richard, Mont. Canadiens	Right Wing	Gordie Howe, Detroit

1950–51

Terry Sawchuk, Detroit	Goal	Chuck Rayner, N.Y. Rangers
Red Kelly, Detroit	Defense	Jim Thomson, Toronto
Bill Quackenbush, Boston	Defense	Leo Reise, Detroit
Ted Lindsay, Detroit	Left Wing	Sid Smith, Toronto
Milt Schmidt, Boston	Center (tie)	Sid Abel, Detroit
		Ted Kennedy, Toronto
Gordie Howe, Detroit	Right Wing	Maurice Richard, Mont. Canadiens

1951–52

Terry Sawchuk, Detroit	Goal	Jim Henry, Boston
Red Kelly, Detroit	Defense	Hy Buller, N.Y. Rangers
Doug Harvey, Mont. Canadiens	Defense	Jim Thomson, Toronto
Ted Lindsay, Detroit	Left Wing	Sid Smith, Toronto
Elmer Lach, Mont. Canadiens	Center	Milt Schmidt, Boston
Gordie Howe, Detroit	Right Wing	Maurice Richard, Mont. Canadiens

1952–53

Terry Sawchuk, Detroit	Goal	Gerry McNeil, Mont. Canadiens
Red Kelly, Detroit	Defense	Bill Quackenbush, Boston
Doug Harvey, Mont. Canadiens	Defense	Bill Gadsby, Chicago
Ted Lindsay, Detroit	Left Wing	Bert Olmstead, Mont. Canadiens
Fleming Mackell, Boston	Center	Alex Delvecchio, Detroit
Gordie Howe, Detroit	Right Wing	Maurice Richard, Mont. Canadiens

1953–54

Harry Lumley, Toronto	Goal	Terry Sawchuk, Detroit
Red Kelly, Detroit	Defense	Bill Gadsby, Chicago
Doug Harvey, Mont. Canadiens	Defense	Tim Horton, Toronto
Ted Lindsay, Detroit	Left Wing	Ed Sandford, Boston
Kenny Mosdell, Mont. Canadiens	Center	Ted Kennedy, Toronto
Gordie Howe, Detroit	Right Wing	Maurice Richard, Mont. Canadiens

1954–55

Harry Lumley, Toronto	Goal	Terry Sawchuk, Detroit
Doug Harvey, Mont. Canadiens	Defense	Bob Goldham, Detroit
Red Kelly, Detroit	Defense	Fernie Flaman, Boston
Sid Smith, Toronto	Left Wing	Danny Lewicki, N.Y. Rangers
Jean Beliveau, Mont. Canadiens	Center	Kenny Mosdell, Mont. Canadiens
Maurice Richard, Mont. Canadiens	Right Wing	Bernie Geoffrion, Mont. Canadiens

1955–56

Jacques Plante, Mont. Canadiens	Goal	Glenn Hall, Detroit
Doug Harvey, Mont. Canadiens	Defense	Red Kelly, Detroit
Bill Gadsby, N.Y. Rangers	Defense	Tom Johnson, Mont. Canadiens
Ted Lindsay, Detroit	Left Wing	Bert Olmstead, Mont. Canadiens
Jean Beliveau, Mont. Canadiens	Center	Tod Sloan, Toronto
Maurice Richard, Mont. Canadiens	Right Wing	Gordie Howe, Detroit

1956–57

Glenn Hall, Detroit	Goal	Jacques Plante, Mont. Canadiens
Doug Harvey, Mont. Canadiens	Defense	Fernie Flaman, Boston
Red Kelly, Detroit	Defense	Bill Gadsby, N.Y. Rangers
Ted Lindsay, Detroit	Left Wing	Real Chevrefils, Boston
Jean Beliveau, Mont. Canadiens	Center	Ed Litzenberger, Chicago
Gordie Howe, Detroit	Right Wing	Maurice Richard, Mont. Canadiens

1957–58

Glenn Hall, Chicago	Goal	Jacques Plante, Mont. Canadiens
Doug Harvey, Mont. Canadiens	Defense	Fernie Flaman, Boston
Bill Gadsby, N.Y. Rangers	Defense	Marcel Pronovost, Detroit
Dickie Moore, Mont. Canadiens	Left Wing	Camille Henry, N.Y. Rangers
Henri Richard, Mont. Canadiens	Center	Jean Beliveau, Mont. Canadiens
Gordie Howe, Detroit	Right Wing	Andy Bathgate, N.Y. Rangers

1958–59

Jacques Plante, Mont. Canadiens	Goal	Terry Sawchuk, Detroit
Tom Johnson, Mont. Canadiens	Defense	Marcel Pronovost, Detroit
Bill Gadsby, N.Y. Rangers	Defense	Doug Harvey, Mont. Canadiens
Dickie Moore, Mont. Canadiens	Left Wing	Alex Delvecchio, Detroit
Jean Beliveau, Mont. Canadiens	Center	Henri Richard, Mont. Canadiens
Andy Bathgate, N.Y. Rangers	Right Wing	Gordie Howe, Detroit

1959–60

Glenn Hall, Chicago	Goal	Jacques Plante, Mont. Canadiens
Doug Harvey, Mont. Canadiens	Defense	Allan Stanley, Toronto
Marcel Pronovost, Detroit	Defense	Pierre Pilote, Chicago
Bobby Hull, Chicago	Left Wing	Dean Prentice, N.Y. Rangers
Jean Beliveau, Mont. Canadiens	Center	Bronco Horvath, Boston
Gordie Howe, Detroit	Right Wing	Bernie Geoffrion, Mont. Canadiens

1960–61

Johnny Bower, Toronto	Goal	Glenn Hall, Chicago
Doug Harvey, Mont. Canadiens	Defense	Allan Stanley, Toronto
Marcel Pronovost, Detroit	Defense	Pierre Pilote, Chicago
Frank Mahovlich, Toronto	Left Wing	Dickie Moore, N.Y. Rangers
Jean Beliveau, Mont. Canadiens	Center	Henri Richard, Mont. Canadiens
Bernie Geoffrion, Mont. Canadiens	Right Wing	Gordie Howe, Detroit

1961–62

Jacques Plante, Mont. Canadiens	Goal	Glenn Hall, Chicago
Doug Harvey, Mont. Canadiens	Defense	Carl Brewer, Toronto
Jean-Guy Talbot, Mont. Canadiens	Defense	Pierre Pilote, Chicago
Bobby Hull, Chicago	Left Wing	Frank Mahovlich, Toronto
Stan Mikita, Chicago	Center	Dave Keon, Toronto
Andy Bathgate, N.Y. Rangers	Right Wing	Gordie Howe, Detroit

1962–63

Glenn Hall, Chicago	Goal	Terry Sawchuk, Detroit
Pierre Pilote, Chicago	Defense	Tim Horton, Toronto
Carl Brewer, Toronto	Defense	Elmer Vasko, Chicago
Frank Mahovlich, Toronto	Left Wing	Bobby Hull, Chicago
Stan Mikita, Chicago	Center	Henri Richard, Mont. Canadiens
Gordie Howe, Detroit	Right Wing	Andy Bathgate, N.Y. Rangers

1963–64

Glenn Hall, Chicago	Goal	Charlie Hodge, Mont. Canadiens
Pierre Pilote, Chicago	Defense	Elmer Vasko, Chicago
Tim Horton, Toronto	Defense	Jacques Laperriere, Mont. Canadiens
Bobby Hull, Chicago	Left Wing	Frank Mahovlich, Toronto
Stan Mikita, Chicago	Center	Jean Beliveau, Mont. Canadiens
Ken Wharram, Chicago	Right Wing	Gordie Howe, Detroit

1964–65

Roger Crozier, Detroit	Goal	Charlie Hodge, Mont. Canadiens
Pierre Pilote, Chicago	Defense	Bill Gadsby, Detroit
Jacques Laperriere, Mont. Canadiens	Defense	Carl Brewer, Toronto
Bobby Hull, Chicago	Left Wing	Frank Mahovlich, Toronto
Norm Ullman, Detroit	Center	Stan Mikita, Chicago
Claude Provost, Mont. Canadiens	Right Wing	Gordie Howe, Detroit

1965–66

Glenn Hall, Chicago	Goal	Gump Worsley, Mont. Canadiens
Jacques Laperriere, Mont. Canadiens	Defense	Allan Stanley, Toronto
Pierre Pilote, Chicago	Defense	Pat Stapleton, Chicago
Bobby Hull, Chicago	Left Wing	Frank Mahovlich, Toronto
Stan Mikita, Chicago	Center	Jean Beliveau, Mont. Canadiens
Gordie Howe, Detroit	Right Wing	Bobby Rousseau, Mont. Canadiens

1966–67

Ed Giacomin, N.Y. Rangers	Goal	Glenn Hall, Chicago
Pierre Pilote, Chicago	Defense	Tim Horton, Toronto
Harry Howell, N.Y. Rangers	Defense	Bobby Orr, Boston
Bobby Hull, Chicago	Left Wing	Don Marshall, N.Y. Rangers
Stan Mikita, Chicago	Center	Norm Ullman, Detroit
Ken Wharram, Chicago	Right Wing	Gordie Howe, Detroit

1967–68

Gump Worsley, Mont. Canadiens	Goal	Ed Giacomin, N.Y. Rangers
Bobby Orr, Boston	Defense	Ted Green, Boston
Tim Horton, Toronto	Defense	Ted Harris, Mont. Canadiens
Bobby Hull, Chicago	Left Wing	Johnny Bucyk, Boston
Stan Mikita, Chicago	Center	Phil Esposito, Boston
Gordie Howe, Detroit	Right Wing	Rod Gilbert, N.Y. Rangers

1968–69

Glenn Hall, St. Louis	Goal	Ed Giacomin, N.Y. Rangers
Bobby Orr, Boston	Defense	Ted Green, Boston
Tim Horton, Toronto	Defense	Jacques Laperriere, Mont. Canadiens
Bobby Hull, Chicago	Left Wing	Frank Mahovlich, Detroit
Phil Esposito, Boston	Center	Stan Mikita, Chicago
Gordie Howe, Detroit	Right Wing	Yvan Cournoyer, Mont. Canadiens

1969–70

Tony Esposito, Chicago	Goal	Ed Giacomin, N.Y. Rangers
Bobby Orr, Boston	Defense	Carl Brewer, Detroit
Brad Park, N.Y. Rangers	Defense	Jacques Laperriere, Mont. Canadiens
Bobby Hull, Chicago	Left Wing	Frank Mahovlich, Detroit
Phil Esposito, Boston	Center	Stan Mikita, Chicago
Gordie Howe, Detroit	Right Wing	John McKenzie, Boston

1970–71

Ed Giacomin, N.Y. Rangers	Goal	Jacques Plante, Toronto
Bobby Orr, Boston	Defense	Brad Park, N.Y. Rangers
J.C. Tremblay, Mont. Canadiens	Defense	Pat Stapleton, Chicago
Johnny Bucyk, Boston	Left Wing	Bobby Hull, Chicago
Phil Esposito, Boston	Center	Dave Keon, Toronto
Ken Hodge, Boston	Right Wing	Yvan Cournoyer, Mont. Canadiens

1971–72

Tony Esposito, Chicago	Goal	Ken Dryden, Mont. Canadiens
Bobby Orr, Boston	Defense	Bill White, Chicago
Brad Park, N.Y. Rangers	Defense	Pat Stapleton, Chicago
Bobby Hull, Chicago	Left Wing	Vic Hadfield, N.Y. Rangers
Phil Esposito, Boston	Center	Jean Ratelle, N.Y. Rangers
Rod Gilbert, N.Y. Rangers	Right Wing	Yvan Cournoyer, Mont. Canadiens

1972–73

Ken Dryden, Mont. Canadiens	Goal	Tony Esposito, Chicago
Bobby Orr, Boston	Defense	Brad Park, N.Y. Rangers
Guy Lapointe, Mont. Canadiens	Defense	Bill White, Chicago
Frank Mahovlich, Mont. Canadiens	Left Wing	Dennis Hull, Chicago
Phil Esposito, Boston	Center	Bobby Clarke, Philadelphia
Mickey Redmond, Detroit	Right Wing	Yvan Cournoyer, Mont. Canadiens

1973–74

Bernie Parent, Philadelphia	Goal	Tony Esposito, Chicago
Bobby Orr, Boston	Defense	Bill White, Chicago
Brad Park, N.Y. Rangers	Defense	Barry Ashbee, Philadelphia
Richard Martin, Buffalo	Left Wing	Wayne Cashman, Boston
Phil Esposito, Boston	Center	Bobby Clarke, Philadelphia
Ken Hodge, Boston	Right Wing	Mickey Redmond, Detroit

1974–75

Bernie Parent, Philadelphia	Goal	Rogie Vachon, Los Angeles
Bobby Orr, Boston	Defense	Guy Lapointe, Mont. Canadiens
Denis Potvin, N.Y. Islanders	Defense	Borje Salming, Toronto
Richard Martin, Buffalo	Left Wing	Steve Vickers, N.Y. Rangers
Bobby Clarke, Philadelphia	Center	Phil Esposito, Boston
Guy Lafleur, Mont. Canadiens	Right Wing	Rene Robert, Buffalo

1975–76

Ken Dryden, Mont. Canadiens	Goal	Chico Resch, N.Y. Islanders
Denis Potvin, N.Y. Islanders	Defense	Borje Salming, Toronto
Brad Park, Boston	Defense	Guy Lapointe, Mont. Canadiens
Bill Barber, Philadelphia	Left Wing	Richard Martin, Buffalo
Bobby Clarke, Philadelphia	Center	Gil Perreault, Buffalo
Guy Lafleur, Mont. Canadiens	Right Wing	Reggie Leach, Philadelphia

1976–77

Ken Dryden, Mont. Canadiens	Goal	Rogie Vachon, Los Angeles
Larry Robinson, Mont. Canadiens	Defense	Denis Potvin, N.Y. Islanders
Borje Salming, Toronto	Defense	Guy Lapointe, Mont. Canadiens
Steve Shutt, Mont. Canadiens	Left Wing	Richard Martin, Buffalo
Marcel Dionne, Los Angeles	Center	Gil Perreault, Buffalo
Guy Lafleur, Mont. Canadiens	Right Wing	Lanny McDonald, Toronto

1977–78

Ken Dryden, Mont. Canadiens	Goal	Don Edwards, Buffalo
Denis Potvin, N.Y. Islanders	Defense	Larry Robinson, Mont. Canadiens
Brad Park, Boston	Defense	Borje Salming, Toronto
Clark Gillies, N.Y. Islanders	Left Wing	Steve Shutt, Mont. Canadiens
Bryan Trottier, N.Y. Islanders	Center	Darryl Sittler, Toronto
Guy Lafleur, Mont. Canadiens	Right Wing	Mike Bossy, N.Y. Islanders

1978–79

Ken Dryden, Mont. Canadiens	Goal	Chico Resch, N.Y. Islanders
Denis Potvin, N.Y. Islanders	Defense	Borje Salming, Toronto
Larry Robinson, Mont. Canadiens	Defense	Serge Savard, Mont. Canadiens
Clark Gillies, N.Y. Islanders	Left Wing	Bill Barber, Philadelphia
Bryan Trottier, N.Y. Islanders	Center	Marcel Dionne, Los Angeles
Guy Lafleur, Mont. Canadiens	Right Wing	Mike Bossy, N.Y. Islanders

1979–80

Tony Esposito, Chicago	Goal	Don Edwards, Buffalo
Larry Robinson, Mont. Canadiens	Defense	Borje Salming, Toronto
Ray Bourque, Boston	Defense	Jim Schoenfeld, Buffalo
Charlie Simmer, Los Angeles	Left Wing	Steve Shutt, Mont. Canadiens
Marcel Dionne, Los Angeles	Center	Wayne Gretzky, Edmonton
Guy Lafleur, Mont. Canadiens	Right Wing	Danny Gare, Buffalo

1980–81

Mike Liut, St. Louis	Goal	Mario Lessard, Los Angeles
Denis Potvin, N.Y. Islanders	Defense	Larry Robinson, Mont. Canadiens
Randy Carlyle, Pittsburgh	Defense	Ray Bourque, Boston
Charlie Simmer, Los Angeles	Left Wing	Bill Barber, Philadelphia
Wayne Gretzky, Edmonton	Center	Marcel Dionne, Los Angeles
Mike Bossy, N.Y. Islanders	Right Wing	Dave Taylor, Los Angeles

1981–82

Billy Smith, N.Y. Islanders	Goal	Grant Fuhr, Edmonton
Doug Wilson, Chicago	Defense	Paul Coffey, Edmonton
Ray Bourque, Boston	Defense	Brian Engblom, Mont. Canadiens
Mark Messier, Edmonton	Left Wing	John Tonelli, N.Y. Islanders
Wayne Gretzky, Edmonton	Center	Bryan Trottier, N.Y. Islanders
Mike Bossy, N.Y. Islanders	Right Wing	Rick Middleton, Boston

1982–83

Pete Peeters, Boston	Goal	Rollie Melanson, N.Y. Islanders
Mark Howe, Philadelphia	Defense	Ray Bourque, Boston
Rod Langway, Washington	Defense	Paul Coffey, Edmonton
Mark Messier, Edmonton	Left Wing	Michel Goulet, Quebec
Wayne Gretzky, Edmonton	Center	Denis Savard, Chicago
Mike Bossy, N.Y. Islanders	Right Wing	Lanny McDonald, Calgary

The Prince of Wales Trophy

No prize in the NHL's trophy room has had as checkered a past as the Prince of Wales Trophy. Donated to the league in 1924 by His Royal Highness, the Prince of Wales, the trophy was originally awarded to the winner of the NHL's league playoffs. From 1928 to 1938, it went to the team finishing first in the league's American Division. From 1939, when the league reverted to one combined section, to 1967 it was given to the team finishing in first place in the regular season.

When the NHL expanded in 1967–68, it again became a divisional trophy for the team finishing first in the Eastern Division. The realignment of 1974–75 created the Wales Conference, and until 1980–81 the trophy was awarded to the team with the highest point total in the conference during the regular season. Since 1981–82, it has honored the team winning the Wales Conference playoffs.

1924–25	Montreal Canadiens
1925–26	Montreal Maroons
1926–27	Ottawa Senators
1927–28	Boston Bruins
1928–29	Boston Bruins
1929–30	Boston Bruins
1930–31	Boston Bruins
1931–32	New York Rangers
1932–33	Boston Bruins
1933–34	Detroit Red Wings
1934–35	Boston Bruins
1935–36	Detroit Red Wings
1936–37	Detroit Red Wings
1937–38	Boston Bruins
1938–39	Boston Bruins
1939–40	Boston Bruins
1940–41	Boston Bruins
1941–42	New York Rangers
1942–43	Detroit Red Wings
1943–44	Montreal Canadiens
1944–45	Montreal Canadiens
1945–46	Montreal Canadiens
1946–47	Montreal Canadiens
1947–48	Toronto Maple Leafs
1948–49	Detroit Red Wings
1949–50	Detroit Red Wings
1950–51	Detroit Red Wings
1951–52	Detroit Red Wings
1952–53	Detroit Red Wings
1953–54	Detroit Red Wings
1954–55	Detroit Red Wings
1955–56	Montreal Canadiens
1956–57	Detroit Red Wings
1957–58	Montreal Canadiens
1958–59	Montreal Canadiens
1959–60	Montreal Canadiens
1960–61	Montreal Canadiens
1961–62	Montreal Canadiens
1962–63	Montreal Canadiens
1963–64	Montreal Canadiens
1964–65	Detroit Red Wings
1965–66	Montreal Canadiens
1966–67	Chicago Black Hawks
1967–68	Montreal Canadiens
1968–69	Montreal Canadiens
1969–70	Chicago Black Hawks
1970–71	Boston Bruins
1971–72	Boston Bruins
1972–73	Montreal Canadiens
1973–74	Boston Bruins
1974–75	Buffalo Sabres
1975–76	Montreal Canadiens
1976–77	Montreal Canadiens
1977–78	Montreal Canadicns
1978–79	Montreal Canadiens
1979–80	Buffalo Sabres
1980–81	Montreal Canadiens
1981–82	New York Islanders
1982–83	New York Islanders

The Campbell Bowl

Following its tradition of honoring its own, the NHL produced a piece of silverware to commemorate Clarence Sutherland Campbell, president of the league from 1946 through 1977. The bowl was originally presented to the regular–season champions of the Western Division from 1968 through 1974. From 1974 to 1981, it went to the regular–season leaders of the Campbell Conference. Beginning in the 1981–82 season, this was changed so that it now honors the playoff champion of that conference. Like its cousin, the Prince of Wales Trophy, it is little noted by the fans and is vastly overshadowed by the Stanley Cup.

1967–68	Philadelphia Flyers
1968–69	St. Louis Blues
1969–70	St. Louis Blues
1970–71	Chicago Black Hawks
1971–72	Chicago Black Hawks
1972–73	Chicago Black Hawks
1973–74	Philadelphia Flyers
1974–75	Philadelphia Flyers
1975–76	Philadelphia Flyers
1976–77	Philadelphia Flyers
1977–78	New York Islanders
1978–79	New York Islanders
1979–80	Philadelphia Flyers
1980–81	New York Islanders
1981–82	Vancouver Canucks
1982–83	Edmonton Oilers

The O'Brien Trophy

All but forgotten by NHL archivists, the O'Brien Trophy was one of the earliest of all hockey trophies. Hockey entrepreneur M.J. O'Brien conceived the trophy when professional hockey was still in its infancy. It was originally given to the team winning the National Hockey Association championship. When the NHA ceased operations in 1917 and was replaced by the NHL, the O'Brien Trophy was given to the NHL's champion. From 1927–28 until 1938–39, the trophy went to the winner of the Canadian Division title. From then on until the trophy was discontinued following the 1950 playoffs, it was a consolation prize for the loser of the Stanley Cup finals. The trophy was then returned to its trustee.

1909–10	Montreal Wanderers
1910–11	Ottawa Senators
1911–12	Quebec Bulldogs
1912–13	Quebec Bulldogs
1913–14	Toronto
1914–15	Ottawa Senators
1915–16	Montreal Canadiens
1916–17	Montreal Canadiens
1917–18	Toronto Arenas
1918–19	Montreal Canadiens
1919–20	Ottawa Senators
1920–21	Ottawa Senators
1921–22	Toronto St. Patricks
1922–23	Ottawa Senators
1923–24	Montreal Canadiens
1924–25	Montreal Canadiens
1925–26	Montreal Maroons
1926–27	Ottawa Senators
1927–28	Montreal Canadiens
1928–29	Montreal Canadiens
1929–30	Montreal Maroons
1930–31	Montreal Canadiens
1931–32	Montreal Canadiens
1932–33	Toronto Maple Leafs
1933–34	Toronto Maple Leafs
1934–35	Toronto Maple Leafs
1935–36	Montreal Maroons
1936–37	Montreal Canadiens
1937–38	Toronto Maple Leafs
1938–39	Toronto Maple Leafs
1939–40	Toronto Maple Leafs
1940–41	Detroit Red Wings
1941–42	Detroit Red Wings
1942–43	Boston Bruins
1943–44	Chicago Black Hawks
1944–45	Detroit Red Wings
1945–46	Boston Bruins
1946–47	Montreal Canadiens
1947–48	Detroit Red Wings
1948–49	Detroit Red Wings
1949–50	New York Rangers

The Hockey Hall of Fame (Canada)

The Hockey Hall of Fame, located at the Canadian National Exhibition in Toronto, opened on August 26, 1961. Several earlier attempts to open such a Hall of Fame failed; this one succeeded thanks to contributions from the six clubs in existence at the time: the Rangers, Bruins, Red Wings, Black Hawks, Maple Leafs, and Canadiens. The building is administered and maintained by the Canadian National Exhibition Association. The Hall features exhibits provided and financed by the NHL, with cooperative support from the Canadian Amateur Hockey Association.

Selections were made to the Hall long before the construction was underway. When the first selections were made in 1945, it was hoped that the building could be constructed in Kingston, Ontario, where some historians believe the game was first played. However, the project never got underway, and the site in Toronto was eventually agreed upon.

Any person who is or has been distinguished in hockey as a player, executive, or referee is eligible for election. Player and referee candidates have normally completed their active careers three years prior to election, but in exceptional cases this waiting period can be shortened by the Hockey Hall of Fame Governing Committee. Candidates for election as executives are nominated only by the Governing Committee, and upon election are known as Builders. Candidates are chosen on the basis of playing ability, integrity, character, and their contribution to their team and the game of hockey in general.

To date, 170 players, nine referees, and 63 builders have been elected to the Hall of Fame. They are all listed below. The year in parentheses after each name is the year in which they were inducted.

PLAYERS

Sid Abel (1969)
Jack Adams (1959)
Syl Apps (1961)
George Armstrong (1975)
Ace Bailey (1975)
Dan Bain (1945)
Hobey Baker (1945)
Marty Barry (1965)
Andy Bathgate (1978)
Jean Beliveau (1972)
Clint Benedict (1965)
Doug Bentley (1964)
Max Bentley (1966)
Toe Blake (1966)
Dickie Boon (1952)
Butch Bouchard (1966)
Frank Boucher (1958)
George Boucher (1960)
Johnny Bower (1976)
Russell Bowie (1945)
Frankie Brimsek (1966)
Harry Broadbent (1962)
Turk Broda (1967)
Johnny Bucyk (1981)
Billy Burch (1974)
Harry Cameron (1962)
King Clancy (1958)
Dit Clapper (1945)
Sprague Cleghorn (1958)
Neil Colville (1967)
Charlie Conacher (1961)
Alex Connell (1958)
Bill Cook (1952)
Art Coulter (1974)
Yvan Cournoyer (1982)
Bill Cowley (1968)
Rusty Crawford (1962)
Jack Darragh (1962)
Scotty Davidson (1950)
Hap Day (1961)
Alex Delvecchio (1977)
Cy Denneny (1959)
Gordie Drillon (1975)
Charles Drinkwater (1952)
Ken Dryden (1983)
Tom Dunderdale (1974)
Bill Durnan (1964)
Red Dutton (1958)
Babe Dye (1970)
Art Farrell (1965)
Frank Foyston (1958)
Frank Frederickson (1958)
Bill Gadsby (1970)
Charlie Gardiner (1945)
Herb Gardiner (1958)
Jimmy Gardner (1962)
Bernie Geoffrion (1972)
Eddie Gerard (1945)
Rod Gilbert (1982)
Billy Gilmour (1962)
Moose Goheen (1962)
Ebbie Goodfellow (1963)
Mike Grant (1950)
Shorty Green (1962)
Si Griffis (1950)
George Hainsworth (1961)
Glenn Hall (1975)
Joe Hall (1961)
Doug Harvey (1973)
George Hay (1958)
Riley Hern (1962)
Bryan Hextall (1969)
Harry Holmes (1972)
Tom Hooper (1962)

Red Horner (1965)
Tim Horton (1977)
Gordie Howe (1972)
Sid Howe (1965)
Harry Howell (1979)
Bobby Hull (1983)
Bouse Hutton (1962)
Harry Hyland (1962)
Dick Irvin (1958)
Busher Jackson (1971)
Ernest Johnson (1952)
Ching Johnson (1958)
Tom Johnson (1970)
Aurel Joliat (1945)
Duke Keats (1958)
Red Kelly (1969)
Ted Kennedy (1966)
Elmer Lach (1966)
Newsy Lalonde (1950)
Jack Laviolette (1962)
Hugh Lehman (1958)
Percy LeSeuer (1961)
Ted Lindsay (1966)
Harry Lumley (1980)
Duncan MacKay (1952)
Frank Mahovlich (1981)
Joe Malone (1950)
Sylvio Mantha (1960)
Jack Marshall (1965)
Fred Maxwell (1962)
Frank McGee (1945)
Billy McGimsee (1962)
George McNamara (1958)
Stan Mikita (1983)
Dickie Moore (1974)
Paddy Moran (1958)
Howie Morenz (1945)
Bill Mosienko (1965)
Frank Nighbor (1945)
Reg Noble (1962)
Harry Oliver (1967)
Bobby Orr (1979)
Lester Patrick (1945)
Lynn Patrick (1980)
Tommy Phillips (1945)
Pierre Pilote (1975)
Pit Pitre (1962)
Jacques Plante (1978)
Babe Pratt (1966)
Joe Primeau (1963)
Marcel Pronovost (1978)
Harvey Pulford (1945)
Bill Quackenbush (1976)
Frank Rankin (1961)
Chuck Rayner (1973)
Kenny Reardon (1966)
Henri Richard (1979)
Maurice Richard (1961)
George Richardson (1950)
Gordon Roberts (1971)
Art Ross (1945)
Blair Russel (1965)
Ernest Russell (1965)
Jack Ruttan (1962)
Terry Sawchuk (1971)
Fred Scanlan (1965)
Milt Schmidt (1961)
Sweeney Schriner (1962)
Earl Seibert (1963)
Oliver Seibert (1961)
Eddie Shore (1945)
Babe Siebert (1964)
Joe Simpson (1962)
Alfred Smith (1962)
Hooley Smith (1972)
Thomas Smith (1973)
Allan Stanley (1981)
Russell Stanley (1962)
Jack Stewart (1964)
Nels Stewart (1962)
Bruce Stuart (1961)
Hod Stuart (1945)
Cyclone Taylor (1945)
Tiny Thompson (1959)
Col. Harry Trihey (1950)
Norm Ullman (1982)
Georges Vezina (1945)
Jack Walker (1960)
Marty Walsh (1962)
Harry Watson (1962)
Cooney Weiland (1971)
Harry Westwick (1962)
Fred Whitcroft (1962)
Gord Wilson (1962)
Gump Worsley (1980)
Roy Worters (1969)

REFEREES

John George Ashley (1981)
William L. Chadwick (1964)
Chaucer Elliott (1961)
Robert W. Hewitson (1963)
Fred J. "Mickey" Ion (1961)
Michael J. Rodden (1962)
J. Cooper Smeaton (1961)
Roy Alvin "Red" Storey (1967)
Frank Joseph Udvari (1973)

BUILDERS

Charles Francis Adams (1960)
Weston W. Adams (1972)
Frank Ahearn (1962)
Bunny Ahearne (1977)
Sir Montague Allan (1945)
Harold Ballard (1977)
John P. Bickell (1978)
George V. Brown (1961)
Walter A. Brown (1962)
Frank Buckland (1975)
Jack Butterfield (1980)
Frank Calder (1945)
Angus Campbell (1964)
Clarence Campbell (1966)
Joseph Cattarinich (1977)
Leo Dandurand (1963)
Francis P. Dilio (1964)
George S. Dudley (1958)
James A. Dunn (1968)
Emile Francis (1982)
Dr. John L. Gibson (1976)
Tommy Gorman (1963)
Charles Hay (1974)
James C. Hendy (1968)
Foster Hewitt (1965)
William A. Hewitt (1945)
Fred J. Hume (1962)
Thomas N. Ivan (1974)
William M. Jennings (1975)
Gordon Juckes (1979)
Gen. John R. Kilpatrick (1960)

George A. Leader (1969)
Robert LeBel (1970)
Thomas F. Lockhart (1965)
Paul Loicq (1961)
Major Frederic McLaughlin (1963)
Hon. Hartland de Montarville Molson (1973)
Francis Nelson (1945)
Bruce A. Norris (1969)
James Norris, Sr. (1958)
James D. Norris (1962)
William M. Northey (1945)
John A. O'Brien (1962)
Frank Patrick (1958)
Allan W. Pickard (1958)
Sam Pollock (1978)
Sen. Donat Raymond (1958)
John R. Robertson (1945)
Claude C. Robinson (1945)
Philip D. Ross (1976)
Frank J. Selke, Sr. (1976)
Harry Sinden (1983)
Frank D. Smith (1962)
Conn Smythe (1958)
Lord Stanley of Preston (1945)
Cap. James T. Sutherland (1945)
Anatoli V. Tarasov (1974)
Lloyd Turner (1958)
William Thayer Tutt (1978)
Carl P. Voss (1974)
Fred C. Waghorne (1961)
Arthur M. Wirtz (1971)
William W. Wirtz (1976)

The United States Hockey Hall of Fame

The rise of the American athlete in hockey was saluted with the opening of the Untied States Hockey Hall of Fame in Eveleth, Minnesota on June 23, 1973. Like its Canadian counterpart, the American Hall inducts new members on an annual basis. Inductees must have made a significant contribution to hockey in the United States.

PLAYERS

Taffy Abel
Hobey Baker
Earl Bartholome
Peter Bessone
Frankie Brimsek
Ray Chaisson
John P. Chase
Robert Cleary
William Cleary
Anthony Conroy
Cully Dahlstrom
Victor DesJardins
Bob Dill
Doug Everett
John B. Garrison
Moose Goheen
Austin Harding
Stewart Iglehart
Virgil Johnson
Mike Karakas
Myles J. Lane
Joseph Linder
Sam L. LoPresti
John Mariucci
John Mayasich
Jack McCartan
William Moe
Fred Moseley
Hub Nelson
Eddie Olson
George Owen, Jr.
Winth Palmer
Fido Purpur
William Riley
Doc Romnes
Thomas Williams
Coddy Winters

COACHES

Oscar Almquist
Malcolm K. Gordon
Victor Heyliger
Edward J. Jeremiah
John Kelley
Jack Riley
Clifford R. Thompson
William Stewart
Ralph Winsor

ADMINISTRATORS

George V. Brown
Walter A. Brown
Walter Bush
Donald Clark
Doc Gibson
William M. Jennings
Nick Kahler
Thomas F. Lockhart
Cal Marvin
Robert Ridder
William Thayer Tutt
Lyle Z. Wright

REFEREE

William Chadwick

All-Time Leaders

The All-Time Leaders section provides information on individual all-time single season, career, and Stanley Cup playoff records since the founding of the National Hockey League in 1917. Included for all the various categories are the leaders among players and goaltenders.

The NHL does not recognize WHA records as official. For this reason, we have chosen to list the leaders both for the NHL and for the combined NHL-WHA listings.

Individual All-Time Single Season Leaders

The top 25 men are shown for all categories. If required by ties, one additional player is shown. If ties would require more than one additional player to be shown, none of the last tied group is listed. All of the information is self-explanatory.

Goals against Average. Until the 1942–43 season, the NHL played sudden-death overtime to settle tie games. It abandoned the practice that season, not to pick it up again until the 1983–84 season.

From 1917–18 through 1966–67, the official goals against averages for goaltenders were calculated by dividing goals allowed (excluding empty net goals) by games played. This method was justifiable for the years that employed overtime, because the games did not necessarily last exactly 60 minutes. There is a basic inconsistency, however, in listing the same goals against average for a goaltender who allowed one goal in five minutes as for one who allowed one goal in 60. For the years from 1942–43 to the present, therefore, we have recalculated goaltenders goals against averages to indicate the number of goals allowed per 60 minutes.

To qualify as a leader in goals against average, a goaltender must have played in at least 40% of his team's scheduled games for that season.

Individual Career Leaders

For all categories, all players who have met the indicated minimum criterion are listed. As with the single season leaders, there are separate listings for NHL and combined NHL-WHA careers.

The following are the minimums required for listing in each category:

Years Played: 20
Games: 1,000
Goals: 300
Assists: 500
Points: 800
Penalty Minutes: 1,400
Goals against Average: 2.60, minimum 5 years
Shutouts: 40
Goalies' Penalty Minutes: 100

Stanley Cup Playoff Leaders

The Stanley Cup Playoff leaders listed are for the years since the Stanley Cup became the championship of professional ice hockey. There are no listings in this section for WHA playoff leaders.

Single Season Leaders. For each category listed, the "single season" listed consists of all levels of playoffs, from preliminary rounds through the Stanley Cup finals. The top 15 players and goaltenders are listed. If required by ties, one additional player is listed. If ties would require listing more than one additional player, none of the last tied group is listed.

Career Leaders. As with the regular season career leaders, all men who have surpassed the minimum criterion for each category area are listed. The minimums for each category are as follows:

Goals: 40
Assists: 60
Points: 95
Penalty Minutes: 200
Goals against Average: 2.50, minimum 3 years
Shutouts: 6
Stanley Cup Championships: 5

GOALS

1.	Wayne Gretzky 1981–82	92
2.	Phil Esposito 1970–71	76
3.	Wayne Gretzky 1982–83	71
4.	Mike Bossy 1978–79	69
5.	Phil Esposito 1973–74	68
5.	Mike Bossy 1980–81	68
7.	Phil Esposito 1971–72	66
7.	Lanny McDonald 1982–83	66
9.	Mike Bossy 1981–82	64
10.	Phil Esposito 1974–75	61
10.	Reggie Leach 1975–76	61
12.	Steve Shutt 1976–77	60
12.	Guy Lafleur 1977–78	60
12.	Dennis Maruk 1981–82	60
12.	Mike Bossy 1982–83	60
16.	Marcel Dionne 1978–79	59
17.	Bobby Hull 1968–69	58
17.	Marcel Dionne 1980–81	58
19.	Michel Goulet 1982–83	57
20.	Guy Lafleur 1975–76	56
20.	Guy Lafleur 1976–77	56
20.	Charlie Simmer 1979–80	56
20.	Danny Gare 1979–80	56
20.	Blaine Stoughton 1979–80	56
20.	Charlie Simmer 1980–81	56
20.	Marcel Dionne 1982–83	56

ASSISTS

1.	Wayne Gretzky 1982–83	125
2.	Wayne Gretzky 1981–82	120
3.	Wayne Gretzky 1980–81	109
4.	Bobby Orr 1970–71	102
5.	Peter Stastny 1981–82	93
6.	Bobby Orr 1973–74	90
7.	Bobby Clarke 1974–75	89
7.	Bobby Clarke 1975–76	89
7.	Bobby Orr 1974–75	89
10.	Denis Savard 1981–82	87
10.	Bobby Orr 1969–70	87
10.	Bryan Trottier 1978–79	87
13.	Wayne Gretzky 1979–80	86
14.	Denis Savard 1982–83	85
15.	Marcel Dionne 1979–80	84
16.	Mike Bossy 1981–82	83
17.	Pete Mahovlich 1974–75	82
17.	Kent Nilsson 1980–81	82
19.	Bobby Orr 1971–72	80
19.	Guy Lafleur 1976–77	80

POINTS

1.	Wayne Gretzky 1981–82	212
2.	Wayne Gretzky 1982–83	196
3.	Wayne Gretzky 1980–81	164
4.	Phil Esposito 1970–71	152
5.	Mike Bossy 1981–82	147
6.	Phil Esposito 1973–74	145
7.	Bobby Orr 1970–71	139
8.	Wayne Gretzky 1979–80	137
8.	Marcel Dionne 1979–80	137
10.	Guy Lafleur 1976–77	136
10.	Dennis Maruk 1981–82	136
12.	Bobby Orr 1974–75	135
12.	Marcel Dionne 1980–81	135
14.	Bryan Trottier 1978–79	134
15.	Phil Esposito 1971–72	133
16.	Guy Lafleur 1977–78	132
17.	Kent Nilsson 1980–81	131
18.	Phil Esposito 1972–73	130
18.	Marcel Dionne 1978–79	130
20.	Guy Lafleur 1978–79	129
20.	Bryan Trottier 1981–82	129
22.	Phil Esposito 1974–75	127
23.	Phil Esposito 1968–69	126
23.	Mike Bossy 1978–79	126
25.	Guy Lafleur 1975–76	125
25.	Guy Lafleur 1979–80	125

PENALTY MINUTES

1.	Dave Schultz 1974–75	472
2.	Paul Baxter 1981–82	409
3.	Dave Schultz 1977–78	405
4.	Steve Durbano 1975–76	370
5.	Tiger Williams 1977–78	351
6.	Dave Schultz 1973–74	348
7.	Tiger Williams 1980–81	343
8.	Tiger Williams 1979–80	341
9.	Tiger Williams 1976–77	338
10.	Bryan Watson 1975–76	322
10.	Pat Price 1981–82	322
12.	Dave Schultz 1975–76	307
13.	Bob Gassoff 1975–76	306
13.	Paul Holmgren 1980–81	306
15.	Al Secord 1981–82	303
16.	Dennis Polonich 1975–76	302
17.	Tiger Williams 1975–76	299
18.	Tiger Williams 1978–79	298
19.	Keith Magnuson 1970–71	291
20.	Willi Plett 1981–82	288
21.	Jim Mann 1979–80	287
22.	Steve Durbano 1973–74	284
23.	Randy Holt 1978–79	282
24.	Tiger Williams 1981–82	278
25.	Andre Dupont 1974–75	276

GOALS AGAINST AVE.

1.	George Hainsworth 1928–29	0.98
2.	George Hainsworth 1927–28	1.09
3.	Alex Connell 1925–26	1.17
4.	Tiny Thompson 1928–29	1.18
5.	Roy Worters 1928–29	1.21
6.	Alex Connell 1927–28	1.30
7.	Clarence Dolson 1928–29	1.43
8.	Wilf Cude 1933–34	1.47
9.	John Roach 1928–29	1.48
10.	Clint Benedict 1926–27	1.51
11.	George Hainsworth 1926–27	1.52
11.	Alex Connell 1928–29	1.52
13.	Clint Benedict 1928–29	1.54
14.	Lorne Chabot 1926–27	1.56
14.	Lorne Chabot 1928–29	1.56
16.	Alex Connell 1926–27	1.57
17.	Frankie Brimsek 1938–39	1.58
18.	Hal Winkler 1927–28	1.59
19.	Davie Kerr 1939–40	1.60
20.	Roy Worters 1930–31	1.68
21.	Tiny Thompson 1935–36	1.71
22.	Clint Benedict 1927–28	1.73
22.	Roy Worters 1927–28	1.73
22.	Chuck Gardiner 1933–34	1.73
25.	Hal Winkler 1926–27	1.74

SHUTOUTS

1.	George Hainsworth 1928–29	22
2.	Alex Connell 1925–26	15
2.	Alex Connell 1927–28	15
2.	Hal Winkler 1927–28	15
2.	Tony Esposito 1969–70	15
6.	George Hainsworth 1926–27	14
7.	Clint Benedict 1926–27	13
7.	George Hainsworth 1927–28	13
7.	John Roach 1928–29	13
7.	Roy Worters 1928–29	13
7.	Harry Lumley 1953–54	13
7.	Alex Connell 1926–27	13
13.	Tiny Thompson 1928–29	12
13.	Lorne Chabot 1928–29	12
13.	Chuck Gardiner 1930–31	12
13.	Terry Sawchuk 1951–52	12
13.	Terry Sawchuk 1953–54	12
13.	Terry Sawchuk 1954–55	12
13.	Glenn Hall 1955–56	12
13.	Bernie Parent 1973–74	12
13.	Bernie Parent 1974–75	12

PENALTY MINUTES BY GOALTENDERS

1.	Gerry Cheevers 1979–80	62
2.	Andy Brown 1973–74	60
3.	Billy Smith 1978–79	54
4.	Al Smith 1980–81	51
5.	Gerry Cheevers 1976–77	46
6.	Glen Hanlon 1979–80	43
7.	Billy Smith 1972–73	42
7.	Dan Bouchard 1974–75	42
9.	Al Smith 1970–71	41
9.	Billy Smith 1982–83	41
11.	Terry Sawchuk 1957–58	39
11.	Billy Smith 1979–80	39
13.	Doug Favell 1967–68	37
13.	Phil Myre 1979–80	37
15.	Dan Bouchard 1981–82	36
16.	Billy Smith 1977–78	35
16.	Marco Baron 1981–82	35
16.	Greg Stefan 1982–83	35
19.	Dan Bouchard 1979–80	34
20.	Gary Smith 1974–75	33
20.	Billy Smith 1980–81	33
22.	Pete Peeters 1982–83	33
23.	Doug Favell 1971–72	32
24.	Glen Hanlon 1978–79	30
24.	Rich Sevigny 1980–81	30

YEARS PLAYED

1. Gordie Howe 26
2. Alex Delvecchio 24
3. Tim Horton 23
3. John Bucyk 23
5. Stan Mikita 22
5. Doug Mohns 22
5. Dean Prentice 22
8. Harry Howell 21
8. Allan Stanley 21
8. George Armstrong 21
8. Eric Nesterenko 21
8. Jean Ratelle 21
8. Ron Stewart 21
14. Jean Beliveau 20
14. Red Kelly 20
14. Bill Gadsby 20
14. Marcel Pronovost 20
14. Henri Richard 20
14. Norm Ullman 20

GAMES

1. Gordie Howe 1767
2. Alex Delvecchio 1549
3. John Bucyk 1540
4. Tim Horton 1446
5. Harry Howell 1411
6. Norm Ullman 1410
7. Stan Mikita 1394
8. Doug Mohns 1390
9. Dean Prentice 1378
10. Ron Stewart 1353
11. Red Kelly 1316
12. Dave Keon 1296
13. Phil Esposito 1282
14. Jean Ratelle 1281
15. Henri Richard 1256
16. Bill Gadsby 1248
17. Allan Stanley 1244
18. Ed Westfall 1227
19. Eric Nesterenko 1219
20. Marcel Pronovost 1206
21. George Armstrong 1187
22. Frank Mahovlich 1181
23. Don Marshall 1176
24. Leo Boivin 1150
25. Bob Nevin 1128
26. Murray Oliver 1127
27. Jean Beliveau 1125
28. Doug Harvey 1113
29. Garry Unger 1105
30. Pit Martin 1101
31. Carol Vadnais 1087
32. Bob Pulford 1079
33. Bobby Clarke 1071
34. Andy Bathgate 1069
35. Ted Lindsay 1068
36. Terry Harper 1066
37. Rod Gilbert 1065
38. Bobby Hull 1063
39. Jean-Guy Talbot 1056
40. Eddie Shack 1047
41. Ron Ellis 1034
42. Ralph Backstrom 1032
43. Dick Duff 1030
44. Wayne Cashman 1027
45. Jim Neilson 1023
46. Jim Roberts 1006
47. Claude Provost 1005
48. Vic Hadfield 1002

GOALS

1. Gordie Howe 801
2. Phil Esposito 717
3. Bobby Hull 610
4. John Bucyk 556
5. Maurice Richard 544
5. Marcel Dionne 544
7. Stan Mikita 541
8. Frank Mahovlich 533
9. Jean Beliveau 507
10. Jean Ratelle 491
11. Norm Ullman 490
12. Guy Lafleur 486
13. Alex Delvecchio 456
14. Darryl Sittler 446
15. Yvan Cournoyer 428
16. Gil Perreault 421
17. Garry Unger 413
18. Rod Gilbert 406
19. Bill Barber 398
20. Dave Keon 396
21. Bernie Geoffrion 393
22. Steve Shutt 392
23. Jean Pronovost 391
23. Dean Prentice 391
25. Lanny McDonald 385
26. Rick Martin 384
27. Reggie Leach 381
28. Ted Lindsay 379
29. Jacques Lemaire 366
30. Mike Bossy 365
31. Henri Richard 358
32. Rick Kehoe 353
33. Andy Bathgate 349
34. Bobby Clarke 341
35. Rick MacLeish 339
36. Butch Goring 338
37. Ron Ellis 332
38. Ken Hodge 328
39. Nels Stewart 324
39. Pit Martin 324
41. Vic Hadfield 323
42. Rick Middleton 313
43. Bryan Trottier 312
44. Ivan Boldirev 307
44. Bob Nevin 307
46. Danny Gare 306
47. Dennis Hull 303

ASSISTS

1. Gordie Howe 1049
2. Stan Mikita 926
3. Phil Esposito 873
4. Alex Delvecchio 825
5. John Bucyk 813
6. Bobby Clarke 809
7. Jean Ratelle 776
8. Marcel Dionne 743
9. Norm Ullman 739
10. Jean Beliveau 712
11. Henri Richard 688
12. Guy Lafleur 685
13. Gil Perreault 656
14. Bobby Orr 645
15. Andy Bathgate 624
16. Rod Gilbert 615
17. Brad Park 600
18. Dave Keon 590
19. Darryl Sittler 585
20. Frank Mahovlich 570
21. Bobby Hull 560
22. Red Kelly 542
23. Bryan Trottier 537
24. Denis Potvin 528
25. Wayne Cashman 516

POINTS

1. Gordie Howe 1850
2. Phil Esposito 1590
3. Stan Mikita 1467
4. John Bucyk 1369
5. Marcel Dionne 1287
6. Alex Delvecchio 1281
7. Jean Ratelle 1267
8. Norm Ullman 1229
9. Jean Beliveau 1219
10. Guy Lafleur 1171
11. Bobby Hull 1170
12. Bobby Clarke 1150
13. Frank Mahovlich 1103
14. Gil Perreault 1077
15. Henri Richard 1046
16. Darryl Sittler 1031
17. Rod Gilbert 1021
18. Dave Keon 986
19. Andy Bathgate 973
20. Maurice Richard 965
21. Bobby Orr 915
22. Yvan Cournoyer 863
23. Dean Prentice 860
24. Ted Lindsay 851
25. Bryan Trottier 849
26. Jacques Lemaire 835
27. Bill Barber 829
28. Red Kelly 823
29. Bernie Geoffrion 822
30. Pit Martin 809
31. Garry Unger 804
32. Butch Goring 801
33. Ken Hodge 800

PENALTY MINUTES

1. Tiger Williams 2700
2. Dave Schultz 2294
3. Bryan Watson 2214
4. Andre Dupont 1986
5. Garry Howatt 1822
6. Carol Vadnais 1813
7. Ted Lindsay 1808
8. Terry O'Reilly 1803
9. Phil Russell 1757
10. Gordie Howe 1685
11. Tim Horton 1611
12. Bill Gadsby 1539
13. Jerry Korab 1518
14. Paul Holmgren 1495
15. Bob Baun 1493
16. Dan Maloney 1489
17. Reggie Fleming 1468
18. Bob Kelly 1454
19. Keith Magnuson 1442
20. Eddie Shack 1437
21. Willi Plett 1435
22. Dave Hutchison 1413

GOALS AGAINST AVE.

1. George Hainsworth 1.91
2. Alex Connell 1.91
3. Chuck Gardiner 2.02
4. Lorne Chabot 2.04
5. Tiny Thompson 2.08
6. Davie Kerr 2.17
7. Ken Dryden 2.24
8. Roy Worters 2.27
9. Norm Smith 2.32
10. Clint Benedict 2.32
11. Flat Walsh 2.32
12. Bill Durnan 2.36
13. Gerry McNeil 2.36
14. Jacques Plante 2.38
15. John Roach 2.46
16. Glenn Hall 2.51
17. Terry Sawchuk 2.52
18. Johnny Bower 2.52
19. Turk Broda 2.55
20. Bernie Parent 2.56

SHUTOUTS

1. Terry Sawchuk 103
2. George Hainsworth 94
3. Glenn Hall 84
4. Jacques Plante 82
5. Tiny Thompson 81
5. Alex Connell 81
7. Tony Esposito 75
8. Lorne Chabot 73
9. Harry Lumley 71
10. Roy Worters 66
11. Turk Broda 62
12. Clint Benedict 58
12. John Roach 58
14. Bernie Parent 55
15. Ed Giacomin 54
16. Davie Kerr 51
16. Rogie Vachon 51
18. Ken Dryden 46
19. Gump Worsley 43
20. Chuck Gardiner 42
21. Frankie Brimsek 40

PENALTY MINUTES BY GOALTENDERS

1. Billy Smith 327
2. Gerry Cheevers 206
3. Dan Bouchard 194
4. Terry Sawchuk 188
5. Doug Favell 152
6. Gary Smith 146
7. Gump Worsley 145
8. Al Smith 135
9. Gilles Gilbert 110
10. Glen Hanlon 109
11. Bernie Parent 108
12. Phil Myre 101

GOALS

	Player	Season	Goals
1.	Wayne Gretzky	1981–82	92
2.	Bobby Hull	1974–75	77
3.	Phil Esposito	1970–71	76
4.	Real Cloutier	1978–79	75
5.	Marc Tardif	1975–76	71
5.	Wayne Gretzky	1982–83	71
7.	Anders Hedberg	1976–77	70
8.	Mike Bossy	1978–79	69
9.	Phil Esposito	1973–74	68
9.	Mike Bossy	1980–81	68
11.	Phil Esposito	1971–72	66
11.	Real Cloutier	1976–77	66
11.	Lanny McDonald	1982–83	66
14.	Marc Tardif	1977–78	65
14.	Morris Lukowich	1978–79	65
16.	Mike Bossy	1981–82	64
17.	Anders Hedberg	1977–78	63
18.	Phil Esposito	1974–75	61
18.	Reggie Leach	1975–76	61
20.	Real Cloutier	1975–76	60
20.	Steve Shutt	1976–77	60
20.	Mark Napier	1976–77	60
20.	Guy Lafleur	1977–78	60
20.	Dennis Maruk	1981–82	60
20.	Mike Bossy	1982–83	60

ASSISTS

	Player	Season	Assists
1.	Wayne Gretzky	1982–83	125
2.	Wayne Gretzky	1981–82	120
3.	Wayne Gretzky	1980–81	109
4.	Andre Lacroix	1974–75	106
5.	Bobby Orr	1970–71	102
6.	Ulf Nilsson	1974–75	94
7.	Peter Stastny	1981–82	93
8.	Bobby Orr	1973–74	90
9.	Bobby Clarke	1974–75	89
9.	Bobby Orr	1974–75	89
9.	Bobby Clarke	1975–76	89
9.	Ulf Nilsson	1977–78	89
9.	Marc Tardif	1977–78	89
14.	Bobby Orr	1969–70	87
14.	Bryan Trottier	1978–79	87
14.	Denis Savard	1981–82	87
17.	Wayne Gretzky	1979–80	86
18.	Ulf Nilsson	1976–77	85
18.	Denis Savard	1982–83	85
20.	Marcel Dionne	1979–80	84
21.	Mike Bossy	1981–82	83
22.	Pete Mahovlich	1974–75	82
22.	Andre Lacroix	1976–77	82
22.	Kent Nilsson	1980–81	82

POINTS

	Player	Season	Points
1.	Wayne Gretzky	1981–82	212
2.	Wayne Gretzky	1982–83	196
3.	Wayne Gretzky	1980–81	164
4.	Marc Tardif	1977–78	154
5.	Phil Esposito	1970–71	152
6.	Marc Tardif	1975–76	148
7.	Andre Lacroix	1974–75	147
7.	Mike Bossy	1981–82	147
9.	Phil Esposito	1973–74	145
10.	Bobby Hull	1974–75	142
11.	Real Cloutier	1977–78	141
12.	Bobby Orr	1970–71	139
13.	Wayne Gretzky	1979–80	137
13.	Marcel Dionne	1979–80	137
15.	Guy Lafleur	1976–77	136
15.	Dennis Maruk	1981–82	136
17.	Bryan Trottier	1978–79	134
17.	Bobby Orr	1974–75	135
17.	Marcel Dionne	1980–81	135
19.	Bryan Trottier	1978–79	134
20.	Phil Esposito	1971–72	133
21.	Guy Lafleur	1977–78	132
22.	Anders Hedberg	1976–77	131
22.	Kent Nilsson	1980–81	131
24.	Phil Esposito	1972–73	130
24.	Marcel Dionne	1978–79	130

PENALTY MINUTES

	Player	Season	PIM
1.	Dave Schultz	1974–75	472
2.	Paul Baxter	1981–82	409
3.	Dave Schultz	1977–78	405
4.	Steve Durbano	1975–76	370
5.	Curt Brackenbury	1975–76	365
6.	Kim Clackson	1975–76	351
6.	Tiger Williams	1977–78	351
8.	Dave Schultz	1973–74	348
9.	Tiger Williams	1980–81	343
10.	Tiger Williams	1981–82	341
11.	Tiger Williams	1976–77	338
12.	Bryan Watson	1975–76	322
12.	Pat Price	1981–82	322
14.	Dave Schultz	1975–76	307
15.	Bob Gassoff	1975–76	306
15.	Paul Holmgren	1980–81	306
17.	Al Secord	1981–82	303
18.	Dennis Polonich	1975–76	302
19.	Tiger Williams	1975–76	299
20.	Tiger Williams	1978–79	298
21.	Keith Magnuson	1970–71	291
22.	Willi Plett	1981–82	288
23.	Jim Mann	1979–80	287
24.	Steve Durbano	1973–74	284
24.	Steve Durbano	1977–78	284

GOALS AGAINST AVE.

	Player	Season	GAA
1.	George Hainsworth	1928–29	0.98
2.	George Hainsworth	1927–28	1.09
3.	Alex Connell	1925–26	1.17
4.	Tiny Thompson	1928–29	1.18
5.	Roy Worters	1928–29	1.21
6.	Alex Connell	1927–28	1.30
7.	Clarence Dolson	1928–29	1.43
8.	Wilf Cude	1933–34	1.47
9.	John Roach	1928–29	1.48
10.	Clint Benedict	1926–27	1.51
11.	George Hainsworth	1926–27	1.52
11.	Alex Connell	1928–29	1.52
13.	Clint Benedict	1928–29	1.54
14.	Lorne Chabot	1926–27	1.56
14.	Lorne Chabot	1928–29	1.56
16.	Alex Connell	1926–27	1.57
17.	Frankie Brimsek	1938–39	1.58
18.	Hal Winkler	1927–28	1.59
19.	Davie Kerr	1939–40	1.60
20.	Roy Worters	1930–31	1.68
21.	Tiny Thompson	1935–36	1.71
22.	Clint Benedict	1927–28	1.73
22.	Roy Worters	1927–28	1.73
22.	Chuck Gardiner	1933–34	1.73
25.	Hal Winkler	1926–27	1.74

SHUTOUTS

	Player	Season	Shutouts
1.	George Hainsworth	1928–29	22
2.	Alex Connell	1926–26	15
2.	Alex Connell	1927–28	15
2.	Hal Winkler	1927–28	15
2.	Tony Esposito	1969–70	15
6.	George Hainsworth	1926–27	14
7.	Clint Benedict	1926–27	13
7.	George Hainsworth	1927–28	13
7.	John Roach	1928–29	13
7.	Roy Worters	1928–29	13
7.	Harry Lumley	1953–54	13
7.	Alex Connell	1926–27	13
13.	Tiny Thompson	1928–29	12
13.	Lorne Chabot	1928–29	12
13.	Chuck Gardiner	1930–31	12
13.	Terry Sawchuk	1951–52	12
13.	Terry Sawchuk	1953–54	12
13.	Terry Sawchuk	1954–55	12
13.	Glenn Hall	1955–56	12
13.	Bernie Parent	1973–74	12
13.	Bernie Parent	1974–75	12

PENALTY MINUTES BY GOALTENDERS

	Player	Season	PIM
1.	Andy Brown	1974–75	75
2.	Gerry Cheevers	1979–80	62
3.	Andy Brown	1973–74	60
4.	Gerry Cheevers	1974–75	59
5.	Serge Aubry	1972–73	54
5.	Billy Smith	1978–79	54
7.	Al Smith	1980–81	51
8.	Gerry Cheevers	1976–77	46
9.	Glen Hanlon	1979–80	43
10.	Billy Smith	1972–73	42
10.	Dan Bouchard	1974–75	42
10.	Gary Inness	1977–78	42
13.	Al Smith	1970–71	41
13.	Billy Smith	1982–83	41
15.	Terry Sawchuk	1957–58	39
15.	Al Smith	1972–73	39
15.	Billy Smith	1979–80	39
18.	Doug Favell	1967–68	37
18.	Phil Myre	1979–80	37
20.	Bernie Parent	1972–73	36
20.	Dan Bouchard	1981–82	36
22.	Billy Smith	1977–78	35
22.	Al Smith	1978–79	35
22.	Marco Baron	1981–82	35
22.	Greg Stefan	1982–83	35

YEARS PLAYED

1.	Gordie Howe	32
2.	Alex Delvecchio	24
2.	Harry Howell	24
2.	Tim Horton	24
5.	John Bucyk	23
5.	Bobby Hull	23
7.	Dave Keon	22
7.	Frank Mahovlich	22
7.	Stan Mikita	22
7.	Doug Mohns	22
7.	Eric Nesterenko	22
7.	Dean Prentice	22
7.	Norm Ullman	22
14.	George Armstrong	21
14.	Ralph Backstrom	21
14.	Jean Ratelle	21
14.	Allan Stanley	21
14.	Ron Stewart	21
19.	Jean Beliveau	20
19.	Bill Gadsby	20
19.	Red Kelly	20
19.	Marcel Pronovost	20
19.	Henri Richard	20
19.	J.C. Tremblay	20

GAMES

1.	Gordie Howe	2186
2.	Dave Keon	1597
3.	Harry Howell	1581
4.	Norm Ullman	1554
5.	Alex Delvecchio	1549
6.	John Bucyk	1540
7.	Bobby Hull	1474
8.	Tim Horton	1446
9.	Frank Mahovlich	1418
10.	Stan Mikita	1394
11.	Doug Mohns	1390
12.	Dean Prentice	1378
13.	Ron Stewart	1353
14.	Ralph Backstrom	1336
15.	Red Kelly	1316
16.	Phil Esposito	1282
17.	Jean Ratelle	1281
18.	Henri Richard	1256
19.	J.C. Tremblay	1249
20.	Bill Gadsby	1248
20.	Eric Nesterenko	1248
22.	Allan Stanley	1244
23.	Ed Westfall	1227
24.	Marcel Pronovost	1206
25.	Claude Larose	1195
26.	George Armstrong	1187
27.	Don Marshall	1176
28.	John McKenzie	1168
29.	Leo Boivin	1150
30.	Bob Nevin	1141
31.	Murray Oliver	1127
32.	Jean Beliveau	1125
33.	Doug Harvey	1113
34.	Garry Unger	1105
35.	Pit Martin	1101

GOALS

1.	Gordie Howe	975
2.	Bobby Hull	913
3.	Phil Esposito	717
4.	Frank Mahovlich	622
5.	John Bucyk	556
6.	Maurice Richard	544
6.	Marcel Dionne	544
8.	Stan Mikita	541
9.	Norm Ullman	537
10.	Marc Tardif	510
11.	Jean Beliveau	507
12.	Dave Keon	498
13.	Jean Ratelle	491
14.	Guy Lafleur	486
15.	Alex Delvecchio	456
16.	Darryl Sittler	446
17.	Yvan Cournoyer	428
18.	Gil Perreault	421
19.	Garry Unger	413
20.	Rod Gilbert	406
21.	Real Cloutier	405
22.	Bill Barber	398
23.	Bernie Geoffrion	393
24.	Steve Shutt	392
25.	Jean Pronovost	391
25.	Dean Prentice	391
27.	Lanny McDonald	385
28.	Rick Martin	384
29.	Reggie Leach	381
30.	Ted Lindsay	379
31.	Ralph Backstrom	378
32.	Paul Henderson	376
33.	John McKenzie	369
34.	Jacques Lemaire	366
35.	Mike Bossy	365
36.	Henri Richard	358
37.	Anders Hedberg	356
38.	Rick Kehoe	353
39.	Andy Bathgate	350
40.	Bobby Clarke	341
41.	Rick MacLeish	339
42.	Butch Goring	338
43.	Mike Walton	337
44.	Ron Ellis	332
45.	Andre Lacroix	330
46.	Ken Hodge	328
47.	Nels Stewart	324
48.	Pit Martin	324
49.	Vic Hadfield	323
50.	Blaine Stoughton	319
51.	Wayne Gretzky	315
52.	Rick Middleton	313
53.	Bryan Trottier	312
54.	Bob Nevin	310
55.	Serge Bernier	308
56.	Ivan Boldirev	307
57.	Danny Gare	306
58.	Bill Flett	305
59.	Dennis Hull	303
60.	Wayne Connelly	300

ASSISTS

1.	Gordie Howe	1383
2.	Stan Mikita	926
3.	Bobby Hull	895
4.	Phil Esposito	873
5.	Alex Delvecchio	825
6.	Norm Ullman	822
7.	John Bucyk	813
8.	Bobby Clarke	809
9.	Dave Keon	779
10.	Jean Ratelle	776
11.	Marcel Dionne	743
12.	Frank Mahovlich	713
13.	Jean Beliveau	712
14.	Henri Richard	688
15.	Guy Lafleur	685
16.	Andre Lacroix	666
17.	J.C. Tremblay	664
18.	Gil Perreault	656
19.	Bobby Orr	645
20.	Andy Bathgate	624
21.	Rod Gilbert	615
22.	Brad Park	600
23.	Darryl Sittler	585
24.	Marc Tardif	557
25.	Red Kelly	542
26.	Bryan Trottier	537
27.	Denis Potvin	528
28.	John McKenzie	518
29.	Wayne Cashman	516
30.	Ralph Backstrom	514
31.	Wayne Gretzky	504

POINTS

1.	Gordie Howe	2358
2.	Bobby Hull	1808
3.	Phil Esposito	1590
4.	Stan Mikita	1467
5.	John Bucyk	1369
6.	Norm Ullman	1359
7.	Frank Mahovlich	1335
8.	Marcel Dionne	1287
9.	Alex Delvecchio	1281
10.	Dave Keon	1277
11.	Jean Ratelle	1267
12.	Jean Beliveau	1219
13.	Guy Lafleur	1171
14.	Bobby Clarke	1150
15.	Gil Perreault	1077
16.	Marc Tardif	1067
17.	Henri Richard	1046
18.	Darryl Sittler	1031
19.	Rod Gilbert	1021
20.	Andre Lacroix	996
21.	Andy Bathgate	980
22.	Maurice Richard	965
23.	Bobby Orr	915
24.	Ralph Backstrom	892
25.	John McKenzie	887
26.	Yvan Cournoyer	863
27.	Dean Prentice	860
28.	Ted Lindsay	851
29.	Real Cloutier	850
30.	Bryan Trottier	849
31.	Jacques Lemaire	835
32.	Bill Barber	829
33.	Red Kelly	823
34.	Bernie Geoffrion	822
35.	Pit Martin	809
36.	Garry Unger	804
37.	Butch Goring	801
38.	Ken Hodge	800

PENALTY MINUTES

1.	Tiger Williams	2700
2.	Dave Schultz	2294
3.	Bryan Watson	2270
4.	Gordie Howe	2084
5.	Andre Dupont	1986
6.	Paul Baxter	1958
7.	Garry Howatt	1822
8.	Carol Vadnais	1813
9.	Ted Lindsay	1808
10.	Terry O'Reilly	1803
11.	Phil Russell	1757
12.	Paul Holmgren	1616
13.	Tim Horton	1611
14.	Reggie Fleming	1610
15.	Dave Hutchison	1567
16.	Bill Gadsby	1539
17.	John McKenzie	1534
18.	Jerry Korab	1518
19.	Bob Baun	1493
20.	Dan Maloney	1489
21.	Bob Kelly	1454
22.	Keith Magnuson	1442
23.	Eddie Shack	1437
24.	Willi Plett	1435

GOALS AGAINST AVE.

1.	George Hainsworth	1.91
2.	Alex Connell	1.91
3.	Chuck Gardiner	2.02
4.	Lorne Chabot	2.04
5.	Tiny Thompson	2.08
6.	Davie Kerr	2.17
7.	Ken Dryden	2.24
8.	Roy Worters	2.27
9.	Norm Smith	2.32
10.	Clint Benedict	2.32
11.	Flat Walsh	2.32
12.	Bill Durnan	2.31
13.	Gerry McNeil	2.36
14.	Jacques Plante	2.38
15.	John Roach	2.46
16.	Glenn Hall	2.51
17.	Terry Sawchuk	2.52
18.	Johnny Bower	2.52
19.	Turk Broda	2.55
20.	Bernie Parent	2.56

SHUTOUTS

1.	Terry Sawchuk	103
2.	George Hainsworth	94
3.	Glenn Hall	84
4.	Jacques Plante	83
5.	Tiny Thompson	81
5.	Alex Connell	81
7.	Tony Esposito	75
8.	Lorne Chabot	73
9.	Harry Lumley	71
10.	Roy Worters	66
11.	Turk Broda	62
12.	Clint Benedict	58
12.	John Roach	58
14.	Bernie Parent	55
15.	Ed Giacomin	54
16.	Davie Kerr	51
16.	Rogie Vachon	51
18.	Ken Dryden	46
19.	Gump Worsley	43
20.	Chuck Gardiner	42
21.	Frankie Brimsek	40

PENALTY MINUTES BY GOALTENDERS

1.	Gerry Cheevers	340
2.	Billy Smith	327
3.	Al Smith	264
4.	Dan Bouchard	194
5.	Terry Sawchuk	188
6.	Doug Favell	152
7.	Gary Smith	146
8.	Gump Worsley	145
9.	Bernie Parent	144
10.	Andy Brown	139
11.	Gilles Gilbert	110
12.	Glen Hanlon	109
13.	Phil Myre	101

GOALS

1.	Reggie Leach 1975–76	19
2.	Mike Bossy 1980–81	17
2.	Steve Payne 1980–81	17
2.	Mike Bossy 1981–82	17
2.	Mike Bossy 1982–83	17
6.	Yvan Cournoyer 1972–73	15
6.	Mark Messier 1982–83	15
8.	Frank Mahovlich 1970–71	14
8.	Barry Pederson 1982–83	14
10.	Phil Esposito 1969–70	13
10.	Rick MacLeish 1973–74	13
12.	Maurice Richard 1943–44	12
12.	Jean Beliveau 1955–56	12
12.	Guy Lafleur 1974–75	12
12.	Bill Barber 1979–80	12
12.	Bryan Trottier 1979–80	12
12.	Wayne Gretzky 1982–83	12

ASSISTS

1.	Wayne Gretzky 1982–83	26
2.	Bryan Trottier 1981–82	23
3.	Rick Middleton 1982–83	22
4.	Bob Bourne 1982–83	20
5.	Bobby Orr 1971–72	19
6.	Ken Linseman 1979–80	18
6.	Mike Bossy 1980–81	18
6.	Bryan Trottier 1980–81	18
6.	Barry Pederson 1982–83	18
10.	Guy Lafleur 1976–77	17
10.	Larry Robinson 1977–78	17
10.	Denis Potvin 1980–81	17
10.	Bryan Trottier 1979–80	17
10.	Bobby Smith 1980–81	17

POINTS

1.	Wayne Gretzky 1982–83	38
2.	Mike Bossy 1980–81	35
3.	Rick Middleton 1982–83	33
4.	Barry Pederson 1982–83	32
5.	Bryan Trottier 1979–80	29
5.	Steve Payne 1980–81	29
5.	Bryan Trottier 1980–81	29
5.	Bryan Trottier 1981–82	29
9.	Bob Bourne 1982–83	28
10.	Phil Esposito 1969–70	27
10.	Frank Mahovlich 1970–71	27
10.	Mike Bossy 1981–82	27
13.	Guy Lafleur 1976–77	26
13.	Mike Bossy 1982–83	26

PENALTY MINUTES

1.	Dave Schultz 1973–74	139
2.	Tiger Williams 1981–82	116
3.	Ed Hospodar 1980–81	93
4.	Dave Schultz 1975–76	90
5.	Willi Plett 1980–81	89
6.	Gord Lane 1979–80	85
7.	Garry Howatt 1979–80	84
8.	Dave Schultz 1974–75	83
9.	John Ferguson 1968–69	80
10.	Barclay Plager 1967–68	73
11.	Derek Sanderson 1969–70	72
12.	Mel Bridgman 1979–80	70
13.	Bob Plager 1967–68	69
14.	Andre Dupont 1973–74	67
14.	Ken Linseman 1980–81	67

GOALS AGAINST AVE.

1.	Tiny Thompson 1928–29	0.60
2.	Terry Sawchuk 1951–52	0.63
3.	Alex Connell 1926–27	0.67
4.	John Roach 1928–29	0.83
5.	Clint Benedict 1927–28	0.89
6.	Georges Vezina 1923–24	1.00
6.	Clint Benedict 1925–26	1.00
6.	George Hainsworth 1929–30	1.00
6.	John Roach 1930–31	1.00
10.	Turk Broda 1950–51	1.06
11.	Davie Kerr 1936–37	1.11
12.	Alex Connell 1934–35	1.14
13.	Norm Smith 1936–37	1.20
14.	Clint Benedict 1922–23	1.25
14.	Lorne Chabot 1928–29	1.25
14.	Flat Walsh 1930–31	1.25

SHUTOUTS

1.	Clint Benedict 1925–26	4
1.	Clint Benedict 1927–28	4
1.	Davie Kerr 1936–37	4
1.	Frank McCool 1944–45	4
1.	Terry Sawchuk 1951–52	4
1.	Bernie Parent 1974–75	4
1.	Ken Dryden 1976–77	4
8.	Clint Benedict 1922–23	3
8.	John Roach 1928–29	3
8.	Tiny Thompson 1928–29	3
8.	George Hainsworth 1929–30	3
8.	Davie Kerr 1939–40	3
8.	Turk Broda 1949–50	3
8.	Harry Lumley 1949–50	3
8.	Jacques Plante 1959–60	3
8.	Jacques Plante 1968–69	3

GOALS

1.	Maurice Richard	82
2.	Jean Beliveau	79
3.	Mike Bossy	69
4.	Yvan Cournoyer	64
5.	Gordie Howe	63
6.	Bobby Hull	62
7.	Jacques Lemaire	61
7.	Phil Esposito	61
9.	Stan Mikita	59
10.	Bernie Geoffrion	58
11.	Guy Lafleur	57
12.	Rick MacLeish	54
13.	Bill Barber	53
14.	Frank Mahovlich	51
15.	Henri Richard	49
15.	Denis Potvin	49
17.	Ted Lindsay	47
17.	Reggie Leach	47
19.	Dickie Moore	46
20.	Steve Shutt	43
21.	Bryan Trottier	42
22.	John Bucyk	41

ASSISTS

1.	Jean Beliveau	97
2.	Denis Potvin	94
3.	Gordie Howe	92
3.	Bryan Trottier	92
5.	Stan Mikita	91
6.	Brad Park	87
7.	Henri Richard	80
8.	Jacques Lemaire	78
9.	Phil Esposito	76
9.	Bobby Clarke	76
11.	Guy Lafleur	73
12.	Alex Delvecchio	69
13.	Bobby Hull	67
13.	Frank Mahovlich	67
15.	Jean Ratelle	66
15.	Bobby Orr	66
17.	Gil Perreault	65
18.	Dickie Moore	64
18.	Doug Harvey	64
20.	Yvan Cournoyer	63
21.	John Bucyk	62

POINTS

1.	Jean Beliveau	176
2.	Gordie Howe	160
3.	Stan Mikita	150
4.	Denis Potvin	143
5.	Jacques Lemaire	139
6.	Phil Esposito	137
7.	Bryan Trottier	134
8.	Guy Lafleur	130
9.	Bobby Hull	129
9.	Henri Richard	129
11.	Yvan Cournoyer	127
12.	Maurice Richard	126
13.	Mike Bossy	123
14.	Brad Park	122
15.	Frank Mahovlich	118
15.	Bernie Geoffrion	118
17.	Bobby Clarke	116
18.	Dickie Moore	110
19.	Bill Barber	108
20.	Rick MacLeish	107
21.	Alex Delvecchio	104
22.	John Bucyk	103
23.	Jean Ratelle	98
24.	Ted Lindsay	96
25.	Gil Perreault	95

PENALTY MINUTES

1.	Dave Schultz	412
2.	Tiger Williams	408
3.	Andre Dupont	352
4.	Terry O'Reilly	312
5.	Garry Howatt	289
6.	John Ferguson	260
7.	Wayne Cashman	250
8.	Mel Bridgman	248
9.	Ted Harris	230
10.	Willi Plett	229
11.	Clark Gillies	228
12.	Gordie Howe	220
13.	Jean Beliveau	211
14.	Al Secord	210
15.	Brad Park	206

GOALS AGAINST AVE.

1.	Alex Connell	1.19
2.	Chuck Gardiner	1.37
3.	Lorne Chabot	1.50
4.	Davie Kerr	1.74
5.	Earl Robertson	1.75
6.	Clint Benedict	1.80
7.	John Roach	1.88
8.	Tiny Thompson	1.88
9.	Gerry McNeil	1.89
10.	George Hainsworth	1.93
11.	Turk Broda	1.98
12.	Bill Durnan	2.08
13.	Jacques Plante	2.17
14.	Charlie Hodge	2.31
15.	Wilf Cude	2.32
16.	Ken Dryden	2.40
17.	Bernie Parent	2.43
18.	Chuck Rayner	2.43

SHUTOUTS

1.	Clint Benedict	15
1.	Jacques Plante	15
3.	Turk Broda	13
4.	Terry Sawchuk	12
5.	Ken Dryden	10
6.	John Roach	8
6.	Davie Kerr	8
6.	George Hainsworth	8
9.	Tiny Thompson	7
9.	Harry Lumley	7
9.	Gerry Cheevers	7
12.	Glenn Hall	6
12.	Tony Esposito	6
12.	Bernie Parent	6

STANLEY CUP CHAMPIONS

1.	Henri Richard	11
2.	Jean Beliveau	10
3.	Claude Provost	9
4.	Yvan Cournoyer	8
4.	Red Kelly	8
4.	Jacques Lemaire	8
4.	Maurice Richard	8
8.	Serge Savard	7
8.	Jean-Guy Talbot	7
10.	Ralph Backstrom	6
10.	Ken Dryden	6
10.	Dick Duff	6
10.	Bernie Geoffrion	6
10.	Doug Harvey	6
10.	Tom Johnson	6
10.	Frank Mahovlich	6
10.	Dickie Moore	6
10.	Jacques Plante	6
19.	Pierre Bouchard	5
19.	Turk Broda	5
19.	Cy Denneny	5
19.	John Ferguson	5
19.	Terry Harper	5
19.	Ted Harris	5
19.	Rejean Houle	5
19.	Ted Kennedy	5
19.	Guy Lafleur	5
19.	Jacques Laperriere	5
19.	Guy Lapointe	5
19.	Claude Larose	5
19.	Don Marshall	5
19.	Don Metz	5
19.	Bert Olmstead	5
19.	Marcel Pronovost	5
19.	Jim Roberts	5
19.	Larry Robinson	5
19.	Dollard St. Laurent	5
19.	Steve Shutt	5
19.	J.C. Tremblay	5
19.	Bob Turner	5
19.	Harry Watson	5

Player Register

The Player Register is an alphabetical listing of every man who has played professional ice hockey in the National Hockey League or World Hockey Association, except goaltenders, who are listed in the Goaltender Register. Included are biographical facts about the players, their complete scoring records year by year, their performance in the Stanley Cup and WHA playoffs, and information about any trades or sales in which they may have been involved.

All information or abbreviations that may appear unfamiliar are explained below.

Year	TEAM & LEAGUE	GP	G	A	PTS	PIM

John Doe

DOE, JOHN LEE (Slim) 5'11", 185 lbs.
B. Jan 26, 1961, Brantford, Ont. Center, Shoots L
Won Hart Trophy, 1979-80, 1980-81, 1981-82
Won Lady Byng Trophy, 1979-80
Won Art Ross Trophy, 1980-81, 1981-82

Year	TEAM & LEAGUE	GP	G	A	PTS	PIM
1978-79	**IND W**	8	3	3	6	0
	EDM W	72	43	61	104	19
	2 Team Total:	80	46	64	110	19
1979-80	**EDM N**	79	51	**86**	**137**	21
1980-81		80	55	**109**	**164**	28
1981-82		80	**92**[1]	**120**[1]	**212**[1]	26
4 yrs.	**N Totals:**	239	198	315	513	75
	W Totals:	80	46	64	110	19
PLAYOFFS						
1978-79	**EDM W**	13	**10**	10	**20**	2
1979-80	**EDM N**	3	2	1	3	0
1980-81*		9	7	14	21	4
1981-82		5	5	7	12	8
4 yrs.	**N Totals:**	17	14	22	36	12
	W Totals:	13	10	10	20	2

Reclaimed by **Edmonton** as under-age junior prior to Expansion Draft, June 9, 1979. Claimed as priority selection by **Edmonton**, June 9, 1979.

John Doe	This shortened version of the player's name is the name by which the player is best known. All the players in this section are arranged in alphabetical order by the last name portion of this name.
DOE, JOHN LEE	The player's full name.
(Slim)	The player's nickname. Any name or names appearing in parentheses are nicknames.
B. Jan 26, 1961, Brantford, Ont.	Date and place of birth.

Won Hart Trophy, etc.	The major trophies awarded by the league that have been won by Doe during his career. (For a complete listing of the winners of all awards, see the Awards and Achievements section.)
5′11″, 185 lbs.	Doe's height and average playing weight.
Center	The primary position played by the player.
Shoots L	The player's main shooting style.

Column Headings Information

GP Games Played
G Goals Scored
A Assists
PTS Points
PIM Penalties in Minutes

The following are the team abbreviations used in this section. For a more detailed listing of the teams involved, including team nicknames, please see the introduction to the Teams and their Players section.

ALTA Alberta
ATL Atlanta
BIRM Birmingham
BOS Boston
BUF Buffalo
CALG Calgary
CALIF California
CHI Chicago
CIN Cincinnati
CLEVE Cleveland
COLO Colorado
DET Detroit
EDM Edmonton
HAMIL Hamilton
HART Hartford
HOUS Houston
IND Indianapolis
KC Kansas City
LA Los Angeles
MINN Minnesota
MON (M) Montreal (Maroons)
MON (W) Montreal (Wanderers)
MONT Montreal (Canadiens)
NE New England
NJ New Jersey
NY New York (Raiders)
NYA New York (Americans)
NYI New York (Islanders)
NYR New York (Rangers)
OAK Oakland
OTTA Ottawa
PHI Philadelphia
PHOE Phoenix
PITT Pittsburgh
QUE Quebec
SD San Diego
STL St. Louis
TOR Toronto
VAN Vancouver
WASH Washington
WINN Winnipeg

In addition, there were three teams in the WHA that moved during the course of the season. These clubs are abbreviated as follows:

D-O Denver-Ottawa
M-B Michigan-Baltimore
NY-NJ New York-New Jersey

Blank space appearing beneath a team and league indicates that a player remained with the same club. Doe played with Edmonton in the NHL in 1980–81 and 1981–82.

Two Team Total. Doe played with two teams in the 1978–79 season. In addition to his record with each team, his combined total for the two teams is listed.

Total Playing Years. This information, which appears as the first item in the player's lifetime total, indicates the total number of years in which the player played in at least one game. NHL and WHA years are combined for this total.

League Totals. Separate totals are given for each player's career totals in the NHL and WHA.

League Leaders. Statistics that appear in boldface indicate that the player led his league in that category for the season. Doe, for example, led the NHL in assists and points in 1979–80.

All-Time Single Season Leaders. These are indicated by a small superscript "1" next to the player's statistic. Doe set all-time NHL records in goals, assists, and points during the 1981–82 season.

Trade Information. The text appearing below a player's record indicates any player transactions (drafts, trades, sales, free agent signings) he has been involved with in his NHL career. The team to which the player moves in a given transaction is listed in boldface. Trade information is listed back to the 1949–50 season. Research is continuing to fill in the gaps in our information.

Playoff Records. Complete information is given for every year in which the player participated in the Stanley Cup or WHA playoffs.

Cup Championships. An asterisk (*) appearing beside a given year indicates that the player's team won the Stanley Cup in that year. There is no similar designation for WHA championships. In the example above, Doe's team won the Stanley Cup in 1980–81.

For some players in the early NHL years and the WHA, we have been unable to find the proper division of an individual's statistics between his two (or more) teams in a year. In such cases we have listed the player's full season totals under his last team, and credited him with zero games for the other teams. Research into these questions continues.

Bruce Abbey

ABBEY, BRUCE 6'1", 185 lbs.
B. Aug. 18, 1951 Defense

YEAR	TEAM & LEAGUE	GP	G	A	PTS	PIM
1975-76	**CIN** W	17	1	0	1	12

Reg Abbott

ABBOTT, REGINALD 5'10½", 155 lbs.
B. Feb. 4, 1930, Winnipeg, Man. Center, Shoots L

YEAR	TEAM & LEAGUE	GP	G	A	PTS	PIM
1952-53	**MONT** N	3	0	0	0	0

Gerry Abel

ABEL, GERALD SCOTT 6'2", 168 lbs.
B. Dec. 25, 1944, Detroit, Mich. Left Wing, Shoots L

YEAR	TEAM & LEAGUE	GP	G	A	PTS	PIM
1966-67	**DET** N	1	0	0	0	0

Sid Abel

ABEL, SIDNEY GERALD 5'11", 190 lbs.
B. Feb. 22, 1918, Melville, Sask. Center, Shoots L
Won Hart Trophy, 1948-49
Hall of Fame, 1969

YEAR	TEAM & LEAGUE	GP	G	A	PTS	PIM
1938-39	**DET** N	15	1	1	2	0
1939-40		24	1	5	6	4
1940-41		47	11	22	33	29
1941-42		48	18	31	49	45
1942-43		49	18	24	42	33
1945-46		7	0	2	2	0
1946-47		60	19	29	48	29
1947-48		60	14	30	44	69
1948-49		60	**28**	26	54	49
1949-50		70	34	35	69	46
1950-51		69	23	38	61	30
1951-52		62	17	36	53	32
1952-53	**CHI** N	39	5	4	9	6
1953-54		3	0	0	0	4
14 yrs.	N Totals:	613	189	283	472	376

PLAYOFFS

YEAR	TEAM & LEAGUE	GP	G	A	PTS	PIM
1938-39	**DET** N	3	1	1	2	2
1939-40		5	0	3	3	21
1940-41		9	2	2	4	2
1941-42		12	4	2	6	6
1942-43*		10	5	8	13	4
1945-46		3	0	0	0	0
1946-47		5	1	1	2	2
1947-48		10	0	3	3	16
1948-49		11	3	3	6	6
1949-50*		14	6	2	8	6
1950-51		6	4	3	7	0
1951-52*		7	2	2	4	12
1952-53	**CHI** N	1	0	0	0	0
13 yrs.	N Totals:	96	28	30	58	77

Sold to **Chicago** by Detroit, July 29, 1952.

Taffy Abel

ABEL, CLARENCE JOHN 6'1", 225 lbs.
B. May 28, 1900, Sault Ste. Marie, Mich. Defense, Shoots L

YEAR	TEAM & LEAGUE	GP	G	A	PTS	PIM
1926-27	**NYR** N	44	8	4	12	78
1927-28		22	0	1	1	28
1928-29		44	2	1	3	41
1929-30	**CHI** N	38	3	3	6	42
1930-31		40	0	1	1	45
1931-32		48	3	3	6	34
1932-33		45	0	4	4	63
1933-34		46	2	1	3	28
8 yrs.	N Totals:	327	18	18	36	359

PLAYOFFS

YEAR	TEAM & LEAGUE	GP	G	A	PTS	PIM
1926-27	**NYR** N	2	0	1	1	8
1927-28*		9	1	0	1	14
1928-29		6	0	0	0	8
1929-30	**CHI** N	2	0	0	0	10
1930-31		9	0	0	0	8
1931-32		2	0	0	0	2
1933-34*		8	0	0	0	8

Taffy Abel continued

YEAR	TEAM & LEAGUE	GP	G	A	PTS	PIM
7 yrs.	N Totals:	38	1	1	2	58

Dennis Abgrall

ABGRALL, DENNIS HARVEY 6'1", 180 lbs.
B. Apr. 24, 1953, Tisdale, Sask. Right Wing, Shoots R

YEAR	TEAM & LEAGUE	GP	G	A	PTS	PIM
1975-76	**LA** N	13	0	2	2	4
1976-77	**CIN** W	80	23	39	62	22
1977-78		65	13	11	24	13
3 yrs.	N Totals:	13	0	2	2	4
	W Totals:	145	36	50	86	35

PLAYOFFS

YEAR	TEAM & LEAGUE	GP	G	A	PTS	PIM
1976-77	**CIN** W	4	2	0	2	5

Thommy Abrahamsson

ABRAHAMSSON, THOMMY 6'2", 190 lbs.
B. Apr. 12, 1947, Ulmea, Sweden Defense, Shoots L

YEAR	TEAM & LEAGUE	GP	G	A	PTS	PIM
1974-75	**NE** W	76	8	22	30	46
1975-76		63	14	21	35	47
1976-77		64	6	24	30	33
1980-81	**HART** N	32	6	11	17	16
4 yrs.	N Totals:	32	6	11	17	16
	W Totals:	203	28	67	95	126

PLAYOFFS

YEAR	TEAM & LEAGUE	GP	G	A	PTS	PIM
1975-76	**NE** W	17	2	4	6	15
1976-77		5	0	3	3	0
2 yrs.	W Totals:	22	2	7	9	15

Signed as free agent by **Hartford** May 23, 1980.

Gene Achtymichuk

ACHTYMICHUK, EUGENE EDWARD 5'11", 170 lbs.
B. Sept. 7, 1932, Lamont, Alta. Center, Shoots L

YEAR	TEAM & LEAGUE	GP	G	A	PTS	PIM
1951-52	**MONT** N	1	0	0	0	0
1956-57		3	0	0	0	0
1957-58		16	3	5	8	2
1958-59	**DET** N	12	0	0	0	0
4 yrs.	N Totals:	32	3	5	8	2

Drafted by **Detroit** from Montreal, June 3, 1958.

Doug Acomb

ACOMB, DOUGLAS RAYMOND 5'10", 165 lbs.
B. May 15, 1949, Toronto, Ont. Center, Shoots L

YEAR	TEAM & LEAGUE	GP	G	A	PTS	PIM
1969-70	**TOR** N	2	0	1	1	0

Keith Acton

ACTON, KEITH EDWARD 5'8", 167 lbs.
B. Apr. 15, 1958, Newmarket, Ont. Center, Shoots L

YEAR	TEAM & LEAGUE	GP	G	A	PTS	PIM
1979-80	**MONT** N	2	0	1	1	4
1980-81		61	15	24	39	74
1981-82		78	36	52	88	88
1982-83		78	24	26	50	63
4 yrs.	N Totals:	219	75	103	178	229

PLAYOFFS

YEAR	TEAM & LEAGUE	GP	G	A	PTS	PIM
1980-81	**MONT** N	2	0	0	0	6
1981-82		5	0	4	4	16
1982-83		3	0	0	0	0
3 yrs.	N Totals:	10	0	4	4	22

Jim Adair

ADAIR, JAMES 5'11", 180 lbs.
B. Sept. 28, 1948, Brockville, Ont. Center, Shoots L

YEAR	TEAM & LEAGUE	GP	G	A	PTS	PIM
1973-74	**VAN** W	70	12	17	29	10

Douglas Adam

ADAM, DOUGLAS PATRICK 5'10½", 165 lbs.
B. Sept. 7, 1923, Toronto, Ont. Left Wing, Shoots L

YEAR	TEAM & LEAGUE		GP	G	A	PTS	PIM
1949-50	NYR	N	4	0	1	1	0

Russ Adam

ADAM, RUSS 5'11", 185 lbs.
B. May 5, 1961, Windsor, Ont. Forward

YEAR	TEAM & LEAGUE		GP	G	A	PTS	PIM
1982-83	TOR	N	8	1	2	3	11

Greg Adams

ADAMS, GREG 6'1", 190 lbs.
B. May 31, 1960, Duncan, B.C. Left Wing, Shoots L

YEAR	TEAM & LEAGUE		GP	G	A	PTS	PIM
1980-81	PHI	N	6	3	0	3	8
1981-82			33	4	15	19	105
1982-83	HART	N	79	10	13	23	216
3 yrs.		N Totals:	118	17	28	45	329

Traded to **Hartford** with Ken Linseman, a first round choice (David Jensen) and a third round choice (Dave McLean) in the 1983 Amateur Draft by Philadelphia for Mark Howe and Hartford's third choice (Derrick Smith) in the 1983 Amateur Draft, Aug. 19, 1982.

Jack Adams

ADAMS, JOHN ELLIS 5'10", 163 lbs.
B. May 5, 1920, Calgary, Alta. Left Wing, Shoots L

YEAR	TEAM & LEAGUE		GP	G	A	PTS	PIM
1940-41	MONT	N	42	6	12	18	11
PLAYOFFS							
1940-41	MONT	N	3	0	0	0	0

Jack Adams

ADAMS, JOHN JAMES
B. June 14, 1895, Fort William, Ont. Center
Hall of Fame, 1959

YEAR	TEAM & LEAGUE		GP	G	A	PTS	PIM
1917-18	TOR	N	8	0	0	0	15
1918-19			17	3	3	6	17
1922-23			23	19	9	28	42
1923-24			22	13	3	16	**49**
1924-25			27	21	8	29	66
1925-26			36	21	5	26	52
1926-27	OTTA	N	40	5	1	6	66
7 yrs.		N Totals:	173	82	29	111	307
PLAYOFFS							
1917-18*	TOR	N	2	2	0	2	3
1924-25			2	1	0	1	7
1926-27			6	0	0	0	2
3 yrs.		N Totals:	10	3	0	3	12

Stewart Adams

ADAMS, STEWART
B. Unknown Left Wing

YEAR	TEAM & LEAGUE		GP	G	A	PTS	PIM
1929-30	CHI	N	24	4	6	10	16
1930-31			37	5	13	18	18
1931-32			26	0	5	5	26
1932-33	TOR	N	19	0	2	2	0
4 yrs.		N Totals:	106	9	26	35	60
PLAYOFFS							
1929-30	CHI	N	2	0	0	0	6
1930-31			9	3	3	6	8
2 yrs.		N Totals:	11	3	3	6	14

Ray Adduono

ADDUONO, RAYMOND 5'9", 175 lbs.
B. Jan. 21, 1947, Fort William, Ont. Center, Shoots L

YEAR	TEAM & LEAGUE		GP	G	A	PTS	PIM
1973-74	CLEVE	W	2	0	0	0	0
1974-75	SD	W	78	15	59	74	23
1975-76			80	23	67	90	22
1976-77	MINN	W	40	4	19	23	17
	SD	W	13	2	5	7	5
	2 team total		53	6	24	30	22
1977-78	IND	W	8	1	2	3	0

Ray Adduono continued

YEAR	TEAM & LEAGUE		GP	G	A	PTS	PIM
5 yrs.		W Totals:	221	45	152	197	67
PLAYOFFS							
1974-75	SD	W	10	5	9	14	13
1975-76			11	4	7	11	6
1976-77			7	3	2	5	19
3 yrs.		W Totals:	28	12	18	30	38

Rick Adduono

ADDUONO, RICK 5'11", 182 lbs.
B. Dec. 5, 1955, Thunder Bay, Ont. Center, Shoots L

YEAR	TEAM & LEAGUE		GP	G	A	PTS	PIM
1975-76	BOS	N	1	0	0	0	0
1978-79	BIRM	W	80	20	33	53	67
1979-80	ATL	N	3	0	0	0	2
3 yrs.		N Totals:	4	0	0	0	2
		W Totals:	80	20	33	53	67

Signed as free agent by **Atlanta** Oct. 9, 1979.

Bruce Affleck

AFFLECK, ROBERT BRUCE 6', 205 lbs.
B. May 5, 1964, Salmon Arm, B.C. Defense, Shoots L

YEAR	TEAM & LEAGUE		GP	G	A	PTS	PIM
1974-75	STL	N	13	0	2	2	4
1975-76			80	4	26	30	20
1976-77			80	5	20	25	24
1977-78			75	4	14	18	26
1978-79			26	1	3	4	12
1979-80	VAN	N	5	0	1	1	0
6 yrs.		N Totals:	279	14	66	80	86
PLAYOFFS							
1974-75	STL	N	1	0	0	0	0
1975-76			3	0	0	0	0
1976-77			4	0	0	0	0
3 yrs.		N Totals:	8	0	0	0	0

Traded to **St. Louis** by California for Frank Spring, Jan. 9, 1975. Sold by St. Louis with Gord Buynak to **Vancouver** Nov. 6, 1979. Sold to **St. Louis** by Vancouver with Gord Buynak, Feb. 28, 1980.

Kevin Ahearn

AHEARN, KEVIN 5'10", 160 lbs.
B. June 20, 1948, Milton, Mass. Left Wing, Shoots L

YEAR	TEAM & LEAGUE		GP	G	A	PTS	PIM
1972-73	NE	W	78	20	22	42	18
PLAYOFFS							
1972-73	NE	W	14	1	2	3	9

Fred Ahern

AHERN, FREDERICK VINCENT JR. 6', 180 lbs.
B. Feb. 12, 1952, Boston, Mass. Right Wing, Shoots R

YEAR	TEAM & LEAGUE		GP	G	A	PTS	PIM
1974-75	CALIF	N	3	2	1	3	0
1975-76			44	17	8	25	43
1976-77	CLEVE	N	25	4	4	8	20
1977-78			36	3	4	7	48
	COLO	N	38	5	13	18	19
	2 team total		74	8	17	25	67
4 yrs.		N Totals:	146	31	30	61	130
PLAYOFFS							
1977-78	COLO	N	2	0	1	1	2

Traded to **Colorado** by Cleveland with Ralph Klassen for Rick Jodzio and Chuck Arnason, Jan. 9, 1978. Sold to **Cleveland** by Colorado, May 11, 1978. Put on **Minnesota** Reserve List after Cleveland-Minnesota Dispersal Draft, June 15, 1978.

Ahlin

AHLIN
B. Unknown Forward

YEAR	TEAM & LEAGUE		GP	G	A	PTS	PIM
1937-38	CHI	N	1	0	0	0	0

Chris Ahrens

AHRENS, CHRIS ALFRED 6', 185 lbs.
B. July 31, 1952, San Bernadino, Ca. Defense, Shoots R

YEAR	TEAM & LEAGUE		GP	G	A	PTS	PIM
1973-74	**MINN**	**N**	3	0	1	1	0
1974-75			44	0	2	2	7
1975-76			2	0	0	0	2
1976-77			2	0	0	0	5
1977-78			1	0	0	0	0
	EDM	**W**	4	0	0	0	15
	2 team total		5	0	0	0	15
5 yrs.		**N Totals:**	52	0	3	3	14
		W Totals:	4	0	0	0	15

PLAYOFFS

YEAR	TEAM & LEAGUE		GP	G	A	PTS	PIM
1972-73	**MINN**	**N**	1	0	0	0	0

Lloyd Ailsby

AILSBY, LLOYD HAROLD 5'11", 194 lbs.
B. May 11, 1917, Lac Pelletier, Sask. Defense, Shoots L

YEAR	TEAM & LEAGUE		GP	G	A	PTS	PIM
1951-52	**NYR**	**N**	3	0	0	0	2

Clint Albright

ALBRIGHT, CLINTON HOWARD 6'2", 180 lbs.
B. Feb. 28, 1926, Winnipeg, Man. Center, Shoots L

YEAR	TEAM & LEAGUE		GP	G	A	PTS	PIM
1948-49	**NYR**	**N**	59	14	5	19	19

Gary Aldcorn

ALDCORN, GARY WILLIAM 5'11", 180 lbs.
B. Mar. 7, 1935, Shaunavon, Sask. Shoots L

YEAR	TEAM & LEAGUE		GP	G	A	PTS	PIM
1956-57	**TOR**	**N**	22	5	1	6	4
1957-58			59	10	14	24	12
1958-59			5	0	3	3	2
1959-60	**DET**	**N**	70	22	29	51	32
1960-61			49	2	6	8	16
	BOS	**N**	21	2	3	5	12
	2 team total		70	4	9	13	28
5 yrs.		**N Totals:**	226	41	56	97	78

PLAYOFFS

YEAR	TEAM & LEAGUE		GP	G	A	PTS	PIM
1959-60	**DET**	**N**	6	1	2	3	4

Drafted by **Detroit** from Toronto, June 10, 1959. Traded to **Boston** with Murray Oliver and Tom McCarthy by Detroit, for Vic Stasiuk and Leo Labine, Jan., 1961.

Claire Alexander

ALEXANDER, CLAIRE ARTHUR 6'1", 175 lbs.
B. June 16, 1945, Collingwood, Ont. Defense, Shoots R

YEAR	TEAM & LEAGUE		GP	G	A	PTS	PIM
1974-75	**TOR**	**N**	42	7	11	18	12
1975-76			33	2	6	8	6
1976-77			48	1	12	13	12
1977-78	**VAN**	**N**	32	8	18	26	6
1978-79	**EDM**	**W**	54	8	23	31	16
5 yrs.		**N Totals:**	155	18	47	65	36
		W Totals:	54	8	23	31	16

PLAYOFFS

YEAR	TEAM & LEAGUE		GP	G	A	PTS	PIM
1974-75	**TOR**	**N**	7	0	0	0	0
1975-76			9	2	4	6	4
2 yrs.		**N Totals:**	16	2	4	6	4

Sold to **Vancouver** by Toronto, Jan. 29, 1978.

Art Alexandre

ALEXANDRE, ARTHUR
Forward, Shoots R

YEAR	TEAM & LEAGUE		GP	G	A	PTS	PIM
1931-32	**MONT**	**N**	10	0	2	2	8
1932-33			1	0	0	0	0
2 yrs.		**N Totals:**	11	0	2	2	8

PLAYOFFS

YEAR	TEAM & LEAGUE		GP	G	A	PTS	PIM
1931-32	**MONT**	**N**	4	0	0	0	0

George Allen

ALLEN, GEORGE TRENHOLM 5'10", 162 lbs.
B. July 27, 1914, Bayfield, N.B. Defense, Shoots L

YEAR	TEAM & LEAGUE		GP	G	A	PTS	PIM
1938-39	**NYR**	**N**	19	6	6	12	10
1939-40	**CHI**	**N**	48	10	12	22	26
1940-41			44	14	17	31	22
1941-42			43	7	13	20	31
1942-43			47	10	14	24	26
1943-44			45	17	24	41	36
1945-46			44	11	15	26	16
1946-47	**MONT**	**N**	49	7	14	21	12
8 yrs.		**N Totals:**	339	82	115	197	179

PLAYOFFS

YEAR	TEAM & LEAGUE		GP	G	A	PTS	PIM
1938-39	**NYR**	**N**	7	0	0	0	4
1939-40	**CHI**	**N**	2	0	0	0	0
1940-41			5	2	2	4	10
1941-42			3	1	1	2	0
1943-44			9	5	4	9	8
1945-46			4	0	0	0	4
1946-47	**MONT**	**N**	11	1	3	4	6
7 yrs.		**N Totals:**	41	9	10	19	32

Jeff Allen

ALLEN, JEFFREY

YEAR	TEAM & LEAGUE		GP	G	A	PTS	PIM
1977-78	**CLEVE**	**N**	4	0	0	0	2
	CIN	**W**	2	0	0	0	0
	2 team total		6	0	0	0	2

Keith Allen

ALLEN, COURTNEY KEITH (Bingo) 5'11", 190 lbs.
B. Aug. 21, 1923, Saskatoon, Sask. Defense, Shoots L

YEAR	TEAM & LEAGUE		GP	G	A	PTS	PIM
1953-54	**DET**	**N**	10	0	4	4	2
1954-55			18	0	0	0	6
2 yrs.		**N Totals:**	28	0	4	4	8

PLAYOFFS

YEAR	TEAM & LEAGUE		GP	G	A	PTS	PIM
1953-54*	**DET**	**N**	5	0	0	0	0

Viv Allen

ALLEN, VIVAN MARINER (Squee) 5'6", 140 lbs.
B. Sept. 9, 1916, Bayfield, N.B. Right Wing, Shoots R

YEAR	TEAM & LEAGUE		GP	G	A	PTS	PIM
1940-41	**NYA**	**N**	6	0	1	1	0

Steve Alley

ALLEY, STEVE 6', 185 lbs.
B. Dec. 29, 1953, Anoka, Minn. Left Wing, Shoots L

YEAR	TEAM & LEAGUE		GP	G	A	PTS	PIM
1977-78	**BIRM**	**W**	27	8	12	20	11
1978-79			78	17	24	41	36
1979-80	**HART**	**N**	7	1	1	2	0
1980-81			8	2	2	4	11
4 yrs.		**N Totals:**	15	3	3	6	11
		W Totals:	105	25	36	61	47

PLAYOFFS

YEAR	TEAM & LEAGUE		GP	G	A	PTS	PIM
1977-78	**BIRM**	**W**	5	1	0	1	5
1979-80	**HART**	**N**	3	0	1	1	0
2 yrs.		**N Totals:**	3	0	1	1	0
		W Totals:	5	1	0	1	5

Mike Allison

ALLISON, MICHAEL EARNEST 6', 200 lbs.
B. Mar. 28, 1961, Fort Frances, Ont. Left Wing, Shoots R

YEAR	TEAM & LEAGUE		GP	G	A	PTS	PIM
1980-81	**NYR**	**N**	75	26	38	64	83
1981-82			48	7	15	22	74
1982-83			39	11	9	20	37
3 yrs.		**N Totals:**	162	44	62	106	194

PLAYOFFS

YEAR	TEAM & LEAGUE		GP	G	A	PTS	PIM
1980-81	**NYR**	**N**	14	3	1	4	20
1981-82			10	1	3	4	18
1982-83			8	0	5	5	10

Mike Allison continued

YEAR	TEAM & LEAGUE		GP	G	A	PTS	PIM
3 yrs.		N Totals:	32	4	9	13	48

Ray Allison

ALLISON, RAYMOND PETER 6', 199 lbs.
B. Mar. 4, 1959, Cranbrook, B.C. Right Wing, Shoots R

YEAR	TEAM & LEAGUE		GP	G	A	PTS	PIM
1979-80	HART	N	64	16	12	28	13
1980-81			6	1	0	1	0
1981-82	PHI	N	51	17	37	54	104
1982-83			67	21	30	51	57
4 yrs.		N Totals:	188	55	79	134	174
PLAYOFFS							
1979-80	HART	N	2	0	1	1	0
1981-82	PHI	N	3	2	0	2	2
1982-83			3	0	1	1	12
3 yrs.		N Totals:	8	2	2	4	14

Traded to **Philadelphia** by Hartford with Fred Arthur and Hartford's first (Ron Sutter), second (later transferred to Toronto, Peter Ihnacak), and third round (Miroslav Dvorak) choices in the 1982 Entry Draft for Rick MacLeish, Blake Wesley, Don Gillen and Philadelphia's first (Paul Lawless), second (Mark Paterson) and third-round (Kevin Dineen) choices in the 1982 Entry Draft, July 3, 1981.

Bill Allum

ALLUM, WILLIAM JAMES DOUGLAS 5'11", 194 lbs.
B. Oct. 9, 1916, Winnipeg, Man. Defense, Shoots L

YEAR	TEAM & LEAGUE		GP	G	A	PTS	PIM
1940-41	NYR	N	1	0	1	1	0

Dave Amadio

AMADIO, DAVID A. 6'1", 205 lbs.
B. Apr. 23, 1939, Glace Bay, N.S. Defense, Shoots R

YEAR	TEAM & LEAGUE		GP	G	A	PTS	PIM
1957-58	DET	N	2	0	0	0	2
1967-68	LA	N	58	4	6	10	101
1968-69			65	1	5	6	60
3 yrs.		N Totals:	125	5	11	16	163
PLAYOFFS							
1967-68	LA	N	7	0	2	2	8
1968-69			9	1	0	1	10
2 yrs.		N Totals:	16	1	2	3	18

Mike Amodeo

AMODEO, MICHAEL 5'10", 190 lbs.
B. June 22, 1952, Toronto, Ont. Defense, Shoots L

YEAR	TEAM & LEAGUE		GP	G	A	PTS	PIM
1972-73	OTTA	W	61	1	14	15	77
1973-74	TOR	W	76	0	11	11	82
1974-75			64	1	13	14	50
1975-76			31	4	8	12	35
1977-78	WINN	W	3	1	1	2	0
1978-79			64	4	18	22	29
1979-80	WINN	N	19	0	0	0	2
7 yrs.		N Totals:	19	0	0	0	2
		W Totals:	299	11	65	76	273
PLAYOFFS							
1972-73	OTTA	W	5	0	1	1	10
1973-74	TOR	W	12	0	2	2	26
1974-75			3	0	1	1	4
1977-78	WINN	W	7	1	3	4	19
4 yrs.		W Totals:	27	1	7	8	59

Bill Anderson

ANDERSON, WILLIAM
B. Dec. 13, 1912, Tilsonberg, Ont. Defense

YEAR	TEAM & LEAGUE		GP	G	A	PTS	PIM
PLAYOFFS							
1942-43	BOS	N	1	0	0	0	0

Dale Anderson

ANDERSON, DALE NORMAN 6'3", 190 lbs.
B. Mar. 5, 1932, Regina, Sask. Defense, Shoots L

YEAR	TEAM & LEAGUE		GP	G	A	PTS	PIM
1956-57	DET	N	13	0	0	0	6
PLAYOFFS							
1956-57	DET	N	2	0	0	0	0

Doug Anderson

ANDERSON, DOUGLAS 5'7", 157 lbs.
B. Oct. 20, 1927, Edmonton, Alta. Center, Shoots L

YEAR	TEAM & LEAGUE		GP	G	A	PTS	PIM
PLAYOFFS							
1952-53*	MONT	N	2	0	0	0	0

Earl Anderson

ANDERSON, EARL ORLIN 6', 185 lbs.
B. Feb. 24, 1951, Roseau, Minn. Right Wing, Shoots R

YEAR	TEAM & LEAGUE		GP	G	A	PTS	PIM
1974-75	DET	N	45	7	3	10	12
	BOS	N	19	2	4	6	4
	2 team total		64	9	7	16	16
1975-76			5	0	1	1	2
1976-77			40	10	11	21	4
3 yrs.		N Totals:	109	19	19	38	22
PLAYOFFS							
1974-75	BOS	N	3	0	1	1	0
1976-77			2	0	0	0	0
2 yrs.		N Totals:	5	0	1	1	0

Traded to **Boston** by Detroit with Hank Nowak for Walt McKechnie and Boston's third choice (Clark Hamilton) in 1975 Amateur Draft, Feb. 18, 1975.

Glenn Anderson

ANDERSON, GLENN CHRIS (Andy) 5'11", 175 lbs.
B. Oct. 2, 1960, Vancouver, B.C. Right Wing, Shoots L

YEAR	TEAM & LEAGUE		GP	G	A	PTS	PIM
1980-81	EDM	N	58	30	23	53	24
1981-82			80	38	67	105	71
1982-83			72	48	56	104	70
3 yrs.		N Totals:	210	116	146	262	165
PLAYOFFS							
1980-81	EDM	N	9	5	7	12	12
1981-82			5	2	5	7	8
1982-83			16	10	10	20	32
3 yrs.		N Totals:	30	17	22	39	52

Jim Anderson

ANDERSON, JAMES WILLIAM 5'9", 170 lbs.
B. Dec. 1, 1930, Pembroke, Ont. Left Wing, Shoots L

YEAR	TEAM & LEAGUE		GP	G	A	PTS	PIM
1967-68	LA	N	7	1	2	3	2
PLAYOFFS							
1968-69	LA	N	4	0	0	0	2

John Anderson

ANDERSON, JOHN MURRAY 5'11", 190 lbs.
B. Mar. 28, 1957, Toronto, Ont. Right Wing, Shoots R

YEAR	TEAM & LEAGUE		GP	G	A	PTS	PIM
1977-78	TOR	N	17	1	2	3	2
1978-79			71	15	11	26	10
1979-80			74	25	28	53	22
1980-81			75	17	26	43	31
1981-82			69	31	26	57	30
1982-83			80	31	49	80	24
6 yrs.		N Totals:	386	120	142	262	119
PLAYOFFS							
1977-78	TOR	N	2	0	0	0	0
1978-79			6	0	2	2	0
1979-80			3	1	1	2	0
1980-81			2	0	0	0	0
1982-83			4	2	4	6	0

John Anderson continued

YEAR	TEAM & LEAGUE		GP	G	A	PTS	PIM
5 yrs.		N Totals:	17	3	7	10	0

Murray Anderson

ANDERSON, MURRAY CRAIG 5'10", 175 lbs.
B. Aug. 28, 1949, The Pas, Man. Defense, Shoots L

YEAR	TEAM & LEAGUE		GP	G	A	PTS	PIM
1974-75	**WASH**	**N**	40	0	1	1	68

Sold to **Minnesota** by Montreal, May 29, 1973. Drafted by **Washington** from Minnesota in Expansion Draft, June 12, 1974.

Perry Anderson

ANDERSON, PERRY LYNN 6', 194 lbs.
B. Oct. 14, 1961, Barrie, Ont. Left Wing, Shoots L

YEAR	TEAM & LEAGUE		GP	G	A	PTS	PIM
1981-82	**STL**	**N**	5	1	2	3	0
1982-83			18	5	2	7	14
2 yrs.		**N Totals:**	23	6	4	10	14

PLAYOFFS

YEAR	TEAM & LEAGUE		GP	G	A	PTS	PIM
1981-82	**STL**	**N**	10	2	0	2	4

Ron Anderson

ANDERSON, RONALD CHESTER (Goings) 6', 180 lbs.
B. July 29, 1945, Red Deer, Alta. Right Wing, Shoots R

YEAR	TEAM & LEAGUE		GP	G	A	PTS	PIM
1967-68	**DET**	**N**	18	2	0	2	13
1968-69			7	0	0	0	8
	LA	**N**	56	3	5	8	26
	2 team total		63	3	5	8	34
1969-70	**STL**	**N**	59	9	9	18	36
1970-71	**BUF**	**N**	74	14	12	26	44
1971-72			37	0	4	4	19
1972-73	**ALTA**	**W**	73	14	15	29	43
1973-74	**EDM**	**W**	19	5	2	7	6
7 yrs.		**N Totals:**	251	28	30	58	146
		W Totals:	92	19	17	36	49

PLAYOFFS

YEAR	TEAM & LEAGUE		GP	G	A	PTS	PIM
1969-70	**STL**	**N**	1	0	0	0	0

Traded by Detroit to **Los Angeles** for Poul Popeil, Nov. 12, 1968. Drafted by **St. Louis** from Los Angeles, June 11, 1969. Traded to **Buffalo** by St. Louis for Craig Cameron, Oct. 2, 1970.

Ron Anderson

ANDERSON, RONALD HENRY 5'10", 165 lbs.
B. Jan. 21, 1950, Moncton, N.B. Right Wing, Shoots R

YEAR	TEAM & LEAGUE		GP	G	A	PTS	PIM
1974-75	**WASH**	**N**	28	9	7	16	8

Drafted by **Washington** from Boston in Expansion Draft, June 12, 1974.

Ron Anderson

ANDERSON, RONALD FRANK 6', 190 lbs.
B. Nov. 15, 1948, Dryden, Ont. Defense, Shoots L

YEAR	TEAM & LEAGUE		GP	G	A	PTS	PIM
1972-73	**CHI**	**W**	74	3	26	29	34
1973-74			2	0	0	0	0
1974-75	**CLEVE**	**W**	39	0	9	9	10
3 yrs.		**W Totals:**	115	3	35	38	44

Russ Anderson

ANDERSON, RUSSELL VINCENT 6'3", 210 lbs.
B. Feb. 12, 1955, Minneapolis, Minn. Defense, Shoots L

YEAR	TEAM & LEAGUE		GP	G	A	PTS	PIM
1976-77	**PITT**	**N**	66	2	11	13	81
1977-78			74	2	16	18	150
1978-79			72	3	13	16	93
1979-80			76	5	22	27	150
1980-81			34	3	14	17	112
1981-82			31	0	1	1	98
	HART	**N**	25	1	3	4	85
	2 team total		56	1	4	5	183
1982-83			57	0	6	6	171
7 yrs.		**N Totals:**	435	16	86	102	940

Russ Anderson continued

PLAYOFFS

YEAR	TEAM & LEAGUE		GP	G	A	PTS	PIM
1976-77	**PITT**	**N**	3	0	1	1	14
1978-79			2	0	0	0	0
1979-80			5	0	2	2	14
3 yrs.		**N Totals:**	10	0	3	3	28

Traded to **Hartford** by Pittsburgh with an eighth-round choice in 1983 Entry Draft for Rick MacLeish, Dec. 29, 1981. Signed as a free agent by **Los Angeles** Sept. 6, 1983.

Tom Anderson

ANDERSON, THOMAS LINTON (Cowboy) 5'10", 180 lbs.
B. July 9, 1910, Edinburgh, Scotland Left Wing, Shoots L
Won Hart Trophy, 1941-42

YEAR	TEAM & LEAGUE		GP	G	A	PTS	PIM
1934-35	**DET**	**N**	27	5	2	7	16
1935-36	**NYA**	**N**	24	3	2	5	20
1936-37			45	10	15	25	24
1937-38			45	4	21	25	22
1938-39			47	13	27	40	14
1939-40			48	12	19	31	22
1940-41			35	3	12	15	8
1941-42			48	12	29	41	64
8 yrs.		**N Totals:**	319	62	127	189	190

PLAYOFFS

YEAR	TEAM & LEAGUE		GP	G	A	PTS	PIM
1935-36	**NYA**	**N**	5	0	0	0	60
1937-38			6	1	4	5	2
1938-39			2	0	0	0	0
1939-40			3	1	3	4	0
4 yrs.		**N Totals:**	16	2	7	9	62

Kent-Erik Andersson

ANDERSSON, KENT-ERIK 6'2", 185 lbs.
B. May 24, 1951, Orebro, Sweden Right Wing, Shoots R

YEAR	TEAM & LEAGUE		GP	G	A	PTS	PIM
1977-78	**MINN**	**N**	73	15	18	33	4
1978-79			41	9	4	13	4
1979-80			61	9	10	19	8
1980-81			77	17	24	41	22
1981-82			70	9	12	21	18
1982-83	**NYR**	**N**	71	8	20	28	14
6 yrs.		**N Totals:**	393	67	88	155	70

PLAYOFFS

YEAR	TEAM & LEAGUE		GP	G	A	PTS	PIM
1979-80	**MINN**	**N**	13	2	4	6	2
1980-81			19	2	4	6	2
1981-82			4	0	2	2	0
1982-83	**NYR**	**N**	9	0	0	0	0
4 yrs.		**N Totals:**	45	4	10	14	4

Traded by Minnesota with Mark Johnson to **Hartford** for Jordy Douglas and Hartford's fifth round choice in the 1984 Amateur Draft, Oct. 1, 1982. Traded to **New York Rangers** by Hartford for Ed Hospodar, Oct. 1, 1982.

Steve Andrascik

ANDRASCIK, STEVE GEORGE 5'11", 200 lbs.
B. Nov. 6, 1948, Sherridon, Man. Right Wing, Shoots R

YEAR	TEAM & LEAGUE		GP	G	A	PTS	PIM
1974-75	**IND**	**W**	20	2	4	6	16
	M-B	**W**	57	4	7	11	42
	2 team total		77	6	11	17	58
1975-76	**CIN**	**W**	20	3	2	5	21
2 yrs.		**W Totals:**	97	9	13	22	79

PLAYOFFS

YEAR	TEAM & LEAGUE		GP	G	A	PTS	PIM
1971-72	**NYR**	**N**	1	0	0	0	0

Traded to **N.Y. Rangers** by Detroit for Don Luce, Nov. 2, 1970. Traded to **Pittsburgh** by N.Y. Rangers to complete earlier deal (March 2, 1973) in which N.Y. Rangers acquired Sheldon Kannegiesser.

Paul Andrea

ANDREA, PAUL LAWRENCE 5'10", 174 lbs.
B. July 31, 1941, North Sydney, N.S. Right Wing, Shoots L

YEAR	TEAM & LEAGUE		GP	G	A	PTS	PIM
1965-66	**NYR**	**N**	4	1	1	2	0
1967-68	**PITT**	**N**	65	11	21	32	2
1968-69			25	7	6	13	2

Paul Andrea continued

YEAR	TEAM & LEAGUE	GP	G	A	PTS	PIM
1970-71	CALIF N	9	1	0	1	4
	BUF N	47	11	21	32	4
	2 team total	56	12	21	33	8
1972-73	CLEVE W	66	21	30	51	12
1973-74		69	15	18	33	14
6 yrs.	N Totals:	150	31	49	80	12
	W Totals:	135	36	48	84	26
PLAYOFFS						
1972-73	CLEVE W	9	2	8	10	2
1973-74		5	1	0	1	0
2 yrs.	W Totals:	14	3	8	11	2

Traded to **Pittsburgh** with George Konik, Dunc McCallum and amateur Frank Francis by N.Y. Rangers for Larry Jeffrey, June 6, 1967. Drafted by **Oakland** from Vancouver (WHL) in Intra-League Draft, June 9, 1970. Claimed on waivers by **Buffalo** from California (Oakland), Nov. 4, 1970.

Lloyd Andrews

ANDREWS, LLOYD
B. Unknown — Forward

YEAR	TEAM & LEAGUE	GP	G	A	PTS	PIM
1921-22	TOR N	11	0	0	0	0
1922-23		23	5	4	9	10
1923-24		12	2	1	3	0
1924-25		7	1	0	1	0
4 yrs.	N Totals:	53	8	5	13	10
PLAYOFFS						
1921-22*	TOR N	7	2	0	2	5

Dave Andreychuk

ANDREYCHUK, DAVE — 6'3", 195 lbs.
B. Sept. 29, 1963, Hamilton, Ont. — Center, Shoots R

YEAR	TEAM & LEAGUE	GP	G	A	PTS	PIM
1982-83	BUF N	43	14	23	37	16
PLAYOFFS						
1982-83	BUF N	4	1	0	1	4

Ron Andruff

ANDRUFF, RONALD NICHOLAS — 6', 185 lbs.
B. July 10, 1953, Port Alberni, B.C. — Center, Shoots R

YEAR	TEAM & LEAGUE	GP	G	A	PTS	PIM
1974-75	MONT N	5	0	0	0	2
1975-76		1	0	0	0	0
1976-77	COLO N	66	4	18	22	21
1977-78		78	15	18	33	31
1978-79		3	0	0	0	0
5 yrs.	N Totals:	153	19	36	55	54
PLAYOFFS						
1977-78	COLO N	2	0	0	0	0

Sent to **Colorado** by Montreal with Sean Shanahan, Sept. 13, 1976. As completion of deal, Montreal switched first round selections with Colorado in the 1980 Entry Draft. (Montreal selected Doug Wickenheiser, Colorado selected Paul Gagne.)

Lou Angotti

ANGOTTI, LOUIS FREDERICK — 5'8", 170 lbs.
B. Jan. 16, 1938, Toronto, Ont. — Center, Shoots R

YEAR	TEAM & LEAGUE	GP	G	A	PTS	PIM
1964-65	NYR N	70	9	8	17	20
1965-66		21	2	2	4	2
	CHI N	30	4	10	14	12
	2 team total	51	6	12	18	14
1966-67		63	6	12	18	21
1967-68	PHI N	70	12	37	49	35
1968-69	PITT N	71	17	20	37	36
1969-70	CHI N	70	12	26	38	25
1970-71		65	9	16	25	19
1971-72		65	5	10	15	23
1972-73		77	15	22	37	26
1973-74	STL N	51	12	23	35	9
1974-75	CHI W	26	2	5	7	9
11 yrs.	N Totals:	653	103	186	289	228
	W Totals:	26	2	5	7	9
PLAYOFFS						
1965-66	CHI N	6	0	0	0	2

Lou Angotti continued

YEAR	TEAM & LEAGUE	GP	G	A	PTS	PIM
1966-67		6	2	1	3	2
1967-68	PHI N	7	0	0	0	2
1969-70	CHI N	8	0	0	0	0
1970-71		16	3	3	6	9
1971-72		6	0	0	0	0
1972-73		16	3	4	7	2
7 yrs.	N Totals:	65	8	8	16	17

Sold by N.Y. Rangers to **Chicago** Jan. 7, 1966. Drafted by **Philadelphia** from Chicago in Expansion Draft, June 6, 1967. Traded to **St. Louis** by Philadelphia with Ian Campbell for Darryl Edestrand and Gerry Melnyk, June 11, 1968. Traded to **Pittsburgh** by St. Louis for Ab McDonald, June ll, 1968. Traded to **St. Louis** by Pittsburgh with Pittsburgh's first choice (Gene Carr) in the 1971 Amateur Draft for Ron Schock and Craig Cameron, June 6, 1969. Drafted by **Chicago** from St. Louis, June 11, 1969. Drafted by **St. Louis** from Chicago in Intra-League Draft, June 12, 1973.

Hubie Anslow

ANSLOW, HUBERT WALLACE — 5'11", 173 lbs.
B. Mar. 23, 1926, Pembroke, Ont. — Left Wing, Shoots L

YEAR	TEAM & LEAGUE	GP	G	A	PTS	PIM
1947-48	NYR N	2	0	0	0	0

Mike Antonovich

ANTONOVICH, MICHAEL J — 5'8", 165 lbs.
B. Oct. 18, 1951, Calumet, Minn. — Center, Shoots L

YEAR	TEAM & LEAGUE	GP	G	A	PTS	PIM
1972-73	MINN W	75	20	19	39	46
1973-74		68	21	29	50	4
1974-75		67	24	26	50	20
1975-76	MINN N	12	0	2	2	8
	MINN W	57	25	21	46	18
	2 team total	69	25	23	48	26
1976-77	MINN W	42	27	21	48	28
	EDM W	7	1	1	2	0
	NE W	26	12	9	21	10
	3 team total	75	40	31	71	38
1977-78		75	32	35	67	32
1978-79		69	20	27	47	35
1979-80	HART N	5	0	1	1	2
1981-82	MINN N	2	0	0	0	0
1982-83	NJ N	30	7	7	14	11
10 yrs.	N Totals:	49	7	10	17	21
	W Totals:	486	182	188	370	193
PLAYOFFS						
1972-73	MINN W	5	2	0	2	0
1973-74		11	1	4	5	4
1974-75		12	1	4	5	2
1976-77	NE W	5	2	2	4	4
1977-78		14	10	7	17	4
1978-79		10	5	3	8	14
6 yrs.	W Totals:	57	21	20	41	28

Syl Apps

APPS, SYLVANUS MARSHALL — 6', 195 lbs.
B. Aug. 1, 1947, Toronto, Ont. — Center, Shoots R

YEAR	TEAM & LEAGUE	GP	G	A	PTS	PIM
1970-71	NYR N	31	1	2	3	11
	PITT N	31	9	16	25	21
	2 team total	62	10	18	28	32
1971-72		72	15	44	59	78
1972-73		77	29	56	85	18
1973-74		75	24	61	85	37
1974-75		79	24	55	79	43
1975-76		80	32	67	99	24
1976-77		72	18	43	61	20
1977-78		9	0	7	7	0
	LA N	70	19	26	45	18
	2 team total	79	19	33	52	18
1978-79		80	7	30	37	29
1979-80		51	5	16	21	12
10 yrs.	N Totals:	727	183	423	606	311
PLAYOFFS						
1971-72	PITT N	4	1	0	1	2
1974-75		9	2	3	5	9
1975-76		3	0	1	1	0
1976-77		3	1	0	1	12
1977-78	LA N	2	0	1	1	0

Syl Apps continued

YEAR	TEAM & LEAGUE		GP	G	A	PTS	PIM
1978-79			2	1	0	1	0
6 yrs.		N Totals:	23	5	5	10	23

Traded to **Pittsburgh** by N.Y. Rangers for Glen Sather, Jan. 26, 1971. Traded to **Los Angeles** by Pittsburgh with Hartland Monahan for Dave Schultz, Gene Carr and Los Angeles' fourth-round choice (Shane Pearsall) in the 1978 Amateur Draft, Nov. 2, 1977.

Syl Apps

APPS, CHARLES JOSEPH SYLVANUS 6', 173 lbs.
B. Jan. 18, 1915, Paris, Ont. Center, Shoots L
Won Lady Byng Trophy, 1941-42
Won Calder Trophy, 1936-37
Hall of Fame, 1961

YEAR	TEAM & LEAGUE		GP	G	A	PTS	PIM
1936-37	**TOR**	N	48	16	**29**	45	10
1937-38			47	21	**29**	50	9
1938-39			44	15	25	40	4
1939-40			27	13	17	30	5
1940-41			41	20	24	44	6
1941-42			38	18	23	41	0
1942-43			29	23	17	40	2
1945-46			40	24	16	40	2
1946-47			54	25	24	49	6
1947-48			55	26	27	53	12
10 yrs.		N Totals:	423	201	231	432	56
PLAYOFFS							
1936-37	**TOR**	N	2	0	1	1	0
1937-38			7	1	4	5	0
1938-39			10	2	6	8	10
1939-40			10	5	2	7	2
1940-41			7	3	2	5	2
1941-42*			13	5	8	13	2
1946-47*			11	5	1	6	0
1947-48*			9	4	4	8	0
8 yrs.		N Totals:	69	25	28	53	16

Al Arbour

ARBOUR, ALGER JOSEPH 6'1", 180 lbs.
B. Nov. 1, 1932, Sudbury, Ont. Defense, Shoots L
Won Jack Adams Award, 1978-79

YEAR	TEAM & LEAGUE		GP	G	A	PTS	PIM
1953-54	**DET**	N	36	0	1	1	18
1956-57			44	1	6	7	38
1957-58			69	1	6	7	104
1958-59	**CHI**	N	70	2	10	12	86
1959-60			57	1	5	6	66
1960-61			53	3	2	5	40
1961-62	**TOR**	N	52	1	5	6	68
1962-63			4	1	0	1	4
1963-64			6	0	1	1	0
1965-66			4	0	1	1	2
1967-68	**STL**	N	74	1	10	11	50
1968-69			67	1	6	7	50
1969-70			68	0	3	3	85
1970-71			22	0	2	2	6
14 yrs.		N Totals:	626	12	58	70	617
PLAYOFFS							
1955-56	**DET**	N	4	0	1	1	0
1956-57			5	0	0	0	6
1957-58			4	0	1	1	4
1958-59	**CHI**	N	6	1	2	3	26
1959-60			4	0	0	0	4
1960-61*			7	0	0	0	2
1961-62*	**TOR**	N	8	0	0	0	6
1964-65			1	0	0	0	2
1967-68	**STL**	N	14	0	3	3	10
1968-69			12	0	0	0	10
1969-70			14	0	1	1	16
1970-71			6	0	0	0	6
12 yrs.		N Totals:	85	1	8	9	92

Drafted by **Chicago** from Detroit, June, 1958. Drafted by **Toronto** from Chicago, June, 1961. Drafted by **St. Louis** from Toronto in Expansion Draft, June 6, 1967.

Amos Arbour

ARBOUR, AMOS
B. Unknown Forward

YEAR	TEAM & LEAGUE		GP	G	A	PTS	PIM
1918-19	**MONT**	N	1	0	0	0	0
1919-20			20	22	4	26	10
1920-21			22	14	3	17	40
1921-22	**HAMIL**	N	23	8	3	11	6
1922-23			23	6	1	7	6
1923-24	**TOR**	N	20	1	2	3	4
6 yrs.		N Totals:	109	51	13	64	66

Jack Arbour

ARBOUR, JOHN A.
B. Unknown Forward

YEAR	TEAM & LEAGUE		GP	G	A	PTS	PIM
1926-27	**DET**	N	37	4	1	5	46
1928-29	**TOR**	N	10	1	0	1	10
2 yrs.		N Totals:	47	5	1	6	56

John Arbour

ARBOUR, JOHN GILBERT 5'11", 195 lbs.
B. Sept. 28, 1945, Niagara Falls, Ont. Defense, Shoots L

YEAR	TEAM & LEAGUE		GP	G	A	PTS	PIM
1965-66	**BOS**	N	2	0	0	0	0
1967-68			4	0	1	1	11
1968-69	**PITT**	N	17	0	2	2	35
1970-71	**VAN**	N	13	0	0	0	12
	STL	N	53	1	6	7	81
	2 team total		66	1	6	7	93
1971-72			17	0	0	0	10
1972-73	**MINN**	W	76	6	27	33	188
1973-74			77	6	43	49	192
1974-75			71	11	43	54	67
1975-76	**D-O**	W	34	2	13	15	49
	MINN	W	7	0	4	4	14
	2 team total		41	2	17	19	63
1976-77			33	3	19	22	22
	CALG	W	37	1	15	16	38
	2 team total		70	4	34	38	60
10 yrs.		N Totals:	106	1	9	10	149
		W Totals:	335	29	164	193	570
PLAYOFFS							
1970-71	**STL**	N	5	0	0	0	0
1972-73	**MINN**	W	5	0	1	1	12
1973-74			11	3	6	9	27
1974-75			12	0	6	6	23
4 yrs.		N Totals:	5	0	0	0	0
		W Totals:	28	3	13	16	62

Sold to **Pittsburgh** by Boston with Jean Pronovost, May 21, 1968. Sold to **Vancouver** by Pittsburgh, June 10, 1970. Sold to **St. Louis** by Vancouver, Dec. 3, 1970.

Ty Arbour

ARBOUR, ERNEST
B. Unknown Forward

YEAR	TEAM & LEAGUE		GP	G	A	PTS	PIM
1926-27	**PITT**	N	40	7	8	15	10
1927-28			7	0	0	0	0
	CHI	N	32	5	5	10	32
	2 team total		39	5	5	10	32
1928-29			42	3	4	7	32
1929-30			44	10	8	18	26
1930-31			38	3	3	6	12
5 yrs.		N Totals:	203	28	28	56	112
PLAYOFFS							
1929-30	**CHI**	N	2	1	0	1	0
1930-31			9	1	0	1	6
2 yrs.		N Totals:	11	2	0	2	6

Michel Archambault

ARCHAMBAULT, MICHEL JOSEPH 5'8", 160 lbs.
B. Sept. 27, 1950, St. Hyacinthe, Que. Left Wing, Shoots L

YEAR	TEAM & LEAGUE		GP	G	A	PTS	PIM
1972-73	**QUE**	W	57	12	25	37	36
1976-77	**CHI**	N	3	0	0	0	0

Michel Archambault *continued*

YEAR	TEAM	LEAGUE	GP	G	A	PTS	PIM
2 yrs.		**N Totals:**	3	0	0	0	0
		W Totals:	57	12	25	37	36

Ronald Areshenkoff

ARESHENKOFF, RONALD 6', 175 lbs.
B. June 13, 1957, Grand Forks, B.C. Center, Shoots L

YEAR	TEAM	LEAGUE	GP	G	A	PTS	PIM
1979-80	**EDM**	**N**	4	0	0	0	0

Claimed by **Edmonton** from Buffalo in Expansion Draft, June 13, 1979. Traded to **Philadelphia** along with Edmonton's tenth round choice in 1980 Entry Draft (Bob O'Brien) by Edmonton for Barry Dean, June 11, 1980.

Bob Armstrong

ARMSTRONG, ROBERT RICHARD 6'1", 180 lbs.
B. Apr. 17, 1931, Toronto, Ont. Defense, Shoots R

YEAR	TEAM	LEAGUE	GP	G	A	PTS	PIM
1950-51	**BOS**	**N**	2	0	0	0	2
1952-53			55	0	8	8	45
1953-54			64	2	10	12	81
1954-55			57	1	3	4	38
1955-56			68	0	12	12	122
1956-57			57	1	15	16	79
1957-58			47	1	4	5	66
1958-59			60	1	9	10	50
1959-60			69	5	14	19	96
1960-61			54	0	10	10	72
1961-62			9	2	1	3	20
11 yrs.		**N Totals:**	542	13	86	99	671

PLAYOFFS

YEAR	TEAM	LEAGUE	GP	G	A	PTS	PIM
1951-52	**BOS**	**N**	5	0	0	0	2
1952-53			11	1	1	2	10
1953-54			4	0	1	1	0
1954-55			5	0	0	0	2
1956-57			10	0	3	3	10
1958-59			7	0	2	2	4
6 yrs.		**N Totals:**	42	1	7	8	28

George Armstrong

ARMSTRONG, GEORGE EDWARD (The Chief)
6'1", 194 lbs.
B. July 6, 1930, Bowlands, Ont. Right Wing, Shoots R
Hall of Fame, 1975

YEAR	TEAM	LEAGUE	GP	G	A	PTS	PIM
1949-50	**TOR**	**N**	2	0	0	0	0
1951-52			20	3	3	6	30
1952-53			52	14	11	25	54
1953-54			63	17	15	32	60
1954-55			66	10	18	28	80
1955-56			67	16	32	48	97
1956-57			54	18	26	44	37
1957-58			59	17	25	42	93
1958-59			59	20	16	36	37
1959-60			70	23	28	51	60
1960-61			47	14	19	33	21
1961-62			70	21	32	53	27
1962-63			70	19	24	43	27
1963-64			66	20	17	37	14
1964-65			59	15	22	37	14
1965-66			70	16	35	51	12
1966-67			70	9	24	33	26
1967-68			62	13	21	34	4
1968-69			53	11	16	27	10
1969-70			49	13	15	28	12
1970-71			59	7	18	25	6
21 yrs.		**N Totals:**	1187	296	417	713	721

PLAYOFFS

YEAR	TEAM	LEAGUE	GP	G	A	PTS	PIM
1951-52	**TOR**	**N**	4	0	0	0	2
1953-54			5	1	0	1	2
1954-55			4	1	0	1	40
1955-56			5	4	2	6	0
1958-59			12	0	4	4	10
1959-60			10	1	4	5	4
1960-61			5	1	1	2	0
1961-62*			12	7	5	12	2
1962-63*			10	3	6	9	4

George Armstrong *continued*

YEAR	TEAM	LEAGUE	GP	G	A	PTS	PIM
1963-64*			14	5	8	13	10
1964-65			6	1	0	1	4
1965-66			4	0	1	1	4
1966-67*			9	2	1	3	6
1968-69			4	0	0	0	0
1970-71			6	0	2	2	0
15 yrs.		**N Totals:**	110	26	34	60	88

Murray Armstrong

ARMSTRONG, MURRAY ALEXANDER 5'10", 170 lbs.
B. Jan. 1, 1916, Manor, Sask. Center, Shoots L

YEAR	TEAM	LEAGUE	GP	G	A	PTS	PIM
1937-38	**TOR**	**N**	9	0	0	0	0
1938-39			3	0	1	1	0
1939-40	**NYA**	**N**	47	16	20	36	12
1940-41			48	10	14	24	6
1941-42			45	6	22	28	15
1943-44	**DET**	**N**	28	12	22	34	4
1944-45			50	15	24	39	31
1945-46			40	8	18	26	4
8 yrs.		**N Totals:**	270	67	121	188	72

PLAYOFFS

YEAR	TEAM	LEAGUE	GP	G	A	PTS	PIM
1937-38	**TOR**	**N**	3	0	0	0	0
1939-40	**NYA**	**N**	3	0	0	0	0
1943-44	**DET**	**N**	5	0	2	2	0
1944-45			14	4	2	6	2
1945-46			5	0	2	2	0
5 yrs.		**N Totals:**	30	4	6	10	2

Red Armstrong

ARMSTRONG, NORMAN GERRARD 5'11", 205 lbs.
B. Oct. 17, 1938, Owen Sound, Ont. Shoots L

YEAR	TEAM	LEAGUE	GP	G	A	PTS	PIM
1962-63	**TOR**	**N**	7	1	1	2	2

Chuck Arnason

ARNASON, ERNEST CHARLES 5'10", 185 lbs.
B. July 15, 1951, Dauphin, Man. Right Wing, Shoots R

YEAR	TEAM	LEAGUE	GP	G	A	PTS	PIM
1971-72	**MONT**	**N**	17	3	0	3	4
1972-73			19	1	1	2	2
1973-74	**ATL**	**N**	33	7	6	13	13
	PITT	**N**	41	13	5	18	4
	2 team total		74	20	11	31	17
1974-75			78	26	32	58	32
1975-76			30	7	3	10	14
	KC	**N**	39	14	10	24	21
	2 team total		69	21	13	34	35
1976-77	**COLO**	**N**	61	13	10	23	10
1977-78			29	4	8	12	10
	CLEVE	**N**	40	21	13	34	8
	2 team total		69	25	21	46	18
1978-79	**MINN**	**N**	1	0	0	0	0
	WASH	**N**	13	0	2	2	4
	2 team total		14	0	2	2	4
8 yrs.		**N Totals:**	401	109	90	199	122

PLAYOFFS

YEAR	TEAM	LEAGUE	GP	G	A	PTS	PIM
1974-75	**PITT**	**N**	9	2	4	6	4

Traded to **Atlanta** by Montreal for Atlanta's first choice (Rick Chartraw) in 1974 Amateur Draft, May 29, 1973. Traded to **Pittsburgh** by Atlanta with Bob Paradise for Al McDonough, Jan. 4, 1974. Traded to **Kansas City** by Pittsburgh with Steve Durbano and Pittsburgh's first choice (Paul Gardner) in 1976 Amateur Draft for Simon Nolet, Ed Gilbert and Kansas City's first choice (Blair Chapman) in same draft, Jan. 9, 1976. Traded to **Cleveland** by Colorado with Rick Jodzio for Fred Ahern and Ralph Klassen, Jan. 9, 1978. Put on **Minnesota** Reserve list after Cleveland-Minnesota Dispersal Draft, June 15, 1978. Traded to **Washington** by Minnesota for cash and future considerations, March 12, 1979. Traded to **Minnesota** by Washington for return of future considerations, April 24, 1979. Traded to **Vancouver** by Minnesota for future considerations, July 19, 1979.

Danny Arndt

ARNDT, DANIEL 5'10", 170 lbs.
B. Mar. 26, 1955, Saskatoon, Sask. Left Wing

YEAR	TEAM	LEAGUE	GP	G	A	PTS	PIM
1975-76	**NE**	**W**	69	8	8	16	10
1976-77			46	8	14	22	11
	EDM	**W**	1	0	0	0	0
	2 team total		47	8	14	22	11

Danny Arndt continued

YEAR	TEAM & LEAGUE		GP	G	A	PTS	PIM
1977-78	**BIRM**	W	4	0	1	1	0
3 yrs.		**W Totals:**	120	16	23	39	21
PLAYOFFS							
1975-76	**NE**	W	8	0	0	0	0

Scott Arniel

ARNIEL, SCOTT 6'1", 170 lbs.
B. Sept. 17, 1962, Cornwall, Ont. Center, Shoots L

YEAR	TEAM & LEAGUE		GP	G	A	PTS	PIM
1981-82	**WINN**	N	17	1	8	9	14
1982-83			75	13	5	18	46
2 yrs.		**N Totals:**	92	14	13	27	60
PLAYOFFS							
1981-82	**WINN**	N	3	0	0	0	0
1982-83			2	0	0	0	0
2 yrs.		**N Totals:**	5	0	0	0	0

Fred Arthur

ARTHUR, FREDERICK EDWARD 6'5", 210 lbs.
B. Mar. 6, 1961, Toronto, Ont. Defense, Shoots L

YEAR	TEAM & LEAGUE		GP	G	A	PTS	PIM
1980-81	**HART**	N	3	0	0	0	0
1981-82	**PHI**	N	74	1	7	8	47
2 yrs.		**N Totals:**	77	1	7	8	47
PLAYOFFS							
1981-82	**PHI**	N	4	0	0	0	2

Traded to **Philadelphia** by Hartford with Ray Allison and Hartford's first (Ron Sutter) and third-round (Miroslav Dvorak) choices in the 1982 Entry Draft for Rick MacLeish, Blake Wesley, Don Gillen and Philadelphia's first (Paul Lawless), second (Mark Paterson) and third-round (Kevin Dineen) choices in the 1982 Entry Draft, July 3, 1981.

John Arundel

ARUNDEL, JOHN O'GORMAN 5'11", 181 lbs.
B. Nov. 4, 1927, Winnipeg, Man. Defense, Shoots L

YEAR	TEAM & LEAGUE		GP	G	A	PTS	PIM
1949-50	**TOR**	N	3	0	0	0	0

Bob Ash

ASH, ROBERT JOHN (Squeaky) 5'9", 170 lbs.
B. Sept. 29, 1943, Broadview, Sask. Defense, Shoots L

YEAR	TEAM & LEAGUE		GP	G	A	PTS	PIM
1972-73	**WINN**	W	75	3	14	17	39
1973-74			60	2	18	20	30
1974-75	**IND**	W	64	1	14	15	19
3 yrs.		**W Totals:**	199	6	46	52	88
PLAYOFFS							
1972-73	**WINN**	W	13	1	3	4	4
1973-74			4	0	1	1	2
2 yrs.		**W Totals:**	17	1	4	5	6

Barry Ashbee

ASHBEE, WILLIAM BARRY 5'10", 180 lbs.
B. July 28, 1939, Weston, Ont. Defense, Shoots R

YEAR	TEAM & LEAGUE		GP	G	A	PTS	PIM
1965-66	**BOS**	N	14	0	3	3	14
1970-71	**PHI**	N	64	4	23	27	44
1971-72			73	6	14	20	75
1972-73			64	1	17	18	106
1973-74			69	4	13	17	52
5 yrs.		**N Totals:**	284	15	70	85	291
PLAYOFFS							
1972-73	**PHI**	N	11	0	4	4	20
1973-74*			6	0	0	0	2
2 yrs.		**N Totals:**	17	0	4	4	22

Sold to **Philadelphia** by Hershey (AHL), May 22, 1970.

Don Ashby

ASHBY, DONALD ALAN (Ash) 6'1", 185 lbs.
B. Mar. 8, 1955, Kamloops, B.C. Center, Shoots L

YEAR	TEAM & LEAGUE		GP	G	A	PTS	PIM
1975-76	**TOR**	N	50	6	15	21	10
1976-77			76	19	23	42	24
1977-78			12	1	2	3	0
1978-79			3	0	0	0	0
	COLO	N	12	2	3	5	0
	2 team total		15	2	3	5	0
1979-80			11	0	1	1	4
	EDM	N	18	10	9	19	0
	2 team total		29	10	10	20	4
1980-81			6	2	3	5	2
6 yrs.		**N Totals:**	188	40	56	96	40
PLAYOFFS							
1976-77	**TOR**	N	9	1	0	1	4
1979-80	**EDM**	N	3	0	0	0	0
2 yrs.		**N Totals:**	12	1	0	1	4

Traded to **Colorado** by Toronto with Trevor Johansen for Paul Gardner, March 13, 1979. Traded to **Edmonton** by Colorado for Bobby Schmautz, Feb. 25, 1980.

Brent Ashton

ASHTON, BRENT KENNETH 6'1", 210 lbs.
B. May 18, 1960, Saskatoon, Sask. Left Wing, Shoots L

YEAR	TEAM & LEAGUE		GP	G	A	PTS	PIM
1979-80	**VAN**	N	47	5	14	19	11
1980-81			77	18	11	29	57
1981-82	**COLO**	N	80	24	36	60	76
1982-83	**NJ**	N	76	14	19	33	47
4 yrs.		**N Totals:**	280	61	80	141	191
PLAYOFFS							
1979-80	**VAN**	N	4	1	0	1	6
1980-81			3	0	0	0	2
2 yrs.		**N Totals:**	7	1	0	1	8

Traded to **Winnipeg** by Vancouver with Vancouver's fourth round choice (Tom Martin) in the 1982 Entry Draft as compensation for the signing of Ivan Hlinka, July 15, 1981.

Ron Ashton

ASHTON, RONALD 6'2", 210 lbs.
B. May 11, 1954, Regina, Sask. Left Wing, Shoots L

YEAR	TEAM & LEAGUE		GP	G	A	PTS	PIM
1974-75	**WINN**	W	36	1	3	4	66

Frank Ashworth

ASHWORTH, FRANK 5'9", 165 lbs.
B. Oct. 16, 1927, Moose Jaw, Sask. Center, Shoots L

YEAR	TEAM & LEAGUE		GP	G	A	PTS	PIM
1946-47	**CHI**	N	18	5	4	9	2

Duke Asmundson

ASMUNDSON, DUKE 6'2", 195 lbs.
B. Aug. 17, 1943, Vita, Man. Defense, Shoots R

YEAR	TEAM & LEAGUE		GP	G	A	PTS	PIM
1972-73	**WINN**	W	76	2	14	16	54
1973-74			72	5	14	19	85
1974-75			38	4	15	19	53
1975-76			72	5	11	16	19
4 yrs.		**W Totals:**	258	16	54	70	211
PLAYOFFS							
1972-73	**WINN**	W	12	1	2	3	8
1973-74			4	0	1	1	2
1975-76			13	3	2	5	11
3 yrs.		**W Totals:**	29	4	5	9	21

Oscar Asmundson

ASMUNDSON, OSCAR 5'11½", 170 lbs.
B. Nov. 17, 1908, Red Deer, Alta. Center, Shoots R

YEAR	TEAM & LEAGUE		GP	G	A	PTS	PIM
1932-33	**NYR**	N	48	5	10	15	20
1933-34			46	2	6	8	8
1934-35	**DET**	N	3	0	0	0	0
	STL	N	11	4	7	11	2
	2 team total		14	4	7	11	2

YEAR	TEAM & LEAGUE		GP	G	A	PTS	PIM
1936-37	**NYA**	**N**	2	0	0	0	0
1937-38	**MONT**	**N**	2	0	0	0	0
5 yrs.		**N Totals:**	112	11	23	34	30
PLAYOFFS							
1932-33*	**NYR**	**N**	8	0	2	2	4
1933-34			1	0	0	0	0
2 yrs.		**N Totals:**	9	0	2	2	4

Walt Atanas

ATANAS, WALTER (Ants) 5'8½", 168 lbs.
B. Dec. 22, 1922, Hamilton, Ont. Right Wing, Shoots R

YEAR	TEAM & LEAGUE		GP	G	A	PTS	PIM
1944-45	**NYR**	**N**	49	13	8	21	40

Steve Atkinson

ATKINSON, STEVEN JOHN 5'11", 170 lbs.
B. Oct. 16, 1948, Toronto, Ont. Right Wing, Shoots R

YEAR	TEAM & LEAGUE		GP	G	A	PTS	PIM
1968-69	**BOS**	**N**	1	0	0	0	0
1970-71	**BUF**	**N**	57	20	18	38	12
1971-72			67	14	10	24	26
1972-73			61	9	9	18	36
1973-74			70	6	10	16	22
1974-75	**WASH**	**N**	46	11	4	15	8
1975-76	**TOR**	**W**	52	2	6	8	22
7 yrs.		**N Totals:**	302	60	51	111	104
		W Totals:	52	2	6	8	22
PLAYOFFS							
1972-73	**BUF**	**N**	1	0	0	0	0

Claimed on waivers by **Buffalo** from Boston, Nov. 1, 1970. Drafted by **Washington** from Buffalo in Expansion Draft, June 12, 1974.

Bob Attwell

ATTWELL, ROBERT ALLAN 6', 192 lbs.
B. Dec. 26, 1959, Spokane, Wash. Right Wing, Shoots R

YEAR	TEAM & LEAGUE		GP	G	A	PTS	PIM
1979-80	**COLO**	**N**	7	1	1	2	0
1980-81			15	0	4	4	0
2 yrs.		**N Totals:**	22	1	5	6	0

Ron Attwell

ATTWELL, RONALD ALLAN 6'2", 208 lbs.
B. Feb. 9, 1935, Humber Summit, Ont. Center, Shoots R

YEAR	TEAM & LEAGUE		GP	G	A	PTS	PIM
1967-68	**STL**	**N**	18	1	7	8	6
	NYR	**N**	3	0	0	0	2
	2 team total		21	1	7	8	8

Sold by Montreal with Pat Quinn to **St. Louis** June 14, 1967. Traded by St. Louis with Ron Stewart to **N.Y. Rangers** for Red Berenson and Barclay Plager, Nov. 29, 1967.

Norm Aubin

AUBIN, NORMAND 6', 185 lbs.
B. July 26, 1960, St. Leonard, Que. Center, Shoots L

YEAR	TEAM & LEAGUE		GP	G	A	PTS	PIM
1981-82	**TOR**	**N**	43	14	12	26	22
1982-83			26	4	1	5	8
2 yrs.		**N Totals:**	69	18	13	31	30
PLAYOFFS							
1982-83	**TOR**	**N**	1	0	0	0	0

Pierre Aubry

AUBRY, PIERRE 5'10", 175 lbs.
B. Apr. 15, 1960, Cap De La Madeleine, Que Left Wing, Shoots L

YEAR	TEAM & LEAGUE		GP	G	A	PTS	PIM
1980-81	**QUE**	**N**	1	0	0	0	0
1981-82			62	10	13	23	27
1982-83			77	7	9	16	48
3 yrs.		**N Totals:**	140	17	22	39	75
PLAYOFFS							
1981-82	**QUE**	**N**	15	1	1	2	30
1982-83			2	0	0	0	0
2 yrs.		**N Totals:**	17	1	1	2	30

Signed as free agent by **Quebec** Oct. 10, 1980.

Ossie Aubuchon

AUBUCHON, OSCAR 5'10", 175 lbs.
B. Jan. 1, 1917, St. Hyacinthe, Que. Left Wing, Shoots L

YEAR	TEAM & LEAGUE		GP	G	A	PTS	PIM
1942-43	**BOS**	**N**	3	3	0	3	0
1943-44			9	1	0	1	0
	NYR	**N**	38	15	12	27	4
	2 team total		47	16	12	28	4
2 yrs.		**N Totals:**	50	19	12	31	4
PLAYOFFS							
1942-43	**BOS**	**N**	6	1	0	1	0

Les Auge

AUGE, LES 6'1", 190 lbs.
B. May 16, 1953, St. Paul, Minn. Defense, Shoots L

YEAR	TEAM & LEAGUE		GP	G	A	PTS	PIM
1980-81	**COLO**	**N**	6	0	3	3	4

Larry Aurie

AURIE, LAURENCE 5'6", 148 lbs.
B. Sudbury, Ont. Right Wing, Shoots R

YEAR	TEAM & LEAGUE		GP	G	A	PTS	PIM
1927-28	**DET**	**N**	44	13	3	16	43
1928-29			37	1	1	2	26
1929-30			43	14	5	19	28
1930-31			41	12	6	18	23
1931-32			48	12	8	20	18
1932-33			47	12	11	23	25
1933-34			48	16	19	35	36
1934-35			48	17	19	36	24
1935-36			44	16	18	34	17
1936-37			45	**23**	20	43	20
1937-38			47	10	9	19	19
1938-39			1	1	0	1	0
12 yrs.		**N Totals:**	493	147	119	266	279
PLAYOFFS							
1928-29	**DET**	**N**	2	1	0	1	2
1931-32			2	0	0	0	0
1932-33			4	1	0	1	4
1933-34			9	3	7	10	2
1935-36*			7	1	2	3	2
5 yrs.		**N Totals:**	24	6	9	15	10

Don Awrey

AWREY, DONALD WILLIAM 6', 195 lbs.
B. July 18, 1943, Kitchener, Ont. Defense, Shoots L

YEAR	TEAM & LEAGUE		GP	G	A	PTS	PIM
1963-64	**BOS**	**N**	16	1	0	1	4
1964-65			47	2	3	5	41
1965-66			70	4	3	7	74
1966-67			4	1	0	1	6
1967-68			74	3	12	15	150
1968-69			73	0	13	13	149
1969-70			73	3	10	13	120
1970-71			74	4	21	25	141
1971-72			34	1	8	9	52
1972-73			78	2	17	19	90
1973-74	**STL**	**N**	75	5	16	21	51
1974-75			20	0	8	8	4
	MONT	**N**	56	1	11	12	58
	2 team total		76	1	19	20	62
1975-76			72	0	12	12	29
1976-77	**PITT**	**N**	79	1	12	13	40
1977-78	**NYR**	**N**	78	2	8	10	38
1978-79	**COLO**	**N**	56	1	4	5	18
16 yrs.		**N Totals:**	979	31	158	189	1065
PLAYOFFS							
1967-68	**BOS**	**N**	4	0	1	1	4
1968-69			10	0	1	1	28
1969-70*			14	0	5	5	32
1970-71			7	0	0	0	17
1971-72*			15	0	4	4	45
1972-73			4	0	0	0	6
1974-75	**MONT**	**N**	11	0	6	6	12
1976-77	**PITT**	**N**	3	0	1	1	0
1977-78	**NYR**	**N**	3	0	0	0	6
9 yrs.		**N Totals:**	71	0	18	18	150

Traded to **St. Louis** by Boston for Jake Rathwell, St. Louis' second choice in 1974 Amateur Draft (Mark Howe) and cash, Oct. 5, 1973. Traded to **Montreal** by St. Louis for Chuck Lefley, Nov. 28, 1974. Traded to **Pittsburgh** by Montreal for Pittsburgh's third choice (Richard David) in 1978 Amateur Draft and other future considerations, August 11, 1976. Negotiating rights traded to **Washington** by Pittsburgh for Bob Paradise, Oct. 1, 1977. Signed as a free agent by **N.Y. Rangers** Oct. 4, 1977. Compensation to Washington in form of cash.

Vern Ayres

AYRES, THOMAS VERNON 6'2", 220 lbs.
B. Apr. 27, 1909, Toronto, Ont. Defense, Shoots L

YEAR	TEAM & LEAGUE		GP	G	A	PTS	PIM
1930-31	**NYA**	**N**	26	2	1	3	54
1931-32			45	2	4	6	82
1932-33			48	0	3	3	97
1933-34	**MON(M)**	**N**	17	0	0	0	19
1934-35	**STL**	**N**	47	2	2	4	60
1935-36	**NYR**	**N**	28	0	4	4	38
6 yrs.		**N Totals:**	211	6	14	20	350

Pete Babando

BABANDO, PETER JOSEPH 5'9", 187 lbs.
B. May 10, 1925, Braeburn, Pa. Left Wing, Shoots L

YEAR	TEAM & LEAGUE		GP	G	A	PTS	PIM
1947-48	**BOS**	**N**	60	23	11	34	52
1948-49			58	19	14	33	34
1949-50	**DET**	**N**	56	6	6	12	25
1950-51	**CHI**	**N**	70	18	19	37	36
1951-52			49	11	14	25	29
1952-53			28	5	4	9	10
	NYR	**N**	30	4	5	9	8
	2 team total		58	9	9	18	18
6 yrs.		**N Totals:**	351	86	73	159	194
PLAYOFFS							
1947-48	**BOS**	**N**	5	1	1	2	2
1948-49			4	0	0	0	2
1949-50*	**DET**	**N**	8	2	2	4	2
3 yrs.		**N Totals:**	17	3	3	6	6

Traded to **Detroit** by Boston with Clare Martin, Lloyd Durham and Jim Peters for Bill Quackenbush and Pete Horeck, Aug. 16, 1949. Traded to **Chicago** by Detroit with Harry Lumley, Jack Stewart, Al Dewsbury and Don Morrison for Jim Henry, Bob Goldham, Gaye Stewart and Metro Prystai, July 13, 1950. Sold to **N.Y. Rangers** by Chicago, Jan. 9, 1953. Traded to **Montreal** by N.Y. Rangers with Ed Slowinski for Ivan Irwin, Aug. 17, 1953.

Mitch Babin

BABIN, MITCH 6'2", 195 lbs.
B. Nov. 1, 1954, Kapuskasing, Ont. Center, Shoots L

YEAR	TEAM & LEAGUE		GP	G	A	PTS	PIM
1975-76	**STL**	**N**	8	0	0	0	0

John Baby

BABY, JOHN GEORGE 6', 195 lbs.
B. May 18, 1957, Sudbury, Ont. Defense, Shoots R

YEAR	TEAM & LEAGUE		GP	G	A	PTS	PIM
1977-78	**CLEVE**	**N**	24	2	7	9	26
1978-79	**MINN**	**N**	2	0	1	1	0
2 yrs.		**N Totals:**	26	2	8	10	26

Put on **Minnesota** Reserve List after Cleveland-Minnesota Dispersal Draft, June 15, 1978. Claimed by **Quebec** from Minnesota in Expansion Draft, June 13, 1979.

Dave Babych

BABYCH, DAVID MICHAEL 6'2", 205 lbs.
B. May 23, 1961, Edmonton, Alta. Defense, Shoots L

YEAR	TEAM & LEAGUE		GP	G	A	PTS	PIM
1980-81	**WINN**	**N**	69	6	38	44	90
1981-82			79	19	49	68	92
1982-83			79	13	61	74	56
3 yrs.		**N Totals:**	227	38	148	186	238
PLAYOFFS							
1981-82	**WINN**	**N**	4	1	2	3	29
1982-83			3	0	0	0	0
2 yrs.		**N Totals:**	7	1	2	3	29

Wayne Babych

BABYCH, WAYNE JOSEPH 5'11", 191 lbs.
B. June 6, 1958, Edmonton, Alta. Right Wing, Shoots R

YEAR	TEAM & LEAGUE		GP	G	A	PTS	PIM
1978-79	**STL**	**N**	67	27	36	63	75
1979-80			59	26	35	61	49
1980-81			78	54	42	96	93
1981-82			51	19	25	44	51
1982-83			71	16	23	39	62
5 yrs.		**N Totals:**	326	142	161	303	330
PLAYOFFS							
1979-80	**STL**	**N**	3	1	2	3	2
1980-81			11	2	0	2	8
1981-82			7	3	2	5	8
3 yrs.		**N Totals:**	21	6	4	10	18

Mike Backman

BACKMAN, MICHAEL CHARLES 5'10", 175 lbs.
B. Feb. 2, 1955, Halifax, N.S. Right Wing, Shoots R

YEAR	TEAM & LEAGUE		GP	G	A	PTS	PIM
1981-82	**NYR**	**N**	3	0	2	2	4
1982-83			7	1	3	4	6
2 yrs.		**N Totals:**	10	1	5	6	10
PLAYOFFS							
1981-82	**NYR**	**N**	1	0	0	0	2
1982-83			9	2	2	4	0
2 yrs.		**N Totals:**	10	2	2	4	2

Peter Backor

BACKOR, PETER 6', 185 lbs.
B. Apr. 29, 1919, Fort William, Ont. Defense, Shoots L

YEAR	TEAM & LEAGUE		GP	G	A	PTS	PIM
1944-45	**TOR**	**N**	36	4	5	9	6

Ralph Backstrom

BACKSTROM, RALPH GERALD 5'10", 170 lbs.
B. Sept. 18, 1937, Kirkland Lake, Ont. Center, Shoots L
Won Calder Trophy, 1958-59

YEAR	TEAM & LEAGUE		GP	G	A	PTS	PIM
1956-57	**MONT**	**N**	3	0	0	0	0
1957-58			2	0	1	1	0
1958-59			64	18	22	40	19
1959-60			64	13	15	28	24
1960-61			69	12	20	32	44
1961-62			66	27	38	65	29
1962-63			70	23	12	35	51
1963-64			70	8	21	29	41
1964-65			70	25	30	55	41
1965-66			67	22	20	42	10
1966-67			69	14	27	41	39
1967-68			70	20	25	45	14
1968-69			72	13	28	41	16
1969-70			72	19	24	43	20
1970-71			16	1	4	5	0
	LA	**N**	33	14	13	27	8
	2 team total		49	15	17	32	8
1971-72			76	23	29	52	22
1972-73			63	20	29	49	6
	CHI	**N**	16	6	3	9	2
	2 team total		79	26	32	58	8
1973-74	**CHI**	**W**	78	33	50	83	26
1974-75			70	15	24	39	28
1975-76	**D-O**	**W**	41	21	29	50	14
	NE	**W**	38	14	19	33	6
	2 team total		79	35	48	83	20
1976-77			77	17	31	48	30
21 yrs.		**N Totals:**	1032	278	361	639	386
		W Totals:	304	100	153	253	104
PLAYOFFS							
1958-59*	**MONT**	**N**	11	3	5	8	12
1959-60*			7	0	3	3	2
1960-61			5	0	0	0	4
1961-62			5	0	1	1	6
1962-63			5	0	0	0	2
1963-64			7	2	1	3	8
1964-65*			13	2	3	5	10
1965-66*			10	3	4	7	4
1966-67			10	5	2	7	6
1967-68*			13	4	3	7	4

Ralph Backstrom continued

YEAR	TEAM & LEAGUE		GP	G	A	PTS	PIM
1968-69*			14	3	4	7	10
1972-73	**CHI**	**N**	16	5	6	11	0
1973-74	**CHI**	**W**	18	5	14	19	4
1975-76	**NE**	**W**	17	5	4	9	8
1976-77			3	0	0	0	0
15 yrs.		**N Totals:**	116	27	32	59	68
		W Totals:	38	10	18	28	12

Traded to **Los Angeles** by Montreal for Gord Labossiere and Ray Fortin, Jan. 26, 1971. Traded to **Chicago** by Los Angeles for Dan Maloney, Feb. 26, 1973.

Ace Bailey

BAILEY, IRVINE 5'10", 160 lbs.
B. July 3, 1903, Bracebridge, Ont. Right Wing, Shoots R
Won Art Ross Trophy, 1928-29
Hall of Fame, 1975

YEAR	TEAM & LEAGUE		GP	G	A	PTS	PIM
1926-27	**TOR**	**N**	42	15	13	28	82
1927-28			43	9	3	12	72
1928-29			44	**22**	10	**32**	78
1929-30			43	22	21	43	69
1930-31			40	23	19	42	46
1931-32			41	8	5	13	62
1932-33			47	10	8	18	52
1933-34			13	2	3	5	11
8 yrs.		**N Totals:**	313	111	82	193	472

PLAYOFFS

YEAR	TEAM & LEAGUE		GP	G	A	PTS	PIM
1928-29	**TOR**	**N**	4	2	1	3	4
1930-31			2	1	1	2	0
1931-32*			7	0	1	1	4
1932-33			8	0	1	1	4
4 yrs.		**N Totals:**	21	3	4	7	12

Ace Bailey

BAILEY, GARNET EDWARD 5'11", 192 lbs.
B. June 13, 1948, Lloydminster, Sask. Left Wing, Shoots L

YEAR	TEAM & LEAGUE		GP	G	A	PTS	PIM
1968-69	**BOS**	**N**	8	3	3	6	10
1969-70			58	11	11	22	82
1970-71			36	0	6	6	44
1971-72			73	9	13	22	64
1972-73			57	8	13	21	89
	DET	**N**	13	2	11	13	16
	2 team total		70	10	24	34	105
1973-74			45	9	14	23	33
	STL	**N**	22	7	3	10	20
	2 team total		67	16	17	33	53
1974-75			49	15	26	41	113
	WASH	**N**	22	4	13	17	8
	2 team total		71	19	39	58	121
1975-76			67	13	19	32	75
1976-77			78	19	27	46	51
1977-78			40	7	12	19	28
1978-79	**EDM**	**W**	38	5	4	9	22
11 yrs.		**N Totals:**	568	107	171	278	633
		W Totals:	38	5	4	9	22

PLAYOFFS

YEAR	TEAM & LEAGUE		GP	G	A	PTS	PIM
1968-69	**BOS**	**N**	1	0	0	0	2
1970-71			1	0	0	0	10
1971-72*			13	2	4	6	16
1978-79	**EDM**	**W**	2	0	0	0	4
4 yrs.		**N Totals:**	15	2	4	6	28
		W Totals:	2	0	0	0	4

Traded to **Detroit** by Boston with a player to be named later (Murray Wing, June 4, 1973) for Gary Doak, Mar. 1, 1973. Traded to **St. Louis** by Detroit with Ted Harris and Bill Collins for Chris Evans, Bryan Watson, and Jean Hamel, Feb. 14, 1974. Traded to **Washington** by St. Louis with Stan Gilbertson for Denis Dupere, Feb. 10, 1975.

Bob Bailey

BAILEY, ROBERT ALLAN 6', 197 lbs.
B. May 29, 1931, Kenora, Ont. Right Wing, Shoots R

YEAR	TEAM & LEAGUE		GP	G	A	PTS	PIM
1953-54	**TOR**	**N**	48	2	7	9	70
1954-55			32	4	2	6	52
1955-56			6	0	0	0	6
1957-58	**CHI**	**N**	28	3	6	9	38
	DET	**N**	36	6	6	12	41
	2 team total		64	9	12	21	79
4 yrs.		**N Totals:**	150	15	21	36	207

Bob Bailey continued

PLAYOFFS

YEAR	TEAM & LEAGUE		GP	G	A	PTS	PIM
1953-54	**TOR**	**N**	5	0	2	2	4
1954-55			1	0	0	0	0
1956-57	**DET**	**N**	5	0	2	2	2
1957-58			4	0	0	0	16
4 yrs.		**N Totals:**	15	0	4	4	22

Purchased from Toronto by **Detroit** Sept. 22, 1956. Drafted by **Chicago** from Detroit, June 5, 1957. Traded to **Detroit** by Chicago with Jack McIntyre, Nick Mickoski and Hec Lalande for Earl Reibel, Billy Dea, Lorne Ferguson and Bill Dineen, Dec. 17, 1957.

Reid Bailey

BAILEY, REID 6'2", 200 lbs.
B. May 28, 1956, Toronto, Ont. Defense, Shoots L

YEAR	TEAM & LEAGUE		GP	G	A	PTS	PIM
1980-81	**PHI**	**N**	17	1	3	4	55
1981-82			10	0	0	0	23
1982-83	**TOR**	**N**	1	0	0	0	2
3 yrs.		**N Totals:**	28	1	3	4	80

PLAYOFFS

YEAR	TEAM & LEAGUE		GP	G	A	PTS	PIM
1980-81	**PHI**	**N**	12	0	2	2	23
1981-82			2	0	0	0	0
1982-83	**TOR**	**N**	2	0	0	0	2
3 yrs.		**N Totals:**	16	0	2	2	25

Signed as free agent by **Philadelphia** Nov. 20, 1978.

Ken Baird

BAIRD, KENNETH STEWART 6', 190 lbs.
B. Feb. 1, 1951, Flin Flon, Man. Defense, Shoots L

YEAR	TEAM & LEAGUE		GP	G	A	PTS	PIM
1971-72	**CALIF**	**N**	10	0	2	2	15
1972-73	**ALTA**	**W**	75	14	15	29	112
1973-74	**EDM**	**W**	68	17	19	36	115
1974-75			77	30	28	59	151
1975-76			48	13	24	37	87
1976-77			2	1	2	3	0
	CALG	**W**	7	0	0	0	2
	2 team total		9	1	2	3	2
1977-78	**EDM**	**W**	0	0	0	0	0
	WINN	**W**	55	16	11	27	31
	2 team total		55	16	11	27	31
7 yrs.		**N Totals:**	10	0	2	2	15
		W Totals:	332	91	99	191	498

PLAYOFFS

YEAR	TEAM & LEAGUE		GP	G	A	PTS	PIM
1973-74	**EDM**	**W**	5	1	1	2	7
1975-76			4	3	1	4	16
1977-78	**WINN**	**W**	7	0	4	4	7
3 yrs.		**W Totals:**	16	4	6	10	30

Bill Baker

BAKER, WILLIAM ROBERT 6'1", 195 lbs.
B. Nov. 29, 1956, Grand Rapids, Mich. Defense, Shoots L

YEAR	TEAM & LEAGUE		GP	G	A	PTS	PIM
1980-81	**MONT**	**N**	11	0	0	0	32
	COLO	**N**	13	0	3	3	12
	2 team total		24	0	3	3	44
1981-82			14	0	3	3	12
	STL	**N**	35	3	5	8	50
	2 team total		49	3	8	11	62
1982-83	**NYR**	**N**	70	4	14	18	64
3 yrs.		**N Totals:**	143	7	25	32	170

PLAYOFFS

YEAR	TEAM & LEAGUE		GP	G	A	PTS	PIM
1981-82	**STL**	**N**	4	0	0	0	0
1982-83	**NYR**	**N**	2	0	0	0	0
2 yrs.		**N Totals:**	6	0	0	0	0

Traded to **Colorado** by Montreal for Colorado's third-round choice in the 1983 Entry Draft, Mar. 10, 1981. Traded to **St. Louis** for Joe Micheletti and Dick Lamby, Dec. 4, 1981. Acquired by **New York Rangers** in Waiver Draft, Oct. 4, 1982.

Doug Baldwin

BALDWIN, DOUGLAS 6', 175 lbs.
B. Nov. 2, 1922, Winnipeg, Man. Defense, Shoots L

YEAR	TEAM & LEAGUE		GP	G	A	PTS	PIM
1945-46	**TOR**	**N**	15	0	1	1	6
1946-47	**DET**	**N**	4	0	0	0	0
1947-48	**CHI**	**N**	5	0	0	0	2
3 yrs.		**N Totals:**	24	0	1	1	8

Earl Balfour

BALFOUR, EARL FREDERICK 6'1", 180 lbs.
B. Jan. 4, 1933, Toronto, Ont. Left Wing, Shoots L

YEAR	TEAM & LEAGUE		GP	G	A	PTS	PIM
1951-52	**TOR**	**N**	3	0	0	0	2
1953-54			17	0	1	1	6
1955-56			59	14	5	19	40
1957-58			1	0	0	0	0
1958-59	**CHI**	**N**	70	10	8	18	10
1959-60			70	3	5	8	16
1960-61			68	3	3	6	4
7 yrs.		**N Totals:**	288	30	22	52	78

PLAYOFFS

YEAR	TEAM & LEAGUE		GP	G	A	PTS	PIM
1951-52	**TOR**	**N**	1	0	0	0	0
1955-56			3	0	1	1	2
1958-59	**CHI**	**N**	6	0	2	2	0
1959-60			4	0	0	0	0
1960-61			12	0	0	0	2
5 yrs.		**N Totals:**	26	0	3	3	4

Drafted from Toronto by **Chicago** June 4, 1958. Drafted by **Boston** from Chicago, June 14, 1961.

Murray Balfour

BALFOUR, MURRAY 5'9", 178 lbs.
B. Aug. 24, 1936, Regina, Sask. Right Wing, Shoots R

YEAR	TEAM & LEAGUE		GP	G	A	PTS	PIM
1956-57	**MONT**	**N**	2	0	0	0	2
1957-58			3	1	1	2	4
1959-60	**CHI**	**N**	61	18	12	30	55
1960-61			70	21	27	48	123
1961-62			49	15	15	30	72
1962-63			65	10	23	33	35
1963-64			41	2	10	12	36
1964-65	**BOS**	**N**	15	0	2	2	26
8 yrs.		**N Totals:**	306	67	90	157	353

PLAYOFFS

YEAR	TEAM & LEAGUE		GP	G	A	PTS	PIM
1959-60	**CHI**	**N**	4	1	0	1	0
1960-61*			12	5	5	10	2
1961-62			12	1	1	2	15
1962-63			6	0	2	2	12
1963-64			7	2	2	4	4
5 yrs.		**N Totals:**	41	9	10	19	33

Purchased by **Chicago** from Montreal, June 9, 1959. Traded to **Boston** by Chicago with Mike Draper for Matt Ravlich and Jerry Toppazzini, June 9, 1964.

Terry Ball

BALL, TERRY JAMES 5'8", 165 lbs.
B. Nov. 29, 1944, Selkirk, Man. Defense, Shoots R

YEAR	TEAM & LEAGUE		GP	G	A	PTS	PIM
1967-68	**PHI**	**N**	1	0	0	0	0
1969-70			61	7	18	25	20
1970-71	**BUF**	**N**	2	0	0	0	0
1971-72			10	0	1	1	6
1972-73	**MINN**	**W**	76	6	34	40	66
1973-74			71	8	28	36	34
1974-75			76	8	37	45	36
1975-76	**CLEVE**	**W**	23	2	15	17	18
	CIN	**W**	36	3	14	17	12
	2 team total		59	5	29	34	30
1976-77	**BIRM**	**W**	23	1	6	7	8
9 yrs.		**N Totals:**	74	7	19	26	26
		W Totals:	305	28	134	162	174

PLAYOFFS

YEAR	TEAM & LEAGUE		GP	G	A	PTS	PIM
1972-73	**MINN**	**W**	5	1	2	3	4
1973-74			11	1	2	3	6
1974-75			12	3	4	7	4

Terry Ball continued

YEAR	TEAM & LEAGUE		GP	G	A	PTS	PIM
3 yrs.		**W Totals:**	28	5	8	13	14

Drafted by **Philadelphia** from N.Y. Rangers in Expansion Draft, June 6, 1967. Traded to **Pittsburgh** by Philadelphia for George Swarbrick, June 11, 1970. Traded to **Buffalo** by Pittsburgh for Jean-Guy Legace, Jan. 24, 1971.

Dave Balon

BALON, DAVID ALEXANDER 5'10", 172 lbs.
B. Aug. 2, 1937, Wakaw, Sask. Left Wing, Shoots L

YEAR	TEAM & LEAGUE		GP	G	A	PTS	PIM
1959-60	**NYR**	**N**	3	0	0	0	0
1960-61			13	1	2	3	8
1961-62			30	4	11	15	11
1962-63			70	11	13	24	72
1963-64	**MONT**	**N**	70	24	18	42	80
1964-65			63	18	23	41	61
1965-66			45	3	7	10	24
1966-67			48	11	8	19	31
1967-68	**MINN**	**N**	73	15	32	47	84
1968-69	**NYR**	**N**	75	10	21	31	57
1969-70			76	33	37	70	100
1970-71			78	36	24	60	34
1971-72			16	4	5	9	2
	VAN	**N**	59	19	19	38	21
	2 team total		75	23	24	47	23
1972-73			57	3	2	5	22
1973-74	**QUE**	**W**	9	0	0	0	2
15 yrs.		**N Totals:**	776	192	222	414	607
		W Totals:	9	0	0	0	2

PLAYOFFS

YEAR	TEAM & LEAGUE		GP	G	A	PTS	PIM
1961-62	**NYR**	**N**	6	2	3	5	2
1963-64	**MONT**	**N**	7	1	1	2	25
1964-65*			10	0	0	0	10
1965-66*			9	2	3	5	8
1966-67			9	0	2	2	6
1967-68	**MINN**	**N**	14	4	9	13	14
1968-69	**NYR**	**N**	4	1	0	1	0
1969-70			6	1	1	2	32
1970-71			13	3	2	5	4
9 yrs.		**N Totals:**	78	14	21	35	101

Traded to **Montreal** by N.Y. Rangers with Leon Rochefort, Len Ronson, and Gump Worsley for Phil Goyette, Don Marshall, and Jacques Plante, June 4, 1963. Drafted by **Minnesota** from Montreal in Expansion Draft, June 6, 1967. Traded to **N.Y. Rangers** by Minnesota for Wayne Hillman, Dan Seguin and Joey Johnston, June 12, 1968. Traded to **Vancouver** by N.Y. Rangers with Wayne Connelly and Ron Stewart for Gary Doak and Jim Wiste, Nov. 16, 1971.

Bryon Baltimore

BALTIMORE, BRYON DON 6'2", 200 lbs.
B. Aug. 26, 1952, Whitehorse, Yukon Defense, Shoots R

YEAR	TEAM & LEAGUE		GP	G	A	PTS	PIM
1974-75	**CHI**	**W**	77	8	12	20	110
1975-76	**D-O**	**W**	41	1	8	9	32
	IND	**W**	37	1	10	11	30
	2 team total		78	2	18	20	62
1976-77			55	0	15	15	63
1977-78			22	1	7	8	47
	CIN	**W**	28	2	9	11	23
	2 team total		50	3	16	19	70
1978-79	**IND**	**W**	2	1	1	2	2
	CIN	**W**	69	4	10	14	83
	2 team total		71	5	11	16	85
1979-80	**EDM**	**N**	2	0	0	0	4
6 yrs.		**N Totals:**	2	0	0	0	4
		W Totals:	331	18	72	90	390

PLAYOFFS

YEAR	TEAM & LEAGUE		GP	G	A	PTS	PIM
1975-76	**IND**	**W**	7	0	1	1	4
1976-77			9	0	0	0	5
1978-79	**CIN**	**W**	3	0	0	0	2
3 yrs.		**W Totals:**	19	0	1	1	11

Stanley Baluik

BALUIK, STANLEY 5'8", 160 lbs.
B. Oct. 5, 1935, Port Arthur, Ont. Center, Shoots L

YEAR	TEAM & LEAGUE		GP	G	A	PTS	PIM
1959-60	BOS	N	7	0	0	0	2

Jeff Bandura

BANDURA, JEFFREY MITCHELL JOSEPH 6'1", 195 lbs.
B. Feb. 4, 1957, White Rick, B.C. Defense, Shoots R

YEAR	TEAM & LEAGUE		GP	G	A	PTS	PIM
1980-81	NYR	N	2	0	1	1	0

Traded to **N.Y. Rangers** by Vancouver with Jere Gillis for Mario Marois and Jim Mayer, Nov. 11, 1980.

Andy Barbe

BARBE, ANDRE JOSEPH 6', 175 lbs.
B. July 27, 1923, Coniston, Ont. Right Wing, Shoots R

YEAR	TEAM & LEAGUE		GP	G	A	PTS	PIM
1950-51	TOR	N	1	0	0	0	2

Bill Barber

BARBER, WILLIAM CHARLES 6', 190 lbs.
B. July 11, 1952, Callander, Ont. Left Wing, Shoots L

YEAR	TEAM & LEAGUE		GP	G	A	PTS	PIM
1972-73	PHI	N	69	30	34	64	46
1973-74			75	34	35	69	54
1974-75			79	34	37	71	66
1975-76			80	50	62	112	104
1976-77			73	20	35	55	62
1977-78			80	41	31	72	34
1978-79			79	34	46	80	22
1979-80			79	40	32	72	17
1980-81			80	43	42	85	69
1981-82			80	45	44	89	85
1982-83			66	27	33	60	28
11 yrs.		N Totals:	840	398	431	829	587

PLAYOFFS

YEAR	TEAM & LEAGUE		GP	G	A	PTS	PIM
1972-73	PHI	N	11	3	2	5	22
1973-74*			17	3	6	9	18
1974-75*			17	6	9	15	8
1975-76			16	6	7	13	18
1976-77			10	1	4	5	2
1977-78			12	6	3	9	2
1978-79			8	3	4	7	10
1979-80			19	12	9	21	23
1980-81			12	11	5	16	0
1981-82			4	1	5	6	4
1982-83			3	1	1	2	2
11 yrs.		N Totals:	129	53	55	108	109

Butch Barber

BARBER, ROBERT IAN 5'10", 172 lbs.
B. Aug. 31, 1943, Fairview, Alta. Defense, Shoots L

YEAR	TEAM & LEAGUE		GP	G	A	PTS	PIM
1972-73	CHI	W	75	4	19	23	39
1973-74	NY-NJ	W	3	0	0	0	2
2 yrs.		W Totals:	78	4	19	23	41

Bill Barilko

BARILKO, WILLIAM 5'11", 184 lbs.
B. Mar. 25, 1927, Timmins, Ont. Defense, Shoots L

YEAR	TEAM & LEAGUE		GP	G	A	PTS	PIM
1946-47	TOR	N	18	3	7	10	33
1947-48			57	5	9	14	**147**
1948-49			60	5	4	9	95
1949-50			59	7	10	17	85
1950-51			58	6	6	12	96
5 yrs.		N Totals:	252	26	36	62	456

PLAYOFFS

YEAR	TEAM & LEAGUE		GP	G	A	PTS	PIM
1946-47*	TOR	N	11	0	3	3	18
1947-48*			9	1	0	1	17
1948-49*			9	0	1	1	20
1949-50			7	1	1	2	18
1950-51*			11	3	2	5	31
5 yrs.		N Totals:	47	5	7	12	104

Doug Barkley

BARKLEY, DOUGLAS 6'2", 185 lbs.
B. Jan. 6, 1937, Lethbridge, Alta. Defense, Shoots R

YEAR	TEAM & LEAGUE		GP	G	A	PTS	PIM
1957-58	CHI	N	3	0	0	0	0
1959-60			3	0	0	0	2
1962-63	DET	N	70	3	24	27	78
1963-64			67	11	21	32	115
1964-65			67	5	20	25	122
1965-66			43	5	15	20	65
6 yrs.		N Totals:	253	24	80	104	382

PLAYOFFS

YEAR	TEAM & LEAGUE		GP	G	A	PTS	PIM
1962-63	DET	N	11	0	3	3	16
1963-64			14	0	5	5	33
1964-65			5	0	1	1	14
3 yrs.		N Totals:	30	0	9	9	63

Traded to **Detroit** by Chicago for Len Lunde and John McKenzie, June, 1962.

Bob Barlow

BARLOW, ROBERT GEORGE 5'10", 175 lbs.
B. June 17, 1935, Hamilton, Ont. Shoots L

YEAR	TEAM & LEAGUE		GP	G	A	PTS	PIM
1969-70	MINN	N	70	16	17	33	10
1970-71			7	0	0	0	0
1974-75	PHOE	W	51	6	20	26	8
3 yrs.		N Totals:	77	16	17	33	10
		W Totals:	51	6	20	26	8

PLAYOFFS

YEAR	TEAM & LEAGUE		GP	G	A	PTS	PIM
1969-70	MINN	N	6	2	2	4	6

Sold to **Minnesota** by Philadelphia, June 10, 1969.

Blair Barnes

BARNES, BLAIR 5'11", 190 lbs.
B. Sept. 21, 1960, Windsor, Ont. Right Wing, Shoots R

YEAR	TEAM & LEAGUE		GP	G	A	PTS	PIM
1982-83	LA	N	1	0	0	0	0

Traded by Edmonton to **Los Angeles** for Paul Mulvey, June 22, 1982.

Norm Barnes

BARNES, NORMAN LEONARD CHARLES 6', 190 lbs.
B. Aug. 24, 1953, Toronto, Ont. Defense, Shoots L

YEAR	TEAM & LEAGUE		GP	G	A	PTS	PIM
1976-77	PHI	N	1	0	0	0	0
1979-80			59	4	21	25	59
1980-81			22	0	3	3	18
	HART	N	54	1	10	11	82
	2 team total		76	1	13	14	100
1981-82			20	1	4	5	19
4 yrs.		N Totals:	156	6	38	44	178

PLAYOFFS

YEAR	TEAM & LEAGUE		GP	G	A	PTS	PIM
1978-79	PHI	N	2	0	0	0	0
1979-80			10	0	0	0	8
2 yrs.		N Totals:	12	0	0	0	8

Traded to **Hartford** by Philadelphia with Jack McIlhargey for Hartford's second round choice (Peter Ihnacak - transferred to Toronto) in the 1982 Entry Draft, Nov. 21, 1980.

Dave Barr

BARR, DAVID 6'1", 185 lbs.
B. Nov. 30, 1960, Toronto, Ont. Right Wing, Shoots R

YEAR	TEAM & LEAGUE		GP	G	A	PTS	PIM
1981-82	BOS	N	2	0	0	0	0
1982-83			10	1	1	2	7
2 yrs.		N Totals:	12	1	1	2	7

PLAYOFFS

YEAR	TEAM & LEAGUE		GP	G	A	PTS	PIM
1981-82	BOS	N	5	1	0	1	0
1982-83			10	0	0	0	2
2 yrs.		N Totals:	15	1	0	1	2

Signed as free agent by **Boston** Sept. 28, 1981.

Fred Barrett

BARRETT, FREDERICK WILLIAM 6', 194 lbs.
B. Dec. 6, 1950, Ottawa, Ont. Defense, Shoots L

YEAR	TEAM & LEAGUE		GP	G	A	PTS	PIM
1970-71	**MINN**	**N**	57	0	13	13	75
1972-73			46	2	4	6	21
1973-74			40	0	7	7	12
1974-75			62	3	18	21	82
1975-76			79	2	9	11	66
1976-77			60	1	8	9	46
1977-78			79	0	15	15	59
1978-79			45	1	9	10	48
1979-80			80	8	14	22	71
1980-81			62	4	8	12	72
1981-82			69	1	15	16	89
1982-83			51	1	3	4	22
12 yrs.		**N Totals:**	730	23	123	146	663
PLAYOFFS							
1972-73	**MINN**	**N**	6	0	0	0	4
1976-77			2	0	0	0	2
1979-80			14	0	0	0	22
1980-81			14	0	1	1	16
1981-82			4	0	1	1	16
1982-83			4	0	0	0	0
6 yrs.		**N Totals:**	44	0	2	2	60

John Barrett

BARRETT, JOHN DAVID 6'1", 210 lbs.
B. July 1, 1958, Ottawa, Ont. Defense, Shoots L

YEAR	TEAM & LEAGUE		GP	G	A	PTS	PIM
1980-81	**DET**	**N**	56	3	10	13	60
1981-82			69	1	12	13	93
1982-83			79	4	10	14	74
3 yrs.		**N Totals:**	204	8	32	40	227

Doug Barrie

BARRIE, DOUGLAS ROBERT 5'9", 175 lbs.
B. Oct. 2, 1946, Edmonton, Alta. Defense, Shoots R

YEAR	TEAM & LEAGUE		GP	G	A	PTS	PIM
1968-69	**PITT**	**N**	8	1	1	2	8
1970-71	**BUF**	**N**	75	4	23	27	168
1971-72			27	2	5	7	45
	LA	**N**	48	3	13	16	47
	2 team total		75	5	18	23	92
1972-73	**ALTA**	**W**	54	9	22	31	111
1973-74	**EDM**	**W**	69	4	27	31	214
1974-75			78	12	33	45	122
1975-76			79	4	21	25	81
1976-77			70	8	19	27	92
8 yrs.		**N Totals:**	158	10	42	52	268
		W Totals:	350	37	122	159	620
PLAYOFFS							
1973-74	**EDM**	**W**	4	1	0	1	16
1975-76			4	0	1	1	6
1976-77			4	0	0	0	0
3 yrs.		**W Totals:**	12	1	1	2	22

Drafted by **Buffalo** from Pittsburgh in Expansion Draft, June 10, 1970. Traded to **Los Angeles** by Buffalo with Mike Keeler for Mike Byers and Larry Hillman, Dec. 16, 1971.

Ed Barry

BARRY, EDWARD THOMAS 5'10", 180 lbs.
B. Oct. 12, 1919, Wellesley, Mass. Left Wing, Shoots L

YEAR	TEAM & LEAGUE		GP	G	A	PTS	PIM
1946-47	**BOS**	**N**	19	1	3	4	2

Marty Barry

BARRY, MARTIN J. 5'11", 175 lbs.
B. Dec. 8, 1905, Quebec City, Que. Center, Shoots L
Won Lady Byng Trophy, 1936-37
Hall of Fame, 1965

YEAR	TEAM & LEAGUE		GP	G	A	PTS	PIM
1927-28	**NYA**	**N**	9	1	0	1	2
1929-30	**BOS**	**N**	44	18	15	33	8
1930-31			44	20	11	31	26
1931-32			48	21	17	38	22
1932-33			47	24	13	37	40
1933-34			48	27	12	39	12

Marty Barry continued

YEAR	TEAM & LEAGUE		GP	G	A	PTS	PIM
1934-35			48	20	20	40	33
1935-36	**DET**	**N**	48	21	19	40	16
1936-37			47	17	27	44	6
1937-38			48	9	20	29	34
1938-39			48	13	28	41	4
1939-40	**MONT**	**N**	30	4	10	14	2
12 yrs.		**N Totals:**	509	195	192	387	205
PLAYOFFS							
1929-30	**BOS**	**N**	6	3	3	6	14
1930-31			5	1	1	2	4
1932-33			5	2	2	4	6
1934-35			4	0	0	0	2
1935-36*	**DET**	**N**	7	2	4	6	6
1936-37*			10	4	7	11	2
1938-39			6	3	1	4	0
7 yrs.		**N Totals:**	43	15	18	33	34

Ray Barry

BARRY, WILLIAM RAYMOND 5'11", 170 lbs.
B. Oct. 4, 1928, Boston, Mass. Center, Shoots L

YEAR	TEAM & LEAGUE		GP	G	A	PTS	PIM
1951-52	**BOS**	**N**	18	1	2	3	6

Jim Bartlett

BARTLETT, JAMES BAKER 5'9", 165 lbs.
B. May 27, 1932, Verdun, Que. Left Wing, Shoots L

YEAR	TEAM & LEAGUE		GP	G	A	PTS	PIM
1954-55	**MONT**	**N**	2	0	0	0	4
1955-56	**NYR**	**N**	12	0	1	1	8
1958-59			70	11	9	20	118
1959-60			44	8	4	12	48
1960-61	**BOS**	**N**	63	15	9	24	95
5 yrs.		**N Totals:**	191	34	23	57	273
PLAYOFFS							
1954-55	**MONT**	**N**	2	0	0	0	0

Drafted by **N.Y. Rangers** from Montreal, June, 1955. Drafted from N.Y. Rangers by **Boston** June 8, 1960.

Cliff Barton

BARTON, CLIFFORD JOHN 5'7", 155 lbs.
B. Sept. 3, 1907, Sault Ste. Marie, Mich. Right Wing, Shoots R

YEAR	TEAM & LEAGUE		GP	G	A	PTS	PIM
1929-30	**PITT**	**N**	39	4	2	6	4
1930-31	**PHI**	**N**	43	6	7	13	18
1939-40	**NYR**	**N**	3	0	0	0	0
3 yrs.		**N Totals:**	85	10	9	19	22

Jamie Bateman

BATEMAN, JAMES 6'1", 185 lbs.
B. Sept. 16, 1954, Thetford Mines, Que. Defense, Shoots L

YEAR	TEAM & LEAGUE		GP	G	A	PTS	PIM
1974-75	**SD**	**W**	24	0	3	3	96
1975-76			17	1	0	1	4
2 yrs.		**W Totals:**	41	1	3	4	100

Frank Bathe

BATHE, FRANCIS LENARD 6'1", 190 lbs.
B. Sept. 27, 1954, Oshawa, Ont. Defense, Shoots L

YEAR	TEAM & LEAGUE		GP	G	A	PTS	PIM
1974-75	**DET**	**N**	19	0	3	3	31
1975-76			7	0	1	1	9
1977-78	**PHI**	**N**	1	0	0	0	0
1978-79			21	1	3	4	76
1979-80			47	0	7	7	111
1980-81			44	0	3	3	175
1981-82			28	1	3	4	68
1982-83			57	1	8	9	72
8 yrs.		**N Totals:**	224	3	28	31	542
PLAYOFFS							
1978-79	**PHI**	**N**	6	1	0	1	12
1979-80			1	0	0	0	0
1980-81			12	0	3	3	16
1981-82			4	0	0	0	2
1982-83			3	0	0	0	12
5 yrs.		**N Totals:**	26	1	3	4	42

Signed as free agent by **Philadelphia** Oct. 6, 1977.

Andy Bathgate

BATHGATE, ANDREW JAMES 6', 180 lbs.
B. Aug. 28, 1932, Winnipeg, Man. Right Wing, Shoots R
Won Hart Trophy, 1958-59
Hall of Fame, 1978

YEAR	TEAM	LEAGUE	GP	G	A	PTS	PIM
1952-53	**NYR**	**N**	18	0	1	1	6
1953-54			20	2	2	4	18
1954-55			70	20	20	40	37
1955-56			70	19	**47**	66	59
1956-57			70	27	50	77	60
1957-58			65	30	48	78	42
1958-59			70	40	48	88	48
1959-60			70	26	**48**	74	28
1960-61			70	29	48	77	22
1961-62			70	28	**56**	**84**	44
1962-63			70	35	46	81	54
1963-64			56	16	43	59	26
	TOR	**N**	15	3	15	18	8
	2 team total		71	19	**58**	77	34
1964-65			55	16	29	45	34
1965-66	**DET**	**N**	70	15	32	47	25
1966-67			60	8	23	31	24
1967-68	**PITT**	**N**	74	20	39	59	55
1970-71			76	15	29	44	34
1974-75	**VAN**	**W**	11	1	6	7	2
18 yrs.	**N Totals:**		1069	349	624	973	624
	W Totals:		11	1	6	7	2

PLAYOFFS

YEAR	TEAM	LEAGUE	GP	G	A	PTS	PIM
1955-56	**NYR**	**N**	5	1	2	3	2
1956-57			5	2	0	2	7
1957-58			6	5	3	8	6
1961-62			6	1	2	3	4
1963-64*	**TOR**	**N**	14	5	4	9	25
1964-65			6	1	0	1	6
1965-66	**DET**	**N**	12	6	3	9	6
7 yrs.	**N Totals:**		54	21	14	35	56

Traded by N.Y. Rangers with Don McKenney to **Toronto** for Dick Duff, Bob Nevin, Arnie Brown, Bill Collins, and Rod Seiling, Feb. 22, 1964. Traded to **Detroit** by Toronto with Billy Harris and Gary Jarrett for Marcel Pronovost, Ed Joyal, Larry Jeffrey, Lowell MacDonald, and Autry Erickson, May 20, 1965. Drafted by **Pittsburgh** from Detroit in Expansion Draft, June 6, 1967.

Frank Bathgate

BATHGATE, FRANK 5'10", 162 lbs.
B. Feb. 14, 1930, Winnipeg, Man. Center, Shoots R

YEAR	TEAM	LEAGUE	GP	G	A	PTS	PIM
1952-53	**NYR**	**N**	2	0	0	0	2

Bobby Bauer

BAUER, ROBERT THEODORE 5'6", 150 lbs.
B. Feb. 16, 1915, Waterloo, Ont. Right Wing, Shoots R
Won Lady Byng Trophy, 1939–40, 1940–41, 1946-47

YEAR	TEAM	LEAGUE	GP	G	A	PTS	PIM
1935-36	**BOS**	**N**	1	0	0	0	0
1936-37			1	1	0	1	0
1937-38			48	20	14	34	9
1938-39			48	13	18	31	4
1939-40			48	17	26	43	2
1940-41			48	17	22	39	2
1941-42			36	13	22	35	11
1945-46			39	11	10	21	4
1946-47			58	30	24	54	4
1951-52			1	1	1	2	0
10 yrs.	**N Totals:**		328	123	137	260	36

PLAYOFFS

YEAR	TEAM	LEAGUE	GP	G	A	PTS	PIM
1936-37	**BOS**	**N**	1	0	0	0	0
1937-38			3	0	0	0	2
1938-39*			12	3	2	5	0
1939-40			6	1	0	1	2
1940-41*			11	2	2	4	0
1945-46			10	4	3	7	2
1946-47			5	1	1	2	0
7 yrs.	**N Totals:**		48	11	8	19	6

Mike Baumgartner

BAUMGARTNER, MICHAEL EDWARD 6'2", 195 lbs.
B. Jan. 30, 1949, Roseau, Mn. Defense, Shoots L

YEAR	TEAM	LEAGUE	GP	G	A	PTS	PIM
1974-75	**KC**	**N**	17	0	0	0	0

Traded to **Atlanta** by Chicago for Lynn Powis, Aug. 30, 1973. Sold to **Montreal** by Atlanta, May 27, 1974. Sold to **Kansas City** by Montreal, Aug. 22, 1974.

Bob Baun

BAUN, ROBERT NEIL 5'9", 182 lbs.
B. Sept. 9, 1936, Lanigan, Sask. Defense, Shoots R

YEAR	TEAM	LEAGUE	GP	G	A	PTS	PIM
1956-57	**TOR**	**N**	20	0	5	5	37
1957-58			67	1	9	10	91
1958-59			51	1	8	9	87
1959-60			61	8	9	17	59
1960-61			70	1	14	15	70
1961-62			65	4	11	15	94
1962-63			48	4	8	12	65
1963-64			52	4	14	18	113
1964-65			70	0	18	18	160
1965-66			44	0	6	6	68
1966-67			54	2	8	10	83
1967-68	**OAK**	**N**	67	3	10	13	81
1968-69	**DET**	**N**	76	4	16	20	121
1969-70			71	1	18	19	112
1970-71			11	0	3	3	24
	TOR	**N**	58	1	17	18	123
	2 team total		69	1	20	21	147
1971-72			74	2	12	14	101
1972-73			5	1	1	2	4
17 yrs.	**N Totals:**		964	37	187	224	1493

PLAYOFFS

YEAR	TEAM	LEAGUE	GP	G	A	PTS	PIM
1958-59	**TOR**	**N**	12	0	0	0	24
1959-60			10	1	0	1	17
1960-61			3	0	0	0	8
1961-62*			12	0	3	3	19
1962-63*			10	0	3	3	6
1963-64*			14	2	3	5	42
1964-65			6	0	1	1	14
1965-66			4	0	1	1	8
1966-67*			10	0	0	0	4
1969-70	**DET**	**N**	4	0	0	0	6
1970-71	**TOR**	**N**	6	0	1	1	19
1971-72			5	0	0	0	4
12 yrs.	**N Totals:**		96	3	12	15	171

Drafted by **Oakland** from Toronto in Expansion Draft, June 6, 1967. Traded to **Detroit** by Oakland with Ron Harris for Gary Jarrett, Doug Roberts, Howie Young, and Chris Worthy, May 27, 1968. Claimed on waivers by **Buffalo** from Detroit, Nov. 3, 1970. Traded to **St. Louis** by Buffalo for Larry Keenan and Jean-Guy Talbot, Nov. 4, 1970. Traded to **Toronto** by St. Louis for Brit Selby, Nov. 13, 1970.

Paul Baxter

BAXTER, PAUL GORDON 5'11", 200 lbs.
B. Oct. 25, 1955, Winnipeg, Man. Defense, Shoots R

YEAR	TEAM	LEAGUE	GP	G	A	PTS	PIM
1974-75	**CLEVE**	**W**	5	0	0	0	37
1975-76			67	3	7	10	201
1976-77	**QUE**	**W**	66	6	17	23	244
1977-78			76	6	29	35	240
1978-79			76	10	36	46	240
1979-80	**QUE**	**N**	61	7	13	20	145
1980-81	**PITT**	**N**	51	5	14	19	204
1981-82			76	9	34	43	**409**
1982-83			75	11	21	32	238
9 yrs.	**N Totals:**		263	32	82	114	996
	W Totals:		290	25	89	114	962

PLAYOFFS

YEAR	TEAM	LEAGUE	GP	G	A	PTS	PIM
1975-76	**CLEVE**	**W**	3	0	0	0	10
1976-77	**QUE**	**W**	12	2	2	4	35
1977-78			11	4	7	11	42
1978-79			4	0	2	2	7
1980-81	**PITT**	**N**	5	0	1	1	28
1981-82			5	0	0	0	14
6 yrs.	**N Totals:**		10	0	1	1	42
	W Totals:		30	6	11	17	94

Reclaimed by **Pittsburgh** from Quebec prior to Expansion Draft, June 9,

1979. Claimed as priority selection by **Quebec** June 9, 1979. Signed by **Pittsburgh** as free agent from Quebec, Aug. 7, 1980. Quebec received Kim Clackson as compensation.

Sandy Beadle

BEADLE, SANDY JAMES 6'2", 185 lbs.
B. July 12, 1960, Regina, Sask. Left Wing, Shoots L

YEAR	TEAM & LEAGUE		GP	G	A	PTS	PIM
1980-81	**WINN**	**N**	6	1	0	1	2

Frank Beaton

BEATON, ALEXANDER FRANCIS (Seldom)
5'10", 200 lbs.
B. Apr. 28, 1953, Antigonish, N.S. Left Wing, Shoots L

YEAR	TEAM & LEAGUE		GP	G	A	PTS	PIM
1975-76	**CIN**	**W**	29	2	3	5	61
1976-77	**EDM**	**W**	68	4	9	13	**274**
1977-78	**BIRM**	**W**	56	6	9	15	279
1978-79	**NYR**	**N**	2	0	0	0	0
1979-80			23	1	1	2	43
5 yrs.		**N Totals:**	25	1	1	2	43
		W Totals:	153	12	21	33	614

PLAYOFFS

YEAR	TEAM & LEAGUE		GP	G	A	PTS	PIM
1976-77	**EDM**	**W**	5	0	2	2	21
1977-78	**BIRM**	**W**	5	2	0	2	10
2 yrs.		**W Totals:**	10	2	2	4	31

Signed as free agent by **N.Y. Rangers** July 21, 1978.

Red Beattie

BEATTIE, JOHN 5'9", 170 lbs.
B. Oct. 2, 1907, Ibstock, England Left Wing, Shoots L

YEAR	TEAM & LEAGUE		GP	G	A	PTS	PIM
1930-31	**BOS**	**N**	32	10	11	21	25
1931-32			2	0	0	0	0
1932-33			48	8	12	20	12
1933-34			48	9	13	22	26
1934-35			48	9	18	27	27
1935-36			48	14	18	32	27
1936-37			48	8	7	15	10
1937-38			14	0	0	0	0
	DET	**N**	11	1	2	3	0
	NYA	**N**	19	3	4	7	5
	3 team total		44	4	6	10	5
1938-39			17	0	0	0	5
9 yrs.		**N Totals:**	335	62	85	147	137

PLAYOFFS

YEAR	TEAM & LEAGUE		GP	G	A	PTS	PIM
1930-31	**BOS**	**N**	4	0	0	0	0
1932-33			5	0	0	0	2
1934-35			4	1	0	1	2
1936-37			3	1	0	1	0
1937-38	**NYA**	**N**	6	2	2	4	2
5 yrs.		**N Totals:**	22	4	2	6	6

Norm Beaudin

BEAUDIN, NORMAN JOSEPH ANDREW
5'8", 170 lbs.
B. Nov. 28, 1941, Montmartre, Sask. Right Wing, Shoots R

YEAR	TEAM & LEAGUE		GP	G	A	PTS	PIM
1967-68	**STL**	**N**	13	1	1	2	4
1970-71	**MINN**	**N**	12	0	1	1	0
1972-73	**WINN**	**W**	78	38	65	103	15
1973-74			74	27	28	55	8
1974-75			77	16	31	47	8
1975-76			80	16	31	47	38
6 yrs.		**N Totals:**	25	1	2	3	4
		W Totals:	309	97	155	252	69

PLAYOFFS

YEAR	TEAM & LEAGUE		GP	G	A	PTS	PIM
1972-73	**WINN**	**W**	14	13	15	28	2
1973-74			4	3	1	4	2
1975-76			13	2	3	5	10
3 yrs.		**W Totals:**	31	18	19	37	14

Drafted by **St. Louis** from Detroit in Expansion Draft, June 6, 1967.

Serge Beaudoin

BEAUDOIN, SERGE 6'2", 215 lbs.
B. Nov. 30, 1952, Montreal, Que. Defense, Shoots L

YEAR	TEAM & LEAGUE		GP	G	A	PTS	PIM
1973-74	**VAN**	**W**	26	1	11	12	37
1974-75			4	0	0	0	2
1975-76	**PHOE**	**W**	76	0	21	21	102
1976-77			77	6	24	30	136
1977-78	**CIN**	**W**	0	0	0	0	0
	BIRM	**W**	77	8	26	34	115
	2 team total		77	8	26	34	115
1978-79			72	5	21	26	127
1979-80	**ATL**	**N**	3	0	0	0	0
7 yrs.		**N Totals:**	3	0	0	0	0
		W Totals:	332	20	103	123	519

PLAYOFFS

YEAR	TEAM & LEAGUE		GP	G	A	PTS	PIM
1975-76	**PHOE**	**W**	5	1	0	1	10
1977-78	**BIRM**	**W**	5	1	0	1	46
2 yrs.		**W Totals:**	10	2	0	2	56

Signed as free agent with **Atlanta** August, 1979.

Alain Beaule

BEAULE, ALAIN 6', 195 lbs.
B. Apr. 7, 1946, St.-Romain, Que. Defense, Shoots L

YEAR	TEAM & LEAGUE		GP	G	A	PTS	PIM
1973-74	**QUE**	**W**	78	4	36	40	93
1974-75			22	4	7	11	19
	WINN	**W**	54	0	14	14	24
	2 team total		76	4	21	25	43
2 yrs.		**W Totals:**	154	8	57	65	136

Don Beaupre

BEAUPRE, DONALD WILLIAM 5'8", 150 lbs.
B. Sept. 19, 1961, Waterloo, Ont. Shoots L

PLAYOFFS

YEAR	TEAM & LEAGUE		GP	G	A	PTS	PIM
1980-81	**MINN**	**N**	6	0	0	0	0

Barry Beck

BECK, BARRY DAVID (Bubba) 6'3", 216 lbs.
B. June 3, 1957, Vancouver, B.C. Defense, Shoots L

YEAR	TEAM & LEAGUE		GP	G	A	PTS	PIM
1977-78	**COLO**	**N**	75	22	38	60	89
1978-79			63	14	28	42	91
1979-80			10	1	5	6	8
	NYR	**N**	61	14	45	59	98
	2 team total		71	15	50	65	106
1980-81			75	11	23	34	231
1981-82			60	9	29	38	111
1982-83			66	12	22	34	112
6 yrs.		**N Totals:**	410	83	190	273	740

PLAYOFFS

YEAR	TEAM & LEAGUE		GP	G	A	PTS	PIM
1977-78	**COLO**	**N**	2	0	1	1	0
1979-80	**NYR**	**N**	9	1	4	5	6
1980-81			14	5	8	13	32
1981-82			10	1	5	6	14
1982-83			9	2	4	6	8
5 yrs.		**N Totals:**	44	9	22	31	60

Traded to **N.Y. Rangers** by Colorado for Pat Hickey, Lucien DeBlois, Mike McEwen, Dean Turner, and future considerations (Bobby Crawford), Nov. 2, 1979.

Bob Beckett

BECKETT, ROBERT OWEN 6', 185 lbs.
B. Apr. 8, 1936, Unionville, Ont. Center, Shoots L

YEAR	TEAM & LEAGUE		GP	G	A	PTS	PIM
1956-57	**BOS**	**N**	18	0	3	3	2
1957-58			9	0	0	0	2
1961-62			32	7	2	9	14
1963-64			7	0	1	1	0
4 yrs.		**N Totals:**	66	7	6	13	18

James Bedard

BEDARD, JAMES LEO 6', 180 lbs.
B. Nov. 19, 1927, Admiral, Sask. Defense, Shoots L

YEAR	TEAM & LEAGUE		GP	G	A	PTS	PIM
1949-50	**CHI**	**N**	5	0	0	0	2
1950-51			17	1	1	2	6
2 yrs.		**N Totals:**	22	1	1	2	8

Jim Bedard

BEDARD, JAMES ARTHUR 5'10", 181 lbs.
B. Nov. 14, 1956, Niagara Falls, Ont. Shoots L

YEAR	TEAM & LEAGUE		GP	G	A	PTS	PIM
1977-78	**WASH**	**N**	43	0	2	2	4

John Bednarski

BEDNARSKI, JOHN SEVERN 5'10", 195 lbs.
B. July 4, 1952, Thunder Bay, Ont. Defense, Shoots L

YEAR	TEAM & LEAGUE		GP	G	A	PTS	PIM
1974-75	**NYR**	**N**	35	1	10	11	37
1975-76			59	1	8	9	77
1976-77			5	0	0	0	0
1979-80	**EDM**	**N**	1	0	0	0	0
4 yrs.		**N Totals:**	100	2	18	20	114
PLAYOFFS							
1974-75	**NYR**	**N**	1	0	0	0	17

Signed as free agent by **Edmonton** July, 1979. Signed as free agent by **Buffalo** June 26, 1980.

Ed Beers

BEERS, EDWARD JOSEPH 6'2", 200 lbs.
B. Oct. 12, 1959, Merritt, B.C. Left Wing, Shoots L

YEAR	TEAM & LEAGUE		GP	G	A	PTS	PIM
1981-82	**CALG**	**N**	5	1	1	2	21
1982-83			41	11	15	26	21
2 yrs.		**N Totals:**	46	12	16	28	42
PLAYOFFS							
1982-83	**CALG**	**N**	8	1	1	2	27

Dick Behling

BEHLING, RICHARD CLARENCE
B. Mar. 16, 1916, Kitchener, Ont. Defense, Shoots R

YEAR	TEAM & LEAGUE		GP	G	A	PTS	PIM
1940-41	**DET**	**N**	3	0	0	0	0
1942-43			2	1	0	1	2
2 yrs.		**N Totals:**	5	1	0	1	2

Frank Beisler

BEISLER, FRANK
B. New Haven, Conn. Defense

YEAR	TEAM & LEAGUE		GP	G	A	PTS	PIM
1936-37	**NYA**	**N**	1	0	0	0	0
1939-40			1	0	0	0	0
2 yrs.		**N Totals:**	2	0	0	0	0

Alain Belanger

BELANGER, ALAIN 6'1", 190 lbs.
B. Jan. 18, 1956, St. Janvier, Que. Right Wing, Shoots R

YEAR	TEAM & LEAGUE		GP	G	A	PTS	PIM
1977-78	**TOR**	**N**	9	0	1	1	6

Danny Belisle

BELISLE, DANIEL GEORGE 5'10", 175 lbs.
B. May 9, 1937, South Porcupine, Ont. Right Wing, Shoots R

YEAR	TEAM & LEAGUE		GP	G	A	PTS	PIM
1960-61	**NYR**	**N**	4	2	0	2	0

Jean Beliveau

BELIVEAU, JEAN ARTHUR (Le Gros Bill)
6'3", 205 lbs.
B. Aug. 31, 1931, Trois Rivieres, Que. Center, Shoots L
Won Hart Trophy, 1955–56 , 1963-64
Won Art Ross Trophy, 1955-56
Won Conn Smythe Trophy, 1964-65
Hall of Fame, 1972

YEAR	TEAM & LEAGUE		GP	G	A	PTS	PIM
1950-51	**MONT**	**N**	2	1	1	2	0
1952-53			3	5	0	5	0
1953-54			44	13	21	34	22
1954-55			70	37	36	73	58
1955-56			70	**47**	41	**88**	143

Jean Beliveau continued

YEAR	TEAM & LEAGUE		GP	G	A	PTS	PIM
1956-57			69	33	51	84	105
1957-58			55	27	32	59	93
1958-59			64	**45**	46	91	67
1959-60			60	34	40	74	57
1960-61			69	32	**58**	90	57
1961-62			43	18	23	41	36
1962-63			69	18	**49**	67	68
1963-64			68	28	50	78	42
1964-65			58	20	23	43	76
1965-66			67	29	**48**	77	50
1966-67			53	12	26	38	22
1967-68			59	31	37	68	28
1968-69			69	33	49	82	55
1969-70			63	19	30	49	10
1970-71			70	25	51	76	40
20 yrs.		**N Totals:**	1125	507	712	1219	1029
PLAYOFFS							
1953-54	**MONT**	**N**	10	2	8	10	4
1954-55			12	6	7	13	18
1955-56*			10	12	7	19	22
1956-57*			10	6	6	12	15
1957-58*			10	4	8	12	10
1958-59*			3	1	4	5	4
1959-60*			8	5	2	7	6
1960-61			6	0	5	5	0
1961-62			6	2	1	3	4
1962-63			5	2	1	3	2
1963-64			5	2	0	2	18
1964-65*			13	8	8	16	34
1965-66*			10	5	5	10	6
1966-67			10	6	5	11	26
1967-68*			10	7	4	11	6
1968-69*			14	5	10	15	8
1970-71*			20	6	16	22	28
17 yrs.		**N Totals:**	162	79	97	176	211

Billy Bell

BELL, BILLY
B. June 10, 1891, Lachine, Que. Center

YEAR	TEAM & LEAGUE		GP	G	A	PTS	PIM
1917-18	**MON(W)**	**N**	2	0	0	0	0
	MONT	**N**	6	1	0	1	3
	2 team total		8	1	0	1	3
1918-19			1	0	0	0	0
1920-21			4	0	0	0	0
1921-22			6	1	0	1	0
	OTTA	**N**	17	1	1	2	4
	2 team total		23	2	1	3	4
1922-23	**MONT**	**N**	15	0	0	0	0
1923-24			10	0	0	0	0
6 yrs.		**N Totals:**	61	3	1	4	7
PLAYOFFS							
1921-22	**OTTA**	**N**	1	0	0	0	0
1922-23	**MONT**	**N**	2	0	0	0	0
1923-24*			5	0	0	0	0
3 yrs.		**N Totals:**	8	0	0	0	0

Harry Bell

BELL, HARRY 5'8½", 180 lbs.
B. Oct. 31, 1925, Regina, Sask. Defense, Shoots R

YEAR	TEAM & LEAGUE		GP	G	A	PTS	PIM
1946-47	**NYR**	**N**	1	0	1	1	0

Joe Bell

BELL, JOSEPH 5'10", 170 lbs.
B. Nov. 27, 1923, Portage la Prairie, Man.
Left Wing, Shoots L

YEAR	TEAM & LEAGUE		GP	G	A	PTS	PIM
1942-43	**NYR**	**N**	15	2	5	7	6
1946-47			47	6	4	10	12
2 yrs.		**N Totals:**	62	8	9	17	18

Neil Belland

BELLAND, NEIL 5'11", 175 lbs.
B. Apr. 3, 1961, Parry Sound, Ont. Defense, Shoots L

YEAR	TEAM & LEAGUE		GP	G	A	PTS	PIM
1981-82	**VAN**	**N**	28	3	6	9	16
1982-83			14	2	4	6	4

Neil Belland continued

YEAR	TEAM	LEAGUE	GP	G	A	PTS	PIM
2 yrs.		N Totals:	42	5	10	15	20
PLAYOFFS							
1981-82	**VAN**	**N**	17	1	7	8	16

Signed as free agent by **Vancouver** Oct. 1, 1980.

Pete Bellefeuille

BELLEFEUILLE, PETER
B. Unknown — Right Wing

YEAR	TEAM	LEAGUE	GP	G	A	PTS	PIM
1925-26	**TOR**	**N**	36	14	2	16	22
1926-27			13	0	0	0	12
	DET	**N**	18	6	0	6	14
	2 team total		31	6	0	6	26
1928-29			1	1	0	1	0
1929-30			26	5	2	7	10
4 yrs.		N Totals:	94	26	4	30	58

Andy Bellemer

BELLEMER, ANDREW
B. July 3, 1904, Penetang, Ont. — Forward

YEAR	TEAM	LEAGUE	GP	G	A	PTS	PIM
1932-33	**MON(M)**	**N**	15	0	0	0	0

Brian Bellows

BELLOWS, BRIAN — 5'11", 194 lbs.
B. Sept. 1, 1964, St. Catherines, Ont. — Right Wing, Shoots R

YEAR	TEAM	LEAGUE	GP	G	A	PTS	PIM
1982-83	**MINN**	**N**	78	35	30	65	27
PLAYOFFS							
1982-83	**MINN**	**N**	9	5	4	9	18

Lin Bend

BEND, JOHN LINTHWAITE — 5'9½", 165 lbs.
B. Dec. 20, 1922, Poplar Point, Man. — Center, Shoots L

YEAR	TEAM	LEAGUE	GP	G	A	PTS	PIM
1942-43	**NYR**	**N**	8	3	1	4	2

Bill Bennett

BENNETT, WILLIAM — 6'5", 235 lbs.
B. May 31, 1953, Warwick, R.I. — Left Wing, Shoots L

YEAR	TEAM	LEAGUE	GP	G	A	PTS	PIM
1978-79	**BOS**	**N**	7	1	4	5	2
1979-80	**HART**	**N**	24	3	3	6	63
2 yrs.		N Totals:	31	4	7	11	65

Claimed by **Hartford** from Boston in Expansion Draft, June 13, 1979.

Curt Bennett

BENNETT, CURT ALEXANDER — 6'3", 195 lbs.
B. Mar. 27, 1948, Regina,Sask. — Center, Shoots L

YEAR	TEAM	LEAGUE	GP	G	A	PTS	PIM
1970-71	**STL**	**N**	4	2	0	2	0
1971-72			31	3	5	8	30
1972-73	**NYR**	**N**	16	0	1	1	11
	ATL	**N**	52	18	17	35	9
	2 team total		68	18	18	36	20
1973-74			71	17	24	41	34
1974-75			80	31	33	64	40
1975-76			80	34	31	65	61
1976-77			76	22	25	47	36
1977-78			25	3	7	10	10
	STL	**N**	50	7	17	24	54
	2 team total		75	10	24	34	64
1978-79			74	14	19	33	62
1979-80	**ATL**	**N**	21	1	3	4	0
10 yrs.		N Totals:	580	152	182	334	347
PLAYOFFS							
1970-71	**STL**	**N**	2	0	0	0	0
1971-72			10	0	0	0	12
1973-74	**ATL**	**N**	4	0	1	1	34
1975-76			2	0	0	0	4
1976-77			3	1	0	1	7
5 yrs.		N Totals:	21	1	1	2	57

Traded to **N.Y. Rangers** by St. Louis with goaltender Peter McDuffe to complete earlier trade (May 24) in which St. Louis received Steve Durbano, June 7, 1972. Traded to **Atlanta** by N.Y. Rangers for Ron Harris, Nov. 29, 1972. Traded to **St. Louis** by Atlanta with Phil Myre and Barry Gibbs for Yves Belanger, Dick Redmond, Bob MacMillan and St. Louis' second round choice (Mike Perovich) in 1979 Entry Draft, Dec. 12, 1977. Traded to **Atlanta** by St. Louis for Bobby Simpson, May 24, 1979. Claimed by **Atlanta** as fill in Expansion Draft, June 13, 1979.

Frank Bennett

BENNETT, FRANK
B. Unknown — Forward

YEAR	TEAM	LEAGUE	GP	G	A	PTS	PIM
1943-44	**DET**	**N**	7	0	1	1	2

Harvey Bennett

BENNETT, HARVEY A., JR. — 6'4", 215 lbs.
B. Aug. 9, 1952, Cranston, R.I. — Center, Shoots L

YEAR	TEAM	LEAGUE	GP	G	A	PTS	PIM
1974-75	**PITT**	**N**	7	0	0	0	0
1975-76			25	3	3	6	53
	WASH	**N**	49	12	10	22	39
	2 team total		74	15	13	28	92
1976-77			18	2	6	8	34
	PHI	**N**	51	12	8	20	60
	2 team total		69	14	14	28	94
1977-78			2	1	0	1	0
	MINN	**N**	64	11	10	21	91
	2 team total		66	12	10	22	91
1978-79	**STL**	**N**	52	3	9	12	63
5 yrs.		N Totals:	268	44	46	90	340
PLAYOFFS							
1976-77	**PHI**	**N**	4	0	0	0	2

Traded to **Washington** by Pittsburgh for Stan Gilbertson, Dec. 16, 1975. Sold to **Philadelphia** by Washington, Nov. 24, 1976. Traded to **Minnesota** by Philadelphia for Blake Dunlop and Minnesota's third-round choice (Gord Salt) in the 1978 Amateur Draft, Oct. 28, 1977. Traded to **St. Louis** by Minnesota for St. Louis' second round choice in the 1981 Entry Draft, Aug. 8, 1978.

John Bennett

BENNETT, JOHN — 6'1", 175 lbs.
B. Jan. 19, 1950, Cranston, R.I. — Left Wing, Shoots R

YEAR	TEAM	LEAGUE	GP	G	A	PTS	PIM
1972-73	**PHI**	**W**	34	4	6	10	18

Max Bennett

BENNETT, MAXWELL
B. Nov. 4, 1912, Cobalt, Ont. — Right Wing, Shoots R

YEAR	TEAM	LEAGUE	GP	G	A	PTS	PIM
1935-36	**MONT**	**N**	1	0	0	0	0

Wendall Bennett

BENNETT, WENDALL — 6'2", 180 lbs.
B. Mar. 24, 1950, Loon Lake, Sask. — Right Wing, Shoots R

YEAR	TEAM	LEAGUE	GP	G	A	PTS	PIM
1974-75	**PHOE**	**W**	67	4	15	19	92
PLAYOFFS							
1974-75	**PHOE**	**W**	5	1	2	3	6

Jim Benning

BENNING, JAMES — 6', 183 lbs.
B. Apr. 29, 1963, Edmonton, Alta. — Defense, Shoots L

YEAR	TEAM	LEAGUE	GP	G	A	PTS	PIM
1981-82	**TOR**	**N**	74	7	24	31	46
1982-83			74	5	17	22	47
2 yrs.		N Totals:	148	12	41	53	93
PLAYOFFS							
1982-83	**TOR**	**N**	4	1	1	2	2

Joe Benoit

BENOIT, JOSEPH — 5'9½", 160 lbs.
B. Mar. 37, 1916, St. Albert, Alta. — Right Wing, Shoots R

YEAR	TEAM	LEAGUE	GP	G	A	PTS	PIM
1940-41	**MONT**	**N**	45	16	16	32	32
1941-42			46	20	16	36	27
1942-43			49	30	27	57	23
1945-46			39	9	10	19	8
1946-47			6	0	0	0	4

Joe Benoit continued

YEAR	TEAM & LEAGUE		GP	G	A	PTS	PIM
5 yrs.		N Totals:	185	75	69	144	94
PLAYOFFS							
1940-41	**MONT**	**N**	3	4	0	4	2
1941-42			3	1	0	1	5
1942-43			5	1	3	4	4
3 yrs.		N Totals:	11	6	3	9	11

Bill Benson

BENSON, WILLIAM LLOYD 5'11", 165 lbs.
B. July 29, 1920, Winnipeg, Man. Center, Shoots L

YEAR	TEAM & LEAGUE		GP	G	A	PTS	PIM
1940-41	**NYA**	**N**	22	3	4	7	4
1941-42			45	8	21	29	31
2 yrs.		N Totals:	67	11	25	36	35

Bobby Benson

BENSON, ROBERT
B. Buffalo, N.Y. Defense

YEAR	TEAM & LEAGUE		GP	G	A	PTS	PIM
1924-25	**BOS**	**N**	8	0	1	1	4

Doug Bentley

BENTLEY, DOUGLAS WAGNER 5'8", 145 lbs.
B. Sept. 3, 1916, Delisle, Sask. Left Wing, Shoots L
Won Art Ross Trophy, 1942-43
Hall of Fame, 1964

YEAR	TEAM & LEAGUE		GP	G	A	PTS	PIM
1939-40	**CHI**	**N**	39	12	7	19	12
1940-41			47	8	20	28	12
1941-42			38	12	14	26	11
1942-43			50	**33**	40	**73**	18
1943-44			50	**38**	39	77	22
1945-46			36	19	21	40	16
1946-47			52	21	34	55	18
1947-48			60	20	**37**	57	16
1948-49			58	23	**43**	66	38
1949-50			64	20	33	53	28
1950-51			44	9	23	32	20
1951-52			8	2	3	5	4
1953-54	**NYR**	**N**	20	2	10	12	2
13 yrs.		N Totals:	566	219	324	543	217
PLAYOFFS							
1939-40	**CHI**	**N**	2	0	0	0	0
1940-41			5	1	1	2	4
1941-42			3	0	1	1	4
1943-44			9	8	4	12	4
1945-46			4	0	2	2	0
5 yrs.		N Totals:	23	9	8	17	12

Purchased by **N.Y. Rangers** from Chicago, June 30, 1953.

Max Bentley

BENTLEY, MAXWELL HERBERT LLOYD
5'8½", 158 lbs.
B. Mar. 1, 1920, Delisle, Sask. Center, Shoots L
Won Hart Trophy, 1945-46
Won Art Ross Trophy, 1945–46 , 1946-47
Won Lady Byng Trophy, 1942-43
Hall of Fame, 1966

YEAR	TEAM & LEAGUE		GP	G	A	PTS	PIM
1940-41	**CHI**	**N**	36	7	10	17	6
1941-42			39	13	17	30	19
1942-43			47	26	44	70	2
1945-46			47	30	31	**61**	6
1946-47			60	29	43	**72**	12
1947-48			6	3	3	6	0
	TOR	**N**	53	23	25	48	10
	2 team total		59	26	28	54	10
1948-49			60	19	22	41	18
1949-50			69	23	18	41	14
1950-51			67	21	41	62	34
1951-52			69	24	17	41	40
1952-53			36	12	11	23	16
1953-54	**NYR**	**N**	57	14	18	32	15
12 yrs.		N Totals:	646	244	300	544	192
PLAYOFFS							
1940-41	**CHI**	**N**	5	1	3	4	2

Max Bentley continued

YEAR	TEAM & LEAGUE		GP	G	A	PTS	PIM
1941-42			3	2	0	2	0
1945-46			4	1	0	1	4
1947-48*	**TOR**	**N**	9	4	7	11	0
1948-49*			9	4	3	7	2
1949-50			7	3	3	6	0
1950-51*			11	2	11	13	4
1951-52			4	1	0	1	2
8 yrs.		N Totals:	52	18	27	45	14

Purchased by **N.Y. Rangers** from Toronto, Aug. 11, 1953.

Reggie Bentley

BENTLEY, REGINALD
B. May 3, 1914, Delisle, Sask. Right Wing, Shoots L

YEAR	TEAM & LEAGUE		GP	G	A	PTS	PIM
1942-43	**CHI**	**N**	11	1	2	3	2

Jim Benzelock

BENZELOCK, JAMES JOHN (The Big Cat)
5'11", 187 lbs.
B. June 21, 1947, Winnipeg, Man. Right Wing, Shoots R

YEAR	TEAM & LEAGUE		GP	G	A	PTS	PIM
1972-73	**ALTA**	**W**	26	1	1	2	10
	CHI	**W**	43	9	12	21	23
	2 team total		69	10	13	23	33
1973-74			53	6	7	13	19
1974-75			10	0	2	2	14
1975-76	**QUE**	**W**	34	2	5	7	6
4 yrs.		W Totals:	166	18	27	45	72
PLAYOFFS							
1973-74	**CHI**	**W**	18	2	2	4	36
1975-76	**QUE**	**W**	3	0	0	0	0
2 yrs.		W Totals:	21	2	2	4	36

Red Berenson

BERENSON, GORDON ARTHUR (The Red Baron)
6', 195 lbs.
B. Dec. 8, 1939, Regina, Sask. Center, Shoots L

YEAR	TEAM & LEAGUE		GP	G	A	PTS	PIM
1961-62	**MONT**	**N**	4	1	2	3	4
1962-63			37	2	6	8	15
1963-64			69	7	9	16	12
1964-65			3	1	2	3	0
1965-66			23	3	4	7	12
1966-67	**NYR**	**N**	30	0	5	5	2
1967-68			19	2	1	3	2
	STL	**N**	55	22	29	51	22
	2 team total		74	24	30	54	24
1968-69			76	35	47	82	43
1969-70			67	33	39	72	38
1970-71			45	16	26	42	12
	DET	**N**	24	5	12	17	4
	2 team total		69	21	38	59	16
1971-72			78	28	41	69	16
1972-73			78	13	30	43	8
1973-74			76	24	42	66	28
1974-75			27	3	3	6	8
	STL	**N**	44	12	19	31	12
	2 team total		71	15	22	37	20
1975-76			72	20	27	47	47
1976-77			80	21	28	49	8
1977-78			80	13	25	38	12
17 yrs.		N Totals:	987	261	397	658	305
PLAYOFFS							
1961-62	**MONT**	**N**	5	2	0	2	0
1962-63			5	0	0	0	0
1963-64			7	0	0	0	4
1964-65*			9	0	1	1	2
1966-67	**NYR**	**N**	4	0	1	1	2
1967-68	**STL**	**N**	18	5	2	7	9
1968-69			12	7	3	10	20
1969-70			16	7	5	12	8
1974-75			2	1	0	1	0
1975-76			3	1	2	3	0
1976-77			4	0	0	0	4
11 yrs.		N Totals:	85	23	14	37	49

Fred Bergdinon

BERGDINON, FRED
B. Quebec City, Que. Forward

YEAR	TEAM & LEAGUE		GP	G	A	PTS	PIM
1925-26	**BOS**	**N**	2	0	0	0	0

Michel Bergeron

BERGERON, MICHEL 5'10", 170 lbs.
B. Nov. 11, 1954, Chicoutimi, Que. Right Wing, Shoots R

YEAR	TEAM & LEAGUE		GP	G	A	PTS	PIM
1974-75	**DET**	**N**	25	10	7	17	10
1975-76			72	32	27	59	48
1976-77			74	21	12	33	98
1977-78			3	1	0	1	0
	NYI	**N**	25	9	6	15	2
	2 team total		28	10	6	16	2
1978-79	**WASH**	**N**	30	7	6	13	7
5 yrs.		**N Totals:**	229	80	58	138	165

Traded to **N.Y. Islanders** by Detroit for Andre St. Laurent, Oct. 20, 1977. Traded to **Washington** by by N.Y. Islanders for Washington's second-round choice (Tomas Jonsson) in the 1979 Entry Draft, Oct. 19, 1978.

Yves Bergeron

BERGERON, YVES 5'9", 165 lbs.
B. Jan. 11, 1952, Malartic, Que. Right Wing, Shoots R

YEAR	TEAM & LEAGUE		GP	G	A	PTS	PIM
1972-73	**QUE**	**W**	65	14	19	33	32
1974-75	**PITT**	**N**	2	0	0	0	0
1976-77			1	0	0	0	0
3 yrs.		**N Totals:**	3	0	0	0	0
		W Totals:	65	14	19	33	32

Bob Bergloff

BERGLOFF, ROBERT 6'1", 185 lbs.
B. July 26, 1958, Dickinson, N.Dak. Defense, Shoots R

YEAR	TEAM & LEAGUE		GP	G	A	PTS	PIM
1982-83	**MINN**	**N**	2	0	0	0	5

Gary Bergman

BERGMAN, GARY GUNNAR 5'11", 185 lbs.
B. Oct. 7, 1938, Kenora, Ont. Defense, Shoots L

YEAR	TEAM & LEAGUE		GP	G	A	PTS	PIM
1964-65	**DET**	**N**	58	4	7	11	85
1965-66			61	3	16	19	96
1966-67			70	5	30	35	129
1967-68			74	13	28	41	109
1968-69			76	7	30	37	80
1969-70			69	6	17	23	122
1970-71			68	8	25	33	149
1971-72			75	6	32	38	138
1972-73			68	3	28	31	71
1973-74			1	0	6	6	18
	MINN	**N**	57	3	23	26	66
	2 team total		58	3	29	32	84
1974-75	**DET**	**N**	76	5	25	30	104
1975-76	**KC**	**N**	75	5	33	38	82
12 yrs.		**N Totals:**	828	68	300	368	1249
PLAYOFFS							
1964-65	**DET**	**N**	5	0	1	1	4
1965-66			12	0	3	3	14
1969-70			4	0	1	1	2
3 yrs.		**N Totals:**	21	0	5	5	20

Drafted by **Detroit** from Montreal, June 10, 1964. Traded to **Minnesota** by Detroit for Ted Harris, Nov. 7, 1973. Traded to **Detroit** by Minnesota for Detroit's third choice (Alex Pirus) in 1975 Amateur Draft, Oct. 1, 1974.

Thommie Bergman

BERGMAN, LARS RUDOLF THOMMIE 6'2", 200 lbs.
B. Dec. 10, 1947, Munkfors, Sweden Defense, Shoots L

YEAR	TEAM & LEAGUE		GP	G	A	PTS	PIM
1972-73	**DET**	**N**	75	9	12	21	70
1973-74			43	0	3	3	21
1974-75			18	0	1	1	27
	WINN	**W**	49	4	15	19	70
	2 team total		67	4	16	20	97
1975-76			81	11	30	41	111
1976-77			42	2	24	26	37
1977-78			65	5	28	33	43
	DET	**N**	14	1	6	7	16
	2 team total		79	6	34	40	59

Thommie Bergman continued

YEAR	TEAM & LEAGUE		GP	G	A	PTS	PIM
1978-79			68	10	17	27	64
1979-80			28	1	5	6	45
8 yrs.		**N Totals:**	246	21	44	65	243
		W Totals:	237	22	97	119	261
PLAYOFFS							
1975-76	**WINN**	**W**	13	3	10	13	8
1977-78	**DET**	**N**	7	0	2	2	2
2 yrs.		**N Totals:**	7	0	2	2	2
		W Totals:	13	3	10	13	8

Louis Berlinquette

BERLINQUETTE, LOUIS
Left Wing

YEAR	TEAM & LEAGUE		GP	G	A	PTS	PIM
1917-18	**MONT**	**N**	20	2	0	2	9
1918-19			18	5	3	8	9
1919-20			24	7	7	14	36
1920-21			24	12	**9**	21	24
1921-22			24	12	5	17	8
1922-23			24	2	3	5	4
1924-25	**MON(M)**	**N**	29	4	2	6	22
1925-26	**PITT**	**N**	30	0	0	0	8
8 yrs.		**N Totals:**	193	44	29	73	120
PLAYOFFS							
1917-18	**MONT**	**N**	2	0	0	0	0
1918-19			2	1	0	1	9
1922-23			2	0	1	1	0
1925-26	**PITT**	**N**	2	0	0	0	0
4 yrs.		**N Totals:**	8	1	1	2	9

Jean Bernier

BERNIER, JEAN 5'10", 170 lbs.
B. July 21, 1954, St. Hyacinthe, Que. Defense, Shoots L

YEAR	TEAM & LEAGUE		GP	G	A	PTS	PIM
1974-75	**QUE**	**W**	34	1	13	14	13
1975-76			81	4	26	30	10
1976-77			72	2	13	15	23
1977-78			74	10	32	42	4
4 yrs.		**W Totals:**	261	17	84	101	50
PLAYOFFS							
1974-75	**QUE**	**W**	9	0	1	1	2
1975-76			4	0	1	1	0
1976-77			9	0	2	2	0
1977-78			10	3	4	7	2
4 yrs.		**W Totals:**	32	3	8	11	4

Rights sold to **Atlanta** by Chicago, Oct. 5, 1978.

Serge Bernier

BERNIER, SERGE JOSEPH 6'1", 190 lbs.
B. Apr. 29, 1947, Padoue, Que. Center, Shoots R

YEAR	TEAM & LEAGUE		GP	G	A	PTS	PIM
1968-69	**PHI**	**N**	1	0	0	0	2
1969-70			1	0	1	1	0
1970-71			77	23	28	51	77
1971-72			44	12	11	23	51
	LA	**N**	26	11	11	22	12
	2 team total		70	23	22	45	63
1972-73			75	22	46	68	43
1973-74	**QUE**	**W**	74	37	49	86	107
1974-75			76	54	68	122	75
1975-76			70	34	68	102	91
1976-77			74	43	53	96	94
1977-78			58	26	52	78	48
1978-79			65	36	46	82	71
1979-80	**QUE**	**N**	32	8	14	22	31
1980-81			46	2	8	10	18
13 yrs.		**N Totals:**	302	78	119	197	234
		W Totals:	417	230	336	566	486
PLAYOFFS							
1970-71	**PHI**	**N**	4	1	1	2	0
1974-75	**QUE**	**W**	16	8	8	16	6
1975-76			5	2	6	8	6
1976-77			17	14	22	36	10
1977-78			11	4	10	14	17
1978-79			1	0	0	0	2

Serge Bernier continued

YEAR	TEAM & LEAGUE		GP	G	A	PTS	PIM
1980-81	**QUE**	**N**	1	0	0	0	0
7 yrs.		**N Totals:**	5	1	1	2	0
		W Totals:	50	28	46	74	41

Traded to **Los Angeles** by Philadelphia with Bill Lesuk and Jim Johnson for Bill Flett, Ed Joyal, Jean Potvin, and Ross Lonsberry, Jan. 28, 1972.

Bob Berry

BERRY, ROBERT VICTOR 6', 190 lbs.
B. Nov. 29, 1943, Montreal, Que. Left Wing, Shoots L

YEAR	TEAM & LEAGUE		GP	G	A	PTS	PIM
1968-69	**MONT**	**N**	2	0	0	0	0
1970-71	**LA**	**N**	77	25	38	63	52
1971-72			78	17	22	39	44
1972-73			78	36	28	64	75
1973-74			77	23	33	56	56
1974-75			80	25	23	48	60
1975-76			80	20	22	42	37
1976-77			69	13	25	38	20
8 yrs.		**N Totals:**	541	159	191	350	344
PLAYOFFS							
1973-74	**LA**	**N**	5	0	0	0	0
1974-75			3	1	2	3	2
1975-76			9	1	1	2	0
1976-77			9	0	3	3	4
4 yrs.		**N Totals:**	26	2	6	8	6

Sold to **Los Angeles** by Montreal, Oct. 8, 1970.

Doug Berry

BERRY, DOUGLAS ALAN 6'1", 190 lbs.
B. June 3, 1957, New Westminster, B.C. Center, Shoots L

YEAR	TEAM & LEAGUE		GP	G	A	PTS	PIM
1978-79	**EDM**	**W**	29	6	3	9	4
1979-80	**COLO**	**N**	75	7	23	30	16
1980-81			46	3	10	13	8
3 yrs.		**N Totals:**	121	10	33	43	24
		W Totals:	29	6	3	9	4

Reclaimed by **Colorado** from Edmonton prior to Expansion Draft, June 9, 1979.

Fred Berry

BERRY, FREDERICK ALLAN 5'9", 175 lbs.
B. Mar. 26, 1956, Edmonton, Alta. Center, Shoots L

YEAR	TEAM & LEAGUE		GP	G	A	PTS	PIM
1976-77	**DET**	**N**	3	0	0	0	0

Ken Berry

BERRY, KENNETH E 5'9", 165 lbs.
B. June 21, 1960, New Westminster, B.C.
Left Wing, Shoots L

YEAR	TEAM & LEAGUE		GP	G	A	PTS	PIM
1981-82	**EDM**	**N**	15	2	3	5	9

Traded to **Edmonton** by Vancouver with Garry Lariviere for Blair MacDonald and Lars-Gunnar Petersson, Mar. 10, 1981.

Phil Besler

BESLER, PHILIP
B. Dec. 9, 1911, Melville,Sask. Right Wing, Shoots R

YEAR	TEAM & LEAGUE		GP	G	A	PTS	PIM
1935-36	**BOS**	**N**	8	0	0	0	0
1938-39	**CHI**	**N**	17	1	3	4	16
	DET	**N**	5	0	1	1	2
	2 team total		22	1	4	5	18
2 yrs.		**N Totals:**	30	1	4	5	18

Pete Bessone

BESSONE, PETER 5'10½", 200 lbs.
B. Jan. 13, 1913, New Bedford, Mass. Defense, Shoots L

YEAR	TEAM & LEAGUE		GP	G	A	PTS	PIM
1937-38	**DET**	**N**	6	0	1	1	6

John Bethel

BETHEL, JOHN CHARLES 5'11", 185 lbs.
B. Nov. 5, 1957, Montreal, Que. Left Wing, Shoots L

YEAR	TEAM & LEAGUE		GP	G	A	PTS	PIM
1979-80	**WINN**	**N**	17	0	2	2	4

Signed as free agent by **Winnipeg** Nov. 12, 1979.

Sam Bettio

BETTIO, SILVIO ANGELO 5'8", 175 lbs.
B. Dec. 1, 1928, Copper Cliff, Ont. Left Wing, Shoots L

YEAR	TEAM & LEAGUE		GP	G	A	PTS	PIM
1949-50	**BOS**	**N**	44	9	12	21	32

Nick Beverley

BEVERLEY, NICHOLAS GERALD 6'2", 185 lbs.
B. Apr. 21, 1947, Toronto, Ont. Defense, Shoots R

YEAR	TEAM & LEAGUE		GP	G	A	PTS	PIM
1966-67	**BOS**	**N**	2	0	0	0	0
1969-70			2	0	0	0	2
1971-72			1	0	0	0	0
1972-73			76	1	10	11	26
1973-74			10	0	0	0	0
	PITT	**N**	67	2	14	16	21
	2 team total		77	2	14	16	21
1974-75	**NYR**	**N**	54	3	15	18	19
1975-76			63	1	8	9	46
1976-77			9	0	0	0	2
	MINN	**N**	52	2	17	19	6
	2 team total		61	2	17	19	8
1977-78			57	7	14	21	18
1978-79	**LA**	**N**	7	0	3	3	0
	COLO	**N**	52	2	4	6	6
	2 team total		59	2	7	9	6
1979-80			46	0	9	9	10
11 yrs.		**N Totals:**	498	18	94	112	156
PLAYOFFS							
1972-73	**BOS**	**N**	4	0	0	0	0
1974-75	**NYR**	**N**	3	0	1	1	0
2 yrs.		**N Totals:**	7	0	1	1	0

Traded to **Pittsburgh** by Boston for Darryl Edestrand, Oct. 25, 1973. Traded to **N.Y. Rangers** by Pittsburgh for Vic Hadfield, May 27, 1974. Traded to **Minnesota** by N.Y. Rangers with Bill Fairbairn for Bill Goldsworthy, Nov. 11, 1976. Claimed on waivers by **Los Angeles** from Minnesota, Sept. 5, 1978. Traded to **Colorado** by Los Angeles for Colorado's fourth-round choice in the 1982 Entry Draft, Nov. 18, 1978. Claimed by **Hartford** from Colorado in Expansion Draft, June 13, 1979. Signed as a free agent by **Colorado** Sept. 15, 1979.

Dwight Bialowas

BIALOWAS, DWIGHT JOSEPH 6', 185 lbs.
B. Sept. 8, 1952, Regina, Sask. Defense, Shoots R

YEAR	TEAM & LEAGUE		GP	G	A	PTS	PIM
1973-74	**ATL**	**N**	11	0	0	0	2
1974-75			37	3	9	12	20
	MINN	**N**	40	2	10	12	2
	2 team total		77	5	19	24	22
1975-76			58	5	18	23	22
1976-77			18	1	9	10	0
4 yrs.		**N Totals:**	164	11	46	57	46

Traded to **Minnesota** by Atlanta with Dean Talafous for Barry Gibbs, Jan. 3, 1975.

Wayne Bianchin

BIANCHIN, WAYNE RICHARD 5'10", 180 lbs.
B. Sept. 6, 1953, Nanaimo, B.C. Left Wing, Shoots L

YEAR	TEAM & LEAGUE		GP	G	A	PTS	PIM
1973-74	**PITT**	**N**	69	12	13	25	38
1974-75			2	0	0	0	0
1975-76			14	1	5	6	4
1976-77			79	28	6	34	28
1977-78			61	20	13	33	40
1978-79			40	7	4	11	20
1979-80	**EDM**	**N**	11	0	0	0	7
7 yrs.		**N Totals:**	276	68	41	109	137
PLAYOFFS							
1976-77	**PITT**	**N**	3	0	1	1	6

Claimed by **Edmonton** from Pittsburgh in Expansion Draft, June 13, 1979.

Todd Bidner

BIDNER, RICHARD TODD 6'2", 205 lbs.
B. July 5, 1961, Petrolia, Ont. Left Wing, Shoots L

YEAR	TEAM & LEAGUE		GP	G	A	PTS	PIM
1981-82	WASH	N	12	2	1	3	7

Traded to **Edmonton** by Washington for Doug Hicks, Mar. 9, 1982.

Larry Bignell

BIGNELL, LARRY IRVIN 6', 170 lbs.
B. Jan. 7, 1950, Edmonton, Alta. Defense, Shoots L

YEAR	TEAM & LEAGUE		GP	G	A	PTS	PIM
1973-74	PITT	N	20	0	3	3	2
1975-76	D-O	W	41	5	5	10	43
2 yrs.		N Totals:	20	0	3	3	2
		W Totals:	41	5	5	10	43
PLAYOFFS							
1974-75	PITT	N	3	0	0	0	2

Gilles Bilodeau

BILODEAU, GILLES 6'1", 220 lbs.
B. July 31, 1955, St. Prime, Que. Left Wing, Shoots L

YEAR	TEAM & LEAGUE		GP	G	A	PTS	PIM
1975-76	TOR	W	14	0	1	1	38
1976-77	BIRM	W	34	2	6	8	133
1977-78			59	2	2	4	258
1978-79	QUE	W	36	3	6	9	141
1979-80	QUE	N	9	0	1	1	25
5 yrs.		N Totals:	9	0	1	1	25
		W Totals:	143	7	15	22	570
PLAYOFFS							
1977-78	BIRM	W	3	0	0	0	27
1978-79	QUE	W	3	0	0	0	25
2 yrs.		W Totals:	6	0	0	0	52

Yvon Bilodeau

BILODEAU, YVON 6'3", 210 lbs.
B. Jan. 18, 1951, Vimy, Alta. Defense, Shoots L

YEAR	TEAM & LEAGUE		GP	G	A	PTS	PIM
1975-76	CALG	W	4	0	0	0	2

Jack Bionda

BIONDA, JACK ARTHUR 6', 175 lbs.
B. Sept. 18, 1933, Huntsville, Ont. Defense, Shoots L

YEAR	TEAM & LEAGUE		GP	G	A	PTS	PIM
1955-56	TOR	N	13	0	1	1	18
1956-57	BOS	N	35	2	3	5	43
1957-58			42	1	4	5	50
1958-59			3	0	1	1	2
4 yrs.		N Totals:	93	3	9	12	113
PLAYOFFS							
1956-57	BOS	N	10	0	1	1	14
1958-59			1	0	0	0	0
2 yrs.		N Totals:	11	0	1	1	14

Drafted by **N.Y. Rangers** from Toronto, June 6, 1956.

Milt Black

BLACK, MILTON 6', 190 lbs.
B. June 20, 1949, Winnipeg, Man. Right Wing, Shoots R

YEAR	TEAM & LEAGUE		GP	G	A	PTS	PIM
1972-73	WINN	W	77	18	16	34	31
1973-74			47	6	9	15	14
1974-75			65	4	6	10	10
3 yrs.		W Totals:	189	28	31	59	55
PLAYOFFS							
1972-73	WINN	W	14	1	3	4	2

Stephen Black

BLACK, STEPHEN 6', 185 lbs.
B. Mar. 31, 1927, Fort William, Ont. Left Wing, Shoots L

YEAR	TEAM & LEAGUE		GP	G	A	PTS	PIM
1949-50	DET	N	69	7	14	21	53
1950-51			5	0	0	0	2
	CHI	N	39	4	6	10	22
	2 team total		44	4	6	10	24

Stephen Black continued

YEAR	TEAM & LEAGUE		GP	G	A	PTS	PIM
2 yrs.		N Totals:	113	11	20	31	77
PLAYOFFS							
1949-50*	DET	N	13	0	0	0	13

Traded to **Chicago** by Detroit with Lee Fogolin for Bert Olmstead and Vic Stasiuk, Dec. 10, 1950.

Bob Blackburn

BLACKBURN, ROBERT JOHN 5'11", 198 lbs.
B. Feb. 1, 1938, Rouyn, Que. Defense, Shoots L

YEAR	TEAM & LEAGUE		GP	G	A	PTS	PIM
1968-69	NYR	N	11	0	0	0	0
1969-70	PITT	N	60	4	7	11	51
1970-71			64	4	5	9	54
3 yrs.		N Totals:	135	8	12	20	105
PLAYOFFS							
1969-70	PITT	N	6	0	0	0	4

Drafted by **Pittsburgh** from N.Y. Rangers, June 11, 1969.

Don Blackburn

BLACKBURN, JOHN DONALD 6', 190 lbs.
B. May 14, 1938, Kirkland Lake, Ont. Left Wing, Shoots L

YEAR	TEAM & LEAGUE		GP	G	A	PTS	PIM
1962-63	BOS	N	6	0	5	5	4
1967-68	PHI	N	67	9	20	29	23
1968-69			48	7	9	16	36
1969-70	NYR	N	3	0	0	0	0
1970-71			1	0	0	0	0
1972-73	NYI	N	56	7	10	17	20
	MINN	N	4	0	0	0	4
	2 team total		60	7	10	17	24
1973-74	NE	W	75	20	39	59	18
1974-75			50	18	32	50	10
1975-76			21	2	3	5	6
9 yrs.		N Totals:	185	23	44	67	87
		W Totals:	146	40	74	114	34
PLAYOFFS							
1967-68	PHI	N	7	3	0	3	8
1968-69			4	0	0	0	0
1969-70	NYR	N	1	0	0	0	0
1973-74	NE	W	7	2	4	6	4
1974-75			5	1	2	3	2
5 yrs.		N Totals:	12	3	0	3	8
		W Totals:	12	3	6	9	6

Drafted by **Toronto** from Montreal, June 15, 1966. Drafted by **Philadelphia** from Toronto in Expansion Draft, June 6, 1967. Traded to **N.Y. Rangers** by Philadelphia with Leon Rochefort for Reg Fleming, June 6, 1969. Drafted by **N.Y. Islanders** in Intra-league Draft, June 6, 1972. Sold to **Minnesota** by N.Y. Islanders, March 1, 1973.

Hank Blade

BLADE, HENRY GORDON 6', 182 lbs.
B. Apr. 28, 1921, Peterborough, Ont. Center, Shoots L

YEAR	TEAM & LEAGUE		GP	G	A	PTS	PIM
1946-47	CHI	N	18	1	3	4	2
1947-48			6	1	0	1	0
2 yrs.		N Totals:	24	2	3	5	2

Tom Bladon

BLADON, THOMAS GEORGE (Bomber) 6'1", 195 lbs.
B. Dec. 29, 1952, Edmonton, Alta. Defense, Shoots R

YEAR	TEAM & LEAGUE		GP	G	A	PTS	PIM
1972-73	PHI	N	78	11	31	42	26
1973-74			70	12	22	34	37
1974-75			76	9	20	29	54
1975-76			80	14	23	37	68
1976-77			80	10	43	53	39
1977-78			79	11	24	35	57
1978-79	PITT	N	78	4	23	27	64
1979-80			57	2	6	8	35
1980-81	EDM	N	1	0	0	0	0
	WINN	N	9	0	5	5	10
	DET	N	2	0	0	0	2
	3 team total		12	0	5	5	12
9 yrs.		N Totals:	610	73	197	270	392

Tom Bladon continued

PLAYOFFS

YEAR	TEAM & LEAGUE		GP	G	A	PTS	PIM
1972-73	**PHI**	**N**	11	0	4	4	2
1973-74*			16	4	6	10	25
1974-75*			13	1	3	4	12
1975-76			16	2	6	8	14
1976-77			10	1	3	4	4
1977-78			12	0	2	2	11
1978-79	**PITT**	**N**	7	0	4	4	2
1979-80			1	0	1	1	0
8 yrs.		**N Totals:**	86	8	29	37	70

Traded to **Pittsburgh** by Philadelphia with Ross Lonsberry and Orest Kindrachuk for Pittsburgh's first round choice (Behn Wilson) in the 1978 Amateur Draft and other considerations, June 14, 1978. Signed as free agent by **Edmonton** July 10, 1980. Signed as free agent by **Winnipeg** Dec. 13, 1980. Signed as free agent by **Detroit** Jan. 14, 1981.

Jacques Blain

BLAIN, JACQUES 5'11", 180 lbs.
B. July 19, 1947, Gatineau, Que. Forward, Shoots L

YEAR	TEAM & LEAGUE		GP	G	A	PTS	PIM
1972-73	**QUE**	**W**	69	1	10	11	78

Gary Blaine

BLAINE, GARY JAMES 5'11", 190 lbs.
B. Apr. 19, 1933, St. Boniface, Man. Defense, Shoots R

YEAR	TEAM & LEAGUE		GP	G	A	PTS	PIM
1954-55	**MONT**	**N**	1	0	0	0	0

Andy Blair

BLAIR, ANDREW DRYDEN 6'1", 180 lbs.
B. Feb. 27, 1908, Winnipeg, Man. Center, Shoots L

YEAR	TEAM & LEAGUE		GP	G	A	PTS	PIM
1928-29	**TOR**	**N**	44	12	15	27	41
1929-30			42	11	10	21	27
1930-31			44	11	8	19	32
1931-32			48	9	14	23	35
1932-33			43	6	9	15	38
1933-34			47	14	9	23	35
1934-35			45	6	14	20	22
1935-36			45	5	4	9	60
1936-37	**CHI**	**N**	44	0	3	3	33
9 yrs.		**N Totals:**	402	74	86	160	323

PLAYOFFS

YEAR	TEAM & LEAGUE		GP	G	A	PTS	PIM
1928-29	**TOR**	**N**	4	3	0	3	2
1930-31			2	1	0	1	0
1931-32*			7	2	2	4	6
1932-33			9	0	2	2	4
1933-34			5	0	2	2	16
1934-35			2	0	0	0	2
1935-36			9	0	0	0	2
7 yrs.		**N Totals:**	38	6	6	12	32

Chuck Blair

BLAIR, CHARLES 5'10", 175 lbs.
B. July 23, 1928, Edinburgh, Scotland Right Wing, Shoots R

YEAR	TEAM & LEAGUE		GP	G	A	PTS	PIM
1948-49	**TOR**	**N**	1	0	0	0	0
1950-51			2	0	0	0	0
2 yrs.		**N Totals:**	3	0	0	0	0

George Blair

BLAIR, GEORGE (Dusty) 5'8", 160 lbs.
B. Sept. 15, 1929, South Porcupine, Ont. Center

YEAR	TEAM & LEAGUE		GP	G	A	PTS	PIM
1950-51	**TOR**	**N**	2	0	0	0	0

Mike Blaisdell

BLAISDELL, MICHAEL WALTER (Blazer) 6'1", 196 lbs.
B. Nov. 8, 1960, Moose Jaw, Sask. Right Wing, Shoots R

YEAR	TEAM & LEAGUE		GP	G	A	PTS	PIM
1980-81	**DET**	**N**	32	3	6	9	10
1981-82			80	23	32	55	48
1982-83			80	18	23	41	22
3 yrs.		**N Totals:**	192	44	61	105	80

Traded by Detroit to **New York Rangers** with Willie Huber and Mark Osborne for Ron Duguay, Eddie Mio, and Ed Johnstone, June 13, 1983.

Mickey Blake

BLAKE, FRANCIS JOSEPH 5'10", 186 lbs.
B. Oct. 31, 1912, Barriefield, Ont. Defense

YEAR	TEAM & LEAGUE		GP	G	A	PTS	PIM
1934-35	**STL**	**N**	8	1	1	2	2
1935-36	**BOS**	**N**	7	0	0	0	2
	TOR	**N**	1	0	0	0	0
	2 team total		8	0	0	0	2
2 yrs.		**N Totals:**	16	1	1	2	4

Toe Blake

BLAKE, HECTOR 5'9½", 165 lbs.
B. Aug. 21, 1912, Victoria Mines, Ont. Left Wing, Shoots L
Won Hart Trophy, 1938-39
Won Art Ross Trophy, 1938-39
Won Lady Byng Trophy, 1945-46
Hall of Fame, 1966

YEAR	TEAM & LEAGUE		GP	G	A	PTS	PIM
1932-33	**MON(M)**	**N**	1	0	0	0	0
1934-35			8	0	0	0	0
1935-36	**MONT**	**N**	11	1	2	3	28
1936-37			43	10	12	22	12
1937-38			43	17	16	33	33
1938-39			48	24	23	**47**	10
1939-40			48	17	19	36	48
1940-41			48	12	20	32	49
1941-42			48	17	28	45	19
1942-43			48	23	36	59	26
1943-44			41	26	33	59	10
1944-45			49	29	38	67	25
1945-46			50	29	21	50	2
1946-47			60	21	29	50	6
1947-48			32	9	15	24	4
15 yrs.		**N Totals:**	578	235	292	527	272

PLAYOFFS

YEAR	TEAM & LEAGUE		GP	G	A	PTS	PIM
1936-37	**MONT**	**N**	5	1	0	1	0
1937-38			3	3	1	4	2
1938-39			3	1	1	2	2
1940-41			3	0	3	3	5
1941-42			3	0	3	3	2
1942-43			5	4	3	7	0
1943-44*			9	7	11	18	2
1944-45			6	0	2	2	5
1945-46*			9	7	6	13	5
1946-47			11	2	7	9	0
10 yrs.		**N Totals:**	57	25	37	62	23

Bernie Blanchette

BLANCHETTE, BERNARD ROBERT 6', 165 lbs.
B. July 11, 1947, N. Battleford, Sask. Right Wing, Shoots R

YEAR	TEAM & LEAGUE		GP	G	A	PTS	PIM
1972-73	**ALTA**	**W**	23	5	4	9	2
	CHI	**W**	24	2	3	5	8
	2 team total		47	7	7	14	10

Rick Blight

BLIGHT, RICHARD DEREK 6'2", 195 lbs.
B. Oct. 17, 1955, Portage La Prairie, Man. Right Wing, Shoots R

YEAR	TEAM & LEAGUE		GP	G	A	PTS	PIM
1975-76	**VAN**	**N**	74	25	31	56	29
1976-77			78	28	40	68	32
1977-78			80	25	38	63	33
1978-79			56	5	10	15	16
1979-80			33	12	6	18	54
1980-81			3	1	0	1	4
1982-83	**LA**	**N**	2	0	0	0	2
7 yrs.		**N Totals:**	326	96	125	221	170

PLAYOFFS

YEAR	TEAM & LEAGUE		GP	G	A	PTS	PIM
1975-76	**VAN**	**N**	2	0	1	1	0
1978-79			3	0	4	4	2
2 yrs.		**N Totals:**	5	0	5	5	2

Russ Blinco

BLINCO, RUSSELL PERCIVAL (Beaver) 5'10", 171 lbs.
B. Mar. 12, 1908, Grand Mere, Que. Center
Won Calder Trophy, 1933-34

YEAR	TEAM & LEAGUE		GP	G	A	PTS	PIM
1933-34	**MON(M)**	**N**	31	14	9	23	2

Russ Blinco continued

YEAR	TEAM & LEAGUE		GP	G	A	PTS	PIM
1934-35			48	13	14	27	4
1935-36			46	13	10	23	10
1936-37			48	6	12	18	2
1937-38			47	10	9	19	4
1938-39	**CHI**	**N**	48	3	12	15	2
6 yrs.		**N Totals:**	268	59	66	125	24
PLAYOFFS							
1933-34	**MON(M)**	**N**	4	0	1	1	0
1934-35*			7	2	2	4	2
1935-36			3	0	0	0	0
1936-37			5	1	0	1	2
4 yrs.		**N Totals:**	19	3	3	6	4

Ken Block

BLOCK, KENNETH RICHARD 5'10", 184 lbs.
B. Mar. 18, 1944, Grunthal, Man. Defense, Shoots L

YEAR	TEAM & LEAGUE		GP	G	A	PTS	PIM
1970-71	**VAN**	**N**	1	0	0	0	0
1972-73	**NY**	**W**	78	5	53	58	43
1973-74	**NY-NJ**	**W**	74	3	43	46	22
1974-75	**SD**	**W**	36	1	11	12	12
	IND	**W**	37	0	17	17	18
	2 team total		73	1	28	29	30
1975-76			79	1	25	26	28
1976-77			52	3	10	13	25
1977-78			77	1	25	26	34
1978-79			22	2	3	5	10
8 yrs.		**N Totals:**	1	0	0	0	0
		W Totals:	455	16	187	203	192
PLAYOFFS							
1976-77	**IND**	**W**	9	0	2	2	6

Drafted by **Los Angeles** from N.Y. Rangers in Expansion Draft, June 6, 1967. Traded to **Toronto** by Los Angeles for Red Kelly, June 8, 1967.

Timo Blomqvist

BLOMQVIST, TIMO 6', 198 lbs.
B. Jan. 23, 1961, Helsinki, Finland Defense, Shoots R

YEAR	TEAM & LEAGUE		GP	G	A	PTS	PIM
1981-82	**WASH**	**N**	44	1	11	12	62
1982-83			61	1	17	18	67
2 yrs.		**N Totals:**	105	2	28	30	129
PLAYOFFS							
1982-83	**WASH**	**N**	3	0	0	0	16

Mike Bloom

BLOOM, MICHAEL CARROLL 6'3", 205 lbs.
B. Apr. 12, 1952, Ottawa, Ont. Left Wing, Shoots L

YEAR	TEAM & LEAGUE		GP	G	A	PTS	PIM
1974-75	**WASH**	**N**	67	7	19	26	84
	DET	**N**	13	4	8	12	10
	2 team total		80	11	27	38	94
1975-76			76	13	17	30	99
1976-77			45	6	3	9	22
3 yrs.		**N Totals:**	201	30	47	77	215

Drafted by **Washington** from Boston in Expansion Draft, June 12, 1974. Traded to **Detroit** by Washington for Blair Stewart, March 9, 1975.

John Blum

BLUM, JOHN 6'3", 205 lbs.
B. Oct. 8, 1959, Minneapolis, Minn. Defense, Shoots R

YEAR	TEAM & LEAGUE		GP	G	A	PTS	PIM
1982-83	**EDM**	**N**	5	0	3	3	24

Signed as free agent by **Edmonton** May 5, 1981.

Gregg Boddy

BODDY, GREGG ALLEN 6'2", 200 lbs.
B. Mar. 19, 1949, Ponoka, Alta. Defense, Shoots L

YEAR	TEAM & LEAGUE		GP	G	A	PTS	PIM
1971-72	**VAN**	**N**	40	2	5	7	45
1972-73			74	3	11	14	50
1973-74			53	2	10	12	59
1974-75			72	11	12	23	56
1975-76			34	5	6	11	33
1976-77	**SD**	**W**	0	0	0	0	0
	EDM	**W**	64	2	19	21	60
	2 team total		64	2	19	21	60

Gregg Boddy continued

YEAR	TEAM & LEAGUE		GP	G	A	PTS	PIM
6 yrs.		**N Totals:**	273	23	44	67	243
		W Totals:	64	2	19	21	60
PLAYOFFS							
1974-75	**VAN**	**N**	3	0	0	0	0
1976-77	**EDM**	**W**	4	1	2	3	14
2 yrs.		**N Totals:**	3	0	0	0	0
		W Totals:	4	1	2	3	14

Traded to **Montreal** by Los Angeles with Leon Rochefort and Wayne Thomas for Larry Mickey, Lucien Grenier and goaltender Jack Norris, May 22, 1970. Traded to **Vancouver** for cash and Vancouver's third draft choice (Jim Cahoon) in 1971 Amateur Draft, May 25, 1971.

Gus Bodnar

BODNAR, AUGUST 5'10", 160 lbs.
B. Aug. 24, 1925, Fort William, Ont. Center, Shoots R
Won Calder Trophy, 1943-44

YEAR	TEAM & LEAGUE		GP	G	A	PTS	PIM
1943-44	**TOR**	**N**	50	22	40	62	18
1944-45			49	8	36	44	18
1945-46			49	14	23	37	14
1946-47			39	4	6	10	10
1947-48	**CHI**	**N**	46	13	22	35	23
1948-49			50	19	26	45	14
1949-50			70	11	28	39	6
1950-51			44	8	12	20	8
1951-52			69	14	26	40	26
1952-53			66	16	13	29	26
1953-54			44	6	15	21	20
	BOS	**N**	15	3	3	6	10
	2 team total		59	9	18	27	30
1954-55			67	4	4	8	14
12 yrs.		**N Totals:**	658	142	254	396	207
PLAYOFFS							
1943-44	**TOR**	**N**	5	0	0	0	0
1944-45*			13	3	1	4	4
1946-47			1	0	0	0	0
1952-53	**CHI**	**N**	7	1	1	2	2
1953-54	**BOS**	**N**	1	0	0	0	0
1954-55			5	0	1	1	4
6 yrs.		**N Totals:**	32	4	3	7	10

Traded to **Boston** by Chicago for Jerry Toppazzini, Feb. 16, 1954.

Ron Boehm

BOEHM, RONALD JOHN 5'7", 160 lbs.
B. Aug. 14, 1943, Saskatoon, Sask. Left Wing, Shoots L

YEAR	TEAM & LEAGUE		GP	G	A	PTS	PIM
1967-68	**OAK**	**N**	16	2	1	3	10

Drafted by **Oakland** from N.Y. Rangers in Expansion Draft, June 6, 1967. Sold to **N.Y. Rangers** by Oakland, Sept. 13, 1968.

Garth Boesch

BOESCH, GARTH VERNON 6', 180 lbs.
B. Oct. 7, 1920, Milestone, Sask. Defense, Shoots R

YEAR	TEAM & LEAGUE		GP	G	A	PTS	PIM
1946-47	**TOR**	**N**	35	4	5	9	47
1947-48			45	2	7	9	52
1948-49			59	1	10	11	43
1949-50			58	2	6	8	63
4 yrs.		**N Totals:**	197	9	28	37	205
PLAYOFFS							
1946-47*	**TOR**	**N**	11	0	2	2	6
1947-48*			8	2	1	3	2
1948-49*			9	0	2	2	6
1949-50			6	0	0	0	4
4 yrs.		**N Totals:**	34	2	5	7	18

Marc Boileau

BOILEAU, MARC CLAUDE 5'11", 170 lbs.
B. Sept. 3, 1932, Pointe Claire, Que. Center, Shoots L

YEAR	TEAM & LEAGUE		GP	G	A	PTS	PIM
1961-62	**DET**	**N**	54	5	6	11	8

Rene Boileau

BOILEAU, RENE

B. Unknown — Forward

YEAR	TEAM	LEAGUE	GP	G	A	PTS	PIM
1925-26	**NYA**	**N**	7	0	0	0	2

Fred Boimistruck

BOIMISTRUCK, FREDERICK — 5'11", 191 lbs.

B. Nov. 4, 1962, Sudbury, Ont. — Defense, Shoots R

YEAR	TEAM	LEAGUE	GP	G	A	PTS	PIM
1981-82	**TOR**	**N**	57	2	11	13	32
1982-83			26	2	3	5	13
2 yrs.		**N Totals:**	83	4	14	18	45

Serge Boisvert

BOISVERT, SERGE — 5'9", 172 lbs.

B. June 1, 1959, Drummondville, Ont. — Forward, Shoots R

YEAR	TEAM	LEAGUE	GP	G	A	PTS	PIM
1982-83	**TOR**	**N**	17	0	2	2	4

Leo Boivin

BOIVIN, LEO JOSEPH — 5'7", 190 lbs.

B. Aug. 2, 1932, Prescott, Ont. — Defense, Shoots L

YEAR	TEAM	LEAGUE	GP	G	A	PTS	PIM
1951-52	**TOR**	**N**	2	0	1	1	4
1952-53			70	2	13	15	97
1953-54			58	1	6	7	81
1954-55			7	0	0	0	8
	BOS	**N**	59	6	11	17	105
	2 team total		66	6	11	17	113
1955-56			68	4	16	20	80
1956-57			55	2	8	10	55
1957-58			33	0	4	4	54
1958-59			70	5	16	21	94
1959-60			70	4	21	25	66
1960-61			57	6	17	23	50
1961-62			65	5	18	23	89
1962-63			62	2	24	26	48
1963-64			65	10	14	24	42
1964-65			67	3	10	13	68
1965-66			46	0	5	5	34
	DET	**N**	16	0	5	5	16
	2 team total		62	0	10	10	50
1966-67			69	4	17	21	0
1967-68	**PITT**	**N**	73	9	13	22	74
1968-69			41	5	13	18	26
	MINN	**N**	28	1	6	7	16
	2 team total		69	6	19	25	42
1969-70			69	3	12	15	30
19 yrs.		**N Totals:**	1150	72	250	322	1137

PLAYOFFS

YEAR	TEAM	LEAGUE	GP	G	A	PTS	PIM
1953-54	**TOR**	**N**	5	0	0	0	2
1954-55	**BOS**	**N**	5	0	1	1	4
1956-57			10	2	3	5	12
1957-58			12	0	3	3	21
1958-59			7	1	2	3	4
1965-66	**DET**	**N**	12	0	1	1	16
1969-70	**PITT**	**N**	3	0	0	0	0
7 yrs.		**N Totals:**	54	3	10	13	59

Traded to **Toronto** by Boston with Fern Flaman, Ken Smith and Phil Maloney for Bill Ezinicki and Vic Lynn, Nov. 16, 1950. Traded to **Boston** by Toronto for Joe Klukay, Nov., 1954. Traded by Boston to **Detroit** for Gary Doak, Bill Lesuk, and extra amateur draft choice (Steve Atkinson), Feb. 18, 1966. Drafted by **Pittsburgh** from Detroit in Expansion Draft, June 6, 1967. Traded to **Minnesota** by Pittsburgh for Duane Rupp, Jan. 24, 1969.

Mike Boland

BOLAND, MICHAEL ANTHONY — 5'10", 185 lbs.

B. Dec. 16, 1949, Montreal, Que. — Right Wing, Shoots R

YEAR	TEAM	LEAGUE	GP	G	A	PTS	PIM
1972-73	**OTTA**	**W**	41	1	15	16	44
1974-75	**PHI**	**N**	2	0	0	0	0
2 yrs.		**N Totals:**	2	0	0	0	0
		W Totals:	41	1	15	16	44

PLAYOFFS

YEAR	TEAM	LEAGUE	GP	G	A	PTS	PIM
1972-73	**OTTA**	**W**	1	0	0	0	12

Mike Boland

BOLAND, MICHAEL JOHN — 6', 190 lbs.

B. Oct. 29, 1954, London, Ont. — Defense, Shoots R

YEAR	TEAM	LEAGUE	GP	G	A	PTS	PIM
1974-75	**KC**	**N**	1	0	0	0	0
1978-79	**BUF**	**N**	22	1	2	3	29
2 yrs.		**N Totals:**	23	1	2	3	29

PLAYOFFS

YEAR	TEAM	LEAGUE	GP	G	A	PTS	PIM
1978-79	**BUF**	**N**	3	1	0	1	2

Signed as free agent by **Buffalo** Jan. 5, 1979.

Ivan Boldirev

BOLDIREV, IVAN — 6', 190 lbs.

B. Aug. 15, 1949, Zranjanin, Yugoslavia — Center, Shoots L

YEAR	TEAM	LEAGUE	GP	G	A	PTS	PIM
1970-71	**BOS**	**N**	2	0	0	0	0
1971-72			11	0	2	2	6
	CALIF	**N**	57	16	23	39	54
	2 team total		68	16	25	41	60
1972-73			56	11	23	34	58
1973-74			78	25	31	56	22
1974-75	**CHI**	**N**	80	24	43	67	54
1975-76			78	28	34	62	33
1976-77			80	24	38	62	40
1977-78			80	35	45	80	34
1978-79			66	29	35	64	25
	ATL	**N**	13	6	8	14	6
	2 team total		79	35	43	78	31
1979-80			52	16	24	40	20
	VAN	**N**	27	16	11	27	14
	2 team total		79	32	35	67	34
1980-81			72	26	33	59	34
1981-82			78	33	40	73	45
1982-83			39	5	20	25	12
	DET	**N**	33	13	17	30	14
	2 team total		72	18	37	55	26
13 yrs.		**N Totals:**	902	307	427	734	471

PLAYOFFS

YEAR	TEAM	LEAGUE	GP	G	A	PTS	PIM
1974-75	**CHI**	**N**	8	4	2	6	2
1975-76			4	0	1	1	0
1976-77			2	0	1	1	0
1977-78			4	0	2	2	2
1978-79	**ATL**	**N**	2	0	2	2	2
1979-80	**VAN**	**N**	4	0	2	2	0
1980-81			1	1	1	2	0
1981-82			17	8	3	11	4
8 yrs.		**N Totals:**	42	13	14	27	10

Traded to **California** by Boston for Richard Leduc and Chris Oddleifson, Nov. 17, 1971. Traded to **Chicago** by California for Len Frig and Mike Christie, May 24, 1974. Traded to **Atlanta** by Chicago with Phil Russell and Darcy Rota for Tom Lysiak, Pat Ribble, Greg Fox, Harold Phillipoff, and Miles Zaharko, Mar. 13, 1979. Traded to **Vancouver** by Atlanta with Darcy Rota for Don Lever and Brad Smith, Feb. 8, 1980. Traded by Vancouver to **Detroit** for Mark Kirton, Jan. 17, 1983.

Danny Bolduc

BOLDUC, DANIEL GEORGE — 5'9", 180 lbs.

B. Apr. 6, 1953, Waterville, Me. — Left Wing, Shoots L

YEAR	TEAM	LEAGUE	GP	G	A	PTS	PIM
1975-76	**NE**	**W**	14	2	5	7	14
1976-77			33	8	3	11	15
1977-78			41	5	5	10	22
1978-79	**DET**	**N**	56	16	13	29	14
1979-80			44	6	5	11	19
5 yrs.		**N Totals:**	100	22	18	40	33
		W Totals:	88	15	13	28	51

PLAYOFFS

YEAR	TEAM	LEAGUE	GP	G	A	PTS	PIM
1975-76	**NE**	**W**	16	1	6	7	4
1977-78			14	2	4	6	4
2 yrs.		**W Totals:**	30	3	10	13	8

Miche Bolduc

BOLDUC, MICHEL 6'2", 210 lbs.
B. Mar. 13, 1961, Angegardien, Que. Defense, Shoots L

YEAR	TEAM & LEAGUE		GP	G	A	PTS	PIM
1981-82	**QUE**	**N**	3	0	0	0	0
1982-83			7	0	0	0	6
2 yrs.		**N Totals:**	10	0	0	0	6

Buzz Boll

BOLL, FRANK 5'10", 166 lbs.
B. Mar. 6, 1911, Filmore, Sask. Left Wing

YEAR	TEAM & LEAGUE		GP	G	A	PTS	PIM
1933-34	**TOR**	**N**	42	12	8	20	21
1934-35			47	14	4	18	4
1935-36			44	15	13	28	14
1936-37			25	6	3	9	12
1937-38			44	14	11	25	18
1938-39			11	0	0	0	0
1939-40	**NYA**	**N**	47	5	10	15	18
1940-41			46	12	14	26	16
1941-42			48	11	15	26	23
1942-43	**BOS**	**N**	43	25	27	52	20
1943-44			39	19	25	44	2
11 yrs.		**N Totals:**	436	133	130	263	148
PLAYOFFS							
1933-34	**TOR**	**N**	5	0	0	0	9
1934-35			5	0	0	0	0
1935-36			9	**7**	3	**10**	2
1936-37			2	0	0	0	0
1937-38			7	0	0	0	2
1939-40	**NYA**	**N**	1	0	0	0	0
6 yrs.		**N Totals:**	29	7	3	10	13

Larry Bolonchuk

BOLONCHUK, LARRY KENNETH MITCHELL
5'10", 190 lbs.
B. Feb. 26, 1952, Winnipeg, Man. Defense, Shoots L

YEAR	TEAM & LEAGUE		GP	G	A	PTS	PIM
1972-73	**VAN**	**N**	15	0	0	0	6
1975-76	**WASH**	**N**	1	0	1	1	0
1976-77			9	0	0	0	12
1977-78			49	3	8	11	79
4 yrs.		**N Totals:**	74	3	9	12	97

Drafted by **Washington** from Vancouver in Expansion Draft, June 12, 1974.

Hughie Bolton

BOLTON, HUGH EDWARD 6'3", 190 lbs.
B. Apr. 15, 1929, Toronto, Ont. Defense, Shoots R

YEAR	TEAM & LEAGUE		GP	G	A	PTS	PIM
1949-50	**TOR**	**N**	2	0	0	0	2
1950-51			13	1	3	4	2
1951-52			60	3	13	16	73
1952-53			9	0	0	0	10
1953-54			9	0	0	0	10
1954-55			69	2	19	21	55
1955-56			67	4	16	20	65
1956-57			6	0	0	0	0
8 yrs.		**N Totals:**	235	10	51	61	217
PLAYOFFS							
1951-52	**TOR**	**N**	3	0	0	0	4
1953-54			5	0	1	1	4
1954-55			4	0	3	3	6
1955-56			5	0	1	1	0
4 yrs.		**N Totals:**	17	0	5	5	14

Dan Bonar

BONAR, DANIEL (Kato) 5'9", 175 lbs.
B. Sept. 23, 1956, Brandon, Man. Center, Shoots R

YEAR	TEAM & LEAGUE		GP	G	A	PTS	PIM
1980-81	**LA**	**N**	71	11	15	26	57
1981-82			79	13	23	36	111
1982-83			20	1	1	2	40
3 yrs.		**N Totals:**	170	25	39	64	208
PLAYOFFS							
1980-81	**LA**	**N**	4	1	1	2	11

Dan Bonar continued

YEAR	TEAM & LEAGUE		GP	G	A	PTS	PIM
1981-82			10	2	3	5	11
2 yrs.		**N Totals:**	14	3	4	7	22

Signed as free agent by **Los Angeles** Aug. 7, 1978.

Kerry Bond

BOND, JOHN KERRY 6', 190 lbs.
B. July 18, 1945, Sudbury, Ont. Left Wing, Shoots L

YEAR	TEAM & LEAGUE		GP	G	A	PTS	PIM
1974-75	**IND**	**W**	71	22	15	37	23
1975-76			15	2	0	2	9
2 yrs.		**W Totals:**	86	24	15	39	32
PLAYOFFS							
1975-76	**IND**	**W**	7	1	0	1	11

Marcel Bonin

BONIN, MARCEL 5'9", 175 lbs.
B. Sept. 12, 1932, Montreal, Que. Left Wing, Shoots L

YEAR	TEAM & LEAGUE		GP	G	A	PTS	PIM
1952-53	**DET**	**N**	37	4	9	13	14
1953-54			2	0	0	0	0
1954-55			69	16	20	36	53
1955-56	**BOS**	**N**	67	9	9	18	49
1957-58	**MONT**	**N**	66	15	24	39	37
1958-59			57	13	30	43	38
1959-60			59	17	34	51	59
1960-61			65	16	35	51	45
1961-62			33	7	14	21	41
9 yrs.		**N Totals:**	455	97	175	272	336
PLAYOFFS							
1952-53	**DET**	**N**	5	0	1	1	0
1954-55*			11	0	2	2	4
1957-58*	**MONT**	**N**	9	0	1	1	12
1958-59*			11	10	5	15	4
1959-60*			8	1	4	5	12
1960-61			6	0	1	1	29
6 yrs.		**N Totals:**	50	11	14	25	61

Traded to **Boston** by Detroit with Lorne Davis, Terry Sawchuk and Vic Stasiuk for Gilles Boisvert, Real Chevrefils, Norm Corcoran, Warren Godfrey, and Ed Sandford, June, 1955. Drafted by **Montreal** from Boston, June, 1957.

Jim Boo

BOO, JAMES MCQUAID 6'1", 200 lbs.
B. Nov. 12, 1954, Rolla, Mo. Defense, Shoots R

YEAR	TEAM & LEAGUE		GP	G	A	PTS	PIM
1977-78	**MINN**	**N**	6	0	0	0	22

Signed as free agent by **Minnesota** July 1, 1978.

Buddy Boone

BOONE, CARL GEORGE 5'7", 158 lbs.
B. Sept. 11, 1932, Kirkland Lake, Ont. Right Wing, Shoots R

YEAR	TEAM & LEAGUE		GP	G	A	PTS	PIM
1957-58	**BOS**	**N**	34	5	3	8	28
PLAYOFFS							
1956-57	**BOS**	**N**	10	1	0	1	12
1957-58			12	1	1	2	13
2 yrs.		**N Totals:**	22	2	1	3	25

George Boothman

BOOTHMAN, GEORGE EDWARD 6'2", 175 lbs.
B. Sept. 25, 1916, Calgary, Alta. Defense, Shoots R

YEAR	TEAM & LEAGUE		GP	G	A	PTS	PIM
1942-43	**TOR**	**N**	9	1	1	2	4
1943-44			49	16	18	34	14
2 yrs.		**N Totals:**	58	17	19	36	18
PLAYOFFS							
1943-44	**TOR**	**N**	5	2	1	3	2

Chris Bordeleau

BORDELEAU, CHRISTIAN GERARD 5'8", 172 lbs.
B. Sept. 23, 1947, Noranda, Que. Center, Shoots L

YEAR	TEAM & LEAGUE		GP	G	A	PTS	PIM
1968-69	**MONT**	**N**	13	1	3	4	4
1969-70			48	2	13	15	18
1970-71	**STL**	**N**	78	21	32	53	48
1971-72			41	8	9	17	6
	CHI	**N**	25	6	8	14	6
	2 team total		66	14	17	31	12
1972-73	**WINN**	**W**	78	47	54	101	12
1973-74			75	26	49	75	22
1974-75			18	8	8	16	0
	QUE	**W**	53	15	33	48	24
	2 team total		71	23	41	64	24
1975-76			74	37	72	109	42
1976-77			72	32	75	107	34
1977-78			26	9	22	31	28
1978-79			16	5	12	17	0
11 yrs.		**N Totals:**	205	38	65	103	82
		W Totals:	412	179	325	504	162

PLAYOFFS

YEAR	TEAM & LEAGUE		GP	G	A	PTS	PIM
1968-69*	**MONT**	**N**	6	1	0	1	0
1970-71	**STL**	**N**	5	0	1	1	17
1971-72	**CHI**	**N**	8	3	6	9	0
1972-73	**WINN**	**W**	12	5	8	13	4
1973-74			3	3	2	5	0
1974-75	**QUE**	**W**	15	2	13	15	2
1975-76			5	1	1	2	4
1976-77			8	4	5	9	0
1977-78			10	1	5	6	6
9 yrs.		**N Totals:**	19	4	7	11	17
		W Totals:	53	16	34	50	16

Sold to **St. Louis** by Montreal, May 22, 1970. Traded to **Chicago** by St. Louis for Danny O'Shea, Feb. 8, 1972. Sold to **St. Louis** by Chicago, Sept. 15, 1972. Reclaimed by **St. Louis** from Quebec prior to Expansion Draft, June 9, 1979.

J.P. Bordeleau

BORDELEAU, JEAN-PIERRE 6', 170 lbs.
B. June 13, 1949, Norando, Que. Right Wing, Shoots R

YEAR	TEAM & LEAGUE		GP	G	A	PTS	PIM
1971-72	**CHI**	**N**	3	0	2	2	2
1972-73			73	15	15	30	6
1973-74			64	11	9	20	11
1974-75			59	7	8	15	4
1975-76			76	12	18	30	6
1976-77			60	15	14	29	20
1977-78			76	15	25	40	32
1978-79			63	15	21	36	34
1979-80			45	7	14	21	28
9 yrs.		**N Totals:**	519	97	126	223	143

PLAYOFFS

YEAR	TEAM & LEAGUE		GP	G	A	PTS	PIM
1969-70	**CHI**	**N**	1	0	0	0	0
1972-73			14	1	0	1	4
1973-74			11	0	2	2	2
1974-75			7	2	2	4	2
1975-76			4	0	0	0	0
1976-77			2	0	0	0	2
1977-78			4	0	1	1	0
1978-79			4	0	1	1	2
1979-80			1	0	0	0	0
9 yrs.		**N Totals:**	48	3	6	9	12

Paul Bordeleau

BORDELEAU, PAULIN JOSEPH 5'9", 162 lbs.
B. Jan. 29, 1953, Noranda, Que. Right Wing, Shoots R

YEAR	TEAM & LEAGUE		GP	G	A	PTS	PIM
1973-74	**VAN**	**N**	68	11	13	24	20
1974-75			67	17	31	48	21
1975-76			48	5	12	17	6
1976-77	**QUE**	**W**	80	42	41	83	52
1977-78			77	42	23	65	29
1978-79			77	17	12	29	44
6 yrs.		**N Totals:**	183	33	56	89	47
		W Totals:	234	101	76	177	125

PLAYOFFS

YEAR	TEAM & LEAGUE		GP	G	A	PTS	PIM
1974-75	**VAN**	**N**	5	2	1	3	0

Paul Bordeleau continued

YEAR	TEAM & LEAGUE		GP	G	A	PTS	PIM
1976-77	**QUE**	**W**	16	12	9	21	12
1977-78			11	4	6	10	2
1978-79			4	1	0	1	0
4 yrs.		**N Totals:**	5	2	1	3	0
		W Totals:	31	17	15	32	14

Don Borgeson

BORGESON, DONALD 5'11", 175 lbs.
B. May 20, 1945, N. Battlefield, Sask. Left Wing, Shoots L

YEAR	TEAM & LEAGUE		GP	G	A	PTS	PIM
1974-75	**PHOE**	**W**	74	29	28	57	38
1975-76	**D-O**	**W**	40	21	16	37	26
	NE	**W**	31	9	8	17	4
	2 team total		71	30	24	54	30
2 yrs.		**W Totals:**	145	59	52	111	68

PLAYOFFS

YEAR	TEAM & LEAGUE		GP	G	A	PTS	PIM
1974-75	**PHOE**	**W**	5	0	1	1	2
1975-76	**NE**	**W**	3	1	1	2	0
2 yrs.		**W Totals:**	8	1	2	3	2

Jack Borotsik

BOROTSIK, JACK 5'9", 178 lbs.
B. Nov. 26, 1949, Brandon, Man. Center, Shoots L

YEAR	TEAM & LEAGUE		GP	G	A	PTS	PIM
1974-75	**STL**	**N**	1	0	0	0	0

Laurie Boschman

BOSCHMAN, LAURIE JOSEPH 6', 185 lbs.
B. June 4, 1960, Major, Sask. Center, Shoots L

YEAR	TEAM & LEAGUE		GP	G	A	PTS	PIM
1979-80	**TOR**	**N**	80	16	32	48	78
1980-81			53	14	19	33	178
1981-82			54	9	19	28	150
	EDM	**N**	11	2	3	5	37
	2 team total		65	11	22	33	187
1982-83			62	8	12	20	183
	WINN	**N**	12	3	5	8	33
	2 team total		74	11	17	28	216
4 yrs.		**N Totals:**	272	52	90	142	659

PLAYOFFS

YEAR	TEAM & LEAGUE		GP	G	A	PTS	PIM
1979-80	**TOR**	**N**	3	1	1	2	18
1980-81			3	0	0	0	7
1981-82	**EDM**	**N**	3	0	1	1	4
1982-83	**WINN**	**N**	3	0	1	1	12
4 yrs.		**N Totals:**	12	1	3	4	41

Traded to **Edmonton** by Toronto for Walt Poddubny and Phil Drouilliard, Mar. 8, 1982. Traded to **Winnipeg** by Edmonton for Willy Lindstrom, March 8, 1983.

Mike Bossy

BOSSY, MICHAEL (Boss) 6', 186 lbs.
B. Jan. 22, 1957, Montreal, Que. Right Wing, Shoots R
Won Lady Byng Trophy, 1982-83
Won Calder Trophy, 1977-78
Won Conn Smythe Trophy, 1981-82

YEAR	TEAM & LEAGUE		GP	G	A	PTS	PIM
1977-78	**NYI**	**N**	73	53	38	91	6
1978-79			80	**69**	57	126	25
1979-80			75	51	41	92	12
1980-81			79	**68**	51	119	32
1981-82			80	64	83	147	22
1982-83			79	60	58	118	20
6 yrs.		**N Totals:**	466	365	328	693	117

PLAYOFFS

YEAR	TEAM & LEAGUE		GP	G	A	PTS	PIM
1977-78	**NYI**	**N**	7	2	2	4	2
1978-79			10	6	2	8	2
1979-80*			16	10	13	23	8
1980-81*			18	17	18	35	4
1981-82*			19	17	10	27	0
1982-83*			19	17	9	26	10
6 yrs.		**N Totals:**	89	69	54	123	26

Helge Bostrom

BOSTROM, HELGE 5'7½", 185 lbs.
B. Jan. 9, 1894, Gimley, Man. Defense, Shoots L

YEAR	TEAM & LEAGUE	GP	G	A	PTS	PIM
1929-30	CHI N	20	0	1	1	8
1930-31		42	2	2	4	32
1931-32		14	0	0	0	4
1932-33		20	1	0	1	14
4 yrs.	N Totals:	96	3	3	6	58
PLAYOFFS						
1929-30	CHI N	2	0	0	0	0
1930-31		9	0	0	0	16
1931-32		2	0	0	0	0
3 yrs.	N Totals:	13	0	0	0	16

Mark Botell

BOTELL, MARK 6'4", 212 lbs.
B. Aug. 27, 1961, Scarborough, Ont. Defense, Shoots L

YEAR	TEAM & LEAGUE	GP	G	A	PTS	PIM
1981-82	PHI N	32	4	10	14	31

Tim Bothwell

BOTHWELL, TIMOTHY 6'3", 190 lbs.
B. May 6, 1955, Vancouver, B.C. Defense, Shoots L

YEAR	TEAM & LEAGUE	GP	G	A	PTS	PIM
1978-79	NYR N	1	0	0	0	2
1979-80		45	4	6	10	20
1980-81		3	0	1	1	0
1981-82		13	0	3	3	10
1982-83	STL N	61	4	11	15	34
5 yrs.	N Totals:	123	8	21	29	66
PLAYOFFS						
1979-80	NYR N	9	0	0	0	8

Acquired by **St. Louis** from N.Y. Rangers in Waiver Draft, Oct. 4, 1982.

Cam Botting

BOTTING, CAMERON ALLEN 6'2", 205 lbs.
B. Mar. 10, 1954, Kingston, Ont. Right Wing, Shoots R

YEAR	TEAM & LEAGUE	GP	G	A	PTS	PIM
1975-76	ATL N	2	0	1	1	0

Henry Boucha

BOUCHA, HENRY CHARLES 6', 185 lbs.
B. June 1, 1951, Warroad, Mn. Center, Shoots R

YEAR	TEAM & LEAGUE	GP	G	A	PTS	PIM
1971-72	DET N	16	1	0	1	2
1972-73		73	14	14	28	82
1973-74		70	19	12	31	32
1974-75	MINN N	51	15	14	29	23
1975-76	KC N	28	4	7	11	14
	MINN W	36	15	20	35	47
	2 team total	64	19	27	46	61
1976-77	COLO N	9	0	2	2	4
6 yrs.	N Totals:	247	53	49	102	157
	W Totals:	36	15	20	35	47

Traded to **Minnesota** by Detroit for Danny Grant, Aug. 27, 1974. Rights traded to **Kansas City** by Minnesota for Kansas City's second choice (Steve Christoff) in 1978 Amateur Draft, Dec. 9, 1974.

Emile Bouchard

BOUCHARD, EMILE JOSEPH (Butch) 6'2", 205 lbs.
B. Sept. 11, 1920, Montreal, Que. Defense, Shoots R
Hall of Fame, 1966

YEAR	TEAM & LEAGUE	GP	G	A	PTS	PIM
1941-42	MONT N	44	0	6	6	38
1942-43		45	2	16	18	47
1943-44		35	5	14	19	52
1944-45		50	11	23	34	34
1945-46		45	7	10	17	52
1946-47		60	5	7	12	60
1947-48		60	4	6	10	78
1948-49		27	3	3	6	42
1949-50		69	1	7	8	88
1950-51		52	3	10	13	80
1951-52		60	3	9	12	45
1952-53		58	2	8	10	55
1953-54		70	1	10	11	89
1954-55		70	2	15	17	81

Emile Bouchard continued

YEAR	TEAM & LEAGUE	GP	G	A	PTS	PIM
1955-56		36	0	0	0	22
15 yrs.	N Totals:	781	49	144	193	863
PLAYOFFS						
1941-42	MONT N	3	1	1	2	0
1942-43		5	0	1	1	4
1943-44*		9	1	3	4	4
1944-45		6	3	4	7	4
1945-46*		9	2	1	3	17
1946-47		11	0	3	3	21
1948-49		7	0	0	0	6
1949-50		5	0	2	2	2
1950-51		11	1	1	2	2
1951-52		11	0	2	2	14
1952-53*		12	1	1	2	6
1953-54		11	2	1	3	4
1954-55		12	0	1	1	37
1955-56*		1	0	0	0	0
14 yrs.	N Totals:	113	11	21	32	121

Dick Bouchard

BOUCHARD, RICHARD 5'8", 155 lbs.
B. Dec. 2, 1934, Lettelier, Man. Right Wing, Shoots R

YEAR	TEAM & LEAGUE	GP	G	A	PTS	PIM
1954-55	NYR N	1	0	0	0	0

Edmond Bouchard

BOUCHARD, EDMOND
B. Trois Rivieres, Que. Forward

YEAR	TEAM & LEAGUE	GP	G	A	PTS	PIM
1921-22	MONT N	18	1	4	5	4
1922-23	HAMIL N	20	5	**12**	17	32
1923-24		20	5	0	5	2
1924-25		29	2	2	4	14
1925-26	NYA N	34	3	1	4	10
1926-27		38	2	1	3	12
1927-28		39	1	0	1	27
1928-29		6	0	0	0	2
	PITT N	12	0	0	0	2
	2 team total	18	0	0	0	4
8 yrs.	N Totals:	216	19	20	39	105

Pierre Bouchard

BOUCHARD, PIERRE 6'2", 205 lbs.
B. Feb. 20, 1948, Longueuil, Que. Defense, Shoots L

YEAR	TEAM & LEAGUE	GP	G	A	PTS	PIM
1970-71	MONT N	51	0	3	3	50
1971-72		60	3	5	8	39
1972-73		41	0	7	7	69
1973-74		60	1	14	15	25
1974-75		79	3	9	12	65
1975-76		66	1	11	12	50
1976-77		73	4	11	15	52
1977-78		59	4	6	10	29
1978-79	WASH N	1	0	0	0	0
1979-80		54	5	9	14	16
1980-81		50	3	7	10	28
1981-82		1	0	0	0	10
12 yrs.	N Totals:	595	24	82	106	433
PLAYOFFS						
1970-71*	MONT N	13	0	1	1	10
1971-72		1	0	0	0	0
1972-73*		17	1	3	4	2
1973-74		6	0	2	2	4
1974-75		10	0	2	2	10
1975-76*		13	2	0	2	8
1976-77*		6	0	1	1	6
1977-78*		10	0	1	1	5
8 yrs.	N Totals:	76	3	10	13	45

Claimed by **Washington** from Montreal in Waiver Draft, Oct. 9, 1978.

Billy Boucher

BOUCHER, WILLIAM
B. Ottawa, Ont. Right Wing

YEAR	TEAM & LEAGUE	GP	G	A	PTS	PIM
1921-22	MONT N	24	17	5	22	18
1922-23		24	23	4	27	**52**
1923-24		23	16	6	22	33

YEAR	TEAM & LEAGUE		GP	G	A	PTS	PIM

Billy Boucher continued

YEAR	TEAM	LEAGUE	GP	G	A	PTS	PIM
1924-25			30	18	13	31	**92**
1925-26			34	8	5	13	112
1926-27			21	4	0	4	14
	BOS	N	14	2	0	2	12
	2 team total		35	6	0	6	26
1927-28	NYA	N	43	5	2	7	58
7 yrs.		N Totals:	213	93	35	128	391
PLAYOFFS							
1922-23	MONT	N	2	1	0	1	2
1923-24*			5	6	2	8	14
1924-25			6	2	1	3	17
1926-27	BOS	N	8	0	0	0	2
4 yrs.		N Totals:	21	9	3	12	35

Frank Boucher

BOUCHER, FRANK (Raffles) 5'8½", 185 lbs.
B. Oct. 7, 1901, Ottawa, Ont. Center, Shoots L
Won Lady Byng Trophy, 1927–28, 1928–29, 1929–30, 1930–31, 1932–33, 1933–34, 1934-35
Hall of Fame, 1958

YEAR	TEAM	LEAGUE	GP	G	A	PTS	PIM
1921-22	OTTA	N	24	9	1	10	4
1926-27	NYR	N	44	13	15	28	17
1927-28			44	23	12	35	14
1928-29			44	10	**16**	26	8
1929-30			42	26	**36**	62	16
1930-31			44	12	27	39	20
1931-32			48	12	23	35	18
1932-33			46	7	**28**	35	4
1933-34			48	14	30	44	4
1934-35			48	13	32	45	2
1935-36			48	11	18	29	2
1936-37			44	7	13	20	5
1937-38			18	0	1	1	2
1943-44			15	4	10	14	2
14 yrs.		N Totals:	557	161	262	423	118
PLAYOFFS							
1921-22	OTTA	N	2	0	0	0	0
1926-27	NYR	N	2	0	0	0	4
1927-28*			9	7	1	8	2
1928-29			6	1	0	1	0
1929-30			3	1	1	2	0
1930-31			4	0	2	2	0
1931-32			7	3	6	9	0
1932-33*			8	2	2	4	6
1933-34			2	0	0	0	0
1934-35			4	0	3	3	0
1936-37			9	2	3	5	0
11 yrs.		N Totals:	56	16	18	34	12

George Boucher

BOUCHER, GEORGE
B. Ottawa, Ont. Forward
Hall of Fame, 1960

YEAR	TEAM	LEAGUE	GP	G	A	PTS	PIM
1917-18	OTTA	N	22	9	0	9	27
1918-19			17	5	2	7	21
1919-20			22	10	4	14	34
1920-21			23	12	5	17	43
1921-22			23	12	8	20	10
1922-23			23	15	9	24	44
1923-24			21	14	5	19	28
1924-25			28	15	4	19	80
1925-26			32	8	4	12	64
1926-27			40	8	3	11	115
1927-28			43	7	5	12	78
1928-29			29	3	1	4	60
	MON(M)	N	12	1	1	2	10
	2 team total		41	4	2	6	70
1929-30			37	2	6	8	50
1930-31			30	0	0	0	25
1931-32	CHI	N	43	1	5	6	50
15 yrs.		N Totals:	445	122	62	184	739
PLAYOFFS							
1918-19	OTTA	N	5	2	1	3	9
1919-20*			5	2	0	2	0
1920-21*			7	5	0	5	18
1921-22			2	0	0	0	4
1922-23*			8	2	1	3	8

George Boucher continued

YEAR	TEAM	LEAGUE	GP	G	A	PTS	PIM
1923-24			2	0	1	1	4
1925-26			2	0	0	0	10
1926-27*			6	0	0	0	26
1927-28			2	0	0	0	4
1929-30	MON(M)	N	3	0	0	0	2
1931-32	CHI	N	2	0	1	1	0
11 yrs.		N Totals:	44	11	4	15	85

Robert Boucher

BOUCHER, ROBERT
B. Ottawa, Ont. Forward

YEAR	TEAM	LEAGUE	GP	G	A	PTS	PIM
1923-24	MONT	N	12	0	0	0	0

Bruce Boudreau

BOUDREAU, BRUCE ALLAN 5'9", 175 lbs.
B. Jan. 9, 1955, Toronto, Ont. Center, Shoots L

YEAR	TEAM	LEAGUE	GP	G	A	PTS	PIM
1975-76	MINN	W	30	3	6	9	4
1976-77	TOR	N	15	2	5	7	4
1977-78			40	11	18	29	12
1978-79			26	4	3	7	2
1979-80			2	0	0	0	2
1980-81			39	10	14	24	18
1981-82			12	0	2	2	6
7 yrs.		N Totals:	134	27	42	69	44
		W Totals:	30	3	6	9	4
PLAYOFFS							
1976-77	TOR	N	3	0	0	0	0
1980-81			2	1	0	1	0
1982-83			4	1	0	1	4
3 yrs.		N Totals:	9	2	0	2	4

Claimed by **Toronto** as fill in Expansion Draft, June 13, 1979.

Michel Boudreau

BOUDREAU, MICHEL
Defense

YEAR	TEAM	LEAGUE	GP	G	A	PTS	PIM
1972-73	PHI	W	33	7	7	14	4
1973-74	VAN	W	3	1	0	1	0
2 yrs.		W Totals:	36	8	7	15	4

Andre Boudrias

BOUDRIAS, ANDRE G. 5'8", 165 lbs.
B. Sept. 19, 1943, Montreal, Que. Left Wing, Shoots L

YEAR	TEAM	LEAGUE	GP	G	A	PTS	PIM
1963-64	MONT	N	4	1	4	5	2
1964-65			1	0	0	0	2
1966-67			2	0	1	1	0
1967-68	MINN	N	74	18	35	53	42
1968-69			53	4	9	13	6
	CHI	N	20	4	10	14	4
	2 team total		73	8	19	27	10
1969-70	STL	N	50	3	14	17	20
1970-71	VAN	N	77	25	41	66	16
1971-72			78	27	34	61	26
1972-73			77	30	40	70	24
1973-74			78	16	59	75	18
1974-75			77	16	62	78	46
1975-76			71	7	31	38	10
1976-77	QUE	W	74	12	31	43	12
1977-78			66	10	17	27	22
14 yrs.		N Totals:	662	151	340	491	216
		W Totals:	140	22	48	70	34
PLAYOFFS							
1967-68	MINN	N	14	3	6	9	8
1969-70	STL	N	14	2	4	6	4
1974-75	VAN	N	5	1	0	1	0
1975-76			1	0	0	0	0
1976-77	QUE	W	17	3	12	15	6
1977-78			11	0	2	2	4
6 yrs.		N Totals:	34	6	10	16	12
		W Totals:	28	3	14	17	10

Traded to **Minnesota** by Montreal with Bob Charlebois and amateur Bernard Cote for Minnesota's first choice (Chuck Arnason) in 1971 Amateur Draft, June 6, 1967. Traded to **Chicago** by Minnesota with Mike McMahon for Tom Reid and Bill Orban, Feb. 14, 1969. Drafted by **St. Louis** from Chicago,

June 11, 1969. Sold to **Vancouver** by St. Louis, June 10, 1970.

Barry Boughner

BOUGHNER, BARRY MICHAEL 5'10", 180 lbs.
B. Jan. 29, 1948, Delhi, Ont. Left Wing, Shoots L

YEAR	TEAM & LEAGUE		GP	G	A	PTS	PIM
1969-70	OAK	N	4	0	0	0	2
1970-71	CALIF	N	16	0	0	0	9
2 yrs.		N Totals:	20	0	0	0	11

Dan Bourbonnais

BOURBONNAIS, DAN 5'10", 181 lbs.
B. Mar. 3, 1962, Winnipeg, Man. Left Wing, Shoots L

YEAR	TEAM & LEAGUE		GP	G	A	PTS	PIM
1981-82	HART	N	24	3	9	12	11

Rick Bourbonnais

BOURBONNAIS, RICK 6', 186 lbs.
B. Apr. 20, 1955, Toronto, Ont. Right Wing, Shoots R

YEAR	TEAM & LEAGUE		GP	G	A	PTS	PIM
1975-76	STL	N	7	0	0	0	8
1976-77			33	6	8	14	10
1977-78			31	3	7	10	11
3 yrs.		N Totals:	71	9	15	24	29
PLAYOFFS							
1976-77	STL	N	4	0	1	1	0

Conrad Bourcier

BOURCIER, CONRAD 5'7", 145 lbs.
B. May 28, 1915, Montreal, Que. Center, Shoots L

YEAR	TEAM & LEAGUE		GP	G	A	PTS	PIM
1935-36	MONT	N	6	0	0	0	0

Jean Bourcier

BOURCIER, JEAN-LOUIS 5'11", 175 lbs.
B. Jan. 3, 1911, Montreal, Que. Left Wing, Shoots L

YEAR	TEAM & LEAGUE		GP	G	A	PTS	PIM
1935-36	MONT	N	9	0	1	1	0

Leo Bourgeault

BOURGEAULT, LEO A. 5'6", 165 lbs.
B. Jan. 17, 1903, Sturgeon Falls, Ont. Defense, Shoots L

YEAR	TEAM & LEAGUE		GP	G	A	PTS	PIM
1926-27	TOR	N	22	0	0	0	44
	NYR	N	20	2	1	3	28
	2 team total		42	2	1	3	72
1927-28			37	7	0	7	7
1928-29			44	2	3	5	59
1929-30			44	7	6	13	54
1930-31			10	0	1	1	12
	OTTA	N	28	0	4	4	28
	2 team total		38	0	5	5	40
1932-33			35	1	1	2	18
	MONT	N	15	1	1	2	9
	2 team total		50	2	2	4	27
1933-34			48	4	3	7	10
1934-35			4	0	0	0	0
8 yrs.		N Totals:	307	24	20	44	269
PLAYOFFS							
1926-27	NYR	N	2	0	0	0	4
1927-28*			9	0	0	0	8
1928-29			6	0	0	0	0
1929-30			3	1	1	2	6
1932-33	MONT	N	2	0	0	0	0
1933-34			2	0	0	0	0
6 yrs.		N Totals:	24	1	1	2	18

Charles Bourgeois

BOURGEOIS, CHARLES 6'4", 205 lbs.
B. Nov. 11, 1959, Moncton, N.B. Defense, Shoots R

YEAR	TEAM & LEAGUE		GP	G	A	PTS	PIM
1981-82	CALG	N	54	2	13	15	112
1982-83			15	2	3	5	21
2 yrs.		N Totals:	69	4	16	20	133
PLAYOFFS							
1981-82	CALG	N	3	0	0	0	7

Charles Bourgeois continued

Signed as free agent by **Calgary** April 19, 1981.

Bob Bourne

BOURNE, ROBERT GLEN (Bournie) 6'3", 200 lbs.
B. June 21, 1954, Kindersley, Sask. Center, Shoots L

YEAR	TEAM & LEAGUE		GP	G	A	PTS	PIM
1974-75	NYI	N	77	16	23	39	12
1975-76			14	2	3	5	13
1976-77			75	16	19	35	30
1977-78			80	30	33	63	31
1978-79			80	30	31	61	48
1979-80			73	15	25	40	52
1980-81			78	35	41	76	62
1981-82			76	27	26	53	77
1982-83			77	20	42	62	55
9 yrs.		N Totals:	630	191	243	434	380
PLAYOFFS							
1974-75	NYI	N	9	1	2	3	4
1976-77			8	2	0	2	4
1977-78			7	2	3	5	2
1978-79			10	1	3	4	6
1979-80*			21	10	10	20	10
1980-81*			14	4	6	10	19
1981-82*			19	9	7	16	36
1982-83*			20	8	20	28	14
8 yrs.		N Totals:	108	37	51	88	95

Traded to **N.Y. Islanders** by Kansas City for Bart Crashley and the rights to Larry Hornung, Sept. 13, 1974.

Ray Bourque

BOURQUE, RAYMOND JEAN 5'11", 197 lbs.
B. Dec. 28, 1960, Montreal, Que. Defense, Shoots L
Won Calder Trophy, 1979-80

YEAR	TEAM & LEAGUE		GP	G	A	PTS	PIM
1979-80	BOS	N	80	17	48	65	73
1980-81			67	27	29	56	96
1981-82			65	17	49	66	51
1982-83			65	22	51	73	20
4 yrs.		N Totals:	277	83	177	260	240
PLAYOFFS							
1979-80	BOS	N	10	2	9	11	27
1980-81			3	0	1	1	2
1981-82			9	1	5	6	16
1982-83			17	8	15	23	10
4 yrs.		N Totals:	39	11	30	41	55

Pat Boutette

BOUTETTE, PATRICK MICHAEL 5'8", 175 lbs.
B. Mar. 1, 1952, Windsor, Ont. Right Wing, Shoots L

YEAR	TEAM & LEAGUE		GP	G	A	PTS	PIM
1975-76	TOR	N	77	10	22	32	140
1976-77			80	18	18	36	107
1977-78			80	17	19	36	120
1978-79			80	14	19	33	136
1979-80			32	0	4	4	17
	HART	N	47	13	31	44	75
	2 team total		79	13	35	48	92
1980-81			80	28	52	80	160
1981-82	PITT	N	80	23	51	74	230
1982-83			80	27	29	56	152
8 yrs.		N Totals:	636	150	245	395	1137
PLAYOFFS							
1975-76	TOR	N	10	1	4	5	16
1976-77			9	0	4	4	17
1977-78			13	3	3	6	40
1978-79			6	2	2	4	22
1979-80	HART	N	3	1	0	1	6
1981-82	PITT	N	5	3	1	4	8
6 yrs.		N Totals:	46	10	14	24	109

Traded to **Hartford** by Toronto for Bob Stephenson, Dec. 24, 1979. Traded to **Pittsburgh** by Hartford with Kevin McLelland, June 29, 1981, as compensation for Hartford's signing of Greg Millen as a free agent, June 15, 1981.

Paul Boutilier

BOUTILIER, PAUL ANDRE 5'11", 188 lbs.
B. May 3, 1963, Sydney, N.S. Defense, Shoots L

YEAR	TEAM & LEAGUE		GP	G	A	PTS	PIM
1981-82	NYI	N	1	0	0	0	0
1982-83			29	4	5	9	24
2 yrs.		N Totals:	30	4	5	9	24
PLAYOFFS							
1982-83*	NYI	N	2	0	0	0	2

Clarence Bowcher

BOWCHER, CLARENCE
B. Sudbury, Ont. Defense

YEAR	TEAM & LEAGUE		GP	G	A	PTS	PIM
1926-27	NYA	N	11	0	1	1	4
1927-28			36	2	1	3	106
2 yrs.		N Totals:	47	2	2	4	110

Brian Bowles

BOWLES, BRIAN EARL 5'11", 185 lbs.
B. Feb. 18, 1952, Drummondville, Que. Defense, Shoots R

YEAR	TEAM & LEAGUE		GP	G	A	PTS	PIM
1975-76	CLEVE	W	3	0	0	0	0

Kirk Bowman

BOWMAN, ROBERT KIRK 5'9", 178 lbs.
B. Sept. 30, 1952, Leamington, Ont. Left Wing, Shoots L

YEAR	TEAM & LEAGUE		GP	G	A	PTS	PIM
1973-74	LA	W	10	0	2	2	0
1976-77	CHI	N	55	10	13	23	6
1977-78			33	1	4	5	13
3 yrs.		N Totals:	88	11	17	28	19
		W Totals:	10	0	2	2	0
PLAYOFFS							
1976-77	CHI	N	2	1	0	1	0
1977-78			3	0	0	0	0
1978-79			2	0	0	0	0
3 yrs.		N Totals:	7	1	0	1	0

Scotty Bowman

BOWMAN, RALPH B. 5'11", 190 lbs.
B. June 20, 1911, Winnipeg, Man. Defense, Shoots L

YEAR	TEAM & LEAGUE		GP	G	A	PTS	PIM
1933-34	OTTA	N	46	0	2	2	64
1934-35	STL	N	31	2	2	4	51
	DET	N	13	1	3	4	21
	2 team total		44	3	5	8	72
1935-36			48	3	2	5	44
1936-37			37	0	1	1	24
1937-38			45	0	2	2	26
1938-39			43	2	3	5	26
1939-40			11	0	2	2	4
7 yrs.		N Totals:	274	8	17	25	260
PLAYOFFS							
1935-36*	DET	N	7	2	1	3	2
1936-37*			10	0	1	1	4
1938-39			5	0	0	0	0
3 yrs.		N Totals:	22	2	2	4	6

Jack Bownass

BOWNASS, JOHN 6'1", 200 lbs.
B. July 27, 1930, Winnipeg, Man. Defense, Shoots L

YEAR	TEAM & LEAGUE		GP	G	A	PTS	PIM
1957-58	MONT	N	4	0	1	1	0
1958-59	NYR	N	35	1	2	3	20
1959-60			37	2	5	7	34
1961-62			4	0	0	0	4
4 yrs.		N Totals:	80	3	8	11	58

Rick Bowness

BOWNESS, RICHARD GARY 6'1", 185 lbs.
B. Jan. 25, 1955, Moncton, N.B. Right Wing, Shoots R

YEAR	TEAM & LEAGUE		GP	G	A	PTS	PIM
1975-76	ATL	N	5	0	0	0	0
1976-77			28	0	4	4	29
1977-78	DET	N	61	8	11	19	76

Rick Bowness continued

YEAR	TEAM & LEAGUE		GP	G	A	PTS	PIM
1978-79	STL	N	24	1	3	4	30
1979-80			10	1	2	3	11
1980-81	WINN	N	45	8	17	25	45
6 yrs.		N Totals:	173	18	37	55	191
PLAYOFFS							
1977-78	DET	N	4	0	0	0	2
1981-82	WINN	N	1	0	0	0	0
2 yrs.		N Totals:	5	0	0	0	2

Sold to **Detroit** by Atlanta, Aug. 18, 1977. Sold to **St. Louis** by Detroit, Oct. 10, 1978. Traded to **Winnipeg** by St. Louis for Craig Norwich, June 19, 1980.

Bill Boyd

BOYD, WILLIAM G. 5'10", 185 lbs.
B. May 15, 1898, Belleville, Ont. Right Wing, Shoots R

YEAR	TEAM & LEAGUE		GP	G	A	PTS	PIM
1926-27	NYR	N	41	4	1	5	40
1927-28			43	4	0	4	11
1928-29			11	0	0	0	5
1929-30	NYA	N	43	7	6	13	16
4 yrs.		N Totals:	138	15	7	22	72
PLAYOFFS							
1927-28*	NYR	N	9	0	0	0	2

Bob Boyd

BOYD, ROBERT (Boydie) 6', 190 lbs.
B. Nov. 27, 1951, Toronto, Ont. Defense, Shoots R

YEAR	TEAM & LEAGUE		GP	G	A	PTS	PIM
1973-74	MINN	W	41	1	14	15	14
1974-75			13	0	0	0	21
2 yrs.		W Totals:	54	1	14	15	35
PLAYOFFS							
1973-74	MINN	W	7	0	0	0	4

Irwin Boyd

BOYD, IRWIN (Yank) 5'10", 152 lbs.
B. Nov. 13, 1908, Ardmore, Pa. Right Wing, Shoots R

YEAR	TEAM & LEAGUE		GP	G	A	PTS	PIM
1931-32	BOS	N	30	10	10	20	31
1934-35	DET	N	42	2	3	5	14
1942-43	BOS	N	20	6	5	11	6
1943-44			5	0	1	1	0
4 yrs.		N Totals:	97	18	19	37	51
PLAYOFFS							
1931-32	BOS	N	10	0	0	0	0
1942-43			5	0	1	1	4
2 yrs.		N Totals:	15	0	1	1	4

Jim Boyd

BOYD, JAMES 5'9", 180 lbs.
B. June 4, 1949, Calgary, Alta. Center, Shoots L

YEAR	TEAM & LEAGUE		GP	G	A	PTS	PIM
1974-75	PHOE	W	76	26	44	70	18
1975-76			80	23	34	57	44
1976-77	CALG	W	13	0	2	2	6
3 yrs.		W Totals:	169	49	80	129	68
PLAYOFFS							
1974-75	PHOE	W	5	1	1	2	2
1975-76			5	3	2	5	2
2 yrs.		W Totals:	10	4	3	7	4

Randy Boyd

BOYD, RANDY KEITH 5'11", 192 lbs.
B. Jan. 23, 1962, Coniston, Ont. Defense, Shoots L

YEAR	TEAM & LEAGUE		GP	G	A	PTS	PIM
1981-82	PITT	N	23	0	2	2	49
1982-83			56	4	14	18	71
2 yrs.		N Totals:	79	4	16	20	120
PLAYOFFS							
1981-82	PITT	N	3	0	0	0	11

Wally Boyer

BOYER, WALTER 5'8", 165 lbs.
B. Sept. 27, 1937, Cowan, Man. Center, Shoots L

YEAR	TEAM & LEAGUE		GP	G	A	PTS	PIM
1965-66	TOR	N	46	4	17	21	23
1966-67	CHI	N	42	5	6	11	15
1967-68	OAK	N	74	13	20	33	44
1968-69	PITT	N	62	10	19	29	17
1969-70			72	11	12	23	34
1970-71			68	11	30	41	30
1971-72			1	0	1	1	0
1972-73	WINN	W	69	6	28	34	27
8 yrs.		N Totals:	365	54	105	159	163
		W Totals:	69	6	28	34	27
PLAYOFFS							
1965-66	TOR	N	4	0	1	1	0
1966-67	CHI	N	1	0	0	0	0
1969-70	PITT	N	10	1	2	3	0
1972-73	WINN	W	14	4	2	6	4
4 yrs.		N Totals:	15	1	3	4	0
		W Totals:	14	4	2	6	4

Claimed in draft by **Mont. Canadiens** from Toronto, then drafted by **Chicago** from Montreal, June 15, 1966. Drafted by **Oakland** from Chicago in Expansion Draft, June 6, 1967. Traded to **Montreal** by Oakland with Alain Caron and Oakland's first-round choices in the 1968 (Jim Pritchard) and 1970 (Ray Martyniuk) Amateur Drafts for Norm Ferguson and Stan Fuller, May 21, 1968. Traded to **Pittsburgh** by Montreal for Al MacNeil, June 12, 1968.

Dean Boylan

BOYLAN, DEAN 6', 185 lbs.
B. Jan. 28, 1951, Boston, Mass. Defense, Shoots R

YEAR	TEAM & LEAGUE		GP	G	A	PTS	PIM
1973-74	NY-NJ	W	61	1	5	6	112
1974-75	SD	W	3	0	0	0	10
2 yrs.		W Totals:	64	1	5	6	122

Steve Bozek

BOZEK, STEVEN MICHAEL 5'11", 170 lbs.
B. Nov. 26, 1960, Kelowna, B.C. Center, Shoots R

YEAR	TEAM & LEAGUE		GP	G	A	PTS	PIM
1981-82	LA	N	71	33	23	56	68
1982-83			53	13	13	26	14
2 yrs.		N Totals:	124	46	36	82	82
PLAYOFFS							
1981-82	LA	N	10	4	1	5	6

Traded to **Calgary** by Los Angeles for Kevin Lavallee and Carl Mokosak, June 20, 1983.

John Brackenborough

BRACKENBOROUGH, JOHN
B. Unknown Center

YEAR	TEAM & LEAGUE		GP	G	A	PTS	PIM
1925-26	BOS	N	7	0	0	0	0

Curt Brackenbury

BRACKENBURY, JOHN CURTIS 5'10", 197 lbs.
B. Jan. 31, 1952, Kapuskasing, Ont. Right Wing, Shoots R

YEAR	TEAM & LEAGUE		GP	G	A	PTS	PIM
1973-74	CHI	W	4	0	1	1	11
1974-75	MINN	W	7	0	0	0	22
1975-76			59	4	9	13	254
	QUE	W	15	4	5	9	111
	2 team total		74	8	14	22	**365**
1976-77			77	16	13	29	146
1977-78			33	4	9	13	54
1978-79			70	13	13	26	155
1979-80	QUE	N	63	6	8	14	55
1980-81	EDM	N	58	2	7	9	153
1981-82			14	0	2	2	12
1982-83	STL	N	6	1	0	1	6
10 yrs.		N Totals:	141	9	17	26	226
		W Totals:	265	41	50	91	753
PLAYOFFS							
1974-75	MINN	W	12	0	2	2	59
1975-76	QUE	W	5	0	0	0	18

Curt Brackenbury continued

YEAR	TEAM & LEAGUE		GP	G	A	PTS	PIM
1976-77			17	3	5	8	51
1977-78			10	1	1	2	31
1978-79			4	1	1	2	2
1980-81	EDM	N	2	0	0	0	0
6 yrs.		N Totals:	2	0	0	0	0
		W Totals:	48	5	9	14	161

Claimed by **Edmonton** from Quebec in Waiver Draft, Oct. 10, 1980.

Barton Bradley

BRADLEY, BARTON WILLIAM 5'7½", 150 lbs.
B. July 29, 1930, Fort William, Ont. Center, Shoots L

YEAR	TEAM & LEAGUE		GP	G	A	PTS	PIM
1949-50	BOS	N	1	0	0	0	0

Brian Bradley

BRADLEY, BRIAN JAMES 5'10", 185 lbs.
B. Dec. 14, 1944, Sudbury, Ont. Left Wing, Shoots L

YEAR	TEAM & LEAGUE		GP	G	A	PTS	PIM
1972-73	NY	W	78	22	33	55	20
1973-74	NY-NJ	W	78	15	23	38	12
1974-75	SD	W	24	4	5	9	6
3 yrs.		W Totals:	180	41	61	102	38
PLAYOFFS							
1974-75	SD	W	6	0	1	1	2

Walter Bradley

BRADLEY, WALTER LYLE 5'9", 160 lbs.
B. July 31, 1943, Lloydminster, Sask. Center, Shoots R

YEAR	TEAM & LEAGUE		GP	G	A	PTS	PIM
1973-74	CALIF	N	4	1	0	1	2
1976-77	CLEVE	N	2	0	0	0	0
2 yrs.		N Totals:	6	1	0	1	2

Rick Bragnalo

BRAGNALO, RICHARD JAMES 5'8", 160 lbs.
B. Dec. 1, 1951, Thunder Bay, Ont. Center, Shoots L

YEAR	TEAM & LEAGUE		GP	G	A	PTS	PIM
1975-76	WASH	N	19	2	10	12	8
1976-77			80	11	12	23	16
1977-78			44	2	13	15	22
1978-79			2	0	0	0	0
4 yrs.		N Totals:	145	15	35	50	46

Andy Brannigan

BRANNIGAN, ANDREW JOHN 5'11", 190 lbs.
B. Apr. 11, 1922, Winnipeg, Man. Defense, Shoots L

YEAR	TEAM & LEAGUE		GP	G	A	PTS	PIM
1940-41	NYA	N	6	1	0	1	5
1941-42			20	0	2	2	26
2 yrs.		N Totals:	26	1	2	3	31

Per-Olov Brasar

BRASAR, PER-OLOV 5'10", 180 lbs.
B. Sept. 30, 1950, Falun, Sweden Left Wing, Shoots L

YEAR	TEAM & LEAGUE		GP	G	A	PTS	PIM
1977-78	MINN	N	77	20	37	57	6
1978-79			68	6	28	34	6
1979-80			22	1	14	15	0
	VAN	N	48	9	10	19	7
	2 team total		70	10	24	34	7
1980-81			80	22	41	63	8
1981-82			53	6	12	18	6
5 yrs.		N Totals:	348	64	142	206	33
PLAYOFFS							
1979-80	VAN	N	4	1	2	3	0
1980-81			3	0	0	0	0
1981-82			6	0	0	0	0
3 yrs.		N Totals:	13	1	2	3	0

Traded to **Vancouver** by Minnesota for Vancouver's second-round choice (Mike Sands) in the 1981 Entry Draft, Dec. 10, 1979.

Duane Bray

BRAY, DUANE GEORGE 6'2", 195 lbs.
B. Sept. 24, 1954, Flin Flon, Man. Defense, Shoots L

YEAR	TEAM & LEAGUE		GP	G	A	PTS	PIM
1976-77	PHOE	W	46	2	6	8	62

Russ Brayshaw

BRAYSHAW, RUSSELL AMBROSE 5'10", 170 lbs.
B. Jan. 17, 1918, Saskatoon, Sask. Left Wing, Shoots L

YEAR	TEAM & LEAGUE		GP	G	A	PTS	PIM
1944-45	CHI	N	43	5	9	14	24

Gary Bredin

BREDIN, GARY BLAINE 6', 185 lbs.
B. May 25, 1948, Edmonton, Alta. Right Wing, Shoots R

YEAR	TEAM & LEAGUE		GP	G	A	PTS	PIM
1974-75	IND	W	10	3	2	5	8
	M-B	W	67	15	21	36	29
	2 team total		77	18	23	41	37
1975-76	D-O	W	16	4	3	7	2
	SD	W	50	4	5	9	10
	2 team total		66	8	8	16	12
2 yrs.		W Totals:	143	26	31	57	49

Traded to **Vancouver** by Detroit with John Cunniff for Irv Spencer and Bob Dillabough, June 8, 1971.

Ken Breitenbach

BREITENBACH, KEN 6'1", 190 lbs.
B. Jan. 9, 1955, Welland, Ont. Defense, Shoots L

YEAR	TEAM & LEAGUE		GP	G	A	PTS	PIM
1975-76	BUF	N	7	0	0	0	6
1976-77			31	0	5	5	18
1978-79			30	1	8	9	25
3 yrs.		N Totals:	68	1	13	14	49
PLAYOFFS							
1975-76	BUF	N	1	0	0	0	0
1976-77			4	0	0	0	0
1978-79			3	0	1	1	4
3 yrs.		N Totals:	8	0	1	1	4

Doug Brennan

BRENNAN, DOUGLAS R. 5'10½", 180 lbs.
B. Jan. 10, 1905, Peterborough, Ont. Defense, Shoots L

YEAR	TEAM & LEAGUE		GP	G	A	PTS	PIM
1931-32	NYR	N	38	4	3	7	40
1932-33			48	5	4	9	94
1933-34			37	0	0	0	18
3 yrs.		N Totals:	123	9	7	16	152
PLAYOFFS							
1931-32	NYR	N	7	1	0	1	10
1932-33			8	0	0	0	11
1933-34			1	0	0	0	0
3 yrs.		N Totals:	16	1	0	1	21

Tom Brennan

BRENNAN, THOMAS E 5'8½", 155 lbs.
B. Jan. 22, 1922, Philadelphia, Pa. Right Wing, Shoots R

YEAR	TEAM & LEAGUE		GP	G	A	PTS	PIM
1943-44	BOS	N	21	2	1	3	2
1944-45			1	0	1	1	0
2 yrs.		N Totals:	22	2	2	4	2

John Brenneman

BRENNEMAN, JOHN GARY 5'10", 175 lbs.
B. Jan. 5, 1943, Fort Erie, Ont. Left Wing, Shoots L

YEAR	TEAM & LEAGUE		GP	G	A	PTS	PIM
1964-65	CHI	N	17	1	0	1	2
	NYR	N	22	3	3	6	6
	2 team total		39	4	3	7	8
1965-66			11	0	0	0	14
1966-67	TOR	N	41	6	4	10	4
1967-68	DET	N	9	0	2	2	0
	OAK	N	31	10	8	18	14
	2 team total		40	10	10	20	14
1968-69	CALIF	N	21	1	2	3	6
5 yrs.		N Totals:	152	21	19	40	46

Traded to **N.Y. Rangers** by Chicago with Doug Robinson and Wayne Hillman for Camille Henry, Don Johns, Billy Taylor and Wally Chevrier, Feb. 4, 1965. Claimed in draft by **Toronto** from N.Y. Rangers, June 15, 1966. Drafted by **St. Louis** from Toronto in Expansion Draft, June 6, 1967. Traded by St. Louis to **Detroit** for Craig Cameron, Larry Hornung, and Don Giesebrecht, Oct. 19, 1967. Traded by Detroit with Ted Hampson and Bert Marshall to **Oakland** for Kent Douglas, Jan. 9, 1968.

Joe Bretto

BRETTO, JOSEPH 6'1", 248 lbs.
B. Nov. 29, 1912, Hibbing, Minn. Defense, Shoots L

YEAR	TEAM & LEAGUE		GP	G	A	PTS	PIM
1944-45	CHI	N	3	0	0	0	4

Carl Brewer

BREWER, CARL THOMAS 5'10", 180 lbs.
B. Oct. 21, 1938, Toronto, Ont. Defense, Shoots L

YEAR	TEAM & LEAGUE		GP	G	A	PTS	PIM
1957-58	TOR	N	2	0	0	0	0
1958-59			69	3	21	24	125
1959-60			67	4	19	23	**150**
1960-61			51	1	14	15	92
1961-62			67	1	22	23	89
1962-63			70	2	23	25	168
1963-64			57	4	9	13	114
1964-65			70	4	23	27	**177**
1969-70	DET	N	70	2	37	39	51
1970-71	STL	N	19	2	9	11	29
1971-72			42	2	16	18	40
1973-74	TOR	W	77	2	23	25	42
1979-80	TOR	N	20	0	5	5	2
13 yrs.		N Totals:	604	25	198	223	1037
		W Totals:	77	2	23	25	42
PLAYOFFS							
1958-59	TOR	N	12	0	6	6	40
1959-60			10	2	3	5	16
1960-61			5	0	0	0	4
1961-62*			8	0	2	2	22
1962-63*			10	0	1	1	12
1963-64*			12	0	1	1	30
1964-65			6	1	2	3	12
1969-70	DET	N	4	0	0	0	2
1970-71	STL	N	5	0	2	2	8
1973-74	TOR	W	12	0	4	4	11
10 yrs.		N Totals:	72	3	17	20	146
		W Totals:	12	0	4	4	11

Traded to **Detroit** by Toronto with Garry Unger and Pete Stemkowski for Paul Henderson, Norm Ullman and Floyd Smith, March 3, 1968. Traded to **St. Louis** by Detroit for Mike Lowe, Ab McDonald and Bob Wall, Feb. 18, 1971. Signed as free agent by **Toronto** Jan. 2, 1980.

Andy Brickley

BRICKLEY, ANDY 6', 190 lbs.
B. Aug. 9, 1961, Melrose, Mass. Left Wing, Shoots L

YEAR	TEAM & LEAGUE		GP	G	A	PTS	PIM
1982-83	PHI	N	3	1	1	2	0

Archie Briden

BRIDEN, E. ARCHIBALD
B. Forward

YEAR	TEAM & LEAGUE		GP	G	A	PTS	PIM
1926-27	DET	N	42	5	2	7	36
1929-30	PITT	N	30	4	3	7	20
2 yrs.		N Totals:	72	9	5	14	56

Mel Bridgman

BRIDGMAN, MELVIN JOHN 6', 190 lbs.
B. Apr. 28, 1955, Trenton, Ont. Center, Shoots L

YEAR	TEAM & LEAGUE		GP	G	A	PTS	PIM
1975-76	PHI	N	80	23	27	50	86
1976-77			70	19	38	57	120
1977-78			76	16	32	48	203
1978-79			76	24	35	59	184
1979-80			74	16	31	47	136
1980-81			77	14	37	51	195
1981-82			9	7	5	12	0
	CALG	N	63	26	49	75	94
	2 team total		72	33	54	87	94
1982-83			79	19	31	50	103
8 yrs.		N Totals:	604	164	285	449	1121

Mel Bridgman continued

PLAYOFFS

YEAR	TEAM	LEAGUE	GP	G	A	PTS	PIM
1975-76	**PHI**	**N**	16	6	8	14	31
1976-77			7	1	0	1	8
1977-78			12	1	7	8	36
1978-79			8	1	2	3	17
1979-80			19	2	9	11	70
1980-81			12	2	4	6	39
1981-82	**CALG**	**N**	3	2	0	2	14
1982-83			9	3	4	7	33
8 yrs.		**N Totals:**	86	18	34	52	248

Traded to **Calgary** by Philadelphia for Brad Marsh, Nov. 11, 1981. Traded by Calgary with Phil Russell to **New Jersey** for Joel Quenneville and Steve Tambellini, June 20, 1983.

Michel Briere

BRIERE, MICHEL EDOUARD 5'10", 165 lbs.
B. Oct. 21, 1949, Malartic, Que. Center, Shoots L

YEAR	TEAM	LEAGUE	GP	G	A	PTS	PIM
1969-70	**PITT**	**N**	76	12	32	44	20

PLAYOFFS

YEAR	TEAM	LEAGUE	GP	G	A	PTS	PIM
1969-70	**PITT**	**N**	10	5	3	8	17

Doug Brindley

BRINDLEY, DOUGLAS ALLEN 6'1", 175 lbs.
B. June 8, 1949, Walkerton, Ont. Center, Shoots L

YEAR	TEAM	LEAGUE	GP	G	A	PTS	PIM
1970-71	**TOR**	**N**	3	0	0	0	0
1972-73	**CLEVE**	**W**	73	15	11	26	6
1973-74			30	13	9	22	13
3 yrs.		**N Totals:**	3	0	0	0	0
		W Totals:	103	28	20	48	19

PLAYOFFS

YEAR	TEAM	LEAGUE	GP	G	A	PTS	PIM
1973-74	**CLEVE**	**W**	5	0	1	1	2

Milt Brink

BRINK, MILTON
B. U.S.A. Forward

YEAR	TEAM	LEAGUE	GP	G	A	PTS	PIM
1936-37	**CHI**	**N**	5	0	0	0	0

Gerry Brisson

BRISSON, GERALD 5'9", 155 lbs.
B. Sept. 3, 1937, Boniface, Man. Right Wing, Shoots L

YEAR	TEAM	LEAGUE	GP	G	A	PTS	PIM
1962-63	**MONT**	**N**	4	0	2	2	4

Punch Broadbent

BROADBENT, HARRY
B. July 13, 1892, Ottawa, Ont. Right Wing, Shoots R
Won Art Ross Trophy, 1921-22
Hall of Fame, 1962

YEAR	TEAM	LEAGUE	GP	G	A	PTS	PIM
1918-19	**OTTA**	**N**	8	4	2	6	12
1919-20			20	19	4	23	39
1920-21			9	4	1	5	6
1921-22			24	**32**	**14**	**46**	24
1922-23			24	14	0	14	32
1923-24			22	9	4	13	44
1924-25	**MON(M)**	**N**	30	15	4	19	75
1925-26			36	12	5	17	112
1926-27			42	11	4	15	42
1927-28	**OTTA**	**N**	43	3	2	5	62
1928-29	**NYA**	**N**	44	1	4	5	59
11 yrs.		**N Totals:**	302	124	44	168	507

PLAYOFFS

YEAR	TEAM	LEAGUE	GP	G	A	PTS	PIM
1918-19	**OTTA**	**N**	5	2	0	2	12
1919-20*			4	0	0	0	0
1920-21*			7	2	0	2	6
1921-22			2	0	0	0	6
1922-23*			8	6	1	7	12
1923-24			2	0	0	0	2
1925-26*	**MON(M)**	**N**	8	2	0	2	36
1926-27			2	0	0	0	0
1927-28	**OTTA**	**N**	2	0	0	0	0
1928-29	**NYA**	**N**	2	0	0	0	2

Punch Broadbent continued

YEAR	TEAM	LEAGUE	GP	G	A	PTS	PIM
10 yrs.		**N Totals:**	42	12	1	13	76

Connie Broden

BRODEN, CONNELL 5'8", 160 lbs.
B. Apr. 6, 1932, Montreal, Que. Center, Shoots L

YEAR	TEAM	LEAGUE	GP	G	A	PTS	PIM
1955-56	**MONT**	**N**	3	0	0	0	2
1957-58			3	2	1	3	0
2 yrs.		**N Totals:**	6	2	1	3	2

PLAYOFFS

YEAR	TEAM	LEAGUE	GP	G	A	PTS	PIM
1956-57*	**MONT**	**N**	6	0	1	1	0
1957-58*			1	0	0	0	0
2 yrs.		**N Totals:**	7	0	1	1	0

Gord Brooks

BROOKS, GORDON JOHN 5'8", 168 lbs.
B. Sept. 11, 1950, Cobourg, Ont. Right Wing, Shoots R

YEAR	TEAM	LEAGUE	GP	G	A	PTS	PIM
1971-72	**STL**	**N**	2	0	0	0	0
1973-74			30	6	8	14	12
1974-75	**WASH**	**N**	38	1	10	11	25
3 yrs.		**N Totals:**	70	7	18	25	37

Drafted by **Washington** from St. Louis in Expansion Draft, June 12, 1974.

Bernie Brophy

BROPHY, BERNARD
B. Collingwood, Ont. Forward

YEAR	TEAM	LEAGUE	GP	G	A	PTS	PIM
1925-26	**MON(M)**	**N**	10	0	0	0	0
1928-29	**DET**	**N**	37	2	4	6	23
1929-30			17	1	9	10	2
3 yrs.		**N Totals:**	64	3	13	16	25

PLAYOFFS

YEAR	TEAM	LEAGUE	GP	G	A	PTS	PIM
1928-29	**DET**	**N**	2	0	0	0	2

Willie Brossart

BROSSART, WILLIAM 6', 190 lbs.
B. May 29, 1949, Allan, Sask. Defense, Shoots L

YEAR	TEAM	LEAGUE	GP	G	A	PTS	PIM
1970-71	**PHI**	**N**	1	0	0	0	0
1971-72			42	0	4	4	12
1972-73			4	0	1	1	0
1973-74	**TOR**	**N**	17	0	1	1	20
1974-75			4	0	0	0	2
	WASH	**N**	12	1	0	1	14
	2 team total		16	1	0	1	16
1975-76			49	0	8	8	40
6 yrs.		**N Totals:**	129	1	14	15	88

PLAYOFFS

YEAR	TEAM	LEAGUE	GP	G	A	PTS	PIM
1973-74	**TOR**	**N**	1	0	0	0	0

Sold to **Toronto** by Philadelphia, May 23, 1973. Traded to **Washington** by Toronto with Tim Ecclestone for Rod Seiling, Nov. 2, 1974.

Aaron Broten

BROTEN, AARON 5'10", 175 lbs.
B. Nov. 14, 1960, Roseau, Minn. Left Wing, Shoots L

YEAR	TEAM	LEAGUE	GP	G	A	PTS	PIM
1980-81	**COLO**	**N**	2	0	0	0	0
1981-82			58	15	24	39	6
1982-83	**NJ**	**N**	73	16	39	55	28
3 yrs.		**N Totals:**	133	31	63	94	34

Neal Broten

BROTEN, NEAL LAMOY 5'9", 160 lbs.
B. Nov. 29, 1959, Roseau, Minn. Center, Shoots L

YEAR	TEAM	LEAGUE	GP	G	A	PTS	PIM
1980-81	**MINN**	**N**	3	2	0	2	12
1981-82			73	38	60	98	42
1982-83			79	32	45	77	43
3 yrs.		**N Totals:**	155	72	105	177	97

PLAYOFFS

YEAR	TEAM	LEAGUE	GP	G	A	PTS	PIM
1980-81	**MINN**	**N**	19	1	7	8	9

Neal Broten continued

YEAR	TEAM & LEAGUE		GP	G	A	PTS	PIM
1981-82			4	0	2	2	0
1982-83			9	1	6	7	10
3 yrs.		**N Totals:**	32	2	15	17	19

Adam Brown

BROWN, ADAM 5'10", 175 lbs.
B. Feb. 4, 1920, Johnstone, Scotland Left Wing, Shoots L

YEAR	TEAM & LEAGUE		GP	G	A	PTS	PIM
1941-42	**DET**	**N**	28	6	9	15	15
1943-44			50	24	18	42	56
1945-46			48	20	11	31	27
1946-47			22	8	5	13	28
	CHI	**N**	42	11	25	36	59
	2 team total		64	19	30	49	87
1947-48			32	7	10	17	41
1948-49			58	8	12	20	69
1949-50			25	2	2	4	16
1950-51			53	10	12	22	16
1951-52	**BOS**	**N**	33	8	9	17	6
9 yrs.		**N Totals:**	391	104	113	217	333
PLAYOFFS							
1941-42	**DET**	**N**	12	0	2	2	4
1942-43*			6	1	1	2	2
1943-44			5	1	1	2	0
1945-46			5	1	1	2	0
4 yrs.		**N Totals:**	28	3	5	8	6

Sold to **Chicago** by Boston, Aug. 20, 1951.

Arnie Brown

BROWN, STEWART ARNOLD 5'11", 185 lbs.
B. Jan. 28, 1942, Oshawa, Ont. Defense, Shoots L

YEAR	TEAM & LEAGUE		GP	G	A	PTS	PIM
1961-62	**TOR**	**N**	2	0	0	0	0
1963-64			4	0	0	0	6
1964-65	**NYR**	**N**	58	1	11	12	145
1965-66			64	1	7	8	106
1966-67			69	2	10	12	61
1967-68			74	1	25	26	83
1968-69			74	10	12	22	48
1969-70			73	15	21	36	78
1970-71			48	3	12	15	24
	DET	**N**	27	2	6	8	30
	2 team total		75	5	18	23	54
1971-72			77	2	23	25	84
1972-73	**NYI**	**N**	48	4	8	12	27
	ATL	**N**	15	1	0	1	17
	2 team total		63	5	8	13	44
1973-74			48	2	6	8	29
1974-75	**M-B**	**W**	50	3	4	7	27
	VAN	**W**	10	0	1	1	13
	2 team total		60	3	5	8	40
13 yrs.		**N Totals:**	681	44	141	185	738
		W Totals:	60	3	5	8	40
PLAYOFFS							
1966-67	**NYR**	**N**	4	0	0	0	6
1967-68			6	0	1	1	8
1968-69			4	0	1	1	0
1969-70			4	0	4	4	9
1970-71			11	0	1	1	0
1973-74	**ATL**	**N**	4	0	0	0	0
6 yrs.		**N Totals:**	33	0	7	7	23

Traded by Toronto Rod Seiling, Bob Nevin, Dick Duff, and Bill Collins to **N.Y. Rangers** for Andy Bathgate and Don McKenney, Feb. 22, 1964. Traded to **Detroit** by N.Y. Rangers with Mike Robitaille and Tom Miller for Bruce MacGregor and Larry Brown, Feb. 2, 1970. Traded to **N.Y. Islanders** by detroit with Gerry Gray for Denis DeJordy and Don McLaughlin, Oct. 4, 1972. Traded to **Atlanta** by N.Y. Islanders for Ernie Hicke, Feb. 13, 1973.

Bob Brown

BROWN, ROBERT 6'1", 195 lbs.
B. Dec. 18, 1950, Toronto, Ont. Defense, Shoots R

YEAR	TEAM & LEAGUE		GP	G	A	PTS	PIM
1972-73	**PHI**	**W**	4	0	0	0	2
	NY	**W**	17	0	4	4	6
	2 team total		21	0	4	4	8
1973-74	**NY-NJ**	**W**	59	7	13	20	38

Bob Brown continued

YEAR	TEAM & LEAGUE		GP	G	A	PTS	PIM
2 yrs.		**W Totals:**	80	7	17	24	46

Connie Brown

BROWN, PATRICK CORNELIUS 5'7", 168 lbs.
B. Jan. 11, 1917, Vankleek Hill, Ont. Center, Shoots L

YEAR	TEAM & LEAGUE		GP	G	A	PTS	PIM
1938-39	**DET**	**N**	20	1	0	1	0
1939-40			36	8	3	11	2
1940-41			3	1	2	3	0
1941-42			9	0	3	3	4
1942-43			23	5	16	21	6
5 yrs.		**N Totals:**	91	15	24	39	12
PLAYOFFS							
1939-40	**DET**	**N**	5	2	1	3	0
1940-41			9	0	2	2	0
2 yrs.		**N Totals:**	14	2	3	5	0

Dave Brown

BROWN, DAVE 6'5", 205 lbs.
B. Oct. 12, 1962, Saskatoon, Sask. Right Wing, Shoots R

YEAR	TEAM & LEAGUE		GP	G	A	PTS	PIM
1982-83	**PHI**	**N**	2	0	0	0	5

Fred Brown

BROWN, FREDERICK
B. Kingston, Ont. Forward

YEAR	TEAM & LEAGUE		GP	G	A	PTS	PIM
1927-28	**MON(M)**	**N**	19	1	0	1	0
PLAYOFFS							
1927-28	**MON(M)**	**N**	9	0	0	0	0

George Brown

BROWN, GEORGE ALLAN 5'11½", 185 lbs.
B. May 17, 1912, Winnipeg, Man. Center, Shoots L

YEAR	TEAM & LEAGUE		GP	G	A	PTS	PIM
1936-37	**MONT**	**N**	27	4	6	10	10
1937-38			34	1	7	8	14
1938-39			18	1	9	10	10
3 yrs.		**N Totals:**	79	6	22	28	34
PLAYOFFS							
1936-37	**MONT**	**N**	4	0	0	0	0
1937-38			3	0	0	0	2
2 yrs.		**N Totals:**	7	0	0	0	2

Gerry Brown

BROWN, GERALD 5'10½", 176 lbs.
B. July 7, 1917, Edmonton, Alta. Left Wing, Shoots L

YEAR	TEAM & LEAGUE		GP	G	A	PTS	PIM
1941-42	**DET**	**N**	13	4	4	8	0
1945-46			10	0	1	1	2
2 yrs.		**N Totals:**	23	4	5	9	2
PLAYOFFS							
1941-42	**DET**	**N**	12	2	1	3	4

Harold Brown

BROWN, HAROLD FRASER 5'10", 160 lbs.
B. Sept. 14, 1920, Brandon, Man. Right Wing, Shoots L

YEAR	TEAM & LEAGUE		GP	G	A	PTS	PIM
1945-46	**NYR**	**N**	13	2	1	3	2

Jim Brown

BROWN, JIM 6'4", 210 lbs.
B. Mar. 1, 1960, Phoenix, Ariz. Defense, Shoots R

YEAR	TEAM & LEAGUE		GP	G	A	PTS	PIM
1982-83	**LA**	**N**	3	0	1	1	5

Keith Brown

BROWN, KEITH JEFFREY 6'1", 192 lbs.
B. May 6, 1960, Corner Brook, Nfld. Defense, Shoots R

YEAR	TEAM & LEAGUE		GP	G	A	PTS	PIM
1979-80	**CHI**	**N**	76	2	18	20	27
1980-81			80	9	34	43	80

Keith Brown continued

YEAR	TEAM & LEAGUE		GP	G	A	PTS	PIM
1981-82			33	4	20	24	26
1982-83			50	4	27	31	20
4 yrs.		**N Totals:**	239	19	99	118	153
PLAYOFFS							
1979-80	**CHI**	**N**	6	0	0	0	4
1980-81			3	0	2	2	2
1981-82			4	0	2	2	5
1982-83			7	0	0	0	11
4 yrs.		**N Totals:**	20	0	4	4	22

Larry Brown

BROWN, LARRY WAYNE 6'2", 210 lbs.
B. Apr. 14, 1947, Brandon, Man. Defense, Shoots L

YEAR	TEAM & LEAGUE		GP	G	A	PTS	PIM
1969-70	**NYR**	**N**	15	0	3	3	8
1970-71	**DET**	**N**	33	1	4	5	8
	NYR	**N**	31	1	1	2	10
	2 team total		64	2	5	7	18
1971-72	**PHI**	**N**	12	0	0	0	2
1972-73	**LA**	**N**	55	0	7	7	46
1973-74			45	0	4	4	14
1974-75			78	1	15	16	50
1975-76			74	2	5	7	33
1976-77			55	1	6	7	24
1977-78			57	1	8	9	23
9 yrs.		**N Totals:**	455	7	53	60	218
PLAYOFFS							
1970-71	**NYR**	**N**	11	0	1	1	0
1973-74	**LA**	**N**	2	0	0	0	0
1974-75			3	0	2	2	0
1975-76			9	0	0	0	2
1976-77			9	0	1	1	6
1977-78			1	0	0	0	2
6 yrs.		**N Totals:**	35	0	4	4	10

Traded to **Detroit** by N.Y. Rangers for Pete Stemkowski, Oct. 31, 1970. Traded to **N.Y. Rangers** by Detroit with Bruce MacGregor for Arnie Brown, Mike Robitaille, and Tom Miller, Feb. 2, 1971. Drafted by **Philadelphia** from N.Y. Rangers in Intra-league Draft, June 8, 1971. Claimed on waivers by **Los Angeles** from Philadelphia, Jan. 28, 1972. Claimed by **Edmonton** from Los Angeles in Expansion Draft, June 13, 1979.

Stan Brown

BROWN, STANLEY 5'9½", 150 lbs.
B. May 9, 1898, North Bay, Ont. Forward, Shoots L

YEAR	TEAM & LEAGUE		GP	G	A	PTS	PIM
1926-27	**NYR**	**N**	24	6	2	8	14
1927-28	**DET**	**N**	24	2	0	2	4
2 yrs.		**N Totals:**	48	8	2	10	18
PLAYOFFS							
1926-27	**NYR**	**N**	2	0	0	0	0

Wayne Brown

BROWN, WAYNE HEWETSON 5'8", 150 lbs.
B. Nov. 16, 1930, Deloro, Ont. Right Wing, Shoots L

YEAR	TEAM & LEAGUE		GP	G	A	PTS	PIM
PLAYOFFS							
1953-54	**BOS**	**N**	4	0	0	0	2

Cecil Browne

BROWNE, CECIL
B. Unknown Left Wing, Shoots L

YEAR	TEAM & LEAGUE		GP	G	A	PTS	PIM
1927-28	**CHI**	**N**	13	2	0	2	4

Jeff Brownschidle

BROWNSCHIDLE, JEFFREY PAUL 6'2", 205 lbs.
B. Mar. 1, 1959, Buffalo, N.Y. Defense, Shoots R

YEAR	TEAM & LEAGUE		GP	G	A	PTS	PIM
1981-82	**HART**	**N**	3	0	1	1	2
1982-83			4	0	0	0	0
2 yrs.		**N Totals:**	7	0	1	1	2

Signed as free agent by **Hartford** June 9, 1981.

Jack Brownschidle

BROWNSCHIDLE, JOHN J. JR. 6'2", 195 lbs.
B. Oct. 2, 1955, Buffalo, N.Y. Defense, Shoots L

YEAR	TEAM & LEAGUE		GP	G	A	PTS	PIM
1977-78	**STL**	**N**	40	2	15	17	23
1978-79			64	10	24	34	14
1979-80			77	12	32	44	8
1980-81			71	5	23	28	12
1981-82			80	5	33	38	26
1982-83			72	1	22	23	30
6 yrs.		**N Totals:**	404	35	149	184	113
PLAYOFFS							
1979-80	**STL**	**N**	3	0	0	0	0
1980-81			11	0	3	3	2
1981-82			8	0	2	2	14
1982-83			4	0	0	0	2
4 yrs.		**N Totals:**	26	0	5	5	18

Jeff Brubaker

BRUBAKER, JEFFREY J. 6'2", 210 lbs.
B. Feb. 24, 1958, Hagerstown, Md. Left Wing, Shoots L

YEAR	TEAM & LEAGUE		GP	G	A	PTS	PIM
1978-79	**NE**	**W**	12	0	0	0	19
1979-80	**HART**	**N**	3	0	1	1	2
1980-81			43	5	3	8	93
1981-82	**MONT**	**N**	3	0	1	1	32
4 yrs.		**N Totals:**	49	5	5	10	127
		W Totals:	12	0	0	0	19
PLAYOFFS							
1978-79	**NE**	**W**	3	0	0	0	12
1981-82	**MONT**	**N**	2	0	0	0	27
2 yrs.		**N Totals:**	2	0	0	0	27
		W Totals:	3	0	0	0	12

Claimed by **Montreal** from Hartford in 1981 Waiver Draft, Oct. 5, 1982.

Gordie Bruce

BRUCE, ARTHUR GORDON 5'11", 195 lbs.
B. May 9, 1919, Ottawa, Ont. Left Wing, Shoots L

YEAR	TEAM & LEAGUE		GP	G	A	PTS	PIM
1940-41	**BOS**	**N**	8	0	1	1	2
1941-42			15	4	8	12	11
1945-46			5	0	0	0	0
3 yrs.		**N Totals:**	28	4	9	13	13
PLAYOFFS							
1940-41	**BOS**	**N**	2	0	0	0	0
1941-42			5	2	3	5	4
2 yrs.		**N Totals:**	7	2	3	5	4

Morley Bruce

BRUCE, MORLEY
B. Unknown Defense

YEAR	TEAM & LEAGUE		GP	G	A	PTS	PIM
1917-18	**OTTA**	**N**	7	0	0	0	0
1919-20			21	1	0	1	2
1920-21			21	3	1	4	23
1921-22			23	4	0	4	2
4 yrs.		**N Totals:**	72	8	1	9	27
PLAYOFFS							
1919-20*	**OTTA**	**N**	5	0	0	0	0
1920-21*			7	0	0	0	3
1921-22			1	0	0	0	0
3 yrs.		**N Totals:**	13	0	0	0	3

James Brumwell

BRUMWELL, JAMES MURRAY 6'1", 190 lbs.
B. Mar. 31, 1960, Calgray, Alta. Defense, Shoots L

YEAR	TEAM & LEAGUE		GP	G	A	PTS	PIM
1980-81	**MINN**	**N**	1	0	0	0	0
1981-82			21	0	3	3	18
1982-83	**NJ**	**N**	59	5	14	19	34
3 yrs.		**N Totals:**	81	5	17	22	52
PLAYOFFS							
1981-82	**MINN**	**N**	2	0	0	0	2

James Brumwell continued

Signed as free agent by **Minnesota** Aug. 7, 1980. Acquired by **New Jersey** from Minnesota in Waiver Draft, Oct. 4, 1982.

Eddie Bruneteau

BRUNETEAU, EDWARD ERNEST HENRY
5'9", 172 lbs.
B. Aug. 1, 1919, St. Boniface, Man. Right Wing, Shoots R

YEAR	TEAM & LEAGUE		GP	G	A	PTS	PIM
1940-41	DET	N	12	1	1	2	2
1943-44			2	0	1	1	0
1944-45			42	12	13	25	6
1945-46			46	17	12	29	11
1946-47			60	9	14	23	14
1947-48			18	1	1	2	2
1948-49			1	0	0	0	0
7 yrs.		N Totals:	181	40	42	82	35
PLAYOFFS							
1944-45	DET	N	14	5	2	7	0
1945-46			4	1	0	1	0
1946-47			4	1	4	5	0
1947-48			6	0	0	0	5
4 yrs.		N Totals:	28	7	6	13	5

Mud Bruneteau

BRUNETEAU, MODERE
5'11", 185 lbs.
B. Nov. 28, 1914, St. Boniface, Man. Right Wing, Shoots R

YEAR	TEAM & LEAGUE		GP	G	A	PTS	PIM
1935-36	DET	N	24	2	0	2	2
1936-37			42	9	7	16	18
1937-38			24	3	6	9	16
1938-39			20	3	7	10	0
1939-40			48	10	14	24	10
1940-41			45	11	17	28	12
1941-42			48	14	19	33	8
1942-43			50	23	22	45	2
1943-44			39	35	18	53	4
1944-45			43	23	24	47	6
1945-46			28	6	4	10	2
11 yrs.		N Totals:	411	139	138	277	80
PLAYOFFS							
1935-36*	DET	N	7	2	2	4	4
1936-37*			10	2	0	2	6
1938-39			6	0	0	0	0
1939-40			5	3	2	5	0
1940-41			9	2	1	3	2
1941-42			12	5	1	6	6
1942-43*			9	5	4	9	0
1943-44			5	1	2	3	2
1944-45			14	3	2	5	2
9 yrs.		N Totals:	77	23	14	37	22

Bill Brydge

BRYDGE, WILLIAM H.
5'9", 195 lbs.
B. Iroquois Falls, Ont. Defense, Shoots R

YEAR	TEAM & LEAGUE		GP	G	A	PTS	PIM
1926-27	TOR	N	41	6	3	9	76
1928-29	DET	N	31	2	2	4	59
1929-30	NYA	N	41	2	6	8	64
1930-31			43	2	5	7	70
1931-32			48	2	8	10	77
1932-33			48	4	15	19	60
1933-34			48	6	7	13	44
1934-35			47	2	6	8	29
1935-36			21	0	0	0	27
9 yrs.		N Totals:	368	26	52	78	506
PLAYOFFS							
1928-29	DET	N	2	0	0	0	4

Glenn Brydson

BRYDSON, GLENN
5'9½", 170 lbs.
B. Nov. 7, 1910, Swansea, Ont. Right Wing, Shoots R

YEAR	TEAM & LEAGUE		GP	G	A	PTS	PIM
1930-31	MON(M)	N	14	0	0	0	4
1931-32			47	12	13	25	44
1932-33			48	11	17	28	26
1933-34			37	4	5	9	19

Glenn Brydson continued

YEAR	TEAM & LEAGUE		GP	G	A	PTS	PIM
1934-35	STL	N	48	11	18	29	45
1935-36	NYR	N	30	4	12	16	9
	CHI	N	22	6	4	10	30
	2 team total		52	10	16	26	39
1936-37			34	7	7	14	20
1937-38			19	1	3	4	6
8 yrs.		N Totals:	299	56	79	135	203
PLAYOFFS							
1930-31	MON(M)	N	2	0	0	0	0
1931-32			4	0	0	0	4
1932-33			2	0	0	0	0
1933-34			1	0	0	0	0
1935-36	CHI	N	2	0	0	0	4
5 yrs.		N Totals:	11	0	0	0	8

Gord Brydson

BRYDSON, GORDON
B. Unknown Forward

YEAR	TEAM & LEAGUE		GP	G	A	PTS	PIM
1929-30	TOR	N	8	2	0	2	8

Jiri Bubla

BUBLA, JIRI
5'11", 200 lbs.
B. Jan. 27, 1950, Usti Nad Labem, Czech.
Defense, Shoots R

YEAR	TEAM & LEAGUE		GP	G	A	PTS	PIM
1981-82	VAN	N	23	1	1	2	16
1982-83			72	2	28	30	59
2 yrs.		N Totals:	95	3	29	32	75
PLAYOFFS							
1982-83	VAN	N	1	0	0	0	5

N rights obtained by **Vancouver** from Colorado when Vancouver sent Brent Ashton and their fourth-round choice in 1982 Entry Draft (Tom Martin) to Winnipeg. (Winnipeg traded Ashton and their third-round choice in 1982 Entry Draft (Dave Kasper) to Colorado for Lucien DeBlois, July 15, 1981.)

Al Buchanan

BUCHANAN, ALLASTER WILLIAM
5'8", 160 lbs.
B. May 17, 1927, Winnipeg, Man. Left Wing, Shoots L

YEAR	TEAM & LEAGUE		GP	G	A	PTS	PIM
1948-49	TOR	N	3	0	1	1	2
1949-50			1	0	0	0	0
2 yrs.		N Totals:	4	0	1	1	2

Bucky Buchanan

BUCHANAN, RALPH LEONARD (Bucky)
5'8½", 172 lbs.
B. Dec. 28, 1922, Montreal, Que. Center, Shoots R

YEAR	TEAM & LEAGUE		GP	G	A	PTS	PIM
1948-49	NYR	N	2	0	0	0	0

Mike Buchanan

BUCHANAN, MICHAEL MURRAY
6'1", 185 lbs.
B. Mar. 1, 1932, Sault Ste. Marie, Ont. Defense, Shoots L

YEAR	TEAM & LEAGUE		GP	G	A	PTS	PIM
1951-52	CHI	N	1	0	0	0	0

Ron Buchanan

BUCHANAN, RONALD LEONARD
6'3", 178 lbs.
B. Nov. 15, 1944, Montreal, Que. Center, Shoots L

YEAR	TEAM & LEAGUE		GP	G	A	PTS	PIM
1966-67	BOS	N	3	0	0	0	0
1969-70	STL	N	2	0	0	0	0
1972-73	CLEVE	W	75	37	44	81	20
1973-74			49	18	27	45	2
1974-75			4	2	0	2	2
	EDM	W	22	6	9	15	4
	IND	W	32	16	15	31	16
	3 team total		58	24	24	48	22
1975-76			23	4	7	11	4
6 yrs.		N Totals:	5	0	0	0	0
		W Totals:	205	83	102	185	48
PLAYOFFS							
1972-73	CLEVE	W	9	7	3	10	0
1973-74			5	0	0	0	2
2 yrs.		W Totals:	14	7	3	10	2

Drafted by **Philadelphia** from Boston, June 12, 1968. Sold to **St. Louis** by Philadelphia, May 14, 1969.

John Bucyk

BUCYK, JOHN PAUL (Chief) 6', 215 lbs.

B. May 12, 1935, Edmonton, Alta. Left Wing, Shoots L

Won Lady Byng Trophy, 1970–71, 1973-74

Hall of Fame, 1981

YEAR	TEAM & LEAGUE		GP	G	A	PTS	PIM
1955-56	**DET**	**N**	38	1	8	9	20
1956-57			66	10	11	21	41
1957-58	**BOS**	**N**	68	21	31	52	57
1958-59			69	24	36	60	36
1959-60			56	16	36	52	26
1960-61			70	19	20	39	48
1961-62			67	20	40	60	32
1962-63			69	27	39	66	36
1963-64			62	18	36	54	36
1964-65			68	26	29	55	24
1965-66			63	27	30	57	12
1966-67			59	18	30	48	12
1967-68			72	30	39	69	8
1968-69			70	24	42	66	18
1969-70			76	31	38	69	13
1970-71			78	51	65	116	8
1971-72			78	32	51	83	4
1972-73			78	40	53	93	12
1973-74			76	31	44	75	8
1974-75			78	29	52	81	10
1975-76			77	36	47	83	20
1976-77			49	20	23	43	12
1977-78			53	5	13	18	4
23 yrs.		**N Totals:**	1540	556	813	1369	497

PLAYOFFS

YEAR	TEAM & LEAGUE		GP	G	A	PTS	PIM
1955-56	**DET**	**N**	10	1	1	2	8
1956-57			5	0	1	1	0
1957-58	**BOS**	**N**	12	0	4	4	16
1958-59			7	2	4	6	6
1967-68			3	0	2	2	0
1968-69			10	5	6	11	0
1969-70*			14	11	8	19	2
1970-71			7	2	5	7	0
1971-72*			15	9	11	20	6
1972-73			5	0	3	3	0
1973-74			16	8	10	18	4
1974-75			3	1	0	1	0
1975-76			12	2	7	9	0
1976-77			5	0	0	0	0
14 yrs.		**N Totals:**	124	41	62	103	42

Traded to **Boston** by Detroit for Terry Sawchuk, July 24, 1957.

Brad Buetow

BUETOW, BRADFORD 6'3", 196 lbs.

B. Oct. 28, 1950, St. Paul, Minn. Forward, Shoots L

YEAR	TEAM & LEAGUE		GP	G	A	PTS	PIM
1973-74	**CLEVE**	**W**	25	0	0	0	4

Doug Buhr

BUHR, DOUGLAS LEONARD 6'3", 215 lbs.

B. June 29, 1949, Vancouver, B.C. Left Wing, Shoots L

YEAR	TEAM & LEAGUE		GP	G	A	PTS	PIM
1974-75	**KC**	**N**	6	0	2	2	4

Tony Bukovich

BUKOVICH, ANTHONY JOHN 5'11", 160 lbs.

B. Aug. 30, 1918, Painesdale, Mich. Center, Shoots L

YEAR	TEAM & LEAGUE		GP	G	A	PTS	PIM
1943-44	**DET**	**N**	30	0	1	1	0
1944-45			14	7	2	9	6
2 yrs.		**N Totals:**	44	7	3	10	6

PLAYOFFS

YEAR	TEAM & LEAGUE		GP	G	A	PTS	PIM
1944-45	**DET**	**N**	6	0	1	1	0

Mike Bullard

BULLARD, MICHAEL BRIAN 5'10", 183 lbs.

B. Mar. 10, 1961, Ottawa, Ont. Center, Shoots L

YEAR	TEAM & LEAGUE		GP	G	A	PTS	PIM
1980-81	**PITT**	**N**	15	1	2	3	19
1981-82			75	36	27	63	91
1982-83			57	22	22	44	60
3 yrs.		**N Totals:**	147	59	51	110	170

PLAYOFFS

YEAR	TEAM & LEAGUE		GP	G	A	PTS	PIM
1980-81	**PITT**	**N**	4	3	3	6	0
1981-82			5	1	1	2	4
2 yrs.		**N Totals:**	9	4	4	8	4

Hy Buller

BULLER, HYMAN (The Blueline Blaster) 5'11", 185 lbs.

B. Mar. 15, 1926, Montreal, Que. Defense, Shoots L

YEAR	TEAM & LEAGUE		GP	G	A	PTS	PIM
1943-44	**DET**	**N**	7	0	3	3	4
1944-45			2	0	0	0	2
1951-52	**NYR**	**N**	68	12	23	35	96
1952-53			70	7	18	25	73
1953-54			41	3	14	17	40
5 yrs.		**N Totals:**	188	22	58	80	215

Signed as a free agent by **N.Y. Rangers** May 14, 1951. Traded to **Montreal** by N.Y. Rangers for Dick Gamble and Eddie Dorohoy, June 8, 1954.

Ted Bulley

BULLEY, EDWARD H. 6'1", 192 lbs.

B. Mar. 25, 1955, Windsor, Ont. Left Wing, Shoots L

YEAR	TEAM & LEAGUE		GP	G	A	PTS	PIM
1976-77	**CHI**	**N**	2	0	0	0	0
1977-78			79	23	28	51	141
1978-79			75	27	23	50	153
1979-80			66	14	17	31	136
1980-81			68	18	16	34	95
1981-82			59	12	18	30	120
1982-83	**WASH**	**N**	39	4	9	13	47
7 yrs.		**N Totals:**	388	98	111	209	692

PLAYOFFS

YEAR	TEAM & LEAGUE		GP	G	A	PTS	PIM
1977-78	**CHI**	**N**	4	1	1	2	2
1978-79			2	0	0	0	0
1979-80			7	2	3	5	10
1981-82			15	2	1	3	12
1982-83	**WASH**	**N**	1	0	0	0	0
5 yrs.		**N Totals:**	29	5	5	10	24

Traded by Chicago with Dave Hutchison to **Washington** for Washington's sixth choice (Jari Torkki) in the 1983 Amateur Draft and fifth choice in the 1984 Draft, August 24, 1982.

Billy Burch

BURCH, WILLIAM 6', 200 lbs.

B. Nov. 20, 1900, Yonkers, N.Y. Center, Shoots L

Won Hart Trophy, 1924-25

Won Lady Byng Trophy, 1926-27

Hall of Fame, 1974

YEAR	TEAM & LEAGUE		GP	G	A	PTS	PIM
1922-23	**HAMIL**	**N**	10	6	2	8	2
1923-24			24	16	2	18	4
1924-25			27	20	4	24	10
1925-26	**NYA**	**N**	36	22	3	25	33
1926-27			44	19	8	27	40
1927-28			33	10	2	12	34
1928-29			44	11	5	16	45
1929-30			35	7	3	10	22
1930-31			44	14	8	22	35
1931-32			48	14	11	25	71
1932-33	**BOS**	**N**	23	3	1	4	4
	CHI	**N**	24	2	0	2	2
	2 team total		47	5	1	6	6
11 yrs.		**N Totals:**	392	144	49	193	302

PLAYOFFS

YEAR	TEAM & LEAGUE		GP	G	A	PTS	PIM
1928-29	**NYA**	**N**	2	0	0	0	0

Fred Burchell

BURCHELL, FREDERICK (Skippy) 5'6", 145 lbs.
B. Jan. 9, 1931, Montreal, Que. Center, Shoots L

YEAR	TEAM & LEAGUE		GP	G	A	PTS	PIM
1950-51	**MONT**	**N**	2	0	0	0	0
1953-54			2	0	0	0	2
2 yrs.		**N Totals:**	4	0	0	0	2

Glen Burdon

BURDON, GLEN WILLIAM 6'2", 178 lbs.
B. Aug. 4, 1954, Regina, Sask. Center, Shoots L

YEAR	TEAM & LEAGUE		GP	G	A	PTS	PIM
1974-75	**KC**	**N**	11	0	2	2	0

Bill Burega

BUREGA, WILLIAM 6'1", 200 lbs.
B. Mar. 13, 1932, Winnipeg, Man. Defense, Shoots L

YEAR	TEAM & LEAGUE		GP	G	A	PTS	PIM
1955-56	**BOS**	**N**	4	0	1	1	4

Don Burgess

BURGESS, DONALD RUBIN 6', 170 lbs.
B. June 8, 1946, Port Edward, Ont. Left Wing, Shoots L

YEAR	TEAM & LEAGUE		GP	G	A	PTS	PIM
1972-73	**PHI**	**W**	74	20	22	42	15
1973-74	**VAN**	**W**	78	30	36	66	8
1974-75			62	11	18	29	19
1975-76	**SD**	**W**	73	14	11	25	35
1976-77			77	20	22	42	8
1977-78	**IND**	**W**	79	11	12	23	2
1978-79			3	1	1	2	0
7 yrs.		**W Totals:**	446	107	122	229	87
PLAYOFFS							
1972-73	**PHI**	**W**	4	1	0	1	0
1975-76	**SD**	**W**	11	1	7	8	4
1976-77			7	2	2	4	0
3 yrs.		**W Totals:**	22	4	9	13	4

Eddie Burke

BURKE, EDWARD A.
B. June 3, 1907, Toronto, Ont. Forward

YEAR	TEAM & LEAGUE		GP	G	A	PTS	PIM
1931-32	**BOS**	**N**	16	3	0	3	12
1932-33	**NYA**	**N**	15	2	0	2	4
1933-34			46	20	10	30	24
1934-35			29	4	10	14	15
4 yrs.		**N Totals:**	106	29	20	49	55

Marty Burke

BURKE, MARTIN ALPHONSUS 5'7½", 160 lbs.
B. Jan. 28, 1905, Toronto, Ont. Left Wing, Shoots L

YEAR	TEAM & LEAGUE		GP	G	A	PTS	PIM
1927-28	**MONT**	**N**	11	0	0	0	10
	PITT	**N**	35	2	1	3	51
	2 team total		46	2	1	3	61
1928-29	**MONT**	**N**	44	4	2	6	68
1929-30			44	2	11	13	71
1930-31			44	2	5	7	91
1931-32			48	3	6	9	50
1932-33			29	2	5	7	36
	OTTA	**N**	16	0	0	0	10
	2 team total		45	2	5	7	46
1933-34	**MONT**	**N**	45	1	4	5	28
1934-35	**CHI**	**N**	47	2	2	4	29
1935-36			40	0	3	3	49
1936-37			41	1	3	4	28
1937-38			12	0	0	0	8
	MONT	**N**	38	0	5	5	31
	2 team total		50	0	5	5	39
11 yrs.		**N Totals:**	494	19	47	66	560
PLAYOFFS							
1927-28	**PITT**	**N**	2	1	0	1	2
1928-29	**MONT**	**N**	3	0	0	0	8
1929-30*			6	0	1	1	6
1930-31*			10	1	2	3	10
1931-32			4	0	0	0	12
1933-34			2	0	1	1	2
1934-35	**CHI**	**N**	2	0	0	0	2

Marty Burke continued

YEAR	TEAM & LEAGUE		GP	G	A	PTS	PIM
1935-36			2	0	0	0	2
8 yrs.		**N Totals:**	31	2	4	6	44

Roy Burmeister

BURMEISTER, ROY 5'10", 155 lbs.
B. Collingwood, Ont. Left Wing, Shoots L

YEAR	TEAM & LEAGUE		GP	G	A	PTS	PIM
1929-30	**NYA**	**N**	40	1	1	2	0
1930-31			11	0	0	0	0
1931-32			16	3	2	5	2
3 yrs.		**N Totals:**	67	4	3	7	2

Kelly Burnett

BURNETT, JAMES KELVIN 5'10", 160 lbs.
B. June 16, 1926, Lachine, Que. Center, Shoots L

YEAR	TEAM & LEAGUE		GP	G	A	PTS	PIM
1952-53	**NYR**	**N**	3	1	0	1	0

Bobby Burns

BURNS, ROBERT 5'9½", 155 lbs.
B. Apr. 5, 1905, Gore Bay, Ont. Left Wing, Shoots L

YEAR	TEAM & LEAGUE		GP	G	A	PTS	PIM
1927-28	**CHI**	**N**	1	0	0	0	0
1928-29			7	0	0	0	6
1929-30			12	1	0	1	2
3 yrs.		**N Totals:**	20	1	0	1	8

Charlie Burns

BURNS, CHARLES FREDERICK 5'11", 170 lbs.
B. Feb. 14, 1936, Detroit, Mi. Center, Shoots L

YEAR	TEAM & LEAGUE		GP	G	A	PTS	PIM
1958-59	**DET**	**N**	70	9	11	20	32
1959-60	**BOS**	**N**	62	10	17	27	46
1960-61			62	15	26	41	16
1961-62			70	11	17	28	43
1962-63			68	12	10	22	13
1967-68	**OAK**	**N**	73	9	26	35	20
1968-69	**PITT**	**N**	76	13	38	51	22
1969-70	**MINN**	**N**	50	3	13	16	10
1970-71			76	9	19	28	13
1971-72			77	11	14	25	24
1972-73			65	4	7	11	13
11 yrs.		**N Totals:**	749	106	198	304	252
PLAYOFFS							
1969-70	**MINN**	**N**	6	1	0	1	2
1970-71			12	3	3	6	2
1971-72			7	1	1	2	2
1972-73			6	0	0	0	0
4 yrs.		**N Totals:**	31	5	4	9	6

Drafted by **Boston** from Detroit, June, 1959. Drafted by **Pittsburgh** from Oakland, June 12, 1968. Drafted by **Minnesota** from Pittsburgh, June 11, 1969.

Gary Burns

BURNS, GARY 6'1", 190 lbs.
B. Jan. 16, 1955, Cambridge, Mass. Center, Shoots L

YEAR	TEAM & LEAGUE		GP	G	A	PTS	PIM
1980-81	**NYR**	**N**	11	2	2	4	18
PLAYOFFS							
1980-81	**NYR**	**N**	1	0	0	0	2
1981-82			4	0	0	0	4
2 yrs.		**N Totals:**	5	0	0	0	6

Signed as free agent by **Boston** Oct. 10, 1979.

Norm Burns

BURNS, NORMAN 6', 195 lbs.
B. Feb. 20, 1918, Youngstown, Alta. Center, Shoots R

YEAR	TEAM & LEAGUE		GP	G	A	PTS	PIM
1941-42	**NYR**	**N**	11	0	4	4	2

Robin Burns

BURNS, ROBERT ARTHUR 6', 195 lbs.
B. Aug. 27, 1946, Montreal, Que. Left Wing, Shoots L

YEAR	TEAM & LEAGUE		GP	G	A	PTS	PIM
1970-71	**PITT**	**N**	10	0	3	3	4
1971-72			5	0	0	0	8
1972-73			26	0	2	2	20
1974-75	**KC**	**N**	71	18	15	33	70
1975-76			78	13	18	31	37
5 yrs.		**N Totals:**	190	31	38	69	139

Sold to **Pittsburgh** by Montreal, Oct. 2, 1970. Drafted by **Kansas City** from Pittsburgh in Expansion Draft, June 12, 1974.

Dave Burrows

BURROWS, DAVID JAMES 6'1", 190 lbs.
B. Jan. 11, 1949, Toronto, Ont. Defense, Shoots L

YEAR	TEAM & LEAGUE		GP	G	A	PTS	PIM
1971-72	**PITT**	**N**	77	2	10	12	48
1972-73			78	3	24	27	46
1973-74			71	3	14	17	30
1974-75			78	2	15	17	49
1975-76			80	7	22	29	51
1976-77			69	3	6	9	29
1977-78			67	4	15	19	24
1978-79	**TOR**	**N**	65	2	11	13	28
1979-80			80	3	16	19	42
1980-81			6	0	0	0	2
	PITT	**N**	53	0	2	2	28
	2 team total		59	0	2	2	30
10 yrs.		**N Totals:**	724	29	135	164	377

PLAYOFFS

YEAR	TEAM & LEAGUE		GP	G	A	PTS	PIM
1971-72	**PITT**	**N**	4	0	0	0	4
1974-75			9	1	1	2	12
1975-76			3	0	0	0	0
1976-77			3	0	2	2	0
1978-79	**TOR**	**N**	6	0	1	1	7
1979-80			3	0	1	1	2
1980-81	**PITT**	**N**	1	0	0	0	0
7 yrs.		**N Totals:**	29	1	5	6	25

Drafted by **Pittsburgh** from Chicago in Intra-League Draft June 8, 1971. Traded to **Toronto** by Pittsburgh for Randy Carlyle and George Ferguson, June 14, 1978. Traded to **Pittsburgh** by Toronto with Paul Gardner for Kim Davis and Paul Marshall, Nov. 18, 1980.

Bert Burry

BURRY, BERTHOLD
B. Unknown Defense

YEAR	TEAM & LEAGUE		GP	G	A	PTS	PIM
1932-33	**OTTA**	**N**	4	0	0	0	0

Cummy Burton

BURTON, CUMMING SCOTT 5'10", 175 lbs.
B. May 12, 1936, Sudbury, Ont. Right Wing, Shoots R

YEAR	TEAM & LEAGUE		GP	G	A	PTS	PIM
1955-56	**DET**	**N**	3	0	0	0	0
1957-58			26	0	1	1	12
1958-59			14	0	1	1	9
3 yrs.		**N Totals:**	43	0	2	2	21

PLAYOFFS

YEAR	TEAM & LEAGUE		GP	G	A	PTS	PIM
1955-56	**DET**	**N**	3	0	0	0	0

Nelson Burton

BURTON, NELSON 6', 205 lbs.
B. Nov. 6, 1957, Sydney, N.S. Left Wing, Shoots L

YEAR	TEAM & LEAGUE		GP	G	A	PTS	PIM
1977-78	**WASH**	**N**	5	1	0	1	8
1978-79			3	0	0	0	13
2 yrs.		**N Totals:**	8	1	0	1	21

Traded to **Quebec** by Washington for goaltender Dave Parro, June 15, 1979. Traded to **Minnnesota** by Quebec for Danny Chicoine, June 9, 1981.

Eddie Bush

BUSH, EDWARD WEBSTER 6'1", 195 lbs.
B. July 11, 1918, Collingwood, Ont. Defense, Shoots R

YEAR	TEAM & LEAGUE		GP	G	A	PTS	PIM
1938-39	**DET**	**N**	9	0	0	0	0
1941-42			18	4	6	10	50
2 yrs.		**N Totals:**	27	4	6	10	50

PLAYOFFS

YEAR	TEAM & LEAGUE		GP	G	A	PTS	PIM
1941-42	**DET**	**N**	12	1	6	7	23

Rod Buskas

BUSKAS, ROD 6'1", 197 lbs.
B. Jan. 7, 1961, Wetaskiwin, Alta. Defense, Shoots R

YEAR	TEAM & LEAGUE		GP	G	A	PTS	PIM
1982-83	**PITT**	**N**	41	2	2	4	102

Mike Busniuk

BUSNIUK, MICHAEL 6'3", 200 lbs.
B. Dec. 13, 1951, Thunder Bay, Ont. Defense, Shoots R

YEAR	TEAM & LEAGUE		GP	G	A	PTS	PIM
1979-80	**PHI**	**N**	71	2	18	20	93
1980-81			72	1	5	6	204
2 yrs.		**N Totals:**	143	3	23	26	297

PLAYOFFS

YEAR	TEAM & LEAGUE		GP	G	A	PTS	PIM
1979-80	**PHI**	**N**	19	2	4	6	23
1980-81			6	0	1	1	11
2 yrs.		**N Totals:**	25	2	5	7	34

Signed as free agent by **Philadelphia** Oct. 21, 1977.

Ron Busniuk

BUSNIUK, RONALD EDWARD 5'11", 180 lbs.
B. Aug. 13, 1948, Fort William, Ont. Right Wing, Shoots R

YEAR	TEAM & LEAGUE		GP	G	A	PTS	PIM
1972-73	**BUF**	**N**	1	0	0	0	0
1973-74			5	0	3	3	4
1974-75	**MINN**	**W**	73	2	21	23	176
1975-76			60	2	11	13	150
	NE	**W**	11	0	3	3	55
	2 team total		71	2	14	16	205
1976-77			0	0	0	0	0
	EDM	**W**	84	3	11	14	224
	2 team total		84	3	11	14	224
1977-78			59	2	18	20	157
6 yrs.		**N Totals:**	6	0	3	3	4
		W Totals:	287	9	64	73	762

PLAYOFFS

YEAR	TEAM & LEAGUE		GP	G	A	PTS	PIM
1974-75	**MINN**	**W**	12	2	1	3	63
1975-76	**NE**	**W**	17	0	2	2	14
1976-77	**EDM**	**W**	5	0	2	2	37
1977-78			5	0	0	0	18
4 yrs.		**W Totals:**	39	2	5	7	132

Sold to **Buffalo** by Montreal, June 8, 1972. Drafted by **Detroit** from Buffalo in Intra-League Draft, June 10, 1974.

Walt Buswell

BUSWELL, WALTER GERARD 5'11", 170 lbs.
B. Nov. 6, 1907, Montreal, Que. Defense, Shoots L

YEAR	TEAM & LEAGUE		GP	G	A	PTS	PIM
1932-33	**DET**	**N**	46	2	4	6	16
1933-34			47	1	2	3	8
1934-35			47	1	3	4	32
1935-36	**MONT**	**N**	44	0	2	2	34
1936-37			44	0	4	4	30
1937-38			48	2	15	17	24
1938-39			46	3	7	10	10
1939-40			46	1	3	4	10
8 yrs.		**N Totals:**	368	10	40	50	164

PLAYOFFS

YEAR	TEAM & LEAGUE		GP	G	A	PTS	PIM
1932-33	**DET**	**N**	4	0	0	0	4
1933-34			9	0	1	1	2
1936-37	**MONT**	**N**	5	0	0	0	2
1937-38			3	0	0	0	0
1938-39			3	2	0	2	2

Walt Buswell continued

YEAR	TEAM & LEAGUE	GP	G	A	PTS	PIM
5 yrs.	N Totals:	24	2	1	3	10

Garth Butcher

BUTCHER, GARTH 6', 194 lbs.
B. Jan. 8, 1963, Regina, Sask. Defense, Shoots R

YEAR	TEAM & LEAGUE	GP	G	A	PTS	PIM
1981-82	**VAN N**	5	0	0	0	9
1982-83		55	1	13	14	104
2 yrs.	**N Totals:**	60	1	13	14	113
PLAYOFFS						
1981-82	**VAN N**	1	0	0	0	0
1982-83		3	1	0	1	2
2 yrs.	**N Totals:**	4	1	0	1	2

Dick Butler

BUTLER, JOHN RICHARD 5'7", 175 lbs.
B. June 2, 1926, Delisle, Sask. Right Wing, Shoots L

YEAR	TEAM & LEAGUE	GP	G	A	PTS	PIM
1947-48	**CHI N**	7	2	0	2	0

Jerry Butler

BUTLER, JEROME PATRICK (Bugsy) 6', 180 lbs.
B. Feb. 27, 1951, Sarnia, Ont. Right Wing, Shoots R

YEAR	TEAM & LEAGUE	GP	G	A	PTS	PIM
1972-73	**NYR N**	8	1	0	1	4
1973-74		26	6	10	16	24
1974-75		78	17	16	33	102
1975-76	**STL N**	66	17	24	41	75
1976-77		80	12	20	32	65
1977-78		9	0	2	2	6
	TOR N	73	9	7	16	49
	2 team total	82	9	9	18	55
1978-79		76	8	7	15	52
1979-80		55	7	8	15	29
	VAN N	23	4	4	8	21
	2 team total	78	11	12	23	50
1980-81		80	12	15	27	60
1981-82		25	3	1	4	15
10 yrs.	**N Totals:**	599	96	114	210	502
PLAYOFFS						
1973-74	**NYR N**	12	0	2	2	25
1974-75		3	1	0	1	16
1975-76	**STL N**	3	0	0	0	0
1976-77		4	0	0	0	14
1977-78	**TOR N**	13	1	1	2	18
1978-79		6	0	0	0	4
1979-80	**VAN N**	4	0	0	0	2
1980-81		3	1	0	1	0
8 yrs.	**N Totals:**	48	3	3	6	79

Traded to **St. Louis** by N.Y. Rangers with Ted Irvine and Bert Wilson for Bill Collins and goalie John Davidson, June 18, 1975. Traded to **Toronto** by St. Louis for Inge Hammarstrom, Nov. 1, 1977. Traded to **Vancouver** by Toronto with Tiger Williams for Bill Derlago and Rick Vaive, Feb. 18, 1980.

Bill Butters

BUTTERS, WILLIAM JOSEPH 5'9", 192 lbs.
B. Jan. 10, 1951, St. Paul, Minn. Defense, Shoots R

YEAR	TEAM & LEAGUE	GP	G	A	PTS	PIM
1974-75	**MINN W**	24	2	2	4	58
1975-76		59	0	15	15	120
	HOUS W	14	0	4	4	18
	2 team total	73	0	19	19	138
1976-77	**MINN W**	42	0	7	7	133
	EDM W	7	0	2	2	17
	NE W	26	1	8	9	65
	3 team total	75	1	17	18	215
1977-78		45	1	13	14	69
	MINN N	23	1	0	1	30
	2 team total	68	2	13	15	99
1978-79		49	0	4	4	47
5 yrs.	**N Totals:**	72	1	4	5	77
	W Totals:	217	4	51	55	480
PLAYOFFS						
1974-75	**MINN W**	12	1	0	1	21

Bill Butters continued

YEAR	TEAM & LEAGUE	GP	G	A	PTS	PIM
1975-76	**HOUS W**	17	0	3	3	51
1976-77	**NE W**	5	0	1	1	15
3 yrs.	**W Totals:**	34	1	4	5	87

Signed as free agent by **Minnesota** Feb. 16, 1978.

Gord Buttrey

BUTTREY, GORDON 5'7", 167 lbs.
B. Mar. 17, 1926, Regina, Sask. Forward

YEAR	TEAM & LEAGUE	GP	G	A	PTS	PIM
1943-44	**CHI N**	10	0	0	0	0
PLAYOFFS						
1943-44	**CHI N**	10	0	0	0	0

Gordon Buynak

BUYNAK, GORDON 6'1", 180 lbs.
B. Mar. 19, 1954, Detroit, Mich. Defense, Shoots L

YEAR	TEAM & LEAGUE	GP	G	A	PTS	PIM
1974-75	**STL N**	4	0	0	0	2

Sold by St. Louis with Bruce Affleck to **Vancouver** Nov. 6, 1979. Sold to **St. Louis** with Bruce Affleck by Vancouver, Feb. 28, 1980.

Brian Bye

BYE, BRIAN 5'10", 180 lbs.
B. June 27, 1954, Brantford, Ont. Center, Shoots L

YEAR	TEAM & LEAGUE	GP	G	A	PTS	PIM
1975-76	**SD W**	1	0	0	0	0

Gord Byers

BYERS, GORDON CHARLES 5'9½", 182 lbs.
B. Mar. 11, 1930, Eganville, Ont. Defense, Shoots R

YEAR	TEAM & LEAGUE	GP	G	A	PTS	PIM
1949-50	**BOS N**	1	0	1	1	0

Jerry Byers

BYERS, JERRY WILLIAM 5'11", 170 lbs.
B. Mar. 29, 1952, Kentville, N.S. Left Wing, Shoots L

YEAR	TEAM & LEAGUE	GP	G	A	PTS	PIM
1972-73	**MINN N**	14	0	2	2	6
1973-74		10	0	0	0	0
1974-75	**ATL N**	12	1	1	2	4
1977-78	**NYR N**	7	2	1	3	0
4 yrs.	**N Totals:**	43	3	4	7	10

Traded to **Atlanta** by Minnesota with Buster Harvey for John Flesch and Don Martineau, May 27, 1974. Traded to **N.Y. Rangers** by Atlanta for goaltender Curt Ridley, Sept. 9, 1975.

Mike Byers

BYERS, MICHAEL ARTHUR 5'10", 185 lbs.
B. Sept. 11, 1946, Toronto, Ont. Right Wing, Shoots R

YEAR	TEAM & LEAGUE	GP	G	A	PTS	PIM
1967-68	**TOR N**	10	2	2	4	0
1968-69		5	0	0	0	2
	PHI N	5	0	2	2	0
	2 team total	10	0	2	2	2
1970-71	**LA N**	72	27	18	45	14
1971-72		28	4	5	9	11
	BUF N	46	9	7	16	12
	2 team total	74	13	12	25	23
1972-73	**LA W**	56	19	17	36	20
	NE W	19	6	4	10	4
	2 team total	75	25	21	46	24
1973-74		78	29	21	50	6
1974-75		72	22	26	48	10
1975-76		21	4	3	7	0
	CIN W	20	3	3	6	0
	2 team total	41	7	6	13	0
8 yrs.	**N Totals:**	166	42	34	76	39
	W Totals:	266	83	74	157	40
PLAYOFFS						
1968-69	**PHI N**	4	0	1	1	0
1972-73	**NE W**	12	6	5	11	6
1973-74		7	2	4	6	12
1974-75		6	2	2	4	2
4 yrs.	**N Totals:**	4	0	1	1	0
	W Totals:	25	10	11	21	20

Traded to **Philadelphia** by Toronto with Bill Sutherland and Gerry Meehan for Brit Selby and Forbes Kennedy, March 2, 1969. Traded to **Los Angeles** by Philadelphia for Brent Hughes, May 21, 1970. Traded to **Buffalo** by Los

Angeles with Larry Hillman for Doug Barrie and Mike Keeler, Dec. 16, 1971.

Brian Cadle

CADLE, BRIAN 6'1½", 170 lbs.
B. Sept. 13, 1948, Vancouver, B.C. Left Wing, Shoots L

YEAR	TEAM & LEAGUE		GP	G	A	PTS	PIM
1972-73	**WINN**	**W**	56	4	4	8	39

Jack Caffery

CAFFERY, JOHN 6', 175 lbs.
B. June 30, 1934, Kingston, Ont. Center, Shoots R

YEAR	TEAM & LEAGUE		GP	G	A	PTS	PIM
1954-55	**TOR**	**N**	3	0	0	0	0
1956-57	**BOS**	**N**	47	2	2	4	20
1957-58			7	1	0	1	2
3 yrs.		**N Totals:**	57	3	2	5	22
PLAYOFFS							
1956-57	**BOS**	**N**	10	1	0	1	4

Drafted by **Boston** from Toronto, June 5, 1956.

Terry Caffery

CAFFERY, TERRANCE MICHAEL 5'9", 165 lbs.
B. Apr. 1, 1949, Toronto, Ont. Center, Shoots R

YEAR	TEAM & LEAGUE		GP	G	A	PTS	PIM
1969-70	**CHI**	**N**	6	0	0	0	0
1970-71	**MINN**	**N**	8	0	0	0	0
1972-73	**NE**	**W**	74	39	61	100	14
1974-75			67	15	37	52	12
1975-76			2	0	0	0	0
	CALG	**W**	21	5	13	18	4
	2 team total		23	5	13	18	4
5 yrs.		**N Totals:**	14	0	0	0	0
		W Totals:	164	59	111	170	30
PLAYOFFS							
1970-71	**MINN**	**N**	1	0	0	0	0
1972-73	**NE**	**W**	8	3	7	10	0
2 yrs.		**N Totals:**	1	0	0	0	0
		W Totals:	8	3	7	10	0

Traded to **Minnesota** by Chicago with Doug Mohns for Danny O'Shea, Feb. 23, 1971.

Larry Cahan

CAHAN, LARRY (Hank) 6', 195 lbs.
B. Dec. 25, 1933, Fort William, Ont. Defense, Shoots R

YEAR	TEAM & LEAGUE		GP	G	A	PTS	PIM
1954-55	**TOR**	**N**	58	0	6	6	64
1955-56			21	0	2	2	46
1956-57	**NYR**	**N**	61	5	4	9	65
1957-58			34	1	1	2	20
1958-59			16	1	0	1	8
1961-62			57	2	7	9	85
1962-63			56	6	14	20	47
1963-64			53	4	8	12	80
1964-65			26	0	5	5	32
1967-68	**OAK**	**N**	74	9	15	24	80
1968-69	**LA**	**N**	72	3	11	14	76
1969-70			70	4	8	12	50
1970-71			67	3	11	14	45
1972-73	**CHI**	**W**	75	1	10	11	44
1973-74			3	0	0	0	2
15 yrs.		**N Totals:**	665	38	92	130	698
		W Totals:	78	1	10	11	46
PLAYOFFS							
1954-55	**TOR**	**N**	4	0	0	0	0
1956-57	**NYR**	**N**	3	0	0	0	2
1957-58			5	0	0	0	4
1961-62			6	0	0	0	10
1968-69	**LA**	**N**	11	1	1	2	22
5 yrs.		**N Totals:**	29	1	1	2	38

Drafted by **N.Y. Rangers** from Toronto, June 6, 1956. Drafted by **Oakland** from N.Y. Rangers in Expansion Draft, June 6, 1967. Put on **Montreal** reserve list from Oakland, June 12, 1968. Traded to **Los Angeles** by Montreal for Brian Smith and Yves Locas, July 1, 1968.

Chuck Cahill

CAHILL, CHARLES
B. Unknown Forward

YEAR	TEAM & LEAGUE		GP	G	A	PTS	PIM
1925-26	**BOS**	**N**	31	0	1	1	4
1926-27			1	0	0	0	0
2 yrs.		**N Totals:**	32	0	1	1	4

Herbert Cain

CAIN, HERBERT 5'11½", 180 lbs.
B. Dec. 24, 1912, Newmarket, Ont. Left Wing, Shoots L
Won Art Ross Trophy, 1943-44

YEAR	TEAM & LEAGUE		GP	G	A	PTS	PIM
1933-34	**MON(M)**	**N**	31	4	5	9	14
1934-35			44	20	7	27	13
1935-36			47	5	13	18	16
1936-37			43	13	17	30	18
1937-38			47	11	19	30	10
1938-39	**MONT**	**N**	45	13	14	27	26
1939-40	**BOS**	**N**	48	21	10	31	30
1940-41			40	8	10	18	6
1941-42			35	8	10	18	2
1942-43			45	18	18	36	19
1943-44			48	36	46	**82**	4
1944-45			50	32	13	45	16
1945-46			48	17	12	29	4
13 yrs.		**N Totals:**	571	206	194	400	178
PLAYOFFS							
1933-34	**MON(M)**	**N**	4	0	0	0	0
1934-35*			4	1	0	1	2
1935-36			3	0	1	1	0
1936-37			5	1	1	2	0
1938-39	**MONT**	**N**	3	0	0	0	2
1939-40	**BOS**	**N**	6	1	3	4	2
1940-41*			11	3	2	5	5
1941-42			5	1	0	1	0
1942-43			7	4	2	6	0
1944-45			7	5	2	7	0
1945-46			9	0	2	2	2
11 yrs.		**N Totals:**	64	16	13	29	13

Jim Cain

CAIN, JAMES F. (Dutch)
B. Newmarket, Ont. Defense

YEAR	TEAM & LEAGUE		GP	G	A	PTS	PIM
1924-25	**MON(M)**	**N**	28	4	0	4	27
1925-26			10	0	0	0	0
	TOR	**N**	23	0	0	0	8
	2 team total		33	0	0	0	8
2 yrs.		**N Totals:**	61	4	0	4	35

Don Cairns

CAIRNS, DONALD 6'1", 195 lbs.
B. Oct. 8, 1955, Calgary, Alta. Left Wing, Shoots L

YEAR	TEAM & LEAGUE		GP	G	A	PTS	PIM
1975-76	**KC**	**N**	7	0	0	0	0
1976-77	**COLO**	**N**	2	0	1	1	2
2 yrs.		**N Totals:**	9	0	1	1	2

Eric Calder

CALDER, ERIC 6'1", 184 lbs.
B. July 26, 1963, Kitchener, Ont. Defense, Shoots R

YEAR	TEAM & LEAGUE		GP	G	A	PTS	PIM
1981-82	**WASH**	**N**	1	0	0	0	0
1982-83			1	0	0	0	0
2 yrs.		**N Totals:**	2	0	0	0	0

Norm Calladine

CALLADINE, NORMAN 5'9", 155 lbs.
B. Peterborough, Ont. Center

YEAR	TEAM & LEAGUE		GP	G	A	PTS	PIM
1942-43	**BOS**	**N**	3	0	1	1	0
1943-44			49	16	27	43	8
1944-45			11	3	1	4	0
3 yrs.		**N Totals:**	63	19	29	48	8

Drew Callander

CALLANDER, LEONARD DREW 6'2", 188 lbs.
B. Aug. 17, 1956, Regina, Sask. Center, Shoots R

YEAR	TEAM	LEAGUE	GP	G	A	PTS	PIM
1976-77	PHI	N	2	1	0	1	0
1977-78			1	0	0	0	0
1978-79			15	2	1	3	5
	VAN	N	17	2	0	2	2
	2 team total		32	4	1	5	7
1979-80			4	1	1	2	0
4 yrs.		N Totals:	39	6	2	8	7

Traded to **Vancouver** by Philadelphia with Kevin McCarthy for Dennis Ververgaert, Dec. 29, 1978.

Brett Callighen

CALLIGHEN, BRETT (Key) 5'11", 182 lbs.
B. May 15, 1953, Toronto, Ont. Center, Shoots L

YEAR	TEAM	LEAGUE	GP	G	A	PTS	PIM
1976-77	NE	W	33	6	10	16	41
	EDM	W	29	9	16	25	48
	2 team total		62	15	26	41	89
1977-78			80	20	30	50	112
1978-79			71	31	39	70	79
1979-80	EDM	N	59	23	35	58	72
1980-81			55	25	35	60	32
1981-82			46	8	19	27	28
6 yrs.		N Totals:	160	56	89	145	132
		W Totals:	213	66	95	161	280

PLAYOFFS

YEAR	TEAM	LEAGUE	GP	G	A	PTS	PIM
1976-77	EDM	W	5	4	1	5	7
1977-78			5	0	2	2	16
1978-79			13	5	10	15	15
1979-80	EDM	N	3	0	2	2	0
1980-81			9	4	4	8	6
1981-82			2	0	0	0	2
6 yrs.		N Totals:	14	4	6	10	8
		W Totals:	23	9	13	22	38

Patsy Callighen

CALLIGHEN, FRANCIS CHARLES WINSLOW
5'6", 175 lbs.
B. Feb. 13, 1906, Toronto, Ont. Left Wing, Shoots L

YEAR	TEAM	LEAGUE	GP	G	A	PTS	PIM
1927-28	NYR	N	36	0	0	0	32

PLAYOFFS

YEAR	TEAM	LEAGUE	GP	G	A	PTS	PIM
1927-28*	NYR	N	9	0	0	0	0

Tony Camazzola

CAMAZZOLA, ANTHOMY BERT 6'2", 210 lbs.
B. Sept. 11, 1962, Vancouver, B.C. Defense, Shoots L

YEAR	TEAM	LEAGUE	GP	G	A	PTS	PIM
1981-82	WASH	N	3	0	0	0	0

Al Cameron

CAMERON, ALAN RICHARD 6', 205 lbs.
B. Oct. 21, 1955, Edmonton, Alta. Defense, Shoots L

YEAR	TEAM	LEAGUE	GP	G	A	PTS	PIM
1975-76	DET	N	38	2	8	10	49
1976-77			80	3	13	16	112
1977-78			63	2	7	9	94
1978-79			9	0	3	3	8
1979-80	WINN	N	63	3	11	14	72
1980-81			29	1	2	3	21
6 yrs.		N Totals:	282	11	44	55	356

PLAYOFFS

YEAR	TEAM	LEAGUE	GP	G	A	PTS	PIM
1977-78	DET	N	7	0	1	1	2

Claimed by **Winnipeg** from Detroit in Expansion Draft, June 13, 1979.

Scotty Cameron

CAMERON, ANGUS 6'1½", 175 lbs.
B. Nov. 5, 1921, Prince Albert, Sask. Center, Shoots L

YEAR	TEAM	LEAGUE	GP	G	A	PTS	PIM
1942-43	NYR	N	35	8	11	19	0

Billy Cameron

CAMERON, WILLIAM
B. Timmins, Ont. Right Wing

YEAR	TEAM	LEAGUE	GP	G	A	PTS	PIM
1923-24	MONT	N	18	0	0	0	2
1925-26	NYA	N	21	0	0	0	0
2 yrs.		N Totals:	39	0	0	0	2

PLAYOFFS

YEAR	TEAM	LEAGUE	GP	G	A	PTS	PIM
1923-24*	MONT	N	6	0	0	0	0

Craig Cameron

CAMERON, CRAIG LAUDER 6', 200 lbs.
B. July 19, 1945, Edmonton, Alta. Right Wing, Shoots R

YEAR	TEAM	LEAGUE	GP	G	A	PTS	PIM
1966-67	DET	N	1	0	0	0	0
1967-68	STL	N	32	7	2	9	8
1968-69			72	11	5	16	40
1970-71			78	14	6	20	32
1971-72	MINN	N	64	2	1	3	11
1972-73	NYI	N	72	19	14	33	27
1973-74			78	15	14	29	28
1974-75			37	1	3	7	10
	MINN	N	40	10	7	17	12
	2 team total		77	11	10	24	22
1975-76			78	8	10	18	34
9 yrs.		N Totals:	552	87	62	152	202

PLAYOFFS

YEAR	TEAM	LEAGUE	GP	G	A	PTS	PIM
1967-68	STL	N	14	1	0	1	11
1968-69			2	0	0	0	0
1970-71			6	2	0	2	4
1971-72	MINN	N	5	0	1	1	0
4 yrs.		N Totals:	27	3	1	4	15

Traded by Detroit with Larry Hornung and Don Giesebrecht to **St. Louis** for John Brenneman, Oct. 9, 1967. Traded to **Pittsburgh** by St. Louis with Ron Schock for Lou Angotti and Pittsburgh's first choice (Gene Carr) in the 1971 Amateur Draft, June 6, 1969. Put on **Los Angeles** reserve list from Pittsburgh in Intra-League Draft, June 9, 1970. Drafted by **Buffalo** from Los Angeles in Expansion Draft, June 10, 1970. Traded to **St. Louis** by Buffalo for Ron Anderson, Oct. 2, 1970. Claimed on waivers by **Minnesota** from St. Louis, Oct. 1, 1971. Drafted by **N.Y. Islanders** from Minnesota in Expansion Draft, June 6, 1972. Traded to **Minnesota** by N.Y. Islanders for Jude Drouin, Jan. 7, 1972.

Dave Cameron

CAMERON, DAVID WILLIAM 6', 185 lbs.
B. July 29, 1958, Charlottetown, P.E.I. Center, Shoots L

YEAR	TEAM	LEAGUE	GP	G	A	PTS	PIM
1981-82	COLO	N	66	11	12	23	103
1982-83	NJ	N	35	5	4	9	50
2 yrs.		N Totals:	101	16	16	32	153

Traded to **Colorado** by N.Y. Islanders with Bob Lorimer for Colorado's first round choice (Pat Lafontaine) in 1983 Entry Draft, Oct. 1, 1981.

Harry Cameron

CAMERON, HARRY
B. Feb. 6, 1890, Pembroke, Ont. Defense
Hall of Fame, 1962

YEAR	TEAM	LEAGUE	GP	G	A	PTS	PIM
1917-18	TOR	N	20	17	0	17	17
1918-19			7	7	2	9	23
	OTTA	N	7	4	1	5	12
	2 team total		14	11	3	14	35
1919-20	TOR	N	7	3	1	4	0
	MONT	N	16	8	5	13	11
	2 team total		23	11	6	17	11
1920-21	TOR	N	24	18	9	27	55
1921-22			24	19	8	27	18
1922-23			22	9	6	15	18
6 yrs.		N Totals:	127	85	32	117	154

PLAYOFFS

YEAR	TEAM	LEAGUE	GP	G	A	PTS	PIM
1917-18*	TOR	N	7	3	0	3	9
1918-19	OTTA	N	5	4	0	4	6
1920-21	TOR	N	2	0	0	0	0
1921-22*			7	0	0	0	19
4 yrs.		N Totals:	21	7	0	7	34

Bryan Campbell

CAMPBELL, BRYAN ALBERT 6', 175 lbs.
B. Mar. 27, 1944, Sudbury, Ont. Center, Shoots L

YEAR	TEAM & LEAGUE		GP	G	A	PTS	PIM
1967-68	LA	N	43	6	15	21	16
1968-69			18	2	1	3	4
1969-70			31	4	4	8	4
	CHI	N	14	1	1	2	2
	2 team total		45	5	5	10	6
1970-71			78	17	37	54	26
1971-72			75	5	13	18	22
1972-73	PHI	W	75	25	48	73	85
1973-74	VAN	W	76	27	62	89	50
1974-75			78	29	34	63	24
1975-76	CIN	W	77	22	50	72	24
1976-77	IND	W	8	1	4	5	6
	EDM	W	66	12	42	54	18
	2 team total		74	13	46	59	24
1977-78			53	7	13	20	12
11 yrs.		N Totals:	259	35	71	106	74
		W Totals:	433	123	253	376	219

PLAYOFFS

YEAR	TEAM & LEAGUE		GP	G	A	PTS	PIM
1968-69	LA	N	6	2	1	3	0
1969-70	CHI	N	8	1	2	3	0
1970-71			4	0	1	1	0
1971-72			4	0	0	0	2
1972-73	PHI	W	3	0	1	1	8
1976-77	EDM	W	5	3	1	4	0
6 yrs.		N Totals:	22	3	4	7	2
		W Totals:	8	3	2	5	8

Drafted by **N.Y. Rangers** from Detroit, June 15, 1966. Drafted by **Los Angeles** from N.Y. Rangers in Expansion Draft, June 6, 1967. Traded to **Chicago** by Los Angeles with Bill White and goaltender Gerry Desjardins for Gilles Marotte, Jim Stanfield, and goaltender Denis DeJordy, Feb. 20, 1970.

Colin Campbell

CAMPBELL, COLIN JOHN (Soupy) 5'9", 190 lbs.
B. Jan. 28, 1953, London, Ont. Defense, Shoots L

YEAR	TEAM & LEAGUE		GP	G	A	PTS	PIM
1973-74	VAN	W	78	3	20	23	191
1974-75	PITT	N	59	4	15	19	172
1975-76			64	7	10	17	105
1976-77	COLO	N	54	3	8	11	67
1977-78	PITT	N	55	1	9	10	103
1978-79			65	2	18	20	137
1979-80	EDM	N	72	2	11	13	196
1980-81	VAN	N	42	1	8	9	75
1981-82			47	0	8	8	131
1982-83	DET	N	53	1	7	8	74
10 yrs.		N Totals:	511	21	94	115	1060
		W Totals:	78	3	20	23	191

PLAYOFFS

YEAR	TEAM & LEAGUE		GP	G	A	PTS	PIM
1974-75	PITT	N	9	1	3	4	21
1975-76			3	0	0	0	0
1978-79			7	1	4	5	30
1979-80	EDM	N	3	0	0	0	11
1980-81	VAN	N	3	0	1	1	9
1981-82			16	2	2	4	89
6 yrs.		N Totals:	41	4	10	14	160

Services transferred to **Colorado** from Pittsburgh for 1976-77 season as part compensation for earlier deal in which Pittsburgh received goaltender Denis Herron from Kansas City (Colorado) for Simon Nolet and goaltender Michel Plasse, Sept. 1, 1976. Claimed by **Edmonton** from Pittsburgh in Expansion Draft, June 13, 1979. Claimed by **Vancouver** from **Edmonton** in Waiver Draft, Oct. 10, 1980. Signed as a free agent by **Detroit** from Vancouver, June 26, 1982.

Dave Campbell

CAMPBELL, DAVID
B. Apr. 27, 1896, Lachute, Que. Defense

YEAR	TEAM & LEAGUE		GP	G	A	PTS	PIM
1920-21	MONT	N	3	0	0	0	0

Don Campbell

CAMPBELL, DONALD WILLIAM
B. July 12, 1925, Drumheller, Alta. Forward, Shoots L

YEAR	TEAM & LEAGUE		GP	G	A	PTS	PIM
1943-44	CHI	N	17	1	3	4	8

Scott Campbell

CAMPBELL, SCOTT 6'3", 205 lbs.
B. June 22, 1957, Toronto, Ont. Defense, Shoots L

YEAR	TEAM & LEAGUE		GP	G	A	PTS	PIM
1977-78	HOUS	W	75	8	29	37	116
1978-79	WINN	W	74	3	15	18	**248**
1979-80	WINN	N	63	3	17	20	136
1980-81			14	1	4	5	55
1981-82	STL	N	3	0	0	0	52
5 yrs.		N Totals:	80	4	21	25	243
		W Totals:	149	11	44	55	364

PLAYOFFS

YEAR	TEAM & LEAGUE		GP	G	A	PTS	PIM
1977-78	HOUS	W	6	1	1	2	8
1978-79	WINN	W	10	0	2	2	25
2 yrs.		W Totals:	16	1	3	4	33

Reclaimed by **St. Louis** from Winnipeg prior to Expansion Draft, June 9, 1979. Claimed as priority selection by **Winnipeg** June 9, 1979. Traded to **St. Louis** by Winnipeg with John Markell for Bryan Maxwell, Ed Staniowski and Paul MacLean, July 3, 1981.

Spiff Campbell

CAMPBELL, EARL
B. Unknown Forward

YEAR	TEAM & LEAGUE		GP	G	A	PTS	PIM
1923-24	OTTA	N	18	4	1	5	6
1924-25			30	0	0	0	0
1925-26	NYA	N	29	1	0	1	6
3 yrs.		N Totals:	77	5	1	6	12

PLAYOFFS

YEAR	TEAM & LEAGUE		GP	G	A	PTS	PIM
1923-24	OTTA	N	1	0	0	0	6

Wade Campbell

CAMPBELL, WADE 6'4", 220 lbs.
B. Feb. 1, 1961, Peace River, Alta. Defense

YEAR	TEAM & LEAGUE		GP	G	A	PTS	PIM
1982-83	WINN	N	42	1	2	3	0

Signed by **Winnipeg** as a free agent, Oct. 19, 1982.

Dick Campeau

CAMPEAU, RYCHARD 6', 165 lbs.
B. Apr. 9, 1952, Montreal, Que. Forward, Shoots R

YEAR	TEAM & LEAGUE		GP	G	A	PTS	PIM
1972-73	PHI	W	75	1	18	19	72
1973-74	VAN	W	7	0	0	0	2
2 yrs.		W Totals:	82	1	18	19	74

PLAYOFFS

YEAR	TEAM & LEAGUE		GP	G	A	PTS	PIM
1972-73	PHI	W	4	1	0	1	17

Tod Campeau

CAMPEAU, JEAN CLAUDE 5'11", 175 lbs.
B. June 4, 1923, St. Jerome, Que. Center, Shoots L

YEAR	TEAM & LEAGUE		GP	G	A	PTS	PIM
1943-44	MONT	N	2	0	0	0	0
1947-48			14	2	2	4	4
1948-49			26	3	7	10	12
3 yrs.		N Totals:	42	5	9	14	16

PLAYOFFS

YEAR	TEAM & LEAGUE		GP	G	A	PTS	PIM
1948-49	MONT	N	1	0	0	0	0

Leo Carbol

CARBOL, LEO 5'10½", 170 lbs.
B. June 5, 1910, Ottawa, Ont. Defense, Shoots R

YEAR	TEAM & LEAGUE		GP	G	A	PTS	PIM
1942-43	CHI	N	6	0	1	1	4

Guy Carbonneau

CARBONNEAU, GUY 5'10", 165 lbs.
B. Mar. 18, 1960, Sept Isles, Que. Center, Shoots R

YEAR	TEAM & LEAGUE		GP	G	A	PTS	PIM
1980-81	**MONT**	**N**	2	0	1	1	0
1982-83			77	18	29	47	68
2 yrs.		**N Totals:**	79	18	30	48	68
PLAYOFFS							
1982-83	**MONT**	**N**	3	0	0	0	2

Jim Cardiff

CARDIFF, GARRY JAMES 5'9", 165 lbs.
B. Aug. 29, 1944, Dauphin, Man. Defense, Shoots L

YEAR	TEAM & LEAGUE		GP	G	A	PTS	PIM
1972-73	**PHI**	**W**	78	3	24	27	185
1973-74	**VAN**	**W**	78	1	21	22	188
1974-75			44	0	2	2	25
3 yrs.		**W Totals:**	200	4	47	51	398

Claude Cardin

CARDIN, CLAUDE 5'7", 160 lbs.
B. Feb. 17, 1941, Sorel, Que. Left Wing, Shoots R

YEAR	TEAM & LEAGUE		GP	G	A	PTS	PIM
1967-68	**STL**	**N**	1	0	0	0	0

Steve Cardwell

CARDWELL, STEPHEN MICHAEL 5'11", 190 lbs.
B. Aug. 13, 1950, Toronto, Ont. Left Wing, Shoots L

YEAR	TEAM & LEAGUE		GP	G	A	PTS	PIM
1970-71	**PITT**	**N**	5	0	1	1	15
1971-72			28	7	7	14	18
1972-73			20	2	2	4	2
1973-74	**MINN**	**W**	77	23	23	46	100
1974-75	**CLEVE**	**W**	75	9	13	22	127
5 yrs.		**N Totals:**	53	9	10	19	35
		W Totals:	152	32	36	68	227
PLAYOFFS							
1971-72	**PITT**	**N**	4	0	0	0	2
1973-74	**MINN**	**W**	10	0	0	0	20
1974-75	**CLEVE**	**W**	5	0	1	1	14
3 yrs.		**N Totals:**	4	0	0	0	2
		W Totals:	15	0	1	1	34

George Carey

CAREY, GEORGE
B. Unknown Right Wing

YEAR	TEAM & LEAGUE		GP	G	A	PTS	PIM
1919-20	**QUE**	**N**	20	11	5	16	4
1920-21	**HAMIL**	**N**	20	7	1	8	8
1921-22			23	3	2	5	2
1922-23			5	1	0	1	0
1923-24	**TOR**	**N**	4	0	0	0	0
5 yrs.		**N Totals:**	72	22	8	30	14

Wayne Carleton

CARLETON, KENNETH WAYNE 6'2", 215 lbs.
B. Aug. 4, 1946, Sudbury, Ont. Left Wing, Shoots L

YEAR	TEAM & LEAGUE		GP	G	A	PTS	PIM
1965-66	**TOR**	**N**	2	0	1	1	0
1966-67			5	1	0	1	14
1967-68			65	8	11	19	34
1968-69			12	1	3	4	6
1969-70			7	0	1	1	6
	BOS	**N**	42	6	19	25	23
	2 team total		49	6	20	26	29
1970-71			69	22	24	46	44
1971-72	**CALIF**	**N**	76	17	14	31	45
1972-73	**OTTA**	**W**	75	42	49	91	42
1973-74	**TOR**	**W**	78	37	55	92	31
1974-75	**NE**	**W**	73	35	39	74	50
1975-76			35	12	21	33	6
	EDM	**W**	26	5	16	21	6
	2 team total		61	17	37	54	12
1976-77	**BIRM**	**W**	3	1	0	1	0
12 yrs.		**N Totals:**	278	55	73	128	172
		W Totals:	290	132	180	312	135
PLAYOFFS							
1969-70*	**BOS**	**N**	14	2	4	6	14

Wayne Carleton continued

YEAR	TEAM & LEAGUE		GP	G	A	PTS	PIM
1970-71			4	0	0	0	0
1972-73	**OTTA**	**W**	3	3	3	6	4
1973-74	**TOR**	**W**	12	2	12	14	4
1974-75	**NE**	**W**	6	2	5	7	14
1975-76	**EDM**	**W**	4	1	1	2	2
6 yrs.		**N Totals:**	18	2	4	6	14
		W Totals:	25	8	21	29	24

Traded to **Boston** by Toronto for Jim Harrison, Dec. 10, 1969. Drafted by **California** from Boston in Intra-league Draft, June 8, 1971.

Brian Carlin

CARLIN, BRIAN JOHN 5'10", 175 lbs.
B. June 13, 1950, Calgary, Alta. Left Wing, Shoots L

YEAR	TEAM & LEAGUE		GP	G	A	PTS	PIM
1971-72	**LA**	**N**	5	1	0	1	0
1972-73	**ALTA**	**W**	65	12	22	34	6
1973-74	**EDM**	**W**	5	1	0	1	0
3 yrs.		**N Totals:**	5	1	0	1	0
		W Totals:	70	13	22	35	6

Jack Carlson

CARLSON, JACK (The Big Bopper) 6'3", 205 lbs.
B. Aug. 23, 1954, Virginia, Minn. Right Wing, Shoots L

YEAR	TEAM & LEAGUE		GP	G	A	PTS	PIM
1974-75	**MINN**	**W**	32	5	5	10	85
1975-76			58	8	10	18	189
	EDM	**W**	10	1	1	2	31
	2 team total		68	9	11	20	220
1976-77	**MINN**	**W**	36	4	3	7	55
	NE	**W**	35	7	5	12	81
	2 team total		71	11	8	19	136
1977-78			67	9	20	29	192
1978-79			34	2	7	9	61
	MINN	**N**	16	3	0	3	40
	2 team total		50	5	7	12	101
1980-81			43	7	2	9	108
1981-82			57	8	4	12	103
1982-83	**STL**	**N**	54	6	1	7	58
8 yrs.		**N Totals:**	170	24	7	31	309
		W Totals:	272	36	51	87	694
PLAYOFFS							
1974-75	**MINN**	**W**	10	1	2	3	41
1975-76	**EDM**	**W**	4	0	0	0	4
1976-77	**NE**	**W**	5	1	1	2	9
1977-78			9	1	1	2	14
1980-81	**MINN**	**N**	15	1	2	3	50
1981-82			1	0	0	0	15
1982-83	**STL**	**N**	4	0	0	0	5
7 yrs.		**N Totals:**	20	1	2	3	70
		W Totals:	28	3	4	7	68

Rights traded to **Minnesota** by Detroit for future considerations, July 27, 1978. Traded by New England (W) to **Minnesota** for future considerations, Feb. 1, 1979. Acquired by **St. Louis** from Minnesota in Waiver Draft, Oct. 4, 1982.

Jeff Carlson

CARLSON, JEFFREY 6'3", 210 lbs.
B. July 20, 1953, Virginia, Minn. Right Wing, Shoots R

YEAR	TEAM & LEAGUE		GP	G	A	PTS	PIM
1975-76	**MINN**	**W**	7	0	1	1	14

Steve Carlson

CARLSON, STEVEN 6'3", 180 lbs.
B. Aug. 26, 1955, Virginia, Minn. Center, Shoots L

YEAR	TEAM & LEAGUE		GP	G	A	PTS	PIM
1975-76	**MINN**	**W**	10	0	1	1	23
1976-77			21	5	8	13	8
	NE	**W**	31	4	9	13	40
	2 team total		52	9	17	26	48
1977-78			38	6	7	13	11
1978-79	**EDM**	**W**	73	18	22	40	50
1979-80	**LA**	**N**	52	9	12	21	23
5 yrs.		**N Totals:**	52	9	12	21	23
		W Totals:	173	33	47	80	132
PLAYOFFS							
1976-77	**NE**	**W**	5	0	0	0	9
1977-78			13	2	7	9	2

Steve Carlson continued

YEAR	TEAM	LEAGUE	GP	G	A	PTS	PIM
1978-79	**EDM**	**W**	11	1	1	2	12
1979-80	**LA**	**N**	4	1	1	2	7
4 yrs.		**N Totals:**	4	1	1	2	7
		W Totals:	29	3	8	11	23

Rights transferred to **Los Angeles** by Detroit for Steve Short, Dec. 6, 1978. Reclaimed by **Los Angeles** from **Edmonton** prior to Expansion Draft, June 9, 1979. Claimed by **Los Angeles** as fill in Expansion Draft, June 13, 1979.

Randy Carlyle

CARLYLE, RANDOLPH ROBERT 5'10", 200 lbs.
B. Apr. 19, 1956, Sudbury, Ont. Defense, Shoots L
Won Norris Trophy, 1980-81

YEAR	TEAM	LEAGUE	GP	G	A	PTS	PIM
1976-77	**TOR**	**N**	45	0	5	5	51
1977-78			49	2	11	13	31
1978-79	**PITT**	**N**	70	13	34	47	78
1979-80			67	8	28	36	45
1980-81			76	16	67	83	136
1981-82			73	11	64	75	131
1982-83			61	15	41	56	110
7 yrs.		**N Totals:**	441	65	250	315	582

PLAYOFFS

YEAR	TEAM	LEAGUE	GP	G	A	PTS	PIM
1976-77	**TOR**	**N**	9	0	1	1	20
1977-78			7	0	1	1	8
1978-79	**PITT**	**N**	7	0	0	0	12
1979-80			5	1	0	1	4
1980-81			5	4	5	9	9
1981-82			5	1	3	4	16
6 yrs.		**N Totals:**	38	6	10	16	69

Traded to **Pittsburgh** by Toronto with George Ferguson for Dave Burrows, June 14, 1978.

Steve Carlyle

CARLYLE, STEVEN 5'10", 180 lbs.
B. Mar. 10, 1950, Lacombe, Alta. Defense, Shoots L

YEAR	TEAM	LEAGUE	GP	G	A	PTS	PIM
1972-73	**ALTA**	**W**	67	7	10	17	35
1973-74	**EDM**	**W**	50	2	13	15	18
1974-75			73	4	25	29	46
1975-76			28	0	11	11	10
4 yrs.		**W Totals:**	218	13	59	72	109

PLAYOFFS

YEAR	TEAM	LEAGUE	GP	G	A	PTS	PIM
1973-74	**EDM**	**W**	5	0	1	1	4

Alain Caron

CARON, ALAIN LUC 5'10", 175 lbs.
B. Apr. 27, 1938, Dolbeau, Que. Right Wing, Shoots R

YEAR	TEAM	LEAGUE	GP	G	A	PTS	PIM
1967-68	**OAK**	**N**	58	9	13	22	18
1968-69	**MONT**	**N**	2	0	0	0	0
1972-73	**QUE**	**W**	68	36	27	63	14
1973-74			59	31	15	46	10
1974-75			21	7	3	10	2
	M-B	**W**	47	8	5	13	4
	2 team total		68	15	8	23	6
5 yrs.		**N Totals:**	60	9	13	22	18
		W Totals:	195	82	50	132	30

Drafted by **Oakland** in Expansion Draft, June 6, 1967. Traded to **Montreal** by Oakland with Wally Boyer and Oakland's first-round draft choices in the 1968 (Jim Pritchard) and 1970 (Ray Martyniuk) Amateur Drafts for Norm Ferguson and Stan Fuller, May 21, 1968.

Bobby Carpenter

CARPENTER, ROBERT 5'11", 178 lbs.
B. July 13, 1963, Beverly, Mass. Center, Shoots L

YEAR	TEAM	LEAGUE	GP	G	A	PTS	PIM
1981-82	**WASH**	**N**	80	32	35	67	69
1982-83			80	32	37	69	64
2 yrs.		**N Totals:**	160	64	72	136	133

PLAYOFFS

YEAR	TEAM	LEAGUE	GP	G	A	PTS	PIM
1982-83	**WASH**	**N**	4	1	0	1	2

Eddie Carpenter

CARPENTER, EVERARD LORNE
B. Hartford, Mich. Defense

YEAR	TEAM	LEAGUE	GP	G	A	PTS	PIM
1919-20	**QUE**	**N**	24	8	3	11	19
1920-21	**HAMIL**	**N**	20	2	1	3	4
2 yrs.		**N Totals:**	44	10	4	14	23

Al Carr

CARR, ALFRED GEORGE ROBERT (Red) 5'8", 178 lbs.
B. Winnipeg, Man. Left Wing, Shoots L

YEAR	TEAM	LEAGUE	GP	G	A	PTS	PIM
1943-44	**TOR**	**N**	5	0	1	1	4

Gene Carr

CARR, EUGENE WILLIAM 5'11", 185 lbs.
B. Sept. 17, 1951, Nanaimo, B.C. Center, Shoots L

YEAR	TEAM	LEAGUE	GP	G	A	PTS	PIM
1971-72	**STL**	**N**	15	3	2	5	9
	NYR	**N**	59	8	8	16	25
	2 team total		74	11	10	21	34
1972-73			50	9	10	19	50
1973-74			29	1	5	6	15
	LA	**N**	21	6	11	17	36
	2 team total		50	7	16	23	51
1974-75			80	7	32	39	103
1975-76			38	8	11	19	16
1976-77			68	15	12	27	25
1977-78			5	2	0	2	4
	PITT	**N**	70	17	37	54	76
	2 team total		75	19	37	56	80
1978-79	**ATL**	**N**	30	3	8	11	6
8 yrs.		**N Totals:**	465	79	136	215	365

PLAYOFFS

YEAR	TEAM	LEAGUE	GP	G	A	PTS	PIM
1971-72	**NYR**	**N**	16	1	3	4	21
1972-73			1	0	1	1	0
1973-74	**LA**	**N**	5	2	1	3	14
1974-75			3	1	2	3	29
1976-77			9	1	1	2	2
1978-79	**ATL**	**N**	1	0	0	0	0
6 yrs.		**N Totals:**	35	5	8	13	66

Traded to **N.Y. Rangers** by St. Louis with Jim Lorentz and Wayne Connelly for Jack Egers, Andre Dupont and Mike Murphy, Nov. 15, 1971. Traded to **Los Angeles** by N.Y. Rangers for Los Angeles' first choice (Ron Duguay) in 1977 Amateur Draft, Feb. 15, 1974. Traded to **Pittsburgh** by Los Angeles with Dave Schultz and Los Angeles' fourth-round choice (Shane Pearsall) in the 1978 Amateur Draft for Syl Apps and Hartland Monahan, Nov. 2, 1977. Signed as free agent by **Atlanta** June 6, 1978.

Lorne Carr

CARR, LORNE BELL 5'8", 161 lbs.
B. July 2, 1910, Stoughton, Sask. Right Wing, Shoots R

YEAR	TEAM	LEAGUE	GP	G	A	PTS	PIM
1933-34	**NYR**	**N**	14	0	0	0	0
1934-35	**NYA**	**N**	48	17	14	31	14
1935-36			44	8	10	18	4
1936-37			47	18	16	34	22
1937-38			48	16	7	23	12
1938-39			47	19	18	37	16
1939-40			48	8	17	25	17
1940-41			48	13	19	32	10
1941-42	**TOR**	**N**	47	16	17	33	4
1942-43			50	27	33	60	15
1943-44			50	36	38	74	9
1944-45			47	11	25	36	7
1945-46			42	5	8	13	2
13 yrs.		**N Totals:**	580	194	222	416	132

PLAYOFFS

YEAR	TEAM	LEAGUE	GP	G	A	PTS	PIM
1935-36	**NYA**	**N**	5	1	1	2	0
1937-38			6	3	1	4	2
1938-39			2	0	0	0	0
1939-40			3	0	0	0	0
1941-42*	**TOR**	**N**	13	3	2	5	6
1942-43			6	1	2	3	0
1943-44			5	0	1	1	0
1944-45*			13	2	2	4	5
8 yrs.		**N Totals:**	53	10	9	19	13

Carr

CARR
B. Unknown

YEAR	TEAM	LEAGUE	GP	G	A	PTS	PIM
1919-20	QUE	N	1	0	0	0	0

Larry Carriere

CARRIERE, LARRY 6'1", 190 lbs.
B. Jan. 30, 1952, Montreal, Que. Defense, Shoots L

YEAR	TEAM	LEAGUE	GP	G	A	PTS	PIM
1972-73	BUF	N	40	2	8	10	52
1973-74			77	6	24	30	103
1974-75			80	1	11	12	111
1975-76	ATL	N	75	4	15	19	96
1976-77			25	2	3	5	16
	VAN	N	49	1	9	10	55
	2 team total		74	3	12	15	71
1977-78			7	0	3	3	12
	LA	N	2	0	0	0	0
	BUF	N	9	0	0	0	18
	3 team total		18	0	3	3	30
1979-80	TOR	N	2	0	1	1	0
7 yrs.		N Totals:	366	16	74	90	463
PLAYOFFS							
1972-73	BUF	N	6	0	1	1	8
1974-75			17	0	2	2	32
1975-76	ATL	N	2	0	0	0	2
1979-80	TOR	N	2	0	0	0	0
4 yrs.		N Totals:	27	0	3	3	42

Traded to **Atlanta** by Buffalo with Buffalo's first choice (Greg Carroll) in 1976 Amateur Draft (later traded to Washington) and cash for Jacques Richard, Oct. 1, 1975. Traded to **Vancouver** by Atlanta with Hilliard Graves for John Gould and Los Angeles' second round choice (Brian Hill), Vancouver property via earlier deal, in 1977 Amateur Draft, Dec. 2, 1976. Traded to **Los Angeles** by Vancouver for Sheldon Kannegiesser, Nov. 21, 1977. Signed as a free agent by **Buffalo** March 12, 1978. Signed as free agent by **Toronto** Apr. 5, 1980.

Gene Carrigan

CARRIGAN, EUGENE 6'1", 200 lbs.
B. July 5, 1907, Edmonton, Alta. Center, Shoots L

YEAR	TEAM	LEAGUE	GP	G	A	PTS	PIM
1930-31	NYR	N	33	2	0	2	13
1934-35	STL	N	4	0	1	1	0
2 yrs.		N Totals:	37	2	1	3	13
PLAYOFFS							
1933-34	DET	N	4	0	0	0	0

Billy Carroll

CARROLL, WILLIAM ALLAN 5'10", 191 lbs.
B. Jan. 19, 1959, Toronto, Ont. Center, Shoots L

YEAR	TEAM	LEAGUE	GP	G	A	PTS	PIM
1980-81	NYI	N	18	4	4	8	6
1981-82			72	9	20	29	32
1982-83			71	1	11	12	24
3 yrs.		N Totals:	161	14	35	49	62
PLAYOFFS							
1980-81*	NYI	N	18	3	9	12	4
1981-82*			19	2	2	4	8
1982-83*			20	1	1	2	2
3 yrs.		N Totals:	57	6	12	18	14

George Carroll

CARROLL, GEORGE
B. Unknown Defense

YEAR	TEAM	LEAGUE	GP	G	A	PTS	PIM
1924-25	MON(M)	N	4	0	0	0	0
	BOS	N	11	0	0	0	9
	2 team total		15	0	0	0	9

Greg Carroll

CARROLL, GREGORY JOHN 6', 185 lbs.
B. Nov. 10, 1956, Gimli, Man. Center, Shoots L

YEAR	TEAM	LEAGUE	GP	G	A	PTS	PIM
1976-77	CIN	W	77	15	39	54	53
1977-78	NE	W	48	9	14	23	27
	CIN	W	26	6	13	19	36
	2 team total		74	15	27	42	63

Greg Carroll continued

YEAR	TEAM	LEAGUE	GP	G	A	PTS	PIM
1978-79	WASH	N	24	5	6	11	12
	DET	N	36	2.	9	11	8
	2 team total		60	7	15	22	20
1979-80	HART	N	71	13	19	32	24
4 yrs.		N Totals:	131	20	34	54	44
		W Totals:	151	30	66	96	116
PLAYOFFS							
1976-77	CIN	W	4	1	2	3	0

Claimed on waivers by **Detroit** from Washington, Jan. 6, 1979. Signed by **Hartford** as free agent, Oct. 30, 1979.

Dwight Carruthers

CARRUTHERS, GORDON DWIGHT 5'9", 185 lbs.
B. Nov. 7, 1944, Lashburn, Sask. Defense, Shoots R

YEAR	TEAM	LEAGUE	GP	G	A	PTS	PIM
1965-66	DET	N	1	0	0	0	0
1967-68	PHI	N	1	0	0	0	0
2 yrs.		N Totals:	2	0	0	0	0

Bill Carse

CARSE, WILLIAM ALEXANDER 5'8", 165 lbs.
B. May 29, 1914, Edmonton, Alta. Center, Shoots L

YEAR	TEAM	LEAGUE	GP	G	A	PTS	PIM
1938-39	NYR	N	1	0	1	1	0
1939-40	CHI	N	48	10	13	23	10
1940-41			32	5	15	20	12
1941-42			43	13	14	27	16
4 yrs.		N Totals:	124	28	43	71	38
PLAYOFFS							
1938-39	NYR	N	6	1	1	2	0
1939-40	CHI	N	2	1	0	1	0
1940-41			5	0	0	0	0
1941-42			3	1	1	2	0
4 yrs.		N Totals:	16	3	2	5	0

Bob Carse

CARSE, ROBERT ALLISON 5'9", 170 lbs.
B. July 19, 1919, Edmonton, Alta. Left Wing, Shoots L

YEAR	TEAM	LEAGUE	GP	G	A	PTS	PIM
1939-40	CHI	N	22	3	5	8	11
1940-41			43	9	9	18	9
1941-42			33	7	16	23	10
1942-43			47	10	22	32	6
1947-48	MONT	N	22	3	3	6	16
5 yrs.		N Totals:	167	32	55	87	52
PLAYOFFS							
1939-40	CHI	N	2	0	0	0	0
1940-41			5	0	0	0	2
1941-42			3	0	2	2	0
3 yrs.		N Totals:	10	0	2	2	2

Bill Carson

CARSON, WILLIAM J.
B. Nov. 25, 1900, Bracebridge, Ont. Forward

YEAR	TEAM	LEAGUE	GP	G	A	PTS	PIM
1926-27	TOR	N	40	16	6	22	41
1927-28			32	20	6	26	36
1928-29			24	7	6	13	45
	BOS	N	19	4	2	6	10
	2 team total		43	11	8	19	55
1929-30			44	7	4	11	24
4 yrs.		N Totals:	159	54	24	78	156
PLAYOFFS							
1928-29*	BOS	N	5	2	0	2	8
1929-30			6	1	0	1	6
2 yrs.		N Totals:	11	3	0	3	14

Frank Carson

CARSON, FRANK R. 5'7", 165 lbs.
B. Jan. 12, 1902, Bracebridge, Ont. Right Wing, Shoots R

YEAR	TEAM	LEAGUE	GP	G	A	PTS	PIM
1925-26	MON(M)	N	16	2	1	3	6
1926-27			43	2	3	5	12
1927-28			19	0	1	1	10
1930-31	NYA	N	43	6	7	13	36

Frank Carson continued

YEAR	TEAM & LEAGUE	GP	G	A	PTS	PIM
1931-32	**DET N**	30	10	14	24	31
1932-33		47	12	13	25	35
1933-34		47	10	9	19	36
7 yrs.	**N Totals:**	245	42	48	90	166
PLAYOFFS						
1925-26*	**MON(M) N**	8	0	0	0	0
1926-27		2	0	0	0	2
1931-32	**DET N**	2	0	0	0	2
1932-33		4	0	1	1	0
1933-34		7	0	1	1	5
5 yrs.	**N Totals:**	23	0	2	2	9

Gerry Carson

CARSON, GERALD (Stub) 5'10", 175 lbs.
B. Oct. 10, 1905, Parry Sound, Ont. Defense, Shoots L

YEAR	TEAM & LEAGUE	GP	G	A	PTS	PIM
1928-29	**MONT N**	26	0	0	0	4
	NYR N	14	0	0	0	5
	2 team total	40	0	0	0	9
1929-30	**MONT N**	35	1	0	1	8
1932-33		48	5	2	7	53
1933-34		48	5	1	6	51
1934-35		48	0	5	5	56
1936-37	**MON(M) N**	42	1	3	4	28
6 yrs.	**N Totals:**	261	12	11	23	205
PLAYOFFS						
1928-29	**NYR N**	5	0	0	0	0
1929-30*	**MONT N**	6	0	0	0	0
1932-33		2	0	0	0	2
1933-34		2	0	0	0	2
1934-35		2	0	0	0	4
1936-37	**MON(M) N**	5	0	0	0	4
6 yrs.	**N Totals:**	22	0	0	0	12

Lindsay Carson

CARSON, LINDSAY WARREN 6'2", 190 lbs.
B. Nov. 21, 1960, Oxbow, Sask. Center, Shoots L

YEAR	TEAM & LEAGUE	GP	G	A	PTS	PIM
1981-82	**PHI N**	18	0	1	1	32
1982-83		78	18	19	37	68
2 yrs.	**N Totals:**	96	18	20	38	100
PLAYOFFS						
1982-83	**PHI N**	1	0	0	0	0

Billy Carter

CARTER, WILLIAM 5'11", 155 lbs.
B. Dec. 2, 1937, Cornwall, Ont. Center, Shoots L

YEAR	TEAM & LEAGUE	GP	G	A	PTS	PIM
1957-58	**MONT N**	1	0	0	0	0
1960-61	**BOS N**	8	0	0	0	2
1961-62	**MONT N**	7	0	0	0	4
3 yrs.	**N Totals:**	16	0	0	0	6

Lyle Carter

CARTER, LYLE DWIGHT 6'1", 185 lbs.
B. Apr. 29, 1945, Truro, N.S. Shoots L

YEAR	TEAM & LEAGUE	GP	G	A	PTS	PIM
1971-72	**CALIF N**	15	0	0	0	2

Ron Carter

CARTER, RONALD 6'1", 205 lbs.
B. Mar. 14, 1958, Montreal, Que. Right Wing, Shoots L

YEAR	TEAM & LEAGUE	GP	G	A	PTS	PIM
1979-80	**EDM N**	2	0	0	0	0

Jean Cartier

CARTIER, JEAN-YVES 5'9", 180 lbs.
B. Verdun, Que. Defense, Shoots L

YEAR	TEAM & LEAGUE	GP	G	A	PTS	PIM
1972-73	**QUE W**	15	0	3	3	8

Joe Carveth

CARVETH, JOSEPH GORDON 5'10", 180 lbs.
B. Mar. 21, 1918, Regina, Sask. Right Wing, Shoots R

YEAR	TEAM & LEAGUE	GP	G	A	PTS	PIM
1940-41	**DET N**	19	2	1	3	2
1941-42		29	6	11	17	2
1942-43		43	18	18	36	6
1943-44		46	21	35	56	6
1944-45		50	26	28	54	10
1945-46		48	17	18	35	18
1946-47	**BOS N**	51	21	15	36	10
1947-48		22	8	9	17	2
	MONT N	35	1	10	11	6
	2 team total	57	9	19	28	8
1948-49		60	15	22	37	8
1949-50		11	1	1	2	2
	DET N	60	13	17	30	13
	2 team total	71	14	18	32	15
1950-51		30	1	4	5	0
11 yrs.	**N Totals:**	504	150	189	339	85
PLAYOFFS						
1941-42	**DET N**	9	4	0	4	0
1942-43*		10	6	2	8	4
1943-44		5	2	1	3	8
1944-45		14	5	6	11	2
1945-46		5	0	1	1	0
1946-47	**BOS N**	5	2	1	3	0
1948-49	**MONT N**	7	0	1	1	8
1949-50*	**DET N**	14	2	4	6	6
8 yrs.	**N Totals:**	69	21	16	37	28

Traded to **Detroit** by Montreal for Calum MacKay, Nov. 11, 1949.

Wayne Cashman

CASHMAN, WAYNE JOHN (Cash) 6'1", 208 lbs.
B. June 24, 1945, Kingston, Ont. Left Wing, Shoots R

YEAR	TEAM & LEAGUE	GP	G	A	PTS	PIM
1964-65	**BOS N**	1	0	0	0	0
1967-68		12	0	4	4	2
1968-69		51	8	23	31	49
1969-70		70	9	26	35	79
1970-71		77	21	58	79	100
1971-72		74	23	29	52	103
1972-73		76	29	39	68	100
1973-74		78	30	59	89	111
1974-75		42	11	22	33	24
1975-76		80	28	43	71	87
1976-77		65	15	37	52	76
1977-78		76	24	38	62	69
1978-79		75	27	40	67	63
1979-80		44	11	21	32	19
1980-81		77	25	35	60	80
1981-82		64	12	31	43	59
1982-83		65	4	11	15	20
17 yrs.	**N Totals:**	1027	277	516	793	1041
PLAYOFFS						
1967-68	**BOS N**	1	0	0	0	0
1968-69		6	0	1	1	0
1969-70*		14	5	4	9	50
1970-71		7	3	2	5	15
1971-72*		15	4	7	11	42
1972-73		5	1	1	2	4
1973-74		16	5	9	14	46
1974-75		1	0	2	2	0
1975-76		11	1	5	6	16
1976-77		14	1	8	9	18
1977-78		15	4	6	10	13
1978-79		10	4	5	9	8
1979-80		10	3	3	6	32
1980-81		3	0	1	1	0
1981-82		9	0	2	2	6
1982-83		8	0	1	1	0
16 yrs.	**N Totals:**	145	31	57	88	250

Tom Cassidy

CASSIDY, THOMAS E.J. 5'11", 180 lbs.
B. Mar. 15, 1952, Blind River, Ont. Center, Shoots L

YEAR	TEAM & LEAGUE		GP	G	A	PTS	PIM
1977-78	**PITT**	**N**	26	3	4	7	15

Sold to **Los Angeles** by California, March 2, 1974. Signed as free agent by **Boston** Oct. 30, 1976. Signed as free agent by **Pittsburgh** Oct. 11, 1977.

Tony Cassolato

CASSOLATO, ANTHONY GERALD 5'11", 183 lbs.
B. May 7, 1956, Guelph, Ont. Right Wing, Shoots R

YEAR	TEAM & LEAGUE		GP	G	A	PTS	PIM
1976-77	**SD**	**W**	43	13	12	25	26
1977-78	**BIRM**	**W**	77	18	25	43	59
1978-79			64	13	7	20	62
1979-80	**WASH**	**N**	9	0	2	2	0
1980-81			2	0	0	0	0
1981-82			12	1	4	5	4
6 yrs.		**N Totals:**	23	1	6	7	4
		W Totals:	184	44	44	88	147
PLAYOFFS							
1976-77	**SD**	**W**	3	0	0	0	4
1977-78	**BIRM**	**W**	4	0	0	0	4
2 yrs.		**W Totals:**	7	0	0	0	8

Ray Ceresino

CERESINO, RAYMOND 5'8½", 160 lbs.
B. Apr. 24, 1929, Port Arthur, Ont. Right Wing, Shoots R

YEAR	TEAM & LEAGUE		GP	G	A	PTS	PIM
1948-49	**TOR**	**N**	12	1	1	2	2

John Chad

CHAD, JOHN 5'10", 167 lbs.
B. Sept. 16, 1919, Provost, Alta. Right Wing, Shoots R

YEAR	TEAM & LEAGUE		GP	G	A	PTS	PIM
1939-40	**CHI**	**N**	22	8	3	11	11
1940-41			45	7	18	25	16
1945-46			13	0	1	1	2
3 yrs.		**N Totals:**	80	15	22	37	29
PLAYOFFS							
1939-40	**CHI**	**N**	2	0	0	0	0
1940-41			5	0	0	0	2
1945-46			3	0	1	1	0
3 yrs.		**N Totals:**	10	0	1	1	2

Bill Chalmers

CHALMERS, WILLIAM (Chick) 6', 180 lbs.
B. Jan. 24, 1934, Stratford, Ont. Center, Shoots L

YEAR	TEAM & LEAGUE		GP	G	A	PTS	PIM
1953-54	**NYR**	**N**	1	0	0	0	0

Murph Chamberlain

CHAMBERLAIN, ERWIN GROVES 5'11", 172 lbs.
B. Feb. 14, 1915, Shawville, Que. Center, Shoots L

YEAR	TEAM & LEAGUE		GP	G	A	PTS	PIM
1937-38	**TOR**	**N**	43	4	12	16	51
1938-39			48	10	16	26	32
1939-40			40	5	17	22	63
1940-41	**MONT**	**N**	45	10	15	25	75
1941-42			26	6	3	9	30
	NYA	**N**	11	6	9	15	16
	2 team total		37	12	12	24	46
1942-43	**BOS**	**N**	45	9	24	33	67
1943-44	**MONT**	**N**	47	15	32	47	85
1944-45			32	2	12	14	38
1945-46			40	12	14	26	42
1946-47			49	10	10	20	97
1947-48			30	6	3	9	62
1948-49			54	5	8	13	111
12 yrs.		**N Totals:**	510	100	175	275	769
PLAYOFFS							
1937-38	**TOR**	**N**	5	0	0	0	2
1938-39			10	2	5	7	4
1939-40			3	0	0	0	0
1940-41	**MONT**	**N**	3	0	2	2	11
1942-43	**BOS**	**N**	6	1	1	2	12
1943-44*	**MONT**	**N**	9	5	3	8	12

Murph Chamberlain continued

YEAR	TEAM & LEAGUE		GP	G	A	PTS	PIM
1944-45			6	1	1	2	10
1945-46*			9	4	2	6	18
1946-47			11	1	3	4	19
1948-49			4	0	0	0	8
10 yrs.		**N Totals:**	66	14	17	31	96

Andre Champagne

CHAMPAGNE, ANDRE JOSEPH ORIUS 6', 190 lbs.
B. Sept. 19, 1943, Ottawa, Ont. Left Wing, Shoots L

YEAR	TEAM & LEAGUE		GP	G	A	PTS	PIM
1962-63	**TOR**	**N**	2	0	0	0	0

Art Chapman

CHAPMAN, ARTHUR 5'10", 170 lbs.
B. May 29, 1906, Winnipeg, Man. Center, Shoots L

YEAR	TEAM & LEAGUE		GP	G	A	PTS	PIM
1930-31	**BOS**	**N**	44	7	7	14	22
1931-32			48	11	14	25	18
1932-33			46	3	6	9	19
1933-34			21	3	2	5	6
	NYA	**N**	25	2	8	10	9
	2 team total		46	5	10	15	15
1934-35			47	9	**34**	43	4
1935-36			48	10	**28**	38	14
1936-37			43	8	23	31	36
1937-38			45	2	27	29	8
1938-39			45	3	19	22	2
1939-40			26	4	6	10	2
10 yrs.		**N Totals:**	438	62	174	236	140
PLAYOFFS							
1930-31	**BOS**	**N**	5	0	1	1	7
1932-33			5	0	0	0	2
1935-36	**NYA**	**N**	5	0	3	3	0
1937-38			6	0	1	1	0
1938-39			2	0	0	0	0
1939-40			2	1	0	1	0
6 yrs.		**N Totals:**	25	1	5	6	9

Blair Chapman

CHAPMAN, BLAIR DOUGLAS 6'1", 190 lbs.
B. June 13, 1956, Lloydminster, Sask. Right Wing, Shoots R

YEAR	TEAM & LEAGUE		GP	G	A	PTS	PIM
1976-77	**PITT**	**N**	80	14	23	37	16
1977-78			75	24	20	44	37
1978-79			71	10	8	18	18
1979-80			1	0	0	0	0
	STL	**N**	63	25	26	51	28
	2 team total		64	25	26	51	28
1980-81			55	20	26	46	41
1981-82			18	6	11	17	8
1982-83			39	7	11	18	10
7 yrs.		**N Totals:**	402	106	125	231	158
PLAYOFFS							
1976-77	**PITT**	**N**	3	1	1	2	7
1978-79			7	1	0	1	2
1979-80	**STL**	**N**	3	0	0	0	0
1980-81			9	2	5	7	6
1981-82			3	0	0	0	0
5 yrs.		**N Totals:**	25	4	6	10	15

Traded to **St. Louis** by Pittsburgh for Bob Stewart, Nov. 13, 1979.

Bob Charlebois

CHARLEBOIS, ROBERT RICHARD 6', 175 lbs.
B. May 27, 1944, Cornwall, Ont. Left Wing, Shoots L

YEAR	TEAM & LEAGUE		GP	G	A	PTS	PIM
1967-68	**MINN**	**N**	7	1	0	1	0
1972-73	**OTTA**	**W**	78	24	40	64	28
1973-74	**NE**	**W**	74	4	7	11	6
1974-75			8	1	0	1	0
1975-76			28	3	3	6	0
5 yrs.		**N Totals:**	7	1	0	1	0
		W Totals:	188	32	50	82	34
PLAYOFFS							
1972-73	**OTTA**	**W**	5	1	1	2	4
1973-74	**NE**	**W**	7	0	0	0	4

Bob Charlebois continued

YEAR	TEAM	LEAGUE	GP	G	A	PTS	PIM
1974-75			4	1	0	1	0
3 yrs.		W Totals:	16	2	1	3	8

Traded by Montreal with Andre Boudrias and amateur Bernard Cote to **Minnesota** for Minnesota's first choice (Chuck Arnason) in the 1971 Amateur Draft, June 6, 1967.

Guy Charron

CHARRON, GUY JOSEPH JEAN 5'10", 180 lbs.
B. Jan. 24, 1949, Verdin, Que. Center, Shoots L

YEAR	TEAM	LEAGUE	GP	G	A	PTS	PIM
1969-70	**MONT**	**N**	5	0	0	0	0
1970-71			15	2	2	4	4
	DET	**N**	24	8	4	12	4
	2 team total		39	10	6	16	8
1971-72			64	9	16	25	84
1972-73			75	18	18	36	23
1973-74			76	25	30	55	10
1974-75			26	1	10	11	6
	KC	**N**	51	13	29	42	21
	2 team total		77	14	39	53	27
1975-76			78	27	44	71	12
1976-77	**WASH**	**N**	80	36	46	82	10
1977-78			80	38	35	73	12
1978-79			80	28	42	70	24
1979-80			33	11	20	31	6
1980-81			47	5	13	18	2
12 yrs.		N Totals:	734	221	309	530	218

Traded to **Detroit** by Montreal with Mickey Redmond and Bill Collins for Frank Mahovlich, Jan. 13, 1971. Traded to **Kansas City** by Detroit with Claude Houde for Bart Crashley, Ted Snell and Larry Giroux, Dec. 14, 1974. Signed as free agent by **Washington** from Colorado, Sept. 1, 1976.

Dave Chartier

CHARTIER, DAVID 5'9", 170 lbs.
B. Feb. 15, 1961, St. Lazare, Man. Center, Shoots R

YEAR	TEAM	LEAGUE	GP	G	A	PTS	PIM
1980-81	**WINN**	**N**	1	0	0	0	0

Rick Chartraw

CHARTRAW, RAYMOND RICHARD (Charty) 6'2", 210 lbs.
B. July 13, 1954, Caracas, Venezuela Defense, Shoots R

YEAR	TEAM	LEAGUE	GP	G	A	PTS	PIM
1974-75	**MONT**	**N**	12	0	0	0	6
1975-76			16	1	3	4	25
1976-77			43	3	4	7	59
1977-78			68	4	12	16	64
1978-79			62	5	11	16	29
1979-80			66	5	7	12	35
1980-81			14	0	0	0	4
	LA	**N**	21	1	6	7	28
	2 team total		35	1	6	7	32
1981-82			33	2	8	10	56
1982-83			31	3	5	8	31
	NYR	**N**	26	2	2	4	37
	2 team total		57	5	7	12	68
9 yrs.		N Totals:	392	26	58	84	374

PLAYOFFS

YEAR	TEAM	LEAGUE	GP	G	A	PTS	PIM
1975-76*	**MONT**	**N**	2	0	0	0	0
1976-77*			13	2	1	3	17
1977-78*			10	1	1	2	10
1978-79*			16	2	1	3	24
1979-80			10	2	2	4	0
1980-81	**LA**	**N**	4	0	1	1	4
1981-82			10	0	2	2	17
1982-83	**NYR**	**N**	9	0	2	2	6
8 yrs.		N Totals:	74	7	10	17	78

Traded to **Los Angeles** by Montreal for Los Angeles' second round choice in either the 1983 or 1984 Entry Draft. Claimed on waivers by **N.Y. Rangers** from Los Angeles, Jan. 13, 1983.

Claude Chartre

CHARTRE, CLAUDE 6', 180 lbs.
B. Dec. 21, 1949, Grande-Riviere, Que. Center, Shoots L

YEAR	TEAM	LEAGUE	GP	G	A	PTS	PIM
1972-73	**NY**	**W**	12	2	3	5	0
1973-74	**NY-NJ**	**W**	5	0	0	0	0
1974-75	**M-B**	**W**	1	0	0	0	0

Claude Chartre continued

YEAR	TEAM	LEAGUE	GP	G	A	PTS	PIM
3 yrs.		W Totals:	18	2	3	5	0

Lude Check

CHECK, LUDIC 154 lbs.
B. May 22, 1919, Brandon, Man. Forward

YEAR	TEAM	LEAGUE	GP	G	A	PTS	PIM
1943-44	**DET**	**N**	1	0	0	0	0
1944-45	**CHI**	**N**	26	6	2	8	4
2 yrs.		N Totals:	27	6	2	8	4

Mike Chernoff

CHERNOFF, MICHAEL TERENCE 5'9", 175 lbs.
B. May 13, 1946, Yorkton, Sask. Left Wing, Shoots L

YEAR	TEAM	LEAGUE	GP	G	A	PTS	PIM
1968-69	**MINN**	**N**	1	0	0	0	0
1973-74	**VAN**	**W**	36	11	10	21	4
1974-75			3	0	0	0	0
3 yrs.		N Totals:	1	0	0	0	0
		W Totals:	39	11	10	21	4

Richard Chernomaz

CHERNOMAZ, RICHARD 5'9", 175 lbs.
B. Sept. 1, 1963, Selkirk, Man. Right Wing, Shoots R

YEAR	TEAM	LEAGUE	GP	G	A	PTS	PIM
1981-82	**COLO**	**N**	2	0	0	0	0

Dick Cherry

CHERRY, RICHARD JOHN 6', 200 lbs.
B. Mar. 28, 1937, Kingston, Ont. Defense, Shoots L

YEAR	TEAM	LEAGUE	GP	G	A	PTS	PIM
1956-57	**BOS**	**N**	6	0	0	0	4
1968-69	**PHI**	**N**	71	9	6	15	18
1969-70			68	3	4	7	23
3 yrs.		N Totals:	145	12	10	22	45

PLAYOFFS

YEAR	TEAM	LEAGUE	GP	G	A	PTS	PIM
1968-69	**PHI**	**N**	4	1	0	1	4

Drafted by **Philadelphia** from Boston in Expansion Draft, June 6, 1967. Put on **Boston** reserve list from Philadelphia in Intra-League Draft, June 9, 1970.

Don Cherry

CHERRY, DONALD STEWART (Grapes) 5'11", 180 lbs.
B. Feb. 5, 1934, Kingston, Ont. Defense, Shoots L
Won Jack Adams Award, 1975-76

PLAYOFFS

YEAR	TEAM	LEAGUE	GP	G	A	PTS	PIM
1954-55	**BOS**	**N**	1	0	0	0	0

Real Chevrefils

CHEVREFILS, REAL 5'10", 175 lbs.
B. May 2, 1932, Timmins, Ont. Left Wing, Shoots L

YEAR	TEAM	LEAGUE	GP	G	A	PTS	PIM
1951-52	**BOS**	**N**	33	8	17	25	8
1952-53			69	19	14	33	44
1953-54			14	4	1	5	2
1954-55			64	18	22	40	30
1955-56	**DET**	**N**	38	3	4	7	24
	BOS	**N**	25	11	8	19	10
	2 team total		63	14	12	26	34
1956-57			70	31	17	48	38
1957-58			44	9	9	18	21
1958-59			30	1	5	6	8
8 yrs.		N Totals:	387	104	97	201	185

PLAYOFFS

YEAR	TEAM	LEAGUE	GP	G	A	PTS	PIM
1951-52	**BOS**	**N**	7	1	1	2	6
1952-53			7	0	1	1	6
1954-55			5	2	1	3	4
1956-57			10	2	1	3	4
1957-58			1	0	0	0	0
5 yrs.		N Totals:	30	5	4	9	20

Traded to **Detroit** by Boston with Ed Sandford, Norm Corcoran, Gilles Boisvert and Warren Godfrey for Marcel Bonin, Terry Sawchuk, Vic Stasiuk and Lorne Davis, June 3, 1955. Traded to **Boston** by Detroit with Jerry Toppazzini for Lorne Ferguson and Murray Costello, Jan. 17, 1956.

Dan Chicoine

CHICOINE, DANIEL 5'11", 192 lbs.
B. Nov. 30, 1957, Chatham, Ont. Right Wing, Shoots R

YEAR	TEAM & LEAGUE		GP	G	A	PTS	PIM
1977-78	CLEVE	N	6	0	0	0	0
1978-79	MINN	N	1	0	0	0	0
1979-80			24	1	2	3	12
3 yrs.		N Totals:	31	1	2	3	12
PLAYOFFS							
1979-80	MINN	N	1	0	0	0	0

Put on **Minnesota** Reserve List after Cleveland-Minnesota Dispersal Draft, June 15, 1978. Claimed by **Minnesota** as fill in Expansion Draft, June 13, 1979. Traded to **Quebec** by Minnesota for Nelson Burton, June 9, 1981.

Rick Chinnick

CHINNICK, RICHARD VAUGHN 5'11", 180 lbs.
B. Aug. 15, 1953, Chatham, Ont. Right Wing, Shoots L

YEAR	TEAM & LEAGUE		GP	G	A	PTS	PIM
1973-74	MINN	N	1	0	1	1	0
1974-75			3	0	1	1	0
2 yrs.		N Totals:	4	0	2	2	0

Traded to **Detroit** by Minnesota for Dennis Hextall, Nov. 21, 1975.

Jack Chipchase

CHIPCHASE, JOHN ALBERT 5'11", 205 lbs.
B. Apr. 5, 1945, Seaforth, Ont. Defense, Shoots L

YEAR	TEAM & LEAGUE		GP	G	A	PTS	PIM
1972-73	PHI	W	4	0	0	0	2

Ron Chipperfield

CHIPPERFIELD, RONALD JAMES (The Magnificent 7) 5'11", 180 lbs.
B. Mar. 28, 1954, Brandon, Man. Center, Shoots R

YEAR	TEAM & LEAGUE		GP	G	A	PTS	PIM
1974-75	VAN	W	78	19	20	39	30
1975-76	CALG	W	75	42	41	83	32
1976-77			81	27	27	54	32
1977-78	EDM	W	80	33	52	85	48
1978-79			55	32	37	69	47
1979-80	EDM	N	67	18	19	37	24
	QUE	N	12	4	4	8	8
	2 team total		79	22	23	45	32
1980-81			4	0	1	1	2
7 yrs.		N Totals:	83	22	24	46	34
		W Totals:	369	153	177	330	189
PLAYOFFS							
1975-76	CALG	W	10	5	4	9	6
1977-78	EDM	W	5	1	1	2	0
1978-79			13	9	10	19	8
3 yrs.		W Totals:	28	15	15	30	14

Traded to **Quebec** by Edmonton for Ron Low, March 11, 1980.

Art Chisholm

CHISHOLM, ARTHUR
Center

YEAR	TEAM & LEAGUE		GP	G	A	PTS	PIM
1960-61	BOS	N	3	0	0	0	0

Lex Chisholm

CHISHOLM, ALEXANDER
B. Galt, Ont. Center

YEAR	TEAM & LEAGUE		GP	G	A	PTS	PIM
1939-40	TOR	N	28	6	8	14	11
1940-41			26	4	0	4	8
2 yrs.		N Totals:	54	10	8	18	19
PLAYOFFS							
1940-41	TOR	N	3	1	0	1	0

Marc Chorney

CHORNEY, MARC 6', 200 lbs.
B. Nov. 8, 1959, Sudbury, Ont. Defense, Shoots L

YEAR	TEAM & LEAGUE		GP	G	A	PTS	PIM
1980-81	PITT	N	8	1	6	7	14
1981-82			60	1	6	7	63
1982-83			67	3	5	8	66

Marc Chorney continued

YEAR	TEAM & LEAGUE		GP	G	A	PTS	PIM
3 yrs.		N Totals:	135	5	17	22	143
PLAYOFFS							
1980-81	PITT	N	2	0	1	1	2
1981-82			5	0	0	0	0
2 yrs.		N Totals:	7	0	1	1	2

Gene Chouinard

CHOUINARD, EUGENE
B. Unknown Defense

YEAR	TEAM & LEAGUE		GP	G	A	PTS	PIM
1927-28	OTTA	N	8	0	0	0	0

Guy Chouinard

CHOUINARD, GUY CAMIL 5'11", 182 lbs.
B. Oct. 20, 1956, Quebec City, Queb. Center, Shoots R

YEAR	TEAM & LEAGUE		GP	G	A	PTS	PIM
1974-75	ATL	N	5	0	0	0	2
1975-76			4	0	2	2	2
1976-77			80	17	33	50	8
1977-78			73	28	30	58	8
1978-79			80	50	57	107	14
1979-80			76	31	46	77	22
1980-81	CALG	N	52	31	52	83	24
1981-82			64	23	57	80	12
1982-83			80	13	59	72	18
9 yrs.		N Totals:	514	193	336	529	110
PLAYOFFS							
1975-76	ATL	N	2	0	0	0	0
1976-77			3	2	0	2	0
1977-78			2	1	0	1	0
1978-79			2	1	2	3	0
1979-80			4	1	3	4	4
1980-81	CALG	N	16	3	14	17	4
1981-82			3	0	1	1	0
1982-83			9	1	6	7	4
8 yrs.		N Totals:	41	9	26	35	12

Dave Christian

CHRISTIAN, DAVID 5'11", 170 lbs.
B. May 12, 1959, Warroad, Minn. Center, Shoots R

YEAR	TEAM & LEAGUE		GP	G	A	PTS	PIM
1979-80	WINN	N	15	8	10	18	2
1980-81			80	28	43	71	22
1981-82			80	25	51	76	28
1982-83			55	18	26	44	23
4 yrs.		N Totals:	230	79	130	209	75
PLAYOFFS							
1981-82	WINN	N	4	0	1	1	2
1982-83			3	0	0	0	0
2 yrs.		N Totals:	7	0	1	1	2

Traded to **Washington** by Winnipeg for Washington's first round choice in the 1983 Amateur Draft (Robby Dollas), June 8, 1983.

Keith Christiansen

CHRISTIANSEN, KEITH (Huffer) 5'6", 155 lbs.
B. Apr. 8, 1947, Fort Frances, Ont. Center, Shoots R

YEAR	TEAM & LEAGUE		GP	G	A	PTS	PIM
1972-73	MINN	W	64	12	30	42	24
1973-74			74	11	25	36	36
2 yrs.		W Totals:	138	23	55	78	60
PLAYOFFS							
1972-73	MINN	W	5	1	0	1	0
1973-74			10	0	1	1	2
2 yrs.		W Totals:	15	1	1	2	2

Mike Christie

CHRISTIE, MICHAEL HUNT 6', 190 lbs.
B. Dec. 20, 1949, Big Spring, Tx. Defense, Shoots L

YEAR	TEAM & LEAGUE		GP	G	A	PTS	PIM
1974-75	CALIF	N	34	0	14	14	76
1975-76			78	3	18	21	152
1976-77	CLEVE	N	79	6	27	33	79

Mike Christie continued

YEAR	TEAM & LEAGUE		GP	G	A	PTS	PIM
1977-78			34	1	6	7	49
	COLO	N	35	2	8	10	28
	2 team total		69	3	14	17	77
1978-79			68	1	10	11	88
1979-80			74	1	17	18	78
1980-81			1	0	0	0	0
	VAN	N	9	1	1	2	0
	2 team total		10	1	1	2	0
7 yrs.		N Totals:	412	15	101	116	550
PLAYOFFS							
1977-78	COLO	N	2	0	0	0	0

Traded to **California** by Chicago with Len Frig for Ivan Boldirev, May 24, 1974. Traded to **Colorado** by Cleveland for Dennis O'Brien, Jan. 12, 1978. Sold to **Vancouver** by Colorado, Dec. 6, 1980.

Steve Christoff

CHRISTOFF, STEVE 6'1", 180 lbs.
B. Jan. 23, 1958, Richfield, Minn. Center, Shoots L

YEAR	TEAM & LEAGUE		GP	G	A	PTS	PIM
1979-80	MINN	N	20	8	7	15	19
1980-81			56	26	13	39	58
1981-82			69	26	29	55	14
1982-83	CALG	N	45	9	8	17	4
4 yrs.		N Totals:	190	69	57	126	95
PLAYOFFS							
1979-80	MINN	N	14	8	4	12	7
1980-81			18	8	8	16	16
1981-82			2	0	0	0	2
1982-83	CALG	N	1	0	0	0	0
4 yrs.		N Totals:	35	16	12	28	25

Traded to **Calgary** by Minnesota with Bill Nyrop and Minnesota's second choice (Dave Reierson) in 1982 Entry Draft for Willi Plett and Calgary's fourth choice (Dusan Pasek) in 1982 Entry Draft, June 7, 1982. Traded by Calgary with a second round choice in the 1983 Amateur Draft (acquired earlier from Montreal, Frantisek Musil) to **Minnesota** for Mike Eaves and Keith Hanson, June 6, 1983.

Bob Chrystal

CHRYSTAL, ROBERT HARRY 6', 180 lbs.
B. Apr. 30, 1930, Winnipeg, Man. Defense, Shoots L

YEAR	TEAM & LEAGUE		GP	G	A	PTS	PIM
1953-54	NYR	N	64	5	5	10	44
1954-55			68	6	9	15	68
2 yrs.		N Totals:	132	11	14	25	112

Drafted by **Chicago** from N.Y. Rangers, June 4, 1957.

Jack Church

CHURCH, JOHN 5'11", 180 lbs.
B. May 24, 1915, Kamsack, Sask. Defense, Shoots R

YEAR	TEAM & LEAGUE		GP	G	A	PTS	PIM
1938-39	TOR	N	3	0	2	2	2
1939-40			31	1	4	5	62
1940-41			11	0	1	1	22
1941-42			27	0	4	4	28
	NYA	N	15	1	2	3	12
	2 team total		42	1	6	7	40
1942-43			15	1	3	4	10
1945-46	BOS	N	43	2	6	8	28
6 yrs.		N Totals:	145	5	22	27	164
PLAYOFFS							
1938-39	TOR	N	1	0	0	0	0
1939-40			10	1	1	2	6
1940-41			5	0	0	0	8
1945-46	BOS	N	9	0	0	0	4
4 yrs.		N Totals:	25	1	1	2	18

Dino Ciccarelli

CICCARELLI, DINO 5'11", 185 lbs.
B. Aug. 2, 1960, Sarnia, Ont. Right Wing, Shoots R

YEAR	TEAM & LEAGUE		GP	G	A	PTS	PIM
1980-81	MINN	N	32	18	12	30	29
1981-82			76	55	51	106	138
1982-83			77	37	38	75	94
3 yrs.		N Totals:	185	110	101	211	261

Dino Ciccarelli continued

YEAR	TEAM & LEAGUE		GP	G	A	PTS	PIM
PLAYOFFS							
1980-81	MINN	N	19	14	7	21	25
1981-82			4	3	1	4	2
1982-83			9	4	6	10	11
3 yrs.		N Totals:	32	21	14	35	38

Signed as free agent by **Minnesota** Sept. 23, 1979.

Hank Ciesla

CIESLA, HENRY EDWARD 6'2", 190 lbs.
B. Oct. 15, 1934, St. Catharines, Ont. Center, Shoots L

YEAR	TEAM & LEAGUE		GP	G	A	PTS	PIM
1955-56	CHI	N	70	8	23	31	22
1956-57			70	10	8	18	28
1957-58	NYR	N	60	2	6	8	16
1958-59			69	6	14	20	21
4 yrs.		N Totals:	269	26	51	77	87
PLAYOFFS							
1957-58	NYR	N	6	0	2	2	0

Sold by Chicago to **N.Y. Rangers** Sept. 20, 1957.

Joe Cirella

CIRELLA, JOE 6'2", 193 lbs.
B. May 9, 1963, Hamilton, Ont. Defense, Shoots R

YEAR	TEAM & LEAGUE		GP	G	A	PTS	PIM
1981-82	COLO	N	65	7	12	19	52
1982-83	NJ	N	2	0	1	1	4
2 yrs.		N Totals:	67	7	13	20	56

Kim Clackson

CLACKSON, KIMBLE GERALD 5'11", 195 lbs.
B. Feb. 13, 1955, Saskatoon, Sask. Defense, Shoots R

YEAR	TEAM & LEAGUE		GP	G	A	PTS	PIM
1975-76	IND	W	77	1	12	13	351
1976-77			71	3	8	11	168
1977-78	WINN	W	52	2	7	9	203
1978-79			71	0	12	12	210
1979-80	PITT	N	46	0	3	3	166
1980-81	QUE	N	61	0	5	5	204
6 yrs.		N Totals:	107	0	8	8	370
		W Totals:	271	6	39	45	932
PLAYOFFS							
1975-76	IND	W	6	0	0	0	25
1976-77			9	0	1	1	24
1977-78	WINN	W	9	0	1	1	61
1978-79			9	0	5	5	28
1979-80	PITT	N	3	0	0	0	37
1980-81	QUE	N	5	0	0	0	33
6 yrs.		N Totals:	8	0	0	0	70
		W Totals:	33	0	7	7	138

Reclaimed by **Pittsburgh** from Winnipeg prior to Expansion Draft, June 9, 1979. Claimed by **Pittsburgh** as fill in Expansion Draft, June 13, 1979. Sent to **Quebec** by Pittsburgh, Aug. 7, 1980, as compensation for Pittsburgh's signing of free agent Paul Baxter.

King Clancy

CLANCY, FRANCIS MICHAEL 5'9", 184 lbs.
B. Feb. 25, 1903, Ottawa, Ont. Defense, Shoots L
Hall of Fame, 1958

YEAR	TEAM & LEAGUE		GP	G	A	PTS	PIM
1921-22	OTTA	N	24	4	5	9	19
1922-23			24	3	1	4	20
1923-24			24	9	8	17	18
1924-25			29	14	5	19	61
1925-26			35	8	4	12	80
1926-27			44	9	10	19	78
1927-28			39	8	7	15	73
1928-29			44	13	2	15	89
1929-30			44	17	23	40	83
1930-31	TOR	N	44	7	14	21	63
1931-32			48	10	9	19	61
1932-33			48	13	12	25	79
1933-34			46	11	17	28	62
1934-35			47	5	16	21	53
1935-36			47	5	10	15	61
1936-37			6	1	0	1	4

King Clancy continued

YEAR	TEAM & LEAGUE		GP	G	A	PTS	PIM
16 yrs.		N Totals:	593	137	143	280	904
PLAYOFFS							
1921-22	OTTA	N	2	0	0	0	2
1922-23*			8	1	0	1	4
1923-24			2	0	0	0	6
1925-26			2	1	0	1	4
1926-27*			6	1	1	2	14
1927-28			2	0	0	0	0
1929-30			2	0	1	1	2
1930-31	TOR	N	2	1	0	1	2
1931-32*			7	2	1	3	14
1932-33			9	0	3	3	14
1933-34			3	0	0	0	0
1934-35			7	1	0	1	8
1935-36			9	2	2	4	10
13 yrs.		N Totals:	61	9	8	17	80

Terry Clancy

CLANCY, TERRANCE JOHN 6', 195 lbs.
B. Apr. 2, 1943, Ottawa, Ont. Right Wing, Shoots L

YEAR	TEAM & LEAGUE		GP	G	A	PTS	PIM
1967-68	OAK	N	7	0	0	0	2
1968-69	TOR	N	2	0	0	0	0
1969-70			52	6	5	11	31
1972-73			32	0	1	1	6
4 yrs.		N Totals:	93	6	6	12	39

Dit Clapper

CLAPPER, AUBREY VICTOR 6'2", 195 lbs.
B. Feb. 9, 1907, Newmarket, Ont. Right Wing, Shoots R
Hall of Fame, 1945

YEAR	TEAM & LEAGUE		GP	G	A	PTS	PIM
1927-28	BOS	N	40	4	1	5	20
1928-29			40	9	2	11	48
1929-30			44	41	20	61	48
1930-31			43	22	8	30	50
1931-32			48	17	22	39	21
1932-33			48	14	14	28	42
1933-34			48	10	12	22	6
1934-35			48	21	16	37	21
1935-36			44	12	13	25	14
1936-37			48	17	8	25	25
1937-38			46	6	9	15	24
1938-39			42	13	13	26	22
1939-40			44	10	18	28	25
1940-41			48	8	18	26	24
1941-42			32	3	12	15	31
1942-43			38	5	18	23	12
1943-44			50	6	25	31	13
1944-45			46	8	14	22	16
1945-46			30	2	3	5	0
1946-47			6	0	0	0	0
20 yrs.		N Totals:	833	228	246	474	462
PLAYOFFS							
1927-28	BOS	N	2	0	0	0	2
1928-29*			5	1	0	1	0
1929-30			6	4	0	4	4
1930-31			5	2	4	6	4
1932-33			5	1	1	2	2
1934-35			3	1	0	1	0
1935-36			2	0	1	1	0
1936-37			3	2	0	2	5
1937-38			3	0	0	0	12
1938-39*			11	0	1	1	6
1939-40			5	0	2	2	2
1940-41*			11	0	5	5	4
1941-42			5	0	0	0	0
1942-43			9	2	3	5	9
1944-45			7	0	0	0	0
1945-46			4	0	0	0	0
16 yrs.		N Totals:	86	13	17	30	50

Andy Clark

CLARK, ANDREW
B. Unknown Defense

YEAR	TEAM & LEAGUE		GP	G	A	PTS	PIM
1927-28	BOS	N	5	0	0	0	0

Dan Clark

CLARK, DANIEL 6'1", 195 lbs.
B. Nov. 3, 1957, Toronto, Ont. Defense, Shoots L

YEAR	TEAM & LEAGUE		GP	G	A	PTS	PIM
1978-79	NYR	N	4	0	1	1	6

Claimed by **N.Y. Rangers** as Re-Entry in 1978 Amateur Draft, June 15, 1978.

Gordie Clark

CLARK, GORDON CORSON 5'10", 180 lbs.
B. May 31, 1952, Glasgow, Scotland Right Wing, Shoots R

YEAR	TEAM & LEAGUE		GP	G	A	PTS	PIM
1974-75	BOS	N	1	0	0	0	0
1975-76			7	0	1	1	0
1978-79	CIN	W	21	3	3	6	2
3 yrs.		N Totals:	8	0	1	1	0
		W Totals:	21	3	3	6	2
PLAYOFFS							
1975-76	BOS	N	1	0	0	0	0

Bobby Clarke

CLARKE, ROBERT EARLE 5'10", 185 lbs.
B. Aug. 13, 1949, Flin Flon, Man. Center, Shoots L
Won Hart Trophy, 1972–73, 1974–75, 1975-76
Won Selke Trophy, 1982-83
Won Masterton Trophy, 1971-72

YEAR	TEAM & LEAGUE		GP	G	A	PTS	PIM
1969-70	PHI	N	76	15	31	46	68
1970-71			77	27	36	63	78
1971-72			78	35	46	81	87
1972-73			78	37	67	104	80
1973-74			77	35	52	87	113
1974-75			80	27	**89**	116	125
1975-76			76	30	**89**	119	136
1976-77			80	27	63	90	71
1977-78			71	21	68	89	83
1978-79			80	16	57	73	68
1979-80			76	12	57	69	65
1980-81			80	19	46	65	140
1981-82			62	17	46	63	154
1982-83			80	23	62	85	115
14 yrs.		N Totals:	1071	341	809	1150	1383
PLAYOFFS							
1970-71	PHI	N	4	0	0	0	2
1972-73			11	2	6	8	6
1973-74*			17	5	11	16	42
1974-75*			17	4	12	16	16
1975-76			16	2	14	16	28
1976-77			10	5	5	10	8
1977-78			12	4	7	11	8
1978-79			8	2	4	6	8
1979-80			19	8	12	20	16
1980-81			12	3	3	6	6
1981-82			4	4	2	6	4
1982-83			3	1	0	1	2
12 yrs.		N Totals:	133	40	76	116	146

Jim Clarke

CLARKE, JAMES 6'3", 215 lbs.
B. Aug. 11, 1954, Toronto, Ont. Defense, Shoots L

YEAR	TEAM & LEAGUE		GP	G	A	PTS	PIM
1975-76	PHOE	W	59	1	9	10	57
PLAYOFFS							
1975-76	PHOE	W	1	0	0	0	0

Ray Clearwater

CLEARWATER, RAYMOND WESLEY 5'11", 175 lbs.
B. Nov. 10, 1942, Winnipeg, Man. Defense, Shoots L

YEAR	TEAM & LEAGUE		GP	G	A	PTS	PIM
1972-73	CLEVE	W	78	11	36	47	41
1973-74			68	12	23	35	47

YEAR	TEAM & LEAGUE		GP	G	A	PTS	PIM

Ray Clearwater continued

YEAR	TEAM	LEAGUE	GP	G	A	PTS	PIM
1974-75			66	4	18	22	51
1976-77	**MINN**	**W**	2	0	0	0	2
4 yrs.		**W Totals:**	214	27	77	104	141
PLAYOFFS							
1972-73	**CLEVE**	**W**	9	1	2	3	8
1973-74			5	0	0	0	2
1974-75			4	1	1	2	0
3 yrs.		**W Totals:**	18	2	3	5	10

Odie Cleghorn

CLEGHORN, OGILVIE
B. Montreal, Que. — Right Wing

YEAR	TEAM	LEAGUE	GP	G	A	PTS	PIM
1918-19	**MONT**	**N**	17	**23**	6	29	22
1919-20			21	19	3	22	30
1920-21			21	5	4	9	8
1921-22			23	21	3	24	26
1922-23			24	19	7	26	14
1923-24			23	3	3	6	14
1924-25			30	3	2	5	14
1925-26	**PITT**	**N**	17	3	1	4	4
1926-27			4	0	0	0	0
1927-28			2	0	0	0	0
10 yrs.		**N Totals:**	182	96	29	125	132
PLAYOFFS							
1918-19	**MONT**	**N**	10	9	1	10	11
1922-23			2	0	0	0	2
1923-24*			6	0	1	1	0
1924-25			5	0	1	1	0
1925-26	**PITT**	**N**	1	0	0	0	0
5 yrs.		**N Totals:**	24	9	3	12	13

Sprague Cleghorn

CLEGHORN, SPRAGUE
B. Montreal, Que. — Defense
Hall of Fame, 1958

YEAR	TEAM	LEAGUE	GP	G	A	PTS	PIM
1918-19	**OTTA**	**N**	18	6	6	12	27
1919-20			21	16	5	21	62
1920-21			3	2	1	3	9
	TOR	**N**	13	3	4	7	26
	2 team total		16	5	5	10	35
1921-22	**MONT**	**N**	24	17	7	24	**63**
1922-23			24	9	4	13	34
1923-24			23	8	3	11	39
1924-25			27	8	1	9	82
1925-26	**BOS**	**N**	28	6	5	11	49
1926-27			44	7	1	8	84
1927-28			37	2	2	4	14
10 yrs.		**N Totals:**	262	84	39	123	489
PLAYOFFS							
1918-19	**OTTA**	**N**	5	2	2	4	5
1919-20*			5	0	1	1	**9**
1920-21*			6	1	2	3	21
1922-23	**MONT**	**N**	1	0	0	0	0
1923-24*			6	2	1	3	2
1924-25			6	1	2	3	4
1926-27	**BOS**	**N**	8	0	1	1	8
1927-28			2	0	0	0	0
8 yrs.		**N Totals:**	39	6	9	15	49

Bill Clement

CLEMENT, WILLIAM H. — 6'1", 194 lbs.
B. Dec. 20, 1950, Thurso, Que. — Center, Shoots L

YEAR	TEAM	LEAGUE	GP	G	A	PTS	PIM
1971-72	**PHI**	**N**	49	9	14	23	39
1972-73			73	14	14	28	51
1973-74			39	9	8	17	34
1974-75			68	21	16	37	42
1975-76	**WASH**	**N**	46	10	17	27	20
	ATL	**N**	31	13	14	27	29
	2 team total		77	23	31	54	49
1976-77			67	17	26	43	27
1977-78			70	20	30	50	34
1978-79			65	12	23	35	14
1979-80			64	7	14	21	32
1980-81	**CALG**	**N**	78	12	20	32	33
1981-82			69	4	12	16	28

YEAR	TEAM & LEAGUE		GP	G	A	PTS	PIM

Bill Clement continued

YEAR	TEAM	LEAGUE	GP	G	A	PTS	PIM
11 yrs.		**N Totals:**	719	148	208	356	383
PLAYOFFS							
1972-73	**PHI**	**N**	2	0	0	0	0
1973-74*			4	1	0	1	4
1974-75*			12	1	0	1	8
1975-76	**ATL**	**N**	2	0	1	1	0
1976-77			3	1	1	2	0
1977-78			2	0	0	0	2
1978-79			2	0	0	0	0
1979-80			4	0	0	0	4
1980-81	**CALG**	**N**	16	2	1	3	6
1981-82			3	0	0	0	2
10 yrs.		**N Totals:**	50	5	3	8	26

Traded to **Washington** by Philadelphia with Don Maclean and Philadelphia's first choice (Alex Forsythe) in 1975 Amateur Draft for Washington's first choice (Mel Bridgman) in same draft, June 4, 1975. Traded to **Atlanta** by Washington for Gerry Meehan, Jean Lemieux and Buffalo's first choice (Greg Carroll) in 1976 Amateur Draft (Atlanta property via an earlier deal), Jan. 22, 1976.

Ron Climie

CLIMIE, RONALD MALCOMB — 5'11", 180 lbs.
B. Mar. 5, 1950, Hamilton, Ont. — Left Wing, Shoots L

YEAR	TEAM	LEAGUE	GP	G	A	PTS	PIM
1972-73	**OTTA**	**W**	31	12	19	31	2
1973-74	**EDM**	**W**	76	38	36	74	22
1974-75			49	15	27	42	15
	NE	**W**	25	8	4	12	12
	2 team total		74	23	31	54	27
1975-76			65	25	20	45	17
1976-77			3	0	0	0	0
5 yrs.		**W Totals:**	249	98	106	204	68
PLAYOFFS							
1972-73	**OTTA**	**W**	4	1	0	1	2
1973-74	**EDM**	**W**	5	0	0	0	0
1974-75	**NE**	**W**	6	3	0	3	0
3 yrs.		**W Totals:**	15	4	0	4	2

Bruce Cline

CLINE, BRUCE — 5'7", 137 lbs.
B. Nov. 14, 1931, Massawippi, Que. — Right Wing, Shoots R

YEAR	TEAM	LEAGUE	GP	G	A	PTS	PIM
1956-57	**NYR**	**N**	30	2	3	5	10

Steve Clippingdale

CLIPPINGDALE, STEVE — 6'2", 195 lbs.
B. Apr. 29, 1956, Vancouver, B.C. — Left Wing, Shoots L

YEAR	TEAM	LEAGUE	GP	G	A	PTS	PIM
1976-77	**LA**	**N**	16	1	2	3	9
1979-80	**WASH**	**N**	3	0	0	0	0
2 yrs.		**N Totals:**	19	1	2	3	9
PLAYOFFS							
1976-77	**LA**	**N**	1	0	0	0	0

Traded to **Washington** by Los Angeles for Mike Marson, June 11, 1979.

Real Cloutier

CLOUTIER, REAL — 5'10", 185 lbs.
B. July 30, 1956, St. Emile, Que. — Right Wing, Shoots R

YEAR	TEAM	LEAGUE	GP	G	A	PTS	PIM
1974-75	**QUE**	**W**	63	26	27	53	36
1975-76			80	60	54	114	27
1976-77			76	66	75	**141**	39
1977-78			73	56	73	129	19
1978-79			77	**75**	54	**129**	48
1979-80	**QUE**	**N**	67	42	47	89	12
1980-81			34	15	16	31	18
1981-82			67	37	60	97	34
1982-83			68	28	39	67	30
9 yrs.		**N Totals:**	236	122	162	284	94
		W Totals:	369	283	283	566	169
PLAYOFFS							
1974-75	**QUE**	**W**	12	4	3	7	2
1975-76			5	4	5	9	0
1976-77			17	14	13	27	10

Real Cloutier *continued*

YEAR	TEAM & LEAGUE		GP	G	A	PTS	PIM
1977-78			10	9	7	16	15
1978-79			4	2	2	4	4
1980-81	**QUE**	**N**	3	0	0	0	10
1981-82			16	7	5	12	10
1982-83			4	0	0	0	0
8 yrs.		**N Totals:**	23	7	5	12	20
		W Totals:	48	33	30	63	31

Traded to **Buffalo** with Quebec's first round choice in the 1983 Amateur Draft (Adam Creighton) for Tony McKegney, Andre Savard, Jean Sauve, and Buffalo's third round choice in the 1983 Amateur Draft (Liro Jarvi), June 8, 1983.

Rejean Cloutier

CLOUTIER, REJEAN 6', 180 lbs.
B. Feb. 15, 1960, Windsor, Que. Defense, Shoots L

YEAR	TEAM & LEAGUE		GP	G	A	PTS	PIM
1979-80	**DET**	**N**	3	0	1	1	0

Roland Cloutier

CLOUTIER, ROLAND 5'8", 157 lbs.
B. Oct. 6, 1957, Rouyn-Noranda, Que. Center, Shoots L

YEAR	TEAM & LEAGUE		GP	G	A	PTS	PIM
1977-78	**DET**	**N**	1	0	0	0	0
1978-79			19	6	6	12	2
1979-80	**QUE**	**N**	14	2	3	5	0
3 yrs.		**N Totals:**	34	8	9	17	2

Claimed by **Quebec** from Detroit in Expansion Draft, June 13, 1979.

Wally Clune

CLUNE, WALTER JAMES 5'9", 150 lbs.
B. Feb. 20, 1930, Toronto, Ont. Defense, Shoots R

YEAR	TEAM & LEAGUE		GP	G	A	PTS	PIM
1955-56	**MONT**	**N**	5	0	0	0	6

Gary Coalter

COALTER, GARY MERRITT CHARLES 5'10", 185 lbs.
B. July 8, 1950, Toronto, Ont. Right Wing, Shoots R

YEAR	TEAM & LEAGUE		GP	G	A	PTS	PIM
1973-74	**CALIF**	**N**	4	0	0	0	0
1974-75	**KC**	**N**	30	2	4	6	2
2 yrs.		**N Totals:**	34	2	4	6	2

Sold to **California** by N.Y. Rangers, May 11, 1973. Drafted by **Kansas City** from California in Expansion Draft, June 12, 1974.

Brian Coates

COATES, BRIAN JAMES (Coatesy) 6', 196 lbs.
B. Sept. 22, 1952, Carmen, Man. Left Wing, Shoots L

YEAR	TEAM & LEAGUE		GP	G	A	PTS	PIM
1973-74	**CHI**	**W**	50	10	3	13	14
1974-75			35	12	9	21	26
1975-76	**IND**	**W**	59	11	16	27	24
1976-77			16	1	5	6	4
1977-78	**CIN**	**W**	42	8	10	18	18
5 yrs.		**W Totals:**	202	42	43	85	86
PLAYOFFS							
1973-74	**CHI**	**W**	17	0	3	3	35
1975-76	**IND**	**W**	4	0	0	0	6
2 yrs.		**W Totals:**	21	0	3	3	41

Steve Coates

COATES, STEPHEN JOHN 5'9", 172 lbs.
B. July 2, 1950, Toronto, Ont. Right Wing, Shoots R

YEAR	TEAM & LEAGUE		GP	G	A	PTS	PIM
1976-77	**DET**	**N**	5	1	0	1	24

Traded to **Detroit** by Philadelphia with Terry Murray, Bob Ritchie and Dave Kelly for Rick Lapointe and Mike Korney, Feb. 17, 1977.

Glen Cochrane

COCHRANE, GLEN MACLEOD 6'2", 200 lbs.
B. Jan. 29, 1958, Cranbrook, B.C. Defense, Shoots L

YEAR	TEAM & LEAGUE		GP	G	A	PTS	PIM
1978-79	**PHI**	**N**	1	0	0	0	0
1980-81			31	1	8	9	219
1981-82			63	6	12	18	329
1982-83			77	2	22	24	237

Glen Cochrane *continued*

YEAR	TEAM & LEAGUE		GP	G	A	PTS	PIM
4 yrs.		**N Totals:**	172	9	42	51	785
PLAYOFFS							
1980-81	**PHI**	**N**	6	1	1	2	18
1981-82			2	0	0	0	2
1982-83			3	0	0	0	4
3 yrs.		**N Totals:**	11	1	1	2	24

Paul Coffey

COFFEY, PAUL DOUGLAS (Coff) 6'1", 185 lbs.
B. June 1, 1961, Weston, Ont. Defense, Shoots L

YEAR	TEAM & LEAGUE		GP	G	A	PTS	PIM
1980-81	**EDM**	**N**	74	9	23	32	130
1981-82			80	29	60	89	106
1982-83			80	29	67	96	87
3 yrs.		**N Totals:**	234	67	150	217	323
PLAYOFFS							
1980-81	**EDM**	**N**	9	4	3	7	22
1981-82			5	1	1	2	6
1982-83			16	7	7	14	15
3 yrs.		**N Totals:**	30	12	11	23	43

Hughie Coflin

COFLIN, HUGH ALEXANDER 6', 190 lbs.
B. Dec. 15, 1928, Blaine Lake, Sask. Defense, Shoots L

YEAR	TEAM & LEAGUE		GP	G	A	PTS	PIM
1950-51	**CHI**	**N**	31	0	3	3	33

Traded to **Detroit** by Chicago with $75,000 for George Gee, Jim Peters, Clare Martin, Rags Raglan, Max McNab and Jim McFadden, Aug. 20, 1951.

Hal Colborne

COLBORNE, HAL
Forward

YEAR	TEAM & LEAGUE		GP	G	A	PTS	PIM
1973-74	**EDM**	**W**	2	0	0	0	0

Jim Cole

COLE, JAMES
Forward

YEAR	TEAM & LEAGUE		GP	G	A	PTS	PIM
1976-77	**WINN**	**W**	2	0	1	1	0

Tom Colley

COLLEY, THOMAS 5'9", 162 lbs.
B. Aug. 21, 1953, Toronto, Ont. Center, Shoots L

YEAR	TEAM & LEAGUE		GP	G	A	PTS	PIM
1974-75	**MINN**	**N**	1	0	0	0	2

Norm Collings

COLLINGS, NORMAN (Dodger)
B. Bradford, Ont. Forward

YEAR	TEAM & LEAGUE		GP	G	A	PTS	PIM
1934-35	**MONT**	**N**	1	0	1	1	0

Gary Collins

COLLINS, RANLEIGH GARY 5'11", 190 lbs.
B. Sept. 27, 1935, Toronto, Ont. Center, Shoots L

YEAR	TEAM & LEAGUE		GP	G	A	PTS	PIM
PLAYOFFS							
1958-59	**TOR**	**N**	2	0	0	0	0

Bill Collins

COLLINS, WILLIAM EARL 6', 178 lbs.
B. July 13, 1943, Ottawa, Ont. Right Wing, Shoots R

YEAR	TEAM & LEAGUE		GP	G	A	PTS	PIM
1967-68	**MINN**	**N**	71	9	11	20	41
1968-69			75	9	10	19	24
1969-70			74	29	9	38	48
1970-71	**MONT**	**N**	40	6	2	8	39
	DET	**N**	36	5	16	21	10
	2 team total		76	11	18	29	49
1971-72			71	15	25	40	38
1972-73			78	21	21	42	44
1973-74			54	13	15	28	37
	STL	**N**	12	2	2	4	14
	2 team total		66	15	17	32	51
1974-75			70	22	15	37	34

Bill Collins continued

YEAR	TEAM & LEAGUE		GP	G	A	PTS	PIM
1975-76	NYR	N	50	4	4	8	38
1976-77	PHI	N	9	1	1	2	4
	WASH	N	54	11	14	25	26
	2 team total		63	12	15	27	30
1977-78			74	10	9	19	18
11 yrs.		N Totals:	768	157	154	311	415
PLAYOFFS							
1967-68	MINN	N	10	2	4	6	4
1969-70			6	0	1	1	8
1974-75	STL	N	2	1	0	1	0
3 yrs.		N Totals:	18	3	5	8	12

Drafted by **Minnesota** from N.Y. Rangers in Expansion Draft, June 6, 1967. Traded to **Montreal** by Minnesota for Jude Drouin, June 10, 1970. Traded to **Detroit** by Montreal with Guy Charron and Mickey Redmond for Frank Mahovlich, Jan. 13, 1971. Traded to **St. Louis** by Detroit with Ted Harris and Garnet Bailey for Chris Evans, Bryan Watson and Jean Hamel, Feb. 14, 1974. Traded to **N.Y. Rangers** by St. Louis with goaltender John Davidson for Ted Irvine, Bert Wilson, and Jerry Butler, June 18, 1975. Signed as a free agent by **Philadelphia** from N.Y. Rangers, Oct. 20, 1976. Sold to **Washington** by Philadelphia, Dec. 4, 1976.

Bob Collyard

COLLYARD, ROBERT LEANDER 5'9", 170 lbs.
B. Oct. 16, 1949, Hibbing, Mn. Center, Shoots L

YEAR	TEAM & LEAGUE		GP	G	A	PTS	PIM
1973-74	STL	N	10	1	3	4	4

Drafted by **Washington** from St. Louis in Expansion Draft, June 12, 1974.

Mac Colville

COLVILLE, MATTHEW LAMONT 5'8½", 175 lbs.
B. Jan. 8, 1916, Edmonton, Alta. Right Wing, Shoots R

YEAR	TEAM & LEAGUE		GP	G	A	PTS	PIM
1935-36	NYR	N	18	1	4	5	6
1936-37			46	7	12	19	10
1937-38			48	14	14	28	18
1938-39			48	7	21	28	26
1939-40			47	7	14	21	12
1940-41			47	14	17	31	18
1941-42			46	14	16	30	26
1945-46			39	7	6	13	8
1946-47			14	0	0	0	8
9 yrs.		N Totals:	353	71	104	175	132
PLAYOFFS							
1936-37	NYR	N	9	1	2	3	2
1937-38			3	0	2	2	0
1938-39			7	1	2	3	4
1939-40*			12	3	2	5	6
1940-41			3	1	1	2	2
1941-42			6	3	1	4	0
6 yrs.		N Totals:	40	9	10	19	14

Neil Colville

COLVILLE, NEIL MCNEIL 6', 175 lbs.
B. Aug. 4, 1914, Edmonton, Alta. Center, Shoots R
Hall of Fame, 1967

YEAR	TEAM & LEAGUE		GP	G	A	PTS	PIM
1935-36	NYR	N	1	0	0	0	0
1936-37			45	10	18	28	33
1937-38			45	17	19	36	11
1938-39			47	18	19	37	12
1939-40			48	19	19	38	22
1940-41			48	14	28	42	28
1941-42			48	8	25	33	37
1944-45			4	0	1	1	2
1945-46			49	5	4	9	25
1946-47			60	4	16	20	16
1947-48			55	4	12	16	25
1948-49			14	0	5	5	2
12 yrs.		N Totals:	464	99	166	265	213
PLAYOFFS							
1936-37	NYR	N	9	3	3	6	0
1937-38			3	0	1	1	0
1938-39			7	0	2	2	2
1939-40*			12	2	7	9	19
1940-41			3	1	1	2	0
1941-42			6	0	5	5	6
1947-48			6	1	0	1	6
7 yrs.		N Totals:	46	7	19	26	33

Les Colwill

COLWILL, LESLIE JOHN 5'11", 170 lbs.
B. Jan. 1, 1935, Divide, Sask. Right Wing, Shoots R

YEAR	TEAM & LEAGUE		GP	G	A	PTS	PIM
1958-59	NYR	N	69	7	6	13	16

Rey Comeau

COMEAU, REYNALD XAVIER 5'8", 173 lbs.
B. Oct. 25, 1948, Montreal, Que. Center, Shoots L

YEAR	TEAM & LEAGUE		GP	G	A	PTS	PIM
1971-72	MONT	N	4	0	0	0	0
1972-73	ATL	N	77	21	21	42	19
1973-74			78	11	23	34	16
1974-75			75	14	20	34	40
1975-76			79	17	22	39	42
1976-77			80	15	18	33	16
1977-78			79	10	22	32	20
1978-79	COLO	N	70	8	10	18	16
1979-80			22	2	5	7	6
9 yrs.		N Totals:	564	98	141	239	175
PLAYOFFS							
1973-74	ATL	N	4	2	1	3	6
1976-77			3	0	0	0	2
1977-78			2	0	0	0	0
3 yrs.		N Totals:	9	2	1	3	8

Drafted by **Vancouver** from Montreal in Intra-League Draft, June 8, 1971. Sold to **Montreal** by Vancouver, Sept. 14, 1971. Sold to **Atlanta** by Montreal, June 16, 1972. Signed as free agent by **Colorado** June 23, 1978; Atlanta received cash as compensation.

Brian Conacher

CONACHER, BRIAN KENNEDY 6'3", 197 lbs.
B. Aug. 31, 1941, Toronto, Ont. Left Wing, Shoots L

YEAR	TEAM & LEAGUE		GP	G	A	PTS	PIM
1961-62	TOR	N	1	0	0	0	0
1965-66			2	0	0	0	2
1966-67			66	14	13	27	47
1967-68			64	11	14	25	31
1971-72	DET	N	22	3	1	4	4
1972-73	OTTA	W	69	8	19	27	32
6 yrs.		N Totals:	155	28	28	56	84
		W Totals:	69	8	19	27	32
PLAYOFFS							
1966-67*	TOR	N	12	3	2	5	21
1972-73	OTTA	W	5	1	3	4	4
2 yrs.		N Totals:	12	3	2	5	21
		W Totals:	5	1	3	4	4

Charlie Conacher

CONACHER, CHARLES WILLIAM (The Bomber)
6'1", 195 lbs.
B. Dec. 20, 1910, Toronto, Ont. Right Wing, Shoots R
Won Art Ross Trophy, 1933-34 , 1934-35
Hall of Fame, 1961

YEAR	TEAM & LEAGUE		GP	G	A	PTS	PIM
1929-30	TOR	N	38	20	9	29	48
1930-31			37	**31**	12	43	78
1931-32			44	**34**	14	48	66
1932-33			40	14	19	33	64
1933-34			42	**32**	20	**52**	38
1934-35			47	**36**	21	**57**	24
1935-36			44	**23**	15	38	74
1936-37			15	3	5	8	16
1937-38			19	7	9	16	6
1938-39	DET	N	40	8	15	23	29
1939-40	NYA	N	48	10	18	28	41
1940-41			46	7	16	23	32
12 yrs.		N Totals:	460	225	173	398	516
PLAYOFFS							
1930-31	TOR	N	2	0	1	1	4
1931-32*			7	6	2	8	6
1932-33			9	1	1	2	10
1933-34			5	3	2	5	0
1934-35			7	1	4	5	6
1935-36			9	3	2	5	12
1936-37			2	0	0	0	5
1938-39	DET	N	5	2	5	7	2

Charlie Conacher continued

YEAR	TEAM	LEAGUE	GP	G	A	PTS	PIM
1939-40	**NYA**	**N**	3	1	1	2	8
9 yrs.		**N Totals:**	49	17	18	35	53

Jim Conacher

CONACHER, JAMES 5'10", 155 lbs.
B. May 5, 1921, Motherwell, Scotland Center, Shoots L

YEAR	TEAM	LEAGUE	GP	G	A	PTS	PIM
1945-46	**DET**	**N**	20	1	5	6	6
1946-47			33	16	13	29	2
1947-48			60	17	23	40	2
1948-49			4	1	0	1	2
	CHI	**N**	55	25	23	48	41
	2 team total		59	**26**	23	49	43
1949-50			66	13	20	33	14
1950-51			52	10	27	37	16
1951-52			5	0	1	1	0
	NYR	**N**	16	1	1	2	2
	2 team total		21	1	2	3	2
1952-53			17	1	4	5	2
8 yrs.		**N Totals:**	328	85	117	202	87
PLAYOFFS							
1945-46	**DET**	**N**	5	1	1	2	0
1946-47			5	2	1	3	2
1947-48			9	2	0	2	2
3 yrs.		**N Totals:**	19	5	2	7	4

Claimed on waivers by **N.Y. Rangers** from Chicago, Oct. 26, 1951.

Lionel Conacher

CONACHER, LIONEL PRETORIA 6'1", 195 lbs.
B. May 24, 1901, Toronto, Ont. Defense, Shoots L

YEAR	TEAM	LEAGUE	GP	G	A	PTS	PIM
1925-26	**PITT**	**N**	33	9	4	13	64
1926-27			9	0	0	0	12
	NYA	**N**	30	8	9	17	81
	2 team total		39	8	9	17	93
1927-28			35	11	6	17	82
1928-29			44	5	2	7	132
1929-30			40	4	6	10	3
1930-31	**MON(M)**	**N**	36	4	3	7	57
1931-32			45	7	9	16	60
1932-33			47	7	21	28	61
1933-34	**CHI**	**N**	48	10	13	23	87
1934-35	**MON(M)**	**N**	38	2	6	8	44
1935-36			46	7	7	14	65
1936-37			47	6	19	25	64
12 yrs.		**N Totals:**	498	80	105	185	812
PLAYOFFS							
1925-26	**PITT**	**N**	2	0	0	0	0
1928-29	**NYA**	**N**	2	0	0	0	10
1930-31	**MON(M)**	**N**	2	0	0	0	2
1931-32			4	0	0	0	8
1932-33			2	0	1	1	0
1933-34*	**CHI**	**N**	8	2	0	2	4
1934-35*	**MON(M)**	**N**	7	0	0	0	14
1935-36			3	0	0	0	0
1936-37			5	0	1	1	2
9 yrs.		**N Totals:**	35	2	2	4	40

Pat Conacher

CONACHER, PAT 5'8", 185 lbs.
B. May 1, 1959, Edmonton, Alta. Center, Shoots L

YEAR	TEAM	LEAGUE	GP	G	A	PTS	PIM
1979-80	**NYR**	**N**	17	0	5	5	4
1982-83			5	0	1	1	4
2 yrs.		**N Totals:**	22	0	6	6	8
PLAYOFFS							
1979-80	**NYR**	**N**	3	0	1	1	2
1982-83			1	0	0	0	0
2 yrs.		**N Totals:**	4	0	1	1	2

Pete Conacher

CONACHER, CHARLES WILLIAM, JR. 5'10", 165 lbs.
B. July 29, 1932, Toronto, Ont. Left Wing, Shoots L

YEAR	TEAM	LEAGUE	GP	G	A	PTS	PIM
1951-52	**CHI**	**N**	2	0	1	1	0
1952-53			41	5	6	11	7

Pete Conacher continued

YEAR	TEAM	LEAGUE	GP	G	A	PTS	PIM
1953-54			70	19	9	28	23
1954-55			18	2	4	6	2
	NYR	**N**	52	10	7	17	10
	2 team total		70	12	11	23	12
1955-56			41	11	11	22	10
1957-58	**TOR**	**N**	5	0	1	1	5
6 yrs.		**N Totals:**	229	47	39	86	57
PLAYOFFS							
1952-53	**CHI**	**N**	2	0	0	0	0
1955-56	**NYR**	**N**	5	0	0	0	0
2 yrs.		**N Totals:**	7	0	0	0	0

Traded to **N.Y. Rangers** by Chicago with Bill Gadsby for Rich Lamoureux, Allan Stanley and Nick Mickoski, Nov. 23, 1954. Drafted by **Toronto** from N.Y. Rangers, June 4, 1957.

Roy Conacher

CONACHER, ROY GORDON 6'1", 175 lbs.
B. Oct. 5, 1916, Toronto, Ont. Left Wing, Shoots L
Won Art Ross Trophy, 1948-49

YEAR	TEAM	LEAGUE	GP	G	A	PTS	PIM
1938-39	**BOS**	**N**	47	**26**	11	37	12
1939-40			31	18	12	30	9
1940-41			41	24	14	38	7
1941-42			43	24	13	37	12
1945-46			4	2	1	3	0
1946-47	**DET**	**N**	60	30	24	54	6
1947-48	**CHI**	**N**	52	22	27	49	4
1948-49			60	26	42	**68**	8
1949-50			70	25	31	56	16
1950-51			70	26	24	50	16
1951-52			12	3	1	4	0
11 yrs.		**N Totals:**	490	226	200	426	90
PLAYOFFS							
1938-39*	**BOS**	**N**	12	6	4	10	12
1939-40			6	2	1	3	0
1940-41*			11	1	5	6	0
1941-42			5	2	1	3	0
1945-46			3	0	0	0	0
1946-47	**DET**	**N**	5	4	4	8	2
6 yrs.		**N Totals:**	42	15	15	30	14

Hugh Conn

CONN, HUGH MAITLAND (Red) 170 lbs.
B. Oct. 25, 1908, Hartley, Man. Forward, Shoots L

YEAR	TEAM	LEAGUE	GP	G	A	PTS	PIM
1933-34	**NYA**	**N**	48	4	17	21	12
1934-35			48	5	11	16	10
2 yrs.		**N Totals:**	96	9	28	37	22

Gary Connelly

CONNELLY, GARY NORMAN 6', 186 lbs.
B. Dec. 22, 1950, Rouyn, Que. Right Wing, Shoots R

YEAR	TEAM	LEAGUE	GP	G	A	PTS	PIM
1973-74	**CHI**	**W**	4	0	1	1	2

Wayne Connelly

CONNELLY, WAYNE FRANCIS 5'10", 170 lbs.
B. Dec. 16, 1939, Rouyn, Que. Right Wing, Shoots R

YEAR	TEAM	LEAGUE	GP	G	A	PTS	PIM
1960-61	**MONT**	**N**	3	0	0	0	0
1961-62	**BOS**	**N**	61	8	12	20	34
1962-63			18	2	6	8	2
1963-64			26	2	3	5	12
1966-67			64	13	17	30	12
1967-68	**MINN**	**N**	74	35	21	56	40
1968-69			55	14	16	30	11
	DET	**N**	19	4	9	13	0
	2 team total		74	18	25	43	11
1969-70			76	23	36	59	10
1970-71			51	8	13	21	12
	STL	**N**	28	5	16	21	9
	2 team total		79	13	29	42	21
1971-72			15	5	5	10	2
	VAN	**N**	53	14	20	34	12
	2 team total		68	19	25	44	14
1972-73	**MINN**	**W**	78	40	30	70	16
1973-74			78	42	53	95	16
1974-75			76	38	33	71	16
1975-76			59	24	23	47	19
	CLEVE	**W**	12	5	2	7	4
	2 team total		71	29	25	54	23

Wayne Connelly continued

YEAR	TEAM & LEAGUE		GP	G	A	PTS	PIM
1976-77	**CALG**	**W**	25	5	6	11	4
	EDM	**W**	38	13	15	28	18
	2 team total		63	18	21	39	22
15 yrs.		**N Totals:**	543	133	174	307	156
		W Totals:	366	167	162	329	93
PLAYOFFS							
1967-68	**MINN**	**N**	14	8	3	11	2
1969-70	**DET**	**N**	4	1	3	4	2
1970-71	**STL**	**N**	6	2	1	3	0
1972-73	**MINN**	**W**	5	1	3	4	0
1973-74			11	6	7	13	4
1974-75			12	8	4	12	10
1975-76	**CLEVE**	**W**	3	1	0	1	2
1976-77	**EDM**	**W**	5	0	1	1	0
8 yrs.		**N Totals:**	24	11	7	18	4
		W Totals:	36	16	15	31	16

Sold to **Boston** by Montreal, June 10, 1961. Drafted by **Minnesota** from Boston in Expansion Draft, June 6, 1967. Traded to **Detroit** with Garry Unger for Red Berenson and Tim Ecclestone, Feb. 6, 1971. Traded to **N.Y. Rangers** by St. Louis with Gene Carr and Jim Lorentz for Andre Dupont, Jack Egers and Mike Murphy, Nov. 15, 1971. Traded to **Vancouver** by N.Y. Rangers with Dave Balon and Ron Stewart for Gary Doak and Jim Wiste, Nov. 16, 1971.

Bert Connolly

CONNOLLY, ALBERT PATRICK 5'11½", 174 lbs.
B. Apr. 22, 1909, Montreal, Que. Left Wing, Shoots L

YEAR	TEAM & LEAGUE		GP	G	A	PTS	PIM
1934-35	**NYR**	**N**	47	10	11	21	23
1935-36			25	2	2	4	10
1937-38	**CHI**	**N**	15	1	2	3	4
3 yrs.		**N Totals:**	87	13	15	28	37
PLAYOFFS							
1934-35	**NYR**	**N**	4	1	0	1	0
1937-38*	**CHI**	**N**	10	0	0	0	0
2 yrs.		**N Totals:**	14	1	0	1	0

Cam Connor

CONNOR, CAMERON DUNCAN 6'2", 200 lbs.
B. Aug. 10, 1954, Winnipeg, Man. Right Wing, Shoots L

YEAR	TEAM & LEAGUE		GP	G	A	PTS	PIM
1974-75	**PHOE**	**W**	57	9	19	28	168
1975-76			73	18	21	39	295
1976-77	**HOUS**	**W**	76	35	32	67	224
1977-78			68	21	16	37	217
1978-79	**MONT**	**N**	23	1	3	4	39
1979-80	**EDM**	**N**	38	7	13	20	136
	NYR	**N**	12	0	3	3	37
	2 team total		50	7	16	23	173
1980-81			15	1	3	4	44
1982-83			1	0	0	0	0
8 yrs.		**N Totals:**	89	9	22	31	256
		W Totals:	274	83	88	171	904
PLAYOFFS							
1974-75	**PHOE**	**W**	5	0	0	0	2
1975-76			5	1	0	1	21
1976-77	**HOUS**	**W**	11	3	4	7	47
1977-78			2	1	0	1	22
1978-79*	**MONT**	**N**	8	1	0	1	0
1979-80	**NYR**	**N**	2	0	0	0	2
1981-82			10	4	0	4	16
7 yrs.		**N Totals:**	20	5	0	5	18
		W Totals:	23	5	4	9	92

Claimed by **Edmonton** from Montreal in Expansion Draft, June 13, 1979. Traded to **N.Y. Rangers** by Edmonton with Edmonton's third choice in 1981 Entry Draft (Peter Sundstrum) for Don Murdoch, Mar. II, 1980.

Harry Connor

CONNOR, HAROLD
B. Ottawa, Ont. Forward

YEAR	TEAM & LEAGUE		GP	G	A	PTS	PIM
1927-28	**BOS**	**N**	42	9	1	10	26
1928-29	**NYA**	**N**	43	6	2	8	83
1929-30	**OTTA**	**N**	25	1	2	3	22
	BOS	**N**	13	0	0	0	4
	2 team total		38	1	2	3	26
1930-31	**OTTA**	**N**	11	0	0	0	4

Harry Connor continued

YEAR	TEAM & LEAGUE		GP	G	A	PTS	PIM
4 yrs.		**N Totals:**	134	16	5	21	139
PLAYOFFS							
1927-28	**BOS**	**N**	2	0	0	0	0
1928-29	**NYA**	**N**	2	0	0	0	2
1929-30	**BOS**	**N**	6	0	0	0	0
3 yrs.		**N Totals:**	10	0	0	0	2

Bobby Connors

CONNORS, ROBERT
Defense

YEAR	TEAM & LEAGUE		GP	G	A	PTS	PIM
1926-27	**NYA**	**N**	6	1	0	1	0
1928-29	**DET**	**N**	41	13	3	16	68
1929-30			31	3	7	10	42
3 yrs.		**N Totals:**	78	17	10	27	110
PLAYOFFS							
1928-29	**DET**	**N**	2	0	0	0	10

Mike Conroy

CONROY, MICHAEL 6', 180 lbs.
B. Aug. 28, 1951, North Bay, Ont. Left Wing, Shoots L

YEAR	TEAM & LEAGUE		GP	G	A	PTS	PIM
1975-76	**CLEVE**	**W**	4	0	1	1	0

Charlie Constantin

CONSTANTIN, CHARLES 6'1", 192 lbs.
B. Apr. 17, 1954, Montreal, Que. Left Wing, Shoots L

YEAR	TEAM & LEAGUE		GP	G	A	PTS	PIM
1974-75	**QUE**	**W**	20	2	4	6	9
1975-76			41	8	7	15	77
1976-77			77	14	19	33	93
1977-78			0	0	0	0	0
	IND	**W**	54	4	5	9	50
	2 team total		54	4	5	9	50
4 yrs.		**W Totals:**	192	28	35	63	229
PLAYOFFS							
1975-76	**QUE**	**W**	5	0	1	1	4
1976-77			15	0	1	1	15
2 yrs.		**W Totals:**	20	0	2	2	19

Joe Contini

CONTINI, JOSEPH MARIO 5'10", 178 lbs.
B. Jan. 29, 1957, Galt, Ont. Center, Shoots L

YEAR	TEAM & LEAGUE		GP	G	A	PTS	PIM
1977-78	**COLO**	**N**	37	12	9	21	28
1978-79			30	5	12	17	6
1980-81	**MINN**	**N**	1	0	0	0	0
3 yrs.		**N Totals:**	68	17	21	38	34
PLAYOFFS							
1977-78	**COLO**	**N**	2	0	0	0	0

Claimed by **Colorado** as fill in Expansion Draft, June 13, 1979. Signed as free agent by **Minnesota** Feb. 1, 1980.

Eddie Convey

CONVEY, EDWARD
B. Toronto, Ont. Forward

YEAR	TEAM & LEAGUE		GP	G	A	PTS	PIM
1930-31	**NYA**	**N**	2	0	0	0	0
1931-32			21	1	0	1	21
1932-33			13	0	1	1	12
3 yrs.		**N Totals:**	36	1	1	2	33

Bill Cook

COOK, WILLIAM OSSER 5'10", 170 lbs.
B. Oct. 9, 1896, Brantford, Ont. Right Wing, Shoots R
Won Art Ross Trophy, 1926-27 , 1932-33
Hall of Fame, 1952

YEAR	TEAM & LEAGUE		GP	G	A	PTS	PIM
1926-27	**NYR**	**N**	44	**33**	4	**37**	58
1927-28			43	18	6	24	42
1928-29			43	15	8	23	41
1929-30			44	29	30	59	56
1930-31			44	30	12	42	39

Bill Cook continued

YEAR	TEAM & LEAGUE		GP	G	A	PTS	PIM
1931-32			48	34	14	48	33
1932-33			48	**28**	22	**50**	51
1933-34			48	13	13	26	21
1934-35			48	21	15	36	23
1935-36			21	1	4	5	16
1936-37			21	1	4	5	6
11 yrs.		**N Totals:**	452	223	132	355	386
PLAYOFFS							
1926-27	**NYR**	**N**	2	1	0	1	10
1927-28*			9	2	3	5	24
1928-29			6	0	0	0	6
1929-30			4	0	1	1	9
1930-31			4	3	0	3	2
1931-32			7	3	4	7	2
1932-33*			8	3	2	5	4
1933-34			2	0	0	0	2
1934-35			4	1	2	3	7
9 yrs.		**N Totals:**	46	13	12	25	66

Bob Cook

COOK, ROBERT ARTHUR 6', 190 lbs.
B. Jan. 6, 1946, Sudbury, Ont. Right Wing, Shoots R

YEAR	TEAM & LEAGUE		GP	G	A	PTS	PIM
1970-71	**VAN**	**N**	2	0	0	0	0
1972-73	**DET**	**N**	13	3	1	4	4
	NYI	**N**	33	8	6	14	14
	2 team total		46	11	7	18	18
1973-74			22	2	1	3	4
1974-75	**MINN**	**N**	2	0	1	1	0
4 yrs.		**N Totals:**	72	13	9	22	22

Sold to **Detroit** by Vancouver, Nov. 21, 1971. Traded to **N.Y. Islanders** by Detroit with Ralph Stewart for Ken Murray and Brian Lavender, Jan. 17, 1973. Sold to **Minnesota** by N.Y. Islanders, Jan. 5, 1975.

Bud Cook

COOK, ALEXANDER LEONE LALLY 5'9½", 160 lbs.
B. Nov. 20, 1907, Kingston, Ont. Center, Shoots L

YEAR	TEAM & LEAGUE		GP	G	A	PTS	PIM
1931-32	**BOS**	**N**	28	4	4	8	14
1933-34	**OTTA**	**N**	19	1	0	1	8
1934-35	**STL**	**N**	4	0	0	0	0
3 yrs.		**N Totals:**	51	5	4	9	22

Bun Cook

COOK, FREDERICK JOSEPH 5'11", 180 lbs.
B. Sept. 18, 1903, Kingston, Ont. Left Wing, Shoots L

YEAR	TEAM & LEAGUE		GP	G	A	PTS	PIM
1926-27	**NYR**	**N**	44	14	9	23	42
1927-28			44	14	14	28	28
1928-29			43	13	5	18	70
1929-30			43	24	18	42	55
1930-31			44	18	17	35	72
1931-32			45	14	20	34	43
1932-33			48	22	15	37	35
1933-34			48	18	15	33	36
1934-35			48	13	21	34	26
1935-36			26	4	5	9	12
1936-37	**BOS**	**N**	40	4	5	9	8
11 yrs.		**N Totals:**	473	158	144	302	427
PLAYOFFS							
1926-27	**NYR**	**N**	2	0	0	0	6
1927-28*			9	2	1	3	10
1928-29			6	1	0	1	8
1929-30			4	2	0	2	4
1930-31			4	0	0	0	11
1931-32			7	6	2	8	12
1932-33*			8	2	0	2	4
1933-34			2	0	0	0	2
1934-35			4	2	0	2	0
9 yrs.		**N Totals:**	46	15	3	18	57

Lloyd Cook

COOK, LLOYD
B. Unknown Defense, Shoots L

YEAR	TEAM & LEAGUE		GP	G	A	PTS	PIM
1924-25	**BOS**	**N**	4	1	0	1	0

Tom Cook

COOK, THOMAS JOHN 5'7", 140 lbs.
B. May 7, 1907, Fort William, Ont. Center, Shoots L

YEAR	TEAM & LEAGUE		GP	G	A	PTS	PIM
1929-30	**CHI**	**N**	41	14	16	30	16
1930-31			44	15	14	29	34
1931-32			48	12	13	25	36
1932-33			47	12	14	26	30
1934-35			47	13	18	31	33
1935-36			47	4	8	12	20
1936-37			17	0	2	2	0
1937-38	**MON(M)**	**N**	20	2	4	6	0
8 yrs.		**N Totals:**	311	72	89	161	169
PLAYOFFS							
1929-30	**CHI**	**N**	2	0	1	1	4
1930-31			9	1	3	4	9
1931-32			2	0	0	0	2
1933-34*			8	1	0	1	0
1934-35			2	0	0	0	2
1935-36			1	0	0	0	0
6 yrs.		**N Totals:**	24	2	4	6	17

Carson Cooper

COOPER, CARSON E.
B. Cornwall, Ont. Forward

YEAR	TEAM & LEAGUE		GP	G	A	PTS	PIM
1924-25	**BOS**	**N**	12	5	3	8	4
1925-26			36	28	3	31	10
1926-27			10	0	0	0	0
	MONT	**N**	14	9	3	12	16
	2 team total		24	9	3	12	16
1927-28	**DET**	**N**	43	15	2	17	32
1928-29			44	18	9	27	14
1929-30			44	18	18	36	14
1930-31			43	14	14	28	10
1931-32			48	3	5	8	11
8 yrs.		**N Totals:**	294	110	57	167	111
PLAYOFFS							
1926-27	**MONT**	**N**	3	0	0	0	0
1928-29	**DET**	**N**	2	0	0	0	2
1931-32			2	0	0	0	0
3 yrs.		**N Totals:**	7	0	0	0	2

Ed Cooper

COOPER, EDWARD WILLIAM 5'10", 188 lbs.
B. Aug. 28, 1960, Loon Lake, Sask. Left Wing, Shoots L

YEAR	TEAM & LEAGUE		GP	G	A	PTS	PIM
1980-81	**COLO**	**N**	47	7	7	14	46
1981-82			2	1	0	1	0
2 yrs.		**N Totals:**	49	8	7	15	46

Traded to **Edmonton** by Colorado for Stan Weir, Mar. 9, 1982.

Hal Cooper

COOPER, HAROLD WALLACE 5'5", 155 lbs.
B. Aug. 29, 1915, New Liskeard, Ont. Right Wing, Shoots R

YEAR	TEAM & LEAGUE		GP	G	A	PTS	PIM
1944-45	**NYR**	**N**	8	0	0	0	2

Joe Cooper

COOPER, JOSEPH 6'1½", 200 lbs.
B. Dec. 14, 1914, Winnipeg, Man. Defense, Shoots R

YEAR	TEAM & LEAGUE		GP	G	A	PTS	PIM
1935-36	**NYR**	**N**	1	0	0	0	0
1936-37			48	0	3	3	42
1937-38			46	3	2	5	56
1938-39	**CHI**	**N**	17	3	3	6	10
1939-40			44	4	7	11	59
1940-41			45	5	5	10	66
1941-42			47	6	14	20	58
1943-44			13	1	0	1	17
1944-45			50	4	17	21	50
1945-46			50	2	7	9	46
1946-47	**NYR**	**N**	59	2	8	10	38
11 yrs.		**N Totals:**	420	30	66	96	442
PLAYOFFS							
1936-37	**NYR**	**N**	9	1	1	2	12

Joe Cooper continued

YEAR	TEAM & LEAGUE	GP	G	A	PTS	PIM
1939-40	**CHI** N	2	0	0	0	6
1940-41		5	1	0	1	8
1941-42		3	0	2	2	2
1943-44		9	1	1	2	18
1945-46		4	0	1	1	14
6 yrs.	N Totals:	32	3	5	8	60

Bob Copp

COPP, ROBERT ALONZO 5'11½", 180 lbs.
B. Nov. 15, 1918, Port Elgin, N.B. Defense, Shoots L

YEAR	TEAM & LEAGUE	GP	G	A	PTS	PIM
1942-43	**TOR** N	38	3	9	12	24
1950-51		2	0	0	0	2
2 yrs.	N Totals:	40	3	9	12	26

Bert Corbeau

CORBEAU, ALBERT
Defense

YEAR	TEAM & LEAGUE	GP	G	A	PTS	PIM
1917-18	**MONT** N	20	8	0	8	22
1918-19		16	2	1	3	51
1919-20		23	11	5	16	59
1920-21		24	12	1	13	**86**
1921-22		22	4	7	11	26
1922-23	**HAMIL** N	21	10	3	13	36
1923-24	**TOR** N	24	8	6	14	**55**
1924-25		30	4	3	7	67
1925-26		36	5	5	10	**121**
1926-27		41	1	2	3	88
10 yrs.	N Totals:	257	65	33	98	611

PLAYOFFS

YEAR	TEAM & LEAGUE	GP	G	A	PTS	PIM
1917-18	**MONT** N	2	1	0	1	5
1918-19		10	1	0	1	5
1924-25	**TOR** N	2	0	0	0	6
3 yrs.	N Totals:	14	2	0	2	16

Michael Corbett

CORBETT, MICHAEL CHARLES 6'2", 200 lbs.
B. Oct. 4, 1942, Toronto, Ont. Right Wing, Shoots L

PLAYOFFS

YEAR	TEAM & LEAGUE	GP	G	A	PTS	PIM
1967-68	**LA** N	2	0	1	1	2

Norm Corcoran

CORCORAN, NORMAN 6', 165 lbs.
B. Aug. 15, 1931, Toronto, Ont. Center, Shoots R

YEAR	TEAM & LEAGUE	GP	G	A	PTS	PIM
1949-50	**BOS** N	1	0	0	0	0
1952-53		1	0	0	0	0
1954-55		2	0	0	0	2
1955-56	**DET** N	2	0	0	0	0
	CHI N	23	1	3	4	19
	2 team total	25	1	3	4	19
4 yrs.	N Totals:	29	1	3	4	21

PLAYOFFS

YEAR	TEAM & LEAGUE	GP	G	A	PTS	PIM
1954-55	**BOS** N	4	0	0	0	6

Traded to **Detroit** by Boston with Ed Sandford, Real Chevrefils, Gilles Boisvert and Warren Godfrey for Marcel Bonin, Terry Sawchuk, Vic Stasiuk and Lorne Davis, June, 1955. Claimed on waivers by **Chicago** from Detroit, Jan. 17, 1956.

Michel Cormier

CORMIER, MICHEL 5'9", 170 lbs.
B. Dec. 22, 1945, Trois Rivieres, Que. Left Wing, Shoots L

YEAR	TEAM & LEAGUE	GP	G	A	PTS	PIM
1974-75	**PHOE** W	78	36	38	74	26
1975-76		46	21	15	36	4
1976-77		58	13	16	29	22
3 yrs.	W Totals:	182	70	69	139	52

PLAYOFFS

YEAR	TEAM & LEAGUE	GP	G	A	PTS	PIM
1974-75	**PHOE** W	5	1	0	1	2

Roger Cormier

CORMIER, ROGER
B. Unknown Forward

YEAR	TEAM & LEAGUE	GP	G	A	PTS	PIM
1925-26	**MONT** N	1	0	0	0	0

Charlie Corrigan

CORRIGAN, CHARLES HUBERT PATRICK 6'1½", 192 lbs.
B. Moosomin, Sask. Right Wing, Shoots R

YEAR	TEAM & LEAGUE	GP	G	A	PTS	PIM
1937-38	**TOR** N	3	0	0	0	0
1940-41	**NYA** N	16	2	2	4	2
2 yrs.	N Totals:	19	2	2	4	2

Mike Corrigan

CORRIGAN, MICHAEL DOUGLAS 5'10", 175 lbs.
B. Jan. 11, 1946, Ottawa, Ont. Left Wing, Shoots L

YEAR	TEAM & LEAGUE	GP	G	A	PTS	PIM
1967-68	**LA** N	5	0	0	0	2
1969-70		36	6	4	10	30
1970-71	**VAN** N	76	21	28	49	103
1971-72		19	3	4	7	27
	LA N	56	12	22	34	93
	2 team total	75	15	26	41	120
1972-73		37	37	30	67	146
1973-74		75	16	26	42	119
1974-75		80	13	21	34	61
1975-76		71	22	21	43	71
1976-77	**PITT** N	73	14	27	41	36
1977-78		25	8	12	20	10
10 yrs.	N Totals:	553	152	195	347	698

PLAYOFFS

YEAR	TEAM & LEAGUE	GP	G	A	PTS	PIM
1973-74	**LA** N	3	0	1	1	4
1974-75		3	0	0	0	4
1975-76		9	2	2	4	12
1976-77	**PITT** N	2	0	0	0	0
4 yrs.	N Totals:	17	2	3	5	20

Drafted by **Los Angeles** from Toronto in Expansion Draft, June 6, 1967. Drafted by **Vancouver** from Los Angeles in Expansion Draft, June 10, 1970. Claimed on waivers by **Los Angeles** from Vancouver, Nov. 22, 1971. Traded to **Pittsburgh** by Los Angeles for Pittsburgh's fifth round choice (Julian Baretta) in 1977 Amateur Draft, Oct. 18, 1976.

Fred Corriveau

CORRIVEAU, FRED ANDRE 5'8", 135 lbs.
B. May 15, 1928, Grand Mere, Que. Right Wing, Shoots L

YEAR	TEAM & LEAGUE	GP	G	A	PTS	PIM
1953-54	**MONT** N	3	0	1	1	0

Keith Cory

CORY, KEITH ROSS 6'2", 195 lbs.
B. Feb. 4, 1957, Calgary, Alta. Defense, Shoots L

YEAR	TEAM & LEAGUE	GP	G	A	PTS	PIM
1979-80	**WINN** N	46	2	9	11	32
1980-81		5	0	1	1	9
2 yrs.	N Totals:	51	2	10	12	41

Jacques Cossete

COSSETE, JACQUES 5'9", 185 lbs.
B. June 20, 1954, Rouyn-Noranda, Que. Right Wing, Shoots R

YEAR	TEAM & LEAGUE	GP	G	A	PTS	PIM
1975-76	**PITT** N	7	0	2	2	9
1977-78		19	1	2	3	4
1978-79		38	7	2	9	16
3 yrs.	N Totals:	64	8	6	14	29

PLAYOFFS

YEAR	TEAM & LEAGUE	GP	G	A	PTS	PIM
1978-79	**PITT** N	3	0	1	1	4

Les Costello

COSTELLO, LESTER JOHN THOMAS 5'8", 158 lbs.
B. Feb. 16, 1928, South Porcupine, Ont. Left Wing, Shoots L

YEAR	TEAM & LEAGUE	GP	G	A	PTS	PIM
1948-49	**TOR** N	15	2	3	5	11

PLAYOFFS

YEAR	TEAM & LEAGUE	GP	G	A	PTS	PIM
1947-48*	**TOR** N	5	2	2	4	2

Les Costello continued

YEAR	TEAM & LEAGUE		GP	G	A	PTS	PIM
1949-50			1	0	0	0	0
2 yrs.		N Totals:	6	2	2	4	2

Murray Costello

COSTELLO, MURRAY 6'3", 190 lbs.
B. Feb. 24, 1934, South Porcupine, Ont. Center, Shoots R

YEAR	TEAM & LEAGUE		GP	G	A	PTS	PIM
1953-54	CHI	N	40	3	0	5	6
1954-55	BOS	N	54	4	11	15	25
1955-56			41	6	6	12	19
	DET	N	24	0	0	0	4
	2 team total		65	6	6	12	23
1956-57			3	0	0	0	0
4 yrs.		N Totals:	162	13	17	32	54
PLAYOFFS							
1954-55	BOS	N	1	0	0	0	2
1955-56	DET	N	4	0	0	0	0
2 yrs.		N Totals:	5	0	0	0	2

Traded to **Boston** by Chicago for Frank Martin, Oct. 4, 1954. Traded to **Detroit** by Boston with Lorne Ferguson for Real Chevrefils and Jerry Toppazzini, Jan. 17, 1956.

Charlie Cotch

COTCH, CHARLES
B. Unknown Forward

YEAR	TEAM & LEAGUE		GP	G	A	PTS	PIM
1924-25	HAMIL	N	11	1	0	1	0

Alain Cote

COTE, ALAIN 5'10", 203 lbs.
B. May 3, 1957, Matane, Que. Left Wing, Shoots L

YEAR	TEAM & LEAGUE		GP	G	A	PTS	PIM
1977-78	QUE	W	27	3	5	8	8
1978-79			79	14	13	27	23
1979-80	QUE	N	41	5	11	16	13
1980-81			51	8	18	26	64
1981-82			79	15	16	31	82
1982-83			79	12	28	40	45
6 yrs.		N Totals:	250	40	73	113	204
		W Totals:	106	17	18	35	31
PLAYOFFS							
1977-78	QUE	W	11	1	2	3	0
1978-79			4	0	0	0	2
1980-81	QUE	N	4	0	0	0	6
1981-82			16	1	2	3	8
1982-83			4	0	3	3	0
5 yrs.		N Totals:	24	1	5	6	14
		W Totals:	15	1	2	3	2

Reclaimed by **Montreal** from Quebec prior to Expansion Draft, June 9, 1979. Claimed by **Quebec** from Montreal in Expansion Draft, June 13, 1979.

Ray Cote

COTE, RAYMOND 5'11", 170 lbs.
B. May 31, 1961, Pincher Creek, Alta. Center, Shoots R

YEAR	TEAM & LEAGUE		GP	G	A	PTS	PIM
PLAYOFFS							
1982-83	EDM	N	14	3	2	5	4

Roger Cote

COTE, REGENT 5'9", 184 lbs.
B. Dec. 22, 1939, Belleterre, Que. Defense, Shoots L

YEAR	TEAM & LEAGUE		GP	G	A	PTS	PIM
1972-73	ALTA	W	61	3	5	8	46
1973-74	EDM	W	59	0	3	3	34
1974-75	IND	W	36	0	6	6	24
3 yrs.		W Totals:	156	3	14	17	104
PLAYOFFS							
1973-74	EDM	W	2	0	0	0	0

Baldy Cotton

COTTON, HAROLD 5'10", 155 lbs.
B. Nov. 5, 1902, Nanticoke, Ont. Left Wing

YEAR	TEAM & LEAGUE		GP	G	A	PTS	PIM
1925-26	PITT	N	33	7	1	8	22
1926-27			37	5	0	5	17
1927-28			42	9	3	12	40
1928-29			32	3	2	5	38
	TOR	N	11	1	2	3	8
	2 team total		43	4	4	8	46
1929-30			41	21	17	38	47
1930-31			43	12	17	29	45
1931-32			48	5	13	18	41
1932-33			48	10	11	21	29
1933-34			47	8	14	22	46
1934-35			47	11	14	25	36
1935-36	NYA	N	45	7	9	16	23
1936-37			29	2	0	2	23
12 yrs.		N Totals:	503	101	103	204	415
PLAYOFFS							
1925-26	PITT	N	1	1	0	1	0
1927-28			2	1	1	2	2
1928-29	TOR	N	4	0	0	0	2
1930-31			2	0	0	0	2
1931-32*			7	2	2	4	8
1932-33			9	0	3	3	6
1933-34			5	0	2	2	0
1934-35			7	0	0	0	17
1935-36	NYA	N	5	0	1	1	9
9 yrs.		N Totals:	42	4	9	13	46

Jack Coughlin

COUGHLIN, JAMES
B. Unknown Forward

YEAR	TEAM & LEAGUE		GP	G	A	PTS	PIM
1917-18	TOR	N	6	2	0	2	0
1919-20	QUE	N	8	0	0	0	0
	MONT	N	3	0	0	0	0
	2 team total		11	0	0	0	0
1920-21	HAMIL	N	2	0	0	0	0
3 yrs.		N Totals:	19	2	0	2	0

Tim Coulis

COULIS, TIM 6', 197 lbs.
B. Feb. 24, 1958, Kenora, Ont. Left Wing, Shoots L

YEAR	TEAM & LEAGUE		GP	G	A	PTS	PIM
1979-80	WASH	N	19	1	2	3	27

Traded to **Toronto** by Washington with Robert Picard and Washington's second-round choice in the 1980 Entry Draft (Bob McGill) for Mike Palmateer and Toronto's third-round choice in 1980 Entry Draft (Torrie Robertson), June 11, 1980.

D'Arcy Coulson

COULSON, D'ARCY
B. Unknown Forward

YEAR	TEAM & LEAGUE		GP	G	A	PTS	PIM
1930-31	PHI	N	28	0	0	0	103

Art Coulter

COULTER, ARTHUR EDMUND 5'11", 185 lbs.
B. May 31, 1909, Winnipeg, Man. Defense, Shoots R
Hall of Fame, 1974

YEAR	TEAM & LEAGUE		GP	G	A	PTS	PIM
1931-32	CHI	N	13	0	1	1	23
1932-33			46	3	2	5	53
1933-34			46	5	2	7	59
1934-35			48	4	8	12	68
1935-36			25	0	2	2	18
	NYR	N	23	1	5	6	26
	2 team total		48	1	7	8	44
1936-37			47	1	5	6	27
1937-38			43	5	10	15	90
1938-39			44	4	8	12	58
1939-40			48	1	9	10	68
1940-41			35	5	14	19	42
1941-42			47	1	16	17	31
11 yrs.		N Totals:	465	30	82	112	563
PLAYOFFS							
1931-32	CHI	N	2	1	0	1	0

Art Coulter continued

YEAR	TEAM & LEAGUE		GP	G	A	PTS	PIM
1933-34*			8	1	0	1	10
1934-35			2	0	0	0	5
1936-37	**NYR**	**N**	9	0	3	3	15
1938-39			7	1	1	2	6
1939-40*			12	1	0	1	21
1940-41			3	0	0	0	0
1941-42			6	0	1	1	4
8 yrs.		**N Totals:**	49	4	5	9	61

Tommy Coulter

COULTER, THOMAS

B. Unknown — Forward

YEAR	TEAM & LEAGUE		GP	G	A	PTS	PIM
1933-34	**CHI**	**N**	2	0	0	0	0

Norm Cournoyer

COURNOYER, NORMAND — 5'10", 170 lbs.

B. Mar. 17, 1951, Drummondville, Que. — Center, Shoots L

YEAR	TEAM & LEAGUE		GP	G	A	PTS	PIM
1973-74	**CLEVE**	**W**	13	3	5	8	6
1976-77	**SD**	**W**	19	1	2	3	8
2 yrs.		**W Totals:**	32	4	7	11	14

Yvan Cournoyer

COURNOYER, YVAN SERGE (The Roadrunner) — 5'7", 178 lbs.

B. Nov. 22, 1943, Drummondville, Que. — Right Wing, Shoots L

Won Conn Smythe Trophy, 1972-73

Hall of Fame, 1982

YEAR	TEAM & LEAGUE		GP	G	A	PTS	PIM
1963-64	**MONT**	**N**	5	4	0	4	0
1964-65			55	7	10	17	10
1965-66			65	18	11	29	8
1966-67			69	25	15	40	14
1967-68			64	28	32	60	23
1968-69			76	43	44	87	31
1969-70			72	27	36	63	23
1970-71			65	37	36	73	21
1971-72			73	47	36	83	15
1972-73			67	40	39	79	18
1973-74			67	40	33	73	18
1974-75			76	29	45	74	32
1975-76			71	32	36	68	20
1976-77			60	25	28	53	8
1977-78			68	24	29	53	12
1978-79			15	2	5	7	2
16 yrs.		**N Totals:**	968	428	435	863	255

PLAYOFFS

YEAR	TEAM & LEAGUE		GP	G	A	PTS	PIM
1964-65*	**MONT**	**N**	12	3	1	4	0
1965-66*			10	2	3	5	2
1966-67			10	2	3	5	6
1967-68*			13	6	8	14	4
1968-69*			14	4	7	11	5
1970-71*			20	10	12	22	6
1971-72			6	2	1	3	2
1972-73*			17	15	10	25	2
1973-74			6	5	2	7	2
1974-75			11	5	6	11	4
1975-76*			13	3	6	9	4
1977-78*			15	7	4	11	10
12 yrs.		**N Totals:**	147	64	63	127	47

Billy Couture

COUTURE, WILFRED (COUTU)

B. Sault Ste. Marie, Ont. — Defense

YEAR	TEAM & LEAGUE		GP	G	A	PTS	PIM
1917-18	**MONT**	**N**	19	2	0	2	30
1918-19			15	1	1	2	18
1919-20			17	4	0	4	30
1920-21	**HAMIL**	**N**	24	8	4	12	74
1921-22	**MONT**	**N**	23	4	3	7	4
1922-23			24	5	2	7	37
1923-24			16	3	1	4	8
1924-25			28	3	2	5	49
1925-26			33	2	4	6	95
1926-27	**BOS**	**N**	41	1	1	2	25
10 yrs.		**N Totals:**	240	33	18	51	370

Billy Couture continued

PLAYOFFS

YEAR	TEAM & LEAGUE		GP	G	A	PTS	PIM
1917-18	**MONT**	**N**	2	0	0	0	0
1918-19			10	0	0	0	6
1922-23			1	0	0	0	2
1923-24*			6	0	0	0	2
1924-25			6	1	0	1	14
1926-27	**BOS**	**N**	7	1	0	1	4
6 yrs.		**N Totals:**	32	2	0	2	28

Doc Couture

COUTURE, GERALD JOSEPH WILFRED ARTHUR — 6'2", 185 lbs.

B. Aug. 6, 1925, Saskatoon, Sask. — Center, Shoots R

YEAR	TEAM & LEAGUE		GP	G	A	PTS	PIM
1945-46	**DET**	**N**	43	3	7	10	18
1946-47			30	5	10	15	0
1947-48			19	3	6	9	2
1948-49			51	19	10	29	6
1949-50			70	24	7	31	21
1950-51			53	7	6	13	2
1951-52	**MONT**	**N**	10	0	1	1	4
1952-53	**CHI**	**N**	70	19	18	37	22
1953-54			40	6	5	11	14
9 yrs.		**N Totals:**	386	86	70	156	89

PLAYOFFS

YEAR	TEAM & LEAGUE		GP	G	A	PTS	PIM
1944-45	**DET**	**N**	2	0	0	0	0
1945-46			5	0	2	2	0
1946-47			1	0	0	0	0
1948-49			10	2	0	2	2
1949-50*			14	5	4	9	2
1950-51			6	1	1	2	0
1952-53	**CHI**	**N**	7	1	0	1	0
7 yrs.		**N Totals:**	45	9	7	16	4

Traded to **Montreal** by Detroit for Bert Hirschfield, June 19, 1951. Sold to **Chicago** by Montreal, Sept. 22, 1952.

Rosie Couture

COUTURE, ROSARIO (Lolo) — 5'11", 164 lbs.

B. July 24, 1905, Boniface, Man. — Right Wing, Shoots R

YEAR	TEAM & LEAGUE		GP	G	A	PTS	PIM
1928-29	**CHI**	**N**	43	1	3	4	22
1929-30			43	8	8	16	63
1930-31			44	8	11	19	30
1931-32			48	9	9	18	8
1932-33			46	10	7	17	26
1933-34			48	5	8	13	21
1934-35			27	7	9	16	14
1935-36	**MONT**	**N**	10	0	1	1	0
8 yrs.		**N Totals:**	309	48	56	104	184

PLAYOFFS

YEAR	TEAM & LEAGUE		GP	G	A	PTS	PIM
1929-30	**CHI**	**N**	2	0	0	0	2
1930-31			9	0	3	3	2
1931-32			2	0	0	0	2
1933-34*			8	1	2	3	4
1934-35			2	0	0	0	5
5 yrs.		**N Totals:**	23	1	5	6	15

Tommy Cowan

COWAN, THOMAS

B. Unknown — Defense

YEAR	TEAM & LEAGUE		GP	G	A	PTS	PIM
1930-31	**PHI**	**N**	1	0	0	0	0

Robert Cowick

COWICK, ROBERT BRUCE — 6'1", 200 lbs.

B. Aug. 18, 1951, Victoria, B.C. — Left Wing, Shoots L

YEAR	TEAM & LEAGUE		GP	G	A	PTS	PIM
1974-75	**WASH**	**N**	65	5	6	11	41
1975-76	**STL**	**N**	5	0	0	0	2
2 yrs.		**N Totals:**	70	5	6	11	43

PLAYOFFS

YEAR	TEAM & LEAGUE		GP	G	A	PTS	PIM
1973-74*	**PHI**	**N**	8	0	0	0	9

Drafted by **Washington** from Philadelphia in Expansion Draft, June 12, 1974. Claimed on waivers by **St. Louis** from Washington, May 27, 1975.

Bill Cowley

COWLEY, WILLIAM 5'10", 165 lbs.
B. June 12, 1912, Bristol, Que. Center
Won Hart Trophy, 1940–41, 1942-43
Won Art Ross Trophy, 1940-41
Hall of Fame, 1968

YEAR	TEAM & LEAGUE	GP	G	A	PTS	PIM
1934-35	STL N	41	5	7	12	10
1935-36	BOS N	48	11	10	21	17
1936-37		46	13	22	35	35
1937-38		48	17	22	39	8
1938-39		34	8	**34**	42	2
1939-40		48	13	27	40	24
1940-41		46	17	**45**	**62**	16
1941-42		28	4	23	27	6
1942-43		48	27	**45**	72	10
1943-44		36	30	41	71	12
1944-45		49	25	40	65	12
1945-46		26	12	12	24	6
1946-47		51	13	25	38	16
13 yrs.	N Totals:	549	195	353	548	174

PLAYOFFS

YEAR	TEAM & LEAGUE	GP	G	A	PTS	PIM
1935-36	BOS N	2	2	1	3	2
1936-37		3	0	3	3	0
1937-38		3	2	0	2	0
1938-39*		12	3	11	14	2
1939-40		6	1	0	1	7
1940-41*		2	0	0	0	0
1941-42		5	0	3	3	5
1942-43		9	1	7	8	4
1944-45		7	3	3	6	0
1945-46		10	1	3	4	2
1946-47		5	0	2	2	0
11 yrs.	N Totals:	64	13	33	46	22

Danny Cox

COX, DANIEL SMITH 5'10", 180 lbs.
B. Oct. 12, 1903, Little Current, Ont. Left Wing, Shoots L

YEAR	TEAM & LEAGUE	GP	G	A	PTS	PIM
1926-27	TOR N	14	0	1	1	4
1927-28		41	9	6	15	27
1928-29		42	12	7	19	14
1929-30		19	1	5	6	18
	OTTA N	23	3	1	4	2
	2 team total	42	4	6	10	20
1930-31		44	9	12	21	12
1931-32	DET N	47	4	6	10	23
1932-33	OTTA N	47	4	7	11	8
1933-34		29	0	4	4	0
	NYR N	13	5	0	5	2
	2 team total	42	5	4	9	2
1934-35	STL N	10	0	0	0	0
9 yrs.	N Totals:	329	47	49	96	110

PLAYOFFS

YEAR	TEAM & LEAGUE	GP	G	A	PTS	PIM
1928-29	TOR N	4	0	1	1	4
1929-30	OTTA N	2	0	0	0	0
1931-32	DET N	2	0	0	0	2
1933-34	NYR N	2	0	0	0	0
4 yrs.	N Totals:	10	0	1	1	6

Bart Crashley

CRASHLEY, WILLIAM BARTON 6', 180 lbs.
B. June 15, 1946, Toronto, Ont. Defense, Shoots R

YEAR	TEAM & LEAGUE	GP	G	A	PTS	PIM
1965-66	DET N	1	0	0	0	0
1966-67		2	0	0	0	2
1967-68		57	2	14	16	18
1968-69		1	0	0	0	0
1972-73	LA W	70	18	27	45	10
1973-74		78	4	26	30	16
1974-75	KC N	27	3	6	9	10
	DET N	48	2	15	17	14
	2 team total	75	5	21	26	24
1975-76	LA N	4	0	1	1	6
8 yrs.	N Totals:	140	7	36	43	50
	W Totals:	148	22	53	75	26

PLAYOFFS

YEAR	TEAM & LEAGUE	GP	G	A	PTS	PIM
1972-73	LA W	6	0	2	2	2

Traded to **Montreal** by Detroit with Pete Mahovlich for Garry Monahan and Doug Piper, June 6, 1969. Drafted by **N.Y. Islanders** from Montreal in Expansion Draft, June 6, 1972. Traded to **Kansas City** by N.Y. Islanders with the rights to Larry Hornung for Bob Bourne, Sept. 16, 1974. Traded to **Detroit** by Kansas City with Ted Snell and Larry Giroux for Guy Charron and Claude Houde, Dec. 14, 1974. Traded to **Los Angeles** by Detroit with the rights to Marcel Dionne for Dan Maloney, Terry Harper, and Los Angeles' second choice, later transferred to Minnesota (Jimmy Roberts), in the 1976 Amateur Draft, June 23, 1975.

Murray Craven

CRAVEN, MURRAY 6'1", 165 lbs.
B. July 20, 1964, Medicine Hat, Alta. Center, Shoots L

YEAR	TEAM & LEAGUE	GP	G	A	PTS	PIM
1982-83	DET N	31	4	7	11	6

Bob Crawford

CRAWFORD, ROBERT REMI 5'11", 177 lbs.
B. Apr. 6, 1959, Belleville, Ont. Right Wing, Shoots R

YEAR	TEAM & LEAGUE	GP	G	A	PTS	PIM
1979-80	STL N	8	1	0	1	2
1981-82		3	0	1	1	0
1982-83		27	5	9	14	2
3 yrs.	N Totals:	38	6	10	16	4

PLAYOFFS

YEAR	TEAM & LEAGUE	GP	G	A	PTS	PIM
1982-83	STL N	4	0	0	0	0

Bobby Crawford

CRAWFORD, BOBBY 5'8", 178 lbs.
B. May 27, 1960, New York, N.Y. Center, Shoots R

YEAR	TEAM & LEAGUE	GP	G	A	PTS	PIM
1980-81	COLO N	15	1	3	4	6
1982-83	DET N	1	0	C	0	0
2 yrs.	N Totals:	16	1	3	4	6

Signed as free agent by **N.Y. Rangers** Nov. 16, 1979. Traded to **Colorado** by N.Y. Rangers, Jan. 15, 1980, to complete deal of Nov. 2, 1979, in which N.Y. Rangers traded Pat Hickey, Lucien DeBlois, Mike McEwen and Dean Turner to Colorado for Barry Beck.

Jack Crawford

CRAWFORD, JACK SHEA 5'11", 200 lbs.
B. Oct. 26, 1916, Dublin, Ont. Defense, Shoots R

YEAR	TEAM & LEAGUE	GP	G	A	PTS	PIM
1937-38	BOS N	2	0	0	0	0
1938-39		38	4	8	12	12
1939-40		36	1	4	5	26
1940-41		45	2	8	10	27
1941-42		43	2	9	11	37
1942-43		49	5	18	23	24
1943-44		34	4	16	20	8
1944-45		40	5	19	24	10
1945-46		48	7	9	16	10
1946-47		58	1	17	18	16
1947-48		45	3	11	14	10
1948-49		55	2	13	15	14
1949-50		46	2	8	10	8
13 yrs.	N Totals:	539	38	140	178	202

PLAYOFFS

YEAR	TEAM & LEAGUE	GP	G	A	PTS	PIM
1938-39*	BOS N	12	1	1	2	9
1939-40		6	0	0	0	0
1940-41*		11	0	2	2	7
1941-42		5	0	1	1	4
1942-43		6	1	1	2	10
1944-45		7	0	5	5	0
1945-46		10	1	2	3	4
1946-47		2	1	0	1	0
1947-48		4	0	1	1	2
1948-49		3	0	0	0	0
10 yrs.	N Totals:	66	4	13	17	36

Marc Crawford

CRAWFORD, MARC JOSEPH 5'11", 183 lbs.
B. Feb. 13, 1961, Belleville, Ont. Left Wing, Shoots L

YEAR	TEAM & LEAGUE	GP	G	A	PTS	PIM
1981-82	VAN N	40	4	8	12	29
1982-83		41	4	5	9	28
2 yrs.	N Totals:	81	8	13	21	57

PLAYOFFS

YEAR	TEAM & LEAGUE	GP	G	A	PTS	PIM
1981-82	VAN N	15	1	0	1	11

Marc Crawford continued

YEAR	TEAM & LEAGUE		GP	G	A	PTS	PIM
1982-83			3	0	1	1	25
2 yrs.		N Totals:	18	1	1	2	36

Rusty Crawford

CRAWFORD, RUSSELL
B. Nov. 7, 1885, Cardinal, Ont. — Left Wing
Hall of Fame, 1962

YEAR	TEAM & LEAGUE		GP	G	A	PTS	PIM
1917-18	OTTA	N	11	1	0	1	9
	TOR	N	9	2	0	2	24
	2 team total		20	3	0	3	33
1918-19			18	7	3	10	51
2 yrs.		N Totals:	38	10	3	13	84
PLAYOFFS							
1917-18*	TOR	N	2	2	1	3	0

Dave Creighton

CREIGHTON, DAVID THEODORE — 6'1", 181 lbs.
B. June 24, 1930, Port Arthur, Ont. — Center, Shoots L

YEAR	TEAM & LEAGUE		GP	G	A	PTS	PIM
1948-49	BOS	N	12	1	3	4	0
1949-50			64	18	13	31	13
1950-51			56	5	4	9	4
1951-52			49	20	17	37	18
1952-53			69	20	20	40	27
1953-54			69	20	20	40	27
1954-55	TOR	N	14	2	1	3	8
	CHI	N	49	7	7	14	6
	2 team total		63	9	8	17	14
1955-56	NYR	N	70	20	31	51	43
1956-57			70	18	21	39	42
1957-58			70	17	35	52	40
1958-59	TOR	N	34	3	9	12	4
1959-60			14	1	5	6	4
12 yrs.		N Totals:	640	152	186	338	236
PLAYOFFS							
1948-49	BOS	N	3	0	0	0	0
1950-51			5	0	1	1	0
1951-52			7	2	1	3	2
1952-53			11	4	5	9	10
1953-54			4	0	0	0	0
1955-56	NYR	N	5	0	0	0	4
1956-57			5	2	2	4	2
1957-58			6	3	3	6	2
1958-59	TOR	N	5	0	1	1	0
9 yrs.		N Totals:	51	11	13	24	20

Traded to **Toronto** by Boston for Fern Flaman, July 20, 1954. Sold to **Chicago** by Toronto, Nov. 16, 1954. Traded to **Detroit** by Chicago with Jerry Toppazzini, John McCormack and Gord Hollingworth for Tony Leswick, Glen Skov, Johnny Wilson and Benny Woit, June 3, 1955. Traded to **N.Y. Rangers** by Detroit with Bronco Horvath for Billy Dea and Aggie Kukulowicz, Aug. 18, 1955. Drafted from New York by **Montreal** June 4, 1958.

Jimmy Creighton

CREIGHTON, JAMES
B. Unknown — Forward

YEAR	TEAM & LEAGUE		GP	G	A	PTS	PIM
1930-31	DET	N	11	1	0	1	2

Dave Cressman

CRESSMAN, DAVID GREGORY — 6'1", 180 lbs.
B. Jan. 2, 1950, Kitchener, Ont. — Left Wing, Shoots L

YEAR	TEAM & LEAGUE		GP	G	A	PTS	PIM
1974-75	MINN	N	5	2	0	2	4
1975-76			80	4	8	12	33
2 yrs.		N Totals:	85	6	8	14	37

Glen Cressman

CRESSMAN, GLEN — 5'8½", 155 lbs.
B. Aug. 29, 1934, Petersburg, Ont. — Center, Shoots R

YEAR	TEAM & LEAGUE		GP	G	A	PTS	PIM
1956-57	MONT	N	4	0	0	0	2

Terry Crisp

CRISP, TERRY ARTHUR — 5'10", 180 lbs.
B. May 28, 1943, Parry Sound, Ont. — Center, Shoots L

YEAR	TEAM & LEAGUE		GP	G	A	PTS	PIM
1965-66	BOS	N	3	0	0	0	0
1967-68	STL	N	74	9	20	29	10
1968-69			57	6	9	15	14
1969-70			26	5	6	11	2
1970-71			54	5	11	16	13
1971-72			75	13	18	31	12
1972-73	NYI	N	54	4	16	20	6
	PHI	N	12	1	5	6	2
	2 team total		66	5	21	26	8
1973-74			71	10	21	31	28
1974-75			71	8	19	27	20
1975-76			38	6	9	15	28
1976-77			2	0	0	0	0
11 yrs.		N Totals:	537	67	134	201	135
PLAYOFFS							
1967-68	STL	N	18	1	5	6	6
1968-69			12	3	4	7	20
1969-70			16	2	3	5	2
1970-71			6	1	0	1	2
1971-72			11	1	3	4	2
1972-73	PHI	N	11	3	2	5	2
1973-74*			17	2	2	4	4
1974-75*			9	2	4	6	0
1975-76			10	0	5	5	2
9 yrs.		N Totals:	110	15	28	43	40

Drafted by **St. Louis** from Boston in Expansion Draft, June 6, 1967. Drafted by **N.Y. Islanders** from St. Louis in Expansion Draft, June 6, 1972. Traded to **Philadelphia** by N.Y. Islanders for Jean Potvin and a player to be named later (Glen Irwin, May 18, 1973), March 5, 1973.

Glen Critch

CRITCH, GLEN
Defense

YEAR	TEAM & LEAGUE		GP	G	A	PTS	PIM
1975-76	IND	W	3	0	0	0	0

Maurice Croghen

CROGHEN, MAURICE
B. Nov. 19, 1914, Montreal, Que. — Forward

YEAR	TEAM & LEAGUE		GP	G	A	PTS	PIM
1937-38	MON(M)	N	16	0	0	0	4

Mike Crombeen

CROMBEEN, MICHAEL JOSEPH — 5'11", 192 lbs.
B. Apr. 16, 1957, Sarnia, Ont. — Right Wing, Shoots R

YEAR	TEAM & LEAGUE		GP	G	A	PTS	PIM
1977-78	CLEVE	N	43	3	4	7	13
1978-79	STL	N	37	3	8	11	34
1979-80			71	10	12	22	20
1980-81			66	9	14	23	58
1981-82			71	19	8	27	32
1982-83			80	6	11	17	20
6 yrs.		N Totals:	368	50	57	107	177
PLAYOFFS							
1979-80	STL	N	2	0	0	0	0
1980-81			11	3	0	3	8
1981-82			10	3	1	4	20
1982-83			4	0	1	1	4
4 yrs.		N Totals:	27	6	2	8	32

Claimed by **St. Louis** in Cleveland-Minnesota Dispersal Draft, June 15, 1978.

Jim Cross

CROSS, JAMES
B. Unknown — Defense

YEAR	TEAM & LEAGUE		GP	G	A	PTS	PIM
1977-78	EDM	W	2	0	0	0	0

Stan Crossett

CROSSETT, STANLEY
B. Unknown — Forward

YEAR	TEAM & LEAGUE		GP	G	A	PTS	PIM
1930-31	**PHI**	**N**	21	0	0	0	10

Doug Crossman

CROSSMAN, DOUGLAS — 6'2", 190 lbs.
B. May 30, 1960, Peterborough, Ont. — Defense, Shoots L

YEAR	TEAM & LEAGUE		GP	G	A	PTS	PIM
1980-81	**CHI**	**N**	9	0	2	2	2
1981-82			70	12	28	40	24
1982-83			80	13	40	53	46
3 yrs.		**N Totals:**	159	25	70	95	72
PLAYOFFS							
1981-82	**CHI**	**N**	11	0	3	3	4
1982-83			13	3	7	10	6
2 yrs.		**N Totals:**	24	3	10	13	10

Traded to **Philadelphia** by Chicago with Chicago's second round choice in the 1984 Amateur Draft for Behn Wilson, June 8, 1983.

Gary Croteau

CROTEAU, GARY PAUL — 6', 202 lbs.
B. June 20, 1946, Sudbury, Ont. — Left Wing, Shoots L

YEAR	TEAM & LEAGUE		GP	G	A	PTS	PIM
1968-69	**LA**	**N**	11	5	1	6	6
1969-70	**DET**	**N**	10	0	2	2	2
	LA	**N**	3	0	0	0	0
	2 team total		13	0	2	2	2
1970-71	**CALIF**	**N**	74	15	28	43	12
1971-72			73	12	12	24	11
1972-73			47	6	15	21	8
1973-74			76	14	21	35	16
1974-75	**KC**	**N**	77	8	11	19	16
1975-76			79	19	14	33	12
1976-77	**COLO**	**N**	78	24	27	51	14
1977-78			62	17	22	39	24
1978-79			79	23	18	41	18
1979-80			15	1	4	5	4
12 yrs.		**N Totals:**	684	144	175	319	143
PLAYOFFS							
1968-69	**LA**	**N**	11	3	2	5	8

Traded to **Detroit** by Los Angeles with Dale Rolfe and Larry Johnston for Brian Gibbons and Garry Monahan, Feb. 20, 1970. Drafted by **Oakland** from Detroit in Intra-League Draft, June 9, 1970. Drafted by **Kansas City** from California in Expansion Draft, June 12, 1974.

Bruce Crowder

CROWDER, BRUCE — 6', 180 lbs.
B. Mar. 25, 1957, Essex, Ont. — Right Wing, Shoots R

YEAR	TEAM & LEAGUE		GP	G	A	PTS	PIM
1981-82	**BOS**	**N**	63	16	11	27	31
1982-83			80	21	19	40	58
2 yrs.		**N Totals:**	143	37	30	67	89
PLAYOFFS							
1981-82	**BOS**	**N**	11	5	3	8	9
1982-83			17	3	1	4	34
2 yrs.		**N Totals:**	28	8	4	12	43

Signed as free agent by **Boston** Sept. 29, 1981.

Keith Crowder

CROWDER, KEITH SCOTT — 6', 190 lbs.
B. Jan. 6, 1959, Windsor, Ont. — Right Wing, Shoots R

YEAR	TEAM & LEAGUE		GP	G	A	PTS	PIM
1978-79	**BIRM**	**W**	5	1	0	1	17
1980-81	**BOS**	**N**	47	13	12	25	172
1981-82			71	23	21	44	101
1982-83			74	35	39	74	105
4 yrs.		**N Totals:**	192	71	72	143	378
		W Totals:	5	1	0	1	17
PLAYOFFS							
1980-81	**BOS**	**N**	3	2	0	2	9
1981-82			11	2	2	4	14
1982-83			17	1	6	7	52

Keith Crowder continued

YEAR	TEAM & LEAGUE		GP	G	A	PTS	PIM
3 yrs.		**N Totals:**	31	5	8	13	75

Paul Crowley

CROWLEY, PAUL — 5'9", 182 lbs.
B. Dec. 26, 1955, Montreal, Que. — Right Wing, Shoots R

YEAR	TEAM & LEAGUE		GP	G	A	PTS	PIM
1975-76	**TOR**	**W**	4	0	0	0	0

Signed as free agent by **Buffalo** Oct. 17, 1977.

Joe Crozier

CROZIER, JOSEPH RICHARD — 6', 180 lbs.
B. Feb. 19, 1929, Winnipeg, Man. — Defense, Shoots R

YEAR	TEAM & LEAGUE		GP	G	A	PTS	PIM
1959-60	**TOR**	**N**	5	0	3	3	2

Nels Crutchfield

CRUTCHFIELD, NELSON — 6'1", 175 lbs.
B. July 12, 1911, Knowlton, P.Q. — Center, Shoots L

YEAR	TEAM & LEAGUE		GP	G	A	PTS	PIM
1934-35	**MONT**	**N**	41	5	5	10	20
PLAYOFFS							
1934-35	**MONT**	**N**	2	0	1	1	22

Steve Cuddie

CUDDIE, STEVEN ROSS — 5'10", 190 lbs.
B. June 18, 1950, Toronto, Ont. — Defense, Shoots R

YEAR	TEAM & LEAGUE		GP	G	A	PTS	PIM
1972-73	**WINN**	**W**	77	7	13	20	121
1973-74	**TOR**	**W**	74	5	18	23	65
1974-75			70	5	16	21	49
3 yrs.		**W Totals:**	221	17	47	64	235
PLAYOFFS							
1972-73	**WINN**	**W**	12	0	1	1	10
1973-74	**TOR**	**W**	8	1	4	5	14
1974-75			6	0	4	4	8
3 yrs.		**W Totals:**	26	1	9	10	32

Barry Cullen

CULLEN, CHARLES FRANCIS — 6', 175 lbs.
B. June 16, 1935, Ottawa, Ont. — Right Wing, Shoots R

YEAR	TEAM & LEAGUE		GP	G	A	PTS	PIM
1955-56	**TOR**	**N**	3	0	0	0	4
1956-57			51	6	10	16	30
1957-58			70	16	25	41	37
1958-59			40	6	8	14	17
1959-60	**DET**	**N**	55	4	9	13	23
5 yrs.		**N Totals:**	219	32	52	84	111
PLAYOFFS							
1958-59	**TOR**	**N**	2	0	0	0	0
1959-60	**DET**	**N**	4	0	0	0	2
2 yrs.		**N Totals:**	6	0	0	0	2

Traded to **Detroit** by Toronto for Johnny Wilson and Frank Roggeveen, June 9, 1959. Drafted by **New York** from Toronto, June 10, 1959.

Brian Cullen

CULLEN, BRIAN JOSEPH — 5'10", 164 lbs.
B. Nov. 11, 1933, Ottawa, Ont. — Center, Shoots L

YEAR	TEAM & LEAGUE		GP	G	A	PTS	PIM
1954-55	**TOR**	**N**	27	3	5	8	6
1955-56			21	2	6	8	8
1956-57			46	8	12	20	27
1957-58			67	20	23	43	29
1958-59			59	4	14	18	10
1959-60	**NYR**	**N**	64	8	21	29	6
1960-61			42	11	19	30	6
7 yrs.		**N Totals:**	326	56	100	156	92
PLAYOFFS							
1954-55	**TOR**	**N**	4	1	0	1	0
1955-56			5	1	0	1	2
1958-59			10	1	0	1	0
3 yrs.		**N Totals:**	19	3	0	3	2

Ray Cullen

CULLEN, RAYMOND MURRAY 5'11", 180 lbs.
B. Sept. 20, 1941, Ottawa, Ont. Center, Shoots R

YEAR	TEAM & LEAGUE		GP	G	A	PTS	PIM
1965-66	NYR	N	8	1	3	4	0
1966-67	DET	N	28	8	8	16	8
1967-68	MINN	N	67	28	25	53	18
1968-69			67	26	38	64	44
1969-70			74	17	28	45	8
1970-71	VAN	N	71	12	21	33	42
6 yrs.		N Totals:	315	92	123	215	120
PLAYOFFS							
1967-68	MINN	N	14	2	6	8	2
1969-70			6	1	4	5	0
2 yrs.		N Totals:	20	3	10	13	2

Drafted by **Detroit** from N.Y. Rangers, June 15, 1966. Drafted by **Minnesota** from Detroit in Expansion Draft, June 6, 1967. Drafted by **Vancouver** from Minnesota in Expansion Draft, June 10, 1970.

Barry Cummins

CUMMINS, BARRY KENNETH 5'9", 175 lbs.
B. Jan. 25, 1949, Regina, Sask. Defense, Shoots L

YEAR	TEAM & LEAGUE		GP	G	A	PTS	PIM
1973-74	CALIF	N	36	1	2	3	39

Randy Cunneyworth

CUNNEYWORTH, RANDOLPH WILLIAM 6', 177 lbs.
B. May 10, 1961, Etobicoke, Ont. Center, Shoots L

YEAR	TEAM & LEAGUE		GP	G	A	PTS	PIM
1980-81	BUF	N	1	0	0	0	2
1981-82			20	2	4	6	47
2 yrs.		N Totals:	21	2	4	6	49

John Cunniff

CUNNIFF, JOHN PAUL 5'9", 175 lbs.
B. July 9, 1944, South Boston, Mass. Left Wing, Shoots L

YEAR	TEAM & LEAGUE		GP	G	A	PTS	PIM
1972-73	NE	W	33	3	5	8	16
1973-74			30	7	5	12	14
1975-76	QUE	W	2	0	0	0	5
3 yrs.		W Totals:	65	10	10	20	35
PLAYOFFS							
1972-73	NE	W	13	1	1	2	2
1973-74			5	1	1	2	0
2 yrs.		W Totals:	18	2	2	4	2

Bob Cunningham

CUNNINGHAM, ROBERT GORDON 5'11", 168 lbs.
B. Feb. 26, 1941, Welland, Ont. Center, Shoots L

YEAR	TEAM & LEAGUE		GP	G	A	PTS	PIM
1960-61	NYR	N	3	0	1	1	0
1961-62			1	0	0	0	0
2 yrs.		N Totals:	4	0	1	1	0
PLAYOFFS							
1972-73	OTTA	W	5	1	1	2	2

Gary Cunningham

CUNNINGHAM, GARY 6', 184 lbs.
B. Aug. 28, 1950, Welland, Ont. Defense, Shoots L

YEAR	TEAM & LEAGUE		GP	G	A	PTS	PIM
1973-74	EDM	W	2	0	0	0	0

Jim Cunningham

CUNNINGHAM, JAMES 5'11", 185 lbs.
B. Aug. 15, 1956, St. Paul, Minn. Left Wing, Shoots L

YEAR	TEAM & LEAGUE		GP	G	A	PTS	PIM
1977-78	PHI	N	1	0	0	0	4

Claimed by **Winnipeg** from Philadelphia in Expansion Draft, June 13, 1979.

Les Cunningham

CUNNINGHAM, LESLIE ROY 5'8", 165 lbs.
B. Oct. 4, 1913, Calgary, Alta. Center, Shoots L

YEAR	TEAM & LEAGUE		GP	G	A	PTS	PIM
1936-37	NYA	N	23	1	8	9	19
1939-40	CHI	N	37	6	11	17	2
2 yrs.		N Totals:	60	7	19	26	21
PLAYOFFS							
1939-40	CHI	N	1	0	0	0	2

Rick Cunningham

CUNNINGHAM, RICK 5'10", 190 lbs.
B. Mar. 3, 1951, Toronto, Ont. Defense, Shoots R

YEAR	TEAM & LEAGUE		GP	G	A	PTS	PIM
1972-73	OTTA	W	78	9	32	41	121
1973-74	TOR	W	75	2	19	21	88
1974-75			71	7	18	25	117
1975-76			36	5	14	19	57
4 yrs.		W Totals:	260	23	83	106	383
PLAYOFFS							
1973-74	TOR	W	11	0	4	4	31
1974-75			5	0	1	1	0
2 yrs.		W Totals:	16	0	5	5	31

Bill Cupolo

CUPOLO, WILLIAM DONALD 5'8", 170 lbs.
B. Jan. 8, 1924, Niagara Falls, Ont. Right Wing, Shoots R

YEAR	TEAM & LEAGUE		GP	G	A	PTS	PIM
1944-45	BOS	N	47	11	13	24	10
PLAYOFFS							
1944-45	BOS	N	7	1	2	3	0

Glen Currie

CURRIE, GLEN 6'1", 177 lbs.
B. July 18, 1958, Montreal, Que. Center, Shoots L

YEAR	TEAM & LEAGUE		GP	G	A	PTS	PIM
1979-80	WASH	N	32	2	0	2	2
1980-81			40	5	13	18	16
1981-82			43	7	7	14	14
1982-83			68	11	28	39	20
4 yrs.		N Totals:	183	25	48	73	52
PLAYOFFS							
1982-83	WASH	N	4	0	3	3	4

Hugh Currie

CURRIE, HUGH ROY 6', 190 lbs.
B. Oct. 22, 1925, Saskatoon, Sask. Defense, Shoots R

YEAR	TEAM & LEAGUE		GP	G	A	PTS	PIM
1950-51	MONT	N	1	0	0	0	0

Tony Currie

CURRIE, TONY 5'11", 166 lbs.
B. Nov. 12, 1957, Sydney Mines, N.S. Right Wing, Shoots R

YEAR	TEAM & LEAGUE		GP	G	A	PTS	PIM
1977-78	STL	N	22	4	5	9	4
1978-79			36	4	15	19	0
1979-80			40	19	14	33	4
1980-81			61	23	32	55	38
1981-82			48	18	22	40	17
	VAN	N	12	5	3	8	2
	2 team total		60	23	25	48	19
1982-83			8	1	1	2	0
6 yrs.		N Totals:	227	74	92	166	65
PLAYOFFS							
1979-80	STL	N	2	0	0	0	0
1980-81			11	4	12	16	4
1981-82	VAN	N	3	0	0	0	10
3 yrs.		N Totals:	16	4	12	16	14

Traded to **Vancouver** by St. Louis with Jim Nill, Rick Heinz and St. Louis' fourth round choice (Shawn Kilroy) in 1982 Entry Draft for Glen Hanlon, Mar. 9, 1982.

Floyd Curry

CURRY, FLOYD JAMES (Busher) 5'11", 175 lbs.
B. Aug. 11, 1925, Chapleau, Ont. Right Wing, Shoots R

YEAR	TEAM & LEAGUE		GP	G	A	PTS	PIM
1947-48	**MONT**	**N**	31	1	5	6	0
1949-50			49	8	8	16	8
1950-51			69	13	14	27	23
1951-52			64	20	18	38	10
1952-53			68	16	6	22	10
1953-54			70	13	8	21	22
1954-55			68	11	10	21	36
1955-56			70	14	18	32	10
1956-57			70	7	9	16	20
1957-58			42	2	3	5	8
10 yrs.		**N Totals:**	601	105	99	204	147
PLAYOFFS							
1948-49	**MONT**	**N**	2	0	0	0	2
1949-50			5	1	0	1	2
1950-51			11	0	2	2	2
1951-52			11	4	3	7	6
1952-53*			12	2	1	3	2
1953-54			11	4	0	4	4
1954-55			12	8	4	12	4
1955-56*			10	1	5	6	12
1956-57*			10	3	2	5	2
1957-58*			7	0	0	0	2
10 yrs.		**N Totals:**	91	23	17	40	38

Tony Curtale

CURTALE, TONY 6', 183 lbs.
B. Jan. 29, 1962, Detroit, Mich. Defense, Shoots L

YEAR	TEAM & LEAGUE		GP	G	A	PTS	PIM
1980-81	**CALG**	**N**	2	0	0	0	0

Paul Curtis

CURTIS, PAUL EDWIN 6', 185 lbs.
B. Sept. 29, 1947, Peterborough, Ont. Defense, Shoots L

YEAR	TEAM & LEAGUE		GP	G	A	PTS	PIM
1969-70	**MONT**	**N**	1	0	0	0	0
1970-71	**LA**	**N**	64	1	13	14	82
1971-72			64	1	12	13	57
1972-73			27	0	5	5	16
	STL	**N**	29	1	4	5	6
	2 team total		56	1	9	10	22
1974-75	**M-B**	**W**	76	4	15	19	32
5 yrs.		**N Totals:**	185	3	34	37	161
		W Totals:	76	4	15	19	32
PLAYOFFS							
1972-73	**STL**	**N**	5	0	0	0	2

Drafted by **Los Angeles** from Montreal in Intra-League Draft, June 9, 1970. Traded to **St. Louis** by Los Angeles for Frank St. Marseille, Jan. 22, 1973. Traded to **Buffalo** by St. Louis for Jake Rathwell, June 14, 1973. Traded to **N.Y. Rangers** by Buffalo for Real Lemieux, Jan. 21, 1974.

Ian Cushenan

CUSHENAN, IAN ROBERTSON 6'1", 195 lbs.
B. Nov. 29, 1933, Hamilton, Ont. Defense, Shoots L

YEAR	TEAM & LEAGUE		GP	G	A	PTS	PIM
1956-57	**CHI**	**N**	11	0	0	0	13
1957-58			61	2	8	10	67
1958-59	**MONT**	**N**	35	1	2	3	28
1959-60	**NYR**	**N**	17	0	1	1	12
1963-64	**DET**	**N**	5	0	0	0	4
5 yrs.		**N Totals:**	129	3	11	14	124

Drafted from Montreal by **New York** June 10, 1959. Signed as a free agent by **Detroit** Aug. 5, 1963. Traded to **Chicago** by Detroit with John Miszuk and Art Stratton for Aut Erickson and Ron Murphy, June 9, 1964.

Jean Cusson

CUSSON, JEAN 5'10", 175 lbs.
B. Oct. 5, 1942, Verdun, Que. Left Wing, Shoots L

YEAR	TEAM & LEAGUE		GP	G	A	PTS	PIM
1967-68	**OAK**	**N**	2	0	0	0	0

Denis Cyr

CYR, DENIS
Forward

YEAR	TEAM & LEAGUE		GP	G	A	PTS	PIM
1980-81	**CALG**	**N**	10	1	4	5	0
1981-82			45	12	10	22	13
1982-83			11	1	1	2	0
	CHI	**N**	41	7	8	15	2
	2 team total		52	8	9	17	2
3 yrs.		**N Totals:**	107	21	23	44	15
PLAYOFFS							
1982-83	**CHI**	**N**	1	0	0	0	0

Traded by Calgary to **Chicago** for the rights to Carey Wilson, Nov. 8, 1982.

Paul Cyr

CYR, PAUL 5'10", 184 lbs.
B. Oct. 31, 1963, Port Alberni, B.C. Left Wing, Shoots L

YEAR	TEAM & LEAGUE		GP	G	A	PTS	PIM
1982-83	**BUF**	**N**	36	15	12	27	59
PLAYOFFS							
1982-83	**BUF**	**N**	10	1	3	4	6

Cully Dahlstrom

DAHLSTROM, CARL S. 5'1½", 175 lbs.
B. July 3, 1913, Minneapolis, Minn. Center, Shoots L
Won Calder Trophy, 1937-38

YEAR	TEAM & LEAGUE		GP	G	A	PTS	PIM
1937-38	**CHI**	**N**	48	10	9	19	11
1938-39			48	6	14	20	2
1939-40			45	11	19	30	15
1940-41			40	11	14	25	6
1941-42			33	13	14	27	6
1942-43			38	11	13	24	10
1943-44			50	20	22	42	8
1944-45			40	6	13	19	0
8 yrs.		**N Totals:**	342	88	118	206	58
PLAYOFFS							
1937-38*	**CHI**	**N**	10	3	1	4	2
1939-40			2	0	0	0	0
1940-41			5	3	3	6	2
1941-42			3	0	0	0	0
1943-44			9	0	4	4	0
5 yrs.		**N Totals:**	29	6	8	14	4

Alain Daigle

DAIGLE, ROLAND ALAIN 5'10", 180 lbs.
B. Aug. 24, 1954, Cap-de-la-Madeleine,Que.
Right Wing, Shoots R

YEAR	TEAM & LEAGUE		GP	G	A	PTS	PIM
1974-75	**CHI**	**N**	52	5	4	9	6
1975-76			71	15	9	24	15
1976-77			73	12	8	20	11
1977-78			53	6	6	12	95
1978-79			74	11	14	25	55
1979-80			66	7	9	16	22
6 yrs.		**N Totals:**	389	56	50	106	204
PLAYOFFS							
1974-75	**CHI**	**N**	2	0	0	0	0
1975-76			4	0	0	0	0
1976-77			1	0	0	0	0
1977-78			4	0	1	1	0
1978-79			4	0	0	0	0
1979-80			2	0	0	0	0
6 yrs.		**N Totals:**	17	0	1	1	0

Bob Dailey

DAILEY, ROBERT SCOTT 6'5", 220 lbs.
B. May 3, 1953, Kingston, Ont. Defense, Shoots R

YEAR	TEAM & LEAGUE		GP	G	A	PTS	PIM
1973-74	**VAN**	**N**	76	7	17	24	143
1974-75			70	12	36	48	103
1975-76			67	15	24	39	119
1976-77			44	4	16	20	52
	PHI	**N**	32	5	14	19	38
	2 team total		76	9	30	39	90
1977-78			76	21	36	57	62

Bob Dailey continued

YEAR	TEAM & LEAGUE		GP	G	A	PTS	PIM
1978-79			70	9	30	39	63
1979-80			61	13	26	39	71
1980-81			53	7	27	34	141
1981-82			12	1	5	6	22
9 yrs.		**N Totals:**	561	94	231	325	814
PLAYOFFS							
1974-75	**VAN**	**N**	5	1	3	4	14
1975-76			2	1	1	2	0
1976-77	**PHI**	**N**	10	4	9	13	15
1977-78			12	1	5	6	22
1978-79			8	1	2	3	14
1979-80			19	4	13	17	22
1980-81			7	0	1	1	18
7 yrs.		**N Totals:**	63	12	34	46	105

Traded to **Philadelphia** by Vancouver for Larry Goodenough and Jack McIlhargey, Jan. 20, 1977.

Frank Daley

DALEY, FRANKLIN
B. Unknown — Defense

YEAR	TEAM & LEAGUE		GP	G	A	PTS	PIM
1928-29	**DET**	**N**	5	0	0	0	0
PLAYOFFS							
1928-29	**DET**	**N**	2	0	0	0	0

Pat Daley

DALEY, PATRICK LLOYD — 6'1", 176 lbs.
B. Mar. 27, 1959, Marieville, France — Left Wing, Shoots L

YEAR	TEAM & LEAGUE		GP	G	A	PTS	PIM
1979-80	**WINN**	**N**	5	1	0	1	4
1980-81			7	0	0	0	9
2 yrs.		**N Totals:**	12	1	0	1	13

Bob D'Alvise

D'ALVISE, ROBERT — 5'11", 185 lbs.
B. Dec. 23, 1952, Etobicoke, Ont. — Center, Shoots L

YEAR	TEAM & LEAGUE		GP	G	A	PTS	PIM
1975-76	**TOR**	**W**	59	5	8	13	10

Bunny Dame

DAME, AURELIA N.
B. Edmonton, Alta. — Left Wing

YEAR	TEAM & LEAGUE		GP	G	A	PTS	PIM
1941-42	**MONT**	**N**	34	2	5	7	4

Hank Damore

DAMORE, HENRY JOHN (Lou Costello) — 5'5½", 200 lbs.
B. July 17, 1919, Niagara Falls, Ont. — Center, Shoots L

YEAR	TEAM & LEAGUE		GP	G	A	PTS	PIM
1943-44	**NYR**	**N**	4	1	0	1	2

John Danby

DANBY, JOHN — 5'10", 165 lbs.
B. July 20, 1948, Toronto, Ont. — Center, Shoots R

YEAR	TEAM & LEAGUE		GP	G	A	PTS	PIM
1972-73	**NE**	**W**	77	14	23	37	10
1973-74			72	2	2	4	6
1975-76			1	0	0	0	0
3 yrs.		**W Totals:**	150	16	25	41	16
PLAYOFFS							
1973-74	**NE**	**W**	7	1	0	1	0
1974-75			4	0	1	1	0
2 yrs.		**W Totals:**	11	1	1	2	0

Dan Daoust

DAOUST, DAN (Dangerous) — 5'10", 160 lbs.
B. Feb. 29, 1960, Kirkland Lake, Ont. — Center, Shoots L

YEAR	TEAM & LEAGUE		GP	G	A	PTS	PIM
1982-83	**MONT**	**N**	4	0	1	1	4
	TOR	**N**	48	18	33	51	31
	2 team total		52	18	34	52	35

Traded to **Toronto** by Montreal for Toronto's third round choice in the 1984 Amateur Draft, Dec. 17, 1982.

Harry Darragh

DARRAGH, HAROLD EDWARD (Howl) — 5'1", 145 lbs.
B. Sept. 13, 1903, Ottawa, Ont. — Forward, Shoots R

YEAR	TEAM & LEAGUE		GP	G	A	PTS	PIM
1925-26	**PITT**	**N**	35	10	7	17	6
1926-27			42	12	3	15	4
1927-28			44	13	2	15	16
1928-29			43	9	3	12	6
1929-30			42	15	17	32	6
1930-31	**PHI**	**N**	10	1	1	2	2
	BOS	**N**	25	2	4	6	4
	2 team total		35	3	5	8	6
1931-32	**TOR**	**N**	48	5	10	15	6
1932-33			9	1	2	3	0
8 yrs.		**N Totals:**	298	68	49	117	50
PLAYOFFS							
1925-26	**PITT**	**N**	2	1	0	1	0
1927-28			2	0	1	1	0
1930-31	**BOS**	**N**	5	0	1	1	2
1931-32*	**TOR**	**N**	7	0	1	1	2
4 yrs.		**N Totals:**	16	1	3	4	4

Jack Darragh

DARRAGH, JOHN PROCTOR
B. Dec. 4, 1890, Ottawa, Ont. — Right Wing, Shoots R
Hall of Fame, 1962

YEAR	TEAM & LEAGUE		GP	G	A	PTS	PIM
1917-18	**OTTA**	**N**	18	14	0	14	3
1918-19			14	12	1	13	27
1919-20			22	22	5	27	22
1920-21			24	11	8	19	20
1922-23			24	7	7	14	14
1923-24			18	2	0	2	2
6 yrs.		**N Totals:**	120	68	21	89	88
PLAYOFFS							
1918-19	**OTTA**	**N**	5	3	0	3	0
1919-20*			5	5	**2**	**7**	3
1920-21*			7	5	0	5	6
1922-23*			2	1	0	1	2
1923-24			2	0	0	0	2
5 yrs.		**N Totals:**	21	14	2	16	13

Richard David

DAVID, RICHARD — 6', 194 lbs.
B. Apr. 8, 1958, Notre Dame Sallette, Que — Left Wing, Shoots L

YEAR	TEAM & LEAGUE		GP	G	A	PTS	PIM
1978-79	**QUE**	**W**	14	0	4	4	4
1979-80	**QUE**	**N**	10	0	0	0	1
1981-82			5	1	1	2	4
1982-83			16	3	3	6	4
4 yrs.		**N Totals:**	31	4	4	8	9
		W Totals:	14	0	4	4	4
PLAYOFFS							
1981-82	**QUE**	**N**	1	0	0	0	0

Blair Davidson

DAVIDSON, BLAIR — 5'10", 185 lbs.
B. Oct. 4, 1955, Cartwright, Man. — Defense, Shoots L

YEAR	TEAM & LEAGUE		GP	G	A	PTS	PIM
1976-77	**PHOE**	**W**	2	0	0	0	2

Bob Davidson

DAVIDSON, ROBERT E. — 5'11", 185 lbs.
B. Feb. 10, 1912, Toronto, Ont. — Forward, Shoots L

YEAR	TEAM & LEAGUE		GP	G	A	PTS	PIM
1934-35	**TOR**	**N**	5	0	0	0	6
1935-36			35	4	4	8	32
1936-37			46	8	7	15	43
1937-38			48	3	17	20	52
1938-39			47	4	10	14	29
1939-40			48	8	18	26	56
1940-41			37	3	6	9	39
1941-42			37	6	20	26	39
1942-43			50	13	23	36	20
1943-44			47	19	28	47	21
1944-45			50	17	18	35	49
1945-46			41	9	9	18	12

Bob Davidson continued

YEAR	TEAM & LEAGUE		GP	G	A	PTS	PIM
12 yrs.		N Totals:	491	94	160	254	398
PLAYOFFS							
1935-36	TOR	N	9	1	3	4	2
1936-37			2	0	0	0	5
1937-38			7	0	2	2	10
1938-39			10	1	1	2	6
1939-40			10	0	3	3	16
1940-41			7	0	2	2	7
1941-42*			13	1	2	3	20
1942-43			6	1	2	3	7
1943-44			5	0	0	0	4
1944-45*			13	1	2	3	2
10 yrs.		N Totals:	82	5	17	22	79

Gord Davidson

DAVIDSON, GORDON JOHN 5'11", 188 lbs.
B. Aug. 5, 1918, Stratton, Ont. Defense, Shoots L

YEAR	TEAM & LEAGUE		GP	G	A	PTS	PIM
1942-43	NYR	N	35	2	3	5	4
1943-44			16	1	3	4	4
2 yrs.		N Totals:	51	3	6	9	8

Bob Davie

DAVIE, ROBERT HOWARD (Pinkie) 6', 170 lbs.
B. Sept. 12, 1912, Beausejour, Man. Defense, Shoots R

YEAR	TEAM & LEAGUE		GP	G	A	PTS	PIM
1933-34	BOS	N	9	0	0	0	6
1934-35			30	0	1	1	17
1935-36			2	0	0	0	2
3 yrs.		N Totals:	41	0	1	1	25

Ken Davies

DAVIES, KENNETH GEORGE (Buck) 5'6", 160 lbs.
B. Aug. 10, 1922, Bowmanville, Ont. Center, Shoots L

YEAR	TEAM & LEAGUE		GP	G	A	PTS	PIM
PLAYOFFS							
1947-48	NYR	N	1	0	0	0	0

Bill Davis

DAVIS, WILLIAM LLOYD 6'1", 195 lbs.
B. Aug. 22, 1954, Lindsay, Ont. Defense, Shoots L

YEAR	TEAM & LEAGUE		GP	G	A	PTS	PIM
1977-78	WINN	W	12	0	0	0	2
1978-79			5	1	2	3	0
2 yrs.		W Totals:	17	1	2	3	2

Bob Davis

DAVIS, ROBERT
B. Unknown Forward

YEAR	TEAM & LEAGUE		GP	G	A	PTS	PIM
1932-33	DET	N	3	0	0	0	0

Kelly Davis

DAVIS, KELLY 6', 175 lbs.
B. Sept. 23, 1958, Grande Prairie, Alta. Defense, Shoots L

YEAR	TEAM & LEAGUE		GP	G	A	PTS	PIM
1978-79	CIN	W	18	0	1	1	20

Reclaimed by **N.Y. Islanders** from Cincinnati (W) prior to Expansion Draft, June 9, 1979.

Kim Davis

DAVIS, KIM 5'11", 170 lbs.
B. Oct. 31, 1957, Flin Flon, Man. Center, Shoots L

YEAR	TEAM & LEAGUE		GP	G	A	PTS	PIM
1977-78	PITT	N	1	0	0	0	0
1978-79			1	1	0	1	0
1979-80			24	3	7	10	4
1980-81			8	1	0	1	4
	TOR	N	2	0	0	0	4
	2 team total		10	1	0	1	8
4 yrs.		N Totals:	36	5	7	12	12
PLAYOFFS							
1979-80	PITT	N	4	0	0	0	0

Traded to **Toronto** by Pittsburgh with Paul Marshall for Paul Gardner and Dave Burrows, Nov. 18, 1980.

Lorne Davis

DAVIS, LORNE AUSTIN 5'11", 190 lbs.
B. July 20, 1930, Regina, Sask. Right Wing, Shoots R

YEAR	TEAM & LEAGUE		GP	G	A	PTS	PIM
1951-52	MONT	N	3	1	1	2	2
1953-54			37	6	4	10	2
1954-55	DET	N	30	0	5	5	6
1955-56	BOS	N	15	0	1	1	0
1959-60			10	1	1	2	10
5 yrs.		N Totals:	95	8	12	20	20
PLAYOFFS							
1952-53*	MONT	N	7	1	1	2	2
1953-54			11	2	0	2	8
2 yrs.		N Totals:	18	3	1	4	10

Traded to **Chicago** by Detroit for Ike Hildebrand, Oct. 14, 1954. Traded to **Detroit** by Chicago for Metro Prystai, Nov. 9, 1954. Traded to **Boston** by Detroit with Terry Sawchuk, Vic Stasiuk and Marcel Bonin, for Ed Sandford, Real Chevrefils, Norm Corcoran, Gilles Boisvert and Warren Godfrey, June, 1955.

Mal Davis

DAVIS, MALCOLM STERLING 5'11", 180 lbs.
B. Oct. 10, 1956, Lockeport, N.S. Left Wing, Shoots L

YEAR	TEAM & LEAGUE		GP	G	A	PTS	PIM
1978-79	DET	N	6	0	0	0	0
1980-81			5	2	0	2	0
1982-83	BUF	N	24	8	12	20	0
3 yrs.		N Totals:	35	10	12	22	0
PLAYOFFS							
1982-83	BUF	N	6	1	0	1	0

Signed as free agent by **Detroit** Oct. 12, 1978.

Murray Davison

DAVISON, MURRAY 6'2", 190 lbs.
B. June 10, 1938, Brantford, Ont. Defense, Shoots R

YEAR	TEAM & LEAGUE		GP	G	A	PTS	PIM
1965-66	BOS	N	1	0	0	0	0

Robert Dawes

DAWES, ROBERT JAMES 6'1", 170 lbs.
B. Nov. 29, 1924, Saskatoon, Sask. Defense, Shoots L

YEAR	TEAM & LEAGUE		GP	G	A	PTS	PIM
1946-47	TOR	N	1	0	0	0	0
1948-49			5	1	0	1	0
1949-50			11	1	2	3	2
1950-51	MONT	N	15	0	5	5	4
4 yrs.		N Totals:	32	2	7	9	6
PLAYOFFS							
1948-49*	TOR	N	9	0	0	0	2
1950-51*			1	0	0	0	0
2 yrs.		N Totals:	10	0	0	0	2

Hap Day

DAY, CLARENCE HENRY 5'11", 175 lbs.
B. June 1, 1901, Owen Sound, Ont. Left Wing
Hall of Fame, 1961

YEAR	TEAM & LEAGUE		GP	G	A	PTS	PIM
1924-25	TOR	N	26	10	12	22	33
1925-26			36	14	2	16	26
1926-27			44	11	5	16	50
1927-28			22	9	8	17	48
1928-29			44	6	6	12	84
1929-30			43	7	14	21	77
1930-31			44	1	13	14	56
1931-32			47	7	8	15	33
1932-33			47	6	14	20	46
1933-34			48	9	10	19	35
1934-35			45	2	4	6	38
1935-36			44	1	13	14	41
1936-37			48	3	4	7	20
1937-38	NYA	N	44	0	3	3	14
14 yrs.		N Totals:	582	86	116	202	601

Hap Day continued

YEAR	TEAM & LEAGUE		GP	G	A	PTS	PIM
PLAYOFFS							
1924-25	**TOR**	**N**	2	0	0	0	0
1928-29			4	1	0	1	2
1930-31			2	0	3	3	7
1931-32*			7	3	3	6	6
1932-33			9	0	1	1	21
1933-34			5	0	0	0	6
1934-35			7	0	0	0	4
1935-36			9	0	0	0	8
1936-37			2	0	0	0	0
1937-38	**NYA**	**N**	6	0	0	0	0
10 yrs.	**N Totals:**		53	4	7	11	54

Billy Dea

DEA, WILLIAM FRASER 5'8", 175 lbs.
B. Apr. 3, 1933, Edmonton, Alta. Left Wing, Shoots L

YEAR	TEAM & LEAGUE		GP	G	A	PTS	PIM
1953-54	**NYR**	**N**	14	1	1	2	2
1956-57	**DET**	**N**	69	15	15	30	14
1957-58			29	4	4	8	6
	CHI	**N**	34	5	8	13	4
	2 team total		63	9	12	21	10
1967-68	**PITT**	**N**	73	16	12	28	6
1968-69			68	10	8	18	4
1969-70	**DET**	**N**	70	10	3	13	6
1970-71			42	6	3	9	2
7 yrs.	**N Totals:**		399	67	54	121	44
PLAYOFFS							
1956-57	**DET**	**N**	5	2	0	2	2
1966-67	**CHI**	**N**	2	0	0	0	2
1969-70	**DET**	**N**	4	0	1	1	2
3 yrs.	**N Totals:**		11	2	1	3	6

Traded to **Detroit** by N.Y. Rangers with Aggie Kukulowicz and cash for Dave Creighton and Bronco Horvath, Aug. 18, 1955. Traded to **Chicago** by Detroit with Bill Dineen, Lorne Ferguson, and Earl Reibel for Nick Mickoski, Bob Bailey, Hec Lalande and Jack McIntyre, Dec. 17, 1957. Drafted by **Pittsburgh** from Chicago in Expansion Draft, June 6, 1967. Traded to **Detroit** by Pittsburgh for Mike McMahon, Oct. 28, 1969.

Don Deacon

DEACON, DONALD JOHN 5'9", 190 lbs.
B. June 2, 1913, Regina, Sask. Left Wing, Shoots L

YEAR	TEAM & LEAGUE		GP	G	A	PTS	PIM
1936-37	**DET**	**N**	4	0	0	0	2
1938-39			8	1	3	4	2
1939-40			18	5	1	6	2
3 yrs.	**N Totals:**		30	6	4	10	6
PLAYOFFS							
1938-39	**DET**	**N**	2	2	1	3	0

Butch Deadmarsh

DEADMARSH, ERNEST CHARLES 5'10", 185 lbs.
B. Apr. 5, 1950, Trail, B.C. Left Wing, Shoots L

YEAR	TEAM & LEAGUE		GP	G	A	PTS	PIM
1970-71	**BUF**	**N**	10	0	0	0	9
1971-72			12	1	1	2	4
1972-73			34	1	1	2	26
	ATL	**N**	19	1	0	1	8
	2 team total		53	2	1	3	34
1973-74			42	6	1	7	89
1974-75	**KC**	**N**	20	3	2	5	19
	VAN	**W**	38	7	8	15	128
	2 team total		58	10	10	20	147
1975-76	**CALG**	**W**	79	26	28	54	196
1976-77	**MINN**	**W**	35	9	4	13	51
	CALG	**W**	38	13	17	30	77
	2 team total		73	22	21	43	128
1977-78	**EDM**	**W**	0	0	0	0	0
	CIN	**W**	65	8	9	17	118
	2 team total		65	8	9	17	118
8 yrs.	**N Totals:**		137	12	5	17	155
	W Totals:		255	63	66	129	570
PLAYOFFS							
1973-74	**ATL**	**N**	4	0	0	0	17
1975-76	**CALG**	**W**	8	0	1	1	14

Butch Deadmarsh continued

YEAR	TEAM & LEAGUE		GP	G	A	PTS	PIM
2 yrs.	**N Totals:**		4	0	0	0	17
	W Totals:		8	0	1	1	14

Traded to **Atlanta** by Buffalo for Norm Gratton, Feb. 14, 1973. Drafted by **Kansas City** from Atlanta in Expansion Draft, June 12, 1974.

Barry Dean

DEAN, BARRY JAMES 6'1", 195 lbs.
B. Feb. 26, 1955, Maple Creek, Sask. Left Wing, Shoots L

YEAR	TEAM & LEAGUE		GP	G	A	PTS	PIM
1975-76	**PHOE**	**W**	71	9	25	34	110
1976-77	**COLO**	**N**	79	14	25	39	92
1977-78	**PHI**	**N**	56	7	18	25	34
1978-79			30	4	13	17	20
4 yrs.	**N Totals:**		165	25	56	81	146
	W Totals:		71	9	25	34	110

Traded to **Philadelphia** by Colorado for Mark Suzor, Aug. 5, 1977. Claimed by **Philadelphia** as fill in Expansion Draft, June 13, 1979. Traded to **Edmonton** by Philadelphia for Ron Areshenkoff and Edmonton's tenth-round choice in 1980 Entry Draft (Bob O'Brien), June 11, 1980.

Nelson Debenedet

DEBENEDET, NELSON FLAVIO 6'1", 195 lbs.
B. Dec. 31, 1947, Cordenons, Italy Left Wing, Shoots L

YEAR	TEAM & LEAGUE		GP	G	A	PTS	PIM
1973-74	**DET**	**N**	15	4	1	5	2
1974-75	**PITT**	**N**	31	6	3	9	11
2 yrs.	**N Totals:**		46	10	4	14	13

Traded to **Pittsburgh** by Detroit for Hank Nowak and Pittsburgh's third choice (Dan Mandryk) in 1974 Amateur Draft, May 27, 1974.

Lucien Deblois

DEBLOIS, LUCIEN 5'11", 200 lbs.
B. June 21, 1957, Joliette, Que. Right Wing, Shoots R

YEAR	TEAM & LEAGUE		GP	G	A	PTS	PIM
1977-78	**NYR**	**N**	71	22	8	30	27
1978-79			62	11	17	28	26
1979-80			6	3	1	4	7
	COLO	**N**	70	24	19	43	36
	2 team total		76	27	20	47	43
1980-81			74	26	16	42	78
1981-82	**WINN**	**N**	65	25	27	52	87
1982-83			79	27	27	54	69
6 yrs.	**N Totals:**		427	138	115	253	330
PLAYOFFS							
1977-78	**NYR**	**N**	3	0	0	0	2
1978-79			9	2	0	2	4
1981-82	**WINN**	**N**	4	2	1	3	4
1982-83			3	0	0	0	5
4 yrs.	**N Totals:**		19	4	1	5	15

Traded to **Colorado** by N.Y. Rangers with Pat Hickey, Mike McEwen, Dean Turner and future considerations (Bobby Crawford) for Barry Beck, Nov. 2, 1979. Traded to **Winnipeg** by Colorado for Brent Ashton and Winnipeg's third-round choice (Dave Kasper) in the 1982 Entry Draft, July 15, 1981.

Dave Debol

DEBOL, DAVID 5'11", 175 lbs.
B. Mar. 27, 1956, St. Clair Shores, Mich.
Center, Shoots R

YEAR	TEAM & LEAGUE		GP	G	A	PTS	PIM
1977-78	**CIN**	**W**	9	3	2	5	2
1978-79			59	10	27	37	9
1979-80	**HART**	**N**	48	12	14	26	4
1980-81			44	14	12	26	0
4 yrs.	**N Totals:**		92	26	26	52	4
	W Totals:		68	13	29	42	11
PLAYOFFS							
1979-80	**HART**	**N**	3	0	0	0	0

Armand Delmonte

DELMONTE, ARMAND ROMEO (Dutch) 5'10", 190 lbs.
B. Jan. 4, 1925, Timmons, Ont. Center, Shoots R

YEAR	TEAM & LEAGUE		GP	G	A	PTS	PIM
1945-46	**BOS**	**N**	1	0	0	0	0

Gilbert Delorme

DELORME, GILBERT 5'11", 202 lbs.
B. Nov. 25, 1962, Boucherville, Que. Defense, Shoots R

YEAR	TEAM & LEAGUE		GP	G	A	PTS	PIM
1981-82	**MONT**	**N**	60	3	8	11	55
1982-83			78	12	21	33	89
2 yrs.		**N Totals:**	138	15	29	44	144
PLAYOFFS							
1982-83	**MONT**	**N**	3	0	0	0	2

Ron Delorme

DELORME, RONALD ELMER (Chief) 6'2", 185 lbs.
B. Sept. 3, 1955, North Battleford, Sask. Center, Shoots R

YEAR	TEAM & LEAGUE		GP	G	A	PTS	PIM
1975-76	**D-O**	**W**	22	1	3	4	28
1976-77	**COLO**	**N**	29	6	4	10	23
1977-78			63	10	11	21	40
1978-79			77	20	8	28	68
1979-80			75	19	24	43	76
1980-81			65	11	16	27	70
1981-82	**VAN**	**N**	59	9	8	17	177
1982-83			56	5	8	13	87
8 yrs.		**N Totals:**	424	80	79	159	541
		W Totals:	22	1	3	4	28
PLAYOFFS							
1977-78	**COLO**	**N**	2	0	0	0	10
1981-82	**VAN**	**N**	14	0	2	2	31
1982-83			4	0	0	0	10
3 yrs.		**N Totals:**	20	0	2	2	51

Claimed by **Vancouver** from Colorado, in Waiver Draft, Oct. 5, 1981.

Valentine Delory

DELORY, VALENTINE 5'10", 160 lbs.
B. Feb. 14, 1927, Toronto, Ont. Left Wing, Shoots L

YEAR	TEAM & LEAGUE		GP	G	A	PTS	PIM
1948-49	**NYR**	**N**	1	0	0	0	0

Guy Delparte

DELPARTE, GUY PHILIPP 5'9", 178 lbs.
B. Aug. 30, 1949, Prince Albert, Sask. Left Wing, Shoots L

YEAR	TEAM & LEAGUE		GP	G	A	PTS	PIM
1976-77	**COLO**	**N**	48	1	8	9	18

Signed as free agent by **Colorado** Oct. 4, 1976.

Alex Delvecchio

DELVECCHIO, ALEX PETER 6', 195 lbs.
B. Dec. 4, 1931, Fort William, Ont. Center, Shoots L
Won Lady Byng Trophy, 1958–59, 1965–66, 1968-69
Hall of Fame, 1977

YEAR	TEAM & LEAGUE		GP	G	A	PTS	PIM
1950-51	**DET**	**N**	1	0	0	0	0
1951-52			65	15	22	37	22
1952-53			70	16	43	59	28
1953-54			69	11	18	29	34
1954-55			69	17	31	48	37
1955-56			70	25	26	51	24
1956-57			48	16	25	41	8
1957-58			70	21	38	59	22
1958-59			70	19	35	54	6
1959-60			70	19	28	47	8
1960-61			70	27	35	62	26
1961-62			70	26	43	69	18
1962-63			70	20	44	64	8
1963-64			70	23	30	53	11
1964-65			68	25	42	67	16
1965-66			70	31	38	69	16
1966-67			70	17	38	55	10
1967-68			74	22	48	70	14
1968-69			72	25	58	83	8
1969-70			73	21	47	68	24
1970-71			77	21	34	55	6
1971-72			75	20	45	65	22
1972-73			77	18	53	71	13
1973-74			11	1	4	5	2
24 yrs.		**N Totals:**	1549	456	825	1281	383
PLAYOFFS							
1951-52*	**DET**	**N**	8	0	3	3	4

Alex Delvecchio continued

YEAR	TEAM & LEAGUE		GP	G	A	PTS	PIM
1952-53			6	2	4	6	2
1953-54*			12	2	7	9	7
1954-55*			11	7	8	15	2
1955-56			10	7	3	10	2
1956-57			5	3	2	5	2
1957-58			4	0	1	1	0
1959-60			6	2	6	8	0
1960-61			11	4	5	9	0
1962-63			11	3	6	9	2
1963-64			14	3	8	11	0
1964-65			7	2	3	5	4
1965-66			12	0	11	11	4
1969-70			4	0	2	2	0
14 yrs.		**N Totals:**	121	35	69	104	29

Ab DeMarco

DEMARCO, ALBERT GEORGE 6', 168 lbs.
B. May 10, 1916, North Bay, Ont. Center, Shoots R

YEAR	TEAM & LEAGUE		GP	G	A	PTS	PIM
1938-39	**CHI**	**N**	2	1	0	1	0
1939-40			17	0	5	5	17
1942-43	**TOR**	**N**	4	0	1	1	0
	BOS	**N**	3	4	1	5	0
	2 team total		7	4	2	6	0
1943-44			3	0	0	0	0
	NYR	**N**	36	14	19	33	2
	2 team total		39	14	19	33	2
1944-45			50	24	30	54	10
1945-46			50	20	27	47	20
1946-47			44	9	10	19	4
7 yrs.		**N Totals:**	209	72	93	165	53
PLAYOFFS							
1939-40	**CHI**	**N**	2	0	0	0	0
1942-43	**BOS**	**N**	9	3	0	3	2
2 yrs.		**N Totals:**	11	3	0	3	2

Ab DeMarco

DEMARCO, ALBERT THOMAS 6', 170 lbs.
B. Feb. 27, 1949, Cleveland, Oh. Defense, Shoots R

YEAR	TEAM & LEAGUE		GP	G	A	PTS	PIM
1969-70	**NYR**	**N**	3	0	0	0	0
1970-71			2	0	1	1	0
1971-72			48	4	7	11	4
1972-73			51	4	13	17	15
	STL	**N**	14	4	9	13	2
	2 team total		65	8	22	30	17
1973-74			23	3	9	12	11
	PITT	**N**	34	7	12	19	4
	2 team total		57	10	21	31	15
1974-75			8	2	1	3	4
	VAN	**N**	61	10	14	24	21
	2 team total		69	12	15	27	25
1975-76			34	3	8	11	2
	LA	**N**	30	4	3	7	6
	2 team total		64	7	11	18	8
1976-77			33	3	3	6	6
1977-78	**EDM**	**W**	47	6	8	14	20
1978-79	**BOS**	**N**	3	0	0	0	0
10 yrs.		**N Totals:**	344	44	80	124	75
		W Totals:	47	6	8	14	20
PLAYOFFS							
1969-70	**NYR**	**N**	5	0	0	0	2
1971-72			4	0	1	1	0
1972-73	**STL**	**N**	4	1	1	2	2
1974-75	**VAN**	**N**	2	0	0	0	0
1975-76	**LA**	**N**	9	0	0	0	11
1976-77			1	0	0	0	2
1977-78	**EDM**	**W**	1	0	0	0	0
7 yrs.		**N Totals:**	25	1	2	3	17
		W Totals:	1	0	0	0	0

Traded to **St. Louis** by N.Y. Rangers for Mike Murphy, March 2, 1973. Traded to **Pittsburgh** by St. Louis with Steve Durbano and Bob Kelly for Bryan Watson, Greg Polis, and Pittsburgh's second choice (Bob Hess) in 1974 Amateur Draft Draft, Jan. 17, 1974. Traded to **Vancouver** by Pittsburgh for Barry Wilkins, Nov. 4, 1974. Traded to **Los Angeles** by Vancouver for Los Angeles' second choice (later transferred to Atlanta, Brian Hill) in 1977 Amateur Draft, Jan. 14, 1976. Traded to **Atlanta** by Los Angeles for Randy Manery, May 23, 1977. Signed as free agent by **Boston** Oct. 23, 1978.

Tony Demers

DEMERS, ANTONIO 5'9", 180 lbs.
B. July 22, 1917, Chambly Basin, Que. Right Wing, Shoots R

YEAR	TEAM	LEAGUE	GP	G	A	PTS	PIM
1937-38	MONT	N	6	0	0	0	0
1939-40			14	2	3	5	2
1940-41			46	13	10	23	17
1941-42			7	3	4	7	4
1942-43			9	2	5	7	0
1943-44	NYR	N	1	0	0	0	0
6 yrs.		N Totals:	83	20	22	42	23

PLAYOFFS

YEAR	TEAM	LEAGUE	GP	G	A	PTS	PIM
1940-41	MONT	N	3	0	0	0	0

Johnny Denis

DENIS, JEAN PAUL 5'8", 170 lbs.
B. Feb. 28, 1924, Montreal, Que. Right Wing, Shoots R

YEAR	TEAM	LEAGUE	GP	G	A	PTS	PIM
1946-47	NYR	N	6	0	1	1	0
1949-50			4	0	1	1	2
2 yrs.		N Totals:	10	0	2	2	2

Lulu Denis

DENIS, LOUIS GILBERT 5'8", 140 lbs.
B. June 7, 1928, Vonda, Sask. Right Wing, Shoots R

YEAR	TEAM	LEAGUE	GP	G	A	PTS	PIM
1949-50	MONT	N	2	0	1	1	0
1950-51			1	0	0	0	0
2 yrs.		N Totals:	3	0	1	1	0

Corbett Denneny

DENNENY, CORBETT
B. Left Wing

YEAR	TEAM	LEAGUE	GP	G	A	PTS	PIM
1917-18	TOR	N	21	20	0	20	8
1918-19			16	7	3	10	15
1919-20			23	23	**12**	35	18
1920-21			20	17	6	23	27
1921-22			24	19	7	26	28
1922-23			1	1	0	1	0
1923-24	HAMIL	N	23	0	0	0	6
1926-27	TOR	N	29	7	1	8	24
1927-28	CHI	N	19	5	0	5	12
9 yrs.		N Totals:	176	99	29	128	138

PLAYOFFS

YEAR	TEAM	LEAGUE	GP	G	A	PTS	PIM
1917-18*	TOR	N	7	3	2	5	3
1920-21			2	0	0	0	0
1921-22*			7	3	2	5	2
3 yrs.		N Totals:	16	6	4	10	5

Cy Denneny

DENNENY, CYRIL
B. Dec. 23, 1897, Farran's point, Ont. Left Wing
Won Art Ross Trophy, 1923-24
Hall of Fame, 1959

YEAR	TEAM	LEAGUE	GP	G	A	PTS	PIM
1917-18	OTTA	N	22	36	0	36	34
1918-19			18	18	4	22	43
1919-20			22	16	2	18	21
1920-21			24	34	5	39	0
1921-22			22	27	12	39	18
1922-23			24	21	10	31	20
1923-24			21	**22**	1	**23**	10
1924-25			28	27	**15**	42	16
1925-26			36	24	12	36	18
1926-27			42	17	6	23	16
1927-28			44	3	0	3	12
1928-29	BOS	N	23	1	2	3	2
12 yrs.		N Totals:	326	246	69	315	210

PLAYOFFS

YEAR	TEAM	LEAGUE	GP	G	A	PTS	PIM
1918-19	OTTA	N	5	2	0	2	0
1919-20*			5	0	0	0	3
1920-21*			7	4	2	6	20
1921-22			2	2	0	2	4
1922-23*			8	3	1	4	6
1923-24			2	2	0	2	2
1925-26			2	0	0	0	4

Cy Denneny continued

YEAR	TEAM	LEAGUE	GP	G	A	PTS	PIM
1926-27*			6	5	0	5	0
1927-28			2	0	0	0	0
1928-29*	BOS	N	2	0	0	0	0
10 yrs.		N Totals:	41	18	3	21	39

Norm Dennis

DENNIS, NORMAN MARSHALL 5'10", 175 lbs.
B. Dec. 10, 1942, Aurora, Ont. Center, Shoots L

YEAR	TEAM	LEAGUE	GP	G	A	PTS	PIM
1968-69	STL	N	2	0	0	0	2
1969-70			5	3	0	3	5
1970-71			4	0	0	0	0
1971-72			1	0	0	0	4
4 yrs.		N Totals:	12	3	0	3	11

PLAYOFFS

YEAR	TEAM	LEAGUE	GP	G	A	PTS	PIM
1969-70	STL	N	2	0	0	0	2
1970-71			3	0	0	0	0
2 yrs.		N Totals:	5	0	0	0	2

Sold to **St. Louis** by Montreal, Oct. 29, 1968. Traded to **N.Y. Rangers** by St. Louis with Don Borgeson for Bob Kelly, Sept. 8, 1973.

Gerry Denoird

DENOIRD, GERALD
B. Unknown Forward

YEAR	TEAM	LEAGUE	GP	G	A	PTS	PIM
1922-23	TOR	N	15	0	0	0	0

Brian Derkson

DERKSON, BRIAN 5'10", 190 lbs.
B. Nov. 29, 1951, Borden, Sask. Defense, Shoots L

YEAR	TEAM	LEAGUE	GP	G	A	PTS	PIM
1973-74	LA	W	1	0	0	0	2

Bill Derlago

DERLAGO, WILLIAM ANTHONY 5'10", 194 lbs.
B. Aug. 25, 1958, Birtle, Man. Center, Shoots L

YEAR	TEAM	LEAGUE	GP	G	A	PTS	PIM
1978-79	VAN	N	9	4	4	8	2
1979-80			54	11	15	26	27
	TOR	N	23	5	12	17	13
	2 team total		77	16	27	43	40
1980-81			80	35	39	74	26
1981-82			75	34	50	84	42
1982-83			58	13	24	37	27
5 yrs.		N Totals:	299	102	144	246	137

PLAYOFFS

YEAR	TEAM	LEAGUE	GP	G	A	PTS	PIM
1979-80	TOR	N	3	0	0	0	4
1980-81			3	1	0	1	2
1982-83			4	3	0	3	2
3 yrs.		N Totals:	10	4	0	4	8

Traded to **Toronto** by Vancouver with Rick Vaive for Tiger Williams and Jerry Butler, Feb. 18, 1980.

Gerard Desaulniers

DESAULNIERS, GERARD 5'11", 152 lbs.
B. Dec. 31, 1928, Shawinigan Falls, Que.
Center, Shoots L

YEAR	TEAM	LEAGUE	GP	G	A	PTS	PIM
1950-51	MONT	N	3	0	1	1	2
1952-53			2	0	1	1	2
1953-54			3	0	0	0	0
3 yrs.		N Totals:	8	0	2	2	4

Andre Deschamps

DESCHAMPS, ANDRE 5'11", 180 lbs.
B. Aug. 13, 1953, Valleyfield, Que. Left Wing, Shoots L

YEAR	TEAM	LEAGUE	GP	G	A	PTS	PIM
1976-77	CALG	W	9	1	2	3	19

Norm Descoteaux

DESCOTEAUX, JOSEPH NORMAND 5'9", 170 lbs.
B. Jan. 3, 1948, Montreal, Que. Defense, Shoots L

YEAR	TEAM & LEAGUE		GP	G	A	PTS	PIM
1972-73	**QUE**	**W**	2	0	1	1	0
1973-74			35	1	6	7	6
2 yrs.		**W Totals:**	37	1	7	8	6

Joffre Desilets

DESILETS, JOFFRE WILFRID 5'10½", 170 lbs.
B. Apr. 16, 1915, Capreol, Ont. Right Wing

YEAR	TEAM & LEAGUE		GP	G	A	PTS	PIM
1935-36	**MONT**	**N**	38	7	6	13	0
1936-37			48	7	12	19	17
1937-38			32	6	7	13	6
1938-39	**CHI**	**N**	48	11	13	24	28
1939-40			26	6	7	13	6
5 yrs.		**N Totals:**	192	37	45	82	57

PLAYOFFS

YEAR	TEAM & LEAGUE		GP	G	A	PTS	PIM
1936-37	**MONT**	**N**	5	1	0	1	0
1937-38			2	0	0	0	7
2 yrs.		**N Totals:**	7	1	0	1	7

Ken Desjardine

DESJARDINE, KENNETH FREDERICK 6', 180 lbs.
B. Aug. 23, 1947, Toronto, Ont. Defense, Shoots L

YEAR	TEAM & LEAGUE		GP	G	A	PTS	PIM
1972-73	**QUE**	**W**	38	2	6	8	36
1973-74			70	2	10	12	44
1974-75	**IND**	**W**	46	0	8	8	68
1975-76	**CALG**	**W**	1	0	0	0	0
4 yrs.		**W Totals:**	155	4	24	28	148

Vic Desjardins

DESJARDINS, VICTOR ARTHUR 5'9", 160 lbs.
B. July 4, 1900, Soo, Mich. Center, Shoots R

YEAR	TEAM & LEAGUE		GP	G	A	PTS	PIM
1930-31	**CHI**	**N**	39	3	12	15	11
1931-32	**NYR**	**N**	48	3	3	6	16
2 yrs.		**N Totals:**	87	6	15	21	27

PLAYOFFS

YEAR	TEAM & LEAGUE		GP	G	A	PTS	PIM
1930-31	**CHI**	**N**	9	0	0	0	0
1931-32	**NYR**	**N**	7	0	0	0	0
2 yrs.		**N Totals:**	16	0	0	0	0

Jacques Deslauriers

DESLAURIERS, JACQUES 6', 170 lbs.
B. Sept. 3, 1928, Montreal, Que. Defense, Shoots L

YEAR	TEAM & LEAGUE		GP	G	A	PTS	PIM
1955-56	**MONT**	**N**	2	0	0	0	0

Kevin Devine

DEVINE, KEVIN 5'9", 173 lbs.
B. Dec. 9, 1954, Charlottetown, P.E.I. Left Wing, Shoots L

YEAR	TEAM & LEAGUE		GP	G	A	PTS	PIM
1974-75	**SD**	**W**	46	4	10	14	48
1975-76			80	21	28	49	102
1976-77			81	30	20	50	114
1977-78	**IND**	**W**	76	19	23	42	141
1978-79	**QUE**	**W**	5	0	0	0	6
1982-83	**NYI**	**N**	2	0	1	1	8
6 yrs.		**N Totals:**	2	0	1	1	8
		W Totals:	288	74	81	155	411

PLAYOFFS

YEAR	TEAM & LEAGUE		GP	G	A	PTS	PIM
1974-75	**SD**	**W**	10	1	0	1	14
1975-76			11	3	1	4	36
1976-77			7	1	3	4	14
3 yrs.		**W Totals:**	28	5	4	9	64

Signed as free agent by **N.Y. Islanders** Oct. 9, 1981.

Pete Devlin

DEVLIN, PETER
Defense

PLAYOFFS

YEAR	TEAM & LEAGUE		GP	G	A	PTS	PIM
1975-76	**NE**	**W**	1	0	0	0	0

Tom Dewar

DEWAR, THOMAS
B. June 10, 1913, Frobisher, Sask. Defense

YEAR	TEAM & LEAGUE		GP	G	A	PTS	PIM
1943-44	**NYR**	**N**	9	0	2	2	4

Al Dewsbury

DEWSBURY, ALBERT PERCY 6'2", 202 lbs.
B. Apr. 12, 1926, Goderich, Ont. Defense, Shoots L

YEAR	TEAM & LEAGUE		GP	G	A	PTS	PIM
1946-47	**DET**	**N**	23	2	1	3	12
1949-50			11	2	2	4	2
1950-51	**CHI**	**N**	67	5	14	19	79
1951-52			69	7	17	24	99
1952-53			69	5	17	22	97
1953-54			69	6	15	21	44
1954-55			2	0	1	1	10
1955-56			37	3	12	15	22
8 yrs.		**N Totals:**	347	30	79	109	365

PLAYOFFS

YEAR	TEAM & LEAGUE		GP	G	A	PTS	PIM
1946-47	**DET**	**N**	2	0	0	0	4
1947-48			1	0	0	0	0
1949-50*			4	0	3	3	8
1952-53	**CHI**	**N**	7	1	2	3	4
4 yrs.		**N Totals:**	14	1	5	6	16

Traded to **Chicago** by Detroit with Harry Lumley, Jack Stewart, Don Morrison and Pete Babando for Jim Henry, Bob Goldham, Gaye Stewart and Metro Prystai, July 13, 1950.

Michel Deziel

DEZIEL, MICHEL 5'11", 180 lbs.
B. Jan. 13, 1954, Sorel, Que. Defense

PLAYOFFS

YEAR	TEAM & LEAGUE		GP	G	A	PTS	PIM
1974-75	**BUF**	**N**	1	0	0	0	0

Marcel Dheere

DHEERE, MARCEL ALBERT (Ching) 5'7", 175 lbs.
B. Dec. 19, 1920, St. Boniface, Man. Left Wing, Shoots L

YEAR	TEAM & LEAGUE		GP	G	A	PTS	PIM
1942-43	**MONT**	**N**	11	1	2	3	2

PLAYOFFS

YEAR	TEAM & LEAGUE		GP	G	A	PTS	PIM
1942-43	**MONT**	**N**	5	0	0	0	6

Edward Diachuk

DIACHUK, EDWARD 6'1", 195 lbs.
B. Aug. 16, 1936, Vegreville, Alta. Left Wing, Shoots L

YEAR	TEAM & LEAGUE		GP	G	A	PTS	PIM
1960-61	**DET**	**N**	12	0	0	0	19

Harry Dick

DICK, HARRY 5'11½", 210 lbs.
B. Nov. 22, 1922, Port Colborne, Ont. Defense, Shoots L

YEAR	TEAM & LEAGUE		GP	G	A	PTS	PIM
1946-47	**CHI**	**N**	12	0	1	1	12

Ernie Dickens

DICKENS, ERNEST LESLIE 6', 175 lbs.
B. June 25, 1921, Winnipeg, Man. Defense, Shoots L

YEAR	TEAM & LEAGUE		GP	G	A	PTS	PIM
1941-42	**TOR**	**N**	10	2	2	4	6
1945-46			15	1	3	4	6
1947-48	**CHI**	**N**	54	5	15	20	30
1948-49			59	2	3	5	14
1949-50			70	0	13	13	22
1950-51			70	2	8	10	20
6 yrs.		**N Totals:**	278	12	44	56	98

PLAYOFFS

YEAR	TEAM & LEAGUE		GP	G	A	PTS	PIM
1941-42*	**TOR**	**N**	13	0	0	0	4

Herb Dickenson

DICKENSON, JOHN HERBERT 5'11", 175 lbs.
B. June 11, 1931, Hamilton, Ont. Left Wing, Shoots L

YEAR	TEAM & LEAGUE		GP	G	A	PTS	PIM
1951-52	**NYR**	**N**	37	14	13	27	8
1952-53			11	4	4	8	2
2 yrs.		**N Totals:**	48	18	17	35	10

Bob Dill

DILL, ROBERT EDWARD 5'8", 185 lbs.
B. Apr. 25, 1920, St. Paul, Minn. Defense, Shoots L

YEAR	TEAM & LEAGUE		GP	G	A	PTS	PIM
1943-44	**NYR**	**N**	28	6	10	16	66
1944-45			48	9	5	14	69
2 yrs.		**N Totals:**	76	15	15	30	135

Bob Dillabough

DILLABOUGH, ROBERT WELLINGTON 5'10", 180 lbs.
B. Apr. 27, 1941, Belleville, Ont. Center, Shoots L

YEAR	TEAM & LEAGUE		GP	G	A	PTS	PIM
1961-62	**DET**	**N**	5	0	0	0	2
1964-65			4	0	0	0	2
1965-66	**BOS**	**N**	53	7	13	20	18
1966-67			60	6	12	18	14
1967-68	**PITT**	**N**	47	7	12	19	18
1968-69			14	0	0	0	2
	CALIF	**N**	48	7	12	19	4
	2 team total		62	7	12	19	6
1969-70	**OAK**	**N**	52	5	5	10	16
1972-73	**CLEVE**	**W**	72	8	8	16	8
8 yrs.		**N Totals:**	283	32	54	86	76
		W Totals:	72	8	8	16	8

PLAYOFFS

YEAR	TEAM & LEAGUE		GP	G	A	PTS	PIM
1962-63	**DET**	**N**	1	0	0	0	0
1963-64			1	0	0	0	0
1964-65			4	0	0	0	0
1968-69	**CALIF**	**N**	7	3	0	3	0
1969-70	**OAK**	**N**	4	0	0	0	0
1972-73	**CLEVE**	**W**	9	1	0	1	0
6 yrs.		**N Totals:**	17	3	0	3	0
		W Totals:	9	1	0	1	0

Traded by Detroit with Albert Langlois, Ron Harris, and Parker MacDonald to **Boston** for Ab McDonald, Bob McCord, and Ken Stephanson, May 31, 1965. Drafted by **Pittsburgh** from Boston in Expansion Draft, June 6, 1967. Traded to **Oakland** by Pittsburgh for Billy Harris, Nov. 29, 1968. Drafted by **Vancouver** from Oakland in Expansion Draft, June 10, 1970. Traded to **Detroit** by Vancouver with Irv Spencer for John Cunniff and Gary Bredin, June 8, 1971.

Ceece Dillon

DILLON, CECIL GRAHAM 5'10½", 173 lbs.
B. Apr. 26, 1908, Toledo, Ohio Forward, Shoots L

YEAR	TEAM & LEAGUE		GP	G	A	PTS	PIM
1930-31	**NYR**	**N**	25	7	3	10	8
1931-32			48	23	15	38	22
1932-33			48	21	10	31	12
1933-34			48	13	26	39	10
1934-35			48	25	9	34	4
1935-36			48	18	14	32	12
1936-37			48	20	11	31	13
1937-38			48	21	18	39	6
1938-39			48	12	15	27	6
1939-40	**DET**	**N**	44	7	10	17	12
10 yrs.		**N Totals:**	453	167	131	298	105

PLAYOFFS

YEAR	TEAM & LEAGUE		GP	G	A	PTS	PIM
1930-31	**NYR**	**N**	4	0	1	1	2
1931-32			7	2	1	3	4
1932-33*			8	8	2	10	6
1933-34			2	0	1	1	2
1934-35			4	2	1	3	0
1936-37			9	0	3	3	0
1937-38			3	1	0	1	0
1938-39			1	0	0	0	0
1939-40	**DET**	**N**	5	1	0	1	0
9 yrs.		**N Totals:**	43	14	9	23	14

Gary Dillon

DILLON, GARY KEVIN 5'10", 173 lbs.
B. Feb. 28, 1959, Toronto, Ont. Center, Shoots L

YEAR	TEAM & LEAGUE		GP	G	A	PTS	PIM
1980-81	**COLO**	**N**	13	1	1	2	29

Signed as free agent by **Quebec** Oct. 7, 1981.

Wayne Dillon

DILLON, GERALD WAYNE (Tommy) 6', 185 lbs.
B. May 25, 1955, Toronto, Ont. Center, Shoots L

YEAR	TEAM & LEAGUE		GP	G	A	PTS	PIM
1973-74	**TOR**	**W**	71	30	35	65	13
1974-75			77	29	66	95	22
1975-76	**NYR**	**N**	79	21	24	45	10
1976-77			78	17	29	46	33
1977-78			59	5	13	18	15
1978-79	**BIRM**	**W**	64	12	27	39	43
1979-80	**WINN**	**N**	13	0	0	0	2
7 yrs.		**N Totals:**	229	43	66	109	60
		W Totals:	212	71	128	199	78

PLAYOFFS

YEAR	TEAM & LEAGUE		GP	G	A	PTS	PIM
1973-74	**TOR**	**W**	12	5	6	11	9
1974-75			6	4	4	8	4
1977-78	**NYR**	**N**	3	0	1	1	0
3 yrs.		**N Totals:**	3	0	1	1	0
		W Totals:	18	9	10	19	13

Traded to **Winnipeg** by N.Y. Rangers for future considerations, July 25, 1979.

Ray DiLorenzi

DILORENZI, RAYMOND (The Hawk) 5'10", 185 lbs.
Right Wing

YEAR	TEAM & LEAGUE		GP	G	A	PTS	PIM
1974-75	**VAN**	**W**	3	0	0	0	0
1975-76	**CALG**	**W**	39	8	12	20	4
2 yrs.		**W Totals:**	42	8	12	20	4

Bill Dineen

DINEEN, WILLIAM PATRICK 5'11", 180 lbs.
B. Sept. 18, 1932, Arvida, Que. Right Wing, Shoots R

YEAR	TEAM & LEAGUE		GP	G	A	PTS	PIM
1953-54	**DET**	**N**	70	17	8	25	34
1954-55			69	10	9	19	36
1955-56			70	12	7	19	30
1956-57			51	6	7	13	12
1957-58			22	2	4	6	2
	CHI	**N**	41	4	9	13	10
	2 team total		63	6	13	19	12
5 yrs.		**N Totals:**	323	51	44	95	124

PLAYOFFS

YEAR	TEAM & LEAGUE		GP	G	A	PTS	PIM
1953-54*	**DET**	**N**	12	0	0	0	2
1954-55*			11	0	1	1	8
1955-56			10	1	0	1	8
1956-57			4	0	0	0	0
4 yrs.		**N Totals:**	37	1	1	2	18

Traded to **Chicago** by Detroit with Billy Dea, Lorne Ferguson, and Earl Reibel for Nick Mickoski, Bob Bailey, Hec Lalande, and Jack McIntyre, Dec. 17, 1957.

Gary Dineen

DINEEN, GARY DANIEL PATRICK 5'10", 175 lbs.
B. Sept. 18, 1932, Montreal, Que. Center, Shoots L

YEAR	TEAM & LEAGUE		GP	G	A	PTS	PIM
1968-69	**MINN**	**N**	4	0	1	1	0

Gord Dineen

DINEEN, GORD 5'11", 180 lbs.
B. Sept. 21, 1962, Toronto, Ont. Defense, Shoots R

YEAR	TEAM & LEAGUE		GP	G	A	PTS	PIM
1982-83	**NYI**	**N**	2	0	0	0	4

Chuck Dinsmore

DINSMORE, CHARLES A. (Dinny)
B. July 23, 1903, Toronto, Ont. Forward

YEAR	TEAM & LEAGUE		GP	G	A	PTS	PIM
1924-25	MON(M)	N	30	2	1	3	26
1925-26			33	3	1	4	18
1926-27			31	1	0	1	6
1929-30			8	0	0	0	0
4 yrs.		N Totals:	102	6	2	8	50
PLAYOFFS							
1925-26*	MON(M)	N	8	0	0	0	4
1929-30			4	0	0	0	0
2 yrs.		N Totals:	12	0	0	0	4

Marcel Dionne

DIONNE, MARCEL ELPHEGE (Lou) 5'8", 185 lbs.
B. Aug. 3, 1951, Drummondville, Que. Center, Shoots R
Won Art Ross Trophy, 1979-80
Won Lady Byng Trophy, 1974–75 , 1976-77

YEAR	TEAM & LEAGUE		GP	G	A	PTS	PIM
1971-72	DET	N	78	28	49	77	14
1972-73			77	40	50	90	21
1973-74			74	24	54	78	10
1974-75			80	47	74	121	14
1975-76	LA	N	80	40	54	94	38
1976-77			80	53	69	122	12
1977-78			70	36	43	79	36
1978-79			80	59	71	130	30
1979-80			80	53	84	**137**	32
1980-81			80	58	77	135	70
1981-82			78	50	67	117	50
1982-83			80	56	51	107	22
12 yrs.		N Totals:	937	544	743	1287	349
PLAYOFFS							
1975-76	LA	N	9	6	1	7	0
1976-77			9	5	9	14	2
1977-78			2	0	0	0	0
1978-79			2	0	1	1	0
1979-80			4	0	3	3	4
1980-81			4	1	3	4	7
1981-82			10	7	4	11	0
7 yrs.		N Totals:	40	19	21	40	13

Acquired as free agent by **Los Angeles** from Detroit with Bart Crashley for Terry Harper, Dan Maloney and Los Angeles' second choice (later transferred to Minnesota) in 1976 Amateur Draft, June 23, 1975.

Gary Doak

DOAK, GARY WALTER 5'11", 191 lbs.
B. Feb. 25, 1946, Goderich, Ont. Defense, Shoots R

YEAR	TEAM & LEAGUE		GP	G	A	PTS	PIM
1965-66	DET	N	4	0	0	0	12
	BOS	N	20	0	8	8	28
	2 team total		24	0	8	8	40
1966-67			29	0	1	1	50
1967-68			59	2	9	11	100
1968-69			22	3	3	6	37
1969-70			44	1	7	8	63
1970-71	VAN	N	77	2	10	12	112
1971-72			6	0	1	1	23
	NYR	N	49	1	10	11	23
	2 team total		55	1	11	12	46
1972-73	DET	N	44	0	5	5	51
	BOS	N	5	0	0	0	2
	2 team total		49	0	5	5	53
1973-74			69	0	4	4	44
1974-75			40	0	0	0	30
1975-76			58	1	6	7	60
1976-77			76	3	13	16	107
1977-78			61	4	13	17	50
1978-79			63	6	11	17	28
1979-80			52	0	5	5	45
1980-81			11	0	0	0	12
16 yrs.		N Totals:	789	23	106	129	877
PLAYOFFS							
1967-68	BOS	N	4	0	0	0	4
1969-70*			8	0	0	0	9
1971-72	NYR	N	12	0	0	0	46
1972-73	BOS	N	2	0	0	0	2

Gary Doak continued

YEAR	TEAM & LEAGUE		GP	G	A	PTS	PIM
1974-75			3	0	0	0	4
1975-76			12	1	0	1	22
1976-77			14	0	2	2	26
1977-78			12	1	0	1	4
1978-79			7	0	2	2	4
1979-80			4	0	0	0	0
10 yrs.		N Totals:	78	2	4	6	121

Traded to **Boston** by Detroit with Bill Lesuk and extra amateur draft choice (Steve Atkinson) for Leo Boivin, Feb. 18, 1966. Drafted by **Vancouver** from Boston in Expansion Draft, June 10, 1970. Traded to **N.Y. Rangers** by Vancouver with Jim Wiste for Dave Balon, Wayne Connelly and Ron Stewart, Nov. 16, 1971. Traded to **Detroit** by N.Y. Rangers with Rick Newell for Joe Zanussi and Detroit's first choice (Albert Blanchard) in the 1972 Amateur Draft, May 24, 1972. Traded to **Boston** by Detroit for Garnet Bailey and a player to be named later (Murray Wing, June 4, 1973), March 1, 1973.

Bob Dobek

DOBEK, ROBERT 6', 175 lbs.
B. Oct. 4, 1952, Detroit, Mich. Center, Shoots L

YEAR	TEAM & LEAGUE		GP	G	A	PTS	PIM
1975-76	SD	W	14	3	1	4	2
1976-77			58	7	17	24	17
2 yrs.		W Totals:	72	10	18	28	19
PLAYOFFS							
1975-76	SD	W	11	1	2	3	0
1976-77			5	0	0	0	4
2 yrs.		W Totals:	16	1	2	3	4

Jim Dobson

DOBSON, JAMES 6'1", 176 lbs.
B. Feb. 29, 1960, Winnipeg, Man. Right Wing, Shoots R

YEAR	TEAM & LEAGUE		GP	G	A	PTS	PIM
1979-80	MINN	N	1	0	0	0	0
1980-81			1	0	0	0	0
1981-82			6	0	0	0	4
	COLO	N	3	0	0	0	2
	2 team total		9	0	0	0	6
3 yrs.		N Totals:	11	0	0	0	6

Sold to **Colorado** by Minnesota, Dec. 31, 1981.

Fred Doherty

DOHERTY, FREDERICK
B. Unknown Forward

YEAR	TEAM & LEAGUE		GP	G	A	PTS	PIM
1918-19	MONT	N	3	0	0	0	0

Gary Donaldson

DONALDSON, GARY
Defense

YEAR	TEAM & LEAGUE		GP	G	A	PTS	PIM
1973-74	CHI	N	1	0	0	0	0
1976-77	HOUS	W	5	0	0	0	6
2 yrs.		N Totals:	1	0	0	0	0
		W Totals:	5	0	0	0	6

Babe Donnelly

DONNELLY (Babe)
B. Dec. 22, 1895, Sault Ste. Marie, Ont. Defense

YEAR	TEAM & LEAGUE		GP	G	A	PTS	PIM
1926-27	MON(M)	N	34	0	1	1	14
PLAYOFFS							
1926-27	MON(M)	N	2	0	0	0	0

John Donnelly

DONNELLY, JOHN 6', 190 lbs.
B. Sept. 28, 1948 Defense

YEAR	TEAM & LEAGUE		GP	G	A	PTS	PIM
1972-73	OTTA	W	15	1	1	2	44

Pat Donnelly

DONNELLY, PATRICK 5'10", 170 lbs.
B. Feb. 24, 1953 Center

YEAR	TEAM & LEAGUE		GP	G	A	PTS	PIM
1975-76	CIN	W	23	5	7	12	4

Peter Donnelly

DONNELLY, PETER 5'8", 155 lbs.
B. June 14, 1948, Detroit, Mich. Shoots R

YEAR	TEAM & LEAGUE		GP	G	A	PTS	PIM
1973-74	VAN	W	52	0	1	1	9

Red Doran

DORAN, LLOYD GEORGE 6', 175 lbs.
B. Jan. 10, 1921, South Porcupine, Ont. Center, Shoots L

YEAR	TEAM & LEAGUE		GP	G	A	PTS	PIM
1946-47	DET	N	24	3	2	5	10

Red Doran

DORAN, JOHN MICHAEL 6', 195 lbs.
B. May 24, 1911, Belleville, Ont. Defense, Shoots L

YEAR	TEAM & LEAGUE		GP	G	A	PTS	PIM
1933-34	NYA	N	39	1	4	5	40
1935-36			25	4	2	6	44
1936-37			21	0	1	1	10
1937-38	DET	N	7	0	0	0	10
1939-40	MONT	N	6	0	3	3	6
5 yrs.		N Totals:	98	5	10	15	110
PLAYOFFS							
1935 36	NYA	N	3	0	0	0	0

Ken Doraty

DORATY, KENNETH EDWARD 5'7", 133 lbs.
B. June 23, 1906, Stittsville, Ont. Forward, Shoots R

YEAR	TEAM & LEAGUE		GP	G	A	PTS	PIM
1926-27	CHI	N	18	0	0	0	0
1932-33	TOR	N	38	5	11	16	16
1933-34			34	9	10	19	6
1934-35			11	1	4	5	0
1937-38	DET	N	2	0	1	1	2
5 yrs.		N Totals:	103	15	26	41	24
PLAYOFFS							
1932-33	TOR	N	9	5	0	5	2
1933-34			5	2	2	4	0
1934-35			1	0	0	0	0
3 yrs.		N Totals:	15	7	2	9	2

Andre Dore

DORE, ANDRE HECTOR 6'2", 200 lbs.
B. Feb. 2, 1958, Montreal, Que. Defense, Shoots R

YEAR	TEAM & LEAGUE		GP	G	A	PTS	PIM
1978-79	NYR	N	2	0	0	0	0
1979-80			2	0	0	0	0
1980-81			15	1	3	4	15
1981-82			56	4	16	20	64
1982-83			39	3	12	15	39
	STL	N	38	2	15	17	25
	2 team total		77	5	27	32	64
5 yrs.		N Totals:	152	10	46	56	143
PLAYOFFS							
1981-82	NYR	N	10	1	1	2	16
1982-83	STL	N	4	0	1	1	8
2 yrs.		N Totals:	14	1	2	3	24

Traded to **St. Louis** by New York Rangers for Glen Hanlon and Vaclav Nedomansky, Jan. 4, 1983.

Jim Dorey

DOREY, ROBERT JAMES 6'1", 190 lbs.
B. Aug. 17, 1947, Kingston, Ont. Defense, Shoots L

YEAR	TEAM & LEAGUE		GP	G	A	PTS	PIM
1968-69	TOR	N	61	8	22	30	200
1969-70			46	6	11	17	99
1970-71			74	7	22	29	198
1971-72			50	4	19	23	56
	NYR	N	1	0	0	0	0
	2 team total		51	4	19	23	56
1972-73	NE	W	75	7	56	63	95
1973-74			77	6	40	46	134
1974-75			31	5	17	22	43
	TOR	W	43	11	23	34	69
	2 team total		74	16	40	56	112
1975-76			74	9	51	60	134
1976-77	QUE	W	73	13	34	47	102

Jim Dorey continued

YEAR	TEAM & LEAGUE		GP	G	A	PTS	PIM
1977-78			26	1	9	10	23
1978-79			32	0	2	2	17
11 yrs.		N Totals:	232	25	74	99	553
		W Totals:	431	52	232	284	617
PLAYOFFS							
1968-69	TOR	N	4	0	1	1	21
1970-71			6	0	1	1	19
1971-72	NYR	N	1	0	0	0	0
1972-73	NE	W	15	3	16	19	41
1973-74			6	0	6	6	26
1974-75	TOR	W	6	2	6	8	2
1976-77	QUE	W	10	0	2	2	28
1977-78			11	0	3	3	34
1978-79			3	0	0	0	0
9 yrs.		N Totals:	11	0	2	2	40
		W Totals:	51	5	33	38	131

Traded to **N.Y. Rangers** by Toronto for Pierre Jarry, Feb. 20, 1972.

Gary Dornhoefer

DORNHOEFER, GERHARDT OTTO 6'1", 190 lbs.
B. Feb. 2, 1943, Kitchener, Ont. Right Wing, Shoots R

YEAR	TEAM & LEAGUE		GP	G	A	PTS	PIM
1963-64	BOS	N	32	12	10	22	20
1964-65			20	0	1	1	13
1965-66			10	0	1	1	2
1967-68	PHI	N	65	13	30	43	134
1968-69			60	8	16	24	80
1969-70			65	26	29	55	96
1970-71			57	20	20	40	93
1971-72			75	17	32	49	183
1972-73			77	30	49	79	168
1973-74			57	11	39	50	125
1974-75			69	17	27	44	102
1975-76			74	28	35	63	128
1976-77			79	25	34	59	85
1977-78			47	7	5	12	62
14 yrs.		N Totals:	787	214	328	542	1291
PLAYOFFS							
1967-68	PHI	N	3	0	0	0	15
1968-69			4	0	1	1	20
1970-71			2	0	0	0	4
1972-73			11	3	3	6	16
1973-74*			14	5	6	11	43
1974-75*			17	5	5	10	33
1975-76			16	3	4	7	43
1976-77			9	1	0	1	22
1977-78			4	0	0	0	7
9 yrs.		N Totals:	80	17	19	36	203

Drafted by **Philadelphia** from Boston in Expansion Draft, June 6, 1967.

Dave Dornseif

DORNSEIF, DAVID 6'3", 205 lbs.
B. Aug. 12, 1956, Edina, Minn. Defense, Shoots L

YEAR	TEAM & LEAGUE		GP	G	A	PTS	PIM
1977-78	IND	W	3	0	1	1	0
1978-79	CIN	W	1	0	0	0	0
2 yrs.		W Totals:	4	0	1	1	0

Eddie Dorohoy

DOROHOY, EDWARD (The Great Gabbo, Pistol) 5'9", 150 lbs.
B. Mar. 13, 1929, Medicine Hat, Alta. Center, Shoots L

YEAR	TEAM & LEAGUE		GP	G	A	PTS	PIM
1948-49	MONT	N	16	0	0	0	6

Traded to **N.Y. Rangers** by Montreal with Dick Gamble for Hy Buller, June 8, 1954.

Jordy Douglas

DOUGLAS, JORDAN PAUL 6', 195 lbs.
B. Jan. 20, 1958, Winnipeg, Man. Left Wing, Shoots L

YEAR	TEAM & LEAGUE		GP	G	A	PTS	PIM
1978-79	NE	W	51	6	10	16	15
1979-80	HART	N	77	33	24	57	39
1980-81			55	13	9	22	29
1981-82			30	10	7	17	44
1982-83	MINN	N	68	13	14	27	30

Jordy Douglas continued

YEAR	TEAM	LEAGUE	GP	G	A	PTS	PIM
5 yrs.		**N Totals:**	230	69	54	123	142
		W Totals:	51	6	10	16	15
PLAYOFFS							
1978-79	**NE**	**W**	10	4	0	4	23
1982-83	**MINN**	**N**	5	0	0	0	2
2 yrs.		**N Totals:**	5	0	0	0	2
		W Totals:	10	4	0	4	23

Reclaimed by **Toronto** prior to Expansion Draft, June 9, 1979. Claimed as a priority selection by **Hartford** June 9, 1979. Traded to **Minnesota** by Hartford with a fifth round choice in 1984 Amateur Draft for Mark Johnson and Kent-Erik Andersson, Oct. 1, 1982.

Kent Douglas

DOUGLAS, KENT GEMMELL 5'10", 189 lbs.
B. Feb. 6, 1936, Cobalt, Ont. Defense, Shoots L
Won Calder Trophy, 1962-63

YEAR	TEAM	LEAGUE	GP	G	A	PTS	PIM
1962-63	**TOR**	**N**	70	7	15	22	105
1963-64			43	0	1	1	29
1964-65			67	5	23	28	129
1965-66			64	6	14	20	97
1966-67			39	2	12	14	48
1967-68	**OAK**	**N**	40	4	11	15	80
	DET	**N**	36	7	10	17	46
	2 team total		76	11	21	32	126
1968-69			69	2	29	31	97
1972-73	**NY**	**W**	60	3	15	18	74
8 yrs.		**N Totals:**	428	33	115	148	631
		W Totals:	60	3	15	18	74
PLAYOFFS							
1962-63*	**TOR**	**N**	10	1	1	2	2
1964-65			5	0	1	1	19
1965-66			4	0	1	1	12
3 yrs.		**N Totals:**	19	1	3	4	33

Drafted by **Oakland** from Toronto in Expansion Draft, June 6, 1967. Traded to **Detroit** by Oakland for John Brenneman, Ted Hampson, and Bert Marshall, Jan. 9, 1968.

Les Douglas

DOUGLAS, LESLIE GORDON 5'9", 165 lbs.
B. Dec. 5, 1918, Perth, Ont. Center, Shoots L

YEAR	TEAM	LEAGUE	GP	G	A	PTS	PIM
1940-41	**DET**	**N**	18	1	2	3	2
1942-43			21	5	8	13	4
1945-46			1	0	0	0	0
1946-47			12	0	2	2	2
4 yrs.		**N Totals:**	52	6	12	18	8
PLAYOFFS							
1942-43*	**DET**	**N**	10	3	2	5	0

Dave Downie

DOWNIE, DAVID M. 5'7½", 168 lbs.
B. Mar. 11, 1909, Burke's Falls, Ont. Center, Shoots R

YEAR	TEAM	LEAGUE	GP	G	A	PTS	PIM
1932-33	**TOR**	**N**	11	0	1	1	2

Bruce Draper

DRAPER, BRUCE 5'10", 157 lbs.
B. Oct. 2, 1940, Toronto, Ont. Forward

YEAR	TEAM	LEAGUE	GP	G	A	PTS	PIM
1962-63	**TOR**	**N**	1	0	0	0	0

Gordie Drillon

DRILLON, GORDON 6'2", 178 lbs.
B. Oct. 23, 1914, Moncton, N.B. Left Wing, Shoots L
Won Art Ross Trophy, 1937-38
Won Lady Byng Trophy, 1937-38
Hall of Fame, 1975

YEAR	TEAM	LEAGUE	GP	G	A	PTS	PIM
1936-37	**TOR**	**N**	41	16	17	33	2
1937-38			48	**26**	26	**52**	4
1938-39			40	18	16	34	15
1939-40			43	21	19	40	13
1940-41			42	23	21	44	2
1941-42			48	23	18	41	6
1942-43	**MONT**	**N**	49	28	22	50	14

Gordie Drillon continued

YEAR	TEAM	LEAGUE	GP	G	A	PTS	PIM
7 yrs.		**N Totals:**	311	155	139	294	56
PLAYOFFS							
1936-37	**TOR**	**N**	2	0	0	0	0
1937-38			7	7	1	8	2
1938-39			10	7	6	13	4
1939-40			10	3	1	4	0
1940-41			7	3	2	5	2
1941-42*			9	2	3	5	2
1942-43	**MONT**	**N**	5	4	2	6	0
7 yrs.		**N Totals:**	50	26	15	41	10

Pete Driscoll

DRISCOLL, PETER JOHN (Drisk) 6', 190 lbs.
B. Oct. 27, 1954, Kingston, Ont. Left Wing, Shoots L

YEAR	TEAM	LEAGUE	GP	G	A	PTS	PIM
1974-75	**VAN**	**W**	21	3	2	5	40
1975-76	**CALG**	**W**	75	16	18	34	127
1976-77			76	23	29	52	120
1977-78	**QUE**	**W**	21	3	7	10	28
	IND	**W**	56	25	21	46	130
	2 team total		77	28	28	56	158
1978-79			8	3	1	4	17
	EDM	**W**	69	17	23	40	115
	2 team total		77	20	24	44	132
1979-80	**EDM**	**N**	39	1	5	6	54
1980-81			21	2	3	5	43
7 yrs.		**N Totals:**	60	3	8	11	97
		W Totals:	326	90	101	191	577
PLAYOFFS							
1975-76	**CALG**	**W**	10	2	5	7	41
1978-79	**EDM**	**W**	13	1	6	7	8
1979-80	**EDM**	**N**	3	0	0	0	0
3 yrs.		**N Totals:**	3	0	0	0	0
		W Totals:	23	3	11	14	49

Rene Drolet

DROLET, RENE GEORGES 5'7", 155 lbs.
B. Nov. 13, 1944, Quebec, Que. Right Wing, Shoots R

YEAR	TEAM	LEAGUE	GP	G	A	PTS	PIM
1971-72	**PHI**	**N**	1	0	0	0	0
1974-75	**DET**	**N**	1	0	0	0	0
2 yrs.		**N Totals:**	2	0	0	0	0

Claimed by Tidewater **(Detroit)** from Philadelphia in Reverse Draft, June 13, 1974.

Clarence Drouillard

DROUILLARD, CLARENCE JOSEPH 5'7", 150 lbs.
B. Mar. 2, 1914, Windsor, Ont. Center, Shoots L

YEAR	TEAM	LEAGUE	GP	G	A	PTS	PIM
1937-38	**DET**	**N**	10	0	1	1	0

Jude Drouin

DROUIN, JUDE 5'9", 165 lbs.
B. Oct. 28, 1948, Mont-Louis, Que. Center, Shoots R

YEAR	TEAM	LEAGUE	GP	G	A	PTS	PIM
1968-69	**MONT**	**N**	9	0	1	1	0
1969-70			3	0	0	0	2
1970-71	**MINN**	**N**	75	16	52	68	49
1971-72			63	13	43	56	31
1972-73			78	27	46	73	61
1973-74			65	19	24	43	30
1974-75			38	4	18	22	16
	NYI	**N**	40	14	18	32	6
	2 team total		78	18	36	54	22
1975-76			76	21	41	62	58
1976-77			78	24	29	53	27
1977-78			56	5	17	22	12
1979-80	**WINN**	**N**	78	8	16	24	50
1980-81			7	0	0	0	4
12 yrs.		**N Totals:**	666	151	305	456	346
PLAYOFFS							
1970-71	**MINN**	**N**	12	5	7	12	10
1971-72			7	4	4	8	6
1972-73			6	1	3	4	0
1974-75	**NYI**	**N**	17	6	12	18	6

Jude Drouin continued

YEAR	TEAM & LEAGUE		GP	G	A	PTS	PIM
1975-76			13	6	9	15	0
1976-77			12	5	6	11	6
1977-78			5	0	0	0	5
7 yrs.		**N Totals:**	72	27	41	68	33

Traded to **Minnesota** by Montreal for Bill Collins, June 10, 1970. Traded to **N.Y. Islanders** by Minnesota for Craig Cameron, Jan. 7, 1975. Signed as a free agent by **Winnipeg** Oct. 5, 1979.

Polly Drouin

DROUIN, EMILE PAUL 5'7", 160 lbs.
B. J Verdun, Que. Left Wing, Shoots L

YEAR	TEAM & LEAGUE		GP	G	A	PTS	PIM
1935-36	**MONT**	**N**	30	1	8	9	19
1936-37			31	7	13	20	8
1937-38			28	7	11	18	2
1938-39			42	4	11	15	51
1939-40			21	4	7	11	0
1940-41			21	4	7	11	0
6 yrs.		**N Totals:**	173	27	57	84	80
PLAYOFFS							
1937-38	**MONT**	**N**	1	0	0	0	0
1938-39			3	0	1	1	5
1940-41			1	0	0	0	0
3 yrs.		**N Totals:**	5	0	1	1	5

John Drummond

DRUMMOND, JOHN S.
B. Oct. 20, 1918, Toronto, Ont. Defense

YEAR	TEAM & LEAGUE		GP	G	A	PTS	PIM
1944-45	**NYR**	**N**	2	0	0	0	0

Herb Drury

DRURY, HERBERT 5'7", 165 lbs.
Forward

YEAR	TEAM & LEAGUE		GP	G	A	PTS	PIM
1925-26	**PITT**	**N**	33	6	2	8	40
1926-27			41	5	1	6	48
1927-28			42	6	4	10	44
1928-29			43	5	4	9	49
1929-30			26	2	0	2	12
1930-31	**PHI**	**N**	22	0	2	2	10
6 yrs.		**N Totals:**	207	24	13	37	203
PLAYOFFS							
1925-26	**PITT**	**N**	2	1	0	1	0
1927-28			2	0	1	1	0
2 yrs.		**N Totals:**	4	1	1	2	0

Gilles Dube

DUBE, JOSEPH GILLES 5'10", 165 lbs.
B. June 2, 1927, Sherbrooke, Que. Left Wing, Shoots L

YEAR	TEAM & LEAGUE		GP	G	A	PTS	PIM
1949-50	**MONT**	**N**	12	1	2	3	2
PLAYOFFS							
1953-54*	**DET**	**N**	2	0	0	0	0

Norm Dube

DUBE, NORMAND G. 5'11", 185 lbs.
B. Sept. 12, 1951, Sherbrooke, Que. Left Wing, Shoots L

YEAR	TEAM & LEAGUE		GP	G	A	PTS	PIM
1974-75	**KC**	**N**	56	8	10	18	54
1975-76			1	0	0	0	0
1976-77	**QUE**	**W**	39	15	18	33	8
1977-78			73	16	31	47	17
1978-79			36	2	13	15	4
5 yrs.		**N Totals:**	57	8	10	18	54
		W Totals:	148	33	62	95	29
PLAYOFFS							
1976-77	**QUE**	**W**	14	3	12	15	11
1977-78			10	2	2	4	6
2 yrs.		**W Totals:**	24	5	14	19	17

Drafted by **Kansas City** from Los Angeles in Expansion Draft, June 12, 1974.

Mike Dubois

DUBOIS, MICHEL JEAN CLAUDE (Plywood) 5'11", 181 lbs.
B. Nov. 7, 1954, Montreal, Que. Defense, Shoots L

YEAR	TEAM & LEAGUE		GP	G	A	PTS	PIM
1975-76	**IND**	**W**	34	2	2	4	104
	QUE	**W**	21	0	3	3	23
	2 team total		55	2	5	7	127
1976-77			4	0	0	0	0
2 yrs.		**W Totals:**	59	2	5	7	127
PLAYOFFS							
1975-76	**QUE**	**W**	1	0	0	0	0
1976-77			2	0	1	1	0
2 yrs.		**W Totals:**	3	0	1	1	0

Gaetan Duchesne

DUCHESNE, GAETAN 5'11", 177 lbs.
B. July 11, 1961, Quebec City, Que. Left Wing, Shoots L

YEAR	TEAM & LEAGUE		GP	G	A	PTS	PIM
1981-82	**WASH**	**N**	74	9	14	23	46
1982-83			77	18	19	37	52
2 yrs.		**N Totals:**	151	27	33	60	98
PLAYOFFS							
1982-83	**WASH**	**N**	4	1	1	2	4

Rick Dudley

DUDLEY, RICHARD CLARENCE (Duds) 6', 190 lbs.
B. Jan. 31, 1949, Toronto, Ont. Left Wing, Shoots L

YEAR	TEAM & LEAGUE		GP	G	A	PTS	PIM
1972-73	**BUF**	**N**	6	0	1	1	7
1973-74			67	13	13	26	71
1974-75			78	31	39	70	116
1975-76	**CIN**	**W**	74	43	38	81	156
1976-77			77	41	47	88	102
1977-78			72	30	41	71	156
1978-79			47	17	20	37	102
	BUF	**N**	24	5	6	11	2
	2 team total		71	22	26	48	104
1979-80			66	11	22	33	58
1980-81			38	10	13	23	10
	WINN	**N**	30	5	5	10	28
	2 team total		68	15	18	33	38
9 yrs.		**N Totals:**	309	75	99	174	292
		W Totals:	270	131	146	277	516
PLAYOFFS							
1974-75	**BUF**	**N**	10	3	1	4	26
1976-77	**CIN**	**W**	4	0	1	1	7
1978-79	**BUF**	**N**	3	1	1	2	2
1979-80			12	3	0	3	41
4 yrs.		**N Totals:**	25	7	2	9	69
		W Totals:	4	0	1	1	7

Claimed on waivers by **Winnipeg** from Buffalo, Jan. 12, 1981.

Dick Duff

DUFF, TERRANCE RICHARD 5'9", 166 lbs.
B. Feb. 18, 1936, Kirkland Lake, Ont. Left Wing, Shoots L

YEAR	TEAM & LEAGUE		GP	G	A	PTS	PIM
1954-55	**TOR**	**N**	3	0	0	0	2
1955-56			69	18	19	37	74
1956-57			70	26	14	40	50
1957-58			65	26	23	49	79
1958-59			69	29	24	53	73
1959-60			67	19	22	41	51
1960-61			67	16	17	33	54
1961-62			51	17	20	37	37
1962-63			69	16	19	35	56
1963-64			52	7	7	14	59
	NYR	**N**	14	4	4	8	2
	2 team total		66	11	11	22	61
1964-65			29	3	9	12	20
	MONT	**N**	40	9	7	16	16
	2 team total		69	12	16	28	36
1965-66			63	21	24	45	78
1966-67			51	12	11	23	23
1967-68			66	25	21	46	21
1968-69			68	19	21	40	55
1969-70			17	1	1	2	4
	LA	**N**	32	5	8	13	8
	2 team total		49	6	9	15	12
1970-71			7	1	0	1	0
	BUF	**N**	53	7	13	20	12
	2 team total		60	8	13	21	12

YEAR	TEAM	LEAGUE	GP	G	A	PTS	PIM
1971-72			8	2	2	4	0
18 yrs.		**N Totals:**	1030	283	286	569	774
PLAYOFFS							
1955-56	**TOR**	**N**	5	1	4	5	2
1958-59			12	4	3	7	8
1959-60			10	2	4	6	6
1960-61			5	0	1	1	2
1961-62*			12	3	10	13	20
1962-63*			10	4	1	5	2
1964-65*	**MONT**	**N**	13	3	6	9	17
1965-66*			10	2	5	7	2
1966-67			10	2	3	5	4
1967-68*			13	3	4	7	4
1968-69*			14	6	8	14	11
11 yrs.		**N Totals:**	114	30	49	79	78

Traded to **N.Y. Rangers** by Toronto with Bob Nevin, Arnie Brown, Bill Collins, and Rod Seiling for Andy Bathgate and Don McKenney, Feb. 22, 1964. Traded to **Mont. Canadiens** by N.Y. Rangers for Bill Hicke, Dec. 22, 1964. Sold to **Los Angeles** by Montreal, Jan. 23, 1970. Traded to **Buffalo** by Los Angeles with Eddie Shack for Mike McMahon, Dec. 1, 1970.

Guy Dufour

DUFOUR, GUY 5'11", 185 lbs.
B. Feb. 9, 1946, LaTuque, Que. Right Wing, Shoots R

YEAR	TEAM	LEAGUE	GP	G	A	PTS	PIM
1972-73	**QUE**	**W**	9	3	2	5	2
1973-74			74	27	23	50	30
2 yrs.		**W Totals:**	83	30	25	55	32

Luc Dufour

DUFOUR, LUC 5'11", 179 lbs.
B. Feb. 13, 1963, Chicoutimi, Que. Left Wing, Shoots L

YEAR	TEAM	LEAGUE	GP	G	A	PTS	PIM
1982-83	**BOS**	**N**	73	14	11	25	107
PLAYOFFS							
1982-83	**BOS**	**N**	17	1	0	1	30

Marc Dufour

DUFOUR, MARC 6', 175 lbs.
B. Sept. 11, 1941, Trois Rivieres, Que. Right Wing, Shoots R

YEAR	TEAM	LEAGUE	GP	G	A	PTS	PIM
1963-64	**NYR**	**N**	10	1	0	1	2
1964-65			2	0	0	0	0
1968-69	**LA**	**N**	2	0	0	0	0
3 yrs.		**N Totals:**	14	1	0	1	2

Drafted by **Los Angeles** from N.Y. Rangers in Expansion Draft, June 6, 1967.

Jack Duggan

DUGGAN, JAMES
B. Unknown Defense

YEAR	TEAM	LEAGUE	GP	G	A	PTS	PIM
1925-26	**OTTA**	**N**	27	0	0	0	0
PLAYOFFS							
1925-26	**OTTA**	**N**	2	0	0	0	0

Ron Duguay

DUGUAY, RONALD (Doogie) 6'2", 210 lbs.
B. July 6, 1957, Sudbury, Ont. Center, Shoots R

YEAR	TEAM	LEAGUE	GP	G	A	PTS	PIM
1977-78	**NYR**	**N**	71	20	20	40	43
1978-79			79	27	36	63	35
1979-80			73	28	22	50	37
1980-81			50	17	21	38	83
1981-82			72	40	36	76	82
1982-83			72	19	25	44	58
6 yrs.		**N Totals:**	417	151	160	311	338
PLAYOFFS							
1977-78	**NYR**	**N**	3	1	1	2	2
1978-79			18	5	4	9	11
1979-80			9	5	2	7	11
1980-81			14	8	9	17	16
1981-82			10	5	1	6	31
1982-83			9	2	2	4	28

Ron Duguay continued

YEAR	TEAM	LEAGUE	GP	G	A	PTS	PIM
6 yrs.		**N Totals:**	63	26	19	45	99

Traded to **Detroit** with Ed Mio and Eddie Johnstone by New York Rangers for Mike Blaisdell, Willie Huber, and Mark Osborne, June 13, 1983.

Lorne Duguid

DUGUID, LORNE 5'11", 185 lbs.
B. Apr. 4, 1910, Bolton, Ont. Left Wing

YEAR	TEAM	LEAGUE	GP	G	A	PTS	PIM
1931-32	**MON(M)**	**N**	13	0	0	0	6
1932-33			48	4	7	11	38
1933-34			5	0	1	1	0
1934-35	**DET**	**N**	34	3	3	6	9
1935-36			5	0	0	0	0
	BOS	**N**	29	1	4	5	2
	2 team total		34	1	4	5	2
1936-37			1	1	0	1	2
6 yrs.		**N Totals:**	135	9	15	24	57
PLAYOFFS							
1932-33	**MON(M)**	**N**	2	0	0	0	4

Woody Dumart

DUMART, WOODROW WILSON CLARENCE 6'1", 200 lbs.
B. Dec. 23, 1916, Kitchener, Ont. Left Wing, Shoots L

YEAR	TEAM	LEAGUE	GP	G	A	PTS	PIM
1935-36	**BOS**	**N**	1	0	0	0	0
1936-37			17	4	4	8	2
1937-38			48	13	14	27	6
1938-39			45	14	15	29	2
1939-40			48	22	21	43	16
1940-41			40	18	15	33	2
1941-42			35	14	15	29	8
1945-46			50	22	12	34	2
1946-47			60	24	28	52	12
1947-48			59	21	16	37	14
1948-49			59	11	12	23	6
1949-50			69	14	25	39	14
1950-51			70	20	21	41	7
1951-52			39	5	8	13	0
1952-53			62	5	9	14	2
1953-54			69	4	3	7	6
16 yrs.		**N Totals:**	771	211	218	429	99
PLAYOFFS							
1936-37	**BOS**	**N**	3	0	0	0	0
1937-38			3	0	0	0	0
1938-39*			12	1	3	4	6
1939-40			6	1	0	1	0
1940-41*			11	1	3	4	9
1945-46			10	4	3	7	0
1946-47			5	1	1	2	8
1947-48			5	0	0	0	0
1948-49			5	3	0	3	0
1950-51			6	1	2	3	0
1951-52			7	0	1	1	0
1952-53			11	0	2	2	0
1953-54			4	0	0	0	0
13 yrs.		**N Totals:**	88	12	15	27	23

Art Duncan

DUNCAN, ARTHUR
Defense

YEAR	TEAM	LEAGUE	GP	G	A	PTS	PIM
1926-27	**DET**	**N**	34	3	2	5	26
1927-28	**TOR**	**N**	43	7	5	12	97
1928-29			39	4	4	8	53
1929-30			38	4	5	9	49
1930-31			2	0	0	0	0
5 yrs.		**N Totals:**	156	18	16	34	225
PLAYOFFS							
1928-29	**TOR**	**N**	4	0	0	0	4
1930-31			1	0	0	0	0
2 yrs.		**N Totals:**	5	0	0	0	4

YEAR	TEAM & LEAGUE		GP	G	A	PTS	PIM

Frank Dunlap

DUNLAP, FRANK
B. Unknown — Forward

YEAR	TEAM	LEAGUE	GP	G	A	PTS	PIM
1943-44	TOR	N	15	0	1	1	2

Blake Dunlop

DUNLOP, BLAKE ROBERT — 5'10", 170 lbs.
B. Apr. 4, 1953, Hamilton, Ont. — Center, Shoots R
Won Masterton Trophy, 1980-81

YEAR	TEAM	LEAGUE	GP	G	A	PTS	PIM
1973-74	MINN	N	12	0	0	0	2
1974-75			52	9	18	27	8
1975-76			33	9	11	20	8
1976-77			3	0	1	1	0
1977-78	PHI	N	3	0	1	1	0
1978-79			66	20	28	48	16
1979-80	STL	N	72	18	27	45	28
1980-81			80	20	67	87	40
1981-82			77	25	53	78	32
1982-83			78	22	44	66	14
10 yrs.	N Totals:		476	123	250	373	148

PLAYOFFS

YEAR	TEAM	LEAGUE	GP	G	A	PTS	PIM
1978-79	PHI	N	8	1	1	2	4
1979-80	STL	N	3	0	2	2	2
1980-81			11	0	3	3	4
1981-82			10	2	2	4	4
1982-83			4	1	1	2	0
5 yrs.	N Totals:		36	4	9	13	14

Traded to **Philadelphia** by Minnesota with Minnesota's third-round choice (Gord Salt) in the 1978 Amateur Draft for Harvey Bennett, Oct. 28, 1977. Traded to **St. Louis** by Philadelphia with Rick LaPointe for goalie Phil Myre, June 7, 1979.

Dave Dunn

DUNN, DAVID GEORGE — 6'2", 200 lbs.
B. Aug. 19, 1948, Moosomin, Sask. — Defense, Shoots L

YEAR	TEAM	LEAGUE	GP	G	A	PTS	PIM
1973-74	VAN	N	68	11	22	33	76
1974-75			1	0	0	0	11
	TOR	N	72	3	11	14	142
	2 team total		73	3	11	14	153
1975-76			43	0	8	8	84
1976-77	WINN	W	40	3	11	14	129
1977-78			66	6	20	26	79
5 yrs.	N Totals:		184	14	41	55	313
	W Totals:		106	9	31	40	208

PLAYOFFS

YEAR	TEAM	LEAGUE	GP	G	A	PTS	PIM
1974-75	TOR	N	7	1	1	2	24
1975-76			3	0	0	0	17
1976-77	WINN	W	20	4	4	8	23
1977-78			9	1	2	3	0
4 yrs.	N Totals:		10	1	1	2	41
	W Totals:		29	5	6	11	23

Traded to **Toronto** by Vancouver for Garry Monahan and John Grisdale, Oct. 16, 1974.

Richie Dunn

DUNN, RICHARD L. — 6', 192 lbs.
B. May 12, 1957, Boston, Mass. — Defense, Shoots L

YEAR	TEAM	LEAGUE	GP	G	A	PTS	PIM
1977-78	BUF	N	25	0	3	3	16
1978-79			24	0	3	3	14
1979-80			80	7	31	38	61
1980-81			79	7	42	49	34
1981-82			72	7	19	26	73
1982-83	CALG	N	80	3	11	14	47
6 yrs.	N Totals:		360	24	109	133	245

PLAYOFFS

YEAR	TEAM	LEAGUE	GP	G	A	PTS	PIM
1977-78	BUF	N	1	0	0	0	2
1979-80			14	2	8	10	8
1980-81			8	0	5	5	6
1981-82			4	0	1	1	0
1982-83	CALG	N	9	1	1	2	8
5 yrs.	N Totals:		36	3	15	18	24

Signed as free agent by **Buffalo** Oct. 3, 1977. Traded to **Calgary** by Buffalo along with Don Edwards and Buffalo's second round choice in 1982 Entry Draft (Richard Kromm) for Calgary's first round choice (Paul Cyr) and second round choice (Jens Johansson) in the 1982 Entry Draft and Calgary's second round choice in 1983 Entry Draft. Traded to **Hartford** by Calgary with Joel Quenneville for Mickey Volcan, July 6, 1983.

Denis Dupere

DUPERE, DENIS GILLES — 6'1", 200 lbs.
B. June 21, 1948, Jonquiere, Que. — Left Wing, Shoots L

YEAR	TEAM	LEAGUE	GP	G	A	PTS	PIM
1970-71	TOR	N	20	1	2	3	4
1971-72			77	7	10	17	4
1972-73			61	13	23	36	10
1973-74			34	8	9	17	8
1974-75	WASH	N	53	20	15	35	8
	STL	N	22	3	6	9	8
	2 team total		75	23	21	44	16
1975-76	KC	N	43	6	8	14	16
1976-77	COLO	N	57	7	11	18	4
1977-78			54	15	15	30	4
8 yrs.	N Totals:		421	80	99	179	66

PLAYOFFS

YEAR	TEAM	LEAGUE	GP	G	A	PTS	PIM
1970-71	TOR	N	6	0	0	0	0
1971-72			5	0	0	0	0
1973-74			3	0	0	0	0
1977-78	COLO	N	2	1	0	1	0
4 yrs.	N Totals:		16	1	0	1	0

Traded to **Toronto** by N.Y. Rangers with Guy Trottier (via Intra-League Draft, 1970) for Tim Horton, March 3, 1970. Drafted by **Washington** from Toronto in Expansion Draft, June 12, 1974. Traded to **St. Louis** by Washington for Garnet Bailey and Stan Gilbertson, Feb. 10, 1975. Traded to **Kansas City** by St. Louis with Craig Patrick and cash for Lynn Powis and Kansas City's second choice (Brian Sutter) in the 1976 Amateur Draft, June 18, 1975.

Andre Dupont

DUPONT, ANDRE (Moose) — 6', 202 lbs.
B. July 27, 1949, Trois-Rivieres, Que. — Defense, Shoots L

YEAR	TEAM	LEAGUE	GP	G	A	PTS	PIM
1970-71	NYR	N	7	1	2	3	21
1971-72	STL	N	60	3	10	13	147
1972-73			25	1	6	7	51
	PHI	N	46	3	20	23	164
	2 team total		71	4	26	30	215
1973-74			75	3	20	23	216
1974-75			80	11	21	32	276
1975-76			75	9	27	36	214
1976-77			69	10	19	29	168
1977-78			69	2	12	14	225
1978-79			77	3	9	12	135
1979-80			58	1	7	8	107
1980-81	QUE	N	63	5	8	13	93
1981-82			60	4	12	16	100
1982-83			46	3	12	15	69
13 yrs.	N Totals:		810	59	185	244	1986

PLAYOFFS

YEAR	TEAM	LEAGUE	GP	G	A	PTS	PIM
1971-72	STL	N	11	1	0	1	20
1972-73	PHI	N	11	1	2	3	29
1973-74*			16	4	3	7	67
1974-75*			17	3	2	5	49
1975-76			15	2	2	4	46
1976-77			10	1	1	2	35
1977-78			12	2	1	3	13
1978-79			8	0	0	0	17
1979-80			19	0	4	4	50
1980-81	QUE	N	1	0	0	0	0
1981-82			16	0	3	3	18
1982-83			4	0	0	0	8
12 yrs.	N Totals:		140	14	18	32	352

As an amateur, traded to **N.Y. Rangers** by St. Louis for Phil Goyette, June 10, 1969. Traded to **St. Louis** by N.Y. Rangers with Jack Egers and Mike Murphy for Gene Carr, Jim Lorentz and Wayne Connelly, Nov. 15, 1971. Traded to **Philadelphia** by St. Louis with St. Louis' third round choice (Bob Stumpf) in the 1973 Amateur Draft for Brent Hughes and Pierre Plante, Dec. 14, 1972. Traded to **Quebec** by Philadelphia for cash and Quebec's seventh-round choice (Vladmir Svitek) in the 1981 Entry Draft, Sept. 15, 1980.

Jerome Dupont

DUPONT, JEROME 6'3", 190 lbs.
B. Feb. 21, 1962, Ottawa, Ont. Defense, Shoots L

YEAR	TEAM & LEAGUE		GP	G	A	PTS	PIM
1981-82	CHI	N	34	0	4	4	51
1982-83			1	0	0	0	0
2 yrs.		N Totals:	35	0	4	4	51

Norm Dupont

DUPONT, NORMAND 5'11", 180 lbs.
B. May 5, 1957, Montreal, Que. Left Wing, Shoots L

YEAR	TEAM & LEAGUE		GP	G	A	PTS	PIM
1979-80	MONT	N	35	1	3	4	4
1980-81	WINN	N	80	27	26	53	8
1981-82			62	13	25	38	22
1982-83			39	7	16	23	6
4 yrs.		N Totals:	216	48	70	118	40
PLAYOFFS							
1979-80	MONT	N	8	1	1	2	0
1981-82	WINN	N	4	2	0	2	0
1982-83			1	1	1	2	0
3 yrs.		N Totals:	13	4	2	6	0

Traded to **Winnipeg** by Montreal for Winnipeg's second round choice (David Maley) in the 1982 Entry Draft, Sept. 26, 1980.

Rich Dupras

DUPRAS, RICHARD 6', 185 lbs.
B. Jan. 1, 1950, Montreal, Que. Center, Shoots L

YEAR	TEAM & LEAGUE		GP	G	A	PTS	PIM
1973-74	TOR	W	2	0	0	0	0

Steve Durbano

DURBANO, HARRY STEVEN 6'1", 210 lbs.
B. Dec. 12, 1951, Toronto, Ont. Defense, Shoots L

YEAR	TEAM & LEAGUE		GP	G	A	PTS	PIM
1972-73	STL	N	49	3	18	21	231
1973-74			36	4	5	9	146
	PITT	N	33	4	14	18	138
	2 team total		69	8	19	27	284
1974-75			1	0	1	1	10
1975-76			32	0	8	8	161
	KC	N	37	1	11	12	209
	2 team total		69	1	19	20	370
1976-77	COLO	N	19	0	2	2	129
1977-78	BIRM	W	45	6	4	10	**284**
1978-79	STL	N	13	1	1	2	103
7 yrs.		N Totals:	220	13	60	73	1127
		W Totals:	45	6	4	10	284
PLAYOFFS							
1972-73	STL	N	5	0	2	2	8
1977-78	BIRM	W	4	0	2	2	16
2 yrs.		N Totals:	5	0	2	2	8
		W Totals:	4	0	2	2	16

Traded to **St. Louis** by N.Y. Rangers for Peter McDuffe and Curt Bennett, May 24, 1972. Traded to **Pittsburgh** by St. Louis with Ab DeMarco and Bob Kelly for Bryan Watson, Greg Polis and Pittsburgh's second choice (Bob Hess) in 1974 Amateur Draft, Jan. 17, 1974. Traded to **Kansas City** by Pittsburgh with Chuck Arnason and Pittsburgh's first round choice (Paul Gardner) in 1976 Amateur Draft for Simon Nolet, Ed Gilbert and Kansas City's first round choice (Blair Chapman) in same draft, Jan. 9, 1976. Signed as free agent by **Detroit** July 14, 1977. Signed as free agent by **St. Louis** Aug. 11, 1978.

Vitezslav Duris

DURIS, VITEZSLAV (Slava) 6'1", 185 lbs.
B. Jan. 5, 1595, Pizen, Czechoslavakia Defense, Shoots L

YEAR	TEAM & LEAGUE		GP	G	A	PTS	PIM
1980-81	TOR	N	57	1	12	13	50
1982-83			32	2	8	10	12
2 yrs.		N Totals:	89	3	20	23	62
PLAYOFFS							
1980-81	TOR	N	3	0	1	1	2

Signed as free agent by **Toronto** Sept. 25, 1980.

Norm Dussault

DUSSAULT, NORMAND JOSEPH 5'7½", 165 lbs.
B. Sept. 26, 1925, Springfield, Mass. Center, Shoots L

YEAR	TEAM & LEAGUE		GP	G	A	PTS	PIM
1947-48	MONT	N	28	5	10	15	4
1948-49			47	9	8	17	6
1949-50			67	13	24	37	22
1950-51			64	4	20	24	15
4 yrs.		N Totals:	206	31	62	93	47
PLAYOFFS							
1948-49	MONT	N	2	0	0	0	0
1949-50			5	3	1	4	0
2 yrs.		N Totals:	7	3	1	4	0

Duke Dutkowski

DUTKOWSKI, LAUDAS JOSEPH 5'10", 185 lbs.
B. Aug. 30, 1902, Regina, Sask. Defense, Shoots L

YEAR	TEAM & LEAGUE		GP	G	A	PTS	PIM
1926-27	CHI	N	28	3	2	5	16
1929-30			44	7	10	17	42
1930-31			25	1	3	4	28
	NYA	N	12	1	1	2	12
	2 team total		37	2	4	6	40
1932-33			48	4	7	11	43
1933-34			9	0	1	1	11
	CHI	N	5	0	0	0	2
	NYR	N	29	0	6	6	18
	3 team total		43	0	7	7	31
5 yrs.		N Totals:	200	16	30	46	172
PLAYOFFS							
1926-27	CHI	N	2	0	0	0	0
1929-30			2	0	0	0	6
1933-34	NYR	N	2	0	0	0	0
3 yrs.		N Totals:	6	0	0	0	6

Red Dutton

DUTTON, MERVYN A. 6', 185 lbs.
B. Jan. 3, 1898, Russell, Man. Defense, Shoots R
Hall of Fame, 1958

YEAR	TEAM & LEAGUE		GP	G	A	PTS	PIM
1926-27	MON(M)	N	44	4	4	8	108
1927-28			42	7	6	13	94
1928-29			44	1	3	4	**139**
1929-30			43	3	13	16	98
1930-31	NYA	N	44	1	11	12	71
1931-32			47	3	5	8	**107**
1932-33			43	0	2	2	74
1933-34			48	2	8	10	65
1934-35			48	3	7	10	46
1935-36			46	5	8	13	69
10 yrs.		N Totals:	449	29	67	96	871
PLAYOFFS							
1926-27	MON(M)	N	2	0	0	0	4
1927-28			9	1	0	1	27
1929-30			4	0	0	0	2
1935-36	NYA	N	3	0	0	0	0
4 yrs.		N Totals:	18	1	0	1	33

Miroslav Dvorak

DVORAK, MIROSLAV 5'10", 198 lbs.
B. Oct. 11, 1951, Czechoslovakia Defense, Shoots L

YEAR	TEAM & LEAGUE		GP	G	A	PTS	PIM
1982-83	PHI	N	80	4	33	37	20
PLAYOFFS							
1982-83	PHI	N	3	0	1	1	0

Mike Dwyer

DWYER, MICHAEL 5'11", 172 lbs.
B. Sept. 16, 1957, Brampton, Ont. Left Wing, Shoots L

YEAR	TEAM & LEAGUE		GP	G	A	PTS	PIM
1978-79	COLO	N	12	2	3	5	2
1979-80			10	0	0	0	19
1980-81	CALG	N	4	0	1	1	4
1981-82			5	0	2	2	0
4 yrs.		N Totals:	31	2	6	8	25

Mike Dwyer continued

PLAYOFFS

YEAR	TEAM	LEAGUE	GP	G	A	PTS	PIM
1980-81	**CALG**	**N**	1	1	0	1	0

Signed as free agent by **Calgary** Oct. 17, 1980.

Henry Dyck

DYCK, HENRY RICHARD 5'7½", 155 lbs.
B. Sept. 5, 1911, Herbert, Sask. Center, Shoots L

YEAR	TEAM	LEAGUE	GP	G	A	PTS	PIM
1943-44	**NYR**	**N**	1	0	0	0	0

Babe Dye

DYE, CECIL
B. May 13, 1898, Hamilton, Ont. Right Wing, Shoots R
Won Art Ross Trophy, 1922–23, 1924-25
Hall of Fame, 1970

YEAR	TEAM	LEAGUE	GP	G	A	PTS	PIM
1919-20	**TOR**	**N**	21	12	3	15	0
1920-21	**HAMIL**	**N**	1	2	0	2	0
	TOR	**N**	23	33	2	35	32
	2 team total		24	**35**	2	37	32
1921-22			24	30	7	37	18
1922-23			22	**26**	11	**37**	19
1923-24			19	17	2	19	23
1924-25			29	**38**	6	**44**	41
1925-26			31	18	5	23	26
1926-27	**CHI**	**N**	41	25	5	30	14
1927-28			11	0	0	0	0
1928-29	**NYA**	**N**	42	1	0	1	17
1930-31	**TOR**	**N**	6	0	0	0	0
11 yrs.		**N Totals:**	270	202	41	243	190

PLAYOFFS

YEAR	TEAM	LEAGUE	GP	G	A	PTS	PIM
1920-21	**TOR**	**N**	2	0	0	0	9
1921-22*			7	9	2	11	7
1924-25			2	0	0	0	0
1926-27	**CHI**	**N**	2	0	0	0	2
1928-29	**NYA**	**N**	2	0	0	0	0
5 yrs.		**N Totals:**	15	9	2	11	18

John Dyte

DYTE, JOHN LEONARD 6', lbs.
B. Oct. 13, 1918, Kingston, Ont.

YEAR	TEAM	LEAGUE	GP	G	A	PTS	PIM
1943-44	**CHI**	**N**	27	1	0	1	31

Mike Eagles

EAGLES, MIKE 5'10", 180 lbs.
B. Mar. 7, 1963, Sussex, N.B. Center, Shoots L

YEAR	TEAM	LEAGUE	GP	G	A	PTS	PIM
1982-83	**QUE**	**N**	2	0	0	0	2

Bruce Eakin

EAKIN, BRUCE 5'11", 185 lbs.
B. Sept. 28, 1962, Winnipeg, Man. Center, Shoots L

YEAR	TEAM	LEAGUE	GP	G	A	PTS	PIM
1981-82	**CALG**	**N**	1	0	0	0	0

Tom Earl

EARL, WARREN THOMAS 6', 180 lbs.
B. Sept. 24, 1947, Niagara Falls, Ont. Right Wing, Shoots R

YEAR	TEAM	LEAGUE	GP	G	A	PTS	PIM
1972-73	**NE**	**W**	77	10	13	23	4
1973-74			78	10	10	20	29
1974-75			72	3	8	11	20
1975-76			66	8	11	19	26
1976-77			54	9	14	23	37
5 yrs.		**W Totals:**	347	40	56	96	116

PLAYOFFS

YEAR	TEAM	LEAGUE	GP	G	A	PTS	PIM
1972-73	**NE**	**W**	15	2	3	5	10
1973-74			7	0	2	2	2
1974-75			6	1	1	2	12
1975-76			17	0	5	5	4
1976-77			1	0	0	0	0
5 yrs.		**W Totals:**	46	3	11	14	28

Jeff Eatough

EATOUGH, JEFF 5'9", 168 lbs.
B. June 2, 1963, Toronto, Ont. Right Wing, Shoots R

YEAR	TEAM	LEAGUE	GP	G	A	PTS	PIM
1981-82	**BUF**	**N**	1	0	0	0	0

Mike Eaves

EAVES, MICHAEL GORDON 5'10", 180 lbs.
B. June 10, 1956, Denver, Colo. Center, Shoots R

YEAR	TEAM	LEAGUE	GP	G	A	PTS	PIM
1978-79	**MINN**	**N**	3	0	0	0	0
1979-80			56	18	28	46	4
1980-81			48	10	24	34	18
1981-82			25	11	10	21	0
1982-83			75	16	16	32	21
5 yrs.		**N Totals:**	207	55	78	133	43

PLAYOFFS

YEAR	TEAM	LEAGUE	GP	G	A	PTS	PIM
1979-80	**MINN**	**N**	15	2	5	7	4
1982-83			9	0	0	0	0
2 yrs.		**N Totals:**	24	2	5	7	4

As an amateur, rights traded to **Cleveland** by St. Louis for Len Frig, Aug. 17, 1977. Rights transferred to **Minnesota** Reserve List after Cleveland-Minnesota Dispersal Draft, June 15, 1978. Traded by Minnesota with Keith Hanson to **Calgary** for Steve Christoff and Calgary's second round choice (Frantisek Musil, choice acquired earlier from Montreal), June 6, 1983.

Murray Eaves

EAVES, MURRAY 5'10", 185 lbs.
B. May 10, 1960, Calgary, Alta. Center, Shoots R

YEAR	TEAM	LEAGUE	GP	G	A	PTS	PIM
1980-81	**WINN**	**N**	12	1	2	3	5
1981-82			2	0	0	0	0
1982-83			26	2	7	9	2
3 yrs.		**N Totals:**	40	3	9	12	7

Tim Ecclestone

ECCLESTONE, TIMOTHY JAMES 5'10", 195 lbs.
B. Sept. 24, 1947, Toronto, Ont. Left Wing, Shoots R

YEAR	TEAM	LEAGUE	GP	G	A	PTS	PIM
1967-68	**STL**	**N**	50	6	8	14	36
1968-69			68	11	23	34	31
1969-70			65	16	21	37	59
1970-71			47	15	24	39	34
	DET	**N**	27	4	10	14	13
	2 team total		74	19	34	53	47
1971-72			72	18	35	53	33
1972-73			78	18	30	48	28
1973-74			14	0	5	5	6
	TOR	**N**	46	9	14	23	32
	2 team total		60	9	19	28	38
1974-75			5	1	1	2	0
	ATL	**N**	62	13	21	34	34
	2 team total		67	14	22	36	34
1975-76			69	6	21	27	30
1976-77			78	9	18	27	26
1977-78			11	0	2	2	2
11 yrs.		**N Totals:**	692	126	233	359	364

PLAYOFFS

YEAR	TEAM	LEAGUE	GP	G	A	PTS	PIM
1967-68	**STL**	**N**	12	1	2	3	2
1968-69			12	2	2	4	20
1969-70			16	3	4	7	48
1973-74	**TOR**	**N**	4	0	1	1	0
1976-77	**ATL**	**N**	3	0	2	2	6
1977-78			1	0	0	0	0
6 yrs.		**N Totals:**	48	6	11	17	76

Traded to **St. Louis** by N.Y. Rangers with Gary Sabourin, Bob Plager, and Gord Kannegiesser for Rod Seiling, June 6, 1967. Traded to **Detroit** by St. Louis with Red Berenson for Garry Unger and Wayne Connelly, Feb. 6, 1971. Traded to **Toronto** by Detroit for Pierre Jarry, Nov. 29, 1973. Traded to **Washington** by Toronto with Willie Brossart for Rod Seiling, Nov. 2, 1974. Sold to **Atlanta** by Washington, Nov. 2, 1974.

Rolf Edberg

EDBERG, ROLF ARNE 5'10", 175 lbs.
B. Sept. 29, 1950, Stockholm, Sweden Center, Shoots L

YEAR	TEAM	LEAGUE	GP	G	A	PTS	PIM
1978-79	**WASH**	**N**	76	14	27	41	6
1979-80			63	23	23	46	12

Rolf Edberg continued

YEAR	TEAM & LEAGUE		GP	G	A	PTS	PIM
1980-81			45	8	8	16	6
3 yrs.		**N Totals:**	184	45	58	103	24

Frank Eddolls

EDDOLLS, FRANK HERBERT 5'8", 180 lbs.
B. July 5, 1921, Lachine, Que. Defense, Shoots L

YEAR	TEAM & LEAGUE		GP	G	A	PTS	PIM
1944-45	**MONT**	**N**	43	5	8	13	20
1945-46			8	0	1	1	6
1946-47			6	0	0	0	0
1947-48	**NYR**	**N**	58	6	13	19	16
1948-49			34	4	2	6	10
1949-50			58	2	6	8	20
1950-51			68	3	8	11	24
1951-52			42	3	5	8	18
8 yrs.		**N Totals:**	317	23	43	66	114
PLAYOFFS							
1944-45	**MONT**	**N**	3	0	0	0	0
1945-46*			8	0	1	1	2
1946-47			6	0	0	0	4
1947-48	**NYR**	**N**	2	0	0	0	0
1949-50			11	0	1	1	4
5 yrs.		**N Totals:**	30	0	2	2	10

Darryl Edestrand

EDESTRAND, DARRYL 5'11", 185 lbs.
B. Nov. 6, 1945, Strathroy, Ont. Defense, Shoots L

YEAR	TEAM & LEAGUE		GP	G	A	PTS	PIM
1967-68	**STL**	**N**	12	0	0	0	2
1969-70	**PHI**	**N**	2	0	0	0	6
1971-72	**PITT**	**N**	77	10	23	33	52
1972-73			78	15	24	39	88
1973-74			3	0	0	0	0
	BOS	**N**	52	3	8	11	20
	2 team total		55	3	8	11	20
1974-75			68	1	9	10	56
1975-76			77	4	17	21	103
1976-77			17	0	3	3	16
1977-78			1	0	0	0	6
	LA	**N**	13	0	2	2	15
	2 team total		14	0	2	2	21
1978-79			55	1	4	5	46
10 yrs.		**N Totals:**	455	34	90	124	410
PLAYOFFS							
1971-72	**PITT**	**N**	4	0	2	2	0
1973-74	**BOS**	**N**	16	1	2	3	15
1974-75			3	0	1	1	7
1975-76			12	1	3	4	23
1976-77			3	0	0	0	2
1977-78	**LA**	**N**	2	1	1	2	4
1978-79			2	0	0	0	6
7 yrs.		**N Totals:**	42	3	9	12	57

Drafted by **St. Louis** from Toronto in Expansion Draft, June 6, 1967. Traded to **Philadelphia** by St. Louis with Gerry Melnyk for Lou Angotti and Ian Campbell, June 11, 1968. Sold to Hershey **(Pittsburgh)** by Quebec **(Philadelphia)** June 15, 1970. Traded to **Boston** by Pittsburgh for Nick Beverley, Oct. 25, 1973. Sold to **Los Angeles** by Boston, March 13, 1978. Claimed by **Los Angeles** as fill in Expansion Draft, June 13, 1979.

Garry Edmundson

EDMUNDSON, GARRY FRANK 6', 173 lbs.
B. May 6, 1932, Sexsmith, Alta. Left Wing, Shoots L

YEAR	TEAM & LEAGUE		GP	G	A	PTS	PIM
1951-52	**MONT**	**N**	1	0	0	0	0
1959-60	**TOR**	**N**	39	4	6	10	47
1960-61			3	0	0	0	0
3 yrs.		**N Totals:**	43	4	6	10	47
PLAYOFFS							
1951-52	**MONT**	**N**	2	0	0	0	4
1959-60	**TOR**	**N**	9	0	1	1	4
2 yrs.		**N Totals:**	11	0	1	1	8

Tom Edur

EDUR, TOOMAS 6'1", 185 lbs.
B. Nov. 18, 1954, Toronto, Ont. Defense, Shoots R

YEAR	TEAM & LEAGUE		GP	G	A	PTS	PIM
1973-74	**CLEVE**	**W**	76	7	31	38	26
1974-75			61	3	20	23	28
1975-76			80	7	28	35	62
1976-77	**COLO**	**N**	80	7	25	32	39
1977-78			20	5	7	12	10
	PITT	**N**	58	5	38	43	18
	2 team total		78	10	45	55	28
5 yrs.		**N Totals:**	158	17	70	87	67
		W Totals:	217	17	79	96	116
PLAYOFFS							
1973-74	**CLEVE**	**W**	5	1	2	3	0
1974-75			5	2	0	2	0
1975-76			3	0	3	3	0
3 yrs.		**W Totals:**	13	3	5	8	0

Playing rights sold to **Colorado** by Boston, Sept. 7, 1976. Traded to **Pittsburgh** by Colorado for Dennis Owchar, Dec. 2, 1977.

Pat Egan

EGAN, MARTIN JOSEPH (Boxcar) 5'10", 190 lbs.
B. Apr. 25, 1918, Blackie, Alta. Defense, Shoots R

YEAR	TEAM & LEAGUE		GP	G	A	PTS	PIM
1939-40	**NYA**	**N**	10	4	3	7	6
1940-41			39	4	9	13	51
1941-42			48	8	20	28	**124**
1943-44	**DET**	**N**	23	4	15	19	40
	BOS	**N**	25	11	13	24	55
	2 team total		48	15	28	43	95
1944-45			48	7	15	22	**86**
1945-46			41	8	10	18	32
1946-47			60	7	18	25	89
1947-48			60	8	11	19	81
1948-49			60	6	18	24	92
1949-50	**NYR**	**N**	70	5	11	16	50
1950-51			70	5	10	15	70
11 yrs.		**N Totals:**	554	77	153	230	776
PLAYOFFS							
1939-40	**NYA**	**N**	2	0	0	0	4
1944-45	**BOS**	**N**	7	2	0	2	6
1945-46			10	3	0	3	8
1946-47			5	0	2	2	6
1947-48			5	1	1	2	2
1948-49			5	0	0	0	16
1949-50	**NYR**	**N**	12	3	1	4	6
7 yrs.		**N Totals:**	46	9	4	13	48

Jack Egers

EGERS, JOHN RICHARD 6'1", 175 lbs.
B. Jan. 28, 1949, Sudbury, Ont. Right Wing, Shoots L

YEAR	TEAM & LEAGUE		GP	G	A	PTS	PIM
1969-70	**NYR**	**N**	6	3	0	3	2
1970-71			60	7	10	17	50
1971-72			17	2	1	3	14
	STL	**N**	63	21	25	46	34
	2 team total		80	23	26	49	48
1972-73			78	24	24	48	26
1973-74			6	0	1	1	6
	NYR	**N**	28	1	3	4	6
	2 team total		34	1	4	5	12
1974-75	**WASH**	**N**	14	3	2	5	8
1975-76			12	3	3	6	8
7 yrs.		**N Totals:**	284	64	69	133	154
PLAYOFFS							
1969-70	**NYR**	**N**	5	3	1	4	10
1970-71			3	0	0	0	2
1971-72	**STL**	**N**	11	1	4	5	14
1972-73			5	0	1	1	2
1973-74	**NYR**	**N**	8	1	0	1	4
5 yrs.		**N Totals:**	32	5	6	11	32

Traded to **St. Louis** by N.Y. Rangers with Andre Dupont and Mike Murphy for Gene Carr, Jim Lorentz and Wayne Connelly, Nov. 15, 1971. Traded to **N.Y. Rangers** by St. Louis for Glen Sather and Rene Villemore, Oct. 28, 1972. Drafted by **Washington** from N.Y. Rangers in Expansion Draft, June 12, 1974.

Gerry Ehman

EHMAN, GERALD JOSEPH 6', 190 lbs.
B. Nov. 3, 1932, Cudworth, Sask. Right Wing, Shoots R

YEAR	TEAM & LEAGUE	GP	G	A	PTS	PIM
1957-58	**BOS N**	1	1	0	1	0
1958-59	**DET N**	8	0	1	1	4
	TOR N	36	12	13	25	12
	2 team total	44	12	14	26	16
1959-60		69	12	16	28	26
1960-61		14	1	1	2	2
1963-64		4	1	1	2	0
1967-68	**OAK N**	73	19	25	44	20
1968-69	**CALIF N**	70	21	24	45	12
1969-70	**OAK N**	76	11	19	30	8
1970-71	**CALIF N**	78	18	18	36	16
9 yrs.	**N Totals:**	429	96	118	214	100

PLAYOFFS

YEAR	TEAM & LEAGUE	GP	G	A	PTS	PIM
1958-59	**TOR N**	12	6	7	13	8
1959-60		9	0	0	0	0
1963-64*		9	1	0	1	4
1968-69	**CALIF N**	7	2	2	4	0
1969-70	**OAK N**	4	1	1	2	0
5 yrs.	**N Totals:**	41	10	10	20	12

Drafted by **Detroit** from Boston, June 4, 1958. Claimed on waivers by **Toronto** from Detroit, Dec., 1959. Traded to **Oakland** by Toronto for Bryan Hextall and J.P. Parise, Oct. 3, 1967.

Anders Eldebrink

ELDEBRINK, ANDERS 5'11", 187 lbs.
B. Dec. 11, 1960, kalix, Sweden Defense, Shoots R

YEAR	TEAM & LEAGUE	GP	G	A	PTS	PIM
1981-82	**VAN N**	38	1	8	9	21
1982-83		5	1	1	2	0
	QUE N	12	1	2	3	8
	2 team total	17	2	3	5	8
2 yrs.	**N Totals:**	55	3	11	14	29

PLAYOFFS

YEAR	TEAM & LEAGUE	GP	G	A	PTS	PIM
1981-82	**VAN N**	13	0	0	0	10
1982-83	**QUE N**	1	0	0	0	0
2 yrs.	**N Totals:**	14	0	0	0	10

Signed as free agent by **Vancouver** May 16, 1981. Traded by Vancouver to **Quebec** for John Garrett, Feb. 4, 1983.

Boris Elik

ELIK, BORIS 5'10", 190 lbs.
B. Oct. 17, 1929, Geraldton, Ont. Left Wing, Shoots L

YEAR	TEAM & LEAGUE	GP	G	A	PTS	PIM
1962-63	**DET N**	3	0	0	0	0

Fred Elliott

ELLIOTT, FRED H.
B. Unknown Right Wing

YEAR	TEAM & LEAGUE	GP	G	A	PTS	PIM
1928-29	**OTTA N**	43	2	0	2	6

Ron Ellis

ELLIS, RONALD JOHN EDWARD 5'9", 195 lbs.
B. Jan. 8, 1945, Lindsay, Ont. Right Wing, Shoots R

YEAR	TEAM & LEAGUE	GP	G	A	PTS	PIM
1963-64	**TOR N**	1	0	0	0	0
1964-65		62	23	16	39	14
1965-66		70	19	23	42	24
1966-67		67	22	23	45	14
1967-68		74	28	20	48	8
1968-69		72	25	21	46	12
1969-70		76	35	19	54	14
1970-71		78	24	29	53	10
1971-72		78	23	24	47	17
1972-73		78	22	29	51	22
1973-74		70	23	25	48	12
1974-75		79	32	29	61	25
1977-78		80	26	24	50	17
1978-79		63	16	12	28	10
1979-80		59	12	11	23	6
1980-81		27	2	3	5	2
16 yrs.	**N Totals:**	1034	332	308	640	207

Ron Ellis continued

PLAYOFFS

YEAR	TEAM & LEAGUE	GP	G	A	PTS	PIM
1964-65	**TOR N**	6	3	0	3	2
1965-66		4	0	0	0	2
1966-67*		12	2	1	3	4
1968-69		4	2	1	3	2
1970-71		6	1	1	2	2
1971-72		5	1	1	2	4
1973-74		4	2	1	3	0
1974-75		7	3	0	3	2
1977-78		13	3	2	5	0
1978-79		6	1	1	2	2
1979-80		3	0	0	0	0
11 yrs.	**N Totals:**	70	18	8	26	20

Claimed by **Toronto** as fill in Expansion Draft, June 13, 1979.

Kari Eloranta

ELORANTA, KARI 6'2", 200 lbs.
B. Apr. 29, 1956, Lahti, Finland Defense, Shoots L

YEAR	TEAM & LEAGUE	GP	G	A	PTS	PIM
1981-82	**CALG N**	19	0	5	5	14
	STL N	12	1	7	8	6
	2 team total	31	1	12	13	20
1982-83	**CALG N**	80	4	40	44	43
2 yrs.	**N Totals:**	111	5	52	57	63

PLAYOFFS

YEAR	TEAM & LEAGUE	GP	G	A	PTS	PIM
1981-82	**STL N**	5	0	0	0	0
1982-83	**CALG N**	9	1	3	4	17
2 yrs.	**N Totals:**	14	1	3	4	17

Signed as free agent by **Calgary** June, 1981. Traded to **St. Louis** by Calgary for future considerations, Mar. 18, 1982.

Eddie Emberg

EMBERG, EDWARD
B. Nov. 18, 1921, Montreal, Que. Forward

PLAYOFFS

YEAR	TEAM & LEAGUE	GP	G	A	PTS	PIM
1944-45	**MONT N**	2	1	0	1	0

Hap Emms

EMMS, LEIGHTON 6', 190 lbs.
B. Jan. 12, 1905, Barrie, Ont. Left Wing, Shoots L

YEAR	TEAM & LEAGUE	GP	G	A	PTS	PIM
1926-27	**MON(M) N**	8	0	0	0	0
1927-28		8	0	1	1	10
1930-31	**NYA N**	44	5	4	9	56
1931-32		13	1	0	1	11
	DET N	20	6	9	15	27
	2 team total	33	7	9	16	38
1932-33		41	9	13	22	63
1933-34		47	7	7	14	51
1934-35	**BOS N**	11	1	1	2	8
	NYA N	28	2	2	4	19
	2 team total	39	3	3	6	27
1935-36		31	1	5	6	12
1936-37		47	4	8	12	48
1937-38		22	1	3	4	6
10 yrs.	**N Totals:**	320	37	53	90	311

PLAYOFFS

YEAR	TEAM & LEAGUE	GP	G	A	PTS	PIM
1931-32	**DET N**	2	0	0	0	2
1932-33		4	0	0	0	8
1933-34		8	0	0	0	2
3 yrs.	**N Totals:**	14	0	0	0	12

Brian Engblom

ENGBLOM, BRIAN 6'2", 200 lbs.
B. Jan. 27, 1955, Winnipeg, Man. Defense, Shoots L

YEAR	TEAM & LEAGUE	GP	G	A	PTS	PIM
1977-78	**MONT N**	28	1	2	3	23
1978-79		62	3	11	14	60
1979-80		70	3	20	23	43
1980-81		80	3	25	28	96
1981-82		76	4	29	33	76
1982-83	**WASH N**	73	5	22	27	59
6 yrs.	**N Totals:**	389	19	109	128	357

Brian Engblom continued

YEAR	TEAM & LEAGUE		GP	G	A	PTS	PIM
PLAYOFFS							
1976-77*	MONT	N	2	0	0	0	2
1977-78*			5	0	0	0	2
1978-79*			16	0	1	1	11
1979-80			10	2	4	6	6
1980-81			3	1	0	1	4
1981-82			5	0	2	2	14
1982-83	WASH	N	4	0	2	2	2
7 yrs.		N Totals:	45	3	9	12	41

Traded by Montreal with Rod Langway, Doug Jarvis, and Craig Laughlin to **Washington** for Rick Green and Ryan Walter, Sept. 9, 1982.

Jerry Engele

ENGELE, JEROME WILFRED 6', 197 lbs.
B. Nov. 26, 1950, Humboldt, Sask. Defense, Shoots L

YEAR	TEAM & LEAGUE		GP	G	A	PTS	PIM
1975-76	MINN	N	17	0	1	1	16
1976-77			31	1	7	8	41
1977-78			52	1	5	6	105
3 yrs.		N Totals:	100	2	13	15	162
PLAYOFFS							
1976-77	MINN	N	2	0	1	1	0

Sent to **Montreal** as compensation for Minnesota's signing of free agent Mike Polich, Sept. 6, 1978.

Aut Erickson

ERICKSON, AUTRY RAYMOND 6', 188 lbs.
B. Jan. 25, 1938, Lethbridge, Alta. Defense, Shoots L

YEAR	TEAM & LEAGUE		GP	G	A	PTS	PIM
1959-60	BOS	N	58	1	6	7	29
1960-61			68	2	6	8	65
1962-63	CHI	N	3	0	0	0	8
1963-64			31	0	1	1	34
1967-68	OAK	N	66	4	11	15	46
1969-70	OAK	N	1	0	0	0	0
6 yrs.		N Totals:	227	7	24	31	182
PLAYOFFS							
1963-64	CHI	N	6	0	0	0	0
1966-67*	TOR	N	1	0	0	0	2
2 yrs.		N Totals:	7	0	0	0	2

Drafted by **Boston** from Chicago, June, 1959. Drafted by **Chicago** from Boston, June, 1961. Traded by Chicago with Ron Murphy to **Detroit** for John Miszuk, Art Stratton, and Ian Cushenan, June 10, 1964. Traded by Detroit with Marcel Pronovost, Larry Jeffrey, Ed Joyal, and Lowell MacDonald to **Toronto** for Billy Harris, Andy Bathgate, and Gary Jarrett, May 20, 1965. Drafted by **Oakland** from Toronto in Expansion Draft, June 6, 1967.

Grant Erickson

ERICKSON, GRANT 5'9", 165 lbs.
B. Apr. 28, 1947, Pierceland, Sask. Left Wing, Shoots L

YEAR	TEAM & LEAGUE		GP	G	A	PTS	PIM
1968-69	BOS	N	2	1	0	1	0
1969-70	MINN	N	4	0	0	0	4
1972-73	CLEVE	W	77	15	29	44	23
1973-74			78	23	27	50	26
1974-75			78	12	15	27	24
1975-76	PHOE	W	33	4	4	8	6
6 yrs.		N Totals:	6	1	0	1	4
		W Totals:	266	54	75	129	79
PLAYOFFS							
1972-73	CLEVE	W	9	2	1	3	2
1973-74			5	0	2	2	0
1975-76	PHOE	W	5	0	2	2	0
3 yrs.		W Totals:	19	2	5	7	2

Rolie Eriksson

ERIKSSON, BENGT ROLAND 6'3", 190 lbs.
B. Mar. 1, 1954, Storatuna, Sweden Center, Shoots L

YEAR	TEAM & LEAGUE		GP	G	A	PTS	PIM
1976-77	MINN	N	80	25	44	69	10
1977-78			78	21	39	60	12
1978-79	VAN	N	35	2	12	14	4
	WINN	W	33	5	10	15	2
	2 team total		68	7	22	29	6

Rolie Eriksson continued

YEAR	TEAM & LEAGUE		GP	G	A	PTS	PIM
3 yrs.		N Totals:	193	48	95	143	26
		W Totals:	33	5	10	15	2
PLAYOFFS							
1976-77	MINN	N	2	1	0	1	0
1978-79	WINN	W	10	1	4	5	0
2 yrs.		N Totals:	2	1	0	1	0
		W Totals:	10	1	4	5	0

Signed as free agent by **Vancouver** June 7, 1978.

Thomas Erikkson

ERIKKSON, THOMAS 6'2", 182 lbs.
B. Oct. 16, 1959, Stockholm, Sweden Defense, Shoots L

YEAR	TEAM & LEAGUE		GP	G	A	PTS	PIM
1980-81	PHI	N	24	1	10	11	14
1981-82			1	0	0	0	4
2 yrs.		N Totals:	25	1	10	11	18
PLAYOFFS							
1980-81	PHI	N	7	0	2	2	6

Phil Esposito

ESPOSITO, PHILIP ANTHONY (Espo) 6'1", 205 lbs.
B. Feb. 20, 1942, Sault Ste. Marie, Ont. Center, Shoots L
Won Hart Trophy, 1968–69, 1973-74
Won Art Ross Trophy, 1968–69, 1970–71, 1971–72, 1972–73, 1973-74

YEAR	TEAM & LEAGUE		GP	G	A	PTS	PIM
1963-64	CHI	N	27	3	2	5	2
1964-65			70	23	32	55	44
1965-66			69	27	26	53	49
1966-67			69	21	40	61	40
1967-68	BOS	N	74	35	**49**	84	21
1968-69			74	49	**77**	**126**	79
1969-70			76	**43**	56	99	50
1970-71			78	**76**	76	**152**	71
1971-72			76	**66**	67	**133**	76
1972-73			78	**55**	**75**	**130**	87
1973-74			78	**68**	77	**145**	58
1974-75			79	**61**	66	127	62
1975-76			12	6	10	16	8
	NYR	N	62	29	38	67	28
	2 team total		74	35	48	83	36
1976-77			80	34	46	80	52
1977-78			79	38	43	81	53
1978-79			80	42	36	78	14
1979-80			80	34	44	78	73
1980-81			41	7	13	20	20
18 yrs.		N Totals:	1282	717	873	1590	887
PLAYOFFS							
1963-64	CHI	N	4	0	0	0	0
1964-65			13	3	3	6	15
1965-66			6	1	1	2	2
1966-67			6	0	0	0	4
1967-68	BOS	N	4	0	3	3	0
1968-69			10	8	10	18	8
1969-70*			14	13	14	27	16
1970-71			7	3	7	10	6
1971-72*			15	9	15	24	24
1972-73			2	0	1	1	2
1973-74			16	9	5	14	25
1974-75			3	4	1	5	0
1977-78	NYR	N	3	0	1	1	5
1978-79			18	8	12	20	20
1979-80			9	3	3	6	8
15 yrs.		N Totals:	130	61	76	137	135

Traded to **Boston** by Chicago with Ken Hodge and Fred Stanfield for Gilles Marotte, Pit Martin and Jack Norris, May 15, 1967. Traded to **N.Y. Rangers** by Boston with Carol Vadnais for Brad Park, Jean Ratelle, and Joe Zanussi, Nov. 7, 1975.

Chris Evans

EVANS, CHRISTOPHER BRUCE 5'9", 180 lbs.
B. Sept. 14, 1946, Toronto, Ont. Defense, Shoots L

YEAR	TEAM & LEAGUE		GP	G	A	PTS	PIM
1969-70	TOR	N	2	0	0	0	0
1971-72	BUF	N	61	6	18	24	98
	STL	N	2	0	0	0	0
	2 team total		63	6	18	24	98
1972-73			77	9	12	21	31

Chris Evans continued

YEAR	TEAM & LEAGUE	GP	G	A	PTS	PIM
1973-74		54	4	7	11	8
	DET N	23	0	2	2	2
	2 team total	77	4	9	13	10
1974-75	**KC N**	2	0	2	2	2
	STL N	20	0	1	1	2
	2 team total	22	0	3	3	4
1975-76	**CALG W**	75	3	20	23	50
1976-77		81	7	27	34	60
1977-78	**BIRM W**	0	0	0	0	0
	QUE W	48	1	4	5	26
	2 team total	48	1	4	5	26
8 yrs.	**N Totals:**	241	19	42	61	143
	W Totals:	204	11	51	62	136
PLAYOFFS						
1971-72	**STL N**	7	1	0	1	4
1972-73		5	0	1	1	4
1975-76	**CALG W**	10	5	5	10	4
3 yrs.	**N Totals:**	12	1	1	2	8
	W Totals:	10	5	5	10	4

Sold to Phoenix by Toronto, May 22, 1970. Drafted by **St. Louis** from Phoenix in Inter-League Draft, June 9, 1970. Drafted by **Buffalo** from St. Louis in Expansion Draft, June 10, 1970. Traded to **St. Louis** by Buffalo for George Morrison and St. Louis' second round choice (Larry Carriere) in the 1972 Amateur Draft, Mar. 5 1972. Traded to **Detroit** by St. Louis with Bryan Watson and Jean Hamel for Ted Harris, Bill Collins and Garnet Bailey, Feb. 14, 1974. Drafted by **Kansas City** from Detroit in Expansion Draft June 12, 1974. Traded to **St. Louis** by Kansas City with Kansas City's fourth choice (goaltender Mike Liut) in 1976 Amateur Draft for Larry Giroux, Oct. 29, 1974

Daryl Evans

EVANS, DARYL TOMAS (Reggie) 5'8", 185 lbs.
B. Jan. 12, 1961, Toronto, Ont. Left Wing, Shoots L

YEAR	TEAM & LEAGUE	GP	G	A	PTS	PIM
1981-82	**LA N**	14	2	6	8	2
1982-83		80	18	22	40	21
2 yrs.	**N Totals:**	94	20	28	48	23
PLAYOFFS						
1981-82	**LA N**	10	5	8	13	12

Jack Evans

EVANS, WILLIAM JOHN 6'1", 194 lbs.
B. Apr. 21, 1928, Garnant, South Wales Defense, Shoots L

YEAR	TEAM & LEAGUE	GP	G	A	PTS	PIM
1948-49	**NYR N**	3	0	0	0	4
1949-50		2	0	0	0	2
1950-51		49	1	0	1	95
1951-52		52	1	6	7	83
1953-54		44	4	4	8	73
1954-55		47	0	5	5	91
1955-56		70	2	9	11	104
1956-57		70	3	6	9	110
1957-58		70	4	8	12	108
1958-59	**CHI N**	70	1	8	9	75
1959-60		68	0	4	4	60
1960-61		69	0	8	8	58
1961-62		70	3	14	17	80
1962-63		68	0	8	8	46
14 yrs.	**N Totals:**	752	19	80	99	989
PLAYOFFS						
1955-56	**NYR N**	5	1	0	1	18
1956-57		5	0	1	1	4
1957-58		6	0	0	0	17
1958-59	**CHI N**	6	0	0	0	10
1959-60		4	0	0	0	4
1960-61*		12	1	1	2	14
1961-62		12	0	0	0	26
1962-63		6	0	0	0	4
8 yrs.	**N Totals:**	56	2	2	4	97

Drafted by **Chicago** from N.Y. Rangers, June, 1958.

John Evans

EVANS, JOHN PAUL 5'9", 170 lbs.
B. May 2, 1954, Toronto, Ont. Center, Shoots L

YEAR	TEAM & LEAGUE	GP	G	A	PTS	PIM
1978-79	**PHI N**	44	6	5	11	12
1980-81		1	0	0	0	2

John Evans continued

YEAR	TEAM & LEAGUE	GP	G	A	PTS	PIM
1982-83		58	8	20	28	20
3 yrs.	**N Totals:**	103	14	25	39	34

Traded to **Philadelphia** by Los Angeles to complete earlier deal (Steve Short, June 17, 1977), Nov. 3, 1977.

Paul Evans

EVANS, PAUL EDWARD VINCENT 5'11", 175 lbs.
B. Feb. 24, 1955, Peterborough, Ont. Center, Shoots L

YEAR	TEAM & LEAGUE	GP	G	A	PTS	PIM
1976-77	**TOR N**	7	1	1	2	19
1977-78		4	0	0	0	2
2 yrs.	**N Totals:**	11	1	1	2	21
PLAYOFFS						
1976-77	**TOR N**	2	0	0	0	0
1982-83	**PHI N**	1	0	0	0	0
2 yrs.	**N Totals:**	3	0	0	0	0

Stewart Evans

EVANS, STEWART 5'10", 170 lbs.
B. June 19, 1908, Ottawa, Ont. Shoots L

YEAR	TEAM & LEAGUE	GP	G	A	PTS	PIM
1930-31	**DET N**	43	1	4	5	14
1932-33		48	2	6	8	74
1933-34		17	0	0	0	20
	MON(M) N	27	4	2	6	35
	2 team total	44	4	2	6	55
1934-35		46	5	7	12	54
1935-36		47	3	5	8	57
1936-37		48	6	7	13	54
1937-38		48	5	11	16	59
1938-39	**MONT N**	43	2	7	9	58
8 yrs.	**N Totals:**	367	28	49	77	425
PLAYOFFS						
1932-33	**DET N**	4	0	0	0	6
1933-34	**MON(M) N**	4	0	0	0	4
1934-35*		7	0	0	0	8
1935-36		3	0	0	0	0
1936-37		5	0	0	0	0
1938-39	**MONT N**	3	0	0	0	2
6 yrs.	**N Totals:**	26	0	0	0	20

Bill Evo

EVO, WILLIAM 6'2", 187 lbs.
B. Feb. 21, 1954, Royal Oak, Mich. Right Wing, Shoots L

YEAR	TEAM & LEAGUE	GP	G	A	PTS	PIM
1974-75	**M-B W**	49	13	9	22	32
1975-76	**EDM W**	8	0	4	4	0
	CLEVE W	40	1	5	6	32
	2 team total	48	1	9	10	32
2 yrs.	**W Totals:**	97	14	18	32	64

Bill Ezinicki

EZINICKI, WILLIAM (Wild Bill) 5'10", 170 lbs.
B. Mar. 11, 1924, Winnipeg, Man. Right Wing, Shoots R

YEAR	TEAM & LEAGUE	GP	G	A	PTS	PIM
1944-45	**TOR N**	8	1	4	5	17
1945-46		24	4	8	12	29
1946-47		60	17	20	37	93
1947-48		60	11	20	31	97
1948-49		52	13	15	28	**145**
1949-50		67	10	12	22	**144**
1950-51	**BOS N**	53	16	19	35	119
1951-52		28	5	5	10	47
1954-55	**NYR N**	16	2	2	4	22
9 yrs.	**N Totals:**	368	79	105	184	713
PLAYOFFS						
1946-47*	**TOR N**	11	0	2	2	30
1947-48*		9	3	1	4	6
1948-49*		9	1	4	5	20
1949-50		5	0	0	0	13
1950-51	**BOS N**	6	1	1	2	18
5 yrs.	**N Totals:**	40	5	8	13	87

Traded to **Boston** by Toronto with Vic Lynn for Fern Flaman, Ken Smith, Phil Maloney and Leo Boivin, Nov. 16, 1950. Sold to **Toronto** by Boston, Sept. 14, 1952. Purchased by **N.Y. Rangers** from Toronto, Feb. 12, 1955.

Trevor Fahey

FAHEY, JOHN TREVOR 6', 180 lbs.
B. Jan. 4, 1944, New Waterford, N.S. Left Wing, Shoots L

YEAR	TEAM & LEAGUE		GP	G	A	PTS	PIM
1964-65	NYR	N	1	0	0	0	0

Bill Fairbairn

FAIRBAIRN, WILLIAM JOHN (Magnet) 5'10", 195 lbs.
B. Jan. 7, 1947, Brandon, Man. Right Wing, Shoots R

YEAR	TEAM & LEAGUE		GP	G	A	PTS	PIM
1968-69	NYR	N	1	0	0	0	0
1969-70			76	23	33	56	23
1970-71			56	7	23	30	32
1971-72			78	22	36	58	53
1972-73			78	30	33	63	23
1973-74			78	18	44	62	12
1974-75			80	24	37	61	10
1975-76			80	13	15	28	8
1976-77			9	1	2	3	0
	MINN	N	51	9	20	29	2
	2 team total		60	10	22	32	2
1977-78			6	0	1	1	0
	STL	N	60	14	16	30	10
	2 team total		66	14	17	31	10
1978-79			5	1	0	1	0
11 yrs.		N Totals:	658	162	260	422	173
PLAYOFFS							
1969-70	NYR	N	6	0	1	1	10
1970-71			4	0	0	0	0
1971-72			16	5	7	12	11
1972-73			10	1	8	9	2
1973-74			13	3	5	8	6
1974-75			3	4	0	4	13
1976-77	MINN	N	2	0	1	1	0
7 yrs.		N Totals:	54	13	22	35	42

Traded to **Minnesota** by N.Y. Rangers with Nick Beverley for Bill Goldsworthy, Nov. 11, 1976. Claimed on waivers by **St. Louis** from Minnesota, Oct. 24, 1977.

Bob Falkenberg

FALKENBERG, ROBERT ARTHUR (Steady)
6', 205 lbs.
B. Jan. 1, 1946, Stettler, Alta. Defense, Shoots L

YEAR	TEAM & LEAGUE		GP	G	A	PTS	PIM
1966-67	DET	N	16	1	1	2	10
1967-68			20	0	3	3	10
1968-69			5	0	0	0	0
1970-71			9	0	1	1	6
1971-72			4	0	0	0	0
1972-73	ALTA	W	76	6	23	29	44
1973-74	EDM	W	78	3	14	17	32
1974-75	SD	W	78	2	18	20	42
1975-76			79	3	13	16	31
1976-77			64	0	6	6	34
1977-78	EDM	W	2	0	0	0	0
11 yrs.		N Totals:	54	1	5	6	26
		W Totals:	377	14	74	88	183
PLAYOFFS							
1973-74	EDM	W	5	0	2	2	14
1974-75	SD	W	10	0	1	1	4
1975-76			11	1	2	3	6
1976-77			2	0	0	0	0
4 yrs.		W Totals:	28	1	5	6	24

Craig Falkman

FALKMAN, CRAIG 5'11", 190 lbs.
B. Aug. 1, 1943, St. Paul, Minn. Right Wing, Shoots R

YEAR	TEAM & LEAGUE		GP	G	A	PTS	PIM
1972-73	MINN	W	45	1	5	6	12

Dick Farda

FARDA, RICHARD 5'9", 175 lbs.
B. Nov. 8, 1945, Brno, Czechoslovakia Center, Shoots L

YEAR	TEAM & LEAGUE		GP	G	A	PTS	PIM
1974-75	TOR	W	66	6	25	31	2
1975-76			63	19	35	54	8
1976-77	BIRM	W	48	9	26	35	2

Dick Farda continued

YEAR	TEAM & LEAGUE		GP	G	A	PTS	PIM
3 yrs.		W Totals:	177	34	86	120	12

Walt Farrant

FARRANT, WALTER LESLIE (Whitey) 5'10", 155 lbs.
B. Aug. 12, 1912, Toronto, Ont. Right Wing, Shoots R

YEAR	TEAM & LEAGUE		GP	G	A	PTS	PIM
1943-44	CHI	N	1	0	0	0	0

Dave Farrish

FARRISH, DAVID ALLAN 6', 190 lbs.
B. Aug. 1, 1956, Wingham, Ont. Defense, Shoots L

YEAR	TEAM & LEAGUE		GP	G	A	PTS	PIM
1976-77	NYR	N	80	2	17	19	102
1977-78			66	3	5	8	62
1978-79			71	1	19	20	61
1979-80	QUE	N	4	0	0	0	0
	TOR	N	20	1	8	9	30
	2 team total		24	1	8	9	30
1980-81			74	2	18	20	90
1982-83			56	4	24	28	38
6 yrs.		N Totals:	371	13	91	104	383
PLAYOFFS							
1977-78	NYR	N	3	0	0	0	0
1978-79			7	0	2	2	14
1979-80	TOR	N	3	0	0	0	10
1980-81			1	0	0	0	0
4 yrs.		N Totals:	14	0	2	2	24

Claimed by **Quebec** from N.Y. Rangers in Expansion Draft, June 13, 1979. Traded to **Toronto** by Quebec with Terry Martin for Reggie Thomas, Dec. 13, 1979.

Gordie Fashoway

FASHOWAY, GORDON 5'11", 180 lbs.
B. June 16, 1926, Portage La Prairie, Man.
Forward, Shoots L

YEAR	TEAM & LEAGUE		GP	G	A	PTS	PIM
1950-51	CHI	N	13	3	2	5	14

Mario Faubert

FAUBERT, MARIO 6'1", 175 lbs.
B. Dec. 2, 1954, Valleyfield, Que. Defense, Shoots R

YEAR	TEAM & LEAGUE		GP	G	A	PTS	PIM
1974-75	PITT	N	10	1	0	1	0
1975-76			21	1	8	9	10
1976-77			47	2	11	13	32
1977-78			18	0	6	6	11
1979-80			49	5	13	18	31
1980-81			72	8	44	52	118
1981-82			14	4	8	12	14
7 yrs.		N Totals:	231	21	90	111	216
PLAYOFFS							
1976-77	PITT	N	3	1	0	1	2
1979-80			2	0	1	1	0
1980-81			5	1	1	2	4
3 yrs.		N Totals:	10	2	2	4	6

Alex Faulkner

FAULKNER, ALEX 5'8", 165 lbs.
B. May 21, 1936, Bishop Falls, Nfld. Center, Shoots L

YEAR	TEAM & LEAGUE		GP	G	A	PTS	PIM
1961-62	TOR	N	1	0	0	0	0
1962-63	DET	N	70	10	10	20	6
1963-64			30	5	7	12	9
3 yrs.		N Totals:	101	15	17	32	15
PLAYOFFS							
1962-63	DET	N	8	5	0	5	2
1963-64			4	0	0	0	0
2 yrs.		N Totals:	12	5	0	5	2

Drafted by **Detroit** from Toronto, June, 1962.

Dave Feamster

FEAMSTER, DAVID ALLAN 5'11", 180 lbs.
B. Sept. 10, 1958, Detroit, Mich. Defense, Shoots L

YEAR	TEAM & LEAGUE		GP	G	A	PTS	PIM
1981-82	**CHI**	**N**	29	0	2	2	29
1982-83			78	6	12	18	69
2 yrs.		**N Totals:**	107	6	14	20	98
PLAYOFFS							
1981-82	**CHI**	**N**	15	2	4	6	53
1982-83			13	1	0	1	4
2 yrs.		**N Totals:**	28	3	4	7	57

Tony Featherstone

FEATHERSTONE, ANTHONY JAMES 5'11", 187 lbs.
B. July 31, 1949, Toronto, Ont. Right Wing, Shoots R

YEAR	TEAM & LEAGUE		GP	G	A	PTS	PIM
1969-70	**OAK**	**N**	9	0	1	1	17
1970-71	**CALIF**	**N**	67	8	8	16	44
1973-74	**MINN**	**N**	54	9	12	21	4
1974-75	**TOR**	**W**	76	25	38	63	26
1975-76			32	4	7	11	5
5 yrs.		**N Totals:**	130	17	21	38	65
		W Totals:	108	29	45	74	31
PLAYOFFS							
1969-70	**OAK**	**N**	2	0	0	0	0
1974-75	**TOR**	**W**	6	2	1	3	2
2 yrs.		**N Totals:**	2	0	0	0	0
		W Totals:	6	2	1	3	2

Sold to **Montreal** by California, Oct. 4, 1971. Sold to **N.Y. Islanders** by Montreal, June 12, 1972. Sold to **Montreal** by N.Y. Islanders, Dec. 7, 1972. Traded to **Minnesota** by Montreal for a player to be named later, May 29, 1973.

Bernie Federko

FEDERKO, BERNARD ALLAN 6', 178 lbs.
B. May 12, 1956, Foam Lake, Sask. Center, Shoots L

YEAR	TEAM & LEAGUE		GP	G	A	PTS	PIM
1976-77	**STL**	**N**	31	14	9	23	15
1977-78			72	17	24	41	27
1978-79			74	31	64	95	14
1979-80			79	38	56	94	24
1980-81			78	31	73	104	47
1981-82			74	30	62	92	70
1982-83			75	24	60	84	24
7 yrs.		**N Totals:**	483	185	348	533	221
PLAYOFFS							
1976-77	**STL**	**N**	4	1	1	2	2
1979-80			3	1	0	1	2
1980-81			11	8	10	18	2
1981-82			10	3	15	18	10
1982-83			4	2	3	5	0
5 yrs.		**N Totals:**	32	15	29	44	16

Mike Federko

FEDERKO, MICHAEL
Forward

YEAR	TEAM & LEAGUE		GP	G	A	PTS	PIM
1976-77	**HOUS**	**W**	4	0	0	0	0

Tony Feltrin

FELTRIN, ANTHOMY LOUIS 5'11", 185 lbs.
B. Dec. 6, 1961, Ladysmith, B.C. Defense, Shoots L

YEAR	TEAM & LEAGUE		GP	G	A	PTS	PIM
1980-81	**PITT**	**N**	2	0	0	0	0
1981-82			4	0	0	0	4
1982-83			32	3	3	6	40
3 yrs.		**N Totals:**	38	3	3	6	44

David Fenyves

FENYVES, DAVID 5'11", 188 lbs.
B. Apr. 29, 1960, Dunnville, Ont. Defense, Shoots L

YEAR	TEAM & LEAGUE		GP	G	A	PTS	PIM
1982-83	**BUF**	**N**	24	0	8	8	14
PLAYOFFS							
1982-83	**BUF**	**N**	4	0	0	0	0

David Fenyves continued

Signed as free agent by **Buffalo** Oct. 31, 1979.

Tom Fergus

FERGUS, THOMAS JOSEPH 6', 179 lbs.
B. June 16, 1962, Chicago, Ill. Center, Shoots L

YEAR	TEAM & LEAGUE		GP	G	A	PTS	PIM
1981-82	**BOS**	**N**	61	15	24	39	12
1982-83			80	28	35	63	39
2 yrs.		**N Totals:**	141	43	59	102	51
PLAYOFFS							
1981-82	**BOS**	**N**	6	3	0	3	0
1982-83			15	2	2	4	15
2 yrs.		**N Totals:**	21	5	2	7	15

Ferguson

FERGUSON
B. Unknown Forward

YEAR	TEAM & LEAGUE		GP	G	A	PTS	PIM
1939-40	**CHI**	**N**	1	0	0	0	0

George Ferguson

FERGUSON, GEORGE 6', 195 lbs.
B. Aug. 22, 1952, Trenton, Ont. Center, Shoots R

YEAR	TEAM & LEAGUE		GP	G	A	PTS	PIM
1972-73	**TOR**	**N**	72	10	13	23	34
1973-74			16	0	4	4	4
1974-75			69	19	30	49	61
1975-76			79	12	32	44	76
1976-77			50	9	15	24	24
1977-78			73	7	16	23	37
1978-79	**PITT**	**N**	80	21	29	50	37
1979-80			73	21	28	49	56
1980-81			79	25	18	43	42
1981-82			71	22	31	53	45
1982-83			7	0	0	0	2
	MINN	**N**	65	8	12	20	14
	2 team total		72	8	12	20	16
11 yrs.		**N Totals:**	734	154	228	382	432
PLAYOFFS							
1973-74	**TOR**	**N**	3	0	1	1	2
1974-75			7	1	0	1	7
1975-76			10	2	4	6	2
1976-77			9	0	3	3	7
1977-78			13	5	1	6	7
1978-79	**PITT**	**N**	7	2	1	3	0
1979-80			5	0	3	3	4
1980-81			5	2	6	8	9
1981-82			5	0	1	1	0
1982-83	**MINN**	**N**	9	0	3	3	4
10 yrs.		**N Totals:**	73	12	23	35	42

Traded to **Pittsburgh** by Toronto with Randy Carlyle for Dave Burrows, June 14, 1978. Traded by Pittsburgh with a first round choice in the 1983 Amateur Draft (Brian Lawton) to **Minnesota** for Ron Meighan and Anders Hakansson, Oct. 28, 1982.

John Ferguson

FERGUSON, JOHN BOWIE (Fergie) 5'11", 190 lbs.
B. Sept. 5, 1938, Vancouver, B.C. Left Wing, Shoots L

YEAR	TEAM & LEAGUE		GP	G	A	PTS	PIM
1963-64	**MONT**	**N**	59	18	27	45	125
1964-65			69	17	27	44	156
1965-66			65	11	14	25	153
1966-67			67	20	22	42	**177**
1967-68			61	15	18	33	117
1968-69			71	29	23	52	45
1969-70			48	19	13	32	139
1970-71			60	16	14	30	32
8 yrs.		**N Totals:**	500	145	158	303	944
PLAYOFFS							
1963-64	**MONT**	**N**	7	0	1	1	25
1964-65*			13	3	1	4	28
1965-66*			10	2	0	2	44
1966-67			10	4	2	6	22
1967-68*			13	3	5	8	25
1968-69*			14	4	3	7	80

John Ferguson continued

YEAR	TEAM & LEAGUE		GP	G	A	PTS	PIM
1970-71*			18	4	6	10	36
7 yrs.		**N Totals:**	85	20	18	38	260

Lorne Ferguson

FERGUSON, LORNE ROBERT (Fergie) 6', 185 lbs.
B. May 26, 1930, Palmerston, Ont. Left Wing, Shoots L

YEAR	TEAM & LEAGUE		GP	G	A	PTS	PIM
1949-50	**BOS**	**N**	3	1	1	2	0
1950-51			70	16	17	33	31
1951-52			27	3	4	7	14
1954-55			69	20	14	34	24
1955-56			32	7	5	12	18
	DET	**N**	31	8	7	15	12
	2 team total		63	15	12	27	30
1956-57			70	13	10	23	26
1957-58			15	1	3	4	0
	CHI	**N**	38	6	9	15	24
	2 team total		53	7	12	19	24
1958-59			67	7	10	17	44
8 yrs.		**N Totals:**	422	82	80	162	193
PLAYOFFS							
1950-51	**BOS**	**N**	6	1	0	1	2
1954-55			4	1	0	1	2
1955-56	**DET**	**N**	10	1	2	3	12
1956-57			5	1	0	1	6
1958-59	**CHI**	**N**	6	2	1	3	2
5 yrs.		**N Totals:**	31	6	3	9	24

Traded to **Detroit** by Boston with Murray Costello, for Real Chevrefils and Jerry Toppazzini, Jan. 17, 1956. Traded to **Chicago** by Detroit with Earl Reibel, Billy Dea and Bill Dineen for Nick Mickoski, Jack McIntyre, Bob Bailey and Hec Lalande, Dec. 17, 1957.

Norm Ferguson

FERGUSON, NORMAN GERARD 5'8", 165 lbs.
B. Oct. 16, 1945, Sydney, N.S. Right Wing, Shoots R

YEAR	TEAM & LEAGUE		GP	G	A	PTS	PIM
1968-69	**CALIF**	**N**	76	34	20	54	31
1969-70	**OAK**	**N**	72	11	9	20	19
1970-71	**CALIF**	**N**	77	14	20	34	13
1971-72			77	14	20	34	13
1972-73	**NY**	**W**	56	28	40	68	8
1973-74	**NY-NJ**	**W**	75	15	21	36	12
1974-75	**SD**	**W**	78	36	33	69	6
1975-76			79	37	37	74	12
1976-77			77	39	32	71	5
1977-78	**EDM**	**W**	71	26	21	47	2
10 yrs.		**N Totals:**	302	73	69	142	76
		W Totals:	436	181	184	365	45
PLAYOFFS							
1968-69	**CALIF**	**N**	7	1	4	5	7
1969-70	**OAK**	**N**	3	0	0	0	0
1974-75	**SD**	**W**	10	6	5	11	0
1975-76			4	2	0	2	9
1976-77			7	2	4	6	0
1977-78	**EDM**	**W**	5	0	0	0	0
6 yrs.		**N Totals:**	10	1	4	5	7
		W Totals:	26	10	9	19	9

Traded to **Oakland** by Montreal with Stan Fuller for Alain Caron, Wally Boyer and Oakland's first round choices in the 1968 (Jim Pritchard) and 1970 (goaltender Ray Martyniuk) Amateur Drafts, May 21, 1968. Drafted by **N.Y. Islanders** from California in Expansion Draft, June 6, 1972.

Mike Fidler

FIDLER, MICHAEL EDWARD 5'11", 195 lbs.
B. Aug. 19, 1956, Everett, Mass. Left Wing, Shoots L

YEAR	TEAM & LEAGUE		GP	G	A	PTS	PIM
1976-77	**CLEVE**	**N**	46	17	16	33	17
1977-78			78	23	28	51	38
1978-79	**MINN**	**N**	59	23	26	49	42
1979-80			24	5	4	9	13
1980-81			20	5	12	17	6
	HART	**N**	38	9	9	18	4
	2 team total		58	14	21	35	10
1981-82			2	0	1	1	0
1982-83	**CHI**	**N**	4	2	1	3	4
7 yrs.		**N Totals:**	271	84	97	181	124

Protected by Minnesota prior to Cleveland-Minnesota Dispersal Draft, June 15, 1978. Traded to **Hartford** by Minnesota for Gordie Roberts, Dec. 16, 1980. Signed as free agent by **Boston** Dec. 1, 1981.

Wilf Field

FIELD, WILFRED SPENCE 5'11", 185 lbs.
B. Apr. 29, 1915, Winnipeg, Man. Defense, Shoots L

YEAR	TEAM & LEAGUE		GP	G	A	PTS	PIM
1936-37	**NYA**	**N**	1	0	0	0	0
1938-39			43	1	3	4	37
1939-40			45	1	3	4	28
1940-41			36	5	6	11	31
1941-42			41	6	9	15	23
1944-45	**MONT**	**N**	9	1	0	1	10
	CHI	**N**	39	3	4	7	22
	2 team total		48	4	4	8	32
6 yrs.		**N Totals:**	214	17	25	42	151
PLAYOFFS							
1938-39	**NYA**	**N**	2	0	0	0	2
1939-40			3	0	0	0	0
2 yrs.		**N Totals:**	5	0	0	0	2

Guy Fielder

FIELDER, GUYLE ABNER 5'9", 165 lbs.
B. Nov. 21, 1930, Potlatch, Ida. Center, Shoots L

YEAR	TEAM & LEAGUE		GP	G	A	PTS	PIM
1950-51	**CHI**	**N**	30	0	0	0	0
1957-58	**DET**	**N**	6	0	0	0	2
2 yrs.		**N Totals:**	36	0	0	0	2
PLAYOFFS							
1952-53	**DET**	**N**	4	0	0	0	0
1953-54	**BOS**	**N**	2	0	0	0	2
2 yrs.		**N Totals:**	6	0	0	0	2

Sold to **Detroit** by Chicago with Steve Hrymnak and Red Almas, Sept. 23, 1952. Sold by Detroit to **Boston** Sept. 24, 1953. Purchased from Boston by **Detroit** June 5, 1957.

Bob Fillion

FILLION, LOUIS ROBERT 5'9½", 170 lbs.
B. July 12, 1921, Thetford Mines, Que. Left Wing, Shoots L

YEAR	TEAM & LEAGUE		GP	G	A	PTS	PIM
1943-44	**MONT**	**N**	41	7	23	30	14
1944-45			31	6	8	14	12
1945-46			50	10	6	16	12
1946-47			57	6	3	9	16
1947-48			32	4	9	13	8
1948-49			59	3	9	12	14
1949-50			57	1	3	4	8
7 yrs.		**N Totals:**	327	37	61	98	84
PLAYOFFS							
1943-44*	**MONT**	**N**	3	0	0	0	0
1944-45			1	3	0	3	0
1945-46*			9	4	3	7	6
1946-47			8	0	0	0	0
1948-49			7	0	1	1	4
1949-50			5	0	0	0	0
6 yrs.		**N Totals:**	33	7	4	11	10

Marcel Fillion

FILLION, MARCEL 5'7", 175 lbs.
B. May 28, 1923, Thetford Mines, Que. Left Wing, Shoots L

YEAR	TEAM & LEAGUE		GP	G	A	PTS	PIM
1944-45	**BOS**	**N**	1	0	0	0	0

Tommy Filmore

FILMORE, THOMAS 5'11½", 189 lbs.
B. Thamesford, Ont. Right Wing, Shoots R

YEAR	TEAM & LEAGUE		GP	G	A	PTS	PIM
1930-31	**DET**	**N**	40	6	2	8	10
1931-32			9	0	0	0	2
	NYA	**N**	31	8	6	14	12
	2 team total		40	8	6	14	14
1932-33			33	1	4	5	9
1933-34	**BOS**	**N**	3	0	0	0	0
4 yrs.		**N Totals:**	116	15	12	27	33

Lloyd Finkbeiner

FINKBEINER, LLOYD

Forward

YEAR	TEAM & LEAGUE		GP	G	A	PTS	PIM
1940-41	NYA	N	1	0	0	0	0

Sid Finney

FINNEY, JOSEPH SIDNEY — 5'10", 160 lbs.
B. May 1, 1929, Banbridge, Ireland — Center, Shoots L

YEAR	TEAM & LEAGUE		GP	G	A	PTS	PIM
1951-52	CHI	N	26	6	5	11	0
1952-53			18	4	2	6	4
1953-54			6	0	0	0	0
3 yrs.		N Totals:	50	10	7	17	4
PLAYOFFS							
1952-53	CHI	N	7	0	2	2	0

Ed Finnigan

FINNIGAN, EDWARD
B. Shawville, Que. — Forward

YEAR	TEAM & LEAGUE		GP	G	A	PTS	PIM
1935-36	BOS	N	3	0	0	0	0

Frank Finnigan

FINNIGAN, FRANK — 5'9", 165 lbs.
B. July 9, 1903, Shawville, Ont. — Right Wing, Shoots R

YEAR	TEAM & LEAGUE		GP	G	A	PTS	PIM
1923-24	OTTA	N	4	0	0	0	0
1924-25			29	0	0	0	20
1925-26			36	2	0	2	24
1926-27			35	15	1	16	52
1927-28			43	20	5	25	34
1928-29			44	15	4	19	71
1929-30			43	21	15	36	46
1930-31			44	9	8	17	40
1931-32	TOR	N	47	8	13	21	45
1932-33	OTTA	N	44	4	14	18	37
1933-34			48	10	10	20	10
1934-35	STL	N	34	5	5	10	10
	TOR	N	11	2	0	2	2
	2 team total		45	7	5	12	12
1935-36			48	2	6	8	10
1936-37			48	2	7	9	4
14 yrs.		N Totals:	558	115	88	203	405
PLAYOFFS							
1925-26	OTTA	N	2	0	0	0	0
1926-27*			6	3	0	3	2
1927-28			2	0	1	1	4
1929-30			2	0	0	0	2
1931-32*	TOR	N	7	2	3	5	8
1934-35			7	1	2	3	2
1935-36			9	0	3	3	0
1936-37			2	0	0	0	0
8 yrs.		N Totals:	37	6	9	15	18

Ron Fischer

FISCHER, RONALD ALEXANDER — 6'2", 195 lbs.
B. Apr. 12, 1959, Merritt, B.C. — Defense, Shoots R

YEAR	TEAM & LEAGUE		GP	G	A	PTS	PIM
1981-82	BUF	N	15	0	7	7	6
1982-83			3	0	0	0	0
2 yrs.		N Totals:	18	0	7	7	6

Signed as free agent by **Buffalo** Mar. 19, 1981.

Alvin Fisher

FISHER, ALVIN

Forward

YEAR	TEAM & LEAGUE		GP	G	A	PTS	PIM
1924-25	TOR	N	9	1	0	1	4

Dunc Fisher

FISHER, DUNCAN ROBERT — 5'8", 165 lbs.
B. Aug. 30, 1927, Regina, Sask. — Right Wing, Shoots R

YEAR	TEAM & LEAGUE		GP	G	A	PTS	PIM
1948-49	NYR	N	60	9	16	25	40
1949-50			70	12	21	33	42
1950-51			12	0	0	0	0
	BOS	N	57	9	20	29	20
	2 team total		69	9	20	29	20

Dunc Fisher continued

YEAR	TEAM & LEAGUE		GP	G	A	PTS	PIM
1951-52			65	15	12	27	2
1952-53			7	0	1	1	0
1958-59	DET	N	8	0	0	0	0
6 yrs.		N Totals:	279	45	70	115	104
PLAYOFFS							
1947-48	NYR	N	1	0	1	1	0
1949-50			12	3	3	6	14
1950-51	BOS	N	6	1	0	1	0
1951-52			2	0	0	0	0
4 yrs.		N Totals:	21	4	4	8	14

Traded to **Boston** by N.Y. Rangers for Ed Harrison and Zellio Toppazzini, Nov. 16, 1950.

Joe Fisher

FISHER, JOSEPH H. — 6', 175 lbs.
B. July 4, 1916, Medicine Hat, Alta. — Right Wing, Shoots R

YEAR	TEAM & LEAGUE		GP	G	A	PTS	PIM
1939-40	DET	N	34	2	4	6	2
1940-41			28	5	8	13	11
1941-42			3	0	0	0	0
1942-43			1	1	0	1	0
4 yrs.		N Totals:	66	8	12	20	13
PLAYOFFS							
1939-40	DET	N	5	1	1	2	0
1940-41			9	1	0	1	6
1942-43*			1	0	0	0	0
3 yrs.		N Totals:	15	2	1	3	6

John Fisher

FISHER, JOHN

Defense

YEAR	TEAM & LEAGUE		GP	G	A	PTS	PIM
1972-73	ALTA	W	40	0	5	5	0

Bob Fitchner

FITCHNER, ROBERT DOUGLAS — 6', 190 lbs.
B. Dec. 22, 1950, Sudbury, Ont. — Center, Shoots L

YEAR	TEAM & LEAGUE		GP	G	A	PTS	PIM
1973-74	EDM	W	31	1	2	3	21
1974-75	IND	W	78	11	19	30	96
1975-76			52	15	16	31	112
	QUE	W	21	7	9	16	22
	2 team total		73	22	25	47	134
1976-77			81	9	30	39	105
1977-78			72	15	28	43	76
1978-79			79	10	35	45	69
1979-80	QUE	N	70	11	20	31	59
1980-81			8	1	0	1	0
8 yrs.		N Totals:	78	12	20	32	59
		W Totals:	414	68	139	207	501
PLAYOFFS							
1975-76	QUE	W	5	1	0	1	8
1976-77			17	3	3	6	16
1977-78			11	1	6	7	10
1978-79			4	1	3	4	0
1980-81	QUE	N	3	0	0	0	10
5 yrs.		N Totals:	3	0	0	0	10
		W Totals:	37	6	12	18	34

Sandy Fitzpatrick

FITZPATRICK, ALEXANDER STEWART — 6'1", 195 lbs.
B. Dec. 22, 1944, Paisley, Scotland — Center, Shoots L

YEAR	TEAM & LEAGUE		GP	G	A	PTS	PIM
1964-65	NYR	N	4	0	0	0	2
1967-68	MINN	N	18	3	6	9	6
2 yrs.		N Totals:	22	3	6	9	8
PLAYOFFS							
1967-68	MINN	N	12	0	0	0	0

Drafted by **Minnesota** from N.Y. Rangers in Expansion Draft, June 6, 1967.

Ross Fitzpatrick

FITZPATRICK, ROSS 6'1", 195 lbs.
B. Oct. 7, 1960, Penticton, B.C. Left Wing, Shoots L

YEAR	TEAM	LEAGUE	GP	G	A	PTS	PIM
1982-83	PHI	N	1	0	0	0	0

Fernie Flaman

FLAMAN, FERDINAND CHARLES 5'10", 190 lbs.
B. Jan. 25, 1927, Dysart, Sask. Defense, Shoots R

YEAR	TEAM	LEAGUE	GP	G	A	PTS	PIM
1944-45	BOS	N	1	0	0	0	0
1945-46			1	0	0	0	0
1946-47			23	1	4	5	41
1947-48			56	4	6	10	69
1948-49			60	4	12	16	62
1949-50			69	2	5	7	122
1950-51			14	1	1	2	37
	TOR	N	39	2	6	8	64
	2 team total		53	3	7	10	101
1951-52			61	0	7	7	110
1952-53			66	2	6	8	110
1953-54			62	0	8	8	84
1954-55	BOS	N	70	4	14	18	**150**
1955-56			62	4	17	21	70
1956-57			68	6	25	31	108
1957-58			66	0	15	15	71
1958-59			70	0	21	21	101
1959-60			60	2	18	20	112
1960-61			62	2	9	11	59
17 yrs.		N Totals:	910	34	174	208	1370

PLAYOFFS

YEAR	TEAM	LEAGUE	GP	G	A	PTS	PIM
1946-47	BOS	N	5	0	0	0	8
1947-48			5	0	0	0	12
1948-49			5	0	1	1	8
1950-51*	TOR	N	9	1	0	1	8
1951-52			4	0	2	2	18
1953-54			2	0	0	0	0
1954-55	BOS	N	4	1	0	1	2
1956-57			10	0	3	3	19
1957-58			12	2	2	4	10
1958-59			7	0	0	0	8
10 yrs.		N Totals:	63	4	8	12	93

Traded to **Toronto** by Boston with Ken Smith, Leo Boivin and Phil Maloney for Bill Ezinicki and Vic Lynn, Nov. 16, 1950. Traded to **Boston** by Toronto for Dave Creighton, July 20, 1954.

Reggie Fleming

FLEMING, REGINALD STEPHEN 5'10", 185 lbs.
B. Apr. 21, 1936, Montreal, Que. Left Wing, Shoots L

YEAR	TEAM	LEAGUE	GP	G	A	PTS	PIM
1959-60	MONT	N	3	0	0	0	2
1960-61	CHI	N	66	4	4	8	145
1961-62			70	7	9	16	71
1962-63			64	7	7	14	99
1963-64			61	3	6	9	140
1964-65	BOS	N	67	18	23	41	136
1965-66			34	4	6	10	42
	NYR	N	35	10	14	24	124
	2 team total		69	14	20	34	**166**
1966-67			61	15	16	31	146
1967-68			73	17	7	24	132
1968-69			72	8	12	20	138
1969-70	PHI	N	65	9	18	27	134
1970-71	BUF	N	78	6	10	16	159
1972-73	CHI	W	74	23	45	68	93
1973-74			45	2	12	14	49
14 yrs.		N Totals:	749	108	132	240	1468
		W Totals:	119	25	57	82	142

PLAYOFFS

YEAR	TEAM	LEAGUE	GP	G	A	PTS	PIM
1960-61*	CHI	N	12	1	0	1	12
1961-62			12	2	2	4	27
1962-63			6	0	0	0	27
1963-64			7	0	0	0	18
1966-67	NYR	N	4	0	2	2	11
1967-68			6	0	2	2	4
1968-69			3	0	0	0	7
1973-74	CHI	W	12	0	4	4	12
8 yrs.		N Totals:	50	3	6	9	106
		W Totals:	12	0	4	4	12

Sold to **Chicago** by Montreal with Cecil Hoekstra, June 7, 1960. Traded to **Boston** by Chicago with Ab McDonald for Doug Mohns, June 8, 1964. Traded to **N.Y. Rangers** by Boston for Leon Rochefort and Don Blackburn, June 6, 1969. Drafted by **Buffalo** from Philadelphia in Expansion Draft, June 10, 1970.

Flesch

FLESCH
B. Unknown Forward

YEAR	TEAM	LEAGUE	GP	G	A	PTS	PIM
1920-21	HAMIL	N	1	0	0	0	0

John Flesch

FLESCH, JOHN PATRICK 6'2", 200 lbs.
B. July 15, 1953, Sudbury, Ont. Left Wing, Shoots L

YEAR	TEAM	LEAGUE	GP	G	A	PTS	PIM
1974-75	MINN	N	57	8	15	23	47
1975-76			33	3	2	5	47
1977-78	PITT	N	29	7	5	12	19
1979-80	COLO	N	5	0	1	1	4
4 yrs.		N Totals:	124	18	23	41	117

Traded to **Minnesota** by Atlanta with Don Martineau for Buster Harvey and Jerry Byers, May 27, 1974. Signed as a free agent by **Pittsburgh** Feb. 4, 1978. Signed as free agent by **Colorado** Jan. 13, 1980.

Bill Flett

FLETT, WILLIAM MYER (Cowboy) 6'1", 205 lbs.
B. July 21, 1943, Vermillion, Alta. Right Wing, Shoots R

YEAR	TEAM	LEAGUE	GP	G	A	PTS	PIM
1967-68	LA	N	73	26	20	46	97
1968-69			72	24	25	49	53
1969-70			69	14	18	32	70
1970-71			64	13	24	37	57
1971-72			45	7	12	19	18
	PHI	N	31	11	10	21	26
	2 team total		76	18	22	40	44
1972-73			69	43	31	74	53
1973-74			67	17	27	44	51
1974-75	TOR	N	77	15	25	40	38
1975-76	ATL	N	78	23	17	40	30
1976-77			24	4	4	8	6
	EDM	W	48	34	20	54	20
	2 team total		72	38	24	62	26
1977-78			74	41	28	69	34
1978-79			73	28	36	64	14
1979-80	EDM	N	20	5	2	7	2
13 yrs.		N Totals:	689	202	215	417	501
		W Totals:	195	103	84	187	68

PLAYOFFS

YEAR	TEAM	LEAGUE	GP	G	A	PTS	PIM
1967-68	LA	N	7	1	2	3	8
1968-69			10	3	4	7	11
1972-73	PHI	N	11	3	4	7	0
1973-74*			17	0	6	6	21
1974-75	TOR	N	5	0	0	0	2
1975-76	ATL	N	2	0	0	0	0
1976-77	EDM	W	5	0	2	2	2
1978-79			10	5	2	7	2
8 yrs.		N Totals:	52	7	16	23	42
		W Totals:	15	5	4	9	4

Drafted by **Los Angeles** from Toronto in Expansion Draft, June 6. 1967. Traded to **Philadelphia** by Los Angeles with Ed Joyal, Jean Potvin and Ross Lonsberry for Bill Lesuk, Jim Johnson and Serge Bernier, Jan 28, 1972. Traded to **Toronto** by Philadelphia for Dave Fortier and Randy Osburn, May 27, 1974. Claimed on waivers by **Atlanta** from Toronto, May 20, 1975.

Rob Flockhart

FLOCKHART, ROBERT WALTER 6', 185 lbs.
B. Feb. 6, 1956, Sicamous, B.C. Right Wing, Shoots L

YEAR	TEAM	LEAGUE	GP	G	A	PTS	PIM
1976-77	VAN	N	5	0	0	0	0
1977-78			24	0	1	1	9
1978-79			14	1	1	2	0
1979-80	MINN	N	10	1	3	4	2
1980-81			2	0	0	0	0
5 yrs.		N Totals:	55	2	5	7	11

PLAYOFFS

YEAR	TEAM	LEAGUE	GP	G	A	PTS	PIM
1979-80	MINN	N	1	1	0	1	2

Signed as free agent by **Minnesota** Oct. 12, 1979.

Ron Flockhart

FLOCKHART, RONALD (Flocky) 5'11", 174 lbs.
B. Oct. 10, 1960, Smithers, B.C. Center, Shoots L

YEAR	TEAM & LEAGUE		GP	G	A	PTS	PIM
1980-81	PHI	N	14	3	7	10	11
1981-82			72	33	39	72	44
1982-83			73	29	31	60	49
3 yrs.		N Totals:	159	65	77	142	104
PLAYOFFS							
1980-81	PHI	N	3	1	0	1	2
1981-82			4	0	1	1	2
1982-83			2	1	1	2	2
3 yrs.		N Totals:	9	2	2	4	6

Signed as free agent by **Philadelphia** July 2, 1980.

Larry Floyd

FLOYD, LARRY 5'8", 177 lbs.
B. May 1, 1961, Peterborough, Ont. Center, Shoots L

YEAR	TEAM & LEAGUE		GP	G	A	PTS	PIM
1982-83	NJ	N	5	1	0	1	2

Signed by **New Jersey** as a free agent, Sept., 1982.

Lee Fogolin

FOGOLIN, LEE JOSEPH (Fogey) 6', 204 lbs.
B. Feb. 7, 1955, Chicago, Ill. Defense, Shoots R

YEAR	TEAM & LEAGUE		GP	G	A	PTS	PIM
1974-75	BUF	N	5	2	2	4	59
1975-76			58	0	9	9	64
1976-77			71	3	15	18	100
1977-78			76	0	23	23	98
1978-79			74	3	19	22	103
1979-80	EDM	N	80	5	10	15	104
1980-81			80	13	17	30	139
1981-82			80	4	25	29	159
1982-83			72	0	18	18	92
9 yrs.		N Totals:	596	30	138	168	918
PLAYOFFS							
1974-75	BUF	N	8	0	0	0	6
1975-76			9	0	4	4	23
1976-77			4	0	0	0	2
1977-78			6	0	2	2	23
1978-79			3	0	0	0	4
1979-80	EDM	N	3	0	0	0	4
1980-81			9	0	0	0	12
1981-82			5	1	1	2	14
1982-83			16	0	5	5	36
9 yrs.		N Totals:	63	1	12	13	124

Claimed by **Edmonton** from Buffalo in Expansion Draft, June 13, 1979.

Lee Fogolin

FOGOLIN, LIDIO JOHN 5'11", 200 lbs.
B. Feb. 27, 1926, Fort William, Ont. Defense, Shoots L

YEAR	TEAM & LEAGUE		GP	G	A	PTS	PIM
1948-49	DET	N	43	1	2	3	59
1949-50			64	4	8	12	63
1950-51			19	0	1	1	16
	CHI	N	35	3	10	13	63
	2 team total		54	3	11	14	79
1951-52			69	0	9	9	96
1952-53			70	2	8	10	79
1953-54			68	0	1	1	95
1954-55			9	0	1	1	16
1955-56			51	0	8	8	88
8 yrs.		N Totals:	428	10	48	58	575
PLAYOFFS							
1947-48	DET	N	2	0	1	1	6
1948-49			9	0	0	0	4
1949-50*			10	0	0	0	16
1952-53	CHI	N	7	0	1	1	4
4 yrs.		N Totals:	28	0	2	2	30

Traded to **Chicago** by Detroit with Steve Black for Bert Olmstead and Vic Stasiuk, Dec. 10, 1950.

Peter Folco

FOLCO, PETER KEVIN 6', 185 lbs.
B. Aug. 13, 1953, Montreal, Que. Defense, Shoots L

YEAR	TEAM & LEAGUE		GP	G	A	PTS	PIM
1973-74	VAN	N	2	0	0	0	0
1975-76	TOR	W	19	1	8	9	15
1976-77	BIRM	W	2	0	0	0	0
3 yrs.		N Totals:	2	0	0	0	0
		W Totals:	21	1	8	9	15

Gerry Foley

FOLEY, GERALD JAMES 6', 172 lbs.
B. Sept. 22, 1932, Ware, Mass. Right Wing, Shoots R

YEAR	TEAM & LEAGUE		GP	G	A	PTS	PIM
1954-55	TOR	N	4	0	0	0	8
1956-57	NYR	N	69	7	9	16	48
1957-58			68	2	5	7	43
1968-69	LA	N	1	0	0	0	0
4 yrs.		N Totals:	142	9	14	23	99
PLAYOFFS							
1956-57	NYR	N	3	0	0	0	0
1957-58			6	0	1	1	2
2 yrs.		N Totals:	9	0	1	1	2

Drafted with Parker MacDonald by **New York** from Toronto, June 5, 1956.

Rick Foley

FOLEY, GILBERT ANTHONY 6'4", 225 lbs.
B. Sept. 22, 1945, Niagara Falls, Ont. Defense, Shoots L

YEAR	TEAM & LEAGUE		GP	G	A	PTS	PIM
1970-71	CHI	N	2	0	1	1	8
1971-72	PHI	N	58	11	25	36	168
1973-74	DET	N	7	0	0	0	4
1975-76	TOR	W	11	1	2	3	6
4 yrs.		N Totals:	67	11	26	37	180
		W Totals:	11	1	2	3	6
PLAYOFFS							
1970-71	CHI	N	4	0	1	1	4

Traded to **Philadelphia** by Chicago for Andre Lacroix, Oct. 15, 1971. Traded to **Detroit** by Philadelphia for Serge Lajeunesse, May 15, 1973.

Mike Foligno

FOLIGNO, MICHAEL ANTHONY 6'2", 195 lbs.
B. Jan. 29, 1959, Sudbury, Ont. Right Wing, Shoots R

YEAR	TEAM & LEAGUE		GP	G	A	PTS	PIM
1979-80	DET	N	80	36	35	71	109
1980-81			80	28	35	63	210
1981-82			26	13	13	26	140
	BUF	N	56	20	31	51	149
	2 team total		82	33	44	77	289
1982-83			66	22	25	47	135
4 yrs.		N Totals:	308	119	139	258	743
PLAYOFFS							
1981-82	BUF	N	4	2	0	2	9
1982-83			10	2	3	5	39
2 yrs.		N Totals:	14	4	3	7	48

Traded to **Buffalo** by Detroit with Dale McCourt and Brent Peterson for Danny Gare, Jim Schoenfeld and Derek Smith, Dec. 2, 1981.

Bill Folk

FOLK, WILLIAM JOSEPH 6', 190 lbs.
B. July 11, 1927, Regina, Sask. Defense, Shoots L

YEAR	TEAM & LEAGUE		GP	G	A	PTS	PIM
1951-52	DET	N	8	0	0	0	2
1952-53			4	0	0	0	2
2 yrs.		N Totals:	12	0	0	0	4

Len Fontaine

FONTAINE, LEONARD JOSEPH 5'7", 165 lbs.
B. Feb. 25, 1948, Quebec City, Que. Right Wing, Shoots R

YEAR	TEAM & LEAGUE		GP	G	A	PTS	PIM
1972-73	DET	N	39	8	10	18	6
1973-74			7	0	1	1	4
1974-75	M-B	W	21	1	8	9	6

Len Fontaine continued

YEAR	TEAM & LEAGUE		GP	G	A	PTS	PIM
3 yrs.		N Totals:	46	8	11	19	10
		W Totals:	21	1	8	9	6

Jon Fontas

FONTAS, JON 5'10", 185 lbs.
B. Apr. 16, 1955, Arlington, Mass. Center, Shoots R

YEAR	TEAM & LEAGUE		GP	G	A	PTS	PIM
1979-80	**MINN**	**N**	1	0	0	0	0
1980-81			1	0	0	0	0
2 yrs.		N Totals:	2	0	0	0	0

Val Fonteyne

FONTEYNE, VALERE RONALD 5'9", 155 lbs.
B. Dec. 2, 1933, Wetaskiwin, Alta. Left Wing, Shoots L

YEAR	TEAM & LEAGUE		GP	G	A	PTS	PIM
1959-60	**DET**	**N**	69	4	7	11	2
1960-61			66	6	11	17	4
1961-62			70	5	5	10	4
1962-63			67	6	14	20	2
1963-64	**NYR**	**N**	69	7	18	25	4
1964-65			27	0	1	1	2
	DET	**N**	16	2	6	8	6
	2 team total		43	2	7	9	8
1965-66			59	5	10	15	0
1966-67			28	1	1	2	0
1967-68	**PITT**	**N**	69	6	28	34	0
1968-69			74	12	17	29	2
1969-70			68	11	15	26	2
1970-71			70	4	9	13	0
1971-72			68	6	13	19	0
1972-73	**ALTA**	**W**	77	7	32	39	2
1973-74	**EDM**	**W**	72	9	13	22	2
15 yrs.		N Totals:	820	75	155	230	28
		W Totals:	149	16	45	61	4

PLAYOFFS

YEAR	TEAM & LEAGUE		GP	G	A	PTS	PIM
1959-60	**DET**	**N**	6	0	4	4	0
1960-61			11	2	3	5	0
1962-63			11	0	0	0	2
1964-65			5	0	1	1	0
1965-66			12	1	0	1	4
1969-70	**PITT**	**N**	10	0	2	2	0
1971-72			4	0	0	0	2
1973-74	**EDM**	**W**	5	1	0	1	0
8 yrs.		N Totals:	59	3	10	13	8
		W Totals:	5	1	0	1	0

Drafted by **N.Y. Rangers** from Detroit, June, 1963. Claimed on waivers by **Detroit** Feb. 8, 1965. Drafted by **Pittsburgh** from Detroit in Expansion Draft, June 6, 1967.

Louie Fontinato

FONTINATO, LOUIS (Leaping Louie) 6'1", 195 lbs.
B. Jan. 20, 1932, Guelph, Ont. Defense, Shoots L

YEAR	TEAM & LEAGUE		GP	G	A	PTS	PIM
1954-55	**NYR**	**N**	27	2	2	4	60
1955-56			70	3	15	18	**202**
1956-57			70	3	12	15	139
1957-58			70	3	8	11	**152**
1958-59			64	7	6	13	149
1959-60			64	2	11	13	137
1960-61			53	2	3	5	100
1961-62	**MONT**	**N**	54	2	13	15	**167**
1962-63			63	2	8	10	141
9 yrs.		N Totals:	535	26	78	104	1247

PLAYOFFS

YEAR	TEAM & LEAGUE		GP	G	A	PTS	PIM
1955-56	**NYR**	**N**	4	0	0	0	6
1956-57			5	0	0	0	7
1957-58			6	0	1	1	6
1961-62	**MONT**	**N**	6	0	1	1	23
4 yrs.		N Totals:	21	0	2	2	42

Dave Forbes

FORBES, DAVID STEPHEN 5'10", 180 lbs.
B. Nov. 16, 1948, Montreal, Que. Left Wing, Shoots L

YEAR	TEAM & LEAGUE		GP	G	A	PTS	PIM
1973-74	**BOS**	**N**	63	10	16	26	41
1974-75			69	18	12	30	80
1975-76			79	16	13	29	52
1976-77			73	9	11	20	47
1977-78	**WASH**	**N**	77	11	11	22	119
1978-79			2	0	1	1	2
	CIN	**W**	73	6	5	11	83
	2 team total		75	6	6	12	85
6 yrs.		N Totals:	363	64	64	128	341
		W Totals:	73	6	5	11	83

PLAYOFFS

YEAR	TEAM & LEAGUE		GP	G	A	PTS	PIM
1973-74	**BOS**	**N**	16	0	2	2	6
1974-75			3	0	0	0	0
1975-76			12	1	1	2	5
1976-77			14	0	1	1	2
1978-79	**CIN**	**W**	3	0	1	1	7
5 yrs.		N Totals:	45	1	4	5	13
		W Totals:	3	0	1	1	7

Claimed by **Washingon** from Boston in waiver Draft, Oct. 10, 1977.

Mike Forbes

FORBES, MICHAEL D. 6'2", 200 lbs.
B. Sept. 20, 1957, Brampton, Ont. Defense, Shoots R

YEAR	TEAM & LEAGUE		GP	G	A	PTS	PIM
1977-78	**BOS**	**N**	32	0	4	4	15
1979-80	**EDM**	**N**	2	0	0	0	0
1981-82			16	1	7	8	26
3 yrs.		N Totals:	50	1	11	12	41

Claimed by **Edmonton** from Boston in Expansion Draft, June 13, 1979.

Mike Ford

FORD, MICHAEL ALFRED 6'1", 185 lbs.
B. July 26, 1952, Ottawa, Ont. Defense, Shoots R

YEAR	TEAM & LEAGUE		GP	G	A	PTS	PIM
1974-75	**WINN**	**W**	73	12	22	34	68
1975-76			81	13	43	56	70
1976-77	**CALG**	**W**	76	8	34	42	34
1977-78	**WINN**	**W**	3	0	0	0	0
4 yrs.		W Totals:	233	33	99	132	172

PLAYOFFS

YEAR	TEAM & LEAGUE		GP	G	A	PTS	PIM
1975-76	**WINN**	**W**	12	1	12	13	8
1976-77			20	3	13	16	12
1977-78			2	1	0	1	0
3 yrs.		W Totals:	34	5	25	30	20

Connie Forey

FOREY, CONLEY MICHAEL 6'2", 185 lbs.
B. Oct. 18, 1950, Montreal, Que. Left Wing, Shoots L

YEAR	TEAM & LEAGUE		GP	G	A	PTS	PIM
1973-74	**STL**	**N**	4	0	0	0	2

Drafted by **N.Y. Rangers** from Hershey (AHL) in Inter-League Draft, June 6, 1972.

Jack Forsey

FORSEY, JOHN
B. Unknown Forward

YEAR	TEAM & LEAGUE		GP	G	A	PTS	PIM
1942-43	**TOR**	**N**	19	7	9	16	10

PLAYOFFS

YEAR	TEAM & LEAGUE		GP	G	A	PTS	PIM
1942-43	**TOR**	**N**	3	0	1	1	0

Gus Forslund

FORSLUND, GUSTAV 150 lbs.
B. Apr. 25, 1908, Sweden Forward, Shoots R

YEAR	TEAM & LEAGUE		GP	G	A	PTS	PIM
1932-33	**OTTA**	**N**	48	4	9	13	2

YEAR	TEAM & LEAGUE		GP	G	A	PTS	PIM

Alex Forsyth

FORSYTH, ALEX 6'2", 195 lbs.
B. Jan. 6, 1955, Galt, Ont. Center, Shoots L

YEAR	TEAM	LG	GP	G	A	PTS	PIM
1976-77	WASH	N	1	0	0	0	0

Charles Fortier

FORTIER, CHARLES
B. Unknown Forward

YEAR	TEAM	LG	GP	G	A	PTS	PIM
1923-24	MONT	N	1	0	0	0	0

Dave Fortier

FORTIER, DAVID EDWARD 5'11", 190 lbs.
B. June 17, 1951, Sudbury, Ont. Defense, Shoots L

YEAR	TEAM	LG	GP	G	A	PTS	PIM
1972-73	TOR	N	23	1	4	5	63
1974-75	NYI	N	65	6	12	18	79
1975-76			59	0	2	2	68
1976-77	VAN	N	58	1	3	4	125
1977-78	IND	W	54	1	15	16	86
5 yrs.		N Totals:	205	8	21	29	335
		W Totals:	54	1	15	16	86

PLAYOFFS

YEAR	TEAM	LG	GP	G	A	PTS	PIM
1974-75	NYI	N	14	0	2	2	33
1975-76			6	0	0	0	0
2 yrs.		N Totals:	20	0	2	2	33

Traded to **Philadelphia** by Toronto with Randy Osborn for Bill Flett, May 27, 1974. Drafted by **N.Y. Islanders** from Philadelphia in Intra-league Draft, June 10, 1974. Sold with Ralph Stewart to **Vancouver** by N.Y. Islanders, Oct. 6, 1976.

Florent Fortier

FORTIER, FLORENT
Defense

YEAR	TEAM	LG	GP	G	A	PTS	PIM
1975-76	QUE	W	4	1	1	2	0

PLAYOFFS

YEAR	TEAM	LG	GP	G	A	PTS	PIM
1975-76	QUE	W	1	0	0	0	0

Ray Fortin

FORTIN, RAYMOND HENRI 5'8", 180 lbs.
B. Mar. 11, 1941, Drummondville, Que. Defense, Shoots L

YEAR	TEAM	LG	GP	G	A	PTS	PIM
1967-68	STL	N	24	0	2	2	8
1968-69			11	1	0	1	6
1969-70			57	1	4	5	19
3 yrs.		N Totals:	92	2	6	8	33

PLAYOFFS

YEAR	TEAM	LG	GP	G	A	PTS	PIM
1967-68	STL	N	3	0	0	0	2
1969-70			3	0	0	0	6
2 yrs.		N Totals:	6	0	0	0	8

Traded by St. Louis to **Los Angeles** for Bob Wall, May 11, 1970. Traded to **Montreal** by Los Angeles with Gord Labossiere for Ralph Backstrom, Jan. 26, 1971.

Joe Fortunato

FORTUNATO, JOSEPH 5'10", 170 lbs.
B. Jan. 1, 1955, Bari, Italy Left Wing, Shoots L

YEAR	TEAM	LG	GP	G	A	PTS	PIM
1976-77	EDM	W	1	0	0	0	0

Dwight Foster

FOSTER, DWIGHT ALEXANDER (Dewey)
5'10", 190 lbs.
B. Apr. 2, 1957, Toronto, Ont. Center, Shoots R

YEAR	TEAM	LG	GP	G	A	PTS	PIM
1977-78	BOS	N	14	2	1	3	6
1978-79			44	11	13	24	14
1979-80			57	10	28	38	42
1980-81			77	24	28	52	62
1981-82	COLO	N	70	12	19	31	41
1982-83	NJ	N	4	0	0	0	2
	DET	N	58	17	22	39	58
	2 team total		62	17	22	39	60
6 yrs.		N Totals:	324	76	111	187	225

Dwight Foster continued

PLAYOFFS

YEAR	TEAM	LG	GP	G	A	PTS	PIM
1978-79	BOS	N	11	1	3	4	0
1979-80			9	3	5	8	2
1980-81			3	1	1	2	0
3 yrs.		N Totals:	23	5	9	14	2

Signed as free agent with **Colorado** July 21, 1981. As compensation, Boston received Colorado's second-round choice (Brian Curran) in the 1982 Entry Draft and switched first round choices in the same draft. Boston claimed Gord Kluzak, while Colorado selected Ken Daneyko. Sold to **Detroit** by New Jersey, Oct. 29, 1982.

Herb Foster

FOSTER, HERBERT 5'9½", 168 lbs.
B. Aug. 9, 1913, Brockville, Ont. Left Wing, Shoots L

YEAR	TEAM	LG	GP	G	A	PTS	PIM
1940-41	NYR	N	4	1	0	1	5
1947-48			1	0	0	0	0
2 yrs.		N Totals:	5	1	0	1	5

Harry Foster

FOSTER, HAROLD C. (Yip) 198 lbs.
B. Nov. 25, 1907, Guelph, Ont. Defense, Shoots L

YEAR	TEAM	LG	GP	G	A	PTS	PIM
1929-30	NYR	N	31	0	0	0	10
1931-32	BOS	N	34	1	2	3	12
1933-34	DET	N	6	0	0	0	2
1934-35			12	2	0	2	8
4 yrs.		N Totals:	83	3	2	5	32

Nick Fotiu

FOTIU, NICHOLAS EVLAMPIOS 6'2", 200 lbs.
B. May 25, 1952, Staten Island, N.Y. Left Wing, Shoots L

YEAR	TEAM	LG	GP	G	A	PTS	PIM
1974-75	NE	W	61	2	2	4	144
1975-76			49	3	2	5	94
1976-77	NYR	N	70	4	8	12	174
1977-78			59	2	7	9	105
1978-79			71	3	5	8	190
1979-80	HART	N	74	10	8	18	107
1980-81			42	4	3	7	79
	NYR	N	27	5	6	11	91
	2 team total		69	9	9	18	170
1981-82			70	8	10	18	151
1982-83			72	8	13	21	90
9 yrs.		N Totals:	485	44	60	104	987
		W Totals:	110	5	4	9	238

PLAYOFFS

YEAR	TEAM	LG	GP	G	A	PTS	PIM
1974-75	NE	W	4	2	0	2	27
1975-76			16	3	2	5	57
1977-78	NYR	N	3	0	0	0	5
1978-79			4	0	0	0	6
1979-80	HART	N	3	0	0	0	6
1980-81	NYR	N	2	0	0	0	4
1981-82			10	0	2	2	6
1982-83			5	0	1	1	6
8 yrs.		N Totals:	27	0	3	3	33
		W Totals:	20	5	2	7	84

Signed as free agent by **N.Y. Rangers** July 23, 1976. Claimed by **Hartford** from Rangers in Expansion Draft, June 13, 1979. Traded to **N.Y. Rangers** by Hartford for Rangers' fifth round draft choice (Bill Maguire) in 1981 Entry Draft, Jan. 15, 1981.

Jimmy Fowler

FOWLER, JAMES WILLIAM 5'11", 168 lbs.
B. Apr. 6, 1915, Toronto, Ont. Defense, Shoots L

YEAR	TEAM	LG	GP	G	A	PTS	PIM
1936-37	TOR	N	48	7	11	18	22
1937-38			48	10	12	22	8
1938-39			39	1	6	7	9
3 yrs.		N Totals:	135	18	29	47	39

PLAYOFFS

YEAR	TEAM	LG	GP	G	A	PTS	PIM
1936-37	TOR	N	2	0	0	0	0
1937-38			7	0	2	2	0
1938-39			9	0	1	1	2
3 yrs.		N Totals:	18	0	3	3	2

Tom Fowler

FOWLER, THOMAS 5'11", 165 lbs.
B. May 18, 1924, Winnipeg, Man. Center, Shoots L

YEAR	TEAM & LEAGUE	GP	G	A	PTS	PIM
1946-47	CHI N	24	0	1	1	18

Greg Fox

FOX, GREGORY BRENT 6'2", 190 lbs.
B. Aug. 12, 1953, Port McNeil, B.C. Defense, Shoots L

YEAR	TEAM & LEAGUE	GP	G	A	PTS	PIM
1977-78	ATL N	16	1	2	3	25
1978-79		64	0	12	12	70
	CHI N	14	0	5	5	16
	2 team total	78	0	17	17	86
1979-80		71	4	11	15	73
1980-81		75	3	16	19	112
1981-82		79	2	19	21	137
1982-83		76	0	13	13	81
6 yrs.	N Totals:	395	10	78	88	514

PLAYOFFS

YEAR	TEAM & LEAGUE	GP	G	A	PTS	PIM
1977-78	ATL N	2	0	1	1	8
1978-79	CHI N	4	0	1	1	0
1979-80		7	0	0	0	8
1980-81		3	0	1	1	2
1981-82		15	1	3	4	27
1982-83		13	0	3	3	22
6 yrs.	N Totals:	44	1	9	10	67

Traded to **Chicago** by Atlanta with Tom Lysiak, Harold Phillipoff, Pat Ribble, and Miles Zaharko for Ivan Boldirev, Darcy Rota and Phil Russell, Mar. 13, 1979.

Jimmy Fox

FOX, JAMES CHARLES 5'8", 170 lbs.
B. May 18, 1960, Coniston, Ont. Right Wing, Shoots R

YEAR	TEAM & LEAGUE	GP	G	A	PTS	PIM
1980-81	LA N	71	18	25	43	8
1981-82		77	30	38	68	23
1982-83		77	28	40	68	8
3 yrs.	N Totals:	225	76	103	179	39

PLAYOFFS

YEAR	TEAM & LEAGUE	GP	G	A	PTS	PIM
1980-81	LA N	4	0	100	100	0
1981-82		9	1	4	5	0
2 yrs.	N Totals:	13	1	104	105	0

Frank Foyston

FOYSTON, FRANK
B. Feb. 2, 1891 Center, Shoots L
Hall of Fame, 1958

YEAR	TEAM & LEAGUE	GP	G	A	PTS	PIM
1926-27	DET N	41	10	5	15	16
1927-28		23	7	2	9	16
2 yrs.	N Totals:	64	17	7	24	32

Bob Frampton

FRAMPTON, ROBERT PERCY JAMES 5'10", 175 lbs.
B. Jan. 20, 1929, Toronto, Ont. Left Wing, Shoots L

YEAR	TEAM & LEAGUE	GP	G	A	PTS	PIM
1949-50	MONT N	2	0	0	0	0

PLAYOFFS

YEAR	TEAM & LEAGUE	GP	G	A	PTS	PIM
1949-50	MONT N	3	0	0	0	0

Lou Franceschetti

FRANCESCHETTI, LOU 5'11", 180 lbs.
B. Apr. 28, 1958, Toronto, Ont. Right Wing, Shoots L

YEAR	TEAM & LEAGUE	GP	G	A	PTS	PIM
1981-82	WASH N	30	2	10	12	23

Bobby Francis

FRANCIS, ROBERT 5'9", 175 lbs.
B. Dec. 5, 1958, North Battleford, Sask. Center, Shoots R

YEAR	TEAM & LEAGUE	GP	G	A	PTS	PIM
1982-83	DET N	14	2	0	2	0

Ron Francis

FRANCIS, RONALD 5'11", 175 lbs.
B. Mar. 1, 1963, Sault Ste. Marie, Ont. Center, Shoots L

YEAR	TEAM & LEAGUE	GP	G	A	PTS	PIM
1981-82	HART N	59	25	43	68	51
1982-83		79	31	59	90	60
2 yrs.	N Totals:	138	56	102	158	111

Archie Fraser

FRASER, ARCHIBALD MCKAY
B. Feb. 9, 1914, Souris, Man. Forward

YEAR	TEAM & LEAGUE	GP	G	A	PTS	PIM
1943-44	NYR N	3	0	1	1	0

Curt Fraser

FRASER, CURT M. (Frazz) 6', 190 lbs.
B. Jan. 12, 1958, Cincinnati, Ohio Left Wing, Shoots L

YEAR	TEAM & LEAGUE	GP	G	A	PTS	PIM
1978-79	VAN N	78	16	19	35	116
1979-80		78	17	25	42	143
1980-81		77	25	24	49	118
1981-82		79	28	39	67	175
1982-83		36	6	7	13	99
	CHI N	38	6	13	19	77
	2 team total	74	12	20	32	176
5 yrs.	N Totals:	386	98	127	225	728

PLAYOFFS

YEAR	TEAM & LEAGUE	GP	G	A	PTS	PIM
1978-79	VAN N	3	0	2	2	6
1979-80		4	0	0	0	2
1980-81		3	1	0	1	2
1981-82		17	3	7	10	98
1982-83	CHI N	13	4	4	8	18
5 yrs.	N Totals:	40	8	13	21	126

Traded by Chicago to **Vancouver** for Tony Tanti, Jan. 6, 1983.

Gord Fraser

FRASER, GORDON
B. Pembroke, Ont. Defense

YEAR	TEAM & LEAGUE	GP	G	A	PTS	PIM
1926-27	CHI N	43	14	6	20	89
1927-28		11	1	1	2	10
	DET N	30	3	1	4	50
	2 team total	41	4	2	6	60
1928-29		13	0	0	0	12
1929-30	MONT N	10	0	0	0	4
	PITT N	30	6	4	10	37
	2 team total	40	6	4	10	41
1930-31	PHI N	7	0	0	0	22
5 yrs.	N Totals:	144	24	12	36	224

PLAYOFFS

YEAR	TEAM & LEAGUE	GP	G	A	PTS	PIM
1926-27	CHI N	2	1	0	1	6

Harry Fraser

FRASER, JAMES HARVEY 5'10", 168 lbs.
B. Oct. 14, 1918, Souris, Man. Center, Shoots R

YEAR	TEAM & LEAGUE	GP	G	A	PTS	PIM
1944-45	CHI N	21	5	4	9	0

Jack Fraser

FRASER
Forward

YEAR	TEAM & LEAGUE	GP	G	A	PTS	PIM
1923-24	HAMIL N	1	0	0	0	0

Rick Fraser

FRASER, RICHARD 5'10", 177 lbs.
B. Oct. 7, 1954, Sarnia, Ont. Defense, Shoots R

YEAR	TEAM & LEAGUE	GP	G	A	PTS	PIM
1974-75	IND W	4	0	0	0	2

Frank Frederickson

FREDERICKSON, FRANK 5'11", 175 lbs.
B. Winnipeg, Man. Center
Hall of Fame, 1958

YEAR	TEAM & LEAGUE	GP	G	A	PTS	PIM
1926-27	DET N	16	4	6	10	12
	BOS N	28	14	7	21	33
	2 team total	44	18	13	31	45
1927-28		44	10	4	14	83

Frank Frederickson continued

YEAR	TEAM & LEAGUE		GP	G	A	PTS	PIM
1928-29			12	3	1	4	24
	PITT	**N**	31	3	7	10	28
	2 team total		43	6	8	14	52
1929-30			9	4	7	11	20
1930-31	**DET**	**N**	25	1	2	3	6
5 yrs.		**N Totals:**	165	39	34	73	206
PLAYOFFS							
1926-27	**BOS**	**N**	8	2	4	6	22
1927-28			2	0	1	1	4
2 yrs.		**N Totals:**	10	2	5	7	26

John French

FRENCH, JOHN GEORGE 5'11", 175 lbs.
B. Aug. 25, 1950, Orillia, Ont. Left Wing, Shoots L

YEAR	TEAM & LEAGUE		GP	G	A	PTS	PIM
1972-73	**NE**	**W**	74	24	35	59	43
1973-74			77	24	48	72	31
1974-75			75	12	41	53	28
1975-76	**SD**	**W**	76	25	39	64	16
1976-77			44	14	21	35	6
1977-78	**IND**	**W**	74	9	8	17	6
6 yrs.		**W Totals:**	420	108	192	300	130
PLAYOFFS							
1972-73	**NE**	**W**	15	3	11	14	2
1973-74			7	4	2	6	2
1974-75			4	1	2	3	0
1975-76	**SD**	**W**	11	4	7	11	0
1976-77			7	2	3	5	2
5 yrs.		**W Totals:**	44	14	25	39	6

Sold to **California** by Montreal, June 8, 1972. Put on **Minnesota** Reserve List after Cleveland-Minnesota Dispersal Draft, June 15, 1978.

Irv Frew

FREW, IRVINE 5'9½", 180 lbs.
B. Aug. 16, 1907, Kilsyth, Scotland Defense, Shoots R

YEAR	TEAM & LEAGUE		GP	G	A	PTS	PIM
1933-34	**MON(M)**	**N**	30	2	1	3	41
1934-35	**STL**	**N**	47	0	2	2	89
1935-36	**MONT**	**N**	18	0	2	2	16
3 yrs.		**N Totals:**	95	2	5	7	146
PLAYOFFS							
1933-34	**MON(M)**	**N**	4	0	0	0	6

Dan Fridgen

FRIDGEN, DAN 5'11", 180 lbs.
B. May 18, 1959, Arnprior, Ont. Left Wing, Shoots L

YEAR	TEAM & LEAGUE		GP	G	A	PTS	PIM
1981-82	**HART**	**N**	2	0	1	1	0
1982-83			11	2	2	4	2
2 yrs.		**N Totals:**	13	2	3	5	2

Signed as free agent by **Hartford** April, 1982.

Ron Friest

FRIEST, RONALD 6', 185 lbs.
B. Nov. 4, 1958, Windsor, Ont. Left Wing, Shoots L

YEAR	TEAM & LEAGUE		GP	G	A	PTS	PIM
1980-81	**MINN**	**N**	4	1	0	1	10
1981-82			10	0	0	0	31
1982-83			50	6	7	13	150
3 yrs.		**N Totals:**	64	7	7	14	191
PLAYOFFS							
1981-82	**MINN**	**N**	2	0	0	0	5
1982-83			4	1	0	1	2
2 yrs.		**N Totals:**	6	1	0	1	7

Signed as free agent by **Minnesota** June 26, 1980.

Len Frig

FRIG, LEONARD ELROY 5'11", 190 lbs.
B. Oct. 23, 1950, Lethbridge, Alta. Defense, Shoots R

YEAR	TEAM & LEAGUE		GP	G	A	PTS	PIM
1973-74	**CHI**	**N**	66	4	10	14	35
1974-75	**CALIF**	**N**	80	3	17	20	127

Len Frig continued

YEAR	TEAM & LEAGUE		GP	G	A	PTS	PIM
1975-76			62	3	12	15	55
1976-77	**CLEVE**	**N**	66	2	7	9	213
1977-78	**STL**	**N**	30	1	3	4	45
1979-80			7	0	2	2	2
6 yrs.		**N Totals:**	311	13	51	64	477
PLAYOFFS							
1972-73	**CHI**	**N**	4	1	1	2	0
1973-74			7	1	0	1	0
1979-80	**STL**	**N**	3	0	0	0	0
3 yrs.		**N Totals:**	14	2	1	3	0

Traded to **California** by Chicago with Mike Christie for Ivan Boldirev, May 24, 1974. Traded to **St. Louis** by Cleveland for the professional rights to Mike Eaves, Aug. 17, 1977.

Harry Frost

FROST, HAROLD 5'11", 165 lbs.
B. Aug. 17, 1914, Kerr Lake, Ont. Right Wing, Shoots R

YEAR	TEAM & LEAGUE		GP	G	A	PTS	PIM
1938-39	**BOS**	**N**	3	0	0	0	0
PLAYOFFS							
1938-39*	**BOS**	**N**	1	0	0	0	0

Miroslav Frycer

FRYCER, MIROSLAV 6', 198 lbs.
B. Sept. 27, 1959, Ostrava, Czechoslovakia
Right Wing, Shoots R

YEAR	TEAM & LEAGUE		GP	G	A	PTS	PIM
1981-82	**QUE**	**N**	49	20	17	37	47
	TOR	**N**	10	4	6	10	31
	2 team total		59	24	23	47	78
1982-83			67	25	30	55	90
2 yrs.		**N Totals:**	126	49	53	102	168
PLAYOFFS							
1982-83	**TOR**	**N**	4	2	5	7	0

Signed as free agent by **Quebec** April 21, 1980. Traded to **Toronto** by Quebec along with Quebec's seventh round choice (Jeff Triano) in 1982 Entry Draft for Wilf Paiement, Mar. 9, 1982.

Bob Fryday

FRYDAY, ROBERT GEORGE 5'10", 155 lbs.
B. Dec. 5, 1928, Toronto, Ont. Right Wing, Shoots R

YEAR	TEAM & LEAGUE		GP	G	A	PTS	PIM
1949-50	**MONT**	**N**	2	1	0	1	0
1951-52			3	0	0	0	0
2 yrs.		**N Totals:**	5	1	0	1	0

Frye

FRYE
B. Unknown Defense

YEAR	TEAM & LEAGUE		GP	G	A	PTS	PIM
1927-28	**CHI**	**N**	10	0	0	0	0

Robbie Ftorek

FTOREK, ROBERT BRIAN (Britz) 5'10", 155 lbs.
B. Jan. 2, 1952, Needham, Mass. Center, Shoots L

YEAR	TEAM & LEAGUE		GP	G	A	PTS	PIM
1972-73	**DET**	**N**	3	0	0	0	0
1973-74			12	2	5	7	4
1974-75	**PHOE**	**W**	53	31	37	68	29
1975-76			80	41	72	113	109
1976-77			80	46	71	117	86
1977-78	**CIN**	**W**	80	59	50	109	54
1978-79			80	39	**77**	116	87
1979-80	**QUE**	**N**	52	18	33	51	28
1980-81			78	24	49	73	104
1981-82			19	1	8	9	4
	NYR	**N**	30	8	24	32	24
	2 team total		49	9	32	41	28
1982-83			61	12	19	31	41
11 yrs.		**N Totals:**	255	65	138	203	205
		W Totals:	373	216	307	523	365
PLAYOFFS							
1974-75	**PHOE**	**W**	5	2	5	7	2
1975-76			5	1	3	4	2
1978-79	**CIN**	**W**	3	3	2	5	6
1980-81	**QUE**	**N**	5	1	2	3	17

Robbie Ftorek continued

YEAR	TEAM	LEAGUE	GP	G	A	PTS	PIM
1981-82	**NYR**	**N**	10	7	4	11	11
1982-83			4	1	0	1	0
6 yrs.		**N Totals:**	19	9	6	15	28
		W Totals:	13	6	10	16	10

Traded to **N.Y. Rangers** by Quebec along with Quebec's eighth round choice (Bryan Glynn) in 1982 Entry Draft for Jere Gillis and Dean Talafous (later Pat Hickey), Dec. 30, 1981.

Lawrence Fullan

FULLAN, LAWRENCE 5'11", 185 lbs.
B. Aug. 11, 1949, Toronto, Ont. Left Wing, Shoots L

YEAR	TEAM	LEAGUE	GP	G	A	PTS	PIM
1974-75	**WASH**	**N**	4	1	0	1	0

Drafted by **Washington** from Montreal in Expansion Draft, June 12, 1974.

Bill Gadsby

GADSBY, WILLIAM ALEXANDER 6', 185 lbs.
B. Aug. 8, 1927, Calgary, Alta. Defense, Shoots L
Hall of Fame, 1970

YEAR	TEAM	LEAGUE	GP	G	A	PTS	PIM
1946-47	**CHI**	**N**	48	8	10	18	31
1947-48			60	6	10	16	66
1948-49			50	3	10	13	85
1949-50			70	10	24	34	138
1950-51			25	3	7	10	32
1951-52			59	7	15	22	87
1952-53			68	2	20	22	84
1953-54			70	12	29	41	108
1954-55			18	3	5	8	17
	NYR	**N**	52	8	8	16	44
	2 team total		70	11	13	24	61
1955-56			70	9	42	51	84
1956-57			70	4	37	41	72
1957-58			65	14	32	46	48
1958-59			70	5	46	51	56
1959-60			65	9	22	31	60
1960-61			65	9	26	35	49
1961-62	**DET**	**N**	70	7	30	37	88
1962-63			70	4	24	28	116
1963-64			64	2	16	18	80
1964-65			61	0	12	12	122
1965-66			58	5	12	17	72
20 yrs.		**N Totals:**	1248	130	437	567	1539

PLAYOFFS

YEAR	TEAM	LEAGUE	GP	G	A	PTS	PIM
1952-53	**CHI**	**N**	7	0	1	1	4
1955-56	**NYR**	**N**	5	1	3	4	4
1956-57			5	1	2	3	2
1957-58			6	0	3	3	4
1962-63	**DET**	**N**	11	1	4	5	36
1963-64			14	0	4	4	22
1964-65			7	0	3	3	8
1965-66			12	1	3	4	12
8 yrs.		**N Totals:**	67	4	23	27	92

Traded to **N.Y. Rangers** by Chicago with Pete Conacher for Allan Stanley, Nick Mickoski, and Richard Lamoureux, Nov., 1954. Traded to **Detroit** by N.Y. Rangers for Leslie Hunt, June, 1961.

Jody Gage

GAGE, JOSEPH WILLIAM 5'11", 182 lbs.
B. Nov. 29, 1959, Toronto, Ont. Right Wing, Shoots R

YEAR	TEAM	LEAGUE	GP	G	A	PTS	PIM
1980-81	**DET**	**N**	16	2	2	4	22
1981-82			31	9	10	19	2
2 yrs.		**N Totals:**	47	11	12	23	24

Art Gagne

GAGNE, ARTHUR E.
Right Wing, Shoots R

YEAR	TEAM	LEAGUE	GP	G	A	PTS	PIM
1926-27	**MONT**	**N**	44	14	3	17	42
1927-28			44	20	10	30	75
1928-29			44	7	3	10	52
1929-30	**BOS**	**N**	6	0	1	1	6
	OTTA	**N**	33	6	4	10	32
	2 team total		39	6	5	11	38
1930-31			44	19	11	30	50
1931-32	**DET**	**N**	13	1	1	2	0

Art Gagne continued

YEAR	TEAM	LEAGUE	GP	G	A	PTS	PIM
6 yrs.		**N Totals:**	228	67	33	100	257

PLAYOFFS

YEAR	TEAM	LEAGUE	GP	G	A	PTS	PIM
1926-27	**MONT**	**N**	4	0	0	0	0
1927-28			2	1	1	2	4
1928-29			3	0	0	0	12
1929-30	**OTTA**	**N**	2	1	0	1	4
4 yrs.		**N Totals:**	11	2	1	3	20

Paul Gagne

GAGNE, PAUL 5'10", 178 lbs.
B. Feb. 6, 1962, Iroquois Falls, Ont. Left Wing, Shoots L

YEAR	TEAM	LEAGUE	GP	G	A	PTS	PIM
1980-81	**COLO**	**N**	61	25	16	41	12
1981-82			59	10	12	22	17
1982-83	**NJ**	**N**	53	14	15	29	13
3 yrs.		**N Totals:**	173	49	43	92	42

Pierre Gagne

GAGNE, PIERRE REYNALD 6', 180 lbs.
B. June 5, 1940, North Bay, Ont. Left Wing, Shoots L

YEAR	TEAM	LEAGUE	GP	G	A	PTS	PIM
1959-60	**BOS**	**N**	2	0	0	0	0

Germain Gagnon

GAGNON, GERMAIN 6', 172 lbs.
B. Dec. 9, 1942, Chicoutimi, Que. Left Wing, Shoots L

YEAR	TEAM	LEAGUE	GP	G	A	PTS	PIM
1971-72	**MONT**	**N**	4	0	0	0	0
1972-73	**NYI**	**N**	63	12	29	41	31
1973-74			62	8	14	22	8
	CHI	**N**	14	3	14	17	4
	2 team total		76	11	28	39	12
1974-75			80	16	35	51	21
1975-76			5	0	0	0	2
	KC	**N**	31	1	9	10	6
	2 team total		36	1	9	10	8
5 yrs.		**N Totals:**	259	40	101	141	72

PLAYOFFS

YEAR	TEAM	LEAGUE	GP	G	A	PTS	PIM
1973-74	**CHI**	**N**	11	2	2	4	2
1974-75			8	0	1	1	0
2 yrs.		**N Totals:**	19	2	3	5	2

Traded to **N.Y. Islanders** by Montreal Canadiens to complete earlier deal (June 6, 1972) in which Islanders received goaltender Denis DeJordy, Tony Featherstone, Murray Anderson and amateurs Chico Resch and Alec Campbell for cash and other considerations, June 26, 1972. Traded to **Chicago** by N.Y. Islanders for cash and a player to be named later (Walt Ledingham, May 24, 1974), March 7, 1974. Claimed on waivers by **Kansas City** from Chicago, Oct. 28, 1975.

Johnny Gagnon

GAGNON, JOHNNY (The Black Cat) 5'5", 140 lbs.
B. June 8, 1905, Chicoutimi, Que. Right Wing, Shoots R

YEAR	TEAM	LEAGUE	GP	G	A	PTS	PIM
1930-31	**MONT**	**N**	41	18	7	25	43
1931-32			48	19	18	37	40
1932-33			48	12	23	35	64
1933-34			48	9	15	24	25
1934-35	**BOS**	**N**	24	1	1	2	9
	MONT	**N**	23	1	5	6	2
	2 team total		47	2	6	8	11
1935-36			48	7	9	16	42
1936-37			48	20	16	36	38
1937-38			47	13	17	30	9
1938-39			45	12	22	34	23
1939-40			10	4	5	9	0
	NYA	**N**	24	4	3	7	0
	2 team total		34	8	8	16	0
10 yrs.		**N Totals:**	454	120	141	261	295

PLAYOFFS

YEAR	TEAM	LEAGUE	GP	G	A	PTS	PIM
1930-31*	**MONT**	**N**	10	6	2	8	8
1931-32			4	1	1	2	4
1932-33			2	0	2	2	0
1933-34			2	1	0	1	2
1934-35			2	0	1	1	2
1936-37			5	2	1	3	9
1937-38			3	1	3	4	2

Johnny Gagnon continued

YEAR	TEAM	LEAGUE	GP	G	A	PTS	PIM
1938-39			3	0	2	2	10
1939-40	**NYA**	**N**	1	1	0	1	0
9 yrs.		**N Totals:**	32	12	12	24	37

Bob Gainey

GAINEY, ROBERT MICHAEL 6'2", 190 lbs.
B. Dec. 13, 1953, Peterborough, Ont. Left Wing, Shoots L
Won Conn Smythe Trophy, 1978-79
Won Selke Trophy, 1977-78, 1978-79, 1979-80, 1980-81

YEAR	TEAM	LEAGUE	GP	G	A	PTS	PIM
1973-74	**MONT**	**N**	66	3	7	10	34
1974-75			80	17	20	37	49
1975-76			78	15	13	28	57
1976-77			80	14	19	33	41
1977-78			66	15	16	31	57
1978-79			79	20	18	38	44
1979-80			64	14	19	33	32
1980-81			78	23	24	47	36
1981-82			79	21	24	45	24
1982-83			80	12	18	30	43
10 yrs.		**N Totals:**	750	154	178	332	417
PLAYOFFS							
1973-74	**MONT**	**N**	6	0	0	0	6
1974-75			11	2	4	6	4
1975-76*			13	1	3	4	20
1976-77*			14	4	1	5	25
1977-78*			15	2	7	9	14
1978-79*			16	6	10	16	10
1979-80			10	1	1	2	4
1980-81			3	0	0	0	2
1981-82			5	0	1	1	8
1982-83			3	0	0	0	4
10 yrs.		**N Totals:**	96	16	27	43	97

Dutch Gainor

GAINOR, NORMAN 6'1", 170 lbs.
B. Apr. 10, 1904, Calgary, Alta. Center, Shoots L

YEAR	TEAM	LEAGUE	GP	G	A	PTS	PIM
1927-28	**BOS**	**N**	41	8	4	12	35
1928-29			39	14	5	19	30
1929-30			43	18	31	49	39
1930-31			32	8	3	11	14
1931-32	**NYR**	**N**	46	3	9	12	9
1932-33	**OTTA**	**N**	2	0	0	0	0
1934-35	**MON(M)**	**N**	40	0	4	4	2
7 yrs.		**N Totals:**	243	51	56	107	129
PLAYOFFS							
1927-28	**BOS**	**N**	2	0	0	0	6
1928-29*			5	2	0	2	4
1929-30			6	0	0	0	0
1930-31			5	0	1	1	2
1931-32	**NYR**	**N**	7	0	0	0	2
5 yrs.		**N Totals:**	25	2	1	3	14

Michel Galarneau

GALARNEAU, MICHEL 6'1", 172 lbs.
B. Mar. 1, 1961, Montreal, Que. Center, Shoots R

YEAR	TEAM	LEAGUE	GP	G	A	PTS	PIM
1980-81	**HART**	**N**	30	2	6	8	9
1981-82			10	0	0	0	4
1982-83			38	5	4	9	21
3 yrs.		**N Totals:**	78	7	10	17	34

Perk Galbraith

GALBRAITH, PERCIVAL 5'10", 162 lbs.
B. Toronto, Ont. Left Wing, Shoots L

YEAR	TEAM	LEAGUE	GP	G	A	PTS	PIM
1926-27	**BOS**	**N**	42	9	8	17	26
1927-28			42	6	5	11	26
1928-29			38	2	1	3	44
1929-30			44	7	9	16	38
1930-31			43	2	3	5	28
1931-32			47	2	1	3	28
1932-33			47	1	2	3	28
1933-34	**OTTA**	**N**	2	0	0	0	0
	BOS	**N**	42	0	2	2	5
	2 team total		44	0	2	2	5

Perk Galbraith continued

YEAR	TEAM	LEAGUE	GP	G	A	PTS	PIM
8 yrs.		**N Totals:**	347	29	31	60	223
PLAYOFFS							
1926-27	**BOS**	**N**	8	3	3	6	2
1927-28			2	0	1	1	6
1928-29*			5	0	0	0	2
1929-30			6	1	3	4	8
1930-31			5	0	0	0	6
1932-33			5	0	0	0	0
6 yrs.		**N Totals:**	31	4	7	11	24

John Gallagher

GALLAGHER, JOHN JAMES PATRICK 5'11", 188 lbs.
B. Jan. 19, 1909, Kenora, Ont. Shoots L

YEAR	TEAM	LEAGUE	GP	G	A	PTS	PIM
1930-31	**MON(M)**	**N**	35	4	2	6	35
1931-32			19	1	0	1	18
1932-33			6	1	0	1	0
	DET	**N**	35	3	6	9	48
	2 team total		41	4	6	10	48
1933-34			1	0	0	0	0
1936-37	**NYA**	**N**	9	0	0	0	8
	DET	**N**	11	1	0	1	4
	2 team total		20	1	0	1	12
1937-38	**NYA**	**N**	47	3	6	9	18
1938-39			41	1	5	6	22
7 yrs.		**N Totals:**	204	14	19	33	153
PLAYOFFS							
1930-31	**MON(M)**	**N**	2	0	0	0	0
1932-33	**DET**	**N**	4	1	1	2	4
1936-37*			10	1	0	1	17
1937-38	**NYA**	**N**	6	0	2	2	6
4 yrs.		**N Totals:**	22	2	3	5	27

Gordon Gallant

GALLANT, GORDON 5'11", 175 lbs.
B. Oct. 27, 1950, Shediac, N.B. Left Wing, Shoots L

YEAR	TEAM	LEAGUE	GP	G	A	PTS	PIM
1973-74	**MINN**	**W**	72	7	15	22	**223**
1974-75			66	10	13	23	**203**
1975-76	**QUE**	**W**	64	4	15	19	297
1976-77	**MINN**	**W**	71	10	16	26	126
4 yrs.		**W Totals:**	273	31	59	90	849
PLAYOFFS							
1973-74	**MINN**	**W**	11	1	2	3	67
1974-75			1	1	0	1	0
1975-76	**QUE**	**W**	2	0	0	0	31
3 yrs.		**W Totals:**	14	2	2	4	98

Signed as free agent by **St. Louis,** June 30, 1978.

Jamie Gallimore

GALLIMORE, JAMES 6', 180 lbs.
B. Nov. 28, 1957, Edmonton, Alta. Right Wing, Shoots R

YEAR	TEAM	LEAGUE	GP	G	A	PTS	PIM
1977-78	**MINN**	**N**	2	0	0	0	0

Don Gallinger

GALLINGER, DONALD C. 6', 170 lbs.
B. Apr. 10, 1925, Port Colborne, Ont. Center, Shoots L

YEAR	TEAM	LEAGUE	GP	G	A	PTS	PIM
1942-43	**BOS**	**N**	48	14	20	34	16
1943-44			23	13	5	18	6
1945-46			50	17	23	40	18
1946-47			47	11	19	30	12
1947-48			54	10	21	31	37
5 yrs.		**N Totals:**	222	65	88	153	89
PLAYOFFS							
1942-43	**BOS**	**N**	9	3	1	4	10
1945-46			10	2	4	6	2
1946-47			4	0	0	0	7
3 yrs.		**N Totals:**	23	5	5	10	19

Dick Gamble

GAMBLE, RICHARD FRANK 6', 178 lbs.
B. Nov. 16, 1928, Moncton, N.B. Left Wing, Shoots L

YEAR	TEAM & LEAGUE		GP	G	A	PTS	PIM
1950-51	MONT	N	1	0	0	0	0
1951-52			64	23	17	40	8
1952-53			69	11	13	24	26
1953-54			32	4	8	12	18
1954-55	CHI	N	14	2	0	2	6
1955-56	MONT	N	12	0	3	3	8
1965-66	TOR	N	2	1	0	1	0
1966-67			1	0	0	0	0
8 yrs.		N Totals:	195	41	41	82	66

PLAYOFFS

YEAR	TEAM & LEAGUE		GP	G	A	PTS	PIM
1951-52	MONT	N	7	0	2	2	0
1952-53*			5	1	0	1	2
1954-55			2	0	0	0	2
3 yrs.		N Totals:	14	1	2	3	4

Traded to **N.Y. Rangers** by Montreal with Eddie Dorohoy for Hy Buller, June 8, 1954. Purchased by **Chicago** from N.Y. Rangers, Oct. 9, 1954. Sold to **Montreal** by Chicago, Nov. 23, 1954.

Gary Gambucci

GAMBUCCI, GARY ALLAN 5'9", 175 lbs.
B. Sept. 27, 1946, Hibbing, Minn. Center, Shoots L

YEAR	TEAM & LEAGUE		GP	G	A	PTS	PIM
1971-72	MINN	N	9	1	0	1	0
1973-74			42	1	7	8	9
1974-75	MINN	W	67	19	18	37	19
1975-76			45	10	6	16	14
4 yrs.		N Totals:	51	2	7	9	9
		W Totals:	112	29	24	53	33

PLAYOFFS

YEAR	TEAM & LEAGUE		GP	G	A	PTS	PIM
1974-75	MINN	W	12	4	0	4	6

Dave Gans

GANS, DAVE 5'11", 178 lbs.
B. June 6, 1964, Brantford, Ont. Center, Shoots L

YEAR	TEAM & LEAGUE		GP	G	A	PTS	PIM
1982-83	LA	N	3	0	0	0	0

Herb Gardiner

GARDINER, HERBERT
B. Winnipeg, Man. Defense
Won Hart Trophy, 1926-27
Hall of Fame, 1958

YEAR	TEAM & LEAGUE		GP	G	A	PTS	PIM
1926-27	MONT	N	44	6	6	12	26
1927-28			44	4	3	7	26
1928-29	CHI	N	5	0	0	0	0
	MONT	N	8	0	0	0	0
	2 team total		13	0	0	0	0
3 yrs.		N Totals:	101	10	9	19	52

PLAYOFFS

YEAR	TEAM & LEAGUE		GP	G	A	PTS	PIM
1926-27	MONT	N	2	0	0	0	10
1927-28			2	0	1	1	4
1928-29			3	0	0	0	0
3 yrs.		N Totals:	7	0	1	1	14

Cal Gardner

GARDNER, CALVIN PEARLY (Finger) 6'1", 175 lbs.
B. Oct. 30, 1924, Transcona, Man. Center, Shoots L

YEAR	TEAM & LEAGUE		GP	G	A	PTS	PIM
1945-46	NYR	N	16	8	2	10	2
1946-47			52	13	16	29	30
1947-48			58	7	18	25	71
1948-49	TOR	N	53	13	22	35	35
1949-50			30	7	19	26	12
1950-51			66	23	28	51	42
1951-52			70	15	26	41	40
1952-53	CHI	N	70	11	24	35	60
1953-54	BOS	N	70	14	20	34	62
1954-55			70	16	22	38	40
1955-56			70	15	21	36	57
1956-57			70	12	20	32	66
12 yrs.		N Totals:	695	154	238	392	517

Cal Gardner continued

PLAYOFFS

YEAR	TEAM & LEAGUE		GP	G	A	PTS	PIM
1947-48	NYR	N	5	0	0	0	0
1948-49*	TOR	N	9	2	5	7	0
1949-50			7	1	0	1	4
1950-51*			11	1	1	2	4
1951-52			3	0	0	0	2
1952-53	CHI	N	7	0	2	2	4
1953-54	BOS	N	4	1	1	2	0
1954-55			5	0	0	0	4
1956-57			10	2	1	3	2
9 yrs.		N Totals:	61	7	10	17	20

Traded to **Chicago** by Toronto with Al Rollins, Ray Hannigan and Gus Mortson for Harry Lumley, Sept. 11, 1952. Purchased by **Boston** from Toronto, June 26, 1953.

Dave Gardner

GARDNER, DAVID CALVIN 6', 183 lbs.
B. Aug. 23, 1952, Toronto, Ont. Center, Shoots R

YEAR	TEAM & LEAGUE		GP	G	A	PTS	PIM
1972-73	MONT	N	5	1	1	2	0
1973-74			31	1	10	11	2
	STL	N	15	5	2	7	6
	2 team total		46	6	12	18	8
1974-75			8	0	2	2	0
	CALIF	N	64	16	20	36	6
	2 team total		72	16	22	38	6
1975-76			74	16	32	48	8
1976-77	CLEVE	N	76	16	22	38	9
1977-78			75	19	25	44	10
1979-80	PHI	N	2	1	1	2	0
7 yrs.		N Totals:	350	75	115	190	41

Traded to **St. Louis** by Montreal for St. Louis' first choice (Doug Risebrough) in 1974 Amateur Draft, March 9, 1974. Traded to **California** by St. Louis with Butch Williams for Craig Patrick and Stan Gilbertson, Nov. 11, 1974. Put on **Minnesota** Reserve List after Cleveland-Minnesota Dispersal Draft, June 15, 1978. Sent to **Los Angeles** by Minnesota with Rick Hampton and Steve Jensen as compensation for Minnesota's signing of free agent Gary Sargent from Los Angeles, July 15, 1978. Signed as free agent by **Philadelphia** Jan. 21, 1980.

Paul Gardner

GARDNER, PAUL MALONE 6', 193 lbs.
B. Mar. 5, 1956, Fort Erie, Ont. Center, Shoots L

YEAR	TEAM & LEAGUE		GP	G	A	PTS	PIM
1976-77	COLO	N	60	30	29	59	25
1977-78			46	30	22	52	39
1978-79			64	23	26	49	32
	TOR	N	11	7	2	9	0
	2 team total		75	30	28	58	32
1979-80			45	11	13	24	10
1980-81	PITT	N	62	34	40	74	59
1981-82			59	36	33	69	28
1982-83			70	28	27	55	12
7 yrs.		N Totals:	417	199	192	391	205

PLAYOFFS

YEAR	TEAM & LEAGUE		GP	G	A	PTS	PIM
1978-79	TOR	N	6	0	1	1	4
1980-81	PITT	N	5	1	0	1	8
1981-82			5	1	5	6	2
3 yrs.		N Totals:	16	2	6	8	14

Traded to **Toronto** by Colorado for Don Ashby and Trever Johansen, March 13, 1979. Traded to **Pittsburgh** by Toronto with Dave Burrows for Kim Davis and Paul Marshall, Nov. 8, 1980.

Bill Gardner

GARDNER, WILLIAM SCOTT 5'10", 170 lbs.
B. May 19, 1960, Toronto, Ont. Center, Shoots L

YEAR	TEAM & LEAGUE		GP	G	A	PTS	PIM
1980-81	CHI	N	1	0	0	0	0
1981-82			69	8	15	23	20
1982-83			77	15	25	40	12

Bill Gardner continued

YEAR	TEAM & LEAGUE		GP	G	A	PTS	PIM
3 yrs.		N Totals:	147	23	40	63	32
PLAYOFFS							
1981-82	CHI	N	15	1	4	5	6
1982-83			13	1	0	1	9
2 yrs.		N Totals:	28	2	4	6	15

Danny Gare

GARE, DANIEL MIRL 5'9", 175 lbs.
B. May 14, 1954, Nelson, B.C. Right Wing, Shoots R

YEAR	TEAM & LEAGUE		GP	G	A	PTS	PIM
1974-75	BUF	N	78	31	31	62	75
1975-76			79	50	23	73	129
1976-77			35	11	15	26	73
1977-78			69	39	38	77	95
1978-79			79	27	40	67	90
1979-80			76	**56**	33	89	90
1980-81			73	46	39	85	109
1981-82			22	7	14	21	25
	DET	N	36	13	9	22	74
	2 team total		58	20	23	43	99
1982-83			79	26	35	61	107
9 yrs.		N Totals:	626	306	277	583	867
PLAYOFFS							
1974-75	BUF	N	17	7	6	13	19
1975-76			9	5	2	7	21
1976-77			4	0	0	0	18
1977-78			8	4	6	10	37
1978-79			3	0	0	0	9
1979-80			14	4	7	11	35
1980-81			3	3	0	3	8
7 yrs.		N Totals:	58	23	21	44	147

Traded to **Detroit** by Buffalo with Jim Schoenfeld and Derek Smith for Mike Foligno, Dale McCourt and Brent Peterson, Dec. 2, 1981.

Ray Gariepy

GARIEPY, RAYMOND 5'8½", 180 lbs.
B. Sept. 4, 1928, Toronto, Ont. Defense, Shoots L

YEAR	TEAM & LEAGUE		GP	G	A	PTS	PIM
1953-54	BOS	N	35	1	6	7	39
1955-56	TOR	N	1	0	0	0	4
2 yrs.		N Totals:	36	1	6	7	43

Purchased by **Toronto** from Boston, Sept. 23, 1955.

Scott Garland

GARLAND, STEPHEN SCOTT 6'1", 185 lbs.
B. May 16, 1952, Regina, Sask. Center, Shoots R

YEAR	TEAM & LEAGUE		GP	G	A	PTS	PIM
1975-76	TOR	N	16	4	3	7	8
1976-77			69	9	20	29	83
1978-79	LA	N	6	0	1	1	24
3 yrs.		N Totals:	91	13	24	37	115
PLAYOFFS							
1975-76	TOR	N	7	1	2	3	35

Traded to **Los Angeles** by Toronto with Brian Glennie, Kurt Walker, a second round choice (Mark Hardy) in 1979 Amateur Draft and future considerations for Dave Hutchison and Lorne Stamler, June 14, 1978.

J.C. Garneau

GARNEAU, JEAN CLAUDE 5'9", 165 lbs.
B. Oct. 19, 1943, Quebec City, Que. Left Wing, Shoots L

YEAR	TEAM & LEAGUE		GP	G	A	PTS	PIM
1974-75	QUE	W	17	0	5	5	27

Bob Garner

GARNER, ROBERT WILLIAM 5'11", 180 lbs.
B. Aug. 17, 1958, Weston, Ont. Center, Shoots L

YEAR	TEAM & LEAGUE		GP	G	A	PTS	PIM
1982-83	PITT	N	1	0	0	0	0

Red Garrett

GARRETT, DUDLEY 5'11½", 190 lbs.
B. July 24, 1924, Toronto, Ont. Defense, Shoots L

YEAR	TEAM & LEAGUE		GP	G	A	PTS	PIM
1942-43	NYR	N	23	1	1	2	18

Mike Gartner

GARTNER, MICHAEL ALFRED 5'11", 180 lbs.
B. Oct. 29, 1959, Ottawa, Ont. Center, Shoots L

YEAR	TEAM & LEAGUE		GP	G	A	PTS	PIM
1978-79	CIN	W	78	27	25	52	123
1979-80	WASH	N	77	36	32	68	66
1980-81			80	48	46	94	100
1981-82			80	35	45	80	121
1982-83			73	38	38	76	54
5 yrs.		N Totals:	310	157	161	318	341
		W Totals:	78	27	25	52	123
PLAYOFFS							
1978-79	CIN	W	3	0	0	0	2
1982-83	WASH	N	4	0	0	0	4
2 yrs.		N Totals:	4	0	0	0	4
		W Totals:	3	0	0	0	2

Ron Garwasiuk

GARWASIUK, RONALD VICTOR 5'8", 160 lbs.
B. Feb. 17, 1949, St. Paul, Alta. Left Wing, Shoots L

YEAR	TEAM & LEAGUE		GP	G	A	PTS	PIM
1973-74	LA	W	51	6	13	19	100

Bob Gassoff

GASSOFF, ROBERT ALLEN 5'10", 195 lbs.
B. Apr. 17, 1953, Quesnel, B.C. Defense, Shoots L

YEAR	TEAM & LEAGUE		GP	G	A	PTS	PIM
1973-74	STL	N	28	0	3	3	84
1974-75			60	4	14	18	222
1975-76			80	1	12	13	306
1976-77			77	6	18	24	254
4 yrs.		N Totals:	245	11	47	58	866
PLAYOFFS							
1974-75	STL	N	2	0	0	0	0
1975-76			3	0	0	0	6
1976-77			4	0	1	1	10
3 yrs.		N Totals:	9	0	1	1	16

Brad Gassoff

GASSOFF, HOWARD BRADLEY 5'11", 195 lbs.
B. Nov. 13, 1955, Quesnel, B.C. Left Wing, Shoots L

YEAR	TEAM & LEAGUE		GP	G	A	PTS	PIM
1975-76	VAN	N	4	0	0	0	5
1976-77			37	6	4	10	35
1977-78			47	9	6	15	70
1978-79			34	4	7	11	53
4 yrs.		N Totals:	122	19	17	36	163
PLAYOFFS							
1978-79	VAN	N	3	0	0	0	0

Marty Gateman

GATEMAN, JOHN MARTIN 6', 185 lbs.
B. Dec. 7, 1952, Southampton, Ont. Defense, Shoots L

YEAR	TEAM & LEAGUE		GP	G	A	PTS	PIM
1975-76	NE	W	12	0	1	1	6

Steve Gatzos

GATZOS, STEVE 5'11", 182 lbs.
B. June 22, 1961, Toronto, Ont. Right Wing, Shoots R

YEAR	TEAM & LEAGUE		GP	G	A	PTS	PIM
1981-82	PITT	N	16	6	8	14	14
1982-83			44	6	7	13	52
2 yrs.		N Totals:	60	12	15	27	66
PLAYOFFS							
1981-82	PITT	N	1	0	0	0	0

Andre Gaudette

GAUDETTE, ANDRE 5'7", 165 lbs.
B. Dec. 16, 1947, Sherbrooke, Que. Center, Shoots L

YEAR	TEAM & LEAGUE		GP	G	A	PTS	PIM
1972-73	QUE	W	78	27	44	71	12
1973-74			78	24	44	68	16
1974-75			67	10	17	27	6
3 yrs.		W Totals:	223	61	105	166	34
PLAYOFFS							
1974-75	QUE	W	9	0	1	1	0

Armand Gaudreault

GAUDREAULT, ARMAND GERARD 5'9", 155 lbs.
B. July 14, 1921, Lac St. Jean, Que. Left Wing, Shoots L

YEAR	TEAM & LEAGUE		GP	G	A	PTS	PIM
1944-45	BOS	N	44	15	9	24	27
PLAYOFFS							
1944-45	BOS	N	7	0	2	2	8

Leo Gaudreault

GAUDREAULT, LEO 5'9½", 152 lbs.
B. Chicoutimi, Que. Left Wing, Shoots L

YEAR	TEAM & LEAGUE		GP	G	A	PTS	PIM
1927-28	MONT	N	32	6	2	8	24
1928-29			11	0	0	0	4
1932-33			24	2	2	4	2
3 yrs.		N Totals:	67	8	4	12	30

Jean Gaulin

GAULIN, JEAN-MARC 5'10", 182 lbs.
B. Mar. 3, 1692, Balve, Germany Right Wing, Shoots R

YEAR	TEAM & LEAGUE		GP	G	A	PTS	PIM
1982-83	QUE	N	1	0	0	0	0

Art Gauthier

GAUTHIER, ARTHUR
B. Unknown Forward

YEAR	TEAM & LEAGUE		GP	G	A	PTS	PIM
1926-27	MONT	N	13	0	0	0	0
PLAYOFFS							
1926-27	MONT	N	1	0	0	0	0

Fern Gauthier

GAUTHIER, RENE FERNAND 5'11", 175 lbs.
B. Aug. 31, 1919, Chicoutimi, Que. Right Wing, Shoots R

YEAR	TEAM & LEAGUE		GP	G	A	PTS	PIM
1943-44	NYR	N	33	14	10	24	0
1944-45	MONT	N	50	18	13	31	23
1945-46	DET	N	30	9	8	17	6
1946-47			40	1	12	13	2
1947-48			35	1	5	6	2
1948-49			41	3	2	5	2
6 yrs.		N Totals:	229	46	50	96	35
PLAYOFFS							
1944-45	MONT	N	4	0	0	0	0
1945-46	DET	N	5	3	0	3	2
1946-47			3	1	0	1	0
1947-48			10	1	1	2	5
4 yrs.		N Totals:	22	5	1	6	7

Jean Gauthier

GAUTHIER, JEAN PHILIPPE 6'1", 200 lbs.
B. Mar. 29, 1937, Montreal, Que. Defense, Shoots R

YEAR	TEAM & LEAGUE		GP	G	A	PTS	PIM
1960-61	MONT	N	4	0	1	1	8
1961-62			12	0	1	1	10
1962-63			65	1	17	18	46
1963-64			1	0	0	0	2
1965-66			2	0	0	0	0
1966-67			2	0	0	0	2
1967-68	PHI	N	65	5	7	12	74
1968-69	BOS	N	11	0	2	2	8
1969-70	MONT	N	4	0	1	1	0
1972-73	NY	W	31	2	1	3	21
10 yrs.		N Totals:	166	6	29	35	150
		W Totals:	31	2	1	3	21

Jean Gauthier continued

YEAR	TEAM & LEAGUE		GP	G	A	PTS	PIM
PLAYOFFS							
1962-63	MONT	N	5	0	0	0	12
1964-65*			2	0	0	0	4
1967-68	PHI	N	7	1	3	4	6
3 yrs.		N Totals:	14	1	3	4	22

Drafted by **Philadelphia** from Montreal in Expansion Draft, June 6, 1967. Drafted by **Boston** from Philadelphia, June 12, 1968. Claimed by Cleveland **(Montreal)** from Oklahoma City (Boston) in Reverse Draft, June 12, 1969.

Bob Gavin

GAVIN, ROBERT STEWART 5'11", 185 lbs.
B. Mar. 15, 1960, Ottawa, Ont. Left Wing, Shoots L

YEAR	TEAM & LEAGUE		GP	G	A	PTS	PIM
1980-81	TOR	N	14	1	2	3	13
1981-82			38	5	6	11	29
1982-83			63	6	5	11	44
3 yrs.		N Totals:	115	12	13	25	86
PLAYOFFS							
1982-83	TOR	N	4	0	0	0	0

George Gee

GEE, GEORGE 5'11", 180 lbs.
B. June 28, 1922, Stratford, Ont. Center, Shoots L

YEAR	TEAM & LEAGUE		GP	G	A	PTS	PIM
1945-46	CHI	N	35	14	15	29	12
1946-47			60	20	20	40	26
1947-48			60	14	25	39	18
1948-49			4	0	2	2	4
	DET	N	47	7	11	18	27
	2 team total		51	7	13	20	31
1949-50			69	17	21	38	42
1950-51			70	17	20	37	19
1951-52	CHI	N	70	18	31	49	39
1952-53			67	18	21	39	99
1953-54			69	10	16	26	59
9 yrs.		N Totals:	551	135	182	317	345
PLAYOFFS							
1945-46	CHI	N	4	1	1	2	4
1948-49	DET	N	10	1	3	4	22
1949-50*			14	3	6	9	0
1950-51			6	0	1	1	0
1952-53	CHI	N	7	1	2	3	6
5 yrs.		N Totals:	41	6	13	19	32

Traded to **Chicago** by Detroit with Jim McFadden, Max McNab, Jim Peters, Clare Martin and Rags Raglan for Hugh Coflin and $75,000, Aug. 20, 1951.

Gary Geldart

GELDART, GARY DANIEL 5'8", 155 lbs.
B. June 14, 1950, Moncton, N.B. Defense, Shoots L

YEAR	TEAM & LEAGUE		GP	G	A	PTS	PIM
1970-71	MINN	N	4	0	0	0	5

Sold to **Montreal** by Minnesota, May 29, 1973.

Sam Gellard

GELLARD, SAMUEL 6', 190 lbs.
B. Mar. 14, 1950, Port of Spain, Trinidad
Left Wing, Shoots L

YEAR	TEAM & LEAGUE		GP	G	A	PTS	PIM
1972-73	PHI	W	5	0	0	0	0
1973-74	VAN	W	23	7	4	11	15
2 yrs.		W Totals:	28	7	4	11	15

Jean Guy Gendron

GENDRON, JEAN GUY 5'9", 165 lbs.
B. Aug. 30, 1934, Montreal, Que. Left Wing, Shoots L

YEAR	TEAM & LEAGUE		GP	G	A	PTS	PIM
1955-56	NYR	N	63	5	7	12	38
1956-57			70	9	6	15	40
1957-58			70	10	17	27	68
1958-59	BOS	N	60	15	9	24	57
1959-60			67	24	11	35	64
1960-61			13	1	7	8	24
	MONT	N	53	9	12	21	51
	2 team total		66	10	19	29	75
1961-62	NYR	N	69	14	11	25	71

YEAR	TEAM & LEAGUE		GP	G	A	PTS	PIM

Jean Guy Gendron continued

YEAR	TEAM	LEAGUE	GP	G	A	PTS	PIM
1962-63	**BOS**	N	66	21	22	43	42
1963-64			54	5	13	18	43
1967-68	**PHI**	N	1	0	1	1	2
1968-69			74	20	35	55	65
1969-70			71	23	21	44	54
1970-71			76	20	16	36	46
1971-72			56	6	13	19	36
1972-73	**QUE**	W	63	17	33	50	113
1973-74			64	11	8	19	42
16 yrs.		**N Totals:**	863	182	201	383	701
		W Totals:	127	28	41	69	155
PLAYOFFS							
1955-56	**NYR**	N	5	2	1	3	2
1956-57			5	0	1	1	6
1957-58			6	1	0	1	11
1958-59	**BOS**	N	7	1	0	1	18
1960-61	**MONT**	N	5	0	0	0	2
1961-62	**NYR**	N	6	3	1	4	2
1968-69	**PHI**	N	4	0	0	0	6
1970-71			4	0	1	1	0
8 yrs.		**N Totals:**	42	7	4	11	47

Drafted by **Boston** with Gord Redahl from New York, June 4, 1958. Traded to **Montreal** by Boston, for Andre Pronovost, Nov. 27, 1960. Drafted by **Boston** from N.Y. Rangers, June, 1962. Put on **Montreal** reserve list from Philadelphia, June 11, 1969. Sold to **Philadelphia** by Montreal, June 12, 1969. Drafted by **New York** from Montreal, June 14, 1961. Drafted by **Boston** from New York, June 6, 1962.

Bernie Geoffrion

GEOFFRION, BERNARD (Boom Boom) 5'11", 185 lbs.
B. Feb. 16, 1931, Montreal, Que. Right Wing, Shoots R
Won Hart Trophy, 1960-61
Won Art Ross Trophy, 1954–55, 1960-61
Won Calder Trophy, 1951-52
Hall of Fame, 1972

YEAR	TEAM	LEAGUE	GP	G	A	PTS	PIM
1950-51	**MONT**	N	18	8	6	14	9
1951-52			67	30	24	54	66
1952-53			65	22	17	39	37
1953-54			54	29	25	54	87
1954-55			70	**38**	37	**75**	57
1955-56			59	29	33	62	66
1956-57			41	19	21	40	18
1957-58			42	27	23	50	51
1958-59			59	22	44	66	30
1959-60			59	30	41	71	36
1960-61			64	**50**	45	**95**	29
1961-62			62	23	36	59	36
1962-63			51	23	18	41	73
1963-64			55	21	18	39	41
1966-67	**NYR**	N	58	17	25	42	42
1967-68			59	5	16	21	11
16 yrs.		**N Totals:**	883	393	429	822	689
PLAYOFFS							
1950-51	**MONT**	N	11	1	1	2	6
1951-52			11	3	1	4	6
1952-53*			12	6	4	10	12
1953-54			11	6	5	11	18
1954-55			12	8	5	13	8
1955-56*			10	5	9	14	6
1956-57*			10	11	7	18	2
1957-58*			10	6	5	11	2
1958-59*			11	5	8	13	10
1959-60*			8	2	10	12	4
1960-61			4	2	1	3	0
1961-62			5	0	1	1	6
1962-63			5	0	1	1	4
1963-64			7	1	1	2	4
1966-67	**NYR**	N	4	2	0	2	0
1967-68			1	0	1	1	0
16 yrs.		**N Totals:**	132	58	60	118	88

Claimed on waivers by **N.Y. Rangers** from Montreal, June 9, 1966.

Danny Geoffrion

GEOFFRION, DANIEL 5'10", 185 lbs.
B. Jan. 24, 1958, Montreal, Que. Right Wing, Shoots R

YEAR	TEAM	LEAGUE	GP	G	A	PTS	PIM
1978-79	**QUE**	W	77	12	14	26	74
1979-80	**MONT**	N	32	0	6	6	12
1980-81	**WINN**	N	78	20	26	46	82
1981-82			1	0	0	0	5
4 yrs.		**N Totals:**	111	20	32	52	99
		W Totals:	77	12	14	26	74
PLAYOFFS							
1978-79	**QUE**	W	4	1	2	3	2
1979-80	**MONT**	N	2	0	0	0	7
2 yrs.		**N Totals:**	2	0	0	0	7
		W Totals:	4	1	2	3	2

Reclaimed by **Montreal** from Quebec prior to Expansion Draft, June 9, 1979. Claimed by **Quebec** from Montreal in Waiver Draft, Oct. 8, 1980. Sold to **Winnipeg** by Quebec, Oct. 8, 1980.

Wes George

GEORGE, WESLEY 6'2", 220 lbs.
B. Sept. 26, 1958, Young, Sask. Left Wing, Shoots L

YEAR	TEAM	LEAGUE	GP	G	A	PTS	PIM
1978-79	**IND**	W	9	4	2	6	23
	EDM	W	3	0	0	0	11
	2 team total		12	4	2	6	34

Gerry Geran

GERAN, GERALD PIERCE
B. Aug. 3, 1896, Holyoke, Mass. Forward

YEAR	TEAM	LEAGUE	GP	G	A	PTS	PIM
1917-18	**MON(W)**	N	4	0	0	0	0
1925-26	**BOS**	N	33	5	1	6	6
2 yrs.		**N Totals:**	37	5	1	6	6

Eddie Gerard

GERARD, EDDIE
B. Feb. 22, 1890 Forward
Hall of Fame, 1945

YEAR	TEAM	LEAGUE	GP	G	A	PTS	PIM
1917-18	**OTTA**	N	21	13	0	13	12
1918-19			18	4	6	10	17
1919-20			21	9	3	12	19
1920-21			24	11	4	15	18
1921-22			21	7	9	16	16
1922-23			23	6	8	14	24
6 yrs.		**N Totals:**	128	50	30	80	106
PLAYOFFS							
1918-19	**OTTA**	N	5	3	0	3	3
1919-20*			5	2	1	3	6
1920-21*			7	1	0	1	33
1921-22			3	0	0	0	8
1922-23*			7	1	0	1	2
5 yrs.		**N Totals:**	27	7	1	8	52

Ray Getliffe

GETLIFFE, RAY 5'11", 175 lbs.
B. Apr. 3, 1914, Galt, Ont. Center, Shoots L

YEAR	TEAM	LEAGUE	GP	G	A	PTS	PIM
1935-36	**BOS**	N	1	0	0	0	2
1936-37			48	16	15	31	28
1937-38			36	11	13	24	16
1938-39			43	10	12	22	11
1939-40	**MONT**	N	46	11	12	23	29
1940-41			39	15	10	25	25
1941-42			45	11	15	26	35
1942-43			50	18	28	46	56
1943-44			44	28	25	53	44
1944-45			41	16	7	23	34
10 yrs.		**N Totals:**	393	136	137	273	280
PLAYOFFS							
1935-36	**BOS**	N	2	0	0	0	0
1936-37			3	2	1	3	2
1937-38			3	0	1	1	2
1938-39*			11	1	1	2	2
1940-41	**MONT**	N	3	1	1	2	0
1941-42			3	0	0	0	0
1942-43			5	0	1	1	8
1943-44*			9	5	4	9	16
1944-45			6	0	1	1	0
9 yrs.		**N Totals:**	45	9	10	19	30

Mario Giallonardo

GIALLONARDO, MARIO 5'11", 201 lbs.
B. Sept. 23, 1957, Toronto, Ont. Defense, Shoots L

YEAR	TEAM	LEAGUE	GP	G	A	PTS	PIM
1979-80	**COLO**	**N**	8	0	1	1	2
1980-81			15	0	2	2	4
2 yrs.		**N Totals:**	23	0	3	3	6

Signed as free agent by **Colorado** Dec. 21, 1978.

Brian Gibbons

GIBBONS, BRIAN 6'3", 190 lbs.
B. July 7, 1947, St. John's, Nfld. Defense, Shoots L

YEAR	TEAM	LEAGUE	GP	G	A	PTS	PIM
1972-73	**OTTA**	**W**	73	7	35	42	62
1973-74	**TOR**	**W**	78	4	31	35	84
1974-75			73	4	22	26	105
1975-76	**D-O**	**W**	2	0	0	0	0
4 yrs.		**W Totals:**	226	15	88	103	251
PLAYOFFS							
1972-73	**OTTA**	**W**	5	1	2	3	12
1973-74	**TOR**	**W**	12	2	5	7	10
2 yrs.		**W Totals:**	17	3	7	10	22

Traded to **Los Angeles** by Detroit with Garry Monahan for Dale Rolfe, Gary Croteau, and Larry Johnston, Feb. 20, 1970.

Gerry Gibbons

GIBBONS, GERARD 6'3", 185 lbs.
B. Jan. 17, 1953, St. John's, Nfld. Defense, Shoots L

YEAR	TEAM	LEAGUE	GP	G	A	PTS	PIM
1973-74	**TOR**	**W**	26	1	4	5	23
1975-76			5	1	0	1	7
2 yrs.		**W Totals:**	31	2	4	6	30
PLAYOFFS							
1973-74	**TOR**	**W**	1	0	0	0	0

Barry Gibbs

GIBBS, BARRY PAUL 5'11", 195 lbs.
B. Sept. 28, 1948, Lloydminster, Sask. Defense, Shoots R

YEAR	TEAM	LEAGUE	GP	G	A	PTS	PIM
1967-68	**BOS**	**N**	16	0	0	0	2
1968-69			8	0	0	0	2
1969-70	**MINN**	**N**	56	3	13	16	182
1970-71			63	5	15	20	132
1971-72			75	4	20	24	128
1972-73			63	10	24	34	54
1973-74			76	9	29	38	82
1974-75			37	4	20	24	22
	ATL	**N**	39	3	13	16	39
	2 team total		76	7	33	40	61
1975-76			76	8	21	29	92
1976-77			66	1	16	17	63
1977-78			27	1	5	6	24
	STL	**N**	51	6	12	18	45
	2 team total		78	7	17	24	69
1978-79			75	2	27	29	46
1979-80	**LA**	**N**	63	2	9	11	32
13 yrs.		**N Totals:**	791	58	224	282	945
PLAYOFFS							
1969-70	**MINN**	**N**	6	1	0	1	7
1970-71			12	0	1	1	47
1971-72			7	1	1	2	9
1972-73			5	1	0	1	0
1975-76	**ATL**	**N**	2	1	0	1	2
1976-77			3	0	0	0	2
1979-80	**LA**	**N**	1	0	0	0	0
7 yrs.		**N Totals:**	36	4	2	6	67

Traded to **Minnesota** by Boston with Tommy Williams for Minnesota's first choice in the 1969 Amateur Draft (Don Tannahill) and Fred O'Donnell, May 7, 1969. Traded to **Atlanta** by Minnesota for Dean Talafous and Dwight Biolawas, Jan. 3, 1975. Traded to **St. Louis** by Atlanta with Phil Myre and Curt Bennett for Yves Belanger, Dick Redmond, Bob MacMillan, and St. Louis' second round choice (Mike Perovich) in 1979 Entry Draft, Dec. 12, 1977. Traded to **N.Y. Islanders** by St. Louis with Terry Richardson for future considerations, June 9, 1979. Traded to **Los Angeles** by N.Y. Islanders, Aug. 16, 1979. Los Angeles sent Tom Williams to St. Louis to complete the three-team trade of June 9 and Aug. 16, 1979.

Doug Gibson

GIBSON, DOUGLAS JOHN 5'10", 175 lbs.
B. Sept. 28, 1953, Peterborough, Ont. Center, Shoots L

YEAR	TEAM	LEAGUE	GP	G	A	PTS	PIM
1973-74	**BOS**	**N**	2	0	0	0	0
1975-76			50	7	18	25	0
1977-78	**WASH**	**N**	11	2	1	3	0
3 yrs.		**N Totals:**	63	9	19	28	0
PLAYOFFS							
1973-74	**BOS**	**N**	1	0	0	0	0

Claimed on waivers by **Washington** from Boston, May 29, 1977.

Jack Gibson

GIBSON, JAMES 6', 185 lbs.
B. Aug. 18, 1948, Picton, Ont. Left Wing, Shoots L

YEAR	TEAM	LEAGUE	GP	G	A	PTS	PIM
1972-73	**OTTA**	**W**	59	22	13	35	48
1973-74	**TOR**	**W**	61	16	9	25	60
1975-76			2	0	0	0	0
3 yrs.		**W Totals:**	122	38	22	60	108
PLAYOFFS							
1972-73	**OTTA**	**W**	1	1	0	1	5
1973-74	**TOR**	**W**	12	1	3	4	11
2 yrs.		**W Totals:**	13	2	3	5	16

John Gibson

GIBSON, JOHN WILLIAM 6'3", 208 lbs.
B. June 2, 1959, St, Catharines, Ont. Defense, Shoots L

YEAR	TEAM	LEAGUE	GP	G	A	PTS	PIM
1978-79	**WINN**	**W**	9	0	1	1	5
1980-81	**LA**	**N**	4	0	0	0	21
1981-82			6	0	0	0	18
	TOR	**N**	27	0	2	2	67
	2 team total		33	0	2	2	85
3 yrs.		**N Totals:**	37	0	2	2	106
		W Totals:	9	0	1	1	5

Traded to **Toronto** by Los Angeles with Billy Harris for Ian Turnbull, Nov. ll, 1981.

Gus Giesebrecht

GIESEBRECHT, ROY 6', 177 lbs.
B. Sept. 16, 1918, Pembroke, Ont. Center, Shoots L

YEAR	TEAM	LEAGUE	GP	G	A	PTS	PIM
1938-39	**DET**	**N**	28	10	10	20	2
1939-40			30	4	7	11	2
1940-41			43	7	18	25	7
1941-42			34	6	16	22	2
4 yrs.		**N Totals:**	135	27	51	78	13
PLAYOFFS							
1938-39	**DET**	**N**	6	0	2	2	0
1940-41			9	2	1	3	0
1941-42			2	0	0	0	0
3 yrs.		**N Totals:**	17	2	3	5	0

Ed Gilbert

GILBERT, EDWARD FERGUSON 6', 185 lbs.
B. Mar. 12, 1952, Hamilton, Ont. Center, Shoots L

YEAR	TEAM	LEAGUE	GP	G	A	PTS	PIM
1974-75	**KC**	**N**	80	16	22	38	14
1975-76			41	4	8	12	8
	PITT	**N**	38	1	1	2	0
	2 team total		79	5	9	14	8
1976-77			7	0	0	0	0
1978-79	**CIN**	**W**	29	3	3	6	40
4 yrs.		**N Totals:**	166	21	31	52	22
		W Totals:	29	3	3	6	40

Drafted by **Kansas City** from Montreal in Expansion Draft, June 12, 1974. Traded to **Pittsburgh** by Kansas City with Simon Nolet and Kansas City's first round choice (Blair Chapman) in 1976 Amateur Draft for Steve Durbano, Chuck Arnason and Pittsburgh's first round choice (Greg Carroll) in same draft, Jan. 9, 1976.

YEAR	TEAM & LEAGUE		GP	G	A	PTS	PIM

Greg Gilbert

GILBERT, GREG SCOTT 6'1", 194 lbs.
B. Jan. 22, 1962, Mississauga, Ont. Left Wing, Shoots L

YEAR	TEAM	LEAGUE	GP	G	A	PTS	PIM
1981-82	**NYI**	**N**	1	1	0	1	0
1982-83			45	8	11	19	30
2 yrs.		**N Totals:**	46	9	11	20	30
PLAYOFFS							
1981-82*	**NYI**	**N**	4	1	1	2	2
1982-83*			10	1	0	1	14
2 yrs.		**N Totals:**	14	2	1	3	16

Jean Gilbert

GILBERT, JEANNOT ELMOURT 5'9", 170 lbs.
B. Dec. 29, 1940, Port Alfred, Que. Center, Shoots L

YEAR	TEAM	LEAGUE	GP	G	A	PTS	PIM
1962-63	**BOS**	**N**	5	0	0	0	4
1964-65			4	0	0	0	0
1973-74	**QUE**	**W**	75	17	39	56	20
1974-75			58	7	21	28	12
4 yrs.		**N Totals:**	9	0	0	0	4
		W Totals:	133	24	60	84	32
PLAYOFFS							
1974-75	**QUE**	**W**	11	3	6	9	2

Drafted by **Pittsburgh** from Boston in Expansion Draft, June 6, 1967.

Rod Gilbert

GILBERT, RODRIGUE GABRIEL 5'9", 180 lbs.
B. July 1, 1941, Montreal, Que. Right Wing, Shoots R
Won Masterton Trophy, 1975-76
Hall of Fame, 1982

YEAR	TEAM	LEAGUE	GP	G	A	PTS	PIM
1960-61	**NYR**	**N**	1	0	1	1	2
1961-62			1	0	0	0	0
1962-63			70	11	20	31	20
1963-64			70	24	40	64	62
1964-65			70	25	36	61	52
1965-66			34	10	15	25	20
1966-67			64	28	18	46	12
1967-68			73	29	48	77	12
1968-69			66	28	49	77	22
1969-70			72	16	37	53	22
1970-71			78	30	31	61	65
1971-72			73	43	54	97	64
1972-73			76	25	59	84	25
1973-74			75	36	41	77	20
1974-75			76	36	61	97	22
1975-76			70	36	50	86	32
1976-77			77	27	48	75	50
1977-78			19	2	7	9	6
18 yrs.		**N Totals:**	1065	406	615	1021	508
PLAYOFFS							
1961-62	**NYR**	**N**	4	2	3	5	4
1966-67			4	2	2	4	6
1967-68			6	5	0	5	4
1968-69			4	1	0	1	2
1969-70			6	4	5	9	0
1970-71			13	4	6	10	8
1971-72			16	7	8	15	11
1972-73			10	5	1	6	2
1973-74			13	3	5	8	4
1974-75			3	1	3	4	2
10 yrs.		**N Totals:**	79	34	33	67	43

Stan Gilbertson

GILBERTSON, STANLEY FRANK 6', 175 lbs.
B. Oct. 29, 1944, Duluth, Mn. Left Wing, Shoots L

YEAR	TEAM	LEAGUE	GP	G	A	PTS	PIM
1971-72	**CALIF**	**N**	78	16	16	32	47
1972-73			66	6	15	21	19
1973-74			76	18	12	30	39
1974-75			15	1	4	5	2
	STL	**N**	22	1	4	5	4
	WASH	**N**	25	11	7	18	12
	3 team total		62	13	15	28	18
1975-76			31	13	14	27	6
	PITT	**N**	49	13	8	21	6
	2 team total		80	26	22	48	12

Stan Gilbertson continued

YEAR	TEAM	LEAGUE	GP	G	A	PTS	PIM
1976-77			67	6	9	15	13
6 yrs.		**N Totals:**	429	85	89	174	148
PLAYOFFS							
1975-76	**PITT**	**N**	3	1	1	2	2

Drafted by **California** from Boston in Intra-League Draft, June 8, 1971. Traded to **St. Louis** by California with Craig Patrick for Dave Gardner and Warren Williams, Nov. 11, 1974. Traded to **Washington** by St. Louis with Garnet Bailey for Denis Dupere, Feb. 10, 1975. Traded to **Pittsburgh** by Washington for Harvey Bennett, Dec. 16, 1975.

Curt Giles

GILES, CURT (Pengy) 5'8", 180 lbs.
B. Nov. 30, 1958, Humboldt, Sask. Defense, Shoots L

YEAR	TEAM	LEAGUE	GP	G	A	PTS	PIM
1979-80	**MINN**	**N**	37	2	7	9	31
1980-81			67	5	22	27	56
1981-82			74	3	12	15	87
1982-83			76	2	21	23	70
4 yrs.		**N Totals:**	254	12	62	74	244
PLAYOFFS							
1979-80	**MINN**	**N**	12	2	4	6	10
1980-81			19	1	4	5	14
1981-82			4	0	0	0	2
1982-83			5	0	2	2	6
4 yrs.		**N Totals:**	40	3	10	13	32

Randy Gilhen

GILHEN, RANDY 5'10", 190 lbs.
B. June 13, 1963, Zweibucken, West Germany
Right Wing, Shoots L

YEAR	TEAM	LEAGUE	GP	G	A	PTS	PIM
1982-83	**HART**	**N**	2	0	1	1	0

Don Gillen

GILLEN, DONALD 6'3", 222 lbs.
B. Dec. 24, 1960, Dodsland, Sask. Right Wing, Shoots R

YEAR	TEAM	LEAGUE	GP	G	A	PTS	PIM
1979-80	**PHI**	**N**	1	1	0	1	0
1981-82	**HART**	**N**	34	1	4	5	22
2 yrs.		**N Totals:**	35	2	4	6	22

Traded to **Hartford** by Philadelphia with Rick MacLeish, Blake Wesley and Philadelphia's first (Paul Lawless), second (Mark Paterson) and third round (Kevin Dineen) choices in the 1982 Entry Draft for Ray Allison, Fred Arthur and Hartford's first (Ron Sutter) and third round (Miroslav Dvorak) choices in the 1982 Entry Draft, July 3, 1981.

Ferrand Gillie

GILLIE, FERRAND
B. Cornwall, Ont. Forward

YEAR	TEAM	LEAGUE	GP	G	A	PTS	PIM
1928-29	**DET**	**N**	1	0	0	0	0

Clark Gillies

GILLIES, CLARK (Jethro) 6'3", 215 lbs.
B. Apr. 7, 1954, Moose Jaw, Sask. Left Wing, Shoots L

YEAR	TEAM	LEAGUE	GP	G	A	PTS	PIM
1974-75	**NYI**	**N**	80	25	22	47	66
1975-76			80	34	27	61	96
1976-77			70	33	22	55	93
1977-78			80	35	50	85	76
1978-79			75	35	56	91	68
1979-80			73	19	35	54	49
1980-81			80	33	45	78	99
1981-82			79	38	39	77	75
1982-83			70	21	20	41	76
9 yrs.		**N Totals:**	687	273	316	589	698
PLAYOFFS							
1974-75	**NYI**	**N**	17	4	2	6	36
1975-76			13	2	4	6	16
1976-77			12	4	4	8	15
1977-78			7	2	0	2	15
1978-79			10	1	2	3	11
1979-80*			21	6	10	16	63
1980-81*			18	6	9	15	28
1981-82*			19	8	6	14	34
1982-83*			8	0	2	2	10

Clark Gillies continued

YEAR	TEAM & LEAGUE		GP	G	A	PTS	PIM
9 yrs.		N Totals:	125	33	39	72	228

Bill Gilligan

GILLIGAN, WILLIAM 5'11", 175 lbs.
B. Aug. 5, 1954, Beverly, Ma. Center, Shoots R

YEAR	TEAM & LEAGUE		GP	G	A	PTS	PIM
1977-78	**CIN**	**W**	54	10	14	24	59
1978-79			74	17	26	43	54
2 yrs.		**W Totals:**	128	27	40	67	113
PLAYOFFS							
1978-79	**CIN**	**W**	3	1	0	1	0

Jere Gillis

GILLIS, JERE ALAN 6', 190 lbs.
B. Jan. 18, 1957, Bend, Ore. Left Wing, Shoots L

YEAR	TEAM & LEAGUE		GP	G	A	PTS	PIM
1977-78	**VAN**	**N**	79	23	18	41	35
1978-79			78	13	12	25	33
1979-80			67	13	17	30	108
1980-81			11	0	4	4	4
	NYR	**N**	35	10	10	20	4
	2 team total		46	10	14	24	8
1981-82			26	3	9	12	16
	QUE	**N**	12	2	1	3	0
	2 team total		38	5	10	15	16
1982-83	**BUF**	**N**	3	0	0	0	0
6 yrs.		**N Totals:**	311	64	71	135	200
PLAYOFFS							
1978-79	**VAN**	**N**	1	0	1	1	0
1980-81	**NYR**	**N**	14	2	5	7	9
2 yrs.		**N Totals:**	15	2	6	8	9

Traded to **N.Y. Rangers** by Vancouver with Jeff Bandura for Mario Marois and Jim Mayer, Nov. 11, 1980. Traded to **Quebec** by N.Y. Rangers with Dean Talafous (replaced by Pat Hickey) for Robbie Ftorek and Quebec's eighth round choice (Brian Glynn) in 1982 Entry Draft, Dec. 30, 1981. Signed as a free agent by **Buffalo** Sept. 11, 1982.

Mike Gillis

GILLIS, MICHAEL DAVID 6'1", 195 lbs.
B. Dec. 1, 1958, Sudbury, Ont. Left Wing, Shoots L

YEAR	TEAM & LEAGUE		GP	G	A	PTS	PIM
1978-79	**COLO**	**N**	30	1	7	8	6
1979-80			40	4	5	9	22
1980-81			51	11	7	18	54
	BOS	**N**	17	2	4	6	15
	2 team total		68	13	11	24	69
1981-82			53	9	8	17	54
1982-83			5	0	1	1	0
5 yrs.		**N Totals:**	196	27	32	59	151
PLAYOFFS							
1980-81	**BOS**	**N**	1	0	0	0	0
1981-82			11	1	2	3	6
1982-83			12	1	3	4	2
3 yrs.		**N Totals:**	24	2	5	7	8

Claimed by **Colorado** as fill in Expansion Draft, June 13, 1979. Traded to **Boston** by Colorado for Bob Miller, Feb. 18, 1981.

Paul Gillis

GILLIS, PAUL 5'11", 195 lbs.
B. Dec. 31, 1963, Toronto, Ont. Center, Shoots L

YEAR	TEAM & LEAGUE		GP	G	A	PTS	PIM
1982-83	**QUE**	**N**	7	0	2	2	2

Tom Gilmore

GILMORE, THOMAS MCCRACKEN 5'11", 190 lbs.
B. May 14, 1948, Flin Flon, Man. Left Wing, Shoots L

YEAR	TEAM & LEAGUE		GP	G	A	PTS	PIM
1972-73	**LA**	**W**	71	17	18	35	191
1973-74	**EDM**	**W**	57	19	23	42	164
1974-75			74	12	19	31	84
3 yrs.		**W Totals:**	202	48	60	108	439

Tom Gilmore continued

YEAR	TEAM & LEAGUE		GP	G	A	PTS	PIM
PLAYOFFS							
1972-73	**LA**	**W**	5	1	3	4	2
1973-74	**EDM**	**W**	5	1	4	5	15
2 yrs.		**W Totals:**	10	2	7	9	17

Dave Gilmour

GILMOUR, DAVID DONALD 5'9", 165 lbs.
B. Kingston, Ont. Left Wing, Shoots L

YEAR	TEAM & LEAGUE		GP	G	A	PTS	PIM
1975-76	**CALG**	**W**	1	0	0	0	0

Gaston Gingras

GINGRAS, GASTON REGINALD 6', 191 lbs.
B. Feb. 13, 1959, Temiscamingue, Que. Defense, Shoots L

YEAR	TEAM & LEAGUE		GP	G	A	PTS	PIM
1978-79	**BIRM**	**W**	60	13	21	34	35
1979-80	**MONT**	**N**	34	3	7	10	18
1980-81			55	5	16	21	22
1981-82			34	6	18	24	28
1982-83			22	1	8	9	8
	TOR	**N**	45	10	18	28	10
	2 team total		67	11	26	37	18
5 yrs.		**N Totals:**	190	25	67	92	86
		W Totals:	60	13	21	34	35
PLAYOFFS							
1979-80	**MONT**	**N**	10	1	6	7	8
1980-81			1	1	0	1	0
1981-82			5	0	1	1	0
1982-83	**TOR**	**N**	3	1	2	3	2
4 yrs.		**N Totals:**	19	3	9	12	10

Traded to **Toronto** by Montreal for future considerations, Dec. 17, 1982.

Bob Girard

GIRARD, ROBERT 6', 180 lbs.
B. Apr. 12, 1949, Montreal, Que. Left Wing, Shoots L

YEAR	TEAM & LEAGUE		GP	G	A	PTS	PIM
1975-76	**CALIF**	**N**	80	16	26	42	54
1976-77	**CLEVE**	**N**	68	11	10	21	33
1977-78			25	0	4	4	11
	WASH	**N**	52	9	14	23	6
	2 team total		77	9	18	27	17
1978-79			79	9	15	24	36
1979-80			1	0	0	0	0
5 yrs.		**N Totals:**	305	45	69	114	140

Traded to **Washington** by Cleveland with Cleveland's second-round choice (Paul MacKinnon) in the 1978 Amateur Draft for Walt McKechnie, Dec. 9, 1977. Claimed by **Washington** as fill in Expansion Draft, June 13, 1979.

Kenny Girard

GIRARD, KENNETH 6', 184 lbs.
B. Dec. 8, 1936, Toronto, Ont. Right Wing, Shoots R

YEAR	TEAM & LEAGUE		GP	G	A	PTS	PIM
1956-57	**TOR**	**N**	3	0	1	1	2
1957-58			3	0	0	0	0
1959-60			1	0	0	0	0
3 yrs.		**N Totals:**	7	0	1	1	2

Art Giroux

GIROUX, ARTHUR JOSEPH 5'1", 165 lbs.
B. June 6, 1907, Strathmore, Alta. Right Wing, Shoots R

YEAR	TEAM & LEAGUE		GP	G	A	PTS	PIM
1932-33	**MONT**	**N**	40	5	2	7	14
1934-35	**BOS**	**N**	10	1	0	1	0
1935-36	**DET**	**N**	4	0	2	2	0
3 yrs.		**N Totals:**	54	6	4	10	14
PLAYOFFS							
1932-33	**MONT**	**N**	2	0	0	0	0

Larry Giroux

GIROUX, LARRY DOUGLAS 6', 190 lbs.
B. Aug. 28, 1951, Weyburn, Sask. Defense, Shoots R

YEAR	TEAM & LEAGUE		GP	G	A	PTS	PIM
1973-74	**STL**	**N**	74	5	17	22	59
1974-75	**KC**	**N**	21	0	6	6	24
	DET	**N**	39	2	20	22	60
	2 team total		60	2	26	28	84

Larry Giroux continued

YEAR	TEAM & LEAGUE		GP	G	A	PTS	PIM
1975-76			10	1	1	2	25
1976-77			2	0	0	0	2
1977-78			5	0	3	3	4
1978-79	**STL**	**N**	73	5	22	27	111
1979-80			3	0	0	0	4
	HART	**N**	47	2	5	7	44
	2 team total		50	2	5	7	48
7 yrs.		**N Totals:**	274	15	74	89	333
PLAYOFFS							
1977-78	**DET**	**N**	2	0	0	0	2
1979-80	**HART**	**N**	3	0	0	0	2
2 yrs.		**N Totals:**	5	0	0	0	4

Traded to **Kansas City** by St. Louis for Chris Evans and Kansas City's fourth choice (Mike Liut) in 1976 Amateur Draft, Oct. 29, 1974. Traded to **Detroit** by Kansas City with **Hartford** Dec. 13, 1978. Dec. 14, 1974. Claimed by **St. Louis** from Detroit in League Waiver Draft, Oct. 9, 1978. Signed as free agent with **Hartford,** Dec. 13, 1978.

Pierre Giroux

GIROUX, PIERRE-YVES RICHARD 5'11", 186 lbs.
B. Nov. 17, 1955, Brownsburg, Que. Center, Shoots R

YEAR	TEAM & LEAGUE		GP	G	A	PTS	PIM
1982-83	**LA**	**N**	6	1	0	1	17

Signed by **Los Angeles** as a free agent, Jan., 1982.

Rejean Giroux

GIROUX, REJEAN GERARD 5'11", 160 lbs.
B. Sept. 13, 1952, Quebec City, Que. Right Wing, Shoots R

YEAR	TEAM & LEAGUE		GP	G	A	PTS	PIM
1972-73	**QUE**	**W**	59	10	12	22	41
1973-74			12	5	6	11	14
2 yrs.		**W Totals:**	71	15	18	33	55

Dan Givens

GIVENS, DANIEL

YEAR	TEAM & LEAGUE		GP	G	A	PTS	PIM
1974-75	**VAN**	**W**	1	0	0	0	0

Bob Gladney

GLADNEY, ROBERT LAWRENCE 5'11", 184 lbs.
B. Aug. 27, 1957, Come-By-Chance, Nfld.
Defense, Shoots L

YEAR	TEAM & LEAGUE		GP	G	A	PTS	PIM
1982-83	**LA**	**N**	1	0	0	0	2

Traded to **Los Angeles** by Toronto, along with Toronto's sixth round choice in the 1983 Entry Draft for Don Luce, Aug. 10, 1981.

Jean Gladu

GLADU, JOSEPH JEAN PAUL 5'10½", 180 lbs.
B. June 20, 1921, St. Hyacinthe, Que. Left Wing, Shoots L

YEAR	TEAM & LEAGUE		GP	G	A	PTS	PIM
1944-45	**BOS**	**N**	40	6	14	20	2
PLAYOFFS							
1944-45	**BOS**	**N**	7	2	2	4	0

Brian Glennie

GLENNIE, BRIAN ALEXANDER 6'1", 200 lbs.
B. Aug. 29, 1946, Toronto, Ont. Defense, Shoots L

YEAR	TEAM & LEAGUE		GP	G	A	PTS	PIM
1969-70	**TOR**	**N**	52	1	14	15	50
1970-71			54	0	8	8	31
1971-72			61	2	8	10	44
1972-73			44	1	10	11	54
1973-74			65	4	18	22	100
1974-75			63	1	7	8	110
1975-76			69	0	8	8	75
1976-77			69	1	10	11	73
1977-78			77	2	15	17	62
1978-79	**LA**	**N**	18	2	2	4	22
10 yrs.		**N Totals:**	572	14	100	114	621
PLAYOFFS							
1970-71	**TOR**	**N**	3	0	0	0	0
1971-72			5	0	0	0	25
1973-74			3	0	0	0	10
1975-76			6	0	1	1	15

Brian Glennie continued

YEAR	TEAM & LEAGUE		GP	G	A	PTS	PIM
1976-77			2	0	0	0	0
1977-78			13	0	0	0	16
6 yrs.		**N Totals:**	32	0	1	1	66

Traded to **Los Angeles** by Toronto with Kurt Walker, Scott Garland, Toronto's second round choice (Mark Hardy) in the 1979 Entry Draft and future considerations for Dave Hutchison and Lorne Stamler, June 14, 1978.

Brian Glenwright

GLENWRIGHT, BRIAN JOSEPH (Wimpy)
6'3", 206 lbs.
B. Oct. 8, 1949, Windsor, Ont. Left Wing, Shoots L

YEAR	TEAM & LEAGUE		GP	G	A	PTS	PIM
1972-73	**CHI**	**W**	50	2	5	7	0
1973-74	**LA**	**W**	15	3	2	5	0
2 yrs.		**W Totals:**	65	5	7	12	0

Allan Globensky

GLOBENSKY, ALLAN 6'1", 190 lbs.
B. Apr. 17, 1951, Montreal, Que. Defense, Shoots R

YEAR	TEAM & LEAGUE		GP	G	A	PTS	PIM
1972-73	**QUE**	**W**	3	0	0	0	0
1974-75			5	0	0	0	5
1975-76			34	1	2	3	13
3 yrs.		**W Totals:**	42	1	2	3	18
PLAYOFFS							
1974-75	**QUE**	**W**	2	1	0	1	0

Lorry Gloeckner

GLOECKNER, LORRY 6'2", 210 lbs.
B. Jan. 25, 1956, Kindersley, Sask. Defense, Shoots L

YEAR	TEAM & LEAGUE		GP	G	A	PTS	PIM
1978-79	**DET**	**N**	13	0	2	2	6

Signed as free agent by **Detroit** Oct. 12, 1978.

Dan Gloor

GLOOR, DANIEL HAROLD 5'9", 170 lbs.
B. Dec. 4, 1952, Stratford, Ont. Center, Shoots L

YEAR	TEAM & LEAGUE		GP	G	A	PTS	PIM
1973-74	**VAN**	**N**	2	0	0	0	0

Fred Glover

GLOVER, FREDERICK AUSTIN 5'9", 175 lbs.
B. Jan. 5, 1928, Toronto, Ont. Right Wing, Shoots R

YEAR	TEAM & LEAGUE		GP	G	A	PTS	PIM
1949-50	**DET**	**N**	7	0	0	0	0
1951-52			54	9	9	18	25
1952-53	**CHI**	**N**	31	4	2	6	37
3 yrs.		**N Totals:**	92	13	11	24	62
PLAYOFFS							
1948-49	**DET**	**N**	1	0	0	0	0
1950-51			2	0	0	0	0
2 yrs.		**N Totals:**	3	0	0	0	0

Sold to **Chicago** by Detroit with Enio Sclisizzi, Aug. 14, 1952.

Howie Glover

GLOVER, HOWARD EDWARD 5'11", 195 lbs.
B. Feb. 14, 1935, Toronto, Ont. Right Wing, Shoots R

YEAR	TEAM & LEAGUE		GP	G	A	PTS	PIM
1958-59	**CHI**	**N**	13	0	1	1	2
1960-61	**DET**	**N**	66	21	8	29	46
1961-62			39	7	8	15	44
1963-64	**NYR**	**N**	25	1	0	1	9
1968-69	**MONT**	**N**	1	0	0	0	0
5 yrs.		**N Totals:**	144	29	17	46	101
PLAYOFFS							
1960-61	**DET**	**N**	11	1	2	3	2

Traded to **Detroit** by Chicago for Jim Morrison, June, 7, 1960. Drafted by **New York** from Detroit, June 5, 1963.

Ernie Godden

GODDEN, ERNIE ALFRED 5'7", 154 lbs.
B. Mar. 13, 1961, Keswick, Ont. Center, Shoots L

YEAR	TEAM & LEAGUE		GP	G	A	PTS	PIM
1981-82	TOR	N	5	1	1	2	6

Warren Godfrey

GODFREY, WARREN 6'1", 190 lbs.
B. Mar. 23, 1931, Toronto, Ont. Defense, Shoots L

YEAR	TEAM & LEAGUE		GP	G	A	PTS	PIM
1952-53	BOS	N	60	1	13	14	40
1953-54			70	5	9	14	71
1954-55			62	1	17	18	58
1955-56	DET	N	67	2	6	8	86
1956-57			69	1	8	9	103
1957-58			67	2	16	18	56
1958-59			69	6	4	10	44
1959-60			69	5	9	14	60
1960-61			63	3	16	19	62
1961-62			69	4	13	17	84
1962-63	BOS	N	66	2	9	11	56
1963-64	DET	N	4	0	0	0	2
1964-65			11	0	0	0	8
1965-66			26	0	4	4	22
1966-67			2	0	0	0	0
1967-68			12	0	1	1	0
16 yrs.		N Totals:	786	32	125	157	752
PLAYOFFS							
1952-53	BOS	N	11	0	1	1	2
1953-54			4	0	0	0	4
1954-55			3	0	0	0	0
1956-57	DET	N	5	0	0	0	6
1957-58			4	0	0	0	0
1959-60			6	1	0	1	10
1960-61			11	0	2	2	18
1964-65			4	0	1	1	2
1965-66			4	0	0	0	0
9 yrs.		N Totals:	52	1	4	5	42

Traded to **Detroit** by Boston with Gilles Boisvert, Real Chevrefils, Norm Corcoran and Ed Sandford for Marcel Bonin, Lorne Davis, Terry Sawchuk, and Vic Stasiuk, June, 1955. Drafted by **Boston** from Detroit, June, 1962. Traded to **Detroit** by Boston for Gerry Odrowski, Oct. 10, 1963.

Eddy Godin

GODIN, JOSEPH ALAIN EDDY 5'10", 187 lbs.
B. Mar. 29, 1957, Donnacona, Que. Right Wing, Shoots L

YEAR	TEAM & LEAGUE		GP	G	A	PTS	PIM
1977-78	WASH	N	18	3	3	6	6
1978-79			9	0	3	3	6
2 yrs.		N Totals:	27	3	6	9	12

Claimed by **Washington** as fill in Expansion Draft, June 13, 1979.

Sammy Godin

GODIN, HOGOMER GABRIEL 5'9½", 156 lbs.
B. Sept. 20, 1909, Rockland, Ont. Right Wing, Shoots R

YEAR	TEAM & LEAGUE		GP	G	A	PTS	PIM
1927-28	OTTA	N	24	0	0	0	0
1928-29			23	2	1	3	21
1933-34	MONT	N	36	2	2	4	15
3 yrs.		N Totals:	83	4	3	7	36

Peter Goegan

GOEGAN, PETER JOHN 6'1", 200 lbs.
B. Mar. 6, 1934, Fort William, Ont. Defense, Shoots L

YEAR	TEAM & LEAGUE		GP	G	A	PTS	PIM
1957-58	DET	N	14	0	2	2	28
1958-59			67	1	11	12	109
1959-60			21	3	0	3	6
1960-61			67	5	29	34	48
1961-62			39	5	5	10	24
	NYR	N	7	0	2	2	6
	2 team total		46	5	7	12	30
1962-63	DET	N	62	1	8	9	48
1963-64			12	0	0	0	8
1964-65			4	1	0	1	2
1965-66			13	0	2	2	14
1966-67			31	2	6	8	12
1967-68	MINN	N	45	1	2	3	30

Peter Goegan continued

YEAR	TEAM & LEAGUE		GP	G	A	PTS	PIM
11 yrs.		N Totals:	382	19	67	86	335
PLAYOFFS							
1957-58	DET	N	4	0	0	0	18
1959-60			6	1	0	1	13
1960-61			11	0	1	1	18
1962-63			11	0	2	2	12
1965-66			1	0	0	0	0
5 yrs.		N Totals:	33	1	3	4	61

Traded to **N.Y. Rangers** for Noel Price, Feb. 16, 1962. Traded to **Detroit** by N.Y. Rangers for Noel Price, Oct. 8, 1962. Drafted by **Minnesota** from Detroit in Expansion Draft, June 6, 1967.

Bob Goldham

GOLDHAM, ROBERT JOHN 6'1", 195 lbs.
B. May 12, 1922, Georgetown, Ont. Defense, Shoots R

YEAR	TEAM & LEAGUE		GP	G	A	PTS	PIM
1941-42	TOR	N	19	4	7	11	25
1945-46			49	7	14	21	44
1946-47			11	1	1	2	10
1947-48	CHI	N	38	2	9	11	38
1948-49			60	1	10	11	43
1949-50			67	2	10	12	57
1950-51	DET	N	61	5	8	13	31
1951-52			69	0	14	14	24
1952-53			70	1	13	14	32
1953-54			69	1	15	16	50
1954-55			69	1	16	17	14
1955-56			68	3	16	19	32
12 yrs.		N Totals:	650	28	133	161	400
PLAYOFFS							
1941-42*	TOR	N	13	2	2	4	31
1950-51	DET	N	6	0	1	1	0
1951-52*			8	0	1	1	8
1952-53			6	1	1	2	2
1953-54*			12	0	2	2	2
1954-55*			11	0	4	4	4
1955-56			10	0	3	3	4
7 yrs.		N Totals:	66	3	14	17	51

Traded to **Detroit** by Chicago with Jim Henry, Gaye Stewart and Metro Prystai for Harry Lumley, Jack Stewart, Al Dewsbury, Don Morrison and Pete Babando, July 13, 1950.

Bill Goldsworthy

GOLDSWORTHY, WILLIAM ALFRED 6', 190 lbs.
B. Aug. 24, 1944, Kitchener, Ont. Right Wing, Shoots R

YEAR	TEAM & LEAGUE		GP	G	A	PTS	PIM
1964-65	BOS	N	2	0	0	0	0
1965-66			13	3	1	4	6
1966-67			18	3	5	8	21
1967-68	MINN	N	68	14	19	33	68
1968-69			68	14	10	24	110
1969-70			75	36	29	65	89
1970-71			77	34	31	65	85
1971-72			78	31	31	62	59
1972-73			75	27	33	60	97
1973-74			74	48	26	74	73
1974-75			71	37	35	72	77
1975-76			68	24	22	46	47
1976-77			16	2	3	5	6
	NYR	N	61	10	12	22	43
	2 team total		77	12	15	27	49
1977-78			7	0	1	1	12
	IND	W	32	8	10	18	10
	2 team total		39	8	11	19	22
1978-79	EDM	W	17	4	2	6	14
15 yrs.		N Totals:	771	283	258	541	793
		W Totals:	49	12	12	24	24
PLAYOFFS							
1967-68	MINN	N	14	8	7	15	12
1969-70			6	4	3	7	6
1970-71			7	2	4	6	6
1971-72			7	2	3	5	6
1972-73			6	2	2	4	0
1978-79	EDM	W	4	1	1	2	11
6 yrs.		N Totals:	40	18	19	37	30
		W Totals:	4	1	1	2	11

Drafted by **Minnesota** from Boston in Expansion Draft, June 6, 1967. Traded to **N.Y. Rangers** by Minnesota for Bill Fairbairn and Nick Beverley, Nov. 11, 1976.

Leroy Goldsworthy

GOLDSWORTHY, LEROY D. 6', 190 lbs.
B. Oct. 18, 1908, Two Harbors, Minn. Right Wing, Shoots L

YEAR	TEAM & LEAGUE		GP	G	A	PTS	PIM
1929-30	NYR	N	44	4	1	5	16
1930-31	DET	N	13	1	0	1	2
1932-33			26	3	6	9	6
1933-34	CHI	N	28	3	3	6	0
1934-35			7	0	0	0	2
	MONT	N	33	20	9	29	13
	2 team total		40	20	9	29	15
1935-36			47	15	11	26	8
1936-37	BOS	N	47	8	6	14	8
1937-38			45	9	10	19	14
1938-39	NYA	N	47	3	11	14	10
9 yrs.		N Totals:	337	66	57	123	79

PLAYOFFS

YEAR	TEAM & LEAGUE		GP	G	A	PTS	PIM
1929-30	NYR	N	4	0	0	0	2
1932-33	DET	N	2	0	0	0	0
1933-34*	CHI	N	8	0	0	0	0
1934-35	MONT	N	2	1	0	1	0
1936-37	BOS	N	3	0	0	0	0
1937-38			3	0	0	0	2
6 yrs.		N Totals:	22	1	0	1	4

Bill Goldthorpe

GOLDTHORPE, WILLIAM 5'11", 173 lbs.
B. June 20, 1953, Thunder Bay, Ont. Left Wing, Shoots L

YEAR	TEAM & LEAGUE		GP	G	A	PTS	PIM
1974-75	M-B	W	7	0	0	0	26
1975-76	SD	W	14	1	0	1	30
	D-O	W	12	0	0	0	31
	2 team total		26	1	0	1	61
2 yrs.		W Totals:	33	1	0	1	87

PLAYOFFS

YEAR	TEAM & LEAGUE		GP	G	A	PTS	PIM
1973-74	MINN	W	3	0	0	0	25

Glenn Goldup

GOLDUP, GLENN MICHAEL 6', 190 lbs.
B. Apr. 26, 1953, St. Catharines, Ont. Right Wing, Shoots L

YEAR	TEAM & LEAGUE		GP	G	A	PTS	PIM
1973-74	MONT	N	6	0	0	0	0
1974-75			9	0	1	1	2
1975-76			3	0	0	0	2
1976-77	LA	N	28	7	6	13	29
1977-78			66	14	18	32	66
1978-79			73	15	22	37	89
1979-80			55	10	11	21	78
1980-81			49	6	9	15	35
1981-82			2	0	0	0	0
9 yrs.		N Totals:	291	52	67	119	301

PLAYOFFS

YEAR	TEAM & LEAGUE		GP	G	A	PTS	PIM
1976-77	LA	N	8	2	2	4	2
1977-78			2	1	0	1	11
1978-79			2	0	1	1	9
1979-80			4	1	0	1	0
4 yrs.		N Totals:	16	4	3	7	22

Traded to **Los Angeles** by Montreal with Montreal's third choice in 1978 Amateur Draft (later transferred to Detroit, Doug Derkson) for Los Angeles' third choice in 1977 (Moe Robinson) and first choice (Danny Geoffrion) in 1978 Amateur Drafts, June 12, 1976.

Hank Goldup

GOLDUP, HENRY G. 5'11", 175 lbs.
B. Oct. 29, 1918, Kingston, Ont. Left Wing, Shoots L

YEAR	TEAM & LEAGUE		GP	G	A	PTS	PIM
1940-41	TOR	N	26	10	5	15	9
1941-42			44	12	18	30	13
1942-43			8	1	7	8	4
	NYR	N	36	11	20	31	33
	2 team total		44	12	27	39	37
1944-45			48	17	25	42	25
1945-46			19	6	1	7	11
5 yrs.		N Totals:	181	57	76	133	95

Hank Goldup continued

PLAYOFFS

YEAR	TEAM & LEAGUE		GP	G	A	PTS	PIM
1939-40	TOR	N	10	5	1	6	4
1940-41			7	0	0	0	0
1941-42*			9	0	0	0	2
3 yrs.		N Totals:	26	5	1	6	6

Frank Golembrosky

GOLEMBROSKY, FRANK ALEXANDER 6', 190 lbs.
B. May 3, 1945, Calgary, Alta. Right Wing, Shoots R

YEAR	TEAM & LEAGUE		GP	G	A	PTS	PIM
1972-73	PHI	W	8	0	0	0	0
	QUE	W	52	8	12	20	44
	2 team total		60	8	12	20	44

Bill Gooden

GOODEN, WILLIAM FRANCIS CHARLES 5'9", 175 lbs.
B. Sept. 8, 1924, Winnipeg, Man. Left Wing, Shoots L

YEAR	TEAM & LEAGUE		GP	G	A	PTS	PIM
1942-43	NYR	N	12	0	3	3	0
1943-44			41	9	8	17	15
2 yrs.		N Totals:	53	9	11	20	15

Larry Goodenough

GOODENOUGH, LARRY J 6', 195 lbs.
B. Jan. 19, 1953, Toronto, Ont. Defense, Shoots R

YEAR	TEAM & LEAGUE		GP	G	A	PTS	PIM
1974-75	PHI	N	20	3	9	12	0
1975-76			77	8	34	42	83
1976-77			32	4	13	17	21
	VAN	N	30	2	4	6	27
	2 team total		62	6	17	23	48
1977-78			42	1	6	7	28
1978-79			36	4	9	13	18
1979-80			5	0	2	2	2
6 yrs.		N Totals:	242	22	77	99	179

PLAYOFFS

YEAR	TEAM & LEAGUE		GP	G	A	PTS	PIM
1974-75*	PHI	N	5	0	4	4	2
1975-76			16	3	11	14	6
1978-79	VAN	N	1	0	0	0	2
3 yrs.		N Totals:	22	3	15	18	10

Traded to **Vancouver** by Philadelphia with Jack McIlhargey for Bob Dailey, Jan. 20, 1977. Signed as free agent with **Los Angeles** Dec. 5, 1980. Traded to **Chicago** with a third round choice in the 1984 Amateur Draft by Los Angeles for Terry Ruskowski, Oct. 24, 1982.

Ebbie Goodfellow

GOODFELLOW, EBENEZER 6', 180 lbs.
B. Apr. 9, 1907, Ottawa, Ont. Center, Shoots L
Won Hart Trophy, 1939-40
Hall of Fame, 1963

YEAR	TEAM & LEAGUE		GP	G	A	PTS	PIM
1929-30	DET	N	44	17	17	34	54
1930-31			44	25	23	48	32
1931-32			48	14	16	30	56
1932-33			40	12	8	20	47
1933-34			48	13	13	26	45
1934-35			48	12	24	36	44
1935-36			48	5	18	23	69
1936-37			48	9	16	25	43
1937-38			29	0	7	7	18
1938-39			48	8	8	16	36
1939-40			43	11	17	28	31
1940-41			47	5	17	22	35
1941-42			8	2	2	4	2
1942-43			11	1	4	5	4
14 yrs.		N Totals:	554	134	190	324	516

PLAYOFFS

YEAR	TEAM & LEAGUE		GP	G	A	PTS	PIM
1931-32	DET	N	2	0	0	0	0
1932-33			4	1	0	1	11
1933-34			9	4	3	7	12
1935-36*			7	1	0	1	4
1936-37*			9	2	2	4	12
1938-39			6	0	0	0	8
1939-40			5	0	2	2	9
1940-41			3	0	1	1	9

Ebbie Goodfellow continued

YEAR	TEAM	LEAGUE	GP	G	A	PTS	PIM
8 yrs.		N Totals:	45	8	8	16	65

Don Gordon

GORDON, DONALD JAMES (Gordo) 5'11", 184 lbs.
B. Apr. 17, 1948, Timmins, Ont. Right Wing, Shoots R

YEAR	TEAM	LEAGUE	GP	G	A	PTS	PIM
1973-74	LA	W	29	8	6	14	24
	CHI	W	23	5	4	9	9
	2 team total		52	13	10	23	33
1974-75			42	4	5	9	10
2 yrs.		W Totals:	94	17	15	32	43
PLAYOFFS							
1973-74	CHI	W	18	4	8	12	4

Fred Gordon

GORDON, FREDERICK
B. Unknown Forward

YEAR	TEAM	LEAGUE	GP	G	A	PTS	PIM
1926-27	DET	N	36	5	5	10	28
1927-28	BOS	N	41	3	2	5	40
2 yrs.		N Totals:	77	8	7	15	68
PLAYOFFS							
1927-28	BOS	N	1	0	0	0	0

Jackie Gordon

GORDON, JOHN 5'8½", 154 lbs.
B. Mar. 3, 1928, Winnipeg, Man. Center, Shoots R

YEAR	TEAM	LEAGUE	GP	G	A	PTS	PIM
1948-49	NYR	N	31	3	9	12	0
1949-50			1	0	0	0	0
1950-51			4	0	1	1	0
3 yrs.		N Totals:	36	3	10	13	0
PLAYOFFS							
1949-50	NYR	N	9	1	1	2	7

Tom Gorence

GORENCE, THOMAS 6', 180 lbs.
B. Mar. 11, 1957, St. Paul, Minn. Right Wing, Shoots R

YEAR	TEAM	LEAGUE	GP	G	A	PTS	PIM
1978-79	PHI	N	42	13	6	19	10
1979-80			51	8	13	21	15
1980-81			79	24	18	42	46
1981-82			66	5	8	13	8
1982-83			53	7	7	14	10
5 yrs.		N Totals:	291	57	52	109	89
PLAYOFFS							
1978-79	PHI	N	7	3	1	4	0
1979-80			15	3	3	6	18
1980-81			12	3	2	5	29
1981-82			3	0	0	0	0
4 yrs.		N Totals:	37	9	6	15	47

Traded to **Hartford** by Philadelphia for future considerations, Sept. 9, 1983.

Butch Goring

GORING, ROBERT THOMAS 5'9", 166 lbs.
B. Oct. 22, 1949, St. Boniface, Man. Center, Shoots L
Won Lady Byng Trophy, 1977-78
Won Conn Smythe Trophy, 1980-81
Won Masterton Trophy, 1977-78

YEAR	TEAM	LEAGUE	GP	G	A	PTS	PIM
1969-70	LA	N	59	13	23	36	8
1970-71			19	2	5	7	2
1971-72			74	21	29	50	2
1972-73			67	28	31	59	2
1973-74			70	28	33	61	2
1974-75			60	27	33	60	6
1975-76			80	33	40	73	8
1976-77			78	30	55	85	6
1977-78			80	37	36	73	2
1978-79			80	36	51	87	16
1979-80			69	20	48	68	12
	NYI	N	12	6	5	11	2
	2 team total		81	26	53	79	14

Butch Goring continued

YEAR	TEAM	LEAGUE	GP	G	A	PTS	PIM
1980-81			78	23	37	60	0
1981-82			67	15	17	32	10
1982-83			75	19	20	39	8
14 yrs.		N Totals:	968	338	463	801	86
PLAYOFFS							
1973-74	LA	N	5	0	1	1	0
1974-75			3	0	0	0	0
1975-76			9	2	3	5	4
1976-77			9	7	5	12	0
1977-78			2	0	0	0	2
1978-79			2	0	0	0	0
1979-80*	NYI	N	21	7	12	19	2
1980-81*			18	10	10	20	6
1981-82*			19	6	5	11	12
1982-83*			20	4	8	12	4
10 yrs.		N Totals:	108	36	44	80	30

Traded to **N.Y. Islanders** by Los Angeles for Billy Harris and Dave Lewis, Mar. 10, 1980.

Dave Gorman

GORMAN, DAVID PETER 5'11", 185 lbs.
B. Apr. 8, 1955, Oshawa, Ont. Right Wing, Shoots R

YEAR	TEAM	LEAGUE	GP	G	A	PTS	PIM
1974-75	PHOE	W	13	3	5	8	10
1975-76			67	11	20	31	28
1976-77			5	0	0	0	0
	BIRM	W	52	9	13	22	38
	2 team total		57	9	13	22	38
1977-78			63	19	21	40	93
1978-79			60	14	24	38	18
1979-80	ATL	N	3	0	0	0	0
6 yrs.		N Totals:	3	0	0	0	0
		W Totals:	260	56	83	139	187
PLAYOFFS							
1975-76	PHOE	W	5	0	2	2	24
1977-78	BIRM	W	4	1	1	2	0
2 yrs.		W Totals:	9	1	3	4	24

Signed as free agent by **Buffalo** June 30, 1981.

Ed Gorman

GORMAN, EDWIN
B. Unknown Defense, Shoots L

YEAR	TEAM	LEAGUE	GP	G	A	PTS	PIM
1924-25	OTTA	N	30	11	3	14	49
1925-26			23	2	1	3	12
1926-27			41	1	0	1	17
1927-28	TOR	N	19	0	1	1	30
4 yrs.		N Totals:	113	14	5	19	108
PLAYOFFS							
1925-26	OTTA	N	2	0	0	0	2
1926-27*			6	0	0	0	0
2 yrs.		N Totals:	8	0	0	0	2

Benoit Gosselin

GOSSELIN, BENOIT 5'11", 190 lbs.
B. July 19, 1957, Montreal, Que. Left Wing, Shoots L

YEAR	TEAM	LEAGUE	GP	G	A	PTS	PIM
1977-78	NYR	N	7	0	0	0	33

Signed as free agent by **Winnipeg** Sept. 25, 1979.

Rich Gosselin

GOSSELIN, RICHARD
Center

YEAR	TEAM	LEAGUE	GP	G	A	PTS	PIM
1978-79	WINN	W	3	0	0	0	0

Johnny Gottselig

GOTTSELIG, JOHN 5'11", 158 lbs.
B. June 24, 1905, Odessa, Russia Left Wing, Shoots L

YEAR	TEAM	LEAGUE	GP	G	A	PTS	PIM
1928-29	CHI	N	42	5	3	8	26
1929-30			39	21	4	25	28
1930-31			42	20	12	32	14
1931-32			43	14	15	29	50
1932-33			42	11	11	22	6

Johnny Gottselig continued

YEAR	TEAM & LEAGUE		GP	G	A	PTS	PIM
1933-34			48	16	14	30	4
1934-35			48	19	18	37	16
1935-36			40	14	15	29	4
1936-37			47	9	21	30	10
1937-38			48	13	19	32	22
1938-39			48	16	23	39	15
1939-40			38	8	15	23	7
1940-41			8	1	4	5	5
1942-43			10	2	6	8	12
1943-44			45	8	15	23	6
1944-45			1	0	0	0	0
16 yrs.		N Totals:	589	177	195	372	225
PLAYOFFS							
1929-30	CHI	N	2	0	0	0	4
1930-31			9	3	3	6	4
1931-32			2	0	0	0	2
1933-34*			8	4	3	7	4
1934-35			2	0	0	0	0
1935-36			2	0	2	2	0
1937-38*			10	5	3	8	4
1939-40			2	0	1	1	0
1943-44			6	1	1	2	2
9 yrs.		N Totals:	43	13	13	26	20

Bob Gould

GOULD, ROBERT 5'11", 195 lbs.
B. Sept. 2, 1957, Petrolia, Ont. Right Wing, Shoots R

YEAR	TEAM & LEAGUE		GP	G	A	PTS	PIM
1979-80	ATL	N	1	0	0	0	0
1980-81	CALG	N	3	0	0	0	0
1981-82			16	3	0	3	4
	WASH	N	60	18	13	31	69
	2 team total		76	21	13	34	73
1982-83			80	22	18	40	43
4 yrs.		N Totals:	160	43	31	74	116
PLAYOFFS							
1980-81	CALG	N	11	3	1	4	4
1982-83	WASH	N	4	5	0	5	4
2 yrs.		N Totals:	15	8	1	9	8

Traded to **Washington** by Calgary along with Randy Holt for Pat Ribble and Washington's second round choice in 1983 Entry Draft, Nov. 25, 1981.

John Gould

GOULD, JOHN MILTON 5'11", 197 lbs.
B. Apr. 11, 1949, Beeton, Ont. Right Wing, Shoots L

YEAR	TEAM & LEAGUE		GP	G	A	PTS	PIM
1971-72	BUF	N	2	1	0	1	0
1972-73			8	0	1	1	0
1973-74			30	4	2	6	2
	VAN	N	45	9	10	19	8
	2 team total		75	13	12	25	10
1974-75			78	34	31	65	27
1975-76			70	32	27	59	16
1976-77			25	7	8	15	2
	ATL	N	54	8	15	23	8
	2 team total		79	15	23	38	10
1977-78			75	19	28	47	21
1978-79			61	8	7	15	18
1979-80	BUF	N	52	9	9	18	11
9 yrs.		N Totals:	500	131	138	269	113
PLAYOFFS							
1974-75	VAN	N	5	2	2	4	0
1975-76			2	1	0	1	0
1976-77	ATL	N	3	0	0	0	2
1977-78			2	0	0	0	2
1978-79			2	0	0	0	0
5 yrs.		N Totals:	14	3	2	5	4

Traded to **Vancouver** by Buffalo with Tracy Pratt for Jerry Korab, Dec. 27, 1973. Traded to **Atlanta** by Vancouver with Los Angeles' second round choice (Brian Hill), Vancouver property via earlier deal, in 1977 Amateur Draft for Hilliard Graves and Larry Carriere, Dec. 2, 1976. Claimed by **Edmonton** from Atlanta in Expansion Draft, June 13, 1979. Traded to **Buffalo** by Edmonton for Alex Tidey, Nov. 13, 1979.

Larry Gould

GOULD, LARRY STEPHEN 5'9", 170 lbs.
B. Aug. 16, 1952, Alliston, Ont. Left Wing, Shoots L

YEAR	TEAM & LEAGUE		GP	G	A	PTS	PIM
1973-74	VAN	N	2	0	0	0	0

Michel Goulet

GOULET, MICHEL 6'1", 195 lbs.
B. Apr. 21, 1960, Peribonqua, Que. Right Wing, Shoots R

YEAR	TEAM & LEAGUE		GP	G	A	PTS	PIM
1978-79	BIRM	W	78	28	30	58	64
1979-80	QUE	N	77	22	32	54	48
1980-81			76	32	39	71	45
1981-82			80	42	42	84	48
1982-83			80	57	48	105	51
5 yrs.		N Totals:	313	153	161	314	192
		W Totals:	78	28	30	58	64
PLAYOFFS							
1980-81	QUE	N	4	3	4	7	7
1981-82			16	8	5	13	6
1982-83			4	0	0	0	6
3 yrs.		N Totals:	24	11	9	20	19

Red Goupille

GOUPILLE, CLIFFORD 6', 190 lbs.
B. Sept. 2, 1915, Trois Rivieres, Que. Defense, Shoots R

YEAR	TEAM & LEAGUE		GP	G	A	PTS	PIM
1935-36	MONT	N	4	0	0	0	0
1936-37			4	0	0	0	0
1937-38			47	4	5	9	44
1938-39			18	0	2	2	24
1939-40			48	2	10	12	48
1940-41			48	3	6	9	81
1941-42			47	1	5	6	51
1942-43			6	2	0	2	8
8 yrs.		N Totals:	222	12	28	40	256
PLAYOFFS							
1937-38	MONT	N	3	2	0	2	4
1940-41			2	0	0	0	0
1941-42			3	0	0	0	2
3 yrs.		N Totals:	8	2	0	2	6

Gerry Goyer

GOYER, GERALD FRANCIS 6'1", 196 lbs.
B. Oct. 20, 1936, Belleville, Ont. Center, Shoots L

YEAR	TEAM & LEAGUE		GP	G	A	PTS	PIM
1967-68	CHI	N	40	1	2	3	4
PLAYOFFS							
1967-68	CHI	N	3	0	0	0	2

Phil Goyette

GOYETTE, JOSEPH GEORGES PHILIPE 5'11", 170 lbs.
B. Oct. 31, 1933, Lachine, Que. Center, Shoots L
Won Lady Byng Trophy, 1969-70

YEAR	TEAM & LEAGUE		GP	G	A	PTS	PIM
1956-57	MONT	N	14	3	4	7	0
1957-58			70	9	37	46	8
1958-59			63	10	18	28	8
1959-60			65	21	22	43	4
1960-61			62	7	4	11	4
1961-62			69	7	27	34	18
1962-63			32	5	8	13	2
1963-64	NYR	N	67	24	41	65	15
1964-65			52	12	34	46	6
1965-66			60	11	31	42	6
1966-67			70	12	49	61	6
1967-68			73	25	40	65	10
1968-69			67	13	32	45	8
1969-70	STL	N	72	29	49	78	16
1970-71	BUF	N	59	15	46	61	6
1971-72			37	3	21	24	14
	NYR	N	8	1	4	5	0
	2 team total		45	4	25	29	14
16 yrs.		N Totals:	940	207	467	674	131
PLAYOFFS							
1956-57*	MONT	N	10	2	1	3	4

Phil Goyette continued

YEAR	TEAM & LEAGUE		GP	G	A	PTS	PIM
1957-58*			10	4	1	5	4
1958-59*			10	0	4	4	0
1959-60*			8	2	1	3	4
1960-61			6	3	3	6	0
1961-62			6	1	4	5	2
1962-63			2	0	0	0	0
1966-67	**NYR**	**N**	4	1	0	1	0
1967-68			6	0	1	1	4
1968-69			3	0	0	0	0
1969-70	**STL**	**N**	16	3	11	14	6
1971-72	**NYR**	**N**	13	1	3	4	2
12 yrs.		**N Totals:**	94	17	29	46	26

Traded to **N.Y. Rangers** by Montreal with Don Marshall and Jacques Plante for Dave Balon, Leon Rochefort, Len Ronson, and Gump Worsley, June 4, 1963. Traded to **St. Louis** by N.Y. Rangers for Andre Dupont, June 10, 1969. Drafted by **Buffalo** from St. Louis in Expansion Draft, June 10, 1970.

Tony Graboski

GRABOSKI, ANTHONY RUDEL 5'10", 170 lbs.
B. May 9, 1916, Timmins, Ont. Forward

YEAR	TEAM & LEAGUE		GP	G	A	PTS	PIM
1940-41	**MONT**	**N**	34	4	3	7	6
1941-42			23	2	5	7	8
1942-43			9	0	2	2	4
3 yrs.		**N Totals:**	66	6	10	16	18
PLAYOFFS							
1940-41	**MONT**	**N**	2	0	0	0	0

Bob Gracie

GRACIE, ROBERT J. 5'8½", 155 lbs.
B. Nov. 8, 1910, North Bay, Ont. Left Wing, Shoots L

YEAR	TEAM & LEAGUE		GP	G	A	PTS	PIM
1930-31	**TOR**	**N**	8	4	2	6	4
1931-32			48	13	8	21	29
1932-33			48	9	13	22	27
1933-34	**BOS**	**N**	24	2	6	8	16
	NYA	**N**	24	4	6	10	4
	2 team total		48	6	12	18	20
1934-35			14	2	1	3	4
	MON(M)	**N**	32	10	8	18	11
	2 team total		46	12	9	21	15
1935-36			46	11	14	25	31
1936-37			48	11	25	36	18
1937-38			48	12	19	31	32
1938-39	**MONT**	**N**	7	0	1	1	4
	CHI	**N**	31	4	6	10	27
	2 team total		38	4	7	11	31
9 yrs.		**N Totals:**	378	82	109	191	207
PLAYOFFS							
1930-31	**TOR**	**N**	2	0	0	0	0
1931-32*			7	3	1	4	0
1932-33			9	0	1	1	0
1934-35*	**MON(M)**	**N**	7	0	2	2	2
1935-36			3	0	1	1	0
1936-37			5	1	2	3	2
6 yrs.		**N Totals:**	33	4	7	11	4

Thomas Gradin

GRADIN, THOMAS 5'11", 176 lbs.
B. Feb. 18, 1956, Solleftea, Sweden Center, Shoots R

YEAR	TEAM & LEAGUE		GP	G	A	PTS	PIM
1978-79	**VAN**	**N**	76	20	31	51	22
1979-80			80	30	45	75	22
1980-81			79	21	48	69	34
1981-82			76	37	49	86	32
1982-83			80	32	54	86	61
5 yrs.		**N Totals:**	391	140	227	367	171
PLAYOFFS							
1978-79	**VAN**	**N**	3	4	1	5	4
1979-80			4	0	2	2	0
1980-81			3	1	3	4	0
1981-82			17	9	10	19	10
1982-83			4	1	3	4	2
5 yrs.		**N Totals:**	31	15	19	34	16

Rights traded to **Vancouver** by Chicago for Vancouver's second round choice (Steve Ludzik) in the 1980 Entry Draft, June 15, 1978.

Leth Graham

GRAHAM, LETH
B. Unknown Left Wing

YEAR	TEAM & LEAGUE		GP	G	A	PTS	PIM
1920-21	**OTTA**	**N**	13	0	0	0	0
1921-22			2	2	0	2	0
1922-23	**HAMIL**	**N**	4	1	0	1	0
1923-24	**OTTA**	**N**	3	0	0	0	0
1924-25			3	0	0	0	0
1925-26			10	0	0	0	0
6 yrs.		**N Totals:**	35	3	0	3	0
PLAYOFFS							
1920-21*	**OTTA**	**N**	1	0	0	0	0

Pat Graham

GRAHAM, PATRICK THOMAS 6'1", 190 lbs.
B. May 25, 1961, Toronto, Ont. Left Wing, Shoots L

YEAR	TEAM & LEAGUE		GP	G	A	PTS	PIM
1981-82	**PITT**	**N**	42	6	8	14	55
1982-83			20	1	5	6	16
2 yrs.		**N Totals:**	62	7	13	20	71
PLAYOFFS							
1981-82	**PITT**	**N**	4	0	0	0	2

Rod Graham

GRAHAM, RODNEY DOUGLAS 5'11", 185 lbs.
B. Aug. 19, 1946, London, Ont. Left Wing, Shoots L

YEAR	TEAM & LEAGUE		GP	G	A	PTS	PIM
1974-75	**BOS**	**N**	14	2	1	3	7

Ted Graham

GRAHAM, EDWARD DIXON 5'10", 173 lbs.
B. June 30, 1906, Owen Sound, Ont. Shoots L

YEAR	TEAM & LEAGUE		GP	G	A	PTS	PIM
1927-28	**CHI**	**N**	16	1	0	1	8
1929-30			26	1	2	3	23
1930-31			42	0	7	7	38
1931-32			48	0	3	3	40
1932-33			47	3	8	11	57
1933-34	**MON(M)**	**N**	19	2	1	3	10
	DET	**N**	28	1	0	1	29
	2 team total		47	3	1	4	39
1934-35			24	0	2	2	26
	STL	**N**	13	0	0	0	2
	2 team total		37	0	2	2	28
1935-36	**BOS**	**N**	48	4	1	5	37
1936-37			1	0	0	0	0
	NYA	**N**	31	2	1	3	30
	2 team total		32	2	1	3	30
9 yrs.		**N Totals:**	343	14	25	39	300
PLAYOFFS							
1929-30	**CHI**	**N**	2	0	0	0	8
1930-31			8	0	0	0	14
1931-32			2	0	0	0	2
1933-34	**DET**	**N**	9	3	1	4	8
1935-36	**BOS**	**N**	2	0	0	0	2
5 yrs.		**N Totals:**	23	3	1	4	34

Danny Grant

GRANT, DANIEL FREDERICK 5'10", 188 lbs.
B. Feb. 21, 1946, Fredericton, N.B. Left Wing, Shoots L
Won Calder Trophy, 1968-69

YEAR	TEAM & LEAGUE		GP	G	A	PTS	PIM
1965-66	**MONT**	**N**	1	0	0	0	0
1967-68			22	3	4	7	10
1968-69	**MINN**	**N**	75	34	31	65	46
1969-70			76	29	28	57	23
1970-71			78	34	23	57	46
1971-72			78	18	25	43	18
1972-73			78	32	35	67	12
1973-74			78	29	35	64	16
1974-75	**DET**	**N**	80	50	37	87	28
1975-76			39	10	13	23	20
1976-77			42	2	10	12	4
1977-78			13	2	2	4	0
	LA	**N**	41	10	19	29	2
	2 team total		54	12	21	33	2
1978-79			35	10	11	21	8

Danny Grant continued

YEAR	TEAM & LEAGUE		GP	G	A	PTS	PIM
13 yrs.		N Totals:	736	263	273	536	233
PLAYOFFS							
1967-68*	MONT	N	10	0	3	3	5
1969-70	MINN	N	6	0	2	2	4
1970-71			12	5	5	10	8
1971-72			7	2	1	3	0
1972-73			6	3	1	4	0
1977-78	LA	N	2	0	2	2	2
6 yrs.		N Totals:	43	10	14	24	19

Traded to **Minnesota** by Montreal with Claude Larose for a first round choice (Dave Gardner) in the 1972 Amateur Draft and a player to be named at the end of the 1970-71 season (Marshall Johnston) and cash, June 10, 1968. Traded to **Detroit** by Minnesota for Henry Boucha, Aug. 27, 1974. Traded to **Los Angeles** by Detroit for Montreal's third round choice (Doug Derkson, Los Angeles property via earlier deal) and the rights to Barry Long, Jan. 9, 1978.

Bill Gratton

GRATTON, WILLIAM 6'3", 200 lbs.
B. Brantford, Ont. Left Wing, Shoots L

YEAR	TEAM & LEAGUE		GP	G	A	PTS	PIM
1975-76	CALG	W	6	0	1	1	2

Jean Gratton

GRATTON, JEAN-GUY LIONEL 5'9", 169 lbs.
B. Mar. 8, 1947, St.Ann Des Plaines, Que. Right Wing, Shoots R

YEAR	TEAM & LEAGUE		GP	G	A	PTS	PIM
1972-73	WINN	W	71	15	12	27	37
1973-74			68	12	21	33	13
1974-75			49	4	8	12	2
3 yrs.		W Totals:	188	31	41	72	52
PLAYOFFS							
1972-73	WINN	W	12	1	1	2	4
1973-74			2	0	0	0	0
2 yrs.		W Totals:	14	1	1	2	4

Drafted by **Boston** with Gord Redahl from New York, June 4, 1958. Traded to **Montreal** by Boston for Andre Pronovost, Nov. 27, 1960. Drafted by **N.Y. Rangers** from Montreal, June 14, 1961. Drafted by **Boston** from N.Y. Rangers, June 6, 1962. Put on **Montreal** reserve list from Boston, June 11, 1969. Sold to **Philadelphia** by Montreal, June 12, 1969.

Norm Gratton

GRATTON, NORMAND LIONEL 5'11", 165 lbs.
B. Dec. 22, 1950, LaSalle, Que. Left Wing, Shoots L

YEAR	TEAM & LEAGUE		GP	G	A	PTS	PIM
1971-72	NYR	N	3	0	1	1	0
1972-73	ATL	N	29	3	6	9	12
	BUF	N	21	6	5	11	12
	2 team total		50	9	11	20	24
1973-74			57	6	12	18	16
1974-75			25	3	6	9	2
	MINN	N	34	14	12	26	8
	2 team total		59	17	18	35	10
1975-76			32	7	3	10	14
5 yrs.		N Totals:	201	39	45	84	64
PLAYOFFS							
1972-73	BUF	N	6	0	1	1	2

Drafted by **Atlanta** from N.Y. Rangers in Expansion Draft, June 6, 1972. Traded to **Buffalo** by Atlanta for Butch Deadmarsh, Feb. 14, 1973. Traded to **Minnesota** by Buffalo with Buffalo's third choice in 1976 Amateur Draft for Fred Stanfield, Jan. 27, 1975.

John Gravel

GRAVEL, JOHN
B. Oct. 27, 1943, Montreal, Que. Defense

YEAR	TEAM & LEAGUE		GP	G	A	PTS	PIM
1972-73	PHI	W	8	1	3	4	0

Leo Gravelle

GRAVELLE, JOSEPH GERARD LEO (The Gazelle) 5'8½", 158 lbs.
B. June 10, 1925, Aylmer, Que. Right Wing, Shoots R

YEAR	TEAM & LEAGUE		GP	G	A	PTS	PIM
1946-47	MONT	N	53	16	14	30	12

Leo Gravelle continued

YEAR	TEAM & LEAGUE		GP	G	A	PTS	PIM
1947-48			15	0	0	0	0
1948-49			36	4	6	10	6
1949-50			70	19	10	29	18
1950-51			31	4	2	6	0
	DET	N	18	1	2	3	6
	2 team total		49	5	4	9	6
5 yrs.		N Totals:	223	44	34	78	42
PLAYOFFS							
1946-47	MONT	N	6	2	0	2	2
1948-49			7	2	1	3	0
1949-50			4	0	0	0	0
3 yrs.		N Totals:	17	4	1	5	2

Traded to **Detroit** by Montreal for Bert Olmstead, Dec. 19, 1950.

Hilliard Graves

GRAVES, HILLIARD DONALD 5'11", 175 lbs.
B. Oct. 18, 1950, Saint John, N.B. Right Wing, Shoots R

YEAR	TEAM & LEAGUE		GP	G	A	PTS	PIM
1970-71	CALIF	N	14	0	0	0	0
1972-73			75	27	25	52	34
1973-74			64	11	18	29	48
1974-75	ATL	N	67	10	19	29	30
1975-76			80	19	30	49	16
1976-77			25	8	5	13	17
	VAN	N	54	10	20	30	17
	2 team total		79	18	25	43	34
1977-78			80	21	26	47	18
1978-79			62	11	15	26	14
1979-80	WINN	N	35	1	5	6	15
9 yrs.		N Totals:	556	118	163	281	209
PLAYOFFS							
1975-76	ATL	N	2	0	0	0	0

Traded to **Atlanta** by California for John Stewart, July 18, 1974. Traded to **Vancouver** by Atlanta with Larry Carriere for John Gould and Los Angeles' second round choice (Brian Hill), Vancouver property via earlier deal, in 1977 Amateur Draft, Dec. 2, 1976. Claimed by **Winnipeg** from Vancouver in Expansion Draft, June 13, 1979.

Alex Gray

GRAY, ALEXANDER 5'10", 170 lbs.
B. June 21, 1899, Glasgow, Scotland Right Wing, Shoots R

YEAR	TEAM & LEAGUE		GP	G	A	PTS	PIM
1927-28	NYR	N	43	7	0	7	28
1928-29	TOR	N	7	0	0	0	2
2 yrs.		N Totals:	50	7	0	7	30
PLAYOFFS							
1927-28*	NYR	N	9	1	0	1	0
1928-29	TOR	N	4	0	0	0	0
2 yrs.		N Totals:	13	1	0	1	0

John Gray

GRAY, JOHN GORDON 5'10", 185 lbs.
B. Aug. 13, 1949, Little Current, Ont. Left Wing, Shoots L

YEAR	TEAM & LEAGUE		GP	G	A	PTS	PIM
1974-75	PHOE	W	75	35	33	68	107
1975-76			79	35	45	80	136
1976-77			28	10	10	20	59
	HOUS	W	47	21	20	41	25
	2 team total		75	31	30	61	84
1977-78			77	35	23	58	80
1978-79	WINN	W	57	10	15	25	51
5 yrs.		W Totals:	363	146	146	292	458
PLAYOFFS							
1974-75	PHOE	W	5	2	3	5	12
1975-76			5	1	1	2	7
1976-77	HOUS	W	6	0	1	1	8
1977-78			6	0	3	3	10
1978-79	WINN	W	1	0	0	0	0
5 yrs.		W Totals:	23	3	8	11	37

Terry Gray

GRAY, TERRENCE STANLEY 6', 175 lbs.
B. Mar. 21, 1938, Montreal, Que. Right Wing, Shoots R

YEAR	TEAM & LEAGUE		GP	G	A	PTS	PIM
1961-62	BOS	N	42	8	7	15	15
1963-64	MONT	N	4	0	0	0	6
1967-68	LA	N	65	12	16	28	22
1968-69	STL	N	8	4	0	4	4
1969-70			28	2	5	7	17
5 yrs.		N Totals:	147	26	28	54	64
PLAYOFFS							
1967-68	LA	N	7	0	2	2	10
1968-69	STL	N	11	3	2	5	8
1969-70			16	2	1	3	4
1970-71			1	0	0	0	0
4 yrs.		N Totals:	35	5	5	10	22

Drafted by **Los Angeles** from Detroit in Expansion Draft, June 6, 1967. Traded to **St. Louis** by Los Angeles for Traded to **Montreal** by Chicago with Glen Skov for Ab McDonald, June 7, 1960. Drafted by **Los Angeles** from Detroit in Expansion Draft, June 6, 1967. Traded to **St. Louis** by Los Angeles for Myron Stankiewicz, June 11, 1968.

Green

GREEN
B. Unknown Forward

YEAR	TEAM & LEAGUE		GP	G	A	PTS	PIM
1928-29	DET	N	2	0	0	0	0

Red Green

GREEN, REDVERS
B. Sudbury, Ont. Left Wing

YEAR	TEAM & LEAGUE		GP	G	A	PTS	PIM
1923-24	HAMIL	N	23	11	0	11	20
1924-25			30	19	4	23	63
1925-26	NYA	N	35	13	4	17	42
1926-27			44	10	4	14	53
1927-28			40	6	1	7	67
1928-29	BOS	N	25	0	0	0	16
6 yrs.		N Totals:	197	59	13	72	261

Rick Green

GREEN, RICHARD DOUGLAS 6'3", 207 lbs.
B. Feb. 20, 1956, Belleville, Ont. Defense, Shoots L

YEAR	TEAM & LEAGUE		GP	G	A	PTS	PIM
1976-77	WASH	N	45	3	12	15	16
1977-78			60	5	14	19	67
1978-79			71	8	33	41	62
1979-80			71	4	20	24	52
1980-81			65	8	23	31	91
1981-82			65	3	25	28	93
1982-83	MONT	N	66	2	24	26	58
7 yrs.		N Totals:	443	33	151	184	439
PLAYOFFS							
1982-83	MONT	N	3	0	0	0	2

Traded by Washington with Ryan Walter to **Montreal** for Doug Jarvis, Craig Laughlin, Rod Langway, and Brian Engblom, Sept. 9, 1982.

Ted Green

GREEN, EDWARD JOSEPH (Terrible Ted)
5'10", 200 lbs.
B. Mar. 23, 1940, Eriksdale, Man. Defense, Shoots R

YEAR	TEAM & LEAGUE		GP	G	A	PTS	PIM
1960-61	BOS	N	1	0	0	0	2
1961-62			66	3	8	11	116
1962-63			70	1	11	12	117
1963-64			70	4	10	14	145
1964-65			70	8	27	35	156
1965-66			27	5	13	18	113
1966-67			47	6	10	16	67
1967-68			72	7	36	43	133
1968-69			65	8	38	46	99
1970-71			78	5	37	42	60
1971-72			54	1	16	17	21
1972-73	NE	W	78	16	30	46	47
1973-74			75	7	26	33	42
1974-75			57	6	14	20	29

Ted Green continued

YEAR	TEAM & LEAGUE		GP	G	A	PTS	PIM
1975-76	WINN	W	79	5	23	28	73
1976-77			70	4	21	25	45
1977-78			73	4	22	26	52
1978-79			20	0	2	2	16
18 yrs.		N Totals:	620	48	206	254	1029
		W Totals:	452	42	138	180	304
PLAYOFFS							
1967-68	BOS	N	4	1	1	2	11
1968-69			10	2	7	9	18
1970-71			7	1	0	1	25
1971-72*			10	0	0	0	0
1972-73	NE	W	12	1	5	6	25
1973-74			7	0	4	4	7
1975-76	WINN	W	11	0	2	2	16
1976-77			20	1	3	4	12
1977-78			8	0	2	2	2
9 yrs.		N Totals:	31	4	8	12	54
		W Totals:	58	2	16	18	62

Wilf Green

GREEN, WILFRED THOMAS (Shorty)
B. July 17, 1896, Sudbury, Ont. Right Wing, Shoots R
Hall of Fame, 1962

YEAR	TEAM & LEAGUE		GP	G	A	PTS	PIM
1923-24	HAMIL	N	22	7	2	9	19
1924-25			28	18	1	19	75
1925-26	NYA	N	32	6	4	10	40
1926-27			25	2	1	3	17
4 yrs.		N Totals:	107	33	8	41	151

Randy Gregg

GREGG, RANDOLPH 6'4", 215 lbs.
B. Feb. 19, 1956, Edmonton, Alta. Defense, Shoots L

YEAR	TEAM & LEAGUE		GP	G	A	PTS	PIM
1982-83	EDM	N	80	6	22	28	54
PLAYOFFS							
1981-82	EDM	N	4	0	2	2	12
1982-83			16	2	4	6	13
2 yrs.		N Totals:	20	2	6	8	25

Bruce Greig

GREIG, BRUCE 6'2", 220 lbs.
B. May 9, 1953, High River, Alta. Left Wing, Shoots L

YEAR	TEAM & LEAGUE		GP	G	A	PTS	PIM
1973-74	CALIF	N	1	0	0	0	4
1974-75			8	0	1	1	42
1976-77	CALG	W	7	1	1	2	10
1977-78	CIN	W	32	3	1	4	57
1978-79	IND	W	21	3	7	10	64
5 yrs.		N Totals:	9	0	1	1	46
		W Totals:	60	7	9	16	131

Lucien Grenier

GRENIER, LUCIEN S. J. 5'10", 163 lbs.
B. Nov. 3, 1946, Malartic, Que. Right Wing, Shoots L

YEAR	TEAM & LEAGUE		GP	G	A	PTS	PIM
1969-70	MONT	N	23	2	3	5	2
1970-71	LA	N	68	9	7	16	12
1971-72			59	3	4	7	4
3 yrs.		N Totals:	150	14	14	28	18
PLAYOFFS							
1968-69*	MONT	N	2	0	0	0	0

Traded to **Los Angeles** by Montreal with Larry Mickey and goaltender Jack Norris for Leon Rochefort, Gregg Boddy and and goaltender Wayne Thomas, May 22, 1970. Drafted by **Atlanta** from Los Angeles in Expansion Draft, June 6, 1972.

Richard Grenier

GRENIER, RICHARD 5'11", 170 lbs.
B. Sept. 18, 1952, Montreal, Que. Center, Shoots L

YEAR	TEAM & LEAGUE		GP	G	A	PTS	PIM
1972-73	NYI	N	10	1	1	2	2
1976-77	QUE	W	34	11	9	20	4
2 yrs.		N Totals:	10	1	1	2	2
		W Totals:	34	11	9	20	4

Ron Greschner

GRESCHNER, RONALD S. (Gresh) 6'2", 185 lbs.
B. Dec. 22, 1954, Goodsoil, Sask. Defense, Shoots L

YEAR	TEAM & LEAGUE		GP	G	A	PTS	PIM
1974-75	**NYR**	**N**	70	8	37	45	93
1975-76			77	6	21	27	93
1976-77			80	11	36	47	89
1977-78			78	24	48	72	100
1978-79			60	17	36	53	66
1979-80			76	21	37	58	103
1980-81			74	27	41	68	112
1981-82			29	5	11	16	16
1982-83			10	3	5	8	0
9 yrs.		**N Totals:**	554	122	272	394	672
PLAYOFFS							
1974-75			3	0	1	1	2
1977-78	**NYR**	**N**	3	0	0	0	2
1978-79			18	7	5	12	16
1979-80			9	0	6	6	10
1980-81			14	4	8	12	17
1982-83			8	2	2	4	12
6 yrs.		**N Totals:**	52	13	21	34	57
		W Totals:	3	0	1	1	2

Gary Gresdal

GRESDAL, GARY EDWARD 6', 195 lbs.
B. Kingston, Ont. Left Wing, Shoots L

YEAR	TEAM & LEAGUE		GP	G	A	PTS	PIM
1975-76	**QUE**	**W**	2	0	1	1	5

Wayne Gretzky

GRETZKY, WAYNE (The Great) 5'11", 165 lbs.
B. Jan. 26, 1961, Brantford, Ont. Center, Shoots L
Won Hart Trophy, 1979–80 , 1980–81, 1981–82 , 1982-83
Won Art Ross Trophy, 1980–81, 1981–82 , 1982-83
Won Lady Byng Trophy, 1979-80

YEAR	TEAM & LEAGUE		GP	G	A	PTS	PIM
1978-79	**IND**	**W**	8	3	3	6	0
	EDM	**W**	52	43	61	104	19
	2 team total		60	46	64	110	19
1979-80	**EDM**	**N**	79	51	**86**	**137**	21
1980-81			80	55	**109**	**164**	28
1981-82			80	**92**[1]	**120**	**212**[1]	26
1982-83			80	**71**	**125**[1]	**196**	59
5 yrs.		**N Totals:**	319	269	440	709	134
		W Totals:	60	46	64	110	19
PLAYOFFS							
1978-79	**EDM**	**W**	13	10	10	20	2
1979-80	**EDM**	**N**	3	2	1	3	0
1980-81			9	7	14	21	4
1981-82			5	5	7	12	8
1982-83			16	12	26	38	4
5 yrs.		**N Totals:**	33	26	48	74	16
		W Totals:	13	10	10	20	2

Reclaimed by **Edmonton** as an under-age junior prior to Expansion Draft, June 9, 1979. Claimed as priority selection by **Edmonton** June 9, 1979.

Don Grierson

GRIERSON, DONALD JAMES 6', 185 lbs.
B. June 18, 1947, North Bay, Ont. Right Wing, Shoots R

YEAR	TEAM & LEAGUE		GP	G	A	PTS	PIM
1972-73	**HOUS**	**W**	78	22	22	44	83
1973-74			65	11	18	29	45
2 yrs.		**W Totals:**	143	33	40	73	128
PLAYOFFS							
1973-74	**HOUS**	**W**	14	1	5	6	23

Chris Grigg

GRIGG, CHRISTOPHER (Gouler, Fig) 6'1", 174 lbs.
B. Feb. 2, 1953, Ottawa, Ont. Shoots L

YEAR	TEAM & LEAGUE		GP	G	A	PTS	PIM
1975-76	**D-O**	**W**	2	0	0	0	0

George Grigor

GRIGOR, GEORGE (Shorty)
B. Edinburgh, Scotland Forward

YEAR	TEAM & LEAGUE		GP	G	A	PTS	PIM
1943-44	**CHI**	**N**	2	1	0	1	0
PLAYOFFS							
1943-44	**CHI**	**N**	1	0	0	0	0

John Grisdale

GRISDALE, JOHN RUSSELL 6', 195 lbs.
B. Aug. 23, 1948, Geraldton, Ont. Defense, Shoots R

YEAR	TEAM & LEAGUE		GP	G	A	PTS	PIM
1972-73	**TOR**	**N**	49	1	7	8	76
1974-75			2	0	0	0	4
	VAN	**N**	58	1	12	13	91
	2 team total		60	1	12	13	95
1975-76			38	2	6	8	54
1976-77			20	0	2	2	20
1977-78			42	0	9	9	47
1978-79			41	0	3	3	54
6 yrs.		**N Totals:**	250	4	39	43	346
PLAYOFFS							
1974-75	**VAN**	**N**	5	0	1	1	13
1975-76			2	0	0	0	0
1978-79			3	0	0	0	2
3 yrs.		**N Totals:**	10	0	1	1	15

Traded to **Vancouver** by Toronto with Garry Monahan for Dave Dunn, Oct. 16, 1974.

Lloyd Gronsdahl

GRONSDAHL, LLOYD GILFORD (Gabby) 5'9", 170 lbs.
B. May 10, 1921, Norquay, Sask. Right Wing, Shoots R

YEAR	TEAM & LEAGUE		GP	G	A	PTS	PIM
1941-42	**BOS**	**N**	10	1	2	3	0

Lloyd Gross

GROSS, LLOYD GEORGE 5'8½", 175 lbs.
B. Oct. 15, 1907, Kitchener, Ont. Left Wing, Shoots L

YEAR	TEAM & LEAGUE		GP	G	A	PTS	PIM
1926-27	**TOR**	**N**	16	1	1	2	0
1933-34	**NYA**	**N**	21	7	3	10	10
	BOS	**N**	6	1	0	1	6
	DET	**N**	13	1	1	2	2
	3 team total		40	9	4	13	18
1934-35			6	1	0	1	2
3 yrs.		**N Totals:**	62	11	5	16	20
PLAYOFFS							
1933-34	**DET**	**N**	1	0	0	0	0

Don Grosso

GROSSO, DONALD 5'11½", 170 lbs.
B. Apr. 12, 1915, Saulte Ste. Marie, Ont. Left Wing, Shoots L

YEAR	TEAM & LEAGUE		GP	G	A	PTS	PIM
1939-40	**DET**	**N**	28	2	3	5	11
1940-41			45	8	7	15	14
1941-42			48	23	30	53	13
1942-43			50	15	17	32	10
1943-44			42	16	31	47	13
1944-45			20	6	10	16	6
	CHI	**N**	21	9	6	15	4
	2 team total		41	15	16	31	10
1945-46			47	7	10	17	17
1946-47	**BOS**	**N**	33	0	2	2	2
8 yrs.		**N Totals:**	334	86	116	202	90
PLAYOFFS							
1938-39	**DET**	**N**	5	0	0	0	0
1939-40			5	0	0	0	0
1940-41			9	1	4	5	0
1941-42			12	8	6	14	19
1942-43*			10	4	2	6	10
1943-44			5	1	0	1	0
1945-46	**CHI**	**N**	4	0	0	0	17
7 yrs.		**N Totals:**	50	14	12	26	46

Len Grosvenar

GROSVENAR, LEONARD
B. Ottawa, Ont. — Forward

YEAR	TEAM & LEAGUE		GP	G	A	PTS	PIM
1927-28	**OTTA**	**N**	41	1	2	3	18
1928-29			42	3	2	5	16
1929-30			14	0	3	3	19
1930-31			34	5	4	9	25
1931-32	**NYA**	**N**	12	0	0	0	0
1932-33	**MONT**	**N**	4	0	0	0	0
6 yrs.		**N Totals:**	147	9	11	20	78

PLAYOFFS

YEAR	TEAM & LEAGUE		GP	G	A	PTS	PIM
1927-28	**OTTA**	**N**	2	0	0	0	2
1932-33	**MONT**	**N**	2	0	0	0	0
2 yrs.		**N Totals:**	4	0	0	0	2

Danny Gruen

GRUEN, DANIEL PATRICK — 5'11", 190 lbs.
B. June 26, 1952, Thunder Bay, Ont. — Left Wing, Shoots L

YEAR	TEAM & LEAGUE		GP	G	A	PTS	PIM
1972-73	**DET**	**N**	2	0	0	0	0
1973-74			18	1	3	4	7
1974-75	**M-B**	**W**	34	10	16	26	73
	WINN	**W**	32	9	12	21	21
	2 team total		66	19	28	47	94
1975-76	**CLEVE**	**W**	80	26	24	50	72
1976-77	**MINN**	**W**	34	10	9	19	19
	CALG	**W**	1	1	0	1	0
	COLO	**N**	29	8	10	18	12
	3 team total		64	19	19	38	31
5 yrs.		**N Totals:**	49	9	13	22	19
		W Totals:	181	56	61	117	185

PLAYOFFS

YEAR	TEAM & LEAGUE		GP	G	A	PTS	PIM
1975-76	**CLEVE**	**W**	3	0	1	1	0

Playing rights purchased by **Colorado** from Detroit, Feb. 1, 1977. Signed as free agent by **Detroit** Aug. 17, 1977.

Scott Gruhl

GRUHL, SCOTT KENNETH — 5'11", 185 lbs.
B. Sept. 13, 1959, Port Colborne, Ont. — Left Wing, Shoots L

YEAR	TEAM & LEAGUE		GP	G	A	PTS	PIM
1981-82	**LA**	**N**	7	2	1	3	2
1982-83			7	0	2	2	4
2 yrs.		**N Totals:**	14	2	3	5	6

Signed as free agent by **Los Angeles** Oct. 11, 1979.

Bob Gryp

GRYP, ROBERT DOUGLAS — 6'1", 190 lbs.
B. May 6, 1950, Chatham, Ont. — Left Wing, Shoots L

YEAR	TEAM & LEAGUE		GP	G	A	PTS	PIM
1973-74	**BOS**	**N**	1	0	0	0	0
1974-75	**WASH**	**N**	27	5	8	13	21
1975-76			46	6	5	11	12
3 yrs.		**N Totals:**	74	11	13	24	33

Drafted by **Washington** from Boston in Expansion Draft, June 12, 1974.

Jocelyn Guevremont

GUEVREMONT, JOCELYN MARCEL — 6'2", 200 lbs.
B. Mar. 1, 1951, Montreal, Que. — Defense, Shoots R

YEAR	TEAM & LEAGUE		GP	G	A	PTS	PIM
1971-72	**VAN**	**N**	75	13	38	51	44
1972-73			78	16	26	42	46
1973-74			72	15	24	39	34
1974-75			2	0	0	0	0
	BUF	**N**	64	7	25	32	32
	2 team total		66	7	25	32	32
1975-76			80	12	40	52	57
1976-77			80	9	29	38	46
1977-78			66	7	28	35	46
1978-79			34	3	8	11	8
1979-80	**NYR**	**N**	20	2	5	7	6
9 yrs.		**N Totals:**	571	84	223	307	319

PLAYOFFS

YEAR	TEAM & LEAGUE		GP	G	A	PTS	PIM
1974-75	**BUF**	**N**	17	0	6	6	14

Jocelyn Guevremont continued

YEAR	TEAM & LEAGUE		GP	G	A	PTS	PIM
1975-76			9	0	5	5	2
1976-77			6	3	4	7	0
1977-78			8	1	2	3	2
4 yrs.		**N Totals:**	40	4	17	21	18

Traded to **Buffalo** by Vancouver with Bryan McSheffrey for Gerry Meehan and Mike Robitaille, Oct. 14, 1974. Traded to **N.Y. Rangers** by Buffalo for New York's third round choice (Jacques Cloutier) in the 1979 Entry Draft and third round choice in the 1980 Entry Draft (Sean McKenna), Mar. 12, 1979. Claimed by **N.Y. Rangers** as fill in Expansion Draft, June 13, 1979.

Aldo Guidolin

GUIDOLIN, ALDO — 6', 180 lbs.
B. June 6, 1932, Forks of Credit, Ont. — Defense, Shoots R

YEAR	TEAM & LEAGUE		GP	G	A	PTS	PIM
1952-53	**NYR**	**N**	30	4	4	8	24
1953-54			68	2	6	8	51
1954-55			70	2	5	7	34
1955-56			14	1	0	1	8
4 yrs.		**N Totals:**	182	9	15	24	117

Bep Guidolin

GUIDOLIN, ARMAND — 5'8", 175 lbs.
B. Dec. 9, 1925, Thorold, Ont. — Left Wing, Shoots L

YEAR	TEAM & LEAGUE		GP	G	A	PTS	PIM
1942-43	**BOS**	**N**	42	7	15	22	43
1943-44			47	17	25	42	58
1945-46			50	15	17	32	62
1946-47			56	10	13	23	73
1947-48	**DET**	**N**	58	12	10	22	78
1948-49			4	0	0	0	0
	CHI	**N**	56	4	17	21	116
	2 team total		60	4	17	21	116
1949-50			70	17	34	51	42
1950-51			69	12	22	34	56
1951-52			67	13	18	31	78
9 yrs.		**N Totals:**	519	107	171	278	606

PLAYOFFS

YEAR	TEAM & LEAGUE		GP	G	A	PTS	PIM
1942-43	**BOS**	**N**	9	0	4	4	12
1945-46			10	5	2	7	13
1946-47			3	0	1	1	6
1947-48	**DET**	**N**	2	0	0	0	4
4 yrs.		**N Totals:**	24	5	7	12	35

Bobby Guindon

GUINDON, ROBERT PIERRE — 5'9", 175 lbs.
B. Nov. 19, 1950, Labelle, Que. — Left Wing, Shoots L

YEAR	TEAM & LEAGUE		GP	G	A	PTS	PIM
1972-73	**QUE**	**W**	71	28	28	56	31
1973-74			77	31	39	70	30
1974-75			69	12	18	30	23
1975-76	**WINN**	**W**	39	3	3	6	14
1976-77			69	10	17	27	19
1977-78			77	20	22	42	18
1978-79			71	8	18	26	21
1979-80	**WINN**	**N**	6	0	1	1	0
8 yrs.		**N Totals:**	6	0	1	1	0
		W Totals:	473	112	145	257	156

PLAYOFFS

YEAR	TEAM & LEAGUE		GP	G	A	PTS	PIM
1974-75	**QUE**	**W**	15	7	6	13	10
1975-76	**WINN**	**W**	13	3	3	6	9
1976-77			20	4	4	8	9
1977-78			9	8	5	13	5
1978-79			7	2	1	3	0
5 yrs.		**W Totals:**	64	24	19	43	33

Pierre Guite

GUITE, PIERRE — 6'2", 190 lbs.
B. Apr. 17, 1952, Montreal, Que. — Left Wing, Shoots L

YEAR	TEAM & LEAGUE		GP	G	A	PTS	PIM
1972-73	**QUE**	**W**	65	10	8	18	136
1973-74			72	14	20	34	106
1974-75			22	14	8	22	59
	M-B	**W**	13	5	4	9	11
	2 team total		35	19	12	31	70
1975-76	**CIN**	**W**	52	20	24	44	80
1976-77			27	10	8	18	32
	QUE	**W**	35	2	6	8	67
	2 team total		62	12	14	26	99

YEAR	TEAM & LEAGUE		GP	G	A	PTS	PIM
1977-78			18	4	5	9	15
	EDM	W	60	12	21	33	71
	2 team total		78	16	26	42	86
1978-79			12	1	1	2	8
7 yrs.		W Totals:	376	92	105	197	585
PLAYOFFS							
1976-77	QUE	W	17	5	0	5	9
1977-78	EDM	W	5	1	1	2	20
2 yrs.		W Totals:	22	6	1	7	29

Bud Gulka

GULKA, WALTER Forward

YEAR	TEAM & LEAGUE		GP	G	A	PTS	PIM
1974-75	VAN	W	5	1	0	1	10

Bengt-Ake Gustafsson

GUSTAFSSON, BENGT-AKE 6', 185 lbs.
B. Mar. 23, 1958, Karlskoga, Sweden Right Wing, Shoots L

YEAR	TEAM & LEAGUE		GP	G	A	PTS	PIM
1979-80	WASH	N	80	22	38	60	17
1980-81			72	21	34	55	26
1981-82			70	26	34	60	40
1982-83			67	22	42	64	16
4 yrs.		N Totals:	289	91	148	239	99
PLAYOFFS							
1978-79	EDM	W	2	1	2	3	0
1982-83	WASH	N	4	0	1	1	4
2 yrs.		N Totals:	4	0	1	1	4
		W Totals:	2	1	2	3	0

Reclaimed by **Washington** from Edmonton prior to Expansion Draft, June 9, 1979.

Peter Gustavsson

GUSTAVSSON, PETER 6'1", 188 lbs.
B. Mar. 30, 1958, Bollebydg, Sweden Left Wing, Shoots L

YEAR	TEAM & LEAGUE		GP	G	A	PTS	PIM
1981-82	COLO	N	2	0	0	0	0

Signed as free agent by **Colorado** May 11, 1981.

Derek Haas

HAAS, DEREK 6', 170 lbs.
B. May 1, 1955, Trail, B.C. Left Wing, Shoots L

YEAR	TEAM & LEAGUE		GP	G	A	PTS	PIM
1975-76	CALG	W	30	5	9	14	6
PLAYOFFS							
1975-76	CALG	W	1	0	0	0	0

Marc Habscheid

HABSCHEID, MARC JOSEPH 5'10", 167 lbs.
B. Mar. 1, 1963, Swift Current, Sask. Center, Shoots R

YEAR	TEAM & LEAGUE		GP	G	A	PTS	PIM
1981-82	EDM	N	7	1	3	4	2
1982-83			32	3	10	13	14
2 yrs.		N Totals:	39	4	13	17	16

Lloyd Haddon

HADDON, LLOYD WARD 6', 195 lbs.
B. Aug. 10, 1938, Sarnia, Ont. Defense, Shoots L

YEAR	TEAM & LEAGUE		GP	G	A	PTS	PIM
1959-60	DET	N	8	0	0	0	2
PLAYOFFS							
1959-60	DET	N	1	0	0	0	0

Vic Hadfield

HADFIELD, VICTOR EDWARD 6', 190 lbs.
B. Oct. 4, 1940, Oakville, Ont. Left Wing, Shoots L

YEAR	TEAM & LEAGUE		GP	G	A	PTS	PIM
1961-62	NYR	N	44	3	1	4	22
1962-63			36	5	6	11	32
1963-64			69	14	11	25	**151**
1964-65			70	18	20	38	102
1965-66			67	16	19	35	112
1966-67			69	13	20	33	80
1967-68			59	20	19	39	45
1968-69			73	26	40	66	108
1969-70			71	20	34	54	69

Vic Hadfield continued

YEAR	TEAM & LEAGUE		GP	G	A	PTS	PIM
1970-71			63	22	22	44	38
1971-72			78	50	56	106	142
1972-73			63	28	34	62	60
1973-74			77	27	28	55	75
1974-75	PITT	N	78	31	42	73	72
1975-76			76	30	35	65	46
1976-77			9	0	2	2	0
16 yrs.		N Totals:	1002	323	389	712	1154
PLAYOFFS							
1961-62	NYR	N	4	0	0	0	2
1966-67			4	1	0	1	17
1967-68			6	1	2	3	6
1968-69			4	2	1	3	2
1970-71			13	8	5	13	46
1971-72			16	7	9	16	22
1972-73			9	2	2	4	11
1973-74			6	1	0	1	0
1974-75	PITT	N	9	4	2	6	0
1975-76			3	1	0	1	11
10 yrs.		N Totals:	74	27	21	48	117

Drafted by **N.Y. Rangers** from Chicago, June 14, 1961. Traded to **Pittsburgh** by N.Y. Rangers for Nick Beverley, May 27, 1974.

Jim Haggarty

HAGGARTY, JAMES 5'11", 167 lbs.
B. Apr. 14, 1914, Port Arthur, Ont. Left Wing

YEAR	TEAM & LEAGUE		GP	G	A	PTS	PIM
1941-42	MONT	N	5	1	1	2	0
PLAYOFFS							
1941-42	MONT	N	3	2	1	3	0

Matti Hagman

HAGMAN, MATTI RISTO TAPIO (Hakki) 6'1", 184 lbs.
B. Sept. 21, 1955, Helsinki, Finland Center, Shoots L

YEAR	TEAM & LEAGUE		GP	G	A	PTS	PIM
1976-77	BOS	N	75	11	17	28	0
1977-78			15	4	1	5	6
	QUE	W	53	25	31	56	16
	2 team total		68	29	32	61	22
1980-81	EDM	N	75	20	33	53	16
1981-82			72	21	38	59	18
4 yrs.		N Totals:	237	56	89	145	40
		W Totals:	53	25	31	56	16
PLAYOFFS							
1976-77	BOS	N	9	0	1	1	0
1980-81	EDM	N	9	4	1	5	6
1981-82			3	1	0	1	0
3 yrs.		N Totals:	21	5	2	7	6

Signed as free agent by **Edmonton** Sept. 11, 1980.

Adam Haidy

HAIDY, GORDON ADAM 5'10½", 185 lbs.
B. Apr. 11, 1928, Winnipeg, Man. Right Wing, Shoots R

YEAR	TEAM & LEAGUE		GP	G	A	PTS	PIM
PLAYOFFS							
1949-50*	DET	N	1	0	0	0	0

Bill Hajt

HAJT, WILLIAM ALBERT 6'3", 204 lbs.
B. Nov. 18, 1951, Borden, Sask. Defense, Shoots L

YEAR	TEAM & LEAGUE		GP	G	A	PTS	PIM
1973-74	BUF	N	6	0	2	2	0
1974-75			76	3	26	29	68
1975-76			80	6	21	27	48
1976-77			79	6	20	26	56
1977-78			76	4	18	22	30
1978-79			40	3	8	11	20
1979-80			75	4	12	16	24
1980-81			68	2	19	21	42
1981-82			65	2	9	11	44
1982-83			72	3	12	15	26
10 yrs.		N Totals:	637	33	147	180	358
PLAYOFFS							
1974-75	BUF	N	17	1	4	5	18

Bill Hajt continued

YEAR	TEAM & LEAGUE		GP	G	A	PTS	PIM
1975-76			9	0	1	1	15
1976-77			6	0	1	1	4
1977-78			8	0	0	0	2
1979-80			14	0	5	5	4
1980-81			8	0	2	2	17
1981-82			2	0	0	0	0
1982-83			10	0	0	0	4
8 yrs.		**N Totals:**	74	1	13	14	64

Anders Hakansson

HAKANSSON, ANDERS 6'2", 191 lbs.
B. Apr. 27, 1956, Munfors, Sweden Left Wing, Shoots L

YEAR	TEAM & LEAGUE		GP	G	A	PTS	PIM
1981-82	**MINN**	**N**	72	12	4	16	29
1982-83			5	0	0	0	9
	PITT	**N**	62	9	12	21	26
	2 team total		67	9	12	21	35
2 yrs.		**N Totals:**	139	21	16	37	64

PLAYOFFS

YEAR	TEAM & LEAGUE		GP	G	A	PTS	PIM
1981-82	**MINN**	**N**	3	0	0	0	2

Signed as free agent by **Minnesota** July, 1981. Traded by Minnesota with Ron Meighan to **Pittsburgh** for George Ferguson and Pittsburgh's first round choice in the 1983 Amateur Draft (Brian Lawton), Oct. 28, 1982.

Slim Halderson

HALDERSON, HAROLD 6'3", 200 lbs.
B. Jan. 6, 1900, Winnipeg, Man. Defense, Shoots R

YEAR	TEAM & LEAGUE		GP	G	A	PTS	PIM
1926-27	**DET**	**N**	18	2	0	2	29
	TOR	**N**	26	1	2	3	36
	2 team total		44	3	2	5	65

Larry Hale

HALE, LARRY JAMES 6'1", 180 lbs.
B. Oct. 9, 1941, Summerland, B.C. Defense, Shoots L

YEAR	TEAM & LEAGUE		GP	G	A	PTS	PIM
1968-69	**PHI**	**N**	67	3	16	19	28
1969-70			53	1	9	10	28
1970-71			70	1	11	12	34
1971-72			6	0	1	1	0
1972-73	**HOUS**	**W**	68	4	26	30	65
1973-74			69	2	14	16	39
1974-75			76	2	18	20	40
1975-76			77	2	12	14	30
1976-77			67	0	14	14	18
1977-78			56	2	11	13	22
10 yrs.		**N Totals:**	196	5	37	42	90
		W Totals:	413	12	95	107	214

PLAYOFFS

YEAR	TEAM & LEAGUE		GP	G	A	PTS	PIM
1968-69	**PHI**	**N**	4	0	0	0	10
1970-71			4	0	0	0	2
1972-73	**HOUS**	**W**	10	1	2	3	2
1973-74			14	3	2	5	6
1974-75			13	0	4	4	0
1975-76			17	0	5	5	8
1976-77			11	0	2	2	6
7 yrs.		**N Totals:**	8	0	0	0	12
		W Totals:	65	4	15	19	22

Drafted by **Philadelphia** from Minnesota, June 12, 1968. Drafted by **Atlanta** from Philadelphia in Expansion Draft, June 6, 1972.

Len Haley

HALEY, LEONARD 5'7", 168 lbs.
B. Sept. 15, 1931, Edmonton, Alta. Right Wing, Shoots R

YEAR	TEAM & LEAGUE		GP	G	A	PTS	PIM
1959-60	**DET**	**N**	27	1	2	3	12
1960-61			3	1	0	1	2
2 yrs.		**N Totals:**	30	2	2	4	14

PLAYOFFS

YEAR	TEAM & LEAGUE		GP	G	A	PTS	PIM
1959-60	**DET**	**N**	6	1	3	4	6

Bob Hall

HALL, ROBERT
B. Unknown Forward

YEAR	TEAM & LEAGUE		GP	G	A	PTS	PIM
1925-26	**NYA**	**N**	8	0	0	0	0

Del Hall

HALL, DEL ALLISON 5'10", 170 lbs.
B. May 7, 1949, Peterborough, Ont. Center, Shoots L

YEAR	TEAM & LEAGUE		GP	G	A	PTS	PIM
1971-72	**CALIF**	**N**	1	0	0	0	0
1972-73			6	0	0	0	0
1973-74			2	2	0	2	2
1975-76	**PHOE**	**W**	80	47	44	91	10
1976-77			80	38	41	79	30
1977-78	**CIN**	**W**	0	0	0	0	0
	EDM	**W**	26	4	3	7	4
	2 team total		26	4	3	7	4
6 yrs.		**N Totals:**	9	2	0	2	2
		W Totals:	186	89	88	177	44

PLAYOFFS

YEAR	TEAM & LEAGUE		GP	G	A	PTS	PIM
1975-76	**PHOE**	**W**	5	2	3	5	0

Gary Hall

HALL, GARY WAYNE 5'8", 170 lbs.
B. May 22, 1939, Melita, Man. Left Wing, Shoots L

YEAR	TEAM & LEAGUE		GP	G	A	PTS	PIM
1960-61	**NYR**	**N**	4	0	0	0	0

Joe Hall

HALL, JOSEPH HENRY (Bad Joe)
B. Staffordshire, England Forward, Shoots R
Hall of Fame, 1961

YEAR	TEAM & LEAGUE		GP	G	A	PTS	PIM
1917-18	**MONT**	**N**	20	8	0	8	**60**
1918-19			17	7	1	8	**85**
2 yrs.		**N Totals:**	37	15	1	16	145

PLAYOFFS

YEAR	TEAM & LEAGUE		GP	G	A	PTS	PIM
1917-18	**MONT**	**N**	2	0	2	2	6
1918-19			10	0	0	0	**25**
2 yrs.		**N Totals:**	12	0	2	2	31

Murray Hall

HALL, MURRAY WINSTON 6', 175 lbs.
B. Nov. 24, 1940, Kirkland Lake, Ont. Center, Shoots R

YEAR	TEAM & LEAGUE		GP	G	A	PTS	PIM
1961-62	**CHI**	**N**	2	0	0	0	0
1963-64			23	2	0	2	4
1965-66	**DET**	**N**	1	0	0	0	0
1966-67			12	4	3	7	4
1967-68	**MINN**	**N**	17	2	1	3	10
1970-71	**VAN**	**N**	77	21	38	59	22
1971-72			32	6	6	12	6
1972-73	**HOUS**	**W**	76	28	42	70	84
1973-74			78	30	28	58	25
1974-75			78	18	29	47	28
1975-76			80	20	26	46	18
11 yrs.		**N Totals:**	164	35	48	83	46
		W Totals:	312	96	125	221	155

PLAYOFFS

YEAR	TEAM & LEAGUE		GP	G	A	PTS	PIM
1962-63	**CHI**	**N**	4	0	0	0	0
1964-65	**DET**	**N**	1	0	0	0	0
1972-73	**HOUS**	**W**	10	4	4	8	18
1973-74			14	9	6	15	6
1974-75			13	7	3	10	8
1975-76			17	1	4	5	0
6 yrs.		**N Totals:**	5	0	0	0	0
		W Totals:	54	21	17	38	32

Drafted by **Detroit** from Chicago, June 10, 1964. Sold on May 8, 1967 to **Chicago** by Detroit with Albert LeBrun to complete trade of Dec. 20, 1966 in which Detroit acquired Howie Young from Chicago. Drafted by **Minnesota** from Chicago in Expansion Draft, June 6, 1967. Sold to **Toronto** by Minnesota, May 9, 1968.

Milt Halliday

HALLIDAY, MILTON

Defense

YEAR	TEAM & LEAGUE	GP	G	A	PTS	PIM
1926-27	**OTTA N**	38	1	0	1	4
1927-28		13	0	0	0	2
1928-29		16	0	0	0	0
3 yrs.	**N Totals:**	67	1	0	1	6
PLAYOFFS						
1926-27*	**OTTA N**	6	0	0	0	0

Mats Hallin

HALLIN, MATS 6'2", 202 lbs.
B. Mar. 9, 1958, Eskilstuna, Sweden Left Wing, Shoots L

YEAR	TEAM & LEAGUE	GP	G	A	PTS	PIM
1982-83	**NYI N**	30	7	7	14	26
PLAYOFFS						
1982-83*	**NYI N**	7	1	0	1	6

Signed as free agent by **N.Y. Islanders** June 12, 1981.

Doug Halward

HALWARD, DOUGLAS ROBERT (Hawk) 6'1", 184 lbs.
B. Nov. 1, 1955, Toronto, Ont. Defense, Shoots L

YEAR	TEAM & LEAGUE	GP	G	A	PTS	PIM
1975-76	**BOS N**	22	1	5	6	6
1976-77		18	2	4	4	6
1977-78		25	0	2	2	2
1978-79	**LA N**	27	1	5	6	13
1979-80		63	11	45	56	52
1980-81		51	4	15	19	96
	VAN N	7	0	1	1	4
	2 team total	58	4	16	20	100
1981-82		37	4	13	17	40
1982-83		75	19	33	52	83
8 yrs.	**N Totals:**	325	42	121	163	302
PLAYOFFS						
1975-76	**BOS N**	1	0	0	0	0
1976-77		6	0	0	0	4
1978-79	**LA N**	1	0	0	0	12
1980-81	**VAN N**	2	0	1	1	6
1981-82		15	2	4	6	44
1982-83		4	1	0	1	21
6 yrs.	**N Totals:**	29	3	5	8	87

Traded to **Los Angeles** by Boston for future considerations on Sept. 18, 1978. Claimed by **Los Angeles** as fill in Expansion Draft, June 13, 1979. Traded to **Vancouver** by Los Angeles for Vancouver's fifth round choice (Ulf Isaacson) in 1982 Entry Draft, Mar. 8, 1981.

Gilles Hamel

HAMEL, GILLES 6'3", 183 lbs.
B. Mar. 18, 1960, Asbestos, Que. Left Wing, Shoots L

YEAR	TEAM & LEAGUE	GP	G	A	PTS	PIM
1980-81	**BUF N**	51	10	9	19	53
1981-82		16	2	7	9	2
1982-83		66	22	20	42	26
3 yrs.	**N Totals:**	133	34	36	70	81
PLAYOFFS						
1980-81	**BUF N**	5	0	1	1	4
1982-83		9	2	2	4	2
2 yrs.	**N Totals:**	14	2	3	5	6

Herb Hamel

HAMEL, HERBERT (Hap)
B. Unknown Forward

YEAR	TEAM & LEAGUE	GP	G	A	PTS	PIM
1930-31	**TOR N**	2	0	0	0	14

Jean Hamel

HAMEL, JEAN 5'11", 195 lbs.
B. June 6, 1952, Asbestos, Que. Defense, Shoots L

YEAR	TEAM & LEAGUE	GP	G	A	PTS	PIM
1972-73	**STL N**	55	2	7	9	24
1973-74		23	1	1	2	6
	DET N	22	0	3	3	40
	2 team total	45	1	4	5	46

Jean Hamel continued

YEAR	TEAM & LEAGUE	GP	G	A	PTS	PIM
1974-75		80	5	19	24	136
1975-76		77	3	9	12	129
1976-77		71	1	10	11	63
1977-78		32	2	6	8	34
1978-79		52	2	4	6	72
1979-80		49	1	4	5	43
1980-81		68	5	7	12	57
1981-82	**QUE N**	40	1	6	7	32
1982-83		51	2	7	9	38
11 yrs.	**N Totals:**	620	25	83	108	674
PLAYOFFS						
1972-73	**STL N**	2	0	0	0	0
1977-78	**DET N**	7	0	0	0	10
1981-82	**QUE N**	5	0	0	0	16
1982-83		4	0	0	0	2
4 yrs.	**N Totals:**	18	0	0	0	28

Traded to **Detroit** by St. Louis with Chris Evans and Bryan Watson for Ted Harris, Bill Collins and Garnet Bailey, Feb. 14, 1974. Claimed as fill by **Detroit** in Expansion Draft, June 13, 1979. Signed as free agent by **Quebec** Oct. 6, 1981.

Pierre Hamel

HAMEL, PIERRE 5'9", 170 lbs.
B. Sept. 16, 1952, Montreal, Que. Shoots L

YEAR	TEAM & LEAGUE	GP	G	A	PTS	PIM
1979-80	**WINN N**	35	0	2	2	10

Claimed by **Winnipeg** from Toronto in Expansion Draft, June 13, 1979.

Red Hamill

HAMILL, ROBERT GEORGE 5'11", 180 lbs.
B. Jan. 11, 1917, Toronto, Ont. Left Wing, Shoots L

YEAR	TEAM & LEAGUE	GP	G	A	PTS	PIM
1937-38	**BOS N**	6	0	1	1	2
1938-39		7	0	1	1	0
1939-40		28	10	8	18	16
1940-41		8	0	1	1	0
1941-42		9	6	3	9	2
	CHI N	34	18	9	27	21
	2 team total	43	24	12	36	23
1942-43		50	28	16	44	44
1945-46		38	20	17	37	23
1946-47		60	21	19	40	12
1947-48		60	11	13	24	18
1948-49		57	8	4	12	16
1949-50		59	6	2	8	6
1950-51		2	0	0	0	0
12 yrs.	**N Totals:**	418	128	94	222	160
PLAYOFFS						
1938-39*	**BOS N**	11	0	0	0	8
1939-40		5	0	1	1	5
1941-42	**CHI N**	3	0	1	1	0
1945-46		4	1	0	1	7
4 yrs.	**N Totals:**	23	1	2	3	20

Al Hamilton

HAMILTON, ALLAN GUY 6'1", 195 lbs.
B. Aug. 20, 1946, Flin Flon, Man. Defense, Shoots R

YEAR	TEAM & LEAGUE	GP	G	A	PTS	PIM
1965-66	**NYR N**	4	0	0	0	0
1967-68		2	0	0	0	0
1968-69		16	0	0	0	0
1969-70		59	0	5	5	54
1970-71	**BUF N**	69	2	28	30	71
1971-72		76	4	30	34	105
1972-73	**ALTA W**	78	11	50	61	124
1973-74	**EDM W**	77	14	45	59	104
1974-75		25	1	13	14	42
1975-76		54	2	32	34	78
1976-77		81	8	37	45	60
1977-78		59	11	43	54	46
1978-79		80	6	38	44	38
1979-80	**EDM N**	31	4	15	19	20
14 yrs.	**N Totals:**	257	10	78	88	250
	W Totals:	454	53	258	311	492
PLAYOFFS						
1968-69	**NYR N**	1	0	0	0	0
1969-70		5	0	0	0	2
1973-74	**EDM W**	4	1	1	2	15

Al Hamilton continued

YEAR	TEAM & LEAGUE		GP	G	A	PTS	PIM
1975-76			4	0	1	1	6
1976-77			5	0	4	4	4
1978-79			13	4	5	9	4
1979-80	**EDM**	**N**	1	0	0	0	0
7 yrs.		**N Totals:**	7	0	0	0	2
		W Totals:	26	5	11	16	29

Drafted by **Buffalo** from N.Y. Rangers in Expansion Draft, June 10, 1970.

Chuck Hamilton

HAMILTON, CHARLES 5'11", 175 lbs.
B. Jan. 18, 1939, Kirkland Lake, Ont. Left Wing, Shoots L

YEAR	TEAM & LEAGUE		GP	G	A	PTS	PIM
1961-62	**MONT**	**N**	1	0	0	0	0
1972-73	**STL**	**N**	3	0	2	2	2
2 yrs.		**N Totals:**	4	0	2	2	2

Sold to **Montreal** by Detroit, June 11, 1969.

Jack Hamilton

HAMILTON, JOHN MCIVOR 5'7", 170 lbs.
B. June 2, 1925, Trenton, Ont. Center, Shoots L

YEAR	TEAM & LEAGUE		GP	G	A	PTS	PIM
1942-43	**TOR**	**N**	49	4	22	26	60
1943-44			49	20	17	37	4
1945-46			40	7	9	16	12
3 yrs.		**N Totals:**	138	31	48	79	76

PLAYOFFS

YEAR	TEAM & LEAGUE		GP	G	A	PTS	PIM
1942-43	**TOR**	**N**	6	1	1	2	0
1943-44			5	1	0	1	0
2 yrs.		**N Totals:**	11	2	1	3	0

Jim Hamilton

HAMILTON, JAMES 6', 180 lbs.
B. Jan. 18, 1957, Barrie, Ont. Right Wing, Shoots L

YEAR	TEAM & LEAGUE		GP	G	A	PTS	PIM
1977-78	**PITT**	**N**	25	2	4	6	2
1978-79			2	0	0	0	0
1979-80			10	2	0	2	0
1980-81			20	1	6	7	18
1981-82			11	5	3	8	2
1982-83			5	0	2	2	2
6 yrs.		**N Totals:**	73	10	15	25	24

PLAYOFFS

YEAR	TEAM & LEAGUE		GP	G	A	PTS	PIM
1978-79	**PITT**	**N**	5	3	0	3	0
1980-81			1	0	0	0	0
2 yrs.		**N Totals:**	6	3	0	3	0

Reg Hamilton

HAMILTON, REGINALD 5'11", 180 lbs.
B. Apr. 29, 1914, Toronto, Ont. Defense, Shoots L

YEAR	TEAM & LEAGUE		GP	G	A	PTS	PIM
1935-36	**TOR**	**N**	7	0	0	0	0
1936-37			39	3	7	10	32
1937-38			45	1	4	5	43
1938-39			48	0	7	7	54
1939-40			23	2	2	4	23
1940-41			45	3	12	15	59
1941-42			22	0	4	4	27
1942-43			11	1	1	2	**68**
1943-44			39	4	12	16	32
1944-45			50	3	12	15	41
1945-46	**CHI**	**N**	48	1	7	8	31
1946-47			10	0	3	3	2
12 yrs.		**N Totals:**	387	18	71	89	412

PLAYOFFS

YEAR	TEAM & LEAGUE		GP	G	A	PTS	PIM
1936-37	**TOR**	**N**	2	0	1	1	2
1937-38			7	0	1	1	2
1938-39			10	0	0	0	4
1939-40			10	0	0	0	0
1940-41			7	1	2	3	13
1942-43			6	1	1	2	9
1943-44			5	1	0	1	8
1944-45*			13	3	0	3	14
1945-46	**CHI**	**N**	4	0	1	1	2

Reg Hamilton continued

YEAR	TEAM & LEAGUE		GP	G	A	PTS	PIM
9 yrs.		**N Totals:**	64	6	6	12	54

Inge Hammarstrom

HAMMARSTROM, HANS INGE 6', 180 lbs.
B. Jan. 20, 1948, Sundsvall, Sweden Left Wing, Shoots L

YEAR	TEAM & LEAGUE		GP	G	A	PTS	PIM
1973-74	**TOR**	**N**	66	20	23	43	14
1974-75			69	21	20	41	23
1975-76			76	19	21	40	21
1976-77			78	24	17	41	16
1977-78			3	1	1	2	6
	STL	**N**	70	19	19	38	4
	2 team total		73	20	20	40	10
1978-79			65	12	22	34	8
6 yrs.		**N Totals:**	427	116	123	239	92

PLAYOFFS

YEAR	TEAM & LEAGUE		GP	G	A	PTS	PIM
1973-74	**TOR**	**N**	4	1	0	1	0
1974-75			7	1	3	4	4
1976-77			2	0	0	0	0
3 yrs.		**N Totals:**	13	2	3	5	4

Traded to **St. Louis** by Toronto for Jerry Butler, Nov. 1, 1977.

Gord Hampson

HAMPSON, GORD 6'3", 210 lbs.
B. Feb. 13, 1959, Vancouver, B.C. Left Wing, Shoots L

YEAR	TEAM & LEAGUE		GP	G	A	PTS	PIM
1982-83	**CALG**	**N**	4	0	0	0	5

Signed by **Calgary** as a free agent, June, 1981.

Ted Hampson

HAMPSON, EDWARD GEORGE 5'8", 173 lbs.
B. Dec. 11, 1936, Togo, Sask. Center, Shoots L
Won Masterton Trophy, 1968-69

YEAR	TEAM & LEAGUE		GP	G	A	PTS	PIM
1959-60	**TOR**	**N**	41	2	8	10	17
1960-61	**NYR**	**N**	69	6	14	20	4
1961-62			68	4	24	28	10
1962-63			46	4	2	6	2
1963-64	**DET**	**N**	7	0	1	1	0
1964-65			1	0	0	0	0
1966-67			65	13	35	48	4
1967-68			37	9	18	27	10
	OAK	**N**	34	8	19	27	4
	2 team total		71	17	37	54	14
1968-69	**CALIF**	**N**	76	26	49	75	6
1969-70	**OAK**	**N**	76	17	35	52	10
1970-71	**CALIF**	**N**	60	10	20	30	14
	MINN	**N**	18	4	6	10	4
	2 team total		78	14	26	40	18
1971-72			78	5	14	19	6
1972-73	**MINN**	**W**	77	17	45	62	20
1973-74			77	17	38	55	9
1974-75			78	17	36	53	6
1975-76			59	5	15	20	14
	QUE	**W**	14	4	10	14	2
	2 team total		73	9	25	34	16
16 yrs.		**N Totals:**	676	108	245	353	91
		W Totals:	305	60	144	204	51

PLAYOFFS

YEAR	TEAM & LEAGUE		GP	G	A	PTS	PIM
1961-62	**NYR**	**N**	6	0	1	1	0
1968-69	**CALIF**	**N**	7	3	4	7	2
1969-70	**OAK**	**N**	4	1	1	2	0
1970-71	**MINN**	**N**	11	3	3	6	0
1971-72			7	0	1	1	2
1972-73	**MINN**	**W**	5	3	1	4	0
1973-74			11	4	4	8	8
1974-75			12	1	7	8	0
1975-76	**QUE**	**W**	5	0	2	2	10
9 yrs.		**N Totals:**	35	7	10	17	4
		W Totals:	33	8	14	22	18

Claimed on waivers by **Toronto** from N.Y. Rangers, Sept. 18, 1959. Drafted By **N.Y. Rangers** from Toronto, June 8, 1960. Drafted by **Detroit** from N.Y. Rangers, June 4, 1963. Traded to **Oakland** by Detroit with John Brenneman and Bert Marshall for Kent Douglas, Jan. 9, 1968. Traded to **Minnesota** by California with Wayne Muloin for Tom Williams and Dick Redmond, Mar. 7, 1971. Drafted by **N.Y. Islanders** from Minnesota in Expansion Draft, June

YEAR	TEAM & LEAGUE		GP	G	A	PTS	PIM

6, 1972. Signed as free agent by **Minnesota** Jan. 1, 1979.

Rick Hampton

HAMPTON, RICHARD CHARLES 6', 190 lbs.
B. June 14, 1956, King, Ont. Defense, Shoots L

YEAR	TEAM	LEAGUE	GP	G	A	PTS	PIM
1974-75	**CALIF**	**N**	78	8	17	25	59
1975-76			73	14	37	51	54
1976-77	**CLEVE**	**N**	57	16	24	40	13
1977-78			77	18	18	36	19
1978-79	**LA**	**N**	49	3	17	20	22
1979-80			3	0	0	0	0
6 yrs.		**N Totals:**	337	59	113	172	167
PLAYOFFS							
1978-79	**LA**	**N**	2	0	0	0	0

Protected by **Minnesota** prior to Cleveland-Minnesota Dispersal Draft, June 14, 1978. Sent to **Los Angeles** by Minnesota with Steve Jensen and Dave Gardner as compensation for Minnesota's signing free agent Gary Sargent from Los Angeles, July, 1978.

Alf Handrahan

HANDRAHAN, JOHN ALFRED 5'9", 185 lbs.
B. Dec. 27, 1949, Alberton, P.E.I. Right Wing, Shoots R

YEAR	TEAM	LEAGUE	GP	G	A	PTS	PIM
1977-78	**CIN**	**W**	14	1	3	4	42

Merv Haney

HANEY, MERVYN
Forward

YEAR	TEAM	LEAGUE	GP	G	A	PTS	PIM
1972-73	**OTTA**	**W**	7	0	1	1	4

Al Hangsleben

HANGSLEBEN, ALAN (Hank) 6'1", 195 lbs.
B. Feb. 22, 1953, Warroad, Man. Defense, Shoots L

YEAR	TEAM	LEAGUE	GP	G	A	PTS	PIM
1974-75	**NE**	**W**	26	0	4	4	8
1975-76			78	2	23	25	62
1976-77			74	13	9	22	79
1977-78			79	11	18	29	140
1978-79			77	10	19	29	148
1979-80	**HART**	**N**	37	3	15	18	69
	WASH	**N**	37	10	7	17	45
	2 team total		74	13	22	35	114
1980-81			76	5	19	24	198
1981-82			17	1	1	2	19
	LA	**N**	18	2	6	8	65
	2 team total		35	3	7	10	84
8 yrs.		**N Totals:**	185	21	48	69	396
		W Totals:	334	36	73	109	437
PLAYOFFS							
1974-75	**NE**	**W**	6	0	3	3	19
1975-76			13	2	3	5	20
1976-77			4	0	0	0	9
1977-78			14	1	4	5	37
1978-79			10	1	2	3	12
5 yrs.		**W Totals:**	47	4	12	16	97

Reclaimed by **Montreal** from Hartford prior to Expansion Draft, June 9, 1979. Claimed by **Hartford** from Montreal in Expansion Draft, June 13, 1979. Traded to **Washington** by Hartford for Tom Rowe, Jan. 17, 1980. Signed as free agent by **Los Angeles** Jan. 4, 1982.

Craig Hanmer

HANMER, CRAIG 6'2", 210 lbs.
B. Jan. 6, 1956, St. Paul, Minn. Defense, Shoots L

YEAR	TEAM	LEAGUE	GP	G	A	PTS	PIM
1974-75	**IND**	**W**	27	1	0	1	15

John Hanna

HANNA, JOHN 6', 195 lbs.
B. Apr. 5, 1935, Sydney, N.S. Defense, Shoots R

YEAR	TEAM	LEAGUE	GP	G	A	PTS	PIM
1958-59	**NYR**	**N**	70	1	10	11	83
1959-60			61	4	8	12	87
1960-61			46	1	8	9	34
1963-64	**MONT**	**N**	6	0	0	0	2
1967-68	**PHI**	**N**	15	0	0	0	0
1972-73	**CLEVE**	**W**	66	6	20	26	68

YEAR	TEAM & LEAGUE		GP	G	A	PTS	PIM

John Hanna continued

YEAR	TEAM	LEAGUE	GP	G	A	PTS	PIM
6 yrs.		**N Totals:**	198	6	26	32	206
		W Totals:	66	6	20	26	68

Traded to **Montreal** by New York for Al Langlois, June 13, 1961.

David Hannan

HANNAN, DAVID 5'10", 173 lbs.
B. Nov. 26, 1961, Sudbury, Ont. Center, Shoots L

YEAR	TEAM	LEAGUE	GP	G	A	PTS	PIM
1981-82	**PITT**	**N**	1	0	0	0	0
1982-83			74	11	22	33	127
2 yrs.		**N Totals:**	75	11	22	33	127

Gord Hannigan

HANNIGAN, JOHN GORDON 5'7", 163 lbs.
B. Jan. 19, 1929, Schumacher, Ont. Center, Shoots L

YEAR	TEAM	LEAGUE	GP	G	A	PTS	PIM
1952-53	**TOR**	**N**	65	17	18	35	51
1953-54			38	4	4	8	18
1954-55			13	0	2	2	8
1955-56			48	8	7	15	40
4 yrs.		**N Totals:**	164	29	31	60	117
PLAYOFFS							
1953-54	**TOR**	**N**	5	2	0	2	4
1955-56			4	0	0	0	4
2 yrs.		**N Totals:**	9	2	0	2	8

Pat Hannigan

HANNIGAN, PATRICK EDWARD 5'10", 190 lbs.
B. Mar. 5, 1936, Timmins, Ont. Right Wing, Shoots R

YEAR	TEAM	LEAGUE	GP	G	A	PTS	PIM
1959-60	**TOR**	**N**	1	0	0	0	0
1960-61	**NYR**	**N**	53	11	9	20	24
1961-62			56	8	14	22	34
1967-68	**PHI**	**N**	65	11	15	26	36
1968-69			7	0	1	1	22
5 yrs.		**N Totals:**	182	30	39	69	116
PLAYOFFS							
1961-62	**NYR**	**N**	4	0	0	0	2
1967-68	**PHI**	**N**	7	1	2	3	9
2 yrs.		**N Totals:**	11	1	2	3	11

Traded to **N.Y. Rangers** by Toronto with Johnny Wilson for Eddie Shack, Nov., 1960. Drafted by **Philadelphia** from Chicago in Expansion Draft, June 6, 1967.

Ray Hannigan

HANNIGAN, RAYMOND JAMES
B. July 14, 1927, Schumacher, Ont. Forward

YEAR	TEAM	LEAGUE	GP	G	A	PTS	PIM
1948-49	**TOR**	**N**	3	0	0	0	2

Traded to **Chicago** with Al Rollins, Cal Gardner and Gus Mortson by Toronto for Harry Lumley, Sept. 11, 1952.

Ritchie Hansen

HANSEN, RICHARD JOHN 5'10", 197 lbs.
B. Oct. 30, 1955, Bronx, N.Y. Center, Shoots L

YEAR	TEAM	LEAGUE	GP	G	A	PTS	PIM
1976-77	**NYI**	**N**	4	1	0	1	0
1977-78			2	0	0	0	0
1978-79			12	1	6	7	4
1981-82	**STL**	**N**	2	0	2	2	2
4 yrs.		**N Totals:**	20	2	8	10	6

Sent to **Minnesota** by N.Y. Islanders as compensation for Islanders' signing free agent Jean Potvin, June 10, 1979. Traded to **St. Louis** by Minnesota with Bryan Maxwell for St. Louis' second round choice (Dave Reierson) in 1982 Entry Draft.

Ron Hansis

HANSIS, RONALD LOUIS 6'2", 195 lbs.
B. Nov. 12, 1952, Brownsville, Tex. Right Wing, Shoots R

YEAR	TEAM	LEAGUE	GP	G	A	PTS	PIM
1976-77	**HOUS**	**W**	22	4	3	7	6
1977-78			78	13	9	22	51

Ron Hansis continued

YEAR	TEAM & LEAGUE		GP	G	A	PTS	PIM
2 yrs.		W Totals:	100	17	12	29	57
PLAYOFFS							
1976-77	HOUS	W	8	1	1	2	4
1977-78			6	1	1	2	4
2 yrs.		W Totals:	14	2	2	4	8

Dave Hanson

HANSON, DAVID 6', 190 lbs.
B. Apr. 12, 1954, Cumberland, Wisc. Defense, Shoots L

YEAR	TEAM & LEAGUE		GP	G	A	PTS	PIM
1976-77	MINN	W	1	0	0	0	9
	NE	W	7	0	2	2	35
	2 team total		8	0	2	2	44
1977-78	BIRM	W	42	7	16	23	241
1978-79			53	6	22	28	212
	DET	N	11	0	0	0	26
	2 team total		64	6	22	28	238
1979-80	MINN	N	22	1	1	2	39
4 yrs.		N Totals:	33	1	1	2	65
		W Totals:	103	13	40	53	497
PLAYOFFS							
1976-77	NE	W	1	0	0	0	0
1977-78	BIRM	W	5	0	1	1	48
2 yrs.		W Totals:	6	0	1	1	48

Signed as free agent by **Detroit** Oct. 4, 1977. Traded to **Minnesota** by Detroit for future considerations, Jan. 3, 1980.

Emil Hanson

HANSON, EMIL 5'10", 180 lbs.
B. Nov. 18, 1907, Centerville, S.Dak. Defense, Shoots L

YEAR	TEAM & LEAGUE		GP	G	A	PTS	PIM
1932-33	DET	N	7	0	0	0	6

Ossie Hanson

HANSON, OSCAR
B. U.S.A. Defense

YEAR	TEAM & LEAGUE		GP	G	A	PTS	PIM
1937-38	CHI	N	7	0	0	0	0

Nick Harbaruk

HARBARUK, MIKOLAJ NICKOLAS 6', 195 lbs.
B. Aug. 16, 1943, Drohiczyn, Poland Right Wing, Shoots R

YEAR	TEAM & LEAGUE		GP	G	A	PTS	PIM
1969-70	PITT	N	74	5	17	22	56
1970-71			78	13	12	25	108
1971-72			78	12	17	29	46
1972-73			78	10	15	25	47
1973-74	STL	N	56	5	14	19	16
1974-75	IND	W	78	20	23	43	52
1975-76			76	23	19	42	24
1976-77			27	2	2	4	2
8 yrs.		N Totals:	364	45	75	120	273
		W Totals:	181	45	44	89	78
PLAYOFFS							
1969-70	PITT	N	10	3	0	3	20
1971-72			4	0	1	1	0
1975-76	IND	W	7	2	0	2	10
1976-77			6	1	1	2	0
4 yrs.		N Totals:	14	3	1	4	20
		W Totals:	13	3	1	4	10

Drafted by **Pittsburgh** from Vancouver in Inter-League Draft, June 10, 1969. Traded to **St. Louis** by Pittsburgh for goaltender Bob Johnson, Oct. 4, 1973.

Joe Hardy

HARDY, JOCELYN JOSEPH (Gypsy Joe) 6', 175 lbs.
B. Dec. 5, 1945, Kenogami, Que. Center, Shoots L

YEAR	TEAM & LEAGUE		GP	G	A	PTS	PIM
1969-70	OAK	N	23	5	4	9	20
1970-71	CALIF	N	40	4	10	14	31
1972-73	CLEVE	W	72	17	33	50	80
1973-74	CHI	W	77	24	35	59	55
1974-75			17	1	6	7	8
	IND	W	32	2	17	19	36
	SD	W	12	2	3	5	22
	3 team total		61	5	26	31	66

Joe Hardy continued

YEAR	TEAM & LEAGUE		GP	G	A	PTS	PIM
5 yrs.		N Totals:	63	9	14	23	51
		W Totals:	210	46	94	140	201
PLAYOFFS							
1969-70	OAK	N	4	0	0	0	0
1972-73	CLEVE	W	7	0	2	2	0
1973-74	CHI	W	17	4	8	12	13
3 yrs.		N Totals:	4	0	0	0	0
		W Totals:	24	4	10	14	13

Mark Hardy

HARDY, MARK LEA 5'11", 190 lbs.
B. Feb. 1, 1959, Semaden, Switzerland Defense, Shoots L

YEAR	TEAM & LEAGUE		GP	G	A	PTS	PIM
1979-80	LA	N	15	0	1	1	10
1980-81			77	5	20	25	77
1981-82			77	6	39	45	130
1982-83			74	5	34	39	101
4 yrs.		N Totals:	243	16	94	110	318
PLAYOFFS							
1979-80	LA	N	4	1	1	2	9
1980-81			4	1	2	3	4
1981-82			10	1	2	3	9
3 yrs.		N Totals:	18	3	5	8	22

Jim Hargreaves

HARGREAVES, JAMES ALBERT (Cement-Head) 5'11", 185 lbs.
B. May 2, 1950, Winnipeg, Man. Defense, Shoots R

YEAR	TEAM & LEAGUE		GP	G	A	PTS	PIM
1970-71	VAN	N	7	0	1	1	33
1972-73			59	1	6	7	72
1973-74	WINN	W	53	1	4	5	50
1974-75	IND	W	37	2	5	7	30
	SD	W	41	8	10	18	45
	2 team total		78	10	15	25	75
1975-76			43	1	1	2	26
5 yrs.		N Totals:	66	1	7	8	105
		W Totals:	174	12	20	32	151
PLAYOFFS							
1974-75	SD	W	10	1	0	1	6
1975-76			5	0	0	0	2
2 yrs.		W Totals:	15	1	0	1	8

Ted Hargreaves

HARGREAVES, EDWARD 5'11", 175 lbs.
B. Weyburn, Sask. Left Wing, Shoots L

YEAR	TEAM & LEAGUE		GP	G	A	PTS	PIM
1973-74	WINN	W	74	7	12	19	15
PLAYOFFS							
1973-74	WINN	W	4	0	1	1	10

Derek Harker

HARKER, DEREK 6', 185 lbs.
B. Jan. 7, 1951, Edmonton, Alta. Defense, Shoots L

YEAR	TEAM & LEAGUE		GP	G	A	PTS	PIM
1972-73	ALTA	W	1	0	0	0	0
	PHI	W	28	0	5	5	46
	2 team total		29	0	5	5	46

Glen Harmon

HARMON, DAVID GLEN 5'8½", 165 lbs.
B. Jan. 2, 1921, Holland, Man. Defense, Shoots L

YEAR	TEAM & LEAGUE		GP	G	A	PTS	PIM
1942-43	MONT	N	27	5	9	14	25
1943-44			43	5	16	21	36
1944-45			42	5	8	13	41
1945-46			49	7	10	17	28
1946-47			57	5	9	14	53
1947-48			56	10	4	14	52
1948-49			59	8	12	20	44
1949-50			62	3	16	19	28
1950-51			57	2	12	14	27
9 yrs.		N Totals:	452	50	96	146	334

Glen Harmon continued

PLAYOFFS

YEAR	TEAM	LEAGUE	GP	G	A	PTS	PIM
1942-43	**MONT**	**N**	5	0	1	1	2
1943-44*			9	1	2	3	4
1944-45			6	1	0	1	2
1945-46*			9	1	4	5	0
1946-47			11	1	1	2	4
1948-49			7	1	1	2	4
1949-50			5	0	1	1	21
1950-51			1	0	0	0	0
8 yrs.		**N Totals:**	53	5	10	15	37

John Harms

HARMS, JOHN 5'8", 160 lbs.
B. Apr. 25, 1925, Saskatoon, Sask. Right Wing, Shoots R

YEAR	TEAM	LEAGUE	GP	G	A	PTS	PIM
1943-44	**CHI**	**N**	1	0	0	0	0
1944-45			43	5	5	10	21
2 yrs.		**N Totals:**	44	5	5	10	21

PLAYOFFS

YEAR	TEAM	LEAGUE	GP	G	A	PTS	PIM
1943-44	**CHI**	**N**	3	3	0	3	2

Happy Harnott

HARNOTT, WALTER HERBERT 5'7", 170 lbs.
B. Sept. 24, 1909, Montreal, Que. Forward

YEAR	TEAM	LEAGUE	GP	G	A	PTS	PIM
1933-34	**BOS**	**N**	6	0	0	0	6

Terry Harper

HARPER, TERRANCE VICTOR 6'1", 197 lbs.
B. Jan. 27, 1940, Regina, Sask. Defense, Shoots R

YEAR	TEAM	LEAGUE	GP	G	A	PTS	PIM
1962-63	**MONT**	**N**	14	1	1	2	10
1963-64			70	2	15	17	149
1964-65			62	0	7	7	93
1965-66			69	1	11	12	91
1966-67			56	0	16	16	99
1967-68			57	3	8	11	66
1968-69			21	0	3	3	37
1969-70			75	4	18	22	109
1970-71			78	1	21	22	116
1971-72			52	2	12	14	35
1972-73	**LA**	**N**	77	1	8	9	74
1973-74			77	0	17	17	119
1974-75			80	5	21	26	120
1975-76	**DET**	**N**	69	8	25	33	59
1976-77			52	4	8	12	28
1977-78			80	2	17	19	85
1978-79			51	0	6	6	58
1979-80	**STL**	**N**	11	1	5	6	6
1980-81	**COLO**	**N**	15	0	2	2	8
19 yrs.		**N Totals:**	1066	35	221	256	1362

PLAYOFFS

YEAR	TEAM	LEAGUE	GP	G	A	PTS	PIM
1962-63	**MONT**	**N**	5	1	0	1	8
1963-64			7	0	0	0	6
1964-65*			13	0	0	0	19
1965-66*			10	2	3	5	18
1966-67			10	0	1	1	15
1967-68*			13	0	1	1	8
1968-69*			11	0	0	0	8
1970-71*			20	0	6	6	28
1971-72			5	1	1	2	6
1973-74	**LA**	**N**	5	0	0	0	16
1974-75			3	0	0	0	2
1977-78	**DET**	**N**	7	0	1	1	4
1979-80	**STL**	**N**	3	0	0	0	2
13 yrs.		**N Totals:**	112	4	13	17	140

Traded to **Los Angeles** by Montreal for Los Angeles' second choice (Gary MacGregor) in 1974 Amateur Draft, first choice (Pierre Mondou) and third choice (Paul Woods) in 1975 Amateur Draft, and first choice (Rod Shutt) in 1976 Amateur Draft, Aug. 22, 1972. Traded to **Detroit** by Los Angeles with Dan Maloney and Los Angeles' second choice (later transferred to Minnesota, Jimmy Roberts) in 1976 Amateur Draft for Bart Crashley and the rights to Marcel Dionne, June 23, 1975. Signed as free agent with **St. Louis** March 10, 1980. Signed as free agent with **Colorado** Feb. 12, 1981.

Tim Harrer

HARRER, TIM 6', 180 lbs.
B. May 10, 1957, Bloomington, Minn. Right Wing, Shoots R

YEAR	TEAM	LEAGUE	GP	G	A	PTS	PIM
1982-83	**CALG**	**N**	3	0	0	0	2

Hago Harrington

HARRINGTON, LELAND K. 5'8", 163 lbs.
B. Melrose, Mass. Left Wing, Shoots L

YEAR	TEAM	LEAGUE	GP	G	A	PTS	PIM
1925-26	**BOS**	**N**	26	7	2	9	6
1927-28			22	1	0	1	7
1932-33	**MONT**	**N**	24	1	1	2	2
3 yrs.		**N Totals:**	72	9	3	12	15

PLAYOFFS

YEAR	TEAM	LEAGUE	GP	G	A	PTS	PIM
1927-28	**BOS**	**N**	2	0	0	0	0
1932-33	**MONT**	**N**	2	1	0	1	2
2 yrs.		**N Totals:**	4	1	0	1	2

Billy Harris

HARRIS, WILLIAM EDWARD 6', 165 lbs.
B. July 29, 1935, Toronto, Ont. Center, Shoots L

YEAR	TEAM	LEAGUE	GP	G	A	PTS	PIM
1955-56	**TOR**	**N**	70	9	13	22	8
1956-57			23	4	6	10	6
1957-58			68	16	28	44	32
1958-59			70	22	30	52	29
1959-60			70	13	25	38	29
1960-61			66	12	27	39	30
1961-62			67	15	10	25	14
1962-63			65	8	24	32	22
1963-64			67	6	12	18	17
1964-65			48	1	6	7	0
1967-68	**OAK**	**N**	62	12	17	29	2
1968-69	**CALIF**	**N**	19	0	4	4	2
	PITT	**N**	54	7	13	20	8
	2 team total		73	7	17	24	10
12 yrs.		**N Totals:**	749	125	215	340	199

PLAYOFFS

YEAR	TEAM	LEAGUE	GP	G	A	PTS	PIM
1955-56	**TOR**	**N**	5	1	1	4	0
1958-59			12	3	4	7	16
1959-60			9	0	3	3	4
1960-61			5	1	0	1	0
1961-62*			12	2	1	3	2
1962-63*			10	0	1	1	0
1963-64*			9	1	1	2	4
1964-65			9	1	1	2	4
8 yrs.		**N Totals:**	71	9	12	23	30

Traded to **Detroit** by Toronto with Andy Bathgate and Gary Jarrett for Marcel Pronovost, Larry Jeffrey, Ed Joyal, Lowell MacDonald, and Autry Erickson, May 20, 1965. Drafted by **Oakland** from Detroit in Expansion Draft, June 6, 1967. Traded to **Pittsburgh** by Oakland for Bob Dillabough, Nov. 29, 1968.

Billy Harris

HARRIS, WILLIAM EDWARD 6'2", 195 lbs.
B. Jan. 29, 1952, Toronto, Ont. Right Wing, Shoots L

YEAR	TEAM	LEAGUE	GP	G	A	PTS	PIM
1972-73	**NYI**	**N**	78	28	22	50	35
1973-74			78	23	27	50	34
1974-75			80	25	37	62	34
1975-76			80	32	38	70	54
1976-77			80	24	43	67	44
1977-78			80	22	38	60	40
1978-79			80	15	39	54	18
1979-80			67	15	15	30	37
	LA	**N**	11	4	3	7	6
	2 team total		78	19	18	37	43
1980-81			80	20	29	49	36
1981-82			16	1	3	4	6
	TOR	**N**	2	2	0	2	4
	2 team total		18	3	3	6	10
1982-83			76	11	19	30	26
11 yrs.		**N Totals:**	808	222	313	535	374

Billy Harris continued

YEAR	TEAM	LEAGUE	GP	G	A	PTS	PIM
PLAYOFFS							
1974-75	**NYI**	**N**	17	3	7	10	12
1975-76			13	5	2	7	10
1976-77			12	7	7	14	8
1977-78			7	0	0	0	4
1978-79			10	2	1	3	10
1979-80	**LA**	**N**	4	0	0	0	2
1980-81			4	2	1	3	0
1982-83	**TOR**	**N**	4	0	1	1	2
8 yrs.		**N Totals:**	71	19	19	38	48

Traded to **Los Angeles** by N.Y. Islanders with Dave Lewis for Butch Goring, Mar. 10, 1980. Traded to **Toronto** by Los Angeles with John Gibson for Ian Turnbull, Nov. 11, 1981.

Duke Harris

HARRIS, GEORGE FRANCIS (The Duker)

6', 204 lbs.

B. Feb. 25, 1942, Sarnia, Ont. Right Wing, Shoots R

YEAR	TEAM	LEAGUE	GP	G	A	PTS	PIM
1967-68	**MINN**	**N**	22	1	4	5	4
	TOR	**N**	4	0	0	0	0
	2 team total		26	1	4	5	4
1972-73	**HOUS**	**W**	75	30	12	42	14
1973-74	**CHI**	**W**	64	14	16	30	20
1974-75			54	9	19	28	18
4 yrs.		**N Totals:**	26	1	4	5	4
		W Totals:	193	53	47	100	52
PLAYOFFS							
1972-73	**HOUS**	**W**	10	1	1	2	4
1973-74	**CHI**	**W**	18	6	6	12	2
2 yrs.		**W Totals:**	28	7	7	14	6

Hugh Harris

HARRIS, HUGH THOMAS 6'1", 195 lbs.

B. June 7, 1948, Toronto, Ont. Center, Shoots L

YEAR	TEAM	LEAGUE	GP	G	A	PTS	PIM
1972-73	**BUF**	**N**	60	12	26	38	17
1973-74	**NE**	**W**	75	24	28	52	78
1974-75	**PHOE**	**W**	22	10	10	20	15
	VAN	**W**	58	23	34	57	19
	2 team total		80	33	44	77	34
1975-76	**CALG**	**W**	30	5	9	14	19
	IND	**W**	41	12	27	39	23
	2 team total		71	17	36	53	42
1976-77			46	21	35	56	21
1977-78			19	1	7	8	6
	CIN	**W**	45	11	23	34	30
	2 team total		64	12	30	42	36
6 yrs.		**N Totals:**	60	12	26	38	17
		W Totals:	336	107	173	280	211
PLAYOFFS							
1972-73	**BUF**	**N**	3	0	0	0	0
1973-74	**NE**	**W**	7	0	4	4	11
1975-76	**IND**	**W**	7	2	5	7	8
1976-77			2	0	0	0	0
4 yrs.		**N Totals:**	3	0	0	0	0
		W Totals:	16	2	9	11	19

Drafted by **Buffalo** from Montreal in Intra-League Draft, June 8, 1971.

Ron Harris

HARRIS, RONALD THOMAS 5'9", 190 lbs.

B. June 30, 1942, Verdun, Que. Defense, Shoots R

YEAR	TEAM	LEAGUE	GP	G	A	PTS	PIM
1962-63	**DET**	**N**	1	0	1	1	0
1963-64			3	0	0	0	7
1965-66			24	1	4	5	6
1967-68	**OAK**	**N**	54	4	6	10	60
1968-69	**DET**	**N**	73	3	13	16	91
1969-70			72	2	19	21	99
1970-71			42	2	8	10	65
1971-72			61	1	10	11	80
1972-73	**ATL**	**N**	24	2	4	6	8
	NYR	**N**	46	3	10	13	17
	2 team total		70	5	14	19	25
1973-74			63	2	12	14	25
1974-75			34	1	7	8	22
1975-76			3	0	1	1	0
12 yrs.		**N Totals:**	500	21	95	116	480
PLAYOFFS							
1969-70	**DET**	**N**	4	0	0	0	8
1972-73	**NYR**	**N**	10	0	3	3	2
1973-74			11	3	0	3	14
1974-75			3	1	0	1	9
4 yrs.		**N Totals:**	28	4	3	7	33

Smokey Harris

HARRIS, FREDERICK HENRY

Left Wing, Shoots L

YEAR	TEAM	LEAGUE	GP	G	A	PTS	PIM
1924-25	**BOS**	**N**	6	3	1	4	8
1930-31			34	2	4	6	20
2 yrs.		**N Totals:**	40	5	5	10	28
PLAYOFFS							
1930-31	**BOS**	**N**	2	0	0	0	0

Ted Harris

HARRIS, EDWARD ALEXANDER 6'2", 183 lbs.

B. July 18, 1936, Winnipeg, Man. Defense, Shoots L

YEAR	TEAM	LEAGUE	GP	G	A	PTS	PIM
1963-64	**MONT**	**N**	4	0	1	1	0
1964-65			68	1	14	15	107
1965-66			53	0	13	13	81
1966-67			65	2	16	18	86
1967-68			67	5	16	21	78
1968-69			76	7	18	25	102
1969-70			74	3	17	20	116
1970-71	**MINN**	**N**	78	2	13	15	130
1971-72			78	2	15	17	77
1972-73			78	7	23	30	893
1973-74			12	0	1	1	4
	DET	**N**	41	0	11	11	66
	STL	**N**	24	0	4	4	16
	3 team total		77	0	16	16	86
1974-75	**PHI**	**N**	70	1	6	7	48
12 yrs.		**N Totals:**	788	30	168	198	1804
PLAYOFFS							
1964-65*	**MONT**	**N**	13	0	5	5	45
1965-66*			10	0	0	0	38
1966-67			10	0	1	1	19
1967-68*			13	0	4	4	22
1968-69*			14	1	2	3	34
1970-71	**MINN**	**N**	12	0	4	4	36
1971-72			7	0	1	1	17
1972-73			5	0	1	1	15
1974-75*	**PHI**	**N**	16	0	4	4	4
9 yrs.		**N Totals:**	100	1	22	23	230

Transferred from Montreal reserve list to **Minnesota** in Intra-league Draft, June 9, 1970. Traded to **Detroit** by Minnesota for Gary Bergman, Nov. 7, 1973. Traded to **St. Louis** by Detroit with Bill Collins and Ace Bailey for Chris Evans, Bryan Watson and Jean Hamel, Feb. 14, 1974. Sold to **Philadelphia** by St. Louis, Sept. 16, 1974.

Fran Harrison

HARRISON, FRANCIS EDWARD 6', 170 lbs.

B. July 25, 1927, Mimico, Ont. Left Wing, Shoots L

YEAR	TEAM	LEAGUE	GP	G	A	PTS	PIM
1947-48	**BOS**	**N**	52	6	7	13	8
1948-49			59	5	5	10	20
1949-50			70	14	12	26	23
1950-51			9	1	0	1	0
	NYR	**N**	4	1	0	1	2
	2 team total		13	2	0	2	2
4 yrs.		**N Totals:**	194	27	24	51	53
PLAYOFFS							
1947-48	**BOS**	**N**	5	1	0	1	2
1948-49			4	0	0	0	0
2 yrs.		**N Totals:**	9	1	0	1	2

Traded to **N.Y. Rangers** by Boston with Zellio Toppazzini for Dunc Fisher, Nov. 16, 1950.

Jim Harrison

HARRISON, JAMES DAVID 5'11", 185 lbs.
B. July 9, 1947, Bonnyville, Alta. Center, Shoots R

YEAR	TEAM & LEAGUE		GP	G	A	PTS	PIM
1968-69	**BOS**	**N**	16	1	2	3	21
1969-70			23	3	1	4	16
	TOR	**N**	31	7	10	17	36
	2 team total		54	10	11	21	52
1970-71			78	13	20	33	108
1971-72			66	19	17	36	104
1972-73	**ALTA**	**W**	66	39	47	86	93
1973-74	**EDM**	**W**	46	24	45	69	99
1974-75	**CLEVE**	**W**	60	20	22	42	106
1975-76			59	34	38	72	62
1976-77	**CHI**	**N**	60	18	23	41	97
1977-78			26	2	8	10	13
1978-79			21	4	5	9	22
1979-80	**EDM**	**N**	3	0	0	0	0
12 yrs.		**N Totals:**	324	67	86	153	417
		W Totals:	231	117	152	269	360

PLAYOFFS

YEAR	TEAM & LEAGUE		GP	G	A	PTS	PIM
1970-71	**TOR**	**N**	6	0	1	1	33
1971-72			5	1	0	1	10
1974-75	**CLEVE**	**W**	5	1	2	3	4
1975-76			3	0	1	1	9
1976-77	**CHI**	**N**	2	0	0	0	0
5 yrs.		**N Totals:**	13	1	1	2	43
		W Totals:	8	1	3	4	13

Traded to **Toronto** by Boston for Wayne Carleton, Dec. 10, 1969. Rights traded to **Chicago** by Toronto for Chicago's second-round choice (Robert Gladney) in the 1977 Amateur Draft, Sept. 28, 1976. Transferred to **Edmonton** by Chicago, Sept. 24, 1979. Transferred by Edmonton to **Chicago** Nov. 6, 1979.

Paul Harrison

HARRISON, PAUL DOUGLAS 6'1", 175 lbs.
B. Feb. 11, 1955, Timmons, Ont. Shoots L

PLAYOFFS

YEAR	TEAM & LEAGUE		GP	G	A	PTS	PIM
1980-81	**TOR**	**N**	1	0	0	0	0

Traded to **Toronto** by Minnesota for Toronto's fourth round choice (Terry Tait) in the 1981 Entry Draft, June 14, 1978. Claimed on waivers by **Buffalo** Feb. 8, 1982.

Dick Hart

HART, RICHARD EDWARD 6', 195 lbs.
B. Oct. 5, 1952, Boston, Mass. Defense, Shoots L

YEAR	TEAM & LEAGUE		GP	G	A	PTS	PIM
1976-77	**BIRM**	**W**	4	0	0	0	0

Gerry Hart

HART, GERALD WILLIAM 5'9", 190 lbs.
B. Jan. 1, 1948, Flin Flon, Man. Defense, Shoots L

YEAR	TEAM & LEAGUE		GP	G	A	PTS	PIM
1968-69	**DET**	**N**	1	0	0	0	2
1969-70			3	0	0	0	2
1970-71			64	2	7	9	148
1971-72			3	0	0	0	0
1972-73	**NYI**	**N**	47	1	11	12	158
1973-74			70	1	10	11	61
1974-75			71	4	14	18	143
1975-76			80	6	18	24	151
1976-77			80	4	18	22	98
1977-78			78	2	23	25	94
1978-79			50	2	14	16	78
1979-80	**QUE**	**N**	71	3	23	26	59
1980-81			6	0	0	0	10
	STL	**N**	63	4	11	15	132
	2 team total		69	4	11	15	142
1981-82			35	0	1	1	102
1982-83			8	0	0	0	2
15 yrs.		**N Totals:**	730	29	150	179	1240

PLAYOFFS

YEAR	TEAM & LEAGUE		GP	G	A	PTS	PIM
1974-75	**NYI**	**N**	17	2	2	4	42
1975-76			13	1	3	4	24
1976-77			12	0	2	2	23
1977-78			7	0	0	0	6
1978-79			9	0	2	2	10
1980-81	**STL**	**N**	10	0	0	0	27
1981-82			10	0	3	3	33
7 yrs.		**N Totals:**	78	3	12	15	165

Drafted by **N.Y. Islanders** from Detroit in Expansion Draft, June 6, 1972. Claimed by **Quebec** from N.Y. Islanders in Expansion Draft, June 13, 1979. Signed by **St. Louis** from Quebec as a free agent, Nov. 12, 1980.

Gizzy Hart

HART, WILFRED HAROLD 5'9", 171 lbs.
B. June 1, 1903, Weyburn, Sask. Left Wing

YEAR	TEAM & LEAGUE		GP	G	A	PTS	PIM
1926-27	**DET**	**N**	6	0	0	0	0
	MONT	**N**	32	3	3	6	8
	2 team total		38	3	3	6	8
1927-28			44	3	2	5	4
1932-33			18	0	3	3	0
3 yrs.		**N Totals:**	100	6	8	14	12

PLAYOFFS

YEAR	TEAM & LEAGUE		GP	G	A	PTS	PIM
1926-27	**MONT**	**N**	4	0	0	0	0
1927-28			2	0	0	0	0
1932-33			2	0	1	1	0
3 yrs.		**N Totals:**	8	0	1	1	0

Craig Hartsburg

HARTSBURG, CRAIG 6'1", 190 lbs.
B. June 29, 1959, Stratford, Ont. Defense, Shoots L

YEAR	TEAM & LEAGUE		GP	G	A	PTS	PIM
1978-79	**BIRM**	**W**	77	9	40	49	73
1979-80	**MINN**	**N**	79	14	30	44	81
1980-81			74	13	30	43	124
1981-82			76	17	60	77	117
1982-83			78	12	50	62	109
5 yrs.		**N Totals:**	307	56	170	226	431
		W Totals:	77	9	40	49	73

PLAYOFFS

YEAR	TEAM & LEAGUE		GP	G	A	PTS	PIM
1979-80	**MINN**	**N**	15	3	1	4	17
1980-81			19	3	12	15	16
1981-82			4	1	2	3	14
1982-83			9	3	8	11	7
4 yrs.		**N Totals:**	47	10	23	33	54

Doug Harvey

HARVEY, DOUGLAS NORMAN 5'11", 180 lbs.
B. Dec. 19, 1924, Montreal, Que. Defense, Shoots L
Won Norris Trophy, 1954–55 , 1955–56 , 1956–57 , 1957–58 , 1959–60 , 1960–61 , 1961–62
Hall of Fame, 1973

YEAR	TEAM & LEAGUE		GP	G	A	PTS	PIM
1947-48	**MONT**	**N**	35	4	4	8	32
1948-49			55	3	13	16	87
1949-50			70	4	20	24	76
1950-51			70	5	24	29	93
1951-52			68	6	23	29	82
1952-53			69	4	30	34	67
1953-54			68	8	29	37	110
1954-55			70	6	**43**	49	58
1955-56			62	5	39	44	60
1956-57			70	6	44	50	92
1957-58			68	9	32	41	131
1958-59			61	4	16	20	61
1959-60			66	6	21	27	45
1960-61			58	6	33	39	0
1961-62	**NYR**	**N**	69	6	24	30	42
1962-63			68	4	35	39	92
1963-64			14	0	2	2	10
1966-67	**DET**	**N**	2	0	0	0	0
1968-69	**STL**	**N**	70	2	20	22	30
19 yrs.		**N Totals:**	1113	88	452	540	1168

PLAYOFFS

YEAR	TEAM & LEAGUE		GP	G	A	PTS	PIM
1948-49	**MONT**	**N**	7	0	1	1	10
1949-50			5	0	2	2	10
1950-51			11	0	5	5	12
1951-52			11	0	3	3	8
1952-53*			12	0	5	5	8
1953-54			10	0	2	2	12
1954-55			12	0	8	8	6
1955-56*			10	2	5	7	10
1956-57*			10	0	7	7	10
1957-58*			10	2	9	11	16
1958-59*			11	1	11	12	22

YEAR	TEAM & LEAGUE		GP	G	A	PTS	PIM

Doug Harvey continued

YEAR	TEAM & LEAGUE		GP	G	A	PTS	PIM
1959-60*			8	3	0	3	6
1960-61			6	0	1	1	8
1961-62	**NYR**	**N**	6	0	1	1	2
1967-68	**STL**	**N**	8	0	4	4	12
15 yrs.		**N Totals:**	137	8	64	72	152

Sold to **N.Y. Rangers** by Montreal, June, 1961. Signed as a free agent with **Detroit** January, 1967. Signed as a free agent with **St. Louis** April, 1968.

Fred Harvey

HARVEY, FREDERIC JOHN CHARLES (Buster) 6', 185 lbs.
B. Apr. 2, 1950, Fredericton, N.B. Right Wing, Shoots R

YEAR	TEAM & LEAGUE		GP	G	A	PTS	PIM
1970-71	**MINN**	**N**	59	12	8	20	36
1972-73			68	21	34	55	16
1973-74			72	16	17	33	14
1974-75	**ATL**	**N**	79	17	27	44	16
1975-76			1	0	0	0	0
	KC	**N**	39	5	12	17	6
	DET	**N**	35	8	9	17	25
	3 team total		75	13	21	34	31
1976-77			54	11	11	22	18
6 yrs.		**N Totals:**	407	90	118	208	131
PLAYOFFS							
1970-71	**MINN**	**N**	7	0	0	0	4
1971-72			1	0	1	1	17
1972-73			6	0	2	2	4
3 yrs.		**N Totals:**	14	0	3	3	25

Traded to **Atlanta** by Minnesota with Jerry Byers for John Flesch and Don Martineau, May 27, 1974. Traded to **Kansas City** by Atlanta for Richard Lemieux and Kansas City's (Colorado's) second choice (Miles Zaharko) in 1977 Amateur Draft, Oct. 13, 1975. Traded to **Detroit** by Kansas City for Phil Roberto, Jan. 14, 1976.

Lionel Harvey

HARVEY, LIONEL HUGH 6', 175 lbs.
B. June 25, 1949, Kingston, Ont. Left Wing, Shoots L

YEAR	TEAM & LEAGUE		GP	G	A	PTS	PIM
1974-75	**KC**	**N**	8	0	0	0	2
1975-76			10	1	1	2	2
2 yrs.		**N Totals:**	18	1	1	2	4

Mike Harvey

HARVEY, MICHEL 5'10½", 182 lbs.
B. Jan. 31, 1938, Alma, Que. Center, Shoots L

YEAR	TEAM & LEAGUE		GP	G	A	PTS	PIM
1972-73	**QUE**	**W**	40	6	13	19	14

Bob Hassard

HASSARD, ROBERT HARRY 6', 165 lbs.
B. Mar. 26, 1929, Lloydminster, Sask. Center, Shoots R

YEAR	TEAM & LEAGUE		GP	G	A	PTS	PIM
1949-50	**TOR**	**N**	1	0	0	0	0
1950-51			12	0	1	1	0
1952-53			70	8	23	31	14
1953-54			26	1	4	5	4
1954-55	**CHI**	**N**	17	0	0	0	4
5 yrs.		**N Totals:**	126	9	28	37	22

Purchased by **Chicago** from Toronto, Sept. 10, 1954.

Ed Hatoum

HATOUM, EDWARD 5'10", 185 lbs.
B. Dec. 7, 1947, Beirut, Lebanon Right Wing, Shoots R

YEAR	TEAM & LEAGUE		GP	G	A	PTS	PIM
1968-69	**DET**	**N**	16	2	1	3	2
1969-70			5	0	2	2	2
1970-71	**VAN**	**N**	26	1	3	4	21
1972-73	**CHI**	**W**	15	1	1	2	2
1973-74	**VAN**	**W**	37	3	12	15	8
5 yrs.		**N Totals:**	47	3	6	9	25
		W Totals:	52	4	13	17	10

Drafted by **Vancouver** from Detroit in Expansion Draft, June 10, 1970.

Dale Hawerchuk

HAWERCHUK, DALE 5'11", 170 lbs.
B. Apr. 4, 1963, Toronto, Ont. Center, Shoots L
Won Calder Trophy, 1981-82

YEAR	TEAM & LEAGUE		GP	G	A	PTS	PIM
1981-82	**WINN**	**N**	80	45	58	103	47
1982-83			79	40	51	91	31
2 yrs.		**N Totals:**	159	85	109	194	78
PLAYOFFS							
1981-82	**WINN**	**N**	4	1	7	8	5
1982-83			3	1	4	5	8
2 yrs.		**N Totals:**	7	2	11	13	13

Alan Haworth

HAWORTH, ALLAN JOSEPH GORDON 5'10", 188 lbs.
B. Sept. 1, 1960, Drummondville, Que. Center, Shoots R

YEAR	TEAM & LEAGUE		GP	G	A	PTS	PIM
1980-81	**BUF**	**N**	49	16	20	36	34
1981-82			57	21	18	39	30
1982-83	**WASH**	**N**	74	23	27	50	34
3 yrs.		**N Totals:**	180	60	65	125	98
PLAYOFFS							
1980-81	**BUF**	**N**	7	4	4	8	2
1981-82			3	0	1	1	2
1982-83	**WASH**	**N**	4	0	0	0	2
3 yrs.		**N Totals:**	14	4	5	9	6

Traded to **Washington** by Buffalo along with Buffalo's third round choice in 1982 Entry Draft (Milan Novy) for Washington's second round choice (Mike Anderson) and fourth round choice (Timo Jutila) in 1982 Entry Draft, June 9, 1982. Traded by Buffalo with Buffalo's third round choice in the 1982 Amateur Draft (Milan Novy) to **Washington** for Washington's second round (Mike Anderson) and fourth round choices (Timo Jutila) in the 1982 Amateur Draft, June 9, 1982.

Gord Haworth

HAWORTH, GORDON JOSEPH 5'10", 165 lbs.
B. Feb. 20, 1932, Drummondville, Que. Center, Shoots L

YEAR	TEAM & LEAGUE		GP	G	A	PTS	PIM
1952-53	**NYR**	**N**	2	0	1	1	0

Neil Hawryliw

HAWRYLIW, NEIL 5'11", 185 lbs.
B. Nov. 9, 1955, Fielding, Sask. Right Wing, Shoots L

YEAR	TEAM & LEAGUE		GP	G	A	PTS	PIM
1981-82	**NYI**	**N**	1	0	0	0	0

Signed as free agent by **N.Y. Islanders** Oct. 10, 1978.

Billy Hay

HAY, WILLIAM CHARLES (Red) 6'3", 197 lbs.
B. Dec. 8, 1935, Saskatoon, Sask. Center, Shoots L
Won Calder Trophy, 1959-60

YEAR	TEAM & LEAGUE		GP	G	A	PTS	PIM
1959-60	**CHI**	**N**	70	18	37	55	31
1960-61			69	11	48	59	45
1961-62			60	11	52	63	34
1962-63			64	12	33	45	36
1963-64			70	23	33	56	30
1964-65			69	11	26	37	36
1965-66			68	20	31	51	20
1966-67			36	7	13	20	33
8 yrs.		**N Totals:**	506	113	273	386	265
PLAYOFFS							
1959-60	**CHI**	**N**	4	1	2	3	2
1960-61*			12	2	5	7	20
1961-62			12	3	7	10	18
1962-63			6	3	2	5	6
1963-64			7	3	1	4	4
1964-65			14	3	1	4	4
1965-66			6	0	2	2	4
1966-67			6	0	1	1	4
8 yrs.		**N Totals:**	67	15	21	36	62

Sold to **Chicago** by Montreal, April, 1959.

George Hay

HAY, GEORGE
B. Jan. 10, 1898, Listowel, Ont. — Left Wing
Hall of Fame, 1958

YEAR	TEAM & LEAGUE		GP	G	A	PTS	PIM
1926-27	**CHI**	**N**	37	14	8	22	12
1927-28	**DET**	**N**	42	22	13	35	20
1928-29			42	11	8	19	14
1929-30			42	18	15	33	8
1930-31			44	8	10	18	24
1932-33			34	1	6	7	6
1933-34			1	0	0	0	0
7 yrs.	**N Totals:**		242	74	60	134	84

PLAYOFFS

YEAR	TEAM & LEAGUE		GP	G	A	PTS	PIM
1926-27	**CHI**	**N**	2	1	2	3	12
1928-29	**DET**	**N**	2	1	0	1	2
1932-33			4	0	1	1	0
3 yrs.	**N Totals:**		8	2	3	5	14

Jim Hay

HAY, JAMES (Red-Eye) — 5'11", 185 lbs.
B. May 15, 1931, Saskatoon, Sask. — Defense, Shoots R

YEAR	TEAM & LEAGUE		GP	G	A	PTS	PIM
1952-53	**DET**	**N**	42	1	4	5	2
1953-54			12	0	0	0	0
1954-55			20	0	1	1	20
3 yrs.	**N Totals:**		74	1	5	6	22

PLAYOFFS

YEAR	TEAM & LEAGUE		GP	G	A	PTS	PIM
1952-53	**DET**	**N**	4	0	0	0	0
1954-55*			5	1	0	1	0
2 yrs.	**N Totals:**		9	1	0	1	0

Peter Hayek

HAYEK, PETER — 5'10", 198 lbs.
B. Nov. 16, 1957, Minneapolis, Minn. — Defense, Shoots L

YEAR	TEAM & LEAGUE		GP	G	A	PTS	PIM
1981-82	**MINN**	**N**	1	0	0	0	0

Hayes

HAYES
B. Unknown — Forward

YEAR	TEAM & LEAGUE		GP	G	A	PTS	PIM
1929-30	**DET**	**N**	1	0	0	0	0

Chris Hayes

HAYES, CHRISTOPHER JOSEPH — 5'10", 180 lbs.
B. Aug. 24, 1946, Rouyn, Que. — Left Wing, Shoots L

PLAYOFFS

YEAR	TEAM & LEAGUE		GP	G	A	PTS	PIM
1971-72*	**BOS**	**N**	1	0	0	0	0

Paul Haynes

HAYNES, PAUL — 5'10", 160 lbs.
B. Mar. 1, 1910, Montreal, Que. — Center, Shoots L

YEAR	TEAM & LEAGUE		GP	G	A	PTS	PIM
1930-31	**MON(M)**	**N**	19	1	0	1	0
1931-32			11	1	0	1	0
1932-33			47	16	25	41	18
1933-34			45	5	4	9	18
1934-35			11	1	2	3	0
	BOS	**N**	37	4	3	7	8
	2 team total		48	5	5	10	8
1935-36	**MONT**	**N**	48	5	19	24	24
1936-37			47	8	18	26	24
1937-38			48	13	22	35	25
1938-39			47	5	33	38	27
1939-40			23	2	8	10	8
1940-41			7	0	0	0	12
11 yrs.	**N Totals:**		390	61	134	195	164

PLAYOFFS

YEAR	TEAM & LEAGUE		GP	G	A	PTS	PIM
1931-32	**MON(M)**	**N**	4	0	0	0	0
1932-33			2	0	0	0	2
1933-34	**MONT**	**N**	4	0	1	1	2
1934-35	**BOS**	**N**	4	0	0	0	0
1936-37	**MONT**	**N**	5	2	3	5	0
1937-38			3	0	4	4	5
1938-39			3	0	0	0	4

Paul Haynes continued

YEAR	TEAM & LEAGUE		GP	G	A	PTS	PIM
7 yrs.	**N Totals:**		25	2	8	10	13

Steve Hazlett

HAZLETT, STEVEN — 5'9", 170 lbs.
B. Dec. 12, 1957, Sarnia, Ont. — Left Wing, Shoots L

YEAR	TEAM & LEAGUE		GP	G	A	PTS	PIM
1979-80	**VAN**	**N**	1	0	0	0	0

Galen Head

HEAD, GALEN RUSSELL — 5'10", 170 lbs.
B. Apr. 6, 1947, Grand Prairie, Alta. — Right Wing, Shoots R

YEAR	TEAM & LEAGUE		GP	G	A	PTS	PIM
1967-68	**DET**	**N**	1	0	0	0	0

Curley Headley

HEADLEY, FERN JAMES — 5'11", 175 lbs.
B. Mar. 2, 1901, Christie, N.D. — Defense

YEAR	TEAM & LEAGUE		GP	G	A	PTS	PIM
1924-25	**BOS**	**N**	11	0	1	1	2
	MONT	**N**	16	1	0	1	0
	2 team total		27	1	1	2	2

PLAYOFFS

YEAR	TEAM & LEAGUE		GP	G	A	PTS	PIM
1924-25	**MONT**	**N**	5	0	0	0	0

Dick Healey

HEALEY, RICHARD THOMAS — 5'10", 170 lbs.
B. Mar. 12, 1938, Vancouver, B.C. — Defense, Shoots L

YEAR	TEAM & LEAGUE		GP	G	A	PTS	PIM
1960-61	**DET**	**N**	1	0	0	0	2

Mark Heaslip

HEASLIP, MARK PATRICK — 5'10", 190 lbs.
B. Dec. 26, 1951, Duluth, Minn. — Right Wing, Shoots R

YEAR	TEAM & LEAGUE		GP	G	A	PTS	PIM
1976-77	**NYR**	**N**	19	1	0	1	31
1977-78			29	5	10	15	34
1978-79	**LA**	**N**	69	4	9	13	45
3 yrs.	**N Totals:**		117	10	19	29	110

PLAYOFFS

YEAR	TEAM & LEAGUE		GP	G	A	PTS	PIM
1977-78	**NYR**	**N**	3	0	0	0	0
1978-79	**LA**	**N**	2	0	0	0	2
2 yrs.	**N Totals:**		5	0	0	0	2

Traded to **N.Y. Rangers** by Los Angeles for John Campbell, May 28, 1976. Signed as free agent by **Los Angeles** June 14, 1978. Claimed by **Winnipeg** from Los Angeles in Expansion Draft, June 13, 1979.

Murray Heatley

HEATLEY, MURRAY (Mole) — 5'8", 180 lbs.
B. Nov. 7, 1948, Calgary, Alta. — Right Wing, Shoots R

YEAR	TEAM & LEAGUE		GP	G	A	PTS	PIM
1973-74	**MINN**	**W**	71	26	32	58	23
1974-75			22	5	9	14	31
	IND	**W**	29	15	8	23	25
	2 team total		51	20	17	37	56
1975-76			34	2	5	7	7
3 yrs.	**W Totals:**		156	48	54	102	86

PLAYOFFS

YEAR	TEAM & LEAGUE		GP	G	A	PTS	PIM
1973-74	**MINN**	**W**	10	1	0	1	2

Paul Heaver

HEAVER, PAUL GERHARD — 6'1", 195 lbs.
B. Paddington, England — Defense, Shoots R

YEAR	TEAM & LEAGUE		GP	G	A	PTS	PIM
1975-76	**TOR**	**W**	66	2	12	14	83
1976-77	**BIRM**	**W**	5	0	0	0	0
2 yrs.	**W Totals:**		71	2	12	14	83

Andy Hebenton

HEBENTON, ANDREW ALEXANDER — 5'9", 182 lbs.
B. Oct. 3, 1929, Winnipeg, Man. — Right Wing, Shoots L
Won Lady Byng Trophy, 1956-57

YEAR	TEAM & LEAGUE		GP	G	A	PTS	PIM
1955-56	**NYR**	**N**	70	24	14	38	8

Andy Hebenton continued

YEAR	TEAM & LEAGUE		GP	G	A	PTS	PIM
1956-57	BOS	N	70	21	23	44	10
1957-58	NYR	N	70	21	24	45	17
1958-59			70	33	29	62	8
1959-60			70	19	27	46	4
1960-61			70	26	28	54	10
1961-62			70	18	24	42	10
1962-63			70	15	22	37	8
1963-64	BOS	N	70	12	11	23	8
9 yrs.		N Totals:	630	189	202	391	83
PLAYOFFS							
1955-56	NYR	N	5	1	0	1	2
1956-57			5	2	0	2	2
1957-58			6	2	3	5	4
1961-62			6	1	2	3	0
4 yrs.		N Totals:	22	6	5	11	8

Drafted by **Boston** from New York, June 5, 1963. Traded by Boston with Orland Kurtenbach and Pat Stapleton to **Toronto** for Ron Stewart, June 8, 1967.

Anders Hedberg

HEDBERG, ANDERS 5'11", 175 lbs.
B. Feb. 25, 1951, Ornskoldsvik, Sweden Right Wing, Shoots L

YEAR	TEAM & LEAGUE		GP	G	A	PTS	PIM
1974-75	WINN	W	65	53	47	100	45
1975-76			76	50	55	105	48
1976-77			68	**70**	61	131	48
1977-78			77	63	59	122	60
1978-79	NYR	N	80	33	45	78	33
1979-80			80	32	39	71	21
1980-81			80	30	40	70	52
1981-82			4	0	1	1	0
1982-83			78	25	34	59	12
9 yrs.		N Totals:	322	120	159	279	118
		W Totals:	286	236	222	458	201
PLAYOFFS							
1975-76	WINN	W	13	13	6	19	15
1976-77			20	13	16	29	13
1977-78			9	9	6	15	2
1978-79	NYR	N	18	4	5	9	12
1979-80			9	3	2	5	7
1980-81			14	8	8	16	6
1982-83			9	4	8	12	4
7 yrs.		N Totals:	50	19	23	42	29
		W Totals:	42	35	28	63	30

Signed as free agent by **N.Y. Rangers** June 5, 1978.

Frank Heffernan

HEFFERNAN, FRANK
B. Unknown Forward

YEAR	TEAM & LEAGUE		GP	G	A	PTS	PIM
1919-20	TOR	N	17	0	0	0	4

Gerry Heffernan

HEFFERNAN, GERALD J. 5'9", 160 lbs.
B. July 24, 1916, Montreal, Que. Right Wing, Shoots R

YEAR	TEAM & LEAGUE		GP	G	A	PTS	PIM
1941-42	MONT	N	40	5	15	20	15
1943-44			43	28	20	48	12
2 yrs.		N Totals:	83	33	35	68	27
PLAYOFFS							
1941-42	MONT	N	2	2	1	3	0
1942-43			2	0	0	0	0
1943-44*			7	1	2	3	8
3 yrs.		N Totals:	11	3	3	6	8

Howie Heggedal

HEGGEDAL, HOWARD
B. Sept. 15, 1949 Right Wing

YEAR	TEAM & LEAGUE		GP	G	A	PTS	PIM
1972-73	LA	W	8	2	1	3	0
PLAYOFFS							
1972-73	LA	W	1	0	0	0	0

Bill Heindl

HEINDL, WILLIAM WAYNE 5'10", 175 lbs.
B. May 13, 1946, Sherbrooke, Que. Left Wing, Shoots L

YEAR	TEAM & LEAGUE		GP	G	A	PTS	PIM
1970-71	MINN	N	12	1	1	2	0
1971-72			2	0	0	0	0
1972-73	NYR	N	4	1	0	1	0
1973-74	CLEVE	W	67	4	14	18	4
4 yrs.		N Totals:	18	2	1	3	0
		W Totals:	67	4	14	18	4
PLAYOFFS							
1973-74	CLEVE	W	5	0	1	1	2

Drafted by **Atlanta** from Minnesota in Expansion Draft, June 6, 1972.

Lionel Heinrich

HEINRICH, LIONEL GRANT 5'10", 180 lbs.
B. Apr. 20, 1934, Churchbridge, Sask. Left Wing, Shoots L

YEAR	TEAM & LEAGUE		GP	G	A	PTS	PIM
1955-56	BOS	N	35	1	1	2	33

Earl Heiskala

HEISKALA, EARL WALDEMAR 6', 185 lbs.
B. Nov. 30, 1942, Kirkland Lake, Ont. Left Wing, Shoots L

YEAR	TEAM & LEAGUE		GP	G	A	PTS	PIM
1968-69	PHI	N	21	3	3	6	51
1969-70			65	8	7	15	171
1970-71			41	2	1	3	72
1972-73	LA	W	70	12	17	29	150
1973-74			24	2	6	8	45
5 yrs.		N Totals:	127	13	11	24	294
		W Totals:	94	14	23	37	195
PLAYOFFS							
1972-73	LA	W	5	1	1	2	4

Peter Helander

HELANDER, PETER 6'1", 185 lbs.
B. Dec. 4, 1951, Stockholm, Sweden Defense, Shoots L

YEAR	TEAM & LEAGUE		GP	G	A	PTS	PIM
1982-83	LA	N	7	0	1	1	0

Ott Heller

HELLER, EHRHARDT HENRY 6', 195 lbs.
B. June 2, 1910, Kitchener, Ont. Defense, Shoots R

YEAR	TEAM & LEAGUE		GP	G	A	PTS	PIM
1931-32	NYR	N	21	2	2	4	9
1932-33			40	5	7	12	31
1933-34			48	2	5	7	29
1934-35			47	3	11	14	31
1935-36			43	2	11	13	40
1936-37			48	5	12	17	42
1937-38			48	2	14	16	68
1938-39			48	0	23	23	42
1939-40			47	5	14	19	26
1940-41			48	2	16	18	42
1941-42			35	6	5	11	22
1942-43			45	4	14	18	14
1943-44			50	8	27	35	29
1944-45			45	7	12	19	26
1945-46			34	2	3	5	14
15 yrs.		N Totals:	647	55	176	231	465
PLAYOFFS							
1931-32	NYR	N	7	3	1	4	8
1933-34			2	0	0	0	0
1934-35			4	0	1	1	4
1936-37			9	0	0	0	11
1937-38			3	0	1	1	2
1938-39			7	0	1	1	10
1939-40*			12	0	3	3	12
1940-41			3	0	1	1	4
1941-42			6	0	0	0	0
9 yrs.		N Totals:	53	3	8	11	51

Harry Helman

HELMAN, HAROLD

Defense

YEAR	TEAM & LEAGUE	GP	G	A	PTS	PIM
1922-23	OTTA N	24	0	0	0	5
1923-24		17	1	0	1	2
1924-25		1	0	0	0	0
3 yrs.	N Totals:	42	1	0	1	7
PLAYOFFS						
1922-23*	OTTA N	4	0	0	0	0

Tony Hemmerling

HEMMERLING, ELMER CHARLES 5'11", 178 lbs.
B. May 11, 1913, Landis, Sask. Left Wing, Shoots L

YEAR	TEAM & LEAGUE	GP	G	A	PTS	PIM
1935-36	NYA N	6	0	0	0	0
1936-37		18	3	3	6	4
2 yrs.	N Totals:	24	3	3	6	4

Archie Henderson

HENDERSON, ARCHIE 6'6", 218 lbs.
B. Feb. 17, 1957, Calgary, Alta. Right Wing, Shoots R

YEAR	TEAM & LEAGUE	GP	G	A	PTS	PIM
1980-81	WASH N	7	1	0	1	28
1981-82	MINN N	1	0	0	0	0
1982-83	HART N	15	2	1	3	64
3 yrs.	N Totals:	23	3	1	4	92

Signed as free agent by **Minnesota** July 15, 1981. Signed as a free agent by **Hartford** Aug. 9, 1982.

Murray Henderson

HENDERSON, JOHN MURRAY (Moe) 6', 180 lbs.
B. Sept. 5, 1921, Toronto, Ont. Defense, Shoots L

YEAR	TEAM & LEAGUE	GP	G	A	PTS	PIM
1944-45	BOS N	5	0	1	1	4
1945-46		48	4	11	15	30
1946-47		57	5	12	17	63
1947-48		49	6	8	14	50
1948-49		60	2	9	11	28
1949-50		64	3	8	11	42
1950-51		66	4	7	11	37
1951-52		56	0	6	6	51
8 yrs.	N Totals:	405	24	62	86	305
PLAYOFFS						
1944-45	BOS N	7	0	1	1	2
1945-46		10	1	1	2	4
1946-47		4	0	0	0	4
1947-48		3	1	0	1	5
1948-49		5	0	1	1	2
1950-51		5	0	0	0	2
1951-52		7	0	0	0	4
7 yrs.	N Totals:	41	2	3	5	23

Paul Henderson

HENDERSON, PAUL GARNET 5'11", 180 lbs.
B. Jan. 28, 1943, Kincardine, Ont. Left Wing, Shoots R

YEAR	TEAM & LEAGUE	GP	G	A	PTS	PIM
1962-63	DET N	2	0	0	0	9
1963-64		32	3	3	6	6
1964-65		70	8	13	21	30
1965-66		69	22	24	46	34
1966-67		46	21	19	40	10
1967-68		50	13	20	33	35
	TOR N	13	5	6	11	8
	2 team total	63	18	26	44	43
1968-69		74	27	32	59	16
1969-70		67	20	22	42	18
1970-71		72	30	30	60	34
1971-72		73	38	20	58	32
1972-73		40	18	16	34	18
1973-74		69	24	31	55	40
1974-75	TOR W	58	30	33	63	18
1975-76		65	26	29	55	22
1976-77	BIRM W	81	23	25	48	30
1977-78		80	37	29	66	22
1978-79		76	24	27	51	20
1979-80	ATL N	30	7	6	13	6

Paul Henderson continued

YEAR	TEAM & LEAGUE	GP	G	A	PTS	PIM
18 yrs.	N Totals:	707	236	242	478	296
	W Totals:	360	140	143	283	112
PLAYOFFS						
1963-64	DET N	14	2	3	5	6
1964-65		7	0	2	2	0
1965-66		12	3	3	6	10
1968-69	TOR N	4	0	1	1	0
1970-71		6	5	1	6	4
1971-72		5	1	2	3	6
1973-74		4	0	2	2	2
1977-78	BIRM W	5	1	1	2	0
1979-80	ATL N	4	0	0	0	0
9 yrs.	N Totals:	56	11	14	25	28
	W Totals:	5	1	1	2	0

Traded to **Toronto** by Detroit with Norm Ullman and Floyd Smith for Frank Mahovlich, Pete Stemkowski, Garry Unger and the rights to Carl Brewer, March 3, 1968. Signed as free agent by **Atlanta** Sept. 17, 1979.

John Hendrickson

HENDRICKSON, JOHN GUNNARD 5'11", 175 lbs.
B. Dec. 5, 1936, Kingston, Ont. Defense, Shoots R

YEAR	TEAM & LEAGUE	GP	G	A	PTS	PIM
1957-58	DET N	1	0	0	0	0
1958-59		3	0	0	0	2
1961-62		1	0	0	0	2
3 yrs.	N Totals:	5	0	0	0	4

Lorne Henning

HENNING, LORNE EDWARD 5'11", 185 lbs.
B. Feb. 22, 1952, Melfort, Sask. Center, Shoots L

YEAR	TEAM & LEAGUE	GP	G	A	PTS	PIM
1972-73	NYI N	63	7	19	26	14
1973-74		60	12	15	27	6
1974-75		60	5	6	11	6
1975-76		80	7	10	17	16
1976-77		80	13	18	31	10
1977-78		79	12	15	27	16
1978-79		73	13	20	33	14
1979-80		39	3	6	9	6
1980-81		9	1	2	3	24
9 yrs.	N Totals:	543	73	111	184	112
PLAYOFFS						
1974-75	NYI N	17	0	2	2	0
1975-76		13	2	0	2	2
1976-77		12	0	1	1	0
1977-78		7	0	0	0	4
1978-79		10	2	0	2	0
1979-80*		21	3	4	7	2
1980-81*		1	0	0	0	0
7 yrs.	N Totals:	81	7	7	14	8

Camille Henry

HENRY, CAMILLE JOSEPH WILFRID (The Eel)
5'8", 152 lbs.
B. Jan. 31, 1933, Quebec City, Que. Center, Shoots L
Won Lady Byng Trophy, 1957-58
Won Calder Trophy, 1953-54

YEAR	TEAM & LEAGUE	GP	G	A	PTS	PIM
1953-54	NYR N	66	24	15	39	10
1954-55		21	5	2	7	4
1956-57		36	14	15	29	2
1957-58		70	32	24	56	2
1958-59		70	23	35	58	2
1959-60		49	12	15	27	6
1960-61		53	28	25	53	8
1961-62		60	23	15	38	8
1962-63		60	37	23	60	8
1963-64		68	29	26	55	8
1964-65		48	21	15	36	20
	CHI N	22	5	3	8	2
	2 team total	70	26	18	44	22
1967-68	NYR N	36	8	12	20	0
1968-69	STL N	64	17	22	39	8
1969-70		4	1	2	3	0
14 yrs.	N Totals:	727	279	249	528	88
PLAYOFFS						
1956-57	NYR N	5	2	3	5	0

Camille Henry continued

YEAR	TEAM	LEAGUE	GP	G	A	PTS	PIM
1957-58			6	1	4	5	5
1961-62			5	0	0	0	0
1964-65	CHI	N	14	1	0	1	2
1967-68	NYR	N	6	0	0	0	0
1968-69	STL	N	11	2	5	7	0
6 yrs.		N Totals:	47	6	12	18	7

Traded to **Chicago** by N.Y. Rangers with Don Johns, Wally Chevrier, and Billy Taylor for Doug Robinson, Wayne Hillman, and John Brenneman, Feb. 4, 1965. Traded to **N.Y. Rangers** by Chicago for Paul Shmyr, Aug. 17, 1967. Traded to **St. Louis** by N.Y. Rangers with Bill Plager and Robbie Irons for Don Caley and Wayne Rivers, June 13, 1968.

Pierre Henry

HENRY, PIERRE 5'10", 180 lbs.
B. Mar. 10, 1952, Montreal, Que. Left Wing, Shoots L

YEAR	TEAM	LEAGUE	GP	G	A	PTS	PIM
1972-73	PHI	W	19	2	3	5	13

Jimmy Herberts

HERBERTS, JIMMY
B. Collingwood, Ont. Forward

YEAR	TEAM	LEAGUE	GP	G	A	PTS	PIM
1924-25	BOS	N	30	17	5	22	50
1925-26			36	26	5	31	47
1926-27			35	15	7	22	51
1927-28	TOR	N	43	15	4	19	64
1928-29	DET	N	40	9	5	14	34
1929-30			26	1	3	4	4
6 yrs.		N Totals:	210	83	29	112	250
PLAYOFFS							
1926-27	BOS	N	8	3	0	3	33
1928-29	DET	N	1	0	0	0	2
2 yrs.		N Totals:	9	3	0	3	35

Art Herchenratter

HERCHENRATTER, ARTHUR 6', 185 lbs.
B. Nov. 24, 1917, Kitchener, Ont. Left Wing, Shoots L

YEAR	TEAM	LEAGUE	GP	G	A	PTS	PIM
1940-41	DET	N	10	1	2	3	2

Fred Hergerts

HERGERTS, FREDERICK 6'½", 190 lbs.
B. Jan. 29, 1913, Calgary, Alta. Center, Shoots R

YEAR	TEAM	LEAGUE	GP	G	A	PTS	PIM
1934-35	NYA	N	18	2	4	6	2
1935-36			1	0	0	0	0
2 yrs.		N Totals:	19	2	4	6	2

Philip Hergesheimer

HERGESHEIMER, PHILIP 5'10", 175 lbs.
B. July 9, 1914, Winnipeg, Man. Right Wing, Shoots R

YEAR	TEAM	LEAGUE	GP	G	A	PTS	PIM
1939-40	CHI	N	41	9	11	20	6
1940-41			47	9	11	20	9
1941-42			23	3	11	14	2
	BOS	N	3	0	0	0	2
	2 team total		26	3	11	14	4
1942-43	CHI	N	9	1	3	4	0
4 yrs.		N Totals:	123	22	36	58	19
PLAYOFFS							
1939-40	CHI	N	2	0	0	0	0
1940-41			5	0	0	0	2
2 yrs.		N Totals:	7	0	0	0	2

Wally Hergesheimer

HERGESHEIMER, WALTER E. (Hergie) 5'8", 155 lbs.
B. Jan. 8, 1927, Winnipeg, Man. Right Wing, Shoots R

YEAR	TEAM	LEAGUE	GP	G	A	PTS	PIM
1951-52	NYR	N	68	26	12	38	6
1952-53			70	30	29	59	10
1953-54			66	27	16	43	42
1954-55			14	4	2	6	4
1955-56			70	22	18	40	26
1956-57	CHI	N	41	2	8	10	12
1958-59	NYR	N	22	3	0	3	6

Wally Hergesheimer continued

YEAR	TEAM	LEAGUE	GP	G	A	PTS	PIM
7 yrs.		N Totals:	351	114	85	199	106
PLAYOFFS							
1955-56	NYR	N	5	1	0	1	0

Purchased by **Chicago** from N.Y. Rangers, Sept. 19, 1956.

Red Heron

HERON, ROBERT GEATREX 5'11", 170 lbs.
B. Dec. 31, 1917, Toronto, Ont. Center, Shoots L

YEAR	TEAM	LEAGUE	GP	G	A	PTS	PIM
1938-39	TOR	N	6	0	0	0	0
1939-40			42	11	12	23	12
1940-41			35	9	5	14	12
1941-42	NYA	N	11	0	1	1	2
	MONT	N	12	1	1	2	12
	2 team total		23	1	2	3	14
4 yrs.		N Totals:	106	21	19	40	38
PLAYOFFS							
1939-40	TOR	N	9	2	0	2	55
1940-41			7	0	2	2	0
2 yrs.		N Totals:	16	2	2	4	55

Don Herriman

HERRIMAN, DONALD 5'10", 165 lbs.
B. Jan. 2, 1946, Sault Ste. Marie, Ont. Left Wing, Shoots L

YEAR	TEAM	LEAGUE	GP	G	A	PTS	PIM
1972-73	PHI	W	78	24	48	72	63
1973-74	NY-NJ	W	44	11	21	32	59
1974-75	EDM	W	33	1	2	3	21
3 yrs.		W Totals:	155	36	71	107	143
PLAYOFFS							
1972-73	PHI	W	4	1	0	1	14

Bob Hess

HESS, ROBERT GEORGE 5'11", 180 lbs.
B. May 19, 1955, Middleton, N.S. Defense, Shoots L

YEAR	TEAM	LEAGUE	GP	G	A	PTS	PIM
1974-75	STL	N	76	9	30	39	58
1975-76			78	9	23	32	58
1976-77			53	4	18	22	14
1977-78			55	2	12	14	16
1978-79			27	3	4	7	14
1980-81			4	0	0	0	4
1981-82	BUF	N	33	0	8	8	14
7 yrs.		N Totals:	326	27	95	122	178
PLAYOFFS							
1974-75	STL	N	10	0	0	0	2
1975-76			1	0	1	1	0
1976-77			1	0	0	0	0
1980-81	BUF	N	1	1	0	1	0
4 yrs.		N Totals:	13	1	1	2	2

Traded to **Buffalo** by St. Louis with St. Louis' fourth-round choice (Anders Wickenberg) in the 1981 Entry Draft for Bill Stewart, Oct. 30, 1980.

Obs Heximer

HEXIMER, ORVILLE RUSSELL 5'7", 159 lbs.
B. Feb. 16, 1910, Niagara Falls, Ont. Left Wing, Shoots L

YEAR	TEAM	LEAGUE	GP	G	A	PTS	PIM
1929-30	NYR	N	19	1	0	1	4
1932-33	BOS	N	48	7	5	12	24
1934-35	NYA	N	18	5	2	7	0
3 yrs.		N Totals:	85	13	7	20	28
PLAYOFFS							
1932-33	BOS	N	5	0	0	0	2

Bryan Hextall

HEXTALL, BRYAN 5'10", 180 lbs.
B. July 31, 1913, Grenfell, Sask. Right Wing, Shoots L
Won Art Ross Trophy, 1941-42
Hall of Fame, 1969

YEAR	TEAM	LEAGUE	GP	G	A	PTS	PIM
1936-37	NYR	N	1	0	1	1	0
1937-38			48	17	4	21	6

Bryan Hextall continued

YEAR	TEAM	LEAGUE	GP	G	A	PTS	PIM
1938-39			48	20	15	35	18
1939-40			48	**24**	15	39	52
1940-41			48	**26**	18	44	16
1941-42			48	24	32	**56**	30
1942-43			50	27	32	59	28
1943-44			50	21	33	54	41
1945-46			3	0	1	1	0
1946-47			60	21	10	31	12
1947-48			43	8	14	22	18
11 yrs.		N Totals:	447	188	175	363	221
PLAYOFFS							
1937-38	NYR	N	3	2	0	2	0
1938-39			7	0	1	1	4
1939-40*			12	4	3	7	11
1940-41			3	0	1	1	0
1941-42			6	1	1	2	4
1947-48			6	1	3	4	0
6 yrs.		N Totals:	37	8	9	17	19

Bryan Hextall

HEXTALL, BRYAN LEE 5'11", 185 lbs.
B. May 23, 1941, Winnipeg, Man. Center, Shoots L

YEAR	TEAM	LEAGUE	GP	G	A	PTS	PIM
1962-63	NYR	N	21	0	2	2	10
1969-70	PITT	N	66	12	19	31	87
1970-71			76	16	32	48	133
1971-72			78	20	24	44	126
1972-73			78	21	33	54	113
1973-74			37	2	7	9	39
	ATL	N	40	2	4	6	55
	2 team total		77	4	11	15	94
1974-75			74	18	16	34	62
1975-76	DET	N	21	0	4	4	29
	MINN	N	58	8	20	28	84
	2 team total		79	8	24	32	113
8 yrs.		N Totals:	549	99	161	260	738
PLAYOFFS							
1969-70	PITT	N	10	0	1	1	34
1971-72			4	0	2	2	9
1973-74	ATL	N	4	0	1	1	16
3 yrs.		N Totals:	18	0	4	4	59

Drafted by **Oakland** from N.Y. Rangers in Expansion Draft, June 6, 1967. Sold to **Toronto** by Oakland, Oct. 12, 1967. Sold to **Pittsburgh** by Toronto, May 20, 1969. Claimed on waivers by **Atlanta** from Pittsburgh, Jan. 6, 1974. Traded to **Detroit** by Atlanta for Dave Kryskow, June 5, 1975. Traded to **Minnesota** by Detroit for Rick Chinnick, Nov. 21, 1975.

Dennis Hextall

HEXTALL, DENNIS HAROLD 5'11", 175 lbs.
B. Apr. 17, 1943, Winnipeg, Man. Center, Shoots L

YEAR	TEAM	LEAGUE	GP	G	A	PTS	PIM
1968-69	NYR	N	13	1	4	5	25
1969-70	LA	N	28	5	7	12	40
1970-71	CALIF	N	78	21	31	52	**217**
1971-72	MINN	N	36	6	10	16	49
1972-73			78	30	52	82	140
1973-74			78	20	62	82	138
1974-75			80	17	57	74	147
1975-76			59	11	35	46	93
	DET	N	17	5	9	14	71
	2 team total		76	16	44	60	164
1976-77			78	14	32	46	158
1977-78			78	16	33	49	195
1978-79			20	4	8	12	33
	WASH	N	26	2	9	11	43
	2 team total		46	6	17	23	76
1979-80			15	1	1	2	49
12 yrs.		N Totals:	684	153	350	503	1398
PLAYOFFS							
1967-68	NYR	N	2	0	0	0	0
1971-72	MINN	N	7	0	2	2	19
1972-73			6	2	0	2	16
1977-78	DET	N	7	1	1	2	10
4 yrs.		N Totals:	22	3	3	6	45

Traded to **Los Angeles** by N.Y. Rangers with Leon Rochefort for Real Lemieux, June 9, 1969. Sold to **California** by Los Angeles on May 22, 1970. Traded to **Minnesota** by California for Joey Johnston and Walt McKechnie, May 20, 1971. Traded to **Detroit** by Minnesota for Bill Hogaboam and Jimmy Roberts (Los Angeles' second-round choice in 1976 Amateur Draft transferred to Detroit via earlier deal), Feb. 27, 1976. Signed as free agent by **Washington** Feb. 7, 1979.

Vic Heyliger

HEYLIGER, VICTOR 5'8½", 175 lbs.
B. Sept. 26, 1919, Boston, Mass. Center

YEAR	TEAM	LEAGUE	GP	G	A	PTS	PIM
1937-38	CHI	N	8	0	0	0	0
1943-44			26	2	3	5	2
2 yrs.		N Totals:	34	2	3	5	2

Bill Hicke

HICKE, WILLIAM LAWRENCE 5'8", 170 lbs.
B. Mar. 31, 1938, Regina, Sask. Right Wing, Shoots L

YEAR	TEAM	LEAGUE	GP	G	A	PTS	PIM
1959-60	MONT	N	43	3	10	13	17
1960-61			70	18	27	45	31
1961-62			70	20	31	51	42
1962-63			70	17	22	39	39
1963-64			48	11	9	20	41
1964-65			17	0	1	1	6
	NYR	N	40	6	11	17	26
	2 team total		57	6	12	18	32
1965-66			49	9	18	27	21
1966-67			48	3	4	7	11
1967-68	OAK	N	52	21	19	40	32
1968-69	CALIF	N	67	25	36	61	68
1969-70	OAK	N	69	15	29	44	14
1970-71	CALIF	N	74	18	17	35	41
1971-72	PITT	N	12	2	0	2	6
1972-73	ALTA	W	73	14	24	38	20
14 yrs.		N Totals:	729	168	234	402	395
		W Totals:	73	14	24	38	20
PLAYOFFS							
1958-59*	MONT	N	1	0	0	0	0
1959-60*			7	1	2	3	0
1960-61			5	2	0	2	19
1961-62			6	0	2	2	14
1962-63			5	0	0	0	0
1963-64			7	0	2	2	2
1968-69	CALIF	N	7	0	3	3	4
1969-70	OAK	N	4	0	1	1	2
8 yrs.		N Totals:	42	3	10	13	41

Traded to **N.Y. Rangers** by Mont. Canadiens for Dick Duff, Dec. 22, 1964. Drafted by **Oakland** from N.Y. Rangers in Expansion Draft, June 6, 1967. Sold to **Pittsburgh** by California, Sept. 7, 1971. Sold to **Detroit** by Pittsburgh, Nov. 22, 1971.

Ernie Hicke

HICKE, ERNEST ALLAN 5'11", 180 lbs.
B. Nov. 7, 1947, Regina, Sask. Left Wing, Shoots L

YEAR	TEAM	LEAGUE	GP	G	A	PTS	PIM
1970-71	CALIF	N	78	22	25	47	62
1971-72			68	11	12	23	55
1972-73	ATL	N	58	14	23	37	37
	NYI	N	1	0	0	0	0
	2 team total		59	14	23	37	37
1973-74			55	6	7	13	26
1974-75			20	2	6	8	40
	MINN	N	42	15	13	28	51
	2 team total		62	17	19	36	91
1975-76			80	23	19	42	77
1976-77			77	30	20	50	41
1977-78	LA	N	41	9	15	24	18
8 yrs.		N Totals:	520	132	140	272	407
PLAYOFFS							
1976-77	MINN	N	2	1	0	1	0

Traded to **Oakland** by Montreal with Montreal's first choice (Chris Oddleifson) in 1970 Amateur Draft for Francois Lacombe and Oakland's first choice (Guy Lafleur) in 1971 Amateur Draft and cash, May 22, 1970. Drafted by **Atlanta** from California in Expansion Draft, June 6, 1972. Traded to **N.Y. Islanders** by Atlanta with a player to be named later (Billy MacMillan, May 29, 1973), for Arnie Brown, Feb. 13, 1973. Traded to **Minnesota** by N.Y. Islanders with Doug Rombough for J.P. Parise, Jan. 5, 1975. Signed as free agent by **Los Angeles** Sept. 16, 1977.

YEAR	TEAM & LEAGUE		GP	G	A	PTS	PIM

Greg Hickey

HICKEY, GREG (H) 5'10", 160 lbs.
B. Mar. 8, 1955, Toronto, Ont. Left Wing, Shoots L

YEAR	TEAM	LEAGUE	GP	G	A	PTS	PIM
1977-78	NYR	N	1	0	0	0	0

Pat Hickey

HICKEY, PATRICK JOSEPH (Hitch) 5'1", 190 lbs.
B. May 15, 1953, Brantford, Ont. Left Wing, Shoots L

YEAR	TEAM	LEAGUE	GP	G	A	PTS	PIM
1973-74	TOR	W	78	26	29	55	52
1974-75			74	34	34	68	50
1975-76	NYR	N	70	14	22	36	36
1976-77			80	23	17	40	35
1977-78			80	40	33	73	47
1978-79			80	34	41	75	56
1979-80			7	2	2	4	10
	COLO	N	24	7	9	16	10
	TOR	N	45	22	16	38	16
	3 team total		76	31	27	58	36
1980-81			72	16	33	49	49
1981-82			1	0	0	0	0
	NYR	N	53	15	14	29	32
	QUE	N	7	0	1	1	4
	3 team total		61	15	15	30	36
1982-83	STL	N	1	0	0	0	0
10 yrs.		N Totals:	520	173	188	361	295
		W Totals:	152	60	63	123	102

PLAYOFFS

YEAR	TEAM	LEAGUE	GP	G	A	PTS	PIM
1973-74	TOR	W	12	3	3	6	12
1974-75			5	0	1	1	4
1977-78	NYR	N	3	2	0	2	0
1978-79			18	1	7	8	6
1979-80	TOR	N	3	0	0	0	2
1980-81			2	0	0	0	0
1981-82	QUE	N	15	1	3	4	21
7 yrs.		N Totals:	41	4	10	14	29
		W Totals:	17	3	4	7	16

Traded to **Colorado** by N.Y. Rangers with Lucien DeBlois, Mike McEwen, Dean Turner and future considerations (Bobby Sheehan) for Barry Beck, Nov. 2, 1979. Traded to **Toronto** by Colorado with Wilf Paiement for Lanny McDonald and Joel Quenneville, Dec. 29, 1979. Traded to **N.Y. Rangers** by Toronto for Rangers' fifth-round choice (Sylvain Charland) in 1982 Entry Draft, Oct. 16, 1981. Rights transferred to **Quebec** by N.Y. Rangers on Mar. 8, 1982, as compensation when Dean Talafous retired. Traded by Quebec to **St. Louis** for Rick LaPointe, August 4, 1982.

Doug Hicks

HICKS, DOUGLAS ALLAN (Hicksy) 6', 185 lbs.
B. May 28, 1550, Cold Lake, Alta. Defense, Shoots L

YEAR	TEAM	LEAGUE	GP	G	A	PTS	PIM
1974-75	MINN	N	80	6	12	18	51
1975-76			80	5	13	18	54
1976-77			79	5	14	19	68
1977-78			61	2	9	11	51
	CHI	N	13	1	7	8	31
	2 team total		74	3	16	19	82
1978-79			44	1	8	9	15
1979-80	EDM	N	78	9	31	40	52
1980-81			59	5	16	21	76
1981-82			49	3	20	23	55
	WASH	N	12	0	1	1	11
	2 team total		61	3	21	24	66
1982-83			6	0	0	0	7
9 yrs.		N Totals:	561	37	131	168	471

PLAYOFFS

YEAR	TEAM	LEAGUE	GP	G	A	PTS	PIM
1976-77	MINN	N	2	0	0	0	7
1977-78	CHI	N	4	1	0	1	2
1979-80	EDM	N	3	0	0	0	2
1980-81			9	1	1	2	4
4 yrs.		N Totals:	18	2	1	3	15

Traded to **Chicago** by Minnesota for a player to be named later (Pierre Plante, May 4, 1978), Mar. 14, 1978. Claimed by **Edmonton** from Chicago in Expansion Draft, June 13, 1979. Traded to **Washington** by Edmonton for Todd Bidner, Mar. 9, 1982.

Glenn Hicks

HICKS, GLENN 5'10", 177 lbs.
B. Aug. 28, 1958, Red Deer, Alta. Left Wing, Shoots L

YEAR	TEAM	LEAGUE	GP	G	A	PTS	PIM
1978-79	WINN	W	69	6	10	16	48
1979-80	DET	N	50	1	2	3	43
1980-81			58	5	10	15	84
3 yrs.		N Totals:	108	6	12	18	127
		W Totals:	69	6	10	16	48

PLAYOFFS

YEAR	TEAM	LEAGUE	GP	G	A	PTS	PIM
1978-79	WINN	W	7	1	1	2	4

Reclaimed by **Detroit** from Winnipeg prior to Expansion Draft, June 9, 1979.

Hal Hicks

HICKS, HAROLD H.
B. Dec. 10, 1900, Ottawa, Ont. Defense

YEAR	TEAM	LEAGUE	GP	G	A	PTS	PIM
1928-29	MON(M)	N	44	2	0	2	27
1929-30	DET	N	44	3	2	5	35
1930-31			22	2	0	2	10
3 yrs.		N Totals:	110	7	2	9	72

Wayne Hicks

HICKS, WAYNE WILSON 5'10", 190 lbs.
B. Apr. 9, 1937, Aberdeen, Wash. Right Wing, Shoots R

YEAR	TEAM	LEAGUE	GP	G	A	PTS	PIM
1960-61	CHI	N	1	0	0	0	0
1962-63	BOS	N	65	7	9	16	14
1963-64	MONT	N	2	0	0	0	0
1967-68	PHI	N	32	2	7	9	6
	PITT	N	15	4	7	11	2
	2 team total		47	6	14	20	8
4 yrs.		N Totals:	115	13	23	36	22

PLAYOFFS

YEAR	TEAM	LEAGUE	GP	G	A	PTS	PIM
1959-60	CHI	N	1	0	1	1	0
1960-61*			1	0	0	0	2
2 yrs.		N Totals:	2	0	1	1	2

Traded to **Montreal** by Chicago for Al MacNeil, May, 1962. Sold to **Pittsburgh** by Philadelphia, Feb. 27, 1968.

Paul Higgins

HIGGINS, PAUL 6'1", 190 lbs.
B. Jan. 13, 1962, St. John, N.B. Right Wing, Shoots R

YEAR	TEAM	LEAGUE	GP	G	A	PTS	PIM
1981-82	TOR	N	3	0	0	0	17
1982-83			22	0	0	0	135
2 yrs.		N Totals:	25	0	0	0	152

PLAYOFFS

YEAR	TEAM	LEAGUE	GP	G	A	PTS	PIM
1982-83	TOR	N	1	0	0	0	0

Tim Higgins

HIGGINS, TIM RAY 6', 181 lbs.
B. Feb. 7, 1958, Ottawa, Ont. Right Wing, Shoots R

YEAR	TEAM	LEAGUE	GP	G	A	PTS	PIM
1978-79	CHI	N	36	7	16	23	30
1979-80			74	13	12	25	50
1980-81			78	24	35	59	86
1981-82			74	20	30	50	85
1982-83			64	14	9	23	63
5 yrs.		N Totals:	326	78	102	180	314

PLAYOFFS

YEAR	TEAM	LEAGUE	GP	G	A	PTS	PIM
1978-79	CHI	N	4	0	0	0	0
1979-80			7	0	3	3	10
1980-81			3	0	0	0	0
1981-82			12	3	1	4	15
1982-83			13	1	3	4	10
5 yrs.		N Totals:	39	4	7	11	35

Ike Hildebrand

HILDEBRAND, ISAAC BRUCE 5'8", 155 lbs.
B. May 27, 1927, Winnipeg, Man. Right Wing, Shoots R

YEAR	TEAM & LEAGUE		GP	G	A	PTS	PIM
1953-54	**NYR**	**N**	31	6	7	13	12
	CHI	**N**	7	1	4	5	4
	2 team total		38	7	11	18	16
1954-55			3	0	0	0	0
2 yrs.		**N Totals:**	41	7	11	18	16

Sold by N.Y. Rangers to Vancouver (WHL), Jan. 7, 1954. Sold by Vancouver to **Chicago** Jan. 20, 1954. Traded to **Detroit** by Chicago for Lorne Davis, Oct. 14, 1954.

Al Hill

HILL, ALLAN DOUGLAS 6'1", 175 lbs.
B. Apr. 22, 1955, Nanaimo, B.C. Left Wing, Shoots L

YEAR	TEAM & LEAGUE		GP	G	A	PTS	PIM
1976-77	**PHI**	**N**	9	2	4	6	27
1977-78			3	0	0	0	2
1978-79			31	5	11	16	28
1979-80			61	16	10	26	53
1980-81			57	10	15	25	45
1981-82			41	6	13	19	58
6 yrs.		**N Totals:**	202	39	53	92	213

PLAYOFFS

YEAR	TEAM & LEAGUE		GP	G	A	PTS	PIM
1978-79	**PHI**	**N**	7	1	0	1	2
1979-80			19	3	5	8	19
1980-81			12	2	4	6	18
1981-82			3	0	0	0	0
4 yrs.		**N Totals:**	41	6	9	15	39

Brian Hill

HILL, BRIAN NELSON 6', 175 lbs.
B. Jan. 12, 1957, Regina, Sask. Right Wing, Shoots R

YEAR	TEAM & LEAGUE		GP	G	A	PTS	PIM
1979-80	**HART**	**N**	19	1	1	2	4

Claimed by **Hartford** from Atlanta in Expansion Draft, June 13, 1979.

Mel Hill

HILL, JOHN MELVIN (Sudden Death) 5'10", 175 lbs.
B. Feb. 15, 1914, Glenboro, Man. Right Wing, Shoots R

YEAR	TEAM & LEAGUE		GP	G	A	PTS	PIM
1937-38	**BOS**	**N**	8	2	0	2	2
1938-39			44	10	10	20	16
1939-40			37	9	11	20	19
1940-41			41	5	4	9	4
1941-42	**NYA**	**N**	47	14	23	37	10
1942-43	**TOR**	**N**	49	17	27	44	47
1943-44			17	9	10	19	6
1944-45			45	18	17	35	14
1945-46			35	5	7	12	10
9 yrs.		**N Totals:**	323	89	109	198	128

PLAYOFFS

YEAR	TEAM & LEAGUE		GP	G	A	PTS	PIM
1938-39*	**BOS**	**N**	12	6	3	9	12
1939-40			2	0	0	0	0
1940-41*			10	1	1	2	0
1942-43	**TOR**	**N**	6	3	0	3	0
1944-45*			13	2	3	5	6
5 yrs.		**N Totals:**	43	12	7	19	18

Dutch Hiller

HILLER, WILBERT CARL 5'8", 170 lbs.
B. Kitchener, Ont. Left Wing, Shoots L

YEAR	TEAM & LEAGUE		GP	G	A	PTS	PIM
1937-38	**NYR**	**N**	9	0	1	1	2
1938-39			48	10	19	29	22
1939-40			48	13	18	31	57
1940-41			45	8	10	18	20
1941-42	**DET**	**N**	7	0	0	0	0
	BOS	**N**	43	7	10	17	19
	2 team total		50	7	10	17	19
1942-43	**MONT**	**N**	42	8	6	14	4
1943-44	**NYR**	**N**	50	18	22	40	15
1944-45	**MONT**	**N**	48	20	16	36	20
1945-46			45	7	11	18	4
9 yrs.		**N Totals:**	385	91	113	204	163

Dutch Hiller continued

PLAYOFFS

YEAR	TEAM & LEAGUE		GP	G	A	PTS	PIM
1937-38	**NYR**	**N**	1	0	0	0	0
1938-39			7	1	0	1	9
1939-40*			12	2	4	6	2
1940-41			3	0	0	0	0
1941-42	**BOS**	**N**	5	0	1	1	0
1942-43	**MONT**	**N**	5	1	0	1	4
1944-45			6	1	1	2	4
1945-46*			9	4	2	6	2
8 yrs.		**N Totals:**	48	9	8	17	21

Randy Hillier

HILLIER, RANDY GEORGE 6', 178 lbs.
B. Mar. 30, 1960, Toronto, Ont. Defense, Shoots R

YEAR	TEAM & LEAGUE		GP	G	A	PTS	PIM
1981-82	**BOS**	**N**	25	0	8	8	29
1982-83			70	0	10	10	99
2 yrs.		**N Totals:**	95	0	18	18	128

PLAYOFFS

YEAR	TEAM & LEAGUE		GP	G	A	PTS	PIM
1981-82	**BOS**	**N**	8	0	1	1	16
1982-83			3	0	0	0	4
2 yrs.		**N Totals:**	11	0	1	1	20

Floyd Hillman

HILLMAN, FLOYD ARTHUR 5'11", 170 lbs.
B. Nov. 19, 1933, Ruthven, Ont. Defense, Shoots L

YEAR	TEAM & LEAGUE		GP	G	A	PTS	PIM
1956-57	**BOS**	**N**	6	0	0	0	10

Larry Hillman

HILLMAN, LARRY MORLEY 6', 181 lbs.
B. Feb. 5, 1937, Kirkland Lake, Ont. Defense, Shoots L

YEAR	TEAM & LEAGUE		GP	G	A	PTS	PIM
1954-55	**DET**	**N**	6	0	0	0	2
1955-56			47	0	3	3	53
1956-57			16	1	2	3	4
1957-58	**BOS**	**N**	70	3	19	22	60
1958-59			55	3	10	13	19
1959-60			2	0	1	1	2
1960-61	**TOR**	**N**	62	3	10	13	59
1961-62			5	0	0	0	4
1962-63			5	0	0	0	2
1963-64			33	0	4	4	31
1964-65			2	0	0	0	2
1965-66			48	3	25	28	34
1966-67			67	4	19	23	40
1967-68			55	3	17	20	13
1968-69	**MINN**	**N**	12	1	5	6	0
	MONT	**N**	25	0	5	5	17
	2 team total		37	1	10	11	17
1969-70	**PHI**	**N**	76	5	26	31	73
1970-71			73	3	13	16	39
1971-72	**LA**	**N**	22	1	2	3	11
	BUF	**N**	43	1	11	12	58
	2 team total		65	2	13	15	69
1972-73			78	5	24	29	56
1973-74	**CLEVE**	**W**	44	5	21	26	37
1974-75			77	0	16	16	83
1975-76	**WINN**	**W**	71	1	12	13	62
22 yrs.		**N Totals:**	802	36	196	232	579
		W Totals:	192	6	49	55	182

PLAYOFFS

YEAR	TEAM & LEAGUE		GP	G	A	PTS	PIM
1954-55*	**DET**	**N**	3	0	0	0	0
1955-56			10	0	1	1	6
1957-58	**BOS**	**N**	11	0	2	2	6
1958-59			7	0	1	1	0
1960-61	**TOR**	**N**	5	0	0	0	0
1963-64*			11	0	0	0	2
1965-66			4	1	1	2	6
1966-67*			12	1	2	3	0
1968-69*	**MONT**	**N**	1	0	0	0	0
1970-71	**PHI**	**N**	4	0	2	2	2
1972-73	**BUF**	**N**	6	0	0	0	8
1974-75	**CLEVE**	**W**	5	1	3	4	8
1975-76	**WINN**	**W**	12	0	2	2	32
13 yrs.		**N Totals:**	74	2	9	11	30
		W Totals:	17	1	5	6	40

Drafted by **Toronto** from Detroit, June 8, 1960.

Wayne Hillman

HILLMAN, WAYNE JAMES 6'1", 205 lbs.
B. Nov. 13, 1938, Kirkland Lake, Ont. Defense, Shoots L

YEAR	TEAM & LEAGUE		GP	G	A	PTS	PIM
1961-62	CHI	N	19	0	2	2	14
1962-63			67	3	5	8	74
1963-64			59	1	4	5	31
1964-65			19	0	1	1	8
	NYR	N	22	1	8	9	26
	2 team total		41	1	9	10	34
1965-66			68	3	17	20	70
1966-67			67	2	12	14	43
1967-68			62	0	5	5	46
1968-69	MINN	N	50	0	8	8	32
1969-70	PHI	N	68	3	5	8	69
1970-71			69	5	7	12	47
1971-72			47	0	3	3	21
1972-73			74	0	10	10	33
1973-74	CLEVE	W	66	1	7	8	51
1974-75			60	2	9	11	37
14 yrs.		N Totals:	691	18	87	105	514
		W Totals:	126	3	16	19	88

PLAYOFFS

YEAR	TEAM & LEAGUE		GP	G	A	PTS	PIM
1960-61*	CHI	N	1	0	0	0	0
1962-63			6	0	2	2	2
1963-64			7	0	1	1	15
1966-67	NYR	N	4	0	0	0	2
1967-68			2	0	0	0	0
1972-73	PHI	N	8	0	0	0	0
1973-74	CLEVE	W	5	0	0	0	16
1974-75			5	0	2	2	2
8 yrs.		N Totals:	28	0	3	3	19
		W Totals:	10	0	2	2	18

Traded to **N.Y. Rangers** with Doug Robinson and John Brenneman by Chicago for Camille Henry, Don Johns, Billy Taylor, and Wally Chevrier, Feb. 4, 1965. Traded to **Minnesota** by N.Y. Rangers with Dan Seguin and Joey Johnston for Dave Balon, June 12, 1968. Traded to **Philadelphia** by Minnesota for John Miszuk, May 14, 1969.

John Hilworth

HILWORTH, JOHN 6'4", 205 lbs.
B. May 23, 1957, Jasper, Alta. Defense, Shoots R

YEAR	TEAM & LEAGUE		GP	G	A	PTS	PIM
1977-78	DET	N	5	0	0	0	12
1978-79			37	1	1	2	66
1979-80			15	0	0	0	11
3 yrs.		N Totals:	57	1	1	2	89

Normie Himes

HIMES, NORMAN 5'9", 145 lbs.
B. Apr. 13, 1903, Galt, Ont. Shoots R

YEAR	TEAM & LEAGUE		GP	G	A	PTS	PIM
1926-27	NYA	N	42	9	2	11	14
1927-28			44	14	5	19	22
1928-29			44	10	0	10	25
1929-30			44	28	22	50	15
1930-31			44	15	9	24	18
1931-32			48	7	21	28	9
1932-33			48	9	25	34	12
1933-34			48	9	16	25	10
1934-35			40	5	13	18	2
9 yrs.		N Totals:	402	106	113	219	127

PLAYOFFS

YEAR	TEAM & LEAGUE		GP	G	A	PTS	PIM
1928-29	NYA	N	2	0	0	0	0

David Hindmarch

HINDMARCH, DAVID 5'11", 182 lbs.
B. Oct. 15, 1958, Vancouver, B.C. Right Wing, Shoots R

YEAR	TEAM & LEAGUE		GP	G	A	PTS	PIM
1980-81	CALG	N	1	1	0	1	0
1981-82			9	3	0	3	0
1982-83			60	11	12	23	23
3 yrs.		N Totals:	70	15	12	27	23

PLAYOFFS

YEAR	TEAM & LEAGUE		GP	G	A	PTS	PIM
1980-81	CALG	N	6	0	0	0	2
1982-83			4	0	0	0	4

David Hindmarch continued

YEAR	TEAM & LEAGUE		GP	G	A	PTS	PIM
2 yrs.		N Totals:	10	0	0	0	6

Andre Hinse

HINSE, JOSEPH CHARLES ANDRE 5'9", 172 lbs.
B. Apr. 19, 1945, Trois-Rivieres, Que. Left Wing, Shoots L

YEAR	TEAM & LEAGUE		GP	G	A	PTS	PIM
1967-68	TOR	N	4	0	0	0	0
1973-74	HOUS	W	69	24	56	80	39
1974-75			75	39	47	86	12
1975-76			70	35	38	73	6
1976-77			0	0	0	0	0
	PHOE	W	42	4	10	14	12
	2 team total		42	4	10	14	12
5 yrs.		N Totals:	4	0	0	0	0
		W Totals:	256	102	151	253	69

PLAYOFFS

YEAR	TEAM & LEAGUE		GP	G	A	PTS	PIM
1973-74	HOUS	W	14	8	9	17	18
1974-75			11	5	4	9	8
1975-76			17	2	3	5	2
3 yrs.		W Totals:	42	15	16	31	28

Dan Hinton

HINTON, DANIEL ANTHONY 6'1", 175 lbs.
B. May 24, 1953, Toronto, Ont. Left Wing, Shoots L

YEAR	TEAM & LEAGUE		GP	G	A	PTS	PIM
1976-77	CHI	N	14	0	0	0	16

Bert Hirschfeld

HIRSCHFELD, JOHN ALBERT 5'10", 165 lbs.
B. Mar. 1, 1929, Halifax, N.S. Left Wing, Shoots L

YEAR	TEAM & LEAGUE		GP	G	A	PTS	PIM
1949-50	MONT	N	13	1	2	3	2
1950-51			20	0	2	2	0
2 yrs.		N Totals:	33	1	4	5	2

PLAYOFFS

YEAR	TEAM & LEAGUE		GP	G	A	PTS	PIM
1949-50	MONT	N	5	1	0	1	0

Traded to **Detroit** by Montreal for Doc Couture, June 19, 1951.

Jamie Hislop

HISLOP, JAMES DONALD 5'10", 180 lbs.
B. Jan. 20, 1954, Sarnia, Ont. Right Wing, Shoots R

YEAR	TEAM & LEAGUE		GP	G	A	PTS	PIM
1976-77	CIN	W	46	7	19	26	6
1977-78			80	24	43	67	17
1978-79			80	30	40	70	45
1979-80	QUE	N	80	19	20	39	6
1980-81			50	19	22	41	15
	CALG	N	29	6	9	15	11
	2 team total		79	25	31	56	26
1981-82			80	16	25	41	35
1982-83			79	14	19	33	17
7 yrs.		N Totals:	318	74	95	169	84
		W Totals:	206	61	102	163	68

PLAYOFFS

YEAR	TEAM & LEAGUE		GP	G	A	PTS	PIM
1976-77	CIN	W	4	0	1	1	5
1978-79			3	2	4	6	0
1980-81	CALG	N	16	3	0	3	5
1981-82			3	0	0	0	0
1982-83			9	0	2	2	6
5 yrs.		N Totals:	28	3	2	5	11
		W Totals:	7	2	5	7	5

Traded to **Quebec** by Winnipeg with Barry Legge for Barry Melrose, June 28, 1979. Traded to **Calgary** by Quebec for goaltender Daniel Bouchard, Jan. 30, 1981.

Lionel Hitchman

HITCHMAN, LIONEL 6', 167 lbs.
B. Toronto, Ont. Defense, Shoots L

YEAR	TEAM & LEAGUE		GP	G	A	PTS	PIM
1922-23	OTTA	N	3	0	1	1	12
1923-24			24	2	6	8	24
1924-25			12	0	0	0	2
	BOS	N	18	3	0	3	22
	2 team total		30	3	0	3	24
1925-26			36	7	4	11	70

Lionel Hitchman continued

YEAR	TEAM	LEAGUE	GP	G	A	PTS	PIM
1926-27			41	3	6	9	70
1927-28			44	5	3	8	87
1928-29			38	1	0	1	64
1929-30			39	2	7	9	39
1930-31			41	0	2	2	40
1931-32			48	4	3	7	36
1932-33			45	0	1	1	34
1933-34			27	1	0	1	4
12 yrs.		**N Totals:**	416	28	33	61	504
PLAYOFFS							
1922-23*	**OTTA**	**N**	7	1	0	1	4
1923-24			2	0	0	0	4
1926-27	**BOS**	**N**	8	1	0	1	16
1927-28			2	0	0	0	2
1928-29*			5	0	1	1	22
1929-30			6	1	0	1	12
1930-31			5	0	0	0	0
1932-33			5	1	0	1	0
8 yrs.		**N Totals:**	40	4	1	5	60

Ivan Hlinka

HLINKA, IVAN 6'2", 219 lbs.
B. Jan. 26, 1950, Most, Czechoslovakia Center, Shoots L

YEAR	TEAM	LEAGUE	GP	G	A	PTS	PIM
1981-82	**VAN**	**N**	72	23	37	60	16
1982-83			65	19	44	63	12
2 yrs.		**N Totals:**	137	42	81	123	28
PLAYOFFS							
1981-82	**VAN**	**N**	12	2	6	8	4
1982-83			4	1	4	5	4
2 yrs.		**N Totals:**	16	3	10	13	8

N rights obtained by **Vancouver** from Winnipeg for Brent Ashton and Vancouver's fourth round choice in the 1982 Entry Draft (Tom Martin), July 15, 1981.

Mike Hobin

HOBIN, MICHAEL 5'11", 180 lbs.
B. Sarnia, Ont. Center, Shoots L

YEAR	TEAM	LEAGUE	GP	G	A	PTS	PIM
1975-76	**PHOE**	**W**	9	1	1	2	2
1976-77			68	17	18	35	14
2 yrs.		**W Totals:**	77	18	19	37	16
PLAYOFFS							
1975-76	**PHOE**	**W**	1	0	0	0	0

Ken Hodge

HODGE, KENNETH RAYMOND 6'2", 210 lbs.
B. June 25, 1944, Birmingham, England Right Wing, Shoots R

YEAR	TEAM	LEAGUE	GP	G	A	PTS	PIM
1965-66	**CHI**	**N**	63	6	17	23	47
1966-67			68	10	25	35	59
1967-68	**BOS**	**N**	74	25	31	56	31
1968-69			75	45	45	90	75
1969-70			72	25	29	54	87
1970-71			78	43	62	105	113
1971-72			60	16	40	56	81
1972-73			73	37	44	81	58
1973-74			76	50	55	105	43
1974-75			72	23	43	66	90
1975-76			72	25	36	61	42
1976-77	**NYR**	**N**	78	21	41	62	43
1977-78			18	2	4	6	8
13 yrs.		**N Totals:**	879	328	472	800	777
PLAYOFFS							
1965-66	**CHI**	**N**	5	0	0	0	8
1966-67			6	0	0	0	4
1967-68	**BOS**	**N**	4	3	0	3	2
1968-69			10	5	7	12	4
1969-70*			14	3	10	13	17
1970-71			7	2	5	7	6
1971-72*			15	9	8	17	62
1972-73			5	1	0	1	7
1973-74			16	6	10	16	16
1974-75			3	1	1	2	0
1975-76			12	4	6	10	4

Ken Hodge continued

YEAR	TEAM	LEAGUE	GP	G	A	PTS	PIM
11 yrs.		**N Totals:**	97	34	47	81	130

Traded to **Boston** by Chicago with Phil Esposito and Fred Stanfield for Gilles Marotte, Pit Martin and Jack Norris, May 15, 1967. Traded to **N.Y. Rangers** by Boston for Rick Middleton, May 26, 1976.

Rick Hodgson

HODGSON, RICHARD 6', 175 lbs.
B. May 23, 1956, Medicine Hat, Alta. Right Wing, Shoots R

YEAR	TEAM	LEAGUE	GP	G	A	PTS	PIM
1979-80	**HART**	**N**	6	0	0	0	6
PLAYOFFS							
1979-80	**HART**	**N**	1	0	0	0	0

Claimed by **Hartford** from Atlanta in Expansion Draft, June 13, 1979.

Ted Hodgson

HODGSON, EDWARD JAMES 5'11", 175 lbs.
B. June 30, 1945, Hobbema, Alta. Right Wing, Shoots R

YEAR	TEAM	LEAGUE	GP	G	A	PTS	PIM
1966-67	**BOS**	**N**	4	0	0	0	0
1972-73	**CLEVE**	**W**	74	15	23	38	93
1973-74			10	0	2	2	6
	LA	**W**	23	3	9	12	22
	2 team total		33	3	11	14	28
3 yrs.		**N Totals:**	4	0	0	0	0
		W Totals:	107	18	34	52	121
PLAYOFFS							
1972-73	**CLEVE**	**W**	9	1	3	4	13

Sold to **N.Y. Rangers** by Salt Lake, May 22, 1970. Sold to **Buffalo** by N.Y. Rangers, June 10, 1970.

Cecil Hoekstra

HOEKSTRA, CECIL THOMAS 6'1", 175 lbs.
B. Apr. 2, 1935, Winnipeg, Man. Center, Shoots L

YEAR	TEAM	LEAGUE	GP	G	A	PTS	PIM
1959-60	**MONT**	**N**	4	0	0	0	0

Purchased with Reggie Fleming by **Chicago** from Montreal, June 7, 1960.

Ed Hoekstra

HOEKSTRA, EDWARD ADRIAN 5'11", 170 lbs.
B. Nov. 4, 1937, Winnipeg, Man. Center, Shoots R

YEAR	TEAM	LEAGUE	GP	G	A	PTS	PIM
1967-68	**PHI**	**N**	70	15	21	36	6
1972-73	**HOUS**	**W**	78	11	28	39	12
1973-74			19	2	0	2	0
3 yrs.		**N Totals:**	70	15	21	36	6
		W Totals:	97	13	28	41	12
PLAYOFFS							
1967-68	**PHI**	**N**	7	0	1	1	0
1972-73	**HOUS**	**W**	9	1	2	3	0
2 yrs.		**N Totals:**	7	0	1	1	0
		W Totals:	9	1	2	3	0

Phil Hoene

HOENE, PHIL GEORGE 5'9", 175 lbs.
B. Mar. 15, 1949, Duluth, Mn. Left Wing, Shoots L

YEAR	TEAM	LEAGUE	GP	G	A	PTS	PIM
1972-73	**LA**	**N**	4	0	1	1	0
1973-74			31	2	3	5	22
1974-75			2	0	0	0	0
3 yrs.		**N Totals:**	37	2	4	6	22

Vic Hoffinger

HOFFINGER, VICTOR
B. Unknown Defense

YEAR	TEAM	LEAGUE	GP	G	A	PTS	PIM
1927-28	**CHI**	**N**	18	0	1	1	18
1928-29			10	0	0	0	12
2 yrs.		**N Totals:**	28	0	1	1	30

Mike Hoffman

HOFFMAN, MIKE 5'11", 190 lbs.
B. Feb. 26, 1923, Cambridge, Ont. Left Wing, Shoots L

YEAR	TEAM & LEAGUE		GP	G	A	PTS	PIM
1982-83	HART	N	2	0	1	1	0

Bob Hoffmeyer

HOFFMEYER, ROBERT FRANK 6', 182 lbs.
B. July 27, 1955, Dodsland, Sask. Defense, Shoots L

YEAR	TEAM & LEAGUE		GP	G	A	PTS	PIM
1977-78	CHI	N	5	0	1	1	12
1978-79			6	0	2	2	5
1981-82	PHI	N	57	7	20	27	142
1982-83			35	2	11	13	40
4 yrs.		N Totals:	103	9	34	43	199
PLAYOFFS							
1981-82	PHI	N	2	0	1	1	25
1982-83			1	0	0	0	0
2 yrs.		N Totals:	3	0	1	1	25

Acquired by **Edmonton** from Philadelphia in Waiver Draft, Oct. 4, 1982. Traded to **Philadelphia** by Edmonton for Peter Dineen, Oct. 22, 1982. Signed as a free agent by **New Jersey** Sept. 3, 1983.

Bill Hogaboam

HOGABOAM, WILLIAM HAROLD 5'11", 170 lbs.
B. May 9, 1949, Swift Current, Sask. Center, Shoots R

YEAR	TEAM & LEAGUE		GP	G	A	PTS	PIM
1972-73	ATL	N	2	0	0	0	0
	DET	N	4	1	0	1	2
	2 team total		6	1	0	1	2
1973-74			47	18	23	41	12
1974-75			60	14	27	41	16
1975-76			50	21	16	37	30
	MINN	N	18	7	7	14	6
	2 team total		68	28	23	51	36
1976-77			73	10	15	25	16
1977-78			8	1	2	3	4
1978-79			10	1	1	2	0
	DET	N	18	4	6	10	4
	2 team total		28	5	7	12	4
1979-80			42	3	12	15	10
8 yrs.		N Totals:	332	80	109	189	100
PLAYOFFS							
1976-77	MINN	N	2	0	0	0	0

Traded to **Detroit** by Atlanta for Leon Rochefort, Nov. 28, 1972. Traded to **Minnesota** by Detroit with Jimmy Roberts (Los Angeles' second-round choice in 1976 Amateur Draft transferred to Detroit via earlier deal), for Dennis Hextall, Feb. 27, 1976. Signed as free agent by **Detroit** Feb. 12, 1979.

Dale Hoganson

HOGANSON, DALE GORDON 5'10", 190 lbs.
B. July 8, 1949, North Battleford, Sask. Defense, Shoots L

YEAR	TEAM & LEAGUE		GP	G	A	PTS	PIM
1969-70	LA	N	49	1	7	8	37
1970-71			70	4	10	14	52
1971-72			10	1	2	3	14
	MONT	N	21	0	0	0	2
	2 team total		31	1	2	3	16
1972-73			25	0	2	2	2
1973-74	QUE	W	62	8	33	41	27
1974-75			78	9	35	44	47
1975-76			45	3	14	17	18
1976-77	BIRM	W	81	7	48	55	48
1977-78			43	1	12	13	29
1978-79	QUE	W	69	2	19	21	17
1979-80	QUE	N	77	4	36	40	31
1980-81			61	3	14	17	32
1981-82			30	0	6	6	16
13 yrs.		N Totals:	343	13	77	90	186
		W Totals:	378	30	161	191	186
PLAYOFFS							
1974-75	QUE	W	13	1	3	4	4
1975-76			5	1	3	4	2
1977-78	BIRM	W	5	0	0	0	7
1978-79	QUE	W	4	0	0	0	2
1980-81	QUE	N	5	0	3	3	10
1981-82			6	0	0	0	2

Dale Hoganson continued

YEAR	TEAM & LEAGUE		GP	G	A	PTS	PIM
6 yrs.		N Totals:	11	0	3	3	12
		W Totals:	27	2	6	8	15

Traded to **Montreal** by Los Angeles with goaltender Denis DeJordy, Noel Price, and Doug Robinson for Rogie Vachon, Nov. 4, 1971. Playing rights sold to **Atlanta** by Montreal, May 29, 1973.

Terry Holbrook

HOLBROOK, TERRY EUGENE 6', 185 lbs.
B. July 11, 1950, Petrolia, Ont. Right Wing, Shoots R

YEAR	TEAM & LEAGUE		GP	G	A	PTS	PIM
1972-73	MINN	N	21	2	3	5	0
1973-74			22	1	3	4	4
1974-75	CLEVE	W	78	10	13	23	7
1975-76			15	1	2	3	6
4 yrs.		N Totals:	43	3	6	9	4
		W Totals:	93	11	15	26	13
PLAYOFFS							
1972-73	MINN	N	6	0	0	0	0
1974-75	CLEVE	W	5	0	1	1	0
1975-76			3	0	0	0	0
3 yrs.		N Totals:	6	0	0	0	0
		W Totals:	8	0	1	1	0

Bill Holden

HOLDEN, WILLIAM

YEAR	TEAM & LEAGUE		GP	G	A	PTS	PIM
1973-74	WINN	W	1	0	0	0	0

Jerry Holland

HOLLAND, JERRY ALLAN 5'10", 190 lbs.
B. Aug. 25, 1954, Beaverlodge, Alta. Left Wing, Shoots L

YEAR	TEAM & LEAGUE		GP	G	A	PTS	PIM
1974-75	NYR	N	1	1	0	1	0
1975-76			36	7	4	11	6
1977-78	EDM	W	22	2	1	3	14
3 yrs.		N Totals:	37	8	4	12	6
		W Totals:	22	2	1	3	14

Flash Hollett

HOLLETT, FRANK WILLIAM 6', 180 lbs.
B. Apr. 13, 1912, North Sydney, N.S. Defense, Shoots L

YEAR	TEAM & LEAGUE		GP	G	A	PTS	PIM
1933-34	TOR	N	4	0	0	0	4
	OTTA	N	30	7	4	11	21
	2 team total		34	7	4	11	25
1934-35	TOR	N	48	10	16	26	38
1935-36			11	1	4	5	8
	BOS	N	6	1	2	3	2
	2 team total		17	2	6	8	10
1936-37			47	3	7	10	22
1937-38			48	4	10	14	54
1938-39			47	10	17	27	35
1939-40			44	10	18	28	18
1940-41			42	9	15	24	23
1941-42			48	19	14	33	41
1942-43			50	19	25	44	19
1943-44			25	9	7	16	4
	DET	N	27	6	12	18	34
	2 team total		52	15	19	34	38
1944-45			50	20	21	41	39
1945-46			38	4	9	13	16
13 yrs.		N Totals:	565	132	181	313	378
PLAYOFFS							
1934-35	TOR	N	7	0	0	0	6
1936-37	BOS	N	3	0	0	0	2
1937-38			3	0	1	1	0
1938-39*			12	1	3	4	2
1939-40			5	1	2	3	2
1940-41*			11	3	4	7	8
1941-42			5	0	1	1	2
1942-43			9	0	9	9	4
1943-44	DET	N	5	0	0	0	6
1944-45			14	3	4	7	6
1945-46			5	0	2	2	0

Flash Hollett continued

YEAR	TEAM	LEAGUE	GP	G	A	PTS	PIM
11 yrs.		N Totals:	79	8	26	34	38

Gord Hollingworth

HOLLINGWORTH, GORDON 5'11½", 185 lbs.
B. July 24, 1933, Verdun, Que. Defense, Shoots L

YEAR	TEAM	LEAGUE	GP	G	A	PTS	PIM
1954-55	**CHI**	**N**	70	3	9	12	135
1955-56	**DET**	**N**	41	0	2	2	28
1956-57			25	0	1	1	16
1957-58			27	1	2	3	22
4 yrs.		N Totals:	163	4	14	18	201
PLAYOFFS							
1955-56	**DET**	**N**	3	0	0	0	2

Purchased by **Chicago** from Montreal for $15,000, Oct. 3, 1954. Traded to **Detroit** by Chicago with Jerry Toppazzini, John McCormack and Dave Creighton for Tony Leswick, Glen Skov, Johnny Wilson and Benny Woit, June 3, 1955.

Bill Holmes

HOLMES, WILLIAM
B. Weyburn, Sask. Forward

YEAR	TEAM	LEAGUE	GP	G	A	PTS	PIM
1925-26	**MONT**	**N**	9	1	0	1	2
1926-27	**NYA**	**N**	1	0	0	0	0
1929-30			42	5	4	9	33
3 yrs.		N Totals:	52	6	4	10	35

Chuck Holmes

HOLMES, CHARLES FRANK 6', 185 lbs.
B. Sept. 21, 1934, Edmonton, Alta. Right Wing, Shoots R

YEAR	TEAM	LEAGUE	GP	G	A	PTS	PIM
1958-59	**DET**	**N**	15	0	3	3	6
1961-62			8	1	0	1	4
2 yrs.		N Totals:	23	1	3	4	10

Lou Holmes

HOLMES, LOUIS 150 lbs.
B. Jan. 29, 1911, England Forward, Shoots L

YEAR	TEAM	LEAGUE	GP	G	A	PTS	PIM
1931-32	**CHI**	**N**	41	1	4	5	6
1932-33			18	0	0	0	0
2 yrs.		N Totals:	59	1	4	5	6
PLAYOFFS							
1931-32	**CHI**	**N**	2	0	0	0	2

Warren Holmes

HOLMES, WARREN 6'1", 185 lbs.
B. Feb. 18, 1957, Beeton, Ont. Center, Shoots L

YEAR	TEAM	LEAGUE	GP	G	A	PTS	PIM
1981-82	**LA**	**N**	3	0	2	2	0
1982-83			39	8	16	24	7
2 yrs.		N Totals:	42	8	18	26	7

Paul Holmgren

HOLMGREN, PAUL HOWARD 6'3", 210 lbs.
B. Dec. 2, 1955, St. Paul, Minn. Right Wing, Shoots R

YEAR	TEAM	LEAGUE	GP	G	A	PTS	PIM
1975-76	**MINN**	**W**	51	14	16	30	121
	PHI	**N**	1	0	0	0	2
	2 team total		52	14	16	30	123
1976-77			59	14	12	26	201
1977-78			62	16	18	34	190
1978-79			57	19	10	29	168
1979-80			74	30	35	65	**267**
1980-81			77	22	37	59	306
1981-82			41	9	22	31	183
1982-83			77	19	24	43	178
8 yrs.		N Totals:	448	129	158	287	1495
		W Totals:	51	14	16	30	121
PLAYOFFS							
1976-77	**PHI**	**N**	10	1	1	2	25
1977-78			12	1	4	5	26
1978-79			8	1	5	6	22

Paul Holmgren continued

YEAR	TEAM	LEAGUE	GP	G	A	PTS	PIM
1979-80			18	10	10	20	47
1980-81			12	5	9	14	49
1981-82			4	1	2	3	6
1982-83			3	0	0	0	6
7 yrs.		N Totals:	67	19	31	50	181

John Holota

HOLOTA, JOHN PAUL 5'6", 160 lbs.
B. Feb. 25, 1921, Hamilton, Ont. Center, Shoots L

YEAR	TEAM	LEAGUE	GP	G	A	PTS	PIM
1942-43	**DET**	**N**	12	2	0	2	0
1945-46			3	0	0	0	0
2 yrs.		N Totals:	15	2	0	2	0

Greg Holst

HOLST, GREG 5'10", 170 lbs.
B. Feb. 21, 1954, Montreal, Que. Center, Shoots L

YEAR	TEAM	LEAGUE	GP	G	A	PTS	PIM
1975-76	**NYR**	**N**	2	0	0	0	0
1976-77			5	0	0	0	0
1977-78			4	0	0	0	0
3 yrs.		N Totals:	11	0	0	0	0

Gary Holt

HOLT, GARETH RAY 5'9", 175 lbs.
B. Jan. 1, 1952, Sarnia, Ont. Left Wing, Shoots L

YEAR	TEAM	LEAGUE	GP	G	A	PTS	PIM
1973-74	**CALIF**	**N**	1	0	0	0	0
1974-75			1	0	1	1	0
1975-76			48	6	5	11	50
1976-77	**CLEVE**	**N**	2	0	1	1	2
1977-78	**STL**	**N**	49	7	4	11	81
5 yrs.		N Totals:	101	13	11	24	133

Signed as free agent by **St. Louis** Oct. 20, 1977.

Randy Holt

HOLT, STEWART RANDALL 5'11", 184 lbs.
B. Jan. 15, 1953, Pembroke, Ont. Defense, Shoots R

YEAR	TEAM	LEAGUE	GP	G	A	PTS	PIM
1974-75	**CHI**	**N**	12	0	1	1	13
1975-76			12	0	0	0	13
1976-77			12	0	3	3	14
1977-78			6	0	0	0	20
	CLEVE	**N**	48	1	4	5	229
	2 team total		54	1	4	5	249
1978-79	**VAN**	**N**	22	1	3	4	80
	LA	**N**	36	0	6	6	202
	2 team total		58	1	9	10	282
1979-80			42	0	1	1	94
1980-81	**CALG**	**N**	48	0	5	5	165
1981-82			8	0	0	0	9
	WASH	**N**	53	2	6	8	250
	2 team total		61	2	6	8	259
1982-83			70	0	8	8	**275**
9 yrs.		N Totals:	369	4	37	41	1364
PLAYOFFS							
1976-77	**CHI**	**N**	2	0	0	0	7
1978-79	**LA**	**N**	2	0	0	0	4
1980-81	**CALG**	**N**	13	2	2	4	52
1982-83	**WASH**	**N**	4	0	1	1	20
4 yrs.		N Totals:	21	2	3	5	83

Traded to **Cleveland** by Chicago for Reg Kerr, Nov. 23, 1977. Claimed by **Vancouver** in Cleveland-Minnesota Dispersal Draft, June 15, 1978. Traded to **Los Angeles** by Vancouver for Don Kozak, Dec. 31, 1978. Traded to **Calgary** by Los Angeles with Bert Wilson for Garry Unger, June 6, 1980. Traded to **Washington** by Calgary with Bobby Gould for Washington's second round choice in 1983 Entry Draft (later transferred to Montreal, Todd Francis) and Pat Ribble, Nov. 25, 1981.

Toots Holway

HOLWAY, ALBERT ROBERT 6'1½", 190 lbs.
B. Sept. 24, 1902, Toronto, Ont. Defense, Shoots L

YEAR	TEAM	LEAGUE	GP	G	A	PTS	PIM
1923-24	**TOR**	**N**	6	1	0	1	0
1924-25			25	2	2	4	20
1925-26			12	0	0	0	0
	MON(M)	**N**	17	0	0	0	6
	2 team total		29	0	0	0	6

Toots Holway continued

YEAR	TEAM & LEAGUE		GP	G	A	PTS	PIM
1926-27			13	0	0	0	10
1928-29	PITT	N	40	4	0	4	20
5 yrs.		N Totals:	113	7	2	9	56
PLAYOFFS							
1924-25	TOR	N	2	0	0	0	0
1925-26*	MON(M)	N	6	0	0	0	2
2 yrs.		N Totals:	8	0	0	0	2

Ron Homenuke

HOMENUKE, RONALD WAYNE 5'10", 180 lbs.
B. Jan. 5, 1952, Hazelton, B.C. Right Wing, Shoots R

YEAR	TEAM & LEAGUE		GP	G	A	PTS	PIM
1972-73	VAN	N	1	0	0	0	0

Ralph Hopiavouri

HOPIAVOURI, RALPH 5'10", 185 lbs.
B. July 15, 1951, Kirkland Lake, Ont. Defense, Shoots R

YEAR	TEAM & LEAGUE		GP	G	A	PTS	PIM
1972-73	CLEVE	W	29	4	5	9	44
1973-74			13	0	2	2	6
1974-75	IND	W	28	2	8	10	21
3 yrs.		W Totals:	70	6	15	21	71
PLAYOFFS							
1972-73	CLEVE	W	8	0	1	1	6
1973-74			4	0	1	1	0
2 yrs.		W Totals:	12	0	2	2	6

Dean Hopkins

HOPKINS, DEAN ROBERT 6'1", 205 lbs.
B. June 6, 1959, Cobourg, Ont. Right Wing, Shoots R

YEAR	TEAM & LEAGUE		GP	G	A	PTS	PIM
1979-80	LA	N	60	8	6	14	39
1980-81			67	8	18	26	118
1981-82			41	2	13	15	102
1982-83			49	5	12	17	43
4 yrs.		N Totals:	217	23	49	72	302
PLAYOFFS							
1979-80	LA	N	4	0	1	1	5
1980-81			4	1	0	1	9
1981-82			10	0	4	4	15
3 yrs.		N Totals:	18	1	5	6	29

Larry Hopkins

HOPKINS, LARRY HAROLD 6'1", 214 lbs.
B. Mar. 17, 1954, Oshawa, Ont. Left Wing, Shoots L

YEAR	TEAM & LEAGUE		GP	G	A	PTS	PIM
1977-78	TOR	N	2	0	0	0	0
1979-80	WINN	N	5	0	0	0	0
1981-82			41	10	15	25	22
1982-83			12	3	1	4	4
4 yrs.		N Totals:	60	13	16	29	26
PLAYOFFS							
1981-82	WINN	N	4	0	0	0	2
1982-83			2	0	0	0	0
2 yrs.		N Totals:	6	0	0	0	2

Signed by **Winnipeg** as free agent, Aug. 15, 1979.

Doug Horbul

HORBUL, DOUGLAS GEORGE 5'9", 170 lbs.
B. July 27, 1952, Nokomis, Sask. Left Wing, Shoots L

YEAR	TEAM & LEAGUE		GP	G	A	PTS	PIM
1974-75	KC	N	4	1	0	1	2

Drafted by **Kansas City** from N.Y. Rangers in Expansion Draft, June 12, 1974.

Mike Hordy

HORDY, MICHAEL 5'10", 180 lbs.
B. Oct. 10, 1956, Thunder Bay, Ont. Defense, Shoots L

YEAR	TEAM & LEAGUE		GP	G	A	PTS	PIM
1978-79	NYI	N	2	0	0	0	0
1979-80			9	0	0	0	7
2 yrs.		N Totals:	11	0	0	0	7

Pete Horeck

HORECK, PETER 5'9", 160 lbs.
B. June 15, 1923, Massey, Ont. Right Wing, Shoots L

YEAR	TEAM & LEAGUE		GP	G	A	PTS	PIM
1944-45	CHI	N	50	20	16	36	44
1945-46			50	20	21	41	34
1946-47			18	4	6	10	12
	DET	N	38	12	13	25	49
	2 team total		56	16	19	35	61
1947-48			50	12	17	29	44
1948-49			60	14	18	32	46
1949-50	BOS	N	34	5	5	10	22
1950-51			66	10	13	23	57
1951-52	CHI	N	60	9	11	20	22
8 yrs.		N Totals:	426	106	120	226	330
PLAYOFFS							
1945-46	CHI	N	4	0	0	0	2
1946-47	DET	N	5	2	0	2	6
1947-48			10	3	7	10	12
1948-49			11	1	1	2	10
1950-51	BOS	N	4	0	0	0	13
5 yrs.		N Totals:	34	6	8	14	43

Traded to **Boston** by Detroit with Bill Quackenbush for Pete Babando, Clare Martin, Lloyd Durham and Jim Peters, Aug. 16, 1949.

Shorty Horne

HORNE, GEORGE
Forward

YEAR	TEAM & LEAGUE		GP	G	A	PTS	PIM
1925-26	MON(M)	N	13	0	0	0	2
1926-27			2	0	0	0	0
1928-29	TOR	N	39	9	3	12	32
3 yrs.		N Totals:	54	9	3	12	34
PLAYOFFS							
1928-29	TOR	N	4	0	0	0	4

Red Horner

HORNER, REGINALD 6', 190 lbs.
B. May 28, 1909, Lynden, Ont. Defense, Shoots R
Hall of Fame, 1965

YEAR	TEAM & LEAGUE		GP	G	A	PTS	PIM
1928-29	TOR	N	22	0	0	0	30
1929-30			33	2	7	9	96
1930-31			42	1	11	12	71
1931-32			42	7	9	16	97
1932-33			48	3	8	11	**144**
1933-34			40	11	10	21	**146**
1934-35			46	4	8	12	**125**
1935-36			43	2	9	11	**167**
1936-37			48	3	9	12	**124**
1937-38			47	4	20	24	**92**
1938-39			48	4	10	14	**85**
1939-40			31	1	9	10	**87**
12 yrs.		N Totals:	490	42	110	152	1264
PLAYOFFS							
1928-29	TOR	N	4	1	0	1	2
1930-31			2	0	0	0	0
1931-32*			7	2	2	4	20
1932-33			9	1	0	1	10
1933-34			5	1	0	1	6
1934-35			7	0	1	1	4
1935-36			9	1	2	3	**22**
1936-37			2	0	0	0	7
1937-38			7	0	1	1	14
1938-39			10	1	2	3	26
1939-40			9	0	2	2	55
11 yrs.		N Totals:	71	7	10	17	166

Larry Hornung

HORNUNG, LAWRENCE JOHN 6′, 190 lbs.
B. Oct. 10, 1945, Gravelburg, Sask. Defense, Shoots L

YEAR	TEAM	LEAGUE	GP	G	A	PTS	PIM
1970-71	**STL**	**N**	1	0	0	0	0
1971-72			47	2	9	11	10
1972-73	**WINN**	**W**	77	13	45	58	28
1973-74			51	4	19	23	18
1974-75			69	7	25	32	21
1975-76			76	3	18	21	26
1976-77	**EDM**	**W**	21	2	1	3	0
	SD	**W**	58	4	9	13	8
	2 team total		79	6	10	16	8
1977-78	**WINN**	**W**	19	1	4	5	2
8 yrs.		**N Totals:**	48	2	9	11	10
		W Totals:	371	34	121	155	103

PLAYOFFS

YEAR	TEAM	LEAGUE	GP	G	A	PTS	PIM
1971-72	**STL**	**N**	11	0	2	2	2
1972-73	**WINN**	**W**	14	2	9	11	0
1973-74			4	0	0	0	0
1975-76			13	0	3	3	6
1976-77	**SD**	**W**	6	0	0	0	0
5 yrs.		**N Totals:**	11	0	2	2	2
		W Totals:	37	2	12	14	6

Traded to **St. Louis** by Detroit with Craig Cameron and Don Giesebrect for John Brenneman, Oct. 9, 1967. Drafted by **N.Y. Islanders** from St. Louis in Expansion Draft, June 6, 1972.

Bill Horton

HORTON, WILLIAM HARLEY 6′, 195 lbs.
B. Sept. 5, 1946, Lindsay, Ont. Defense, Shoots L

YEAR	TEAM	LEAGUE	GP	G	A	PTS	PIM
1972-73	**CLEVE**	**W**	74	2	17	19	55
1973-74	**LA**	**W**	60	0	9	9	46
1974-75	**IND**	**W**	59	2	9	11	30
3 yrs.		**W Totals:**	193	4	35	39	131

PLAYOFFS

YEAR	TEAM	LEAGUE	GP	G	A	PTS	PIM
1972-73	**CLEVE**	**W**	9	0	1	1	10

Tim Horton

HORTON, MILES GILBERT 5′10″, 180 lbs.
B. Jan. 12, 1930, Cochrane, Ont. Defense, Shoots R
Hall of Fame, 1977

YEAR	TEAM	LEAGUE	GP	G	A	PTS	PIM
1949-50	**TOR**	**N**	1	0	0	0	2
1951-52			4	0	0	0	8
1952-53			70	2	14	16	85
1953-54			70	7	24	31	94
1954-55			67	5	9	14	84
1955-56			35	0	5	5	36
1956-57			66	6	19	25	72
1957-58			53	6	20	26	39
1958-59			70	5	21	26	76
1959-60			70	3	29	32	69
1960-61			57	6	15	21	75
1961-62			70	10	28	38	88
1962-63			70	6	19	25	69
1963-64			70	9	20	29	71
1964-65			70	12	16	28	95
1965-66			70	6	22	28	76
1966-67			70	8	17	25	70
1967-68			69	4	23	27	82
1968-69			74	11	29	40	107
1969-70			59	3	19	22	91
	NYR	**N**	15	1	5	6	16
	2 team total		74	4	24	28	107
1970-71			78	2	18	20	57
1971-72	**PITT**	**N**	44	2	9	11	40
1972-73	**BUF**	**N**	69	1	16	17	56
1973-74			55	0	6	6	53
24 yrs.		**N Totals:**	1446	115	403	518	1611

PLAYOFFS

YEAR	TEAM	LEAGUE	GP	G	A	PTS	PIM
1949-50	**TOR**	**N**	1	0	0	0	2
1953-54			5	1	1	2	4
1955-56			2	0	0	0	4
1958-59			12	0	3	3	16
1959-60			10	0	1	1	6
1960-61			5	0	0	0	0
1961-62*			12	3	13	16	16

Tim Horton continued

YEAR	TEAM	LEAGUE	GP	G	A	PTS	PIM
1962-63*			10	1	3	4	10
1963-64*			14	0	4	4	20
1964-65			6	0	2	2	13
1965-66			4	1	0	1	12
1966-67*			12	3	5	8	25
1968-69			4	0	0	0	7
1969-70	**NYR**	**N**	6	1	1	2	28
1970-71			13	1	4	5	14
1971-72	**PITT**	**N**	4	0	1	1	2
1972-73	**BUF**	**N**	6	0	1	1	4
17 yrs.		**N Totals:**	126	11	39	50	183

Traded to **N.Y. Rangers** by Toronto for Guy Trottier (via 1970 Intra-League Draft) and Denis Dupere, March 3, 1970. Drafted by **Pittsburgh** from N.Y. Rangers in Intra-League Draft, June 8, 1971. Drafted by **Buffalo** from Pittsburgh in Intra-League Draft, June 5, 1972.

Bronco Horvath

HORVATH, BRONCO JOSEPH 5′10″, 185 lbs.
B. Mar. 12, 1930, Port Colborne, Ont. Center, Shoots L

YEAR	TEAM	LEAGUE	GP	G	A	PTS	PIM
1955-56	**NYR**	**N**	66	12	17	29	40
1956-57			7	1	2	3	4
	MONT	**N**	1	0	0	0	0
	2 team total		8	1	2	3	4
1957-58	**BOS**	**N**	67	30	36	66	71
1958-59			45	19	20	39	58
1959-60			68	**39**	41	80	60
1960-61			47	15	15	30	15
1961-62	**CHI**	**N**	68	17	29	46	21
1962-63	**NYR**	**N**	41	7	15	22	34
	TOR	**N**	9	0	4	4	12
	2 team total		50	7	19	26	46
1967-68	**MINN**	**N**	14	1	6	7	4
9 yrs.		**N Totals:**	433	141	185	326	319

PLAYOFFS

YEAR	TEAM	LEAGUE	GP	G	A	PTS	PIM
1955-56	**NYR**	**N**	5	1	2	3	4
1957-58	**BOS**	**N**	12	5	3	8	8
1958-59			7	2	3	5	0
1961-62	**CHI**	**N**	12	4	1	5	6
4 yrs.		**N Totals:**	36	12	9	21	18

Traded to **N.Y. Rangers** by Detroit with Dave Creighton for Billy Dea and Aggie Kukulowicz, Aug., 1955. Sold to **Mont. Canadiens** by N.Y. Rangers, Nov., 1956. Drafted by **Boston** from Montreal, June 5, 1957. Drafted by **Chicago** from Boston, June, 1961. Drafted by **N.Y. Rangers** from Chicago, June, 1962. Claimed on waivers by **Toronto** from N.Y. Rangers, June 19, 1963.

Ed Hospodar

HOSPODAR, EDWARD DAVID (Boxcar) 6′2″, 210 lbs.
B. Feb. 9, 1959, Bowling Green, Ohio Defense, Shoots R

YEAR	TEAM	LEAGUE	GP	G	A	PTS	PIM
1979-80	**NYR**	**N**	20	0	1	1	76
1980-81			61	5	14	19	214
1981-82			41	3	8	11	152
1982-83	**HART**	**N**	72	1	9	10	199
4 yrs.		**N Totals:**	194	9	32	41	641

PLAYOFFS

YEAR	TEAM	LEAGUE	GP	G	A	PTS	PIM
1979-80	**NYR**	**N**	7	1	0	1	42
1980-81			12	2	0	2	93
2 yrs.		**N Totals:**	19	3	0	3	135

Traded to **Hartford** by New York Rangers for Kent-Erik Andersson, Oct. 1, 1982.

Greg Hotham

HOTHAM, GREGORY 5′11″, 183 lbs.
B. Mar. 7, 1956, London, Ont. Defense, Shoots R

YEAR	TEAM	LEAGUE	GP	G	A	PTS	PIM
1979-80	**TOR**	**N**	46	3	10	13	10
1980-81			11	1	1	2	11
1981-82			3	0	0	0	0
	PITT	**N**	25	4	6	10	16
	2 team total		28	4	6	10	16
1982-83			58	2	30	32	39
4 yrs.		**N Totals:**	143	10	47	57	76

PLAYOFFS

YEAR	TEAM	LEAGUE	GP	G	A	PTS	PIM
1981-82	**PITT**	**N**	5	0	3	3	6

Greg Hotham continued

Traded to **Pittsburgh** by Toronto for Pittsburgh's sixth round choice (Craig Kales) in 1982 Entry Draft, Feb. 3, 1982.

Claude Houde

HOUDE, CLAUDE DANIEL 6'1", 190 lbs.
B. Nov. 18, 1948, Drummondville, Que. Defense, Shoots L

YEAR	TEAM	LEAGUE	GP	G	A	PTS	PIM
1974-75	**KC**	**N**	34	3	4	7	20
1975-76			25	0	2	2	20
2 yrs.		**N Totals:**	59	3	6	9	40

Traded to **Detroit** by N.Y. Rangers for Brian Lavender, Feb. 24, 1974. Traded to **Kansas City** by Detroit with Guy Charron for Bart Crashley, Ted Snell and Larry Giroux, Dec. 14, 1974.

Rejean Houle

HOULE, REJEAN (Reggie) 5'11", 168 lbs.
B. Oct. 25, 1949, Rouyn, Que. Left Wing, Shoots L

YEAR	TEAM	LEAGUE	GP	G	A	PTS	PIM
1969-70	**MONT**	**N**	9	0	1	1	0
1970-71			66	10	9	19	28
1971-72			77	11	17	28	21
1972-73			72	13	35	48	36
1973-74	**QUE**	**W**	69	27	35	62	17
1974-75			64	40	52	92	37
1975-76			81	51	52	103	61
1976-77	**MONT**	**N**	65	22	30	52	24
1977-78			76	30	28	58	50
1978-79			66	17	34	51	43
1979-80			60	18	27	45	68
1980-81			77	27	31	58	83
1981-82			51	11	32	43	34
1982-83			16	2	3	5	8
14 yrs.		**N Totals:**	635	161	247	408	395
		W Totals:	214	118	139	257	115

PLAYOFFS

YEAR	TEAM	LEAGUE	GP	G	A	PTS	PIM
1970-71*	**MONT**	**N**	20	2	5	7	20
1971-72			6	0	0	0	2
1972-73*			17	3	6	9	0
1974-75	**QUE**	**W**	15	10	6	16	2
1975-76			5	2	0	2	8
1976-77*	**MONT**	**N**	6	0	1	1	4
1977-78*			15	3	8	11	14
1978-79*			7	1	5	6	2
1979-80			10	4	5	9	12
1980-81			3	1	0	1	6
1981-82			5	0	4	4	6
1982-83			1	0	0	0	0
12 yrs.		**N Totals:**	90	14	34	48	66
		W Totals:	20	12	6	18	10

Phil Housley

HOUSLEY, PHIL 5'10", 180 lbs.
B. Mar. 9, 1964, St. Paul, Minn. Defense

YEAR	TEAM	LEAGUE	GP	G	A	PTS	PIM
1982-83	**BUF**	**N**	77	19	47	66	39

PLAYOFFS

YEAR	TEAM	LEAGUE	GP	G	A	PTS	PIM
1982-83	**BUF**	**N**	10	3	4	7	2

Ken Houston

HOUSTON, KENNETH LYLE 6'2", 207 lbs.
B. Sept. 15, 1953, Dresden, Ont. Right Wing, Shoots R

YEAR	TEAM	LEAGUE	GP	G	A	PTS	PIM
1975-76	**ATL**	**N**	38	5	6	11	11
1976-77			78	20	24	44	35
1977-78			74	22	16	38	51
1978-79			80	21	31	52	135
1979-80			80	23	31	54	100
1980-81	**CALG**	**N**	42	15	15	30	93
1981-82			70	22	22	44	91
1982-83	**WASH**	**N**	71	25	14	39	93
8 yrs.		**N Totals:**	533	153	159	312	609

PLAYOFFS

YEAR	TEAM	LEAGUE	GP	G	A	PTS	PIM
1975-76	**ATL**	**N**	2	0	0	0	0
1976-77			3	0	0	0	4
1977-78			2	0	0	0	0
1978-79			1	1	0	1	16
1979-80			4	1	1	2	10
1980-81	**CALG**	**N**	16	7	8	15	28
1981-82			3	1	0	1	4
1982-83	**WASH**	**N**	4	1	0	1	4
8 yrs.		**N Totals:**	35	11	9	20	66

Traded to **Washington** by Calgary with Pat Riggin for Howard Walker, George White, Washington's sixth round choice (Mats Kihlstron) in 1982 Entry Draft, third round choice (Perry Berezan) in 1983 Entry Draft, and second round choice in 1984 Entry Draft, June 9, 1982. Traded to **Washington** by Calgary with Pat Riggin for Howard Walker and George White, June 9, 1982. In addition, Washington transferred the following Amateur Draft Choices: a sixth round choice (acquired earlier from Quebec, Mats Kihlstron) in 1982, a third round choice in 1983 (Barry Perezan), and a second round choice in 1984.

Frank Howard

HOWARD, JACK FRANCIS
B. Oct. 15, 1915, London, Ont. Defense

YEAR	TEAM	LEAGUE	GP	G	A	PTS	PIM
1936-37	**TOR**	**N**	2	0	0	0	0

Garry Howatt

HOWATT, GARRY ROBERT CHARLES (Howie) 5'9", 175 lbs.
B. Sept. 26, 1952, Grand Center, Alta. Left Wing, Shoots L

YEAR	TEAM	LEAGUE	GP	G	A	PTS	PIM
1972-73	**NYI**	**N**	8	0	1	1	18
1973-74			78	6	11	17	204
1974-75			77	18	30	48	121
1975-76			80	21	13	34	197
1976-77			70	13	15	28	182
1977-78			61	7	12	19	146
1978-79			75	16	12	28	205
1979-80			77	8	11	19	219
1980-81			70	4	15	19	174
1981-82	**HART**	**N**	80	18	32	50	242
1982-83	**NJ**	**N**	38	1	4	5	114
11 yrs.		**N Totals:**	714	112	156	268	1822

PLAYOFFS

YEAR	TEAM	LEAGUE	GP	G	A	PTS	PIM
1974-75	**NYI**	**N**	17	3	3	6	59
1975-76			13	5	5	10	23
1976-77			12	1	1	2	28
1977-78			7	0	1	1	62
1978-79			9	0	1	1	18
1979-80*			21	3	1	4	84
1980-81*			8	0	2	2	15
7 yrs.		**N Totals:**	87	12	14	26	289

Traded to **Hartford** by N.Y. Islanders for Hartford's fifth round choice in 1983 Entry Draft, Oct. 2, 1981. Traded by Hartford with Rick Meagher to **New Jersey** for Merlin Malinowski and the rights to Scott Fusco, Oct. 15, 1982.

Gordie Howe

HOWE, GORDON 6', 205 lbs.
B. Mar. 31, 1928, Floral, Sask. Right Wing, Shoots R
Won Hart Trophy, 1951–52, 1952–53, 1956–57 , 1957–58 , 1959–60 , 1962-63
Won Art Ross Trophy,1950–51 , 1951–52 , 1952–53, 1953–54 1956–57 , 1962-63
Hall of Fame, 1972

YEAR	TEAM	LEAGUE	GP	G	A	PTS	PIM
1946-47	**DET**	**N**	58	7	15	22	52
1947-48			60	16	28	44	63
1948-49			40	12	25	37	57
1949-50			70	35	33	68	69
1950-51			70	**43**	**43**	**86**	74
1951-52			70	**47**	39	**86**	78
1952-53			70	**49**	**46**	**95**	57
1953-54			70	33	**48**	**81**	109
1954-55			64	29	33	62	68
1955-56			70	38	41	79	100
1956-57			70	**44**	45	**89**	72
1957-58			64	33	44	77	40
1958-59			70	32	46	78	57
1959-60			70	28	45	73	46
1960-61			64	23	49	72	30
1961-62			70	33	44	77	54
1962-63			70	**38**	48	**86**	100
1963-64			69	26	47	73	70
1964-65			70	29	47	76	104

Gordie Howe continued

YEAR	TEAM & LEAGUE	GP	G	A	PTS	PIM
1965-66		70	29	46	75	83
1966-67		69	25	40	65	53
1967-68		74	39	43	82	53
1968-69		76	44	59	103	58
1969-70		76	31	40	71	58
1970-71		63	23	29	52	38
1973-74	**HOUS** W	70	31	69	100	46
1974-75		75	34	65	99	84
1975-76		78	32	70	102	76
1976-77		62	24	44	68	57
1977-78	**NE** W	76	34	62	96	85
1978-79		58	19	24	43	51
1979-80	**HART** N	80	15	26	41	42
32 yrs.	**N Totals:**	1767	801	1049	1850	1685
	W Totals:	419	174	334	508	399

PLAYOFFS

YEAR	TEAM & LEAGUE	GP	G	A	PTS	PIM
1946-47	**DET** N	5	0	0	0	18
1947-48		10	1	1	2	11
1948-49		11	8	3	11	19
1949-50*		1	0	0	0	7
1950-51		6	4	3	7	4
1951-52*		8	2	5	7	2
1952-53		6	2	5	7	2
1953-54*		12	4	5	9	31
1954-55*		11	9	11	20	24
1955-56		10	3	9	12	8
1956-57		5	2	5	7	6
1957-58		4	1	1	2	0
1959-60		6	1	5	6	4
1960-61		11	4	11	15	10
1962-63		11	7	9	16	22
1963-64		14	9	10	19	16
1964-65		7	4	2	6	20
1965-66		12	4	6	10	12
1969-70		4	2	0	2	2
1973-74	**HOUS** W	13	3	14	17	34
1974-75		13	8	12	20	20
1975-76		17	4	8	12	31
1976-77		11	5	3	8	11
1977-78	**NE** W	14	5	5	10	15
1978-79		10	3	1	4	4
1979-80	**HART** N	3	1	1	2	2
26 yrs.	**N Totals:**	157	68	92	160	220
	W Totals:	78	28	43	71	115

Mark Howe

HOWE, MARK STEVEN 5'11", 180 lbs.
B. May 28, 1955, Detroit, Mich. Left Wing, Shoots L

YEAR	TEAM & LEAGUE	GP	G	A	PTS	PIM
1973-74	**HOUS** W	76	38	41	79	20
1974-75		74	36	40	76	30
1975-76		72	39	37	76	38
1976-77		57	23	52	75	46
1977-78	**NE** W	70	30	61	91	32
1978-79		77	42	65	107	32
1979-80	**HART** N	74	24	56	80	20
1980-81		63	19	46	65	54
1981-82		76	8	45	53	18
1982-83	**PHI** N	76	20	47	67	18
10 yrs.	**N Totals:**	289	71	194	265	110
	W Totals:	426	208	296	504	198

PLAYOFFS

YEAR	TEAM & LEAGUE	GP	G	A	PTS	PIM
1973-74	**HOUS** W	14	9	10	19	4
1974-75		13	10	12	22	0
1975-76		17	6	10	16	18
1976-77		11	4	10	14	2
1977-78	**NE** W	14	8	7	15	18
1978-79		6	4	2	6	6
1979-80	**HART** N	3	1	2	3	2
1982-83	**PHI** N	3	0	2	2	4
8 yrs.	**N Totals:**	6	1	4	5	6
	W Totals:	75	41	51	92	48

Reclaimed by **Boston** from Hartford prior to Expansion Draft, June 9, 1979. Claimed as priority selection by **Hartford** June 9, 1979. Traded by Hartford with their third round choice in the 1983 Amateur Draft (Derrick Smith) to **Philadelphia** for Ken Linseman, Greg Adams, and Philadelphia's first (David Jensen) and third (Dave McLean) round choices in the 1982 Amateur Draft, August 19, 1982.

Marty Howe

HOWE, MARTY GORDON 6'1", 195 lbs.
B. Feb. 18, 1954, Detroit, Mich. Defense, Shoots L

YEAR	TEAM & LEAGUE	GP	G	A	PTS	PIM
1973-74	**HOUS** W	73	4	20	24	90
1974-75		75	13	21	34	89
1975-76		80	14	23	37	81
1976-77		80	17	28	45	103
1977-78	**NE** W	75	10	10	20	66
1978-79		66	9	15	24	31
1979-80	**HART** N	6	0	1	1	4
1980-81		12	0	1	1	25
1981-82		13	0	4	4	2
1982-83	**BOS** N	78	1	11	12	24
10 yrs.	**N Totals:**	109	1	17	18	55
	W Totals:	449	67	117	184	460

PLAYOFFS

YEAR	TEAM & LEAGUE	GP	G	A	PTS	PIM
1973-74	**HOUS** W	14	1	5	6	31
1974-75		11	0	2	2	11
1975-76		16	4	4	8	12
1976-77		11	3	1	4	10
1977-78	**NE** W	14	1	1	2	13
1978-79		9	0	1	1	8
1979-80	**HART** N	3	1	1	2	0
1982-83	**BOS** N	12	0	1	1	9
8 yrs.	**N Totals:**	15	1	2	3	9
	W Totals:	75	9	14	23	85

Rights traded to **Detroit** by Montreal for cash and future considerations, Feb. 25, 1977. Loaned to **Boston** by Hartford, Oct. 1, 1982. Returned to **Hartford** by Boston, August, 1983.

Syd Howe

HOWE, SYDNEY HARRIS 5'9", 165 lbs.
B. Oct. 28, 1911, Ottawa, Ont. Center, Shoots L
Hall of Fame, 1965

YEAR	TEAM & LEAGUE	GP	G	A	PTS	PIM
1929-30	**OTTA** N	14	1	1	2	2
1930-31	**PHI** N	44	9	11	20	20
1931-32	**TOR** N	3	0	0	0	0
1932-33	**OTTA** N	48	12	12	24	17
1933-34		41	13	7	20	18
1934-35	**STL** N	36	14	13	27	23
	DET N	14	8	12	20	11
	2 team total	50	22	25	47	34
1935-36		48	16	14	30	26
1936-37		42	17	10	27	10
1937-38		47	8	19	27	14
1938-39		48	16	20	36	11
1939-40		48	14	23	37	17
1940-41		48	20	24	44	8
1941-42		48	16	19	35	6
1942-43		50	20	35	55	10
1943-44		40	32	28	60	6
1944-45		46	17	36	53	6
1945-46		26	4	7	11	9
17 yrs.	**N Totals:**	691	237	291	528	214

PLAYOFFS

YEAR	TEAM & LEAGUE	GP	G	A	PTS	PIM
1929-30	**OTTA** N	2	0	0	0	0
1935-36*	**DET** N	7	3	3	6	2
1936-37*		10	2	5	7	0
1938-39		6	3	1	4	4
1939-40		5	2	2	4	2
1940-41		9	1	7	8	0
1941-42		12	3	5	8	0
1942-43*		7	1	2	3	0
1943-44		5	2	2	4	0
1944-45		7	0	0	0	2
10 yrs.	**N Totals:**	70	17	27	44	10

Vic Howe

HOWE, VICTOR STANLEY 6', 172 lbs.
B. Nov. 2, 1929, Saskatoon, Sask. Right Wing, Shoots R

YEAR	TEAM & LEAGUE	GP	G	A	PTS	PIM
1950-51	**NYR** N	3	1	0	1	0
1953-54		1	0	0	0	0
1954-55		29	2	4	6	10
3 yrs.	**N Totals:**	33	3	4	7	10

Harry Howell

HOWELL, HENRY VERNON 6'1", 200 lbs.
B. Dec. 28, 1932, Hamilton, Ont. Defense, Shoots L
Won Norris Trophy, 1966-67
Hall of Fame, 1979

YEAR	TEAM & LEAGUE		GP	G	A	PTS	PIM
1952-53	**NYR**	**N**	67	3	8	11	46
1953-54			67	7	9	16	58
1954-55			70	2	14	16	87
1955-56			70	3	15	18	77
1956-57			65	2	10	12	70
1957-58			70	4	7	11	62
1958-59			70	4	10	14	101
1959-60			67	7	6	13	58
1960-61			70	7	10	17	62
1961-62			66	6	15	21	89
1962-63			70	5	20	25	55
1963-64			70	5	31	36	75
1964-65			68	2	20	22	63
1965-66			70	4	29	33	92
1966-67			70	12	28	40	54
1967-68			74	5	24	29	62
1968-69			56	4	7	11	36
1969-70	**OAK**	**N**	55	4	16	20	52
1970-71	**CALIF**	**N**	28	0	9	9	14
	LA	**N**	18	3	8	11	4
	2 team total		46	3	17	20	18
1971-72			77	1	17	18	53
1972-73			73	4	11	15	28
1973-74	**NY-NJ**	**W**	65	3	23	26	24
1974-75	**SD**	**W**	74	4	10	14	28
1975-76	**CALG**	**W**	31	0	3	3	6
24 yrs.		**N Totals:**	1411	94	324	418	1298
		W Totals:	170	7	36	43	58

PLAYOFFS

YEAR	TEAM & LEAGUE		GP	G	A	PTS	PIM
1955-56	**NYR**	**N**	5	0	1	1	4
1956-57			5	1	0	1	6
1957-58			6	1	0	1	8
1961-62			6	0	1	1	8
1966-67			4	0	0	0	4
1967-68			6	1	0	1	0
1968-69			2	0	0	0	0
1969-70	**OAK**	**N**	4	0	1	1	2
1974-75	**SD**	**W**	5	1	0	1	10
1975-76	**CALG**	**W**	2	0	0	0	2
10 yrs.		**N Totals:**	38	3	3	6	32
		W Totals:	7	1	0	1	12

Sold to **Oakland** by N.Y. Rangers, June 10, 1969. Sold to **Los Angeles** by California, Feb. 5, 1971.

Ron Howell

HOWELL, RONALD
B. Dec. 4, 1935,

YEAR	TEAM & LEAGUE		GP	G	A	PTS	PIM
1954-55	**NYR**	**N**	3	0	0	0	4
1955-56			1	0	0	0	0
2 yrs.		**N Totals:**	4	0	0	0	4

Don Howse

HOWSE, DONALD GORDON 6', 182 lbs.
B. July 28, 1952, Grand Falls, Nfld. Left Wing, Shoots L

YEAR	TEAM & LEAGUE		GP	G	A	PTS	PIM
1979-80	**LA**	**N**	33	2	5	7	6

PLAYOFFS

YEAR	TEAM & LEAGUE		GP	G	A	PTS	PIM
1979-80	**LA**	**N**	2	0	0	0	0

Dave Hoyda

HOYDA, DAVID ALLAN 6', 206 lbs.
B. May 20, 1957, Edmonton, Alta. Left Wing, Shoots L

YEAR	TEAM & LEAGUE		GP	G	A	PTS	PIM
1977-78	**PHI**	**N**	41	1	3	4	119
1978-79			67	3	13	16	138
1979-80	**WINN**	**N**	15	1	1	2	35
1980-81			9	1	0	1	7
4 yrs.		**N Totals:**	132	6	17	23	299

PLAYOFFS

YEAR	TEAM & LEAGUE		GP	G	A	PTS	PIM
1977-78	**PHI**	**N**	9	0	0	0	17
1978-79			3	0	0	0	0

Dave Hoyda continued

YEAR	TEAM & LEAGUE		GP	G	A	PTS	PIM
2 yrs.		**N Totals:**	12	0	0	0	17

Claimed by **Winnipeg** from Philadelphia in Expansion Draft, June 13, 1979.

Dave Hrechkosy

HRECHKOSY, DAVID JOHN 6'2", 216 lbs.
B. Nov. 1, 1951, Winnipeg, Man. Left Wing, Shoots L

YEAR	TEAM & LEAGUE		GP	G	A	PTS	PIM
1973-74	**CALIF**	**N**	2	0	0	0	0
1974-75			72	29	14	43	25
1975-76			38	9	5	14	14
	STL	**N**	13	3	3	6	0
	2 team total		51	12	8	20	14
1976-77			15	1	2	3	2
4 yrs.		**N Totals:**	140	42	24	66	41

PLAYOFFS

YEAR	TEAM & LEAGUE		GP	G	A	PTS	PIM
1975-76	**STL**	**N**	3	1	0	1	2

Traded to **St. Louis** by California for St. Louis' fifth round choice (Cal Sandbeck) in 1976 Amateur Draft plus the return of California's previously-traded third round choice (Reg Kerr) in 1977 Amateur Draft, Mar. 9, 1976.

Jim Hrycuik

HRYCUIK, JAMES PETER 5'10", 178 lbs.
B. Oct. 7, 1949, Rosthern, Sask. Center, Shoots L

YEAR	TEAM & LEAGUE		GP	G	A	PTS	PIM
1974-75	**WASH**	**N**	21	5	5	10	12

Steve Hrymnak

HRYMNAK, STEFAN 5'10½", 178 lbs.
B. Mar. 3, 1926, Port Arthur, Ont. Defense, Shoots L

YEAR	TEAM & LEAGUE		GP	G	A	PTS	PIM
1951-52	**CHI**	**N**	18	2	1	3	4

PLAYOFFS

YEAR	TEAM & LEAGUE		GP	G	A	PTS	PIM
1952-53	**DET**	**N**	2	0	0	0	0

Sold to **Detroit** by Chicago with Guy Fielder and Red Almas, Sept. 23, 1952.

Tim Hrynewich

HRYNEWICH, TIM 5'11", 187 lbs.
B. Oct. 2, 1963, Leamington, Ont. Left Wing, Shoots L

YEAR	TEAM & LEAGUE		GP	G	A	PTS	PIM
1982-83	**PITT**	**N**	30	2	3	5	48

Rolly Huard

HUARD, ROLAND
B. Unknown Forward

YEAR	TEAM & LEAGUE		GP	G	A	PTS	PIM
1930-31	**TOR**	**N**	1	1	0	1	0

Willie Huber

HUBER, WILHELM HEINRICH (Hubie) 6'5", 228 lbs.
B. Jan. 15, 1958, Strasskirchen, Germany
Defense, Shoots R

YEAR	TEAM & LEAGUE		GP	G	A	PTS	PIM
1978-79	**DET**	**N**	68	7	24	31	114
1979-80			76	17	23	40	164
1980-81			80	15	34	49	130
1981-82			74	15	30	45	98
1982-83			74	14	29	43	106
5 yrs.		**N Totals:**	372	68	140	208	612

Traded by Detroit with Mike Blaisdell and Mark Osborne to **N.Y. Rangers** for Ron Duguay, Ed Mio, and Eddie Johnstone, June 13, 1983.

Greg Hubick

HUBICK, GREGORY WAYNE 5'11", 183 lbs.
B. Nov. 12, 1951, Strasbourg, Sask. Defense, Shoots L

YEAR	TEAM & LEAGUE		GP	G	A	PTS	PIM
1975-76	**TOR**	**N**	72	6	8	14	10
1979-80	**VAN**	**N**	5	0	1	1	0
2 yrs.		**N Totals:**	77	6	9	15	10

Traded to **Toronto** by Montreal for Toronto's second choice (Doug Jarvis) in 1975 Amateur Draft, June 26, 1975. Signed as free agent by **Vancouver** Sept. 7, 1979.

Fran Huck

HUCK, ANTHONY FRANCIS 5'7", 165 lbs.
B. Dec. 4, 1945, Regina, Sask. Center, Shoots R

YEAR	TEAM & LEAGUE		GP	G	A	PTS	PIM
1969-70	**MONT**	**N**	2	0	0	0	0
1970-71			5	1	2	3	0
	STL	**N**	29	7	8	15	18
	2 team total		34	8	10	18	18
1972-73			58	16	20	36	20
1973-74	**WINN**	**W**	74	26	48	74	68
1974-75	**MINN**	**W**	78	22	45	67	26
1975-76			59	17	32	49	27
1976-77	**WINN**	**W**	12	2	2	4	10
1977-78			5	0	0	0	2
8 yrs.		**N Totals:**	94	24	30	54	38
		W Totals:	228	67	127	194	133
PLAYOFFS							
1970-71	**STL**	**N**	6	1	2	3	2
1972-73			5	2	2	4	0
1973-74	**WINN**	**W**	4	0	0	0	2
1974-75	**MINN**	**W**	12	3	13	16	6
1976-77	**WINN**	**W**	7	0	2	2	6
5 yrs.		**N Totals:**	11	3	4	7	2
		W Totals:	23	3	15	18	14

Traded to **St. Louis** by Montreal for St. Louis' second choice (Michel Deguise) in 1971 Amateur Draft, Jan. 28, 1971.

Fred Hucul

HUCUL, FREDERICK ALBERT 5'11", 188 lbs.
B. Dec. 5, 1931, Tubrose, Sask. Defense, Shoots L

YEAR	TEAM & LEAGUE		GP	G	A	PTS	PIM
1950-51	**CHI**	**N**	3	1	0	1	2
1951-52			34	3	7	10	37
1952-53			57	5	7	12	25
1953-54			27	0	3	3	19
1967-68	**STL**	**N**	43	2	13	15	30
5 yrs.		**N Totals:**	164	11	30	41	113
PLAYOFFS							
1952-53	**CHI**	**N**	6	1	0	1	10

Drafted by **St. Louis** from Toronto in Expansion Draft, June 6, 1967.

Charlie Huddy

HUDDY, CHARLES WILLIAM 6', 200 lbs.
B. June 2, 1959, Toronto, Ont. Defense, Shoots L

YEAR	TEAM & LEAGUE		GP	G	A	PTS	PIM
1980-81	**EDM**	**N**	12	2	5	7	6
1981-82			41	4	11	15	46
1982-83			76	20	37	57	58
3 yrs.		**N Totals:**	129	26	53	79	110
PLAYOFFS							
1981-82	**EDM**	**N**	5	1	2	3	14
1982-83			15	1	6	7	10
2 yrs.		**N Totals:**	20	2	8	10	24

Dave Hudson

HUDSON, DAVID RICHARD 6', 175 lbs.
B. Dec. 28, 1949, St. Thomas, Ont. Center, Shoots L

YEAR	TEAM & LEAGUE		GP	G	A	PTS	PIM
1972-73	**NYI**	**N**	69	12	19	31	17
1973-74			63	2	10	12	7
1974-75	**KC**	**N**	70	9	32	41	27
1975-76			74	11	20	31	12
1976-77	**COLO**	**N**	73	15	21	36	14
1977-78			60	10	22	32	12
6 yrs.		**N Totals:**	409	59	124	183	89
PLAYOFFS							
1977-78	**COLO**	**N**	2	1	1	2	0

Drafted by **N.Y. Islanders** from Chicago in Expansion Draft, June 6, 1972. Drafted by **Kansas City** from N.Y. Islanders in Expansion Draft, June 12, 1974.

Lex Hudson

HUDSON, ALEXANDER 6'3", 184 lbs.
B. Dec. 31, 1955, Winnipeg, Man. Defense, Shoots L

YEAR	TEAM & LEAGUE		GP	G	A	PTS	PIM
1978-79	**PITT**	**N**	2	0	0	0	0
PLAYOFFS							
1978-79	**PITT**	**N**	2	0	0	0	0

Ron Hudson

HUDSON, RONALD 5'10", 175 lbs.
B. Apr. 18, 1911, Timmons, Ont. Right Wing, Shoots R

YEAR	TEAM & LEAGUE		GP	G	A	PTS	PIM
1937-38	**DET**	**N**	33	5	2	7	2
1939-40			1	0	0	0	0
2 yrs.		**N Totals:**	34	5	2	7	2

Al Huggins

HUGGINS, ALLAN
B. Toronto, Ont. Forward

YEAR	TEAM & LEAGUE		GP	G	A	PTS	PIM
1930-31	**MON(M)**	**N**	20	1	1	2	2

Al Hughes

HUGHES, ALBERT
B. Collingwood, Ont. Forward

YEAR	TEAM & LEAGUE		GP	G	A	PTS	PIM
1930-31	**NYA**	**N**	42	5	7	12	14
1931-32			18	1	1	2	8
2 yrs.		**N Totals:**	60	6	8	14	22

Brent Hughes

HUGHES, BRENTON ALEXANDER 6', 205 lbs.
B. June 17, 1943, Bowmanville, Ont. Defense, Shoots L

YEAR	TEAM & LEAGUE		GP	G	A	PTS	PIM
1967-68	**LA**	**N**	44	4	10	14	36
1968-69			42	2	19	21	73
1969-70			52	1	7	8	108
1970-71	**PHI**	**N**	30	1	10	11	21
1971-72			63	2	20	22	35
1972-73			29	2	11	13	32
	STL	**N**	8	1	1	2	0
	2 team total		37	3	12	15	32
1973-74			2	0	0	0	0
	DET	**N**	69	1	21	22	92
	2 team total		71	1	21	22	92
1974-75	**KC**	**N**	66	1	18	19	43
1975-76	**SD**	**W**	78	7	28	35	63
1976-77			62	4	13	17	48
1977-78	**BIRM**	**W**	80	9	35	44	48
1978-79			48	3	3	6	21
12 yrs.		**N Totals:**	405	15	117	132	440
		W Totals:	268	23	79	102	180
PLAYOFFS							
1967-68	**LA**	**N**	7	0	0	0	10
1968-69			7	0	0	0	2
1970-71	**PHI**	**N**	4	0	0	0	6
1975-76	**SD**	**W**	10	1	5	6	6
1976-77			7	1	4	5	0
1977-78	**BIRM**	**W**	5	0	0	0	12
6 yrs.		**N Totals:**	18	0	0	0	18
		W Totals:	22	2	9	11	18

Drafted by **Los Angeles** from Detroit in Expansion Draft, June 6, 1967. Traded to **Philadelphia** by Los Angeles for Mike Byers, May 20, 1970. Traded to **St. Louis** by Philadelphia with Pierre Plante for Andre Dupont and St. Louis' third round choice (Bob Stumpf) in 1973 Amateur Draft, Dec. 14, 1972. Sold to **Detroit** by St. Louis, Oct. 27, 1973. Drafted by **Kansas City** from Detroit in Expansion Draft, June 12, 1974.

Frank Hughes

HUGHES, FRANK 5'10", 180 lbs.
B. Oct. 1, 1949, Fernie, B.C. Left Wing, Shoots L

YEAR	TEAM & LEAGUE		GP	G	A	PTS	PIM
1971-72	**CALIF**	**N**	5	0	0	0	0
1972-73	**HOUS**	**W**	76	22	19	41	41
1973-74			73	42	42	84	47
1974-75			76	48	35	83	35
1975-76			80	31	45	76	26
1976-77			27	3	8	11	2
	PHOE	**W**	48	24	29	53	20
	2 team total		75	27	37	64	22
1977-78	**HOUS**	**W**	11	3	2	5	2

Frank Hughes continued

YEAR	TEAM & LEAGUE		GP	G	A	PTS	PIM
7 yrs.		N Totals:	5	0	0	0	0
		W Totals:	391	173	180	353	173
PLAYOFFS							
1972-73	HOUS	W	10	4	4	8	2
1973-74			14	9	5	14	9
1974-75			13	6	6	12	2
1975-76			17	5	1	6	20
4 yrs.		W Totals:	54	24	16	40	33

Drafted by **California** from Toronto in Intra-League Draft, June 8, 1971. Drafted by **Atlanta** from California in Expansion Draft, June 6, 1971.

Howie Hughes

HUGHES, HOWARD DUNCAN 5'9", 180 lbs.
B. Apr. 4, 1939, St. Boniface, Man. Right Wing, Shoots L

YEAR	TEAM & LEAGUE		GP	G	A	PTS	PIM
1967-68	LA	N	74	9	14	23	20
1968-69			73	16	14	30	10
1969-70			21	0	4	4	0
3 yrs.		N Totals:	168	25	32	57	30

Drafted by **Los Angeles** from Montreal in Expansion Draft, June 6, 1967.

Jack Hughes

HUGHES, JOHN F. 6'1", 205 lbs.
B. July 20, 1957, Somerville, Mass. Defense, Shoots R

YEAR	TEAM & LEAGUE		GP	G	A	PTS	PIM
1980-81	COLO	N	38	2	5	7	91

John Hughes

HUGHES, JOHN SPENCER 5'11", 200 lbs.
B. Mar. 18, 1954, Charlottetown, P.E.I. Defense, Shoots L

YEAR	TEAM & LEAGUE		GP	G	A	PTS	PIM
1974-75	PHOE	W	72	4	25	29	201
1975-76	CIN	W	79	3	34	37	204
1976-77			79	3	27	30	113
1977-78	HOUS	W	79	3	25	28	130
1978-79	IND	W	22	3	4	7	48
	EDM	W	41	2	15	17	82
	2 team total		63	5	19	24	130
1979-80	VAN	N	52	2	11	13	181
1980-81	EDM	N	18	0	3	3	30
1981-82	COLO	N	8	0	0	0	17
8 yrs.		N Totals:	78	2	14	16	228
		W Totals:	372	18	130	148	778
PLAYOFFS							
1976-77	CIN	W	4	0	0	0	8
1977-78	HOUS	W	6	1	1	2	6
1978-79	EDM	W	13	1	0	1	35
1979-80	VAN	N	4	0	0	0	10
1980-81	NYR	N	3	0	1	1	6
5 yrs.		N Totals:	7	0	1	1	16
		W Totals:	23	2	1	3	49

Reclaimed by **Vancouver** from Edmonton prior to Expansion Draft, June 9, 1979. Claimed on waivers by **Edmonton** from Vancouver, Dec. 15, 1980. Traded to **N.Y. Rangers** by Edmonton for Ray Markham, Mar. 10, 1981.

Pat Hughes

HUGHES, PATRICK 6'1", 180 lbs.
B. Mar. 25, 1955, Calgary, Alta. Right Wing, Shoots R

YEAR	TEAM & LEAGUE		GP	G	A	PTS	PIM
1977-78	MONT	N	3	0	0	0	2
1978-79			41	9	8	17	22
1979-80	PITT	N	78	18	14	32	78
1980-81			58	10	9	19	161
	EDM	N	2	0	0	0	0
	2 team total		60	10	9	19	161
1981-82			68	24	22	46	99
1982-83			80	25	20	45	85
6 yrs.		N Totals:	330	86	73	159	447
PLAYOFFS							
1978-79*	MONT	N	8	1	2	3	4
1979-80	PITT	N	5	0	0	0	21
1980-81	EDM	N	5	0	0	0	4
1981-82			5	2	1	3	6
1982-83			16	2	5	7	14

Pat Hughes continued

YEAR	TEAM & LEAGUE		GP	G	A	PTS	PIM
5 yrs.		N Totals:	39	5	8	13	49

Traded to **Pittsburgh** by Montreal with Robert Holland for Denis Herron and Pittsburgh's second round choice (Jocelyn Gauvreau) in the 1982 Entry Draft, Aug. 30, 1979. Traded to **Edmonton** by Pittsburgh, for Pat Price, Mar. 10, 1981.

Rusty Hughes

HUGHES, J.
Defense

YEAR	TEAM & LEAGUE		GP	G	A	PTS	PIM
1929-30	DET	N	40	0	1	1	48

Bobby Hull

HULL, ROBERT MARVIN (The Golden Jet) 5'10", 193 lbs.
B. Jan. 3, 1939, Pointe Anne, Ont. Left Wing, Shoots L
Won Hart Trophy, 1964–65, 1965-66
Won Art Ross Trophy, 1959–60, 1961–62, 1965-66
Won Lady Byng Trophy, 1964-65
Hall of Fame, 1983

YEAR	TEAM & LEAGUE		GP	G	A	PTS	PIM
1957-58	CHI	N	70	13	34	47	62
1958-59			70	18	32	50	50
1959-60			70	**39**	42	**81**	68
1960-61			67	31	25	56	43
1961-62			70	**50**	34	**84**	35
1962-63			65	31	31	62	27
1963-64			70	**43**	44	87	50
1964-65			61	39	32	71	32
1965-66			65	**54**	43	**97**	70
1966-67			66	**52**	28	80	52
1967-68			71	**44**	31	75	39
1968-69			74	**58**	49	107	48
1969-70			61	38	29	67	8
1970-71			78	44	52	96	32
1971-72			78	50	43	93	24
1972-73	WINN	W	63	51	52	103	37
1973-74			75	53	42	95	38
1974-75			78	**77**	65	142	41
1975-76			80	53	70	123	30
1976-77			34	21	32	53	14
1977-78			77	46	71	117	23
1978-79			4	2	3	5	0
1979-80	WINN	N	18	4	6	10	0
	HART	N	9	2	5	7	0
	2 team total		27	6	11	17	0
23 yrs.		N Totals:	1063	610	560	1170	640
		W Totals:	411	303	335	638	183
PLAYOFFS							
1958-59	CHI	N	6	1	1	2	2
1959-60			3	1	0	1	2
1960-61*			12	4	10	14	4
1961-62			12	8	6	14	12
1962-63			5	8	2	10	4
1963-64			7	2	5	7	2
1964-65			14	10	7	17	27
1965-66			3	2	2	4	10
1966-67			6	4	2	6	0
1967-68			11	4	6	10	15
1969-70			8	3	8	11	2
1970-71			18	11	14	25	16
1971-72			8	4	4	8	6
1972-73	WINN	W	14	9	16	25	16
1973-74			4	1	1	2	4
1975-76			13	12	8	20	4
1976-77			20	13	9	22	2
1977-78			9	8	3	11	12
1979-80	HART	N	3	0	0	0	0
19 yrs.		N Totals:	116	62	67	129	102
		W Totals:	60	43	37	80	38

Dennis Hull

HULL, DENNIS WILLIAM 5'11", 195 lbs.
B. Nov. 19, 1944, Pointe Anne, Ont. Left Wing, Shoots L

YEAR	TEAM & LEAGUE		GP	G	A	PTS	PIM
1964-65	CHI	N	55	10	4	14	18
1965-66			25	1	5	6	6
1966-67			70	25	17	42	33
1967-68			74	18	15	33	34
1968-69			72	30	34	64	25

Dennis Hull continued

YEAR	TEAM & LEAGUE		GP	G	A	PTS	PIM
1969-70			76	17	35	52	31
1970-71			78	40	26	66	16
1971-72			78	30	39	69	10
1972-73			78	39	51	90	27
1973-74			74	29	39	68	15
1974-75			69	16	21	37	10
1975-76			80	27	39	66	28
1976-77			75	16	17	33	2
1977-78	**DET**	**N**	55	5	9	14	6
14 yrs.		**N Totals:**	959	303	351	654	261
PLAYOFFS							
1964-65	**CHI**	**N**	6	0	0	0	0
1967-68			11	1	3	4	6
1969-70			8	5	2	7	0
1970-71			18	7	6	13	2
1971-72			8	4	2	6	4
1972-73			16	9	15	24	4
1973-74			10	6	3	9	0
1974-75			5	0	2	2	0
1975-76			4	0	0	0	0
1976-77			2	1	0	1	0
1977-78	**DET**	**N**	7	0	0	0	2
11 yrs.		**N Totals:**	95	33	33	66	18

Traded to **Detroit** by Chicago for Detroit's fourth round draft choice (Carey Wilson) in 1980 Amateur Draft, Dec. 2, 1977.

Steve Hull

HULL, STEVEN 5'10", 180 lbs.
B. Aug. 29, 1952, Ottawa, Ont. Left Wing, Shoots R

YEAR	TEAM & LEAGUE		GP	G	A	PTS	PIM
1975-76	**CALG**	**W**	58	11	15	26	6
1976-77			2	0	2	2	0
2 yrs.		**W Totals:**	60	11	17	28	6

Fred Hunt

HUNT, FREDRICK TENNYSON (Fritz) 5'8", 160 lbs.
B. Jan. 17, 1919, Brantford, Ont. Right Wing, Shoots R

YEAR	TEAM & LEAGUE		GP	G	A	PTS	PIM
1940-41	**NYA**	**N**	15	2	5	7	0
1944-45	**NYR**	**N**	44	13	9	22	6
2 yrs.		**N Totals:**	59	15	14	29	6

Dale Hunter

HUNTER, DALE ROBERT 5'9", 190 lbs.
B. July 31, 1060, Oil Springs, Ont. Center, Shoots L

YEAR	TEAM & LEAGUE		GP	G	A	PTS	PIM
1980-81	**QUE**	**N**	80	19	44	63	226
1981-82			80	22	50	72	272
1982-83			80	17	46	63	206
3 yrs.		**N Totals:**	240	58	140	198	704
PLAYOFFS							
1980-81	**QUE**	**N**	5	4	2	6	34
1981-82			16	3	7	10	52
1982-83			4	2	1	3	24
3 yrs.		**N Totals:**	25	9	10	19	110

Dave Hunter

HUNTER, DAVID (Hunts) 5'11", 195 lbs.
B. Jan. 1, 1958, Petrolia, Ont. Left Wing, Shoots L

YEAR	TEAM & LEAGUE		GP	G	A	PTS	PIM
1978-79	**EDM**	**W**	72	7	25	32	134
1979-80	**EDM**	**N**	80	12	31	43	103
1980-81			78	12	16	28	98
1981-82			63	16	22	38	63
1982-83			80	13	18	31	120
5 yrs.		**N Totals:**	301	53	87	140	384
		W Totals:	72	7	25	32	134
PLAYOFFS							
1978-79	**EDM**	**W**	13	2	3	5	32
1979-80	**EDM**	**N**	3	0	0	0	7
1980-81			9	0	0	0	28
1981-82			5	0	1	1	26
1982-83			16	4	7	11	60
5 yrs.		**N Totals:**	33	4	8	12	121
		W Totals:	13	2	3	5	32

Claimed by **Edmonton** from Montreal in Expansion Draft, June 22, 1979.

Mark Hunter

HUNTER, MARK 6', 194 lbs.
B. Nov. 12, 1962, Petrolia, Ont. Right Wing, Shoots R

YEAR	TEAM & LEAGUE		GP	G	A	PTS	PIM
1981-82	**MONT**	**N**	71	18	11	29	143
1982-83			31	8	8	16	73
2 yrs.		**N Totals:**	102	26	19	45	216
PLAYOFFS							
1981-82	**MONT**	**N**	5	0	0	0	20

Tim Hunter

HUNTER, TIMOTHY ROBERT 6'2", 186 lbs.
B. Sept. 10, 1960, Calgary, Alta. Defense, Shoots R

YEAR	TEAM & LEAGUE		GP	G	A	PTS	PIM
1981-82	**CALG**	**N**	2	0	0	0	9
1982-83			16	1	0	1	54
2 yrs.		**N Totals:**	18	1	0	1	63
PLAYOFFS							
1982-83	**CALG**	**N**	9	1	0	1	70

Larry Huras

HURAS, LARRY ROBERT 6'2", 200 lbs.
B. July 8, 1955, Listowel, Ont. Defense, Shoots L

YEAR	TEAM & LEAGUE		GP	G	A	PTS	PIM
1976-77	**NYR**	**N**	1	0	0	0	0

Signed as free agent by **St. Louis** Oct. 12, 1977.

Bob Hurlburt

HURLBURT, ROBERT GEORGE 5'11", 185 lbs.
B. May 1, 1950, Toronto, Ont. Left Wing, Shoots L

YEAR	TEAM & LEAGUE		GP	G	A	PTS	PIM
1974-75	**VAN**	**N**	1	0	0	0	2

Paul Hurley

HURLEY, PAUL MICHAEL 5'11", 185 lbs.
B. July 12, 1946, Melrose, Ma. Defense, Shoots R

YEAR	TEAM & LEAGUE		GP	G	A	PTS	PIM
1968-69	**BOS**	**N**	1	0	1	1	0
1972-73	**NE**	**W**	78	3	15	18	58
1973-74			52	3	11	14	21
1974-75			75	3	26	29	36
1975-76			10	0	14	14	20
	EDM	**W**	26	1	4	5	14
	2 team total		36	1	18	19	34
1976-77	**CALG**	**W**	34	0	6	6	32
6 yrs.		**N Totals:**	1	0	1	1	0
		W Totals:	275	10	76	86	181
PLAYOFFS							
1972-73	**NE**	**W**	15	0	7	7	14
1974-75			6	0	1	1	4
1975-76	**EDM**	**W**	4	0	0	0	0
3 yrs.		**W Totals:**	25	0	8	8	18

Ron Hurst

HURST, RONALD 5'9", 175 lbs.
B. May 18, 1931, Toronto, Ont. Right Wing, Shoots R

YEAR	TEAM & LEAGUE		GP	G	A	PTS	PIM
1955-56	**TOR**	**N**	50	7	5	12	62
1956-57			14	2	2	4	8
2 yrs.		**N Totals:**	64	9	7	16	70
PLAYOFFS							
1955-56	**TOR**	**N**	3	0	2	2	4

Ron Huston

HUSTON, RONALD EARLE 5'9", 170 lbs.
B. Apr. 8, 1945, Manitou, Man. Center, Shoots R

YEAR	TEAM & LEAGUE		GP	G	A	PTS	PIM
1973-74	**CALIF**	**N**	23	3	10	13	0
1974-75			23	3	10	13	0
1975-76	**PHOE**	**W**	79	22	44	66	4
1976-77			80	20	39	59	10
4 yrs.		**N Totals:**	46	6	20	26	0
		W Totals:	159	42	83	125	14
PLAYOFFS							
1975-76	**PHOE**	**W**	5	1	1	2	0

Ronald Hutchinson

HUTCHINSON, RONALD WAYNE 5'10", 175 lbs.
B. Oct. 24, 1936, Flin Flon, Man. Center, Shoots L

YEAR	TEAM & LEAGUE		GP	G	A	PTS	PIM
1960-61	NYR	N	9	0	0	0	0

Dave Hutchison

HUTCHISON, DAVID JOSEPH 6'3", 205 lbs.
B. May 2, 1952, London, Ont. Defense, Shoots L

YEAR	TEAM & LEAGUE		GP	G	A	PTS	PIM
1972-73	PHI	W	28	0	2	2	3
1973-74	VAN	W	69	0	13	13	151
1974-75	LA	N	68	0	6	6	133
1975-76			50	0	10	10	181
1976-77			70	6	11	17	220
1977-78			44	0	10	10	71
1978-79	TOR	N	79	4	15	19	235
1979-80			31	1	6	7	28
	CHI	N	38	0	5	5	73
	2 team total		69	1	11	12	101
1980-81			59	2	9	11	124
1981-82			66	5	18	23	246
1982-83	NJ	N	32	1	4	5	102
11 yrs.		N Totals:	537	19	94	113	1413
		W Totals:	97	0	15	15	154

PLAYOFFS

YEAR	TEAM & LEAGUE		GP	G	A	PTS	PIM
1974-75	LA	N	2	0	0	0	22
1975-76			9	0	3	3	29
1976-77			9	1	4	5	17
1978-79	TOR	N	6	0	3	3	23
1979-80	CHI	N	6	0	0	0	12
1980-81			2	0	0	0	2
1981-82			14	1	2	3	44
7 yrs.		N Totals:	48	2	12	14	149

Traded to **Toronto** by Los Angeles with Lorne Stamler for Brian Glennie, Kurt Walker, Scott Garland, Toronto's second round choice (Mark Hardy) in 1979 Entry Draft, and future considerations, June 14, 1979. Traded to **Chicago** by Toronto for Pat Ribble, Jan. 10, 1980. Traded by Chicago with Ted Bulley to **Washington** for Washington's sixth round choice (Jari Torkki) in the 1983 Amateur Draft, and fifth choice in the 1984 Draft, August 24, 1982. Acquired by **New Jersey** from Washington in Waiver Draft, Oct. 4, 1982.

William Hutton

HUTTON, WILLIAM DAVID 5'10½", 165 lbs.
B. Jan. 28, 1910, Calgary, Alta. Defense, Shoots R

YEAR	TEAM & LEAGUE		GP	G	A	PTS	PIM
1929-30	BOS	N	16	2	0	2	2
	OTTA	N	18	0	1	1	0
	2 team total		34	2	1	3	2
1930-31	BOS	N	9	0	0	0	2
	PHI	N	21	1	1	2	4
	2 team total		30	1	1	2	6
2 yrs.		N Totals:	64	3	2	5	8

PLAYOFFS

YEAR	TEAM & LEAGUE		GP	G	A	PTS	PIM
1929-30	OTTA	N	2	0	0	0	0

Harry Hyland

HYLAND, HAROLD
B. Jan. 2, 1889, Montreal, Que. Right Wing
Hall of Fame, 1962

YEAR	TEAM & LEAGUE		GP	G	A	PTS	PIM
1917-18	MON(W)	N	4	6	0	6	6
	OTTA	N	12	8	0	8	3
	2 team total		16	14	0	14	9

Mike Hyndman

HYNDMAN, MICHAEL ANTHONY 6'1", 205 lbs.
B. Dec. 8, 1945, Quebec City, Que. Right Wing, Shoots R

YEAR	TEAM & LEAGUE		GP	G	A	PTS	PIM
1973-74	LA	W	8	0	1	1	0

PLAYOFFS

YEAR	TEAM & LEAGUE		GP	G	A	PTS	PIM
1972-73	LA	W	6	0	3	3	17

Dave Hynes

HYNES, DAVID E. 5'9", 182 lbs.
B. Apr. 17, 1951, Cambridge, Mass. Left Wing, Shoots L

YEAR	TEAM & LEAGUE		GP	G	A	PTS	PIM
1973-74	BOS	N	3	0	0	0	0
1974-75			19	4	0	4	2
1976-77	NE	W	22	5	4	9	4
3 yrs.		N Totals:	22	4	0	4	2
		W Totals:	22	5	4	9	4

Peter Ihnacak

IHNACAK, PETER 5'11", 180 lbs.
B. Czechoslovakia Forward

YEAR	TEAM & LEAGUE		GP	G	A	PTS	PIM
1982-83	TOR	N	80	28	38	66	44

Brent Imlach

IMLACH, BRENT
B. Nov. 16, 1946, Toronto, Ont. Forward

YEAR	TEAM & LEAGUE		GP	G	A	PTS	PIM
1965-66	TOR	N	2	0	0	0	2
1966-67			1	0	0	0	0
2 yrs.		N Totals:	3	0	0	0	2

Earl Ingarfield

INGARFIELD, EARL THOMPSON 5'11", 185 lbs.
B. Oct. 25, 1934, Lethbridge, Alta. Center, Shoots L

YEAR	TEAM & LEAGUE		GP	G	A	PTS	PIM
1958-59	NYR	N	35	1	2	3	10
1959-60			20	1	2	3	2
1960-61			66	13	21	34	18
1961-62			70	26	31	57	18
1962-63			69	19	24	43	40
1963-64			63	15	11	26	26
1964-65			69	15	13	28	40
1965-66			68	20	16	36	35
1966-67			67	12	22	34	12
1967-68	PITT	N	50	15	22	37	12
1968-69			40	8	15	23	4
	CALIF	N	26	8	15	23	8
	2 team total		66	16	30	46	12
1969-70	OAK	N	54	21	24	45	10
1970-71	CALIF	N	49	5	8	13	4
13 yrs.		N Totals:	746	179	226	405	239

PLAYOFFS

YEAR	TEAM & LEAGUE		GP	G	A	PTS	PIM
1961-62	NYR	N	6	3	2	5	2
1966-67			4	1	0	1	2
1968-69	CALIF	N	7	4	6	10	2
1969-70	OAK	N	4	1	0	1	4
4 yrs.		N Totals:	21	9	8	17	10

Traded to **Mont. Canadiens** by N.Y. Rangers with Noel Price, Gord Labossiere, and Dave McComb for Cesare Maniago and Garry Peters, June 8, 1965. Drafted by **N.Y. Rangers** from Montreal, June 9, 1965. Drafted by **Pittsburgh** from N.Y. Rangers in Expansion Draft, June 6, 1967. Traded to **Oakland** by Pittsburgh with Gene Ubriaco and Dick Mattiussi for Bryan Watson, George Swarbrick, and Tracy Pratt, Jan. 30, 1969.

Earl Ingarfield

INGARFIELD, EARL THOMPSON, JR. 5'10", 175 lbs.
B. Jan. 30, 1959, Manhasset, N.Y. Center, Shoots L

YEAR	TEAM & LEAGUE		GP	G	A	PTS	PIM
1979-80	ATL	N	1	0	0	0	0
1980-81	CALG	N	16	2	3	5	6
	DET	N	22	2	1	3	16
	2 team total		38	4	4	8	22
2 yrs.		N Totals:	39	4	4	8	22

PLAYOFFS

YEAR	TEAM & LEAGUE		GP	G	A	PTS	PIM
1979-80	ATL	N	2	0	1	1	0

Traded to **Detroit** by Calgary for Dan Labraaten, Feb. 3, 1981.

Lee Inglis

INGLIS, LEE 5'10", 190 lbs.
B. Aug. 31, 1947, Latchford, Ont. Left Wing, Shoots L

YEAR	TEAM & LEAGUE		GP	G	A	PTS	PIM
1973-74	NY-NJ	W	5	0	0	0	0
1974-75	SD	W	5	0	2	2	0

Lee Inglis continued

YEAR	TEAM & LEAGUE		GP	G	A	PTS	PIM
2 yrs.		W Totals:	10	0	2	2	0

Bill Inglis

INGLIS, WILLIAM JOHN 5'9", 160 lbs.
B. May 11, 1943, Ottawa, Ont. Center, Shoots L

YEAR	TEAM & LEAGUE		GP	G	A	PTS	PIM
1967-68	**LA**	**N**	12	1	1	2	0
1968-69			10	0	1	1	0
1970-71	**BUF**	**N**	14	0	1	1	4
3 yrs.		**N Totals:**	36	1	3	4	4
PLAYOFFS							
1968-69	**LA**	**N**	11	1	2	3	4

Drafted by **Los Angeles** from Montreal in Expansion Draft, June 6, 1967. Put on **Montreal** reserve list from Los Angeles in Intra-league Draft, June 9, 1970. Drafted by **Buffalo** from Montreal (AHL) in Inter-League Draft, June 9, 1970.

Johnny Ingoldsby

INGOLDSBY, JOHN GORDON (Ding) 6'2", 210 lbs.
B. June 21, 1924, Toronto, Ont. Right Wing, Shoots R

YEAR	TEAM & LEAGUE		GP	G	A	PTS	PIM
1942-43	**TOR**	**N**	8	0	1	1	0
1943-44			21	5	0	5	15
2 yrs.		**N Totals:**	29	5	1	6	15

Frank Ingram

INGRAM, FRANK 5'7½", 185 lbs.
B. Sept. 17, 1907, Graven, Sask. Right Wing, Shoots R

YEAR	TEAM & LEAGUE		GP	G	A	PTS	PIM
1924-25	**BOS**	**N**	1	0	0	0	0
1929-30	**CHI**	**N**	37	6	10	16	28
1930-31			43	17	4	21	37
1931-32			21	1	2	3	4
4 yrs.		**N Totals:**	102	24	16	40	69
PLAYOFFS							
1929-30	**CHI**	**N**	2	0	0	0	0
1930-31			9	0	1	1	2
2 yrs.		**N Totals:**	11	0	1	1	2

Ron Ingram

INGRAM, RONALD WALTER 5'11", 185 lbs.
B. July 5, 1933, Toronto, Ont. Defense, Shoots R

YEAR	TEAM & LEAGUE		GP	G	A	PTS	PIM
1956-57	**CHI**	**N**	45	1	6	7	21
1963-64	**DET**	**N**	50	3	6	9	50
	NYR	**N**	16	1	3	4	8
	2 team total		66	4	9	13	58
1964-65			3	0	0	0	2
3 yrs.		**N Totals:**	114	5	15	20	81
PLAYOFFS							
1962-63	**CHI**	**N**	2	0	0	0	0

Traded by Chicago along with Roger Crozier to **Detroit** for Howie Young, June 5, 1963. Traded by Detroit to **N.Y. Rangers** for Albert Langlois, Feb. 14, 1964.

Dave Inkpen

INKPEN, DAVID 6', 185 lbs.
B. Sept. 4, 1954, Edmonton, Alta. Defense, Shoots R

YEAR	TEAM & LEAGUE		GP	G	A	PTS	PIM
1975-76	**CIN**	**W**	80	4	24	28	95
1976-77			48	3	14	17	61
	IND	**W**	32	4	12	16	20
	2 team total		80	7	26	33	81
1977-78	**EDM**	**W**	19	0	1	1	16
	QUE	**W**	24	0	1	1	20
	IND	**W**	24	1	9	10	24
	3 team total		67	1	11	12	60
1978-79			25	1	8	9	22
	NE	**W**	41	0	7	7	15
	2 team total		66	1	15	16	37
4 yrs.		**W Totals:**	293	13	76	89	273
PLAYOFFS							
1976-77	**IND**	**W**	9	0	2	2	8

Dave Inkpen continued

YEAR	TEAM & LEAGUE		GP	G	A	PTS	PIM
1978-79	**NE**	**W**	5	0	1	1	4
2 yrs.		**W Totals:**	14	0	3	3	12

Dick Irvin

IRVIN, RICHARD
B. July 19, 1892, Limestone Ridge, Ont. Forward
Hall of Fame, 1958

YEAR	TEAM & LEAGUE		GP	G	A	PTS	PIM
1926-27	**CHI**	**N**	44	**18**	18	36	34
1927-28			14	5	4	9	12
1928-29			36	6	1	7	30
3 yrs.		**N Totals:**	94	29	23	52	76
PLAYOFFS							
1926-27	**CHI**	**N**	2	2	0	2	4

Ted Irvine

IRVINE, EDWARD AMOS 6'2", 195 lbs.
B. Dec. 8, 1944, Winnipeg, Man. Left Wing, Shoots L

YEAR	TEAM & LEAGUE		GP	G	A	PTS	PIM
1963-64	**BOS**	**N**	1	0	0	0	0
1967-68	**LA**	**N**	73	18	22	40	26
1968-69			76	15	24	39	47
1969-70			58	11	13	24	28
	NYR	**N**	17	0	3	3	10
	2 team total		75	11	16	27	38
1970-71			76	20	18	38	137
1971-72			78	15	21	36	66
1972-73			53	8	12	20	54
1973-74			75	26	20	46	105
1974-75			79	17	17	34	66
1975-76	**STL**	**N**	69	10	13	23	80
1976-77			69	14	14	28	38
11 yrs.		**N Totals:**	724	154	177	331	657
PLAYOFFS							
1967-68	**LA**	**N**	6	1	3	4	2
1968-69			11	5	1	6	7
1969-70	**NYR**	**N**	6	1	2	3	8
1970-71			12	1	2	3	28
1971-72			16	4	5	9	19
1972-73			10	1	3	4	20
1973-74			13	3	5	8	16
1974-75			3	0	1	1	11
1975-76	**STL**	**N**	3	0	2	2	2
1976-77			3	0	0	0	2
10 yrs.		**N Totals:**	83	16	24	40	115

Drafted by **Los Angeles** from Boston in Expansion Draft, June 6, 1967. Traded to **N.Y. Rangers** by Los Angeles for Real Lemieux and Juha Widing, Feb. 28, 1970. Traded to **St. Louis** by N.Y. Rangers with Bert Wilson and Jerry Butler for Bill Collins and goaltender John Davidson, June 18, 1975.

Glen Irwin

IRWIN, GLEN MAC 5'11", 195 lbs.
B. Mar. 1, 1951, Edmonton, Alta. Defense, Shoots R

YEAR	TEAM & LEAGUE		GP	G	A	PTS	PIM
1974-75	**HOUS**	**W**	70	2	11	13	153
1975-76			72	3	8	11	116
1976-77			44	2	4	6	168
1977-78			3	0	0	0	0
	IND	**W**	20	0	0	0	72
	2 team total		23	0	0	0	72
1978-79			24	0	1	1	124
5 yrs.		**W Totals:**	233	7	24	31	633
PLAYOFFS							
1974-75	**HOUS**	**W**	13	0	2	2	8
1975-76			5	0	0	0	9
2 yrs.		**W Totals:**	18	0	2	2	17

Traded to **N.Y. Islanders** by Philadelphia, May 18, 1973 to complete deal in which N.Y. Islanders acquired Jean Potvin for Terry Crisp, Mar. 5, 1973.

Ivan Irwin

IRWIN, IVAN DUANE (Ivan the Terrible) 6'2", 185 lbs.
B. Mar. 13, 1927, Chicago, Ill. Defense, Shoots L

YEAR	TEAM	LEAGUE	GP	G	A	PTS	PIM
1952-53	**MONT**	**N**	4	0	1	1	0
1953-54	**NYR**	**N**	56	2	12	14	109
1954-55			60	0	13	13	85
1955-56			34	0	1	1	20
1957-58			1	0	0	0	0
5 yrs.		**N Totals:**	155	2	27	29	214

PLAYOFFS

YEAR	TEAM	LEAGUE	GP	G	A	PTS	PIM
1955-56	**NYR**	**N**	5	0	0	0	8

Traded to **N.Y. Rangers** by Montreal for Pete Babando and Ed Slowinski, Aug. 17, 1953.

Ulf Isaksson

ISAKSSON, ULF 6'1", 185 lbs.
B. Mar. 19, 1954, Norfunda, Sweden Left Wing, Shoots L

YEAR	TEAM	LEAGUE	GP	G	A	PTS	PIM
1982-83	**LA**	**N**	50	7	15	22	10

Larry Israelson

ISRAELSON, LAWRENCE 6'1", 180 lbs.
B. Wetaskiwin, Sask. Left Wing

YEAR	TEAM	LEAGUE	GP	G	A	PTS	PIM
1974-75	**VAN**	**W**	46	12	9	21	10
1975-76	**CALG**	**W**	57	10	22	32	26
1976-77			2	0	0	0	0
3 yrs.		**W Totals:**	105	22	31	53	36

PLAYOFFS

YEAR	TEAM	LEAGUE	GP	G	A	PTS	PIM
1975-76	**CALG**	**W**	3	0	0	0	0

Art Jackson

JACKSON, ARTHUR M. 5'7½", 165 lbs.
B. Dec. 15, 1915, Toronto, Ont. Center, Shoots L

YEAR	TEAM	LEAGUE	GP	G	A	PTS	PIM
1934-35	**TOR**	**N**	20	1	3	4	4
1935-36			48	5	15	20	14
1936-37			14	2	0	2	2
1937-38	**BOS**	**N**	48	9	3	12	24
1938-39	**NYA**	**N**	48	12	13	25	15
1939-40	**BOS**	**N**	45	7	18	25	6
1940-41			47	17	15	32	10
1941-42			47	6	18	24	25
1942-43			50	22	31	53	20
1943-44			49	21	38	59	8
1944-45			19	5	8	13	10
	TOR	**N**	31	9	13	22	6
	2 team total		50	14	21	35	16
11 yrs.		**N Totals:**	466	116	175	291	144

PLAYOFFS

YEAR	TEAM	LEAGUE	GP	G	A	PTS	PIM
1935-36	**TOR**	**N**	8	0	3	3	2
1937-38	**BOS**	**N**	3	0	0	0	0
1938-39	**NYA**	**N**	2	0	0	0	2
1939-40	**BOS**	**N**	5	1	2	3	0
1940-41*			11	1	3	4	16
1941-42			5	0	1	1	0
1942-43			9	6	3	9	7
1944-45*	**TOR**	**N**	8	0	0	0	0
8 yrs.		**N Totals:**	51	8	12	20	27

Busher Jackson

JACKSON, RALPH HARVEY 5'11", 195 lbs.
B. Jan. 19, 1911, Toronto, Ont. Shoots L
Won Art Ross Trophy, 1931-32
Hall of Fame, 1971

YEAR	TEAM	LEAGUE	GP	G	A	PTS	PIM
1929-30	**TOR**	**N**	32	12	6	18	29
1930-31			43	18	13	31	81
1931-32			48	28	25	**53**	63
1932-33			48	27	17	44	43
1933-34			38	20	18	38	38
1934-35			42	22	22	44	27
1935-36			47	11	11	22	19
1936-37			46	21	19	40	12
1937-38			48	17	17	34	18
1938-39			42	10	17	27	12

Busher Jackson continued

YEAR	TEAM	LEAGUE	GP	G	A	PTS	PIM
1939-40	**NYA**	**N**	43	12	8	20	10
1940-41			46	8	18	26	4
1941-42	**BOS**	**N**	27	5	7	12	18
1942-43			44	19	15	34	38
1943-44			42	11	21	32	25
15 yrs.		**N Totals:**	636	241	234	475	437

PLAYOFFS

YEAR	TEAM	LEAGUE	GP	G	A	PTS	PIM
1930-31	**TOR**	**N**	2	0	0	0	0
1931-32*			7	5	2	**7**	13
1932-33			9	3	1	4	2
1933-34			5	1	0	1	8
1934-35			7	3	2	5	2
1935-36			9	3	2	5	4
1936-37			2	1	0	1	2
1937-38			6	1	0	1	8
1938-39			7	0	1	1	2
1939-40	**NYA**	**N**	3	0	1	1	2
1941-42	**BOS**	**N**	5	0	1	1	0
1942-43			9	1	2	3	10
12 yrs.		**N Totals:**	71	18	12	30	53

Don Jackson

JACKSON, DONALD CLINTON 6'3", 210 lbs.
B. Sept. 2, 1956, Minneapolis, Minn. Defense, Shoots L

YEAR	TEAM	LEAGUE	GP	G	A	PTS	PIM
1977-78	**MINN**	**N**	2	0	0	0	2
1978-79			5	0	0	0	2
1979-80			10	0	4	4	12
1980-81			10	0	3	3	19
1981-82	**EDM**	**N**	8	0	0	0	18
1982-83			71	2	8	10	136
6 yrs.		**N Totals:**	106	2	15	17	189

PLAYOFFS

YEAR	TEAM	LEAGUE	GP	G	A	PTS	PIM
1979-80	**MINN**	**N**	1	0	0	0	0
1982-83			16	3	3	6	30
2 yrs.		**N Totals:**	1	0	0	0	0
		W Totals:	16	3	3	6	30

Hal Jackson

JACKSON, HAROLD RUSSELL 5'11", 175 lbs.
B. Aug. 1, 1917, Cedar Springs, Ont. Defense, Shoots R

YEAR	TEAM	LEAGUE	GP	G	A	PTS	PIM
1936-37	**CHI**	**N**	40	1	3	4	6
1937-38			4	0	0	0	0
1940-41	**DET**	**N**	1	0	0	0	0
1942-43			4	0	4	4	6
1943-44			50	7	12	19	76
1944-45			50	5	6	11	45
1945-46			36	3	4	7	36
1946-47			37	1	5	6	39
8 yrs.		**N Totals:**	222	17	34	51	208

PLAYOFFS

YEAR	TEAM	LEAGUE	GP	G	A	PTS	PIM
1937-38*	**CHI**	**N**	1	0	0	0	2
1942-43*	**DET**	**N**	6	0	1	1	4
1943-44			5	0	0	0	11
1944-45			14	1	1	2	10
1945-46			5	0	0	0	6
5 yrs.		**N Totals:**	31	1	2	3	33

Jim Jackson

JACKSON, JIM 5'10", 190 lbs.
B. Feb. 1, 1960, Oshana, Ont. Forward, Shoots L

YEAR	TEAM	LEAGUE	GP	G	A	PTS	PIM
1982-83	**CALG**	**N**	48	8	12	20	7

PLAYOFFS

YEAR	TEAM	LEAGUE	GP	G	A	PTS	PIM
1982-83	**CALG**	**N**	8	2	1	3	2

John Jackson

JACKSON, JOHN ALEXANDER 5'10", 185 lbs.
B. May 3, 1925, Windsor, Ont. Defense, Shoots R

YEAR	TEAM	LEAGUE	GP	G	A	PTS	PIM
1946-47	**CHI**	**N**	48	2	5	7	38

Lloyd Jackson

JACKSON, LLOYD EDGAR 5'9", 150 lbs.
B. Jan. 7, 1912, Ottawa, Ont. Center, Shoots L

YEAR	TEAM & LEAGUE		GP	G	A	PTS	PIM
1936-37	NYA	N	14	1	1	2	0

Stan Jackson

JACKSON, STANTON
B. Unknown Left Wing

YEAR	TEAM & LEAGUE		GP	G	A	PTS	PIM
1921-22	TOR	N	1	0	0	0	0
1923-24			21	1	1	2	6
1924-25			4	0	0	0	0
	BOS	N	24	5	0	5	36
	2 team total		28	5	0	5	36
1925-26			28	3	3	6	30
1926-27	OTTA	N	8	0	0	0	2
5 yrs.		N Totals:	86	9	4	13	74

Walt Jackson

JACKSON, WALTER (Red) 160 lbs.
B. June 3, 1908, Instock, England Forward, Shoots L

YEAR	TEAM & LEAGUE		GP	G	A	PTS	PIM
1932-33	NYA	N	35	10	2	12	6
1933-34			46	6	9	15	12
1934-35			1	0	0	0	0
3 yrs.		N Totals:	82	16	11	27	18

Gary Jackwith

JACKWITH, GARY 6', 200 lbs.
B. May 30, 1948, Lynn, Mass. Defense, Shoots L

YEAR	TEAM & LEAGUE		GP	G	A	PTS	PIM
1975-76	SD	W	2	0	0	0	0

Paul Jacobs

JACOBS, PAUL
B. Unknown Forward

YEAR	TEAM & LEAGUE		GP	G	A	PTS	PIM
1918-19	TOR	N	1	0	0	0	0

Tim Jacobs

JACOBS, TIMOTHY JAMES 5'10", 180 lbs.
B. Mar. 28, 1952, Espanola, Ont. Defense, Shoots L

YEAR	TEAM & LEAGUE		GP	G	A	PTS	PIM
1975-76	CALIF	N	46	0	10	10	35

Jeff Jacques

JACQUES, JEFF 5'11", 180 lbs.
B. Apr. 4, 1953, Preston, Ont. Center, Shoots R

YEAR	TEAM & LEAGUE		GP	G	A	PTS	PIM
1974-75	TOR	W	39	12	8	20	26
1975-76			81	17	33	50	113
1976-77	BIRM	W	79	21	27	48	92
3 yrs.		W Totals:	199	50	68	118	231
PLAYOFFS							
1974-75	TOR	W	6	0	4	4	2

Mike Jakubo

JAKUBO, MICHAEL PAUL 6', 190 lbs.
B. July 7, 1947, Sudbury, Ont. Center, Shoots L

YEAR	TEAM & LEAGUE		GP	G	A	PTS	PIM
1972-73	LA	W	7	0	0	0	0

Kari Jalonen

JALONEN, KARI 6'3", 190 lbs.
B. Jan. 6, 1960, Oulu, Finland Center, Shoots R

YEAR	TEAM & LEAGUE		GP	G	A	PTS	PIM
1982-83	CALG	N	25	9	3	12	4
PLAYOFFS							
1982-83	CALG	N	5	1	0	1	0

Gerry James

JAMES, GERALD EDWIN 5'11", 191 lbs.
B. Oct. 22, 1934, Regina, Sask. Right Wing, Shoots R

YEAR	TEAM & LEAGUE		GP	G	A	PTS	PIM
1954-55	TOR	N	1	0	0	0	0
1955-56			46	3	3	6	50
1956-57			53	4	12	16	90

Gerry James continued

YEAR	TEAM & LEAGUE		GP	G	A	PTS	PIM
1957-58			15	3	2	5	61
1959-60			34	4	9	13	56
5 yrs.		N Totals:	149	14	26	40	257
PLAYOFFS							
1955-56	TOR	N	5	1	0	1	8
1959-60			10	0	0	0	0
2 yrs.		N Totals:	15	1	0	1	8

Val James

JAMES, VALMORE 6'2", 205 lbs.
B. Feb. 14, 1957, Ocala, Fla. Left Wing, Shoots L

YEAR	TEAM & LEAGUE		GP	G	A	PTS	PIM
1981-82	BUF	N	7	0	0	0	16
PLAYOFFS							
1981-82	BUF	N	3	0	0	0	0

Jim Jamieson

JAMIESON, JAMES 5'8", 170 lbs.
B. Mar. 21, 1922, Brantford, Ont. Defense, Shoots L

YEAR	TEAM & LEAGUE		GP	G	A	PTS	PIM
1943-44	NYR	N	1	0	1	1	0

Lou Jankowski

JANKOWSKI, LOUIS CASIMER 6', 184 lbs.
B. June 27, 1931, Regina, Sask. Left Wing, Shoots R

YEAR	TEAM & LEAGUE		GP	G	A	PTS	PIM
1950-51	DET	N	1	0	1	1	0
1952-53			22	1	2	3	0
1953-54	CHI	N	68	15	13	28	7
1954-55			36	3	2	5	8
4 yrs.		N Totals:	127	19	18	37	15
PLAYOFFS							
1952-53	DET	N	1	0	0	0	0

Purchased by **Chicago** from Detroit with Larry Zeidel and Larry Wilson, Aug. 12, 1953.

Doug Jarrett

JARRETT, DOUGLAS WILLIAM 6'1", 205 lbs.
B. Apr. 22, 1944, London, Ont. Defense, Shoots L

YEAR	TEAM & LEAGUE		GP	G	A	PTS	PIM
1964-65	CHI	N	46	2	15	17	34
1965-66			66	4	12	16	71
1966-67			70	5	21	26	76
1967-68			74	4	19	23	48
1968-69			69	0	13	13	58
1969-70			72	4	20	24	78
1970-71			51	1	12	13	46
1971-72			78	6	23	29	68
1972-73			49	2	11	13	18
1973-74			67	5	11	16	45
1974-75			79	5	21	26	66
1975-76	NYR	N	45	0	4	4	19
1976-77			9	0	0	0	4
13 yrs.		N Totals:	775	38	182	220	631
PLAYOFFS							
1964-65	CHI	N	11	1	0	1	10
1965-66			5	0	1	1	9
1966-67			6	0	3	3	8
1967-68			11	4	0	4	9
1969-70			8	1	0	1	4
1970-71			18	1	6	7	14
1971-72			8	0	2	2	16
1972-73			15	0	3	3	2
1973-74			10	0	1	1	6
1974-75			7	0	0	0	4
10 yrs.		N Totals:	99	7	16	23	82

Traded to **N.Y. Rangers** by Chicago for Gilles Villemure, Oct. 28, 1975.

Gary Jarrett

JARRETT, GARY WALTER 5'8", 170 lbs.
B. Sept. 3, 1942, Toronto, Ont. Left Wing, Shoots L

YEAR	TEAM & LEAGUE		GP	G	A	PTS	PIM
1960-61	TOR	N	1	0	0	0	0
1966-67	DET	N	4	0	0	0	0

Gary Jarrett continued

YEAR	TEAM & LEAGUE		GP	G	A	PTS	PIM
1967-68			68	18	21	39	20
1968-69	**CALIF**	**N**	63	22	23	45	22
1969-70	**OAK**	**N**	75	12	19	31	31
1970-71	**CALIF**	**N**	74	15	19	34	40
1971-72			55	5	10	15	18
1972-73	**CLEVE**	**W**	77	40	39	79	79
1973-74			75	31	39	70	68
1974-75			77	17	24	41	70
1975-76			69	16	17	33	22
11 yrs.		**N Totals:**	340	72	92	164	131
		W Totals:	298	104	119	223	239
PLAYOFFS							
1968-69	**CALIF**	**N**	7	2	1	3	4
1969-70	**OAK**	**N**	4	1	0	1	5
1972-73	**CLEVE**	**W**	9	8	3	11	19
1973-74			5	1	1	2	13
1974-75			5	0	1	1	0
1975-76			3	0	3	3	2
6 yrs.		**N Totals:**	11	3	1	4	9
		W Totals:	22	9	8	17	34

Traded to **Detroit** by Toronto with Billy Harris and Andy Bathgate for Lowell Macdonald, Marcel Pronovost, Ed Joyal, Larry Jeffrey and Aut Erickson, May 20, 1965. Traded to **Oakland** by Detroit with Doug Roberts, Howie Young and Chris Worthy, for Bob Baun and Ron Harris, May 27, 1968.

Pierre Jarry

JARRY, PIERRE JOSEPH REYNALD 5'11", 182 lbs.
B. Mar. 30, 1949, Montreal, Que. Left Wing, Shoots L

YEAR	TEAM & LEAGUE		GP	G	A	PTS	PIM
1971-72	**NYR**	**N**	34	3	3	6	20
	TOR	**N**	17	3	4	7	13
	2 team total		51	6	7	13	33
1972-73			74	19	18	37	42
1973-74			12	2	8	10	10
	DET	**N**	52	15	23	38	17
	2 team total		64	17	31	48	27
1974-75			39	8	13	21	4
1975-76	**MINN**	**N**	59	21	18	39	32
1976-77			21	8	13	21	2
1977-78			35	9	17	26	2
	EDM	**W**	18	4	10	14	4
	2 team total		53	13	27	40	6
7 yrs.		**N Totals:**	343	88	117	205	142
		W Totals:	18	4	10	14	4
PLAYOFFS							
1971-72	**TOR**	**N**	5	0	1	1	0
1977-78	**EDM**	**W**	5	1	0	1	4
2 yrs.		**N Totals:**	5	0	1	1	0
		W Totals:	5	1	0	1	4

Traded to **Toronto** by N.Y. Rangers for Jim Dorey, Feb. 20, 1972. Traded to **Detroit** by Toronto for Tim Ecclestone, Nov. 29, 1973. Traded to **Minnesota** by Detroit for Don Martineau, Nov. 25, 1975.

Doug Jarvis

JARVIS, DOUGLAS 5'9", 165 lbs.
B. Mar. 24, 1955, Peterborough, Ont. Center, Shoots L

YEAR	TEAM & LEAGUE		GP	G	A	PTS	PIM
1975-76	**MONT**	**N**	80	5	30	35	16
1976-77			80	16	22	38	14
1977-78			80	11	28	39	23
1978-79			80	10	13	23	16
1979-80			80	13	11	24	28
1980-81			80	16	22	38	34
1981-82			80	20	28	48	20
1982-83	**WASH**	**N**	80	8	22	30	10
8 yrs.		**N Totals:**	640	99	176	275	161
PLAYOFFS							
1975-76*	**MONT**	**N**	13	2	1	3	2
1976-77*			14	0	7	7	2
1977-78*			15	3	5	8	12
1978-79*			12	1	3	4	4
1979-80			10	4	4	8	2
1980-81			3	0	0	0	0
1981-82			5	1	0	1	4
1982-83	**WASH**	**N**	4	0	1	1	0
8 yrs.		**N Totals:**	76	11	21	32	26

Traded to **Montreal** by Toronto for Greg Hubick, June 26, 1975. Traded by Montreal with Rod Langway, Craig Laughlin, and Brian Engblom to **Washington** for Ryan Walter and Rick Green, Sept. 9, 1982.

Jim Jarvis

JARVIS, JAMES (Bud) 5'6", 165 lbs.
B. Dec. 7, 1907, Fort William, Ont. Left Wing, Shoots L

YEAR	TEAM & LEAGUE		GP	G	A	PTS	PIM
1929-30	**PITT**	**N**	41	11	8	19	32
1930-31	**PHI**	**N**	43	5	7	12	30
1936-37	**TOR**	**N**	24	1	0	1	0
3 yrs.		**N Totals:**	108	17	15	32	62

Wes Jarvis

JARVIS, WESLEY 5'11", 185 lbs.
B. May 30, 1958, Toronto, Ont. Center, Shoots L

YEAR	TEAM & LEAGUE		GP	G	A	PTS	PIM
1979-80	**WASH**	**N**	63	11	15	26	8
1980-81			55	9	14	23	30
1981-82			26	1	12	13	18
1982-83	**MINN**	**N**	3	0	0	0	2
4 yrs.		**N Totals:**	147	21	41	62	58

Traded to **Minnesota** with Rollie Boutin by Washington for Robbie Moore, Aug. 5, 1982.

Larry Jeffrey

JEFFREY, LAWRENCE JOSEPH 5'11", 189 lbs.
B. Oct. 12, 1940, Zurich, Ont. Left Wing, Shoots L

YEAR	TEAM & LEAGUE		GP	G	A	PTS	PIM
1961-62	**DET**	**N**	18	5	3	8	20
1962-63			53	5	11	16	62
1963-64			58	10	18	28	87
1964-65			41	4	2	6	48
1965-66	**TOR**	**N**	20	1	1	2	22
1966-67			56	11	17	28	27
1967-68	**NYR**	**N**	47	2	4	6	15
1968-69			75	1	6	7	12
8 yrs.		**N Totals:**	368	39	62	101	293
PLAYOFFS							
1962-63	**DET**	**N**	9	3	3	6	8
1963-64			14	1	6	7	28
1964-65			2	0	0	0	0
1966-67*	**TOR**	**N**	6	0	1	1	4
1967-68	**NYR**	**N**	3	0	0	0	0
1968-69			4	0	0	0	2
6 yrs.		**N Totals:**	38	4	10	14	42

Traded by Detroit with Marcel Pronovost, Ed Joyal, Autry Erickson, and Lowell MacDonald to **Toronto** for Andy Bathgate, Billy Harris, and Gary Jarrett, May 20, 1965. Drafted by **Pittsburgh** from Toronto in Expansion Draft, June 6, 1967. Traded to **N.Y. Rangers** by Pittsburgh for George Konik, Paul Andrea, Duncan McCallum, and Frank Francis, June 6, 1967. Traded to **Detroit** by N.Y. Rangers for Sandy Snow and Terry Sawchuk, June 17, 1969.

Roger Jenkins

JENKINS, JOSEPH ROGER 5'11", 173 lbs.
B. Nov. 18, 1911, Appleton, Wisc. Defense, Shoots R

YEAR	TEAM & LEAGUE		GP	G	A	PTS	PIM
1930-31	**TOR**	**N**	21	0	0	0	12
	CHI	**N**	10	0	1	1	2
	2 team total		31	0	1	1	14
1932-33			45	3	10	13	42
1933-34			48	2	2	4	63
1934-35	**MONT**	**N**	45	4	6	10	63
1935-36	**BOS**	**N**	42	2	6	8	51
1936-37	**MONT**	**N**	10	0	0	0	8
	MON(M)	**N**	1	0	0	0	0
	NYA	**N**	26	1	4	5	6
	3 team total		37	1	4	5	14
1937-38	**CHI**	**N**	39	1	8	9	26
1938-39			14	1	1	2	2
	NYA	**N**	27	1	1	2	4
	2 team total		41	2	2	4	6
8 yrs.		**N Totals:**	328	15	39	54	279
PLAYOFFS							
1930-31	**CHI**	**N**	3	0	0	0	0
1933-34*			8	0	0	0	0
1934-35	**MONT**	**N**	2	1	0	1	2
1935-36	**BOS**	**N**	2	0	1	1	2
1937-38*	**CHI**	**N**	10	0	6	6	8

Roger Jenkins continued

YEAR	TEAM	LEAGUE	GP	G	A	PTS	PIM
5 yrs.		N Totals:	25	1	7	8	12

Bill Jennings

JENNINGS, JOSEPH WILLIAM 5'9½", 165 lbs.
B. June 28, 1917, Toronto, Ont. Right Wing, Shoots R

YEAR	TEAM	LEAGUE	GP	G	A	PTS	PIM
1940-41	DET	N	12	1	5	6	2
1941-42			16	2	1	3	6
1942-43			8	3	3	6	2
1943-44			33	6	11	17	10
1944-45	BOS	N	39	20	13	33	25
5 yrs.		N Totals:	108	32	33	65	45
PLAYOFFS							
1940-41	DET	N	9	2	2	4	0
1943-44			4	0	0	0	0
1944-45	BOS	N	7	2	2	4	6
3 yrs.		N Totals:	20	4	4	8	6

Steve Jensen

JENSEN, STEVEN ALLAN 6'2", 190 lbs.
B. Apr. 14, 1955, Minneapolis, Minn. Left Wing, Shoots L

YEAR	TEAM	LEAGUE	GP	G	A	PTS	PIM
1975-76	MINN	N	19	7	6	13	6
1976-77			78	22	23	45	62
1977-78			74	13	17	30	73
1978-79	LA	N	72	23	8	31	57
1979-80			76	21	15	36	13
1980-81			74	19	19	38	88
1981-82			45	8	19	27	19
7 yrs.		N Totals:	438	113	107	220	318
PLAYOFFS							
1976-77	MINN	N	2	0	1	1	0
1978-79	LA	N	2	0	0	0	0
1979-80			4	0	0	0	2
1980-81			4	0	2	2	7
4 yrs.		N Totals:	12	0	3	3	9

Ed Jeremiah

JEREMIAH, EDWARD
B. Worcester, Mass. Defense

YEAR	TEAM	LEAGUE	GP	G	A	PTS	PIM
1931-32	NYA	N	9	0	1	1	0
	BOS	N	6	0	0	0	0
	2 team total		15	0	1	1	0

Frank Jerwa

JERWA, FRANK 6'1", 179 lbs.
B. Feb. 28, 1910, Bankhead, Alta. Left Wing, Shoots L

YEAR	TEAM	LEAGUE	GP	G	A	PTS	PIM
1931-32	BOS	N	29	4	5	9	14
1932-33			34	3	4	7	23
1933-34			7	0	0	0	2
1934-35			5	0	0	0	0
	STL	N	16	4	7	11	14
	2 team total		21	4	7	11	14
4 yrs.		N Totals:	91	11	16	27	53

Joe Jerwa

JERWA, JOSEPH 5'2", 185 lbs.
B. Jan. 22, 1909, Bankhead, Alta. Defense, Shoots L

YEAR	TEAM	LEAGUE	GP	G	A	PTS	PIM
1930-31	NYR	N	33	4	7	11	72
1931-32	BOS	N	6	0	0	0	8
1933-34			3	0	0	0	8
1935-36	NYA	N	48	9	12	21	65
1936-37	BOS	N	26	3	5	8	30
	NYA	N	22	6	8	14	27
	2 team total		48	9	13	22	57
1937-38			47	3	14	17	53
1938-39			48	4	12	16	52
7 yrs.		N Totals:	233	29	58	87	315
PLAYOFFS							
1930-31	NYR	N	4	0	0	0	8
1935-36	NYA	N	5	2	3	5	2
1937-38			6	0	0	0	8

Joe Jerwa continued

YEAR	TEAM	LEAGUE	GP	G	A	PTS	PIM
1938-39			2	0	0	0	2
4 yrs.		N Totals:	17	2	3	5	20

Jaroslav Jirik

JIRIK, JAROSLAV 5'11", 170 lbs.
B. Dec. 10, 1939, Vojnuv Mestac, Czech.
Right Wing, Shoots R

YEAR	TEAM	LEAGUE	GP	G	A	PTS	PIM
1969-70	STL	N	3	0	0	0	0

Rosario Joanette

JOANETTE, ROSARIO (Ticroute) 5'11", 168 lbs.
B. July 27, 1919, Valleyfield, Que. Center, Shoots R

YEAR	TEAM	LEAGUE	GP	G	A	PTS	PIM
1944-45	MONT	N	2	0	1	1	4

Rick Jodzio

JODZIO, RICHARD JOSEPH 6'1", 190 lbs.
B. June 3, 1954, Edmonton, Alta. Left Wing, Shoots L

YEAR	TEAM	LEAGUE	GP	G	A	PTS	PIM
1974-75	VAN	W	44	1	3	4	159
1975-76	CALG	W	47	10	7	17	137
1976-77			46	4	6	10	61
1977-78	COLO	N	32	0	5	5	28
	CLEVE	N	38	2	3	5	43
	2 team total		70	2	8	10	71
4 yrs.		N Totals:	70	2	8	10	71
		W Totals:	137	15	16	31	357
PLAYOFFS							
1975-76	CALG	W	2	0	0	0	14

Trevor Johansen

JOHANSEN, TREVOR DANIEL 5'9", 200 lbs.
B. Mar. 30, 1957, Thunder Bay, Ont. Defense, Shoots R

YEAR	TEAM	LEAGUE	GP	G	A	PTS	PIM
1977-78	TOR	N	79	2	14	16	82
1978-79			40	1	4	5	48
	COLO	N	11	1	3	4	16
	2 team total		51	2	7	9	64
1979-80			62	3	8	11	45
1980-81			35	0	7	7	18
1981-82	LA	N	46	3	7	10	69
	TOR	N	13	1	3	4	4
	2 team total		59	4	10	14	73
5 yrs.		N Totals:	286	11	46	57	282
PLAYOFFS							
1977-78	TOR	N	13	0	3	3	21

Traded to **Colorado** by Toronto with Don Ashby for Paul Gardner, Mar. 13, 1979. Claimed on waivers by **Toronto** from Los Angeles, Feb. 19, 1982.

Bjorn Johansson

JOHANSSON, BJORN 6', 195 lbs.
B. Jan. 15, 1956, Orebro, Sweden Defense, Shoots L

YEAR	TEAM	LEAGUE	GP	G	A	PTS	PIM
1976-77	CLEVE	N	10	1	1	2	4
1977-78			5	0	0	0	6
2 yrs.		N Totals:	15	1	1	2	10

Don Johns

JOHNS, DONALD ERNEST 5'11", 190 lbs.
B. Dec. 13, 1937, Brantford, Ont. Defense, Shoots R

YEAR	TEAM	LEAGUE	GP	G	A	PTS	PIM
1960-61	NYR	N	63	1	7	8	34
1962-63			6	0	4	4	6
1963-64			57	1	9	10	26
1964-65			22	0	1	1	4
1965-66	MONT	N	1	0	0	0	0
1967-68	MINN	N	4	0	0	0	6
6 yrs.		N Totals:	153	2	21	23	76

Traded to **Chicago** by N.Y. Rangers with Camille Henry, Billy Taylor, and Wally Chevrier for Doug Robinson, Wayne Hillman, and John Brenneman, Feb. 4, 1965. Sold to **Minnesota** by Montreal, Oct. 5, 1967.

Al Johnson

JOHNSON, ALLAN EDMUND 5'11", 185 lbs.
B. Mar. 30, 1935, Winnipeg, Man. Right Wing, Shoots R

YEAR	TEAM	LEAGUE	GP	G	A	PTS	PIM
1956-57	MONT	N	2	0	1	1	2
1960-61	DET	N	70	16	21	37	14
1961-62			31	5	6	11	14
1962-63			2	0	0	0	0
4 yrs.		N Totals:	105	21	28	49	30
PLAYOFFS							
1960-61	DET	N	11	2	2	4	6

Ching Johnson

JOHNSON, IVAN WILFRED (Ching-A-Ling Chinaman) 5'11", 210 lbs.
B. Dec. 7, 1898, Winnipeg, Man. Defense, Shoots L
Hall of Fame, 1958

YEAR	TEAM	LEAGUE	GP	G	A	PTS	PIM
1926-27	NYR	N	27	3	2	5	66
1927-28			43	10	6	16	146
1928-29			9	0	0	0	14
1929-30			30	3	3	6	82
1930-31			44	2	6	8	77
1931-32			47	3	10	13	106
1932-33			48	8	9	17	127
1933-34			48	2	6	8	86
1934-35			26	2	3	5	34
1935-36			47	5	3	8	58
1936-37			34	0	0	0	2
1937-38	NYA	N	32	0	0	0	10
12 yrs.		N Totals:	435	38	48	86	808
PLAYOFFS							
1926-27	NYR	N	2	0	0	0	8
1927-28*			9	1	1	2	46
1928-29			6	0	0	0	26
1929-30			4	0	0	0	14
1930-31			4	1	0	1	17
1931-32			7	2	0	2	24
1932-33*			8	1	0	1	14
1933-34			2	0	0	0	4
1934-35			3	0	0	0	2
1936-37			9	0	1	1	4
1937-38	NYA	N	6	0	0	0	2
11 yrs.		N Totals:	60	5	2	7	161

Danny Johnson

JOHNSON, DANIEL DOUGLAS 5'11", 170 lbs.
B. Oct. 1, 1944, Winnipegosis, Man. Center, Shoots L

YEAR	TEAM	LEAGUE	GP	G	A	PTS	PIM
1969-70	TOR	N	1	0	0	0	0
1970-71	VAN	N	66	15	11	26	16
1971-72			11	1	3	4	0
	DET	N	43	2	5	7	8
	2 team total		54	3	8	11	8
1972-73	WINN	W	76	19	23	42	17
1973-74			78	16	21	37	20
1974-75			78	18	14	32	25
6 yrs.		N Totals:	121	18	19	37	24
		W Totals:	232	53	58	111	62
PLAYOFFS							
1972-73	WINN	W	14	4	1	5	0
1973-74			4	1	0	1	5
2 yrs.		W Totals:	18	5	1	6	5

Drafted by **Vancouver** from Toronto in Expansion Draft June 10, 1970. Claimed on waivers by **Detroit** from Vancouver, Nov. 22, 1971.

Earl Johnson

JOHNSON, EARL O. 6', 185 lbs.
B. June 28, 1931, Fort Frances, Ont. Center, Shoots L

YEAR	TEAM	LEAGUE	GP	G	A	PTS	PIM
1953-54	DET	N	1	0	0	0	0

Jim Johnson

JOHNSON, NORMAN JAMES (J.J.) 5'9", 190 lbs.
B. Nov. 7, 1942, Winnipeg, Man. Center, Shoots L

YEAR	TEAM	LEAGUE	GP	G	A	PTS	PIM
1964-65	NYR	N	1	0	0	0	0
1965-66			5	1	0	1	0
1966-67			2	0	0	0	0
1967-68	PHI	N	13	2	1	3	2
1968-69			69	17	27	44	20
1969-70			72	18	30	48	17
1970-71			66	16	29	45	16
1971-72			46	13	15	28	12
	LA	N	28	8	9	17	6
	2 team total		74	21	24	45	18
1972-73	MINN	W	33	9	14	23	12
1973-74			71	15	39	54	30
1974-75			11	1	3	15	0
	IND	W	42	7	15	22	12
	2 team total		53	8	18	37	12
11 yrs.		N Totals:	302	75	111	186	73
		W Totals:	157	32	71	114	54
PLAYOFFS							
1968-69	PHI	N	3	0	0	0	2
1970-71			4	0	2	2	0
1972-73	MINN	W	5	2	1	3	2
1973-74			11	1	4	5	4
4 yrs.		N Totals:	7	0	2	2	2
		W Totals:	16	3	5	8	6

Mark Johnson

JOHNSON, MARK 5'9", 160 lbs.
B. Sept. 22, 1957, Madison, Wisc. Left Wing, Shoots L

YEAR	TEAM	LEAGUE	GP	G	A	PTS	PIM
1979-80	PITT	N	17	3	5	8	4
1980-81			73	10	23	33	50
1981-82			46	10	11	21	30
	MINN	N	10	2	2	4	10
	2 team total		56	12	13	25	40
1982-83	HART	N	73	31	38	69	28
4 yrs.		N Totals:	219	56	79	135	122
PLAYOFFS							
1979-80	PITT	N	5	2	2	4	0
1980-81			5	2	1	3	6
1981-82	MINN	N	4	2	0	2	0
3 yrs.		N Totals:	14	6	3	9	6

Traded to **Minnesota** by Pittsburgh for Minnesota's second round choice (Tim Hrynewich) in 1982 Entry Draft, Mar. 2, 1982. Traded by Minnesota with Kent-Erik Andersson to **Hartford** for Jordy Douglas and Hartford's fifth round choice in the 1984 Amateur Draft, Oct. 1, 1982.

Norm Johnson

JOHNSON, NORMAN B.
B. Nov. 27, 1932, Moose Jaw, Sask. Forward, Shoots L

YEAR	TEAM	LEAGUE	GP	G	A	PTS	PIM
1957-58	BOS	N	15	2	3	5	8
1958-59	CHI	N	7	1	0	1	8
2 yrs.		N Totals:	22	3	3	6	16
PLAYOFFS							
1957-58	BOS	N	12	4	0	4	6
1959-60	CHI	N	2	0	0	0	0
2 yrs.		N Totals:	14	4	0	4	6

Claimed on waivers by **Chicago** from Boston, Jan., 1959. Drafted by **Philadelphia** from N.Y. Rangers in Expansion Draft, June 6, 1967. Traded to **Los Angeles** by Philadelphia with Bill Lesuk and Serge Bernier for Bill Flett, Ed Joyal, Jean Potvin, and Ross Lonsberry, Jan. 28, 1972.

Odd Johnson

JOHNSON, WILLIAM ODD (JOHANSEN) 6', 163 lbs.
B. July 27, 1928, Port Arthur, Ont. Center, Shoots R

YEAR	TEAM	LEAGUE	GP	G	A	PTS	PIM
1949-50	TOR	N	1	0	0	0	0

Terry Johnson

JOHNSON, TERRANCE 6'3", 210 lbs.
B. Nov. 28, 1958, Calgary, Alta. Defense, Shoots L

YEAR	TEAM & LEAGUE		GP	G	A	PTS	PIM
1979-80	**QUE**	**N**	3	0	0	0	2
1980-81			13	0	1	1	46
1981-82			6	0	1	1	5
1982-83			3	0	0	0	2
4 yrs.		**N Totals:**	25	0	2	2	55
PLAYOFFS							
1980-81	**QUE**	**N**	2	0	0	0	0

Tom Johnson

JOHNSON, THOMAS CHRISTIAN 6', 180 lbs.
B. Feb. 18, 1928, Baldur, Man. Defense, Shoots L
Won Norris Trophy, 1958-59
Hall of Fame, 1970

YEAR	TEAM & LEAGUE		GP	G	A	PTS	PIM
1947-48	**MONT**	**N**	1	0	0	0	0
1950-51			70	2	8	10	128
1951-52			67	0	7	7	76
1952-53			70	3	8	11	63
1953-54			70	7	11	18	85
1954-55			70	6	19	25	74
1955-56			64	3	10	13	75
1956-57			70	4	11	15	59
1957-58			66	3	18	21	75
1958-59			70	10	29	39	76
1959-60			64	4	25	29	59
1960-61			70	1	15	16	54
1961-62			62	1	17	18	45
1962-63			43	3	5	8	28
1963-64	**BOS**	**N**	70	4	21	25	33
1964-65			51	0	9	9	30
16 yrs.		**N Totals:**	978	51	213	264	960
PLAYOFFS							
1949-50	**MONT**	**N**	1	0	0	0	0
1950-51			11	0	0	0	6
1951-52			11	1	0	1	2
1952-53*			12	2	3	5	8
1953-54			11	1	2	3	30
1954-55			12	2	0	2	22
1955-56*			10	0	2	2	8
1956-57*			10	0	2	2	13
1957-58*			2	0	0	0	0
1958-59*			11	2	3	5	8
1959-60*			8	0	1	1	4
1960-61			6	0	1	1	8
1961-62			6	0	1	1	0
13 yrs.		**N Totals:**	111	8	15	23	109

Claimed on waivers by **Boston** from Mont. Canadiens, June 4, 1963.

Virg Johnson

JOHNSON, VIRGIL 5'8½", 165 lbs.
B. Mar. 4, 1912, Minneapolis, Minn. Defense, Shoots L

YEAR	TEAM & LEAGUE		GP	G	A	PTS	PIM
1937-38	**CHI**	**N**	25	1	0	1	2
1943-44			48	1	8	9	23
1944-45			2	0	1	1	2
3 yrs.		**N Totals:**	75	2	9	11	27
PLAYOFFS							
1937-38*	**CHI**	**N**	10	0	0	0	0
1943-44			9	0	3	3	4
2 yrs.		**N Totals:**	19	0	3	3	4

Bernie Johnston

JOHNSTON, BERNARD 5'11", 185 lbs.
B. Sept. 15, 1956, Toronto, Ont. Center, Shoots R

YEAR	TEAM & LEAGUE		GP	G	A	PTS	PIM
1979-80	**HART**	**N**	32	8	13	21	8
1980-81			25	4	11	15	8
2 yrs.		**N Totals:**	57	12	24	36	16
PLAYOFFS							
1979-80	**HART**	**N**	3	0	1	1	0

Signed as free agent by **Philadelphia** Sept. 28, 1977. Claimed by **Hartford** from Philadelphia in Expansion Draft, June 13, 1979.

George Johnston

JOHNSTON, GEORGE JOSEPH (Wingy) 5'8", 160 lbs.
B. July 30, 1920, St. Charles, Man. Right Wing, Shoots R

YEAR	TEAM & LEAGUE		GP	G	A	PTS	PIM
1941-42	**CHI**	**N**	2	2	0	2	0
1942-43			30	10	7	17	0
1945-46			16	5	4	9	2
1946-47			10	3	1	4	0
4 yrs.		**N Totals:**	58	20	12	32	2

Jay Johnston

JOHNSTON, JOHN 5'11", 180 lbs.
B. Feb. 28, 1958, Hamilton, Ont. Defense, Shoots L

YEAR	TEAM & LEAGUE		GP	G	A	PTS	PIM
1980-81	**WASH**	**N**	2	0	0	0	9
1981-82			6	0	0	0	0
2 yrs.		**N Totals:**	8	0	0	0	9

Joey Johnston

JOHNSTON, JOSEPH JOHN 5'10", 180 lbs.
B. Mar. 3, 1949, Peterborough, Ont. Left Wing, Shoots L

YEAR	TEAM & LEAGUE		GP	G	A	PTS	PIM
1968-69	**MINN**	**N**	12	1	0	1	6
1971-72	**CALIF**	**N**	77	15	18	33	107
1972-73			71	28	21	49	62
1973-74			78	27	40	67	67
1974-75			62	14	23	37	72
1975-76	**CHI**	**N**	32	0	5	5	6
6 yrs.		**N Totals:**	332	85	107	192	320

Traded to **Minnesota** by N.Y. Rangers with Wayne Hillman and Dan Seguin for Dave Balon, June 12, 1968. Traded to **California** by Minnesota with Walt McKechnie for Dennis Hextall, May 20, 1971. Traded to **Chicago** by California for Jim Pappin and Chicago's third choice in 1977 Amateur Draft (Randy Ireland), June 1, 1975.

Larry Johnston

JOHNSTON, LAWRENCE ROY 5'11", 195 lbs.
B. July 20, 1943, Kitchener, Ont. Defense, Shoots R

YEAR	TEAM & LEAGUE		GP	G	A	PTS	PIM
1967-68	**LA**	**N**	4	0	0	0	4
1971-72	**DET**	**N**	65	4	20	24	111
1972-73			73	1	12	13	169
1973-74			65	2	12	14	139
1974-75	**M-B**	**W**	49	0	9	9	93
	KC	**N**	16	0	7	7	10
	2 team total		65	0	16	16	103
1975-76			72	2	10	12	112
1976-77	**COLO**	**N**	25	0	3	3	35
7 yrs.		**N Totals:**	320	9	64	73	580
		W Totals:	49	0	9	9	93
PLAYOFFS							
1969-70	**MINN**	**N**	6	0	0	0	2

Traded to **Detroit** by Los Angeles with Dale Rolfe and Gary Croteau for Garry Monahan and Brian Gibbons, Feb. 20, 1970. Removed outright from Detroit reserve list, Sept. 3, 1974. Signed as a free agent by **Kansas City** from Baltimore (W), March 1, 1975.

Marsh Johnston

JOHNSTON, LAWRENCE MARSHALL 5'11", 175 lbs.
B. June 6, 1941, Birch Hills, Sask. Defense, Shoots R

YEAR	TEAM & LEAGUE		GP	G	A	PTS	PIM
1967-68	**MINN**	**N**	6	0	0	0	6
1968-69			13	0	0	0	2
1969-70			28	0	5	5	14
1970-71			1	0	0	0	0
1971-72	**CALIF**	**N**	74	2	10	12	4
1972-73			78	10	20	30	14
1973-74			50	2	16	18	24
7 yrs.		**N Totals:**	250	14	51	65	64

Randy Johnston

JOHNSTON, RANDY JOHN 6', 190 lbs.
B. June 2, 1958, Brampton, Ont. Defense, Shoots L

YEAR	TEAM & LEAGUE		GP	G	A	PTS	PIM
1979-80	**NYI**	**N**	4	0	0	0	4

Eddie Johnstone

JOHNSTONE, EDWARD LAVERN — 5'9", 175 lbs.
B. Mar. 2, 1954, Brandon, Man. — Right Wing, Shoots R

YEAR	TEAM & LEAGUE		GP	G	A	PTS	PIM
1974-75	**M-B**	**W**	23	4	4	8	43
1975-76	**NYR**	**N**	10	2	1	3	4
1977-78			53	13	13	26	44
1978-79			30	5	3	8	27
1979-80			78	14	21	35	60
1980-81			80	30	38	68	100
1981-82			68	30	28	58	57
1982-83			52	15	21	36	27
8 yrs.		**N Totals:**	371	109	125	234	319
		W Totals:	23	4	4	8	43
PLAYOFFS							
1978-79	**NYR**	**N**	17	5	0	5	10
1979-80			9	0	1	1	25
1980-81			8	2	2	4	4
1981-82			10	2	6	8	25
1982-83			9	4	1	5	19
5 yrs.		**N Totals:**	53	13	10	23	83

Claimed by **N.Y. Rangers** as fill in Expansion Draft, June 13, 1979. Traded to **Detroit** with Ed Mio and Ron Duguay by N.Y. Rangers for Mike Blaisdell, Mark Osborne, and Willie Huber, June 13, 1983.

Ross Johnstone

JOHNSTONE, ROBERT ROSS — 6', 185 lbs.
B. Apr. 7, 1926, Montreal, Que. — Defense, Shoots L

YEAR	TEAM & LEAGUE		GP	G	A	PTS	PIM
1943-44	**TOR**	**N**	18	2	0	2	6
1944-45			24	3	4	7	8
2 yrs.		**N Totals:**	42	5	4	9	14
PLAYOFFS							
1943-44	**TOR**	**N**	3	0	0	0	0

Aurel Joliat

JOLIAT, AUREL — 5'6", 136 lbs.
B. Aug. 29, 1901, Ottawa, Ont. — Left Wing, Shoots L
Won Hart Trophy, 1933-34
Hall of Fame, 1945

YEAR	TEAM & LEAGUE		GP	G	A	PTS	PIM
1922-23	**MONT**	**N**	24	13	9	22	31
1923-24			24	15	5	20	19
1924-25			24	**29**	11	40	85
1925-26			35	17	9	26	52
1926-27			43	14	4	18	79
1927-28			44	28	11	39	105
1928-29			44	12	5	17	59
1929-30			42	19	12	31	40
1930-31			43	13	22	35	73
1931-32			48	15	24	39	46
1932-33			48	18	21	39	53
1933-34			48	22	15	37	27
1934-35			48	17	12	29	18
1935-36			48	15	8	23	16
1936-37			47	17	15	32	30
1937-38			44	6	7	13	24
16 yrs.		**N Totals:**	654	270	190	460	757
PLAYOFFS							
1922-23	**MONT**	**N**	2	1	1	2	8
1923-24*			6	4	4	8	10
1924-25			5	2	2	4	21
1926-27			4	1	0	1	10
1927-28			2	0	0	0	4
1928-29			3	1	1	2	10
1929-30*			6	0	2	2	6
1930-31*			10	0	4	4	12
1931-32			4	2	0	2	4
1932-33			2	2	1	3	2
1933-34			3	0	1	1	0
1934-35			2	1	0	1	0
1936-37			5	0	3	3	2
13 yrs.		**N Totals:**	54	14	19	33	89

Bobby Joliat

JOLIAT, RENE
B. Unknown — Forward

YEAR	TEAM & LEAGUE		GP	G	A	PTS	PIM
1924-25	**MONT**	**N**	1	0	0	0	0

Greg Joly

JOLY, GREGORY JAMES — 6'1", 185 lbs.
B. May 30, 1954, Calgary, Alta. — Defense, Shoots L

YEAR	TEAM & LEAGUE		GP	G	A	PTS	PIM
1974-75	**WASH**	**N**	44	1	7	8	44
1975-76			54	8	17	25	28
1976-77	**DET**	**N**	53	1	11	12	14
1977-78			79	7	20	27	73
1978-79			20	0	4	4	6
1979-80			59	3	10	13	45
1980-81			17	0	2	2	10
1981-82			37	1	5	6	0
1982-83			2	0	0	0	0
9 yrs.		**N Totals:**	365	21	76	97	220
PLAYOFFS							
1977-78	**DET**	**N**	5	0	0	0	8

Traded to **Detroit** by Washington for Bryan Watson, Nov. 30, 1976.

Yvan Joly

JOLY, YVAN RENE — 5'8", 170 lbs.
B. Feb. 6, 1960, Hawkesbury, Ont. — Right Wing, Shoots R

YEAR	TEAM & LEAGUE		GP	G	A	PTS	PIM
1980-81	**MONT**	**N**	1	0	0	0	0
1982-83			1	0	0	0	0
2 yrs.		**N Totals:**	2	0	0	0	0
PLAYOFFS							
1979-80	**MONT**	**N**	10	0	0	0	0

Stan Jonathan

JONATHAN, STANLEY CARL — 5'8", 175 lbs.
B. Sept. 5, 1955, Oshweken, Ont. — Left Wing, Shoots L

YEAR	TEAM & LEAGUE		GP	G	A	PTS	PIM
1975-76	**BOS**	**N**	1	0	0	0	0
1976-77			69	17	13	30	69
1977-78			68	27	25	52	116
1978-79			33	6	9	15	96
1979-80			79	21	19	40	208
1980-81			74	14	24	38	192
1981-82			67	6	17	23	57
1982-83			1	0	0	0	0
	PITT	**N**	19	0	3	3	13
	2 team total		20	0	3	3	13
8 yrs.		**N Totals:**	411	91	110	201	751
PLAYOFFS							
1976-77	**BOS**	**N**	14	4	2	6	24
1977-78			15	0	1	1	36
1978-79			11	4	1	5	12
1979-80			9	0	0	0	29
1980-81			3	0	0	0	30
1981-82			11	0	0	0	6
6 yrs.		**N Totals:**	63	8	4	12	137

Traded by Boston to **Pittsburgh** for future considerations, Nov. 8, 1982.

Bob Jones

JONES, ROBERT CHARLES — 6'1", 192 lbs.
B. Nov. 27, 1945, Espanola, Ont. — Left Wing, Shoots L

YEAR	TEAM & LEAGUE		GP	G	A	PTS	PIM
1968-69	**NYR**	**N**	2	0	0	0	0
1972-73	**LA**	**W**	20	2	7	9	8
	NY	**W**	56	11	12	23	24
	2 team total		76	13	19	32	32
1973-74	**NY-NJ**	**W**	78	17	28	45	20
1974-75	**M-B**	**W**	5	0	1	1	8
1975-76	**IND**	**W**	2	0	0	0	0
5 yrs.		**N Totals:**	2	0	0	0	0
		W Totals:	161	30	48	78	60

Buck Jones

JONES, ALVIN BERNARD 6', 180 lbs.
B. Aug. 17, 1918, Owen Sound, Ont. Defense, Shoots R

YEAR	TEAM & LEAGUE		GP	G	A	PTS	PIM
1938-39	DET	N	11	0	1	1	6
1939-40			2	0	0	0	0
1941-42			21	2	1	3	8
1942-43	TOR	N	16	0	0	0	22
4 yrs.		N Totals:	50	2	2	4	36
PLAYOFFS							
1938-39	DET	N	6	0	1	1	10
1942-43*			6	0	0	0	8
2 yrs.		N Totals:	12	0	1	1	18

Jim Jones

JONES, JAMES WILLIAM 5'10", 185 lbs.
B. July 27, 1949, Espanola, Ont. Defense, Shoots L

YEAR	TEAM & LEAGUE		GP	G	A	PTS	PIM
1971-72	CALIF	N	2	0	0	0	0
1973-74	CHI	W	1	0	0	0	0
2 yrs.		N Totals:	2	0	0	0	0
		W Totals:	1	0	0	0	0

Jimmy Jones

JONES, JAMES HARRISON 5'9", 177 lbs.
B. Jan. 2, 1953, Woodbridge, Ont. Center, Shoots R

YEAR	TEAM & LEAGUE		GP	G	A	PTS	PIM
1973-74	VAN	W	18	3	2	5	23
1974-75			63	11	7	18	39
1977-78	TOR	N	78	4	9	13	23
1978-79			69	9	9	18	45
1979-80			1	0	0	0	0
5 yrs.		N Totals:	148	13	18	31	68
		W Totals:	81	14	9	23	62
PLAYOFFS							
1977-78	TOR	N	13	1	5	6	7
1978-79			6	0	0	0	4
2 yrs.		N Totals:	19	1	5	6	11

Signed as free agent by **Toronto** Oct. 25, 1977. Claimed by **Toronto** as fill in Expansion Draft, June 13, 1979.

Ron Jones

JONES, RONALD PERRY 6'1", 190 lbs.
B. Apr. 11, 1951, Vermillion, Alta. Defense, Shoots L

YEAR	TEAM & LEAGUE		GP	G	A	PTS	PIM
1971-72	BOS	N	1	0	0	0	0
1972-73			7	0	0	0	2
1973-74	PITT	N	25	0	3	3	15
1974-75	WASH	N	19	1	1	2	16
1975-76			2	0	0	0	0
5 yrs.		N Totals:	54	1	4	5	33

Drafted by **Pittsburgh** from Boston in Intra-League Draft, June 12, 1973. Traded to **Washington** by Pittsburgh for Pete Laframboise, Jan. 21, 1975.

Tomas Jonsson

JONSSON, TOMAS 5'10", 176 lbs.
B. Apr. 12, 1960, Falun, Sweden Defense, Shoots L

YEAR	TEAM & LEAGUE		GP	G	A	PTS	PIM
1981-82	NYI	N	70	9	25	34	51
1982-83			72	13	35	48	50
2 yrs.		N Totals:	142	22	60	82	101
PLAYOFFS							
1981-82*	NYI	N	10	0	2	2	21
1982-83*			20	2	10	12	18
2 yrs.		N Totals:	30	2	12	14	39

Ric Jordan

JORDAN, RICHARD 6'3", 200 lbs.
B. Mar. 31, 1950, Toronto, Ont. Defense, Shoots L

YEAR	TEAM & LEAGUE		GP	G	A	PTS	PIM
1972-73	NE	W	34	1	5	6	12
1973-74			34	0	3	3	14
1974-75	QUE	W	56	6	8	14	75
1975-76			54	4	7	11	75
1976-77	CALG	W	5	0	0	0	4

Ric Jordan continued

YEAR	TEAM & LEAGUE		GP	G	A	PTS	PIM
5 yrs.		W Totals:	183	11	23	34	180
PLAYOFFS							
1973-74	NE	W	7	0	0	0	6

Eddie Joyal

JOYAL, EDWARD ABEL 6', 180 lbs.
B. May 8, 1940, Edmonton, Alta. Center, Shoots L

YEAR	TEAM & LEAGUE		GP	G	A	PTS	PIM
1962-63	DET	N	14	2	8	10	0
1963-64			47	10	7	17	17
1964-65			46	8	14	22	4
1965-66	TOR	N	14	0	2	2	2
1967-68	LA	N	74	23	34	57	20
1968-69			73	33	19	52	24
1969-70			59	18	22	40	8
1970-71			68	20	21	41	14
1971-72			44	11	3	14	27
	PHI	N	26	3	4	7	8
	2 team total		70	14	7	21	35
1972-73	ALTA	W	71	22	16	38	16
1973-74	EDM	W	45	8	10	18	2
1974-75			78	22	25	47	2
1975-76			45	5	4	9	6
13 yrs.		N Totals:	465	128	134	262	124
		W Totals:	239	57	55	112	26
PLAYOFFS							
1962-63	DET	N	11	1	0	1	2
1963-64			14	2	3	5	10
1964-65			7	1	1	2	4
1967-68	LA	N	7	4	1	5	2
1968-69			11	3	3	6	0
1973-74	EDM	W	5	2	0	2	4
6 yrs.		N Totals:	50	11	8	19	18
		W Totals:	5	2	0	2	4

Traded by Detroit with Marcel Pronovost, Lowell MacDonald, Larry Jeffrey and Aut Erickson to **Toronto** for Andy Bathgate, Billy Harris and Gary Jarrett, May 20, 1965. Drafted by **Los Angeles** from Toronto in Expansion Draft, June 6, 1967. Traded to **Philadelphia** by Los Angeles with Bill Flett, Jean Potvin and Ross Lonsberry for Bill Lesuk, Jim Johnson and Serge Bernier, Jan. 28, 1972.

Bing Juckes

JUCKES, WINSTON BRYAN 5'10", 165 lbs.
B. June 14, 1926, Hamiota, Man. Left Wing, Shoots L

YEAR	TEAM & LEAGUE		GP	G	A	PTS	PIM
1947-48	NYR	N	2	0	0	0	0
1949-50			14	2	1	3	6
2 yrs.		N Totals:	16	2	1	3	6

Dan Justin

JUSTIN, DANIEL SY (Justy) 6'1", 201 lbs.
B. Jan. 12, 1955, Palo Alto, Calif. Defense, Shoots L

YEAR	TEAM & LEAGUE		GP	G	A	PTS	PIM
1975-76	CIN	W	17	0	0	0	2
1976-77			6	0	2	2	4
2 yrs.		W Totals:	23	0	2	2	6

Bill Juzda

JUZDA, WILLIAM (The Fireman, The Beast) 5'8", 203 lbs.
B. Oct. 29, 1920, Winnipeg, Man. Defense, Shoots R

YEAR	TEAM & LEAGUE		GP	G	A	PTS	PIM
1940-41	NYR	N	5	0	0	0	2
1941-42			45	4	8	12	29
1945-46			32	1	3	4	17
1946-47			45	3	5	8	60
1947-48			60	3	9	12	70
1948-49	TOR	N	38	1	2	3	23
1949-50			62	1	14	15	23
1950-51			65	0	9	9	64
1951-52			46	1	4	5	65
9 yrs.		N Totals:	398	14	54	68	353
PLAYOFFS							
1941-42	NYR	N	6	0	1	1	4
1947-48			6	0	0	0	9

YEAR	TEAM & LEAGUE		GP	G	A	PTS	PIM

Bill Juzda continued

YEAR	TEAM & LEAGUE		GP	G	A	PTS	PIM
1948-49*	TOR	N	9	0	2	2	8
1949-50			7	0	0	0	16
1950-51*			11	0	0	0	7
1951-52			3	0	0	0	2
6 yrs.		N Totals:	42	0	3	3	46

Bob Kabel

KABEL, ROBERT GERALD 6', 183 lbs.
B. Dec. 11, 1934, Dauphin, Mn. Center, Shoots L

YEAR	TEAM & LEAGUE		GP	G	A	PTS	PIM
1959-60	NYR	N	44	5	11	16	32
1960-61			4	0	2	2	2
2 yrs.		N Totals:	48	5	13	18	34

Ed Kachur

KACHUR, EDWARD CHARLES 5'8", 170 lbs.
B. Apr. 22, 1934, Fort William, Ont. Right Wing, Shoots R

YEAR	TEAM & LEAGUE		GP	G	A	PTS	PIM
1956-57	CHI	N	34	5	7	12	21
1957-58			62	5	7	12	14
2 yrs.		N Totals:	96	10	14	24	35

Vern Kaiser

KAISER, VERNON CHARLES 6', 180 lbs.
B. Sept. 28, 1925, Preston, Ont. Left Wing, Shoots L

YEAR	TEAM & LEAGUE		GP	G	A	PTS	PIM
1950-51	MONT	N	50	7	5	12	33
PLAYOFFS							
1950-51	MONT	N	2	0	0	0	0

Jeff Kalbfleish

KALBFLEISH, WALTER MORRIS 5'10", 175 lbs.
B. Dec. 18, 1911, New Hamburg, Ont. Defense, Shoots R

YEAR	TEAM & LEAGUE		GP	G	A	PTS	PIM
1933-34	OTTA	N	22	0	4	4	20
1934-35	STL	N	3	0	0	0	6
1935-36	NYA	N	4	0	0	0	2
1936-37			6	0	0	0	4
	BOS	N	1	0	0	0	0
	2 team total		7	0	0	0	4
4 yrs.		N Totals:	36	0	4	4	32
PLAYOFFS							
1935-36	NYA	N	5	0	0	0	2

Alex Kaleta

KALETA, ALEXANDER (Killer) 5'11", 175 lbs.
B. Nov. 29, 1919, Canmore, Alta. Left Wing, Shoots L

YEAR	TEAM & LEAGUE		GP	G	A	PTS	PIM
1941-42	CHI	N	48	7	21	28	24
1945-46			49	19	27	46	17
1946-47			57	24	20	44	37
1947-48			52	10	16	26	40
1948-49	NYR	N	56	12	19	31	18
1949-50			67	17	14	31	40
1950-51			58	3	4	7	26
7 yrs.		N Totals:	387	92	121	213	202
PLAYOFFS							
1941-42	CHI	N	3	1	2	3	0
1945-46			4	0	1	1	2
1949-50	NYR	N	10	0	3	3	0
3 yrs.		N Totals:	17	1	6	7	2

Anders Kallur

KALLUR, ANDERS (Andy) 5'11", 183 lbs.
B. July 6, 1952, Ludvika, Sweden Right Wing, Shoots L

YEAR	TEAM & LEAGUE		GP	G	A	PTS	PIM
1979-80	NYI	N	76	22	30	52	16
1980-81			78	36	28	64	32
1981-82			58	18	22	40	18
1982-83			55	6	8	14	33
4 yrs.		N Totals:	267	82	88	170	99
PLAYOFFS							
1980-81*	NYI	N	12	4	3	7	10

Anders Kallur continued

YEAR	TEAM & LEAGUE		GP	G	A	PTS	PIM
1981-82*			19	1	6	7	8
1982-83*			20	3	12	15	12
3 yrs.		N Totals:	51	8	21	29	30

Signed as free agent by **N.Y. Islanders** Aug. 15, 1979.

Max Kaminsky

KAMINSKY, MAX 5'10½", 160 lbs.
B. Apr. 19, 1913, Niagara Falls, Ont. Center, Shoots L

YEAR	TEAM & LEAGUE		GP	G	A	PTS	PIM
1933-34	OTTA	N	38	9	17	26	14
1934-35	STL	N	11	0	0	0	0
	BOS	N	38	12	15	27	4
	2 team total		49	12	15	27	4
1935-36			37	1	2	3	20
1936-37	MON(M)	N	6	0	0	0	0
4 yrs.		N Totals:	130	22	34	56	38
PLAYOFFS							
1934-35	BOS	N	4	0	0	0	0

Bingo Kampman

KAMPMAN, RUDOLPH 5'9½", 187 lbs.
B. Mar. 12, 1914, Kitchener, Ont. Defense, Shoots R

YEAR	TEAM & LEAGUE		GP	G	A	PTS	PIM
1937-38	TOR	N	32	1	2	3	56
1938-39			41	2	8	10	52
1939-40			39	6	9	15	59
1940-41			39	1	4	5	53
1941-42			38	4	7	11	67
5 yrs.		N Totals:	189	14	30	44	287
PLAYOFFS							
1937-38	TOR	N	7	0	1	1	6
1938-39			10	1	1	2	20
1939-40			10	0	0	0	0
1940-41			7	0	0	0	0
1941-42*			13	0	2	2	12
5 yrs.		N Totals:	47	1	4	5	38

Frank Kane

KANE, FRANCIS JOSEPH (Red) 5'11", 190 lbs.
B. Jan. 19, 1923, Stratford, Ont. Defense, Shoots L

YEAR	TEAM & LEAGUE		GP	G	A	PTS	PIM
1943-44	DET	N	2	0	0	0	0

Gord Kannegiesser

KANNEGIESSER, GORDON CAMERON 6', 190 lbs.
B. Dec. 21, 1945, North Bay, Ont. Defense, Shoots L

YEAR	TEAM & LEAGUE		GP	G	A	PTS	PIM
1967-68	STL	N	19	0	1	1	13
1971-72			4	0	0	0	2
1972-73	HOUS	W	45	0	10	10	32
1973-74			78	0	20	20	26
1974-75	IND	W	4	1	4	5	4
5 yrs.		N Totals:	23	0	1	1	15
		W Totals:	127	1	34	35	62
PLAYOFFS							
1972-73	HOUS	W	9	0	1	1	11
1973-74			3	0	2	2	2
2 yrs.		W Totals:	12	0	3	3	13

Traded to **St. Louis** with Gary Sabourin, Bob Plager and Tim Ecclestone for Rod Seiling, June 6. 1967.

Sheldon Kannegiesser

KANNEGIESSER, SHELDON BRUCE 6', 198 lbs.
B. Aug. 15, 1947, North Bay, Ont. Defense, Shoots L

YEAR	TEAM & LEAGUE		GP	G	A	PTS	PIM
1970-71	PITT	N	18	0	2	2	29
1971-72			54	2	4	6	47
	STL	N	4	0	0	0	2
	2 team total		58	2	4	6	49
1972-73	PITT	N	3	0	0	0	0
1973-74	NYR	N	12	1	3	4	6
	LA	N	51	3	17	20	49
	2 team total		63	4	20	24	55
1974-75			74	2	23	25	57
1975-76			70	4	9	13	36
1976-77			39	1	1	2	28

YEAR	TEAM & LEAGUE		GP	G	A	PTS	PIM

Sheldon Kannegiesser continued

YEAR	TEAM	LEAGUE	GP	G	A	PTS	PIM
1977-78	**VAN**	**N**	42	1	7	8	36
8 yrs.		**N Totals:**	367	14	66	80	290

PLAYOFFS

YEAR	TEAM	LEAGUE	GP	G	A	PTS	PIM
1972-73	**NYR**	**N**	1	0	0	0	2
1973-74	**LA**	**N**	5	0	1	1	0
1974-75			3	0	1	1	4
1975-76			9	0	0	0	4
4 yrs.		**N Totals:**	18	0	2	2	10

Traded to **N.Y. Rangers** by Pittsburgh, March 2, 1973 for a player to be named later (Steve Andrascik, May 16, 1973). Traded to **Los Angeles** by N.Y. Rangers with Mike Murphy and Tom Williams for Gilles Marotte and Real Lemieux, Nov. 30, 1973. Traded to **Vancouver** by Los Angeles for Larry Carriere, Nov. 21, 1977.

Al Karlander

KARLANDER, ALLAN DAVID 5'8", 170 lbs.
B. Nov. 5, 1946, Lac La Hache, B.C. Center, Shoots L

YEAR	TEAM	LEAGUE	GP	G	A	PTS	PIM
1969-70	**DET**	**N**	41	5	10	15	6
1970-71			23	1	4	5	10
1971-72			71	15	20	35	29
1972-73			77	15	22	37	25
1973-74	**NE**	**W**	77	20	41	61	46
1974-75			48	7	14	21	2
1975-76	**IND**	**W**	79	19	26	45	36
1976-77			65	17	28	45	23
8 yrs.		**N Totals:**	212	36	56	92	70
		W Totals:	269	63	109	172	107

PLAYOFFS

YEAR	TEAM	LEAGUE	GP	G	A	PTS	PIM
1969-70	**DET**	**N**	4	0	1	1	0
1973-74	**NE**	**W**	7	1	3	4	2
1974-75			5	0	3	3	0
1975-76	**IND**	**W**	3	0	0	0	4
1976-77			6	2	1	3	0
5 yrs.		**N Totals:**	4	0	1	1	0
		W Totals:	21	3	7	10	6

Steve Kasper

KASPER, STEPHEN NEIL 5'8", 159 lbs.
B. Sept. 28, 1961, Montreal, Que. Center, Shoots L
Won Selke Trophy, 1981-82

YEAR	TEAM	LEAGUE	GP	G	A	PTS	PIM
1980-81	**BOS**	**N**	76	21	35	56	94
1981-82			73	20	31	51	72
1982-83			24	2	6	8	24
3 yrs.		**N Totals:**	173	43	72	115	190

PLAYOFFS

YEAR	TEAM	LEAGUE	GP	G	A	PTS	PIM
1980-81	**BOS**	**N**	3	0	1	1	0
1981-82			11	3	6	9	22
1982-83			12	2	1	3	10
3 yrs.		**N Totals:**	26	5	8	13	32

Dennis Kassian

KASSIAN, DENNIS 5'11", 170 lbs.
B. July 14, 1941, Vegreville, Alta. Left Wing, Shoots L

YEAR	TEAM	LEAGUE	GP	G	A	PTS	PIM
1972-73	**ALTA**	**W**	50	6	7	13	14

Mike Kaszycki

KASZYCKI, MICHAEL 5'9", 190 lbs.
B. Feb. 27, 1956, Milton, Ont. Center, Shoots L

YEAR	TEAM	LEAGUE	GP	G	A	PTS	PIM
1977-78	**NYI**	**N**	58	13	29	42	24
1978-79			71	16	18	34	37
1979-80			16	1	4	5	15
	WASH	**N**	28	7	10	17	10
	TOR	**N**	25	4	4	8	10
	3 team total		69	12	18	30	35
1980-81			6	0	2	2	2
1982-83			22	1	13	14	10
5 yrs.		**N Totals:**	226	42	80	122	108

PLAYOFFS

YEAR	TEAM	LEAGUE	GP	G	A	PTS	PIM
1977-78	**NYI**	**N**	7	1	3	4	4
1979-80	**TOR**	**N**	2	0	0	0	2

Mike Kaszycki continued

YEAR	TEAM	LEAGUE	GP	G	A	PTS	PIM
2 yrs.		**N Totals:**	9	1	3	4	6

Traded to **Washington** by N.Y. Islanders for Gord Lane, Dec. 7, 1979. Traded to **Toronto** by Washington for Pat Ribble, Feb. 16, 1980.

Ed Kea

KEA, ADRIAN JOSEPH 6'3", 199 lbs.
B. Jan. 19, 1948, Weesp, Holland Defense, Shoots L

YEAR	TEAM	LEAGUE	GP	G	A	PTS	PIM
1973-74	**ATL**	**N**	3	0	2	2	0
1974-75			50	1	9	10	39
1975-76			78	8	19	27	101
1976-77			72	4	21	25	63
1977-78			60	3	23	26	40
1978-79			53	6	18	24	40
1979-80	**STL**	**N**	69	3	16	19	79
1980-81			74	3	18	21	60
1981-82			78	2	14	16	62
1982-83			46	0	5	5	24
10 yrs.		**N Totals:**	583	30	145	175	508

PLAYOFFS

YEAR	TEAM	LEAGUE	GP	G	A	PTS	PIM
1975-76	**ATL**	**N**	2	0	0	0	7
1976-77			3	0	1	1	2
1977-78			1	0	0	0	0
1978-79			2	0	0	0	0
1979-80	**STL**	**N**	3	0	0	0	2
1980-81			11	1	2	3	12
1981-82			10	1	1	2	16
7 yrs.		**N Totals:**	32	2	4	6	39

Traded to **St. Louis** by Atlanta with Don Laurence and Atlanta's second round choice (Hakan Nordin) in 1981 Entry Draft for Garry Unger, Oct. 10, 1979.

Doug Keans

KEANS, DOUGLAS FREDERICK 5'7", 174 lbs.
B. Jan. 7, 1958, Pembroke, Ont. Shoots L

PLAYOFFS

YEAR	TEAM	LEAGUE	GP	G	A	PTS	PIM
1979-80	**LA**	**N**	1	0	0	0	0

Dennis Kearns

KEARNS, DENNIS MCALEER 5'9", 185 lbs.
B. Sept. 27, 1945, Kinston, Ont. Defense, Shoots L

YEAR	TEAM	LEAGUE	GP	G	A	PTS	PIM
1971-72	**VAN**	**N**	73	3	26	29	59
1972-73			72	4	33	37	51
1973-74			52	4	13	17	30
1974-75			49	1	11	12	31
1975-76			80	5	46	51	48
1976-77			80	5	55	60	60
1977-78			80	4	43	47	27
1978-79			78	3	31	34	28
1979-80			67	1	18	19	24
1980-81			46	1	14	15	28
10 yrs.		**N Totals:**	677	31	290	321	386

PLAYOFFS

YEAR	TEAM	LEAGUE	GP	G	A	PTS	PIM
1974-75	**VAN**	**N**	4	0	0	0	4
1975-76			2	0	1	1	0
1978-79			3	1	1	2	2
1979-80			2	0	0	0	2
4 yrs.		**N Totals:**	11	1	2	3	8

Drafted by **Vancouver** from Chicago in Intra-league Draft, June 8, 1971.

Jack Keating

KEATING, JOHN R.
B. St. John, N.B. Forward

YEAR	TEAM	LEAGUE	GP	G	A	PTS	PIM
1931-32	**NYA**	**N**	22	5	3	8	6
1932-33			13	0	2	2	11
2 yrs.		**N Totals:**	35	5	5	10	17

John Keating

KEATING, JOHN THOMAS (Red) 6', 180 lbs.
B. Oct. 9, 1916, Kitchener, Ont. Left Wing, Shoots L

YEAR	TEAM & LEAGUE		GP	G	A	PTS	PIM
1938-39	**DET**	**N**	1	0	1	1	2
1939-40			10	2	0	2	2
2 yrs.		**N Totals:**	11	2	1	3	4

Mike Keating

KEATING, MICHAEL JOSEPH 6', 185 lbs.
B. Jan. 21, 1957, Toronto, Ont. Left Wing, Shoots L

YEAR	TEAM & LEAGUE		GP	G	A	PTS	PIM
1977-78	**NYR**	**N**	1	0	0	0	0

Duke Keats

KEATS, GORDON BLANCHARD
B. Mar. 1, 1895, Montreal, Que. Center, Shoots R
Hall of Fame, 1958

YEAR	TEAM & LEAGUE		GP	G	A	PTS	PIM
1926-27	**DET**	**N**	40	16	8	24	52
1927-28			5	0	2	2	6
	CHI	**N**	32	14	8	22	55
	2 team total		37	14	10	24	61
1928-29			3	0	1	1	0
3 yrs.		**N Totals:**	80	30	19	49	113

Mike Keeler

KEELER, MICHAEL JOHN 5'10", 185 lbs.
B. May 21, 1950, Toronto, Ont. Defense, Shoots R

YEAR	TEAM & LEAGUE		GP	G	A	PTS	PIM
1973-74	**NE**	**W**	1	0	0	0	0
PLAYOFFS							
1973-74	**NE**	**W**	1	0	0	0	0

Butch Keeling

KEELING, MELVILLE SIDNEY 6', 180 lbs.
B. Aug. 10, 1905, Owen Sound, Ont. Left Wing, Shoots L

YEAR	TEAM & LEAGUE		GP	G	A	PTS	PIM
1926-27	**TOR**	**N**	30	11	2	13	29
1927-28			43	10	6	16	52
1928-29	**NYR**	**N**	43	6	3	9	35
1929-30			44	19	7	26	34
1930-31			44	13	9	22	35
1931-32			48	17	3	20	38
1932-33			47	8	6	14	22
1933-34			48	15	5	20	20
1934-35			47	15	4	19	14
1935-36			47	13	5	18	22
1936-37			48	22	4	26	18
1937-38			39	8	9	17	12
12 yrs.		**N Totals:**	528	157	63	220	331
PLAYOFFS							
1928-29	**NYR**	**N**	6	3	0	3	2
1929-30			4	0	3	3	8
1930-31			4	1	1	2	0
1931-32			7	2	1	3	12
1932-33*			8	0	2	2	8
1933-34			2	0	0	0	0
1934-35			4	2	1	3	0
1936-37			9	3	2	5	2
1937-38			3	0	1	1	0
9 yrs.		**N Totals:**	47	11	11	22	32

Larry Keenan

KEENAN, LAWRENCE CHRISTOPHER 5'10", 177 lbs.
B. Oct. 1, 1940, North Bay, Ont. Left Wing, Shoots L

YEAR	TEAM & LEAGUE		GP	G	A	PTS	PIM
1961-62	**TOR**	**N**	2	0	0	0	0
1967-68	**STL**	**N**	40	12	8	20	4
1968-69			47	5	9	14	6
1969-70			56	10	23	33	8
1970-71			9	1	3	4	0
	BUF	**N**	51	7	20	27	6
	2 team total		60	8	23	31	6
1971-72			15	2	0	2	2
	PHI	**N**	14	1	1	2	2
	2 team total		29	3	1	4	4
6 yrs.		**N Totals:**	234	38	64	102	28

Larry Keenan continued

YEAR	TEAM & LEAGUE		GP	G	A	PTS	PIM
PLAYOFFS							
1967-68	**STL**	**N**	18	4	5	9	4
1968-69			12	4	5	9	8
1969-70			16	7	6	13	0
3 yrs.		**N Totals:**	46	15	16	31	12

Drafted by **St. Louis** from Toronto in Expansion Draft, June 16, 1967. Traded to **Buffalo** by St. Louis with Jean-Guy Talbot for Bob Baun, Nov. 4, 1970. Traded to **Philadelphia** by Buffalo for Larry Mickey, Nov. 16, 1971.

Rick Kehoe

KEHOE, RICK THOMAS 5'11", 180 lbs.
B. July 15, 1951, Windsor, Ont. Right Wing, Shoots R
Won Lady Byng Trophy, 1980-81

YEAR	TEAM & LEAGUE		GP	G	A	PTS	PIM
1971-72	**TOR**	**N**	38	8	8	16	4
1972-73			77	33	42	75	20
1973-74			69	18	22	40	8
1974-75	**PITT**	**N**	76	32	31	63	22
1975-76			71	29	47	76	6
1976-77			80	30	27	57	10
1977-78			70	29	21	50	10
1978-79			57	27	18	45	2
1979-80			79	30	30	60	4
1980-81			80	55	33	88	6
1981-82			71	33	52	85	8
1982-83			75	29	36	65	12
12 yrs.		**N Totals:**	843	353	367	720	112
PLAYOFFS							
1971-72	**TOR**	**N**	2	0	0	0	2
1974-75	**PITT**	**N**	9	0	2	2	0
1975-76			3	0	0	0	0
1976-77			3	0	2	2	0
1978-79			7	0	2	2	0
1979-80			5	2	5	7	0
1980-81			5	0	3	3	0
1981-82			5	2	3	5	2
8 yrs.		**N Totals:**	39	4	17	21	4

Traded to **Pittsburgh** by Toronto for Blaine Stoughton and future considerations, Sept. 13, 1974.

Ralph Keller

KELLER, RALPH 5'9", 175 lbs.
B. Feb. 6, 1936, Wilkie, Sask. Defense, Shoots L

YEAR	TEAM & LEAGUE		GP	G	A	PTS	PIM
1962-63	**NYR**	**N**	3	1	0	1	6

Christer Kellgren

KELLGREN, CHRISTER 6', 173 lbs.
B. Aug. 15, 1958, Goteborg, Sweden Right Wing, Shoots L

YEAR	TEAM & LEAGUE		GP	G	A	PTS	PIM
1981-82	**COLO**	**N**	5	0	0	0	0

Signed as free agent by **Colorado** May 11, 1981.

Bob Kelly

KELLY, JOHN ROBERT (Battleship) 6'2", 195 lbs.
B. June 6, 1946, Fort William, Ont. Left Wing, Shoots L

YEAR	TEAM & LEAGUE		GP	G	A	PTS	PIM
1973-74	**STL**	**N**	37	9	8	17	45
	PITT	**N**	30	7	10	17	78
	2 team total		67	16	18	34	123
1974-75			69	27	24	51	120
1975-76			77	25	30	55	149
1976-77			74	10	21	31	115
1977-78	**CHI**	**N**	75	7	11	18	20
1978-79			63	2	5	7	85
6 yrs.		**N Totals:**	425	87	109	196	612
PLAYOFFS							
1974-75	**PITT**	**N**	9	5	3	8	17
1975-76			3	0	0	0	2
1976-77			3	1	0	1	4
1977-78	**CHI**	**N**	4	0	0	0	8
1978-79			4	0	0	0	9
5 yrs.		**N Totals:**	23	6	3	9	40

Traded to **St. Louis** by N.Y. Rangers for Norm Dennis and Don Borgeson, Sept. 8, 1973. Traded to **Pittsburgh** by St. Louis with Steve Durbano and Ab DeMarco for Bryan Watson, Greg Polis and Pittsburgh's second choice

(Bob Hess) in 1974 Amateur Draft, Jan. 17, 1974. Signed as free agent by **Chicago** Aug. 17, 1977. Claimed by **Edmonton** from Chicago in Expansion Draft, June 13, 1979.

Bob Kelly

KELLY, ROBERT JAMES (Hound) 5'10", 200 lbs.
B. Nov. 25, 1950, Oakville, Ont. Left Wing, Shoots L

YEAR	TEAM & LEAGUE		GP	G	A	PTS	PIM
1970-71	**PHI**	**N**	76	14	18	32	70
1971-72			78	14	15	29	157
1972-73			77	10	11	21	238
1973-74			65	4	10	14	130
1974-75			67	11	18	29	99
1975-76			79	12	8	20	125
1976-77			73	22	24	46	117
1977-78			74	19	13	32	95
1978-79			71	7	31	38	132
1979-80			75	15	20	35	122
1980-81	**WASH**	**N**	80	26	36	62	157
1981-82			16	0	4	4	12
12 yrs.		**N Totals:**	831	154	208	362	1454

PLAYOFFS

YEAR	TEAM & LEAGUE		GP	G	A	PTS	PIM
1970-71	**PHI**	**N**	4	1	0	1	2
1972-73			11	0	1	1	8
1973-74*			5	0	0	0	0
1974-75*			16	3	3	6	15
1975-76			16	0	2	2	44
1976-77			10	0	1	1	18
1977-78			12	3	5	8	26
1978-79			8	1	1	2	10
1979-80			19	1	1	2	38
9 yrs.		**N Totals:**	101	9	14	23	161

Traded to **Washington** by Philadelphia for Washington's third-round choice (Bill Campbell) in the 1982 Entry Draft, Aug. 21, 1980.

Dave Kelly

KELLY, DAVID LESLIE 6'2", 205 lbs.
B. Sept. 20, 1952, Chatham, Ont. Right Wing, Shoots R

YEAR	TEAM & LEAGUE		GP	G	A	PTS	PIM
1976-77	**DET**	**N**	16	2	0	2	4

Traded to **Detroit** by Philadelphia with Terry Murray, Bob Ritchie and Steve Coates for Rick LaPointe and Mike Korney, Feb. 17, 1977.

John Kelly

KELLY, JOHN PAUL (Jeep) 6', 212 lbs.
B. Nov. 15, 1959, Edmonton, Alta. Left Wing, Shoots L

YEAR	TEAM & LEAGUE		GP	G	A	PTS	PIM
1979-80	**LA**	**N**	40	2	5	7	28
1980-81			19	3	6	9	8
1981-82			70	12	11	23	100
1982-83			65	16	15	31	52
4 yrs.		**N Totals:**	194	33	37	70	188

PLAYOFFS

YEAR	TEAM & LEAGUE		GP	G	A	PTS	PIM
1979-80	**LA**	**N**	3	0	0	0	2
1980-81			4	0	1	1	25
1981-82			10	1	0	1	14
3 yrs.		**N Totals:**	17	1	1	2	41

Pep Kelly

KELLY, REGIS J. 5'6½", 152 lbs.
B. Jan. 9, 1914, North Bay, Ont. Shoots R

YEAR	TEAM & LEAGUE		GP	G	A	PTS	PIM
1934-35	**TOR**	**N**	47	11	8	19	14
1935-36			42	11	8	19	24
1936-37			16	2	0	2	8
	CHI	**N**	29	13	4	17	0
	2 team total		45	15	4	19	8
1937-38	**TOR**	**N**	43	9	10	19	25
1938-39			48	11	11	22	12
1939-40			34	11	9	20	15
1940-41	**CHI**	**N**	22	5	3	8	7
1941-42	**NYA**	**N**	8	1	0	1	0
8 yrs.		**N Totals:**	289	74	53	127	105

PLAYOFFS

YEAR	TEAM & LEAGUE		GP	G	A	PTS	PIM
1934-35	**TOR**	**N**	7	2	0	2	4
1935-36			9	2	3	5	4

Pep Kelly continued

YEAR	TEAM & LEAGUE		GP	G	A	PTS	PIM
1937-38			7	2	2	4	2
1938-39			10	1	0	1	0
1939-40			6	0	1	1	0
5 yrs.		**N Totals:**	39	7	6	13	10

Pete Kelly

KELLY, PETER CAMERON 5'10½", 170 lbs.
B. May 22, 1913, St. Vital, Man. Right Wing, Shoots R

YEAR	TEAM & LEAGUE		GP	G	A	PTS	PIM
1934-35	**STL**	**N**	25	3	10	13	14
1935-36	**DET**	**N**	48	6	8	14	30
1936-37			48	5	4	9	12
1937-38			9	0	1	1	2
1938-39			32	4	9	13	4
1940-41	**NYA**	**N**	10	3	5	8	2
1941-42			8	0	1	1	4
7 yrs.		**N Totals:**	180	21	38	59	68

PLAYOFFS

YEAR	TEAM & LEAGUE		GP	G	A	PTS	PIM
1935-36*	**DET**	**N**	7	1	1	2	2
1936-37*			8	2	0	2	6
1938-39			4	0	0	0	0
3 yrs.		**N Totals:**	19	3	1	4	8

Red Kelly

KELLY, LEONARD PATRICK 6', 195 lbs.
B. July 9, 1927, Simcoe, Ont. Center, Shoots L
Won Lady Byng Trophy, 1950–51, 1952–53, 1953–54 , 1960-61
Won Norris Trophy, 1953-54
Hall of Fame, 1969

YEAR	TEAM & LEAGUE		GP	G	A	PTS	PIM
1947-48	**DET**	**N**	60	6	14	20	13
1948-49			59	5	11	16	10
1949-50			70	15	25	40	9
1950-51			70	17	37	54	24
1951-52			67	16	31	47	16
1952-53			70	19	27	46	8
1953-54			62	16	33	49	18
1954-55			70	15	30	45	28
1955-56			70	16	34	50	39
1956-57			70	10	25	35	18
1957-58			61	13	18	31	26
1958-59			67	8	13	21	34
1959-60			50	6	12	18	10
	TOR	**N**	18	6	5	11	8
	2 team total		68	12	17	29	18
1960-61			64	20	50	70	12
1961-62			58	22	27	49	6
1962-63			66	20	40	60	8
1963-64			70	11	34	45	16
1964-65			70	18	28	46	8
1965-66			63	8	24	32	12
1966-67			61	14	24	38	4
20 yrs.		**N Totals:**	1316	281	542	823	327

PLAYOFFS

YEAR	TEAM & LEAGUE		GP	G	A	PTS	PIM
1947-48	**DET**	**N**	10	3	2	5	2
1948-49			11	1	1	2	6
1949-50*			14	1	3	4	2
1950-51			6	0	1	1	0
1951-52*			5	1	0	1	0
1952-53			6	0	4	4	0
1953-54*			12	5	1	6	4
1954-55*			11	2	4	6	17
1955-56			10	2	4	6	2
1956-57			5	1	0	1	0
1957-58			4	0	1	1	2
1959-60	**TOR**	**N**	10	3	8	11	2
1960-61			2	1	0	1	0
1961-62*			12	4	6	10	0
1962-63*			10	2	6	8	6
1963-64*			14	4	9	13	4
1964-65			6	3	2	5	2
1965-66			4	0	2	2	0
1966-67*			12	0	5	5	2
19 yrs.		**N Totals:**	164	33	59	92	51

Traded to **Toronto** by Detroit in exchange for Marc Reaume, Feb., 1960.

Kevin Kemp

KEMP, KEVIN GLEN 6', 188 lbs.
B. May 3, 1954, Ottawa,Ont. Defense, Shoots L

YEAR	TEAM & LEAGUE		GP	G	A	PTS	PIM
1980-81	**HART**	**N**	3	0	0	0	4

Claimed by **Hartford** from Toronto in Expansion Draft, June 13, 1979.

Stan Kemp

KEMP, STANLEY 5'9", 165 lbs.
B. Mar. 2, 1924, Hamilton, Ont. Defense, Shoots R

YEAR	TEAM & LEAGUE		GP	G	A	PTS	PIM
1948-49	**TOR**	**N**	1	0	0	0	2

William Kendall

KENDALL, WILLIAM 5'8", 168 lbs.
B. Apr. 1, 1901, Winnipeg, Man. Shoots R

YEAR	TEAM & LEAGUE		GP	G	A	PTS	PIM
1933-34	**CHI**	**N**	20	3	0	3	0
1934-35			47	6	4	10	16
1935-36			23	2	1	3	0
1936-37			17	3	0	3	6
	TOR	**N**	15	2	4	6	4
	2 team total		32	5	4	9	10
1937-38	**CHI**	**N**	10	0	1	1	2
5 yrs.		**N Totals:**	132	16	10	26	28

PLAYOFFS

YEAR	TEAM & LEAGUE		GP	G	A	PTS	PIM
1933-34*	**CHI**	**N**	1	0	0	0	0
1934-35			2	0	0	0	0
1935-36			2	0	0	0	0
3 yrs.		**N Totals:**	5	0	0	0	0

Dean Kennedy

KENNEDY, DEAN 6'2", 190 lbs.
B. Jan. 18, 1963, Redver, Sask. Defense, Shoots R

YEAR	TEAM & LEAGUE		GP	G	A	PTS	PIM
1982-83	**LA**	**N**	55	0	12	12	97

Forbes Kennedy

KENNEDY, FORBES TAYLOR 5'8", 185 lbs.
B. Aug. 18, 1935, Dorchester, N.B. Center, Shoots L

YEAR	TEAM & LEAGUE		GP	G	A	PTS	PIM
1956-57	**CHI**	**N**	69	8	13	21	102
1957-58	**DET**	**N**	70	11	16	27	135
1958-59			67	1	4	5	49
1959-60			17	1	2	3	8
1961-62			14	1	0	1	8
1962-63	**BOS**	**N**	49	12	18	30	46
1963-64			70	8	17	25	95
1964-65			52	6	4	10	41
1965-66			50	4	6	10	55
1967-68	**PHI**	**N**	73	10	18	28	130
1968-69			59	8	7	15	195
	TOR	**N**	13	0	3	3	24
	2 team total		72	8	10	18	**219**
11 yrs.		**N Totals:**	603	70	108	178	888

PLAYOFFS

YEAR	TEAM & LEAGUE		GP	G	A	PTS	PIM
1957-58	**DET**	**N**	4	1	0	1	12
1967-68	**PHI**	**N**	7	1	4	5	14
1968-69	**TOR**	**N**	1	0	0	0	38
3 yrs.		**N Totals:**	12	2	4	6	64

Sold to **Chicago** by Mont. Canadiens, May, 1956. Traded to **Detroit** by Chicago with John Wilson, William Preston, and Henry Bassen for Ted Lindsay and Glenn Hall, July, 1957. Traded to **Boston** by Detroit for Andre Pronovost, Dec., 1962. Drafted by **Philadelphia** from Boston in Expansion Draft, June 6, 1967. Traded to **Toronto** by Philadelphia with Brit Selby for Gerry Meehan and Mike Byers, Mar. 2, 1969. Sold to **Pittsburgh** by Toronto, May 30, 1969. Put on **N.Y. Rangers** reserve list from Pittsburgh, June 11, 1969.

Jamie Kennedy

KENNEDY, JAMES ROY 5'8½", 175 lbs.
B. Sept. 7, 1946, Dorchester, N.B. Right Wing, Shoots R

YEAR	TEAM & LEAGUE		GP	G	A	PTS	PIM
1972-73	**NY**	**W**	54	4	6	10	11

Ted Kennedy

KENNEDY, THEODORE (Teeder) 5'11", 180 lbs.
B. Dec. 12, 1925, Humberstone, Ont. Center, Shoots R
Won Hart Trophy, 1954-55
Hall of Fame, 1966

YEAR	TEAM & LEAGUE		GP	G	A	PTS	PIM
1942-43	**TOR**	**N**	2	0	1	1	0
1943-44			49	26	23	49	2
1944-45			49	29	25	54	14
1945-46			21	3	2	5	4
1946-47			60	28	32	60	27
1947-48			60	25	21	46	32
1948-49			59	18	21	39	25
1949-50			53	20	24	44	34
1950-51			63	18	**43**	61	32
1951-52			70	19	33	52	33
1952-53			43	14	23	37	42
1953-54			67	15	23	38	78
1954-55			70	10	42	52	74
1956-57			30	6	16	22	35
14 yrs.		**N Totals:**	696	231	329	560	432

PLAYOFFS

YEAR	TEAM & LEAGUE		GP	G	A	PTS	PIM
1943-44	**TOR**	**N**	5	1	1	2	4
1944-45*			13	7	2	9	12
1946-47*			11	4	5	9	4
1947-48*			9	8	6	14	0
1948-49*			9	2	6	8	2
1949-50			7	1	2	3	8
1950-51*			11	4	5	9	6
1951-52			4	0	0	0	4
1953-54			5	1	1	2	2
1954-55			4	1	3	4	0
10 yrs.		**N Totals:**	78	29	31	60	42

Murray Kennett

KENNETT, MURRAY 5'10", 175 lbs.
B. June 28, 1952, Kamloops, B.C. Defense, Shoots L

YEAR	TEAM & LEAGUE		GP	G	A	PTS	PIM
1974-75	**IND**	**W**	28	1	3	4	8
	EDM	**W**	50	4	14	18	17
	2 team total		78	5	17	22	25
1975-76			28	3	4	7	14
2 yrs.		**W Totals:**	106	8	21	29	39

Eddie Kenny

KENNY, WILLIAM ERNEST 6'2", 195 lbs.
B. Aug. 20, 1907, Vermilion, Alta. Defense, Shoots L

YEAR	TEAM & LEAGUE		GP	G	A	PTS	PIM
1930-31	**NYR**	**N**	6	0	0	0	0
1934-35	**CHI**	**N**	5	0	0	0	18
2 yrs.		**N Totals:**	11	0	0	0	18

Murray Keogan

KEOGAN, MURRAY 5'10", 175 lbs.
B. Jan. 14, 1950, Biggar, Sask. Center, Shoots L

YEAR	TEAM & LEAGUE		GP	G	A	PTS	PIM
1974-75	**PHOE**	**W**	78	35	29	64	68
1975-76			8	0	2	2	4
	CALG	**W**	38	7	11	18	19
	2 team total		46	7	13	20	23
2 yrs.		**W Totals:**	124	42	42	84	91

PLAYOFFS

YEAR	TEAM & LEAGUE		GP	G	A	PTS	PIM
1974-75	**PHOE**	**W**	5	0	1	1	0

Dave Keon

KEON, DAVID MICHAEL 5'9", 167 lbs.
B. Mar. 22, 1940, Noranda, Que. Center, Shoots L
Won Lady Byng Trophy, 1961–62, 1962-63
Won Calder Trophy, 1960-61
Won Conn Smythe Trophy, 1966-67

YEAR	TEAM & LEAGUE		GP	G	A	PTS	PIM
1960-61	**TOR**	**N**	70	20	25	45	6
1961-62			64	26	35	61	2
1962-63			68	28	28	56	2
1963-64			70	23	37	60	6
1964-65			65	21	29	50	10
1965-66			69	24	30	54	4
1966-67			66	19	33	52	2
1967-68			67	11	37	48	4

Dave Keon continued

YEAR	TEAM & LEAGUE		GP	G	A	PTS	PIM
1968-69			75	27	34	61	12
1969-70			72	32	30	62	6
1970-71			76	38	38	76	4
1971-72			72	18	30	48	4
1972-73			76	37	36	73	2
1973-74			74	25	28	53	7
1974-75			78	16	43	59	4
1975-76	**MINN**	**W**	57	26	38	64	4
	IND	**W**	12	3	7	10	2
	2 team total		69	29	45	74	6
1976-77	**MINN**	**W**	42	13	38	51	2
	NE	**W**	34	14	25	39	8
	2 team total		76	27	63	90	10
1977-78			77	24	38	62	2
1978-79			79	22	43	65	2
1979-80	**HART**	**N**	76	10	52	62	10
1980-81			80	13	34	47	26
1981-82			78	8	11	19	6
22 yrs.		**N Totals:**	1296	396	590	986	117
		W Totals:	301	102	189	291	20

PLAYOFFS

YEAR	TEAM & LEAGUE		GP	G	A	PTS	PIM
1960-61	**TOR**	**N**	5	1	1	2	0
1961-62*			12	5	3	8	0
1962-63*			10	7	5	12	0
1963-64*			14	7	2	9	2
1964-65			6	2	2	4	2
1965-66			4	0	2	2	0
1966-67*			12	3	5	8	0
1968-69			4	1	3	4	2
1970-71			6	3	2	5	0
1971-72			5	2	3	5	0
1973-74			4	1	2	3	0
1974-75			7	0	5	5	0
1975-76	**IND**	**W**	7	2	2	4	2
1976-77	**NE**	**W**	5	3	1	4	0
1977-78			14	5	11	16	4
1978-79			10	3	9	12	2
1979-80	**HART**	**N**	3	0	1	1	0
17 yrs.		**N Totals:**	92	32	36	68	6
		W Totals:	36	13	23	36	8

Reg Kerr

KERR, REGINALD JOHN 5'10", 179 lbs.
B. Oct. 16, 1957, Oxbow, Sask. Left Wing, Shoots L

YEAR	TEAM & LEAGUE		GP	G	A	PTS	PIM
1977-78	**CLEVE**	**N**	7	0	2	2	7
	CHI	**N**	2	0	2	2	0
	2 team total		9	0	4	4	7
1978-79			73	16	24	40	50
1979-80			49	9	8	17	17
1980-81			70	30	30	60	56
1981-82			59	11	28	39	39
5 yrs.		**N Totals:**	260	66	94	160	169

PLAYOFFS

YEAR	TEAM & LEAGUE		GP	G	A	PTS	PIM
1978-79	**CHI**	**N**	4	1	0	1	5
1980-81			3	0	0	0	2
2 yrs.		**N Totals:**	7	1	0	1	7

Tim Kerr

KERR, TIMOTHY 6'3", 215 lbs.
B. Jan. 5, 1960, Windsor, Ont. Center, Shoots R

YEAR	TEAM & LEAGUE		GP	G	A	PTS	PIM
1980-81	**PHI**	**N**	68	22	23	45	84
1981-82			61	21	30	51	138
1982-83			24	11	8	19	6
3 yrs.		**N Totals:**	153	54	61	115	228

PLAYOFFS

YEAR	TEAM & LEAGUE		GP	G	A	PTS	PIM
1980-81	**PHI**	**N**	10	1	3	4	2
1981-82			4	0	2	2	2
1982-83			2	2	0	2	0
3 yrs.		**N Totals:**	16	3	5	8	4

Signed as free agent with **Philadelphia** Oct. 25, 1979.

Doug Kerslake

KERSLAKE, DOUGLAS 5'11", 200 lbs.
B. Mar. 23, 1950, Saskatoon, Sask. Right Wing, Shoots R

YEAR	TEAM & LEAGUE		GP	G	A	PTS	PIM
1974-75	**EDM**	**W**	10	4	0	4	10
1975-76			13	1	1	2	4
2 yrs.		**W Totals:**	23	5	1	6	14

Rick Kessell

KESSELL, RICHARD JOHN 5'10", 175 lbs.
B. July 27, 1949, Toronto, Ont. Center, Shoots L

YEAR	TEAM & LEAGUE		GP	G	A	PTS	PIM
1969-70	**PITT**	**N**	8	1	2	3	2
1970-71			6	0	2	2	2
1971-72			3	0	1	1	0
1972-73			67	1	13	14	0
1973-74	**CALIF**	**N**	51	2	6	8	4
5 yrs.		**N Totals:**	135	4	24	28	8

Claimed by Salt Lake (**California** from Pittsburgh in Reverse Draft, June 13, 1973.

Veli-Pekka Ketola

KETOLA, VELI-PEKKA 6'3", 220 lbs.
B. Mar. 28, 1948, Pori, Finland Center, Shoots L

YEAR	TEAM & LEAGUE		GP	G	A	PTS	PIM
1974-75	**WINN**	**W**	74	23	28	51	25
1975-76			80	32	36	68	32
1976-77			64	25	29	54	59
	CALG	**W**	17	4	6	10	2
	2 team total		81	29	35	64	61
1981-82	**COLO**	**N**	44	9	5	14	4
4 yrs.		**N Totals:**	44	9	5	14	4
		W Totals:	235	84	99	183	118

PLAYOFFS

YEAR	TEAM & LEAGUE		GP	G	A	PTS	PIM
1975-76	**WINN**	**W**	13	7	5	12	2

Signed as free agent by **Colorado** July 8, 1981.

Kerry Ketter

KETTER, KERRY KENNETH 6'1", 202 lbs.
B. Sept. 20, 1947, Prince George, B.C. Defense, Shoots L

YEAR	TEAM & LEAGUE		GP	G	A	PTS	PIM
1972-73	**ATL**	**N**	41	0	2	2	58
1975-76	**EDM**	**W**	48	1	9	10	20
2 yrs.		**N Totals:**	41	0	2	2	58
		W Totals:	48	1	9	10	20

Traded to **Montreal** by Detroit with cash for Leon Rochefort, May 25, 1971. Drafted by **Atlanta** from Montreal in Expansion Draft, June 6, 1972. Drafted by **Kansas City** from Atlanta in Expansion Draft, June 12, 1974.

Udo Kiessling

KIESSLING, UDO 5'10", 180 lbs.
B. May 21, 1955, Crimmitschau, Germany
Defense, Shoots L

YEAR	TEAM & LEAGUE		GP	G	A	PTS	PIM
1981-82	**MINN**	**N**	1	0	0	0	2

Signed as free agent by **Minnesota** Mar. 5, 1982.

Brian Kilrea

KILREA, BRIAN BLAIR 5'11", 182 lbs.
B. Oct. 21, 1934, Ottawa, Ont. Center, Shoots R

YEAR	TEAM & LEAGUE		GP	G	A	PTS	PIM
1957-58	**DET**	**N**	1	0	0	0	0
1967-68	**LA**	**N**	25	3	5	8	12
2 yrs.		**N Totals:**	26	3	5	8	12

Hec Kilrea

KILREA, HECTOR J. 5'7½", 175 lbs.
B. June 11, 1907, Blackburn, Ont. Left Wing, Shoots L

YEAR	TEAM & LEAGUE		GP	G	A	PTS	PIM
1925-26	**OTTA**	**N**	35	5	0	5	12
1926-27			42	11	7	18	48
1927-28			42	19	4	23	66
1928-29			38	5	7	12	36
1929-30			44	36	22	58	72
1930-31			44	14	8	22	44
1931-32	**DET**	**N**	47	13	3	16	28
1932-33	**OTTA**	**N**	48	14	8	22	26

Hec Kilrea continued

YEAR	TEAM	LEAGUE	GP	G	A	PTS	PIM
1933-34	TOR	N	43	10	13	23	15
1934-35			46	11	13	24	16
1935-36	DET	N	48	6	17	23	37
1936-37			48	6	9	15	20
1937-38			47	9	9	18	10
1938-39			47	8	9	17	8
1939-40			12	0	0	0	0
15 yrs.		N Totals:	631	167	129	296	438
PLAYOFFS							
1925-26	OTTA	N	2	0	0	0	0
1926-27*			6	1	1	2	4
1927-28			2	1	0	1	0
1929-30			2	0	0	0	4
1931-32	DET	N	2	0	0	0	0
1933-34	TOR	N	5	2	0	2	2
1934-35			6	0	0	0	4
1935-36*	DET	N	7	0	3	3	2
1936-37			10	3	1	4	2
1938-39			6	1	2	3	0
10 yrs.		N Totals:	48	8	7	15	18

Ken Kilrea

KILREA, KENNETH 6', 170 lbs.
B. Jan. 16, 1919, Ottawa, Ont. Left Wing, Shoots L

YEAR	TEAM	LEAGUE	GP	G	A	PTS	PIM
1938-39	DET	N	1	0	0	0	0
1939-40			40	10	8	18	4
1940-41			12	2	0	2	0
1941-42			21	3	12	15	4
1943-44			14	1	3	4	0
5 yrs.		N Totals:	88	16	23	39	8
PLAYOFFS							
1938-39	DET	N	3	1	1	2	4
1939-40			5	1	1	2	0
1943-44			2	0	0	0	0
3 yrs.		N Totals:	10	2	2	4	4

Wally Kilrea

KILREA, WALTER CHARLES 5'7", 150 lbs.
B. Feb. 18, 1909, Ottawa, Ont. Shoots R

YEAR	TEAM	LEAGUE	GP	G	A	PTS	PIM
1929-30	OTTA	N	42	4	2	6	4
1930-31	PHI	N	44	8	12	20	22
1931-32	NYA	N	48	3	8	11	18
1932-33	OTTA	N	32	4	5	9	14
	MON(M)	N	6	1	7	8	2
	2 team total		38	5	12	17	16
1933-34			44	3	1	4	7
1934-35	DET	N	2	0	0	0	0
1935-36			44	4	10	14	10
1936-37			48	8	13	21	6
1937-38			5	0	0	0	4
9 yrs.		N Totals:	315	35	58	93	87
PLAYOFFS							
1929-30	OTTA	N	2	0	0	0	0
1932-33	MON(M)	N	2	0	0	0	0
1933-34			4	0	0	0	0
1935-36*	DET	N	7	2	2	4	2
1936-37*			10	0	2	2	4
5 yrs.		N Totals:	25	2	4	6	6

Orest Kindrachuk

KINDRACHUK, OREST 5'10", 175 lbs.
B. Sept. 14, 1950, Nanton, Alta. Center, Shoots L

YEAR	TEAM	LEAGUE	GP	G	A	PTS	PIM
1972-73	PHI	N	2	0	0	0	0
1973-74			71	11	30	41	85
1974-75			60	10	21	31	72
1975-76			76	26	49	75	101
1976-77			78	15	36	51	79
1977-78			73	17	45	62	128
1978-79	PITT	N	79	18	42	60	84
1979-80			51	17	29	46	63
1980-81			13	3	9	12	34
1981-82	WASH	N	4	1	0	1	2
10 yrs.		N Totals:	507	118	261	379	648

Orest Kindrachuk continued

YEAR	TEAM	LEAGUE	GP	G	A	PTS	PIM
PLAYOFFS							
1973-74*	PHI	N	17	5	4	9	17
1974-75*			14	0	2	2	12
1975-76			16	4	7	11	4
1976-77			10	2	1	3	0
1977-78			12	5	5	10	13
1978-79	PITT	N	7	4	1	5	7
6 yrs.		N Totals:	76	20	20	40	53

Traded to **Pittsburgh** by Philadelphia with Tom Bladon and Ross Lonsberry for Pittsburgh's first choice (Behn Wilson) in the 1978 Amateur Draft and other considerations, June 14, 1978. Signed as free agent by **Washington** Sept. 4, 1981.

Frank King

KING, FRANK EDWARD 5'11", 185 lbs.
B. Mar. 7, 1929, Toronto, Ont. Center, Shoots L

YEAR	TEAM	LEAGUE	GP	G	A	PTS	PIM
1950-51	MONT	N	10	1	0	1	2

Steve King

KING, STEPHEN 5'10", 185 lbs.
B. Sept. 8, 1948, Toronto, Ont. Right Wing, Shoots R

YEAR	TEAM	LEAGUE	GP	G	A	PTS	PIM
1972-73	OTTA	W	69	18	34	52	28
1973-74	TOR	W	67	14	22	36	26
2 yrs.		W Totals:	136	32	56	88	54
PLAYOFFS							
1972-73	OTTA	W	5	0	1	1	7
1973-74	TOR	W	12	0	3	3	11
2 yrs.		W Totals:	17	0	4	4	18

Wayne King

KING, WAYNE GORDON 5'10", 185 lbs.
B. Sept. 4, 1951, Midland, Ont. Center, Shoots R

YEAR	TEAM	LEAGUE	GP	G	A	PTS	PIM
1973-74	CALIF	N	2	0	0	0	0
1974-75			25	4	7	11	8
1975-76			46	1	11	12	26
3 yrs.		N Totals:	73	5	18	23	34

Brian Kinsella

KINSELLA, BRIAN EDWARD 5'11", 180 lbs.
B. Feb. 11, 1954, Barrie, Ont. Center, Shoots R

YEAR	TEAM	LEAGUE	GP	G	A	PTS	PIM
1975-76	WASH	N	4	0	1	1	0
1976-77			6	0	0	0	0
2 yrs.		N Totals:	10	0	1	1	0

Ray Kinsella

KINSELLA, THOMAS RAYMOND
B. Jan. 27, 1911, Ottawa, Ont. Forward

YEAR	TEAM	LEAGUE	GP	G	A	PTS	PIM
1930-31	OTTA	N	14	0	0	0	0

Bobby Kirk

KIRK, ROBERT H. 5'9", 180 lbs.
B. Aug. 8, 1910, Belfast, Ireland Right Wing, Shoots R

YEAR	TEAM	LEAGUE	GP	G	A	PTS	PIM
1937-38	NYR	N	39	4	8	12	14

Gavin Kirk

KIRK, GAVIN 5'10", 165 lbs.
B. Dec. 6, 1951, London, England Center, Shoots L

YEAR	TEAM	LEAGUE	GP	G	A	PTS	PIM
1972-73	OTTA	W	78	28	40	68	54
1973-74	TOR	W	78	20	48	68	44
1974-75			78	15	58	73	69
1975-76			62	29	38	67	32
	CALG	W	15	7	8	15	14
	2 team total		77	36	46	82	46
1976-77	BIRM	W	29	9	18	27	34
	EDM	W	52	8	28	36	16
	2 team total		81	17	46	63	50
1978-79	BIRM	W	30	1	5	6	16
6 yrs.		W Totals:	422	117	243	360	279
PLAYOFFS							
1972-73	OTTA	W	5	2	3	5	12

Gavin Kirk continued

YEAR	TEAM & LEAGUE		GP	G	A	PTS	PIM
1973-74	**TOR**	**W**	12	2	4	6	4
1974-75			6	5	6	11	2
1975-76	**CALG**	**W**	10	4	6	10	19
1976-77	**EDM**	**W**	5	1	0	1	4
5 yrs.		**W Totals:**	38	14	19	33	41

Bob Kirkpatrick

KIRKPATRICK, ROBERT DRYNAN 5'10", 165 lbs.
B. Jan. 20, 1191, Regina, Sask. Center, Shoots L

YEAR	TEAM & LEAGUE		GP	G	A	PTS	PIM
1942-43	**NYR**	**N**	49	12	12	24	6

Mark Kirton

KIRTON, MARK ROBERT (Kirt) 5'10", 170 lbs.
B. Feb. 3, 1958, Regina, Sask. Center, Shoots L

YEAR	TEAM & LEAGUE		GP	G	A	PTS	PIM
1979-80	**TOR**	**N**	2	1	0	1	2
1980-81			11	0	0	0	0
	DET	**N**	50	18	13	31	24
	2 team total		61	18	13	31	24
1981-82			74	14	28	42	62
1982-83			10	1	1	2	6
	VAN	**N**	31	4	6	10	4
	2 team total		41	5	7	12	10
4 yrs.		**N Totals:**	178	38	48	86	98
PLAYOFFS							
1982-83	**VAN**	**N**	4	1	2	3	7

Traded to **Detroit** by Toronto for Jim Rutherford, Dec. 4, 1980. Traded by Detroit to **Vancouver** for Ivan Boldirev, Jan. 17, 1983.

Kelly Kisio

KISIO, KELLY W. 5'9", 170 lbs.
B. Sept. 18, 1959, Peace River, Sask. Right Wing, Shoots L

YEAR	TEAM & LEAGUE		GP	G	A	PTS	PIM
1982-83	**DET**	**N**	15	4	3	7	0

Bill Kitchen

KITCHEN, WILLIAM 6'1", 195 lbs.
B. Oct. 2, 1960, Schomberg, Ont. Defense, Shoots L

YEAR	TEAM & LEAGUE		GP	G	A	PTS	PIM
1981-82	**MONT**	**N**	1	0	0	0	7
1982-83			8	0	0	0	4
2 yrs.		**N Totals:**	9	0	0	0	11
PLAYOFFS							
1981-82	**MONT**	**N**	3	0	1	1	0

Hobie Kitchen

KITCHEN, CHAPMAN H.
B. Toronto, Ont. Defense

YEAR	TEAM & LEAGUE		GP	G	A	PTS	PIM
1925-26	**MON(M)**	**N**	30	5	2	7	16
1926-27	**DET**	**N**	18	0	2	2	42
2 yrs.		**N Totals:**	48	5	4	9	58

Mike Kitchen

KITCHEN, MICHAEL ELWIN 5'10", 175 lbs.
B. Feb. 1, 1956, Newmarket, Ont. Defense, Shoots L

YEAR	TEAM & LEAGUE		GP	G	A	PTS	PIM
1976-77	**COLO**	**N**	60	1	8	9	36
1977-78			61	2	17	19	45
1978-79			53	1	4	5	28
1979-80			42	1	6	7	25
1980-81			75	1	7	8	100
1981-82			63	1	8	9	60
1982-83	**NJ**	**N**	77	4	8	12	52
7 yrs.		**N Totals:**	431	11	58	69	346
PLAYOFFS							
1977-78	**COLO**	**N**	2	0	0	0	2

Ralph Klassen

KLASSEN, RALPH L 5'11", 175 lbs.
B. Sept. 15, 1955, Humboldt, Sask. Center, Shoots L

YEAR	TEAM & LEAGUE		GP	G	A	PTS	PIM
1975-76	**CALIF**	**N**	71	6	15	21	26
1976-77	**CLEVE**	**N**	80	14	18	32	23
1977-78			13	2	1	3	6
	COLO	**N**	44	6	9	15	8
	2 team total		57	8	10	18	14
1978-79			64	6	13	19	12
1979-80	**STL**	**N**	80	9	16	25	10
1980-81			66	6	12	18	23
1981-82			45	3	7	10	6
1982-83			29	0	2	2	6
8 yrs.		**N Totals:**	492	52	93	145	120
PLAYOFFS							
1977-78	**COLO**	**N**	2	0	0	0	0
1979-80	**STL**	**N**	3	0	0	0	0
1980-81			11	2	0	2	2
1981-82			10	2	2	4	10
4 yrs.		**N Totals:**	26	4	2	6	12

Traded to **Colorado** by Cleveland with Fred Ahern for Rick Jodzio and Chuck Arnason, Jan. 9 1978. Claimed from **Colorado** by Hartford in 1979 Expansion Draft, June 13, 1979. Traded to **N.Y. Islanders** by Hartford for Terry Richardson, June, 14, 1979. Sent to **St. Louis** by N.Y. Islanders, June 14, 1979, as part of trade in which N.Y. Islanders received Barry Gibbs and Terry Richardson from St. Louis, June 9, 1979.

Bill Klatt

KLATT, WILLIAM GERALD 5'11", 185 lbs.
B. Oct. 16, 1947, St. Paul, Mn. Right Wing, Shoots R

YEAR	TEAM & LEAGUE		GP	G	A	PTS	PIM
1972-73	**MINN**	**W**	78	36	22	58	22
1973-74			65	14	6	20	12
2 yrs.		**W Totals:**	143	50	28	78	34
PLAYOFFS							
1972-73	**MINN**	**W**	5	1	3	4	5
1973-74			11	3	2	5	18
2 yrs.		**W Totals:**	16	4	5	9	23

Jim Klein

KLEIN, JAMES LLOYD (Dede) 6', 185 lbs.
B. Jan. 13, 1910, Saskatoon, Alta. Left Wing, Shoots L

YEAR	TEAM & LEAGUE		GP	G	A	PTS	PIM
1928-29	**BOS**	**N**	14	1	0	1	5
1931-32			6	1	0	1	0
1932-33	**NYA**	**N**	15	2	2	4	4
1933-34			48	13	9	22	34
1934-35			30	7	3	10	9
1935-36			42	4	8	12	14
1936-37			11	2	1	3	2
1937-38			3	0	1	1	0
8 yrs.		**N Totals:**	169	30	24	54	68
PLAYOFFS							
1935-36	**NYA**	**N**	5	0	0	0	2

Scot Kleinendorst

KLEINENDORST, SCOT 6'3", 205 lbs.
B. Jan. 16, 1960, Grand Rapids, Mich. Defense, Shoots L

YEAR	TEAM & LEAGUE		GP	G	A	PTS	PIM
1982-83	**NYR**	**N**	30	2	9	11	8
PLAYOFFS							
1982-83	**NYR**	**N**	6	0	2	2	2

Ike Klingbeil

KLINGBEIL, ERNEST
B. U.S.A. Forward

YEAR	TEAM & LEAGUE		GP	G	A	PTS	PIM
1936-37	**CHI**	**N**	5	1	2	3	2

Joe Klukay

KLUKAY, JOSEPH FRANCIS (Duke of Paducah)

6', 175 lbs.

B. Nov. 6, 1922, Sault Ste. Marie, Ont. Left Wing, Shoots L

YEAR	TEAM & LEAGUE		GP	G	A	PTS	PIM
1946-47	TOR	N	55	9	20	29	12
1947-48			59	15	15	30	28
1948-49			45	11	10	21	11
1949-50			70	15	16	31	11
1950-51			70	14	16	30	16
1951-52			43	4	8	12	6
1952-53	BOS	N	70	13	16	29	20
1953-54			70	20	17	37	27
1954-55			10	0	0	0	4
	TOR	N	56	8	8	16	44
	2 team total		66	8	8	16	48
1955-56			18	0	1	1	2
10 yrs.		N Totals:	566	109	127	236	181

PLAYOFFS

YEAR	TEAM & LEAGUE		GP	G	A	PTS	PIM
1942-43	TOR	N	1	0	0	0	0
1946-47*			11	1	0	1	0
1947-48*			9	1	1	2	2
1948-49*			9	2	3	5	4
1949-50			7	3	0	3	4
1950-51*			11	3	4	7	0
1951-52			4	1	1	2	0
1952-53	BOS	N	11	1	2	3	9
1953-54			4	0	0	0	0
1954-55	TOR	N	4	0	0	0	4
10 yrs.		N Totals:	71	12	11	23	23

Sold to **Boston** by Toronto, Sept. 16, 1952. Traded to **Toronto** by Boston for Leo Boivin, Nov. 9, 1954.

Gord Kluzak

KLUZAK, GORD 6'4", 220 lbs.

B. Mar. 4, 1964, Climax, Sask. Defense, Shoots L

YEAR	TEAM & LEAGUE		GP	G	A	PTS	PIM
1982-83	BOS	N	70	1	6	7	105

PLAYOFFS

YEAR	TEAM & LEAGUE		GP	G	A	PTS	PIM
1982-83	BOS	N	17	1	4	5	54

Bill Knibbs

KNIBBS, WILLIAM ARTHUR 6'1", 180 lbs.

B. Jan. 24, 1942, Toronto, Ont. Center, Shoots L

YEAR	TEAM & LEAGUE		GP	G	A	PTS	PIM
1964-65	BOS	N	53	7	10	17	4

Darrel Knibbs

KNIBBS, DARREL 6'1", 185 lbs.

B. Sept. 21, 1949, Medicine Hat, Alta. Right Wing, Shoots R

YEAR	TEAM & LEAGUE		GP	G	A	PTS	PIM
1972-73	CHI	W	41	3	8	11	0

Bill Knott

KNOTT, WILLIAM EARL (Nick) 6'1½", 200 lbs.

B. July 23, 1920, Kingston, Ont. Defense, Shoots L

YEAR	TEAM & LEAGUE		GP	G	A	PTS	PIM
1941-42	NYA	N	14	3	1	4	9

Bill Knox

KNOX, PAUL WILLIAM

Right Wing

YEAR	TEAM & LEAGUE		GP	G	A	PTS	PIM
1954-55	TOR	N	1	0	0	0	0

Keith Kokkola

KOKKOLA, KEITH VICTOR (Coke, Bear) 6'3", 204 lbs.

B. May 4, 1949, Windsor, Ont. Defense, Shoots L

YEAR	TEAM & LEAGUE		GP	G	A	PTS	PIM
1974-75	CHI	W	33	0	2	2	69
1975-76	D-O	W	16	0	3	3	40
1976-77	BIRM	W	5	0	0	0	21
3 yrs.		W Totals:	54	0	5	5	130

Neil Komadoski

KOMADOSKI, NEIL GEORGE 6', 200 lbs.

B. Nov. 5, 1951, Winnipeg, Man. Defense, Shoots L

YEAR	TEAM & LEAGUE		GP	G	A	PTS	PIM
1972-73	LA	N	62	1	8	9	67
1973-74			68	2	4	6	43
1974-75			75	4	12	16	69
1975-76			80	3	15	18	165
1976-77			68	3	9	12	109
1977-78			25	0	6	6	24
	STL	N	33	2	8	10	73
	2 team total		58	2	14	16	97
1978-79			42	1	2	3	30
1979-80			49	0	12	12	52
8 yrs.		N Totals:	502	16	76	92	632

PLAYOFFS

YEAR	TEAM & LEAGUE		GP	G	A	PTS	PIM
1973-74	LA	N	2	0	0	0	12
1974-75			3	0	0	0	2
1975-76			9	0	0	0	18
1976-77			9	0	2	2	15
4 yrs.		N Totals:	23	0	2	2	47

Traded to **St. Louis** by Los Angeles for St. Louis' second round choice in the 1980 Entry Draft, Jan. 14, 1978. Claimed by **St. Louis** as fill in Expansion Draft, June 13, 1979.

George Konik

KONIK, GEORGE SAMUEL 5'10", 200 lbs.

B. May 4, 1938, Flin Flon, Man. Left Wing, Shoots L

YEAR	TEAM & LEAGUE		GP	G	A	PTS	PIM
1967-68	PITT	N	52	7	8	15	26
1972-73	MINN	W	54	4	12	16	34
2 yrs.		N Totals:	52	7	8	15	26
		W Totals:	54	4	12	16	34

Traded to **Pittsburgh** by N.Y. Rangers with Paul Andrea, Duncan McCallum, and Frank Francis for Larry Jeffrey, June 6, 1967.

Stephen Konroyd

KONROYD, STEPHEN MARK 6'1", 195 lbs.

B. Feb. 10, 1961, Scarborough, Ont. Defense, Shoots L

YEAR	TEAM & LEAGUE		GP	G	A	PTS	PIM
1980-81	CALG	N	4	0	0	0	4
1981-82			63	3	14	17	78
1982-83			79	4	13	17	73
3 yrs.		N Totals:	146	7	27	34	155

PLAYOFFS

YEAR	TEAM & LEAGUE		GP	G	A	PTS	PIM
1981-82	CALG	N	3	0	0	0	12
1982-83			9	2	1	3	18
2 yrs.		N Totals:	12	2	1	3	30

Chris Kontos

KONTOS, CHRIS 6'1", 195 lbs.

B. Dec. 10, 1963, Toronto, Ont. Center, Shoots L

YEAR	TEAM & LEAGUE		GP	G	A	PTS	PIM
1982-83	NYR	N	44	8	7	15	33

Russ Kopak

KOPAK, RUSSELL 5'10", 158 lbs.

B. Apr. 26, 1924, Edmonton, Alta. Center, Shoots L

YEAR	TEAM & LEAGUE		GP	G	A	PTS	PIM
1943-44	BOS	N	24	7	9	16	0

Jerry Korab

KORAB, GERALD JOSEPH (Kong) 6'3", 218 lbs.

B. Sept. 15, 1948, Sault Ste. Marie, Ont. Defense, Shoots L

YEAR	TEAM & LEAGUE		GP	G	A	PTS	PIM
1970-71	CHI	N	46	4	14	18	152
1971-72			73	9	5	14	95
1972-73			77	12	15	27	94
1973-74	VAN	N	31	4	7	11	64
	BUF	N	45	6	12	18	73
	2 team total		76	10	19	29	137
1974-75			79	12	44	56	184
1975-76			65	13	28	41	85
1976-77			77	14	33	47	120
1977-78			77	7	34	41	119
1978-79			78	11	40	51	104
1979-80			43	1	10	11	74
	LA	N	11	1	2	3	34
	2 team total		54	2	12	14	108

Jerry Korab continued

YEAR	TEAM & LEAGUE		GP	G	A	PTS	PIM
1980-81			78	9	43	52	139
1981-82			50	5	13	18	91
1982-83			72	3	26	29	90
13 yrs.		N Totals:	902	111	326	437	1518
PLAYOFFS							
1970-71	CHI	N	7	1	0	1	20
1971-72			8	0	1	1	20
1972-73			15	0	0	0	22
1974-75	BUF	N	16	3	2	5	32
1975-76			9	1	3	4	12
1976-77			6	2	4	6	8
1977-78			8	0	5	5	6
1978-79			3	1	0	1	4
1979-80	LA	N	3	0	1	1	11
1980-81			4	0	0	0	33
1981-82			10	0	2	2	26
11 yrs.		N Totals:	89	8	18	26	194

Traded to **Vancouver** by Chicago with Gary Smith for Dale Tallon, May 14, 1973. Traded to **Buffalo** by Vancouver for John Gould and Tracy Pratt, Dec. 27, 1973. Traded to **Los Angeles** by Buffalo for Los Angeles' first choice (Phil Housley) in 1982 Entry Draft, Mar. 10, 1980.

Jim Korn

KORN, JAMES A 6'3", 210 lbs.
B. July 28, 1957, Hopkins, Minn. Defense, Shoots L

YEAR	TEAM & LEAGUE		GP	G	A	PTS	PIM
1979-80	DET	N	63	5	13	18	108
1980-81			63	5	15	20	246
1981-82			59	1	7	8	124
	TOR	N	11	1	3	4	44
	2 team total		70	2	10	12	168
1982-83			80	8	21	29	238
4 yrs.		N Totals:	276	20	59	79	760
PLAYOFFS							
1982-83	TOR	N	3	0	0	0	26

Teaded to **Toronto** by Detroit for Toronto's fourth round choice (Craig Core) in 1982 Entry Draft and Toronto's fifth round choice (Joey Kocur) in 1983 Entry Draft, Mar. 8, 1982.

Mike Korney

KORNEY, MICHAEL WAYNE 6'3", 195 lbs.
B. Sept. 15, 1953, Dauphin, Man. Right Wing, Shoots R

YEAR	TEAM & LEAGUE		GP	G	A	PTS	PIM
1973-74	DET	N	2	0	0	0	0
1974-75			30	8	2	10	18
1975-76			27	1	7	8	23
1978-79	NYR	N	18	0	1	1	18
4 yrs.		N Totals:	77	9	10	19	59

Traded to **Philadelphia** by Detroit with Rick LaPointe for Terry Murray, Bob Ritchie, Steve Coates and Dave Kelly, Feb. 17, 1977. Signed as free agent by **St. Louis** July 29, 1978. Traded to **Montreal** by St. Louis for the rights to Gord McTavish, Oct. 7, 1978. Claimed by **N.Y. Rangers** from Montreal in League Waiver Draft, Oct. 9, 1978. Instead of receiving cash, Montreal elected to claim Dan Newman from N.Y. Rangers.

Cliff Koroll

KOROLL, CLIFFORD EUGENE 6', 195 lbs.
B. Oct. 1, 1946, Canora, Sask. Right Wing, Shoots R

YEAR	TEAM & LEAGUE		GP	G	A	PTS	PIM
1969-70	CHI	N	73	18	19	37	44
1970-71			72	16	34	50	85
1971-72			76	22	23	45	51
1972-73			77	33	24	57	38
1973-74			78	21	25	46	32
1974-75			80	27	32	59	27
1975-76			80	25	33	58	29
1976-77			80	15	26	41	8
1977-78			73	16	15	31	19
1978-79			78	12	19	31	20
1979-80			47	3	4	7	6
11 yrs.		N Totals:	814	208	254	462	359
PLAYOFFS							
1969-70	CHI	N	8	1	4	5	9
1970-71			18	7	9	16	18
1971-72			8	0	0	0	11
1972-73			16	4	6	10	6

Cliff Koroll continued

YEAR	TEAM & LEAGUE		GP	G	A	PTS	PIM
1973-74			11	2	5	7	13
1974-75			8	3	5	8	8
1975-76			4	1	0	1	0
1976-77			2	0	0	0	0
1977-78			4	1	0	1	0
1978-79			4	0	0	0	0
1979-80			2	0	0	0	2
11 yrs.		N Totals:	85	19	29	48	67

Dick Kotanen

KOTANEN, RICHARD 5'11", 190 lbs.
B. Nov. 18, 1925, Strathmore, Alta. Defense, Shoots R

YEAR	TEAM & LEAGUE		GP	G	A	PTS	PIM
1948-49	DET	N	1	0	1	1	0
1950-51	NYR	N	1	0	0	0	0
2 yrs.		N Totals:	2	0	1	1	0

Chris Kotsopoulos

KOTSOPOULOS, CHRISTOPHER 6'3", 215 lbs.
B. Nov. 27, 1958, Toronto, Ont. Defense, Shoots R

YEAR	TEAM & LEAGUE		GP	G	A	PTS	PIM
1980-81	NYR	N	54	4	12	16	153
1981-82	HART	N	68	13	20	33	147
1982-83			68	6	24	30	125
3 yrs.		N Totals:	190	23	56	79	425
PLAYOFFS							
1980-81	NYR	N	14	0	3	3	63

Traded to **Hartford** by N.Y. Rangers along with Gerry McDonald and Doug Sulliman for Mike Rogers and future considerations, Oct. 2, 1981.

Joe Kowal

KOWAL, JOSEPH DOUGLAS 6'5", 212 lbs.
B. Feb. 3, 1956, Toronto, Ont. Left Wing, Shoots L

YEAR	TEAM & LEAGUE		GP	G	A	PTS	PIM
1976-77	BUF	N	16	0	5	5	6
1977-78			6	0	0	0	7
2 yrs.		N Totals:	22	0	5	5	13
PLAYOFFS							
1977-78	BUF	N	2	0	0	0	0

Don Kozak

KOZAK, DONALD 5'9", 184 lbs.
B. Feb. 2, 1952, Saskatoon, Sask. Right Wing, Shoots R

YEAR	TEAM & LEAGUE		GP	G	A	PTS	PIM
1972-73	LA	N	72	14	6	20	104
1973-74			76	21	14	35	54
1974-75			77	16	15	31	64
1975-76			62	20	24	44	94
1976-77			79	15	17	32	89
1977-78			43	8	5	13	45
1978-79	VAN	N	28	2	5	7	30
7 yrs.		N Totals:	437	96	86	182	480
PLAYOFFS							
1973-74	LA	N	5	0	0	0	33
1974-75			3	1	1	2	7
1975-76			9	1	0	1	12
1976-77			9	4	1	5	17
1978-79	VAN	N	3	1	0	1	0
5 yrs.		N Totals:	29	7	2	9	69

Traded to **Vancouver** by Los Angeles for Randy Holt, Dec. 31, 1978. Claimed by **Hartford** from Vancouver in Expansion Draft, June 13, 1979.

Les Kozak

KOZAK, LESLIE PAUL 6', 185 lbs.
B. Oct. 28, 1940

YEAR	TEAM & LEAGUE		GP	G	A	PTS	PIM
1961-62	TOR	N	12	1	0	1	2

Stephen Kraftcheck

KRAFTCHECK, STEPHEN S. 5'10½", 185 lbs.
B. Mar. 3, 1929, Tinturn, Ont. Defense, Shoots R

YEAR	TEAM	LEAGUE	GP	G	A	PTS	PIM
1950-51	BOS	N	22	0	0	0	8
1951-52	NYR	N	58	8	9	17	30
1952-53			69	2	9	11	45
1958-59	TOR	N	8	1	0	1	0
4 yrs.		N Totals:	157	11	18	29	83
PLAYOFFS							
1950-51	BOS	N	6	0	0	0	7

Sold to **N.Y. Rangers** by Boston with Ed Reigle, May 14, 1951.

Skip Krake

KRAKE, PHILIP GORDON 5'11", 170 lbs.
B. Oct. 14, 1943, North Battleford, Sask.
Center, Shoots R

YEAR	TEAM	LEAGUE	GP	G	A	PTS	PIM
1963-64	BOS	N	2	0	0	0	0
1965-66			2	0	0	0	0
1966-67			15	6	2	8	4
1967-68			68	5	7	12	13
1968-69	LA	N	30	3	9	12	11
1969-70			58	5	17	22	86
1970-71	BUF	N	74	4	5	9	68
1972-73	CLEVE	W	26	9	10	19	61
1973-74			69	20	36	56	94
1974-75			71	15	23	38	108
1975-76	EDM	W	41	8	8	16	55
11 yrs.		N Totals:	249	23	40	63	182
		W Totals:	207	52	77	129	318
PLAYOFFS							
1967-68	BOS	N	4	0	0	0	2
1968-69	LA	N	6	1	0	1	15
1972-73	CLEVE	W	9	1	2	3	27
1973-74			5	0	1	1	39
1974-75			5	1	1	2	0
5 yrs.		N Totals:	10	1	0	1	17
		W Totals:	19	2	4	6	66

Traded to **Los Angeles** by Boston, May 20, 1968, for Los Angeles' first choice (Reg Leach) in 1970 Amateur Draft. Drafted by **Buffalo** from Los Angeles in Expansion Draft, June 10, 1970.

Reggie Krezanski

KREZANSKI, REGINALD 5'10", 200 lbs.
B. Jan. 1, 1948, New Westminster, B.C. Defense

YEAR	TEAM	LEAGUE	GP	G	A	PTS	PIM
1974-75	SD	W	2	0	0	0	2

Joe Krol

KROL, JOSEPH 5'11½", 173 lbs.
B. Aug. 13, 1915, Winnipeg, Man. Left Wing, Shoots L

YEAR	TEAM	LEAGUE	GP	G	A	PTS	PIM
1936-37	NYR	N	1	0	0	0	0
1938-39			1	1	1	2	0
1941-42	NYA	N	24	9	3	12	8
3 yrs.		N Totals:	26	10	4	14	8

Kevin Krook

KROOK, KEVIN BRADLEY 5'11", 187 lbs.
B. Apr. 5, 1958, Cold Lake, Alta. Defense, Shoots L

YEAR	TEAM	LEAGUE	GP	G	A	PTS	PIM
1978-79	COLO	N	3	0	0	0	2

Jim Krulicki

KRULICKI, JAMES JOHN 5'11", 180 lbs.
B. Mar. 9, 1948, Kitchener, Ont. Left Wing, Shoots L

YEAR	TEAM	LEAGUE	GP	G	A	PTS	PIM
1970-71	NYR	N	27	0	2	2	6
	DET	N	14	0	1	1	0
	2 team total		41	0	3	3	6

Traded to **Detroit** by N.Y. Rangers for Dale Rolfe, Mar. 2, 1971.

Pat Krupicka

KRUPICKA, JARDA 5'9", 160 lbs.
B. Mar. 15, 1946, Brno, Czechoslovakia Right Wing

YEAR	TEAM	LEAGUE	GP	G	A	PTS	PIM
1972-73	LA	W	6	1	0	1	2
	NY	W	30	1	2	3	4
	2 team total		36	2	2	4	6

Mike Krushelnyski

KRUSHELNYSKI, MICHAEL 6'2", 200 lbs.
B. Apr. 27, 1960, Montreal, Que. Center, Shoots L

YEAR	TEAM	LEAGUE	GP	G	A	PTS	PIM
1981-82	BOS	N	17	3	3	6	2
1982-83			79	23	42	65	43
2 yrs.		N Totals:	96	26	45	71	45
PLAYOFFS							
1981-82	BOS	N	1	0	0	0	2
1982-83			17	8	6	14	12
2 yrs.		N Totals:	18	8	6	14	14

Dave Kryskow

KRYSKOW, DAVID ROY 5'10", 175 lbs.
B. Dec. 25, 1951, Edmonton, Alta. Left Wing, Shoots L

YEAR	TEAM	LEAGUE	GP	G	A	PTS	PIM
1972-73	CHI	N	11	1	0	1	0
1973-74			72	7	12	19	22
1974-75	WASH	N	51	9	15	24	83
	DET	N	18	1	4	5	4
	2 team total		69	10	19	29	87
1975-76	ATL	N	79	15	25	40	65
1976-77	CALG	W	45	16	17	33	47
1977-78	WINN	W	71	20	21	41	16
6 yrs.		N Totals:	231	33	56	89	174
		W Totals:	116	36	38	74	63
PLAYOFFS							
1972-73	CHI	N	3	2	0	2	0
1973-74			7	0	0	0	2
1975-76	ATL	N	2	0	0	0	2
1977-78	WINN	W	9	4	4	8	2
4 yrs.		N Totals:	12	2	0	2	4
		W Totals:	9	4	4	8	2

Drafted by **Washington** from Chicago in Expansion Draft, June 12, 1974. Traded to **Detroit** by Washington for Jack Lynch, Feb. 8, 1975. Traded to **Atlanta** by Detroit for Bryan Hextall, June 5, 1975.

Edward Kryzanowski

KRYZANOWSKI, EDWARD LLOYD 5'10½", 178 lbs.
B. Nov. 14, 1925, Fort Francis, Ont. Defense, Shoots R

YEAR	TEAM	LEAGUE	GP	G	A	PTS	PIM
1948-49	BOS	N	36	1	3	4	10
1949-50			59	6	10	16	12
1950-51			69	3	6	9	10
1951-52			70	5	3	8	33
1952-53	CHI	N	5	0	0	0	0
5 yrs.		N Totals:	239	15	22	37	65
PLAYOFFS							
1948-49	BOS	N	5	0	1	1	2
1950-51			6	0	0	0	2
1951-52			7	0	0	0	0
3 yrs.		N Totals:	18	0	1	1	4

Sold to **Chicago** by Boston with Vic Lynn, Aug. 14, 1952.

Gord Kuhn

KUHN, GORDON (Doggie)
B. Truro, N.S. Forward

YEAR	TEAM	LEAGUE	GP	G	A	PTS	PIM
1932-33	NYA	N	12	1	1	2	4

Adolph Kukulowicz

KUKULOWICZ, ADOLPH FRANK (Aggie)
6'2", 175 lbs.
B. Apr. 2, 1933, Winnipeg, Man. Center, Shoots L

YEAR	TEAM	LEAGUE	GP	G	A	PTS	PIM
1952-53	NYR	N	3	1	0	1	0
1953-54			1	0	0	0	0

YEAR	TEAM & LEAGUE		GP	G	A	PTS	PIM

Adolph Kukulowicz continued

2 yrs.		N Totals:	4	1	0	1	0

Traded to **Detroit** with Billy Dea by N.Y. Rangers, for Dave Creighton and Bronco Horvath, Aug. 18, 1955.

Stewart Kulak

KULAK, STEWART 5'10", 179 lbs.
B. Mar. 10, 1963, Edmonton, Alta. Right Wing, Shoots R

YEAR	TEAM	LEAGUE	GP	G	A	PTS	PIM
1982-83	VAN	N	4	1	1	2	0

Arnie Kullman

KULLMAN, ARNOLD EDWIN 5'6½", 175 lbs.
B. Oct. 9, 1927, Winnipeg, Man. Center, Shoots L

YEAR	TEAM	LEAGUE	GP	G	A	PTS	PIM
1947-48	BOS	N	1	0	0	0	0
1949-50			12	0	1	1	11
2 yrs.		N Totals:	13	0	1	1	11

Eddie Kullman

KULLMAN, EDWARD GEORGE 5'7", 170 lbs.
B. Dec. 12, 1923, Winnipeg, Man. Right Wing, Shoots R

YEAR	TEAM	LEAGUE	GP	G	A	PTS	PIM
1947-48	NYR	N	51	15	17	32	32
1948-49			18	5	4	9	14
1950-51			70	14	18	32	88
1951-52			64	11	10	21	59
1952-53			70	8	10	18	61
1953-54			70	4	10	14	44
6 yrs.		N Totals:	343	57	69	126	298
PLAYOFFS							
1947-48	NYR	N	6	1	0	1	2

Alan Kuntz

KUNTZ, ALAN ROBERT 5'11", 165 lbs.
B. June 4, 1919, Toronto, Ont. Left Wing, Shoots L

YEAR	TEAM	LEAGUE	GP	G	A	PTS	PIM
1941-42	NYR	N	31	10	11	21	10
1945-46			14	0	1	1	2
2 yrs.		N Totals:	45	10	12	22	12
PLAYOFFS							
1941-42	NYR	N	6	1	0	1	2

Murray Kuntz

KUNTZ, MURRAY ROBERT 5'10", 180 lbs.
B. Dec. 19, 1945, Ottawa, Ont. Left Wing, Shoots L

YEAR	TEAM	LEAGUE	GP	G	A	PTS	PIM
1974-75	STL	N	7	1	2	3	0

Jari Kurri

KURRI, JARI 6'1", 185 lbs.
B. May 18, 1960, Helsinki, Finland Left Wing, Shoots R

YEAR	TEAM	LEAGUE	GP	G	A	PTS	PIM
1980-81	EDM	N	75	32	43	75	40
1981-82			71	32	54	86	32
1982-83			80	45	59	104	22
3 yrs.		N Totals:	226	109	156	265	94
PLAYOFFS							
1980-81	EDM	N	9	5	7	12	4
1981-82			5	2	5	7	10
1982-83			16	8	15	23	8
3 yrs.		N Totals:	30	15	27	42	22

Orland Kurtenbach

KURTENBACH, ORLAND JOHN 6'2", 195 lbs.
B. Sept. 7, 1936, Cudworth, Sask. Center, Shoots L

YEAR	TEAM	LEAGUE	GP	G	A	PTS	PIM
1960-61	NYR	N	10	0	6	6	2
1961-62	BOS	N	8	0	0	0	6
1963-64			70	12	25	37	91
1964-65			64	6	20	26	86
1965-66	TOR	N	70	9	6	15	54
1966-67	NYR	N	60	11	25	36	58
1967-68			73	15	20	35	82

Orland Kurtenbach continued

YEAR	TEAM	LEAGUE	GP	G	A	PTS	PIM
1968-69			2	0	0	0	2
1969-70			53	4	10	14	47
1970-71	VAN	N	52	21	32	53	84
1971-72			78	24	37	61	48
1972-73			47	9	19	28	38
1973-74			52	8	13	21	30
13 yrs.		N Totals:	639	119	213	332	628
PLAYOFFS							
1965-66	TOR	N	4	0	0	0	20
1966-67	NYR	N	3	0	2	2	0
1967-68			6	1	0	1	26
1969-70			6	1	2	3	24
4 yrs.		N Totals:	19	2	4	6	70

Drafted by **Boston** from New York, June 14, 1961. Traded by Boston with Pat Stapleton and Andy Hebenton to **Toronto** for Ron Stewart, June 8, 1965. Drafted by **N.Y. Rangers** from Toronto, June 15, 1966. Drafted by **Vancouver** from N.Y. Rangers in Expansion Draft, June 10, 1970.

Mervin Kuryluk

KURYLUK, MERVIN 5'11", 185 lbs.
B. Aug. 10, 1937, Yorkton, Sask. Left Wing, Shoots L

YEAR	TEAM	LEAGUE	GP	G	A	PTS	PIM
PLAYOFFS							
1961-62	CHI	N	2	0	0	0	0

George Kuzmicz

KUZMICZ, GEORGE 6'1", 200 lbs.
B. May 24, 1952, Montreal, Que. Defense, Shoots L

YEAR	TEAM	LEAGUE	GP	G	A	PTS	PIM
1974-75	TOR	W	34	0	12	12	22
1975-76			1	0	0	0	0
2 yrs.		W Totals:	35	0	12	12	22

Ken Kuzyk

KUZYK, KENNETH MICHAEL 6'1", 195 lbs.
B. Aug. 11, 1953, Toronto, Ont. Right Wing, Shoots R

YEAR	TEAM	LEAGUE	GP	G	A	PTS	PIM
1976-77	CLEVE	N	13	0	5	5	2
1977-78			28	5	4	9	6
2 yrs.		N Totals:	41	5	9	14	8

Put on **Minnesota** reserve list after Cleveland-Minnesota Dispersal Draft, June 15, 1978. Claimed by **Quebec** from Minnesota in Expansion Draft, June 13, 1979. Signed as free agent by **Minnesota** Feb. 1, 1980.

King Kwong

KWONG, LARRY 5'6", 150 lbs.
B. June 17, 1923, Vernon, B.C. Right Wing, Shoots R

YEAR	TEAM	LEAGUE	GP	G	A	PTS	PIM
1947-48	NYR	N	1	0	0	0	0

Bill Kyle

KYLE, WILLIAM MILLER 6'1", 175 lbs.
B. Dec. 23, 1924, Dysart, Sask. Center, Shoots R

YEAR	TEAM	LEAGUE	GP	G	A	PTS	PIM
1949-50	NYR	N	2	0	0	0	0
1950-51			1	0	3	3	0
2 yrs.		N Totals:	3	0	3	3	0

Gus Kyle

KYLE, WALTER LAWRENCE 6'1", 202 lbs.
B. Sept. 11, 1923, Dysart, Sask. Defense, Shoots L

YEAR	TEAM	LEAGUE	GP	G	A	PTS	PIM
1949-50	NYR	N	70	3	5	8	143
1950-51			64	2	3	5	92
1951-52	BOS	N	69	1	12	13	**127**
3 yrs.		N Totals:	203	6	20	26	362
PLAYOFFS							
1949-50	NYR	N	12	1	2	3	30
1951-52	BOS	N	2	0	0	0	4
2 yrs.		N Totals:	14	1	2	3	34

Traded to **Boston** by N.Y. Rangers with Pentti Lund for Paul Ronty, Sept. 20, 1951.

Jim Kyte

KYTE, JIM 6'5", 210 lbs.
B. Mar. 21, 1964, Ottawa, Ont. Defense, Shoots L

YEAR	TEAM & LEAGUE	GP	G	A	PTS	PIM
1982-83	WINN N	2	0	0	0	0

Mike Labadie

LABADIE, MICHEL 5'11", 170 lbs.
B. Aug. 17, 1932, St. Francis Assisi, Que.
Right Wing, Shoots R

YEAR	TEAM & LEAGUE	GP	G	A	PTS	PIM
1952-53	NYR N	3	0	0	0	0

Neil Labatte

LABATTE, NEIL JOSEPH HENRY 6'2", 178 lbs.
B. Apr. 24, 1957, Toronto, Ont. Defense, Shoots L

YEAR	TEAM & LEAGUE	GP	G	A	PTS	PIM
1978-79	STL N	22	0	2	2	13
1981-82		4	0	0	0	6
2 yrs.	N Totals:	26	0	2	2	19

Moe L'Abbe

L'ABBE, MAURICE JOSEPH 5'9", 170 lbs.
B. Aug. 12, 1947, Montreal, Que. Right Wing, Shoots L

YEAR	TEAM & LEAGUE	GP	G	A	PTS	PIM
1972-73	CHI N	5	0	1	1	0

Leo Labine

LABINE, LEO GERALD 5'10", 178 lbs.
B. July 22, 1931, Haileybury, Ont. Right Wing, Shoots R

YEAR	TEAM & LEAGUE	GP	G	A	PTS	PIM
1951-52	BOS N	15	2	4	6	9
1952-53		51	8	15	23	69
1953-54		68	16	19	35	57
1954-55		67	24	18	42	75
1955-56		68	16	18	34	104
1956-57		67	18	29	47	128
1957-58		62	7	14	21	18
1958-59		70	9	23	32	74
1959-60		63	16	28	44	58
1960-61		40	7	12	19	34
	DET N	24	2	9	11	32
	2 team total	64	9	21	30	66
1961-62		48	3	4	7	30
11 yrs.	N Totals:	643	128	193	321	688

PLAYOFFS

YEAR	TEAM & LEAGUE	GP	G	A	PTS	PIM
1951-52	BOS N	5	0	1	1	4
1952-53		7	2	1	3	19
1953-54		4	0	1	1	28
1954-55		5	2	1	3	11
1956-57		10	2	3	5	14
1957-58		11	0	2	2	10
1958-59		7	2	1	3	12
1960-61	DET N	11	3	2	5	4
8 yrs.	N Totals:	60	11	12	23	102

Traded to **Detroit** by Boston with Vic Stasiuk in exchange for Gary Aldcorn, Murray Oliver and Thomas McCarthy, Jan., 1961

Gord Labossierre

LABOSSIERRE, GORDON WILLIAM 6'1", 180 lbs.
B. Jan. 2, 1940, St. Boniface, Man. Center, Shoots R

YEAR	TEAM & LEAGUE	GP	G	A	PTS	PIM
1963-64	NYR N	15	0	0	0	12
1964-65		1	0	0	0	0
1967-68	LA N	68	13	27	40	31
1968-69		48	10	18	28	12
1970-71		45	11	10	21	16
	MINN N	29	8	4	12	4
	2 team total	74	19	14	33	20
1971-72		9	2	3	5	0
1972-73	HOUS W	77	36	60	96	56
1973-74		67	19	36	55	30
1974-75		76	23	34	57	40
1975-76		80	24	32	56	18
10 yrs.	N Totals:	215	44	62	106	75
	W Totals:	300	102	162	264	144

PLAYOFFS

YEAR	TEAM & LEAGUE	GP	G	A	PTS	PIM
1967-68	LA N	7	2	3	5	24
1970-71	MINN N	3	0	0	0	4

Gord Labossierre continued

YEAR	TEAM & LEAGUE	GP	G	A	PTS	PIM
1972-73	HOUS W	6	1	4	5	8
1973-74		14	7	9	16	20
1974-75		13	6	7	13	4
1975-76		17	2	8	10	14
6 yrs.	N Totals:	10	2	3	5	28
	W Totals:	50	16	28	44	46

Drafted by **Los Angeles** from Montreal in Expansion Draft, June 6, 1967. Traded to **Montreal** by Los Angeles with Ray Fortin for Ralph Backstrom, then traded to **Minnesota** by Montreal for Rey Comeau, Jan. 26, 1971. Sold to **N.Y. Islanders** by Minnesota, June 6, 1972.

Max Labovitch

LABOVITCH, MAXWELL 5'10", 165 lbs.
B. Jan. 18, 1924, Winnipeg, Man. Right Wing, Shoots R

YEAR	TEAM & LEAGUE	GP	G	A	PTS	PIM
1943-44	NYR N	5	0	0	0	4

Dan Labraaten

LABRAATEN, DANIEL 6', 190 lbs.
B. June 9, 1951, Leksland, Sweden Left Wing, Shoots R

YEAR	TEAM & LEAGUE	GP	G	A	PTS	PIM
1976-77	WINN W	64	24	27	51	21
1977-78		47	18	16	34	30
1978-79	DET N	78	19	19	38	8
1979-80		76	30	27	57	8
1980-81		44	3	8	11	12
	CALG N	27	9	7	16	13
	2 team total	71	12	15	27	25
1981-82		43	10	12	22	6
6 yrs.	N Totals:	268	71	73	144	47
	W Totals:	111	42	43	85	51

PLAYOFFS

YEAR	TEAM & LEAGUE	GP	G	A	PTS	PIM
1976-77	WINN W	20	7	17	24	15
1977-78		4	1	1	2	8
1980-81	CALG N	5	1	0	1	4
1981-82		3	0	0	0	0
4 yrs.	N Totals:	8	1	0	1	4
	W Totals:	24	8	18	26	23

Signed as free agent by **Detroit** Oct. 12, 1978. Traded to **Calgary** by Detroit for Earl Ingarfield Jr., Feb. 3, 1981.

Yvon Labre

LABRE, YVON JULES 5'10", 190 lbs.
B. Nov. 29, 1949, Sudbury, Ont. Defense, Shoots L

YEAR	TEAM & LEAGUE	GP	G	A	PTS	PIM
1970-71	PITT N	21	1	1	2	19
1973-74		16	1	2	3	13
1974-75	WASH N	76	4	23	27	182
1975-76		80	2	20	22	146
1976-77		62	3	11	14	169
1977-78		22	0	8	8	41
1978-79		51	1	13	14	80
1979-80		18	0	5	5	38
1980-81		25	2	4	6	100
9 yrs.	N Totals:	371	14	87	101	788

Drafted by **Washington** from Pittsburgh in Expansion Draft, June 12, 1974.

Guy Labrie

LABRIE, GUY 6', 185 lbs.
B. Aug. 11, 1920, St. Charles Bel'chas,Que
Defense, Shoots L

YEAR	TEAM & LEAGUE	GP	G	A	PTS	PIM
1943-44	BOS N	15	2	7	9	2
1944-45	NYR N	27	2	2	4	14
2 yrs.	N Totals:	42	4	9	13	16

Elmer Lach

LACH, ELMER 5'10", 170 lbs.
B. Jan. 22, 1918, Nokomis, Sask. Center, Shoots L
Won Hart Trophy, 1944-45
Won Art Ross Trophy, 1944-45, 1947-48
Hall of Fame, 1966

YEAR	TEAM & LEAGUE	GP	G	A	PTS	PIM
1940-41	MONT N	43	7	14	21	16
1941-42		1	0	1	1	0
1942-43		45	18	40	58	14
1943-44		48	24	48	72	23
1944-45		50	26	**54**	**80**	37

Elmer Lach continued

YEAR	TEAM	LEAGUE	GP	G	A	PTS	PIM
1945-46			50	13	**34**	47	34
1946-47			31	14	16	30	22
1947-48			60	30	31	**61**	72
1948-49			36	11	18	29	59
1949-50			64	15	33	48	33
1950-51			65	21	24	45	45
1951-52			70	15	**50**	65	36
1952-53			53	16	25	41	56
1953-54			48	5	20	25	28
14 yrs.		N Totals:	664	215	408	623	475
PLAYOFFS							
1940-41	MONT	N	3	1	0	1	0
1942-43			5	2	4	6	6
1943-44*			9	2	11	13	4
1944-45			6	4	4	8	2
1945-46*			9	5	12	17	4
1948-49			1	0	0	0	4
1949-50			5	1	2	3	4
1950-51			11	2	2	4	2
1951-52			11	1	2	3	4
1952-53*			12	1	6	7	6
1953-54			4	0	2	2	0
11 yrs.		N Totals:	76	19	45	64	36

Milt Lach

LACH, MILTON

Forward

YEAR	TEAM	LEAGUE	GP	G	A	PTS	PIM
PLAYOFFS							
1973-74	WINN	W	4	1	1	2	8

LaChance

LACHANCE

B. Unknown — Forward

YEAR	TEAM	LEAGUE	GP	G	A	PTS	PIM
1926-27	MONT	N	1	0	0	0	0

Michel LaChance

LACHANCE, MICHEL — 6', 190 lbs.

B. Apr. 11, 1955, Quebec, Que. — Defense, Shoots R

YEAR	TEAM	LEAGUE	GP	G	A	PTS	PIM
1978-79	COLO	N	21	0	4	4	22

Signed as free agent by **Colorado** Oct. 12, 1978.

Francois Lacombe

LACOMBE, FRANCOIS — 5'10", 175 lbs.

B. Feb. 24, 1948, Lachine, Que. — Defense, Shoots L

YEAR	TEAM	LEAGUE	GP	G	A	PTS	PIM
1968-69	CALIF	N	72	2	16	18	50
1969-70	OAK	N	2	0	0	0	0
1970-71	BUF	N	1	0	1	1	2
1972-73	QUE	W	61	10	18	28	123
1973-74			71	9	26	35	41
1974-75			55	7	17	24	54
1975-76	CALG	W	71	3	28	31	62
1976-77	QUE	W	81	5	22	27	86
1977-78			22	1	7	8	12
1978-79			78	3	21	24	44
1979-80	QUE	N	3	0	0	0	2
11 yrs.		N Totals:	78	2	17	19	54
		W Totals:	439	38	139	177	422
PLAYOFFS							
1968-69	CALIF	N	3	1	0	1	0
1974-75	QUE	W	15	0	2	2	14
1975-76	CALG	W	8	0	0	0	2
1976-77	QUE	W	17	4	3	7	16
1977-78			10	1	4	5	2
1978-79			4	0	1	1	2
6 yrs.		N Totals:	3	1	0	1	0
		W Totals:	54	5	10	15	36

Traded to **Oakland** by Montreal with Michel Jacques and cash for Lyle Bradley, May 21, 1968. Traded to **Montreal** by Oakland with cash and Oakland's first choice (Guy Lafleur) in 1971 Amateur Draft for Ernie Hicke and Montreal's first choice (Chris Oddleifson) in 1970 Amateur Draft. Drafted by **Buffalo** from Montreal in Expansion Draft, June 10, 1970.

Andre Lacroix

LACROIX, ANDRE JOSEPH — 5'8", 175 lbs.

B. June 5, 1945, Lauzon, Que. — Center, Shoots L

YEAR	TEAM	LEAGUE	GP	G	A	PTS	PIM
1967-68	PHI	N	18	6	8	14	6
1968-69			75	24	32	56	4
1969-70			74	22	36	58	14
1970-71			78	20	22	42	12
1971-72	CHI	N	51	4	7	11	6
1972-73	PHI	W	78	50	74	**124**	83
1973-74	NY-NJ	W	78	31	**80**	111	54
1974-75	SD	W	78	41	**106**	**147**	63
1975-76			80	29	72	101	42
1976-77			81	32	82	114	79
1977-78	HOUS	W	78	36	77	113	57
1978-79	NE	W	78	32	56	88	34
1979-80	HART	N	29	3	14	17	2
13 yrs.		N Totals:	325	79	119	198	44
		W Totals:	551	251	547	798	412
PLAYOFFS							
1967-68	PHI	N	7	2	3	5	0
1968-69			4	0	0	0	0
1970-71			4	0	2	2	0
1971-72	CHI	N	1	0	0	0	0
1972-73	PHI	W	4	0	2	2	18
1974-75	SD	W	10	3	9	12	2
1975-76			11	4	6	10	4
1976-77			7	1	6	7	6
1977-78	HOUS	W	6	2	2	4	0
1978-79	NE	W	10	4	4	8	0
10 yrs.		N Totals:	16	2	5	7	0
		W Totals:	48	14	29	43	30

Traded to **Chicago** by Philadelphia for Rick Foley, Oct. 15, 1971.

Pierre Lacroix

LACROIX, PIERRE — 5'11", 185 lbs.

B. Apr. 11, 1959, Quebec City, Que. — Defense, Shoots L

YEAR	TEAM	LEAGUE	GP	G	A	PTS	PIM
1979-80	QUE	N	76	9	21	30	45
1980-81			61	5	34	39	54
1981-82			68	4	23	27	74
1982-83			13	0	5	5	6
	HART	N	56	6	25	31	18
	2 team total		69	6	30	36	24
4 yrs.		N Totals:	274	24	108	132	197
PLAYOFFS							
1980-81	QUE	N	5	0	2	2	10
1981-82			3	0	0	0	0
2 yrs.		N Totals:	8	0	2	2	10

Traded by Quebec to **Hartford** for Trevor Wesley, Dec. 3, 1982.

Randy Ladouceur

LADOUCEUR, RANDY — 6'2", 220 lbs.

B. June 30, 1960, Brockville, Ont. — Defense, Shoots L

YEAR	TEAM	LEAGUE	GP	G	A	PTS	PIM
1982-83	DET	N	27	0	4	4	16

Guy Lafleur

LAFLEUR, GUY DAMIEN (The Flower) — 6', 175 lbs.

B. Sept. 20, 1951, Thurso, Que. — Right Wing, Shoots R

Won Hart Trophy, 1976-77, 1977-78

Won Art Ross Trophy, 1975-76, 1976-77, 1977-78

Won Conn Smythe Trophy, 1976-77

YEAR	TEAM	LEAGUE	GP	G	A	PTS	PIM
1971-72	MONT	N	73	29	35	64	48
1972-73			69	28	27	55	51
1973-74			73	21	35	56	29
1974-75			70	53	66	119	37
1975-76			80	56	69	**125**	36
1976-77			80	56	**80**	**136**	20
1977-78			78	**60**	72	**132**	26
1978-79			80	52	77	129	28
1979-80			74	50	75	125	12
1980-81			51	27	43	70	29
1981-82			66	27	57	84	24
1982-83			68	27	49	76	12
12 yrs.		N Totals:	862	486	685	1171	352

Guy Lafleur continued

PLAYOFFS

YEAR	TEAM & LEAGUE		GP	G	A	PTS	PIM
1971-72	MONT	N	6	1	4	5	2
1972-73*			17	3	5	8	9
1973-74			6	0	1	1	4
1974-75			11	12	7	19	15
1975-76*			13	7	10	17	2
1976-77*			14	9	17	26	6
1977-78*			15	10	11	21	16
1978-79*			16	10	13	23	0
1979-80			3	3	1	4	0
1980-81			3	0	1	1	2
1981-82			5	2	1	3	4
1982-83			3	0	2	2	2
12 yrs.		N Totals:	112	57	73	130	62

Rene Lafleur

LAFLEUR, RENE
B. Unknown — Forward

YEAR	TEAM & LEAGUE		GP	G	A	PTS	PIM
1924-25	MONT	N	1	0	0	0	0

Ernie LaForce

LAFORCE, ERNEST
B. June 23, 1916, Montreal, Que. — Defense

YEAR	TEAM & LEAGUE		GP	G	A	PTS	PIM
1942-43	MONT	N	1	0	0	0	0

Claude LaForge

LAFORGE, CLAUDE ROGER — 5'9", 172 lbs.
B. July 1, 1936, Sorel, Que. — Left Wing, Shoots L

YEAR	TEAM & LEAGUE		GP	G	A	PTS	PIM
1957-58	MONT	N	4	0	0	0	0
1958-59	DET	N	57	2	5	7	18
1960-61			10	1	0	1	2
1961-62			38	10	9	19	20
1963-64			17	2	3	5	4
1964-65			1	0	0	0	2
1967-68	PHI	N	63	9	16	25	36
1968-69			2	0	0	0	0
8 yrs.		N Totals:	192	24	33	57	82

PLAYOFFS

YEAR	TEAM & LEAGUE		GP	G	A	PTS	PIM
1967-68	PHI	N	5	1	2	3	15

Sold to **Detroit** by Mont. Canadiens, June, 1958.

Pete Laframboise

LAFRAMBOISE, PETER ALFRED — 6'2", 185 lbs.
B. Jan. 18, 1950, Ottawa, Ont. — Center, Shoots L

YEAR	TEAM & LEAGUE		GP	G	A	PTS	PIM
1971-72	CALIF	N	5	0	0	0	0
1972-73			77	16	25	41	26
1973-74			65	7	7	14	14
1974-75	WASH	N	45	5	10	15	22
	PITT	N	35	5	13	18	8
	2 team total		80	10	23	33	30
1976-77	EDM	W	17	0	5	5	12
5 yrs.		N Totals:	227	33	55	88	70
		W Totals:	17	0	5	5	12

PLAYOFFS

YEAR	TEAM & LEAGUE		GP	G	A	PTS	PIM
1974-75	PITT	N	9	1	0	1	0

Drafted by **Washington** from California in Expansion Draft, June 12, 1974. Traded to **Pittsburgh** by Washington for Jan. 21, 1975.

Adie LaFrance

LAFRANCE, ADELARD
B. Jan. 13, 1912, Chapleau, Ont. — Forward

YEAR	TEAM & LEAGUE		GP	G	A	PTS	PIM
1933-34	MONT	N	3	0	0	0	2

PLAYOFFS

YEAR	TEAM & LEAGUE		GP	G	A	PTS	PIM
1933-34	MONT	N	2	0	0	0	0

Leo Lafrance

LAFRANCE, LEO — Forward

YEAR	TEAM & LEAGUE		GP	G	A	PTS	PIM
1926-27	MONT	N	4	0	0	0	0
1927-28			15	1	0	1	2
	CHI	N	14	1	0	1	4
	2 team total		29	2	0	2	6
2 yrs.		N Totals:	33	2	0	2	6

Roger Lafreniere

LAFRENIERE, ROGER JOSEPH — 6', 190 lbs.
B. July 24, 1942, Montreal, Que. — Left Wing, Shoots L

YEAR	TEAM & LEAGUE		GP	G	A	PTS	PIM
1962-63	DET	N	3	0	0	0	4
1972-73	STL	N	10	0	0	0	0
2 yrs.		N Totals:	13	0	0	0	4

Jean-Guy Lagace

LAGACE, JEAN-GUY — 5'10", 185 lbs.
B. Feb. 5, 1945, L'Abord a Plouffe, Que. — Defense, Shoots R

YEAR	TEAM & LEAGUE		GP	G	A	PTS	PIM
1968-69	PITT	N	17	0	1	1	14
1970-71	BUF	N	3	0	0	0	2
1972-73	PITT	N	31	1	5	6	32
1973-74			31	2	6	8	34
1974-75			21	1	8	9	39
	KC	N	19	2	9	11	22
	2 team total		40	3	17	20	61
1975-76			69	3	10	13	108
6 yrs.		N Totals:	191	9	39	48	251

Drafted by **Minnesota** from Pittsburgh in Intra-League Draft, June 9, 1970. Drafted by **Buffalo** from Minnesota in Expansion Draft, June 10, 1970. Traded to **Kansas City** by Pittsburgh with goaltender Denis Herron for goaltender Michel Plasse, Jan. 10, 1975.

Michel Lagace

LAGACE, MICHEL — Forward

YEAR	TEAM & LEAGUE		GP	G	A	PTS	PIM
1968-69	PITT	N	17	0	1	1	14

Pierre Lagace

LAGACE, PIERRE — 6'2", 210 lbs.
B. Oct. 27, 1957, Montreal, Que. — Left Wing, Shoots L

YEAR	TEAM & LEAGUE		GP	G	A	PTS	PIM
1976-77	BIRM	W	78	2	25	27	110
1977-78	QUE	W	17	2	4	6	2
1978-79			21	0	1	1	12
3 yrs.		W Totals:	116	4	30	34	124

PLAYOFFS

YEAR	TEAM & LEAGUE		GP	G	A	PTS	PIM
1977-78	QUE	W	1	0	0	0	0
1978-79			3	0	1	1	2
2 yrs.		W Totals:	4	0	1	1	2

Floyd Lahache

LAHACHE, FLOYD — 5'10", 185 lbs.
B. Sept. 17, 1957, Caughnawaga, Que. — Defense

YEAR	TEAM & LEAGUE		GP	G	A	PTS	PIM
1977-78	CIN	W	11	0	3	3	13

Tom Laidlaw

LAIDLAW, THOMAS — 6'2", 215 lbs.
B. Apr. 15, 1958, Brampton, Ont. — Defense, Shoots L

YEAR	TEAM & LEAGUE		GP	G	A	PTS	PIM
1980-81	NYR	N	80	6	23	29	120
1981-82			79	3	18	21	104
1982-83			80	0	10	10	75
3 yrs.		N Totals:	239	9	51	60	299

PLAYOFFS

YEAR	TEAM & LEAGUE		GP	G	A	PTS	PIM
1980-81	NYR	N	14	1	4	5	18
1981-82			10	0	3	3	14
1982-83			9	1	1	2	10
3 yrs.		N Totals:	33	2	8	10	42

Bill Laing

LAING, WILLIAM — 6'2", 190 lbs.
B. Mar. 24, 1953, Harris, Sask. — Center, Shoots L

YEAR	TEAM & LEAGUE		GP	G	A	PTS	PIM
1974-75	EDM	W	43	2	4	6	32
1975-76			54	8	12	20	67

Bill Laing continued

YEAR	TEAM & LEAGUE	GP	G	A	PTS	PIM
2 yrs.	**W Totals:**	97	10	16	26	99

Robbie Laird

LAIRD, ROBBIE 5'9", 165 lbs.
B. Dec. 29, 1954, Regina, Sask. Left Wing, Shoots L

YEAR	TEAM & LEAGUE	GP	G	A	PTS	PIM
1979-80	**MINN N**	1	0	0	0	0

Signed by **Minnesota** as free agent, Sept. 15, 1979.

Serge Lajeunesse

LAJEUNESSE, SERGE 5'10", 185 lbs.
B. June 11, 1950, Montreal, Que. Right Wing, Shoots R

YEAR	TEAM & LEAGUE	GP	G	A	PTS	PIM
1970-71	**DET N**	62	1	3	4	55
1971-72		7	0	0	0	20
1972-73		28	0	1	1	26
1973-74	**PHI N**	1	0	0	0	0
1974-75		5	0	0	0	2
5 yrs.	**N Totals:**	103	1	4	5	103

Traded to **Philadelphia** by Detroit for Rick Foley, May 15, 1973.

Hec Lalande

LALANDE, HECTOR 5'9", 157 lbs.
B. Nov. 24, 1934, North Bay, Ont. Center, Shoots L

YEAR	TEAM & LEAGUE	GP	G	A	PTS	PIM
1953-54	**CHI N**	2	0	0	0	2
1955-56		65	8	18	26	70
1956-57		50	11	17	28	38
1957-58		22	2	2	4	10
	DET N	12	0	2	2	2
	2 team total	34	2	4	6	12
4 yrs.	**N Totals:**	151	21	39	60	122

Traded to **Detroit** by Chicago with Jack McIntyre, Nick Mickoski and Bob Bailey for Earl Reibel, Billy Dea, Lorne Ferguson and Bill Dineen, Dec. 17, 1957.

Bobby Lalonde

LALONDE, ROBERT PATRICK 5'5", 155 lbs.
B. Mar. 27, 1951, Montreal, Que. Center, Shoots L

YEAR	TEAM & LEAGUE	GP	G	A	PTS	PIM
1971-72	**VAN N**	27	1	5	6	2
1972-73		77	20	27	47	32
1973-74		36	3	4	7	18
1974-75		74	17	30	47	48
1975-76		71	14	36	50	46
1976-77		68	17	15	32	39
1977-78	**ATL N**	73	14	23	37	28
1978-79		78	24	32	56	24
1979-80		3	0	1	1	2
	BOS N	71	10	25	35	28
	2 team total	74	10	26	36	30
1980-81		62	4	12	16	31
1981-82	**CALG N**	1	0	0	0	0
11 yrs.	**N Totals:**	641	124	210	334	298
PLAYOFFS						
1974-75	**VAN N**	5	0	0	0	0
1975-76		1	0	0	0	2
1977-78	**ATL N**	1	1	0	1	0
1978-79		2	1	0	1	0
1979-80	**BOS N**	4	0	1	1	2
1980-81		3	2	1	3	2
6 yrs.	**N Totals:**	16	4	2	6	6

Signed as free agent by **Atlanta** Sept. 20, 1977. Claimed by **Atlanta** as fill in Expansion Draft, June 13, 1979. Traded to **Boston** by Atlanta for future considerations, Oct. 23, 1979.

Newsy Lalonde

LALONDE, EDWARD C.
B. Oct. 31, 1887, Cornwall, Ont. Center, Shoots R
Won Art Ross Trophy, 1918–19, 1920-21
Hall of Fame, 1950

YEAR	TEAM & LEAGUE	GP	G	A	PTS	PIM
1917-18	**MONT N**	14	23	0	23	16
1918-19		17	**23**	**9**	**32**	40

Newsy Lalonde continued

YEAR	TEAM & LEAGUE	GP	G	A	PTS	PIM
1919-20		23	36	6	42	33
1920-21		24	33	8	**41**	36
1921-22		20	9	4	13	11
1926-27	**NYA N**	1	0	0	0	2
6 yrs.	**N Totals:**	99	124	27	151	138
PLAYOFFS						
1917-18	**MONT N**	2	5	0	5	11
1918-19		10	17	1	18	8
2 yrs.	**N Totals:**	12	22	1	23	19

Rick Lalonde

LALONDE, RICHARD 6', 202 lbs.
B. Feb. 19, 1955, Ottawa, Ont. Defense, Shoots R

YEAR	TEAM & LEAGUE	GP	G	A	PTS	PIM
1975-76	**SD W**	2	0	0	0	0

Ron Lalonde

LALONDE, RONALD LEO 5'10", 170 lbs.
B. Oct. 30, 1952, Toronto, Ont. Center, Shoots L

YEAR	TEAM & LEAGUE	GP	G	A	PTS	PIM
1972-73	**PITT N**	9	0	0	0	2
1973-74		73	10	17	27	14
1974-75		24	0	3	3	0
	WASH N	50	12	14	26	27
	2 team total	74	12	17	29	27
1975-76		80	9	19	28	19
1976-77		76	12	17	29	24
1977-78		67	1	5	6	16
1978-79		18	1	3	4	4
7 yrs.	**N Totals:**	397	45	78	123	106

Traded to **Washington** by Pittsburgh for Lew Morrison, Dec. 14, 1974. Claimed by **Washington** as fill in Expansion Draft, June 13, 1979.

Joe Lamb

LAMB, JOSEPH GORDON 5'9½", 170 lbs.
B. June 18, 1906, Sussex, N.B. Right Wing, Shoots R

YEAR	TEAM & LEAGUE	GP	G	A	PTS	PIM
1927-28	**MON(M) N**	21	8	5	13	39
1928-29		30	4	1	5	44
	OTTA N	5	0	0	0	8
	2 team total	35	4	1	5	52
1929-30		44	29	20	49	**119**
1930-31		44	11	14	25	91
1931-32	**NYA N**	48	14	11	25	71
1932-33	**BOS N**	42	11	8	19	68
1933-34		48	10	15	25	47
1934-35	**MONT N**	7	3	2	5	4
	STL N	31	11	12	23	19
	2 team total	38	14	14	28	23
1935-36	**MON(M) N**	35	0	3	3	12
1936-37	**NYA N**	48	3	9	12	53
1937-38		27	1	0	1	20
	DET N	14	3	1	4	6
	2 team total	41	4	1	5	26
11 yrs.	**N Totals:**	444	108	101	209	601
PLAYOFFS						
1927-28	**MON(M) N**	8	1	0	1	32
1929-30	**OTTA N**	2	0	0	0	11
1932-33	**BOS N**	5	0	1	1	6
1935-36	**MON(M) N**	3	0	0	0	2
4 yrs.	**N Totals:**	18	1	1	2	51

Yvon Lambert

LAMBERT, YVON PIERRE 6', 195 lbs.
B. May 20, 1950, Drummondville, Que. Left Wing, Shoots L

YEAR	TEAM & LEAGUE	GP	G	A	PTS	PIM
1972-73	**MONT N**	1	0	0	0	0
1973-74		60	6	10	16	42
1974-75		80	32	35	67	74
1975-76		80	32	35	67	28
1976-77		79	24	28	52	50
1977-78		77	18	22	40	20
1978-79		79	26	40	66	26
1979-80		77	21	32	53	23
1980-81		73	22	32	54	39
1981-82	**BUF N**	77	25	39	64	38
10 yrs.	**N Totals:**	683	206	273	479	340

Yvon Lambert continued

PLAYOFFS

YEAR	TEAM & LEAGUE		GP	G	A	PTS	PIM
1973-74	**MONT**	**N**	5	0	0	0	7
1974-75			11	4	2	6	0
1975-76*			12	2	3	5	18
1976-77*			14	3	3	6	12
1977-78*			15	2	4	6	6
1978-79*			16	5	6	11	16
1979-80			10	8	4	12	4
1980-81			3	0	0	0	2
1981-82	**BUF**	**N**	4	3	0	3	2
9 yrs.		**N Totals:**	90	27	22	49	67

Claimed in Reverse Draft by **Montreal** from Detroit, June 9, 1971. Claimed by **Buffalo** from Montreal in 1981 Waiver Draft.

Dick Lamby

LAMBY, RICHARD A. 6'1", 200 lbs.
B. May 3, 1955, Auburn, Mass. Defense, Shoots R

YEAR	TEAM & LEAGUE		GP	G	A	PTS	PIM
1978-79	**STL**	**N**	9	0	4	4	12
1979-80			12	0	1	1	10
1980-81			1	0	0	0	0
3 yrs.		**N Totals:**	22	0	5	5	22

Traded to **Colorado** by St. Louis along with Joe Micheletti for Bill Baker, Dec. 4, 1981.

Jean Lamirande

LAMIRANDE, JEAN PAUL 5'8", 170 lbs.
B. Aug. 21, 1923, Shawinigan Falls, Que. Defense, Shoots R

YEAR	TEAM & LEAGUE		GP	G	A	PTS	PIM
1946-47	**NYR**	**N**	14	1	1	2	14
1947-48			18	0	1	1	6
1949-50			16	4	3	7	6
1954-55	**MONT**	**N**	1	0	0	0	0
4 yrs.		**N Totals:**	49	5	5	10	26

PLAYOFFS

YEAR	TEAM & LEAGUE		GP	G	A	PTS	PIM
1947-48	**NYR**	**N**	6	0	0	0	4
1949-50			2	0	0	0	0
2 yrs.		**N Totals:**	8	0	0	0	4

Purchased by **Montreal** from N.Y. Rangers, Sept. 25, 1954.

Leo Lamoureux

LAMOUREUX, LEO 5'11", 175 lbs.
B. Oct. 1, 1906, Espenola, Ont. Defense, Shoots L

YEAR	TEAM & LEAGUE		GP	G	A	PTS	PIM
1941-42	**MONT**	**N**	1	0	0	0	0
1942-43			46	2	16	18	43
1943-44			44	8	23	31	32
1944-45			49	2	22	24	38
1945-46			45	5	7	12	18
1946-47			50	2	11	13	14
6 yrs.		**N Totals:**	235	19	79	98	145

PLAYOFFS

YEAR	TEAM & LEAGUE		GP	G	A	PTS	PIM
1943-44*	**MONT**	**N**	9	0	3	3	8
1944-45			6	1	1	2	2
1945-46*			9	0	2	2	2
1946-47			4	0	0	0	4
4 yrs.		**N Totals:**	28	1	6	7	16

Mike Lampman

LAMPMAN, MICHAEL DAVID 6'2", 195 lbs.
B. Apr. 20, 1950, Hamilton, Ont. Left Wing, Shoots L

YEAR	TEAM & LEAGUE		GP	G	A	PTS	PIM
1972-73	**STL**	**N**	18	2	3	5	2
1973-74			15	1	0	1	0
	VAN	**N**	14	1	0	1	0
	2 team total		29	2	0	2	0
1975-76	**WASH**	**N**	27	7	12	19	28
1976-77			22	6	5	11	4
4 yrs.		**N Totals:**	96	17	20	37	34

Traded to **Vancouver** by St. Louis for John Wright, Dec. 10, 1973. Drafted by **Washington** from Vancouver in Expansion Draft, June 12, 1974.

Jack Lancien

LANCIEN, JOHN GORDON 6', 188 lbs.
B. June 14, 1923, Regina, Sask. Defense, Shoots L

YEAR	TEAM & LEAGUE		GP	G	A	PTS	PIM
1946-47	**NYR**	**N**	1	0	0	0	0
1949-50			43	1	4	5	27
1950-51			19	0	1	1	8
3 yrs.		**N Totals:**	63	1	5	6	35

PLAYOFFS

YEAR	TEAM & LEAGUE		GP	G	A	PTS	PIM
1947-48	**NYR**	**N**	2	0	0	0	2
1949-50			4	0	1	1	0
2 yrs.		**N Totals:**	6	0	1	1	2

Gord Lane

LANE, GORDON 6'1", 186 lbs.
B. Mar. 31, 1953, Brandon, Man. Defense, Shoots L

YEAR	TEAM & LEAGUE		GP	G	A	PTS	PIM
1975-76	**WASH**	**N**	3	1	0	1	12
1976-77			80	2	15	17	207
1977-78			69	2	9	11	195
1978-79			64	3	15	18	147
1979-80			19	2	4	6	53
	NYI	**N**	55	2	14	16	152
	2 team total		74	4	18	22	205
1980-81			60	3	9	12	24
1981-82			51	0	13	13	98
1982-83			44	3	4	7	87
8 yrs.		**N Totals:**	445	18	83	101	975

PLAYOFFS

YEAR	TEAM & LEAGUE		GP	G	A	PTS	PIM
1979-80*	**NYI**	**N**	21	1	3	4	85
1980-81*			12	1	5	6	32
1981-82*			19	0	4	4	61
1982-83*			18	1	2	3	32
4 yrs.		**N Totals:**	70	3	14	17	210

Signed as free agent by **Washington** Oct. 5, 1976. Traded to **N.Y. Islanders** by Washington for Mike Kaszycki, Dec. 7, 1979.

Myles Lane

LANE, MYLES J. 6', 180 lbs.
B. Oct. 2, 1905, Melrose, Mass. Defense, Shoots L

YEAR	TEAM & LEAGUE		GP	G	A	PTS	PIM
1928-29	**NYR**	**N**	24	1	0	1	22
	BOS	**N**	5	1	0	1	2
	2 team total		29	2	0	2	24
1929-30			3	0	0	0	0
1933-34			28	2	1	3	17
3 yrs.		**N Totals:**	60	4	1	5	41

PLAYOFFS

YEAR	TEAM & LEAGUE		GP	G	A	PTS	PIM
1928-29*	**BOS**	**N**	4	0	0	0	0
1929-30			6	0	0	0	0
2 yrs.		**N Totals:**	10	0	0	0	0

Steve Langdon

LANGDON, STEPHEN MURRAY 5'11", 175 lbs.
B. Dec. 23, 1953, Toronto, Ont. Left Wing, Shoots L

YEAR	TEAM & LEAGUE		GP	G	A	PTS	PIM
1974-75	**BOS**	**N**	1	0	1	1	0
1975-76			4	0	0	0	2
1977-78			2	0	0	0	0
3 yrs.		**N Totals:**	7	0	1	1	2

PLAYOFFS

YEAR	TEAM & LEAGUE		GP	G	A	PTS	PIM
1975-76	**BOS**	**N**	4	0	0	0	0

Pete Langelle

LANGELLE, PETER 5'10", 170 lbs.
B. Nov. 4, 1917, Winnipeg, Man. Center, Shoots L

YEAR	TEAM & LEAGUE		GP	G	A	PTS	PIM
1938-39	**TOR**	**N**	2	1	0	1	0
1939-40			39	7	14	21	2
1940-41			48	4	15	19	0
1941-42			48	10	22	32	9
4 yrs.		**N Totals:**	137	22	51	73	11

PLAYOFFS

YEAR	TEAM & LEAGUE		GP	G	A	PTS	PIM
1938-39	**TOR**	**N**	11	1	2	3	2

Pete Langelle continued

YEAR	TEAM & LEAGUE		GP	G	A	PTS	PIM
1939-40			10	0	3	3	0
1940-41			7	1	1	2	0
1941-42*			13	3	3	6	2
4 yrs.		N Totals:	41	5	9	14	4

Dave Langevin

LANGEVIN, DAVID (The Bammer) 6'2", 200 lbs.
B. May 15, 1954, St. Paul, Minn. Defense, Shoots L

YEAR	TEAM & LEAGUE		GP	G	A	PTS	PIM
1976-77	EDM	W	77	7	16	23	94
1977-78			62	6	22	28	90
1978-79			77	6	21	27	76
1979-80	NYI	N	76	3	13	16	100
1980-81			75	1	16	17	122
1981-82			73	1	20	21	82
1982-83			73	4	17	21	64
7 yrs.		N Totals:	297	9	66	75	368
		W Totals:	216	19	59	78	260
PLAYOFFS							
1976-77	EDM	W	5	2	1	3	9
1977-78			5	0	2	2	10
1978-79			13	0	1	1	25
1979-80*	NYI	N	21	0	3	3	32
1980-81*			18	0	3	3	25
1981-82*			19	2	4	6	16
1982-83*			8	0	2	2	2
7 yrs.		N Totals:	66	2	12	14	75
		W Totals:	23	2	4	6	44

Reclaimed by **N.Y. Islanders** from Edmonton prior to Expansion Draft, June 9,1979.

Joseph Langlais

LANGLAIS, JOSEPH ALFRED ALAIN 5'10", 175 lbs.
B. Oct. 9, 1950, Chicoutimi, Que. Left Wing, Shoots L

YEAR	TEAM & LEAGUE		GP	G	A	PTS	PIM
1973-74	MINN	N	14	3	3	6	8
1974-75			11	1	1	2	2
2 yrs.		N Totals:	25	4	4	8	10

Al Langlois

LANGLOIS, ALBERT (Junior) 6', 205 lbs.
B. Nov. 6, 1934, Magog, Que. Defense, Shoots L

YEAR	TEAM & LEAGUE		GP	G	A	PTS	PIM
1957-58	MONT	N	1	0	0	0	0
1958-59			48	0	3	3	26
1959-60			67	1	14	15	48
1960-61			61	1	12	13	56
1961-62	NYR	N	69	7	18	25	90
1962-63			60	2	14	16	62
1963-64			44	4	2	6	32
	DET	N	17	1	6	7	13
	2 team total		61	5	8	13	45
1964-65			65	1	12	13	107
1965-66	BOS	N	65	4	10	14	54
9 yrs.		N Totals:	497	21	91	112	488
PLAYOFFS							
1957-58*	MONT	N	7	0	1	1	4
1958-59*			7	0	0	0	4
1959-60*			8	0	3	3	18
1960-61			5	0	0	0	6
1961-62	NYR	N	6	0	1	1	2
1963-64	DET	N	14	0	0	0	12
1964-65			6	1	0	1	4
7 yrs.		N Totals:	53	1	5	6	50

Traded to **N.Y. Rangers** by Montreal Canadiens in exchange for John Hanna, June 13, 1961. Traded by New York to **Detroit** in exchange for Ron Ingram, Feb. 14, 1964. Traded by Detroit with Ron Harris, Parker MacDonald and Bob Dillabough to **Boston** for Ab McDonald, Bob McCord and Ken Stephenson, May 31, 1965.

Charlie Langlois

LANGLOIS, CHARLIE
B. Aug. 25, 1894, Latbiniere, Que. Defense

YEAR	TEAM & LEAGUE		GP	G	A	PTS	PIM
1924-25	HAMIL	N	30	6	1	7	59

Charlie Langlois continued

YEAR	TEAM & LEAGUE		GP	G	A	PTS	PIM
1925-26	NYA	N	36	9	1	10	76
1926-27			9	2	0	2	8
	PITT	N	37	5	1	6	36
	2 team total		46	7	1	8	44
1927-28			8	0	0	0	8
	MONT	N	32	0	0	0	14
	2 team total		40	0	0	0	22
4 yrs.		N Totals:	152	22	3	25	201
PLAYOFFS							
1927-28	MONT	N	2	0	0	0	0

Rod Langway

LANGWAY, ROD CORRY 6'3", 215 lbs.
B. May 3, 1957, Maaq, Taiwan Defense, Shoots L
Won Norris Trophy, 1982-83

YEAR	TEAM & LEAGUE		GP	G	A	PTS	PIM
1977-78	BIRM	W	52	3	18	21	52
1978-79	MONT	N	45	3	4	7	30
1979-80			77	7	29	36	81
1980-81			80	11	34	45	120
1981-82			66	5	34	39	116
1982-83	WASH	N	80	3	29	32	75
6 yrs.		N Totals:	348	29	130	159	422
		W Totals:	52	3	18	21	52
PLAYOFFS							
1977-78	BIRM	W	4	0	0	0	9
1978-79*	MONT	N	8	0	0	0	16
1979-80			10	3	3	6	2
1980-81			3	0	0	0	6
1981-82			5	0	3	3	18
1982-83	WASH	N	4	0	0	0	0
6 yrs.		N Totals:	30	3	6	9	42
		W Totals:	4	0	0	0	9

Claimed by **Montreal** as fill in Expansion Draft, June 13, 1979. Traded by Montreal with Doug Jarvis, Craig Laughlin, and Brian Engblom to **Washington** for Rick Green and Ryan Walter, Sept. 9, 1982.

Ted Lanyon

LANYON, THEODORE 5'11", 170 lbs.
B. June 11, 1939, Winnipeg, Man. Defense, Shoots L

YEAR	TEAM & LEAGUE		GP	G	A	PTS	PIM
1967-68	PITT	N	5	0	0	0	4

Rick Lanz

LANZ, RICK ROMAN 6'1", 195 lbs.
B. Sept. 16, 1961, Karlovyvary, Czech. Defense, Shoots R

YEAR	TEAM & LEAGUE		GP	G	A	PTS	PIM
1980-81	VAN	N	76	7	22	29	40
1981-82			39	3	11	14	48
1982-83			74	10	38	48	46
3 yrs.		N Totals:	189	20	71	91	134
PLAYOFFS							
1980-81	VAN	N	3	0	0	0	4
1982-83			4	2	1	3	0
2 yrs.		N Totals:	7	2	1	3	4

Jacques Laperriere

LAPERRIERE, JOSEPH JACQUES HUGUES
6'2", 190 lbs.
B. Nov. 22, 1941, Rouyn, Que. Defense, Shoots L
Won Norris Trophy, 1965-66
Won Calder Trophy, 1963-64

YEAR	TEAM & LEAGUE		GP	G	A	PTS	PIM
1962-63	MONT	N	6	0	2	2	2
1963-64			65	2	28	30	102
1964-65			67	5	22	27	92
1965-66			57	6	25	31	85
1966-67			61	0	20	20	48
1967-68			72	4	21	25	84
1968-69			69	5	26	31	45
1969-70			73	6	31	37	98
1970-71			49	0	16	16	20
1971-72			73	3	25	28	50
1972-73			57	7	16	23	34
1973-74			42	2	10	12	14

Jacques Laperriere continued

YEAR	TEAM & LEAGUE	GP	G	A	PTS	PIM
12 yrs.	N Totals:	691	40	242	282	674
PLAYOFFS						
1962-63	MONT N	5	0	1	1	4
1963-64		7	1	1	2	8
1964-65*		6	1	1	2	16
1966-67		9	0	1	1	9
1967-68*		13	1	3	4	20
1968-69*		14	1	3	4	28
1970-71*		20	4	9	13	12
1971-72		4	0	0	0	2
1972-73*		10	1	3	4	2
9 yrs.	N Totals:	88	9	22	31	101

Camille Lapierre

LAPIERRE, CAMILLE 5'10", 160 lbs.
B. Feb. 8, 1951, Chicoutimi, Que. Center, Shoots L

YEAR	TEAM & LEAGUE	GP	G	A	PTS	PIM
1972-73	PHI W	24	5	9	14	2
1973-74	VAN W	9	0	3	3	0
2 yrs.	W Totals:	33	5	12	17	2
PLAYOFFS						
1972-73	PHI W	4	0	2	2	0

Guy Lapointe

LAPOINTE, GUY GERARD 6', 200 lbs.
B. Mar. 18, 1948, Montreal, Que. Defense, Shoots L

YEAR	TEAM & LEAGUE	GP	G	A	PTS	PIM
1968-69	MONT N	1	0	0	0	2
1969-70		5	0	0	0	4
1970-71		78	15	29	44	107
1971-72		69	11	38	49	58
1972-73		76	19	35	54	117
1973-74		71	13	40	53	63
1974-75		80	28	47	75	88
1975-76		77	21	47	68	78
1976-77		77	13	29	42	53
1977-78		49	130	290	420	19
1978-79		69	13	42	55	43
1979-80		45	6	20	26	29
1980-81		33	1	9	10	79
1981-82		47	1	19	20	72
	STL N	8	0	6	6	4
	2 team total	55	1	25	26	76
1982-83		54	3	23	26	43
15 yrs.	N Totals:	839	274	674	948	859
PLAYOFFS						
1970-71	CHI N	20	4	5	9	34
1971-72	MONT N	6	0	1	1	0
1972-73*		17	6	7	13	20
1973-74		6	0	2	2	4
1974-75		11	6	4	10	4
1975-76*		13	3	3	6	12
1976-77*		12	3	9	12	4
1977-78*		14	1	6	7	16
1978-79*		10	2	6	8	10
1979-80		2	0	0	0	0
1980-81		1	0	0	0	17
1981-82	STL N	7	1	0	1	8
1982-83		4	0	1	1	9
13 yrs.	N Totals:	123	26	44	70	138

Traded to **St. Louis** by Montreal for St. Louis' second round choice (Sergio Momesso) in 1983 Entry Draft, Mar. 9, 1982. Signed as a free agent by **Boston** Aug. 16, 1983.

Rick Lapointe

LAPOINTE, RICHARD PAUL 6'2", 200 lbs.
B. Aug. 2, 1955, Victoria, B.C. Defense, Shoots L

YEAR	TEAM & LEAGUE	GP	G	A	PTS	PIM
1975-76	DET N	80	10	23	33	95
1976-77		49	2	11	13	80
	PHI N	22	1	8	9	39
	2 team total	71	3	19	22	119
1977-78		47	4	16	20	91
1978-79		77	3	18	21	53
1979-80	STL N	80	6	19	25	87

Rick Lapointe continued

YEAR	TEAM & LEAGUE	GP	G	A	PTS	PIM
1980-81		80	8	25	33	124
1981-82		71	2	20	22	127
1982-83	QUE N	43	2	9	11	59
8 yrs.	N Totals:	549	38	149	187	755
PLAYOFFS						
1976-77	PHI N	10	0	0	0	7
1977-78		12	0	3	3	19
1978-79		7	0	1	1	14
1979-80	STL N	3	0	1	1	6
1980-81		8	2	2	4	12
1981-82		3	0	0	0	6
6 yrs.	N Totals:	43	2	7	9	64

Traded to **Philadelphia** by Detroit with Mike Korney for Terry Murray, Bob Ritchie, Steve Coates and Dave Kelly, Feb. 17, 1977. Traded to **St. Louis** by Philadelphia with Blake Dunlop for goaltender Phil Myre, June 7, 1979. Traded to **Quebec** by St. Louis for Pat Hickey, Aug. 4, 1982.

Edgar Laprade

LAPRADE, EDGAR LOUIS 5'8", 157 lbs.
B. Oct. 10, 1919, Mine Center, Ont. Center, Shoots R
Won Lady Byng Trophy, 1949-50
Won Calder Trophy, 1945-46

YEAR	TEAM & LEAGUE	GP	G	A	PTS	PIM
1945-46	NYR N	49	15	19	34	0
1946-47		58	15	25	40	9
1947-48		59	13	34	47	7
1948-49		56	18	12	30	12
1949-50		60	22	22	44	2
1950-51		42	10	13	23	0
1951-52		70	9	29	38	8
1952-53		11	2	1	3	2
1953-54		35	1	6	7	2
1954-55		60	3	11	14	0
10 yrs.	N Totals:	500	108	172	280	42
PLAYOFFS						
1947-48	NYR N	6	1	4	5	0
1949-50		12	3	5	8	4
2 yrs.	N Totals:	18	4	9	13	4

Ben LaPrairie

LAPRAIRIE, BENJAMIN (Bun)
B. Unknown Defense

YEAR	TEAM & LEAGUE	GP	G	A	PTS	PIM
1936-37	CHI N	7	0	0	0	0

Garry Lariviere

LARIVIERE, GARRY JOSEPH 6', 190 lbs.
B. Dec. 6, 1954, St. Catharines, Ont. Defense, Shoots R

YEAR	TEAM & LEAGUE	GP	G	A	PTS	PIM
1974-75	PHOE W	4	0	1	1	28
1975-76		79	7	17	24	100
1976-77		61	7	23	30	48
	QUE W	15	0	3	3	8
	2 team total	76	7	26	33	56
1977-78		80	7	49	56	78
1978-79		50	5	33	38	54
1979-80	QUE N	75	2	19	21	56
1980-81		52	3	13	16	50
	EDM N	13	0	2	2	6
	2 team total	65	3	15	18	56
1981-82		62	1	21	22	41
1982-83		17	0	2	2	14
9 yrs.	N Totals:	219	6	57	63	167
	W Totals:	289	26	126	152	316
PLAYOFFS						
1974-75	PHOE W	1	0	0	0	0
1975-76		5	0	2	2	2
1976-77	QUE W	17	0	10	10	10
1977-78		11	3	2	5	4
1978-79		4	0	1	1	2
1980-81	EDM N	9	0	3	3	8
1981-82		4	0	1	1	0
1982-83		1	0	1	1	0
8 yrs.	N Totals:	14	0	5	5	8
	W Totals:	38	3	15	18	18

Reclaimed by **N.Y. Islanders** from Quebec prior to Expansion Draft, June 9, 1979. Claimed as priority selection by **Quebec** June 9, 1979. Traded to **Vancouver** by Quebec for Mario Marois, Mar.10, 1981. Traded to **Edmon-**

ton by Vancouver with the rights to Lars Gunnar Pettersson for Blair MacDonald and the rights to Ken Berry, Mar.10, 1981.

Jeff Larmer

LARMER, JEFF 5'10", 172 lbs.
B. Nov. 10, 1962, Peterborough, Ont. Left Wing, Shoots L

YEAR	TEAM & LEAGUE		GP	G	A	PTS	PIM
1981-82	COLO	N	8	1	1	2	8
1982-83	NJ	N	65	21	24	45	21
2 yrs.		N Totals:	73	22	25	47	29

Steve Larmer

LARMER, STEVEN DONALD 5'10", 185 lbs.
B. June 16, 1961, Peterborough, Ont. Right Wing, Shoots L
Won Calder Trophy, 1982-83

YEAR	TEAM & LEAGUE		GP	G	A	PTS	PIM
1980-81	CHI	N	4	0	1	1	0
1981-82			3	0	0	0	0
1982-83			80	43	47	90	28
3 yrs.		N Totals:	87	43	48	91	28
PLAYOFFS							
1982-83	CHI	N	11	5	7	12	8

Wildor Larochelle

LAROCHELLE, WILDOR 5'8", 158 lbs.
B. Oct. 23, 1906, Sorel, Que. Shoots R

YEAR	TEAM & LEAGUE		GP	G	A	PTS	PIM
1925-26	MONT	N	33	2	1	3	10
1926-27			41	0	1	1	6
1927-28			40	3	1	4	30
1928-29			2	0	0	0	0
1929-30			44	14	11	25	28
1930-31			40	8	5	13	35
1931-32			48	18	8	26	16
1932-33			47	11	4	15	27
1933-34			48	16	11	27	27
1934-35			48	9	19	28	12
1935-36			13	0	2	2	6
	CHI	N	27	2	1	3	8
	2 team total		40	2	3	5	14
1936-37			43	9	10	19	6
12 yrs.		N Totals:	474	92	74	166	211
PLAYOFFS							
1926-27	MONT	N	4	0	0	0	0
1927-28			2	0	0	0	0
1929-30*			6	1	0	1	12
1930-31*			10	1	2	3	8
1931-32			4	2	1	3	4
1932-33			2	1	0	1	0
1933-34			2	1	1	2	0
1934-35			2	0	0	0	0
1935-36	CHI	N	2	0	0	0	0
9 yrs.		N Totals:	34	6	4	10	24

Claude Larose

LAROSE, CLAUDE 5'10", 170 lbs.
B. May 17, 1955, St. Jean, Que. Left Wing, Shoots L

YEAR	TEAM & LEAGUE		GP	G	A	PTS	PIM
1975-76	CIN	W	79	28	24	52	19
1976-77			81	30	46	76	8
1977-78			51	11	20	31	6
	IND	W	28	14	16	30	12
	2 team total		79	25	36	61	18
1978-79			13	5	8	13	0
1979-80	NYR	N	25	4	7	11	2
5 yrs.		N Totals:	25	4	7	11	2
		W Totals:	252	88	114	202	45
PLAYOFFS							
1976-77	CIN	W	4	2	1	3	0
1981-82	NYR	N	2	0	0	0	0
2 yrs.		N Totals:	2	0	0	0	0
		W Totals:	4	2	1	3	0

Charles Larose

LAROSE, CHARLES BONNER
B. Unknown

YEAR	TEAM & LEAGUE		GP	G	A	PTS	PIM
1925-26	BOS	N	6	0	0	0	0

Claude Larose

LAROSE, CLAUDE 6', 170 lbs.
Right Wing, Shoots R

YEAR	TEAM & LEAGUE		GP	G	A	PTS	PIM
1962-63	MONT	N	4	0	0	0	0
1963-64			21	1	1	2	43
1964-65			68	21	16	37	82
1965-66			64	15	18	33	67
1966-67			69	19	16	35	82
1967-68			42	2	9	11	28
1968-69	MINN	N	67	25	37	62	106
1969-70			75	24	23	47	109
1970-71	MONT	N	64	10	13	23	90
1971-72			76	20	18	38	64
1972-73			73	11	23	34	30
1973-74			39	17	7	24	52
1974-75			8	1	2	3	6
	STL	N	56	10	17	27	38
	2 team total		64	11	19	30	44
1975-76			67	13	25	38	48
1976-77			80	29	19	48	22
1977-78			69	8	13	21	20
16 yrs.		N Totals:	942	226	257	483	887
PLAYOFFS							
1963-64	MONT	N	2	1	0	1	0
1964-65*			13	0	1	1	14
1965-66*			6	0	1	1	31
1966-67			10	1	5	6	15
1967-68*			12	3	2	5	8
1969-70	MINN	N	6	1	1	2	25
1970-71*	MONT	N	11	1	0	1	10
1971-72			6	2	1	3	23
1972-73*			17	3	4	7	6
1973-74			5	0	2	2	11
1974-75	STL	N	2	1	1	2	0
1975-76			3	0	0	0	0
1976-77			4	1	0	1	0
13 yrs.		N Totals:	97	14	18	32	143

Paul Larose

LAROSE, PAUL 5'8", 155 lbs.
B. Jan. 11, 1950, Noranda, Que. Right Wing, Shoots R

YEAR	TEAM & LEAGUE		GP	G	A	PTS	PIM
1972-73	QUE	W	28	0	7	7	7
1974-75	M-B	W	5	1	1	2	2
2 yrs.		W Totals:	33	1	8	9	9

Ray Larose

LAROSE, RAY
B. Nov. 20, 1941, Quebec City, Que. Defense, Shoots L

YEAR	TEAM & LEAGUE		GP	G	A	PTS	PIM
1972-73	HOUS	W	67	1	10	11	25
1973-74	NY-NJ	W	18	0	1	1	20
2 yrs.		W Totals:	85	1	11	12	45

Pierre Larouche

LAROUCHE, PIERRE (Lucky Pierre) 5'11", 175 lbs.
B. Nov. 16, 1955, Taschereau, Que. Center, Shoots R

YEAR	TEAM & LEAGUE		GP	G	A	PTS	PIM
1974-75	PITT	N	79	31	37	68	52
1975-76			76	53	58	111	33
1976-77			65	29	34	63	14
1977-78			20	6	5	11	0
	MONT	N	44	17	32	49	11
	2 team total		64	23	37	60	11
1978-79			36	9	13	22	4
1979-80			73	50	41	91	16
1980-81			61	25	28	53	28
1981-82			22	9	12	21	0
	HART	N	45	25	25	50	12
	2 team total		67	34	37	71	12
1982-83			38	18	22	40	8
9 yrs.		N Totals:	559	272	307	579	178

Pierre Larouche continued

PLAYOFFS

YEAR	TEAM & LEAGUE		GP	G	A	PTS	PIM
1974-75	**PITT**	N	9	2	5	7	2
1975-76			3	0	1	1	0
1976-77			3	0	3	3	0
1977-78*	**MONT**	N	5	2	1	3	4
1978-79*			6	1	3	4	0
1979-80			9	1	7	8	2
1980-81			2	0	2	2	0
7 yrs.	**N Totals:**		37	6	22	28	8

Traded to **Montreal** from Pittsburgh with a player to be named later (Peter Marsh, Dec. 15, 1977) for Pete Mahovlich and Peter Lee, Nov. 29, 1977. Traded to **Hartford** by Montreal in exchange for a switch in first round selections in 1984 Entry Draft, a switch in third round selections in 1985 Entry Draft, and Hartford's second round choice in 1984 Entry Draft, Dec. 21, 1981. Signed as a free agent by **N.Y. Rangers** Sept. 13, 1983.

Norman Larson

LARSON, NORMAN 6', 175 lbs.
B. Oct. 13, 1920, Moose Jaw, Sask. Right Wing, Shoots R

YEAR	TEAM & LEAGUE		GP	G	A	PTS	PIM
1940-41	**NYA**	N	48	9	9	18	6
1941-42			40	16	9	25	6
1946-47	**NYR**	N	1	0	0	0	0
3 yrs.	**N Totals:**		89	25	18	43	12

Reed Larson

LARSON, REED DAVID 6', 188 lbs.
B. July 30, 1956, Minneapolis, Minn. Defense, Shoots R

YEAR	TEAM & LEAGUE		GP	G	A	PTS	PIM
1976-77	**DET**	N	14	0	1	1	23
1977-78			75	19	41	60	95
1978-79			79	18	49	67	169
1979-80			80	22	44	66	101
1980-81			78	27	31	58	153
1981-82			80	21	39	60	112
1982-83			80	22	52	74	104
7 yrs.	**N Totals:**		486	129	257	386	757

PLAYOFFS

YEAR	TEAM & LEAGUE		GP	G	A	PTS	PIM
1977-78	**DET**	N	7	0	2	2	4

Don Larway

LARWAY, JOHN DONALD 6'1", 192 lbs.
B. Feb. 2, 1954, Oar Lake, Man. Right Wing, Shoots R

YEAR	TEAM & LEAGUE		GP	G	A	PTS	PIM
1974-75	**HOUS**	W	76	21	13	34	59
1975-76			79	30	20	50	56
1976-77			75	11	13	24	112
1977-78			69	24	35	59	52
1978-79	**IND**	W	25	8	10	18	39
5 yrs.	**W Totals:**		324	94	91	185	318

PLAYOFFS

YEAR	TEAM & LEAGUE		GP	G	A	PTS	PIM
1974-75	**HOUS**	W	13	3	1	4	8
1975-76			16	7	5	12	21
1976-77			3	1	0	1	0
1977-78			6	1	2	3	4
4 yrs.	**W Totals:**		38	12	8	20	33

Signed as free agent by **Detroit** Sept. 4, 1979.

Phil Latreille

LATREILLE, PHILIPPE
B. Apr. 20, 1938, Montreal, Que.

YEAR	TEAM & LEAGUE		GP	G	A	PTS	PIM
1960-61	**NYR**	N	4	0	0	0	2

Marty Lauder

LAUDER, MARTIN
B. Unknown Defense

YEAR	TEAM & LEAGUE		GP	G	A	PTS	PIM
1927-28	**BOS**	N	3	0	0	0	2

Craig Laughlin

LAUGHLIN, CRAIG 5'11", 198 lbs.
B. Sept. 19, 1957, Toronto, Ont. Right Wing, Shoots R

YEAR	TEAM & LEAGUE		GP	G	A	PTS	PIM
1981-82	**MONT**	N	36	12	11	23	33
1982-83	**WASH**	N	75	17	27	44	41
2 yrs.	**N Totals:**		111	29	38	67	74

PLAYOFFS

YEAR	TEAM & LEAGUE		GP	G	A	PTS	PIM
1981-82	**MONT**	N	3	0	1	1	0
1982-83	**WASH**	N	4	1	0	1	0
2 yrs.	**N Totals:**		7	1	1	2	0

Traded by Montreal with Doug Jarvis, Rod Langway, and Brian Engblom to **Washington** for Rick Green and Ryan Walter, Sept. 9, 1982.

Mike Laughton

LAUGHTON, MICHAEL FREDERIC 6'2", 185 lbs.
B. Feb. 21, 1944, Nelson, B.C. Center, Shoots L

YEAR	TEAM & LEAGUE		GP	G	A	PTS	PIM
1967-68	**OAK**	N	35	2	6	8	38
1968-69	**CALIF**	N	53	20	23	43	12
1969-70	**OAK**	N	76	16	19	35	39
1970-71	**CALIF**	N	25	1	0	1	2
1972-73	**NY**	W	67	16	20	36	44
1973-74	**NY-NJ**	W	71	20	18	38	34
1974-75	**SD**	W	65	7	9	16	22
7 yrs.	**N Totals:**		189	39	48	87	91
	W Totals:		203	43	47	90	100

PLAYOFFS

YEAR	TEAM & LEAGUE		GP	G	A	PTS	PIM
1968-69	**CALIF**	N	7	3	2	5	0
1969-70	**OAK**	N	4	0	1	1	0
1974-75	**SD**	W	10	4	1	5	0
3 yrs.	**N Totals:**		11	3	3	6	0
	W Totals:		10	4	1	5	0

Drafted by **Oakland** from Toronto in Expansion Draft, June 6, 1967. Sold to **Montreal** by California, Aug. 31, 1971.

Red Laurence

LAURENCE, DONALD 5'9", 173 lbs.
B. June 27, 1957, Galt, Ont. Center, Shoots R

YEAR	TEAM & LEAGUE		GP	G	A	PTS	PIM
1978-79	**ATL**	N	59	14	20	34	6
1979-80	**STL**	N	20	1	2	3	8
2 yrs.	**N Totals:**		79	15	22	37	14

Traded to **St. Louis** by Atlanta with Ed Kea and Atlanta's second-round choice (Hakan Nordin) in 1981 Entry Draft for Garry Unger, Oct. 10, 1979.

Kevin Lavallee

LAVALLEE, KEVIN A. 5'8", 180 lbs.
B. Sept. 16, 1961, Sudbury, Ont. Left Wing, Shoots L

YEAR	TEAM & LEAGUE		GP	G	A	PTS	PIM
1980-81	**CALG**	N	77	15	20	35	16
1981-82			75	32	29	61	30
1982-83			60	19	16	35	17
3 yrs.	**N Totals:**		212	66	65	131	63

PLAYOFFS

YEAR	TEAM & LEAGUE		GP	G	A	PTS	PIM
1980-81	**CALG**	N	8	2	3	5	4
1981-82			3	0	0	0	7
1982-83			8	1	3	4	0
3 yrs.	**N Totals:**		19	3	6	9	11

Traded by Calgary with Carl Mokosak to **Los Angeles** for Steve Bozek, June 20, 1983.

Brian Lavender

LAVENDER, BRIAN JAMES 6', 180 lbs.
B. Apr. 20, 1947, Edmonton, Alta. Left Wing, Shoots L

YEAR	TEAM & LEAGUE		GP	G	A	PTS	PIM
1971-72	**STL**	N	46	5	11	16	54
1972-73	**NYI**	N	43	6	6	12	47
	DET	N	26	2	2	4	14
	2 team total		69	8	8	16	61
1973-74			4	0	0	0	11
1974-75	**CALIF**	N	65	3	7	10	48
1975-76	**D-O**	W	37	2	0	2	7

Brian Lavender continued

YEAR	TEAM & LEAGUE		GP	G	A	PTS	PIM
5 yrs.		**N Totals:**	184	16	26	42	174
		W Totals:	37	2	0	2	7
PLAYOFFS							
1971-72	**STL**	**N**	3	0	0	0	2

Drafted by **Minnesota** from Montreal in Intra-league Draft, June 8, 1971. Drafted from Minnesota by Denver Spurs **(St. Louis)** in Reverse Draft, June, 1971. Sold to **N.Y. Islanders** by St. Louis, Sept. 1, 1972. Traded to **Detroit** by N.Y. Islanders with Ken Murray for Ralph Stewart and Bob Cook, Jan. 17, 1973. Traded to **N.Y. Rangers** by Detroit for Claude Houde, Feb. 28, 1974. Traded to **California** by N.Y. Rangers for Hartland Monahan, Sept. 23, 1974.

Jack Laviolette

LAVIOLETTE, JEAN-BAPTISTE
B. July 19, 1879 — Defense
Hall of Fame, 1962

YEAR	TEAM & LEAGUE		GP	G	A	PTS	PIM
1917-18	**MONT**	**N**	18	2	0	2	6
PLAYOFFS							
1917-18	**MONT**	**N**	2	0	0	0	0

Paul Lawless

LAWLESS, PAUL — 6', 186 lbs.
B. July 2, 1964, Scarborough, Ont. — Left Wing, Shoots L

YEAR	TEAM & LEAGUE		GP	G	A	PTS	PIM
1982-83	**HART**	**N**	47	6	9	15	4

Danny Lawson

LAWSON, DANIEL MICHAEL — 5'11", 180 lbs.
B. Oct. 30, 1947, Toronto, Ont. — Right Wing, Shoots R

YEAR	TEAM & LEAGUE		GP	G	A	PTS	PIM
1967-68	**DET**	**N**	1	0	0	0	0
1968-69			44	5	7	12	21
	MINN	**N**	18	3	3	6	4
	2 team total		62	8	10	18	25
1969-70			45	9	8	17	19
1970-71			33	1	5	6	2
1971-72	**BUF**	**N**	78	10	6	16	15
1972-73	**PHI**	**W**	78	**61**	45	106	35
1973-74	**VAN**	**W**	78	55	33	88	14
1974-75			78	33	43	76	19
1975-76	**CALG**	**W**	80	44	52	96	46
1976-77			64	24	19	43	26
	WINN	**W**	14	6	7	13	2
	2 team total		78	30	26	56	28
10 yrs.		**N Totals:**	219	28	29	57	61
		W Totals:	392	223	199	422	142
PLAYOFFS							
1969-70	**MINN**	**N**	6	0	1	1	2
1970-71			10	0	0	0	0
1972-73	**PHI**	**W**	4	0	1	1	0
1975-76	**CALG**	**W**	9	4	4	8	19
1976-77	**WINN**	**W**	13	2	4	6	6
5 yrs.		**N Totals:**	16	0	1	1	2
		W Totals:	26	6	9	15	25

Traded to **Minnesota** by Detroit for Wayne Connelly, Feb. 15, 1969. Drafted by **Buffalo** from Minnesota in Intra-league Draft, June 8, 1971.

Hal Laycoe

LAYCOE, HAROLD RICHARDSON — 6'1", 175 lbs.
B. June 23, 1922, Sutherland, Sask. — Defense, Shoots L

YEAR	TEAM & LEAGUE		GP	G	A	PTS	PIM
1945-46	**NYR**	**N**	17	0	2	2	6
1946-47			58	1	12	13	25
1947-48	**MONT**	**N**	14	1	2	3	4
1948-49			51	3	5	8	31
1949-50			30	0	2	2	21
1950-51			38	0	2	2	25
	BOS	**N**	6	1	1	2	4
	2 team total		44	1	3	4	29
1951-52			70	5	7	12	61
1952-53			54	2	10	12	36
1953-54			58	3	16	19	29
1954-55			5	1	0	1	34
1955-56			65	5	5	10	16
11 yrs.		**N Totals:**	466	22	64	86	292

Hal Laycoe continued

YEAR	TEAM & LEAGUE		GP	G	A	PTS	PIM
PLAYOFFS							
1948-49	**MONT**	**N**	7	0	1	1	13
1949-50			2	0	0	0	0
1950-51	**BOS**	**N**	6	0	1	1	5
1951-52			7	1	1	2	11
1952-53			11	0	2	2	10
1953-54			2	0	0	0	0
1954-55			5	1	0	1	0
7 yrs.		**N Totals:**	40	2	5	7	39

Traded to **Boston** by Montreal for Ross Lowe, Feb. 14, 1951.

Larry Leach

LEACH, LAWRENCE RAYMOND — 6'2", 180 lbs.
B. June 18, 1936, Lloydminster, Sask. — Center, Shoots L

YEAR	TEAM & LEAGUE		GP	G	A	PTS	PIM
1958-59	**BOS**	**N**	29	4	12	16	26
1959-60			69	7	12	19	47
1961-62			28	2	5	7	18
3 yrs.		**N Totals:**	126	13	29	42	91
PLAYOFFS							
1958-59	**BOS**	**N**	7	1	1	2	8

Reggie Leach

LEACH, REGINALD JOSEPH (Rifle) — 6', 195 lbs.
B. Apr. 23, 1950, Riverton, Man. — Right Wing, Shoots R
Won Conn Smythe Trophy, 1975-76

YEAR	TEAM & LEAGUE		GP	G	A	PTS	PIM
1970-71	**BOS**	**N**	23	2	4	6	0
1971-72			56	7	13	20	12
	CALIF	**N**	16	6	7	13	7
	2 team total		72	13	20	33	19
1972-73			76	23	12	35	45
1973-74			78	22	24	46	34
1974-75	**PHI**	**N**	80	45	33	78	63
1975-76			80	**61**	30	91	41
1976-77			77	32	14	46	23
1977-78			72	24	28	52	24
1978-79			76	34	20	54	20
1979-80			76	50	26	76	28
1980-81			79	34	36	70	59
1981-82			66	26	21	47	18
1982-83	**DET**	**N**	78	15	17	32	13
13 yrs.		**N Totals:**	933	381	285	666	387
PLAYOFFS							
1970-71	**BOS**	**N**	3	0	0	0	0
1974-75*	**PHI**	**N**	17	8	2	10	6
1975-76			16	19	5	24	8
1976-77			10	4	5	9	0
1977-78			12	2	2	4	0
1978-79			8	5	1	6	0
1979-80			19	9	7	16	6
1980-81			9	0	0	0	2
8 yrs.		**N Totals:**	94	47	22	69	22

Traded to **California** by Boston with Rick Smith and Bob Stewart for Carol Vadnais and Don O'Donoghue, Feb. 23, 1972. Traded to **Philadelphia** by California for Larry Wright, Al MacAdam and Philadelphia's first choice (Ron Chipperfield) in 1974 Amateur Draft, May 24, 1974. (Rights for Chipperfield traded back to **Philadelphia** by California for George Pesut, Dec. 11, 1974.) Signed as a free agent by **Detroit** Aug. 25, 1982.

Fern LeBlanc

LEBLANC, FERNAND — 5'9", 170 lbs.
B. Jan. 12, 1956, Gaspesie, Que. — Center, Shoots L

YEAR	TEAM & LEAGUE		GP	G	A	PTS	PIM
1976-77	**DET**	**N**	3	0	0	0	0
1977-78			2	0	0	0	0
1978-79			29	5	6	11	0
3 yrs.		**N Totals:**	34	5	6	11	0

J.P. LeBlanc

LEBLANC, JEAN-PAUL — 5'10", 175 lbs.
B. Oct. 20, 1946, Durham, Que. — Center, Shoots L

YEAR	TEAM & LEAGUE		GP	G	A	PTS	PIM
1968-69	**CHI**	**N**	60	1	2	3	0
1972-73	**LA**	**W**	77	19	50	69	49
1973-74			78	20	46	66	58

J.P. LeBlanc continued

YEAR	TEAM & LEAGUE		GP	G	A	PTS	PIM
1974-75	M-B	W	78	16	33	49	100
1975-76	D-O	W	15	1	5	6	25
	DET	N	46	4	9	13	39
	2 team total		61	5	14	19	64
1976-77			74	7	11	18	40
1977-78			3	0	2	2	4
1978-79			24	2	6	8	4
8 yrs.		N Totals:	207	14	30	44	87
		W Totals:	248	56	134	190	232
PLAYOFFS							
1972-73	LA	W	6	0	5	5	2
1977-78	DET	N	2	0	0	0	0
2 yrs.		N Totals:	2	0	0	0	0
		W Totals:	6	0	5	5	2

Traded to **Detroit** by Chicago for Detroit's second round choice (Jean Savard) in 1977 Amateur Draft, Nov. 20, 1975.

Al LeBrun

LEBRUN, ALBERT IVAN 6', 195 lbs.
B. Dec. 1, 1940, Timmins, Ont. Defense, Shoots R

YEAR	TEAM & LEAGUE		GP	G	A	PTS	PIM
1960-61	NYR	N	4	0	2	2	4
1965-66			2	0	0	0	0
2 yrs.		N Totals:	6	0	2	2	4

Drafted by **Detroit** from N.Y. Rangers, June 15, 1966. Sold to **Chicago** by Detroit with Murray Hall to complete trade of Dec. 20, 1966, in which Detroit acquired Howie Young from Chicago, May 8, 1967.

Bill Lecaine

LECAINE, WILLIAM JOSEPH 6', 172 lbs.
B. Mar. 11, 1940, Moose Jaw, Sask. Left Wing, Shoots R

YEAR	TEAM & LEAGUE		GP	G	A	PTS	PIM
1968-69	PITT	N	4	0	0	0	0

Jack Leclair

LECLAIR, JOHN LOUIS 5'10", 175 lbs.
B. May 30, 1929, Quebec City, Que. Center, Shoots L

YEAR	TEAM & LEAGUE		GP	G	A	PTS	PIM
1954-55	MONT	N	59	11	22	33	12
1955-56			54	6	8	14	30
1956-57			47	3	10	13	14
3 yrs.		N Totals:	160	20	40	60	56
PLAYOFFS							
1954-55	MONT	N	12	5	0	5	2
1955-56*			8	1	1	2	4
2 yrs.		N Totals:	20	6	1	7	6

Rene Leclerc

LECLERC, RENALD 5'11", 165 lbs.
B. Nov. 12, 1947, Ville-de-Vanier, Que. Right Wing, Shoots R

YEAR	TEAM & LEAGUE		GP	G	A	PTS	PIM
1968-69	DET	N	43	2	3	5	62
1970-71			44	8	8	16	30
1972-73	QUE	W	60	24	28	52	111
1973-74			58	17	27	44	84
1974-75			73	18	32	50	85
1975-76			42	15	17	32	35
	IND	W	40	18	21	39	52
	2 team total		82	33	38	71	87
1976-77			68	25	30	55	43
1977-78			60	12	15	27	31
1978-79			22	5	7	12	12
	QUE	W	23	0	0	0	8
	2 team total		45	5	7	12	20
9 yrs.		N Totals:	87	10	11	21	92
		W Totals:	446	134	177	311	461
PLAYOFFS							
1974-75	QUE	W	14	7	7	14	41
1975-76	IND	W	7	2	5	7	7
1976-77			9	1	1	2	4
1978-79	QUE	W	4	0	0	0	0
4 yrs.		W Totals:	34	10	13	23	52

Doug Lecuyer

LECUYER, DOUGLAS J. 5'9", 179 lbs.
B. Mar. 10, 1958, Wainwright, Alta. Left Wing, Shoots L

YEAR	TEAM & LEAGUE		GP	G	A	PTS	PIM
1978-79	CHI	N	2	1	0	1	0
1979-80			53	3	10	13	69
1980-81			14	0	0	0	41
	WINN	N	45	6	17	23	66
	2 team total		59	6	17	23	107
1982-83	PITT	N	12	1	4	5	12
4 yrs.		N Totals:	126	11	31	42	188
PLAYOFFS							
1979-80	CHI	N	7	4	0	4	15

Traded to **Winnipeg** by Chicago with Tim Trimper for Peter Marsh, Dec. 1, 1980. Acquired by **Pittsburgh** from Winnipeg in Waiver Draft, Oct. 4, 1982.

Walt Ledingham

LEDINGHAM, WALTER NORMAN 5'11", 180 lbs.
B. Oct. 26, 1950, Weyburn, Sask. Left Wing, Shoots L

YEAR	TEAM & LEAGUE		GP	G	A	PTS	PIM
1972-73	CHI	N	9	0	1	1	4
1974-75	NYI	N	2	0	1	1	0
1976-77			4	0	0	0	0
3 yrs.		N Totals:	15	0	2	2	4

Traded to **N.Y. Islanders** by Chicago, May 24, 1974, to complete deal of March 7, 1974 in which Chicago acquired Germain Gagnon.

Albert LeDuc

LEDUC, ALBERT (Battleship) 5'9", 180 lbs.
B. Nov. 22, 1902, Valleyfield, Que. Shoots R

YEAR	TEAM & LEAGUE		GP	G	A	PTS	PIM
1925-26	MONT	N	32	10	3	13	62
1926-27			43	5	2	7	62
1927-28			42	8	5	13	73
1928-29			43	9	2	11	79
1929-30			44	6	8	14	90
1930-31			44	8	6	14	82
1931-32			41	5	3	8	60
1932-33			48	5	3	8	62
1933-34	OTTA	N	34	1	3	4	34
	NYR	N	10	0	0	0	6
	2 team total		44	1	3	4	40
1934-35	MONT	N	4	0	0	0	4
10 yrs.		N Totals:	385	57	35	92	614
PLAYOFFS							
1926-27	MONT	N	4	0	0	0	2
1927-28			2	1	0	1	5
1928-29			3	1	0	1	4
1929-30*			6	1	3	4	8
1930-31*			7	0	2	2	9
1931-32			4	1	1	2	2
1932-33			2	1	0	1	2
1933-34	NYR	N	2	0	0	0	0
8 yrs.		N Totals:	30	5	6	11	32

Bob LeDuc

LEDUC, ROBERT JOSEPH 5'10", 185 lbs.
B. May 24, 1944, Sudbury, Ont. Left Wing, Shoots L

YEAR	TEAM & LEAGUE		GP	G	A	PTS	PIM
1972-73	OTTA	W	77	22	33	55	71
1973-74	TOR	W	61	22	29	51	29
1974-75			19	3	4	7	9
3 yrs.		W Totals:	157	47	66	113	109
PLAYOFFS							
1972-73	OTTA	W	5	0	2	2	4
1973-74	TOR	W	12	4	6	10	42
2 yrs.		W Totals:	17	4	8	12	46

Rich LeDuc

LEDUC, RICHARD HENRI 5'11", 170 lbs.
B. Aug. 24, 1951, Ile Perrot, Que. Center, Shoots L

YEAR	TEAM & LEAGUE		GP	G	A	PTS	PIM
1972-73	BOS	N	5	1	1	2	2
1973-74			28	3	3	6	12
1974-75	CLEVE	W	78	34	31	65	122
1975-76			79	36	22	58	76

Rich LeDuc continued

YEAR	TEAM & LEAGUE		GP	G	A	PTS	PIM
1976-77	**CIN**	**W**	81	52	55	107	75
1977-78			54	27	31	58	44
	IND	**W**	28	10	15	25	38
	2 team total		82	37	46	83	82
1978-79			13	5	9	14	14
	QUE	**W**	61	30	32	62	30
	2 team total		74	35	41	76	44
1979-80	**QUE**	**N**	75	21	27	48	49
1980-81			22	3	7	10	6
9 yrs.		**N Totals:**	130	28	38	66	69
		W Totals:	394	194	195	389	399

PLAYOFFS

YEAR	TEAM & LEAGUE		GP	G	A	PTS	PIM
1973-74	**BOS**	**N**	5	0	0	0	9
1974-75	**CLEVE**	**W**	5	0	2	2	2
1975-76			3	2	1	3	2
1976-77	**CIN**	**W**	4	1	3	4	16
1978-79	**QUE**	**W**	4	0	2	2	0
5 yrs.		**N Totals:**	5	0	0	0	9
		W Totals:	16	3	8	11	20

Traded to **Boston** by California with Chris Oddleifson for Ivan Boldirev, Nov. 17, 1971.

Bobby Lee

LEE, ROBERT

B. Unknown — Defense

YEAR	TEAM & LEAGUE		GP	G	A	PTS	PIM
1942-43	**MONT**	**N**	1	0	0	0	0

Peter Lee

LEE, PETER JOHN — 5'9", 180 lbs.

B. Jan. 2, 1956, Ellesmere, England — Right Wing, Shoots R

YEAR	TEAM & LEAGUE		GP	G	A	PTS	PIM
1977-78	**PITT**	**N**	60	5	13	18	19
1978-79			80	32	26	58	24
1979-80			74	16	29	45	20
1980-81			80	30	34	64	88
1981-82			74	18	16	34	98
1982-83			63	13	13	26	10
6 yrs.		**N Totals:**	431	114	131	245	259

PLAYOFFS

YEAR	TEAM & LEAGUE		GP	G	A	PTS	PIM
1978-79	**PITT**	**N**	7	0	3	3	0
1979-80			4	0	1	1	0
1980-81			5	0	4	4	4
1981-82			3	0	0	0	0
4 yrs.		**N Totals:**	19	0	8	8	4

Traded to **Pittsburgh** by Montreal with Pete Mahovlich for Pierre Larouche and a player to be named later (Peter Marsh, Dec. 15, 1977), Nov. 29, 1977.

Gary Leeman

LEEMAN, GARY — 5'11", 168 lbs.

B. Feb. 19, 1964, Toronto, Ont. — Defense, Shoots L

PLAYOFFS

YEAR	TEAM & LEAGUE		GP	G	A	PTS	PIM
1982-83	**TOR**	**N**	2	0	0	0	2

Bryan Lefley

LEFLEY, BRYAN ANDREW — 6', 184 lbs.

B. Oct. 18, 1948, Gross Isle, Man. — Defense, Shoots R

YEAR	TEAM & LEAGUE		GP	G	A	PTS	PIM
1972-73	**NYI**	**N**	63	3	7	10	56
1973-74			7	0	0	0	0
1974-75	**KC**	**N**	29	0	3	3	6
1976-77	**COLO**	**N**	58	0	6	6	27
1977-78			71	4	13	17	12
5 yrs.		**N Totals:**	228	7	29	36	101

PLAYOFFS

YEAR	TEAM & LEAGUE		GP	G	A	PTS	PIM
1977-78	**COLO**	**N**	2	0	0	0	0

Drafted by **N.Y. Islanders** from N.Y. Rangers in Expansion Draft, June 6, 1972. Drafted by **Kansas City** from N.Y. Islanders in Expansion Draft, June 12, 1974.

Chuck Lefley

LEFLEY, CHARLES THOMAS — 6'2", 185 lbs.

B. Jan. 20, 1950, Winnipeg, Man. — Left Wing, Shoots L

YEAR	TEAM & LEAGUE		GP	G	A	PTS	PIM
1970-71	**MONT**	**N**	1	0	0	0	0
1971-72			16	0	2	2	0
1972-73			65	21	25	46	22
1973-74			74	23	31	54	34
1974-75			18	1	2	3	4
	STL	**N**	57	23	26	49	24
	2 team total		75	24	28	52	28
1975-76			75	43	42	85	41
1976-77			71	11	30	41	12
1979-80			28	6	6	12	0
1980-81			2	0	0	0	0
9 yrs.		**N Totals:**	407	128	164	292	137

PLAYOFFS

YEAR	TEAM & LEAGUE		GP	G	A	PTS	PIM
1970-71*	**MONT**	**N**	20	0	1	1	0
1972-73*			17	3	5	8	6
1973-74			6	0	1	1	0
1974-75	**STL**	**N**	2	0	0	0	2
1975-76			2	2	1	3	0
1976-77			1	0	1	1	2
6 yrs.		**N Totals:**	48	5	9	14	10

Traded to **St. Louis** by Montreal for Don Awrey, Nov. 28, 1974.

Roger Leger

LEGER, ROGER — 5'11", 210 lbs.

B. Mar. 26, 1919, L'Annonciation, Que. — Defense, Shoots R

YEAR	TEAM & LEAGUE		GP	G	A	PTS	PIM
1943-44	**NYR**	**N**	7	1	2	3	2
1946-47	**MONT**	**N**	49	4	18	22	12
1947-48			48	4	14	18	26
1948-49			28	6	7	13	10
1949-50			55	3	12	15	21
5 yrs.		**N Totals:**	187	18	53	71	71

PLAYOFFS

YEAR	TEAM & LEAGUE		GP	G	A	PTS	PIM
1946-47	**MONT**	**N**	11	0	6	6	10
1948-49			5	0	1	1	2
1949-50			4	0	0	0	2
3 yrs.		**N Totals:**	20	0	7	7	14

Barry Legge

LEGGE, BARRY GRAHAM — 6', 186 lbs.

B. Oct. 22, 1954, Winnipeg, Man. — Defense, Shoots L

YEAR	TEAM & LEAGUE		GP	G	A	PTS	PIM
1974-75	**M-B**	**W**	36	3	18	21	20
1975-76	**D-O**	**W**	40	6	8	14	15
	CLEVE	**W**	35	0	7	7	22
	2 team total		75	6	15	21	37
1976-77	**MINN**	**W**	2	0	0	0	0
	CIN	**W**	74	7	22	29	39
	2 team total		76	7	22	29	39
1977-78			78	7	17	24	114
1978-79			80	3	8	11	131
1979-80	**QUE**	**N**	31	0	3	3	18
1980-81	**WINN**	**N**	38	0	6	6	69
1981-82			38	1	2	3	57
8 yrs.		**N Totals:**	107	1	11	12	144
		W Totals:	345	26	80	106	341

PLAYOFFS

YEAR	TEAM & LEAGUE		GP	G	A	PTS	PIM
1975-76	**CLEVE**	**W**	3	0	1	1	12
1976-77	**CIN**	**W**	4	0	0	0	0
1978-79			3	0	4	4	0
3 yrs.		**W Totals:**	10	0	5	5	12

Traded to **Quebec** by Winnipeg with Jamie Hislop for Barry Melrose, June 28, 1979. Sold to **Winnipeg** by Quebec, May 26, 1980.

Randy Legge

LEGGE, NORMAN RANDALL 5'11", 184 lbs.
B. Dec. 16, 1945, Newmarket, Ont. Defense, Shoots R

YEAR	TEAM & LEAGUE		GP	G	A	PTS	PIM
1972-73	NYR	N	12	0	2	2	2
1974-75	M-B	W	78	1	14	15	69
1975-76	WINN	W	1	0	0	0	0
	CLEVE	W	44	1	8	9	28
	2 team total		45	1	8	9	28
1976-77	SD	W	69	1	9	10	69
4 yrs.		N Totals:	12	0	2	2	2
		W Totals:	192	3	31	34	166
PLAYOFFS							
1975-76	CLEVE	W	3	0	0	0	0
1976-77	SD	W	7	0	0	0	18
2 yrs.		W Totals:	10	0	0	0	18

Antero Lehtonen

LEHTONEN, ANTERO 6', 185 lbs.
B. Apr. 12, 1954, Tampere, Finland Left Wing, Shoots L

YEAR	TEAM & LEAGUE		GP	G	A	PTS	PIM
1979-80	WASH	N	65	9	12	21	14

Signed by **Washington** as free agent, Sept. 16, 1979.

Henri Lehvonen

LEHVONEN, HENRI 6', 185 lbs.
B. Aug. 26, 1950, Sarnia, Ont. Defense, Shoots L

YEAR	TEAM & LEAGUE		GP	G	A	PTS	PIM
1974-75	KC	N	4	0	0	0	0

Edward Leier

LEIER, EDWARD 5'11", 165 lbs.
B. Nov. 3, 1927, Poland Center, Shoots R

YEAR	TEAM & LEAGUE		GP	G	A	PTS	PIM
1949-50	CHI	N	5	0	1	1	0
1950-51			11	2	0	2	2
2 yrs.		N Totals:	16	2	1	3	2

Mikko Leinonen

LEINONEN, MIKKO 6', 175 lbs.
B. July 15, 1955, Tampere, Finland Center, Shoots L

YEAR	TEAM & LEAGUE		GP	G	A	PTS	PIM
1981-82	NYR	N	53	11	20	31	18
1982-83			78	17	34	51	23
2 yrs.		N Totals:	131	28	54	82	41
PLAYOFFS							
1981-82	NYR	N	7	1	6	7	20
1982-83			7	1	3	4	4
2 yrs.		N Totals:	14	2	9	11	24

Signed as free agent by **N.Y. Rangers** Sept., 1981.

Bobby Leiter

LEITER, ROBERT EDWARD 5'9", 164 lbs.
B. Mar. 22, 1941, Winnipeg, Man. Center, Shoots L

YEAR	TEAM & LEAGUE		GP	G	A	PTS	PIM
1962-63	BOS	N	51	9	13	22	34
1963-64			56	6	13	19	43
1964-65			18	3	1	4	6
1965-66			9	2	1	3	2
1968-69			1	0	0	0	0
1971-72	PITT	N	78	14	17	31	18
1972-73	ATL	N	78	26	34	60	19
1973-74			78	26	26	52	10
1974-75			52	10	18	28	8
1975-76			26	2	3	5	4
	CALG	W	51	17	17	34	8
	2 team total		77	19	20	39	12
10 yrs.		N Totals:	447	98	126	224	144
		W Totals:	51	17	17	34	8
PLAYOFFS							
1971-72	PITT	N	4	3	0	3	0
1973-74	ATL	N	4	0	0	0	2
1975-76	CALG	W	3	2	0	2	0
3 yrs.		N Totals:	8	3	0	3	2
		W Totals:	3	2	0	2	0

Drafted by **Atlanta** from Pittsburgh in Expansion Draft, June 6, 1972.

Jacques Lemaire

LEMAIRE, JACQUES GERARD 5'10", 180 lbs.
B. Sept. 7, 1945, LaSalle, Que. Center, Shoots L

YEAR	TEAM & LEAGUE		GP	G	A	PTS	PIM
1967-68	MONT	N	69	22	20	42	16
1968-69			75	29	34	63	29
1969-70			69	32	28	60	16
1970-71			78	28	28	56	18
1971-72			77	32	49	81	26
1972-73			77	44	51	95	16
1973-74			66	29	38	67	10
1974-75			80	36	56	92	20
1975-76			61	20	32	52	20
1976-77			75	34	41	75	22
1977-78			75	36	61	97	14
1978-79			50	24	31	55	10
12 yrs.		N Totals:	852	366	469	835	217
PLAYOFFS							
1967-68*	MONT	N	13	7	6	13	6
1968-69*			14	4	2	6	6
1970-71*			20	9	10	19	17
1971-72			6	2	1	3	2
1972-73*			17	7	13	20	2
1973-74			6	0	4	4	2
1974-75			11	5	7	12	4
1975-76*			13	3	3	6	2
1976-77*			14	7	12	19	6
1977-78*			15	6	8	14	10
1978-79*			16	11	12	23	6
11 yrs.		N Totals:	145	61	78	139	63

Moe Lemay

LEMAY, MAURICE 5'11", 186 lbs.
B. Feb. 18, 1962, Saskatoon, Sask. Left Wing, Shoots L

YEAR	TEAM & LEAGUE		GP	G	A	PTS	PIM
1981-82	VAN	N	5	1	2	3	0
1982-83			44	11	9	20	41
2 yrs.		N Totals:	49	12	11	23	41

Rejean Lemelin

LEMELIN, REJEAN 5'11", 160 lbs.
B. Nov. 19, 1954, Sherbrooke, Que. Shoots L

YEAR	TEAM & LEAGUE		GP	G	A	PTS	PIM
PLAYOFFS							
1980-81	CALG	N	6	0	0	0	0

Signed as free agent by **Atlanta** Aug. 17, 1978.

Roger Lemelin

LEMELIN, ROGER MARCEL 6'3", 215 lbs.
B. Feb. 6, 1954, Iroquois Falls, Ont. Defense, Shoots R

YEAR	TEAM & LEAGUE		GP	G	A	PTS	PIM
1974-75	KC	N	8	0	1	1	6
1975-76			11	0	0	0	0
2 yrs.		N Totals:	19	0	1	1	6

Alain Lemieux

LEMIEUX, ALAIN 6', 185 lbs.
B. May 24, 1961, Montreal, Que. Center, Shoots L

YEAR	TEAM & LEAGUE		GP	G	A	PTS	PIM
1981-82	STL	N	3	0	1	1	0
1982-83			42	9	25	34	18
2 yrs.		N Totals:	45	9	26	35	18
PLAYOFFS							
1982-83	STL	N	4	0	1	1	0

Jacques Lemieux

LEMIEUX, JACQUES 6'2", 185 lbs.
B. Apr. 8, 1943, Matane, Que. Forward, Shoots R

YEAR	TEAM & LEAGUE		GP	G	A	PTS	PIM
1967-68	LA	N	16	0	3	3	8
1968-69			75	11	29	40	68
2 yrs.		N Totals:	91	11	32	43	76
PLAYOFFS							
1968-69	LA	N	1	0	0	0	0

Dick Lemieux

LEMIEUX, RICHARD BERNARD 5'8", 160 lbs.
B. Apr. 19, 1951, Temiscamingue So., Que.
Center, Shoots L

YEAR	TEAM & LEAGUE		GP	G	A	PTS	PIM
1971-72	STL	N	42	7	9	16	4
1972-73	VAN	N	78	17	35	52	41
1973-74			72	5	17	22	23
1974-75	KC	N	79	10	20	30	64
1975-76			2	0	0	0	0
	ATL	N	1	0	1	1	0
	2 team total		3	0	1	1	0
1976-77	CALG	W	33	6	11	17	9
6 yrs.		N Totals:	274	39	82	121	132
		W Totals:	33	6	11	17	9
PLAYOFFS							
1975-76	ATL	N	2	0	0	0	0

Drafted by **Kansas City** from Vancouver in Expansion Draft, June 12, 1974. Traded to **Atlanta** by Kansas City with Kansas City's second round choice (Don Laurence) in 1977 Amateur Draft for Buster Harvey, Oct. 13, 1975.

Jean Lemieux

LEMIEUX, JEAN 6'1", 180 lbs.
B. May 31, 1952, Noranda, Que. Defense, Shoots R

YEAR	TEAM & LEAGUE		GP	G	A	PTS	PIM
1969-70	LA	N	3	0	1	1	0
1973-74	ATL	N	32	3	5	8	6
1974-75			75	3	24	27	19
1975-76			33	4	9	13	10
	WASH	N	33	6	14	20	2
	2 team total		66	10	23	33	12
1976-77			15	4	4	8	2
1977-78			16	3	7	10	0
6 yrs.		N Totals:	207	23	64	87	39
PLAYOFFS							
1973-74	ATL	N	3	1	1	2	0

Traded to **Washington** by Atlanta with Gerry Meehan and Buffalo's first choice (Greg Carroll) in 1976 Amateur Draft (which was Atlanta's property via an earlier deal) for Bill Clement, Jan. 22, 1976. Signed as free agent by **Montreal** Aug. 8, 1978.

Real Lemieux

LEMIEUX, REAL GASTON 5'11", 180 lbs.
B. Jan. 3, 1945, Victoriaville, Que. Left Wing, Shoots L

YEAR	TEAM & LEAGUE		GP	G	A	PTS	PIM
1966-67	DET	N	1	0	0	0	0
1967-68	LA	N	74	12	23	35	60
1969-70	NYR	N	55	4	6	10	51
	LA	N	18	2	4	6	0
	2 team total		73	6	10	16	51
1970-71			43	3	6	9	22
1971-72			78	13	25	38	28
1972-73			74	5	10	15	19
1973-74			20	0	0	0	0
	NYR	N	7	0	0	0	0
	BUF	N	11	1	1	2	4
	3 team total		38	1	1	2	4
7 yrs.		N Totals:	381	40	75	115	184
PLAYOFFS							
1967-68	LA	N	7	1	1	2	0
1968-69			11	1	3	4	10
2 yrs.		N Totals:	18	2	4	6	10

Drafted by **Los Angeles** from Detroit in Expansion Draft, June 6, 1967. Traded to **N.Y. Rangers** by Los Angeles for Leon Rochefort and Dennis Hextall, June 9, 1969. Traded to **Los Angeles** by N.Y. Rangers with Juha Widing for Ted Irvine, Feb. 28, 1970. Traded to **N.Y. Rangers** by Los Angeles with Gilles Marotte for Sheldon Kannegiesser, Mike Murphy and Tom Williams, Nov. 30, 1973. Traded to **Buffalo** by N.Y. Rangers for Paul Curtis, Jan. 21, 1974.

Hec Lepine

LEPINE, HECTOR
B. Unknown Forward

YEAR	TEAM & LEAGUE		GP	G	A	PTS	PIM
1925-26	MONT	N	33	5	2	7	2

Pit Lepine

LEPINE, ALFRED
B. July 30, 1901, Ste. Anne Bellevue, Que.
Center, Shoots L

YEAR	TEAM & LEAGUE		GP	G	A	PTS	PIM
1925-26	MONT	N	27	9	1	10	18
1926-27			44	16	1	17	20
1927-28			20	4	1	5	6
1928-29			44	6	1	7	48
1929-30			44	24	9	33	47
1930-31			44	17	7	24	63
1931-32			48	19	11	30	32
1932-33			46	8	8	16	45
1933-34			48	10	8	18	44
1934-35			48	12	19	31	16
1935-36			32	6	10	16	4
1936-37			34	7	8	15	15
1937-38			47	5	14	19	24
13 yrs.		N Totals:	526	143	98	241	382
PLAYOFFS							
1926-27	MONT	N	4	0	0	0	2
1927-28			1	0	0	0	0
1928-29			3	0	0	0	2
1929-30*			6	2	2	4	6
1930-31*			10	4	2	6	6
1931-32			3	1	0	1	4
1932-33			2	0	0	0	0
1933-34			2	0	0	0	0
1934-35			2	0	0	0	2
1936-37			5	0	1	1	0
1937-38			3	0	0	0	0
11 yrs.		N Totals:	41	7	5	12	22

Gaston Leroux

LEROUX, GASTON
B. Unknown Forward

YEAR	TEAM & LEAGUE		GP	G	A	PTS	PIM
1935-36	MONT	N	2	0	0	0	0

Gerry Leroux

LEROUX, GERALD 5'7", 160 lbs.
B. June 9, 1958, St. Bernardin, Ont. Left Wing, Shoots L

YEAR	TEAM & LEAGUE		GP	G	A	PTS	PIM
1978-79	IND	W	10	0	3	3	2

Art Lesieur

LESIEUR, ARTHUR 5'10½", 191 lbs.
B. Sept. 13, 1907, Fall River, Mass. Defense, Shoots R

YEAR	TEAM & LEAGUE		GP	G	A	PTS	PIM
1928-29	MONT	N	15	0	0	0	0
	CHI	N	2	0	0	0	0
	2 team total		17	0	0	0	0
1930-31	MONT	N	21	2	0	2	14
1931-32			24	1	2	3	12
1935-36			38	1	0	1	24
4 yrs.		N Totals:	100	4	2	6	50
PLAYOFFS							
1930-31*	MONT	N	10	0	0	0	4
1931-32			4	0	0	0	0
2 yrs.		N Totals:	14	0	0	0	4

Bill Lesuk

LESUK, WILLIAM ANTON 5'9", 187 lbs.
B. Nov. 1, 1946, Moose Jaw, Sask. Left Wing, Shoots L

YEAR	TEAM & LEAGUE		GP	G	A	PTS	PIM
1968-69	BOS	N	5	0	1	1	0
1969-70			3	0	0	0	0
1970-71	PHI	N	78	17	19	36	81
1971-72			45	7	6	13	31
	LA	N	27	4	10	14	14
	2 team total		72	11	16	27	45
1972-73			67	6	14	20	90
1973-74			35	2	1	3	32
1974-75	WASH	N	79	8	11	19	77
1975-76	WINN	W	81	15	21	36	92
1976-77			78	14	27	41	85
1977-78			80	9	18	27	48
1978-79			79	17	15	32	44
1979-80	WINN	N	49	0	1	1	43

Bill Lesuk continued

YEAR	TEAM & LEAGUE		GP	G	A	PTS	PIM
12 yrs.		N Totals:	388	44	63	107	368
		W Totals:	318	55	81	136	269
PLAYOFFS							
1968-69	BOS	N	1	0	0	0	0
1969-70*			2	0	0	0	0
1970-71	PHI	N	4	1	0	1	8
1973-74	LA	N	2	0	0	0	4
1975-76	WINN	W	13	2	2	4	8
1976-77			18	2	1	3	22
1977-78			9	2	5	7	12
1978-79			10	1	3	4	6
8 yrs.		N Totals:	9	1	0	1	12
		W Totals:	50	7	11	18	48

Drafted by **Philadelphia** from Boston in Intra-League Draft, June 9, 1970. Traded to **Los Angeles** by Philadelphia with Jim Johnson and Serge Bernier for Bill Flett, Ed Joyal, Jean Potvin and Ross Lonsberry, Jan. 28, 1972. Sold to **Washington** by Los Angeles July 29, 1974.

Jack Leswick

LESWICK, JACK

Forward

YEAR	TEAM & LEAGUE		GP	G	A	PTS	PIM
1933-34	CHI	N	47	1	7	8	16

Peter Leswick

LESWICK, PETER JOHN 5'6", 145 lbs.
B. July 12, 1918, Saskatoon, Sask. Right Wing, Shoots R

YEAR	TEAM & LEAGUE		GP	G	A	PTS	PIM
1936-37	NYA	N	1	1	0	1	0
1944-45	BOS	N	2	0	0	0	0
2 yrs.		N Totals:	3	1	0	1	0

Tony Leswick

LESWICK, ANTHONY JOSEPH (Tough Tony) 5'6", 160 lbs.
B. Mar. 17, 1923, Humboldt, Sask. Left Wing, Shoots R

YEAR	TEAM & LEAGUE		GP	G	A	PTS	PIM
1945-46	NYR	N	50	15	9	24	9
1946-47			59	27	14	41	51
1947-48			60	24	16	40	76
1948-49			60	13	14	27	70
1949-50			69	19	25	44	70
1950-51			70	15	11	26	112
1951-52	DET	N	70	9	10	19	93
1952-53			70	15	12	27	87
1953-54			70	6	18	24	90
1954-55			70	10	17	27	137
1955-56	CHI	N	70	11	11	22	71
1957-58	DET	N	22	1	2	3	2
12 yrs.		N Totals:	740	165	159	324	868
PLAYOFFS							
1947-48	NYR	N	6	3	2	5	8
1949-50			12	2	4	6	12
1951-52*	DET	N	8	3	1	4	22
1952-53			6	1	0	1	11
1953-54*			12	3	1	4	18
1954-55*			11	1	2	3	20
1957-58			4	0	0	0	0
7 yrs.		N Totals:	59	13	10	23	91

Traded to **Detroit** by N.Y. Rangers for Gaye Stewart, June 19, 1951. Traded to **Chicago** by Detroit with Glen Skov, Johnny Wilson and Benny Woit for Jerry Toppazzini, John McCormack, Dave Creighton and Gord Hollingworth, June 3, 1955.

Joseph Levandoski

LEVANDOSKI, JOSEPH THOMAS 5'10", 185 lbs.
B. Mar. 17, 1921, Cobalt, Ont. Right Wing, Shoots R

YEAR	TEAM & LEAGUE		GP	G	A	PTS	PIM
1946-47	NYR	N	8	1	1	2	0

Norm Leveille

LEVEILLE, NORMAND 5'10", 175 lbs.
B. Jan. 10, 1963, Montreal, Que. Left Wing, Shoots L

YEAR	TEAM & LEAGUE		GP	G	A	PTS	PIM
1981-82	BOS	N	66	14	19	33	49
1982-83			9	3	6	9	0

Norm Leveille continued

YEAR	TEAM & LEAGUE		GP	G	A	PTS	PIM
2 yrs.		N Totals:	75	17	25	42	49

Don Lever

LEVER, DONALD RICHARD (Cleaver) 5'11", 175 lbs.
B. Nov. 14, 1952, S. Porcupine, Ont. Center, Shoots L

YEAR	TEAM & LEAGUE		GP	G	A	PTS	PIM
1972-73	VAN	N	78	12	26	38	49
1973-74			78	23	25	48	28
1974-75			80	38	30	68	49
1975-76			80	25	40	65	43
1976-77			80	27	30	57	28
1977-78			75	17	32	49	58
1978-79			71	23	21	44	17
1979-80			51	21	17	38	32
	ATL	N	28	14	16	30	4
	2 team total		79	35	33	68	36
1980-81	CALG	N	62	26	31	57	56
1981-82			23	8	11	19	6
	COLO	N	59	22	28	50	70
	2 team total		82	30	39	69	76
1982-83	NJ	N	79	23	30	53	68
11 yrs.		N Totals:	844	279	337	616	508
PLAYOFFS							
1974-75	VAN	N	5	0	1	1	4
1975-76			2	0	0	0	0
1978-79			3	2	1	3	2
1979-80	ATL	N	4	1	1	2	0
1980-81	CALG	N	16	4	7	11	20
5 yrs.		N Totals:	30	7	10	17	26

Traded to **Atlanta** by Vancouver with Brad Smith for Ivan Boldirev and Darcy Rota, Feb. 8, 1980. Traded to **Colorado** by Calgary along with Bob MacMillan for Lanny McDonald and Colorado's fourth round choice in 1982 Entry Draft (later transferred to N.Y. Islanders, Mikko Makela) Nov. 25, 1981.

Craig Levie

LEVIE, CRAIG DEAN 5'11", 190 lbs.
B. Aug. 17, 1959, Calgary, Alta. Defense, Shoots R

YEAR	TEAM & LEAGUE		GP	G	A	PTS	PIM
1981-82	WINN	N	40	4	9	13	48
1982-83			22	4	5	9	31
2 yrs.		N Totals:	62	8	14	22	79

Claimed by **Winnipeg** from Montreal in 1981 Waiver Draft, Oct. 5, 1981. Traded to **Minnesota** by Winnipeg with the rights to college player Tom Ward for Tim Young, Sept. 3, 1983.

Alex Levinsky

LEVINSKY, ALEXANDER (Mine Boy) 5'10", 184 lbs.
B. Feb. 2, 1910, Syracuse, N.Y. Defense, Shoots R

YEAR	TEAM & LEAGUE		GP	G	A	PTS	PIM
1930-31	TOR	N	8	0	1	1	2
1931-32			47	5	5	10	29
1932-33			48	5	11	16	61
1933-34			47	5	11	16	38
1934-35	NYR	N	21	0	4	4	6
	CHI	N	23	3	4	7	16
	2 team total		44	3	8	11	22
1935-36			48	1	7	8	69
1936-37			48	0	8	8	32
1937-38			48	3	2	5	18
1938-39			29	1	3	4	16
9 yrs.		N Totals:	367	23	56	79	287
PLAYOFFS							
1930-31	TOR	N	2	0	0	0	0
1931-32*			7	0	0	0	6
1932-33			9	1	0	1	14
1933-34			5	0	0	0	0
1934-35	CHI	N	2	0	0	0	0
1935-36			2	0	1	1	0
1937-38*			7	1	0	1	0
7 yrs.		N Totals:	34	2	1	3	20

Tapio Levo

LEVO, TAPIO 6'2", 200 lbs.
B. Sept. 24, 1956, Pori, Finland Defense, Shoots L

YEAR	TEAM & LEAGUE		GP	G	A	PTS	PIM
1981-82	**COLO**	**N**	34	9	13	22	14
1982-83	**NJ**	**N**	73	7	40	47	22
2 yrs.		**N Totals:**	107	16	53	69	36

Signed as free agent by **Colorado** July 8, 1981.

Danny Lewicki

LEWICKI, DANIEL 5'9", 165 lbs.
B. Mar. 12, 1931, Fort William, Ont. Left Wing, Shoots L

YEAR	TEAM & LEAGUE		GP	G	A	PTS	PIM
1950-51	**TOR**	**N**	61	16	18	34	26
1951-52			51	4	9	13	26
1952-53			4	1	3	4	2
1953-54			7	0	1	1	12
1954-55	**NYR**	**N**	70	29	24	53	8
1955-56			70	18	27	45	26
1956-57			70	18	20	38	47
1957-58			70	11	19	30	26
1958-59	**CHI**	**N**	58	8	14	22	4
9 yrs.		**N Totals:**	461	105	135	240	177

PLAYOFFS

YEAR	TEAM & LEAGUE		GP	G	A	PTS	PIM
1950-51*	**TOR**	**N**	9	0	0	0	0
1955-56	**NYR**	**N**	5	0	3	3	0
1956-57			5	0	1	1	2
1957-58			6	0	0	0	6
1958-59	**CHI**	**N**	3	0	0	0	0
5 yrs.		**N Totals:**	28	0	4	4	8

Sold to **N.Y. Rangers** by Toronto, July 20, 1954. Drafted by **Montreal** from N.Y. Rangers, June 4, 1958.

Bob Lewis

LEWIS, ROBERT DALE 6', 190 lbs.
B. July 28, 1952, Edmonton, Alta. Left Wing, Shoots L

YEAR	TEAM & LEAGUE		GP	G	A	PTS	PIM
1975-76	**NYR**	**N**	8	0	0	0	0

Drafted by **N.Y. Rangers** from Los Angeles in Intra-league Draft, June 17, 1975. Signed as free agent by **Atlanta** Sept. 11, 1979.

Dave Lewis

LEWIS, DAVID RODNEY (Lewie) 6'2", 205 lbs.
B. July 3, 1953, Kindersley, Sask. Defense, Shoots L

YEAR	TEAM & LEAGUE		GP	G	A	PTS	PIM
1973-74	**NYI**	**N**	66	2	15	17	58
1974-75			78	5	14	19	98
1975-76			73	0	19	19	54
1976-77			79	4	24	28	44
1977-78			77	3	11	14	58
1978-79			79	5	18	23	43
1979-80			62	5	16	21	54
	LA	**N**	11	1	1	2	12
	2 team total		73	6	17	23	66
1980-81			67	1	12	13	98
1981-82			64	1	13	14	75
1982-83			79	2	10	12	53
10 yrs.		**N Totals:**	735	29	153	182	647

PLAYOFFS

YEAR	TEAM & LEAGUE		GP	G	A	PTS	PIM
1974-75	**NYI**	**N**	17	0	1	1	28
1975-76			13	0	1	1	44
1976-77			12	1	6	7	4
1977-78			7	0	1	1	11
1978-79			10	0	0	0	4
1979-80	**LA**	**N**	4	0	1	1	2
1980-81			4	0	2	2	4
1981-82			10	0	4	4	36
8 yrs.		**N Totals:**	77	1	16	17	133

Traded to **Los Angeles** by N.Y. Islanders with Billy Harris for Butch Goring, Mar. 10, 1980.

Douglas Lewis

LEWIS, DOUGLAS 5'8", 155 lbs.
B. Mar. 3, 1921, Winnipeg, Man. Left Wing, Shoots L

YEAR	TEAM & LEAGUE		GP	G	A	PTS	PIM
1946-47	**MONT**	**N**	3	0	0	0	0

Herbie Lewis

LEWIS, HERBERT 5'9", 160 lbs.
B. Apr. 17, 1907, Calgary, Alta. Left Wing, Shoots L

YEAR	TEAM & LEAGUE		GP	G	A	PTS	PIM
1928-29	**DET**	**N**	37	9	5	14	33
1929-30			44	20	11	31	36
1930-31			44	15	6	21	38
1931-32			48	5	14	19	21
1932-33			48	20	14	34	20
1933-34			43	16	15	31	15
1934-35			48	16	27	43	26
1935-36			45	14	23	37	25
1936-37			45	14	18	32	14
1937-38			42	13	18	31	12
1938-39			39	6	10	16	8
11 yrs.		**N Totals:**	483	148	161	309	248

PLAYOFFS

YEAR	TEAM & LEAGUE		GP	G	A	PTS	PIM
1931-32	**DET**	**N**	2	0	0	0	0
1932-33			4	1	0	1	0
1933-34			9	5	2	7	2
1935-36*			7	2	3	5	0
1936-37*			10	4	3	7	4
1938-39			6	1	2	3	0
6 yrs.		**N Totals:**	38	13	10	23	6

Rick Ley

LEY, RICHARD NORMAN 5'9", 185 lbs.
B. Nov. 2, 1948, Orillia, Ont. Defense, Shoots L

YEAR	TEAM & LEAGUE		GP	G	A	PTS	PIM
1968-69	**TOR**	**N**	38	1	11	12	39
1969-70			48	2	13	15	102
1970-71			76	4	16	20	151
1971-72			67	1	14	15	124
1972-73	**NE**	**W**	76	3	27	30	108
1973-74			72	6	35	41	148
1974-75			62	6	36	42	50
1975-76			67	8	30	38	78
1976-77			55	2	21	23	102
1977-78			73	3	41	44	95
1978-79			73	7	20	27	135
1979-80	**HART**	**N**	65	4	16	20	92
1980-81			16	0	2	2	20
13 yrs.		**N Totals:**	310	12	72	84	528
		W Totals:	478	35	210	245	716

PLAYOFFS

YEAR	TEAM & LEAGUE		GP	G	A	PTS	PIM
1968-69	**TOR**	**N**	3	0	0	0	9
1970-71			6	0	2	2	4
1971-72			5	0	0	0	7
1972-73	**NE**	**W**	15	3	7	10	24
1973-74			7	1	5	6	18
1974-75			6	1	1	2	32
1975-76			17	1	4	5	49
1976-77			5	0	4	4	4
1977-78			14	1	8	9	4
1978-79			9	0	4	4	11
10 yrs.		**N Totals:**	14	0	2	2	20
		W Totals:	73	7	33	40	142

Reclaimed by **Toronto** from Hartford prior to Expansion Draft, June 9, 1979. Claimed by **Hartford** from Toronto in Expansion Draft, June 13, 1979.

Nick Libett

LIBETT, LYNN NICHOLAS 6'1", 195 lbs.
B. Dec. 9, 1945, Stratford, Ont. Left Wing, Shoots L

YEAR	TEAM & LEAGUE		GP	G	A	PTS	PIM
1967-68	**DET**	**N**	22	2	1	3	12
1968-69			75	10	14	24	34
1969-70			76	20	20	40	39
1970-71			78	16	13	29	25
1971-72			77	31	22	53	50
1972-73			78	19	34	53	56
1973-74			67	24	24	48	37

Nick Libett continued

YEAR	TEAM	LEAGUE	GP	G	A	PTS	PIM
1974-75			80	23	28	51	39
1975-76	KC	N	80	20	26	46	71
1976-77	DET	N	80	14	27	41	25
1977-78			80	23	22	45	46
1978-79			68	15	19	34	20
1979-80	PITT	N	78	14	12	26	14
1980-81			43	6	6	12	4
14 yrs.		N Totals:	982	237	268	505	472
PLAYOFFS							
1969-70	DET	N	4	2	0	2	2
1977-78			7	3	1	4	0
1979-80	PITT	N	5	1	1	2	0
3 yrs.		N Totals:	16	6	2	8	2

Traded to **Pittsburgh** by Detroit for Peter Mahovlich, Aug. 3, 1979.

Anthony Licari

LICARI, ANTHONY 5'7", 147 lbs.
B. Apr. 9, 1921, Ottawa, Ont. Right Wing

YEAR	TEAM	LEAGUE	GP	G	A	PTS	PIM
1946-47	DET	N	9	0	1	1	0

Bob Liddington

LIDDINGTON, ROBERT ALLEN 6', 175 lbs.
B. Sept. 15, 1948, Calgary, Alta. Left Wing, Shoots L

YEAR	TEAM	LEAGUE	GP	G	A	PTS	PIM
1970-71	TOR	N	11	0	1	1	2
1972-73	CHI	W	78	20	11	31	24
1973-74			73	26	21	47	20
1974-75			78	23	18	41	27
1975-76	D-O	W	35	7	8	15	14
	HOUS	W	2	0	0	0	2
	2 team total		37	7	8	15	16
1976-77	PHOE	W	80	20	24	44	28
6 yrs.		N Totals:	11	0	1	1	2
		W Totals:	346	96	82	178	115
PLAYOFFS							
1973-74	CHI	W	18	6	5	11	11

Len Lilyholm

LILYHOLM, LEONARD 5'8", 163 lbs.
B. Apr. 1, 1941, Minneapolis, Minn. Left Wing, Shoots R

YEAR	TEAM	LEAGUE	GP	G	A	PTS	PIM
1972-73	MINN	W	77	8	13	21	37
PLAYOFFS							
1972-73	MINN	W	5	1	0	1	0

Lars Lindgren

LINDGREN, LARS 6'1", 208 lbs.
B. Oct. 12, 1952, Pitea, Sweden Defense, Shoots L

YEAR	TEAM	LEAGUE	GP	G	A	PTS	PIM
1978-79	VAN	N	64	2	19	21	68
1979-80			73	5	30	35	66
1980-81			52	4	18	22	32
1981-82			75	5	16	21	74
1982-83			64	6	14	20	48
5 yrs.		N Totals:	328	22	97	119	288
PLAYOFFS							
1978-79	VAN	N	3	0	0	0	6
1979-80			2	0	1	1	0
1981-82			16	2	4	6	6
1982-83			4	1	1	2	2
4 yrs.		N Totals:	25	3	6	9	14

Signed as free agent by **Vancouver** June 5, 1978.

Mats Lindh

LINDH, MATS 6'1", 180 lbs.
B. Sept. 12, 1947 Defense, Shoots L

YEAR	TEAM	LEAGUE	GP	G	A	PTS	PIM
1975-76	WINN	W	65	19	15	34	12
1976-77			73	14	17	31	2
2 yrs.		W Totals:	138	33	32	65	14
PLAYOFFS							
1975-76	WINN	W	13	2	2	4	4

Mats Lindh continued

YEAR	TEAM	LEAGUE	GP	G	A	PTS	PIM
1976-77			20	2	7	9	2
2 yrs.		W Totals:	33	4	9	13	6

Ted Lindsay

LINDSAY, ROBERT BLAKE THEODORE 5'8", 160 lbs.
B. July 29, 1925, Renfrew, Ont. Left Wing, Shoots L
Won Art Ross Trophy, 1949-50
Hall of Fame, 1966

YEAR	TEAM	LEAGUE	GP	G	A	PTS	PIM
1944-45	DET	N	45	17	6	23	43
1945-46			47	7	10	17	14
1946-47			59	27	15	42	57
1947-48			60	**33**	19	52	95
1948-49			50	26	28	54	97
1949-50			69	23	**55**	**78**	141
1950-51			67	24	35	59	110
1951-52			70	30	39	69	123
1952-53			70	32	39	71	111
1953-54			70	26	36	62	110
1954-55			49	19	19	38	85
1955-56			67	27	23	50	**161**
1956-57			70	30	**55**	85	103
1957-58	CHI	N	68	15	24	39	110
1958-59			70	22	36	58	**184**
1959-60			68	7	19	26	91
1964-65	DET	N	69	14	14	28	173
17 yrs.		N Totals:	1068	379	472	851	1808
PLAYOFFS							
1944-45	DET	N	14	2	0	2	6
1945-46			5	0	1	1	0
1946-47			5	2	2	4	10
1947-48			10	3	1	4	6
1948-49			11	2	6	8	31
1949-50*			13	4	4	8	16
1950-51			6	0	1	1	8
1951-52*			8	5	2	7	8
1952-53			6	4	4	8	6
1953-54*			12	4	4	8	14
1954-55*			11	7	12	19	12
1955-56			10	6	3	9	22
1956-57			5	2	4	6	8
1958-59	CHI	N	6	2	4	6	13
1959-60			4	1	1	2	0
1964-65	DET	N	7	3	0	3	34
16 yrs.		N Totals:	133	47	49	96	194

Traded to **Chicago** with Glenn Hall by Detroit for Johnny Wilson, Hank Bassen, Forbes Kennedy and Bill Preston, July 23, 1957. Rights purchased by **Detroit** from Chicago, Oct. 14, 1964.

Doug Lindskog

LINDSKOG, DOUGLAS 6'1", 186 lbs.
B. Aug. 12, 1955, Red Deer, Alta. Left Wing, Shoots L

YEAR	TEAM	LEAGUE	GP	G	A	PTS	PIM
1976-77	CALG	W	2	0	0	0	2

Willy Lindstrom

LINDSTROM, BO MORGAN WILLY (Willy the Wisp) 6', 180 lbs.
B. May 5, 1961, Brunns, Sweden Right Wing, Shoots L

YEAR	TEAM	LEAGUE	GP	G	A	PTS	PIM
1975-76	WINN	W	81	23	36	59	32
1976-77			79	44	36	80	37
1977-78			77	30	30	60	42
1978-79			79	26	36	62	22
1979-80	WINN	N	79	23	26	49	20
1980-81			72	22	13	35	45
1981-82			74	32	27	59	33
1982-83			63	20	25	45	8
	EDM	N	10	6	5	11	2
	2 team total		73	26	30	56	10
8 yrs.		N Totals:	298	103	96	199	108
		W Totals:	316	123	138	261	133
PLAYOFFS							
1975-76	WINN	W	13	4	7	11	2
1976-77			20	9	6	15	22
1977-78			8	3	4	7	17

Willy Lindstrom continued

YEAR	TEAM	LEAGUE	GP	G	A	PTS	PIM
1978-79			10	10	5	15	9
1981-82	**WINN**	**N**	4	2	1	3	2
1982-83	**EDM**	**N**	16	2	11	13	4
6 yrs.		**N Totals:**	20	4	12	16	6
		W Totals:	51	26	22	48	50

Signed as free agent by **Winnipeg** July 25, 1979. Traded to **Edmonton** by Winnipeg for Laurie Boschman, March 8, 1983.

Ken Linseman

LINSEMAN, KEN (The Rat) 5'11", 175 lbs.
B. Aug. 11, 1958, Kingston, Ont. Center, Shoots L

YEAR	TEAM	LEAGUE	GP	G	A	PTS	PIM
1977-78	**BIRM**	**W**	71	38	38	76	126
1978-79	**PHI**	**N**	30	5	20	25	23
1979-80			80	22	57	79	107
1980-81			51	17	30	47	150
1981-82			79	24	68	92	275
1982-83	**EDM**	**N**	72	33	42	75	181
6 yrs.		**N Totals:**	312	101	217	318	736
		W Totals:	71	38	38	76	126
PLAYOFFS							
1977-78	**BIRM**	**W**	5	2	2	4	15
1978-79	**PHI**	**N**	8	2	6	8	22
1979-80			17	4	18	22	40
1980-81			12	4	16	20	67
1981-82			4	1	2	3	6
1982-83	**EDM**	**N**	16	6	8	14	22
6 yrs.		**N Totals:**	57	17	50	67	157
		W Totals:	5	2	2	4	15

Traded to **Hartford** with Greg Adams and a first (David Jensen) and third (Dave McLean) round choice in the 1983 Amateur Draft by Philadelphia for Mark Howe and Hartford's third choice (Derrick Smith) in 1983 Amateur Draft, Aug. 19, 1982. Traded to **Edmonton** by Hartford with Don Nachbur for Risto Siltanen and Brent Loney, August 19, 1982.

Carl Liscombe

LISCOMBE, CARL 5'8", 170 lbs.
B. May 17, 1915, Perth, Ont. Left Wing, Shoots L

YEAR	TEAM	LEAGUE	GP	G	A	PTS	PIM
1937-38	**DET**	**N**	42	14	10	24	30
1938-39			47	8	18	26	13
1939-40			30	2	7	9	4
1940-41			31	10	10	20	0
1941-42			47	13	17	30	30
1942-43			50	19	23	42	19
1943-44			50	36	37	73	17
1944-45			42	23	9	32	18
1945-46			44	12	9	21	2
9 yrs.		**N Totals:**	383	137	140	277	133
PLAYOFFS							
1938-39	**DET**	**N**	6	0	0	0	2
1940-41			8	4	3	7	12
1941-42			12	6	6	12	2
1942-43*			10	6	8	14	2
1943-44			5	1	0	1	2
1944-45			14	4	2	6	0
1945-46			4	1	0	1	0
7 yrs.		**N Totals:**	59	22	19	41	20

Ed Litzenberger

LITZENBERGER, EDWARD C.J. 6'3", 194 lbs.
B. July 15, 1932, Neudorf, Sask. Right Wing, Shoots R
Won Calder Trophy, 1954-55

YEAR	TEAM	LEAGUE	GP	G	A	PTS	PIM
1952-53	**MONT**	**N**	2	1	0	1	2
1953-54			3	0	0	0	0
1954-55			29	7	4	11	12
	CHI	**N**	44	16	24	40	28
	2 team total		73	23	28	51	40
1955-56			70	10	29	39	36
1956-57			70	32	32	64	48
1957-58			70	32	30	62	63
1958-59			70	33	44	77	37
1959-60			52	12	18	30	15
1960-61			62	10	22	32	14
1961-62	**DET**	**N**	32	8	12	20	4
	TOR	**N**	37	10	10	20	14
	2 team total		69	18	22	40	18

Ed Litzenberger continued

YEAR	TEAM	LEAGUE	GP	G	A	PTS	PIM
1962-63			58	5	13	18	10
1963-64			19	2	0	2	0
12 yrs.		**N Totals:**	618	178	238	416	283
PLAYOFFS							
1958-59	**CHI**	**N**	6	3	5	8	8
1959-60			4	0	1	1	4
1960-61*			10	1	3	4	2
1961-62*	**TOR**	**N**	10	0	2	2	4
1962-63*			9	1	2	3	6
1963-64*			1	0	0	0	10
6 yrs.		**N Totals:**	40	5	13	18	34

Sold to **Chicago** by Mont. Canadiens, Dec., 1954. Traded to **Detroit** by Chicago for Gerry Melnyk and Brian Smith, June, 1961. Claimed on waivers by **Toronto** from Detroit, Dec., 1961.

Owen Lloyd

LLOYD, OWEN 5'11", 194 lbs.
B. Apr. 30, 1957, Vancouver, B.C. Defense, Shoots L

YEAR	TEAM	LEAGUE	GP	G	A	PTS	PIM
1977-78	**EDM**	**W**	3	0	1	1	4

Jacques Locas

LOCAS, JACQUES 5'11", 175 lbs.
B. Feb. 12, 1926, Pointe aux Trembles, Que
Center, Shoots R

YEAR	TEAM	LEAGUE	GP	G	A	PTS	PIM
1947-48	**MONT**	**N**	56	7	8	15	66
1948-49			3	0	0	0	0
2 yrs.		**N Totals:**	59	7	8	15	66

Jacques Locas

LOCAS, JACQUES ROMEO 5'8", 170 lbs.
B. Jan. 7, 1954, St. Jerome, Que. Center, Shoots L

YEAR	TEAM	LEAGUE	GP	G	A	PTS	PIM
1974-75	**M-B**	**W**	12	1	4	5	4
	IND	**W**	11	0	1	1	2
	2 team total		23	1	5	6	6
1975-76	**CIN**	**W**	80	27	46	73	70
1976-77			45	18	13	31	27
	CALG	**W**	22	3	4	7	2
	2 team total		67	21	17	38	29
1977-78	**CIN**	**W**	17	0	2	2	6
4 yrs.		**W Totals:**	187	49	70	119	111

Bill Lochead

LOCHEAD, WILLIAM ALEXANDER 6'1", 190 lbs.
B. Oct. 13, 1954, Forest, Ont. Left Wing, Shoots R

YEAR	TEAM	LEAGUE	GP	G	A	PTS	PIM
1974-75	**DET**	**N**	65	16	12	28	34
1975-76			53	9	11	20	22
1976-77			61	16	14	30	39
1977-78			77	20	16	36	47
1978-79			40	4	7	11	20
	COLO	**N**	27	4	2	6	14
	2 team total		67	8	9	17	34
1979-80	**NYR**	**N**	7	0	0	0	4
6 yrs.		**N Totals:**	330	69	62	131	180
PLAYOFFS							
1977-78	**DET**	**N**	7	3	0	3	6

Norm Locking

LOCKING, NORMAN WESLEY 6', 165 lbs.
B. May 24, 1911, Owen Sound, Ont. Left Wing, Shoots L

YEAR	TEAM	LEAGUE	GP	G	A	PTS	PIM
1934-35	**CHI**	**N**	35	2	5	7	19
1935-36			13	0	1	1	7
2 yrs.		**N Totals:**	48	2	6	8	26
PLAYOFFS							
1934-35	**CHI**	**N**	1	0	0	0	0

Dan Lodboa

LODBOA, DANIEL STEPHEN (Boa) 5'9", 178 lbs.
B. Sept. 25, 1946, Thorold, Ont. Left Wing, Shoots L

YEAR	TEAM	LEAGUE	GP	G	A	PTS	PIM
1972-73	**CHI**	**W**	58	15	18	33	16

Mark Lofthouse

LOFTHOUSE, MARK 6'1", 185 lbs.
B. Apr. 21, 1957, New Westminster, B.C. Right Wing, Shoots R

YEAR	TEAM & LEAGUE		GP	G	A	PTS	PIM
1977-78	**WASH**	**N**	18	2	1	3	8
1978-79			52	13	10	23	10
1979-80			68	15	18	33	20
1980-81			3	1	1	2	4
1981-82	**DET**	**N**	12	3	4	7	13
1982-83			28	8	4	12	18
6 yrs.		**N Totals:**	181	42	38	80	73

Traded to **Detroit** by Washington for Al Jensen, July 23, 1981.

Dave Logan

LOGAN, DAVID GEORGE 5'10", 190 lbs.
B. July 2, 1954, Montreal, Que. Defense, Shoots L

YEAR	TEAM & LEAGUE		GP	G	A	PTS	PIM
1975-76	**CHI**	**N**	2	0	0	0	0
1976-77			34	0	2	2	61
1977-78			54	1	5	6	77
1978-79			76	1	14	15	176
1979-80			12	2	3	5	34
	VAN	**N**	33	1	5	6	109
	2 team total		45	3	8	11	143
1980-81			7	0	0	0	13
6 yrs.		**N Totals:**	218	5	29	34	470
PLAYOFFS							
1977-78	**CHI**	**N**	4	0	0	0	8
1978-79			4	0	0	0	2
1979-80	**VAN**	**N**	4	0	0	0	0
3 yrs.		**N Totals:**	12	0	0	0	10

Traded to **Vancouver** by Chicago with Harold Phillipoff for Ron Sedlbauer, Dec. 21, 1979. Signed as a free agent by **Philadelphia** Mar. 6, 1981.

Claude Loiselle

LOISELLE, CLAUDE 5'11", 171 lbs.
B. May 29, 1963, Ottawa, Ont. Center, Shoots L

YEAR	TEAM & LEAGUE		GP	G	A	PTS	PIM
1981-82	**DET**	**N**	4	1	0	1	2
1982-83			18	2	0	2	15
2 yrs.		**N Totals:**	22	3	0	3	17

Mark Lomenda

LOMENDA, MARK WESLEY THOMAS 6', 186 lbs.
B. Apr. 14, 1954, Esterhazy, Sask. Right Wing, Shoots R

YEAR	TEAM & LEAGUE		GP	G	A	PTS	PIM
1974-75	**CHI**	**W**	69	16	33	49	21
1975-76	**D-O**	**W**	37	6	16	22	11
	IND	**W**	2	0	0	0	0
	2 team total		39	6	16	22	11
1976-77			56	9	12	21	14
3 yrs.		**W Totals:**	164	31	61	92	46
PLAYOFFS							
1976-77	**IND**	**W**	9	3	1	4	17

Barry Long

LONG, BARRY KENNETH 6'2", 210 lbs.
B. Jan. 3, 1949, Brantford, Ont. Defense, Shoots L

YEAR	TEAM & LEAGUE		GP	G	A	PTS	PIM
1972-73	**LA**	**N**	70	2	13	15	48
1973-74			60	3	19	22	118
1974-75	**EDM**	**W**	78	20	40	60	116
1975-76			78	10	32	42	66
1976-77			2	0	1	1	2
	WINN	**W**	71	9	38	47	54
	2 team total		73	9	39	48	56
1977-78			78	7	24	31	42
1978-79			79	5	36	41	42
1979-80	**DET**	**N**	80	0	17	17	38
1980-81	**WINN**	**N**	65	6	17	23	42
1981-82			5	0	2	2	4
10 yrs.		**N Totals:**	280	11	68	79	250
		W Totals:	386	51	171	222	322
PLAYOFFS							
1973-74	**LA**	**N**	5	0	1	1	18
1975-76	**EDM**	**W**	4	0	0	0	4

Barry Long continued

YEAR	TEAM & LEAGUE		GP	G	A	PTS	PIM
1976-77	**WINN**	**W**	20	1	5	6	10
1977-78			9	0	5	5	6
1978-79			10	2	3	5	0
5 yrs.		**N Totals:**	5	0	1	1	18
		W Totals:	43	3	13	16	20

Drafted by **Los Angeles** from Chicago in Intra-League Draft, June 5, 1972. Rights traded to **Detroit** by Los Angeles with Montreal's third round choice (Doug Derkson) in the 1978 Amateur Draft (Los Angeles' property via earlier deal) for Danny Grant, Jan. 9, 1979. Reclaimed by **Detroit** from Winnipeg prior to Expansion Draft, June 9, 1979. Sold to **Winnipeg** by Detroit, Oct. 31, 1980.

Stanley Long

LONG, STANLEY GORDON 5'11", 190 lbs.
B. Nov. 6, 1929, Owen Sound, Ont. Defense, Shoots L

YEAR	TEAM & LEAGUE		GP	G	A	PTS	PIM
PLAYOFFS							
1951-52	**MONT**	**N**	3	0	0	0	0

Ted Long

LONG, EDWARD 6'1", 185 lbs.
B. Jan. 26, 1955, Woodstock, Ont. Defense, Shoots L

YEAR	TEAM & LEAGUE		GP	G	A	PTS	PIM
1976-77	**CIN**	**W**	1	0	0	0	0

Ross Lonsberry

LONSBERRY, DAVID ROSS 5'11", 195 lbs.
B. Feb. 7, 1947, Humboldt, Sask. Left Wing, Shoots L

YEAR	TEAM & LEAGUE		GP	G	A	PTS	PIM
1966-67	**BOS**	**N**	8	0	0	0	2
1967-68			19	2	2	4	12
1968-69			6	0	0	0	2
1969-70	**LA**	**N**	76	20	22	42	118
1970-71			76	25	28	53	80
1971-72			50	9	14	23	39
	PHI	**N**	32	7	7	14	22
	2 team total		82	16	21	37	61
1972-73			77	21	29	50	59
1973-74			75	32	19	51	48
1974-75			80	24	25	49	99
1975-76			80	19	28	47	87
1976-77			75	23	32	55	43
1977-78			78	18	30	48	45
1978-79	**PITT**	**N**	80	24	22	46	38
1979-80			76	15	18	33	36
1980-81			80	17	33	50	76
15 yrs.		**N Totals:**	968	256	309	565	806
PLAYOFFS							
1972-73	**PHI**	**N**	11	4	3	7	9
1973-74*			17	4	9	13	18
1974-75*			17	4	3	7	10
1975-76			16	4	3	7	2
1976-77			10	1	2	3	29
1977-78			12	2	2	4	6
1978-79	**PITT**	**N**	7	0	2	2	9
1979-80			5	2	1	3	2
1980-81			5	0	0	0	2
9 yrs.		**N Totals:**	100	21	25	46	87

Traded to **Los Angeles** by Boston with Eddie Shack for Los Angeles' first choices in the 1971 (Ron Jones) and 1973 (Andre Savard) Amateur Drafts and Ken Turlik, May 14, 1969. Traded to **Philadelphia** by Los Angeles with Bill Flett, Ed Joyal, and Jean Potvin for Bill Lesuk, Jim Johnson and Serge Bernier, Jan. 28, 1972. Traded to **Pittsburgh** by Philadelphia with Tom Bladon and Orest Kindrachuk for Pittsburgh's first choice (Behn Wilson) in the 1978 Amateur Draft and other considerations, June 14, 1978.

Jim Lorentz

LORENTZ, JAMES PETER 6', 180 lbs.
B. May 1, 1947, Waterloo, Ont. Center, Shoots L

YEAR	TEAM & LEAGUE		GP	G	A	PTS	PIM
1968-69	**BOS**	**N**	11	1	3	4	6
1969-70			68	7	16	23	30
1970-71	**STL**	**N**	76	19	21	40	34
1971-72			12	0	1	1	12
	NYR	**N**	7	0	0	0	0
	BUF	**N**	33	10	14	24	12
	3 team total		52	10	15	25	24
1972-73			78	27	35	62	30

Jim Lorentz continued

YEAR	TEAM & LEAGUE		GP	G	A	PTS	PIM
1973-74			78	23	31	54	28
1974-75			72	25	45	70	18
1975-76			75	17	24	41	18
1976-77			79	23	33	56	8
1977-78			70	9	15	24	12
10 yrs.		N Totals:	659	161	238	399	208
PLAYOFFS							
1969-70*	BOS	N	11	1	0	1	4
1970-71	STL	N	6	0	1	1	4
1972-73	BUF	N	6	0	3	3	2
1974-75			16	6	4	10	6
1975-76			9	1	2	3	6
1976-77			6	4	0	4	8
6 yrs.		N Totals:	54	12	10	22	30

Traded to **St. Louis** by Boston for St. Louis' first choice (Ron Plumb) in the 1970 Amateur Draft, May 22, 1970. Traded to **N.Y. Rangers** by St. Louis with Gene Carr and Wayne Connelly for Jack Egers, Andre Dupont and Mike Murphy, Nov. 15, 1971. Traded to **Buffalo** by N.Y. Rangers for Buffalo's second choice (Larry Sacharuk) in 1972 Amateur Draft, Jan. 14, 1972.

Bob Lorimer

LORIMER, ROBERT ROY — 6'1", 190 lbs.
B. Aug. 25, 1953, Toronto, Ont. — Defense, Shoots R

YEAR	TEAM & LEAGUE		GP	G	A	PTS	PIM
1976-77	NYI	N	1	0	1	1	0
1977-78			5	1	0	1	0
1978-79			67	3	18	21	42
1979-80			74	3	16	19	53
1980-81			73	1	12	13	77
1981-82	COLO	N	79	5	15	20	68
1982-83	NJ	N	66	3	10	13	42
7 yrs.		N Totals:	365	16	72	88	282
PLAYOFFS							
1978-79	NYI	N	10	1	3	4	15
1979-80*			21	1	3	4	41
1980-81*			18	1	4	5	27
3 yrs.		N Totals:	49	3	10	13	83

Traded to **Colorado** by N.Y. Islanders along with Dave Cameron for Colorado's first round choice in 1983 Entry Draft, Oct. 1, 1981.

Rod Lorrain

LORRAIN, RODRIGUE — 5'5", 156 lbs.
B. Buckingham, Que. — Right Wing, Shoots R

YEAR	TEAM & LEAGUE		GP	G	A	PTS	PIM
1935-36	MONT	N	1	0	0	0	2
1936-37			47	3	6	9	8
1937-38			48	13	19	32	14
1938-39			38	10	9	19	0
1939-40			41	1	5	6	6
1941-42			4	1	0	1	0
6 yrs.		N Totals:	179	28	39	67	30
PLAYOFFS							
1936-37	MONT	N	5	0	0	0	0
1937-38			3	0	0	0	0
1938-39			3	0	3	3	0
3 yrs.		N Totals:	11	0	3	3	0

Clem Loughlin

LOUGHLIN, CLEMENT — 6', 180 lbs.
B. Nov. 15, 1894, Carroll, Man. — Defense

YEAR	TEAM & LEAGUE		GP	G	A	PTS	PIM
1926-27	DET	N	34	7	3	10	40
1927-28			43	1	2	3	21
1928-29	CHI	N	24	0	1	1	16
3 yrs.		N Totals:	101	8	6	14	77

Wilf Loughlin

LOUGHLIN, WILF
B. Unknown

YEAR	TEAM & LEAGUE		GP	G	A	PTS	PIM
1923-24	TOR	N	14	0	0	0	2

Dwayne Lowdermilk

LOWDERMILK, DWAYNE KENNETH — 6', 201 lbs.
B. Jan. 9, 1958, Burnaby, B.C. — Defense, Shoots R

YEAR	TEAM & LEAGUE		GP	G	A	PTS	PIM
1980-81	WASH	N	2	0	1	1	2

Kevin Lowe

LOWE, KEVIN HUGH (Vicious) — 6'2", 197 lbs.
B. Apr. 15, 1959, Hawksbury, Ont. — Defense, Shoots L

YEAR	TEAM & LEAGUE		GP	G	A	PTS	PIM
1979-80	EDM	N	64	2	19	21	70
1980-81			79	10	24	34	94
1981-82			80	9	31	40	63
1982-83			80	6	34	40	43
4 yrs.		N Totals:	303	27	108	135	270
PLAYOFFS							
1979-80	EDM	N	3	0	1	1	0
1980-81			9	0	2	2	11
1981-82			5	0	3	3	0
1982-83			16	1	8	9	10
4 yrs.		N Totals:	33	1	14	15	21

Norm Lowe

LOWE, NORMAN E. (Odie) — 5'8", 140 lbs.
B. Apr. 15, 1928, Winnipeg, Man. — Center, Shoots R

YEAR	TEAM & LEAGUE		GP	G	A	PTS	PIM
1948-49	NYR	N	1	0	0	0	0
1949-50			3	1	1	2	0
2 yrs.		N Totals:	4	1	1	2	0

Ross Lowe

LOWE, ROSS ROBERT — 6'1", 180 lbs.
B. Sept. 21, 1928, Oshawa, Ont. — Forward, Shoots L

YEAR	TEAM & LEAGUE		GP	G	A	PTS	PIM
1949-50	BOS	N	3	0	0	0	0
1950-51			40	5	3	8	34
	MONT	N	3	0	0	0	6
	2 team total		43	5	3	8	40
1951-52			31	1	5	6	42
3 yrs.		N Totals:	77	6	8	14	82
PLAYOFFS							
1950-51	MONT	N	2	0	0	0	0

Traded to **Montreal** by Boston for Hal Laycoe, Feb. 14, 1951. Drafted with Jim Bartlett from Montreal by **N.Y. Rangers** June 1, 1955.

Frock Lowery

LOWERY, FREDERICK JOHN
B. Ottawa, Ont. — Defense

YEAR	TEAM & LEAGUE		GP	G	A	PTS	PIM
1924-25	MON(M)	N	28	0	0	0	6
1925-26			10	0	0	0	2
	PITT	N	16	1	0	1	2
	2 team total		26	1	0	1	4
2 yrs.		N Totals:	54	1	0	1	10
PLAYOFFS							
1925-26	PITT	N	2	0	0	0	6

Eddie Lowrey

LOWREY, EDDIE
Forward

YEAR	TEAM & LEAGUE		GP	G	A	PTS	PIM
1917-18	OTTA	N	11	0	0	0	3
1918-19			10	0	0	0	3
1920-21	HAMIL	N	3	0	0	0	0
3 yrs.		N Totals:	24	0	0	0	6

Gerry Lowrey

LOWREY, GERALD — 5'8", 150 lbs.
B. Ottawa, Ont. — Left Wing, Shoots L

YEAR	TEAM & LEAGUE		GP	G	A	PTS	PIM
1927-28	TOR	N	25	6	5	11	29
1928-29			28	3	9	12	24
	PITT	N	16	2	3	5	6
	2 team total		44	5	12	17	30
1929-30			44	16	14	30	30
1930-31	PHI	N	42	13	14	27	27

Gerry Lowrey continued

YEAR	TEAM & LEAGUE		GP	G	A	PTS	PIM
1931-32	**CHI**	**N**	48	8	3	11	32
1932-33	**OTTA**	**N**	6	0	0	0	0
6 yrs.		**N Totals:**	209	48	48	96	148
PLAYOFFS							
1931-32	**CHI**	**N**	2	1	0	1	2

Danny Lucas

LUCAS, DANIEL KENNETH 6'1", 197 lbs.
B. Feb. 28, 1958, Powell River, B.C. Right Wing, Shoots L

YEAR	TEAM & LEAGUE		GP	G	A	PTS	PIM
1978-79	**PHI**	**N**	6	1	0	1	0

Dave Lucas

LUCAS, DAVID CHARLES
B. Mar. 22, 1932, Downeyville, Ont. Defense, Shoots L

YEAR	TEAM & LEAGUE		GP	G	A	PTS	PIM
1962-63	**DET**	**N**	1	0	0	0	0

Don Luce

LUCE, DONALD HAROLD 6'2", 185 lbs.
B. Oct. 2, 1948, London, Ont. Center, Shoots L
Won Masterton Trophy, 1974-75

YEAR	TEAM & LEAGUE		GP	G	A	PTS	PIM
1969-70	**NYR**	**N**	12	1	2	3	8
1970-71			9	0	1	1	0
	DET	**N**	58	3	11	14	18
	2 team total		67	3	12	15	18
1971-72	**BUF**	**N**	78	11	8	19	38
1972-73			78	18	25	43	32
1973-74			75	26	30	56	44
1974-75			80	33	43	76	45
1975-76			77	21	49	70	42
1976-77			80	26	43	69	16
1977-78			78	26	35	61	24
1978-79			79	26	35	61	14
1979-80			80	14	29	43	30
1980-81			61	15	13	28	19
	LA	**N**	10	1	0	1	2
	2 team total		71	16	13	29	21
1981-82	**TOR**	**N**	39	4	4	8	32
13 yrs.		**N Totals:**	894	225	328	553	364
PLAYOFFS							
1969-70	**NYR**	**N**	5	0	1	1	4
1972-73	**BUF**	**N**	6	1	1	2	2
1974-75			16	5	8	13	19
1975-76			9	4	3	7	6
1976-77			6	3	1	4	2
1977-78			8	0	2	2	6
1978-79			3	1	1	2	0
1979-80			14	3	3	6	11
1980-81	**LA**	**N**	4	0	2	2	2
9 yrs.		**N Totals:**	71	17	22	39	52

Traded to **Detroit** by N.Y. Rangers for Steve Andrascik, Nov. 2, 1970. Traded to **Buffalo** by Detroit with Mike Robitaille for goaltender Joe Daley, May 25, 1971. **Los Angeles** by Buffalo for cash and Los Angeles' sixth choice (Jeff Parker) in 1982 Entry Draft, Mar. 10, 1981. Traded to **Toronto** by Los Angeles for Bob Gladney and Toronto's sixth round choice in the 1983 Entry Draft, Aug. 10, 1981.

Jan Ludvig

LUDVIG, JAN 5'10", 185 lbs.
B. Sept. 17, 1961, Liberec, Czechoslovakia
Right Wing, Shoots R

YEAR	TEAM & LEAGUE		GP	G	A	PTS	PIM
1982-83	**NJ**	**N**	51	7	10	17	30

Signed by **New Jersey** as a free agent, Oct. 28, 1982.

Craig Ludwig

LUDWIG, CRAIG LEE 6'3", 212 lbs.
B. Mar. 15, 1961, Rhinelander, Wis. Defense, Shoots L

YEAR	TEAM & LEAGUE		GP	G	A	PTS	PIM
1982-83	**MONT**	**N**	80	0	25	25	59
PLAYOFFS							
1982-83	**MONT**	**N**	3	0	0	0	2

Steve Ludzik

LUDZIK, STEVEN 5'11", 170 lbs.
B. Apr. 3, 1961, Toronto, Ont. Center, Shoots L

YEAR	TEAM & LEAGUE		GP	G	A	PTS	PIM
1981-82	**CHI**	**N**	8	2	1	3	2
1982-83			66	6	19	25	63
2 yrs.		**N Totals:**	74	8	20	28	65
PLAYOFFS							
1982-83	**CHI**	**N**	13	3	5	8	20

Bernie Lukowich

LUKOWICH, BERNARD JOSEPH 6', 190 lbs.
B. Mar. 18, 1952, North Battleford, Sask.
Right Wing, Shoots R

YEAR	TEAM & LEAGUE		GP	G	A	PTS	PIM
1973-74	**PITT**	**N**	53	9	10	19	32
1974-75	**STL**	**N**	26	4	5	9	2
1975-76	**CALG**	**W**	15	5	2	7	18
3 yrs.		**N Totals:**	79	13	15	28	34
		W Totals:	15	5	2	7	18
PLAYOFFS							
1974-75	**STL**	**N**	2	0	0	0	0
1975-76	**CALG**	**W**	10	4	3	7	8
2 yrs.		**N Totals:**	2	0	0	0	0
		W Totals:	10	4	3	7	8

Traded to **St. Louis** by Pittsburgh for Bob Stumpf, Jan. 20, 1975.

Morris Lukowich

LUKOWICH, MORRIS (Luke) 5'9", 170 lbs.
B. June 1, 1956, Saskatoon, Sask. Left Wing, Shoots L

YEAR	TEAM & LEAGUE		GP	G	A	PTS	PIM
1976-77	**CALG**	**W**	6	0	1	1	0
	HOUS	**W**	62	27	18	45	67
	2 team total		68	27	19	46	67
1977-78			80	40	35	75	131
1978-79	**WINN**	**W**	80	65	34	99	119
1979-80	**WINN**	**N**	78	35	39	74	77
1980-81			80	33	34	67	90
1981-82			77	43	49	92	102
1982-83			69	22	21	43	67
7 yrs.		**N Totals:**	304	133	143	276	336
		W Totals:	228	132	88	220	317
PLAYOFFS							
1976-77	**HOUS**	**W**	11	6	4	10	19
1977-78			6	1	2	3	17
1978-79	**WINN**	**W**	10	8	7	15	21
1981-82	**WINN**	**N**	4	0	2	2	16
4 yrs.		**N Totals:**	4	0	2	2	16
		W Totals:	27	15	13	28	57

Reclaimed by **Pittsburgh** from Winnipeg prior to Expansion Draft, June 9, 1979. Claimed as priority selection by **Winnipeg** June 9, 1979.

Chuck Luksa

LUKSA, CHARLES 6'1", 197 lbs.
B. July 15, 1954, Toronto, Ont. Defense, Shoots L

YEAR	TEAM & LEAGUE		GP	G	A	PTS	PIM
1978-79	**CIN**	**W**	78	8	12	20	116
1979-80	**HART**	**N**	8	0	1	1	4
2 yrs.		**N Totals:**	8	0	1	1	4
		W Totals:	78	8	12	20	116
PLAYOFFS							
1978-79	**CIN**	**W**	3	0	0	0	7

Signed as free agent by **Hartford** Aug. 3, 1979.

Dave Lumley

LUMLEY, DAVID (Lummer) 6', 185 lbs.
B. Sept. 1, 1954, Toronto, Ont. Right Wing, Shoots R

YEAR	TEAM & LEAGUE		GP	G	A	PTS	PIM
1978-79	MONT	N	3	0	0	0	0
1979-80	EDM	N	80	20	38	58	138
1980-81			53	7	9	16	74
1981-82			66	32	42	74	96
1982-83			72	13	24	37	158
5 yrs.		N Totals:	274	72	113	185	466
PLAYOFFS							
1979-80	EDM	N	3	1	0	1	12
1980-81			7	1	0	1	4
1981-82			5	2	1	3	21
1982-83			16	0	0	0	19
4 yrs.		N Totals:	31	4	1	5	56

Traded to **Edmonton** by Montreal with Dan Newman for Edmonton's second round choice (Ric Nattress) in 1980 Entry Draft, June 13, 1979.

Larry Lund

LUND, LAWRENCE 6', 190 lbs.
B. Sept. 9, 1940, Penticton, B.C. Center, Shoots R

YEAR	TEAM & LEAGUE		GP	G	A	PTS	PIM
1972-73	HOUS	W	77	21	45	66	120
1973-74			75	33	53	86	109
1974-75			78	33	75	108	68
1975-76			73	24	49	73	50
1976-77			80	29	38	67	36
1977-78			76	9	17	26	36
6 yrs.		W Totals:	459	149	277	426	419
PLAYOFFS							
1972-73	HOUS	W	10	3	7	10	24
1973-74			14	9	14	23	56
1974-75			13	5	13	18	13
1975-76			5	1	1	2	4
1976-77			11	2	8	10	17
1977-78			6	0	2	2	2
6 yrs.		W Totals:	59	20	45	65	116

Penny Lund

LUND, PENTTI ALEXANDER 6', 185 lbs.
B. Dec. 6, 1925, Helsinki, Finland Right Wing, Shoots R
Won Calder Trophy, 1948-49

YEAR	TEAM & LEAGUE		GP	G	A	PTS	PIM
1948-49	NYR	N	59	14	16	30	16
1949-50			64	18	9	27	16
1950-51			59	4	16	20	6
1951-52	BOS	N	23	0	5	5	0
1952-53			54	8	9	17	2
5 yrs.		N Totals:	259	44	55	99	40
PLAYOFFS							
1946-47	BOS	N	1	0	0	0	0
1947-48			2	0	0	0	0
1949-50	NYR	N	12	6	5	11	0
1951-52	BOS	N	2	1	0	1	0
1952-53			2	0	0	0	0
5 yrs.		N Totals:	19	7	5	12	0

Traded to **Boston** by N.Y. Rangers with Gus Kyle for Paul Ronty, Sept. 20, 1951.

Brian Lundbert

LUNDBERT, BRIAN 5'11", 190 lbs.
B. June 5, 1960, Burnaby, B.C. Defense, Shoots R

YEAR	TEAM & LEAGUE		GP	G	A	PTS	PIM
1982-83	PITT	N	1	0	0	0	2

Len Lunde

LUNDE, LEONARD MELVIN 6'1", 194 lbs.
B. Nov. 13, 1936, Campbell River, B.C. Center, Shoots R

YEAR	TEAM & LEAGUE		GP	G	A	PTS	PIM
1958-59	DET	N	68	14	12	26	15
1959-60			66	6	17	23	10
1960-61			53	6	12	18	10
1961-62			23	2	9	11	4
1962-63	CHI	N	60	6	22	28	30
1965-66			24	4	7	11	4
1967-68	MINN	N	7	0	1	1	0
1970-71	VAN	N	20	1	3	4	2
1973-74	EDM	W	71	26	22	48	8
9 yrs.		N Totals:	321	39	83	122	75
		W Totals:	71	26	22	48	8
PLAYOFFS							
1959-60	DET	N	6	1	2	3	0
1960-61			10	2	0	2	0
1962-63	CHI	N	4	0	0	0	2
1973-74	EDM	W	5	0	1	1	0
4 yrs.		N Totals:	20	3	2	5	2
		W Totals:	5	0	1	1	0

Traded to **Chicago** by Detroit with John McKenzie for Doug Barkley, June 5, 1962. Drafted by **Minnesota** from Chicago in Expansion Draft, June 6, 1967.

Bengt Lundholm

LUNDHOLM, BENGT 6', 165 lbs.
B. Aug. 4, 1955, Falun, Sweden Left Wing, Shoots L

YEAR	TEAM & LEAGUE		GP	G	A	PTS	PIM
1981-82	WINN	N	66	14	30	44	10
1982-83			58	14	28	42	16
2 yrs.		N Totals:	124	28	58	86	26
PLAYOFFS							
1981-82	WINN	N	4	1	1	2	2
1982-83			3	0	1	1	2
2 yrs.		N Totals:	7	1	2	3	4

Signed as free agent by **Winnipeg** June 19, 1981.

Joe Lundrigan

LUNDRIGAN, JOSEPH ROCHE 5'11", 180 lbs.
B. Sept. 12, 1948, Corner Brook, Nfld. Defense, Shoots L

YEAR	TEAM & LEAGUE		GP	G	A	PTS	PIM
1972-73	TOR	N	49	2	8	10	20
1974-75	WASH	N	3	0	0	0	2
2 yrs.		N Totals:	52	2	8	10	22

Drafted by **Washington** from Toronto in Expansion Draft, June 12, 1974.

Tord Lundstrom

LUNDSTROM, TORD 5'11", 176 lbs.
B. Mar. 4, 1945, Kiruna, Sweden Left Wing, Shoots L

YEAR	TEAM & LEAGUE		GP	G	A	PTS	PIM
1973-74	DET	N	11	1	1	2	0

Pat Lundy

LUNDY, PATRICK ANTHONY 5'10½", 168 lbs.
B. May 31, 1924, Saskatoon, Sask. Center, Shoots R

YEAR	TEAM & LEAGUE		GP	G	A	PTS	PIM
1945-46	DET	N	4	3	2	5	2
1946-47			59	17	17	34	10
1947-48			11	4	1	5	6
1948-49			15	4	3	7	4
1950-51	CHI	N	61	9	9	18	9
5 yrs.		N Totals:	150	37	32	69	31
PLAYOFFS							
1945-46	DET	N	2	1	0	1	0
1947-48			5	1	1	2	0
1948-49			4	0	0	0	0
3 yrs.		N Totals:	11	2	1	3	0

Sold to **Chicago** by Detroit, Oct. 1, 1950.

Gilles Lupien

LUPIEN, GILLES 6'6", 210 lbs.
B. Apr. 20, 1954, Lachute, Que. Defense, Shoots L

YEAR	TEAM & LEAGUE		GP	G	A	PTS	PIM
1977-78	MONT	N	46	1	3	4	108
1978-79			72	1	9	10	124
1979-80			56	1	7	8	109
1980-81	PITT	N	31	0	1	1	34
	HART	N	20	2	4	6	39
	2 team total		51	2	5	7	73
1981-82			1	0	1	1	2
5 yrs.		N Totals:	226	5	25	30	416
PLAYOFFS							
1977-78*	MONT	N	8	0	0	0	17
1978-79*			13	0	0	0	2
1979-80			4	0	0	0	2
3 yrs.		N Totals:	25	0	0	0	21

Claimed by **Montreal** as fill in Expansion Draft, June 13, 1979. Traded to **Pittsburgh** by Montreal for Pittsburgh's third round choice in 1983 Entry Draft, Sept. 26, 1980. Traded to **Hartford** by Pittsburgh for Hartford's sixth round choice (Paul Edwards) in 1981 Entry Draft, Feb. 20, 1981.

Gary Lupul

LUPUL, GARY JOHN (Loopy) 5'9", 172 lbs.
B. Apr. 4, 1959, Powell River, B.C. Center, Shoots L

YEAR	TEAM & LEAGUE		GP	G	A	PTS	PIM
1979-80	VAN	N	51	9	11	20	24
1980-81			7	0	2	2	2
1981-82			41	10	7	17	26
1982-83			40	18	10	28	46
4 yrs.		N Totals:	139	37	30	67	98
PLAYOFFS							
1979-80	VAN	N	4	1	0	1	0
1981-82			10	2	3	5	4
1982-83			4	1	3	4	0
3 yrs.		N Totals:	18	4	6	10	4

Signed as free agent by **Vancouver** Sept. 14, 1979.

George Lyle

LYLE, GEORGE 6'2", 210 lbs.
B. Nov. 24, 1953, Edmonton, Alta. Left Wing, Shoots L

YEAR	TEAM & LEAGUE		GP	G	A	PTS	PIM
1976-77	NE	W	75	39	33	72	62
1977-78			68	30	24	54	74
1978-79			59	17	18	35	54
1979-80	DET	N	27	7	4	11	2
1980-81			31	10	14	24	28
1981-82			11	1	2	3	0
	HART	N	14	2	12	14	9
	2 team total		25	3	14	17	9
1982-83			16	4	6	10	8
7 yrs.		N Totals:	99	24	38	62	47
		W Totals:	202	86	75	161	190
PLAYOFFS							
1976-77	NE	W	5	1	0	1	4
1977-78			12	2	1	3	13
1978-79			9	3	5	8	25
3 yrs.		W Totals:	26	6	6	12	42

Reclaimed by **Detroit** from Hartford prior to Expansion Draft, June 9, 1979. Claimed on waivers by **Hartford** Nov. 13, 1981.

Jack Lynch

LYNCH, JOHN ALAN 6'2", 180 lbs.
B. May 25, 1952, Toronto, Ont. Defense, Shoots R

YEAR	TEAM & LEAGUE		GP	G	A	PTS	PIM
1972-73	PITT	N	47	1	18	19	40
1973-74			17	0	7	7	21
	DET	N	35	3	9	12	27
	2 team total		52	3	16	19	48
1974-75			50	2	15	17	46
	WASH	N	20	1	5	6	16
	2 team total		70	3	20	23	62
1975-76			79	9	13	22	78
1976-77			75	5	25	30	90
1977-78			29	1	8	9	4

Jack Lynch continued

YEAR	TEAM & LEAGUE		GP	G	A	PTS	PIM
1978-79			30	2	6	8	14
7 yrs.		N Totals:	382	24	106	130	336

Traded to **Detroit** by Pittsburgh with Jim Rutherford for Ron Stackhouse, Jan. 18, 1974. Traded to **Washington** by Detroit for Dave Kryskow, Feb. 8, 1975.

Vic Lynn

LYNN, VICTOR IVAN 5'9½", 185 lbs.
B. Jan. 26, 1925, Saskatoon, Sask. Defense, Shoots L

YEAR	TEAM & LEAGUE		GP	G	A	PTS	PIM
1943-44	DET	N	3	0	0	0	4
1945-46	MONT	N	2	0	0	0	0
1946-47	TOR	N	31	6	14	20	44
1947-48			60	12	22	34	53
1948-49			52	7	9	16	36
1949-50			70	7	13	20	36
1950-51	BOS	N	56	14	6	20	69
1951-52			12	2	2	4	4
1952-53	CHI	N	29	0	10	10	23
1953-54			11	0	1	1	2
10 yrs.		N Totals:	326	48	77	125	271
PLAYOFFS							
1946-47*	TOR	N	11	4	1	5	16
1947-48*			9	2	5	7	20
1948-49*			8	0	1	1	2
1949-50			7	0	2	2	2
1950-51	BOS	N	5	0	0	0	2
1952-53	CHI	N	7	1	1	2	4
6 yrs.		N Totals:	47	7	10	17	46

Traded to **Boston** by Toronto with Bill Ezinicki for Fern Flaman, Ken Smith, Phil Maloney and Leo Boivin, Nov. 16, 1950. Sold to **Chicago** by Boston with Ed Kryzanowski, Aug. 14, 1952.

Steve Lyon

LYON, STEVEN 5'10", 169 lbs.
B. May 16, 1952, Toronto, Ont. Defense, Shoots R

YEAR	TEAM & LEAGUE		GP	G	A	PTS	PIM
1976-77	PITT	N	3	0	0	0	2

Peaches Lyons

LYONS, RONALD
B. Unknown Left Wing

YEAR	TEAM & LEAGUE		GP	G	A	PTS	PIM
1930-31	BOS	N	2	0	0	0	2
	PHI	N	22	2	4	6	8
	BOS	N	12	0	0	0	19
	3 team total		36	2	4	6	29
PLAYOFFS							
1930-31	BOS	N	5	0	0	0	0

Tom Lysiak

LYSIAK, THOMAS JAMES 6'1", 195 lbs.
B. Apr. 22, 1953, High Prairie, Alta. Center, Shoots L

YEAR	TEAM & LEAGUE		GP	G	A	PTS	PIM
1973-74	ATL	N	77	19	45	64	54
1974-75			77	25	52	77	73
1975-76			80	31	51	82	60
1976-77			79	30	51	81	52
1977-78			80	27	42	69	54
1978-79			52	23	35	58	36
	CHI	N	14	0	10	10	14
	2 team total		66	23	45	68	50
1979-80			77	26	43	69	31
1980-81			72	21	55	76	20
1981-82			71	32	50	82	84
1982-83			61	23	38	61	29
10 yrs.		N Totals:	740	257	472	729	507
PLAYOFFS							
1973-74	ATL	N	4	0	2	2	0
1975-76			2	0	0	0	2
1976-77			3	1	3	4	8
1977-78			2	1	0	1	2
1978-79	CHI	N	4	0	0	0	2
1979-80			7	4	4	8	0
1980-81			3	0	3	3	0
1981-82			15	6	9	15	13

Tom Lysiak continued

YEAR	TEAM & LEAGUE		GP	G	A	PTS	PIM
1982-83			13	6	7	13	8
9 yrs.		N Totals:	53	18	28	46	35

Traded to **Chicago** by Atlanta with Harold Phillipoff, Pat Ribble, Greg Fox and Miles Zaharko for Ivan Boldirev, Phil Russell and Darcy Rota, Mar. 13, 1979.

Al MacAdam

MACADAM, REGINALD ALAN 6', 180 lbs.
B. Mar. 16, 1952, Charlottetown, P.E.I. Right Wing, Shoots L
Won Masterton Trophy, 1979-80

YEAR	TEAM & LEAGUE		GP	G	A	PTS	PIM
1973-74	PHI	N	5	0	0	0	0
1974-75	CALIF	N	80	18	25	43	55
1975-76			80	32	31	63	49
1976-77	CLEVE	N	80	22	41	63	68
1977-78			80	16	32	48	43
1978-79	MINN	N	69	24	34	58	30
1979-80			80	42	51	93	24
1980-81			78	21	39	60	94
1981-82			79	18	43	61	37
1982-83			73	11	22	33	60
10 yrs.		N Totals:	704	204	318	522	460
PLAYOFFS							
1973-74*	PHI	N	1	0	0	0	0
1979-80	MINN	N	15	7	9	16	4
1980-81			19	9	10	19	4
1981-82			4	1	0	1	4
1982-83			9	2	1	3	2
5 yrs.		N Totals:	48	19	20	39	14

Traded to **California** by Philadelphia with Larry Wright and Philadelphia's first choice (Ron Chipperfield) in 1974 Amateur Draft for Reggie Leach, May 24, 1974. Protected by **Minnesota** prior to Cleveland-Minnesota Dispersal Draft, June 15, 1978.

Paul MacDermid

MACDERMID, PAUL 5'11", 188 lbs.
B. Apr. 14, 1963, Chesley, Ont. Center, Shoots R

YEAR	TEAM & LEAGUE		GP	G	A	PTS	PIM
1981-82	HART	N	3	1	0	1	2
1982-83			7	0	0	0	2
2 yrs.		N Totals:	10	1	0	1	4

Blair MacDonald

MACDONALD, BLAIR JOSEPH (B.J.) 5'10", 180 lbs.
B. Nov. 17, 1953, Cornwall, Ont. Right Wing, Shoots R

YEAR	TEAM & LEAGUE		GP	G	A	PTS	PIM
1972-73	HOUS	W	71	20	20	40	78
1973-74	EDM	W	78	21	24	45	34
1974-75			72	22	24	46	14
1975-76			25	7	5	12	8
	IND	W	56	20	11	31	14
	2 team total		81	27	16	43	22
1976-77			81	34	30	64	28
1977-78	EDM	W	80	34	34	68	11
1978-79			80	34	37	71	44
1979-80	EDM	N	80	46	48	94	6
1980-81			51	19	24	43	27
	VAN	N	12	5	9	14	10
	2 team total		63	24	33	57	37
1981-82			59	18	15	33	20
1982-83			17	3	4	7	2
11 yrs.		N Totals:	219	91	100	191	65
		W Totals:	543	192	185	377	231
PLAYOFFS							
1973-74	EDM	W	5	4	2	6	2
1975-76	IND	W	7	0	0	0	0
1976-77			9	7	8	15	4
1977-78	EDM	W	5	1	1	2	0
1978-79			13	8	10	18	6
1979-80	EDM	N	3	0	3	3	0
1980-81	VAN	N	3	0	1	1	2
1981-82			3	0	0	0	0
1982-83			2	0	2	2	0
9 yrs.		N Totals:	11	0	6	6	2
		W Totals:	39	20	21	41	12

Traded to **Vancouver** by Edmonton with the rights to Ken Berry for Garry Lariviere and the rights to Lars Gunnar Petterson, Mar 10, 1981.

Kilby MacDonald

MACDONALD, JAMES ALLEN KILBY 5'11½", 178 lbs.
B. Sept. 6, 1914, Ottawa, Ont. Left Wing, Shoots L
Won Calder Trophy, 1939-40

YEAR	TEAM & LEAGUE		GP	G	A	PTS	PIM
1939-40	NYR	N	44	15	13	28	19
1940-41			47	5	6	11	12
1943-44			24	7	9	16	4
1944-45			36	9	6	15	12
4 yrs.		N Totals:	151	36	34	70	47
PLAYOFFS							
1939-40*	NYR	N	12	0	2	2	4
1940-41			3	1	0	1	0
2 yrs.		N Totals:	15	1	2	3	4

Lowell MacDonald

MACDONALD, LOWELL WILSON 5'11", 185 lbs.
B. Aug. 30, 1941, New Glasgow, N.S. Right Wing, Shoots R
Won Masterton Trophy, 1972-73

YEAR	TEAM & LEAGUE		GP	G	A	PTS	PIM
1961-62	DET	N	1	0	0	0	2
1962-63			26	2	1	3	8
1963-64			10	1	4	5	0
1964-65			9	2	1	3	0
1967-68	LA	N	74	21	24	45	12
1968-69			58	14	14	28	10
1970-71	PITT	N	10	0	1	1	0
1972-73			78	34	41	75	8
1973-74			78	43	39	82	14
1974-75			71	27	33	60	24
1975-76			69	30	43	73	12
1976-77			3	1	1	2	0
1977-78			19	5	8	13	2
13 yrs.		N Totals:	506	180	210	390	92
PLAYOFFS							
1967-68	LA	N	7	3	4	7	2
1968-69			7	2	3	5	0
1974-75	PITT	N	9	4	2	6	4
1975-76			3	1	0	1	0
1976-77			3	1	2	3	4
5 yrs.		N Totals:	29	11	11	22	10

Traded by Detroit with Marcel Pronovost, Ed Joyal, Larry Jeffrey, and Aut Erickson to **Toronto** for Andy Bathgate, Billy Harris, and Gary Jarrett, May 20, 1965. Drafted by **Los Angeles** from Toronto in Expansion Draft, June 6, 1967. Drafted by **Pittsburgh** from Los Angeles in Intra-league Draft, June 9, 1970.

Parker MacDonald

MACDONALD, CALVIN PARKER 5'11", 184 lbs.
B. June 14, 1933, Sydney, N.S. Left Wing, Shoots L

YEAR	TEAM & LEAGUE		GP	G	A	PTS	PIM
1952-53	TOR	N	1	0	0	0	0
1954-55			62	8	3	11	36
1956-57	NYR	N	45	7	8	15	24
1957-58			70	8	10	18	30
1959-60			4	0	0	0	0
1960-61	DET	N	70	14	12	26	6
1961-62			32	5	7	12	8
1962-63			69	33	28	61	32
1963-64			68	21	25	46	25
1964-65			69	13	33	46	38
1965-66	BOS	N	29	6	4	10	6
	DET	N	37	5	12	17	24
	2 team total		66	11	16	27	30
1966-67			16	3	5	8	2
1967-68	MINN	N	69	19	23	42	22
1968-69			35	2	9	11	0
14 yrs.		N Totals:	676	144	179	323	253
PLAYOFFS							
1954-55	TOR	N	4	0	0	0	4
1956-57	NYR	N	1	1	1	2	0
1957-58			6	1	2	3	2
1960-61	DET	N	9	1	0	1	0
1962-63			11	3	2	5	2
1963-64			14	3	3	6	2
1964-65			7	1	1	2	6
1965-66			9	0	0	0	2
1967-68	MINN	N	14	4	5	9	2

Parker MacDonald continued

YEAR	TEAM & LEAGUE		GP	G	A	PTS	PIM
9 yrs.		**N Totals:**	75	14	14	28	20

Drafted with Gerry Foley from Toronto by **New York** June 5, 1956. Drafted by **Detroit** from N.Y. Rangers, June, 1960. Traded by Detroit to **Boston** with Albert Langlois, Ron Harris, and Bob Dillabough for Ab McDonald, Bob McCord, and Ken Stephanson, May 31, 1965. Traded by Boston to **Detroit** for Pit Martin, Dec. 30, 1965. Drafted by **Minnesota** from Detroit in Expansion Draft, June 6, 1967.

Kim MacDougall

MACDOUGALL, KIM — 5'11", 180 lbs.
B. Aug. 29, 1954, Regina, Sask. — Defense, Shoots L

YEAR	TEAM & LEAGUE		GP	G	A	PTS	PIM
1974-75	**MINN**	**N**	1	0	0	0	0

Hub Macey

MACEY, HUBERT — 5'8", 178 lbs.
B. Apr. 13, 1921, Big River, Sask. — Center, Shoots L

YEAR	TEAM & LEAGUE		GP	G	A	PTS	PIM
1941-42	**NYR**	**N**	9	3	5	8	0
1942-43			9	3	3	6	0
1946-47	**MONT**	**N**	12	0	1	1	0
3 yrs.		**N Totals:**	30	6	9	15	0
PLAYOFFS							
1941-42	**NYR**	**N**	1	0	0	0	0
1946-47	**MONT**	**N**	7	0	0	0	0
2 yrs.		**N Totals:**	8	0	0	0	0

Bruce MacGregor

MACGREGOR, BRUCE CAMERON — 5'10", 180 lbs.
B. Apr. 26, 1941, Edmonton, Alta. — Right Wing, Shoots R

YEAR	TEAM & LEAGUE		GP	G	A	PTS	PIM
1960-61	**DET**	**N**	12	0	1	1	0
1961-62			65	6	12	18	16
1962-63			67	11	11	22	12
1963-64			63	11	21	32	15
1964-65			66	21	20	41	19
1965-66			70	20	14	34	28
1966-67			70	28	19	47	14
1967-68			71	15	24	39	13
1968-69			69	18	23	41	14
1969-70			73	15	23	38	24
1970-71			47	6	16	22	18
	NYR	**N**	27	12	13	25	4
	2 team total		74	18	29	47	22
1971-72			75	19	21	40	22
1972-73			52	14	12	26	12
1973-74			66	17	27	44	6
1974-75	**EDM**	**W**	72	24	28	52	10
1975-76			63	13	10	23	13
16 yrs.		**N Totals:**	893	213	257	470	217
		W Totals:	135	37	38	75	23
PLAYOFFS							
1960-61	**DET**	**N**	8	1	2	3	6
1962-63			10	1	4	5	10
1963-64			14	5	2	7	12
1964-65			7	0	2	2	2
1965-66			12	1	4	5	2
1969-70			4	1	0	1	2
1970-71	**NYR**	**N**	13	0	4	4	2
1971-72			16	2	6	8	4
1972-73			10	2	2	4	2
1973-74			13	6	2	8	2
10 yrs.		**N Totals:**	107	19	28	47	44

Traded to **N.Y. Rangers** by Detroit with Larry Brown for Arnie Brown, Mike Robitaille, and Tom Miller, Feb. 2, 1971.

Gary MacGregor

MACGREGOR, GARY GEORGE (Mac) — 5'11", 176 lbs.
B. Sept. 21, 1954, Kingston, Ont. — Center, Shoots L

YEAR	TEAM & LEAGUE		GP	G	A	PTS	PIM
1974-75	**CHI**	**W**	78	44	34	78	26
1975-76	**D-O**	**W**	38	16	14	30	18
	CLEVE	**W**	35	5	3	8	6
	2 team total		73	21	17	38	24
1976-77	**NE**	**W**	30	8	8	16	4
	IND	**W**	16	0	5	5	4
	2 team total		46	8	13	21	8

Gary MacGregor continued

YEAR	TEAM & LEAGUE		GP	G	A	PTS	PIM
1977-78	**EDM**	**W**	37	11	2	13	29
1978-79	**IND**	**W**	17	8	4	12	0
5 yrs.		**W Totals:**	251	92	70	162	87
PLAYOFFS							
1975-76	**CLEVE**	**W**	3	0	0	0	4

Randy MacGregor

MACGREGOR, RANDY KENNETH — 5'9", 175 lbs.
B. July 9, 1953, Cobourg, Ont. — Right Wing, Shoots L

YEAR	TEAM & LEAGUE		GP	G	A	PTS	PIM
1981-82	**HART**	**N**	2	1	1	2	2

Garth MacGuigan

MACGUIGAN, GARTH LESLIE — 6', 191 lbs.
B. Feb. 16, 1956, Charlottetown, P.E.I. — Center, Shoots L

YEAR	TEAM & LEAGUE		GP	G	A	PTS	PIM
1979-80	**NYI**	**N**	2	0	0	0	0

Al MacInnis

MACINNIS, ALLAN — 6', 180 lbs.
B. July 11, 1963, Inverness, N.S. — Defense, Shoots R

YEAR	TEAM & LEAGUE		GP	G	A	PTS	PIM
1981-82	**CALG**	**N**	2	0	0	0	0
1982-83			14	1	3	4	9
2 yrs.		**N Totals:**	16	1	3	4	9

Ian MacIntosh

MACINTOSH, IAN
B. Unknown — Forward

YEAR	TEAM & LEAGUE		GP	G	A	PTS	PIM
1952-53	**NYR**	**N**	4	0	0	0	4

Don MacIver

MACIVER, DONALD — 6', 200 lbs.
B. May 3, 1955, Montreal, Que. — Defense, Shoots L

YEAR	TEAM & LEAGUE		GP	G	A	PTS	PIM
1979-80	**WINN**	**N**	6	0	0	0	2

Signed as free agent by **Winnipeg** Oct. 16, 1979.

Blair Mackasey

MACKASEY, BLAIR — 6'2", 200 lbs.
B. Dec. 13, 1955, Hamilton, Ont. — Defense, Shoots R

YEAR	TEAM & LEAGUE		GP	G	A	PTS	PIM
1976-77	**TOR**	**N**	1	0	0	0	2

Playing rights transferred to **Toronto** from Washington, Sept. 27, 1976.

Calum MacKay

MACKAY, CALUM (Baldy) — 5'9", 185 lbs.
B. Jan. 1, 1927, Toronto, Ont. — Left Wing, Shoots L

YEAR	TEAM & LEAGUE		GP	G	A	PTS	PIM
1946-47	**DET**	**N**	5	0	0	0	0
1948-49			1	0	0	0	0
1949-50	**MONT**	**N**	52	8	10	18	44
1950-51			70	18	10	28	69
1951-52			12	0	1	1	8
1953-54			47	10	13	23	54
1954-55			50	14	21	35	39
7 yrs.		**N Totals:**	237	50	55	105	214
PLAYOFFS							
1949-50	**MONT**	**N**	5	0	1	1	2
1950-51			11	1	0	1	0
1952-53*			7	1	3	4	10
1953-54			3	0	1	1	0
1954-55			12	3	8	11	8
5 yrs.		**N Totals:**	38	5	13	18	20

Traded to **Montreal** by Detroit for Joe Carveth, Nov. 11, 1949.

Dave MacKay

MACKAY, DAVID
B. Edmonton, Alta. — Defense

YEAR	TEAM & LEAGUE		GP	G	A	PTS	PIM
1940-41	**CHI**	**N**	29	3	0	3	26
PLAYOFFS							
1940-41	**CHI**	**N**	5	0	1	1	2

Mickey MacKay

MACKAY, DUNCAN
B. May 21, 1894, Chesley, Ont. — Center
Hall of Fame, 1952

YEAR	TEAM & LEAGUE		GP	G	A	PTS	PIM
1926-27	CHI	N	36	14	8	22	23
1927-28			35	17	4	21	23
1928-29	PITT	N	10	1	0	1	2
	BOS	N	30	8	2	10	18
	2 team total		40	9	2	11	20
1929-30			40	4	5	9	13
4 yrs.		N Totals:	151	44	19	63	79
PLAYOFFS							
1926-27	CHI	N	2	0	0	0	0
1928-29*	BOS	N	3	0	0	0	2
1929-30			6	0	0	0	4
3 yrs.		N Totals:	11	0	0	0	6

Murdo MacKay

MACKAY, MURDO JOHN — 5'11½", 175 lbs.
B. Aug. 8, 1917, Fort William, Ont. — Center, Shoots R

YEAR	TEAM & LEAGUE		GP	G	A	PTS	PIM
1945-46	MONT	N	5	0	1	1	0
1947-48			14	0	2	2	0
2 yrs.		N Totals:	19	0	3	3	0
PLAYOFFS							
1946-47	MONT	N	9	0	1	1	0
1947-48			6	1	1	2	0
2 yrs.		N Totals:	15	1	2	3	0

Mac MacKell

MACKELL, FLEMING DAVID — 5'8", 167 lbs.
B. Apr. 30, 1929, Montreal, Que. — Center, Shoots L

YEAR	TEAM & LEAGUE		GP	G	A	PTS	PIM
1947-48	TOR	N	3	0	0	0	2
1948-49			11	1	1	2	0
1949-50			36	7	13	20	0
1950-51			70	12	13	25	40
1951-52			32	2	8	10	16
	BOS	N	30	1	8	9	24
	2 team total		62	3	16	19	40
1952-53			65	27	17	44	63
1953-54			67	15	32	47	60
1954-55			60	11	24	35	76
1955-56			52	7	9	16	59
1956-57			65	22	17	39	73
1957-58			70	20	40	60	72
1958-59			57	17	23	40	28
1959-60			47	7	15	22	19
13 yrs.		N Totals:	665	149	220	369	532
PLAYOFFS							
1948-49*	TOR	N	9	2	4	6	2
1949-50			7	1	1	2	11
1950-51*			11	2	3	5	9
1951-52	BOS	N	5	2	1	3	12
1952-53			11	2	7	9	7
1953-54			4	1	1	2	8
1954-55			4	0	1	1	0
1956-57			10	5	3	8	4
1957-58			12	5	14	19	12
1958-59			7	2	6	8	8
10 yrs.		N Totals:	80	22	41	63	73

Traded to **Boston** by Toronto for Jim Morrison, Jan. 9, 1952.

Al MacKenzie

MACKENZIE, ALAN — 5'10", 165 lbs.
B. Feb. 2, 1952, Windsor, Ont. — Defense, Shoots R

YEAR	TEAM & LEAGUE		GP	G	A	PTS	PIM
1973-74	CHI	W	2	0	0	0	0

Barry MacKenzie

MACKENZIE, JOHN BARRY — 6', 190 lbs.
B. Aug. 16, 1941, Toronto, Ont. — Defense, Shoots L

YEAR	TEAM & LEAGUE		GP	G	A	PTS	PIM
1968-69	MINN	N	6	0	1	1	6

Bill MacKenzie

MACKENZIE, WILLIAM KENNETH — 5'11", 175 lbs.
B. Dec. 12, 1911, Winnipeg, Man — Defense, Shoots R

YEAR	TEAM & LEAGUE		GP	G	A	PTS	PIM
1932-33	CHI	N	35	4	4	8	13
1933-34	MON(M)	N	48	4	3	7	20
1934-35			5	0	0	0	0
	NYR	N	15	1	0	1	10
	2 team total		20	1	0	1	10
1936-37	MON(M)	N	10	0	1	1	16
	MONT	N	39	4	3	7	22
	2 team total		49	4	4	8	38
1937-38			11	0	0	0	4
	CHI	N	35	1	2	3	20
	2 team total		46	1	2	3	24
1938-39			48	1	0	1	14
1939-40			20	0	1	1	14
7 yrs.		N Totals:	266	15	14	29	133
PLAYOFFS							
1933-34	MON(M)	N	4	0	0	0	0
1934-35	NYR	N	3	0	0	0	0
1936-37	MONT	N	5	1	0	1	0
1937-38*	CHI	N	7	0	1	1	11
4 yrs.		N Totals:	19	1	1	2	11

Shawn MacKenzie

MACKENZIE, SHAWN — 5'10", 175 lbs.
B. Aug. 22, 1962, Bedford, N.S. — Shoots R

YEAR	TEAM & LEAGUE		GP	G	A	PTS	PIM
1982-83	NJ	N	6	0	0	0	0

Reggie Mackey

MACKEY, REGINALD — 5'7", 155 lbs.
B. May 7, 1900, Ottawa, Ont. — Defense, Shoots L

YEAR	TEAM & LEAGUE		GP	G	A	PTS	PIM
1926-27	NYR	N	34	0	0	0	16
PLAYOFFS							
1926-27	NYR	N	1	0	0	0	0

Howie Mackie

MACKIE, HOWARD — 5'8", 175 lbs.
B. Aug. 30, 1913, Kitchener, Ont. — Defense

YEAR	TEAM & LEAGUE		GP	G	A	PTS	PIM
1936-37	DET	N	13	1	0	1	4
1937-38			7	0	0	0	0
2 yrs.		N Totals:	20	1	0	1	4
PLAYOFFS							
1936-37*	DET	N	8	0	0	0	0

Paul MacKinnon

MACKINNON, PAUL — 6', 190 lbs.
B. Nov. 6, 1958, Brantford, Ont. — Defense, Shoots R

YEAR	TEAM & LEAGUE		GP	G	A	PTS	PIM
1978-79	WINN	W	73	2	15	17	70
1979-80	WASH	N	63	1	11	12	22
1980-81			14	0	0	0	22
1981-82			39	2	9	11	35
1982-83			19	2	2	4	8
5 yrs.		N Totals:	135	5	22	27	87
		W Totals:	73	2	15	17	70
PLAYOFFS							
1978-79	WINN	W	10	2	5	7	4

Reclaimed by **Washington** from Winnipeg prior to Expansion Draft, June 9, 1979.

Paul MacLean

MACLEAN, PAUL — 6', 189 lbs.
B. Mar. 9, 1958, Grostenquin, France — Right Wing, Shoots R

YEAR	TEAM & LEAGUE		GP	G	A	PTS	PIM
1980-81	STL	N	1	0	0	0	0
1981-82	WINN	N	74	36	25	61	106
1982-83			80	32	44	76	121
3 yrs.		N Totals:	155	68	69	137	227
PLAYOFFS							
1980-81	STL	N	10	0	0	0	0
1981-82	WINN	N	4	3	2	5	20

YEAR	TEAM & LEAGUE		GP	G	A	PTS	PIM

Paul MacLean continued

YEAR	TEAM & LEAGUE		GP	G	A	PTS	PIM
1982-83			3	1	2	3	6
3 yrs.		N Totals:	17	4	4	8	26

Traded to **Winnipeg** by St. Louis with Bryan Maxwell and Ed Staniowski for Scott Campbell and John Markell, July 3, 1981.

Rick MacLeish

MACLEISH, RICHARD GEORGE 5'11", 185 lbs.
B. Jan. 3, 1950, Lindsay, Ont. Center, Shoots L

YEAR	TEAM & LEAGUE		GP	G	A	PTS	PIM
1970-71	PHI	N	26	2	4	6	19
1971-72			17	1	2	3	9
1972-73			78	50	50	100	69
1973-74			78	32	45	77	42
1974-75			80	38	41	79	50
1975-76			51	22	23	45	16
1976-77			79	49	48	97	42
1977-78			76	31	39	70	33
1978-79			71	26	32	58	47
1979-80			78	31	35	66	28
1980-81			78	38	36	74	25
1981-82	HART	N	34	6	16	22	16
	PITT	N	40	13	12	25	28
	2 team total		74	19	28	47	44
1982-83			6	0	5	5	2
13 yrs.		N Totals:	792	339	388	727	426
PLAYOFFS							
1970-71	PHI	N	4	1	0	1	0
1972-73			10	3	4	7	2
1973-74*			17	13	9	22	20
1974-75*			17	11	9	20	8
1976-77			10	4	9	13	2
1977-78			12	7	9	16	4
1978-79			7	0	1	1	0
1979-80			19	9	6	15	2
1980-81			12	5	5	10	0
1981-82	PITT	N	5	1	1	2	0
10 yrs.		N Totals:	113	54	53	107	38

Traded to **Philadelphia** by Boston with Danny Schock for Mike Walton, Feb. 1, 1971. Traded to **Hartford** by Philadelphia with Don Gillen, Blake Wesley and Philadelphia's first (Paul Lawless), second (Mark Paterson), and third round choices (Kevin Dineen) in 1982 Entry Draft for Ray Allison, Fred Arthur and Hartford's first (Ron Sutter), and third-round choices (Miroslav Dvorak) in the 1982 Entry Draft, July 3, 1981. Traded to **Pittsburgh** by Hartford for Ross Anderson and Pittsburgh's eighth round choice in 1983 Entry Draft, Dec. 29, 1981.

Brian MacLellan

MACLELLAN, BRIAN 6'3", 212 lbs.
B. Oct. 27, 1958, Guelph, Ont. Left Wing, Shoots L

YEAR	TEAM & LEAGUE		GP	G	A	PTS	PIM
1982-83	LA	N	8	0	3	3	7

Signed by **Los Angeles** as a free agent, Apr., 1982.

Billy MacMillan

MACMILLAN, WILLIAM STEWART 5'10", 180 lbs.
B. Mar. 7, 1943, Charlottetown, P.E.I. Right Wing, Shoots L

YEAR	TEAM & LEAGUE		GP	G	A	PTS	PIM
1970-71	TOR	N	76	22	19	41	42
1971-72			61	10	7	17	39
1972-73	ATL	N	78	10	15	25	52
1973-74	NYI	N	55	4	9	13	16
1974-75			69	13	12	25	12
1975-76			64	9	7	16	10
1976-77			43	6	8	14	13
7 yrs.		N Totals:	446	74	77	151	184
PLAYOFFS							
1970-71	TOR	N	6	0	3	3	2
1971-72			5	0	0	0	0
1974-75	NYI	N	17	0	1	1	23
1975-76			13	4	2	6	8
1976-77			12	2	0	2	7
5 yrs.		N Totals:	53	6	6	12	40

Drafted by **Atlanta** from Toronto in Expansion Draft, June 6, 1972. Traded to **N.Y. Islanders** by Atlanta, May 29, 1973, to complete earlier deal in which Atlanta acquired Arnie Brown for Ernie Hicke (Feb. 13, 1972).

Bob MacMillan

MACMILLAN, ROBERT LEA 5'11", 185 lbs.
B. Dec. 3, 1952, Charlottetown, P.E.I. Right Wing, Shoots L
Won Lady Byng Trophy, 1978-79

YEAR	TEAM & LEAGUE		GP	G	A	PTS	PIM
1972-73	MINN	W	75	13	27	40	48
1973-74			78	14	34	48	81
1974-75	NYR	N	22	1	2	3	4
1975-76	STL	N	80	20	32	52	41
1976-77			80	19	39	58	11
1977-78			28	7	12	19	23
	ATL	N	52	31	21	52	26
	2 team total		80	38	33	71	49
1978-79			79	37	71	108	14
1979-80			77	22	39	61	10
1980-81	CALG	N	77	28	35	63	47
1981-82			23	4	7	11	14
	COLO	N	57	18	32	50	27
	2 team total		80	22	39	61	41
1982-83	NJ	N	71	19	29	48	8
11 yrs.		N Totals:	646	206	319	525	225
		W Totals:	153	27	61	88	129
PLAYOFFS							
1972-73	MINN	W	5	0	3	3	0
1973-74			11	2	3	5	4
1975-76	STL	N	3	0	1	1	0
1976-77			4	0	1	1	0
1977-78	ATL	N	2	0	2	2	0
1978-79			2	0	1	1	0
1979-80			4	0	0	0	9
1980-81	CALG	N	16	8	6	14	7
8 yrs.		N Totals:	31	8	11	19	16
		W Totals:	16	2	6	8	4

Traded to **St. Louis** by N.Y. Rangers for Larry Sacharuk, Sept. 21, 1975. Traded to **Atlanta** by St. Louis with Yves Belanger, Dick Redmond and St. Louis' second round choice (Mike Perovich) in the 1979 Entry Draft for Barry Gibbs, Curt Bennett and Phil Myre, Dec. 12, 1977. Traded to **Colorado** by Calgary along with Don Lever for Lanny McDonald and Colorado's fourth round choice in 1983 Entry Draft, Nov. 25, 1981.

John MacMillan

MACMILLAN, JOHN STEWART 5'9", 185 lbs.
B. Oct. 25, 1935, Lethbridge, Alta. Right Wing, Shoots L

YEAR	TEAM & LEAGUE		GP	G	A	PTS	PIM
1960-61	TOR	N	31	3	5	8	8
1961-62			32	1	0	1	8
1962-63			6	1	1	2	6
1963-64			13	0	0	0	10
	DET	N	20	0	3	3	6
	2 team total		33	0	3	3	16
1964-65			3	0	1	1	0
5 yrs.		N Totals:	105	5	10	15	38
PLAYOFFS							
1960-61	TOR	N	4	0	0	0	0
1961-62*			3	0	0	0	0
1962-63*			1	0	0	0	0
1963-64	DET	N	4	0	1	1	2
4 yrs.		N Totals:	12	0	1	1	2

Sold by Toronto to **Detroit** Dec. 3, 1963.

Al MacNeil

MACNEIL, ALLISTER WENCES 5'10", 180 lbs.
B. Sept. 27, 1935, Sydney, N.S. Defense, Shoots L

YEAR	TEAM & LEAGUE		GP	G	A	PTS	PIM
1955-56	TOR	N	1	0	0	0	2
1956-57			53	4	8	12	84
1957-58			13	0	0	0	9
1959-60			4	0	0	0	2
1961-62	MONT	N	61	1	7	8	74
1962-63	CHI	N	70	2	19	21	100
1963-64			70	5	19	24	7
1964-65			69	3	7	10	119
1965-66			51	0	1	1	34
1966-67	NYR	N	58	0	4	4	44
1967-68	PITT	N	74	2	10	12	58
11 yrs.		N Totals:	524	17	75	92	533
PLAYOFFS							
1961-62	MONT	N	5	0	0	0	2

Al MacNeil continued

YEAR	TEAM & LEAGUE		GP	G	A	PTS	PIM
1962-63	CHI	N	4	0	1	1	4
1963-64			7	0	2	2	25
1964-65			14	0	1	1	34
1965-66			3	0	0	0	0
1966-67	NYR	N	4	0	0	0	2
6 yrs.		N Totals:	37	0	4	4	67

Traded to **Mont. Canadiens** by Toronto for Stan Smrke, June, 1960. Traded to **Chicago** by Mont. Canadiens for Wayne Hicks, May, 1962. Claimed in draft by **Montreal** from Chicago, then drafted by **N.Y. Rangers** from Montreal, June 15, 1966. Drafted by **Pittsburgh** from N.Y. Rangers in Expansion Draft, June 6, 1967. Traded to **Mont. Canadiens** by Pittsburgh for Wally Boyer, June 12, 1968.

Bernie MacNeil

MACNEIL, STEPHEN BERNARD 5'11", 190 lbs.
B. Mar. 7, 1950, Sudbury, Ont. Left Wing, Shoots L

YEAR	TEAM & LEAGUE		GP	G	A	PTS	PIM
1972-73	LA	W	42	4	7	11	48
1973-74	STL	N	4	0	0	0	0
1975-76	CIN	W	77	15	12	27	83
3 yrs.		N Totals:	4	0	0	0	0
		W Totals:	119	19	19	38	131

Jamie Macoun

MACOUN, JAMIE 6'2", 200 lbs.
B. Aug. 17, 1963, Newmarket, Ont. Defense, Shoots R

YEAR	TEAM & LEAGUE		GP	G	A	PTS	PIM
1982-83	CALG	N	22	1	4	5	25
PLAYOFFS							
1982-83	CALG	N	9	0	2	2	8

Bud MacPherson

MACPHERSON, JAMES ALBERT 6'3", 205 lbs.
B. Mar. 21, 1927, Edmonton, Alta. Defense, Shoots L

YEAR	TEAM & LEAGUE		GP	G	A	PTS	PIM
1948-49	MONT	N	3	0	0	0	2
1950-51			62	0	16	16	40
1951-52			54	2	1	3	24
1952-53			59	2	3	5	67
1953-54			41	0	5	5	41
1954-55			30	1	8	9	55
1956-57			10	0	0	0	4
7 yrs.		N Totals:	259	5	33	38	233
PLAYOFFS							
1950-51	MONT	N	11	0	2	2	8
1951-52			11	0	0	0	0
1952-53*			4	0	1	1	9
1953-54			3	0	0	0	4
4 yrs.		N Totals:	29	0	3	3	21

Sold by Montreal to **Chicago** with Ken Mosdell and Eddie Mazur for $55,-000 with option to recall at end of season, May 24, 1956. Returned to **Montreal** by Chicago, Oct. 10, 1956.

Ralph MacSweyn

MACSWEYN, DONALD RALPH 5'11", 195 lbs.
B. Sept. 8, 1942, Hawkesbury, Ont. Defense, Shoots R

YEAR	TEAM & LEAGUE		GP	G	A	PTS	PIM
1967-68	PHI	N	4	0	0	0	0
1968-69			24	0	4	4	6
1969-70			17	0	0	0	4
1971-72			2	0	1	1	0
1972-73	LA	W	78	0	23	23	39
1973-74			13	0	3	3	6
	VAN	W	56	2	18	20	52
	2 team total		69	2	21	23	58
6 yrs.		N Totals:	47	0	5	5	10
		W Totals:	147	2	44	46	97
PLAYOFFS							
1968-69	PHI	N	4	0	0	0	4
1970-71			4	0	0	0	2
1972-73	LA	W	6	1	2	3	4
3 yrs.		N Totals:	8	0	0	0	6
		W Totals:	6	1	2	3	4

Craig MacTavish

MACTAVISH, CRAIG 6', 185 lbs.
B. Aug. 15, 1958, London, Ont. Center, Shoots L

YEAR	TEAM & LEAGUE		GP	G	A	PTS	PIM
1979-80	BOS	N	46	11	17	28	8
1980-81			24	3	5	8	13
1981-82			2	0	1	1	0
1982-83			75	10	20	30	18
4 yrs.		N Totals:	147	24	43	67	39
PLAYOFFS							
1979-80	BOS	N	10	3	2	5	7
1982-83			17	3	1	4	18
2 yrs.		N Totals:	27	6	3	9	25

Connie Madigan

MADIGAN, CORNELIUS DENNIS 5'10", 185 lbs.
B. Oct. 4, 1934, Port Arthur, Ont. Defense, Shoots L

YEAR	TEAM & LEAGUE		GP	G	A	PTS	PIM
1972-73	STL	N	20	0	3	3	25
PLAYOFFS							
1972-73	STL	N	5	0	0	0	4

Dean Magee

MAGEE, DEAN 6'2", 210 lbs.
B. Apr. 29, 1955, Rocky Mtn. House, Alta. Left Wing, Shoots L

YEAR	TEAM & LEAGUE		GP	G	A	PTS	PIM
1977-78	MINN	N	7	0	0	0	4
1978-79	IND	W	5	0	1	1	10
2 yrs.		N Totals:	7	0	0	0	4
		W Totals:	5	0	1	1	10

Darryl Maggs

MAGGS, DARRYL JOHN 6'2", 195 lbs.
B. Apr. 6, 1949, Victoria, B.C. Defense, Shoots R

YEAR	TEAM & LEAGUE		GP	G	A	PTS	PIM
1971-72	CHI	N	59	7	4	11	4
1972-73			17	0	0	0	4
	CALIF	N	54	7	15	22	46
	2 team total		71	7	15	22	50
1973-74	CHI	W	78	8	22	30	148
1974-75			77	6	27	33	137
1975-76	D-O	W	42	4	23	27	42
	IND	W	36	5	16	21	40
	2 team total		78	9	39	48	82
1976-77			81	16	55	71	114
1977-78			0	0	0	0	0
	CIN	W	62	8	20	28	37
	2 team total		62	8	20	28	37
1978-79			27	4	14	18	22
1979-80	TOR	N	5	0	0	0	0
9 yrs.		N Totals:	135	14	19	33	54
		W Totals:	403	51	177	228	540
PLAYOFFS							
1971-72	CHI	N	4	0	0	0	0
1973-74	CHI	W	18	3	5	8	71
1975-76	IND	W	7	1	0	1	20
1976-77			9	1	4	5	4
4 yrs.		N Totals:	4	0	0	0	0
		W Totals:	34	5	9	14	95

Traded to **California** by Chicago for Dick Redmond, Dec. 5, 1972.

Marc Magnan

MAGNAN, MARC 5'11", 195 lbs.
B. Feb. 17, 1962, Beaumont, Alta. Forward

YEAR	TEAM & LEAGUE		GP	G	A	PTS	PIM
1982-83	TOR	N	4	0	1	1	5

Keith Magnuson

MAGNUSON, KEITH ARLEN 6', 185 lbs.
B. Apr. 27, 1947, Saskatoon, Sask. Defense, Shoots R

YEAR	TEAM & LEAGUE		GP	G	A	PTS	PIM
1969-70	CHI	N	76	0	24	24	**213**
1970-71			76	3	20	23	**291**
1971-72			74	2	19	21	201
1972-73			77	0	19	19	140
1973-74			57	2	11	13	105

Keith Magnuson continued

YEAR	TEAM & LEAGUE		GP	G	A	PTS	PIM
1974-75			48	2	12	14	117
1975-76			48	1	6	7	99
1976-77			37	1	6	7	86
1977-78			67	2	4	6	145
1978-79			26	1	4	5	41
1979-80			3	0	0	0	4
11 yrs.		**N Totals:**	589	14	125	139	1442
PLAYOFFS							
1969-70	**CHI**	**N**	8	1	2	3	17
1970-71			18	0	2	2	63
1971-72			8	0	1	1	29
1972-73			7	0	2	2	4
1973-74			11	1	0	1	17
1974-75			8	1	2	3	15
1975-76			4	0	0	0	12
1977-78			4	0	0	0	7
8 yrs.		**N Totals:**	68	3	9	12	164

Claimed by **Chicago** as fill in Expansion Draft, June 13, 1979.

John Mahaffy

MAHAFFY, JOHN 5'7", 165 lbs.
B. July 18, 1919, Montreal, Que. Center, Shoots L

YEAR	TEAM & LEAGUE		GP	G	A	PTS	PIM
1942-43	**MONT**	**N**	9	2	5	7	4
1943-44	**NYR**	**N**	28	9	20	29	0
2 yrs.		**N Totals:**	37	11	25	36	4
PLAYOFFS							
1944-45	**MONT**	**N**	1	0	1	1	0

Frank Mahovlich

MAHOVLICH, FRANCIS WILLIAM (Big M) 6', 205 lbs.
B. Jan. 10, 1938, Timmins, Ont. Left Wing, Shoots L
Won Calder Trophy, 1957-58
Hall of Fame, 1981

YEAR	TEAM & LEAGUE		GP	G	A	PTS	PIM
1956-57	**TOR**	**N**	3	1	0	1	2
1957-58			67	20	16	36	67
1958-59			63	22	27	49	94
1959-60			70	18	21	39	61
1960-61			70	48	36	84	131
1961-62			70	33	38	71	87
1962-63			67	36	37	73	56
1963-64			70	26	29	55	66
1964-65			59	23	28	51	76
1965-66			68	32	24	56	68
1966-67			63	18	28	46	44
1967-68			50	19	17	36	30
	DET	**N**	13	7	9	16	2
	2 team total		63	26	26	52	32
1968-69			76	49	29	78	38
1969-70			74	38	32	70	59
1970-71			35	14	18	32	30
	MONT	**N**	38	17	24	41	11
	2 team total		73	31	42	73	41
1971-72			76	43	53	96	36
1972-73			78	38	55	93	51
1973-74			71	31	49	80	47
1974-75	**TOR**	**W**	73	38	44	82	27
1975-76			75	34	55	89	14
1976-77	**BIRM**	**W**	17	3	20	23	12
1977-78			72	14	24	38	22
22 yrs.		**N Totals:**	1181	533	570	1103	1056
		W Totals:	237	89	143	232	75
PLAYOFFS							
1958-59	**TOR**	**N**	12	6	5	11	18
1959-60			10	3	1	4	27
1960-61			5	1	1	2	6
1961-62*			12	6	6	12	29
1962-63*			9	0	2	2	8
1963-64*			14	4	11	15	20
1964-65			6	0	3	3	9
1965-66			4	1	0	1	10
1966-67*			12	3	7	10	8
1969-70	**DET**	**N**	4	0	0	0	2
1970-71*	**MONT**	**N**	20	14	13	27	18
1971-72			6	3	2	5	2
1972-73*			17	9	14	23	6

Frank Mahovlich continued

YEAR	TEAM & LEAGUE		GP	G	A	PTS	PIM
1973-74			6	1	2	3	0
1974-75	**TOR**	**W**	6	3	0	3	2
1977-78	**BIRM**	**W**	3	1	1	2	0
16 yrs.		**N Totals:**	137	51	67	118	163
		W Totals:	9	4	1	5	2

Traded to **Detroit** by Toronto with Garry Unger, Pete Stemkowski, and the rights to Carl Brewer for Paul Henderson, Norm Ullman, and Floyd Smith, March 3, 1968. Traded to **Montreal** by Detroit for Mickey Redmond, Guy Charron, and Bill Collins, Jan. 13, 1971.

Pete Mahovlich

MAHOVLICH, PETER JOSEPH (Little M) 6'5", 210 lbs.
B. Oct. 10, 1946, Timmins, Ont. Center, Shoots L

YEAR	TEAM & LEAGUE		GP	G	A	PTS	PIM
1965-66	**DET**	**N**	3	0	1	1	0
1966-67			34	1	3	4	16
1967-68			15	6	4	10	13
1968-69			30	2	2	4	21
1969-70	**MONT**	**N**	36	9	8	17	51
1970-71			78	35	26	61	181
1971-72			75	35	32	67	103
1972-73			61	21	38	59	49
1973-74			78	36	37	73	122
1974-75			80	35	82	117	64
1975-76			80	34	71	105	76
1976-77			76	15	47	62	45
1977-78			17	3	5	8	4
	PITT	**N**	57	25	36	61	37
	2 team total		74	28	41	69	41
1978-79			60	14	39	53	39
1979-80	**DET**	**N**	80	16	50	66	69
1980-81			24	1	4	5	26
16 yrs.		**N Totals:**	884	288	485	773	916
PLAYOFFS							
1970-71*	**MONT**	**N**	20	10	6	16	43
1971-72			6	0	2	2	12
1972-73*			17	4	9	13	22
1973-74			6	2	1	3	4
1974-75			11	6	10	16	10
1975-76*			13	4	8	12	24
1976-77*			13	4	5	9	19
1978-79	**PITT**	**N**	2	0	1	1	0
8 yrs.		**N Totals:**	88	30	42	72	134

Traded to **Montreal** by Detroit with Bart Crashley for Garry Monahan and Doug Piper, June 6, 1969. Traded to **Pittsburgh** by Montreal with Peter Lee for Pierre Larouche and a player to be named later (Peter Marsh, Dec. 5, 1977), Nov. 29, 1977. Traded to **Detroit** by Pittsburgh for Nick Libett, Aug. 3, 1979.

Frank Mailley

MAILLEY, FRANK
B. Unknown Defense

YEAR	TEAM & LEAGUE		GP	G	A	PTS	PIM
1942-43	**MONT**	**N**	1	0	0	0	0

Jim Mair

MAIR, JAMES MCKAY 5'9", 170 lbs.
B. May 15, 1946, Schumacher, Ont. Defense, Shoots R

YEAR	TEAM & LEAGUE		GP	G	A	PTS	PIM
1970-71	**PHI**	**N**	2	0	0	0	0
1971-72			2	0	0	0	0
1972-73	**NYI**	**N**	49	2	11	13	41
	VAN	**N**	15	1	0	1	8
	2 team total		64	3	11	14	49
1973-74			6	1	3	4	0
1974-75			2	0	1	1	0
5 yrs.		**N Totals:**	76	4	15	19	49
PLAYOFFS							
1970-71	**PHI**	**N**	4	1	2	3	4

Drafted by **N.Y. Islanders** from Philadelphia in Expansion Draft, June 6, 1972. Claimed by **Vancouver** on waivers from N.Y. Islanders, Feb. 19, 1973.

Fern Majeau

MAJEAU, FERNAND — 5'8½", 155 lbs.
B. May 3, 1916, Verdun, Que. — Forward, Shoots L

YEAR	TEAM & LEAGUE		GP	G	A	PTS	PIM
1943-44	**MONT**	**N**	44	20	18	38	39
1944-45			12	2	6	8	4
2 yrs.		**N Totals:**	56	22	24	46	43
PLAYOFFS							
1943-44*	**MONT**	**N**	1	0	0	0	0

Chico Maki

MAKI, RONALD PATRICK — 5'10", 170 lbs.
B. Aug. 17, 1939, Sault Ste. Marie, Ont. — Right Wing, Shoots R

YEAR	TEAM & LEAGUE		GP	G	A	PTS	PIM
1961-62	**CHI**	**N**	16	4	6	10	2
1962-63			65	7	17	24	35
1963-64			68	8	14	22	70
1964-65			65	16	24	40	58
1965-66			68	17	31	48	41
1966-67			56	9	29	38	14
1967-68			60	8	16	24	4
1968-69			66	7	21	28	30
1969-70			75	10	24	34	27
1970-71			72	22	26	48	18
1971-72			61	13	34	47	22
1972-73			77	13	19	32	10
1973-74			69	9	26	35	12
1975-76			22	0	6	6	2
14 yrs.		**N Totals:**	840	143	293	436	345
PLAYOFFS							
1960-61*	**CHI**	**N**	1	0	0	0	0
1962-63			6	0	1	1	2
1963-64			7	0	0	0	15
1964-65			14	3	9	12	8
1965-66			3	1	1	2	0
1966-67			6	0	0	0	0
1967-68			2	1	0	1	2
1969-70			8	2	2	4	2
1970-71			18	6	5	11	6
1971-72			8	1	4	5	4
1972-73			16	2	8	10	0
1973-74			11	0	1	1	2
1975-76			4	0	0	0	0
13 yrs.		**N Totals:**	104	16	31	47	41

Wayne Maki

MAKI, WAYNE — 5'11", 185 lbs.
B. Nov. 10, 1944, Sault Ste. Marie, Ont. — Left Wing, Shoots L

YEAR	TEAM & LEAGUE		GP	G	A	PTS	PIM
1967-68	**CHI**	**N**	49	5	5	10	32
1968-69			1	0	0	0	0
1969-70	**STL**	**N**	16	2	1	3	4
1970-71	**VAN**	**N**	78	25	38	63	99
1971-72			76	22	25	47	43
1972-73			26	3	10	13	6
6 yrs.		**N Totals:**	246	57	79	136	184

Drafted by **St. Louis** from Chicago, June 11, 1969. Drafted by **Vancouver** from St. Louis in Expansion Draft, June 10, 1970.

Karl Makkonen

MAKKONEN, KARL — 6', 190 lbs.
B. Jan. 20, 1955, Pori, Finland — Right Wing, Shoots R

YEAR	TEAM & LEAGUE		GP	G	A	PTS	PIM
1979-80	**EDM**	**N**	9	2	2	4	0

Signed by **Edmonton** as free agent, June 23, 1979.

Merlin Malinowski

MALINOWSKI, MERLIN TRAVIS (Magician) — 6', 190 lbs.
B. Sept. 27, 1958, N. Battleford, Sask. — Center, Shoots L

YEAR	TEAM & LEAGUE		GP	G	A	PTS	PIM
1978-79	**COLO**	**N**	54	6	17	23	10
1979-80			10	2	4	6	2
1980-81			69	25	37	62	61
1981-82			69	13	28	41	32
1982-83	**NJ**	**N**	5	3	2	5	0
	HART	**N**	75	5	23	28	16
	2 team total		80	8	25	33	16
5 yrs.		**N Totals:**	282	54	111	165	121

Merlin Malinowski continued

Traded by New Jersey with the rights to Scott Fusco to **Hartford** for Garry Howatt and Rick Meagher, Oct. 15, 1982.

Cliff Malone

MALONE, CLIFFORD — 5'10", 155 lbs.
B. Sept. 4, 1925, Quebec City, Que. — Right Wing, Shoots R

YEAR	TEAM & LEAGUE		GP	G	A	PTS	PIM
1951-52	**MONT**	**N**	3	0	0	0	0

Greg Malone

MALONE, WILLIAM GREGORY — 6', 190 lbs.
B. Mar. 8, 1956, Fredericton, N.B. — Center, Shoots L

YEAR	TEAM & LEAGUE		GP	G	A	PTS	PIM
1976-77	**PITT**	**N**	66	18	19	37	43
1977-78			78	18	43	61	80
1978-79			80	35	30	65	52
1979-80			51	19	32	51	46
1980-81			62	21	29	50	68
1981-82			78	15	24	39	125
1982-83			80	17	44	61	82
7 yrs.		**N Totals:**	495	143	221	364	496
PLAYOFFS							
1976-77	**PITT**	**N**	3	1	1	2	2
1978-79			7	0	1	1	10
1980-81			5	2	3	5	16
1981-82			3	0	0	0	4
4 yrs.		**N Totals:**	18	3	5	8	32

Joe Malone

MALONE, M. JOSEPH
B. Feb. 28, 1890, Sillery, Que. — Forward, Shoots L
Won Art Ross Trophy, 1917–18, 1919-20
Hall of Fame, 1950

YEAR	TEAM & LEAGUE		GP	G	A	PTS	PIM
1917-18	**MONT**	**N**	20	**44**	0	**44**	12
1918-19			8	7	1	8	3
1919-20	**QUE**	**N**	24	**39**	6	**45**	12
1920-21	**HAMIL**	**N**	20	30	4	34	2
1921-22			24	25	7	32	4
1922-23	**MONT**	**N**	20	1	0	1	2
1923-24			9	0	0	0	0
7 yrs.		**N Totals:**	125	146	18	164	35
PLAYOFFS							
1917-18	**MONT**	**N**	2	1	0	1	0
1918-19			5	6	1	7	0
1922-23			2	0	0	0	0
3 yrs.		**N Totals:**	9	7	1	8	0

Dan Maloney

MALONEY, DANIEL CHARLES — 6'2", 195 lbs.
B. Sept. 24, 1950, Barrie, Ont. — Left Wing, Shoots L

YEAR	TEAM & LEAGUE		GP	G	A	PTS	PIM
1970-71	**CHI**	**N**	74	12	14	26	174
1972-73			57	13	17	30	63
	LA	**N**	14	4	7	11	18
	2 team total		71	17	24	41	81
1973-74			65	15	17	32	113
1974-75			80	27	39	66	165
1975-76	**DET**	**N**	77	27	39	66	203
1976-77			34	13	13	26	64
1977-78			66	16	29	45	151
	TOR	**N**	13	3	4	7	25
	2 team total		79	19	33	52	176
1978-79			77	17	36	53	157
1979-80			71	17	16	33	102
1980-81			65	20	21	41	183
1981-82			44	8	7	15	71
11 yrs.		**N Totals:**	737	192	259	451	1489
PLAYOFFS							
1970-71	**CHI**	**N**	10	0	1	1	8
1973-74	**LA**	**N**	5	0	0	0	2
1974-75			3	0	0	0	2
1977-78	**TOR**	**N**	13	1	3	4	17
1978-79			6	3	3	6	2

Dan Maloney continued

YEAR	TEAM & LEAGUE		GP	G	A	PTS	PIM
1980-81			3	0	0	0	4
6 yrs.		N Totals:	40	4	7	11	35

Traded to **Los Angeles** by Chicago for Ralph Backstrom, Feb. 16, 1973. Traded to **Detroit** by Los Angeles with Terry Harper and Los Angeles' second choice (later transferred to Minnesota, Jimmy Roberts) in 1976 Amateur Draft for Bart Crashley and the rights to Marcel Dionne, June 23, 1975. Traded to **Toronto** by Detroit with Detroit's second round choice (Craig Muni) in the 1980 Entry Draft for Errol Thompson and Toronto's first-round choice (Brent Peterson) and second round choice (Al Jensen) in the 1978 Amateur Draft and Toronto's first-round choice (Mike Blaisdell) in the 1980 Entry Draft, Mar. 13, 1978.

Dave Maloney

MALONEY, DAVID WILFRED — 6'1", 195 lbs.
B. July 31, 1956, Kitchener, Ont. — Defense, Shoots L

YEAR	TEAM & LEAGUE		GP	G	A	PTS	PIM
1974-75	NYR	N	4	0	2	2	0
1975-76			21	1	3	4	66
1976-77			66	3	18	21	100
1977-78			56	2	19	21	63
1978-79			76	11	17	28	151
1979-80			77	12	25	37	186
1980-81			79	11	36	47	132
1981-82			64	13	36	49	105
1982-83			78	8	42	50	132
9 yrs.		N Totals:	521	61	198	259	935
PLAYOFFS							
1977-78	NYR	N	3	0	0	0	11
1978-79			17	3	4	7	45
1979-80			8	2	1	3	8
1980-81			2	0	2	2	9
1981-82			10	1	4	5	6
1982-83			7	1	6	7	10
6 yrs.		N Totals:	47	7	17	24	89

Don Maloney

MALONEY, DONALD MICHAEL — 6'1", 190 lbs.
B. Sept. 5, 1958, Lindsay, Ont. — Left Wing, Shoots L

YEAR	TEAM & LEAGUE		GP	G	A	PTS	PIM
1978-79	NYR	N	28	9	17	26	39
1979-80			79	25	48	73	97
1980-81			61	29	23	52	99
1981-82			54	22	36	58	73
1982-83			78	29	40	69	88
5 yrs.		N Totals:	300	114	164	278	396
PLAYOFFS							
1978-79	NYR	N	18	7	13	20	19
1979-80			9	0	4	4	10
1980-81			13	1	6	7	13
1981-82			10	5	5	10	10
1982-83			5	0	1	1	0
5 yrs.		N Totals:	55	13	29	42	52

Phil Maloney

MALONEY, PHILIP FRANCIS — 5'9", 170 lbs.
B. Oct. 6, 1927, Ottawa, Ont. — Center, Shoots L

YEAR	TEAM & LEAGUE		GP	G	A	PTS	PIM
1949-50	BOS	N	70	15	31	46	6
1950-51			13	2	0	2	2
	TOR	N	1	1	0	1	0
	2 team total		14	3	0	3	2
1952-53			29	2	6	8	2
1959-60	CHI	N	21	6	4	10	0
4 yrs.		N Totals:	134	26	41	67	10
PLAYOFFS							
1958-59	CHI	N	6	0	0	0	0

Traded to **Toronto** by Boston with Fern Flaman, Ken Smith and Leo Boivin for Bill Ezinicki and Vic Lynn, Nov. 16, 1950. Drafted by **N.Y. Rangers** from Toronto, June 4, 1957.

Ray Maluta

MALUTA, RAYMOND WILLIAM — 5'8", 173 lbs.
B. July 24, 1954, Flin Flon, Man. — Defense, Shoots L

YEAR	TEAM & LEAGUE		GP	G	A	PTS	PIM
1975-76	BOS	N	2	0	0	0	2
1976-77			23	2	3	5	4

Ray Maluta continued

YEAR	TEAM & LEAGUE		GP	G	A	PTS	PIM
2 yrs.		N Totals:	25	2	3	5	6
PLAYOFFS							
1975-76	BOS	N	2	0	0	0	0

Tom Manastersky

MANASTERSKY, TIMOTHY — 5'9", 185 lbs.
B. Mar. 7, 1929, Montreal, Que. — Defense, Shoots R

YEAR	TEAM & LEAGUE		GP	G	A	PTS	PIM
1950-51	MONT	N	6	0	0	0	11

Gus Mancuso

MANCUSO, FELIX
B. Apr. 11, 1914, Niagara Falls, Ont.

YEAR	TEAM & LEAGUE		GP	G	A	PTS	PIM
1937-38	MONT	N	17	1	1	2	4
1938-39			2	0	0	0	0
1939-40			2	0	0	0	0
1942-43	NYR	N	21	6	8	14	13
4 yrs.		N Totals:	42	7	9	16	17

Dan Mandich

MANDICH, DAN — 6'3", 205 lbs.
B. June 12, 1960, Brantford, Ont. — Defense, Shoots R

YEAR	TEAM & LEAGUE		GP	G	A	PTS	PIM
1982-83	MINN	N	67	3	4	7	169
PLAYOFFS							
1982-83	MINN	N	7	0	0	0	2

Kris Manery

MANERY, KRIS FRANKLIN — 6', 185 lbs.
B. Sept. 24, 1954, Leamington, Ont. — Right Wing, Shoots R

YEAR	TEAM & LEAGUE		GP	G	A	PTS	PIM
1977-78	CLEVE	N	78	22	27	49	14
1978-79	MINN	N	60	17	19	36	16
1979-80			28	3	4	7	16
	VAN	N	21	2	1	3	15
	WINN	N	16	6	4	10	6
	3 team total		65	11	9	20	37
1980-81			47	13	9	22	24
4 yrs.		N Totals:	250	63	64	127	91

Put on **Minnesota** Reserve list after Cleveland-Minnesota Dispersal Draft, June 15, 1978. Traded to **Vancouver** by Minnesota for Vancouver's second round choice (later transferred to Montreal, Kent Carlson) in the 1982 Entry Draft, Jan. 4, 1980. Claimed on waivers by **Winnipeg** from Vancouver, Feb. 27, 1980.

Randy Manery

MANERY, RANDY NEAL — 6', 185 lbs.
B. Jan. 10, 1949, Leamington, Ont. — Defense, Shoots R

YEAR	TEAM & LEAGUE		GP	G	A	PTS	PIM
1970-71	DET	N	2	0	0	0	0
1971-72			1	0	0	0	0
1972-73	ATL	N	78	5	30	35	44
1973-74			78	8	29	37	75
1974-75			68	5	27	32	48
1975-76			80	7	32	39	42
1976-77			73	5	24	29	33
1977-78	LA	N	79	6	27	33	61
1978-79			71	8	27	35	64
1979-80			52	6	10	16	48
10 yrs.		N Totals:	582	50	206	256	415
PLAYOFFS							
1973-74	ATL	N	4	0	2	2	4
1975-76			2	0	0	0	0
1976-77			3	0	0	0	0
1977-78	LA	N	2	0	0	0	2
1978-79			2	0	0	0	6
5 yrs.		N Totals:	13	0	2	2	12

Drafted by **Atlanta** from Detroit in Expansion Draft, June 6, 1972. Traded to **Los Angeles** by Atlanta for Ab DeMarco, May 23, 1977.

Jack Mann

MANN, JOHN E. K. 5'7", 180 lbs.

B. July 27, 1919, Winnipeg, Man. Center, Shoots L

YEAR	TEAM & LEAGUE		GP	G	A	PTS	PIM
1943-44	NYR	N	3	0	0	0	0
1944-45			6	3	4	7	0
2 yrs.		N Totals:	9	3	4	7	0

Jim Mann

MANN, JAMES EDWARD 6', 202 lbs.

B. Apr. 17, 1959, Montreal, Que. Right Wing, Shoots R

YEAR	TEAM & LEAGUE		GP	G	A	PTS	PIM
1979-80	WINN	N	72	3	5	8	**287**
1980-81			37	3	3	6	105
1981-82			37	3	2	5	79
1982-83			40	0	1	1	73
4 yrs.		N Totals:	186	9	11	20	544
PLAYOFFS							
1981-82	WINN	N	3	0	0	0	7
1982-83			1	0	0	0	0
2 yrs.		N Totals:	4	0	0	0	7

Ken Mann

MANN, KENNETH ROSS 5'11", 200 lbs.

B. Sept. 5, 1953, Hamilton, Ont. Right Wing, Shoots R

YEAR	TEAM & LEAGUE		GP	G	A	PTS	PIM
1975-76	DET	N	1	0	0	0	0

Norm Mann

MANN, NORMAN THOMAS 5'10", 155 lbs.

B. Mar. 3, 1914, Bradford, England Right Wing, Shoots R

YEAR	TEAM & LEAGUE		GP	G	A	PTS	PIM
1938-39	TOR	N	16	0	0	0	2
1940-41			15	0	3	3	2
2 yrs.		N Totals:	31	0	3	3	4
PLAYOFFS							
1940-41	TOR	N	1	0	0	0	0

Ren Manners

MANNERS, RENNISON

B. Unknown Forward

YEAR	TEAM & LEAGUE		GP	G	A	PTS	PIM
1929-30	PITT	N	33	3	2	5	14
1930-31	PHI	N	4	0	0	0	0
2 yrs.		N Totals:	37	3	2	5	14

Bob Manno

MANNO, ROBERT JOHN 6', 185 lbs.

B. Oct. 31, 1956, Niagara Falls, Ont. Defense, Shoots L

YEAR	TEAM & LEAGUE		GP	G	A	PTS	PIM
1976-77	VAN	N	2	0	0	0	0
1977-78			49	5	14	19	29
1978-79			52	5	16	21	42
1979-80			40	3	14	17	14
1980-81			20	0	11	11	30
1981-82	TOR	N	72	9	41	50	67
6 yrs.		N Totals:	235	22	96	118	182
PLAYOFFS							
1978-79	VAN	N	3	0	1	1	4
1979-80			4	1	0	1	6
1980-81			3	0	0	0	2
3 yrs.		N Totals:	10	1	1	2	12

Ray Manson

MANSON, RAYMOND CLIFTON 5'11", 180 lbs.

B. Dec. 3, 1926, St. Boniface, Man. Left Wing, Shoots L

YEAR	TEAM & LEAGUE		GP	G	A	PTS	PIM
1947-48	BOS	N	1	0	0	0	0
1948-49	NYR	N	1	0	1	1	0
2 yrs.		N Totals:	2	0	1	1	0

George Mantha

MANTHA, LEON-GEORGES 5'8½", 162 lbs.

B. Nov. 29, 1908, Lachine, Que. Left Wing, Shoots L

YEAR	TEAM & LEAGUE		GP	G	A	PTS	PIM
1928-29	MONT	N	31	0	0	0	8
1929-30			44	5	2	7	16
1930-31			44	11	6	17	25
1931-32			48	1	7	8	8
1932-33			43	3	6	9	10
1933-34			44	6	9	15	12
1934-35			42	12	10	22	14
1935-36			35	1	12	13	14
1936-37			47	13	14	27	17
1937-38			47	23	19	42	12
1938-39			25	5	5	10	6
1939-40			42	9	11	20	6
1940-41			6	0	1	1	0
13 yrs.		N Totals:	498	85	102	191	148
PLAYOFFS							
1928-29	MONT	N	3	0	0	0	0
1929-30*			6	0	0	0	0
1930-31*			10	5	1	6	4
1931-32			4	0	1	1	8
1934-35			2	0	0	0	4
1936-37			5	0	0	0	0
1937-38			3	1	0	1	0
1938-39			3	0	0	0	0
8 yrs.		N Totals:	36	6	2	8	16

Moe Mantha

MANTHA, MAURICE WILLIAM 6'2", 197 lbs.

B. Jan. 21, 1961, Lakewood, Ohio Defense, Shoots L

YEAR	TEAM & LEAGUE		GP	G	A	PTS	PIM
1980-81	WINN	N	58	2	23	25	35
1981-82			25	0	12	12	28
1982-83			21	2	7	9	6
3 yrs.		N Totals:	104	4	42	46	69
PLAYOFFS							
1981-82	WINN	N	4	1	3	4	16
1982-83			2	2	2	4	0
2 yrs.		N Totals:	6	3	5	8	16

Sylvio Mantha

MANTHA, SYLVIO 5'10", 178 lbs.

B. Apr. 14, 1902, Montreal, Que. Defense, Shoots R

Hall of Fame, 1960

YEAR	TEAM & LEAGUE		GP	G	A	PTS	PIM
1923-24	MONT	N	24	1	0	1	9
1924-25			30	2	0	2	16
1925-26			34	2	1	3	66
1926-27			43	10	5	15	77
1927-28			43	4	11	15	61
1928-29			44	9	4	13	56
1929-30			44	13	11	24	**108**
1930-31			44	4	7	11	75
1931-32			47	5	5	10	62
1932-33			48	4	7	11	50
1933-34			48	4	6	10	24
1934-35			47	3	11	14	36
1935-36			42	2	4	6	25
1936-37	BOS	N	4	0	0	0	2
14 yrs.		N Totals:	542	63	72	142	667
PLAYOFFS							
1923-24*	MONT	N	5	0	0	0	0
1924-25			6	0	0	0	2
1926-27			4	1	0	1	4
1927-28			2	0	0	0	6
1928-29			3	0	0	0	0
1929-30*			6	2	1	3	18
1930-31*			10	2	1	3	26
1931-32			4	0	1	1	8
1932-33			2	0	1	1	2
1933-34			2	0	0	0	2
1934-35			2	0	0	0	2
11 yrs.		N Totals:	46	5	4	9	70

Pete Mara

MARA, PETER JOHN 5'7", 167 lbs.
B. July 5, 1947, Point Edward, Ont. Center, Shoots L

YEAR	TEAM & LEAGUE		GP	G	A	PTS	PIM
1974-75	CHI	W	57	17	21	38	16
1975-76	D-O	W	40	3	7	10	8
2 yrs.		W Totals:	97	20	28	48	24

Buddy Maracle

MARACLE, HENRY ELMER
B. Sept. 8, 1904, Ayr, Ont. Forward

YEAR	TEAM & LEAGUE		GP	G	A	PTS	PIM
1930-31	NYR	N	11	1	3	4	4

PLAYOFFS

YEAR	TEAM & LEAGUE		GP	G	A	PTS	PIM
1930-31	NYR	N	4	0	0	0	0

Milan Marcetta

MARCETTA, MILAN 6'1", 195 lbs.
B. Sept. 19, 1936, Cadomin, Alta. Center, Shoots L

YEAR	TEAM & LEAGUE		GP	G	A	PTS	PIM
1967-68	MINN	N	36	4	12	16	6
1968-69			18	3	2	5	4
2 yrs.		N Totals:	54	7	14	21	10

PLAYOFFS

YEAR	TEAM & LEAGUE		GP	G	A	PTS	PIM
1966-67*	TOR	N	3	0	0	0	0
1967-68	MINN	N	14	7	7	14	4
2 yrs.		N Totals:	17	7	7	14	4

Sold to **Minnesota** by Toronto, Dec. 27, 1967.

Mush March

MARCH, HAROLD 5'5", 154 lbs.
B. Oct. 18, 1908, Silton, Sask. Right Wing, Shoots R

YEAR	TEAM & LEAGUE		GP	G	A	PTS	PIM
1928-29	CHI	N	35	3	3	6	6
1929-30			43	8	7	15	48
1930-31			44	11	6	17	36
1931-32			48	12	13	25	36
1932-33			48	9	11	20	38
1933-34			48	4	13	17	26
1934-35			47	13	17	30	48
1935-36			48	16	19	35	48
1936-37			37	11	6	17	31
1937-38			41	11	17	28	16
1938-39			46	10	11	21	29
1939-40			45	9	14	23	49
1940-41			44	8	9	17	16
1941-42			48	6	26	32	22
1942-43			50	7	29	36	46
1943-44			48	10	27	37	16
1944-45			38	5	5	10	12
17 yrs.		N Totals:	758	153	233	386	523

PLAYOFFS

YEAR	TEAM & LEAGUE		GP	G	A	PTS	PIM
1930-31	CHI	N	9	3	1	4	11
1931-32			2	0	0	0	2
1933-34*			8	2	2	4	6
1934-35			2	0	0	0	0
1935-36	BOS	N	2	2	3	5	0
1937-38*	CHI	N	10	2	4	6	12
1939-40			2	1	0	1	2
1940-41			5	2	3	5	0
1941-42			3	0	2	2	4
1943-44			5	0	0	0	4
10 yrs.		N Totals:	48	12	15	27	41

Brian Marchinko

MARCHINKO, BRIAN NICHOLAS WAYNE 6', 180 lbs.
B. Aug. 2, 1948, Weyburn, Sask. Center, Shoots R

YEAR	TEAM & LEAGUE		GP	G	A	PTS	PIM
1970-71	TOR	N	2	0	0	0	0
1971-72			3	0	0	0	0
1972-73	NYI	N	36	2	6	8	0
1973-74			6	0	0	0	0
4 yrs.		N Totals:	47	2	6	8	0

Drafted by **N.Y. Islanders** from Toronto in Expansion Draft, June 6, 1972.

Lou Marcon

MARCON, LOUIS ANGELO 5'9", 178 lbs.
B. May 28, 1935, Fort William, Ont. Defense, Shoots R

YEAR	TEAM & LEAGUE		GP	G	A	PTS	PIM
1958-59	DET	N	31	0	1	1	12
1959-60			38	0	3	3	30
1962-63			1	0	0	0	0
3 yrs.		N Totals:	70	0	4	4	42

Don Marcotte

MARCOTTE, DONALD MICHEL 5'10", 185 lbs.
B. Apr. 15, 1947, Asbestos, Que. Left Wing, Shoots L

YEAR	TEAM & LEAGUE		GP	G	A	PTS	PIM
1965-66	BOS	N	1	0	0	0	0
1968-69			7	1	0	1	2
1969-70			35	9	3	12	14
1970-71			75	15	13	28	30
1971-72			47	6	4	10	12
1972-73			78	24	31	55	49
1973-74			78	24	26	50	18
1974-75			80	31	33	64	76
1975-76			58	16	20	36	24
1976-77			80	27	18	45	20
1977-78			77	20	34	54	16
1978-79			79	20	27	47	10
1979-80			32	4	11	15	0
1980-81			72	20	13	33	32
1981-82			69	13	21	34	14
15 yrs.		N Totals:	868	230	254	484	317

PLAYOFFS

YEAR	TEAM & LEAGUE		GP	G	A	PTS	PIM
1969-70*	BOS	N	14	2	0	2	11
1970-71			4	0	0	0	0
1971-72*			14	3	0	3	6
1972-73			5	1	1	2	0
1973-74			16	4	2	6	8
1974-75			3	1	0	1	0
1975-76			12	4	2	6	8
1976-77			14	5	6	11	10
1977-78			15	5	4	9	8
1978-79			11	5	3	8	10
1979-80			10	2	3	5	4
1980-81			3	2	2	4	6
1981-82			11	0	4	4	10
13 yrs.		N Totals:	132	34	27	61	81

Hector Marini

MARINI, HECTOR (The Wrecker) 6'1", 204 lbs.
B. Jan. 27, 1957, Timmins, Ont. Right Wing, Shoots R

YEAR	TEAM & LEAGUE		GP	G	A	PTS	PIM
1978-79	NYI	N	1	0	0	0	2
1980-81			14	4	7	11	39
1981-82			30	4	9	13	53
1982-83	NJ	N	77	17	28	45	105
4 yrs.		N Totals:	122	25	44	69	199

PLAYOFFS

YEAR	TEAM & LEAGUE		GP	G	A	PTS	PIM
1978-79	NYI	N	1	0	0	0	0
1980-81*			9	3	6	9	14
2 yrs.		N Totals:	10	3	6	9	14

Traded to **New Jersey** by New York Islanders for future considerations, Oct. 1, 1982.

Frank Mario

MARIO, FRANK GEORGE 5'8", 170 lbs.
B. Feb. 25, 1921, Esterhazy, Sask. Center, Shoots L

YEAR	TEAM & LEAGUE		GP	G	A	PTS	PIM
1941-42	BOS	N	9	1	1	2	0
1944-45			44	8	18	26	24
2 yrs.		N Totals:	53	9	19	28	24

John Mariucci

MARIUCCI, JOHN 5'10", 200 lbs.
B. May 8, 1916, Eveleth, Mn. Defense, Shoots L

YEAR	TEAM & LEAGUE		GP	G	A	PTS	PIM
1940-41	CHI	N	23	0	5	5	33
1941-42			47	5	8	13	44
1945-46			50	3	8	11	58
1946-47			52	2	9	11	110
1947-48			51	1	4	5	63

John Mariucci continued

YEAR	TEAM & LEAGUE		GP	G	A	PTS	PIM
5 yrs.		N Totals:	223	11	34	45	308
PLAYOFFS							
1940-41	CHI	N	4	0	2	2	16
1941-42			3	0	0	0	0
1945-46			4	0	1	1	10
3 yrs.		N Totals:	11	0	3	3	26

John Markell

MARKELL, JOHN RICHARD 5'11", 185 lbs.
B. Mar. 10, 1956, Cornwall, Ont. Left Wing, Shoots L

YEAR	TEAM & LEAGUE		GP	G	A	PTS	PIM
1979-80	WINN	N	38	10	7	17	21
1980-81			14	1	3	4	15
2 yrs.		N Totals:	52	11	10	21	36

Signed by **Winnipeg** as a free agent, April 16, 1979. Traded to **St. Louis** by Winnipeg with Scott Campbell for Ed Staniowski, Bryan Maxwell and Paul MacLean, July 3, 1981.

Gus Marker

MARKER, AUGUST SOLBERG
B. Aug. 1, 1907, Wetaskewin, Alta. Forward

YEAR	TEAM & LEAGUE		GP	G	A	PTS	PIM
1932-33	DET	N	15	1	1	2	8
1933-34			7	1	0	1	2
1934-35	MON(M)	N	42	11	4	15	18
1935-36			47	7	12	19	10
1936-37			48	10	12	22	22
1937-38			48	9	15	24	35
1938-39	TOR	N	43	9	6	15	14
1939-40			42	10	9	19	15
1940-41			27	4	5	9	10
1941-42	NYA	N	17	2	5	7	2
10 yrs.		N Totals:	336	64	69	133	136
PLAYOFFS							
1933-34	DET	N	3	1	1	2	2
1934-35*	MON(M)	N	7	1	1	2	4
1935-36			3	1	0	1	2
1936-37			5	0	1	1	0
1938-39	TOR	N	10	2	2	4	0
1939-40			10	1	3	4	23
1940-41			7	0	0	0	5
7 yrs.		N Totals:	45	6	8	14	36

Ray Markham

MARKHAM, RAYMOND JOSEPH 6'3", 220 lbs.
B. Jan. 23, 1958, Windsor, Ont. Center, Shoots R

YEAR	TEAM & LEAGUE		GP	G	A	PTS	PIM
1979-80	NYR	N	14	1	1	2	21
PLAYOFFS							
1979-80	NYR	N	7	1	0	1	24

Traded to **Edmonton** by N.Y. Rangers for John Hughes, Mar. 10, 1981.

Jack Markle

MARKLE, JOHN A.
B. Thessalon, Ont. Forward

YEAR	TEAM & LEAGUE		GP	G	A	PTS	PIM
1935-36	TOR	N	8	0	1	1	0

Jack Marks

MARKS, JOHN 6'2", 195 lbs.
B. Mar. 28, 1948, Winnipeg, Man. Defense, Shoots L

YEAR	TEAM & LEAGUE		GP	G	A	PTS	PIM
1917-18	MON(W)	N	1	0	0	0	0
	TOR	N	5	0	0	0	0
	2 team total		6	0	0	0	0
1919-20	QUE	N	1	0	0	0	4
2 yrs.		N Totals:	7	0	0	0	4

John Marks

MARKS, JOHN GARRISON 6'2", 200 lbs.
B. Mar. 22, 1948, Hamiota, Man. Left Wing, Shoots L

YEAR	TEAM & LEAGUE		GP	G	A	PTS	PIM
1972-73	CHI	N	55	3	10	13	21
1973-74			76	13	18	31	22
1974-75			80	17	30	47	56
1975-76			80	21	23	44	43
1976-77			80	7	15	22	41
1977-78			80	15	22	37	26
1978-79			80	21	24	45	35
1979-80			74	6	15	21	51
1980-81			39	8	6	14	28
1981-82			13	1	0	1	7
10 yrs.		N Totals:	657	112	163	275	330
PLAYOFFS							
1972-73	CHI	N	16	1	2	3	2
1973-74			11	2	0	2	8
1974-75			8	2	6	8	34
1975-76			4	0	0	0	10
1976-77			2	0	0	0	4
1977-78			4	0	1	1	0
1978-79			4	0	0	0	2
1979-80			4	0	0	0	0
1980-81			3	0	0	0	0
1981-82			1	0	0	0	0
10 yrs.		N Totals:	57	5	9	14	60

Mario Marois

MAROIS, MARIO 5'11", 170 lbs.
B. Dec. 15, 1957, Ancienne Lorette, Que. Defense, Shoots L

YEAR	TEAM & LEAGUE		GP	G	A	PTS	PIM
1977-78	NYR	N	8	1	1	2	15
1978-79			71	5	26	31	153
1979-80			79	8	23	31	142
1980-81			8	1	2	3	46
	VAN	N	50	4	12	16	115
	QUE	N	11	0	7	7	20
	3 team total		69	5	21	26	181
1981-82			71	11	32	43	161
1982-83			36	2	12	14	108
6 yrs.		N Totals:	334	32	115	147	760
PLAYOFFS							
1977-78	NYR	N	1	0	0	0	5
1978-79			18	0	6	6	29
1979-80			9	0	2	2	8
1980-81	QUE	N	5	0	1	1	6
1981-82			13	1	2	3	44
5 yrs.		N Totals:	46	1	11	12	92

Traded to **Vancouver** by N.Y. Rangers with Jim Mayer for Jere Gillis and Jeff Bandura, Nov. 11, 1980. Traded to **Quebec** by Vancouver for Garry Lariviere, Mar. 10, 1981.

Gilles Marotte

MAROTTE, JEAN GILLES (Captain Crunch)
5'9", 205 lbs.
B. June 7, 1945, Montreal, Que. Defense, Shoots L

YEAR	TEAM & LEAGUE		GP	G	A	PTS	PIM
1965-66	BOS	N	51	3	17	20	52
1966-67			67	7	8	15	65
1967-68	CHI	N	73	0	21	21	122
1968-69			68	5	29	34	120
1969-70			51	5	13	18	52
	LA	N	21	0	6	6	0
	2 team total		72	5	19	24	52
1970-71			78	6	27	33	96
1971-72			72	10	24	34	83
1972-73			78	6	39	45	7
1973-74			22	1	11	12	23
	NYR	N	46	2	17	19	28
	2 team total		68	3	28	31	51
1974-75			77	4	32	36	69
1975-76			57	4	17	21	34
1976-77	STL	N	47	3	4	7	26
1977-78	CIN	W	0	0	0	0	0
	IND	W	73	3	20	23	76
	2 team total		73	3	20	23	76
13 yrs.		N Totals:	808	56	265	321	777
		W Totals:	73	3	20	23	76

Gilles Marotte continued

PLAYOFFS

YEAR	TEAM & LEAGUE		GP	G	A	PTS	PIM
1967-68	**CHI**	**N**	11	3	1	4	14
1973-74	**NYR**	**N**	12	0	1	1	6
1974-75			3	0	1	1	4
1976-77	**STL**	**N**	3	0	0	0	2
4 yrs.		**N Totals:**	29	3	3	6	26

Traded to **Chicago** by Boston with Pit Martin and Jack Norris for Phil Esposito, Ken Hodge, and Fred Stanfield, May 15, 1967. Traded to **Los Angeles** by Chicago with Jim Stanfield and Denis DeJordy for Brian Campbell, Bill White, and goaltender Gerry Desjardins, Feb. 10, 1970. Traded to **N.Y. Rangers** by Los Angeles with Real Lemieux for Sheldon Kannegiesser, Mike Murphy, and Tom Williams, Nov. 30, 1973. Claimed on waivers by **St. Louis** from N.Y. Rangers, Oct. 12, 1976.

Mark Marquess

MARQUESS, CLARENCE EMMETT 5'8", 160 lbs.
B. Mar. 26, 1925, Bassano, Alta. Right Wing, Shoots R

YEAR	TEAM & LEAGUE		GP	G	A	PTS	PIM
1946-47	**BOS**	**N**	27	5	4	9	27

PLAYOFFS

YEAR	TEAM & LEAGUE		GP	G	A	PTS	PIM
1946-47	**BOS**	**N**	4	0	0	0	0

Pete Marrin

MARRIN, PETER 5'10", 160 lbs.
B. Aug. 8, 1953, Toronto, Ont. Center, Shoots R

YEAR	TEAM & LEAGUE		GP	G	A	PTS	PIM
1973-74	**TOR**	**W**	31	1	4	5	4
1974-75			4	3	1	4	0
1975-76			64	22	16	38	16
1976-77	**BIRM**	**W**	79	23	37	60	36
1977-78			80	28	43	71	53
1978-79			20	4	11	15	18
6 yrs.		**W Totals:**	278	81	112	193	127

PLAYOFFS

YEAR	TEAM & LEAGUE		GP	G	A	PTS	PIM
1973-74	**TOR**	**W**	3	0	1	1	0
1974-75			6	0	4	4	2
1977-78	**BIRM**	**W**	5	0	3	3	2
3 yrs.		**W Totals:**	14	0	8	8	4

Brad Marsh

MARSH, CHARLES BRADLEY 6'3", 210 lbs.
B. Mar. 31, 1958, London, Ont. Defense, Shoots L

YEAR	TEAM & LEAGUE		GP	G	A	PTS	PIM
1978-79	**ATL**	**N**	80	0	19	19	101
1979-80			80	2	9	11	119
1980-81	**CALG**	**N**	80	1	12	13	87
1981-82			17	0	1	1	10
	PHI	**N**	66	2	22	24	106
	2 team total		83	2	23	25	116
1982-83			68	2	11	13	52
5 yrs.		**N Totals:**	391	7	74	81	475

PLAYOFFS

YEAR	TEAM & LEAGUE		GP	G	A	PTS	PIM
1978-79	**ATL**	**N**	2	0	0	0	17
1979-80			4	0	1	1	2
1980-81	**CALG**	**N**	16	0	5	5	8
1981-82	**PHI**	**N**	4	0	0	0	2
1982-83			2	0	1	1	0
5 yrs.		**N Totals:**	28	0	7	7	29

Claimed by **Atlanta** as fill in Expansion Draft, June 13, 1979. Traded to **Philadelphia** by Calgary for Mel Bridgman, Nov. 11, 1981.

Gary Marsh

MARSH, GARY ARTHUR 5'9", 172 lbs.
B. Mar. 9, 1946, Toronto, Ont. Left Wing, Shoots L

YEAR	TEAM & LEAGUE		GP	G	A	PTS	PIM
1967-68	**DET**	**N**	6	1	3	4	4
1968-69	**TOR**	**N**	1	0	0	0	0
2 yrs.		**N Totals:**	7	1	3	4	4

Put on **Toronto** reserve list from Detroit, June 12, 1968.

Jim Marsh

MARSH, DONALD JAMES 6', 180 lbs.
B. July 9, 1951, Quesnel, B.C. Defense, Shoots L

YEAR	TEAM & LEAGUE		GP	G	A	PTS	PIM
1976-77	**BIRM**	**W**	1	0	0	0	0

Pete Marsh

MARSH, PETER 6'1", 180 lbs.
B. Dec. 21, 1956, Halifax, N.S. Right Wing, Shoots L

YEAR	TEAM & LEAGUE		GP	G	A	PTS	PIM
1976-77	**CIN**	**W**	76	23	28	51	52
1977-78			74	25	25	50	123
1978-79			80	43	23	66	95
1979-80	**WINN**	**N**	57	18	20	38	59
1980-81			24	6	7	13	9
	CHI	**N**	29	4	6	10	20
	2 team total		53	10	13	23	29
1981-82			57	10	18	28	47
1982-83			68	6	14	20	55
7 yrs.		**N Totals:**	235	44	65	109	190
		W Totals:	230	91	76	167	270

PLAYOFFS

YEAR	TEAM & LEAGUE		GP	G	A	PTS	PIM
1976-77	**CIN**	**W**	4	2	0	2	0
1978-79			3	1	0	1	0
1980-81	**CHI**	**N**	2	1	1	2	2
1981-82			12	0	2	2	31
1982-83			12	0	2	2	0
5 yrs.		**N Totals:**	26	1	5	6	33
		W Totals:	7	3	0	3	0

Rights transferred to **Montreal** Reserve List by Pittsburgh, Dec. 15, 1977, to complete earlier deal when Pittsburgh sent Pierre Larouche to Montreal for Peter Mahovlich and Peter Lee, Nov. 29, 1977. Reclaimed by **Montreal** from Cincinnati prior to Expansion Draft, June 9, 1979. Claimed by **Winnipeg** from Montreal in Expansion Draft, June 13, 1979. Traded to **Chicago** by Winnipeg for Doug Lecuyer and Tim Trimper, Dec. l, 1980.

Bert Marshall

MARSHALL, ALBERT LEROY 6'3", 205 lbs.
B. Nov. 22, 1943, Kamloops, B.C. Defense, Shoots L

YEAR	TEAM & LEAGUE		GP	G	A	PTS	PIM
1965-66	**DET**	**N**	61	0	19	19	45
1966-67			57	0	10	10	0
1967-68			37	1	5	6	56
	OAK	**N**	20	0	4	4	18
	2 team total		57	1	9	10	74
1968-69	**CALIF**	**N**	68	3	15	18	81
1969-70	**OAK**	**N**	72	1	15	16	109
1970-71	**CALIF**	**N**	32	2	6	8	48
1971-72			66	0	14	14	68
1972-73			55	2	6	8	71
	NYR	**N**	8	0	0	0	14
	2 team total		63	2	6	8	85
1973-74	**NYI**	**N**	69	1	7	8	84
1974-75			77	2	28	30	58
1975-76			71	0	16	16	72
1976-77			72	4	21	25	61
1977-78			58	0	7	7	44
1978-79			45	1	8	9	29
14 yrs.		**N Totals:**	868	17	181	198	858

PLAYOFFS

YEAR	TEAM & LEAGUE		GP	G	A	PTS	PIM
1965-66	**DET**	**N**	12	1	3	4	16
1968-69	**CALIF**	**N**	7	0	7	7	20
1969-70	**OAK**	**N**	4	0	1	1	12
1972-73	**NYR**	**N**	6	0	1	1	8
1974-75	**NYI**	**N**	17	2	5	7	16
1975-76			13	1	3	4	12
1976-77			6	0	0	0	6
1977-78			7	0	2	2	9
8 yrs.		**N Totals:**	72	4	22	26	99

Traded to **Oakland** by Detroit with John Brenneman and Ted Hampson for Kent Douglas, Jan. 9, 1968. Traded to **N.Y. Rangers** by California, March 4, 1973, for cash and future considerations (Dave Hrechkosy and Gary Coalter, May 17, 1973). Drafted by **N.Y. Islanders** from N.Y. Rangers in Intra-League Draft, June 12, 1973.

Don Marshall

MARSHALL, DONALD ROBERT 5'10", 166 lbs.
B. Mar. 23, 1932, Verdun, Que. Left Wing, Shoots L

YEAR	TEAM & LEAGUE		GP	G	A	PTS	PIM
1951-52	**MONT**	**N**	1	0	0	0	0
1954-55			39	5	3	8	9
1955-56			66	4	1	5	10
1956-57			70	12	8	20	6
1957-58			68	22	19	41	14
1958-59			70	10	22	32	12
1959-60			70	16	22	38	4
1960-61			70	14	17	31	8
1961-62			66	18	28	46	12
1962-63			65	13	20	33	6
1963-64	**NYR**	**N**	70	11	12	23	8
1964-65			69	20	15	35	2
1965-66			69	26	28	54	6
1966-67			70	24	22	46	4
1967-68			70	19	30	49	2
1968-69			74	20	19	39	12
1969-70			57	9	15	24	6
1970-71	**BUF**	**N**	62	20	29	49	6
1971-72	**TOR**	**N**	50	2	14	16	0
19 yrs.		**N Totals:**	1176	265	324	589	127

PLAYOFFS

YEAR	TEAM & LEAGUE		GP	G	A	PTS	PIM
1954-55	**MONT**	**N**	12	1	1	2	2
1955-56*			10	1	0	1	0
1956-57*			10	1	3	4	2
1957-58*			10	0	2	2	4
1958-59*			11	0	2	2	2
1959-60*			8	2	2	4	0
1960-61			6	0	2	2	0
1961-62			6	0	1	1	2
1962-63			5	0	0	0	0
1966-67	**NYR**	**N**	4	0	1	1	2
1967-68			6	2	1	3	0
1968-69			4	1	0	1	0
1969-70			1	0	0	0	0
1971-72	**TOR**	**N**	1	0	0	0	0
14 yrs.		**N Totals:**	94	8	15	23	14

Traded to **New York** from Montreal with Jacques Plante and Phil Goyette for Dave Balon, Leon Rochefort, Len Ronson, and Gump Worsley, June 4, 1963. Drafted by **Buffalo** from N.Y. Rangers in Expansion Draft, June 10, 1970. Drafted by **Toronto** from Buffalo in Intra-League Draft, June 8, 1971.

Paul Marshall

MARSHALL, PAUL A. 6'2", 182 lbs.
B. Sept. 7, 1960, Toronto, Ont. Left Wing, Shoots L

YEAR	TEAM & LEAGUE		GP	G	A	PTS	PIM
1979-80	**PITT**	**N**	46	9	12	21	9
1980-81			13	3	0	3	400
	TOR	**N**	13	0	2	2	2
	2 team total		26	3	2	5	402
1981-82			10	2	2	4	2
1982-83	**HART**	**N**	13	1	2	3	0
4 yrs.		**N Totals:**	95	15	18	33	413

PLAYOFFS

YEAR	TEAM & LEAGUE		GP	G	A	PTS	PIM
1979-80	**PITT**	**N**	1	0	0	0	0

Traded to **Toronto** by Pittsburgh with Kim Davis for Dave Burrows and Paul Gardner, Nov. 18, 1980. Traded by Toronto to **Hartford** for future considerations Oct. 5, 1982.

Willie Marshall

MARSHALL, WILLMOTT CHARLES 5'10", 160 lbs.
B. Dec. 1, 1931, Kirkland Lake, Ont. Center, Shoots L

YEAR	TEAM & LEAGUE		GP	G	A	PTS	PIM
1952-53	**TOR**	**N**	2	0	0	0	0
1954-55			16	1	14	15	0
1955-56			6	0	0	0	0
1958-59			9	0	1	1	2
4 yrs.		**N Totals:**	33	1	15	16	2

Mike Marson

MARSON, MICHAEL ROBERT 5'9", 200 lbs.
B. July 24, 1955, Scarborough, Ont. Left Wing, Shoots L

YEAR	TEAM & LEAGUE		GP	G	A	PTS	PIM
1974-75	**WASH**	**N**	76	16	12	28	59
1975-76			57	4	7	11	50
1976-77			10	0	1	1	18
1977-78			46	4	4	8	101
1978-79			4	0	0	0	0
1979-80	**LA**	**N**	3	0	0	0	5
6 yrs.		**N Totals:**	196	24	24	48	233

Traded to **Los Angeles** by Washington for Steve Clippingdale, June 11, 1979.

Clare Martin

MARTIN, CLARE GEORGE 5'11", 180 lbs.
B. Feb. 25, 1922, Waterloo, Ont. Defense, Shoots R

YEAR	TEAM & LEAGUE		GP	G	A	PTS	PIM
1941-42	**BOS**	**N**	13	0	1	1	4
1946-47			6	3	0	3	0
1947-48			59	5	13	18	34
1949-50	**DET**	**N**	64	2	5	7	14
1950-51			50	1	6	7	12
1951-52	**CHI**	**N**	31	1	2	3	8
	NYR	**N**	14	0	1	1	6
	2 team total		45	1	3	4	14
6 yrs.		**N Totals:**	237	12	28	40	78

PLAYOFFS

YEAR	TEAM & LEAGUE		GP	G	A	PTS	PIM
1941-42	**BOS**	**N**	5	0	0	0	0
1946-47			5	0	1	1	0
1947-48			5	0	0	0	6
1949-50*	**DET**	**N**	10	0	1	1	0
1950-51			2	0	0	0	0
5 yrs.		**N Totals:**	27	0	2	2	6

Traded to **Detroit** by Boston with Pete Babando, Lloyd Durham and Jim Peters for Bill Quackenbush and Pete Horeck, Aug. 16, 1949. Traded to **Chicago** by Detroit with Jim McFadden, George Gee, Rags Raglan, Jim Peters and Max McNab for Hugh Coflin and $75,000, Aug. 20, 1951. Sold to **N.Y. Rangers** by Chicago, Dec. 28, 1951.

Frank Martin

MARTIN, FRANCIS WILLIAM 6'1", 194 lbs.
B. May 1, 1933, Cayuga, Ont. Defense, Shoots L

YEAR	TEAM & LEAGUE		GP	G	A	PTS	PIM
1952-53	**BOS**	**N**	14	0	2	2	6
1953-54			68	3	17	20	38
1954-55	**CHI**	**N**	66	4	8	12	35
1955-56			61	3	11	14	21
1956-57			70	1	8	9	12
1957-58			3	0	0	0	10
6 yrs.		**N Totals:**	282	11	46	57	122

PLAYOFFS

YEAR	TEAM & LEAGUE		GP	G	A	PTS	PIM
1952-53	**BOS**	**N**	6	0	1	1	2
1953-54			4	0	1	1	0
2 yrs.		**N Totals:**	10	0	2	2	2

Traded to **Chicago** by Boston for Murray Costello, Oct. 4, 1954.

Jack Martin

MARTIN, JACK 5'11", 184 lbs.
B. Nov. 29, 1940, St. Catharines, Ont.

YEAR	TEAM & LEAGUE		GP	G	A	PTS	PIM
1960-61	**TOR**	**N**	1	0	0	0	0

Pit Martin

MARTIN, HUBERT JACQUES 5'9", 170 lbs.
B. Dec. 9, 1943, Noranda, Que. Center, Shoots R
Won Masterton Trophy, 1969-70

YEAR	TEAM & LEAGUE		GP	G	A	PTS	PIM
1961-62	**DET**	**N**	1	0	1	1	0
1963-64			50	9	12	21	21
1964-65			58	8	9	17	32
1965-66			10	1	1	2	0
	BOS	**N**	41	16	11	27	10
	2 team total		51	17	12	29	10
1966-67			70	20	22	42	40
1967-68	**CHI**	**N**	63	16	19	35	36

Pit Martin continued

YEAR	TEAM & LEAGUE		GP	G	A	PTS	PIM
1968-69			76	23	38	61	73
1969-70			73	30	33	63	61
1970-71			62	22	33	55	40
1971-72			78	24	51	75	56
1972-73			78	29	61	90	30
1973-74			78	30	47	77	43
1974-75			70	19	26	45	34
1975-76			80	32	39	71	44
1976-77			75	17	36	53	22
1977-78			7	1	1	2	12
	VAN	**N**	67	15	31	46	36
	2 team total		74	16	32	48	48
1978-79			64	12	14	26	24
17 yrs.		**N Totals:**	1101	324	485	809	614

PLAYOFFS

YEAR	TEAM & LEAGUE		GP	G	A	PTS	PIM
1963-64	**DET**	**N**	14	1	4	5	14
1964-65			3	0	1	1	2
1967-68	**CHI**	**N**	11	3	6	9	2
1969-70			8	3	3	6	4
1970-71			17	2	7	9	12
1971-72			8	4	2	6	4
1972-73			15	10	6	16	6
1973-74			7	2	0	2	4
1974-75			8	1	1	2	2
1975-76			4	1	0	1	4
1976-77			2	0	0	0	0
1978-79	**VAN**	**N**	3	0	1	1	2
12 yrs.		**N Totals:**	100	27	31	58	56

Traded to **Boston** by Detroit for Parker MacDonald, Dec. 30, 1965. Traded to **Chicago** by Boston with Gilles Marotte and Jack Norris for Phil Esposito, Ken Hodge and Fred Stanfield, May 15, 1967. Traded to **Vancouver** by Chicago for future considerations (goaltender Murray Bannerman, May 27, 1978), Nov. 4, 1977.

Rick Martin

MARTIN, RICHARD LIONEL 5'11", 179 lbs.
B. July 26, 1951, Verdun, Que. Left Wing, Shoots L

YEAR	TEAM & LEAGUE		GP	G	A	PTS	PIM
1971-72	**BUF**	**N**	73	44	30	74	36
1972-73			75	37	36	73	79
1973-74			78	52	34	86	38
1974-75			68	52	43	95	72
1975-76			80	49	37	86	67
1976-77			66	36	29	65	58
1977-78			65	28	35	63	16
1978-79			73	32	21	53	35
1979-80			80	45	34	79	16
1980-81			23	7	14	21	20
	LA	**N**	1	1	1	2	0
	2 team total		24	8	15	23	20
1981-82			3	1	3	4	2
11 yrs.		**N Totals:**	685	384	317	701	439

PLAYOFFS

YEAR	TEAM & LEAGUE		GP	G	A	PTS	PIM
1972-73	**BUF**	**N**	6	3	2	5	12
1974-75			17	7	8	15	20
1975-76			9	4	7	11	12
1976-77			6	2	1	3	9
1977-78			7	2	4	6	13
1978-79			3	0	3	3	0
1979-80			14	6	4	10	8
1980-81	**LA**	**N**	1	0	0	0	0
8 yrs.		**N Totals:**	63	24	29	53	74

Traded to **Los Angeles** by Buffalo for Los Angeles' third round choice (Colin Chisholm) in 1981 Entry Draft and Los Angeles' first round choice (Tom Barrasso) in 1983 Entry Draft, Mar. 10, 1981.

Ron Martin

MARTIN, RONALD D. 130 lbs.
B. Aug. 22, 1909, Calgary, Alta. Forward, Shoots R

YEAR	TEAM & LEAGUE		GP	G	A	PTS	PIM
1932-33	**NYA**	**N**	47	5	7	12	6
1933-34			47	8	9	17	30
2 yrs.		**N Totals:**	94	13	16	29	36

Terry Martin

MARTIN, TERENCE GEORGE 5'11", 175 lbs.
B. Oct. 25, 1955, Barrie, Ont. Left Wing, Shoots L

YEAR	TEAM & LEAGUE		GP	G	A	PTS	PIM
1975-76	**BUF**	**N**	1	0	0	0	0
1976-77			62	11	12	23	8
1977-78			21	3	2	5	9
1978-79			64	6	8	14	33
1979-80	**QUE**	**N**	3	0	0	0	0
	TOR	**N**	37	6	15	21	2
	2 team total		40	6	15	21	2
1980-81			69	23	14	37	32
1981-82			72	25	24	49	39
1982-83			76	14	13	27	28
8 yrs.		**N Totals:**	405	88	88	176	151

PLAYOFFS

YEAR	TEAM & LEAGUE		GP	G	A	PTS	PIM
1976-77	**BUF**	**N**	3	0	2	2	5
1977-78			8	2	0	2	5
1979-80	**TOR**	**N**	3	2	0	2	7
1980-81			3	0	0	0	0
1982-83			4	0	0	0	9
5 yrs.		**N Totals:**	21	4	2	6	26

Claimed by **Quebec** from Buffalo in Expansion Draft, June 13, 1979. Traded to **Toronto** by Quebec with Dave Farrish for Reggie Thomas, Dec. 13, 1979.

Tom Martin

MARTIN, THOMAS RAYMOND 5'9", 170 lbs.
B. Oct. 16, 1947, Toronto, Ont. Right Wing, Shoots R

YEAR	TEAM & LEAGUE		GP	G	A	PTS	PIM
1967-68	**TOR**	**N**	3	1	0	1	0
1972-73	**OTTA**	**W**	75	19	27	46	27
1973-74	**TOR**	**W**	74	25	32	57	14
1974-75			64	14	17	31	18
4 yrs.		**N Totals:**	3	1	0	1	0
		W Totals:	213	58	76	134	59

PLAYOFFS

YEAR	TEAM & LEAGUE		GP	G	A	PTS	PIM
1972-73	**OTTA**	**W**	5	0	5	5	2
1973-74	**TOR**	**W**	12	7	3	10	2
1974-75			5	1	5	6	0
3 yrs.		**W Totals:**	22	8	13	21	4

Drafted by **Boston** from Phoenix (WHL) in Inter-League Draft, June 9, 1970.

Don Martineau

MARTINEAU, DONALD JEAN 6', 190 lbs.
B. Apr. 25, 1952, Kimberley, B.C. Right Wing, Shoots R

YEAR	TEAM & LEAGUE		GP	G	A	PTS	PIM
1973-74	**ATL**	**N**	4	0	0	0	2
1974-75	**MINN**	**N**	76	6	9	15	61
1975-76	**DET**	**N**	9	0	1	1	0
1976-77			1	0	0	0	0
4 yrs.		**N Totals:**	90	6	10	16	63

Traded to **Minnesota** by Atlanta with John Flesch for Buster Harvey and Jerry Byers, May 28, 1974. Traded to **Detroit** by Minnesota for Pierre Jarry, Nov. 25, 1975.

Dennis Maruk

MARUK, DENNIS JOHN 5'8", 165 lbs.
B. Nov. 17, 1955, Toronto, Ont. Center, Shoots L

YEAR	TEAM & LEAGUE		GP	G	A	PTS	PIM
1975-76	**CALIF**	**N**	80	30	32	62	44
1976-77	**CLEVE**	**N**	80	28	50	78	68
1977-78			76	36	35	71	50
1978-79	**MINN**	**N**	2	0	0	0	0
	WASH	**N**	76	31	59	90	71
	2 team total		78	31	59	90	71
1979-80			27	10	17	27	8
1980-81			80	50	47	97	87
1981-82			80	60	76	136	128
1982-83			80	31	50	81	71
8 yrs.		**N Totals:**	581	276	366	642	527

PLAYOFFS

YEAR	TEAM & LEAGUE		GP	G	A	PTS	PIM
1982-83	**WASH**	**N**	4	1	1	2	2

Protected by **Minnesota** prior to Cleveland-Minnesota Dispersal Draft, June 15, 1978. Traded to **Washington** by Minnesota for Pittsburgh's first round choice (Tom McCarthy) in 1979 Entry Draft (Washington property via earlier deal), Oct. 18, 1978.

Paul Masnick

MASNICK, PAUL ANDREW — 5'9", 165 lbs.
B. Apr. 14, 1931, Regina, Sask. — Center, Shoots R

YEAR	TEAM & LEAGUE		GP	G	A	PTS	PIM
1950-51	MONT	N	43	4	1	5	14
1951-52			15	1	2	3	2
1952-53			53	10	7	17	44
1953-54			50	5	21	26	57
1954-55			11	0	0	0	0
	CHI	N	11	1	0	1	8
	MONT	N	8	0	1	1	0
	3 team total		30	1	1	2	8
1957-58	TOR	N	41	2	9	11	14
6 yrs.		N Totals:	232	23	41	64	139
PLAYOFFS							
1950-51	MONT	N	11	2	1	3	4
1951-52			6	1	0	1	12
1952-53*			6	1	0	1	7
1953-54			10	0	4	4	4
4 yrs.		N Totals:	33	4	5	9	27

Traded to **Chicago** by Montreal for a player to be named later (Al Dewsbury), Nov. 9, 1954. Returned to **Montreal** Dec. 10, 1954. Purchased from Montreal by **Toronto** Sept. 30, 1957.

Charley Mason

MASON, CHARLES C. (Dutch) — 5'10", 160 lbs.
B. Feb. 1, 1912, Seaforth, Ont. — Forward

YEAR	TEAM & LEAGUE		GP	G	A	PTS	PIM
1934-35	NYR	N	46	5	9	14	14
1935-36			28	1	5	6	30
1937-38	NYA	N	2	0	0	0	0
1938-39	DET	N	6	0	1	1	0
	CHI	N	13	1	3	4	0
	2 team total		19	1	4	5	0
4 yrs.		N Totals:	95	7	18	25	44
PLAYOFFS							
1934-35	NYR	N	4	0	1	1	0

George Massecar

MASSECAR, GEORGE
B. Niagara Falls, Ont. — Left Wing, Shoots L

YEAR	TEAM & LEAGUE		GP	G	A	PTS	PIM
1929-30	NYA	N	43	7	3	10	18
1930-31			43	4	7	11	16
1931-32			14	1	1	2	12
3 yrs.		N Totals:	100	12	11	23	46

Jamie Masters

MASTERS, JAMES EDWARD — 6'1", 195 lbs.
B. Apr. 14, 1955, Toronto, Ont. — Defense, Shoots R

YEAR	TEAM & LEAGUE		GP	G	A	PTS	PIM
1975-76	STL	N	7	0	0	0	0
1976-77			16	1	7	8	2
1978-79			10	0	6	6	0
3 yrs.		N Totals:	33	1	13	14	2
PLAYOFFS							
1975-76	STL	N	1	0	0	0	0
1976-77			1	0	0	0	0
2 yrs.		N Totals:	2	0	0	0	0

Claimed by **Quebec** from St. Louis in Expansion Draft, June 13, 1979.

Bill Masterton

MASTERTON, WILLIAM (Bat) — 6', 189 lbs.
B. Aug. 13, 1938, Winnipeg, Man. — Center

YEAR	TEAM & LEAGUE		GP	G	A	PTS	PIM
1967-68	MINN	N	38	4	8	12	4

Frank Mathers

MATHERS, FRANK SYDNEY — 6'½", 182 lbs.
B. Mar. 29, 1924, Winnipeg, Man. — Defense, Shoots L

YEAR	TEAM & LEAGUE		GP	G	A	PTS	PIM
1948-49	TOR	N	15	1	2	3	2
1949-50			6	0	1	1	2
1951-52			2	0	0	0	0
3 yrs.		N Totals:	23	1	3	4	4

Joe Matte

MATTE, JOSEPH
B. Bourget, Ont. — Defense

YEAR	TEAM & LEAGUE		GP	G	A	PTS	PIM
1919-20	TOR	N	16	8	2	10	12
1920-21	HAMIL	N	19	7	**9**	16	27
1921-22			20	3	3	6	4
1925-26	BOS	N	3	0	0	0	0
	MONT	N	6	0	0	0	0
	2 team total		9	0	0	0	0
4 yrs.		N Totals:	64	18	14	32	43

Joe Matte

MATTE, JOSEPH
B. Mar. 3, 1909, Ottawa, Ont. — Defense

YEAR	TEAM & LEAGUE		GP	G	A	PTS	PIM
1942-43	CHI	N	12	0	2	2	8

Roland Matte

MATTE, ROLAND — 5'10½", 178 lbs.
B. Mar. 15, 1909, Bourget, Ont. — Defense, Shoots R

YEAR	TEAM & LEAGUE		GP	G	A	PTS	PIM
1929-30	DET	N	12	0	1	1	0

Dick Mattiussi

MATTIUSSI, RICHARD ARTHUR — 5'10", 185 lbs.
B. May 1, 1938, Smooth Rock Falls, Ont. — Defense, Shoots L

YEAR	TEAM & LEAGUE		GP	G	A	PTS	PIM
1967-68	PITT	N	32	0	2	2	18
1968-69			12	0	2	2	14
	CALIF	N	24	1	9	10	16
	2 team total		36	1	11	12	30
1969-70	OAK	N	65	4	10	14	38
1970-71	CALIF	N	67	3	8	11	38
4 yrs.		N Totals:	200	8	31	39	124
PLAYOFFS							
1968-69	CALIF	N	7	0	1	1	6
1969-70	OAK	N	1	0	0	0	0
2 yrs.		N Totals:	8	0	1	1	6

Traded to **Oakland** by Pittsburgh with Earl Ingarfield and Gene Ubriaco for Bryan Watson, George Swarbrick and Tracy Pratt, Jan. 30, 1969.

Johnny Matz

MATZ, JEAN
B. Unknown — Forward

YEAR	TEAM & LEAGUE		GP	G	A	PTS	PIM
1924-25	MONT	N	30	3	2	5	0
PLAYOFFS							
1924-25	MONT	N	5	0	0	0	2

Larry Mavety

MAVETY, LAWRENCE DOUGLAS (Mav, Moose) — 5'11", 196 lbs.
B. May 29, 1942, Woodstock, Ont. — Defense, Shoots R

YEAR	TEAM & LEAGUE		GP	G	A	PTS	PIM
1972-73	LA	W	2	1	0	1	2
	PHI	W	4	0	0	0	14
	CHI	W	67	9	40	49	73
	3 team total		73	10	40	50	89
1973-74			77	15	36	51	157
1974-75			57	10	22	32	126
	TOR	W	17	0	9	9	24
	2 team total		74	10	31	41	150
1975-76	D-O	W	14	0	4	4	14
1976-77	IND	W	10	2	2	4	8
5 yrs.		W Totals:	248	37	113	150	418
PLAYOFFS							
1973-74	CHI	W	18	4	8	12	46
1974-75	TOR	W	6	0	3	3	6
2 yrs.		W Totals:	24	4	11	15	52

Wayne Maxner

MAXNER, WAYNE DOUGLAS 5'11", 170 lbs.
B. Sept. 27, 1942, Halifax, N.S. Left Wing, Shoots L

YEAR	TEAM & LEAGUE		GP	G	A	PTS	PIM
1964-65	**BOS**	**N**	54	7	6	13	42
1965-66			8	1	3	4	6
2 yrs.		**N Totals:**	62	8	9	17	48

Brad Maxwell

MAXWELL, BRAD ROBERT 6'2", 181 lbs.
B. July 8, 1957, Brandon, Man. Defense, Shoots R

YEAR	TEAM & LEAGUE		GP	G	A	PTS	PIM
1977-78	**MINN**	**N**	75	18	29	47	100
1978-79			70	9	28	37	145
1979-80			58	7	30	37	12
1980-81			27	3	13	16	98
1981-82			51	10	21	31	96
1982-83			77	11	28	39	157
6 yrs.		**N Totals:**	358	58	149	207	608

PLAYOFFS

YEAR	TEAM & LEAGUE		GP	G	A	PTS	PIM
1979-80	**MINN**	**N**	11	0	8	8	20
1980-81			18	3	11	14	35
1981-82			4	0	3	3	13
1982-83			9	5	6	11	23
4 yrs.		**N Totals:**	42	8	28	36	91

Bryan Maxwell

MAXWELL, BRYAN CLIFFORD (Maxie) 6'3", 210 lbs.
B. Sept. 7, 1955, North Bay, Ont. Defense, Shoots L

YEAR	TEAM & LEAGUE		GP	G	A	PTS	PIM
1975-76	**CLEVE**	**W**	73	3	14	17	177
1976-77	**CIN**	**W**	34	1	8	9	29
1977-78	**NE**	**W**	17	2	1	3	11
	MINN	**N**	18	2	5	7	41
	2 team total		35	4	6	10	52
1978-79			25	1	6	7	46
1979-80	**STL**	**N**	57	1	11	12	112
1980-81			40	3	10	13	137
1981-82	**WINN**	**N**	45	1	9	10	110
1982-83			54	7	13	20	131
8 yrs.		**N Totals:**	239	15	54	69	577
		W Totals:	124	6	23	29	217

PLAYOFFS

YEAR	TEAM & LEAGUE		GP	G	A	PTS	PIM
1975-76	**CLEVE**	**W**	2	0	0	0	4
1976-77	**CIN**	**W**	4	0	0	0	29
1979-80	**STL**	**N**	1	0	0	0	9
1980-81			11	0	1	1	54
1982-83	**WINN**	**N**	3	1	0	1	23
5 yrs.		**N Totals:**	15	1	1	2	86
		W Totals:	6	0	0	0	33

Traded to **St. Louis** by Minnesota with Ritchie Hansen for St. Louis' second round choice (Dave Reierson) in the 1982 Entry Draft, June 10, 1979. Traded to **Winnipeg** by St. Louis with Paul MacLean and Ed Staniowski for Scott Campbell and John Markell, July 3, 1981.

Kevin Maxwell

MAXWELL, KEVIN (Maxi) 5'9", 165 lbs.
B. Mar. 30, 1960, Edmonton, Alta. Center, Shoots R

YEAR	TEAM & LEAGUE		GP	G	A	PTS	PIM
1980-81	**MINN**	**N**	6	0	3	3	7
1981-82			12	1	4	5	8
	COLO	**N**	34	5	5	10	44
	2 team total		46	6	9	15	52
2 yrs.		**N Totals:**	52	6	12	18	59

PLAYOFFS

YEAR	TEAM & LEAGUE		GP	G	A	PTS	PIM
1980-81	**MINN**	**N**	16	3	4	7	24

Sold to **Colorado** by Minnesota, Dec. 31, 1981.

Wally Maxwell

MAXWELL, WALTER
B. Aug. 24, 1933, Ottawa, Ont. Forward

YEAR	TEAM & LEAGUE		GP	G	A	PTS	PIM
1952-53	**TOR**	**N**	2	0	0	0	0

Gilles Mayer

MAYER, GILLES 5'6", 135 lbs.
B. Aug. 24, 1930, Ottawa, Ont. Shoots L

YEAR	TEAM & LEAGUE		GP	G	A	PTS	PIM
1949-50	**TOR**	**N**	1	0	0	0	0

Jim Mayer

MAYER, JAMES PATRICK 6', 190 lbs.
B. Oct. 30, 1954, Capreol, Ont. Right Wing, Shoots R

YEAR	TEAM & LEAGUE		GP	G	A	PTS	PIM
1976-77	**CALG**	**W**	21	2	3	5	0
1977-78	**NE**	**W**	51	11	9	20	21
1978-79	**EDM**	**W**	2	0	0	0	0
1979-80	**NYR**	**N**	4	0	0	0	0
4 yrs.		**N Totals:**	4	0	0	0	0
		W Totals:	74	13	12	25	21

Reclaimed by **N.Y. Rangers** from Edmonton prior to Expansion Draft, June 9, 1979. Traded to **Vancouver** by N.Y. Rangers with Mario Marois for Jere Gillis and Jeff Bandura, Nov. 11, 1980.

Shep Mayer

MAYER, SHEPPARD E.
B. Sturgeon Falls, Ont. Forward

YEAR	TEAM & LEAGUE		GP	G	A	PTS	PIM
1942-43	**TOR**	**N**	12	1	2	3	4

Eddie Mazur

MAZUR, EDWARD JOSEPH (Spider) 6'2", 186 lbs.
B. July 25, 1929, Winnipeg, Man. Left Wing, Shoots L

YEAR	TEAM & LEAGUE		GP	G	A	PTS	PIM
1953-54	**MONT**	**N**	67	7	14	21	95
1954-55			25	1	5	6	21
1956-57	**CHI**	**N**	15	0	1	1	4
3 yrs.		**N Totals:**	107	8	20	28	120

PLAYOFFS

YEAR	TEAM & LEAGUE		GP	G	A	PTS	PIM
1950-51	**MONT**	**N**	2	0	0	0	0
1951-52			5	2	0	2	4
1952-53*			7	2	2	4	11
1953-54			11	0	3	3	7
4 yrs.		**N Totals:**	25	4	5	9	22

Sold to **Chicago** by Montreal with Ken Mosdell and Bud MacPherson for $55,000, with option to recall at end of season, May 24, 1956.

John Mazur

MAZUR, JOHN

YEAR	TEAM & LEAGUE		GP	G	A	PTS	PIM
1977-78	**HOUS**	**W**	1	0	0	0	0

Gary McAdam

MCADAM, GARY 5'11", 175 lbs.
B. Dec. 31, 1955, Smith Falls, Ont. Right Wing, Shoots L

YEAR	TEAM & LEAGUE		GP	G	A	PTS	PIM
1975-76	**BUF**	**N**	31	1	2	3	2
1976-77			73	13	16	29	17
1977-78			79	19	22	41	44
1978-79			40	6	5	11	13
	PITT	**N**	28	5	9	14	2
	2 team total		68	11	14	25	15
1979-80			78	19	22	41	63
1980-81			34	3	9	12	30
	DET	**N**	40	5	14	19	27
	2 team total		74	8	23	31	57
1981-82	**CALG**	**N**	46	12	15	27	18
1982-83	**BUF**	**N**	4	1	0	1	0
8 yrs.		**N Totals:**	453	84	114	198	216

PLAYOFFS

YEAR	TEAM & LEAGUE		GP	G	A	PTS	PIM
1975-76	**BUF**	**N**	1	0	0	0	0
1976-77			6	1	0	1	0
1977-78			8	2	2	4	7
1978-79	**PITT**	**N**	7	2	1	3	0
1979-80			5	1	2	3	9
1981-82	**CALG**	**N**	3	0	0	0	0
6 yrs.		**N Totals:**	30	6	5	11	16

Traded to **Pittsburgh** by Buffalo for Dave Schultz, Feb. 6, 1979. Traded to **Detroit** by Pittsburgh for Errol Thompson, Jan. 8, 1981. Traded to **Calgary** by Detroit along with Detroit's fourth round choice in 1983 Entry Draft for Eric Vail, Nov. 10,1981. Signed as a free agent by **New Jersey** Sept. 3, 1983.

Sam McAdam

MCADAM, SAMUEL 5'8", 175 lbs.
B. May 31, 1908, Sterling, Scotland Center, Shoots L

YEAR	TEAM & LEAGUE		GP	G	A	PTS	PIM
1930-31	NYR	N	5	0	0	0	0

Hazen McAndrew

MCANDREW, HAZEN BERNARD 5'9½", 175 lbs.
B. Aug. 7, 1917, Mayo, Que. Defense, Shoots L

YEAR	TEAM & LEAGUE		GP	G	A	PTS	PIM
1941-42	NYA	N	7	0	1	1	6

Bob McAneeley

MCANEELEY, ROBERT WILLIAM 5'9", 180 lbs.
B. Nov. 7, 1950, Cranbrook, B.C. Center, Shoots L

YEAR	TEAM & LEAGUE		GP	G	A	PTS	PIM
1972-73	ALTA	W	51	5	7	12	24
1973-74	EDM	W	52	12	11	23	49
1975-76			71	12	16	28	60
3 yrs.		W Totals:	174	29	34	63	133
PLAYOFFS							
1973-74	EDM	W	4	1	0	1	0
1975-76			3	1	0	1	0
2 yrs.		W Totals:	7	2	0	2	0

Ted McAneeley

MCANEELEY, EDWARD JOSEPH 5'9", 185 lbs.
B. Nov. 7, 1950, Cranbrook, B.C. Defense, Shoots L

YEAR	TEAM & LEAGUE		GP	G	A	PTS	PIM
1972-73	CALIF	N	77	4	13	17	75
1973-74			72	4	20	24	62
1974-75			9	0	2	2	4
1975-76	EDM	W	79	2	17	19	71
4 yrs.		N Totals:	158	8	35	43	141
		W Totals:	79	2	17	19	71
PLAYOFFS							
1975-76	EDM	W	4	0	0	0	0

Jud McAtee

MCATEE, JEROME F. 5'9", 170 lbs.
B. Feb. 5, 1920, Stratford, Ont. Left Wing, Shoots L

YEAR	TEAM & LEAGUE		GP	G	A	PTS	PIM
1942-43	DET	N	1	0	0	0	0
1943-44			1	0	2	2	0
1944-45			44	15	11	26	6
3 yrs.		N Totals:	46	15	13	28	6
PLAYOFFS							
1944-45	DET	N	14	2	1	3	0

Norm McAtee

MCATEE, NORMAN JEROME 5'8", 165 lbs.
B. June 28, 1921, Stratford, Ont. Center, Shoots L

YEAR	TEAM & LEAGUE		GP	G	A	PTS	PIM
1946-47	BOS	N	13	0	1	1	0

George McAvoy

MCAVOY, GEORGE 6', 190 lbs.
B. June 21, 1931, Edmonton, Alta. Defense, Shoots L

YEAR	TEAM & LEAGUE		GP	G	A	PTS	PIM
PLAYOFFS							
1954-55	MONT	N	4	0	0	0	0

Cliff McBride

MCBRIDE, CLIFFORD
B. Unknown Defense

YEAR	TEAM & LEAGUE		GP	G	A	PTS	PIM
1928-29	MON(M)	N	1	0	0	0	0
1929-30	TOR	N	1	0	0	0	0
2 yrs.		N Totals:	2	0	0	0	0

Jim McBurney

MCBURNEY, JAMES
B. Jan. 3, 1933, Sault Ste. Marie, Ont. Forward

YEAR	TEAM & LEAGUE		GP	G	A	PTS	PIM
1952-53	CHI	N	1	0	1	1	0

Stan McCabe

MCCABE, STANLEY
B. Ottawa, Ont. Defense

YEAR	TEAM & LEAGUE		GP	G	A	PTS	PIM
1929-30	DET	N	25	7	3	10	23
1930-31			44	2	1	3	22
1932-33	MON(M)	N	1	0	0	0	0
1933-34			8	0	0	0	4
4 yrs.		N Totals:	78	9	4	13	49

Bert McCaffrey

MCCAFFREY, BERT
B. Listowel, Que. Defense

YEAR	TEAM & LEAGUE		GP	G	A	PTS	PIM
1924-25	TOR	N	30	9	6	15	12
1925-26			36	14	7	21	42
1926-27			43	5	5	10	43
1927-28			8	1	1	2	9
	PITT	N	36	6	3	9	14
	2 team total		44	7	4	11	23
1928-29			42	1	0	1	34
1929-30			15	3	4	7	12
	MONT	N	28	1	3	4	26
	2 team total		43	4	7	11	38
1930-31			22	2	1	3	10
7 yrs.		N Totals:	260	42	30	72	202
PLAYOFFS							
1924-25	TOR	N	2	1	0	1	6
1927-28	PITT	N	2	0	0	0	0
1929-30*	MONT	N	6	1	1	2	6
3 yrs.		N Totals:	10	2	1	3	12

John McCahill

MCCAHILL, JOHN WALTER 6'1", 215 lbs.
B. Dec. 2, 1955, Sarnia, Ont. Defense, Shoots R

YEAR	TEAM & LEAGUE		GP	G	A	PTS	PIM
1977-78	COLO	N	1	0	0	0	0

Signed as free agent by **Colorado** May 17, 1978.

Douglas McCaig

MCCAIG, DOUGLAS 6', 180 lbs.
B. Feb. 24, 1919, Guelph, Ont. Defense, Shoots R

YEAR	TEAM & LEAGUE		GP	G	A	PTS	PIM
1941-42	DET	N	9	0	1	1	6
1945-46			6	0	1	1	12
1946-47			47	2	4	6	64
1947-48			29	3	3	6	37
1948-49			1	0	0	0	0
	CHI	N	55	1	3	4	60
	2 team total		56	1	3	4	60
1949-50			64	0	4	4	49
1950-51			53	2	5	7	29
7 yrs.		N Totals:	264	8	21	29	257
PLAYOFFS							
1941-42	DET	N	2	0	0	0	6
1946-47			5	0	1	1	4
2 yrs.		N Totals:	7	0	1	1	10

Traded to **Detroit** by Chicago for Max Quackenbush, Sept. 18, 1951.

Dunc McCallum

MCCALLUM, DUNCAN SELBIE 6'1", 193 lbs.
B. Mar. 29, 1940, Flin Flon, Man. Defense, Shoots R

YEAR	TEAM & LEAGUE		GP	G	A	PTS	PIM
1965-66	NYR	N	2	0	0	0	2
1967-68	PITT	N	32	0	2	2	36
1968-69			62	5	13	18	81
1969-70			14	0	0	0	16
1970-71			77	9	20	29	95
1972-73	HOUS	W	69	9	20	29	112
1974-75	CHI	W	31	0	10	10	24

Dunc McCallum continued

YEAR	TEAM & LEAGUE		GP	G	A	PTS	PIM
7 yrs.	N Totals:		187	14	35	49	230
	W Totals:		100	9	30	39	136
PLAYOFFS							
1969-70	PITT	N	10	1	2	3	12
1972-73	HOUS	W	10	2	3	5	6
2 yrs.	N Totals:		10	1	2	3	12
	W Totals:		10	2	3	5	6

Traded to **Pittsburgh** by N.Y. Rangers with George Konik, Paul Andrea, and Frank Francis for Larry Jeffrey, June 6, 1967.

Eddie McCalmon

MCCALMON, EDWARD

Right Wing

YEAR	TEAM & LEAGUE		GP	G	A	PTS	PIM
1927-28	CHI	N	23	2	0	2	8
1930-31	PHI	N	16	3	0	3	6
2 yrs.	N Totals:		39	5	0	5	14

Rick McCann

MCCANN, RICHARD LEO 5'9", 178 lbs.

B. May 27, 1944, Hamilton, Ont. Center, Shoots L

YEAR	TEAM & LEAGUE		GP	G	A	PTS	PIM
1967-68	DET	N	3	0	0	0	0
1968-69			3	0	0	0	0
1969-70			18	0	1	1	4
1970-71			5	0	0	0	0
1971-72			1	0	0	0	0
1974-75			13	1	3	4	2
6 yrs.	N Totals:		43	1	4	5	6

Dan McCarthy

MCCARTHY, DANIEL 5'9", 185 lbs.

B. Apr. 7, 1958, St. Mary's, Ont. Center, Shoots L

YEAR	TEAM & LEAGUE		GP	G	A	PTS	PIM
1980-81	NYR	N	5	4	0	4	4

Traded to **Minnesota** by New York Rangers for Shawn Dineen, August 24, 1982.

Kevin McCarthy

MCCARTHY, KEVIN 5'11", 195 lbs.

B. July 14, 1957, Winnipeg, Man. Defense, Shoots R

YEAR	TEAM & LEAGUE		GP	G	A	PTS	PIM
1977-78	PHI	N	62	2	15	17	32
1978-79			22	1	2	3	21
	VAN	N	1	0	0	0	0
	2 team total		23	1	2	3	21
1979-80			79	15	30	45	70
1980-81			80	16	37	53	85
1981-82			71	6	39	45	84
1982-83			74	12	28	40	88
6 yrs.	N Totals:		389	52	151	203	380
PLAYOFFS							
1977-78	PHI	N	10	0	1	1	8
1979-80	VAN	N	4	1	0	1	0
1980-81			3	0	1	1	0
1982-83			4	1	1	2	12
4 yrs.	N Totals:		21	2	3	5	20

Traded to **Vancouver** by Philadelphia with Drew Callander for Dennis Ververgaert, Dec. 29, 1978.

Tom McCarthy

MCCARTHY, THOMAS

B. Unknown Right Wing, Shoots L

YEAR	TEAM & LEAGUE		GP	G	A	PTS	PIM
1919-20	QUE	N	12	11	2	13	0
1920-21	HAMIL	N	22	8	1	9	10
2 yrs.	N Totals:		34	19	3	22	10

Tom McCarthy

MCCARTHY, THOMAS PATRICK FRANCIS 6'1", 190 lbs.

B. Sept. 15, 1934, Toronto, Ont. Left Wing, Shoots L

YEAR	TEAM & LEAGUE		GP	G	A	PTS	PIM
1956-57	DET	N	3	0	0	0	0
1957-58			18	2	1	3	4
1958-59			15	2	3	5	4
1960-61	BOS	N	24	4	5	9	0
4 yrs.	N Totals:		60	8	9	17	8

Traded to **Boston** by Detroit with Murray Oliver and Gary Aldcorn for Leo Labine and Vic Stasiuk, Jan., 1961.

Tom McCarthy

MCCARTHY, THOMAS JOSEPH (Jug) 6'2", 200 lbs.

B. July 31, 1960, Toronto, Ont. Left Wing, Shoots L

YEAR	TEAM & LEAGUE		GP	G	A	PTS	PIM
1979-80	MINN	N	68	16	20	36	39
1980-81			62	23	25	48	62
1981-82			40	12	30	42	36
1982-83			80	28	48	76	59
4 yrs.	N Totals:		250	79	123	202	196
PLAYOFFS							
1979-80	MINN	N	15	5	6	11	20
1980-81			8	0	3	3	6
1981-82			4	0	2	2	4
1982-83			9	2	4	6	9
4 yrs.	N Totals:		36	7	15	22	39

Walt McCartney

MCCARTNEY, WALTER

B. Unknown Defense

YEAR	TEAM & LEAGUE		GP	G	A	PTS	PIM
1932-33	MONT	N	2	0	0	0	0

Ted McCaskill

MCCASKILL, EDWARD JOEL 6'1", 195 lbs.

B. Oct. 29, 1936, Kapuskasing, Ont. Center, Shoots L

YEAR	TEAM & LEAGUE		GP	G	A	PTS	PIM
1967-68	MINN	N	4	0	2	2	0
1972-73	LA	W	73	11	11	22	150
1973-74			18	2	2	4	63
3 yrs.	N Totals:		4	0	2	2	0
	W Totals:		91	13	13	26	213
PLAYOFFS							
1972-73	LA	W	6	2	3	5	12

Rob McClanahan

MCCLANAHAN, ROB 5'10", 180 lbs.

B. Jan. 9, 1958, St. Paul, Minn. Center, Shoots R

YEAR	TEAM & LEAGUE		GP	G	A	PTS	PIM
1979-80	BUF	N	13	2	5	7	0
1980-81			53	3	12	15	38
1981-82	HART	N	17	0	3	3	11
	NYR	N	22	5	9	14	10
	2 team total		39	5	12	17	21
1982-83			78	22	26	48	46
4 yrs.	N Totals:		183	32	55	87	105
PLAYOFFS							
1979-80	BUF	N	10	0	1	1	4
1980-81			5	0	1	1	13
1981-82	NYR	N	10	2	5	7	2
1982-83			9	2	5	7	12
4 yrs.	N Totals:		34	4	12	16	31

Claimed by **Hartford** from Buffalo in 1981 Waiver Draft, Oct. 5, 1981. Traded to **N.Y. Rangers** by Hartford for N.Y. Rangers' tenth round choice in 1983 Entry Draft (Reine Karlsson), Feb. 2, 1982.

Kevin McClelland

MCCLELLAND, KEVIN WILLIAM 6', 180 lbs.

B. July 4, 1962, Oshawa, Ont. Center, Shoots R

YEAR	TEAM & LEAGUE		GP	G	A	PTS	PIM
1981-82	PITT	N	10	1	4	5	4
1982-83			38	5	4	9	73
2 yrs.	N Totals:		48	6	8	14	77
PLAYOFFS							
1981-82	PITT	N	5	1	1	2	5

Kevin McClelland continued

Acquired by **Pittsburgh** along with Pat Boutette from Hartford as compensation for Greg Millen, June 29, 1981.

Bob McCord

MCCORD, ROBERT LOMER — 6'1", 202 lbs.
B. Mar. 30, 1934, Matheson, Ont. — Defense, Shoots R

YEAR	TEAM & LEAGUE		GP	G	A	PTS	PIM
1963-64	**BOS**	**N**	65	1	9	10	49
1964-65			43	0	6	6	26
1965-66	**DET**	**N**	9	0	2	2	16
1966-67			14	1	2	3	27
1967-68			3	0	0	0	2
	MINN	**N**	70	3	9	12	39
	2 team total		73	3	9	12	41
1968-69			69	4	17	21	70
1972-73	**STL**	**N**	43	1	13	14	33
7 yrs.		**N Totals:**	316	10	58	68	262
PLAYOFFS							
1967-68	**MINN**	**N**	14	2	5	7	10

Traded by Boston with Ab McDonald and Ken Stephenson to **Detroit** for Al Langlois, Ron Harris, Parker MacDonald and Bob Dillabough, May 31, 1965. Traded to **Minnesota** by Detroit for Jean Guy Talbot, Oct. 19, 1967. Drafted by **Montreal** from Minnesota in Intra-league Draft, June 9, 1970.

Dennis McCord

MCCORD, DENNIS FREDERICK — 5'10", 190 lbs.
B. July 28, 1951, Chatham, Ont. — Defense, Shoots L

YEAR	TEAM & LEAGUE		GP	G	A	PTS	PIM
1973-74	**VAN**	**N**	3	0	0	0	6

John McCormack

MCCORMACK, JOHN RONALD (Goose) — 6', 185 lbs.
B. Aug. 2, 1925, Edmonton, Alta. — Center, Shoots L

YEAR	TEAM & LEAGUE		GP	G	A	PTS	PIM
1947-48	**TOR**	**N**	3	0	1	1	0
1948-49			1	0	0	0	0
1949-50			34	6	5	11	0
1950-51			46	6	7	13	2
1951-52	**MONT**	**N**	54	2	10	12	4
1952-53			59	1	9	10	9
1953-54			51	5	10	15	12
1954-55	**CHI**	**N**	63	5	7	12	8
8 yrs.		**N Totals:**	311	25	49	74	35
PLAYOFFS							
1949-50	**TOR**	**N**	6	1	0	1	0
1952-53*	**MONT**	**N**	9	0	0	0	0
1953-54			7	0	1	1	0
3 yrs.		**N Totals:**	22	1	1	2	0

Sold to **Toronto** by Montreal, Sept. 23, 1951. Drafted by **Chicago** from Montreal, Sept. 16, 1954. Traded to **Detroit** by Chicago with Jerry Toppazzini, Dave Creighton and Gord Hollingworth for Tony Leswick, Glen Skov, Johnny Wilson and Benny Woit, June 3, 1955.

Dale McCourt

MCCOURT, DALE ALLEN — 5'10", 180 lbs.
B. Jan. 26, 1957, Falconbridge, Ont. — Center, Shoots R

YEAR	TEAM & LEAGUE		GP	G	A	PTS	PIM
1977-78	**DET**	**N**	76	33	39	72	10
1978-79			79	28	43	71	14
1979-80			80	30	51	81	7
1980-81			80	30	56	86	50
1981-82			26	13	14	27	12
	BUF	**N**	52	20	22	42	12
	2 team total		78	33	36	69	24
1982-83			62	20	32	52	10
6 yrs.		**N Totals:**	455	174	257	431	115
PLAYOFFS							
1977-78	**DET**	**N**	7	4	2	6	2
1981-82	**BUF**	**N**	4	2	3	5	0
1982-83			10	3	2	5	4
3 yrs.		**N Totals:**	21	9	7	16	6

Sent to **Los Angeles** by Detroit as compensation for Detroit's signing free agent Rogie Vachon, Aug. 8, 1978. Remained with Detroit, pending outcome of litigation. Traded to **Detroit** by Los Angeles for Andre St. Laurent and Detroit's first-round choice (Larry Murphy) in the 1980 Entry Draft and Detroit's first-round choice (Doug Smith) in the 1981 Entry Draft. Traded to **Buffalo** by Detroit along with Mike Foligno and Brent Peterson for Danny Gare, Jim Schoenfeld and Derek Smith, Dec. 2, 1981.

Bill McCreary

MCCREARY, WILLIAM EDWARD — 5'10", 172 lbs.
B. Dec. 2, 1934, Sundridge, Ont. — Left Wing, Shoots L

YEAR	TEAM & LEAGUE		GP	G	A	PTS	PIM
1953-54	**NYR**	**N**	2	0	0	0	2
1954-55			8	0	2	2	0
1957-58	**DET**	**N**	3	1	0	1	2
1962-63	**MONT**	**N**	14	2	3	5	0
1964-65			9	0	3	3	4
1967-68	**STL**	**N**	70	13	13	26	22
1968-69			71	13	17	30	50
1969-70			73	15	17	32	16
1970-71			68	9	10	19	16
9 yrs.		**N Totals:**	318	53	65	118	112
PLAYOFFS							
1961-62	**MONT**	**N**	1	0	0	0	0
1967-68	**STL**	**N**	15	3	2	5	0
1968-69			12	1	5	6	14
1969-70			15	1	7	8	0
1970-71			6	1	2	3	0
5 yrs.		**N Totals:**	49	6	16	22	14

Drafted by **Detroit** from N.Y. Rangers, June 5, 1956. Traded to **St. Louis** by Mont. Canadiens for Claude Cardin and Phil Obendorf, June 14, 1967.

Bill McCreary

MCCREARY, WILLIAM — 6', 190 lbs.
B. Apr. 15, 1960, Springfield, Mass. — Right Wing, Shoots R

YEAR	TEAM & LEAGUE		GP	G	A	PTS	PIM
1980-81	**TOR**	**N**	12	1	0	1	4

Keith McCreary

MCCREARY, VERNON KEITH — 5'10", 180 lbs.
B. June 19, 1940, Sundridge, Ont. — Right Wing, Shoots L

YEAR	TEAM & LEAGUE		GP	G	A	PTS	PIM
1967-68	**PITT**	**N**	70	14	12	26	44
1968-69			70	25	23	48	42
1969-70			60	18	8	26	67
1970-71			59	21	12	33	24
1971-72			33	4	4	8	22
1972-73	**ATL**	**N**	77	20	21	41	21
1973-74			76	18	19	37	62
1974-75			78	11	10	21	8
8 yrs.		**N Totals:**	523	131	109	240	290
PLAYOFFS							
1969-70	**PITT**	**N**	10	0	4	4	4
1971-72			1	0	0	0	2
1973-74	**ATL**	**N**	4	0	0	0	0
3 yrs.		**N Totals:**	15	0	4	4	6

Drafted by **Pittsburgh** from Montreal in Expansion Draft June 6, 1967. Drafted by **Atlanta** from Pittsburgh in Expansion Draft, June 6, 1972.

Pat McCreavy

MCCREAVY, PATRICK JOSEPH — 5'11", 165 lbs.
B. Jan. 16, 1918, Owen Sound, Ont. — Center, Shoots R

YEAR	TEAM & LEAGUE		GP	G	A	PTS	PIM
1938-39	**BOS**	**N**	5	0	0	0	0
1939-40			2	0	0	0	2
1940-41			8	0	1	1	2
1941-42			6	0	1	1	0
	DET	**N**	34	5	8	13	0
	2 team total		40	5	9	14	0
4 yrs.		**N Totals:**	55	5	10	15	4
PLAYOFFS							
1940-41*	**BOS**	**N**	9	2	2	4	5
1941-42	**DET**	**N**	11	1	1	2	4
2 yrs.		**N Totals:**	20	3	3	6	9

YEAR	TEAM & LEAGUE		GP	G	A	PTS	PIM

Johnny McCreedy

MCCREEDY, JOHN 5'8½", 160 lbs.
B. Mar. 23, 1911, Winnipeg, Man. Right Wing, Shoots R

YEAR	TEAM	LEAGUE	GP	G	A	PTS	PIM
1941-42	TOR	N	47	15	8	23	14
1944-45			17	2	4	6	11
2 yrs.		N Totals:	64	17	12	29	25
PLAYOFFS							
1941-42*	TOR	N	13	4	3	7	6
1944-45*			8	0	0	0	10
2 yrs.		N Totals:	21	4	3	7	16

Brad McCrimmon

MCCRIMMON, BYRON BRAD 5'11", 193 lbs.
B. Mar. 29, 1959, Dodsland, Sask. Defense, Shoots L

YEAR	TEAM	LEAGUE	GP	G	A	PTS	PIM
1979-80	BOS	N	72	5	11	16	94
1980-81			78	11	18	29	148
1981-82			78	1	8	9	83
1982-83	PHI	N	79	4	21	25	61
4 yrs.		N Totals:	307	21	58	79	386
PLAYOFFS							
1979-80	BOS	N	10	1	1	2	28
1980-81			3	0	1	1	2
1981-82			2	0	0	0	2
1982-83	PHI	N	3	0	0	0	4
4 yrs.		N Totals:	18	1	2	3	36

Traded to **Philadelphia** by Boston for goaltender Pete Peeters. June 9, 1982. Traded to **Philadelphia** by Boston for Pete Peeters, June 9, 1982.

Jim McCrimmon

MCCRIMMON, JOHN JAMES 6'1", 210 lbs.
B. May 29, 1953, Ponoka, Alta. Defense, Shoots R

YEAR	TEAM	LEAGUE	GP	G	A	PTS	PIM
1973-74	EDM	W	75	2	3	5	106
1974-75			34	1	5	6	50
	STL	N	2	0	0	0	0
	2 team total		36	1	5	6	50
1975-76	CALG	W	5	0	0	0	2
3 yrs.		N Totals:	2	0	0	0	0
		W Totals:	114	3	8	11	158

Bob McCulley

MCCULLEY, ROBERT
B. Unknown Forward

YEAR	TEAM	LEAGUE	GP	G	A	PTS	PIM
1934-35	MONT	N	1	0	0	0	0

Don McCulloch

MCCULLOCH, DONALD 6'2", 190 lbs.
B. Mar. 23, 1951, Little Current, Sask. Defense, Shoots L

YEAR	TEAM	LEAGUE	GP	G	A	PTS	PIM
1974-75	VAN	W	51	1	9	10	42

Brian McCutcheon

MCCUTCHEON, BRIAN KENNETH 5'10", 180 lbs
B. Aug. 3, 1949, Toronto, Ont. Left Wing, Shoots L

YEAR	TEAM	LEAGUE	GP	G	A	PTS	PIM
1974-75	DET	N	17	3	1	4	2
1975-76			8	0	0	0	5
1976-77			12	0	0	0	0
3 yrs.		N Totals:	37	3	1	4	7

Darwin McCutcheon

MCCUTCHEON, DARWIN 6'4", 190 lbs.
B. Apr. 19, 1962, Listowel, Ont. Defense, Shoots L

YEAR	TEAM	LEAGUE	GP	G	A	PTS	PIM
1981-82	TOR	N	1	0	0	0	2

Jeff McDill

MCDILL, JEFFREY DONALD 5'11", 190 lbs.
B. Mar. 16, 1956, Thunder Bay, Ont. Right Wing, Shoots R

YEAR	TEAM	LEAGUE	GP	G	A	PTS	PIM
1976-77	CHI	N	1	0	0	0	0

Signed as free agent by **N.Y. Rangers** Oct. 13, 1978.

Bill McDonagh

MCDONAGH, WILLIAM JAMES 5'9", 150 lbs.
B. Apr. 30, 1928, Rouyn, Que. Left Wing, Shoots L

YEAR	TEAM	LEAGUE	GP	G	A	PTS	PIM
1949-50	NYR	N	4	0	0	0	2

Ab McDonald

MCDONALD, ALVIN BRIAN 6'2", 194 lbs.
B. Feb. 18, 1936, Winnipeg, Man. Left Wing, Shoots L

YEAR	TEAM	LEAGUE	GP	G	A	PTS	PIM
1958-59	MONT	N	69	13	23	36	35
1959-60			68	9	13	22	26
1960-61	CHI	N	61	17	16	33	22
1961-62			65	22	18	40	8
1962-63			69	20	41	61	12
1963-64			70	14	32	46	19
1964-65	BOS	N	60	9	9	18	6
1965-66	DET	N	43	6	16	22	6
1966-67			12	2	0	2	2
1967-68	PITT	N	74	22	21	43	38
1968-69	STL	N	68	21	21	42	12
1969-70			64	25	30	55	8
1970-71			20	0	5	5	6
1971-72	DET	N	19	2	3	5	0
1972-73	WINN	W	77	17	24	41	16
1973-74			70	12	17	29	8
16 yrs.		N Totals:	762	182	248	430	200
		W Totals:	147	29	41	70	24
PLAYOFFS							
1957-58*	MONT	N	2	0	0	0	2
1958-59*			11	1	1	2	6
1960-61*	CHI	N	8	2	2	4	0
1961-62			12	6	6	12	0
1962-63			6	2	3	5	9
1963-64			7	2	2	4	0
1965-66	DET	N	10	1	4	5	2
1968-69	STL	N	12	2	1	3	10
1969-70			16	5	10	15	13
1972-73	WINN	W	14	2	5	7	2
1973-74			4	0	1	1	2
11 yrs.		N Totals:	84	21	29	50	42
		W Totals:	18	2	6	8	4

Traded to **Chicago** by Montreal for Terry Gray and Glen Skov, June 7, 1960. Traded to **Boston** by Chicago with Reggie Fleming for Doug Mohns, June 8, 1964. Traded by Boston with Bob McCord and Ken Stephenson to **Detroit** for Parker MacDonald, Albert Langlois, Ron Harris and Bob Dillabough, May 31, 1965. Drafted by **Pittsburgh** from Detroit in Expansion Draft, June 6, 1967. Traded to **St. Louis** with Bob Wall and Mike Lowe, May 12, 1971, to complete deal in which St. Louis acquired Carl Brewer (Feb. 22, 1971).

Brian McDonald

MCDONALD, BRIAN HAROLD 5'11", 190 lbs.
B. Mar. 23, 1945, Toronto, Ont. Right Wing, Shoots R

YEAR	TEAM	LEAGUE	GP	G	A	PTS	PIM
1970-71	BUF	N	12	0	0	0	29
1972-73	HOUS	W	71	20	20	40	78
1973-74	LA	W	56	22	30	52	54
1974-75	M-B	W	18	3	5	8	15
	IND	W	47	14	15	29	19
	2 team total		65	17	20	37	34
1975-76			62	15	18	33	54
1976-77			50	15	13	28	48
6 yrs.		N Totals:	12	0	0	0	29
		W Totals:	304	89	101	190	268
PLAYOFFS							
1967-68	CHI	N	8	0	0	0	2
1972-73	HOUS	W	10	3	0	3	16
1975-76	IND	W	7	0	1	1	12
1976-77			9	3	4	7	33
4 yrs.		N Totals:	8	0	0	0	2
		W Totals:	26	6	5	11	61

Bucko McDonald

MCDONALD, WILFRID KENNEDY 5'9½", 205 lbs.
B. Oct. 31, 1911, Fergus, Ont. Defense, Shoots L

YEAR	TEAM	LEAGUE	GP	G	A	PTS	PIM
1934-35	DET	N	16	1	2	3	8
1935-36			48	4	6	10	32
1936-37			47	3	5	8	20

Bucko McDonald continued

YEAR	TEAM & LEAGUE		GP	G	A	PTS	PIM
1937-38			47	3	7	10	14
1938-39			14	0	0	0	2
	TOR	**N**	33	3	3	6	20
	2 team total		47	3	3	6	22
1939-40			34	2	5	7	13
1940-41			31	6	11	17	12
1941-42			48	2	19	21	24
1942-43			40	2	11	13	39
1943-44			9	2	4	6	8
	NYR	**N**	41	5	6	11	14
	2 team total		50	7	10	17	22
1944-45			40	2	9	11	0
11 yrs.		**N Totals:**	448	35	88	123	206

PLAYOFFS

YEAR	TEAM & LEAGUE		GP	G	A	PTS	PIM
1935-36*	**DET**	**N**	7	3	0	3	10
1936-37*			10	0	0	0	2
1938-39	**TOR**	**N**	10	0	0	0	4
1939-40			10	0	0	0	0
1940-41			7	2	0	2	2
1941-42*			13	0	1	1	2
1942-43			6	1	0	1	4
7 yrs.		**N Totals:**	63	6	1	7	24

Butch McDonald

MCDONALD, BYRON RUSSELL 6′, 185 lbs.
B. Nov. 21, 1916, Moose Jaw, Sask. Left Wing, Shoots L

YEAR	TEAM & LEAGUE		GP	G	A	PTS	PIM
1939-40	**DET**	**N**	37	1	6	7	2
1944-45			3	1	1	2	0
	CHI	**N**	26	6	13	19	0
	2 team total		29	7	14	21	0
2 yrs.		**N Totals:**	66	8	20	28	2

PLAYOFFS

YEAR	TEAM & LEAGUE		GP	G	A	PTS	PIM
1939-40	**DET**	**N**	5	0	2	2	10

Gerry McDonald

MCDONALD, GIRARD J. 6′3″, 190 lbs.
B. Mar. 18, 1958, Weymouth, Mass. Defense, Shoots R

YEAR	TEAM & LEAGUE		GP	G	A	PTS	PIM
1981-82	**HART**	**N**	3	0	0	0	0

Traded to **Hartford** by N.Y. Rangers along with Chris Kotsopoulos and Doug Sulliman for Mike Rogers and Hartford's tenth round choice (Simo Saarinen) in 1982 Entry Draft, Oct. 2, 1981.

Jack McDonald

MCDONALD, JOHN
B. Unknown Left Wing

YEAR	TEAM & LEAGUE		GP	G	A	PTS	PIM
1917-18	**MON(W)**	**N**	4	3	0	3	0
	MONT	**N**	8	9	0	9	9
	2 team total		12	12	0	12	9
1918-19			18	8	4	12	9
1919-20	**QUE**	**N**	24	7	6	13	4
1920-21	**MONT**	**N**	9	0	0	0	0
	TOR	**N**	8	0	1	1	0
	2 team total		17	0	1	1	0
1921-22	**MONT**	**N**	2	0	0	0	0
5 yrs.		**N Totals:**	73	27	11	38	22

PLAYOFFS

YEAR	TEAM & LEAGUE		GP	G	A	PTS	PIM
1917-18	**MONT**	**N**	2	1	0	1	0
1918-19			10	1	0	1	5
2 yrs.		**N Totals:**	12	2	0	2	5

John McDonald

MCDONALD, ALBERT JOHN 5′11½″, 205 lbs.
B. Nov. 24, 1921, Swan River, Man. Right Wing, Shoots R

YEAR	TEAM & LEAGUE		GP	G	A	PTS	PIM
1943-44	**NYR**	**N**	43	10	9	19	6

Lanny McDonald

MCDONALD, LANNY KING 6′, 190 lbs.
B. Feb. 16, 1953, Hanna, Alta. Right Wing, Shoots R
Won Masterton Trophy, 1982-83

YEAR	TEAM & LEAGUE		GP	G	A	PTS	PIM
1973-74	**TOR**	**N**	70	14	16	30	43
1974-75			64	17	27	44	86
1975-76			75	37	56	93	70

Lanny McDonald continued

YEAR	TEAM & LEAGUE		GP	G	A	PTS	PIM
1976-77			80	46	44	90	77
1977-78			74	47	40	87	54
1978-79			79	43	42	85	32
1979-80			35	15	15	30	10
	COLO	**N**	46	25	20	45	43
	2 team total		81	40	35	75	53
1980-81			80	35	46	81	56
1981-82			16	6	9	15	20
	CALG	**N**	55	34	33	67	37
	2 team total		71	40	42	82	57
1982-83			80	66	32	98	90
10 yrs.		**N Totals:**	754	385	380	765	618

PLAYOFFS

YEAR	TEAM & LEAGUE		GP	G	A	PTS	PIM
1974-75	**TOR**	**N**	7	0	0	0	2
1975-76			10	4	4	8	4
1976-77			9	10	7	17	6
1977-78			13	3	4	7	10
1978-79			6	3	2	5	0
1981-82	**CALG**	**N**	3	0	1	1	6
1982-83			7	3	4	7	19
7 yrs.		**N Totals:**	55	23	22	45	47

Traded to **Colorado** by Toronto with Joel Quenneville for Pat Hickey and Wilf Paiement, Dec. 29, 1979. Traded to **Calgary** by Colorado along with Colorado's fourth round choice in 1983 Entry Draft for Bob MacMillan and Don Lever, Nov. 25, 1981.

Bob McDonald

MCDONALD, ROBERT
B. Jan. 4, 1923, Toronto, Ont. Forward

YEAR	TEAM & LEAGUE		GP	G	A	PTS	PIM
1943-44	**NYR**	**N**	1	0	0	0	0

Terry McDonald

MCDONALD, TERRY GRANT 6′1″, 180 lbs.
B. Jan. 1, 1956, Coquitlam, B.C. Defense, Shoots L

YEAR	TEAM & LEAGUE		GP	G	A	PTS	PIM
1975-76	**KC**	**N**	8	0	1	1	6

Joe McDonnell

MCDONNELL, JOSEPH PATRICK 6′2″, 200 lbs.
B. May 11, 1961, Kitchener, Ont. Defense, Shoots R

YEAR	TEAM & LEAGUE		GP	G	A	PTS	PIM
1981-82	**VAN**	**N**	7	0	1	1	12

Signed as free agent by **Vancouver** Sept. 22, 1980.

Moylan McDonnell

MCDONNELL, MOYLAN
B. Unknown Defense

YEAR	TEAM & LEAGUE		GP	G	A	PTS	PIM
1920-21	**HAMIL**	**N**	20	1	1	2	0

Al McDonough

MCDONOUGH, JAMES ALLISON 6′1″, 175 lbs.
B. June 6, 1950, Hamilton, Ont. Right Wing, Shoots R

YEAR	TEAM & LEAGUE		GP	G	A	PTS	PIM
1970-71	**LA**	**N**	6	2	1	3	0
1971-72			31	3	2	5	8
	PITT	**N**	37	7	11	18	8
	2 team total		68	10	13	23	16
1972-73			78	35	41	76	26
1973-74			37	14	22	36	12
	ATL	**N**	35	10	9	19	15
	2 team total		72	24	31	55	27
1974-75	**CLEVE**	**W**	78	34	30	64	27
1975-76			80	23	22	45	19
1976-77	**MINN**	**W**	42	9	21	30	6
1977-78	**DET**	**N**	12	2	2	4	4
8 yrs.		**N Totals:**	236	73	88	161	73
		W Totals:	200	66	73	139	52

PLAYOFFS

YEAR	TEAM & LEAGUE		GP	G	A	PTS	PIM
1971-72	**PITT**	**N**	4	0	1	1	0
1973-74	**ATL**	**N**	4	0	0	0	2
1974-75	**CLEVE**	**W**	5	2	1	3	2
1975-76			3	1	0	1	0
4 yrs.		**N Totals:**	8	0	1	1	2
		W Totals:	8	3	1	4	2

Mike McDougal

MCDOUGAL, MICHAEL GEORGE 6'2", 205 lbs.
B. Apr. 30, 1958, Port Huron, Mich. Right Wing, Shoots L

YEAR	TEAM & LEAGUE		GP	G	A	PTS	PIM
1978-79	**NYR**	**N**	1	0	0	0	0
1980-81			2	0	0	0	0
1981-82	**HART**	**N**	3	0	0	0	0
1982-83			55	8	10	18	43
4 yrs.		**N Totals:**	61	8	10	18	43

Jim McElmury

MCELMURY, JAMES DONALD 6', 190 lbs.
B. Oct. 3, 1949, St. Paul, Minn. Defense, Shoots L

YEAR	TEAM & LEAGUE		GP	G	A	PTS	PIM
1972-73	**MINN**	**N**	7	0	1	1	2
1974-75	**KC**	**N**	78	5	17	22	25
1975-76			38	2	6	8	6
1976-77	**COLO**	**N**	55	7	23	30	16
1977-78			2	0	0	0	0
5 yrs.		**N Totals:**	180	14	47	61	49

Sold to **Los Angeles** by Minnesota, March 1, 1974. Signed as a free agent by Kansas City, June 27, 1974.

Mike McEwen

MCEWEN, MICHAEL TODD (Q) 6'1", 185 lbs.
B. Aug. 10, 1956, Hornepayne, Ont. Defense, Shoots L

YEAR	TEAM & LEAGUE		GP	G	A	PTS	PIM
1976-77	**NYR**	**N**	80	14	29	43	38
1977-78			57	5	13	18	52
1978-79			80	20	38	58	35
1979-80			9	1	7	8	8
	COLO	**N**	67	11	40	51	33
	2 team total		76	12	47	59	41
1980-81			65	11	35	46	84
	NYI	**N**	13	0	3	3	10
	2 team total		78	11	38	49	94
1981-82			73	10	39	49	50
1982-83			42	2	11	13	16
7 yrs.		**N Totals:**	486	74	215	289	326
PLAYOFFS							
1978-79	**NYR**	**N**	18	2	11	13	8
1980-81*	**NYI**	**N**	17	6	8	14	6
1981-82*			15	3	7	10	18
1982-83*			12	0	2	2	4
4 yrs.		**N Totals:**	62	11	28	39	36

Traded to **Colorado** by N.Y. Rangers with Pat Hickey, Lucien DeBlois, Dean Turner, and future considerations (Bobby Crawford), for Barry Beck, Nov. 2, 1979. Traded to **N.Y. Islanders** by Colorado with Jari Kaarela for Chico Resch and Steve Tambellini, Mar. 10, 1981.

Jim McFadden

MCFADDEN, JAMES ALEXANDER 5'7", 178 lbs.
B. Apr. 15, 1920, Belfast, Ireland Center, Shoots L
Won Calder Trophy, 1947-48

YEAR	TEAM & LEAGUE		GP	G	A	PTS	PIM
1947-48	**DET**	**N**	60	24	24	48	12
1948-49			55	12	20	32	10
1949-50			68	14	16	30	8
1950-51			70	14	18	32	10
1951-52	**CHI**	**N**	70	10	24	34	14
1952-53			70	23	21	44	29
1953-54			19	3	3	6	6
7 yrs.		**N Totals:**	412	100	126	226	89
PLAYOFFS							
1947-48	**DET**	**N**	10	5	3	8	10
1948-49			8	0	1	1	6
1949-50*			14	2	3	5	8
1950-51			6	0	0	0	2
1952-53	**CHI**	**N**	7	3	0	3	4
5 yrs.		**N Totals:**	45	10	7	17	30

Traded to **Chicago** by Detroit with George Gee, Max McNab, Clare Martin, Jim Peters and Rags Raglan for Hugh Coflin and $75,000, Aug. 20, 1951.

George McFarland

MCFARLAND, GEORGE
B. Unknown Defense

YEAR	TEAM & LEAGUE		GP	G	A	PTS	PIM
1926-27	**CHI**	**N**	2	0	0	0	0

Don McFayden

MCFAYDEN, DONALD P. 5'9", 163 lbs.
B. Mar. 24, 1907, Grossfield, Alta. Forward, Shoots L

YEAR	TEAM & LEAGUE		GP	G	A	PTS	PIM
1932-33	**CHI**	**N**	48	5	9	14	20
1933-34			46	1	3	4	20
1934-35			37	2	5	7	4
1935-36			48	4	16	20	33
4 yrs.		**N Totals:**	179	12	33	45	77
PLAYOFFS							
1933-34*	**CHI**	**N**	8	2	2	4	5
1934-35			2	0	0	0	0
1935-36			2	0	0	0	0
3 yrs.		**N Totals:**	12	2	2	4	5

Jim McGeough

MCGEOUGH, JAMES 5'8", 161 lbs.
B. Apr. 13, 1963, Regina, Sask. Center, Shoots L

YEAR	TEAM & LEAGUE		GP	G	A	PTS	PIM
1981-82	**WASH**	**N**	4	0	0	0	0

John McGibbon

MCGIBBON, JOHN IRVING
B. Unknown

YEAR	TEAM & LEAGUE		GP	G	A	PTS	PIM
1942-43	**MONT**	**N**	1	0	0	0	2

Bob McGill

MCGILL, ROBERT PAUL 6', 202 lbs.
B. Apr. 27, 1962, Edmonton, Alta. Defense, Shoots R

YEAR	TEAM & LEAGUE		GP	G	A	PTS	PIM
1981-82	**TOR**	**N**	68	1	10	11	263
1982-83			30	0	0	0	146
2 yrs.		**N Totals:**	98	1	10	11	409

Jack McGill

MCGILL, JOHN 5'10", 150 lbs.
B. Nov. 3, 1910, Ottawa, Ont. Forward, Shoots L

YEAR	TEAM & LEAGUE		GP	G	A	PTS	PIM
1934-35	**MONT**	**N**	44	9	1	10	34
1935-36			46	13	7	20	28
1936-37			44	5	2	7	9
3 yrs.		**N Totals:**	134	27	10	37	71
PLAYOFFS							
1934-35	**MONT**	**N**	2	2	0	2	0
1936-37			1	0	0	0	0
2 yrs.		**N Totals:**	3	2	0	2	0

Jack McGill

MCGILL, JOHN GEORGE (Big Jack) 6'1", 180 lbs.
B. Sept. 19, 1921, Edmonton, Alta. Center, Shoots L

YEAR	TEAM & LEAGUE		GP	G	A	PTS	PIM
1941-42	**BOS**	**N**	13	8	11	19	2
1944-45			14	4	2	6	0
1945-46			46	6	14	20	21
1946-47			24	5	9	14	19
4 yrs.		**N Totals:**	97	23	36	59	42
PLAYOFFS							
1941-42	**BOS**	**N**	5	4	1	5	6
1944-45			7	3	3	6	0
1945-46			10	0	0	0	0
1946-47			5	0	0	0	11
4 yrs.		**N Totals:**	27	7	4	11	17

Dick McGlynn

MCGLYNN, RICHARD ANTHONY 6'2", 185 lbs.
B. July 19, 1948, Medford, Mass. Defense, Shoots R

YEAR	TEAM & LEAGUE		GP	G	A	PTS	PIM
1972-73	**CHI**	**W**	30	0	0	0	12

Sandy McGregor

MCGREGOR, DONALD ALEXANDER 5'11", 165 lbs.
B. Mar. 30, 1939, Toronto, Ont. Right Wing, Shoots R

YEAR	TEAM & LEAGUE		GP	G	A	PTS	PIM
1963-64	**NYR**	**N**	2	0	0	0	2

Mickey McGuire

MCGUIRE, FRANK S.
Forward

YEAR	TEAM & LEAGUE		GP	G	A	PTS	PIM
1926-27	**PITT**	**N**	32	3	0	3	6
1927-28			4	0	0	0	0
2 yrs.		**N Totals:**	36	3	0	3	6

Duke McGurry

MCGURRY, FRANCIS J.
Forward

YEAR	TEAM & LEAGUE		GP	G	A	PTS	PIM
1925-26	**PITT**	**N**	36	13	4	17	32
1926-27			33	3	3	6	23
1927-28			43	5	3	8	60
1928-29			39	0	1	1	12
4 yrs.		**N Totals:**	151	21	11	32	127
PLAYOFFS							
1925-26	**PITT**	**N**	2	0	2	2	4
1927-28			2	0	0	0	0
2 yrs.		**N Totals:**	4	0	2	2	4

Jack McIlhargey

MCILHARGEY, JOHN CECIL 6', 190 lbs.
B. Mar. 7, 1952, Edmonton, Alta. Defense, Shoots L

YEAR	TEAM & LEAGUE		GP	G	A	PTS	PIM
1974-75	**PHI**	**N**	2	0	0	0	11
1975-76			57	1	2	3	205
1976-77			40	2	1	3	164
	VAN	**N**	21	1	7	8	61
	2 team total		61	3	8	11	225
1977-78			69	3	5	8	172
1978-79			53	2	4	6	129
1979-80			24	0	2	2	41
	PHI	**N**	26	0	4	4	95
	2 team total		50	0	6	6	136
1980-81			3	0	0	0	22
	HART	**N**	48	1	6	7	142
	2 team total		51	1	6	7	164
1981-82			50	1	5	6	60
8 yrs.		**N Totals:**	393	11	36	47	1102
PLAYOFFS							
1975-76	**PHI**	**N**	15	0	3	3	41
1978-79	**VAN**	**N**	3	0	0	0	2
1979-80	**PHI**	**N**	9	0	0	0	250
3 yrs.		**N Totals:**	27	0	3	3	293

Traded to **Vancouver** by Philadelphia with Larry Goodenough for Bob Dailey, Jan. 20, 1977. Sold to **Philadelphia** by Vancouver, Jan. 2, 1980. Traded to **Hartford** by Philadelphia with Norm Barnes for Hartford's second round choice (later transferred to Toronto, Gary Leeman) in the 1982 Entry Draft, Nov. 21, 1980.

Bert McInenly

MCINENLY, BERTRAM H. 5'9", 160 lbs.
B. May 6, 1906, Quebec, Que. Shoots L

YEAR	TEAM & LEAGUE		GP	G	A	PTS	PIM
1930-31	**DET**	**N**	44	3	5	8	48
1931-32			17	0	1	1	16
	NYA	**N**	30	12	6	18	44
	2 team total		47	12	7	19	60
1932-33	**OTTA**	**N**	30	2	2	4	8
1933-34			2	0	0	0	0
	BOS	**N**	7	0	0	0	4
	2 team total		9	0	0	0	4
1934-35			33	2	1	3	24
1935-36			3	0	0	0	0
6 yrs.		**N Totals:**	166	19	15	34	144
PLAYOFFS							
1934-35	**BOS**	**N**	4	0	0	0	2

Bruce McIntosh

MCINTOSH, BRUCE 6', 178 lbs.
B. Mar. 17, 1949, Minneapolis, Minn. Defense, Shoots L

YEAR	TEAM & LEAGUE		GP	G	A	PTS	PIM
1972-73	**MINN**	**N**	2	0	0	0	0

Paul McIntosh

MCINTOSH, PAUL 5'10", 177 lbs.
B. Mar. 13, 1954, Listowel, Ont. Defense, Shoots R

YEAR	TEAM & LEAGUE		GP	G	A	PTS	PIM
1974-75	**BUF**	**N**	6	0	1	1	5
1975-76			42	0	1	1	61
2 yrs.		**N Totals:**	48	0	2	2	66
PLAYOFFS							
1974-75	**BUF**	**N**	1	0	0	0	0
1975-76			1	0	0	0	7
2 yrs.		**N Totals:**	2	0	0	0	7

Jack McIntyre

MCINTYRE, JOHN ARCHIBALD 5'11", 190 lbs.
B. Sept. 8, 1930, Brussels, Ont. Left Wing, Shoots L

YEAR	TEAM & LEAGUE		GP	G	A	PTS	PIM
1949-50	**BOS**	**N**	1	0	1	1	0
1951-52			52	12	19	31	18
1952-53			70	7	15	22	31
1953-54	**CHI**	**N**	23	8	3	11	4
1954-55			65	16	13	29	40
1955-56			46	10	5	15	14
1956-57			70	18	14	32	32
1957-58			27	0	4	4	10
	DET	**N**	41	15	7	22	4
	2 team total		68	15	11	26	14
1958-59			55	15	14	29	14
1959-60			49	8	7	15	6
10 yrs.		**N Totals:**	499	109	102	211	173
PLAYOFFS							
1950-51	**BOS**	**N**	2	0	0	0	0
1951-52			7	1	2	3	2
1952-53			10	4	2	6	2
1957-58	**DET**	**N**	4	1	1	2	0
1959-60			6	1	1	2	0
5 yrs.		**N Totals:**	29	7	6	13	4

Purchased by **Chicago** from Boston, Jan. 20, 1954. Traded to **Detroit** by Chicago with Nick Mickoski, Bob Bailey and Hec Lalande for Earl Reibel, Billy Dea, Lorne Ferguson and Bill Dineen on Dec. 17, 1957.

Larry McIntyre

MCINTYRE, LAWRENCE ALBERT 6'1", 190 lbs.
B. July 13, 1949, Moose Jaw, Sask. Defense, Shoots L

YEAR	TEAM & LEAGUE		GP	G	A	PTS	PIM
1969-70	**TOR**	**N**	1	0	0	0	0
1972-73			40	0	3	3	26
2 yrs.		**N Totals:**	41	0	3	3	26

Traded to **Vancouver** by Toronto with Murray Heatley for Dunc Wilson, May 29, 1973.

Doug McKay

MCKAY, ALVIN DOUGLAS 5'9", 165 lbs.
B. May 28, 1929, Hamilton,Ont. Left Wing, Shoots L

YEAR	TEAM & LEAGUE		GP	G	A	PTS	PIM
PLAYOFFS							
1949-50*	**DET**	**N**	1	0	0	0	0

Ray McKay

MCKAY, RAY OWEN 6'4", 183 lbs.
B. Aug. 22, 1946, Edmonton, Alta. Defense, Shoots L

YEAR	TEAM & LEAGUE		GP	G	A	PTS	PIM
1968-69	**CHI**	**N**	9	0	1	1	12
1969-70			17	0	0	0	23
1970-71			2	0	0	0	0
1971-72	**BUF**	**N**	39	0	3	3	18
1972-73			1	0	0	0	0
1973-74	**CALIF**	**N**	72	2	12	14	49
1974-75	**EDM**	**W**	69	8	20	28	47
1975-76	**CLEVE**	**W**	68	3	10	13	44
1976-77	**MINN**	**W**	42	2	9	11	28
	BIRM	**W**	19	0	1	1	11
	2 team total		61	2	10	12	39

Ray McKay continued

YEAR	TEAM & LEAGUE		GP	G	A	PTS	PIM
1977-78	**EDM**	**W**	14	1	4	5	4
10 yrs.		**N Totals:**	140	2	16	18	102
		W Totals:	212	14	44	58	134
PLAYOFFS							
1969-70	**CHI**	**N**	1	0	0	0	0
1975-76	**CLEVE**	**W**	3	0	0	0	4
1977-78	**EDM**	**W**	4	0	1	1	4
3 yrs.		**N Totals:**	1	0	0	0	0
		W Totals:	7	0	1	1	8

Drafted by **Buffalo** from Chicago in Intra-league Draft, June 8, 1971. Drafted by **California** from Buffalo in Intra-League Draft, June 12, 1973.

Walt McKechnie

MCKECHNIE, WALTER THOMAS JOHN 6'2", 200 lbs.
B. June 19, 1947, London, Ont. Center, Shoots L

YEAR	TEAM & LEAGUE		GP	G	A	PTS	PIM
1967-68	**MINN**	**N**	4	0	0	0	0
1968-69			58	5	9	14	22
1969-70			20	1	3	4	21
1970-71			30	3	1	4	34
1971-72	**CALIF**	**N**	56	11	20	31	40
1972-73			78	16	38	54	58
1973-74			63	23	29	52	14
1974-75	**BOS**	**N**	53	3	3	6	8
	DET	**N**	23	6	11	17	6
	2 team total		76	9	14	23	14
1975-76			80	26	56	82	85
1976-77			80	25	34	59	50
1977-78	**WASH**	**N**	16	4	1	5	0
	CLEVE	**N**	53	12	22	34	12
	2 team total		69	16	23	39	12
1978-79	**TOR**	**N**	79	25	36	61	18
1979-80			54	7	36	43	4
	COLO	**N**	17	0	4	4	2
	2 team total		71	7	40	47	6
1980-81			53	15	23	38	18
1981-82	**DET**	**N**	73	18	37	55	35
1982-83			64	14	29	43	42
16 yrs.		**N Totals:**	954	214	392	606	469
PLAYOFFS							
1967-68	**MINN**	**N**	9	3	2	5	0
1978-79	**TOR**	**N**	6	4	3	7	9
2 yrs.		**N Totals:**	15	7	5	12	9

Traded to **California** by Minnesota with Joey Johnston for Dennis Hextall, May 20, 1971. Put on **N.Y. Rangers'** reserve list from California in Intra-League Draft, June 10, 1974. Traded to **Boston** by N.Y. Rangers for Derek Sanderson, June 12, 1974. Traded to **Detroit** by Boston with Boston's third choice (Clarke Hamilton) in 1975 Amateur Draft for Hank Nowak and Earl Anderson, Feb. 18, 1975. Traded to **Washington** by Detroit with Detroit's 1978 (John Johnston) third-round Amateur Draft choice and 1979 second-round (Errol Rausse) Entry Draft choice for the rights to goaltender Ron Low and Washington's 1979 third-round (Borris Fistric) Entry Draft choice. Traded to **Cleveland** by Washington for Bob Girard and Cleveland's second round choice (Paul MacKinnon) in the 1978 Amateur Draft, Dec. 9, 1977. Put on **Minnesota** Reserve List after Cleveland-Minnesota Dispersal Draft, June 15,1978. Traded to **Toronto** by Minnesota for Toronto's third round choice (Randy Velischek) in the 1980 Entry Draft, Oct. 5, 1978. Traded to **Colorado** by Toronto for Colorado's third round choice (Fred Boimistruck) in the 1980 Entry Draft, Mar. 3, 1980. Signed by **Detroit** as free agent, Oct. 1, 1981.

Ian McKegney

MCKEGNEY, IAN ROBERT 5'11", 165 lbs.
B. May 7, 1947, Sarnia, Ont. Defense, Shoots L

YEAR	TEAM & LEAGUE		GP	G	A	PTS	PIM
1976-77	**CHI**	**N**	3	0	0	0	2

Tony McKegney

MCKEGNEY, ANTHONY SYIIYD 6'1", 198 lbs.
B. Feb. 15, 1958, Montreal, Que. Left Wing, Shoots L

YEAR	TEAM & LEAGUE		GP	G	A	PTS	PIM
1978-79	**BUF**	**N**	52	8	14	22	10
1979-80			80	23	29	52	24
1980-81			80	37	32	69	24
1981-82			73	23	29	52	41
1982-83			78	36	37	73	18
5 yrs.		**N Totals:**	363	127	141	268	117
PLAYOFFS							
1978-79	**BUF**	**N**	2	0	1	1	0
1979-80			14	3	4	7	2
1980-81			8	5	3	8	2
1981-82			4	0	0	0	2
1982-83			10	3	1	4	4
5 yrs.		**N Totals:**	38	11	9	20	10

Tony McKegney continued

Traded by Buffalo with Jean Sauve, Andre Savard, and Buffalo's third pick in the 1983 Amateur Draft (Liro Jarvi) to **Quebec** for Real Cloutier and Quebec's first pick in the 1983 Amateur Draft (Adam Creighton), June 8, 1983.

Jack McKell

MCKELL
Defense

YEAR	TEAM & LEAGUE		GP	G	A	PTS	PIM
1919-20	**OTTA**	**N**	21	2	0	2	20
1920-21			21	2	1	3	22
2 yrs.		**N Totals:**	42	4	1	5	42
PLAYOFFS							
1919-20*	**OTTA**	**N**	5	0	0	0	0
1920-21*			7	0	0	0	0
2 yrs.		**N Totals:**	12	0	0	0	0

Alex McKendry

MCKENDRY, ALEXANDER 6'4", 200 lbs.
B. Nov. 21, 1956, Midland, Ont. Left Wing, Shoots L

YEAR	TEAM & LEAGUE		GP	G	A	PTS	PIM
1977-78	**NYI**	**N**	4	0	0	0	2
1978-79			4	0	0	0	0
1979-80			2	0	0	0	2
1980-81	**CALG**	**N**	36	3	6	9	19
4 yrs.		**N Totals:**	46	3	6	9	23
PLAYOFFS							
1979-80*	**NYI**	**N**	6	2	2	4	0

Traded to **Calgary** by N.Y. Islanders for Calgary's third round choice (Ron Handy) in the 1981 Entry Draft, Oct. 9, 1980.

Sean McKenna

MCKENNA, SEAN MICHAEL 6', 186 lbs.
B. Mar. 7, 1962, Asbestos, Que. Right Wing, Shoots R

YEAR	TEAM & LEAGUE		GP	G	A	PTS	PIM
1981-82	**BUF**	**N**	3	0	1	1	2
1982-83			46	10	14	24	4
2 yrs.		**N Totals:**	49	10	15	25	6

Don McKenney

MCKENNEY, DONALD HAMILTON 6', 175 lbs.
B. Apr. 30, 1934, Smith Falls, Ont. Center, Shoots L
Won Lady Byng Trophy, 1959-60

YEAR	TEAM & LEAGUE		GP	G	A	PTS	PIM
1954-55	**BOS**	**N**	69	22	20	42	34
1955-56			65	10	24	34	20
1956-57			69	21	39	60	31
1957-58			70	28	30	58	59
1958-59			70	32	30	62	20
1959-60			70	20	**49**	69	28
1960-61			68	26	23	49	22
1961-62			70	22	33	55	10
1962-63			41	14	19	33	2
	NYR	**N**	21	8	16	24	4
	2 team total		62	22	35	57	6
1963-64			55	9	17	26	6
	TOR	**N**	15	9	17	26	2
	2 team total		70	18	34	52	8
1964-65			52	6	13	19	6
1965-66	**DET**	**N**	24	1	6	7	0
1967-68	**STL**	**N**	39	9	20	29	4
13 yrs.		**N Totals:**	798	237	356	593	248
PLAYOFFS							
1954-55	**BOS**	**N**	5	1	2	3	4
1956-57			10	1	5	6	4
1957-58			12	9	8	17	0
1958-59			7	2	5	7	0
1963-64*	**TOR**	**N**	12	4	8	12	0
1964-65			6	0	0	0	0
1967-68	**STL**	**N**	6	1	1	2	2

YEAR	TEAM & LEAGUE		GP	G	A	PTS	PIM

Don McKenney continued

YEAR	TEAM	LEAGUE	GP	G	A	PTS	PIM
7 yrs.		N Totals:	58	18	29	47	10

Traded to **N.Y. Rangers** by Boston for Dean Prentice, Feb. 1963. Traded by N.Y. Rangers to **Toronto** with Andy Bathgate for Dick Duff, Bob Nevin, Arnie Brown, Bill Collins, and Rod Seiling, Feb. 22, 1964. Claimed on waivers by **Detroit** from Toronto, June 8, 1965. Drafted by **St. Louis** from Detroit in Expansion Draft, June 6, 1967.

Jim McKenny

MCKENNY, JAMES CLAUDE 6', 185 lbs.
B. Dec. 1, 1946, Ottawa, Ont. Defense, Shoots R

YEAR	TEAM	LEAGUE	GP	G	A	PTS	PIM
1965-66	**TOR**	**N**	2	0	0	0	2
1966-67			6	1	0	1	0
1967-68			5	1	0	1	0
1968-69			7	0	0	0	2
1969-70			73	11	33	44	34
1970-71			68	4	26	30	42
1971-72			76	5	31	36	27
1972-73			77	11	41	52	55
1973-74			77	14	28	42	36
1974-75			66	8	35	43	31
1975-76			46	10	19	29	19
1976-77			76	14	31	45	36
1977-78			15	2	2	4	8
1978-79	**MINN**	**N**	10	1	1	2	2
14 yrs.		**N Totals:**	604	82	247	329	294

PLAYOFFS

YEAR	TEAM	LEAGUE	GP	G	A	PTS	PIM
1970-71	**TOR**	**N**	6	2	1	3	2
1971-72			5	3	0	3	2
1973-74			4	0	2	2	0
1974-75			7	0	1	1	2
1975-76			6	2	3	5	2
1976-77			9	0	2	2	2
6 yrs.		**N Totals:**	37	7	9	16	10

Sold to **Minnesota** by Toronto, May 10, 1978. As completion of deal, Toronto received the rights to Owen Lloyd, Oct. 25, 1978.

Bill McKenzie

MCKENZIE, WILLIAM IAN 5'11", 180 lbs.
B. Mar. 12, 1949, St. Thomas, Ont. Shoots R

YEAR	TEAM	LEAGUE	GP	G	A	PTS	PIM
1974-75	**DET**	**N**	13	0	0	0	0
1975-76	**KC**	**N**	22	0	1	1	4
2 yrs.		**N Totals:**	35	0	1	1	4

Traded to **Kansas City** by Detroit with Gary Bergman for goaltender Peter McDuffe and Glen Burdon, Aug. 22, 1975.

Brian McKenzie

MCKENZIE, BRIAN STEWART 5'10", 165 lbs.
B. Mar. 16, 1951, St. Catharines, Ont. Left Wing, Shoots L

YEAR	TEAM	LEAGUE	GP	G	A	PTS	PIM
1971-72	**PITT**	**N**	6	1	1	2	4
1973-74	**EDM**	**W**	78	18	20	38	66
1974-75	**IND**	**W**	9	1	0	1	6
3 yrs.		**N Totals:**	6	1	1	2	4
		W Totals:	87	19	20	39	72

PLAYOFFS

YEAR	TEAM	LEAGUE	GP	G	A	PTS	PIM
1973-74	**EDM**	**W**	5	0	1	1	0

John McKenzie

MCKENZIE, JOHN ALBERT 5'9", 175 lbs.
B. Dec. 12, 1937, High River, Alta. Right Wing, Shoots R

YEAR	TEAM	LEAGUE	GP	G	A	PTS	PIM
1958-59	**CHI**	**N**	32	3	4	7	22
1959-60	**DET**	**N**	59	8	12	20	50
1960-61			16	3	1	4	13
1963-64	**CHI**	**N**	45	9	9	18	50
1964-65			51	8	10	18	46
1965-66	**NYR**	**N**	35	6	5	11	36
	BOS	**N**	36	13	9	22	36
	2 team total		71	19	14	33	72
1966-67			69	17	19	36	98
1967-68			74	28	38	66	107
1968-69			60	29	27	56	99
1969-70			72	29	41	70	114

YEAR	TEAM & LEAGUE		GP	G	A	PTS	PIM

John McKenzie continued

YEAR	TEAM	LEAGUE	GP	G	A	PTS	PIM
1970-71			65	31	46	77	120
1971-72			77	22	47	69	126
1972-73	**PHI**	**W**	60	28	50	78	157
1973-74	**VAN**	**W**	45	14	38	52	71
1974-75			74	23	37	60	82
1975-76	**MINN**	**W**	57	21	26	47	48
	CIN	**W**	12	3	10	13	6
	2 team total		69	24	36	60	54
1976-77	**MINN**	**W**	40	17	13	30	52
	NE	**W**	34	11	19	30	25
	2 team total		74	28	32	60	77
1977-78			79	27	29	56	61
1978-79			76	19	28	47	115
19 yrs.		**N Totals:**	691	206	268	474	917
		W Totals:	477	163	250	413	617

PLAYOFFS

YEAR	TEAM	LEAGUE	GP	G	A	PTS	PIM
1958-59	**CHI**	**N**	2	0	0	0	2
1959-60	**DET**	**N**	2	0	0	0	0
1963-64	**CHI**	**N**	4	0	1	1	6
1964-65			11	0	1	1	6
1967-68	**BOS**	**N**	4	1	1	2	8
1968-69			10	2	2	4	17
1969-70*			14	5	12	17	35
1970-71			7	2	3	5	22
1971-72*			15	5	12	17	37
1972-73	**PHI**	**W**	4	3	1	4	8
1976-77	**NE**	**W**	5	2	1	3	8
1977-78			14	6	6	12	16
1978-79			10	3	7	10	10
13 yrs.		**N Totals:**	69	15	32	47	133
		W Totals:	33	14	15	29	42

Drafted from Chicago by **Detroit** June 10, 1959. Traded to **Chicago** by Detroit with Len Lunde for Doug Barkley, June 6, 1962. Traded to **N.Y. Rangers** by Chicago with Ray Cullen for Tracy Pratt, Dick Meissner, Dave Richardson and Mel Pearson, June 4, 1965. Traded to **Boston** by N.Y. Rangers for Reggie Fleming, Jan. 10, 1966. Sold to **Philadelphia** by Boston, Aug. 3, 1972.

Alex McKinnon

MCKINNON, ALEX
B. Sudbury, Ont. Defense

YEAR	TEAM	LEAGUE	GP	G	A	PTS	PIM
1924-25	**HAMIL**	**N**	30	8	2	10	45
1925-26	**NYA**	**N**	30	5	3	8	34
1926-27			42	2	1	3	29
1927-28			43	3	3	6	71
1928-29	**CHI**	**N**	44	1	1	2	56
5 yrs.		**N Totals:**	189	19	10	29	235

Bob McKinnon

MCKINNON, ROBERT
B. Unknown Forward

YEAR	TEAM	LEAGUE	GP	G	A	PTS	PIM
1928-29	**CHI**	**N**	2	0	0	0	0

John McKinnon

MCKINNON, JOHN DOUGLAS 5'8", 170 lbs.
B. July 15, 1902, Guysborough, N.S. Shoots R

YEAR	TEAM	LEAGUE	GP	G	A	PTS	PIM
1925-26	**MONT**	**N**	2	0	0	0	0
1927-28	**PITT**	**N**	41	3	3	6	46
1928-29			42	1	0	1	44
1929-30			43	10	7	17	42
1930-31	**PHI**	**N**	38	1	1	2	46
5 yrs.		**N Totals:**	166	15	11	26	178

PLAYOFFS

YEAR	TEAM	LEAGUE	GP	G	A	PTS	PIM
1927-28	**PITT**	**N**	2	0	0	0	4

Don McLean

MCLEAN, ROBERT DONALD 6'1", 200 lbs.
B. Jan. 19, 1954, Niagara Falls, Ont. Defense, Shoots R

YEAR	TEAM	LEAGUE	GP	G	A	PTS	PIM
1975-76	**WASH**	**N**	9	0	0	0	6

Traded to **Washington** by Philadelphia with Bill Clement and Philadelphia's first choice (Alex Forsythe) in 1975 Amateur Draft for Washington's first choice (Mel Bridgman) in same draft, June 4, 1975.

Fred McLean

MCLEAN, FRED
B. Unknown — Forward

YEAR	TEAM & LEAGUE		GP	G	A	PTS	PIM
1919-20	QUE	N	7	0	0	0	2
1920-21	HAMIL	N	2	0	0	0	0
2 yrs.		N Totals:	9	0	0	0	2

Jack McLean

MCLEAN, JACK — 5'8", 165 lbs.
B. Jan. 1, 1923, Winnipeg, Man. — Center, Shoots R

YEAR	TEAM & LEAGUE		GP	G	A	PTS	PIM
1942-43	TOR	N	27	9	8	17	33
1943-44			32	3	15	18	30
1944-45			8	2	1	3	13
3 yrs.		N Totals:	67	14	24	38	76
PLAYOFFS							
1942-43	TOR	N	6	2	2	4	2
1943-44			3	0	0	0	6
1944-45*			4	0	0	0	0
3 yrs.		N Totals:	13	2	2	4	8

John McLellan

MCLELLAN, DANIEL JOHN — 5'11", 150 lbs.
B. Aug. 6, 1928, South Porcupine, Ont. — Center, Shoots L

YEAR	TEAM & LEAGUE		GP	G	A	PTS	PIM
1951-52	TOR	N	2	0	0	0	0

Scott McLellan

MCLELLAN, DAVID SCOTT — 6'1", 175 lbs.
B. Feb. 10, 1963, Toronto, Ont. — Right Wing, Shoots R

YEAR	TEAM & LEAGUE		GP	G	A	PTS	PIM
1982-83	BOS	N	2	0	0	0	0

Roly McLenahan

MCLENAHAN, ROLAND JOSEPH — 5'7", 170 lbs.
B. Oct. 26, 1921, Fredericton, N.B. — Defense, Shoots L

YEAR	TEAM & LEAGUE		GP	G	A	PTS	PIM
1945-46	DET	N	9	2	1	3	10
PLAYOFFS							
1945-46	DET	N	2	0	0	0	0

Al McLeod

MCLEOD, ALLAN SIDNEY — 5'11", 200 lbs.
B. June 17, 1949, Medicine Hat, Alta. — Defense, Shoots L

YEAR	TEAM & LEAGUE		GP	G	A	PTS	PIM
1973-74	DET	N	26	2	2	4	24
1974-75	PHOE	W	77	3	16	19	98
1975-76			80	2	17	19	82
1976-77	PHOE	W	29	1	5	6	35
	HOUS	W	51	7	21	28	20
	2 team total		80	8	26	34	55
1977-78	HOUS	W	80	2	22	24	54
1978-79	IND	W	25	0	11	11	22
6 yrs.		N Totals:	26	2	2	4	24
		W Totals:	342	15	92	107	311
PLAYOFFS							
1974-75	PHOE	W	5	0	4	4	4
1975-76			5	0	2	2	4
1976-77	HOUS	W	10	1	3	4	9
1977-78			6	1	0	1	2
4 yrs.		W Totals:	26	2	9	11	19

Don McLeod

MCLEOD, DONALD MARTIN — 6', 190 lbs.
B. Aug. 24, 1946, Trail, B.C. — Shoots L

YEAR	TEAM & LEAGUE		GP	G	A	PTS	PIM
1975-76	CALG	W	63	0	13	13	4

Jack McLeod

MCLEOD, ROBERT JOHN — 5'8½", 150 lbs.
B. Apr. 30, 1930, Regina, Sask. — Right Wing, Shoots R

YEAR	TEAM & LEAGUE		GP	G	A	PTS	PIM
1949-50	NYR	N	38	6	9	15	2
1950-51			41	5	10	15	2
1951-52			13	2	3	5	2
1952-53			3	0	0	0	2
1954-55			11	1	1	2	2

Jack McLeod continued

YEAR	TEAM & LEAGUE		GP	G	A	PTS	PIM
5 yrs.		N Totals:	106	14	23	37	10
PLAYOFFS							
1949-50	NYR	N	7	0	0	0	0

Jim McLeod

MCLEOD, JAMES BRADLEY — 5'8", 170 lbs.
B. Apr. 7, 1937, Port Arthur, Ont. — Shoots L

YEAR	TEAM & LEAGUE		GP	G	A	PTS	PIM
1971-72	STL	N	16	0	1	1	0
1972-73	CHI	W	54	0	1	1	2
2 yrs.		N Totals:	16	0	1	1	0
		W Totals:	54	0	1	1	2

Mike McMahon

MCMAHON, MICHAEL CLARENCE — 5'8", 215 lbs.
B. Feb. 1, 1915, Brockville, Ont. — Defense, Shoots L

YEAR	TEAM & LEAGUE		GP	G	A	PTS	PIM
1943-44	MONT	N	42	7	17	24	**98**
1945-46			13	0	1	1	2
	BOS	N	2	0	0	0	2
	2 team total		15	0	1	1	4
2 yrs.		N Totals:	57	7	18	25	102
PLAYOFFS							
1942-43	MONT	N	5	0	0	0	14
1943-44*			8	1	2	3	16
2 yrs.		N Totals:	13	1	2	3	30

Mike McMahon

MCMAHON, MICHAEL — 5'11", 175 lbs.
B. Aug. 30, 1941, Quebec City, Que. — Defense, Shoots L

YEAR	TEAM & LEAGUE		GP	G	A	PTS	PIM
1963-64	NYR	N	18	0	1	1	16
1964-65			1	0	0	0	0
1965-66			41	0	12	12	34
1967-68	MINN	N	74	14	33	47	71
1968-69			43	0	11	11	0
	CHI	N	20	0	8	8	6
	2 team total		63	0	19	19	6
1969-70	DET	N	2	0	0	0	0
	PITT	N	12	1	3	4	19
	2 team total		14	1	3	4	19
1970-71	BUF	N	12	0	0	0	4
1971-72	NYR	N	1	0	0	0	0
1972-73	MINN	W	75	12	39	51	87
1973-74			71	10	35	45	82
1974-75			54	5	15	20	42
1975-76	SD	W	69	2	12	14	38
12 yrs.		N Totals:	224	15	68	83	150
		W Totals:	269	29	101	130	249
PLAYOFFS							
1967-68	MINN	N	14	3	7	10	4
1972-73	MINN	W	5	0	5	5	2
1973-74			11	1	7	8	9
1974-75			7	0	1	1	0
1975-76	SD	W	9	0	1	1	2
5 yrs.		N Totals:	14	3	7	10	4
		W Totals:	32	1	14	15	13

Claimed in draft by **Montreal** from N.Y. Rangers, June 15, 1966. Sold to **Minnesota** by Montrel, June 14, 1967. Traded to **Chicago** by Minnesota with Andre Boudrias for Tom Reid and Bill Orban, Feb. 14, 1969. Traded to **Pittsburgh** by Detroit for Billy Dea, Oct. 28, 1969. Drafted by **Buffalo** from Pittsburgh in Expansion Draft, June 10, 1970. Traded to **Los Angeles** by Buffalo for Eddie Shack and Dick Duff, Nov. 25, 1970.

Bob McManama

MCMANAMA, ROBERT S. — 6', 180 lbs.
B. Oct. 7, 1951, Belmont, Mass. — Center, Shoots R

YEAR	TEAM & LEAGUE		GP	G	A	PTS	PIM
1973-74	PITT	N	47	5	14	19	18
1974-75			40	5	9	14	6
1975-76			12	1	2	3	4
	NE	W	37	3	10	13	28
	2 team total		49	4	12	16	32
3 yrs.		N Totals:	99	11	25	36	28
		W Totals:	37	3	10	13	28

Bob McManama continued

YEAR	TEAM & LEAGUE		GP	G	A	PTS	PIM
PLAYOFFS							
1974-75	PITT	N	8	0	1	1	6
1975-76	NE	W	12	4	3	7	4
2 yrs.		N Totals:	8	0	1	1	6
		W Totals:	12	4	3	7	4

Sammy McManus

MCMANUS, A. SAMUEL
B. Belfast, Ireland — Left Wing, Shoots L

YEAR	TEAM & LEAGUE		GP	G	A	PTS	PIM
1934-35	MON(M)	N	25	0	1	1	8
1936-37	BOS	N	1	0	0	0	0
2 yrs.		N Totals:	26	0	1	1	8
PLAYOFFS							
1934-35*	MON(M)	N	1	0	0	0	0

Jim McMasters

MCMASTERS, JAMES DEAN — 5'10", 195 lbs.
B. Sept. 20, 1952, High River, Alta. — Defense, Shoots L

YEAR	TEAM & LEAGUE		GP	G	A	PTS	PIM
1972-73	CLEVE	W	74	1	7	8	37
1973-74			9	0	0	0	4
2 yrs.		W Totals:	83	1	7	8	41
PLAYOFFS							
1972-73	CLEVE	W	9	0	1	1	6

Dale McMullen

MCMULLEN, DALE — Left Wing

YEAR	TEAM & LEAGUE		GP	G	A	PTS	PIM
1977-78	EDM	W	1	0	0	0	0

Max McNab

MCNAB, MAXWELL DOUGLAS — 6'2", 170 lbs.
B. June 21, 1924, Watson, Sask. — Center, Shoots L

YEAR	TEAM & LEAGUE		GP	G	A	PTS	PIM
1947-48	DET	N	12	2	2	4	2
1948-49			51	10	13	23	14
1949-50			65	4	4	8	8
3 yrs.		N Totals:	128	16	19	35	24
PLAYOFFS							
1947-48	DET	N	3	0	0	0	2
1948-49			10	0	1	1	2
1949-50*			10	0	0	0	0
1950-51			2	0	0	0	0
4 yrs.		N Totals:	25	0	1	1	4

Traded to **Chicago** by Detroit with Jim McFadden, George Gee, Jim Peters, Clare Martin and Rags Raglan for Hugh Coflin and $75,000, Aug. 20, 1951.

Pete McNab

MCNAB, PETER MAXWELL — 6'3", 203 lbs.
B. May 8, 1952, Vancouver, B.C. — Center, Shoots L

YEAR	TEAM & LEAGUE		GP	G	A	PTS	PIM
1973-74	BUF	N	22	3	6	9	2
1974-75			53	22	21	43	8
1975-76			79	24	32	56	16
1976-77	BOS	N	80	38	48	86	11
1977-78			79	41	39	80	4
1978-79			76	35	45	80	10
1979-80			74	40	38	78	10
1980-81			80	37	46	83	24
1981-82			80	36	40	76	19
1982-83			74	22	52	74	23
10 yrs.		N Totals:	697	298	367	665	127
PLAYOFFS							
1974-75	BUF	N	17	2	6	8	4
1975-76			8	0	0	0	0
1976-77	BOS	N	14	5	3	8	2
1977-78			15	8	11	19	2
1978-79			11	5	3	8	0
1979-80			10	8	6	14	2
1980-81			3	3	0	3	0
1981-82			11	6	8	14	6

Pete McNab continued

YEAR	TEAM & LEAGUE		GP	G	A	PTS	PIM
1982-83			15	3	5	8	4
9 yrs.		N Totals:	104	40	42	82	20

Signed as free agent by **Boston** from Buffalo, June 11, 1976.

Sid McNabney

MCNABNEY, SIDNEY — 5'7", 150 lbs.
B. Jan. 15, 1929, Toronto, Ont. — Center, Shoots L

YEAR	TEAM & LEAGUE		GP	G	A	PTS	PIM
PLAYOFFS							
1950-51	MONT	N	5	0	1	1	2

Howard McNamara

MCNAMARA, HOWARD — 240 lbs.
B. Unknown — Defense

YEAR	TEAM & LEAGUE		GP	G	A	PTS	PIM
1919-20	MONT	N	11	1	0	1	2

Mike McNamara

MCNAMARA, MICHAEL
B. Mar. 28, 1949, — Forward

YEAR	TEAM & LEAGUE		GP	G	A	PTS	PIM
1972-73	QUE	W	19	0	0	0	5

Pete McNamee

MCNAMEE, PETER CHARLES — 5'11", 198 lbs.
B. Sept. 11, 1950, Jamaica, West Indies — Defense, Shoots L

YEAR	TEAM & LEAGUE		GP	G	A	PTS	PIM
1973-74	VAN	W	3	0	0	0	0
1974-75			11	2	1	3	15
	PHOE	W	55	9	19	28	77
	2 team total		66	11	20	31	92
1975-76			14	1	2	3	32
	SD	W	51	1	3	4	27
	2 team total		65	2	5	7	59
1976-77			41	3	6	9	38
4 yrs.		W Totals:	175	16	31	47	189
PLAYOFFS							
1974-75	PHOE	W	5	1	0	1	2
1975-76	SD	W	11	0	1	1	28
1976-77			2	0	0	0	2
3 yrs.		W Totals:	18	1	1	2	32

Signed by **Colorado** as free agent, Aug. 16, 1979.

George McNaughton

MCNAUGHTON, GEORGE
B. Unknown — Forward

YEAR	TEAM & LEAGUE		GP	G	A	PTS	PIM
1919-20	QUE	N	1	0	0	0	0

Billy McNeill

MCNEILL, WILLIAM RONALD — 5'10", 185 lbs.
B. Jan. 26, 1936, Edmonton, Alta. — Right Wing, Shoots R

YEAR	TEAM & LEAGUE		GP	G	A	PTS	PIM
1956-57	DET	N	64	5	10	15	34
1957-58			35	5	10	15	29
1958-59			54	2	5	7	32
1959-60			47	5	13	18	33
1962-63			42	3	7	10	12
1963-64			15	1	1	2	2
6 yrs.		N Totals:	257	21	46	67	142
PLAYOFFS							
1957-58	DET	N	4	1	1	2	4

Drafted by **New York** from Detroit, June 8, 1960.

Stu McNeill

MCNEILL, STUART
B. Sept. 25, 1938, Port Arthur, Ont. — Forward

YEAR	TEAM & LEAGUE		GP	G	A	PTS	PIM
1957-58	DET	N	2	0	0	0	0
1958-59			3	1	1	2	2
1959-60			5	0	0	0	0
3 yrs.		N Totals:	10	1	1	2	2

George McPhee

MCPHEE, GEORGE 5'9", 170 lbs.
B. July 2, 1958, Guelph, Ont. Left Wing, Shoots L

PLAYOFFS

YEAR	TEAM	LEAGUE	GP	G	A	PTS	PIM
1982-83	NYR	N	9	3	3	6	6

Basil McRae

MCRAE, BASIL PAUL 6'2", 205 lbs.
B. Jan. 1, 1961, Beaverton, Ont. Left Wing, Shoots L

YEAR	TEAM	LEAGUE	GP	G	A	PTS	PIM
1981-82	QUE	N	20	4	3	7	69
1982-83			22	1	1	2	59
2 yrs.		N Totals:	42	5	4	9	128

PLAYOFFS

YEAR	TEAM	LEAGUE	GP	G	A	PTS	PIM
1981-82	QUE	N	9	1	0	1	34

Bryan McSheffrey

MCSHEFFREY, BRYAN GERALD 6'2", 205 lbs.
B. Sept. 25, 1952, Ottawa, Ont. Right Wing, Shoots R

YEAR	TEAM	LEAGUE	GP	G	A	PTS	PIM
1972-73	VAN	N	33	4	4	8	10
1973-74			54	9	3	12	34
1974-75	BUF	N	3	0	0	0	0
3 yrs.		N Totals:	90	13	7	20	44

Traded to **Buffalo** by Vancouver with Jocelyn Guevremont for Gerry Meehan and Mike Robitaille, Oct. 14, 1974.

Jim McTaggart

MCTAGGART, JAMES 5'11", 197 lbs.
B. Mar. 31, 1960, Weyburn, Sask. Defense, Shoots L

YEAR	TEAM	LEAGUE	GP	G	A	PTS	PIM
1980-81	WASH	N	52	1	6	7	185
1981-82			19	2	4	6	20
2 yrs.		N Totals:	71	3	10	13	205

Signed as free agent by **Washington** Nov. 9, 1979. Traded by Edmonton with Ron Low to **New Jersey** for Lindsay Middlebrook and Paul Miller, Feb. 23, 1983.

Gordon McTavish

MCTAVISH, GORDON 6'4", 200 lbs.
B. June 3, 1954, Guelph, Ont. Center, Shoots R

YEAR	TEAM	LEAGUE	GP	G	A	PTS	PIM
1978-79	STL	N	1	0	0	0	0
1979-80	WINN	N	10	1	3	4	2
2 yrs.		N Totals:	11	1	3	4	2

Traded to **St. Louis** by Montreal for Mike Korney, Oct. 7, 1978. Claimed by **Winnipeg** from St. Louis in Expansion Draft, June 13, 1979.

Charley McVeigh

MCVEIGH, CHARLES (Rabbit) 5'6", 145 lbs.
B. Mar. 29, 1898, Kenora, Ont. Left Wing

YEAR	TEAM	LEAGUE	GP	G	A	PTS	PIM
1926-27	CHI	N	43	12	4	16	23
1927-28			43	6	7	13	10
1928-29	NYA	N	44	6	2	8	16
1929-30			40	14	14	28	32
1930-31			44	5	11	16	23
1931-32			48	12	15	27	16
1932-33			40	7	12	19	10
1933-34			48	15	12	27	4
1934-35			47	7	11	18	4
9 yrs.		N Totals:	397	84	88	172	138

PLAYOFFS

YEAR	TEAM	LEAGUE	GP	G	A	PTS	PIM
1926-27	CHI	N	2	0	0	0	0
1928-29	NYA	N	2	0	0	0	2
2 yrs.		N Totals:	4	0	0	0	2

Jack McVicar

MCVICAR, JOHN (Slim)
Defense, Shoots R

YEAR	TEAM	LEAGUE	GP	G	A	PTS	PIM
1930-31	MON(M)	N	40	2	4	6	35
1931-32			48	0	0	0	28

Jack McVicar continued

YEAR	TEAM	LEAGUE	GP	G	A	PTS	PIM
2 yrs.		N Totals:	88	2	4	6	63

PLAYOFFS

YEAR	TEAM	LEAGUE	GP	G	A	PTS	PIM
1930-31	MON(M)	N	2	0	0	0	2

Rick Meagher

MEAGHER, RICHARD 5'10", 175 lbs.
B. Nov. 4, 1953, Belleville, Ont. Center, Shoots R

YEAR	TEAM	LEAGUE	GP	G	A	PTS	PIM
1979-80	MONT	N	2	0	0	0	0
1980-81	HART	N	27	7	10	17	19
1981-82			65	24	19	43	51
1982-83			4	0	0	0	0
	NJ	N	57	15	14	29	11
	2 team total		61	15	14	29	11
4 yrs.		N Totals:	155	46	43	89	81

Traded to **Hartford** by Montreal for an exchange of 1981 Entry Draft choices, Montreal receiving Hartford's third round (Dieter Hegen) and fifth round (Steve Rooney) choices and Hartford receiving Montreal's third round (Paul MacDermid) and fifth round (Dans Bourbonnais) choices, June 5, 1980. Traded by Hartford with Garry Howatt to **New Jersey** for Merlin Malinowski and the rights to Scott Fusco, Oct. 15, 1982.

Gerry Meehan

MEEHAN, GERALD MARCUS 6'2", 200 lbs.
B. Sept. 3, 1946, Toronto, Ont. Center, Shoots L

YEAR	TEAM	LEAGUE	GP	G	A	PTS	PIM
1968-69	TOR	N	25	0	2	2	2
	PHI	N	12	0	3	3	4
	2 team total		37	0	5	5	6
1970-71	BUF	N	77	24	31	55	8
1971-72			77	19	27	46	12
1972-73			77	31	29	60	21
1973-74			72	20	26	46	17
1974-75			3	0	1	1	2
	VAN	N	57	10	15	25	4
	ATL	N	14	4	10	14	0
	3 team total		74	14	26	40	6
1975-76			48	7	20	27	8
	WASH	N	32	16	15	31	10
	2 team total		80	23	35	58	18
1976-77			80	28	36	64	13
1977-78			78	19	24	43	10
1978-79			18	2	4	6	0
	CIN	W	2	0	0	0	0
	2 team total		20	2	4	6	0
10 yrs.		N Totals:	670	180	243	423	111
		W Totals:	2	0	0	0	0

PLAYOFFS

YEAR	TEAM	LEAGUE	GP	G	A	PTS	PIM
1968-69	PHI	N	4	0	0	0	0
1972-73	BUF	N	6	0	1	1	0
2 yrs.		N Totals:	10	0	1	1	0

Traded to **Philadelphia** by Toronto with Mike Byers for Brit Selby and Forbes Kennedy, March 2, 1969. Drafted by **Buffalo** from Philadelphia in Expansion Draft, June 10, 1970. Traded to **Vancouver** by Buffalo with Mike Robitaille for Jocelyn Guevremont and Bryan McSheffrey, Oct. 14, 1974. Traded to **Atlanta** by Vancouver for Bob Murray, March 9, 1975. Traded to **Washington** by Atlanta with Jean Lemieux and Buffalo's first choice (Greg Carroll) in 1976 Amateur Draft (which was Atlanta's property via an earlier deal) for Bill Clement, Jan. 22, 1976.

Brent Meeke

MEEKE, BRENT ALAN 5'11", 172 lbs.
B. Apr. 10, 1952, Toronto, Ont. Defense, Shoots L

YEAR	TEAM	LEAGUE	GP	G	A	PTS	PIM
1972-73	CALIF	N	3	0	0	0	0
1973-74			18	1	9	10	4
1974-75			4	0	0	0	0
1975-76			1	0	0	0	0
1976-77	CLEVE	N	49	8	13	21	4
5 yrs.		N Totals:	75	9	22	31	8

Howie Meeker

MEEKER, HOWARD WILLIAM 5'8½", 165 lbs.
B. Nov. 4, 1924, Kitchener, Ont. Right Wing, Shoots R
Won Calder Trophy, 1946-47

YEAR	TEAM	LEAGUE	GP	G	A	PTS	PIM
1946-47	TOR	N	55	27	18	45	76

Howie Meeker continued

YEAR	TEAM & LEAGUE		GP	G	A	PTS	PIM
1947-48			58	14	20	34	62
1948-49			30	7	7	14	56
1949-50			70	18	22	40	35
1950-51			49	6	14	20	24
1951-52			54	9	14	23	50
1952-53			25	1	7	8	26
1953-54			5	1	0	1	0
8 yrs.		N Totals:	346	83	102	185	329
PLAYOFFS							
1946-47*	TOR	N	11	3	3	6	6
1947-48*			9	2	4	6	15
1949-50			7	0	1	1	4
1950-51*			11	1	1	2	14
1951-52			4	0	0	0	11
5 yrs.		N Totals:	42	6	9	15	50

Mike Meeker

MEEKER, MICHAEL THOMAS 5'11", 195 lbs.
B. Feb. 23, 1958, Kingston, Ont. Right Wing, Shoots R

YEAR	TEAM & LEAGUE		GP	G	A	PTS	PIM
1978-79	PITT	N	4	0	0	0	5

Harry Meeking

MEEKING, HARRY
B. Nov. 4, 1894, Kitchener, Ont. Left Wing

YEAR	TEAM & LEAGUE		GP	G	A	PTS	PIM
1917-18	TOR	N	20	10	0	10	19
1918-19			14	7	3	10	22
1926-27	DET	N	6	0	0	0	4
	BOS	N	23	1	0	1	2
	2 team total		29	1	0	1	6
3 yrs.		N Totals:	63	18	3	21	47
PLAYOFFS							
1917-18*	TOR	N	7	1	2	3	24
1926-27	BOS	N	8	0	0	0	0
2 yrs.		N Totals:	15	1	2	3	24

Paul Meger

MEGER, PAUL CARL 5'7", 160 lbs.
B. Feb. 17, 1929, Watrous, Sask. Left Wing, Shoots L

YEAR	TEAM & LEAGUE		GP	G	A	PTS	PIM
1950-51	MONT	N	17	2	4	6	6
1951-52			69	24	18	42	44
1952-53			69	9	17	26	38
1953-54			44	4	9	13	24
1954-55			13	0	4	4	6
5 yrs.		N Totals:	212	39	52	91	118
PLAYOFFS							
1949-50	MONT	N	2	0	0	0	2
1950-51			11	1	3	4	4
1951-52			11	0	3	3	2
1952-53*			5	1	2	3	4
1953-54			6	1	0	1	4
5 yrs.		N Totals:	35	3	8	11	16

Ron Meighan

MEIGHAN, RONALD JAMES 6'3", 194 lbs.
B. May 26, 1963, Montreal, Que. Defense, Shoots R

YEAR	TEAM & LEAGUE		GP	G	A	PTS	PIM
1981-82	MINN	N	7	1	1	2	2
1982-83	PITT	N	41	2	6	8	16
2 yrs.		N Totals:	48	3	7	10	18

Traded by Minnesota with Anders Hakansson to **Pittsburgh** for George Ferguson and Pittsburgh's first round choice in the 1983 Amateur Draft (Brian Lawton), Oct. 28, 1982.

Barrie Meissner

MEISSNER, BARRIE MICHAEL 5'9", 165 lbs.
B. July 26, 1946, Unity, Sask. Left Wing, Shoots L

YEAR	TEAM & LEAGUE		GP	G	A	PTS	PIM
1967-68	MINN	N	1	0	0	0	2
1968-69			5	0	1	1	2
2 yrs.		N Totals:	6	0	1	1	4

Traded to **Minnesota** by Mont. Canadiens with Bill Plager and Leo Thiffault for Bryan Watson, June 6, 1967.

Dick Meissner

MEISSNER, RICHARD DONALD 5'11", 200 lbs.
B. Jan. 6, 1940, Kindersley, Sask. Right Wing, Shoots R

YEAR	TEAM & LEAGUE		GP	G	A	PTS	PIM
1959-60	BOS	N	60	5	6	11	22
1960-61			9	0	1	1	2
1961-62			66	3	3	6	13
1963-64	NYR	N	35	3	5	8	0
1964-65			1	0	0	0	0
5 yrs.		N Totals:	171	11	15	26	37

Drafted by **New York** from Boston, June 4, 1963.

Roger Melin

MELIN, ROGER ALF 6'4", 198 lbs.
B. Apr. 25, 1956, Enkoping, Sweden Left Wing, Shoots L

YEAR	TEAM & LEAGUE		GP	G	A	PTS	PIM
1980-81	MINN	N	1	0	0	0	0
1981-82			2	0	0	0	0
2 yrs.		N Totals:	3	0	0	0	0

Signed as free agent by **Minnesota** Mar. 23, 1981.

Tom Mellor

MELLOR, THOMAS ROBERT 6'1", 185 lbs.
B. Jan. 27, 1950, Cranston, R.I. Defense, Shoots R

YEAR	TEAM & LEAGUE		GP	G	A	PTS	PIM
1973-74	DET	N	25	2	4	6	25
1974-75			1	0	0	0	0
2 yrs.		N Totals:	26	2	4	6	25

Gerry Melnyk

MELNYK, MICHAEL GERALD 5'10", 180 lbs.
B. Sept. 16, 1934, Edmonton, Alta. Center, Shoots R

YEAR	TEAM & LEAGUE		GP	G	A	PTS	PIM
1959-60	DET	N	63	10	10	20	12
1960-61			70	9	16	25	2
1961-62	CHI	N	63	5	16	21	6
1967-68	STL	N	73	15	35	50	14
4 yrs.		N Totals:	269	39	77	116	34
PLAYOFFS							
1955-56	DET	N	6	0	0	0	0
1959-60			6	3	0	3	0
1960-61			11	1	0	1	2
1961-62	CHI	N	7	0	0	0	2
1964-65			6	0	0	0	0
1967-68	STL	N	17	2	6	8	2
6 yrs.		N Totals:	53	6	6	12	6

Traded to **Chicago** by Detroit with Brian Smith for Ed Litzenberger, June, 1961. Drafted by **St. Louis** from Chicago in Expansion Draft, June 6, 1967.

Larry Melnyk

MELNYK, LAWRENCE JOSEPH 6', 180 lbs.
B. Feb. 21, 1960, New Westminster, B.C.
Defense, Shoots L

YEAR	TEAM & LEAGUE		GP	G	A	PTS	PIM
1980-81	BOS	N	26	0	4	4	39
1981-82			48	0	8	8	84
1982-83			1	0	0	0	0
3 yrs.		N Totals:	75	0	12	12	123
PLAYOFFS							
1981-82	BOS	N	11	0	3	3	40
1982-83			11	0	0	0	9
2 yrs.		N Totals:	22	0	3	3	49

Denis Meloche

MELOCHE, DENIS PHILIPPE 5'9", 175 lbs.
B. June 19, 1952, Montreal, Que. Center, Shoots L

YEAR	TEAM & LEAGUE		GP	G	A	PTS	PIM
1972-73	PHI	W	4	1	1	2	0
1973-74	VAN	W	41	6	13	19	18
2 yrs.		W Totals:	45	7	14	21	18

YEAR	TEAM & LEAGUE		GP	G	A	PTS	PIM

Chris Meloff

MELOFF, CHRISTOPHER 5'11", 180 lbs.
B. May 7, 1952, Toronto, Ont. Defense, Shoots L

YEAR	TEAM	LG	GP	G	A	PTS	PIM
1972-73	OTTA	W	21	1	6	7	40

Barry Melrose

MELROSE, BARRY 6', 205 lbs.
B. July 15, 1956, Kelvington, Sask. Defense, Shoots R

YEAR	TEAM	LG	GP	G	A	PTS	PIM
1976-77	CIN	W	29	1	4	5	8
1977-78			69	2	9	11	113
1978-79			80	2	14	16	222
1979-80	WINN	N	74	4	6	10	124
1980-81			18	1	1	2	40
	TOR	N	57	2	5	7	166
	2 team total		75	3	6	9	206
1981-82			64	1	5	6	186
1982-83			52	2	5	7	68
7 yrs.		N Totals:	265	10	22	32	584
		W Totals:	178	5	27	32	343
PLAYOFFS							
1976-77	CIN	W	2	0	0	0	2
1978-79			3	0	1	1	8
1980-81	TOR	N	3	0	1	1	15
1982-83			4	0	1	1	23
4 yrs.		N Totals:	7	0	2	2	38
		W Totals:	5	0	1	1	10

Traded to **Winnipeg** by Quebec for Barry Legge and Jamie Hislop, June 28, 1979. Claimed on waivers by **Toronto** from Winnipeg, Nov. 30, 1980. Signed as a free agent by **Detroit** Sept. 6, 1983.

Hill Menard

MENARD, HILLARY
B. Jan. 15, 1934, Timmins, Ont. Defense

YEAR	TEAM	LG	GP	G	A	PTS	PIM
1953-54	CHI	N	1	0	0	0	0

Howie Menard

MENARD, HOWARD HUBERT 5'8", 160 lbs.
B. Apr. 28, 1942, Timmins, Ont. Center, Shoots R

YEAR	TEAM	LG	GP	G	A	PTS	PIM
1963-64	DET	N	3	0	0	0	0
1967-68	LA	N	35	9	15	24	32
1968-69			56	10	17	27	31
1969-70	CHI	N	19	2	3	5	8
	OAK	N	38	2	7	9	16
	2 team total		57	4	10	14	24
4 yrs.		N Totals:	151	23	42	65	87
PLAYOFFS							
1967-68	LA	N	7	0	5	5	24
1968-69			11	3	2	5	12
1969-70	OAK	N	1	0	0	0	0
3 yrs.		N Totals:	19	3	7	10	36

Drafted by **Chicago** from Los Angeles, June 11, 1969. Traded to **Oakland** by Chicago for Gene Ubriaco, Dec. 15, 1969. Drafted by **Buffalo** from Oakland in Expansion Draft, June 10, 1970.

Vic Mercredi

MERCREDI, VICTOR DENNIS 5'11", 185 lbs.
B. Mar. 31, 1953, Yellowknife, N.W.T. Center, Shoots R

YEAR	TEAM	LG	GP	G	A	PTS	PIM
1974-75	ATL	N	2	0	0	0	0
1975-76	CALG	W	3	0	0	0	29
2 yrs.		N Totals:	2	0	0	0	0
		W Totals:	3	0	0	0	29

Greg Meredith

MEREDITH, GREGORY PAUL 6'1", 210 lbs.
B. Feb. 23, 1958, Toronto, Ont. Right Wing, Shoots R

YEAR	TEAM	LG	GP	G	A	PTS	PIM
1980-81	CALG	N	3	1	0	1	0
1982-83			35	5	4	9	8
2 yrs.		N Totals:	38	6	4	10	8
PLAYOFFS							
1982-83	CALG	N	5	3	1	4	4

Glenn Merkosky

MERKOSKY, GLENN 5'9", 175 lbs.
B. Apr. 8, 1960, Edmonton, Alta. Center, Shoots L

YEAR	TEAM	LG	GP	G	A	PTS	PIM
1981-82	HART	N	7	0	0	0	2
1982-83	NJ	N	34	4	10	14	20
2 yrs.		N Totals:	41	4	10	14	22

Signed as free agent with **Hartford** Aug. 10, 1980.

Bill Meronek

MERONEK, WILLIAM (Smiley)
B. Apr. 15, 1917, Stoney Mountain, Man.
Forward

YEAR	TEAM	LG	GP	G	A	PTS	PIM
1939-40	MONT	N	7	2	2	4	0
1942-43			12	3	6	9	0
2 yrs.		N Totals:	19	5	8	13	0
PLAYOFFS							
1942-43	MONT	N	1	0	0	0	0

Barry Merrell

MERRELL, BARRY
Defense

YEAR	TEAM	LG	GP	G	A	PTS	PIM
1976-77	EDM	W	10	1	3	4	0

Wayne Merrick

MERRICK, LEONARD WAYNE (Bones) 6'1", 195 lbs.
B. Apr. 23, 1952, Sarnia, Ont. Center, Shoots L

YEAR	TEAM	LG	GP	G	A	PTS	PIM
1972-73	STL	N	50	10	11	21	10
1973-74			64	20	23	43	32
1974-75			76	28	37	65	57
1975-76			19	7	8	15	0
	CALIF	N	56	25	27	52	36
	2 team total		75	32	35	67	36
1976-77	CLEVE	N	80	18	38	56	25
1977-78			18	2	5	7	8
	NYI	N	37	10	14	24	8
	2 team total		55	12	19	31	16
1978-79			75	20	21	41	24
1979-80			70	13	22	35	16
1980-81			71	16	15	31	30
1981-82			68	12	27	39	20
1982-83			59	4	12	16	27
11 yrs.		N Totals:	743	185	260	445	293
PLAYOFFS							
1972-73	STL	N	5	0	1	1	2
1974-75			2	1	1	2	0
1977-78	NYI	N	7	1	0	1	0
1978-79			10	2	3	5	2
1979-80*			21	2	4	6	2
1980-81*			18	6	12	18	8
1981-82*			19	6	6	12	6
1982-83*			19	1	3	4	10
8 yrs.		N Totals:	101	19	30	49	30

Traded to **California** by St. Louis for Larry Patey and California's third round choice (Reg Kerr) in 1977 Amateur Draft (later returned to California in another deal), Nov. 24, 1975. Traded to **N.Y. Islanders** by Cleveland with Darcy Regier and Cleveland's fourth round choice in the 1978 Amateur Draft (later cancelled by Cleveland-Minnesota merger) for J.P. Parise and Jean Potvin, Jan. 10, 1978.

Horace Merrill

MERRILL, HORACE
Defense

YEAR	TEAM	LG	GP	G	A	PTS	PIM
1917-18	OTTA	N	4	0	0	0	0
1919-20			7	0	0	0	0
2 yrs.		N Totals:	11	0	0	0	0

Mark Messier

MESSIER, MARK DOUGLAS (Mess) 6', 190 lbs.
B. Jan. 18, 1961, Edmonton, Alta. Left Wing, Shoots L

YEAR	TEAM	LG	GP	G	A	PTS	PIM
1978-79	IND	W	5	0	0	0	0
	CIN	W	47	1	10	11	58
	2 team total		52	1	10	11	58

Mark Messier continued

YEAR	TEAM	LEAGUE	GP	G	A	PTS	PIM
1979-80	**EDM**	**N**	75	12	21	33	120
1980-81			72	23	40	63	102
1981-82			78	50	38	88	119
1982-83			77	48	58	106	72
5 yrs.		**N Totals:**	302	133	157	290	413
		W Totals:	52	1	10	11	58
PLAYOFFS							
1979-80	**EDM**	**N**	3	1	2	3	2
1980-81			9	2	5	7	13
1981-82			5	1	2	3	8
1982-83			15	15	6	21	14
4 yrs.		**N Totals:**	32	19	15	34	37

Paul Messier

MESSIER, PAUL EDMOND 6'1", 184 lbs.
B. Jan. 27, 1958, Nottingham, England Center, Shoots R

YEAR	TEAM	LEAGUE	GP	G	A	PTS	PIM
1978-79	**COLO**	**N**	9	0	0	0	4

Gerry Methe

METHE, GERALD PAUL 5'10", 170 lbs.
B. Dec. 12, 1951, Willowdale, Ont. Left Wing, Shoots L

YEAR	TEAM	LEAGUE	GP	G	A	PTS	PIM
1974-75	**NE**	**W**	5	0	1	1	4

Don Metz

METZ, DONALD MAURICE 5'9½", 165 lbs.
B. Jan. 10, 1916, Wilcox, Sask. Right Wing, Shoots R

YEAR	TEAM	LEAGUE	GP	G	A	PTS	PIM
1939-40	**TOR**	**N**	10	1	1	2	4
1940-41			31	4	10	14	6
1941-42			25	2	3	5	8
1945-46			7	1	0	1	0
1946-47			40	4	9	13	10
1947-48			26	4	6	10	2
1948-49			33	4	6	10	12
7 yrs.		**N Totals:**	172	20	35	55	42
PLAYOFFS							
1939-40	**TOR**	**N**	2	0	0	0	0
1940-41			5	1	1	2	2
1941-42*			13	4	3	7	0
1944-45*			11	0	1	1	4
1946-47*			11	2	3	5	4
1947-48*			2	0	0	0	0
1948-49*			3	0	0	0	0
7 yrs.		**N Totals:**	47	7	8	15	10

Nick Metz

METZ, NICHOLAS J. 5'11", 160 lbs.
B. Feb. 16, 1914, Wilcox, Sask. Left Wing, Shoots L

YEAR	TEAM	LEAGUE	GP	G	A	PTS	PIM
1934-35	**TOR**	**N**	18	2	2	4	4
1935-36			38	14	6	20	14
1936-37			48	9	11	20	19
1937-38			48	15	7	22	12
1938-39			47	11	10	21	15
1939-40			31	6	5	11	2
1940-41			47	14	21	35	10
1941-42			30	11	9	20	20
1944-45			50	22	13	35	26
1945-46			41	11	11	22	4
1946-47			60	12	16	28	15
1947-48			60	4	8	12	8
12 yrs.		**N Totals:**	518	131	119	250	149
PLAYOFFS							
1934-35	**TOR**	**N**	6	1	1	2	0
1936-37			2	0	0	0	0
1937-38			7	0	2	2	0
1938-39			10	3	3	6	6
1939-40			9	1	3	4	9
1940-41			7	3	4	7	0
1941-42*			13	4	4	8	12
1944-45*			7	1	1	2	2
1946-47*			6	4	2	6	0
1947-48*			9	2	0	2	2
10 yrs.		**N Totals:**	76	19	20	39	31

Art Michaluk

MICHALUK, ARTHUR 6', 182 lbs.
B. May 4, 1923, Canmore, Alta. Defense, Shoots R

YEAR	TEAM	LEAGUE	GP	G	A	PTS	PIM
1947-48	**CHI**	**N**	5	0	0	0	0

John Michaluk

MICHALUK, JOHN JR. 5'10", 155 lbs.
B. Nov. 2, 1928, Canmore, Alta. Forward, Shoots L

YEAR	TEAM	LEAGUE	GP	G	A	PTS	PIM
1950-51	**CHI**	**N**	1	0	0	0	0

Dave Michayluk

MICHAYLUK, DAVID 5'10", 180 lbs.
B. May 18, 1962, Wakaw, Sask. Right Wing, Shoots L

YEAR	TEAM	LEAGUE	GP	G	A	PTS	PIM
1981-82	**PHI**	**N**	1	0	0	0	0
1982-83			13	2	6	8	8
2 yrs.		**N Totals:**	14	2	6	8	8

Joe Micheletti

MICHELETTI, JOSEPH ROBERT 6'1", 185 lbs.
B. Oct. 24, 1954, Hibbing, Minn. Defense, Shoots L

YEAR	TEAM	LEAGUE	GP	G	A	PTS	PIM
1976-77	**CALG**	**W**	14	3	3	6	10
1977-78	**EDM**	**W**	56	14	34	48	56
1978-79			72	14	33	47	85
1979-80	**STL**	**N**	54	2	16	18	29
1980-81			63	4	27	31	53
1981-82			20	3	11	14	28
	COLO	**N**	21	2	6	8	4
	2 team total		41	5	17	22	32
6 yrs.		**N Totals:**	158	11	60	71	114
		W Totals:	142	31	70	101	151
PLAYOFFS							
1977-78	**EDM**	**W**	5	0	2	2	4
1978-79			13	0	9	9	2
1980-81	**STL**	**N**	11	1	11	12	10
3 yrs.		**N Totals:**	11	1	11	12	10
		W Totals:	18	0	11	11	6

Claimed by **Edmonton** from Montreal in 1979 Expansion Draft, June 22, 1979. Traded to **St. Louis** by Edmonton for Tom Roulston and Risto Siltanen, Aug. 7, 1979. Traded to **Colorado** by St. Louis with Dick Lamby for Bill Baker, Dec. 4, 1981.

Larry Mickey

MICKEY, ROBERT LAWRENCE 5'11", 180 lbs.
B. Oct. 21, 1943, Lacombe, Alta. Right Wing, Shoots R

YEAR	TEAM	LEAGUE	GP	G	A	PTS	PIM
1964-65	**CHI**	**N**	1	0	0	0	0
1965-66	**NYR**	**N**	7	0	0	0	2
1966-67			8	0	0	0	0
1967-68			4	0	2	2	0
1968-69	**TOR**	**N**	55	8	19	27	43
1969-70	**MONT**	**N**	21	4	4	8	4
1970-71	**LA**	**N**	65	6	12	18	46
1971-72	**PHI**	**N**	14	1	2	3	8
	BUF	**N**	4	0	1	1	0
	2 team total		18	1	3	4	8
1972-73			77	15	9	24	47
1973-74			13	3	4	7	8
1974-75			23	2	0	2	2
11 yrs.		**N Totals:**	292	39	53	92	160
PLAYOFFS							
1968-69	**TOR**	**N**	3	0	0	0	5
1972-73	**BUF**	**N**	6	1	0	1	5
2 yrs.		**N Totals:**	9	1	0	1	10

Nick Mickoski

MICKOSKI, NICHOLAS 6'1", 193 lbs.
B. Dec. 7, 1927, Winnipeg, Man. Left Wing, Shoots L

YEAR	TEAM	LEAGUE	GP	G	A	PTS	PIM
1948-49	**NYR**	**N**	54	13	9	22	20
1949-50			45	10	10	20	10
1950-51			64	20	15	35	12
1951-52			43	7	13	20	20
1952-53			70	19	16	35	39
1953-54			68	19	16	35	22

Nick Mickoski continued

YEAR	TEAM	LEAGUE	GP	G	A	PTS	PIM
1954-55			18	0	14	14	6
	CHI	**N**	52	10	19	29	42
	2 team total		70	10	33	43	48
1955-56			70	19	20	39	52
1956-57			70	16	20	36	24
1957-58			28	5	6	11	20
	DET	**N**	37	8	12	20	30
	2 team total		65	13	18	31	50
1958-59			66	11	15	26	20
1959-60	**BOS**	**N**	18	1	0	1	2
12 yrs.		**N Totals:**	703	158	185	343	319
PLAYOFFS							
1947-48	**NYR**	**N**	2	0	1	1	0
1949-50			12	1	5	6	2
1957-58	**DET**	**N**	4	0	0	0	4
3 yrs.		**N Totals:**	18	1	6	7	6

Traded to **Chicago** by N.Y. Rangers with Allan Stanley and Rich Lamoureux for Bill Gadsby and Pete Conacher, Nov. 23, 1954. Traded to **Detroit** by Chicago with Jack McIntyre, Bob Bailey and Hec Lalande for Bill Dineen, Billy Dea, Earl Reibel and Lorne Ferguson, Dec. 17, 1957.

Rick Middleton

MIDDLETON, RICHARD DAVID (Slick) 5'11", 170 lbs.
B. Dec. 4, 1953, Toronto, Ont. Right Wing, Shoots R
Won Lady Byng Trophy, 1981-82

YEAR	TEAM	LEAGUE	GP	G	A	PTS	PIM
1974-75	**NYR**	**N**	47	22	18	40	19
1975-76			77	24	26	50	14
1976-77	**BOS**	**N**	72	20	22	42	2
1977-78			79	25	35	60	8
1978-79			71	38	48	86	7
1979-80			80	40	52	92	24
1980-81			80	44	59	103	16
1981-82			75	51	43	94	12
1982-83			80	49	47	96	8
9 yrs.		**N Totals:**	661	313	350	663	110
PLAYOFFS							
1974-75	**NYR**	**N**	3	0	0	0	2
1976-77	**BOS**	**N**	13	5	4	9	0
1977-78			15	5	2	7	0
1978-79			11	4	8	12	0
1979-80			10	4	2	6	5
1980-81			3	0	1	1	2
1981-82			11	6	9	15	0
1982-83			17	11	22	33	6
8 yrs.		**N Totals:**	83	35	48	83	15

Traded to **Boston** by N.Y. Rangers for Ken Hodge, May 26, 1976.

Rudy Migay

MIGAY, RUDOLPH JOSEPH 5'10", 175 lbs.
B. Nov. 18, 1928, Fort William, Ont. Center, Shoots L

YEAR	TEAM	LEAGUE	GP	G	A	PTS	PIM
1949-50	**TOR**	**N**	18	1	5	6	8
1951-52			19	2	1	3	12
1952-53			40	5	4	9	22
1953-54			70	8	15	23	60
1954-55			67	8	16	24	66
1955-56			70	12	16	28	52
1956-57			66	15	20	35	51
1957-58			48	7	14	21	18
1958-59			19	1	1	2	4
1959-60			1	0	0	0	0
10 yrs.		**N Totals:**	418	59	92	151	293
PLAYOFFS							
1953-54	**TOR**	**N**	5	1	0	1	4
1954-55			3	0	0	0	10
1955-56			5	0	0	0	6
1958-59			2	0	0	0	0
4 yrs.		**N Totals:**	15	1	0	1	20

John Migneault

MIGNEAULT, JOHN 5'11", 180 lbs.
B. Feb. 14, 1949, Thompkins, Sask. Left Wing, Shoots L

YEAR	TEAM	LEAGUE	GP	G	A	PTS	PIM
1972-73	**PHI**	**W**	54	10	8	18	38
1973-74	**VAN**	**W**	74	21	26	47	27
1974-75			14	4	2	6	12
	PHOE	**W**	47	6	13	19	16
	2 team total		61	10	15	25	28

John Migneault continued

YEAR	TEAM	LEAGUE	GP	G	A	PTS	PIM
1975-76			68	8	12	20	14
4 yrs.		**W Totals:**	257	49	61	110	107
PLAYOFFS							
1975-76	**PHOE**	**W**	3	0	0	0	0

Stan Mikita

MIKITA, STANLEY (Stosh) 5'9", 169 lbs.
B. May 20, 1940, Skolce, Czechoslovakia
Center, Shoots R
Won Hart Trophy, 1966–67, 1967–68
Won Art Ross Trophy, 1963–64, 1964–65, 1966–67, 1967–68
Won Lady Byng Trophy, 1966–67, 1967–68
Hall of Fame, 1983

YEAR	TEAM	LEAGUE	GP	G	A	PTS	PIM
1958-59	**CHI**	**N**	3	0	1	1	4
1959-60			67	8	18	26	119
1960-61			66	19	34	53	100
1961-62			70	25	52	77	97
1962-63			65	31	45	76	69
1963-64			70	39	**50**	**89**	**149**
1964-65			70	28	**59**	87	154
1965-66			68	30	**48**	78	58
1966-67			70	35	**62**	**97**	12
1967-68			72	40	47	**87**	14
1968-69			74	30	67	97	52
1969-70			76	39	47	86	50
1970-71			74	24	48	72	85
1971-72			74	26	39	65	46
1972-73			57	27	56	83	32
1973-74			76	30	50	80	46
1974-75			79	36	50	86	48
1975-76			48	16	41	57	37
1976-77			57	19	30	49	20
1977-78			76	18	41	59	35
1978-79			65	19	36	55	34
1979-80			17	2	5	7	12
22 yrs.		**N Totals:**	1394	541	926	1467	1273
PLAYOFFS							
1959-60	**CHI**	**N**	3	0	1	1	2
1960-61*			12	6	5	11	21
1961-62			12	6	15	21	19
1962-63			6	3	2	5	2
1963-64			7	3	6	9	8
1964-65			14	3	7	10	53
1965-66			6	1	2	3	2
1966-67			6	2	2	4	2
1967-68			11	5	7	12	6
1969-70			8	4	6	10	2
1970-71			18	5	13	18	16
1971-72			8	3	1	4	4
1972-73			15	7	13	20	8
1973-74			11	5	6	11	8
1974-75			8	3	4	7	12
1975-76			4	0	0	0	4
1976-77			2	0	1	1	0
1977-78			4	3	0	3	0
18 yrs.		**N Totals:**	155	59	91	150	169

Bill Mikkelson

MIKKELSON, WILLIAM ROBERT 6', 190 lbs.
B. May 21, 1948, Neepawa, Man. Defense, Shoots L

YEAR	TEAM	LEAGUE	GP	G	A	PTS	PIM
1971-72	**LA**	**N**	15	0	1	1	6
1972-73	**NYI**	**N**	72	1	10	11	45
1974-75	**WASH**	**N**	59	3	7	10	52
1976-77			1	0	0	0	2
4 yrs.		**N Totals:**	147	4	18	22	105

Drafted by **N.Y. Islanders** from Los Angeles in Expansion Draft, June 6, 1972. Drafted by **Washington** from N.Y. Islanders in Expansion Draft, June 12, 1974. Sold to **Washington** by Los Angeles, May 24, 1975.

Jim Mikol

MIKOL, JOHN STANLEY 6', 175 lbs.
B. June 11, 1938, Kitchener, Ont. Defense, Shoots R

YEAR	TEAM	LEAGUE	GP	G	A	PTS	PIM
1962-63	**TOR**	**N**	4	0	1	1	2
1964-65	**NYR**	**N**	30	1	3	4	6
2 yrs.		**N Totals:**	34	1	4	5	8

Tom Milani

MILANI, THOMAS 5′6″, 170 lbs.
B. Apr. 13, 1952, Thunder Bay, Ont. Right Wing, Shoots R

YEAR	TEAM & LEAGUE	GP	G	A	PTS	PIM
1976-77	**MINN W**	2	0	0	0	0

Mike Milbury

MILBURY, MICHAEL JAMES 6′1″, 202 lbs.
B. June 17, 1952, Brighton, Mass. Defense, Shoots L

YEAR	TEAM & LEAGUE	GP	G	A	PTS	PIM
1975-76	**BOS N**	3	0	0	0	9
1976-77		77	6	18	24	166
1977-78		80	8	30	38	151
1978-79		74	1	34	35	149
1979-80		72	10	13	23	59
1980-81		77	0	18	18	222
1981-82		51	2	10	12	71
1982-83		78	9	15	24	216
8 yrs.	**N Totals:**	512	36	138	174	1043
PLAYOFFS						
1975-76	**BOS N**	11	0	0	0	290
1976-77		13	2	2	4	47
1977-78		15	1	8	9	27
1978-79		11	1	7	8	7
1979-80		10	0	2	2	50
1980-81		2	0	1	1	10
1981-82		11	0	4	4	6
7 yrs.	**N Totals:**	73	4	24	28	437

Hib Milks

MILKS, HIBBERT 5′11″, 165 lbs.
B. Apr. 1, 1902, Eardley, Ont. Left Wing, Shoots L

YEAR	TEAM & LEAGUE	GP	G	A	PTS	PIM
1925-26	**PITT N**	36	14	5	19	17
1926-27		44	16	6	22	18
1927-28		44	18	3	21	34
1928-29		42	9	3	12	22
1929-30		40	13	11	24	36
1930-31	**PHI N**	44	17	6	23	42
1931-32	**NYR N**	45	0	4	4	12
1932-33	**OTTA N**	18	0	3	3	0
8 yrs.	**N Totals:**	313	87	41	128	181
PLAYOFFS						
1925-26	**PITT N**	2	0	0	0	0
1927-28		2	0	0	0	2
1931-32	**NYR N**	7	0	0	0	0
3 yrs.	**N Totals:**	11	0	0	0	2

Hugh Millar

MILLAR, HUGH ALEXANDER 5′8½″, 200 lbs.
B. Apr. 3, 1921, Edmonton, Alta. Defense, Shoots L

YEAR	TEAM & LEAGUE	GP	G	A	PTS	PIM
1946-47	**DET N**	4	0	0	0	0
PLAYOFFS						
1946-47	**DET N**	1	0	0	0	0

Bill Miller

MILLER, WILLIAM 6′, 160 lbs.
B. Aug. 1, 1911, Campbellton, N.B. Center, Shoots R

YEAR	TEAM & LEAGUE	GP	G	A	PTS	PIM
1934-35	**MON(M) N**	22	3	0	3	2
1935-36		8	0	0	0	0
	MONT N	17	1	2	3	2
	2 team total	25	1	2	3	2

Bill Miller continued

YEAR	TEAM & LEAGUE	GP	G	A	PTS	PIM
1936-37		48	3	1	4	12
3 yrs.	**N Totals:**	95	7	3	10	16
PLAYOFFS						
1934-35*	**MON(M) N**	7	0	0	0	0
1936-37	**MONT N**	5	0	0	0	0
2 yrs.	**N Totals:**	12	0	0	0	0

Bob Miller

MILLER, ROBERT 5′11″, 185 lbs.
B. Sept. 28, 1956, Medford, Mass. Center, Shoots L

YEAR	TEAM & LEAGUE	GP	G	A	PTS	PIM
1977-78	**BOS N**	76	20	20	40	41
1978-79		77	15	33	48	30
1979-80		80	16	25	41	53
1980-81		30	4	4	8	19
	COLO N	22	5	1	6	15
	2 team total	52	9	5	14	34
1981-82		56	11	20	31	27
5 yrs.	**N Totals:**	341	71	103	174	185
PLAYOFFS						
1977-78	**BOS N**	13	0	3	3	15
1978-79		11	1	1	2	8
1979-80		10	3	2	5	4
3 yrs.	**N Totals:**	34	4	6	10	27

Traded to **Colorado** by Boston for Mike Gillis, Feb. 18, 1981.

Earl Miller

MILLER, EARL
B. Regina, Sask. Forward

YEAR	TEAM & LEAGUE	GP	G	A	PTS	PIM
1927-28	**CHI N**	22	1	1	2	32
1928-29		15	1	1	2	24
1929-30		38	11	5	16	50
1930-31		17	3	4	7	8
1931-32		9	0	0	0	0
	TOR N	15	3	3	6	10
	2 team total	24	3	3	6	10
5 yrs.	**N Totals:**	116	19	14	33	124
PLAYOFFS						
1929-30	**CHI N**	2	1	0	1	6
1930-31		1	0	0	0	0
1931-32*	**TOR N**	7	0	0	0	0
3 yrs.	**N Totals:**	10	1	0	1	6

Jack Miller

MILLER, JACK LESLIE 5′8″, 155 lbs.
B. Sept. 16, 1925, Delisle, Sask. Left Wing, Shoots L

YEAR	TEAM & LEAGUE	GP	G	A	PTS	PIM
1949-50	**CHI N**	6	0	0	0	0
1950-51		11	0	0	0	4
2 yrs.	**N Totals:**	17	0	0	0	4

Paul Miller

MILLER, PAUL EDWARD 5′10″, 170 lbs.
B. Aug. 21, 1959, Billerica, Mass. Center, Shoots L

YEAR	TEAM & LEAGUE	GP	G	A	PTS	PIM
1981-82	**COLO N**	3	0	3	3	0

Signed as free agent by **Colorado** Nov. 20, 1981. Traded by New Jersey with Lindsay Middlebrook to **Edmonton** for Ron Low and Jim McTaggart, Feb. 23, 1983.

Perry Miller

MILLER, PERRY ELVIN 6′1″, 194 lbs.
B. June 24, 1952, Winnipeg, Man. Defense, Shoots L

YEAR	TEAM & LEAGUE	GP	G	A	PTS	PIM
1974-75	**WINN W**	67	9	19	28	133
1975-76		47	7	6	13	41
	MINN W	13	1	4	5	7
	2 team total	60	8	10	18	48
1976-77	**WINN W**	74	14	31	45	124
1977-78	**DET N**	62	4	17	21	120
1978-79		75	5	23	28	156
1979-80		16	0	3	3	41
1980-81		64	1	8	9	70

Perry Miller continued

YEAR	TEAM & LEAGUE		GP	G	A	PTS	PIM
7 yrs.		N Totals:	217	10	51	61	387
		W Totals:	201	31	60	91	305
PLAYOFFS							
1976-77	**WINN**	W	20	4	6	10	27

Signed as free agent by **Detroit** July 8, 1977.

Tom Miller

MILLER, THOMAS WILLIAM 6', 187 lbs.
B. Mar. 31, 1947, Kitchener, Ont. Center, Shoots L

YEAR	TEAM & LEAGUE		GP	G	A	PTS	PIM
1970-71	**DET**	N	29	1	7	8	9
1972-73	**NYI**	N	69	13	17	30	21
1973-74			19	2	1	3	4
1974-75			1	0	0	0	0
4 yrs.		N Totals:	118	16	25	41	34

Traded to **Detroit** by N.Y. Rangers with Arnie Brown and Mike Robitaille for Bruce MacGregor and Larry Brown, Feb. 23, 1971. Drafted by **Buffalo** from Detroit in Intra-league Draft, June 8, 1971. Drafted by **N.Y. Islanders** from Buffalo in Expansion Draft, June 6, 1972.

Warren Miller

MILLER, WARREN 5'11", 180 lbs.
B. Jan. 1, 1954, St. Paul, Minn. Right Wing, Shoots R

YEAR	TEAM & LEAGUE		GP	G	A	PTS	PIM
1975-76	**CALG**	W	3	0	0	0	0
1976-77			80	23	32	55	51
1977-78	**EDM**	W	18	2	4	6	18
	QUE	W	60	14	24	38	50
	2 team total		78	16	28	44	68
1978-79	**NE**	W	77	26	23	49	44
1979-80	**NYR**	N	55	7	6	13	17
1980-81	**HART**	N	77	22	22	44	37
1981-82			74	10	12	22	68
1982-83			56	1	10	11	15
8 yrs.		N Totals:	262	40	50	90	137
		W Totals:	238	65	83	148	163
PLAYOFFS							
1975-76	**CALG**	W	10	1	0	1	28
1977-78	**QUE**	W	11	0	2	2	0
1978-79	**NE**	W	10	0	8	8	28
1979-80	**NYR**	N	6	1	0	1	0
4 yrs.		N Totals:	6	1	0	1	0
		W Totals:	31	1	10	11	56

Reclaimed by **N.Y. Rangers** from Hartford prior to Expansion Draft, June 9, 1979. Sold by N.Y. Rangers to **Hartford** Aug. 7, 1980.

Gerry Minor

MINOR, GERALD (Bucky) 5'8", 178 lbs.
B. Oct. 27, 1958, Regina, Sask. Center, Shoots L

YEAR	TEAM & LEAGUE		GP	G	A	PTS	PIM
1979-80	**VAN**	N	5	0	1	1	2
1980-81			74	10	14	24	108
1981-82			13	0	1	1	6
1982-83			39	1	5	6	57
4 yrs.		N Totals:	131	11	21	32	173
PLAYOFFS							
1980-81	**VAN**	N	3	0	0	0	8
1981-82			9	1	3	4	17
2 yrs.		N Totals:	12	1	3	4	25

John Miszuk

MISZUK, JOHN STANLEY 6', 200 lbs.
B. Sept. 29, 1940, Naliboki, Poland Defense, Shoots L

YEAR	TEAM & LEAGUE		GP	G	A	PTS	PIM
1963-64	**DET**	N	42	0	2	2	30
1965-66	**CHI**	N	2	1	1	2	2
1966-67			3	0	0	0	0
1967-68	**PHI**	N	74	5	17	22	79
1968-69			66	1	13	14	70
1969-70	**MINN**	N	50	0	6	6	51
1974-75	**M-B**	W	66	2	19	21	56
1975-76	**CALG**	W	69	2	21	23	66
1976-77			79	2	26	28	57
9 yrs.		N Totals:	237	7	39	46	232
		W Totals:	214	6	66	72	179

John Miszuk continued

YEAR	TEAM & LEAGUE		GP	G	A	PTS	PIM
PLAYOFFS							
1963-64	**DET**	N	3	0	0	0	2
1965-66	**CHI**	N	3	0	0	0	4
1966-67			2	0	0	0	2
1967-68	**PHI**	N	7	0	3	3	11
1968-69			4	0	0	0	0
1975-76	**CALG**	W	10	0	1	1	10
6 yrs.		N Totals:	19	0	3	3	19
		W Totals:	10	0	1	1	10

Traded to **Chicago** by Detroit with Art Stratton and Ian Cushenan for Ron Murphy and Aut Erickson, June, 1964. Drafted by **Philadelphia** from Chicago in Expansion Draft, June 6, 1967. Traded to **Minnesota** by Philadelphia for Wayne Hillman, May 14, 1969.

Bill Mitchell

MITCHELL, WILLIAM LAWSON 5'10", 185 lbs.
B. Sept. 6, 1912, Toronto, Ont. Defense, Shoots R

YEAR	TEAM & LEAGUE		GP	G	A	PTS	PIM
1963-64	**DET**	N	1	0	0	0	0

Herb Mitchell

MITCHELL, HERBERT
Defense

YEAR	TEAM & LEAGUE		GP	G	A	PTS	PIM
1924-25	**BOS**	N	27	3	0	3	24
1925-26			26	3	0	3	14
2 yrs.		N Totals:	53	6	0	6	38

Red Mitchell

MITCHELL, WILLIAM DICKIE 5'10", 185 lbs.
B. Feb. 22, 1930, Port Dalhousie, Ont. Defense, Shoots R

YEAR	TEAM & LEAGUE		GP	G	A	PTS	PIM
1941-42	**CHI**	N	1	0	0	0	4
1942-43			42	1	1	2	47
1944-45			40	3	4	7	16
3 yrs.		N Totals:	83	4	5	9	67

Billy Moe

MOE, WILLIAM 5'11", 185 lbs.
B. Oct. 2, 1916, Danvers, Mass. Defense, Shoots R

YEAR	TEAM & LEAGUE		GP	G	A	PTS	PIM
1944-45	**NYR**	N	35	2	4	6	14
1945-46			48	4	4	8	14
1946-47			59	4	10	14	44
1947-48			59	1	15	16	31
1948-49			60	0	9	9	60
5 yrs.		N Totals:	261	11	42	53	163
PLAYOFFS							
1947-48	**NYR**	N	1	0	0	0	0

Traded to **Boston** by New York for Pat Egan, Oct. 7, 1949.

Lyle Moffat

MOFFAT, LYLE GORDON 5'10", 180 lbs.
B. Mar. 19, 1948, Calgary, Alta. Left Wing, Shoots L

YEAR	TEAM & LEAGUE		GP	G	A	PTS	PIM
1972-73	**TOR**	N	1	0	0	0	0
1974-75			22	2	7	9	13
1975-76	**CLEVE**	W	33	4	7	11	33
	WINN	W	42	13	9	22	44
	2 team total		75	17	16	33	77
1976-77			74	13	11	24	90
1977-78			57	9	16	25	39
1978-79			70	14	18	32	38
1979-80	**WINN**	N	74	10	9	19	38
7 yrs.		N Totals:	97	12	16	28	51
		W Totals:	276	53	61	114	244
PLAYOFFS							
1975-76	**WINN**	W	13	3	3	6	9
1976-77			17	2	0	2	6
1977-78			9	5	7	12	9
1978-79			10	3	1	4	22
4 yrs.		W Totals:	49	13	11	24	46

Ron Moffatt

MOFFATT, RONALD

B. West Hope, N.D. Forward

YEAR	TEAM	LEAGUE	GP	G	A	PTS	PIM
1932-33	**DET**	**N**	24	1	1	2	6
1933-34			5	0	0	0	2
1934-35			7	0	0	0	0
3 yrs.		**N Totals:**	36	1	1	2	8
PLAYOFFS							
1932-33	**DET**	**N**	4	0	0	0	0
1933-34			3	0	0	0	0
2 yrs.		**N Totals:**	7	0	0	0	0

Mike Moher

MOHER, MIKE 5'10", 180 lbs.

B. Mar. 26, 1962, Manitouwadge, Ont. Right Wing, Shoots R

YEAR	TEAM	LEAGUE	GP	G	A	PTS	PIM
1982-83	**NJ**	**N**	9	0	1	1	28

Doug Mohns

MOHNS, DOUGLAS ALLEN 6', 184 lbs.

B. Dec. 13, 1933, Capreol, Ont. Defense, Shoots L

YEAR	TEAM	LEAGUE	GP	G	A	PTS	PIM
1953-54	**BOS**	**N**	70	13	14	27	27
1954-55			70	14	18	32	82
1955-56			64	10	8	18	48
1956-57			68	6	34	40	89
1957-58			54	5	16	21	28
1958-59			47	6	24	30	40
1959-60			65	20	25	45	62
1960-61			65	12	21	33	63
1961-62			69	16	29	45	74
1962-63			68	7	23	30	63
1963-64			70	9	17	26	95
1964-65	**CHI**	**N**	49	13	20	33	84
1965-66			70	22	27	49	63
1966-67			61	25	35	60	58
1967-68			65	24	29	53	33
1968-69			65	22	19	41	47
1969-70			66	6	27	33	46
1970-71			39	4	6	10	16
	MINN	**N**	17	2	5	7	14
	2 team total		56	6	11	17	30
1971-72			78	6	30	36	82
1972-73			67	4	13	17	52
1973-74	**ATL**	**N**	28	0	3	3	10
1974-75	**WASH**	**N**	75	2	19	21	54
22 yrs.		**N Totals:**	1390	248	462	710	1230
PLAYOFFS							
1953-54	**BOS**	**N**	4	1	0	1	4
1954-55			5	0	0	0	4
1956-57			10	2	3	5	2
1957-58			12	3	10	13	18
1958-59			4	0	2	2	12
1964-65	**CHI**	**N**	14	3	4	7	21
1965-66			5	1	0	1	4
1966-67			5	0	5	5	8
1967-68			11	1	5	6	12
1969-70			8	0	2	2	15
1970-71	**MINN**	**N**	6	2	2	4	10
1971-72			4	1	2	3	10
1972-73			6	0	1	1	2
13 yrs.		**N Totals:**	94	14	36	50	122

Traded to **Chicago** by Boston for Reg Fleming and Ab McDonald, June 8, 1964. Traded to **Minnesota** by Chicago with Terry Caffery for Danny O'-Shea, Feb. 22, 1971. Drafted by **Atlanta** from Minnesota in Intra-league Draft, June 12, 1973. Sold to **Washington** by Atlanta, June 20, 1974.

Lloyd Mohns

MOHNS, WARREN LLOYD 5'9", 185 lbs.

B. July 31, 1921, Petawawa, Ont. Defense, Shoots R

YEAR	TEAM	LEAGUE	GP	G	A	PTS	PIM
1943-44	**NYR**	**N**	1	0	0	0	0

Carl Mokosak

MOKOSAK, CARL 6'1", 200 lbs.

B. Apr. 12, 1962, Fort Saskatchewan, Alta. Left Wing, Shoots L

YEAR	TEAM	LEAGUE	GP	G	A	PTS	PIM
1981-82	**CALG**	**N**	1	0	1	1	0
1982-83			41	7	6	13	87
2 yrs.		**N Totals:**	42	7	7	14	87

Signed as free agent by **Calgary** July 21, 1981. Traded by Calgary with Kevin Lavallee to **Los Angeles** for Steve Bozek, June 13, 1983.

Lars Molin

MOLIN, LARS 6', 165 lbs.

B. May 7, 1956, Ornskoldsvik, Sweden Left Wing, Shoots L

YEAR	TEAM	LEAGUE	GP	G	A	PTS	PIM
1981-82	**VAN**	**N**	72	15	31	46	10
1982-83			58	12	27	39	23
2 yrs.		**N Totals:**	130	27	58	85	33
PLAYOFFS							
1981-82	**VAN**	**N**	17	2	9	11	7

Signed as free agent by **Vancouver** May 18, 1981.

Mike Moller

MOLLER, MICHAEL JOHN 6', 189 lbs.

B. June 16, 1962, Calgary, Alta. Right Wing, Shoots R

YEAR	TEAM	LEAGUE	GP	G	A	PTS	PIM
1980-81	**BUF**	**N**	5	2	2	4	0
1981-82			9	0	0	0	0
1982-83			49	6	12	18	14
3 yrs.		**N Totals:**	63	8	14	22	14
PLAYOFFS							
1980-81	**BUF**	**N**	3	0	1	1	0

Randy Moller

MOLLER, RANDY 6'2", 205 lbs.

B. Aug. 23, 1963, Red Deer, Alta. Defense, Shoots R

YEAR	TEAM	LEAGUE	GP	G	A	PTS	PIM
1982-83	**QUE**	**N**	75	2	12	14	145
PLAYOFFS							
1981-82	**QUE**	**N**	1	0	0	0	2
1982-83			4	1	0	1	4
2 yrs.		**N Totals:**	5	1	0	1	6

Larry Molyneaux

MOLYNEAUX, LAWRENCE 5'11½", 208 lbs.

B. July 8, 1912, Sutton West, Ont. Defense

YEAR	TEAM	LEAGUE	GP	G	A	PTS	PIM
1937-38	**NYR**	**N**	2	0	0	0	2
1938-39			43	0	1	1	18
2 yrs.		**N Totals:**	45	0	1	1	20
PLAYOFFS							
1937-38	**NYR**	**N**	3	0	0	0	8

Garry Monahan

MONAHAN, GARRY MICHAEL 6', 185 lbs.

B. Oct. 20, 1946, Barrie, Ont. Left Wing, Shoots L

YEAR	TEAM	LEAGUE	GP	G	A	PTS	PIM
1967-68	**MONT**	**N**	11	0	0	0	8
1968-69			3	0	0	0	0
1969-70	**DET**	**N**	51	3	4	7	24
	LA	**N**	21	0	3	3	13
	2 team total		72	3	7	10	37
1970-71	**TOR**	**N**	78	15	22	37	79
1971-72			78	14	17	31	47
1972-73			78	13	18	31	53
1973-74			78	9	16	25	70
1974-75			1	0	0	0	0
	VAN	**N**	78	14	20	34	51
	2 team total		79	14	20	34	51
1975-76			66	16	17	33	39
1976-77			76	18	26	44	48
1977-78			67	10	19	29	28
1978-79	**TOR**	**N**	62	4	7	11	25

YEAR	TEAM & LEAGUE		GP	G	A	PTS	PIM

Garry Monahan continued

YEAR	TEAM	LEAGUE	GP	G	A	PTS	PIM
12 yrs.		N Totals:	748	116	169	285	485
PLAYOFFS							
1970-71	**TOR**	**N**	6	2	0	2	2
1971-72			5	0	0	0	0
1973-74			4	0	1	1	7
1974-75	**VAN**	**N**	5	1	0	1	2
1975-76			2	0	0	0	2
5 yrs.		N Totals:	22	3	1	4	13

Traded to **Detroit** by Montreal with Doug Piper for Pete Mahovlich and Bart Cashley, June 6, 1969. Traded to **Los Angeles** by Detroit with Brian Gibbons for Dale Rolfe, Gary Croteau and Larry Johnston, Feb. 20, 1970. Traded to **Toronto** by Los Angeles with Brian Murphy for Bob Pulford, Sept. 3, 1970. Traded to **Vancouver** by Toronto with John Grisdale for Dave Dunn, Oct. 16, 1974. Sold to **Toronto** by Vancouver, Sept. 13, 1978.

Hartland Monahan

MONAHAN, HARTLAND PATRICK 5'11", 197 lbs.
B. Mar. 29, 1951, Montreal, Que. Right Wing, Shoots R

YEAR	TEAM	LEAGUE	GP	G	A	PTS	PIM
1973-74	**CALIF**	**N**	1	0	0	0	0
1974-75	**NYR**	**N**	6	0	1	1	4
1975-76	**WASH**	**N**	80	17	29	46	35
1976-77			79	23	27	50	37
1977-78	**PITT**	**N**	7	2	0	2	0
	LA	**N**	64	10	9	19	45
	2 team total		71	12	9	21	45
1979-80	**STL**	**N**	72	5	12	17	36
1980-81			25	4	2	6	4
7 yrs.		N Totals:	334	61	80	141	161
PLAYOFFS							
1977-78	**LA**	**N**	2	0	0	0	0
1979-80	**STL**	**N**	3	0	0	0	0
1980-81			1	0	0	0	4
3 yrs.		N Totals:	6	0	0	0	4

Traded to **N.Y. Rangers** by California for Brian Lavender, Sept. 23, 1974. Drafted by **Washington** from N.Y. Rangers in Intra-league Draft, June 17, 1975. Traded to **Pittsburgh** by Washington for Pittsburgh's first round choice (Tom McCarthy) in the 1979 Entry Draft (later transferred to Minnesota), Oct. 17, 1977. Traded to **Los Angeles** by Pittsburgh with Syl Apps for Dave Schultz, Gene Carr and Los Angeles' fourth round choice (Shane Pearsall) in the 1978 Amateur Draft, Nov. 2, 1977. Claimed by **Quebec** from Los Angeles in Expansion Draft, June 13, 1979. Sold by **St. Louis** by Quebec, June 13, 1979.

Armand Mondou

MONDOU, ARMAND 5'10", 175 lbs.
B. June 27, 1905, Yanaska, Que. Left Wing, Shoots L

YEAR	TEAM	LEAGUE	GP	G	A	PTS	PIM
1928-29	**MONT**	**N**	32	3	4	7	6
1929-30			44	3	5	8	24
1930-31			40	5	4	9	10
1931-32			47	6	12	18	22
1932-33			24	1	3	4	15
1933-34			48	5	3	8	4
1934-35			45	9	15	24	6
1935-36			36	7	11	18	10
1936-37			7	1	1	2	0
1937-38			7	2	4	6	0
1938-39			34	3	7	10	2
1939-40			21	2	2	4	0
12 yrs.		N Totals:	385	47	71	118	99
PLAYOFFS							
1928-29	**MONT**	**N**	3	0	0	0	2
1929-30*			6	1	1	2	6
1930-31*			8	0	0	0	0
1931-32			4	1	2	3	2
1933-34			4	0	1	1	0
1934-35			2	0	1	1	0
1936-37			5	0	0	0	0
1938-39			3	1	0	1	2
8 yrs.		N Totals:	35	3	5	8	12

YEAR	TEAM & LEAGUE		GP	G	A	PTS	PIM

Pierre Mondou

MONDOU, PIERRE 5'11", 175 lbs.
B. Nov. 27, 1955, Sorel, Que. Center, Shoots R

YEAR	TEAM	LEAGUE	GP	G	A	PTS	PIM
1977-78	**MONT**	**N**	71	19	30	49	8
1978-79			77	31	41	72	26
1979-80			75	30	36	66	12
1980-81			57	17	24	41	16
1981-82			73	35	33	68	57
1982-83			76	29	37	66	31
6 yrs.		N Totals:	429	161	201	362	150
PLAYOFFS							
1976-77*	**MONT**	**N**	3	0	0	0	0
1977-78*			15	3	7	10	4
1978-79*			16	3	6	9	4
1979-80			4	1	4	5	4
1980-81			3	0	1	1	0
1981-82			5	2	5	7	8
1982-83			3	0	1	1	2
7 yrs.		N Totals:	49	9	24	33	22

Bob Mongrain

MONGRAIN, ROBERT 5'10", 165 lbs.
B. Aug. 31, 1959, La Sarre, Que. Center, Shoots L

YEAR	TEAM	LEAGUE	GP	G	A	PTS	PIM
1979-80	**BUF**	**N**	34	4	6	10	4
1980-81			4	0	0	0	2
1981-82			24	6	4	10	6
3 yrs.		N Totals:	62	10	10	20	12
PLAYOFFS							
1979-80	**BUF**	**N**	9	1	2	3	2
1981-82			1	0	0	0	0
2 yrs.		N Totals:	10	1	2	3	2

Signed by **Buffalo** as free agent, Sept. 16, 1979.

Larry Mononen

MONONEN, LAURI ILMARI 6', 185 lbs.
B. Mar. 22, 1950, Joensuu, Finland Right Wing, Shoots L

YEAR	TEAM	LEAGUE	GP	G	A	PTS	PIM
1975-76	**PHOE**	**W**	75	15	21	36	19
1976-77			67	21	29	50	0
2 yrs.		W Totals:	142	36	50	86	19
PLAYOFFS							
1975-76	**PHOE**	**W**	5	1	3	4	2

Hank Monteith

MONTEITH, HENRY GEORGE 5'10", 180 lbs.
B. Oct. 2, 1945, Stratford, Ont. Left Wing, Shoots L

YEAR	TEAM	LEAGUE	GP	G	A	PTS	PIM
1968-69	**DET**	**N**	34	1	9	10	6
1969-70			9	0	0	0	4
1970-71			34	4	3	7	0
3 yrs.		N Totals:	77	5	12	17	10
PLAYOFFS							
1969-70	**DET**	**N**	4	0	0	0	0

Alfie Moore

MOORE, ALFRED ERNEST
B. Toronto, Ont.

YEAR	TEAM	LEAGUE	GP	G	A	PTS	PIM
1938-39	**NYA**	**N**	2	0	0	0	0
PLAYOFFS							
1938-39	**NYA**	**N**	2	0	0	0	0

Dickie Moore

MOORE, RICHARD WINSTON 5'10", 185 lbs.
B. Jan. 6, 1931, Montreal, Que. Right Wing, Shoots R
Won Art Ross Trophy, 1957-58, 1958-59
Hall of Fame, 1974

YEAR	TEAM	LEAGUE	GP	G	A	PTS	PIM
1951-52	**MONT**	**N**	33	18	15	33	44
1952-53			18	2	6	8	19
1953-54			13	1	4	5	12

Dickie Moore continued

YEAR	TEAM & LEAGUE		GP	G	A	PTS	PIM
1954-55			67	16	20	36	32
1955-56			70	11	39	50	55
1956-57			70	29	29	58	56
1957-58			70	**36**	48	**84**	65
1958-59			70	41	**55**	**96**	61
1959-60			62	22	42	64	54
1960-61			57	35	34	69	62
1961-62			57	19	22	41	54
1962-63			67	24	26	50	61
1964-65	**TOR**	**N**	38	2	4	6	68
1967-68	**STL**	**N**	27	5	3	8	9
14 yrs.		**N Totals:**	719	261	347	608	652
PLAYOFFS							
1951-52	**MONT**	**N**	11	1	1	2	12
1952-53*			12	3	2	5	13
1953-54			11	5	8	13	8
1954-55			12	1	5	6	22
1955-56*			10	3	6	9	12
1956-57*			10	3	7	10	4
1957-58*			10	4	7	11	4
1958-59*			11	5	12	17	8
1959-60*			8	6	4	10	4
1960-61			6	3	1	4	4
1961-62			6	4	2	6	8
1962-63			5	0	1	1	2
1964-65	**TOR**	**N**	5	1	1	2	6
1967-68	**STL**	**N**	18	7	7	14	15
14 yrs.		**N Totals:**	135	46	64	110	122

Drafted by **Toronto** from Mont. Canadiens, June 10, 1964.

Amby Moran

MORAN, AMBROSE JASON

Defense

YEAR	TEAM & LEAGUE		GP	G	A	PTS	PIM
1926-27	**MONT**	**N**	12	0	0	0	10
1927-28	**CHI**	**N**	23	1	1	2	14
2 yrs.		**N Totals:**	35	1	1	2	24

Brian Morenz

MORENZ, BRIAN (Mr. Versatility) 5'10", 185 lbs.
B. May 11, 1949, Brampton, Ont. Center, Shoots L

YEAR	TEAM & LEAGUE		GP	G	A	PTS	PIM
1972-73	**NY**	**W**	30	7	1	8	23
1973-74	**NY-NJ**	**W**	75	20	30	50	44
1974-75	**SD**	**W**	78	20	19	39	76
1975-76			40	6	7	13	22
4 yrs.		**W Totals:**	223	53	57	110	165
PLAYOFFS							
1974-75	**SD**	**W**	10	0	3	3	6
1975-76			11	2	1	3	11
2 yrs.		**W Totals:**	21	2	4	6	17

Howie Morenz

MORENZ, HOWARTH (Stratford Flash, Meteor)
5'9", 165 lbs.
B. June 21, 1902, Mitchell, Ont. Center, Shoots L
Won Hart Trophy, 1927–28, 1930–31, 1931-32
Won Art Ross Trophy, 1927–28, 1930–31
Hall of Fame, 1945

YEAR	TEAM & LEAGUE		GP	G	A	PTS	PIM
1923-24	**MONT**	**N**	24	13	3	16	20
1924-25			30	27	7	34	31
1925-26			31	23	3	26	39
1926-27			44	25	7	32	49
1927-28			43	**33**	**18**	**51**	66
1928-29			42	17	10	27	47
1929-30			44	40	10	50	72
1930-31			39	28	23	**51**	49
1931-32			48	24	25	49	46
1932-33			46	14	21	35	32
1933-34			39	8	13	21	21
1934-35	**CHI**	**N**	48	8	26	34	21
1935-36			23	4	10	14	20
	NYR	**N**	19	2	5	7	6
	2 team total		42	6	15	21	26
1936-37	**MONT**	**N**	30	4	16	20	12
14 yrs.		**N Totals:**	550	270	197	467	531

Howie Morenz continued

YEAR	TEAM & LEAGUE		GP	G	A	PTS	PIM
PLAYOFFS							
1923-24*	**MONT**	**N**	6	7	2	9	10
1924-25			6	7	1	8	10
1926-27			4	1	0	1	4
1927-28			2	0	0	0	12
1928-29			3	0	0	0	6
1929-30*			6	3	0	3	10
1930-31*			10	1	4	5	10
1931-32			4	1	0	1	4
1932-33			2	0	3	3	2
1933-34			2	1	1	2	0
1934-35	**CHI**	**N**	2	0	0	0	0
11 yrs.		**N Totals:**	47	21	11	32	68

Angelo Moretto

MORETTO, ANGELO JOSEPH 6'3", 212 lbs.
B. Sept. 18, 1953, Toronto, Ont. Center, Shoots L

YEAR	TEAM & LEAGUE		GP	G	A	PTS	PIM
1976-77	**CLEVE**	**N**	5	1	2	3	2
1978-79	**IND**	**W**	18	3	1	4	2
2 yrs.		**N Totals:**	5	1	2	3	2
		W Totals:	18	3	1	4	2

Put on **Minnesota** Reserve List after Cleveland-Minnesota Dispersal Draft, June 15, 1978.

Ron Morgan

MORGAN, RONALD 5'11", 190 lbs.
B. Toronto, Ont. Left Wing, Shoots L

YEAR	TEAM & LEAGUE		GP	G	A	PTS	PIM
1973-74	**CLEVE**	**W**	4	0	1	1	7
PLAYOFFS							
1973-74	**CLEVE**	**W**	2	1	0	1	0

Pete Morin

MORIN, PETER
B. Dec. 8, 1915, Lachine, Que. Forward

YEAR	TEAM & LEAGUE		GP	G	A	PTS	PIM
1941-42	**MONT**	**N**	31	10	12	22	7
PLAYOFFS							
1941-42	**MONT**	**N**	1	0	0	0	0

Wayne Morin

MORIN, WAYNE 5'10", 185 lbs.
B. May 13, 1955, Progress, B.C. Defense, Shoots R

YEAR	TEAM & LEAGUE		GP	G	A	PTS	PIM
1976-77	**CALG**	**W**	13	2	0	2	25

Bernie Morris

MORRIS, BERNARD
B. Unknown Defense

YEAR	TEAM & LEAGUE		GP	G	A	PTS	PIM
1924-25	**BOS**	**N**	6	2	0	2	0

Billy Morris

MORRIS, WILLIAM JOHN 6', 185 lbs.
B. June 26, 1949, Toronto, Ont. Left Wing, Shoots L

YEAR	TEAM & LEAGUE		GP	G	A	PTS	PIM
1974-75	**EDM**	**W**	36	4	8	12	6

Moe Morris

MORRIS, ELWIN GORDON 5'7", 185 lbs.
B. Jan. 3, 1921, Toronto, Ont. Defense, Shoots L

YEAR	TEAM & LEAGUE		GP	G	A	PTS	PIM
1943-44	**TOR**	**N**	50	12	21	33	22
1944-45			29	0	2	2	18
1945-46			38	1	5	6	10
1948-49	**NYR**	**N**	18	0	1	1	8
4 yrs.		**N Totals:**	135	13	29	42	58
PLAYOFFS							
1943-44	**TOR**	**N**	5	1	2	3	2
1944-45*			13	3	0	3	14
2 yrs.		**N Totals:**	18	4	2	6	16

Pete Morris

MORRIS, PETER 5'8", 165 lbs.
B. June 29, 1955, Edmonton, Alta. Left Wing, Shoots L

YEAR	TEAM & LEAGUE		GP	G	A	PTS	PIM
1975-76	**EDM**	**W**	75	7	13	20	34
1976-77			3	0	0	0	2
2 yrs.		**W Totals:**	78	7	13	20	36
PLAYOFFS							
1975-76	**EDM**	**W**	3	0	1	1	7

Rick Morris

MORRIS, RICHARD IAN (Quick Rick) 5'11", 176 lbs.
B. July 5, 1946, Hamilton, Ont. Left Wing, Shoots L

YEAR	TEAM & LEAGUE		GP	G	A	PTS	PIM
1972-73	**CHI**	**W**	76	31	17	48	84
1973-74			76	17	16	33	140
1974-75			78	15	13	28	110
1975-76	**D-O**	**W**	40	9	16	25	58
	EDM	**W**	33	11	15	26	52
	2 team total		73	20	31	51	110
1976-77			79	18	17	35	76
1977-78			0	0	0	0	0
	QUE	**W**	30	1	6	7	47
	2 team total		30	1	6	7	47
6 yrs.		**W Totals:**	412	102	100	202	567
PLAYOFFS							
1973-74	**CHI**	**W**	18	4	3	7	42
1976-77	**EDM**	**W**	5	0	1	1	4
2 yrs.		**W Totals:**	23	4	4	8	46

Dave Morrison

MORRISON, DAVID STUART 6', 186 lbs.
B. June 12, 1962, Toronto, Ont. Right Wing, Shoots R

YEAR	TEAM & LEAGUE		GP	G	A	PTS	PIM
1980-81	**LA**	**N**	3	0	0	0	0
1981-82			4	0	0	0	0
1982-83			24	3	3	6	4
3 yrs.		**N Totals:**	31	3	3	6	4

Don Morrison

MORRISON, DONALD MACRAE 5'10", 165 lbs.
B. July 14, 1923, Saskatoon, Sask. Center, Shoots R

YEAR	TEAM & LEAGUE		GP	G	A	PTS	PIM
1947-48	**DET**	**N**	40	10	15	25	6
1948-49			13	0	1	1	0
1950-51	**CHI**	**N**	59	8	12	20	6
3 yrs.		**N Totals:**	112	18	28	46	12
PLAYOFFS							
1947-48	**DET**	**N**	3	0	1	1	0

Traded to **Chicago** by Detroit with Harry Lumley, Jack Stewart, Al Dewsbury and Pete Babando for Jim Henry, Bob Goldham, Gaye Stewart and Metro Prystai, July 13, 1950.

Doug Morrison

MORRISON, DOUGLAS 5'11", 185 lbs.
B. Feb. 1, 1960, Vancouver, B.C. Right Wing, Shoots R

YEAR	TEAM & LEAGUE		GP	G	A	PTS	PIM
1979-80	**BOS**	**N**	1	0	0	0	0
1980-81			18	7	3	10	13
1981-82			3	0	0	0	0
3 yrs.		**N Totals:**	22	7	3	10	13

Gary Morrison

MORRISON, GARY 6'2", 200 lbs.
B. Nov. 8, 1955, Detroit, Mich. Right Wing, Shoots R

YEAR	TEAM & LEAGUE		GP	G	A	PTS	PIM
1979-80	**PHI**	**N**	3	0	2	2	0
1980-81			33	1	13	14	68
1981-82			7	0	0	0	2
3 yrs.		**N Totals:**	43	1	15	16	70
PLAYOFFS							
1979-80	**PHI**	**N**	5	0	1	1	2

George Morrison

MORRISON, GEORGE HAROLD 6'1", 170 lbs.
B. Dec. 24, 1948, Toronto, Ont. Left Wing, Shoots L

YEAR	TEAM & LEAGUE		GP	G	A	PTS	PIM
1970-71	**STL**	**N**	73	15	10	25	6
1971-72			42	2	11	13	7
1972-73	**MINN**	**W**	70	16	24	40	20
1973-74			73	40	38	78	37
1974-75			76	31	29	60	30
1975-76	**CALG**	**W**	79	25	32	57	13
1976-77			63	11	19	30	10
7 yrs.		**N Totals:**	115	17	21	38	13
		W Totals:	361	123	142	265	110
PLAYOFFS							
1970-71	**STL**	**N**	3	0	0	0	0
1972-73	**MINN**	**W**	5	1	1	2	2
1973-74			11	5	5	10	12
1974-75			12	5	9	14	0
1975-76	**CALG**	**W**	10	3	2	5	0
5 yrs.		**N Totals:**	3	0	0	0	0
		W Totals:	38	14	17	31	14

Traded to **Buffalo** by St. Louis with St. Louis' second choice (Larry Carriere) in 1972 Amateur Draft for Chris Evans, March 5, 1972.

Jim Morrison

MORRISON, JAMES STUART HUNTER 5'10", 183 lbs.
B. Oct. 11, 1931, Montreal Que. Defense, Shoots L

YEAR	TEAM & LEAGUE		GP	G	A	PTS	PIM
1951-52	**BOS**	**N**	14	0	2	2	2
	TOR	**N**	17	0	1	1	4
	2 team total		31	0	3	3	6
1952-53			56	1	8	9	36
1953-54			60	11	9	20	51
1954-55			70	5	12	17	84
1955-56			63	2	17	19	77
1956-57			63	3	17	20	44
1957-58			70	3	21	24	62
1958-59	**BOS**	**N**	70	8	17	25	42
1959-60	**DET**	**N**	70	3	23	26	62
1960-61	**NYR**	**N**	19	1	6	7	6
1969-70	**PITT**	**N**	59	5	15	20	40
1970-71			73	0	10	10	32
12 yrs.		**N Totals:**	704	42	158	200	542
PLAYOFFS							
1951-52	**TOR**	**N**	2	0	0	0	0
1953-54			5	0	0	0	4
1954-55			4	0	1	1	4
1955-56			5	0	0	0	4
1958-59	**BOS**	**N**	6	0	6	6	13
1959-60	**DET**	**N**	6	0	2	2	0
1969-70	**PITT**	**N**	8	0	3	3	10
7 yrs.		**N Totals:**	36	0	12	12	35

Traded to **Toronto** by Boston for Fleming Mackell, Jan. 9, 1952. Traded to **Boston** by Toronto for Allan Stanley, Oct. 8, 1958. Traded to **Detroit** by Boston for Nick Mickoski, Aug. 25, 1959. Traded to **Chicago** by Detroit for Howie Glover, June 7, 1960. Drafted by **New York** from Chicago, June 8, 1960.

John Morrison

MORRISON, JOHN W.
B. Selkirk, Man.

YEAR	TEAM & LEAGUE		GP	G	A	PTS	PIM
1925-26	**NYA**	**N**	18	0	0	0	0

Traded to **Detroit** by N.Y. Rangers with Reg Sinclair for Leo Reise, Jr., Aug. 18, 1952.

Kevin Morrison

MORRISON, KEVIN GREGORY JOSEPH
5'11", 202 lbs.
B. Oct. 28, 1949, Sydney, N.S. Defense, Shoots L

YEAR	TEAM & LEAGUE		GP	G	A	PTS	PIM
1973-74	**NY-NJ**	**W**	78	24	43	67	132
1974-75	**SD**	**W**	78	20	61	81	143
1975-76			80	22	43	65	56
1976-77			75	8	30	38	68
1977-78	**IND**	**W**	75	17	40	57	49

Kevin Morrison continued

YEAR	TEAM & LEAGUE		GP	G	A	PTS	PIM
1978-79			5	0	2	2	0
	QUE	**W**	27	2	5	7	14
	2 team total		32	2	7	9	14
1979-80	**COLO**	**N**	41	4	11	15	23
7 yrs.		**N Totals:**	41	4	11	15	23
		W Totals:	418	93	224	317	462
PLAYOFFS							
1974-75	**SD**	**W**	10	0	7	7	2
1975-76			11	1	5	6	12
1976-77			7	1	3	4	8
3 yrs.		**W Totals:**	28	2	15	17	22

Lew Morrison

MORRISON, HENRY LEWIS 6', 185 lbs.
B. Feb. 11, 1948, Gainsborough, Sask. Right Wing, Shoots R

YEAR	TEAM & LEAGUE		GP	G	A	PTS	PIM
1969-70	**PHI**	**N**	66	9	10	19	19
1970-71			78	5	7	12	25
1971-72			73	5	5	10	26
1972-73	**ATL**	**N**	78	6	9	15	19
1973-74			52	1	4	5	0
1974-75	**WASH**	**N**	18	0	4	4	6
	PITT	**N**	52	7	5	12	4
	2 team total		70	7	9	16	10
1975-76			78	4	5	9	8
1976-77			76	2	1	3	0
1977-78			8	0	2	2	0
9 yrs.		**N Totals:**	579	39	52	91	107
PLAYOFFS							
1970-71	**PHI**	**N**	4	0	0	0	2
1974-75	**PITT**	**N**	9	0	0	0	0
1975-76			3	0	0	0	0
1976-77			1	0	0	0	0
4 yrs.		**N Totals:**	17	0	0	0	2

Drafted by **Atlanta** from Philadelphia in Expansion Draft, June 6, 1972. Drafted by **Washington** from Atlanta in Expansion Draft, June 12, 1974. Traded to **Pittsburgh** by Washington for Ron Lalonde, Dec. 14, 1974.

Mark Morrison

MORRISON, MARK 5'8", 150 lbs.
B. Mar. 11, 1963, Prince George, B.C. Center, Shoots R

YEAR	TEAM & LEAGUE		GP	G	A	PTS	PIM
1981-82	**NYR**	**N**	9	1	1	2	0

Roderick Morrison

MORRISON, RODERICK FINLAY 5'9", 160 lbs.
B. Oct. 7, 1925, Saskatoon, Sask. Right Wing, Shoots R

YEAR	TEAM & LEAGUE		GP	G	A	PTS	PIM
1947-48	**DET**	**N**	34	8	7	15	4
PLAYOFFS							
1947-48	**DET**	**N**	3	0	0	0	0

Dave Morrow

MORROW, DAVE 6', 190 lbs.
B. Apr. 21, 1957, Edmonton, Alta. Center, Shoots L

YEAR	TEAM & LEAGUE		GP	G	A	PTS	PIM
1978-79	**IND**	**W**	10	2	10	12	29

Ken Morrow

MORROW, KENNETH 6'4", 210 lbs.
B. Oct. 17, 1956, Davison, Mich. Defense, Shoots R

YEAR	TEAM & LEAGUE		GP	G	A	PTS	PIM
1979-80	**NYI**	**N**	18	0	3	3	4
1980-81			80	2	11	13	20
1981-82			75	1	18	19	56
1982-83			79	5	11	16	44
4 yrs.		**N Totals:**	252	8	43	51	124
PLAYOFFS							
1979-80*	**NYI**	**N**	20	1	2	3	12
1980-81*			18	3	4	7	8
1981-82*			19	0	4	4	8
1982-83*			19	5	7	12	18
4 yrs.		**N Totals:**	76	9	17	26	46

Gus Mortson

MORTSON, JAMES ANGUS GERALD 5'11", 190 lbs.
B. Jan. 24, 1925, New Liskeard, Ont. Defense, Shoots L

YEAR	TEAM & LEAGUE		GP	G	A	PTS	PIM
1946-47	**TOR**	**N**	60	5	13	18	**133**
1947-48			58	7	11	18	118
1948-49			60	2	13	15	85
1949-50			68	3	14	17	85
1950-51			60	3	10	13	**142**
1951-52			65	1	10	11	106
1952-53	**CHI**	**N**	68	5	18	23	88
1953-54			68	5	13	18	**132**
1954-55			65	2	11	13	133
1955-56			52	5	10	15	87
1956-57			70	5	18	23	**147**
1957-58			67	3	10	13	62
1958-59	**DET**	**N**	36	0	1	1	22
13 yrs.		**N Totals:**	797	46	152	198	1340
PLAYOFFS							
1946-47*	**TOR**	**N**	11	1	3	4	22
1947-48*			5	1	2	3	2
1948-49*			9	2	1	3	5
1949-50			7	0	0	0	18
1950-51*			11	0	1	1	4
1951-52			4	0	0	0	8
1952-53	**CHI**	**N**	7	1	1	2	6
7 yrs.		**N Totals:**	54	5	8	13	65

Traded to **Chicago** by Toronto with Al Rollins, Cal Gardner and Ray Hannigan for Harry Lumley, Sept. 11, 1952.

Keke Mortson

MORTSON, CLELAND LINDSAY 5'9", 170 lbs.
B. Mar. 29, 1934, Arntfeld, Que. Right Wing, Shoots R

YEAR	TEAM & LEAGUE		GP	G	A	PTS	PIM
1972-73	**HOUS**	**W**	67	13	16	29	95
1977-78			6	0	1	1	7
2 yrs.		**W Totals:**	73	13	17	30	102
PLAYOFFS							
1972-73	**HOUS**	**W**	10	0	3	3	16
1977-78			2	0	1	1	0
2 yrs.		**W Totals:**	12	0	4	4	16

Kenny Mosdell

MOSDELL, KENNETH 6'1", 170 lbs.
B. July 13, 1922, Montreal, Que. Center, Shoots L

YEAR	TEAM & LEAGUE		GP	G	A	PTS	PIM
1941-42	**NYA**	**N**	41	7	9	16	16
1944-45	**MONT**	**N**	31	12	6	18	16
1945-46			13	2	1	3	8
1946-47			54	5	10	15	50
1947-48			23	1	0	1	19
1948-49			60	17	9	26	59
1949-50			67	15	12	27	42
1950-51			66	13	18	31	24
1951-52			44	5	11	16	19
1952-53			63	5	14	19	27
1953-54			67	22	24	46	64
1954-55			70	22	32	54	82
1955-56			67	13	17	30	48
1956-57	**CHI**	**N**	25	2	4	6	10
1957-58	**MONT**	**N**	2	0	1	1	0
15 yrs.		**N Totals:**	693	141	168	309	484
PLAYOFFS							
1945-46*	**MONT**	**N**	9	4	1	5	6
1946-47			4	2	0	2	4
1948-49			7	1	1	2	4
1949-50			5	0	0	0	12
1950-51			11	1	1	2	4
1951-52			2	1	0	1	0
1952-53*			7	3	2	5	4
1953-54			11	1	0	1	4
1954-55			12	2	7	9	8
1955-56*			9	1	1	2	2
1958-59*			2	0	0	0	0
11 yrs.		**N Totals:**	79	16	13	29	48

Sold to **Chicago** with Eddie Mazur and Bud MacPherson by Montreal for $55,000, with option to recall at end of season, May, 24, 1956. Returned to **Montreal** by Chicago, Sept. 20, 1957.

Wayne Mosdell

MOSDELL, WAYNE KENNETH 6'3", 185 lbs.
B. Dec. 4, 1944, Montreal, Que. Defense, Shoots R

YEAR	TEAM & LEAGUE		GP	G	A	PTS	PIM
1972-73	**PHI**	**W**	8	0	1	1	12

Bill Mosienko

MOSIENKO, WILLIAM (Mosi) 5'8", 160 lbs.
B. Nov. 2, 1921, Winnipeg, Man. Right Wing, Shoots R
Won Lady Byng Trophy, 1944-45
Hall of Fame, 1965

YEAR	TEAM & LEAGUE		GP	G	A	PTS	PIM
1941-42	**CHI**	**N**	12	6	8	14	4
1942-43			2	2	0	2	0
1943-44			50	32	38	70	10
1944-45			50	28	26	54	0
1945-46			40	18	30	48	12
1946-47			59	25	27	52	2
1947-48			40	16	8	24	0
1948-49			60	17	25	42	6
1949-50			69	18	28	46	10
1950-51			65	21	15	36	18
1951-52			70	31	22	53	10
1952-53			65	17	20	37	8
1953-54			65	15	19	34	17
1954-55			64	12	15	27	24
14 yrs.	**N Totals:**		711	259	281	539	121

PLAYOFFS

YEAR	TEAM & LEAGUE		GP	G	A	PTS	PIM
1941-42	**CHI**	**N**	3	2	0	2	0
1943-44			8	2	2	4	6
1945-46			4	2	0	2	2
1952-53			7	4	2	6	7
4 yrs.	**N Totals:**		22	10	4	14	15

Darwin Mott

MOTT, DARWIN 5'9", 165 lbs.
B. Aug. 19, 1950, Creelman, Sask. Left Wing, Shoots L

YEAR	TEAM & LEAGUE		GP	G	A	PTS	PIM
1972-73	**PHI**	**W**	1	0	0	0	0

Morris Mott

MOTT, MORRIS KENNETH 5'10", 165 lbs.
B. May 25, 1946, Creelman, Sask. Right Wing, Shoots L

YEAR	TEAM & LEAGUE		GP	G	A	PTS	PIM
1972-73	**CALIF**	**N**	70	6	7	13	8
1973-74			77	9	17	26	33
1974-75			52	3	8	11	8
1976-77	**WINN**	**W**	2	0	1	1	5
4 yrs.	**N Totals:**		199	18	32	50	49
	W Totals:		2	0	1	1	5

Alex Motter

MOTTER, ALEX MOTTER 6', 175 lbs.
B. June 20, 1913, Melville, Sask. Center, Shoots L

YEAR	TEAM & LEAGUE		GP	G	A	PTS	PIM
1934-35	**BOS**	**N**	5	0	0	0	0
1935-36			23	1	4	5	4
1937-38	**DET**	**N**	33	5	17	22	6
1938-39			42	5	11	16	17
1939-40			37	7	12	19	28
1940-41			47	13	12	25	18
1941-42			30	2	4	6	20
1942-43			50	6	4	10	42
8 yrs.	**N Totals:**		267	39	64	103	135

PLAYOFFS

YEAR	TEAM & LEAGUE		GP	G	A	PTS	PIM
1934-35	**BOS**	**N**	4	0	0	0	0
1935-36			2	0	0	0	0
1938-39	**DET**	**N**	4	0	1	1	0
1939-40			5	1	1	2	15
1940-41			9	1	3	4	4
1941-42			11	1	3	4	20
1942-43*			5	0	1	1	2
7 yrs.	**N Totals:**		40	3	9	12	41

Bob Mowat

MOWAT, ROBERT 5'9", 170 lbs.
B. Oct. 5, 1949, Kamloops, B.C. Right Wing, Shoots R

YEAR	TEAM & LEAGUE		GP	G	A	PTS	PIM
1974-75	**PHOE**	**W**	53	9	10	19	34

Jim Moxey

MOXEY, JAMES GEORGE 6'1", 190 lbs.
B. May 28, 1953, Toronto, Ont. Right Wing, Shoots L

YEAR	TEAM & LEAGUE		GP	G	A	PTS	PIM
1974-75	**CALIF**	**N**	47	5	4	9	14
1975-76			44	10	16	26	33
1976-77	**CLEVE**	**N**	35	7	7	14	20
	LA	**N**	1	0	0	0	2
	2 team total		36	7	7	14	22
3 yrs.	**N Totals:**		127	22	27	49	69

Traded to **Los Angeles** by Cleveland with Gary Simmons for Juha Widing and Gary Edwards, Jan. 22, 1977.

Richard Mulhern

MULHERN, RICHARD SYDNEY 6'1", 188 lbs.
B. Mar. 1, 1955, Edmonton, Alta. Defense, Shoots L

YEAR	TEAM & LEAGUE		GP	G	A	PTS	PIM
1975-76	**ATL**	**N**	12	1	0	1	4
1976-77			79	12	32	44	80
1977-78			79	9	23	32	47
1978-79			37	3	12	15	22
	LA	**N**	36	2	9	11	23
	2 team total		73	5	21	26	45
1979-80			15	0	3	3	16
	TOR	**N**	26	0	10	10	11
	2 team total		41	0	13	13	27
1980-81	**WINN**	**N**	19	0	4	4	14
6 yrs.	**N Totals:**		303	27	93	120	217

PLAYOFFS

YEAR	TEAM & LEAGUE		GP	G	A	PTS	PIM
1976-77	**ATL**	**N**	3	0	2	2	5
1977-78			2	0	1	1	0
1978-79	**LA**	**N**	1	0	0	0	0
1979-80	**TOR**	**N**	1	0	0	0	0
4 yrs.	**N Totals:**		7	0	3	3	5

Traded to **Los Angeles** by Atlanta with Atlanta's second round choice (Dave Morrison) in the 1980 Entry Draft for Bob Murdoch and Los Angeles' second round choice (Tony Curtale) in the 1980 Entry Draft, Jan. 16, 1979. Claimed on waivers by **Toronto** from Los Angeles, Feb. 10, 1980. Sold to **Winnipeg** by Toronto, Dec. 2, 1980.

Brian Mullen

MULLEN, BRIAN 5'10", 180 lbs.
B. Mar. 16, 1962, New York, N.Y. Defense, Shoots L

YEAR	TEAM & LEAGUE		GP	G	A	PTS	PIM
1982-83	**WINN**	**N**	80	24	26	50	14

PLAYOFFS

YEAR	TEAM & LEAGUE		GP	G	A	PTS	PIM
1982-83	**WINN**	**N**	3	1	0	1	0

Joe Mullen

MULLEN, JOSEPH 5'9", 180 lbs.
B. Feb. 26, 1957, New York, N.Y. Right Wing, Shoots R

YEAR	TEAM & LEAGUE		GP	G	A	PTS	PIM
1981-82	**STL**	**N**	45	25	34	59	4
1982-83			49	17	30	47	6
2 yrs.	**N Totals:**		94	42	64	106	10

PLAYOFFS

YEAR	TEAM & LEAGUE		GP	G	A	PTS	PIM
1979-80	**STL**	**N**	1	0	0	0	0
1981-82			10	7	11	18	4
2 yrs.	**N Totals:**		11	7	11	18	4

Signed by **St. Louis** as free agent, Aug. 16, 1979.

Johnny Muloin

MULOIN, JOHN WAYNE 5'8", 176 lbs.
B. Dec. 24, 1941, Toronto, Ont. Defense, Shoots L

YEAR	TEAM & LEAGUE		GP	G	A	PTS	PIM
1963-64	**DET**	**N**	3	0	1	1	2
1969-70	**OAK**	**N**	71	3	6	9	53
1970-71	**CALIF**	**N**	67	0	14	14	32
	MINN	**N**	7	0	0	0	6
	2 team total		74	0	14	14	38

Johnny Muloin continued

YEAR	TEAM & LEAGUE	GP	G	A	PTS	PIM
1972-73	**CLEVE W**	70	2	13	15	62
1973-74		76	3	7	10	39
1974-75		78	4	17	21	5
1975-76		27	0	5	5	12
	EDM W	10	1	1	2	0
	2 team total	37	1	6	7	12
7 yrs.	**N Totals:**	148	3	21	24	93
	W Totals:	261	10	43	53	118
PLAYOFFS						
1969-70	**OAK N**	4	0	0	0	0
1970-71	**MINN N**	7	0	0	0	2
1972-73	**CLEVE W**	9	1	3	4	14
1973-74		5	1	0	1	0
1974-75		5	0	1	1	4
1975-76	**EDM W**	1	0	0	0	0
6 yrs.	**N Totals:**	11	0	0	0	2
	W Totals:	20	2	4	6	18

Traded to **Minnesota** by California with Ted Hampson for Tom Williams and Dick Redmond, March 7, 1971.

Grant Mulvey

MULVEY, GRANT MICHAEL 6'3", 200 lbs.
B. Sept. 17, 1956, Sudbury, Ont. Right Wing, Shoots R

YEAR	TEAM & LEAGUE	GP	G	A	PTS	PIM
1974-75	**CHI N**	74	7	4	11	36
1975-76		64	11	17	28	72
1976-77		80	10	14	24	111
1977-78		78	14	24	38	135
1978-79		80	19	15	34	99
1979-80		80	39	26	65	122
1980-81		42	18	14	32	81
1981-82		73	30	19	49	141
1982-83		3	0	0	0	0
9 yrs.	**N Totals:**	574	148	133	281	797
PLAYOFFS						
1974-75	**CHI N**	6	2	0	2	6
1975-76		4	0	0	0	2
1976-77		2	1	0	1	2
1977-78		4	2	2	4	0
1978-79		1	0	0	0	2
1979-80		7	1	1	2	8
1980-81		3	0	0	0	0
1981-82		15	4	2	6	50
8 yrs.	**N Totals:**	42	10	5	15	70

Paul Mulvey

MULVEY, PAUL JOSEPH 6'4", 220 lbs.
B. Sept. 27, 1958, Sudbury, Ont. Left Wing, Shoots L

YEAR	TEAM & LEAGUE	GP	G	A	PTS	PIM
1978-79	**WASH N**	55	7	4	11	81
1979-80		77	15	19	34	240
1980-81		55	7	14	21	166
1981-82	**PITT N**	27	1	7	8	76
	LA N	11	0	7	7	50
	2 team total	38	1	14	15	126
4 yrs.	**N Totals:**	225	30	51	81	613

Claimed on waivers by **Los Angeles** Dec. 30, 1981. Traded to **Edmonton** by Los Angeles for Blair Barnes, June 22, 1982.

Harry Mummery

MUMMERY, HARRY 245 lbs.
Defense, Shoots L

YEAR	TEAM & LEAGUE	GP	G	A	PTS	PIM
1917-18	**TOR N**	18	3	0	3	24
1918-19		13	2	0	2	27
1919-20	**QUE N**	24	9	6	15	42
1920-21	**MONT N**	24	15	5	20	68
1921-22	**HAMIL N**	20	4	2	6	20
1922-23		7	0	0	0	4
6 yrs.	**N Totals:**	106	33	13	46	185
PLAYOFFS						
1917-18*	**TOR N**	7	0	4	4	18

Craig Muni

MUNI, CRAIG 6'2", 201 lbs.
B. July 19, 1962, Toronto, Ont. Defense, Shoots L

YEAR	TEAM & LEAGUE	GP	G	A	PTS	PIM
1981-82	**TOR N**	3	0	0	0	2
1982-83		2	0	1	1	0
2 yrs.	**N Totals:**	5	0	1	1	2

Dunc Munro

MUNRO, DUNCAN B.
B. Toronto, Ont. Defense

YEAR	TEAM & LEAGUE	GP	G	A	PTS	PIM
1924-25	**MON(M) N**	27	5	1	6	14
1925-26		33	4	6	10	55
1926-27		44	6	5	11	42
1927-28		43	5	2	7	35
1928-29		1	0	0	0	0
1929-30		36	7	2	9	10
1930-31		4	0	1	1	0
1931-32	**MONT N**	48	1	1	2	14
8 yrs.	**N Totals:**	236	28	18	46	170
PLAYOFFS						
1925-26*	**MON(M) N**	6	1	0	1	6
1926-27		2	0	0	0	4
1927-28		9	0	2	2	8
1929-30		4	2	0	2	4
1931-32	**MONT N**	2	0	0	0	2
5 yrs.	**N Totals:**	23	3	2	5	24

Gerry Munro

MUNRO, GERALD
B. Nov. 20, 1897, Sault Ste. Marie, Ont. Defense

YEAR	TEAM & LEAGUE	GP	G	A	PTS	PIM
1924-25	**MON(M) N**	29	1	0	1	22
1925-26	**TOR N**	4	0	0	0	0
2 yrs.	**N Totals:**	33	1	0	1	22

Bob Murdoch

MURDOCH, ROBERT JOHN 6', 190 lbs.
B. Nov. 20, 1946, Kirkland Lake, Ont. Defense, Shoots R

YEAR	TEAM & LEAGUE	GP	G	A	PTS	PIM
1970-71	**MONT N**	1	0	2	2	2
1971-72		11	1	1	2	8
1972-73		69	2	22	24	55
1973-74	**LA N**	76	8	20	28	85
1974-75		80	13	29	42	116
1975-76		80	6	29	35	103
1976-77		70	9	23	32	79
1977-78		76	2	17	19	68
1978-79		32	3	12	15	46
	ATL N	35	5	11	16	24
	2 team total	67	8	23	31	70
1979-80		80	5	16	21	48
1980-81	**CALG N**	74	3	19	22	54
1981-82		73	3	17	20	76
12 yrs.	**N Totals:**	757	60	218	278	764
PLAYOFFS						
1970-71*	**MONT N**	2	0	0	0	0
1971-72		1	0	0	0	0
1972-73*		13	0	3	3	10
1973-74	**LA N**	5	0	0	0	2
1974-75		3	0	1	1	4
1975-76		9	0	5	5	15
1976-77		9	2	3	5	14
1977-78		2	0	1	1	5
1978-79	**ATL N**	2	0	0	0	4
1979-80		4	1	1	2	2
1980-81	**CALG N**	16	1	4	5	36
1981-82		3	0	0	0	0
12 yrs.	**N Totals:**	69	4	18	22	92

Traded to **Minnesota** by Montreal for Marshall Johnston, May 25, 1971. Claimed by **Montreal** from Minnesota in Intra-league Draft, June 8, 1971. Traded to **Los Angeles** by Montreal with Randy Rota for Los Angeles' first choice (Mario Tremblay) in 1974 Amateur Draft and cash, May 29, 1973. Traded to **Atlanta** by Los Angeles with Los Angeles' second-round choice (Tony Curtale) in the 1980 Entry Draft, for Richard Mulhern and Atlanta's second-round choice (Dave Morrison) in the 1980 Entry Draft, Jan. 16, 1979.

Bob Murdoch

MURDOCH, ROBERT LOVELL 5'11", 191 lbs.
B. Jan. 29, 1954, Cranbrook, B.C. Right Wing, Shoots R

YEAR	TEAM & LEAGUE		GP	G	A	PTS	PIM
1975-76	CALIF	N	78	22	27	49	53
1976-77	CLEVE	N	57	23	19	42	30
1977-78			71	14	26	40	27
1978-79	STL	N	54	13	13	26	17
4 yrs.		N Totals:	260	72	85	157	127

Put on **Minnesota** reserve list after Cleveland-Minnesota Dispersal Draft, June 15, 1978. Sold to **St. Louis** by Minnesota, Aug. 8, 1978. Claimed by **St. Louis** as fill in Expansion Draft, June 13, 1979.

Don Murdoch

MURDOCH, DONALD WALTER (Murder) 5'11", 180 lbs.
B. Oct. 25, 1956, Cranbrook, B.C. Right Wing, Shoots R

YEAR	TEAM & LEAGUE		GP	G	A	PTS	PIM
1976-77	NYR	N	59	32	24	56	47
1977-78			66	27	28	55	41
1978-79			40	15	22	37	6
1979-80			56	23	19	42	16
	EDM	N	10	5	2	7	4
	2 team total		66	28	21	49	20
1980-81			40	10	9	19	18
1981-82	DET	N	49	9	13	22	23
6 yrs.		N Totals:	320	121	117	238	155
PLAYOFFS							
1977-78	NYR	N	3	1	3	4	4
1978-79			18	7	5	12	12
1979-80	EDM	N	3	2	0	2	0
3 yrs.		N Totals:	24	10	8	18	16

Traded to **Edmonton** by N.Y. Rangers for Cam Connor and Edmonton's third choice (Peter Sundstrum) in 1981 Entry Draft, Mar. 11, 1980.

Murray Murdoch

MURDOCH, JOHN MURRAY 5'10", 180 lbs.
B. May 19, 1904, Lucknow, Ont. Left Wing, Shoots L

YEAR	TEAM & LEAGUE		GP	G	A	PTS	PIM
1926-27	NYR	N	44	6	4	10	12
1927-28			44	7	3	10	14
1928-29			44	8	6	14	18
1929-30			44	13	13	26	22
1930-31			44	7	7	14	8
1931-32			48	5	16	21	32
1932-33			48	5	11	16	23
1933-34			48	14	15	29	14
1934-35			48	2	9	11	9
1935-36			48	0	14	14	16
1936-37			48	0	14	14	16
11 yrs.		N Totals:	508	67	112	179	184
PLAYOFFS							
1926-27	NYR	N	2	0	0	0	0
1927-28*			9	2	1	3	12
1928-29			6	0	0	0	2
1929-30			4	3	0	3	6
1930-31			4	0	2	2	0
1931-32			7	0	2	2	0
1932-33*			8	3	4	7	2
1933-34			4	0	2	2	4
1934-35			4	0	2	2	4
1935-36			9	1	1	2	0
1936-37			9	1	1	2	0
11 yrs.		N Totals:	66	10	15	25	30

Brian Murphy

MURPHY, BRIAN 6'3", 195 lbs.
B. Aug. 20, 1947, Toronto, Ont. Center, Shoots L

YEAR	TEAM & LEAGUE		GP	G	A	PTS	PIM
1974-75	DET	N	1	0	0	0	0

Traded to **Toronto** with Garry Monahan for Bob Pulford, Sept. 3, 1970.

Larry Murphy

MURPHY, LAWRENCE THOMAS 6'1", 210 lbs.
B. Mar. 8, 1961, Scarborough, Ont. Defense, Shoots R

YEAR	TEAM & LEAGUE		GP	G	A	PTS	PIM
1980-81	LA	N	80	16	60	76	79
1981-82			79	22	44	66	95
1982-83			77	14	48	62	81
3 yrs.		N Totals:	236	52	152	204	255
PLAYOFFS							
1980-81	LA	N	4	3	0	3	2
1981-82			10	2	8	10	12
2 yrs.		N Totals:	14	5	8	13	14

Mike Murphy

MURPHY, MICHAEL JOHN (Murph) 6', 188 lbs.
B. Sept. 12, 1950, Toronto, Ont. Right Wing, Shoots R

YEAR	TEAM & LEAGUE		GP	G	A	PTS	PIM
1971-72	STL	N	63	20	23	43	19
1972-73			64	18	27	45	48
	NYR	N	15	4	4	8	5
	2 team total		79	22	31	53	53
1973-74			16	2	1	3	0
	LA	N	53	13	16	29	38
	2 team total		69	15	17	32	38
1974-75			78	30	38	68	44
1975-76			80	26	42	68	61
1976-77			76	25	36	61	58
1977-78			72	20	36	56	48
1978-79			64	16	29	45	38
1979-80			80	27	22	49	29
1980-81			68	16	23	39	54
1981-82			28	5	10	15	20
1982-83			74	16	11	27	52
12 yrs.		N Totals:	831	238	318	556	514
PLAYOFFS							
1971-72	STL	N	11	2	3	5	6
1972-73	NYR	N	10	0	0	0	0
1973-74	LA	N	5	0	4	4	0
1974-75			3	3	0	3	4
1975-76			9	1	4	5	6
1976-77			9	4	9	13	4
1977-78			2	0	0	0	0
1978-79			2	0	1	1	0
1979-80			4	1	0	1	2
1980-81			1	0	1	1	0
1981-82			10	2	1	3	32
11 yrs.		N Totals:	66	13	23	36	54

Traded to **St. Louis** by N.Y. Rangers with Jack Egers and Andre Dupont for Gene Carr, Jim Lorentz and Wayne Connelly, Nov. 15, 1971. Traded to **N.Y. Rangers** by St. Louis for Ab DeMarco, Mar. 2, 1973. Traded to **Los Angeles** by N.Y. Rangers with Sheldon Kannegiesser and Tom Williams for Gilles Marotte and Real Lemieux, Nov. 30, 1973.

Ron Murphy

MURPHY, ROBERT RONALD 5'11", 185 lbs.
B. Apr. 10, 1933, Hamilton, Ont. Left Wing, Shoots L

YEAR	TEAM & LEAGUE		GP	G	A	PTS	PIM
1952-53	NYR	N	15	3	1	4	0
1953-54			27	1	3	4	20
1954-55			66	14	16	30	36
1955-56			66	16	28	44	71
1956-57			33	7	12	19	14
1957-58	CHI	N	69	11	17	28	32
1958-59			59	17	30	47	52
1959-60			63	15	21	36	18
1960-61			70	21	19	40	30
1961-62			60	12	16	28	41
1962-63			68	18	16	34	28
1963-64			70	11	8	19	32
1964-65	DET	N	58	20	19	39	32
1965-66			32	10	7	17	10
	BOS	N	2	0	1	1	0
	2 team total		34	10	8	18	10
1966-67			39	11	16	27	6
1967-68			12	0	1	1	4
1968-69			60	16	38	54	26
1969-70			20	2	5	7	8
18 yrs.		N Totals:	889	205	274	479	460

Ron Murphy *continued*

PLAYOFFS

YEAR	TEAM & LEAGUE	GP	G	A	PTS	PIM
1955-56	**NYR** N	5	0	1	1	2
1956-57		5	0	0	0	0
1959-60	**CHI** N	4	1	0	1	0
1960-61*		12	2	1	3	0
1962-63		1	0	0	0	0
1963-64		7	0	1	1	8
1964-65	**DET** N	5	0	1	1	4
1967-68	**BOS** N	4	0	0	0	0
1968-69		10	4	4	8	12
9 yrs.	**N Totals:**	53	7	8	15	26

Traded to **Chicago** by N.Y. Rangers for Henry Ciesla, June, 1957. Traded to **Detroit** by Chicago with Autry Erickson for Art Stratton, John Miszuk, and Ian Cushenan, June 9, 1964. Traded by Detroit to **Boston** for Dean Prentice, Feb. 18, 1966.

Allan Murray

MURRAY, ALLAN 5'7½", 165 lbs.
B. Nov. 10, 1908, Stratford, Ont. Defense, Shoots L

YEAR	TEAM & LEAGUE	GP	G	A	PTS	PIM
1933-34	**NYA** N	48	1	1	2	20
1934-35		43	2	1	3	36
1935-36		48	1	0	1	33
1936-37		39	0	2	2	22
1937-38		46	0	1	1	34
1938-39		19	0	0	0	8
1939-40		34	1	4	5	10
7 yrs.	**N Totals:**	277	5	9	14	163

PLAYOFFS

YEAR	TEAM & LEAGUE	GP	G	A	PTS	PIM
1935-36	**NYA** N	5	0	0	0	2
1937-38		6	0	0	0	6
1939-40		3	0	0	0	0
3 yrs.	**N Totals:**	14	0	0	0	8

Bob Murray

MURRAY, ROBERT FREDERICK 5'10", 183 lbs.
B. Nov. 26, 1954, Kingston, Ont. Defense, Shoots R

YEAR	TEAM & LEAGUE	GP	G	A	PTS	PIM
1975-76	**CHI** N	64	1	2	3	44
1976-77		77	10	11	21	71
1977-78		70	14	17	31	41
1978-79		79	19	32	51	38
1979-80		74	16	34	50	60
1980-81		77	13	47	60	93
1981-82		45	8	22	30	48
1982-83		79	7	32	39	71
8 yrs.	**N Totals:**	565	88	197	285	466

PLAYOFFS

YEAR	TEAM & LEAGUE	GP	G	A	PTS	PIM
1976-77	**CHI** N	2	0	1	1	2
1977-78		4	1	4	5	2
1978-79		4	1	0	1	6
1979-80		7	2	4	6	6
1980-81		3	0	0	0	2
1981-82		15	1	6	7	16
1982-83		13	2	3	5	10
7 yrs.	**N Totals:**	48	7	18	25	44

Bob Murray

MURRAY, ROBERT JOHN 6'1", 195 lbs.
B. July 16, 1948, Burlington, Ont. Defense, Shoots R

YEAR	TEAM & LEAGUE	GP	G	A	PTS	PIM
1973-74	**ATL** N	62	0	3	3	34
1974-75		42	3	3	6	22
	VAN N	13	1	5	6	8
	2 team total	55	4	8	12	30
1975-76		65	2	5	7	28
1976-77		12	0	0	0	6
4 yrs.	**N Totals:**	194	6	16	22	98

PLAYOFFS

YEAR	TEAM & LEAGUE	GP	G	A	PTS	PIM
1973-74	**ATL** N	4	1	0	1	2
1974-75	**VAN** N	5	0	1	1	13
1975-76		5	0	1	1	13
3 yrs.	**N Totals:**	14	1	2	3	28

Traded to **Atlanta** by Montreal for Atlanta's third choice (Pierre Lagace) in 1977 Amateur Draft, May 29, 1973. Traded to **Vancouver** by Atlanta for Gerry Meehan, Mar. 9, 1975.

Jim Murray

MURRAY, JAMES ARNOLD 6'1", 165 lbs.
B. Nov. 25, 1943, Virden, Man. Defense, Shoots L

YEAR	TEAM & LEAGUE	GP	G	A	PTS	PIM
1967-68	**LA** N	30	0	2	2	14

Traded to **Los Angeles** by N.Y. Rangers with Trevor Fahey and Ken Turlik for Barclay Plager, June 16, 1967.

Ken Murray

MURRAY, KENNETH RICHARD 6', 180 lbs.
B. Jan. 22, 1948, Toronto, Ont. Defense, Shoots R

YEAR	TEAM & LEAGUE	GP	G	A	PTS	PIM
1969-70	**TOR** N	1	0	1	1	2
1970-71		4	0	0	0	0
1972-73	**NYI** N	39	0	4	4	59
	DET N	31	1	1	2	36
	2 team total	70	1	5	6	95
1974-75	**KC** N	8	0	2	2	14
1975-76		23	0	2	2	24
5 yrs.	**N Totals:**	106	1	10	11	135

Drafted by **Buffalo** from Toronto in Intra-League Draft, June 8, 1971. Drafted by **N.Y. Islanders** from Buffalo in Expansion Draft, June 6, 1972. Traded to **Detroit** by N.Y. Islanders with Brian Lavender for Ralph Stewart and Bob Cook, Jan. 17, 1973. Drafted by **Kansas City** from Detroit in Expansion Draft, June 12, 1974. Sold to **Los Angeles** by Kansas City, Feb. 10, 1975.

Leo Murray

MURRAY, LEONARD
B. Feb. 15, 1902, Portage La Prairie, Man.
Center, Shoots L

YEAR	TEAM & LEAGUE	GP	G	A	PTS	PIM
1932-33	**MONT** N	6	0	0	0	2

Randy Murray

MURRAY, RANDALL 6'1", 195 lbs.
B. Aug. 24, 1945, Chatham, Ont. Defense, Shoots R

YEAR	TEAM & LEAGUE	GP	G	A	PTS	PIM
1969-70	**TOR** N	3	0	0	0	2

Terry Murray

MURRAY, TERENCE RODNEY 6'2", 190 lbs.
B. July 20, 1950, Shawville, Que. Defense, Shoots R

YEAR	TEAM & LEAGUE	GP	G	A	PTS	PIM
1972-73	**CALIF** N	23	0	3	3	4
1973-74		58	0	12	12	48
1974-75		9	0	2	2	8
1975-76	**PHI** N	3	0	0	0	2
1976-77		36	0	13	13	14
	DET N	23	0	7	7	10
	2 team total	59	0	20	20	24
1978-79	**PHI** N	5	0	0	0	0
1980-81		71	1	17	18	53
1981-82	**WASH** N	74	3	22	25	60
8 yrs.	**N Totals:**	302	4	76	80	199

PLAYOFFS

YEAR	TEAM & LEAGUE	GP	G	A	PTS	PIM
1975-76	**PHI** N	6	0	1	1	0
1980-81		12	2	1	3	10
2 yrs.	**N Totals:**	18	2	2	4	10

Signed as free agent by **Philadelphia** Sept. 26, 1975. Traded to **Detroit** by Philadelphia with Bob Ritchie, Steve Coates and Dave Kelly for Rick LaPointe and Mike Korney, Feb. 17, 1977. Sold to **Detroit** by Philadelphia, Feb. 18, 1977. Sold to **Philadelphia** by Detroit, Nov. 1, 1977. Claimed by **Washington** from Philadelphia in 1981 Waiver Draft.

Troy Murray

MURRAY, TROY NORMAN 5'11", 180 lbs.
B. July 31, 1962, Calgary, Alta. Center, Shoots R

YEAR	TEAM & LEAGUE	GP	G	A	PTS	PIM
1981-82	**CHI** N	1	0	0	0	0
1982-83		54	8	8	16	27
2 yrs.	**N Totals:**	55	8	8	16	27

PLAYOFFS

YEAR	TEAM & LEAGUE	GP	G	A	PTS	PIM
1981-82	**CHI** N	7	1	0	1	5

Troy Murray continued

YEAR	TEAM & LEAGUE		GP	G	A	PTS	PIM
1982-83			2	0	0	0	0
2 yrs.		**N Totals:**	9	1	0	1	5

Hap Myers

MYERS, HAROLD ROBERT 5'11", 195 lbs.
B. July 28, 1947, Edmonton, Alta. Defense, Shoots L

YEAR	TEAM & LEAGUE		GP	G	A	PTS	PIM
1970-71	**BUF**	**N**	13	0	0	0	6

Murray Myers

MYERS, MURRAY 6', 185 lbs.
B. Feb. 9, 1952, Yellow Grass, Sask. Right Wing, Shoots R

YEAR	TEAM & LEAGUE		GP	G	A	PTS	PIM
1972-73	**PHI**	**W**	7	0	0	0	0
1973-74	**VAN**	**W**	61	22	20	42	28
1974-75			24	1	1	2	4
1975-76	**CIN**	**W**	56	14	15	29	12
4 yrs.		**W Totals:**	148	37	36	73	44

Vic Myles

MYLES, VICTOR ROBERT 6'1", 208 lbs.
B. Nov. 12, 1915, Fairlight, Sask. Defense, Shoots R

YEAR	TEAM & LEAGUE		GP	G	A	PTS	PIM
1942-43	**NYR**	**N**	45	6	9	15	57

Don Nachbaur

NACHBAUR, DONALD KENNETH 6'2", 200 lbs.
B. Jan. 30, 1959, Kitimat, B.C. Center, Shoots L

YEAR	TEAM & LEAGUE		GP	G	A	PTS	PIM
1980-81	**HART**	**N**	77	16	17	33	139
1981-82			77	5	21	26	117
1982-83	**EDM**	**N**	4	0	0	0	17
3 yrs.		**N Totals:**	158	21	38	59	273
PLAYOFFS							
1982-83	**EDM**	**N**	2	0	0	0	7

Traded to **Edmonton** by Hartford with Ken Linseman for Risto Siltanen and Brent Loney, August 19, 1982.

Jim Nahrgang

NAHRGANG, JAMES HERBERT 6', 185 lbs.
B. Apr. 17, 1951, Millbank, Ont. Defense, Shoots R

YEAR	TEAM & LEAGUE		GP	G	A	PTS	PIM
1974-75	**DET**	**N**	1	0	0	0	0
1975-76			3	0	1	1	0
1976-77			53	5	11	16	34
3 yrs.		**N Totals:**	57	5	12	17	34

Lou Nanne

NANNE, LOUIS VINCENT (Sweet Lou from the Soo) 6', 185 lbs.
B. June 2, 1941, Sault Ste. Marie, Ont. Defense, Shoots R

YEAR	TEAM & LEAGUE		GP	G	A	PTS	PIM
1967-68	**MINN**	**N**	2	0	1	1	0
1968-69			41	2	12	14	47
1969-70			74	3	20	23	75
1970-71			68	5	11	16	22
1971-72			78	21	28	49	27
1972-73			74	15	20	35	39
1973-74			76	11	21	32	46
1974-75			49	6	9	15	35
1975-76			79	3	14	17	45
1976-77			68	2	20	22	12
1977-78			26	0	1	1	8
11 yrs.		**N Totals:**	635	68	157	225	356
PLAYOFFS							
1969-70	**MINN**	**N**	5	0	2	2	2
1970-71			12	3	6	9	4
1971-72			7	0	0	0	2
1972-73			6	1	2	3	0
1976-77			2	0	0	0	2
5 yrs.		**N Totals:**	32	4	10	14	10

Richard Nantais

NANTAIS, RICHARD FRANCOIS 5'11", 188 lbs.
B. Oct. 27, 1954, Repentigny, Que. Left Wing, Shoots L

YEAR	TEAM & LEAGUE		GP	G	A	PTS	PIM
1974-75	**MINN**	**N**	18	4	1	5	9
1975-76			5	0	0	0	17
1976-77			40	1	3	4	53
3 yrs.		**N Totals:**	63	5	4	9	79

Mark Napier

NAPIER, ROBERT MARK 5'10", 182 lbs.
B. Jan. 28, 1957, Toronto, Ont. Right Wing, Shoots L

YEAR	TEAM & LEAGUE		GP	G	A	PTS	PIM
1975-76	**TOR**	**W**	78	43	50	93	20
1976-77	**BIRM**	**W**	80	60	36	96	24
1977-78			79	33	32	65	90
1978-79	**MONT**	**N**	54	11	20	31	11
1979-80			76	16	33	49	7
1980-81			79	35	36	71	24
1981-82			80	40	41	81	14
1982-83			73	40	27	67	6
8 yrs.		**N Totals:**	362	142	157	299	62
		W Totals:	237	136	118	254	134
PLAYOFFS							
1977-78	**BIRM**	**W**	5	0	2	2	14
1978-79*	**MONT**	**N**	12	3	2	5	2
1979-80			10	2	6	8	0
1980-81			3	0	0	0	2
1981-82			5	3	2	5	0
1982-83			3	0	0	0	0
6 yrs.		**N Totals:**	33	8	10	18	4
		W Totals:	5	0	2	2	14

Mats Naslund

NASLUND, MATS 5'7", 158 lbs.
B. Oct. 31, 1959, Timra, Sweden Left Wing, Shoots L

YEAR	TEAM & LEAGUE		GP	G	A	PTS	PIM
1982-83	**MONT**	**N**	74	26	45	71	10
PLAYOFFS							
1982-83	**MONT**	**N**	3	1	0	1	0

Ralph Nattrass

NATTRASS, RALPH WILLIAM 6', 200 lbs.
B. May 26, 1925, Gainsboro, Sask. Defense, Shoots R

YEAR	TEAM & LEAGUE		GP	G	A	PTS	PIM
1946-47	**CHI**	**N**	35	4	5	9	34
1947-48			60	5	12	17	79
1948-49			60	4	10	14	99
1949-50			68	5	11	16	96
4 yrs.		**N Totals:**	223	18	38	56	308

Ric Nattress

NATTRESS, RIC 6'2", 208 lbs.
B. May 25, 1962, Hamilton, Ont. Defense, Shoots R

YEAR	TEAM & LEAGUE		GP	G	A	PTS	PIM
1982-83	**MONT**	**N**	40	1	3	4	19
PLAYOFFS							
1982-83	**MONT**	**N**	3	0	0	0	10

Robbie Neale

NEALE, ROBERT 6', 185 lbs.
B. Apr. 17, 1953, Brandon, Man. Center, Shoots L

YEAR	TEAM & LEAGUE		GP	G	A	PTS	PIM
1973-74	**CLEVE**	**W**	43	8	9	17	30
1974-75			9	1	3	4	4
	WINN	**W**	7	0	2	2	4
	2 team total		16	1	5	6	8
2 yrs.		**W Totals:**	59	9	14	23	38
PLAYOFFS							
1973-74	**CLEVE**	**W**	5	0	0	0	4

Victor Nechaev

NECHAEV, VICTOR — 6'1", 183 lbs.
B. Jan. 28, 1955, Kuib.-Vost., Siberia — Center, Shoots L

YEAR	TEAM & LEAGUE		GP	G	A	PTS	PIM
1982-83	**LA**	**N**	3	1	0	1	0

Ned Nedomansky

NEDOMANSKY, VACLAV (Big Ned) — 6'2", 205 lbs.
B. Mar. 14, 1944, Hodonin, Czechoslavakia — Right Wing, Shoots L

YEAR	TEAM & LEAGUE		GP	G	A	PTS	PIM
1974-75	**TOR**	**W**	78	41	40	81	19
1975-76			81	56	42	98	8
1976-77	**BIRM**	**W**	81	36	33	69	10
1977-78			12	2	3	5	6
	DET	**N**	63	11	17	28	2
	2 team total		75	13	20	33	8
1978-79			80	38	35	73	19
1979-80			79	35	39	74	13
1980-81			74	12	20	32	30
1981-82			68	12	28	40	22
1982-83	**NYR**	**N**	1	1	0	1	0
	STL	**N**	22	2	9	11	2
	NYR	**N**	34	11	8	19	0
	3 team total		57	14	17	31	2
9 yrs.		**N Totals:**	421	122	156	278	88
		W Totals:	252	135	118	253	43
PLAYOFFS							
1974-75	**TOR**	**W**	6	3	1	4	9
1977-78	**DET**	**N**	7	3	5	8	0
2 yrs.		**N Totals:**	7	3	5	8	0
		W Totals:	6	3	1	4	9

Signed as free agent by **Detroit** Nov. 18, 1977. Signed as a free agent by **N.Y. Rangers** Oct. 5, 1982. Acquired by **St. Louis** from N.Y. Rangers on waivers, Oct. 13, 1982. Traded to **N.Y. Rangers** by St. Louis with Glen Hanlon for Andre Dore, Jan. 4, 1983.

Greg Neeld

NEELD, GREGORY — 6', 192 lbs.
B. Feb. 25, 1955, Vancouver, B.C. — Defense

YEAR	TEAM & LEAGUE		GP	G	A	PTS	PIM
1975-76	**TOR**	**W**	17	0	1	1	18

Bob Neely

NEELY, ROBERT BARRY — 6'1", 210 lbs.
B. Nov. 9, 1953, Sarnia, Ont. — Left Wing, Shoots L

YEAR	TEAM & LEAGUE		GP	G	A	PTS	PIM
1973-74	**TOR**	**N**	54	5	7	12	98
1974-75			57	5	16	21	61
1975-76			69	9	13	22	89
1976-77			70	17	16	33	16
1977-78			11	0	1	1	0
	COLO	**N**	22	3	6	9	2
	2 team total		33	3	7	10	2
5 yrs.		**N Totals:**	283	39	59	98	266
PLAYOFFS							
1973-74	**TOR**	**N**	4	1	3	4	0
1974-75			3	0	0	0	2
1975-76			10	3	1	4	7
1976-77			9	1	3	4	6
4 yrs.		**N Totals:**	26	5	7	12	15

Sold to **Colorado** by Toronto, Jan. 9, 1978. Sold to **Toronto** by Colorado, May 30, 1978.

Jim Neilson

NEILSON, JAMES ANTHONY (Chief) — 6'2", 205 lbs.
B. Nov. 28, 1941, Big River, Sask. — Defense, Shoots L

YEAR	TEAM & LEAGUE		GP	G	A	PTS	PIM
1962-63	**NYR**	**N**	69	5	11	16	38
1963-64			69	5	24	29	93
1964-65			62	0	13	13	58
1965-66			65	4	19	23	84
1966-67			61	4	11	15	65
1967-68			67	6	29	35	60
1968-69			76	10	34	44	95
1969-70			62	3	20	23	75
1970-71			77	8	24	32	69
1971-72			78	7	30	37	56
1972-73			52	4	16	20	35

Jim Neilson continued

YEAR	TEAM & LEAGUE		GP	G	A	PTS	PIM
1973-74			72	4	7	11	38
1974-75	**CALIF**	**N**	72	3	17	20	56
1975-76			26	1	6	7	20
1976-77	**CLEVE**	**N**	47	3	17	20	42
1977-78			68	2	21	23	20
1978-79	**EDM**	**W**	35	0	5	5	18
17 yrs.		**N Totals:**	1023	69	299	368	904
		W Totals:	35	0	5	5	18
PLAYOFFS							
1966-67	**NYR**	**N**	4	1	0	1	0
1967-68			6	1	1	2	4
1968-69			4	0	3	3	5
1969-70			6	0	1	1	8
1970-71			13	0	3	3	30
1971-72			10	0	3	3	8
1972-73			10	0	4	4	2
1973-74			12	0	1	1	4
8 yrs.		**N Totals:**	65	2	16	18	61

Drafted by **California** from N.Y. Rangers in Intra-League Draft, June 10, 1974. Put on **Minnesota** Reserve List after Cleveland-Minnesota Dispersal Draft, June 15, 1978.

Gordie Nelson

NELSON, GORDON WILLIAM — 5'7", 180 lbs.
B. May 10, 1947, Kinistino, Sask. — Defense, Shoots L

YEAR	TEAM & LEAGUE		GP	G	A	PTS	PIM
1969-70	**TOR**	**N**	3	0	0	0	11

Eric Nesterenko

NESTERENKO, ERIC PAUL — 6'2", 197 lbs.
B. Oct. 31, 1933, Flin Flon, Man. — Right Wing, Shoots R

YEAR	TEAM & LEAGUE		GP	G	A	PTS	PIM
1951-52	**TOR**	**N**	1	0	0	0	0
1952-53			35	10	6	16	27
1953-54			68	14	9	23	70
1954-55			62	15	15	30	99
1955-56			40	4	6	10	65
1956-57	**CHI**	**N**	24	8	15	23	32
1957-58			70	20	18	38	104
1958-59			70	16	18	34	81
1959-60			61	13	23	36	71
1960-61			68	19	19	38	125
1961-62			68	15	14	29	97
1962-63			67	12	15	27	103
1963-64			70	7	19	26	93
1964-65			56	14	16	30	63
1965-66			67	15	25	40	58
1966-67			68	14	23	37	38
1967-68			71	11	25	36	37
1968-69			72	15	17	32	29
1969-70			67	16	18	34	26
1970-71			76	8	15	23	28
1971-72			38	4	8	12	27
1973-74	**LA**	**W**	29	2	5	7	8
22 yrs.		**N Totals:**	1219	250	324	574	1273
		W Totals:	29	2	5	7	8
PLAYOFFS							
1953-54	**TOR**	**N**	5	0	1	1	9
1954-55			4	0	1	1	6
1958-59	**CHI**	**N**	6	2	2	4	8
1959-60			4	0	0	0	2
1960-61*			11	2	3	5	6
1961-62			12	0	5	5	22
1962-63			6	2	3	5	8
1963-64			7	2	1	3	8
1964-65			14	2	2	4	16
1965-66			6	1	0	1	4
1966-67			6	1	2	3	2
1967-68			10	0	1	1	2
1969-70			7	1	2	3	4
1970-71			18	0	1	1	19
1971-72			8	0	0	0	11
15 yrs.		**N Totals:**	124	13	24	37	127

Purchased by **Chicago** from Toronto, along with Harry Lumley, for $40,-000, May 21, 1956.

Lance Nethery

NETHERY, LANCE 6'1", 185 lbs.
B. June 28, 1957, Toronto, Ont. Center, Shoots L

YEAR	TEAM & LEAGUE		GP	G	A	PTS	PIM
1980-81	**NYR**	**N**	33	11	12	23	12
1981-82			5	0	0	0	0
	EDM	**N**	3	0	2	2	2
	2 team total		8	0	2	2	2
2 yrs.		**N Totals:**	41	11	14	25	14
PLAYOFFS							
1980-81	**NYR**	**N**	14	5	3	8	9

Traded to **Edmonton** by N.Y. Rangers for Ed Mio, Dec. 11, 1981.

Ray Neufeld

NEUFELD, RAYMOND MATTHEW 6'2", 215 lbs.
B. Apr. 15, 1959, St. Boniface, Man. Right Wing, Shoots R

YEAR	TEAM & LEAGUE		GP	G	A	PTS	PIM
1979-80	**HART**	**N**	8	1	0	1	0
1980-81			52	5	10	15	44
1981-82			19	4	3	7	4
1982-83			80	26	31	57	86
4 yrs.		**N Totals:**	159	36	44	80	134
PLAYOFFS							
1979-80	**HART**	**N**	2	1	0	1	0

Mike Neville

NEVILLE, MICHAEL R.
B. Toronto, Ont. Forward

YEAR	TEAM & LEAGUE		GP	G	A	PTS	PIM
1917-18	**TOR**	**N**	1	1	0	1	0
1924-25			12	1	0	1	4
1925-26			33	3	3	6	8
1930-31	**NYA**	**N**	16	1	0	1	2
4 yrs.		**N Totals:**	62	6	3	9	14
PLAYOFFS							
1924-25	**TOR**	**N**	2	0	0	0	0

Bob Nevin

NEVIN, ROBERT FRANK 6', 190 lbs.
B. Mar. 18, 1938, South Porcupine, Ont. Right Wing, Shoots R

YEAR	TEAM & LEAGUE		GP	G	A	PTS	PIM
1957-58	**TOR**	**N**	4	0	0	0	0
1958-59			2	0	0	0	2
1960-61			68	21	37	58	13
1961-62			69	15	30	45	10
1962-63			58	12	21	33	4
1963-64			49	7	12	19	26
	NYR	**N**	14	5	4	9	9
	2 team total		63	12	16	28	35
1964-65			64	16	14	30	28
1965-66			69	29	33	62	10
1966-67			67	20	24	44	6
1967-68			74	28	30	58	20
1968-69			71	31	25	56	14
1969-70			68	18	19	37	8
1970-71			78	21	25	46	10
1971-72	**MINN**	**N**	72	15	19	34	6
1972-73			66	5	13	18	0
1973-74	**LA**	**N**	78	20	30	50	12
1974-75			80	31	41	72	19
1975-76			77	13	42	55	14
1976-77	**EDM**	**W**	13	3	2	5	0
19 yrs.		**N Totals:**	1128	307	419	726	211
		W Totals:	13	3	2	5	0
PLAYOFFS							
1960-61	**TOR**	**N**	5	1	0	1	2
1961-62*			12	2	4	6	6
1962-63*			10	3	0	3	2
1966-67	**NYR**	**N**	4	0	3	3	2
1967-68			6	0	3	3	4
1968-69			4	0	2	2	0
1969-70			6	1	1	2	2
1970-71			13	5	3	8	0
1971-72	**MINN**	**N**	7	1	1	2	0
1973-74	**LA**	**N**	5	1	0	1	2
1974-75			3	0	0	0	0

Bob Nevin continued

YEAR	TEAM & LEAGUE		GP	G	A	PTS	PIM
1975-76			9	2	1	3	4
12 yrs.		**N Totals:**	84	16	18	34	24

Traded by Toronto to **N.Y. Rangers** with Dick Duff, Arnie Brown, Bill Collins and Rod Seiling for Andy Bathgate and Don McKenney, Feb. 22, 1964. Traded to **Minnesota** by N.Y. Rangers (May 25, 1971) for a player to be named later (Bobby Rousseau, June 8, 1971). Claimed by **Los Angeles** from Minnesota in Reverse Draft, June 13, 1973.

John Newberry

NEWBERRY, JOHN 6', 190 lbs.
B. Apr. 8, 1962, Port Alberni, B.C. Shoots L

YEAR	TEAM & LEAGUE		GP	G	A	PTS	PIM
PLAYOFFS							
1982-83	**MONT**	**N**	2	0	0	0	0

Rick Newell

NEWELL, GORDON RICHARD 5'11", 180 lbs.
B. Feb. 18, 1948, Winnipeg, Man. Defense, Shoots L

YEAR	TEAM & LEAGUE		GP	G	A	PTS	PIM
1972-73	**DET**	**N**	3	0	0	0	0
1973-74			4	0	0	0	0
1974-75	**PHOE**	**W**	25	0	4	4	39
3 yrs.		**N Totals:**	7	0	0	0	0
		W Totals:	25	0	4	4	39
PLAYOFFS							
1974-75	**PHOE**	**W**	5	0	1	1	2

Traded to **Detroit** by N.Y. Rangers with Gary Doak for Joe Zanussi and Detroit's first choice (Albert Blanchard) in 1972 Amateur Draft, May 24, 1972.

Dan Newman

NEWMAN, DANIEL KENNETH 6'1", 195 lbs.
B. Jan. 26, 1952, Windsor, Ont. Left Wing, Shoots L

YEAR	TEAM & LEAGUE		GP	G	A	PTS	PIM
1976-77	**NYR**	**N**	41	9	8	17	37
1977-78			59	5	13	18	22
1978-79	**MONT**	**N**	6	0	2	2	4
1979-80	**EDM**	**N**	10	3	1	4	0
4 yrs.		**N Totals:**	116	17	24	41	63
PLAYOFFS							
1977-78	**NYR**	**N**	3	0	0	0	4

Claimed by **Montreal** from N.Y. Rangers after Rangers claimed Mike Korney from Montreal in League Waiver Draft, Oct. 9, 1978. Traded to **Edmonton** by Montreal with Dave Lumley for Edmonton's second round choice in the 1980 Entry Draft, June 18, 1979. Traded to **Boston** by Edmonton for Bobby Schmautz, Dec. 10, 1979.

John Newman

NEWMAN, JOHN
B. Unknown Defense

YEAR	TEAM & LEAGUE		GP	G	A	PTS	PIM
1930-31	**DET**	**N**	8	1	1	2	0

Bernie Nicholls

NICHOLLS, BERNARD IRVINE 6', 185 lbs.
B. June 24, 1961, Haliburton, Ont. Center, Shoots R

YEAR	TEAM & LEAGUE		GP	G	A	PTS	PIM
1981-82	**LA**	**N**	22	14	18	32	27
1982-83			71	28	22	50	124
2 yrs.		**N Totals:**	93	42	40	82	151
PLAYOFFS							
1981-82	**LA**	**N**	10	4	0	4	23

Al Nicholson

NICHOLSON, ALLAN DOUGLAS 6'1", 180 lbs.
B. Apr. 26, 1936, Estevan, Sask. Left Wing, Shoots L

YEAR	TEAM & LEAGUE		GP	G	A	PTS	PIM
1955-56	**BOS**	**N**	14	0	0	0	4
1956-57			5	0	1	1	0
2 yrs.		**N Totals:**	19	0	1	1	4

Edward Nicholson

NICHOLSON, EDWARD GEORGE 5'7", 171 lbs.
B. Sept. 9, 1923, Portsmouth, Ont. Defense, Shoots L

YEAR	TEAM & LEAGUE		GP	G	A	PTS	PIM
1947-48	**DET**	**N**	1	0	0	0	0

Graeme Nicholson

NICHOLSON, GRAEME BUTTE 6', 186 lbs.
B. Jan. 13, 1958, North Bay, Ont. Defense, Shoots R

YEAR	TEAM & LEAGUE		GP	G	A	PTS	PIM
1981-82	**COLO**	**N**	41	2	7	9	51
1982-83	**NYR**	**N**	10	0	0	0	0
2 yrs.		**N Totals:**	51	2	7	9	51

Signed as free agent by **Colorado** Sept. 2, 1981. Acquired by **N.Y. Rangers** in Waiver Draft, Oct. 4, 1982.

John Nicholson

NICHOLSON, JOHN IVAN 5'9½", 170 lbs.
B. Sept. 9, 1914, Charlottetown, P.E.I. Left Wing, Shoots L

YEAR	TEAM & LEAGUE		GP	G	A	PTS	PIM
1937-38	**CHI**	**N**	2	1	0	1	0

Neil Nicholson

NICHOLSON, NEIL ANDREWS 5'11", 180 lbs.
B. Sept. 12, 1949, Saint John, N.B. Defense, Shoots R

YEAR	TEAM & LEAGUE		GP	G	A	PTS	PIM
1972-73	**NYI**	**N**	30	3	1	4	23
1973-74			8	0	0	0	0
1977-78			1	0	0	0	0
3 yrs.		**N Totals:**	39	3	1	4	23
PLAYOFFS							
1969-70	**OAK**	**N**	2	0	0	0	0

Drafted by **N.Y. Islanders** from Salt Lake (WHL) in Inter-league Draft, June 6, 1972.

Paul Nicholson

NICHOLSON, PAUL 6', 190 lbs.
B. Feb. 16, 1954, London, Ont. Left Wing, Shoots L

YEAR	TEAM & LEAGUE		GP	G	A	PTS	PIM
1974-75	**WASH**	**N**	39	4	5	9	7
1975-76			14	0	2	2	9
1976-77			9	0	1	1	2
3 yrs.		**N Totals:**	62	4	8	12	18

Jim Niekamp

NIEKAMP, JAMES LAWRENCE 6', 170 lbs.
B. Mar. 11, 1946, Detroit, Mich. Defense, Shoots R

YEAR	TEAM & LEAGUE		GP	G	A	PTS	PIM
1970-71	**DET**	**N**	24	0	2	2	27
1971-72			5	0	0	0	0
1972-73	**LA**	**W**	78	7	22	29	155
1973-74			76	2	19	21	95
1974-75	**PHOE**	**W**	71	2	26	28	66
1975-76			79	4	14	18	77
1976-77			79	1	15	16	91
7 yrs.		**N Totals:**	29	0	2	2	27
		W Totals:	383	16	96	112	484
PLAYOFFS							
1972-73	**LA**	**W**	6	2	1	3	10
1975-76	**PHOE**	**W**	5	1	0	1	0
2 yrs.		**W Totals:**	11	3	1	4	10

Traded to **Vancouver** by Detroit for Ralph Stewart, March 6, 1972.

Frank Nighbor

NIGHBOR, FRANK (Dutch)
B. Jan. 26, 1893, Pembroke, Ont. Center
Won Hart Trophy, 1923-24
Won Lady Byng Trophy, 1924–25, 1925-26
Hall of Fame, 1945

YEAR	TEAM & LEAGUE		GP	G	A	PTS	PIM
1917-18	**OTTA**	**N**	9	11	0	11	3
1918-19			18	18	4	22	27
1919-20			23	26	7	33	18
1920-21			24	18	3	21	10
1921-22			20	7	9	16	16
1922-23			22	11	5	16	16

Frank Nighbor continued

YEAR	TEAM & LEAGUE		GP	G	A	PTS	PIM
1923-24			20	10	3	13	14
1924-25			26	5	2	7	18
1925-26			35	12	**13**	25	40
1926-27			39	6	6	12	26
1927-28			42	8	5	13	46
1928-29			32	1	4	5	22
1929-30			19	0	1	1	8
	TOR	**N**	22	2	0	2	2
	2 team total		41	2	1	3	10
13 yrs.		**N Totals:**	351	135	62	197	266
PLAYOFFS							
1918-19	**OTTA**	**N**	2	0	3	3	0
1919-20*			5	6	1	7	3
1920-21*			7	1	3	4	2
1921-22			2	2	0	2	4
1922-23*			8	1	2	3	10
1923-24			2	0	1	1	2
1925-26			2	0	0	0	2
1926-27*			6	1	0	1	2
1927-28			2	0	0	0	2
9 yrs.		**N Totals:**	36	11	10	21	27

Frank Nigro

NIGRO, FRANK 5'9", 182 lbs.
B. Feb. 11, 1960, Richmond Hill, Ont. Forward

YEAR	TEAM & LEAGUE		GP	G	A	PTS	PIM
1982-83	**TOR**	**N**	51	6	15	21	23
PLAYOFFS							
1982-83	**TOR**	**N**	3	0	0	0	2

Chris Nilan

NILAN, CHRISTOPHER JOHN 6', 200 lbs.
B. Feb. 9, 1958, Boston, Mass. Right Wing, Shoots R

YEAR	TEAM & LEAGUE		GP	G	A	PTS	PIM
1979-80	**MONT**	**N**	15	0	2	2	50
1980-81			57	7	8	15	262
1981-82			49	7	4	11	204
1982-83			66	6	8	14	213
4 yrs.		**N Totals:**	187	20	22	42	729
PLAYOFFS							
1979-80	**MONT**	**N**	5	0	0	0	2
1980-81			2	0	0	0	0
1981-82			5	1	1	2	22
1982-83			3	0	0	0	5
4 yrs.		**N Totals:**	15	1	1	2	29

Jim Nill

NILL, JAMES EDWARD 6', 175 lbs.
B. Apr. 11, 1958, Hanna, Alta. Right Wing, Shoots R

YEAR	TEAM & LEAGUE		GP	G	A	PTS	PIM
1981-82	**STL**	**N**	61	9	12	21	127
	VAN	**N**	8	1	2	3	5
	2 team total		69	10	14	24	132
1982-83			65	7	15	22	136
2 yrs.		**N Totals:**	134	17	29	46	268
PLAYOFFS							
1981-82	**VAN**	**N**	16	4	3	7	67
1982-83			4	0	0	0	6
2 yrs.		**N Totals:**	20	4	3	7	73

Traded to **Vancouver** by St. Louis with Tony Currie, Rick Heinz and St. Louis' fourth round choice (Shawn Kilroy) in 1982 Entry Draft for Glen Hanlon, Mar. 9, 1982.

Kent Nilsson

NILSSON, KENT 6'1", 185 lbs.
B. Aug. 31, 1956, Nynashamn, Sweden Center, Shoots L

YEAR	TEAM & LEAGUE		GP	G	A	PTS	PIM
1977-78	**WINN**	**W**	80	42	65	107	8
1978-79			78	39	68	107	8
1979-80	**ATL**	**N**	80	40	53	93	10
1980-81	**CALG**	**N**	80	49	82	131	26
1981-82			41	26	29	55	8
1982-83			80	46	58	104	10
6 yrs.		**N Totals:**	281	161	222	383	54
		W Totals:	158	81	133	214	16

Kent Nilsson continued

PLAYOFFS

YEAR	TEAM & LEAGUE		GP	G	A	PTS	PIM
1977-78	**WINN**	**W**	9	2	8	10	10
1978-79			10	3	11	14	4
1979-80	**ATL**	**N**	4	0	0	0	2
1980-81	**CALG**	**N**	14	3	9	12	2
1981-82			3	0	3	3	2
1982-83			9	1	11	12	2
6 yrs.		**N Totals:**	30	4	23	27	8
		W Totals:	19	5	19	24	14

Reclaimed by **Atlanta** from Winnipeg prior to Expansion Draft, June 9, 1979.

Ulf Nilsson

NILSSON, ULF GOSTA 5'11", 175 lbs.
B. May 11, 1950, Nynashamn, Sweden Center, Shoots R

YEAR	TEAM & LEAGUE		GP	G	A	PTS	PIM
1974-75	**WINN**	**W**	78	26	94	120	79
1975-76			78	38	76	114	84
1976-77			71	39	**85**	124	89
1977-78			73	37	**89**	126	89
1978-79	**NYR**	**N**	59	27	39	66	21
1979-80			50	14	44	58	20
1980-81			51	14	25	39	42
1982-83			10	2	4	6	2
8 yrs.		**N Totals:**	170	57	112	169	85
		W Totals:	300	140	344	484	341

PLAYOFFS

YEAR	TEAM & LEAGUE		GP	G	A	PTS	PIM
1975-76	**WINN**	**W**	13	7	19	26	6
1976-77			20	6	21	27	33
1977-78			9	1	13	14	12
1978-79	**NYR**	**N**	2	0	0	0	2
1979-80			9	0	6	6	2
1980-81			14	8	8	16	23
6 yrs.		**N Totals:**	25	8	14	22	27
		W Totals:	42	14	53	67	51

Signed as free agent by **N.Y. Rangers** June 5, 1978.

Lou Nistico

NISTICO, LOUIS 5'7", 170 lbs.
B. Jan. 25, 1953, Thunder Bay, Ont. Center, Shoots L

YEAR	TEAM & LEAGUE		GP	G	A	PTS	PIM
1973-74	**TOR**	**W**	13	1	3	4	14
1974-75			29	11	11	22	75
1975-76			65	12	22	34	120
1976-77	**BIRM**	**W**	79	20	36	56	166
1977-78	**COLO**	**N**	3	0	0	0	0
5 yrs.		**N Totals:**	3	0	0	0	0
		W Totals:	186	44	72	116	375

PLAYOFFS

YEAR	TEAM & LEAGUE		GP	G	A	PTS	PIM
1974-75	**TOR**	**W**	6	6	1	7	19

Reg Noble

NOBLE, REGINALD 5'8", 180 lbs.
B. June 23, 1895 Left Wing, Shoots L
Hall of Fame, 1962

YEAR	TEAM & LEAGUE		GP	G	A	PTS	PIM
1917-18	**TOR**	**N**	20	28	0	28	23
1918-19			17	11	3	14	35
1919-20			24	24	7	31	51
1920-21			24	20	6	26	54
1921-22			24	17	8	25	10
1922-23			24	12	10	22	41
1923-24			23	12	3	15	23
1924-25			3	1	0	1	4
	MON(M)	**N**	27	7	6	13	58
	2 team total		30	8	6	14	62
1925-26			30	9	9	18	36
1926-27			44	3	3	6	12
1927-28	**DET**	**N**	44	6	8	14	63
1928-29			44	6	4	10	52
1929-30			43	6	4	10	72
1930-31			44	2	5	7	42
1931-32			48	3	3	6	72
1932-33			5	0	0	0	6
	MON(M)	**N**	27	0	0	0	16
	2 team total		32	0	0	0	22
16 yrs.		**N Totals:**	515	167	79	246	670

Reg Noble continued

PLAYOFFS

YEAR	TEAM & LEAGUE		GP	G	A	PTS	PIM
1917-18*	**TOR**	**N**	7	2	1	3	3
1920-21			2	0	0	0	0
1921-22*			7	0	2	2	20
1925-26*	**MON(M)**	**N**	8	0	0	0	10
1926-27			2	0	0	0	2
1928-29	**DET**	**N**	2	0	0	0	2
1931-32			2	0	0	0	0
7 yrs.		**N Totals:**	30	2	3	5	37

Claude Noel

NOEL, CLAUDE 5'11", 165 lbs.
B. Oct. 31, 1955, Kirkland Lake, Ont. Center, Shoots L

YEAR	TEAM & LEAGUE		GP	G	A	PTS	PIM
1979-80	**WASH**	**N**	7	0	0	0	0

Pat Nolan

NOLAN, PATRICK
B. Unknown Forward

YEAR	TEAM & LEAGUE		GP	G	A	PTS	PIM
1921-22	**TOR**	**N**	2	0	0	0	0

Ted Nolan

NOLAN, THEODORE JOHN 6', 185 lbs.
B. Apr. 7, 1958, Sault Ste. Marie, Ont. Center, Shoots L

YEAR	TEAM & LEAGUE		GP	G	A	PTS	PIM
1981-82	**DET**	**N**	41	4	13	17	45

Simon Nolet

NOLET, SIMON LAURENT 5'9", 185 lbs.
B. Nov. 23, 1941, St. Odilon, Que, Right Wing, Shoots R

YEAR	TEAM & LEAGUE		GP	G	A	PTS	PIM
1967-68	**PHI**	**N**	4	0	0	0	2
1968-69			35	4	10	14	8
1969-70			56	22	22	44	36
1970-71			74	9	19	28	42
1971-72			67	23	20	43	22
1972-73			70	16	20	36	6
1973-74			52	19	17	36	13
1974-75	**KC**	**N**	72	26	32	58	30
1975-76			41	10	15	25	16
	PITT	**N**	39	9	8	17	2
	2 team total		80	19	23	42	18
1976-77	**COLO**	**N**	52	12	19	31	10
10 yrs.		**N Totals:**	562	150	182	332	187

PLAYOFFS

YEAR	TEAM & LEAGUE		GP	G	A	PTS	PIM
1967-68	**PHI**	**N**	1	0	0	0	0
1970-71			4	2	1	3	0
1972-73			11	3	1	4	4
1973-74*			15	1	1	2	4
1975-76	**PITT**	**N**	3	0	0	0	0
5 yrs.		**N Totals:**	34	6	3	9	8

Drafted by **Kansas City** from Philadelphia in Expansion Draft, June 12, 1974. Traded to **Pittsburgh** by Kansas City with Ed Gilbert and Kansas City's first round choice (Blair Chapman) in 1976 Amateur Draft for Steve Durbano, Chuck Arnason and Pittsburgh's first round choice (Paul Gardner) in same draft, Jan. 9, 1975. Traded to **Denver** by Pittsburgh with goaltender Michel Plasse as compensation for Pittsburgh's signing of goaltender Denis Herron as free agent, Aug. 7, 1976.

Joe Noris

NORIS, JOSEPH S. 6', 185 lbs.
B. Oct. 26, 1951, Denver, Colo. Defense, Shoots R

YEAR	TEAM & LEAGUE		GP	G	A	PTS	PIM
1971-72	**PITT**	**N**	35	2	5	7	20
1972-73	**STL**	**N**	2	0	0	0	0
1973-74	**BUF**	**N**	18	0	0	0	2
1975-76	**SD**	**W**	80	28	40	68	24
1976-77			73	35	57	92	30
1977-78	**BIRM**	**W**	45	9	19	28	6
6 yrs.		**N Totals:**	55	2	5	7	22
		W Totals:	198	72	116	188	60

PLAYOFFS

YEAR	TEAM & LEAGUE		GP	G	A	PTS	PIM
1975-76	**SD**	**W**	11	2	4	6	6
1976-77			7	2	1	3	6

Joe Noris continued

YEAR	TEAM	LEAGUE	GP	G	A	PTS	PIM
2 yrs.		**W Totals:**	18	4	5	9	12

Traded to **St. Louis** by Pittsburgh for Jim Shires, Jan. 8, 1973. Drafted by **Buffalo** from St. Louis in Intra-League Draft, June 12, 1973.

Rod Norrish

NORRISH, ROD 5'10", 185 lbs.
B. Nov. 27, 1951, Saskatoon, Sask. Left Wing, Shoots L

YEAR	TEAM	LEAGUE	GP	G	A	PTS	PIM
1973-74	**MINN**	**N**	9	2	1	3	0
1974-75			12	1	2	3	2
2 yrs.		**N Totals:**	21	3	3	6	2

Baldy Northcott

NORTHCOTT, LAWRENCE 6', 184 lbs.
B. Sept. 7, 1908, Calgary, Alta. Left Wing, Shoots L

YEAR	TEAM	LEAGUE	GP	G	A	PTS	PIM
1928-29	**MON(M)**	**N**	6	0	0	0	0
1929-30			41	10	1	11	6
1930-31			22	7	3	10	15
1931-32			47	19	6	25	33
1932-33			47	22	21	43	30
1933-34			47	20	13	33	27
1934-35			47	9	14	23	44
1935-36			48	15	21	36	41
1936-37			48	15	14	29	18
1937-38			47	11	12	23	50
1938-39	**CHI**	**N**	46	5	7	12	9
11 yrs.		**N Totals:**	446	133	112	245	273

PLAYOFFS

YEAR	TEAM	LEAGUE	GP	G	A	PTS	PIM
1929-30	**MON(M)**	**N**	4	0	0	0	4
1930-31			2	0	1	1	0
1931-32			4	1	2	3	4
1932-33			2	0	0	0	4
1933-34			4	2	0	2	0
1934-35*			7	4	1	5	0
1935-36			3	0	0	0	0
1936-37			5	1	1	2	2
8 yrs.		**N Totals:**	31	8	5	13	14

Craig Norwich

NORWICH, CRAIG RICHARD 5'11", 175 lbs.
B. Dec. 15, 1955, New York, N.Y. Defense, Shoots L

YEAR	TEAM	LEAGUE	GP	G	A	PTS	PIM
1977-78	**CIN**	**W**	65	7	23	30	48
1978-79			80	6	51	57	73
1979-80	**WINN**	**N**	70	10	35	45	36
1980-81	**STL**	**N**	23	4	12	16	14
	COLO	**N**	11	3	11	14	10
	2 team total		34	7	23	30	24
4 yrs.		**N Totals:**	104	17	58	75	60
		W Totals:	145	13	74	87	121

PLAYOFFS

YEAR	TEAM	LEAGUE	GP	G	A	PTS	PIM
1978-79	**CIN**	**W**	3	0	1	1	4

Traded to **St. Louis** by Winnipeg for Rick Bowness, June 19, 1980. Claimed on waivers by **Colorado** from St. Louis, Feb. 2, 1981.

Lee Norwood

NORWOOD, LEE CHARLES 6', 190 lbs.
B. Feb. 2, 1960, Oakland, Cal. Defense, Shoots L

YEAR	TEAM	LEAGUE	GP	G	A	PTS	PIM
1980-81	**QUE**	**N**	11	1	1	2	9
1981-82			2	0	0	0	2
	WASH	**N**	26	7	10	17	125
	2 team total		28	7	10	17	127
1982-83			8	0	1	1	14
3 yrs.		**N Totals:**	47	8	12	20	150

PLAYOFFS

YEAR	TEAM	LEAGUE	GP	G	A	PTS	PIM
1980-81	**QUE**	**N**	3	0	0	0	2

Traded to **Washington** by Quebec for Tim Tookey and Washington's seventh round choice (Daniel Poudrier) in 1982 Entry Draft, Feb. 1, 1982.

Milan Novy

NOVY, MILAN 5'10", 196 lbs.
B. Sept. 23, 1951, Kladno, Czechoslovakia Center, Shoots L

YEAR	TEAM	LEAGUE	GP	G	A	PTS	PIM
1982-83	**WASH**	**N**	73	18	30	48	16

PLAYOFFS

YEAR	TEAM	LEAGUE	GP	G	A	PTS	PIM
1982-83	**WASH**	**N**	2	0	0	0	0

Hank Nowak

NOWAK, HENRY STANLEY 6'1", 195 lbs.
B. Nov. 24, 1950, Oshawa, Ont. Left Wing, Shoots L

YEAR	TEAM	LEAGUE	GP	G	A	PTS	PIM
1973-74	**PITT**	**N**	13	0	0	0	11
1974-75	**DET**	**N**	56	8	14	22	69
	BOS	**N**	21	4	7	11	26
	2 team total		77	12	21	33	95
1975-76			66	7	3	10	41
1976-77			24	7	5	12	14
4 yrs.		**N Totals:**	180	26	29	55	161

PLAYOFFS

YEAR	TEAM	LEAGUE	GP	G	A	PTS	PIM
1974-75	**BOS**	**N**	3	1	0	1	0
1975-76			10	0	0	0	8
2 yrs.		**N Totals:**	13	1	0	1	8

Claimed in Reverse Draft by Hershey (AHL) from Philadelphia, June 8, 1972. Sold to **Pittsburgh** by Hershey (AHL), May 22, 1973. Traded to **Detroit** by Pittsburgh with Pittsburgh's third choice (Dan Mandryk) in 1974 Amateur Draft for Nelson Debenedet, May 27, 1974. Traded to **Boston** by Detroit with Earl Anderson for Walt McKechnie and Boston's third choice (Clarke Hamilton) in 1975 Amateur Draft, Feb. 18, 1975.

Kevin Nugent

NUGENT, KEVIN 6'5", 230 lbs.
B. June 7, 1955, Little Falls, Mn. Right Wing, Shoots R

YEAR	TEAM	LEAGUE	GP	G	A	PTS	PIM
1978-79	**IND**	**W**	25	2	8	10	20

Mike Nykoluk

NYKOLUK, MICHAEL 5'11", 212 lbs.
B. Dec. 11, 1934, Toronto, Ont. Right Wing, Shoots R

YEAR	TEAM	LEAGUE	GP	G	A	PTS	PIM
1956-57	**TOR**	**N**	32	3	1	4	20

Gary Nylund

NYLUND, GARY 6'4", 200 lbs.
B. Oct. 28, 1963, Surrey, B.C. Defense, Shoots L

YEAR	TEAM	LEAGUE	GP	G	A	PTS	PIM
1982-83	**TOR**	**N**	16	0	3	3	16

Bill Nyrop

NYROP, WILLIAM D 6'2", 205 lbs.
B. July 23, 1952, Washington, D.C. Defense, Shoots L

YEAR	TEAM	LEAGUE	GP	G	A	PTS	PIM
1975-76	**MONT**	**N**	19	0	3	3	8
1976-77			74	3	19	22	21
1977-78			72	5	21	26	37
1981-82	**MINN**	**N**	42	4	8	12	35
4 yrs.		**N Totals:**	207	12	51	63	101

PLAYOFFS

YEAR	TEAM	LEAGUE	GP	G	A	PTS	PIM
1975-76*	**MONT**	**N**	13	0	3	3	12
1976-77*			8	1	0	1	4
1977-78*			12	0	4	4	6
1981-82	**MINN**	**N**	2	0	0	0	0
4 yrs.		**N Totals:**	35	1	7	8	22

Traded to **Calgary** by Minnesota with Steve Christoff and Minnesota's second choice (Dave Reierson) in 1982 Entry Draft for Willi Plett and Calgary's fourth choice (Dusan Pasek) in 1982 Entry Draft, June 7, 1962.

Bobby Nystrom

NYSTROM, THORE ROBERT 6'1", 200 lbs.
B. Oct. 10, 1952, Stockholm, Sweden Right Wing, Shoots R

YEAR	TEAM	LEAGUE	GP	G	A	PTS	PIM
1972-73	**NYI**	**N**	11	1	1	2	10
1973-74			71	21	20	41	118
1974-75			76	27	28	55	122
1975-76			80	23	25	48	106
1976-77			80	29	27	56	91

Bobby Nystrom continued

YEAR	TEAM & LEAGUE		GP	G	A	PTS	PIM
1977-78			80	30	29	59	94
1978-79			78	19	20	39	113
1979-80			67	21	18	39	94
1980-81			79	14	30	44	145
1981-82			74	22	25	47	103
1982-83			74	10	20	30	98
11 yrs.		N Totals:	770	217	243	460	1094
PLAYOFFS							
1974-75	NYI	N	17	1	3	4	27
1975-76			13	3	6	9	30
1976-77			12	0	2	2	7
1977-78			7	3	1	4	14
1978-79			10	3	2	5	4
1979-80*			20	9	9	18	50
1980-81*			18	6	6	12	20
1981-82*			15	5	5	10	32
1982-83*			20	7	6	13	15
9 yrs.		N Totals:	132	37	40	77	199

Russell Oatman

OATMAN, WARREN RUSSELL 5'10", 195 lbs.
B. Feb. 19, 1905, Tilsonburg, Ont. Forward, Shoots L

YEAR	TEAM & LEAGUE		GP	G	A	PTS	PIM
1926-27	DET	N	14	3	0	3	12
	MON(M)	N	28	8	4	12	30
	2 team total		42	11	4	15	42
1927-28			44	7	4	11	36
1928-29			11	1	0	1	12
	NYR	N	27	1	1	2	10
	2 team total		38	2	1	3	22
3 yrs.		N Totals:	124	20	9	29	100
PLAYOFFS							
1926-27	MON(M)	N	2	0	0	0	0
1927-28			9	1	0	1	18
1928-29	NYR	N	6	0	0	0	0
3 yrs.		N Totals:	17	1	0	1	18

Dennis O'Brien

O'BRIEN, DENNIS FRANCIS 6', 195 lbs.
B. June 10, 1949, Port Hope, Ont. Defense, Shoots L

YEAR	TEAM & LEAGUE		GP	G	A	PTS	PIM
1970-71	MINN	N	27	3	2	5	29
1971-72			70	3	6	9	108
1972-73			74	3	11	14	75
1973-74			77	5	12	17	166
1974-75			56	6	10	16	125
1975-76			78	1	14	15	187
1976-77			75	6	18	24	114
1977-78			13	0	2	2	32
	COLO	N	16	0	2	2	12
	CLEVE	N	23	0	3	3	31
	BOS	N	16	2	3	5	2
	4 team total		68	2	10	12	77
1978-79			64	2	8	10	107
1979-80			3	0	0	0	2
10 yrs.		N Totals:	592	31	91	122	990
PLAYOFFS							
1970-71	MINN	N	9	0	0	0	200
1971-72			3	0	0	0	11
1972-73			6	1	0	1	38
1976-77			2	0	0	0	4
1977-78	BOS	N	14	0	0	0	28
5 yrs.		N Totals:	34	1	0	1	281

Claimed on waivers by **Colorado** from Minnesota, Dec. 2, 1977. Traded to **Cleveland** by Colorado for Mike Christie, Jan. 12, 1978. Claimed on waivers by **Boston** from Cleveland, Mar. 10, 1978. Claimed by **Boston** as fill in Expansion Draft, June 13, 1979.

Obie O'Brien

O'BRIEN, ELLARD JOHN 6'3", 183 lbs.
B. May 27, 1930, St. Catharines, Ont. Left Wing, Shoots L

YEAR	TEAM & LEAGUE		GP	G	A	PTS	PIM
1955-56	BOS	N	2	0	0	0	0

Jack O'Callahan

O'CALLAHAN, JACK 6'1", 185 lbs.
B. July 24, 1957, Charlestown, Mass. Defense, Shoots R

YEAR	TEAM & LEAGUE		GP	G	A	PTS	PIM
1982-83	CHI	N	39	0	11	11	46
PLAYOFFS							
1982-83	CHI	N	5	0	2	2	2

Mike O'Connell

O'CONNELL, MICHAEL THOMAS 5'9", 180 lbs.
B. Nov. 25, 1955, Chicago, Ill. Defense, Shoots R

YEAR	TEAM & LEAGUE		GP	G	A	PTS	PIM
1977-78	CHI	N	6	1	1	2	2
1978-79			48	4	22	26	20
1979-80			78	8	22	30	52
1980-81			34	5	16	21	32
	BOS	N	48	10	22	32	42
	2 team total		82	15	38	53	74
1981-82			80	5	35	40	75
1982-83			80	14	39	53	42
6 yrs.		N Totals:	374	47	157	204	265
PLAYOFFS							
1978-79	CHI	N	4	0	0	0	4
1979-80			7	0	1	1	0
1980-81	BOS	N	3	1	3	4	2
1981-82			11	2	2	4	20
1982-83			17	3	5	8	12
5 yrs.		N Totals:	42	6	11	17	38

Traded to **Boston** by Chicago for Al Secord, Dec. 18, 1980.

Tim O'Connell

O'CONNELL, TIMOTHY 5'11", 170 lbs.
B. Oct. 26, 1963, Chicago, Ill. Right Wing, Shoots R

YEAR	TEAM & LEAGUE		GP	G	A	PTS	PIM
1976-77	SD	W	16	0	3	3	4

Buddy O'Connor

O'CONNOR, HERBERT WILLIAM 5'7", 145 lbs.
B. June 21, 1916, Montreal, Que. Shoots L
Won Hart Trophy, 1947-48
Won Lady Byng Trophy, 1947-48

YEAR	TEAM & LEAGUE		GP	G	A	PTS	PIM
1941-42	MONT	N	36	9	16	25	4
1942-43			50	15	43	58	2
1943-44			44	12	42	54	6
1944-45			50	21	23	44	2
1945-46			45	11	11	22	2
1946-47			46	10	20	30	6
1947-48	NYR	N	60	24	36	60	8
1948-49			46	11	24	35	0
1949-50			66	11	22	33	4
1950-51			66	16	20	36	0
10 yrs.		N Totals:	509	140	257	397	34
PLAYOFFS							
1941-42	MONT	N	3	0	1	1	0
1942-43			5	4	5	9	0
1943-44*			8	1	2	3	2
1944-45			2	0	0	0	0
1945-46*			9	2	3	5	0
1946-47			8	3	4	7	0
1947-48	NYR	N	6	1	4	5	0
1949-50			12	4	2	6	4
8 yrs.		N Totals:	53	15	21	36	6

Chris Oddleifson

ODDLEIFSON, CHRISTOPHER ROY 6'2", 185 lbs.
B. Sept. 7, 1950, Brandon, Man. Center, Shoots L

YEAR	TEAM & LEAGUE		GP	G	A	PTS	PIM
1972-73	BOS	N	6	0	0	0	0
1973-74			49	10	11	21	25
	VAN	N	21	3	5	8	19
	2 team total		70	13	16	29	44
1974-75			60	16	35	51	54
1975-76			80	16	46	62	88
1976-77			80	14	26	40	81
1977-78			78	17	22	39	64
1978-79			67	11	26	37	51

Chris Oddleifson *continued*

YEAR	TEAM & LEAGUE		GP	G	A	PTS	PIM
1979-80			75	8	20	28	76
1980-81			8	0	0	0	6
9 yrs.		N Totals:	524	95	191	286	464
PLAYOFFS							
1974-75	VAN	N	5	0	3	3	2
1975-76			2	1	2	3	0
1978-79			3	0	1	1	2
1979-80			4	0	0	0	4
4 yrs.		N Totals:	14	1	6	7	8

Traded to **Boston** by California with Richard Leduc for Ivan Boldirev, Nov. 17, 1971. Traded to **Vancouver** by Boston with Fred O'Donnell for Bobby Schmautz, Feb. 7, 1974.

Fred O'Donnell

O'DONNELL, FREDERICK JAMES 5'10", 175 lbs.
B. Dec. 6, 1949, Kingston, Ont. Right Wing, Shoots R

YEAR	TEAM & LEAGUE		GP	G	A	PTS	PIM
1972-73	BOS	N	72	10	4	14	55
1973-74			43	5	7	12	43
1974-75	NE	W	76	21	15	36	84
1975-76			79	11	11	22	81
4 yrs.		N Totals:	115	15	11	26	98
		W Totals:	155	32	26	58	165
PLAYOFFS							
1972-73	BOS	N	5	0	1	1	5
1975-76	NE	W	17	2	5	7	20
2 yrs.		N Totals:	5	0	1	1	5
		W Totals:	17	2	5	7	20

Traded to **Vancouver** by Boston with Chris Oddleifson for Bobby Schmautz, Feb. 7, 1974.

Don O'Donoghue

O'DONOGHUE, DONALD FRANCIS 5'10", 180 lbs.
B. Sept. 27, 1949, Kingston, Ont. Right Wing, Shoots R

YEAR	TEAM & LEAGUE		GP	G	A	PTS	PIM
1969-70	OAK	N	68	5	6	11	21
1970-71	CALIF	N	43	11	9	20	10
1971-72			14	2	2	4	4
1972-73	PHI	W	74	16	23	39	43
1973-74	VAN	W	49	8	6	14	20
1974-75			4	0	0	0	0
1975-76	CIN	W	20	1	8	9	0
7 yrs.		N Totals:	125	18	17	35	35
		W Totals:	147	25	37	62	63
PLAYOFFS							
1969-70	OAK	N	3	0	0	0	0
1972-73	PHI	W	4	0	1	1	0
2 yrs.		N Totals:	3	0	0	0	0
		W Totals:	4	0	1	1	0

Traded to **Boston** by California with Carol Vadnais for Reggie Leach, Rick Smith, and Bob Stewart, Feb. 23, 1972.

Gerry Odrowski

ODROWSKI, GERALD BERNARD (Snowy) 5'11", 190 lbs.
B. Oct. 4, 1938, Trout Creek, Ont. Defense, Shoots L

YEAR	TEAM & LEAGUE		GP	G	A	PTS	PIM
1960-61	DET	N	68	1	4	5	45
1961-62			69	1	6	7	24
1962-63			1	0	0	0	0
1967-68	OAK	N	42	4	6	10	10
1968-69	CALIF	N	74	5	1	6	24
1971-72	STL	N	55	1	2	3	8
1972-73	LA	W	78	6	31	37	89
1973-74			77	4	32	36	48
1974-75	PHOE	W	77	5	38	43	77
1975-76	MINN	W	37	1	12	13	10
	WINN	W	13	0	1	1	6
	2 team total		50	1	13	14	16
10 yrs.		N Totals:	309	12	19	31	111
		W Totals:	282	16	114	130	230
PLAYOFFS							
1960-61	DET	N	10	0	0	0	4
1962-63			2	0	0	0	2

Gerry Odrowski *continued*

YEAR	TEAM & LEAGUE		GP	G	A	PTS	PIM
1968-69	CALIF	N	7	0	1	1	2
1971-72	STL	N	11	0	0	0	8
1972-73	LA	W	6	1	2	3	6
1974-75	PHOE	W	5	0	2	2	0
6 yrs.		N Totals:	30	0	1	1	16
		W Totals:	11	1	4	5	6

Gerry O'Flaherty

O'FLAHERTY, GERARD JOSEPH 5'10", 182 lbs.
B. Aug. 31, 1950, Pittsburgh, Pa. Left Wing, Shoots L

YEAR	TEAM & LEAGUE		GP	G	A	PTS	PIM
1971-72	TOR	N	2	0	0	0	0
1972-73	VAN	N	78	13	17	30	29
1973-74			78	22	20	42	18
1974-75			80	25	17	42	37
1975-76			68	20	18	38	47
1976-77			72	12	12	24	20
1977-78			59	6	11	17	15
1978-79	ATL	N	1	1	0	1	2
8 yrs.		N Totals:	438	99	95	194	168
PLAYOFFS							
1974-75	VAN	N	5	2	2	4	6
1975-76			2	0	0	0	0
2 yrs.		N Totals:	7	2	2	4	6

Drafted by **Vancouver** from Toronto in Intra-league Draft, June 5, 1972. Signed as free agent by **Minnesota** July 15, 1978. Sold to **Atlanta** by Minnesota, Oct. 10, 1978.

John O'Flaherty

O'FLAHERTY, JOHN BENEDICT (Peanuts) 5'7", 154 lbs.
B. Apr. 10, 1918, Toronto, Ont. Right Wing, Shoots R

YEAR	TEAM & LEAGUE		GP	G	A	PTS	PIM
1940-41	NYA	N	10	4	0	4	0
1941-42			11	1	1	2	0
2 yrs.		N Totals:	21	5	1	6	0

Brian Ogilvie

OGILVIE, BRIAN HUGH 5'11", 186 lbs.
B. Jan. 30, 1952, Stettler, Alta. Center, Shoots R

YEAR	TEAM & LEAGUE		GP	G	A	PTS	PIM
1972-73	CHI	N	12	1	2	3	18
1974-75	STL	N	20	5	5	10	4
1975-76			9	2	1	3	2
1976-77			3	0	0	0	0
1977-78			32	6	8	14	12
1978-79			14	1	5	6	7
6 yrs.		N Totals:	90	15	21	36	43

Drafted by **St. Louis** from Chicago in Intra-League Draft, June 10, 1974.

George O'Grady

O'GRADY, GEORGE
B. Unknown Forward

YEAR	TEAM & LEAGUE		GP	G	A	PTS	PIM
1917-18	MON(W)	N	4	0	0	0	0

John Ogrodnick

OGRODNICK, JOHN 6', 190 lbs.
B. June 20, 1959, Ottawa, Ont. Right Wing, Shoots L

YEAR	TEAM & LEAGUE		GP	G	A	PTS	PIM
1979-80	DET	N	41	8	24	32	8
1980-81			80	35	35	70	14
1981-82			80	28	26	54	28
1982-83			80	41	44	85	30
4 yrs.		N Totals:	281	112	129	241	80

Wally Olds

OLDS, WALTER RAYMOND 6'2", 200 lbs.
B. Aug. 17, 1949, Warroad, Minn. Defense, Shoots R

YEAR	TEAM & LEAGUE		GP	G	A	PTS	PIM
1972-73	NY	W	61	5	7	12	4
1975-76	CALG	W	28	0	5	5	6
2 yrs.		W Totals:	89	5	12	17	10
PLAYOFFS							
1975-76	CALG	W	9	0	2	2	4

Harry Oliver

OLIVER, HAROLD — 5'8", 155 lbs.
B. Oct. 26, 1898, Selkirk, Man. — Right Wing, Shoots R
Hall of Fame, 1967

YEAR	TEAM & LEAGUE		GP	G	A	PTS	PIM
1926-27	BOS	N	44	18	6	24	17
1927-28			44	13	5	18	20
1928-29			43	17	6	23	24
1929-30			42	16	5	21	12
1930-31			43	16	14	30	18
1931-32			44	13	7	20	22
1932-33			47	11	7	18	10
1933-34			48	5	9	14	6
1934-35	NYA	N	48	7	9	16	4
1935-36			48	9	16	25	12
1936-37			22	2	1	3	2
11 yrs.	N Totals:		473	127	85	212	147
PLAYOFFS							
1926-27	BOS	N	8	4	2	6	4
1927-28			2	2	0	2	2
1928-29*			5	1	1	2	8
1929-30			6	2	1	3	6
1930-31			4	0	0	0	2
1932-33			5	0	0	0	0
1935-36	NYA	N	5	1	2	3	0
7 yrs.	N Totals:		35	10	6	16	22

Murray Oliver

OLIVER, MURRAY CLIFFORD — 5'9", 170 lbs.
B. Nov. 14, 1937, Hamilton, Ont. — Center, Shoots L

YEAR	TEAM & LEAGUE		GP	G	A	PTS	PIM
1957-58	DET	N	1	0	1	1	0
1959-60			54	20	19	39	6
1960-61			49	11	12	23	8
	BOS	N	21	6	10	16	8
	2 team total		70	17	22	39	16
1961-62			70	17	29	46	21
1962-63			65	22	40	62	38
1963-64			70	24	44	68	41
1964-65			65	20	23	43	76
1965-66			70	18	42	60	30
1966-67			65	9	26	35	16
1967-68	TOR	N	74	16	21	37	18
1968-69			76	14	36	50	16
1969-70			76	14	33	47	16
1970-71	MINN	N	61	9	23	32	8
1971-72			77	27	29	56	16
1972-73			75	11	31	42	10
1973-74			78	17	20	37	4
1974-75			80	19	15	34	24
17 yrs.	N Totals:		1127	274	454	728	356
PLAYOFFS							
1959-60	DET	N	6	1	0	1	4
1968-69	TOR	N	4	1	2	3	0
1970-71	MINN	N	12	7	4	11	0
1971-72			7	0	6	6	4
1972-73			6	0	4	4	2
5 yrs.	N Totals:		35	9	16	25	10

Traded to **Boston** by Detroit with Gary Aldcorn and Tom McCarthy for Leo Labine and Vic Stasiuk, Jan., 1961. Traded to **Toronto** by Boston with cash for Eddie Shack, May 15, 1967. Traded to **Minnesota** by Toronto for Brian Conacher, Terry O'Malley and cash, May 22, 1970.

Bert Olmstead

OLMSTEAD, MURRAY BERT — 6'2", 183 lbs.
B. Sept. 4, 1926, Scepter, Sask. — Left Wing, Shoots L

YEAR	TEAM & LEAGUE		GP	G	A	PTS	PIM
1948-49	CHI	N	9	0	2	2	4
1949-50			70	20	29	49	40
1950-51			15	2	1	3	0
	MONT	N	39	16	22	38	40
	2 team total		54	18	23	41	40
1951-52			69	7	28	35	49
1952-53			69	17	28	45	83
1953-54			70	15	37	52	85
1954-55			70	10	**48**	58	103
1955-56			70	14	**56**	70	94
1956-57			64	15	33	48	74
1957-58			57	9	28	37	71
1958-59	TOR	N	70	10	31	41	74

Bert Olmstead continued

YEAR	TEAM & LEAGUE		GP	G	A	PTS	PIM
1959-60			53	15	21	36	63
1960-61			67	18	34	52	84
1961-62			56	13	23	36	10
14 yrs.	N Totals:		848	181	421	602	874
PLAYOFFS							
1950-51	MONT	N	11	2	3	5	9
1951-52			11	0	1	1	4
1952-53*			12	2	2	4	4
1953-54			11	0	1	1	19
1954-55			12	0	4	4	21
1955-56*			10	4	10	14	8
1956-57*			10	0	9	9	13
1957-58*			9	0	3	3	0
1958-59	TOR	N	12	4	2	6	13
1959-60			10	3	4	7	0
1960-61			3	1	2	3	10
1961-62*			4	0	1	1	0
12 yrs.	N Totals:		115	16	42	58	101

Traded to **Detroit** by Chicago with Vic Stasiuk for Lee Fogolin and Steve Black, Dec. 10, 1950. Traded to **Montreal** for Leo Gravelle by Detroit, Dec. 19, 1950. Drafted by **Toronto** from Montreal, June 4, 1958.

Dennis Olson

OLSON, DENNIS — 6', 182 lbs.
B. Nov. 9, 1934, Kenora, Ont. — Center, Shoots R

YEAR	TEAM & LEAGUE		GP	G	A	PTS	PIM
1957-58	DET	N	4	0	0	0	0

Paul O'Neil

O'NEIL, PAUL JOSEPH — 6'1", 177 lbs.
B. Aug. 24, 1953, Boston, Ma. — Center, Shoots R

YEAR	TEAM & LEAGUE		GP	G	A	PTS	PIM
1973-74	VAN	N	5	0	0	0	0
1975-76	BOS	N	1	0	0	0	0
1978-79	BIRM	W	1	0	0	0	0
3 yrs.	N Totals:		6	0	0	0	0
	W Totals:		1	0	0	0	0

Signed as free agent by **Boston** Oct. 10, 1975.

Jim O'Neill

O'NEILL, JAMES BEATON (Peggy) — 5'8", 160 lbs.
B. Apr. 3, 1913, Semans, Sask. — Center, Shoots R

YEAR	TEAM & LEAGUE		GP	G	A	PTS	PIM
1933-34	BOS	N	25	2	2	4	15
1934-35			48	2	11	13	35
1935-36			48	2	11	13	49
1936-37			20	0	2	2	6
1940-41	MONT	N	12	0	3	3	0
1941-42			12	0	1	1	4
6 yrs.	N Totals:		165	6	30	36	109
PLAYOFFS							
1934-35	BOS	N	4	0	0	0	9
1935-36			1	1	1	2	4
1940-41	MONT	N	3	0	0	0	0
1941-42			3	0	0	0	0
4 yrs.	N Totals:		11	1	1	2	13

Tom O'Neill

O'NEILL, THOMAS (Windy) — 5'10", 155 lbs.
B. Sept. 28, 1923, Deseronto, Ont. — Right Wing, Shoots R

YEAR	TEAM & LEAGUE		GP	G	A	PTS	PIM
1943-44	TOR	N	33	8	7	15	29
1944-45			33	2	5	7	24
2 yrs.	N Totals:		66	10	12	22	53
PLAYOFFS							
1943-44	TOR	N	4	0	0	0	6

Bill Orban

ORBAN, WILLIAM TERRANCE — 6', 175 lbs.
B. Feb. 20, 1944, Regina, Sask. — Left Wing, Shoots L

YEAR	TEAM & LEAGUE		GP	G	A	PTS	PIM
1967-68	CHI	N	39	3	2	5	17
1968-69			45	4	6	10	33
	MINN	N	21	1	5	6	10
	2 team total		66	5	11	16	43
1969-70			9	0	2	2	7

Bill Orban continued

YEAR	TEAM & LEAGUE		GP	G	A	PTS	PIM
3 yrs.		**N Totals:**	114	8	15	23	67
PLAYOFFS							
1967-68	**CHI**	**N**	3	0	0	0	0

Traded to **Minnesota** by Chicago with Tom Reid for Andre Boudrias and Mike McMahon, Feb. 14, 1969. Put on **Chicago** reserve list from Los Angeles via Intra-League Draft, June 5, 1972.

Willie O'Ree

O'REE, WILLIAM 5'10", 175 lbs.
B. Oct. 15, 1935, Fredericton, N.B. Left Wing, Shoots L

YEAR	TEAM & LEAGUE		GP	G	A	PTS	PIM
1957-58	**BOS**	**N**	2	0	0	0	0
1960-61			43	4	10	14	26
2 yrs.		**N Totals:**	45	4	10	14	26

Terry O'Reilly

O'REILLY, JOSEPH JAMES TERENCE 6'1", 199 lbs.
B. June 7, 1951, Niagara Falls, Ont. Right Wing, Shoots R

YEAR	TEAM & LEAGUE		GP	G	A	PTS	PIM
1971-72	**BOS**	**N**	1	1	0	1	0
1972-73			72	5	22	27	109
1973-74			76	11	24	35	94
1974-75			68	15	20	35	146
1975-76			80	23	27	50	150
1976-77			79	14	41	55	147
1977-78			77	29	61	90	211
1978-79			80	26	51	77	205
1979-80			71	19	42	61	265
1980-81			77	8	35	43	223
1981-82			70	22	30	52	213
1982-83			19	6	14	20	40
12 yrs.		**N Totals:**	770	179	367	546	1803
PLAYOFFS							
1972-73	**BOS**	**N**	5	0	0	0	2
1973-74			16	2	5	7	38
1974-75			3	0	0	0	17
1975-76			12	3	1	4	25
1976-77			14	5	6	11	28
1977-78			15	5	10	15	40
1978-79			11	0	6	6	25
1979-80			10	3	6	9	69
1980-81			3	1	2	3	12
1981-82			11	5	4	9	56
10 yrs.		**N Totals:**	100	24	40	64	312

Jimmy Orlando

ORLANDO, JAMES V. 5'11", 185 lbs.
B. Feb. 27, 1916, Montreal, Que. Defense, Shoots L

YEAR	TEAM & LEAGUE		GP	G	A	PTS	PIM
1936-37	**DET**	**N**	10	0	1	1	8
1937-38			6	0	0	0	4
1939-40			48	1	3	4	54
1940-41			48	1	10	11	**99**
1941-42			48	1	7	8	111
1942-43			40	4	3	7	**99**
6 yrs.		**N Totals:**	200	7	24	31	375
PLAYOFFS							
1939-40	**DET**	**N**	5	0	0	0	15
1940-41			9	0	2	2	31
1941-42			12	0	4	4	45
1942-43*			10	0	3	3	14
4 yrs.		**N Totals:**	36	0	9	9	105

Dave Orleski

ORLESKI, DAVID EUGENE 6'3", 210 lbs.
B. Dec. 26, 1959, Edmonton, Alta. Left Wing, Shoots L

YEAR	TEAM & LEAGUE		GP	G	A	PTS	PIM
1980-81	**MONT**	**N**	1	0	0	0	0
1981-82			1	0	0	0	0
2 yrs.		**N Totals:**	2	0	0	0	0

Bill Orr

ORR, WILLIAM LINDSAY 5'10", 185 lbs.
B. June 12, 1948, South Porcupine, Ont. Defense, Shoots R

YEAR	TEAM & LEAGUE		GP	G	A	PTS	PIM
1973-74	**TOR**	**W**	46	3	9	12	16
PLAYOFFS							
1973-74	**TOR**	**W**	12	1	0	1	6

Bobby Orr

ORR, ROBERT GORDON 6', 199 lbs.
B. Mar. 20, 1948, Parry Sound, Ont. Defense, Shoots L
Won Hart Trophy, 1969–70, 1970–71, 1971-72
Won Art Ross Trophy, 1969–70, 1974-75
Won Norris Trophy, 1967–68, 1968–69, 1969–70, 1970–71, 1971–72, 1972–73, 1973–74, 1974–75
Won Calder Trophy, 1966-67
Won Conn Smythe Trophy, 1969–70, 1971-72
Hall of Fame, 1979

YEAR	TEAM & LEAGUE		GP	G	A	PTS	PIM
1966-67	**BOS**	**N**	61	13	28	41	102
1967-68			46	11	20	31	63
1968-69			67	21	43	64	133
1969-70			76	33	**87**	**120**	125
1970-71			78	37	**102**	139	91
1971-72			76	37	**80**	117	106
1972-73			63	29	72	101	99
1973-74			74	32	**90**	122	82
1974-75			80	46	**89**	**135**	101
1975-76			10	5	13	18	22
1976-77	**CHI**	**N**	20	4	19	23	25
1978-79			6	2	2	4	4
12 yrs.		**N Totals:**	657	270	645	915	953
PLAYOFFS							
1967-68	**BOS**	**N**	4	0	2	2	2
1968-69			10	1	7	8	10
1969-70*			14	9	11	20	14
1970-71			7	5	7	12	25
1971-72*			15	5	19	24	19
1972-73			5	1	1	2	7
1973-74			16	4	14	18	28
1974-75			3	1	5	6	2
8 yrs.		**N Totals:**	74	26	66	92	107

Signed as free agent by **Chicago** June 24, 1976.

Mark Osborne

OSBORNE, MARK ANATOLE (Ozzie) 6'1", 185 lbs.
B. Aug. 13, 1961, Toronto, Ont. Left Wing, Shoots L

YEAR	TEAM & LEAGUE		GP	G	A	PTS	PIM
1981-82	**DET**	**N**	80	26	41	67	61
1982-83			80	19	24	43	83
2 yrs.		**N Totals:**	160	45	65	110	144

Traded by Detroit with Mike Blaisdell and Willie Huber to **N.Y. Rangers** for Ron Duguay, Ed Mio, and Eddie Johnstone, June 13, 1983.

Randy Osburn

OSBURN, RANDOULF ALLAN 6', 190 lbs.
B. Nov. 26, 1952, Collingwood, Ont. Left Wing, Shoots L

YEAR	TEAM & LEAGUE		GP	G	A	PTS	PIM
1972-73	**TOR**	**N**	26	0	2	2	0
1974-75	**PHI**	**N**	1	0	0	0	0
2 yrs.		**N Totals:**	27	0	2	2	0

Traded to **Philadelphia** by Toronto with Dave Fortier for Bill Flett, May 27, 1974.

Danny O'Shea

O'SHEA, DANIEL PATRICK 6'1", 190 lbs.
B. June 15, 1945, Toronto, Ont. Center, Shoots L

YEAR	TEAM & LEAGUE		GP	G	A	PTS	PIM
1968-69	**MINN**	**N**	74	15	34	49	57
1969-70			75	10	24	34	82
1970-71			59	14	12	26	16
	CHI	**N**	18	4	7	11	10
	2 team total		77	18	19	37	26
1971-72			48	6	9	15	28
	STL	**N**	20	3	3	6	11
	2 team total		68	9	12	21	39
1972-73			75	12	26	38	30
1974-75	**MINN**	**W**	76	16	25	41	47

Danny O'Shea continued

YEAR	TEAM & LEAGUE		GP	G	A	PTS	PIM
6 yrs.		N Totals:	369	64	115	179	234
		W Totals:	76	16	25	41	47
PLAYOFFS							
1969-70	MINN	N	6	1	0	1	8
1970-71	CHI	N	18	2	5	7	15
1971-72	STL	N	10	0	2	2	36
1972-73			5	0	0	0	2
4 yrs.		N Totals:	39	3	7	10	61

Traded to **Chicago** by Minnesota for Doug Mohns and Terry Caffery, Feb. 22, 1971. Traded to **St. Louis** by Chicago for Chris Bordeleau, Feb. 8, 1972.

Kevin O'Shea

O'SHEA, KEVIN WILLIAM 6'2", 205 lbs.
B. May 28, 1947, Toronto, Ont. Right Wing, Shoots R

YEAR	TEAM & LEAGUE		GP	G	A	PTS	PIM
1970-71	BUF	N	41	4	4	8	8
1971-72			52	6	9	15	44
	STL	N	4	0	0	0	2
	2 team total		56	6	9	15	46
1972-73			36	3	5	8	31
1974-75	MINN	W	68	10	10	20	42
4 yrs.		N Totals:	133	13	18	31	85
		W Totals:	68	10	10	20	42
PLAYOFFS							
1971-72	STL	N	11	2	1	3	6
1972-73			1	0	0	0	0
2 yrs.		N Totals:	12	2	1	3	6

Claimed on waivers by **St. Louis** from Buffalo Mar. 3, 1972.

Eddie Ouelette

OUELETTE, ADELARD EDWARD 5'8", 172 lbs.
B. Mar. 9, 1911, Ottawa, Ont. Center, Shoots L

YEAR	TEAM & LEAGUE		GP	G	A	PTS	PIM
1935-36	CHI	N	43	3	2	5	11
PLAYOFFS							
1935-36	CHI	N	1	0	0	0	0

Gerry Ouellette

OUELLETTE, GERALD ADRIAN 5'8", 170 lbs.
B. Nov. 1, 1938, Grand Falls, N.B. Right Wing, Shoots R

YEAR	TEAM & LEAGUE		GP	G	A	PTS	PIM
1960-61	BOS	N	39	5	4	9	0

Francois Ouimet

OUIMET, FRANCOIS 5'10", 175 lbs.
B. Oct. 14, 1951, Montreal, Que. Defense, Shoots L

YEAR	TEAM & LEAGUE		GP	G	A	PTS	PIM
1975-76	MINN	W	9	0	2	2	2
1976-77	CIN	W	16	1	8	9	10
2 yrs.		W Totals:	25	1	10	11	12

Dennis Owchar

OWCHAR, DENNIS 5'11", 190 lbs.
B. Mar. 28, 1953, Dryden, Ont. Defense, Shoots R

YEAR	TEAM & LEAGUE		GP	G	A	PTS	PIM
1974-75	PITT	N	46	6	11	17	67
1975-76			54	5	12	17	19
1976-77			46	5	18	23	37
1977-78			22	2	8	10	23
	COLO	N	60	8	23	31	25
	2 team total		82	10	31	41	48
1978-79			50	3	13	16	27
1979-80			10	1	0	1	2
6 yrs.		N Totals:	288	30	85	115	200
PLAYOFFS							
1974-75	PITT	N	6	0	1	1	4
1975-76			2	0	0	0	2
1977-78	COLO	N	2	1	0	1	2
3 yrs.		N Totals:	10	1	1	2	8

Traded to **Colorado** by Pittsburgh for Tom Edur, Dec. 2, 1977.

George Owen

OWEN, GEORGE 5'11", 190 lbs.
B. D Hamilton, Ont. Defense, Shoots L

YEAR	TEAM & LEAGUE		GP	G	A	PTS	PIM
1928-29	BOS	N	26	5	4	9	48
1929-30			42	9	4	13	31
1930-31			37	12	13	25	33
1931-32			45	12	10	22	29
1932-33			42	6	2	8	10
5 yrs.		N Totals:	192	44	33	77	151
PLAYOFFS							
1928-29*	BOS	N	5	0	0	0	0
1929-30			6	0	2	2	6
1930-31			5	2	3	5	13
1932-33			5	0	0	0	6
4 yrs.		N Totals:	21	2	5	7	25

Clayton Pachal

PACHAL, CLAYTON 5'10", 185 lbs.
B. Apr. 21, 1956, Yorkton, Sask. Left Wing, Shoots L

YEAR	TEAM & LEAGUE		GP	G	A	PTS	PIM
1976-77	BOS	N	1	0	0	0	12
1977-78			10	0	0	0	14
1978-79	COLO	N	24	2	3	5	69
3 yrs.		N Totals:	35	2	3	5	95

Traded to **Colorado** by Boston for Mark Suzor, Oct. 11, 1978.

Al Paddock

PADDOCK, ALVIN JOHN 6'1", 185 lbs.
B. June 9, 1954, Brandon, Man. Left Wing, Shoots L

YEAR	TEAM & LEAGUE		GP	G	A	PTS	PIM
1975-76	WASH	N	8	1	1	2	12
1976-77	PHI	N	5	0	0	0	9
1979-80			32	3	7	10	36
1980-81	QUE	N	32	2	5	7	25
1982-83	PHI	N	10	2	1	3	4
5 yrs.		N Totals:	87	8	14	22	86
PLAYOFFS							
1979-80	PHI	N	3	2	0	2	0
1980-81	QUE	N	2	0	0	0	0
2 yrs.		N Totals:	5	2	0	2	0

Traded to **Philadelphia** by Washington, Sept. 1, 1976 to complete earlier deal in which Washington acquired Bob Sirois from Philadelphia, Dec. 15, 1975. Sold to **Quebec** by Philadelphia, Aug. 11, 1980. Signed as a free agent by **New Jersey** Sept. 3, 1983.

Pierre Paiement

PAIEMENT, PIERRE
Defense

YEAR	TEAM & LEAGUE		GP	G	A	PTS	PIM
1972-73	PHI	W	8	1	0	1	18

Rosaire Paiement

PAIEMENT, JOSEPH WILFRED ROSAIRE (Rosey) 5'11", 170 lbs.
B. Aug. 12, 1945, Earlton, Ont. Right Wing, Shoots R

YEAR	TEAM & LEAGUE		GP	G	A	PTS	PIM
1967-68	PHI	N	7	1	0	1	11
1968-69			27	2	4	6	52
1969-70			9	1	1	2	11
1970-71	VAN	N	78	34	28	62	152
1971-72			69	10	9	19	117
1972-73	CHI	W	78	33	36	69	135
1973-74			78	30	43	73	87
1974-75			78	26	48	74	97
1975-76	NE	W	80	28	43	71	89
1976-77			13	5	2	7	12
	IND	W	67	18	25	43	91
	2 team total		80	23	27	50	103
1977-78			61	6	24	30	81
11 yrs.		N Totals:	190	48	42	90	343
		W Totals:	455	146	221	367	592
PLAYOFFS							
1967-68	PHI	N	3	3	0	3	0
1973-74	CHI	W	18	9	6	15	16
1975-76	NE	W	17	4	11	15	41
1976-77	IND	W	9	0	5	5	15

Rosaire Paiement continued

YEAR	TEAM & LEAGUE		GP	G	A	PTS	PIM
4 yrs.		N Totals:	3	3	0	3	0
		W Totals:	44	13	22	35	72

Drafted by **Vancouver** from Philadelphia in Expansion Draft, June 10, 1970.

Wilf Paiement

PAIEMENT, WILFRID, JR. 6'1", 205 lbs.
B. Oct. 16, 1955, Earlton, Ont. Right Wing, Shoots R

YEAR	TEAM & LEAGUE		GP	G	A	PTS	PIM
1974-75	**KC**	**N**	78	26	13	39	101
1975-76			57	21	22	43	121
1976-77	**COLO**	**N**	78	41	40	81	101
1977-78			80	31	56	87	114
1978-79			65	24	36	60	80
1979-80			34	10	16	26	41
	TOR	**N**	41	20	28	48	72
	2 team total		75	30	44	74	113
1980-81			77	40	57	97	145
1981-82			69	18	40	58	203
	QUE	**N**	8	7	6	13	18
	2 team total		77	25	46	71	221
1982-83			80	26	38	64	170
9 yrs.		N Totals:	667	264	352	616	1166
PLAYOFFS							
1977-78	**COLO**	**N**	2	0	0	0	7
1979-80	**TOR**	**N**	3	0	2	2	17
1980-81			3	0	0	0	2
1981-82	**QUE**	**N**	14	6	6	12	28
1982-83			4	0	1	1	4
5 yrs.		N Totals:	26	6	9	15	58

Traded to **Toronto** by Colorado with Pat Hickey for Lanny McDonald and Joel Quenneville, Dec. 29, 1979. Traded to **Quebec** by Toronto for Miroslav Frycer and Quebec's seventh round choice (Jeff Triano) in 1982 Entry Draft, Mar. 6, 1982.

Peter Palangio

PALANGIO, PETER ALBERT 5'11", 175 lbs.
B. Oct. 10, 1908, North Bay, Ont. Left Wing, Shoots L

YEAR	TEAM & LEAGUE		GP	G	A	PTS	PIM
1926-27	**MONT**	**N**	6	0	0	0	0
1927-28	**DET**	**N**	14	3	0	3	8
1928-29	**MONT**	**N**	2	0	0	0	0
1936-37	**CHI**	**N**	30	8	9	17	16
1937-38			19	2	1	3	4
5 yrs.		N Totals:	71	13	10	23	28
PLAYOFFS							
1926-27	**MONT**	**N**	4	0	0	0	0
1937-38*	**CHI**	**N**	3	0	0	0	0
2 yrs.		N Totals:	7	0	0	0	0

Aldo Palazzari

PALAZZARI, ALDO 5'7", 168 lbs.
B. July 25, 1918, Eveleth, Minn. Right Wing, Shoots L

YEAR	TEAM & LEAGUE		GP	G	A	PTS	PIM
1943-44	**BOS**	**N**	23	6	3	9	4
	NYR	**N**	12	2	0	2	0
	2 team total		35	8	3	11	4

Doug Palazzari

PALAZZARI, DOUGLAS JOHN 5'5", 170 lbs.
B. Nov. 3, 1952, Eveleth, Minn. Center, Shoots L

YEAR	TEAM & LEAGUE		GP	G	A	PTS	PIM
1974-75	**STL**	**N**	73	14	17	31	19
1976-77			12	1	0	1	0
1977-78			3	1	0	1	0
1978-79			20	2	3	5	4
4 yrs.		N Totals:	108	18	20	38	23
PLAYOFFS							
1974-75	**STL**	**N**	2	0	0	0	0

Brad Palmer

PALMER, BRAD DONALD 6', 185 lbs.
B. Sept. 14, 1961, Duncan, B.C. Left Wing, Shoots L

YEAR	TEAM & LEAGUE		GP	G	A	PTS	PIM
1980-81	**MINN**	**N**	23	4	4	8	22
1981-82			72	22	23	45	18
1982-83	**BOS**	**N**	73	6	11	17	18
3 yrs.		N Totals:	168	32	38	70	58
PLAYOFFS							
1980-81	**MINN**	**N**	19	8	5	13	4
1981-82			3	0	0	0	12
1982-83	**BOS**	**N**	7	1	0	1	0
3 yrs.		N Totals:	29	9	5	14	16

Traded to **Boston** by Minnesota with Minnesota's first round choice (Dave Donnelly) in 1982 Amateur Draft for past consideration involving the 1982 Amateur Draft, June 9, 1982.

Rob Palmer

PALMER, ROBERT ROSS 5'11", 190 lbs.
B. Sept. 10, 1956, Sarnia, Ont. Defense, Shoots R

YEAR	TEAM & LEAGUE		GP	G	A	PTS	PIM
1977 78	**LA**	**N**	48	0	3	3	27
1978-79			78	4	41	45	26
1979-80			78	4	36	40	18
1980-81			13	0	4	4	13
1981-82			5	0	2	2	0
1982-83	**NJ**	**N**	60	1	10	11	21
6 yrs.		N Totals:	282	9	96	105	105
PLAYOFFS							
1977-78	**LA**	**N**	2	0	0	0	0
1978-79			2	0	0	0	2
1979-80			4	1	2	3	4
3 yrs.		N Totals:	8	1	2	3	6

Rob Palmer

PALMER, ROBERT HAZEN 6', 190 lbs.
B. Oct. 2, 1952, Detroit, Mich. Center, Shoots L

YEAR	TEAM & LEAGUE		GP	G	A	PTS	PIM
1973-74	**CHI**	**N**	1	0	0	0	0
1974-75			13	0	2	2	2
1975-76			2	0	1	1	0
3 yrs.		N Totals:	16	0	3	3	2

Ed Panagabko

PANAGABKO, EDWIN ARNOLD 5'8", 170 lbs.
B. May 17, 1934, Norquay, Sask. Center, Shoots L

YEAR	TEAM & LEAGUE		GP	G	A	PTS	PIM
1955-56	**BOS**	**N**	28	0	3	3	38
1956-57			1	0	0	0	0
2 yrs.		N Totals:	29	0	3	3	38

Joe Papike

PAPIKE, JOSEPH 6', 175 lbs.
B. Mar. 28, 1915, Eveleth, Minn Right Wing, Shoots R

YEAR	TEAM & LEAGUE		GP	G	A	PTS	PIM
1940-41	**CHI**	**N**	10	2	2	4	2
1941-42			9	1	0	1	0
1944-45			2	0	1	1	2
3 yrs.		N Totals:	21	3	3	6	4
PLAYOFFS							
1940-41	**CHI**	**N**	5	0	2	2	0

Jim Pappin

PAPPIN, JAMES JOSEPH 6'1", 190 lbs.
B. Sept. 10, 1939, Sudbury, Ont. Right Wing, Shoots R

YEAR	TEAM & LEAGUE		GP	G	A	PTS	PIM
1963-64	**TOR**	**N**	50	11	8	19	33
1964-65			44	9	9	18	33
1965-66			7	0	3	3	8
1966-67			64	21	11	32	89
1967-68			58	13	15	28	37
1968-69	**CHI**	**N**	75	30	40	70	49
1969-70			66	28	25	53	68
1970-71			58	22	23	45	40
1971-72			64	27	21	48	38

Jim Pappin continued

YEAR	TEAM & LEAGUE	GP	G	A	PTS	PIM
1972-73		76	41	51	92	82
1973-74		78	32	41	73	76
1974-75		71	36	27	63	94
1975-76	**CALIF N**	32	6	13	19	12
1976-77	**CLEVE N**	24	2	8	10	8
14 yrs.	**N Totals:**	767	278	295	573	667
PLAYOFFS						
1963-64*	**TOR N**	11	0	0	0	0
1966-67*		12	7	8	15	12
1969-70	**CHI N**	8	3	2	5	6
1970-71		18	10	4	14	24
1971-72		8	2	5	7	4
1972-73		16	8	7	15	24
1973-74		11	3	6	9	29
1974-75		8	0	2	2	2
8 yrs.	**N Totals:**	92	33	34	67	101

Traded to **Chicago** by Toronto for Pierre Pilote, May 23, 1968. Traded to **California** by Chicago with Chicago's third choice (Guy Lash) in 1977 Amateur Draft for Joey Johnston, June 1, 1975.

Bob Paradise

PARADISE, ROBERT HARVEY 6'1", 205 lbs.
B. Apr. 22, 1944, St. Paul, Minn. Defense, Shoots L

YEAR	TEAM & LEAGUE	GP	G	A	PTS	PIM
1971-72	**MINN N**	6	0	0	0	6
1972-73	**ATL N**	71	1	7	8	103
1973-74		18	0	1	1	13
	PITT N	38	2	7	9	39
	2 team total	56	2	8	10	52
1974-75		78	3	15	18	109
1975-76		9	0	0	0	4
	WASH N	48	0	8	8	42
	2 team total	57	0	8	8	46
1976-77		22	0	5	5	20
1977-78	**PITT N**	64	2	10	12	53
1978-79		14	0	1	1	4
8 yrs.	**N Totals:**	368	8	54	62	393
PLAYOFFS						
1971-72	**MINN N**	4	0	0	0	0
1974-75	**PITT N**	6	0	1	1	17
1978-79		2	0	0	0	0
3 yrs.	**N Totals:**	12	0	1	1	17

Dick Paradise

PARADISE, RICHARD JOHN 5'11", 194 lbs.
B. Apr. 21, 1945, St. Paul, Minn. Defense, Shoots L

YEAR	TEAM & LEAGUE	GP	G	A	PTS	PIM
1972-73	**MINN W**	77	3	15	18	189
1973-74		67	2	7	9	71
2 yrs.	**W Totals:**	144	5	22	27	260
PLAYOFFS						
1972-73	**MINN W**	5	0	1	1	2
1973-74		7	0	0	0	6
2 yrs.	**W Totals:**	12	0	1	1	8

George Pargeter

PARGETER, GEORGE WILLIAM 5'7", 168 lbs.
B. Feb. 24, 1923, Calgary, Alta. Left Wing, Shoots L

YEAR	TEAM & LEAGUE	GP	G	A	PTS	PIM
1946-47	**MONT N**	4	0	0	0	0

J.P. Parise

PARISE, JEAN-PAUL 5'9", 175 lbs.
B. Dec. 11, 1941, Smooth Rock Falls, Ont. Left Wing

YEAR	TEAM & LEAGUE	GP	G	A	PTS	PIM
1965-66	**BOS N**	3	0	0	0	0
1966-67		18	2	2	4	10
1967-68	**TOR N**	1	0	1	1	0
	MINN N	42	11	15	26	27
	2 team total	43	11	16	27	27
1968-69		76	22	27	49	53
1969-70		74	24	48	72	72
1970-71		73	11	23	34	60
1971-72		71	19	18	37	70
1972-73		78	27	48	75	96
1973-74		78	18	37	55	42

J.P. Parise continued

YEAR	TEAM & LEAGUE	GP	G	A	PTS	PIM
1974-75		38	9	16	25	40
	NYI N	41	14	16	30	22
	2 team total	79	23	32	55	62
1975-76		80	22	35	57	80
1976-77		80	25	31	56	46
1977-78		39	12	16	28	12
	CLEVE N	40	9	13	22	27
	2 team total	79	21	29	50	39
1978-79	**MINN N**	57	13	9	22	45
14 yrs.	**N Totals:**	889	238	355	593	702
PLAYOFFS						
1967-68	**MINN N**	14	2	5	7	10
1969-70		6	3	2	5	2
1970-71		12	3	3	6	22
1971-72		7	3	3	6	6
1972-73		6	0	0	0	9
1974-75	**NYI N**	17	8	8	16	22
1975-76		13	4	6	10	10
1976-77		11	4	4	8	6
8 yrs.	**N Totals:**	86	27	31	58	87

Drafted by **Oakland** from Boston in Expansion Draft, June 6, 1967. Sold to **Toronto** by Oakland, Oct. 3, 1967. Sold to **Minnesota** by Toronto, Dec. 27, 1967. Traded to **N.Y. Islanders** by Minnesota for Ernie Hicke and Doug Rombough, Jan. 5, 1975. Traded to **Cleveland** by N.Y. Islanders with Jean Potvin and a fourth round choice in the 1978 Amateur Draft (later cancelled by Cleveland-Minnesota merger) for Wayne Merrick and Darcy Regnier, Jan. 10, 1976. Put on **Minnesota** reserve list after Cleveland-Minnesota Dispersal Draft, June 15, 1978.

Mike Parizeau

PARIZEAU, MICHEL GERARD 5'10", 165 lbs.
B. Apr. 9, 1948, Montreal, Que. Center, Shoots L

YEAR	TEAM & LEAGUE	GP	G	A	PTS	PIM
1971-72	**STL N**	20	1	2	3	8
	PHI N	38	2	12	14	10
	2 team total	58	3	14	17	18
1972-73	**QUE W**	75	25	48	73	50
1973-74		78	26	34	60	39
1974-75		78	28	46	74	69
1975-76		58	12	27	39	20
	IND W	23	13	15	28	22
	2 team total	81	25	42	67	42
1976-77		75	18	37	55	39
1977-78		70	13	27	40	47
1978-79		22	4	9	13	4
	CIN W	30	3	9	12	28
	2 team total	52	7	18	25	32
8 yrs.	**N Totals:**	58	3	14	17	18
	W Totals:	509	142	252	394	318
PLAYOFFS						
1974-75	**QUE W**	15	2	4	6	10
1975-76	**IND W**	7	4	4	8	6
1976-77		8	3	6	9	8
1978-79	**CIN W**	3	1	0	1	0
4 yrs.	**W Totals:**	33	10	14	24	24

Drafted by **St. Louis** from N.Y. Rangers in Intra-League Draft, June 8, 1971. Claimed on waivers by **Philadelphia** from St. Louis, Dec. 3, 1971.

Brad Park

PARK, DOUGLAS BRADFORD 6', 200 lbs.
B. July 6, 1948, Toronto, Ont. Defense, Shoots L

YEAR	TEAM & LEAGUE	GP	G	A	PTS	PIM
1968-69	**NYR N**	54	3	23	26	70
1969-70		60	11	26	37	98
1970-71		68	7	37	44	114
1971-72		75	24	49	73	130
1972-73		52	10	43	53	51
1973-74		78	25	57	82	148
1974-75		65	13	44	57	104
1975-76		13	2	4	6	23
	BOS N	43	16	37	53	95
	2 team total	56	18	41	59	118
1976-77		77	12	55	67	67
1977-78		80	22	57	79	79
1978-79		40	7	32	39	10
1979-80		32	5	16	21	27
1980-81		78	14	52	66	111
1981-82		75	14	42	56	82
1982-83		76	10	26	36	82

Brad Park continued

YEAR	TEAM & LEAGUE	GP	G	A	PTS	PIM
15 yrs.	N Totals:	966	195	600	795	1291
PLAYOFFS						
1968-69	NYR N	4	0	2	2	7
1969-70		5	1	2	3	11
1970-71		13	0	4	4	42
1971-72		16	4	7	11	21
1972-73		10	2	5	7	8
1973-74		13	4	8	12	38
1974-75		3	1	4	5	2
1975-76	BOS N	11	3	8	11	14
1976-77		14	2	10	12	4
1977-78		15	9	11	20	14
1978-79		11	1	4	5	8
1979-80		10	3	6	9	4
1980-81		3	1	3	4	11
1981-82		11	1	4	5	4
1982-83		16	3	9	12	18
15 yrs.	N Totals:	155	35	87	122	206

Traded to **Boston** by N.Y. Rangers with Jean Ratelle and Joe Zanussi for Phil Esposito and Carol Vadnais, Nov. 7, 1975. Signed as a free agent by **Detroit** Aug. 9, 1983.

Ernie Parkes

PARKES, ERNEST
B. Unknown — Right Wing, Shoots R

YEAR	TEAM & LEAGUE	GP	G	A	PTS	PIM
1924-25	MON(M) N	17	0	0	0	2

George Parsons

PARSONS, GEORGE HENRY — 5'11½", 174 lbs.
B. June 28, 1914, Toronto, Ont. — Left Wing, Shoots L

YEAR	TEAM & LEAGUE	GP	G	A	PTS	PIM
1936-37	TOR N	5	0	0	0	0
1937-38		30	5	6	11	6
1938-39		29	7	7	14	11
3 yrs.	N Totals:	64	12	13	25	17
PLAYOFFS						
1937-38	TOR N	7	3	2	5	11

Rusty Patenaude

PATENAUDE, EDGAR ARNOLD — 5'9", 175 lbs.
B. Oct. 17, 1949, Williams Lake, B.C. — Right Wing, Shoots R

YEAR	TEAM & LEAGUE	GP	G	A	PTS	PIM
1972-73	ALTA W	77	29	27	56	59
1973-74	EDM W	71	20	23	43	55
1974-75		56	20	16	36	38
1975-76		77	42	30	72	88
1976-77		73	25	16	41	57
1977-78	IND W	76	23	19	42	71
6 yrs.	W Totals:	430	159	131	290	368
PLAYOFFS						
1973-74	EDM W	4	0	2	2	2
1975-76		4	1	4	5	12
1976-77		2	0	0	0	8
3 yrs.	W Totals:	10	1	6	7	22

Joe Paterson

PATERSON, JOSEPH — 6'1", 208 lbs.
B. June 25, 1960, Toronto, Ont. — Left Wing, Shoots L

YEAR	TEAM & LEAGUE	GP	G	A	PTS	PIM
1980-81	DET N	38	2	5	7	53
1981-82		3	0	0	0	0
1982-83		33	2	1	3	14
3 yrs.	N Totals:	74	4	6	10	67

Mark Paterson

PATERSON, MARK — 6', 190 lbs.
B. Feb. 2, 1964, Ottawa, Ont. — Defense, Shoots L

YEAR	TEAM & LEAGUE	GP	G	A	PTS	PIM
1982-83	HART N	2	0	0	0	0

Rick Paterson

PATERSON, RICHARD — 5'9", 187 lbs.
B. Feb. 10, 1958, Kingston, Ont. — Defense, Shoots R

YEAR	TEAM & LEAGUE	GP	G	A	PTS	PIM
1979-80	CHI N	11	0	2	2	0
1980-81		49	8	2	10	18
1981-82		48	4	7	11	8
1982-83		79	14	9	23	14
4 yrs.	N Totals:	187	26	20	46	40
PLAYOFFS						
1978-79	CHI N	1	0	1	1	0
1979-80		7	0	0	0	5
1980-81		2	1	0	1	0
1981-82		15	3	2	5	21
1982-83		13	1	1	2	4
5 yrs.	N Totals:	38	5	4	9	30

Doug Patey

PATEY, DOUGLAS EDWARD — 5'11", 180 lbs.
B. Dec. 28, 1956, Toronto, Ont. — Right Wing, Shoots R

YEAR	TEAM & LEAGUE	GP	G	A	PTS	PIM
1976-77	WASH N	37	3	1	4	6
1977-78		2	0	1	1	0
1978-79		6	1	0	1	2
3 yrs.	N Totals:	45	4	2	6	8

Claimed by **Edmonton** from Washington in Expansion Draft, June 13, 1979.

Larry Patey

PATEY, LAWRENCE JAMES — 6'1", 185 lbs.
B. Mar. 19, 1953, Toronto, Ont. — Center, Shoots L

YEAR	TEAM & LEAGUE	GP	G	A	PTS	PIM
1973-74	CALIF N	1	0	0	0	0
1974-75		79	25	20	45	68
1975-76		18	4	4	8	23
	STL N	53	8	6	14	26
	2 team total	71	12	10	22	49
1976-77		80	21	29	50	41
1977-78		80	17	17	34	29
1978-79		78	15	19	34	60
1979-80		78	17	17	34	76
1980-81		80	22	23	45	107
1981-82		70	14	12	26	97
1982-83		67	9	12	21	80
10 yrs.	N Totals:	684	152	159	311	607
PLAYOFFS						
1975-76	STL N	3	1	1	2	2
1976-77		4	1	0	1	0
1979-80		3	1	0	1	2
1980-81		11	2	4	6	30
1981-82		10	2	4	6	13
1982-83		4	1	0	1	4
6 yrs.	N Totals:	35	8	9	17	51

Traded to **St. Louis** by California, with California's third round choice (Reg Kerr) in 1977 Amateur Draft for Wayne Merrick, Nov. 24, 1975.

Craig Patrick

PATRICK, CRAIG — 6', 185 lbs.
B. May 20, 1946, Detroit, Mich. — Right Wing, Shoots L

YEAR	TEAM & LEAGUE	GP	G	A	PTS	PIM
1971-72	CALIF N	59	8	3	11	12
1972-73		71	20	22	42	6
1973-74		59	10	20	30	17
1974-75		14	2	1	3	0
	STL N	43	6	9	15	6
	2 team total	57	8	10	18	6
1975-76	KC N	80	17	18	35	14
1976-77	MINN W	30	6	11	17	6
	WASH N	28	7	10	17	2
	2 team total	58	13	21	34	8
1977-78		44	1	7	8	4
1978-79		3	1	1	2	0
8 yrs.	N Totals:	401	72	91	163	61
	W Totals:	30	6	11	17	6
PLAYOFFS						
1974-75	STL N	2	0	1	1	0

Traded to **St. Louis** by California with Stan Gilbertson for Warren Williams and Dave Gardner, Nov. 11, 1974. Traded to **Kansas City** by St. Louis with Denis Dupere and cash for Lynn Powis and Kansas City's second choice (Brian Sutter) in 1976 Amateur Draft, June 18, 1975. Signed as free agent by **Washington** from Colorado, Feb. 1, 1977.

Glenn Patrick

PATRICK, GLENN CURTISS 6'2", 195 lbs.
B. Apr. 26, 1950, New York, N.Y. Defense, Shoots L

YEAR	TEAM & LEAGUE		GP	G	A	PTS	PIM
1973-74	**STL**	**N**	1	0	0	0	2
1974-75	**CALIF**	**N**	2	0	0	0	0
1976-77	**CLEVE**	**N**	35	2	3	5	70
	EDM	**W**	23	0	4	4	62
	2 team total		58	2	7	9	132
3 yrs.		**N Totals:**	38	2	3	5	72
		W Totals:	23	0	4	4	62
PLAYOFFS							
1976-77	**EDM**	**W**	2	0	0	0	0

Traded to **California** by St. Louis for Ron Serafini, July 18, 1974.

Lester Patrick

PATRICK, LESTER 6'1", 180 lbs.
B. Dec. 30, 1883, Drummondville, Que. Defense
Hall of Fame, 1945

YEAR	TEAM & LEAGUE		GP	G	A	PTS	PIM
1926-27	**NYR**	**N**	1	0	0	0	0

Lynn Patrick

PATRICK, LYNN 6'1", 192 lbs.
B. Feb. 3, 1912, Victoria, B.C. Left Wing, Shoots L
Hall of Fame, 1980

YEAR	TEAM & LEAGUE		GP	G	A	PTS	PIM
1934-35	**NYR**	**N**	48	9	13	22	17
1935-36			48	11	14	25	29
1936-37			45	8	16	24	23
1937-38			48	15	19	34	24
1938-39			35	8	21	29	25
1939-40			48	12	16	28	34
1940-41			48	20	24	44	12
1941-42			47	**32**	22	54	18
1942-43			50	22	39	61	58
1945-46			38	8	6	14	30
10 yrs.		**N Totals:**	455	145	190	335	270
PLAYOFFS							
1934-35	**NYR**	**N**	4	2	2	4	0
1936-37			9	3	0	3	2
1937-38			3	0	1	1	2
1938-39			7	1	1	2	0
1939-40*			12	2	2	4	4
1940-41			3	1	0	1	14
1941-42			6	1	0	1	0
7 yrs.		**N Totals:**	44	10	6	16	22

Muzz Patrick

PATRICK, FREDERICK MURRAY 6'2", 200 lbs.
B. June 28, 1915, Victoria, B.C. Defense, Shoots L

YEAR	TEAM & LEAGUE		GP	G	A	PTS	PIM
1937-38	**NYR**	**N**	1	0	2	2	0
1938-39			48	1	10	11	64
1939-40			46	2	4	6	44
1940-41			47	2	8	10	21
1945-46			24	0	2	2	4
5 yrs.		**N Totals:**	166	5	26	31	133
PLAYOFFS							
1937-38	**NYR**	**N**	3	0	0	0	2
1938-39			7	1	0	1	17
1939-40*			12	3	0	3	13
1940-41			3	0	0	0	2
4 yrs.		**N Totals:**	25	4	0	4	34

Steve Patrick

PATRICK, STEPHEN GARY 6'4", 206 lbs.
B. Feb. 4, 1961, Winnipeg, Man. Right Wing, Shoots R

YEAR	TEAM & LEAGUE		GP	G	A	PTS	PIM
1980-81	**BUF**	**N**	30	1	7	8	25
1981-82			41	8	8	16	64
1982-83			56	9	13	22	26

Steve Patrick continued

YEAR	TEAM & LEAGUE		GP	G	A	PTS	PIM
3 yrs.		**N Totals:**	127	18	28	46	115
PLAYOFFS							
1980-81	**BUF**	**N**	5	0	1	1	6
1982-83			2	0	0	0	0
2 yrs.		**N Totals:**	7	0	1	1	6

Denis Patry

PATRY, DENIS 5'8", 165 lbs.
B. Dec. 3, 1953, Asbestos, Que. Right Wing, Shoots R

YEAR	TEAM & LEAGUE		GP	G	A	PTS	PIM
1974-75	**QUE**	**W**	3	1	2	3	2

Dennis Patterson

PATTERSON, DENNIS G. 5'8", 175 lbs.
B. Jan. 9, 1950, Peterborough, Ont. Defense, Shoots L

YEAR	TEAM & LEAGUE		GP	G	A	PTS	PIM
1974-75	**KC**	**N**	66	1	5	6	39
1975-76			69	5	16	21	28
1976-77	**EDM**	**W**	23	0	2	2	2
1979-80	**PHI**	**N**	3	0	1	1	0
4 yrs.		**N Totals:**	138	6	22	28	67
		W Totals:	23	0	2	2	2

Drafted by **Kansas City** from Minnesota in Expansion Draft, June 12, 1974. Signed as a free agent with **Philadelphia** Aug. 8, 1979.

Pat Patterson

PATTERSON, GEORGE 6'1", 176 lbs.
B. May 22, 1906, Kingston, Ont. Right Wing

YEAR	TEAM & LEAGUE		GP	G	A	PTS	PIM
1926-27	**TOR**	**N**	17	4	2	6	17
1927-28			12	1	0	1	17
	MONT	**N**	16	0	1	1	0
	2 team total		28	1	1	2	17
1928-29			44	4	5	9	34
1929-30	**NYA**	**N**	44	13	4	17	24
1930-31			44	8	6	14	67
1931-32			20	6	0	6	26
1932-33			48	12	7	19	26
1933-34			13	3	0	3	6
	BOS	**N**	10	0	1	1	2
	2 team total		23	3	1	4	8
1934-35	**DET**	**N**	7	0	1	1	0
	STL	**N**	14	0	0	0	2
	2 team total		21	0	1	1	2
9 yrs.		**N Totals:**	289	51	27	78	221
PLAYOFFS							
1928-29	**MONT**	**N**	3	0	0	0	2

Arthur Paul

PAUL, ARTHUR STEWART (Butch) 5'11", 160 lbs.
B. Sept. 11, 1943, Rocky Mtn. House, Alta.
Center, Shoots R

YEAR	TEAM & LEAGUE		GP	G	A	PTS	PIM
1964-65	**DET**	**N**	3	0	0	0	0

Rollie Paulus

PAULUS, ROLAND
B. Unknown
Defense

YEAR	TEAM & LEAGUE		GP	G	A	PTS	PIM
1925-26	**MONT**	**N**	33	0	0	0	0

Mark Pavelich

PAVELICH, MARK (Pav) 5'8", 170 lbs.
B. Feb. 28, 1958, Eveleth, Minn. Center, Shoots R

YEAR	TEAM & LEAGUE		GP	G	A	PTS	PIM
1981-82	**NYR**	**N**	79	33	43	76	67
1982-83			78	37	38	75	52
2 yrs.		**N Totals:**	157	70	81	151	119
PLAYOFFS							
1981-82	**NYR**	**N**	6	1	5	6	0
1982-83			9	4	5	9	12
2 yrs.		**N Totals:**	15	5	10	15	12

Signed as free agent by **N.Y. Rangers** June, 1981.

Marty Pavelich

PAVELICH, MARTIN NICHOLAS 5'10", 170 lbs.

B. Nov. 6, 1927, Sault Ste. Marie, Ont. Left Wing, Shoots L

YEAR	TEAM & LEAGUE		GP	G	A	PTS	PIM
1947-48	**DET**	**N**	41	4	8	12	10
1948-49			60	10	16	26	40
1949-50			65	8	15	23	58
1950-51			67	9	20	29	41
1951-52			68	17	19	36	54
1952-53			64	13	20	33	49
1953-54			65	9	20	29	57
1954-55			70	15	15	30	59
1955-56			70	5	13	18	38
1956-57			64	3	13	16	48
10 yrs.		**N Totals:**	634	93	159	252	454
PLAYOFFS							
1947-48	**DET**	**N**	10	2	2	4	6
1948-49			9	0	1	1	8
1949-50*			14	4	2	6	13
1950-51			6	0	1	1	2
1951-52*			8	2	2	4	2
1952-53			6	2	1	3	7
1953-54*			12	2	2	4	4
1954-55*			11	1	3	4	12
1955-56			10	0	1	1	14
1956-57			5	0	0	0	6
10 yrs.		**N Totals:**	91	13	15	28	74

Jim Pavese

PAVESE, JAMES PETER 6'2", 204 lbs.

B. May 8, 1962, New York, N.Y. Defense, Shoots L

YEAR	TEAM & LEAGUE		GP	G	A	PTS	PIM
1981-82	**STL**	**N**	42	2	9	11	101
1982-83			24	0	2	2	45
2 yrs.		**N Totals:**	66	2	11	13	146
PLAYOFFS							
1981-82	**STL**	**N**	3	0	3	3	2
1982-83			4	0	0	0	6
2 yrs.		**N Totals:**	7	0	3	3	8

Evariste Payer

PAYER, EVARISTE P.

B. Unknown Forward

YEAR	TEAM & LEAGUE		GP	G	A	PTS	PIM
1917-18	**MONT**	**N**	1	0	0	0	0

Jean Payette

PAYETTE, JEAN LAURENT 6', 170 lbs.

B. Mar. 29, 1946, Cornwall, Ont. Center, Shoots L

YEAR	TEAM & LEAGUE		GP	G	A	PTS	PIM
1972-73	**QUE**	**W**	71	15	29	44	46
1973-74			41	4	11	15	6
2 yrs.		**W Totals:**	112	19	40	59	52

Steve Payne

PAYNE, STEVEN JOHN 6'2", 205 lbs.

B. Aug. 16, 1958, Toronto, Ont. Left Wing, Shoots L

YEAR	TEAM & LEAGUE		GP	G	A	PTS	PIM
1978-79	**MINN**	**N**	70	23	17	40	29
1979-80			80	42	43	85	40
1980-81			76	30	28	58	88
1981-82			74	33	45	78	76
1982-83			80	30	39	69	53
5 yrs.		**N Totals:**	380	158	172	330	286
PLAYOFFS							
1979-80	**MINN**	**N**	15	7	7	14	9
1980-81			19	17	12	29	6
1981-82			4	4	2	6	2
1982-83			9	3	6	9	19
4 yrs.		**N Totals:**	47	31	27	58	36

Gene Peacosh

PEACOSH, EUGENE (Peco) 5'11", 190 lbs.

B. Sept. 28, 1948, Sherridon, Man. Left Wing, Shoots L

YEAR	TEAM & LEAGUE		GP	G	A	PTS	PIM
1972-73	**NY**	**W**	67	37	34	71	25
1973-74	**NY-NJ**	**W**	68	21	32	53	17
1974-75	**SD**	**W**	78	43	36	79	22
1975-76			79	37	33	70	35
1976-77	**EDM**	**W**	11	5	4	9	14
	IND	**W**	64	22	26	48	21
	2 team total		75	27	30	57	35
5 yrs.		**W Totals:**	367	165	165	330	134
PLAYOFFS							
1974-75	**SD**	**W**	10	7	5	12	4
1975-76			11	2	1	3	21
1976-77	**IND**	**W**	9	3	3	6	2
3 yrs.		**W Totals:**	30	12	9	21	27

Mel Pearson

PEARSON, GEORGE ALEXANDER MELVIN 5'10", 175 lbs.

B. Apr. 29, 1938, Flin Flon, Man. Left Wing, Shoots L

YEAR	TEAM & LEAGUE		GP	G	A	PTS	PIM
1959-60	**NYR**	**N**	23	1	5	6	13
1961-62			3	0	0	0	2
1962-63			5	1	0	1	6
1964-65			5	0	0	0	4
1967-68	**PITT**	**N**	2	0	1	1	0
1972-73	**MINN**	**W**	70	8	12	20	12
6 yrs.		**N Totals:**	38	2	6	8	25
		W Totals:	70	8	12	20	12
PLAYOFFS							
1972-73	**MINN**	**W**	5	2	0	2	0

Drafted by **Pittsburgh** from Chicago in Expansion Draft, June 6, 1967.

Barry Pederson

PEDERSON, BARRY ALAN 5'11", 171 lbs.

B. Mar. 13, 1961, Big River, Sask. Center, Shoots R

YEAR	TEAM & LEAGUE		GP	G	A	PTS	PIM
1980-81	**BOS**	**N**	9	1	4	5	6
1981-82			80	44	48	92	53
1982-83			77	46	61	107	47
3 yrs.		**N Totals:**	166	91	113	204	106
PLAYOFFS							
1981-82	**BOS**	**N**	11	7	11	18	2
1982-83			17	14	18	32	21
2 yrs.		**N Totals:**	28	21	29	50	23

Bert Peer

PEER, BERTRAM

B. Unknown Defense

YEAR	TEAM & LEAGUE		GP	G	A	PTS	PIM
1939-40	**DET**	**N**	1	0	0	0	0

Johnny Peirson

PEIRSON, JOHN FREDERICK 5'11", 170 lbs.

B. July 21, 1925, Winnipeg, Man. Right Wing, Shoots R

YEAR	TEAM & LEAGUE		GP	G	A	PTS	PIM
1946-47	**BOS**	**N**	5	0	0	0	0
1947-48			15	4	2	6	0
1948-49			59	22	21	43	45
1949-50			57	27	25	52	49
1950-51			70	19	19	38	43
1951-52			68	20	30	50	30
1952-53			49	14	15	29	32
1953-54			68	21	19	40	55
1955-56			33	11	14	25	10
1956-57			68	13	26	39	41
1957-58			53	2	2	4	10
11 yrs.		**N Totals:**	545	153	173	326	315
PLAYOFFS							
1947-48	**BOS**	**N**	4	2	3	5	0
1948-49			5	3	1	4	4
1950-51			2	1	1	2	2
1951-52			7	0	2	2	4

YEAR	TEAM & LEAGUE		GP	G	A	PTS	PIM

Johnny Peirson continued

YEAR	TEAM	LEAGUE	GP	G	A	PTS	PIM
1952-53			11	3	6	9	2
1953-54			4	0	0	0	2
1956-57			10	0	3	3	12
1957-58			5	0	1	1	0
8 yrs.		**N Totals:**	48	9	17	26	26

Andre Peloffy

PELOFFY, ANDRE CHARLES 5'8", 160 lbs.
B. Feb. 25, 1951, Sete, France Center, Shoots L

YEAR	TEAM	LEAGUE	GP	G	A	PTS	PIM
1974-75	**WASH**	**N**	9	0	0	0	2
1977-78	**NE**	**W**	10	2	0	2	2
2 yrs.		**N Totals:**	9	0	0	0	2
		W Totals:	10	2	0	2	2

PLAYOFFS

YEAR	TEAM	LEAGUE	GP	G	A	PTS	PIM
1977-78	**NE**	**W**	2	0	0	0	0

Sold to **Washington** by N.Y. Rangers, July 29, 1974.

Mike Pelyk

PELYK, MICHAEL JOSEPH 6'1", 188 lbs.
B. Sept. 29, 1947, Toronto, Ont. Defense, Shoots L

YEAR	TEAM	LEAGUE	GP	G	A	PTS	PIM
1967-68	**TOR**	**N**	24	0	3	3	55
1968-69			65	3	9	12	146
1969-70			35	1	3	4	37
1970-71			73	5	21	26	54
1971-72			46	1	4	5	44
1972-73			72	3	16	19	118
1973-74			71	12	19	31	94
1974-75	**VAN**	**W**	75	14	26	40	121
1975-76	**CIN**	**W**	75	10	23	33	117
1976-77	**TOR**	**N**	13	0	2	2	4
1977-78			41	1	11	12	14
11 yrs.		**N Totals:**	440	26	88	114	566
		W Totals:	150	24	49	73	238

PLAYOFFS

YEAR	TEAM	LEAGUE	GP	G	A	PTS	PIM
1968-69	**TOR**	**N**	4	0	0	0	8
1970-71			6	0	0	0	10
1971-72			5	0	0	0	8
1973-74			4	0	0	0	4
1976-77			9	0	2	2	4
1977-78			12	0	1	1	7
6 yrs.		**N Totals:**	40	0	3	3	41

Cliff Pennington

PENNINGTON, CLIFFORD 6', 170 lbs.
B. Apr. 18, 1940, Winnipeg, Man. Center, Shoots R

YEAR	TEAM	LEAGUE	GP	G	A	PTS	PIM
1960-61	**MONT**	**N**	4	1	0	1	0
1961-62	**BOS**	**N**	70	9	32	41	2
1962-63			27	7	10	17	4
3 yrs.		**N Totals:**	101	17	42	59	6

Dwayne Pentland

PENTLAND, DWAYNE WILBERT 5'10", 180 lbs.
B. Feb. 8, 1953, Vancouver, B.C. Defense, Shoots L

YEAR	TEAM	LEAGUE	GP	G	A	PTS	PIM
1976-77	**HOUS**	**W**	29	1	2	3	6

PLAYOFFS

YEAR	TEAM	LEAGUE	GP	G	A	PTS	PIM
1976-77	**HOUS**	**W**	2	0	0	0	0

Jim Peplinski

PEPLINSKI, JAMES DESMOND (Pep) 6'2", 201 lbs.
B. Oct. 24, 1960, Renfrew, Ont. Right Wing, Shoots R

YEAR	TEAM	LEAGUE	GP	G	A	PTS	PIM
1980-81	**CALG**	**N**	80	13	25	38	108
1981-82			74	30	37	67	115
1982-83			80	15	26	41	134
3 yrs.		**N Totals:**	234	58	88	146	357

PLAYOFFS

YEAR	TEAM	LEAGUE	GP	G	A	PTS	PIM
1980-81	**CALG**	**N**	16	2	3	5	41
1981-82			3	1	0	1	13
1982-83			8	1	1	2	45

YEAR	TEAM & LEAGUE		GP	G	A	PTS	PIM

Jim Peplinski continued

YEAR	TEAM	LEAGUE	GP	G	A	PTS	PIM
3 yrs.		**N Totals:**	27	4	4	8	99

Ross Perkins

PERKINS, ROSS HAROLD 5'10", 176 lbs.
B. Nov. 4, 1946, Tisdale, Sask. Center, Shoots R

YEAR	TEAM	LEAGUE	GP	G	A	PTS	PIM
1972-73	**ALTA**	**W**	71	21	37	58	19
1973-74	**EDM**	**W**	78	16	40	56	43
1974-75			76	7	16	23	33
3 yrs.		**W Totals:**	225	44	93	137	95

PLAYOFFS

YEAR	TEAM	LEAGUE	GP	G	A	PTS	PIM
1973-74	**EDM**	**W**	5	1	3	4	2

Fred Perlini

PERLINI, FREDERICK 6'2", 175 lbs.
B. Apr. 12, 1962, Sault Ste. Marie, Ont. Center, Shoots L

YEAR	TEAM	LEAGUE	GP	G	A	PTS	PIM
1981-82	**TOR**	**N**	7	2	3	5	0

Fern Perreault

PERREAULT, FERNAND 6', 180 lbs.
B. Mar. 31, 1927, Chambly Basin, Que. Left Wing, Shoots L

YEAR	TEAM	LEAGUE	GP	G	A	PTS	PIM
1947-48	**NYR**	**N**	2	0	0	0	0
1949-50			1	0	0	0	0
2 yrs.		**N Totals:**	3	0	0	0	0

Gil Perreault

PERREAULT, GILBERT 6', 202 lbs.
B. Nov. 13, 1960, Victoriaville, Que. Center, Shoots L
Won Lady Byng Trophy, 1972-73
Won Calder Trophy, 1970-71

YEAR	TEAM	LEAGUE	GP	G	A	PTS	PIM
1970-71	**BUF**	**N**	78	38	34	72	19
1971-72			76	26	48	74	24
1972-73			78	28	60	88	10
1973-74			55	18	33	51	10
1974-75			68	39	57	96	36
1975-76			80	44	69	113	36
1976-77			80	39	56	95	30
1977-78			79	41	48	89	20
1978-79			79	27	58	85	20
1979-80			80	40	66	106	57
1980-81			56	20	39	59	56
1981-82			62	31	42	73	40
1982-83			77	30	46	76	34
13 yrs.		**N Totals:**	948	421	656	1077	392

PLAYOFFS

YEAR	TEAM	LEAGUE	GP	G	A	PTS	PIM
1972-73	**BUF**	**N**	6	3	7	10	2
1974-75			17	6	9	15	10
1975-76			9	4	4	8	4
1976-77			6	1	8	9	4
1977-78			8	3	2	5	0
1978-79			3	1	0	1	2
1979-80			14	10	11	21	8
1980-81			8	2	10	12	2
1981-82			4	0	7	7	0
1982-83			10	0	7	7	8
10 yrs.		**N Totals:**	85	30	65	95	40

Brian Perry

PERRY, BRIAN THOMAS 5'11", 180 lbs.
B. Apr. 6, 1944, Aldershot, England Center, Shoots L

YEAR	TEAM	LEAGUE	GP	G	A	PTS	PIM
1968-69	**CALIF**	**N**	61	10	21	31	10
1969-70	**OAK**	**N**	34	6	8	14	14
1970-71	**BUF**	**N**	1	0	0	0	0
1972-73	**NY**	**W**	74	13	20	33	30

Brian Perry continued

YEAR	TEAM & LEAGUE		GP	G	A	PTS	PIM
1973-74	**NY-NJ**	**W**	71	20	11	31	19
5 yrs.		**N Totals:**	96	16	29	45	24
		W Totals:	145	33	31	64	49
PLAYOFFS							
1968-69	**CALIF**	**N**	6	1	1	2	4
1969-70	**OAK**	**N**	2	0	0	0	0
1974-75	**SD**	**W**	6	1	2	3	6
3 yrs.		**N Totals:**	8	1	1	2	4
		W Totals:	6	1	2	3	6

Drafted by **Buffalo** from Oakland in Expansion Draft, June 10, 1970.

Stefan Persson

PERSSON, STEFAN (Steff) 6'1", 189 lbs.
B. Dec. 22, 1954, Bjurholm, Sweden Defense, Shoots L

YEAR	TEAM & LEAGUE		GP	G	A	PTS	PIM
1977-78	**NYI**	**N**	66	6	50	56	54
1978-79			78	10	56	66	57
1979-80			73	4	35	39	76
1980-81			80	9	52	61	82
1981-82			70	6	37	43	99
1982-83			70	4	25	29	71
6 yrs.		**N Totals:**	437	39	255	294	439
PLAYOFFS							
1977-78	**NYI**	**N**	7	0	2	2	6
1978-79			10	0	4	4	8
1979-80*			21	5	10	15	16
1980-81*			7	0	5	5	6
1981-82*			13	1	14	15	9
1982-83*			18	1	5	6	18
6 yrs.		**N Totals:**	76	7	40	47	63

George Pesut

PESUT, GEORGE MATHEW 6'1", 185 lbs.
B. June 17, 1953, Saskatoon, Sask. Defense, Shoots L

YEAR	TEAM & LEAGUE		GP	G	A	PTS	PIM
1974-75	**CALIF**	**N**	47	0	13	13	73
1975-76			45	3	9	12	57
1976-77	**CALG**	**W**	17	2	0	2	2
3 yrs.		**N Totals:**	92	3	22	25	130
		W Totals:	17	2	0	2	2

Traded to **California** by Philadelphia for the rights to Ron Chipperfield, Dec. 11, 1974.

Frank Peters

PETERS, FRANKLIN J.
B. June 5, 1905, Rouses Point, N.Y. Defense

YEAR	TEAM & LEAGUE		GP	G	A	PTS	PIM
1930-31	**NYR**	**N**	43	0	0	0	59
PLAYOFFS							
1930-31	**NYR**	**N**	4	0	0	0	2

Garry Peters

PETERS, GARRY LORNE 5'10", 180 lbs.
B. Regina, Sask. Center, Shoots L

YEAR	TEAM & LEAGUE		GP	G	A	PTS	PIM
1964-65	**MONT**	**N**	13	0	2	2	6
1965-66	**NYR**	**N**	63	7	3	10	42
1966-67	**MONT**	**N**	4	0	1	1	2
1967-68	**PHI**	**N**	31	7	5	12	22
1968-69			66	8	6	14	49
1969-70			59	6	10	16	69
1970-71			73	6	7	13	69
1971-72	**BOS**	**N**	2	0	0	0	2
1972-73	**NY**	**W**	23	2	7	9	24
1973-74	**NY-NJ**	**W**	34	2	5	7	18
10 yrs.		**N Totals:**	311	34	34	68	261
		W Totals:	57	4	12	16	42
PLAYOFFS							
1968-69	**PHI**	**N**	4	1	1	2	16
1970-71			4	1	1	2	15
1971-72*	**BOS**	**N**	1	0	0	0	0
3 yrs.		**N Totals:**	9	2	2	4	31

Jim Peters

PETERS, JAMES MELDRUM 5'11", 165 lbs.
B. Oct. 2, 1922, Verdun, Que. Right Wing, Shoots R

YEAR	TEAM & LEAGUE		GP	G	A	PTS	PIM
1945-46	**MONT**	**N**	47	11	19	30	10
1946-47			60	11	13	24	27
1947-48			22	1	3	4	6
	BOS	**N**	37	12	15	27	38
	2 team total		59	13	18	31	44
1948-49			60	16	15	31	8
1949-50	**DET**	**N**	70	14	16	30	20
1950-51			68	17	21	38	14
1951-52	**CHI**	**N**	70	15	21	36	15
1952-53			69	22	19	41	16
1953-54			46	6	4	10	21
	DET	**N**	26	0	4	4	10
	2 team total		72	6	8	14	31
9 yrs.		**N Totals:**	575	125	150	275	185
PLAYOFFS							
1945-46*	**MONT**	**N**	9	3	1	4	6
1946-47			11	1	2	3	10
1947-48	**BOS**	**N**	5	1	2	3	2
1948-49			4	0	1	1	0
1949-50*	**DET**	**N**	8	0	2	2	0
1950-51			6	0	0	0	0
1952-53	**CHI**	**N**	7	0	1	1	4
1953-54*	**DET**	**N**	10	0	0	0	0
8 yrs.		**N Totals:**	60	5	9	14	22

Traded to **Detroit** by Boston with Pete Babando, Clare Martin and Lloyd Durham for Bill Quackenbush and Pete Horeck, Aug. 16, 1949. Traded to **Chicago** by Detroit with Jim McFadden, George Gee, Clare Martin, Rags Raglan and Max McNab for Hugh Coflin and $75,000, Aug. 20, 1951. Traded to **Detroit** by Chicago for rights to two unnamed juniors, Jan. 25, 1954.

Jimmy Peters

PETERS, JAMES STEPHEN JR. 6'2", 185 lbs.
B. June 20, 1944, Montreal, Que. Center, Shoots L

YEAR	TEAM & LEAGUE		GP	G	A	PTS	PIM
1964-65	**DET**	**N**	1	0	0	0	0
1965-66			6	1	1	2	2
1966-67			2	0	0	0	0
1967-68			45	5	6	11	8
1968-69	**LA**	**N**	76	10	15	25	28
1969-70			74	15	9	24	10
1972-73			77	4	5	9	0
1973-74			25	2	0	2	0
1974-75			3	0	0	0	0
9 yrs.		**N Totals:**	309	37	36	73	48
PLAYOFFS							
1968-69	**LA**	**N**	11	0	2	2	2

Traded to **Los Angeles** by Detroit for Terry Sawchuk, Oct. 10, 1968.

Steve Peters

PETERS, STEVEN ALAN 5'11", 186 lbs.
B. Jan. 23, 1960, Peterborough, Ont. Center, Shoots L

YEAR	TEAM & LEAGUE		GP	G	A	PTS	PIM
1979-80	**COLO**	**N**	2	0	1	1	0

Brent Peterson

PETERSON, BRENT RONALD 6', 190 lbs.
B. Feb. 15, 1958, Calgary, Alta. Center, Shoots R

YEAR	TEAM & LEAGUE		GP	G	A	PTS	PIM
1978-79	**DET**	**N**	5	0	0	0	0
1979-80			18	1	2	3	2
1980-81			53	6	18	24	24
1981-82			15	1	0	1	6
	BUF	**N**	46	9	5	14	43
	2 team total		61	10	5	15	49
1982-83			75	13	24	37	38
5 yrs.		**N Totals:**	212	30	49	79	113
PLAYOFFS							
1981-82	**BUF**	**N**	4	1	0	1	12
1982-83			10	1	2	3	28
2 yrs.		**N Totals:**	14	2	2	4	40

Traded to **Buffalo** by Detroit along with Mike Foligno and Dale McCourt for

Danny Gare, Jim Schoenfeld and Derek Smith, Dec. 2, 1981.

Michel Petit

PETIT, MICHEL 6'1", 191 lbs.
B. Feb. 12, 1964, St. Malo, Que. Defense, Shoots R

YEAR	TEAM & LEAGUE		GP	G	A	PTS	PIM
1982-83	**VAN**	**N**	2	0	0	0	0

Jorgen Pettersson

PETTERSSON, JORGEN 6'2", 185 lbs.
B. July 11, 1956, Gothenburg, Sweden Left Wing, Shoots L

YEAR	TEAM & LEAGUE		GP	G	A	PTS	PIM
1980-81	**STL**	**N**	62	37	36	73	24
1981-82			77	38	31	69	28
1982-83			74	35	38	73	4
3 yrs.		**N Totals:**	213	110	105	215	56
PLAYOFFS							
1980-81	**STL**	**N**	11	4	3	7	0
1981-82			7	1	2	3	0
1982-83			4	1	1	2	0
3 yrs.		**N Totals:**	22	6	6	12	0

Signed as free agent with **St. Louis** May 8, 1980.

Eric Pettinger

PETTINGER, ERIC (Cowboy) 6', 175 lbs.
B. Regina, Sask. Left Wing, Shoots L

YEAR	TEAM & LEAGUE		GP	G	A	PTS	PIM
1928-29	**BOS**	**N**	17	0	0	0	17
	TOR	**N**	25	3	3	6	24
	2 team total		42	3	3	6	41
1929-30			43	4	9	13	40
1930-31	**OTTA**	**N**	12	0	0	0	2
3 yrs.		**N Totals:**	97	7	12	19	83
PLAYOFFS							
1928-29	**TOR**	**N**	4	1	0	1	8

Gord Pettinger

PETTINGER, GORDON ROBINSON 6', 175 lbs.
B. Nov. 17, 1911, Regina, Sask. Center, Shoots L

YEAR	TEAM & LEAGUE		GP	G	A	PTS	PIM
1932-33	**NYR**	**N**	35	1	2	3	18
1933-34	**DET**	**N**	48	3	14	17	14
1934-35			13	2	3	5	2
1935-36			33	8	7	15	6
1936-37			48	7	15	22	13
1937-38			11	1	3	4	4
	BOS	**N**	35	7	10	17	10
	2 team total		46	8	13	21	14
1938-39			48	11	14	25	8
1939-40			21	2	6	8	2
8 yrs.		**N Totals:**	292	42	74	116	77
PLAYOFFS							
1932-33*	**NYR**	**N**	8	0	0	0	0
1933-34	**DET**	**N**	9	1	0	1	2
1935-36*			7	2	2	4	0
1936-37*			10	0	2	2	2
1937-38	**BOS**	**N**	3	0	0	0	0
1938-39*			12	1	1	2	7
6 yrs.		**N Totals:**	49	4	5	9	11

Jean Phaneuf

PHANEUF, JEAN-LUC 5'8", 165 lbs.
B. Oct. 26, 1955, Montreal, Que. Center, Shoots R

YEAR	TEAM & LEAGUE		GP	G	A	PTS	PIM
1975-76	**TOR**	**W**	48	8	8	16	4
1976-77	**BIRM**	**W**	30	2	7	9	2
2 yrs.		**W Totals:**	78	10	15	25	6

Harold Phillipoff

PHILLIPOFF, HAROLD 6'3", 220 lbs.
B. July 15, 1956, Kamsack, Sask. Left Wing, Shoots L

YEAR	TEAM & LEAGUE		GP	G	A	PTS	PIM
1977-78	**ATL**	**N**	67	17	36	53	128
1978-79			51	9	17	26	113
	CHI	**N**	14	0	4	4	6
	2 team total		65	9	21	30	119

Harold Phillipoff continued

YEAR	TEAM & LEAGUE		GP	G	A	PTS	PIM
1979-80			9	0	0	0	20
3 yrs.		**N Totals:**	141	26	57	83	267
PLAYOFFS							
1977-78	**ATL**	**N**	2	0	1	1	2
1978-79	**CHI**	**N**	4	0	1	1	7
2 yrs.		**N Totals:**	6	0	2	2	9

Traded to **Chicago** by Atlanta with Tom Lysiak, Pat Ribble, Greg Fox and Miles Zaharko for Ivan Boldirev, Phil Russell and Darcy Rota, Mar. 13, 1979. Traded to **Vancouver** by Chicago with Dave Logan for Ron Sedlbauer, Dec. 21, 1979.

Bat Phillips

PHILLIPS, W.J.
B. Carleton Place, Ont. Right Wing

YEAR	TEAM & LEAGUE		GP	G	A	PTS	PIM
1929-30	**MON(M)**	**N**	27	1	1	2	6
PLAYOFFS							
1929-30	**MON(M)**	**N**	4	0	0	0	2

Bill Phillips

PHILLIPS, MERLYN J. 5'7", 160 lbs.
B. Thesselon, Ont. Forward, Shoots R

YEAR	TEAM & LEAGUE		GP	G	A	PTS	PIM
1925-26	**MON(M)**	**N**	12	3	1	4	6
1926-27			43	15	1	16	45
1927-28			41	7	5	12	33
1928-29			42	6	5	11	41
1929-30			42	13	10	23	38
1930-31			42	6	1	7	38
1931-32			47	1	1	2	11
1932-33			2	0	0	0	0
	NYA	**N**	26	1	7	8	10
	2 team total		28	1	7	8	10
8 yrs.		**N Totals:**	297	52	31	83	222
PLAYOFFS							
1925-26*	**MON(M)**	**N**	8	1	1	2	4
1926-27			2	0	0	0	0
1927-28			9	2	1	3	13
1929-30			4	0	0	0	6
1930-31			1	0	0	0	2
1931-32			4	0	0	0	2
6 yrs.		**N Totals:**	28	3	2	5	27

Charlie Phillips

PHILLIPS, CHARLES
B. May 10, 1917, Toronto, Ont. Defense

YEAR	TEAM & LEAGUE		GP	G	A	PTS	PIM
1942-43	**MONT**	**N**	17	0	0	0	6

Adrien Picard

PICARD, ADRIEN ROGER 6', 200 lbs.
B. Jan. 13, 1935, Montreal, Que. Right Wing, Shoots R

YEAR	TEAM & LEAGUE		GP	G	A	PTS	PIM
1967-68	**STL**	**N**	15	2	2	4	21

Bob Picard

PICARD, ROBERT RENE JOSEPH 6'2", 211 lbs.
B. May 25, 1957, Montreal, Que. Defense, Shoots L

YEAR	TEAM & LEAGUE		GP	G	A	PTS	PIM
1977-78	**WASH**	**N**	75	10	27	37	101
1978-79			77	21	44	65	85
1979-80			78	11	43	54	122
1980-81	**TOR**	**N**	59	6	19	25	68
	MONT	**N**	8	2	2	4	6
	2 team total		67	8	21	29	74
1981-82			62	2	26	28	106
1982-83			64	7	31	38	60
6 yrs.		**N Totals:**	423	59	192	251	548
PLAYOFFS							
1980-81	**MONT**	**N**	1	0	0	0	0
1981-82			5	1	1	2	7
1982-83			3	0	0	0	0
3 yrs.		**N Totals:**	9	1	1	2	7

Traded to **Toronto** by Washington with Tom Coulis and Washington's second round draft choice in 1980 Entry Draft (Bob McGill) for Mike Palmateer and Toronto's third round choice in 1980 Entry Draft (Torrie

Robertson), June 11, 1980. Traded to **Montreal** by Toronto for Michel Larocque, Mar. 10, 1981.

Noel Picard

PICARD, JEAN-NOEL YVES 6'1", 185 lbs.
B. Dec. 25, 1938, Montreal, Que. Shoots R

YEAR	TEAM & LEAGUE		GP	G	A	PTS	PIM
1964-65	**MONT**	**N**	16	0	7	7	33
1967-68	**STL**	**N**	66	1	10	11	142
1968-69			67	5	19	24	131
1969-70			39	1	4	5	88
1970-71			75	3	8	11	119
1971-72			15	1	5	6	50
1972-73			16	1	0	1	10
	ATL	**N**	41	0	10	10	43
	2 team total		57	1	10	11	53
7 yrs.		**N Totals:**	335	12	63	75	616
PLAYOFFS							
1964-65*	**MONT**	**N**	3	0	1	1	0
1967-68	**STL**	**N**	13	0	3	3	46
1968-69			12	1	4	5	30
1969-70			16	0	2	2	65
1970-71			6	1	1	2	26
5 yrs.		**N Totals:**	50	2	11	13	167

Drafted by **St. Louis** from Montreal in Expansion Draft, June 6, 1967. Claimed on waivers by **Atlanta** from St. Louis, Nov. 25, 1972.

Dave Pichette

PICHETTE, DAVID 6'3", 200 lbs.
B. Feb. 4, 1960, Grand Falls, Nfld. Defense, Shoots L

YEAR	TEAM & LEAGUE		GP	G	A	PTS	PIM
1980-81	**QUE**	**N**	46	4	16	20	62
1981-82			67	7	30	37	152
1982-83			53	3	21	24	49
3 yrs.		**N Totals:**	166	14	67	81	263
PLAYOFFS							
1980-81	**QUE**	**N**	1	0	0	0	14
1981-82			16	2	4	6	22
1982-83			2	0	1	1	0
3 yrs.		**N Totals:**	19	2	5	7	36

Signed as free agent with **Quebec** Oct. 31, 1979.

Hal Picketts

PICKETTS, FREDERIC HAROLD 180 lbs.
B. Apr. 22, 1909, Asquith, Sask. Forward, Shoots R

YEAR	TEAM & LEAGUE		GP	G	A	PTS	PIM
1933-34	**NYA**	**N**	48	3	1	4	32

Harry Pidhirny

PIDHIRNY, HARRY 5'11", 155 lbs.
B. Mar. 5, 1928, Toronto, Ont. Center, Shoots L

YEAR	TEAM & LEAGUE		GP	G	A	PTS	PIM
1957-58	**BOS**	**N**	2	0	0	0	0

Randy Pierce

PIERCE, RANDOLPH STEPHEN 5'11", 187 lbs.
B. Nov. 23, 1957, Arnprior, Ont. Right Wing, Shoots R

YEAR	TEAM & LEAGUE		GP	G	A	PTS	PIM
1977-78	**COLO**	**N**	35	9	10	19	15
1978-79			70	19	17	36	35
1979-80			75	16	23	39	100
1980-81			55	9	21	30	52
1981-82			5	0	0	0	4
1982-83	**NJ**	**N**	3	0	0	0	0
6 yrs.		**N Totals:**	243	53	71	124	206
PLAYOFFS							
1977-78	**COLO**	**N**	2	0	0	0	0

Alf Pike

PIKE, ALFRED G. 6', 187 lbs.
B. Sept. 15, 1917, Winnipeg, Man. Center, Shoots L

YEAR	TEAM & LEAGUE		GP	G	A	PTS	PIM
1939-40	**NYR**	**N**	47	8	9	17	38
1940-41			48	6	13	19	23
1941-42			34	8	19	27	16

Alf Pike continued

YEAR	TEAM & LEAGUE		GP	G	A	PTS	PIM
1942-43			41	6	16	22	48
1945-46			33	7	9	16	18
1946-47			31	7	11	18	2
6 yrs.		**N Totals:**	234	42	77	119	145
PLAYOFFS							
1939-40*	**NYR**	**N**	12	3	1	4	6
1940-41			3	0	1	1	2
1941-42			6	1	0	1	4
3 yrs.		**N Totals:**	21	4	2	6	12

Pierre Pilote

PILOTE, PIERRE PAUL 5'10", 178 lbs.
B. Dec. 11, 1931, Kenogami, Que. Defense, Shoots L
Won Norris Trophy, 1962–63, 1963–64, 1964-65
Hall of Fame, 1975

YEAR	TEAM & LEAGUE		GP	G	A	PTS	PIM
1955-56	**CHI**	**N**	20	3	5	8	34
1956-57			70	3	14	17	117
1957-58			70	6	24	30	91
1958-59			70	7	30	37	79
1959-60			70	7	38	45	100
1960-61			70	6	29	35	**165**
1961-62			59	7	35	42	97
1962-63			59	8	18	26	57
1963-64			70	7	46	53	84
1964-65			68	14	45	59	162
1965-66			51	2	34	36	60
1966-67			70	6	46	52	90
1967-68			74	1	36	37	69
1968-69	**TOR**	**N**	69	3	18	21	46
14 yrs.		**N Totals:**	890	80	418	498	1251
PLAYOFFS							
1958-59	**CHI**	**N**	6	0	2	2	10
1959-60			4	0	1	1	8
1960-61*			12	3	12	15	8
1961-62			12	0	7	7	8
1962-63			6	0	8	8	8
1963-64			7	2	6	8	6
1964-65			12	0	7	7	22
1965-66			6	0	2	2	10
1966-67			6	2	4	6	6
1967-68			11	1	3	4	12
1968-69	**TOR**	**N**	4	0	1	1	4
11 yrs.		**N Totals:**	86	8	53	61	102

Traded to **Toronto** by Chicago for Jim Pappin, May 23, 1968.

Gerry Pinder

PINDER, ALLEN GERALD 5'8", 165 lbs.
B. Sept. 15, 1948, Saskatoon, Sask. Left Wing, Shoots R

YEAR	TEAM & LEAGUE		GP	G	A	PTS	PIM
1969-70	**CHI**	**N**	75	19	20	39	41
1970-71			74	13	18	31	35
1971-72	**CALIF**	**N**	74	23	31	54	59
1972-73	**CLEVE**	**W**	78	30	36	66	21
1973-74			73	23	33	56	90
1974-75			74	13	28	41	71
1975-76			79	21	30	51	118
1976-77	**SD**	**W**	44	6	13	19	36
1977-78	**EDM**	**W**	5	0	1	1	0
9 yrs.		**N Totals:**	223	55	69	124	135
		W Totals:	353	93	141	234	336
PLAYOFFS							
1969-70	**CHI**	**N**	8	0	4	4	4
1970-71			9	0	0	0	2
1972-73	**CLEVE**	**W**	9	2	9	11	30
1973-74			1	0	0	0	0
1974-75			5	3	1	4	6
1975-76			3	0	0	0	4
6 yrs.		**N Totals:**	17	0	4	4	6
		W Totals:	18	5	10	15	40

Traded to **California** by Chicago with goaltender Gerry Desjardins and Kerry Bond for Gary Smith, Sept. 9, 1971.

Alex Pirus

PIRUS, JOSEPH ALEXANDER 6'1", 205 lbs.
B. Aug. 14, 1959, Toronto, Ont. Right Wing, Shoots R

YEAR	TEAM & LEAGUE		GP	G	A	PTS	PIM
1976-77	**MINN**	N	79	20	17	37	47
1977-78			61	9	6	15	38
1978-79			15	1	3	4	9
1979-80	**DET**	N	4	0	2	2	0
4 yrs.		N Totals:	159	30	28	58	94

PLAYOFFS

YEAR	TEAM & LEAGUE		GP	G	A	PTS	PIM
1976-77	**MINN**	N	2	0	1	1	2

Sold to **Detroit** by Minnesota, Jan. 3, 1980. Sold to **Minnesota** by Detroit, June 6, 1980. Traded to **N.Y. Islanders** by Minnesota for future considerations, July 4, 1980.

Didier Pitre

PITRE, DIDIER (Cannonball) 200 lbs.
B. Sault Ste. Marie, Ont. Defense
Hall of Fame, 1962

YEAR	TEAM & LEAGUE		GP	G	A	PTS	PIM
1917-18	**MONT**	N	19	17	0	17	9
1918-19			17	14	4	18	9
1919-20			22	15	7	22	6
1920-21			23	15	1	16	23
1921-22			23	2	3	5	12
1922-23			23	1	2	3	0
6 yrs.		N Totals:	127	64	17	81	59

PLAYOFFS

YEAR	TEAM & LEAGUE		GP	G	A	PTS	PIM
1917-18	**MONT**	N	2	0	0	0	10
1918-19			10	2	2	4	3
1922-23			2	0	0	0	0
3 yrs.		N Totals:	14	2	2	4	13

Ed Pizunski

PIZUNSKI, EDWARD 5'11", 185 lbs.
B. Oct. 8, 1954, Toronto, Ont. Defense, Shoots L

YEAR	TEAM & LEAGUE		GP	G	A	PTS	PIM
1975-76	**D-O**	W	1	0	0	0	0

Signed as free agent by **N.Y. Islanders** Oct. 27, 1976.

Barclay Plager

PLAGER, BARCLAY GRAHAM 5'11", 175 lbs.
B. Mar. 26, 1941, Kirkland Lake, Ont. Defense, Shoots L

YEAR	TEAM & LEAGUE		GP	G	A	PTS	PIM
1967-68	**STL**	N	49	5	15	20	**153**
1968-69			61	4	26	30	120
1969-70			75	6	26	32	128
1970-71			69	4	20	24	172
1971-72			78	7	22	29	176
1972-73			68	8	25	33	102
1973-74			72	6	20	26	99
1974-75			76	4	24	28	96
1975-76			64	0	8	8	67
1976-77			2	0	1	1	2
10 yrs.		N Totals:	614	44	187	231	1115

PLAYOFFS

YEAR	TEAM & LEAGUE		GP	G	A	PTS	PIM
1967-68	**STL**	N	18	2	5	7	73
1968-69			12	0	4	4	31
1969-70			13	0	2	2	20
1970-71			6	0	3	3	10
1971-72			11	1	4	5	21
1972-73			5	0	1	1	0
1974-75			2	0	1	1	14
1975-76			1	0	0	0	13
8 yrs.		N Totals:	68	3	20	23	182

Traded to **N.Y. Rangers** by Los Angeles for Trevor Fahey, Ken Turlik, and Jim Murray, June 16, 1967. Traded to **St. Louis** by N.Y. Rangers with Red Berenson for Ron Stewart and Ron Attwell, Nov. 29, 1967.

Bill Plager

PLAGER, WILLIAM RONALD 5'9", 175 lbs.
B. July 6, 1945, Kirkland Lake, Ont. Defense, Shoots R

YEAR	TEAM & LEAGUE		GP	G	A	PTS	PIM
1967-68	**MINN**	N	42	0	2	2	30
1968-69	**STL**	N	2	0	0	0	2

Bill Plager continued

YEAR	TEAM & LEAGUE		GP	G	A	PTS	PIM
1969-70			24	1	4	5	30
1970-71			36	0	3	3	45
1971-72			65	1	11	12	64
1972-73	**ATL**	N	76	2	11	13	92
1973-74	**MINN**	N	1	0	0	0	2
1974-75			7	0	0	0	8
1975-76			20	0	3	3	21
9 yrs.		N Totals:	273	4	34	38	294

PLAYOFFS

YEAR	TEAM & LEAGUE		GP	G	A	PTS	PIM
1967-68	**MINN**	N	12	0	2	2	8
1968-69	**STL**	N	4	0	0	0	4
1969-70			3	0	0	0	0
1970-71			1	0	0	0	2
1971-72			11	0	0	0	12
5 yrs.		N Totals:	31	0	2	2	26

Traded to **Minnesota** by Montreal with Leo Thiffault and Barrie Meissner for Bryan Watson, June 6, 1967. Put on **N.Y. Rangers** reserve list from Minnesota, June 12, 1968. Traded to **St. Louis** by N.Y. Rangers with Camille Henry and Robbie Irons for Don Caley and Wayne Rivers, June 13, 1968. Drafted by **Atlanta** from St. Louis in Expansion Draft, June 6, 1972. Put on **Minnesota** reserve list from Atlanta in Intra-league Draft, June 12, 1973.

Bob Plager

PLAGER, ROBERT BRYANT 5'11", 195 lbs.
B. Mar. 11, 1943, Kirkland Lake, Ont. Defense, Shoots L

YEAR	TEAM & LEAGUE		GP	G	A	PTS	PIM
1964-65	**NYR**	N	10	0	0	0	18
1965-66			18	0	5	5	22
1966-67			1	0	0	0	0
1967-68	**STL**	N	53	2	5	7	86
1968-69			32	0	7	7	43
1969-70			64	3	11	14	113
1970-71			70	1	19	20	114
1971-72			50	4	7	11	81
1972-73			77	2	31	33	107
1973-74			61	3	10	13	48
1974-75			73	1	14	15	53
1975-76			63	3	8	11	90
1976-77			54	1	9	10	23
1977-78			18	0	0	0	4
14 yrs.		N Totals:	644	20	126	146	802

PLAYOFFS

YEAR	TEAM & LEAGUE		GP	G	A	PTS	PIM
1967-68	**STL**	N	18	1	2	3	69
1968-69			9	0	4	4	47
1969-70			16	0	3	3	46
1970-71			6	0	2	2	4
1971-72			11	1	4	5	5
1972-73			5	0	2	2	2
1974-75			2	0	0	0	20
1975-76			3	0	0	0	2
1976-77			4	0	0	0	0
9 yrs.		N Totals:	74	2	17	19	195

Gerry Plamondon

PLAMONDON, GERARD ROGER 5'7½", 170 lbs.
B. Jan. 5, 1925, Sherbrooke, Que. Left Wing, Shoots L

YEAR	TEAM & LEAGUE		GP	G	A	PTS	PIM
1945-46	**MONT**	N	6	0	2	2	2
1947-48			3	1	1	2	0
1948-49			27	5	5	10	8
1949-50			37	1	5	6	0
1950-51			1	0	0	0	0
5 yrs.		N Totals:	74	7	13	20	10

PLAYOFFS

YEAR	TEAM & LEAGUE		GP	G	A	PTS	PIM
1945-46*	**MONT**	N	1	0	0	0	0
1948-49*			7	5	1	6	0
1949-50			3	0	1	1	2
3 yrs.		N Totals:	11	5	2	7	2

Michel Plante

PLANTE, MICHEL 5'10", 170 lbs.
B. Jan. 19, 1952, Drummondville, Que. Left Wing, Shoots L

YEAR	TEAM & LEAGUE		GP	G	A	PTS	PIM
1972-73	**PHI**	W	70	13	12	25	35
1973-74	**VAN**	W	22	3	2	5	2
2 yrs.		W Totals:	92	16	14	30	37

Pierre Plante

PLANTE, PIERRE RENALD 6'1", 190 lbs.
B. May 14, 1951, Valleyfield, Que. Right Wing, Shoots R

YEAR	TEAM & LEAGUE		GP	G	A	PTS	PIM
1971-72	PHI	N	24	1	0	1	15
1972-73			2	0	3	3	0
	STL	N	49	12	13	25	56
	2 team total		51	12	16	28	56
1973-74			78	26	28	54	85
1974-75			80	34	32	66	125
1975-76			74	14	19	33	77
1976-77			76	18	20	38	77
1977-78	CHI	N	77	10	18	28	59
1978-79	NYR	N	70	6	25	31	37
1979-80	QUE	N	69	4	14	18	68
9 yrs.		N Totals:	599	125	172	297	599
PLAYOFFS							
1972-73	STL	N	5	2	0	2	15
1974-75			2	0	0	0	8
1975-76			3	0	0	0	6
1976-77			4	0	0	0	2
1977-78	CHI	N	1	0	0	0	0
1978-79	NYR	N	18	0	6	6	20
6 yrs.		N Totals:	33	2	6	8	51

Traded to **St. Louis** by Philadelphia with Brent Hughes for Andre Dupont and St. Louis' third round choice (Bob Stumpf) in 1973 Amateur Draft, Dec. 14, 1972. Traded to **Chicago** by St. Louis for Dick Redmond, Aug. 9, 1977. Traded to **Minnesota** by Chicago, May 4, 1978 to complete an earlier deal (Doug Hicks, March 14, 1978). Claimed on waivers by **Detroit** from Minnesota, Sept. 13, 1978. Claimed by **N.Y. Rangers** from Detroit in League Waiver Draft, Oct. 9, 1978. Claimed by **Quebec** from N.Y. Rangers in Expansion Draft, June 13, 1979.

Mark Plantery

PLANTERY, MARK P. 6'1", 185 lbs.
B. Aug. 14, 1959, St. Catharines, Ont. Defense, Shoots L

YEAR	TEAM & LEAGUE		GP	G	A	PTS	PIM
1980-81	WINN	N	25	1	5	6	14

Signed as free agent by **Winnipeg** Oct. 5, 1979.

Hugh Plaxton

PLAXTON, HUGH JOHN 184 lbs.
B. May 16, 1904, Barrie, Ont. Left Wing, Shoots L

YEAR	TEAM & LEAGUE		GP	G	A	PTS	PIM
1932-33	MON(M)	N	15	1	2	3	4

Larry Playfair

PLAYFAIR, LAWRENCE WILLIAM 6'4", 201 lbs.
B. June 23, 1958, Fort St. James, B.C. Defense, Shoots L

YEAR	TEAM & LEAGUE		GP	G	A	PTS	PIM
1978-79	BUF	N	26	0	3	3	60
1979-80			79	2	10	12	145
1980-81			75	3	9	12	169
1981-82			77	6	10	16	258
1982-83			79	4	13	17	180
5 yrs.		N Totals:	336	15	45	60	812
PLAYOFFS							
1979-80	BUF	N	14	0	2	2	29
1980-81			8	0	0	0	26
1981-82			4	0	0	0	22
1982-83			5	0	1	1	11
4 yrs.		N Totals:	31	0	3	3	88

Claimed by **Buffalo** as fill in Expansion Draft, June 13, 1979.

Larry Pleau

PLEAU, LAWRENCE WINSLOW 6'1", 190 lbs.
B. Jan. 29, 1947, Lynn, Ma. Center, Shoots L

YEAR	TEAM & LEAGUE		GP	G	A	PTS	PIM
1969-70	MONT	N	20	1	0	1	0
1970-71			19	1	5	6	8
1971-72			55	7	10	17	14
1972-73	NE	W	78	39	48	87	42
1973-74			77	26	43	69	35
1974-75			78	30	34	64	50
1975-76			75	29	45	74	21
1976-77			78	11	21	32	22
1977-78			54	16	18	34	4

Larry Pleau continued

YEAR	TEAM & LEAGUE		GP	G	A	PTS	PIM
1978-79			28	6	6	12	6
10 yrs.		N Totals:	94	9	15	24	22
		W Totals:	468	157	215	372	180
PLAYOFFS							
1971-72	MONT	N	4	0	0	0	0
1972-73	NE	W	15	12	7	19	15
1973-74			2	2	0	2	0
1974-75			6	2	3	5	14
1975-76			14	5	7	12	0
1976-77			5	1	0	1	0
1977-78			14	5	4	9	8
1978-79			10	2	1	3	0
8 yrs.		N Totals:	4	0	0	0	0
		W Totals:	66	29	22	51	37

Willi Plett

PLETT, WILLI 6'3", 205 lbs.
B. June 7, 1955, Paraguay Right Wing, Shoots R
Won Calder Trophy, 1976-77

YEAR	TEAM & LEAGUE		GP	G	A	PTS	PIM
1975-76	ATL	N	4	0	0	0	0
1976-77			64	33	23	56	123
1977-78			78	22	21	43	171
1978-79			74	23	20	43	213
1979-80			76	13	19	32	231
1980-81	CALG	N	78	38	30	68	239
1981-82			78	21	36	57	288
1982-83	MINN	N	71	25	14	39	170
8 yrs.		N Totals:	523	175	163	338	1435
PLAYOFFS							
1976-77	ATL	N	3	1	0	1	19
1978-79			2	1	0	1	29
1979-80			4	1	0	1	15
1980-81	CALG	N	15	8	4	12	89
1981-82			3	1	2	3	39
1982-83	MINN	N	9	1	3	4	38
6 yrs.		N Totals:	36	13	9	22	229

Traded to **Minnesota** by Calgary along with Calgary's fourth choice (Dusan Pasek) in 1982 Entry Draft for Steve Christoff, Bill Nyrop and Minnesota's second choice (Dave Reierson) in 1982 Entry Draft, June 7, 1982.

Rob Plumb

PLUMB, ROBERT EDWIN 5'8", 166 lbs.
B. Aug. 29, 1957, Kingston, Ont. Left Wing, Shoots L

YEAR	TEAM & LEAGUE		GP	G	A	PTS	PIM
1977-78	DET	N	7	2	1	3	0

Ron Plumb

PLUMB, RONALD WILLIAM 5'10", 175 lbs.
B. July 17, 1950, Kingston, Ont. Defense, Shoots L

YEAR	TEAM & LEAGUE		GP	G	A	PTS	PIM
1972-73	PHI	W	78	10	41	51	66
1973-74	VAN	W	75	6	32	38	40
1974-75	SD	W	78	10	38	48	56
1975-76	CIN	W	80	10	36	46	31
1976-77			79	11	58	69	52
1977-78			54	13	34	47	45
	NE	W	27	1	9	10	18
	2 team total		81	14	43	57	63
1978-79			78	4	16	20	33
1979-80	HART	N	26	3	4	7	14
8 yrs.		N Totals:	26	3	4	7	14
		W Totals:	549	65	264	329	341
PLAYOFFS							
1972-73	PHI	W	4	0	2	2	13
1974-75	SD	W	10	2	3	5	19
1976-77	CIN	W	4	1	2	3	0
1977-78	NE	W	14	1	5	6	16
1978-79			9	1	3	4	0
5 yrs.		W Totals:	41	5	15	20	48

YEAR	TEAM & LEAGUE		GP	G	A	PTS	PIM

Harvie Pocza

POCZA, HARVIE D. 6'2", 198 lbs.
B. Sept. 22, 1959, Lethbridge, Alta. Left Wing, Shoots L

YEAR	TEAM	LEAGUE	GP	G	A	PTS	PIM
1979-80	**WASH**	**N**	1	0	0	0	0
1981-82			2	0	0	0	0
2 yrs.		**N Totals:**	3	0	0	0	0

Walt Poddubny

PODDUBNY, WALTER MICHAEL 6'1", 203 lbs.
B. Feb. 14, 1960, Thunder Bay, Ont. Center, Shoots L

YEAR	TEAM	LEAGUE	GP	G	A	PTS	PIM
1981-82	**EDM**	**N**	4	0	0	0	8
	TOR	**N**	11	3	4	7	8
	2 team total		15	3	4	7	16
1982-83			72	28	31	59	71
2 yrs.		**N Totals:**	87	31	35	66	87
PLAYOFFS							
1982-83	**TOR**	**N**	4	3	1	4	0

Traded to **Toronto** by Edmonton along with Phil Drouilliard for Laurie Boschman, Mar. 8, 1982.

Nellie Podolsky

PODOLSKY, NELSON 5'10", 170 lbs.
B. Dec. 19, 1925, Winnipeg, Man. Left Wing, Shoots L

YEAR	TEAM	LEAGUE	GP	G	A	PTS	PIM
1948-49	**DET**	**N**	1	0	0	0	0
PLAYOFFS							
1948-49	**DET**	**N**	7	0	0	0	4

Anthony Poeta

POETA, ANTHONY JOSEPH 5'5", 168 lbs.
B. Mar. 4, 1933, North Bay, Ont. Right Wing, Shoots L

YEAR	TEAM	LEAGUE	GP	G	A	PTS	PIM
1951-52	**CHI**	**N**	1	0	0	0	0

Bud Poile

POILE, NORMAN ROBERT 6', 185 lbs.
B. Feb. 10, 1924, Fort William, Ont. Center, Shoots R

YEAR	TEAM	LEAGUE	GP	G	A	PTS	PIM
1942-43	**TOR**	**N**	48	16	19	35	24
1943-44			11	6	8	14	9
1945-46			9	1	8	9	0
1946-47			59	19	17	36	19
1947-48			4	2	0	2	0
	CHI	**N**	54	23	29	52	14
	2 team total		58	25	29	54	14
1948-49			4	0	0	0	2
	DET	**N**	56	21	21	42	6
	2 team total		60	21	21	42	8
1949-50	**NYR**	**N**	27	3	6	9	8
	BOS	**N**	39	16	14	30	6
	2 team total		66	19	20	39	14
7 yrs.		**N Totals:**	311	107	122	229	88
PLAYOFFS							
1942-43	**TOR**	**N**	6	2	4	6	4
1946-47*			7	2	0	2	2
1948-49	**DET**	**N**	10	0	1	1	2
3 yrs.		**N Totals:**	23	4	5	9	8

Sold to **N.Y. Rangers** by Detroit, Aug. 16, 1949. Sold to **Boston** by N.Y. Rangers for cash and a player to be named later, Dec. 4, 1949.

Don Poile

POILE, DONALD B.
B. June 1, 1932, Fort William, Ont. Center, Shoots L

YEAR	TEAM	LEAGUE	GP	G	A	PTS	PIM
1954-55	**DET**	**N**	4	0	0	0	0
1957-58			62	7	9	16	12
2 yrs.		**N Totals:**	66	7	9	16	12
PLAYOFFS							
1957-58	**DET**	**N**	4	0	0	0	0

Gordie Poirer

POIRER, GORDON ARTHUR
B. Oct. 27, 1914, Maple Creek, Sask. Center, Shoots L

YEAR	TEAM	LEAGUE	GP	G	A	PTS	PIM
1939-40	**MONT**	**N**	10	0	1	1	0

Tom Polanic

POLANIC, THOMAS JOSEPH 6'3", 205 lbs.
B. Apr. 2, 1943, Toronto, Ont. Defense, Shoots L

YEAR	TEAM	LEAGUE	GP	G	A	PTS	PIM
1969-70	**MINN**	**N**	16	0	2	2	53
1970-71			3	0	0	0	0
2 yrs.		**N Totals:**	19	0	2	2	53
PLAYOFFS							
1969-70	**MINN**	**N**	5	1	1	2	4

Nick Polano

POLANO, NICHOLAS 6', 187 lbs.
B. Mar. 25, 1941, Sudbury, Ont. Defense, Shoots L

YEAR	TEAM	LEAGUE	GP	G	A	PTS	PIM
1972-73	**PHI**	**W**	17	0	3	3	24

John Polich

POLICH, JOHN 6'1½", 200 lbs.
B. July 8, 1916, Hibbing, Minn. Right Wing, Shoots R

YEAR	TEAM	LEAGUE	GP	G	A	PTS	PIM
1939-40	**NYR**	**N**	1	0	0	0	0
1940-41			2	0	1	1	0
2 yrs.		**N Totals:**	3	0	1	1	0

Mike Polich

POLICH, MICHAEL D. 5'8", 165 lbs.
B. Dec. 19, 1952, Hibbing, Minn. Left Wing, Shoots L

YEAR	TEAM	LEAGUE	GP	G	A	PTS	PIM
1977-78	**MONT**	**N**	1	0	0	0	0
1978-79	**MINN**	**N**	73	6	10	16	18
1979-80			78	10	14	24	20
1980-81			74	8	5	13	19
4 yrs.		**N Totals:**	226	24	29	53	57
PLAYOFFS							
1976-77*	**MONT**	**N**	5	0	0	0	0
1979-80	**MINN**	**N**	15	2	1	3	2
1980-81			3	0	0	0	0
3 yrs.		**N Totals:**	23	2	1	3	2

Signed as free agent by **Minnesota** Sept. 6, 1978. As compensation, Montreal received Jerre Engele.

Greg Polis

POLIS, GREGORY LINN 6', 195 lbs.
B. Aug. 8, 1950, Westlock, Alta. Left Wing, Shoots L

YEAR	TEAM	LEAGUE	GP	G	A	PTS	PIM
1970-71	**PITT**	**N**	61	18	15	33	40
1971-72			76	30	19	49	38
1972-73			78	26	23	49	36
1973-74			41	14	13	27	32
	STL	**N**	37	8	12	20	24
	2 team total		78	22	25	47	56
1974-75	**NYR**	**N**	76	26	15	41	55
1975-76			79	15	21	36	77
1976-77			77	16	23	39	44
1977-78			37	7	16	23	12
1978-79			6	1	1	2	8
	WASH	**N**	19	12	6	18	6
	2 team total		25	13	7	20	14
1979-80			28	1	5	6	19
10 yrs.		**N Totals:**	615	174	169	343	391
PLAYOFFS							
1971-72	**PITT**	**N**	4	0	2	2	0
1974-75	**NYR**	**N**	3	0	0	0	6
2 yrs.		**N Totals:**	7	0	2	2	6

Traded to **St. Louis** by Pittsburgh with Bryan Watson and Pittsburgh's second choice (Bob Hess) in 1974 Amateur Draft for Steve Durbano, Ab DeMarco, and Bob Kelly, Jan. 17, 1974. Traded to **N.Y. Rangers** by St. Louis for Larry Sacharuk, Aug. 29, 1974. Claimed on waivers by **Washington** from N.Y. Rangers, Jan. 15, 1979.

Daniel Poliziani

POLIZIANI, DANIEL 5'11", 160 lbs.
B. Jan. 8, 1935, Sydney, N.S. Right Wing, Shoots R

YEAR	TEAM & LEAGUE		GP	G	A	PTS	PIM
1958-59	BOS	N	1	0	0	0	0
PLAYOFFS							
1958-59	BOS	N	3	0	0	0	0

Dennis Polonich

POLONICH, DENNIS DANIEL 5'6", 170 lbs.
B. Dec. 4, 1953, Foam Lake, Sask. Center, Shoots R

YEAR	TEAM & LEAGUE		GP	G	A	PTS	PIM
1974-75	DET	N	4	0	0	0	0
1975-76			57	11	12	23	302
1976-77			79	18	28	46	274
1977-78			79	16	19	35	254
1978-79			62	10	12	22	208
1979-80			66	2	8	10	127
1980-81			32	2	2	4	77
1982-83			11	0	1	1	0
8 yrs.		N Totals:	390	59	82	141	1242
PLAYOFFS							
1977-78	DET	N	7	1	0	1	19

Larry Popein

POPEIN, LAWRENCE THOMAS (Pope) 5'9", 165 lbs.
B. Aug. 11, 1930, Yorkton, Sask. Center, Shoots L

YEAR	TEAM & LEAGUE		GP	G	A	PTS	PIM
1954-55	NYR	N	70	11	17	28	27
1955-56			64	14	25	39	37
1956-57			67	11	19	30	20
1957-58			70	12	22	34	22
1958-59			61	13	21	34	28
1959-60			66	14	22	36	16
1960-61			4	0	1	1	0
1967-68	OAK	N	47	5	14	19	12
8 yrs.		N Totals:	449	80	141	221	162
PLAYOFFS							
1955-56	NYR	N	5	0	1	1	2
1956-57			5	0	3	3	0
1957-58			6	1	0	1	4
3 yrs.		N Totals:	16	1	4	5	6

Jan Popiel

POPIEL, JAN VALDEMAR (Pope, Poper) 5'9", 183 lbs.
B. Oct. 9, 1947, Virum, Denmark Left Wing, Shoots L

YEAR	TEAM & LEAGUE		GP	G	A	PTS	PIM
1972-73	CHI	W	76	31	34	65	77
1973-74			63	22	17	39	36
1974-75			60	18	22	40	74
1975-76	D-O	W	1	0	0	0	0
	HOUS	W	67	4	7	11	59
	2 team total		68	4	7	11	59
1976-77	PHOE	W	28	3	2	5	8
5 yrs.		W Totals:	295	78	82	160	254
PLAYOFFS							
1973-74	CHI	N	18	8	5	13	12
1975-76	HOUS	W	8	1	1	2	4
2 yrs.		N Totals:	18	8	5	13	12
		W Totals:	8	1	1	2	4

Poul Popiel

POPIEL, POUL PETER 5'8", 170 lbs.
B. Feb. 28, 1943, Sollested, Denmark Defense, Shoots L

YEAR	TEAM & LEAGUE		GP	G	A	PTS	PIM
1965-66	BOS	N	3	0	1	1	2
1967-68	LA	N	1	0	0	0	0
1968-69	DET	N	62	2	13	15	82
1969-70			32	0	4	4	31
1970-71	VAN	N	78	10	22	32	61
1971-72			38	1	1	2	36
1972-73	HOUS	W	74	16	48	64	158
1973-74			78	7	41	48	126
1974-75			78	11	53	64	22
1975-76			78	10	36	46	71
1976-77			80	12	56	68	87

Poul Popiel continued

YEAR	TEAM & LEAGUE		GP	G	A	PTS	PIM
1977-78			80	6	31	37	53
1979-80	EDM	N	10	0	0	0	0
13 yrs.		N Totals:	224	13	41	54	212
		W Totals:	468	62	265	327	517
PLAYOFFS							
1967-68	LA	N	3	1	0	1	4
1969-70	DET	N	1	0	0	0	0
1972-73	HOUS	W	10	2	9	11	23
1973-74			14	1	14	15	22
1974-75			13	1	10	11	34
1975-76			17	3	5	8	16
1976-77			11	0	7	7	10
1977-78			6	0	2	2	13
8 yrs.		N Totals:	4	1	0	1	4
		W Totals:	71	7	47	54	118

Drafted by **Los Angeles** from Boston in Expansion Draft, June 6, 1967. Traded to **Detroit** by Los Angeles for Ron Anderson, Nov, 12, 1968. Drafted by **Vancouver** from Detroit in Expansion Draft, June 10, 1970.

Jack Portland

PORTLAND, JOHN FRED 6'2", 185 lbs.
B. July 30, 1912, Waubaushene, Ont. Defense, Shoots L

YEAR	TEAM & LEAGUE		GP	G	A	PTS	PIM
1933-34	MONT	N	31	0	2	2	10
1934-35			5	0	0	0	2
	BOS	N	15	1	1	2	2
	2 team total		20	1	1	2	4
1935-36			2	0	0	0	0
1936-37			46	2	4	6	58
1937-38			48	0	5	5	26
1938-39			48	4	5	9	46
1939-40			28	0	5	5	16
	CHI	N	16	1	4	5	20
	2 team total		44	1	9	10	36
1940-41			5	0	0	0	4
	MONT	N	42	2	7	9	34
	2 team total		47	2	7	9	38
1941-42			46	2	9	11	53
1942-43			49	3	14	17	52
10 yrs.		N Totals:	381	15	56	71	323
PLAYOFFS							
1933-34	MONT	N	2	0	0	0	0
1936-37	BOS	N	3	0	0	0	4
1937-38			3	0	0	0	4
1938-39*			12	0	0	0	11
1939-40	CHI	N	2	0	0	0	2
1940-41	MONT	N	3	0	1	1	2
1941-42			3	0	0	0	0
1942-43			5	1	2	3	2
8 yrs.		N Totals:	33	1	3	4	25

Jukka Porvari

PORVARI, JUKKA 5'11", 175 lbs.
B. Jan. 19, 1954, Tampere, Finland Right Wing, Shoots L

YEAR	TEAM & LEAGUE		GP	G	A	PTS	PIM
1981-82	COLO	N	31	2	6	8	0
1982-83	NJ	N	8	1	3	4	4
2 yrs.		N Totals:	39	3	9	12	4

Signed as free agent by **Colorado** July 8, 1981.

Denis Potvin

POTVIN, DENIS CHARLES (Bear) 6', 204 lbs.
B. Oct. 29, 1953, Ottawa, Ont. Defense, Shoots L
Won Norris Trophy, 1975–76, 1977–78, 1978-79
Won Calder Trophy, 1973-74

YEAR	TEAM & LEAGUE		GP	G	A	PTS	PIM
1973-74	NYI	N	77	17	37	54	175
1974-75			79	21	55	76	105
1975-76			78	31	67	98	100
1976-77			80	25	55	80	103
1977-78			80	30	64	94	81
1978-79			73	31	70	101	58
1979-80			31	8	33	41	44
1980-81			74	20	56	76	104
1981-82			60	24	37	61	83
1982-83			69	12	54	66	60
10 yrs.		N Totals:	701	219	528	747	913

Denis Potvin continued

PLAYOFFS

YEAR	TEAM	LEAGUE	GP	G	A	PTS	PIM
1974-75	NYI	N	17	5	9	14	30
1975-76			13	5	14	19	32
1976-77			12	6	4	10	20
1977-78			7	2	2	4	6
1978-79			10	4	7	11	8
1979-80*			21	6	13	19	24
1980-81*			18	8	17	25	16
1981-82*			19	5	16	21	30
1982-83*			20	8	12	20	22
9 yrs.		N Totals:	137	49	94	143	188

Jean Potvin

POTVIN, JEAN RENE 5'11", 188 lbs.
B. Mar. 25, 1949, Hull, Que. Defense, Shoots R

YEAR	TEAM	LEAGUE	GP	G	A	PTS	PIM
1970-71	LA	N	4	1	3	4	2
1971-72			39	2	3	5	35
	PHI	N	29	3	12	15	6
	2 team total		68	5	15	20	41
1972-73			35	3	9	12	10
	NYI	N	10	0	3	3	12
	2 team total		45	3	12	15	22
1973-74			78	5	23	28	100
1974-75			73	9	24	33	59
1975-76	MONT	N	78	17	55	72	74
1976-77	NYI	N	79	10	36	46	26
1977-78			34	1	10	11	30
	CLEVE	N	40	3	14	17	30
	2 team total		74	4	24	28	60
1978-79	MINN	N	64	5	16	21	65
1979-80	NYI	N	32	2	13	15	26
1980-81			18	2	3	5	25
11 yrs.		N Totals:	613	63	224	287	500

PLAYOFFS

YEAR	TEAM	LEAGUE	GP	G	A	PTS	PIM
1974-75	NYI	N	15	2	4	6	9
1975-76			13	0	1	1	2
1976-77			11	0	4	4	6
3 yrs.		N Totals:	39	2	9	11	17

Traded to **Philadelphia** by Los Angeles with Bill Flett, Ed Joyal and Ross Lonsberry for Bill Lesuk, Jim Johnson and Serge Bernier, Jan. 28, 1972. Traded to **N.Y. Islanders** by Philadelphia with a player to be named later (Glen Irwin, May 18, 1973) for Terry Crisp, March 5, 1973. Traded to **Cleveland** by N.Y. Islanders with J.P. Parise and N.Y. Islanders' fourth round choice (later cancelled by Cleveland-Minnesota merger) in the 1978 Amateur Draft for Wayne Merrick and Darcy Regier, Jan. 10, 1978. Put on **Minnesota** Reserve List after Cleveland-Minnesota Dispersal Draft, June 15, 1978. Signed as free agent by **N.Y. Islanders** from Minnesota, June 10, 1979. Minnesota received Ritchie Hansen as compensation.

Dan Poulin

POULIN, DANIEL 5'11", 185 lbs.
B. Sept. 19, 1957, Robertsville, Que. Defense, Shoots R

YEAR	TEAM	LEAGUE	GP	G	A	PTS	PIM
1981-82	MINN	N	3	1	1	2	2
1982-83	PHI	N	2	2	0	2	2
2 yrs.		N Totals:	5	3	1	4	4

Signed as free agent with **Minnesota** June 16, 1980.

Dave Poulin

POULIN, DAVID 5'11", 180 lbs.
B. Dec. 17, 1958, Timmins, Ont. Center, Shoots L

PLAYOFFS

YEAR	TEAM	LEAGUE	GP	G	A	PTS	PIM
1982-83	PHI	N	3	1	3	4	9

Jaroslav Pouzar

POUZAR, JAROSLAV 5'11", 202 lbs.
B. Jan. 23, 1952, Czechoslovakia Left Wing, Shoots L

YEAR	TEAM	LEAGUE	GP	G	A	PTS	PIM
1982-83	EDM	N	74	15	18	33	57

PLAYOFFS

YEAR	TEAM	LEAGUE	GP	G	A	PTS	PIM
1982-83	EDM	N	1	2	0	2	0

Ray Powell

POWELL, RAYMOND HENRY 6', 170 lbs.
B. Nov. 16, 1925, Timmins, Ont. Center, Shoots L

YEAR	TEAM	LEAGUE	GP	G	A	PTS	PIM
1950-51	CHI	N	31	7	15	22	2

Jeff Powis

POWIS, GEOFFREY CHARLES 6', 179 lbs.
B. June 14, 1945, Winnipeg, Man. Center, Shoots L

YEAR	TEAM	LEAGUE	GP	G	A	PTS	PIM
1967-68	CHI	N	2	0	0	0	0

Lynn Powis

POWIS, TREVOR LYNN 6', 176 lbs.
B. July 7, 1949, Maryfield, Sask. Center, Shoots L

YEAR	TEAM	LEAGUE	GP	G	A	PTS	PIM
1973-74	CHI	N	57	8	13	21	6
1974-75	KC	N	73	11	20	31	19
1975-76	CALG	W	21	4	10	14	2
1976-77			63	30	30	60	40
1977-78	IND	W	0	0	0	0	0
	WINN	W	69	16	25	41	18
	2 team total		69	16	25	41	18
5 yrs.		N Totals:	130	19	33	52	25
		W Totals:	153	50	65	115	60

PLAYOFFS

YEAR	TEAM	LEAGUE	GP	G	A	PTS	PIM
1973-74	CHI	N	1	0	0	0	0
1975-76	CALG	W	10	5	4	9	2
1977-78	WINN	W	3	2	1	3	7
3 yrs.		N Totals:	1	0	0	0	0
		W Totals:	13	7	5	12	9

Sold to **Atlanta** by Montreal, June 9, 1972. Traded to **Chicago** by Atlanta for Mike Baumgartner, Aug. 30, 1973. Drafted by **Kansas City** from Chicago in Expansion Draft, June 12, 1974. Traded to **St. Louis** by Kansas City with Kansas City's second choice (Brian Sutter) in 1976 Amateur Draft for Craig Patrick and Denis Dupere, June 18, 1975.

Babe Pratt

PRATT, WALTER 6'3", 210 lbs.
B. Jan. 7, 1916, Stony Mountain, Man. Defense, Shoots L
Won Hart Trophy, 1943-44
Hall of Fame, 1966

YEAR	TEAM	LEAGUE	GP	G	A	PTS	PIM
1935-36	NYR	N	17	1	1	2	16
1936-37			47	8	7	15	23
1937-38			47	5	14	19	56
1938-39			48	2	19	21	20
1939-40			48	4	13	17	61
1940-41			47	3	17	20	52
1941-42			47	4	24	28	45
1942-43			4	0	2	2	6
	TOR	N	40	12	25	37	44
	2 team total		44	12	27	39	50
1943-44			50	17	40	57	30
1944-45			50	18	23	41	39
1945-46			41	5	20	25	36
1946-47	BOS	N	31	4	4	8	25
12 yrs.		N Totals:	517	83	209	292	453

PLAYOFFS

YEAR	TEAM	LEAGUE	GP	G	A	PTS	PIM
1936-37	NYR	N	9	3	1	4	11
1937-38			2	0	0	0	2
1938-39			7	1	2	3	9
1939-40*			12	3	1	4	18
1940-41			3	1	1	2	6
1941-42			6	1	3	4	24
1942-43	TOR	N	6	1	2	3	8
1943-44			5	0	3	3	4
1944-45*			13	2	4	6	8
9 yrs.		N Totals:	63	12	17	29	90

Jack Pratt

PRATT, JOHN
B. Edinburgh, Scotland Defense

YEAR	TEAM	LEAGUE	GP	G	A	PTS	PIM
1930-31	BOS	N	32	2	0	2	36
1931-32			5	0	0	0	6
2 yrs.		N Totals:	37	2	0	2	42

PLAYOFFS

YEAR	TEAM	LEAGUE	GP	G	A	PTS	PIM
1930-31	BOS	N	4	0	0	0	0

Kelly Pratt

PRATT, KELLY EDWARD 5'9", 170 lbs.
B. Feb. 8, 1953, High Prairie, Alta. Right Wing, Shoots R

YEAR	TEAM & LEAGUE		GP	G	A	PTS	PIM
1973-74	WINN	W	46	4	6	10	50
1974-75	PITT	N	22	0	6	6	15
2 yrs.		N Totals:	22	0	6	6	15
		W Totals:	46	4	6	10	50

Tracy Pratt

PRATT, TRACY ARNOLD 6'2", 195 lbs.
B. Mar. 8, 1943, New York, N.Y. Defense, Shoots L

YEAR	TEAM & LEAGUE		GP	G	A	PTS	PIM
1967-68	OAK	N	34	0	5	5	90
1968-69	PITT	N	18	0	5	5	34
1969-70			65	5	7	12	124
1970-71	BUF	N	76	1	7	8	179
1971-72			27	0	10	10	52
1972-73			74	1	15	16	116
1973-74			33	0	7	7	52
	VAN	N	45	3	8	11	44
	2 team total		78	3	15	18	96
1974-75			79	5	17	22	145
1975-76			52	1	5	6	72
1976-77	COLO	N	66	1	10	11	110
	TOR	N	11	0	1	1	8
	2 team total		77	1	11	12	118
10 yrs.		N Totals:	580	17	97	114	1026
PLAYOFFS							
1969-70	PITT	N	10	0	1	1	51
1972-73	BUF	N	6	0	0	0	6
1974-75	VAN	N	3	0	0	0	5
1975-76			2	0	0	0	0
1976-77	TOR	N	4	0	0	0	0
5 yrs.		N Totals:	25	0	1	1	62

Drafted by **Oakland** from Chicago in Expansion Draft, June 6, 1967. Traded to **Pittsburgh** by Oakland with George Swarbrick and Bryan Watson for Earl Ingarfield, Dick Mattiussi and Gene Ubriaco, Jan. 30, 1969. Drafted by **Buffalo** from Pittsburgh in Expansion Draft, June 19, 1970. Traded to **Vancouver** by Buffalo with John Gould for Jerry Korab, Dec. 27, 1973. Traded to **Toronto** by Colorado for Toronto's third choice (Randy Pierce) in 1977 Amateur Draft, March 8, 1977.

Bill Prentice

PRENTICE, WILLIAM 6'1", 196 lbs.
B. Aug. 3, 1950, Oshawa, Ont. Defense, Shoots L

YEAR	TEAM & LEAGUE		GP	G	A	PTS	PIM
1972-73	HOUS	W	3	0	1	1	0
1973-74			55	1	2	3	35
1974-75			17	0	3	3	19
1975-76	IND	W	38	4	2	6	92
	QUE	W	21	2	5	7	89
	2 team total		59	6	7	13	181
1976-77	EDM	W	3	0	0	0	2
1977-78	IND	W	21	1	1	2	28
6 yrs.		W Totals:	158	8	14	22	265
PLAYOFFS							
1973-74	HOUS	W	10	0	0	0	5
1975-76	QUE	W	5	0	0	0	17
2 yrs.		W Totals:	15	0	0	0	22

Dean Prentice

PRENTICE, DEAN SUTHERLAND 5'11", 180 lbs.
B. Schumacher, Ont. Left Wing, Shoots L

YEAR	TEAM & LEAGUE		GP	G	A	PTS	PIM
1952-53	NYR	N	55	6	3	9	20
1953-54			52	4	13	17	18
1954-55			70	16	15	31	21
1955-56			70	24	18	42	44
1956-57			68	19	23	42	38
1957-58			38	13	9	22	14
1958-59			70	17	33	50	11
1959-60			70	32	34	66	43
1960-61			56	20	25	45	17
1961-62			68	22	38	60	20
1962-63			49	13	25	38	18
	BOS	N	19	6	9	15	4
	2 team total		68	19	34	53	22
1963-64			70	23	16	39	37

Dean Prentice continued

YEAR	TEAM & LEAGUE		GP	G	A	PTS	PIM
1964-65			31	14	9	23	12
1965-66			50	7	22	29	10
	DET	N	19	6	9	15	8
	2 team total		69	13	31	44	18
1966-67			68	23	22	45	18
1967-68			69	17	38	55	42
1968-69			74	14	20	34	18
1969-70	PITT	N	75	26	25	51	14
1970-71			69	21	17	38	18
1971-72	MINN	N	71	20	27	47	14
1972-73			73	26	16	42	22
1973-74			24	2	3	5	4
22 yrs.		N Totals:	1378	391	469	860	485
PLAYOFFS							
1955-56	NYR	N	5	1	0	1	2
1956-57			5	0	2	2	4
1957-58			6	1	3	4	4
1961-62			3	0	2	2	0
1965-66	DET	N	12	5	5	10	4
1969-70	PITT	N	10	2	5	7	8
1971-72	MINN	N	7	3	0	3	0
1972-73			6	1	0	1	16
8 yrs.		N Totals:	54	13	17	30	38

Traded to **Boston** by N.Y. Rangers for Don McKenney, Feb. 6, 1963.

Eric Prentice

PRENTICE, ERIC DAYTON
B. Aug. 22, 1926, Schumacher, Ont. Defense

YEAR	TEAM & LEAGUE		GP	G	A	PTS	PIM
1943-44	TOR	N	5	0	0	0	4

Rich Preston

PRESTON, RICHARD JOHN (Cool Hand Luke) 6', 185 lbs.
B. May 22, 1952, Regina, Sask. Right Wing, Shoots R

YEAR	TEAM & LEAGUE		GP	G	A	PTS	PIM
1974-75	HOUS	W	78	20	21	41	10
1975-76			77	22	33	55	33
1976-77			80	38	41	79	54
1977-78			73	25	25	50	52
1978-79	WINN	W	80	28	32	60	88
1979-80	CHI	N	80	31	30	61	70
1980-81			47	7	14	21	24
1981-82			75	15	28	43	30
1982-83			79	25	28	53	64
9 yrs.		N Totals:	281	78	100	178	188
		W Totals:	388	133	152	285	237
PLAYOFFS							
1974-75	HOUS	W	13	1	6	7	6
1975-76			17	4	6	10	8
1976-77			11	3	5	8	10
1978-79	WINN	W	10	8	5	13	15
1979-80	CHI	N	7	0	3	3	2
1980-81			3	0	1	1	0
1981-82			15	2	4	6	21
1982-83			13	2	7	9	25
8 yrs.		N Totals:	38	4	15	19	48
		W Totals:	51	16	22	38	39

Claimed by **Chicago** from Winnipeg in Expansion Draft, June 13, 1979.

Yves Preston

PRESTON, YVES 5'11", 180 lbs.
B. June 14, 1956, Montreal, Que. Left Wing, Shoots L

YEAR	TEAM & LEAGUE		GP	G	A	PTS	PIM
1978-79	PHI	N	9	3	1	4	0
1980-81			19	4	2	6	4
2 yrs.		N Totals:	28	7	3	10	4

Signed as free agent by **Philadelphia** Oct. 9, 1978.

Price

PRICE
B. Unknown Forward

YEAR	TEAM & LEAGUE		GP	G	A	PTS	PIM
1919-20	OTTA	N	1	0	0	0	0

Jack Price

PRICE, JOHN REES 5'9", 185 lbs.
B. May 8, 1932, Goderich, Ont. Defense, Shoots L

YEAR	TEAM & LEAGUE		GP	G	A	PTS	PIM
1951-52	**CHI**	**N**	1	0	0	0	0
1952-53			10	0	0	0	2
1953-54			46	4	6	10	22
3 yrs.		**N Totals:**	57	4	6	10	24
PLAYOFFS							
1952-53	**CHI**	**N**	4	0	0	0	0

Traded to **Toronto** by Chicago for Ray Timgren, Oct. 4, 1954.

Noel Price

PRICE, NOEL 6', 185 lbs.
B. Dec. 9, 1935, Brockville, Ont. Defense, Shoots L

YEAR	TEAM & LEAGUE		GP	G	A	PTS	PIM
1957-58	**TOR**	**N**	1	0	0	0	5
1958-59			28	0	0	0	4
1959-60	**NYR**	**N**	6	0	0	0	0
1960-61			1	0	0	0	2
1961-62	**DET**	**N**	20	0	1	1	6
1965-66	**MONT**	**N**	15	0	6	6	8
1966-67			24	0	3	3	8
1967-68	**PITT**	**N**	70	6	27	33	48
1968-69			73	2	18	20	79
1970-71	**LA**	**N**	62	1	19	20	29
1972-73	**ATL**	**N**	54	1	13	14	38
1973-74			62	0	13	13	38
1974-75			80	4	14	18	82
1975-76			3	0	0	0	2
14 yrs.		**N Totals:**	499	14	114	128	349
PLAYOFFS							
1958-59	**TOR**	**N**	5	0	0	0	2
1965-66*	**MONT**	**N**	3	0	1	1	0
1973-74	**ATL**	**N**	4	0	0	0	6
3 yrs.		**N Totals:**	12	0	1	1	8

Traded to **Detroit** by N.Y. Rangers for Peter Goegan, Feb. 16, 1962. Traded to **N.Y. Rangers** by Detroit for Peter Goegan, Oct. 8, 1962. Traded by N.Y. Rangers with Gord Labossiere, Earl Ingarfield, and Dave McComb to **Montreal** for Garry Peters and Cesare Maniago, June 8, 1965. Drafted by **Pittsburgh** from Montreal on Expansion Draft, June 6, 1967. Traded to **Montreal** by Los Angeles with goaltender Denis DeJordy, Dale Hoganson and Doug Robinson for goaltender Rogie Vachon, Nov. 4, 1977. Sold to **Atlanta** by Montreal, Aug. 14, 1972.

Pat Price

PRICE, SHAUN PATRICK (Pricey) 6'2", 200 lbs.
B. Mar. 24, 1955, Nelson, B.C. Defense, Shoots L

YEAR	TEAM & LEAGUE		GP	G	A	PTS	PIM
1974-75	**VAN**	**W**	69	5	29	34	54
1975-76	**NYI**	**N**	4	0	2	2	2
1976-77			71	3	22	25	25
1977-78			52	2	10	12	27
1978-79			55	3	11	14	50
1979-80	**EDM**	**N**	75	11	21	32	134
1980-81			59	8	24	32	193
	PITT	**N**	13	0	10	10	33
	2 team total		72	8	34	42	226
1981-82			77	7	31	38	322
1982-83			38	1	11	12	104
	QUE	**N**	14	1	2	3	28
	2 team total		52	2	13	15	132
9 yrs.		**N Totals:**	458	36	144	180	918
		W Totals:	69	5	29	34	54
PLAYOFFS							
1976-77	**NYI**	**N**	10	0	1	1	2
1977-78			5	0	1	1	2
1978-79			7	0	1	1	25
1979-80	**EDM**	**N**	3	0	0	0	11
1980-81	**PITT**	**N**	5	1	1	2	21
1981-82			5	0	0	0	28
1982-83	**QUE**	**N**	4	0	0	0	14
7 yrs.		**N Totals:**	39	1	4	5	103

Claimed by **Edmonton** from N.Y. Islanders in Expansion Draft, June 13, 1979. Traded to **Pittsburgh** by Edmonton for Pat Hughes, Mar. 10, 1981. Claimed by **Quebec** on waivers from Pittsburgh, Dec. 1, 1982.

Tom Price

PRICE, THOMAS EDWARD 6'1", 190 lbs.
B. July 12, 1954, Toronto, Ont. Defense, Shoots L

YEAR	TEAM & LEAGUE		GP	G	A	PTS	PIM
1974-75	**CALIF**	**N**	3	0	0	0	4
1975-76			5	0	0	0	0
1976-77	**CLEVE**	**N**	2	0	0	0	0
	PITT	**N**	7	0	2	2	4
	2 team total		9	0	2	2	4
1977-78			10	0	0	0	0
1978-79			2	0	0	0	4
5 yrs.		**N Totals:**	29	0	2	2	12

Signed as free agent by **Pittsburgh** from Cleveland, Feb. 28, 1977.

Joe Primeau

PRIMEAU, JOE 5'11", 153 lbs.
B. Jan. 24, 1906, Lindsay, Ont. Center
Won Lady Byng Trophy, 1931-32
Hall of Fame, 1963

YEAR	TEAM & LEAGUE		GP	G	A	PTS	PIM
1927-28	**TOR**	**N**	2	0	0	0	0
1928-29			6	0	1	1	2
1929-30			43	5	21	26	28
1930-31			38	9	**32**	41	18
1931-32			46	13	**37**	50	25
1932-33			48	11	21	32	4
1933-34			45	14	**32**	46	8
1934-35			37	10	20	30	16
1935-36			45	4	13	17	10
9 yrs.		**N Totals:**	310	66	177	243	111
PLAYOFFS							
1930-31	**TOR**	**N**	2	0	0	0	0
1931-32*			7	0	6	6	2
1932-33			8	0	1	1	4
1933-34			5	2	4	6	6
1934-35			7	0	3	3	0
1935-36			9	3	4	7	0
6 yrs.		**N Totals:**	38	5	18	23	12

Kev Primeau

PRIMEAU, KEVIN
Right Wing, Shoots R

YEAR	TEAM & LEAGUE		GP	G	A	PTS	PIM
1977-78	**EDM**	**W**	7	0	1	1	2
1980-81	**VAN**	**N**	2	0	0	0	4
2 yrs.		**N Totals:**	2	0	0	0	4
		W Totals:	7	0	1	1	2
PLAYOFFS							
1977-78	**EDM**	**W**	2	0	0	0	2

Ellie Pringle

PRINGLE, ELLIS
B. Toronto, Ont. Defense

YEAR	TEAM & LEAGUE		GP	G	A	PTS	PIM
1930-31	**NYA**	**N**	6	0	0	0	0

Jim Pritchard

PRITCHARD, JAMES GEORGE 5'9", 175 lbs.
B. Feb. 14, 1948, Winnipeg, Man. Defense, Shoots L

YEAR	TEAM & LEAGUE		GP	G	A	PTS	PIM
1974-75	**CHI**	**W**	2	0	0	0	0

Dick Proceviat

PROCEVIAT, RICHARD PETER (Pro, Herman, Goodyear)
6', 179 lbs.
B. June 25, 1946, Whitemouth, Man. Defense, Shoots L

YEAR	TEAM & LEAGUE		GP	G	A	PTS	PIM
1972-73	**CHI**	**W**	53	4	14	18	33
1973-74			77	2	20	22	55
1974-75			11	0	3	3	11
	IND	**W**	52	1	28	29	51
	2 team total		63	1	31	32	62
1975-76			73	7	13	20	31
1976-77			55	2	12	14	33
5 yrs.		**W Totals:**	321	16	90	106	214
PLAYOFFS							
1973-74	**CHI**	**W**	13	0	4	4	10

Dick Proceviat continued

YEAR	TEAM & LEAGUE	GP	G	A	PTS	PIM
1975-76	**IND W**	7	0	0	0	2
2 yrs.	**W Totals:**	20	0	4	4	12

Goldie Prodgers

PRODGERS, GEORGE

Forward

YEAR	TEAM & LEAGUE	GP	G	A	PTS	PIM
1919-20	**TOR N**	16	8	6	14	2
1920-21	**HAMIL N**	23	18	8	26	8
1921-22		24	15	4	19	4
1922-23		23	13	3	16	13
1923-24		23	9	1	10	6
1924-25		1	0	0	0	0
1925-26	**MONT N**	24	0	0	0	0
7 yrs.	**N Totals:**	134	63	22	85	33

Andre Pronovost

PRONOVOST, JOSEPH ARMAND ANDRE

5'9½", 165 lbs.

B. July 9, 1936, Shawinigan Falls, Que. Left Wing, Shoots L

YEAR	TEAM & LEAGUE	GP	G	A	PTS	PIM
1956-57	**MONT N**	64	10	11	21	58
1957-58		66	16	12	28	55
1958-59		70	9	14	23	48
1959-60		69	12	19	31	61
1960-61		21	1	5	6	4
	BOS N	47	11	11	22	30
	2 team total	68	12	16	28	34
1961-62		70	15	8	23	70
1962-63		21	0	2	2	4
	DET N	47	13	5	18	20
	2 team total	68	13	7	20	24
1963-64		70	7	16	23	23
1964-65		3	0	1	1	0
1967-68	**MINN N**	8	0	0	0	0
10 yrs.	**N Totals:**	556	94	104	198	373

PLAYOFFS

YEAR	TEAM & LEAGUE	GP	G	A	PTS	PIM
1956-57*	**MONT N**	8	1	0	1	4
1957-58*		10	2	0	2	16
1958-59*		11	2	1	3	6
1959-60*		8	1	2	3	C
1962-63	**DET N**	11	1	4	5	6
1963-64		14	4	3	7	26
1967-68	**MINN N**	8	0	1	1	0
7 yrs.	**N Totals:**	70	11	11	22	58

Traded to **Boston** by Mont. Canadiens for Jean-Guy Gendron, Nov., 1960. Traded to **Detroit** by Boston for Forbes Kennedy, Dec., 1962. Drafted by **Minnesota** from Detroit in Expansion Draft, June 6, 1967.

Jean Pronovost

PRONOVOST, JOSEPH JEAN DENIS 185 lbs.

B. Dec. 18, 1945, Shawinigan Falls, Que.

Right Wing, Shoots R

YEAR	TEAM & LEAGUE	GP	G	A	PTS	PIM
1968-69	**PITT N**	76	16	25	41	41
1969-70		72	20	21	41	45
1970-71		78	21	24	45	35
1971-72		68	30	23	53	12
1972-73		66	21	22	43	16
1973-74		77	40	32	72	22
1974-75		78	43	32	75	37
1975-76		80	52	52	104	24
1976-77		79	33	31	64	24
1977-78		79	40	25	65	50
1978-79	**ATL N**	75	28	39	67	30
1979-80		80	24	19	43	12
1980-81	**WASH N**	80	22	36	58	67
1981-82		10	1	2	3	4
14 yrs.	**N Totals:**	998	391	383	774	419

PLAYOFFS

YEAR	TEAM & LEAGUE	GP	G	A	PTS	PIM
1969-70	**PITT N**	10	3	4	7	2

Jean Pronovost continued

YEAR	TEAM & LEAGUE	GP	G	A	PTS	PIM
1971-72		4	1	1	2	0
1974-75		9	3	3	6	6
1975-76		3	0	0	0	2
1976-77		3	2	1	3	2
1978-79	**ATL N**	2	2	0	2	0
1979-80		4	0	0	0	2
7 yrs.	**N Totals:**	35	11	9	20	14

Sold to **Pittsburgh** by Boston, May 21, 1968. Traded to **Atlanta** by Pittsburgh for Gregg Sheppard, Sept. 6, 1978. Sold to **Washington** by Calgary, July 1, 1980.

Marcel Pronovost

PRONOVOST, RENE MARCEL 6', 190 lbs.

B. June 15, 1930, Lac la Tortue, Que. Defense, Shoots L

Hall of Fame, 1978

YEAR	TEAM & LEAGUE	GP	G	A	PTS	PIM
1950-51	**DET N**	37	1	6	7	20
1951-52		69	7	11	18	50
1952-53		68	8	19	27	72
1953-54		57	6	12	18	50
1954-55		70	9	25	34	90
1955-56		68	4	13	17	46
1956-57		70	7	9	16	38
1957-58		62	2	18	20	52
1958-59		69	11	21	32	44
1959-60		69	7	17	24	38
1960-61		70	6	11	17	44
1961-62		70	4	14	18	30
1962-63		69	4	9	13	48
1963-64		67	3	17	20	20
1964-65		68	1	15	16	45
1965-66	**TOR N**	54	2	8	10	34
1966-67		58	2	12	14	28
1967-68		70	3	17	20	48
1968-69		34	1	2	3	20
1969-70		7	0	1	1	4
20 yrs.	**N Totals:**	1206	88	257	345	821

PLAYOFFS

YEAR	TEAM & LEAGUE	GP	G	A	PTS	PIM
1949-50*	**DET N**	9	0	1	1	10
1950-51		6	0	0	0	0
1951-52*		8	0	1	1	10
1952-53		6	0	0	0	6
1953-54*		12	2	3	5	12
1954-55*		11	1	3	4	6
1955-56		10	0	2	2	8
1956-57		5	0	0	0	6
1957-58		4	0	1	1	4
1959-60		6	1	1	2	2
1960-61		9	2	3	5	0
1962-63		11	1	4	5	8
1963-64		14	4	3	7	26
1964-65		7	0	3	3	4
1965-66	**TOR N**	4	0	0	0	6
1966-67*		12	1	0	1	8
16 yrs.	**N Totals:**	134	12	25	37	116

Traded by Detroit with Autry Erickson, Larry Jeffrey, Ed Joyal, and Lowell MacDonald to **Toronto** for Andy Bathgate, Billy Harris, and Gary Jarrett, May 20, 1965.

Brian Propp

PROPP, BRIAN PHILIP 5'9", 185 lbs.

B. Feb. 15, 1959, Lanigan, Sask. Left Wing, Shoots L

YEAR	TEAM & LEAGUE	GP	G	A	PTS	PIM
1979-80	**PHI N**	80	34	41	75	54
1980-81		79	26	40	66	110
1981-82		80	44	47	91	117
1982-83		80	40	42	82	72
4 yrs.	**N Totals:**	319	144	170	314	353

PLAYOFFS

YEAR	TEAM & LEAGUE	GP	G	A	PTS	PIM
1979-80	**PHI N**	19	5	10	15	29
1980-81		12	6	6	12	32
1981-82		4	2	2	4	4
1982-83		3	1	2	3	8
4 yrs.	**N Totals:**	38	14	20	34	73

Claude Provost

PROVOST, JOSEPH ANTOINE CLAUDE

5'9", 175 lbs.

B. Sept. 17, 1933, Montreal, Que. — Right Wing, Shoots R

Won Masterton Trophy, 1967-68

YEAR	TEAM & LEAGUE		GP	G	A	PTS	PIM
1955-56	MONT	N	60	13	16	29	30
1956-57			67	16	14	30	24
1957-58			70	19	32	51	71
1958-59			69	16	22	38	37
1959-60			70	17	29	46	42
1960-61			49	11	4	15	32
1961-62			70	33	29	62	22
1962-63			67	20	30	50	26
1963-64			68	15	17	32	37
1964-65			70	27	37	64	28
1965-66			70	19	36	55	38
1966-67			64	11	13	24	16
1967-68			73	14	30	44	26
1968-69			73	13	15	28	18
1969-70			65	10	11	21	22
15 yrs.	N Totals:		1005	254	335	589	469

PLAYOFFS

YEAR	TEAM & LEAGUE		GP	G	A	PTS	PIM
1955-56*	MONT	N	10	3	3	6	12
1956-57*			10	0	1	1	8
1957-58*			10	1	3	4	8
1958-59*			11	6	2	8	2
1959-60*			8	1	1	2	0
1960-61			6	1	3	4	4
1961-62			6	2	2	4	2
1962-63			5	0	1	1	2
1963-64			7	2	2	4	22
1964-65*			13	2	6	8	12
1965-66*			10	2	3	5	2
1966-67			7	1	1	2	0
1967-68*			13	2	8	10	10
1968-69*			10	2	2	4	2
14 yrs.	N Totals:		126	25	38	63	86

Sold to **Los Angeles** by Montreal, June 8, 1971.

Metro Prystai

PRYSTAI, METRO

5'9", 170 lbs.

B. Nov. 7, 1927, Yorkton, Sask. — Center, Shoots L

YEAR	TEAM & LEAGUE		GP	G	A	PTS	PIM
1947-48	CHI	N	54	7	11	18	25
1948-49			59	12	7	19	19
1949-50			65	29	22	51	31
1950-51	DET	N	62	20	17	37	27
1951-52			69	21	22	43	16
1952-53			70	16	34	50	12
1953-54			70	12	15	27	26
1954-55			12	2	3	5	9
	CHI	N	57	11	13	24	28
	2 team total		69	13	16	29	37
1955-56			8	1	3	4	8
	DET	N	63	12	16	28	10
	2 team total		71	13	19	32	18
1956-57			70	7	15	22	16
1957-58			15	1	1	2	4
11 yrs.	N Totals:		674	151	179	330	231

PLAYOFFS

YEAR	TEAM & LEAGUE		GP	G	A	PTS	PIM
1950-51	DET	N	3	1	0	1	0
1951-52*			8	2	5	7	0
1952-53			6	4	4	8	2
1953-54*			12	2	3	5	0
1955-56			9	1	2	3	6
1956-57			5	2	0	2	0
6 yrs.	N Totals:		43	12	14	26	8

Traded to **Detroit** by Chicago with Jim Henry, Bob Goldham, and Gaye Stewart for Harry Lumley, Jack Stewart, Al Dewsbury, Don Morrison and Pete Babando, July 13, 1950. Traded to **Chicago** by Detroit for Lorne Davis, Nov. 9, 1954. Traded to **Detroit** by Chicago for Ed Sandford, Oct. 24, 1955.

Al Pudas

PUDAS, ALBERT

B. Unknown — Left Wing, Shoots L

YEAR	TEAM & LEAGUE		GP	G	A	PTS	PIM
1926-27	TOR	N	3	0	0	0	0

Bob Pulford

PULFORD, ROBERT JESSE — 5'11", 188 lbs.

B. Mar. 31, 1936, Newton Robinson, Ont.

Left Wing, Shoots L

Won Jack Adams Award, 1974-75

YEAR	TEAM & LEAGUE		GP	G	A	PTS	PIM
1956-57	TOR	N	65	11	11	22	32
1957-58			70	14	17	31	48
1958-59			70	23	14	37	53
1959-60			70	24	28	52	81
1960-61			40	11	18	29	41
1961-62			70	18	21	39	98
1962-63			70	19	25	44	49
1963-64			70	18	30	48	73
1964-65			65	19	20	39	46
1965-66			70	28	28	56	51
1966-67			67	17	28	45	28
1967-68			74	20	30	50	40
1968-69			72	11	23	34	20
1969-70			74	18	19	37	31
1970-71	LA	N	59	17	26	43	53
1971-72			73	13	24	37	48
16 yrs.	N Totals:		1079	281	362	643	792

PLAYOFFS

YEAR	TEAM & LEAGUE		GP	G	A	PTS	PIM
1958-59	TOR	N	12	4	4	8	8
1959-60			10	4	1	5	10
1960-61			5	0	0	0	8
1961-62*			12	7	1	8	24
1962-63*			10	2	5	7	14
1963-64*			14	5	3	8	20
1964-65			6	1	1	2	16
1965-66			4	1	1	2	12
1966-67*			12	1	10	11	12
1968-69			4	0	0	0	2
10 yrs.	N Totals:		89	25	26	51	126

Traded by Toronto to **Los Angeles** for Garry Monahan and Brian Murphy, Sept. 3, 1970.

Dave Pulkkinen

PULKKINEN, DAVID JOEL JOHN — 6', 175 lbs.

B. May 18, 1949, Kapuskasing, Ont. — Defense, Shoots R

YEAR	TEAM & LEAGUE		GP	G	A	PTS	PIM
1972-73	NYI	N	2	0	0	0	0

Rich Pumple

PUMPLE, RICHARD — 6'3", 200 lbs.

B. Feb. 11, 1948, Kirkland Lake, Ont. — Left Wing, Shoots L

YEAR	TEAM & LEAGUE		GP	G	A	PTS	PIM
1972-73	CLEVE	W	77	21	20	41	45
1973-74			17	2	2	4	16
1974-75	IND	W	34	4	8	12	29
3 yrs.	W Totals:		128	27	30	57	90

PLAYOFFS

YEAR	TEAM & LEAGUE		GP	G	A	PTS	PIM
1972-73	CLEVE	W	9	3	5	8	11

Fido Purpur

PURPUR, CLIFFORD

B. Oct. 26, 1916, Grand Forks, N.D.

YEAR	TEAM & LEAGUE		GP	G	A	PTS	PIM
1934-35	STL	N	25	2	1	3	8
1941-42	CHI	N	8	0	0	0	0
1942-43			50	13	16	29	14
1943-44			40	9	10	19	13
1944-45			21	2	7	9	11
5 yrs.	N Totals:		144	26	34	60	46

PLAYOFFS

YEAR	TEAM & LEAGUE		GP	G	A	PTS	PIM
1943-44	CHI	N	9	1	1	2	0
1944-45	DET	N	7	0	1	1	4
2 yrs.	N Totals:		16	1	2	3	4

Jean Pusie

PUSIE, JEAN BAPTISTE 6', 205 lbs.
B. Oct. 15, 1910, Montral, Que. Defense, Shoots L

YEAR	TEAM & LEAGUE		GP	G	A	PTS	PIM
1930-31	MONT	N	6	0	0	0	0
1931-32			1	0	0	0	0
1933-34	NYR	N	19	0	2	2	17
1934-35	BOS	N	4	1	0	1	0
1935-36	MONT	N	31	0	2	2	11
5 yrs.		N Totals:	61	1	4	5	28
PLAYOFFS							
1930-31*	MONT	N	3	0	0	0	0
1934-35	BOS	N	4	0	0	0	0
2 yrs.		N Totals:	7	0	0	0	0

Nelson Pyatt

PYATT, FREDERICK NELSON 6', 175 lbs.
B. Sept. 9, 1953, Port Arthur, Ont. Center, Shoots L

YEAR	TEAM & LEAGUE		GP	G	A	PTS	PIM
1973-74	DET	N	5	0	0	0	0
1974-75			9	0	0	0	0
	WASH	N	16	6	4	10	21
	2 team total		25	6	4	10	21
1975-76			77	26	23	49	14
1976-77	COLO	N	77	23	22	45	20
1977-78			71	9	12	21	8
1978-79			28	2	2	4	2
1979-80			13	5	0	5	2
7 yrs.		N Totals:	296	71	63	134	67

Bill Quackenbush

QUACKENBUSH, HUBERT GEORGE 5'11", 180 lbs.
B. Mar. 2, 1922, Toronto, Ont. Defense, Shoots L
Won Lady Byng Trophy, 1948-49
Hall of Fame, 1976

YEAR	TEAM & LEAGUE		GP	G	A	PTS	PIM
1942-43	DET	N	10	1	1	2	4
1943-44			43	4	14	18	6
1944-45			50	7	14	21	10
1945-46			48	11	10	21	6
1946-47			44	5	17	22	6
1947-48			58	6	16	22	17
1948-49			60	6	17	23	0
1949-50	BOS	N	70	8	17	25	4
1950-51			70	5	24	29	12
1951-52			69	2	17	19	6
1952-53			69	2	16	18	6
1953-54			45	0	17	17	6
1954-55			68	2	20	22	8
1955-56			70	3	22	25	4
14 yrs.		N Totals:	774	62	222	284	95
PLAYOFFS							
1943-44	DET	N	2	1	0	1	0
1944-45			14	0	2	2	2
1945-46			5	0	1	1	0
1946-47			5	0	0	0	6
1947-48			10	0	2	2	0
1948-49			11	1	1	2	0
1950-51	BOS	N	6	0	1	1	0
1951-52			7	0	3	3	0
1952-53			11	0	4	4	4
1953-54			4	0	0	0	0
1954-55			5	0	5	5	0
11 yrs.		N Totals:	80	2	19	21	12

Traded to **Boston** by Detroit with Pete Horeck for Pete Babando, Clare Martin, Lloyd Durham and Jim Peters, Aug. 16, 1949.

Max Quackenbush

QUACKENBUSH, MAXWELL JOSEPH 6'2", 180 lbs.
B. Aug. 29, 1928, Toronto, Ont. Defense, Shoots L

YEAR	TEAM & LEAGUE		GP	G	A	PTS	PIM
1950-51	BOS	N	47	4	6	10	26
1951-52	CHI	N	14	0	1	1	4
2 yrs.		N Totals:	61	4	7	11	30
PLAYOFFS							
1950-51	BOS	N	6	0	0	0	4

Traded to **Chicago** by Detroit for Doug McCaig, Sept. 18, 1951.

Joel Quenneville

QUENNEVILLE, JOEL NORMAN (Herbie) 6', 188 lbs.
B. Sept. 15, 1958, Windsor, Ont. Defense, Shoots L

YEAR	TEAM & LEAGUE		GP	G	A	PTS	PIM
1978-79	TOR	N	61	2	9	11	60
1979-80			32	1	4	5	24
	COLO	N	35	5	7	12	26
	2 team total		67	6	11	17	50
1980-81			71	10	24	34	86
1981-82			64	5	10	15	55
1982-83	NJ	N	74	5	12	17	46
5 yrs.		N Totals:	337	28	66	94	297
PLAYOFFS							
1978-79	TOR	N	6	0	1	1	4

Traded to **Colorado** by Toronto with Lanny McDonald for Pat Hickey and Wilf Paiement, Dec. 29, 1979. Traded to **Calgary** by New Jersey with Steve Tambellini for Mel Bridgman and Phil Russell, June 20, 1983. Traded to **Hartford** by Calgary with Richie Dunn for Mickey Volcan, July 6, 1983.

Leo Quenneville

QUENNEVILLE, LEONARD 5'10", 170 lbs.
B. June 15, 1900, Anicet, Que. Forward, Shoots L

YEAR	TEAM & LEAGUE		GP	G	A	PTS	PIM
1929-30	NYR	N	25	0	3	3	10
PLAYOFFS							
1929-30	NYR	N	3	0	0	0	0

John Quilty

QUILTY, JOHN FRANCIS 5'10", 175 lbs.
B. Jan. 21, 1921, Ottawa, Ont. Center, Shoots L
Won Calder Trophy, 1940-41

YEAR	TEAM & LEAGUE		GP	G	A	PTS	PIM
1940-41	MONT	N	48	18	16	34	31
1941-42			48	12	12	24	44
1946-47			3	1	1	2	0
1947-48			20	2	3	5	4
	BOS	N	6	3	2	5	2
	2 team total		26	5	5	10	6
4 yrs.		N Totals:	125	36	34	70	81
PLAYOFFS							
1940-41	MONT	N	3	0	2	2	0
1941-42			3	0	1	1	0
1946-47			7	3	2	5	9
3 yrs.		N Totals:	13	3	5	8	9

Pat Quinn

QUINN, JOHN BRIAN PATRICK 6'3", 215 lbs.
B. Jan. 29, 1943, Hamilton, Ont. Defense, Shoots L
Won Jack Adams Award, 1979-80

YEAR	TEAM & LEAGUE		GP	G	A	PTS	PIM
1968-69	TOR	N	40	2	7	9	95
1969-70			59	0	5	5	88
1970-71	VAN	N	76	2	11	13	149
1971-72			57	2	3	5	63
1972-73	ATL	N	78	2	18	20	113
1973-74			77	5	27	32	94
1974-75			80	2	19	21	156
1975-76			80	2	11	13	134
1976-77			59	1	12	13	58
9 yrs.		N Totals:	606	18	113	131	950
PLAYOFFS							
1968-69	TOR	N	4	0	0	0	13
1973-74	ATL	N	4	0	0	0	6
1975-76			2	0	1	1	2
1976-77			1	0	0	0	0
4 yrs.		N Totals:	11	0	1	1	21

Claimed in draft by **Montreal** from Detroit, June 15, 1966. Sold to **St. Louis** by Montreal with Ron Attwell, June 14, 1967. Sold to **Toronto** by St. Louis, March 25, 1968. Drafted by **Vancouver** from Toronto in Expansion Draft, June 10, 1970. Drafted by **Atlanta** from Vancouver in Expansion Draft, June 6, 1972.

Yip Radley

RADLEY, HARRY JOHN 5'11½", 198 lbs.
B. June 27, 1910, Ottawa, Ont. Defense, Shoots L

YEAR	TEAM & LEAGUE	GP	G	A	PTS	PIM
1930-31	NYA N	1	0	0	0	0
1936-37	MON(M) N	17	0	1	1	13
2 yrs.	N Totals:	18	0	1	1	13

Rags Raglan

RAGLAN, CLARENCE ELDON 6'1", 177 lbs.
B. Sept. 4, 1927, Pembroke, Ont. Defense, Shoots L

YEAR	TEAM & LEAGUE	GP	G	A	PTS	PIM
1950-51	DET N	33	3	1	4	14
1951-52	CHI N	35	0	5	5	28
1952-53		32	1	3	4	10
3 yrs.	N Totals:	100	4	9	13	52
PLAYOFFS						
1952-53	CHI N	3	0	0	0	0

Traded to **Chicago** by Detroit with Jim McFadden, George Gee, Jim Peters, Clare Martin and Max McNab for Hugh Coflin and $75,000, Aug. 20, 1951.

Don Raleigh

RALEIGH, JAMES DONALD (Bones) 5'11", 150 lbs.
B. June 27, 1926, Kenora, Ont. Center, Shoots L

YEAR	TEAM & LEAGUE	GP	G	A	PTS	PIM
1943-44	NYR N	15	2	2	4	2
1947-48		52	15	18	33	2
1948-49		41	10	16	26	8
1949-50		70	12	25	37	11
1950-51		64	15	24	39	18
1951-52		70	19	42	61	14
1952-53		55	4	18	22	2
1953-54		70	15	30	45	16
1954-55		69	8	32	40	19
1955-56		29	1	12	13	4
10 yrs.	N Totals:	535	101	219	320	96
PLAYOFFS						
1947-48	NYR N	6	2	0	2	2
1949-50		12	4	5	9	4
2 yrs.	N Totals:	18	6	5	11	6

Rob Ramage

RAMAGE, GEORGE ROBB 6'2", 195 lbs.
B. Jan. 11, 1959, Byron, Ont. Defense, Shoots L

YEAR	TEAM & LEAGUE	GP	G	A	PTS	PIM
1978-79	BIRM W	80	12	36	48	165
1979-80	COLO N	75	8	20	28	135
1980-81		79	20	42	62	193
1981-82		80	13	29	42	201
1982-83	STL N	78	16	35	51	193
5 yrs.	N Totals:	312	57	126	183	722
	W Totals:	80	12	36	48	165
PLAYOFFS						
1982-83	STL N	4	0	3	3	22

Traded to **St. Louis** by New Jersey for St. Louis' first round choice (Rocky Trottier) in 1982 Entry Draft and first round choice (John MacLean) in 1983 Entry Draft, June 9, 1982. Traded by New Jersey to **St. Louis** for St. Louis' first round choice in the 1982 Amateur Draft (Rocky Trottier) and St. Louis' first round choice in 1983 (John McLean), June 9, 1982.

Beattie Ramsay

RAMSAY, BEATTIE
Defense

YEAR	TEAM & LEAGUE	GP	G	A	PTS	PIM
1927-28	TOR N	43	0	2	2	10

Craig Ramsay

RAMSAY, CRAIG EDWARD (Rammer) 5'10", 176 lbs.
B. Mar. 17, 1951, Weston, Ont. Left Wing, Shoots L

YEAR	TEAM & LEAGUE	GP	G	A	PTS	PIM
1971-72	BUF N	57	6	10	16	0
1972-73		76	11	17	28	15
1973-74		78	20	26	46	0
1974-75		80	26	38	64	26
1975-76		80	22	49	71	34
1976-77		80	20	41	61	20
1977-78		80	28	43	71	18
1978-79		80	26	31	57	10

Craig Ramsay continued

YEAR	TEAM & LEAGUE	GP	G	A	PTS	PIM
1979-80		80	21	39	60	18
1980-81		80	24	35	59	12
1981-82		80	16	35	51	8
1982-83		64	11	18	29	7
12 yrs.	N Totals:	915	231	382	613	168
PLAYOFFS						
1972-73	BUF N	6	1	1	2	0
1974-75		17	5	7	12	2
1975-76		9	1	2	3	2
1976-77		6	0	4	4	0
1977-78		8	3	1	4	9
1978-79		3	1	0	1	2
1979-80		10	0	6	6	4
1980-81		8	2	4	6	4
1981-82		4	1	1	2	0
1982-83		10	2	3	5	4
10 yrs.	N Totals:	81	16	29	45	27

Les Ramsey

RAMSEY, LES
B. Montreal, Que. Left Wing, Shoots L

YEAR	TEAM & LEAGUE	GP	G	A	PTS	PIM
1944-45	CHI N	11	2	2	4	2

Mike Ramsey

RAMSEY, MICHAEL ALLEN 6'3", 190 lbs.
B. Dec. 3, 1960, Minneapolis, Minn. Defense, Shoots L

YEAR	TEAM & LEAGUE	GP	G	A	PTS	PIM
1979-80	BUF N	13	1	6	7	6
1980-81		72	3	14	17	56
1981-82		80	7	23	30	56
1982-83		77	8	30	38	55
4 yrs.	N Totals:	242	19	73	92	173
PLAYOFFS						
1979-80	BUF N	13	1	2	3	12
1980-81		8	0	3	3	20
1981-82		4	1	1	2	14
1982-83		10	4	4	8	15
4 yrs.	N Totals:	35	6	10	16	61

Wayne Ramsey

RAMSEY, WAYNE 6', 185 lbs.
B. Jan. 31, 1957, Hamiota, Man. Defense, Shoots L

YEAR	TEAM & LEAGUE	GP	G	A	PTS	PIM
1977-78	BUF N	2	0	0	0	0

Ken Randall

RANDALL, KEN
Right Wing

YEAR	TEAM & LEAGUE	GP	G	A	PTS	PIM
1917-18	TOR N	20	12	0	12	55
1918-19		14	7	6	13	27
1919-20		21	10	7	17	43
1920-21		21	6	1	7	58
1921-22		24	10	6	16	20
1922-23		24	3	5	8	51
1923-24	HAMIL N	24	7	1	8	18
1924-25		30	8	0	8	49
1925-26	NYA N	34	4	2	6	94
1926-27		3	0	0	0	0
10 yrs.	N Totals:	215	67	28	95	415
PLAYOFFS						
1917-18*	TOR N	7	1	0	1	**24**
1920-21		2	0	0	0	14
1921-22*		5	1	0	1	11
3 yrs.	N Totals:	14	2	0	2	49

George Ranieri

RANIERI, GEORGE DOMINIC 5'8", 190 lbs.
B. Jan. 14, 1936, Toronto, Ont. Left Wing, Shoots L

YEAR	TEAM & LEAGUE	GP	G	A	PTS	PIM
1956-57	BOS N	2	0	0	0	0

Jean Ratelle

RATELLE, JOSEPH GILBERT YVON JEAN

6'1", 180 lbs.

B. Oct. 3, 1940, Lac St. Jean, Que. — Center, Shoots L

Won Lady Byng Trophy, 1971-72, 1975-76

Won Masterton Trophy, 1970-71

YEAR	TEAM & LEAGUE		GP	G	A	PTS	PIM
1960-61	**NYR**	**N**	3	2	1	3	0
1961-62			31	4	8	12	4
1962-63			48	11	9	20	8
1963-64			15	0	7	7	6
1964-65			54	14	21	35	14
1965-66			67	21	30	51	10
1966-67			41	6	5	11	4
1967-68			74	32	46	78	18
1968-69			75	32	46	78	26
1969-70			75	32	42	74	28
1970-71			78	26	46	72	14
1971-72			63	46	63	109	4
1972-73			78	41	53	94	12
1973-74			68	28	39	67	16
1974-75			79	36	55	91	26
1975-76			13	5	10	15	2
	BOS	**N**	67	31	59	90	16
	2 team total		80	36	69	105	18
1976-77			78	33	61	94	22
1977-78			80	25	59	84	10
1978-79			80	27	45	72	12
1979-80			67	28	45	73	8
1980-81			47	11	26	37	16
21 yrs.		**N Totals:**	1281	491	776	1267	276

PLAYOFFS

YEAR	TEAM & LEAGUE		GP	G	A	PTS	PIM
1966-67	**NYR**	**N**	4	0	0	0	2
1967-68			6	0	4	4	2
1968-69			4	1	0	1	0
1969-70			6	1	3	4	0
1970-71			13	2	9	11	8
1971-72			6	0	1	1	0
1972-73			10	2	7	9	0
1973-74			13	2	4	6	0
1974-75			3	1	5	6	2
1975-76	**BOS**	**N**	12	8	8	16	4
1976-77			14	5	12	17	4
1977-78			15	3	7	10	0
1978-79			11	7	6	13	2
1979-80			3	0	0	0	0
1980-81			3	0	0	0	0
15 yrs.		**N Totals:**	123	32	66	98	24

Traded to **Boston** by N.Y. Rangers with Brad Park and Joe Zanussi for Phil Esposito and Carol Vadnais, Nov. 7, 1975.

John Rathwell

RATHWELL, JOHN DONALD — 6', 190 lbs.

B. Aug. 12, 1947, Temiscamingue, Que. — Right Wing, Shoots L

YEAR	TEAM & LEAGUE		GP	G	A	PTS	PIM
1974-75	**BOS**	**N**	1	0	0	0	0

Errol Rausse

RAUSSE, ERROL A. — 5'10", 181 lbs.

B. May 18, 1959, Quesnel, B.C. — Left Wing, Shoots L

YEAR	TEAM & LEAGUE		GP	G	A	PTS	PIM
1979-80	**WASH**	**N**	24	6	2	8	0
1980-81			5	1	1	2	0
1981-82			2	0	0	0	0
3 yrs.		**N Totals:**	31	7	3	10	0

Pekka Rautakallio

RAUTAKALLIO, PEKKA — 5'11", 185 lbs.

B. July 25, 1953, Pori, Finland — Defense, Shoots L

YEAR	TEAM & LEAGUE		GP	G	A	PTS	PIM
1975-76	**PHOE**	**W**	73	11	39	50	8
1976-77			78	4	31	35	8
1979-80	**ATL**	**N**	79	5	25	30	18
1980-81	**CALG**	**N**	76	11	45	56	64
1981-82			80	17	51	68	40
5 yrs.		**N Totals:**	235	33	121	154	122
		W Totals:	151	15	70	85	16

PLAYOFFS

YEAR	TEAM & LEAGUE		GP	G	A	PTS	PIM
1975-76	**PHOE**	**W**	5	0	2	2	0
1979-80	**ATL**	**N**	4	0	1	1	2
1980-81	**CALG**	**N**	16	2	4	6	6
1981-82			3	0	0	0	0
4 yrs.		**N Totals:**	23	2	5	7	8
		W Totals:	5	0	2	2	0

Signed by **Atlanta** as a free agent, June 5, 1979.

Matt Ravlich

RAVLICH, MATHEW JOSEPH — 5'10", 185 lbs.

B. July 12, 1938, Sault Ste. Marie, Ont. — Defense, Shoots L

YEAR	TEAM & LEAGUE		GP	G	A	PTS	PIM
1962-63	**BOS**	**N**	2	1	0	1	0
1964-65	**CHI**	**N**	61	3	16	19	80
1965-66			62	0	16	16	78
1966-67			62	0	3	3	39
1968-69			60	2	12	14	57
1969-70	**DET**	**N**	46	0	6	6	33
	LA	**N**	21	3	7	10	34
	2 team total		67	3	13	16	67
1970-71			66	3	16	19	41
1971-72	**BOS**	**N**	26	0	1	1	2
1972-73			5	0	1	1	0
9 yrs.		**N Totals:**	411	12	78	90	364

PLAYOFFS

YEAR	TEAM & LEAGUE		GP	G	A	PTS	PIM
1964-65	**CHI**	**N**	14	1	4	5	14
1965-66			6	0	1	1	2
1967-68			4	0	0	0	0
3 yrs.		**N Totals:**	24	1	5	6	16

Traded to **Chicago** by Boston with Jerry Toppazzini for Murray Balfour and Mike Draper, June 9, 1964.

Armand Raymond

RAYMOND, ARMAND

B. Jan. 12, 1913 — Defense, Shoots L

YEAR	TEAM & LEAGUE		GP	G	A	PTS	PIM
1937-38	**MONT**	**N**	11	0	1	1	10
1939-40			11	0	1	1	0
2 yrs.		**N Totals:**	22	0	2	2	10

Paul Raymond

RAYMOND, PAUL MARCEL — 5'7½", 138 lbs.

B. Feb. 27, 1913, Montreal, Que. — Right Wing, Shoots R

YEAR	TEAM & LEAGUE		GP	G	A	PTS	PIM
1932-33	**MONT**	**N**	16	0	0	0	0
1933-34			29	1	0	1	2
1934-35			20	1	1	2	0
1937-38			11	0	2	2	4
4 yrs.		**N Totals:**	76	2	3	5	6

PLAYOFFS

YEAR	TEAM & LEAGUE		GP	G	A	PTS	PIM
1933-34	**MONT**	**N**	2	0	0	0	0
1937-38			3	0	0	0	2
2 yrs.		**N Totals:**	5	0	0	0	2

Mel Read

READ, MELVIN DEAN — 5'6", 165 lbs.

B. Apr. 10, 1924, Montreal, Que. — Center, Shoots L

YEAR	TEAM & LEAGUE		GP	G	A	PTS	PIM
1946-47	**NYR**	**N**	1	0	0	0	0

Ken Reardon

REARDON, KENNETH JOSEPH — 5'10", 180 lbs.

B. Apr. 1, 1921, Winnipeg, Man. — Defense, Shoots L

Hall of Fame, 1966

YEAR	TEAM & LEAGUE		GP	G	A	PTS	PIM
1940-41	**MONT**	**N**	34	2	8	10	41
1941-42			41	3	12	15	93
1945-46			43	5	4	9	45
1946-47			52	5	17	22	84
1947-48			58	7	15	22	129
1948-49			46	3	13	16	103
1949-50			67	1	27	28	109
7 yrs.		**N Totals:**	341	26	96	122	604

PLAYOFFS

YEAR	TEAM & LEAGUE		GP	G	A	PTS	PIM
1940-41	**MONT**	**N**	3	0	0	0	4

Ken Reardon continued

YEAR	TEAM & LEAGUE		GP	G	A	PTS	PIM
1941-42			3	0	0	0	4
1945-46*			9	1	1	2	4
1946-47			7	1	2	3	20
1948-49			7	0	0	0	18
1949-50			2	0	2	2	12
6 yrs.		N Totals:	31	2	5	7	62

Terry Reardon

REARDON, TERRANCE GEORGE 5'10", 170 lbs.
B. Apr. 6, 1919, Winnipeg, Man. Defense, Shoots R

YEAR	TEAM & LEAGUE		GP	G	A	PTS	PIM
1938-39	BOS	N	4	0	0	0	0
1940-41			34	6	5	11	19
1941-42	MONT	N	33	17	17	34	14
1942-43			13	6	6	12	2
1945-46	BOS	N	49	12	11	23	21
1946-47			60	6	14	20	17
6 yrs.		N Totals:	193	47	53	100	73
PLAYOFFS							
1939-40	BOS	N	1	0	1	1	0
1940-41*			11	2	4	6	6
1941-42	MONT	N	3	2	2	4	2
1945-46	BOS	N	10	4	0	4	2
1946-47			5	0	3	3	2
5 yrs.		N Totals:	30	8	10	18	12

Marc Reaume

REAUME, MARC AVELLIN 6'1", 185 lbs.
B. Feb. 7, 1934, Lasalle, Que. Defense, Shoots L

YEAR	TEAM & LEAGUE		GP	G	A	PTS	PIM
1954-55	TOR	N	1	0	0	0	4
1955-56			48	0	12	12	50
1956-57			66	6	14	20	81
1957-58			68	1	7	8	49
1958-59			51	1	5	6	57
1959-60			36	0	1	1	6
	DET	N	9	0	1	1	2
	2 team total		45	0	2	2	8
1960-61			38	0	1	1	8
1963-64	MONT	N	3	0	0	0	2
1970-71	VAN	N	27	0	2	2	4
9 yrs.		N Totals:	347	8	43	51	263
PLAYOFFS							
1954-55	TOR	N	4	0	0	0	2
1955-56			5	0	2	2	6
1958-59			10	0	0	0	0
1959-60	DET	N	2	0	0	0	0
4 yrs.		N Totals:	21	0	2	2	8

Traded by Toronto to **Detroit** for Red Kelly, Feb. 10, 1960. Drafted by **Toronto** from Detroit, June 9, 1964.

Billy Reay

REAY, WILLIAM 5'7", 155 lbs.
B. Aug. 21, 1918, Winnipeg, Man. Center, Shoots L

YEAR	TEAM & LEAGUE		GP	G	A	PTS	PIM
1943-44	DET	N	2	2	0	2	2
1944-45			2	0	0	0	0
1945-46	MONT	N	44	17	12	29	10
1946-47			59	22	20	42	17
1947-48			60	6	14	20	24
1948-49			60	22	23	45	33
1949-50			68	19	26	45	48
1950-51			60	6	18	24	24
1951-52			68	7	34	41	20
1952-53			56	4	15	19	26
10 yrs.		N Totals:	479	105	162	267	204
PLAYOFFS							
1945-46*	MONT	N	9	1	2	3	4
1946-47			11	6	1	7	14
1948-49			7	1	5	6	4
1949-50			4	0	1	1	0
1950-51			11	3	3	6	10
1951-52			10	2	2	4	7
1952-53*			11	0	2	2	4
7 yrs.		N Totals:	63	13	16	29	43

Gord Redahl

REDAHL, GORDON 5'11½", 170 lbs.
B. Aug. 28, 1935, Kinistino, Sask. Right Wing, Shoots L

YEAR	TEAM & LEAGUE		GP	G	A	PTS	PIM
1958-59	BOS	N	18	0	1	1	2

Drafted with Jean-Guy Gendron by **Boston** from New York, June 4, 1958.

George Redding

REDDING, GEORGE
B. Unknown Defense

YEAR	TEAM & LEAGUE		GP	G	A	PTS	PIM
1924-25	BOS	N	27	3	2	5	10
1925-26			8	0	0	0	0
2 yrs.		N Totals:	35	3	2	5	10

Dick Redmond

REDMOND, RICHARD JOHN 5'11", 178 lbs.
B. Aug. 14, 1949, Kirkland Lake, Ont. Defense, Shoots L

YEAR	TEAM & LEAGUE		GP	G	A	PTS	PIM
1969-70	MINN	N	7	0	1	1	4
1970-71			9	0	2	2	16
	CALIF	N	11	2	4	6	12
	2 team total		20	2	6	8	28
1971-72			74	10	35	45	76
1972-73			24	3	13	16	22
	CHI	N	52	9	19	28	4
	2 team total		76	12	32	44	26
1973-74			76	17	42	59	69
1974-75			80	14	43	57	90
1975-76			53	9	27	36	25
1976-77			80	22	25	47	30
1977-78	STL	N	28	4	11	15	16
	ATL	N	42	7	11	18	16
	2 team total		70	11	22	33	32
1978-79	BOS	N	64	7	26	33	21
1979-80			76	14	33	47	39
1980-81			78	15	20	35	60
1981-82			17	0	0	0	4
13 yrs.		N Totals:	771	133	312	445	504
PLAYOFFS							
1972-73	CHI	N	13	4	2	6	2
1973-74			11	1	7	8	8
1974-75			8	2	3	5	0
1975-76			4	0	2	2	4
1976-77			2	0	1	1	0
1977-78	ATL	N	2	1	0	1	0
1978-79	BOS	N	11	1	3	4	2
1979-80			10	0	3	3	9
1980-81			3	0	1	1	2
1981-82			2	0	0	0	0
10 yrs.		N Totals:	66	9	22	31	27

Traded to **California** by Minnesota with Tom Williams for Ted Hampson and Wayne Muloin, Mar. 7, 1971. Traded to **Chicago** by California with Bobby Sheehan for Darryl Maggs, Dec. 5, 1972. Traded to **St. Louis** by Chicago for Pierre Plante, Aug. 9, 1977. Traded to **Atlanta** by St. Louis with Yves Belanger, Bob MacMillan and St. Louis' second round choice (Mike Perovich) in the 1979 Entry Draft for Phil Myre, Curt Bennett, and Barry Gibbs, Dec. 12, 1977. Traded to **Boston** by Atlanta for Gregg Sheppard, Sept. 6, 1978.

Mickey Redmond

REDMOND, MICHAEL EDWARD 5'11", 185 lbs.
B. Dec. 27, 1947, Kirkland Lake, Ont. Right Wing, Shoots R

YEAR	TEAM & LEAGUE		GP	G	A	PTS	PIM
1967-68	MONT	N	41	6	5	11	4
1968-69			65	9	15	24	12
1969-70			75	27	27	54	61
1970-71			40	14	16	30	35
	DET	N	21	6	8	14	7
	2 team total		61	20	24	44	42
1971-72			78	42	28	70	34
1972-73			76	52	41	93	24
1973-74			76	51	26	77	14
1974-75			29	15	12	27	18
1975-76			37	11	17	28	10
9 yrs.		N Totals:	538	233	195	428	219
PLAYOFFS							
1967-68*	MONT	N	2	0	0	0	0
1968-69*			14	2	3	5	2

Mickey Redmond continued

YEAR	TEAM & LEAGUE		GP	G	A	PTS	PIM
2 yrs.		N Totals:	16	2	3	5	2

Traded to **Detroit** by Montreal with Guy Charron and Bill Collins for Frank Mahovlich, Jan. 13, 1971.

Bill Reed

REED, WILLIAM ERNEST 5'11", 190 lbs.
B. May 25, 1954, Toronto, Ont. Defense, Shoots R

YEAR	TEAM & LEAGUE		GP	G	A	PTS	PIM
1974-75	M-B	W	11	0	0	0	12
1975-76	CALG	W	29	0	5	5	14
2 yrs.		W Totals:	40	0	5	5	26

Mark Reeds

REEDS, MARK 5'10", 188 lbs.
B. Jan. 24, 1960, Burlington, Ont. Right Wing, Shoots R

YEAR	TEAM & LEAGUE		GP	G	A	PTS	PIM
1981-82	STL	N	9	1	3	4	0
1982-83			20	5	14	19	6
2 yrs.		N Totals:	29	6	17	23	6
PLAYOFFS							
1981-82	STL	N	10	0	1	1	2
1982-83			4	1	0	1	2
2 yrs.		N Totals:	14	1	1	2	4

Bill Regan

REGAN, WILLIAM DONALD
B. Dec. 11, 1908, Creighton Mines, Ont. Defense

YEAR	TEAM & LEAGUE		GP	G	A	PTS	PIM
1929-30	NYR	N	10	0	0	0	4
1930-31			42	2	1	3	49
1932-33	NYA	N	15	1	1	2	14
3 yrs.		N Totals:	67	3	2	5	67
PLAYOFFS							
1929-30	NYR	N	4	0	0	0	0
1930-31			4	0	0	0	2
2 yrs.		N Totals:	8	0	0	0	2

Larry Regan

REGAN, LAWRENCE EMMETT 5'9", 178 lbs.
B. Aug. 9, 1930, North Bay, Ont. Right Wing, Shoots R
Won Calder Trophy, 1956-57

YEAR	TEAM & LEAGUE		GP	G	A	PTS	PIM
1956-57	BOS	N	69	14	19	33	29
1957-58			59	11	28	39	22
1958-59			36	5	6	11	10
	TOR	N	32	4	21	25	2
	2 team total		68	9	27	36	12
1959-60			47	4	16	20	6
1960-61			37	3	5	8	2
5 yrs.		N Totals:	280	41	95	136	71
PLAYOFFS							
1956-57	BOS	N	8	0	2	2	10
1957-58			12	3	8	11	6
1958-59	TOR	N	8	1	1	2	2
1959-60			10	3	3	6	0
1960-61			4	0	0	0	0
5 yrs.		N Totals:	42	7	14	21	18

Claimed on waivers by **Toronto** from Boston, Jan. 7, 1959.

Darcy Regier

REGIER, DARCY JOHN 5'11", 191 lbs.
B. Nov. 27, 1956, Swift Current, Sask. Defense, Shoots L

YEAR	TEAM & LEAGUE		GP	G	A	PTS	PIM
1977-78	CLEVE	N	15	0	1	1	28
1982-83	NYI	N	6	0	0	0	7
2 yrs.		N Totals:	21	0	1	1	35

Traded to **N.Y. Islanders** by Cleveland with Wayne Merrick for Jean-Paul Parise, Jean Potvin and N.Y. Islander's fourth round choice (later cancelled by Cleveland-Minnesota merger) in the 1978 Amateur Draft, Jan. 10, 1978.

Earl Reibel

REIBEL, EARL 5'8", 160 lbs.
B. July 21, 1930, Kitchener, Ont. Center, Shoots R
Won Lady Byng Trophy, 1955-56

YEAR	TEAM & LEAGUE		GP	G	A	PTS	PIM
1953-54	DET	N	69	15	33	48	18
1954-55			70	25	41	66	15
1955-56			68	17	39	56	10
1956-57			70	13	23	36	6
1957-58			29	4	5	9	4
	CHI	N	40	4	12	16	6
	2 team total		69	8	17	25	10
1958-59	BOS	N	63	6	8	14	16
6 yrs.		N Totals:	409	84	161	245	75
PLAYOFFS							
1953-54*	DET	N	9	1	3	4	0
1954-55*			11	5	7	12	2
1955-56			10	0	2	2	2
1956-57			5	0	2	2	0
1958-59	BOS	N	4	0	0	0	0
5 yrs.		N Totals:	39	6	14	20	4

Traded to **Chicago** by Detroit with Billy Dea, Lorne Ferguson and Bill Dineen for Nick Mickoski, Jack McIntyre, Bob Bailey and Hec Lalande on Dec. 17, 1957. Drafted from Chicago by **Boston** June 4, 1958.

Craig Reichmuth

REICHMUTH, CRAIG RICHARD 5'11", 185 lbs.
B. Sept. 22, 1947, Russell, Man. Left Wing, Shoots L

YEAR	TEAM & LEAGUE		GP	G	A	PTS	PIM
1972-73	NY	W	73	13	14	27	127
1973-74	NY-NJ	W	72	10	8	18	114
1974-75	SD	W	28	2	1	3	58
	M-B	W	16	0	2	2	23
	2 team total		44	2	3	5	81
3 yrs.		W Totals:	189	25	25	50	322

Dave Reid

REID, DAVID
B. Jan. 11, 1934, Toronto, Ont. Forward

YEAR	TEAM & LEAGUE		GP	G	A	PTS	PIM
1952-53	TOR	N	2	0	0	0	0
1954-55			1	0	0	0	0
1955-56			4	0	0	0	0
3 yrs.		N Totals:	7	0	0	0	0

Gerry Reid

REID, GERALD ROLAND 6', 160 lbs.
B. Oct. 13, 1928, Owen Sound, Ont. Center, Shoots R

YEAR	TEAM & LEAGUE		GP	G	A	PTS	PIM
PLAYOFFS							
1948-49	DET	N	2	0	0	0	2

Gordie Reid

REID, GORDON J.
B. Mount Albert, Ont. Defense

YEAR	TEAM & LEAGUE		GP	G	A	PTS	PIM
1936-37	NYA	N	1	0	0	0	2

Reg Reid

REID, REGINALD S.
B. Unknown Forward

YEAR	TEAM & LEAGUE		GP	G	A	PTS	PIM
1924-25	TOR	N	28	2	0	2	2
1925-26			12	0	0	0	2
2 yrs.		N Totals:	40	2	0	2	4
PLAYOFFS							
1924-25	TOR	N	2	0	0	0	0

Tom Reid

REID, ALLAN THOMAS 6'1", 200 lbs.
B. June 24, 1946, Fort Erie, Ont. Defense, Shoots L

YEAR	TEAM & LEAGUE		GP	G	A	PTS	PIM
1967-68	CHI	N	57	0	4	4	25
1968-69			30	0	3	3	12
	MINN	N	18	0	4	4	38
	2 team total		48	0	7	7	50
1969-70			66	1	7	8	51
1970-71			73	3	14	17	62
1971-72			78	6	15	21	107
1972-73			60	1	13	14	50

Tom Reid continued

YEAR	TEAM & LEAGUE		GP	G	A	PTS	PIM
1973-74			76	4	19	23	81
1974-75			74	1	5	6	103
1975-76			69	0	15	15	52
1976-77			65	0	8	8	52
1977-78			36	1	6	7	21
11 yrs.		N Totals:	702	17	113	130	654
PLAYOFFS							
1967-68	CHI	N	9	0	0	0	2
1969-70	MINN	N	6	0	1	1	4
1970-71			12	0	6	6	20
1971-72			7	1	4	5	17
1972-73			6	0	2	2	4
1976-77			2	0	0	0	2
6 yrs.		N Totals:	42	1	13	14	49

Ed Reigle

REIGLE, EDMOND (Rags) 5'8", 180 lbs.
B. June 19, 1924, Winnipeg, Man. Defense, Shoots L

YEAR	TEAM & LEAGUE		GP	G	A	PTS	PIM
1950-51	BOS	N	17	0	2	2	25

Sold to **N.Y. Rangers** by Boston with Steve Kraftcheck, May 14, 1951.

Paul Reinhart

REINHART, PAUL 5'11", 216 lbs.
B. Jan. 8, 1960, Kitchener, Ont. Defense, Shoots L

YEAR	TEAM & LEAGUE		GP	G	A	PTS	PIM
1979-80	ATL	N	79	9	38	47	31
1980-81	CALG	N	74	18	49	67	52
1981-82			62	13	48	61	17
1982-83			78	17	58	75	28
4 yrs.		N Totals:	293	57	193	250	128
PLAYOFFS							
1980-81	CALG	N	16	1	14	15	16
1981-82			3	0	1	1	2
1982-83			9	6	3	9	2
3 yrs.		N Totals:	28	7	18	25	20

Ollie Reinikka

REINIKKA, OLIVER M.
Forward, Shoots R

YEAR	TEAM & LEAGUE		GP	G	A	PTS	PIM
1926-27	NYR	N	16	0	0	0	0

Leo Reise

REISE, LEO CHARLES, JR.
B. June 7, 1922, Stoney Creek, Ont. Defense

YEAR	TEAM & LEAGUE		GP	G	A	PTS	PIM
1945-46	CHI	N	6	0	0	0	6
1946-47			17	0	0	0	18
	DET	N	31	4	6	10	14
	2 team total		48	4	6	10	32
1947-48			58	5	4	9	30
1948-49			59	3	7	10	60
1949-50			70	4	17	21	46
1950-51			68	5	16	21	67
1951-52			54	0	11	11	34
1952-53	NYR	N	61	4	15	19	53
1953-54			70	3	5	8	71
9 yrs.		N Totals:	494	28	81	109	399
PLAYOFFS							
1946-47	DET	N	5	0	1	1	4
1947-48			10	2	1	3	12
1948-49			11	1	0	1	4
1949-50*			14	2	0	2	19
1950-51			6	2	3	5	2
1951-52*			6	1	0	1	27
6 yrs.		N Totals:	52	8	5	13	68

Traded to **N.Y. Rangers** by Detroit for Reg Sinclair and John Morrison, Aug. 18, 1952.

Leo Reise

REISE, LEO CHARLES, SR. 5'11", 175 lbs.
B. June 1, 1892, Pembroke, Ont. Defense, Shoots R

YEAR	TEAM & LEAGUE		GP	G	A	PTS	PIM
1920-21	HAMIL	N	6	2	0	2	8
1921-22			24	9	14	23	8
1922-23			24	6	6	12	35
1923-24			4	0	0	0	0
1926-27	NYA	N	40	7	6	13	24
1927-28			43	8	1	9	62
1928-29			44	4	1	5	32
1929-30			24	3	1	4	12
	NYR	N	12	0	1	1	8
	2 team total		36	3	2	5	20
8 yrs.		N Totals:	221	39	30	69	189
PLAYOFFS							
1928-29	NYA	N	2	0	0	0	0
1929-30			4	0	0	0	16
2 yrs.		N Totals:	6	0	0	0	16

Mark Renaud

RENAUD, MARK JOSEPH 5'11", 180 lbs.
B. Feb. 21, 1959, Windsor, Ont. Defense, Shoots L

YEAR	TEAM & LEAGUE		GP	G	A	PTS	PIM
1979-80	HART	N	13	0	2	2	4
1980-81			4	1	0	1	0
1981-82			48	1	17	18	39
1982-83			77	3	28	31	37
4 yrs.		N Totals:	142	5	47	52	80

Seppio Repo

REPO, SEPPIO (The Fox) 5'10", 180 lbs.
B. Sept. 21, 1947, Turku, Finland Center, Shoots R

YEAR	TEAM & LEAGUE		GP	G	A	PTS	PIM
1976-77	PHOE	W	80	29	31	60	10

Brad Rhiness

RHINESS, BRADFORD 5'9", 165 lbs.
B. Nov. 6, 1956, Huntsville, Ont. Center, Shoots L

YEAR	TEAM & LEAGUE		GP	G	A	PTS	PIM
1976-77	SD	W	58	9	14	23	14
1977-78	IND	W	12	3	3	6	2
2 yrs.		W Totals:	70	12	17	29	16
PLAYOFFS							
1976-77	SD	W	5	0	1	1	0

Pat Ribble

RIBBLE, PATRICK WAYNE 6'4", 210 lbs.
B. Apr. 26, 1954, Leamington, Ont. Defense, Shoots L

YEAR	TEAM & LEAGUE		GP	G	A	PTS	PIM
1975-76	ATL	N	3	0	0	0	0
1976-77			23	2	2	4	31
1977-78			80	5	12	17	68
1978-79			66	5	16	21	69
	CHI	N	12	1	3	4	8
	2 team total		78	6	19	25	77
1979-80			23	1	2	3	14
	TOR	N	13	0	2	2	2
	WASH	N	19	1	5	6	30
	3 team total		55	2	9	11	46
1980-81			67	3	15	18	103
1981-82			12	1	2	3	14
	CALG	N	3	0	0	0	2
	2 team total		15	1	2	3	16
1982-83			28	0	1	1	18
8 yrs.		N Totals:	349	19	60	79	359
PLAYOFFS							
1976-77	ATL	N	2	0	0	0	6
1977-78			2	0	1	1	2
1978-79	CHI	N	4	0	0	0	4
3 yrs.		N Totals:	8	0	1	1	12

Traded to **Chicago** by Atlanta with Tom Lysiak, Harold Phillipoff, Greg Fox and Miles Zaharko for Ivan Boldirev, Phil Russell and Darcy Rota, Mar. 13, 1979. Traded to **Toronto** by Chicago for Dave Hutchison, Jan. 10, 1980. Traded to **Washington** by Toronto for Mike Kaszycki, Feb. 16, 1980. Traded to **Calgary** by Washington along with Washington's second round choice in 1983 Entry Draft (later transferred to Montreal, Todd Francis) for Randy Holt and Bobby Gould, Nov. 25, 1981.

Henri Richard

RICHARD, JOSEPH HENRI (The Pocket Rocket)

5'7", 160 lbs.
B. Feb. 29, 1936, Montreal, Que. Center, Shoots R
Won Masterton Trophy, 1973-74
Hall of Fame, 1979

YEAR	TEAM	LEAGUE	GP	G	A	PTS	PIM
1955-56	**MONT**	**N**	64	19	21	40	46
1956-57			63	18	36	54	71
1957-58			67	28	**52**	80	56
1958-59			63	21	30	51	33
1959-60			70	30	43	73	66
1960-61			70	24	44	68	91
1961-62			54	21	29	50	48
1962-63			67	23	**50**	73	57
1963-64			66	14	39	53	73
1964-65			53	23	29	52	43
1965-66			62	22	39	61	47
1966-67			65	21	34	55	28
1967-68			54	9	19	28	16
1968-69			64	15	37	52	45
1969-70			62	16	36	52	61
1970-71			75	12	37	49	46
1971-72			75	12	32	44	48
1972-73			71	8	35	43	21
1973-74			75	19	36	55	28
1974-75			16	3	10	13	4
20 yrs.		**N Totals:**	1256	358	688	1046	928
PLAYOFFS							
1955-56*	**MONT**	**N**	10	4	4	8	21
1956-57*			10	2	6	8	10
1957-58*			10	1	7	8	11
1958-59*			11	3	8	11	13
1959-60*			8	3	9	12	9
1960-61			6	2	4	6	22
1962-63			5	1	1	2	2
1963-64			7	1	1	2	9
1964-65*			13	7	4	11	24
1965-66*			8	1	4	5	2
1966-67			10	4	6	10	2
1967-68*			13	4	4	8	4
1968-69*			14	2	4	6	8
1970-71*			20	5	7	12	20
1971-72			6	0	3	3	4
1972-73*			17	6	4	10	14
1973-74			6	2	2	4	2
1974-75			6	1	2	3	4
18 yrs.		**N Totals:**	180	49	80	129	181

Jacques Richard

RICHARD, JACQUES

5'11", 175 lbs.
B. Oct. 7, 1952, Quebec City, Que. Left Wing, Shoots L

YEAR	TEAM	LEAGUE	GP	G	A	PTS	PIM
1972-73	**ATL**	**N**	74	13	18	31	32
1973-74			78	27	16	43	45
1974-75			63	17	12	29	31
1975-76	**BUF**	**N**	73	12	23	35	31
1976-77			12	0	0	2	16
1978-79			61	10	15	25	26
1979-80	**QUE**	**N**	14	3	12	15	4
1980-81			78	52	51	103	39
1981-82			59	15	26	41	77
1982-83			35	9	14	23	6
10 yrs.		**N Totals:**	547	158	187	347	307
PLAYOFFS							
1973-74	**ATL**	**N**	4	0	0	0	2
1975-76	**BUF**	**N**	9	1	1	2	7
1978-79			3	1	0	1	0
1980-81	**QUE**	**N**	5	2	4	6	14
1981-82			10	1	0	1	9
1982-83			4	0	0	0	2
6 yrs.		**N Totals:**	35	5	5	10	34

Traded to **Buffalo** by Atlanta for Larry Carriere and Buffalo's first choice (Greg Carroll) in 1976 Amateur Draft (later traded to Washington) and cash, Oct. 1, 1975. Signed as free agent with **Quebec** Feb. 12, 1980.

Maurice Richard

RICHARD, JOSEPH HENRI MAURICE (The Rocket)

5'10", 195 lbs.
B. Aug. 4, 1921, Montreal, Que. Right Wing, Shoots L
Won Hart Trophy, 1946-47
Hall of Fame, 1961

YEAR	TEAM	LEAGUE	GP	G	A	PTS	PIM
1942-43	**MONT**	**N**	16	5	6	11	4
1943-44			46	32	22	54	45
1944-45			50	**50**	23	73	46
1945-46			50	27	21	48	50
1946-47			60	**45**	26	71	69
1947-48			53	28	25	53	89
1948-49			59	20	18	38	110
1949-50			70	**43**	22	65	114
1950-51			65	42	24	66	97
1951-52			48	27	17	44	44
1952-53			70	28	33	61	**112**
1953-54			70	**37**	30	67	**112**
1954-55			67	**38**	36	74	125
1955-56			70	38	33	71	89
1956-57			63	33	29	62	74
1957-58			28	15	19	34	28
1958-59			42	17	21	38	27
1959-60			51	19	16	35	50
18 yrs.		**N Totals:**	978	544	421	965	1285
PLAYOFFS							
1943-44*	**MONT**	**N**	9	12	5	17	10
1944-45			6	6	2	8	10
1945-46*			9	7	4	11	15
1946-47			10	6	5	11	44
1948-49			7	2	1	3	14
1949-50			5	1	1	2	6
1950-51			11	9	4	13	13
1951-52			11	4	2	6	6
1952-53*			12	7	1	8	2
1953-54			11	3	0	3	22
1955-56*			10	5	9	14	24
1956-57*			10	8	3	11	8
1957-58*			10	11	4	15	10
1958-59*			4	0	0	0	2
1959-60*			8	1	3	4	2
15 yrs.		**N Totals:**	133	82	44	126	188

Dave Richardson

RICHARDSON, DAVID GEORGE 5'8", 175 lbs.
B. Dec. 11, 1940, St. Boniface, Man. Left Wing, Shoots L

YEAR	TEAM	LEAGUE	GP	G	A	PTS	PIM
1963-64	**NYR**	**N**	34	3	1	4	21
1964-65			7	0	1	1	4
1965-66	**CHI**	**N**	3	0	0	0	2
1967-68	**DET**	**N**	1	0	0	0	0
4 yrs.		**N Totals:**	45	3	2	5	27

Drafted by **Minnesota** from Chicago in Expansion Draft, June 6, 1967.

Glen Richardson

RICHARDSON, GLEN GORDON 6'2", 200 lbs.
B. Sept. 20, 1955, Barrie, Ont. Left Wing, Shoots L

YEAR	TEAM	LEAGUE	GP	G	A	PTS	PIM
1975-76	**VAN**	**N**	24	3	6	9	19

Ken Richardson

RICHARDSON, KENNETH WILLIAM 6', 190 lbs.
B. Apr. 12, 1951, North Bay, Ont. Center, Shoots L

YEAR	TEAM	LEAGUE	GP	G	A	PTS	PIM
1974-75	**STL**	**N**	21	5	7	12	12
1977-78			12	2	5	7	2
1978-79			16	1	1	2	2
3 yrs.		**N Totals:**	49	8	13	21	16

Steve Richardson

RICHARDSON, STEPHEN JOHN 6'1", 185 lbs.
B. May 4, 1949, Olds, Alta. Center, Shoots L

YEAR	TEAM	LEAGUE	GP	G	A	PTS	PIM
1974-75	**IND**	**W**	19	1	4	5	16
	M-B	**W**	47	8	18	26	58
	2 team total		66	9	22	31	74
1975-76	**NE**	**W**	6	0	0	0	0
2 yrs.		**W Totals:**	72	9	22	31	74

Bob Richer

RICHER, ROBERT ROGER 5'10", 175 lbs.
B. Apr. 5, 1951, Cowansville, Que. Center, Shoots L

YEAR	TEAM & LEAGUE		GP	G	A	PTS	PIM
1972-73	BUF	N	3	0	0	0	0

Dave Richter

RICHTER, DAVID 6'5", 210 lbs.
B. Apr. 8, 1960, St. Boniface, Man. Defense, Shoots R

YEAR	TEAM & LEAGUE		GP	G	A	PTS	PIM
1981-82	MINN	N	3	0	0	0	11
1982-83			6	0	0	0	4
2 yrs.		N Totals:	9	0	0	0	15

Heikki Riihiranta

RIIHIRANTA, HEIKKI 5'11", 190 lbs.
B. Oct. 4, 1948, Helsinki, Finland Left Wing, Shoots L

YEAR	TEAM & LEAGUE		GP	G	A	PTS	PIM
1974-75	WINN	W	64	8	14	22	30
1975-76			70	1	8	9	26
1976-77			53	1	16	17	28
3 yrs.		W Totals:	187	10	38	48	84
PLAYOFFS							
1975-76	WINN	W	4	0	4	4	6

Bill Riley

RILEY, JAMES WILLIAM 5'11", 195 lbs.
B. Sept. 20, 1950, Amherst, N.S. Right Wing, Shoots R

YEAR	TEAM & LEAGUE		GP	G	A	PTS	PIM
1974-75	WASH	N	1	0	0	0	0
1976-77			43	13	14	27	124
1977-78			57	13	12	25	125
1978-79			24	2	2	4	64
1979-80	WINN	N	14	3	2	5	7
5 yrs.		N Totals:	139	31	30	61	320

Claimed by **Winnipeg** from Washington in Expansion Draft, June 13, 1979.

Jack Riley

RILEY, JACK 5'10½", 160 lbs.
B. Dec. 29, 1910, Berckenia, Ireland Center, Shoots L

YEAR	TEAM & LEAGUE		GP	G	A	PTS	PIM
1932-33	DET	N	1	0	0	0	0
1933-34	MONT	N	48	6	11	17	4
1934-35			47	4	11	15	4
1935-36	BOS	N	8	0	0	0	0
4 yrs.		N Totals:	104	10	22	32	8
PLAYOFFS							
1933-34	MONT	N	2	0	1	1	0
1934-35			2	0	2	2	0
2 yrs.		N Totals:	4	0	3	3	0

Jim Riley

RILEY, JAMES NORMAN
B. May 25, 1897, Bayfield, N.B. Left Wing, Shoots L

YEAR	TEAM & LEAGUE		GP	G	A	PTS	PIM
1926-27	DET	N	17	0	2	2	14

Ron Riley

RILEY, RONALD
B. July 20, 1948, Forward

YEAR	TEAM & LEAGUE		GP	G	A	PTS	PIM
1972-73	OTTA	W	22	0	5	5	2

Howard Riopelle

RIOPELLE, HOWARD JOSEPH (Rip) 5'11", 165 lbs.
B. Jan. 30, 1922, Ottawa, Ont. Left Wing, Shoots L

YEAR	TEAM & LEAGUE		GP	G	A	PTS	PIM
1947-48	MONT	N	55	5	2	7	12
1948-49			48	10	6	16	34
1949-50			66	12	8	20	27
3 yrs.		N Totals:	169	27	16	43	73
PLAYOFFS							
1948-49	MONT	N	7	1	1	2	2
1949-50			1	0	0	0	0

Howard Riopelle continued

YEAR	TEAM & LEAGUE		GP	G	A	PTS	PIM
2 yrs.		N Totals:	8	1	1	2	2

Gerry Rioux

RIOUX, GERARD 5'11", 195 lbs.
B. Feb. 17, 1959, Iroquois Falls, Ont. Right Wing, Shoots R

YEAR	TEAM & LEAGUE		GP	G	A	PTS	PIM
1979-80	WINN	N	8	0	0	0	6

Pierre Rioux

RIOUX, PIERRE 5'9", 165 lbs.
B. Feb. 1, 1962, Quebec City, Que. Right Wing, Shoots L

YEAR	TEAM & LEAGUE		GP	G	A	PTS	PIM
1982-83	CALG	N	14	1	2	3	4

Vic Ripley

RIPLEY, VICTOR MERRICK 5'7½", 170 lbs.
B. May 30, 1906, Elgin, Ont. Left Wing, Shoots L

YEAR	TEAM & LEAGUE		GP	G	A	PTS	PIM
1928-29	CHI	N	34	11	2	13	31
1929-30			40	8	8	16	33
1930-31			37	8	4	12	9
1931-32			46	12	6	18	47
1932-33			15	2	4	6	6
	BOS	N	23	2	5	7	21
	2 team total		38	4	9	13	27
1933-34			14	2	1	3	6
	NYR	N	34	5	12	17	10
	2 team total		48	7	13	20	16
1934-35			4	0	2	2	2
	STL	N	31	1	5	6	8
	2 team total		35	1	7	8	10
7 yrs.		N Totals:	278	51	49	100	173
PLAYOFFS							
1929-30	CHI	N	2	0	0	0	2
1930-31			9	2	1	3	4
1931-32			2	0	0	0	0
1932-33	BOS	N	5	1	0	1	0
1933-34	NYR	N	2	1	0	1	4
5 yrs.		N Totals:	20	4	1	5	10

Doug Risebrough

RISEBROUGH, DOUGLAS 5'11", 180 lbs.
B. Jan. 29, 1954, Guelph, Ont. Center, Shoots L

YEAR	TEAM & LEAGUE		GP	G	A	PTS	PIM
1974-75	MONT	N	64	15	32	47	198
1975-76			80	16	28	44	180
1976-77			78	22	38	60	132
1977-78			72	18	23	41	97
1978-79			48	10	15	25	62
1979-80			44	8	10	18	81
1980-81			48	13	21	34	93
1981-82			59	15	18	33	116
1982-83	CALG	N	71	21	37	58	138
9 yrs.		N Totals:	564	138	222	360	1097
PLAYOFFS							
1974-75	MONT	N	11	3	5	8	37
1975-76*			13	0	3	3	20
1976-77*			12	2	3	5	16
1977-78*			15	2	2	4	17
1978-79*			15	1	6	7	32
1980-81			3	1	0	1	0
1981-82			5	2	1	3	11
1982-83	CALG	N	9	1	3	4	18
8 yrs.		N Totals:	83	12	23	35	151

Traded by Montreal with a second round choice (sent to Minnesota by Calgary) in the 1983 Amateur Draft to **Calgary** for Calgary's second choice in the 1983 Amateur Draft (Todd Francis--draft choice acquired earlier from Washington) and third round choice in the 1984 Draft, Sept. 9, 1982.

Gary Rissling

RISSLING, GARY DANIEL 5'9", 175 lbs.
B. Aug. 8, 1956, Saskatoon, Sask. Left Wing, Shoots L

YEAR	TEAM & LEAGUE		GP	G	A	PTS	PIM
1978-79	WASH	N	26	3	3	6	127
1979-80			11	0	1	1	49
1980-81	PITT	N	25	1	0	1	143

Gary Rissling continued

YEAR	TEAM & LEAGUE		GP	G	A	PTS	PIM
1981-82			16	0	0	0	55
1982-83			40	5	4	9	128
5 yrs.		**N Totals:**	118	9	8	17	502
PLAYOFFS							
1980-81	**PITT**	**N**	5	0	1	1	4

Signed as free agent by **Washington** Dec. 4, 1978. Traded to **Pittsburgh** by Washington for Pittsburgh's fifth round choice (Peter Sidorkiewicz) in the 1981 Entry Draft.

Bob Ritchie

RITCHIE, ROBERT 5'10", 170 lbs.
B. Feb. 20, 1955, Laverlochere, Que. Left Wing, Shoots L

YEAR	TEAM & LEAGUE		GP	G	A	PTS	PIM
1976-77	**PHI**	**N**	1	0	0	0	0
	DET	**N**	17	6	2	8	10
	2 team total		18	6	2	8	10
1977-78			11	2	2	4	0
2 yrs.		**N Totals:**	29	8	4	12	10

Traded to **Detroit** by Philadelphia with Terry Murray, Steve Coates and Dave Kelly for Rick LaPointe and Mike Korney, Feb. 17, 1977.

Dave Ritchie

RITCHIE, DAVID
B. Unknown Forward

YEAR	TEAM & LEAGUE		GP	G	A	PTS	PIM
1917-18	**MON(W)**	**N**	4	5	0	5	3
	OTTA	**N**	13	4	0	4	9
	2 team total		17	9	0	9	12
1918-19	**TOR**	**N**	4	0	0	0	9
1919-20	**QUE**	**N**	21	6	3	9	18
1920-21	**MONT**	**N**	5	0	0	0	0
1924-25			5	0	0	0	0
1925-26			2	0	0	0	0
6 yrs.		**N Totals:**	54	15	3	18	39
PLAYOFFS							
1924-25	**MONT**	**N**	1	0	0	0	0

Alex Ritson

RITSON, ALEXANDER CLIVE 5'11", 172 lbs.
B. Mar. 7, 1922, Peace River, Alta. Center, Shoots L

YEAR	TEAM & LEAGUE		GP	G	A	PTS	PIM
1944-45	**NYR**	**N**	1	0	0	0	0

Alan Rittinger

RITTINGER, ALAN 5'9", 155 lbs.
B. Jan. 28, 1925, Regina, Sask. Left Wing, Shoots R

YEAR	TEAM & LEAGUE		GP	G	A	PTS	PIM
1943-44	**BOS**	**N**	19	3	7	10	0

Bob Rivard

RIVARD, JOSEPH ROBERT 5'8", 155 lbs.
B. Aug. 1, 1939, Sherbrooke, Que. Left Wing, Shoots L

YEAR	TEAM & LEAGUE		GP	G	A	PTS	PIM
1967-68	**PITT**	**N**	27	5	12	17	4

Drafted by **Pittsburgh** from Montreal in Expansion Draft, June 6, 1967.

Gus Rivers

RIVERS, GUS
B. Nov. 19, 1909, Minnipeg, Man. Forward

YEAR	TEAM & LEAGUE		GP	G	A	PTS	PIM
1929-30	**MONT**	**N**	19	1	0	1	2
1930-31			44	2	5	7	6
1931-32			25	1	0	1	4
3 yrs.		**N Totals:**	88	4	5	9	12
PLAYOFFS							
1929-30*	**MONT**	**N**	6	1	0	1	2
1930-31*			10	1	0	1	0
2 yrs.		**N Totals:**	16	2	0	2	2

Wayne Rivers

RIVERS, JOHN WAYNE 5'10", 180 lbs.
B. Feb. 1, 1942, Hamilton, Ont. Right Wing, Shoots R

YEAR	TEAM & LEAGUE		GP	G	A	PTS	PIM
1961-62	**DET**	**N**	2	0	0	0	0
1963-64	**BOS**	**N**	12	2	7	9	6
1964-65			58	6	17	23	72
1965-66			2	1	1	2	2
1966-67			8	2	1	3	59
1967-68	**STL**	**N**	22	4	4	8	8
1968-69	**NYR**	**N**	4	0	0	0	0
1972-73	**NY**	**W**	75	37	40	77	47
1973-74	**NY-NJ**	**W**	73	30	27	57	20
1974-75	**SD**	**W**	78	54	53	107	52
1975-76			71	19	25	44	24
1976-77			60	18	31	49	40
12 yrs.		**N Totals:**	108	15	30	45	147
		W Totals:	357	158	176	334	183
PLAYOFFS							
1974-75	**SD**	**W**	5	3	1	4	8
1975-76			11	4	4	8	4
1976-77			7	1	1	2	2
3 yrs.		**W Totals:**	23	8	6	14	14

Drafted by **Boston** from Detroit, June, 1963. Drafted by **St. Louis** from Boston in Expansion Draft, June 6, 1967. Traded to **N.Y. Rangers** by St. Louis with Don Caley for Camille Henry, Bill Plager and Robbie Irons, June 13, 1968.

Garth Rizzuto

RIZZUTO, GARTH ALEXANDER 5'11", 180 lbs.
B. Sept. 11, 1947, Trail, B.C. Center, Shoots L

YEAR	TEAM & LEAGUE		GP	G	A	PTS	PIM
1970-71	**VAN**	**N**	37	3	4	7	16
1972-73	**WINN**	**W**	61	10	10	20	32
1973-74			41	3	4	7	8
3 yrs.		**N Totals:**	37	3	4	7	16
		W Totals:	102	13	14	27	40
PLAYOFFS							
1972-73	**WINN**	**W**	14	0	1	1	14

Mickey Roach

ROACH, M. R.
B. Boston, Mass. Center

YEAR	TEAM & LEAGUE		GP	G	A	PTS	PIM
1919-20	**TOR**	**N**	20	10	2	12	4
1920-21			8	1	0	1	2
	HAMIL	**N**	14	8	7	15	0
	2 team total		22	9	7	16	2
1921-22			24	14	3	17	7
1922-23			23	17	8	25	8
1923-24			21	5	3	8	0
1924-25			30	6	4	10	4
1925-26	**NYA**	**N**	25	3	0	3	4
1926-27			42	11	0	11	14
8 yrs.		**N Totals:**	207	75	27	102	43

Claude Robert

ROBERT, CLAUDE 5'11", 175 lbs.
B. Aug. 10, 1928, Montreal, Que. Left Wing, Shoots L

YEAR	TEAM & LEAGUE		GP	G	A	PTS	PIM
1950-51	**MONT**	**N**	23	1	0	1	9

Rene Robert

ROBERT, RENE PAUL 5'10", 184 lbs.
B. Dec. 31, 1948, Trois-Rivieres, Que. Right Wing, Shoots R

YEAR	TEAM & LEAGUE		GP	G	A	PTS	PIM
1970-71	**TOR**	**N**	5	0	0	0	0
1971-72	**PITT**	**N**	49	7	11	18	42
	BUF	**N**	12	6	3	9	2
	2 team total		61	13	14	27	44
1972-73			75	40	43	83	83
1973-74			76	21	44	65	71
1974-75			74	40	60	100	75
1975-76			72	35	52	87	53
1976-77			80	33	40	73	46
1977-78			67	25	48	73	25
1978-79			68	22	40	62	46
1979-80	**COLO**	**N**	69	28	35	63	79

YEAR	TEAM & LEAGUE		GP	G	A	PTS	PIM

Rene Robert continued

YEAR	TEAM & LEAGUE		GP	G	A	PTS	PIM
1980-81			28	8	11	19	30
	TOR	N	14	6	7	13	8
	2 team total		42	14	18	32	38
1981-82			55	13	24	37	37
12 yrs.		N Totals:	744	284	418	702	597
PLAYOFFS							
1972-73	BUF	N	6	5	3	8	2
1974-75			16	5	8	13	16
1975-76			9	3	2	5	6
1976-77			6	5	2	7	20
1977-78			7	2	0	2	23
1978-79			3	2	2	4	4
1980-81	TOR	N	3	0	2	2	2
7 yrs.		N Totals:	50	22	19	41	73

Drafted by **Buffalo** from Toronto and later removed by Buffalo and claimed by **Pittsburgh** in Intra-League Draft, June 8, 1971. Traded to **Buffalo** by Pittsburgh for Eddie Shack, Mar. 4, 1972. Traded to **Colorado** by Buffalo for John Van Boxmeer, Oct. 5, 1979. Traded to **Toronto** by Colorado for Toronto's third round choice (Ullrich Hiemer) in the 1981 Entry Draft, Jan. 30, 1981.

Sammy Robert

ROBERT, SAMUEL
B. Unknown
Forward

YEAR	TEAM & LEAGUE		GP	G	A	PTS	PIM
1917-18	OTTA	N	1	0	0	0	0

Phil Roberto

ROBERTO, PHILLIP JOSEPH 6'1", 190 lbs.
B. Jan. 1, 1949, Niagara Falls, Ont. Right Wing, Shoots R

YEAR	TEAM & LEAGUE		GP	G	A	PTS	PIM
1969-70	MONT	N	8	0	1	1	8
1970-71			39	14	7	21	76
1971-72			27	3	2	5	22
	STL	N	49	12	13	25	76
	2 team total		76	15	15	30	98
1972-73			77	20	22	42	99
1973-74			15	1	1	2	10
1974-75			7	0	2	2	2
	DET	N	46	13	27	40	30
	2 team total		53	13	29	42	32
1975-76			37	1	7	8	68
	KC	N	37	7	15	22	42
	2 team total		74	8	22	30	110
1976-77	COLO	N	22	1	5	6	23
	CLEVE	N	21	3	4	7	8
	2 team total		43	4	9	13	31
1977-78	BIRM	W	53	8	20	28	91
9 yrs.		N Totals:	385	75	106	181	464
		W Totals:	53	8	20	28	91
PLAYOFFS							
1970-71*	MONT	N	15	0	1	1	36
1971-72	STL	N	11	7	6	13	29
1972-73			5	2	1	3	4
1977-78	BIRM	W	4	1	0	1	20
4 yrs.		N Totals:	31	9	8	17	69
		W Totals:	4	1	0	1	20

Traded to **St. Louis** by Montreal for Jim Roberts, Dec. 13, 1971. Traded to **Detroit** by St. Louis with St. Louis' third choice (Blair Davidson) in 1975 Amateur Draft for Red Berenson, Dec. 30, 1974. Traded to **Kansas City** by Detroit for Buster Harvey, Jan. 14, 1976. Signed as a free agent by **Cleveland** from Colorado, Dec. 24, 1976.

Doug Roberts

ROBERTS, DOUGLAS WILLIAM 6'2", 190 lbs.
B. Oct. 28, 1942, Detroit, Mich. Defense, Shoots L

YEAR	TEAM & LEAGUE		GP	G	A	PTS	PIM
1965-66	DET	N	1	0	0	0	0
1966-67			13	3	1	4	25
1967-68			36	8	9	17	12
1968-69	CALIF	N	76	1	19	20	79
1969-70	OAK	N	76	6	25	31	107
1970-71	CALIF	N	78	4	13	17	94
1971-72	BOS	N	3	1	0	1	0
1972-73			45	4	7	11	7
1973-74			7	0	1	1	2
	DET	N	57	12	25	37	33
	2 team total		64	12	26	38	35
1974-75			26	4	4	8	8

YEAR	TEAM & LEAGUE		GP	G	A	PTS	PIM

Doug Roberts continued

YEAR	TEAM & LEAGUE		GP	G	A	PTS	PIM
1975-76	NE	W	76	4	13	17	51
1976-77			64	3	18	21	33
12 yrs.		N Totals:	418	43	104	147	367
		W Totals:	140	7	31	38	84
PLAYOFFS							
1968-69	CALIF	N	7	0	1	1	34
1969-70	OAK	N	4	0	2	2	6
1972-73	BOS	N	5	2	0	2	6
1975-76	NE	W	17	1	1	2	8
1976-77			2	0	0	0	0
5 yrs.		N Totals:	16	2	3	5	46
		W Totals:	19	1	1	2	8

Gordie Roberts

ROBERTS, GORDON 6', 188 lbs.
B. Oct. 2, 1957, Detroit, Mich. Defense, Shoots L

YEAR	TEAM & LEAGUE		GP	G	A	PTS	PIM
1975-76	NE	W	77	3	19	22	102
1976-77			77	13	33	46	169
1977-78			78	15	46	61	118
1978-79			79	11	46	57	113
1979-80	HART	N	80	8	28	36	89
1980-81			27	2	11	13	81
	MINN	N	50	6	31	37	94
	2 team total		77	8	42	50	175
1981-82			79	4	30	34	119
1982-83			80	3	41	44	103
8 yrs.		N Totals:	316	23	141	164	486
		W Totals:	311	42	144	186	502
PLAYOFFS							
1975-76	NE	W	17	2	9	11	36
1976-77			5	2	2	4	6
1977-78			14	0	5	5	29
1978-79			10	0	4	4	10
1979-80	HART	N	3	1	1	2	2
1980-81	MINN	N	19	1	5	6	17
1981-82			4	0	3	3	27
1982-83			9	1	5	6	14
8 yrs.		N Totals:	35	3	14	17	60
		W Totals:	46	4	20	24	81

Traded to **Minnesota** by Hartford for Mike Fidler, Dec. 16, 1980.

Jim Roberts

ROBERTS, JAMES WILFRED 5'10", 185 lbs.
B. Apr. 9, 1940, Toronto, Ont. Right Wing, Shoots R

YEAR	TEAM & LEAGUE		GP	G	A	PTS	PIM
1963-64	MONT	N	15	0	1	1	2
1964-65			70	3	10	13	40
1965-66			70	5	5	10	20
1966-67			63	3	0	3	16
1967-68	STL	N	74	14	23	37	66
1968-69			72	14	19	33	81
1969-70			76	13	17	30	51
1970-71			72	13	18	31	77
1971-72			26	5	7	12	8
	MONT	N	51	7	15	22	49
	2 team total		77	12	22	34	57
1972-73			77	14	18	32	28
1973-74			67	8	16	24	39
1974-75			79	5	13	18	52
1975-76			74	13	8	21	35
1976-77			45	5	14	19	18
1977-78	STL	N	75	4	10	14	39
15 yrs.		N Totals:	1006	126	194	320	621
PLAYOFFS							
1963-64	MONT	N	7	0	1	1	14
1964-65*			13	0	0	0	30
1965-66*			10	1	1	2	10
1966-67			4	1	0	1	0
1967-68	STL	N	18	4	1	5	20
1968-69			12	1	4	5	10
1969-70			16	2	3	5	29
1970-71			6	2	1	3	11
1971-72	MONT	N	6	1	0	1	0
1972-73*			17	0	2	2	22
1973-74			6	0	0	0	4
1974-75			11	2	2	4	2

Jim Roberts *continued*

YEAR	TEAM & LEAGUE		GP	G	A	PTS	PIM
1975-76*			13	3	1	4	2
1976-77*			14	3	0	3	6
14 yrs.		**N Totals:**	153	20	16	36	160

Drafted by **St. Louis** from Montreal in Expansion Draft, June 6, 1967. Traded to **Montreal** by St. Louis for Phil Roberto, Dec. 13, 1971. Traded to **St. Louis** by Montreal for St. Louis' third round 1979 Amateur Draft choice, Aug. 18, 1977.

Jimmy Roberts

ROBERTS, JAMES DREW 6'1", 198 lbs.
B. June 8, 1956, Toronto, Ont. Left Wing, Shoots L

YEAR	TEAM & LEAGUE		GP	G	A	PTS	PIM
1976-77	**MINN**	**N**	53	11	8	19	14
1977-78			42	4	14	18	19
1978-79			11	2	1	3	0
3 yrs.		**N Totals:**	106	17	23	40	33
PLAYOFFS							
1976-77	**MINN**	**N**	2	0	0	0	0

Claimed by **Winnipeg** from Minnesota in Expansion Draft, June 13, 1979.

Fred Robertson

ROBERTSON, FRED 5'10", 198 lbs.
B. Oct. 22, 1910, Carlisle, England Shoots L

YEAR	TEAM & LEAGUE		GP	G	A	PTS	PIM
1931-32	**TOR**	**N**	8	0	0	0	23
1933-34			2	0	0	0	0
	DET	**N**	24	1	0	1	12
	2 team total		26	1	0	1	12
2 yrs.		**N Totals:**	34	1	0	1	35
PLAYOFFS							
1931-32*	**TOR**	**N**	7	0	0	0	0

Geordie Robertson

ROBERTSON, GEORDIE 6', 163 lbs.
B. Aug. 1, 1959, Victoria, B.C. Right Wing, Shoots R

YEAR	TEAM & LEAGUE		GP	G	A	PTS	PIM
1982-83	**BUF**	**N**	5	1	2	3	7

George Robertson

ROBERTSON, GEORGE THOMAS (Robbie)
B. May 11, 1928, Winnipeg, Man. Center, Shoots L

YEAR	TEAM & LEAGUE		GP	G	A	PTS	PIM
1947-48	**MONT**	**N**	1	0	0	0	0
1948-49			30	2	5	7	6
2 yrs.		**N Totals:**	31	2	5	7	6

Joe Robertson

ROBERTSON, JOSEPH DUNBAR 5'11", 180 lbs.
B. Mar. 10, 1948, Windsor, N.S. Center, Shoots L

YEAR	TEAM & LEAGUE		GP	G	A	PTS	PIM
1974-75	**IND**	**W**	18	4	4	8	23
	MINN	**W**	11	1	4	5	4
	2 team total		29	5	8	13	27

Torrie Robertson

ROBERTSON, TORRIE ANDREW 5'11", 185 lbs.
B. Aug. 2, 1961, Victoria, B.C. Left Wing, Shoots L

YEAR	TEAM & LEAGUE		GP	G	A	PTS	PIM
1980-81	**WASH**	**N**	3	0	0	0	0
1981-82			54	8	13	21	204
1982-83			5	2	0	2	4
3 yrs.		**N Totals:**	62	10	13	23	208

Florrie Robidoux

ROBIDOUX, FLORENT 6'3", 190 lbs.
B. May 5, 1960, Treheme, Man. Left Wing, Shoots L

YEAR	TEAM & LEAGUE		GP	G	A	PTS	PIM
1980-81	**CHI**	**N**	39	6	2	8	75
1981-82			4	1	2	3	0

Florrie Robidoux *continued*

YEAR	TEAM & LEAGUE		GP	G	A	PTS	PIM
2 yrs.		**N Totals:**	43	7	4	11	75

Signed as free agent with **Chicago** Oct. 20, 1979.

Doug Robinson

ROBINSON, DOUGLAS GARNET 6'2", 197 lbs.
B. Aug. 27, 1940, St. Catharines, Ont. Left Wing, Shoots L

YEAR	TEAM & LEAGUE		GP	G	A	PTS	PIM
1964-65	**CHI**	**N**	40	2	9	11	8
	NYR	**N**	21	8	14	22	2
	2 team total		61	10	23	33	10
1965-66			51	8	12	20	8
1966-67			1	0	0	0	0
1967-68	**LA**	**N**	34	9	9	18	6
1968-69			31	2	10	12	2
1970-71			61	15	13	28	8
6 yrs.		**N Totals:**	239	44	67	111	34
PLAYOFFS							
1963-64	**CHI**	**N**	4	0	0	0	0
1967-68	**LA**	**N**	7	4	3	7	0
2 yrs.		**N Totals:**	11	4	3	7	0

Traded to **N.Y. Rangers** with Wayne Hillman and John Brenneman by Chicago for Camille Henry, Don Johns, Billy Taylor and Wally Chevrier, Feb. 4, 1965. Drafted by **Los Angeles** from N.Y. Rangers in Expansion Draft, June 6, 1967. Traded to **Montreal** by Los Angeles with Denis DeJordy, Dale Hoganson, and Noel Price for Rogie Vachon, Nov. 4, 1971.

Earl Robinson

ROBINSON, EARL HENRY 5'10", 160 lbs.
B. Mar. 11, 1907, Montreal, Que. Right Wing, Shoots R

YEAR	TEAM & LEAGUE		GP	G	A	PTS	PIM
1928-29	**MON(M)**	**N**	33	2	1	3	2
1929-30			35	1	2	3	10
1931-32			28	0	3	3	2
1932-33			43	15	9	24	6
1933-34			47	12	16	28	14
1934-35			47	17	18	35	23
1935-36			40	6	14	20	27
1936-37			48	16	18	34	19
1937-38			38	4	7	11	13
1938-39	**CHI**	**N**	48	9	6	15	13
1939-40	**MONT**	**N**	11	1	4	5	4
11 yrs.		**N Totals:**	418	83	98	181	133
PLAYOFFS							
1929-30	**MON(M)**	**N**	4	0	0	0	0
1932-33			2	0	0	0	0
1933-34			4	2	0	2	0
1934-35*			7	2	2	4	0
1935-36			3	0	0	0	0
1936-37			5	1	2	3	0
6 yrs.		**N Totals:**	25	5	4	9	0

Larry Robinson

ROBINSON, LAURENCE CLARK 6'3", 210 lbs.
B. June 2, 1951, Winchester, Ont. Defense, Shoots L
Won Norris Trophy, 1976–77 , 1979-80
Won Conn Smythe Trophy, 1977-78

YEAR	TEAM & LEAGUE		GP	G	A	PTS	PIM
1972-73	**MONT**	**N**	36	2	4	6	20
1973-74			78	6	20	26	66
1974-75			80	14	47	61	76
1975-76			80	10	30	40	59
1976-77			77	19	66	85	45
1977-78			80	13	52	65	39
1978-79			67	16	45	61	33
1979-80			72	14	61	75	39
1980-81			65	12	38	50	37
1981-82			71	12	47	59	41
1982-83			71	14	49	63	33
11 yrs.		**N Totals:**	777	132	459	591	488
PLAYOFFS							
1972-73*	**MONT**	**N**	11	1	4	5	9
1973-74			6	0	1	1	26
1974-75			11	0	4	4	27
1975-76*			13	3	3	6	10

Larry Robinson continued

YEAR	TEAM & LEAGUE	GP	G	A	PTS	PIM
1976-77*		14	2	10	12	12
1977-78*		15	4	17	21	6
1978-79*		16	6	9	15	8
1979-80		10	0	4	4	2
1980-81		3	0	1	1	2
1981-82		5	0	1	1	8
1982-83		3	0	0	0	2
11 yrs.	**N Totals:**	107	16	54	70	112

Moe Robinson

ROBINSON, MORRIS 6'4", 175 lbs.
B. May 29, 1957, Winchester, Ont. Defense, Shoots L

YEAR	TEAM & LEAGUE	GP	G	A	PTS	PIM
1979-80	**MONT N**	1	0	0	0	0

Mike Robitaille

ROBITAILLE, MICHAEL JAMES DAVID 5'11", 195 lbs.
B. Feb. 12, 1948, Midland, Ont. Defense, Shoots R

YEAR	TEAM & LEAGUE	GP	G	A	PTS	PIM
1969-70	**NYR N**	4	0	0	0	8
1970-71		11	1	1	2	7
	DET N	23	4	8	12	22
	2 team total	34	5	9	14	29
1971-72	**BUF N**	31	2	10	12	22
1972-73		65	4	17	21	40
1973-74		71	2	18	20	60
1974-75		3	0	1	1	0
	VAN N	63	2	22	24	31
	2 team total	66	2	23	25	31
1975-76		71	8	19	27	69
1976-77		40	0	9	9	21
8 yrs.	**N Totals:**	382	23	105	128	280

PLAYOFFS

YEAR	TEAM & LEAGUE	GP	G	A	PTS	PIM
1972-73	**BUF N**	6	0	0	0	0
1974-75	**VAN N**	5	0	1	1	2
1975-76		2	0	0	0	2
3 yrs.	**N Totals:**	13	0	1	1	4

Traded to **Detroit** by N.Y. Rangers with Arnie Brown and Tom Miller for Bruce MacGregor and Larry Brown, Feb. 2, 1971. Traded to **Buffalo** by Detroit with Don Luce for Joe Daley, May 25, 1971. Traded to **Vancouver** by Buffalo with Gerry Meehan for Jocelyn Guevremont and Bryan McSheffrey, Oct. 14, 1974.

Desse Roche

ROCHE, MICHAEL PATRICK DESMOND 5'6½", 188 lbs.
B. Feb. 1, 1909, Kemptville, Ont. Right Wing, Shoots R

YEAR	TEAM & LEAGUE	GP	G	A	PTS	PIM
1930-31	**MON(M) N**	20	0	1	1	6
1932-33		5	0	0	0	0
	OTTA N	16	3	6	9	6
	2 team total	21	3	6	9	6
1933-34		44	14	10	24	22
1934-35	**STL N**	7	0	0	0	10
	MONT N	5	0	1	1	0
	DET N	15	3	0	3	0
	3 team total	27	3	1	4	10
4 yrs.	**N Totals:**	112	20	18	38	44

Earl Roche

ROCHE, EARL 5'11", 175 lbs.
B. Feb. 22, 1910, Prescott, Ont. Left Wing, Shoots L

YEAR	TEAM & LEAGUE	GP	G	A	PTS	PIM
1930-31	**MON(M) N**	42	2	0	2	18
1932-33		5	0	0	0	0
	BOS N	3	0	0	0	0
	OTTA N	20	4	5	9	6
	3 team total	28	4	5	9	6
1933-34		44	13	16	29	22
1934-35	**STL N**	19	3	3	6	2
	DET N	13	3	3	6	0
	2 team total	32	6	6	12	2
4 yrs.	**N Totals:**	146	25	27	52	48

PLAYOFFS

YEAR	TEAM & LEAGUE	GP	G	A	PTS	PIM
1930-31	**MON(M) N**	2	0	0	0	0

Ernest Roche

ROCHE, ERNEST CHARLES 6'1", 170 lbs.
B. Feb. 4, 1930, Montreal, Que. Defense, Shoots L

YEAR	TEAM & LEAGUE	GP	G	A	PTS	PIM
1950-51	**MONT N**	4	0	0	0	2

Dave Rochefort

ROCHEFORT, DAVID JOSEPH 6', 180 lbs.
B. July 22, 1946, Red Deer, Alta. Center, Shoots L

YEAR	TEAM & LEAGUE	GP	G	A	PTS	PIM
1966-67	**DET N**	1	0	0	0	0

Leon Rochefort

ROCHEFORT, LEON JOSEPH FERNAND 6', 185 lbs.
B. May 4, 1939, Cap-de-la-Madeleine,Que. Right Wing, Shoots R

YEAR	TEAM & LEAGUE	GP	G	A	PTS	PIM
1960-61	**NYR N**	1	0	0	0	0
1962-63		23	5	4	9	6
1963-64	**MONT N**	3	0	0	0	0
1964-65		9	2	0	2	0
1965-66		1	0	1	1	0
1966-67		27	9	7	16	6
1967-68	**PHI N**	74	21	21	42	16
1968-69		65	14	21	35	10
1969-70	**LA N**	76	9	23	32	14
1970-71	**MONT N**	57	5	10	15	4
1971-72	**DET N**	64	17	12	29	10
1972-73		20	2	4	6	2
	ATL N	54	9	18	27	10
	2 team total	74	11	22	33	12
1973-74		56	10	12	22	13
1974-75	**VAN N**	76	18	11	29	2
1975-76		11	0	3	3	0
15 yrs.	**N Totals:**	617	121	147	268	93

PLAYOFFS

YEAR	TEAM & LEAGUE	GP	G	A	PTS	PIM
1965-66*	**MONT N**	4	1	1	2	4
1966-67		10	1	1	2	4
1967-68	**PHI N**	7	2	0	2	2
1968-69		3	0	0	0	0
1970-71*	**MONT N**	10	0	0	0	6
1974-75	**VAN N**	5	0	2	2	0
6 yrs.	**N Totals:**	39	4	4	8	16

Traded by N.Y. Rangers to **Montreal** with Dave Balon, Len Ronson and Lorne Worsley for Phil Goyette, Don Marshall and Jacques Plante, June 4, 1963. Drafted by **Philadelphia** from Montreal in Expansion Draft, June 6, 1967. Traded to **N.Y. Rangers** by Philadelphia with Don Blackburn for Reg Fleming, June 6, 1969. Traded to **Los Angeles** by N.Y. Rangers with Dennis Hextall for Real Lemieux, June 9, 1969. Traded to **Montreal** by Los Angeles with Wayne Thomas and Gregg Boddy for Larry Mickey, Lucien Grenier and Jack Norris, May 22, 1970. Traded to **Detroit** by Montreal for Kerry Ketter and cash, May 25, 1971. Traded to **Atlanta** by Detroit for Bill Hogaboam, Nov. 28, 1972. Sold to **Vancouver** by Atlanta, Oct. 4, 1974.

Normand Rochefort

ROCHEFORT, NORMAND 6'1", 200 lbs.
B. Jan. 28, 1961, Trois-Rivieres, Que. Defense, Shoots L

YEAR	TEAM & LEAGUE	GP	G	A	PTS	PIM
1980-81	**QUE N**	56	3	7	10	51
1981-82		72	4	14	18	115
1982-83		62	6	17	23	40
3 yrs.	**N Totals:**	190	13	38	51	206

PLAYOFFS

YEAR	TEAM & LEAGUE	GP	G	A	PTS	PIM
1980-81	**QUE N**	5	0	0	0	4
1981-82		16	0	2	2	10
1982-83		1	0	0	0	2
3 yrs.	**N Totals:**	22	0	2	2	16

Frank Rochon

ROCHON, FRANCOIS JEAN 5'11", 181 lbs.
B. Apr. 18, 1953, Montreal, Que. Left Wing, Shoots L

YEAR	TEAM & LEAGUE	GP	G	A	PTS	PIM
1973-74	**CHI W**	71	12	11	23	27
1974-75		69	27	29	56	19
1975-76	**D-O W**	41	11	10	21	10
	IND W	19	6	2	8	31
	2 team total	60	17	12	29	41
1976-77		57	15	8	23	8

YEAR	TEAM & LEAGUE		GP	G	A	PTS	PIM

Frank Rochon continued

YEAR	TEAM	LEAGUE	GP	G	A	PTS	PIM
4 yrs.		W Totals:	257	71	60	131	95
PLAYOFFS							
1973-74	CHI	W	9	2	1	3	0
1976-77	IND	W	5	0	1	1	0
2 yrs.		W Totals:	14	2	2	4	0

Harvey Rockburn

ROCKBURN, HARVEY

Defense

YEAR	TEAM	LEAGUE	GP	G	A	PTS	PIM
1929-30	DET	N	36	4	0	4	97
1930-31			42	0	1	1	**118**
1932-33	OTTA	N	16	0	1	1	39
3 yrs.		N Totals:	94	4	2	6	254

Eddie Rodden

RODDEN, EDDIE

B. Mar. 22, 1901, Toronto, Ont. Forward

YEAR	TEAM	LEAGUE	GP	G	A	PTS	PIM
1926-27	CHI	N	20	3	3	6	92
1927-28			9	0	2	2	6
	TOR	N	25	3	6	9	36
	2 team total		34	3	8	11	42
1928-29	BOS	N	20	0	0	0	10
1930-31	NYR	N	24	0	3	3	8
4 yrs.		N Totals:	98	6	14	20	152
PLAYOFFS							
1926-27	CHI	N	2	0	1	1	0

Alfred Rogers

ROGERS, ALFRED JOHN 5'11", 175 lbs.

B. Apr. 10, 1953, Paradise Hills, Sask. Right Wing, Shoots R

YEAR	TEAM	LEAGUE	GP	G	A	PTS	PIM
1973-74	MINN	N	10	2	4	6	0
1974-75			4	0	0	0	0
1975-76	EDM	W	44	9	8	17	34
3 yrs.		N Totals:	14	2	4	6	0
		W Totals:	44	9	8	17	34

Mike Rogers

ROGERS, MICHAEL 5'9", 170 lbs.

B. Oct. 24, 1954, Calgary, Alta. Center, Shoots L

YEAR	TEAM	LEAGUE	GP	G	A	PTS	PIM
1974-75	EDM	W	78	35	48	83	2
1975-76			44	12	15	27	10
	NE	W	36	18	14	32	10
	2 team total		80	30	29	59	20
1976-77			78	25	57	82	10
1977-78			80	28	43	71	46
1978-79			80	27	45	72	31
1979-80	HART	N	80	44	61	105	10
1980-81			80	40	65	105	32
1981-82	NYR	N	80	38	65	103	43
1982-83			71	29	47	76	28
9 yrs.		N Totals:	311	151	238	389	113
		W Totals:	396	145	222	367	109
PLAYOFFS							
1975-76	NE	W	17	5	8	13	2
1976-77			5	1	1	2	2
1977-78			14	5	6	11	8
1978-79			10	2	6	8	2
1979-80	HART	N	3	0	3	3	0
1981-82	NYR	N	9	1	6	7	2
1982-83			1	0	0	0	0
7 yrs.		N Totals:	13	1	9	10	2
		W Totals:	46	13	21	34	14

Traded to **N.Y. Rangers** by Hartford along with Hartford's tenth round choice (Simo Saarinen) in 1982 Entry Draft for Chris Kotsopolous, Gerry McDonald, and Doug Sulliman, Oct. 2, 1981.

Dale Rolfe

ROLFE, DALE ROLAND CARL 6'4", 210 lbs.

B. Apr. 30, 1940, Timmins, Ont. Defense, Shoots L

YEAR	TEAM	LEAGUE	GP	G	A	PTS	PIM
1959-60	BOS	N	3	0	0	0	0
1967-68	LA	N	68	3	13	16	84
1968-69			75	3	19	22	85
1969-70			55	1	9	10	77
	DET	N	20	2	9	11	12
	2 team total		75	3	18	21	89
1970-71			44	3	9	12	48
	NYR	N	14	0	7	7	23
	2 team total		58	3	16	19	71
1971-72			68	2	14	16	67
1972-73			72	7	25	32	14
1973-74			48	3	12	15	56
1974-75			42	1	8	9	30
9 yrs.		N Totals:	509	25	125	150	496
PLAYOFFS							
1967-68	LA	N	7	0	1	1	14
1968-69			10	0	4	4	8
1969-70	DET	N	4	0	2	2	8
1970-71	NYR	N	13	0	1	1	14
1971-72			16	4	3	7	16
1972-73			8	0	5	5	6
1973-74			13	1	8	9	23
7 yrs.		N Totals:	71	5	24	29	89

Traded to **Detroit** by Los Angeles with Gary Croteau and Larry Johnston for Brian Gibbons and Garry Monahan, Feb. 20, 1970. Traded to **N.Y. Rangers** by Detroit for Jim Krulicki, March 2, 1971.

Jerry Rollins

ROLLINS, JERRY ALLAN 6'3", 195 lbs.

B. Mar. 22, 1955, New Westminster, B.C. Defense, Shoots R

YEAR	TEAM	LEAGUE	GP	G	A	PTS	PIM
1975-76	TOR	W	52	5	7	12	185
1976-77	BIRM	W	0	0	0	0	0
	PHOE	W	71	4	10	14	186
	2 team total		71	4	10	14	186
1978-79	IND	W	7	0	1	1	7
3 yrs.		W Totals:	130	9	18	27	378

Larry Romanchych

ROMANCHYCH, LARRY BRIAN 6'1", 180 lbs.

B. Sept. 7, 1949, Vancouver, B.C. Right Wing, Shoots R

YEAR	TEAM	LEAGUE	GP	G	A	PTS	PIM
1970-71	CHI	N	10	0	2	2	2
1972-73	ATL	N	70	18	30	48	39
1973-74			73	22	29	51	33
1974-75			53	8	12	20	16
1975-76			67	16	19	35	8
1976-77			25	4	5	9	4
6 yrs.		N Totals:	298	68	97	165	102
PLAYOFFS							
1973-74	ATL	N	4	2	2	4	4
1975-76			2	0	0	0	0
1976-77			1	0	0	0	0
3 yrs.		N Totals:	7	2	2	4	4

Doug Rombough

ROMBOUGH, DOUGLAS GEORGE 6'3", 215 lbs.

B. July 8, 1950, Fergus, Ont. Center, Shoots L

YEAR	TEAM	LEAGUE	GP	G	A	PTS	PIM
1972-73	BUF	N	5	2	0	2	0
1973-74			46	6	9	15	27
	NYI	N	12	3	1	4	8
	2 team total		58	9	10	19	35
1974-75			28	5	6	11	6
	MINN	N	40	6	9	15	33
	2 team total		68	11	15	26	39
1975-76			19	2	2	4	6
4 yrs.		N Totals:	150	24	27	51	80

Traded to **N.Y. Islanders** by Buffalo for Brian Spencer, March 10, 1974. Traded to **Minnesota** by N.Y. Islanders with Ernie Hicke for J.P. Parise, Jan. 5, 1975.

Lorne Rombough

ROMBOUGH, LORNE DAVID 5'11", 190 lbs.
B. Apr. 2, 1948 Left Wing, Shoots L

YEAR	TEAM & LEAGUE		GP	G	A	PTS	PIM
1973-74	LA	W	3	1	2	3	0

Doc Romnes

ROMNES, ELWIN NELSON 5'11", 156 lbs.
B. Jan. 1, 1909, White Bear, Minn. Forward, Shoots L
Won Lady Byng Trophy, 1935-36

YEAR	TEAM & LEAGUE		GP	G	A	PTS	PIM
1930-31	CHI	N	30	5	7	12	8
1931-32			18	0	1	1	6
1932-33			47	10	12	22	2
1933-34			47	8	21	29	6
1934-35			35	10	14	24	8
1935-36			48	13	25	38	6
1936-37			28	4	14	18	2
1937-38			44	10	22	32	4
1938-39			12	0	4	4	0
	TOR	N	36	7	16	23	0
	2 team total		48	7	20	27	0
1939-40	NYA	N	14	0	1	1	0
10 yrs.		N Totals:	359	67	137	204	42

PLAYOFFS

YEAR	TEAM & LEAGUE		GP	G	A	PTS	PIM
1930-31	CHI	N	9	1	1	2	2
1931-32			2	0	0	0	0
1933-34*			8	2	7	9	0
1934-35			2	0	0	0	0
1935-36			2	1	2	3	0
1937-38*			10	2	4	6	2
1938-39	TOR	N	10	1	4	5	0
7 yrs.		N Totals:	43	7	18	25	4

Skene Ronan

RONAN, ERSKINE
B. Unknown Defense

YEAR	TEAM & LEAGUE		GP	G	A	PTS	PIM
1918-19	OTTA	N	11	0	0	0	0

Len Ronson

RONSON, LEONARD KEITH 5'9", 175 lbs.
B. July 8, 1936, Brantford, Ont. Left Wing, Shoots L

YEAR	TEAM & LEAGUE		GP	G	A	PTS	PIM
1960-61	NYR	N	13	2	1	3	10
1968-69	CALIF	N	5	0	0	0	0
2 yrs.		N Totals:	18	2	1	3	10

Traded to **Montreal** by New York with Gump Worsley, Dave Balon and Leon Rochefort for Jacques Plante, Don Marshall and Phil Goyette, June 4, 1963.

Paul Ronty

RONTY, PAUL 6', 160 lbs.
B. June 12, 1928, Toronto, Ont. Center, Shoots L

YEAR	TEAM & LEAGUE		GP	G	A	PTS	PIM
1947-48	BOS	N	24	3	11	14	0
1948-49			60	20	29	49	11
1949-50			70	23	36	59	8
1950-51			70	10	22	32	20
1951-52	NYR	N	65	12	32	43	16
1952-53			70	16	38	54	20
1953-54			70	13	33	46	18
1954-55			55	4	11	15	8
	MONT	N	4	0	0	0	2
	2 team total		59	4	11	15	10
8 yrs.		N Totals:	488	101	212	312	103

PLAYOFFS

YEAR	TEAM & LEAGUE		GP	G	A	PTS	PIM
1947-48	BOS	N	5	0	4	4	0
1948-49			5	1	2	3	2
1950-51			6	0	1	1	2
1954-55	MONT	N	5	0	0	0	2
4 yrs.		N Totals:	21	1	7	8	6

Traded to **N.Y. Rangers** by Boston for Gus Kyle and Pentti Lund, Sept. 20, 1951. Sold to **Montreal** by N.Y. Rangers, Feb. 23, 1955.

Bill Root

ROOT, WILLIAM JOHN 6', 197 lbs.
B. Sept. 6, 1959, Toronto, Ont. Defense, Shoots R

YEAR	TEAM & LEAGUE		GP	G	A	PTS	PIM
1982-83	MONT	N	46	2	3	5	24

Bob Roselle

ROSELLE, ROBERT 6'2", 185 lbs.
B. Oct. 17, 1950, Montreal, Que. Left Wing, Shoots L

YEAR	TEAM & LEAGUE		GP	G	A	PTS	PIM
1975-76	IND	W	1	0	0	0	0

Art Ross

ROSS, ARTHUR
B. Jan. 13, 1886, Naughton, Ont. Defense
Hall of Fame, 1945

YEAR	TEAM & LEAGUE		GP	G	A	PTS	PIM
1917-18	MON(W)	N	3	1	0	1	12

Jim Ross

ROSS, JAMES 6'3", 190 lbs.
B. May 20, 1926, Edinburgh, Scotland Defense, Shoots R

YEAR	TEAM & LEAGUE		GP	G	A	PTS	PIM
1951-52	NYR	N	51	2	9	11	25
1952-53			11	0	2	2	4
2 yrs.		N Totals:	62	2	11	13	29

Roland Rossignol

ROSSIGNOL, ROLAND 168 lbs.
B. Oct. 18, 1921, Edmonton, N.B. Right Wing, Shoots R

YEAR	TEAM & LEAGUE		GP	G	A	PTS	PIM
1943-44	DET	N	1	0	1	1	0
1944-45	MONT	N	5	2	2	4	2
1945-46	DET	N	8	1	2	3	4
3 yrs.		N Totals:	14	3	5	8	6

PLAYOFFS

YEAR	TEAM & LEAGUE		GP	G	A	PTS	PIM
1944-45	MONT	N	1	0	0	0	2

Darcy Rota

ROTA, DARCY IRWIN 5'11", 180 lbs.
B. Feb. 16, 1953, Vancouver, B.C. Left Wing, Shoots L

YEAR	TEAM & LEAGUE		GP	G	A	PTS	PIM
1974-75	CHI	N	78	22	22	44	93
1975-76			79	20	17	37	73
1976-77			76	24	22	46	82
1977-78			78	17	20	37	67
1978-79			63	13	17	30	77
	ATL	N	13	9	5	14	21
	2 team total		76	22	22	44	98
1979-80			44	10	8	18	49
	VAN	N	26	5	6	11	29
	2 team total		70	15	14	29	78
1980-81			80	25	31	56	124
1981-82			51	20	20	40	139
1982-83			73	42	39	81	88
9 yrs.		N Totals:	661	207	207	414	842

PLAYOFFS

YEAR	TEAM & LEAGUE		GP	G	A	PTS	PIM
1973-74	CHI	N	11	3	0	3	11
1974-75			7	0	1	1	24
1975-76			4	1	0	1	2
1976-77	CHI	N	2	0	0	0	0
1977-78			4	0	0	0	2
1978-79	ATL	N	2	0	1	1	26
1979-80	VAN	N	4	2	0	2	8
1980-81			3	2	1	3	14
1981-82			17	6	3	9	54
1982-83			3	0	0	0	6
10 yrs.		N Totals:	53	13	6	19	145
		W Totals:	4	1	0	1	2

Traded to **Atlanta** by Chicago with Ivan Boldirev and Phil Russell for Tom Lysiak, Pat Ribble, Harold Phillipoff, Greg Fox and Miles Zaharko, Mar. 13, 1979. Traded to **Vancouver** by Atlanta with Ivan Boldirev for Don Lever and Brad Smith, Feb. 8, 1980.

Randy Rota

ROTA, RANDOLPH FRANK 5'8", 170 lbs.
B. Aug. 16, 1950, Creston, B.C. Left Wing, Shoots L

YEAR	TEAM & LEAGUE		GP	G	A	PTS	PIM
1972-73	**MONT**	**N**	2	1	1	2	0
1973-74	**LA**	**N**	58	10	6	16	16
1974-75	**KC**	**N**	80	15	18	33	30
1975-76			71	12	14	26	14
1976-77	**EDM**	**W**	40	9	6	15	8
1977-78			53	8	22	30	12
6 yrs.	**N Totals:**		211	38	39	77	60
	W Totals:		93	17	28	45	20

PLAYOFFS

YEAR	TEAM & LEAGUE		GP	G	A	PTS	PIM
1973-74	**LA**	**N**	5	0	1	1	0
1976-77	**EDM**	**W**	5	3	2	5	0
1977-78			5	1	1	2	4
3 yrs.	**N Totals:**		5	0	1	1	0
	W Totals:		10	4	3	7	4

Sold to **Montreal** by California, Oct. 8, 1971. Traded to **Los Angeles** by Montreal with Bob Murdoch for Los Angeles' first choice (Mario Tremblay) in 1974 Amateur Draft and cash, May 29, 1973. Drafted by **Kansas City** from Los Angeles in Expansion Draft, June 12, 1974.

Sam Rothschild

ROTHSCHILD, SAM
B. Oct. 16, 1899, Sudbury, Ont. Forward

YEAR	TEAM & LEAGUE		GP	G	A	PTS	PIM
1924-25	**MON(M)**	**N**	27	5	4	9	4
1925-26			33	2	1	3	8
1926-27			21	1	1	2	8
1927-28	**PITT**	**N**	5	0	0	0	0
	NYA	**N**	5	0	0	0	4
	2 team total		10	0	0	0	4
4 yrs.	**N Totals:**		91	8	6	14	24

PLAYOFFS

YEAR	TEAM & LEAGUE		GP	G	A	PTS	PIM
1925-26*	**MON(M)**	**N**	8	0	0	0	0
1926-27			2	0	0	0	0
2 yrs.	**N Totals:**		10	0	0	0	0

Mike Rouleau

ROULEAU, MICHEL 5'10", 176 lbs.
B. Sept. 28, 1944, Hull, Que. Center, Shoots L

YEAR	TEAM & LEAGUE		GP	G	A	PTS	PIM
1972-73	**PHI**	**W**	6	0	1	1	15
	QUE	**W**	52	7	14	21	142
	2 team total		58	7	15	22	157
1973-74			4	0	4	4	2
1974-75			19	1	7	8	63
	M-B	**W**	7	0	3	3	25
	SD	**W**	27	5	6	11	42
	3 team total		53	6	16	22	130
3 yrs.	**W Totals:**		115	13	35	48	289

Rolly Roulston

ROULSTON, WILLIAM ORVILLE 6', 180 lbs.
B. Apr. 12, 1911, Toronto, Ont. Defense, Shoots L

YEAR	TEAM & LEAGUE		GP	G	A	PTS	PIM
1935-36	**DET**	**N**	1	0	0	0	0
1936-37			21	0	5	5	10
1937-38			2	0	1	1	0
3 yrs.	**N Totals:**		24	0	6	6	10

Tom Roulston

ROULSTON, THOMAS 6'1", 184 lbs.
B. Nov. 20, 1957, Winnipeg, Man. Center, Shoots R

YEAR	TEAM & LEAGUE		GP	G	A	PTS	PIM
1980-81	**EDM**	**N**	11	1	1	2	2
1981-82			35	11	3	14	22
1982-83			67	19	21	40	24
3 yrs.	**N Totals:**		113	31	25	56	48

PLAYOFFS

YEAR	TEAM & LEAGUE		GP	G	A	PTS	PIM
1981-82	**EDM**	**N**	5	1	0	1	2
1982-83			16	1	2	3	0
2 yrs.	**N Totals:**		21	2	2	4	2

Traded to **Edmonton** with Risto Siltanen by St. Louis for Joe Micheletti, Aug. 7, 1979.

Bobby Rousseau

ROUSSEAU, JOSEPH JEAN-PAUL ROBERT 5'10", 178 lbs.
B. July 26, 1940, Montreal, Que. Right Wing, Shoots R
Won Calder Trophy, 1961-62

YEAR	TEAM & LEAGUE		GP	G	A	PTS	PIM
1960-61	**MONT**	**N**	15	1	2	3	4
1961-62			70	21	24	45	26
1962-63			62	19	18	37	15
1963-64			70	25	31	56	32
1964-65			66	12	35	47	26
1965-66			70	30	**48**	78	20
1966-67			68	19	44	63	58
1967-68			74	19	46	65	47
1968-69			76	30	40	70	59
1969-70			72	24	34	58	30
1970-71	**MINN**	**N**	63	4	20	24	12
1971-72	**NYR**	**N**	78	21	36	57	12
1972-73			78	8	37	45	14
1973-74			72	10	41	51	4
1974-75			8	2	2	4	0
15 yrs.	**N Totals:**		942	245	458	703	359

PLAYOFFS

YEAR	TEAM & LEAGUE		GP	G	A	PTS	PIM
1961-62	**MONT**	**N**	6	0	2	2	0
1962-63			5	0	1	1	2
1963-64			7	1	1	2	2
1964-65*			13	5	8	13	24
1965-66*			10	4	4	8	6
1966-67			10	1	7	8	4
1967-68*			13	2	4	6	8
1968-69*			14	3	2	5	8
1970-71	**MINN**	**N**	12	2	6	8	0
1971-72	**NYR**	**N**	16	6	11	17	7
1972-73			10	2	3	5	4
1973-74			12	1	8	9	4
12 yrs.	**N Totals:**		128	27	57	84	69

Traded to **Minnesota** by Montreal for Claude Larose, June 10, 1970. Traded to **N.Y. Rangers** by Minnesota (June 8, 1971) to complete deal of May 25, 1971 by which Minnesota acquired Bob Nevin.

Dunc Rousseau

ROUSSEAU, DUNCAN FRANKLIN 6', 195 lbs.
B. Feb. 10, 1945, Bissett, Man. Left Wing, Shoots L

YEAR	TEAM & LEAGUE		GP	G	A	PTS	PIM
1972-73	**WINN**	**W**	74	16	17	33	75
1973-74			60	10	8	18	39
2 yrs.	**W Totals:**		134	26	25	51	114

PLAYOFFS

YEAR	TEAM & LEAGUE		GP	G	A	PTS	PIM
1972-73	**WINN**	**W**	14	3	72	5	2
1973-74			4	0	0	0	0
2 yrs.	**W Totals:**		18	3	72	5	2

Guy Rousseau

ROUSSEAU, GUY 5'5", 140 lbs.
B. Dec. 21, 1934, Montreal, Que. Left Wing, Shoots L

YEAR	TEAM & LEAGUE		GP	G	A	PTS	PIM
1954-55	**MONT**	**N**	2	0	1	1	0
1956-57			2	0	0	0	2
2 yrs.	**N Totals:**		4	0	1	1	2

Drafted from Montreal by **Toronto** June 8, 1960.

Roland Rousseau

ROUSSEAU, ROLAND (Roly) 5'8", 160 lbs.
B. Dec. 1, 1929, Montreal, Que. Defense, Shoots L

YEAR	TEAM & LEAGUE		GP	G	A	PTS	PIM
1952-53	**MONT**	**N**	2	0	0	0	0

Bobby Rowe

ROWE, BOBBY
B. Unknown Defense, Shoots L

YEAR	TEAM & LEAGUE		GP	G	A	PTS	PIM
1924-25	**BOS**	**N**	4	1	0	1	0

Ron Rowe

ROWE, RONALD NICKOLAS 5'8", 170 lbs.
B. Nov. 30, 1925, Toronto, Ont. Left Wing, Shoots L

YEAR	TEAM & LEAGUE		GP	G	A	PTS	PIM
1947-48	**NYR**	**N**	5	1	0	1	0

Tom Rowe

ROWE, THOMAS JOHN 6', 190 lbs.
B. May 23, 1956, Lynn, Mass. Right Wing, Shoots R

YEAR	TEAM & LEAGUE		GP	G	A	PTS	PIM
1976-77	**WASH**	**N**	12	1	2	3	2
1977-78			63	13	8	21	82
1978-79			69	31	30	61	137
1979-80			41	10	17	27	76
	HART	**N**	20	6	4	10	30
	2 team total		61	16	21	37	106
1980-81			74	13	28	41	190
1981-82			20	4	0	4	18
	WASH	**N**	6	1	1	2	18
	2 team total		26	5	1	6	36
1982-83	**DET**	**N**	51	6	10	16	44
7 yrs.		**N Totals:**	356	85	100	185	597

PLAYOFFS

YEAR	TEAM & LEAGUE		GP	G	A	PTS	PIM
1979-80	**HART**	**N**	3	2	0	2	0

Traded to **Hartford** by Washington for Alan Hangsleben, Jan. 17, 1980. Signed as a free agent by **Washington** Jan. 31, 1982. Signed as a free agent by **Detroit** Aug. 9, 1982. Signed as a free agent by **Edmonton** Aug. 23, 1983.

Pierre Roy

ROY, PIERRE 6', 175 lbs.
B. Mar. 12, 1952, Amos, Que. Defense, Shoots L

YEAR	TEAM & LEAGUE		GP	G	A	PTS	PIM
1972-73	**QUE**	**W**	64	7	12	19	169
1973-74			44	2	7	9	137
1974-75			61	1	18	19	118
1975-76			78	6	30	36	258
1976-77			29	3	5	8	50
	CIN	**W**	39	3	12	15	126
	2 team total		68	6	17	23	176
1978-79	**NE**	**W**	1	0	0	0	2
6 yrs.		**W Totals:**	316	22	84	106	860

PLAYOFFS

YEAR	TEAM & LEAGUE		GP	G	A	PTS	PIM
1974-75	**QUE**	**W**	15	0	9	9	40
1975-76			5	1	2	3	29
1976-77	**CIN**	**W**	3	0	1	1	7
3 yrs.		**W Totals:**	23	1	12	13	76

Gino Rozzini

ROZZINI, GINO 5'8", 150 lbs.
B. Oct. 24, 1918, Shawinigan Falls, Que. Center, Shoots L

YEAR	TEAM & LEAGUE		GP	G	A	PTS	PIM
1944-45	**BOS**	**N**	31	5	10	15	20

PLAYOFFS

YEAR	TEAM & LEAGUE		GP	G	A	PTS	PIM
1944-45	**BOS**	**N**	6	1	2	3	6

Bernard Ruelle

RUELLE, BERNARD 5'9", 165 lbs.
B. Nov. 23, 1920, Houghton, Mich. Left Wing, Shoots L

YEAR	TEAM & LEAGUE		GP	G	A	PTS	PIM
1943-44	**DET**	**N**	2	1	0	1	0

Lindy Ruff

RUFF, LINDY CAMERON 6'2", 190 lbs.
B. Feb. 17, 1960, Warburg, Alta. Defense, Shoots L

YEAR	TEAM & LEAGUE		GP	G	A	PTS	PIM
1979-80	**BUF**	**N**	63	5	14	19	38
1980-81			65	8	18	26	121
1981-82			79	16	32	48	194
1982-83			60	12	17	29	130
4 yrs.		**N Totals:**	267	41	81	122	483

PLAYOFFS

YEAR	TEAM & LEAGUE		GP	G	A	PTS	PIM
1979-80	**BUF**	**N**	8	1	1	2	19
1980-81			6	3	1	4	23
1981-82			4	0	0	0	28
1982-83			10	4	2	6	47

Lindy Ruff continued

YEAR	TEAM & LEAGUE		GP	G	A	PTS	PIM
4 yrs.		**N Totals:**	28	8	4	12	117

Kent Ruhnke

RUHNKE, KENT 6'1", 180 lbs.
Right Wing, Shoots R

YEAR	TEAM & LEAGUE		GP	G	A	PTS	PIM
1975-76	**BOS**	**N**	2	0	1	1	0
1976-77	**WINN**	**W**	51	11	11	22	2
1977-78			21	8	9	17	2
3 yrs.		**N Totals:**	2	0	1	1	0
		W Totals:	72	19	20	39	4

PLAYOFFS

YEAR	TEAM & LEAGUE		GP	G	A	PTS	PIM
1977-78	**WINN**	**W**	5	2	0	2	0

Paul Runge

RUNGE, PAUL 5'11", 167 lbs.
B. Sept. 10, 1908, Edmonton, Alta. Left Wing, Shoots L

YEAR	TEAM & LEAGUE		GP	G	A	PTS	PIM
1930-31	**BOS**	**N**	2	0	0	0	0
1931-32			14	0	1	1	8
1933-34	**MON(M)**	**N**	4	0	0	0	0
1934-35	**MONT**	**N**	3	0	0	0	2
1935-36			12	0	2	2	4
	BOS	**N**	33	8	2	10	14
	2 team total		45	8	4	12	18
1936-37	**MONT**	**N**	4	1	0	1	2
	MON(M)	**N**	30	4	10	14	6
	2 team total		34	5	10	15	8
1937-38			41	5	7	12	21
7 yrs.		**N Totals:**	143	18	22	40	57

PLAYOFFS

YEAR	TEAM & LEAGUE		GP	G	A	PTS	PIM
1935-36	**BOS**	**N**	2	0	0	0	2
1936-37	**MON(M)**	**N**	5	0	0	0	4
2 yrs.		**N Totals:**	7	0	0	0	6

Reijo Ruotsalainen

RUOTSALAINEN, REIJO (Rexie, Ray, Double R, Ho)
5'8", 170 lbs.
B. Apr. 1, 1960, Oulu, Finland Defense, Shoots R

YEAR	TEAM & LEAGUE		GP	G	A	PTS	PIM
1981-82	**NYR**	**N**	78	18	38	56	27
1982-83			77	16	53	69	22
2 yrs.		**N Totals:**	155	34	91	125	49

PLAYOFFS

YEAR	TEAM & LEAGUE		GP	G	A	PTS	PIM
1981-82	**NYR**	**N**	10	4	5	9	2
1982-83			9	4	2	6	6
2 yrs.		**N Totals:**	19	8	7	15	8

Duane Rupp

RUPP, DUANE FRANKLIN 6'1", 185 lbs.
B. Mar. 29, 1938, Macnutt, Sask. Defense, Shoots L

YEAR	TEAM & LEAGUE		GP	G	A	PTS	PIM
1962-63	**NYR**	**N**	2	0	0	0	0
1964-65	**TOR**	**N**	2	0	0	0	0
1965-66			2	0	1	1	0
1966-67			2	0	0	0	0
1967-68			71	1	8	9	42
1968-69	**MINN**	**N**	29	2	1	3	8
	PITT	**N**	30	3	10	13	24
	2 team total		59	5	11	16	32
1969-70			64	2	14	16	18
1970-71			59	5	28	33	34
1971-72			34	4	18	22	32
1972-73			78	7	13	20	68
1974-75	**VAN**	**W**	72	3	26	29	45
1975-76	**CALG**	**W**	42	0	16	16	33
12 yrs.		**N Totals:**	373	24	93	117	226
		W Totals:	114	3	42	45	78

PLAYOFFS

YEAR	TEAM & LEAGUE		GP	G	A	PTS	PIM
1969-70	**PITT**	**N**	6	2	2	4	2
1971-72			4	0	0	0	6
1975-76	**CALG**	**W**	7	0	2	2	0

Duane Rupp continued

YEAR	TEAM & LEAGUE		GP	G	A	PTS	PIM
3 yrs.		N Totals:	10	2	2	4	8
		W Totals:	7	0	2	2	0

Traded by N.Y. Rangers with Ed Ehrenverth to **Toronto** for Lou Angotti and Ed Lawson, June 25, 1964. Put on **Minnesota** reserve list from Toronto, June 12, 1968. Traded to **Pittsburgh** by Minnesota for Leo Boivin, Jan. 24, 1969.

Terry Ruskowski

RUSKOWSKI, TERENCE WALLACE (Roscoe) 5'10", 178 lbs.
B. Dec. 31, 1954, Prince Albert, Sask. Center, Shoots L

YEAR	TEAM & LEAGUE		GP	G	A	PTS	PIM
1974-75	HOUS	W	71	10	36	46	134
1975-76			65	14	35	49	100
1976-77			80	24	60	84	146
1977-78			78	15	57	72	170
1978-79	WINN	W	75	20	66	86	211
1979-80	CHI	N	74	15	55	70	252
1980-81			72	8	51	59	225
1981-82			60	7	30	37	120
1982-83			5	0	2	2	12
	LA	N	71	14	30	44	127
	2 team total		76	14	32	46	139
9 yrs.		N Totals:	282	44	168	212	736
		W Totals:	369	83	254	337	761
PLAYOFFS							
1974-75	HOUS	W	13	4	2	6	15
1975-76			16	6	10	16	64
1976-77			11	6	11	17	67
1977-78			4	1	1	2	5
1978-79	WINN	W	8	1	12	13	23
1979-80	CHI	N	4	0	0	0	22
1980-81			3	0	2	2	11
1981-82			11	1	2	3	53
8 yrs.		N Totals:	18	1	4	5	86
		W Totals:	52	18	36	54	174

Reclaimed by **Chicago** from Winnipeg prior to Expansion Draft, June 9, 1979. Traded to **Los Angeles** by Chicago for Larry Goodenough and Los Angeles' third round choice in the 1984 Amateur Draft, Oct. 24, 1982.

Bob Russell

RUSSELL, ROBERT 5'9", 167 lbs.
B. Feb. 5, 1955, Toronto, Ont. Center, Shoots L

YEAR	TEAM & LEAGUE		GP	G	A	PTS	PIM
1975-76	EDM	W	58	13	18	31	19
1976-77			57	7	6	13	41
2 yrs.		W Totals:	115	20	24	44	60
PLAYOFFS							
1975-76	EDM	W	4	1	0	1	0
1976-77			1	0	0	0	0
2 yrs.		W Totals:	5	1	0	1	0

Church Russell

RUSSELL, CHURCHILL DAVIDSON 5'11", 175 lbs.
B. Mar. 16, 1923, Winnipeg, Man. Left Wing, Shoots L

YEAR	TEAM & LEAGUE		GP	G	A	PTS	PIM
1945-46	NYR	N	17	0	5	5	2
1946-47			54	20	8	28	8
1947-48			19	0	3	3	2
3 yrs.		N Totals:	90	20	16	36	12

Phil Russell

RUSSELL, PHILIP DOUGLAS 6'2", 200 lbs.
B. July 21, 1952, Edmonton, Alta. Defense, Shoots L

YEAR	TEAM & LEAGUE		GP	G	A	PTS	PIM
1972-73	CHI	N	76	6	19	25	156
1973-74			75	10	25	35	184
1974-75			80	5	24	29	260
1975-76			74	9	29	38	194
1976-77			76	9	36	45	233
1977-78			57	6	20	26	139
1978-79			66	8	23	31	122
	ATL	N	13	1	6	7	28
	2 team total		79	9	29	38	150
1979-80			80	5	31	36	115
1980-81	CALG	N	80	6	23	29	104

Phil Russell continued

YEAR	TEAM & LEAGUE		GP	G	A	PTS	PIM
1981-82			71	4	25	29	110
1982-83			78	13	18	31	112
11 yrs.		N Totals:	826	82	279	361	1757
PLAYOFFS							
1972-73	CHI	N	16	0	3	3	49
1973-74			9	0	1	1	41
1974-75			8	1	3	4	23
1975-76			4	0	1	1	17
1976-77			2	0	1	1	2
1978-79	ATL	N	2	0	0	0	9
1979-80			4	0	1	1	6
1980-81	CALG	N	16	2	7	9	29
1981-82			3	0	1	1	2
1982-83			9	1	4	5	24
10 yrs.		N Totals:	73	4	22	26	202

Traded to **Atlanta** by Chicago with Ivan Boldirev and Darcy Rota for Harold Phillipoff, Tom Lysiak, Pat Ribble, Greg Fox and Miles Zaharko, Mar. 13, 1979. Traded by Calgary with Mel Bridgman to **New Jersey** for Joel Quenneville and Steve Tambellini, June 20, 1983.

Terry Ryan

RYAN, TERRANCE CLINTON JOHN 5'10", 178 lbs.
B. Sept. 10, 1952, Grand Falls, Nfld. Center, Shoots L

YEAR	TEAM & LEAGUE		GP	G	A	PTS	PIM
1972-73	MINN	W	76	13	6	19	13
PLAYOFFS							
1972-73	MINN	W	5	0	2	2	0

Allen Rycroft

RYCROFT, ALLEN BRUCE 5'9", 170 lbs.
B. Jan. 9, 1950, Beaver Lodge, Alta. Right Wing, Shoots R

YEAR	TEAM & LEAGUE		GP	G	A	PTS	PIM
1972-73	CLEVE	W	7	0	2	2	0

Blaine Rydman

RYDMAN, BLAINE 6'2", 195 lbs.
B. Dec. 16, 1949, Weyburn, Sask. Forward, Shoots L

YEAR	TEAM & LEAGUE		GP	G	A	PTS	PIM
1972-73	NY	W	2	0	0	0	4
	MINN	W	29	0	1	1	65
	2 team total		31	0	1	1	69
1973-74			8	0	0	0	21
2 yrs.		W Totals:	39	0	1	1	90

Bob Sabourin

SABOURIN, ROBERT 5'9", 205 lbs.
B. Mar. 17, 1933, Sudbury, Ont. Right Wing, Shoots L

YEAR	TEAM & LEAGUE		GP	G	A	PTS	PIM
1951-52	TOR	N	1	0	0	0	2

Gary Sabourin

SABOURIN, GARY BRUCE 5'11", 180 lbs.
B. Dec. 4, 1943, Parry Sound, Ont. Right Wing, Shoots R

YEAR	TEAM & LEAGUE		GP	G	A	PTS	PIM
1967-68	STL	N	50	13	10	23	50
1968-69			75	25	23	48	58
1969-70			72	28	14	42	61
1970-71			59	14	17	31	56
1971-72			77	28	17	45	52
1972-73			76	21	27	48	30
1973-74			54	7	23	30	27
1974-75	TOR	N	55	5	18	23	26
1975-76	CALIF	N	76	21	28	49	33
1976-77	CLEVE	N	33	7	11	18	4
10 yrs.		N Totals:	627	169	188	357	397
PLAYOFFS							
1967-68	STL	N	18	4	2	6	30
1968-69			12	6	5	11	12
1969-70			16	5	0	5	10
1971-72			11	3	3	6	6
1972-73			5	1	1	2	0
5 yrs.		N Totals:	62	19	11	30	58

Traded to **St. Louis** by N.Y. Rangers with Bob Plager, Gord Kannegiesser and Tim Ecclestone for Rod Seiling, June 6, 1967. Traded to **Toronto** by St. Louis for goaltender Ed Johnston, May 27, 1974. Traded to **California** by Toronto for Stan Weir, June 20, 1975.

Larry Sacharuk

SACHARUK, LAWRENCE (Satch) 6', 200 lbs.
B. Sept. 16, 1952, Saskatoon, Sask. Shoots R

YEAR	TEAM & LEAGUE		GP	G	A	PTS	PIM
1972-73	**NYR**	**N**	8	1	0	1	0
1973-74			23	2	4	6	4
1974-75	**STL**	**N**	76	20	22	42	24
1975-76	**NYR**	**N**	42	6	7	13	14
1976-77			2	0	0	0	0
1978-79	**IND**	**W**	15	2	9	11	25
6 yrs.	**N Totals:**		151	29	33	62	42
	W Totals:		15	2	9	11	25
PLAYOFFS							
1974-75	**STL**	**N**	2	1	1	2	2

Traded to **St. Louis** by N.Y. Rangers with Rangers' first round choice (Lucien DeBlois) in 1977 Amateur Draft for Greg Polis, Aug. 29, 1974. Traded to **N.Y. Rangers** by St. Louis for Bob MacMillan, Sept. 20, 1975. (St. Louis later returned to N.Y. Rangers the first round draft choice they had secured in the Greg Polis deal in exchange for Derek Sanderson).

Rocky Saganiuk

SAGANIUK, ROCKY 5'8", 185 lbs.
B. Oct. 15, 1957, Myrnam, Alta. Right Wing, Shoots R

YEAR	TEAM & LEAGUE		GP	G	A	PTS	PIM
1978-79	**TOR**	**N**	16	3	5	8	9
1979-80			75	24	23	47	52
1980-81			71	12	18	30	52
1981-82			65	17	16	33	49
1982-83			3	0	0	0	2
5 yrs.	**N Totals:**		230	56	62	118	164
PLAYOFFS							
1978-79	**TOR**	**N**	3	1	0	1	5
1979-80			3	0	0	0	10
2 yrs.	**N Totals:**		6	1	0	1	15

Andre St. Laurent

ST. LAURENT, ANDRE (Andy) 5'10", 178 lbs.
B. Feb. 16, 1953, Rouyn-Noranda, Que. Center, Shoots R

YEAR	TEAM & LEAGUE		GP	G	A	PTS	PIM
1973-74	**NYI**	**N**	42	5	9	14	78
1974-75			78	14	27	41	60
1975-76			67	9	17	26	56
1976-77			72	10	13	23	55
1977-78			2	0	0	0	2
	DET	**N**	77	31	39	70	108
	2 team total		79	31	39	70	110
1978-79			76	18	31	49	124
1979-80	**LA**	**N**	77	6	24	30	88
1980-81			22	10	6	16	63
1981-82			16	2	4	6	28
	PITT	**N**	18	8	5	13	4
	2 team total		34	10	9	19	32
1982-83			70	13	9	22	105
10 yrs.	**N Totals:**		617	126	184	310	771
PLAYOFFS							
1974-75	**NYI**	**N**	15	2	2	4	6
1975-76			13	1	5	6	15
1976-77			12	1	2	3	6
1977-78	**DET**	**N**	7	1	1	2	4
1979-80	**LA**	**N**	4	1	0	1	0
1980-81			3	0	1	1	9
1981-82	**PITT**	**N**	5	2	1	3	8
7 yrs.	**N Totals:**		59	8	12	20	48

Traded to **Detroit** by N.Y. Islanders for Michel Bergeron, Oct. 20, 1977. Traded to **Los Angeles** by Detroit with Detroit's first round choice (Larry Murphy) in the 1980 Entry Draft and Detroit's first round choice (Doug Smith) in the 1981 Entry Draft for Dale McCourt, Aug. 22, 1979. Claimed on waivers by **Pittsburgh** from Los Angeles, Feb. 23, 1982.

Dollard St. Laurent

ST. LAURENT, DOLLARD HERVE 5'11", 180 lbs.
B. May 12, 1929, Verdun, Que. Defense, Shoots L

YEAR	TEAM & LEAGUE		GP	G	A	PTS	PIM
1950-51	**MONT**	**N**	3	0	0	0	0
1951-52			40	3	10	13	30
1952-53			54	2	6	8	34
1953-54			53	3	12	15	43
1954-55			58	3	14	17	24
1955-56			46	4	9	13	58

Dollard St. Laurent continued

YEAR	TEAM & LEAGUE		GP	G	A	PTS	PIM
1956-57			64	1	11	12	49
1957-58			65	3	20	23	68
1958-59	**CHI**	**N**	70	4	8	12	28
1959-60			68	4	13	17	60
1960-61			67	2	17	19	58
1961-62			64	0	13	13	44
12 yrs.	**N Totals:**		652	29	133	162	496
PLAYOFFS							
1951-52	**MONT**	**N**	9	0	3	3	6
1952-53*			12	0	3	3	4
1953-54			10	1	2	3	8
1954-55			12	0	5	5	12
1955-56*			4	0	0	0	2
1956-57*			7	0	1	1	13
1957-58*			5	0	0	0	10
1958-59			6	0	1	1	2
1959-60			4	0	1	1	0
1960-61*	**CHI**	**N**	11	1	2	3	12
1961-62			12	0	4	4	18
11 yrs.	**N Totals:**		92	2	22	24	87

Purchased by **Chicago** from Montreal, June 3, 1958.

Frank St. Marseille

ST. MARSEILLE, FRANCIS LEO 5'11", 180 lbs.
B. Dec. 14, 1939, Levack, Ont. Right Wing, Shoots R

YEAR	TEAM & LEAGUE		GP	G	A	PTS	PIM
1967-68	**STL**	**N**	57	16	16	32	12
1968-69			72	12	26	38	22
1969-70			74	16	43	59	18
1970-71			77	19	32	51	26
1971-72			78	16	36	52	32
1972-73			45	7	18	25	8
	LA	**N**	29	7	4	11	2
	2 team total		74	14	22	36	10
1973-74			78	14	36	50	40
1974-75			80	17	36	53	46
1975-76			68	10	16	26	20
1976-77			49	6	22	28	16
10 yrs.	**N Totals:**		707	140	285	425	242
PLAYOFFS							
1967-68	**STL**	**N**	18	5	8	13	0
1968-69			12	3	3	6	2
1969-70			15	6	7	13	4
1970-71			6	2	1	3	4
1971-72			11	3	5	8	6
1973-74	**LA**	**N**	5	0	0	0	0
1974-75			3	0	1	1	0
1975-76			9	0	0	0	0
1976-77			9	1	0	1	2
9 yrs.	**N Totals:**		88	20	25	45	18

Traded to **Los Angeles** by St. Louis for Paul Curtis, Jan. 22, 1973.

Claude St. Sauveur

ST. SAUVEUR, CLAUDE 6', 170 lbs.
B. Jan. 2, 1952, Sherbrooke, Que. Left Wing, Shoots L

YEAR	TEAM & LEAGUE		GP	G	A	PTS	PIM
1973-74	**VAN**	**W**	70	38	30	68	55
1974-75			76	24	23	47	32
1975-76	**ATL**	**N**	79	24	24	48	23
1976-77	**CALG**	**W**	17	0	3	3	2
	EDM	**W**	15	5	7	12	2
	2 team total		32	5	10	15	4
1977-78	**IND**	**W**	72	36	42	78	24
1978-79			17	4	2	6	12
	CIN	**W**	16	4	5	9	4
	2 team total		33	8	7	15	16
6 yrs.	**N Totals:**		79	24	24	48	23
	W Totals:		283	111	112	223	131
PLAYOFFS							
1975-76	**ATL**	**N**	2	0	0	0	0
1976-77	**EDM**	**W**	5	1	0	1	0
2 yrs.	**N Totals:**		2	0	0	0	0
	W Totals:		5	1	0	1	0

Sold to **Atlanta** by California, Sept. 23, 1975.

Don Saleski

SALESKI, DONALD PATRICK (Big Bird) 6'3", 205 lbs.
B. Oct. 10, 1949, Moose Jaw, Sask. Right Wing, Shoots R

YEAR	TEAM & LEAGUE		GP	G	A	PTS	PIM
1971-72	PHI	N	1	0	0	0	0
1972-73			78	12	9	21	205
1973-74			77	15	25	40	131
1974-75			63	10	18	28	107
1975-76			78	21	26	47	68
1976-77			74	22	16	38	33
1977-78			70	27	18	45	44
1978-79			35	11	5	16	14
	COLO	N	16	2	0	2	4
	2 team total		51	13	5	18	18
1979-80			51	8	8	16	23
9 yrs.		N Totals:	543	128	125	253	629
PLAYOFFS							
1972-73	PHI	N	11	1	2	3	4
1973-74*			17	2	7	9	24
1974-75*			17	2	3	5	25
1975-76			16	6	5	11	47
1976-77			10	0	0	0	12
1977-78			11	2	0	2	19
6 yrs.		N Totals:	82	13	17	30	131

Traded to **Colorado** by Philadelphia for future considerations, Mar. 3, 1979.

Borje Salming

SALMING, ANDERS BORJE (B.J.) 6'1", 195 lbs.
B. Apr. 17, 1951, Kiruna, Sweden Defense, Shoots L

YEAR	TEAM & LEAGUE		GP	G	A	PTS	PIM
1973-74	TOR	N	76	5	34	39	48
1974-75			60	12	25	37	34
1975-76			79	16	41	57	70
1976-77			76	12	66	78	46
1977-78			80	16	60	76	70
1978-79			78	17	56	73	76
1979-80			74	19	52	71	94
1980-81			72	5	61	66	154
1981-82			69	12	44	56	170
1982-83			69	7	38	45	104
10 yrs.		N Totals:	733	121	477	598	866
PLAYOFFS							
1973-74	TOR	N	4	0	1	1	4
1974-75			7	0	4	4	6
1975-76			10	3	4	7	9
1976-77			9	3	6	9	6
1977-78			6	2	2	4	6
1978-79			6	0	1	1	8
1979-80			3	1	1	2	2
1980-81			3	0	2	2	4
1982-83			4	1	4	5	10
9 yrs.		N Totals:	52	10	25	35	55

Signed as free agent by **Toronto** May 12, 1975.

John Salovaara

SALOVAARA, JOHN BARRY 5'8", 175 lbs.
B. Jan. 7, 1948, Toronto, Ont. Defense, Shoots R

YEAR	TEAM & LEAGUE		GP	G	A	PTS	PIM
1974-75	DET	N	27	0	2	2	18
1975-76			63	2	11	13	52
2 yrs.		N Totals:	90	2	13	15	70

Dave Salvian

SALVIAN, DAVID CLIFFORD 5'10", 170 lbs.
B. Sept. 9, 1955, Toronto, Ont. Right Wing, Shoots L

YEAR	TEAM & LEAGUE		GP	G	A	PTS	PIM
PLAYOFFS							
1976-77	NYI	N	1	0	1	1	2

Philip Samis

SAMIS, PHILIP LAWRENCE 5'10", 180 lbs.
B. Dec. 28, 1927, Edmonton, Alta. Defense, Shoots R

YEAR	TEAM & LEAGUE		GP	G	A	PTS	PIM
1949-50	TOR	N	2	0	0	0	0

Philip Samis continued

YEAR	TEAM & LEAGUE		GP	G	A	PTS	PIM
PLAYOFFS							
1947-48*	TOR	N	5	0	1	1	2

Cal Sandbeck

SANDBECK, CALVIN WAYNE 6'1", 218 lbs.
B. Jan. 28, 1956, Int'l. Falls, Minn. Defense, Shoots L

YEAR	TEAM & LEAGUE		GP	G	A	PTS	PIM
1977-78	EDM	W	11	1	2	3	39
1978-79			6	0	0	0	2
2 yrs.		W Totals:	17	1	2	3	41
PLAYOFFS							
1977-78	EDM	W	5	0	0	0	10

Reclaimed by **Minnesota** from Edmonton prior to Expansion Draft, July 9, 1979.

Frank Sanders

SANDERS, FRANKLIN 6'3", 230 lbs.
B. Mar. 8, 1949, North St. Paul, Minn. Defense, Shoots R

YEAR	TEAM & LEAGUE		GP	G	A	PTS	PIM
1972-73	MINN	W	77	8	8	16	94
PLAYOFFS							
1972-73	MINN	W	4	0	1	1	0

Derek Sanderson

SANDERSON, DEREK MICHAEL (Turk) 6', 185 lbs.
B. June 16, 1946, Niagara Falls, Ont. Center, Shoots L
Won Calder Trophy, 1967-68

YEAR	TEAM & LEAGUE		GP	G	A	PTS	PIM
1965-66	BOS	N	2	0	0	0	0
1966-67			2	0	0	0	0
1967-68			71	24	25	49	98
1968-69			63	26	22	48	146
1969-70			50	18	23	41	118
1970-71			71	29	34	63	130
1971-72			78	25	33	58	108
1972-73	PHI	W	8	3	3	6	69
	BOS	N	25	5	10	15	38
	2 team total		33	8	13	21	107
1973-74			29	8	12	20	48
1974-75	NYR	N	75	25	25	50	106
1975-76			8	0	0	0	4
	STL	N	65	24	43	67	59
	2 team total		73	24	43	67	63
1976-77			32	8	13	21	26
	VAN	N	16	7	9	16	30
	2 team total		48	15	22	37	56
1977-78	PITT	N	13	3	1	4	0
13 yrs.		N Totals:	600	202	250	452	911
		W Totals:	8	3	3	6	69
PLAYOFFS							
1967-68	BOS	N	4	0	2	2	9
1968-69			9	8	2	10	36
1969-70*			14	5	4	9	72
1970-71			7	2	1	3	13
1971-72*			11	1	1	2	44
1972-73			5	1	2	3	13
1974-75	NYR	N	3	0	0	0	0
1975-76	STL	N	3	1	0	1	0
8 yrs.		N Totals:	56	18	12	30	187

Traded to **N.Y. Rangers** by Boston for Walt McKechnie, June 12, 1974. Obtained by **St. Louis** from N.Y. Rangers when Blues returned Rangers' first round choice (Lucien DeBlois) in 1977 Amateur Draft which they had secured in an earlier deal, Oct. 30, 1975. Sold to **Vancouver** by St. Louis, Feb. 18, 1977. Signed as a free agent by Pittsburgh, March 14, 1978.

Ed Sandford

SANDFORD, EDWARD MICHAEL (Sandy) 6'1", 190 lbs.
B. Aug. 20, 1928, New Toronto, Ont. Left Wing, Shoots R

YEAR	TEAM & LEAGUE		GP	G	A	PTS	PIM
1947-48	BOS	N	59	10	15	25	25
1948-49			56	16	20	36	57
1949-50			17	1	4	5	6
1950-51			51	10	13	23	33
1951-52			65	13	12	25	54
1952-53			61	14	21	35	44

Ed Sandford continued

YEAR	TEAM & LEAGUE		GP	G	A	PTS	PIM
1953-54			70	16	31	47	42
1954-55			60	14	20	34	38
1955-56	**DET**	**N**	4	0	0	0	0
	CHI	**N**	57	12	9	21	56
	2 team total		61	12	9	21	56
9 yrs.		**N Totals:**	500	106	145	251	355
PLAYOFFS							
1947-48	**BOS**	**N**	5	1	0	1	0
1948-49			5	1	3	4	2
1950-51			6	0	1	1	4
1951-52			7	2	2	4	0
1952-53			11	8	3	11	11
1953-54			3	0	1	1	4
1954-55			5	1	1	2	6
7 yrs.		**N Totals:**	42	13	11	24	27

Traded to **Chicago** by Detroit for Metro Prystai, Oct. 24, 1955. Traded to **Detroit** by Boston with Real Chevrefils, Norm Corcoran, Gilles Boisvert and Warren Godfrey for Marcel Bonin, Terry Sawchuk, Vic Stasiuk and Lorne Davis, June 3, 1955.

Charlie Sands

SANDS, CHARLIE 5'9", 160 lbs.
B. Mar. 23, 1911, Fort William, Ont. Center, Shoots R

YEAR	TEAM & LEAGUE		GP	G	A	PTS	PIM
1932-33	**TOR**	**N**	3	0	3	3	0
1933-34			45	8	8	16	2
1934-35	**BOS**	**N**	43	15	12	27	0
1935-36			41	6	4	10	8
1936-37			46	18	5	23	6
1937-38			46	17	12	29	12
1938-39			39	7	5	12	10
1939-40	**MONT**	**N**	47	9	20	29	10
1940-41			43	5	13	18	4
1941-42			39	11	16	27	6
1942-43			31	3	9	12	0
1943-44	**NYR**	**N**	9	0	2	2	0
12 yrs.		**N Totals:**	432	99	109	208	58
PLAYOFFS							
1932-33	**TOR**	**N**	9	2	2	4	2
1933-34			4	1	0	1	0
1934-35	**BOS**	**N**	4	0	0	0	0
1935-36			2	0	0	0	0
1936-37			3	1	2	3	0
1937-38			3	1	1	2	0
1938-39*			12	0	0	0	0
1940-41	**MONT**	**N**	2	1	0	1	0
1941-42			3	0	1	1	2
1942-43			2	0	0	0	0
10 yrs.		**N Totals:**	44	6	6	12	4

Nick Sanza

SANZA, NICHOLAS 5'11", 178 lbs.
B. Feb. 6, 1955 Defense

YEAR	TEAM & LEAGUE		GP	G	A	PTS	PIM
1975-76	**D-O**	**W**	1	0	0	0	0

Gary Sargent

SARGENT, GARY ALAN (Sarge) 5'10", 198 lbs.
B. Feb. 8, 1954, Red Lake, Minn. Defense, Shoots L

YEAR	TEAM & LEAGUE		GP	G	A	PTS	PIM
1975-76	**LA**	**N**	63	8	16	24	36
1976-77			80	14	40	54	65
1977-78			72	7	34	41	52
1978-79	**MINN**	**N**	79	12	32	44	39
1979-80			52	13	21	34	22
1980-81			23	4	7	11	36
1981-82			15	0	5	5	18
1982-83			18	3	6	9	5
8 yrs.		**N Totals:**	402	61	161	222	273
PLAYOFFS							
1976-77	**LA**	**N**	9	3	4	7	6
1977-78			2	0	0	0	0
1979-80	**MINN**	**N**	4	2	1	3	2
1982-83			5	0	2	2	0
4 yrs.		**N Totals:**	20	5	7	12	8

Signed as free agent by **Minnesota** June 30, 1978. As compensation, Los Angeles received Rick Hampton, Steve Jensen and Dave Gardner.

Craig Sarner

SARNER, CRAIG BRIAN 5'11", 185 lbs.
B. June 20, 1949, St. Paul, Minn. Right Wing, Shoots L

YEAR	TEAM & LEAGUE		GP	G	A	PTS	PIM
1974-75	**BOS**	**N**	7	0	0	0	0
1975-76	**MINN**	**W**	1	0	0	0	0
2 yrs.		**N Totals:**	7	0	0	0	0
		W Totals:	1	0	0	0	0

Dick Sarrazin

SARRAZIN, RICHARD 6', 185 lbs.
B. Jan. 22, 1946, St.Gabriel Brandon, Que.
Right Wing, Shoots R

YEAR	TEAM & LEAGUE		GP	G	A	PTS	PIM
1968-69	**PHI**	**N**	54	16	30	46	14
1969-70			18	1	1	2	4
1971-72			28	3	4	7	4
1972-73	**NE**	**W**	35	4	7	11	0
	CHI	**W**	33	3	8	11	2
	2 team total		68	7	15	22	2
4 yrs.		**N Totals:**	100	20	35	55	22
		W Totals:	68	7	15	22	2
PLAYOFFS							
1968-69	**PHI**	**N**	4	0	0	0	0

Fred Saskamoose

SASKAMOOSE, FRED 5'9", 165 lbs.
B. Dec. 24, 1934, Sandy Lake Reserve,Sask.
Center, Shoots R

YEAR	TEAM & LEAGUE		GP	G	A	PTS	PIM
1953-54	**CHI**	**N**	11	0	0	0	6

Glen Sather

SATHER, GLEN CAMERON (Slats) 5'11", 180 lbs.
B. Sept. 2, 1943, High River, Alta. Left Wing, Shoots L

YEAR	TEAM & LEAGUE		GP	G	A	PTS	PIM
1966-67	**BOS**	**N**	5	0	0	0	0
1967-68			65	8	12	20	34
1968-69			76	4	11	15	67
1969-70	**PITT**	**N**	76	12	14	26	114
1970-71			46	8	3	11	96
	NYR	**N**	33	2	0	2	52
	2 team total		79	10	3	13	148
1971-72			76	5	9	14	77
1972-73			77	11	15	26	64
1973-74			2	0	0	0	0
	STL	**N**	69	15	29	44	82
	2 team total		71	15	29	44	82
1974-75	**MONT**	**N**	63	6	10	16	44
1975-76	**MINN**	**N**	72	9	10	19	94
1976-77	**EDM**	**W**	81	19	34	53	77
11 yrs.		**N Totals:**	660	80	113	193	724
		W Totals:	81	19	34	53	77
PLAYOFFS							
1967-68	**BOS**	**N**	3	0	0	0	0
1968-69			10	0	0	0	18
1969-70	**PITT**	**N**	10	0	2	2	17
1970-71	**NYR**	**N**	13	0	1	1	18
1971-72			16	0	1	1	22
1972-73			9	0	0	0	7
1974-75	**MONT**	**N**	11	1	1	2	4
1976-77	**EDM**	**W**	5	1	1	2	2
8 yrs.		**N Totals:**	72	1	5	6	86
		W Totals:	5	1	1	2	2

Drafted by **Pittsburgh** from Boston June 11, 1969. Traded to **N.Y. Rangers** by Pittsburgh for Syl Apps Jr., Jan. 26, 1971. Traded to **St. Louis** by N.Y. Rangers with Rene Villemure for Jack Egers, Oct. 28, 1973. Traded to **Montreal** by St. Louis (June 14, 1974) to complete earlier deal (May 27, 1974) in which St. Louis acquired Rick Wilson and Montreal's fifth choice (Don Wheldon) for St. Louis' fourth choice (Barry Legge) in 1974 Amateur Draft. Traded to **Minnesota** by Montreal for cash and Minnesota's third choice (Alain Cote) in 1977 Amateur Draft, July 9, 1975.

Bernie Saunders

SAUNDERS, BERNARD 6', 190 lbs.
B. June 21, 1956, Montreal, Que. Left Wing, Shoots R

YEAR	TEAM & LEAGUE		GP	G	A	PTS	PIM
1979-80	**QUE**	**N**	4	0	0	0	0
1980-81			6	0	1	1	8

YEAR	TEAM & LEAGUE		GP	G	A	PTS	PIM

Bernie Saunders continued

2 yrs.		N Totals:	10	0	1	1	8

Signed as free agent by **Quebec** May 29, 1979.

Bud Saunders

SAUNDERS, EDWARD 5'10½", 168 lbs.
B. Aug. 29, 1912, Ottawa, Ont. Right Wing

1933-34	OTTA	N	19	1	3	4	4

Jean Sauve

SAUVE, JEAN-FRANCOIS (Frankie) 5'6", 175 lbs.
B. Jan. 23, 1960, Ste. Genevieve, Que. Center, Shoots L

1980-81	BUF	N	20	5	9	14	12
1981-82			69	19	36	55	49
1982-83			9	0	4	4	9
3 yrs.		N Totals:	98	24	49	73	70
PLAYOFFS							
1980-81	BUF	N	5	2	0	2	0
1981-82			2	0	2	2	0
2 yrs.		N Totals:	7	2	2	4	0

Signed as free agent with **Buffalo** Nov. 1, 1979. Traded by Buffalo with Tony McKegney, Andre Savard, and Buffalo's third choice (Liro Jarvi) in the 1983 Amateur Draft to **Quebec** for Real Cloutier and Quebec's first pick in the 1983 Amateur Draft (Adam Creighton), June 8, 1983.

Tony Savage

SAVAGE, GORDON 5'11", 170 lbs.
B. July 18, 1906, Calgary, Alta. Defense, Shoots L

1934-35	BOS	N	8	0	0	0	2
	MONT	N	41	1	5	6	4
	2 team total		49	1	5	6	6
PLAYOFFS							
1934-35	MONT	N	2	0	0	0	0

Andre Savard

SAVARD, ANDRE 6'1", 185 lbs.
B. Sept. 2, 1953, Temiscamingue, Que. Center, Shoots L

1973-74	BOS	N	72	16	14	30	39
1974-75			77	19	25	44	45
1975-76			79	17	23	40	60
1976-77	BUF	N	80	25	35	60	30
1977-78			80	19	20	39	40
1978-79			65	18	22	40	20
1979-80			33	3	10	13	16
1980-81			79	31	43	74	63
1981-82			62	18	20	38	24
1982-83			68	16	25	41	28
10 yrs.		N Totals:	695	182	237	419	365
PLAYOFFS							
1973-74	BOS	N	16	3	2	5	24
1974-75			3	1	1	2	2
1975-76			12	1	4	5	9
1976-77	BUF	N	6	0	1	1	2
1977-78			6	0	0	0	4
1978-79			3	0	2	2	2
1979-80			8	1	1	2	2
1980-81			8	4	2	6	17
1981-82			4	0	1	1	5
1982-83			10	0	4	4	8
10 yrs.		N Totals:	76	10	18	28	75

Signed as free agent by **Buffalo** from Boston, June 11, 1976. Traded by Buffalo with Tony McKegney, Jean Sauve, and Buffalo's third round choice in the 1983 Amateur Draft (Liro Jarvi) to **Quebec** for Real Cloutier and Quebec's first round choice (Adam Creighton) in the 1983 Amateur Draft, June 8, 1983.

Denis Savard

SAVARD, DENIS JOSEPH 5'10", 170 lbs.
B. Feb. 4, 1961, Pointe Gatineau, Que. Center, Shoots R

1980-81	CHI	N	76	28	47	75	47
1981-82			80	32	87	119	82
1982-83			78	35	85	120	99
3 yrs.		N Totals:	234	95	219	314	228
PLAYOFFS							
1980-81	CHI	N	3	0	0	0	0
1981-82			15	11	7	18	52
1982-83			13	8	9	17	22
3 yrs.		N Totals:	31	19	16	35	74

Jean Savard

SAVARD, JEAN 5'11", 172 lbs.
B. Apr. 26, 1957, Verdun, Que. Center, Shoots R

1977-78	CHI	N	31	7	11	18	2
1978-79			11	0	1	1	9
1979-80	HART	N	1	0	0	0	2
3 yrs.		N Totals:	43	7	12	19	13

Claimed by **Hartford** from Chicago in Expansion Draft, June 13, 1979.

Serge Savard

SAVARD, SERGE A. (The Senator) 6'2", 210 lbs.
B. Jan. 22, 1946, Montreal, Que. Defense, Shoots L
Won Conn Smythe Trophy, 1968-69
Won Masterton Trophy, 1978-79

1966-67	MONT	N	2	0	0	0	0
1967-68			67	2	13	15	34
1968-69			74	8	23	31	73
1969-70			64	12	19	31	38
1970-71			37	5	10	15	30
1971-72			23	1	8	9	16
1972-73			74	7	32	39	58
1973-74			67	4	14	18	49
1974-75			80	20	40	60	64
1975-76			71	8	39	47	38
1976-77			78	9	33	42	35
1977-78			77	8	34	42	24
1978-79			80	7	26	33	30
1979-80			46	5	8	13	18
1980-81			77	4	13	17	30
1981-82	WINN	N	47	2	5	7	26
1982-83			76	4	16	20	29
17 yrs.		N Totals:	1040	106	333	439	592
PLAYOFFS							
1967-68*	MONT	N	6	2	0	2	0
1968-69*			14	4	6	10	24
1971-72			6	0	0	0	10
1972-73*			17	3	8	11	22
1973-74			6	1	1	2	4
1974-75			11	1	7	8	2
1975-76*			13	3	6	9	6
1976-77*			14	2	7	9	2
1977-78*			15	1	7	8	8
1978-79*			16	2	7	9	6
1979-80			2	0	0	0	0
1980-81			3	0	0	0	0
1981-82	WINN	N	4	0	0	0	2
1982-83			3	0	0	0	2
14 yrs.		N Totals:	130	19	49	68	88

Claimed by **Winnipeg** from Montreal in Waiver Draft Oct. 5, 1981. Traded to **Montreal** by Winnipeg for Montreal's third round choice in the 1983 Amateur Draft (Peter Taglianetti), March 10, 1983.

Peter Scamurra

SCAMURRA, PETER VINCENT 6'3", 185 lbs.
B. Feb. 23, 1955, Buffalo, N.Y. Defense, Shoots L

1975-76	WASH	N	58	2	13	15	33
1976-77			21	0	2	2	8
1978-79			30	3	5	8	12
1979-80			23	3	5	8	6

Peter Scamurra continued

YEAR	TEAM	LEAGUE	GP	G	A	PTS	PIM
4 yrs.		**N Totals:**	132	8	25	33	59

Butch Schaeffer

SCHAEFFER, PAUL

Defense

YEAR	TEAM	LEAGUE	GP	G	A	PTS	PIM
1936-37	**CHI**	**N**	5	0	0	0	6

Kevin Schamehorn

SCHAMEHORN, KEVIN DEAN 5'9", 185 lbs.
B. July 28, 1956, Calgary, Alta. Right Wing, Shoots R

YEAR	TEAM	LEAGUE	GP	G	A	PTS	PIM
1976-77	**DET**	**N**	3	0	0	0	9
1979-80			2	0	0	0	4
1980-81	**LA**	**N**	5	0	0	0	4
3 yrs.		**N Totals:**	10	0	0	0	17

Signed as free agent with **Los Angeles** Oct. 18, 1980.

Ted Scharf

SCHARF, EDWARD WILSON 5'11", 185 lbs.
B. Dec. 3, 1948, Penticton, Ont. Right Wing, Shoots L

YEAR	TEAM	LEAGUE	GP	G	A	PTS	PIM
1972-73	**NY**	**W**	29	2	2	4	72
1973-74	**NY-NJ**	**W**	63	4	2	6	107
1974-75	**SD**	**W**	67	3	1	4	94
1975-76	**IND**	**W**	74	7	14	21	56
1976-77	**EDM**	**W**	5	0	2	2	14
5 yrs.		**W Totals:**	238	16	21	37	343

PLAYOFFS

YEAR	TEAM	LEAGUE	GP	G	A	PTS	PIM
1975-76	**IND**	**W**	7	0	0	0	5

John Schella

SCHELLA, JOHN EDWARD 6', 180 lbs.
B. May 9, 1947, Port Arthur, Ont. Defense, Shoots R

YEAR	TEAM	LEAGUE	GP	G	A	PTS	PIM
1970-71	**VAN**	**N**	38	0	5	5	58
1971-72			77	2	13	15	166
1972-73	**HOUS**	**W**	77	2	24	26	**239**
1973-74			73	12	19	31	170
1974-75			78	10	42	52	176
1975-76			74	6	32	38	106
1976-77			20	0	6	6	28
1977-78			63	9	20	29	125
8 yrs.		**N Totals:**	115	2	18	20	224
		W Totals:	385	39	143	182	844

PLAYOFFS

YEAR	TEAM	LEAGUE	GP	G	A	PTS	PIM
1972-73	**HOUS**	**W**	10	0	2	2	12
1973-74			14	2	6	8	42
1974-75			13	0	8	8	12
1975-76			17	1	6	7	38
1976-77			6	1	2	3	6
1977-78			6	0	1	1	33
6 yrs.		**W Totals:**	66	4	25	29	143

Drafted by **Vancouver** from Montreal in Expansion Draft, June 10, 1970. Drafted by **N.Y. Islanders** from Vancouver in Expansion Draft, June 6, 1972.

Chuck Scherza

SCHERZA, CHARLES 5'10", 190 lbs.
B. Feb. 15, 1923, Brandon, Man. Center, Shoots R

YEAR	TEAM	LEAGUE	GP	G	A	PTS	PIM
1943-44	**BOS**	**N**	10	1	1	2	4
	NYR	**N**	24	3	2	5	13
	2 team total		34	4	3	7	17
1944-45			22	2	3	5	18
2 yrs.		**N Totals:**	56	6	6	12	35

Ken Schinkel

SCHINKEL, KENNETH CALVIN 5'10", 172 lbs.
B. Nov. 27, 1932, Jansen, Sask. Right Wing, Shoots R

YEAR	TEAM	LEAGUE	GP	G	A	PTS	PIM
1959-60	**NYR**	**N**	69	13	16	29	27
1960-61			38	2	6	8	18
1961-62			65	7	21	28	17

Ken Schinkel continued

YEAR	TEAM	LEAGUE	GP	G	A	PTS	PIM
1962-63			69	6	9	15	15
1963-64			4	0	0	0	0
1966-67			20	6	3	9	0
1967-68	**PITT**	**N**	57	14	25	39	19
1968-69			76	18	34	52	18
1969-70			72	20	25	45	19
1970-71			50	15	19	34	6
1971-72			74	15	30	45	10
1972-73			42	11	10	21	16
12 yrs.		**N Totals:**	636	127	198	325	165

PLAYOFFS

YEAR	TEAM	LEAGUE	GP	G	A	PTS	PIM
1961-62	**NYR**	**N**	2	1	0	1	0
1966-67			4	0	1	1	0
1969-70	**PITT**	**N**	10	4	1	5	4
1971-72			3	2	0	2	0
4 yrs.		**N Totals:**	19	7	2	9	4

Drafted by **Pittsburgh** from N.Y. Rangers in Expansion Draft, June 6, 1967.

Andy Schliebener

SCHLIEBENER, ANDREAS 6', 190 lbs.
B. Aug. 16, 1962, Ottawa, Ont. Defense, Shoots L

YEAR	TEAM	LEAGUE	GP	G	A	PTS	PIM
1981-82	**VAN**	**N**	22	0	1	1	10

PLAYOFFS

YEAR	TEAM	LEAGUE	GP	G	A	PTS	PIM
1981-82	**VAN**	**N**	3	0	0	0	0

Bobby Schmautz

SCHMAUTZ, ROBERT JAMES 5'9", 172 lbs.
B. Mar. 28, 1945, Saskatoon, Sask. Right Wing, Shoots R

YEAR	TEAM	LEAGUE	GP	G	A	PTS	PIM
1967-68	**CHI**	**N**	13	3	2	5	6
1968-69			63	9	7	16	37
1970-71	**VAN**	**N**	26	5	5	10	14
1971-72			60	12	13	25	82
1972-73			77	38	33	71	137
1973-74			49	26	19	45	58
	BOS	**N**	27	7	13	20	31
	2 team total		76	33	32	65	89
1974-75			56	21	30	51	63
1975-76			75	28	34	62	116
1976-77			57	23	29	52	62
1977-78			54	27	27	54	87
1978-79			65	20	22	42	77
1979-80			20	8	6	14	8
	EDM	**N**	29	8	8	16	20
	COLO	**N**	20	9	4	13	53
	3 team total		69	25	18	43	81
1980-81	**VAN**	**N**	73	27	34	61	137
13 yrs.		**N Totals:**	764	271	286	557	988

PLAYOFFS

YEAR	TEAM	LEAGUE	GP	G	A	PTS	PIM
1967-68	**CHI**	**N**	11	2	3	5	2
1973-74	**BOS**	**N**	16	3	6	9	44
1974-75			3	1	5	6	6
1975-76			11	2	8	10	13
1976-77			14	11	1	12	10
1977-78			15	7	8	15	11
1978-79			11	2	2	4	6
1980-81	**VAN**	**N**	3	0	0	0	0
8 yrs.		**N Totals:**	84	28	33	61	92

Put on **St. Louis** reserve list from Chicago in Intra-league Draft, June 11, 1969. Traded to **Montreal** by St. Louis with Norm Beaudin for Ernie Wakely, June 27, 1969. Traded to **Boston** by Vancouver for Fred O'Donnell and Chris Oddleifson, Feb. 7, 1974. Traded to **Edmonton** Boston for Dan Newman, Dec. 10, 1979. Traded to **Colorado** by Edmonton for Don Ashby, Feb. 25, 1980. Signed as free agent with **Vancouver** Oct. 2, 1980.

Cliff Schmautz

SCHMAUTZ, CLIFFORD HARVEY 5'7", 161 lbs.
B. Mar. 17, 1939, Saskatoon, Sask. Right Wing, Shoots R

YEAR	TEAM	LEAGUE	GP	G	A	PTS	PIM
1970-71	**BUF**	**N**	26	5	7	12	10
	PHI	**N**	30	8	12	20	23
	2 team total		56	13	19	32	33

Claimed on waivers by **Philadelphia** from Buffalo, Dec. 28, 1970.

Clarence Schmidt

SCHMIDT, CLARENCE 5'11", 165 lbs.
B. Williams, Minn. Right Wing, Shoots R

YEAR	TEAM & LEAGUE		GP	G	A	PTS	PIM
1943-44	**BOS**	**N**	7	1	0	1	2

Jackie Schmidt

SCHMIDT, JOHN R. 5'10", 155 lbs.
B. Nov. 11, 1924, Odessa, Sask. Left Wing, Shoots L

YEAR	TEAM & LEAGUE		GP	G	A	PTS	PIM
1942-43	**BOS**	**N**	45	6	7	13	6
PLAYOFFS							
1942-43	**BOS**	**N**	5	0	0	0	0

Joseph Schmidt

SCHMIDT, JOSEPH 5'9½", 157 lbs.
B. Nov. 5, 1926, Odessa, Sask. Left Wing, Shoots L

YEAR	TEAM & LEAGUE		GP	G	A	PTS	PIM
1943-44	**BOS**	**N**	2	0	0	0	0

Milt Schmidt

SCHMIDT, MILTON CONRAD 5'11", 180 lbs.
B. Mar. 5, 1918, Kitchener, Ont. Center, Shoots L
Won Hart Trophy, 1950-51
Won Art Ross Trophy, 1939-40
Hall of Fame, 1961

YEAR	TEAM & LEAGUE		GP	G	A	PTS	PIM
1936-37	**BOS**	**N**	26	2	8	10	15
1937-38			44	13	14	27	15
1938-39			41	15	17	32	13
1939-40			48	22	**30**	**52**	37
1940-41			45	13	25	38	23
1941-42			36	14	21	35	34
1945-46			48	13	18	31	21
1946-47			59	27	35	62	40
1947-48			33	9	17	26	28
1948-49			44	10	22	32	25
1949-50			68	19	22	41	41
1950-51			62	22	39	61	33
1951-52			69	21	29	50	57
1952-53			68	11	23	34	30
1953-54			64	14	18	32	28
1954-55			23	4	8	12	26
16 yrs.		**N Totals:**	778	229	346	575	466
PLAYOFFS							
1936-37	**BOS**	**N**	3	0	0	0	0
1937-38			3	0	0	0	0
1938-39*			12	3	3	6	2
1939-40			6	0	0	0	0
1940-41*			11	5	6	11	9
1945-46			10	3	5	8	2
1946-47			5	3	1	4	4
1947-48			5	2	5	7	2
1948-49			4	0	2	2	8
1950-51			6	0	1	1	7
1951-52			7	2	1	3	0
1952-53			10	5	1	6	6
1953-54			4	1	0	1	20
13 yrs.		**N Totals:**	86	24	25	49	60

Werner Schnarr

SCHNARR, WERNER
B. Unknown Forward

YEAR	TEAM & LEAGUE		GP	G	A	PTS	PIM
1924-25	**BOS**	**N**	24	0	0	0	0
1925-26			1	0	0	0	0
2 yrs.		**N Totals:**	25	0	0	0	0

Buzz Schneider

SCHNEIDER, WILLIAM 5'11", 175 lbs.
B. Sept. 14, 1954, Babbitt, Minn. Left Wing, Shoots L

YEAR	TEAM & LEAGUE		GP	G	A	PTS	PIM
1976-77	**BIRM**	**W**	4	0	0	0	2

Danny Schock

SCHOCK, DANIEL PATRICK 5'11", 180 lbs.
B. Dec. 30, 1948, Terrace Bay, Ont. Left Wing, Shoots L

YEAR	TEAM & LEAGUE		GP	G	A	PTS	PIM
1970-71	**BOS**	**N**	6	0	0	0	0
	PHI	**N**	14	1	2	3	0
	2 team total		20	1	2	3	0
PLAYOFFS							
1969-70*	**BOS**	**N**	1	0	0	0	0

Traded to **Philadelphia** by Boston with Rick MacLeish for Mike Walton, Feb. 1, 1971.

Ron Schock

SCHOCK, RONALD LAWRENCE 5'11", 180 lbs.
B. Dec. 19, 1943, Chapleau, Ont. Center, Shoots L

YEAR	TEAM & LEAGUE		GP	G	A	PTS	PIM
1963-64	**BOS**	**N**	5	1	2	3	0
1964-65			33	4	7	11	14
1965-66			24	2	2	4	6
1966-67			66	10	20	30	8
1967-68	**STL**	**N**	55	9	9	18	17
1968-69			67	12	27	39	14
1969-70	**PITT**	**N**	76	8	21	29	40
1970-71			71	14	26	40	20
1971-72			77	17	29	46	22
1972-73			78	13	36	49	23
1973-74			77	14	29	43	22
1974-75			80	23	63	86	36
1975-76			80	18	44	62	28
1976-77			80	17	32	49	10
1977-78	**BUF**	**N**	40	4	4	8	0
15 yrs.		**N Totals:**	909	166	351	517	260
PLAYOFFS							
1967-68	**STL**	**N**	12	1	2	3	0
1968-69			12	1	2	3	6
1969-70	**PITT**	**N**	10	1	6	7	7
1971-72			4	1	0	1	6
1974-75			9	0	4	4	10
1975-76			3	0	1	1	0
1976-77			3	0	1	1	0
1977-78	**BUF**	**N**	2	0	0	0	0
8 yrs.		**N Totals:**	55	4	16	20	29

Drafted by **St. Louis** from Boston in Expansion Draft, June 6, 1967. Traded to **Pittsburgh** by St. Louis with Craig Cameron for Lou Angotti and Pittsburgh's first choice in the 1971 Amateur Draft (Gene Carr), June 6, 1969. Traded to **Buffalo** by Pittsburgh for Brian Spencer, Sept. 20, 1977.

Jim Schoenfeld

SCHOENFELD, JAMES GRANT (Schony) 6'2", 210 lbs.
B. Sept. 4, 1952, Galt, Ont. Defense, Shoots L

YEAR	TEAM & LEAGUE		GP	G	A	PTS	PIM
1972-73	**BUF**	**N**	66	4	15	19	178
1973-74			28	1	8	9	56
1974-75			68	1	19	20	184
1975-76			56	2	22	24	114
1976-77			65	7	25	32	97
1977-78			60	2	20	22	89
1978-79			46	8	17	25	67
1979-80			77	9	27	36	72
1980-81			71	8	25	33	110
1981-82			13	3	2	5	30
	DET	**N**	39	5	9	14	69
	2 team total		52	8	11	19	99
1982-83			57	1	10	11	18
11 yrs.		**N Totals:**	646	51	199	250	1084
PLAYOFFS							
1972-73	**BUF**	**N**	6	2	1	3	4
1974-75			17	1	4	5	38
1975-76			9	0	3	3	33
1976-77			6	0	0	0	12
1977-78			8	0	1	1	28
1978-79			3	0	1	1	0
1979-80			14	0	3	3	10
1980-81			8	0	0	0	14
8 yrs.		**N Totals:**	71	3	13	16	139

Traded to **Detroit** by Buffalo along with Danny Gare and Derek Smith for Mike Foligno, Dale McCourt and Brent Peterson Dec. 2, 1981. Signed as a free agent by **Boston** Aug. 20, 1983.

Dwight Schofield

SCHOFIELD, DWIGHT 6'1", 210 lbs.
B. Mar. 25, 1956, Waltham, Mass. Defense, Shoots L

YEAR	TEAM & LEAGUE		GP	G	A	PTS	PIM
1976-77	DET	N	3	1	0	1	2
1982-83	MONT	N	2	0	0	0	7
2 yrs.		N Totals:	5	1	0	1	9

Jim Schraefel

SCHRAEFEL, JAMES 6'1", 180 lbs.
B. Aug. 23, 1948, Dauphin, Man. Center, Shoots L

YEAR	TEAM & LEAGUE		GP	G	A	PTS	PIM
1973-74	EDM	W	34	1	1	2	0
PLAYOFFS							
1973-74	EDM	W	5	0	3	3	0

Sweeney Schriner

SCHRINER, DAVID
B. Nov. 30, 1911, Calgary, Alta. Left Wing
Won Art Ross Trophy, 1935–36, 1936-37
Won Calder Trophy, 1934-35
Hall of Fame, 1962

YEAR	TEAM & LEAGUE		GP	G	A	PTS	PIM
1934-35	NYA	N	48	18	22	40	6
1935-36			48	19	26	**45**	8
1936-37			48	21	25	**46**	17
1937-38			48	21	17	38	22
1938-39			48	13	31	44	20
1939-40	TOR	N	39	11	15	26	10
1940-41			48	24	14	38	6
1941-42			47	20	16	36	21
1942-43			37	19	17	36	13
1944-45			26	27	15	42	10
1945-46			47	13	6	19	15
11 yrs.		N Totals:	484	206	204	410	148
PLAYOFFS							
1935-36	NYA	N	5	3	1	4	2
1937-38			6	1	0	1	0
1938-39			2	0	0	0	30
1939-40	TOR	N	10	1	3	4	4
1940-41			7	2	1	3	4
1941-42*			13	6	3	9	10
1942-43			4	2	2	4	0
1944-45*			13	3	1	4	4
8 yrs.		N Totals:	60	18	11	29	54

Dave Schultz

SCHULTZ, DAVID WILLIAM (The Hammer)
6'1", 190 lbs.
B. Oct. 14, 1949, Waldheim, Sask. Left Wing, Shoots L

YEAR	TEAM & LEAGUE		GP	G	A	PTS	PIM
1971-72	PHI	N	1	0	0	0	0
1972-73			76	9	12	21	**259**
1973-74			73	20	16	36	**348**
1974-75			76	9	17	26	**472**[1]
1975-76			71	13	19	32	307
1976-77	LA	N	76	10	20	30	232
1977-78			8	2	0	2	27
	PITT	N	66	9	25	34	378
	2 team total		74	11	25	36	**405**
1978-79			47	4	9	13	157
	BUF	N	28	2	3	5	86
	2 team total		75	6	12	18	243
1979-80			13	1	0	1	28
9 yrs.		N Totals:	535	79	121	200	2294
PLAYOFFS							
1972-73	PHI	N	11	1	0	1	51
1973-74*			17	2	4	6	139
1974-75*			17	2	3	5	83
1975-76			16	2	2	4	90
1976-77	LA	N	9	1	1	2	45
1978-79	BUF	N	3	0	2	2	4
6 yrs.		N Totals:	73	8	12	20	412

Maynard Schurman

SCHURMAN, MAYNARD F. (M.F.) 6'3", 205 lbs.
B. July 16, 1957, Summerdale, P.E.I. Left Wing, Shoots L

YEAR	TEAM & LEAGUE		GP	G	A	PTS	PIM
1979-80	HART	N	7	0	0	0	0

Rod Schutt

SCHUTT, RODNEY 5'10", 185 lbs.
B. Oct. 13, 1956, Bancroft, Ont. Left Wing, Shoots L

YEAR	TEAM & LEAGUE		GP	G	A	PTS	PIM
1977-78	MONT	N	2	0	0	0	0
1978-79	PITT	N	74	24	21	45	33
1979-80			73	18	21	39	43
1980-81			80	25	35	60	55
1981-82			35	9	12	21	42
1982-83			5	0	0	0	0
6 yrs.		N Totals:	269	76	89	165	173
PLAYOFFS							
1978-79	PITT	N	7	2	0	2	4
1979-80			5	2	1	3	6
1980-81			5	3	3	6	16
1981-82			5	1	2	3	0
4 yrs.		N Totals:	22	8	6	14	26

Traded to **Pittsburgh** by Montreal for Pittsburgh's first round choice (Mark Hunter) in the 1981 Entry Draft, Oct. 18, 1978.

Enio Sclisizzi

SCLISIZZI, ENIO JAMES 5'10", 168 lbs.
B. Aug. 1, 1925, Milton, Ont. Left Wing, Shoots L

YEAR	TEAM & LEAGUE		GP	G	A	PTS	PIM
1947-48	DET	N	4	1	0	1	0
1948-49			50	9	8	17	24
1949-50			4	0	0	0	2
1951-52			9	2	1	3	0
1952-53	CHI	N	14	0	2	2	0
5 yrs.		N Totals:	81	12	11	23	26
PLAYOFFS							
1946-47	DET	N	1	0	0	0	0
1947-48			6	0	0	0	4
1948-49			6	0	0	0	2
3 yrs.		N Totals:	13	0	0	0	6

Sold to **Chicago** by Detroit with Fred Glover, Aug. 14, 1952.

Ganton Scott

SCOTT , GANTON
B. Unknown Right Wing

YEAR	TEAM & LEAGUE		GP	G	A	PTS	PIM
1922-23	TOR	N	17	0	0	0	0
1923-24			4	0	0	0	0
	HAMIL	N	4	0	0	0	0
	2 team total		8	0	0	0	0
1924-25	MON(M)	N	28	1	1	2	0
1926-27	TOR	N	1	0	0	0	0
4 yrs.		N Totals:	54	1	1	2	0

Laurie Scott

SCOTT, LAWRENCE 5'6", 155 lbs.
B. June 19, 1900, South River, Ont. Forward, Shoots L

YEAR	TEAM & LEAGUE		GP	G	A	PTS	PIM
1926-27	NYA	N	39	6	2	8	22
1927-28	NYR	N	23	0	1	1	6
2 yrs.		N Totals:	62	6	3	9	28

Howard Scruton

SCRUTON, HOWARD 6'3", 190 lbs.
B. Oct. 6, 1962, Toronto, Ont. Defense, Shoots L

YEAR	TEAM & LEAGUE		GP	G	A	PTS	PIM
1982-83	LA	N	4	0	4	4	9

Signed by **Los Angeles** as a free agent, Aug. 5, 1981.

Al Secord

SECORD, ALAN (Big Al) 6'1", 205 lbs.
B. Mar. 3, 1958, Sudbury, Ont. Left Wing, Shoots L

YEAR	TEAM & LEAGUE		GP	G	A	PTS	PIM
1978-79	BOS	N	71	16	7	23	125

Al Secord continued

YEAR	TEAM & LEAGUE	GP	G	A	PTS	PIM
1979-80		77	23	16	39	170
1980-81		18	0	3	3	42
	CHI N	41	13	9	22	145
	2 team total	59	13	12	25	187
1981-82		80	44	31	75	303
1982-83		80	54	32	86	180
5 yrs.	**N Totals:**	367	150	98	248	965
PLAYOFFS						
1978-79	**BOS N**	4	0	0	0	4
1979-80		10	0	3	3	65
1980-81	**CHI N**	3	4	0	4	14
1981-82		15	2	5	7	61
1982-83		12	4	7	11	66
5 yrs.	**N Totals:**	44	10	15	25	210

Traded to **Chicago** by Boston for Mike O'Connell, Dec. 18, 1980.

Ron Sedlbauer

SEDLBAUER, RONALD ANDREW 6'3", 200 lbs.
B. Oct. 22, 1954, Burlington, Ont. Left Wing, Shoots L

YEAR	TEAM & LEAGUE	GP	G	A	PTS	PIM
1974-75	**VAN N**	26	3	4	7	17
1975-76		56	19	13	32	66
1976-77		70	18	20	38	29
1977-78		62	18	12	30	25
1978-79		79	40	16	56	26
1979-80		32	10	4	14	7
	CHI N	45	13	10	23	14
	2 team total	77	23	14	37	21
1980-81		39	12	3	15	12
	TOR N	21	10	4	14	14
	2 team total	60	22	7	29	26
7 yrs.	**N Totals:**	430	143	86	229	210
PLAYOFFS						
1974-75	**VAN N**	5	0	0	0	10
1975-76		2	0	0	0	0
1978-79		3	0	1	1	9
1979-80	**CHI N**	7	1	1	2	6
1980-81	**TOR N**	2	0	1	1	2
5 yrs.	**N Totals:**	19	1	3	4	27

Traded to **Chicago** by Vancouver for Dave Logan and Harold Phillipoff, Dec. 21, 1979. Purchased by **Toronto** from Chicago, Feb. 18, 1981.

Dan Seguin

SEGUIN, DANIEL G. 5'8", 165 lbs.
B. June 7, 1948, Sudbury, Ont. Left Wing, Shoots L

YEAR	TEAM & LEAGUE	GP	G	A	PTS	PIM
1970-71	**MINN N**	11	1	1	2	4
	VAN N	25	0	5	5	46
	2 team total	36	1	6	7	50
1973-74		1	1	0	1	0
2 yrs.	**N Totals:**	37	2	6	8	50

Claimed on waivers by **Vancouver** from Minnesota, Nov. 23, 1970.

Earl Seibert

SEIBERT, EARL 6'2", 198 lbs.
B. Dec. 7, 1911, Kitchener, Ont. Defense
Hall of Fame, 1963

YEAR	TEAM & LEAGUE	GP	G	A	PTS	PIM
1931-32	**NYR N**	44	4	6	10	88
1932-33		45	2	3	5	92
1933-34		48	13	10	23	66
1934-35		48	6	19	25	86
1935-36		15	3	3	6	6
	CHI N	29	2	6	8	21
	2 team total	44	5	9	14	27
1936-37		43	9	6	15	46
1937-38		48	8	13	21	38
1938-39		48	4	11	15	57
1939-40		36	3	7	10	35
1940-41		46	3	17	20	52
1941-42		46	7	14	21	52
1942-43		44	5	27	32	48
1943-44		50	8	25	33	40
1944-45		22	7	8	15	13
	DET N	25	5	9	14	10
	2 team total	47	12	17	29	23
1945-46		18	0	3	3	18
15 yrs.	**N Totals:**	655	89	187	276	768

Earl Seibert continued

YEAR	TEAM & LEAGUE	GP	G	A	PTS	PIM
PLAYOFFS						
1931-32	**NYR N**	7	1	2	3	4
1932-33*		8	1	0	1	14
1933-34		2	0	0	0	4
1934-35		4	0	0	0	6
1935-36	**CHI N**	2	2	0	2	0
1937-38*		10	5	2	7	12
1939-40		2	0	1	1	8
1940-41		5	0	0	0	12
1941-42		3	0	0	0	0
1943-44		9	0	2	2	2
1944-45	**DET N**	14	2	1	3	4
11 yrs.	**N Totals:**	66	11	8	19	66

Ric Seiling

SEILING, RICHARD JAMES 6'1", 178 lbs.
B. Dec. 15, 1957, Elmire, Ont. Right Wing, Shoots R

YEAR	TEAM & LEAGUE	GP	G	A	PTS	PIM
1977-78	**BUF N**	80	19	19	38	33
1978-79		78	20	22	42	56
1979-80		80	25	35	60	54
1980-81		74	30	27	57	80
1981-82		57	22	25	47	58
1982-83		75	19	22	41	41
6 yrs.	**N Totals:**	444	135	150	285	322
PLAYOFFS						
1977-78	**BUF N**	8	0	2	2	7
1978-79		3	0	1	1	2
1979-80		14	5	4	9	6
1980-81		8	2	2	4	2
1981-82		4	1	1	2	2
1982-83		10	2	3	5	6
6 yrs.	**N Totals:**	47	10	13	23	25

Rod Seiling

SEILING, RODNEY ALBERT (Sod) 6', 195 lbs.
B. Nov. 14, 1944, Elmira, Ont. Defense, Shoots L

YEAR	TEAM & LEAGUE	GP	G	A	PTS	PIM
1962-63	**TOR N**	1	0	1	1	0
1963-64	**NYR N**	2	0	1	1	0
1964-65		68	4	22	26	44
1965-66		52	5	10	15	24
1966-67		12	1	1	2	6
1967-68		71	5	11	16	44
1968-69		73	4	17	21	75
1969-70		76	5	21	26	68
1970-71		68	5	22	27	34
1971-72		78	5	36	41	62
1972-73		72	9	33	42	36
1973-74		68	7	23	30	32
1974-75		4	0	1	1	0
	WASH N	1	0	0	0	0
	TOR N	60	5	12	17	40
	3 team total	65	5	13	18	40
1975-76		77	3	16	19	46
1976-77	**STL N**	79	3	26	29	36
1977-78		78	1	11	12	40
1978-79		3	0	1	1	4
	ATL N	36	0	4	4	12
	2 team total	39	0	5	5	16
17 yrs.	**N Totals:**	979	62	269	331	603
PLAYOFFS						
1967-68	**NYR N**	6	0	2	2	4
1968-69		4	1	0	1	2
1969-70		2	0	0	0	0
1970-71		13	1	0	1	12
1971-72		16	1	4	5	10
1973-74		13	0	2	2	19
1974-75	**TOR N**	7	0	0	0	0
1975-76		10	0	1	1	6
1976-77	**STL N**	4	0	0	0	2
1978-79	**ATL N**	2	0	0	0	0
10 yrs.	**N Totals:**	77	3	9	12	55

Traded to **N.Y. Rangers** by Toronto with Dick Duff, Bob Nevin, Arnie Brown and Bill Collins for Andy Bathgate and Don McKenney, Feb. 22, 1964. Drafted by **St. Louis** from N.Y Rangers in Expansion Draft, June 6, 1967. Traded to **N.Y. Rangers** by St. Louis for Gary Sabourin, Bob Plager, Gord Kannegiesser and Tim Ecclestone, June 6, 1967. Claimed on waivers by

Washington from N.Y. Rangers, Oct. 29, 1974. Traded to **Toronto** by Washington for Tim Ecclestone and Willie Brossart, Nov. 2, 1974. Signed as free agent by **St. Louis** from Toronto, Sept. 9, 1976. As compensation, Toronto received cash and St. Louis' second round choice (Joel Quenneville) in the 1978 Amateur Draft. Sold to **Atlanta** by St. Louis, Nov. 4, 1978.

Brit Selby

SELBY, ROBERT BRITON 5'10", 175 lbs.
B. Mar. 27, 1945, Kingston, Ont. Left Wing, Shoots L
Won Calder Trophy, 1965-66

YEAR	TEAM & LEAGUE		GP	G	A	PTS	PIM
1964-65	**TOR**	**N**	3	2	0	2	2
1965-66			61	14	13	27	26
1966-67			6	1	1	2	0
1967-68	**PHI**	**N**	56	15	15	30	24
1968-69			63	10	13	23	23
	TOR	**N**	14	2	2	4	19
	2 team total		77	12	15	27	42
1969-70			74	10	13	23	40
1970-71			11	0	1	1	6
	STL	**N**	53	1	4	5	23
	2 team total		64	1	5	6	29
1971-72			6	0	0	0	8
1972-73	**QUE**	**W**	7	0	1	1	4
	NE	**W**	65	13	29	42	48
	2 team total		72	13	30	43	52
1973-74	**TOR**	**W**	64	9	17	26	21
1974-75			17	1	4	5	0
11 yrs.		**N Totals:**	347	55	62	117	171
		W Totals:	153	23	51	74	73

PLAYOFFS

YEAR	TEAM & LEAGUE		GP	G	A	PTS	PIM
1965-66	**TOR**	**N**	4	0	0	0	0
1967-68	**PHI**	**N**	7	1	1	2	4
1968-69	**TOR**	**N**	4	0	0	0	4
1970-71	**STL**	**N**	1	0	0	0	0
1972-73	**NE**	**W**	13	3	4	7	13
1973-74	**TOR**	**W**	10	1	3	4	2
6 yrs.		**N Totals:**	16	1	1	2	8
		W Totals:	23	4	7	11	15

Drafted by **Philadelphia** from Toronto in Expansion Draft, June 6, 1967. Traded to **Toronto** by Philadelphia with Forbes Kennedy for Gerry Meehan and Mike Byers, March 2, 1969. Traded to **St. Louis** by Toronto for Bob Baun, Nov. 13, 1970.

Steve Self

SELF, STEVEN 5'9", 170 lbs.
B. May 9, 1950, Peterborough, Ont. Center, Shoots L

YEAR	TEAM & LEAGUE		GP	G	A	PTS	PIM
1976-77	**WASH**	**N**	3	0	0	0	0

Brad Selwood

SELWOOD, BRADLEY WAYNE 6'1", 200 lbs.
B. Mar. 18, 1948, Leamington, Ont. Defense, Shoots L

YEAR	TEAM & LEAGUE		GP	G	A	PTS	PIM
1970-71	**TOR**	**N**	28	2	10	12	13
1971-72			72	4	17	21	58
1972-73	**NE**	**W**	75	13	21	34	114
1973-74			76	9	28	37	91
1974-75			77	4	35	39	117
1975-76			40	2	10	12	28
1976-77			41	4	12	16	71
1977-78			80	6	25	31	88
1978-79			42	4	12	16	47
1979-80	**LA**	**N**	63	1	13	14	82
10 yrs.		**N Totals:**	163	7	40	47	153
		W Totals:	431	42	143	185	556

PLAYOFFS

YEAR	TEAM & LEAGUE		GP	G	A	PTS	PIM
1971-72	**TOR**	**N**	5	0	0	0	4
1972-73	**NE**	**W**	15	3	5	8	22
1973-74			7	0	2	2	11
1974-75			5	1	0	1	11
1975-76			17	2	2	4	27
1976-77			5	0	0	0	2
1977-78			14	0	3	3	8
1979-80	**LA**	**N**	1	0	0	0	0
8 yrs.		**N Totals:**	6	0	0	0	4
		W Totals:	63	6	12	18	81

Put on **Montreal** reserve list from Toronto via Intra-league Draft, June 5, 1972. Traded to **Los Angeles** by Montreal for switch of fourth-round choices in the 1982 Entry Draft, Sept. 14, 1979.

YEAR TEAM & LEAGUE GP G A PTS PIM

Dave Semenko

SEMENKO, DAVID (Sam) 6'3", 200 lbs.
B. July 12, 1957, Winnipeg, Man. Left Wing, Shoots L

YEAR	TEAM & LEAGUE		GP	G	A	PTS	PIM
1977-78	**EDM**	**W**	65	6	6	12	140
1978-79			77	10	14	24	158
1979-80	**EDM**	**N**	67	6	7	13	135
1980-81			58	11	8	19	80
1981-82			59	12	12	24	194
1982-83			75	12	15	27	141
6 yrs.		**N Totals:**	259	41	42	83	550
		W Totals:	142	16	20	36	298

PLAYOFFS

YEAR	TEAM & LEAGUE		GP	G	A	PTS	PIM
1977-78	**EDM**	**W**	5	0	0	0	8
1978-79			11	4	2	6	29
1979-80	**EDM**	**N**	3	0	0	0	2
1980-81			8	0	0	0	5
1981-82			4	0	0	0	2
1982-83			15	1	1	2	69
6 yrs.		**N Totals:**	30	1	1	2	78
		W Totals:	16	4	2	6	37

Reclaimed by **Minnesota** from Edmonton prior to Expansion Draft, June 9, 1979. Traded to **Edmonton** by Minnesota for Edmonton's second (Neal Broten) and third (Kevin Maxwell) round draft picks in 1979 Entry Draft, Aug. 9, 1979.

George Senick

SENICK, GEORGE 5'10", 175 lbs.
B. Sept. 16, 1929, Saskatoon, Sask. Left Wing, Shoots L

YEAR	TEAM & LEAGUE		GP	G	A	PTS	PIM
1952-53	**NYR**	**N**	13	2	3	5	8

Dick Sentes

SENTES, RICHARD JAMES 5'11", 180 lbs.
B. Jan. 10, 1947, Regina, Sask. Right Wing, Shoots L

YEAR	TEAM & LEAGUE		GP	G	A	PTS	PIM
1972-73	**OTTA**	**W**	73	22	19	41	78
1973-74	**TOR**	**W**	64	26	34	60	46
1974-75	**SD**	**W**	74	44	41	85	52
1975-76	**CALG**	**W**	72	25	24	49	33
1976-77			29	10	14	24	8
	SD	**W**	24	10	11	21	16
	2 team total		53	20	25	45	24
5 yrs.		**W Totals:**	336	137	143	280	233

PLAYOFFS

YEAR	TEAM & LEAGUE		GP	G	A	PTS	PIM
1972-73	**OTTA**	**W**	5	3	1	4	2
1973-74	**TOR**	**W**	12	7	4	11	19
1974-75	**SD**	**W**	10	0	2	2	0
1975-76	**CALG**	**W**	8	0	1	1	8
1976-77	**SD**	**W**	5	0	4	4	12
5 yrs.		**W Totals:**	40	10	12	22	41

Ron Serafini

SERAFINI, RONALD 5'11", 185 lbs.
B. Oct. 31, 1953, Detroit, Mich. Defense, Shoots R

YEAR	TEAM & LEAGUE		GP	G	A	PTS	PIM
1973-74	**CALIF**	**N**	2	0	0	0	2
1975-76	**CIN**	**W**	16	0	2	2	15
2 yrs.		**N Totals:**	2	0	0	0	2
		W Totals:	16	0	2	2	15

Traded to **St. Louis** by California for Glenn Patrick, July 18, 1974.

Tom Serviss

SERVISS, THOMAS HUGH 5'10", 185 lbs.
B. May 25, 1948, Moose Jaw, Sask. Right Wing, Shoots R

YEAR	TEAM & LEAGUE		GP	G	A	PTS	PIM
1972-73	**LA**	**W**	73	11	26	37	32
1973-74			74	6	15	21	37
1974-75	**M-B**	**W**	61	12	17	29	18
1975-76	**QUE**	**W**	71	7	19	26	12
1976-77	**CALG**	**W**	8	2	1	3	2
5 yrs.		**W Totals:**	287	38	78	116	101

PLAYOFFS

YEAR	TEAM & LEAGUE		GP	G	A	PTS	PIM
1975-76	**QUE**	**W**	5	0	0	0	0

Eddie Shack

SHACK, EDWARD STEVEN PHILLIP (The Entertainer)
6'1", 200 lbs.
B. Feb. 11, 1937, Sudbury, Ont. Right Wing, Shoots L

YEAR	TEAM & LEAGUE		GP	G	A	PTS	PIM
1958-59	**NYR**	**N**	67	7	14	21	109
1959-60			62	8	10	18	110
1960-61			12	1	2	3	17
	TOR	**N**	55	14	14	28	90
	2 team total		67	15	16	31	107
1961-62			44	7	14	21	62
1962-63			63	16	9	25	97
1963-64			64	11	10	21	128
1964-65			67	5	9	14	68
1965-66			63	26	17	43	88
1966-67			63	11	14	25	58
1967-68	**BOS**	**N**	70	23	19	42	107
1968-69			50	11	11	22	74
1969-70	**LA**	**N**	73	22	12	34	113
1970-71			11	2	2	4	8
	BUF	**N**	56	25	17	42	93
	2 team total		67	27	19	46	101
1971-72			50	11	14	25	34
	PITT	**N**	18	5	9	14	12
	2 team total		68	16	23	39	46
1972-73			74	25	20	45	84
1973-74	**TOR**	**N**	59	7	8	15	74
1974-75			26	2	1	3	11
17 yrs.		**N Totals:**	1047	239	226	465	1437
PLAYOFFS							
1960-61	**TOR**	**N**	4	0	0	0	2
1961-62*			9	0	0	0	18
1962-63*			10	2	1	3	11
1963-64*			13	0	1	1	25
1964-65			5	1	0	1	8
1965-66			4	2	1	3	33
1966-67*			8	0	0	0	8
1967-68	**BOS**	**N**	4	0	1	1	6
1968-69			9	0	2	2	23
1971-72	**PITT**	**N**	4	0	1	1	15
1973-74	**TOR**	**N**	4	1	0	1	2
11 yrs.		**N Totals:**	74	6	7	13	151

Traded to **Toronto** by N.Y. Rangers for Pat Hannigan and John Wilson, Nov. 1960. Traded to **Boston** by Toronto for Murray Oliver and cash, May 15, 1967. Traded to **Los Angeles** by Boston with Ross Lonsberry for Ken Turlik and Los Angeles' first-round choices in the 1971 (Ron Jones) and 1973 (Andre Savard) Amateur Drafts, May 14, 1969. Traded to **Pittsburgh** by Buffalo for Rene Robert, March 4, 1972. Sold to **Toronto** by Pittsburgh, July 3, 1973.

Joe Shack

SHACK, JOSEPH 5'10", 170 lbs.
B. Dec. 3, 1915, Winnipeg, Man. Left Wing

YEAR	TEAM & LEAGUE		GP	G	A	PTS	PIM
1942-43	**NYR**	**N**	20	5	9	14	6
1944-45			50	18	4	22	14
2 yrs.		**N Totals:**	70	23	13	36	20

Paul Shakes

SHAKES, PAUL STEVEN 5'10", 172 lbs.
B. Sept. 4, 1952, Collingwood, Ont. Defense, Shoots R

YEAR	TEAM & LEAGUE		GP	G	A	PTS	PIM
1973-74	**CALIF**	**N**	21	0	4	4	12

Sean Shanahan

SHANAHAN, SEAN BRYAN 6'3", 210 lbs.
B. Feb. 8, 1951, Toronto, Ont. Left Wing, Shoots R

YEAR	TEAM & LEAGUE		GP	G	A	PTS	PIM
1975-76	**MONT**	**N**	4	0	0	0	0
1976-77	**COLO**	**N**	30	1	3	4	40
1977-78	**BOS**	**N**	6	0	0	0	7
1978-79	**CIN**	**W**	4	0	0	0	7
4 yrs.		**N Totals:**	40	1	3	4	47
		W Totals:	4	0	0	0	7

Sold to **Colorado** by Montreal with Ron Andruff, Sept. 13, 1976. Signed as a free agent by **Boston** Oct. 13, 1977. Signed as a free agent by **Detroit** June 6, 1978.

Dave Shand

SHAND, DAVID ALISTAIR 6'2", 200 lbs.
B. Aug. 11, 1956, Cold Lake, Alta. Defense, Shoots R

YEAR	TEAM & LEAGUE		GP	G	A	PTS	PIM
1976-77	**ATL**	**N**	55	5	11	16	62
1977-78			80	2	23	25	94
1978-79			79	4	22	26	64
1979-80			74	3	7	10	104
1980-81	**TOR**	**N**	47	0	4	4	60
1982-83			1	0	1	1	2
6 yrs.		**N Totals:**	336	14	68	82	386
PLAYOFFS							
1976-77	**ATL**	**N**	3	0	0	0	33
1977-78			2	0	0	0	4
1978-79			2	0	0	0	20
1979-80			4	0	1	1	0
1980-81	**TOR**	**N**	3	0	0	0	0
1982-83			4	1	0	1	13
6 yrs.		**N Totals:**	18	1	1	2	70

Traded to **Toronto** by Atlanta with Atlanta's (Calgary's) third round choice in 1980 Entry Draft (later traded to Washington) for Toronto's second round choice in 1980 Entry Draft (Kevin Lavallee), June 10, 1980.

Charles Shannon

SHANNON, CHARLES KITCHENER 5'10½", 192 lbs.
B. Mar. 22, 1916, Campbellford, Ont. Defense, Shoots L

YEAR	TEAM & LEAGUE		GP	G	A	PTS	PIM
1939-40	**NYA**	**N**	4	0	0	0	2

Gerry Shannon

SHANNON, GERALD EDMUND 5'11", 170 lbs.
B. Oct. 25, 1910, Campbellford, Ont. Shoots L

YEAR	TEAM & LEAGUE		GP	G	A	PTS	PIM
1933-34	**OTTA**	**N**	48	11	15	26	0
1934-35	**STL**	**N**	25	2	2	4	11
	BOS	**N**	17	1	1	2	4
	2 team total		42	3	3	6	15
1935-36			25	0	1	1	6
1936-37	**MON(M)**	**N**	32	9	7	16	20
1937-38			36	0	3	3	80
5 yrs.		**N Totals:**	183	23	29	52	121
PLAYOFFS							
1934-35	**BOS**	**N**	4	0	0	0	2
1936-37	**MON(M)**	**N**	5	0	1	1	0
2 yrs.		**N Totals:**	9	0	1	1	2

Glen Sharpley

SHARPLEY, GLEN STUART 6', 187 lbs.
B. Sept. 6, 1956, York, Ont. Center, Shoots R

YEAR	TEAM & LEAGUE		GP	G	A	PTS	PIM
1976-77	**MINN**	**N**	80	25	32	57	48
1977-78			79	22	33	55	42
1978-79			80	19	34	53	30
1979-80			51	20	27	47	38
1980-81			28	12	12	24	18
	CHI	**N**	35	10	16	26	12
	2 team total		63	22	28	50	30
1981-82			36	9	7	16	11
6 yrs.		**N Totals:**	389	117	161	278	199
PLAYOFFS							
1976-77	**MINN**	**N**	2	0	0	0	4
1979-80			9	1	6	7	4
1980-81	**CHI**	**N**	1	0	2	2	0
1981-82			15	6	3	9	16
4 yrs.		**N Totals:**	27	7	11	18	24

Traded to **Chicago** by Minnesota for Ken Solheim and Chicago's second round choice (Tom Hirsch) in 1981 Entry Draft, Dec. 29, 1980.

David Shaw

SHAW, DAVID 6'2", 187 lbs.
B. May 25, 1964, St. Thomas, Ont. Defense, Shoots R

YEAR	TEAM & LEAGUE		GP	G	A	PTS	PIM
1982-83	**QUE**	**N**	2	0	0	0	0

Norman Shay

SHAY, NORMAN
B. Unknown — Forward

YEAR	TEAM & LEAGUE		GP	G	A	PTS	PIM
1924-25	**BOS**	**N**	18	1	1	2	14
1925-26			13	1	0	1	2
	TOR	**N**	22	3	1	4	18
	2 team total		35	4	1	5	20
2 yrs.		**N Totals:**	53	5	2	7	34

Pat Shea

SHEA, FRANCIS
B. Oct. 29, 1912, Potlatch, Idaho — Defense

YEAR	TEAM & LEAGUE		GP	G	A	PTS	PIM
1931-32	**CHI**	**N**	14	0	1	1	0

Doug Shedden

SHEDDEN, DOUGLAS — 6', 184 lbs.
B. Apr. 29, 1961, Wallaceburg, Ont. — Center, Shoots R

YEAR	TEAM & LEAGUE		GP	G	A	PTS	PIM
1981-82	**PITT**	**N**	38	10	15	25	12
1982-83			80	24	43	67	54
2 yrs.		**N Totals:**	118	34	58	92	66

Bobby Sheehan

SHEEHAN, ROBERT RICHARD — 5'7", 155 lbs.
B. Jan. 11, 1949, Weymouth, Mass. — Center, Shoots L

YEAR	TEAM & LEAGUE		GP	G	A	PTS	PIM
1969-70	**MONT**	**N**	16	2	1	3	2
1970-71			29	6	5	11	2
1971-72	**CALIF**	**N**	78	20	26	46	12
1972-73	**NY**	**W**	75	35	53	88	17
1973-74	**NY-NJ**	**W**	50	12	8	20	8
	EDM	**W**	10	1	3	4	6
	2 team total		60	13	11	24	14
1974-75			77	19	39	58	8
1975-76	**CHI**	**N**	78	11	20	31	18
1976-77	**DET**	**N**	34	5	4	9	2
1977-78	**IND**	**W**	29	8	7	15	6
1979-80	**COLO**	**N**	30	3	4	7	2
1980-81			41	1	3	4	10
1981-82	**LA**	**N**	4	0	0	0	2
12 yrs.		**N Totals:**	310	48	63	111	50
		W Totals:	241	75	110	185	45

PLAYOFFS

YEAR	TEAM & LEAGUE		GP	G	A	PTS	PIM
1970-71*	**MONT**	**N**	6	0	0	0	0
1973-74	**EDM**	**W**	5	1	3	4	0
1975-76	**CHI**	**N**	4	0	0	0	0
1978-79	**NYR**	**N**	15	4	3	7	8
4 yrs.		**N Totals:**	25	4	3	7	8
		W Totals:	5	1	3	4	0

Sold to **California** by Montreal, May 25, 1971. Traded to **Chicago** by California with Dick Redmond for Darryl Maggs, Dec. 5, 1972. Signed as free agent by **Detroit** from Chicago, Oct. 8, 1976. Signed as free agent by **N.Y. Rangers** Oct. 1, 1978. Traded by N.Y. Rangers (New Haven, AHL) to **Colorado** for future considerations, May 12, 1979. Signed as free agent by **Los Angeles** July 8, 1981.

Tim Sheehy

SHEEHY, TIMOTHY KANE — 6'1", 185 lbs.
B. Sept. 3, 1948, Fort Frances, Ont. — Right Wing, Shoots R

YEAR	TEAM & LEAGUE		GP	G	A	PTS	PIM
1972-73	**NE**	**W**	78	33	38	71	30
1973-74			77	29	29	58	22
1974-75			52	20	13	33	18
	EDM	**W**	29	8	20	28	4
	2 team total		81	28	33	61	22
1975-76			81	34	31	65	17
1976-77			28	15	8	23	4
	BIRM	**W**	50	26	21	47	44
	2 team total		78	41	29	70	48
1977-78			13	4	2	6	5
	DET	**N**	15	0	0	0	0
	NE	**W**	25	8	11	19	12
	3 team total		53	12	13	25	17
1979-80	**HART**	**N**	12	2	1	3	0
7 yrs.		**N Totals:**	27	2	1	3	0
		W Totals:	433	177	173	350	156

PLAYOFFS

YEAR	TEAM & LEAGUE		GP	G	A	PTS	PIM
1972-73	**NE**	**W**	15	9	14	23	13

Tim Sheehy continued

YEAR	TEAM & LEAGUE		GP	G	A	PTS	PIM
1973-74			7	4	2	6	4
1975-76	**EDM**	**W**	4	2	2	4	0
1977-78	**NE**	**W**	13	1	3	4	9
4 yrs.		**W Totals:**	39	16	21	37	26

Doug Shelton

SHELTON, WAYNE DOUGLAS — 5'9", 175 lbs.
B. June 27, 1945, Woodstock, Ont. — Right Wing, Shoots R

YEAR	TEAM & LEAGUE		GP	G	A	PTS	PIM
1967-68	**CHI**	**N**	5	0	1	1	2

Frank Sheppard

SHEPPARD, JOSEPH FRANCIS XAVIER — 5'6", 157 lbs.
B. Oct. 19, 1907, Montreal, Que. — Center, Shoots L

YEAR	TEAM & LEAGUE		GP	G	A	PTS	PIM
1927-28	**DET**	**N**	8	1	1	2	0

Gregg Sheppard

SHEPPARD, GREGORY WAYNE — 5'8", 170 lbs.
B. Apr. 23, 1949, North Battleford, Sask. — Center, Shoots L

YEAR	TEAM & LEAGUE		GP	G	A	PTS	PIM
1972-73	**BOS**	**N**	64	24	26	50	18
1973-74			75	16	31	47	21
1974-75			76	30	48	78	19
1975-76			70	31	43	74	28
1976-77			77	31	36	67	20
1977-78			54	23	36	59	24
1978-79	**PITT**	**N**	60	15	22	37	9
1979-80			76	13	24	37	20
1980-81			47	11	17	28	49
1981-82			58	11	10	21	35
10 yrs.		**N Totals:**	657	205	293	498	243

PLAYOFFS

YEAR	TEAM & LEAGUE		GP	G	A	PTS	PIM
1972-73	**BOS**	**N**	5	2	1	3	0
1973-74			16	11	8	19	4
1974-75			3	3	1	4	5
1975-76			12	5	6	11	6
1976-77			14	5	7	12	8
1977-78			15	2	10	12	6
1978-79	**PITT**	**N**	7	1	2	3	0
1979-80			5	1	1	2	0
1980-81			5	2	4	6	2
9 yrs.		**N Totals:**	82	32	40	72	31

Traded to **Atlanta** by Boston for Dick Redmond; Atlanta then traded Sheppard to **Pittsburgh** for Jean Pronovost, all on Sept. 6, 1978.

Johnny Sheppard

SHEPPARD, JOHN O. — 5'7", 165 lbs.
B. Oct. 19, 1907, Montreal, Que. — Left Wing, Shoots L

YEAR	TEAM & LEAGUE		GP	G	A	PTS	PIM
1926-27	**DET**	**N**	43	13	8	21	60
1927-28			44	10	10	20	40
1928-29	**NYA**	**N**	43	5	4	9	38
1929-30			43	14	15	29	32
1930-31			42	5	8	13	16
1931-32			8	1	0	1	2
1932-33			46	17	9	26	32
1933-34	**BOS**	**N**	4	0	0	0	0
	CHI	**N**	38	3	4	7	4
	2 team total		42	3	4	7	4
8 yrs.		**N Totals:**	311	68	58	126	224

PLAYOFFS

YEAR	TEAM & LEAGUE		GP	G	A	PTS	PIM
1928-29	**NYA**	**N**	2	0	0	0	0
1933-34*	**CHI**	**N**	8	0	0	0	0
2 yrs.		**N Totals:**	10	0	0	0	0

John Sherf

SHERF, JOHN HAROLD — 5'11½", 178 lbs.
B. Apr. 8, 1914, Calumet, Mich. — Left Wing, Shoots L

YEAR	TEAM & LEAGUE		GP	G	A	PTS	PIM
1935-36	**DET**	**N**	1	0	0	0	0
1936-37			1	0	0	0	0
1937-38			6	0	0	0	2
1938-39			3	0	0	0	0
1943-44			8	0	0	0	6

John Sherf continued

YEAR	TEAM & LEAGUE		GP	G	A	PTS	PIM
5 yrs.		N Totals:	19	0	0	0	8
PLAYOFFS							
1936-37*	DET	N	5	0	1	1	2
1938-39			3	0	0	0	0
2 yrs.		N Totals:	8	0	1	1	2

John Sheridan

SHERIDAN, JOHN 6'1", 190 lbs.
B. Sept. 18, 1954, Minneapolis, Minn. Center, Shoots L

YEAR	TEAM & LEAGUE		GP	G	A	PTS	PIM
1974-75	IND	W	58	17	11	28	20
1975-76			11	1	2	3	0
2 yrs.		W Totals:	69	18	13	31	20

Fred Shero

SHERO, FRED ALEXANDER (The Fog) 5'10", 185 lbs.
B. Oct. 23, 1925, Winnipeg, Man. Defense, Shoots L
Won Jack Adams Award, 1973-74

YEAR	TEAM & LEAGUE		GP	G	A	PTS	PIM
1947-48	NYR	N	19	1	0	1	2
1948-49			59	3	6	9	64
1949-50			67	2	8	10	71
3 yrs.		N Totals:	145	6	14	20	137
PLAYOFFS							
1947-48	NYR	N	6	0	1	1	6
1949-50			7	0	1	1	2
2 yrs.		N Totals:	13	0	2	2	8

Jim Sherrit

SHERRIT, JAMES 5'7", 170 lbs.
B. Sept. 29, 1948, Glasgow, Scotland Center, Shoots L

YEAR	TEAM & LEAGUE		GP	G	A	PTS	PIM
1973-74	HOUS	W	76	30	28	58	18
1974-75			77	22	25	47	25
1975-76	D-O	W	40	11	19	30	16
3 yrs.		W Totals:	193	63	72	135	59
PLAYOFFS							
1973-74	HOUS	W	14	5	7	12	2
1974-75			13	3	3	6	6
2 yrs.		W Totals:	27	8	10	18	8

Moose Sherritt

SHERRITT, GORDON EPHRAIM 6'1", 195 lbs.
B. Apr. 8, 1920, Oakville, Man. Defense, Shoots L

YEAR	TEAM & LEAGUE		GP	G	A	PTS	PIM
1943-44	DET	N	8	0	0	0	12

Jack Shewchuk

SHEWCHUK, JOHN MICHAEL 6'1", 190 lbs.
B. June 19, 1917, Brantford, Ont. Defense, Shoots L

YEAR	TEAM & LEAGUE		GP	G	A	PTS	PIM
1938-39	BOS	N	3	0	0	0	2
1939-40			47	2	4	6	55
1940-41			20	2	2	4	8
1941-42			22	2	0	2	14
1942-43			48	2	6	8	50
1944-45			47	1	7	8	31
6 yrs.		N Totals:	187	9	19	28	160
PLAYOFFS							
1939-40	BOS	N	6	0	0	0	0
1941-42			5	0	1	1	7
1942-43			9	0	0	0	12
3 yrs.		N Totals:	20	0	1	1	19

Alex Shibicky

SHIBICKY, ALEX 6', 180 lbs.
B. May 19, 1914, Winnipeg, Man. Right Wing, Shoots R

YEAR	TEAM & LEAGUE		GP	G	A	PTS	PIM
1935-36	NYR	N	18	4	2	6	6
1936-37			47	14	8	22	30
1937-38			43	17	18	35	26
1938-39			48	24	9	33	24
1939-40			43	11	21	32	33
1940-41			40	10	14	24	14

Alex Shibicky continued

YEAR	TEAM & LEAGUE		GP	G	A	PTS	PIM
1941-42			45	20	14	34	16
1945-46			33	10	5	15	12
8 yrs.		N Totals:	317	110	91	201	161
PLAYOFFS							
1936-37	NYR	N	9	1	4	5	0
1937-38			3	2	0	2	2
1938-39			7	3	1	4	2
1939-40*			12	2	5	7	4
1940-41			3	1	0	1	2
1941-42			6	3	2	5	2
6 yrs.		N Totals:	40	12	12	24	12

Al Shields

SHIELDS, ALLEN 6', 188 lbs.
B. May 10, 1907, Ottawa, Ont. Defense, Shoots R

YEAR	TEAM & LEAGUE		GP	G	A	PTS	PIM
1927-28	OTTA	N	6	0	1	1	2
1928-29			42	0	1	1	10
1929-30			44	6	3	9	32
1930-31	PHI	N	43	7	3	10	98
1931-32	NYA	N	48	4	1	5	45
1932-33	OTTA	N	48	4	7	11	119
1933-34			48	4	7	11	44
1934-35	MON(M)	N	43	4	8	12	45
1935-36			45	2	7	9	81
1936-37	NYA	N	27	3	0	3	79
	BOS	N	18	0	4	4	15
	2 team total		45	3	4	7	94
1937-38	MON(M)	N	48	5	7	12	67
11 yrs.		N Totals:	460	39	49	88	637
PLAYOFFS							
1927-28	OTTA	N	2	0	0	0	0
1929-30			2	0	0	0	0
1934-35*	MON(M)	N	7	0	1	1	6
1935-36			3	0	0	0	6
1936-37	BOS	N	3	0	0	0	2
5 yrs.		N Totals:	17	0	1	1	14

Bill Shill

SHILL, WILLIAM ROY 6'1", 175 lbs.
B. Mar. 6, 1923, Toronto, Ont. Right Wing, Shoots R

YEAR	TEAM & LEAGUE		GP	G	A	PTS	PIM
1942-43	BOS	N	7	4	1	5	4
1945-46			45	15	12	27	12
1946-47			27	2	0	2	2
3 yrs.		N Totals:	79	21	13	34	18
PLAYOFFS							
1945-46	BOS	N	7	1	2	3	2

Jack Shill

SHILL, JOHN WALKER 5'8", 175 lbs.
B. Toronto, Ont. Defense, Shoots L

YEAR	TEAM & LEAGUE		GP	G	A	PTS	PIM
1933-34	TOR	N	7	0	1	1	0
1934-35	BOS	N	45	4	4	8	22
1935-36	TOR	N	3	0	1	1	0
1936-37			32	4	4	8	26
1937-38	NYA	N	25	1	3	4	10
	CHI	N	23	4	3	7	8
	2 team total		48	5	6	11	18
1938-39			28	2	4	6	4
6 yrs.		N Totals:	163	15	20	35	70
PLAYOFFS							
1933-34	TOR	N	2	0	0	0	0
1934-35	BOS	N	4	0	0	0	0
1935-36	TOR	N	9	0	3	3	8
1936-37			2	0	0	0	0
1937-38*	CHI	N	10	1	3	4	5
5 yrs.		N Totals:	27	1	6	7	13

Rick Shinske

SHINSKE, RICHARD CHARLES 5'11", 165 lbs.
B. May 31, 1955, Weyburn, Sask. Center, Shoots L

YEAR	TEAM	LEAGUE	GP	G	A	PTS	PIM
1976-77	**CLEVE**	**N**	5	0	0	0	2
1977-78			47	5	12	17	6
1978-79	**STL**	**N**	11	0	4	4	2
3 yrs.		**N Totals:**	63	5	16	21	10

Put on **Minnesota** Reserve List after Cleveland-Minnesota Dispersal Draft, June 15, 1978. Claimed on waivers by **St. Louis** from Minnesota, Aug. 12, 1978. Signed as free agent by **Detroit** Sept. 4, 1979.

Jim Shires

SHIRES, JAMES ARTHUR 6', 180 lbs.
B. Nov. 15, 1945, Edmonton, Alta. Left Wing, Shoots L

YEAR	TEAM	LEAGUE	GP	G	A	PTS	PIM
1970-71	**DET**	**N**	21	2	1	3	22
1971-72	**STL**	**N**	18	0	3	3	8
1972-73	**PITT**	**N**	18	1	2	3	2
3 yrs.		**N Totals:**	57	3	6	9	32

Glen Shirton

SHIRTON, GLEN
Defense

YEAR	TEAM	LEAGUE	GP	G	A	PTS	PIM
1973-74	**CLEVE**	**W**	4	0	0	0	0

Johnny Shmyr

SHMYR, JOHN
B. Jan. 2, 1945, Cudworth, Sask. Defense

YEAR	TEAM	LEAGUE	GP	G	A	PTS	PIM
1972-73	**WINN**	**W**	7	0	0	0	2
1973-74	**LA**	**W**	43	1	3	4	13
1974-75	**VAN**	**W**	39	1	5	6	43
3 yrs.		**W Totals:**	89	2	8	10	58

PLAYOFFS

YEAR	TEAM	LEAGUE	GP	G	A	PTS	PIM
1972-73	**WINN**	**W**	3	0	1	1	2

Paul Shmyr

SHMYR, PAUL 5'11", 170 lbs.
B. Jan. 28, 1946, Cudworth, Sask. Defense, Shoots L

YEAR	TEAM	LEAGUE	GP	G	A	PTS	PIM
1968-69	**CHI**	**N**	3	1	0	1	8
1969-70			24	0	4	4	26
1970-71			58	1	12	13	41
1971-72	**CALIF**	**N**	69	6	21	27	156
1972-73	**CLEVE**	**W**	73	5	43	48	169
1973-74			78	13	31	44	165
1974-75			49	7	14	21	103
1975-76			70	6	44	50	101
1976-77	**SD**	**W**	81	13	37	50	103
1977-78	**EDM**	**W**	80	9	40	49	100
1978-79			80	8	39	47	119
1979-80	**MINN**	**N**	63	3	15	18	84
1980-81			61	1	9	10	79
1981-82	**HART**	**N**	66	1	11	12	134
14 yrs.		**N Totals:**	344	13	72	85	528
		W Totals:	511	61	248	309	860

PLAYOFFS

YEAR	TEAM	LEAGUE	GP	G	A	PTS	PIM
1969-70	**CHI**	**N**	8	1	2	3	0
1970-71			9	0	0	0	17
1972-73	**CLEVE**	**W**	8	1	3	4	19
1973-74			5	0	4	4	31
1974-75			5	2	1	3	15
1976-77	**SD**	**W**	7	0	2	2	8
1977-78	**EDM**	**W**	5	1	3	4	11
1978-79			13	1	5	6	23
1979-80	**MINN**	**N**	14	2	1	3	23
1980-81			3	0	0	0	4
10 yrs.		**N Totals:**	34	3	3	6	44
		W Totals:	43	5	18	23	107

Traded to **Chicago** by N.Y. Rangers for Camille Henry, Aug. 17, 1967. Traded to **California** by Chicago with goalie Gilles Meloche for goalie Gerry Desjardins, Oct. 18, 1971. Playing rights transferred to **Minnesota** Reserve List after Cleveland-Minnesota Dispersal Draft, June 15, 1978. Reclaimed by **Minnesota** from Edmonton prior to Expansion Draft, June 9, 1979.

Eddie Shore

SHORE, EDDIE 5'11", 190 lbs.
B. Nov. 25, 1902, Fort Qu'Appelle, Sask.
Defense
Won Hart Trophy, 1932–33, 1934–35, 1935–36, 1937-38
Hall of Fame, 1945

YEAR	TEAM	LEAGUE	GP	G	A	PTS	PIM
1926-27	**BOS**	**N**	41	12	6	18	130
1927-28			44	11	6	17	**165**
1928-29			39	12	7	19	96
1929-30			43	12	19	31	105
1930-31			44	15	16	31	105
1931-32			44	9	13	22	80
1932-33			48	8	27	35	102
1933-34			30	2	10	12	57
1934-35			48	7	26	33	32
1935-36			46	3	16	19	61
1936-37			19	3	1	4	12
1937-38			47	3	14	17	42
1938-39			46	4	14	18	47
1939-40			4	2	1	3	4
	NYA	**N**	10	2	3	5	9
	2 team total		14	4	4	8	13
14 yrs.		**N Totals:**	553	105	179	284	1047

PLAYOFFS

YEAR	TEAM	LEAGUE	GP	G	A	PTS	PIM
1926-27	**BOS**	**N**	8	1	1	2	46
1927-28			2	0	0	0	8
1928-29*			5	1	1	2	28
1929-30			6	1	0	1	26
1930-31			5	2	1	3	24
1932-33			5	0	1	1	14
1934-35			4	0	1	1	2
1935-36			2	1	1	2	12
1937-38			3	0	1	1	6
1938-39*			12	0	4	4	19
1939-40	**NYA**	**N**	3	0	2	2	2
11 yrs.		**N Totals:**	55	6	13	19	187

Hamby Shore

SHORE, SAM HAMILTON
B. Ottawa, Ont. Left Wing

YEAR	TEAM	LEAGUE	GP	G	A	PTS	PIM
1917-18	**OTTA**	**N**	18	3	0	3	17

Aubrey Shores

SHORES, AUBREY
B. Unknown Forward

YEAR	TEAM	LEAGUE	GP	G	A	PTS	PIM
1930-31	**PHI**	**N**	1	0	0	0	0

Steve Short

SHORT, STEVEN 6'2", 210 lbs.
B. Apr. 6, 1954, Roseville, Minn. Left Wing, Shoots L

YEAR	TEAM	LEAGUE	GP	G	A	PTS	PIM
1977-78	**LA**	**N**	5	0	0	0	2
1978-79	**DET**	**N**	1	0	0	0	0
2 yrs.		**N Totals:**	6	0	0	0	2

Traded to **Los Angeles** by Philadelphia for future considerations (Paul Evans, Nov. 3, 1977), June 17, 1977. Traded to **Detroit** by Los Angeles for the rights to Steve Carlson, Dec. 6, 1978.

Byron Shutt

SHUTT, BYRON 6'1", 195 lbs.
B. Oct. 26, 1955, Toronto, Ont. Left Wing, Shoots L

YEAR	TEAM	LEAGUE	GP	G	A	PTS	PIM
1978-79	**CIN**	**W**	65	10	7	17	115

Steve Shutt

SHUTT, STEPHEN JOHN 5'11", 180 lbs.
B. July 1, 1952, Toronto, Ont. Left Wing, Shoots L

YEAR	TEAM	LEAGUE	GP	G	A	PTS	PIM
1972-73	**MONT**	**N**	50	8	8	16	24
1973-74			70	15	20	35	17
1974-75			77	30	35	65	40
1975-76			80	45	34	79	47
1976-77			80	**60**	45	105	28
1977-78			80	49	37	86	24
1978-79			72	37	40	77	31
1979-80			77	47	42	89	34
1980-81			77	35	38	73	51

Steve Shutt continued

YEAR	TEAM & LEAGUE	GP	G	A	PTS	PIM
1981-82		57	31	24	55	40
1982-83		78	35	22	57	26
11 yrs.	N Totals:	798	392	345	737	362
PLAYOFFS						
1972-73*	MONT N	1	0	0	0	0
1973-74		6	5	3	8	9
1974-75		9	1	6	7	4
1975-76*		13	7	8	15	2
1976-77*		14	8	10	18	2
1977-78*		15	9	8	17	20
1978-79*		11	4	7	11	6
1979-80		10	6	3	9	6
1980-81		3	2	1	3	4
1982-83		3	1	0	1	0
10 yrs.	N Totals:	85	43	46	89	53

Bob Sicinski

SICINSKI, ROBERT STANLEY 5'9", 175 lbs.
B. Nov. 13, 1946, Toronto, Ont. Center, Shoots L

YEAR	TEAM & LEAGUE	GP	G	A	PTS	PIM
1972-73	CHI W	77	25	63	88	18
1973-74		69	11	29	40	8
1974-75	IND W	77	19	34	53	12
1975-76		70	9	34	43	4
1976-77		60	12	24	36	14
5 yrs.	W Totals:	353	76	184	260	56
PLAYOFFS						
1973-74	CHI W	18	6	8	14	0
1975-76	IND W	7	0	0	0	2
1976-77		9	0	3	3	4
3 yrs.	W Totals:	34	6	11	17	6

Babe Siebert

SIEBERT, ALBERT CHARLES 5'10", 182 lbs.
B. Jan. 14, 1904, Plattsville, Ont. Left Wing
Won Hart Trophy, 1936-37
Hall of Fame, 1964

YEAR	TEAM & LEAGUE	GP	G	A	PTS	PIM
1925-26	MON(M) N	35	16	8	24	108
1926-27		44	5	3	8	116
1927-28		40	8	9	17	109
1928-29		40	3	5	8	82
1929-30		40	14	19	33	94
1930-31		43	16	12	28	76
1931-32		48	21	18	39	64
1932-33	NYR N	42	9	10	19	38
1933-34		13	0	1	1	18
	BOS N	19	5	6	11	31
	2 team total	32	5	7	12	49
1934-35		48	6	18	24	80
1935-36		46	12	9	21	66
1936-37	MONT N	44	8	20	28	38
1937-38		37	8	11	19	56
1938-39		44	9	7	16	26
14 yrs.	N Totals:	583	140	156	296	1002
PLAYOFFS						
1925-26*	MON(M) N	8	2	2	4	6
1926-27		2	1	0	1	2
1927-28		9	2	0	2	28
1929-30		2	0	0	0	0
1930-31		2	0	0	0	4
1931-32		4	0	1	1	4
1932-33*	NYR N	8	1	0	1	12
1934-35	BOS N	4	0	0	0	6
1935-36		2	0	1	1	0
1936-37	MONT N	5	1	2	3	2
1937-38		3	1	1	2	0
1938-39		3	0	0	0	0
12 yrs.	N Totals:	52	8	7	15	64

Dave Silk

SILK, DAVID 5'11", 190 lbs.
B. Jan. 1, 1958, Scituate, Mass. Right Wing, Shoots R

YEAR	TEAM & LEAGUE	GP	G	A	PTS	PIM
1979-80	NYR N	2	0	0	0	0
1980-81		59	14	12	26	58
1981-82		64	15	20	35	39

Dave Silk continued

YEAR	TEAM & LEAGUE	GP	G	A	PTS	PIM
1982-83		16	1	1	2	15
4 yrs.	N Totals:	141	30	33	63	112
PLAYOFFS						
1981-82	NYR N	9	2	4	6	4

Mike Siltala

SILTALA, MICHAEL 5'9", 168 lbs.
B. Aug. 5, 1963, Toronto, Ont. Right Wing, Shoots R

YEAR	TEAM & LEAGUE	GP	G	A	PTS	PIM
1981-82	WASH N	3	1	0	1	2

Risto Siltanen

SILTANEN, RISTO (Incredible Hulk) 5'7", 158 lbs.
B. Oct. 31, 1958, Tampere, Finland Defense, Shoots L

YEAR	TEAM & LEAGUE	GP	G	A	PTS	PIM
1978-79	EDM W	20	3	4	7	4
1979-80	EDM N	64	6	29	35	26
1980-81		79	17	36	53	54
1981-82		63	15	48	63	26
1982-83	HART N	74	5	25	30	28
5 yrs.	N Totals:	280	43	138	181	134
	W Totals:	20	3	4	7	4
PLAYOFFS						
1978-79	EDM W	11	0	9	9	4
1979-80	EDM N	2	0	0	0	2
1980-81		9	2	0	2	8
1981-82		5	3	2	5	10
4 yrs.	N Totals:	16	5	2	7	20
	W Totals:	11	0	9	9	4

Reclaimed by **St. Louis** from Edmonton prior to Expansion Draft, June 9, 1979. Traded to **Edmonton** by St. Louis with Tom Roulston for Joe Micheletti, Aug. 19, 1979. Traded to **Hartford** by Edmonton with Brent Loney for Ken Linseman and Don Nachbaur, August 19, 1982.

Charlie Simmer

SIMMER, CHARLES ROBERT (Chaz) 6'3", 195 lbs.
B. Mar. 20, 1954, Terrace Bay, Ont. Left Wing, Shoots L

YEAR	TEAM & LEAGUE	GP	G	A	PTS	PIM
1974-75	CALIF N	35	8	13	21	26
1975-76		21	1	1	2	22
1976-77	CLEVE N	24	2	0	2	16
1977-78	LA N	3	0	0	0	2
1978-79		38	21	27	48	16
1979-80		64	**56**	45	101	65
1980-81		65	56	49	105	62
1981-82		50	15	24	39	42
1982-83		80	29	51	80	51
9 yrs.	N Totals:	380	188	210	398	302
PLAYOFFS						
1978-79	LA N	2	1	0	1	2
1979-80		3	2	0	2	0
1981-82		10	4	7	11	22
3 yrs.	N Totals:	15	7	7	14	24

Signed as free agent by **Los Angeles** Aug. 8, 1977.

Al Simmons

SIMMONS, ALLAN KENNETH 6', 170 lbs.
B. Sept. 25, 1951, Winnipeg, Man. Defense, Shoots R

YEAR	TEAM & LEAGUE	GP	G	A	PTS	PIM
1971-72	CALIF N	1	0	0	0	0
1973-74	BOS N	3	0	0	0	0
1975-76		7	0	1	1	21
3 yrs.	N Totals:	11	0	1	1	21
PLAYOFFS						
1973-74	BOS N	1	0	0	0	0

Sold to **N.Y. Rangers** by Boston, Nov. 14, 1975.

Cully Simon

SIMON, JOHN CULLEN 5'10", 190 lbs.
B. Brockville, Ont. Shoots L

YEAR	TEAM & LEAGUE	GP	G	A	PTS	PIM
1942-43	DET N	34	1	1	2	34
1943-44		46	3	7	10	52

Cully Simon continued

YEAR	TEAM & LEAGUE		GP	G	A	PTS	PIM
1944-45			21	0	2	2	26
	CHI	N	29	0	1	1	9
	2 team total		50	0	3	3	35
3 yrs.		N Totals:	130	4	11	15	121
PLAYOFFS							
1942-43*	DET	N	9	0	1	1	4
1943-44			5	0	0	0	2
2 yrs.		N Totals:	14	0	1	1	6

Thain Simon

SIMON, THAIN ANDREW 6', 200 lbs.
B. Apr. 24, 1922, Brockville, Ont. Defense, Shoots L

YEAR	TEAM & LEAGUE		GP	G	A	PTS	PIM
1946-47	DET	N	3	0	0	0	0

Bobby Simpson

SIMPSON, ROBERT 6', 190 lbs.
B. Nov. 17, 1956, Caughnawaga, Que. Left Wing, Shoots L

YEAR	TEAM & LEAGUE		GP	G	A	PTS	PIM
1976-77	ATL	N	72	13	10	23	45
1977-78			55	10	8	18	49
1979-80	STL	N	18	2	2	4	11
1981-82	PITT	N	26	9	9	18	4
1982-83			4	1	0	1	0
5 yrs.		N Totals:	175	35	29	64	109
PLAYOFFS							
1976-77	ATL	N	2	0	1	1	0
1977-78			2	0	0	0	2
1981-82	PITT	N	2	0	0	0	0
3 yrs.		N Totals:	6	0	1	1	2

Traded to **St. Louis** by Atlanta for Curt Bennett, May 24, 1979. Claimed by **St. Louis** as fill in Expansion Draft, June 13, 1979.

Cliff Simpson

SIMPSON, CLIFFORD VERNON 5'11", 175 lbs.
B. Apr. 4, 1923, Toronto, Ont. Center, Shoots R

YEAR	TEAM & LEAGUE		GP	G	A	PTS	PIM
1946-47	DET	N	6	0	1	1	0
PLAYOFFS							
1946-47	DET	N	1	0	0	0	0
1947-48			1	0	0	0	2
2 yrs.		N Totals:	2	0	0	0	2

Joe Simpson

SIMPSON, JOE (Bullet)
B. Aug. 13, 1893, Selkirk, Man. Defense
Hall of Fame, 1962

YEAR	TEAM & LEAGUE		GP	G	A	PTS	PIM
1925-26	NYA	N	32	2	2	4	2
1926-27			42	4	2	6	39
1927-28			25	2	0	2	32
1928-29			42	3	2	5	29
1929-30			44	8	13	21	41
1930-31			42	2	0	2	13
6 yrs.		N Totals:	227	21	19	40	156
PLAYOFFS							
1928-29	NYA	N	2	0	0	0	0

Tom Simpson

SIMPSON, THOMAS PHILLIP 5'9", 190 lbs.
B. Aug. 15, 1952, Bowmanville, Ont. Right Wing, Shoots R

YEAR	TEAM & LEAGUE		GP	G	A	PTS	PIM
1972-73	OTTA	W	57	10	7	17	44
1973-74	TOR	W	74	33	20	53	27
1974-75			70	52	28	80	48
1975-76			73	20	21	41	15
1976-77	BIRM	W	25	7	6	13	10
	EDM	W	15	3	2	5	16
	2 team total		40	10	8	18	26
5 yrs.		W Totals:	314	125	84	209	160
PLAYOFFS							
1972-73	OTTA	W	5	1	0	1	0
1973-74	TOR	W	12	4	1	5	5

Tom Simpson continued

YEAR	TEAM & LEAGUE		GP	G	A	PTS	PIM
1974-75			5	1	1	2	0
3 yrs.		W Totals:	22	6	2	8	5

Al Sims

SIMS, ALLAN EUGENE 6', 182 lbs.
B. Apr. 18, 1953, Toronto, Ont. Defense, Shoots L

YEAR	TEAM & LEAGUE		GP	G	A	PTS	PIM
1973-74	BOS	N	77	3	9	12	22
1974-75			75	4	8	12	73
1975-76			48	4	3	7	43
1976-77			1	0	0	0	0
1977-78			43	2	8	10	104
1978-79			67	9	20	29	28
1979-80	HART	N	76	10	31	41	30
1980-81			80	16	36	52	68
1981-82	LA	N	8	1	1	2	16
1982-83			1	0	0	0	0
10 yrs.		N Totals:	476	49	116	165	384
PLAYOFFS							
1973-74	BOS	N	16	0	0	0	12
1976-77			2	0	0	0	0
1977-78			8	0	0	0	0
1978-79			11	0	2	2	0
1979-80	HART	N	3	0	0	0	2
5 yrs.		N Totals:	40	0	2	2	14

Claimed by **Hartford** from Boston in Expansion Draft, June 13, 1979. Claimed from Hartford by **Los Angeles** in Waiver Draft, Oct. 5, 1981.

Reg Sinclair

SINCLAIR, REGINALD ALEXANDER 6', 165 lbs.
B. Mar. 6, 1925, Lachine, Que. Right Wing, Shoots R

YEAR	TEAM & LEAGUE		GP	G	A	PTS	PIM
1950-51	NYR	N	70	18	21	39	70
1951-52			69	20	10	30	33
1952-53	DET	N	69	11	12	23	36
3 yrs.		N Totals:	208	49	43	92	139
PLAYOFFS							
1952-53	DET	N	3	1	0	1	0

Traded to **Detroit** by N.Y. Rangers with John Morrison for Leo Reise, Jr., Aug. 18, 1952.

Alex Singbush

SINGBUSH, E. ALEXANDER
B. Winnipeg, Man.

YEAR	TEAM & LEAGUE		GP	G	A	PTS	PIM
1940-41	MONT	N	32	0	5	5	15
PLAYOFFS							
1940-41	MONT	N	3	0	0	0	4

Ilkka Sinisalo

SINISALO, ILKKA 6'1", 190 lbs.
B. July 10, 1958, Helsinki, Finland Left Wing, Shoots L

YEAR	TEAM & LEAGUE		GP	G	A	PTS	PIM
1981-82	PHI	N	66	15	22	37	22
1982-83			61	21	29	50	16
2 yrs.		N Totals:	127	36	51	87	38
PLAYOFFS							
1981-82	PHI	N	4	0	2	2	0
1982-83			3	1	1	2	0
2 yrs.		N Totals:	7	1	3	4	0

Signed as free agent by **Philadelphia** Feb. 17, 1981.

Bob Sirois

SIROIS, ROBERT 6', 178 lbs.
B. Feb. 6, 1954, Montreal, Que. Right Wing, Shoots L

YEAR	TEAM & LEAGUE		GP	G	A	PTS	PIM
1974-75	PHI	N	3	1	0	1	4
1975-76			1	0	0	0	0
	WASH	N	43	10	19	29	6
	2 team total		44	10	19	29	6
1976-77			45	13	22	35	2
1977-78			72	24	37	61	6

Bob Sirois continued

YEAR	TEAM & LEAGUE		GP	G	A	PTS	PIM
1978-79			73	29	25	54	6
1979-80			49	15	17	32	18
6 yrs.		N Totals:	286	92	120	212	42

Traded to **Washington** by Philadelphia for a player to be named later (John Paddock, Sept. 1, 1976), Dec. 15, 1975.

Darryl Sittler

SITTLER, DARRYL GLEN 6', 190 lbs.
B. Sept. 18, 1950, Kitchener, Ont. Center, Shoots L

YEAR	TEAM & LEAGUE		GP	G	A	PTS	PIM
1970-71	**TOR**	**N**	49	10	8	18	37
1971-72			74	15	17	32	44
1972-73			78	29	48	77	69
1973-74			78	38	46	84	55
1974-75			72	36	44	80	47
1975-76			79	41	59	100	90
1976-77			73	38	52	90	89
1977-78			80	45	72	117	100
1978-79			70	36	51	87	69
1979-80			73	40	57	97	62
1980-81			80	43	53	96	77
1981-82			38	18	20	38	24
	PHI	**N**	35	14	18	32	50
	2 team total		73	32	38	70	74
1982-83			80	43	40	83	60
13 yrs.		N Totals:	959	446	585	1031	873
PLAYOFFS							
1970-71	**TOR**	**N**	6	2	1	3	31
1971-72			3	0	0	0	2
1973-74			4	2	1	3	6
1974-75			7	2	1	3	15
1975-76			10	5	7	12	19
1976-77			9	5	16	21	4
1977-78			13	3	8	11	12
1978-79			6	5	4	9	17
1979-80			3	1	2	3	10
1980-81			3	0	0	0	4
1981-82	**PHI**	**N**	4	3	1	4	6
1982-83			3	1	0	1	4
12 yrs.		N Totals:	71	29	41	70	130

Traded to **Philadelphia** by Toronto for Rich Costello, Hartford's second round choice (Peter Ihnacak) in 1982 Entry Draft (Philadelphia property via an earlier deal) and future considerations (Ken Strong), Jan. 20, 1982.

Gary Sittler

SITTLER, GARY 6'1", 187 lbs.
B. Kitchener, Ont. Defense

YEAR	TEAM & LEAGUE		GP	G	A	PTS	PIM
1974-75	**M-B**	**W**	5	1	1	2	14

Lars Sjoberg

SJOBERG, LARS-ERIK (The Shoe, Little General 5'8", 179 lbs.
B. May 5, 1944, Falun, Sweden Defense, Shoots L

YEAR	TEAM & LEAGUE		GP	G	A	PTS	PIM
1974-75	**WINN**	**W**	75	7	53	60	30
1975-76			81	5	36	41	12
1976-77			52	2	38	40	31
1977-78			78	11	39	50	72
1978-79			9	0	3	3	2
1979-80	**WINN**	**N**	79	7	27	34	48
6 yrs.		N Totals:	79	7	27	34	48
		W Totals:	295	25	169	194	147
PLAYOFFS							
1975-76	**WINN**	**W**	13	0	5	5	12
1976-77			20	0	6	6	22
1977-78			9	0	9	9	4
1978-79			10	1	2	3	4
4 yrs.		W Totals:	52	1	22	23	42

Bjorne Skaare

SKAARE, BJORNE 6', 180 lbs.
B. Oct. 29, 1958, Oslo, Norway Center, Shoots L

YEAR	TEAM & LEAGUE		GP	G	A	PTS	PIM
1978-79	**DET**	**N**	1	0	0	0	0

Raymond Skilton

SKILTON, RAYMOND
B. Unknown Defense

YEAR	TEAM & LEAGUE		GP	G	A	PTS	PIM
1917-18	**MON(W)**	**N**	1	0	0	0	0

Alf Skinner

SKINNER, ALFRED
B. Unknown Right Wing, Shoots R

YEAR	TEAM & LEAGUE		GP	G	A	PTS	PIM
1917-18	**TOR**	**N**	19	13	0	13	20
1918-19			17	12	3	15	26
1924-25	**BOS**	**N**	9	0	0	0	6
	MON(M)	**N**	18	1	1	2	22
	2 team total		27	1	1	2	28
1925-26	**PITT**	**N**	7	0	0	0	2
4 yrs.		N Totals:	70	26	4	30	76
PLAYOFFS							
1917-18*	**TOR**	**N**	7	**8**	0	**8**	21

Larry Skinner

SKINNER, LAURENCE FOSTER 5'11", 180 lbs.
B. Apr. 21, 1956, Vancouver, B.C. Center, Shoots L

YEAR	TEAM & LEAGUE		GP	G	A	PTS	PIM
1976-77	**COLO**	**N**	19	4	5	9	6
1977-78			14	3	5	8	0
1978-79			12	3	2	5	2
1979-80			2	0	0	0	0
4 yrs.		N Totals:	47	10	12	22	8
PLAYOFFS							
1977-78	**COLO**	**N**	2	0	0	0	0

Claimed by **Colorado** as fill in Expansion Draft, June 13, 1979.

Glen Skov

SKOV, GLEN FREDERICK 6'1", 185 lbs.
B. Jan. 26, 1931, Wheatley, Ont. Center, Shoots L

YEAR	TEAM & LEAGUE		GP	G	A	PTS	PIM
1949-50	**DET**	**N**	2	0	0	0	0
1950-51			19	7	6	13	13
1951-52			70	12	24	36	48
1952-53			70	12	15	27	54
1953-54			70	17	10	27	95
1954-55			70	14	16	30	53
1955-56	**CHI**	**N**	70	7	20	27	26
1956-57			67	14	28	42	69
1957-58			70	17	18	35	35
1958-59			70	3	5	8	4
1959-60			69	3	4	7	16
1960-61	**MONT**	**N**	3	0	0	0	0
12 yrs.		N Totals:	650	106	146	252	413
PLAYOFFS							
1950-51	**DET**	**N**	6	0	0	0	0
1951-52*			8	1	4	5	16
1952-53			6	1	0	1	2
1953-54*			12	1	2	3	16
1954-55*			11	2	0	2	8
1958-59	**CHI**	**N**	6	2	1	3	4
1959-60			4	0	0	0	2
7 yrs.		N Totals:	53	7	7	14	48

Traded to **Chicago** by Detroit with Tony Leswick, Johnny Wilson and Benny Woit for Jerry Toppazzini, John McCormack, Dave Creighton and Gord Hollingworth, June 3, 1955. Traded with Terry Gray to **Montreal** by Chicago for Ab McDonald, June 7, 1960.

Pete Slater

SLATER, PETER 5'9", 170 lbs.
B. Jan. 31, 1948, Renfrew, Ont. Right Wing, Shoots L

YEAR	TEAM & LEAGUE		GP	G	A	PTS	PIM
1972-73	**LA**	**W**	73	12	12	24	87
1973-74			19	1	1	2	2
2 yrs.		W Totals:	92	13	13	26	89

John Sleaver

SLEAVER, JOHN 6'1", 180 lbs.
B. Aug. 18, 1934, Copper Cliff, Ont. Center, Shoots R

YEAR	TEAM & LEAGUE		GP	G	A	PTS	PIM
1953-54	**CHI**	**N**	12	1	0	1	2
1956-57			12	1	0	1	4
2 yrs.		**N Totals:**	24	2	0	2	6

Mike Sleep

SLEEP, MICHAEL
Defense

YEAR	TEAM & LEAGUE		GP	G	A	PTS	PIM
1975-76	**PHOE**	**W**	9	2	0	2	0
1976-77			13	2	2	4	6
2 yrs.		**W Totals:**	22	4	2	6	6
PLAYOFFS							
1975-76	**PHOE**	**W**	3	0	0	0	0

Louis Sleigher

SLEIGHER, LOUIS 5'11", 195 lbs.
B. Oct. 23, 1958, Nouvelle, Que. Right Wing, Shoots R

YEAR	TEAM & LEAGUE		GP	G	A	PTS	PIM
1978-79	**BIRM**	**W**	62	26	12	38	46
1979-80	**QUE**	**N**	2	0	1	1	0
1981-82			8	0	0	0	0
1982-83			51	14	10	24	49
4 yrs.		**N Totals:**	61	14	11	25	49
		W Totals:	62	26	12	38	46
PLAYOFFS							
1982-83	**QUE**	**N**	4	0	0	0	4

Signed as free agent by **Quebec** Sept. 11, 1980.

Tod Sloan

SLOAN, ALOYSIUS MARTIN 5'10", 175 lbs.
B. Nov. 30, 1927, Vinton, Que. Center, Shoots R

YEAR	TEAM & LEAGUE		GP	G	A	PTS	PIM
1947-48	**TOR**	**N**	1	0	0	0	0
1948-49			29	3	4	7	0
1950-51			70	31	25	56	105
1951-52			68	25	23	48	89
1952-53			70	15	10	25	76
1953-54			67	11	32	43	100
1954-55			63	13	15	28	89
1955-56			70	37	29	66	100
1956-57			52	14	21	35	33
1957-58			59	13	25	38	58
1958-59	**CHI**	**N**	59	27	35	62	79
1959-60			70	20	20	40	54
1960-61			67	11	23	34	48
13 yrs.		**N Totals:**	745	220	262	482	831
PLAYOFFS							
1950-51	**TOR**	**N**	11	4	5	9	18
1951-52			4	0	0	0	10
1953-54			5	1	1	2	24
1954-55			4	0	0	0	2
1955-56			2	0	0	0	5
1958-59	**CHI**	**N**	6	3	5	8	0
1959-60			3	0	0	0	0
1960-61*			12	1	1	2	8
8 yrs.		**N Totals:**	47	9	12	21	67

Purchased from Toronto by **Chicago** June 4, 1958.

Peter Slobodzian

SLOBODZIAN, PETER PAUL 6'1", 185 lbs.
B. Apr. 24, 1918, Dauphin, Man. Defense, Shoots L

YEAR	TEAM & LEAGUE		GP	G	A	PTS	PIM
1940-41	**NYA**	**N**	41	3	2	5	54

Eddie Slowinski

SLOWINSKI, EDWARD STANLEY 6', 200 lbs.
B. Nov. 18, 1922, Winnipeg, Man. Right Wing, Shoots R

YEAR	TEAM & LEAGUE		GP	G	A	PTS	PIM
1947-48	**NYR**	**N**	38	6	5	11	2
1948-49			20	1	1	2	2
1949-50			63	14	23	37	12
1950-51			69	14	18	32	15
1951-52			64	21	22	43	18
1952-53			37	2	5	7	14
6 yrs.		**N Totals:**	291	58	74	132	63
PLAYOFFS							
1947-48	**NYR**	**N**	4	0	0	0	0
1949-50			12	2	6	8	6
2 yrs.		**N Totals:**	16	2	6	8	6

Traded to **Montreal** by N.Y. Rangers with Pete Babando, for Ivan Irwin, Aug. 17, 1953.

Darryl Sly

SLY, DARRYL HAYWARD 5'10", 185 lbs.
B. Apr. 3, 1939, Collingwood, Ont. Defense, Shoots R

YEAR	TEAM & LEAGUE		GP	G	A	PTS	PIM
1965-66	**TOR**	**N**	2	0	0	0	0
1967-68			17	0	0	0	4
1969-70	**MINN**	**N**	29	1	0	1	6
1970-71	**VAN**	**N**	31	0	2	2	10
4 yrs.		**N Totals:**	79	1	2	3	20

Drafted by **Vancouver** from Minnesota in Expansion Draft, June 10, 1970.

Doug Smail

SMAIL, DOUGLAS 5'9", 175 lbs.
B. Sept. 2, 1957, Moose Jaw, Sask. Left Wing, Shoots L

YEAR	TEAM & LEAGUE		GP	G	A	PTS	PIM
1980-81	**WINN**	**N**	30	10	8	18	45
1981-82			72	17	18	35	55
1982-83			80	15	29	44	32
3 yrs.		**N Totals:**	182	42	55	97	132
PLAYOFFS							
1981-82	**WINN**	**N**	4	0	0	0	0
1982-83			3	0	0	0	6
2 yrs.		**N Totals:**	7	0	0	0	6

Signed as free agent by **Winnipeg** May 22, 1980.

Alec Smart

SMART, ALEXANDER
B. May 29, 1918, Brandon, Man. Forward

YEAR	TEAM & LEAGUE		GP	G	A	PTS	PIM
1942-43	**MONT**	**N**	8	2	5	7	0

Dale Smedsmo

SMEDSMO, DALE DARWIN 6'1", 195 lbs.
B. Apr. 23, 1951, Roseau, Minn. Left Wing, Shoots L

YEAR	TEAM & LEAGUE		GP	G	A	PTS	PIM
1972-73	**TOR**	**N**	4	0	0	0	0
1975-76	**CIN**	**W**	66	8	14	22	187
1976-77	**NE**	**W**	15	2	0	2	54
	CIN	**W**	23	0	5	5	43
	2 team total		38	2	5	7	97
1977-78	**IND**	**W**	6	0	3	3	7
4 yrs.		**N Totals:**	4	0	0	0	0
		W Totals:	110	10	22	32	291
PLAYOFFS							
1976-77	**CIN**	**W**	2	0	1	1	0

Don Smillie

SMILLIE, DONALD
B. Unknown Forward

YEAR	TEAM & LEAGUE		GP	G	A	PTS	PIM
1933-34	**BOS**	**N**	12	2	2	4	4

Alex Smith

SMITH, ALEX 5'11½", 176 lbs.
B. Apr. 2, 1902, Liverpool, England Shoots L

YEAR	TEAM & LEAGUE		GP	G	A	PTS	PIM
1924-25	**OTTA**	**N**	7	0	0	0	2
1925-26			36	0	0	0	36
1926-27			43	4	1	5	58
1927-28			44	9	4	13	90
1928-29			42	1	7	8	36
1929-30			44	2	6	8	91
1930-31			44	5	6	11	73
1931-32	**DET**	**N**	48	6	8	14	47

Alex Smith continued

YEAR	TEAM & LEAGUE		GP	G	A	PTS	PIM
1932-33	**OTTA**	**N**	33	2	0	2	42
	BOS	**N**	15	5	4	9	30
	2 team total		48	7	4	11	72
1933-34			48	4	6	10	32
1934-35	**NYA**	**N**	48	3	8	11	46
1937-38	**BOS**	**N**	1	0	0	0	0
12 yrs.		**N Totals:**	453	41	50	91	583
PLAYOFFS							
1925-26	**OTTA**	**N**	2	0	0	0	0
1926-27*			6	0	0	0	8
1927-28			2	0	0	0	4
1929-30			2	0	0	0	4
1931-32	**DET**	**N**	2	0	0	0	4
1932-33	**BOS**	**N**	5	0	2	2	6
6 yrs.		**N Totals:**	19	0	2	2	26

Arthur Smith

SMITH, ARTHUR

Forward

YEAR	TEAM & LEAGUE		GP	G	A	PTS	PIM
1927-28	**TOR**	**N**	15	5	3	8	22
1928-29			43	5	0	5	91
1929-30			43	3	3	6	75
1930-31	**OTTA**	**N**	36	2	4	6	61
4 yrs.		**N Totals:**	137	15	10	25	249
PLAYOFFS							
1928-29	**TOR**	**N**	4	1	1	2	8

Barry Smith

SMITH, BARRY EDWARD 5'11", 178 lbs.
B. Apr. 25, 1955, Surrey, B.C. Center, Shoots L

YEAR	TEAM & LEAGUE		GP	G	A	PTS	PIM
1975-76	**BOS**	**N**	19	1	0	1	2
1979-80	**COLO**	**N**	33	2	3	5	4
1980-81			62	4	4	8	4
3 yrs.		**N Totals:**	114	7	7	14	10

Signed as free agent with **Colorado** Sept. 14, 1979.

Bobby Smith

SMITH, ROBERT DAVID 6'4", 210 lbs.
B. Feb. 12, 1958, North Sydney, N.S. Center, Shoots L
Won Calder Trophy, 1978-79

YEAR	TEAM & LEAGUE		GP	G	A	PTS	PIM
1978-79	**MINN**	**N**	80	30	44	74	39
1979-80			61	27	56	83	24
1980-81			78	29	64	93	73
1981-82			80	43	71	114	82
1982-83			77	24	53	77	81
5 yrs.		**N Totals:**	376	153	288	441	299
PLAYOFFS							
1979-80	**MINN**	**N**	15	1	13	14	9
1980-81			19	8	17	25	13
1981-82			4	2	4	6	5
1982-83			9	6	4	10	17
4 yrs.		**N Totals:**	47	17	38	55	44

Brad Smith

SMITH, BRAD ALLAN (Smitty) 6'1", 195 lbs.
B. Apr. 13, 1958, Windsor, Ont. Right Wing, Shoots R

YEAR	TEAM & LEAGUE		GP	G	A	PTS	PIM
1978-79	**VAN**	**N**	2	0	0	0	2
1979-80			19	1	3	4	50
	ATL	**N**	4	0	0	0	4
	2 team total		23	1	3	4	54
1980-81	**CALG**	**N**	45	7	4	11	65
	DET	**N**	20	5	2	7	93
	2 team total		65	12	6	18	158
1981-82			33	2	0	2	80
1982-83			1	0	0	0	0
5 yrs.		**N Totals:**	124	15	9	24	294

Traded to **Atlanta** by Vancouver with Don Lever for Ivan Boldirev and Darcy Rota, Feb. 8, 1980. Traded to **Detroit** by Calgary for future considerations (Rick Vasko, May 28, 1981), Feb. 24, 1981.

Bri Smith

SMITH, BRIAN

Forward

YEAR	TEAM & LEAGUE		GP	G	A	PTS	PIM
1972-73	**HOUS**	**W**	48	7	6	13	19
PLAYOFFS							
1972-73	**HOUS**	**W**	10	0	2	2	0

Brian Smith

SMITH, BRIAN STUART 6', 180 lbs.
B. Dec. 6, 1937, Creighton Mine, Ont. Left Wing, Shoots L

YEAR	TEAM & LEAGUE		GP	G	A	PTS	PIM
1957-58	**DET**	**N**	4	0	1	1	0
1959-60			31	2	5	7	2
1960-61			26	0	2	2	10
3 yrs.		**N Totals:**	61	2	8	10	12
PLAYOFFS							
1959-60	**DET**	**N**	5	0	0	0	0

Brian Smith

SMITH, BRIAN DESMOND 6', 180 lbs.
B. Sept. 6, 1940, Ottawa, Ont. Left Wing, Shoots L

YEAR	TEAM & LEAGUE		GP	G	A	PTS	PIM
1967-68	**LA**	**N**	58	10	9	19	33
1968-69	**MINN**	**N**	9	0	1	1	0
2 yrs.		**N Totals:**	67	10	10	20	33
PLAYOFFS							
1967-68	**LA**	**N**	7	0	0	0	0

Traded to **Montreal** by Los Angeles with Yves Locas for Larry Cahan, July 1, 1968. Sold to **Minnesota** by Montreal, Nov. 15, 1968.

Carl Smith

SMITH, CARL DAVID
B. Sept. 18, 1917, Cache Bay, Ont. Forward

YEAR	TEAM & LEAGUE		GP	G	A	PTS	PIM
1943-44	**DET**	**N**	7	1	1	2	2

Clint Smith

SMITH, CLINTON JAMES (Snuffy) 5'8", 165 lbs.
B. Dec. 12, 1913, Assiniboia, Sask. Center
Won Lady Byng Trophy, 1938-39, 1943-44

YEAR	TEAM & LEAGUE		GP	G	A	PTS	PIM
1936-37	**NYR**	**N**	2	1	0	1	0
1937-38			48	14	23	37	0
1938-39			48	21	20	41	2
1939-40			41	8	16	24	2
1940-41			48	14	11	25	0
1941-42			47	10	24	34	4
1942-43			47	12	21	33	4
1943-44	**CHI**	**N**	50	23	**49**	72	4
1944-45			50	23	31	54	0
1945-46			50	26	24	50	2
1946-47			52	9	17	26	6
11 yrs.		**N Totals:**	483	161	236	397	24
PLAYOFFS							
1937-38	**NYR**	**N**	3	2	0	2	0
1938-39			7	1	2	3	0
1939-40*			12	1	3	4	2
1940-41			3	0	0	0	0
1941-42			6	0	0	0	0
1943-44	**CHI**	**N**	9	4	8	12	0
1945-46			4	2	1	3	0
7 yrs.		**N Totals:**	44	10	14	24	2

Dallas Smith

SMITH, DALLAS 5'11", 180 lbs.
B. Oct. 10, 1941, Hamiota, Man. Defense, Shoots L

YEAR	TEAM & LEAGUE		GP	G	A	PTS	PIM
1959-60	**BOS**	**N**	5	1	1	2	0
1960-61			70	1	9	10	79
1961-62			7	0	0	0	10
1965-66			2	0	0	0	0
1966-67			33	0	1	1	24
1967-68			74	4	23	27	65
1968-69			75	4	24	28	74
1969-70			75	7	17	24	119

Dallas Smith continued

YEAR	TEAM & LEAGUE	GP	G	A	PTS	PIM
1970-71		73	7	38	45	68
1971-72		78	8	22	30	132
1972-73		78	4	27	31	72
1973-74		77	6	21	27	64
1974-75		79	3	20	23	84
1975-76		77	7	25	32	103
1976-77		58	2	20	22	40
1977-78	**NYR** N	29	1	4	5	23
16 yrs.	**N Totals:**	890	55	252	307	957
PLAYOFFS						
1967-68	**BOS** N	4	0	2	2	0
1968-69		10	0	3	3	16
1969-70*		14	0	3	3	19
1970-71		7	0	3	3	26
1971-72*		15	0	4	4	22
1972-73		5	0	2	2	2
1973-74		16	1	7	8	20
1974-75		3	0	2	2	4
1975-76		11	2	2	4	19
1977-78	**NYR** N	1	0	1	1	0
10 yrs.	**N Totals:**	86	3	29	32	128

Signed as a free agent by **N.Y. Rangers** Dec. 19, 1977.

Dalton Smith

SMITH, DALTON J. (Nakina) 5'10", 150 lbs.
B. June 26, 1915, Cache Bay, Ont. Center, Shoots L

YEAR	TEAM & LEAGUE	GP	G	A	PTS	PIM
1936-37	**NYA** N	1	0	0	0	0
1943-44	**DET** N	10	1	2	3	0
2 yrs.	**N Totals:**	11	1	2	3	0

Derek Smith

SMITH, DEREK ROBERT 5'11", 177 lbs.
B. July 31, 1954, Quebec City, Que. Center, Shoots L

YEAR	TEAM & LEAGUE	GP	G	A	PTS	PIM
1976-77	**BUF** N	5	0	0	0	0
1977-78		35	3	3	6	0
1978-79		43	14	12	26	8
1979-80		79	24	39	63	16
1980-81		69	21	43	64	12
1981-82		12	3	1	4	2
	DET N	49	6	14	20	10
	2 team total	61	9	15	24	12
1982-83		42	7	4	11	12
7 yrs.	**N Totals:**	334	78	116	194	60
PLAYOFFS						
1975-76		1	0	0	0	0
1977-78	**BUF** N	8	3	3	6	7
1979-80		13	5	7	12	4
1980-81		8	1	4	5	2
4 yrs.	**N Totals:**	29	9	14	23	13
	W Totals:	1	0	0	0	0

Traded to **Detroit** by Buffalo along with Danny Gare and Jim Schoenfeld, for Mike Foligno, Dale McCourt and Brent Peterson, Dec. 2, 1981.

Des Smith

SMITH, DESMOND PATRICK 6', 185 lbs.
B. Feb. 22, 1914, Ottawa, Ont. Defense, Shoots L

YEAR	TEAM & LEAGUE	GP	G	A	PTS	PIM
1937-38	**MON(M)** N	41	3	1	4	47
1938-39	**MONT** N	16	3	3	6	8
1939-40	**CHI** N	24	1	4	5	27
	BOS N	18	2	2	4	23
	2 team total	42	3	6	9	50
1940-41		48	6	8	14	61
1941-42		48	7	7	14	70
5 yrs.	**N Totals:**	195	22	25	47	236
PLAYOFFS						
1938-39	**MONT** N	3	0	0	0	4
1939-40	**BOS** N	6	0	0	0	0
1940-41*		11	0	2	2	12
1941-42		5	1	2	3	2
4 yrs.	**N Totals:**	25	1	4	5	18

Don Smith

SMITH, DONALD
Center

YEAR	TEAM & LEAGUE	GP	G	A	PTS	PIM
1919-20	**MONT** N	10	1	0	1	4

Don Smith

SMITH, DONALD ARTHUR 5'10", 165 lbs.
B. May 4, 1929, Regina, Sask. Center, Shoots L

YEAR	TEAM & LEAGUE	GP	G	A	PTS	PIM
1949-50	**NYR** N	11	1	1	2	0
PLAYOFFS						
1949-50	**NYR** N	1	0	0	0	0

Doug Smith

SMITH, DOUGLAS 5'11", 178 lbs.
B. May 17, 1963, Ottawa, Ont. Center, Shoots R

YEAR	TEAM & LEAGUE	GP	G	A	PTS	PIM
1981-82	**LA** N	80	16	14	30	64
1982-83		42	11	11	22	12
2 yrs.	**N Totals:**	122	27	25	52	76
PLAYOFFS						
1981-82	**LA** N	10	3	2	5	11

Floyd Smith

SMITH, FLOYD ROBERT DONALD 5'10", 180 lbs.
B. May 16, 1935, Perth, Ont. Right Wing, Shoots R

YEAR	TEAM & LEAGUE	GP	G	A	PTS	PIM
1954-55	**BOS** N	3	0	1	1	0
1956-57		23	0	0	0	6
1960-61	**NYR** N	29	5	9	14	0
1962-63	**DET** N	51	9	17	26	10
1963-64		52	18	13	31	22
1964-65		67	16	29	45	44
1965-66		66	21	28	49	20
1966-67		54	11	14	25	8
1967-68		57	18	21	39	14
	TOR N	6	6	1	7	0
	2 team total	63	24	22	46	14
1968-69		64	15	19	34	22
1969-70		61	4	14	18	13
1970-71	**BUF** N	77	6	11	17	46
1971-72		6	0	1	1	2
13 yrs.	**N Totals:**	550	108	150	258	187
PLAYOFFS						
1962-63	**DET** N	11	2	3	5	4
1963-64		14	4	3	7	4
1964-65		7	1	3	4	4
1965-66		12	5	2	7	4
1968-69	**TOR** N	4	0	0	0	0
5 yrs.	**N Totals:**	48	12	11	23	16

Drafted by **Detroit** from N.Y. Rangers, June, 1962. Traded to **Toronto** by Detroit with Norm Ullman and Paul Henderson for Frank Mahovlich, Pete Stemkowski, Garry Unger, and the rights to Carl Brewer, Mar. 3, 1968. Sold to **Buffalo** by Toronto, Aug. 31, 1970.

George Smith

SMITH, GEORGE
Forward

YEAR	TEAM & LEAGUE	GP	G	A	PTS	PIM
1921-22	**TOR** N	9	0	0	0	0

Glen Smith

SMITH, GLEN

YEAR	TEAM & LEAGUE	GP	G	A	PTS	PIM
1950-51	**CHI** N	2	0	0	0	0

Glenn Smith

SMITH, GLENN
Defense

YEAR	TEAM & LEAGUE	GP	G	A	PTS	PIM
1922-23	**TOR** N	9	0	0	0	0

Gord Smith

SMITH, GORDON JOSEPH 5'10", 175 lbs.
B. Nov. 17, 1949, Perth, Ont. Defense, Shoots L

YEAR	TEAM & LEAGUE		GP	G	A	PTS	PIM
1974-75	WASH	N	63	3	8	11	56
1975-76			25	1	2	3	28
1976-77			79	1	12	13	92
1977-78			80	4	7	11	78
1978-79			39	0	1	1	22
1979-80	WINN	N	13	0	0	0	8
6 yrs.		N Totals:	299	9	30	39	284

Signed as free agent by **Los Angeles** May 22, 1970. Drafted by **Washington** from Los Angeles in Expansion Draft, June 12, 1974. Claimed by **Winnipeg** from Washington in Expansion Draft, June 13, 1979.

Greg Smith

SMITH, GREGORY JAMES 6', 195 lbs.
B. July 8, 1955, Ponoka, Alta. Defense, Shoots L

YEAR	TEAM & LEAGUE		GP	G	A	PTS	PIM
1975-76	CALIF	N	1	0	1	1	2
1976-77	CLEVE	N	74	9	17	26	65
1977-78			80	7	30	37	92
1978-79	MINN	N	80	5	27	32	147
1979-80			55	5	13	18	103
1980-81			74	5	21	26	126
1981-82	DET	N	69	10	22	32	79
1982-83			73	4	26	30	79
8 yrs.		N Totals:	506	45	157	202	693
PLAYOFFS							
1979-80	MINN	N	12	0	1	1	9
1980-81			19	1	5	6	39
2 yrs.		N Totals:	31	1	6	7	48

Protected by **Minnesota** prior to Cleveland-Minnesota Dispersal Draft, June 15, 1978. Traded by Minnesota to **Detroit** along with the rights to Don Murdoch and Minnesota's first round choice (Murray Craven) in 1982 Entry Draft for Detroit's first round choice (Brian Bellows) in 1982 Entry Draft.

Guy Smith

SMITH, GUY 6'1", 188 lbs.
B. Jan. 2, 1950, Ottawa, Ont. Right Wing, Shoots R

YEAR	TEAM & LEAGUE		GP	G	A	PTS	PIM
1972-73	NE	W	23	3	3	6	6
1973-74			16	1	5	6	25
2 yrs.		W Totals:	39	4	8	12	31
PLAYOFFS							
1972-73	NE	W	11	2	0	2	4

Hooley Smith

SMITH, REGINALD JOSEPH
B. Jan. 7, 1905, Toronto, Ont. Defense
Hall of Fame, 1972

YEAR	TEAM & LEAGUE		GP	G	A	PTS	PIM
1924-25	OTTA	N	30	10	3	13	81
1925-26			28	16	9	25	53
1926-27			43	9	6	15	125
1927-28	MON(M)	N	36	14	5	19	72
1928-29			41	10	9	19	120
1929-30			41	21	9	30	83
1930-31			40	12	14	26	48
1931-32			46	11	33	44	49
1932-33			48	20	21	41	66
1933-34			47	18	19	37	58
1934-35			45	5	22	27	41
1935-36			47	19	19	38	75
1936-37	BOS	N	43	8	10	18	36
1937-38	NYA	N	47	10	10	20	23
1938-39			48	8	11	19	18
1939-40			48	7	8	15	41
1940-41			41	2	7	9	4
17 yrs.		N Totals:	719	200	215	415	993
PLAYOFFS							
1925-26	OTTA	N	2	0	0	0	14
1926-27*			6	1	0	1	16
1927-28	MON(M)	N	9	2	1	3	17
1929-30			4	1	1	2	12

Hooley Smith continued

YEAR	TEAM & LEAGUE		GP	G	A	PTS	PIM
1931-32			4	2	1	3	2
1932-33			2	2	0	2	2
1933-34			4	0	1	1	6
1934-35*			6	0	0	0	14
1935-36			3	0	0	0	2
1936-37	BOS	N	3	0	0	0	0
1937-38	NYA	N	6	0	3	3	0
1938-39			2	0	0	0	14
1939-40			3	3	1	4	2
13 yrs.		N Totals:	54	11	8	19	101

Kenny Smith

SMITH, KENNETH ALVIN 5'7", 150 lbs.
B. May 8, 1924, Moose Jaw, Sask. Left Wing, Shoots L

YEAR	TEAM & LEAGUE		GP	G	A	PTS	PIM
1944-45	BOS	N	49	20	14	34	2
1945-46			23	2	6	8	0
1946-47			60	14	7	21	4
1947-48			60	11	12	23	14
1948-49			59	20	20	40	6
1949-50			66	10	31	41	12
1950-51			14	3	1	4	11
7 yrs.		N Totals:	331	80	91	171	49
PLAYOFFS							
1944-45	BOS	N	7	3	4	7	0
1945-46			8	0	4	4	0
1946-47			5	3	0	3	2
1947-48			5	2	3	5	0
1948-49			5	0	2	2	4
5 yrs.		N Totals:	30	8	13	21	6

Traded to **Toronto** by Boston with Fern Flaman, Leo Boivin and Phil Maloney for Bill Ezinicki and Vic Lynn, Nov. 16, 1950.

Rick Smith

SMITH, RICHARD ALLAN 5'11", 200 lbs.
B. June 29, 1948, Hamilton, Ont. Defense, Shoots L

YEAR	TEAM & LEAGUE		GP	G	A	PTS	PIM
1968-69	BOS	N	47	0	5	5	29
1969-70			69	2	8	10	65
1970-71			67	4	19	23	44
1971-72			61	2	12	14	46
	CALIF	N	17	1	4	5	26
	2 team total		78	3	16	19	72
1972-73			64	9	24	33	77
1973-74	MINN	W	71	10	28	38	98
1974-75			78	9	29	38	112
1975-76			51	1	32	33	50
	STL	N	24	1	7	8	18
	2 team total		75	2	39	41	68
1976-77			18	0	1	1	6
	BOS	N	46	6	16	22	30
	2 team total		64	6	17	23	36
1977-78			79	7	29	36	69
1978-79			65	7	18	25	46
1979-80			78	8	18	26	62
1980-81	DET	N	11	0	2	2	6
	WASH	N	40	5	4	9	36
	2 team total		51	5	6	11	42
13 yrs.		N Totals:	686	52	167	219	560
		W Totals:	200	20	89	109	260
PLAYOFFS							
1968-69	BOS	N	9	0	0	0	6
1969-70*			14	1	3	4	17
1970-71			6	0	0	0	0
1973-74	MINN	W	11	0	1	1	22
1974-75			12	2	7	9	6
1975-76	STL	N	3	0	1	1	4
1976-77	BOS	N	14	0	9	9	14
1977-78			15	1	5	6	18
1978-79			11	0	4	4	12
1979-80			6	1	1	2	2
10 yrs.		N Totals:	78	3	23	26	73
		W Totals:	23	2	8	10	28

Traded to **California** by Boston with Reggie Leach and Bob Stewart for Carol Vadnais and Don O'Donoghue, Feb. 23, 1972. Rights sold to **St. Louis** by California, Oct. 22, 1975. Traded to **Boston** by St. Louis for Joe Zanussi, Dec. 20, 1976. Claimed by **Detroit** from Boston in Waiver Draft, Oct. 10, 1980. Claimed on waivers by **Washington** from Detroit, Nov. 7, 1980.

Roger Smith

SMITH, ROGER — 6', 175 lbs. Defense

YEAR	TEAM & LEAGUE		GP	G	A	PTS	PIM
1925-26	PITT	N	36	9	1	10	22
1926-27			36	4	0	4	6
1927-28			43	1	0	1	30
1928-29			44	4	2	6	49
1929-30			42	2	1	3	55
1930-31	PHI	N	9	0	0	0	0
6 yrs.		N Totals:	210	20	4	24	162
PLAYOFFS							
1925-26	PITT	N	2	1	0	1	0
1927-28			2	2	0	2	0
2 yrs.		N Totals:	4	3	0	3	0

Ron Smith

SMITH, RONALD ROBERT — 6', 185 lbs.
B. Nov. 19, 1952, Port Hope, Ont. — Defense, Shoots R

YEAR	TEAM & LEAGUE		GP	G	A	PTS	PIM
1972-73	NYI	N	11	1	1	2	14

Ross Smith

SMITH, ROSS — 6', 184 lbs.
B. Nov. 20, 1953, Fawcett, Alta. — Left Wing, Shoots L

YEAR	TEAM & LEAGUE		GP	G	A	PTS	PIM
1974-75	IND	W	15	1	6	7	19

Sid Smith

SMITH, SIDNEY JAMES — 5'10", 177 lbs.
B. July 11, 1925, Toronto, Ont. — Left Wing, Shoots L
Won Lady Byng Trophy, 1951-52, 1954-55

YEAR	TEAM & LEAGUE		GP	G	A	PTS	PIM
1946-47	TOR	N	14	2	1	3	0
1947-48			31	7	10	17	10
1948-49			1	0	0	0	0
1949-50			68	22	23	45	6
1950-51			70	30	21	51	10
1951-52			70	27	30	57	6
1952-53			70	20	19	39	6
1953-54			70	22	16	38	28
1954-55			70	33	21	54	14
1955-56			55	4	17	21	8
1956-57			70	17	24	41	4
1957-58			12	2	1	3	2
12 yrs.		N Totals:	601	186	183	369	94
PLAYOFFS							
1947-48*	TOR	N	2	0	0	0	0
1948-49*			6	5	2	7	0
1949-50			7	0	3	3	2
1950-51*			11	7	3	10	0
1951-52			4	0	0	0	0
1953-54			5	1	1	2	0
1954-55			4	3	1	4	0
1955-56			5	1	0	1	0
8 yrs.		N Totals:	44	17	10	27	2

Stan Smith

SMITH, STANFORD GEORGE — 5'10", 165 lbs.
B. Aug. 13, 1917, Coal Creek, B.C. — Center, Shoots L

YEAR	TEAM & LEAGUE		GP	G	A	PTS	PIM
1939-40	NYR	N	1	0	0	0	0
1940-41			8	2	1	3	0
2 yrs.		N Totals:	9	2	1	3	0

Steve Smith

SMITH, STEVEN — 5'9", 202 lbs.
B. Apr. 4, 1963, Trenton, Ont. — Defense, Shoots L

YEAR	TEAM & LEAGUE		GP	G	A	PTS	PIM
1981-82	PHI	N	8	0	1	1	0

Stu Smith

SMITH, STUART GORDON — 6'1", 185 lbs.
B. Mar. 17, 1960, Toronto, Ont. — Defense, Shoots R

YEAR	TEAM & LEAGUE		GP	G	A	PTS	PIM
1979-80	HART	N	4	0	0	0	0
1980-81			38	1	7	8	55
1981-82			17	0	3	3	15

Stu Smith continued

YEAR	TEAM & LEAGUE		GP	G	A	PTS	PIM
1982-83			18	1	0	1	25
4 yrs.		N Totals:	77	2	10	12	95
PLAYOFFS							
1940-41	MONT	N	1	0	0	0	0

Stu Smith

SMITH, STUART ERNEST — Right Wing

YEAR	TEAM & LEAGUE		GP	G	A	PTS	PIM
1940-41	MONT	N	16	2	3	5	2
1941-42			1	0	1	1	0
2 yrs.		N Totals:	17	2	4	6	2

Tommy Smith

SMITH, TOMMY — Left Wing
Hall of Fame, 1973

YEAR	TEAM & LEAGUE		GP	G	A	PTS	PIM
1919-20	QUE	N	10	0	0	0	9

Wayne Smith

SMITH, WAYNE CLIFFORD — 6', 195 lbs.
B. Feb. 12, 1943, Kamsack, Sask. — Defense, Shoots L

YEAR	TEAM & LEAGUE		GP	G	A	PTS	PIM
1966-67	CHI	N	2	1	1	2	2
PLAYOFFS							
1966-67	CHI	N	1	0	0	0	0

John Smrke

SMRKE, JOHN — 5'11", 205 lbs.
B. Feb. 25, 1956, Chicoutimi, Que. — Left Wing, Shoots L

YEAR	TEAM & LEAGUE		GP	G	A	PTS	PIM
1977-78	STL	N	18	2	4	6	11
1978-79			55	6	8	14	20
1979-80	QUE	N	30	3	5	8	2
3 yrs.		N Totals:	103	11	17	28	33

Claimed by **Quebec** from St. Louis in Expansion Draft, June 13, 1979.

Stan Smrke

SMRKE, STANLEY — 5'11", 180 lbs.
B. Sept. 2, 1928, Belgrade, Yugoslavia — Left Wing, Shoots L

YEAR	TEAM & LEAGUE		GP	G	A	PTS	PIM
1956-57	MONT	N	4	0	0	0	0
1957-58			5	0	3	3	0
2 yrs.		N Totals:	9	0	3	3	0

Traded to **Toronto** by Montreal for Al MacNeil, June 7, 1960.

Stan Smyl

SMYL, STANLEY PHILLIP (Steamer) — 5'8", 200 lbs.
B. Jan. 28, 1958, Glendon, Alta. — Right Wing, Shoots R

YEAR	TEAM & LEAGUE		GP	G	A	PTS	PIM
1978-79	VAN	N	62	14	24	38	89
1979-80			77	31	47	78	204
1980-81			80	25	38	63	171
1981-82			80	34	44	78	144
1982-83			74	38	50	88	114
5 yrs.		N Totals:	373	142	203	345	722
PLAYOFFS							
1978-79	VAN	N	2	1	1	2	0
1979-80			4	0	2	2	14
1980-81			3	1	2	3	0
1981-82			17	9	9	18	25
1982-83			4	3	2	5	12
5 yrs.		N Totals:	30	14	16	30	51

Rod Smylie

SMYLIE, RODERICK — Left Wing

YEAR	TEAM & LEAGUE		GP	G	A	PTS	PIM
1920-21	TOR	N	23	2	0	2	2
1921-22			21	0	0	0	2
1922-23			2	0	0	0	0
1923-24	OTTA	N	14	1	1	2	6
1924-25	TOR	N	11	0	0	0	0

Rod Smylie continued

YEAR	TEAM & LEAGUE		GP	G	A	PTS	PIM
1925-26			5	0	0	0	0
6 yrs.		N Totals:	76	3	1	4	10
PLAYOFFS							
1920-21	TOR	N	2	0	0	0	0
1921-22*			6	1	2	3	2
1924-25			2	0	0	0	0
3 yrs.		N Totals:	10	1	2	3	2

Ted Snell

SNELL, HAROLD EDWARD 5'9", 190 lbs.
B. May 28, 1946, Ottawa, Ont. Right Wing, Shoots R

YEAR	TEAM & LEAGUE		GP	G	A	PTS	PIM
1973-74	PITT	N	55	4	12	16	8
1974-75	KC	N	29	3	2	5	8
	DET	N	20	0	4	4	6
	2 team total		49	3	6	9	14
2 yrs.		N Totals:	104	7	18	25	22

Drafted by **Kansas City** from Pittsburgh in Expansion Draft, June 12, 1974. Traded to **Detroit** by Kansas City with Bart Crashley and Larry Giroux for Guy Charron and Claude Houde, Dec. 14, 1974.

Ron Snell

SNELL, RONALD WAYNE 5'10", 158 lbs.
B. Aug. 11, 1948, Regina, Sask. Right Wing, Shoots R

YEAR	TEAM & LEAGUE		GP	G	A	PTS	PIM
1968-69	PITT	N	4	3	1	4	6
1969-70			3	0	1	1	0
1973-74	WINN	W	70	24	25	49	32
1974-75			20	0	0	0	8
4 yrs.		N Totals:	7	3	2	5	6
		W Totals:	90	24	25	49	40
PLAYOFFS							
1973-74	WINN	W	4	0	0	0	0

Harold Snepsts

SNEPSTS, HAROLD JOHN 6'3", 215 lbs.
B. Oct. 24, 1954, Edmonton, Alta. Defense, Shoots L

YEAR	TEAM & LEAGUE		GP	G	A	PTS	PIM
1974-75	VAN	N	27	1	2	3	30
1975-76			78	3	15	18	125
1976-77			79	4	18	22	149
1977-78			75	4	16	20	118
1978-79			76	7	24	31	130
1979-80			79	3	20	23	202
1980-81			76	3	16	19	212
1981-82			68	3	14	17	153
1982-83			46	2	8	10	80
9 yrs.		N Totals:	604	30	133	163	1199
PLAYOFFS							
1975-76	VAN	N	2	0	0	0	4
1978-79			3	0	0	0	0
1979-80			4	0	2	2	8
1980-81			3	0	0	0	8
1981-82			17	0	4	4	50
1982-83			4	1	1	2	8
6 yrs.		N Totals:	33	1	7	8	78

Sandy Snow

SNOW, WILLIAM ALEXANDER 5'11", 175 lbs.
B. Nov. 11, 1946, Glace Bay, N.S. Right Wing, Shoots R

YEAR	TEAM & LEAGUE		GP	G	A	PTS	PIM
1968-69	DET	N	3	0	0	0	2

Traded to **N.Y. Rangers** by Detroit with Terry Sawchuk for Larry Jeffrey, June 8, 1969.

Dennis Sobchuk

SOBCHUK, DENNIS JAMES 6'2", 180 lbs.
B. Jan. 12, 1954, Lang, Sask. Center, Shoots L

YEAR	TEAM & LEAGUE		GP	G	A	PTS	PIM
1974-75	PHOE	W	38	32	45	77	36
1975-76	CIN	W	79	32	40	72	74
1976-77			81	44	52	96	38
1977-78			23	5	9	14	22
	EDM	W	13	6	3	9	4
	2 team total		36	11	12	23	26
1978-79			74	26	37	63	31

Dennis Sobchuk continued

YEAR	TEAM & LEAGUE		GP	G	A	PTS	PIM
1979-80	DET	N	33	4	6	10	0
1982-83	QUE	N	2	1	0	1	2
7 yrs.		N Totals:	35	5	6	11	2
		W Totals:	308	145	186	331	205
PLAYOFFS							
1974-75	PHOE	W	5	4	1	5	2
1976-77	CIN	W	3	0	1	1	2
1977-78	EDM	W	5	1	0	1	4
1978-79			12	6	6	12	4
4 yrs.		W Totals:	25	11	8	19	12

Reclaimed by **Philadelphia** from Edmonton prior to Expansion Draft, June 9, 1979. Claimed as fill by **Philadelphia in Expansion Draft, June 13, 1979. Traded to Detroit** by Philadelphia for Detroit's third round choice (David Michayluk) in the 1981 Entry Draft, Sept. 4, 1979.

Gene Sobchuk

SOBCHUK, EUGENE 5'9", 160 lbs.
B. Feb. 19, 1951, Lang, Sask. Left Wing, Shoots L

YEAR	TEAM & LEAGUE		GP	G	A	PTS	PIM
1973-74	VAN	N	1	0	0	0	0
1974-75	PHOE	W	3	1	0	1	0
1975-76	CIN	W	78	24	19	43	37
3 yrs.		N Totals:	1	0	0	0	0
		W Totals:	81	25	19	44	37

Ken Solheim

SOLHEIM, KENNETH LAWRENCE 6'3", 210 lbs.
B. Mar. 27, 1961, Hythe, Alta. Left Wing, Shoots L

YEAR	TEAM & LEAGUE		GP	G	A	PTS	PIM
1980-81	CHI	N	5	2	0	2	0
	MINN	N	5	2	1	3	0
	2 team total		10	4	1	5	0
1981-82			29	4	5	9	4
1982-83			25	2	4	6	4
	DET	N	10	0	0	0	2
	2 team total		35	2	4	6	6
3 yrs.		N Totals:	74	10	10	20	10
PLAYOFFS							
1980-81	MINN	N	2	1	0	1	0
1981-82			1	0	1	1	2
2 yrs.		N Totals:	3	1	1	2	2

Traded to **Minnesota** by Chicago with Chicago's second round choice (Tom Hirsch) in 1981 Entry Draft, for Glen Sharpley, Dec. 29, 1980. Traded to **Detroit** by Minnesota for future considerations March 8, 1983.

Bob Solinger

SOLINGER, ROBERT EDWARD 5'10", 190 lbs.
B. Dec. 23, 1925, Star City, Sask. Left Wing, Shoots L

YEAR	TEAM & LEAGUE		GP	G	A	PTS	PIM
1951-52	TOR	N	24	5	3	8	4
1952-53			19	1	1	2	2
1953-54			39	3	2	5	2
1954-55			17	1	5	6	11
1959-60	DET	N	1	0	0	0	0
5 yrs.		N Totals:	100	10	11	21	19

Art Somers

SOMERS, ARTHUR 5'5", 167 lbs.
B. Jan. 17, 1904, Winnipeg, Man. Shoots L

YEAR	TEAM & LEAGUE		GP	G	A	PTS	PIM
1929-30	CHI	N	44	11	13	24	74
1930-31			33	3	6	9	33
1931-32	NYR	N	48	11	15	26	45
1932-33			48	7	15	22	28
1933-34			8	1	2	3	5
1934-35			41	0	5	5	4
6 yrs.		N Totals:	222	33	56	89	189
PLAYOFFS							
1929-30	CHI	N	2	0	0	0	2
1930-31			9	0	0	0	0
1931-32	NYR	N	7	0	1	1	8
1932-33*			8	1	4	5	8
1933-34			2	0	0	0	0
1934-35			2	0	0	0	2
6 yrs.		N Totals:	30	1	5	6	20

Roy Sommer

SOMMER, ROY 6', 180 lbs.
B. Apr. 5, 1957, Oakland, Cal. Center, Shoots L

YEAR	TEAM & LEAGUE		GP	G	A	PTS	PIM
1980-81	**EDM**	**N**	3	1	0	1	7

Tom Songin

SONGIN, THOMAS DAVID 6'3", 195 lbs.
B. Dec. 20, 1953, Norwood, Mass. Right Wing, Shoots R

YEAR	TEAM & LEAGUE		GP	G	A	PTS	PIM
1978-79	**BOS**	**N**	17	3	1	4	0
1979-80			17	1	3	4	16
1980-81			9	1	1	2	6
3 yrs.		**N Totals:**	43	5	5	10	22

Signed as free agent by **Boston** Oct. 3, 1978.

Glen Sonmor

SONMOR, GLEN ROBERT 5'11", 165 lbs.
B. Apr. 22, 1929, Moose Jaw, Sask. Left Wing, Shoots L

YEAR	TEAM & LEAGUE		GP	G	A	PTS	PIM
1953-54	**NYR**	**N**	15	2	0	2	17
1954-55			13	0	0	0	4
2 yrs.		**N Totals:**	28	2	0	2	21

John Sorrell

SORRELL, JOHN 6', 152 lbs.
B. Jan. 16, 1904, Chesterville, Ont. Left Wing

YEAR	TEAM & LEAGUE		GP	G	A	PTS	PIM
1930-31	**DET**	**N**	39	9	7	16	10
1931-32			48	8	5	13	22
1932-33			47	14	10	24	11
1933-34			47	21	10	31	8
1934-35			47	20	16	36	12
1935-36			48	13	15	28	8
1936-37			48	8	16	24	4
1937-38			23	3	7	10	0
	NYA	**N**	17	8	2	10	9
	2 team total		40	11	9	20	9
1938-39			48	13	9	22	10
1939-40			48	8	16	24	4
1940-41			30	2	6	8	2
11 yrs.		**N Totals:**	490	127	119	246	100

PLAYOFFS

YEAR	TEAM & LEAGUE		GP	G	A	PTS	PIM
1931-32	**DET**	**N**	2	1	0	1	0
1932-33			4	2	2	4	4
1933-34			8	0	2	2	0
1935-36*			7	3	4	7	0
1936-37*			10	2	4	6	2
1937-38	**NYA**	**N**	6	4	0	4	2
1938-39			2	0	0	0	0
1939-40			3	0	3	3	2
8 yrs.		**N Totals:**	42	12	15	27	10

Emory Sparrow

SPARROW, EMORY
B. Unknown Forward

YEAR	TEAM & LEAGUE		GP	G	A	PTS	PIM
1924-25	**BOS**	**N**	6	0	0	0	4

Fred Speck

SPECK, FREDERICK EDMONDSTONE 5'9", 160 lbs.
B. July 22, 1947, Thorold, Ont. Center, Shoots L

YEAR	TEAM & LEAGUE		GP	G	A	PTS	PIM
1968-69	**DET**	**N**	5	0	0	0	2
1969-70			5	0	0	0	0
1971-72	**VAN**	**N**	18	1	2	3	0
1972-73	**MINN**	**W**	47	13	16	29	52
	LA	**W**	28	3	13	16	22
	2 team total		75	16	29	45	74
1973-74			18	2	5	7	4
1974-75	**M-B**	**W**	30	4	8	12	18
6 yrs.		**N Totals:**	28	1	2	3	2
		W Totals:	123	22	42	64	96

PLAYOFFS

YEAR	TEAM & LEAGUE		GP	G	A	PTS	PIM
1972-73	**LA**	**W**	6	3	2	5	2

Bill Speer

SPEER, FRANCIS WILLIAM 5'11", 200 lbs.
B. Mar. 20, 1942, Lindsay, Ont. Defense, Shoots L

YEAR	TEAM & LEAGUE		GP	G	A	PTS	PIM
1967-68	**PITT**	**N**	68	3	13	16	44
1968-69			34	1	4	5	27
1969-70	**BOS**	**N**	27	1	3	4	4
1970-71			1	0	0	0	4
1972-73	**NY**	**W**	69	3	23	26	40
1973-74	**NY-NJ**	**W**	66	1	3	4	30
6 yrs.		**N Totals:**	130	5	20	25	79
		W Totals:	135	4	26	30	70

PLAYOFFS

YEAR	TEAM & LEAGUE		GP	G	A	PTS	PIM
1969-70*	**BOS**	**N**	8	1	0	1	4

Brian Spencer

SPENCER, BRIAN ROY (Spinner) 5'11", 185 lbs.
B. Sept. 3, 1949, Fort St. James, B.C. Left Wing, Shoots L

YEAR	TEAM & LEAGUE		GP	G	A	PTS	PIM
1969-70	**TOR**	**N**	9	0	0	0	12
1970-71			50	9	15	24	115
1971-72			36	1	5	6	65
1972-73	**NYI**	**N**	78	14	24	38	90
1973-74			54	5	16	21	65
	BUF	**N**	13	3	2	5	4
	2 team total		67	8	18	26	69
1974-75			73	12	29	41	77
1975-76			77	13	26	39	70
1976-77			77	14	15	29	55
1977-78	**PITT**	**N**	79	9	11	20	81
1978-79			7	0	0	0	0
10 yrs.		**N Totals:**	553	80	143	223	634

PLAYOFFS

YEAR	TEAM & LEAGUE		GP	G	A	PTS	PIM
1970-71	**TOR**	**N**	6	0	1	1	17
1974-75	**BUF**	**N**	16	0	4	4	8
1975-76			9	1	0	1	4
1976-77			6	0	0	0	0
4 yrs.		**N Totals:**	37	1	5	6	29

Drafted by **N.Y. Islanders** from Toronto in Expansion Draft, June 6, 1972. Traded to **Buffalo** by N.Y. Islanders for Doug Rombough, March 10, 1974. Traded to **Pittsburgh** by Buffalo for Ron Schock, Sept. 20, 1977.

Irv Spencer

SPENCER, IRVIN JAMES 5'10", 180 lbs.
B. Dec. 4, 1937, Sudbury, Ont. Defense, Shoots L

YEAR	TEAM & LEAGUE		GP	G	A	PTS	PIM
1959-60	**NYR**	**N**	32	1	2	3	20
1960-61			56	1	8	9	30
1961-62			43	2	10	12	31
1962-63	**BOS**	**N**	69	5	17	22	34
1963-64	**DET**	**N**	25	3	0	3	8
1967-68			5	0	1	1	4
1972-73	**PHI**	**W**	54	2	27	29	43
1973-74	**VAN**	**W**	19	0	1	1	6
8 yrs.		**N Totals:**	230	12	38	50	127
		W Totals:	73	2	28	30	49

PLAYOFFS

YEAR	TEAM & LEAGUE		GP	G	A	PTS	PIM
1961-62	**NYR**	**N**	1	0	0	0	2
1963-64	**DET**	**N**	11	0	0	0	0
1964-65			1	0	0	0	4
1965-66			3	0	0	0	2
4 yrs.		**N Totals:**	16	0	0	0	8

Drafted by **N.Y. Rangers** from Montreal, June, 1959. Drafted by **Boston** from N.Y. Rangers, June, 1962. Drafted by **Detroit** from Boston, June, 1963.

Chris Speyer

SPEYER, CHRIS
B. Toronto, Ont. Defense

YEAR	TEAM & LEAGUE		GP	G	A	PTS	PIM
1923-24	**TOR**	**N**	3	0	0	0	0
1924-25			2	0	0	0	0
1933-34	**NYA**	**N**	9	0	0	0	0
3 yrs.		**N Totals:**	14	0	0	0	0

Dan Spring

SPRING, DANIEL JOSEPH 6', 180 lbs.
B. Oct. 31, 1951, Rossland, B.C. Center, Shoots R

YEAR	TEAM & LEAGUE		GP	G	A	PTS	PIM
1973-74	WINN	W	66	8	16	24	8
1974-75			60	19	24	43	22
1975-76	EDM	W	75	12	11	23	8
3 yrs.		W Totals:	201	39	51	90	38
PLAYOFFS							
1973-74	WINN	W	4	0	1	1	0
1975-76	EDM	W	2	1	1	2	0
2 yrs.		W Totals:	6	1	2	3	0

Don Spring

SPRING, DONALD NEIL 5'11", 195 lbs.
B. June 15, 1959, Maracaibo, Venezuela Defense, Shoots L

YEAR	TEAM & LEAGUE		GP	G	A	PTS	PIM
1980-81	WINN	N	80	1	18	19	18
1981-82			78	0	16	16	21
1982-83			80	0	16	16	37
3 yrs.		N Totals:	238	1	50	51	76
PLAYOFFS							
1981-82	WINN	N	4	0	0	0	4
1982-83			2	0	0	0	6
2 yrs.		N Totals:	6	0	0	0	10

Signed as free agent by **Winnipeg** May 22, 1980.

Frank Spring

SPRING, FRANKLIN PATRICK 6'3", 216 lbs.
B. Oct. 19, 1949, Cranbrook, B.C. Right Wing, Shoots R

YEAR	TEAM & LEAGUE		GP	G	A	PTS	PIM
1969-70	BOS	N	1	0	0	0	0
1973-74	STL	N	2	0	0	0	0
1974-75			3	0	0	0	0
	CALIF	N	28	3	8	11	6
	2 team total		31	3	8	11	6
1975-76			1	0	2	2	0
1976-77	CLEVE	N	26	11	10	21	6
1977-78	IND	W	13	2	4	6	2
6 yrs.		N Totals:	61	14	20	34	12
		W Totals:	13	2	4	6	2

Drafted by **Philadelphia** from Boston in Intra-league Draft, June 8, 1971. Sold to **St. Louis** by Philadelphia, Dec. 1, 1973. Traded to **California** by St. Louis for Bruce Affleck, Jan. 9, 1975.

Jesse Spring

SPRING, JESSE
B. Toronto, Ont. Defense

YEAR	TEAM & LEAGUE		GP	G	A	PTS	PIM
1923-24	HAMIL	N	20	3	2	5	8
1924-25			29	2	0	2	11
1925-26	PITT	N	32	5	0	5	23
1926-27	TOR	N	2	0	0	0	0
1928-29	NYA	N	23	0	0	0	0
	PITT	N	5	0	0	0	2
	2 team total		28	0	0	0	2
1929-30	NYA	N	29	0	0	0	0
	PITT	N	22	1	0	1	18
	2 team total		51	1	0	1	18
6 yrs.		N Totals:	162	11	2	13	62
PLAYOFFS							
1925-26	PITT	N	2	0	2	2	2

Andy Spruce

SPRUCE, ANDREW WILLIAM 5'11", 177 lbs.
B. Apr. 17, 1954, London, Ont. Left Wing, Shoots L

YEAR	TEAM & LEAGUE		GP	G	A	PTS	PIM
1976-77	VAN	N	51	9	6	15	37
1977-78	COLO	N	74	19	21	40	43
1978-79			47	3	15	18	31
3 yrs.		N Totals:	172	31	42	73	111
PLAYOFFS							
1977-78	COLO	N	2	0	2	2	0

Signed as free agent by **Colorado** Oct. 5, 1977.

Ron Stackhouse

STACKHOUSE, RONALD LORNE 6'3", 210 lbs.
B. Aug. 26, 1949, Haliburton, Ont. Defense, Shoots R

YEAR	TEAM & LEAGUE		GP	G	A	PTS	PIM
1970-71	CALIF	N	78	8	24	32	73
1971-72			6	1	3	4	8
	DET	N	73	5	25	30	81
	2 team total		79	6	28	34	89
1972-73			78	5	29	34	82
1973-74			33	2	14	16	33
	PITT	N	36	4	15	19	33
	2 team total		69	6	29	35	66
1974-75			72	15	45	60	52
1975-76			80	11	60	71	76
1976-77			80	7	34	41	72
1977-78			50	5	15	20	36
1978-79			75	10	33	43	54
1979-80			78	6	27	33	36
1980-81			74	6	29	35	86
1981-82			76	2	19	21	102
12 yrs.		N Totals:	889	87	372	459	824
PLAYOFFS							
1974-75	PITT	N	9	2	6	8	10
1975-76			3	0	0	0	0
1976-77			3	2	1	3	0
1978-79			7	0	0	0	4
1979-80			5	1	0	1	18
1980-81			4	0	1	1	6
1981-82			1	0	0	0	0
7 yrs.		N Totals:	32	5	8	13	38

Traded to **Detroit** by California for Tom Webster, Oct. 22, 1971. Traded to **Pittsburgh** by Detroit for Jack Lynch and goaltender Jim Rutherford, Jan. 18, 1974.

Ted Stackhouse

STACKHOUSE, THEODORE
B. Unknown Defense

YEAR	TEAM & LEAGUE		GP	G	A	PTS	PIM
1921-22	TOR	N	12	0	0	0	2
PLAYOFFS							
1921-22*	TOR	N	5	0	0	0	0

Butch Stahan

STAHAN, FRANK RALPH
B. Oct. 29, 1915, Minnedosa, Man. Defense

YEAR	TEAM & LEAGUE		GP	G	A	PTS	PIM
PLAYOFFS							
1944-45	MONT	N	3	0	1	1	2

Al Staley

STALEY, ALLAN R. 6', 160 lbs.
B. Sept. 21, 1928, Regina, Sask. Center, Shoots R

YEAR	TEAM & LEAGUE		GP	G	A	PTS	PIM
1948-49	NYR	N	1	0	1	1	0

Lorne Stamler

STAMLER, LORNE ALEXANDER 6', 190 lbs.
B. Aug. 9, 1951, Winnipeg, Man. Left Wing, Shoots L

YEAR	TEAM & LEAGUE		GP	G	A	PTS	PIM
1976-77	LA	N	7	2	1	3	2
1977-78			2	0	0	0	0
1978-79	TOR	N	45	4	3	7	2
1979-80	WINN	N	62	8	7	15	12
4 yrs.		N Totals:	116	14	11	25	16

Traded to **Toronto** by Los Angeles with Dave Hutchison for Brian Glennie, Scott Garland, Kurt Walker and Toronto's second round choice (Mark Hardy) in the 1979 Entry Draft, June 14, 1978. Claimed by **Winnipeg** from Toronto in Expansion Draft, June 13, 1979.

George Standing

STANDING, GEORGE MICHAEL 5'10", 175 lbs.
B. Aug. 3, 1941, Toronto, Ont. Right Wing, Shoots R

YEAR	TEAM & LEAGUE		GP	G	A	PTS	PIM
1967-68	MINN	N	2	0	0	0	0

Fred Stanfield

STANFIELD, FREDERIC WILLIAM 5'10", 185 lbs.
B. May 4, 1944, Toronto, Ont. Center, Shoots L

YEAR	TEAM & LEAGUE		GP	G	A	PTS	PIM
1964-65	**CHI**	**N**	58	7	10	17	14
1965-66			39	2	2	4	2
1966-67			10	1	0	1	0
1967-68	**BOS**	**N**	73	20	44	64	10
1968-69			71	25	29	54	22
1969-70			73	23	35	58	14
1970-71			75	24	52	76	12
1971-72			78	23	56	79	12
1972-73			78	20	58	78	10
1973-74	**MINN**	**N**	71	16	28	44	10
1974-75			40	8	18	26	12
	BUF	**N**	32	12	21	33	4
	2 team total		72	20	39	59	16
1975-76			80	18	30	48	4
1976-77			79	9	14	23	6
1977-78			57	3	8	11	2
14 yrs.		**N Totals:**	914	211	405	616	134

PLAYOFFS

YEAR	TEAM & LEAGUE		GP	G	A	PTS	PIM
1964-65	**CHI**	**N**	14	2	1	3	2
1965-66			5	0	0	0	2
1966-67			1	0	0	0	0
1967-68	**BOS**	**N**	4	0	1	1	0
1968-69			10	2	2	4	0
1969-70*			14	4	12	16	6
1970-71			7	3	4	7	0
1971-72*			15	7	9	16	0
1972-73			5	1	1	2	0
1974-75	**BUF**	**N**	17	2	4	6	0
1975-76			9	0	1	1	0
1976-77			5	0	0	0	0
12 yrs.		**N Totals:**	106	21	35	56	10

Traded to **Boston** by Chicago with Phil Esposito and Ken Hodge for Gilles Marotte, Pit Martin and Jack Norris, May 15, 1967. Traded to **Minnesota** by Boston for goaltender Gilles Gilbert, May 22, 1973. Traded to **Buffalo** by Minnesota for Norm Gratton and Buffalo's third choice (Ron Zanussi) in the 1976 Amateur Draft, Jan. 27, 1975.

Jack Stanfield

STANFIELD, JOHN GORDON 5'11", 176 lbs.
B. May 30, 1942, Toronto, Ont. Left Wing, Shoots L

YEAR	TEAM & LEAGUE		GP	G	A	PTS	PIM
1972-73	**HOUS**	**W**	71	8	12	20	8
1973-74			41	1	3	4	2
2 yrs.		**W Totals:**	112	9	15	24	10

PLAYOFFS

YEAR	TEAM & LEAGUE		GP	G	A	PTS	PIM
1965-66	**CHI**	**N**	1	0	0	0	0
1972-73	**HOUS**	**W**	9	1	0	1	0
1973-74			7	0	0	0	2
3 yrs.		**N Totals:**	1	0	0	0	0
		W Totals:	16	1	0	1	2

Jim Stanfield

STANFIELD, JAMES BOVIARD 5'10", 165 lbs.
B. Jan. 1, 1947, Toronto, Ont. Center, Shoots L

YEAR	TEAM & LEAGUE		GP	G	A	PTS	PIM
1969-70	**LA**	**N**	1	0	0	0	0
1970-71			2	0	0	0	0
1971-72			4	0	1	1	0
3 yrs.		**N Totals:**	7	0	1	1	0

Edward Stankiewicz

STANKIEWICZ, EDWARD 5'9", 175 lbs.
B. Dec. 1, 1929, Kitchener, Ont. Right Wing, Shoots R

YEAR	TEAM & LEAGUE		GP	G	A	PTS	PIM
1953-54	**DET**	**N**	1	0	0	0	2
1955-56			5	0	0	0	0
2 yrs.		**N Totals:**	6	0	0	0	2

Myron Stankiewicz

STANKIEWICZ, MYRON 5'11", 185 lbs.
B. Dec. 4, 1935, Kitchener, Ont. Left Wing, Shoots L

YEAR	TEAM & LEAGUE		GP	G	A	PTS	PIM
1968-69	**STL**	**N**	16	0	2	2	11
	PHI	**N**	19	0	5	5	25
	2 team total		35	0	7	7	36

PLAYOFFS

YEAR	TEAM & LEAGUE		GP	G	A	PTS	PIM
1968-69	**PHI**	**N**	1	0	0	0	0

Claimed on waivers by **Philadelphia** from St. Louis, Jan. 16, 1969.

Allan Stanley

STANLEY, ALLAN HERBERT 6'2", 191 lbs.
B. Mar. 1, 1926, Timmins, Ont. Defense, Shoots L
Hall of Fame, 1981

YEAR	TEAM & LEAGUE		GP	G	A	PTS	PIM
1948-49	**NYR**	**N**	40	2	8	10	22
1949-50			55	4	4	8	58
1950-51			70	7	14	21	75
1951-52			50	5	14	19	52
1952-53			70	5	12	17	52
1953-54			10	0	2	2	11
1954-55			12	0	1	1	2
	CHI	**N**	52	10	15	25	22
	2 team total		64	10	16	26	24
1955-56			59	4	14	18	70
1956-57	**BOS**	**N**	60	6	25	31	45
1957-58			69	6	25	31	37
1958-59	**TOR**	**N**	70	1	22	23	47
1959-60			64	10	23	33	22
1960-61			68	9	25	34	42
1961-62			60	9	26	35	24
1962-63			61	4	15	19	22
1963-64			70	6	21	27	60
1964-65			64	2	15	17	30
1965-66			59	4	14	18	35
1966-67			53	1	12	13	20
1967-68			64	1	13	14	16
1968-69	**PHI**	**N**	64	4	13	17	28
21 yrs.		**N Totals:**	1244	100	333	433	792

PLAYOFFS

YEAR	TEAM & LEAGUE		GP	G	A	PTS	PIM
1949-50	**NYR**	**N**	12	2	5	7	10
1957-58	**BOS**	**N**	12	1	3	4	6
1958-59	**TOR**	**N**	12	0	3	3	2
1959-60			10	2	3	5	2
1960-61			5	0	3	3	0
1961-62*			12	0	3	3	6
1962-63*			10	1	6	7	8
1963-64*			14	1	6	7	20
1964-65			6	0	1	1	12
1965-66			1	0	0	0	0
1966-67*			12	0	2	2	10
1968-69	**PHI**	**N**	3	0	1	1	4
12 yrs.		**N Totals:**	109	7	36	43	80

Traded to **Chicago** by N.Y. Rangers with Nick Mickoski and Richard Lamoureux for Bill Gadsby and Pete Conacher, Nov., 1954. Sold to **Boston** by Chicago, Oct., 1956. Traded to **Toronto** by Boston for Jim Morrison, Oct. 8, 1958.

Barney Stanley

STANLEY, BARNEY
B. Jan. 1, 1893, Paisley, Ont.

YEAR	TEAM & LEAGUE		GP	G	A	PTS	PIM
1927-28	**CHI**	**N**	1	0	0	0	0

Wally Stanowski

STANOWSKI, WALTER 5'11", 180 lbs.
B. Apr. 28, 1919, Winnipeg, Man. Defense, Shoots L

YEAR	TEAM & LEAGUE		GP	G	A	PTS	PIM
1939-40	**TOR**	**N**	27	2	7	9	11
1940-41			47	7	14	21	35
1941-42			24	1	7	8	10
1944-45			34	2	9	11	16
1945-46			45	3	10	13	10
1946-47			51	3	16	19	12
1947-48			54	2	11	13	12
1948-49	**NYR**	**N**	60	1	8	9	16
1949-50			37	1	1	2	10
1950-51			49	1	5	6	28

Wally Stanowski continued

YEAR	TEAM & LEAGUE		GP	G	A	PTS	PIM
10 yrs.		N Totals:	428	23	88	111	160
PLAYOFFS							
1939-40	TOR	N	10	1	0	1	2
1940-41			7	0	3	3	2
1941-42*			13	2	8	10	2
1944-45*			13	0	1	1	5
1946-47*			8	0	0	0	0
1947-48*			9	0	2	2	2
6 yrs.		N Totals:	60	3	14	17	13

Brian Stapleton

STAPLETON, BRIAN 6'2", 190 lbs.
B. Dec. 25, 1951, Fort Erie, Ont. Defense, Shoots R

YEAR	TEAM & LEAGUE		GP	G	A	PTS	PIM
1975-76	WASH	N	1	0	0	0	0

Pat Stapleton

STAPLETON, PATRICK JAMES 5'8", 185 lbs.
B. July 4, 1940, Sarnia, Ont. Defense, Shoots L

YEAR	TEAM & LEAGUE		GP	G	A	PTS	PIM
1961-62	BOS	N	69	2	5	7	42
1962-63			21	0	3	3	8
1965-66	CHI	N	55	4	30	34	52
1966-67			70	3	31	34	54
1967-68			67	4	34	38	34
1968-69			75	6	50	56	44
1969-70			49	4	38	42	28
1970-71			76	7	44	51	30
1971-72			78	3	38	41	47
1972-73			75	10	21	31	14
1973-74	CHI	W	78	6	52	58	44
1974-75			68	4	30	34	38
1975-76	IND	W	80	4	40	44	48
1976-77			81	8	45	53	29
1977-78	CIN	W	65	4	45	49	28
15 yrs.		N Totals:	635	43	294	337	353
		W Totals:	372	26	212	238	187
PLAYOFFS							
1965-66	CHI	N	6	2	3	5	4
1966-67			6	1	1	2	12
1967-68			11	0	4	4	4
1970-71			18	3	14	17	4
1971-72			8	2	2	4	4
1972-73			16	2	15	17	10
1973-74	CHI	W	18	0	13	13	36
1975-76	IND	W	7	0	2	2	2
1976-77			9	2	6	8	0
9 yrs.		N Totals:	65	10	39	49	38
		W Totals:	34	2	21	23	38

Drafted by **Boston** from Chicago, June, 1961. Traded to **Toronto** by Boston with Orland Kurtenbach and Andy Hebenton for Ron Stewart, June 8, 1965. Drafted by **Chicago** from Toronto, June 9, 1965.

Harold Starr

STARR, HAROLD 5'11", 176 lbs.
B. July 6, 1906, Ottawa, Ont. Shoots L

YEAR	TEAM & LEAGUE		GP	G	A	PTS	PIM
1929-30	OTTA	N	27	2	1	3	12
1930-31			36	2	1	3	48
1931-32	MON(M)	N	46	1	2	3	47
1932-33	OTTA	N	31	0	0	0	30
	MONT	N	15	0	0	0	6
	2 team total		46	0	0	0	36
1933-34	MON(M)	N	1	0	0	0	0
1934-35	NYR	N	32	1	1	2	31
1935-36			15	0	0	0	12
7 yrs.		N Totals:	203	6	5	11	186
PLAYOFFS							
1929-30	OTTA	N	2	1	0	1	0
1931-32	MON(M)	N	4	0	0	0	0
1932-33	MONT	N	4	0	0	0	0
1933-34	MON(M)	N	3	0	0	0	0
1934-35	NYR	N	4	0	0	0	2
5 yrs.		N Totals:	17	1	0	1	2

Wilf Starr

STARR, WILFRED 5'11", 190 lbs.
B. July 22, 1909, St. Boniface, Man. Forward, Shoots L

YEAR	TEAM & LEAGUE		GP	G	A	PTS	PIM
1932-33	NYA	N	27	4	3	7	8
1933-34	DET	N	28	2	2	4	17
1934-35			29	1	1	2	0
1935-36			5	1	0	1	0
4 yrs.		N Totals:	89	8	6	14	25
PLAYOFFS							
1933-34	DET	N	7	0	2	2	2

Vic Stasiuk

STASIUK, VICTOR JOHN 6'1", 185 lbs.
B. May 23, 1929, Lethbridge, Alta. Left Wing, Shoots L

YEAR	TEAM & LEAGUE		GP	G	A	PTS	PIM
1949-50	CHI	N	17	1	1	2	2
1950-51			20	5	3	8	6
	DET	N	50	3	10	13	12
	2 team total		70	8	13	21	18
1951-52			58	5	9	14	19
1952-53			3	0	0	0	0
1953-54			42	5	2	7	4
1954-55			59	8	11	19	67
1955-56	BOS	N	59	19	18	37	118
1956-57			64	24	16	40	50
1957-58			70	21	35	56	55
1958-59			70	27	33	60	63
1959-60			69	29	39	68	121
1960-61			46	5	25	30	35
	DET	N	21	10	13	23	16
	2 team total		67	15	38	53	51
1961-62			59	15	28	43	45
1962-63			36	6	11	17	37
14 yrs.		N Totals:	743	183	254	437	650
PLAYOFFS							
1951-52*	DET	N	7	0	2	2	0
1954-55*			11	5	3	8	6
1956-57	BOS	N	10	2	1	3	2
1957-58			12	0	5	5	13
1958-59			7	4	2	6	11
1960-61	DET	N	11	2	5	7	4
1962-63			11	3	0	3	4
7 yrs.		N Totals:	69	16	18	34	40

Traded to **Detroit** by Chicago with Bert Olmstead for Lee Fogolin and Steve Black, Dec. 10, 1950. Traded to **Boston** by Detroit with Marcel Bonin, Lorne Davis and Terry Sawchuk for Gilles Boisvert, Real Chevrefils, Norm Corcoran, Warren Godfrey, and Ed Sandford, June 3, 1955. Traded to **Detroit** by Boston with Leo Labine for Gary Aldcorn, Murray Oliver, and Thomas McCarthy, Jan., 1961.

Anton Stastny

STASTNY, ANTON 5'9", 175 lbs.
B. Aug. 5, 1959, Bratislava, Czech. Left Wing, Shoots L

YEAR	TEAM & LEAGUE		GP	G	A	PTS	PIM
1980-81	QUE	N	80	39	46	85	12
1981-82			68	26	46	72	16
1982-83			79	32	60	92	25
3 yrs.		N Totals:	227	97	152	249	53
PLAYOFFS							
1980-81	QUE	N	5	4	3	7	2
1981-82			16	5	10	15	10
1982-83			4	2	2	4	0
3 yrs.		N Totals:	25	11	15	26	12

Marian Stastny

STASTNY, MARIAN 5'10", 193 lbs.
B. Jan. 8, 1953, Bratislava, Czech. Right Wing, Shoots L

YEAR	TEAM & LEAGUE		GP	G	A	PTS	PIM
1981-82	QUE	N	74	35	54	89	27
1982-83			60	36	43	79	32
2 yrs.		N Totals:	134	71	97	168	59
PLAYOFFS							
1981-82	QUE	N	16	3	14	17	5
1982-83			2	0	0	0	0

Marian Stastny continued

YEAR	TEAM & LEAGUE		GP	G	A	PTS	PIM
2 yrs.		**N Totals:**	18	3	14	17	5

Signed as free agent by **Quebec** Aug. 26, 1980.

Peter Stastny

STASTNY, PETER 5'10", 190 lbs.
B. Sept. 18, 1956, Bratislava, Czech. Center, Shoots L
Won Calder Trophy, 1980-81

YEAR	TEAM & LEAGUE		GP	G	A	PTS	PIM
1980-81	**QUE**	**N**	77	39	70	109	37
1981-82			80	46	93	139	91
1982-83			75	47	77	124	78
3 yrs.		**N Totals:**	232	132	240	372	206
PLAYOFFS							
1980-81	**QUE**	**N**	5	2	8	10	7
1981-82			12	7	11	18	10
1982-83			4	3	2	5	10
3 yrs.		**N Totals:**	21	12	21	33	27

Signed as free agent by **Quebec** Aug. 26, 1980.

Billy Steele

STEELE, WILLIAM 5'7", lbs.
B. Nov. 13, 1952, Edinburgh, Scotland Forward, Shoots R

YEAR	TEAM & LEAGUE		GP	G	A	PTS	PIM
1975-76	**CIN**	**W**	3	2	0	2	0
1976-77			81	9	22	31	21
2 yrs.		**W Totals:**	84	11	22	33	21
PLAYOFFS							
1976-77	**CIN**	**W**	2	0	0	0	0

Frank Steele

STEELE, FRANK
Defense

YEAR	TEAM & LEAGUE		GP	G	A	PTS	PIM
1930-31	**DET**	**N**	1	0	0	0	0

Tom Steen

STEEN, THOMAS 5'10", 195 lbs.
B. June 8, 1960, Tocksmark, Sweden Center, Shoots L

YEAR	TEAM & LEAGUE		GP	G	A	PTS	PIM
1980-81	**WINN**	**N**	42	5	11	16	22
1981-82			73	15	29	44	42
1982-83			75	26	33	59	60
3 yrs.		**N Totals:**	190	46	73	119	124
PLAYOFFS							
1981-82	**WINN**	**N**	4	0	4	4	2
1982-83			3	0	2	2	0
2 yrs.		**N Totals:**	7	0	6	6	2

Signed as free agent by **Winnipeg** Mar. 26, 1980.

Morris Stefaniw

STEFANIW, MORRIS ALEXANDER 5'11", 170 lbs.
B. Jan. 10, 1948, North Battleford, Sask. Center, Shoots L

YEAR	TEAM & LEAGUE		GP	G	A	PTS	PIM
1972-73	**ATL**	**N**	13	1	1	2	2

Drafted by **Atlanta** from N.Y. Rangers in Expansion Draft, June 6, 1972.

Bud Stefanski

STEFANSKI, EDWARD STANLEY MICHAEL
5'10", 170 lbs.
B. Apr. 28, 1955, South Porcupine, Ont. Center, Shoots L

YEAR	TEAM & LEAGUE		GP	G	A	PTS	PIM
1977-78	**NYR**	**N**	1	0	0	0	0

Sold to **Winnipeg** by N.Y. Rangers for future considerations, Oct. 12, 1979.

Pete Stemkowski

STEMKOWSKI, PETER DAVID (Stemmer)
6'1", 210 lbs.
B. Aug. 25, 1943, Winnipeg, Man. Center, Shoots L

YEAR	TEAM & LEAGUE		GP	G	A	PTS	PIM
1963-64	**TOR**	**N**	1	0	0	0	2

Pete Stemkowski continued

YEAR	TEAM & LEAGUE		GP	G	A	PTS	PIM
1964-65			36	5	15	20	33
1965-66			56	4	12	16	55
1966-67			68	13	22	35	75
1967-68			60	7	15	22	82
	DET	**N**	13	3	6	9	4
	2 team total		73	10	21	31	86
1968-69			71	21	31	52	81
1969-70			76	25	24	49	114
1970-71			10	2	2	4	8
	NYR	**N**	68	16	29	45	61
	2 team total		78	18	31	49	69
1971-72			59	11	17	28	53
1972-73			78	22	37	59	71
1973-74			78	25	45	70	74
1974-75			77	24	35	59	63
1975-76			75	13	28	41	49
1976-77			61	2	13	15	8
1977-78	**LA**	**N**	80	13	18	31	33
15 yrs.		**N Totals:**	967	206	349	555	866
PLAYOFFS							
1964-65	**TOR**	**N**	6	0	3	3	7
1965-66			4	0	0	0	26
1966-67*			12	5	7	12	20
1969-70	**DET**	**N**	4	1	1	2	6
1970-71	**NYR**	**N**	13	3	2	5	6
1971-72			16	4	8	12	18
1972-73			10	4	2	6	6
1973-74			13	6	6	12	35
1974-75			3	1	0	1	10
1977-78	**LA**	**N**	2	1	0	1	2
10 yrs.		**N Totals:**	83	25	29	54	136

Traded to **Detroit** by Toronto with Frank Mahovlich, Garry Unger and the rights to Carl Brewer for Norm Ullman, Paul Henderson and Floyd Smith, March 3, 1968. Traded to **N.Y. Rangers** by Detroit for Larry Brown, Oct. 31, 1970. Signed as free agent by **Los Angeles** Aug. 31, 1977. As compensation, N.Y. Rangers received Los Angeles' third round round choice (Dean Turner) in the 1978 Amateur Draft.

Ken Stenlund

STENLUND, KENNETH VERN 6'1", 178 lbs.
B. Apr. 11, 1956, Thunder Bay, Ont. Center, Shoots L

YEAR	TEAM & LEAGUE		GP	G	A	PTS	PIM
1976-77	**CLEVE**	**N**	4	0	0	0	0

Put on **Minnesota** Reserve List after Cleveland-Minnesota Dispersal Draft, June 15, 1978.

Phil Stephens

STEPHENS, PHIL
Defense

YEAR	TEAM & LEAGUE		GP	G	A	PTS	PIM
1917-18	**MON(W)**	**N**	4	1	0	1	3
1921-22	**MONT**	**N**	4	0	0	0	0
2 yrs.		**N Totals:**	8	1	0	1	3

Bob Stephenson

STEPHENSON, ROBERT 6'1", 187 lbs.
B. Feb. 1, 1954, Saskatoon, Sask. Defense, Shoots R

YEAR	TEAM & LEAGUE		GP	G	A	PTS	PIM
1977-78	**BIRM**	**W**	39	7	6	13	33
1978-79			78	23	24	47	72
1979-80	**HART**	**N**	4	0	1	1	0
	TOR	**N**	14	2	2	4	4
	2 team total		18	2	3	5	4
3 yrs.		**N Totals:**	18	2	3	5	4
		W Totals:	117	30	30	60	105

Traded to **Toronto** by Hartford for Pat Boutette, Dec. 24, 1979.

Ken Stephenson

STEPHENSON, KENNETH
Forward

YEAR	TEAM & LEAGUE		GP	G	A	PTS	PIM
1972-73	**OTTA**	**W**	77	3	16	19	93
1973-74	**WINN**	**W**	29	0	7	7	24
2 yrs.		**W Totals:**	106	3	23	26	117
PLAYOFFS							
1972-73	**OTTA**	**W**	5	1	1	2	8
1973-74	**WINN**	**W**	3	0	2	2	10

Ken Stephenson continued

YEAR	TEAM & LEAGUE		GP	G	A	PTS	PIM
2 yrs.		W Totals:	8	1	3	4	18

Ulf Sterner

STERNER, ULF 6'2", 187 lbs.
B. Feb. 11, 1941, Deje, Sweden. Left Wing, Shoots L

YEAR	TEAM & LEAGUE		GP	G	A	PTS	PIM
1964-65	NYR	N	4	0	0	0	0

Mike Stevens

STEVENS, MICHAEL 5'11", 188 lbs.
B. Oct. 13, 1950, Winnipeg, Man. Defense, Shoots L

YEAR	TEAM & LEAGUE		GP	G	A	PTS	PIM
1974-75	PHOE	W	70	2	16	18	69
1975-76	HOUS	W	6	0	0	0	2
2 yrs.		W Totals:	76	2	16	18	71
PLAYOFFS							
1974-75	PHOE	W	5	0	1	1	0

Paul Stevens

STEVENS, PAUL
B. Unknown. Defense

YEAR	TEAM & LEAGUE		GP	G	A	PTS	PIM
1925-26	BOS	N	17	0	0	0	0

Scott Stevens

STEVENS, SCOTT 5'11½", 200 lbs.
B. Apr. 1, 1964, Kitchener, Ont. Defense, Shoots L

YEAR	TEAM & LEAGUE		GP	G	A	PTS	PIM
1982-83	WASH	N	77	9	16	25	195
PLAYOFFS							
1982-83	WASH	N	4	1	0	1	26

Bill Stewart

STEWART, WILLIAM DONALD 6'2", 180 lbs.
B. Oct. 6, 1957, Toronto, Ont. Defense, Shoots R

YEAR	TEAM & LEAGUE		GP	G	A	PTS	PIM
1977-78	BUF	N	13	2	0	2	15
1978-79			68	1	17	18	101
1980-81	STL	N	60	2	21	23	114
1981-82			22	0	5	5	25
1982-83			7	0	0	0	8
5 yrs.		N Totals:	170	5	43	48	263
PLAYOFFS							
1977-78	BUF	N	8	0	2	2	0
1978-79			1	0	1	1	0
1980-81	STL	N	4	1	0	1	11
3 yrs.		N Totals:	13	1	3	4	11

Claimed by **Buffalo** as fill in Expansion Draft, June 13, 1979. Traded to **St. Louis** by Buffalo for Bob Hess, Oct. 30, 1980.

Blair Stewart

STEWART, BLAIR JAMES 5'11", 185 lbs.
B. Mar. 15, 1953, Winnipeg, Man. Left Wing, Shoots L

YEAR	TEAM & LEAGUE		GP	G	A	PTS	PIM
1973-74	DET	N	17	0	4	4	16
1974-75			19	0	5	5	38
	WASH	N	2	1	0	1	2
	2 team total		21	1	5	6	40
1975-76			74	13	14	27	113
1976-77			34	5	2	7	85
1977-78			8	0	1	1	9
1978-79			45	7	12	19	48
1979-80	QUE	N	30	8	6	14	15
7 yrs.		N Totals:	229	34	44	78	326

Traded to **Washington** by Detroit for Mike Bloom, March 9, 1975. Claimed by **Quebec** from Washington in Expansion Draft, June 13, 1979.

Gaye Stewart

STEWART, GAYE 5'11½", 175 lbs.
B. June 28, 1923, Fort William, Ont. Left Wing, Shoots L
Won Calder Trophy, 1942-43

YEAR	TEAM & LEAGUE		GP	G	A	PTS	PIM
1942-43	TOR	N	48	24	23	47	20

Gaye Stewart continued

YEAR	TEAM & LEAGUE		GP	G	A	PTS	PIM
1945-46			50	**37**	15	52	8
1946-47			60	19	14	33	15
1947-48			7	1	0	1	9
	CHI	N	54	26	29	55	74
	2 team total		61	27	29	56	83
1948-49			54	20	18	38	57
1949-50			70	24	19	43	43
1950-51	DET	N	67	18	13	31	18
1951-52	NYR	N	69	15	25	40	22
1952-53			18	1	1	2	8
	MONT	N	5	0	2	2	0
	2 team total		23	1	3	4	8
9 yrs.		N Totals:	502	185	159	344	274
PLAYOFFS							
1941-42*	TOR	N	3	0	0	0	0
1942-43			4	0	2	2	4
1946-47*			11	2	5	7	4
1950-51	DET	N	6	0	2	2	4
1953-54	MONT	N	3	0	0	0	0
5 yrs.		N Totals:	27	2	9	11	12

Traded to **Detroit** by Chicago with Jim Henry, Bob Goldham, and Metro Prystai for Harry Lumley, Jack Stewart, Al Dewsbury, Don Morrison and Pete Babando, July 13, 1950. Traded to **N.Y. Rangers** by Detroit for Tony Leswick, June 19, 1951. Sold to **Montreal** by N.Y. Rangers, Dec. 8, 1952.

Jack Stewart

STEWART, JOHN SHERRATT (Black Jack) 5'11", 185 lbs.
B. May 6, 1917, Pilot Mound, Man. Defense, Shoots L
Hall of Fame, 1964

YEAR	TEAM & LEAGUE		GP	G	A	PTS	PIM
1938-39	DET	N	32	0	1	1	18
1939-40			48	1	0	1	40
1940-41			47	2	6	8	56
1941-42			44	4	7	11	93
1942-43			44	2	9	11	68
1945-46			47	4	11	15	**73**
1946-47			55	5	9	14	83
1947-48			60	5	14	19	83
1948-49			60	4	11	15	96
1949-50			65	3	11	14	86
1950-51	CHI	N	26	0	1	1	49
1951-52			37	1	3	4	12
12 yrs.		N Totals:	565	31	83	114	757
PLAYOFFS							
1939-40	DET	N	5	0	0	0	4
1940-41			9	1	2	3	8
1941-42			12	0	1	1	12
1942-43*			10	1	2	3	35
1945-46			5	0	0	0	14
1946-47			5	0	1	1	12
1947-48			9	1	3	4	6
1948-49			11	1	1	2	32
1949-50*			14	1	4	5	20
9 yrs.		N Totals:	80	5	14	19	143

Traded to **Chicago** by Detroit with Harry Lumley, Pete Babando, Al Dewsbury and Don Morrison for Jim Henry, Metro Prystai, Gaye Stewart and Bob Goldham, July 13, 1950.

John Stewart

STEWART, JOHN ALEXANDER 6', 180 lbs.
B. May 16, 1950, Eriksdale, Man. Left Wing, Shoots L

YEAR	TEAM & LEAGUE		GP	G	A	PTS	PIM
1970-71	PITT	N	15	2	1	3	9
1971-72			25	2	8	10	23
1972-73	ATL	N	68	17	17	34	30
1973-74			74	18	15	33	41
1974-75	CALIF	N	76	19	19	38	55
1975-76	CLEVE	W	79	12	21	33	43
1976-77	MINN	W	15	3	3	6	2
	BIRM	W	1	0	0	0	0
	2 team total		16	3	3	6	2
1977-78			48	13	26	39	52
1978-79			70	24	26	50	108
1979-80	QUE	N	2	0	0	0	0
10 yrs.		N Totals:	260	58	60	118	158
		W Totals:	213	52	76	128	205
PLAYOFFS							
1973-74	ATL	N	4	0	0	0	10

John Stewart continued

YEAR	TEAM	LEAGUE	GP	G	A	PTS	PIM
1975-76	CLEVE	W	3	0	0	0	0
2 yrs.		N Totals:	4	0	0	0	10
		W Totals:	3	0	0	0	0

Drafted by **Atlanta** from Pittsburgh in Expansion Draft, June 6, 1972. Traded to **California** by Atlanta for Hilliard Graves, July 18, 1974.

John Stewart

STEWART, JOHN CHRISTOPHER 5'11", 170 lbs.
B. Jan. 2, 1954, Toronto, Ont. Center, Shoots L

YEAR	TEAM	LEAGUE	GP	G	A	PTS	PIM
1974-75	CLEVE	W	59	4	7	11	8
1975-76			42	2	9	11	15
1976-77	BIRM	W	52	17	24	41	33
3 yrs.		W Totals:	153	23	40	63	56
PLAYOFFS							
1974-75	CLEVE	W	1	0	0	0	0
1977-78	BIRM	W	5	1	1	2	6
2 yrs.		W Totals:	6	1	1	2	6

Ken Stewart

STEWART, KENNETH
B. Port Arthur, Ont. Forward

YEAR	TEAM	LEAGUE	GP	G	A	PTS	PIM
1941-42	CHI	N	6	1	1	2	2

Nels Stewart

STEWART, NELS 6'1", 195 lbs.
B. Dec. 29, 1902 Center
Won Hart Trophy, 1925–26, 1929-30
Won Art Ross Trophy, 1925-26
Hall of Fame, 1962

YEAR	TEAM	LEAGUE	GP	G	A	PTS	PIM
1925-26	MON(M)	N	36	**34**	8	**42**	119
1926-27			44	17	4	21	**133**
1927-28			43	27	7	34	104
1928-29			44	21	8	29	74
1929-30			43	39	16	55	81
1930-31			43	25	14	39	75
1931-32			38	22	11	33	61
1932-33	BOS	N	47	18	18	36	62
1933-34			47	21	17	38	68
1934-35			47	21	18	39	45
1935-36	NYA	N	48	14	15	29	16
1936-37	BOS	N	11	3	2	5	6
	NYA	N	32	20	10	30	31
	2 team total		43	**23**	12	35	37
1937-38			48	19	17	36	29
1938-39			46	16	19	35	43
1939-40			37	7	7	14	6
15 yrs.		N Totals:	654	324	191	515	953
PLAYOFFS							
1925-26*	MON(M)	N	8	6	1	7	24
1926-27			2	0	0	0	4
1927-28			9	2	2	4	17
1929-30			4	1	1	2	2
1930-31			2	1	0	1	6
1931-32			4	0	1	1	2
1932-33	BOS	N	5	2	0	2	4
1934-35			4	0	1	1	0
1935-36	NYA	N	5	1	2	3	4
1937-38			6	2	3	5	2
1938-39			2	0	0	0	0
1939-40			3	0	0	0	0
12 yrs.		N Totals:	54	15	11	26	65

Paul Stewart

STEWART, PAUL G. 6'1", 205 lbs.
B. Mar. 21, 1954, Boston, Mass. Left Wing, Shoots L

YEAR	TEAM	LEAGUE	GP	G	A	PTS	PIM
1976-77	EDM	W	2	0	0	0	2
1977-78	CIN	W	40	1	5	6	241
1978-79			23	2	1	3	45
1979-80	QUE	N	21	2	0	2	74
4 yrs.		N Totals:	21	2	0	2	74
		W Totals:	65	3	6	9	288
PLAYOFFS							
1978-79	CIN	W	3	0	0	0	0

Ralph Stewart

STEWART, RALPH DONALD 6'2", 190 lbs.
B. Dec. 2, 1948, Fort William, Ont. Center, Shoots L

YEAR	TEAM	LEAGUE	GP	G	A	PTS	PIM
1970-71	VAN	N	3	0	1	1	0
1972-73	NYI	N	31	4	10	14	4
1973-74			67	23	20	43	6
1974-75			70	16	24	40	12
1975-76			31	6	7	13	2
1976-77	VAN	N	34	6	8	14	4
1977-78			16	2	3	5	0
7 yrs.		N Totals:	252	57	73	130	28
PLAYOFFS							
1974-75	NYI	N	13	3	3	6	2
1975-76			6	1	1	2	0
2 yrs.		N Totals:	19	4	4	8	2

Drafted by **Vancouver** from Montreal in Expansion Draft, June 10, 1970. Traded to **Detroit** by Vancouver for Jim Niekamp, March 6, 1972. Traded to **N.Y. Islanders** by Detroit with Bob Cook for Ken Murray and Brian Lavender, Jan. 17, 1973. Sold to **Vancouver** by N.Y. Islanders with Dave Fortier, Oct. 6, 1978. Sold to **N.Y. Islanders** by Vancouver, Oct. 1, 1978.

Bob Stewart

STEWART, ROBERT HAROLD 6'1", 205 lbs.
B. Nov. 10, 1950, Charlottetown, P.E.I. Defense, Shoots L

YEAR	TEAM	LEAGUE	GP	G	A	PTS	PIM
1971-72	BOS	N	8	0	0	0	15
	CALIF	N	16	1	2	3	44
	2 team total		24	1	2	3	59
1972-73			63	4	17	21	181
1973-74			47	2	5	7	69
1974-75			67	5	12	17	93
1975-76			76	4	17	21	112
1976-77	CLEVE	N	73	1	12	13	108
1977-78			72	2	15	17	84
1978-79	STL	N	78	5	13	18	47
1979-80			10	0	1	1	4
	PITT	N	65	3	7	10	52
	2 team total		75	3	8	11	56
9 yrs.		N Totals:	575	27	101	128	809
PLAYOFFS							
1979-80	PITT	N	5	1	1	2	2

Traded to **California** by Boston with Reggie Leach and Rick Smith for Carol Vadnais and Don O'Donoghue, Feb. 23, 1972. Claimed by **Minnesota** as fill in Cleveland-Minnesota Dispersal Draft, June 15, 1978. Minnesota then traded Stewart to **St. Louis** for a second round choice in the 1981 Entry Draft and future considerations, also on June 15. Traded to **Pittsburgh** by St. Louis for Blair Chapman, Nov. 13, 1979.

Ron Stewart

STEWART, RONALD GEORGE 6'1", 197 lbs.
B. July 11, 1932, Calgary, Alta. Right Wing, Shoots R

YEAR	TEAM	LEAGUE	GP	G	A	PTS	PIM
1952-53	TOR	N	70	13	22	35	29
1953-54			70	14	11	25	72
1954-55			53	14	5	19	20
1955-56			69	13	14	27	35
1956-57			65	15	20	35	28
1957-58			70	15	24	39	51
1958-59			70	21	13	34	23
1959-60			67	14	20	34	28
1960-61			51	13	12	25	8
1961-62			60	8	9	17	14
1962-63			63	16	16	32	26
1963-64			65	14	5	19	46
1964-65			65	16	11	27	33
1965-66	BOS	N	70	20	16	36	17
1966-67			56	14	10	24	31
1967-68	STL	N	19	7	5	12	11
	NYR	N	55	7	7	14	19
	2 team total		74	14	12	26	30
1968-69			75	18	11	29	20
1969-70			76	14	10	24	14
1970-71			76	5	6	11	19
1971-72	VAN	N	42	3	1	4	10
	NYR	N	13	0	2	2	2
	2 team total		55	3	3	6	12
1972-73			11	0	1	1	0
	NYI	N	22	2	2	4	4
	2 team total		33	2	3	5	4

Ron Stewart continued

YEAR	TEAM & LEAGUE		GP	G	A	PTS	PIM
21 yrs.		N Totals:	1353	276	253	529	560
PLAYOFFS							
1953-54	**TOR**	**N**	5	0	1	1	10
1954-55			4	0	0	0	2
1955-56			5	1	1	2	2
1958-59			12	3	3	6	6
1959-60			10	0	2	2	2
1960-61			5	1	0	1	2
1961-62*			11	1	6	7	4
1962-63*			10	4	0	4	2
1963-64*			14	0	4	4	24
1964-65			6	0	1	1	2
1967-68	**NYR**	**N**	6	1	1	2	2
1968-69			4	0	1	1	0
1969-70			6	0	0	0	2
1970-71			13	1	0	1	0
1971-72			8	2	1	3	0
15 yrs.		N Totals:	119	14	21	35	60

Traded by Toronto to **Boston** for Orland Kurtenbach, Andy Hebenton, and Pat Stapleton, June 8, 1965. Drafted by **St. Louis** from Boston in Expansion Draft, June 6, 1967. Traded to **N.Y. Rangers** by St. Louis with Ron Attwell for Red Berenson and Barclay Plager, Nov. 29, 1967. Traded to **Vancouver** by N.Y. Rangers with Dave Balon and Wayne Connelly for Gary Doak and Jim Wiste, Nov. 16, 1971. Sold to **N.Y. Rangers** by Vancouver, Mar. 5, 1972. Sold to **N.Y. Islanders** by N.Y. Rangers, Nov. 14, 1973.

Jack Stoddard

STODDARD, JOHN EDWARD 6'3", 180 lbs.
B. Sept. 26, 1926, Stoney Creek, Ont. Right Wing, Shoots R

YEAR	TEAM & LEAGUE		GP	G	A	PTS	PIM
1951-52	**NYR**	**N**	20	4	2	6	2
1952-53			60	12	13	25	29
2 yrs.		N Totals:	80	16	15	31	31

Andy Stoesz

STOESZ, ANDREW
Defense

YEAR	TEAM & LEAGUE		GP	G	A	PTS	PIM
PLAYOFFS							
1975-76	**WINN**	**W**	1	0	0	0	0

Roland Stoltz

STOLTZ, ROLAND 6'1", 191 lbs.
B. Aug. 15, 1954, Oeverkalix, Sweden Right Wing, Shoots R

YEAR	TEAM & LEAGUE		GP	G	A	PTS	PIM
1981-82	**WASH**	**N**	14	2	2	4	14

Signed as free agent by **Washington** June 5, 1981.

Steve Stone

STONE, STEPHEN GEORGE 5'8", 170 lbs.
B. Sept. 26, 1952, Toronto, Ont. Right Wing, Shoots R

YEAR	TEAM & LEAGUE		GP	G	A	PTS	PIM
1973-74	**VAN**	**N**	2	0	0	0	0

Blaine Stoughton

STOUGHTON, BLAINE (Stash) 5'11", 185 lbs.
B. Mar. 13, 1953, Gilbert Plains, Man. Left Wing, Shoots R

YEAR	TEAM & LEAGUE		GP	G	A	PTS	PIM
1973-74	**PITT**	**N**	34	5	6	11	8
1974-75	**TOR**	**N**	78	23	14	37	24
1975-76			43	6	11	17	8
1976-77	**CIN**	**W**	81	52	52	104	39
1977-78			30	6	13	19	36
	IND	**W**	47	13	13	26	28
	2 team total		77	19	26	45	64
1978-79			25	9	9	18	16
	NE	**W**	36	9	3	12	2
	2 team total		61	18	12	30	18
1979-80	**HART**	**N**	80	**56**	44	100	16
1980-81			71	43	30	73	56
1981-82			80	52	39	91	57
1982-83			72	45	31	76	27
10 yrs.		N Totals:	458	230	175	405	196
		W Totals:	219	89	90	179	121
PLAYOFFS							
1974-75	**TOR**	**N**	7	4	2	6	2
1976-77	**CIN**	**W**	4	0	3	3	2

Blaine Stoughton continued

YEAR	TEAM & LEAGUE		GP	G	A	PTS	PIM
1978-79	**NE**	**W**	7	4	3	7	4
1979-80	**HART**	**N**	1	0	0	0	0
4 yrs.		N Totals:	8	4	2	6	2
		W Totals:	11	4	6	10	6

Traded to **Toronto** by Pittsburgh with future considerations for Rick Kehoe, Sept. 13, 1974. Claimed by **Hartford** from Toronto in 1979 Expansion Draft, June 13, 1979.

Neil Strain

STRAIN, NEIL GILBERT 5'9", 165 lbs.
B. Feb. 24, 1926, Kenora, Ont. Left Wing, Shoots L

YEAR	TEAM & LEAGUE		GP	G	A	PTS	PIM
1952-53	**NYR**	**N**	52	11	13	24	12

Gord Strate

STRATE, GORDON LYNN 6'1", 190 lbs.
B. May 28, 1935, Edmonton, Alta. Defense, Shoots L

YEAR	TEAM & LEAGUE		GP	G	A	PTS	PIM
1956-57	**DET**	**N**	5	0	0	0	4
1957-58			45	0	0	0	24
1958-59			11	0	0	0	6
3 yrs.		N Totals:	61	0	0	0	34

Art Stratton

STRATTON, ARTHUR 6'1", 175 lbs.
B. Oct. 8, 1935, Winnipeg, Man. Center, Shoots L

YEAR	TEAM & LEAGUE		GP	G	A	PTS	PIM
1959-60	**NYR**	**N**	18	2	5	7	2
1963-64	**DET**	**N**	5	0	3	3	2
1965-66	**CHI**	**N**	2	0	0	0	0
1967-68	**PITT**	**N**	58	16	21	37	16
	PHI	**N**	12	0	4	4	4
	2 team total		70	16	25	41	20
4 yrs.		N Totals:	95	18	33	51	24
PLAYOFFS							
1967-68	**PHI**	**N**	5	0	0	0	0

Traded to **Chicago** by Detroit with Ian Cushenan and John Miszuk for Ron Murphy and Aut Erickson, June 9, 1964. Drafted by **Pittsburgh** from Chicago in Expansion Draft, June 6, 1967. Sold to **Philadelphia** by Pittsburgh, Feb. 27, 1968.

Art Strobel

STROBEL, ARTHUR GEORGE 5'6", 160 lbs.
B. Nov. 28, 1922, Regina, Sask. Left Wing, Shoots L

YEAR	TEAM & LEAGUE		GP	G	A	PTS	PIM
1943-44	**NYR**	**N**	7	0	0	0	0

Ken Strong

STRONG, KEN 5'11", 185 lbs.
B. May 9, 1963, Toronto, Ont. Forward

YEAR	TEAM & LEAGUE		GP	G	A	PTS	PIM
1982-83	**TOR**	**N**	2	0	0	0	0

Todd Strueby

STRUEBY, TODD KENNETH 6'1", 186 lbs.
B. June 15, 1963, Lannigan, Sask. Left Wing, Shoots L

YEAR	TEAM & LEAGUE		GP	G	A	PTS	PIM
1981-82	**EDM**	**N**	3	0	0	0	0
1982-83			1	0	0	0	0
2 yrs.		N Totals:	4	0	0	0	0

Billy Stuart

STUART, WILLIAM (Red)
B. Amherst, N.S. Defense

YEAR	TEAM & LEAGUE		GP	G	A	PTS	PIM
1920-21	**TOR**	**N**	18	2	1	3	4
1921-22			24	3	6	9	16
1922-23			23	7	3	10	16
1923-24			24	4	3	7	16
1924-25			5	0	0	0	0
	BOS	**N**	24	5	2	7	32
	2 team total		29	5	2	7	32
1925-26			33	6	1	7	41
1926-27			43	3	1	4	20
7 yrs.		N Totals:	194	30	17	47	145
PLAYOFFS							
1920-21	**TOR**	**N**	2	0	0	0	0

Billy Stuart continued

YEAR	TEAM & LEAGUE		GP	G	A	PTS	PIM
1921-22*			7	0	0	0	9
1926-27	**BOS**	**N**	8	0	0	0	6
3 yrs.		**N Totals:**	17	0	0	0	15

Robert Stumpf

STUMPF, ROBERT 6'1", 195 lbs.
B. Apr. 25, 1953, Milo, Alta. Right Wing, Shoots R

YEAR	TEAM & LEAGUE		GP	G	A	PTS	PIM
1974-75	**STL**	**N**	7	1	1	2	16
	PITT	**N**	3	0	0	0	4
	2 team total		10	1	1	2	20

Traded to **Pittsburgh** by St. Louis for Bernie Lukowich, Jan. 20, 1975.

Peter Sturgeon

STURGEON, PETER ALEXANDER 6'2", 205 lbs.
B. Feb. 12, 1954, Whitehorse, Yukon Left Wing, Shoots L

YEAR	TEAM & LEAGUE		GP	G	A	PTS	PIM
1979-80	**COLO**	**N**	2	0	0	0	0
1980-81			4	0	1	1	2
2 yrs.		**N Totals:**	6	0	1	1	2

Kai Suikkanen

SUIKKANEN, KAI 6'2", 207 lbs.
B. Sept. 29, 1960, Opiskelija, Finland Defense, Shoots L

YEAR	TEAM & LEAGUE		GP	G	A	PTS	PIM
1981-82	**BUF**	**N**	1	0	0	0	0
1982-83			1	0	0	0	0
2 yrs.		**N Totals:**	2	0	0	0	0

Signed as free agent by **Buffalo** June 1, 1981.

Doug Sulliman

SULLIMAN, SIMON DOUGLAS 5'9", 195 lbs.
B. Aug. 29, 1959, Glace Bay, N.S. Right Wing, Shoots L

YEAR	TEAM & LEAGUE		GP	G	A	PTS	PIM
1979-80	**NYR**	**N**	31	4	7	11	2
1980-81			32	4	1	5	32
1981-82	**HART**	**N**	77	29	40	69	39
1982-83			77	22	19	41	14
4 yrs.		**N Totals:**	217	59	67	126	87
PLAYOFFS							
1980-81	**NYR**	**N**	3	1	0	1	0

Traded to **Hartford** by N.Y. Rangers along with Chris Kotsopoulos and Gerry McDonald for Mike Rogers and Hartford's tenth round choice (Simo Saarinen) in 1982 Entry Draft, Oct. 2, 1981.

Barry Sullivan

SULLIVAN, BARRY CARTER 6', 205 lbs.
B. Sept. 21, 1926, Preston, Ont. Right Wing, Shoots R

YEAR	TEAM & LEAGUE		GP	G	A	PTS	PIM
1947-48	**DET**	**N**	1	0	0	0	0

Bob Sullivan

SULLIVAN, BOB 6', 210 lbs.
B. Nov. 29, 1957, Noranda, Que. Left Wing, Shoots R

YEAR	TEAM & LEAGUE		GP	G	A	PTS	PIM
1982-83	**HART**	**N**	62	18	19	37	18

Signed as a free agent by **Hartford** Sept., 1981.

Frank Sullivan

SULLIVAN, FRANK TAYLOR (Sully) 5'11", 178 lbs.
B. June 16, 1929, Toronto, Ont. Defense, Shoots R

YEAR	TEAM & LEAGUE		GP	G	A	PTS	PIM
1949-50	**TOR**	**N**	1	0	0	0	0
1952-53			5	0	0	0	2
1954-55	**CHI**	**N**	1	0	0	0	0
1955-56			1	0	0	0	0
4 yrs.		**N Totals:**	8	0	0	0	2

Pete Sullivan

SULLIVAN, PETER (Silky) 5'9", 170 lbs.
B. July 25, 1951, Toronto, Ont. Center, Shoots R

YEAR	TEAM & LEAGUE		GP	G	A	PTS	PIM
1975-76	**WINN**	**W**	78	32	39	71	22
1976-77			78	31	52	83	18

Pete Sullivan continued

YEAR	TEAM & LEAGUE		GP	G	A	PTS	PIM
1977-78			77	16	39	55	43
1978-79			80	46	40	86	24
1979-80	**WINN**	**N**	79	24	35	59	20
1980-81			47	4	19	23	20
6 yrs.		**N Totals:**	126	28	54	82	40
		W Totals:	313	125	170	295	107
PLAYOFFS							
1975-76	**WINN**	**W**	13	6	7	13	0
1976-77			20	7	12	19	2
1977-78			9	3	4	7	4
1978-79			10	5	9	14	2
4 yrs.		**W Totals:**	52	21	32	53	8

Claimed by **Winnipeg** in 1979 Expansion Draft, June 22, 1979.

Red Sullivan

SULLIVAN, GEORGE JAMES (Red) 5'11", 160 lbs.
B. Dec. 24, 1929, Peterborough, Ont. Center, Shoots L

YEAR	TEAM & LEAGUE		GP	G	A	PTS	PIM
1949-50	**BOS**	**N**	3	0	1	1	0
1951-52			67	12	12	24	24
1952-53			32	3	8	11	8
1954-55	**CHI**	**N**	70	19	42	61	51
1955-56			63	14	26	40	58
1956-57	**NYR**	**N**	42	6	17	23	36
1957-58			70	11	35	46	61
1958-59			70	21	42	63	56
1959-60			70	12	25	37	81
1960-61			70	9	31	40	66
10 yrs.		**N Totals:**	557	107	239	346	441
PLAYOFFS							
1950-51	**BOS**	**N**	2	0	0	0	2
1951-52			7	0	0	0	0
1952-53			3	0	0	0	0
1956-57	**NYR**	**N**	5	1	2	3	4
1957-58			1	0	0	0	0
5 yrs.		**N Totals:**	18	1	2	3	6

Purchased by **Chicago** from Boston, Sept. 10, 1954.

Bill Summerhill

SUMMERHILL, WILLIAM ARTHUR 5'9", 170 lbs.
B. July 9, 1915, Toronto, Ont. Right Wing, Shoots R

YEAR	TEAM & LEAGUE		GP	G	A	PTS	PIM
1938-39	**MONT**	**N**	43	6	10	16	28
1939-40			13	3	2	5	24
1941-42	**NYA**	**N**	16	5	5	10	18
3 yrs.		**N Totals:**	72	14	17	31	70
PLAYOFFS							
1938-39	**MONT**	**N**	3	0	0	0	2

Patrik Sundstrom

SUNDSTROM, PATRIK 6', 198 lbs.
B. Dec. 14, 1961, Skellefteaa, Sweden Center, Shoots L

YEAR	TEAM & LEAGUE		GP	G	A	PTS	PIM
1982-83	**VAN**	**N**	74	23	23	46	30
PLAYOFFS							
1982-83	**VAN**	**N**	4	0	0	0	2

Al Suomi

SUOMI, ALFRED
B. Unknown Forward

YEAR	TEAM & LEAGUE		GP	G	A	PTS	PIM
1936-37	**CHI**	**N**	5	0	0	0	0

Bill Sutherland

SUTHERLAND, WILLIAM FRASER 5'10", 176 lbs.
B. Nov. 10, 1934, Regina, Sask. Center, Shoots L

YEAR	TEAM & LEAGUE		GP	G	A	PTS	PIM
1967-68	**PHI**	**N**	60	20	9	29	6
1968-69	**TOR**	**N**	44	7	5	.12	14
	PHI	**N**	12	7	3	10	4
	2 team total		56	14	8	22	18
1969-70			51	15	17	32	30
1970-71			1	0	0	0	0
	STL	**N**	68	19	20	39	41
	2 team total		69	19	20	39	41
1971-72			11	2	3	5	2
	DET	**N**	5	0	1	0	2
	2 team total		16	2	4	5	4

YEAR	TEAM & LEAGUE		GP	G	A	PTS	PIM
1972-73	WINN	W	48	6	16	22	34
1973-74			12	4	5	9	6
7 yrs.		N Totals:	252	70	58	127	99
		W Totals:	60	10	21	31	40
PLAYOFFS							
1962-63	MONT	N	2	0	0	0	0
1967-68	PHI	N	7	1	3	4	0
1968-69			4	1	1	2	0
1970-71	STL	N	1	0	0	0	0
1972-73	WINN	W	14	5	9	14	9
1973-74			4	0	0	0	4
6 yrs.		N Totals:	14	2	4	6	0
		W Totals:	18	5	9	14	13

Ron Sutherland

SUTHERLAND, RONALD 5'8½", 180 lbs.
B. Feb. 8, 1913, Regina, Sask. Defense, Shoots L

YEAR	TEAM & LEAGUE		GP	G	A	PTS	PIM
1931-32	BOS	N	2	0	0	0	0

Steve Sutherland

SUTHERLAND, STEPHEN 5'11", 172 lbs.
B. Sept. 1, 1946, Noranda, Que. Left Wing, Shoots L

YEAR	TEAM & LEAGUE		GP	G	A	PTS	PIM
1972-73	LA	W	44	11	6	17	98
1973-74			72	20	12	32	182
1974-75	M-B	W	22	1	5	6	37
	QUE	W	56	14	15	29	114
	2 team total		78	15	20	35	151
1975-76			74	22	19	41	197
1976-77			36	6	9	15	34
1977-78			75	23	10	33	143
6 yrs.		W Totals:	379	97	76	173	805
PLAYOFFS							
1972-73	LA	W	6	0	2	2	8
1974-75	QUE	W	13	0	3	3	34
1975-76			4	2	1	3	17
1976-77			17	5	0	5	16
1977-78			11	2	0	2	37
5 yrs.		W Totals:	51	9	6	15	112

Brent Sutter

SUTTER, BRENT BOLIN (Pup) 5'11", 175 lbs.
B. June 10, 1962, Viking, Alta. Center, Shoots R

YEAR	TEAM & LEAGUE		GP	G	A	PTS	PIM
1980-81	NYI	N	3	2	2	4	0
1981-82			43	21	22	43	114
1982-83			80	21	19	40	128
3 yrs.		N Totals:	126	44	43	87	242
PLAYOFFS							
1981-82*	NYI	N	19	2	6	8	36
1982-83*			20	10	11	21	26
2 yrs.		N Totals:	39	12	17	29	62

Brian Sutter

SUTTER, BRIAN LOUIS ALLEN 5'11", 173 lbs.
B. Oct. 7, 1956, Viking, Alta. Left Wing, Shoots L

YEAR	TEAM & LEAGUE		GP	G	A	PTS	PIM
1976-77	STL	N	35	4	10	14	82
1977-78			78	9	13	22	123
1978-79			77	41	39	80	165
1979-80			71	23	35	58	156
1980-81			78	35	34	69	232
1981-82			74	39	36	75	239
1982-83			79	46	30	76	254
7 yrs.		N Totals:	492	197	197	394	1251
PLAYOFFS							
1976-77	STL	N	4	1	0	1	14
1979-80			3	0	0	0	4
1980-81			11	6	3	9	77
1981-82			10	8	6	14	49
1982-83			4	2	1	3	10
5 yrs.		N Totals:	32	17	10	27	154

Darryl Sutter

SUTTER, DARRYL JOHN 5'11", 176 lbs.
B. Aug. 19, 1958, Viking, Alta. Left Wing, Shoots L

YEAR	TEAM & LEAGUE		GP	G	A	PTS	PIM
1979-80	CHI	N	8	2	0	2	2
1980-81			76	40	22	62	86
1981-82			40	23	12	35	31
1982-83			80	31	30	61	53
4 yrs.		N Totals:	204	96	64	160	172
PLAYOFFS							
1979-80	CHI	N	7	3	1	4	2
1980-81			3	3	1	4	2
1981-82			3	0	1	1	2
1982-83			13	4	6	10	8
4 yrs.		N Totals:	26	10	9	19	14

Duane Sutter

SUTTER, DUANE CALVIN (Dog) 6'1", 185 lbs.
B. Mar. 16, 1960, Viking, Alta. Right Wing, Shoots R

YEAR	TEAM & LEAGUE		GP	G	A	PTS	PIM
1979-80	NYI	N	56	15	9	24	55
1980-81			23	7	11	18	26
1981-82			77	18	35	53	100
1982-83			75	13	19	32	118
4 yrs.		N Totals:	231	53	74	127	299
PLAYOFFS							
1979-80*	NYI	N	21	3	7	10	74
1980-81*			12	3	1	4	10
1981-82*			19	5	5	10	57
1982-83*			20	9	12	21	43
4 yrs.		N Totals:	72	20	25	45	184

Rich Sutter

SUTTER, RICHARD 5'11", 165 lbs.
B. Dec. 2, 1963, Viking, Alta. Right Wing, Shoots R

YEAR	TEAM & LEAGUE		GP	G	A	PTS	PIM
1982-83	PITT	N	4	0	0	0	0

Ron Sutter

SUTTER, RONALD 5'11", 166 lbs.
B. Dec. 2, 1963, Viking, Alta. Center, Shoots R

YEAR	TEAM & LEAGUE		GP	G	A	PTS	PIM
1982-83	PHI	N	10	1	1	2	9

Mark Suzor

SUZOR, MARK JOSEPH 6'1", 212 lbs.
B. Nov. 5, 1956, Windsor, Ont. Defense, Shoots L

YEAR	TEAM & LEAGUE		GP	G	A	PTS	PIM
1976-77	PHI	N	4	0	1	1	4
1977-78	COLO	N	60	4	15	19	56
2 yrs.		N Totals:	64	4	16	20	60

Traded to **Colorado** by Philadelphia for Barry Dean, Aug. 5, 1977. Traded to **Boston** by Colorado for Clayton Pachal, Oct. 11, 1978.

Leif Svensson

SVENSSON, LEIF 6'3", 190 lbs.
B. July 8, 1951, Harnosand, Sweden Defense, Shoots L

YEAR	TEAM & LEAGUE		GP	G	A	PTS	PIM
1978-79	WASH	N	74	2	29	31	28
1979-80			47	4	11	15	21
2 yrs.		N Totals:	121	6	40	46	49

Garry Swain

SWAIN, GARTH FREDERICK ARTHUR 5'9", 164 lbs.
B. Sept. 11, 1947, Welland, Ont. Center, Shoots L

YEAR	TEAM & LEAGUE		GP	G	A	PTS	PIM
1968-69	PITT	N	9	1	1	2	0
1974-75	NE	W	66	7	15	22	18
1975-76			79	10	16	26	46
1976-77			26	5	2	7	6
4 yrs.		N Totals:	9	1	1	2	0
		W Totals:	171	22	33	55	70
PLAYOFFS							
1974-75	NE	W	6	0	3	3	41
1975-76			17	3	2	5	15
1976-77			2	0	0	0	0

Garry Swain continued

YEAR	TEAM & LEAGUE		GP	G	A	PTS	PIM
3 yrs.		**W Totals:**	25	3	5	8	56

George Swarbrick

SWARBRICK, GEORGE RAYMOND 5'10", 180 lbs.
B. Feb. 16, 1942, Moose Jaw, Sask. Right Wing, Shoots R

YEAR	TEAM & LEAGUE		GP	G	A	PTS	PIM
1967-68	**OAK**	**N**	49	13	5	18	62
1968-69	**CALIF**	**N**	50	3	13	16	75
	PITT	**N**	19	1	6	7	26
	2 team total		69	4	19	23	101
1969-70			12	0	1	1	8
1970-71	**PHI**	**N**	2	0	0	0	0
4 yrs.		**N Totals:**	132	17	25	42	171

Bill Sweeney

SWEENEY, WILLIAM 5'10", 165 lbs.
B. Jan. 30, 1937, Guelph, Ont. Center, Shoots L

YEAR	TEAM & LEAGUE		GP	G	A	PTS	PIM
1959-60	**NYR**	**N**	4	1	0	1	0

Cal Swenson

SWENSON, CALVIN BERLE 5'8", 176 lbs.
B. Apr. 16, 1948, Naicam, Sask. Center, Shoots L

YEAR	TEAM & LEAGUE		GP	G	A	PTS	PIM
1972-73	**WINN**	**W**	76	7	21	28	19
1973-74			25	5	4	9	2
2 yrs.		**W Totals:**	101	12	25	37	21
PLAYOFFS							
1972-73	**WINN**	**W**	14	1	5	6	7
1973-74			1	0	0	0	0
2 yrs.		**W Totals:**	15	1	5	6	7

Bob Sykes

SYKES, ROBERT JOHN WILLIAM 6', 200 lbs.
B. Sept. 26, 1951, Sudbury, Ont. Left Wing, Shoots L

YEAR	TEAM & LEAGUE		GP	G	A	PTS	PIM
1974-75	**TOR**	**N**	2	0	0	0	0

Phil Sykes

SYKES, PHIL 6', 185 lbs.
B. May 18, 1959, Dawson Creek, B.C. Left Wing, Shoots L

YEAR	TEAM & LEAGUE		GP	G	A	PTS	PIM
1982-83	**LA**	**N**	7	2	0	2	2

Signed by **Los Angeles** as a free agent, Apr., 1982.

Dave Syvret

SYVRET, DAVID JAMES 6', 190 lbs.
B. Oct. 28, 1954, Hamilton, Ont. Defense, Shoots L

YEAR	TEAM & LEAGUE		GP	G	A	PTS	PIM
1975-76	**TOR**	**W**	50	1	11	12	14
1976-77	**BIRM**	**W**	8	0	0	0	0
2 yrs.		**W Totals:**	58	1	11	12	14

Signed as a free agent by **Cleveland** Oct. 7, 1977.

Joe Szura

SZURA, JOSEPH BOLESLAW 6'2", 198 lbs.
B. Dec. 18, 1938, Fort William, Ont. Center, Shoots L

YEAR	TEAM & LEAGUE		GP	G	A	PTS	PIM
1967-68	**OAK**	**N**	20	1	3	4	10
1968-69	**CALIF**	**N**	70	9	12	21	20
1972-73	**LA**	**W**	72	13	32	45	25
1973-74	**HOUS**	**W**	42	8	7	15	4
4 yrs.		**N Totals:**	90	10	15	25	30
		W Totals:	114	21	39	60	29
PLAYOFFS							
1968-69	**CALIF**	**N**	7	2	3	5	2
1973-74	**HOUS**	**W**	10	0	0	0	0
2 yrs.		**N Totals:**	7	2	3	5	2
		W Totals:	10	0	0	0	0

John Taft

TAFT, JOHN PHILIP 6'2", 185 lbs.
B. Mar. 8, 1954, Minneapolis, Minn. Defense, Shoots L

YEAR	TEAM & LEAGUE		GP	G	A	PTS	PIM
1978-79	**DET**	**N**	15	0	2	2	4

Rudy Tajcnar

TAJCNAR, RUDOLPH 5'11", 225 lbs.
B. Bratislava, Czech. Forward

YEAR	TEAM & LEAGUE		GP	G	A	PTS	PIM
1978-79	**EDM**	**W**	2	0	0	0	0

Dean Talafous

TALAFOUS, DEAN CHARLES 6'4", 190 lbs.
B. Aug. 25, 1953, Duluth, Minn. Right Wing, Shoots R

YEAR	TEAM & LEAGUE		GP	G	A	PTS	PIM
1974-75	**ATL**	**N**	18	1	4	5	13
	MINN	**N**	43	8	17	25	6
	2 team total		61	9	21	30	19
1975-76			79	18	30	48	18
1976-77			80	22	27	49	10
1977-78			75	13	16	29	25
1978-79	**NYR**	**N**	68	13	16	29	29
1979-80			55	10	20	30	26
1980-81			50	13	17	30	28
1981-82			29	6	7	13	8
8 yrs.		**N Totals:**	497	104	154	258	163
PLAYOFFS							
1976-77	**MINN**	**N**	2	0	0	0	0
1979-80	**NYR**	**N**	5	1	2	3	9
1980-81			14	3	5	8	2
3 yrs.		**N Totals:**	21	4	7	11	11

Traded to **Minnesota** by Atlanta with Dwight Bialowas for Barry Gibbs, Jan. 3, 1975. Signed as free agent by **N.Y. Rangers** July 17, 1978. Traded to **Quebec** by N.Y. Rangers along with Jere Gillis for Robbie Ftorek and Quebec's eighth round choice (Brian Glynn) in 1982 Entry Draft.

Jean-Guy Talbot

TALBOT, JEAN-GUY 5'11", 170 lbs.
B. July 11, 1932, Cap Madelaine, Que. Defense, Shoots L

YEAR	TEAM & LEAGUE		GP	G	A	PTS	PIM
1954-55	**MONT**	**N**	3	0	1	1	0
1955-56			66	1	13	14	80
1956-57			59	0	13	13	70
1957-58			55	4	15	19	65
1958-59			69	4	17	21	77
1959-60			69	1	14	15	60
1960-61			70	5	26	31	143
1961-62			70	5	42	47	90
1962-63			70	3	22	25	51
1963-64			66	1	13	14	83
1964-65			67	8	14	22	64
1965-66			59	1	14	15	50
1966-67			68	3	5	8	51
1967-68	**MINN**	**N**	4	0	0	0	4
	DET	**N**	32	0	3	3	10
	STL	**N**	23	0	4	4	2
	3 team total		59	0	7	7	16
1968-69			69	5	4	9	24
1969-70			75	2	15	17	40
1970-71			5	0	0	0	6
	BUF	**N**	57	0	7	7	36
	2 team total		62	0	7	7	42
17 yrs.		**N Totals:**	1056	43	242	285	1006
PLAYOFFS							
1955-56*	**MONT**	**N**	9	0	2	2	4
1956-57*			10	0	2	2	10
1957-58*			10	0	3	3	12
1958-59*			11	0	1	1	10
1959-60*			8	1	1	2	8
1960-61			6	1	1	2	10
1961-62			6	1	1	2	10
1962-63			5	0	0	0	8
1963-64			7	0	2	2	10
1964-65*			13	0	1	1	22
1965-66*			10	0	2	2	8
1966-67			10	0	0	0	0
1967-68	**STL**	**N**	17	0	2	2	8
1968-69			12	0	2	2	6

Jean-Guy Talbot continued

YEAR	TEAM	LEAGUE	GP	G	A	PTS	PIM
1969-70			16	1	6	7	16
15 yrs.		**N Totals:**	150	4	26	30	142

Dale Tallon

TALLON, MICHAEL DALE LEE 6'1", 205 lbs.
B. Oct. 19, 1950, Noranda, Que. Defense, Shoots L

YEAR	TEAM	LEAGUE	GP	G	A	PTS	PIM
1970-71	**VAN**	**N**	78	14	42	56	58
1971-72			69	17	27	44	78
1972-73			75	13	24	37	83
1973-74	**CHI**	**N**	65	15	19	34	36
1974-75			35	5	10	15	28
1975-76			80	15	47	62	101
1976-77			70	5	16	21	65
1977-78			75	4	20	24	66
1978-79	**PITT**	**N**	63	5	24	29	35
1979-80			32	5	9	14	18
10 yrs.		**N Totals:**	642	98	238	336	568
PLAYOFFS							
1973-74	**CHI**	**N**	11	1	3	4	29
1974-75			8	1	3	4	4
1975-76			4	0	1	1	8
1976-77			2	0	1	1	0
1977-78			4	0	2	2	0
1979-80	**PITT**	**N**	4	0	0	0	4
6 yrs.		**N Totals:**	33	2	10	12	45

Traded to **Chicago** by Vancouver for Jerry Korab and goaltender Gary Smith, May 14, 1973. Traded to **Pittsburgh** by Chicago for Pittsburgh's second round choice (Ken Soleheim) in the 1980 Entry Draft, Oct. 9, 1978. Claimed by **Pittsburgh** as fill in Expansion Draft, June 13, 1979.

Steve Tambellini

TAMBELLINI, STEVEN ANTHONY 6', 190 lbs.
B. May 14, 1958, Trail, B.C. Center, Shoots L

YEAR	TEAM	LEAGUE	GP	G	A	PTS	PIM
1978-79	**NYI**	**N**	1	0	0	0	0
1979-80			45	5	8	13	4
1980-81			61	19	17	36	17
	COLO	**N**	13	6	12	18	2
	2 team total		74	25	29	54	19
1981-82			79	29	30	59	14
1982-83	**NJ**	**N**	73	25	18	43	14
5 yrs.		**N Totals:**	272	84	85	169	51

Traded to **Colorado** by N.Y. Islanders with Chico Resch for Mike McEwen and Jari Kaarela, March 10, 1981. Traded to **Calgary** with Joel Quenneville by New Jersey for Mel Bridgman and Phil Russell, June 20, 1983.

Juha Tamminen

TAMMINEN, JUHANI 5'11", 185 lbs.
B. May 26, 1950, Turku, Finland Right Wing, Shoots L

YEAR	TEAM	LEAGUE	GP	G	A	PTS	PIM
1975-76	**CLEVE**	**W**	65	7	14	21	0
1976-77	**PHOE**	**W**	65	10	29	39	22
2 yrs.		**W Totals:**	130	17	43	60	22
PLAYOFFS							
1975-76	**CLEVE**	**W**	1	0	0	0	0

Chris Tanguay

TANGUAY, CHRISTIAN 5'10", 190 lbs.
B. Aug. 4, 1962, Beauport, Que. Right Wing, Shoots R

YEAR	TEAM	LEAGUE	GP	G	A	PTS	PIM
1981-82	**QUE**	**N**	2	0	0	0	0

Don Tannahill

TANNAHILL, DONALD ANDREW 5'11", 175 lbs.
B. Feb. 21, 1949, Penetang, Ont. Left Wing, Shoots L

YEAR	TEAM	LEAGUE	GP	G	A	PTS	PIM
1972-73	**VAN**	**N**	78	22	21	43	21
1973-74			33	8	12	20	4
1974-75	**MINN**	**W**	72	23	30	53	20
1975-76	**CALG**	**W**	78	25	24	49	10
1976-77			72	10	22	32	4
5 yrs.		**N Totals:**	111	30	33	63	25
		W Totals:	222	58	76	134	34
PLAYOFFS							
1974-75	**MINN**	**W**	10	2	4	6	0

Don Tannahill continued

YEAR	TEAM	LEAGUE	GP	G	A	PTS	PIM
1975-76	**CALG**	**W**	10	2	5	7	8
2 yrs.		**W Totals:**	20	4	9	13	8

Drafted by **Vancouver** from Boston in Intra-League Draft, June 5, 1972.

Tony Tanti

TANTI, ANTONY 5'9", 190 lbs.
B. Sept. 7, 1963, Toronto, Ont. Right Wing, Shoots L

YEAR	TEAM	LEAGUE	GP	G	A	PTS	PIM
1981-82	**CHI**	**N**	2	0	0	0	0
1982-83			1	1	0	1	0
	VAN	**N**	39	8	8	16	16
	2 team total		40	9	8	17	16
2 yrs.		**N Totals:**	42	9	8	17	16
PLAYOFFS							
1982-83	**VAN**	**N**	4	0	1	1	0

Traded by Vancouver to **Chicago** for Curt Fraser, Jan. 6, 1983.

Marc Tardif

TARDIF, MARC 6', 180 lbs.
B. June 12, 1949, Granby, Que. Left Wing, Shoots L

YEAR	TEAM	LEAGUE	GP	G	A	PTS	PIM
1969-70	**MONT**	**N**	18	3	2	5	27
1970-71			76	19	30	49	133
1971-72			75	31	22	53	81
1972-73			76	25	25	50	48
1973-74	**LA**	**W**	75	40	30	70	47
1974-75	**M-B**	**W**	23	12	5	17	9
	QUE	**W**	53	38	34	72	70
	2 team total		76	50	39	89	79
1975-76			81	**71**	**77**	**148**	79
1976-77			62	49	60	109	65
1977-78			78	**65**	**89**	**154**	50
1978-79			74	41	55	96	98
1979-80	**QUE**	**N**	58	33	35	68	30
1980-81			63	23	31	54	35
1981-82			75	39	31	70	55
1982-83			76	21	31	52	34
14 yrs.		**N Totals:**	517	194	207	401	443
		W Totals:	446	316	350	666	418
PLAYOFFS							
1970-71*	**MONT**	**N**	20	3	1	4	40
1971-72			6	2	3	5	9
1972-73*			14	6	6	12	6
1974-75	**QUE**	**W**	15	10	11	21	10
1975-76			2	1	0	1	2
1976-77			12	4	10	14	8
1977-78			11	6	9	15	11
1978-79			4	2	6	8	4
1980-81	**QUE**	**N**	5	1	3	4	2
1981-82			13	1	2	3	16
1982-83			4	0	0	0	2
11 yrs.		**N Totals:**	62	13	15	28	75
		W Totals:	44	23	36	59	35

Claimed by **Quebec** from Montreal in 1979 Expansion Draft, June 22, 1979.

Billy Taylor

TAYLOR, WILLIAM GORDON 6'1", 184 lbs.
B. Oct. 14, 1942, Winnipeg, Man. Center, Shoots L

YEAR	TEAM	LEAGUE	GP	G	A	PTS	PIM
1964-65	**NYR**	**N**	2	0	0	0	0

Traded to **Chicago** by N.Y. Rangers with Camille Henry, Don Johns, and Wally Chevrier for Doug Robinson, Wayne Hillman and John Brenneman, Feb. 4, 1965. Drafted by **Minnesota** from Chicago in Expansion Draft, June 6, 1967.

Billy Taylor

TAYLOR, WILLIAM 5'9", 150 lbs.
B. May 3, 1919, Winnipeg, Man. Center, Shoots R

YEAR	TEAM	LEAGUE	GP	G	A	PTS	PIM
1939-40	**TOR**	**N**	29	4	6	10	9
1940-41			47	9	26	35	15
1941-42			48	12	26	38	20
1942-43			50	18	42	60	2
1945-46			48	23	18	41	14

Billy Taylor continued

YEAR	TEAM & LEAGUE		GP	G	A	PTS	PIM
1946-47	**DET**	**N**	60	17	**46**	63	35
1947-48	**BOS**	**N**	39	4	16	20	25
	NYR	**N**	2	0	0	0	0
	2 team total		41	4	16	20	25
7 yrs.		**N Totals:**	323	87	180	267	120
PLAYOFFS							
1939-40	**TOR**	**N**	2	1	0	1	0
1940-41			7	0	3	3	5
1941-42*			13	2	8	10	4
1942-43			6	2	2	4	0
1946-47	**DET**	**N**	5	1	5	6	4
5 yrs.		**N Totals:**	33	6	18	24	13

Bob Taylor

TAYLOR, ROBERT IAN 6'1", 190 lbs.
B. Jan. 24, 1945, Calgary, Alta. Shoots L

YEAR	TEAM & LEAGUE		GP	G	A	PTS	PIM
1929-30	**BOS**	**N**	8	0	0	0	6

Dave Taylor

TAYLOR, DAVID ANDREW 6', 185 lbs.
B. Dec. 4, 1955, Levack, Ont. Right Wing, Shoots R

YEAR	TEAM & LEAGUE		GP	G	A	PTS	PIM
1977-78	**LA**	**N**	64	22	21	43	47
1978-79			78	43	48	91	124
1979-80			61	37	53	90	72
1980-81			72	47	65	112	130
1981-82			78	39	67	106	130
1982-83			46	21	37	58	76
6 yrs.		**N Totals:**	399	209	291	500	579
PLAYOFFS							
1977-78	**LA**	**N**	2	0	0	0	5
1978-79			2	0	0	0	2
1979-80			4	2	1	3	4
1980-81			4	2	2	4	10
1981-82			10	4	6	10	20
5 yrs.		**N Totals:**	22	8	9	17	41

Ted Taylor

TAYLOR, EDWARD WRAY 6', 175 lbs.
B. Feb. 25, 1942, Oak Lake, Man. Left Wing, Shoots L

YEAR	TEAM & LEAGUE		GP	G	A	PTS	PIM
1964-65	**NYR**	**N**	4	0	0	0	4
1965-66			4	0	1	1	2
1966-67	**DET**	**N**	2	0	0	0	0
1967-68	**MINN**	**N**	31	3	5	8	34
1970-71	**VAN**	**N**	56	11	16	27	53
1971-72			69	9	13	22	88
1972-73	**HOUS**	**W**	72	34	42	76	103
1973-74			75	21	23	44	143
1974-75			73	26	27	53	130
1975-76			68	15	26	41	880
1976-77			78	16	35	51	90
1977-78			54	11	11	22	46
12 yrs.		**N Totals:**	166	23	35	58	181
		W Totals:	420	123	164	287	1392
PLAYOFFS							
1972-73	**HOUS**	**W**	10	3	1	4	10
1973-74			14	4	8	12	60
1974-75			11	2	5	7	22
1975-76			11	2	2	4	17
1976-77			11	4	4	8	28
1977-78			6	3	1	4	10
6 yrs.		**W Totals:**	63	18	21	39	147

Traded to **Montreal** by N.Y. Rangers with Garry Peters for Red Berenson, June 13, 1966. Drafted by **Detroit** from Montreal, June 15, 1966. Drafted by **Minnesota** from Detroit in Expansion Draft, June 6, 1967. Drafted by **N.Y. Islanders** from Vancouver in Exapnsion Draft, June 6, 1972.

Harry Taylor

TAYLOR, HARRY 5'8", 165 lbs.
B. Mar. 28, 1926, St. James, Man. Center, Shoots R

YEAR	TEAM & LEAGUE		GP	G	A	PTS	PIM
1946-47	**TOR**	**N**	9	0	2	2	0
1948-49			42	4	7	11	30
1951-52	**CHI**	**N**	15	1	1	2	0
3 yrs.		**N Totals:**	66	5	10	15	30
PLAYOFFS							
1948-49*	**TOR**	**N**	1	0	0	0	0

Mark Taylor

TAYLOR, MARK 5'11", 190 lbs.
B. Jan. 26, 1958, Vancouver, B.C. Center, Shoots L

YEAR	TEAM & LEAGUE		GP	G	A	PTS	PIM
1981-82	**PHI**	**N**	2	0	0	0	0
1982-83			61	8	25	33	24
2 yrs.		**N Totals:**	63	8	25	33	24
PLAYOFFS							
1982-83	**PHI**	**N**	3	0	0	0	0

Ralph Taylor

TAYLOR, RALPH F. 5'9", 180 lbs.
B. Oct. 2, 1905, Toronto, Ont. Defense, Shoots R

YEAR	TEAM & LEAGUE		GP	G	A	PTS	PIM
1927-28	**CHI**	**N**	22	1	1	2	39
1928-29			38	0	0	0	56
1929-30			17	1	0	1	42
	NYR	**N**	22	2	0	2	32
	2 team total		39	3	0	3	74
3 yrs.		**N Totals:**	99	4	1	5	169
PLAYOFFS							
1929-30	**NYR**	**N**	4	0	0	0	10

Skip Teal

TEAL, ALLEN LESLIE
B. July 17, 1933, Ridgeway, Ont. Center

YEAR	TEAM & LEAGUE		GP	G	A	PTS	PIM
1954-55	**BOS**	**N**	1	0	0	0	0

Victor Teal

TEAL, VICTOR (Skeeter) 6'1", 160 lbs.
B. Aug. 10, 1949, St. Catharines, Ont. Right Wing, Shoots R

YEAR	TEAM & LEAGUE		GP	G	A	PTS	PIM
1973-74	**NYI**	**N**	1	0	0	0	0

Greg Tebbut

TEBBUT, GREGORY 6'3", 215 lbs.
B. May 11, 1957, North Vancouver, B.C.
Defense, Shoots L

YEAR	TEAM & LEAGUE		GP	G	A	PTS	PIM
1978-79	**BIRM**	**W**	38	2	5	7	83
1979-80	**QUE**	**N**	2	0	1	1	4
2 yrs.		**N Totals:**	2	0	1	1	4
		W Totals:	38	2	5	7	83

Paul Terbenche

TERBENCHE, PAUL FREDERICK 5'10", 190 lbs.
B. Sept. 16, 1945, Cobourg, Ont. Defense, Shoots L

YEAR	TEAM & LEAGUE		GP	G	A	PTS	PIM
1967-68	**CHI**	**N**	68	3	7	10	8
1970-71	**BUF**	**N**	3	0	0	0	2
1971-72			5	0	0	0	2
1972-73			42	0	7	7	8
1973-74			67	2	12	14	8
1974-75	**VAN**	**W**	60	3	14	17	10
1975-76	**CALG**	**W**	58	2	4	6	22
1976-77			80	9	24	33	30
1977-78	**BIRM**	**W**	11	1	0	1	0
1978-79	**WINN**	**W**	68	3	22	25	12
10 yrs.		**N Totals:**	185	5	26	31	28
		W Totals:	277	18	64	82	74
PLAYOFFS							
1967-68	**CHI**	**N**	6	0	0	0	0
1972-73	**BUF**	**N**	6	0	0	0	0
1975-76	**CALG**	**W**	10	0	6	6	6
1977-78	**HOUS**	**W**	6	1	1	2	0
1978-79	**WINN**	**W**	10	1	1	2	4
5 yrs.		**N Totals:**	12	0	0	0	0
		W Totals:	26	2	8	10	10

Drafted by **Buffalo** from Chicago in Expansion Draft, June 10, 1970. Drafted by **Kansas City** from Buffalo in Expansion Draft, June 12, 1974.

Greg Terrion

TERRION, GREGORY PATRICK 5'11", 190 lbs.
B. May 2, 1960, Peterborough, Ont. Left Wing, Shoots L

YEAR	TEAM & LEAGUE		GP	G	A	PTS	PIM
1980-81	**LA**	**N**	73	12	25	37	99
1981-82			61	15	22	37	23
1982-83	**TOR**	**N**	74	16	16	32	59
3 yrs.		**N Totals:**	208	43	63	106	181

PLAYOFFS

YEAR	TEAM & LEAGUE		GP	G	A	PTS	PIM
1980-81	**LA**	**N**	3	1	0	1	4
1982-83	**TOR**	**N**	4	1	2	3	2
2 yrs.		**N Totals:**	7	2	2	4	6

Traded by Los Angeles to **Toronto** for Toronto's fourth round choice in the 1983 Amateur Draft (Guy Benoit), Oct. 19, 1982.

Orval Tessier

TESSIER, ORVAL ROY 5'8", 160 lbs.
B. June 30, 1933, Cornwall, Ont. Center, Shoots L
Won Jack Adams Award, 1982-83

YEAR	TEAM & LEAGUE		GP	G	A	PTS	PIM
1954-55	**MONT**	**N**	4	0	0	0	0
1955-56	**BOS**	**N**	23	2	3	5	6
1960-61			34	3	4	7	0
3 yrs.		**N Totals:**	61	5	7	12	6

Drafted by **Boston** from Montreal, May 31, 1955.

Jean Tetreault

TETREAULT, JEAN
Defense

YEAR	TEAM & LEAGUE		GP	G	A	PTS	PIM
1975-76	**MINN**	**W**	3	0	0	0	0

Spence Thatchell

THATCHELL, SPENCER HAROLD
B. July 16, 1924, Lloydminster, Sask. Defense

YEAR	TEAM & LEAGUE		GP	G	A	PTS	PIM
1942-43	**NYR**	**N**	1	0	0	0	0

Greg Theberge

THEBERGE, GREGORY RAY 5'10", 187 lbs.
B. Sept. 3, 1959, Peterborough, Ont. Defense, Shoots R

YEAR	TEAM & LEAGUE		GP	G	A	PTS	PIM
1979-80	**WASH**	**N**	12	0	1	1	0
1980-81			1	1	0	1	0
1981-82			57	5	32	37	49
1982-83			70	8	28	36	20
4 yrs.		**N Totals:**	140	14	61	75	69

PLAYOFFS

YEAR	TEAM & LEAGUE		GP	G	A	PTS	PIM
1982-83	**WASH**	**N**	4	0	1	1	0

Gaston Therrien

THERRIEN, GASTON 5'10", 186 lbs.
B. May 27, 1960, Montreal, Que. Defense, Shoots R

YEAR	TEAM & LEAGUE		GP	G	A	PTS	PIM
1980-81	**QUE**	**N**	3	0	1	1	2
1981-82			14	0	7	7	6
1982-83			5	0	0	0	4
3 yrs.		**N Totals:**	22	0	8	8	12

PLAYOFFS

YEAR	TEAM & LEAGUE		GP	G	A	PTS	PIM
1981-82	**QUE**	**N**	9	0	1	1	4

Laurence Thibeault

THIBEAULT, LAURENCE LORRAIN 5'7", 180 lbs.
B. Oct. 2, 1918, Charletone, Ont. Left Wing, Shoots L

YEAR	TEAM & LEAGUE		GP	G	A	PTS	PIM
1944-45	**DET**	**N**	4	0	2	2	0
1945-46	**MONT**	**N**	1	0	0	0	0
2 yrs.		**N Totals:**	5	0	2	2	0

Leo Thiffault

THIFFAULT, LEO EDMUND 5'10", 175 lbs.
B. Dec. 16, 1944, Drummondville, Que. Left Wing, Shoots L

PLAYOFFS

YEAR	TEAM & LEAGUE		GP	G	A	PTS	PIM
1967-68	**MINN**	**N**	5	0	0	0	0

Traded to **Minnesota** by Montreal with Bill Plager and Barrie Meissner for Bryan Watson, June 6, 1967.

Thom

THOM
B. Unknown Forward

YEAR	TEAM & LEAGUE		GP	G	A	PTS	PIM
1940-41	**NYA**	**N**	3	0	0	0	0

Cy Thomas

THOMAS, CYRIL JAMES 5'10½", 185 lbs.
B. Aug. 5, 1926, Dowlais, Wales Shoots L

YEAR	TEAM & LEAGUE		GP	G	A	PTS	PIM
1947-48	**CHI**	**N**	6	1	0	1	8
	TOR	**N**	8	1	2	3	4
	2 team total		14	2	2	4	12

Reg Thomas

THOMAS, REGINALD KENNETH 5'10", 185 lbs.
B. Apr. 21, 1953, Lambeth, Ont. Left Wing, Shoots L

YEAR	TEAM & LEAGUE		GP	G	A	PTS	PIM
1973-74	**LA**	**W**	77	14	21	35	22
1974-75	**M-B**	**W**	50	8	13	21	42
1975-76	**IND**	**W**	80	23	17	40	23
1976-77			79	25	30	55	34
1977-78			49	15	16	31	44
	CIN	**W**	18	4	2	6	12
	2 team total		67	19	18	37	56
1978-79			80	32	39	71	22
1979-80	**QUE**	**N**	39	9	7	16	6
7 yrs.		**N Totals:**	39	9	7	16	6
		W Totals:	433	121	138	259	199

PLAYOFFS

YEAR	TEAM & LEAGUE		GP	G	A	PTS	PIM
1975-76	**IND**	**W**	7	1	0	1	4
1976-77			9	7	9	16	4
1978-79	**CIN**	**W**	3	1	1	2	0
3 yrs.		**W Totals:**	19	9	10	19	8

Claimed by **Edmonton** from Chicago in 1979 Expansion Draft, June 22, 1979. Traded to **Toronto** by Edmonton for Toronto's sixth round choice (Steve Smith) in 1981 Entry Draft. Traded to **Quebec** by Toronto for Dave Parrish and Terry Martin, Dec. 13, 1979.

Cliff Thompson

THOMPSON, CLIFFORD B. 5'11", 185 lbs.
B. Dec. 9, 1918, Winchester, Mass. Defense, Shoots L

YEAR	TEAM & LEAGUE		GP	G	A	PTS	PIM
1941-42	**BOS**	**N**	3	0	0	0	2
1948-49			10	0	1	1	0
2 yrs.		**N Totals:**	13	0	1	1	2

Errol Thompson

THOMPSON, LORAN ERROL 5'8", 180 lbs.
B. May 28, 1950, Summerside, P.E.I. Left Wing, Shoots L

YEAR	TEAM & LEAGUE		GP	G	A	PTS	PIM
1970-71	**TOR**	**N**	1	0	0	0	0
1972-73			68	13	19	32	8
1973-74			56	7	8	15	6
1974-75			65	25	17	42	12
1975-76			75	43	37	80	26
1976-77			41	21	16	37	8
1977-78			59	17	22	39	10
	DET	**N**	14	5	1	6	2
	2 team total		73	22	23	45	12
1978-79			70	23	31	54	26
1979-80			77	34	14	48	22
1980-81			39	14	12	26	52
	PITT	**N**	34	6	8	14	12
	2 team total		73	20	20	40	64
10 yrs.		**N Totals:**	599	208	185	393	184

PLAYOFFS

YEAR	TEAM & LEAGUE		GP	G	A	PTS	PIM
1973-74	**TOR**	**N**	2	0	1	1	0

Errol Thompson continued

YEAR	TEAM & LEAGUE	GP	G	A	PTS	PIM
1974-75		6	0	0	0	9
1975-76		10	3	3	6	0
1976-77		9	2	0	2	0
1977-78	**DET N**	7	2	1	3	2
5 yrs.	**N Totals:**	34	7	5	12	11

Kenneth Thompson

THOMPSON, KENNETH

B. Unknown — Forward

YEAR	TEAM & LEAGUE	GP	G	A	PTS	PIM
1917-18	**MON(W) N**	1	0	0	0	0

Paul Thompson

THOMPSON, PAUL IVAN — 5'10½", 180 lbs.

B. Nov. 2, 1906, Calgary, Alta. — Left Wing, Shoots L

YEAR	TEAM & LEAGUE	GP	G	A	PTS	PIM
1926-27	**NYR N**	43	7	3	10	12
1927-28		41	4	4	8	22
1928-29		44	10	7	17	38
1929-30		44	7	12	19	36
1930-31		44	7	7	14	36
1931-32	**CHI N**	48	8	14	22	34
1932-33		48	13	20	33	27
1933-34		48	20	16	36	17
1934-35		48	16	23	39	20
1935-36		46	17	23	40	19
1936-37		47	17	18	35	28
1937-38		48	22	22	44	14
1938-39		37	5	10	15	33
13 yrs.	**N Totals:**	586	153	179	332	336

PLAYOFFS

YEAR	TEAM & LEAGUE	GP	G	A	PTS	PIM
1926-27	**NYR N**	2	0	0	0	0
1927-28*		8	0	0	0	30
1928-29		6	0	2	2	6
1929-30		4	0	0	0	2
1930-31		4	3	0	3	2
1931-32	**CHI N**	2	0	0	0	2
1933-34*		8	4	3	7	6
1934-35		2	0	0	0	0
1935-36		2	0	3	3	0
1937-38*		10	4	3	7	6
10 yrs.	**N Totals:**	48	11	11	22	54

Bill Thoms

THOMS, BILL — 5'9", 170 lbs.

B. Mar. 5, 1910, Newmarket, Ont. — Center

YEAR	TEAM & LEAGUE	GP	G	A	PTS	PIM
1932-33	**TOR N**	29	3	9	12	15
1933-34		47	8	18	26	24
1934-35		47	9	13	22	19
1935-36		48	**23**	15	38	29
1936-37		48	10	9	19	14
1937-38		48	14	24	38	14
1938-39		12	1	4	5	4
	CHI N	36	6	11	17	16
	2 team total	48	7	15	22	20
1939-40		46	9	13	22	4
1940-41		48	13	19	32	8
1941-42		48	15	30	45	8
1942-43		47	15	28	43	11
1943-44		7	3	5	8	2
1944-45		21	2	6	8	8
	BOS N	17	4	2	6	0
	2 team total	38	6	8	14	8
13 yrs.	**N Totals:**	549	135	206	341	176

PLAYOFFS

YEAR	TEAM & LEAGUE	GP	G	A	PTS	PIM
1932-33	**TOR N**	9	1	1	2	4
1933-34		5	0	2	2	0
1934-35		7	2	0	2	0
1935-36		9	3	**5**	8	0
1936-37		2	0	0	0	0
1937-38		7	0	1	1	0
1939-40	**CHI N**	1	0	0	0	0
1941-42		3	0	1	1	0
1944-45	**BOS N**	1	0	0	0	2
9 yrs.	**N Totals:**	44	6	10	16	6

Bill Thomson

THOMSON, WILLIAM FERGUSON — 5'9", 162 lbs.

B. Mar. 23, 1915, Troon, Scotland — Center, Shoots R

YEAR	TEAM & LEAGUE	GP	G	A	PTS	PIM
1938-39	**DET N**	4	0	0	0	0
1943-44	**CHI N**	1	0	0	0	0
	DET N	5	2	2	4	0
	2 team total	6	2	2	4	0
2 yrs.	**N Totals:**	10	2	2	4	0

PLAYOFFS

YEAR	TEAM & LEAGUE	GP	G	A	PTS	PIM
1943-44	**DET N**	2	0	0	0	0

Floyd Thomson

THOMSON, FLOYD HARVEY — 6', 190 lbs.

B. June 14, 1949, Sudbury, Ont. — Left Wing, Shoots L

YEAR	TEAM & LEAGUE	GP	G	A	PTS	PIM
1971-72	**STL N**	49	4	6	10	48
1972-73		75	14	20	34	71
1973-74		77	11	22	33	58
1974-75		77	9	27	36	106
1975-76		58	8	10	18	25
1976-77		58	7	8	15	11
1977-78		6	1	1	2	4
1979-80		11	2	3	5	18
8 yrs.	**N Totals:**	411	56	97	153	341

PLAYOFFS

YEAR	TEAM & LEAGUE	GP	G	A	PTS	PIM
1972-73	**STL N**	5	0	1	1	2
1974-75		2	0	1	1	0
1976-77		3	0	0	0	4
3 yrs.	**N Totals:**	10	0	2	2	6

Signed as free agent by **St. Louis** Oct 13, 1970.

Jimmy Thomson

THOMSON, JAMES RICHARD — 6', 190 lbs.

B. Feb. 23, 1927, Winnipeg, Man. — Defense, Shoots R

YEAR	TEAM & LEAGUE	GP	G	A	PTS	PIM
1945-46	**TOR N**	5	0	1	1	4
1946-47		60	2	14	16	97
1947-48		59	0	29	29	82
1948-49		60	4	16	20	56
1949-50		70	0	13	13	56
1950-51		69	3	33	36	76
1951-52		70	0	25	25	86
1952-53		69	0	22	22	73
1953-54		61	2	24	26	86
1954-55		70	4	12	16	68
1955-56		62	0	7	7	96
1956-57		62	0	12	12	50
1957-58	**CHI N**	70	4	7	11	75
13 yrs.	**N Totals:**	787	19	215	234	905

PLAYOFFS

YEAR	TEAM & LEAGUE	GP	G	A	PTS	PIM
1946-47*	**TOR N**	11	0	1	1	22
1947-48*		9	1	1	2	9
1948-49*		9	1	5	6	10
1949-50		7	0	2	2	7
1950-51*		11	0	1	1	34
1951-52		4	0	0	0	25
1953-54		3	0	0	0	2
1954-55		4	0	0	0	16
1955-56		5	0	3	3	10
9 yrs.	**N Totals:**	63	2	13	15	135

Claimed on waivers from Toronto by **Chicago** Aug., 1957.

Rhys Thomson

THOMSON, RHYS

B. Aug. 9, 1918, Toronto, Ont. — Defense

YEAR	TEAM & LEAGUE	GP	G	A	PTS	PIM
1939-40	**MONT N**	7	0	0	0	16
1942-43	**TOR N**	18	0	2	2	22
2 yrs.	**N Totals:**	25	0	2	2	38

Joe Thorsteinson

THORSTEINSON, JOSEPH
B. Winnipeg, Man. — Forward

YEAR	TEAM & LEAGUE		GP	G	A	PTS	PIM
1932-33	NYA	N	4	0	0	0	0

Fred Thurier

THURIER, ALFRED MICHAEL — 5'10½", 160 lbs.
B. Jan. 11, 1917, Granby, Que. — Center, Shoots R

YEAR	TEAM & LEAGUE		GP	G	A	PTS	PIM
1940-41	NYA	N	3	2	1	3	0
1941-42			27	7	7	14	4
1944-45	NYR	N	50	16	19	35	14
3 yrs.		N Totals:	80	25	27	52	18

Tom Thurlby

THURLBY, THOMAS NEUMAN — 5'10", 180 lbs.
B. Nov. 9, 1938, Kingston, Ont. — Defense, Shoots L

YEAR	TEAM & LEAGUE		GP	G	A	PTS	PIM
1967-68	OAK	N	20	1	2	3	4

Alex Tidey

TIDEY, ALEXANDER — 6', 188 lbs.
B. Jan. 5, 1955, Vancouver, B.C. — Right Wing, Shoots R

YEAR	TEAM & LEAGUE		GP	G	A	PTS	PIM
1975-76	SD	W	74	16	11	27	46
1976-77	BUF	N	3	0	0	0	0
1977-78			1	0	0	0	0
1979-80	EDM	N	5	0	0	0	8
4 yrs.		N Totals:	9	0	0	0	8
		W Totals:	74	16	11	27	46

PLAYOFFS

YEAR	TEAM & LEAGUE		GP	G	A	PTS	PIM
1975-76	SD	W	11	3	6	9	10
1976-77	BUF	N	2	0	0	0	0
2 yrs.		N Totals:	2	0	0	0	0
		W Totals:	11	3	6	9	10

Traded to **Edmonton** by Buffalo for John Gould, Nov. 13, 1979.

Ray Timgren

TIMGREN, RAYMOND CHARLES — 5'9", 161 lbs.
B. Sept. 29, 1928, Windsor, Ont. — Left Wing, Shoots L

YEAR	TEAM & LEAGUE		GP	G	A	PTS	PIM
1948-49	TOR	N	36	3	12	15	9
1949-50			68	7	18	25	9
1950-51			70	1	9	10	20
1951-52			50	2	4	6	11
1952-53			12	0	0	0	4
1954-55	CHI	N	14	1	1	2	2
	TOR	N	1	0	0	0	2
	2 team total		15	1	1	2	4
6 yrs.		N Totals:	251	14	44	58	57

PLAYOFFS

YEAR	TEAM & LEAGUE		GP	G	A	PTS	PIM
1948-49*	TOR	N	9	3	3	6	2
1949-50			6	0	4	4	2
1950-51*			11	0	1	1	2
1951-52			4	0	1	1	0
4 yrs.		N Totals:	30	3	9	12	6

Traded to **Chicago** by Toronto for Jack Price, Oct. 4, 1954. Loaned to **Toronto** by Chicago, Nov. 16, 1954.

Morris Titanic

TITANIC, MORRIS S. — 6'1", 180 lbs.
B. Jan. 7, 1953, Toronto, Ont. — Left Wing, Shoots L

YEAR	TEAM & LEAGUE		GP	G	A	PTS	PIM
1974-75	BUF	N	17	0	0	0	0
1975-76			2	0	0	0	0
2 yrs.		N Totals:	19	0	0	0	0

Gord Titcomb

TITCOMB, GORDON — 5'11", 186 lbs.
B. Sept. 3, 1953, Dalhousie, N.B. — Forward, Shoots L

YEAR	TEAM & LEAGUE		GP	G	A	PTS	PIM
1974-75	TOR	W	2	0	1	1	0

Walt Tkaczuk

TKACZUK, WALTER ROBERT — 6', 190 lbs.
B. Sept. 29, 1947, Emsdetten, West Germany — Center, Shoots L

YEAR	TEAM & LEAGUE		GP	G	A	PTS	PIM
1967-68	NYR	N	2	0	0	0	0
1968-69			71	12	24	36	28
1969-70			76	27	50	77	38
1970-71			77	26	49	75	48
1971-72			76	24	42	66	65
1972-73			76	27	39	66	59
1973-74			71	21	42	63	58
1974-75			62	11	25	36	34
1975-76			78	8	28	36	56
1976-77			80	12	38	50	38
1977-78			80	26	40	66	30
1978-79			77	15	27	42	38
1979-80			76	12	25	37	36
1980-81			43	6	22	28	28
14 yrs.		N Totals:	945	227	451	678	556

PLAYOFFS

YEAR	TEAM & LEAGUE		GP	G	A	PTS	PIM
1968-69	NYR	N	4	0	1	1	6
1969-70			6	2	1	3	17
1970-71			13	1	5	6	14
1971-72			16	4	6	10	35
1972-73			10	7	2	9	8
1973-74			13	0	5	5	22
1974-75			3	1	2	3	5
1977-78			3	0	2	2	0
1978-79			18	4	7	11	10
1979-80			7	0	1	1	2
10 yrs.		N Totals:	93	19	32	51	119

Mike Toal

TOAL, MICHAEL JAMES (Toaler) — 6', 175 lbs.
B. Mar. 23, 1959, Red Deer, Alta. — Center, Shoots R

YEAR	TEAM & LEAGUE		GP	G	A	PTS	PIM
1979-80	EDM	N	3	0	0	0	0

Glenn Tomalty

TOMALTY, GLENN
Defense

YEAR	TEAM & LEAGUE		GP	G	A	PTS	PIM
1979-80	WINN	N	1	0	0	0	0

John Tomson

TOMSON, JOHN F. — 6'1", 175 lbs.
B. Jan. 31, 1918, Bixbridge, England — Defense, Shoots R

YEAR	TEAM & LEAGUE		GP	G	A	PTS	PIM
1939-40	NYA	N	8	1	1	2	0

PLAYOFFS

YEAR	TEAM & LEAGUE		GP	G	A	PTS	PIM
1938-39	NYA	N	2	0	0	0	0

John Tonelli

TONELLI, JOHN — 6'1", 198 lbs.
B. Mar. 23, 1957, Hamilton, Ont. — Left Wing, Shoots L

YEAR	TEAM & LEAGUE		GP	G	A	PTS	PIM
1975-76	HOUS	W	79	17	14	31	66
1976-77			80	24	31	55	109
1977-78			65	23	41	64	103
1978-79	NYI	N	73	17	39	56	44
1979-80			77	14	30	44	49
1980-81			70	20	32	52	57
1981-82			80	35	58	93	57
1982-83			76	31	40	71	55
8 yrs.		N Totals:	376	117	199	316	262
		W Totals:	224	64	86	150	278

PLAYOFFS

YEAR	TEAM & LEAGUE		GP	G	A	PTS	PIM
1975-76	HOUS	W	17	7	7	14	8
1976-77			11	3	4	7	12
1977-78			6	1	3	4	8
1978-79	NYI	N	10	1	6	7	0
1979-80*			21	7	9	16	18
1980-81*			16	5	8	13	16
1981-82*			19	6	10	16	18
1982-83*			20	7	11	18	20
8 yrs.		N Totals:	86	26	44	70	72
		W Totals:	34	11	14	25	28

Tim Tookey

TOOKEY, TIMOTHY RAYMOND 5'11", 180 lbs.
B. Aug. 29, 1960, Edmonton, Alta. Center, Shoots L

YEAR	TEAM & LEAGUE		GP	G	A	PTS	PIM
1980-81	WASH	N	29	10	13	23	18
1981-82			28	8	8	16	35
1982-83	QUE	N	12	1	6	7	4
3 yrs.		N Totals:	69	19	27	46	57

Traded to **Quebec** by Washington with Washington's seventh round choice (Daniel Poudrier) in 1982 Entry Draft for Lee Norwood, and Quebec's sixth round choice (later transferred to Calgary) in 1982 Entry Draft, Feb. 1, 1982.

Craig Topolinski

TOPOLINSKI, CRAIG
Defense

YEAR	TEAM & LEAGUE		GP	G	A	PTS	PIM
1977-78	EDM	W	1	0	2	2	4

Jerry Toppazzini

TOPPAZZINI, JERRY (Topper) 5'11", 180 lbs.
B. July 29, 1931, Copper Cliff, Ont. Right Wing, Shoots R

YEAR	TEAM & LEAGUE		GP	G	A	PTS	PIM
1952-53	BOS	N	69	10	13	23	36
1953-54			37	0	5	5	24
	CHI	N	14	5	3	8	18
	2 team total		51	5	8	13	42
1954-55			70	9	18	27	20
1955-56	DET	N	40	1	7	8	31
	BOS	N	28	7	7	14	22
	2 team total		68	8	14	22	53
1956-57			55	15	23	38	26
1957-58			64	25	24	49	51
1958-59			70	21	23	44	61
1959-60			69	12	33	45	26
1960-61			67	15	35	50	35
1961-62			70	19	31	50	26
1962-63			65	17	18	35	6
1963-64			65	7	4	11	15
12 yrs.		N Totals:	783	163	244	407	397
PLAYOFFS							
1952-53	BOS	N	11	0	3	3	9
1956-57			10	0	1	1	2
1957-58			12	9	3	12	2
1958-59			1	4	2	6	0
4 yrs.		N Totals:	34	13	9	22	13

Traded to **Chicago** by Boston for Gus Bodnar, Feb., 1954. Traded to **Detroit** by Chicago with Dave Creighton, Gord Hollingsworth and John McCormack for Tony Leswick, Glen Skov, John Wilson, and Benny Woit, June, 1955. Traded to **Boston** by Detroit with Real Chevrefils for Murray Costello and Lorne Ferguson, Jan. 17, 1956. Traded to **Chicago** by Boston with Matt Ravlich for Murray Balfour and Mike Draper, June 9, 1964.

Zellio Toppazzini

TOPPAZZINI, ZELLIO LOUIS PETER (Topper)
5'11", 180 lbs.
B. Jan. 5, 1930, Copper Cliff, Ont. Right Wing, Shoots R

YEAR	TEAM & LEAGUE		GP	G	A	PTS	PIM
1948-49	BOS	N	5	1	1	2	0
1949-50			36	5	5	10	18
1950-51			4	0	1	1	0
	NYR	N	55	14	13	27	27
	2 team total		59	14	14	28	27
1951-52			16	1	1	2	4
1956-57	CHI	N	7	0	0	0	0
5 yrs.		N Totals:	123	21	21	42	49
PLAYOFFS							
1948-49	BOS	N	2	0	0	0	0

Traded to **N.Y. Rangers** by Boston with Ed Harrison for Dunc Fisher, Nov. 16, 1950. Sold to **N. Y. Rangers** by Boston, Oct. 2. 1951. Drafted by **Chicago** from N.Y. Rangers, June 6, 1956.

Bill Touhey

TOUHEY, W. J. 5'9", 155 lbs.
B. Mar. 23, 1906, Ottawa, Ont. Left Wing, Shoots L

YEAR	TEAM & LEAGUE		GP	G	A	PTS	PIM
1927-28	MON(M)	N	29	2	0	2	2
1928-29	OTTA	N	44	9	3	12	28
1929-30			44	10	3	13	24
1930-31			44	15	15	30	8
1931-32	BOS	N	26	5	4	9	12
1932-33	OTTA	N	47	12	7	19	12
1933-34			46	12	8	20	21
7 yrs.		N Totals:	280	65	40	105	107
PLAYOFFS							
1929-30	OTTA	N	2	1	0	1	0

Jacques Toupin

TOUPIN, J. JACQUES
B. Trois Rivieres, Que. Forward

YEAR	TEAM & LEAGUE		GP	G	A	PTS	PIM
1943-44	CHI	N	8	1	2	3	0
PLAYOFFS							
1943-44	CHI	N	4	0	0	0	0

Art Townsend

TOWNSEND, ARTHUR GORDON
Forward

YEAR	TEAM & LEAGUE		GP	G	A	PTS	PIM
1926-27	CHI	N	5	0	0	0	0

Larry Trader

TRADER, LARRY 6'1", 178 lbs.
B. July 7, 1963, Barry's Bay, Ont. Defense, Shoots L

YEAR	TEAM & LEAGUE		GP	G	A	PTS	PIM
1982-83	DET	N	15	0	2	2	6

Wes Trainor

TRAINOR, WESTON THOMAS 5'8", 180 lbs.
B. Sept. 11, 1922, Charlottetown, P.E.I. Left Wing, Shoots R

YEAR	TEAM & LEAGUE		GP	G	A	PTS	PIM
1948-49	NYR	N	17	1	2	3	6

Bobby Trapp

TRAPP, ROBERT
Defense

YEAR	TEAM & LEAGUE		GP	G	A	PTS	PIM
1926-27	CHI	N	44	4	2	6	92
1927-28			38	0	2	2	37
2 yrs.		N Totals:	82	4	4	8	129
PLAYOFFS							
1926-27	CHI	N	2	0	0	0	4

Puss Traub

TRAUB, PERCY
Defense

YEAR	TEAM & LEAGUE		GP	G	A	PTS	PIM
1926-27	CHI	N	42	0	2	2	93
1927-28	DET	N	44	3	1	4	75
1928-29			44	0	0	0	46
3 yrs.		N Totals:	130	3	3	6	214
PLAYOFFS							
1926-27	CHI	N	2	0	0	0	6
1928-29	DET	N	2	0	0	0	0
2 yrs.		N Totals:	4	0	0	0	6

Brock Tredway

TREDWAY, BROCK 6', 180 lbs.
B. June 23, 1959, Highland Creek, Ont. Right Wing, Shoots R

YEAR	TEAM & LEAGUE		GP	G	A	PTS	PIM
PLAYOFFS							
1981-82	LA	N	1	0	0	0	0

Signed as free agent by **Los Angeles** May 11, 1981.

Brent Tremblay

TREMBLAY, BRENT FRANCIS 6'2", 192 lbs.
B. Nov. 1, 1957, North Bay, Ont. Defense, Shoots L

YEAR	TEAM & LEAGUE		GP	G	A	PTS	PIM
1978-79	WASH	N	1	0	0	0	0
1979-80			9	1	0	1	6

Brent Tremblay continued

YEAR	TEAM & LEAGUE		GP	G	A	PTS	PIM
2 yrs.		N Totals:	10	1	0	1	6

Gilles Tremblay

TREMBLAY, JOSEPH JEAN-GILLES 5'10", 175 lbs.
B. Dec. 17, 1938, Montmorency, Que. Left Wing, Shoots L

YEAR	TEAM & LEAGUE		GP	G	A	PTS	PIM
1960-61	**MONT**	N	45	7	11	18	4
1961-62			70	32	22	54	28
1962-63			60	25	24	49	42
1963-64			61	22	15	37	21
1964-65			26	9	7	16	16
1965-66			70	27	21	48	24
1966-67			62	13	19	32	16
1967-68			71	23	28	51	8
1968-69			44	10	15	25	2
9 yrs.		N Totals:	509	168	162	330	161
PLAYOFFS							
1960-61	**MONT**	N	6	1	3	4	0
1961-62			6	1	0	1	2
1962-63			5	2	0	2	0
1963-64			2	0	0	0	0
1965-66*			10	4	5	9	0
1966-67			10	0	1	1	0
1967-68*			9	1	5	6	2
7 yrs.		N Totals:	48	9	14	23	4

J.C. Tremblay

TREMBLAY, JEAN CLAUDE 5'11", 190 lbs.
B. Jan. 22, 1939, Bagotville, Que. Defense, Shoots L

YEAR	TEAM & LEAGUE		GP	G	A	PTS	PIM
1959-60	**MONT**	N	11	0	1	1	0
1960-61			29	1	3	4	18
1961-62			70	3	17	20	18
1962-63			69	1	17	18	10
1963-64			70	5	16	21	24
1964-65			68	3	17	20	22
1965-66			59	6	29	35	8
1966-67			60	8	26	34	14
1967-68			73	4	26	30	18
1968-69			75	7	32	39	18
1969-70			58	2	19	21	7
1970-71			76	11	52	63	23
1971-72			76	6	51	57	24
1972-73	**QUE**	W	76	14	**75**	89	32
1973-74			68	9	44	53	10
1974-75			68	16	56	72	18
1975-76			80	12	**77**	89	16
1976-77			53	4	31	35	16
1977-78			54	5	37	42	26
1978-79			56	6	38	44	8
20 yrs.		N Totals:	794	57	306	363	204
		W Totals:	455	66	358	424	126
PLAYOFFS							
1960-61	**MONT**	N	5	0	0	0	2
1961-62			6	0	2	2	2
1962-63			5	0	0	0	0
1963-64			7	2	1	3	9
1964-65*			13	1	9	10	18
1965-66*			10	2	9	11	2
1966-67			10	2	4	6	2
1967-68*			13	3	6	9	2
1968-69*			13	1	4	5	6
1970-71*			20	3	14	17	15
1971-72			6	0	2	2	0
1974-75	**QUE**	W	11	0	10	10	2
1975-76			5	0	3	3	0
1976-77			17	2	9	11	2
1977-78			1	0	1	1	0
15 yrs.		N Totals:	108	14	51	65	58
		W Totals:	34	2	23	25	4

Marcel Tremblay

TREMBLAY, MARCEL
B. July 4, 1915, Winnipeg, Man. Forward

YEAR	TEAM & LEAGUE		GP	G	A	PTS	PIM
1938-39	**MONT**	N	10	0	2	2	0

Mario Tremblay

TREMBLAY, MARIO 6', 185 lbs.
B. Sept. 2, 1956, Alma, Que. Right Wing, Shoots R

YEAR	TEAM & LEAGUE		GP	G	A	PTS	PIM
1974-75	**MONT**	N	63	21	18	39	108
1975-76			71	11	16	27	88
1976-77			74	18	28	46	61
1977-78			56	10	14	24	44
1978-79			76	30	29	59	74
1979-80			77	16	26	42	105
1980-81			77	25	38	63	123
1981-82			80	33	40	73	66
1982-83			80	30	37	67	87
9 yrs.		N Totals:	654	194	246	440	756
PLAYOFFS							
1974-75	**MONT**	N	11	0	1	1	7
1975-76*			10	0	1	1	27
1976-77*			14	3	0	3	9
1977-78*			5	2	0	2	16
1978-79*			13	3	4	7	13
1979-80			10	0	11	11	14
1980-81			3	0	0	0	9
1981-82			5	4	1	5	24
1982-83			3	0	1	1	7
9 yrs.		N Totals:	74	12	19	31	126

Nels Tremblay

TREMBLAY, NELSON 5'9", 170 lbs.
B. June 2, 1941, Matane, Que. Center, Shoots R

YEAR	TEAM & LEAGUE		GP	G	A	PTS	PIM
1944-45	**MONT**	N	1	0	1	1	0
1945-46			2	0	0	0	0
2 yrs.		N Totals:	3	0	1	1	0
PLAYOFFS							
1944-45	**MONT**	N	2	0	0	0	0

Tom Trevelyn

TREVELYN, THOMAS ARTHUR 5'10½", 185 lbs.
B. Apr. 8, 1949, Toronto, Ont. Center, Shoots L

YEAR	TEAM & LEAGUE		GP	G	A	PTS	PIM
1974-75	**SD**	W	20	0	2	2	4

Tim Trimper

TRIMPER, TIMOTHY EDWARD 5'9", 184 lbs.
B. Sept. 28, 1959, Windsor, Ont. Left Wing, Shoots L

YEAR	TEAM & LEAGUE		GP	G	A	PTS	PIM
1979-80	**CHI**	N	30	6	10	16	10
1980-81	**WINN**	N	56	15	14	29	28
1981-82			74	8	8	16	100
1982-83			5	0	0	0	0
4 yrs.		N Totals:	165	29	32	61	138
PLAYOFFS							
1979-80	**CHI**	N	1	0	0	0	2
1981-82	**WINN**	N	1	0	0	0	0
2 yrs.		N Totals:	2	0	0	0	2

Traded to **Winnipeg** by Chicago with Doug Lecuyer for Peter Marsh, Dec. 1, 1980.

Willie Trognitz

TROGNITZ, RAYMOND WILLIAM 6', 205 lbs.
B. June 11, 1953, Thunder Bay, Ont. Left Wing, Shoots L

YEAR	TEAM & LEAGUE		GP	G	A	PTS	PIM
1977-78	**CIN**	W	29	2	1	3	94

Jerry Troolen

TROOLEN, JEROLD
Defense

YEAR	TEAM & LEAGUE		GP	G	A	PTS	PIM
1972-73	**CHI**	W	2	0	0	0	0

Bryan Trottier

TROTTIER, BRYAN JOHN (Trots) 5'10", 195 lbs.
B. July 18, 1956, Val Marie, Sask.
Won Hart Trophy, 1978-79
Won Art Ross Trophy, 1978-79
Won Calder Trophy, 1975-76
Won Conn Smythe Trophy, 1979-80

YEAR	TEAM & LEAGUE		GP	G	A	PTS	PIM
1975-76	NYI	N	80	32	63	95	21
1976-77			76	30	42	72	34
1977-78			77	46	**77**	123	46
1978-79			76	47	**87**	**134**	50
1979-80			78	42	62	104	68
1980-81			73	31	72	103	74
1981-82			80	50	79	129	88
1982-83			80	34	55	89	68
8 yrs.		N Totals:	620	312	537	849	449
PLAYOFFS							
1975-76	NYI	N	13	1	7	8	8
1976-77			12	2	8	10	2
1977-78			7	0	3	3	4
1978-79			10	2	4	6	13
1979-80*			21	12	17	29	53
1980-81*			18	11	18	29	34
1981-82*			19	6	23	29	40
1982-83*			17	8	12	20	18
8 yrs.		N Totals:	117	42	92	134	172

Dave Trottier

TROTTIER, DAVE 5'10", 170 lbs.
B. June 25, 1906, Pembroke, Ont. Left Wing

YEAR	TEAM & LEAGUE		GP	G	A	PTS	PIM
1928-29	MON(M)	N	37	2	4	6	60
1929-30			41	17	10	27	73
1930-31			43	9	8	17	58
1931-32			48	26	18	44	94
1932-33			48	16	15	31	38
1933-34			48	9	17	26	47
1934-35			34	10	9	19	22
1935-36			46	10	10	20	25
1936-37			43	12	11	23	33
1937-38			47	9	10	19	42
1938-39	DET	N	11	1	1	2	16
11 yrs.		N Totals:	446	121	113	234	508
PLAYOFFS							
1929-30	MON(M)	N	4	0	2	2	8
1930-31			2	0	0	0	6
1931-32			4	1	0	1	2
1932-33			2	0	0	0	6
1933-34			4	0	0	0	6
1934-35*			7	2	1	3	4
1935-36			3	0	0	0	4
1936-37			5	1	0	1	5
8 yrs.		N Totals:	31	4	3	7	41

Guy Trottier

TROTTIER, GUY 5'8", 165 lbs.
B. Apr. 1, 1941, Hull, Que. Right Wing, Shoots R

YEAR	TEAM & LEAGUE		GP	G	A	PTS	PIM
1968-69	NYR	N	2	0	0	0	0
1970-71	TOR	N	61	19	5	24	21
1971-72			52	9	12	21	16
1972-73	OTTA	W	72	26	32	58	25
1973-74	TOR	W	71	27	35	62	58
1974-75			6	2	2	4	2
	M-B	W	17	5	4	9	2
	2 team total		23	7	6	13	4
6 yrs.		N Totals:	115	28	17	45	37
		W Totals:	166	60	73	133	87
PLAYOFFS							
1970-71	TOR	N	5	0	0	0	0
1971-72			4	1	0	1	16
1972-73	OTTA	W	5	1	2	3	0
1973-74	TOR	W	12	5	5	10	4
4 yrs.		N Totals:	9	1	0	1	16
		W Totals:	17	6	7	13	4

Jim Troy

TROY, JAMES EARL 6'2", 200 lbs.
B. Jan. 21, 1953, Boston, Mass. Right Wing, Shoots R

YEAR	TEAM & LEAGUE		GP	G	A	PTS	PIM
1975-76	NE	W	14	0	0	0	0
1976-77			7	0	0	0	7
1977-78	EDM	W	47	2	0	2	124

Jim Troy continued

YEAR	TEAM & LEAGUE		GP	G	A	PTS	PIM
3 yrs.		W Totals:	68	2	0	2	131
PLAYOFFS							
1975-76	NE	W	2	0	0	0	29
1977-78	EDM	W	2	0	0	0	0
2 yrs.		W Totals:	4	0	0	0	29

Lou Trudel

TRUDEL, LOUIS 5'11", 167 lbs.
B. July 21, 1912, Salem, Mass. Left Wing, Shoots L

YEAR	TEAM & LEAGUE		GP	G	A	PTS	PIM
1933-34	CHI	N	31	1	3	4	13
1934-35			47	11	11	22	28
1935-36			47	3	4	7	27
1936-37			45	6	12	18	11
1937-38			42	6	16	22	15
1938-39	MONT	N	31	8	13	21	2
1939-40			47	12	7	19	24
1940-41			16	2	3	5	2
8 yrs.		N Totals:	306	49	69	118	122
PLAYOFFS							
1933-34*	CHI	N	7	0	0	0	2
1934-35			2	0	0	0	0
1935-36			2	0	0	0	2
1937-38*			10	0	3	3	2
1938-39	MONT	N	3	1	0	1	0
5 yrs.		N Totals:	24	1	3	4	6

Rene Trudell

TRUDELL, RENE JOSEPH 5'9", 165 lbs.
B. Jan. 31, 1919, Mariepolis, Man Right Wing, Shoots R

YEAR	TEAM & LEAGUE		GP	G	A	PTS	PIM
1945-46	NYR	N	16	3	5	8	4
1946-47			59	8	16	24	38
1947-48			54	13	7	20	30
3 yrs.		N Totals:	129	24	28	52	72
PLAYOFFS							
1947-48	NYR	N	5	0	0	0	2

Connie Tudin

TUDIN, CORNELL
Defense

YEAR	TEAM & LEAGUE		GP	G	A	PTS	PIM
1941-42	MONT	N	4	0	1	1	4

Rob Tudor

TUDOR, ROBERT ALLAN 5'11", 188 lbs.
B. June 30, 1956, Cupar, Sask. Right Wing, Shoots R

YEAR	TEAM & LEAGUE		GP	G	A	PTS	PIM
1978-79	VAN	N	24	4	4	8	19
1979-80			2	0	0	0	0
1982-83	STL	N	2	0	0	0	0
3 yrs.		N Totals:	28	4	4	8	19
PLAYOFFS							
1978-79	VAN	N	2	0	0	0	0
1979-80			1	0	0	0	0
2 yrs.		N Totals:	3	0	0	0	0

Jim Turkiewicz

TURKIEWICZ, JAMES ROBERT 5'10", 185 lbs.
B. Apr. 13, 1955, Peterborough, Ont. Defense, Shoots L

YEAR	TEAM & LEAGUE		GP	G	A	PTS	PIM
1974-75	TOR	W	78	3	27	30	28
1975-76			77	9	29	38	55
1976-77	BIRM	W	80	6	25	31	54
1977-78			78	3	21	24	45
1978-79			79	3	17	20	52
5 yrs.		W Totals:	392	24	119	143	234
PLAYOFFS							
1974-75	TOR	W	6	0	2	2	0
1977-78	BIRM	W	5	1	1	2	0
2 yrs.		W Totals:	11	1	3	4	0

Gord Turlick

TURLICK, GORDON
B. Sept. 17, 1939, Mickel, B.C. — Forward

YEAR	TEAM & LEAGUE		GP	G	A	PTS	PIM
1959-60	**BOS**	**N**	2	0	0	0	2

Frank Turnbull

TURNBULL, FRANK — 5'8", 155 lbs.
B. Jan. 13, 1953, Trenton, Ont.

YEAR	TEAM & LEAGUE		GP	G	A	PTS	PIM
1975-76	**EDM**	**W**	3	0	0	0	0

Ian Turnbull

TURNBULL, IAN WAYNE — 6', 200 lbs.
B. Dec. 22, 1953, Montreal, Que. — Defense, Shoots L

YEAR	TEAM & LEAGUE		GP	G	A	PTS	PIM
1973-74	**TOR**	**N**	78	8	27	35	74
1974-75			22	6	7	13	44
1975-76			76	20	36	56	90
1976-77			80	22	57	79	84
1977-78			77	14	47	61	77
1978-79			80	12	51	63	80
1979-80			75	11	28	39	90
1980-81			80	19	47	66	104
1981-82			12	0	2	2	8
	LA	**N**	42	11	15	26	81
	2 team total		54	11	17	28	89
1982-83	**PITT**	**N**	6	0	0	0	4
10 yrs.		**N Totals:**	628	123	317	440	736

PLAYOFFS

YEAR	TEAM & LEAGUE		GP	G	A	PTS	PIM
1973-74	**TOR**	**N**	4	0	0	0	8
1974-75			7	0	2	2	4
1975-76			10	2	9	11	29
1976-77			9	4	4	8	10
1977-78			13	6	10	16	10
1978-79			6	0	4	4	27
1979-80			3	0	3	3	2
1980-81			3	1	0	1	4
8 yrs.		**N Totals:**	55	13	32	45	94

Traded to **Los Angeles** by Toronto for Billy Harris and John Gibson, Nov. 11, 1981.

Perry Turnbull

TURNBULL, PERRY JOHN — 6'2", 200 lbs.
B. Mar. 9, 1959, Rimbey, Alta. — Center, Shoots L

YEAR	TEAM & LEAGUE		GP	G	A	PTS	PIM
1979-80	**STL**	**N**	80	16	19	35	124
1980-81			75	34	22	56	209
1981-82			79	33	26	59	161
1982-83			79	32	15	47	172
4 yrs.		**N Totals:**	313	115	82	197	666

PLAYOFFS

YEAR	TEAM & LEAGUE		GP	G	A	PTS	PIM
1979-80	**STL**	**N**	3	1	1	2	2
1981-82			5	3	2	5	11
1982-83			4	1	0	1	14
3 yrs.		**N Totals:**	12	5	3	8	27

Randy Turnbull

TURNBULL, RANDY LAYNE — 5'11", 185 lbs.
B. Feb. 7, 1962, Bentley, Alta. — Defense, Shoots R

YEAR	TEAM & LEAGUE		GP	G	A	PTS	PIM
1981-82	**CALG**	**N**	1	0	0	0	2

Bob Turner

TURNER, ROBERT GEORGE — 6', 178 lbs.
B. Jan. 31, 1934, Regina, Sask. — Defense, Shoots L

YEAR	TEAM & LEAGUE		GP	G	A	PTS	PIM
1955-56	**MONT**	**N**	33	1	4	5	35
1956-57			58	1	4	5	48
1957-58			66	0	3	3	30
1958-59			68	4	24	28	66
1959-60			54	0	9	9	40
1960-61			60	2	2	4	16
1961-62	**CHI**	**N**	69	8	2	10	52
1962-63			70	3	3	6	20
8 yrs.		**N Totals:**	478	19	51	70	307

Bob Turner *continued*

PLAYOFFS

YEAR	TEAM & LEAGUE		GP	G	A	PTS	PIM
1955-56*	**MONT**	**N**	10	0	1	1	10
1956-57*			6	0	1	1	0
1957-58*			10	0	0	0	2
1958-59*			11	0	2	2	20
1959-60*			8	0	0	0	0
1960-61			5	0	0	0	0
1961-62	**CHI**	**N**	12	1	0	1	6
1962-63			6	0	0	0	6
8 yrs.		**N Totals:**	68	1	4	5	44

Traded to **Chicago** by Montreal for Fred Hilts, June 13, 1961.

Dean Turner

TURNER, DEAN CAMERON — 6'2", 215 lbs.
B. June 22, 1958, Dearborn, Mich. — Defense, Shoots L

YEAR	TEAM & LEAGUE		GP	G	A	PTS	PIM
1978-79	**NYR**	**N**	1	0	0	0	0
1979-80	**COLO**	**N**	27	1	0	1	51
1980-81			4	0	0	0	4
1982-83	**LA**	**N**	3	0	0	0	4
4 yrs.		**N Totals:**	35	1	0	1	59

Traded to **Colorado** by N.Y. Rangers with Pat Hickey, Mike McEwen, Lucien DeBlois and future considerations (Bobby Crawford) for Barry Beck, Nov. 2, 1979.

Norman Tustin

TUSTIN, NORMAN ROBERT — 5'11", 175 lbs.
B. Jan. 3, 1919, Regina, Sask. — Left Wing, Shoots L

YEAR	TEAM & LEAGUE		GP	G	A	PTS	PIM
1941-42	**NYR**	**N**	18	2	4	6	0

Audley Tuten

TUTEN, AUDLEY T. — 5'10", 180 lbs.
B. Jan. 14, 1915, Enterprize, Alta. — Defense, Shoots L

YEAR	TEAM & LEAGUE		GP	G	A	PTS	PIM
1941-42	**CHI**	**N**	5	1	1	2	10
1942-43			34	3	7	10	38
2 yrs.		**N Totals:**	39	4	8	12	48

Gene Ubriaco

UBRIACO, EUGENE STEPHEN — 5'8", 157 lbs.
B. Dec. 26, 1937, Sault Ste. Marie, Ont. — Left Wing, Shoots L

YEAR	TEAM & LEAGUE		GP	G	A	PTS	PIM
1967-68	**PITT**	**N**	65	18	15	33	16
1968-69			49	15	11	26	14
	CALIF	**N**	26	4	7	11	14
	2 team total		75	19	18	37	28
1969-70	**OAK**	**N**	16	1	1	2	4
	CHI	**N**	21	1	1	2	2
	2 team total		37	2	2	4	6
3 yrs.		**N Totals:**	177	39	35	74	50

PLAYOFFS

YEAR	TEAM & LEAGUE		GP	G	A	PTS	PIM
1968-69	**CALIF**	**N**	7	2	0	2	2
1969-70	**CHI**	**N**	4	0	0	0	2
2 yrs.		**N Totals:**	11	2	0	2	4

Traded to **Oakland** by Pittsburgh with Earl Ingarfield and Dick Mattiussi for Bryan Watson, George Swarbrick, and Tracy Pratt, Jan. 30, 1969. Traded to **Chicago** by Oakland for Howie Menard, Dec. 15, 1969.

Norm Ullman

ULLMAN, NORMAN VICTOR ALEXANDER
5'10", 185 lbs.
B. Dec. 26, 1935, Provost, Alta. — Center, Shoots L
Hall of Fame, 1982

YEAR	TEAM & LEAGUE		GP	G	A	PTS	PIM
1955-56	**DET**	**N**	66	9	9	18	26
1956-57			64	16	36	52	47
1957-58			69	23	28	51	38
1958-59			69	22	36	58	42
1959-60			70	24	34	58	46
1960-61			70	28	42	70	34
1961-62			70	26	38	64	54
1962-63			70	26	30	56	53
1963-64			61	21	30	51	55
1964-65			70	**42**	41	83	70
1965-66			70	31	41	72	35
1966-67			68	26	44	70	26

Norm Ullman continued

YEAR	TEAM & LEAGUE	GP	G	A	PTS	PIM
1967-68		58	30	25	55	26
	TOR N	13	5	12	17	2
	2 team total	71	35	37	72	28
1968-69		75	35	42	77	41
1969-70		74	18	42	60	37
1970-71		73	34	51	85	24
1971-72		77	23	50	73	26
1972-73		65	20	35	55	10
1973-74		78	22	47	69	12
1974-75		80	9	26	35	8
1975-76	**EDM** W	77	31	56	87	12
1976-77		67	16	27	43	28
22 yrs.	**N Totals:**	1410	490	739	1229	712
	W Totals:	144	47	83	130	40

PLAYOFFS

YEAR	TEAM & LEAGUE	GP	G	A	PTS	PIM
1955-56	**DET** N	10	1	3	4	13
1956-57		5	1	1	2	6
1957-58		4	0	2	2	4
1959-60		6	2	2	4	0
1960-61		11	0	4	4	4
1962-63		11	4	12	16	14
1963-64		14	7	10	17	6
1964-65		7	6	4	10	2
1965-66		12	6	9	15	12
1968-69	**TOR** N	4	1	0	1	0
1970-71		6	0	2	2	2
1971-72		5	1	3	4	2
1973-74		4	1	1	2	0
1974-75		7	0	0	0	2
1975-76	**EDM** W	4	1	3	4	2
1976-77		5	0	3	3	0
16 yrs.	**N Totals:**	106	30	53	83	67
	W Totals:	9	1	6	7	2

Traded to **Toronto** by Detroit with Floyd Smith and Paul Henderson for Frank Mahovlich, Pete Stemkowski, Garry Ungar and the rights to Carl Brewer, Mar. 3, 1968.

Garry Unger

UNGER, GARRY DOUGLAS (Iron Man) 6', 185 lbs.
B. Dec. 7, 1947, Edmonton, Alta. Center, Shoots L

YEAR	TEAM & LEAGUE	GP	G	A	PTS	PIM
1967-68	**TOR** N	15	1	1	2	4
	DET N	13	5	10	15	2
	2 team total	28	6	11	17	6
1968-69		76	24	20	44	33
1969-70		76	42	24	66	67
1970-71		51	13	14	27	63
	STL N	28	15	14	29	41
	2 team total	79	28	28	56	104
1971-72		78	36	34	70	104
1972-73		78	41	39	80	119
1973-74		78	33	35	68	96
1974-75		80	36	44	80	123
1975-76		80	39	44	83	95
1976-77		80	30	27	57	56
1977-78		80	32	20	52	66
1978-79		80	30	26	56	44
1979-80	**ATL** N	79	17	16	33	39
1980-81	**LA** N	58	10	10	20	40
	EDM N	13	0	0	0	6
	2 team total	71	10	10	20	46
1981-82		46	7	13	20	69
1982-83		16	2	0	2	8
16 yrs.	**N Totals:**	1105	413	391	804	1075

PLAYOFFS

YEAR	TEAM & LEAGUE	GP	G	A	PTS	PIM
1969-70	**DET** N	4	0	1	1	6
1970-71	**STL** N	6	3	2	5	20
1971-72		11	4	5	9	35
1972-73		5	1	2	3	2
1974-75		2	1	3	4	6
1975-76		3	2	1	3	7
1976-77		4	0	1	1	2
1979-80	**ATL** N	4	0	3	3	2
1980-81	**EDM** N	8	0	0	0	2
1981-82		4	1	0	1	23
1982-83		1	0	0	0	0
11 yrs.	**N Totals:**	52	12	18	30	105

Traded to **Detroit** by Toronto with Frank Mahovlich, Pete Stemkowski and the rights to Carl Brewer for Norm Ullman, Paul Henderson and Floyd Smith, March 3, 1968. Traded to **St. Louis** by Detroit with Wayne Connelly for Red Berenson and Tim Ecclestone, Feb. 6, 1971. Traded to **Atlanta** by St. Louis for Ed Kea, Don Laurence and Atlanta's second-round choice (Hakan Nordin) in 1981 Entry Entry Draft, Oct. 10, 1979. Traded by Calgary to **Los Angeles** for Bert Wilson and Randy Holt, June 6, 1980. Traded to **Edmonton** by Los Angeles for Edmonton's seventh-round choice (Craig Hurley) in 1981 Entry Draft, Mar. 10, 1981.

Carol Vadnais

VADNAIS, CAROL MARCEL (Vad) 6'1", 210 lbs.
B. Sept. 25, 1945, Montreal, Que. Defense, Shoots L

YEAR	TEAM & LEAGUE	GP	G	A	PTS	PIM
1966-67	**MONT** N	11	0	3	3	35
1967-68		31	1	1	2	31
1968-69	**CALIF** N	76	15	27	42	151
1969-70	**OAK** N	76	24	20	44	212
1970-71	**CALIF** N	42	10	16	26	91
1971-72		52	14	20	34	106
	BOS N	16	4	6	10	37
	2 team total	68	18	26	44	143
1972-73		78	7	24	31	127
1973-74		78	16	43	59	123
1974-75		79	18	56	74	129
1975-76	**BOS** N	12	2	5	7	17
	NYR N	64	20	30	50	104
	2 team total	76	22	35	57	121
1976-77		74	11	37	48	131
1977-78		80	6	40	46	115
1978-79		77	8	37	45	86
1979-80		66	3	20	23	118
1980-81		74	3	20	23	91
1981-82		50	5	6	11	45
1982-83	**NJ** N	51	2	7	9	64
17 yrs.	**N Totals:**	1087	169	418	587	1813

PLAYOFFS

YEAR	TEAM & LEAGUE	GP	G	A	PTS	PIM
1966-67	**MONT** N	1	0	0	0	2
1967-68*		1	0	0	0	2
1968-69	**CALIF** N	7	1	4	5	10
1969-70	**OAK** N	4	2	1	3	15
1971-72*	**BOS** N	15	0	2	2	43
1972-73		5	0	0	0	8
1973-74		16	1	12	13	42
1974-75		3	1	5	6	0
1977-78	**NYR** N	3	0	2	2	16
1978-79		18	2	9	11	13
1979-80		9	1	2	3	6
1980-81		14	1	3	4	26
1981-82		10	1	0	1	4
13 yrs.	**N Totals:**	106	10	40	50	187

Drafted by **Oakland** from Montreal, June 12, 1968. Traded to **Boston** by California with Don O'Donaghue for Reggie Leach, Rick Smith and Bob Stewart, Feb. 23, 1972. Traded to **N.Y. Rangers** by Boston with Phil Esposito for Brad Park, Jean Ratelle and Joe Zanussi, Nov. 7, 1975. Acquired by **New Jersey** from N.Y. Rangers in Waiver Draft, Oct. 4, 1982.

Eric Vail

VAIL, ERIC DOUGLAS (Big Train) 6'2", 210 lbs.
B. Sept. 16, 1530, Timmins, Ont. Left Wing, Shoots L
Won Calder Trophy, 1974-75

YEAR	TEAM & LEAGUE	GP	G	A	PTS	PIM
1973-74	**ATL** N	23	2	9	11	30
1974-75		72	39	21	60	46
1975-76		60	16	31	47	34
1976-77		78	32	39	71	22
1977-78		79	22	36	58	16
1978-79		80	35	48	83	53
1979-80		77	28	25	53	22
1980-81	**CALG** N	64	28	36	64	23
1981-82		6	4	1	5	0
	DET N	52	10	14	24	35
	2 team total	58	14	15	29	35
9 yrs.	**N Totals:**	591	216	260	476	281

PLAYOFFS

YEAR	TEAM & LEAGUE	GP	G	A	PTS	PIM
1973-74	**ATL** N	1	0	0	0	2
1975-76		2	0	0	0	0
1976-77		3	1	3	4	0
1977-78		2	1	1	2	0
1978-79		2	0	1	1	2
1979-80		4	3	1	4	2
1980-81	**CALG** N	6	0	0	0	0

Eric Vail continued

YEAR	TEAM & LEAGUE	GP	G	A	PTS	PIM
7 yrs.	N Totals:	20	5	6	11	6

Traded to **Detroit** by Calgary for Gary McAdam and Detroit's fourth round choice (John Bekkers) in 1983 Entry Draft, Nov. 10, 1981.

Sparky Vail

VAIL, MELVILLE 6', 185 lbs.
B. July 5, 1906, Meaford, Ont. Defense, Shoots R

YEAR	TEAM & LEAGUE	GP	G	A	PTS	PIM
1928-29	**NYR** N	18	3	0	3	16
1929-30		32	1	1	2	2
2 yrs.	N Totals:	50	4	1	5	18
PLAYOFFS						
1928-29	**NYR** N	6	0	0	0	2
1929-30		4	0	0	0	0
2 yrs.	N Totals:	10	0	0	0	2

Rick Vaive

VAIVE, RICK CLAUDE 6', 180 lbs.
B. May 14, 1959, Ottawa, Ont. Right Wing, Shoots R

YEAR	TEAM & LEAGUE	GP	G	A	PTS	PIM
1978-79	**BIRM** W	75	26	33	59	**248**
1979-80	**VAN** N	47	13	8	21	111
	TOR N	22	9	7	16	77
	2 team total	69	22	15	37	188
1980-81		75	33	29	62	229
1981-82		77	54	35	89	157
1982-83		78	51	28	79	105
5 yrs.	N Totals:	299	160	107	267	679
	W Totals:	75	26	33	59	248
PLAYOFFS						
1979-80	**TOR** N	3	1	0	1	11
1980-81		3	1	0	1	4
1982-83		4	2	5	7	6
3 yrs.	N Totals:	10	4	5	9	21

Traded to **Toronto** by Vancouver with Bill Derlago for Tiger Williams and Jerry Butler, Feb. 18, 1980.

Chris Valentine

VALENTINE, CHRISTOPHER WILLIAM
6', 191 lbs.
B. Dec. 6, 1961, Belleville, Ont. Center, Shoots R

YEAR	TEAM & LEAGUE	GP	G	A	PTS	PIM
1981-82	**WASH** N	60	30	37	67	92
1982-83		23	7	10	17	14
2 yrs.	N Totals:	83	37	47	84	106
PLAYOFFS						
1982-83	**WASH** N	2	0	0	0	4

Jack Valiquette

VALIQUETTE, JOHN JOSEPH 6'2", 195 lbs.
B. Mar. 18, 1956, St. Thomas, Ont. Center, Shoots L

YEAR	TEAM & LEAGUE	GP	G	A	PTS	PIM
1974-75	**TOR** N	1	0	0	0	0
1975-76		45	10	23	33	30
1976-77		66	15	30	45	7
1977-78		60	8	13	21	15
1978-79	**COLO** N	76	23	34	57	12
1979-80		77	25	25	50	8
1980-81		25	3	9	12	7
7 yrs.	N Totals:	350	84	134	218	79
PLAYOFFS						
1975-76	**TOR** N	10	2	3	5	2
1977-78		13	1	3	4	2
2 yrs.	N Totals:	23	3	6	9	4

Traded to **Colorado** by Toronto for Colorado's second round choice (Gary Yaremchuk) in 1981 Entry Draft, Oct. 19, 1978.

John Van Boxmeer

VAN BOXMEER, JOHN MARTIN 6', 192 lbs.
B. Nov. 20, 1952, Petrolia, Ont. Defense, Shoots R

YEAR	TEAM & LEAGUE	GP	G	A	PTS	PIM
1973-74	**MONT** N	20	1	4	5	18
1974-75		9	0	2	2	0
1975-76		46	6	11	17	31
1976-77		4	0	1	1	0
	COLO N	41	2	11	13	32
	2 team total	45	2	12	14	32
1977-78		80	12	42	54	87
1978-79		76	9	34	43	46
1979-80	**BUF** N	80	11	40	51	55
1980-81		80	18	51	69	69
1981-82		69	14	54	68	62
1982-83		65	6	21	27	53
10 yrs.	N Totals:	570	79	271	350	453
PLAYOFFS						
1973-74	**MONT** N	1	0	0	0	0
1977-78	**COLO** N	2	0	1	1	2
1979-80	**BUF** N	14	3	5	8	12
1980-81		8	1	8	9	7
1981-82		4	0	1	1	6
1982-83		9	1	0	1	10
6 yrs.	N Totals:	38	5	15	20	37

Traded to **Colorado** by Montreal for cash and Colorado's third choice (Craig Levie) in the 1979 Entry Draft, Nov. 24, 1976. Traded to **Buffalo** by Colorado for Rene Robert, Oct. 5, 1979.

John Van Horlick

VAN HORLICK, JOHN FREDERICK 6', 195 lbs.
B. Feb. 19, 1949, Vancouver, B.C. Defense, Shoots L

YEAR	TEAM & LEAGUE	GP	G	A	PTS	PIM
1975-76	**TOR** W	2	0	0	0	12

Ed Van Impe

VAN IMPE, EDWARD CHARLES 5'10", 205 lbs.
B. May 27, 1940, Saskatoon, Sask. Defense, Shoots L

YEAR	TEAM & LEAGUE	GP	G	A	PTS	PIM
1966-67	**CHI** N	61	8	11	19	111
1967-68	**PHI** N	67	4	13	17	141
1968-69		68	7	12	19	112
1969-70		65	0	10	10	117
1970-71		77	0	11	11	80
1971-72		73	4	9	13	78
1972-73		72	1	11	12	76
1973-74		77	2	16	18	119
1974-75		78	1	17	18	109
1975-76		40	0	8	8	60
	PITT N	12	0	5	5	16
	2 team total	52	0	13	13	76
1976-77		10	0	3	3	6
11 yrs.	N Totals:	700	27	126	153	1025
PLAYOFFS						
1966-67	**CHI** N	6	0	0	0	8
1967-68	**PHI** N	7	0	4	4	11
1968-69		1	0	0	0	17
1970-71		4	0	1	1	8
1972-73		11	0	0	0	16
1973-74*		17	1	2	3	41
1974-75*		17	0	4	4	28
1975-76	**PITT** N	3	0	1	1	2
8 yrs.	N Totals:	66	1	12	13	131

Drafted by **Philadelphia** from Chicago in Expansion Draft, June 6, 1967. Traded to **Pittsburgh** by Philadelphia with Bobby Taylor for Gary Inness and future considerations, Mar. 9, 1976.

Elmer Vasko

VASKO, ELMER (Moose) 6'3", 220 lbs.
B. Dec. 11, 1935, Duparquet, Que. Defense, Shoots L

YEAR	TEAM & LEAGUE	GP	G	A	PTS	PIM
1956-57	**CHI** N	64	3	12	15	31
1957-58		59	6	20	26	51
1958-59		63	6	10	16	52
1959-60		69	3	27	30	110
1960-61		63	4	18	22	40
1961-62		64	2	22	24	87
1962-63		64	4	9	13	70

Elmer Vasko continued

YEAR	TEAM	LEAGUE	GP	G	A	PTS	PIM
1963-64			70	2	18	20	65
1964-65			69	1	10	11	56
1965-66			56	1	7	8	44
1967-68	**MINN**	**N**	70	1	6	7	45
1968-69			72	1	7	8	68
1969-70			3	0	0	0	0
13 yrs.		**N Totals:**	786	34	166	200	719
PLAYOFFS							
1958-59	**CHI**	**N**	6	0	1	1	4
1959-60			4	0	0	0	0
1960-61*			12	1	1	2	23
1961-62			12	0	0	0	4
1962-63			6	0	1	1	8
1963-64			7	0	0	0	4
1964-65			14	1	2	3	20
1965-66			3	0	0	0	4
1967-68	**MINN**	**N**	14	0	2	2	6
9 yrs.		**N Totals:**	78	2	7	9	73

Drafted by **Minnesota** from Chicago in Expansion Draft, June 6, 1967.

Rick Vasko

VASKO, RICHARD JOHN 6', 185 lbs.
B. Jan. 12, 1957, St. Catharines, Ont. Defense, Shoots L

YEAR	TEAM	LEAGUE	GP	G	A	PTS	PIM
1977-78	**DET**	**N**	3	0	0	0	7
1979-80			8	0	0	0	2
1980-81			20	3	7	10	20
3 yrs.		**N Totals:**	31	3	7	10	29

Traded to **Calgary** by Detroit, May 28, 1981, to complete trade in which Detroit received Brad Smith from Calgary, Feb. 24, 1981.

Yvon Vautour

VAUTOUR, YVON 6', 200 lbs.
B. Sept. 10, 1956, St. John, N.B. Right Wing, Shoots R

YEAR	TEAM	LEAGUE	GP	G	A	PTS	PIM
1979-80	**NYI**	**N**	17	3	1	4	24
1980-81	**COLO**	**N**	74	15	19	34	143
1981-82			14	1	2	3	18
1982-83	**NJ**	**N**	52	4	7	11	136
4 yrs.		**N Totals:**	157	23	29	52	321

Claimed by **N.Y. Islanders** as fill in Expansion Draft, June 13, 1979. Claimed by **Colorado** from N.Y. Islanders in Waiver Draft, Oct. 10, 1980.

Greg Vaydik

VAYDIK, GREGORY 6', 185 lbs.
B. Oct. 9, 1955, Yellowknife, N.W.T. Center, Shoots L

YEAR	TEAM	LEAGUE	GP	G	A	PTS	PIM
1976-77	**CHI**	**N**	5	0	0	0	0

Darren Veitch

VEITCH, DARREN WILLIAM 6', 188 lbs.
B. Apr. 24, 1960, Saskatoon, Sask. Defense, Shoots R

YEAR	TEAM	LEAGUE	GP	G	A	PTS	PIM
1980-81	**WASH**	**N**	59	4	21	25	46
1981-82			67	9	44	53	54
1982-83			10	0	8	8	0
3 yrs.		**N Totals:**	136	13	73	86	100

Randy Velischek

VELISCHEK, RANDY 6'1", 200 lbs.
B. Feb. 10, 1962, Montreal, Que. Defense, Shoots L

YEAR	TEAM	LEAGUE	GP	G	A	PTS	PIM
1982-83	**MINN**	**N**	3	0	0	0	2
PLAYOFFS							
1982-83	**MINN**	**N**	9	0	0	0	0

Vic Venasky

VENASKY, VICTOR WILLIAM 5'11", 177 lbs.
B. June 3, 1951, Thunder Bay, Ont. Center, Shoots R

YEAR	TEAM	LEAGUE	GP	G	A	PTS	PIM
1972-73	**LA**	**N**	77	15	19	34	10
1973-74			32	6	5	11	12
1974-75			17	1	2	3	0
1975-76			80	18	26	44	12
1976-77			80	14	26	40	18
1977-78			71	3	10	13	6

Vic Venasky continued

YEAR	TEAM	LEAGUE	GP	G	A	PTS	PIM
1978-79			73	4	13	17	8
7 yrs.		**N Totals:**	430	61	101	162	66
PLAYOFFS							
1975-76	**LA**	**N**	9	0	1	1	6
1976-77			9	1	4	5	6
1977-78			1	0	0	0	0
1978-79			2	0	0	0	0
4 yrs.		**N Totals:**	21	1	5	6	12

Gary Veneruzzo

VENERUZZO, GARY RAYMOND 5'9", 165 lbs.
B. June 28, 1943, Fort William, Ont. Left Wing, Shoots L

YEAR	TEAM	LEAGUE	GP	G	A	PTS	PIM
1967-68	**STL**	**N**	5	1	1	2	0
1971-72			2	0	0	0	0
1972-73	**LA**	**W**	78	43	30	73	34
1973-74			78	39	29	68	68
1974-75	**M-B**	**W**	77	33	27	60	57
1975-76	**CIN**	**W**	14	3	2	5	8
	PHOE	**W**	61	19	24	43	27
	2 team total		75	22	26	48	35
1976-77	**SD**	**W**	40	14	11	25	18
7 yrs.		**N Totals:**	7	1	1	2	0
		W Totals:	348	151	123	274	212
PLAYOFFS							
1967-68	**STL**	**N**	9	0	2	2	2
1972-73	**LA**	**W**	6	3	0	3	4
1975-76	**PHOE**	**W**	5	2	0	2	7
1976-77	**SD**	**W**	7	0	0	0	0
4 yrs.		**N Totals:**	9	0	2	2	2
		W Totals:	18	5	0	5	11

Drafted by **St. Louis** from Toronto in Expansion Draft, June 6, 1967.

Pat Verbeek

VERBEEK, PAT 5'9", 191 lbs.
B. May 24, 1964, Sarnia, Ont. Center, Shoots R

YEAR	TEAM	LEAGUE	GP	G	A	PTS	PIM
1982-83	**NJ**	**N**	6	3	2	5	8

Leigh Verstraete

VERSTRAETE, LEIGH 5'11", 183 lbs.
B. Jan. 6, 1962, Pincher Creek, Alta.

YEAR	TEAM	LEAGUE	GP	G	A	PTS	PIM
1982-83	**TOR**	**N**	3	0	0	0	5

Dennis Ververgaert

VERVERGAERT, DENNIS ANDREW 6', 195 lbs.
B. Mar. 30, 1953, Hamilton, Ont. Right Wing, Shoots R

YEAR	TEAM	LEAGUE	GP	G	A	PTS	PIM
1973-74	**VAN**	**N**	78	26	31	57	25
1974-75			57	19	32	51	25
1975-76			80	37	34	71	53
1976-77			79	27	18	45	38
1977-78			80	21	33	54	23
1978-79			35	9	17	26	13
	PHI	**N**	37	9	7	16	6
	2 team total		72	18	24	42	19
1979-80			58	14	17	31	24
1980-81	**WASH**	**N**	79	14	27	41	40
8 yrs.		**N Totals:**	583	176	216	392	247
PLAYOFFS							
1974-75	**VAN**	**N**	1	0	0	0	0
1975-76			2	1	0	1	4
1978-79	**PHI**	**N**	3	0	2	2	2
1979-80			2	0	0	0	0
4 yrs.		**N Totals:**	8	1	2	3	6

Traded to **Philadelphia** by Vancouver for Drew Callander and Kevin McCarthy, Dec. 31, 1978. Signed as free agent with **Washington** Oct. 6, 1980.

Sid Veysey

VEYSEY, SIDNEY 5'11", 175 lbs.
B. July 30, 1955, Woodstock, B.C. Center, Shoots L

YEAR	TEAM	LEAGUE	GP	G	A	PTS	PIM
1977-78	**VAN**	**N**	1	0	0	0	0

YEAR	TEAM & LEAGUE		GP	G	A	PTS	PIM

Pierre Viau

VIAU, PIERRE 6'2", 187 lbs.
B. Jan. 29, 1952, Montreal, Que. Defense, Shoots L

YEAR	TEAM	LEAGUE	GP	G	A	PTS	PIM
1972-73	**CHI**	**W**	4	0	0	0	0

Steve Vickers

VICKERS, STEPHEN JAMES (Sarge) 6', 185 lbs.
B. Apr. 21, 1951, Toronto, Ont. Left Wing, Shoots L
Won Calder Trophy, 1972-73

YEAR	TEAM	LEAGUE	GP	G	A	PTS	PIM
1972-73	**NYR**	**N**	61	30	23	53	37
1973-74			75	34	24	58	18
1974-75			80	41	48	89	64
1975-76			80	30	53	83	40
1976-77			75	22	31	53	26
1977-78			79	19	44	63	30
1978-79			66	13	34	47	24
1979-80			75	29	33	62	38
1980-81			73	19	39	58	40
1981-82			34	9	11	20	13
10 yrs.	**N Totals:**		698	246	340	586	330

PLAYOFFS

YEAR	TEAM	LEAGUE	GP	G	A	PTS	PIM
1972-73	**NYR**	**N**	10	5	4	9	4
1973-74			13	4	4	8	17
1974-75			3	2	4	6	6
1977-78			3	2	1	3	0
1978-79			18	5	3	8	13
1979-80			9	2	2	4	4
1980-81			12	4	7	11	14
7 yrs.	**N Totals:**		68	24	25	49	58

Alain Vigneault

VIGNEAULT, ALAIN 5'11", 195 lbs.
B. May 14, 1961, Quebec City, Que. Defense, Shoots R

YEAR	TEAM	LEAGUE	GP	G	A	PTS	PIM
1981-82	**STL**	**N**	14	1	2	3	43
1982-83			28	1	3	4	39
2 yrs.	**N Totals:**		42	2	5	7	82

PLAYOFFS

YEAR	TEAM	LEAGUE	GP	G	A	PTS	PIM
1982-83	**STL**	**N**	4	0	1	1	26

Pete Vipond

VIPOND, PETER JOHN 5'10", 175 lbs.
B. Dec. 8, 1949, Oshawa, Ont. Left Wing, Shoots L

YEAR	TEAM	LEAGUE	GP	G	A	PTS	PIM
1972-73	**CALIF**	**N**	3	0	0	0	0

Hannu Virta

VIRTA, HANNU 6', 176 lbs.
B. Mar. 22, 1963, Turku, Finland Defense, Shoots L

YEAR	TEAM	LEAGUE	GP	G	A	PTS	PIM
1981-82	**BUF**	**N**	3	0	1	1	4
1982-83			74	13	24	37	18
2 yrs.	**N Totals:**		77	13	25	38	22

PLAYOFFS

YEAR	TEAM	LEAGUE	GP	G	A	PTS	PIM
1981-82	**BUF**	**N**	4	0	1	1	0
1982-83			10	1	2	3	4
2 yrs.	**N Totals:**		14	1	3	4	4

Vokes

VOKES
B. Unknown Forward

YEAR	TEAM	LEAGUE	GP	G	A	PTS	PIM
1930-31	**CHI**	**N**	4	0	0	0	0

Mickey Volcan

VOLCAN, MICHAEL STEPHEN 6', 190 lbs.
B. Mar. 3, 1962, Edmonton, Alta. Defense, Shoots R

YEAR	TEAM	LEAGUE	GP	G	A	PTS	PIM
1980-81	**HART**	**N**	49	2	11	13	26
1981-82			26	1	5	6	29
1982-83			68	4	13	17	73
3 yrs.	**N Totals:**		143	7	29	36	128

Traded to **Calgary** by Hartford for Joel Quenneville and Richie Dunn, July 6, 1983.

YEAR	TEAM & LEAGUE		GP	G	A	PTS	PIM

Doug Volmar

VOLMAR, DOUGLAS STEVEN 6'1", 215 lbs.
B. Jan. 9, 1945, Cleveland Heights, Ohio
Right Wing, Shoots R

YEAR	TEAM	LEAGUE	GP	G	A	PTS	PIM
1970-71	**DET**	**N**	2	0	1	1	2
1971-72			39	9	5	14	8
1972-73	**LA**	**N**	21	4	2	6	16
1974-75	**SD**	**W**	10	0	100	100	400
4 yrs.	**N Totals:**		62	13	8	21	26
	W Totals:		10	0	100	100	400

PLAYOFFS

YEAR	TEAM	LEAGUE	GP	G	A	PTS	PIM
1969-70	**DET**	**N**	2	1	0	1	0

Drafted by **Los Angeles** from Detroit in Intra-league Draft, June 5, 1972.

Carl Voss

VOSS, CARL 5'8½", 168 lbs.
B. Jan. 6, 1907, Chelsea, Mass. Center, Shoots L
Won Calder Trophy, 1932-33
Hall of Fame, 1974

YEAR	TEAM	LEAGUE	GP	G	A	PTS	PIM
1926-27	**TOR**	**N**	12	0	0	0	0
1928-29			2	0	0	0	0
1932-33	**NYR**	**N**	10	2	1	3	4
	DET	**N**	38	6	14	20	6
	2 team total		48	8	15	23	10
1933-34			8	0	2	2	2
	OTTA	**N**	40	7	16	23	10
	2 team total		48	7	18	25	12
1934-35	**STL**	**N**	48	13	18	31	14
1935-36	**NYA**	**N**	46	3	9	12	10
1936-37	**MON(M)**	**N**	20	0	2	2	4
1937-38			3	0	0	0	0
	CHI	**N**	34	3	8	11	0
	2 team total		37	3	8	11	0
8 yrs.	**N Totals:**		261	34	70	104	50

PLAYOFFS

YEAR	TEAM	LEAGUE	GP	G	A	PTS	PIM
1932-33	**BOS**	**N**	4	1	1	2	0
1935-36	**NYA**	**N**	5	0	0	0	0
1936-37	**MON(M)**	**N**	5	1	0	1	0
1937-38*	**CHI**	**N**	10	3	2	5	0
4 yrs.	**N Totals:**		24	5	3	8	0

Don Waddell

WADDELL, DONALD 5'10", 178 lbs.
B. Aug. 19, 1958, Detroit, Mich. Defense, Shoots L

YEAR	TEAM	LEAGUE	GP	G	A	PTS	PIM
1980-81	**LA**	**N**	1	0	0	0	0

Frank Waite

WAITE, FRANK (Deacon) 5'11", 150 lbs.
B. Apr. 9, 1906, Qu'Appelle, Sask. Forward

YEAR	TEAM	LEAGUE	GP	G	A	PTS	PIM
1930-31	**NYR**	**N**	17	1	3	4	4

Howard Walker

WALKER, HOWARD 6', 205 lbs.
B. Aug. 5, 1958, Grande Prairie, Alta. Defense, Shoots L

YEAR	TEAM	LEAGUE	GP	G	A	PTS	PIM
1980-81	**WASH**	**N**	64	2	11	13	100
1981-82			16	0	2	2	26
1982-83	**CALG**	**N**	3	0	0	0	7
3 yrs.	**N Totals:**		83	2	13	15	133

Signed as free agent with **Washington** June 5, 1980. Traded to **Calgary** with George White by Washington for Pat Riggin and Ken Houston, June 9, 1982. In addition, Washington transferred the following Amateur Draft choices: a sixth round choice (acquired earlier from Quebec, Mats Kihlstron) in 1982, a third round choice in 1983 (Barry Perezan) and a second round choice in 1984.

Jack Walker

WALKER, JACK
Left Wing
Hall of Fame, 1960

YEAR	TEAM	LEAGUE	GP	G	A	PTS	PIM
1926-27	**DET**	**N**	37	3	4	7	6
1927-28			43	2	4	6	12
2 yrs.	**N Totals:**		80	5	8	13	18

Kurt Walker

WALKER, KURT ADRIAN 6'3", 200 lbs.
B. June 10, 1954, Weymouth, Mass. Defense, Shoots R

YEAR	TEAM & LEAGUE	GP	G	A	PTS	PIM
1975-76	TOR N	5	0	0	0	49
1976-77		26	2	3	5	34
1977-78		40	2	2	4	69
3 yrs.	N Totals:	71	4	5	9	152
PLAYOFFS						
1975-76	TOR N	6	0	0	0	24
1977-78		10	0	0	0	10
2 yrs.	N Totals:	16	0	0	0	34

Traded to **Los Angeles** by Toronto with Scott Garland, Brian Glennie, a second round choice (Mark Hardy) in the 1979 Entry Draft and future considerations for Dave Hutchison and Lorne Stamler, June 14, 1978.

Russ Walker

WALKER, RUSSELL 6'2", 185 lbs.
B. May 24, 1953, Red Deer, Alta. Right Wing, Shoots R

YEAR	TEAM & LEAGUE	GP	G	A	PTS	PIM
1973-74	CLEVE W	76	15	14	29	117
1974-75		66	14	11	25	80
1975-76		72	23	15	38	122
1976-77	LA N	16	1	0	1	35
1977-78		1	0	0	0	6
5 yrs.	N Totals:	17	1	0	1	41
	W Totals:	214	52	40	92	319
PLAYOFFS						
1973-74	CLEVE W	5	1	0	1	11
1974-75		5	1	0	1	17
1975-76		3	0	0	0	18
3 yrs.	W Totals:	13	2	0	2	46

Bob Wall

WALL, ROBERT 5'10", 202 lbs.
B. Dec. 1, 1942, Elgin Mills, Ont. Defense, Shoots L

YEAR	TEAM & LEAGUE	GP	G	A	PTS	PIM
1964-65	DET N	1	0	0	0	0
1965-66		8	1	1	2	8
1966-67		31	2	2	4	26
1967-68	LA N	71	5	18	23	66
1968-69		71	13	13	26	16
1969-70		70	5	13	18	26
1970-71	STL N	25	2	4	6	4
1971-72	DET N	45	2	4	6	9
1972-73	ALTA W	78	16	29	45	20
1973-74	EDM W	74	6	31	37	46
1974-75	SD W	33	0	9	9	15
1975-76		68	1	20	21	32
12 yrs.	N Totals:	322	30	55	85	155
	W Totals:	253	23	89	112	113
PLAYOFFS						
1964-65	DET N	1	0	0	0	0
1965-66		6	0	0	0	2
1967-68	LA N	7	0	1	1	0
1968-69		8	0	2	2	0
1973-74	EDM W	5	0	2	2	2
1974-75	SD W	10	0	3	3	2
1975-76		11	1	3	4	4
7 yrs.	N Totals:	22	0	3	3	2
	W Totals:	26	1	8	9	8

Drafted by **Los Angeles** from Detroit in Expansion Draft, June 6, 1967. Traded to **St. Louis** by Los Angeles for Ray Fortin, May 11, 1970. Traded to **Detroit** by St. Louis with Ab McDonald and Mike Lowe (May 12, 1971) to complete deal in which St. Louis acquired Carl Brewer (Feb. 22, 1971).

Peter Wallin

WALLIN, PETER 5'9", 170 lbs.
B. Apr. 30, 1957, Stockholm, Sweden Right Wing, Shoots R

YEAR	TEAM & LEAGUE	GP	G	A	PTS	PIM
1980-81	NYR N	12	1	5	6	2
1981-82		40	2	9	11	12
2 yrs.	N Totals:	52	3	14	17	14
PLAYOFFS						
1980-81	NYR N	14	2	6	8	6

Signed as free agent with **N.Y. Rangers** March 8, 1981.

Brian Walsh

WALSH, BRIAN GERARD 5'8", 172 lbs.
B. Nov. 6, 1954, Cambridge, Mass. Center, Shoots R

YEAR	TEAM & LEAGUE	GP	G	A	PTS	PIM
1976-77	CALG W	5	0	2	2	12

Jim Walsh

WALSH, JAMES 6'1", 185 lbs.
B. Oct. 26, 1956, Norfolk, Va. Defense, Shoots R

YEAR	TEAM & LEAGUE	GP	G	A	PTS	PIM
1981-82	BUF N	4	0	1	1	4

Signed as free agent by **Buffalo** Sept. 5, 1979.

Dave Walter

WALTER, DAVID GEORGE (Wally) 6', 181 lbs.
B. May 6, 1952, Niagara Falls, Ont. Center, Shoots L

YEAR	TEAM & LEAGUE	GP	G	A	PTS	PIM
1973-74	CHI W	4	0	1	1	0
1974-75		6	1	0	1	2
1975-76	SD W	16	1	2	3	6
3 yrs.	W Totals:	26	2	3	5	8

Ryan Walter

WALTER, RYAN WILLIAM 6', 195 lbs.
B. Apr. 23, 1958, New Westminster, B.C.
Center, Shoots L

YEAR	TEAM & LEAGUE	GP	G	A	PTS	PIM
1978-79	WASH N	69	28	28	56	70
1979-80		80	24	42	66	106
1980-81		80	24	44	68	150
1981-82		78	38	49	87	142
1982-83	MONT N	80	29	46	75	40
5 yrs.	N Totals:	387	143	209	352	508
PLAYOFFS						
1982-83	MONT N	3	0	0	0	11

Traded by Washington with Rick Green to **Montreal** for Doug Jarvis, Craig Laughlin, Rod Langway, and Brian Engblom, Sept. 9, 1982.

Ron Walters

WALTERS, RONALD WAYNE 6', 175 lbs.
B. Mar. 9, 1948, Castor, Alta. Right Wing, Shoots R

YEAR	TEAM & LEAGUE	GP	G	A	PTS	PIM
1972-73	ALTA W	78	28	26	54	37
1973-74	LA W	71	14	14	28	28
1974-75	IND W	17	2	1	3	9
3 yrs.	W Totals:	166	44	41	85	74

Bobby Walton

WALTON, ROBERT 5'9", 165 lbs.
B. Aug. 5, 1917, Ottawa, Ont. Center, Shoots R

YEAR	TEAM & LEAGUE	GP	G	A	PTS	PIM
1943-44	MONT N	4	0	0	0	0

Mike Walton

WALTON, MICHAEL ROBERT (Shakey) 5'10", 175 lbs.
B. Jan. 3, 1945, Kirkland Lake, Ont. Center, Shoots L

YEAR	TEAM & LEAGUE	GP	G	A	PTS	PIM
1965-66	TOR N	6	1	3	4	0
1966-67		31	7	12	19	13
1967-68		73	30	29	59	48
1968-69		66	22	21	43	34
1969-70		58	21	34	55	68
1970-71		23	3	10	13	21
	BOS N	23	3	5	8	10
	2 team total	46	6	15	21	31
1971-72		76	28	28	56	45
1972-73		56	25	22	47	37
1973-74	MINN W	78	**57**	60	**117**	88
1974-75		75	48	45	93	33
1975-76		58	31	40	71	27
	VAN N	10	8	8	16	9
	2 team total	68	39	48	87	36
1976-77		40	7	24	31	32
1977-78		65	29	37	66	30
1978-79	STL N	22	7	11	18	6
	BOS N	14	4	2	6	0
	CHI N	26	6	3	9	4
	3 team total	62	17	16	33	10

YEAR	TEAM & LEAGUE		GP	G	A	PTS	PIM
14 yrs.		N Totals:	589	201	249	450	357
		W Totals:	211	136	145	281	148
PLAYOFFS							
1966-67*	TOR	N	12	4	3	7	2
1968-69			4	0	0	0	4
1970-71	BOS	N	5	2	0	2	19
1971-72*			15	6	6	12	13
1972-73			5	1	1	2	2
1973-74	MINN	W	11	10	8	18	16
1974-75			12	10	7	17	10
1975-76	VAN	N	2	0	0	0	5
1978-79	CHI	N	4	1	0	1	0
9 yrs.		N Totals:	47	14	10	24	45
		W Totals:	23	20	15	35	26

Traded to **Philadelphia** by Toronto with goaltender Bruce Gamble and Toronto's first choice (Pierre Plante) in the 1971 Amateur Draft for goaltender Bernie Parent and Philadelphia's second choice (Rick Kehoe) in same draft, Feb. 1, 1971. Philadelphia then traded Walton to **Boston** for Danny Schock and Rick MacLeish, also Feb. 1, 1971. Traded to **Vancouver** by Boston with Chris Oddleifson and Fred O'Donnell for Bobby Schmautz, Feb. 8, 1974. Traded to **St. Louis** by Vancouver for a fourth round draft choice (Harald Luckner) in the 1978 Amateur Draft and future considerations, June 12, 1978. Signed as a free agent by **Boston** Dec. 5, 1978. Signed as a free agent by **Chicago** Jan. 22, 1979.

Rob Walton

WALTON, ROBERT 5'9", 165 lbs.
B. Sept. 3, 1949, Toronto, Ont. Center, Shoots L

YEAR	TEAM & LEAGUE		GP	G	A	PTS	PIM
1973-74	MINN	W	45	8	23	31	24
	VAN	W	28	8	15	23	2
	2 team total		73	16	38	54	26
1974-75			75	24	33	57	28
1975-76	CALG	W	2	0	0	0	0
3 yrs.		W Totals:	150	40	71	111	54

Gord Wappel

WAPPEL, GORDON ALEXANDER 6'2", 203 lbs.
B. July 26, 1958, Regina, Sask. Defense, Shoots L

YEAR	TEAM & LEAGUE		GP	G	A	PTS	PIM
1979-80	ATL	N	2	0	0	0	0
1980-81	CALG	N	7	0	1	1	4
1981-82			11	1	0	1	6
3 yrs.		N Totals:	20	1	1	2	10
PLAYOFFS							
1979-80	ATL	N	2	0	0	0	4

Don Ward

WARD, DONALD JOSEPH 6'2", 210 lbs.
B. Oct. 19, 1935, Sarnia, Ont. Defense, Shoots L

YEAR	TEAM & LEAGUE		GP	G	A	PTS	PIM
1957-58	CHI	N	3	0	0	0	0
1959-60	BOS	N	31	0	1	1	160
2 yrs.		N Totals:	34	0	1	1	160

Jimmy Ward

WARD, JAMES WILLIAM 5'11", 167 lbs.
B. Sept. 1, 1906, Fort William, Ont. Right Wing, Shoots R

YEAR	TEAM & LEAGUE		GP	G	A	PTS	PIM
1927-28	MON(M)	N	44	10	2	12	44
1928-29			44	14	8	22	46
1929-30			43	10	7	17	54
1930-31			42	14	8	22	52
1931-32			48	19	19	38	39
1932-33			48	16	17	33	52
1933-34			48	14	9	23	46
1934-35			42	9	6	15	24
1935-36			48	12	19	31	30
1936-37			41	14	14	28	34
1937-38			48	11	15	26	34
1938-39	MONT	N	36	4	3	7	0
12 yrs.		N Totals:	532	147	127	274	455
PLAYOFFS							
1927-28	MON(M)	N	9	1	1	2	6
1929-30			4	0	1	1	4
1930-31			2	0	0	0	2
1931-32			4	2	1	3	0

Jimmy Ward continued

YEAR	TEAM & LEAGUE		GP	G	A	PTS	PIM
1932-33			2	0	0	0	0
1933-34			4	0	0	0	0
1934-35*			2	1	1	2	0
1935-36			3	0	0	0	6
1938-39	MONT	N	1	0	0	0	0
9 yrs.		N Totals:	31	4	4	8	18

Joe Ward

WARD, JOSEPH MICHAEL 6', 178 lbs.
B. Feb. 11, 1961, Sarnia, Ont. Center, Shoots L

YEAR	TEAM & LEAGUE		GP	G	A	PTS	PIM
1980-81	COLO	N	4	0	0	0	2

Ron Ward

WARD, RONALD LEON 5'10", 180 lbs.
B. Sept. 12, 1944, Cornwall, Ont. Center, Shoots R

YEAR	TEAM & LEAGUE		GP	G	A	PTS	PIM
1969-70	TOR	N	18	0	1	1	2
1971-72	VAN	N	71	2	4	6	4
1972-73	NY	W	77	51	67	118	28
1973-74	VAN	W	7	0	2	2	2
	LA	W	40	14	19	33	16
	CLEVE	W	23	19	7	26	7
	3 team total		70	33	28	61	25
1974-75			73	30	32	62	18
1975-76			75	32	50	82	24
1976-77	MINN	W	41	15	21	36	6
	WINN	W	14	4	7	11	2
	CALG	W	9	5	5	10	0
	3 team total		64	24	33	57	8
7 yrs.		N Totals:	89	2	5	7	6
		W Totals:	359	170	210	380	103
PLAYOFFS							
1973-74	CLEVE	W	5	3	0	3	2
1974-75			5	0	2	2	2
1975-76			3	0	2	2	0
3 yrs.		W Totals:	13	3	4	7	4

Drafted by **Vancouver** from Toronto in Expansion Draft, June 10, 1970.

Eddie Wares

WARES, EDWARD GEORGE 5'10½", 182 lbs.
B. Mar. 19, 1915, Calgary, Alta. Defense, Shoots R

YEAR	TEAM & LEAGUE		GP	G	A	PTS	PIM
1936-37	NYR	N	2	2	0	2	0
1937-38	DET	N	21	9	7	16	2
1938-39			28	8	8	16	10
1939-40			3	2	6	8	19
1940-41			42	10	16	26	34
1941-42			43	9	29	38	31
1942-43			47	12	18	30	10
1945-46	CHI	N	45	4	11	15	34
1946-47			60	4	7	11	21
9 yrs.		N Totals:	291	60	102	162	161
PLAYOFFS							
1938-39	DET	N	6	1	0	1	8
1939-40			5	0	0	0	0
1940-41			9	0	0	0	0
1941-42			12	1	3	4	22
1942-43*			10	3	3	6	4
1945-46	CHI	N	3	0	1	1	0
6 yrs.		N Totals:	45	5	7	12	34

Bob Warner

WARNER, ROBERT NORMAN 5'11", 180 lbs.
B. Dec. 13, 1950, Grimsby, Ont. Defense, Shoots L

YEAR	TEAM & LEAGUE		GP	G	A	PTS	PIM
1976-77	TOR	N	10	1	1	2	4
PLAYOFFS							
1975-76	TOR	N	2	0	0	0	0
1976-77			2	0	0	0	0
2 yrs.		N Totals:	4	0	0	0	0

Jim Warner

WARNER, JAMES 5'11", 180 lbs.
B. Mar. 26, 1954, Minneapolis, Minn. Right Wing, Shoots R

YEAR	TEAM & LEAGUE		GP	G	A	PTS	PIM
1978-79	NE	W	41	6	9	15	20
1979-80	HART	N	32	0	3	3	10
2 yrs.		N Totals:	32	0	3	3	10
		W Totals:	41	6	9	15	20
PLAYOFFS							
1978-79	NE	W	1	0	0	0	0

Steve Warr

WARR, STEVE 5'11", 185 lbs.
B. Jan. 5, 1951, Peterborough, Ont. Defense, Shoots R

YEAR	TEAM & LEAGUE		GP	G	A	PTS	PIM
1972-73	OTTA	W	71	3	8	11	79
PLAYOFFS							
1973-74	TOR	W	2	0	0	0	0

Bill Warwick

WARWICK, WILLIAM HARVEY 5'6½", 165 lbs.
B. Nov. 17, 1924, Regina, Sask. Left Wing, Shoots L

YEAR	TEAM & LEAGUE		GP	G	A	PTS	PIM
1942-43	NYR	N	1	0	1	1	4
1943-44			13	3	2	5	12
2 yrs.		N Totals:	14	3	3	6	16

Knobby Warwick

WARWICK, GRANT DAVID 5'6", 165 lbs.
B. Oct. 11, 1921, Regina, Sask. Right Wing, Shoots R
Won Calder Trophy, 1941-42

YEAR	TEAM & LEAGUE		GP	G	A	PTS	PIM
1941-42	NYR	N	44	16	17	33	36
1942-43			50	17	18	35	31
1943-44			18	8	9	17	14
1944-45			42	20	22	42	25
1945-46			45	19	18	37	19
1946-47			54	20	20	40	24
1947-48			40	17	12	29	30
	BOS	N	18	6	5	11	8
	2 team total		58	23	17	40	38
1948-49			58	22	15	37	14
1949-50	MONT	N	30	2	6	8	19
9 yrs.		N Totals:	399	147	142	289	220
PLAYOFFS							
1941-42	NYR	N	6	0	1	1	2
1947-48	BOS	N	5	0	3	3	4
1948-49			5	2	0	2	0
3 yrs.		N Totals:	16	2	4	6	6

Sold to **Montreal** by Boston, Oct. 10, 1949.

Nick Wasnie

WASNIE, NICHOLAS 5'10½", 174 lbs.
B. Winnipeg, Man. Right Wing, Shoots R

YEAR	TEAM & LEAGUE		GP	G	A	PTS	PIM
1927-28	CHI	N	14	1	0	1	22
1929-30	MONT	N	44	12	11	23	64
1930-31			44	9	2	11	26
1931-32			48	10	2	12	16
1932-33	NYA	N	48	11	12	23	36
1933-34	OTTA	N	37	11	6	17	10
1934-35	STL	N	13	3	1	4	2
7 yrs.		N Totals:	248	57	34	91	176
PLAYOFFS							
1929-30*	MONT	N	6	2	2	4	12
1930-31*			4	4	1	5	8
1931-32			4	0	0	0	0
3 yrs.		N Totals:	14	6	3	9	20

Bryan Watson

WATSON, BRYAN JOSEPH (Bugsy) 5'10", 175 lbs.
B. Nov. 14, 1942, Bancroft, Ont. Defense, Shoots R

YEAR	TEAM & LEAGUE		GP	G	A	PTS	PIM
1963-64	MONT	N	39	0	2	2	18
1964-65			5	0	1	1	7
	DET	N	1	0	0	0	2
	2 team total		6	0	1	1	9
1965-66			70	2	7	9	133
1966-67			48	0	1	1	66
1967-68	MONT	N	12	0	1	1	9
1968-69	CALIF	N	50	2	3	5	97
	PITT	N	18	0	4	4	35
	2 team total		68	2	7	9	132
1969-70			61	1	9	10	189
1970-71			42	2	6	8	119
1971-72			75	3	18	21	**212**
1972-73			69	1	17	18	179
1973-74			38	1	4	5	137
	STL	N	11	0	1	1	19
	DET	N	21	0	4	4	99
	3 team total		70	1	9	10	255
1974-75			70	1	13	14	238
1975-76			79	0	18	18	**322**
1976-77			14	0	1	1	39
	WASH	N	56	1	14	15	91
	2 team total		70	1	15	16	130
1977-78			79	3	11	14	167
1978-79			20	0	1	1	36
	CIN	W	21	0	2	2	56
	2 team total		41	0	3	3	92
16 yrs.		N Totals:	878	17	136	153	2214
		W Totals:	21	0	2	2	56
PLAYOFFS							
1963-64	MONT	N	6	0	0	0	2
1965-66	DET	N	12	2	0	2	30
1969-70	PITT	N	10	0	0	0	17
1971-72			4	0	0	0	21
1978-79	CIN	W	3	0	1	1	2
5 yrs.		N Totals:	32	2	0	2	70
		W Totals:	3	0	1	1	2

Traded to **Chicago** by Montreal for Don Johns, June 8, 1965. Drafted by **Detroit** from Chicago, June 9, 1965. Drafted by **Minnesota** from Detroit in Expansion Draft, June 6, 1967. Traded to **Montreal** by Minnesota for Bill Plager, Leo Thiffault, and Barrie Meissner, June 6, 1967. Traded to **Oakland** by Montreal with cash for Oakland's first choice (Michel Larocque) in 1972 Amateur Draft, June 10, 1968. Traded to **Pittsburgh** by Oakland with George Swarbrick and Tracy Pratt for Earl Ingarfield, Gene Ubriaco and Dick Mattiussi, Jan. 30, 1969. Traded to **St. Louis** by Pittsburgh with Greg Polis and Pittsburgh's second choice (Bob Hess) in 1974 Amateur draft for Steve Durbano, Ab Demarco, and J. Bob Kelly, Jan. 17, 1974. Traded to **Detroit** by St. Louis with Chris Evans and Jean Hamel for Ted Harris, Bill Collins, and Garnet Bailey, Feb. 14, 1974. Traded to **Washington** by Detroit for Greg Joly, Nov. 30, 1976.

Dave Watson

WATSON, DAVID 6'2", 190 lbs.
B. May 19, 1958, Kirkland Lake, Ont. Left Wing, Shoots L

YEAR	TEAM & LEAGUE		GP	G	A	PTS	PIM
1979-80	COLO	N	5	0	0	0	2
1980-81			13	0	1	1	8
2 yrs.		N Totals:	18	0	1	1	10

Harry Watson

WATSON, HARRY PERCIVAL (Whipper) 6'1", 203 lbs.
B. May 6, 1923, Saskatoon, Sask. Left Wing, Shoots L

YEAR	TEAM & LEAGUE		GP	G	A	PTS	PIM
1941-42	NYA	N	47	10	8	18	6
1942-43	DET	N	50	13	18	31	10
1945-46			44	14	10	24	4
1946-47	TOR	N	44	19	15	34	10
1947-48			57	21	20	41	16
1948-49			60	26	19	45	0
1949-50			60	19	16	35	11
1950-51			68	18	19	37	18
1951-52			70	22	17	39	18
1952-53			63	16	8	24	8
1953-54			70	21	7	28	30
1954-55			8	1	1	2	0
	CHI	N	43	14	16	30	4
	2 team total		51	15	17	32	4
1955-56			55	11	14	25	6

Harry Watson continued

YEAR	TEAM & LEAGUE		GP	G	A	PTS	PIM
1956-57			70	11	19	30	9
14 yrs.		N Totals:	809	236	207	443	150
PLAYOFFS							
1942-43*	**DET**	N	7	0	0	0	0
1945-46			5	2	0	2	0
1946-47*	**TOR**	N	11	3	2	5	6
1947-48*			9	5	2	7	9
1948-49*			9	4	2	6	2
1949-50			7	0	0	0	2
1950-51*			5	1	2	3	4
1951-52			4	1	0	1	2
1953-54			5	0	1	1	2
9 yrs.		N Totals:	62	16	9	25	27

Sold to **Chicago** by Toronto, Dec. 10, 1954.

Jim Watson

WATSON, JAMES (Watty) — 6'2", 195 lbs.
B. June 28, 1943, Malartic, Que. — Defense, Shoots L

YEAR	TEAM & LEAGUE		GP	G	A	PTS	PIM
1963-64	**DET**	N	1	0	0	0	0
1965-66			2	0	0	0	4
1967-68			61	0	3	3	87
1968-69			8	0	1	1	4
1969-70			4	0	0	0	0
1970-71	**BUF**	N	78	2	9	11	147
1971-72			66	2	6	8	101
1972-73	**LA**	W	75	5	15	20	123
1973-74			48	0	6	6	28
	CHI	W	23	0	5	5	22
	2 team total		71	0	11	11	50
1974-75			57	3	6	9	31
1975-76	**QUE**	W	28	0	1	1	24
11 yrs.		N Totals:	220	4	19	23	343
		W Totals:	231	8	33	41	228
PLAYOFFS							
1972-73	**LA**	W	4	0	1	1	2
1973-74	**CHI**	W	18	2	3	5	18
2 yrs.		W Totals:	22	2	4	6	20

Jimmy Watson

WATSON, JAMES CHARLES — 6', 195 lbs.
B. Aug. 19, 1952, Smithers, B.C. — Defense, Shoots L

YEAR	TEAM & LEAGUE		GP	G	A	PTS	PIM
1972-73	**PHI**	N	4	0	1	1	5
1973-74			78	2	18	20	44
1974-75			68	7	18	25	72
1975-76			78	2	22	24	28
1976-77			71	3	23	26	35
1977-78			71	5	12	17	62
1978-79			77	9	13	22	52
1979-80			71	5	18	23	51
1980-81			18	2	2	4	6
1981-82			76	3	9	12	99
10 yrs.		N Totals:	612	38	136	174	454
PLAYOFFS							
1972-73	**PHI**	N	2	0	0	0	0
1973-74*			17	1	2	3	41
1974-75*			17	1	8	9	10
1975-76			16	1	8	9	6
1976-77			10	1	2	3	2
1978-79			8	0	2	2	2
1979-80			15	0	4	4	20
1981-82			4	0	1	1	2
8 yrs.		N Totals:	89	4	27	31	83

Joe Watson

WATSON, JOSEPH JOHN — 5'10", 185 lbs.
B. July 6, 1943, Smithers, B.C. — Defense, Shoots L

YEAR	TEAM & LEAGUE		GP	G	A	PTS	PIM
1964-65	**BOS**	N	4	0	1	1	0
1966-67			69	2	13	15	38
1967-68	**PHI**	N	73	5	14	19	56
1968-69			60	2	8	10	14
1969-70			54	3	11	14	28
1970-71			57	3	7	10	50
1971-72			65	3	7	10	38
1972-73			63	2	24	26	46

Joe Watson continued

YEAR	TEAM & LEAGUE		GP	G	A	PTS	PIM
1973-74			74	1	17	18	34
1974-75			80	6	17	23	42
1975-76			78	2	22	24	28
1976-77			77	4	26	30	39
1977-78			65	5	9	14	22
1978-79	**COLO**	N	16	0	2	2	12
14 yrs.		N Totals:	835	38	178	216	447
PLAYOFFS							
1967-68	**PHI**	N	7	1	1	2	28
1968-69			4	0	0	0	0
1970-71			1	0	0	0	0
1972-73			11	0	2	2	12
1973-74*			17	1	4	5	24
1974-75*			17	0	4	4	6
1975-76			16	1	1	2	10
1976-77			10	0	0	0	2
1977-78			1	0	0	0	0
9 yrs.		N Totals:	84	3	12	15	82

Drafted by **Philadelphia** from Boston in Expansion Draft, June 6, 1967. Sold to **Colorado** by Philadelphia, Aug. 31, 1978.

Phil Watson

WATSON, PHILIP HENRY — 5'11", 165 lbs.
B. Apr. 24, 1914, Montreal, Que. — Right Wing, Shoots R

YEAR	TEAM & LEAGUE		GP	G	A	PTS	PIM
1935-36	**NYR**	N	24	0	2	2	24
1936-37			48	11	17	28	22
1937-38			48	7	25	32	52
1938-39			48	15	22	37	42
1939-40			48	7	28	35	42
1940-41			40	11	25	36	49
1941-42			48	15	**37**	52	58
1942-43			46	14	28	42	44
1943-44	**MONT**	N	44	17	32	49	61
1944-45	**NYR**	N	45	11	8	19	24
1945-46			49	12	14	26	43
1946-47			48	6	12	18	17
1947-48			54	18	15	33	54
13 yrs.		N Totals:	590	144	265	409	532
PLAYOFFS							
1936-37	**NYR**	N	9	0	2	2	9
1937-38			3	0	2	2	0
1938-39			7	1	1	2	7
1939-40*			3	3	6	9	16
1940-41			3	0	2	2	9
1941-42			6	1	4	5	8
1943-44*	**MONT**	N	9	3	5	8	16
1947-48	**NYR**	N	5	2	3	5	2
8 yrs.		N Totals:	45	10	25	35	67

Tim Watters

WATTERS, TIMOTHY J. — 5'11", 180 lbs.
B. July 25, 1959, Kamloops, B.C. — Defense, Shoots L

YEAR	TEAM & LEAGUE		GP	G	A	PTS	PIM
1981-82	**WINN**	N	69	2	22	24	97
1982-83			77	5	18	23	98
2 yrs.		N Totals:	146	7	40	47	195
PLAYOFFS							
1981-82	**WINN**	N	4	0	1	1	8
1982-83			3	0	0	0	2
2 yrs.		N Totals:	7	0	1	1	10

Brian Watts

WATTS, BRIAN ALAN — 6', 180 lbs.
B. Sept. 10, 1947, Hagersville, Ont. — Left Wing, Shoots L

YEAR	TEAM & LEAGUE		GP	G	A	PTS	PIM
1975-76	**DET**	N	4	0	0	0	0

Aubrey Webster

WEBSTER, AUBREY — 5'9", 168 lbs.
B. Sept. 25, 1910, Fort William, Ont. — Forward, Shoots R

YEAR	TEAM & LEAGUE		GP	G	A	PTS	PIM
1930-31	**PHI**	N	1	0	0	0	0
1934-35	**MON(M)**	N	4	0	0	0	0
2 yrs.		N Totals:	5	0	0	0	0

Don Webster

WEBSTER, DONALD 5'7", 180 lbs.
B. July 3, 1924, Toronto, Ont. Left Wing, Shoots L

YEAR	TEAM & LEAGUE		GP	G	A	PTS	PIM
1943-44	TOR	N	27	7	6	13	28
PLAYOFFS							
1943-44	TOR	N	5	0	0	0	12

John Webster

WEBSTER, JOHN ROBERT (Chick) 5'10", 160 lbs.
B. Nov. 3, 1920, Toronto, Ont. Center, Shoots L

YEAR	TEAM & LEAGUE		GP	G	A	PTS	PIM
1949-50	NYR	N	14	0	0	0	4

Tom Webster

WEBSTER, THOMAS RONALD 5'10", 170 lbs.
B. Oct. 4, 1948, Kirkland Lake, Ont. Right Wing, Shoots R

YEAR	TEAM & LEAGUE		GP	G	A	PTS	PIM
1968-69	BOS	N	9	0	3	3	9
1969-70			2	0	1	1	2
1970-71	DET	N	78	30	37	67	40
1971-72			4	1	1	2	4
	CALIF	N	8	2	1	3	6
	2 team total		12	3	2	5	10
1972-73	NE	W	77	53	50	103	89
1973-74			64	43	27	70	28
1974-75			66	40	24	64	52
1975-76			55	33	50	83	24
1976-77			70	36	49	85	43
1977-78			20	15	5	20	5
1979-80	DET	N	1	0	0	0	0
11 yrs.		N Totals:	102	33	43	76	61
		W Totals:	352	220	205	425	241
PLAYOFFS							
1968-69	BOS	N	1	0	0	0	0
1972-73	NE	W	15	12	14	26	6
1973-74			3	5	0	5	7
1974-75			3	0	2	2	0
1975-76			17	10	9	19	6
1976-77			5	1	1	2	0
6 yrs.		N Totals:	1	0	0	0	0
		W Totals:	43	28	26	54	19

Drafted by **Buffalo** from Boston in Expansion Draft, June 10, 1970. Traded to **Detroit** by Buffalo for Roger Crozier, June 10, 1970. Traded to **California** by Detroit for Ron Stackhouse, Oct. 22, 1971. Rights transferred to **Minnesota** Reserve List after Cleveland-Minnesota Dispersal Draft, June 15, 1978. Signed by **Detroit** as free agent, Sept. 15, 1979.

Cooney Weiland

WEILAND, RALPH 5'7", 150 lbs.
B. Nov. 5, 1904, Seaforth, Ont. Center
Won Art Ross Trophy, 1929-30
Hall of Fame, 1971

YEAR	TEAM & LEAGUE		GP	G	A	PTS	PIM
1928-29	BOS	N	40	11	7	18	16
1929-30			44	**43**	30	**73**	27
1930-31			44	25	13	38	14
1931-32			47	14	12	26	20
1932-33	OTTA	N	48	16	11	27	4
1933-34			7	2	0	2	4
	DET	N	39	11	19	30	6
	2 team total		46	13	19	32	10
1934-35			48	13	25	38	10
1935-36	BOS	N	48	14	13	27	15
1936-37			48	6	9	15	6
1937-38			48	11	12	23	16
1938-39			47	7	9	16	9
11 yrs.		N Totals:	508	173	160	333	147
PLAYOFFS							
1928-29*	BOS	N	5	2	0	2	2
1929-30			6	1	5	6	2
1930-31			5	6	3	9	2
1933-34	DET	N	9	2	2	4	4
1935-36	BOS	N	2	1	0	1	2
1936-37			3	0	0	0	0
1937-38			3	0	0	0	0
1938-39*			12	0	0	0	0

Cooney Weiland continued

YEAR	TEAM & LEAGUE		GP	G	A	PTS	PIM
8 yrs.		N Totals:	45	12	10	22	12

Stan Weir

WEIR, STANLEY BRIAN (Stash) 6'1", 170 lbs.
B. Mar. 17, 1952, Ponoka, Alta. Center, Shoots L

YEAR	TEAM & LEAGUE		GP	G	A	PTS	PIM
1972-73	CALIF	N	78	15	24	39	16
1973-74			58	9	7	16	10
1974-75			80	18	27	45	12
1975-76	TOR	N	64	19	32	51	22
1976-77			65	11	19	30	14
1977-78			30	12	5	17	4
1978-79	EDM	W	68	31	30	61	20
1979-80	EDM	N	79	33	33	66	40
1980-81			70	12	20	32	40
1981-82			51	3	13	16	13
	COLO	N	10	2	3	5	10
	2 team total		61	5	16	21	23
1982-83	DET	N	57	5	24	29	2
11 yrs.		N Totals:	642	139	207	346	183
		W Totals:	68	31	30	61	20
PLAYOFFS							
1975-76	TOR	N	9	1	3	4	0
1976-77			7	2	1	3	0
1977-78			13	3	1	4	0
1978-79	EDM	W	13	2	5	7	2
1979-80	EDM	N	3	0	0	0	2
1980-81			5	0	0	0	2
6 yrs.		N Totals:	37	6	5	11	4
		W Totals:	13	2	5	7	2

Traded to **Toronto** by California for Gary Sabourin, June 20, 1975. Reclaimed by **Toronto** from Edmonton prior to Expansion Draft, June 9, 1979. Claimed on waivers by **Edmonton** from Toronto, July 4, 1979. Traded to **Colorado** by Edmonton for Ed Cooper, Mar. 9, 1982. Sold to **Detroit** by Edmonton, Sept. 15, 1982.

Wally Weir

WEIR, WALLY 6'2", 200 lbs.
B. June 3, 1954, Verdun, Que. Defense, Shoots L

YEAR	TEAM & LEAGUE		GP	G	A	PTS	PIM
1976-77	QUE	W	69	3	17	20	197
1977-78			13	0	0	0	47
1978-79			68	2	7	9	166
1979-80	QUE	N	73	3	12	15	133
1980-81			54	6	8	14	77
1981-82			62	3	5	8	173
1982-83			58	5	11	16	135
7 yrs.		N Totals:	247	17	36	53	518
		W Totals:	150	5	24	29	410
PLAYOFFS							
1976-77	QUE	W	17	1	5	6	13
1977-78			11	1	2	3	50
1978-79			4	0	1	1	4
1980-81	QUE	N	3	0	0	0	15
1981-82			15	0	0	0	45
1982-83			4	0	1	1	19
6 yrs.		N Totals:	22	0	1	1	79
		W Totals:	32	2	8	10	67

Duke Wellington

WELLINGTON, DUKE
B. Unknown

YEAR	TEAM & LEAGUE		GP	G	A	PTS	PIM
1919-20	QUE	N	1	0	0	0	0

Jay Wells

WELLS, GORDON JAY 6'1", 205 lbs.
B. May 18, 1959, Paris, Ont. Defense, Shoots L

YEAR	TEAM & LEAGUE		GP	G	A	PTS	PIM
1979-80	LA	N	43	0	0	0	113
1980-81			72	5	13	18	155
1981-82			60	1	8	9	145
1982-83			69	3	12	15	167
4 yrs.		N Totals:	244	9	33	42	580

Jay Wells continued

PLAYOFFS

YEAR	TEAM & LEAGUE	GP	G	A	PTS	PIM
1979-80	**LA** **N**	4	0	0	0	11
1980-81		4	0	0	0	27
1981-82		10	1	3	4	41
3 yrs.	**N Totals:**	18	1	3	4	79

John Wensink

WENSINK, JOHN (Wire) 6', 200 lbs.
B. Apr. 1, 1953, Cornwall, Ont. Left Wing, Shoots L

YEAR	TEAM & LEAGUE	GP	G	A	PTS	PIM
1973-74	**STL** **N**	3	0	0	0	0
1976-77	**BOS** **N**	23	4	6	10	32
1977-78		80	16	20	36	181
1978-79		76	28	18	46	106
1979-80		69	9	11	20	110
1980-81	**QUE** **N**	53	6	3	9	124
1981-82	**COLO** **N**	57	5	3	8	152
1982-83	**NJ** **N**	42	2	7	9	135
8 yrs.	**N Totals:**	403	70	68	138	840

PLAYOFFS

YEAR	TEAM & LEAGUE	GP	G	A	PTS	PIM
1976-77	**BOS** **N**	13	0	3	3	8
1977-78		15	2	2	4	54
1978-79		8	0	1	1	19
1979-80		4	0	0	0	5
1980-81	**QUE** **N**	3	0	0	0	0
5 yrs.	**N Totals:**	43	2	6	8	86

Signed as free agent by **Boston** Oct. 12, 1976. Claimed by **Quebec** from Boston in Waiver Draft, Oct. 10, 1980.

Cy Wentworth

WENTWORTH, MARVIN (Cy) 5'9½", 170 lbs.
B. Jan. 24, 1905, Grimsby, Ont. Shoots R

YEAR	TEAM & LEAGUE	GP	G	A	PTS	PIM
1927-28	**CHI** **N**	44	5	5	10	31
1928-29		44	2	1	3	44
1929-30		39	3	4	7	28
1930-31		43	4	4	8	12
1931-32		48	3	10	13	30
1932-33	**MON(M)** **N**	47	4	10	14	48
1933-34		48	2	5	7	31
1934-35		48	4	9	13	28
1935-36		48	4	5	9	24
1936-37		44	3	4	7	29
1937-38		48	4	5	9	32
1938-39	**MONT** **N**	45	0	3	3	12
1939-40		32	1	3	4	6
13 yrs.	**N Totals:**	578	39	68	107	355

PLAYOFFS

YEAR	TEAM & LEAGUE	GP	G	A	PTS	PIM
1930-31	**CHI** **N**	9	1	1	2	16
1931-32		2	0	0	0	0
1932-33	**MON(M)** **N**	2	0	1	1	0
1933-34		4	0	2	2	2
1934-35*		7	3	2	5	0
1935-36		3	0	0	0	0
1936-37		5	1	0	1	0
1938-39	**MONT** **N**	3	0	0	0	4
8 yrs.	**N Totals:**	35	5	6	11	22

Blake Wesley

WESLEY, TREVOR BLAKE 6'1", 200 lbs.
B. July 10, 1959, Red Deer, Alta. Defense, Shoots L

YEAR	TEAM & LEAGUE	GP	G	A	PTS	PIM
1979-80	**PHI** **N**	2	0	1	1	2
1980-81		50	3	7	10	107
1981-82	**HART** **N**	78	9	18	27	123
1982-83		22	0	1	1	46
	QUE **N**	52	4	8	12	84
	2 team total	74	4	9	13	130
4 yrs.	**N Totals:**	204	16	35	51	362

PLAYOFFS

YEAR	TEAM & LEAGUE	GP	G	A	PTS	PIM
1982-83	**QUE** **N**	4	0	0	0	2

Traded to **Hartford** by Philadelphia with Rick MacLeish, Don Gillen and Philadelphia's first (Paul Lawless), second (Mark Paterson) and third-round (Kevin Dineen) choices in the 1982 Entry Draft for Ray Allison, Fred Arthur and Hartford's first (Ron Sutter), second (Peter Ihnacak) and third-round (Miroslav Dvorak) choices in the 1982 Entry Draft, July 3, 1981. Hartford's second round choice (Peter Ihnacak) was transferred to Toronto by Philadelphia on Jan. 20, 1982. Traded by Hartford to **Quebec** for Pierre Lacroix, Dec. 3, 1982.

Steve West

WEST, STEVEN CARTER 5'8", 150 lbs.
B. Mar. 20, 1952, Peterborough, Ont. Center, Shoots L

YEAR	TEAM & LEAGUE	GP	G	A	PTS	PIM
1974-75	**M-B** **W**	50	15	18	33	4
1976-77	**HOUS** **W**	3	0	0	0	2
1977-78		71	11	21	32	23
1978-79	**WINN** **W**	18	3	11	14	6
4 yrs.	**W Totals:**	142	29	50	79	35

PLAYOFFS

YEAR	TEAM & LEAGUE	GP	G	A	PTS	PIM
1975-76	**HOUS** **W**	7	0	1	1	0
1976-77		6	0	0	0	0
1977-78		6	1	0	1	0
1978-79	**WINN** **W**	6	2	3	5	2
4 yrs.	**W Totals:**	25	3	4	7	2

Drafted by **Washington** from Minnesota in Expansion Draft, June 12, 1974.

Ed Westfall

WESTFALL, VERNON EDWIN 6'1", 197 lbs.
B. Sept. 19, 1940, Belleville, Ont. Right Wing, Shoots R
Won Masterton Trophy, 1976-77

YEAR	TEAM & LEAGUE	GP	G	A	PTS	PIM
1961-62	**BOS** **N**	63	2	9	11	53
1962-63		48	1	11	12	34
1963-64		55	1	5	6	35
1964-65		68	12	15	27	65
1965-66		59	9	21	30	42
1966-67		70	12	24	36	26
1967-68		73	14	22	36	38
1968-69		70	18	24	42	22
1969-70		72	14	22	36	28
1970-71		78	25	34	59	48
1971-72		78	18	26	44	19
1972-73	**NYI** **N**	67	15	31	46	25
1973-74		68	19	23	42	28
1974-75		73	22	33	55	28
1975-76		80	25	31	56	27
1976-77		79	14	33	47	8
1977-78		71	5	19	24	14
1978-79		55	5	11	16	4
18 yrs.	**N Totals:**	1227	231	394	625	544

PLAYOFFS

YEAR	TEAM & LEAGUE	GP	G	A	PTS	PIM
1967-68	**BOS** **N**	4	2	0	2	2
1968-69		10	3	7	10	11
1969-70*		14	3	5	8	4
1970-71		7	1	2	3	2
1971-72*		15	4	3	7	10
1974-75	**NYI** **N**	17	5	10	15	12
1975-76		8	2	3	5	0
1976-77		12	1	5	6	0
1977-78		2	0	0	0	0
1978-79		6	1	2	3	0
10 yrs.	**N Totals:**	95	22	37	59	41

Drafted by **N.Y. Islanders** from Boston in Expansion Draft, June 6, 1972.

Pat Westrum

WESTRUM, PATRICK DELVAN 5'10", 185 lbs.
B. Mar. 3, 1948, Minneapolis, Minn. Defense, Shoots L

YEAR	TEAM & LEAGUE	GP	G	A	PTS	PIM
1974-75	**MINN** **W**	23	0	3	3	48
1975-76		54	3	10	13	98
	CALG **W**	9	0	2	2	23
	2 team total	63	3	12	15	121
1976-77	**MINN** **W**	40	1	9	10	42
	BIRM **W**	34	1	11	12	48
	2 team total	74	2	20	22	90
1977-78		77	2	10	12	97
4 yrs.	**W Totals:**	237	7	45	52	356

PLAYOFFS

YEAR	TEAM & LEAGUE	GP	G	A	PTS	PIM
1975-76	**CALG** **W**	6	0	1	1	19
1977-78	**BIRM** **W**	3	0	1	1	0

YEAR	TEAM & LEAGUE		GP	G	A	PTS	PIM

Pat Westrum continued

2 yrs.		W Totals:	9	0	2	2	19

Kenny Wharram

WHARRAM, KENNETH MALCOLM 5'9", 165 lbs.
B. July 2, 1933, Ferris, Ont. Right Wing, Shoots R
Won Lady Byng Trophy, 1963-64

YEAR	TEAM	LEAGUE	GP	G	A	PTS	PIM
1951-52	CHI	N	1	0	0	0	0
1953-54			29	1	7	8	8
1955-56			3	0	0	0	0
1958-59			66	10	9	19	14
1959-60			59	14	11	25	16
1960-61			64	16	29	45	12
1961-62			62	14	23	37	29
1962-63			55	20	18	38	17
1963-64			70	39	32	71	18
1964-65			68	24	20	44	27
1965-66			69	26	17	43	28
1966-67			70	31	34	65	21
1967-68			74	27	42	69	18
1968-69			76	30	39	69	19
14 yrs.		N Totals:	766	252	281	533	227
PLAYOFFS							
1958-59	CHI	N	6	0	2	2	2
1959-60			4	1	1	2	0
1960-61*			12	3	5	8	12
1961-62			12	3	4	7	8
1962-63			6	1	5	6	0
1963-64			7	2	2	4	6
1964-65			12	2	3	5	4
1965-66			6	1	0	1	4
1966-67			6	2	2	4	2
1967-68			9	1	3	4	0
10 yrs.		N Totals:	80	16	27	43	38

Len Wharton

WHARTON, LEONARD
B. Dec. 13, 1927, Winnipeg, Man. Forward

YEAR	TEAM	LEAGUE	GP	G	A	PTS	PIM
1944-45	NYR	N	1	0	0	0	0

Donald Wheldon

WHELDON, DONALD 6'2", 185 lbs.
B. Dec. 28, 1954, Falmouth, Mass. Defense, Shoots R

YEAR	TEAM	LEAGUE	GP	G	A	PTS	PIM
1974-75	STL	N	2	0	0	0	0

Bill Whelton

WHELTON, WILLIAM 6'1", 180 lbs.
B. Aug. 28, 1959, Everett, Mass. Defense, Shoots L

YEAR	TEAM	LEAGUE	GP	G	A	PTS	PIM
1980-81	WINN	N	2	0	0	0	0

Alton White

WHITE, ALTON 5'8½", 175 lbs.
B. May 31, 1945, Amherst, N.S. Right Wing, Shoots R

YEAR	TEAM	LEAGUE	GP	G	A	PTS	PIM
1972-73	NY	W	13	1	4	5	2
	LA	W	57	20	17	37	22
	2 team total		70	21	21	42	24
1973-74			48	8	13	21	13
1974-75	M-B	W	27	9	12	21	8
3 yrs.		W Totals:	145	38	46	84	45

Bill White

WHITE, WILLIAM EARL 6'1", 195 lbs.
B. Aug. 26, 1939, Toronto, Ont. Defense, Shoots R

YEAR	TEAM	LEAGUE	GP	G	A	PTS	PIM
1967-68	LA	N	74	11	27	38	100
1968-69			75	5	28	33	38
1969-70			40	4	11	15	21
	CHI	N	21	0	5	5	18
	2 team total		61	4	16	20	39
1970-71			67	4	21	25	64
1971-72			76	7	22	29	58
1972-73			72	9	38	47	80
1973-74			69	5	31	36	52
1974-75			51	4	23	27	20

Bill White continued

YEAR	TEAM	LEAGUE	GP	G	A	PTS	PIM
1975-76			59	1	9	10	44
9 yrs.		N Totals:	604	50	215	265	495
PLAYOFFS							
1967-68	LA	N	7	2	2	4	4
1968-69			11	1	4	5	8
1969-70	CHI	N	8	1	2	3	8
1970-71			18	1	4	5	20
1971-72			8	0	3	3	6
1972-73			16	1	6	7	10
1973-74			11	1	7	8	14
1974-75			8	0	3	3	4
1975-76			4	0	1	1	2
9 yrs.		N Totals:	91	7	32	39	76

Traded to **Chicago** by Los Angeles with Bryan Campbell and goaltender Gerry Desjardins for Gilles Marotte, Jim Stanfield and Denis DeJordy, Feb. 20, 1970.

Moe White

WHITE, LEONARD A. 5'11", 178 lbs.
B. July 28, 1918, Verdun, Que. Left Wing

YEAR	TEAM	LEAGUE	GP	G	A	PTS	PIM
1945-46	MONT	N	4	0	1	1	2

Sherman White

WHITE, SHERMAN BEVERLY 5'10", 165 lbs.
B. May 12, 1923, Cape Tormentine, N.B.
Center, Shoots L

YEAR	TEAM	LEAGUE	GP	G	A	PTS	PIM
1946-47	NYR	N	1	0	0	0	0
1949-50			3	0	2	2	0
2 yrs.		N Totals:	4	0	2	2	0

Tex White

WHITE, WILFRED 5'11", 155 lbs.

YEAR	TEAM	LEAGUE	GP	G	A	PTS	PIM
1925-26	PITT	N	35	7	1	8	22
1926-27			43	5	4	9	21
1927-28			44	5	1	6	54
1928-29			30	3	4	7	18
	NYA	N	11	2	1	3	8
	2 team total		41	5	5	10	26
1929-30	PITT	N	29	8	1	9	16
1930-31	PHI	N	14	3	0	3	2
6 yrs.		N Totals:	206	33	12	45	141
PLAYOFFS							
1927-28	PITT	N	2	0	0	0	4
1928-29	NYA	N	2	0	0	0	2
2 yrs.		N Totals:	4	0	0	0	6

Tony White

WHITE, ANTHONY RAYMOND 5'10", 175 lbs.
B. June 16, 1954, Grand Falls, Nfld. Left Wing, Shoots L

YEAR	TEAM	LEAGUE	GP	G	A	PTS	PIM
1974-75	WASH	N	5	0	2	2	0
1975-76			80	25	17	42	56
1976-77			72	12	9	21	44
1977-78			1	0	0	0	0
1979-80	MINN	N	6	0	0	0	4
5 yrs.		N Totals:	164	37	28	65	104
PLAYOFFS							
1972-73	LA	W	6	1	0	1	0

Signed as free agent with **Minnesota** Sept. 17, 1979.

Bob Whitelaw

WHITELAW, ROBERT 5'11", 185 lbs.
B. Oct. 5, 1916, Motherwell, Scotland Defense, Shoots L

YEAR	TEAM	LEAGUE	GP	G	A	PTS	PIM
1940-41	DET	N	23	0	2	2	2
1941-42			9	0	0	0	0
2 yrs.		N Totals:	32	0	2	2	2
PLAYOFFS							
1940-41	DET	N	8	0	0	0	0

Bob Whitlock

WHITLOCK, ROBERT ANGUS 5'10", 175 lbs.
B. July 16, 1949, Charlottetown, P.E.I. Center, Shoots R

YEAR	TEAM & LEAGUE	GP	G	A	PTS	PIM
1969-70	MINN N	1	0	0	0	0
1972-73	CHI W	75	23	28	51	53
1973-74		52	16	19	35	44
	LA W	14	4	10	14	4
	2 team total	66	20	29	49	48
1974-75	IND W	73	31	26	57	56
1975-76		30	7	15	22	16
5 yrs.	N Totals:	1	0	0	0	0
	W Totals:	244	81	98	179	173

Doug Wickenheiser

WICKENHEISER, DOUGLAS PETER 6', 200 lbs.
B. Mar. 30, 1961, Regina, Sask. Center, Shoots L

YEAR	TEAM & LEAGUE	GP	G	A	PTS	PIM
1980-81	MONT N	41	7	8	15	20
1981-82		56	12	23	35	43
1982-83		78	25	30	55	49
3 yrs.	N Totals:	175	44	61	105	112

Juha Widing

WIDING, JUHA MARKKU (Whitey) 6'1", 190 lbs.
B. July 4, 1947, Uleaborg, Finland Center, Shoots L

YEAR	TEAM & LEAGUE	GP	G	A	PTS	PIM
1969-70	NYR N	44	7	7	14	10
	LA N	4	0	2	2	2
	2 team total	48	7	9	16	12
1970-71		78	25	40	65	24
1971-72		78	27	28	55	26
1972-73		77	16	54	70	30
1973-74		71	27	30	57	26
1974-75		80	26	34	60	46
1975-76		67	7	15	22	26
1976-77		47	3	8	11	8
	CLEVE N	29	6	8	14	10
	2 team total	76	9	16	25	18
1977-78	EDM W	71	18	24	42	8
9 yrs.	N Totals:	575	144	226	370	208
	W Totals:	71	18	24	42	8

PLAYOFFS

YEAR	TEAM & LEAGUE	GP	G	A	PTS	PIM
1973-74	LA N	5	1	0	1	2
1974-75		3	0	2	2	0
1977-78	EDM W	5	0	1	1	0
3 yrs.	N Totals:	8	1	2	3	2
	W Totals:	5	0	1	1	0

Traded to **Los Angeles** by N.Y. Rangers with Real Lemieux for Ted Irvine, Feb. 28, 1970. Traded to **Cleveland** by Los Angeles with Gary Edwards for Jim Moxey and Gary Simmons, Jan. 22, 1977.

Art Wiebe

WIEBE, WALTER RONALD 5'10", 180 lbs.
B. Sept. 28, 1912, Rosthern, Sask. Defense, Shoots L

YEAR	TEAM & LEAGUE	GP	G	A	PTS	PIM
1932-33	CHI N	3	0	0	0	0
1934-35		42	2	1	3	27
1935-36		46	1	0	1	25
1936-37		45	0	2	2	6
1937-38		44	0	3	3	24
1938-39		47	1	2	3	24
1939-40		40	3	2	5	28
1940-41		46	2	2	4	28
1941-42		44	2	4	6	20
1942-43		33	1	7	8	25
1943-44		21	2	4	6	2
11 yrs.	N Totals:	411	14	27	41	209

PLAYOFFS

YEAR	TEAM & LEAGUE	GP	G	A	PTS	PIM
1934-35	CHI N	2	0	0	0	0
1935-36		2	0	0	0	0
1937-38*		10	0	1	1	2
1939-40		2	1	0	1	2
1940-41		4	0	0	0	0
1941-42		3	0	0	0	0
1943-44		8	0	2	2	4
7 yrs.	N Totals:	31	1	3	4	8

Jim Wiemer

WIEMER, JAMES 6'4", 197 lbs.
B. Jan. 9, 1961, Sudbury, Ont. Left Wing, Shoots L

PLAYOFFS

YEAR	TEAM & LEAGUE	GP	G	A	PTS	PIM
1982-83	BUF N	1	0	0	0	0

Archie Wilcox

WILCOX, ARCHIE 187 lbs.
B. May 9, 1904, Montreal, Que. Defense, Shoots L

YEAR	TEAM & LEAGUE	GP	G	A	PTS	PIM
1929-30	MON(M) N	40	3	5	8	38
1930-31		40	2	2	4	42
1931-32		48	3	3	6	37
1932-33		47	0	3	3	37
1933-34		10	0	0	0	2
	BOS N	16	0	1	1	2
	2 team total	26	0	1	1	4
1934-35	STL N	11	0	0	0	0
6 yrs.	N Totals:	212	8	14	22	158

PLAYOFFS

YEAR	TEAM & LEAGUE	GP	G	A	PTS	PIM
1929-30	MON(M) N	4	1	0	1	4
1930-31		2	0	0	0	2
1931-32		4	0	0	0	4
1932-33		2	0	0	0	0
4 yrs.	N Totals:	12	1	0	1	10

Barry Wilcox

WILCOX, BARRY FREDERICK 6'1", 190 lbs.
B. Apr. 23, 1948, New Westminster, B.C.
Right Wing, Shoots L

YEAR	TEAM & LEAGUE	GP	G	A	PTS	PIM
1972-73	VAN N	31	3	2	5	15
1974-75		2	0	0	0	0
2 yrs.	N Totals:	33	3	2	5	15

Arch Wilder

WILDER, ARCHIBALD 5'9", 155 lbs.
B. Apr. 30, 1917, Melville, Sask. Left Wing, Shoots L

YEAR	TEAM & LEAGUE	GP	G	A	PTS	PIM
1940-41	DET N	18	0	2	2	2

Jim Wiley

WILEY, THOMAS JAMES 6'2", 195 lbs.
B. Apr. 28, 1950, Sault Ste. Marie Center, Shoots L

YEAR	TEAM & LEAGUE	GP	G	A	PTS	PIM
1972-73	PITT N	4	0	1	1	0
1973-74		22	0	3	3	2
1974-75	VAN N	1	0	0	0	0
1975-76		2	0	0	0	2
1976-77		34	4	6	10	4
5 yrs.	N Totals:	63	4	10	14	8

Drafted by **Vancouver** from Pittsburgh in Intra-League Draft, June 10, 1974.

Barry Wilkins

WILKINS, BARRY JAMES 5'11", 190 lbs.
B. Feb. 28, 1947, Toronto, Ont. Defense, Shoots L

YEAR	TEAM & LEAGUE	GP	G	A	PTS	PIM
1966-67	BOS N	1	0	0	0	0
1968-69		1	1	0	1	0
1969-70		6	0	0	0	2
1970-71	VAN N	70	5	18	23	131
1971-72		45	2	5	7	65
1972-73		76	11	17	28	133
1973-74		78	3	28	31	123
1974-75		7	0	1	1	6
	PITT N	59	5	29	34	97
	2 team total	66	5	30	35	103
1975-76		75	0	27	27	106
1976-77	EDM W	51	4	24	28	75
1977-78	IND W	79	2	21	23	79
11 yrs.	N Totals:	418	27	125	152	663
	W Totals:	130	6	45	51	154

PLAYOFFS

YEAR	TEAM & LEAGUE	GP	G	A	PTS	PIM
1974-75	PITT N	3	0	0	0	0
1975-76		3	0	1	1	4

Barry Wilkins continued

YEAR	TEAM & LEAGUE		GP	G	A	PTS	PIM
1976-77	**EDM**	**W**	4	0	1	1	2
3 yrs.		**N Totals:**	6	0	1	1	4
		W Totals:	4	0	1	1	2

Drafted by **Vancouver** from Boston in Expansion Draft, June 10, 1970. Traded to **Pittsburgh** by Vancouver for Ab DeMarco, Nov. 4, 1974. Signed as a free agent by **Colorado** Oct. 11, 1978.

John Wilkinson

WILKINSON, JOHN H.
B. Unknown

YEAR	TEAM & LEAGUE		GP	G	A	PTS	PIM
1943-44	**BOS**	**N**	9	0	0	0	3

Rod Willard

WILLARD, ROD 5'11", 183 lbs.
B. May 1, 1960, Corwall, Ont.

YEAR	TEAM & LEAGUE		GP	G	A	PTS	PIM
1982-83	**TOR**	**N**	1	0	0	0	0

Burr Williams

WILLIAMS, BURR 5'10", 183 lbs.
B. Aug. 30, 1909, Okemah, Okla. Defense, Shoots R

YEAR	TEAM & LEAGUE		GP	G	A	PTS	PIM
1933-34	**DET**	**N**	1	0	1	1	12
1934-35	**STL**	**N**	9	0	0	0	6
	BOS	**N**	7	0	0	0	6
	2 team total		16	0	0	0	12
1936-37	**DET**	**N**	2	0	0	0	4
3 yrs.		**N Totals:**	19	0	1	1	28
PLAYOFFS							
1933-34	**DET**	**N**	2	0	0	0	8

Butch Williams

WILLIAMS, WARREN MILTON 5'11", 195 lbs.
B. Sept. 11, 1952, Duluth, Minn. Right Wing, Shoots R

YEAR	TEAM & LEAGUE		GP	G	A	PTS	PIM
1973-74	**STL**	**N**	31	3	10	13	6
1974-75	**CALIF**	**N**	63	11	21	32	118
1975-76			14	0	4	4	7
1976-77	**EDM**	**W**	29	3	10	13	16
4 yrs.		**N Totals:**	108	14	35	49	131
		W Totals:	29	3	10	13	16

Traded to **California** by St. Louis with Dave Gardner for Craig Patrick and Stan Gilbertson, Nov. 11, 1974.

Fred Williams

WILLIAMS, FREDERICK RICHARD 5'11", 178 lbs.
B. July 1, 1956, Saskatoon, Sask. Center, Shoots L

YEAR	TEAM & LEAGUE		GP	G	A	PTS	PIM
1976-77	**DET**	**N**	44	2	5	7	10

Signed by **Philadelphia** as a free agent, Sept. 15, 1979.

Gord Williams

WILLIAMS, GORDON JAMES 5'11", 190 lbs.
B. Apr. 10, 1960, Saskatoon, Sask. Right Wing, Shoots R

YEAR	TEAM & LEAGUE		GP	G	A	PTS	PIM
1981-82	**PHI**	**N**	1	0	0	0	2
1982-83			1	0	0	0	0
2 yrs.		**N Totals:**	2	0	0	0	2

Tiger Williams

WILLIAMS, DAVID JAMES 5'11", 195 lbs.
B. Feb. 3, 1954, Weyburn, Sask. Left Wing, Shoots L

YEAR	TEAM & LEAGUE		GP	G	A	PTS	PIM
1974-75	**TOR**	**N**	42	10	19	29	187
1975-76			78	21	19	40	299
1976-77			77	18	25	43	**338**
1977-78			78	19	31	50	351
1978-79			77	19	20	39	**298**
1979-80			55	22	18	40	197
	VAN	**N**	23	8	5	13	81
	2 team total		78	30	23	53	278
1980-81			77	35	27	62	**343**
1981-82			77	17	21	38	**341**
1982-83			68	8	13	21	265
9 yrs.		**N Totals:**	652	177	198	375	2700
PLAYOFFS							
1974-75	**TOR**	**N**	7	1	3	4	25
1975-76			10	0	0	0	75
1976-77			9	3	6	9	29
1977-78			12	1	2	3	63
1978-79			6	0	0	0	48
1979-80	**VAN**	**N**	3	0	0	0	20
1980-81			3	0	0	0	20
1981-82			17	3	7	10	116
1982-83			4	0	3	3	12
9 yrs.		**N Totals:**	71	8	21	29	408

Traded to **Vancouver** by Toronto with Jerry Butler for Rick Vaive and Bill Derlago, Feb. 18, 1980.

Tom Williams

WILLIAMS, THOMAS MARK 5'11", 185 lbs.
B. Apr. 17, 1940, Duluth, Minn. Center, Shoots R

YEAR	TEAM & LEAGUE		GP	G	A	PTS	PIM
1961-62	**BOS**	**N**	26	6	6	12	2
1962-63			69	23	20	43	11
1963-64			37	8	15	23	8
1964-65			65	13	21	34	28
1965-66			70	16	22	38	31
1966-67			29	8	13	21	2
1967-68			68	18	32	50	14
1968-69			26	4	7	11	19
1969-70	**MINN**	**N**	75	15	52	67	18
1970-71			41	10	13	23	16
	CALIF	**N**	18	7	10	17	8
	2 team total		59	17	23	40	24
1971-72			32	3	9	12	2
1972-73	**NE**	**W**	69	10	21	31	14
1973-74			70	21	37	58	6
1974-75	**WASH**	**N**	73	22	36	58	12
1975-76			34	8	13	21	6
15 yrs.		**N Totals:**	663	161	269	430	177
		W Totals:	139	31	58	89	20
PLAYOFFS							
1967-68	**BOS**	**N**	4	1	0	1	2
1969-70	**MINN**	**N**	6	1	5	6	0
1972-73	**NE**	**W**	15	6	11	17	2
1973-74			4	0	3	3	10
4 yrs.		**N Totals:**	10	2	5	7	2
		W Totals:	19	6	14	20	12

Traded to **Minnesota** by Boston with Barry Gibbs for Minnesota's first choice in 1969 Amateur Draft (Don Tannahill) and Fred O'Donnell, May 7, 1969. Traded to **California** by Minnesota with Dick Redmond for Ted Hampson and Wayne Muloin, Feb. 23, 1971. Sold to **Boston** by California, Mar. 5, 1972. Sold to **Washington** by Boston, July 22, 1974.

Tommy Williams

WILLIAMS, THOMAS CHARLES 187 lbs.
B. Feb. 7, 1951, Windsor, Ont. Left Wing, Shoots R

YEAR	TEAM & LEAGUE		GP	G	A	PTS	PIM
1971-72	**NYR**	**N**	3	0	0	0	2
1972-73			8	0	1	1	0
1973-74			14	1	2	3	4
	LA	**N**	46	11	17	28	6
	2 team total		60	12	19	31	10
1974-75			74	24	22	46	16
1975-76			70	19	20	39	14
1976-77			80	35	39	74	14
1977-78			58	15	22	37	9
1978-79			44	10	15	25	8
8 yrs.		**N Totals:**	397	115	138	253	73
PLAYOFFS							
1973-74	**LA**	**N**	5	3	1	4	0
1974-75			3	0	0	0	0
1975-76			9	2	2	4	2
1976-77			9	3	4	7	2
1977-78			2	0	0	0	0
1978-79			1	0	0	0	0
6 yrs.		**N Totals:**	29	8	7	15	4

Traded to **Los Angeles** by N.Y. Rangers with Mike Murphy and Sheldon Kannegiesser for Gilles Marotte and Real Lemieux, Nov. 30, 1973. Traded to **St. Louis** by Los Angeles, Aug. 16, 1979, to complete three-team trade among St. Louis, Los Angeles, and N.Y. Islanders, June 9, 1979.

Gary Williamson

WILLIAMSON, GARY ALBERT 5'10", 175 lbs.
B. May 25, 1950, Montreal, Que. Left Wing, Shoots L

YEAR	TEAM & LEAGUE		GP	G	A	PTS	PIM
1973-74	HOUS	W	9	2	6	8	0
PLAYOFFS							
1973-74	HOUS	W	12	0	0	0	0

Hal Willis

WILLIS, HAROLD 6'2", 215 lbs.
B. June 8, 1946, Liverpool, N.S. Defense, Shoots L

YEAR	TEAM & LEAGUE		GP	G	A	PTS	PIM
1972-73	NY	W	74	3	21	24	159
1973-74	LA	W	18	1	2	3	24
2 yrs.		W Totals:	92	4	23	27	183

Don Willson

WILLSON, DONALD
B. Jan. 1, 1914, Chatham, Ont. Forward

YEAR	TEAM & LEAGUE		GP	G	A	PTS	PIM
1937-38	MONT	N	18	2	7	9	0
1938-39			4	0	0	0	0
2 yrs.		N Totals:	22	2	7	9	0
PLAYOFFS							
1937-38	MONT	N	3	0	0	0	0

Behn Wilson

WILSON, BEHN BEVAN 6'3", 210 lbs.
B. Dec. 19, 1958, Toronto, Ont. Defense, Shoots L

YEAR	TEAM & LEAGUE		GP	G	A	PTS	PIM
1978-79	PHI	N	80	13	36	49	197
1979-80			61	9	25	34	212
1980-81			77	16	47	63	237
1981-82			59	13	23	36	135
1982-83			62	8	24	32	92
5 yrs.		N Totals:	339	59	155	214	873
PLAYOFFS							
1978-79	PHI	N	5	1	0	1	8
1979-80			19	4	9	13	66
1980-81			12	2	10	12	36
1981-82			4	1	4	5	10
1982-83			3	0	1	1	2
5 yrs.		N Totals:	43	8	24	32	122

Traded by Philadelphia to **Chicago** for Doug Crossman and Chicago's second round choice in the 1984 Amateur Draft, June 8, 1983.

Bert Wilson

WILSON, BERTWIN HILLIARD 6', 190 lbs.
B. Oct. 17, 1949, Orangeville, Ont. Left Wing, Shoots L

YEAR	TEAM & LEAGUE		GP	G	A	PTS	PIM
1973-74	NYR	N	5	1	1	2	2
1974-75			61	5	1	6	66
1975-76	LA	N	13	0	0	0	17
	STL	N	45	2	3	5	47
	2 team total		58	2	3	5	64
1976-77	LA	N	77	4	3	7	64
1977-78			79	7	16	23	127
1978-79			73	9	10	19	138
1979-80			75	4	3	7	91
1980-81	CALG	N	50	5	7	12	94
8 yrs.		N Totals:	478	37	44	81	646
PLAYOFFS							
1975-76	LA	N	9	0	0	0	24
1976-77			8	0	2	2	12
1977-78			2	0	0	0	2
1979-80			2	0	0	0	4
1980-81	CALG	N	1	0	0	0	0
5 yrs.		N Totals:	22	0	2	2	42

Traded to **St. Louis** by N.Y. Rangers with Ted Irvine and Jerry Butler for Bill Collins and John Davidson, June 18, 1975. Traded to **Los Angeles** by St. Louis with the rights to Curt Brackenbury for cash, Mar. 6, 1976. Traded to **Calgary** by Los Angeles with Randy Holt for Garry Unger, June 6, 1980.

Bob Wilson

WILSON, ROBERT WAYNE 5'9", 178 lbs.
B. Feb. 18, 1934, Sudbury, Ont. Defense, Shoots L

YEAR	TEAM & LEAGUE		GP	G	A	PTS	PIM
1953-54	CHI	N	1	0	0	0	0

Cully Wilson

WILSON, CAROL
Right Wing

YEAR	TEAM & LEAGUE		GP	G	A	PTS	PIM
1919-20	TOR	N	23	21	5	26	**79**
1920-21			8	2	1	3	16
	MONT	N	9	6	1	7	0
	2 team total		17	8	2	10	16
1921-22	HAMIL	N	23	9	7	16	21
1922-23			23	16	3	19	46
1926-27	CHI	N	39	8	4	12	40
5 yrs.		N Totals:	125	62	21	83	202
PLAYOFFS							
1926-27	CHI	N	2	1	0	1	6

Doug Wilson

WILSON, DOUGLAS JR. 6'1", 187 lbs.
B. July 5, 1957, Ottawa, Ont. Defense, Shoots L
Won Norris Trophy, 1981-82

YEAR	TEAM & LEAGUE		GP	G	A	PTS	PIM
1977-78	CHI	N	77	14	20	34	72
1978-79			56	5	21	26	37
1979-80			73	12	49	61	70
1980-81			76	12	39	51	80
1981-82			76	39	46	85	54
1982-83			74	18	51	69	58
6 yrs.		N Totals:	432	100	226	326	371
PLAYOFFS							
1977-78	CHI	N	4	0	0	0	0
1979-80			7	2	8	10	6
1980-81			3	0	3	3	2
1981-82			15	3	10	13	32
1982-83			13	4	11	15	12
5 yrs.		N Totals:	42	9	32	41	52

Gord Wilson

WILSON, GORDON ALLAN 6'1", 185 lbs.
B. Aug. 13, 1932, Port Arthur, Ont. Left Wing, Shoots L

YEAR	TEAM & LEAGUE		GP	G	A	PTS	PIM
PLAYOFFS							
1954-55	BOS	N	2	0	0	0	0

Hub Wilson

WILSON, JAMES 5'10", 180 lbs.
B. May 13, 1909, Ottawa, Ont. Left Wing, Shoots L

YEAR	TEAM & LEAGUE		GP	G	A	PTS	PIM
1931-32	NYA	N	2	0	0	0	0

Jerry Wilson

WILSON, JEROLD 6'2", 200 lbs.
B. Apr. 10, 1937, Edmonton, Alta. Forward, Shoots L

YEAR	TEAM & LEAGUE		GP	G	A	PTS	PIM
1956-57	MONT	N	3	0	0	0	2

Drafted from Montreal by **Toronto** June 4, 1958.

Johnny Wilson

WILSON, JOHN EDWARD (The Iron Man) 5'10", 175 lbs.
B. June 14, 1929, Kincardine, Ont. Left Wing, Shoots L

YEAR	TEAM & LEAGUE		GP	G	A	PTS	PIM
1949-50	DET	N	1	0	0	0	0
1951-52			28	4	5	9	18
1952-53			70	23	19	42	22
1953-54			70	17	17	34	22
1954-55			70	12	15	27	14
1955-56	CHI	N	70	24	9	33	12

Johnny Wilson continued

YEAR	TEAM & LEAGUE		GP	G	A	PTS	PIM
1956-57			70	18	30	48	24
1957-58	DET	N	70	12	27	39	14
1958-59			70	11	17	28	18
1959-60	TOR	N	70	15	16	31	8
1960-61			3	0	1	1	0
	NYR	N	56	14	12	26	24
	2 team total		59	14	13	27	24
1961-62			40	11	3	14	14
12 yrs.		N Totals:	688	161	171	332	190
PLAYOFFS							
1949-50*	DET	N	8	0	1	1	0
1950-51			1	0	0	0	0
1951-52*			8	4	1	5	5
1952-53			6	2	5	7	0
1953-54*			12	3	0	3	0
1954-55*			11	0	1	1	0
1957-58			4	2	1	3	0
1959-60	TOR	N	10	1	2	3	2
1961-62	NYR	N	6	2	2	4	4
9 yrs.		N Totals:	66	14	13	27	11

Traded to **Chicago** by Detroit with Tony Leswick, Glen Skov and Benny Woit for Dave Creighton, Gord Hollingworth, Jerry Toppazzini, and John McCormack, June, 1955. Traded to **Detroit** by Chicago with Forbes Kennedy, William Preston, and Henry Bassen in exchange for Ted Lindsay and Glenn Hall, July, 1957. Traded to **Toronto** by Detroit with Frank Roggeveen for Barry Cullen, June, 1959. Traded to **N.Y. Rangers** by Toronto with Pat Hannigan for Eddie Shack, Nov., 1960.

Larry Wilson

WILSON, LAWRENCE 5'11", 170 lbs.
B. Oct. 23, 1930, Kincardine, Ont. Center, Shoots L

YEAR	TEAM & LEAGUE		GP	G	A	PTS	PIM
1949-50	DET	N	1	0	0	0	2
1951-52			5	0	0	0	4
1952-53			15	0	4	4	6
1953-54	CHI	N	66	9	33	42	22
1954-55			63	12	11	23	39
1955-56			2	0	0	0	2
6 yrs.		N Totals:	152	21	48	69	75
PLAYOFFS							
1949-50*	DET	N	4	0	0	0	0

Purchased by **Chicago** from Detroit with Larry Zeidel and Lou Jankowski, Aug. 12, 1953.

Murray Wilson

WILSON, MURRAY CHARLES 6'1", 185 lbs.
B. Nov. 7, 1951, Toronto, Ont. Left Wing, Shoots L

YEAR	TEAM & LEAGUE		GP	G	A	PTS	PIM
1972-73	MONT	N	52	18	9	27	16
1973-74			72	17	14	31	26
1974-75			73	24	18	42	44
1975-76			59	11	24	35	36
1976-77			60	13	14	27	26
1977-78			12	0	1	1	0
1978-79	LA	N	58	11	15	26	14
7 yrs.		N Totals:	386	94	95	189	162
PLAYOFFS							
1972-73*	MONT	N	16	2	4	6	6
1973-74			5	1	0	1	2
1974-75			5	0	3	3	4
1975-76*			12	1	1	2	6
1976-77*			14	1	6	7	14
1978-79	LA	N	1	0	0	0	0
6 yrs.		N Totals:	53	5	14	19	32

Traded to **Los Angeles** by Montreal with Montreal's first round choice (Jay Wells) in the 1979 Entry Draft for Los Angeles' first round choice in the 1981 Entry Draft, Oct. 5, 1978.

Rik Wilson

WILSON, RICHARD WILLIAM 6', 180 lbs.
B. June 17, 1962, Long Beach, Cal. Defense, Shoots R

YEAR	TEAM & LEAGUE		GP	G	A	PTS	PIM
1981-82	STL	N	48	3	18	21	24
1982-83			56	3	11	14	50
2 yrs.		N Totals:	104	6	29	35	74

Rik Wilson continued

YEAR	TEAM & LEAGUE		GP	G	A	PTS	PIM
PLAYOFFS							
1981-82	STL	N	9	0	3	3	14

Rick Wilson

WILSON, RICHARD GORDON 6'1", 195 lbs.
B. Aug. 10, 1950, Prince Albert, Sask. Defense, Shoots L

YEAR	TEAM & LEAGUE		GP	G	A	PTS	PIM
1973-74	MONT	N	21	0	2	2	6
1974-75	STL	N	76	2	5	7	83
1975-76			65	1	6	7	20
1976-77	DET	N	77	3	13	16	56
4 yrs.		N Totals:	239	6	26	32	165
PLAYOFFS							
1974-75	STL	N	2	0	0	0	0
1975-76			1	0	0	0	0
2 yrs.		N Totals:	3	0	0	0	0

Traded to **St. Louis** by Montreal with Montreal's fifth choice (Don Wheldon) in 1974 Amateur Draft for St. Louis' fourth choice (Barry Legge) in same draft and a player to be named later (Glen Sather, June 14, 1974), May 27, 1974. Traded to **Detroit** by St. Louis, June 16, 1976, to complete earlier deal in which St. Louis acquired Doug Grant (March 9, 1976).

Roger Wilson

WILSON, ROGER SIDNEY 6'2", 210 lbs.
B. Sept. 18, 1946, Sudbury, Ont. Defense, Shoots R

YEAR	TEAM & LEAGUE		GP	G	A	PTS	PIM
1974-75	CHI	N	7	0	2	2	6

Ron Wilson

WILSON, RONALD LEE 5'9", 170 lbs.
B. May 13, 1956, Toronto, Ont. Left Wing, Shoots L

YEAR	TEAM & LEAGUE		GP	G	A	PTS	PIM
1979-80	WINN	N	79	21	36	57	28
1980-81			77	18	33	51	55
1981-82			39	3	13	16	49
1982-83			12	6	3	9	4
4 yrs.		N Totals:	207	48	85	133	136
PLAYOFFS							
1982-83	WINN	N	3	2	2	4	2

Ron Wilson

WILSON, RONALD LAWRENCE 5'11", 175 lbs.
B. May 28, 1955, Windsor, Ont. Right Wing, Shoots R

YEAR	TEAM & LEAGUE		GP	G	A	PTS	PIM
1977-78	TOR	N	13	2	1	3	0
1978-79			46	5	12	17	4
1979-80			5	0	2	2	2
3 yrs.		N Totals:	64	7	15	22	6
PLAYOFFS							
1978-79	TOR	N	3	0	1	1	0
1979-80			3	1	2	3	2
2 yrs.		N Totals:	6	1	3	4	2

Sold to **Winnipeg** by Montreal, Oct. 4, 1979.

Wally Wilson

WILSON, WALLACE LLOYD 5'11", 165 lbs.
B. May 25, 1921, Berwick, N.S. Center, Shoots R

YEAR	TEAM & LEAGUE		GP	G	A	PTS	PIM
1947-48	BOS	N	53	11	8	19	18
PLAYOFFS							
1947-48	BOS	N	1	0	0	0	0

Murray Wing

WING, MURRAY ALLAN 5'11", 180 lbs.
B. Oct. 14, 1950, Thunder Bay, Ont. Defense, Shoots R

YEAR	TEAM & LEAGUE		GP	G	A	PTS	PIM
1973-74	DET	N	1	0	1	1	0

Bob Winograd

WINOGRAD, ROBERT
B. June 6, 1946, Winnipeg, Man. — Defense

YEAR	TEAM & LEAGUE		GP	G	A	PTS	PIM
1972-73	NY	W	52	0	12	12	23
1973-74	NY-NJ	W	7	1	0	1	0
1976-77	SD	W	1	0	0	0	0
3 yrs.		W Totals:	60	1	12	13	23

Eddie Wiseman

WISEMAN, EDWARD RANDALL — 5'7", 160 lbs.
B. Dec. 28, 1912, Newcastle, N.B. — Right Wing, Shoots R

YEAR	TEAM & LEAGUE		GP	G	A	PTS	PIM
1932-33	DET	N	47	8	8	16	16
1933-34			47	5	9	14	13
1934-35			40	11	13	24	14
1935-36			1	0	0	0	0
	NYA	N	42	12	15	27	16
	2 team total		43	12	15	27	16
1936-37			43	14	19	33	12
1937-38			48	18	14	32	32
1938-39			45	12	21	33	8
1939-40			31	5	13	18	8
	BOS	N	18	2	6	8	0
	2 team total		49	7	19	26	8
1940-41			47	16	24	40	10
1941-42			45	12	22	34	8
10 yrs.		N Totals:	454	115	164	279	137
PLAYOFFS							
1932-33	DET	N	2	0	0	0	0
1933-34			9	0	1	1	4
1935-36	NYA	N	4	2	1	3	0
1937-38			6	0	4	4	10
1938-39			2	0	0	0	0
1939-40	BOS	N	6	2	1	3	2
1940-41*			11	6	2	8	0
1941-42			5	0	1	1	0
8 yrs.		N Totals:	45	10	10	20	16

Jim Wiste

WISTE, JAMES ANDREW — 5'10", 185 lbs.
B. Feb. 18, 1946, Moose Jaw, Sask. — Center, Shoots L

YEAR	TEAM & LEAGUE		GP	G	A	PTS	PIM
1968-69	CHI	N	3	0	0	0	0
1969-70			26	0	8	8	8
1970-71	VAN	N	23	1	2	3	0
1972-73	CLEVE	W	70	28	43	71	24
1973-74			76	23	35	58	26
1974-75	IND	W	75	13	28	41	30
1975-76			7	0	2	2	0
7 yrs.		N Totals:	52	1	10	11	8
		W Totals:	228	64	108	172	80
PLAYOFFS							
1972-73	CLEVE	W	9	3	8	11	13
1973-74			5	0	1	1	0
2 yrs.		W Totals:	14	3	9	12	13

Jim Witherspoon

WITHERSPOON, JAMES DOUGLAS — 6'3", 205 lbs.
B. Oct. 3, 1951, Toronto, Ont. — Defense, Shoots R

YEAR	TEAM & LEAGUE		GP	G	A	PTS	PIM
1975-76	LA	N	2	0	0	0	2

Steve Witiuk

WITIUK, STEPHEN — 5'7", 165 lbs.
B. Jan. 8, 1929, Winnipeg, Man. — Right Wing, Shoots R

YEAR	TEAM & LEAGUE		GP	G	A	PTS	PIM
1951-52	CHI	N	33	3	8	11	14

Benny Woit

WOIT, BENEDICT FRANCIS — 5'11", 190 lbs.
B. Jan. 7, 1928, Fort William, Ont. — Defense, Shoots R

YEAR	TEAM & LEAGUE		GP	G	A	PTS	PIM
1950-51	DET	N	2	0	0	0	0
1951-52			58	3	8	11	20
1952-53			70	1	5	6	40
1953-54			70	0	2	2	38
1954-55			62	2	2	4	22

Benny Woit continued

YEAR	TEAM & LEAGUE		GP	G	A	PTS	PIM
1955-56	CHI	N	63	1	8	9	46
1956-57			9	0	0	0	2
7 yrs.		N Totals:	334	7	25	32	168
PLAYOFFS							
1950-51	DET	N	4	0	0	0	2
1951-52*			8	1	1	2	2
1952-53			6	1	3	4	0
1953-54*			12	0	1	1	8
1954-55*			11	0	1	1	6
5 yrs.		N Totals:	41	2	6	8	18

Traded to **Chicago** by Detroit with Tony Leswick, Glen Skov and Johnny Wilson for Jerry Toppazzini, John McCormack, Dave Creighton and Gord Hollingworth, June 3, 1955.

Stephen Wojciechowski

WOJCIECHOWSKI, STEPHEN (WOCHY) — 5'8", 160 lbs.
B. Dec. 25, 1922, Fort William, Ont. — Right Wing, Shoots R

YEAR	TEAM & LEAGUE		GP	G	A	PTS	PIM
1944-45	DET	N	49	19	20	39	17
1946-47			5	0	0	0	0
2 yrs.		N Totals:	54	19	20	39	17
PLAYOFFS							
1944-45	DET	N	6	0	1	1	0

Bennett Wolf

WOLF, BENNETT MARTIN — 6'3", 205 lbs.
B. Oct. 23, 1959, Kitchener, Ont. — Defense, Shoots R

YEAR	TEAM & LEAGUE		GP	G	A	PTS	PIM
1980-81	PITT	N	24	0	1	1	94
1981-82			1	0	0	0	2
1982-83			5	0	0	0	37
3 yrs.		N Totals:	30	0	1	1	133

Mike Wong

WONG, MICHAEL ANTHONY — 6'3", 205 lbs.
B. Jan. 14, 1955, Minneapolis, Minn. — Center, Shoots L

YEAR	TEAM & LEAGUE		GP	G	A	PTS	PIM
1975-76	DET	N	22	1	1	2	12

Robert Wood

WOOD, ROBERT OWEN — 6'1", 185 lbs.
B. July 9, 1930, Lethbridge, Alta. — Defense, Shoots L

YEAR	TEAM & LEAGUE		GP	G	A	PTS	PIM
1950-51	NYR	N	1	0	0	0	0

Paul Woods

WOODS, PAUL WILLIAM (Woodsy) — 5'10", 170 lbs.
B. Apr. 12, 1955, Hespeler, Ont. — Center, Shoots L

YEAR	TEAM & LEAGUE		GP	G	A	PTS	PIM
1977-78	DET	N	80	19	23	42	52
1978-79			80	14	23	37	59
1979-80			79	6	20	26	24
1980-81			67	8	16	24	45
1981-82			75	10	17	27	48
1982-83			63	13	20	33	30
6 yrs.		N Totals:	444	70	119	189	258
PLAYOFFS							
1977-78	DET	N	7	0	5	5	4

Signed as free agent by **Chicago** Aug. 12, 1980.

Bob Woytowich

WOYTOWICH, ROBERT IVAN — 5'11", 195 lbs.
B. Aug. 18, 1941, Winnipeg, Man. — Defense, Shoots R

YEAR	TEAM & LEAGUE		GP	G	A	PTS	PIM
1964-65	BOS	N	21	2	10	12	16
1965-66			68	2	17	19	75
1966-67			64	2	7	9	43
1967-68	MINN	N	66	4	17	21	63
1968-69	PITT	N	71	9	20	29	62
1969-70			68	8	25	33	49
1970-71			78	4	22	26	30
1971-72			31	1	4	5	8
	LA	N	36	0	4	4	6
	2 team total		67	1	8	9	14
1972-73	WINN	W	62	2	4	6	47

Bob Woytowich continued

YEAR	TEAM & LEAGUE		GP	G	A	PTS	PIM
1973-74			72	6	28	34	43
1974-75			24	0	4	4	8
	IND	**W**	42	0	8	8	28
	2 team total		66	0	12	12	36
1975-76			42	1	7	8	14
12 yrs.		**N Totals:**	503	32	126	158	352
		W Totals:	242	9	51	60	140
PLAYOFFS							
1967-68	**MINN**	**N**	14	0	1	1	18
1969-70	**PITT**	**N**	10	1	2	3	2
1972-73	**WINN**	**W**	14	1	1	2	4
1973-74			4	0	0	0	0
4 yrs.		**N Totals:**	24	1	3	4	20
		W Totals:	18	1	1	2	4

Drafted by **Boston** from N.Y. Rangers, June 10, 1964. Drafted by **Minnesota** from Boston in Expansion Draft, June 1967. Traded to **Pittsburgh** by Minnesota for Pittsburgh's first choice (later transferred to Montreal, Dave Gardner) in 1972 Amateur Draft, Oct. 1, 1968. Traded to **Los Angeles** by Pittsburgh for Al McDonough, Jan. 11, 1972.

John Wright

WRIGHT, JOHN GILBERT BRERETON 5′11″, 175 lbs.
B. Nov. 9, 1948, Toronto, Ont. Center, Shoots R

YEAR	TEAM & LEAGUE		GP	G	A	PTS	PIM
1972-73	**VAN**	**N**	71	10	27	37	32
1973-74			20	3	3	6	11
	STL	**N**	32	3	6	9	22
	2 team total		52	6	9	15	33
1974-75	**KC**	**N**	4	0	0	0	2
3 yrs.		**N Totals:**	127	16	36	52	67

Traded to **St. Louis** by Vancouver for Mike Lampman, Dec. 10, 1973. Drafted by **Kansas City** from St. Louis in Expansion Draft, June 12, 1974.

Keith Wright

WRIGHT, KEITH EDWARD 6′, 180 lbs.
B. Apr. 13, 1944, Newmarket, Ont. Left Wing, Shoots L

YEAR	TEAM & LEAGUE		GP	G	A	PTS	PIM
1967-68	**PHI**	**N**	1	0	0	0	0

Larry Wright

WRIGHT, LARRY DALE 6′1″, 180 lbs.
B. Oct. 8, 1951, Regina, Sask. Center, Shoots L

YEAR	TEAM & LEAGUE		GP	G	A	PTS	PIM
1971-72	**PHI**	**N**	27	0	1	1	2
1972-73			9	0	1	1	4
1974-75	**CALIF**	**N**	2	0	0	0	0
1975-76	**PHI**	**N**	2	1	0	1	0
1977-78	**DET**	**N**	66	3	6	9	13
5 yrs.		**N Totals:**	106	4	8	12	19

Traded to **California** by Philadelphia with Al MacAdam and Philadelphia's first choice (Ron Chipperfield) in 1974 Amateur Draft for Reggie Leach, May 24, 1974. Signed as a free agent by **Philadelphia** Sept. 26, 1975. Signed as a free agent by **Detroit** Oct. 22, 1977.

Bus Wycherley

WYCHERLEY, RALPH H. 6′, 185 lbs.
B. Feb. 26, 1920, Saskatoon, Sask. Left Wing, Shoots L

YEAR	TEAM & LEAGUE		GP	G	A	PTS	PIM
1940-41	**NYA**	**N**	26	4	5	9	4
1941-42			2	0	2	2	2
2 yrs.		**N Totals:**	28	4	7	11	6

Duane Wylie

WYLIE, DUANE STEVEN 5′8″, 170 lbs.
B. Nov. 10, 1950, Spokane, Wash. Center, Shoots L

YEAR	TEAM & LEAGUE		GP	G	A	PTS	PIM
1974-75	**CHI**	**N**	6	1	3	4	2
1976-77			8	2	0	2	0
2 yrs.		**N Totals:**	14	3	3	6	2

Signed as a free agent by **Chicago** Oct. 12, 1972.

William Wylie

WYLIE, WILLIAM VANCE (Wiggie) 5′6½″, 145 lbs.
B. July 15, 1928, Galt, Ont. Center, Shoots L

YEAR	TEAM & LEAGUE		GP	G	A	PTS	PIM
1950-51	**NYR**	**N**	1	0	0	0	0

Randy Wyrozub

WYROZUB, WILLIAM RANDALL 5′11″, 170 lbs.
B. Apr. 8, 1950, Lacombe, Alta. Center, Shoots L

YEAR	TEAM & LEAGUE		GP	G	A	PTS	PIM
1970-71	**BUF**	**N**	16	2	2	4	6
1971-72			34	3	4	7	0
1972-73			45	3	3	6	4
1973-74			5	0	1	1	0
1975-76	**IND**	**W**	55	11	14	25	8
5 yrs.		**N Totals:**	100	8	10	18	10
		W Totals:	55	11	14	25	8

Drafted by **Washington** from Buffalo in Expansion Draft, June 12, 1974.

Ken Yackel

YACKEL, KENNETH
B. July 30,1932, St. Paul, Minn. Forward, Shoots R

YEAR	TEAM & LEAGUE		GP	G	A	PTS	PIM
1958-59	**BOS**	**N**	6	0	0	0	2
PLAYOFFS							
1958-59	**BOS**	**N**	2	0	0	0	2

Dale Yakiwchuk

YAKIWCHUK, DALE ALEXANDER 6′4″, 205 lbs.
B. Oct. 17, 1958, Calgary, Alta. Center, Shoots L

YEAR	TEAM & LEAGUE		GP	G	A	PTS	PIM
1978-79	**WINN**	**W**	4	0	0	0	0

Gary Yaremchuk

YAREMCHUK, GARY (Weasel) 6′, 183 lbs.
B. Aug. 15, 1961, Edmonton, Alta. Center, Shoots L

YEAR	TEAM & LEAGUE		GP	G	A	PTS	PIM
1981-82	**TOR**	**N**	18	0	3	3	10
1982-83			3	0	0	0	2
2 yrs.		**N Totals:**	21	0	3	3	12

Bill Young

YOUNG, WILLIAM ANDREW 6′2″, 195 lbs.
B. July 5, 1947, St. Catharines, Ont. Left Wing, Shoots L

YEAR	TEAM & LEAGUE		GP	G	A	PTS	PIM
1972-73	**LA**	**W**	50	14	12	26	46
	MINN	**W**	23	5	6	11	20
	2 team total		73	19	18	37	66
1973-74	**CLEVE**	**W**	53	8	9	17	70
	LA	**W**	16	1	3	4	4
	2 team total		69	9	12	21	74
2 yrs.		**W Totals:**	142	28	30	58	140
PLAYOFFS							
1972-73	**MINN**	**W**	5	1	1	2	4

Brian Young

YOUNG, BRIAN DONALD 6′1″, 183 lbs.
B. Oct. 2, 1958, Jasper, Alta. Defense, Shoots R

YEAR	TEAM & LEAGUE		GP	G	A	PTS	PIM
1980-81	**CHI**	**N**	8	0	2	2	6

Douglas Young

YOUNG, DOUGLAS G. 5′9½″, 190 lbs.
B. Oct. 1, 1908, Medicine Hat, Alta. Shoots R

YEAR	TEAM & LEAGUE		GP	G	A	PTS	PIM
1931-32	**DET**	**N**	47	10	2	12	45
1932-33			48	5	6	11	59
1933-34			48	4	0	4	36
1934-35			48	4	6	10	37
1935-36			48	5	12	17	54
1936-37			10	0	0	0	6
1937-38			48	3	5	8	24
1938-39			44	1	5	6	16
1939-40	**MONT**	**N**	47	3	9	12	22
1940-41			3	0	0	0	4
10 yrs.		**N Totals:**	391	35	45	80	303
PLAYOFFS							
1931-32	**DET**	**N**	2	0	0	0	2
1932-33			4	1	1	2	0
1933-34			9	0	0	0	10
1935-36*			7	0	2	2	0
1938-39			6	0	2	2	4

Douglas Young continued

YEAR	TEAM & LEAGUE		GP	G	A	PTS	PIM
5 yrs.		**N Totals:**	28	1	5	6	16

Howie Young

YOUNG, HOWARD JOHN EDWARD 6', 190 lbs.
B. Aug. 2, 1937, Toronto, Ont. Defense, Shoots R

YEAR	TEAM & LEAGUE		GP	G	A	PTS	PIM
1960-61	**DET**	**N**	29	0	8	8	108
1961-62			30	0	2	2	67
1962-63			64	4	5	9	**273**
1963-64	**CHI**	**N**	39	0	7	7	99
1966-67	**DET**	**N**	44	3	14	17	100
1967-68			62	2	17	19	112
1968-69	**CHI**	**N**	57	3	7	10	67
1970-71	**VAN**	**N**	11	0	2	2	25
1974-75	**PHOE**	**W**	30	3	12	15	44
	WINN	**W**	42	13	10	23	42
	2 team total		72	16	22	38	86
1976-77	**PHOE**	**W**	26	1	3	4	23
10 yrs.		**N Totals:**	336	12	62	74	851
		W Totals:	98	17	25	42	109
PLAYOFFS							
1960-61	**DET**	**N**	11	2	2	4	30
1962-63			8	0	2	2	16
2 yrs.		**N Totals:**	19	2	4	6	46

Traded to **Chicago** by Detroit for Roger Crozier and Ron Ingram, June 5, 1963. Traded to **Detroit** by Chicago for Al Lebrun, Murray Hall, and Rick Morris, Dec. 20, 1966. Traded to **Oakland** by Detroit with Gary Jarrett, Doug Roberts, and Chris Worthy for Bob Baun and Ron Harris, May 27, 1968. Claimed on waivers by **Chicago** from Oakland, Oct. 2, 1968.

Tim Young

YOUNG, TIMOTHY MICHAEL (Blade) 6'2", 176 lbs.
B. Feb. 22, 1955, Scarborough, Ont. Center, Shoots R

YEAR	TEAM & LEAGUE		GP	G	A	PTS	PIM
1975-76	**MINN**	**N**	63	18	33	51	71
1976-77			80	29	66	95	58
1977-78			78	23	35	58	64
1978-79			73	24	32	56	46
1979-80			77	31	43	74	24
1980-81			74	25	41	66	40
1981-82			49	10	31	41	67
1982-83			70	18	35	53	31
8 yrs.		**N Totals:**	564	178	316	494	401
PLAYOFFS							
1976-77	**MINN**	**N**	2	1	1	2	2
1979-80			15	2	5	7	4
1980-81			12	3	14	17	9
1981-82			4	1	1	2	10
1982-83			2	0	2	2	2
5 yrs.		**N Totals:**	35	7	23	30	27

Traded to **Minnesota** by Los Angeles for Minnesota's second round choice (Steve Clippingdale) in 1976 Amateur Draft, Aug. 15, 1975. Traded to **Winnipeg** by Minnesota for Craig Levie and the rights to college player Tom Ward, Sept. 3, 1983.

Warren Young

YOUNG, WARREN 6'3", 195 lbs.
B. Jan. 11, 1956, Toronto, Ont. Center, Shoots L

YEAR	TEAM & LEAGUE		GP	G	A	PTS	PIM
1981-82	**MINN**	**N**	1	0	0	0	0
1982-83			4	1	1	2	0
2 yrs.		**N Totals:**	5	1	1	2	0

Signed as free agent with **Minnesota** Oct. 22, 1981.

Tom Younghans

YOUNGHANS, THOMAS 5'11", lbs.
B. Jan. 22, 1953, St. Paul, Minn. Right Wing, Shoots R

YEAR	TEAM & LEAGUE		GP	G	A	PTS	PIM
1976-77	**MINN**	**N**	78	8	6	14	35
1977-78			72	10	8	18	100
1978-79			76	8	10	18	50
1979-80			79	10	6	16	92
1980-81			74	4	6	10	79
1981-82			3	1	0	1	0
	NYR	**N**	47	3	5	8	17
	2 team total		50	4	5	9	17
6 yrs.		**N Totals:**	429	44	41	85	373
PLAYOFFS							
1976-77	**MINN**	**N**	2	0	0	0	0
1979-80			15	2	1	3	17
1980-81			5	0	0	0	4
1981-82	**NYR**	**N**	2	0	0	0	0
4 yrs.		**N Totals:**	24	2	1	3	21

Signed as free agent by **Minnesota** Sept. 14, 1979. Sold to **N.Y. Rangers** by Minnesota, Oct. 30, 1981.

Marty Zabroski

ZABROSKI, MARTIN
B. Unknown Defense

YEAR	TEAM & LEAGUE		GP	G	A	PTS	PIM
1944-45	**CHI**	**N**	1	0	0	0	0

Miles Zaharko

ZAHARKO, MILES 6', 197 lbs.
B. Apr. 30, 1957, Mannville, Alta. Defense, Shoots L

YEAR	TEAM & LEAGUE		GP	G	A	PTS	PIM
1977-78	**ATL**	**N**	71	1	19	20	26
1978-79	**CHI**	**N**	1	0	0	0	0
1980-81			42	3	11	14	40
1981-82			15	1	2	3	18
4 yrs.		**N Totals:**	129	5	32	37	84
PLAYOFFS							
1977-78	**ATL**	**N**	1	0	0	0	0
1980-81	**CHI**	**N**	2	0	0	0	0
2 yrs.		**N Totals:**	3	0	0	0	0

Traded to **Chicago** by Atlanta with Tom Lysiak, Pat Ribble, Greg Fox and Harold Phillipoff for Ivan Boldirev, Phil Russell and Darcy Rota, March 13, 1979. Claimed by **Chicago** as fill in Expansion Draft, June 13, 1979.

Rod Zaine

ZAINE, RODNEY CARL (Zainer) 5'10", 180 lbs.
B. May 18, 1946, Ottawa, Ont. Center, Shoots L

YEAR	TEAM & LEAGUE		GP	G	A	PTS	PIM
1970-71	**PITT**	**N**	37	8	5	13	21
1971-72	**BUF**	**N**	24	2	1	3	4
1972-73	**CHI**	**W**	74	3	14	17	25
1973-74			78	5	13	18	17
1974-75			68	3	6	9	16
5 yrs.		**N Totals:**	61	10	6	16	25
		W Totals:	220	11	33	44	58
PLAYOFFS							
1973-74	**CHI**	**W**	18	2	1	3	2

Drafted by **Buffalo** from Pittsburgh in Intra-League Draft, June 8, 1971. Drafted by **Atlanta** from Buffalo in Expansion Draft, June 6, 1972.

Joe Zanussi

ZANUSSI, JOSEPH LAWRENCE 5'10", 180 lbs.
B. Sept. 25, 1947, Rossland, B.C. Defense, Shoots R

YEAR	TEAM & LEAGUE		GP	G	A	PTS	PIM
1972-73	**WINN**	**W**	73	4	21	25	53
1973-74			76	3	22	25	53
1974-75	**NYR**	**N**	8	0	2	2	4
1975-76	**BOS**	**N**	60	1	7	8	30
1976-77			8	0	1	1	8
	STL	**N**	11	0	3	3	4
	2 team total		19	0	4	4	12
5 yrs.		**N Totals:**	87	1	13	14	46
		W Totals:	149	7	43	50	106
PLAYOFFS							
1972-73	**WINN**	**W**	14	2	5	7	6
1973-74			4	0	0	0	0
1975-76	**BOS**	**N**	4	0	1	1	2
3 yrs.		**N Totals:**	4	0	1	1	2
		W Totals:	18	2	5	7	6

Traded to **N.Y. Rangers** by Detroit with Detroit's first choice (Albert Blanchard) in the 1972 Amateur Draft for Gary Doak and Rick Newell, May 24, 1972. Traded to **Boston** by N.Y. Rangers with Brad Park and Jean Ratelle for Phil Esposito and Carol Vadnais, Nov. 7, 1975. Traded to **St. Louis** by Boston for Rick Smith, Dec. 20, 1976.

Ron Zanussi

ZANUSSI, RONALD KENNETH 5'11", 180 lbs.
B. Aug. 31, 1956, Toronto, Ont. Right Wing, Shoots R

YEAR	TEAM & LEAGUE		GP	G	A	PTS	PIM
1977-78	MINN	N	68	15	17	32	89
1978-79			63	14	16	30	82
1979-80			72	14	31	45	93
1980-81			41	6	11	17	89
	TOR	N	12	3	0	3	6
	2 team total		53	9	11	20	95
1981-82			43	0	8	8	14
5 yrs.		N Totals:	299	52	83	135	373
PLAYOFFS							
1979-80	MINN	N	14	0	4	4	17
1980-81	TOR	N	3	0	0	0	0
2 yrs.		N Totals:	17	0	4	4	17

Claimed by **Minnesota** as fill in Cleveland-Minnesota Dispersal Draft, June 15, 1978. Traded to **Toronto** by Minnesota, with Minnesota's third round choice (Ernie Godden) in the 1981 Entry Draft for Toronto's second choice (Dave Donnelly) in the 1981 Entry Draft, Mar. 10, 1981.

Larry Zeidel

ZEIDEL, LAZARUS 5'11", 185 lbs.
B. June 1, 1928, Montreal, Que. Defense, Shoots L

YEAR	TEAM & LEAGUE		GP	G	A	PTS	PIM
1951-52	DET	N	19	0	1	1	14
1952-53			9	0	0	0	8
1953-54	CHI	N	64	1	6	7	102
1967-68	PHI	N	57	1	10	11	68
1968-69			9	0	0	0	6
5 yrs.		N Totals:	158	2	17	19	198
PLAYOFFS							
1951-52*	DET	N	5	0	0	0	0
1967-68	PHI	N	7	0	1	1	12
2 yrs.		N Totals:	12	0	1	1	12

Purchased by **Chicago** from Detroit with Lou Jankowski and Larry Wilson, Aug. 12, 1953.

Ed Zeniuk

ZENIUK, EDWARD WILLIAM 5'11", 180 lbs.
B. Mar. 8, 1933, Landis, Sask. Defense, Shoots L

YEAR	TEAM & LEAGUE		GP	G	A	PTS	PIM
1954-55	DET	N	2	0	0	0	0

Lars Zetterstrom

ZETTERSTROM, LARS 6'1", 198 lbs.
B. Nov. 6, 1953, Stockholm, Sweden Defense, Shoots L

YEAR	TEAM & LEAGUE		GP	G	A	PTS	PIM
1978-79	VAN	N	14	0	1	1	2

Signed as free agent by **Vancouver** June 5, 1978. Claimed by **Quebec** from Vancouver in Expansion Draft, June 13, 1979.

Jerry Zrymiak

ZRYMIAK, JERRY 6'1", 195 lbs.
B. Oct. 19, 1948, Regina, Sask. Defense, Shoots R

YEAR	TEAM & LEAGUE		GP	G	A	PTS	PIM
1972-73	LA	W	1	0	0	0	0
1973-74			27	2	8	10	8
1974-75	M-B	W	49	3	9	12	53
1975-76	MINN	W	22	0	8	8	16
	TOR	W	17	0	5	5	11
	2 team total		39	0	13	13	27
1976-77	MINN	W	40	2	10	12	14
5 yrs.		W Totals:	156	7	40	47	102
PLAYOFFS							
1972-73	LA	W	2	1	0	1	2

Wayne Zuk

ZUK, WAYNE DAVID Center, Shoots R

YEAR	TEAM & LEAGUE		GP	G	A	PTS	PIM
1973-74	EDM	W	2	0	0	0	0

Mike Zuke

ZUKE, MICHAEL 6', 180 lbs.
B. Apr. 16, 1954, Sault Ste. Marie, Ont. Center, Shoots R

YEAR	TEAM & LEAGUE		GP	G	A	PTS	PIM
1976-77	IND	W	15	3	4	7	2
1977-78	EDM	W	71	23	34	57	47
1978-79	STL	N	34	9	17	26	18
1979-80			69	22	42	64	30
1980-81			74	24	44	68	57
1981-82			76	13	40	53	41
1982-83			43	8	16	24	14
7 yrs.		N Totals:	296	76	159	235	160
		W Totals:	86	26	38	64	49
PLAYOFFS							
1977-78	EDM	W	5	2	3	5	0
1979-80	STL	N	3	0	0	0	2
1980-81			11	4	5	9	4
1981-82			8	1	1	2	2
1982-83			4	1	0	1	4
5 yrs.		N Totals:	26	6	6	12	12
		W Totals:	5	2	3	5	0

Ruby Zunich

ZUNICH, RALPH
B. Nov. 24, 1910, Calumet, Mich. Defense

YEAR	TEAM & LEAGUE		GP	G	A	PTS	PIM
1943-44	DET	N	2	0	0	0	2

Goaltender Register

The Goaltender Register is an alphabetical listing of every man who has played in goal in the National Hockey League and World Hockey Association. Included are biographical facts about the goalies, complete goaltending records year by year, performance in Stanley Cup and WHA playoffs, and information about any trades or sales in which the goalie may have been involved.

All information or abbreviations that may appear unfamiliar are explained below.

YEAR	TEAM & LEAGUE	GP	MIN	W	L	T	GA	ENG	GAvg.	SO	A	PIM

John Doe

DOE, JOHN LEE (Shakes)
B. Apr 23, 1944, Sault Ste. Marie, Ont.
Won Calder Trophy 1969-70
Won Vezina Trophy 1969-70, 1971-72, 1973-74

5′11″, 185 lbs.
Shoots R

YEAR	TEAM & LEAGUE	GP	MIN	W	L	T	GA	ENG	GAvg.	SO	A	PIM
1968-69	**MONT N**	13	746	6	3	2	34	3	2.73	3	0	0
1969-70	**CHI N**	63	3763	31	23	8	136	4	2.17	**15**[1]	2	2
1970-71		57	3325	30	17	10	126	10	2.27	6	1	0
1971-72		48	2780	26	22	0	82	2	**1.76**	9	1	4
1972-73		56	3340	30	22	4	140	5	2.51	4	2	0
1973-74		70	4143	40	20	10	141	7	2.04	10	1	6
1974-75		71	4219	36	34	1	193	8	2.74	6	1	0
1975-76		68	4003	37	26	5	198	7	2.97	4	1	0
1976-77		69	4067	35	24	10	234	11	3.45	2	2	4
1977-78		64	3840	27	26	11	168	4	2.63	5	4	0
1978-79		63	3780	33	26	4	206	5	3.27	4	1	2
1979-80		69	4140	25	33	1	205	8	2.97	**6**	1	8
1980-81		66	3935	33	23	10	246	2	3.75	0	3	6
	DET N	10	600	4	2	4	30	2	3.00	1	2	0
	2 Team Total	76	4535	37	25	14	276	4	3.65	1	5	6
13 yrs.	**NHL:**	829	49150	411	324	76	2340	82	2.86	74	21	32

PLAYOFFS

YEAR	TEAM & LEAGUE	GP	MIN	W	L	T	GA	ENG	GAvg.	SO	A	PIM
1969-70	**CHI NHL**	8	480	4	4	0	27	2	3.37	0	0	0
1970-71		18	1151	11	7	0	42	1	2.19	2	0	0
1971-72		5	300	1	4	0	16	3	3.20	0	0	0
1972-73		15	895	8	7	0	46	4	3.08	1	0	0
1973-74		10	584	4	6	0	28	2	2.88	2	0	0
1974-75		8	472	3	5	0	34	3	4.32	0	0	0
1975-76*		4	240	0	4	0	13	2	3.25	0	0	0
1976-77		2	120	0	2	0	6	2	3.00	0	0	0
1977-78		4	252	0	4	0	19	3	4.52	0	0	0
1978-79		5	243	1	4	0	14	2	3.46	0	0	0
1979-80		6	373	2	4	0	14	3	2.25	0	0	0
1980-81		3	215	0	3	0	15	2	4.19	0	0	0
1981-82		7	381	3	4	0	16	2	2.52	1	0	0
13 yrs.	**NHL:**	97	5706	37	58	0	290	31	3.50	6	0	0

Drafted by **Chicago** from Montreal in Intra-League Draft, June 11, 1969.

John Doe — This shortened version of the goaltender's name is the name by which he is best known. All the goaltenders in this section are arranged in alphabetical order by the last name portion of this name.

DOE, JOHN LEE — The goaltender's full name.

(Shakes) — The goaltender's nickname. Any name or names in parentheses are nicknames.

B. Apr 23, 1944, Sault Ste. Marie, Ont.	Date and place of birth.
Won Vezina Trophy, etc.	The major trophies awarded by the league that have been won by Doe. This is also where a goal scored by a goaltender will be listed. (For a complete listing of the winners of all awards, see the Awards and Achievements section.)
5′11″, 185 lbs.	The goaltender's height and average playing weight.
Shoots L	The goaltender's main stick-holding style.

Column Headings Information

GP	Games Played	ENG	Empty Net Goals
MIN	Minutes	GAvg.	Goals Against Average
W	Wins	SO	Shutouts
L	Losses	A	Assists
T	Ties	PIM	Penalties in Minutes
GA	Goals Allowed		

The following are the team abbreviations used in this section. For a more detailed listing of the teams involved, including team nicknames, please see the introduction to the Teams and their Players section.

ALTA	Alberta	MON (W)	Montreal (Wanderers)
ATL	Atlanta	MONT	Montreal (Canadiens)
BIRM	Birmingham	NE	New England
BOS	Boston	NJ	New Jersey
BUF	Buffalo	NY	New York (Raiders)
CALG	Calgary	NYA	New York (Americans)
CALIF	California	NYI	New York (Islanders)
CHI	Chicago	NYR	New York (Rangers)
CIN	Cincinnati	OAK	Oakland
CLEVE	Cleveland	OTTA	Ottawa
COLO	Colorado	PHI	Philadelphia
DET	Detroit	PHOE	Phoenix
EDM	Edmonton	PITT	Pittsburgh
HAMIL	Hamilton	QUE	Quebec
HART	Hartford	SD	San Diego
HOUS	Houston	STL	St. Louis
IND	Indianapolis	TOR	Toronto
KC	Kansas City	VAN	Vancouver
LA	Los Angeles	WASH	Washington
MINN	Minnesota	WINN	Winnipeg
MON (M)	Montreal (Maroons)		

In addition, there were three teams in the WHA that moved during the course of the season. These clubs are abbreviated as follows:

D-O Denver-Ottawa
M-B Michigan-Baltimore
NY-NJ New York-New Jersey

Blank space appearing beneath a team and league indicates that a goaltender remained with the same club. Doe played with Chicago in the NHL from 1969–70 through 1980–81.

Won-Lost-Tied Records. If a team employs more than one goaltender during a game, the goaltender of record is the one who was in the nets when the game-winning or game-tying goal was scored.

Empty Net Goals. Goals scored after a goaltender has been removed to permit an extra offensive skater to enter the game are recorded in the records of each goaltender. These goals are not, however, included in the calculation of goals against average.

Goals against Average. From 1917–18 through 1966–67, the NHL's official goals against averages were determined by dividing goals allowed by games played. From 1967–68 on, the averages were calculated on the basis of goals allowed (excluding empty net goals) per 60 minutes played. We have used this latter method to recalculate goals against averages for all years since the elimination of regular-season overtime in 1942–43. It is our belief that this method better reflects the performance of goaltenders who played in parts of a game.

Two Team Total. Doe played with two teams in 1980–81. In addition to his record with each team, his combined total for the two teams is listed.

Total Playing Years. This information, which appears as the first item in the goaltender's lifetime total, indicates the total number of years in which he played in goal for at least one game. NHL and WHA years are combined for this total.

League Totals. Separate totals are given for each goaltender's career totals in the NHL and WHA.

League Leaders. Statistics that appear in boldface print indicate that the goaltender led his league in that category for the season. Doe, for example, led the NHL in Goals against Average in 1971–72.

All-Time Single Season Leaders. These are indicated by a small superscript "1" next to the player's statistic. Doe set an all-time record for shutouts in 1969–70.

Trade Information. The text appearing below a goaltender's record indicates any NHL player transactions (drafts, trades, sales, free agent signings) he has been involved in. The team to which the player moves in a given transaction is listed in boldface. Trade information is listed back to the 1949–50 season. Research is continuing to fill in the gaps in our information.

Playoff Records. Complete information is given for every year in which the goaltender participated in the Stanley Cup or WHA playoffs.

Cup Championships. An asterisk (*) appearing beside a given year indicates that the goaltender's team won the Stanley Cup in that year. There is no similar designation for WHA championships. In the example above, Doe's team won the Stanley Cup in 1975–76.

George Abbott

ABBOTT, GEORGE
B. Unknown

YEAR	TEAM	LEAGUE	GP	MIN	W	L	T	GA	ENG	G AVG	SO	A	PIM
1943-44	**BOS**	**N**	1	60	0	1	0	7	0	7.00	0	0	0

Christer Abrahamsson

ABRAHAMSSON, CHRISTER
B. Apr. 12, 1947, Leksand, Sweden
6'2", 180 lbs. Shoots L

YEAR	TEAM	LEAGUE	GP	MIN	W	L	T	GA	ENG	G AVG	SO	A	PIM
1974-75	**NE**	**W**	15	870	8	6	1	47	0	3.24	1	0	0
1975-76			41	2385	18	18	2	136	0	3.42	2	1	6
1976-77			45	2484	15	22	4	159	0	3.84	0	0	0
3 yrs.		**W Totals:**	101	5739	41	46	7	342	0	3.58	3	1	6
PLAYOFFS													
1975-76	**NE**	**W**	1	1	0	0	0	0	0	0.00	0	0	0
1976-77			2	90	0	1	0	5	0	3.33	0	0	0
2 yrs.		**W Totals:**	3	91	0	1	0	5	0	3.30	0	0	0

John Adams

ADAMS, JOHN MATTHEW
B. July 27, 1946, Port Arthur, Ont.
6', 200 lbs. Shoots L

YEAR	TEAM	LEAGUE	GP	MIN	W	L	T	GA	ENG	G AVG	SO	A	PIM
1972-73	**BOS**	**N**	14	780	9	3	1	39	0	3.00	1	0	0
1974-75	**WASH**	**N**	8	400	0	7	0	46	0	6.90	0	0	2
2 yrs.		**N Totals:**	22	1180	9	10	1	85	0	4.32	1	0	2

Don Aiken

AIKEN, DONALD
B. Jan. 1, 1932, Arlington, Mass.

YEAR	TEAM	LEAGUE	GP	MIN	W	L	T	GA	ENG	G AVG	SO	A	PIM
1957-58	**MONT**	**N**	1	34	0	1	0	6	0	10.59	0	0	0

Andy Aitkenhead

AITKENHEAD, ANDY
B. Mar. 6, 1904, Glasgow, Scotland
145 lbs. Shoots L

YEAR	TEAM	LEAGUE	GP	MIN	W	L	T	GA	ENG	G AVG	SO	A	PIM
1932-33	**NYR**	**N**	48	2970	23	17	8	107	0	2.23	3	0	0
1933-34			48	2990	21	19	8	113	0	2.35	7	0	0
1934-35			10	610	3	7	0	37	0	3.70	1	0	0
3 yrs.		**N Totals:**	106	6570	47	43	16	257	0	2.35	11	0	0
PLAYOFFS													
1932-33*	**NYR**	**N**	8	488	**6**	1	1	13	0	**1.63**	**2**	0	0
1933-34			2	120	0	2	0	2	0	1.00	1	0	0
2 yrs.		**N Totals:**	10	608	6	3	1	15	0	1.48	3	0	0

Red Almas

ALMAS, RALPH CLAYTON
B. Apr. 26, 1924, Saskatoon, Sask.
5'9", 160 lbs. Shoots R

YEAR	TEAM	LEAGUE	GP	MIN	W	L	T	GA	ENG	G AVG	SO	A	PIM
1946-47	**DET**	**N**	1	60	0	1	0	5	0	5.00	0	0	0
1950-51	**CHI**	**N**	1	60	0	1	0	5	0	5.00	0	0	0
1952-53	**DET**	**N**	1	60	0	0	1	3	0	3.00	0	0	0
3 yrs.		**N Totals:**	3	180	0	2	1	13	0	4.33	0	0	0
PLAYOFFS													
1946-47	**DET**	**N**	5	263	1	3	0	13	0	2.97	0	0	0

Sold to **Detroit** by Chicago with Guy Fielder and Steve Hrymnak, Sept. 23, 1952.

Lorne Anderson

ANDERSON, LORNE
B. July 26, 1931, Renfrew, Ont.
5'11", 166 lbs. Shoots L

YEAR	TEAM	LEAGUE	GP	MIN	W	L	T	GA	ENG	G AVG	SO	A	PIM
1951-52	**NYR**	**N**	3	180	1	2	0	18	0	6.00	0	0	0

Yves Archambault

ARCHAMBAULT, YVES
B. June 22, 1952
6', 170 lbs. Shoots L

YEAR	TEAM	LEAGUE	GP	MIN	W	L	T	GA	ENG	G AVG	SO	A	PIM
1972-73	**PHI**	**W**	6	260	1	3	0	17	0	3.92	0	1	0
1973-74	**VAN**	**W**	5	263	1	4	0	27	0	6.16	0	0	0
2 yrs.		**W Totals:**	11	523	2	7	0	44	0	5.05	0	1	0
PLAYOFFS													
1972-73	**PHI**	**W**	3	153	0	2	0	11	0	4.31	0	0	0

Hardy Astrom

ASTROM, HARDY
B. Mar. 29, 1951, Skelleftea, Sweden
6', 170 lbs. Shoots L

YEAR	TEAM	LEAGUE	GP	MIN	W	L	T	GA	ENG	G AVG	SO	A	PIM
1977-78	**NYR**	**N**	4	240	2	2	0	14	0	3.50	0	0	0
1979-80	**COLO**	**N**	49	2574	9	27	6	161	3	3.75	0	0	6
1980-81			30	1642	6	15	6	103	3	3.76	0	1	2
3 yrs.		**N Totals:**	83	4456	17	44	12	278	6	3.74	0	1	8

Rights traded to **Colorado** by N.Y. Rangers for Bill Lochead, July 2, 1979.

Serge Aubry

AUBRY, SERGE
B. Jan. 2, 1942
5'9", 160 lbs. Shoots L

YEAR	TEAM	LEAGUE	GP	MIN	W	L	T	GA	ENG	G AVG	SO	A	PIM
1972-73	**QUE**	**W**	52	3036	25	22	2	182	0	3.60	2	0	**54**
1973-74			26	1395	11	11	2	90	0	3.87	1	1	8
1974-75			31	1762	17	11	0	109	0	3.71	0	1	22
1975-76	**CIN**	**W**	12	549	6	4	0	38	0	4.15	1	1	4
1976-77	**QUE**	**W**	21	769	6	5	0	51	0	3.98	1	1	0
5 yrs.		**W Totals:**	142	7511	65	53	4	470	0	3.75	5	4	88

Serge Aubry continued

YEAR	TEAM & LEAGUE		GP	MIN	W	L	T	GA	ENG	G AVG	SO	A	PIM
PLAYOFFS													
1976-77	**QUE**	**W**	3	18	0	0	0	1	0	3.33	0	0	0

Steve Baker

BAKER, STEVEN
B. May 6, 1957, Boston, Mass.
6'3", 200 lbs.
Shoots L

YEAR	TEAM & LEAGUE		GP	MIN	W	L	T	GA	ENG	G AVG	SO	A	PIM
1979-80	**NYR**	**N**	27	1391	9	8	6	79	1	3.41	1	0	2
1980-81			21	1260	10	6	5	73	2	3.48	2	0	5
1981-82			6	328	1	5	0	33	0	6.04	0	0	0
1982-83			3	102	0	1	0	5	2	2.94	0	0	0
4 yrs.		**N Totals:**	57	3081	20	20	11	190	5	3.70	3	0	7
PLAYOFFS													
1980-81	**NYR**	**N**	14	826	7	7	0	55	0	4.00	0	0	4

Murray Bannerman

BANNERMAN, MURRAY
B. Apr. 27, 1957, Fort Francis, Ont.
5'11", 184 lbs.
Shoots L

YEAR	TEAM & LEAGUE		GP	MIN	W	L	T	GA	ENG	G AVG	SO	A	PIM
1977-78	**VAN**	**N**	1	20	0	0	0	0	0	.00	0	0	0
1980-81	**CHI**	**N**	15	865	2	10	2	62	2	4.30	0	0	0
1981-82			29	1671	11	12	4	116	2	4.17	1	1	0
1982-83			41	2460	24	12	5	127	2	3.10	4	0	0
4 yrs.		**N Totals:**	86	5016	37	34	11	305	6	3.65	5	1	0
PLAYOFFS													
1981-82	**CHI**	**N**	10	555	5	4	0	35	0	3.78	0	1	4
1982-83			8	480	4	4	0	32	1	4.00	0	1	0
2 yrs.		**N Totals:**	18	1035	9	8	0	67	1	3.88	0	2	4

Traded to **Chicago** by Vancouver, May 27, 1978 to complete an earlier deal when Vancouver received Pit Martin, Nov. 4, 1977.

Marco Baron

BARON, JOSEPH MARCO
B. Apr. 8, 1959, Montreal, Que.
5'11", 179 lbs.
Shoots L

YEAR	TEAM & LEAGUE		GP	MIN	W	L	T	GA	ENG	G AVG	SO	A	PIM
1979-80	**BOS**	**N**	1	40	0	0	0	2	0	3.00	0	0	0
1980-81			10	507	3	4	1	24	1	2.84	0	0	7
1981-82			44	2515	22	16	4	144	3	3.44	1	2	35
1982-83			9	516	6	3	0	33	1	3.84	0	0	4
4 yrs.		**N Totals:**	64	3578	31	23	5	203	5	3.40	1	2	46
PLAYOFFS													
1980-81	**BOS**	**N**	1	20	0	1	0	3	0	9.00	0	0	0

Hank Bassen

BASSEN, HENRY (Red)
B. Dec. 6, 1932, Calgary, Alta.
5'10", 170 lbs.
Shoots L

YEAR	TEAM & LEAGUE		GP	MIN	W	L	T	GA	ENG	G AVG	SO	A	PIM
1954-55	**CHI**	**N**	21	1260	4	9	8	63	0	3.00	0	0	0
1955-56			12	720	3	8	1	42	0	3.50	1	0	2
1960-61	**DET**	**N**	35	2120	13	13	8	102	0	2.89	0	1	6
1961-62			27	1620	9	12	6	76	0	2.81	3	0	8
1962-63			17	980	6	5	5	53	0	3.24	0	1	14
1963-64			1	60	0	1	0	4	0	4.00	0	0	0
1965-66			11	406	3	4	0	17	1	2.51	0	0	0
1966-67			8	384	2	4	0	22	0	3.44	1	0	0
1967-68	**PITT**	**N**	25	1299	7	10	3	62	2	2.86	1	0	8
9 yrs.		**N Totals:**	157	8849	47	66	31	441	3	2.99	6	2	38
PLAYOFFS													
1960-61	**DET**	**N**	4	220	1	3	0	9	0	2.45	0	0	0
1965-66			1	54	0	1	0	2	0	2.22	0	0	0
2 yrs.		**N Totals:**	5	274	1	4	0	11	0	2.41	0	0	0

Traded to **Detroit** by Chicago with John Wilson, Forbes Kennedy and William Preston for Ted Lindsay and Glenn Hall, July, 1957. Traded to **Pittsburgh** by Detroit for Roy Edwards, Sept. 7, 1967.

Baz Bastien

BASTIEN, ALDEGE
B. Aug. 29, 1920, Timmins, Ont.
5'7", 160 lbs.
Shoots L

YEAR	TEAM & LEAGUE		GP	MIN	W	L	T	GA	ENG	G AVG	SO	A	PIM
1945-46	**TOR**	**N**	5	300	0	4	1	20	0	4.00	0	0	0

Gary Bauman

BAUMAN, GARY GLENWOOD
B. July 21, 1940, Innisfail, Alta.
5'11", 175 lbs.
Shoots L

YEAR	TEAM & LEAGUE		GP	MIN	W	L	T	GA	ENG	G AVG	SO	A	PIM
1966-67	**MONT**	**N**	2	120	1	1	0	5	0	2.50	0	0	0
1967-68	**MINN**	**N**	26	1294	5	13	5	75	0	3.48	0	0	2
1968-69			7	304	0	4	1	22	0	4.34	0	0	2
3 yrs.		**N Totals:**	35	1718	6	18	6	102	0	3.56	0	0	4

Drafted by **Minnesota** from Mont. Canadiens in Expansion Draft, June 6, 1967.

Don Beaupre

BEAUPRE, DONALD WILLIAM
B. Sept. 19, 1961, Waterloo, Ont.
5'8", 150 lbs.
Shoots L

YEAR	TEAM & LEAGUE		GP	MIN	W	L	T	GA	ENG	G AVG	SO	A	PIM
1980-81	**MINN**	**N**	44	2585	18	14	11	138	4	3.20	0	1	20
1981-82			29	1634	11	8	9	101	3	3.71	0	0	19

Don Beaupre continued

YEAR	TEAM & LEAGUE	GP	MIN	W	L	T	GA	ENG	G AVG	SO	A	PIM
1982-83		36	2011	19	10	5	120	2	3.58	0	2	10
3 yrs.	**N Totals:**	109	6230	48	32	25	359	9	3.46	0	3	49
PLAYOFFS												
1980-81	**MINN N**	6	360	4	2	0	26	0	4.33	0	0	0
1981-82		2	60	0	1	0	4	1	4.00	0	0	2
1982-83		4	245	2	2	0	20	1	4.90	0	0	2
3 yrs.	**N Totals:**	12	665	6	5	0	50	2	4.51	0	0	4

Jim Bedard

BEDARD, JAMES ARTHUR 5'10", 181 lbs.
B. Nov. 14, 1956, Niagara Falls, Ont. Shoots L

YEAR	TEAM & LEAGUE	GP	MIN	W	L	T	GA	ENG	G AVG	SO	A	PIM
1977-78	**WASH N**	43	2492	11	23	7	152	4	3.66	1	2	4
1978-79		30	1740	6	17	6	126	1	4.34	0	0	6
2 yrs.	**N Totals:**	73	4232	17	40	13	278	5	3.94	1	2	10

Yves Belanger

BELANGER, YVES 5'11", 170 lbs.
B. Sept. 30, 1952, Comeau, Que. Shoots L

YEAR	TEAM & LEAGUE	GP	MIN	W	L	T	GA	ENG	G AVG	SO	A	PIM
1974-75	**STL N**	11	640	6	3	2	29	0	2.72	1	1	0
1975-76		31	1763	11	17	1	113	2	3.85	0	2	4
1976-77		3	140	0	3	0	7	0	3.00	0	0	0
1977-78		3	144	0	3	0	15	0	6.25	0	1	0
	ATL N	17	937	7	8	0	55	1	3.52	1	1	0
	2 team total	20	1081	7	11	0	70	1	3.89	1	2	0
1978-79		5	182	1	2	0	21	0	6.92	0	0	0
1979-80	**BOS N**	8	328	2	0	3	19	0	3.48	0	0	0
6 yrs.	**N Totals:**	78	4134	27	36	6	259	3	3.76	2	5	4

Traded to **Atlanta** by St. Louis with Bob MacMillan, Dick Redmond and St. Louis' second round choice (Mike Perovich) in the 1979 Entry Draft for Phil Myre, Curt Bennett, and Barry Gibbs, Dec. 12, 1977. Signed as a free agent by **Boston** , Oct. 8, 1979.

Michel Belhumeur

BELHUMEUR, MICHEL 5'10", 160 lbs.
B. Sept. 2, 1949, Sorel, Que. Shoots L

YEAR	TEAM & LEAGUE	GP	MIN	W	L	T	GA	ENG	G AVG	SO	A	PIM
1972-73	**PHI N**	23	1117	9	7	3	60	1	3.22	0	1	2
1974-75	**WASH N**	35	1812	0	24	3	162	1	5.36	0	2	10
1975-76		7	377	0	5	1	32	0	5.09	0	1	0
3 yrs.	**N Totals:**	65	3306	9	36	7	254	2	4.61	0	4	12
PLAYOFFS												
1972-73	**PHI N**	1	10	0	0	0	1	0	6.00	0	0	0

Gordie Bell

BELL, GORDON 5'10", 164 lbs.
B. Mar. 13, 1925, Portage La Prairie, Man. Shoots L

YEAR	TEAM & LEAGUE	GP	MIN	W	L	T	GA	ENG	G AVG	SO	A	PIM
1945-46	**TOR N**	8	480	3	5	0	31	0	3.88	0	0	0
PLAYOFFS												
1955-56	**NYR N**	2	120	1	1	0	9	0	4.50	0	0	0

Clint Benedict

BENEDICT, CLINTON STEPHEN
B. Ottawa, Ont.
Hall of Fame, 1965

YEAR	TEAM & LEAGUE	GP	MIN	W	L	T	GA	ENG	G AVG	SO	A	PIM
1917-18	**OTTA N**	22	**1337**	9	**13**	0	114	0	5.18	**1**	0	0
1918-19		18	**1113**	**12**	6	0	53	0	**2.94**	**2**	0	3
1919-20		24	1443	**19**	5	0	64	0	**2.67**	**5**	0	2
1920-21		24	**1457**	**13**	11	0	75	0	**3.13**	**2**	0	0
1921-22		24	**1508**	**14**	8	2	84	0	**3.50**	**2**	0	0
1922-23		24	1486	**14**	9	1	54	0	**2.25**	**4**	0	2
1923-24		22	1356	**16**	6	0	45	0	2.05	**3**	0	0
1924-25	**MON(M) N**	30	1843	9	**19**	2	65	0	2.17	2	0	2
1925-26		36	2288	20	11	5	73	0	2.03	6	0	0
1926-27		43	2748	20	19	4	65	0	**1.51**	13	0	0
1927-28		44	2690	24	14	6	76	0	1.73	6	0	0
1928-29		37	2300	14	16	7	57	0	1.54	11	0	0
1929-30		14	752	6	6	1	38	0	2.71	0	0	0
13 yrs.	**N Totals:**	362	22321	190	143	28	863	0	2.32	57	0	9
PLAYOFFS												
1918-19	**OTTA N**	5	300	1	4	0	26	0	5.20	0	0	0
1919-20*		5	**300**	**3**	2	0	11	0	**2.20**	**1**	0	0
1920-21*		7	**420**	**5**	2	0	12	0	**1.71**	**2**	0	0
1921-22		2	120	0	1	0	5	0	2.50	1	0	0
1922-23*		8	**480**	**6**	2	0	10	0	**1.25**	**3**	0	0
1923-24		2	120	0	2	0	5	0	2.50	0	0	0
1925-26*	**MON(M) N**	8	**480**	**5**	1	2	8	0	**1.00**	**4**	0	0
1926-27		2	132	0	1	1	2	0	1.00	0	0	0
1927-28		9	**555**	**5**	3	1	8	0	**0.89**	**4**	0	0
9 yrs.	**N Totals:**	48	2907	25	18	4	87	0	1.80	15	0	0

Harvey Bennett

BENNETT, HARVEY A. 6', 175 lbs. Shoots L

YEAR	TEAM & LEAGUE		GP	MIN	W	L	T	GA	ENG	G AVG	SO	A	PIM
1944-45	BOS	N	24	1470	10	12	2	106	0	4.33	0	0	0

Bill Berglund

BERGLUND, WILLIAM ARTHUR 6'1", 187 lbs.
B. Sept. 24, 1948, Everett, Mass.

YEAR	TEAM & LEAGUE		GP	MIN	W	L	T	GA	ENG	G AVG	SO	A	PIM
1973-74	NE	W	3	180	2	1	0	10	0	3.33	0	0	0
1974-75			2	36	0	0	0	3	0	5.00	0	0	0
2 yrs.		W Totals:	5	216	2	1	0	13	0	3.61	0	0	0

Tim Bernhardt

BERNHARDT, TIMOTHY 5'9", 159 lbs. Shoots L
B. Jan. 17, 1958, Sarnia, Ont.

YEAR	TEAM & LEAGUE		GP	MIN	W	L	T	GA	ENG	G AVG	SO	A	PIM
1982-83	CALG	N	6	280	0	5	0	21	0	4.50	0	0	0

Bill Beveridge

BEVERIDGE, WILLIAM S. 5'8", 170 lbs. Shoots L
B. July 1, 1909, Ottawa, Ont.

YEAR	TEAM & LEAGUE		GP	MIN	W	L	T	GA	ENG	G AVG	SO	A	PIM
1929-30	DET	N	39	2410	14	20	5	109	0	2.79	2	0	0
1930-31	OTTA	N	9	520	0	8	0	32	0	3.56	0	0	0
1932-33			35	2195	7	19	8	95	0	2.71	5	0	0
1933-34			48	3000	13	**29**	6	143	0	2.98	3	0	0
1934-35	STL	N	48	**2990**	11	**31**	6	144	0	3.00	3	0	0
1935-36	MON(M)	N	32	1970	14	13	5	71	0	2.22	1	0	0
1936-37			21	1290	12	6	3	47	0	2.24	1	0	0
1937-38			48	2980	12	**30**	6	149	0	3.10	2	0	0
1942-43	NYR	N	17	1020	4	10	3	89	0	5.24	1	0	0
9 yrs.		N Totals:	297	18375	87	166	42	879	0	2.87	18	0	0
PLAYOFFS													
1936-37	MON(M)	N	5	300	2	3	0	11	0	2.20	0	0	0

Paul Bibeault

BIBEAULT, PAUL 5'9", 160 lbs. Shoots L
B. Apr. 13, 1919, Montreal, Que.

YEAR	TEAM & LEAGUE		GP	MIN	W	L	T	GA	ENG	G AVG	SO	A	PIM
1940-41	MONT	N	4	210	1	2	0	15	0	3.75	0	0	0
1941-42			38	2380	17	19	1	131	0	3.45	1	0	0
1942-43			50	3010	19	**19**	12	191	0	3.81	1	0	0
1943-44	TOR	N	29	1740	13	14	2	87	0	3.00	**5**	0	0
1944-45	BOS	N	26	1530	6	18	2	113	0	4.43	0	0	0
1945-46			16	960	8	4	4	45	0	2.81	2	0	0
	MONT	N	10	600	4	6	0	30	0	3.00	0	0	0
	2 team total		26	1560	12	10	4	75	0	2.88	2	0	0
1946-47	CHI	N	41	2460	0	0	0	170	0	4.15	1	0	2
7 yrs.		N Totals:	214	12890	68	82	21	782	0	3.64	10	0	2
PLAYOFFS													
1941-42	MONT	N	3	180	1	2	0	8	0	2.67	**1**	0	0
1942-43			5	320	1	4	0	18	0	3.38	1	0	0
1943-44	TOR	N	5	300	1	4	0	23	0	4.60	0	0	0
1944-45	BOS	N	7	437	3	4	0	22	0	3.02	0	0	0
4 yrs.		N Totals:	20	1237	6	14	0	71	0	3.44	2	0	0

Andre Binette

BINETTE, ANDRE 5'7", 165 lbs. Shoots L
B. Dec. 2, 1933, Montreal, Que

YEAR	TEAM & LEAGUE		GP	MIN	W	L	T	GA	ENG	G AVG	SO	A	PIM
1954-55	MONT	N	1	60	1	0	0	4	0	4.00	0	0	0

Les Binkley

BINKLEY, LESLIE JOHN 6', 175 lbs. Shoots R
B. June 6, 1936, Owen Sound, Ont.

YEAR	TEAM & LEAGUE		GP	MIN	W	L	T	GA	ENG	G AVG	SO	A	PIM
1967-68	PITT	N	54	3141	20	24	10	151	1	2.88	6	0	0
1968-69			50	2885	10	31	8	158	0	3.29	0	0	0
1969-70			27	1477	10	13	1	79	0	3.21	3	1	0
1970-71			34	1870	11	11	10	89	0	2.86	2	0	0
1971-72			31	1673	7	15	5	98	4	3.51	0	0	2
1972-73	OTTA	W	30	1709	10	17	1	106	1	3.72	0	0	0
1973-74	TOR	W	27	1412	14	9	1	77	0	3.27	1	0	0
1974-75			17	772	6	4	0	46	0	3.58	0	0	0
1975-76			7	335	0	6	0	32	0	5.73	0	0	0
9 yrs.		N Totals:	196	11046	58	94	34	575	5	3.12	11	1	2
		W Totals:	81	4228	30	36	2	261	1	3.70	1	0	0
PLAYOFFS													
1969-70	PITT	N	7	428	5	2	0	15	0	2.10	0	0	0
1972-73	OTTA	W	4	223	1	3	0	17	0	4.57	0	0	0
1973-74	TOR	W	5	182	2	2	0	18	0	5.93	0	0	0
1974-75			1	59	0	1	0	5	0	5.08	0	0	0
4 yrs.		N Totals:	7	428	5	2	0	15	0	2.10	0	0	0
		W Totals:	10	464	3	6	0	40	0	5.17	0	0	0

Richard Bittner

BITTNER, RICHARD J. — 6', 170 lbs.
B. Jan. 12, 1922, New Haven, Conn.

YEAR	TEAM & LEAGUE		GP	MIN	W	L	T	GA	ENG	G AVG	SO	A	PIM
1949-50	BOS	N	1	60	0	0	1	3	0	3.00	0	0	0

Mike Blake

BLAKE, MIKE — 6', 185 lbs.
B. Apr. 6, 1956, Kitchener, Ont.

YEAR	TEAM & LEAGUE		GP	MIN	W	L	T	GA	ENG	G AVG	SO	A	PIM
1981-82	LA	N	2	51	0	0	0	2	0	2.35	0	0	0
1982-83			9	432	4	4	0	30	1	4.17	0	0	2
2 yrs.		N Totals:	11	483	4	4	0	32	1	3.98	0	0	2

Bob Blanchet

BLANCHET, ROBERT — 5'8", 175 lbs.
B. Feb. 24, 1954, Authier-Nord, Que. — Shoots L

YEAR	TEAM & LEAGUE		GP	MIN	W	L	T	GA	ENG	G AVG	SO	A	PIM
1974-75	SD	W	3	179	2	1	0	7	0	2.35	1	0	0
1975-76			1	32	0	1	0	4	0	7.50	0	0	0
2 yrs.		W Totals:	4	211	2	2	0	11	0	3.13	1	0	0

Frank Blum

BLUM, FRANK — 6', 180 lbs.
B. June 29, 1952 — Shoots R

YEAR	TEAM & LEAGUE		GP	MIN	W	L	T	GA	ENG	G AVG	SO	A	PIM
1972-73	OTTA	W	2	28	0	0	0	3	0	6.43	0	0	0
1973-74	TOR	W	5	130	1	0	0	5	0	2.31	0	0	0
2 yrs.		W Totals:	7	158	1	0	0	8	0	3.04	0	0	0
PLAYOFFS													
1973-74	WINN	W	2	120	0	2	0	15	0	7.50	0	0	0

Gilles Boisvert

BOISVERT, GILLES — 5'8", 152 lbs.
B. Feb. 15, 1933, Trois-Rivieres, Que. — Shoots L

YEAR	TEAM & LEAGUE		GP	MIN	W	L	T	GA	ENG	G AVG	SO	A	PIM
1959-60	DET	N	3	180	0	3	0	9	0	3.00	0	0	0

Traded to **Detroit** by Boston with Ed Sandford, Real Chevrefils, Norm Corcoran and Warren Godfrey for Marcel Bonin, Terry Sawchuk, Vic Stasiuk and Lorne Davis, June 3, 1955.

Dan Bouchard

BOUCHARD, DANIEL HECTOR — 6', 175 lbs.
B. Dec. 12, 1950, Val D'Or, Que. — Shoots L

YEAR	TEAM & LEAGUE		GP	MIN	W	L	T	GA	ENG	G AVG	SO	A	PIM
1972-73	ATL	N	34	1944	9	15	10	100	0	3.09	2	1	12
1973-74			46	2660	18	18	8	123	3	2.77	5	0	10
1974-75			40	2400	20	15	5	111	6	2.78	3	0	**42**
1975-76			47	2671	19	17	8	113	2	2.54	2	1	10
1976-77			42	2378	17	17	5	139	2	3.51	1	1	9
1977-78			58	3340	25	12	19	153	0	2.75	2	3	6
1978-79			64	3624	**32**	21	7	201	2	3.33	3	3	17
1979-80			53	3076	23	19	10	163	5	3.18	2	1	34
1980-81	CALG	N	14	760	4	5	3	51	0	4.03	0	4	6
	QUE	N	29	1740	19	5	5	92	4	3.17	2	0	4
	2 team total		43	2500	23	10	8	143	4	3.43	2	4	10
1981-82			60	3572	27	22	11	230	2	3.86	1	3	**36**
1982-83			50	2947	20	21	8	197	1	4.01	1	4	8
11 yrs.		N Totals:	537	31112	233	187	99	1673	27	3.23	24	21	194
PLAYOFFS													
1973-74	ATL	N	1	60	0	1	0	4	0	4.00	0	0	0
1975-76			2	120	0	2	0	3	0	1.50	0	0	0
1976-77			1	60	0	1	0	5	0	5.00	0	0	0
1977-78			2	120	0	2	0	7	1	3.50	0	0	0
1978-79			2	100	0	2	0	9	0	5.40	0	0	4
1979-80			4	241	1	3	0	14	0	3.49	0	0	2
1980-81	QUE	N	5	286	2	3	0	19	1	3.99	**1**	0	14
1981-82			11	677	4	7	0	38	1	3.37	0	0	4
1982-83			4	242	1	3	0	11	0	2.73	0	1	**14**
9 yrs.		N Totals:	32	1906	8	24	0	110	3	3.46	1	1	38

Drafted by **Atlanta** from Boston in Expansion Draft, June 6, 1972. Traded to **Quebec** by Calgary for Jamie Hislop, Jan. 30, 1981.

Claude Bourque

BOURQUE, CLAUDE HENNESSY — 5'6", 140 lbs.
B. Mar. 31, 1915, Oxford, N.S.

YEAR	TEAM & LEAGUE		GP	MIN	W	L	T	GA	ENG	G AVG	SO	A	PIM
1938-39	MONT	N	25	1560	7	13	5	69	0	2.76	2	0	0
1939-40			36	2210	9	24	3	120	0	3.33	3	0	0
	DET	N	1	60	0	1	0	3	0	3.00	0	0	0
	2 team total		37	2270	9	25	3	123	0	3.25	3	0	0
2 yrs.		N Totals:	62	3830	16	38	8	192	0	3.01	5	0	0
PLAYOFFS													
1938-39	MONT	N	3	188	1	2	0	8	0	2.55	1	0	0

Rollie Boutin

BOUTIN, ROLAND — 5'9", 179 lbs.
B. Nov. 6, 1957, Westlock, Alta. — Shoots L

YEAR	TEAM & LEAGUE		GP	MIN	W	L	T	GA	ENG	G AVG	SO	A	PIM
1978-79	WASH	N	2	90	0	1	0	10	1	6.67	0	0	0
1979-80			18	927	7	7	1	54	0	3.50	0	1	6
1980-81			2	120	0	2	0	11	1	5.50	0	0	0
3 yrs.		N Totals:	22	1137	7	10	1	75	2	3.96	0	1	6

Rollie Boutin continued

Traded to **Minnesota** by Washington with Wes Jarvis for Robbie Moore, August 5, 1982.

Lionel Bouvrette

BOUVRETTE, LIONEL
B. June 10, 1914, Hawksbury, Ont.

5'9", 165 lbs.
Shoots L

YEAR	TEAM & LEAGUE		GP	MIN	W	L	T	GA	ENG	G AVG	SO	A	PIM
1942-43	NYR	N	1	60	0	1	0	6	0	6.00	0	0	0

Johnny Bower

BOWER, JOHN WILLIAM (China Wall)
B. Nov. 8, 1924, Prince Albert, Sask.
Won Vezina Trophy, 1960-61
Shared Vezina Trophy, 1964-65
Hall of Fame, 1976

5'11", 189 lbs.
Shoots L

YEAR	TEAM & LEAGUE		GP	MIN	W	L	T	GA	ENG	G AVG	SO	A	PIM
1953-54	NYR	N	70	**4200**	29	31	10	182	0	2.60	5	0	0
1954-55			5	300	2	2	1	13	0	2.60	0	0	0
1956-57			2	120	0	2	0	7	0	3.50	0	0	0
1958-59	TOR	N	39	2340	15	17	7	107	0	2.74	3	0	2
1959-60			66	3960	34	24	8	180	0	2.73	5	0	4
1960-61			58	3480	**33**	15	10	145	0	**2.50**	2	0	0
1961-62			59	3540	32	17	10	152	0	2.58	2	1	4
1962-63			42	2520	20	15	7	110	0	2.62	1	0	2
1963-64			51	3009	24	16	11	106	10	2.11	5	0	4
1964-65			34	2040	13	13	8	81	1	**2.38**	3	0	6
1965-66			35	1998	18	12	5	75	1	**2.25**	3	1	0
1966-67			24	1431	12	9	3	63	2	2.64	2	0	0
1967-68			43	2239	14	18	7	84	4	2.25	4	1	14
1968-69			20	779	5	4	3	37	0	2.85	2	0	0
1969-70			1	60	0	1	0	5	1	5.00	0	0	0
15 yrs.		N Totals:	549	32016	251	196	90	1347	19	2.52	37	3	36
PLAYOFFS													
1958-59	TOR	N	12	**746**	5	7	0	39	0	3.14	0	0	0
1959-60			10	**645**	4	6	0	31	0	2.88	0	0	0
1960-61			3	180	0	3	0	9	0	3.00	0	0	0
1961-62*			10	579	5	4	0	22	0	**2.28**	0	0	0
1962-63*			10	600	**8**	2	0	16	0	**1.60**	**2**	0	0
1963-64*			14	**850**	**8**	6	0	30	0	**2.12**	**2**	0	0
1964-65			5	321	2	3	0	13	0	2.43	0	0	0
1965-66			2	120	0	2	0	8	0	4.00	0	0	0
1966-67*			4	155	2	0	0	5	0	1.94	**1**	0	0
1968-69			4	154	0	2	0	11	0	4.29	0	0	0
10 yrs.		N Totals:	74	4350	34	35	0	184	0	2.54	5	0	0

Drafted by **Toronto** from New York, June 3, 1958.

Andy Brannigan

BRANNIGAN, ANDREW JOHN
B. Apr. 11, 1922, Winnipeg, Man.

5'11", 190 lbs.
Shoots L

YEAR	TEAM & LEAGUE		GP	MIN	W	L	T	GA	ENG	G AVG	SO	A	PIM
1940-41	NYA	N	1	7	0	0	0	0	0	0.00	0	0	0

Frankie Brimsek

BRIMSEK, FRANCIS CHARLES (Mr. Zero)
B. Sept. 26, 1915, Eveleth, Mn.
Won Vezina Trophy, 1938-39, 1941-42
Won Calder Trophy, 1938-39
Hall of Fame, 1966

5'9", 170 lbs.
Shoots L

YEAR	TEAM & LEAGUE		GP	MIN	W	L	T	GA	ENG	G AVG	SO	A	PIM
1938-39	BOS	N	43	2610	**33**	9	1	68	0	**1.58**	**10**	0	0
1939-40			48	2950	**31**	12	5	98	0	2.04	6	0	0
1940-41			48	**3040**	27	8	13	102	0	2.13	**6**	0	0
1941-42			47	2930	24	17	6	115	0	**2.45**	3	0	0
1942-43			50	3000	24	17	9	176	0	3.52	1	0	0
1945-46			34	2040	16	14	4	111	0	3.26	2	0	0
1946-47			60	3600	26	**23**	11	175	0	2.92	3	0	2
1947-48			60	**3600**	23	24	13	168	0	2.80	3	0	0
1948-49			54	3240	26	20	8	147	0	2.72	1	0	2
1949-50	CHI	N	70	**4200**	22	**38**	10	244	0	3.49	5	0	2
10 yrs.		N Totals:	514	31210	252	182	80	1404	0	2.70	40	0	6
PLAYOFFS													
1938-39*	BOS	N	12	**863**	8	4	0	18	0	**1.50**	1	0	0
1939-40			6	360	2	4	0	15	0	2.50	0	0	0
1940-41*			11	678	**8**	3	0	23	0	**2.09**	**1**	0	0
1941-42			5	307	2	3	0	16	0	3.20	0	0	0
1942-43			9	560	4	5	0	33	0	3.54	0	0	0
1945-46			10	**641**	5	5	0	29	0	2.71	0	0	0
1946-47			5	323	1	4	0	16	0	2.97	0	0	0
1947-48			5	317	1	4	0	20	0	3.79	0	0	0
1948-49			5	316	1	4	0	16	0	3.04	0	0	0
9 yrs.		N Totals:	68	4365	32	36	0	186	0	2.56	2	0	0

Sold to **Chicago** by Boston, Sept. 8, 1949.

Turk Broda

BRODA, WALTER
B. May 15, 1914, Brandon, Man.
Won Vezina Trophy, 1940-41, 1947-48
Hall of Fame, 1967

5'9", 180 lbs.
Shoots L

YEAR	TEAM & LEAGUE	GP	MIN	W	L	T	GA	ENG	G AVG	SO	A	PIM
1936-37	**TOR N**	45	2770	**22**	19	4	106	0	2.36	3	0	0
1937-38		48	2980	24	15	9	127	0	2.65	6	0	0
1938-39		48	**2990**	19	20	9	107	0	2.23	8	0	0
1939-40		47	2900	25	17	5	108	0	2.30	4	0	0
1940-41		48	2970	**28**	14	6	99	0	**2.06**	5	0	0
1941-42		48	**2960**	27	18	3	136	0	2.83	**6**	0	0
1942-43		50	3000	22	**19**	9	159	0	3.18	1	0	0
1945-46		15	900	6	6	3	53	0	3.53	0	0	0
1946-47		60	3600	31	19	10	172	0	2.87	4	0	0
1947-48		60	**3600**	**32**	15	13	143	0	**2.38**	5	0	2
1948-49		60	**3600**	22	25	13	161	0	2.68	5	0	0
1949-50		68	4040	30	25	12	167	0	2.48	**9**	0	2
1950-51		31	1827	14	11	5	68	0	2.23	6	0	4
1951-52		1	30	0	1	0	3	0	6.00	0	0	0
14 yrs.	**N Totals:**	629	38167	302	224	101	1609	0	2.53	62	0	8
PLAYOFFS												
1936-37	**TOR N**	2	133	0	2	0	5	0	2.50	0	0	0
1937-38		7	452	3	4	0	13	0	**1.86**	1	0	0
1938-39		10	617	4	5	0	20	0	2.00	**2**	0	0
1939-40		10	657	6	4	0	19	0	1.90	1	0	0
1940-41		7	438	3	4	0	15	0	2.14	0	0	0
1941-42*		13	**780**	**8**	5	0	31	0	2.38	**1**	0	0
1942-43		6	439	2	4	0	20	0	2.73	0	0	0
1946-47*		11	680	**8**	3	0	27	0	2.38	**1**	0	0
1947-48*		9	557	**8**	1	0	20	0	**2.15**	**1**	0	0
1948-49*		9	574	**8**	1	0	15	0	**1.57**	**1**	0	0
1949-50		7	450	3	4	0	10	0	**1.33**	**3**	0	0
1950-51*		9	509	**5**	3	0	9	0	**1.06**	**2**	0	0
1951-52		2	120	0	2	0	7	0	3.50	0	0	0
13 yrs.	**N Totals:**	102	6406	58	42	0	211	0	1.98	13	0	0

Ken Broderick

BRODERICK, KENNETH LORNE
B. Feb. 16, 1942, Toronto, Ont.

5'10", 178 lbs.
Shoots R

YEAR	TEAM & LEAGUE	GP	MIN	W	L	T	GA	ENG	G AVG	SO	A	PIM
1969-70	**MINN N**	7	360	2	4	0	26	0	4.33	0	0	0
1973-74	**BOS N**	5	300	2	2	1	16	1	3.20	0	1	0
1974-75		15	804	7	6	0	32	1	2.39	1	0	0
1976-77	**EDM W**	40	2301	18	18	1	134	0	3.49	**4**	3	2
1977-78		9	497	2	5	0	42	0	5.07	0	0	0
	QUE W	24	1140	9	8	1	83	0	4.37	0	0	0
	2 team total	33	1637	11	13	1	125	0	4.58	0	0	0
5 yrs.	**N Totals:**	27	1464	11	12	1	74	2	3.03	1	1	0
	W Totals:	73	3938	29	31	2	259	0	3.95	4	3	2
PLAYOFFS												
1976-77	**EDM W**	3	179	1	2	0	10	0	3.35	0	0	0
1977-78	**QUE W**	2	48	0	1	0	2	0	2.50	0	0	0
2 yrs.	**W Totals:**	5	227	1	3	0	12	0	3.17	0	0	0

Len Broderick

BRODERICK, LEN
B. Oct. 11, 1930, Toronto, Ont.

YEAR	TEAM & LEAGUE	GP	MIN	W	L	T	GA	ENG	G AVG	SO	A	PIM
1957-58	**MONT N**	1	60	0	0	0	2	0	2.00	0	0	0

Richard Brodeur

BRODEUR, RICHARD (King Richard)
B. Sept. 15, 1952, Longeuil, Que.

5'7", 160 lbs.
Shoots L

YEAR	TEAM & LEAGUE	GP	MIN	W	L	T	GA	ENG	G AVG	SO	A	PIM
1972-73	**QUE W**	24	1288	5	14	2	102	0	4.75	0	0	4
1973-74		30	1607	15	12	1	89	0	3.32	1	1	0
1974-75		51	2938	29	21	0	191	0	3.90	2	0	5
1975-76		69	**3967**	**44**	21	2	244	0	3.69	2	3	0
1976-77		53	2906	29	18	2	167	0	3.45	2	1	0
1977-78		36	1962	18	15	2	121	0	3.70	0	2	0
1978-79		42	2433	25	13	3	126	0	3.11	**3**	3	0
1979-80	**NYI N**	2	80	1	0	0	6	0	4.50	0	0	0
1980-81	**VAN N**	52	3024	17	18	16	177	2	3.51	0	0	0
1981-82		52	3010	20	18	12	168	2	3.35	2	2	0
1982-83		58	3291	21	26	8	208	6	3.79	0	1	2
11 yrs.	**N Totals:**	164	9405	59	62	36	559	10	3.57	2	3	2
	W Totals:	305	17101	165	114	12	1040	0	3.65	10	10	9
PLAYOFFS												
1974-75	**QUE W**	15	**906**	8	7	0	48	0	3.18	1	0	0
1975-76		5	299	1	4	0	22	0	4.41	0	0	0
1976-77		17	1007	**12**	5	0	55	0	3.28	**1**	2	0
1977-78		11	622	5	5	0	38	0	3.67	**1**	0	1
1978-79		3	114	0	2	0	14	0	7.37	0	0	0
1980-81	**VAN N**	3	185	0	3	0	13	0	4.22	0	0	0
1981-82		17	1089	11	6	0	49	1	2.70	0	0	0

Richard Brodeur continued

YEAR	TEAM & LEAGUE	GP	MIN	W	L	T	GA	ENG	G AVG	SO	A	PIM
1982-83		3	193	0	3	0	13	0	4.04	0	0	0
8 yrs.	**N Totals:**	23	1467	11	12	0	75	1	3.07	0	0	0
	W Totals:	51	2948	26	23	0	177	0	3.60	3	2	1

Reclaimed by **N.Y. Islanders** from Quebec prior to Expansion Draft, June 9, 1979. Traded by N.Y. Islanders to **Vancouver** with N.Y. Islanders' fifth-round choice (Moe Lemay) for Vancouver's fifth round choice (Jacques Sylvestre) in the 1981 Entry Draft, Oct. 6, 1980.

Gary Bromley

BROMLEY, GARY BERT
B. Jan. 19, 1950, Edmonton, Alta.
5'10", 160 lbs.
Shoots L

YEAR	TEAM & LEAGUE	GP	MIN	W	L	T	GA	ENG	G AVG	SO	A	PIM
1973-74	**BUF N**	12	598	3	5	3	33	0	3.31	0	0	2
1974-75		50	2787	26	11	11	144	2	3.10	4	4	2
1975-76		1	60	0	1	0	7	0	7.00	0	0	0
1976-77	**CALG W**	28	1237	6	9	2	79	0	3.83	0	0	2
1977-78	**WINN W**	39	2252	25	12	1	124	0	3.30	1	1	0
1978-79	**VAN N**	38	2144	11	19	6	136	1	3.81	2	1	6
1979-80		15	860	8	2	4	43	0	3.00	1	0	2
1980-81		20	978	6	6	4	62	0	3.80	0	1	0
8 yrs.	**N Totals:**	136	7427	54	44	28	425	3	3.43	7	6	12
	W Totals:	67	3489	31	21	3	203	0	3.49	1	1	2
PLAYOFFS												
1977-78	**WINN W**	5	268	4	0	0	7	0	**1.57**	0	0	2
1978-79	**VAN N**	3	180	1	2	0	14	1	4.67	0	0	2
1979-80		4	180	1	3	0	11	1	3.67	0	0	0
3 yrs.	**N Totals:**	7	360	2	5	0	25	2	4.17	0	0	2
	W Totals:	5	268	4	0	0	7	0	1.57	0	0	2

Signed as free agent by **Vancouver** , May 23, 1978.

Arthur Brooks

BROOKS, ARTHUR
B. Unknown

YEAR	TEAM & LEAGUE	GP	MIN	W	L	T	GA	ENG	G AVG	SO	A	PIM
1917-18	**TOR N**	4	220	2	1	0	23	0	5.75	0	0	0

Ross Brooks

BROOKS, DONALD ROSS
B. Oct. 17, 1937, Toronto, Ont.
5'8", 173 lbs.
Shoots L

YEAR	TEAM & LEAGUE	GP	MIN	W	L	T	GA	ENG	G AVG	SO	A	PIM
1972-73	**BOS N**	16	910	11	1	3	40	0	2.64	1	1	0
1973-74		21	1170	16	3	0	46	0	2.36	3	0	2
1974-75		17	967	10	3	3	48	2	2.98	0	0	0
3 yrs.	**N Totals:**	54	3047	37	7	6	134	2	2.64	4	1	2
PLAYOFFS												
1972-73	**BOS N**	1	20	0	0	0	3	0	9.00	0	0	0

Frank Brophy

BROPHY, FRANK
B. Unknown

YEAR	TEAM & LEAGUE	GP	MIN	W	L	T	GA	ENG	G AVG	SO	A	PIM
1919-20	**QUE N**	21	1247	3	**18**	0	148	0	7.05	0	0	0

Andy Brown

BROWN, ANDREW CONRAD
B. Feb. 15, 1944, Hamilton, Ont.
6', 185 lbs.
Shoots L

YEAR	TEAM & LEAGUE	GP	MIN	W	L	T	GA	ENG	G AVG	SO	A	PIM
1971-72	**DET N**	10	560	4	5	1	37	0	3.96	0	1	0
1972-73		7	337	2	1	2	20	0	3.56	0	0	0
	PITT N	9	520	3	4	2	41	0	4.73	0	0	4
	2 team total	16	857	5	5	4	61	0	4.27	0	0	4
1973-74		36	1956	13	16	4	115	0	3.53	1	0	**60**
1974-75	**IND W**	52	2979	15	**35**	0	206	0	4.15	2	1	**75**
1975-76		24	1368	9	11	2	82	0	3.60	1	1	0
1976-77		10	430	1	4	1	26	0	3.63	0	0	0
6 yrs.	**N Totals:**	62	3373	22	26	9	213	0	3.79	1	1	64
	W Totals:	86	4777	25	50	3	314	0	3.94	3	2	75

Traded to **Pittsburgh** by Detroit for cash and Pittsburgh's third round choice (Nelson Pyatt) in 1973 Amateur Draft, Feb. 25, 1973.

Ken Brown

BROWN, KENNETH MURRAY
B. Dec. 19, 1948, Port Arthur, Ont.
5'11", 175 lbs.
Shoots L

YEAR	TEAM & LEAGUE	GP	MIN	W	L	T	GA	ENG	G AVG	SO	A	PIM
1970-71	**CHI N**	1	18	0	0	0	1	0	3.33	0	0	0
1972-73	**ALTA W**	20	1034	10	8	0	63	1	3.66	1	0	2
1974-75	**EDM W**	32	1466	11	11	0	85	0	3.48	2	1	2
3 yrs.	**N Totals:**	1	18	0	0	0	1	0	3.33	0	0	0
	W Totals:	52	2500	21	19	0	148	1	3.55	3	1	4

Bruce Bullock

BULLOCK, BRUCE JOHN
B. May 9, 1949, Toronto, Ont.
5'7", 160 lbs.
Shoots R

YEAR	TEAM & LEAGUE	GP	MIN	W	L	T	GA	ENG	G AVG	SO	A	PIM
1972-73	**VAN N**	14	840	3	8	3	67	0	4.79	0	0	2
1974-75		1	60	0	1	0	4	0	4.00	0	0	0
1976-77		1	27	0	0	0	3	0	6.67	0	0	0
3 yrs.	**N Totals:**	16	927	3	9	3	74	0	4.79	0	0	2

Randy Burchell

BURCHELL, RANDY 6'1", 175 lbs.
B. July 2, 1955, Montreal, Que.

YEAR	TEAM & LEAGUE		GP	MIN	W	L	T	GA	ENG	G AVG	SO	A	PIM
1976-77	IND	W	5	136	1	0	0	8	0	3.53	0	1	0

Steve Buzinski

BUZINSKI, STEPHEN (The Puck Goes Inski)
B. Oct. 15, 1917, Dunblane, Sask.

YEAR	TEAM & LEAGUE		GP	MIN	W	L	T	GA	ENG	G AVG	SO	A	PIM
1942-43	NYR	N	9	560	2	6	1	55	0	5.89	0	0	0

Don Caley

CALEY, DONALD THOMAS 5'10", 165 lbs.
B. Oct. 9, 1945, Dauphin, Man. Shoots L

YEAR	TEAM & LEAGUE		GP	MIN	W	L	T	GA	ENG	G AVG	SO	A	PIM
1967-68	STL	N	1	30	0	0	0	3	0	6.00	0	0	0

Frank Caprice

CAPRICE, FRANK 5'9", 160 lbs.
B. May 2, 1962, Hamilton, Ont. Shoots L

YEAR	TEAM & LEAGUE		GP	MIN	W	L	T	GA	ENG	G AVG	SO	A	PIM
1982-83	VAN	N	1	20	0	0	0	3	0	9.00	0	0	0

Jacques Caron

CARON, JACQUES JOSEPH 6'2", 185 lbs.
B. Apr. 21, 1940, Noranda, Que. Shoots L

YEAR	TEAM & LEAGUE		GP	MIN	W	L	T	GA	ENG	G AVG	SO	A	PIM
1967-68	LA	N	1	60	0	1	0	4	0	4.00	0	0	0
1968-69			3	140	0	1	0	9	0	3.86	0	0	0
1971-72	STL	N	28	1619	14	8	5	68	2	2.52	1	1	0
1972-73			30	1562	8	14	5	92	3	3.53	1	0	0
1973-74	VAN	N	10	465	2	5	1	38	0	4.90	0	0	0
1975-76	CLEVE	W	2	130	1	0	1	8	0	3.69	1	1	0
1976-77	CIN	W	24	1292	13	6	2	61	0	2.83	3	1	0
7 yrs.		N Totals:	72	3846	24	29	11	211	5	3.29	2	1	0
		W Totals:	26	1422	14	6	3	69	0	2.91	4	2	0
PLAYOFFS													
1971-72	STL	N	9	499	4	5	0	26	1	3.13	0	0	2
1972-73			3	140	0	2	0	8	0	3.43	0	0	0
1976-77	CIN	W	1	14	0	1	0	3	0	12.86	0	0	0
3 yrs.		N Totals:	12	639	4	7	0	34	1	3.19	0	0	2
		W Totals:	1	14	0	1	0	3	0	12.86	0	0	0

Claimed by Seattle **(Vancouver)** from St. Louis in Reverse Draft, June 15, 1973.

Lyle Carter

CARTER, LYLE DWIGHT 6'1", 185 lbs.
B. Apr. 29, 1945, Truro, N.S. Shoots L

YEAR	TEAM & LEAGUE		GP	MIN	W	L	T	GA	ENG	G AVG	SO	A	PIM
1971-72	CALIF	N	15	721	4	7	0	50	0	4.16	0	0	2

Lorne Chabot

CHABOT, LORNE (CHABOTSKY) 6'1", 185 lbs.
B. Oct. 5, 1900, Montreal, Que Shoots L
Won Vezina Trophy, 1934-35

YEAR	TEAM & LEAGUE		GP	MIN	W	L	T	GA	ENG	G AVG	SO	A	PIM
1926-27	NYR	N	36	2307	22	9	5	56	0	1.56	10	0	0
1927-28			44	2730	19	16	9	79	0	1.80	11	0	0
1928-29	TOR	N	43	2458	20	18	5	67	0	1.56	12	0	2
1929-30			42	2620	21	12	9	113	0	2.69	**6**	0	0
1930-31			37	2300	21	8	8	80	0	2.16	6	0	0
1931-32			44	2698	22	16	6	106	0	2.41	4	0	2
1932-33			48	2948	24	18	6	111	0	2.31	5	0	2
1933-34	MONT	N	47	2928	21	20	6	101	0	2.15	8	0	2
1934-35	CHI	N	48	2940	26	17	5	88	0	**1.83**	8	0	0
1935-36	MON(M)	N	16	1010	8	3	5	35	0	2.19	2	0	0
1936-37	NYA	N	6	370	2	3	1	25	0	4.17	1	0	0
11 yrs.		N Totals:	411	25309	206	140	65	861	0	2.04	73	0	8
PLAYOFFS													
1926-27	NYR	N	2	120	0	1	1	3	0	1.50	1	0	0
1927-28*			6	321	2	2	1	8	0	1.33	1	0	0
1928-29	TOR	N	4	242	2	2	0	5	0	1.25	0	0	0
1930-31			2	139	0	1	1	4	0	2.00	0	0	0
1931-32*			7	438	**5**	1	1	15	0	**2.14**	0	0	0
1932-33			9	**686**	4	5	0	18	0	2.00	**2**	0	0
1933-34	MONT	N	2	131	0	1	1	4	0	2.00	0	0	0
1934-35	CHI	N	2	124	0	1	1	1	0	0.50	1	0	0
1935-36	MON(M)	N	3	357	0	3	0	6	0	2.00	0	0	0
9 yrs.		N Totals:	37	2558	13	17	6	64	0	1.50	5	0	0

Ed Chadwick

CHADWICK, EDWIN WALTER 5'11", 184 lbs.
B. May 8, 1933, Fergus, Ont. Shoots L

YEAR	TEAM & LEAGUE		GP	MIN	W	L	T	GA	ENG	G AVG	SO	A	PIM
1955-56	TOR	N	5	300	2	0	3	3	0	0.60	2	0	0
1956-57			70	**4200**	21	34	15	192	0	2.74	5	0	0
1957-58			70	**4200**	21	38	11	226	0	3.23	4	0	0
1958-59			31	1800	12	15	4	93	0	3.10	3	0	0
1959-60			4	240	1	2	1	15	0	3.75	0	0	0
1961-62	BOS	N	4	240	0	3	1	22	0	5.50	0	0	0
6 yrs.		N Totals:	184	10980	57	92	35	551	0	3.01	14	0	0

Traded to **Boston** by Toronto for Don Simmons, Jan. 31, 1961.

Bob Champoux

CHAMPOUX, ROBERT JOSEPH
B. Dec. 2, 1942, St. Hilaire, Que.

5'10", 175 lbs.
Shoots L

YEAR	TEAM	LEAGUE	GP	MIN	W	L	T	GA	ENG	G AVG	SO	A	PIM
1973-74	CALIF	N	17	923	2	11	3	80	1	5.20	0	0	0
PLAYOFFS													
1963-64	DET	N	1	40	0	0	0	4	0	6.00	0	0	0

Gerry Cheevers

CHEEVERS, GERALD MICHAEL (Cheesey)
B. Dec. 7, 1940, St. Catharines, Ont.

5'11", 175 lbs.
Shoots L

YEAR	TEAM	LEAGUE	GP	MIN	W	L	T	GA	ENG	G AVG	SO	A	PIM
1961-62	TOR	N	2	120	1	1	0	7	0	3.50	0	0	0
1965-66	BOS	N	7	340	0	4	1	34	0	6.00	0	0	0
1966-67			22	1298	5	11	6	72	0	3.33	1	0	**12**
1967-68			47	2646	23	17	5	125	3	2.83	3	0	0
1968-69			52	3112	28	12	12	145	1	2.80	3	0	14
1969-70			41	2384	24	8	8	108	0	2.72	4	0	4
1970-71			40	2400	27	8	5	109	0	2.73	3	0	4
1971-72			41	2420	27	5	8	101	0	2.50	2	2	25
1972-73	CLEVE	W	52	3144	32	20	0	149	2	**2.84**	**5**	1	30
1973-74			59	**3562**	30	20	6	180	0	3.03	**4**	0	30
1974-75			52	3076	26	24	2	167	0	3.26	**4**	1	**59**
1975-76			28	1570	11	14	1	95	0	3.63	1	0	15
	BOS	N	15	900	8	2	5	41	1	2.73	1	0	2
	2 team total		43	2470	19	16	6	136	1	3.30	2	0	2
1976-77			45	2700	30	10	5	137	0	3.04	3	**4**	**46**
1977-78			21	1086	10	5	2	48	1	2.65	1	1	14
1978-79			43	2509	23	0	10	132	1	3.16	1	2	23
1979-80			42	2479	24	11	7	116	3	2.81	4	0	**62**
16 yrs.		N Totals:	418	24394	230	94	74	1175	10	2.89	26	9	206
		W Totals:	191	11352	99	78	9	591	2	3.12	14	2	134
PLAYOFFS													
1967-68	BOS	N	4	240	0	4	0	15	0	3.75	0	0	0
1968-69			9	572	0	4	0	16	0	1.68	3	0	0
1969-70*			13	**781**	**12**	1	0	29	0	2.23	0	1	2
1970-71			6	360	3	3	0	21	0	3.50	0	0	**4**
1971-72*			8	483	**6**	2	0	21	0	2.61	**2**	0	0
1972-73	CLEVE	W	9	548	5	4	0	22	0	**2.41**	0	0	0
1973-74			5	303	1	4	0	18	0	3.56	0	0	0
1974-75			5	300	1	4	0	23	0	4.60	0	0	0
1975-76	BOS	N	6	392	2	4	0	14	0	2.14	1	0	0
1976-77			14	**858**	8	5	0	44	1	3.08	1	0	4
1977-78			12	731	8	4	0	35	0	2.87	0	0	6
1978-79			6	360	4	2	0	15	1	2.50	0	0	0
1979-80			10	619	4	6	0	32	1	3.10	0	0	0
13 yrs.		N Totals:	88	5396	47	35	0	242	3	2.69	7	1	16
		W Totals:	19	1151	7	12	0	63	0	3.28	0	0	0

Drafted by **Boston** from Toronto, June 9, 1965.

King Clancy

CLANCY, FRANCIS MICHAEL
B. Feb. 25, 1903, Ottawa, Ont.
Hall of Fame, 1958

5'9", 184 lbs.
Shoots L

YEAR	TEAM	LEAGUE	GP	MIN	W	L	T	GA	ENG	G AVG	SO	A	PIM
1932-33	TOR	N	1	1	0	0	0	1	0	1.00	0	0	0

Odie Cleghorn

CLEGHORN, OGILVIE
B. Montreal, Que.

YEAR	TEAM	LEAGUE	GP	MIN	W	L	T	GA	ENG	G AVG	SO	A	PIM
1925-26	PITT	N	1	60	1	0	0	2	0	2.00	0	0	0

Jacques Cloutier

CLOUTIER, JACQUES
B. Jan. 3, 1960, Noranda, Que.

5'7", 154 lbs.
Shoots L

YEAR	TEAM	LEAGUE	GP	MIN	W	L	T	GA	ENG	G AVG	SO	A	PIM
1981-82	BUF	N	7	311	5	1	0	13	1	2.51	0	0	0
1982-83			25	1390	10	7	6	81	0	3.50	0	0	0
2 yrs.		N Totals:	32	1701	15	8	6	94	1	3.32	0	0	0

Les Colvin

COLVIN, LES
B. Feb. 8, 1921, Oshawa, Ont.

5'6", 150 lbs.
Shoots L

YEAR	TEAM	LEAGUE	GP	MIN	W	L	T	GA	ENG	G AVG	SO	A	PIM
1948-49	BOS	N	1	60	0	1	0	4	0	4.00	0	0	0

Charlie Conacher

CONACHER, CHARLES WILLIAM (The Bomber)
B. Dec. 20, 1910, Toronto, Ont.
Won Art Ross Trophy, 1933-34, 1934-35
Hall of Fame, 1961

6'1", 195 lbs.
Shoots R

YEAR	TEAM	LEAGUE	GP	MIN	W	L	T	GA	ENG	G AVG	SO	A	PIM
1932-33	TOR	N	1	2	0	0	0	0	0	0.00	0	0	0
1934-35			1	3	0	0	0	0	0	0.00	0	0	0
1938-39	DET	N	1	4	0	0	0	0	0	0.00	0	0	0
3 yrs.		N Totals:	3	9	0	0	0	0	0	0.00	0	0	0

Alex Connell

CONNELL, ALEX
B. Feb. 8, 1902, Ottawa, Ont.
Hall of Fame, 1958
5'9", 150 lbs.
Shoots R

YEAR	TEAM & LEAGUE		GP	MIN	W	L	T	GA	ENG	G AVG	SO	A	PIM
1924-25	OTTA	N	30	1852	17	12	1	66	0	2.20	**7**	0	0
1925-26			36	2231	**24**	8	1	42	0	**1.17**	**15**	0	0
1926-27			44	2782	**30**	10	4	69	0	1.57	13	0	2
1927-28			44	2760	20	14	10	57	0	1.30	**15**	0	0
1928-29			44	**2820**	14	17	13	67	0	1.52	7	0	0
1929-30			44	**2780**	21	15	8	118	0	2.68	3	0	0
1930-31			36	2190	10	**22**	4	110	0	3.06	3	0	0
1931-32	DET	N	48	**3050**	24	19	5	108	0	2.25	6	0	0
1932-33	OTTA	N	15	845	4	8	2	36	0	2.57	1	0	0
1933-34	NYA	N	1	40	1	0	0	2	0	2.00	0	0	0
1934-35	MON(M)	N	48	2970	24	19	5	92	0	1.92	**9**	0	0
1936-37			27	1710	10	11	6	63	0	2.33	2	0	0
12 yrs.		N Totals:	417	26030	199	155	59	830	0	1.91	81	0	2
PLAYOFFS													
1925-26	OTTA	N	2	120	0	1	1	2	0	**1.00**	0	0	0
1926-27*			6	400	**3**	0	3	4	0	**0.67**	**2**	0	0
1927-28			2	120	0	2	0	3	0	1.50	0	0	0
1929-30			2	120	0	1	1	6	0	3.00	0	0	0
1931-32	DET	N	2	120	0	1	1	3	0	1.50	0	0	0
1934-35*	MON(M)	N	7	429	**6**	0	1	8	0	**1.14**	**2**	0	0
6 yrs.		N Totals:	21	1309	9	5	7	26	0	1.19	4	0	0

Gaye Cooley

COOLEY, GAYE
B. Feb. 8, 1945, North Bay, Ont.
5'10", 185 lbs.
Shoots R

YEAR	TEAM & LEAGUE		GP	MIN	W	L	T	GA	ENG	G AVG	SO	A	PIM
PLAYOFFS													
1975-76	NE	W	1	1	0	0	0	0	0	0.00	0	0	0

Jim Corsi

CORSI, JAMES
B. June 19, 1954, Montreal, Que.
5'10", 180 lbs.
Shoots L

YEAR	TEAM & LEAGUE		GP	MIN	W	L	T	GA	ENG	G AVG	SO	A	PIM
1977-78	QUE	W	23	1089	10	7	0	82	0	4.52	0	1	2
1978-79			40	2291	16	20	1	126	0	3.30	**3**	0	0
1979-80	EDM	N	26	1366	8	14	3	83	3	3.65	0	3	6
3 yrs.		N Totals:	26	1366	8	14	3	83	3	3.65	0	3	6
		W Totals:	63	3380	26	27	1	208	0	3.69	3	1	2

Traded to **Minnesota** by Edmonton for future considerations, March 11, 1980.

Tom Cottringer

COTTRINGER, TOM
B. Feb. 18, 1920, Quebec, Que.
5'8", 162 lbs.
Shoots L

YEAR	TEAM & LEAGUE		GP	MIN	W	L	T	GA	ENG	G AVG	SO	A	PIM
1972-73	PHI	W	2	122	1	1	0	8	0	3.93	0	0	0

Maurice Courteau

COURTEAU, MAURICE LAURENT
B. Feb. 18, 1920, Quebec City, Que.
5'8", 162 lbs.
Shoots L

YEAR	TEAM & LEAGUE		GP	MIN	W	L	T	GA	ENG	G AVG	SO	A	PIM
1943-44	BOS	N	6	360	2	4	0	33	0	5.50	0	0	0

Rick Coutu

COUTU, RICK

YEAR	TEAM & LEAGUE		GP	MIN	W	L	T	GA	ENG	G AVG	SO	A	PIM
1973-74	CHI	W	20	1207	9	10	1	75	0	3.73	0	0	0
1974-75			1	60	0	1	0	5	0	5.00	0	0	0
1975-76	CIN	W	3	149	0	2	0	17	0	6.85	0	0	0
3 yrs.		W Totals:	24	1416	9	13	1	97	0	4.11	0	0	0

Abbie Cox

COX, ABBIE
B. Unknown

YEAR	TEAM & LEAGUE		GP	MIN	W	L	T	GA	ENG	G AVG	SO	A	PIM
1929-30	MON(M)	N	1	60	1	0	0	2	0	2.00	0	0	0
1933-34	DET	N	2	109	0	0	1	5	0	2.50	0	0	0
	NYA	N	1	24	0	1	0	3	0	3.00	0	0	0
	2 team total		3	133	0	1	1	8	0	3.61	0	0	0
1935-36	MONT	N	1	70	0	0	1	1	0	1.00	0	0	0
3 yrs.		N Totals:	5	263	1	1	2	11	0	2.51	0	0	0

Jim Craig

CRAIG, JAMES
B. May 31, 1957, North Easton, Maine
6'1", 190 lbs.
Shoots L

YEAR	TEAM & LEAGUE		GP	MIN	W	L	T	GA	ENG	G AVG	SO	A	PIM
1979-80	ATL	N	4	206	1	2	1	13	0	3.79	0	0	0
1980-81	BOS	N	23	1272	9	7	6	78	1	3.68	0	1	11
2 yrs.		N Totals:	27	1478	10	9	7	91	1	3.69	0	1	11

Jiri Crha

CRHA, JIRI
B. Apr. 13, 1950, Pardubice,Czechoslovakia
5'11", 170 lbs.
Shoots L

YEAR	TEAM & LEAGUE		GP	MIN	W	L	T	GA	ENG	G AVG	SO	A	PIM
1979-80	TOR	N	15	830	8	7	0	50	0	3.61	0	0	4
1980-81			54	3112	20	20	11	211	4	4.07	0	1	8
2 yrs.		N Totals:	69	3942	28	27	11	261	4	3.97	0	1	12

Jiri Crha continued

YEAR	TEAM & LEAGUE		GP	MIN	W	L	T	GA	ENG	G AVG	SO	A	PIM
PLAYOFFS													
1979-80	TOR	N	2	121	0	2	0	10	0	4.96	0	0	0
1980-81			3	65	0	2	0	11	0	10.15	0	0	0
2 yrs.		N Totals:	5	186	0	4	0	21	0	6.77	0	0	0

Roger Crozier

CROZIER, ROGER ALLAN
B. Mar. 16, 1942, Bracebridge, Ont.
Won Calder Trophy, 1964-65
Won Conn Smythe Trophy, 1965-66

5'8", 140 lbs.
Shoots R

YEAR	TEAM & LEAGUE		GP	MIN	W	L	T	GA	ENG	G AVG	SO	A	PIM
1963-64	DET	N	15	900	5	6	4	51	0	3.40	2	0	0
1964-65			70	**4167**	**40**	23	7	168	3	**2.42**	**6**	0	10
1965-66			64	**3734**	28	**24**	12	173	2	2.78	**7**	0	0
1966-67			58	3256	22	**30**	4	182	1	3.35	4	0	0
1967-68			34	1729	9	18	2	95	2	3.30	1	0	2
1968-69			38	1820	11	16	3	101	0	3.33	0	0	2
1969-70			34	1877	16	6	9	83	0	2.65	0	0	0
1970-71	BUF	N	44	2198	9	20	7	135	1	3.69	1	0	0
1971-72			63	3654	13	**34**	14	214	7	3.51	2	0	10
1972-73			49	2633	23	13	7	121	3	2.76	3	0	4
1973-74			12	615	4	3	4	39	0	3.80	0	0	2
1974-75			23	1260	17	2	1	55	0	2.62	3	2	8
1975-76			11	620	8	2	0	27	0	2.61	1	1	0
1976-77	WASH	N	3	103	1	0	0	2	0	1.17	0	0	0
14 yrs.		N Totals:	518	28566	206	197	74	1446	19	3.04	30	3	38
PLAYOFFS													
1963-64	DET	N	2	108	0	1	0	5	0	2.78	0	0	0
1964-65			7	420	3	4	0	23	0	3.29	0	0	0
1965-66			12	**666**	6	5	0	26	0	2.34	**1**	0	0
1969-70			1	34	0	1	0	3	0	5.29	0	0	0
1972-73	BUF	N	4	249	2	2	0	11	1	2.65	0	1	2
1974-75			5	292	3	2	0	14	0	2.88	0	0	0
6 yrs.		N Totals:	31	1769	14	15	0	82	1	2.78	1	1	2

Traded to **Detroit** by Chicago with Ron Ingram for Howie Young, June 5, 1963. Traded to **Buffalo** by Detroit for Tom Webster, June 10, 1970. Sold to **Washington** by Buffalo, March 3, 1977.

Wilf Cude

CUDE, WILFRED
B. July 4, 1910, Barrie, England

5'9", 146 lbs.
Shoots L

YEAR	TEAM & LEAGUE		GP	MIN	W	L	T	GA	ENG	G AVG	SO	A	PIM
1930-31	PHI	N	29	1750	2	**22**	3	127	0	4.38	1	0	0
1931-32	BOS	N	2	120	1	1	0	6	0	3.00	1	0	0
	CHI	N	1	41	0	0	0	9	0	9.00	0	0	0
	2 team total		3	161	1	1	0	15	0	5.59	1	0	0
1933-34	DET	N	29	1860	15	6	8	47	0	1.62	4	0	0
	MONT	N	1	60	1	0	0	0	0	0.00	1	0	0
	2 team total		30	1920	16	6	8	47	0	**1.47**	5	0	0
1934-35			48	2960	19	23	6	145	0	3.02	1	0	0
1935-36			47	2940	11	**26**	10	122	0	2.60	6	0	0
1936-37			44	2730	22	17	5	99	0	2.25	5	0	0
1937-38			47	2990	18	17	12	126	0	2.68	3	0	0
1938-39			23	1440	8	11	4	77	0	3.35	2	0	0
1939-40			7	415	1	5	1	24	0	3.43	0	0	0
1940-41			3	180	2	1	0	13	0	4.33	0	0	0
10 yrs.		N Totals:	281	17486	100	129	49	795	0	2.73	24	0	0
PLAYOFFS													
1933-34	DET	N	9	**653**	4	5	0	21	0	2.33	1	0	0
1934-35	MONT	N	2	120	0	1	1	6	0	3.00	0	0	0
1936-37			5	352	2	3	0	13	0	2.60	0	0	0
1937-38			3	192	1	2	0	11	0	3.67	0	0	0
4 yrs.		N Totals:	19	1317	7	11	1	51	0	2.32	1	0	0

Mike Curran

CURRAN, MICHAEL
B. Apr. 14, 1945, Int'l. Falls, Minn.

5'9", 175 lbs.
Shoots L

YEAR	TEAM & LEAGUE		GP	MIN	W	L	T	GA	ENG	G AVG	SO	A	PIM
1972-73	MINN	W	43	2540	23	17	2	131	3	3.09	4	1	26
1973-74			40	2382	23	14	2	130	0	3.27	2	0	6
1974-75			26	1367	11	10	1	90	0	3.95	0	0	18
1975-76			5	240	2	2	0	22	0	5.50	1	0	2
1976-77			16	848	4	7	3	50	0	3.54	0	0	6
5 yrs.		W Totals:	130	7377	63	50	8	423	3	3.44	7	1	58
PLAYOFFS													
1972-73	MINN	W	2	90	0	2	0	9	0	6.00	0	0	0
1973-74			5	289	2	3	0	14	0	2.91	0	0	0
2 yrs.		W Totals:	7	379	2	5	0	23	0	3.64	0	0	0

Don Cutts

CUTTS, DONALD EDWARD 6'3", 190 lbs.
B. Feb. 24, 1953, Edmonton, Alta. Shoots L

YEAR	TEAM & LEAGUE		GP	MIN	W	L	T	GA	ENG	G AVG	SO	A	PIM
1979-80	EDM	N	6	269	1	2	1	16	1	3.57	0	0	6

Claude Cyr

CYR, CLAUDE
B. Mar. 27, 1939, Montreal, Que.

YEAR	TEAM & LEAGUE		GP	MIN	W	L	T	GA	ENG	G AVG	SO	A	PIM
1958-59	MONT	N	1	20	0	0	0	1	0	3.00	0	0	0

Joe Daley

DALEY, THOMAS JOSEPH 5'10", 160 lbs.
B. Feb. 20, 1943, Winnipeg, Man. Shoots L

YEAR	TEAM & LEAGUE		GP	MIN	W	L	T	GA	ENG	G AVG	SO	A	PIM
1968-69	PITT	N	29	1615	10	13	3	87	2	3.23	2	0	2
1969-70			9	528	1	5	3	26	1	2.95	0	0	0
1970-71	BUF	N	38	2073	12	16	8	128	2	3.70	1	1	12
1971-72	DET	N	29	1620	11	10	5	85	1	3.15	0	0	2
1972-73	WINN	W	29	1718	17	10	1	83	2	2.90	2	1	10
1973-74			41	2454	19	20	1	163	0	3.99	0	1	4
1974-75			51	2902	23	21	4	175	0	3.62	1	1	6
1975-76			62	3612	41	17	1	171	0	**2.84**	**5**	1	**17**
1976-77			65	**3818**	**39**	23	2	206	0	3.24	3	**4**	6
1977-78			37	2075	21	11	1	114	0	3.30	1	2	2
1978-79			23	1256	7	11	3	90	0	4.30	0	0	0
11 yrs.		N Totals:	105	5836	34	44	19	326	6	3.35	3	1	16
		W Totals:	308	17835	167	113	13	1002	2	3.37	12	10	45
PLAYOFFS													
1972-73	WINN	W	7	422	5	2	0	25	0	3.55	0	0	0
1973-74			2	119	0	2	0	8	0	4.03	0	0	0
1975-76			12	671	**10**	1	0	29	0	2.59	1	0	0
1976-77			20	**1186**	11	9	0	71	0	3.59	**1**	0	1
1977-78			5	271	4	1	0	13	0	2.88	0	1	20
1978-79			3	37	0	0	0	3	0	4.86	0	0	0
6 yrs.		W Totals:	49	2706	30	15	0	149	0	3.30	2	1	21

Drafted by **Pittsburgh** from Detroit in Expansion Draft, June 6, 1967. Claimed on waivers by **Buffalo** from Pittsburgh, June 9, 1970. Traded to **Detroit** by Buffalo for Don Luce and Mike Robitaille, May 25, 1971.

Nick Damore

DAMORE, NICHOLAS 5'6", 160 lbs.
B. July 10, 1916, Niagara Falls, Ont. Shoots L

YEAR	TEAM & LEAGUE		GP	MIN	W	L	T	GA	ENG	G AVG	SO	A	PIM
1941-42	BOS	N	1	60	0	1	0	3	0	3.00	0	0	0

John Davidson

DAVIDSON, JOHN ARTHUR 6'3", 205 lbs.
B. Feb. 27, 1953, Ottawa, Ont. Shoots L

YEAR	TEAM & LEAGUE		GP	MIN	W	L	T	GA	ENG	G AVG	SO	A	PIM
1973-74	STL	N	39	2300	13	19	7	118	3	3.08	0	0	10
1974-75			40	2360	17	15	7	144	1	3.66	0	2	8
1975-76	NYR	N	56	3207	22	28	5	212	1	3.97	3	2	8
1976-77			39	2116	14	14	6	125	1	3.54	1	0	6
1977-78			34	1848	14	13	4	98	4	3.18	1	0	10
1978-79			39	2232	20	12	5	131	1	3.52	0	0	12
1979-80			41	2306	20	15	4	122	3	3.17	2	0	0
1980-81			10	560	1	7	1	48	2	5.14	0	0	0
1981-82			1	60	1	0	0	1	0	1.00	0	0	0
1982-83			2	120	1	1	0	5	0	2.50	0	0	0
10 yrs.		N Totals:	301	17109	123	124	39	1004	16	3.52	7	4	54
PLAYOFFS													
1974-75	STL	N	1	60	0	1	0	4	0	4.00	0	0	0
1977-78	NYR	N	2	122	1	1	0	7	0	3.44	0	0	0
1978-79			18	**1106**	11	7	0	42	0	2.28	**1**	0	**6**
1979-80			9	541	4	5	0	21	1	2.33	0	0	0
1981-82			1	33	0	0	0	3	0	5.45	0	0	0
5 yrs.		N Totals:	31	1862	16	14	0	77	1	2.48	1	0	6

Traded to **N.Y. Rangers** by St. Louis with Bill Collins for Ted Irvine, Jerry Butler and Bert Wilson, June 18, 1975.

Robert Decourcy

DECOURCY, ROBERT PHILLIP 5'11", 160 lbs.
B. June 12, 1927, Toronto, Ont. Shoots R

YEAR	TEAM & LEAGUE		GP	MIN	W	L	T	GA	ENG	G AVG	SO	A	PIM
1947-48	NYR	N	1	29	0	1	0	6	0	12.41	0	0	0

Norman Defelice

DEFELICE, NORMAN 5'10", 150 lbs.
B. Jan. 19, 1933, Schumacher, Ont. Shoots L

YEAR	TEAM & LEAGUE		GP	MIN	W	L	T	GA	ENG	G AVG	SO	A	PIM
1956-57	BOS	N	10	600	3	5	2	30	0	3.00	0	0	0

Michel Deguise

DEGUISE, MICHEL 5'8", 150 lbs.
B. June 11, 1951 Shoots L

YEAR	TEAM & LEAGUE		GP	MIN	W	L	T	GA	ENG	G AVG	SO	A	PIM
1973-74	QUE	W	32	1750	12	13	1	96	0	3.29	1	1	0
1975-76			18	835	6	5	2	60	0	4.35	0	1	0
2 yrs.		W Totals:	50	2585	18	18	3	156	0	3.62	1	2	0

Denis DeJordy

DEJORDY, DENIS EMILE
B. Nov. 12, 1938, St. Hyacinthe, Que.
Shared Vezina Trophy, 1966-67
5'9", 185 lbs.
Shoots L

YEAR	TEAM & LEAGUE		GP	MIN	W	L	T	GA	ENG	G AVG	SO	A	PIM
1962-63	CHI	N	5	290	2	1	2	12	0	2.48	0	0	0
1963-64			6	360	2	3	1	19	0	3.17	0	0	0
1964-65			30	1760	16	10	3	74	0	2.52	3	1	0
1966-67			44	2536	22	12	7	104	0	**2.46**	4	0	0
1967-68			50	2838	23	15	11	128	0	2.71	4	0	0
1968-69			53	2981	22	22	7	156	0	3.14	2	1	2
1969-70			10	557	3	5	1	25	0	2.69	0	0	0
	LA	N	21	1147	5	11	4	62	0	3.24	0	0	0
	2 team total		31	1704	8	16	5	87	0	3.06	0	0	0
1970-71			60	3375	18	29	11	214	3	3.80	1	0	0
1971-72			5	291	0	5	0	23	0	4.74	0	0	0
	MONT	N	7	332	3	2	1	25	0	4.52	0	1	0
	2 team total		12	623	3	7	1	48	0	4.62	0	1	0
1972-73	DET	N	24	1331	8	11	3	83	4	3.74	1	0	0
1973-74			1	20	0	1	0	4	0	12.00	0	0	0
11 yrs.		N Totals:	316	17818	124	127	51	929	7	3.13	15	3	2
PLAYOFFS													
1963-64	CHI	N	1	20	0	0	0	2	0	6.00	0	0	0
1964-65			2	80	0	1	0	9	0	6.75	0	0	0
1966-67			4	184	1	2	0	10	0	3.26	0	0	0
1967-68			11	662	5	6	0	34	0	3.08	0	0	0
4 yrs.		N Totals:	18	946	6	9	0	55	0	3.49	0	0	0

Gerry Desjardins

DESJARDINS, GERARD FERDINAND
B. July 22, 1944, Sudbury, Ont.
5'11", 190 lbs.
Shoots L

YEAR	TEAM & LEAGUE		GP	MIN	W	L	T	GA	ENG	G AVG	SO	A	PIM
1968-69	LA	N	60	3499	18	**34**	6	190	0	3.26	4	1	6
1969-70			43	2453	7	29	5	159	1	3.89	3	0	14
	CHI	N	4	240	4	0	0	8	0	2.00	0	1	0
	2 team total		47	2693	11	29	5	167	1	3.72	3	1	14
1970-71			22	1217	12	6	3	49	2	2.42	0	0	6
1971-72			6	360	1	2	3	21	1	3.50	0	0	0
1972-73	NYI	N	44	2498	5	**35**	3	195	0	4.68	0	0	9
1973-74			36	1945	9	17	6	101	1	3.12	0	0	0
1974-75	M-B	W	41	2282	9	28	1	162	0	4.26	0	1	13
	BUF	N	9	540	6	2	1	25	0	2.78	0	0	0
	2 team total		50	2822	15	30	2	187	0	3.98	0	1	13
1975-76			55	3280	29	15	11	161	1	2.95	2	1	2
1976-77			49	2871	31	12	6	126	1	2.63	3	0	2
1977-78			3	111	0	1	0	7	0	3.78	0	0	0
10 yrs.		N Totals:	331	19014	122	153	44	1042	7	3.29	12	3	39
		W Totals:	41	2282	9	28	1	162	0	4.26	0	1	13
PLAYOFFS													
1968-69	LA	N	9	431	3	4	0	28	0	3.90	0	0	0
1971-72	CHI	N	1	60	1	0	0	5	0	5.00	0	0	**4**
1974-75	BUF	N	15	760	7	5	0	43	1	3.39	0	0	0
1975-76			9	563	4	5	0	28	0	2.98	0	0	2
1976-77			1	60	0	1	0	4	0	4.00	0	0	2
5 yrs.		N Totals:	35	1874	15	15	0	108	1	3.46	0	0	8

Traded to **Los Angeles** by Montreal for Los Angeles' first choices in 1969 (transferred to Minnesota) and 1972 (Steve Shutt) Amateur Drafts, June 11, 1968. Traded to **Chicago** by Los Angeles with Bryan Campbell and Bill White for Gilles Marotte, Jim Stanfield and Denis DeJordy, Feb. 20, 1970. Traded to **California** by Chicago with Gerry Pinder and Kerry Bond for goaltender Gary Smith, Sept. 9, 1971. Traded to **Chicago** by California for Paul Shmyr and goaltender Gilles Meloche, Oct. 18, 1971. Drafted by **N.Y. Islanders** from Chicago in Expansion Draft, June 6, 1972. Rights traded to **Buffalo** by N.Y. Islanders for the rights to Jean Lariviere, March 3, 1975.

Bill Dickie

DICKIE, WILLIAM
B. Unknown

YEAR	TEAM & LEAGUE		GP	MIN	W	L	T	GA	ENG	G AVG	SO	A	PIM
1941-42	CHI	N	1	60	1	0	0	3	0	3.00	0	0	0

Connie Dion

DION, CONRAD
B. Aug. 11, 1918, St.Remi de Tingwick, Que
5'4", 140 lbs.
Shoots R

YEAR	TEAM & LEAGUE		GP	MIN	W	L	T	GA	ENG	G AVG	SO	A	PIM
1943-44	DET	N	26	1560	17	7	2	80	0	3.08	1	0	0
1944-45			12	720	6	4	2	39	0	3.25	0	0	0
2 yrs.		N Totals:	38	2280	23	11	4	119	0	3.13	1	0	0
PLAYOFFS													
1943-44	DET	N	5	300	1	4	0	17	0	3.40	0	0	0

Michel Dion

DION, MICHEL
B. Feb. 11, 1954, Granby, Que.
5'10", 184 lbs.
Shoots R

YEAR	TEAM & LEAGUE		GP	MIN	W	L	T	GA	ENG	G AVG	SO	A	PIM
1974-75	IND	W	1	59	0	1	0	4	0	4.07	0	0	0
1975-76			31	1860	14	15	1	85	0	2.74	0	0	2
1976-77			42	2286	17	19	3	128	0	3.36	1	0	0
1977-78	CIN	W	45	2356	21	17	1	140	0	3.57	**4**	0	26
1978-79			30	1681	10	14	2	93	0	3.32	0	0	2
1979-80	QUE	N	50	2773	15	**25**	6	171	4	3.70	2	0	8
1980-81			12	688	0	8	3	61	3	5.32	0	1	0
	WINN	N	14	757	3	6	3	61	1	4.83	0	0	2
	2 team total		26	1445	3	14	6	122	4	5.07	0	1	2

Michel Dion continued

YEAR	TEAM & LEAGUE		GP	MIN	W	L	T	GA	ENG	G AVG	SO	A	PIM
1981-82	**PITT**	**N**	62	3580	25	24	12	226	8	3.79	0	1	4
1982-83			49	2791	12	30	4	198	9	4.26	0	2	8
9 yrs.		**N Totals:**	187	10589	55	93	28	717	25	4.06	2	4	22
		W Totals:	149	8242	62	66	7	450	0	3.28	5	0	30
PLAYOFFS													
1975-76	**IND**	**W**	3	126	0	2	0	5	0	2.38	0	0	0
1976-77			4	245	2	2	0	17	0	4.16	0	0	0
1981-82	**PITT**	**N**	5	304	2	3	0	22	0	4.34	0	0	0
3 yrs.		**N Totals:**	5	304	2	3	0	22	0	4.34	0	0	0
		W Totals:	7	371	2	4	0	22	0	3.56	0	0	0

Sold to **Winnipeg** by Quebec, Feb. 10, 1981. Signed with **Pittsburgh** as free agent, June 30, 1981.

Clarence Dolson

DOLSON, CLARENCE

YEAR	TEAM & LEAGUE		GP	MIN	W	L	T	GA	ENG	G AVG	SO	A	PIM
1928-29	**DET**	**N**	44	2750	19	19	6	63	0	1.43	10	0	0
1929-30			5	320	0	4	0	24	0	4.80	0	0	0
1930-31			44	2750	16	21	7	105	0	2.39	6	0	0
3 yrs.		**N Totals:**	93	5820	35	44	13	192	0	1.98	16	0	0
PLAYOFFS													
1928-29	**DET**	**N**	2	120	0	2	0	7	0	3.50	0	0	0

Peter Donnelly

DONNELLY, PETER
B. June 14, 1948, Detroit, Mich.

5′8″, 155 lbs.
Shoots R

YEAR	TEAM & LEAGUE		GP	MIN	W	L	T	GA	ENG	G AVG	SO	A	PIM
1972-73	**NY**	**W**	47	2606	22	19	2	155	1	3.57	2	0	2
1973-74	**VAN**	**W**	49	2824	22	24	0	179	0	3.80	3	1	9
1975-76	**QUE**	**W**	4	129	0	1	0	10	0	4.65	0	0	0
3 yrs.		**W Totals:**	100	5559	44	44	2	344	1	3.71	5	1	11

Gary Doyle

DOYLE, GARY

YEAR	TEAM & LEAGUE		GP	MIN	W	L	T	GA	ENG	G AVG	SO	A	PIM
1973-74	**EDM**	**W**	1	60	1	0	0	4	0	4.00	0	0	0

Dave Dryden

DRYDEN, DAVID MURRAY
B. Sept. 5, 1941, Hamilton, Ont.

6′2″, 180 lbs.
Shoots R

YEAR	TEAM & LEAGUE		GP	MIN	W	L	T	GA	ENG	G AVG	SO	A	PIM
1961-62	**NYR**	**N**	1	40	0	1	0	3	0	4.50	0	0	0
1965-66	**CHI**	**N**	11	453	3	4	1	23	0	3.05	0	1	0
1967-68			27	1268	0	0	0	69	3	3.26	1	0	0
1968-69			30	1479	0	0	0	79	1	3.20	3	1	0
1970-71	**BUF**	**N**	10	409	3	3	0	23	2	3.37	1	1	0
1971-72			20	1026	3	9	5	68	0	3.98	0	0	0
1972-73			37	2018	14	13	7	89	3	2.65	3	0	0
1973-74			53	2987	23	20	8	148	3	2.97	1	1	4
1974-75	**CHI**	**W**	45	2728	18	26	1	176	0	3.87	1	1	4
1975-76	**EDM**	**W**	62	3567	22	**34**	5	235	0	3.95	1	2	2
1976-77			24	1416	10	13	0	77	0	3.26	1	2	0
1977-78			48	2578	21	23	2	150	0	3.49	2	1	0
1978-79			63	**3531**	**41**	17	2	170	0	**2.89**	**3**	**8**	0
1979-80	**EDM**	**N**	14	744	2	7	3	53	2	4.27	0	0	0
14 yrs.		**N Totals:**	203	10424	48	57	24	555	14	3.19	9	4	4
		W Totals:	242	13820	112	113	10	808	0	3.51	8	14	6
PLAYOFFS													
1965-66	**CHI**	**N**	1	13	0	0	0	0	0	0.00	0	0	0
1972-73	**BUF**	**N**	2	120	0	2	0	9	0	4.50	0	0	0
1975-76	**EDM**	**W**	3	180	0	3	0	15	0	5.00	0	0	0
1977-78			2	91	0	1	0	6	0	3.96	0	0	0
1978-79			13	**687**	6	7	0	42	0	**3.67**	0	0	0
5 yrs.		**N Totals:**	3	133	0	2	0	9	0	4.06	0	0	0
		W Totals:	18	958	6	11	0	63	0	3.95	0	0	0

Sold to **Pittsburgh** by Chicago, June 10, 1970. Sold to **Buffalo** by Pittsburgh, Oct. 9, 1970. Reclaimed by **Buffalo** from Edmonton prior to Expansion Draft, June 9, 1979. Claimed as priority selection by **Edmonton** , June 9, 1979.

Ken Dryden

DRYDEN, KENNETH WAYNE
B. Aug. 8, 1947, Hamilton, Ont.
Won Vezina Trophy, 1972-73, 1975-76
Shared Vezina Trophy, 1976-77, 1977-78, 1978-79
Won Calder Trophy, 1971-72
Won Conn Smythe Trophy, 1970-71
Hall of Fame, 1983

6′4″, 210 lbs.
Shoots L

YEAR	TEAM & LEAGUE		GP	MIN	W	L	T	GA	ENG	G AVG	SO	A	PIM
1970-71	**MONT**	**N**	6	327	6	0	0	9	2	1.65	0	0	0
1971-72			64	**3800**	**39**	8	15	142	2	2.24	8	3	4
1972-73			54	3165	**33**	7	13	119	1	**2.26**	**6**	**4**	2
1974-75			56	3320	30	9	16	149	0	2.69	4	3	0
1975-76			62	3580	**42**	10	8	121	3	**2.03**	**8**	2	0
1976-77			56	3275	**41**	6	8	117	1	**2.14**	**10**	2	0
1977-78			52	3071	37	7	7	105	1	**2.05**	5	2	0

Ken Dryden continued

YEAR	TEAM	LEAGUE	GP	MIN	W	L	T	GA	ENG	G AVG	SO	A	PIM
1978-79			47	2814	30	10	7	108	0	**2.30**	**5**	3	4
8 yrs.		N Totals:	397	23352	258	57	74	870	10	2.24	46	19	10
PLAYOFFS													
1970-71*	MONT	N	20	**1221**	**12**	8	0	61	2	3.00	0	1	0
1971-72			6	360	2	4	0	17	2	2.83	0	0	0
1972-73*			17	**1039**	**12**	5	0	50	2	2.89	1	0	2
1974-75			11	688	6	5	0	29	1	2.53	2	0	0
1975-76*			13	**780**	**12**	1	0	25	1	**1.92**	1	0	0
1976-77*			14	849	**12**	2	0	22	1	**1.55**	**4**	0	0
1977-78*			15	**919**	**12**	3	0	29	0	**1.89**	**2**	0	0
1978-79*			16	990	**12**	4	0	41	0	2.48	0	0	2
8 yrs.		N Totals:	112	6846	80	32	0	274	9	2.40	10	1	4

Michel Dumas

DUMAS, MICHEL
B. July 8, 1949, St. A. de P'briand, Que.
5'9", 180 lbs.
Shoots L

YEAR	TEAM	LEAGUE	GP	MIN	W	L	T	GA	ENG	G AVG	SO	A	PIM
1974-75	CHI	N	3	121	2	0	0	7	0	3.47	0	0	0
1976-77			5	241	0	1	2	17	0	4.23	0	1	0
2 yrs.		N Totals:	8	362	2	1	2	24	0	3.98	0	1	0
PLAYOFFS													
1974-75	CHI	N	1	19	0	0	0	1	0	3.16	0	0	0

Rich Dumas

DUMAS, RICHARD

YEAR	TEAM	LEAGUE	GP	MIN	W	L	T	GA	ENG	G AVG	SO	A	PIM
1974-75	CHI	W	1	1	0	0	0	0	0	0.00	0	0	0

Bob Dupuis

DUPUIS, ROBERT

YEAR	TEAM	LEAGUE	GP	MIN	W	L	T	GA	ENG	G AVG	SO	A	PIM
1979-80	EDM	N	1	60	0	1	0	4	1	4.00	0	0	0

Bill Durnan

DURNAN, WILLIAM
B. Jan. 22, 1916, Toronto, Ont.
Won Vezina Trophy, 1943-44, 1944-45, 1945-46, 1946-47, 1948-49, 1949-50
Hall of Fame, 1964
6', 190 lbs.
Shoots L

YEAR	TEAM	LEAGUE	GP	MIN	W	L	T	GA	ENG	G AVG	SO	A	PIM
1943-44	MONT	N	50	**3000**	**38**	5	7	109	0	**2.18**	2	0	0
1944-45			50	**3000**	**38**	8	4	121	0	**2.42**	1	0	0
1945-46			40	2400	**24**	11	5	104	0	**2.60**	**4**	0	0
1946-47			60	3600	**34**	16	10	138	0	**2.30**	4	0	0
1947-48			59	3505	20	28	10	162	0	2.77	5	0	5
1948-49			60	3600	28	23	9	126	0	**2.10**	**10**	0	0
1949-50			64	3840	26	21	17	141	0	**2.20**	8	1	2
7 yrs.		N Totals:	383	22945	208	112	62	901	0	2.36	34	1	7
PLAYOFFS													
1943-44*	MONT	N	9	**549**	**8**	1	0	14	0	**1.53**	**1**	0	0
1944-45			6	373	2	4	0	15	0	2.41	0	0	0
1945-46*			9	581	**8**	1	0	20	0	**2.07**	0	0	0
1946-47			11	**700**	6	5	0	23	0	**1.97**	**1**	0	0
1948-49			7	468	3	4	0	17	0	2.18	0	0	0
1949-50			3	180	0	3	0	10	0	3.33	0	0	0
6 yrs.		N Totals:	45	2851	27	18	0	99	0	2.08	2	0	0

Ed Dyck

DYCK, EDWIN PAUL
B. Oct. 29, 1950, Warman, Sask.
5'11", 160 lbs.
Shoots L

YEAR	TEAM	LEAGUE	GP	MIN	W	L	T	GA	ENG	G AVG	SO	A	PIM
1971-72	VAN	N	12	573	1	6	2	35	0	3.66	0	0	0
1972-73			25	1297	5	17	1	98	3	4.53	1	0	0
1973-74			12	583	2	5	2	45	0	4.63	0	0	0
1974-75	IND	W	32	1692	3	21	3	123	0	4.36	0	0	6
4 yrs.		N Totals:	49	2453	8	28	5	178	3	4.35	1	0	0
		W Totals:	32	1692	3	21	3	123	0	4.36	0	0	6

Don Edwards

EDWARDS, DONALD LAURIE
B. Sept. 28, 1955, Hamilton, Ont.
Shared Vezina Trophy, 1979-80
5'9", 160 lbs.
Shoots L

YEAR	TEAM	LEAGUE	GP	MIN	W	L	T	GA	ENG	G AVG	SO	A	PIM
1976-77	BUF	N	25	1480	16	7	2	62	1	2.51	2	1	2
1977-78			72	**4209**	**38**	16	7	185	3	2.64	5	3	12
1978-79			54	3160	26	18	9	159	0	3.02	2	2	8
1979-80			49	2920	27	9	12	125	1	2.57	2	1	8
1980-81			45	2700	23	10	12	133	4	**2.96**	**3**	2	0
1981-82			62	3500	26	23	9	205	0	3.51	0	2	2
1982-83	CALG	N	39	2209	16	15	6	148	1	4.02	1	1	0
7 yrs.		N Totals:	346	20178	172	98	57	1017	10	3.02	15	12	32
PLAYOFFS													
1976-77	BUF	N	5	300	2	3	0	15	0	3.00	0	0	0
1977-78			8	482	3	5	0	22	0	2.74	0	0	7

YEAR	TEAM & LEAGUE		GP	MIN	W	L	T	GA	ENG	G AVG	SO	A	PIM

Don Edwards continued

YEAR	TEAM & LEAGUE		GP	MIN	W	L	T	GA	ENG	G AVG	SO	A	PIM
1979-80			6	360	3	3	0	17	1	2.83	1	0	0
1980-81			8	503	4	4	0	28	2	3.34	0	0	0
1981-82			4	214	1	3	0	16	0	4.49	0	0	0
1982-83	**CALG**	**N**	5	226	1	2	0	22	0	5.84	0	0	0
6 yrs.		**N Totals:**	36	2085	14	20	0	120	3	3.45	1	0	7

Traded to **Calgary** by Buffalo with Rich Dunn and Buffalo's second round choice in the 1982 Amateur Draft (Rich Kromm) for Calgary's first round choice (Paul Cyr) and second round choice (Jens Johansson) in the 1982 Amateur Draft and second round choice in the 1983 Amateur Draft (John Tucker), June 9, 1982.

Gary Edwards

EDWARDS, GARY WILLIAM 5'9", 165 lbs.
B. Oct. 5, 1947, Toronto, Ont. Shoots L

YEAR	TEAM & LEAGUE		GP	MIN	W	L	T	GA	ENG	G AVG	SO	A	PIM
1968-69	**STL**	**N**	1	4	0	0	0	0	0	0.00	0	0	0
1969-70			1	60	0	1	0	4	0	4.00	0	0	0
1971-72	**LA**	**N**	44	2503	13	23	5	150	2	3.60	2	0	0
1972-73			27	1560	9	16	1	94	0	3.62	1	1	0
1973-74			18	929	5	7	2	50	1	3.23	1	0	12
1974-75			27	1561	15	3	0	61	1	2.34	3	0	0
1975-76			29	1740	12	13	4	103	1	3.55	0	0	2
1976-77			10	501	0	6	2	39	0	4.67	0	1	2
	CLEVE	**N**	17	999	4	10	3	68	0	4.08	2	0	0
	2 team total		27	1500	4	16	5	107	0	4.28	2	1	2
1977-78			30	1700	6	18	5	128	1	4.52	0	1	4
1978-79	**MINN**	**N**	25	1337	6	11	5	83	0	3.72	0	1	26
1979-80			26	1539	9	7	10	82	1	3.20	0	0	0
1980-81	**EDM**	**N**	15	729	5	3	4	44	0	3.62	0	2	0
1981-82	**PITT**	**N**	6	360	3	2	1	22	0	3.67	1	0	2
	STL	**N**	10	480	1	5	1	45	0	5.63	0	1	0
	2 team total		16	840	4	7	2	67	0	4.79	1	1	2
13 yrs.		**N Totals:**	286	16002	88	125	43	973	7	3.65	10	7	48
PLAYOFFS													
1973-74	**LA**	**N**	1	60	1	0	0	1	0	1.00	0	0	0
1975-76			2	120	1	1	0	9	0	4.50	0	0	0
1979-80	**MINN**	**N**	7	337	3	3	0	22	0	3.92	0	0	2
1980-81	**EDM**	**N**	1	20	0	0	0	2	0	6.00	0	0	0
4 yrs.		**N Totals:**	11	537	5	4	0	34	0	3.80	0	0	2

Drafted by **Buffalo** from St. Louis in Expansion Draft, June 10, 1970. Drafted by **Los Angeles** from Buffalo in Intra-league Draft, June 8, 1971. Traded to **Cleveland** by Los Angeles with Whitey Widing for goaltender Gary Simmons and Jim Moxey, Jan. 22, 1977. Put on **Minnesota** Reserve List after Cleveland-Minnesota Dispersal Draft, June 15, 1978. Traded to **Edmonton** by Minnesota for Edmonton's third round choice in 1982 Entry Draft, Feb. 2, 1981. Traded to **Pittsburgh** by St. Louis for Pittsburgh's eighth round choice in 1984 Entry Draft, Feb. 14, 1982.

Marv Edwards

EDWARDS, MARVIN WAYNE 5'8", 155 lbs.
B. Aug. 15, 1935, St. Catherines, Ont. Shoots L

YEAR	TEAM & LEAGUE		GP	MIN	W	L	T	GA	ENG	G AVG	SO	A	PIM
1968-69	**PITT**	**N**	1	60	0	1	0	3	0	3.00	0	0	0
1969-70	**TOR**	**N**	25	1420	10	9	4	77	1	3.25	1	1	**24**
1972-73	**CALIF**	**N**	21	1207	4	14	2	87	0	4.32	1	1	6
1973-74			14	780	1	10	1	51	0	3.92	0	1	4
4 yrs.		**N Totals:**	61	3467	15	34	7	218	1	3.77	2	3	34

Roy Edwards

EDWARDS, ROY ALLEN 5'8", 165 lbs.
B. Mar. 12, 1937, Seneca Township, Ont. Shoots R

YEAR	TEAM & LEAGUE		GP	MIN	W	L	T	GA	ENG	G AVG	SO	A	PIM
1967-68	**DET**	**N**	41	2177	15	15	8	127	0	3.50	0	0	0
1968-69			40	2099	18	11	6	89	0	2.54	4	0	0
1969-70			47	2683	24	15	6	116	0	2.59	2	1	0
1970-71			37	2104	11	19	7	119	0	3.39	0	0	2
1971-72	**PITT**	**N**	15	847	2	8	4	36	2	2.55	0	1	0
1972-73	**DET**	**N**	52	3012	22	17	7	132	4	2.63	**6**	0	4
1973-74			4	187	0	3	0	18	0	5.78	0	0	0
7 yrs.		**N Totals:**	236	13109	92	88	38	637	6	2.92	12	2	6
PLAYOFFS													
1969-70	**DET**	**N**	4	206	0	3	0	11	2	3.20	0	0	0

Ken Ellacott

ELLACOTT, KENNETH 5'8", 160 lbs.
B. Mar. 3, 1959, Paris, Ont. Shoots L

YEAR	TEAM & LEAGUE		GP	MIN	W	L	T	GA	ENG	G AVG	SO	A	PIM
1982-83	**VAN**	**N**	12	555	2	3	4	41	1	4.43	0	0	0

Tony Esposito

ESPOSITO, ANTHONY JAMES (Tony O) 5'11", 185 lbs.
B. Apr. 23, 1943, Sault Ste. Marie, Ont. Shoots R
Won Vezina Trophy, 1969-70, 1973-74
Shared Vezina Trophy, 1971-72
Won Calder Trophy, 1969-70

YEAR	TEAM & LEAGUE		GP	MIN	W	L	T	GA	ENG	G AVG	SO	A	PIM
1968-69	**MONT**	**N**	13	746	5	3	4	34	0	2.73	2	0	0
1969-70	**CHI**	**N**	63	3763	**38**	17	8	136	0	**2.17**	**15**	2	0
1970-71			57	3325	**35**	14	6	126	0	2.27	6	1	4
1971-72			48	2780	31	10	6	82	0	**1.77**	**9**	1	2
1972-73			56	3340	32	17	7	140	0	2.51	4	2	0

Tony Esposito continued

YEAR	TEAM & LEAGUE		GP	MIN	W	L	T	GA	ENG	G AVG	SO	A	PIM
1973-74			70	4143	34	14	21	141	3	2.04	10	1	0
1974-75			71	**4219**	34	30	7	193	5	2.74	6	1	11
1975-76			68	**4003**	30	23	13	198	4	2.97	4	1	2
1976-77			69	**4067**	25	**36**	8	235	5	3.47	2	0	6
1977-78			64	3840	23	22	14	168	4	2.63	5	**4**	0
1978-79			63	**3780**	24	28	11	206	9	3.27	4	0	2
1979-80			69	**4140**	31	22	16	205	6	2.97	**6**	1	2
1980-81			66	**3935**	29	23	14	246	5	3.75	0	3	0
1981-82			52	3069	19	25	8	231	8	4.52	1	2	0
1982-83			39	2340	23	11	5	135	4	3.46	1	0	0
15 yrs.		N Totals:	868	51490	413	295	148	2476	53	2.89	75	19	29
PLAYOFFS													
1969-70	CHI	N	8	480	4	4	0	27	1	3.38	0	0	0
1970-71			18	1151	11	7	0	42	0	**2.19**	**2**	0	0
1971-72			5	300	2	3	0	16	1	3.20	0	0	0
1972-73			15	895	10	5	0	46	2	3.08	1	0	0
1973-74			10	584	6	4	0	28	2	2.88	**2**	0	0
1974-75			8	472	3	5	0	34	0	4.32	0	0	0
1975-76			4	240	0	4	0	13	0	3.25	0	0	0
1976-77			2	120	0	2	0	6	1	3.00	0	0	0
1977-78			4	252	0	4	0	19	0	4.52	0	0	0
1978-79			4	243	0	4	0	14	0	3.46	0	0	0
1979-80			6	373	3	3	0	14	0	2.25	0	0	0
1980-81			3	215	0	3	0	15	0	4.19	0	0	0
1981-82			7	381	3	3	0	16	0	2.52	**1**	0	0
1982-83			5	311	3	2	0	18	0	3.47	0	0	0
14 yrs.		N Totals:	99	6017	45	53	0	308	7	3.07	6	0	0

Drafted by **Chicago** from Montreal in Intra-league Draft, June 11, 1969.

Claude Evans

EVANS, CLAUDE
B. Apr. 28, 1933, Longueuil, Que.

5'8", 165 lbs.
Shoots L

YEAR	TEAM & LEAGUE		GP	MIN	W	L	T	GA	ENG	G AVG	SO	A	PIM
1954-55	MONT	N	4	220	2	2	0	12	0	3.27	0	0	0
1957-58	BOS	N	1	60	0	0	1	4	0	4.00	0	0	0
2 yrs.		N Totals:	5	280	2	2	1	16	0	3.43	0	0	0

Signed as a free agent by **Boston** , Mar. 6, 1958.

Rocky Farr

FARR, NORMAN RICHARD
B. Apr. 7, 1947, Toronto, Ont.

5'11", 180 lbs.
Shoots R

YEAR	TEAM & LEAGUE		GP	MIN	W	L	T	GA	ENG	G AVG	SO	A	PIM
1972-73	BUF	N	1	29	0	1	0	3	0	6.21	0	0	0
1973-74			11	480	2	4	1	25	0	3.13	0	0	2
1974-75			7	213	0	1	2	14	0	3.94	0	0	0
3 yrs.		N Totals:	19	722	2	6	3	42	0	3.49	0	0	2

Drafted by **Buffalo** from Montreal in Expansion Draft, June 10, 1970. Sold to **Kansas City** by Buffalo, Oct. 1, 1975.

Doug Favell

FAVELL, DOUGLAS ROBERT
B. Apr. 5, 1945, St. Catherines, Ont.

5'10", 172 lbs.
Shoots L

YEAR	TEAM & LEAGUE		GP	MIN	W	L	T	GA	ENG	G AVG	SO	A	PIM
1967-68	PHI	N	37	2192	15	15	6	83	2	2.27	4	0	37
1968-69			21	1195	3	12	5	71	0	3.56	1	0	4
1969-70			15	820	4	5	4	43	1	3.15	1	0	2
1970-71			44	2434	16	15	9	108	3	2.66	2	1	9
1971-72			54	2993	18	25	9	140	5	2.81	5	1	**32**
1972-73			44	2419	20	15	4	114	3	2.83	3	2	4
1973-74	TOR	N	32	1752	14	7	9	79	1	2.71	0	0	20
1974-75			39	2149	12	17	6	145	2	4.05	1	1	10
1975-76			3	160	0	2	1	15	0	5.63	0	0	0
1976-77	COLO	N	30	1614	8	15	3	105	1	3.90	0	0	15
1977-78			47	2663	13	20	11	159	2	3.58	1	2	2
1978-79			7	380	0	5	2	34	1	5.37	0	1	17
12 yrs.		N Totals:	373	20771	123	153	69	1096	21	3.17	18	8	152
PLAYOFFS													
1967-68	PHI	N	2	120	0	2	0	8	0	4.00	0	0	0
1968-69			1	60	0	1	0	5	0	5.00	0	0	0
1970-71			2	120	0	2	0	8	0	4.00	0	0	0
1972-73			11	669	5	6	0	29	1	2.60	1	0	2
1973-74	TOR	N	3	181	0	3	0	10	1	3.31	0	0	0
1977-78	COLO	N	2	120	0	2	0	6	0	3.00	0	0	0
6 yrs.		N Totals:	21	1270	5	16	0	66	2	3.12	1	0	2

Drafted by **Philadelphia** from Boston in Expansion Draft, June 6, 1967. Traded to **Toronto** by Philadelphia, July 27, 1973, to complete deal in which Philadelphia traded its 1973 first-round Amateur Draft Choice (Bob Neely) to Toronto for Toronto's second-round choice in 1973 Amateur Draft (Larry Goodenough) and the rights to goaltender Bernie Parent. Sold to **Colorado** by Toronto, Sept. 15, 1976.

Jake Forbes

FORBES, JAKE
B. Toronto, Ont.

5'6", 140 lbs.
Shoots L

YEAR	TEAM & LEAGUE		GP	MIN	W	L	T	GA	ENG	G AVG	SO	A	PIM
1919-20	TOR	N	5	300	1	4	0	21	0	4.20	0	0	0
1920-21			20	1221	**13**	7	0	78	0	3.90	0	0	0
1922-23	HAMIL	N	24	1469	6	**18**	0	110	0	4.58	0	0	0
1923-24			24	**1483**	9	**15**	0	68	0	2.83	1	0	0
1924-25			30	1833	**19**	10	1	60	0	2.00	6	0	2
1925-26	NYA	N	36	**2241**	12	19	4	86	0	2.39	2	0	0
1926-27			44	2715	17	25	2	91	0	2.07	8	0	0
1927-28			16	980	3	11	2	51	0	3.19	2	0	0
1928-29			1	60	1	0	0	3	0	3.00	0	0	0
1929-30			1	70	0	0	1	1	0	1.00	0	0	0
1930-31	PHI	N	2	120	0	2	0	7	0	3.50	0	0	0
1931-32	NYA	N	6	360	3	3	0	16	0	2.67	0	0	0
1932-33			1	70	0	0	1	2	0	2.00	0	0	0
13 yrs.		N Totals:	210	12922	84	114	11	594	0	2.76	19	0	2
PLAYOFFS													
1920-21	TOR	N	2	120	0	2	0	7	0	3.50	0	0	0

Hec Fowler

FOWLER, NORMAN
B. Unknown

YEAR	TEAM & LEAGUE		GP	MIN	W	L	T	GA	ENG	G AVG	SO	A	PIM
1924-25	BOS	N	7	420	1	6	0	43	0	6.14	0	0	0

Emile Francis

FRANCIS, EMILE (The Cat)
B. Sept. 13, 1926, North Battleford, Sask.
Hall of Fame, 1982

5'6", 145 lbs.
Shoots L

YEAR	TEAM & LEAGUE		GP	MIN	W	L	T	GA	ENG	G AVG	SO	A	PIM
1946-47	CHI	N	19	1140	6	12	1	104	0	5.47	0	0	0
1947-48			54	3240	18	**31**	5	183	0	3.39	1	0	6
1948-49	NYR	N	2	120	2	0	0	4	0	2.00	0	0	0
1949-50			1	60	0	1	0	8	0	8.00	0	0	0
1950-51			5	260	1	1	2	14	0	3.23	0	0	0
1951-52			14	840	4	7	3	42	0	3.00	0	0	0
6 yrs.		N Totals:	95	5660	31	52	11	355	0	3.76	1	0	6

Jim Franks

FRANKS, JAMES REGINALD
B. Nov. 8, 1914, Melville, Sask.

5'11", 156 lbs.
Shoots L

YEAR	TEAM & LEAGUE		GP	MIN	W	L	T	GA	ENG	G AVG	SO	A	PIM
1937-38	DET	N	1	60	1	0	0	3	0	3.00	0	0	0
1942-43	NYR	N	23	1380	5	14	4	103	0	4.48	0	0	0
1943-44	DET	N	18	1080	6	8	3	73	0	4.06	1	0	0
	BOS	N	1	60	0	1	0	6	0	6.00	0	0	0
	2 team total		19	1140	6	9	3	79	0	4.16	1	0	0
3 yrs.		N Totals:	43	2580	12	23	7	185	0	4.30	1	0	0
PLAYOFFS													
1936-37*	DET	N	1	30	0	1	0	2	0	2.00	0	0	0

Ray Frederick

FREDERICK, RAYMOND
B. June 31, 1929, Fort Francis, Ont.

6', 154 lbs.
Shoots L

YEAR	TEAM & LEAGUE		GP	MIN	W	L	T	GA	ENG	G AVG	SO	A	PIM
1954-55	CHI	N	5	300	0	4	1	22	0	4.40	0	0	0

Bob Froese

FROESE, BOB
B. June 30, 1958, St. Catherines, Que.

5'11", 175 lbs.

YEAR	TEAM & LEAGUE		GP	MIN	W	L	T	GA	ENG	G AVG	SO	A	PIM
1982-83	PHI	N	24	1406	17	4	2	59	0	2.52	4	1	2

Grant Fuhr

FUHR, GRANT
B. Sept. 28, 1962, Spruce Grove, Alta.

5'10", lbs.
Shoots L

YEAR	TEAM & LEAGUE		GP	MIN	W	L	T	GA	ENG	G AVG	SO	A	PIM
1981-82	EDM	N	48	2847	**28**	5	14	157	0	3.31	0	**6**	6
1982-83			32	1803	13	12	5	129	0	4.29	0	0	6
2 yrs.		N Totals:	80	4650	41	17	19	286	0	3.69	0	6	12
PLAYOFFS													
1981-82	EDM	N	5	309	2	3	0	26	1	5.05	0	1	0
1982-83			1	11	0	0	0	0	0	0.00	0	0	0
2 yrs.		N Totals:	6	320	2	3	0	26	1	4.88	0	1	0

Bruce Gamble

GAMBLE, BRUCE GEORGE
B. May 24, 1938, Port Arthur, Ont.

5'9", 200 lbs.
Shoots L

YEAR	TEAM & LEAGUE		GP	MIN	W	L	T	GA	ENG	G AVG	SO	A	PIM
1958-59	NYR	N	2	120	0	2	0	6	0	3.00	0	0	0
1960-61	BOS	N	52	3120	12	23	7	195	0	3.75	0	0	**14**
1961-62			28	1680	6	18	4	123	0	4.39	1	0	4
1965-66	TOR	N	10	501	5	2	2	21	0	2.51	2	0	0
1966-67			23	1185	5	10	4	67	1	3.39	0	0	0
1967-68			41	2201	19	13	3	85	3	2.32	5	0	2
1968-69			61	3446	28	20	11	161	3	2.80	3	0	2
1969-70			52	3057	18	23	11	156	1	3.06	5	1	0
1970-71			23	1286	6	14	1	83	2	3.87	2	0	0
	PHI	N	11	660	3	6	2	37	1	3.36	0	0	0
	2 team total		34	1946	9	20	3	120	3	3.70	2	0	0
1971-72			24	1186	7	8	2	58	2	2.93	2	0	0
10 yrs.		N Totals:	327	18442	109	139	47	992	13	3.23	20	1	22

Bruce Gamble continued

YEAR	TEAM	LEAGUE	GP	MIN	W	L	T	GA	ENG	G AVG	SO	A	PIM
PLAYOFFS													
1968-69	**TOR**	**N**	2	86	0	2	0	13	0	9.07	0	0	0
1970-71	**PHI**	**N**	2	120	0	2	0	12	C	6.00	0	0	0
2 yrs.		**N Totals:**	4	206	0	4	0	25	0	7.28	0	0	0

Drafted by **Boston** from N.Y. Rangers, June, 1959. Traded to Springfield (AHL) by Boston with Terry Gray, Randy Miller and Dale Rolfe for Bob McCord, June, 1963. Traded to **Toronto** by Springfield (AHL) for Larry Johnston and Bill Smith, Sept., 1965. Traded to **Philadelphia** by Toronto with Mike Walton and Toronto's first choice (Pierre Plante) in 1971 Amateur Draft for Bernie Parent and Philadelphia's second choice (Rick Kehoe) in same draft, Feb. 1, 1971.

Bert Gardiner

GARDINER, WILBERT
B. Mar. 25, 1913, Saskatoon, Sask.
5'11", 160 lbs.
Shoots L

YEAR	TEAM	LEAGUE	GP	MIN	W	L	T	GA	ENG	G AVG	SO	A	PIM
1935-36	**NYR**	**N**	1	60	1	0	0	1	0	1.00	0	0	0
1940-41	**MONT**	**N**	42	2600	13	**23**	6	119	0	2.83	1	0	0
1941-42			10	620	1	8	1	42	0	4.20	0	0	0
1942-43	**CHI**	**N**	50	**3020**	17	18	15	180	0	3.58	1	0	0
1943-44	**BOS**	**N**	41	2460	17	19	5	212	0	5.17	1	1	0
5 yrs.		**N Totals:**	144	8760	49	68	27	554	0	3.79	3	1	0
PLAYOFFS													
1938-39	**NYR**	**N**	6	433	3	3	0	12	0	2.00	0	0	0
1940-41	**MONT**	**N**	3	214	1	2	0	8	0	2.67	0	0	0
2 yrs.		**N Totals:**	9	647	4	5	0	20	0	1.85	0	0	0

Chuck Gardiner

GARDINER, CHARLES ROBERT
B. Dec. 31, 1904, Edinburgh, Scotland
Won Vezina Trophy, 1931-32, 1933-34
Hall of Fame, 1945
176 lbs.
Shoots R

YEAR	TEAM	LEAGUE	GP	MIN	W	L	T	GA	ENG	G AVG	SO	A	PIM
1927-28	**CHI**	**N**	40	2420	6	32	2	114	0	2.85	3	0	0
1928-29			44	2758	7	**29**	8	85	0	1.93	5	0	2
1929-30			44	2750	21	18	5	111	0	2.52	3	0	0
1930-31			44	2710	24	17	3	78	0	1.77	**12**	0	0
1931-32			48	2989	18	19	11	92	0	**1.92**	4	0	0
1932-33			48	**3010**	16	20	12	101	0	2.10	5	0	0
1933-34			48	3050	20	17	11	83	0	1.73	**10**	0	0
7 yrs.		**N Totals:**	316	19687	112	152	52	664	0	2.02	42	0	2
PLAYOFFS													
1929-30	**CHI**	**N**	2	172	0	1	1	3	0	1.50	0	0	0
1930-31			9	638	5	3	1	14	0	1.56	**2**	0	0
1931-32			2	120	1	1	0	6	0	3.00	**1**	0	0
1933-34*			8	602	**6**	1	1	12	0	**1.50**	**2**	0	0
4 yrs.		**N Totals:**	21	1532	12	6	3	35	0	1.37	5	0	0

George Gardner

GARDNER, GEORGE EDWARD
B. Oct. 8, 1942, Lachine, Que.
5'10", 160 lbs.
Shoots L

YEAR	TEAM	LEAGUE	GP	MIN	W	L	T	GA	ENG	G AVG	SO	A	PIM
1965-66	**DET**	**N**	1	60	1	0	0	1	1	1.00	0	0	0
1966-67			11	560	3	6	0	36	0	3.86	0	0	0
1967-68			12	534	3	2	2	32	0	3.60	0	0	0
1970-71	**VAN**	**N**	18	922	6	8	1	52	1	3.38	0	0	0
1971-72			24	1237	3	14	3	86	1	4.17	0	0	0
1972-73	**LA**	**W**	49	2713	19	22	4	149	0	3.30	1	0	0
1973-74			2	120	0	2	0	13	0	6.50	0	0	0
	VAN	**W**	28	1590	4	21	1	125	0	4.72	0	0	0
	2 team total		30	1710	4	23	1	138	0	4.84	0	0	0
7 yrs.		**N Totals:**	66	3313	16	30	6	207	3	3.75	0	0	0
		W Totals:	79	4423	23	45	5	287	0	3.89	1	0	0
PLAYOFFS													
1972-73	**LA**	**W**	3	116	1	2	0	11	0	5.69	0	0	0

John Garrett

GARRETT, JOHN MURDOCK
B. June 17, 1951, Trenton, Ont.
5'8", 175 lbs.
Shoots R

YEAR	TEAM	LEAGUE	GP	MIN	W	L	T	GA	ENG	G AVG	SO	A	PIM
1973-74	**MINN**	**W**	40	2290	21	18	0	137	0	3.59	1	0	10
1974-75			58	3294	30	23	2	180	0	3.28	2	0	6
1975-76			52	3179	26	22	4	177	0	3.34	2	0	6
	TOR	**W**	9	551	3	6	0	33	0	3.59	1	1	0
	2 team total		61	3730	29	28	4	210	0	3.38	3	1	6
1976-77	**BIRM**	**W**	65	3803	24	**34**	4	224	0	3.53	**4**	3	21
1977-78			58	**3306**	24	**31**	1	210	0	3.81	2	3	26
1978-79	**NE**	**W**	41	2496	20	17	4	149	0	3.58	2	0	6
1979-80	**HART**	**N**	52	3046	16	24	11	202	1	3.98	0	2	12
1980-81			54	3152	15	**27**	12	241	3	4.59	0	1	2
1981-82			16	898	5	6	4	63	1	4.21	0	1	2
	QUE	**N**	12	720	4	5	3	62	0	5.17	0	0	0
	2 team total		28	1618	9	11	7	125	1	4.64	0	1	2
1982-83			17	953	6	8	2	64	3	4.03	0	0	2
	VAN	**N**	17	934	7	6	3	48	2	3.08	1	1	0
	2 team total		34	1887	13	14	5	112	5	3.56	1	1	2
10 yrs.		**N Totals:**	168	9703	53	76	35	680	10	4.20	1	5	18
		W Totals:	323	18919	148	151	15	1110	0	3.52	14	7	75

John Garrett continued

YEAR	TEAM	LEAGUE	GP	MIN	W	L	T	GA	ENG	G AVG	SO	A	PIM
PLAYOFFS													
1973-74	**MINN**	**W**	7	372	4	2	0	25	0	4.03	0	0	0
1974-75			12	726	6	6	0	41	0	3.39	1	0	0
1977-78	**BIRM**	**W**	5	271	1	4	0	26	0	5.76	0	0	0
1978-79	**NE**	**W**	8	447	4	3	0	32	0	4.30	0	0	0
1979-80	**HART**	**N**	1	60	0	1	0	8	0	8.00	0	0	0
1981-82	**QUE**	**N**	5	323	3	2	0	21	0	3.90	0	0	0
1982-83	**VAN**	**N**	1	60	1	0	0	4	0	4.00	0	0	0
7 yrs.		**N Totals:**	7	443	4	3	0	33	0	4.47	0	0	0
		W Totals:	32	1816	15	15	0	124	0	4.10	1	0	0

Reclaimed by **Chicago** from Hartford prior to Expansion Draft, June 9, 1979. Claimed by **Hartford** as priority selection, June 9, 1979. Traded to **Quebec** by Hartford for Michel Plasse and a fourth round choice (Ron Chyzowski) in 1983 Entry Draft, Jan. 12, 1982. Traded by Quebec to **Vancouver** for Anders Eldebrink, Feb. 4, 1983.

Dave Gatherum

GATHERUM, DAVID L. 5'8", 170 lbs.
B. Mar. 28, 1932, Fort William, Ont. Shoots L

YEAR	TEAM	LEAGUE	GP	MIN	W	L	T	GA	ENG	G AVG	SO	A	PIM
1953-54	**DET**	**N**	3	180	2	0	1	3	0	1.00	1	0	0

Paul Gauthier

GAUTHIER, JOSEPH ALPHONSE PAUL 5'5", 125 lbs.
B. Mar. 6, 1915, Winnipeg, Man.

YEAR	TEAM	LEAGUE	GP	MIN	W	L	T	GA	ENG	G AVG	SO	A	PIM
1937-38	**MONT**	**N**	1	70	0	0	1	2	0	2.00	0	0	0

Jack Gelineau

GELINEAU, JOHN EDWARD 6', 180 lbs.
B. Nov. 11, 1924, Toronto, Ont. Shoots L
Won Calder Trophy, 1949-50

YEAR	TEAM	LEAGUE	GP	MIN	W	L	T	GA	ENG	G AVG	SO	A	PIM
1948-49	**BOS**	**N**	4	240	2	2	0	12	0	3.00	0	0	0
1949-50			67	4020	22	30	15	220	0	3.28	3	0	0
1950-51			70	**4200**	22	30	18	197	0	2.81	4	0	4
1953-54	**CHI**	**N**	2	120	0	2	0	18	0	9.00	0	0	0
4 yrs.		**N Totals:**	143	8580	46	64	33	447	0	3.13	7	0	4
PLAYOFFS													
1950-51	**BOS**	**N**	4	260	2	2	0	7	0	1.62	1	0	0

Purchased by **Chicago** from Boston, Nov. 28, 1953.

Ed Giacomin

GIACOMIN, EDWARD 5'11", 180 lbs.
B. June 6, 1939, Sudbury, Ont. Shoots R
Shared Vezina Trophy, 1970-71

YEAR	TEAM	LEAGUE	GP	MIN	W	L	T	GA	ENG	G AVG	SO	A	PIM
1965-66	**NYR**	**N**	36	2096	8	19	7	128	2	3.66	0	0	0
1966-67			68	**3981**	**30**	25	11	173	2	2.61	**9**	0	8
1967-68			66	3940	**36**	20	10	160	0	2.44	**8**	0	4
1968-69			70	**4114**	**37**	23	7	175	0	2.55	7	0	2
1969-70			70	**4148**	35	21	14	163	6	2.36	6	2	2
1970-71			45	2641	27	10	7	95	1	2.16	**8**	0	4
1971-72			44	2551	24	10	9	115	2	2.70	1	3	4
1972-73			43	2580	26	11	6	125	2	2.91	4	2	6
1973-74			56	3286	30	15	10	168	1	3.07	5	1	4
1974-75			37	2069	13	12	8	120	1	3.48	1	0	20
1975-76			4	240	0	3	1	19	0	4.75	0	0	0
	DET	**N**	29	1740	12	14	3	100	1	3.45	2	0	0
	2 team total		33	1980	12	17	4	119	1	3.61	2	0	0
1976-77			33	1791	8	18	3	107	3	3.58	3	1	4
1977-78			9	516	3	5	1	27	0	3.14	0	0	0
13 yrs.		**N Totals:**	610	35693	289	206	97	1675	21	2.82	54	9	58
PLAYOFFS													
1966-67	**NYR**	**N**	4	246	0	4	0	14	0	3.41	0	0	0
1967-68			6	360	2	4	0	18	0	3.00	0	0	0
1968-69			3	180	0	3	0	10	0	3.33	0	0	0
1969-70			5	276	2	3	0	19	0	4.13	0	0	0
1970-71			12	759	7	5	0	28	2	2.21	0	0	2
1971-72			10	**600**	**6**	4	0	27	0	2.70	0	0	2
1972-73			10	539	5	4	0	23	1	2.56	1	0	4
1973-74			13	788	7	6	0	37	2	2.82	0	0	6
1974-75			2	86	0	2	0	4	0	2.79	0	0	4
9 yrs.		**N Totals:**	65	3834	29	35	0	180	5	2.82	1	0	18

Claimed on waivers by **Detroit** from N.Y. Rangers, Oct. 31, 1975.

Gilles Gilbert

GILBERT, GILLES JOSEPH 6'1", 175 lbs.
B. Mar. 31, 1949, St. Esprit, Que. Shoots L

YEAR	TEAM	LEAGUE	GP	MIN	W	L	T	GA	ENG	G AVG	SO	A	PIM
1969-70	**MINN**	**N**	1	60	0	1	0	6	0	6.00	0	0	0
1970-71			17	931	5	9	2	59	0	3.80	0	0	2
1971-72			4	218	1	2	1	11	0	3.03	0	0	0
1972-73			22	1320	10	10	2	67	0	3.05	2	0	4
1973-74	**BOS**	**N**	54	3210	34	12	8	158	0	2.95	6	1	9
1974-75			53	3029	23	17	11	158	4	3.13	3	1	10

Gilles Gilbert continued

YEAR	TEAM & LEAGUE		GP	MIN	W	L	T	GA	ENG	G AVG	SO	A	PIM
1975-76			55	3123	33	8	10	151	0	2.90	3	0	18
1976-77			34	2040	8	18	3	97	3	2.85	1	1	15
1977-78			25	1326	15	6	2	56	0	2.53	2	1	8
1978-79			23	1254	12	8	2	74	1	3.54	0	0	16
1979-80			33	1933	20	9	3	88	1	2.73	1	1	10
1980-81	DET	N	48	2618	11	24	9	175	5	4.01	0	1	12
1981-82			27	1478	6	10	6	105	2	4.26	0	0	2
1982-83			20	1137	4	14	1	85	0	4.49	0	0	4
14 yrs.		N Totals:	416	23677	182	148	60	1290	16	3.27	18	6	110
PLAYOFFS													
1972-73	MINN	N	1	60	0	1	0	4	0	4.00	0	0	0
1973-74	BOS	N	6	977	10	6	0	43	1	2.64	1	1	**8**
1974-75			3	188	1	2	0	12	0	3.83	0	0	0
1975-76			6	360	3	3	0	19	0	3.17	**2**	0	2
1976-77			1	20	0	1	0	3	0	9.00	0	0	0
1978-79			5	314	3	2	0	16	0	3.06	0	0	0
6 yrs.		N Totals:	22	1919	17	15	0	97	1	3.03	3	1	10

Traded to **Boston** by Minnesota for Fred Stanfield, May 22, 1973. Traded to **Detroit** by Boston for Rogie Vachon, July 15, 1980.

Andre Gill

GILL, ANDRE
B. Sept. 19, 1941, Sorel, Que.

5'7", 145 lbs.
Shoots L

YEAR	TEAM & LEAGUE		GP	MIN	W	L	T	GA	ENG	G AVG	SO	A	PIM
1967-68	BOS	N	5	270	3	2	0	13	0	2.89	1	0	0
1972-73	CHI	W	33	1709	4	24	0	118	2	4.14	0	0	6
1973-74			13	803	4	7	2	46	0	3.44	0	0	0
3 yrs.		N Totals:	5	270	3	2	0	13	0	2.89	1	0	0
		W Totals:	46	2512	8	31	2	164	2	3.92	0	0	6
PLAYOFFS													
1973-74	CHI	W	11	614	6	5	0	38	0	3.71	0	0	0

Russ Gillow

GILLOW, RUSSELL
B. Sept. 2, 1940, Hespeler, Ont.

5'10", 165 lbs.
Shoots L

YEAR	TEAM & LEAGUE		GP	MIN	W	L	T	GA	ENG	G AVG	SO	A	PIM
1972-73	LA	W	38	1982	17	13	2	96	3	2.91	2	0	6
1973-74			18	1041	4	13	0	69	0	3.98	1	0	2
1974-75	SD	W	30	1653	15	11	2	94	0	3.41	1	1	4
1975-76			23	1037	1	10	2	74	0	4.28	0	0	0
4 yrs.		W Totals:	109	5713	37	47	6	333	3	3.50	4	1	12
PLAYOFFS													
1972-73	LA	W	5	247	1	2	0	12	0	2.91	0	0	0
1974-75	SD	W	3	79	0	0	0	5	0	3.80	0	0	0
1975-76	CALG	W	1	20	0	0	0	0	0	0.00	0	0	0
3 yrs.		W Totals:	9	346	1	2	0	17	0	2.95	0	0	0

Paul Goodman

GOODMAN, PAUL
B. Nov. 4, 1908, Selkirk, Man.

5'9", 165 lbs.
Shoots L

YEAR	TEAM & LEAGUE		GP	MIN	W	L	T	GA	ENG	G AVG	SO	A	PIM
1939-40	CHI	N	31	1920	16	10	5	62	0	2.00	4	0	0
1940-41			21	1320	7	10	4	55	0	2.62	2	0	0
2 yrs.		N Totals:	52	3240	23	20	9	117	0	2.17	6	0	0
PLAYOFFS													
1937-38*	CHI	N	1	60	0	1	0	5	0	5.00	0	0	0
1939-40			2	127	0	2	0	5	0	2.50	0	0	0
2 yrs.		N Totals:	3	187	0	3	0	10	0	3.21	0	0	0

Ron Grahame

GRAHAME, RONALD IAN
B. June 7, 1950, Victoria, B.C.

5'11", 175 lbs.
Shoots L

YEAR	TEAM & LEAGUE		GP	MIN	W	L	T	GA	ENG	G AVG	SO	A	PIM
1973-74	HOUS	W	4	250	3	0	1	5	0	1.20	1	0	0
1974-75			43	2590	**33**	10	0	131	0	**3.03**	**4**	1	0
1975-76			57	3343	39	17	0	182	0	3.27	3	1	0
1976-77			39	2345	27	10	2	107	0	**2.74**	**4**	1	2
1977-78	BOS	N	40	2328	26	6	7	107	0	2.76	3	1	0
1978-79	LA	N	34	1940	11	19	2	136	0	4.21	0	1	6
1979-80			26	1405	9	11	4	98	1	4.19	2	1	2
1980-81			6	360	3	2	1	28	0	4.67	0	0	0
	QUE	N	8	439	1	5	1	40	1	5.47	0	0	2
	2 team total		14	799	4	7	2	68	1	5.11	0	0	2
8 yrs.		N Totals:	114	6472	50	43	15	409	2	3.79	5	3	10
		W Totals:	143	8528	102	37	3	425	0	2.99	12	3	2
PLAYOFFS													
1974-75	HOUS	W	13	780	**12**	1	0	26	0	**2.00**	**3**	0	0
1975-76			14	817	6	8	0	54	0	3.97	1	0	0
1976-77			9	561	4	5	0	36	0	3.85	0	2	1
1977-78	BOS	N	4	202	2	1	0	7	0	2.08	0	0	0
4 yrs.		N Totals:	4	202	2	1	0	7	0	2.08	0	0	0
		W Totals:	36	2158	22	14	0	116	0	3.23	4	2	1

Ben Grant

GRANT, BENJAMIN CAMERON 5'11", 160 lbs.
B. July 14, 1908, Owen Sound, Ont. Shoots L

YEAR	TEAM & LEAGUE		GP	MIN	W	L	T	GA	ENG	G AVG	SO	A	PIM
1928-29	TOR	N	3	110	1	0	0	4	0	1.33	0	0	0
1929-30			2	130	1	1	0	11	0	5.50	0	0	0
	NYA	N	7	420	3	4	0	25	0	3.57	0	0	0
	2 team total		9	550	4	5	0	36	0	3.93	0	0	0
1930-31	TOR	N	7	430	1	5	1	19	0	2.71	2	0	0
1931-32			5	320	1	2	1	18	0	3.60	1	0	0
1933-34	NYA	N	5	320	1	4	0	18	0	3.60	1	0	0
1943-44	TOR	N	20	1200	9	9	2	83	0	4.15	0	0	0
	BOS	N	1	60	0	1	0	10	0	10.00	0	0	0
	2 team total		21	1260	9	10	2	93	0	4.43	0	0	0
6 yrs.		N Totals:	50	2990	17	26	4	188	0	3.77	4	0	0

Doug Grant

GRANT, DOUG MUNRO 6'1", 200 lbs.
B. July 27, 1948, Corner Brook, N.W.T. Shoots L

YEAR	TEAM & LEAGUE		GP	MIN	W	L	T	GA	ENG	G AVG	SO	A	PIM
1973-74	DET	N	37	2018	15	16	2	140	0	4.16	1	0	2
1974-75			7	380	1	5	0	34	1	5.37	0	0	0
1975-76			2	120	1	1	0	8	0	4.00	0	0	0
1976-77	STL	N	17	960	7	7	3	50	1	3.13	1	0	0
1977-78			9	500	3	3	2	24	0	2.88	0	0	0
1978-79			4	190	0	2	1	23	1	7.26	0	0	0
1979-80			1	31	0	0	0	1	0	1.94	0	0	0
7 yrs.		N Totals:	77	4199	27	34	8	280	3	4.00	2	0	2

Traded to **St. Louis** by Detroit for future considerations (Rick Wilson, June 16, 1976), March 9, 1976.

Gilles Gratton

GRATTON, GILLES (Gratoony the Loony) 5'11", 160 lbs.
B. July 28, 1952, La Salle, Que. Shoots L

YEAR	TEAM & LEAGUE		GP	MIN	W	L	T	GA	ENG	G AVG	SO	A	PIM
1972-73	OTTA	W	51	3021	25	22	3	187	4	3.71	0	1	10
1973-74	TOR	W	57	3200	26	24	3	188	0	3.53	2	4	28
1974-75			53	2881	30	20	1	185	0	3.85	2	4	8
1975-76	STL	N	6	265	2	0	2	11	0	2.49	0	0	2
1976-77	NYR	N	41	2034	11	18	7	143	2	4.22	0	0	13
5 yrs.		N Totals:	47	2299	13	18	9	154	2	4.02	0	0	15
		W Totals:	161	9102	81	66	7	560	4	3.69	4	9	46
PLAYOFFS													
1972-73	OTTA	W	2	87	0	1	0	7	0	4.83	0	0	0
1973-74	TOR	W	10	539	5	3	0	25	0	2.78	0	0	0
1974-75			1	36	0	1	0	5	0	8.33	0	0	0
3 yrs.		W Totals:	13	662	5	5	0	37	0	3.35	0	0	0

Playing rights purchased by **St. Louis** from Buffalo, July 3, 1975. Signed as a free agent by **N.Y. Rangers** , Mar. 24, 1976.

Gerry Gray

GRAY, GERALD ROBERT 6', 168 lbs.
B. Jan. 28, 1948, Brantford, Ont. Shoots L

YEAR	TEAM & LEAGUE		GP	MIN	W	L	T	GA	ENG	G AVG	SO	A	PIM
1970-71	DET	N	7	380	1	4	1	30	0	4.74	0	0	0
1972-73	NYI	N	1	60	0	1	0	5	0	5.00	0	0	0
2 yrs.		N Totals:	8	440	1	5	1	35	0	4.77	0	0	0

Harrison Gray

GRAY, HARRISON LEROY 5'11", 165 lbs.
B. Sept. 5, 1941, Calgary, Alta.

YEAR	TEAM & LEAGUE		GP	MIN	W	L	T	GA	ENG	G AVG	SO	A	PIM
1963-64	DET	N	1	40	0	0	0	5	0	7.50	0	0	0

Chris Grigg

GRIGG, CHRISTOPHER (Gouler, Fig) 6'1", 174 lbs.
B. Feb. 2, 1953, Ottawa, Ont. Shoots L

YEAR	TEAM & LEAGUE		GP	MIN	W	L	T	GA	ENG	G AVG	SO	A	PIM
1975-76	D-O	W	2	80	0	0	0	13	0	9.75	0	0	0

George Hainsworth

HAINSWORTH, GEORGE 5'6", 150 lbs.
B. June 26, 1895, Toronto, Ont. Shoots L
Won Vezina Trophy, 1926-27, 1927-28, 1928-29
Hall of Fame, 1961

YEAR	TEAM & LEAGUE		GP	MIN	W	L	T	GA	ENG	G AVG	SO	A	PIM
1926-27	MONT	N	44	2732	28	14	2	67	0	**1.52**	**14**	0	0
1927-28			44	2730	**26**	11	7	48	0	**1.09**	13	0	0
1928-29			44	2800	22	7	15	43	0	**0.98**[1]	**22**[1]	0	0
1929-30			42	3008	21	14	9	108	0	2.57	4	0	0
1930-31			44	2740	26	10	8	89	0	2.02	8	0	0
1931-32			48	2998	**25**	16	7	110	0	2.29	6	0	2
1932-33			48	2980	18	**25**	5	115	0	2.40	8	0	0
1933-34	TOR	N	48	3010	**26**	13	9	119	0	2.48	3	0	0
1934-35			48	2957	**30**	14	4	111	0	2.31	8	0	0
1935-36			48	3000	23	19	6	106	0	2.21	8	0	0
1936-37			3	190	0	2	1	9	0	3.00	0	0	0
	MONT	N	4	270	2	1	1	12	0	3.00	0	0	0
	2 team total		7	460	2	3	2	21	0	2.74	0	0	0
11 yrs.		N Totals:	465	29415	247	146	74	937	0	1.91	94	0	2
PLAYOFFS													
1926-27	MONT	N	4	252	1	1	2	6	0	1.50	1	0	0

George Hainsworth continued

YEAR	TEAM & LEAGUE		GP	MIN	W	L	T	GA	ENG	G AVG	SO	A	PIM
1927-28			2	128	0	1	1	3	0	1.50	0	0	0
1928-29			3	180	0	3	0	5	0	1.67	0	0	0
1929-30*			6	**481**	**5**	0	1	6	0	**1.00**	**3**	0	0
1930-31*			10	**722**	**6**	4	0	21	0	2.10	**2**	0	0
1931-32			4	300	1	3	0	13	0	3.25	0	0	0
1932-33			2	120	0	1	1	8	0	4.00	0	0	0
1933-34	TOR	N	5	302	2	3	0	11	0	2.20	0	0	0
1934-35			7	**460**	3	4	0	12	0	1.71	**2**	0	0
1935-36			9	541	3	6	0	27	0	3.00	0	0	0
10 yrs.		N Totals:	52	3486	21	26	5	112	0	1.93	8	0	0

Glenn Hall

HALL, GLENN HENRY (Mr. Goalie)
B. Oct. 3, 1931, Humboldt, Sask.
Won Vezina Trophy, 1962-63
Shared Vezina Trophy, 1966-67, 1968-69
Won Calder Trophy, 1955-56
Won Conn Smythe Trophy, 1967-68
Hall of Fame, 1975

6', 160 lbs.
Shoots L

YEAR	TEAM & LEAGUE		GP	MIN	W	L	T	GA	ENG	G AVG	SO	A	PIM
1952-53	DET	N	6	360	4	1	1	10	0	1.67	1	0	0
1954-55			2	120	2	0	0	2	0	1.00	0	0	0
1955-56			70	**4200**	30	24	16	148	0	2.11	**12**	0	14
1956-57			70	**4200**	**38**	20	12	157	0	2.24	4	0	2
1957-58	CHI	N	70	**4200**	24	**39**	7	202	0	2.89	7	0	10
1958-59			70	**4200**	28	29	13	208	0	2.97	1	0	0
1959-60			70	**4200**	28	**29**	13	180	0	2.57	**6**	0	0
1960-61			70	**4200**	29	24	17	180	0	2.57	**6**	1	0
1961-62			70	**4200**	31	26	13	186	0	2.66	**9**	0	12
1962-63			66	3910	**30**	20	16	166	0	2.55	**5**	0	0
1963-64			65	3840	**34**	19	12	148	0	2.31	7	0	2
1964-65			41	2440	18	18	5	99	1	2.43	4	0	2
1965-66			64	3747	**34**	21	7	164	0	2.63	4	2	14
1966-67			32	1664	19	5	5	66	0	2.38	2	0	10
1967-68	STL	N	49	2858	19	21	9	118	0	2.48	5	0	0
1968-69			41	2354	19	12	8	85	2	**2.17**	**8**	2	20
1969-70			18	1010	7	8	3	49	0	2.91	1	0	0
1970-71			32	1761	13	11	8	71	1	2.42	2	1	0
18 yrs.		N Totals:	906	53464	407	327	165	2239	4	2.51	84	6	86
PLAYOFFS													
1955-56	DET	N	10	**604**	5	5	0	28	0	2.78	0	0	0
1956-57			5	300	1	4	0	15	0	3.00	0	0	0
1958-59	CHI	N	6	360	2	4	0	21	0	3.50	0	0	0
1959-60			4	249	0	4	0	14	0	3.37	0	0	0
1960-61*			12	**772**	**8**	4	0	27	0	**2.10**	**2**	0	0
1961-62			12	**720**	**6**	6	0	31	0	2.58	**2**	0	0
1962-63			6	360	2	4	0	25	0	4.17	0	0	0
1963-64			7	408	3	4	0	22	0	3.24	0	0	0
1964-65			13	**760**	**7**	6	0	28	0	2.21	1	0	0
1965-66			6	347	2	4	0	22	0	3.80	0	0	0
1966-67			3	176	1	2	0	8	0	2.73	0	0	0
1967-68	STL	N	18	**1111**	8	10	0	45	0	2.43	**1**	0	0
1968-69			3	131	0	2	0	5	0	2.29	0	0	0
1969-70			7	421	4	3	0	21	0	2.99	0	0	0
1970-71			3	180	0	3	0	9	0	3.00	0	0	0
15 yrs.		N Totals:	115	6899	49	65	0	321	0	2.79	6	0	0

Traded to **Chicago** by Detroit with Ted Lindsay for Johnny Wilson, Forbes Kennedy, William Preston, and Hank Bassen, July, 1957. Drafted by **St. Louis** from Chicago in Expansion Draft, June 6, 1967.

Pierre Hamel

HAMEL, PIERRE
B. Sept. 16, 1952, Montreal, Que.

5'9", 170 lbs.
Shoots L

YEAR	TEAM & LEAGUE		GP	MIN	W	L	T	GA	ENG	G AVG	SO	A	PIM
1974-75	TOR	N	4	195	1	2	0	18	0	5.54	0	0	2
1978-79			1	1	0	0	0	0	0	0.00	0	0	0
1979-80	WINN	N	35	1947	9	19	3	130	0	4.01	0	2	10
1980-81			29	1623	3	20	4	128	2	4.73	0	1	4
4 yrs.		N Totals:	69	3766	13	41	7	276	2	4.40	0	3	16

Claimed by **Winnipeg** from Toronto in Expansion Draft, June 13, 1979.

Glen Hanlon

HANLON, GLEN (Red)
B. Feb. 20, 1957, Brandon, Man.

6', 180 lbs.
Shoots R

YEAR	TEAM & LEAGUE		GP	MIN	W	L	T	GA	ENG	G AVG	SO	A	PIM
1977-78	VAN	N	4	200	1	2	1	9	0	2.70	0	0	2
1978-79			31	1821	12	13	5	94	0	3.10	3	0	30
1979-80			57	3341	17	29	10	193	0	3.47	0	1	43
1980-81			17	798	5	8	0	59	1	4.44	1	1	10
1981-82			28	1610	8	14	5	106	1	3.95	1	0	22
	STL	N	2	76	0	1	0	8	0	6.32	0	0	0
	2 team total		30	1686	8	15	5	114	1	4.06	1	0	22
1982-83			14	671	3	8	1	50	2	4.47	0	0	2
	NYR	N	21	1173	9	10	1	67	1	3.43	0	0	0
	2 team total		35	1844	12	18	2	117	3	3.81	0	0	0
5 yrs.		N Totals:	174	9690	55	85	23	586	5	3.63	5	2	109

Glen Hanlon continued

YEAR	TEAM & LEAGUE		GP	MIN	W	L	T	GA	ENG	G AVG	SO	A	PIM
PLAYOFFS													
1979-80	VAN	N	2	60	0	0	0	3	0	3.00	0	0	0
1981-82	STL	N	3	109	0	2	0	9	0	4.95	0	0	0
1982-83	NYR	N	1	60	0	1	0	5	0	5.00	0	0	**14**
3 yrs.		N Totals:	6	229	0	3	0	17	0	4.45	0	0	14

Traded to **St. Louis** by Vancouver for Tony Currie, Jim Nill, Rick Heinz and St. Louis' fourth round choice (Shawn Kilroy) in 1982 Entry Draft, March 9, 1982. Traded to **New York Rangers** with Vaclav Nedomansky by St. Louis for Andre Dore, Jan. 4, 1983.

Paul Harrison

HARRISON, PAUL DOUGLAS
B. Feb. 11, 1955, Timmons, Ont.
6'1", 175 lbs.
Shoots L

YEAR	TEAM & LEAGUE		GP	MIN	W	L	T	GA	ENG	G AVG	SO	A	PIM
1975-76	MINN	N	6	307	0	0	0	28	0	5.47	0	0	2
1976-77			2	120	0	0	0	11	0	5.50	0	0	0
1977-78			27	1555	6	16	2	99	0	3.82	1	0	10
1978-79	TOR	N	25	1403	8	12	3	82	0	3.51	1	0	10
1979-80			30	1492	9	17	2	110	3	4.42	0	1	4
1981-82	PITT	N	13	700	3	7	0	64	1	5.49	0	0	0
	BUF	N	6	229	2	1	1	14	1	3.67	0	0	2
	2 team total		19	929	5	8	1	78	2	5.04	0	0	2
6 yrs.		N Totals:	109	5806	28	53	8	408	5	4.22	2	1	28
PLAYOFFS													
1978-79	TOR	N	2	91	0	1	0	7	0	4.62	0	0	0
1980-81			1	40	0	0	0	1	0	1.50	0	0	0
1981-82	BUF	N	1	26	0	0	0	1	0	2.31	0	0	0
3 yrs.		N Totals:	4	157	0	1	0	9	0	3.44	0	0	0

Traded to **Toronto** by Minnesota for Toronto's fourth round choice (Terry Tait) in the 1981 Entry Draft, June 14, 1978. Claimed on waivers by **Buffalo** , Feb. 8, 1982.

Brian Hayward

HAYWARD, BRIAN
B. June 25, 1960, Georgetown, Ont.
5'10", 175 lbs.

YEAR	TEAM & LEAGUE		GP	MIN	W	L	T	GA	ENG	G AVG	SO	A	PIM
1982-83	WINN	N	24	1440	10	12	2	89	0	3.71	1	0	0
PLAYOFFS													
1982-83	WINN	N	3	160	0	3	0	14	0	5.25	0	0	0

Don Head

HEAD, DONALD CHARLES
B. June 30, 1933, Mount Denis, Ont.

YEAR	TEAM & LEAGUE		GP	MIN	W	L	T	GA	ENG	G AVG	SO	A	PIM
1961-62	BOS	N	38	2280	9	26	3	161	0	4.24	2	0	14

Clay Hebenton

HEBENTON, CLAY
B. Feb. 24, 1954, Victoria, B.C.

YEAR	TEAM & LEAGUE		GP	MIN	W	L	T	GA	ENG	G AVG	SO	A	PIM
1975-76	PHOE	W	2	80	0	1	0	9	0	6.75	0	0	0
1976-77			56	3129	17	29	3	220	0	4.22	0	0	2
2 yrs.		W Totals:	58	3209	17	30	3	229	0	4.28	0	0	2

Sammy Hebert

HEBERT, SAM

YEAR	TEAM & LEAGUE		GP	MIN	W	L	T	GA	ENG	G AVG	SO	A	PIM
1917-18	TOR	N	2	80	1	1	0	10	0	5.00	0	0	0
1923-24	OTTA	N	2	120	0	2	0	9	0	4.50	0	0	0
2 yrs.		N Totals:	4	200	1	3	0	19	0	5.70	0	0	0

Rick Heinz

HEINZ, RICHARD
B. May 30, 1955, Essex, Ont.
5'10", 165 lbs.
Shoots L

YEAR	TEAM & LEAGUE		GP	MIN	W	L	T	GA	ENG	G AVG	SO	A	PIM
1980-81	STL	N	4	220	2	1	1	8	0	2.18	0	1	0
1981-82			9	433	2	5	0	35	2	4.85	0	0	0
	VAN	N	3	180	2	1	0	9	0	3.00	1	0	0
	2 team total		12	613	4	6	0	44	2	4.31	1	0	0
1982-83	STL	N	9	335	1	5	1	24	1	4.30	1	0	0
3 yrs.		N Totals:	25	1168	7	12	2	76	3	3.90	2	1	0

Traded to **Vancouver** by St. Louis along with Tony Currie, Jim Nill and St. Louis' fourth round choice (Shawn Kilroy) in 1982 Entry Draft for Glen Hanlon, March 9, 1982.

John Henderson

HENDERSON, JOHN DUNCAN (Long John)
B. Mar. 25, 1933, Toronto, Ont.
6'1", 174 lbs.
Shoots L

YEAR	TEAM & LEAGUE		GP	MIN	W	L	T	GA	ENG	G AVG	SO	A	PIM
1954-55	BOS	N	44	2628	15	14	15	109	0	2.49	5	0	0
1955-56			1	60	0	1	0	4	0	4.00	0	0	0
2 yrs.		N Totals:	45	2688	15	15	15	113	0	2.52	5	0	0
PLAYOFFS													
1954-55	BOS	N	2	120	0	2	0	8	0	4.00	0	0	0

Gord Henry

HENRY, GORDON DAVID (Red)
B. Aug. 17, 1926, Owen Sound, Ont.
6', 185 lbs.
Shoots L

YEAR	TEAM & LEAGUE		GP	MIN	W	L	T	GA	ENG	G AVG	SO	A	PIM
1948-49	BOS	N	1	60	1	0	0	0	0	0.00	1	0	0
1949-50			2	120	0	2	0	5	0	2.50	0	0	0
2 yrs.		N Totals:	3	180	1	2	0	5	0	1.67	1	0	0

Gord Henry continued

YEAR	TEAM & LEAGUE		GP	MIN	W	L	T	GA	ENG	G AVG	SO	A	PIM
PLAYOFFS													
1950-51	BOS	N	2	120	0	2	0	10	0	5.00	0	0	0
1952-53			3	163	0	2	0	11	0	4.05	0	0	0
2 yrs.		N Totals:	5	283	0	4	0	21	0	4.45	0	0	0

Jim Henry

HENRY, SAMUEL JAMES (Sugar Jim)
B. Oct. 23, 1920, Winnipeg, Man.

5'9", 165 lbs.
Shoots L

YEAR	TEAM & LEAGUE		GP	MIN	W	L	T	GA	ENG	G AVG	SO	A	PIM
1941-42	NYR	N	48	**2960**	**29**	17	2	143	0	2.98	1	0	0
1945-46			11	623	1	7	2	41	0	3.95	1	0	0
1946-47			2	120	0	2	0	9	0	4.50	0	0	0
1947-48			48	2880	17	18	13	153	0	3.19	2	0	0
1948-49	CHI	N	60	**3600**	21	**31**	8	211	0	3.52	0	0	0
1951-52	BOS	N	70	**4200**	23	34	13	176	0	2.51	7	0	0
1952-53			70	**4200**	28	29	13	172	0	2.46	7	0	0
1953-54			70	**4200**	32	28	10	181	0	2.59	8	0	0
1954-55			26	1532	8	12	6	79	0	3.09	1	0	0
9 yrs.		N Totals:	405	24315	159	178	67	1165	0	2.87	27	0	0
PLAYOFFS													
1941-42	NYR	N	6	360	2	4	0	13	0	**2.17**	**1**	0	0
1951-52	BOS	N	7	448	3	4	0	18	0	2.41	1	0	0
1952-53			9	510	**5**	4	0	26	0	3.06	0	0	0
1953-54			4	240	0	4	0	16	0	4.00	0	0	0
1954-55			3	183	1	2	0	8	0	2.62	0	0	0
5 yrs.		N Totals:	29	1741	11	18	0	81	0	2.79	2	0	0

Traded to **Detroit** by Chicago with Bob Goldham, Gaye Stewart and Metro Prystai for Harry Lumley, Jack Stewart, Al Dewsbury, Don Morrison and Pete Babando, July 13, 1950. Sovld to **Boston** by Detroit, Aug. 20, 1951.

Denis Herron

HERRON, DENIS
B. June 18, 1952, Chambly, Que.
Shared Vezina Trophy, 1980-81
Won Jennings Trophy, 1981-82

5'11", 165 lbs.
Shoots L

YEAR	TEAM & LEAGUE		GP	MIN	W	L	T	GA	ENG	G AVG	SO	A	PIM
1972-73	PITT	N	18	967	6	7	2	55	0	3.41	2	1	0
1973-74			5	260	1	3	0	18	0	4.15	0	0	0
1974-75			3	108	1	1	0	11	0	6.11	0	1	0
	KC	N	22	1280	4	13	4	80	0	3.75	0	1	2
	2 team total		25	1388	5	14	4	91	0	3.93	0	2	2
1975-76			64	3620	11	**39**	11	243	6	4.03	0	0	16
1976-77	PITT	N	34	1920	15	11	5	94	2	2.94	1	1	4
1977-78			60	3534	20	25	15	210	4	3.57	0	1	6
1978-79			56	3208	22	19	12	180	3	3.37	0	2	18
1979-80	MONT	N	34	1909	25	3	3	80	1	2.51	0	0	0
1980-81			25	1147	6	9	6	67	2	3.50	1	2	0
1981-82			27	1547	12	6	8	68	0	2.64	**3**	0	4
1982-83	PITT	N	31	1707	5	18	5	151	0	5.31	1	0	0
11 yrs.		N Totals:	379	21207	128	154	71	1257	18	3.56	8	9	50
PLAYOFFS													
1976-77	PITT	N	3	180	1	2	0	11	2	3.67	0	0	5
1978-79			7	421	2	5	0	24	1	3.42	0	0	0
1979-80	MONT	N	5	300	2	3	0	15	0	3.00	0	0	0
3 yrs.		N Totals:	15	901	5	10	0	50	3	3.33	0	0	5

Traded to **Kansas City** by Pittsburgh with Jean-Guy Lagace for Michel Plasse, Jan. 10, 1975. Signed by **Pittsburgh** as free agent, Aug. 7, 1976. Colorado (Kansas City) received Michel Plasse and Simon Nolet as compensation. Traded to **Montreal** by Pittsburgh with Pittsburgh's second round choice (Jocelyn Gauvreau) in the 1982 Entry Draft for Pat Hughes and Robert Holland, Aug. 30, 1979. Traded by Montreal to **Pittsburgh** for Pittsburgh's third round choice in the 1985 Amateur Draft, Sept. 15, 1982.

Hec Highton

HIGHTON, HECTOR SALISBURY
B. Dec. 10, 1923, Medicine Hat, Alta.

6', 175 lbs.
Shoots R

YEAR	TEAM & LEAGUE		GP	MIN	W	L	T	GA	ENG	G AVG	SO	A	PIM
1943-44	CHI	N	24	1440	10	14	0	108	0	4.50	0	0	0

Normie Himes

HIMES, NORMAN
B. Apr. 13, 1903, Galt, Ont.

5'9", 145 lbs.
Shoots R

YEAR	TEAM & LEAGUE		GP	MIN	W	L	T	GA	ENG	G AVG	SO	A	PIM
1927-28	NYA	N	1	19	0	0	0	0	0	0.00	0	0	0
1928-29			1	60	0	0	1	3	0	3.00	0	0	0
2 yrs.		N Totals:	2	79	0	0	1	3	0	2.28	0	0	0

Charlie Hodge

HODGE, CHARLES EDWARD
B. July 28, 1933, Lachine, Que.
Won Vezina Trophy, 1963-64
Shared Vezina Trophy, 1965-66

5'6", 150 lbs.
Shoots L

YEAR	TEAM & LEAGUE		GP	MIN	W	L	T	GA	ENG	G AVG	SO	A	PIM
1954-55	MONT	N	14	800	7	3	4	31	0	2.33	1	0	0
1957-58			12	720	8	2	2	31	0	2.58	1	0	0
1958-59			2	120	1	1	0	6	0	3.00	0	0	0
1959-60			1	60	0	1	0	3	0	3.00	0	0	0
1960-61			30	1800	19	8	3	76	0	2.53	4	0	0
1963-64			62	3720	33	18	11	140	0	2.26	**8**	0	2

Charlie Hodge continued

YEAR	TEAM & LEAGUE		GP	MIN	W	L	T	GA	ENG	G AVG	SO	A	PIM
1964-65			53	3120	26	16	10	135	0	2.60	3	0	2
1965-66			26	1301	12	7	2	56	0	2.58	1	0	0
1966-67			37	2055	11	15	7	88	0	2.57	3	0	2
1967-68	**OAK**	**N**	58	3311	13	**29**	13	158	0	2.86	3	0	4
1968-69	**CALIF**	**N**	14	781	4	6	1	48	0	3.69	0	0	0
1969-70	**OAK**	**N**	14	738	3	5	2	43	0	3.50	0	0	0
1970-71	**VAN**	**N**	35	1967	15	13	5	112	0	3.42	0	0	0
13 yrs.		**N Totals:**	358	20493	152	124	60	927	0	2.71	24	0	10
PLAYOFFS													
1954-55	**MONT**	**N**	4	84	1	1	0	5	0	3.57	0	0	0
1963-64			7	420	3	4	0	16	0	2.29	1	0	0
1964-65*			5	300	2	3	0	10	0	2.00	1	0	0
3 yrs.		**N Totals:**	16	804	6	8	0	31	0	2.31	2	0	0

Drafted by **Oakland** from Montreal in Expansion Draft, June 6, 1967. Drafted by **Vancouver** from Oakland in Expansion Draft, June 10, 1970.

Paul Hoganson

HOGANSON, PAUL EDWARD
B. Nov. 12, 1949, Toronto, Ont.

5'11", 175 lbs.
Shoots L

YEAR	TEAM & LEAGUE		GP	MIN	W	L	T	GA	ENG	G AVG	SO	A	PIM
1970-71	**PITT**	**N**	2	57	0	1	0	7	0	7.37	0	0	0
1973-74	**LA**	**W**	27	1308	6	16	0	102	0	4.68	0	0	0
1974-75	**M-B**	**W**	32	1776	9	19	2	121	0	4.09	2	0	12
1975-76	**NE**	**W**	4	224	1	2	0	16	0	4.29	0	1	0
	CIN	**W**	45	2392	19	24	0	145	0	3.64	2	1	4
	2 team total		49	2616	20	26	0	161	0	3.69	2	2	4
1976-77			17	823	5	6	1	64	0	4.67	1	0	2
	IND	**W**	11	395	3	2	0	24	0	3.65	0	0	0
	2 team total		28	1218	8	8	1	88	0	4.33	1	0	2
1977-78	**CIN**	**W**	7	326	1	2	1	24	0	4.42	0	0	0
6 yrs.		**N Totals:**	2	57	0	1	0	7	0	7.37	0	0	0
		W Totals:	143	7244	44	71	4	496	0	4.11	5	2	18
PLAYOFFS													
1976-77	**IND**	**W**	5	348	3	2	0	17	0	**2.93**	**1**	0	1

Goran Hogosta

HOGOSTA, GORAN
B. Apr. 15, 1954, Appelbo, Sweden

6'1", 179 lbs.
Shoots L

YEAR	TEAM & LEAGUE		GP	MIN	W	L	T	GA	ENG	G AVG	SO	A	PIM
1977-78	**NYI**	**N**	1	9	0	0	0	0	0	0.00	0	0	0
1979-80	**QUE**	**N**	21	1199	5	12	3	83	3	4.15	1	0	0
2 yrs.		**N Totals:**	22	1208	5	12	3	83	3	4.12	1	0	0

Bill Holden

HOLDEN, WILLIAM

YEAR	TEAM & LEAGUE		GP	MIN	W	L	T	GA	ENG	G AVG	SO	A	PIM
1973-74	**TOR**	**W**	1	10	0	0	0	0	0	0.00	0	0	0

Mark Holden

HOLDEN, MARK
B. June 12, 1957, Weymouth, Mass.

5'10", 165 lbs.
Shoots L

YEAR	TEAM & LEAGUE		GP	MIN	W	L	T	GA	ENG	G AVG	SO	A	PIM
1981-82	**MONT**	**N**	1	20	0	0	0	0	0	0.00	0	0	0
1982-83			2	87	0	1	1	6	0	4.14	0	0	0
2 yrs.		**N Totals:**	3	107	0	1	1	6	0	3.36	0	0	0

Ken Holland

HOLLAND, KENNETH MARK
B. Nov. 10, 1955, Vernon, B. C.

5'8", 160 lbs.
Shoots L

YEAR	TEAM & LEAGUE		GP	MIN	W	L	T	GA	ENG	G AVG	SO	A	PIM
1980-81	**HART**	**N**	1	60	0	1	0	7	0	7.00	0	0	0

Signed as free agent with **Hartford** , July 17, 1980.

Robbie Holland

HOLLAND, ROBERT
B. Sept. 10, 1957, Montreal, Que.

6'1", 182 lbs.
Shoots L

YEAR	TEAM & LEAGUE		GP	MIN	W	L	T	GA	ENG	G AVG	SO	A	PIM
1979-80	**PITT**	**N**	34	1974	10	17	6	126	4	3.83	1	0	2
1980-81			10	539	1	5	3	45	0	5.01	0	0	0
2 yrs.		**N Totals:**	44	2513	11	22	9	171	4	4.08	1	0	2

Traded to **Pittsburgh** by Montreal with Pat Hughes for Denis Herron and Pittsburgh's second-round choice (Jocelyn Gauvreau) in the 1982 Entry Draft, Aug. 30, 1979.

Hap Holmes

HOLMES, HAROLD
B. Aurora, Ont.
Hall of Fame, 1972

YEAR	TEAM & LEAGUE		GP	MIN	W	L	T	GA	ENG	G AVG	SO	A	PIM
1917-18	**TOR**	**N**	16	965	10	6	0	76	0	4.75	0	0	0
1918-19			2	120	0	2	0	9	0	4.50	0	0	0
1926-27	**DET**	**N**	43	2685	12	**27**	4	100	0	2.33	6	0	0
1927-28			44	2740	19	19	6	79	0	1.80	11	0	0
4 yrs.		**N Totals:**	105	6510	41	54	10	264	0	2.43	17	0	0
PLAYOFFS													
1917-18*	**TOR**	**N**	7	**420**	**4**	3	0	26	0	**3.71**	0	0	0

Leif Holmquist

HOLMQUIST, LEIF 5'11", 175 lbs.
B. Sept. 22, 1942, Gayle, Sweden Shoots L

YEAR	TEAM & LEAGUE		GP	MIN	W	L	T	GA	ENG	G AVG	SO	A	PIM
1975-76	IND	W	19	1079	6	9	3	54	0	3.00	0	0	2

Red Horner

HORNER, REGINALD 6', 190 lbs.
B. May 28, 1909, Lynden, Ont. Shoots R
Hall of Fame, 1965

YEAR	TEAM & LEAGUE		GP	MIN	W	L	T	GA	ENG	G AVG	SO	A	PIM
1932-33	TOR	N	1	1	0	0	0	1	0	1.00	0	0	0

Bill Hughes

HUGHES, WILLIAM
B. Nov. 7, 1947, Kirkland Lake, Ont.

YEAR	TEAM & LEAGUE		GP	MIN	W	L	T	GA	ENG	G AVG	SO	A	PIM
1972-73	HOUS	W	3	170	0	1	1	11	1	3.88	0	0	2

Ed Humphreys

HUMPHREYS, EDWARD 6'1", 170 lbs.
B. June 5, 1953, Eston, Sask. Shoots L

YEAR	TEAM & LEAGUE		GP	MIN	W	L	T	GA	ENG	G AVG	SO	A	PIM
1975-76	CALG	W	8	441	2	5	0	27	0	3.67	0	0	0
1976-77	QUE	W	22	1240	12	8	1	74	0	3.58	1	1	0
2 yrs.		W Totals:	30	1681	14	13	1	101	0	3.60	1	1	0
PLAYOFFS													
1975-76	CALG	W	1	20	0	0	0	0	0	0.00	0	0	0

Gary Inness

INNESS, GARY GEORGE 6', 195 lbs.
B. May 28, 1949, Toronto, Ont. Shoots L

YEAR	TEAM & LEAGUE		GP	MIN	W	L	T	GA	ENG	G AVG	SO	A	PIM
1973-74	PITT	N	20	1032	7	10	1	56	1	3.26	0	0	0
1974-75			57	3122	24	18	10	161	4	3.09	2	2	0
1975-76			23	1212	8	9	2	82	1	4.06	0	0	2
	PHI	N	2	120	2	0	0	3	0	1.50	0	0	0
	2 team total		25	1332	10	9	2	85	1	3.83	0	0	2
1976-77			6	210	1	0	2	9	0	2.57	0	1	0
1977-78	IND	W	52	2850	14	30	1	200	0	4.21	0	0	42
1978-79			9	609	3	6	0	51	0	5.02	0	0	9
	WASH	N	37	2107	14	14	8	130	0	3.70	0	2	6
	2 team total		46	2716	17	20	8	181	0	4.00	0	2	15
1979-80			14	727	2	9	2	44	0	3.63	0	0	2
1980-81			3	180	0	1	2	9	1	3.00	0	0	0
8 yrs.		N Totals:	162	8710	58	61	27	494	7	3.40	2	5	10
		W Totals:	61	3459	17	36	1	251	0	4.35	0	0	51
PLAYOFFS													
1974-75	PITT	N	9	540	5	4	0	24	3	2.67	0	0	2

Traded to **Philadelphia** by Pittsburgh for Bobby Taylor and Ed Van Impe, March 9, 1976. Signed as free agent by **Washington** , Dec. 19, 1978.

Randy Ireland

IRELAND, RANDOLPH 6', 165 lbs.
B. Apr. 5, 1957, Rosetown, Sask. Shoots L

YEAR	TEAM & LEAGUE		GP	MIN	W	L	T	GA	ENG	G AVG	SO	A	PIM
1978-79	BUF	N	2	30	0	0	0	3	0	6.00	0	0	0

Claimed as Re-Entry by **Buffalo** in 1978 Amateur Draft, June 15, 1978.

Robbie Irons

IRONS, ROBERT RICHARD 5'8", 150 lbs.
B. Nov. 19, 1946, Toronto, Ont. Shoots L

YEAR	TEAM & LEAGUE		GP	MIN	W	L	T	GA	ENG	G AVG	SO	A	PIM
1968-69	STL	N	1	3	0	0	0	0	0	0.00	0	0	0

Joe Ironstone

IRONSTONE, JOSEPH
B. Unknown

YEAR	TEAM & LEAGUE		GP	MIN	W	L	T	GA	ENG	G AVG	SO	A	PIM
1925-26	NYA	N	1	40	0	1	0	3	0	3.00	0	0	0
1927-28	TOR	N	1	70	1	0	0	0	0	0.00	1	0	0
2 yrs.		N Totals:	2	110	1	1	0	3	0	1.64	1	0	0

Doug Jackson

JACKSON, DOUGLAS 5'10", 150 lbs.
B. Dec. 12, 1924, Winnipeg, Man. Shoots L

YEAR	TEAM & LEAGUE		GP	MIN	W	L	T	GA	ENG	G AVG	SO	A	PIM
1947-48	CHI	N	6	360	2	3	1	42	0	7.00	0	0	0

Percy Jackson

JACKSON, PERCY 5'9", 165 lbs.
B. Sept. 21, 1908, Canmore, Alta.

YEAR	TEAM & LEAGUE		GP	MIN	W	L	T	GA	ENG	G AVG	SO	A	PIM
1931-32	BOS	N	4	232	1	1	1	8	0	2.00	0	0	0
1933-34	NYA	N	1	60	0	1	0	9	0	9.00	0	0	0
1934-35	NYR	N	1	60	0	1	0	8	0	8.00	0	0	0
1935-36	BOS	N	1	40	0	0	0	1	0	1.00	0	0	0
4 yrs.		N Totals:	7	392	1	3	1	26	0	3.98	0	0	0

Steve Janaszak

JANASZAK, STEVEN 6'1", 210 lbs.
B. Jan. 7, 1957, St. Paul, Minn. Shoots R

YEAR	TEAM & LEAGUE		GP	MIN	W	L	T	GA	ENG	G AVG	SO	A	PIM
1979-80	MINN	N	1	60	0	0	1	2	0	2.00	0	0	0
1981-82	COLO	N	2	100	0	1	0	13	0	7.80	0	0	0
2 yrs.		N Totals:	3	160	0	1	1	15	0	5.63	0	0	0

Signed as free agent by **Colorado** , April 14, 1980. Traded to **Calgary** by Colorado for future considerations, Sept. 18, 1981.

Roger Jenkins

JENKINS, JOSEPH ROGER
B. Nov. 18, 1911, Appleton, Wisc.

5'11", 173 lbs.
Shoots R

YEAR	TEAM & LEAGUE		GP	MIN	W	L	T	GA	ENG	G AVG	SO	A	PIM
1938-39	**NYA**	**N**	1	30	0	1	0	7	0	7.00	0	0	0

Al Jensen

JENSEN, ALLAN RAYMOND
B. Nov. 27, 1958, Hamilton, Ont.

5'10", 180 lbs.
Shoots L

YEAR	TEAM & LEAGUE		GP	MIN	W	L	T	GA	ENG	G AVG	SO	A	PIM
1980-81	**DET**	**N**	1	60	0	1	0	7	0	7.00	0	0	0
1981-82	**WASH**	**N**	26	1274	8	8	4	81	0	3.81	0	2	6
1982-83			40	2358	21	12	6	135	0	3.44	1	0	6
3 yrs.		**N Totals:**	67	3692	29	21	10	223	0	3.62	1	2	12
PLAYOFFS													
1982-83	**WASH**	**N**	3	139	1	2	0	10	0	4.32	0	0	0

Traded to **Detroit** by Washington for Mark Lofthouse, July 23, 1981.

Bob Johnson

JOHNSON, ROBERT MARTIN
B. Nov. 12, 1948, Farmington, Mich.

6'1", 185 lbs.
Shoots L

YEAR	TEAM & LEAGUE		GP	MIN	W	L	T	GA	ENG	G AVG	SO	A	PIM
1972-73	**STL**	**N**	12	583	6	5	0	26	0	2.68	0	0	17
1974-75	**PITT**	**N**	12	476	3	4	1	40	0	5.04	0	0	6
1975-76	**D-O**	**W**	24	1334	8	14	1	88	0	3.96	0	0	0
	CLEVE	**W**	18	1043	9	8	0	56	0	3.22	1	0	0
	2 team total		42	2377	17	22	1	144	0	3.63	1	0	0
3 yrs.		**N Totals:**	24	1059	9	9	1	66	0	3.74	0	0	23
		W Totals:	42	2377	17	22	1	144	0	3.63	1	0	0
PLAYOFFS													
1975-76	**CLEVE**	**W**	2	120	0	2	0	8	0	4.00	0	0	0

Traded to **Pittsburgh** by St. Louis for Nick Harbaruk, Oct. 4, 1973.

Eddie Johnston

JOHNSTON, EDWARD JOSEPH
B. Nov. 24, 1935, Montreal, Que.

6', 190 lbs.
Shoots L

YEAR	TEAM & LEAGUE		GP	MIN	W	L	T	GA	ENG	G AVG	SO	A	PIM
1962-63	**BOS**	**N**	49	2880	11	27	11	196	0	4.08	1	0	10
1963-64			70	**4200**	18	**40**	12	211	0	3.01	6	0	0
1964-65			47	2820	12	**31**	4	162	0	3.45	3	0	4
1965-66			33	1743	10	19	2	108	0	3.72	1	0	0
1966-67			34	1880	9	21	2	116	1	3.70	0	1	0
1967-68			28	1524	11	8	5	73	0	2.87	0	0	0
1968-69			24	1440	14	6	4	74	0	3.08	2	1	0
1969-70			37	2176	16	9	11	108	0	2.98	3	2	2
1970-71			38	2280	30	6	2	96	2	2.53	4	1	6
1971-72			38	2260	27	8	3	102	1	2.71	2	4	0
1972-73			45	2510	24	17	1	137	3	3.27	5	1	2
1973-74	**TOR**	**N**	26	1516	12	9	4	78	1	3.09	1	0	0
1974-75	**STL**	**N**	30	1800	12	13	5	93	0	3.10	2	0	0
1975-76			38	2152	11	17	9	130	1	3.62	1	0	0
1976-77			38	2111	13	16	5	108	1	3.07	1	0	0
1977-78			12	650	5	6	7	45	0	4.15	0	0	0
	CHI	**N**	4	240	1	3	0	17	0	4.25	0	0	0
	2 team total		16	890	6	9	7	62	0	4.18	0	0	0
16 yrs.		**N Totals:**	591	34182	236	256	87	1854	10	3.25	32	10	24
PLAYOFFS													
1968-69	**BOS**	**N**	1	65	0	1	0	4	0	3.69	0	0	0
1969-70*			1	60	0	1	0	4	0	4.00	0	0	2
1970-71			1	60	0	1	0	7	0	7.00	0	0	0
1971-72*			7	420	**6**	1	0	13	0	**1.86**	1	0	0
1972-73			3	160	1	2	0	9	0	3.38	0	0	0
1973-74	**TOR**	**N**	1	60	0	1	0	6	0	6.00	0	0	0
1974-75	**STL**	**N**	1	60	0	1	0	5	0	5.00	0	0	0
1976-77			3	138	0	2	0	9	0	3.91	0	0	0
8 yrs.		**N Totals:**	18	1023	7	10	0	57	0	3.34	1	0	2

Traded to **Toronto** by Boston May 22, 1973 to complete earlier deal in which Boston received Jacques Plante and Toronto's third choice (Doug Gibson) in 1973 Amateur Draft for Boston's first round choice (Ian Turnbull) in same draft, Mar. 3, 1973. Traded to **St. Louis** by Toronto for Gary Sabourin, May 27, 1974. Sold to **Chicago** by St. Louis, Jan. 27, 1978.

Joe Junkin

JUNKIN, JOSEPH BRIAN
B. Sept. 8, 1946, Lindsay, Ont.

5'11", 180 lbs.
Shoots L

YEAR	TEAM & LEAGUE		GP	MIN	W	L	T	GA	ENG	G AVG	SO	A	PIM
1968-69	**BOS**	**N**	1	8	0	0	0	0	0	0.00	0	0	0
1973-74	**NY-NJ**	**W**	53	3122	21	**25**	4	197	0	3.79	1	1	7
1974-75	**SD**	**W**	16	839	6	7	0	46	0	3.29	1	1	2
3 yrs.		**N Totals:**	1	8	0	0	0	0	0	0.00	0	0	0
		W Totals:	69	3961	27	32	4	243	0	3.68	2	2	9

Jari Kaarela

KAARELA, JARI PEKKA
B. Aug. 8, 1958, Tampere, Finland

5'10", 165 lbs.
Shoots L

YEAR	TEAM & LEAGUE		GP	MIN	W	L	T	GA	ENG	G AVG	SO	A	PIM
1980-81	COLO	N	5	220	2	2	0	22	0	6.00	0	0	0

Signed as free agent with **Colorado** , Feb. 9, 1981. Traded to **N.Y. Islanders** by Colorado with Mike McEwen for Chico Resch and Steve Tambellini, Mar. 10, 1981.

Hannu Kampurri

KAMPURRI, HANNU

YEAR	TEAM & LEAGUE		GP	MIN	W	L	T	GA	ENG	G AVG	SO	A	PIM
1978-79	EDM	W	2	90	0	1	0	10	0	6.67	0	0	0

Mike Karakas

KARAKAS, MICHAEL
B. Dec. 12, 1911, Aurora, Minn.
Won Calder Trophy, 1935-36

5'11", 147 lbs.
Shoots L

YEAR	TEAM & LEAGUE		GP	MIN	W	L	T	GA	ENG	G AVG	SO	A	PIM
1935-36	CHI	N	48	2990	21	19	8	92	0	1.92	9	0	0
1936-37			48	2978	14	**27**	7	131	0	2.73	5	0	2
1937-38			48	2980	14	25	9	139	0	2.90	1	0	0
1938-39			48	2988	12	**28**	8	132	0	2.75	5	0	2
1939-40			17	1050	7	9	1	58	0	3.41	0	0	0
	MONT	N	5	310	0	4	1	18	0	3.60	0	0	0
	2 team total		22	1360	7	13	2	76	0	3.35	0	0	0
1943-44	CHI	N	26	1560	12	9	5	79	0	3.04	3	0	0
1944-45			48	2880	12	**29**	7	187	0	3.90	**4**	1	0
1945-46			48	2880	22	19	7	166	0	3.46	1	0	5
8 yrs.		N Totals:	336	20616	114	169	53	1002	0	2.92	28	1	9
PLAYOFFS													
1935-36	CHI	N	2	120	1	1	0	7	0	3.50	0	0	0
1937-38*			8	**525**	**6**	2	0	15	0	1.88	**2**	0	0
1943-44			9	**549**	4	5	0	24	0	2.62	**1**	0	0
1945-46			4	240	0	4	0	26	0	6.50	0	0	0
4 yrs.		N Totals:	23	1434	11	12	0	72	0	3.01	3	0	0

Doug Keans

KEANS, DOUGLAS FREDERICK
B. Jan. 7, 1958, Pembroke, Ont.

5'7", 174 lbs.
Shoots L

YEAR	TEAM & LEAGUE		GP	MIN	W	L	T	GA	ENG	G AVG	SO	A	PIM
1979-80	LA	N	10	559	3	3	3	23	3	2.47	0	0	0
1980-81			9	454	2	3	1	37	1	4.89	0	0	7
1981-82			31	1436	8	10	7	103	5	4.30	0	0	0
1982-83			16	304	0	2	2	24	0	4.74	0	1	0
4 yrs.		N Totals:	66	2753	13	18	13	187	9	4.08	0	1	7
PLAYOFFS													
1979-80	LA	N	1	40	0	1	0	7	0	10.50	0	0	0
1981-82			2	32	0	1	0	1	0	1.88	0	0	0
2 yrs.		N Totals:	3	72	0	2	0	8	0	6.67	0	0	0

Don Keenan

KEENAN, DONALD

YEAR	TEAM & LEAGUE		GP	MIN	W	L	T	GA	ENG	G AVG	SO	A	PIM
1958-59	BOS	N	1	60	0	1	0	4	0	4.00	0	0	0

Davie Kerr

KERR, DAVID ALEXANDER
B. Jan. 11, 1910, Toronto, Ont.
Won Vezina Trophy, 1939-40

5'10", 160 lbs.
Shoots R

YEAR	TEAM & LEAGUE		GP	MIN	W	L	T	GA	ENG	G AVG	SO	A	PIM
1930-31	MON(M)	N	28	1649	13	11	4	76	0	2.71	1	0	0
1931-32	NYA	N	1	60	0	1	0	6	0	6.00	0	0	0
1932-33	MON(M)	N	25	1520	14	8	3	58	0	2.32	4	0	0
1933-34			48	**3060**	19	18	11	122	0	2.54	6	0	0
1934-35	NYR	N	37	2290	19	12	6	94	0	2.54	4	0	0
1935-36			47	2980	18	17	12	95	0	2.02	8	0	0
1936-37			48	**3020**	19	20	9	106	0	2.21	4	0	0
1937-38			48	2960	27	15	6	96	0	2.00	**8**	0	0
1938-39			48	2970	26	16	6	105	0	2.19	6	0	0
1939-40			48	**3000**	27	11	10	77	0	**1.60**	**8**	0	0
1940-41			48	3010	21	19	8	125	0	2.60	2	0	0
11 yrs.		N Totals:	426	26519	203	148	75	960	0	2.17	51	0	0
PLAYOFFS													
1930-31	MON(M)	N	2	120	0	2	0	8	0	4.00	0	0	0
1932-33			2	120	0	2	0	5	0	2.50	0	0	0
1933-34			4	240	1	2	1	7	0	1.75	1	0	0
1934-35	NYR	N	4	240	1	1	2	10	0	2.50	0	0	0
1936-37			9	**553**	**6**	3	0	10	0	**1.11**	**4**	0	0
1937-38			3	262	1	2	0	8	0	2.67	0	0	0
1938-39			1	119	0	1	0	2	0	2.00	0	0	0
1939-40*			12	**770**	**8**	4	0	20	0	**1.67**	**3**	0	0
1940-41			3	192	1	2	0	6	0	2.00	0	0	0
9 yrs.		N Totals:	40	2616	18	19	3	76	0	1.74	8	0	0

John Kiely

KIELY, JOHN
B. Aug. 3, 1952

6'3", 190 lbs.
Shoots L

YEAR	TEAM & LEAGUE		GP	MIN	W	L	T	GA	ENG	G AVG	SO	A	PIM
1975-76	CIN	W	22	1087	6	8	1	78	0	4.31	0	1	6

Julian Klymkiw

KLYMKIW, JULIAN
B. July 16, 1933, Winnipeg, Man.

5'11", 180 lbs.
Shoots R

YEAR	TEAM & LEAGUE		GP	MIN	W	L	T	GA	ENG	G AVG	SO	A	PIM
1958-59	NYR	N	1	19	0	0	0	2	0	6.32	0	0	0

Gary Kurt

KURT, GARY DAVID
B. Mar. 9, 1947, Kitchener, Ont.

6'3", 205 lbs.
Shoots L

YEAR	TEAM & LEAGUE		GP	MIN	W	L	T	GA	ENG	G AVG	SO	A	PIM
1971-72	CALIF	N	16	838	1	7	5	60	1	4.30	0	0	0
1972-73	NY	W	36	1881	10	21	0	150	0	4.78	0	1	2
1973-74	NY-NJ	W	20	1089	8	10	0	75	0	4.13	0	1	0
1974-75	PHOE	W	47	2841	25	16	4	156	0	3.29	2	2	2
1975-76			40	2369	18	20	2	147	0	3.72	1	4	4
1976-77			33	1752	11	19	1	162	0	5.55	0	3	6
6 yrs.		N Totals:	16	838	1	7	5	60	1	4.30	0	0	0
		W Totals:	176	9932	72	86	7	690	0	4.17	3	11	14
PLAYOFFS													
1974-75	PHOE	W	4	207	1	2	0	12	0	3.48	0	0	0

Al Lacroix

LACROIX, ALPHONSE
B. Unknown

YEAR	TEAM & LEAGUE		GP	MIN	W	L	T	GA	ENG	G AVG	SO	A	PIM
1925-26	MONT	N	5	280	1	4	0	16	0	3.20	0	0	0

Rich LaFerriere

LAFERRIERE, RICHARD
B. Jan. 3, 1961, Hawksbury, Ont.

5'9", 170 lbs.

YEAR	TEAM & LEAGUE		GP	MIN	W	L	T	GA	ENG	G AVG	SO	A	PIM
1981-82	COLO	N	1	20	0	0	0	1	0	3.00	0	0	0

Bruce Landon

LANDON, NORMAN BRUCE
B. Oct. 5, 1949, Kingston, Ont.

5'10", 180 lbs.
Shoots L

YEAR	TEAM & LEAGUE		GP	MIN	W	L	T	GA	ENG	G AVG	SO	A	PIM
1972-73	NE	W	30	1671	15	11	1	100	0	3.59	1	1	8
1973-74			24	1386	11	9	2	82	0	3.55	0	0	24
1974-75			7	339	2	3	0	19	0	3.36	0	0	0
1975-76			38	2181	14	19	5	126	0	3.47	0	1	0
1976-77			23	1118	8	8	1	59	0	3.17	1	0	4
5 yrs.		W Totals:	122	6695	50	50	9	386	0	3.46	2	2	36
PLAYOFFS													
1973-74	NE	W	1	40	0	0	0	3	0	4.50	0	0	0
1975-76			4	197	3	0	0	7	0	2.13	0	0	0
1976-77			3	152	1	2	0	11	0	4.34	0	0	1
3 yrs.		W Totals:	8	389	4	2	0	21	0	3.24	0	0	1

Norm LaPointe

LAPOINTE, NORMAND
B. Aug. 13, 1955, Laval, Que.

6'1", 180 lbs.
Shoots L

YEAR	TEAM & LEAGUE		GP	MIN	W	L	T	GA	ENG	G AVG	SO	A	PIM
1975-76	CIN	W	12	641	4	6	0	55	0	5.15	0	0	2
1976-77			52	2817	21	25	2	175	0	3.73	2	0	2
1977-78			13	647	5	6	1	50	0	4.64	0	1	4
3 yrs.		W Totals:	77	4105	30	37	3	280	0	4.09	2	1	8
PLAYOFFS													
1976-77	CIN	W	4	273	0	3	0	16	0	3.52	0	0	0

Claimed by **Hartford** from Vancouver in Expansion Draft, June 13, 1979.

Michel Larocque

LAROCQUE, MICHEL RAYMOND (Bunny)
B. Apr. 16, 1952, Hull, Que.
Shared Vezina Trophy, 1976-77, 1977-78, 1978-79, 1980-81

5'10", 185 lbs.
Shoots L

YEAR	TEAM & LEAGUE		GP	MIN	W	L	T	GA	ENG	G AVG	SO	A	PIM
1973-74	MONT	N	27	1431	15	8	2	69	2	2.89	0	2	0
1974-75			25	1480	17	5	0	74	2	3.00	3	1	2
1975-76			22	1220	16	1	3	50	2	2.46	2	2	4
1976-77			26	1525	19	2	4	53	0	2.09	0	0	0
1977-78			30	1729	22	3	4	77	0	2.67	1	4	0
1978-79			34	1986	22	7	4	94	0	2.84	3	3	2
1979-80			39	2259	17	13	8	125	0	3.32	3	2	4
1980-81			28	1623	16	9	3	82	2	3.03	1	1	2
	TOR	N	8	460	3	3	2	40	0	5.22	0	0	0
	2 team total		36	2083	19	12	5	122	2	3.51	1	1	2
1981-82			50	2647	10	24	8	207	4	4.69	0	0	0
1982-83			16	835	3	8	3	68	0	4.89	0	0	0
	PHI	N	2	120	0	1	1	8	0	4.00	0	0	0
	2 team total		18	955	3	9	4	76	0	4.77	0	0	0
10 yrs.		N Totals:	307	17315	160	84	42	947	10	3.28	13	15	14
PLAYOFFS													
1973-74	MONT	N	6	364	2	4	0	18	3	2.97	0	0	0
1978-79*			1	20	0	0	0	0	0	0.00	0	0	0
1979-80			5	300	4	1	0	11	0	2.20	1	0	0
1980-81	TOR	N	2	75	0	1	0	8	0	6.40	0	0	0
4 yrs.		N Totals:	14	759	6	6	0	37	3	2.92	1	0	0

Michel Larocque continued

Traded to **Toronto** by Montreal for Robert Picard, Mar. 10, 1981. Traded by Toronto to **Philadelphia** for Rick St. Croix, Jan. 11, 1983.

Curt Larsson

LARSSON, CURT
B. Dec. 11, 1944

5'11", 171 lbs.
Shoots L

YEAR	TEAM & LEAGUE		GP	MIN	W	L	T	GA	ENG	G AVG	SO	A	PIM
1974-75	WINN	W	26	1514	12	11	1	100	0	3.96	1	1	4
1975-76			23	1287	11	10	1	83	0	3.87	0	1	6
1976-77			19	1019	7	9	0	82	0	4.83	0	1	4
3 yrs.		W Totals:	68	3820	30	30	2	265	0	4.16	1	3	14
PLAYOFFS													
1975-76	WINN	W	2	110	2	0	0	6	0	3.27	0	0	0
1976-77			1	20	0	0	0	1	0	3.00	0	0	0
2 yrs.		W Totals:	3	130	2	0	0	7	0	3.23	0	0	0

Gary Laskowski

LASKOWSKI, GARY
B. June 6, 1959, Ottawa, Ont.

6'1", 175 lbs.
Shoots L

YEAR	TEAM & LEAGUE		GP	MIN	W	L	T	GA	ENG	G AVG	SO	A	PIM
1982-83	LA	N	46	2277	15	20	4	173	3	4.56	0	1	6

Signed as a free agent by **Los Angeles** , Oct. 1, 1982.

Gord Laxton

LAXTON, GORDON
B. Mar. 16, 1955, Montreal, Que.

5'10", 195 lbs.
Shoots L

YEAR	TEAM & LEAGUE		GP	MIN	W	L	T	GA	ENG	G AVG	SO	A	PIM
1975-76	PITT	N	8	414	3	4	0	31	2	4.49	0	0	0
1976-77			6	253	1	3	0	26	0	6.17	0	0	0
1977-78			2	73	0	1	0	9	0	7.40	0	0	0
1978-79			1	60	0	1	0	8	0	8.00	0	0	0
4 yrs.		N Totals:	17	800	4	9	0	74	2	5.55	0	0	0

Albert LeDuc

LEDUC, ALBERT (Battleship)
B. Nov. 22, 1902, Valleyfield, Que.

5'9", 180 lbs.
Shoots R

YEAR	TEAM & LEAGUE		GP	MIN	W	L	T	GA	ENG	G AVG	SO	A	PIM
1931-32	MONT	N	1	2	0	0	0	1	0	1.00	0	0	0

Claude Legris

LEGRIS, CLAUDE
B. Nov. 6, 1956, Verdun, Que.

5'9", 160 lbs.
Shoots L

YEAR	TEAM & LEAGUE		GP	MIN	W	L	T	GA	ENG	G AVG	SO	A	PIM
1980-81	DET	N	3	63	0	1	0	4	0	3.81	0	0	0
1981-82			1	28	0	0	1	0	0	0.00	0	0	0
2 yrs.		N Totals:	4	91	0	1	1	4	0	2.64	0	0	0

Hugh Lehman

LEHMAN, HUGH
B. Oct. 27, 1885, Pembroke, Ont.
Hall of Fame, 1958

YEAR	TEAM & LEAGUE		GP	MIN	W	L	T	GA	ENG	G AVG	SO	A	PIM
1926-27	CHI	N	44	**2797**	19	22	3	116	0	2.64	5	0	0
1927-28			4	250	1	2	1	20	0	5.00	1	0	0
2 yrs.		N Totals:	48	3047	20	24	4	136	0	2.68	6	0	0
PLAYOFFS													
1926-27	CHI	N	2	120	0	1	1	10	0	5.00	0	0	0

Rejean Lemelin

LEMELIN, REJEAN
B. Nov. 19, 1954, Sherbrooke, Que.

5'11", 160 lbs.
Shoots L

YEAR	TEAM & LEAGUE		GP	MIN	W	L	T	GA	ENG	G AVG	SO	A	PIM
1978-79	ATL	N	18	994	8	8	1	55	2	3.32	0	0	4
1979-80			3	150	0	2	0	15	0	6.00	0	0	0
1980-81	CALG	N	29	1629	14	6	7	88	0	3.24	2	1	2
1981-82			34	1866	10	15	6	135	2	4.34	0	1	0
1982-83			39	2211	16	12	8	133	3	3.61	0	5	7
5 yrs.		N Totals:	123	6850	48	43	22	426	7	3.73	2	7	13
PLAYOFFS													
1978-79	ATL	N	1	20	0	0	0	0	0	0.00	0	0	0
1980-81	CALG	N	6	366	3	3	0	22	0	3.61	0	0	0
1982-83			7	327	3	3	0	27	0	4.95	0	0	0
3 yrs.		N Totals:	14	713	6	6	0	49	0	4.12	0	0	0

Signed as free agent by **Atlanta** , Aug. 17, 1978.

Mario Lessard

LESSARD, MARIO
B. June 25, 1954, East Broughton, Que.

5'9", 177 lbs.
Shoots L

YEAR	TEAM & LEAGUE		GP	MIN	W	L	T	GA	ENG	G AVG	SO	A	PIM
1978-79	LA	N	49	2860	23	15	10	148	2	3.10	4	0	6
1979-80			50	2836	18	22	7	185	3	3.91	0	0	6
1980-81			64	3746	**35**	18	11	203	3	3.25	2	1	8
1981-82			52	2933	13	28	8	213	3	4.36	2	2	6
1982-83			19	888	3	10	2	68	0	4.59	1	1	6
5 yrs.		N Totals:	234	13263	92	93	38	817	11	3.70	9	4	32
PLAYOFFS													
1978-79	LA	N	2	126	0	2	0	9	0	4.29	0	0	0
1979-80			4	207	1	2	0	14	0	4.06	0	0	0
1980-81			4	220	1	3	0	20	1	5.45	0	0	0

Mario Lessard continued

YEAR	TEAM & LEAGUE		GP	MIN	W	L	T	GA	ENG	G AVG	SO	A	PIM
1981-82			10	583	4	5	0	41	0	4.22	0	2	2
4 yrs.		N Totals:	20	1136	6	12	0	84	1	4.44	0	2	2

Louis Levasseur

LEVASSEUR, JEAN-LOUIS
B. June 16, 1949, Noranda, Que.

5'10", 160 lbs.
Shoots L

YEAR	TEAM & LEAGUE		GP	MIN	W	L	T	GA	ENG	G AVG	SO	A	PIM
1975-76	MINN	W	4	193	2	1	0	10	0	3.11	0	0	0
1976-77			30	1715	15	11	2	78	0	2.73	2	1	4
	EDM	W	21	1213	6	12	3	88	0	4.35	0	0	0
	2 team total		51	2928	21	23	5	166	0	3.40	2	1	4
1977-78	NE	W	27	1655	14	11	2	91	0	3.30	3	0	2
1978-79	QUE	W	3	140	0	1	1	14	0	6.00	0	0	0
1979-80	MINN	N	1	60	0	1	0	7	0	7.00	0	0	0
5 yrs.		N Totals:	1	60	0	1	0	7	0	7.00	0	0	0
		W Totals:	85	4916	37	36	8	281	0	3.43	5	1	6
PLAYOFFS													
1976-77	EDM	W	2	133	0	2	0	10	0	4.51	0	0	2
1977-78	NE	W	12	**719**	**8**	4	0	31	0	2.59	0	1	2
1978-79	QUE	W	1	59	0	1	0	8	0	8.14	0	0	0
3 yrs.		W Totals:	15	911	8	7	0	49	0	3.23	0	1	4

Alex Levinsky

LEVINSKY, ALEXANDER (Mine Boy)
B. Feb. 2, 1910, Syracuse, N.Y.

5'10", 184 lbs.
Shoots R

YEAR	TEAM & LEAGUE		GP	MIN	W	L	T	GA	ENG	G AVG	SO	A	PIM
1932-33	TOR	N	1	1	0	0	0	1	0	1.00	0	0	0

Pelle Lindbergh

LINDBERGH, PER-ERIK
B. May 24, 1959, Stockholm, Sweden

5'9", 160 lbs.
Shoots L

YEAR	TEAM & LEAGUE		GP	MIN	W	L	T	GA	ENG	G AVG	SO	A	PIM
1981-82	PHI	N	8	480	2	4	2	35	0	4.38	0	0	0
1982-83			40	2334	23	13	3	116	3	2.98	3	4	0
2 yrs.		N Totals:	48	2814	25	17	5	151	3	3.22	3	4	0
PLAYOFFS													
1982-83	PHI	N	3	180	0	3	0	18	0	6.00	0	0	4

Bert Lindsay

LINDSAY, BERT A.

YEAR	TEAM & LEAGUE		GP	MIN	W	L	T	GA	ENG	G AVG	SO	A	PIM
1917-18	MON(W)	N	4	240	1	3	0	35	0	8.75	0	0	0
1918-19	TOR	N	16	1979	5	**11**	0	83	0	5.19	0	0	0
2 yrs.		N Totals:	20	2219	6	14	0	118	0	3.19	0	0	0

Mike Liut

LIUT, MICHAEL
B. Jan. 7, 1956, Weston, Ont

6'2", 195 lbs.
Shoots R

YEAR	TEAM & LEAGUE		GP	MIN	W	L	T	GA	ENG	G AVG	SO	A	PIM
1977-78	CIN	W	27	1215	8	12	0	86	0	4.25	0	1	0
1978-79			54	3181	23	**27**	4	184	0	3.47	**3**	2	9
1979-80	STL	N	64	3661	**32**	23	9	194	1	3.18	2	0	2
1980-81			61	3570	33	14	13	199	2	3.34	1	0	0
1981-82			64	**3691**	**28**	28	7	250	3	4.06	2	2	2
1982-83			68	**3794**	21	27	13	235	0	3.72	1	0	2
6 yrs.		N Totals:	257	14716	114	92	42	878	6	3.58	6	2	6
		W Totals:	81	4396	31	39	4	270	0	3.69	3	3	9
PLAYOFFS													
1978-79	CIN	W	3	179	1	2	0	12	0	4.02	0	0	0
1979-80	STL	N	3	193	0	3	0	12	0	3.73	0	0	0
1980-81			11	685	5	6	0	50	0	4.38	0	0	0
1981-82			10	494	5	3	0	27	0	3.28	0	0	0
1982-83			4	240	1	3	0	15	1	3.75	0	0	0
5 yrs.		N Totals:	28	1612	11	15	0	104	1	3.87	0	0	0
		W Totals:	3	179	1	2	0	12	0	4.02	0	0	0

Reclaimed by **St. Louis** from Cincinnati prior to Expansion Draft, June 9, 1979.

Ken Lockett

LOCKETT, KENNETH RICHARD
B. Aug. 30, 1947, Toronto, Ont.,

6', 160 lbs.
Shoots L

YEAR	TEAM & LEAGUE		GP	MIN	W	L	T	GA	ENG	G AVG	SO	A	PIM
1974-75	VAN	N	25	912	6	7	1	48	2	3.16	2	0	2
1975-76			30	1436	7	8	7	83	1	3.47	0	0	6
1976-77	SD	W	45	1144	18	19	1	148	0	7.76	1	0	0
3 yrs.		N Totals:	55	2348	13	15	8	131	3	3.35	2	0	8
		W Totals:	45	1144	18	19	1	148	0	7.76	1	0	0
PLAYOFFS													
1974-75	VAN	N	1	60	0	1	0	6	0	6.00	0	0	0
1976-77	SD	W	5	260	1	3	0	19	0	4.38	0	0	0
2 yrs.		N Totals:	1	60	0	1	0	6	0	6.00	0	0	0
		W Totals:	5	260	1	3	0	19	0	4.38	0	0	0

Howie Lockhart

LOCKHART, HOWARD (Holes)

YEAR	TEAM & LEAGUE	GP	MIN	W	L	T	GA	ENG	G AVG	SO	A	PIM
1919-20	TOR N	5	268	4	1	0	20	0	4.00	0	0	0
	QUE N	1	60	0	1	0	11	0	11.00	0	0	0
	2 team total	6	328	4	2	0	31	0	5.67	0	0	0
1920-21	HAMIL N	24	1454	7	**17**	0	132	0	5.50	1	0	0
1921-22		24	1409	6	**17**	0	103	0	4.29	0	0	0
1923-24	TOR N	1	60	0	1	0	5	0	5.00	0	0	0
1924-25	BOS N	2	120	0	2	0	11	0	5.50	0	0	0
5 yrs.	N Totals:	57	3371	17	39	0	282	0	5.02	1	0	0

Pete LoPresti

LOPRESTI, PETER JON — 6'1", 195 lbs.
B. May 23, 1954, Virginia, Minn. — Shoots L

YEAR	TEAM & LEAGUE	GP	MIN	W	L	T	GA	ENG	G AVG	SO	A	PIM
1974-75	MINN N	35	1964	9	20	3	137	0	4.19	1	0	2
1975-76		34	1789	7	22	1	123	0	4.13	1	0	0
1976-77		44	2590	13	20	10	156	1	3.61	1	1	4
1977-78		53	3065	12	**35**	6	216	1	4.23	2	0	0
1978-79		7	345	2	4	0	28	0	4.87	0	0	0
1980-81	EDM N	2	105	0	1	0	8	1	4.57	0	0	0
6 yrs.	N Totals:	175	9858	43	102	20	668	3	4.07	5	1	6
PLAYOFFS												
1976-77	MINN N	2	77	0	2	0	6	1	4.68	0	0	0

Claimed by **Edmonton** from Minnesota in Expansion Draft, June 13, 1979.

Sam LoPresti

LOPRESTI, SAMUEL — 5'11", 200 lbs.
B. Jan. 30, 1917, Eveleth, Minn. — Shoots L

YEAR	TEAM & LEAGUE	GP	MIN	W	L	T	GA	ENG	G AVG	SO	A	PIM
1940-41	CHI N	27	1670	9	15	3	84	0	3.11	1	0	0
1941-42		47	2860	21	23	3	152	0	3.23	3	0	0
2 yrs.	N Totals:	74	4530	30	38	6	236	0	3.13	4	0	0
PLAYOFFS												
1940-41	CHI N	5	343	2	3	0	12	0	2.40	0	0	0
1941-42		3	187	1	2	0	5	0	1.67	**1**	0	0
2 yrs.	N Totals:	8	530	3	5	0	17	0	1.92	1	0	0

Ron Loustel

LOUSTEL, RON — 5'11", 185 lbs.
B. Mar. 7, 1962, Winnipeg, Man. — Shoots L

YEAR	TEAM & LEAGUE	GP	MIN	W	L	T	GA	ENG	G AVG	SO	A	PIM
1980-81	WINN N	1	60	0	1	0	10	0	10.00	0	0	0

Ron Low

LOW, RONALD ALBERT — 6'1", 205 lbs.
B. June 21, 1950, Birtle, Man. — Shoots L

YEAR	TEAM & LEAGUE	GP	MIN	W	L	T	GA	ENG	G AVG	SO	A	PIM
1972-73	TOR N	42	2343	12	24	4	152	1	3.89	1	0	4
1974-75	WASH N	48	2588	8	**36**	2	235	0	5.45	1	0	4
1975-76		43	2289	6	31	2	208	3	5.45	0	0	2
1976-77		54	2918	16	27	5	188	1	3.87	0	0	4
1977-78	DET N	32	1816	9	12	9	102	2	3.37	1	1	0
1979-80	QUE N	15	828	5	7	2	51	1	3.70	0	1	0
	EDM N	11	650	8	2	1	37	0	3.42	0	2	0
	2 team total	26	1478	13	9	3	88	1	3.57	0	3	0
1980-81		24	1260	5	13	3	93	2	4.43	0	3	0
1981-82		29	1554	17	7	1	100	2	3.86	0	0	2
1982-83		3	104	0	1	0	10	0	5.77	0	0	0
	NJ N	11	608	2	7	1	41	0	4.05	0	1	4
	2 team total	14	712	2	8	1	51	0	4.30	0	1	4
9 yrs.	N Totals:	312	16958	88	167	30	1217	12	4.31	3	8	20
PLAYOFFS												
1977-78	DET N	4	240	1	3	0	17	0	4.25	0	0	0
1979-80	EDM N	3	212	0	3	0	12	0	3.40	0	0	0
2 yrs.	N Totals:	7	452	1	6	0	29	0	3.85	0	0	0

Drafted by **Washington** from Toronto in Expansion Draft, June 12, 1974. Signed by **Detroit** as free agent, Aug. 17, 1977, with Washington being compensated with Walt McKechnie and Detroit's third round choice (Joey Johnston) in the 1978 Amateur Draft and second-round choice (Errol Rausse) in the 1979 Entry Draft. Detroit also received Washington's third round choice (Boris Fistric) in the 1978 Entry Draft. Claimed by **Quebec** from Detroit in Expansion Draft, June 13, 1979. Traded to **Edmonton** by Quebec for Ron Chipperfield, March 11, 1980. Traded by Edmonton with Jim McTaggart to **New Jersey** for Lindsay Middlebrook and Paul Miller, Feb. 23, 1983.

Pete Lozinski

LOZINSKI, LARRY PETER — 5'11", 175 lbs.
B. Mar. 11, 1958, Hudson Bay, Sask. — Shoots R

YEAR	TEAM & LEAGUE	GP	MIN	W	L	T	GA	ENG	G AVG	SO	A	PIM
1980-81	DET N	30	1459	6	11	7	105	0	4.32	0	1	0

Harry Lumley

LUMLEY, HARRY (Apple Cheeks) — 6', 195 lbs.
B. Nov. 11, 1926, Owen Sound, Ont. — Shoots L
Won Vezina Trophy, 1953-54
Hall of Fame, 1980

YEAR	TEAM & LEAGUE	GP	MIN	W	L	T	GA	ENG	G AVG	SO	A	PIM
1943-44	DET N	2	120	0	2	0	13	0	6.50	0	0	0
	NYR N	1	20	0	0	0	0	0	0.00	0	0	0
	2 team total	3	140	0	2	0	13	0	5.57	0	0	0
1944-45	DET N	37	2220	24	10	3	119	0	3.22	1	0	0

Harry Lumley continued

YEAR	TEAM & LEAGUE		GP	MIN	W	L	T	GA	ENG	G AVG	SO	A	PIM
1945-46			50	**3000**	20	20	10	159	0	3.18	2	0	**6**
1946-47			52	3120	22	20	10	159	0	3.06	3	0	**4**
1947-48			60	3592	30	18	12	147	0	2.46	**7**	0	**8**
1948-49			60	**3600**	**34**	19	7	145	0	2.42	6	0	**12**
1949-50			63	3780	**33**	16	14	148	0	2.35	7	0	**10**
1950-51	CHI	N	64	3785	12	**41**	10	246	0	3.90	3	0	4
1951-52			70	4180	16	**44**	9	241	0	3.46	2	0	2
1952-53	TOR	N	70	4200	27	**30**	13	167	0	2.39	**10**	0	**18**
1953-54			69	4140	32	24	13	128	0	**1.86**	**13**	0	6
1954-55			69	**4140**	24	21	22	134	0	**1.94**	8	0	**9**
1955-56			59	3520	21	28	10	159	0	2.71	3	0	2
1957-58	BOS	N	25	1500	11	10	4	71	0	2.84	3	0	2
1958-59			11	660	8	2	1	27	0	2.45	1	0	0
1959-60			42	2520	18	19	5	147	0	3.50	2	0	12
16 yrs.		N Totals:	804	48097	332	324	143	2210	0	2.76	71	0	95
PLAYOFFS													
1944-45	DET	N	14	**871**	7	7	0	31	0	**2.14**	2	0	0
1945-46			5	310	1	4	0	16	0	3.10	**1**	0	0
1947-48			10	**600**	4	6	0	30	0	3.00	0	0	0
1948-49			11	**726**	4	7	0	26	0	2.15	0	0	0
1949-50*			14	**910**	**8**	6	0	28	0	1.85	**3**	0	0
1953-54	TOR	N	5	321	1	4	0	15	0	2.80	0	0	0
1954-55			4	240	0	4	0	14	0	3.50	0	0	0
1955-56			5	304	1	4	0	14	0	2.76	1	0	0
1957-58	BOS	N	1	60	0	1	0	5	0	5.00	0	0	0
1958-59			7	436	3	4	0	20	0	2.75	0	0	0
10 yrs.		N Totals:	76	4778	29	47	0	199	0	2.50	7	0	0

Traded to **Chicago** by Detroit with Jack Stewart, Al Dewsbury, Don Morrison and Pete Babando for Sugar Jim Henry, Bob Goldham, Gaye Stewart and Metro Prystai, July 13, 1950. Traded to **Toronto** by Chicago for Al Rollins, Gus Mortson, Ray Hannigan and Cal Gardner, Sept. 11, 1952. Purchased from Toronto with Eric Nesterenko by **Chicago** for $40,000, May 21, 1956.

Shawn MacKenzie

MACKENZIE, SHAWN
B. Aug. 22, 1962, Bedford, N.S.
5'10", 175 lbs.
Shoots R

YEAR	TEAM & LEAGUE		GP	MIN	W	L	T	GA	ENG	G AVG	SO	A	PIM
1982-83	NJ	N	6	130	0	1	0	15	0	6.92	0	0	0

Clint Malarchuk

MALARCHUK, CLINT
B. May 1, 1961, Grande, Alta.
5'10", 172 lbs.
Shoots L

YEAR	TEAM & LEAGUE		GP	MIN	W	L	T	GA	ENG	G AVG	SO	A	PIM
1981-82	QUE	N	2	120	0	0	1	14	0	7.00	0	0	0
1982-83			15	900	8	5	2	71	0	4.73	0	0	0
2 yrs.		N Totals:	17	1020	8	5	3	85	0	5.00	0	0	0

Cesare Maniago

MANIAGO, CESARE (Hail Cesare)
B. Jan. 13, 1939, Trail, B.C.
6'3", 195 lbs.
Shoots L

YEAR	TEAM & LEAGUE		GP	MIN	W	L	T	GA	ENG	G AVG	SO	A	PIM
1960-61	TOR	N	7	420	4	2	1	18	0	2.57	0	0	2
1962-63	MONT	N	14	820	5	5	4	42	0	3.07	0	0	2
1965-66	NYR	N	28	1613	9	16	3	94	0	3.50	2	2	2
1966-67			6	219	0	3	1	14	0	3.84	0	0	0
1967-68	MINN	N	52	2877	21	17	9	133	0	2.77	6	0	12
1968-69			64	3599	18	33	10	198	0	3.30	1	0	12
1969-70			50	2887	9	24	16	163	0	3.39	2	0	0
1970-71			40	2380	19	15	6	107	0	2.70	5	1	2
1971-72			43	2539	20	17	4	112	0	2.65	3	0	4
1972-73			47	2736	21	18	6	132	1	2.89	5	0	2
1973-74			40	2378	12	18	10	138	0	3.48	1	0	2
1974-75			37	2129	11	21	4	149	1	4.20	1	0	2
1975-76			47	2704	13	27	5	151	0	3.35	2	0	11
1976-77	VAN	N	47	2699	17	21	9	151	4	3.36	1	1	0
1977-78			46	2570	10	24	8	172	1	4.02	1	0	18
15 yrs.		N Totals:	568	32570	189	261	96	1774	7	3.27	30	4	71
PLAYOFFS													
1960-61	TOR	N	2	145	1	1	0	6	0	2.48	0	0	0
1967-68	MINN	N	14	893	7	7	0	39	0	2.62	0	0	0
1969-70			3	180	1	2	0	6	0	2.00	**1**	0	0
1970-71			8	480	3	5	0	28	1	3.50	0	0	0
1971-72			4	238	1	3	0	12	0	3.03	0	0	0
1972-73			5	309	2	3	0	9	1	**1.75**	**2**	0	2
6 yrs.		N Totals:	36	2245	15	21	0	100	2	2.67	3	0	2

Drafted by **Montreal** from Toronto, June 13, 1961. Traded to **N.Y. Rangers** by Montreal with Garry Peters for Earl Ingarfield, Noel Price, Gord Labossiere and Dave McComb, June 8, 1965. Drafted by **Minnesota** from N.Y. Rangers in Expansion Draft, June 6, 1967. Traded to **Vancouver** by Minnesota for Gary Smith, August 23, 1976.

Jean Marois

MAROIS, JEAN

YEAR	TEAM & LEAGUE		GP	MIN	W	L	T	GA	ENG	G AVG	SO	A	PIM
1943-44	TOR	N	1	60	1	0	0	4	0	4.00	0	0	0

Jean Marois continued

YEAR	TEAM & LEAGUE		GP	MIN	W	L	T	GA	ENG	G AVG	SO	A	PIM
1953-54	**CHI**	**N**	2	120	0	2	0	11	0	5.50	0	0	0
2 yrs.		**N Totals:**	3	180	1	2	0	15	0	5.00	0	0	0

Signed as a free agent by **Chicago** , Nov. 21, 1953.

Seth Martin

MARTIN, SETH
B. May 4, 1933, Rossland, B.C.
5'11", 180 lbs.
Shoots L

YEAR	TEAM & LEAGUE		GP	MIN	W	L	T	GA	ENG	G AVG	SO	A	PIM
1967-68	**STL**	**N**	30	1552	8	10	7	67	0	2.59	1	1	0
PLAYOFFS													
1967-68	**STL**	**N**	2	73	0	0	0	5	0	4.11	0	0	0

Markus Mattsson

MATTSSON, RAINER MARKUS
B. July 30, 1957, Suoneiemi, Finland
6', 180 lbs.
Shoots L

YEAR	TEAM & LEAGUE		GP	MIN	W	L	T	GA	ENG	G AVG	SO	A	PIM
1977-78	**QUE**	**W**	6	266	1	3	0	30	0	6.77	0	0	0
	WINN	**W**	10	511	4	5	0	30	0	3.52	0	0	2
	2 team total		16	777	5	8	0	60	0	4.63	0	0	2
1978-79			52	2990	25	21	3	181	3	3.63	0	1	4
1979-80	**WINN**	**N**	21	1200	5	11	4	65	3	3.25	2	0	2
1980-81			31	1707	3	21	4	128	5	4.50	1	1	2
1982-83	**MINN**	**N**	2	100	1	1	0	6	0	3.60	1	0	0
	LA	**N**	19	899	5	5	4	65	1	4.34	1	1	2
	2 team total		21	999	6	6	4	71	1	4.26	2	1	2
5 yrs.		**N Totals:**	73	3906	14	38	12	264	9	4.06	5	2	6
		W Totals:	68	3767	30	29	3	241	3	3.84	0	1	6

Reclaimed by **N.Y. Islanders** from Winnipeg prior to Expansion Draft, June 9, 1979. Claimed as priority selection by **Winnipeg** , June 9, 1979. Traded to **Los Angeles** by Minnesota for Los Angeles' third round choice in 1984 Amateur Draft, Feb. 1, 1983.

Gilles Mayer

MAYER, GILLES
B. Aug. 24, 1930, Ottawa, Ont.
5'6", 135 lbs.
Shoots L

YEAR	TEAM & LEAGUE		GP	MIN	W	L	T	GA	ENG	G AVG	SO	A	PIM
1949-50	**TOR**	**N**	1	60	0	1	0	2	0	2.00	0	0	0
1953-54			1	60	0	0	1	3	0	3.00	0	0	0
1954-55			1	60	0	1	0	1	0	1.00	0	0	0
1955-56			6	360	1	5	0	19	0	3.17	0	0	0
4 yrs.		**N Totals:**	9	540	1	7	1	25	0	2.78	0	0	0

Ken McAuley

MCAULEY, KENNETH LESLIE (Tubby)
B. Jan. 9, 1921, Edmonton, Alta.
5'10", 190 lbs.
Shoots R

YEAR	TEAM & LEAGUE		GP	MIN	W	L	T	GA	ENG	G AVG	SO	A	PIM
1943-44	**NYR**	**N**	50	2980	6	**39**	5	310	0	6.20	0	0	0
1944-45			46	2760	11	25	10	227	0	4.93	1	0	0
2 yrs.		**N Totals:**	96	5740	17	64	15	537	0	5.61	1	0	0

Jack McCartan

MCCARTAN, JOHN WILLIAM
B. Aug. 5, 1935, St. Paul, Minn.
6'1", 195 lbs.
Shoots L

YEAR	TEAM & LEAGUE		GP	MIN	W	L	T	GA	ENG	G AVG	SO	A	PIM
1959-60	**NYR**	**N**	4	240	2	1	1	7	0	1.75	0	0	0
1960-61			8	440	1	6	1	36	0	4.91	1	0	0
1972-73	**MINN**	**W**	38	2160	15	19	1	129	3	3.58	1	0	19
1973-74			2	42	0	0	0	5	0	7.14	0	0	0
1974-75			2	61	1	0	0	5	0	4.92	0	0	0
5 yrs.		**N Totals:**	12	680	3	7	2	43	0	3.79	1	0	0
		W Totals:	42	2263	16	19	1	139	3	3.69	1	0	19
PLAYOFFS													
1972-73	**MINN**	**W**	4	213	1	2	0	14	0	3.94	0	1	0

Frank McCool

MCCOOL, FRANK (Ulcers)
B. Oct. 27, 1918, Calgary, Alta.
Won Calder Trophy, 1944-45
6', 170 lbs.
Shoots L

YEAR	TEAM & LEAGUE		GP	MIN	W	L	T	GA	ENG	G AVG	SO	A	PIM
1944-45	**TOR**	**N**	50	**3000**	24	22	4	161	0	3.22	**4**	0	0
1945-46			22	1320	10	9	3	81	0	3.68	0	0	2
2 yrs.		**N Totals:**	72	4320	34	31	7	242	0	3.36	4	0	2
PLAYOFFS													
1944-45*	**TOR**	**N**	13	807	**8**	5	0	30	0	2.23	**4**	0	0

Pete McDuffe

MCDUFFE, PETER ARNOLD
B. Feb. 16, 1948, Milton, Ont.
5'9", 180 lbs.
Shoots L

YEAR	TEAM & LEAGUE		GP	MIN	W	L	T	GA	ENG	G AVG	SO	A	PIM
1971-72	**STL**	**N**	10	467	0	6	0	29	0	3.73	0	0	0
1972-73	**NYR**	**N**	1	60	1	0	0	1	0	1.00	0	0	0
1973-74			6	340	3	2	1	18	0	3.18	0	0	0
1974-75	**KC**	**N**	36	2100	7	25	4	148	1	4.23	0	1	0
1975-76	**DET**	**N**	4	240	0	3	1	22	0	5.50	0	0	2
1977-78	**IND**	**W**	12	539	1	6	1	39	0	4.34	0	0	0
6 yrs.		**N Totals:**	57	3207	11	36	6	218	1	4.08	0	1	2
		W Totals:	12	539	1	6	1	39	0	4.34	0	0	0

Pete McDuffe continued

YEAR	TEAM & LEAGUE		GP	MIN	W	L	T	GA	ENG	G AVG	SO	A	PIM
PLAYOFFS													
1971-72	STL	N	1	60	0	1	0	7	0	7.00	0	0	0

Traded to **N.Y. Rangers** by St. Louis with Curt Bennett, June 7, 1972, to complete trade of May 24, 1972 in which St. Louis acquired Steve Durbano. Drafted by **Kansas City** from N.Y. Rangers in Expansion Draft, June 12, 1974. Traded to **Detroit** by Kansas City with Glen Burdon for Gary Bergman and Bill McKenzie, Aug. 22, 1975.

Tom McGrattan

MCGRATTAN, THOMAS
B. Oct. 19, 1927, Brantford, Ont.
6'2", 170 lbs.
Shoots L

YEAR	TEAM & LEAGUE		GP	MIN	W	L	T	GA	ENG	G AVG	SO	A	PIM
1947-48	DET	N	1	8	0	0	0	0	0	0.00	0	0	0

Bill McKenzie

MCKENZIE, WILLIAM IAN
B. Mar. 12, 1949, St. Thomas, Ont.
5'11", 180 lbs.
Shoots R

YEAR	TEAM & LEAGUE		GP	MIN	W	L	T	GA	ENG	G AVG	SO	A	PIM
1973-74	DET	N	13	720	4	4	4	43	0	3.58	1	0	2
1974-75			13	740	1	9	2	58	1	4.70	0	0	2
1975-76	KC	N	22	1120	1	16	1	97	1	5.20	0	0	4
1976-77	COLO	N	5	200	0	2	1	8	0	2.40	0	0	0
1977-78			12	654	3	6	2	42	1	3.85	0	0	2
1979-80			26	1342	9	12	3	78	1	3.49	1	0	2
6 yrs.		N Totals:	91	4776	18	49	13	326	4	4.10	2	0	12

Traded to **Kansas City** by Detroit with Gary Bergman for goaltender Peter McDuffe and Glen Burdon, Aug. 22, 1975.

Murray McLachlan

MCLACHLAN, MURRAY
B. Oct. 20, 1948, London, Ont.
6', 195 lbs.
Shoots L

YEAR	TEAM & LEAGUE		GP	MIN	W	L	T	GA	ENG	G AVG	SO	A	PIM
1970-71	TOR	N	2	25	0	1	0	4	0	9.60	0	0	0

Dave McLelland

MCLELLAND, DAVID
B. Nov. 20, 1952, Penticton, B.C.
5'9", 165 lbs.
Shoots L

YEAR	TEAM & LEAGUE		GP	MIN	W	L	T	GA	ENG	G AVG	SO	A	PIM
1972-73	VAN	N	2	120	1	1	0	10	0	5.00	0	0	0

Don McLeod

MCLEOD, DONALD MARTIN
B. Aug. 24, 1946, Trail, B.C.
6', 190 lbs.
Shoots L

YEAR	TEAM & LEAGUE		GP	MIN	W	L	T	GA	ENG	G AVG	SO	A	PIM
1970-71	DET	N	14	698	3	7	0	60	2	5.16	0	0	0
1971-72	PHI	N	4	181	0	3	1	14	0	4.64	0	0	0
1972-73	HOUS	W	41	2410	19	20	1	145	1	3.61	1	0	6
1973-74			49	2971	**33**	13	3	127	0	**2.56**	3	3	6
1974-75	VAN	W	72	**4184**	**33**	**35**	2	233	0	3.34	1	0	0
1975-76	CALG	W	63	3534	30	27	3	206	0	3.50	1	**13**	4
1976-77			67	3701	25	**34**	5	210	0	3.40	3	9	2
1977-78	QUE	W	7	403	2	4	0	28	0	4.17	0	3	0
	EDM	W	33	1723	15	10	1	102	0	3.55	2	7	2
	2 team total		40	2126	17	14	1	130	0	3.67	2	10	2
8 yrs.		N Totals:	18	879	3	10	1	74	2	5.05	0	0	0
		W Totals:	332	18926	157	143	15	1051	1	3.33	11	35	20
PLAYOFFS													
1972-73	HOUS	W	3	178	0	3	0	8	0	2.70	0	0	0
1973-74			14	**842**	**12**	2	0	35	0	**2.49**	0	0	0
1975-76	CALG	W	10	559	5	5	0	37	0	3.97	0	0	0
1977-78	EDM	W	4	207	1	3	0	16	0	4.64	0	0	0
4 yrs.		W Totals:	31	1786	18	13	0	96	0	3.23	0	0	0

Jim McLeod

MCLEOD, JAMES BRADLEY
B. Apr. 7, 1937, Port Arthur, Ont.
5'8", 170 lbs.
Shoots L

YEAR	TEAM & LEAGUE		GP	MIN	W	L	T	GA	ENG	G AVG	SO	A	PIM
1971-72	STL	N	16	880	6	6	4	44	0	3.00	0	0	0
1972-73	CHI	W	54	2996	22	25	2	166	4	3.32	1	1	2
1973-74	NY-NJ	W	10	517	3	7	0	36	0	4.18	0	0	2
	LA	W	17	969	4	13	0	69	0	4.27	1	0	0
	2 team total		27	1486	7	20	0	105	0	4.24	1	0	2
1974-75	M-B	W	16	694	3	6	1	53	0	4.58	0	0	0
4 yrs.		N Totals:	16	880	6	6	4	44	0	3.00	0	0	0
		W Totals:	97	5176	32	51	3	324	4	3.76	2	1	4

Gerry McNamara

MCNAMARA, GERALD
B. Sept. 22, 1934, Sturgeon Falls, Ont.
6'2", 190 lbs.
Shoots L

YEAR	TEAM & LEAGUE		GP	MIN	W	L	T	GA	ENG	G AVG	SO	A	PIM
1960-61	TOR	N	5	300	2	2	1	13	0	2.60	0	0	2
1969-70			2	23	0	0	0	2	0	5.22	0	0	0
2 yrs.		N Totals:	7	323	2	2	1	15	0	2.79	0	0	2

Gerry McNeil

MCNEIL, GERARD GEORGE
B. Apr. 17, 1926, Quebec, Que.
5'7", 155 lbs.
Shoots L

YEAR	TEAM & LEAGUE		GP	MIN	W	L	T	GA	ENG	G AVG	SO	A	PIM
1947-48	MONT	N	2	95	0	1	1	7	0	4.42	0	0	0
1949-50			6	360	3	1	2	9	0	1.50	1	0	0
1950-51			70	**4200**	25	30	15	184	0	2.63	6	0	0
1951-52			70	**4200**	34	26	10	164	0	2.34	5	0	0
1952-53			66	3960	25	23	18	140	0	2.12	**10**	0	0
1953-54			53	3180	28	19	6	114	0	2.15	6	0	0

Gerry McNeil continued

YEAR	TEAM & LEAGUE	GP	MIN	W	L	T	GA	ENG	G AVG	SO	A	PIM
1956-57		9	540	4	5	0	32	0	3.56	0	0	2
7 yrs.	N Totals:	276	16535	119	105	52	650	0	2.36	28	0	2
PLAYOFFS												
1949-50	MONT N	2	135	1	1	0	5	0	2.22	0	0	0
1950-51		11	**785**	**5**	6	0	25	0	1.91	1	0	0
1951-52		11	**688**	4	7	0	23	0	2.01	1	0	0
1952-53*		8	**486**	**5**	3	0	16	0	**1.98**	**2**	0	0
1953-54		3	190	2	1	0	3	0	0.95	1	0	0
5 yrs.	N Totals:	35	2284	17	18	0	72	0	1.89	5	0	0

Gord McRae

MCRAE, GORDON ALEXANDER
B. Apr. 12, 1948, Sherbrooke, Que

6', 180 lbs.
Shoots L

YEAR	TEAM & LEAGUE	GP	MIN	W	L	T	GA	ENG	G AVG	SO	A	PIM
1972-73	TOR N	11	620	7	3	0	39	0	3.77	0	0	0
1974-75		20	1063	1	13	6	57	0	3.22	0	0	4
1975-76		20	956	6	5	2	59	1	3.70	0	0	0
1976-77		2	120	0	1	1	9	0	4.50	0	0	0
1977-78		18	1040	7	10	1	57	3	3.29	1	0	2
5 yrs.	N Totals:	71	3799	21	32	10	221	4	3.49	1	0	6
PLAYOFFS												
1974-75	TOR N	7	441	2	5	0	21	0	2.86	0	0	0
1975-76		1	13	0	0	0	1	0	4.62	0	0	0
2 yrs.	N Totals:	8	454	2	5	0	22	0	2.91	0	0	0

Rollie Melanson

MELANSON, JOSEPH ROLAND
B. June 28, 1960, Moncton, N.B.
Won Jennings Trophy, 1982-83

5'10", 178 lbs.
Shoots R

YEAR	TEAM & LEAGUE	GP	MIN	W	L	T	GA	ENG	G AVG	SO	A	PIM
1980-81	NYI N	11	620	8	1	1	32	0	3.10	0	0	4
1981-82		36	2115	22	7	6	114	3	3.23	0	0	14
1982-83		44	2460	24	12	5	109	0	2.66	1	3	22
3 yrs.	N Totals:	91	5195	54	20	12	255	3	2.95	1	3	40
PLAYOFFS												
1980-81*	NYI N	3	92	1	0	0	6	0	3.91	0	0	0
1981-82*		3	64	0	1	0	5	0	4.69	0	0	0
1982-83*		5	238	2	2	0	10	0	2.52	**2**	0	0
3 yrs.	N Totals:	11	394	3	3	0	21	0	3.20	2	0	0

Gilles Meloche

MELOCHE, GILLES
B. July 12, 1950, Montreal, Que.

5'10", 170 lbs.
Shoots L

YEAR	TEAM & LEAGUE	GP	MIN	W	L	T	GA	ENG	G AVG	SO	A	PIM
1970-71	CHI N	2	120	2	0	0	6	0	3.00	0	0	0
1971-72	CALIF N	56	3121	16	25	13	173	3	3.33	4	2	6
1972-73		59	**3473**	12	32	14	235	1	4.06	1	2	4
1973-74		47	2800	9	**33**	5	198	2	4.24	1	1	2
1974-75		47	2771	9	27	10	186	4	4.03	1	**6**	14
1975-76		41	2440	12	23	6	140	3	3.44	1	1	0
1976-77	CLEVE N	51	2961	19	24	6	171	0	3.47	2	3	18
1977-78		54	3100	16	27	8	195	1	3.77	1	0	4
1978-79	MINN N	53	3118	20	25	7	173	4	3.33	2	1	25
1979-80		54	3141	27	20	6	160	1	3.06	1	1	4
1980-81		38	2215	17	14	6	120	1	3.25	2	0	2
1981-82		51	3026	26	15	9	175	2	3.47	1	1	6
1982-83		47	2689	20	13	11	160	1	3.57	1	1	0
13 yrs.	N Totals:	600	34975	205	278	101	2092	23	3.59	18	19	85
PLAYOFFS												
1979-80	MINN N	11	564	5	4	0	34	0	3.62	1	0	0
1980-81		13	802	8	5	0	47	1	3.52	0	0	4
1981-82		4	184	1	2	0	8	1	2.61	0	0	2
1982-83		5	319	2	3	0	18	1	3.39	0	0	0
4 yrs.	N Totals:	33	1869	16	14	0	107	3	3.43	1	0	6

Traded to **California** by Chicago with Paul Shmyr for goaltender Gerry Desjardins, Oct. 18, 1971. Protected by **Minnesota** prior to Cleveland-Minnesota Dispersal Draft, June 15, 1978.

Paul Menard

MENARD, PAUL
B. May 22, 1952, Chambord, Que.

5'11", 168 lbs.
Shoots L

YEAR	TEAM & LEAGUE	GP	MIN	W	L	T	GA	ENG	G AVG	SO	A	PIM
1972-73	CHI W	1	45	0	1	0	5	0	6.67	0	0	0

Corr Micalef

MICALEF, CORRADO
B. Apr. 20, 1961, Montreal, Que.

5'8", 172 lbs.
Shoots R

YEAR	TEAM & LEAGUE	GP	MIN	W	L	T	GA	ENG	G AVG	SO	A	PIM
1981-82	DET N	18	809	4	10	1	63	1	4.67	0	0	9
1982-83		34	1756	11	13	5	106	0	3.62	2	1	18
2 yrs.	N Totals:	52	2565	15	23	6	169	1	3.95	2	1	27

Lindsay Middlebrook

MIDDLEBROOK, LINDSAY 5'7", 160 lbs.
B. Sept. 7, 1955, Collingwood, Ont. Shoots R

YEAR	TEAM	LEAGUE	GP	MIN	W	L	T	GA	ENG	G AVG	SO	A	PIM
1979-80	**WINN**	**N**	10	580	2	8	0	40	2	4.14	0	0	0
1980-81			14	653	0	9	3	65	0	5.97	0	0	0
1981-82	**MINN**	**N**	3	140	0	0	2	7	0	3.00	0	0	0
1982-83	**NJ**	**N**	9	412	0	6	1	37	0	5.39	0	1	2
	EDM	**N**	1	60	1	0	0	3	0	3.00	0	0	0
	2 team total		10	472	1	6	1	40	0	5.08	0	1	2
4 yrs.		**N Totals:**	37	1845	3	23	6	152	2	4.94	0	1	2

Claimed by **Winnipeg** from N.Y. Rangers in Expansion Draft, June 13, 1979. Sold to **Minnesota** by Winnipeg, July 31, 1981. Signed as a free agent by **New Jersey** , Sept. 25, 1982. Traded by New Jersey with Paul Miller to **Edmonton** for Ron Low and Jim McTaggart, Feb. 23, 1983.

Joe Millar

MILLAR, JOSEPH 5'11", 175 lbs.
B. Sept. 18, 1929, Winnipeg, Man. Shoots L

YEAR	TEAM	LEAGUE	GP	MIN	W	L	T	GA	ENG	G AVG	SO	A	PIM
1957-58	**BOS**	**N**	6	360	1	3	2	25	0	4.17	0	0	0

Greg Millen

MILLEN, GREG H. 5'9", 160 lbs.
B. June 25, 1957, Toronto, Ont. Shoots R

YEAR	TEAM	LEAGUE	GP	MIN	W	L	T	GA	ENG	G AVG	SO	A	PIM
1978-79	**PITT**	**N**	28	1532	14	11	1	86	2	3.37	2	0	0
1979-80			44	2586	18	18	7	157	2	3.64	2	3	14
1980-81			63	3721	25	**27**	10	258	6	4.16	0	2	6
1981-82	**HART**	**N**	55	3201	11	30	12	229	5	4.29	0	0	2
1982-83			60	3520	14	**38**	6	282	6	4.81	1	2	8
5 yrs.		**N Totals:**	250	14560	82	124	36	1012	21	4.17	5	7	30
PLAYOFFS													
1979-80	**PITT**	**N**	5	300	2	3	0	21	0	4.20	0	0	0
1980-81			5	325	2	3	0	19	1	3.51	0	0	0
2 yrs.		**N Totals:**	10	625	4	6	0	40	1	3.84	0	0	0

Signed as free agent with **Hartford** , June 15, 1981. As compensation, Pittsburgh received Pat Boutette and the rights to Kevin McLelland, June 29, 1981.

Joe Miller

MILLER, JOSEPH 5'9", 170 lbs.
B. Oct. 6, 1900, Morrisburgh, Ont.

YEAR	TEAM	LEAGUE	GP	MIN	W	L	T	GA	ENG	G AVG	SO	A	PIM
1927-28	**NYA**	**N**	28	1721	8	16	4	77	0	2.75	5	0	0
1928-29	**PITT**	**N**	44	2780	9	27	8	80	0	1.82	11	0	0
1929-30			43	2630	5	**35**	3	179	0	4.16	0	0	0
1930-31	**PHI**	**N**	15	850	2	12	1	50	0	3.33	0	0	0
4 yrs.		**N Totals:**	130	7981	24	90	16	386	0	2.90	16	0	0
PLAYOFFS													
1927-28*	**NYR**	**N**	3	180	2	1	0	3	0	1.00	1	0	0

Eddie Mio

MIO, EDWARD 5'10", 180 lbs.
B. Jan. 31, 1954, Windsor, Ont. Shoots L

YEAR	TEAM	LEAGUE	GP	MIN	W	L	T	GA	ENG	G AVG	SO	A	PIM
1977-78	**IND**	**W**	17	900	6	8	0	64	0	4.27	0	0	0
1978-79			5	242	2	2	1	13	2	3.22	1	1	2
	EDM	**W**	22	1068	7	10	0	71	0	3.99	1	1	2
	2 team total		27	1310	9	12	1	84	2	3.85	2	2	4
1979-80	**EDM**	**N**	34	1711	9	13	5	120	2	4.21	1	0	4
1980-81			43	2393	16	15	9	155	4	3.89	0	0	6
1981-82	**NYR**	**N**	25	1500	13	6	5	89	0	3.56	0	0	4
1982-83			41	2365	16	8	6	136	3	3.45	2	3	8
6 yrs.		**N Totals:**	143	7969	54	42	25	500	9	3.76	3	3	22
		W Totals:	44	2210	15	20	1	148	2	4.02	2	2	4
PLAYOFFS													
1978-79	**EDM**	**W**	3	90	0	0	0	6	0	4.00	0	0	0
1981-82	**NYR**	**N**	8	443	4	3	0	28	1	3.79	0	0	0
1982-83			8	480	5	3	0	32	0	4.00	0	0	0
3 yrs.		**N Totals:**	16	923	9	6	0	60	1	3.90	0	0	0
		W Totals:	3	90	0	0	0	6	0	4.00	0	0	0

Reclaimed by **Minnesota** from Edmonton prior to Expansion Draft, June 9, 1970. Claimed as priority selection by **Edmonton** , June 9, 1979. Traded to **N.Y. Rangers** by Edmonton for Lance Nethery, Dec. 11, 1981. Traded to **Detroit** with Ron Duguay and Ed Johnstone by New York Rangers for Mike Blaisdell, Mark Osborne, and Willie Huber, June 13, 1983.

Ivan Mitchell

MITCHELL, IVAN

YEAR	TEAM	LEAGUE	GP	MIN	W	L	T	GA	ENG	G AVG	SO	A	PIM
1919-20	**TOR**	**N**	15	872	7	7	0	65	0	4.33	0	0	0
1920-21			4	240	2	2	0	22	0	5.50	0	0	0
1921-22			2	120	2	0	0	6	0	3.00	0	0	0
3 yrs.		**N Totals:**	21	1232	11	9	0	93	0	4.53	0	0	0

Mike Moffat

MOFFAT, MICHAEL 5'10", 165 lbs.
B. Feb. 4, 1962, Galt, Ont. Shoots L

YEAR	TEAM	LEAGUE	GP	MIN	W	L	T	GA	ENG	G AVG	SO	A	PIM
1981-82	**BOS**	**N**	2	120	2	0	0	6	0	3.00	0	0	0
1982-83			13	673	4	6	1	49	1	4.37	0	0	2
2 yrs.		**N Totals:**	15	793	6	6	1	55	1	4.16	0	0	2

Mike Moffat continued

YEAR	TEAM	LEAGUE	GP	MIN	W	L	T	GA	ENG	G AVG	SO	A	PIM
PLAYOFFS													
1981-82	BOS	N	11	663	6	5	0	38	0	3.44	0	1	8

Andy Moog

MOOG, DONALD ANDREW 5'8", 165 lbs.
B. Feb. 18, 1960, Penticton, B.C. Shoots L

YEAR	TEAM	LEAGUE	GP	MIN	W	L	T	GA	ENG	G AVG	SO	A	PIM
1980-81	EDM	N	7	313	3	3	0	20	0	3.83	0	1	0
1981-82			8	399	3	5	0	32	2	4.81	0	1	2
1982-83			50	2833	33	8	7	167	1	3.54	1	4	16
3 yrs.		N Totals:	65	3545	39	16	7	219	3	3.71	1	6	18
PLAYOFFS													
1980-81	EDM	N	9	526	5	4	0	32	1	3.65	0	0	0
1982-83			16	949	11	5	0	48	2	3.03	0	1	2
2 yrs.		N Totals:	25	1475	16	9	0	80	3	3.25	0	1	2

Alfie Moore

MOORE, ALFRED ERNEST
B. Toronto, Ont.

YEAR	TEAM	LEAGUE	GP	MIN	W	L	T	GA	ENG	G AVG	SO	A	PIM
1936-37	NYA	N	18	1110	7	11	0	64	0	3.56	1	0	0
1938-39			2	120	0	2	0	14	0	7.00	0	0	0
1939-40	DET	N	1	60	0	1	0	3	0	3.00	0	0	0
3 yrs.		N Totals:	21	1290	7	14	0	81	0	3.77	1	0	0
PLAYOFFS													
1937-38*	CHI	N	1	60	1	0	0	1	0	1.00	0	0	0
1938-39	NYA	N	2	120	0	2	0	6	0	3.00	0	0	0
2 yrs.		N Totals:	3	180	1	2	0	7	0	2.33	0	0	0

Robbie Moore

MOORE, ROBERT DAVID 5'5½", 155 lbs.
B. May 3, 1954, Sarnia, Ont. Shoots L

YEAR	TEAM	LEAGUE	GP	MIN	W	L	T	GA	ENG	G AVG	SO	A	PIM
1978-79	PHI	N	5	237	3	0	1	7	0	1.77	2	1	0
1982-83	WASH	N	1	20	0	1	0	1	1	3.00	0	0	0
2 yrs.		N Totals:	6	257	3	1	1	8	1	1.87	2	1	0
PLAYOFFS													
1978-79	PHI	N	5	268	3	2	0	18	0	4.03	0	0	2

Signed as free agent by **Philadelphia** , Nov. 7, 1978. Traded to **Washington** by Minnesota for Rollie Boutin and Wes Jarvis, Aug. 5, 1982.

Jean Morissette

MORISSETTE, JEAN GUY 5'6", 140 lbs.
B. Dec. 19, 1937, Causapscal, Que. Shoots L

YEAR	TEAM	LEAGUE	GP	MIN	W	L	T	GA	ENG	G AVG	SO	A	PIM
1963-64	MONT	N	1	36	0	1	0	4	0	6.67	0	0	0

John Mowers

MOWERS, JOHN THOMAS 5'11", 185 lbs.
B. Oct. 29, 1916, Niagara Falls, Ont. Shoots L
Won Vezina Trophy, 1942-43

YEAR	TEAM	LEAGUE	GP	MIN	W	L	T	GA	ENG	G AVG	SO	A	PIM
1940-41	DET	N	48	**3040**	21	16	11	102	0	2.13	4	0	0
1941-42			47	2880	19	**25**	3	144	0	3.06	5	1	0
1942-43			50	3010	**25**	14	11	124	0	**2.47**	**6**	0	0
1946-47			7	420	0	0	0	29	0	4.14	0	0	0
4 yrs.		N Totals:	152	9350	65	55	25	399	0	2.56	15	1	0
PLAYOFFS													
1940-41	DET	N	9	561	4	5	0	20	0	2.22	0	0	0
1941-42			12	720	7	5	0	38	0	3.17	0	0	0
1942-43*			10	**679**	**8**	2	0	22	0	**1.94**	**2**	0	0
1946-47			1	40	0	1	0	5	0	7.50	0	0	0
4 yrs.		N Totals:	32	2000	19	13	0	85	0	2.55	2	0	0

Jerry Mrazek

MRAZEK, JEROME JOHN 5'9", 160 lbs.
B. Oct. 15, 1951, Prince Albert, Sask. Shoots L

YEAR	TEAM	LEAGUE	GP	MIN	W	L	T	GA	ENG	G AVG	SO	A	PIM
1975-76	PHI	N	1	6	0	0	0	1	0	10.00	0	0	0

Harry Mummery

MUMMERY, HARRY 245 lbs.
B. Unknown Shoots L

YEAR	TEAM	LEAGUE	GP	MIN	W	L	T	GA	ENG	G AVG	SO	A	PIM
1919-20	QUE	N	3	142	1	1	0	18	0	6.00	0	0	0
1921-22	HAMIL	N	1	49	1	0	0	2	0	2.00	0	0	0
2 yrs.		N Totals:	4	191	2	1	0	20	0	6.28	0	0	0

Hal Murphy

MURPHY, HAROLD
B. July 6, 1927, Montreal, Que. Shoots R

YEAR	TEAM	LEAGUE	GP	MIN	W	L	T	GA	ENG	G AVG	SO	A	PIM
1952-53	MONT	N	1	60	1	0	0	4	0	4.00	0	0	0

Tom Murray

MURRAY, THOMAS MICKEY
B. Unknown Shoots R

YEAR	TEAM	LEAGUE	GP	MIN	W	L	T	GA	ENG	G AVG	SO	A	PIM
1929-30	MONT	N	1	60	0	1	0	4	0	4.00	0	0	0

Phil Myre

MYRE, LOUIS PHILIPPE
B. Nov. 1, 1948, Ste.Anne de Bellevue,Que

6'1", 185 lbs.
Shoots L

YEAR	TEAM & LEAGUE		GP	MIN	W	L	T	GA	ENG	G AVG	SO	A	PIM
1969-70	MONT	N	10	503	4	3	2	19	0	2.27	0	0	2
1970-71			30	1677	13	11	4	87	1	3.11	1	1	17
1971-72			9	528	4	5	0	32	0	3.64	0	0	4
1972-73	ATL	N	46	2736	16	23	5	138	1	3.03	2	1	5
1973-74			36	2020	11	16	6	112	0	3.33	0	0	4
1974-75			40	2400	14	16	10	114	0	2.85	5	1	6
1975-76			37	2129	16	16	4	123	0	3.47	1	1	0
1976-77			43	2422	17	17	7	124	0	3.07	3	2	6
1977-78			9	523	2	7	0	43	0	4.93	0	0	2
	STL	N	44	2620	11	25	8	159	2	3.64	1	2	10
	2 team total		53	3143	13	32	8	202	2	3.86	1	2	12
1978-79			39	2259	9	22	8	163	2	4.33	1	0	6
1979-80	PHI	N	41	2367	18	7	15	141	2	3.57	0	0	37
1980-81			16	900	6	5	4	61	1	4.07	0	0	0
	COLO	N	10	580	3	6	1	33	0	3.41	0	0	0
	2 team total		26	1480	9	11	5	94	1	3.81	0	0	0
1981-82			24	1256	2	17	2	112	1	5.35	0	2	0
1982-83	BUF	N	5	300	3	2	0	21	1	4.20	0	0	2
14 yrs.		N Totals:	439	25220	149	198	76	1482	11	3.53	14	10	101
PLAYOFFS													
1973-74	ATL	N	3	186	0	3	0	13	0	4.19	0	0	0
1976-77			2	120	1	1	0	5	1	2.50	0	0	0
1979-80	PHI	N	6	384	5	1	0	16	0	2.50	1	0	0
1982-83	BUF	N	1	57	0	0	0	7	0	7.37	0	0	0
4 yrs.		N Totals:	12	747	6	5	0	41	1	3.29	1	0	0

Drafted by **Atlanta** from Montreal in Expansion Draft, June 6, 1972. Traded to **St. Louis** by Atlanta with Curt Bennett and Barry Gibbs for goaltender Yves Belanger, Dick Redmond, Bob MacMillan and St. Louis' second-round choice (Mike Perovich) in the 1979 Entry Draft, Dec. 12, 1977. Traded to **Philadelphia** by St. Louis for Blake Dunlop and Rick LaPointe, June 7, 1979. Sold to **Colorado** by Philadelphia, Feb. 26, 1981. Signed as a free agent by **Buffalo** , Sept. 11, 1982.

Cam Newton

NEWTON, CAMERON CHARLES
B. Feb. 25, 1950, Peterborough, Ont.

5'11", 170 lbs.
Shoots L

YEAR	TEAM & LEAGUE		GP	MIN	W	L	T	GA	ENG	G AVG	SO	A	PIM
1970-71	PITT	N	5	281	1	3	1	16	0	3.42	0	0	4
1972-73			11	533	3	4	0	35	2	3.94	0	1	2
1973-74	CHI	W	45	2732	25	18	2	143	0	3.14	1	1	0
1974-75			32	1905	12	20	0	126	0	3.97	0	0	0
1975-76	D-O	W	10	573	4	6	0	35	0	3.66	1	0	0
	CLEVE	W	15	896	7	7	1	48	0	3.21	0	1	0
	2 team total		25	1469	11	13	1	83	0	3.39	1	1	0
5 yrs.		N Totals:	16	814	4	7	1	51	2	3.76	0	1	6
		W Totals:	102	6106	48	51	3	352	0	3.46	2	2	0
PLAYOFFS													
1973-74	CHI	W	10	486	2	5	0	34	0	4.20	0	0	0
1975-76	CLEVE	W	1	60	0	1	0	6	0	6.00	0	0	0
2 yrs.		W Totals:	11	546	2	6	0	40	0	4.40	0	0	0

Jack Norris

NORRIS, JACK WAYNE
B. Aug. 5, 1942, Saskatoon, Sask.

5'10", 175 lbs.
Shoots L

YEAR	TEAM & LEAGUE		GP	MIN	W	L	T	GA	ENG	G AVG	SO	A	PIM
1964-65	BOS	N	23	1380	9	12	2	86	1	3.74	1	0	0
1967-68	CHI	N	7	334	2	3	0	22	0	3.95	1	0	0
1968-69			3	100	1	0	0	10	0	6.00	0	0	0
1970-71	LA	N	25	1305	7	11	2	85	1	3.91	0	0	0
1972-73	ALTA	W	64	**3702**	28	**29**	3	189	3	3.06	1	3	2
1973-74	EDM	W	53	2954	23	24	1	158	0	3.21	2	3	0
1974-75	PHOE	W	33	1962	14	15	4	107	0	3.27	1	1	2
1975-76			41	2412	21	14	4	128	0	3.18	1	2	6
8 yrs.		N Totals:	58	3119	19	26	4	203	2	3.91	2	0	0
		W Totals:	191	11030	86	82	12	582	3	3.17	5	9	10
PLAYOFFS													
1973-74	EDM	W	3	111	0	2	0	9	0	4.86	0	0	0
1974-75	PHOE	W	2	100	0	2	0	10	0	6.00	0	0	0
1975-76			5	298	2	3	0	17	0	3.42	0	0	0
3 yrs.		W Totals:	10	509	2	7	0	36	0	4.24	0	0	0

Traded to **Chicago** by Boston with Gilles Marotte and Pit Nartin for Phil Esposito, Ken Hodge and Fred Stanfield, May 15, 1967. Put on **Montreal** reserve list from Chicago June 11, 1969. Traded to **Los Angeles** by Montreal with Larry Mickey and Lucien Grenier for Leon Rochefort, Greg Boddy and Wayne Thomas, May 22, 1970.

Bill Oleschuk

OLESCHUK, WILLIAM STEPHEN
B. July 20, 1955, Edmonton, Alta.

6'3", 194 lbs.
Shoots L

YEAR	TEAM & LEAGUE		GP	MIN	W	L	T	GA	ENG	G AVG	SO	A	PIM
1975-76	KC	N	1	60	0	1	0	4	0	4.00	0	0	0
1977-78	COLO	N	2	100	0	2	0	9	0	5.40	0	0	0
1978-79			40	2118	6	19	8	136	2	3.85	1	0	10
1979-80			12	557	1	6	2	39	0	4.20	0	0	4
4 yrs.		N Totals:	55	2835	7	28	10	188	2	3.98	1	0	14

Dan Olesevich

OLESEVICH, DANIEL
B. Aug. 16, 1937, Port Colburne, Ont.

YEAR	TEAM	LEAGUE	GP	MIN	W	L	T	GA	ENG	G AVG	SO	A	PIM
1961-62	NYR	N	1	40	0	0	1	2	0	3.00	0	0	0

Ted Ouimet

OUIMET, EDWARD JOHN 6', 175 lbs.
B. July 6, 1947, Noranda, Que. Shoots L

YEAR	TEAM	LEAGUE	GP	MIN	W	L	T	GA	ENG	G AVG	SO	A	PIM
1968-69	STL	N	1	60	0	1	0	2	0	2.00	0	0	0
1974-75	NE	W	1	20	0	0	0	3	0	9.00	0	0	0
2 yrs.		N Totals:	1	60	0	1	0	2	0	2.00	0	0	0
		W Totals:	1	20	0	0	0	3	0	9.00	0	0	0

Paul Pageau

PAGEAU, PAUL 5'9", 160 lbs.
B. Oct. 1, 1959, Montreal, Que. Shoots R

YEAR	TEAM	LEAGUE	GP	MIN	W	L	T	GA	ENG	G AVG	SO	A	PIM
1980-81	LA	N	1	60	0	1	0	8	0	8.00	0	0	0

Signed as free agent with **Los Angeles**, May 6, 1980.

Marcel Paille

PAILLE, MARCEL 5'8", 185 lbs.
B. Dec. 8, 1932, Shawinigan Falls, Que. Shoots L

YEAR	TEAM	LEAGUE	GP	MIN	W	L	T	GA	ENG	G AVG	SO	A	PIM
1957-58	NYR	N	33	1980	11	15	7	102	0	3.09	1	0	0
1958-59			1	60	0	0	1	4	0	4.00	0	0	0
1959-60			17	1020	6	9	2	67	0	3.94	1	0	0
1960-61			4	240	2	2	0	16	0	4.00	0	0	0
1961-62			10	600	4	4	2	28	0	2.80	0	0	0
1962-63			3	180	0	1	2	10	0	3.33	0	0	0
1964-65			39	2262	10	21	7	135	1	3.58	0	1	2
1972-73	PHI	W	15	611	2	8	0	49	3	4.81	0	0	0
8 yrs.		N Totals:	107	6342	33	52	21	362	1	3.42	2	1	2
		W Totals:	15	611	2	8	0	49	3	4.81	0	0	0
PLAYOFFS													
1972-73	PHI	W	1	26	0	1	0	5	0	11.54	0	0	0

Mike Palmateer

PALMATEER, MICHAEL (The Popcorn Kid) 5'9", 170 lbs.
B. Jan. 13, 1954, Toronto, Ont. Shoots R

YEAR	TEAM	LEAGUE	GP	MIN	W	L	T	GA	ENG	G AVG	SO	A	PIM
1976-77	TOR	N	50	2877	23	18	8	154	4	3.21	4	2	8
1977-78			63	3760	34	19	9	172	5	2.74	5	1	12
1978-79			58	3396	26	21	10	167	3	2.95	4	**5**	24
1979-80			38	2039	16	14	3	125	2	3.68	2	3	6
1980-81	WASH	N	49	2679	18	19	9	173	5	3.87	2	**8**	17
1981-82			11	584	2	7	2	47	0	4.83	0	1	6
1982-83	TOR	N	53	2965	21	23	7	197	3	3.99	0	3	17
7 yrs.		N Totals:	322	18300	140	121	48	1035	22	3.39	17	23	90
PLAYOFFS													
1976-77	TOR	N	6	360	3	3	0	16	0	2.67	0	0	0
1977-78			13	795	6	7	0	32	0	2.42	2	0	7
1978-79			5	298	2	3	0	17	0	3.42	0	0	**6**
1979-80			1	60	0	1	0	7	0	7.00	0	0	2
1982-83			4	252	1	3	0	17	0	4.05	0	2	0
5 yrs.		N Totals:	29	1765	12	17	0	89	0	3.03	2	2	15

Traded to **Washington** by Toronto with Toronto's third round choice in 1980 Entry Draft (Torrie Robertson) for Robert Picard, Tim Coulis and Washington's second-round choice in 1980 Entry Draft (Bob McGill), June 11, 1980. Sold to **Toronto** by Washington, Sept. 9, 1982.

Bernie Parent

PARENT, BERNARD MARCEL 5'10", 180 lbs.
B. Apr. 3, 1945, Montreal, Que. Shoots L
Won Vezina Trophy, 1973-74, 1974-75
Won Conn Smythe Trophy, 1973-74, 1974-75

YEAR	TEAM	LEAGUE	GP	MIN	W	L	T	GA	ENG	G AVG	SO	A	PIM
1965-66	BOS	N	39	2083	11	20	3	128	0	3.69	1	0	0
1966-67			18	1022	3	11	2	62	2	3.64	0	0	2
1967-68	PHI	N	38	2248	16	17	5	93	1	2.48	4	1	23
1968-69			58	3365	17	23	16	151	3	2.69	1	0	4
1969-70			62	3680	13	29	20	171	7	2.79	3	**3**	14
1970-71			30	1586	9	12	6	73	3	2.76	2	**2**	5
	TOR	N	18	1040	7	7	3	46	1	2.65	1	0	0
	2 team total		48	2626	16	19	9	119	4	2.72	3	2	5
1971-72			47	2715	17	18	9	116	3	2.56	3	1	6
1972-73	PHI	W	63	3653	**33**	28	0	220	5	3.61	2	1	36
1973-74	PHI	N	73	**4314**	**47**	13	12	**136**	2	**1.89**	**12**	3	24
1974-75			68	4041	**44**	14	10	137	1	**2.03**	**12**	0	16
1975-76			11	615	6	2	3	24	0	2.34	0	0	2
1976-77			61	3525	35	13	12	159	2	2.71	5	0	0
1977-78			49	2923	29	6	13	108	1	2.22	**7**	0	4
1978-79			36	1979	16	12	7	89	2	2.70	4	2	8
14 yrs.		N Totals:	608	35136	270	197	121	1493	28	2.55	55	12	108
		W Totals:	63	3653	33	28	0	220	5	3.61	2	1	36
PLAYOFFS													
1967-68	PHI	N	5	355	2	3	0	8	0	**1.35**	0	0	0
1968-69			3	180	0	3	0	12	0	4.00	0	0	0

Bernie Parent continued

YEAR	TEAM & LEAGUE		GP	MIN	W	L	T	GA	ENG	G AVG	SO	A	PIM
1970-71	TOR	N	4	235	2	2	0	9	0	2.30	0	0	0
1971-72			4	243	1	3	0	13	0	3.21	0	0	0
1972-73	PHI	W	1	70	0	1	0	3	0	2.57	0	0	0
1973-74*	PHI	N	17	**1042**	**12**	5	0	35	1	2.02	**2**	0	4
1974-75*			15	**922**	**10**	5	0	29	1	**1.89**	**4**	0	0
1975-76			8	480	4	4	0	27	0	3.38	0	0	0
1976-77			3	123	0	3	0	8	0	3.90	0	0	0
1977-78			12	722	7	5	0	33	2	2.74	0	0	0
10 yrs.		N Totals:	71	4302	38	33	0	174	4	2.43	6	0	4
		W Totals:	1	70	0	1	0	3	0	2.57	0	0	0

Drafted by **Philadelphia** from Boston in Expansion Draft, June 6, 1967. Traded to **Toronto** by Philadelphia with Philadelphia's second choice (Rick Kehoe) in 1971 Amateur Draft for goaltender Bruce Gamble, Mike Walton, and Toronto's first choice (Pierre Plante) in same draft, Feb. 1, 1971. Rights traded to **Philadelphia** by Toronto with Toronto's second round choice (Larry Goodenough) in 1973 Amateur Draft for Philadelphia's first choice (Bob Neely) in same draft, May 15, 1973. Trade completed by **Philadelphia** , July 27, 1973, when Flyers sent goaltender Doug Favell to Toronto.

Bob Parent

PARENT, BOB
B. Feb. 19, 1958, Windsor, Ont.
5'9", 175 lbs.

YEAR	TEAM & LEAGUE		GP	MIN	W	L	T	GA	ENG	G AVG	SO	A	PIM
1981-82	TOR	N	2	120	0	2	0	13	0	6.50	0	0	0
1982-83			1	40	0	0	0	2	0	3.00	0	0	0
2 yrs.		N Totals:	3	160	0	2	0	15	0	5.63	0	0	0

Jim Park

PARK, JAMES
B. June 22, 1952, Toronto, Ont.
6'1", 190 lbs.
Shoots R

YEAR	TEAM & LEAGUE		GP	MIN	W	L	T	GA	ENG	G AVG	SO	A	PIM
1975-76	IND	W	11	572	6	4	0	23	0	2.41	0	1	2
1976-77			31	1727	14	12	4	114	0	3.96	1	1	6
1977-78			12	584	3	7	0	41	0	4.21	0	0	6
3 yrs.		W Totals:	54	2883	23	23	4	178	0	3.70	1	2	14
PLAYOFFS													
1975-76	IND	W	6	294	3	2	0	12	0	2.45	0	0	0

Dave Parro

PARRO, DAVID
B. Apr. 30, 1957, Saskatoon, Sask.
5'10", 155 lbs.
Shoots L

YEAR	TEAM & LEAGUE		GP	MIN	W	L	T	GA	ENG	G AVG	SO	A	PIM
1980-81	WASH	N	18	811	4	7	2	49	2	3.63	1	1	2
1981-82			52	2942	16	26	7	206	4	4.20	1	1	4
1982-83			6	261	1	3	1	19	1	4.37	0	0	0
3 yrs.		N Totals:	76	4014	21	36	10	274	7	4.10	2	2	6

Claimed by **Quebec** from Boston in Expansion Draft, June 13, 1979. Traded to **Washington** by Quebec for Nelson Burton, June 15, 1979.

Lester Patrick

PATRICK, LESTER
B. Dec. 30, 1883, Drummondville, Que.
Hall of Fame, 1945
6'1", 180 lbs.

YEAR	TEAM & LEAGUE		GP	MIN	W	L	T	GA	ENG	G AVG	SO	A	PIM
PLAYOFFS													
1927-28*	NYR	N	1	46	1	0	0	1	0	1.00	0	0	0

Pete Peeters

PEETERS, PETER
B. Aug. 1, 1957, Edmonton, Alta.
Won Vezina Trophy, 1982-83
6', 170 lbs.
Shoots L

YEAR	TEAM & LEAGUE		GP	MIN	W	L	T	GA	ENG	G AVG	SO	A	PIM
1978-79	PHI	N	6	280	1	2	1	16	0	3.43	0	0	6
1979-80			40	2373	29	5	5	108	1	2.73	1	0	28
1980-81			40	2333	22	12	5	115	5	2.96	2	1	8
1981-82			44	2591	23	18	3	160	3	3.71	0	1	19
1982-83	BOS	N	62	3611	**40**	11	9	142	2	**2.36**	**8**	2	33
5 yrs.		N Totals:	192	11188	115	48	23	541	11	2.90	11	4	94
PLAYOFFS													
1979-80	PHI	N	13	799	8	5	0	37	0	2.78	1	0	2
1980-81			3	180	2	1	0	12	0	4.00	0	0	**19**
1981-82			4	220	1	2	0	17	0	4.64	0	0	0
1982-83	BOS	N	17	**1024**	9	8	0	**61**	0	3.57	1	0	8
4 yrs.		N Totals:	37	2223	20	16	0	127	0	3.43	2	0	29

Traded to **Boston** by Philadelphia for Brad McCrimmon, June 9, 1982.

Marcel Pelletier

PELLETIER, MARCEL
B. Dec. 6, 1927, Drummondville, Que.
5'11", 180 lbs.
Shoots R

YEAR	TEAM & LEAGUE		GP	MIN	W	L	T	GA	ENG	G AVG	SO	A	PIM
1950-51	CHI	N	6	355	1	5	0	29	0	4.90	0	0	2
1962-63	NYR	N	2	40	0	1	1	4	0	6.00	0	0	0
2 yrs.		N Totals:	8	395	1	6	1	33	0	5.01	0	0	2

Miche Perreault

PERREAULT, ROBERT 5'8", 170 lbs.
B. Jan. 28, 1931, Trois-Rivieres, Que. Shoots L

YEAR	TEAM & LEAGUE	GP	MIN	W	L	T	GA	ENG	G AVG	SO	A	PIM
1955-56	MONT N	6	360	3	3	0	12	0	2.00	1	0	0
1958-59	DET N	3	180	2	1	0	9	0	3.00	0	0	0
1962-63	BOS N	22	1320	3	12	6	85	0	3.86	1	0	0
1972-73	LA W	1	60	1	0	0	2	0	2.00	0	0	0
4 yrs.	N Totals:	31	1860	8	16	6	106	0	3.42	2	0	0
	W Totals:	1	60	1	0	0	2	0	2.00	0	0	0

Drafted by **Boston** from Detroit, June 6, 1962.

Jim Pettie

PETTIE, JAMES 6', 195 lbs.
B. Oct. 24, 1953, Toronto, Ont. Shoots L

YEAR	TEAM & LEAGUE	GP	MIN	W	L	T	GA	ENG	G AVG	SO	A	PIM
1976-77	BOS N	1	60	1	0	0	3	0	3.00	0	0	0
1977-78		1	60	0	1	0	6	0	6.00	0	0	6
1978-79		19	1037	8	6	2	62	0	3.59	1	0	17
3 yrs.	N Totals:	21	1157	9	7	2	71	0	3.68	1	0	23

Jacques Plante

PLANTE, JOSEPH JACQUES OMER (Jake the Snake) 6', 175 lbs.
B. Jan. 17, 1929, Mont Carmel, Que. Shoots L
Won Hart Trophy, 1961-62
Won Vezina Trophy, 1955-56, 1956-57, 1957-58, 1958-59, 1959-60, 1961-62
Shared Vezina Trophy, 1968-69
Hall of Fame, 1978

YEAR	TEAM & LEAGUE	GP	MIN	W	L	T	GA	ENG	G AVG	SO	A	PIM
1952-53	MONT N	3	180	2	0	1	4	0	1.33	0	0	0
1953-54		17	1020	7	5	5	27	0	1.59	5	0	0
1954-55		52	3080	**31**	13	7	110	0	2.14	5	0	2
1955-56		64	3840	**42**	12	10	**119**	0	**1.86**	7	0	10
1956-57		61	3660	31	18	12	123	0	**2.02**	**9**	0	16
1957-58		57	3386	**34**	14	8	119	0	**2.11**	**9**	0	13
1958-59		67	4000	**38**	16	13	144	0	**2.16**	**9**	1	11
1959-60		69	4140	**40**	17	12	175	0	**2.54**	3	0	2
1960-61		40	2400	22	11	7	112	0	2.80	2	0	2
1961-62		70	**4200**	**42**	14	14	166	0	**2.37**	4	0	**14**
1962-63		56	3320	22	14	9	138	0	**2.49**	**5**	1	2
1963-64	NYR N	65	3900	22	35	8	220	0	3.38	3	0	**6**
1964-65		33	1938	10	17	5	109	1	3.37	2	1	6
1968-69	STL N	37	2139	18	12	6	70	0	1.96	5	0	2
1969-70		32	1839	18	9	5	67	1	2.19	5	2	0
1970-71	TOR N	40	2329	24	11	4	73	2	**1.88**	4	0	2
1971-72		34	1965	16	13	5	86	3	2.63	2	0	2
1972-73		32	1717	8	14	6	87	0	3.04	1	0	0
	BOS N	8	480	7	1	0	16	0	2.00	2	0	0
	2 team total	40	2197	15	15	6	103	0	2.81	4	0	0
1974-75	EDM W	31	1592	15	14	1	88	0	3.32	1	1	2
19 yrs.	N Totals:	837	49533	434	246	137	1965	7	2.38	82	5	90
	W Totals:	31	1592	15	14	1	88	0	3.32	1	1	2
PLAYOFFS												
1952-53*	MONT N	4	240	3	1	0	7	0	1.75	1	0	0
1953-54		8	480	5	3	0	15	0	1.88	**2**	0	0
1954-55		12	639	6	4	0	31	0	2.91	**1**	0	0
1955-56*		10	600	**8**	2	0	18	0	**1.80**	**2**	0	0
1956-57*		10	**616**	**8**	2	0	18	0	**1.75**	1	0	0
1957-58*		10	618	**8**	2	0	20	0	**1.94**	**1**	0	0
1958-59*		11	670	**8**	3	0	28	0	**2.51**	0	0	0
1959-60*		8	489	**8**	0	0	11	0	**1.35**	**3**	0	0
1960-61		6	412	2	4	0	16	0	2.33	0	0	0
1961-62		6	360	2	4	0	19	0	3.17	0	0	0
1962-63		5	300	1	4	0	14	0	2.80	0	0	0
1968-69	STL N	10	**589**	**8**	2	0	14	0	1.43	**3**	0	0
1969-70		6	324	4	1	0	8	0	**1.48**	**1**	0	2
1970-71	TOR N	3	134	0	2	0	7	0	3.13	0	0	0
1971-72		1	60	0	1	0	5	0	5.00	0	0	0
1972-73	BOS N	2	120	0	2	0	10	0	5.00	0	0	0
16 yrs.	N Totals:	112	6651	71	37	0	241	0	2.17	15	0	2

Traded to **New York** with Phil Goyette and Don Marshall by Montreal for Gump Worsley, Len Ronson, Dave Balon and Leon Rochefort, June 4, 1963. Drafted by **St. Louis** from N.Y. Rangers, June 12, 1968.

Michel Plasse

PLASSE, MICHEL PIERRE 5'11", 172 lbs.
B. June 1, 1948, Montreal, Que. Shoots L

YEAR	TEAM & LEAGUE	GP	MIN	W	L	T	GA	ENG	G AVG	SO	A	PIM
1970-71	STL N	1	60	1	0	0	3	0	3.00	0	0	0
1972-73	MONT N	17	932	11	2	3	40	1	2.58	0	0	4
1973-74		15	839	7	4	2	57	0	4.08	0	0	0
1974-75	KC N	24	1420	4	16	3	96	2	4.06	0	1	18
	PITT N	20	1094	9	5	4	73	0	4.00	0	1	6
	2 team total	44	2514	13	21	7	169	2	4.03	0	2	24
1975-76		55	3096	24	19	10	178	1	3.45	2	1	18
1976-77	COLO N	54	2986	12	29	10	190	3	3.82	0	1	0
1977-78		25	1383	3	12	8	90	2	3.90	0	0	12
1978-79		41	2302	9	**29**	2	152	6	3.96	0	0	4
1979-80		6	327	0	3	2	26	0	4.77	0	0	0
1980-81	QUE N	33	1933	10	14	9	118	2	3.66	0	0	0
1981-82		8	388	2	3	1	35	1	5.41	0	1	0
11 yrs.	N Totals:	299	16760	92	136	54	1058	18	3.79	2	5	62

Michel Plasse continued

YEAR	TEAM & LEAGUE		GP	MIN	W	L	T	GA	ENG	G AVG	SO	A	PIM
PLAYOFFS													
1975-76	PITT	N	3	180	1	2	0	8	0	2.67	1	0	0
1980-81	QUE	N	1	15	0	0	0	1	1	4.00	0	0	0
2 yrs.		N Totals:	4	195	1	2	0	9	1	2.77	1	0	0

Sold to **St. Louis** by Montreal, Dec. 11, 1970. Sold to **Montreal** by St. Louis, Aug. 23, 1971. Drafted by **Kansas City** from Montreal in Expansion Draft, June 12, 1974. Traded to **Pittsburgh** by Kansas City for Jean-Guy Lagace and goaltender Denis Herron, January 10, 1975. Traded to **Colorado** by Pittsburgh with Simon Nolet as compensation for Pittsburgh's signing of Denis Herron as free agent, Aug. 7, 1976. Signed as free agent with **Quebec** , Sept. 14, 1980. Traded to **Hartford** by Quebec with a fourth-round choice in the 1983 Entry Draft for John Garrett, Jan. 12, 1982.

Hugh Plaxton

PLAXTON, HUGH JOHN
B. May 16, 1904, Barrie, Ont.

184 lbs.
Shoots L

YEAR	TEAM & LEAGUE		GP	MIN	W	L	T	GA	ENG	G AVG	SO	A	PIM
1932-33	MON(M)	N	1	59	0	1	0	5	0	5.00	0	0	0

Claude Pronovost

PRONOVOST, CLAUDE
B. July 22, 1935, Shawinigan Falls, Que.

5'9", lbs.
Shoots L

YEAR	TEAM & LEAGUE		GP	MIN	W	L	T	GA	ENG	G AVG	SO	A	PIM
1955-56	BOS	N	1	60	1	0	0	0	0	0.00	1	0	2
1958-59	MONT	N	2	60	0	1	0	7	0	7.00	0	0	0
2 yrs.		N Totals:	3	120	1	1	0	7	0	3.50	1	0	2

Cap Raeder

RAEDER, CAP
B. Oct. 8, 1953, Needham, Ma.

5'11", 170 lbs.

YEAR	TEAM & LEAGUE		GP	MIN	W	L	T	GA	ENG	G AVG	SO	A	PIM
1975-76	NE	W	3	100	0	1	0	8	0	4.80	0	0	0
1976-77			26	1328	12	10	1	69	0	3.12	2	0	2
2 yrs.		W Totals:	29	1428	12	11	1	77	0	3.24	2	0	2
PLAYOFFS													
1975-76	NE	W	14	**819**	7	7	0	31	0	**2.27**	**2**	0	0
1976-77			1	60	0	1	0	7	0	7.00	0	0	0
2 yrs.		W Totals:	15	879	7	8	0	38	0	2.59	2	0	0

Chuck Rayner

RAYNER, CLAUDE EARL (Bonnie Prince Charlie)
B. Aug. 11, 1920, Sutherland, Sask.
Won Hart Trophy, 1949-50
Hall of Fame, 1973

5'11", 190 lbs.
Shoots L

YEAR	TEAM & LEAGUE		GP	MIN	W	L	T	GA	ENG	G AVG	SO	A	PIM
1940-41	NYA	N	12	773	2	7	3	44	0	3.67	0	0	0
1941-42			36	2230	13	21	2	129	0	3.58	1	0	0
1945-46	NYR	N	41	2377	12	**21**	7	150	0	3.79	5	0	6
1946-47			58	3480	22	30	6	177	0	3.05	**5**	0	0
1947-48			12	691	4	8	0	42	0	3.65	0	0	0
1948-49			58	3480	16	**31**	11	168	0	2.90	7	0	2
1949-50			69	4140	28	30	11	181	0	2.62	6	0	0
1950-51			66	3940	19	28	19	187	0	2.85	6	0	0
1951-52			53	3180	18	25	10	159	0	3.00	2	0	4
1952-53			20	1200	4	8	8	58	0	2.90	1	0	2
10 yrs.		N Totals:	425	25491	138	209	77	1295	0	3.05	33	0	14
PLAYOFFS													
1947-48	NYR	N	6	360	2	4	0	17	0	2.83	0	0	0
1949-50			12	775	7	5	0	29	0	2.25	1	0	0
2 yrs.		N Totals:	18	1135	9	9	0	46	0	2.43	1	0	0

Greg Redquest

REDQUEST, GREG
B. July 30, 1956, Toronto, Ont.

5'10", 190 lbs.

YEAR	TEAM & LEAGUE		GP	MIN	W	L	T	GA	ENG	G AVG	SO	A	PIM
1977-78	PITT	N	1	13	0	0	0	3	0	13.85	0	0	0

Dave Reece

REECE, DAVID BARRET
B. Sept. 13, 1948, Troy, N.Y.

6'1", 190 lbs.
Shoots L

YEAR	TEAM & LEAGUE		GP	MIN	W	L	T	GA	ENG	G AVG	SO	A	PIM
1975-76	BOS	N	14	777	7	5	2	43	1	3.32	2	0	0

Chico Resch

RESCH, GLENN ALLAN
B. July 10, 1948, Moose Jaw, Sask.
Won Masterton Trophy, 1981-82

5'9", 165 lbs.
Shoots L

YEAR	TEAM & LEAGUE		GP	MIN	W	L	T	GA	ENG	G AVG	SO	A	PIM
1973-74	NYI	N	2	120	1	1	0	6	0	3.00	0	0	0
1974-75			25	1432	12	7	0	59	3	2.47	3	0	0
1975-76			44	2546	23	11	8	88	1	2.07	7	1	0
1976-77			46	2711	26	13	6	103	2	2.28	4	0	0
1977-78			45	2637	28	9	7	112	1	2.55	3	1	12
1978-79			43	2539	26	7	10	106	0	2.50	2	2	6
1979-80			45	2606	23	14	6	132	1	3.04	3	0	4
1980-81			32	1817	18	7	5	93	2	3.07	3	1	0
	COLO	N	8	449	2	4	2	28	0	3.74	0	0	0
	2 team total		40	2266	20	11	7	121	2	3.20	**3**	1	0
1981-82			61	3424	16	**31**	11	230	5	4.03	0	2	8
1982-83	NJ	N	65	3650	15	35	12	242	2	3.98	0	3	6
10 yrs.		N Totals:	416	23931	190	139	67	1199	17	3.01	25	10	36

Chico Resch continued

YEAR	TEAM & LEAGUE		GP	MIN	W	L	T	GA	ENG	G AVG	SO	A	PIM
PLAYOFFS													
1974-75	**NYI**	**N**	12	692	8	4	0	25	1	2.17	1	0	4
1975-76			7	357	3	3	0	18	0	3.03	0	0	0
1976-77			3	144	1	1	0	5	0	2.08	0	0	0
1977-78			7	388	3	4	0	15	0	2.32	0	0	0
1978-79			5	300	2	3	0	11	0	2.20	1	0	0
1979-80*			4	120	0	2	0	9	1	4.50	0	0	0
6 yrs.		**N Totals:**	38	2001	17	17	0	83	2	2.49	2	0	4

Sold to **N.Y. Islanders** by Montreal with Denis DeJordy, Germain Gagnon, Tony Featherstone, Murray Anderson and Alex Campbell, June 26, 1972. Traded to **Colorado** by N.Y. Islanders with Steve Tambellini for Mike McEwen and Jari Kaarela, March 10, 1981.

Herb Rheaume

RHEAUME, HERBERT
B. Unknown

YEAR	TEAM & LEAGUE		GP	MIN	W	L	T	GA	ENG	G AVG	SO	A	PIM
1925-26	**MONT**	**N**	31	1889	10	19	1	92	0	2.97	0	0	0

Nick Ricci

RICCI, JOSEPH NICK 5'10", 160 lbs.
B. June 3, 1959, Niagara Falls, Ont. Shoots L

YEAR	TEAM & LEAGUE		GP	MIN	W	L	T	GA	ENG	G AVG	SO	A	PIM
1979-80	**PITT**	**N**	4	240	2	2	0	14	0	3.50	0	0	0
1980-81			9	540	4	5	0	35	1	3.88	0	0	2
1981-82			3	160	0	3	0	14	2	5.25	0	0	0
3 yrs.		**N Totals:**	16	940	6	10	0	63	3	4.02	0	0	2

Terry Richardson

RICHARDSON, TERRANCE PAUL 6'1", 190 lbs.
B. May 7, 1953, Powell River, B.C. Shoots R

YEAR	TEAM & LEAGUE		GP	MIN	W	L	T	GA	ENG	G AVG	SO	A	PIM
1973-74	**DET**	**N**	9	315	1	4	0	28	0	5.33	0	1	0
1974-75			4	202	1	2	0	23	0	6.83	0	0	0
1975-76			1	60	0	1	0	7	0	7.00	0	0	2
1976-77			5	269	1	3	0	18	0	4.01	0	0	2
1978-79	**STL**	**N**	1	60	0	1	0	9	0	9.00	0	0	0
5 yrs.		**N Totals:**	20	906	3	11	0	85	0	5.63	0	1	4

Signed as free agent by **St. Louis** , July 26, 1978. Traded to **N.Y. Islanders** by St. Louis with Barry Gibbs for future considerations, June 9, 1979. Traded to **Hartford** by N.Y. Islanders for Ralph Klassen, June 14, 1979.

Curt Ridley

RIDLEY, CHARLES CURTIS 6', 190 lbs.
B. Oct. 24, 1951, Minnedosa, Man. Shoots L

YEAR	TEAM & LEAGUE		GP	MIN	W	L	T	GA	ENG	G AVG	SO	A	PIM
1974-75	**NYR**	**N**	2	81	1	1	0	7	0	5.19	0	0	0
1975-76	**VAN**	**N**	9	500	6	0	2	19	0	2.28	1	0	0
1976-77			37	2074	8	21	4	134	2	3.88	0	0	4
1977-78			40	2010	9	17	8	136	1	4.06	0	1	9
1979-80			10	599	2	6	2	39	0	3.91	0	0	0
	TOR	**N**	3	110	0	1	0	8	0	4.36	0	0	2
	2 team total		13	709	2	7	2	47	0	3.98	0	0	2
1980-81			3	124	1	1	0	12	0	5.81	0	0	2
6 yrs.		**N Totals:**	104	5498	27	47	16	355	3	3.87	1	1	17
PLAYOFFS													
1975-76	**VAN**	**N**	2	120	0	2	0	8	0	4.00	0	0	0

Traded to **Atlanta** by N.Y. Rangers for Jerry Byers, Sept. 9, 1975. Traded to **Vancouver** by Atlanta for Vancouver's first round choice (Dave Shand) in 1976 Amateur Draft, Jan. 20, 1976. Sold to **Toronto** by Vancouver, Feb. 10, 1980.

Denis Riggin

RIGGIN, DENIS MELVILLE 5'11", 156 lbs.
B. Apr. 11, 1936, Kincardine, Ont. Shoots L

YEAR	TEAM & LEAGUE		GP	MIN	W	L	T	GA	ENG	G AVG	SO	A	PIM
1959-60	**DET**	**N**	9	540	2	6	1	32	0	3.56	1	0	0
1962-63			9	445	3	4	1	22	0	2.97	0	0	0
2 yrs.		**N Totals:**	18	985	5	10	2	54	0	3.29	1	0	0

Pat Riggin

RIGGIN, PATRICK MICHAEL 5'9", 163 lbs.
B. May 26, 1959, Kincardine, Ont. Shoots R

YEAR	TEAM & LEAGUE		GP	MIN	W	L	T	GA	ENG	G AVG	SO	A	PIM
1978-79	**BIRM**	**W**	46	2511	16	22	5	158	0	3.78	1	3	22
1979-80	**ATL**	**N**	25	1368	11	9	2	73	0	3.20	2	0	0
1980-81	**CALG**	**N**	42	2411	21	16	4	154	3	3.83	0	0	0
1981-82			52	2934	19	19	11	207	1	4.23	2	5	4
1982-83	**WASH**	**N**	38	2161	17	9	9	121	4	3.36	0	0	4
5 yrs.		**N Totals:**	157	8874	68	53	26	555	8	3.75	4	5	8
		W Totals:	46	2511	16	22	5	158	0	3.78	1	3	22
PLAYOFFS													
1980-81	**CALG**	**N**	11	629	6	4	0	37	1	3.53	0	0	0
1981-82			3	194	0	3	0	10	0	3.09	0	0	0
1982-83	**WASH**	**N**	3	101	0	1	0	8	1	4.75	0	0	0
3 yrs.		**N Totals:**	17	924	6	8	0	55	2	3.57	0	0	0

Traded to **Washington** by Calgary along with Ken Houston for Howard Walker, George White, Washington's sixth round choice (Mats Kihlstron) in 1982 Entry Draft, third round choice in 1983 Entry Draft (Parry Berezan) and second round choice in 1984 Entry Draft, June 9, 1982. Traded to **Washington** with Ken Houston by Calgary for Howard Walker and George White, June 9, 1982. In addition Washington transferred the following Amateur Draft choices: a sixth round choice (acquired earlier from Quebec) in 1982 (Mats Kihlstron), a third round choice in 1983 (Barry Perezan), and a second round choice in 1984.

Bob Ring

RING, ROBERT

YEAR	TEAM & LEAGUE		GP	MIN	W	L	T	GA	ENG	G AVG	SO	A	PIM
1965-66	BOS	N	1	34	0	0	0	4	0	7.06	0	0	0

Fern Rivard

RIVARD, FERNAND
B. Jan. 18, 1946, Grand Mere, Que.
5'9", 160 lbs.
Shoots L

YEAR	TEAM & LEAGUE		GP	MIN	W	L	T	GA	ENG	G AVG	SO	A	PIM
1968-69	MINN	N	13	657	0	0	0	48	0	4.38	0	1	0
1969-70			14	800	3	5	5	42	0	3.15	1	0	6
1973-74			13	701	3	6	2	50	0	4.28	1	0	0
1974-75			15	707	3	9	0	50	0	4.24	0	0	4
4 yrs.		N Totals:	55	2865	9	20	7	190	0	3.98	2	1	10

John Roach

ROACH, JOHN ROSS
B. June 23, 1900, Fort Perry, Ont.
5'5", 130 lbs.
Shoots L

YEAR	TEAM & LEAGUE		GP	MIN	W	L	T	GA	ENG	G AVG	SO	A	PIM
1921-22	TOR	N	22	1340	11	10	1	91	0	4.14	0	0	0
1922-23			24	1469	13	10	1	88	0	3.67	1	0	0
1923-24			23	1380	10	13	0	80	0	3.48	1	0	0
1924-25			30	1800	**19**	11	0	84	0	2.80	1	0	0
1925-26			36	2210	12	**21**	3	114	0	3.17	2	0	0
1926-27			44	2764	15	24	5	94	0	2.14	4	0	0
1927-28			43	2690	17	18	8	88	0	2.05	4	0	0
1928-29	NYR	N	44	2760	21	13	10	65	0	1.48	13	0	0
1929-30			44	2770	17	17	10	143	0	3.25	1	0	0
1930-31			44	**2760**	19	16	9	87	0	1.98	7	0	0
1931-32			48	3020	23	17	8	112	0	2.33	**9**	0	0
1932-33	DET	N	48	2970	**25**	15	8	93	0	1.94	10	0	0
1933-34			18	1030	9	8	1	45	0	2.50	1	0	0
1934-35			23	1460	7	11	5	62	0	2.70	4	0	0
14 yrs.		N Totals:	491	30423	218	204	69	1246	0	2.46	58	0	0
PLAYOFFS													
1921-22*	TOR	N	7	**425**	**4**	2	1	13	0	**1.86**	**2**	0	0
1924-25			2	120	0	2	0	5	0	**2.50**	0	0	0
1928-29	NYR	N	6	**392**	3	2	1	5	0	0.83	**3**	0	0
1929-30			4	309	1	2	1	7	0	1.75	0	0	0
1930-31			4	240	2	2	0	4	0	**1.00**	1	0	0
1931-32			7	**480**	3	4	0	27	0	3.86	**1**	0	0
1932-33	DET	N	4	240	2	2	0	8	0	2.00	1	0	0
7 yrs.		N Totals:	34	2206	15	16	3	69	0	1.88	8	0	0

Moe Roberts

ROBERTS, MAURICE
B. Dec. 13, 1907, Waterbury, Conn.
5'9", 165 lbs.
Shoots R

YEAR	TEAM & LEAGUE		GP	MIN	W	L	T	GA	ENG	G AVG	SO	A	PIM
1925-26	BOS	N	2	90	0	1	0	5	0	2.50	0	0	0
1931-32	NYA	N	1	60	1	0	0	1	0	1.00	0	0	0
1933-34			6	336	1	4	0	25	0	4.17	0	0	0
1951-52	CHI	N	1	20	0	0	0	0	0	0.00	0	0	0
4 yrs.		N Totals:	10	506	2	5	0	31	0	3.68	0	0	0

Signed as free agent by **Chicago** , Nov. 25, 1951.

Earl Robertson

ROBERTSON, EARL COOPER
B. Nov. 24, 1910, Bingorgh, Sask.
5'10", 165 lbs.
Shoots L

YEAR	TEAM & LEAGUE		GP	MIN	W	L	T	GA	ENG	G AVG	SO	A	PIM
1937-38	NYA	N	48	**3000**	19	18	11	111	0	2.31	6	0	0
1938-39			46	2850	17	18	10	136	0	2.96	3	0	0
1939-40			48	2960	15	**29**	4	140	0	2.92	6	0	0
1940-41			36	2260	6	22	8	142	0	3.94	1	0	0
1941-42			12	750	3	8	1	46	0	3.83	0	0	0
5 yrs.		N Totals:	190	11820	60	95	34	575	0	2.92	16	0	0
PLAYOFFS													
1936-37*	DET	N	6	340	3	2	0	8	0	1.33	2	0	0
1937-38	NYA	N	6	475	3	3	0	12	0	2.00	0	0	0
1939-40			3	180	0	2	0	9	0	3.00	0	0	0
3 yrs.		N Totals:	15	995	6	7	0	29	0	1.75	2	0	0

Al Rollins

ROLLINS, ELWIN IRA (Ally)
B. Oct. 9, 1926, Vanguard, Sask.
Won Hart Trophy, 1953-54
Won Vezina Trophy, 1950-51
6'2", 175 lbs.
Shoots L

YEAR	TEAM & LEAGUE		GP	MIN	W	L	T	GA	ENG	G AVG	SO	A	PIM
1949-50	TOR	N	2	120	1	1	0	4	0	2.00	1	0	0
1950-51			40	2373	**27**	5	8	70	0	**1.77**	5	0	0
1951-52			70	4170	29	24	16	154	0	2.22	5	0	0
1952-53	CHI	N	70	**4200**	27	28	15	175	0	2.50	6	0	0
1953-54			66	3960	12	**47**	7	213	0	3.23	5	0	**20**
1954-55			44	2640	9	27	8	150	0	3.41	0	0	0
1955-56			58	3480	16	31	11	174	0	3.00	3	0	10
1956-57			70	**4200**	16	**39**	15	225	0	3.21	3	1	0
1959-60	NYR	N	8	480	1	3	4	31	0	3.88	0	0	0
9 yrs.		N Totals:	428	25623	138	205	84	1196	0	2.80	28	1	30

Al Rollins continued

YEAR	TEAM	LEAGUE	GP	MIN	W	L	T	GA	ENG	G AVG	SO	A	PIM
PLAYOFFS													
1950-51*	TOR	N	4	253	3	1	0	6	0	1.42	0	0	0
1951-52			2	120	0	2	0	6	0	3.00	0	0	0
1952-53	CHI	N	7	425	3	4	0	18	0	2.54	0	0	0
3 yrs.		N Totals:	13	798	6	7	0	30	0	2.26	0	0	0

Traded to **Chicago** by Toronto with Ray Hannigan, Cal Gardner and Gus Mortson for Harry Lumley, Sept. 11, 1952.

Roberto Romano

ROMANO, ROBERTO

YEAR	TEAM	LEAGUE	GP	MIN	W	L	T	GA	ENG	G AVG	SO	A	PIM
1982-83	PITT	N	3	155	0	3	0	18	0	6.97	0	0	0

Pat Rupp

RUPP, PATRICK LLOYD
B. Aug. 12, 1942, Detroit, Mich.

YEAR	TEAM	LEAGUE	GP	MIN	W	L	T	GA	ENG	G AVG	SO	A	PIM
1963-64	DET	N	1	60	0	1	0	4	0	4.00	0	0	0

Jim Rutherford

RUTHERFORD, JAMES EARL
B. Feb. 17, 1949, Beeton, Ont.
5'8", 168 lbs.
Shoots L

YEAR	TEAM	LEAGUE	GP	MIN	W	L	T	GA	ENG	G AVG	SO	A	PIM
1970-71	DET	N	29	1498	6	15	3	94	3	3.77	1	0	0
1971-72	PITT	N	40	2160	17	15	5	116	2	3.22	1	0	16
1972-73			49	2660	20	22	5	129	3	2.91	3	0	0
1973-74			26	1432	7	12	4	82	0	3.44	0	1	2
	DET	N	25	1420	9	11	4	86	0	3.63	0	3	2
	2 team total		51	2852	16	23	8	168	0	3.53	0	4	4
1974-75			59	3478	20	29	10	217	1	3.74	2	0	0
1975-76			44	2640	13	25	6	158	4	3.59	4	0	4
1976-77			48	2740	7	34	6	180	1	3.94	0	1	2
1977-78			43	2468	20	17	4	134	1	3.26	1	2	2
1978-79			32	1892	13	14	5	103	2	3.27	1	2	4
1979-80			23	1326	6	13	3	92	1	4.16	1	0	24
1980-81			10	600	2	6	2	43	0	4.30	0	0	0
	TOR	N	18	961	4	10	2	82	2	5.12	0	0	2
	LA	N	3	180	3	0	0	10	0	3.33	0	0	0
	3 team total		31	1741	9	16	4	135	2	4.65	0	0	2
1981-82			7	380	3	3	0	43	0	6.79	0	0	0
1982-83	DET	N	1	60	0	1	0	7	0	7.00	0	0	0
13 yrs.		N Totals:	457	25895	150	227	59	1576	20	3.65	14	9	58
PLAYOFFS													
1971-72	PITT	N	4	240	0	4	0	14	0	3.50	0	0	0
1977-78	DET	N	3	180	2	1	0	12	0	4.00	0	1	0
1980-81	LA	N	1	20	0	0	0	2	0	6.00	0	0	0
3 yrs.		N Totals:	8	440	2	5	0	28	0	3.82	0	1	0

Put on **Pittsburgh** reserve list from Detroit via Intra-League Draft, June 8, 1971. Traded to **Detroit** by Pittsburgh with Jack Lynch for Ron Stackhouse, Jan. 18, 1974. Traded to **Toronto** by Detroit for Mark Kirton, Dec. 4, 1980. Traded to **Los Angeles** by Toronto for Los Angeles' fifth round choice (Barry Brigley) in 1981 Entry Draft, Mar. 10, 1981. Signed by **Detroit** as a free agent, Sept. 27, 1982.

Wayne Rutledge

RUTLEDGE, WAYNE ALVIN
B. Jan. 5, 1942, Barrie, Ont.
6'2", 200 lbs.
Shoots L

YEAR	TEAM	LEAGUE	GP	MIN	W	L	T	GA	ENG	G AVG	SO	A	PIM
1967-68	LA	N	45	2444	20	18	4	117	2	2.87	2	0	4
1968-69			17	921	0	0	0	56	0	3.65	0	0	2
1969-70			20	960	2	12	1	68	0	4.25	0	0	5
1972-73	HOUS	W	36	2163	20	14	2	108	0	3.00	0	0	11
1973-74			25	1509	12	12	1	84	0	3.34	0	1	14
1974-75			35	2098	20	15	0	113	0	3.23	2	0	0
1975-76			25	1456	14	10	0	77	0	3.17	1	0	6
1976-77			42	2512	23	14	4	132	0	3.15	3	3	63
1977-78			12	634	4	7	0	47	0	4.45	0	0	2
9 yrs.		N Totals:	82	4325	22	30	5	241	2	3.34	2	0	11
		W Totals:	175	10372	93	72	7	561	0	3.25	6	4	96
PLAYOFFS													
1967-68	LA	N	3	149	1	1	0	8	0	3.22	0	0	0
1968-69			5	229	1	1	0	12	0	3.14	0	0	0
1972-73	HOUS	W	7	423	4	3	0	20	0	2.84	0	0	0
1975-76			4	200	1	2	0	10	0	3.00	0	0	0
1976-77			2	120	2	0	0	4	0	2.00	0	0	0
1977-78			3	131	1	2	0	8	0	3.66	0	0	2
6 yrs.		N Totals:	8	378	2	2	0	20	0	3.17	0	0	0
		W Totals:	16	874	8	7	0	42	0	2.88	0	0	2

Rick St. Croix

ST. CROIX, RICHARD
B. Jan. 3, 1955, Kenora, Ont.
5'10", 160 lbs.
Shoots L

YEAR	TEAM	LEAGUE	GP	MIN	W	L	T	GA	ENG	G AVG	SO	A	PIM
1977-78	PHI	N	7	395	2	4	1	20	1	3.04	0	0	0
1978-79			2	117	0	1	1	6	0	3.08	0	0	0
1979-80			1	60	1	0	0	2	0	2.00	0	0	0
1980-81			27	1567	13	7	6	65	2	2.49	2	1	0
1981-82			29	1729	13	9	6	112	3	3.89	0	1	2

Rick St. Croix continued

YEAR	TEAM & LEAGUE		GP	MIN	W	L	T	GA	ENG	G AVG	SO	A	PIM
1982-83			16	940	9	5	2	54	2	3.45	0	0	0
	TOR	N	17	920	4	9	2	58	0	3.78	0	0	0
	2 team total		33	1860	13	14	4	112	2	3.61	0	0	0
6 yrs.		N Totals:	99	5728	42	35	18	317	8	3.32	2	2	2
PLAYOFFS													
1980-81	PHI	N	9	541	4	5	0	27	0	2.99	**1**	0	2
1981-82			1	20	0	1	0	1	1	3.00	0	0	0
1982-83	TOR	N	1	1	0	0	0	1	0	60.00	0	0	0
3 yrs.		N Totals:	11	562	4	6	0	29	1	3.10	1	0	2

Traded by Philadelphia to **Toronto** for Michel Larocque, Jan. 11, 1983.

Charlie Sands

SANDS, CHARLIE
B. Mar. 23, 1911, Fort William, Ont.

5'9", 160 lbs.
Shoots R

YEAR	TEAM & LEAGUE		GP	MIN	W	L	T	GA	ENG	G AVG	SO	A	PIM
1939-40	MONT	N	1	25	0	0	0	5	0	5.00	0	0	0

Nick Sanza

SANZA, NICHOLAS
B. Feb. 6, 1955

5'11", 178 lbs.

YEAR	TEAM & LEAGUE		GP	MIN	W	L	T	GA	ENG	G AVG	SO	A	PIM
1975-76	D-O	W	1	20	0	1	0	5	0	15.00	0	0	0

Bob Sauve

SAUVE, ROBERT
B. June 17, 1955, Ste. Genevieve, Que.
Shared Vezina Trophy, 1979-80

5'8", 165 lbs.
Shoots L

YEAR	TEAM & LEAGUE		GP	MIN	W	L	T	GA	ENG	G AVG	SO	A	PIM
1976-77	BUF	N	4	184	1	2	0	11	0	3.59	0	0	0
1977-78			11	480	6	2	0	20	0	2.50	0	1	0
1978-79			29	1610	10	10	7	100	0	3.73	0	0	2
1979-80			32	1880	20	8	4	74	1	**2.36**	4	**4**	2
1980-81			35	2100	16	10	9	111	2	3.17	2	1	0
1981-82	DET	N	41	2365	11	25	4	165	5	4.19	0	0	0
	BUF	N	14	760	6	1	5	35	1	2.76	0	0	2
	2 team total		55	3125	17	26	9	200	6	3.84	0	0	2
1982-83			54	3110	25	20	7	179	0	3.45	1	1	8
7 yrs.		N Totals:	220	12489	95	78	36	695	9	3.34	7	7	14
PLAYOFFS													
1978-79	BUF	N	3	181	1	2	0	9	0	2.98	0	0	0
1979-80			8	501	6	2	0	17	1	**2.04**	**2**	0	2
1982-83			10	545	6	4	0	28	0	3.08	**2**	0	0
3 yrs.		N Totals:	21	1227	13	8	0	54	1	2.64	4	0	2

Traded to **Detroit** by Buffalo for future considerations, Dec. 2, 1981. Signed as free agent by **Buffalo** , June 1, 1982.

Terry Sawchuk

SAWCHUK, TERRANCE GORDON
B. Dec. 28, 1929, Winnipeg, Man.
Won Vezina Trophy, 1951-52, 1952-53, 1954-55
Shared Vezina Trophy, 1964-65
Won Calder Trophy, 1950-51
Hall of Fame, 1971

6', 195 lbs.
Shoots L

YEAR	TEAM & LEAGUE		GP	MIN	W	L	T	GA	ENG	G AVG	SO	A	PIM
1949-50	DET	N	7	420	4	3	0	16	0	2.29	1	0	0
1950-51			70	**4200**	44	13	13	139	0	1.99	**11**	0	2
1951-52			70	**4200**	**44**	14	12	133	0	**1.90**	**12**	0	2
1952-53			63	3780	**32**	15	16	120	0	**1.90**	9	0	5
1953-54			67	4000	**35**	19	13	129	0	1.94	12	0	0
1954-55			68	4040	28	24	26	132	0	1.96	**12**	**1**	0
1955-56	BOS	N	68	4080	22	**33**	13	181	0	2.66	9	0	**20**
1956-57			34	2040	18	10	6	81	0	2.38	2	0	14
1957-58	DET	N	70	**4200**	29	29	12	207	0	2.96	3	0	**39**
1958-59			67	4020	23	**36**	8	209	0	3.12	5	0	**12**
1959-60			58	3480	24	20	14	156	0	2.69	5	0	**22**
1960-61			37	2080	12	16	8	113	0	3.05	2	1	8
1961-62			43	2580	14	21	8	143	0	3.33	5	0	12
1962-63			48	2775	23	16	7	119	0	2.48	3	0	**14**
1963-64			53	3140	24	20	7	138	0	2.60	5	0	0
1964-65	TOR	N	36	2160	17	13	6	92	0	2.56	1	**2**	**24**
1965-66			27	1521	10	11	4	80	1	2.96	1	1	12
1966-67			28	1409	15	5	4	66	0	2.81	2	0	2
1967-68	LA	N	36	1936	11	14	6	99	2	3.07	2	0	0
1968-69	DET	N	13	641	3	4	3	28	0	2.62	0	0	0
1969-70	NYR	N	8	412	3	1	2	20	0	2.91	1	1	0
21 yrs.		N Totals:	971	57114	435	337	188	2401	3	2.52	103	6	188
PLAYOFFS													
1950-51	DET	N	6	463	2	4	0	13	0	1.68	1	0	0
1951-52*			8	480	**8**	0	0	5	0	**0.63**	**4**	0	0
1952-53			6	372	2	4	0	21	0	3.39	1	0	0
1953-54*			12	**751**	**8**	4	0	20	0	**1.60**	**2**	0	0
1954-55*			11	**660**	**8**	3	0	26	0	**2.36**	**1**	0	0
1957-58			4	252	0	4	0	19	0	4.52	0	0	0

Terry Sawchuk continued

YEAR	TEAM & LEAGUE		GP	MIN	W	L	T	GA	ENG	G AVG	SO	A	PIM
1959-60			6	405	2	4	0	20	0	2.96	0	0	0
1960-61			8	465	5	2	0	18	0	2.32	1	0	0
1962-63			11	**660**	5	6	0	36	0	3.27	0	0	0
1963-64			13	695	6	6	0	31	0	2.68	1	0	0
1964-65	TOR	N	1	60	0	1	0	3	0	3.00	0	0	0
1965-66			2	120	0	2	0	6	0	3.00	0	0	0
1966-67*			10	**568**	**6**	4	0	25	0	2.64	0	0	0
1967-68	LA	N	5	280	2	3	0	18	0	3.86	**1**	0	0
1969-70	NYR	N	3	80	0	1	0	6	0	4.50	0	0	0
15 yrs.		N Totals:	106	6311	54	48	0	267	0	2.54	12	0	0

Traded to **Boston** by Detroit with Vic Stasiuk, Marcel Bonin and Lorne Davis for Ed Sandford, Real Chevrefils, Norm Corcoran, Gilles Boisvert and Warren Godfrey, June 3, 1955. Traded to **Detroit** by Boston for John Bucyk, June 10, 1957. Drafted by **Toronto** from Detroit, June 10, 1964. Drafted by **Los Angeles** from Toronto in Expansion Draft, June 6, 1967. Traded to **Detroit** by Los Angeles for Jimmy Peters, Oct. 15, 1968. Traded to **N.Y. Rangers** by Detroit with Sandy Snow for Larry Jeffrey, June 8, 1969.

Joe Schaefer

SCHAEFER, JOSEPH
B. Dec. 21, 1924, Long Island City, N.Y.

YEAR	TEAM & LEAGUE		GP	MIN	W	L	T	GA	ENG	G AVG	SO	A	PIM
1959-60	NYR	N	1	39	0	0	0	5	0	7.69	0	0	0
1960-61			1	47	0	1	0	3	0	3.83	0	0	0
2 yrs.		N Totals:	2	86	0	1	0	8	0	5.58	0	0	0

Rich Sevigny

SEVIGNY, RICHARD
B. Apr. 11, 1957, Montreal, Que.
Shared Vezina Trophy, 1980-81

5'8", 172 lbs.
Shoots L

YEAR	TEAM & LEAGUE		GP	MIN	W	L	T	GA	ENG	G AVG	SO	A	PIM
1979-80	MONT	N	11	632	5	4	2	31	3	2.94	0	0	4
1980-81			33	1777	20	4	3	71	0	2.40	2	0	30
1981-82			19	1027	11	4	2	53	1	3.10	0	0	10
1982-83			38	2130	15	11	8	122	5	3.44	1	1	8
4 yrs.		N Totals:	101	5566	51	23	15	277	9	2.99	3	1	52
PLAYOFFS													
1980-81	MONT	N	3	180	0	3	0	13	2	4.33	0	0	0
1982-83			1	28	0	0	0	0	0	0.00	0	0	0
2 yrs.		N Totals:	4	208	0	3	0	13	2	3.75	0	0	0

Jim Shaw

SHAW, JAMES MORRIS
B. Oct. 18, 1945, Saskatoon, Sask.

6'1", 185 lbs.
Shoots L

YEAR	TEAM & LEAGUE		GP	MIN	W	L	T	GA	ENG	G AVG	SO	A	PIM
1974-75	TOR	W	21	1055	7	9	1	70	0	3.98	0	0	0
1975-76			16	777	4	7	1	63	0	4.86	0	0	0
2 yrs.		W Totals:	37	1832	11	16	2	133	0	4.36	0	0	0
PLAYOFFS													
1974-75	TOR	W	5	262	2	2	0	18	0	4.12	0	0	0

Al Shields

SHIELDS, ALLEN
B. May 10, 1907, Ottawa, Ont.

6', 188 lbs.
Shoots R

YEAR	TEAM & LEAGUE		GP	MIN	W	L	T	GA	ENG	G AVG	SO	A	PIM
1931-32	NYA	N	2	41	0	0	0	9	0	4.50	0	0	0

Don Simmons

SIMMONS, DONALD
B. Sept. 13, 1931, Port Colborne, Ont.

5'10", 150 lbs.
Shoots R

YEAR	TEAM & LEAGUE		GP	MIN	W	L	T	GA	ENG	G AVG	SO	A	PIM
1956-57	BOS	N	26	1560	13	9	4	63	0	2.42	4	0	0
1957-58			38	2228	15	15	7	93	0	2.50	5	0	0
1958-59			58	3480	24	26	8	184	0	3.17	3	0	4
1959-60			28	1680	10	15	3	94	0	3.36	2	0	4
1960-61			18	1080	3	9	6	59	0	3.28	1	0	6
1961-62	TOR	N	9	540	4	4	1	21	0	2.33	1	0	0
1962-63			28	1680	15	8	5	70	0	2.50	1	0	0
1963-64			21	1191	9	9	1	63	0	3.17	3	0	0
1965-66	NYR	N	11	491	3	6	1	37	0	4.52	0	0	0
1967-68			5	300	2	1	2	13	0	2.60	0	0	0
1968-69			5	206	2	2	1	8	0	2.33	0	0	0
11 yrs.		N Totals:	247	14436	100	104	39	705	0	2.93	20	0	14
PLAYOFFS													
1956-57	BOS	N	10	600	5	5	0	29	0	2.90	**2**	0	0
1957-58			11	**671**	6	5	0	27	0	2.41	**1**	0	0
1961-62*	TOR	N	3	165	2	1	0	8	0	2.91	0	0	0
3 yrs.		N Totals:	24	1436	13	11	0	64	0	2.67	3	0	0

Traded to **Toronto** by Boston for Ed Chadwick, Jan., 1961. Drafted by **N.Y. Rangers** from Toronto, June 8, 1965.

Gary Simmons

SIMMONS, GARY BYRNE
B. July 19, 1944, Charlottetown, P.E.I.

6'2", 200 lbs.
Shoots L

YEAR	TEAM & LEAGUE		GP	MIN	W	L	T	GA	ENG	G AVG	SO	A	PIM
1974-75	CALIF	N	34	2029	10	21	3	124	2	3.67	2	1	26
1975-76			40	2360	15	19	5	131	4	3.33	2	0	18
1976-77	CLEVE	N	15	840	2	8	4	51	1	3.64	1	0	0
	LA	N	4	240	1	2	1	16	1	4.00	0	0	0
	2 team total		19	1080	3	10	5	67	2	3.72	1	0	0

Gary Simmons continued

YEAR	TEAM & LEAGUE		GP	MIN	W	L	T	GA	ENG	G AVG	SO	A	PIM
1977-78			14	693	2	7	2	44	1	3.81	0	0	6
4 yrs.		**N Totals:**	107	6162	30	57	15	366	9	3.56	5	1	50
PLAYOFFS													
1976-77	**LA**	**N**	1	20	0	0	0	1	0	3.00	0	0	0

Traded to **Los Angeles** by Cleveland with Jim Moxey for Gary Edwards and Juha Widing, Jan. 22, 1977.

Paul Skidmore

SKIDMORE, PAUL
B. July 22, 1956, Smithtown, N.Y.
6', 185 lbs. Shoots L

YEAR	TEAM & LEAGUE		GP	MIN	W	L	T	GA	ENG	G AVG	SO	A	PIM
1981-82	**STL**	**N**	2	120	1	1	0	6	0	3.00	0	0	0

Warren Skordenski

SKORDENSKI, WARREN
B. Mar. 22, 1960, Winnipeg, Man.
6'1", 180 lbs. Shoots L

YEAR	TEAM & LEAGUE		GP	MIN	W	L	T	GA	ENG	G AVG	SO	A	PIM
1981-82	**CHI**	**N**	1	60	0	1	0	5	1	5.00	0	0	0

Al Smith

SMITH, ALLAN ROBERT
B. Nov. 10, 1945, Toronto, Ont.
6'1", 200 lbs. Shoots L

YEAR	TEAM & LEAGUE		GP	MIN	W	L	T	GA	ENG	G AVG	SO	A	PIM
1965-66	**TOR**	**N**	2	62	2	0	0	2	0	1.94	0	0	0
1966-67			1	60	0	1	0	5	0	5.00	0	0	0
1968-69			7	335	2	2	1	16	0	2.87	0	0	0
1969-70	**PITT**	**N**	46	2555	15	20	8	129	3	3.03	2	0	20
1970-71			46	2472	9	22	9	128	0	3.11	2	0	**41**
1971-72	**DET**	**N**	43	2500	18	20	4	135	4	3.24	4	**4**	23
1972-73	**NE**	**W**	51	3059	31	19	1	162	0	3.18	3	3	39
1973-74			55	3194	30	21	2	164	0	3.08	2	3	33
1974-75			59	3494	33	21	4	202	0	3.47	2	0	18
1975-76	**BUF**	**N**	14	840	9	3	2	43	1	3.07	0	0	0
1976-77			7	265	0	3	0	19	0	4.30	0	0	0
1977-78	**NE**	**W**	55	3246	30	20	3	174	0	**3.22**	2	3	4
1978-79			40	2396	17	17	5	132	0	3.31	1	3	35
1979-80	**HART**	**N**	30	1754	4	10	8	107	2	3.66	2	1	0
1980-81	**COLO**	**N**	37	1909	9	18	4	151	4	4.75	0	2	**51**
15 yrs.		**N Totals:**	233	12752	68	99	36	735	14	3.46	10	7	135
		W Totals:	260	15389	141	98	15	834	0	3.25	10	12	129
PLAYOFFS													
1969-70	**PITT**	**N**	3	180	1	2	0	10	0	3.33	0	0	0
1972-73	**NE**	**W**	15	**909**	**12**	3	0	49	0	3.23	0	1	12
1973-74			7	399	3	4	0	21	0	3.16	**1**	0	0
1974-75			6	366	2	4	0	28	0	4.59	0	0	0
1975-76	**BUF**	**N**	1	17	0	0	0	1	0	3.53	0	0	0
1977-78	**NE**	**W**	3	120	0	2	0	14	0	7.00	0	0	0
1978-79			4	153	1	2	0	12	0	4.71	0	0	0
1979-80	**HART**	**N**	2	120	0	2	0	10	0	5.00	0	0	0
8 yrs.		**N Totals:**	6	317	1	4	0	21	0	3.97	0	0	0
		W Totals:	35	1947	18	15	0	124	0	3.82	1	1	12

Put on **Pittsburgh** reserve list from Toronto via Intra-league Draft, June 8, 1971. Sold to **Colorado** by Hartford, Sept. 4, 1980.

Billy Smith

SMITH, WILLIAM JOHN (The Hatchet Man)
B. Dec. 12, 1950, Perth, Ont.
Won Vezina Trophy, 1981-82
Won Jennings Trophy, 1982-83
Won Conn Smythe Trophy, 1982-83
Scored one goal, 1979–80
5'10", 185 lbs. Shoots L

YEAR	TEAM & LEAGUE		GP	MIN	W	L	T	GA	ENG	G AVG	SO	A	PIM
1971-72	**LA**	**N**	5	300	1	3	1	23	0	4.60	0	0	5
1972-73	**NYI**	**N**	37	2122	7	24	3	147	0	4.16	0	0	**42**
1973-74			46	2615	9	23	12	134	5	3.07	0	0	11
1974-75			58	3368	21	18	1	156	3	2.78	3	0	21
1975-76			39	2254	19	10	9	98	3	2.61	3	1	10
1976-77			36	2089	21	8	6	87	1	2.50	2	1	12
1977-78			38	2154	20	3	8	95	2	2.65	2	0	**35**
1978-79			40	2261	25	8	4	108	0	2.87	1	2	**54**
1979-80			38	2114	15	14	7	104	4	2.95	2	1	39
1980-81			41	2363	22	10	8	129	4	3.28	2	0	33
1981-82			46	2685	32	9	4	133	0	**2.97**	0	1	24
1982-83			41	2340	18	14	7	112	3	2.87	1	0	**41**
12 yrs.		**N Totals:**	465	26665	210	144	70	1326	25	2.98	16	6	327
PLAYOFFS													
1974-75	**NYI**	**N**	6	333	1	4	0	23	1	4.14	0	0	**6**
1975-76			8	437	4	3	0	21	0	2.88	0	0	**11**
1976-77			10	580	7	3	0	27	0	2.79	0	0	**8**
1977-78			1	47	0	0	0	1	0	1.28	0	0	**9**
1978-79			5	315	4	1	0	10	0	**1.90**	**1**	0	4
1979-80*			20	**1198**	**15**	4	0	56	0	2.80	1	0	0
1980-81*			17	**994**	**14**	3	0	42	0	**2.54**	0	1	2
1981-82*			18	**1120**	**15**	3	0	47	0	2.52	**1**	0	**6**

Billy Smith continued

YEAR	TEAM & LEAGUE		GP	MIN	W	L	T	GA	ENG	G AVG	SO	A	PIM
1982-83*			17	962	**13**	3	0	43	0	**2.68**	**2**	1	9
9 yrs.		N Totals:	102	5986	73	24	0	270	1	2.71	5	2	55

Drafted by **N.Y. Islanders** from Los Angeles in Expansion Draft, June 6, 1972.

Gary Smith

SMITH, GARY EDWARD (Suitcase)
B. Feb. 4, 1944, Ottawa, Ont.
Shared Vezina Trophy, 1971-72

6'4", 215 lbs.
Shoots L

YEAR	TEAM & LEAGUE		GP	MIN	W	L	T	GA	ENG	G AVG	SO	A	PIM
1965-66	TOR	N	3	118	0	2	0	7	0	3.56	0	0	0
1966-67			2	115	0	2	0	7	0	3.65	0	0	0
1967-68	OAK	N	21	1129	2	13	4	60	1	3.19	1	1	4
1968-69	CALIF	N	54	2993	0	0	0	148	0	2.97	4	2	7
1969-70	OAK	N	65	3762	19	**34**	12	195	0	3.11	2	1	18
1970-71	CALIF	N	71	**3975**	19	**48**	4	256	3	3.86	2	1	6
1971-72	CHI	N	28	1540	14	5	6	62	0	2.42	5	0	0
1972-73			23	1340	10	10	2	79	0	3.54	0	0	5
1973-74	VAN	N	66	3632	20	**33**	8	208	5	3.44	3	0	0
1974-75			72	3823	32	24	9	197	3	3.09	6	1	33
1975-76			51	2864	20	24	6	167	2	3.50	2	1	**24**
1976-77	MINN	N	36	2090	10	17	8	139	3	3.99	1	0	12
1977-78	WASH	N	17	980	2	12	3	68	2	4.16	0	0	6
	MINN	N	3	180	0	2	1	9	0	3.00	0	0	6
	2 team total		20	1160	2	14	4	77	2	3.98	0	0	12
1978-79	IND	W	11	664	0	10	0	61	0	5.51	0	0	0
	WINN	W	11	626	7	3	0	31	0	2.97	0	3	0
	2 team total		22	1290	7	13	0	92	0	4.28	0	3	0
1979-80	WINN	N	20	1073	4	11	4	73	1	4.08	0	0	25
15 yrs.		N Totals:	532	29614	152	237	67	1675	20	3.39	26	7	146
		W Totals:	22	1290	7	13	0	92	0	4.28	0	3	0
PLAYOFFS													
1968-69	OAK	N	7	420	3	4	0	23	0	3.29	0	0	0
1969-70			4	248	0	4	0	13	0	3.15	0	0	**4**
1971-72	CHI	N	2	120	1	1	0	3	0	1.50	1	0	0
1972-73			2	65	0	1	0	5	0	4.62	0	0	0
1974-75	VAN	N	4	257	1	3	0	14	0	3.27	0	0	0
1976-77	MINN	N	1	43	0	0	0	4	0	5.58	0	0	0
1978-79	WINN	W	10	563	**8**	2	0	35	0	3.73	0	0	0
7 yrs.		N Totals:	20	1153	5	13	0	62	0	3.23	1	0	4
		W Totals:	10	563	8	2	0	35	0	3.73	0	0	0

Drafted by **Oakland** from Toronto in Expansion Draft, June 6, 1967. Traded to **Chicago** by California for goaltender Gerry Desjardins, Gerry Pinder and Kerry Bond, Sept. 9, 1971. Traded to **Vancouver** by Chicago with Jerry Korab for goaltender Cesare Maniago, Aug. 23, 1976. Signed by **Washington** as free agent, Sept. 3, 1977. Sold to **Minnesota** by Washington, Feb. 19, 1978.

Norm Smith

SMITH, NORMAN
B. Mar. 18, 1908, Toronto, Ont.
Won Vezina Trophy, 1936-37

5'7", 165 lbs.

YEAR	TEAM & LEAGUE		GP	MIN	W	L	T	GA	ENG	G AVG	SO	A	PIM
1931-32	MON(M)	N	21	1267	5	12	4	62	0	2.95	0	0	0
1934-35	DET	N	25	1550	12	11	2	52	0	2.08	2	0	0
1935-36			48	**3030**	**24**	16	8	103	0	2.15	6	0	0
1936-37			48	2980	25	14	9	102	0	**2.13**	**6**	0	0
1937-38			47	2930	11	25	11	130	0	2.77	3	0	0
1938-39			4	240	0	4	0	12	0	3.00	0	0	0
1943-44			5	240	3	1	1	11	0	2.75	0	0	0
1944-45			1	60	1	0	0	3	0	3.00	0	0	0
8 yrs.		N Totals:	199	12297	81	83	35	475	0	2.32	17	0	0
PLAYOFFS													
1935-36*	DET	N	7	**598**	**6**	1	0	12	0	**1.71**	**2**	0	0
1936-37*			5	282	3	1	0	6	0	1.20	1	0	0
2 yrs.		N Totals:	12	880	9	2	0	18	0	1.23	3	0	0

Bob Sneddon

SNEDDON, ROBERT ALLAN
B. May 31, 1944, Montreal, Que.

6'2", 190 lbs.
Shoots R

YEAR	TEAM & LEAGUE		GP	MIN	W	L	T	GA	ENG	G AVG	SO	A	PIM
1970-71	CALIF	N	5	225	0	2	0	21	0	5.60	0	0	0

Doug Soetaert

SOETAERT, DOUGLAS HENRY (Soapy)
B. Apr. 21, 1955, Edmonton, Alta.

6', 185 lbs.
Shoots L

YEAR	TEAM & LEAGUE		GP	MIN	W	L	T	GA	ENG	G AVG	SO	A	PIM
1975-76	NYR	N	8	273	2	2	0	24	0	5.27	0	1	0
1976-77			12	570	3	4	1	28	1	2.95	1	0	0
1977-78			6	360	2	2	2	20	0	3.33	0	0	0
1978-79			17	900	5	7	3	57	2	3.80	0	0	4
1979-80			8	435	5	2	0	33	0	4.55	0	0	0
1980-81			39	2320	16	16	7	152	2	3.93	0	0	2
1981-82	WINN	N	39	2157	13	14	8	155	1	4.31	2	2	14
1982-83			44	2533	19	19	6	174	3	4.12	0	1	10
8 yrs.		N Totals:	173	9548	65	66	27	643	9	4.04	3	4	30

Doug Soetaert continued

YEAR	TEAM & LEAGUE		GP	MIN	W	L	T	GA	ENG	G AVG	SO	A	PIM
PLAYOFFS													
1981-82	WINN	N	2	120	1	1	0	8	0	4.00	0	0	0
1982-83			1	20	0	0	0	0	0	0.00	0	0	0
2 yrs.		N Totals:	3	140	1	1	0	8	0	3.43	0	0	0

Red Spooner

SPOONER, ANDY

YEAR	TEAM & LEAGUE		GP	MIN	W	L	T	GA	ENG	G AVG	SO	A	PIM
1929-30	PITT	N	1	60	0	1	0	6	0	6.00	0	0	0

Ed Staniowski

STANIOWSKI, EDWARD 5'9", 170 lbs.
B. July 7, 1955, Moose Jaw, Sask. Shoots L

YEAR	TEAM & LEAGUE		GP	MIN	W	L	T	GA	ENG	G AVG	SO	A	PIM
1975-76	STL	N	11	620	5	3	2	33	0	3.19	0	0	0
1976-77			29	1589	10	15	1	108	1	4.08	0	0	0
1977-78			17	886	1	10	2	57	1	3.86	0	0	0
1978-79			39	2291	9	25	3	146	4	3.82	0	1	2
1979-80			22	1108	2	11	3	80	2	4.33	0	0	2
1980-81			19	1010	10	3	3	72	0	4.28	0	2	0
1981-82	WINN	N	45	2643	20	19	6	174	2	3.95	1	5	4
1982-83			17	827	4	8	0	65	2	4.72	1	1	0
8 yrs.		N Totals:	199	10974	61	94	20	735	12	4.02	2	9	8
PLAYOFFS													
1975-76	STL	N	3	206	1	2	0	7	0	2.04	0	0	0
1976-77			3	102	0	2	0	9	1	5.29	0	0	0
1981-82	WINN	N	2	120	0	2	0	12	0	6.00	0	0	0
3 yrs.		N Totals:	8	428	1	6	0	28	1	3.93	0	0	0

Traded to **Winnipeg** by St. Louis with Bryan Maxwell and Paul MacLean for Scott Campbell and John Markell, July 3, 1981.

Harold Starr

STARR, HAROLD 5'11", 176 lbs.
B. July 6, 1906, Ottawa, Ont. Shoots L

YEAR	TEAM & LEAGUE		GP	MIN	W	L	T	GA	ENG	G AVG	SO	A	PIM
1931-32	MON(M)	N	1	3	0	0	0	0	0	0.00	0	0	0

Greg Stefan

STEFAN, GREG 5'11", 173 lbs.
B. Feb. 11, 1961, Brantford, Ont. Shoots L

YEAR	TEAM & LEAGUE		GP	MIN	W	L	T	GA	ENG	G AVG	SO	A	PIM
1981-82	DET	N	2	120	0	2	0	10	0	5.00	0	0	0
1982-83			35	1847	6	16	9	139	2	4.52	0	0	35
2 yrs.		N Totals:	37	1967	6	18	9	149	2	4.54	0	0	35

Phil Stein

STEIN, PHILLIP J. 5'11", lbs.
B. Sept. 13, 1913, Toronto, Ont. Shoots L

YEAR	TEAM & LEAGUE		GP	MIN	W	L	T	GA	ENG	G AVG	SO	A	PIM
1939-40	TOR	N	1	70	0	0	1	2	0	2.00	0	0	0

Wayne Stephenson

STEPHENSON, FREDERICK WAYNE 5'9", 175 lbs.
B. Jan. 29, 1945, Fort William, Ont. Shoots L

YEAR	TEAM & LEAGUE		GP	MIN	W	L	T	GA	ENG	G AVG	SO	A	PIM
1971-72	STL	N	2	100	0	1	0	9	0	5.40	0	0	0
1972-73			45	2535	18	5	7	128	2	3.03	1	0	0
1973-74			40	2360	13	21	5	123	2	3.13	2	1	2
1974-75	PHI	N	12	639	7	2	0	29	1	2.72	1	0	0
1975-76			66	3819	40	10	11	164	2	2.58	1	0	11
1976-77			21	1065	12	3	2	41	2	2.31	3	0	4
1977-78			26	1482	14	10	1	68	2	2.75	3	0	0
1978-79			40	2187	20	10	5	122	4	3.35	2	1	2
1979-80	WASH	N	56	3146	18	24	10	187	5	3.57	0	0	20
1980-81			20	1010	4	7	5	66	0	3.92	1	0	4
10 yrs.		N Totals:	328	18343	146	93	46	937	20	3.06	14	2	43
PLAYOFFS													
1972-73	STL	N	3	160	1	2	0	14	0	5.25	0	0	0
1974-75*	PHI	N	2	123	2	0	0	4	0	1.95	1	1	0
1975-76			8	494	4	4	0	22	0	2.67	0	0	0
1976-77			9	532	4	3	0	23	1	2.59	1	0	2
1978-79			4	213	0	3	0	16	3	4.51	0	0	5
5 yrs.		N Totals:	26	1522	11	12	0	79	4	3.11	2	1	7

Traded to **Philadelphia** by St. Louis for Philadelphia's second choice (Jamie Masters) in 1975 Amateur Draft and amateur player Randy Andreachuk, Sept. 16, 1974. Traded to **Washington** by Philadelphia for Washington's third-round choice (Barry Tabobondung) in the 1981 Entry Draft, Aug. 16, 1979.

Doug Stevenson

STEVENSON, DOUGLAS 5'8", 170 lbs.
B. Apr. 6, 1924, Regina, Sask. Shoots L

YEAR	TEAM & LEAGUE		GP	MIN	W	L	T	GA	ENG	G AVG	SO	A	PIM
1944-45	NYR	N	4	240	0	4	0	20	0	5.00	0	0	0
	CHI	N	2	120	1	1	0	7	0	3.50	0	0	0
	2 team total		6	360	1	5	0	27	0	4.50	0	0	0
1945-46			2	120	1	1	0	12	0	6.00	0	0	0
2 yrs.		N Totals:	8	480	2	6	0	39	0	4.88	0	0	0

Doc Stewart

STEWART, CHARLES

YEAR	TEAM & LEAGUE		GP	MIN	W	L	T	GA	ENG	G AVG	SO	A	PIM
1924-25	**BOS**	**N**	21	1266	5	16	0	65	0	3.10	2	0	0
1925-26			35	2168	17	14	4	80	0	2.29	6	0	0
1926-27			21	1303	9	11	1	49	0	2.33	2	0	0
3 yrs.		**N Totals:**	77	4737	31	41	5	194	0	2.46	10	0	0

Jim Stewart

STEWART, JIM

YEAR	TEAM & LEAGUE		GP	MIN	W	L	T	GA	ENG	G AVG	SO	A	PIM
1979-80	**BOS**	**N**	1	20	0	1	0	5	0	15.00	0	0	0

Herb Stuart

STUART, HERBERT

YEAR	TEAM & LEAGUE		GP	MIN	W	L	T	GA	ENG	G AVG	SO	A	PIM
1926-27	**DET**	**N**	3	180	0	1	0	5	0	1.67	0	0	0

Danny Sullivan

SULLIVAN, DANIEL

YEAR	TEAM & LEAGUE		GP	MIN	W	L	T	GA	ENG	G AVG	SO	A	PIM
1972-73	**PHI**	**W**	1	60	1	0	0	3	0	3.00	0	0	0
1973-74	**VAN**	**W**	1	60	0	1	0	7	0	7.00	0	0	0
2 yrs.		**W Totals:**	2	120	1	1	0	10	0	5.00	0	0	0

Dave Tataryn

TATARYN, DAVID NATHAN
B. July 17, 1950, Sudbury, Ont.

5'9", 160 lbs.
Shoots L

YEAR	TEAM & LEAGUE		GP	MIN	W	L	T	GA	ENG	G AVG	SO	A	PIM
1975-76	**TOR**	**W**	23	1261	7	12	1	100	0	4.76	0	0	0
1976-77	**NYR**	**N**	2	80	1	1	0	10	0	7.50	0	0	0
2 yrs.		**N Totals:**	2	80	1	1	0	10	0	7.50	0	0	0
		W Totals:	23	1261	7	12	1	100	0	4.76	0	0	0

Bobby Taylor

TAYLOR, ROBERT IAN
B. Jan. 24, 1945, Calgary, Alta.

6'1", 180 lbs.
Shoots L

YEAR	TEAM & LEAGUE		GP	MIN	W	L	T	GA	ENG	G AVG	SO	A	PIM
1971-72	**PHI**	**N**	6	320	1	2	2	16	0	3.00	0	0	0
1972-73			23	1144	8	8	4	78	0	4.09	0	1	0
1973-74			8	366	3	3	0	26	0	4.26	0	0	0
1974-75			3	120	0	2	0	13	0	6.50	0	0	2
1975-76			4	240	3	1	0	15	0	3.75	0	0	2
	PITT	**N**	2	78	0	1	0	7	1	5.38	0	0	0
	2 team total		6	318	3	2	0	22	1	4.15	0	0	2
5 yrs.		**N Totals:**	46	2268	15	17	6	155	1	4.10	0	1	4

Traded to **Pittsburgh** by Philadelphia with Ed Van Impe for Gary Inness and future considerations, Mar. 9, 1976.

Harv Teno

TENO, HARVEY
B. Windsor, Ont.

YEAR	TEAM & LEAGUE		GP	MIN	W	L	T	GA	ENG	G AVG	SO	A	PIM
1938-39	**DET**	**N**	5	300	2	3	0	15	0	3.00	0	0	0

Wayne Thomas

THOMAS, ROBERT WAYNE
B. Oct. 9, 1947, Ottawa, Ont.

6'2", 195 lbs.
Shoots L

YEAR	TEAM & LEAGUE		GP	MIN	W	L	T	GA	ENG	G AVG	SO	A	PIM
1972-73	**MONT**	**N**	10	583	8	1	0	23	0	2.37	1	1	2
1973-74			42	2410	23	12	5	111	1	2.76	1	2	6
1975-76	**TOR**	**N**	64	3684	28	24	12	196	5	3.19	2	0	18
1976-77			33	1803	10	13	6	116	2	3.86	1	1	4
1977-78	**NYR**	**N**	41	2352	12	20	7	141	2	3.60	4	0	9
1978-79			31	1668	15	10	3	101	0	3.63	1	0	0
1979-80			12	668	4	7	0	44	2	3.95	0	0	0
1980-81			10	600	3	6	1	34	2	3.40	0	2	2
8 yrs.		**N Totals:**	243	13768	103	93	34	766	14	3.34	10	6	41
PLAYOFFS													
1975-76	**TOR**	**N**	10	587	5	5	0	34	1	3.48	1	0	0
1976-77			4	202	1	2	0	12	1	3.56	0	0	0
1977-78	**NYR**	**N**	1	60	0	1	0	4	0	4.00	0	0	0
3 yrs.		**N Totals:**	15	849	6	8	0	50	2	3.53	1	0	0

Traded to **Toronto** by Montreal for Toronto's first choice (Peter Lee) in 1976 Amateur Draft, June 17, 1975. Claimed by **N.Y. Rangers** from Toronto in League Waiver Draft, Oct. 10, 1977.

Tiny Thompson

THOMPSON, CECIL
B. May 31, 1905, Sandon, B.C.
Won Vezina Trophy, 1929-30, 1932-33, 1935-36, 1937-38
Hall of Fame, 1959

5'10", 160 lbs.
Shoots R

YEAR	TEAM & LEAGUE		GP	MIN	W	L	T	GA	ENG	G AVG	SO	A	PIM
1928-29	**BOS**	**N**	44	2710	**26**	13	5	52	0	1.18	12	0	0
1929-30			44	2680	**38**	5	1	98	0	**2.23**	3	0	0
1930-31			44	2730	**28**	10	6	90	0	2.05	3	0	0
1931-32			43	2698	13	19	11	103	0	2.40	**9**	0	0
1932-33			48	3000	**25**	15	8	88	0	**1.83**	**11**	0	0
1933-34			48	2980	18	25	5	130	0	2.71	5	0	0
1934-35			48	2970	26	16	6	112	0	2.33	8	0	0
1935-36			48	2930	22	20	6	82	0	**1.71**	**10**	0	0
1936-37			48	2970	23	18	7	110	0	2.29	**6**	0	0
1937-38			48	2970	**30**	11	7	89	0	**1.85**	7	0	0

YEAR	TEAM & LEAGUE		GP	MIN	W	L	T	GA	ENG	G AVG	SO	A	PIM

Tiny Thompson continued

YEAR	TEAM & LEAGUE		GP	MIN	W	L	T	GA	ENG	G AVG	SO	A	PIM
1938-39			5	310	3	1	1	8	0	1.60	0	0	0
	DET	N	39	2396	16	17	6	101	0	2.59	4	0	0
	2 team total		44	2706	19	18	7	109	0	2.42	4	0	0
1939-40			46	2830	16	24	6	120	0	2.61	3	0	0
12 yrs.		N Totals:	553	34174	284	194	75	1183	0	2.08	81	0	0
PLAYOFFS													
1928-29*	BOS	N	5	300	**5**	0	0	3	0	**0.60**	**3**	0	0
1929-30			6	432	3	3	0	12	0	2.00	0	0	0
1930-31			5	348	2	3	0	13	0	2.60	0	0	0
1932-33			5	429	2	3	0	9	0	1.80	0	0	0
1934-35			4	275	1	1	0	7	0	1.75	1	0	0
1935-36			2	120	1	1	0	8	0	4.00	1	0	0
1936-37			3	180	1	2	0	8	0	2.67	1	0	0
1937-38			3	212	0	3	0	6	0	2.00	0	0	0
1938-39	DET	N	6	374	3	3	0	15	0	2.50	1	0	0
1939-40			5	300	2	3	0	12	0	2.40	0	0	0
10 yrs.		N Totals:	44	2970	20	22	0	93	0	1.88	7	0	0

Vince Tremblay

TREMBLAY, VINCENT
B. Oct. 21, 1959, Quebec, Que.
5'11", 185 lbs.
Shoots L

YEAR	TEAM & LEAGUE		GP	MIN	W	L	T	GA	ENG	G AVG	SO	A	PIM
1979-80	TOR	N	10	329	2	1	0	28	1	5.11	0	0	0
1980-81			3	143	0	3	0	16	0	6.71	0	0	0
1981-82			40	2033	10	18	8	153	3	4.52	1	2	2
3 yrs.		N Totals:	53	2505	12	22	8	197	4	4.72	1	2	2

Ted Tucker

TUCKER, TED
B. May 7, 1949, Fort William, Ont.
5'11", 165 lbs.
Shoots L

YEAR	TEAM & LEAGUE		GP	MIN	W	L	T	GA	ENG	G AVG	SO	A	PIM
1973-74	CALIF	N	5	177	1	1	1	10	0	3.39	0	0	0

Gordie Tumilson

TUMILSON, GORDON
B. July 17, 1951, Winnipeg, Man.

YEAR	TEAM & LEAGUE		GP	MIN	W	L	T	GA	ENG	G AVG	SO	A	PIM
1972-73	WINN	W	3	106	0	2	0	10	0	5.66	0	0	0

Frank Turnbull

TURNBULL, FRANK
B. Jan. 13, 1953, Trenton, Ont.
5'8", 155 lbs.

YEAR	TEAM & LEAGUE		GP	MIN	W	L	T	GA	ENG	G AVG	SO	A	PIM
1975-76	EDM	W	3	106	0	1	0	9	0	5.09	0	0	0
1977-78			1	60	0	1	0	6	0	6.00	0	0	0
2 yrs.		W Totals:	4	166	0	2	0	15	0	5.42	0	0	0

Joe Turner

TURNER, JOSEPH
B. Unknown

YEAR	TEAM & LEAGUE		GP	MIN	W	L	T	GA	ENG	G AVG	SO	A	PIM
1941-42	DET	N	1	60	0	0	1	3	0	3.00	0	0	0

Rogie Vachon

VACHON, ROGATIEN ROSAIRE
B. Sept. 8, 1945, Palmarolle, Que.
Shared Vezina Trophy, 1967-68
5'7", 165 lbs.
Shoots L

YEAR	TEAM & LEAGUE		GP	MIN	W	L	T	GA	ENG	G AVG	SO	A	PIM
1966-67	MONT	N	19	1137	11	3	4	47	1	2.48	1	1	0
1967-68			39	2227	23	13	2	92	0	2.48	4	0	2
1968-69			36	2051	22	9	3	98	0	2.87	2	0	2
1969-70			64	3697	31	18	12	162	6	2.63	4	0	0
1970-71			47	2676	23	12	9	118	1	2.65	2	0	0
1971-72			1	20	0	1	0	4	0	12.00	0	0	0
	LA	N	28	1586	6	18	3	107	0	4.05	0	0	0
	2 team total		29	1606	6	19	3	111	0	4.15	0	0	0
1972-73			53	3120	22	20	10	148	3	2.85	4	1	2
1973-74			65	3751	28	26	10	175	5	2.80	5	0	6
1974-75			54	3239	27	14	1	121	2	2.24	6	1	2
1975-76			51	3060	26	20	5	160	1	3.14	5	0	0
1976-77			68	4059	33	23	12	184	1	2.72	8	1	2
1977-78			70	4107	29	27	13	196	4	2.86	4	0	0
1978-79	DET	N	50	2908	10	27	11	189	1	3.90	0	1	21
1979-80			59	3474	20	**30**	8	209	4	3.61	4	3	2
1980-81	BOS	N	53	3021	25	19	6	168	0	3.34	1	1	6
1981-82			38	2165	19	11	6	132	0	3.66	1	1	0
16 yrs.		N Totals:	795	46298	355	291	115	2310	29	2.99	51	10	45
PLAYOFFS													
1966-67	MONT	N	9	555	**6**	3	0	22	0	**2.38**	0	0	0
1967-68*			2	113	1	1	0	4	0	2.12	0	0	0
1968-69*			8	507	7	1	0	12	0	**1.42**	1	0	0
1973-74	LA	N	4	240	0	4	0	7	2	**1.75**	0	0	0
1974-75			3	199	1	2	0	7	0	2.11	0	0	0
1975-76			7	438	4	3	0	17	1	2.33	1	0	0
1976-77			9	520	4	5	0	36	0	4.15	0	0	0
1977-78			2	120	0	2	0	11	0	5.50	0	0	2
1980-81	BOS	N	3	164	0	2	0	16	1	5.85	0	0	0
1981-82			1	20	0	0	0	1	0	3.00	0	0	0
10 yrs.		N Totals:	48	2876	23	23	0	133	4	2.77	2	0	2

Rogie Vachon continued

Traded to **Los Angeles** by Montreal for Denis DeJordy, Noel Price and Doug Robinson, Nov. 4, 1971. Signed as free agent by **Detroit**, Aug. 8, 1978. As compensation, Los Angeles received Dale McCourt. Traded to **Boston** by Detroit for Gilles Gilbert, July 15, 1980.

John Vanbiesbrouck

VANBIESBROUCK, JOHN 5'7", 165 lbs.
B. Sept. 4, 1963, Detroit, Mich.

YEAR	TEAM	LEAGUE	GP	MIN	W	L	T	GA	ENG	G AVG	SO	A	PIM
1981-82	NYR	N	1	60	1	0	0	1	0	1.00	0	0	0

Mike Veisor

VEISOR, MICHAEL DAVID 5'9", 158 lbs.
B. Aug. 25, 1952, Toronto, Ont. Shoots L

YEAR	TEAM	LEAGUE	GP	MIN	W	L	T	GA	ENG	G AVG	SO	A	PIM
1973-74	CHI	N	10	537	7	0	2	20	0	2.23	1	1	0
1974-75			9	460	1	5	1	36	0	4.70	0	0	0
1976-77			3	180	1	2	0	13	0	4.33	0	0	0
1977-78			12	720	3	4	5	31	0	2.58	2	0	0
1978-79			17	1020	5	8	4	60	2	3.53	0	1	0
1979-80			11	660	3	5	3	37	2	3.36	0	0	0
1980-81	HART	N	29	1588	6	13	6	118	3	4.46	1	0	0
1981-82			13	701	5	5	2	53	0	4.54	0	1	0
1982-83			23	1280	5	16	1	118	0	5.53	0	0	2
9 yrs.		N Totals:	127	7146	36	58	24	486	7	4.08	4	3	2
PLAYOFFS													
1973-74	CHI	N	2	80	0	1	0	5	0	3.75	0	0	0
1979-80			1	60	0	1	0	6	0	6.00	0	0	0
2 yrs.		N Totals:	3	140	0	2	0	11	0	4.71	0	0	0

Traded to **Hartford** by Chicago for Hartford's second round choice (Kevin Griffin) in the 1981 Entry Draft, June 19, 1980.

Mike Vernon

VERNON, MIKE 5'9", 150 lbs.
B. Feb. 24, 1963, Calgary, Alta. Shoots L

YEAR	TEAM	LEAGUE	GP	MIN	W	L	T	GA	ENG	G AVG	SO	A	PIM
1982-83	CALG	N	2	100	0	2	0	11	0	6.60	0	0	0

Georges Vezina

VEZINA, GEORGES (The Chicoutimi Cucumber)
B. Chicoutimi, Que.
Hall of Fame, 1945

YEAR	TEAM	LEAGUE	GP	MIN	W	L	T	GA	ENG	G AVG	SO	A	PIM
1917-18	MONT	N	22	1282	**13**	9	0	84	0	**3.82**	**1**	0	0
1918-19			18	1097	10	8	0	78	0	4.33	1	0	0
1919-20			24	**1454**	13	11	0	113	0	4.71	0	0	0
1920-21			24	1436	13	11	0	99	0	4.13	1	0	0
1921-22			24	1468	13	10	1	94	0	3.92	0	0	0
1922-23			24	**1488**	13	9	2	61	0	2.54	2	0	0
1923-24			24	1459	13	11	0	48	0	**2.00**	**3**	0	0
1924-25			30	**1860**	17	11	2	56	0	**1.87**	5	0	0
1925-26			1	20	0	0	0	0	0	0.00	0	0	0
9 yrs.		N Totals:	191	11564	105	80	5	633	0	3.28	13	0	0
PLAYOFFS													
1917-18	MONT	N	2	120	1	1	0	10	0	5.00	0	0	0
1918-19			10	636	**6**	3	0	37	0	**3.70**	**1**	0	0
1922-23			2	120	1	1	0	3	0	1.50	0	0	0
1923-24*			6	**360**	**6**	0	0	6	0	**1.00**	**2**	0	0
1924-25			6	**360**	**5**	1	0	18	0	3.00	**1**	0	0
5 yrs.		N Totals:	26	1596	19	6	0	74	0	2.78	4	0	0

Mario Vien

VIEN, MARIO 5'7", 166 lbs.
B. Aug. 7, 1955 Shoots R

YEAR	TEAM	LEAGUE	GP	MIN	W	L	T	GA	ENG	G AVG	SO	A	PIM
1975-76	TOR	W	26	1228	4	14	3	105	0	5.13	0	0	0

Gilles Villemure

VILLEMURE, GILLES 5'8", 185 lbs.
B. May 30, 1940, Trois Rivieres, Que. Shoots R
Shared Vezina Trophy, 1970-71

YEAR	TEAM	LEAGUE	GP	MIN	W	L	T	GA	ENG	G AVG	SO	A	PIM
1963-64	NYR	N	5	300	0	3	2	18	0	3.60	0	0	0
1967-68			4	200	1	2	0	8	0	2.40	1	0	0
1968-69			4	240	0	1	0	9	0	2.25	0	0	0
1970-71			34	2039	22	8	4	78	1	2.30	4	0	0
1971-72			37	2129	24	7	4	74	1	2.09	3	0	6
1972-73			34	2040	20	12	2	78	2	2.29	3	0	2
1973-74			21	1054	7	7	3	62	2	3.53	0	0	0
1974-75			45	2470	22	14	6	130	0	3.16	2	0	2
1975-76	CHI	N	15	797	2	7	5	57	2	4.29	0	0	0
1976-77			6	312	0	4	1	28	1	5.38	0	0	0
10 yrs.		N Totals:	205	11581	98	65	27	542	9	2.81	13	0	10
PLAYOFFS													
1968-69	NYR	N	1	60	0	1	0	4	0	4.00	0	0	0
1970-71			2	80	0	1	0	6	0	4.50	0	0	0
1971-72			6	360	4	2	0	14	0	2.33	0	0	0
1972-73			2	61	0	1	0	2	0	1.97	0	0	0
1973-74			1	1	0	0	0	0	0	0.00	0	0	0
1974-75			2	94	1	0	0	6	0	3.83	0	0	0
6 yrs.		N Totals:	14	656	5	5	0	32	0	2.93	0	0	0

YEAR	TEAM & LEAGUE		GP	MIN	W	L	T	GA	ENG	G AVG	SO	A	PIM

Gilles Villemure continued

Traded to **Chicago** by N.Y. Rangers for Doug Jarrett, Oct. 28, 1975.

Ernie Wakely

WAKELY, ERNEST ALFRED LINTON
B. Nov. 27, 1940, Flin Flon, Man.

5'11", 160 lbs.
Shoots L

YEAR	TEAM & LEAGUE		GP	MIN	W	L	T	GA	ENG	G AVG	SO	A	PIM
1962-63	MONT	N	1	60	1	0	0	3	0	3.00	0	0	0
1968-69			1	60	0	1	0	4	0	4.00	0	0	0
1969-70	STL	N	30	1651	12	9	4	58	0	**2.11**	4	0	0
1970-71			51	2859	20	14	11	133	0	2.79	3	2	0
1971-72			30	1614	8	18	2	92	2	3.42	1	1	2
1972-73	WINN	W	49	2889	26	19	3	152	0	3.16	2	0	0
1973-74			37	2254	15	18	4	123	0	3.27	3	0	0
1974-75			6	355	3	3	0	16	0	2.70	1	0	0
	SD	W	35	2062	20	12	2	115	0	3.35	2	0	0
	2 team total		41	2417	23	15	2	131	0	3.25	3	0	0
1975-76			67	3824	35	27	4	208	0	3.26	3	0	0
1976-77			46	2506	22	18	3	129	0	3.09	2	0	0
1977-78	CIN	W	6	311	0	5	0	26	0	5.02	0	0	0
	HOUS	W	51	3070	28	18	4	166	0	3.24	2	0	0
	2 team total		57	3381	**28**	23	4	192	0	3.41	2	0	0
1978-79	BIRM	W	37	2060	15	17	1	129	0	3.76	0	0	0
12 yrs.		N Totals:	113	6244	41	42	17	290	2	2.79	8	3	2
		W Totals:	334	19331	164	137	21	1064	0	3.30	15	0	0
PLAYOFFS													
1969-70	STL	N	4	216	0	4	0	17	0	4.72	0	0	0
1970-71			3	180	2	1	0	7	0	2.33	1	0	0
1971-72			3	113	0	1	0	13	0	6.90	0	0	0
1972-73	WINN	W	7	420	4	3	0	22	0	3.14	0	0	0
1974-75	SD	W	10	520	4	6	0	39	0	4.50	0	0	0
1975-76			11	640	5	6	0	39	0	3.66	0	0	0
1976-77			3	160	2	1	0	9	0	3.38	0	0	0
7 yrs.		N Totals:	10	509	2	6	0	37	0	4.36	1	0	0
		W Totals:	31	1740	15	16	0	109	0	3.76	0	0	0

Traded to **St. Louis** by Montreal for Norm Beaudin and Bobby Schmautz, June 27, 1969.

Ed Walsh

WALSH, EDWARD
B. Aug. 18, 1951, Arlington, Mass.

5'10", 180 lbs.
Shoots R

YEAR	TEAM & LEAGUE		GP	MIN	W	L	T	GA	ENG	G AVG	SO	A	PIM
1978-79	EDM	W	3	144	0	2	0	9	0	3.75	0	0	0

Flat Walsh

WALSH, JAMES
B. Mar. 23, 1897, Kinston, Ont.

5'11", 175 lbs.
Shoots L

YEAR	TEAM & LEAGUE		GP	MIN	W	L	T	GA	ENG	G AVG	SO	A	PIM
1926-27	MON(M)	N	1	60	0	1	0	3	0	3.00	0	0	0
1927-28			1	40	0	0	0	1	0	1.00	0	0	0
1928-29	NYA	N	4	260	2	0	2	1	0	0.25	3	0	0
	MON(M)	N	7	450	1	4	2	8	0	1.14	1	0	0
	2 team total		11	710	3	4	4	9	0	0.76	4	0	0
1929-30			30	1897	16	10	4	74	0	2.47	2	0	0
1930-31			16	781	7	7	2	30	0	1.88	2	0	0
1931-32			27	1670	14	10	3	77	0	2.85	2	0	0
1932-33			22	1303	8	11	3	56	0	2.55	2	0	0
7 yrs.		N Totals:	108	6461	48	43	16	250	0	2.32	12	0	0
PLAYOFFS													
1929-30	MON(M)	N	4	312	1	3	0	11	0	2.75	1	0	0
1930-31			4	258	1	1	2	5	0	1.25	1	0	0
2 yrs.		N Totals:	8	570	2	4	2	16	0	1.68	2	0	0

Rick Wamsley

WAMSLEY, RICHARD
B. May 25, 1959, Simcoe, Ont.
Won Jennings Trophy, 1981-82

5'10", 173 lbs.
Shoots R

YEAR	TEAM & LEAGUE		GP	MIN	W	L	T	GA	ENG	G AVG	SO	A	PIM
1980-81	MONT	N	5	253	3	0	1	8	0	1.90	1	0	0
1981-82			38	2206	23	7	7	101	0	2.75	2	2	4
1982-83			46	2583	27	12	5	151	2	3.51	0	1	4
3 yrs.		N Totals:	89	5042	53	19	13	260	2	3.09	3	3	8
PLAYOFFS													
1981-82	MONT	N	5	300	2	3	0	11	0	**2.20**	0	0	2
1982-83			3	152	0	3	0	7	1	2.76	0	0	0
2 yrs.		N Totals:	8	452	2	6	0	18	1	2.39	0	0	2

Jim Watt

WATT, JAMES MAGNUS
B. May 11, 1950, Duluth, Minn.

5'11", 180 lbs.

YEAR	TEAM & LEAGUE		GP	MIN	W	L	T	GA	ENG	G AVG	SO	A	PIM
1973-74	STL	N	1	20	0	0	0	2	0	6.00	0	0	0

Steve Weeks

WEEKS, STEVE
B. June 30, 1958, Scarborough, Ont.
5'11", 165 lbs.
Shoots L

YEAR	TEAM & LEAGUE		GP	MIN	W	L	T	GA	ENG	G AVG	SO	A	PIM
1980-81	NYR	N	1	60	0	1	0	2	0	2.00	0	0	0
1981-82			49	2852	23	16	9	179	3	3.77	1	3	0
1982-83			18	1040	9	5	3	68	0	3.92	0	2	0
3 yrs.		N Totals:	68	3952	32	22	12	249	3	3.78	1	5	0
PLAYOFFS													
1980-81	NYR	N	1	14	0	0	0	1	0	4.29	0	0	0
1981-82			4	127	1	2	0	9	1	4.25	0	0	5
2 yrs.		N Totals:	5	141	1	2	0	10	1	4.26	0	0	5

Carl Wetzel

WETZEL, CARL DAVID
B. Dec. 12, 1938, Detroit, Mich.
6'1", 170 lbs.
Shoots L

YEAR	TEAM & LEAGUE		GP	MIN	W	L	T	GA	ENG	G AVG	SO	A	PIM
1964-65	DET	N	2	33	0	1	0	4	0	7.27	0	0	0
1967-68	MINN	N	5	269	1	2	1	18	0	4.01	0	0	0
1972-73	MINN	W	1	60	0	1	0	3	0	3.00	0	0	0
3 yrs.		N Totals:	7	302	1	3	1	22	0	4.37	0	0	0
		W Totals:	1	60	0	1	0	3	0	3.00	0	0	0

Sold by Mont. Canadiens to **Minnesota**, June 14, 1967.

Bob Whidden

WHIDDEN, ROBERT JOSEPH
B. July 27, 1946, Sudbury, Ont.
5'10", 180 lbs.
Shoots L

YEAR	TEAM & LEAGUE		GP	MIN	W	L	T	GA	ENG	G AVG	SO	A	PIM
1972-73	CLEVE	W	26	1609	11	12	3	88	0	3.28	0	0	5
1973-74			22	1232	7	12	3	80	0	3.90	0	1	2
1974-75			29	1654	9	16	1	89	0	3.23	1	0	2
1975-76			21	1230	7	11	2	70	0	3.41	1	0	2
4 yrs.		W Totals:	98	5725	34	51	9	327	0	3.43	2	1	11

Ian Wilkie

WILKIE, IAN
B. July 20, 1949, Edmonton, Alta.
5'9", 175 lbs.
Shoots R

YEAR	TEAM & LEAGUE		GP	MIN	W	L	T	GA	ENG	G AVG	SO	A	PIM
1972-73	NY	W	5	253	1	3	0	27	0	6.40	0	0	0
1973-74	LA	W	23	1257	11	9	0	82	0	3.91	1	0	2
	EDM	W	5	256	3	1	0	9	0	2.11	0	0	0
	2 team total		28	1513	14	10	0	91	0	3.61	1	0	2
2 yrs.		W Totals:	33	1766	15	13	0	118	0	4.01	1	0	2
PLAYOFFS													
1973-74	EDM	W	1	41	0	1	0	4	0	5.85	0	0	0

Dunc Wilson

WILSON, DUNCAN SHEPHERD
B. Mar. 22, 1948, Toronto, Ont.
5'11", 175 lbs.
Shoots L

YEAR	TEAM & LEAGUE		GP	MIN	W	L	T	GA	ENG	G AVG	SO	A	PIM
1969-70	PHI	N	1	60	0	1	0	3	0	3.00	0	0	0
1970-71	VAN	N	35	1791	3	25	2	128	3	4.29	0	0	18
1971-72			53	2870	16	30	3	173	1	3.62	1	0	15
1972-73			43	2423	13	21	5	159	1	3.94	1	0	6
1973-74	TOR	N	24	1412	9	11	3	68	3	2.89	1	0	6
1974-75			25	1393	8	11	4	86	0	3.70	0	0	6
	NYR	N	3	180	1	2	0	13	0	4.33	0	0	0
	2 team total		28	1573	9	13	4	99	0	3.78	0	0	6
1975-76			20	1080	5	9	3	76	0	4.22	0	0	11
1976-77	PITT	N	45	2627	18	19	8	129	1	2.95	5	0	21
1977-78			21	1180	5	11	3	95	0	4.83	0	0	0
1978-79	VAN	N	17	835	2	10	2	58	1	4.17	0	0	0
10 yrs.		N Totals:	287	15851	80	150	33	988	10	3.74	8	0	83

Drafted by **Vancouver** from Philadelphia in Expansion Draft, June 10, 1970. Traded to **Toronto** by Vancouver for Larry McIntyre and Murray Heatley, May 29, 1973. Claimed on waivers by **N.Y. Rangers** from Toronto, Feb. 15, 1975. Traded to **Pittsburgh** by N.Y. Rangers for Pittsburgh's fourth round choice (Dave Silk) in 1978 Amateur Draft, Oct. 8, 1976. Sold to **Vancouver** by Pittsburgh, Nov. 17, 1978.

Lefty Wilson

WILSON, ROSS INGRAM
B. Oct. 15, 1919, Toronto, Ont.
5'11", 178 lbs.
Shoots L

YEAR	TEAM & LEAGUE		GP	MIN	W	L	T	GA	ENG	G AVG	SO	A	PIM
1953-54	DET	N	1	20	0	0	0	0	0	0.00	0	0	0
1955-56	TOR	N	1	13	0	0	0	0	0	0.00	0	0	0
1957-58	BOS	N	1	52	0	0	1	1	0	1.15	0	0	0
3 yrs.		N Totals:	3	85	0	0	1	1	0	0.71	0	0	0

Hal Winkler

WINKLER, HAROLD LANG
B. Mar. 20, 1892, Gretna, Man.
5'8", 150 lbs.

YEAR	TEAM & LEAGUE		GP	MIN	W	L	T	GA	ENG	G AVG	SO	A	PIM
1926-27	NYR	N	8	514	3	4	1	16	0	2.00	2	0	0
	BOS	N	23	1445	12	9	2	40	0	1.74	4	0	0
	2 team total		31	1959	15	13	3	56	0	1.72	6	0	0
1927-28			44	**2780**	20	13	11	70	0	1.59	**15**	0	0
2 yrs.		N Totals:	75	4739	35	26	14	126	0	1.60	21	0	0
PLAYOFFS													
1926-27	BOS	N	8	**520**	2	2	4	13	0	1.63	**2**	0	0
1927-28			2	120	0	1	1	5	0	2.50	0	0	0
2 yrs.		N Totals:	10	640	2	3	5	18	0	1.69	2	0	0

Bernie Wolfe

WOLFE, BERNARD RONALD
B. Dec. 18, 1951, Montreal,Que.

5'9", 165 lbs.
Shoots L

YEAR	TEAM & LEAGUE	GP	MIN	W	L	T	GA	ENG	G AVG	SO	A	PIM
1975-76	WASH N	40	2134	5	23	7	148	2	4.16	0	0	0
1976-77		37	1779	7	15	9	114	2	3.84	1	1	2
1977-78		25	1328	4	14	4	94	1	4.25	0	0	0
1978-79		18	863	4	9	1	68	0	4.73	0	0	15
4 yrs.	N Totals:	120	6104	20	61	21	424	5	4.17	1	1	17

Wayne Wood

WOOD, WAYNE
B. June 5, 1951, Toronto, Ont

Shoots L

YEAR	TEAM & LEAGUE	GP	MIN	W	L	T	GA	ENG	G AVG	SO	A	PIM
1974-75	VAN W	11	512	4	4	0	30	0	3.52	0	0	0
1975-76	CALG W	19	880	9	3	1	45	0	3.07	1	0	4
	TOR W	13	781	6	7	0	62	0	4.76	0	1	0
	2 team total	32	1661	15	10	1	107	0	3.87	1	1	4
1976-77	BIRM W	23	1132	7	12	0	78	0	4.13	0	0	0
1977-78		32	1551	12	10	2	99	0	3.83	1	3	22
1978-79		6	311	1	3	0	21	0	4.05	0	0	6
5 yrs.	W Totals:	104	5167	39	39	3	335	0	3.89	2	4	32
PLAYOFFS												
1977-78	BIRM W	1	29	0	0	0	3	0	6.21	0	0	0

Alec Woods

WOODS, ALEC
B. Falkirk, Sask.

YEAR	TEAM & LEAGUE	GP	MIN	W	L	T	GA	ENG	G AVG	SO	A	PIM
1936-37	NYA N	1	70	0	1	0	3	0	3.00	0	0	0

Gump Worsley

WORSLEY, LORNE JOHN
B. May 14, 1929, Montreal, Que.
Shared Vezina Trophy, 1965-66, 1967-68
Won Calder Trophy, 1952-53
Hall of Fame, 1980

5'7", 180 lbs.
Shoots L

YEAR	TEAM & LEAGUE	GP	MIN	W	L	T	GA	ENG	G AVG	SO	A	PIM
1952-53	NYR N	50	3000	13	29	8	153	0	3.06	2	0	2
1954-55		65	3900	15	**33**	17	197	0	3.03	4	0	2
1955-56		70	**4200**	32	28	10	203	0	2.90	4	0	2
1956-57		68	4080	26	28	13	220	0	3.24	3	0	**19**
1957-58		37	2220	21	10	6	86	0	2.32	4	0	10
1958-59		67	4001	26	29	12	205	0	3.07	2	0	10
1959-60		41	2301	8	25	8	137	0	3.57	0	0	12
1960-61		58	3473	19	**28**	9	193	0	3.33	1	0	10
1961-62		60	3520	22	**27**	9	174	0	2.97	2	0	12
1962-63		67	**3980**	22	**34**	9	219	0	3.30	2	0	**14**
1963-64	MONT N	8	444	3	2	2	22	0	2.97	1	0	0
1964-65		19	1080	10	7	1	50	0	2.78	1	0	0
1965-66		51	2899	29	14	6	114	3	2.36	2	0	4
1966-67		18	888	9	6	2	47	0	3.18	1	0	4
1967-68		40	2213	19	9	8	73	1	**1.98**	6	0	10
1968-69		30	1703	19	6	4	64	0	2.25	5	0	0
1969-70		6	360	3	1	2	14	0	2.33	0	0	0
	MINN N	8	453	5	1	1	20	0	2.65	1	0	0
	2 team total	14	813	8	2	3	34	0	2.51	1	0	0
1970-71		24	1369	4	10	8	57	0	2.50	0	0	10
1971-72		34	1923	16	10	7	68	0	2.12	2	0	2
1972-73		12	624	6	2	3	30	0	2.88	0	0	22
1973-74		29	1601	8	14	5	86	0	3.22	0	0	0
21 yrs.	N Totals:	862	50232	335	353	150	2432	4	2.90	43	0	145
PLAYOFFS												
1955-56	NYR N	3	180	0	3	0	15	0	5.00	0	0	0
1956-57		5	316	1	4	0	22	0	4.18	0	0	0
1957-58		6	365	2	4	0	28	0	4.60	0	0	0
1961-62		6	384	2	4	0	22	0	3.44	0	0	0
1964-65*	MONT N	8	501	6	2	0	14	0	**1.68**	**2**	0	0
1965-66*		10	600	**8**	2	0	20	0	**2.00**	**1**	0	0
1966-67		2	80	0	1	0	2	0	1.50	0	0	0
1967-68*		12	**669**	**11**	0	0	21	0	1.88	**1**	0	0
1968-69*		7	370	5	1	0	14	0	2.27	0	0	0
1969-70	MINN N	3	180	1	2	0	14	0	4.67	0	0	0
1970-71		4	240	3	1	0	13	0	3.25	0	0	0
1971-72		4	194	2	1	0	7	0	2.16	1	0	0
12 yrs.	N Totals:	70	4079	41	25	0	192	0	2.82	5	0	0

Traded to **Montreal** by New York with Leon Rochefort, Dave Balon and Len Ronson for Jacques Plante, Don Marshall and Phil Goyette, June 4, 1963. Sold to **Minnesota** by Montreal, Feb. 27, 1970.

Roy Worters

WORTERS, ROY (Shrimp)
B. Oct. 19, 1900, Toronto, Ont.
Won Hart Trophy, 1928-29
Won Vezina Trophy, 1930-31
Hall of Fame, 1969

5'3", 135 lbs
Shoots L

YEAR	TEAM & LEAGUE	GP	MIN	W	L	T	GA	ENG	G AVG	SO	A	PIM
1925-26	PITT N	35	2145	18	16	1	68	0	1.94	7	0	0
1926-27		44	2711	15	26	3	108	0	2.45	4	0	0

Roy Worters continued

YEAR	TEAM	LEAGUE	GP	MIN	W	L	T	GA	ENG	G AVG	SO	A	PIM
1927-28			44	2740	19	17	8	76	0	1.73	10	0	0
1928-29	NYA	N	38	2390	16	13	9	46	0	1.21	13	0	0
1929-30			36	2270	11	24	1	135	0	3.75	2	0	0
	MONT	N	1	60	1	0	0	2	0	2.00	0	0	0
	2 team total		37	2330	12	24	1	137	0	3.53	2	0	0
1930-31	NYA	N	44	**2760**	18	16	0	74	0	**1.68**	8	0	0
1931-32			40	2459	12	**20**	7	110	0	2.75	5	0	0
1932-33			47	2970	15	22	10	116	0	2.47	5	0	0
1933-34			36	2240	12	13	10	75	0	2.08	4	0	0
1934-35			48	3000	12	27	9	142	0	2.96	3	0	0
1935-36			48	3000	16	25	7	122	0	2.54	3	0	0
1936-37			23	1430	6	14	3	69	0	3.00	2	0	0
12 yrs.	N Totals:		484	30175	171	233	68	1143	0	2.27	66	0	0
PLAYOFFS													
1925-26	PITT	N	2	120	0	1	1	6	0	3.00	0	0	0
1927-28			2	120	1	1	0	6	0	3.00	0	0	0
1928-29	NYA	N	2	150	0	1	1	1	0	0.50	1	0	0
1935-36			5	300	2	3	0	11	0	2.20	**2**	0	0
4 yrs.	N Totals:		11	690	3	6	2	24	0	2.09	3	0	0

Chris Worthy

WORTHY, CHRISTOPHER JOHN
B. Oct. 23, 1947, Bristol, England

6', 180 lbs.
Shoots L

YEAR	TEAM	LEAGUE	GP	MIN	W	L	T	GA	ENG	G AVG	SO	A	PIM
1968-69	CALIF	N	14	786	4	6	3	54	0	4.12	0	0	2
1969-70	OAK	N	1	60	0	1	0	5	0	5.00	0	0	2
1970-71	CALIF	N	11	480	1	3	1	39	0	4.88	0	0	2
1973-74	EDM	W	29	1452	11	12	1	92	0	3.80	0	0	0
1974-75			29	1660	11	13	3	99	0	3.58	1	0	7
1975-76			24	1256	5	14	0	98	0	4.68	1	0	7
6 yrs.	N Totals:		26	1326	5	10	4	98	0	4.43	0	0	6
	W Totals:		82	4368	27	39	4	289	0	3.97	2	0	14
PLAYOFFS													
1973-74	EDM	W	3	146	1	1	0	8	0	3.29	0	0	0
1975-76			1	60	0	1	0	7	0	7.00	0	0	0
2 yrs.	W Totals:		4	206	1	2	0	15	0	4.37	0	0	0

Douglas Young

YOUNG, DOUGLAS G.
B. Oct. 1, 1908, Medicine Hat, Alta.

5'9½", 190 lbs.
Shoots R

YEAR	TEAM	LEAGUE	GP	MIN	W	L	T	GA	ENG	G AVG	SO	A	PIM
1933-34	DET	N	1	21	0	0	0	1	0	1.00	0	0	0

Lynn Zimmerman

ZIMMERMAN, LYNN BRIAN
B. July 13, 1942, Fort Erie, Ont.

5'7", 155 lbs.
Shoots R

YEAR	TEAM	LEAGUE	GP	MIN	W	L	T	GA	ENG	G AVG	SO	A	PIM
1975-76	D-O	W	8	495	2	5	1	31	0	3.76	0	0	0
1977-78	HOUS	W	20	1166	10	9	0	84	0	4.32	0	0	0
2 yrs.	W Totals:		28	1661	12	14	1	115	0	4.15	0	0	0
PLAYOFFS													
1977-78	HOUS	W	4	239	1	2	0	21	0	5.27	0	0	6

Coaching Register

The Coaching Register is an alphabetical listing of every man who has coached in the National Hockey League or World Hockey Association. Included are facts about the coach and his year-by-year coaching record, along with his team's playoff results.

Like so many other aspects of hockey's evolution, the development of sophisticated coaching techniques took place over a long period of time. In the earliest days the coach invariably doubled as the team's manager and, in some cases, this remained true through the 1930s and 1940s. Jack Adams, autocratic leader of the Detroit Red Wings for whom the award for coach of the year is named, remained in both jobs well into World War II. Many of the early manager-coaches were also players; Lester Patrick is an example of this hardy triple-threat breed.

With the organization of professional hockey many felt it would be better to separate the employer, who signs the paychecks, from the coach, who leads from behind the bench. The Ottawa Senators, the first NHL team to win back-to-back Stanley Cups, were managed by Tommy Gorman but coached by Pete Green. Other teams, though, were still led by one all-powerful head man: Patrick for the New York Rangers, Adams in Detroit, Cecil Hart with the Montreal Canadiens. Today, despite the creation of jobs for varying assistant coaches and even assistant general managers, some managers still prefer to hang onto the coaching reins. Emile Francis is a prototype of this manager-coach in contemporary hockey.

Most of the information in this section is self-explanatory. That which is not is explained below. For an explanation of the demographic information and team abbreviations, see the Player or Goaltender Registers.

Standing. The numbers in this column indicate where the team finished in its league, division, or conference, depending on the configuration of the league at the time. They also indicate any coaching changes that may have been made during the course of a season. There are four possible cases:

Only Coach for the Team that Season. Indicated by a single bold-faced figure that appears in the extreme lefthand column and shows the final standing for the team.

Coach Started Season but Did Not Finish. Indicated by two figures: the first is boldfaced and shows the standing of the team when this coach left; the second shows the final standing of the team.

Coach Finished Season but Did Not Start. Indicated by two figures: the first shows the standing of the team when this coach began; the second is boldfaced and shows the final standing of the team.

Coach Did Not Start or Finish Season. Indicated by three figures: the first shows the standing of the team when this coach started; the second is boldfaced and shows the standing of the team when he left; the third shows the final standing of the team.

Playoff Result. The Playoff Result column is an attempt to reconcile in simplified form the possible results from the varying configurations of playoffs throughout hockey history. Any ambiguities that may remain can be cleared up by referring to the Stanley Cup Playoffs section.

Lost First Round. This phrase is used whenever a team loses in its first playoff action, whether it is in a Semifinal Round, as from 1942–43 through 1966–67, or in an Elimination Round as in the years from 1974–75 to 1980–81.

Lost Quarterfinals. This phrase is used whenever a team loses in a quarterfinal round, provided they won a round prior to the loss. This situation occurs in all years from 1974–75 to the present.

Lost Semifinals. This phrase is used whenever a team loses in a semifinal round, provided they won at least one round prior to the loss. (From 1928–29 through 1937–38, the playoffs consisted of a series between the first place teams from the American and Canadian Divisions with the winner going directly into the finals, and two rounds to determine a finalist from among the second and third place teams. Although the first place playoff was a semifinal, the loser is designated here as "Lost First Round."

Lost League Finals. From 1917–18 through 1925–26, the NHL champion played against the winner of the Pacific Coast Hockey Association or Western Canada Hockey League (later the Western Hockey League) for the Stanley Cup. The loser in the NHL finals for these years only is noted with the phrase "Lost League Finals." The phrase is also used for the coach whose club lost the WHA finals.

Lost Cup Finals. This phrase is used whenever the team lost in the final round of the Stanley Cup Playoffs.

Won WHA Finals. This phrase indicates that the team won the AVCO World Cup for the WHA championship.

Won Stanley Cup. This phrase, in boldface, indicates that the coach won the Stanley Cup championship.

Sid Abel

ABEL, SIDNEY GERALD 5'11", 190 lbs.
B. Feb. 22, 1918, Melville, Sask.
Hall of Fame, 1969

Season	Team	Lg	G	W	L	T		STANDING		PLAYOFF RESULT
1952-53	CHI	N	70	27	28	15		**4**		Lost First Round
1953-54			70	12	51	7		**6**		
1957-58	DET	N	33	16	12	5	4	**3**		Lost First Round
1958-59			70	25	37	8		**6**		
1959-60			70	26	29	15		**4**		Lost First Round
1960-61			70	25	29	16		**4**		Lost Cup Finals
1961-62			70	23	33	14		**5**		
1962-63			70	32	25	13		**4**		Lost Cup Finals
1963-64			70	30	29	11		**4**		Lost Cup Finals
1964-65			70	40	23	7		**1**		Lost First Round
1965-66			70	31	27	12		**4**		Lost Cup Finals
1966-67			70	27	39	4		**5**		
1967-68			74	27	35	12		**6**		
1969-70			73	38	20	15	2	**3**		Lost First Round
1971-72	STL	N	10	3	6	1		**6**	3	
1975-76	KC	N	3	0	3	0	5	**5**	5	
16 yrs.	**N Totals:**		963	382	426	155				

Jack Adams

ADAMS, JOHN JAMES
B. June 14, 1895, Fort William, Ont.
Hall of Fame, 1959

Season	Team	Lg	G	W	L	T		STANDING		PLAYOFF RESULT
1922-23	TOR	N	18	10	7	1	3	**3**		
1927-28	DET	N	44	19	19	6		**4**		
1928-29			44	19	16	9		**3**		Lost First Round
1929-30			44	14	24	6		**4**		
1930-31			44	16	21	7		**4**		
1931-32			48	18	20	10		**3**		Lost First Round
1932-33			48	25	15	8		**2**		Lost Semifinals
1933-34			48	24	14	10		**1**		Lost Cup Finals
1934-35			48	19	22	7		**4**		
1935-36			48	24	16	8		**1**		**Won Stanley Cup**
1936-37			48	25	14	9		**1**		**Won Stanley Cup**
1937-38			48	12	25	11		**4**		
1938-39			48	18	24	6		**5**		Lost Semifinals
1939-40			48	16	26	6		**5**		Lost Semifinals
1940-41			48	21	16	11		**3**		Lost Cup Finals
1941-42			48	19	25	4		**5**		Lost Cup Finals
1942-43			50	25	14	11		**1**		**Won Stanley Cup**
1943-44			50	26	18	6		**2**		Lost First Round
1944-45			50	31	14	5		**2**		Lost Cup Finals
1945-46			50	20	20	10		**4**		Lost First Round
1946-47			60	22	27	11		**4**		Lost First Round
21 yrs.	**N Totals:**		982	423	397	162				3 Cup Champions

Keith Allen

ALLEN, COURTNEY KEITH (Bingo) 5'11", 190 lbs.
B. Aug. 21, 1923, Saskatoon, Sask.

Season	Team	Lg	G	W	L	T		STANDING		PLAYOFF RESULT
1967-68	PHI	N	74	31	32	11		**1**		Lost First Round
1968-69			76	20	35	21		**3**		Lost First Round
2 yrs.	**N Totals:**		150	51	67	32				

Jim Anderson

ANDERSON, JAMES WILLIAM 5'9", 170 lbs.
B. Dec. 1, 1930, Pembroke, Ont.

Season	Team	Lg	G	W	L	T		STANDING		PLAYOFF RESULT
1974-75	WASH	N	54	4	45	5		**5**	5	

Lou Angotti

ANGOTTI, LOUIS FREDERICK 5'8", 170 lbs.
B. Jan. 16, 1938, Toronto, Ont.

Season	Team	Lg	G	W	L	T		STANDING		PLAYOFF RESULT
1973-74	STL	N	23	4	15	4	4	**6**		
1974-75			9	2	5	2		**4**	2	
2 yrs.	**N Totals:**		32	6	20	6				

Al Arbour

ARBOUR, ALGER JOSEPH 6'1", 180 lbs.
B. Nov. 1, 1932, Sudbury, Ont.
Won Jack Adams Award, 1978-79

Season	Team	Lg	G	W	L	T		STANDING		PLAYOFF RESULT
1970-71	STL	N	50	21	15	14		**2**	2	
1971-72			44	19	19	6	6	**3**		Lost Semifinals

Al Arbour continued

Season	Team	Lg	G	W	L	T		STANDING		PLAYOFF RESULT
1972-73			13	2	6	5		**7**	4	
1973-74	NYI	N	78	19	41	18		**8**		
1974-75			80	33	25	22		**3**		Lost Semifinals
1975-76			80	42	21	17		**2**		Lost Semifinals
1976-77			80	47	21	12		**2**		Lost Semifinals
1977-78			80	48	17	15		**1**		Lost First Round
1978-79			80	51	15	14		**1**		Lost Semifinals
1979-80			80	39	28	13		**2**		**Won Stanley Cup**
1980-81			80	48	18	14		**1**		**Won Stanley Cup**
1981-82			80	54	16	10		**1**		**Won Stanley Cup**
1982-83			80	42	26	12		**2**		**Won Stanley Cup**
13 yrs.	**N Totals:**		905	465	268	172				4 Cup Champions

Doug Barkley

BARKLEY, DOUGLAS 6'2", 185 lbs.
B. Jan. 6, 1937, Lethbridge, Alta.

Season	Team	Lg	G	W	L	T		STANDING		PLAYOFF RESULT
1970-71	DET	N	59	13	38	8	6	**7**		
1971-72			11	3	8	0		**7**	5	
1975-76			26	7	15	4		**4**	4	
3 yrs.	**N Totals:**		96	23	61	12				

Andy Bathgate

BATHGATE, ANDREW JAMES 6', 180 lbs.
B. Aug. 28, 1932, Winnipeg, Man.
Hall of Fame, 1978

Season	Team	Lg	G	W	L	T		STANDING		PLAYOFF RESULT
1973-74	VAN	W	59	21	37	1	5	**5**		

Bob Baun

BAUN, ROBERT NEIL 5'9", 182 lbs.
B. Sept. 9, 1936, Lanigan, Sask.

Season	Team	Lg	G	W	L	T		STANDING		PLAYOFF RESULT
1975-76	TOR	W	55	15	35	5		**5**	5	

Andre Beaulieu

BEAULIEU, ANDRE
B. July 30, 1942, Shawinigan Falls, Que.

Season	Team	Lg	G	W	L	T		STANDING		PLAYOFF RESULT
1977-78	MINN	N	32	6	23	3	4	**5**	5	

Danny Belisle

BELISLE, DANIEL GEORGE 5'10", 175 lbs.
B. May 9, 1937, South Porcupine, Ont.

Season	Team	Lg	G	W	L	T		STANDING		PLAYOFF RESULT
1978-79	WASH	N	80	24	41	15		**4**		
1979-80			16	4	10	2		**5**	5	
2 yrs.	**N Totals:**		96	28	51	17				

Red Berenson

BERENSON, GORDON ARTHUR (The Red Baron) 6', 195 lbs.
B. Dec. 8, 1939, Regina, Sask.

Season	Team	Lg	G	W	L	T		STANDING		PLAYOFF RESULT
1979-80	STL	N	52	26	18	8	3	**2**		Lost First Round
1980-81			80	45	18	17		**1**		Lost Quarterfinals
1981-82			69	28	35	6		**3**	3	
3 yrs.	**N Totals:**		201	99	71	31				

Michel Bergeron

BERGERON, MICHEL 5'10", 170 lbs.
B. Nov. 11, 1954, Chicoutimi, Que.

Season	Team	Lg	G	W	L	T		STANDING		PLAYOFF RESULT
1980-81	QUE	N	74	29	29	16	5	**4**		Lost First Round
1981-82			80	33	31	16		**4**		Lost Semifinals
1982-83			80	34	34	12		**4**		Lost First Round
3 yrs.	**N Totals:**		234	96	94	44				

Bob Berry

BERRY, ROBERT VICTOR 6', 190 lbs.
B. Nov. 29, 1943, Montreal, Que.

Season	Team	Lg	G	W	L	T		STANDING		PLAYOFF RESULT
1978-79	LA	N	80	34	34	12		**3**		Lost First Round
1979-80			80	30	36	14		**2**		Lost First Round
1980-81			80	43	24	13		**2**		Lost First Round
1981-82	MONT	N	80	46	17	17		**1**		Lost First Round
1982-83			80	42	24	14		**2**		Lost First Round
5 yrs.	**N Totals:**		400	195	135	70				

Don Blackburn

BLACKBURN, JOHN DONALD 6', 190 lbs.
B. May 14, 1938, Kirkland Lake, Ont.

			G	W	L	T		STANDING		PLAYOFF RESULT
1975-76	NE	W	35	14	18	3	1	**3**	3	
1979-80	HART	N	80	27	34	19		**4**		Lost First Round
1980-81			60	15	29	16		**4**	4	
3 yrs.	N Totals:		140	42	63	35				
	W Totals:		35	14	18	3				

Wren Blair

BLAIR, WREN
B. Oct. 2, 1925, Lindsay, Ont.

			G	W	L	T		STANDING		PLAYOFF RESULT
1967-68	MINN	N	74	27	32	15		**4**		Lost Semifinals
1968-69			11	3	7	1		**5**	6	
			30	9	14	7	6	**6**		
	2 team total		41	12	21	8				
1969-70			32	9	13	10		**2**	3	
3 yrs.	N Totals:		147	48	66	33				

Toe Blake

BLAKE, HECTOR 5'9½", 165 lbs.
B. Aug. 21, 1912, Victoria Mines, Ont.
Hall of Fame, 1966

			G	W	L	T		STANDING		PLAYOFF RESULT
1955-56	MONT	N	70	45	15	10		**1**		**Won Stanley Cup**
1956-57			70	35	23	12		**2**		**Won Stanley Cup**
1957-58			70	43	17	10		**1**		**Won Stanley Cup**
1958-59			70	39	18	13		**1**		**Won Stanley Cup**
1959-60			70	40	18	12		**1**		**Won Stanley Cup**
1960-61			70	41	19	10		**1**		Lost First Round
1961-62			70	42	14	14		**1**		Lost First Round
1962-63			70	28	19	23		**3**		Lost First Round
1963-64			70	36	21	13		**1**		Lost First Round
1964-65			70	36	23	11		**2**		**Won Stanley Cup**
1965-66			70	41	21	8		**1**		**Won Stanley Cup**
1966-67			70	32	25	13		**2**		Lost Cup Finals
1967-68			74	42	22	10		**1**		**Won Stanley Cup**
13 yrs.	N Totals:		914	500	255	159				8 Cup Champions

Marc Boileau

BOILEAU, MARC CLAUDE 5'11", 170 lbs.
B. Sept. 3, 1932, Pointe Claire, Que.

			G	W	L	T		STANDING		PLAYOFF RESULT
1973-74	PITT	N	28	14	10	4	7	**5**		
1974-75			80	37	28	15		**3**		Lost Quarterfinals
1975-76			43	15	23	5		**3**	3	
1976-77	QUE	W	81	47	31	3		**1**		Won WHA Finals
1977-78			59	27	30	2		**5**	4	
5 yrs.	N Totals:		151	66	61	24				
	W Totals:		140	74	61	5				

Leo Boivin

BOIVIN, LEO JOSEPH 5'7", 190 lbs.
B. Aug. 2, 1932, Prescott, Ont.

			G	W	L	T		STANDING		PLAYOFF RESULT
1975-76	STL	N	43	17	17	9	3	**3**		Lost First Round
1977-78			54	11	36	7		**5**	4	
2 yrs.	N Totals:		97	28	53	16				

Frank Boucher

BOUCHER, FRANK (Raffles) 5'8½", 185 lbs.
B. Oct. 7, 1901, Ottawa, Ont.
Hall of Fame, 1958

			G	W	L	T		STANDING		PLAYOFF RESULT
1939-40	NYR	N	48	27	11	10		**2**		**Won Stanley Cup**
1940-41			48	21	19	8		**4**		Lost First Round
1941-42			48	29	17	2		**1**		Lost First Round
1942-43			50	11	31	8		**6**		
1943-44			50	6	39	5		**6**		
1944-45			50	11	29	10		**6**		
1945-46			50	13	28	9		**6**		
1946-47			60	22	32	6		**5**		
1947-48			60	21	26	13		**4**		Lost First Round
1948-49			23	6	11	6		**6**	4	
1953-54			38	12	20	6	5	**5**		
11 yrs.	N Totals:		525	179	263	83				1 Cup Champion

George Boucher

BOUCHER, GEORGE
B. Ottawa, Ont.
Hall of Fame, 1960

			G	W	L	T		STANDING		PLAYOFF RESULT
1930-31	MON(M)	N	12	6	5	1	4	**3**		Lost First Round
1933-34	OTTA	N	48	13	29	6		**5**		
1934-35	STL	N	35	9	20	6	5	**5**		
1949-50	BOS	N	70	22	32	16		**5**		
4 yrs.	N Totals:		165	50	86	29				

Scotty Bowman

BOWMAN, WILLIAM SCOTT
B. Sept. 18, 1933, Montreal, Que.
Won Jack Adams Award, 1976-77

			G	W	L	T		STANDING		PLAYOFF RESULT
1967-68	STL	N	58	23	21	14	6	**3**		Lost Cup Finals
1968-69			76	37	25	14		**1**		Lost Cup Finals
1969-70			76	37	27	12		**1**		Lost Cup Finals
1970-71			28	13	10	5	2	**2**		Lost First Round
1971-72	MONT	N	78	46	16	16		**3**		Lost First Round
1972-73			78	51	10	16		**1**		**Won Stanley Cup**
1973-74			78	45	24	9		**2**		Lost First Round
1974-75			80	47	14	19		**1**		Lost Semifinals
1975-76			80	58	11	11		**1**		**Won Stanley Cup**
1976-77			80	60	8	12		**1**		**Won Stanley Cup**
1977-78			80	59	10	11		**1**		**Won Stanley Cup**
1978-79			80	52	17	11		**1**		**Won Stanley Cup**
1979-80	BUF	N	80	47	17	16		**1**		Lost Semifinals
1981-82			27	14	7	6		**1**	3	
			8	4	3	1	3	**3**		Lost First Round
	2 team total		35	18	10	7				
1982-83			80	38	29	13		**3**		Lost Quarterfinals
15 yrs.	N Totals:		1067	631	249	186				5 Cup Champions

Herb Brooks

BROOKS, HERBERT PAUL
B. Aug. 5, 1937, St. Paul, Minn.

			G	W	L	T		STANDING		PLAYOFF RESULT
1981-82	NYR	N	80	39	27	14		**2**		Lost Quarterfinals
1982-83			80	35	35	10		**4**		Lost Quarterfinals
2 yrs.	N Totals:		160	74	62	24				

John Brophy

BROPHY, JOHN
B. Jan. 20, 1933, Halifax, N.S.

			G	W	L	T		STANDING		PLAYOFF RESULT
1978-79	BIRM	W	80	32	42	6		**6**		

Charlie Burns

BURNS, CHARLES FREDERICK 5'11", 170 lbs.
B. Feb. 14, 1936, Detroit, Mi.

			G	W	L	T		STANDING		PLAYOFF RESULT
1969-70	MINN	N	44	10	22	12	2	**3**		Lost First Round
1974-75			41	12	27	2	4	**4**		
2 yrs.	N Totals:		85	22	49	14				

Eddie Bush

BUSH, EDWARD WEBSTER 6'1", 195 lbs.
B. July 11, 1918, Collingwood, Ont.

			G	W	L	T		STANDING		PLAYOFF RESULT
1975-76	KC	N	32	1	23	8	5	**5**		

Dick Carroll

CARROLL, RICHARD
B. Unknown

			G	W	L	T		STANDING		PLAYOFF RESULT
1917-18	TOR	N	22	13	9	0		**1**		**Won Stanley Cup**
1918-19			18	5	13	0		**3**		
1920-21			24	15	9	0		**1**		Lost League Finals
3 yrs.	N Totals:		64	33	31	0				1 Cup Champion

Gerry Cheevers

CHEEVERS, GERALD MICHAEL (Cheesey) 5'11", 175 lbs.
B. Dec. 7, 1940, St. Catharines, Ont.

			G	W	L	T		STANDING		PLAYOFF RESULT
1980-81	BOS	N	80	37	30	13		**2**		Lost First Round
1981-82			80	43	27	10		**2**		Lost Quarterfinals
1982-83			80	50	20	10		**1**		Lost Semifinals
3 yrs.	N Totals:		240	130	77	33				

Don Cherry

CHERRY, DONALD STEWART (Grapes) 5'11", 180 lbs.
B. Feb. 5, 1934, Kingston, Ont.
Won Jack Adams Award, 1975-76

Year	Team		G	W	L	T		STANDING		PLAYOFF RESULT
1974-75	BOS	N	80	40	26	14		**2**		Lost First Round
1975-76			80	48	15	17		**1**		Lost Semifinals
1976-77			80	49	23	8		**1**		Lost Cup Finals
1977-78			80	51	18	11		**1**		Lost Cup Finals
1978-79			80	43	23	14		**1**		Lost Semifinals
1979-80	COLO	N	80	19	48	13		**6**		
6 yrs.	N Totals:		480	250	153	77				

King Clancy

CLANCY, FRANCIS MICHAEL 5'9", 184 lbs.
B. Feb. 25, 1903, Ottawa, Ont.
Hall of Fame, 1958

Year	Team		G	W	L	T		STANDING		PLAYOFF RESULT
1937-38	MON(M)	N	18	6	11	1		**4**	4	
1953-54	TOR	N	70	32	24	14		**3**		Lost First Round
1954-55			70	24	33	13		**3**		Lost First Round
1955-56			70	24	33	13		**4**		Lost First Round
1966-67			10	7	1	2	4	**3**	3	
1971-72			15	9	3	3	5	**4**		Lost First Round
6 yrs.	N Totals:		253	102	105	46				

Dit Clapper

CLAPPER, AUBREY VICTOR 6'2", 195 lbs.
B. Feb. 9, 1907, Newmarket, Ont.
Hall of Fame, 1945

Year	Team		G	W	L	T		STANDING		PLAYOFF RESULT
1945-46	BOS	N	50	24	18	8		**2**		Lost Cup Finals
1946-47			60	26	23	11		**3**		Lost First Round
1947-48			60	23	24	13		**3**		Lost First Round
1948-49			60	29	23	8		**2**		Lost First Round
4 yrs.	N Totals:		230	102	88	40				

Odie Cleghorn

CLEGHORN, OGILVIE
B. Montreal, Que.

Year	Team		G	W	L	T		STANDING		PLAYOFF RESULT
1925-26	PITT	N	36	19	16	1		**3**		Lost First Round
1926-27			44	15	26	3		**4**		
1927-28			44	19	17	8		**3**		Lost First Round
1928-29			44	9	27	8		**4**		
4 yrs.	N Totals:		168	62	86	20				

Sprague Cleghorn

CLEGHORN, SPRAGUE
B. Montreal, Que.
Hall of Fame, 1958

Year	Team		G	W	L	T		STANDING		PLAYOFF RESULT
1931-32	MON(M)	N	48	19	22	7		**3**		Lost Semifinals

Neil Colville

COLVILLE, NEIL MCNEIL 6', 175 lbs.
B. Aug. 4, 1914, Edmonton, Alta.
Hall of Fame, 1967

Year	Team		G	W	L	T		STANDING		PLAYOFF RESULT
1950-51	NYR	N	70	20	29	21		**5**		
1951-52			23	6	12	5		**6**	5	
2 yrs.	N Totals:		93	26	41	26				

Charlie Conacher

CONACHER, CHARLES WILLIAM (The Bomber)
6'1", 195 lbs.
B. Dec. 20, 1910, Toronto, Ont.
Hall of Fame, 1961

Year	Team		G	W	L	T		STANDING		PLAYOFF RESULT
1947-48	CHI	N	32	13	15	4	6	**6**		
1948-49			60	21	31	8		**5**		
1949-50			70	22	38	10		**6**		
3 yrs.	N Totals:		162	56	84	22				

Lionel Conacher

CONACHER, LIONEL PRETORIA 6'1", 195 lbs.
B. May 24, 1901, Toronto, Ont.

Year	Team		G	W	L	T		STANDING		PLAYOFF RESULT
1929-30	NYA	N	44	14	25	5		**5**		

Bill Cook

COOK, WILLIAM OSSER 5'10", 170 lbs.
B. Oct. 9, 1896, Brantford, Ont.
Hall of Fame, 1952

Year	Team		G	W	L	T		STANDING		PLAYOFF RESULT
1951-52	NYR	N	47	17	22	8	6	**5**		
1952-53			70	17	37	16		**7**		
2 yrs.	N Totals:		117	34	59	24				

Fred Creighton

CREIGHTON, FREDERICK
B. July 14, 1933, Hamiota, Man.

Year	Team		G	W	L	T		STANDING		PLAYOFF RESULT
1974-75	ATL	N	28	12	11	5	4	**4**		
1975-76			80	35	33	12		**3**		Lost First Round
1976-77			80	34	34	12		**3**		Lost First Round
1977-78			80	34	27	19		**3**		Lost First Round
1978-79			80	41	31	8		**4**		Lost First Round
1979-80	BOS	N	73	40	20	13		**2**	2	
6 yrs.	N Totals:		421	196	156	69				

Joe Crozier

CROZIER, JOSEPH RICHARD 6', 180 lbs.
B. Feb. 19, 1929, Winnipeg, Man.

Year	Team		G	W	L	T		STANDING		PLAYOFF RESULT
1971-72	BUF	N	36	8	19	9	6	**6**		
1972-73			78	37	27	14		**4**		Lost First Round
1973-74			78	32	34	12		**5**		
1974-75	VAN	W	78	37	39	2		**4**		
1975-76	CALG	W	80	41	35	4		**3**		Lost Semifinals
1976-77			80	31	42	7		**5**		
1980-81	TOR	N	40	13	22	5		**4**	5	
7 yrs.	N Totals:		232	90	102	40				
	W Totals:		238	109	116	13				

Roger Crozier

CROZIER, ROGER ALLAN 5'8", 140 lbs.
B. Mar. 16, 1942, Bracebridge, Ont.

Year	Team		G	W	L	T		STANDING		PLAYOFF RESULT
1981-82	WASH	N	1	0	1	0	5	**5**	5	

John Cunniff

CUNNIFF, JOHN PAUL 5'9", 175 lbs.
B. July 9, 1944, South Boston, Mass.

Year	Team		G	W	L	T		STANDING		PLAYOFF RESULT
1982-83	HART	N	13	3	9	1	5	**5**		

Leo Dandurand

DANDURAND, LEONARD
B. July 9, 1889, Bourbonnais, Ill.

Year	Team		G	W	L	T		STANDING		PLAYOFF RESULT
1920-21	MONT	N	24	13	11	0		**3**		
1921-22			24	12	11	1		**3**		
1922-23			24	13	9	2		**2**		Lost League Finals
1923-24			24	13	11	0		**2**		**Won Stanley Cup**
1924-25			30	17	11	2		**3**		Lost Cup Finals
1934-35			32	14	15	3	5	**3**		Lost First Round
6 yrs.	N Totals:		158	82	68	8				1 Cup Champion

Hap Day

DAY, CLARENCE HENRY 5'11", 175 lbs.
B. June 1, 1901, Owen Sound, Ont.
Hall of Fame, 1961

Year	Team		G	W	L	T		STANDING		PLAYOFF RESULT
1940-41	TOR	N	48	28	14	6		**2**		Lost First Round
1941-42			48	27	18	3		**2**		**Won Stanley Cup**
1942-43			50	22	19	9		**3**		Lost First Round
1943-44			50	23	23	4		**3**		Lost First Round
1944-45			50	24	22	4		**3**		**Won Stanley Cup**
1945-46			50	19	24	7		**5**		
1946-47			60	31	19	10		**2**		**Won Stanley Cup**
1947-48			60	32	15	13		**1**		**Won Stanley Cup**
1948-49			60	22	25	13		**4**		**Won Stanley Cup**
1949-50			70	31	27	12		**3**		Lost First Round
10 yrs.	N Totals:		546	259	206	81				5 Cup Champions

Billy Dea
DEA, WILLIAM FRASER 5'8", 175 lbs.
B. Apr. 3, 1933, Edmonton, Alta.

Season	Team	Lg	G	W	L	T	Standing	Playoff Result
1981-82	DET	N	11	3	8	0	6 **6**	

Alex Delvecchio
DELVECCHIO, ALEX PETER 6', 195 lbs.
B. Dec. 4, 1931, Fort William, Ont.
Hall of Fame, 1977

Season	Team	Lg	G	W	L	T	Standing	Playoff Result
1973-74	DET	N	66	27	30	9	6 **6**	
1974-75			80	23	45	12	**4**	
1975-76			54	19	29	6	4 **4**	
1976-77			44	13	26	5	**5** 5	
4 yrs.	N Totals:		244	82	130	32		

Jacques Demers
DEMERS, JACQUES
B. Aug. 25, 1944, Montreal, Que.

Season	Team	Lg	G	W	L	T	Standing	Playoff Result
1975-76	IND	W	80	35	39	6	**1**	Lost First Round
1976-77			81	36	37	8	**3**	Lost Semifinals
1977-78	CIN	W	80	35	42	3	**7**	
1978-79	QUE	W	80	41	34	5	**2**	Lost First Round
1979-80	QUE	N	80	25	44	11	**5**	
5 yrs.	N Totals:		80	25	44	11		
	W Totals:		321	147	152	22		

Cy Denneny
DENNENY, CYRIL
B. Dec. 23, 1897, Farran's point, Ont.
Hall of Fame, 1959

Season	Team	Lg	G	W	L	T	Standing	Playoff Result
1928-29	BOS	N	44	26	13	5	**1**	**Won Stanley Cup**
1932-33	OTTA	N	48	11	27	10	**5**	
2 yrs.	N Totals:		92	37	40	15		1 Cup Champion

Bill Dineen
DINEEN, WILLIAM PATRICK 5'11", 180 lbs.
B. Sept. 18, 1932, Arvida, Que.

Season	Team	Lg	G	W	L	T	Standing	Playoff Result
1972-73	HOUS	W	78	39	35	4	**2**	Lost Semifinals
1973-74			78	48	25	5	**1**	Won WHA Finals
1974-75			78	53	25	0	**1**	Won WHA Finals
1975-76			80	53	27	0	**1**	Lost League Finals
1976-77			80	50	24	6	**1**	Lost Semifinals
1977-78			80	42	34	4	**3**	Lost First Round
1978-79	NE	W	80	37	34	9	**4**	Lost Semifinals
7 yrs.	W Totals:		554	322	204	28		

Clare Drake
DRAKE, CLARENCE
B. Oct. 9, 1928, Yorkton, Sask.

Season	Team	Lg	G	W	L	T	Standing	Playoff Result
1975-76	EDM	W	48	18	28	2	**4** 4	

Dick Duff
DUFF, TERRANCE RICHARD 5'9", 166 lbs.
B. Feb. 18, 1936, Kirkland Lake, Ont.

Season	Team	Lg	G	W	L	T	Standing	Playoff Result
1979-80	TOR	N	2	0	2	0	3 **3** 4	

Jules Dugal
DUGAL, JULES
B. Montreal, Que.

Season	Team	Lg	G	W	L	T	Standing	Playoff Result
1938-39	MONT	N	18	9	6	3	7 **6**	Lost First Round

Art Duncan
DUNCAN, ARTHUR

Season	Team	Lg	G	W	L	T	Standing	Playoff Result
1926-27	DET	N	44	12	28	4	**5**	
1930-31	TOR	N	42	21	13	8	1 **2**	Lost First Round
1931-32			5	0	3	2	**4** 2	
3 yrs.	N Totals:		91	33	44	14		

Red Dutton
DUTTON, MERVYN A. 6', 185 lbs.
B. Jan. 3, 1898, Russell, Man.
Hall of Fame, 1958

Season	Team	Lg	G	W	L	T	Standing	Playoff Result
1935-36	NYA	N	48	16	25	7	**3**	Lost Semifinals
1936-37			48	15	29	4	**4**	
1937-38			48	19	18	11	**2**	Lost Semifinals
1938-39			48	17	21	10	**4**	Lost First Round
1939-40			48	15	29	4	**6**	Lost First Round
1940-41			48	8	29	11	**7**	
1941-42			48	16	29	3	**7**	
7 yrs.	N Totals:		336	106	180	50		

Frank Eddolls
EDDOLLS, FRANK HERBERT 5'8", 180 lbs.
B. July 5, 1921, Lachine, Que.

Season	Team	Lg	G	W	L	T	Standing	Playoff Result
1954-55	CHI	N	70	13	40	17	**6**	

Jack Evans
EVANS, WILLIAM JOHN 6'1", 194 lbs.
B. Apr. 21, 1928, Garnant, South Wales

Season	Team	Lg	G	W	L	T	Standing	Playoff Result
1975-76	CALIF	N	80	27	42	11	**4**	
1976-77	CLEVE	N	80	25	42	13	**4**	
1977-78			80	22	45	13	**4**	
3 yrs.	N Totals:		240	74	129	37		

Gordie Fashoway
FASHOWAY, GORDON 5'11", 180 lbs.
B. June 16, 1926, Portage La Prairie, Man.

Season	Team	Lg	G	W	L	T	Standing	Playoff Result
1967-68	OAK	N	10	4	5	1	6 **6**	

John Ferguson
FERGUSON, JOHN BOWIE (Fergie) 5'11", 190 lbs.
B. Sept. 5, 1938, Vancouver, B.C.

Season	Team	Lg	G	W	L	T	Standing	Playoff Result
1975-76	NYR	N	41	14	22	5	4 **4**	
1976-77			80	29	37	14	**4**	
2 yrs.	N Totals:		121	43	59	19		

Maurice Filion
FILION, MAURICE
B. Feb. 12, 1932, Montreal, Que.

Season	Team	Lg	G	W	L	T	Standing	Playoff Result
1972-73	QUE	W	76	32	39	5	4 **5**	
1977-78			21	13	7	1	5 **4**	Lost Semifinals
1980-81	QUE	N	6	1	3	2	**5** 4	
3 yrs.	N Totals:		6	1	3	2		
	W Totals:		97	45	46	6		

Emile Francis
FRANCIS, EMILE (The Cat) 5'6", 145 lbs
B. Sept. 13, 1926, North Battleford, Sask.
Hall of Fame, 1982

Season	Team	Lg	G	W	L	T	Standing	Playoff Result
1965-66	NYR	N	50	13	31	6	5 **6**	
1966-67			70	30	28	12	**4**	Lost First Round
1967-68			74	39	23	12	**2**	Lost First Round
1968-69			33	19	8	6	6 **3**	Lost First Round
1969-70			76	38	22	16	**4**	Lost First Round
1970-71			78	49	18	11	**2**	Lost Semifinals
1971-72			78	48	17	13	**2**	Lost Cup Finals
1972-73			78	47	23	8	**3**	Lost Semifinals
1973-74			37	22	10	5	4 **3**	Lost Semifinals
1974-75			80	37	29	14	**2**	Lost First Round
1976-77	STL	N	80	32	39	9	**1**	Lost First Round
1981-82			11	4	5	2	3 **3**	Lost Quarterfinals
1982-83			32	10	19	3	**3** 4	
13 yrs.	N Totals:		777	388	272	117		

Frank Frederickson
FREDERICKSON, FRANK 5'11", 175 lbs.
B. Winnipeg, Man.
Hall of Fame, 1958

Season	Team	Lg	G	W	L	T	Standing	Playoff Result
1929-30	PITT	N	44	5	36	3	**5**	

Bill Gadsby

GADSBY, WILLIAM ALEXANDER 6', 185 lbs.
B. Aug. 8, 1927, Calgary, Alta.
Hall of Fame, 1970

			G	W	L	T	STANDING	PLAYOFF RESULT
1968-69	**DET**	**N**	76	33	31	12	**5**	
1969-70			3	2	1	0	**2** 3	
2 yrs.	**N Totals:**		79	35	32	12		

Herb Gardiner

GARDINER, HERBERT
B. M Winnipeg, Man.
Hall of Fame, 1958

			G	W	L	T	STANDING	PLAYOFF RESULT
1928-29	**CHI**	**N**	44	7	29	8	**5**	

Jimmy Gardner

GARDNER, JAMES
B. Unknown
Hall of Fame, 1962

			G	W	L	T	STANDING	PLAYOFF RESULT
1924-25	**HAMIL**	**N**	30	19	10	1	**1**	Lost League Finals

Ted Garvin

GARVIN, THEODORE
B. Aug. 30, 1920, Sarnia, Ont.

			G	W	L	T	STANDING	PLAYOFF RESULT
1973-74	**DET**	**N**	12	2	9	1	**6** 6	

Jean Guy Gendron

GENDRON, JEAN GUY 5'9", 165 lbs.
B. Aug. 30, 1934, Montreal, Que.

			G	W	L	T	STANDING	PLAYOFF RESULT
1974-75	**QUE**	**W**	78	46	32	0	**1**	Lost League Finals
1975-76			81	50	27	4	**2**	Lost First Round
2 yrs.	**W Totals:**		159	96	59	4		

Bernie Geoffrion

GEOFFRION, BERNARD (Boom Boom) 5'11", 185 lbs.
B. Feb. 16, 1931, Montreal, Que.
Hall of Fame, 1972

			G	W	L	T	STANDING	PLAYOFF RESULT
1968-69	**NYR**	**N**	43	22	18	3	**6** 3	
1972-73	**ATL**	**N**	78	25	38	15	**7**	
1973-74			78	30	34	14	**4**	Lost First Round
1974-75			52	22	20	10	**4** 4	
1979-80	**MONT**	**N**	30	15	9	6	**1** 1	
5 yrs.	**N Totals:**		281	114	119	48		

Eddie Gerard

GERARD, EDDIE
B. Feb. 22, 1890,
Hall of Fame, 1945

			G	W	L	T	STANDING	PLAYOFF RESULT
1917-18	**OTTA**	**N**	22	9	13	0	**3**	
1924-25	**MON(M)**	**N**	30	9	19	2	**5**	
1925-26			36	20	11	5	**2**	**Won Stanley Cup**
1926-27			44	20	20	4	**3**	Lost First Round
1927-28			44	24	14	6	**2**	Lost Cup Finals
1928-29			44	15	20	9	**5**	
1930-31	**NYA**	**N**	44	18	16	10	**4**	
1931-32			48	16	24	8	**4**	
1932-33	**MON(M)**	**N**	48	22	20	6	**2**	Lost First Round
1933-34			48	19	18	11	**3**	Lost Semifinals
1934-35	**STL**	**N**	13	2	11	0	**5** 5	
11 yrs.	**N Totals:**		421	174	186	61		1 Cup Champion

Dave Gill

GILL, DAVID

			G	W	L	T	STANDING	PLAYOFF RESULT
1926-27	**OTTA**	**N**	44	30	10	4	**1**	**Won Stanley Cup**
1927-28			44	20	14	10	**3**	Lost First Round
1928-29			44	14	17	13	**4**	
3 yrs.	**N Totals:**		132	64	41	27		1 Cup Champion

Fred Glover

GLOVER, FREDERICK AUSTIN 5'9", 175 lbs.
B. Jan. 5, 1928, Toronto, Ont.

			G	W	L	T	STANDING	PLAYOFF RESULT
1968-69	**CALIF**	**N**	76	29	36	11	**2**	Lost First Round
1969-70	**OAK**	**N**	76	22	40	14	**4**	Lost First Round
1970-71	**CALIF**	**N**	78	20	53	5	**7**	
1971-72			3	0	1	2	**5** 6	
	LA	**N**	68	18	42	8	7 **7**	
	2 team total		71	18	43	10		
1972-73	**CALIF**	**N**	66	14	39	13	8 **8**	
1973-74			57	11	38	8	**8** 8	
6 yrs.	**N Totals:**		424	114	249	61		

Bill Goldsworthy

GOLDSWORTHY, WILLIAM ALFRED 6', 190 lbs.
B. Aug. 24, 1944, Kitchener, Ont.

			G	W	L	T	STANDING	PLAYOFF RESULT
1977-78	**IND**	**W**	30	8	17	5	8 **8**	

Ebbie Goodfellow

GOODFELLOW, EBENEZER 6', 180 lbs.
B. Apr. 9, 1907, Ottawa, Ont.
Hall of Fame, 1963

			G	W	L	T	STANDING	PLAYOFF RESULT
1950-51	**CHI**	**N**	70	13	47	10	**6**	
1951-52			70	17	44	9	**6**	
2 yrs.	**N Totals:**		140	30	91	19		

Jackie Gordon

GORDON, JOHN 5'8½", 154 lbs.
B. Mar. 3, 1928, Winnipeg, Man.

			G	W	L	T	STANDING	PLAYOFF RESULT
1970-71	**MINN**	**N**	78	28	34	16	**4**	Lost Semifinals
1971-72			78	37	29	12	**2**	Lost First Round
1972-73			78	37	30	11	**3**	Lost First Round
1973-74			17	3	8	6	**7** 7	
1974-75			39	11	23	5	**4** 4	
5 yrs.	**N Totals:**		290	116	124	50		

Tommy Gorman

GORMAN, THOMAS
B. July 9, 1886, Ottawa, Ont.
Hall of Fame, 1963

			G	W	L	T	STANDING	PLAYOFF RESULT
1925-26	**NYA**	**N**	36	12	20	4	**5**	
1928-29			44	19	13	12	**2**	Lost First Round
1932-33	**CHI**	**N**	25	8	11	6	4 **4**	
1933-34			48	20	17	11	**2**	**Won Stanley Cup**
1934-35	**MON(M)**	**N**	48	24	19	5	**2**	**Won Stanley Cup**
1935-36			48	22	16	10	**1**	Lost First Round
1936-37			48	22	17	9	**2**	Lost Semifinals
1937-38			30	6	19	5	4 **4**	
8 yrs.	**N Totals:**		327	133	132	62		2 Cup Champions

Johnny Gottselig

GOTTSELIG, JOHN 5'11", 158 lbs.
B. June 24, 1905, Odessa, Russia

			G	W	L	T	STANDING	PLAYOFF RESULT
1944-45	**CHI**	**N**	49	13	29	7	3 **5**	
1945-46			50	23	20	7	**3**	Lost First Round
1946-47			60	19	37	4	**6**	
1947-48			28	7	18	3	**6** 6	
4 yrs.	**N Totals:**		187	62	104	21		

Phil Goyette

GOYETTE, JOSEPH GEORGES PHILIPE 5'11", 170 lbs.
B. Oct. 31, 1933, Lachine, Que.

			G	W	L	T	STANDING	PLAYOFF RESULT
1972-73	**NYI**	**N**	50	6	40	4	**8** 8	

Gary Green

GREEN, GARY LEE
B. Aug. 23, 1953, Tillsonburg, Ont.

			G	W	L	T	STANDING	PLAYOFF RESULT
1979-80	**WASH**	**N**	64	23	30	11	5 **5**	
1980-81			80	26	36	18	**5**	
1981-82			13	1	12	0	**5** 5	
3 yrs.	**N Totals:**		157	50	78	29		

Pete Green
GREEN, PETER

Season	Team	Lg	G	W	L	T	Standing	Playoff Result
1919-20	OTTA	N	24	19	5	0	1	Won Stanley Cup
1920-21			24	13	11	0	3	Won Stanley Cup
1921-22			24	14	8	2	1	Lost League Finals
1922-23			24	14	9	1	1	Won Stanley Cup
1923-24			24	16	8	0	1	Lost League Finals
1924-25			30	17	12	1	4	
1925-26			36	24	8	4	1	Lost Semifinals
7 yrs.	N Totals:		186	117	61	8		3 Cup Champions

Wilf Green
GREEN, WILFRED THOMAS (Shorty)
B. July 17, 1896, Sudbury, Ont.
Hall of Fame, 1962

Season	Team	Lg	G	W	L	T	Standing	Playoff Result
1927-28	NYA	N	44	11	27	6	5	

Aldo Guidolin
GUIDOLIN, ALDO 6', 180 lbs.
B. June 6, 1932, Forks of Credit, Ont.

Season	Team	Lg	G	W	L	T	Standing	Playoff Result
1978-79	COLO	N	59	12	39	8	4 4	

Bep Guidolin
GUIDOLIN, ARMAND 5'8", 175 lbs.
B. Dec. 9, 1925, Thorold, Ont.

Season	Team	Lg	G	W	L	T	Standing	Playoff Result
1972-73	BOS	N	26	20	6	0	3 2	Lost First Round
1973-74			78	52	17	9	1	Lost Cup Finals
1974-75	KC	N	80	15	54	11	5	
1975-76			45	11	30	4	5 5	
1976-77	EDM	W	63	25	36	2	5 4	
5 yrs.	N Totals:		229	98	107	24		
	W Totals:		63	25	36	2		

John Hanna
HANNA, JOHN 6', 195 lbs.
B. Apr. 5, 1935, Sydney, N.S.

Season	Team	Lg	G	W	L	T	Standing	Playoff Result
1974-75	CLEVE	W	33	14	18	1	2 2	

Ned Harkness
HARKNESS, EDWARD
B. Sept. 19, 1921, Ottawa, Ont.

Season	Team	Lg	G	W	L	T	Standing	Playoff Result
1970-71	DET	N	19	9	7	3	6 7	

Billy Harris
HARRIS, WILLIAM EDWARD 6', 165 lbs.
B. July 29, 1935, Toronto, Ont.

Season	Team	Lg	G	W	L	T	Standing	Playoff Result
1972-73	OTTA	W	78	35	39	4	4	Lost First Round
1973-74	TOR	W	78	41	33	4	2	Lost Semifinals
1974-75			40	22	17	1	2 2	
3 yrs.	W Totals:		196	98	89	9		

Ted Harris
HARRIS, EDWARD ALEXANDER 6'2", 183 lbs.
B. July 18, 1936, Winnipeg, Man.

Season	Team	Lg	G	W	L	T	Standing	Playoff Result
1975-76	MINN	N	80	20	53	7	4	
1976-77			80	23	39	18	2	Lost First Round
1977-78			19	5	12	2	4 5	
3 yrs.	N Totals:		179	48	104	27		

Cece Hart
HART, CECIL
B. Montreal, Que.

Season	Team	Lg	G	W	L	T	Standing	Playoff Result
1925-26	MONT	N	36	11	24	1	7	
1926-27			44	28	14	2	2	Lost Semifinals
1927-28			44	26	11	7	1	Lost Semifinals
1928-29			44	22	7	15	1	Lost First Round
1929-30			44	21	14	9	2	Won Stanley Cup
1930-31			44	26	10	8	1	Won Stanley Cup
1931-32			48	25	16	7	1	Lost First Round
1936-37			48	24	18	6	1	Lost First Round

Cece Hart continued

Season	Team	Lg	G	W	L	T	Standing	Playoff Result
1937-38			48	18	17	13	3	Lost First Round
1938-39			30	6	18	6	7 6	
10 yrs.	N Totals:		430	207	149	74		2 Cup Champions

Doug Harvey
HARVEY, DOUGLAS NORMAN 5'11", 180 lbs.
B. Dec. 19, 1924, Montreal, Que.
Hall of Fame, 1973

Season	Team	Lg	G	W	L	T	Standing	Playoff Result
1961-62	NYR	N	70	26	32	12	4	Lost First Round

Frank Heffernan
HEFFERNAN, FRANK

Season	Team	Lg	G	W	L	T	Standing	Playoff Result
1919-20	TOR	N	12	5	5	0	3 2	

Camille Henry
HENRY, CAMILLE JOSEPH WILFRID (The Eel) 5'8", 152 lbs.
B. Jan. 31, 1933, Quebec City, Que.

Season	Team	Lg	G	W	L	T	Standing	Playoff Result
1972-73	NY	W	78	33	43	2	6	
1973-74	NY-NJ	W	20	6	12	2	6 6	
2 yrs.	W Totals:		98	39	55	4		

Larry Hillman
HILLMAN, LARRY MORLEY 6', 181 lbs.
B. Feb. 5, 1937, Kirkland Lake, Ont.

Season	Team	Lg	G	W	L	T	Standing	Playoff Result
1977-78	WINN	W	80	20	43	17	3	Won WHA Finals
1978-79			80	25	42	13	2	Won WHA Finals
2 yrs.	W Totals:		160	45	85	30		

Harry Howell
HOWELL, HENRY VERNON 6'1", 200 lbs.
B. Dec. 28, 1932, Hamilton, Ont.
Hall of Fame, 1979

Season	Team	Lg	G	W	L	T	Standing	Playoff Result
1973-74	NY-NJ	W	58	26	30	2	6 6	
1974-75	SD	W	78	43	31	4	2	Lost Semifinals
1978-79	MINN	N	8	2	4	2	4 4	
			3	1	2	0	3 4 4	
	2 team total		11	3	6	2		
3 yrs.	N Totals:		11	3	6	2		
	W Totals:		136	69	61	6		

Sandy Hucul
HUCUL, ALEXANDER KENNETH 6', 200 lbs.
B. Dec. 5, 1933, Eston, Sask.

Season	Team	Lg	G	W	L	T	Standing	Playoff Result
1974-75	PHOE	W	78	39	31	8	4	Lost First Round
1975-76			80	39	35	6	2	Lost First Round
2 yrs.	W Totals:		158	78	66	14		

Bobby Hull
HULL, ROBERT MARVIN (The Golden Jet) 5'10", 193 lbs.
B. Jan. 3, 1939, Pointe Anne, Ont.

Season	Team	Lg	G	W	L	T	Standing	Playoff Result
1972-73	WINN	W	78	43	31	4	1	Lost League Finals
1973-74			78	34	39	5	4	Lost First Round
1974-75			13	4	9	0	4 5 3	
3 yrs.	W Totals:		169	81	79	9		

Bill Hunter
HUNTER, WILLIAM

Season	Team	Lg	G	W	L	T	Standing	Playoff Result
1974-75	EDM	W	19	6	12	1	3 5	
1975-76			33	9	21	3	4 4	Lost First Round
2 yrs.	W Totals:		52	15	33	4		

Punch Imlach

IMLACH, GEORGE
B. Mar. 15, 1918, Toronto, Ont.

Season	Team	Lg	G	W	L	T	Standing	Playoff Result
1958-59	TOR	N	50	22	20	8	6 **4**	Lost Cup Finals
1959-60			70	35	26	9	**2**	Lost Cup Finals
1960-61			70	39	19	12	**2**	Lost First Round
1961-62			70	37	22	11	**2**	**Won Stanley Cup**
1962-63			70	35	23	12	**1**	**Won Stanley Cup**
1963-64			70	33	25	12	**3**	**Won Stanley Cup**
1964-65			70	30	26	14	**4**	Lost First Round
1965-66			70	34	25	11	**3**	Lost First Round
1966-67			49	19	21	9	**4** 3	
			11	6	5	0	3 **3**	**Won Stanley Cup**
	2 team total		60	25	26	9		
1967-68			74	33	31	10	**5**	
1968-69			76	35	26	15	**4**	Lost First Round
1970-71	BUF	N	78	24	39	15	**5**	
1971-72			41	8	23	10	**6** 6	
1979-80	TOR	N	10	5	5	0	3 **4**	Lost First Round
14 yrs.	**N Totals:**		879	395	336	148		4 Cup Champions

Earl Ingarfield

INGARFIELD, EARL THOMPSON 5'11", 185 lbs.
B. Oct. 25, 1934, Lethbridge, Alta.

Season	Team	Lg	G	W	L	T	Standing	Playoff Result
1972-73	NYI	N	28	6	20	2	8 **8**	

Bill Inglis

INGLIS, WILLIAM JOHN 5'9", 160 lbs.
B. May 11, 1943, Ottawa, Ont.

Season	Team	Lg	G	W	L	T	Standing	Playoff Result
1978-79	BUF	N	56	28	18	10	3 **2**	Lost First Round

Ron Ingram

INGRAM, RONALD WALTER 5'11", 185 lbs.
B. July 5, 1933, Toronto, Ont.

Season	Team	Lg	G	W	L	T	Standing	Playoff Result
1975-76	SD	W	80	36	38	6	**3**	Lost Quarterfinals
1976-77			81	40	37	4	**3**	Lost First Round
1977-78	IND	W	51	16	31	4	**8** 8	
3 yrs.	**W Totals:**		212	92	106	14		

Dick Irvin

IRVIN, RICHARD
B. July 19, 1892, Limestone Ridge, Ont.
Hall of Fame, 1958

Season	Team	Lg	G	W	L	T	Standing	Playoff Result
1930-31	CHI	N	44	24	17	3	**2**	Lost Cup Finals
1931-32	TOR	N	43	23	15	5	4 **2**	**Won Stanley Cup**
1932-33			48	24	18	6	**1**	Lost Cup Finals
1933-34			48	26	13	9	**1**	Lost First Round
1934-35			48	30	14	4	**1**	Lost Cup Finals
1935-36			48	23	19	6	**2**	Lost Cup Finals
1936-37			48	22	21	5	**3**	Lost First Round
1937-38			48	24	15	9	**1**	Lost Cup Finals
1938-39			48	19	20	9	**3**	Lost Cup Finals
1939-40			48	25	17	6	**3**	Lost Cup Finals
1940-41	MONT	N	48	16	26	6	**6**	Lost First Round
1941-42			48	18	27	3	**6**	Lost First Round
1942-43			50	19	19	12	**4**	Lost First Round
1943-44			50	38	5	7	**1**	**Won Stanley Cup**
1944-45			50	38	8	4	**1**	Lost First Round
1945-46			50	28	17	5	**1**	**Won Stanley Cup**
1946-47			60	34	16	10	**1**	Lost Cup Finals
1947-48			60	20	29	11	**5**	
1948-49			60	28	23	9	**3**	Lost First Round
1949-50			70	29	22	19	**2**	Lost First Round
1950-51			70	25	30	15	**3**	Lost Cup Finals
1951-52			70	34	26	10	**2**	Lost Cup Finals
1952-53			70	28	23	19	**2**	**Won Stanley Cup**
1953-54			70	35	24	11	**2**	Lost Cup Finals
1954-55			70	41	18	11	**2**	Lost Cup Finals
1955-56	CHI	N	70	19	39	12	**6**	
26 yrs.	**N Totals:**		1437	690	521	226		4 Cup Champions

Tommy Ivan

IVAN, THOMAS N.
B. Jan. 31, 1911, Toronto, Ont.

Tommy Ivan continued

Season	Team	Lg	G	W	L	T	Standing	Playoff Result
1947-48	DET	N	60	30	18	12	**2**	Lost Cup Finals
1948-49			60	34	19	7	**1**	Lost Cup Finals
1949-50			70	37	19	14	**1**	**Won Stanley Cup**
1950-51			70	44	13	13	**1**	Lost First Round
1951-52			70	44	14	12	**1**	**Won Stanley Cup**
1952-53			70	36	16	18	**1**	Lost First Round
1953-54			70	37	19	14	**1**	**Won Stanley Cup**
1956-57	CHI	N	70	16	39	15	**6**	
8 yrs.	**N Totals:**		540	278	157	105		3 Cup Champions

Emil Iverson

IVERSON, EMIL

Season	Team	Lg	G	W	L	T	Standing	Playoff Result
1931-32	CHI	N	48	18	19	11	**2**	Lost First Round
1932-33			23	8	9	6	**4** 4	
2 yrs.	**N Totals:**		71	26	28	17		

Bob Johnson

JOHNSON, ROBERT
B. Mar. 4, 1931, Minneapolis, Minn.

Season	Team	Lg	G	W	L	T	Standing	Playoff Result
1982-83	CALG	N	80	32	34	14	**2**	Lost Quarterfinals

Tom Johnson

JOHNSON, THOMAS CHRISTIAN 6', 180 lbs.
B. Feb. 18, 1928, Baldur, Man.
Hall of Fame, 1970

Season	Team	Lg	G	W	L	T	Standing	Playoff Result
1970-71	BOS	N	78	57	14	7	**1**	Lost First Round
1971-72			78	54	13	11	**1**	**Won Stanley Cup**
1972-73			52	31	16	5	**3** 2	
3 yrs.	**N Totals:**		208	142	43	23		1 Cup Champion

Eddie Johnston

JOHNSTON, EDWARD JOSEPH 6', 190 lbs.
B. Nov. 24, 1935, Montreal, Que.

Season	Team	Lg	G	W	L	T	Standing	Playoff Result
1979-80	CHI	N	80	34	27	19	**1**	Lost Quarterfinals
1980-81	PITT	N	80	30	37	13	**3**	Lost First Round
1981-82			80	31	36	13	**4**	Lost First Round
1982-83			80	18	53	9	**6**	
4 yrs.	**N Totals:**		320	113	153	54		

Marsh Johnston

JOHNSTON, LAWRENCE MARSHALL 5'11", 175 lbs.
B. June 6, 1941, Birch Hills, Sask.

Season	Team	Lg	G	W	L	T	Standing	Playoff Result
1973-74	CALIF	N	21	2	17	2	8 **8**	
1974-75			48	11	28	9	**4** 4	
1981-82	COLO	N	56	15	32	9	5 **5**	
3 yrs.	**N Totals:**		125	28	77	20		

Jack Kelley

KELLEY, JOHN
B. July 10, 1927, Medford, Mass.

Season	Team	Lg	G	W	L	T	Standing	Playoff Result
1972-73	NE	W	78	46	30	2	**1**	Won WHA Finals
1974-75			5	3	2	0	1 **1**	Lost First Round
1975-76			33	14	16	3	**1** 3	
3 yrs.	**W Totals:**		116	63	48	5		

Pat Kelly

KELLY, PATRICK JAMES
B. Sept. 8, 1935, Sioux Lookout, Ont.

Season	Team	Lg	G	W	L	T	Standing	Playoff Result
1976-77	BIRM	W	59	24	32	3	6 **5**	
1977-78	COLO	N	80	19	40	21	**2**	Lost First Round
1978-79			21	3	14	4	**4** 4	
3 yrs.	**N Totals:**		101	22	54	25		
	W Totals:		59	24	32	3		

Red Kelly

KELLY, LEONARD PATRICK 6', 195 lbs.
B. July 9, 1927, Simcoe, Ont.
Hall of Fame, 1969

Season	Team	Lg	G	W	L	T	Standing	Playoff Result
1967-68	LA	N	74	31	33	10	**2**	Lost First Round

Red Kelly continued

			G	W	L	T	STANDING	PLAYOFF RESULT
1968-69			76	24	42	10	**4**	Lost Semifinals
1969-70	**PITT**	**N**	76	26	38	12	**2**	Lost Semifinals
1970-71			78	21	37	20	**6**	
1971-72			78	26	38	14	**4**	Lost First Round
1972-73			42	17	19	6	**5** 5	
1973-74	**TOR**	**N**	80	31	33	16	**4**	Lost First Round
1974-75			80	31	33	16	**3**	Lost Quarterfinals
1975-76			80	34	31	15	**3**	Lost Quarterfinals
1976-77			80	33	32	15	**3**	Lost Quarterfinals
10 yrs.	**N Totals:**		744	274	336	134		

George Kennedy

KENNEDY, GEORGE

B. Unknown

			G	W	L	T	STANDING	PLAYOFF RESULT
1917-18	**MONT**	**N**	22	13	9	0	**2**	Lost League Finals
1918-19			18	10	8	0	**2**	
1919-20			24	13	11	0	**2**	
3 yrs.	**N Totals:**		64	36	28	0		

Ray Kinasewich

KINASEWICH, RAYMOND

B. Sept. 12, 1933, Smokey Lake, Alta.

			G	W	L	T	STANDING	PLAYOFF RESULT
1972-73	**ALTA**	**W**	78	38	37	3	**5**	

Larry Kish

KISH, LAWRENCE

B. Dec. 11, 1941, Welland, Ont.

			G	W	L	T	STANDING	PLAYOFF RESULT
1982-83	**HART**	**N**	49	12	32	5	**5** 5	

Bobby Kromm

KROMM, ROBERT

B. June 8, 1928, Calgary, Alta.

Won Jack Adams Award, 1977-78

			G	W	L	T	STANDING	PLAYOFF RESULT
1975-76	**WINN**	**W**	81	52	27	2	**1**	Won WHA Finals
1976-77			80	46	32	2	**2**	Lost League Finals
1977-78	**DET**	**N**	80	32	34	14	**2**	Lost Quarterfinals
1978-79			80	23	41	16	**4**	
1979-80			71	24	36	11	**5** 5	
5 yrs.	**N Totals:**		231	79	111	41		
	W Totals:		161	98	59	4		

Orland Kurtenbach

KURTENBACH, ORLAND JOHN 6'2", 195 lbs.

B. Sept. 7, 1936, Cudworth, Sask.

			G	W	L	T	STANDING	PLAYOFF RESULT
1976-77	**VAN**	**N**	45	16	19	10	4 **4**	
1977-78			80	20	43	17	**3**	
2 yrs.	**N Totals:**		125	36	62	27		

Newsy Lalonde

LALONDE, EDWARD C.

B. Oct. 31, 1887, Cornwall, Ont.

Hall of Fame, 1950

			G	W	L	T	STANDING	PLAYOFF RESULT
1926-27	**NYA**	**N**	44	17	25	2	**4**	
1929-30	**OTTA**	**N**	44	21	15	8	**3**	Lost First Round
1930-31			44	10	30	4	**5**	
1932-33	**MONT**	**N**	48	18	25	5	**3**	Lost First Round
1933-34			48	22	20	6	**2**	Lost First Round
1934-35			16	5	8	3	**5** 3	
6 yrs.	**N Totals:**		244	93	123	28		

Hal Laycoe

LAYCOE, HAROLD RICHARDSON 6'1", 175 lbs.

B. June 23, 1922, Sutherland, Sask.

			G	W	L	T	STANDING	PLAYOFF RESULT
1969-70	**LA**	**N**	24	5	18	1	**6** 6	
1970-71	**VAN**	**N**	78	24	46	8	**6**	
1971-72			78	20	50	8	**7**	
3 yrs.	**N Totals:**		180	49	114	17		

Bob LeDuc

LEDUC, ROBERT JOSEPH 5'10", 185 lbs.

B. May 24, 1944, Sudbury, Ont.

			G	W	L	T	STANDING	PLAYOFF RESULT
1974-75	**TOR**	**W**	38	21	16	1	2 **2**	Lost First Round

Gilles Leger

LEGER, GILLES

B. July 16, 1941, Cornwall, Ont.

			G	W	L	T	STANDING	PLAYOFF RESULT
1975-76	**TOR**	**W**	26	9	17	0	5 **5**	
1976-77	**BIRM**	**W**	24	7	16	1	**6** 5	
2 yrs.	**W Totals:**		50	16	33	1		

Hugh Lehman

LEHMAN, HUGH

B. Oct. 27, 1885, Pembroke, Ont.

Hall of Fame, 1958

			G	W	L	T	STANDING	PLAYOFF RESULT
1927-28	**CHI**	**N**	21	3	17	1	5 **5**	

Pit Lepine

LEPINE, ALFRED (Pit)

B. July 30, 1901, Ste. Anne Bellevue, Que.

			G	W	L	T	STANDING	PLAYOFF RESULT
1939-40	**MONT**	**N**	48	10	33	5	**7**	

Percy Lesueur

LESUEUR, PERCIVAL

			G	W	L	T	STANDING	PLAYOFF RESULT
1923-24	**HAMIL**	**N**	24	9	15	0	**4**	

Ted Lindsay

LINDSAY, ROBERT BLAKE THEODORE 5'8", 160 lbs.

B. July 29, 1925, Renfrew, Ont.

Hall of Fame, 1966

			G	W	L	T	STANDING	PLAYOFF RESULT
1979-80	**DET**	**N**	9	2	7	0	5 **5**	
1980-81			20	3	14	3	**5** 5	
2 yrs.	**N Totals:**		29	5	21	3		

Clem Loughlin

LOUGHLIN, CLEMENT 6', 180 lbs.

B. Nov. 15, 1894, Carroll, Man.

			G	W	L	T	STANDING	PLAYOFF RESULT
1934-35	**CHI**	**N**	48	26	17	5	**2**	Lost First Round
1935-36			48	21	19	8	**3**	Lost First Round
1936-37			48	14	27	7	**4**	
3 yrs.	**N Totals:**		144	61	63	20		

Parker MacDonald

MACDONALD, CALVIN PARKER 5'11", 184 lbs.

B. June 14, 1933, Sydney, N.S.

			G	W	L	T	STANDING	PLAYOFF RESULT
1973-74	**MINN**	**N**	61	20	30	11	7 **7**	
1981-82	**LA**	**N**	42	13	24	5	**4** 4	
2 yrs.	**N Totals:**		103	33	54	16		

Billy MacMillan

MACMILLAN, WILLIAM STEWART 5'10", 180 lbs.

B. Mar. 7, 1943, Charlottetown, P.E.I.

			G	W	L	T	STANDING	PLAYOFF RESULT
1980-81	**COLO**	**N**	80	22	45	13	**5**	
1982-83	**NJ**	**N**	80	17	49	14	**5**	
2 yrs.	**N Totals:**		160	39	94	27		

Al MacNeil

MACNEIL, ALLISTER WENCES 5'10", 180 lbs.

B. Sept. 27, 1935, Sydney, N.S.

			G	W	L	T	STANDING	PLAYOFF RESULT
1970-71	**MONT**	**N**	55	31	15	9	3 **3**	**Won Stanley Cup**
1979-80	**ATL**	**N**	80	35	32	13	**4**	Lost First Round
1980-81	**CALG**	**N**	80	39	27	14	**3**	Lost Semifinals
1981-82			80	29	34	17	**3**	Lost First Round
4 yrs.	**N Totals:**		295	134	108	53		1 Cup Champion

Keith Magnuson

MAGNUSON, KEITH ARLEN 6′, 185 lbs.
B. Apr. 27, 1947, Saskatoon, Sask.

			G	W	L	T	STANDING	PLAYOFF RESULT
1980-81	CHI	N	80	31	33	16	**2**	Lost First Round
1981-82			52	18	24	10	**4** 4	
2 yrs.	N Totals:		132	49	57	26		

Phil Maloney

MALONEY, PHILIP FRANCIS 5′9″, 170 lbs.
B. Oct. 6, 1927, Ottawa, Ont.

			G	W	L	T	STANDING	PLAYOFF RESULT
1973-74	VAN	N	37	15	18	4	8 **7**	
1974-75			80	38	32	10	**1**	Lost First Round
1975-76			80	33	32	15	**2**	Lost First Round
1976-77			35	9	23	3	**4** 4	
4 yrs.	N Totals:		232	95	105	32		

Sylvio Mantha

MANTHA, SYLVIO 5′10″, 178 lbs.
B. Apr. 14, 1902, Montreal, Que.
Hall of Fame, 1960

			G	W	L	T	STANDING	PLAYOFF RESULT
1935-36	MONT	N	48	11	26	11	**4**	

Bert Marshall

MARSHALL, ALBERT LEROY 6′3″, 205 lbs.
B. Nov. 22, 1943, Kamloops, B.C.

			G	W	L	T	STANDING	PLAYOFF RESULT
1981-82	COLO	N	24	3	17	4	**5** 5	

Wayne Maxner

MAXNER, WAYNE DOUGLAS 5′11″, 170 lbs.
B. Sept. 27, 1942, Halifax, N.S.

			G	W	L	T	STANDING	PLAYOFF RESULT
1980-81	DET	N	60	16	29	15	5 **5**	
1981-82			69	18	39	12	**6** 6	
2 yrs.	N Totals:		129	34	68	27		

Bob McCammon

MCCAMMON, ROBERT
B. Apr. 14, 1941, Kenora, Ont.

			G	W	L	T	STANDING	PLAYOFF RESULT
1978-79	PHI	N	50	22	17	11	**4** 2	
1981-82			8	4	2	2	3 **3**	Lost First Round
1982-83			80	49	23	8	**1**	Lost First Round
3 yrs.	N Totals:		138	75	42	21		

Ted McCaskill

MCCASKILL, EDWARD JOEL 6′1″, 195 lbs.
B. Oct. 29, 1936, Kapuskasing, Ont.

			G	W	L	T	STANDING	PLAYOFF RESULT
1973-74	LA	W	59	20	39	0	6 **6**	

Bill McCreary

MCCREARY, WILLIAM EDWARD 5′10″, 172 lbs.
B. Dec. 2, 1934, Sundridge, Ont.

			G	W	L	T	STANDING	PLAYOFF RESULT
1971-72	STL	N	24	6	14	4	6 **6** 3	
1973-74	VAN	N	41	9	25	7	**8** 7	
1974-75	CALIF	N	32	8	20	4	4 **4**	
3 yrs.	N Totals:		97	23	59	15		

John McKenzie

MCKENZIE, JOHN ALBERT 5′9″, 175 lbs.
B. Dec. 12, 1937, High River, Alta.

			G	W	L	T	STANDING	PLAYOFF RESULT
1972-73	PHI	W	7	1	6	0	**6** 3	
1973-74	VAN	W	7	3	4	0	**4** 5	
2 yrs.	W Totals:		14	4	10	0		

John McLellan

MCLELLAN, DANIEL JOHN 5′11″, 150 lbs.
B. Aug. 6, 1928, South Porcupine, Ont.

			G	W	L	T	STANDING	PLAYOFF RESULT
1969-70	TOR	N	76	29	34	13	**6**	
1970-71			78	37	33	8	**4**	Lost First Round
1971-72			63	24	28	11	**5** 4	

John McLellan continued

			G	W	L	T	STANDING	PLAYOFF RESULT
1972-73			78	27	41	10	**6**	
4 yrs.	N Totals:		295	117	136	42		

Tom McVie

MCVIE, THOMAS
B. June 6, 1935, Trail, B.C.

			G	W	L	T	STANDING	PLAYOFF RESULT
1975-76	WASH	N	44	8	31	5	5 **5**	
1976-77			80	24	42	14	**4**	
1977-78			80	17	49	14	**5**	
1979-80	WINN	N	80	20	49	11	**5**	
1980-81			28	9	9	10	**6** 6	
5 yrs.	N Totals:		312	78	180	54		

Howie Meeker

MEEKER, HOWARD WILLIAM 5′8½″, 165 lbs.
B. Nov. 4, 1924, Kitchener, Ont.

			G	W	L	T	STANDING	PLAYOFF RESULT
1956-57	TOR	N	70	21	34	15	**5**	

Gerry Moore

MOORE, GERALD
B. Nov. 23, 1931, Ottawa, Ont.

			G	W	L	T	STANDING	PLAYOFF RESULT
1974-75	IND	W	78	18	57	3	**4**	

John Muckler

MUCKLER, JOHN
B. Apr. 3, 1934, Midland, Ont.

			G	W	L	T	STANDING	PLAYOFF RESULT
1968-69	MINN	N	35	6	23	6	6 **6** 6	

Pete Muldoon

MULDOON, PETER

			G	W	L	T	STANDING	PLAYOFF RESULT
1926-27	CHI	N	44	19	22	3	**3**	Lost First Round

Dunc Munro

MUNRO, DUNCAN B.
B. Toronto, Ont.

			G	W	L	T	STANDING	PLAYOFF RESULT
1929-30	MON(M)	N	44	23	16	5	**1**	Lost First Round
1930-31			32	14	13	5	**4** 3	
2 yrs.	N Totals:		76	37	29	10		

Bryan Murray

MURRAY, BRYAN
B. Dec. 5, 1942, Shawville, Que.

			G	W	L	T	STANDING	PLAYOFF RESULT
1981-82	WASH	N	66	25	28	13	5 **5**	
1982-83			80	39	25	16	**3**	Lost First Round
2 yrs.	N Totals:		146	64	53	29		

Lou Nanne

NANNE, LOUIS VINCENT (Sweet Lou from the Soo) 6′, 185 lbs.
B. June 2, 1941, Sault Ste. Marie, Ont.

			G	W	L	T	STANDING	PLAYOFF RESULT
1977-78	MINN	N	29	7	18	4	5 **5**	

Harry Neale

NEALE, HAROLD WATSON
B. Mar. 9, 1937, Sarnia, Ont.

			G	W	L	T	STANDING	PLAYOFF RESULT
1973-74	MINN	W	78	44	32	2	**2**	Lost Semifinals
1974-75			78	42	33	3	**3**	Lost Semifinals
1975-76			59	30	25	4	**4**	
	NE	W	12	5	6	1	3 **3**	Lost Semifinals
	2 team total		71	35	31	5		
1976-77			81	35	40	6	**4**	Lost First Round
1977-78			80	44	31	5	**2**	Lost League Finals
1978-79	VAN	N	80	25	42	13	**2**	Lost First Round
1979-80			80	27	37	16	**3**	Lost First Round
1980-81			80	28	32	20	**3**	Lost First Round
1981-82			75	26	33	16	**3** 2	
9 yrs.	N Totals:		315	106	144	65		
	W Totals:		388	200	167	21		

Bill Needham

NEEDHAM, WILLIAM ERIC 5'9", 175 lbs.

B. Jan. 12, 1932, Kirkland Lake, Ont.

Season	Team	Lg	G	W	L	T		STANDING		PLAYOFF RESULT
1972-73	CLEVE	W	78	43	32	3		**2**		Lost Semifinals
1973-74			78	37	32	9		**3**		Lost First Round
2 yrs.	W Totals:		156	80	64	12				

Roger Neilson

NEILSON, ROGER PAUL

B. June 16, 1934, Toronto, Ont.

Season	Team	Lg	G	W	L	T		STANDING		PLAYOFF RESULT
1977-78	TOR	N	80	41	29	10		**3**		Lost Semifinals
1978-79			80	34	33	13		**3**		Lost Quarterfinals
1980-81	BUF	N	80	39	20	21		**1**		Lost Quarterfinals
1981-82	VAN	N	5	4	0	1	3	**2**		Lost Cup Finals
1982-83			80	30	35	15		**3**		Lost First Round
5 yrs.	N Totals:		325	148	117	60				

Mike Nykoluk

NYKOLUK, MICHAEL 5'11", 212 lbs.

B. Dec. 11, 1934, Toronto, Ont.

Season	Team	Lg	G	W	L	T		STANDING		PLAYOFF RESULT
1980-81	TOR	N	40	15	15	10	4	**5**		Lost First Round
1981-82			80	20	44	16		**5**		
1982-83			80	28	40	12		**3**		Lost First Round
3 yrs.	N Totals:		200	63	99	38				

Murray Oliver

OLIVER, MURRAY CLIFFORD 5'9", 170 lbs.

B. Nov. 14, 1937, Hamilton, Ont.

Season	Team	Lg	G	W	L	T		STANDING		PLAYOFF RESULT
1982-83	MINN	N	36	18	11	7	2	**2**		Lost Quarterfinals

Bert Olmstead

OLMSTEAD, MURRAY BERT 6'2", 183 lbs.

B. Sept. 4, 1926, Scepter, Sask.

Season	Team	Lg	G	W	L	T		STANDING		PLAYOFF RESULT
1967-68	OAK	N	64	11	37	16		**6**	6	

Craig Patrick

PATRICK, CRAIG 6', 185 lbs.

B. May 20, 1946, Detroit, Mich.

Season	Team	Lg	G	W	L	T		STANDING		PLAYOFF RESULT
1980-81	NYR	N	59	26	23	10	5	**4**		Lost Semifinals

Frank Patrick

PATRICK, FRANKLIN

B. Dec. 21, 1885, Ottawa, Ont.

Season	Team	Lg	G	W	L	T		STANDING		PLAYOFF RESULT
1934-35	BOS	N	48	26	16	6		**1**		Lost First Round
1935-36			48	22	20	6		**2**		Lost First Round
2 yrs.	N Totals:		96	48	36	12				

Lester Patrick

PATRICK, LESTER 6'1", 180 lbs.

B. Dec. 30, 1883, Drummondville, Que.

Hall of Fame, 1945

Season	Team	Lg	G	W	L	T		STANDING		PLAYOFF RESULT
1926-27	NYR	N	44	25	13	6		**1**		Lost Semifinals
1927-28			44	19	16	9		**2**		**Won Stanley Cup**
1928-29			44	21	13	10		**2**		Lost Cup Finals
1929-30			44	17	17	10		**3**		Lost Semifinals
1930-31			44	19	16	9		**3**		Lost Semifinals
1931-32			48	23	17	8		**1**		Lost Cup Finals
1932-33			48	23	17	8		**3**		**Won Stanley Cup**
1933-34			48	21	19	8		**3**		Lost First Round
1934-35			48	22	20	6		**3**		Lost Semifinals
1935-36			48	19	17	12		**4**		
1936-37			48	19	20	9		**3**		Lost Cup Finals
1937-38			48	27	15	6		**2**		Lost First Round
1938-39			48	26	16	6		**2**		Lost First Round
13 yrs.	N Totals:		604	281	216	107				2 Cup Champions

Lynn Patrick

PATRICK, LYNN 6'1", 192 lbs.

B. Feb. 3, 1912, Victoria, B.C.

Hall of Fame, 1980

Season	Team	Lg	G	W	L	T		STANDING		PLAYOFF RESULT
1948-49	NYR	N	37	12	20	5	6	**6**		
1949-50			70	28	31	11		**4**		Lost Cup Finals
1950-51	BOS	N	70	22	30	18		**4**		Lost First Round
1951-52			70	25	29	16		**4**		Lost First Round
1952-53			70	28	19	13		**3**		Lost Cup Finals
1953-54			70	32	28	10		**4**		Lost First Round
1954-55			30	10	14	6		**4**	4	
1967-68	STL	N	16	4	10	2		**6**	3	
1974-75			2	1	0	1	4	**3**	2	
1975-76			8	3	5	0	3	**3**	3	
10 yrs.	N Totals:		443	165	186	82				

Muzz Patrick

PATRICK, FREDERICK MURRAY 6'2", 200 lbs.

B. June 28, 1915, Victoria, B.C.

Season	Team	Lg	G	W	L	T		STANDING		PLAYOFF RESULT
1953-54	NYR	N	32	17	11	4	5	**5**		
1954-55			70	17	35	18		**5**		
1962-63			34	11	19	4		**5**	5	
3 yrs.	N Totals:		136	45	65	26				

Don Perry

PERRY, DONALD FREDERICK

B. Mar. 16, 1930, Edmonton, Alta.

Season	Team	Lg	G	W	L	T		STANDING		PLAYOFF RESULT
1981-82	LA	N	38	11	17	10	4	**4**		Lost Quarterfinals
1982-83			80	27	41	12		**5**		
2 yrs.	N Totals:		118	38	58	22				

Alf Pike

PIKE, ALFRED G. 6', 187 lbs.

B. Sept. 15, 1917, Winnipeg, Man.

Season	Team	Lg	G	W	L	T		STANDING		PLAYOFF RESULT
1959-60	NYR	N	55	14	29	12	5	**6**		
1960-61			70	22	38	10		**5**		
2 yrs.	N Totals:		125	36	67	22				

Rudy Pilous

PILOUS, RUDOLF 6', 200 lbs.

B. Aug. 11, 1914, Winnipeg, Man.

Season	Team	Lg	G	W	L	T		STANDING		PLAYOFF RESULT
1957-58	CHI	N	70	24	39	7		**5**		
1958-59			70	28	29	13		**3**		Lost First Round
1959-60			70	28	29	13		**3**		Lost First Round
1960-61			70	29	24	17		**3**		**Won Stanley Cup**
1961-62			70	31	26	13		**3**		Lost Cup Finals
1962-63			70	32	21	17		**2**		Lost First Round
1974-75	WINN	W	37	18	17	2		**4**	3	
			28	16	9	3	5	**3**		
	2 team total		65	34	26	5				
7 yrs.	N Totals:		420	172	168	80				1 Cup Champion
	W Totals:		65	34	26	5				

Barclay Plager

PLAGER, BARCLAY GRAHAM 5'11", 175 lbs.

B. Mar. 26, 1941, Kirkland Lake, Ont.

Season	Team	Lg	G	W	L	T		STANDING		PLAYOFF RESULT
1977-78	STL	N	26	9	11	6	5	**4**		
1978-79			80	18	50	12		**3**		
1979-80			28	8	16	4		**3**	2	
1982-83			48	15	21	12	3	**4**		Lost First Round
4 yrs.	N Totals:		182	50	98	34				

Jacques Plante

PLANTE, JOSEPH JACQUES OMER (Jake the Snake) 6', 175 lbs.

B. Jan. 17, 1929, Mont Carmel, Que.

Hall of Fame, 1978

Season	Team	Lg	G	W	L	T		STANDING		PLAYOFF RESULT
1973-74	QUE	W	78	38	36	4		**5**		

Larry Pleau

PLEAU, LAWRENCE WINSLOW 6'1", 190 lbs.
B. Jan. 29, 1947, Lynn, Ma.

			G	W	L	T	STANDING	PLAYOFF RESULT
1980-81	**HART**	**N**	20	6	12	2	4 **4**	Lost First Round
1981-82			80	21	41	18	**5**	
1982-83			18	4	13	1	5 **5** 5	
3 yrs.		**N Totals:**	118	31	66	21		

Nick Polano

POLANO, NICHOLAS 6', 187 lbs.
B. Mar. 25, 1941, Sudbury, Ont.

			G	W	L	T	STANDING	PLAYOFF RESULT
1982-83	**DET**	**N**	80	21	44	15	**5**	

Larry Popein

POPEIN, LAWRENCE THOMAS (Pope) 5'9", 165 lbs.
B. Aug. 11, 1930, Yorkton, Sask.

			G	W	L	T	STANDING	PLAYOFF RESULT
1973-74	**NYR**	**N**	41	18	14	9	**4** 3	

Eddie Powers

POWERS, EDWARD

			G	W	L	T	STANDING	PLAYOFF RESULT
1921-22	**TOR**	**N**	24	13	10	1	**2**	**Won Stanley Cup**
1923-24			24	10	14	0	**3**	
1924-25			30	19	11	0	**2**	Lost First Round
1925-26			36	12	21	3	**6**	
4 yrs.		**N Totals:**	114	54	56	4		1 Cup Champion

Joe Primeau

PRIMEAU, JOE 5'11", 153 lbs.
B. Jan. 24, 1906, Lindsay, Ont.
Hall of Fame, 1963

			G	W	L	T	STANDING	PLAYOFF RESULT
1950-51	**TOR**	**N**	70	41	16	13	**2**	**Won Stanley Cup**
1951-52			70	29	25	16	**3**	Lost First Round
1952-53			70	27	30	13	**5**	
3 yrs.		**N Totals:**	210	97	71	42		1 Cup Champion

Marcel Pronovost

PRONOVOST, RENE MARCEL 6', 190 lbs.
B. June 15, 1930, Lac la Tortue, Que.
Hall of Fame, 1978

			G	W	L	T	STANDING	PLAYOFF RESULT
1972-73	**CHI**	**W**	78	26	50	2	**6**	
1977-78	**BUF**	**N**	80	44	19	17	**2**	Lost Quarterfinals
1978-79			24	8	10	6	**3** 2	
3 yrs.		**N Totals:**	104	52	29	23		
		W Totals:	78	26	50	2		

Bob Pulford

PULFORD, ROBERT JESSE 5'11", 188 lbs.
B. Mar. 31, 1936, Newton Robinson, Ont.
Won Jack Adams Award, 1974-75

			G	W	L	T	STANDING	PLAYOFF RESULT
1972-73	**LA**	**N**	78	31	36	11	**6**	
1973-74			78	33	33	12	**3**	Lost First Round
1974-75			80	42	17	21	**2**	Lost First Round
1975-76			80	38	33	9	**2**	Lost Quarterfinals
1976-77			80	34	31	15	**2**	Lost Quarterfinals
1977-78	**CHI**	**N**	80	32	29	19	**1**	Lost First Round
1978-79			80	29	36	15	**1**	Lost First Round
1981-82			28	12	14	2	4 **4**	Lost Semifinals
8 yrs.		**N Totals:**	584	251	229	104		

Charlie Querrie

QUERRIE, CHARLES
B. Unknown

			G	W	L	T	STANDING	PLAYOFF RESULT
1922-23	**TOR**	**N**	6	3	3	0	**3** 3	

Mike Quinn

QUINN, MICHAEL
B. Unknown

			G	W	L	T	STANDING	PLAYOFF RESULT
1919-20	**QUE**	**N**	24	4	20	0	**4**	

Pat Quinn

QUINN, JOHN BRIAN PATRICK 6'3", 215 lbs.
B. Jan. 29, 1943, Hamilton, Ont.
Won Jack Adams Award, 1979-80

			G	W	L	T	STANDING	PLAYOFF RESULT
1978-79	**PHI**	**N**	30	18	8	4	4 **2**	Lost Quarterfinals
1979-80			80	48	12	20	**1**	Lost Cup Finals
1980-81			80	41	24	15	**2**	Lost Quarterfinals
1981-82			72	34	29	9	**3** 3	
4 yrs.		**N Totals:**	262	141	73	48		

Billy Reay

REAY, WILLIAM 5'7", 155 lbs.
B. Aug. 21, 1918, Winnipeg, Man.

			G	W	L	T	STANDING	PLAYOFF RESULT
1957-58	**TOR**	**N**	70	21	38	11	**6**	
1958-59			20	5	12	3	**6** 4	
1963-64	**CHI**	**N**	70	36	22	12	**2**	Lost First Round
1964-65			70	34	28	8	**3**	Lost Cup Finals
1965-66			70	37	25	8	**2**	Lost First Round
1966-67			70	41	17	12	**1**	Lost First Round
1967-68			74	32	26	16	**4**	Lost Semifinals
1968-69			76	34	33	9	**6**	
1969-70			76	45	22	9	**1**	Lost Semifinals
1970-71			78	49	20	9	**1**	Lost Cup Finals
1971-72			78	46	17	15	**1**	Lost Semifinals
1972-73			78	42	27	9	**1**	Lost Cup Finals
1973-74			78	41	14	23	**2**	Lost Semifinals
1974-75			80	37	35	8	**3**	Lost Quarterfinals
1975-76			80	32	30	18	**1**	Lost First Round
1976-77			34	10	10	5	**2** 3	
16 yrs.		**N Totals:**	1102	542	376	175		

Larry Regan

REGAN, LAWRENCE EMMETT 5'9", 178 lbs.
B. Aug. 9, 1930, North Bay, Ont.

			G	W	L	T	STANDING	PLAYOFF RESULT
1970-71	**LA**	**N**	78	25	40	13	**5**	
1971-72			10	2	7	1	**7** 7	
2 yrs.		**N Totals:**	88	27	47	14		

Maurice Richard

RICHARD, JOSEPH HENRI MAURICE (The Rocket) 5'10", 195 lbs.
B. Aug. 4, 1921, Montreal, Que.
Hall of Fame, 1961

			G	W	L	T	STANDING	PLAYOFF RESULT
1972-73	**QUE**	**W**	2	1	1	0	**4** 5	

Jim Roberts

ROBERTS, JAMES WILFRED 5'10", 185 lbs.
B. Apr. 9, 1940, Toronto, Ont.

			G	W	L	T	STANDING	PLAYOFF RESULT
1981-82	**BUF**	**N**	45	21	15	9	1 **3** 3	

Al Rollins

ROLLINS, ELWIN IRA (Ally) 6'2", 175 lbs.
B. Oct. 9, 1926, Vanguard, Sask.

			G	W	L	T	STANDING	PLAYOFF RESULT
1976-77	**PHOE**	**W**	80	28	48	4	**6**	

Art Ross

ROSS, ARTHUR
B. Jan. 13, 1886, Naughton, Ont.
Hall of Fame, 1945

			G	W	L	T	STANDING	PLAYOFF RESULT
1917-18	**MON(W)**	**N**	6	1	5	0	**4**	
1922-23	**HAMIL**	**N**	24	6	18	0	**4**	
1924-25	**BOS**	**N**	30	6	24	0	**6**	
1925-26			36	17	15	4	**4**	
1926-27			44	21	20	3	**2**	Lost Cup Finals
1927-28			44	20	13	11	**1**	Lost Semifinals
1929-30			44	38	5	1	**1**	Lost Cup Finals
1930-31			44	28	10	6	**1**	Lost First Round
1931-32			48	15	21	12	**4**	
1932-33			48	25	15	8	**1**	Lost First Round
1933-34			48	18	25	5	**4**	
1936-37			48	23	18	7	**2**	Lost First Round
1937-38			48	30	11	7	**1**	Lost First Round
1938-39			48	36	10	2	**1**	**Won Stanley Cup**
1941-42			48	25	17	6	**3**	Lost Semifinals

Art Ross continued

Season	Team	Lg	G	W	L	T		STANDING		PLAYOFF RESULT
1942-43			50	24	17	9		**2**		Lost Semifinals
1943-44			50	19	26	5		**5**		
1944-45			50	16	30	4		**4**		Lost First Round
18 yrs.	**N Totals:**		758	368	300	90				1 Cup Champion

Claude Ruel
RUEL, CLAUDE

B. Sept. 12, 1938, Sherbrooke, Que.

Season	Team	Lg	G	W	L	T		STANDING		PLAYOFF RESULT
1968-69	**MONT**	**N**	76	46	19	11		**1**		**Won Stanley Cup**
1969-70			76	38	22	16		**5**		
1970-71			23	11	8	4		**3**	3	
1979-80			50	32	11	7	1	**1**		Lost Quarterfinals
1980-81			80	45	22	13		**1**		Lost First Round
5 yrs.	**N Totals:**		305	172	82	51				1 Cup Champion

Ron Ryan
RYAN, RONALD

B. July 11, 1938, Welland, Ont.

Season	Team	Lg	G	W	L	T		STANDING		PLAYOFF RESULT
1973-74	**NE**	**W**	78	43	31	4		**1**		Lost First Round
1974-75			73	40	28	5		**1**	1	
2 yrs.	**W Totals:**		151	83	59	9				

Glen Sather
SATHER, GLEN CAMERON (Slats) 5'11", 180 lbs.

B. Sept. 2, 1943, High River, Alta.

Season	Team	Lg	G	W	L	T		STANDING		PLAYOFF RESULT
1976-77	**EDM**	**W**	18	9	7	2	5	**4**		Lost First Round
1977-78			80	38	39	3		**5**		Lost First Round
1978-79			80	48	30	2		**1**		Lost League Finals
1979-80	**EDM**	**N**	80	28	39	13		**4**		Lost First Round
1980-81			62	25	26	11	5	**4**		Lost Quarterfinals
1981-82			80	48	17	15		**1**		Lost First Round
1982-83			80	47	21	12		**1**		Lost Cup Finals
7 yrs.	**N Totals:**		302	148	103	51				
	W Totals:		178	95	76	7				

Ken Schinkel
SCHINKEL, KENNETH CALVIN 5'10", 172 lbs.

B. Nov. 27, 1932, Jansen, Sask.

Season	Team	Lg	G	W	L	T		STANDING		PLAYOFF RESULT
1972-73	**PITT**	**N**	36	15	18	3	5	**5**		
1973-74			50	14	31	5		**7**	5	
1975-76			37	20	10	7	3	**3**		Lost First Round
1976-77			80	34	33	13		**3**		Lost First Round
4 yrs.	**N Totals:**		203	83	92	28				

Milt Schmidt
SCHMIDT, MILTON CONRAD 5'11", 180 lbs.

B. Mar. 5, 1918, Kitchener, Ont.

Hall of Fame, 1961

Season	Team	Lg	G	W	L	T		STANDING		PLAYOFF RESULT
1954-55	**BOS**	**N**	40	13	12	15	4	**4**		Lost First Round
1955-56			70	23	34	13		**5**		
1956-57			70	34	24	12		**3**		Lost Cup Finals
1957-58			70	27	28	15		**4**		Lost Cup Finals
1958-59			70	32	29	9		**2**		Lost First Round
1959-60			70	28	34	8		**5**		
1960-61			70	15	42	13		**6**		
1962-63			56	13	31	12	6	**6**		
1963-64			70	18	40	12		**6**		
1964-65			70	21	43	6		**6**		
1965-66			70	21	43	6		**5**		
1974-75	**WASH**	**N**	7	2	5	0	5	**5**		
1975-76			36	3	28	5		**5**	5	
13 yrs.	**N Totals:**		769	250	393	126				

Tom Shaughnessy
SHAUGHNESSY, THOMAS

B. Unknown

Season	Team	Lg	G	W	L	T		STANDING		PLAYOFF RESULT
1929-30	**CHI**	**N**	21	10	8	3		**2**	2	

Brian Shaw
SHAW, BRIAN

Season	Team	Lg	G	W	L	T		STANDING		PLAYOFF RESULT
1973-74	**EDM**	**W**	78	38	37	3		**3**		Lost First Round
1974-75			59	30	26	3		**3**	5	
2 yrs.	**W Totals:**		137	68	63	6				

Fred Shero
SHERO, FRED ALEXANDER (The Fog) 5'10", 185 lbs.

B. Oct. 23, 1925, Winnipeg, Man.

Won Jack Adams Award, 1973-74

Season	Team	Lg	G	W	L	T		STANDING		PLAYOFF RESULT
1971-72	**PHI**	**N**	78	26	38	14		**5**		
1972-73			78	37	30	11		**2**		Lost Semifinals
1973-74			78	50	16	12		**1**		**Won Stanley Cup**
1974-75			80	51	18	11		**1**		**Won Stanley Cup**
1975-76			80	51	13	16		**1**		Lost Cup Finals
1976-77			80	48	16	16		**1**		Lost Semifinals
1977-78			80	45	20	15		**2**		Lost Semifinals
1978-79	**NYR**	**N**	80	40	29	11		**3**		Lost Cup Finals
1979-80			80	38	32	10		**3**		Lost Quarterfinals
1980-81			21	4	13	4		**5**	4	
10 yrs.	**N Totals:**		735	390	225	120				2 Cup Champions

Joe Simpson
SIMPSON, JOE (Bullet)

B. Aug. 13, 1893, Selkirk, Man.

Hall of Fame, 1962

Season	Team	Lg	G	W	L	T		STANDING		PLAYOFF RESULT
1932-33	**NYA**	**N**	48	15	22	11		**4**		
1933-34			48	15	23	10		**4**		
1934-35			48	12	27	9		**4**		
3 yrs.	**N Totals:**		144	42	72	30				

Harry Sinden
SINDEN, HAROLD JAMES

B. Sept. 14, 1932, Collins Bay, Ont.

Season	Team	Lg	G	W	L	T		STANDING		PLAYOFF RESULT
1966-67	**BOS**	**N**	70	17	43	10		**6**		
1967-68			74	37	27	10		**3**		Lost First Round
1968-69			76	42	18	16		**2**		Lost Semifinals
1969-70			76	40	17	19		**2**		**Won Stanley Cup**
1979-80			7	6	1	0	2	**2**		Lost Quarterfinals
5 yrs.	**N Totals:**		303	142	106	55				1 Cup Champion

Jimmy Skinner
SKINNER, JAMES

B. Jan. 12, 1917, Selkirk, Man.

Season	Team	Lg	G	W	L	T		STANDING		PLAYOFF RESULT
1954-55	**DET**	**N**	70	42	17	11		**1**		**Won Stanley Cup**
1955-56			70	30	24	16		**2**		Lost Cup Finals
1956-57			70	38	20	12		**1**		Lost First Round
1957-58			37	13	17	7		**4**	3	
4 yrs.	**N Totals:**		247	123	78	46				1 Cup Champion

Terry Slater
SLATER, TERRANCE

B. Dec. 5, 1937, Kirkland Lake, Ont.

Season	Team	Lg	G	W	L	T		STANDING		PLAYOFF RESULT
1972-73	**LA**	**W**	78	37	35	6		**3**		Lost First Round
1973-74			19	5	14	0		**6**	6	
1975-76	**CIN**	**W**	80	35	44	1		**4**		
1976-77			81	39	37	5		**2**		Lost First Round
4 yrs.	**W Totals:**		258	116	130	12				

Cooper Smeaton
SMEATON, COOPER

B. July 22, 1890, Carlton Place, Ont.

Hall of Fame, 1961

Season	Team	Lg	G	W	L	T		STANDING		PLAYOFF RESULT
1930-31	**PHI**	**N**	44	4	36	4		**5**		

Alf Smith
SMITH, ALFRED

B. Unknown

Season	Team	Lg	G	W	L	T		STANDING		PLAYOFF RESULT
1918-19	**OTTA**	**N**	18	12	6	0		**1**		Lost League Finals

Floyd Smith

SMITH, FLOYD ROBERT DONALD 5'10", 180 lbs.
B. May 16, 1935, Perth, Ont.

Season	Team	Lg	G	W	L	T	Standing	Playoff Result
1971-72	BUF	N	1	0	1	0	6 **6** 6	
1974-75			80	49	16	15	**1**	Lost Cup Finals
1975-76			80	46	21	13	**2**	Lost Quarterfinals
1976-77			80	48	24	8	**2**	Lost Quarterfinals
1978-79	CIN	W	80	33	41	6	**5**	Lost First Round
1979-80	TOR	N	68	30	33	5	**3** 4	
6 yrs.	N Totals:		309	173	95	41		
	W Totals:		80	33	41	6		

Conn Smythe

SMYTHE, CONN
B. Feb. 1, 1895, Toronto, Ont.
Hall of Fame, 1958

Season	Team	Lg	G	W	L	T	Standing	Playoff Result
1926-27	TOR	N	44	15	24	5	**5**	
1927-28			44	18	18	8	**4**	
1928-29			44	21	18	5	**3**	Lost Semifinals
1929-30			44	17	21	6	**4**	
1930-31			2	1	0	1	**1** 2	
5 yrs.	N Totals:		178	72	81	25		

Glen Sonmor

SONMOR, GLEN ROBERT 5'11", 165 lbs.
B. Apr. 22, 1929, Moose Jaw, Sask.

Season	Team	Lg	G	W	L	T	Standing	Playoff Result
1972-73	MINN	W	79	39	37	3	**4**	Lost First Round
1976-77			42	19	18	5	**4**	
1977-78	BIRM	W	80	36	41	3	**6**	Lost First Round
1978-79	MINN	N	4	2	2	0	4 **3** 4	
			65	23	32	10	4 **4**	
	2 team total		69	25	34	10		
1979-80			80	36	28	16	**3**	Lost Semifinals
1980-81			80	35	28	17	**3**	Lost Cup Finals
1981-82			80	37	23	20	**1**	Lost First Round
1982-83			44	22	13	9	**2** 2	
8 yrs.	N Totals:		353	155	126	72		
	W Totals:		201	94	96	11		

Harry Sproule

SPROULE, HAROLD
B. Unknown

Season	Team	Lg	G	W	L	T	Standing	Playoff Result
1919-20	TOR	N	12	7	5	0	3 **2**	

Barney Stanley

STANLEY, BARNEY
B. Jan. 1, 1893, Paisley, Ont.

Season	Team	Lg	G	W	L	T	Standing	Playoff Result
1927-28	CHI	N	23	4	17	2	**5** 5	

Pat Stapleton

STAPLETON, PATRICK JAMES 5'8", 185 lbs.
B. July 4, 1940, Sarnia, Ont.

Season	Team	Lg	G	W	L	T	Standing	Playoff Result
1973-74	CHI	W	78	38	35	5	**4**	Lost League Finals
1974-75			78	30	47	1	**4**	
1978-79	IND	W	25	5	18	2	**7**	
3 yrs.	W Totals:		181	73	100	8		

Vic Stasiuk

STASIUK, VICTOR JOHN 6'1", 185 lbs.
B. May 23, 1929, Lethbridge, Alta.

Season	Team	Lg	G	W	L	T	Standing	Playoff Result
1969-70	PHI	N	76	17	35	24	**5**	
1970-71			78	28	33	17	**3**	Lost First Round
1971-72	CALIF	N	75	21	38	16	4 **6**	
1972-73	VAN	N	78	22	47	9	**7**	
4 yrs.	N Totals:		307	88	153	66		

Bill Stewart

STEWART, WILLIAM

Season	Team	Lg	G	W	L	T	Standing	Playoff Result
1937-38	CHI	N	48	14	25	9	**3**	**Won Stanley Cup**
1938-39			21	8	10	3	**5** 7	
2 yrs.	N Totals:		69	22	35	12		1 Cup Champion

Ron Stewart

STEWART, RONALD GEORGE 6'1", 197 lbs.
B. July 11, 1932, Calgary, Alta.

Season	Team	Lg	G	W	L	T	Standing	Playoff Result
1975-76	NYR	N	39	15	20	4	**4** 4	
1977-78	LA	N	80	31	34	15	**3**	Lost First Round
2 yrs.	N Totals:		119	46	54	19		

Red Sullivan

SULLIVAN, GEORGE JAMES (Red) 5'11", 160 lbs.
B. Dec. 24, 1929, Peterborough, Ont.

Season	Team	Lg	G	W	L	T	Standing	Playoff Result
1962-63	NYR	N	36	11	17	8	5 **5**	
1963-64			70	22	38	10	**5**	
1964-65			70	20	38	12	**5**	
1965-66			20	5	10	5	**5** 6	
1967-68	PITT	N	74	27	34	13	**5**	
1968-69			76	20	45	11	**5**	
1974-75	WASH	N	19	2	17	0	5 **5** 5	
7 yrs.	N Totals:		365	107	199	59		

Bill Sutherland

SUTHERLAND, WILLIAM FRASER 5'10", 176 lbs.
B. Nov. 10, 1934, Regina, Sask.

Season	Team	Lg	G	W	L	T	Standing	Playoff Result
1980-81	WINN	N	52	8	37	7	6 **6**	

Jean-Guy Talbot

TALBOT, JEAN-GUY 5'11", 170 lbs.
B. July 11, 1932, Cap Madelaine, Que.

Season	Team	Lg	G	W	L	T	Standing	Playoff Result
1972-73	STL	N	65	30	28	7	7 **4**	Lost First Round
1973-74			55	22	25	8	**4** 6	
1975-76	D-O	W	41	14	26	1	**6**	
1977-78	NYR	N	80	30	37	13	**4**	Lost First Round
4 yrs.	N Totals:		200	82	90	28		
	W Totals:		41	14	26	1		

Orval Tessier

TESSIER, ORVAL ROY 5'8", 160 lbs.
B. June 30, 1933, Cornwall, Ont.
Won Jack Adams Award, 1982-83

Season	Team	Lg	G	W	L	T	Standing	Playoff Result
1982-83	CHI	N	80	47	23	10	**1**	Lost Semifinals

Paul Thompson

THOMPSON, PAUL IVAN 5'10½", 180 lbs.
B. Nov. 2, 1906, Calgary, Alta.

Season	Team	Lg	G	W	L	T	Standing	Playoff Result
1938-39	CHI	N	27	4	18	5	5 **7**	
1939-40			48	23	19	6	**4**	Lost First Round
1940-41			48	16	25	7	**5**	Lost Semifinals
1941-42			48	22	23	3	**4**	Lost First Round
1942-43			50	17	18	15	**5**	
1943-44			50	22	23	5	**4**	Lost Cup Finals
1944-45			1	0	1	0	**3** 5	
7 yrs.	N Totals:		272	104	127	41		

Percy Thompson

THOMPSON, PERCIVAL
B. Unknown

Season	Team	Lg	G	W	L	T	Standing	Playoff Result
1920-21	HAMIL	N	24	7	17	0	**4**	
1921-22			24	7	17	0	**4**	
2 yrs.	N Totals:		48	14	34	0		

Bill Tobin

TOBIN, WILLIAM
B. Unknown

Season	Team	Lg	G	W	L	T	Standing	Playoff Result
1929-30	CHI	N	23	11	10	2	2 **2**	Lost First Round

Jack Vivian

VIVIAN, JAMES
B. May 14, 1941, Strathroy, Ont.

Season	Team	Lg	G	W	L	T	Standing	Playoff Result
1974-75	CLEVE	W	45	21	22	2	2 **2**	Lost First Round

Bryan Watson

WATSON, BRYAN JOSEPH (Bugsy) 5'10", 175 lbs.
B. Nov. 14, 1942, Bancroft, Ont.

			G	W	L	T	STANDING	PLAYOFF RESULT
1980-81	**EDM**	**N**	18	4	9	5	**5** 4	

Phil Watson

WATSON, PHILIP HENRY 5'11", 165 lbs.
B. Apr. 24, 1914, Montreal, Que.

			G	W	L	T	STANDING	PLAYOFF RESULT
1955-56	**NYR**	**N**	70	32	28	10	**3**	Lost First Round
1956-57			70	26	30	14	**4**	Lost First Round
1957-58			70	32	25	13	**2**	Lost First Round
1958-59			70	26	32	12	**5**	
1959-60			15	3	9	3	**5** 6	
1961-62	**BOS**	**N**	70	15	47	8	**6**	
1962-63			14	1	8	5	**6** 6	
1972-73	**PHI**	**W**	71	37	34	0	6 **3**	Lost First Round
1973-74	**VAN**	**W**	12	3	9	0	4 **5** 5	
9 yrs.	**N Totals:**		379	135	179	65		
	W Totals:		83	40	43	0		

Tom Watt

WATT, THOMAS
B. June 17, 1935, Toronto, Ont.
Won Jack Adams Award, 1981-82

			G	W	L	T	STANDING	PLAYOFF RESULT
1981-82	**WINN**	**N**	80	33	33	14	**2**	Lost First Round
1982-83			80	33	39	8	**4**	Lost First Round
2 yrs.	**N Totals:**		160	66	72	22		

Cooney Weiland

WEILAND, RALPH 5'7", 150 lbs.
B. Nov. 5, 1904, Seaforth, Ont.
Hall of Fame, 1971

			G	W	L	T	STANDING	PLAYOFF RESULT
1939-40	**BOS**	**N**	48	31	12	5	**1**	Lost First Round
1940-41			48	27	8	13	**1**	**Won Stanley Cup**
2 yrs.	**N Totals:**		96	58	20	18		1 Cup Champion

Bill White

WHITE, WILLIAM EARL 6'1", 195 lbs.
B. Aug. 26, 1939, Toronto, Ont.

			G	W	L	T	STANDING	PLAYOFF RESULT
1976-77	**CHI**	**N**	46	16	24	6	2 **3**	Lost First Round

Johnny Wilson

WILSON, JOHN EDWARD (The Iron Man) 5'10", 175 lbs.
B. June 14, 1929, Kincardine, Ont.

			G	W	L	T	STANDING	PLAYOFF RESULT
1969-70	**LA**	**N**	52	9	34	9	6 **6**	
1971-72	**DET**	**N**	67	30	27	10	7 **5**	
1972-73			78	37	29	12	**5**	
1974-75	**M-B**	**W**	78	21	53	4	**5**	
1975-76	**CLEVE**	**W**	80	35	40	5	**2**	Lost First Round
1976-77	**COLO**	**N**	80	20	46	14	**5**	
1977-78	**PITT**	**N**	80	25	37	18	**4**	
1978-79			80	36	31	13	**2**	Lost Quarterfinals
1979-80			80	30	37	13	**3**	Lost First Round
9 yrs.	**N Totals:**		517	187	241	89		
	W Totals:		158	56	93	9		

Larry Wilson

WILSON, LAWRENCE 5'11", 170 lbs.
B. Oct. 23, 1930, Kincardine, Ont.

			G	W	L	T	STANDING	PLAYOFF RESULT
1976-77	**DET**	**N**	36	3	29	4	5 **5**	

Garry Young

YOUNG, GERALD
B. Jan. 2, 1936, Toronto, Ont.

			G	W	L	T	STANDING	PLAYOFF RESULT
1972-73	**CALIF**	**N**	12	2	7	3	**8** 8	
1974-75	**STL**	**N**	69	32	26	11	3 **2**	Lost First Round
1975-76			29	9	15	5	**3** 3	
3 yrs.	**N Totals:**		110	43	48	19		

The Teams and their Players

The Teams and their Players is a chronological listing of team standings, league leaders, basic team rosters, and player and goaltender records for every National Hockey League and World Hockey Association season. This section, which serves as a cross-reference to the Player Register and Goaltender Register sections, and makes it possible to answer such questions as who was the primary goaltender for the Toronto Maple Leafs in 1942–43, or who were Maurice Richard's linemates in the 1955–56 season. It also gives the yearly league leaders in many statistical categories, and provides such additional information as individuals' shots on goal and shooting percentage since the NHL's expansion in 1967–68, and complete coaching records.

All teams are presented in their order of standing for the season. All abbreviations that may appear unfamiliar are explained below.

	POS	PLAYER	GP	G	A	PTS	SOG	SPct.	PPG	+/–	GOALIE	W	L	T	GAvg.
NYI	LW	C. Gilles	79	38	39	77	200	19.0	8	26	B. Smith	32	9	4	2.97
A. Arbour	C	B. Trottier	80	50	79	129	217	23.0	**18**	48	Melanson	22	7	6	3.23
54-16-10	RW	B. Bourne	76	27	26	53	173	15.6	5	18					
	LW	B. Sutter	43	21	22	43	93	22.6	3	9					
	C	B. Goring	67	15	17	32	63	23.8	1	12					
	RW	M. Bossy	80	64	83	**147**	301	21.3	17	52					
	LW	J. Tonelli	80	35	58	93	165	21.2	5	26					
	RW	B. Nystrom	74	22	25	47	136	16.2	0	8					
	RW	A. Kallur	58	18	22	40	74	**24.3**	2	10					
	RW	H. Marini	30	4	9*	13	14	28.6	1	6					
	F	D. Sutter	77	18	35	53	90	20.0	4	12					
	F	B. Carroll	72	9	20	29	42	21.4	0	–6					
	D	D. Potvin	60	24	37	61	169	14.2	11	31					
	D	M. McEwen	73	10	39	49	161	6.2	1	11					
	D	S. Persson	70	6	37	43	107	5.6	3	4					
	D	T. Jonsson	70	9	25	34	89	10.1	0	–3					
	D	D. Langevin	73	1	20	21	73	1.4	0	8					
	D	K. Morrow	75	1	18	19	91	1.1	0	10					

POS Position
GP Games Played
G Goals Scored
A Assists
PTS Points
SOG Shots on Goal (See below)
SPct. Shooting Percentage
PPG Power Play Goals
+/– Plus-Minus Rating (See below)
W Wins
L Losses
T Ties
GAvg. Goals against Average

The abbreviations for the team rosters appear as listed below. The team's current name is listed as well; past names for teams in that location are listed in parentheses.

NHL

ATL	Atlanta Flames (Moved to Calgary in 1980)	MON (M)	Montreal Maroons
BOS	Boston Bruins	MON (W)	Montreal Wanderers
BUF	Buffalo Sabres	MONT	Montreal Canadiens
CALG	Calgary Flames	NJ	New Jersey Devils
CALIF	California Seals (1968–69 and 1975–76; Golden Seals 1970–75; known as Oakland Seals (OAK) in 1969–70)	NYA	New York Americans
CHI	Chicago Black Hawks	NYI	New York Islanders
CLEVE	Cleveland Barons (Merged with Minnesota in 1978)	NYR	New York Rangers
COLO	Colorado Rockies (Moved to New Jersey in 1982)	OAK	Oakland Seals
DET	Detroit Red Wings (Cougars 1926–29, Falcons 1929–33)	OTTA	Ottawa Senators
EDM	Edmonton Oilers	PHI	Philadelphia Flyers (1967– , or Philadelphia Quakers, 1930–31)
HAMIL	Hamilton Tigers	PITT	Pittsburgh Penguins (1967– , or Pittsburgh Pirates, 1925–1930)
HART	Hartford Whalers	QUE	Quebec Nordiques (1979– , or Quebec Bulldogs, 1919–1920)
KC	Kansas City Scouts (Moved to Colorado in 1976)	STL	St. Louis Blues (1967–?, or St. Louis Eagles, 1934–35)
LA	Los Angeles Kings	TOR	Toronto Maple Leafs (Arenas, 1917–19; St. Patricks, 1919–26)
MINN	Minnesota North Stars	VAN	Vancouver Canucks
		WASH	Washington Capitals
		WINN	Winnipeg Jets

Directly beneath the city abbreviation is the team's won-lost-tied record and the name of the man who coached the team. Teams with more than one coach in a season have their coaches listed in the order in which they coached. (For a detailed explanation of the evolution of the role of coach in professional ice hockey, see the introduction to the Coaching Register.)

Roster Selections. During any given season, as many as 30 different players might play for a single team. In order to present the most meaningful players on each team, we have limited the rosters to 12 players from 1917–18 to 1925–26, 15 players from 1926–27 to 1966–67, and 18 players from 1967–68 on. These rosters may omit such specialty players as enforcers added to a lineup to lend muscle, penalty killers, and similar part–time players. The players selected represent the most important players for that team in that year, as judged by the collective opinion of hockey historians who have studied the era.

Linemates. In many cases throughout this section, the first listed players are three-player combinations of Left Wing, Center, and Right Wing. These represent firm forward line combinations that were kept largely intact through the season.

Early professional teams were often content to employ a basic six-man team for the full 60 minutes of a game, retaining only a few reserves for emergencies. These three-man forward units became renowned throughout the league. The New York Rangers of the late 1920s and 1930s were led by their Cook-Boucher-Cook combination, with Frank Boucher centering for brothers Bill and Bun Cook. Toronto boasted the Kid Line with Joe Primeau centering for Busher Jackson and Charlie Conacher.

In more modern times, with the advent of second and third forward lines, it became more commonplace to juggle lines. Nevertheless, set units remained. Perhaps the most famous were the Montreal Canadiens' Punch Line of Maurice Richard, Elmer Lach, and Toe Blake; and the Detroit Red Wings' Production Line of Gordie Howe, Sid Abel, and Ted Lindsay.

In the post-expansion era, coaches began to utilize as many as four forward lines. Teams coached by Scotty Bowman and Al Arbour saw almost constant line juggling, and the success of their tactics led to wide imitation. Today, it is rare for a forward line, no matter how successful, to last through a season intact.

Multiple Team Players. If a man played for more than one team in a given year, his record as listed is only for the team indicated.

League Leaders. If a player was the league leader in a listed category, his record is marked in boldface. If he was traded during a season in which he led the league in a category, his listed total for a team may not reflect his league leading total. Such records are marked with an asterisk.

Shots on Goal. In the NHL, shots on goal are calculated by official scorers designated by the league. A shot on goal is recorded any time a player takes a shot that either scores a goal or would have been a goal if the goaltender had not stopped it. While the value of shots on goal statistics have always been questioned by serious students of the game, when combined with shooting percentage they provide an important measure of the quantity and quality of the shots taken by a player.

Plus-Minus Rating. Plus-minus ratings are calculated by giving a player a "plus" when he is on ice for an even-strength or shorthanded goal scored by his team, and a "minus" when on ice for an even-strength or shorthanded goal allowed by his team. The plusses and minuses are then totalled to give the player's plus-minus rating.

For years coaches and managers had argued that goals, assists, and points scored did not provide an adequate picture of a player's performance, especially in the case of high scorers who played little defense. For such players, the number of goals scored against his team while he is on ice could well outweigh his scoring contributions. Attempts to keep track of such records were informal and sporadic until the early 1960s, when Emile Francis became general manager of the New York Rangers. Francis formalized what later became the official plus-minus rating. Plus-minus was not recognized as an official statistic by the NHL until 1982; we present here records for individual plus-minus ratings going back to the expansion of 1967–68.

Goalie Won-Lost-Tied Records. If a team employs more than one goaltender in a game, the goaltender of record is the goalie in the nets when the winning goal is scored, regardless of how much time he eventually spends in the nets. Say Philadelphia starts Pelle Lindbergh in a game and falls behind 4–0, then replaces Lindbergh with Bob Froese, whereupon they come back to take a lead of 5–4. If Philadelphia ultimately loses the game 6–5 with Froese still in the nets, Froese will get the loss.

Goals against Average. As noted in the All-Time Leaders section, goals against averages from 1942–43 to 1966–67 have been recalculated to reflect goals per 60 minutes played, rather than being divided by games played as done in the official records. It is our belief that this method better reflects the performance of goal tenders who have played in parts of a game.

Yearly League Leaders

Appearing directly after the roster information are yearly league leaders. The categories generally include the top five players in the league in the given category. If ties would require one additional player to be listed, that player is listed. If the ties would require listing more than one additional player, the entire last tied group is omitted.

For the categories requiring calculation of a percentage (shooting percentage for players, goals against average for goaltenders), the following qualification levels have been used: players must have played in not less than 60% of their team's games, goaltenders in not less than 40% of their team's games.

League Column Headings Information

TEAM	W	L	T	PTS	GF	GA	PPG	PPPct.	SHG	PPGA	PKPct.	SHGA
CAMPBELL CONFERENCE												
NORRIS DIVISION												
MINN	37	23	20	94	**346**	288	89	24.6	11	**49**	81.9	9
WINN*	33	33	14	80	319	332	74	22.6	4	61	75.5	11
STL	32	40	8	72	315	349	76	22.1	10	83	76.8	13
CHI	30	38	12	72	332	363	78	**24.8**	13	93	75.7	12
TOR	20	44	16	56	298	380	58	19.9	10	99	72.7	6
DET	21	47	12	54	270	351	43	16.7	10	75	73.6	6

W	Wins	PPG	Power Play Goals
L	Losses	PPPct.	Power Play Percentage
T	Ties	SHG	Shorthanded Goals
PTS	Points	PPGA	Power Play Goals Against
GF	Goals For	PKPct.	Penalty Killing Percentage
GA	Goals Against	SHGA	Shorthanded Goals Against

League Leaders, Team Information. Statistics that appear in boldface indicate that the team led the league in that particular category for the season. The leaders for Goals Against, Power Play Goals Against, and Shorthanded Goals Against are those teams which allowed the fewest in each category.

Power Play Percentage. The percentage of power play opportunities in which a team scores. Power play percentage equals power play goals divided by power play opportunities.

Penalty Killing Percentage. Penalty Killing Percentage measures a team's ability to prevent goals while its opponent is on a power play. It is calculated by dividing power play goals by opportunities.

Stanley Cup Champion. The team that won the Stanley Cup is noted with an asterisk in the team standings. In the example above, Winnipeg (WINN) won the Stanley Cup.

TEAM	W	L	T	PTS	GF	GA
MONT	13	9	0	26	**115**	**84**
*TOR	13	9	0	26	108	109
OTTA	9	13	0	18	102	114
MON(W)	1	5	0	2	17	35

	POS	PLAYER	GP	G	A	PTS		PLAYER	GP	G	A	PTS	GOALIE	W	L	T	GAvg
MONT	LW	J. Malone	20	**44**	0	**44**	D	J. Hall	20	8	0	8	G. Vezina	**13**	9	0	**3.82**
G. Kennedy	C	N. Lalonde	14	23	0	23	D	B. Corbeau	20	8	0	8					
13–9–0	RW	D. Pitre	19	17	0	17	D	J. Laviolette	18	2	0	2					
	F	J. McDonald	8	9	0	9	D	B. Couture	19	2	0	2					
	F	L. Berlinquette	20	2	0	2	D	E. Payer	1	0	0	0					
	F	B. Bell	6	1	0	1											
TOR	LW	C. Denneny	21	20	0	20	D	H. Cameron	20	17	0	17	H. Holmes	10	6	0	4.75
D. Carroll	C	R. Noble	20	28	0	28	D	K. Randall	20	12	0	12	A. Brooks	2	2	0	5.75
13–9–0	RW	A. Skinner	19	13	0	13	D	H. Mummery	18	3	0	3	S. Hebert	1	1	0	5.00
	F	H. Meeking	20	10	0	10											
	F	R. Crawford	9	2	0	2											
	F	J. Coughlin	6	2	0	2											
	F	M. Neville	1	1	0	1											
	F	J. Marks	5	0	0	0											
	F	J. Adams	8	0	0	0											
OTTA	LW	C. Denneny	22	36	0	36	D	E. Gerard	21	13	0	13	C. Benedict	9	**13**	0	5.18
E. Gerard	C	F. Nighbor	9	11	0	11	D	G. Boucher	22	9	0	9					
9–13–0	RW	J. Darragh	18	14	0	14	D	H. Shore	18	3	0	3					
	F	H. Hyland	12	8	0	8	D	H. Merrill	4	0	0	0					
	F	E. Lowrey	11	0	0	0	D	D. Ritchie	13	4	0	4					
	F	S. Robert	1	0	0	0	D	M. Bruce	7	0	0	0					
MON(W)	F	J. McDonald	4	3	0	3	D	D. Ritchie	4	5	0	5	B. Lindsay	1	5	0	8.75
A. Ross	F	H. Hyland	4	6	0	6	D	P. Stephens	4	1	0	1					
1–5–0	F	G. Geran	4	0	0	0	D	A. Ross	3	1	0	1					
	F	G. O'Grady	4	0	0	0	D	R. Skilton	1	0	0	0					
	F	K. Thompson	1	0	0	0											
	F	B. Bell	2	0	0	0											
	F	J. Marks	1	0	0	0											

GOALS

J. Malone, MONT	44
C. Denneny, OTTA	36
R. Noble, TOR	28
N. Lalonde, MONT	23
C. Denneny, TOR	20

ASSISTS

No official records kept

POINTS

J. Malone, MONT	44
C. Denneny, OTTA	36
R. Noble, TOR	28
N. Lalonde, MONT	23
C. Denneny, TOR	20

PENALTY MINUTES

J. Hall, MONT	60
K. Randall, TOR	55
H. Hyland, OTTA	34
C. Denneny, OTTA	34
R. Crawford, TOR	33

GOALS AGAINST AVE.

G. Vezina, MONT	3.82
H. Holmes, TOR	4.75
C. Benedict, OTTA	5.18

SHUTOUTS

G. Vezina, MONT	1
C. Benedict, OTTA	1

National Hockey League 1918–19

TEAM	W	L	T	PTS	GF	GA
OTTA	12	6	0	24	71	**54**
MONT	10	8	0	20	**88**	78
TOR	5	13	0	10	65	92

	POS	PLAYER	GP	G	A	PTS		PLAYER	GP	G	A	PTS	GOALIE	W	L	T	GAvg
OTTA	LW	C. Denneny	18	18	4	22	D	H. Cameron	7	4	1	5	C. Benedict	**12**	6	0	**2.94**
A. Smith	C	F. Nighbor	18	18	4	22	D	S. Cleghorn	18	6	6	12					
12–6–0	RW	J. Darragh	14	12	1	13	D	E. Gerard	18	4	6	10					
	F	P. Broadbent	8	4	2	6	D	G. Boucher	17	5	2	7					
	F	E. Lowrey	10	0	0	0											
	F	S. Ronan	11	0	0	0											

TEAM	POS	PLAYER	GP	G	A	PTS	POS	PLAYER	GP	G	A	PTS	GOALIE	W	L	T	GAvg
MONT	LW	D. Pitre	17	14	4	18	D	J. Hall	17	7	1	8	G. Vezina	10	8	0	4.33
G. Kennedy	C	O. Cleghorn	17	**23**	6	29	D	B. Corbeau	16	2	1	3					
10–8–0	RW	N. Lalonde	17	**23**	**9**	**32**	D	B. Couture	15	1	1	2					
	F	J. McDonald	18	8	4	12	D	B. Bell	1	0	0	0					
	F	J. Malone	8	7	1	8											
	F	L. Berlinquette	18	5	3	8											
	F	A. Arbour	1	0	0	0											
	F	F. Doherty	3	0	0	0											
TOR	LW	C. Denneny	16	7	3	10	D	K. Randall	14	7	6	13	B. Lindsay	5	**11**	0	5.19
D. Carroll	C	R. Noble	17	11	3	14	D	H. Mummery	13	2	0	2	H. Holmes	0	2	0	4.50
5–13–0	RW	A. Skinner	17	12	3	15	D	D. Ritchie	4	0	0	0					
	F	H. Meeking	14	7	3	10	D	P. Jacobs	1	0	0	0					
	F	J. Adams	17	3	3	6											
	F	R. Crawford	18	7	3	10											

GOALS

N. Lalonde, MONT	23
O. Cleghorn, MONT	23
F. Nighbor, OTTA	18
C. Denneny, OTTA	18
D. Pitre, MONT	14

ASSISTS

N. Lalonde, MONT	9
O. Cleghorn, MONT	6
K. Randall, TOR	6
S. Cleghorn, OTTA	6
E. Gerard, OTTA	6

POINTS

N. Lalonde, MONT	32
O. Cleghorn, MONT	29
F. Nighbor, OTTA	22
C. Denneny, OTTA	22
D. Pitre, MONT	18

PENALTY MINUTES

J. Hall, MONT	85
R. Crawford, TOR	51
B. Corbeau, MONT	51
C. Denneny, OTTA	43
N. Lalonde, MONT	40

GOALS AGAINST AVE.

C. Benedict, OTTA	2.94
G. Vezina, MONT	4.33
B. Lindsay, TOR	5.19

SHUTOUTS

C. Benedict, OTTA	2
G. Vezina, MONT	1

National Hockey League 1919–20

TEAM	W	L	T	PTS	GF	GA
*OTTA	19	5	0	38	121	**64**
MONT	13	11	0	26	**129**	113
TOR	12	12	0	24	119	106
QUE	4	20	0	8	91	177

TEAM	POS	PLAYER	GP	G	A	PTS	POS	PLAYER	GP	G	A	PTS	GOALIE	W	L	T	GAvg
OTTA	LW	C. Denneny	22	16	2	18	D	S. Cleghorn	21	16	5	21	C. Benedict	**19**	5	0	**2.67**
P. Green	C	F. Nighbor	23	26	7	33	D	G. Boucher	22	10	4	14					
19–5–0	RW	J. Darragh	22	22	5	27	D	E. Gerard	21	9	3	12					
	F	P. Broadbent	20	19	4	23	D	J. McKell	21	2	0	2					
	F	Price	1	0	0	0	D	M. Bruce	21	1	0	1					
							D	H. Merrill	7	0	0	0					
MONT	LW	L. Berlinquette	24	7	7	14	D	B. Corbeau	23	11	5	16	G. Vezina	13	11	0	4.71
G. Kennedy	C	N. Lalonde	23	36	6	42	D	H. Cameron	16	8	5	13					
13–11–0	RW	D. Pitre	22	15	7	22	D	B. Couture	17	4	0	4					
	F	O. Cleghorn	21	19	3	22	D	H. McNamara	11	1	0	1					
	F	A. Arbour	20	22	4	26											
	F	D. Smith	10	1	0	1											
TOR	LW	C. Denneny	23	23	**12**	35	D	J. Matte	16	8	2	10	I. Mitchell	7	7	0	4.33
F. Heffernan	C	R. Noble	24	24	7	31	D	K. Randall	21	10	7	17	H. Lockhart	4	1	0	4.00
5–7–0	RW	C. Wilson	23	21	5	26							J. Forbes	1	4	0	4.20
H. Sproule	F	B. Dye	21	12	3	15											
7–5–0	F	G. Prodgers	16	8	6	14											
	F	M. Roach	20	10	2	12											
	F	F. Heffernan	17	0	0	0											
QUE	LW	J. McDonald	24	7	6	13	D	H. Mummery	24	9	6	15	F. Brophy	3	**18**	0	7.05
M. Quinn	C	J. Malone	24	**39**	6	**45**	D	E. Carpenter	24	8	3	11	H. Mummery	1	1	0	6.00
4–20–0	RW	G. Carey	20	11	5	16	D	D. Ritchie	21	6	3	9	H. Lockhart	0	1	0	11.00
	F	T. McCarthy	12	11	2	13	D	F. McLean	7	0	0	0					
	F	T. Smith	10	0	0	0	D	Carr	1	0	0	0					
	F	J. Marks	1	0	0	0											
	F	G. McNaughton	1	0	0	0											

GOALS		ASSISTS		POINTS	
J. Malone, QUE	39	C. Denneny, TOR	12	J. Malone, QUE	48
N. Lalonde, MONT	36	K. Randall, TOR	7	N. Lalonde, MONT	42
F. Nighbor, OTTA	26	F. Nighbor, OTTA	7	C. Denneny, TOR	35
R. Noble, TOR	24	R. Noble, TOR	7	F. Nighbor, OTTA	33
C. Denneny, TOR	23	D. Pitre, MONT	7	R. Noble, TOR	31

PENALTY MINUTES		GOALS AGAINST AVE.		SHUTOUTS	
C. Wilson, TOR	79	C. Benedict, OTTA	2.67	C. Benedict, OTTA	5
S. Cleghorn, OTTA	62	I. Mitchell, TOR	4.33		
B. Corbeau, MONT	59	G. Vezina, MONT	4.71		
R. Noble, TOR	51	F. Brophy, QUE	7.05		
K. Randall, TOR	43				

National Hockey League 1920–21

TEAM	W	L	T	PTS	GF	GA
TOR	15	9	0	30	105	100
*OTTA	14	10	0	28	97	**75**
MONT	13	11	0	26	**112**	99
HAMIL	6	18	0	12	92	132

	POS	PLAYER	GP	G	A	PTS		PLAYER	GP	G	A	PTS	GOALIE	W	L	T	GAvg
TOR	LW	C. Denneny	20	17	6	23	D	H. Cameron	24	18	**9**	27	J. Forbes	13	7	0	3.90
D. Carroll	C	R. Noble	24	20	6	26	D	K. Randall	21	6	1	7	I. Mitchell	2	2	0	5.50
15–9–0	RW	B. Dye	23	33*	2	35	D	B. Stuart	18	2	1	3					
	F	R. Smylie	23	2	0	2	D	S. Cleghorn	13	3	4	7					
	F	J. McDonald	8	0	1	1											
OTTA	LW	C. Denneny	24	34	5	39	D	G. Boucher	23	12	5	17	C. Benedict	**14**	10	0	**3.13**
P. Green	C	F. Nighbor	24	18	3	21	D	S. Cleghorn	3	2	1	3					
14–10–0	RW	J. Darragh	24	11	8	19	D	E. Gerard	24	11	4	15					
	F	P. Broadbent	9	4	1	5	D	M. Bruce	21	3	1	4					
							D	J. McKell	21	2	1	3					
							D	L. Graham	13	0	0	0					
MONT	LW	L. Berlinquette	24	12	**9**	21	D	H. Mummery	24	15	5	20	G. Vezina	13	11	0	4.13
L. Dandurand	C	N. Lalonde	24	33	8	**41**	D	B. Corbeau	24	12	1	13					
13–11–0	RW	D. Pitre	23	15	1	16	D	D. Ritchie	5	0	0	0					
	F	A. Arbour	22	14	3	17	D	B. Bell	4	0	0	0					
	F	O. Cleghorn	21	5	4	9	D	D. Campbell	3	0	0	0					
	F	C. Wilson	9	6	1	7											
HAMIL	F	J. Malone	20	30	4	34	D	G. Prodgers	23	18	8	26	H. Lockhart	7	**17**	0	5.50
P. Thompson	F	M. Roach	14	8	7	15	D	J. Matte	19	7	**9**	16					
7–17–0	F	T. McCarthy	22	8	1	9	D	B. Couture	24	8	4	12					
	F	G. Carey	20	7	1	8	D	E. Carpenter	20	2	1	3					
	F	E. Lowrey	3	0	0	0	D	L. Reise	6	2	0	2					
	F	F. McLean	2	0	0	0	D	M. McDonnell	20	1	1	2					

GOALS		ASSISTS		POINTS	
B. Dye, TOR	35	H. Cameron, TOR	9	N. Lalonde, MONT	41
C. Denneny, OTTA	34	L. Berlinquette, MONT	9	C. Denneny, OTTA	39
N. Lalonde, MONT	33	J. Matte, HAMIL	9	B. Dye, TOR	37
J. Malone, HAMIL	30	N. Lalonde, MONT	8	J. Malone, HAMIL	34
R. Noble, TOR	20	G. Prodgers, HAMIL	8	H. Cameron, TOR	27

PENALTY MINUTES		GOALS AGAINST AVE.		SHUTOUTS	
B. Corbeau, MONT	86	C. Benedict, OTTA	3.13	C. Benedict, OTTA	2
B. Couture, HAMIL	74	J. Forbes, TOR	3.90	G. Vezina, MONT	1
H. Mummery, MONT	68	G. Vezina, MONT	4.13	H. Lockhart, HAMIL	1
K. Randall, TOR	58	H. Lockhart, HAMIL	5.50		
R. Noble, TOR	54				

National Hockey League 1921–22

TEAM	W	L	T	PTS	GF	GA
OTTA	14	8	2	30	**106**	**84**
*TOR	13	10	1	27	98	97
MONT	12	11	1	25	88	94
HAMIL	7	17	0	14	88	105

TEAM	POS	PLAYER	GP	G	A	PTS	POS	PLAYER	GP	G	A	PTS	GOALIE	W	L	T	GAvg
OTTA	LW	C. Denneny	22	27	12	39	D	G. Boucher	23	12	8	20	C. Benedict	**14**	8	2	**3.50**
P. Green	C	F. Nighbor	20	7	9	16	D	E. Gerard	21	7	9	16					
14–8–2	RW	P. Broadbent	24	**32**	**14**	**46**	D	K. Clancy	24	4	5	9					
	F	F. Boucher	24	9	1	10	D	M. Bruce	23	4	0	4					
	F	B. Bell	17	1	1	2	D	L. Graham	2	2	0	2					
TOR	LW	C. Denneny	24	19	7	26	D	H. Cameron	24	19	8	27	J. Roach	11	10	1	4.14
E. Powers	C	R. Noble	24	17	8	25	D	K. Randall	24	10	6	16	I. Mitchell	2	0	0	3.00
13–10–1	RW	B. Dye	24	30	7	37	D	B. Stuart	24	3	6	9					
	F	L. Andrews	11	0	0	0	D	T. Stackhouse	12	0	0	0					
	F	G. Smith	9	0	0	0	D	R. Smylie	21	0	0	0					
	F	S. Jackson	1	0	0	0	D	P. Nolan	2	0	0	0					
MONT	LW	L. Berlinquette	24	12	5	17	D	S. Cleghorn	24	17	7	24	G. Vezina	12	11	1	3.92
L. Dandurand	C	N. Lalonde	20	9	4	13	D	B. Corbeau	22	4	7	11					
12–11–1	RW	B. Boucher	24	17	5	22	D	B. Couture	23	4	3	7					
	F	O. Cleghorn	23	21	3	24	D	P. Stephens	4	0	0	0					
	F	E. Bouchard	18	1	4	5											
	F	D. Pitre	23	2	3	5											
	F	J. McDonald	2	0	0	0											
HAMIL	F	J. Malone	24	25	7	32	D	L. Reise	24	9	14	23	H. Lockhart	6	**17**	0	4.29
P. Thompson	F	M. Roach	24	14	3	17	D	G. Prodgers	24	15	4	19	H. Mummery	1	0	0	2.00
7–17–0	F	C. Wilson	23	9	7	16	D	H. Mummery	20	4	2	6					
	F	A. Arbour	23	8	3	11	D	J. Matte	20	3	3	6					
	F	G. Carey	23	3	2	5											

GOALS	
P. Broadbent, OTTA	32
B. Dye, TOR	30
C. Denneny, OTTA	27
J. Malone, HAMIL	25
O. Cleghorn, MONT	21

ASSISTS	
P. Broadbent, OTTA	14
L. Reise, HAMIL	14
C. Denneny, OTTA	12
E. Gerard, OTTA	9

POINTS	
P. Broadbent, OTTA	46
C. Denneny, OTTA	39
B. Dye, TOR	37
J. Malone, HAMIL	32
H. Cameron, TOR	27

PENALTY MINUTES	
S. Cleghorn, MONT	63
C. Denneny, TOR	28
O. Cleghorn, MONT	26
B. Corbeau, MONT	26
P. Broadbent, OTTA	24

GOALS AGAINST AVE.	
C. Benedict, OTTA	3.50
G. Vezina, MONT	3.92
J. Roach, TOR	4.14
H. Lockhart, HAMIL	4.29

SHUTOUTS	
C. Benedict, OTTA	2

National Hockey League 1922–23

TEAM	W	L	T	PTS	GF	GA
*OTTA	14	9	1	29	77	**54**
MONT	13	9	2	28	73	61
TOR	13	10	1	27	**82**	88
HAMIL	6	18	0	12	81	110

TEAM	POS	PLAYER	GP	G	A	PTS	POS	PLAYER	GP	G	A	PTS	GOALIE	W	L	T	GAvg
OTTA	LW	C. Denneny	24	21	10	31	D	G. Boucher	23	15	9	24	C. Benedict	**14**	9	1	**2.25**
P. Green	C	F. Nighbor	22	11	5	16	D	E. Gerard	23	6	8	14					
14–9–1	RW	P. Broadbent	24	14	0	14	D	K. Clancy	24	3	1	4					
	F	J. Darragh	24	7	7	14	D	L. Hitchman	3	0	1	1					
							D	H. Helman	24	0	0	0					
MONT	LW	A. Joliat	24	13	9	22	D	S. Cleghorn	24	9	4	13	G. Vezina	13	9	2	2.54
L. Dandurand	C	O. Cleghorn	24	19	7	26	D	B. Couture	24	5	2	7					
13–9–2	RW	B. Boucher	24	23	4	27	D	B. Bell	15	0	0	0					
	F	L. Berlinquette	24	2	3	5											
	F	D. Pitre	23	1	2	3											
	F	J. Malone	20	1	0	1											
TOR	LW	R. Noble	24	12	10	22	D	H. Cameron	22	9	6	15	J. Roach	13	10	1	3.67
C. Querrie	C	J. Adams	23	19	9	28	D	B. Stuart	23	7	3	10					
3–3–0	RW	B. Dye	22	**26**	11	**37**	D	K. Randall	24	3	5	8					
J. Adams	F	L. Andrews	23	5	4	9	D	G. Smith	9	0	0	0					
10–7–1	F	C. Denneny	1	1	0	1	D	S. Ganton	17	0	0	0					
	F	G. Denoird	15	0	0	0											
	F	R. Smylie	2	0	0	0											

TEAM	POS	PLAYER	GP	G	A	PTS		PLAYER	GP	G	A	PTS	GOALIE	W	L	T	GAvg
HAMIL	F	M. Roach	23	17	8	25	D	B. Corbeau	21	10	3	13	J. Forbes	6	**18**	0	4.58
A. Ross	F	C. Wilson	23	16	3	19	D	L. Reise	24	6	6	12					
6–18–0	F	E. Bouchard	20	5	**12**	17	D	B. Burch	10	6	2	8					
	F	G. Prodgers	23	13	3	16	D	L. Graham	4	1	0	1					
	F	A. Arbour	23	6	1	7	D	H. Mummery	7	0	0	0					
	F	G. Carey	5	1	0	1											

GOALS		ASSISTS		POINTS	
B. Dye, TOR	26	E. Bouchard, HAMIL	12	B. Dye, TOR	37
B. Boucher, MONT	23	B. Dye, TOR	11	C. Denneny, OTTA	31
C. Denneny, OTTA	21	C. Denneny, OTTA	10	J. Adams, TOR	28
J. Adams, TOR	19	R. Noble, TOR	10	B. Boucher, MONT	27
O. Cleghorn, MONT	19			O. Cleghorn, MONT	26

PENALTY MINUTES		GOALS AGAINST AVE.		SHUTOUTS	
B. Boucher, MONT	52	C. Benedict, OTTA	2.25	C. Benedict, OTTA	4
K. Randall, TOR	51	G. Vezina, MONT	2.54	G. Vezina, MONT	2
C. Wilson, HAMIL	46	J. Roach, TOR	3.67	J. Roach, TOR	1
G. Boucher, OTTA	44	J. Forbes, HAMIL	4.58		
J. Adams, TOR	42				

National Hockey League 1923–24

TEAM	W	L	T	PTS	GF	GA
OTTA	16	8	0	32	**74**	54
*MONT	13	11	0	26	59	**48**
TOR	10	14	0	20	59	85
HAMIL	9	15	0	18	63	68

TEAM	POS	PLAYER	GP	G	A	PTS		PLAYER	GP	G	A	PTS	GOALIE	W	L	T	GAvg
OTTA	LW	C. Denneny	21	**22**	1	**23**	D	G. Boucher	21	14	5	19	C. Benedict	**16**	6	0	2.05
P. Green	C	F. Nighbor	20	10	3	13	D	K. Clancy	24	9	**8**	17	S. Hebert	0	2	0	4.50
16–8–0	RW	P. Broadbent	22	9	4	13	D	L. Hitchman	24	2	6	8					
	F	S. Campbell	18	4	1	5	D	R. Smylie	14	1	1	2					
	F	J. Darragh	18	2	0	2	D	H. Helman	17	1	0	1					
	F	F. Finnigan	4	0	0	0	D	L. Graham	3	0	0	0					
MONT	LW	A. Joliat	24	15	5	20	D	S. Cleghorn	23	8	3	11	G. Vezina	13	11	0	**2.00**
L. Dandurand	C	H. Morenz	24	13	3	16	D	B. Couture	16	3	1	4					
13–11–0	RW	B. Boucher	23	16	6	22	D	S. Mantha	24	1	0	1					
	F	O. Cleghorn	23	3	3	6	D	B. Bell	10	0	0	0					
	F	C. Fortier	1	0	0	0											
	F	J. Malone	9	0	0	0											
	F	R. Boucher	12	0	0	0											
	F	B. Cameron	18	0	0	0											
TOR	LW	R. Noble	23	12	3	15	D	B. Corbeau	24	8	6	14	J. Roach	10	13	0	3.48
E. Powers	C	J. Adams	22	13	3	16	D	B. Stuart	24	4	3	7	H. Lockhart	0	1	0	5.00
10–14–0	RW	B. Dye	19	17	2	19	D	S. Jackson	21	1	1	2					
	F	L. Andrews	12	2	1	3	D	T. Holway	6	1	0	1					
	F	G. Carey	4	0	0	0	D	C. Speyer	3	0	0	0					
							D	W. Loughlin	14	0	0	0					
HAMIL	LW	R. Green	23	11	0	11	D	G. Prodgers	23	9	1	10	J. Forbes	9	**15**	0	2.83
P. Lesueur	C	B. Burch	24	16	2	18	D	K. Randall	24	7	1	8					
9–15–0	RW	W. Green	22	7	2	9	D	J. Spring	20	3	2	5					
	F	M. Roach	21	5	3	8	D	L. Reise	4	0	0	0					
	F	E. Bouchard	20	5	0	5	D	S. Ganton	4	0	0	0					
	F	C. Denneny	23	0	0	0											
	F	J. Fraser	1	0	0	0											

GOALS		ASSISTS		POINTS	
C. Denneny, OTTA	22	K. Clancy, OTTA	8	C. Denneny, OTTA	23
B. Dye, TOR	17	B. Boucher, MONT	6	B. Boucher, MONT	22
B. Boucher, MONT	16	B. Corbeau, TOR	6	A. Joliat, MONT	20
B. Burch, HAMIL	16	L. Hitchman, OTTA	6	B. Dye, TOR	19
A. Joliat, MONT	15	A. Joliat, MONT	5	G. Boucher, OTTA	19

PENALTY MINUTES	
B. Corbeau, TOR	55
J. Adams, TOR	49
P. Broadbent, OTTA	44
S. Cleghorn, MONT	39
B. Boucher, MONT	33

GOALS AGAINST AVE.	
G. Vezina, MONT	2.00
C. Benedict, OTTA	2.05
J. Forbes, HAMIL	2.83
J. Roach, TOR	3.48

SHUTOUTS	
G. Vezina, MONT	3
C. Benedict, OTTA	3
J. Forbes, HAMIL	1
J. Roach, TOR	1

National Hockey League 1924–25

TEAM	W	L	T	PTS	GF	GA
HAMIL	19	10	1	39	90	60
TOR	19	11	0	38	90	84
MONT	17	11	2	36	**93**	**56**
OTTA	17	12	1	35	83	66
MON(M)	9	19	2	20	45	65
BOS	6	24	0	12	49	119

	POS	PLAYER	GP	G	A	PTS		PLAYER	GP	G	A	PTS	GOALIE	W	L	T	GAvg
HAMIL	LW	R. Green	30	19	4	23	D	A. McKinnon	30	8	2	10	J. Forbes	**19**	10	1	2.00
J. Gardner	C	B. Burch	27	20	4	24	D	K. Randall	30	8	0	8					
19–10–1	RW	W. Green	28	18	1	19	D	C. Langlois	30	6	1	7					
	F	M. Roach	30	6	4	10	D	J. Spring	29	2	0	2					
	F	E. Bouchard	29	2	2	4	D	G. Prodgers	1	0	0	0					
	F	C. Cotch	11	1	0	1											
TOR	LW	H. Day	26	10	12	22	D	B. McCaffrey	30	9	6	15	J. Roach	**19**	11	0	2.80
E. Powers	C	J. Adams	27	21	8	29	D	B. Corbeau	30	4	3	7					
19–11–0	RW	B. Dye	29	**38**	6	**44**	D	T. Holway	25	2	2	4					
	F	R. Reid	28	2	0	2	D	C. Speyer	2	0	0	0					
	F	L. Andrews	7	1	0	1	D	R. Smylie	11	0	0	0					
	F	A. Fisher	9	1	0	1											
	F	M. Neville	12	1	0	1											
MONT	LW	A. Joliat	24	29	11	40	D	S. Cleghorn	27	8	1	9	G. Vezina	17	11	2	**1.87**
L. Dandurand	C	H. Morenz	30	27	7	34	D	B. Couture	28	3	2	5					
17–11–2	RW	B. Boucher	30	18	13	31	D	D. Ritchie	5	0	0	0					
	F	O. Cleghorn	30	3	2	5											
	F	J. Matz	30	3	2	5											
	F	S. Mantha	30	2	0	2											
	F	C. Headley	16	1	0	1											
	F	B. Joliat	1	0	0	0											
	F	R. Lafleur	1	0	0	0											
OTTA	LW	C. Denneny	28	27	**15**	42	D	G. Boucher	28	15	4	19	A. Connell	17	12	1	2.20
P. Green	C	F. Nighbor	26	5	2	7	D	K. Clancy	29	14	5	19					
17–12–1	RW	H. Smith	30	10	3	13	D	E. Gorman	30	11	3	14					
	F	F. Finnigan	29	0	0	0	D	L. Graham	3	0	0	0					
	F	S. Campbell	30	0	0	0	D	H. Helman	1	0	0	0					
							D	A. Smith	7	0	0	0					
MON(M)	LW	L. Berlinquette	29	4	2	6	D	D. Munro	27	5	1	6	C. Benedict	9	**19**	2	2.17
E. Gerard	C	R. Noble	27	7	6	13	D	J. Cain	28	4	0	4					
9–19–2	RW	P. Broadbent	30	15	4	19	D	S. Ganton	28	1	1	2					
	F	S. Rothschild	27	5	4	9	D	G. Munro	29	1	0	1					
	F	C. Dinsmore	30	2	1	3											
	F	A. Skinner	18	1	1	2											
	F	E. Parkes	17	0	0	0											
	F	F. Lowery	28	0	0	0											
BOS	F	J. Herberts	30	17	5	22	D	B. Stuart	24	5	2	7	D. Stewart	5	16	0	3.10
A. Ross	F	C. Cooper	12	5	3	8	D	G. Redding	27	3	2	5	H. Fowler	1	6	0	6.14
6–24–0	F	S. Jackson	24	5	0	5	D	L. Hitchman	18	3	0	3	H. Lockhart	0	2	0	5.50
	F	S. Harris	6	3	1	4	D	L. Cook	4	1	0	1					
	F	N. Shay	18	1	1	2	D	B. Rowe	4	1	0	1					
	F	W. Schnarr	24	0	0	0	D	B. Benson	8	0	1	1					

GOALS	
B. Dye, TOR	38
A. Joliat, MONT	29
C. Denneny, OTTA	27
H. Morenz, MONT	27
J. Adams, TOR	21

ASSISTS	
C. Denneny, OTTA	15
B. Boucher, MONT	13
H. Day, TOR	12
A. Joliat, MONT	11
J. Adams, TOR	8

POINTS	
B. Dye, TOR	44
C. Denneny, OTTA	42
A. Joliat, MONT	40
H. Morenz, MONT	34
B. Boucher, MONT	31

PENALTY MINUTES		GOALS AGAINST AVE.		SHUTOUTS	
B. Boucher, MONT	92	G. Vezina, MONT	1.87	A. Connell, OTTA	7
A. Joliat, MONT	85	J. Forbes, HAMIL	2.00	J. Forbes, HAMIL	6
S. Cleghorn, MONT	82	C. Benedict, MON(M)	2.17	G. Vezina, MONT	5
H. Smith, OTTA	81	A. Connell, OTTA	2.20	C. Benedict, MON(M)	2
G. Boucher, OTTA	80	J. Roach, TOR	2.80	D. Stewart, BOS	2

National Hockey League 1925–26

TEAM	W	L	T	PTS	GF	GA
OTTA	24	8	4	52	77	**42**
*MON(M)	20	11	5	45	91	73
PITT	19	16	1	39	82	70
BOS	17	15	4	38	**92**	85
NYA	12	20	4	28	68	89
TOR	12	21	3	27	**92**	114
MONT	11	24	1	23	79	108

	POS	PLAYER	GP	G	A	PTS		PLAYER	GP	G	A	PTS	GOALIE	W	L	T	GAvg
OTTA	LW	C. Denneny	36	24	12	36	D	G. Boucher	32	8	4	12	A. Connell	**24**	8	4	**1.17**
P. Green	C	F. Nighbor	35	12	**13**	25	D	K. Clancy	35	8	4	12					
24–8–4	RW	H. Smith	28	16	9	25	D	E. Gorman	23	2	1	3					
	F	H. Kilrea	35	5	0	5	D	J. Duggan	27	0	0	0					
	F	F. Finnigan	36	2	0	2	D	A. Smith	36	0	0	0					
							D	L. Graham	10	0	0	0					
MON(M)	LW	B. Siebert	35	16	8	24	D	R. Noble	30	9	9	18	C. Benedict	20	11	5	2.03
E. Gerard	C	N. Stewart	36	**34**	8	**42**	D	D. Munro	33	4	6	10					
20–11–5	RW	B. Phillips	12	3	1	4	D	H. Kitchen	30	5	2	7					
	F	P. Broadbent	36	12	5	17	D	T. Holway	17	0	0	0					
	F	C. Dinsmore	33	3	1	4											
	F	F. Carson	16	2	1	3											
	F	S. Rothschild	33	2	1	3											
	F	B. Brophy	10	0	0	0											
PITT	F	H. Milks	36	14	5	19	D	L. Conacher	33	9	4	13	R. Worters	18	16	1	1.94
O. Cleghorn	F	H. Darragh	35	10	7	17	D	R. Smith	36	9	1	10	O. Cleghorn	1	0	0	2.00
19–16–1	F	D. McGurry	36	13	4	17	D	H. Drury	33	6	2	8					
	F	B. Cotton	33	7	1	8	D	J. Spring	32	5	0	5					
	F	T. White	35	7	1	8											
	F	L. Berlinquette	30	0	0	0											
	F	F. Lowery	16	1	0	1											
	F	O. Cleghorn	17	3	1	4											
BOS	F	C. Cooper	36	28	3	31	D	S. Cleghorn	28	6	5	11	D. Stewart	17	14	4	2.29
A. Ross	F	J. Herberts	36	26	5	31	D	L. Hitchman	36	7	4	11	M. Roberts	0	1	0	2.50
17–15–4	F	H. Harrington	26	7	2	9	D	B. Stuart	33	6	1	7					
	F	S. Jackson	28	3	3	6	D	G. Redding	8	0	0	0					
	F	G. Geran	33	5	1	6	D	P. Stevens	17	0	0	0					
	F	H. Mitchell	26	3	0	3											
	F	C. Cahill	31	0	1	1											
NYA	LW	R. Green	35	13	4	17	D	C. Langlois	36	9	1	10	J. Forbes	12	19	4	2.39
T. Gorman	C	B. Burch	36	22	3	25	D	A. McKinnon	30	5	3	8	J. Ironstone	0	1	0	3.00
12–20–4	RW	W. Green	32	6	4	10	D	K. Randall	34	4	2	6					
	F	M. Roach	25	3	0	3	D	J. Simpson	32	2	2	4					
	F	E. Bouchard	34	3	1	4											
	F	B. Cameron	21	0	0	0											
	F	J. Morrison	18	0	0	0											
TOR	LW	H. Day	36	14	2	16	D	B. McCaffrey	36	14	7	21	J. Roach	12	**21**	3	3.17
E. Powers	C	J. Adams	36	21	5	26	D	B. Corbeau	36	5	5	10					
12–21–3	RW	B. Dye	31	18	5	23	D	J. Cain	23	0	0	0					
	F	P. Bellefeuille	36	14	2	16	D	G. Munro	4	0	0	0					
	F	M. Neville	33	3	3	6											
	F	N. Shay	22	3	1	4											
	F	R. Smylie	5	0	0	0											
MONT	LW	A. Joliat	35	17	9	26	D	B. Couture	33	2	4	6	H. Rheaume	10	19	1	2.97
C. Hart	C	H. Morenz	31	23	3	26	D	S. Mantha	34	2	1	3	A. Lacroix	1	4	0	3.20
11–24–1	RW	B. Boucher	34	8	5	13	D	G. Prodgers	24	0	0	0	G. Vezina	0	0	0	0.00
	F	A. LeDuc	32	10	3	13	D	J. McKinnon	2	0	0	0					
	F	H. Lepine	33	5	2	7	D	D. Ritchie	2	0	0	0					
	F	W. Larochelle	33	2	1	3											
	F	B. Holmes	9	1	0	1											
	F	P. Lepine	27	9	1	10											

GOALS		ASSISTS		POINTS	
N. Stewart, MON(M)	34	F. Nighbor, OTTA	13	N. Stewart, MON(M)	42
C. Cooper, BOS	28	C. Denneny, OTTA	12	C. Denneny, OTTA	36
J. Herberts, BOS	26	A. Joliat, MONT	9	J. Herberts, BOS	31
C. Denneny, OTTA	24	H. Smith, OTTA	9	C. Cooper, BOS	31
H. Morenz, MONT	23	R. Noble, MON(M)	9		

PENALTY MINUTES		GOALS AGAINST AVE.		SHUTOUTS	
B. Corbeau, TOR	121	A. Connell, OTTA	1.17	A. Connell, OTTA	15
N. Stewart, MON(M)	119	R. Worters, PITT	1.94	R. Worters, PITT	7
P. Broadbent, MONT	112	C. Benedict, MON(M)	2.03	C. Benedict, MON(M)	6
B. Boucher, MONT	112	D. Stewart, BOS	2.29	D. Stewart, BOS	6
B. Siebert, MON(M)	108	J. Forbes, NYA	2.39	J. Forbes, NYA	2

National Hockey League 1926–27

TEAM	W	L	T	PTS	GF	GA	TEAM	W	L	T	PTS	GF	GA
CANADIAN DIVISION							AMERICAN DIVISION						
*OTTA	30	10	4	64	86	69	NYR	25	13	6	56	95	72
MONT	28	14	2	58	99	**67***	BOS	21	20	3	45	97	89
MON(M)	20	20	4	44	71	68	CHI	19	22	3	41	**115**	116
NYA	17	25	2	36	82	91	PITT	15	26	3	33	79	108
TOR	15	24	5	35	79	94	DET	12	28	4	28	76	105

CANADIAN DIVISION

	POS	PLAYER	GP	G	A	PTS	POS	PLAYER	GP	G	A	PTS	GOALIE	W	L	T	GAvg
OTTA	LW	C. Denneny	42	17	6	23	D	K. Clancy	44	9	10	19	A. Connell	**30**	10	4	1.57
D. Gill	C	F. Nighbor	39	6	6	12	D	G. Boucher	40	8	3	11					
30–10–4	RW	H. Smith	43	9	6	15	D	A. Smith	43	4	1	5					
	F	H. Kilrea	42	11	7	18	D	E. Gorman	41	1	0	1					
	F	F. Finnigan	35	15	1	16											
	F	J. Adams	40	5	1	6											
	F	M. Halliday	38	1	0	1											
	F	S. Jackson	8	0	0	0											
MONT	LW	A. Joliat	43	14	4	18	D	S. Mantha	43	10	5	15	G. Hainsworth	28	14	2	**1.52**
C. Hart	C	H. Morenz	44	25	7	32	D	H. Gardiner	44	6	6	12					
28–14–2	RW	A. Gagne	44	14	3	17	D	A. LeDuc	43	5	2	7					
	LW	G. Hart	32	3	3	6	D	A. Moran	12	0	0	0					
	C	P. Lepine	44	16	1	17	D	A. Gauthier	13	0	0	0					
	RW	W. Larochelle	41	0	1	1	D	P. Palangio	6	0	0	0					
	F	C. Cooper	14	9	3	12											
	F	LaChance	1	0	0	0											
MON(M)	LW	B. Siebert	44	5	3	8	D	D. Munro	44	6	5	11	C. Benedict	20	20	3	**1.51**
E. Gerard	C	N. Stewart	44	17	4	21	D	R. Dutton	44	4	4	8	F. Walsh	0	0	1	3.00
20–20–4	RW	B. Phillips	43	15	1	16	D	R. Noble	44	3	3	6					
	F	P. Broadbent	42	11	4	15	D	B. Donnelly	34	0	1	1					
	F	F. Carson	43	2	3	5	D	T. Holway	13	0	0	0					
	F	S. Rothschild	21	1	1	2											
	F	C. Dinsmore	31	1	0	1											
	F	H. Emms	8	0	0	0											
NYA	LW	R. Green	44	10	4	14	D	L. Conacher	30	8	9	17	J. Forbes	17	25	2	2.07
N. Lalonde	C	B. Burch	44	19	8	27	D	L. Reise	40	7	6	13					
17–25–2	RW	W. Green	25	2	1	3	D	J. Simpson	42	4	2	6					
	F	N. Himes	42	9	2	11	D	A. McKinnon	42	2	1	3					
	F	M. Roach	42	11	0	11	D	C. Bowcher	11	0	1	1					
	F	L. Scott	39	6	2	8	D	B. Connors	6	1	0	1					
	F	E. Bouchard	38	2	1	3											
	F	N. Lalonde	1	0	0	0											
TOR	LW	B. Keeling	30	11	2	13	D	H. Day	44	11	5	16	J. Roach	15	24	5	2.14
C. Smythe	C	B. Carson	40	16	6	22	D	B. McCaffrey	43	5	5	10					
15–24–5	RW	A. Bailey	42	15	13	28	D	S. Halderson	26	1	2	3					
	F	B. Brydge	41	6	3	9	D	B. Corbeau	41	1	2	3					
	F	C. Denneny	29	7	1	8	D	J. Spring	2	0	0	0					
	F	P. Patterson	17	4	2	6											
	F	L. Gross	16	1	1	2											
	F	D. Cox	14	0	1	1											
	F	C. Voss	12	0	0	0											
	F	A. Pudas	3	0	0	0											

AMERICAN DIVISION

TEAM	POS	PLAYER	GP	G	A	PTS	PLAYER	GP	G	A	PTS	GOALIE	W	L	T	GAvg
NYR	LW	B. Cook	44	14	9	23	D S. Brown	24	6	2	8	L. Chabot	22	9	5	1.56
L. Patrick	C	F. Boucher	44	13	15	28	D T. Abel	44	8	4	12	H. Winkler	3	4	1	2.00
25–13–6	RW	B. Cook	44	**33**	4	**37**	D C. Johnson	27	3	2	5					
	LW	P. Thompson	43	7	3	10	D L. Bourgeault	20	2	1	3					
	C	M. Murdoch	44	6	4	10	D R. Mackey	34	0	0	0					
	RW	B. Boyd	41	4	1	5										
	F	O. Reinikka	16	0	0	0										
	F	L. Patrick	1	0	0	0										

TEAM	POS	PLAYER	GP	G	A	PTS	PLAYER	GP	G	A	PTS	GOALIE	W	L	T	GAvg
BOS	LW	P. Galbraith	42	9	8	17	D E. Shore	41	12	6	18	H. Winkler	12	9	2	1.74
A. Ross	C	F. Frederickson	28	14	7	21	D L. Hitchman	41	3	6	9	D. Stewart	9	11	1	2.33
21–20–3	RW	H. Oliver	44	18	6	24	D S. Cleghorn	44	7	1	8					
	F	J. Herberts	35	15	7	22	D B. Stuart	43	3	1	4					
	F	B. Boucher	14	2	0	2	D B. Couture	41	1	1	2					
	F	H. Meeking	23	1	0	1										
	F	C. Cahill	1	0	0	0										

TEAM	POS	PLAYER	GP	G	A	PTS	PLAYER	GP	G	A	PTS	GOALIE	W	L	T	GAvg
CHI	LW	D. Irvin	44	18	**18**	36	D G. Fraser	43	14	6	20	H. Lehman	19	22	3	2.64
P. Muldoon	C	M. MacKay	36	14	8	22	D B. Trapp	44	4	2	6					
19–22–3	RW	B. Dye	41	25	5	30	D D. Dutkowski	28	3	2	5					
	F	G. Hay	37	14	8	22	D P. Traub	42	0	2	2					
	F	C. McVeigh	43	12	4	16	D A. Townsend	5	0	0	0					
	F	C. Wilson	39	8	4	12										
	F	E. Rodden	20	3	3	6										
	F	K. Doraty	18	0	0	0										
	F	G. McFarland	2	0	0	0										

TEAM	POS	PLAYER	GP	G	A	PTS	PLAYER	GP	G	A	PTS	GOALIE	W	L	T	GAvg
PITT	F	H. Milks	44	6	16	22	D C. Langlois	37	5	1	6	R. Worters	15	26	3	2.45
O. Cleghorn	F	T. Arbour	40	7	8	15	D H. Drury	41	5	1	6					
15–26–3	F	H. Darragh	42	12	3	15	D R. Smith	36	4	0	4					
	F	T. White	43	5	4	9										
	F	B. Cotton	37	5	0	5										
	F	M. McGuire	32	3	0	3										
	F	D. McGurry	33	3	3	6										
	F	O. Cleghorn	4	0	0	0										

TEAM	POS	PLAYER	GP	G	A	PTS	PLAYER	GP	G	A	PTS	GOALIE	W	L	T	GAvg
DET	F	D. Keats	40	16	8	24	D A. Briden	42	5	2	7	H. Holmes	12	**27**	4	2.33
A. Duncan	F	J. Sheppard	43	13	8	21	D A. Duncan	34	3	2	5	H. Stuart	0	1	0	1.67
12–28–4	F	F. Foyston	41	10	5	15	D C. Loughlin	34	7	3	10					
	F	F. Gordon	36	5	5	10	D H. Kitchen	18	0	2	2					
	F	J. Walker	37	3	4	7										
	F	P. Bellefeuille	18	6	0	6										
	F	J. Arbour	37	4	1	5										
	F	J. Riley	17	0	2	2										

GOALS		ASSISTS		POINTS	
B. Cook, NYR	33	D. Irvin, CHI	18	B. Cook, NYR	37
B. Dye, CHI	25	F. Boucher, NYR	15	D. Irvin, CHI	36
H. Morenz, MONT	25	F. Frederickson, DET, BOS	13	H. Morenz, MONT	32
B. Burch, NYA	19	A. Bailey, TOR	13	F. Frederickson, DET, BOS	31
		K. Clancy, OTTA	10	B. Dye, CHI	30

PENALTY MINUTES		GOALS AGAINST AVE.		SHUTOUTS	
N. Stewart, MON(M)	133	C. Benedict, MON(M)	1.52	G. Hainsworth, MONT	14
E. Shore, BOS	130	G. Hainsworth, MONT	1.52	C. Benedict, MON(M)	13
H. Smith, OTTA	125	L. Chabot, NYR	1.56	A. Connell, OTTA	13
B. Siebert, MON(M)	116	A. Connell, OTTA	1.57	L. Chabot, NYR	10
G. Boucher, OTTA	115	H. Winkler, NYR, BOS	1.81	J. Forbes, NYA	8

National Hockey League 1927–28

TEAM	W	L	T	PTS	GF	GA	TEAM	W	L	T	PTS	GF	GA
CANADIAN DIVISION							AMERICAN DIVISION						
MONT	26	11	7	59	**116**	**48**	BOS	20	13	11	51	77	70
MON(M)	24	14	6	54	96	77	*NYR	19	16	9	47	94	79
OTTA	20	14	10	50	78	57	PITT	19	17	8	46	67	76
TOR	18	18	8	44	89	88	DET	19	19	6	44	88	79
NYA	11	27	6	28	63	128	CHI	7	34	3	17	68	134

CANADIAN DIVISION

MONT
C. Hart
26–11–7

POS	PLAYER	GP	G	A	PTS		PLAYER	GP	G	A	PTS	GOALIE	W	L	T	GAvg
LW	A. Joliat	44	28	11	39	D	S. Mantha	43	4	11	15	G. Hainsworth	**26**	11	7	**1.09**
C	H. Morenz	43	**18**	**33**	**51**	D	A. LeDuc	42	8	5	13					
RW	A. Gagne	44	20	10	30	D	H. Gardiner	44	4	3	7					
F	L. Gaudreault	32	6	2	8	D	C. Langlois	32	0	0	0					
F	P. Lepine	20	4	1	5											
F	G. Hart	44	3	2	5											
F	W. Larochelle	40	3	1	4											
F	P. Patterson	16	0	1	1											

MON(M)
E. Gerard
24–14–6

POS	PLAYER	GP	G	A	PTS		PLAYER	GP	G	A	PTS	GOALIE	W	L	T	GAvg
LW	B. Siebert	40	8	9	17	D	R. Dutton	42	7	6	13	C. Benedict	24	14	6	1.73
C	N. Stewart	43	27	7	34	D	D. Munro	43	5	2	7	F. Walsh	0	0	0	1.00
RW	H. Smith	36	14	5	19	D	H. Emms	8	0	1	1					
F	J. Lamb	21	8	5	13											
F	B. Phillips	41	7	5	12											
F	J. Ward	44	10	2	12											
F	R. Oatman	44	7	4	11											
F	B. Touhey	29	2	0	2											
F	F. Carson	19	0	1	1											
F	F. Brown	19	1	0	1											

OTTA
D. Gill
20–14–10

POS	PLAYER	GP	G	A	PTS		PLAYER	GP	G	A	PTS	GOALIE	W	L	T	GAvg
LW	H. Kilrea	42	19	4	23	D	K. Clancy	39	8	7	15	A. Connell	20	14	10	1.30
C	F. Nighbor	42	8	5	13	D	A. Smith	44	9	4	13					
RW	F. Finnigan	43	20	5	25	D	G. Boucher	43	7	5	12					
F	P. Broadbent	43	3	2	5	D	A. Shields	6	0	1	1					
F	L. Grosvenar	41	1	2	3	D	M. Halliday	13	0	0	0					
F	C. Denneny	44	3	0	3											
F	S. Godin	24	0	0	0											
F	G. Chouinard	8	0	0	0											

TOR
C. Smythe
18–18–8

POS	PLAYER	GP	G	A	PTS		PLAYER	GP	G	A	PTS	GOALIE	W	L	T	GAvg
LW	B. Keeling	43	10	6	16	D	H. Day	22	9	8	17	J. Roach	17	18	8	2.05
C	B. Carson	32	20	6	26	D	A. Duncan	43	7	5	12	J. Ironstone	1	0	0	0.00
RW	A. Bailey	43	9	3	12	D	B. Ramsay	43	0	2	2					
F	J. Herberts	43	15	4	19	D	E. Gorman	19	0	1	1					
F	D. Cox	41	9	6	15											
F	G. Lowrey	25	6	5	11											
F	E. Rodden	25	3	6	9											
F	A. Smith	15	5	3	8											

NYA
W. Green
11–27–6

POS	PLAYER	GP	G	A	PTS		PLAYER	GP	G	A	PTS	GOALIE	W	L	T	GAvg
LW	R. Green	40	6	1	7	D	L. Conacher	35	11	6	17	J. Miller	8	16	4	2.75
C	N. Himes	44	14	5	19	D	L. Reise	43	8	1	9	J. Forbes	3	11	2	3.19
RW	B. Boucher	43	5	2	7	D	A. McKinnon	43	3	3	6	N. Himes	0	0	0	0.00
F	B. Burch	33	10	2	12	D	C. Bowcher	36	2	1	3					
F	M. Barry	9	1	0	1	D	J. Simpson	25	2	0	2					
F	S. Rothschild	5	0	0	0											

AMERICAN DIVISION

BOS
A. Ross
20–13–11

POS	PLAYER	GP	G	A	PTS		PLAYER	GP	G	A	PTS	GOALIE	W	L	T	GAvg
LW	P. Galbraith	42	6	5	11	D	E. Shore	44	11	6	17	H. Winkler	20	13	11	1.59
C	F. Frederickson	44	10	4	14	D	L. Hitchman	44	5	3	8					
RW	H. Oliver	44	13	5	18	D	D. Clapper	40	4	1	5					
F	D. Norman	41	8	4	12	D	S. Cleghorn	37	2	2	4					
F	H. Connor	42	9	1	10	D	A. Clark	5	0	0	0					
F	F. Gordon	41	3	2	5											
F	H. Harrington	22	1	0	1											
F	M. Lauder	3	0	0	0											

NYR
L. Patrick
19–16–9

POS	PLAYER	GP	G	A	PTS		PLAYER	GP	G	A	PTS	GOALIE	W	L	T	GAvg
LW	B. Cook	44	14	14	28	D	C. Johnson	43	10	6	16	L. Chabot	19	16	9	1.80
C	F. Boucher	44	23	12	35	D	L. Bourgeault	37	7	0	7					
RW	B. Cook	43	18	6	24	D	P. Callighen	36	0	0	0					
LW	P. Thompson	41	4	4	8											
C	M. Murdoch	44	7	3	10											
RW	B. Boyd	43	4	0	4											
F	A. Gray	43	7	0	7											
F	L. Scott	23	0	1	1											

PITT
O. Cleghorn
19–17–8

POS	PLAYER	GP	G	A	PTS		PLAYER	GP	G	A	PTS	GOALIE	W	L	T	GAvg
F	H. Milks	44	18	3	21	D	H. Drury	42	6	4	10	R. Worters	19	17	8	1.73
F	H. Darragh	44	13	2	15	D	J. McKinnon	41	3	3	6					
F	B. Cotton	42	9	3	12	D	M. Burke	35	2	1	3					
F	D. McGurry	43	5	3	8	D	R. Smith	43	1	0	1					
F	T. White	44	5	1	6											
F	M. McGuire	4	0	0	0											
F	O. Cleghorn	2	0	0	0											

TEAM	POS	PLAYER	GP	G	A	PTS	POS	PLAYER	GP	G	A	PTS	GOALIE	W	L	T	GAvg
DET	LW	G. Hay	42	22	13	35	D	R. Noble	44	6	8	14	H. Holmes	19	19	6	1.80
J. Adams	C	J. Sheppard	44	10	10	20	D	G. Fraser	30	3	1	4					
19–19–6	RW	L. Aurie	44	13	3	16	D	P. Traub	44	3	1	4					
	F	C. Cooper	43	15	2	17	D	P. Palangio	14	3	0	3					
	F	F. Foyston	23	7	2	9	D	C. Loughlin	43	1	2	3					
	F	J. Walker	43	2	4	6	D	S. Brown	24	2	0	2					
	F	F. Sheppard	8	1	1	2											
CHI	F	D. Keats	32	14	8	22	D	C. Wentworth	44	5	5	10	C. Gardiner	6	32	2	2.85
B. Stanley	F	M. MacKay	35	17	4	21	D	R. Taylor	22	1	1	2	H. Lehman	1	2	1	5.00
4–17–2	F	C. McVeigh	43	6	7	13	D	A. Moran	23	1	1	2					
H. Lehman	F	T. Arbour	32	5	5	10	D	E. McCalmon	23	2	0	2					
3–17–1	F	D. Irvin	14	5	4	9	D	B. Trapp	38	0	2	2					
	F	C. Denneny	19	5	0	5	D	V. Hoffinger	18	0	1	1					
	F	C. Browne	13	2	0	2											
	F	E. Miller	22	1	1	2											

GOALS		ASSISTS		POINTS	
H. Morenz, MONT	33	H. Morenz, MONT	18	H. Morenz, MONT	51
A. Joliat, MONT	28	B. Cook, NYR	14	A. Joliat, MONT	39
N. Stewart, MON(M)	27	G. Hay, DET	13	F. Boucher, NYR	35
F. Boucher, NYR	23	A. Joliat, MONT	11	G. Hay, DET	35
G. Hay, DET	22	S. Mantha, MONT	11	N. Stewart, MON(M)	34

PENALTY MINUTES		GOALS AGAINST AVE.		SHUTOUTS	
E. Shore, BOS	165	G. Hainsworth, MONT	1.09	H. Winkler, BOS	15
C. Johnson, NYR	146	A. Connell, OTTA	1.30	A. Connell, OTTA	15
B. Siebert, MON(M)	109	H. Winkler, BOS	1.59	G. Hainsworth, MONT	13
C. Bowcher, NYA	106	R. Worters, PITT	1.73	R. Worters, PITT	11
A. Joliat, MONT	105	C. Benedict, MON(M)	1.73	L. Chabot, NYR	11

National Hockey League 1928–29

TEAM	W	L	T	PTS	GF	GA	TEAM	W	L	T	PTS	GF	GA
CANADIAN DIVISION							AMERICAN DIVISION						
MONT	22	7	15	59	71	**43**	*BOS	26	13	5	57	**89**	52
NYA	19	13	12	50	53	53	NYR	21	13	10	52	72	65
TOR	21	18	5	47	85	69	DET	19	16	9	47	72	63
OTTA	14	17	13	41	54	67	PITT	9	27	8	26	46	80
MON(M)	15	20	9	39	67	65	CHI	7	29	8	22	33	85

CANADIAN DIVISION

TEAM	POS	PLAYER	GP	G	A	PTS	POS	PLAYER	GP	G	A	PTS	GOALIE	W	L	T	GAvg
MONT	LW	A. Joliat	44	12	5	17	D	S. Mantha	44	9	4	13	G. Hainsworth	22	7	15	**0.98**
C. Hart	C	H. Morenz	42	17	10	27	D	A. LeDuc	43	9	2	11					
22–7–15	RW	A. Gagne	44	7	3	10	D	M. Burke	44	4	2	6					
	LW	A. Mondou	32	3	4	7	D	H. Gardiner	8	0	0	0					
	C	P. Lepine	44	6	1	7											
	RW	G. Mantha	31	0	0	0											
	F	P. Patterson	44	4	5	9											
	F	W. Larochelle	2	0	0	0											
	F	P. Palangio	2	0	0	0											
	F	L. Gaudreault	11	0	0	0											
NYA	LW	C. McVeigh	44	6	2	8	D	L. Conacher	44	5	2	7	R. Worters	16	13	9	1.21
T. Gorman	C	B. Burch	44	11	5	16	D	J. Simpson	42	3	2	5	F. Walsh	2	0	2	0.25
19–13–12	RW	J. Sheppard	43	5	4	9	D	L. Reise	44	4	1	5	J. Forbes	1	0	0	3.00
	F	T. White	11	2	1	3	D	J. Spring	23	0	0	0	N. Himes	0	0	1	3.00
	F	N. Himes	44	10	0	10											
	F	H. Connor	43	6	2	8											
	F	P. Broadbent	44	1	4	5											
	F	B. Dye	42	1	0	1											

	POS	PLAYER	GP	G	A	PTS		PLAYER	GP	G	A	PTS	GOALIE	W	L	T	GAvg
TOR	LW	D. Cox	42	12	7	19	D	H. Day	44	6	6	12	L. Chabot	20	18	5	1.56
C. Smythe	C	A. Blair	44	12	15	27	D	A. Smith	43	5	0	5	B. Grant	1	0	0	1.33
21–18–5	RW	A. Bailey	44	**22**	10	**32**	D	A. Duncan	39	4	4	8					
	F	S. Horne	39	9	3	12	D	J. Arbour	10	1	0	1					
	F	J. Primeau	6	0	1	1	D	R. Horner	22	0	0	0					
	F	C. Voss	2	0	0	0											
	F	A. Gray	7	0	0	0											
OTTA	LW	H. Kilrea	38	5	7	12	D	K. Clancy	44	13	2	15	A. Connell	14	17	13	1.52
D. Gill	C	F. Nighbor	32	1	4	5	D	A. Smith	42	1	7	8					
14–17–13	RW	F. Finnigan	44	15	4	19	D	A. Shields	42	0	1	1					
	F	B. Touhey	44	9	3	12											
	F	L. Grosvenar	42	3	2	5											
	F	S. Godin	23	2	1	3											
	F	F. Elliott	43	2	0	2											
	F	M. Halliday	16	0	0	0											
MON(M)	LW	B. Siebert	40	3	5	8	D	G. Boucher	12	1	1	2	C. Benedict	14	16	7	1.54
E. Gerard	C	N. Stewart	44	21	8	29	D	R. Dutton	44	1	3	4	F. Walsh	1	4	2	1.14
15–20–9	RW	H. Smith	41	10	9	19	D	H. Hicks	44	2	0	2					
	LW	B. Northcott	6	0	0	0	D	C. McBride	1	0	0	0					
	C	D. Trottier	37	2	4	6											
	RW	J. Ward	44	14	8	22											
	F	B. Phillips	42	6	5	11											
	F	E. Robinson	33	2	1	3											
	F	J. Lamb	30	4	1	5											

AMERICAN DIVISION

	POS	PLAYER	GP	G	A	PTS		PLAYER	GP	G	A	PTS	GOALIE	W	L	T	GAvg
BOS	LW	D. Norman	39	14	5	19	D	E. Shore	39	12	7	19	T. Thompson	**26**	13	5	1.18
C. Denneny	C	C. Weiland	40	11	7	18	D	G. Owen	26	5	4	9					
26–13–5	RW	D. Clapper	40	9	2	11	D	L. Hitchman	38	1	0	1					
	LW	P. Galbraith	38	2	1	3											
	C	H. Oliver	43	17	6	23											
	RW	B. Carson	19	4	2	6											
	F	M. MacKay	30	8	2	10											
	F	C. Denneny	23	1	2	3											
	F	J. Klein	14	1	0	1											
	F	R. Green	25	0	0	0											
	F	E. Rodden	20	0	0	0											
NYR	LW	B. Cook	43	13	5	18	D	L. Bourgeault	44	2	3	5	J. Roach	21	13	10	1.48
L. Patrick	C	F. Boucher	44	10	**16**	26	D	S. Vail	18	3	0	3					
21–13–10	RW	B. Cook	43	15	8	23	D	T. Abel	44	2	1	3					
	F	P. Thompson	44	10	7	17	D	C. Johnson	9	0	0	0					
	F	M. Murdoch	44	8	6	14											
	F	B. Keeling	43	6	3	9											
	F	B. Boyd	11	0	0	0											
DET	F	C. Cooper	44	18	9	27	D	R. Noble	44	6	4	10	C. Dolson	19	16	6	1.43
J. Adams	F	G. Hay	42	11	8	19	D	B. Brydge	31	2	2	4					
19–16–9	F	B. Connors	41	13	3	16	D	G. Fraser	13	0	0	0					
	F	H. Lewis	37	9	5	14	D	P. Traub	44	0	0	0					
	F	J. Herberts	40	9	5	14											
	F	B. Brophy	37	2	4	6											
	F	L. Aurie	37	1	1	2											
	F	P. Bellefeuille	1	1	0	1											
	F	Green	2	0	0	0											
PITT	F	G. Lowrey	16	2	3	5	D	R. Smith	44	4	2	6	J. Miller	9	27	8	1.82
O. Cleghorn	F	F. Frederickson	31	3	7	10	D	T. Holway	40	4	0	4					
9–27–8	F	H. Milks	42	9	3	12	D	B. McCaffrey	42	1	0	1					
	F	H. Darragh	43	9	3	12	D	J. McKinnon	42	1	0	1					
	F	B. Cotton	32	3	2	5	D	H. Drury	43	5	4	9					
	F	D. McGurry	39	0	1	1											
	F	E. Bouchard	12	0	0	0											
CHI	F	V. Ripley	34	11	2	13	D	C. Wentworth	44	2	1	3	C. Gardiner	7	**29**	8	1.93
H. Gardiner	F	J. Gottselig	42	5	3	8	D	A. McKinnon	44	1	1	2					
7–29–8	F	D. Irvin	36	6	1	7	D	C. Loughlin	24	0	1	1					
	F	T. Arbour	42	3	4	7	D	V. Hoffinger	10	0	0	0					
	F	M. March	35	3	3	6	D	R. Taylor	38	0	0	0					
	F	R. Couture	43	1	3	4											
	F	E. Miller	15	1	1	2											
	F	D. Keats	3	0	1	1											
	F	B. Burns	7	0	0	0											

GOALS		ASSISTS		POINTS	
A. Bailey, TOR	22	F. Boucher, NYR	16	A. Bailey, TOR	32
N. Stewart, MON(M)	21	A. Blair, TOR	15	N. Stewart, MON(M)	29
C. Cooper, DET	18	G. Lowrey, TOR, PITT	12	H. Morenz, MONT	27
H. Oliver, BOS	17	A. Bailey, TOR	10	A. Blair, TOR	27
H. Morenz, MONT	17	H. Morenz, MONT	10	C. Cooper, DET	27

PENALTY MINUTES		GOALS AGAINST AVE.		SHUTOUTS	
R. Dutton, MON(M)	139	G. Hainsworth, MONT	0.98	G. Hainsworth, MONT	22
L. Conacher, NYA	132	T. Thompson, BOS	1.18	R. Worters, NYA	13
H. Smith, MON(M)	120	R. Worters, NYA	1.21	J. Roach, NYR	13
E. Shore, BOS	96	C. Dolson, DET	1.43	T. Thompson, BOS	12
		J. Roach, NYR	1.48	L. Chabot, NYR	12

National Hockey League 1929–30

TEAM	W	L	T	PTS	GF	GA
CANADIAN DIVISION						
MON(M)	23	16	5	51	141	114
*MONT	21	14	9	51	142	114
OTTA	21	15	8	50	138	118
TOR	17	21	6	40	116	124
NYA	14	25	5	33	113	161
AMERICAN DIVISION						
BOS	38	5	1	77	**179**	**98**
CHI	21	18	5	47	117	111
NYR	17	17	10	44	136	143
DET	14	24	6	34	117	133
PITT	5	36	3	13	102	185

CANADIAN DIVISION

MON(M) D. Munro 23–16–5

POS	PLAYER	GP	G	A	PTS
LW	B. Siebert	40	14	19	33
C	N. Stewart	43	39	16	55
RW	H. Smith	41	21	9	30
LW	B. Northcott	41	10	1	11
C	D. Trottier	41	17	10	27
RW	J. Ward	43	10	7	17
F	B. Phillips	42	13	10	23
F	E. Robinson	35	1	2	3
F	B. Phillips	27	1	1	2
F	C. Dinsmore	8	0	0	0
D	R. Dutton	43	3	13	16
D	D. Munro	36	7	2	9
D	G. Boucher	37	2	6	8
D	A. Wilcox	40	3	5	8

GOALIE	W	L	T	GAvg
F. Walsh	16	10	4	2.47
C. Benedict	6	6	1	2.71
A. Cox	1	0	0	2.00

MONT C. Hart 21–14–9

POS	PLAYER	GP	G	A	PTS
LW	A. Joliat	42	19	12	31
C	H. Morenz	44	40	10	50
RW	N. Wasnie	44	12	11	23
LW	G. Mantha	44	5	2	7
C	P. Lepine	44	24	9	33
RW	W. Larochelle	44	14	11	25
F	A. Mondou	44	3	5	8
F	G. Carson	35	1	0	1
F	G. Rivers	19	1	0	1
D	A. LeDuc	44	6	8	14
D	M. Burke	44	2	11	13
D	S. Mantha	44	13	11	24

GOALIE	W	L	T	GAvg
G. Hainsworth	20	13	9	2.57
R. Worters	1	0	0	2.00
T. Murray	0	1	0	4.00

OTTA N. Lalonde 21–15–8

POS	PLAYER	GP	G	A	PTS
LW	H. Kilrea	44	36	22	58
C	J. Lamb	44	29	20	49
RW	F. Finnigan	43	21	15	36
F	B. Touhey	44	10	3	13
F	A. Gagne	33	6	4	10
F	W. Kilrea	42	4	2	6
F	W. Hutton	18	0	1	1
F	L. Grosvenar	14	0	3	3
F	H. Starr	27	2	1	3
F	S. Howe	14	1	1	2
D	K. Clancy	44	17	23	40
D	A. Shields	44	6	3	9
D	A. Smith	44	2	6	8

GOALIE	W	L	T	GAvg
A. Connell	21	15	8	2.68

TOR C. Smythe 17–21–6

POS	PLAYER	GP	G	A	PTS
LW	B. Cotton	41	21	17	38
C	A. Blair	42	11	10	21
RW	A. Bailey	43	22	21	43
F	C. Conacher	38	20	9	29
F	J. Primeau	43	5	21	26
F	B. Jackson	32	12	6	18
F	E. Pettinger	43	4	9	13
F	F. Nighbor	22	2	0	2
F	G. Brydson	8	2	0	2
F	C. McBride	1	0	0	0
D	H. Day	43	7	14	21
D	R. Horner	33	2	7	9
D	A. Duncan	38	4	5	9
D	A. Smith	43	3	3	6

GOALIE	W	L	T	GAvg
L. Chabot	16	20	6	2.69
B. Grant	1	1	0	5.50

NYA L. Conacher 14–25–5

POS	PLAYER	GP	G	A	PTS
LW	J. Sheppard	43	14	15	29
C	N. Himes	44	28	22	50
RW	C. McVeigh	40	14	14	28
F	P. Patterson	44	13	4	17
F	B. Boyd	43	7	6	13
F	B. Burch	35	7	3	10
F	G. Massecar	43	7	3	10
F	B. Holmes	42	5	4	9
D	J. Simpson	44	8	13	21
D	L. Conacher	40	4	6	10
D	B. Brydge	41	2	6	8
D	R. Burmeister	40	1	1	2

GOALIE	W	L	T	GAvg
R. Worters	11	21	4	3.75
B. Grant	3	4	0	3.57
J. Forbes	0	0	1	1.00

AMERICAN DIVISION

TEAM	POS	PLAYER	GP	G	A	PTS	POS	PLAYER	GP	G	A	PTS	GOALIE	W	L	T	GAvg
BOS	LW	D. Norman	43	18	31	49	D	E. Shore	43	12	19	31	T. Thompson	**38**	5	1	**2.23**
A. Ross	C	C. Weiland	44	**43**	30	**73**	D	G. Owen	42	9	4	13					
38–5–1	RW	D. Clapper	44	41	20	61	D	L. Hitchman	39	2	7	9					
	LW	P. Galbraith	44	7	9	16	D	M. Lane	3	0	0	0					
	C	M. Barry	44	18	15	33											
	RW	H. Oliver	42	16	5	21											
	F	B. Carson	44	7	4	11											
	F	M. MacKay	40	4	5	9											
	F	B. Taylor	8	0	0	0											
	F	H. Connor	13	0	0	0											
CHI	LW	J. Gottselig	39	21	4	25	D	D. Dutkowski	44	7	10	17	C. Gardiner	21	18	5	2.52
T. Shaughnessy	C	T. Cook	41	14	16	30	D	C. Wentworth	39	3	4	7					
10–8–3	RW	M. March	43	8	7	15	D	T. Abel	38	3	3	6					
B. Tobin	LW	A. Somers	44	11	13	24	D	T. Graham	26	1	2	3					
11–10–2	C	V. Ripley	40	8	8	16											
	RW	R. Couture	43	8	8	16											
	F	T. Arbour	44	10	8	18											
	F	F. Ingram	37	6	10	16											
	F	E. Miller	38	11	5	16											
	F	S. Adams	24	4	6	10											
NYR	LW	B. Cook	43	24	18	42	D	L. Bourgeault	44	7	6	13	J. Roach	17	17	10	3.25
L. Patrick	C	F. Boucher	42	26	**36**	62	D	C. Johnson	30	3	3	6					
17–17–10	RW	B. Cook	44	29	30	59	D	L. Goldsworthy	44	4	1	5					
	F	B. Keeling	44	19	7	26	D	R. Taylor	22	2	0	2					
	F	M. Murdoch	44	13	13	26	D	S. Vail	32	1	1	2					
	F	P. Thompson	44	7	12	19	D	H. Foster	31	0	0	0					
	F	L. Quenneville	25	0	3	3	D	L. Reise	12	0	1	1					
DET	LW	G. Hay	42	18	15	33	D	S. McCabe	25	7	3	10	B. Beveridge	14	20	5	2.79
J. Adams	C	E. Goodfellow	44	17	17	34	D	B. Connors	31	3	7	10	C. Dolson	0	4	1	4.80
14–24–6	RW	C. Cooper	44	18	18	36	D	R. Noble	43	6	4	10					
	F	H. Lewis	44	20	11	31	D	H. Hicks	44	3	2	5					
	F	L. Aurie	43	14	5	19	D	R. Hughes	40	0	1	1					
	F	B. Brophy	17	1	9	10	D	H. Rockburn	36	4	0	4					
	F	P. Bellefeuille	26	5	2	7											
	F	J. Herberts	26	1	3	4											
PITT	F	H. Darragh	42	15	17	32	D	H. Milks	40	13	11	24	J. Miller	5	**35**	3	4.16
F. Frederickson	F	G. Lowrey	44	16	14	30	D	J. McKinnon	43	10	7	17	R. Spooner	0	1	0	6.00
5–36–3	F	J. Jarvis	41	11	8	19	D	G. Fraser	30	6	4	10					
	F	F. Frederickson	9	4	7	11	D	R. Smith	42	2	1	3					
	F	T. White	29	8	1	9	D	H. Drury	26	2	0	2					
	F	A. Briden	30	4	3	7	D	J. Spring	22	1	0	1					
	F	C. Barton	39	4	2	6											
	F	R. Manners	33	3	2	5											

GOALS		ASSISTS		POINTS	
C. Weiland, BOS	43	F. Boucher, NYR	36	C. Weiland, BOS	73
D. Clapper, BOS	41	D. Norman, BOS	31	F. Boucher, NYR	62
H. Morenz, MONT	40	C. Weiland, BOS	30	D. Clapper, BOS	61
N. Stewart, MON(M)	39	B. Cook, NYR	30	B. Cook, NYR	59
H. Kilrea, OTTA	36	K. Clancy, OTTA	23	H. Kilrea, OTTA	58

PENALTY MINUTES		GOALS AGAINST AVE.		SHUTOUTS	
J. Lamb, OTTA	119	T. Thompson, BOS	2.23	L. Chabot, TOR	6
S. Mantha, MONT	108	F. Walsh, MON(M)	2.47	G. Hainsworth, MONT	4
E. Shore, BOS	105	C. Gardiner, CHI	2.52	T. Thompson, BOS	3
R. Dutton, MON(M)	98	G. Hainsworth, MONT	2.57	C. Gardiner, CHI	3
H. Rockburn, DET	97	L. Chabot, TOR	2.69	F. Walsh, MON(M)	2

National Hockey League 1930–31

TEAM	W	L	T	PTS	GF	GA	TEAM	W	L	T	PTS	GF	GA
CANADIAN DIVISION							AMERICAN DIVISION						
*MONT	26	10	8	60	129	89	BOS	28	10	6	62	**143**	90
TOR	22	13	9	53	118	99	NYR	23	17	8	54	134	112
MON(M)	20	18	6	46	105	106	CHI	24	17	3	51	108	78
NYA	18	16	10	46	76	**74**	DET	16	21	7	39	102	105
OTTA	10	30	4	24	91	142	PHI	4	36	4	12	76	184

CANADIAN DIVISION

TEAM	POS	PLAYER	GP	G	A	PTS	POS	PLAYER	GP	G	A	PTS	GOALIE	W	L	T	GAvg
MONT	LW	A. Joliat	43	13	22	35	D	A. LeDuc	44	8	6	14	G. Hainsworth	26	10	8	2.02
C. Hart	C	H. Morenz	39	28	23	**51**	D	S. Mantha	44	4	7	11					
26–10–8	RW	J. Gagnon	41	18	7	25	D	M. Burke	44	2	5	7					
	F	P. Lepine	44	17	7	24	D	B. McCaffrey	22	2	1	3					
	F	G. Mantha	44	11	6	17	D	N. Wasnie	44	9	2	11					
	F	W. Larochelle	40	8	5	13											
	F	A. Lesieur	21	2	0	2											
	F	A. Mondou	40	5	4	9											
	F	G. Rivers	44	2	5	7											
	F	J. Pusie	6	0	0	0											
TOR	LW	B. Jackson	43	18	13	31	D	K. Clancy	44	7	14	21	L. Chabot	21	8	8	2.16
C. Smythe	C	J. Primeau	38	9	**32**	41	D	H. Day	44	1	13	14	B. Grant	1	5	1	2.71
1–0–1	RW	A. Bailey	40	23	19	42	D	R. Horner	42	1	11	12					
A. Duncan	LW	B. Cotton	43	12	17	29	D	A. Levinsky	8	0	1	1					
21–13–8	C	A. Blair	44	11	8	19	D	A. Duncan	2	0	0	0					
	RW	C. Conacher	37	**31**	12	43											
	F	B. Gracie	8	4	2	6											
	F	B. Dye	6	0	0	0											
	F	H. Hamel	2	0	0	0											
MON(M)	LW	B. Siebert	43	16	12	28	D	L. Conacher	36	4	3	7	D. Kerr	13	11	4	2.71
D. Munro	C	N. Stewart	43	25	14	39	D	J. Gallagher	35	4	2	6	F. Walsh	7	7	2	1.88
14–13–5	RW	H. Smith	40	12	14	26	D	A. Wilcox	40	2	2	4					
G. Boucher	F	D. Trottier	43	9	8	17	D	D. Munro	4	0	1	1					
6–5–1	F	J. Ward	42	14	8	22	D	G. Boucher	30	0	0	0					
	F	B. Northcott	22	7	3	10											
	F	B. Phillips	42	6	1	7											
	F	J. McVicar	40	2	4	6											
	F	E. Roche	42	2	0	2											
	F	A. Huggins	20	1	1	2											
NYA	LW	C. McVeigh	44	5	11	16	D	R. Dutton	44	1	11	12	R. Worters	18	16	10	**1.68**
E. Gerard	C	N. Himes	44	15	9	24	D	J. Simpson	42	2	0	2					
18–16–10	RW	P. Patterson	44	8	6	14	D	B. Brydge	43	2	5	7					
	LW	J. Sheppard	42	5	8	13	D	D. Dutkowski	12	1	1	2					
	C	B. Burch	44	14	8	22	D	V. Ayres	26	2	1	3					
	RW	F. Carson	43	6	7	13											
	F	A. Hughes	42	5	7	12											
	F	G. Massecar	43	4	7	11											
	F	H. Emms	44	5	4	9											
	F	M. Neville	16	1	0	1											
OTTA	LW	H. Kilrea	44	14	8	22	D	A. Smith	44	5	6	11	A. Connell	10	**22**	4	3.06
N. Lalonde	C	J. Lamb	44	11	14	25	D	A. Smith	36	2	4	6	B. Beveridge	0	8	0	3.56
10–30–4	RW	F. Finnigan	44	9	8	17	D	L. Bourgeault	28	0	4	4					
	F	A. Gagne	44	19	11	30	D	H. Starr	36	2	1	3					
	F	B. Touhey	44	15	15	30											
	F	D. Cox	44	9	12	21											
	F	L. Grosvenar	34	5	4	9											
	F	H. Connor	11	0	0	0											
	F	R. Kinsella	14	0	0	0											
	F	E. Pettinger	12	0	0	0											

AMERICAN DIVISION

TEAM	POS	PLAYER	GP	G	A	PTS	POS	PLAYER	GP	G	A	PTS	GOALIE	W	L	T	GAvg
BOS	LW	D. Norman	32	8	3	11	D	E. Shore	44	15	16	31	T. Thompson	**28**	10	6	2.05
A. Ross	C	C. Weiland	44	25	13	38	D	G. Owen	37	12	13	25					
28–10–6	RW	D. Clapper	43	22	8	30	D	J. Pratt	32	2	0	2					
	LW	P. Galbraith	43	2	3	5	D	L. Hitchman	41	0	2	2					
	C	M. Barry	44	20	11	31											
	RW	H. Oliver	43	16	14	30											
	F	S. Harris	34	2	4	6											
	F	R. Beattie	32	10	11	21											
	F	A. Chapman	44	7	7	14											
	F	H. Darragh	25	2	4	6											
	F	P. Lyons	12	0	0	0											
NYR	LW	B. Cook	44	18	17	35	D	J. Jerwa	33	4	7	11	J. Roach	19	16	9	1.98
L. Patrick	C	F. Boucher	44	12	27	39	D	C. Johnson	44	2	6	8					
19–16–9	RW	B. Cook	44	30	12	42	D	B. Regan	42	2	1	3					
	F	B. Keeling	44	13	9	22	D	F. Peters	43	0	0	0					
	F	M. Murdoch	44	7	7	14											
	F	P. Thompson	44	7	7	14											
	F	C. Dillon	25	7	3	10											
	F	G. Carrigan	33	2	0	2											
	F	E. Rodden	24	0	3	3											
	F	F. Waite	17	1	3	4											
	F	B. Maracle	11	1	3	4											

	POS	PLAYER	GP	G	A	PTS		PLAYER	GP	G	A	PTS	GOALIE	W	L	T	GAvg
CHI	LW	J. Gottselig	42	20	12	32	D	C. Wentworth	43	4	4	8	C. Gardiner	24	17	3	1.77
D. Irvin	C	T. Cook	44	15	14	29	D	T. Graham	42	0	7	7					
24–17–3	RW	R. Couture	44	8	11	19	D	H. Bostrom	42	2	2	4					
	LW	A. Somers	33	3	6	9	D	T. Abel	40	0	1	1					
	C	V. Ripley	37	8	4	12											
	RW	M. March	44	11	6	17											
	F	F. Ingram	43	17	4	21											
	F	S. Adams	37	5	13	18											
	F	V. Desjardins	39	3	12	15											
	F	D. Romnes	30	5	7	12											
	F	T. Arbour	38	3	3	6											
DET	LW	H. Lewis	44	15	6	21	D	B. McInenly	44	3	5	8	C. Dolson	16	21	7	2.39
J. Adams	C	E. Goodfellow	44	25	23	48	D	R. Noble	44	2	5	7					
16–21–7	RW	C. Cooper	43	14	14	28	D	S. Evans	43	1	4	5					
	F	L. Aurie	41	12	6	18	D	S. McCabe	44	2	1	3					
	F	G. Hay	44	8	10	18	D	H. Rockburn	42	0	1	1					
	F	J. Sorrell	39	9	7	16	D	H. Hicks	22	2	0	2					
	F	T. Filmore	40	6	2	8											
	F	F. Frederickson	25	1	2	3											
	F	J. Newman	8	1	1	2											
	F	J. Creighton	11	1	0	1											
PHI	F	G. Lowrey	42	13	14	27	D	H. Drury	22	0	2	2	W. Cude	2	**22**	3	4.38
C. Smeaton	F	H. Milks	44	17	6	23	D	A. Shields	43	7	3	10	J. Miller	2	12	1	3.33
4–36–4	F	S. Howe	44	9	11	20	D	J. McKinnon	38	1	1	2	J. Forbes	0	2	0	3.50
	F	W. Kilrea	44	8	12	20	D	S. Crossett	21	0	0	0					
	F	C. Barton	43	6	7	13	D	R. Smith	9	0	0	0					
	F	J. Jarvis	43	5	7	12											
	F	T. White	14	3	0	3											
	F	E. McCalmon	16	3	0	3											
	F	W. Hutton	18	0	1	1											

GOALS

C. Conacher, TOR	31
B. Cook, NYR	30
H. Morenz, MONT	28
N. Stewart, MON(M)	25
E. Goodfellow, DET	25
C. Weiland, BOS	25

ASSISTS

J. Primeau, TOR	32
F. Boucher, NYR	27
E. Goodfellow, DET	23
H. Morenz, MONT	23
A. Joliat, MONT	22

POINTS

H. Morenz, MONT	51
E. Goodfellow, DET	48
C. Conacher, TOR	43
A. Bailey, TOR	42
B. Cook, NYR	42

PENALTY MINUTES

H. Rockburn, DET	118
E. Shore, BOS	105
D. Coulson, PHI	103
A. Shields, PHI	98
J. Lamb, OTTA	91
M. Burke, MONT	91

GOALS AGAINST AVE.

R. Worters, NYA	1.68
C. Gardiner, CHI	1.77
J. Roach, NYR	1.98
G. Hainsworth, MONT	2.02
T. Thompson, BOS	2.05

SHUTOUTS

C. Gardiner, CHI	12
G. Hainsworth, MONT	8
R. Worters, NYA	3
J. Roach, NYR	7
L. Chabot, TOR	6
C. Dolson, DET	6

National Hockey League 1931–32

TEAM	W	L	T	PTS	GF	GA
CANADIAN DIVISION						
MONT	25	16	7	57	128	111
*TOR	23	18	7	53	133	127
MON(M)	19	22	7	45	**142**	139
NYA	16	24	8	40	95	142

TEAM	W	L	T	PTS	GF	GA
AMERICAN DIVISION						
NYR	23	17	8	54	134	112
CHI	18	19	11	47	86	**101**
DET	18	20	10	46	95	108
BOS	15	21	12	42	122	117

CANADIAN DIVISION

TEAM	POS	PLAYER	GP	G	A	PTS	PLAYER	GP	G	A	PTS	GOALIE	W	L	T	GAvg
MONT	LW	A. Joliat	48	15	24	39	D S. Mantha	47	5	5	10	G. Hainsworth	**25**	16	7	2.29
C. Hart	C	H. Morenz	48	24	25	49	D M. Burke	48	3	6	9	A. LeDuc	0	0	0	1.00
25–16–7	RW	J. Gagnon	48	19	18	37	D A. LeDuc	41	5	3	8					
	LW	A. Mondou	47	6	12	18	D D. Munro	48	1	1	2					
	C	P. Lepine	48	19	11	30	D A. Lesieur	24	1	2	3					
	RW	W. Larochelle	48	18	8	26										
	F	N. Wasnie	48	10	2	12										
	F	G. Mantha	48	1	7	8										
	F	G. Rivers	25	1	0	1										
	F	A. Alexandre	10	0	2	2										
TOR	LW	B. Jackson	48	28	25	**53**	D K. Clancy	48	10	9	19	L. Chabot	22	16	6	2.41
A. Duncan	C	J. Primeau	46	13	**37**	50	D H. Day	47	7	8	15	B. Grant	1	2	1	3.60
0–3–2	RW	C. Conacher	44	**34**	14	48	D R. Horner	42	7	9	16					
D. Irvin	LW	B. Cotton	48	5	13	18	D A. Levinsky	47	5	5	10					
23–15–5	C	A. Blair	48	9	14	23	D F. Robertson	8	0	0	0					
	RW	A. Bailey	41	8	5	13										
	F	F. Finnigan	47	8	13	21										
	F	B. Gracie	48	13	8	21										
	F	H. Darragh	48	5	10	15										
MON(M)	LW	B. Northcott	47	19	6	25	D L. Conacher	45	7	9	16	F. Walsh	14	10	3	2.85
S. Cleghorn	C	H. Smith	46	11	33	44	D A. Wilcox	48	3	3	6	N. Smith	5	12	4	2.95
19–22–7	RW	J. Ward	48	19	19	38	D H. Starr	46	1	2	3	H. Starr	0	0	0	0.00
	LW	D. Trottier	48	26	18	44	D J. McVicar	48	0	0	0					
	C	P. Haynes	11	1	0	1										
	RW	G. Brydson	47	12	13	25										
	F	B. Siebert	48	21	18	39										
	F	N. Stewart	38	22	11	33										
	F	E. Robinson	28	0	3	3										
	F	B. Phillips	47	1	1	2										
	F	J. Gallagher	19	1	0	1										
NYA	LW	C. McVeigh	48	12	15	27	D B. McInenly	30	12	6	18	R. Worters	12	**20**	8	2.75
E. Gerard	C	N. Himes	48	7	21	28	D B. Brydge	48	2	8	10	J. Forbes	3	3	0	2.67
16–24–8	RW	J. Lamb	48	14	11	25	D R. Dutton	47	3	5	8	A. Shields	0	0	0	4.50
	F	B. Burch	48	14	11	25	D V. Ayres	45	2	4	6	D. Kerr	0	1	0	6.00
	F	T. Filmore	31	8	6	14	D A. Shields	48	4	1	5	M. Roberts	1	0	0	1.00
	F	W. Kilrea	48	3	8	11										
	F	J. Keating	22	5	3	8										
	F	E. Convey	21	1	0	1										
	F	P. Patterson	20	6	0	6										
	F	R. Burmeister	16	3	2	5										

AMERICAN DIVISION

TEAM	POS	PLAYER	GP	G	A	PTS	PLAYER	GP	G	A	PTS	GOALIE	W	L	T	GAvg
NYR	LW	B. Cook	45	14	20	34	D E. Seibert	44	4	6	10	J. Roach	23	17	8	2.33
L. Patrick	C	F. Boucher	48	12	23	35	D C. Johnson	47	3	10	13					
23–17–8	RW	B. Cook	48	**34**	14	48	D H. Milks	45	0	4	4					
	LW	B. Keeling	48	17	3	20	D O. Heller	21	2	2	4					
	C	M. Murdoch	48	5	16	21										
	RW	C. Dillon	48	23	15	38										
	F	A. Somers	48	11	15	26										
	F	D. Norman	46	3	9	12										
	F	V. Desjardins	48	3	3	6										
	F	D. Brennan	38	4	3	7										
CHI	LW	M. March	48	12	13	25	D C. Wentworth	48	3	10	13	C. Gardiner	18	19	11	**1.92**
E. Iverson	C	T. Cook	48	12	13	25	D G. Boucher	43	1	5	6	W. Cude	0	0	0	9.00
18–19–11	RW	J. Gottselig	43	14	15	29	D T. Abel	48	3	3	6					
	F	P. Thompson	48	8	14	22	D T. Graham	48	0	3	3					
	F	V. Ripley	46	12	6	18	D A. Coulter	13	0	1	1					
	F	R. Couture	48	9	9	18										
	F	G. Lowrey	48	8	3	11										
	F	L. Holmes	41	1	4	5										
	F	E. Miller	9	0	0	0										
	F	S. Adams	26	0	5	5										
	F	F. Ingram	21	1	2	3										
DET	LW	H. Kilrea	47	13	3	16	D H. Emms	20	6	9	15	A. Connell	18	20	10	2.25
J. Adams	C	E. Goodfellow	48	14	16	30	D A. Smith	48	6	8	14					
18–20–10	RW	L. Aurie	48	12	8	20	D D. Young	47	10	2	12					
	F	F. Carson	30	10	14	24	D R. Noble	48	3	3	6					
	F	H. Lewis	48	5	14	19										
	F	J. Sorrell	48	8	5	13										
	F	D. Cox	47	4	6	10										
	F	C. Cooper	48	3	5	8										
	F	A. Gagne	13	1	1	2										

TEAM	POS	PLAYER	GP	G	A	PTS	POS	PLAYER	GP	G	A	PTS	GOALIE	W	L	T	GAvg
BOS	LW	P. Galbraith	47	2	1	3	D	E. Shore	44	9	13	22	T. Thompson	13	19	11	2.40
A. Ross	C	M. Barry	48	21	17	38	D	G. Owen	45	12	10	22	P. Jackson	1	1	1	2.00
15–21–12	RW	H. Oliver	44	13	7	20	D	L. Hitchman	48	4	3	7	W. Cude	1	1	0	3.00
	F	D. Clapper	48	17	22	39	D	H. Foster	34	1	2	3					
	F	C. Weiland	47	14	12	26											
	F	A. Chapman	48	11	14	25											
	F	B. Touhey	26	5	4	9											
	F	F. Jerwa	29	4	5	9											
	F	B. Cook	28	4	4	8											
	F	I. Boyd	30	10	10	20											
	F	P. Runge	14	0	1	1											

GOALS		ASSISTS		POINTS	
C. Conacher, TOR	34	J. Primeau, TOR	37	B. Jackson, TOR	53
B. Cook, NYR	34	H. Smith, MON(M)	33	J. Primeau, TOR	50
B. Jackson, TOR	28	B. Jackson, TOR	25	H. Morenz, MONT	49
H. Morenz, MONT	24	H. Morenz, MONT	25	C. Conacher, TOR	48
C. Dillon, NYR	23	A. Joliat, MONT	24	B. Cook, NYR	48

PENALTY MINUTES		GOALS AGAINST AVE.		SHUTOUTS	
R. Dutton, NYA	107	C. Gardiner, CHI	1.92	J. Roach, NYR	9
C. Johnson, NYR	106	A. Connell, DET	2.25	T. Thompson, BOS	9
R. Horner, TOR	97	G. Hainsworth, MONT	2.29	G. Hainsworth, MONT	6
D. Trottier, MON(M)	94	J. Roach, NYR	2.33	A. Connell, DET	6
E. Seibert, NYR	88	L. Chabot, TOR	2.41	R. Worters, NYA	5

National Hockey League 1932–33

TEAM	W	L	T	PTS	GF	GA
CANADIAN DIVISION						
TOR	24	18	6	54	119	111
MON(M)	22	20	6	50	**135**	119
MONT	18	25	5	41	92	115
NYA	15	22	11	41	91	118
OTTA	11	27	10	32	88	131

TEAM	W	L	T	PTS	GF	GA
AMERICAN DIVISION						
BOS	25	15	8	58	124	**88**
DET	25	15	8	58	111	93
*NYR	23	17	8	54	**135**	107
CHI	16	20	12	44	88	101

CANADIAN DIVISION

TEAM	POS	PLAYER	GP	G	A	PTS	POS	PLAYER	GP	G	A	PTS	GOALIE	W	L	T	GAvg
TOR	LW	B. Jackson	48	27	17	44	D	K. Clancy	48	13	12	25	L. Chabot	24	18	6	2.31
D. Irvin	C	J. Primeau	48	11	21	32	D	H. Day	47	6	14	20	C. Conacher	0	0	0	0.00
24–18–6	RW	C. Conacher	40	14	19	33	D	A. Levinsky	48	5	11	16	K. Clancy	0	0	0	1.00
	F	B. Gracie	48	9	13	22	D	R. Horner	48	3	8	11	R. Horner	0	0	0	1.00
	F	B. Cotton	48	10	11	21							A. Levinsky	0	0	0	1.00
	F	A. Bailey	47	10	8	18											
	F	K. Doraty	38	5	11	16											
	F	A. Blair	43	6	9	15											
	F	H. Darragh	9	1	2	3											
	F	B. Thoms	29	3	9	12											
	F	S. Adams	19	0	2	2											
MON(M)	LW	B. Northcott	47	22	21	43	D	L. Conacher	47	7	21	28	D. Kerr	14	8	3	2.32
E. Gerard	C	H. Smith	48	20	21	41	D	C. Wentworth	47	4	10	14	F. Walsh	8	11	3	2.55
22–20–6	RW	J. Ward	48	16	17	33	D	A. Wilcox	47	0	3	3	H. Plaxton	0	1	0	5.00
	LW	D. Trottier	48	16	15	31	D	A. Bellemer	15	0	0	0					
	C	P. Haynes	47	16	25	41	D	R. Noble	27	0	0	0					
	RW	G. Brydson	48	11	17	28											
	F	E. Robinson	43	15	9	24											
	F	L. Duguid	48	4	7	11											
	F	H. Plaxton	15	1	2	3											
	F	W. Kilrea	6	1	7	8											

TEAM	POS	PLAYER	GP	G	A	PTS	POS	PLAYER	GP	G	A	PTS	GOALIE	W	L	T	GAvg
MONT	LW	A. Joliat	48	18	21	39	D	S. Mantha	48	4	7	11	G. Hainsworth	18	**25**	5	2.40
N. Lalonde	C	H. Morenz	46	14	21	35	D	A. LeDuc	48	5	3	8					
18–25–5	RW	J. Gagnon	48	12	23	35	D	G. Carson	48	5	2	7					
	LW	G. Mantha	43	3	6	9	D	L. Bourgeault	15	1	1	2					
	C	P. Lepine	46	8	8	16											
	RW	W. Larochelle	47	11	4	15											
	F	A. Giroux	40	5	2	7											
	F	L. Gaudreault	24	2	2	4											
	F	A. Mondou	24	1	3	4											
	F	H. Harrington	24	1	1	2											
	F	G. Hart	18	0	3	3											
NYA	LW	J. Sheppard	46	17	9	26	D	B. Brydge	48	4	15	19	R. Worters	15	22	10	2.47
J. Simpson	C	N. Himes	48	9	25	34	D	D. Dutkowski	48	4	7	11	J. Forbes	0	0	1	2.00
15–22–11	RW	C. McVeigh	40	7	12	19	D	V. Ayres	48	0	3	3					
	F	N. Wasnie	48	11	12	23	D	R. Dutton	43	0	2	2					
	F	P. Patterson	48	12	7	19											
	F	W. Jackson	35	10	2	12											
	F	R. Martin	47	5	7	12											
	F	B. Phillips	26	1	7	8											
	F	T. Filmore	33	1	4	5											
	F	W. Starr	27	4	3	7											
	F	J. Keating	13	0	2	2											
OTTA	LW	H. Kilrea	48	14	8	22	D	A. Shields	48	4	7	11	B. Beveridge	7	19	8	2.71
C. Denneny	C	C. Weiland	48	16	11	27	D	B. McInenly	30	2	2	4	A. Connell	4	8	2	2.57
11–27–10	RW	S. Howe	48	12	12	24	D	H. Rockburn	16	0	1	1					
	F	B. Touhey	47	12	7	19	D	M. Burke	16	0	0	0					
	F	F. Finnigan	44	4	14	18											
	F	G. Forslund	48	4	9	13											
	F	D. Cox	47	4	7	11											
	F	E. Roche	20	4	5	9											
	F	D. Roche	16	3	6	9											
	F	G. Lowrey	6	0	0	0											

AMERICAN DIVISION

TEAM	POS	PLAYER	GP	G	A	PTS	POS	PLAYER	GP	G	A	PTS	GOALIE	W	L	T	GAvg
BOS	LW	R. Beattie	48	8	12	20	D	E. Shore	48	8	27	35	T. Thompson	**25**	15	8	**1.83**
A. Ross	C	N. Stewart	47	18	18	36	D	G. Owen	42	6	2	8					
25–15–8	RW	D. Clapper	48	14	14	28	D	L. Hitchman	45	0	1	1					
	LW	P. Galbraith	47	1	2	3	D	A. Smith	15	5	4	9					
	C	M. Barry	47	24	13	37											
	RW	H. Oliver	47	11	7	18											
	F	J. Lamb	42	11	8	19											
	F	O. Heximer	48	7	5	12											
	F	A. Chapman	46	3	6	9											
	F	F. Jerwa	34	3	4	7											
	F	V. Ripley	23	2	5	7											
DET	LW	H. Lewis	48	20	14	34	D	D. Young	48	5	6	11	J. Roach	**25**	15	8	1.94
J. Adams	C	C. Voss	38	6	14	20	D	L. Goldsworthy	26	3	6	9					
25–15–8	RW	L. Aurie	47	12	11	23	D	S. Evans	48	2	6	8					
	F	F. Carson	47	12	13	25	D	W. Buswell	46	2	4	6					
	F	H. Emms	41	9	13	22											
	F	E. Goodfellow	40	12	8	20											
	F	E. Wiseman	47	8	8	16											
	F	J. Gallagher	35	3	6	9											
	F	G. Hay	34	1	6	7											
	F	R. Moffatt	24	1	1	2											
	F	G. Marker	15	1	1	2											
NYR	LW	B. Cook	48	22	15	37	D	B. Siebert	42	9	10	19	A. Aitkenhead	23	17	8	2.23
L. Patrick	C	F. Boucher	46	7	**28**	35	D	C. Johnson	48	8	9	17					
23–17–8	RW	B. Cook	48	**28**	22	**50**	D	D. Brennan	48	5	4	9					
	LW	B. Keeling	47	8	6	14	D	E. Seibert	45	2	3	5					
	C	M. Murdoch	48	5	11	16											
	RW	C. Dillon	48	21	10	31											
	F	A. Somers	48	7	15	22											
	F	O. Asmundson	48	5	10	15											
	F	G. Pettinger	35	1	2	3											
CHI	LW	P. Thompson	48	13	20	33	D	T. Graham	47	3	8	11	C. Gardiner	16	20	12	2.10
E. Iverson	C	D. Romnes	47	10	12	22	D	B. MacKenzie	35	4	4	8					
8–9–6	RW	M. March	48	9	11	20	D	A. Coulter	46	3	2	5					
T. Gorman	F	T. Cook	47	12	14	26	D	T. Abel	45	0	4	4					
8–11–6	F	J. Gottselig	42	11	11	22	D	H. Bostrom	20	1	0	1					
	F	R. Couture	46	10	7	17											
	F	D. McFayden	48	5	9	14											
	F	R. Jenkins	45	3	10	13											
	F	B. Burch	24	2	0	2											
	F	L. Holmes	18	0	0	0											

GOALS		ASSISTS		POINTS	
B. Cook, NYR	28	F. Boucher, NYR	28	B. Cook, NYR	50
B. Jackson, TOR	27	E. Shore, BOS	27	B. Jackson, TOR	44
M. Barry, BOS	24	P. Haynes, MON(M)	25	B. Northcott, MON(M)	43
B. Cook, NYR	22	N. Himes, NYA	25	P. Haynes, MON(M)	41
B. Northcott, MON(M)	22	J. Gagnon, MONT	23	H. Smith, MON(M)	41

PENALTY MINUTES		GOALS AGAINST AVE.		SHUTOUTS	
R. Horner, TOR	144	T. Thompson, BOS	1.83	T. Thompson, BOS	11
C. Johnson, NYR	127	J. Roach, DET	1.94	J. Roach, DET	9
A. Shields, OTTA	119	C. Gardiner, CHI	2.10	G. Hainsworth, MONT	7
E. Shore, BOS	102	A. Aitkenhead, NYR	2.23	L. Chabot, TOR	5
V. Ayres, NYA	97	D. Kerr, MON(M)	2.32	C. Gardiner, CHI	5

National Hockey League 1933–34

TEAM	W	L	T	PTS	GF	GA	TEAM	W	L	T	PTS	GF	GA
CANADIAN DIVISION							AMERICAN DIVISION						
TOR	26	13	9	61	**174**	119	DET	24	14	10	58	113	98
MONT	22	20	6	50	99	101	*CHI	20	17	11	51	88	**83**
MON(M)	19	18	11	49	117	122	NYR	21	19	8	50	120	113
NYA	15	23	10	40	104	132	BOS	18	25	5	41	111	130
OTTA	13	29	6	32	115	143							

CANADIAN DIVISION

	POS	PLAYER	GP	G	A	PTS		PLAYER	GP	G	A	PTS	GOALIE	W	L	T	GAvg
TOR	LW	B. Jackson	38	20	18	38	D	K. Clancy	46	11	17	28	G. Hainsworth	**26**	13	9	2.48
D. Irvin	C	J. Primeau	45	14	**32**	46	D	R. Horner	40	11	10	21					
26–13–9	RW	C. Conacher	42	**32**	20	**52**	D	H. Day	48	9	10	19					
	LW	B. Boll	42	12	8	20	D	A. Levinsky	47	5	11	16					
	C	B. Thoms	47	8	18	26											
	RW	H. Kilrea	43	10	13	23											
	F	A. Blair	47	14	9	23											
	F	B. Cotton	47	8	14	22											
	F	K. Doraty	34	9	10	19											
	F	C. Sands	45	8	8	16											
	F	A. Bailey	13	2	3	5											
MONT	LW	G. Mantha	44	6	9	15	D	S. Mantha	48	4	6	10	L. Chabot	21	20	6	2.15
N. Lalonde	C	P. Lepine	48	10	8	18	D	L. Bourgeault	48	4	3	7	W. Cude	1	0	0	0.00*
22–20–6	RW	W. Larochelle	48	16	11	27	D	G. Carson	48	5	1	6					
	LW	A. Joliat	48	22	15	37	D	M. Burke	45	1	4	5					
	C	H. Morenz	39	8	13	21	D	J. Portland	31	0	2	2					
	RW	J. Gagnon	48	9	15	24											
	F	J. Riley	48	6	11	17											
	F	A. Mondou	48	5	3	8											
	F	S. Godin	36	2	2	4											
	F	P. Raymond	29	1	0	1											
MON(M)	LW	B. Northcott	47	20	13	33	D	B. MacKenzie	48	4	3	7	D. Kerr	19	18	11	2.54
E. Gerard	C	H. Smith	47	18	19	37	D	C. Wentworth	48	2	5	7					
19–18–11	RW	J. Ward	48	14	9	23	D	I. Frew	30	2	1	3					
	F	E. Robinson	47	12	16	28	D	V. Ayres	17	0	0	0					
	F	D. Trottier	48	9	17	26											
	F	R. Blinco	31	14	9	23											
	F	H. Cain	31	4	5	9											
	F	G. Brydson	37	4	5	9											
	F	P. Haynes	45	5	4	9											
	F	W. Kilrea	44	3	1	4											
NYA	F	E. Burke	46	20	10	30	D	B. Brydge	48	6	7	13	R. Worters	12	13	10	2.08
J. Simpson	F	N. Himes	48	9	16	25	D	R. Dutton	48	2	8	10	B. Grant	1	4	0	3.60
15–23–10	F	J. Klein	48	13	9	22	D	R. Doran	39	1	4	5	M. Roberts	1	4	0	4.17
	F	H. Conn	48	4	17	21	D	A. Murray	48	1	1	2	A. Connell	1	0	0	2.00
	F	W. Jackson	46	6	9	15	D	C. Speyer	9	0	0	0	A. Cox	0	1	0	3.00
	F	R. Martin	47	8	9	17							P. Jackson	0	1	0	9.00
	F	C. McVeigh	48	15	12	27											
	F	H. Picketts	48	3	1	4											
	F	B. Gracie	24	4	6	10											
	F	A. Chapman	25	2	8	10											

TEAM	POS	PLAYER	GP	G	A	PTS	POS	PLAYER	GP	G	A	PTS	GOALIE	W	L	T	GAvg
OTTA	F	M. Kaminsky	38	9	17	26	D	A. Shields	48	4	7	11	B. Beveridge	13	**29**	6	2.98
G. Boucher	F	B. Touhey	46	12	8	20	D	J. Kalbfleish	22	0	4	4					
13–29–6	F	N. Wasnie	37	11	6	17	D	S. Bowman	46	0	2	2					
	F	D. Roche	44	14	10	24	D	A. LeDuc	34	1	3	4					
	F	C. Voss	40	7	16	23											
	F	B. Saunders	19	1	3	4											
	F	B. Cook	19	1	0	1											

AMERICAN DIVISION

TEAM	POS	PLAYER	GP	G	A	PTS	POS	PLAYER	GP	G	A	PTS	GOALIE	W	L	T	GAvg
DET	LW	H. Lewis	43	16	15	31	D	H. Emms	47	7	7	14	W. Cude	15	6	8	1.62*
J. Adams	C	C. Weiland	39	11	19	30	D	T. Graham	28	1	0	1	J. Roach	9	8	1	2.50
24–14–10	RW	L. Aurie	48	16	19	35	D	D. Young	48	4	0	4	A. Cox	0	0	1	2.50
	LW	J. Sorrell	47	21	10	31	D	W. Buswell	47	1	2	3	D. Young	0	0	0	1.00
	C	E. Goodfellow	48	13	13	26	D	F. Robertson	24	1	0	1					
	RW	E. Wiseman	47	5	9	14											
	F	F. Carson	47	10	9	19											
	F	G. Pettinger	48	3	14	17											
	F	W. STarr	28	2	2	4											
	F	L. Gross	13	1	1	2											
CHI	LW	P. Thompson	48	20	16	36	D	L. Conacher	48	10	13	23	C. Gardiner	20	17	11	1.73
T. Gorman	C	D. Romnes	47	8	21	29	D	A. Coulter	46	5	2	7					
20–17–11	RW	M. March	48	4	13	17	D	R. Jenkins	48	2	2	4					
	LW	J. Gottselig	48	16	14	30											
	C	T. Cook	42	5	9	14											
	RW	R. Couture	48	5	8	13											
	F	J. Leswick	47	1	7	8											
	F	L. Goldsworthy	28	3	3	6											
	F	D. McFayden	46	1	3	4											
	F	L. Trudel	31	1	3	4											
NYR	LW	B. Cook	48	18	15	33	D	E. Seibert	48	13	10	23	A. Aitkenhead	21	19	8	2.35
L. Patrick	C	F. Boucher	48	14	30	44	D	C. Johnson	48	2	6	8					
21–19–8	RW	B. Cook	48	13	13	26	D	O. Heller	48	2	5	7					
	LW	B. Keeling	48	15	5	20	D	D. Dutkowski	29	0	6	6					
	C	M. Murdoch	48	14	15	29	D	D. Brennan	37	0	0	0					
	RW	C. Dillon	48	13	26	39	D	J. Pusie	19	0	2	2					
	F	V. Ripley	34	5	12	17											
	F	O. Asmundson	46	2	6	8											
	F	D. Cox	13	5	0	5											
BOS	LW	R. Beattie	48	9	13	22	D	E. Shore	30	2	10	12	T. Thompson	18	25	5	2.71
A. Ross	C	N. Stewart	47	21	17	38	D	A. Smith	48	4	6	10					
18–25–5	RW	D. Clapper	48	10	12	22	D	M. Lane	28	2	1	3					
	F	M. Barry	48	27	12	39	D	L. Hitchman	27	1	0	1					
	F	J. Lamb	48	10	15	25	D	B. Siebert	19	5	6	11					
	F	H. Oliver	48	5	9	14	D	A. Wilcox	16	0	1	1					
	F	J. O'Neill	25	2	2	4											
	F	P. Galbraith	42	0	2	2											
	F	J. Sheppard	4	0	0	0											
	F	P. Patterson	10	0	1	1											
	F	D. Smillie	12	2	2	4											

GOALS

C. Conacher, TOR	32
M. Barry, BOS	27
A. Joliat, MONT	22
J. Sorrell, DET	21
N. Stewart, BOS	21

ASSISTS

J. Primeau, TOR	32
F. Boucher, NYR	30
C. Dillon, NYR	26
D. Romnes, CHI	21
C. Conacher, TOR	20

POINTS

C. Conacher, TOR	52
J. Primeau, TOR	46
F. Boucher, NYR	44
M. Barry, BOS	39
C. Dillon, NYR	39

PENALTY MINUTES

R. Horner, TOR	146
L. Conacher, CHI	87
C. Johnson, NYR	86
N. Stewart, BOS	68
E. Seibert, NYR	66

GOALS AGAINST AVE.

W. Cude, DET	1.57
C. Gardiner, CHI	1.73
R. Worters, NYA	2.08
L. Chabot, MONT	2.15

SHUTOUTS

C. Gardiner, CHI	10
L. Chabot, MONT	8
A. Aitkenhead, NYR	7
D. Kerr, MON(M)	6
W. Cude, DET, MONT	5

National Hockey League 1934–35

TEAM	W	L	T	PTS	GF	GA
CANADIAN DIVISION						
TOR	30	14	4	64	**157**	111
*MON(M)	24	19	5	53	123	92
MONT	19	23	6	44	110	145
NYA	12	27	9	33	100	142
STL	11	31	6	28	86	144

TEAM	W	L	T	PTS	GF	GA
AMERICAN DIVISION						
BOS	26	16	6	58	129	112
CHI	26	17	5	57	118	**88**
NYR	22	20	6	50	137	139
DET	19	22	7	45	127	114

CANADIAN DIVISION

	POS	PLAYER	GP	G	A	PTS		PLAYER	GP	G	A	PTS	GOALIE	W	L	T	GAvg
TOR	LW	B. Jackson	42	22	22	44	D	K. Clancy	47	5	16	21	G. Hainsworth	**30**	14	4	2.31
D. Irvin	C	J. Primeau	37	10	20	30	D	R. Horner	46	4	8	12	C. Conacher	0	0	0	0.00
30–14–4	RW	C. Conacher	47	**36**	21	**57**	D	H. Day	45	2	4	6					
	F	F. Hollett	48	10	16	26											
	F	B. Cotton	47	11	14	25											
	F	H. Kilrea	46	11	13	24											
	F	B. Thoms	47	9	13	22											
	F	A. Blair	45	6	14	20											
	F	P. Kelly	47	11	8	19											
	F	B. Boll	47	14	4	18											
	F	A. Jackson	20	1	3	4											
MON(M)	LW	D. Trottier	34	10	9	19	D	C. Wentworth	48	4	9	13	A. Connell	24	19	5	1.92
T. Gorman	C	R. Blinco	48	13	14	27	D	A. Shields	43	4	8	12					
24–19–5	RW	E. Robinson	47	17	18	35	D	S. Evans	46	5	7	12					
	LW	H. Cain	44	20	7	27	D	L. Conacher	38	2	6	8					
	C	B. Gracie	32	10	8	18											
	RW	G. Marker	42	11	4	15											
	F	H. Smith	45	5	22	27											
	F	B. Northcott	47	9	14	23											
	F	J. Ward	42	9	6	15											
	F	D. Norman	40	0	4	4											
	F	B. Miller	22	3	0	3											
MONT	LW	A. Joliat	48	17	12	29	D	S. Mantha	47	3	11	14	W. Cude	19	23	6	3.02
N. Lalonde	C	P. Lepine	48	12	19	31	D	N. Crutchfield	41	5	5	10					
5–8–3	RW	W. Larochelle	48	9	19	28	D	R. Jenkins	45	4	6	10					
L. Dandurand	F	L. Goldsworthy	33	20	9	29	D	G. Carson	48	0	5	5					
14–15–3	F	A. Mondou	45	9	15	24	D	T. Savage	41	1	5	6					
	F	G. Mantha	42	12	10	22											
	F	J. Riley	47	4	11	15											
	F	J. McGill	44	9	1	10											
	F	J. Gagnon	23	1	5	6											
	F	P. Raymond	20	1	1	2											
NYA	LW	S. Schriner	48	18	22	40	D	A. Smith	48	3	8	11	R. Worters	12	27	9	2.96
J. Simpson	C	A. Chapman	47	9	**34**	43	D	R. Dutton	48	3	7	10					
12–27–9	RW	L. Carr	48	17	14	31	D	B. Brydge	47	2	6	8					
	F	N. Himes	40	5	13	18	D	H. Emms	28	2	2	4					
	F	C. McVeigh	47	7	11	18	D	A. Murray	43	2	1	3					
	F	H. Oliver	48	7	9	16											
	F	H. Conn	48	5	11	16											
	F	E. Burke	29	4	10	14											
	F	J. Klein	30	7	3	10											
	F	O. Heximer	18	5	2	7											
STL	F	C. Voss	48	13	18	31	D	V. Ayres	47	2	2	4	B. Beveridge	11	**31**	6	3.00
E. Gerard	F	G. Brydson	48	11	18	29	D	F. Purpur	25	2	1	3					
2–11–0	F	J. Lamb	31	11	12	23	D	I. Frew	47	0	2	2					
G. Boucher	F	P. Kelly	25	3	10	13	D	A. Wilcox	11	0	0	0					
9–20–6	F	B. Cowley	41	5	7	12											
	F	O. Asmundson	11	4	7	11											
	F	F. Jerwa	16	4	7	11											
	F	V. Ripley	31	1	5	6											
	F	N. Wasnie	13	3	1	4											
	F	F. Finnigan	34	5	5	10											

AMERICAN DIVISION

	POS	PLAYER	GP	G	A	PTS		PLAYER	GP	G	A	PTS	GOALIE	W	L	T	GAvg
BOS	LW	C. Sands	43	15	12	27	D	E. Shore	48	7	26	33	T. Thompson	26	16	6	2.33
F. Patrick	C	M. Barry	48	20	20	40	D	B. Siebert	48	6	18	24					
26–16–6	RW	D. Clapper	48	21	16	37	D	B. McInenly	33	2	1	3					
	F	N. Stewart	47	21	18	39	D	B. Davie	30	0	1	1					
	F	M. Kaminsky	38	12	15	27	D	A. Giroux	10	1	0	1					
	F	R. Beattie	48	9	18	27											
	F	J. O'Neill	48	2	11	13											
	F	J. Shill	45	4	4	8											
	F	P. Haynes	37	4	3	7											
	F	G. Shannon	17	1	1	2											
CHI	F	P. Thompson	48	16	23	39	D	A. Coulter	48	4	8	12	L. Chabot	26	17	5	**1.83**
C. Loughlin	F	J. Gottselig	48	19	18	37	D	M. Burke	47	2	2	4					
26–17–5	F	H. Morenz	48	8	26	34	D	A. Levinsky	23	3	4	7					
	F	T. Cook	47	13	18	31	D	A. Wiebe	42	2	1	3					
	F	M. March	47	13	17	30											
	F	D. Romnes	35	10	14	24											
	F	L. Trudel	47	11	11	22											
	F	R. Couture	27	7	9	16											
	F	W. Kendall	47	6	4	10											
	F	N. Locking	35	2	5	7											
	F	D. McFayden	37	2	5	7											

TEAM	POS	PLAYER	GP	G	A	PTS	PLAYER	GP	G	A	PTS	GOALIE	W	L	T	GAvg
NYR	F	F. Boucher	48	13	32	45	D E. Seibert	48	6	19	25	D. Kerr	19	12	6	2.54
L. Patrick	F	B. Cook	48	21	15	36	D O. Heller	47	3	11	14	A. Aitkenhead	3	7	0	3.70
22–20–6	F	C. Dillon	48	25	9	34	D C. Johnson	26	2	3	5	P. Jackson	0	1	0	8.00
	F	B. Cook	48	13	21	34	D H. Starr	32	1	1	2					
	F	M. Murdoch	48	2	9	11	D B. MacKenzie	15	1	0	1					
	F	L. Patrick	48	9	13	22										
	F	B. Connolly	47	10	11	21										
	F	B. Keeling	47	15	4	19										
	F	C. Mason	46	5	9	14										
	F	A. Somers	41	0	5	5										
DET	LW	H. Lewis	48	16	27	43	D D. Young	48	4	6	10	N. Smith	12	11	2	2.08
J. Adams	C	C. Weiland	48	13	25	38	D W. Buswell	47	1	3	4	J. Roach	7	11	5	2.70
19–22–7	RW	L. Aurie	48	17	29	46	D B. McDonald	16	1	2	3					
	LW	J. Sorrell	47	20	16	36	D S. Bowman	13	1	3	4					
	C	E. Goodfellow	48	12	24	36										
	RW	E. Wiseman	40	11	13	24										
	F	S. Howe	14	8	12	20										
	F	T. Anderson	27	5	2	7										
	F	L. Duguid	34	3	3	6										
	F	I. Boyd	42	2	3	5										
	F	W. STarr	29	1	1	2										

GOALS		ASSISTS		POINTS	
C. Conacher, TOR	36	A. Chapman, NYR	34	C. Conacher, TOR	57
C. Dillon, NYR	25	F. Boucher, NYR	32	S. Howe, DET, STL	47
S. Howe, DET, STL	22	L. Aurie, DET	29	L. Aurie, DET	46
B. Jackson, TOR	22	H. Lewis, DET	27	F. Boucher, NYR	45
		S. Howe, DET, STL	25	B. Jackson, TOR	44

PENALTY MINUTES		GOALS AGAINST AVE.		SHUTOUTS	
R. Horner, TOR	125	L. Chabot, CHI	1.83	A. Connell, MON(M)	9
I. Frew, STL	89	A. Connell, MON(M)	1.92	L. Chabot, CHI	8
E. Seibert, NYR	86	N. Smith, DET	2.08	G. Hainsworth, TOR	8
B. Siebert, BOS	80	G. Hainsworth, TOR	2.31	T. Thompson, BOS	8
S. Bowman, STL, DET	72	T. Thompson, BOS	2.33	D. Kerr, BOS	8

National Hockey League 1935–36

TEAM	W	L	T	PTS	GF	GA
CANADIAN DIVISION						
MON(M)	22	16	10	54	114	106
TOR	23	19	6	52	**126**	106
NYA	16	25	7	39	109	122
MONT	11	26	11	33	82	123
AMERICAN DIVISION						
*DET	24	16	8	56	124	103
BOS	22	20	6	50	92	**83**
CHI	21	19	8	50	93	92
NYR	19	17	12	50	91	96

CANADIAN DIVISION

TEAM	POS	PLAYER	GP	G	A	PTS	PLAYER	GP	G	A	PTS	GOALIE	W	L	T	GAvg
MON(M)	LW	B. Northcott	48	15	21	36	D L. Conacher	46	7	7	14	B. Beveridge	14	13	5	2.22
T. Gorman	C	H. Smith	47	19	19	38	D S. Evans	47	3	5	8	L. Chabot	8	3	5	2.19
22–16–10	RW	J. Ward	48	12	19	31	D C. Wentworth	48	4	5	9					
	LW	D. Trottier	46	10	10	20										
	C	R. Blinco	46	13	10	23										
	RW	E. Robinson	40	6	14	20										
	F	J. Lamb	35	0	3	3										
	F	B. Gracie	46	11	14	25										
	F	G. Marker	47	7	12	19										
	F	H. Cain	47	5	13	18										
	F	A. Shields	45	2	7	9										

	POS	PLAYER	GP	G	A	PTS		PLAYER	GP	G	A	PTS	GOALIE	W	L	T	GAvg
TOR	LW	B. Jackson	47	11	11	22	D	K. Clancy	47	5	10	15	G. Hainsworth	23	19	6	2.21
D. Irvin	C	A. Jackson	48	5	15	20	D	H. Day	44	1	13	14					
23–19–6	RW	P. Kelly	42	11	8	19	D	R. Horner	43	2	9	11					
	LW	B. Boll	44	15	13	28	D	R. Hamilton	7	0	0	0					
	C	B. Thoms	48	**23**	15	38											
	RW	F. Finnigan	48	2	6	8											
	F	C. Conacher	44	**23**	15	38											
	F	N. Metz	38	14	6	20											
	F	J. Primeau	45	4	13	17											
	F	A. Blair	45	5	4	9											
	F	B. Davidson	35	4	4	8											
NYA	LW	S. Schriner	48	19	26	**45**	D	J. Jerwa	48	9	12	21	R. Worters	16	25	7	2.54
R. Dutton	C	A. Chapman	48	10	**28**	38	D	R. Dutton	46	5	8	13					
16–25–7	RW	L. Carr	44	8	10	18	D	R. Doran	25	4	2	6					
	F	N. Stewart	48	14	15	29	D	A. Murray	48	1	0	1					
	F	E. Wiseman	42	12	15	27	D	B. Brydge	21	0	0	0					
	F	H. Oliver	48	9	16	25											
	F	B. Cotton	45	7	9	16											
	F	J. Klein	42	4	8	12											
	F	C. Voss	46	3	9	12											
	F	H. Emms	31	1	5	6											
MONT	F	L. Goldsworthy	47	15	11	26	D	S. Mantha	42	2	4	6	W. Cude	11	**26**	10	2.60
S. Mantha	F	P. Haynes	48	5	19	24	D	W. Buswell	44	0	2	2	A. Cox	0	0	1	1.00
11–26–11	F	A. Joliat	48	15	8	23	D	A. Lesieur	38	1	0	1					
	F	J. McGill	46	13	7	20	D	I. Frew	18	0	2	2					
	F	A. Mondou	36	7	11	18											
	F	J. Desilets	38	7	6	13											
	F	J. Gagnon	48	7	9	16											
	F	P. Lepine	32	6	10	16											
	F	G. Mantha	35	1	12	13											
	F	P. Drouin	30	1	8	9											
	F	T. Blake	11	1	2	3											

AMERICAN DIVISION

	POS	PLAYER	GP	G	A	PTS		PLAYER	GP	G	A	PTS	GOALIE	W	L	T	GAvg
DET	LW	H. Lewis	45	14	23	37	D	D. Young	48	5	12	17	N. Smith	**24**	16	8	2.15
J. Adams	C	M. Barry	48	21	19	40	D	B. McDonald	48	4	6	10					
24–16–8	RW	L. Aurie	44	16	18	34	D	S. Bowman	48	3	2	5					
	F	S. Howe	48	16	14	30											
	F	J. Sorrell	48	13	15	28											
	F	E. Goodfellow	48	5	18	23											
	F	G. Pettinger	33	8	7	15											
	F	H. Kilrea	48	6	17	23											
	F	P. Kelly	48	6	8	14											
	F	W. Kilrea	44	4	10	14											
	F	M. Bruneteau	24	2	0	2											
BOS	LW	C. Sands	41	6	4	10	D	B. Siebert	46	12	9	21	T. Thompson	22	20	6	**1.71**
F. Patrick	C	C. Weiland	48	14	13	27	D	E. Shore	46	3	16	19	P. Jackson	0	0	0	1.00
22–20–6	RW	D. Clapper	44	12	13	25	D	R. Jenkins	42	2	6	8					
	F	R. Beattie	48	14	18	32	D	A. Motter	23	1	4	5					
	F	B. Cowley	48	11	10	21	D	T. Graham	48	4	1	5					
	F	J. O'Neill	48	2	11	13											
	F	P. Runge	33	8	2	10											
	F	G. Shannon	25	0	1	1											
	F	L. Duguid	29	1	4	5											
CHI	LW	P. Thompson	46	17	23	40	D	A. Levinsky	48	1	7	8	M. Karakas	21	19	8	1.92
C. Loughlin	C	D. Romnes	48	13	25	38	D	E. Seibert	29	2	6	8					
21–19–8	RW	M. March	48	16	19	35	D	A. Wiebe	46	1	0	1					
	F	J. Gottselig	40	14	15	29											
	F	D. McFayden	48	4	16	20											
	F	T. Cook	47	4	8	12											
	F	G. Brydson	22	6	4	10											
	F	L. Trudel	47	3	4	7											
	F	E. Ouelette	43	3	2	5											
	F	W. Larochelle	27	2	1	3											
	F	W. Kendall	23	2	1	3											
NYR	LW	L. Patrick	48	11	14	25	D	O. Heller	43	2	11	13	D. Kerr	18	17	12	2.02
L. Patrick	C	F. Boucher	48	11	18	29	D	C. Johnson	47	5	3	8	B. Gardiner	1	0	0	1.00
19–17–12	RW	C. Dillon	48	18	14	32	D	A. Coulter	23	1	5	6					
	F	B. Keeling	47	13	5	18	D	V. Ayres	28	0	4	4					
	F	M. Murdoch	48	0	14	14	D	W. Pratt	17	1	1	2					
	F	C. Mason	28	1	5	6											
	F	B. Cook	21	1	4	5											
	F	B. Connolly	25	2	2	4											
	F	B. Cook	26	4	5	9											
	F	P. Watson	24	0	2	2											

GOALS		ASSISTS		POINTS	
C. Conacher, TOR	23	A. Chapman, NYA	28	S. Schriner, NYA	45
B. Thoms, TOR	23	S. Schriner, NYA	26	M. Barry, DET	40
M. Barry, DET	21	D. Romnes, CHI	25	P. Thompson, CHI	40
S. Schriner, NYA	19	H. Lewis, DET	23		
H. Smith, MON(M)	19	P. Thompson, CHI	23		

PENALTY MINUTES		GOALS AGAINST AVE.		SHUTOUTS	
R. Horner, TOR	167	T. Thompson, BOS	1.71	T. Thompson, BOS	10
A. Shields, MON(M)	81	M. Karakas, CHI	1.92	M. Karakas, CHI	9
H. Smith, MON(M)	75	D. Kerr, NYR	2.02	D. Kerr, NYR	8
C. Conacher, TOR	74	N. Smith, DET	2.15	G. Hainsworth, TOR	8
R. Dutton, NYA	69	G. Hainsworth, TOR	2.21	N. Smith, DET	6
E. Goodfellow, DET	69			W. Cude, MONT	6

National Hockey League 1936–37

TEAM	W	L	T	PTS	GF	GA	TEAM	W	L	T	PTS	GF	GA
CANADIAN DIVISION							AMERICAN DIVISION						
MONT	24	18	6	54	115	111	*DET	25	14	9	59	**128**	**102**
MON(M)	22	17	9	53	126	110	BOS	23	18	7	53	120	110
TOR	22	21	5	49	119	115	NYR	19	20	9	47	117	106
NYA	15	29	4	34	122	161	CHI	14	27	7	35	99	131

CANADIAN DIVISION

MONT
C. Hart
24–18–6

POS	PLAYER	GP	G	A	PTS	POS	PLAYER	GP	G	A	PTS	GOALIE	W	L	T	GAvg
LW	A. Joliat	47	17	15	32	D	G. Brown	27	4	6	10	W. Cude	22	17	5	2.25
C	H. Morenz	30	4	16	20	D	B. MacKenzie	39	4	3	7	G. Hainsworth	2	1	1	3.00
RW	J. Gagnon	48	20	16	36	D	W. Buswell	44	0	4	4					
LW	T. Blake	43	10	12	22											
C	P. Lepine	34	7	8	15											
RW	G. Mantha	47	13	14	27											
F	B. Siebert	44	8	20	28											
F	J. Desilets	48	7	12	19											
F	P. Haynes	47	8	18	26											
F	R. Lorrain	47	3	6	9											
F	J. McGill	44	5	2	7											

MON(M)
T. Gorman
22–17–9

POS	PLAYER	GP	G	A	PTS	POS	PLAYER	GP	G	A	PTS	GOALIE	W	L	T	GAvg
LW	B. Northcott	48	15	14	29	D	L. Conacher	47	6	19	25	A. Connell	10	11	6	2.33
C	B. Gracie	48	11	25	36	D	S. Evans	48	6	7	13	B. Beveridge	12	6	3	2.24
RW	H. Cain	43	13	17	30	D	C. Wentworth	44	3	4	7					
F	E. Robinson	48	16	18	34	D	G. Carson	42	1	3	4					
F	J. Ward	41	14	14	28											
F	D. Trottier	43	12	11	23											
F	G. Marker	48	10	12	22											
F	R. Blinco	48	6	12	18											
F	G. Shannon	32	9	7	16											
F	P. Runge	30	4	10	14											
F	C. Voss	20	0	2	2											

TOR
D. Irvin
22–21–5

POS	PLAYER	GP	G	A	PTS	POS	PLAYER	GP	G	A	PTS	GOALIE	W	L	T	GAvg
LW	B. Jackson	46	21	19	40	D	J. Fowler	48	7	11	18	T. Broda	22	19	4	2.36
C	S. Apps	48	16	**29**	45	D	R. Horner	48	3	9	12	G. Hainsworth	0	2	1	3.00
RW	G. Drillon	41	16	17	33	D	R. Hamilton	39	3	7	10					
F	N. Metz	48	9	11	20	D	H. Day	48	3	4	7					
F	B. Thoms	48	10	9	19											
F	B. Davidson	46	8	7	15											
F	B. Boll	25	6	3	9											
F	F. Finnigan	48	2	7	9											
F	J. Shill	32	4	4	8											
F	J. Jarvis	24	1	0	1											
F	C. Conacher	15	3	5	8											

NYA
R. Dutton
15–29–4

POS	PLAYER	GP	G	A	PTS	POS	PLAYER	GP	G	A	PTS	GOALIE	W	L	T	GAvg
LW	S. Schriner	48	21	25	**46**	D	H. Emms	47	4	8	12	R. Worters	6	14	3	3.00
C	A. Chapman	43	8	23	31	D	T. Graham	31	2	1	3	A. Moore	7	11	0	3.56
RW	L. Carr	47	18	16	34	D	J. Klein	11	2	1	3	L. Chabot	2	3	1	4.17
F	N. Stewart	32	20*	10	30	D	A. Murray	39	0	2	2	A. Woods	0	1	0	3.00
F	E. Wiseman	43	14	19	33											
F	T. Anderson	45	10	15	25											
F	J. Lamb	48	3	9	12											
F	L. Cunningham	23	1	8	9											
F	T. Hemmerling	18	3	3	6											
F	L. Jackson	14	1	1	2											

AMERICAN DIVISION

TEAM	POS	PLAYER	GP	G	A	PTS		PLAYER	GP	G	A	PTS	GOALIE	W	L	T	GAvg
DET	LW	H. Lewis	45	14	18	32	D	B. McDonald	47	3	5	8	N. Smith	**25**	14	9	**2.13**
J. Adams	C	M. Barry	47	17	27	44	D	S. Bowman	37	0	1	1					
25–14–9	RW	L. Aurie	45	**23**	20	43	D	H. Mackie	13	1	0	1					
	F	S. Howe	42	17	10	27											
	F	E. Goodfellow	48	9	16	25											
	F	J. Sorrell	48	8	16	24											
	F	G. Pettinger	48	7	15	22											
	F	H. Kilrea	48	6	9	15											
	F	W. Kilrea	48	8	13	21											
	F	M. Bruneteau	42	9	7	16											
	F	P. Kelly	48	5	4	9											
BOS	LW	R. Getliffe	48	16	15	31	D	F. Hollett	47	3	7	10	T. Thompson	23	18	7	2.29
A. Ross	C	B. Cowley	46	13	22	35	D	J. Portland	46	2	4	6					
23–18–7	RW	D. Clapper	48	17	8	25	D	A. Shields	18	0	4	4					
	F	C. Sands	46	18	5	23	D	E. Shore	19	3	1	4					
	F	H. Smith	43	8	10	18											
	F	R. Beattie	48	8	7	15											
	F	C. Weiland	48	6	9	15											
	F	L. Goldsworthy	47	8	6	14											
	F	M. Schmidt	26	2	8	10											
	F	B. Cook	40	4	5	9											
	F	J. O'Neill	20	0	2	2											
NYR	LW	L. Patrick	45	8	16	24	D	O. Heller	48	5	12	17	D. Kerr	19	20	9	2.21
L. Patrick	C	M. Murdoch	48	0	14	14	D	W. Pratt	47	8	7	15					
19–20–9	RW	C. Dillon	48	20	11	31	D	A. Coulter	47	1	5	6					
	LW	A. Shibicky	47	14	8	22	D	J. Cooper	48	0	3	3					
	C	N. Colville	45	10	18	28	D	C. Johnson	34	0	0	0					
	RW	M. Colville	46	7	12	19											
	F	F. Boucher	44	7	13	20											
	F	P. Watson	48	11	17	28											
	F	B. Keeling	48	22	4	26											
	F	B. Cook	21	1	4	5											
CHI							D	E. Seibert	43	9	6	15	M. Karakas	14	**27**	7	2.73
C. Loughlin	LW	P. Thompson	47	17	18	35	D	A. Levinsky	48	0	8	8					
14–27–7	C	D. Romnes	28	4	14	18	D	M. Burke	41	1	3	4					
	RW	M. March	37	11	6	17	D	A. Wiebe	45	0	2	2					
	F	J. Gottselig	47	9	21	30											
	F	W. Larochelle	43	9	10	19											
	F	P. Kelly	29	13	4	17											
	F	L. Trudel	45	6	12	18											
	F	G. Brydson	34	7	7	14											
	F	P. Palangio	30	8	9	17											
	F	H. Jackson	40	1	3	4											
	F	A. Blair	44	0	3	3											

GOALS		ASSISTS		POINTS	
L. Aurie, DET	23	S. Apps, TOR	29	S. Schriner, NYA	46
N. Stewart, BOS, NYA	23	M. Barry, DET	27	S. Apps, TOR	45
B. Keeling, NYR	22	B. Gracie, MON(M)	25	M. Barry, DET	44
B. Jackson, TOR	21	S. Schriner, NYA	25	L. Aurie, DET	43
S. Schriner, NYA	21	B. Cowley, BOS	22	B. Jackson, TOR	40

PENALTY MINUTES		GOALS AGAINST AVE.		SHUTOUTS	
R. Horner, TOR	124	N. Smith, DET	2.13	N. Smith, DET	6
A. Shields, NYA, BOS	94	D. Kerr, NYR	2.19	T. Thompson, BOS	6
L. Conacher, MON(M)	64	B. Beveridge, MON(M)	2.24	W. Cude, MONT	5
J. Portland, BOS	58	W. Cude, MONT	2.25	M. Karakas, CHI	5
J. Jerwa, BOS, NYA	57	T. Thompson, BOS	2.29	D. Kerr, NYR	4

National Hockey League 1937–38

TEAM	W	L	T	PTS	GF	GA
CANADIAN DIVISION						
TOR	24	15	9	57	**151**	127
NYA	19	18	11	49	110	111
MONT	18	17	13	49	123	128
MON(M)	12	30	6	30	101	149

TEAM	W	L	T	PTS	GF	GA
AMERICAN DIVISION						
BOS	30	11	7	67	142	**89**
NYR	27	15	6	60	149	96
*CHI	14	25	9	37	97	139
DET	12	25	11	35	99	133

CANADIAN DIVISION

TEAM	POS	PLAYER	GP	G	A	PTS	PLAYER	GP	G	A	PTS	GOALIE	W	L	T	GAvg
TOR	LW	B. Jackson	48	17	17	34	D R. Horner	47	4	20	24	T. Broda	24	15	9	2.65
D. Irvin	C	S. Apps	47	21	**29**	50	D J. Fowler	48	10	12	22					
24–15–9	RW	G. Drillon	48	**26**	26	**52**	D R. Hamilton	45	1	4	5					
	F	B. Thoms	48	14	24	38										
	F	B. Boll	44	14	11	25										
	F	N. Metz	48	15	7	22										
	F	B. Davidson	48	3	17	20										
	F	P. Kelly	43	9	10	19										
	F	M. Chamberlain	43	4	12	16										
	F	B. Kampman	32	1	2	3										
	F	G. Parsons	30	5	6	11										
NYA	LW	S. Schriner	48	21	17	38	D J. Jerwa	47	3	14	17	E. Robertson	19	18	11	2.31
R. Dutton	C	A. Chapman	45	2	27	29	D C. Johnson	32	0	0	0					
19–18–11	RW	L. Carr	48	16	7	23	D H. Emms	22	1	3	4					
	LW	T. Anderson	45	4	21	25	D H. Day	44	0	3	3					
	C	N. Stewart	48	19	17	36	D A. Murray	46	0	1	1					
	RW	E. Wiseman	48	18	14	32										
	F	H. Smith	47	10	10	20										
	F	J. Gallagher	47	3	6	9										
	F	R. Beattie	19	3	4	7										
	F	J. Sorrell	17	8	2	10										
MONT	LW	T. Blake	43	17	16	33	D W. Buswell	48	2	15	17	W. Cude	18	17	12	2.68
C. Hart	C	P. Haynes	48	13	22	35	D R. Goupille	47	4	5	9	P. Gauthier	0	0	1	2.00
18–17–13	RW	J. Gagnon	47	13	17	30	D G. Brown	34	1	7	8					
	F	G. Mantha	47	23	19	42	D M. Burke	38	0	5	5					
	F	R. Lorrain	48	13	19	32										
	F	P. Drouin	28	7	11	18										
	F	B. Siebert	37	8	11	19										
	F	P. Lepine	47	5	14	19										
	F	J. Desilets	32	6	7	13										
	F	A. Joliat	44	6	7	13										
	F	D. Willson	18	2	7	9										
MON(M)	F	B. Gracie	48	12	19	31	D S. Evans	48	5	11	16	B. Beveridge	12	**30**	6	3.10
K. Clancy	F	H. Cain	47	11	19	30	D A. Shields	48	5	7	12					
6–11–1	F	J. Ward	48	11	15	26	D C. Wentworth	48	4	5	9					
T. Gorman	F	G. Marker	48	9	15	24	D G. Shannon	36	0	3	3					
6–19–5	F	B. Northcott	47	11	12	23										
	F	R. Blinco	47	10	9	19										
	F	D. Trottier	47	9	10	19										
	F	P. Runge	41	5	7	12										
	F	E. Robinson	38	4	7	11										
	F	D. Smith	41	3	1	4										
	F	T. Cook	20	2	4	6										

AMERICAN DIVISION

TEAM	POS	PLAYER	GP	G	A	PTS	PLAYER	GP	G	A	PTS	GOALIE	W	L	T	GAvg
BOS	LW	R. Getliffe	36	11	13	24	D E. Shore	47	3	14	17	T. Thompson	**30**	11	7	**1.85**
A. Ross	C	B. Cowley	48	17	22	39	D D. Clapper	46	6	9	15					
30–11–7	RW	C. Sands	46	17	12	29	D F. Hollett	48	4	10	14					
	LW	W. Dumart	48	13	14	27	D J. Portland	48	0	5	5					
	C	M. Schmidt	44	13	14	27										
	RW	B. Bauer	48	20	14	34										
	F	C. Weiland	48	11	12	23										
	F	L. Goldsworthy	45	9	10	19										
	F	G. Pettinger	35	7	10	17										
	F	A. Jackson	48	9	3	12										
NYR	LW	L. Patrick	48	15	19	34	D W. Pratt	47	5	14	19	D. Kerr	27	15	6	2.00
L. Patrick	C	C. Smith	48	14	23	37	D O. Heller	48	2	14	16					
27–15–6	RW	C. Dillon	48	21	18	39	D A. Coulter	43	5	10	15					
	LW	A. Shibicky	43	17	18	35	D J. Cooper	46	3	2	5					
	C	N. Colville	45	17	19	36										
	RW	M. Colville	48	14	14	28										
	F	P. Watson	48	7	25	32										
	F	B. Hextall	48	17	4	21										
	F	B. Keeling	39	8	9	17										
	F	B. Kirk	39	4	8	12										
	F	F. Boucher	18	0	1	1										

	POS	PLAYER	GP	G	A	PTS		PLAYER	GP	G	A	PTS	GOALIE	W	L	T	GAvg
CHI	LW	P. Thompson	48	22	22	44	D	E. Seibert	48	8	13	21	M. Karakas	14	25	9	2.90
B. Stewart	C	D. Romnes	44	10	22	32	D	R. Jenkins	39	1	8	9					
14–25–9	RW	M. March	41	11	17	28	D	A. Levinsky	48	3	2	5					
	C	C. Voss	34	3	8	11	D	A. Wiebe	44	0	3	3					
	F	J. Gottselig	48	13	19	32	D	V. Johnson	25	1	0	1					
	F	L. Trudel	42	6	16	22											
	F	C. Dahlstrom	48	10	9	19											
	F	J. Shill	23	4	3	7											
	F	G. Brydson	19	1	3	4											
	F	B. Connolly	15	1	2	3											
DET	LW	H. Lewis	42	13	18	31	D	A. Motter	33	5	17	22	N. Smith	11	25	11	2.77
J. Adams	C	M. Barry	48	9	20	29	D	B. McDonald	47	3	7	10	J. Franks	1	0	0	3.00
12–25–11	RW	L. Aurie	47	10	9	19	D	D. Young	48	3	5	8					
	F	S. Howe	47	8	19	27	D	S. Bowman	45	0	2	2					
	F	C. Liscombe	42	14	10	24											
	F	H. Kilrea	47	9	9	18											
	F	E. Wares	21	9	7	16											
	F	M. Bruneteau	24	3	6	9											
	F	R. Hudson	33	5	2	7											
	F	E. Goodfellow	29	0	7	7											
	F	C. Drouillard	10	0	1	1											

GOALS		ASSISTS		POINTS	
G. Drillon, TOR	26	S. Apps, TOR	29	G. Drillon, TOR	52
G. Mantha, MONT	23	G. Drillon, TOR	26	S. Apps, TOR	50
P. Thompson, CHI	22	P. Watson, NYR	25	P. Thompson, CHI	44
S. Apps, TOR	21	B. Thoms, TOR	24	G. Mantha, MONT	42
C. Dillon, NYR	21	C. Smith, NYR	23	B. Cowley, BOS	39
S. Schriner, NYA	21			C. Dillon, NYR	39

PENALTY MINUTES		GOALS AGAINST AVE.		SHUTOUTS	
R. Horner, TOR	92	T. Thompson, BOS	1.85	D. Kerr, NYR	8
A. Coulter, NYR	90	D. Kerr, NYR	2.00	T. Thompson, BOS	7
O. Heller, NYR	68	E. Robertson, NYA	2.31	E. Robertson, NYA	6
J. Cooper, NYR	57	T. Broda, TOR	2.64	T. Broda, TOR	6
W. Pratt, NYR	56			W. Cude, MONT	3

National Hockey League 1938–39

TEAM	W	L	T	PTS	GF	GA
*BOS	36	10	2	74	156	**76**
NYR	26	16	6	58	149	105
TOR	19	20	9	47	114	107
NYA	17	21	10	44	119	157
DET	18	24	6	42	**197**	128
MONT	15	24	9	39	115	146
CHI	12	28	8	32	91	132

	POS	PLAYER	GP	G	A	PTS		PLAYER	GP	G	A	PTS	GOALIE	W	L	T	GAvg
BOS	LW	R. Conacher	47	**26**	11	37	D	F. Hollett	47	10	17	27	F. Brimsek	**33**	9	1	**1.58**
A. Ross	C	B. Cowley	34	8	**34**	42	D	D. Clapper	42	13	13	26	T. Thompson	3	1	1	1.60
36–10–2	RW	M. Hill	44	10	10	20	D	E. Shore	46	4	14	18					
	LW	W. Dumart	45	14	15	29	D	J. Crawford	38	4	8	12					
	C	M. Schmidt	41	15	17	32	D	J. Portland	48	4	5	9					
	RW	B. Bauer	48	13	18	31											
	F	G. Pettinger	48	11	14	25											
	F	R. Getliffe	43	10	12	22											
	F	C. Weiland	47	7	9	16											
	F	C. Sands	39	7	5	12											

	POS	PLAYER	GP	G	A	PTS		PLAYER	GP	G	A	PTS	GOALIE	W	L	T	GAvg
NYR	LW	A. Shibicky	48	24	9	33	D	O. Heller	48	0	23	23	D. Kerr	26	16	6	2.19
L. Patrick	C	N. Colville	47	18	19	37	D	W. Pratt	48	2	19	21					
26–16–6	RW	M. Colville	48	7	21	28	D	A. Coulter	44	4	8	12					
	LW	D. Hiller	48	10	19	29	D	L. Molyneaux	43	0	1	1					
	C	P. Watson	48	15	22	37											
	RW	B. Hextall	48	20	15	35											
	F	L. Patrick	35	8	21	29											
	F	C. Smith	48	21	20	41											
	F	C. Dillon	48	12	15	27											
	F	G. Allen	19	6	6	12											
	F	M. Patrick	48	1	10	11											
TOR	LW	B. Jackson	42	10	17	27	D	R. Horner	48	4	10	14	T. Broda	19	20	9	2.23
D. Irvin	C	S. Apps	44	15	25	40	D	J. Fowler	39	1	6	7					
19–20–9	RW	G. Drillon	40	18	16	34	D	R. Hamilton	48	0	7	7					
	F	M. Chamberlain	48	10	16	26	D	B. McDonald	33	3	3	6					
	F	P. Kelly	48	11	11	22											
	F	D. Romnes	36	7	16	23											
	F	N. Metz	47	11	10	21											
	F	G. Marker	43	9	6	15											
	F	B. Davidson	47	4	10	14											
	F	B. Kampman	41	2	8	10											
	F	G. Parsons	29	7	7	14											
NYA	LW	S. Schriner	48	13	31	44	D	J. Jerwa	48	4	12	16	E. Robertson	17	18	10	2.96
R. Dutton	C	A. Chapman	45	3	19	22	D	W. Field	43	1	3	4	A. Moore	0	2	0	7.00
17–21–10	RW	L. Carr	47	19	18	37	D	J. Gallagher	41	1	5	6	R. Jenkins	0	1	0	7.00
	LW	T. Anderson	47	13	27	40	D	L. Goldsworthy	47	3	11	14					
	C	N. Stewart	46	16	19	35											
	RW	E. Wiseman	45	12	21	33											
	F	A. Jackson	48	12	13	25											
	F	J. Sorrell	48	13	9	22											
	F	H. Smith	48	8	11	19											
	F	R. Beattie	17	0	0	0											
DET	F	M. Barry	48	13	28	41	D	A. Motter	42	5	11	16	T. Thompson	16	17	6	2.59
J. Adams	F	S. Howe	48	16	20	36	D	E. Goodfellow	48	8	8	16	H. Teno	2	3	0	3.00
18–24–6	F	C. Liscombe	47	8	18	26	D	S. Bowman	43	2	3	5	N. Smith	0	4	0	3.00
	F	C. Conacher	40	8	15	23	D	D. Young	44	1	5	6	C. Conacher	0	0	0	0.00
	F	H. Kilrea	47	8	9	17	D	J. Stewart	32	0	1	1					
	F	E. Wares	28	8	8	16											
	F	H. Lewis	39	6	10	16											
	F	P. Kelly	32	4	9	13											
	F	M. Bruneteau	20	3	7	10											
MONT	LW	T. Blake	48	24	23	**47**	D	B. Siebert	44	9	7	16	C. Bourque	7	13	5	2.76
C. Hart	C	P. Haynes	47	5	33	38	D	W. Buswell	46	3	7	10	W. Cude	8	11	4	3.35
6–18–6	RW	J. Gagnon	45	12	22	34	D	S. Evans	43	2	7	9					
J. Dugal	F	H. Cain	45	13	14	27	D	C. Wentworth	45	0	3	3					
9–6–3	F	L. Trudel	31	8	13	21	D	G. Brown	18	1	9	10					
	F	R. Lorrain	38	10	9	19											
	F	P. Drouin	42	4	11	15											
	F	B. Summerhill	43	6	10	16											
	F	A. Mondou	34	3	7	10											
	F	J. Ward	36	4	3	7											
CHI	LW	J. Gottselig	48	16	23	39	D	E. Seibert	48	4	11	15	M. Karakas	12	**28**	8	2.75
B. Stewart	C	C. Dahlstrom	48	6	14	20	D	A. Wiebe	47	1	2	3					
8–10–3	RW	M. March	46	10	11	21	D	B. MacKenzie	48	1	0	1					
P. Thompson	F	J. Desilets	48	11	13	24	D	A. Levinsky	29	1	3	4					
4–18–5	F	B. Thoms	36	6	11	17											
	F	P. Thompson	37	5	10	15											
	F	R. Blinco	48	3	12	15											
	F	E. Robinson	48	9	6	15											
	F	B. Northcott	46	5	7	12											
	F	J. Shill	28	2	4	6											
	F	B. Gracie	31	4	6	10											

GOALS

R. Conacher, BOS	26
T. Blake, MONT	24
A. Shibicky, NYR	24
C. Smith, NYR	21
B. Hextall, NYR	20

ASSISTS

B. Cowley, BOS	34
P. Haynes, MONT	33
S. Schriner, NYA	31
M. Barry, DET	28
T. Anderson, NYA	27

POINTS

T. Blake, MONT	47
S. Schriner, NYA	44
B. Cowley, BOS	42
C. Smith, NYR	41
M. Barry, DET	41

PENALTY MINUTES

R. Horner, TOR	85
M. Patrick, NYR	72
A. Coulter, NYR	58
S. Evans, MONT	58
E. Seibert, CHI	57

GOALS AGAINST AVE.

F. Brimsek, BOS	1.58
D. Kerr, NYR	2.19
T. Broda, TOR	2.23
T. Thompson, BOS, DET	2.49

SHUTOUTS

F. Brimsek, BOS	10
T. Broda, TOR	8
D. Kerr, NYR	6
M. Karakas, CHI	5
T. Thompson, BOS, DET	4

TEAM	W	L	T	PTS	GF	GA
BOS	31	12	5	67	**170**	98
*NYR	27	11	10	64	136	**77**
TOR	25	17	6	56	134	110
CHI	23	19	6	52	112	120
DET	16	26	6	38	90	126
NYA	15	29	4	34	196	140
MONT	10	33	5	25	90	167

	POS	PLAYER	GP	G	A	PTS		PLAYER	GP	G	A	PTS	GOALIE	W	L	T	GAvg
BOS	LW	W. Dumart	48	22	21	43	D	D. Clapper	44	10	18	28	F. Brimsek	**31**	12	5	2.04
C. Weiland	C	M. Schmidt	48	22	**30**	**52**	D	F. Hollett	44	10	18	28					
31–12–5	RW	B. Bauer	48	17	26	43	D	J. Shewchuk	47	2	4	6					
	LW	R. Conacher	31	18	12	30	D	J. Crawford	36	1	4	5					
	C	B. Cowley	48	13	27	40	D	D. Smith	18	2	2	4					
	RW	M. Hill	37	9	11	20											
	F	H. Cain	48	21	10	31											
	F	A. Jackson	45	7	18	25											
	F	R. Hamill	28	10	8	18											
	F	G. Pettinger	21	2	6	8											
NYR	LW	D. Hiller	48	13	18	31	D	O. Heller	47	5	14	19	D. Kerr	27	11	10	**1.60**
F. Boucher	C	P. Watson	48	7	28	35	D	A. Pike	47	8	9	17					
27–11–10	RW	B. Hextall	48	**24**	15	39	D	W. Pratt	48	4	13	17					
	LW	A. Shibicky	43	11	21	32	D	A. Coulter	48	1	9	10					
	C	N. Colville	48	19	19	38											
	RW	M. Colville	47	7	14	21											
	F	K. MacDonald	44	15	13	28											
	F	L. Patrick	48	12	16	28											
	F	C. Smith	41	8	16	24											
	F	M. Patrick	46	2	4	6											
TOR	LW	B. Davidson	48	8	18	26	D	R. Horner	31	1	9	10	T. Broda	25	17	5	2.30
D. Irvin	C	S. Apps	27	13	17	30	D	W. Stanowski	27	2	7	9	P. Stein	0	0	1	2.00
25–17–6	RW	G. Drillon	43	21	19	40	D	B. McDonald	34	2	5	7					
	F	S. Schriner	39	11	15	26	D	R. Hamilton	23	2	2	4					
	F	R. Heron	42	11	12	23											
	F	M. Chamberlain	40	5	17	22											
	F	P. Kelly	34	11	9	20											
	F	G. Marker	42	10	9	19											
	F	B. Kampman	39	6	9	15											
	F	L. Chisholm	28	6	8	14											
	F	P. Langelle	39	7	14	21											
CHI	LW	J. Gottselig	38	8	15	23	D	J. Cooper	44	4	7	11	P. Goodman	16	10	5	2.00
P. Thompson	C	C. Dahlstrom	45	11	17	28	D	E. Seibert	36	3	7	10	M. Karakas	7	9	1	3.41
23–19–6	RW	M. March	45	9	14	23	D	A. Wiebe	40	3	2	5					
	F	B. Thoms	46	9	13	22	D	J. Portland	16	1	4	5					
	F	G. Allen	48	10	12	22											
	F	P. Hergesheimer	41	9	11	20											
	F	D. Bentley	39	12	7	19											
	F	L. Cunningham	37	6	11	17											
	F	B. Carse	48	10	13	23											
	F	B. Carse	22	3	5	8											
	F	J. Desilets	26	6	7	13											
DET	F	S. Howe	48	14	23	37	D	E. Goodfellow	43	11	17	28	T. Thompson	16	24	6	2.61
J. Adams	F	M. Bruneteau	48	10	14	24	D	A. Motter	37	7	12	19	A. Moore	0	1	0	3.00
16–26–6	F	K. Kilrea	40	10	8	18	D	S. Bowman	11	0	2	2	C. Bourque	0	1	0	3.00
	F	C. Dillon	44	7	10	17	D	J. Stewart	48	1	0	1					
	F	C. Brown	36	8	3	11											
	F	E. Wares	32	2	6	8											
	F	B. McDonald	37	1	6	7											
	F	G. Giesebrecht	30	4	7	11											
	F	C. Liscombe	30	2	7	9											
	F	J. Fisher	34	2	4	6											
	F	J. Orlando	48	1	3	4											
NYA	LW	B. Jackson	43	12	8	20	D	C. Conacher	48	10	18	28	E. Robertson	15	**29**	4	2.92
R. Dutton	C	M. Armstrong	47	16	20	36	D	H. Smith	48	7	8	15					
15–29–4	RW	L. Carr	48	8	17	25	D	W. Field	45	1	3	4					
	F	T. Anderson	48	12	19	31	D	A. Murray	34	1	4	5					
	F	J. Sorrell	48	8	16	24	D	P. Egan	10	4	3	7					
	F	B. Boll	47	5	10	15	D	E. Shore	10	2	3	5					
	F	N. Stewart	37	7	7	14											
	F	A. Chapman	26	4	6	10											
	F	J. Gagnon	24	4	3	7											

Team	POS	PLAYER	GP	G	A	PTS	POS	PLAYER	GP	G	A	PTS	GOALIE	W	L	T	GAvg
MONT	LW	T. Blake	48	17	19	36	D	C. Wentworth	32	1	3	4	C. Bourque	9	24	3	3.33
P. Lepine	C	R. Getliffe	46	11	12	23	D	D. Young	47	3	9	12	W. Cude	1	5	1	3.43
10–33–5	RW	C. Sands	47	9	20	29	D	W. Buswell	46	1	3	4	M. Karakas	0	4	1	3.60
	F	G. Mantha	42	9	11	20							C. Sands	0	0	0	5.00
	F	L. Trudel	47	12	7	19											
	F	P. Drouin	21	4	7	11											
	F	M. Barry	30	4	10	14											
	F	R. Goupille	48	2	10	12											
	F	R. Lorrain	41	1	5	6											
	F	P. Haynes	23	2	8	10											
	F	A. Mondou	21	2	2	4											

GOALS		ASSISTS		POINTS	
B. Hextall, NYR	24	M. Schmidt, BOS	30	M. Schmidt, BOS	52
W. Dumart, BOS	22	B. Cowley, BOS	27	B. Bauer, BOS	43
M. Schmidt, BOS	22	B. Bauer, BOS	26	W. Dumart, BOS	43
H. Cain, BOS	21	S. Howe, DET	23	B. Cowley, BOS	40
G. Drillon, TOR	21	W. Dumart, BOS	21	G. Drillon, TOR	40

PENALTY MINUTES		GOALS AGAINST AVE.		SHUTOUTS	
R. Horner, TOR	87	D. Kerr, NYR	1.60	D. Kerr, NYR	8
A. Coulter, NYR	68	P. Goodman, CHI	2.00	F. Brimsek, BOS	6
M. Chamberlain, TOR	63	F. Brimsek, BOS	2.04	E. Robertson, NYA	6
J. Church, TOR	62	T. Broda, TOR	2.30	P. Goodman, CHI	4
W. Pratt, NYR	61	T. Thompson, DET	2.61	T. Broda, TOR	4

National Hockey League 1940–41

TEAM	W	L	T	PTS	GF	GA
*BOS	27	8	13	67	**168**	102
TOR	28	14	6	62	145	**99**
DET	21	16	11	53	112	102
NYR	21	19	8	50	143	125
CHI	16	25	7	39	112	139
MONT	16	26	6	38	121	147
NYA	8	29	11	27	99	186

Team	POS	PLAYER	GP	G	A	PTS	POS	PLAYER	GP	G	A	PTS	GOALIE	W	L	T	GAvg
BOS	LW	W. Dumart	40	18	15	33	D	D. Clapper	48	8	18	26	F. Brimsek	27	8	13	2.13
C. Weiland	C	M. Schmidt	45	13	25	38	D	F. Hollett	42	9	15	24					
27–8–13	RW	B. Bauer	48	17	22	39	D	D. Smith	48	6	8	14					
	LW	R. Conacher	41	24	14	38	D	J. Crawford	45	2	8	10					
	C	B. Cowley	46	17	**45**	**62**	D	J. Shewchuk	20	2	2	4					
	RW	M. Hill	41	5	4	9											
	F	E. Wiseman	47	16	24	40											
	F	A. Jackson	47	17	15	32											
	F	H. Cain	40	8	10	18											
	F	T. Reardon	34	6	5	11											
TOR	LW	B. Davidson	37	3	6	9	D	W. Stanowski	47	7	14	21	T. Broda	**28**	14	6	**2.06**
H. Day	C	S. Apps	41	20	24	44	D	B. McDonald	31	6	11	17					
28–14–6	RW	G. Drillon	42	23	21	44	D	R. Hamilton	45	3	12	15					
	LW	S. Schriner	48	24	14	38	D	B. Kampman	39	1	4	5					
	C	B. Taylor	47	9	26	35											
	RW	N. Metz	47	14	21	35											
	F	P. Langelle	48	4	15	19											
	F	H. Goldup	26	10	5	15											
	F	D. Metz	31	4	10	14											
	F	R. Heron	35	9	5	14											
	F	L. Chisholm	26	4	0	4											

	POS	PLAYER	GP	G	A	PTS		PLAYER	GP	G	A	PTS	GOALIE	W	L	T	GAvg
DET	LW	C. Liscombe	31	10	10	20	D	A. Motter	47	13	12	25	J. Mowers	21	16	11	2.13
J. Adams	C	S. Howe	48	20	24	44	D	E. Goodfellow	47	5	17	22					
21–16–11	RW	M. Bruneteau	45	11	17	28	D	J. Orlando	48	1	10	11					
	LW	D. Grosso	45	8	7	15	D	J. Stewart	47	2	6	8					
	C	S. Abel	47	11	22	33	D	B. Whitelaw	23	0	2	2					
	RW	E. Wares	42	10	16	26											
	F	G. Giesebrecht	43	7	18	25											
	F	J. Fisher	28	5	8	13											
	F	B. Jennings	12	1	5	6											
NYR	LW	L. Patrick	48	20	24	44	D	W. Pratt	47	3	17	20	D. Kerr	21	19	8	2.60
F. Boucher	C	P. Watson	40	11	25	36	D	A. Coulter	35	5	14	19					
21–19–8	RW	B. Hextall	48	**26**	18	44	D	A. Pike	48	6	13	19					
	LW	A. Shibicky	40	10	14	24	D	O. Heller	48	2	16	18					
	C	N. Colville	48	14	28	42											
	RW	M. Colville	47	14	17	31											
	F	C. Smith	48	14	11	25											
	F	D. Hiller	45	8	10	18											
	F	K. MacDonald	47	5	6	11											
	F	M. Patrick	47	2	8	10											
	F	S. Smith	8	2	1	3											
CHI	LW	D. Bentley	47	8	20	28	D	G. Allen	44	14	17	31	S. LoPresti	9	15	3	3.11
P. Thompson	C	M. Bentley	36	7	10	17	D	E. Seibert	46	3	17	20	P. Goodman	7	10	4	2.62
16–25–7	RW	M. March	44	8	9	17	D	J. Cooper	45	5	5	10					
	F	B. Thoms	48	13	19	32	D	J. Mariucci	23	0	5	5					
	F	C. Dahlstrom	40	11	14	25	D	A. Wiebe	46	2	2	4					
	F	J. Chad	45	7	18	25											
	F	B. Carse	32	5	15	20											
	F	P. Hergesheimer	47	9	11	20											
	F	B. Carse	43	9	9	18											
	F	P. Kelly	22	5	3	8											
MONT	LW	T. Blake	48	12	20	32	D	K. Reardon	34	2	8	10	B. Gardiner	13	**23**	6	2.83
D. Irvin	C	J. Quilty	48	18	16	34	D	J. Portland	42	2	7	9	P. Bibeault	1	2	0	3.75
16–26–6	RW	J. Benoit	45	16	16	32	D	T. Graboski	34	4	3	7	W. Cude	2	1	0	4.33
	LW	M. Chamberlain	45	10	15	25	D	A. Singbush	32	0	5	5					
	C	E. Lach	43	7	14	21											
	RW	R. Getliffe	39	15	10	25											
	F	T. Demers	46	13	10	23											
	F	J. Adams	42	6	12	18											
	F	C. Sands	43	5	13	18											
	F	P. Drouin	21	4	7	11											
	F	R. Goupille	48	3	6	9											
NYA	LW	B. Jackson	46	8	18	26	D	C. Conacher	46	7	16	23	E. Robertson	6	22	8	3.94
R. Dutton	C	M. Armstrong	48	10	14	24	D	P. Egan	39	4	9	13	C. Rayner	2	7	3	3.67
8–29–11	RW	L. Carr	48	13	19	32	D	W. Field	36	5	6	11	A. Brannigan	0	0	0	0.00
	F	B. Boll	46	12	14	26	D	P. Slobodzian	41	3	2	5					
	F	N. Larson	48	9	9	18											
	F	T. Anderson	35	3	12	15											
	F	B. Wycherley	26	4	5	9											
	F	P. Kelly	10	3	5	8											
	F	J. Sorrell	30	2	6	8											
	F	H. Smith	41	2	7	9											
	F	B. Benson	22	3	4	7											

GOALS		ASSISTS		POINTS	
B. Hextall, NYR	26	B. Cowley, BOS	45	B. Cowley, BOS	62
R. Conacher, BOS	24	N. Colville, NYR	28	S. Apps, TOR	44
S. Schriner, TOR	24	B. Taylor, TOR	26	G. Drillon, TOR	44
G. Drillon, TOR	23	M. Schmidt, BOS	25	B. Hextall, NYR	44
		P. Watson, NYR	25	L. Patrick, NYR	44

PENALTY MINUTES		GOALS AGAINST AVE.		SHUTOUTS	
J. Orlando, DET	99	T. Broda, TOR	2.06	F. Brimsek, BOS	6
R. Goupille, MONT	81	F. Brimsek, BOS	2.13	T. Broda, TOR	4
M. Chamberlain, MONT	75	J. Mowers, DET	2.13	J. Mowers, DET	4
J. Cooper, CHI	66	D. Kerr, NYR	2.60	D. Kerr, NYR	2
D. Smith, BOS	61	P. Goodman, CHI	2.62	P. Goodman, CHI	2

National Hockey League 1941–42

TEAM	W	L	T	PTS	GF	GA
NYR	29	17	2	60	**177**	143
*TOR	27	18	3	57	158	136
BOS	25	17	6	56	160	**118**
CHI	22	23	3	47	145	155
DET	19	25	4	42	140	147
MONT	18	27	3	39	134	173
NYA	16	29	3	35	133	175

	POS	PLAYER	GP	G	A	PTS		PLAYER	GP	G	A	PTS	GOALIE	W	L	T	GAvg
NYR	LW	L. Patrick	47	**32**	22	54	D	W. Pratt	47	4	24	28	J. Henry	**29**	17	2	2.98
F. Boucher	C	P. Watson	48	15	**37**	52	D	A. Coulter	47	1	16	17					
29–17–2	RW	B. Hextall	48	24	32	**56**	D	B. Juzda	45	4	8	12					
	LW	A. Shibicky	45	20	14	34	D	O. Heller	35	6	5	11					
	C	N. Colville	48	8	25	33											
	RW	M. Colville	46	14	16	30											
	F	C. Smith	47	10	24	34											
	F	K. Warwick	44	16	17	33											
	F	A. Pike	34	8	19	27											
	F	A. Kuntz	31	10	11	21											
TOR	LW	B. Davidson	37	6	20	26	D	B. McDonald	48	2	19	21	T. Broda	27	18	3	2.83
H. Day	C	S. Apps	38	18	23	41	D	B. Goldham	19	4	7	11					
27–18–3	RW	G. Drillon	48	23	18	41	D	B. Kampman	38	4	7	11					
	LW	S. Schriner	47	20	16	36	D	W. Stanowski	24	1	7	8					
	C	B. Taylor	48	12	26	38	D	R. Hamilton	22	0	4	4					
	RW	L. Carr	47	16	17	33											
	F	P. Langelle	48	10	22	32											
	F	H. Goldup	44	12	18	30											
	F	J. McCreedy	47	15	8	23											
	F	N. Metz	30	11	9	20											
BOS	LW	W. Dumart	35	14	15	29	D	F. Hollett	48	19	14	33	F. Brimsek	24	17	6	**2.45**
A. Ross	C	M. Schmidt	36	14	21	35	D	D. Clapper	32	3	12	15	N. Damore	1	0	0	3.00
25–17–6	RW	B. Bauer	36	13	22	35	D	D. Smith	48	7	7	14					
	LW	E. Wiseman	45	12	22	34	D	J. Crawford	43	2	9	11					
	C	B. Cowley	28	4	23	27	D	J. Shewchuk	22	2	0	2					
	RW	R. Conacher	43	24	13	37											
	F	A. Jackson	47	6	18	24											
	F	H. Cain	35	8	10	18											
	F	D. Hiller	43	7	10	17											
CHI	LW	D. Bentley	38	12	14	26	D	E. Seibert	46	7	14	21	S. LoPresti	21	23	3	3.23
P. Thompson	C	M. Bentley	39	13	17	30	D	G. Allen	43	7	13	20	B. Dickie	1	0	0	3.00
22–23–3	RW	M. March	48	6	26	32	D	J. Cooper	47	6	14	20					
	LW	A. Kaleta	48	7	21	28	D	J. Mariucci	47	5	8	13					
	C	B. Thoms	48	15	30	45	D	A. Wiebe	44	2	4	6					
	RW	B. Carse	33	7	16	23											
	F	C. Dahlstrom	33	13	14	27											
	F	R. Hamill	34	18	9	27											
	F	B. Carse	43	13	14	27											
	F	B. Mosienko	12	6	8	14											
	F	J. Papike	9	1	0	1											
							D	J. Stewart	44	4	7	11	J. Mowers	19	**25**	3	3.06
DET	LW	D. Grosso	48	23	30	53	D	J. Orlando	48	1	7	8	J. Turner	0	0	1	3.00
J. Adams	C	S. Abel	48	18	31	49	D	A. Motter	30	2	4	6					
19–25–4	RW	E. Wares	43	9	29	38	D	B. Jones	21	2	1	3					
	LW	C. Liscombe	47	13	17	30											
	C	S. Howe	48	16	19	35											
	RW	M. Bruneteau	48	14	19	33											
	F	G. Giesebrecht	34	6	16	22											
	F	J. Carveth	29	6	11	17											
	F	K. Kilrea	21	3	12	15											
	F	A. Brown	28	6	9	15											
	F	P. McCreavy	34	5	8	13											
MONT	LW	T. Blake	48	17	28	45	D	K. Reardon	41	3	12	15	P. Bibeault	17	19	1	3.45
D. Irvin	C	J. Quilty	48	12	12	24	D	J. Portland	46	2	9	11	B. Gardiner	1	8	1	4.20
18–27–3	RW	J. Benoit	46	20	16	36	D	T. Graboski	23	2	5	7					
	LW	P. Morin	31	10	12	22	D	E. Bouchard	44	0	6	6					
	C	B. O'Connor	36	9	16	25	D	R. Goupille	47	1	5	6					
	RW	G. Heffernan	40	5	15	20											
	F	T. Reardon	33	17	17	34											
	F	C. Sands	39	11	16	27											
	F	R. Getliffe	45	11	15	26											
	F	T. Demers	7	3	4	7											
NYA	F	T. Anderson	48	12	29	41	D	P. Egan	48	8	20	28	C. Rayner	13	21	2	3.58
R. Dutton	F	M. Hill	47	14	23	37	D	W. Field	41	6	9	15	E. Robertson	3	8	1	3.83
16–29–3	F	B. Benson	45	8	21	29	D	J. Church	15	1	2	3					
	F	M. Armstrong	45	6	22	28	D	A. Brannigan	20	0	2	2					
	F	B. Boll	48	11	15	26											
	F	N. Larson	40	16	9	25											
	F	H. Watson	47	10	8	18											
	F	M. Chamberlain	11	6	9	15											
	F	K. Mosdell	41	7	9	16											
	F	F. Thurier	27	7	7	14											
	F	J. Krol	24	9	3	12											

GOALS		ASSISTS		POINTS	
L. Patrick, NYR	32	P. Watson, NYR	37	B. Hextall, NYR	56
R. Conacher, BOS	24	B. Hextall, NYR	32	L. Patrick, NYR	54
R. Hamill, BOS, CHI	24	S. Abel, DET	31	D. Grosso, DET	53
B. Hextall, NYR	24	D. Grosso, DET	30	P. Watson, NYR	52
G. Drillon, TOR	23	E. Wares, DET	29	S. Abel, DET	49
D. Grosso, DET	23				

PENALTY MINUTES		GOALS AGAINST AVE.		SHUTOUTS	
P. Egan, NYA	124	F. Brimsek, BOS	2.45	T. Broda, TOR	6
J. Orlando, DET	111	T. Broda, TOR	2.83	J. Mowers, DET	5
J. Stewart, DET	93	J. Henry, NYR	2.98	F. Brimsek, BOS	3
D. Smith, BOS	70	J. Mowers, DET	3.06	S. LoPresti, CHI	3
B. Kampman, TOR	67	S. LoPresti, CHI	3.23	J. Henry, NYR	2

National Hockey League 1942–43

TEAM	W	L	T	PTS	GF	GA
*DET	25	14	11	61	169	**124**
BOS	24	17	9	57	195	176
TOR	22	19	9	53	**198**	159
MONT	19	19	12	50	181	191
CHI	17	18	15	49	179	180
NYR	11	31	8	30	161	253

	POS	PLAYER	GP	G	A	PTS	PLAYER	GP	G	A	PTS	GOALIE	W	L	T	GAvg
DET	LW	S. Howe	50	20	35	55	D J. Stewart	44	2	9	11	J. Mowers	**25**	14	11	**2.47**
J. Adams	C	D. Grosso	50	15	17	32	D A. Motter	50	6	4	10					
25–14–11	RW	M. Bruneteau	50	23	22	45	D J. Orlando	40	4	3	7					
	LW	C. Liscombe	50	19	23	42	D C. Simon	34	1	1	2					
	C	S. Abel	49	18	24	42	D E. Goodfellow	11	1	4	5					
	RW	H. Watson	50	13	18	31										
	C	C. Brown	23	5	16	21										
	C	L. Douglas	21	5	8	13										
	RW	J. Carveth	43	18	18	36										
	RW	E. Wares	47	12	18	30										
BOS	LW	H. Cain	45	18	18	36	D F. Hollett	50	19	25	44	F. Brimsek	24	17	9	3.52
A. Ross	C	B. Cowley	48	27	**45**	72	D D. Clapper	38	5	18	23					
24–17–9	RW	A. Jackson	50	22	31	53	D J. Crawford	49	5	18	23					
	LW	B. Boll	43	25	27	52	D J. Shewchuk	48	2	6	8					
	C	D. Gallinger	48	14	20	34										
	RW	B. Guidolin	42	7	15	22										
	LW	B. Jackson	44	19	15	34										
	C	M. Chamberlain	45	9	24	33										
	RW	J. Schmidt	45	6	7	13										
	RW	B. Shill	7	4	1	5										
	RW	I. Boyd	20	6	5	11										
TOR	LW	S. Schriner	37	19	17	36	D W. Pratt	40	12	25	37	T. Broda	22	**19**	9	3.18
H. Day	C	B. Taylor	50	18	42	60	D B. McDonald	40	2	11	13					
22–19–9	RW	L. Carr	50	27	33	60	D B. Copp	38	3	9	12					
	LW	G. Stewart	48	24	23	47	D R. Hamilton	11	1	1	2					
	C	J. McLean	27	9	8	17	D R. Thomson	18	0	2	2					
	RW	B. Poile	48	16	19	35										
	LW	B. Davidson	50	13	23	36										
	C	S. Apps	29	23	17	40										
	C	J. Hamilton	49	4	22	26										
	RW	M. Hill	49	17	27	44										
MONT	LW	T. Blake	48	23	36	59	D E. Bouchard	45	2	16	18	P. Bibeault	19	**19**	12	3.81
D. Irvin	C	E. Lach	45	18	40	58	D L. Lamoureux	46	2	16	18					
19–19–12	RW	J. Benoit	49	30	27	57	D J. Portland	49	3	14	17					
	LW	R. Getliffe	50	18	28	46	D G. Harmon	27	5	9	14					
	C	B. O'Connor	50	15	43	58	D T. Reardon	13	6	6	12					
	RW	G. Drillon	49	28	22	50										
	LW	D. Hiller	42	8	6	14										
	C	C. Sands	31	3	9	12										
	RW	M. Richard	16	5	6	11										
CHI	LW	D. Bentley	50	**33**	40	**73**	D E. Seibert	44	5	27	32	B. Gardiner	17	18	15	3.58
P. Thompson	C	M. Bentley	47	26	44	70	D G. Allen	47	10	14	24					
17–18–15	RW	B. Thoms	47	15	28	43	D A. Tuten	34	3	7	10					
	LW	R. Hamill	50	28	16	44	D A. Wiebe	33	1	7	8					
	LW	B. Carse	47	10	22	32	D R. Mitchell	42	1	1	2					
	C	C. Dahlstrom	38	11	13	24										
	RW	M. March	50	7	29	36										
	RW	F. Purpur	50	13	16	29										
	RW	R. Bentley	11	1	2	3										
	RW	G. Johnston	30	10	7	17										
	RW	B. Mosienko	2	2	0	2										

	POS	PLAYER	GP	G	A	PTS		PLAYER	GP	G	A	PTS	GOALIE	W	L	T	GAvg
NYR	LW	L. Patrick	50	22	39	61	D	O. Heller	45	4	14	18	J. Franks	5	14	4	4.48
F. Boucher	C	P. Watson	46	14	28	42	D	V. Myles	45	6	9	15	B. Beveridge	4	10	3	5.24
11–31–8	RW	B. Hextall	50	27	32	59	D	G. Davidson	35	2	3	5	S. Buzinski	2	6	1	5.89
	LW	H. Goldup	36	11	20	31	D	R. Garrett	23	1	1	2	L. Bouvrette	0	1	0	6.00
	LW	S. Cameron	35	8	11	19											
	LW	J. Shack	20	5	9	14											
	C	C. Smith	47	12	21	33											
	C	A. Pike	41	6	16	22											
	RW	K. Warwick	50	17	18	35											
	RW	B. Kirkpatrick	49	12	12	24											
	RW	G. Mancuso	21	6	8	14											

GOALS		ASSISTS		POINTS	
D. Bentley, CHI	33	B. Cowley, BOS	45	D. Bentley, CHI	73
J. Benoit, MONT	30	M. Bentley, CHI	44	B. Cowley, BOS	72
G. Drillon, MONT	28	B. O'Connor, MONT	43	M. Bentley, CHI	70
R. Hamill, CHI	28	B. Taylor, TOR	42	L. Patrick, NYR	61
		D. Bentley, CHI	40	L. Carr, TOR	60
		E. Lach, MONT	40	B. Taylor, TOR	60

PENALTY MINUTES		GOALS AGAINST AVE.		SHUTOUTS	
J. Orlando, DET	99	J. Mowers, DET	2.47	J. Mowers, DET	6
R. Hamilton, TOR	68	T. Broda, TOR	3.18	T. Broda, TOR	1
J. Stewart, DET	68	F. Brimsek, BOS	3.52	F. Brimsek, BOS	1
M. Chamberlain, BOS	67	B. Gardiner, CHI	3.58	B. Gardiner, CHI	1
V. Myles, NYR	57	P. Bibeault, MONT	3.81	P. Bibeault, MONT	1

National Hockey League 1943–44

TEAM	W	L	T	PTS	GF	GA
*MONT	38	5	7	83	**234**	**109**
DET	26	18	6	58	214	177
TOR	23	23	4	50	214	174
CHI	22	23	5	49	178	187
BOS	19	26	5	43	223	268
NYR	6	39	5	17	162	310

	POS	PLAYER	GP	G	A	PTS		PLAYER	GP	G	A	PTS	GOALIE	W	L	T	GAvg
MONT	LW	T. Blake	41	26	33	59	D	L. Lamoureux	44	8	23	31	B. Durnan	**38**	5	7	**2.18**
D. Irvin	C	E. Lach	48	24	48	72	D	M. McMahon	42	7	17	24					
38–5–7	RW	M. Richard	46	32	22	54	D	G. Harmon	43	5	16	21					
	LW	M. Chamberlain	47	15	32	47	D	E. Bouchard	35	5	14	19					
	C	R. Getliffe	44	28	25	53											
	RW	P. Watson	44	17	32	49											
	LW	F. Majeau	44	20	18	38											
	C	B. O'Connor	44	12	42	54											
	C	T. Campeau	2	0	0	0											
	RW	G. Heffernan	43	28	20	48											
	RW	B. Fillion	41	7	23	30											
DET	LW	C. Liscombe	50	36	37	73	D	F. Hollett	27	6	12	18	C. Dion	17	7	2	3.08
J. Adams	LW	S. Howe	40	32	28	60	D	B. Quackenbush	43	4	14	18	J. Franks	6	8	3	4.06
26–18–6	LW	A. Brown	50	24	18	42	D	C. Simon	46	3	7	10	N. Smith	3	1	1	2.75
	C	D. Grosso	42	16	31	47	D	H. Jackson	50	7	12	19	H. Lumley	0	2	0	6.50
	C	M. Armstrong	28	12	22	34											
	C	K. Kilrea	14	1	3	4											
	RW	J. Carveth	46	21	35	56											
	RW	M. Bruneteau	39	35	18	53											
	RW	B. Jennings	33	6	11	17											

	POS	PLAYER	GP	G	A	PTS		PLAYER	GP	G	A	PTS	GOALIE	W	L	T	GAvg
TOR	LW	B. Davidson	47	19	28	47	D	W. Pratt	50	17	40	57	P. Bibeault	13	14	2	3.00
H. Day	LW	G. Boothman	49	16	18	34	D	M. Morris	50	12	21	33	B. Grant	9	9	2	4.15
23–23–4	LW	T. O'Neill	33	8	7	15	D	R. Hamilton	39	4	12	16	J. Marois	1	0	0	4.00
	LW	D. Webster	27	7	6	13	D	J. Ingoldsby	21	5	0	5					
	C	G. Bodnar	50	22	40	62											
	C	J. Hamilton	49	20	17	37											
	C	T. Kennedy	49	26	23	49											
	C	J. McLean	32	3	15	18											
	RW	L. Carr	50	36	38	74											
	RW	M. Hill	17	9	10	19											
	RW	B. Poile	11	6	8	14											
CHI	LW	D. Bentley	50	**38**	39	77	D	E. Seibert	50	8	25	33	M. Karakas	12	9	5	3.04
P. Thompson	C	C. Smith	50	23	**49**	72	D	V. Johnson	48	1	8	9	H. Highton	10	14	0	4.50
22–23–5	RW	B. Mosienko	50	32	38	70	D	A. Wiebe	21	2	4	6					
	LW	G. Allen	45	17	24	41	D	J. Dyte	27	1	0	1					
	C	C. Dahlstrom	50	20	22	42	D	J. Cooper	13	1	0	1					
	RW	M. March	48	10	27	37											
	LW	J. Gottselig	45	8	15	23											
	RW	F. Purpur	40	9	10	19											
	RW	V. Heyliger	26	2	3	5											
BOS	LW	H. Cain	48	36	46	**82**	D	P. Egan	25	11	13	24	B. Gardiner	17	19	5	5.17
A. Ross	C	B. Cowley	36	30	41	71	D	D. Clapper	50	6	25	31	M. Courteau	2	4	0	5.50
19–26–5	RW	A. Jackson	49	21	38	59	D	J. Crawford	34	4	16	20	G. Abbott	0	1	0	7.00
	LW	B. Boll	39	19	25	44	D	G. Labrie	15	2	7	9	J. Franks	0	1	0	6.00
	LW	B. Guidolin	47	17	25	42							B. Grant	0	1	0	10.00
	LW	B. Jackson	42	11	21	32											
	C	N. Calladine	49	16	27	43											
	RW	T. Brennan	21	2	1	3											
	RW	R. Kopak	24	7	9	16											
	RW	A. Rittinger	19	3	7	10											
NYR	LW	D. Hiller	50	18	22	40	D	O. Heller	50	8	27	35	K. McAuley	6	**39**	5	6.20
F. Boucher	LW	J. Mahaffy	28	9	20	29	D	B. McDonald	41	5	6	11	H. Lumley	0	0	0	0.00
6–39–5	LW	O. Aubuchon	38	15	12	27	D	B. Dill	28	6	10	16					
	LW	B. Gooden	41	9	8	17											
	LW	B. Warwick	13	3	2	5											
	C	A. DeMarco	36	14	19	33											
	C	J. McDonald	43	10	9	19											
	C	K. MacDonald	24	7	9	16											
	C	F. Boucher	15	4	10	14											
	RW	B. Hextall	50	21	33	54											
	RW	F. Gauthier	33	14	10	24											

GOALS	
D. Bentley, CHI	38
H. Cain, BOS	36
L. Carr, TOR	36
C. Liscombe, DET	36
M. Bruneteau, DET	35

ASSISTS	
C. Smith, CHI	49
E. Lach, MONT	48
H. Cain, BOS	46
B. O'Connor, MONT	42
B. Cowley, BOS	41

POINTS	
H. Cain, BOS	82
D. Bentley, CHI	77
L. Carr, TOR	74
C. Liscombe, DET	73
E. Lach, MONT	72

PENALTY MINUTES	
M. McMahon, MONT	98
P. Egan, DET, BOS	95
M. Chamberlain, MONT	85
B. Dill, NYR	66
P. Watson, MONT	61

GOALS AGAINST AVE.	
B. Durnan, MONT	2.18
P. Bibeault, TOR	3.00
M. Karakas, CHI	3.04
C. Dion, DET	3.08

SHUTOUTS	
P. Bibeault, TOR	5
M. Karakas, CHI	3
B. Durnan, MONT	2
C. Dion, DET	1
J. Franks, DET	1

National Hockey League 1944–45

TEAM	W	L	T	PTS	GF	GA
MONT	38	8	4	80	**228**	**121**
DET	31	14	5	67	218	161
*TOR	24	22	4	52	183	161
BOS	16	30	4	36	179	219
CHI	13	30	7	33	171	174
NYR	11	29	10	32	154	147

TEAM	POS	PLAYER	GP	G	A	PTS		PLAYER	GP	G	A	PTS	GOALIE	W	L	T	GAvg
MONT	LW	T. Blake	49	29	38	67	D	E. Bouchard	50	11	23	34	B. Durnan	**38**	8	4	**2.42**
D. Irvin	C	E. Lach	50	26	**54**	**80**	D	L. Lamoureux	49	2	22	24					
38–8–4	RW	M. Richard	50	**50**	23	73	D	G. Harmon	42	5	8	13					
	LW	D. Hiller	48	20	16	36	D	F. Eddolls	43	5	8	13					
	LW	R. Getliffe	41	16	7	23											
	LW	M. Chamberlain	32	2	12	14											
	LW	F. Majeau	12	2	6	8											
	C	B. O'Connor	50	21	23	44											
	C	K. Mosdell	31	12	6	18											
	RW	F. Gauthier	50	18	13	31											
	RW	B. Fillion	31	6	8	14											
DET	LW	T. Lindsay	45	17	6	23	D	F. Hollett	50	20	21	41	H. Lumley	24	10	3	3.22
J. Adams	C	S. Howe	46	17	36	53	D	E. Seibert	25	5	9	14	C. Dion	6	4	2	3.25
31–14–5	RW	M. Bruneteau	43	23	24	47	D	B. Quackenbush	50	7	14	21	N. Smith	1	0	0	3.00
	LW	C. Liscombe	42	23	9	32	D	H. Jackson	50	5	6	11					
	LW	J. McAtee	44	15	11	26											
	LW	T. Bukovich	14	7	2	9											
	C	M. Armstrong	50	15	24	39											
	RW	J. Carveth	50	26	28	54											
	RW	E. Bruneteau	42	12	13	25											
	RW	Wojciechowski	49	19	20	39											
TOR	LW	S. Schriner	26	27	15	42	D	W. Pratt	50	18	23	41	F. McCool	24	22	4	3.22
H. Day	C	G. Bodnar	49	8	36	44	D	R. Hamilton	50	3	12	15					
24–22–4	RW	L. Carr	47	11	25	36	D	B. Ezinicki	8	1	4	5					
	LW	B. Davidson	50	17	18	35	D	W. Stanowski	34	2	9	11					
	C	T. Kennedy	49	29	25	54	D	R. Johnstone	24	3	4	7					
	RW	M. Hill	45	18	17	35	D	P. Backor	36	4	5	9					
	LW	N. Metz	50	22	13	35											
	C	A. Jackson	31	9	13	22											
	RW	T. O'Neill	33	2	5	7											
	RW	J. McCreedy	17	2	4	6											
BOS	LW	H. Cain	50	32	13	45	D	J. Crawford	40	5	19	24	P. Bibeault	6	18	2	4.43
A. Ross	C	B. Cowley	49	25	40	65	D	P. Egan	48	7	15	22	H. Bennett	10	12	2	4.33
16–30–4	RW	B. Jennings	39	20	13	33	D	J. Shewchuk	47	1	7	8					
	LW	K. Smith	49	20	14	34	D	D. Clapper	46	8	14	22					
	LW	A. Gaudreault	44	15	9	24											
	C	J. Gladu	40	6	14	20											
	C	G. Rozzini	31	5	10	15											
	C	B. Thoms	17	4	2	6											
	C	J. McGill	14	4	2	6											
	RW	F. Mario	44	8	18	26											
	RW	B. Cupolo	47	11	13	24											
CHI	LW	P. Horeck	50	20	16	36	D	J. Cooper	50	4	17	21	M. Karakas	12	**29**	7	3.90
P. Thompson	C	C. Smith	50	23	31	54	D	W. Field	39	3	4	7	D. Stevenson	1	1	0	3.50
0–1–0	RW	B. Mosienko	50	28	26	54	D	R. Mitchell	40	3	4	7					
J. Gottselig	LW	D. Grosso	21	9	6	15	D	C. Simon	29	0	1	1					
13–29–7	LW	R. Brayshaw	43	5	9	14											
	LW	L. Check	26	6	2	8											
	C	B. McDonald	26	6	13	19											
	C	C. Dahlstrom	40	6	13	19											
	C	H. Fraser	21	5	4	9											
	RW	M. March	38	5	5	10											
	RW	J. Harms	43	5	5	10											
NYR	LW	H. Goldup	48	17	25	42	D	O. Heller	45	7	12	19	K. McAuley	11	25	10	4.93
F. Boucher	C	A. DeMarco	50	24	30	54	D	B. Dill	48	9	5	14	D. Stevenson	0	4	0	5.00
11–29–10	RW	K. Warwick	42	20	22	42	D	B. McDonald	40	2	9	11					
	LW	J. Shack	50	18	4	22	D	B. Moe	35	2	4	6					
	LW	J. Mann	6	3	4	7											
	C	F. Thurier	50	16	19	35											
	C	P. Watson	45	11	8	19											
	C	K. MacDonald	36	9	6	15											
	C	C. Scherza	22	2	3	5											
	RW	F. Hunt	44	13	9	22											
	RW	W. Atanas	49	13	8	21											

GOALS	
M. Richard, MONT	50
T. Blake, MONT	29
T. Kennedy, TOR	29
B. Mosienko, CHI	28

ASSISTS	
E. Lach, MONT	54
B. Cowley, BOS	40
T. Blake, MONT	38
G. Bodnar, TOR	36
S. Howe, DET	36

POINTS	
E. Lach, MONT	80
M. Richard, MONT	73
T. Blake, MONT	67
B. Cowley, BOS	65

PENALTY MINUTES	
P. Egan, BOS	86
B. Dill, NYR	69
L. Lamoureux, MONT	58
J. Cooper, CHI	50
B. Davidson, TOR	49

GOALS AGAINST AVE.	
B. Durnan, MONT	2.42
F. McCool, TOR	3.22
H. Lumley, DET	3.22
M. Karakas, CHI	3.90
P. Bibeault, BOS	4.43

SHUTOUTS	
F. McCool, TOR	4
M. Karakas, CHI	4
B. Durnan, MONT	1
H. Lumley, DET	1
K. McAuley, NYR	1

TEAM	W	L	T	PTS	GF	GA
*MONT	28	17	5	61	172	**134**
BOS	24	18	8	56	167	156
CHI	23	20	7	53	**200**	178
DET	20	20	10	50	146	159
TOR	19	24	7	45	174	185
NYR	13	28	9	35	144	191

TEAM	POS	PLAYER	GP	G	A	PTS	POS	PLAYER	GP	G	A	PTS	GOALIE	W	L	T	GAvg
MONT	LW	T. Blake	50	29	21	50	D	E. Bouchard	45	7	10	17	B. Durnan	**24**	11	5	**2.60**
D. Irvin	C	E. Lach	50	13	**34**	47	D	G. Harmon	49	7	10	17	P. Bibeault	4	6	0	3.00
28–17–5	RW	M. Richard	50	27	21	48	D	L. Lamoureux	45	5	7	12					
	LW	D. Hiller	45	7	11	18	D	K. Reardon	43	5	4	9					
	LW	M. Chamberlain	40	12	14	26											
	C	B. Reay	44	17	12	29											
	C	B. O'Connor	45	11	11	22											
	C	K. Mosdell	13	2	1	3											
	RW	J. Peters	47	11	19	30											
	RW	J. Benoit	39	9	10	19											
	RW	B. Fillion	50	10	6	16											
BOS	LW	W. Dumart	50	22	12	34	D	T. Reardon	49	12	11	23	F. Brimsek	16	14	4	3.26
D. Clapper	C	M. Schmidt	48	13	18	31	D	P. Egan	41	8	10	18	P. Bibeault	8	4	4	2.81
24–18–8	RW	B. Bauer	39	11	10	21	D	J. Crawford	48	7	9	16					
	LW	B. Guidolin	50	15	17	32	D	M. Henderson	48	4	11	15					
	LW	H. Cain	48	17	12	29	D	D. Clapper	30	2	3	5					
	LW	K. Smith	23	2	6	8											
	C	D. Gallinger	50	17	23	40											
	C	B. Cowley	26	12	12	24											
	C	J. McGill	46	6	14	20											
	RW	B. Shill	45	15	12	27											
CHI	LW	D. Bentley	36	19	21	40	D	G. Allen	44	11	15	26	M. Karakas	22	19	7	3.46
J. Gottselig	C	M. Bentley	47	30	31	**61**	D	J. Mariucci	50	3	8	11	D. Stevenson	1	1	0	6.00
23–20–7	RW	B. Mosienko	40	18	30	48	D	J. Cooper	50	2	7	9					
	LW	P. Horeck	50	20	21	41	D	E. Wares	45	4	11	15					
	C	C. Smith	50	26	24	50	D	R. Hamilton	48	1	7	8					
	RW	A. Kaleta	49	19	27	46											
	LW	R. Hamill	38	20	17	37											
	LW	D. Grosso	47	7	10	17											
	C	G. Gee	35	14	15	29											
DET	LW	T. Lindsay	47	7	10	17	D	B. Quackenbush	48	11	10	21	H. Lumley	20	20	10	3.18
J. Adams	C	M. Armstrong	40	8	18	26	D	J. Stewart	47	4	11	15					
20–20–10	RW	E. Bruneteau	46	17	12	29	D	H. Jackson	36	3	4	7					
	LW	A. Brown	48	20	11	31	D	F. Hollett	38	4	9	13					
	LW	H. Watson	44	14	10	24	D	E. Seibert	18	0	3	3					
	LW	C. Liscombe	44	12	9	21											
	C	D. Couture	43	3	7	10											
	C	S. Howe	26	4	7	11											
	RW	J. Carveth	48	17	18	35											
	RW	F. Gauthier	30	9	8	17											
TOR	LW	G. Stewart	50	**37**	15	52	D	W. Pratt	41	5	20	25	F. McCool	10	9	3	3.68
H. Day	C	B. Taylor	48	23	18	41	D	B. Goldham	49	7	14	21	T. Broda	6	6	3	3.53
19–24–7	RW	L. Carr	42	5	8	13	D	M. Morris	38	1	5	6	G. Bell	3	5	0	3.88
	LW	N. Metz	41	11	11	22	D	W. Stanowski	45	3	10	13	B. Bastien	0	4	1	4.00
	C	S. Apps	40	24	16	40											
	RW	B. Ezinicki	24	4	8	12											
	LW	S. Schriner	47	13	6	19											
	LW	B. Davidson	41	9	9	18											
	C	G. Bodnar	49	14	23	37											
	C	J. Hamilton	40	7	9	16											
	RW	M. Hill	35	5	7	12											
NYR	LW	T. Leswick	50	15	9	24	D	N. Colville	49	5	4	9	C. Rayner	12	**21**	7	3.79
F. Boucher	C	E. Laprade	49	15	19	34	D	B. Moe	48	4	4	8	J. Henry	1	7	2	3.95
13–28–9	RW	P. Watson	49	12	14	26	D	H. Goldup	19	6	1	7					
	LW	R. Trudell	16	3	5	8	D	B. Juzda	32	1	3	4					
	C	C. Gardner	16	8	2	10											
	RW	C. Russell	17	0	5	5											
	LW	L. Patrick	38	8	6	14											
	LW	A. Pike	33	7	9	16											
	LW	A. Shibicky	33	10	5	15											
	C	A. DeMarco	50	20	27	47											
	RW	K. Warwick	45	19	18	37											

GOALS		ASSISTS		POINTS	
G. Stewart, TOR	37	E. Lach, MONT	34	M. Bentley, CHI	61
M. Bentley, CHI	30	M. Bentley, CHI	31	G. Stewart, TOR	52
T. Blake, MONT	29	B. Mosienko, CHI	30	T. Blake, MONT	50
M. Richard, MONT	27	A. DeMarco, NYR	27	C. Smith, CHI	50
C. Smith, CHI	26	A. Kaleta, CHI	27	M. Richard, MONT	48

PENALTY MINUTES		GOALS AGAINST AVE.		SHUTOUTS	
J. Stewart, DET	73	B. Durnan, MONT	2.60	B. Durnan, MONT	4
B. Guidolin, BOS	62	P. Bibeault, BOS, MONT	2.88	P. Bibeault, BOS, MONT	2
J. Mariucci, CHI	58	H. Lumley, DET	3.18	H. Lumley, DET	2
E. Bouchard, MONT	52	F. Brimsek, BOS	3.26	F. Brimsek, BOS	2
M. Richard, MONT	50	M. Karakas, CHI	3.46	M. Karakas, CHI	1

National Hockey League 1946–47

TEAM	W	L	T	PTS	GF	GA
MONT	34	16	10	78	189	**138**
*TOR	31	19	10	72	**209**	172
BOS	26	23	11	63	190	175
DET	22	27	11	55	190	193
NYR	22	32	6	50	167	186
CHI	19	37	4	42	193	274

TEAM	POS	PLAYER	GP	G	A	PTS	POS	PLAYER	GP	G	A	PTS	GOALIE	W	L	T	GAvg
MONT	LW	T. Blake	60	21	29	50	D	K. Reardon	52	5	17	22	B. Durnan	**34**	16	10	**2.30**
D. Irvin	C	B. O'Connor	46	10	20	30	D	R. Leger	49	4	18	22					
34–16–10	RW	M. Richard	60	**45**	26	71	D	G. Harmon	57	5	9	14					
	LW	M. Chamberlain	49	10	10	20	D	E. Bouchard	60	5	7	12					
	C	B. Reay	59	22	20	42	D	L. Lamoureux	50	2	11	13					
	C	E. Lach	31	14	16	30	D	G. Allen	49	7	14	21					
	C	K. Mosdell	54	5	10	15											
	RW	L. Gravelle	53	16	14	30											
	RW	J. Peters	60	11	13	24											
	RW	B. Fillion	57	6	3	9											
TOR	LW	V. Lynn	31	6	14	20	D	W. Stanowski	51	3	16	19	T. Broda	31	19	10	2.87
H. Day	C	T. Kennedy	60	28	32	60	D	G. Mortson	60	5	13	18					
31–19–10	RW	H. Meeker	55	27	18	45	D	J. Thomson	60	2	14	16					
	LW	N. Metz	60	12	16	28	D	G. Boesch	35	4	5	9					
	C	S. Apps	54	25	24	49											
	RW	B. Ezinicki	60	17	20	37											
	LW	G. Stewart	60	19	14	33											
	LW	H. Watson	44	19	15	34											
	LW	J. Klukay	55	9	20	29											
	RW	B. Poile	59	19	17	36											
BOS	LW	W. Dumart	60	24	28	52	D	P. Egan	60	7	18	25	F. Brimsek	26	**23**	11	2.92
D. Clapper	C	M. Schmidt	59	27	35	62	D	T. Reardon	60	6	14	20					
26–23–11	RW	B. Bauer	58	30	24	54	D	J. Crawford	58	1	17	18					
	LW	B. Guidolin	56	10	13	23	D	M. Henderson	57	5	12	17					
	LW	K. Smith	60	14	7	21	D	W. Pratt	31	4	4	8					
	C	B. Cowley	51	13	25	38	D	F. Flaman	23	1	4	5					
	C	D. Gallinger	47	11	19	30											
	C	J. McGill	24	5	9	14											
	RW	J. Carveth	51	21	15	36											
DET	LW	R. Conacher	60	30	24	54	D	B. Quackenbush	44	5	17	22	H. Lumley	22	20	10	3.06
J. Adams	LW	T. Lindsay	59	27	15	42	D	J. Stewart	55	5	9	14	J. Mowers	0	6	1	4.14
22–27–11	LW	P. Horeck	38	12	13	25	D	L. Reise	31	4	6	10	R. Almas	0	1	0	5.00
	C	B. Taylor	60	17	**46**	63	D	H. Jackson	37	1	5	6					
	C	S. Abel	60	19	29	48	D	D. McCaig	47	2	4	6					
	C	P. Lundy	59	17	17	34											
	C	J. Conacher	33	16	13	29											
	C	D. Couture	30	5	10	15											
	RW	E. Bruneteau	60	9	14	23											
NYR	LW	T. Leswick	59	27	14	41	D	B. Moe	59	4	10	14	C. Rayner	22	30	6	3.05
F. Boucher	C	E. Laprade	58	15	25	40	D	H. Laycoe	58	1	12	13	J. Henry	0	2	0	4.50
22–32–6	RW	B. Hextall	60	21	10	31	D	N. Colville	60	4	16	20					
	LW	R. Trudell	59	8	16	24	D	J. Cooper	59	2	8	10					
	C	C. Gardner	52	13	16	29	D	B. Juzda	45	3	5	8					
	RW	C. Russell	54	20	8	28											
	LW	A. Pike	31	7	11	18											
	LW	K. Warwick	54	20	20	40											
	LW	J. Bell	47	6	4	10											
	C	A. DeMarco	44	9	10	19											
	RW	P. Watson	48	6	12	18											

	POS	PLAYER	GP	G	A	PTS		PLAYER	GP	G	A	PTS	GOALIE	W	L	T	GAvg
CHI	LW	D. Bentley	52	21	34	55	D	B. Gadsby	43	8	10	18	P. Bibeault	13	25	3	4.15
J. Gottselig	C	M. Bentley	60	29	43	**72**	D	J. Mariucci	52	2	9	11	E. Francis	6	12	1	5.47
19–37–4	RW	B. Mosienko	59	25	27	52	D	R. Nattrass	35	4	5	9					
	LW	A. Brown	42	11	25	36	D	J. Jackson	48	2	5	7					
	LW	A. Kaleta	57	24	20	44	D	E. Wares	60	4	7	11					
	LW	R. Hamill	60	21	19	40											
	C	G. Gee	60	20	20	40											
	C	C. Smith	52	9	17	26											
	RW	G. Johnston	10	3	1	4											

GOALS		ASSISTS		POINTS	
M. Richard, MONT	45	B. Taylor, DET	46	M. Bentley, CHI	72
B. Bauer, BOS	30	M. Bentley, CHI	43	M. Richard, MONT	71
R. Conacher, DET	30	M. Schmidt, BOS	35	B. Taylor, DET	63
M. Bentley, CHI	29	D. Bentley, CHI	34	M. Schmidt, BOS	62
T. Kennedy, TOR	28	T. Kennedy, TOR	32	T. Kennedy, TOR	60

PENALTY MINUTES		GOALS AGAINST AVE.		SHUTOUTS	
G. Mortson, TOR	133	B. Durnan, MONT	2.30	C. Rayner, NYR	5
J. Mariucci, CHI	110	T. Broda, TOR	2.87	T. Broda, TOR	4
M. Chamberlain, MONT	97	F. Brimsek, BOS	2.92	F. Brimsek, BOS	3
J. Thomson, TOR	97	C. Rayner, NYR	3.05	H. Lumley, DET	3
B. Ezinicki, TOR	93	H. Lumley, DET	3.06		

National Hockey League 1947–48

TEAM	W	L	T	PTS	GF	GA
*TOR	32	15	13	77	182	**143**
DET	30	18	12	72	187	148
BOS	23	24	13	59	167	168
NYR	21	26	13	55	176	201
MONT	20	29	11	51	147	169
CHI	20	34	6	46	**195**	225

	POS	PLAYER	GP	G	A	PTS		PLAYER	GP	G	A	PTS	GOALIE	W	L	T	GAvg
TOR	LW	H. Watson	57	21	20	41	D	J. Thomson	59	0	29	29	T. Broda	**32**	15	13	**2.38**
H. Day	C	S. Apps	55	26	27	53	D	G. Mortson	58	7	11	18					
32–15–13	RW	B. Ezinicki	60	11	20	31	D	B. Barilko	57	5	9	14					
	LW	V. Lynn	60	12	22	34	D	W. Stanowski	54	2	11	13					
	C	T. Kennedy	60	25	21	46	D	G. Boesch	45	2	7	9					
	RW	H. Meeker	58	14	20	34											
	LW	J. Klukay	59	15	15	30											
	LW	S. Smith	31	7	10	17											
	LW	N. Metz	60	4	8	12											
	C	M. Bentley	53	23	25	48											
DET	LW	T. Lindsay	60	**33**	19	52	D	B. Quackenbush	58	6	16	22	H. Lumley	30	18	12	2.46
T. Ivan	C	S. Abel	60	14	30	44	D	R. Kelly	60	6	14	20	T. McGrattan	0	0	0	0.00
30–18–12	RW	G. Howe	60	16	28	44	D	J. Stewart	60	5	14	19					
	LW	P. Horeck	50	12	17	29	D	L. Reise	58	5	4	9					
	LW	B. Guidolin	58	12	10	22											
	LW	M. Pavelich	41	4	8	12											
	C	J. McFadden	60	24	24	48											
	C	D. Couture	19	3	6	9											
	C	D. Morrison	40	10	15	25											
	RW	R. Morrison	34	8	7	15											
	RW	F. Gauthier	35	1	5	6											
BOS	LW	W. Dumart	59	21	16	37	D	P. Egan	60	8	11	19	F. Brimsek	23	24	13	2.80
D. Clapper	C	M. Schmidt	33	9	17	26	D	J. Crawford	45	3	11	14					
23–24–13	RW	J. Peters	37	12	15	27	D	F. Flaman	56	4	6	10					
	LW	P. Babando	60	23	11	34											
	LW	K. Smith	60	11	12	23											
	C	D. Gallinger	54	10	21	31											
	C	E. Sandford	59	10	15	25											
	C	P. Ronty	24	3	11	14											
	C	W. Wilson	53	11	8	19											
	RW	F. Harrison	52	6	7	13											
	RW	M. Henderson	49	6	8	14											

TEAM	POS	PLAYER	GP	G	A	PTS	PLAYER	GP	G	A	PTS	GOALIE	W	L	T	GAvg
NYR	LW	P. Watson	54	18	15	33	D F. Eddolls	58	6	13	19	J. Henry	17	18	13	3.19
F. Boucher	C	B. O'Connor	60	24	36	60	D N. Colville	55	4	12	16	C. Rayner	4	8	0	3.65
21–26–13	RW	B. Hextall	43	8	14	22	D B. Moe	59	1	15	16	R. Decourcy	0	0	0	12.41
	LW	T. Leswick	60	24	16	40	D B. Juzda	60	3	9	12					
	C	E. Laprade	59	13	34	47										
	RW	E. Kullman	51	15	17	32										
	LW	E. Slowinski	38	6	5	11										
	LW	R. Trudell	54	13	7	20										
	C	D. Raleigh	52	15	18	33										
	C	C. Gardner	58	7	18	25										
	RW	C. Russell	19	0	3	3										
MONT	LW	T. Blake	32	9	15	24	D K. Reardon	58	7	15	22	B. Durnan	20	28	10	2.77
D. Irvin	C	E. Lach	60	30	31	**61**	D R. Leger	48	4	14	18	G. McNeil	0	1	1	4.42
20–29–11	RW	M. Richard	53	28	25	53	D G. Harmon	56	10	4	14					
	LW	N. Dussault	28	5	10	15	D E. Bouchard	60	4	6	10					
	C	B. Reay	60	6	14	20	D D. Harvey	35	4	4	8					
	C	H. Riopelle	55	5	2	7										
	RW	J. Carveth	35	1	10	11										
	RW	B. Fillion	32	4	9	13										
	RW	J. Locas	56	7	8	15										
CHI	LW	R. Conacher	52	22	27	49	D E. Dickens	54	5	15	20	E. Francis	18	**31**	5	3.39
J. Gottselig	C	D. Bentley	60	20	**37**	57	D R. Nattrass	60	5	12	17	D. Jackson	2	3	1	7.00
7–20–2	RW	R. Hamill	60	11	13	24	D B. Gadsby	60	6	10	16					
C. Conacher	LW	G. Stewart	54	26	29	55	D B. Goldham	38	2	9	11					
13–14–4	C	G. Bodnar	46	13	22	35										
	RW	B. Poile	54	23	29	52										
	LW	A. Kaleta	52	10	16	26										
	C	G. Gee	60	14	25	39										
	C	M. Prystai	54	7	11	18										
	RW	B. Mosienko	40	16	8	24										
	RW	A. Brown	32	7	10	17										

GOALS		ASSISTS		POINTS	
T. Lindsay, DET	33	D. Bentley, CHI	37	E. Lach, MONT	61
E. Lach, MONT	30	B. O'Connor, NYR	36	B. O'Connor, NYR	60
M. Richard, MONT	28	E. Laprade, NYR	34	D. Bentley, CHI	57
G. Stewart, TOR, CHI	27	E. Lach, MONT	31	G. Stewart, TOR, CHI	56
M. Bentley, CHI, TOR	26	S. Abel, DET	30	M. Bentley, CHI, TOR	54
S. Apps, TOR	26			B. Poile, TOR, CHI	54

PENALTY MINUTES		GOALS AGAINST AVE.		SHUTOUTS	
B. Barilko, TOR	147	T. Broda, TOR	2.38	H. Lumley, DET	7
K. Reardon, MONT	129	H. Lumley, DET	2.46	T. Broda, TOR	5
G. Mortson, TOR	118	B. Durnan, MONT	2.77	B. Durnan, MONT	5
B. Ezinicki, TOR	97	F. Brimsek, BOS	2.80	F. Brimsek, BOS	3
T. Lindsay, DET	95	J. Henry, NYR	3.19	J. Henry, NYR	2

National Hockey League 1948–49

TEAM	W	L	T	PTS	GF	GA
DET	34	19	7	75	**195**	145
BOS	29	23	8	66	178	163
MONT	28	23	9	65	152	**126**
*TOR	22	25	13	57	147	161
CHI	21	31	8	50	173	211
NYR	18	31	11	47	133	172

TEAM	POS	PLAYER	GP	G	A	PTS	PLAYER	GP	G	A	PTS	GOALIE	W	L	T	GAvg
DET	LW	T. Lindsay	50	24	30	54	D B. Quackenbush	60	6	17	23	H. Lumley	**34**	19	7	2.42
T. Ivan	C	S. Abel	60	**28**	26	54	D R. Kelly	59	5	11	16					
34–19–7	RW	G. Howe	40	12	25	37	D J. Stewart	60	4	11	15					
	LW	P. Horeck	60	14	18	32	D L. Reise	59	3	7	10					
	LW	M. Pavelich	60	10	16	26										
	LW	E. Sclisizzi	50	9	8	17										
	C	J. McFadden	55	12	20	32										
	C	D. Couture	51	19	10	29										
	C	G. Gee	47	7	11	18										
	RW	B. Poile	56	21	21	42										
	RW	M. McNab	51	10	13	23										

	POS	PLAYER	GP	G	A	PTS	POS	PLAYER	GP	G	A	PTS	GOALIE	W	L	T	GAvg
BOS	LW	K. Smith	59	20	20	40	D	P. Egan	60	6	18	24	F. Brimsek	26	20	8	2.72
D. Clapper	C	P. Ronty	60	20	29	49	D	F. Flaman	60	4	12	16	L. Colvin	0	1	0	4.00
29–23–8	RW	J. Peirson	59	22	21	43	D	J. Crawford	55	2	13	15	J. Gelineau	2	2	0	3.00
	LW	P. Babando	58	19	14	33	D	M. Henderson	60	2	9	11	G. Henry	1	0	0	0.00
	LW	W. Dumart	59	11	12	23	D	C. Thompson	10	0	1	1					
	C	E. Sandford	56	16	20	36											
	C	M. Schmidt	44	10	22	32											
	C	D. Creighton	12	1	3	4											
	RW	K. Warwick	58	22	15	37											
	RW	J. Peters	60	16	15	31											
MONT	LW	N. Dussault	47	9	8	17	D	G. Harmon	59	8	12	20	B. Durnan	28	23	9	**2.10**
D. Irvin	C	B. Reay	60	22	23	45	D	K. Reardon	46	3	13	16					
28–23–9	RW	M. Richard	59	20	18	38	D	D. Harvey	55	3	13	16					
	LW	M. Chamberlain	54	5	8	13	D	R. Leger	28	6	7	13					
	LW	G. Plamondon	27	5	5	10											
	C	E. Lach	36	11	18	29											
	C	K. Mosdell	60	17	9	26											
	C	T. Campeau	26	3	7	10											
	C	H. Riopelle	48	10	6	16											
	RW	J. Carveth	60	15	22	37											
	RW	B. Fillion	59	3	9	12											
TOR	LW	H. Watson	60	26	19	45	D	J. Thomson	60	4	16	20	T. Broda	22	25	13	2.68
H. Day	C	C. Gardner	53	13	22	35	D	G. Mortson	60	2	13	15					
22–25–13	RW	B. Ezinicki	52	13	15	28	D	G. Boesch	59	1	10	11					
	LW	V. Lynn	52	7	9	16	D	B. Barilko	60	5	4	9					
	C	T. Kennedy	59	18	21	39	D	B. Juzda	38	1	2	3					
	RW	H. Meeker	30	7	7	14											
	LW	J. Klukay	45	11	10	21											
	LW	R. Timgren	36	3	12	15											
	C	M. Bentley	60	19	22	41											
	RW	D. Metz	33	4	6	10											
CHI	LW	R. Conacher	60	26	42	**68**	D	E. Dickens	59	2	3	5	J. Henry	21	**31**	8	3.52
C. Conacher	C	D. Bentley	58	23	**43**	66	D	R. Nattrass	60	4	10	14					
21–31–8	RW	B. Mosienko	60	17	25	42	D	B. Gadsby	50	3	10	13					
	LW	G. Stewart	54	20	18	38	D	B. Goldham	60	1	10	11					
	LW	B. Guidolin	56	4	17	21											
	LW	R. Hamill	57	8	4	12											
	C	J. Conacher	55	25	23	48											
	C	G. Bodnar	50	19	26	45											
	C	M. Prystai	59	12	7	19											
	RW	A. Brown	58	8	12	20											
	RW	B. Olmstead	9	0	2	2											
NYR	LW	T. Leswick	60	13	14	27	D	A. Stanley	40	2	8	10	C. Rayner	16	**31**	11	2.90
F. Boucher	C	B. O'Connor	46	11	24	35	D	F. Shero	59	3	6	9	E. Francis	2	0	0	2.00
6–11–6	RW	E. Laprade	56	18	12	30	D	B. Moe	60	0	9	9					
L. Patrick	LW	A. Kaleta	56	12	19	31	D	W. Stanowski	60	1	8	9					
12–20–5	LW	E. Slowinski	20	1	1	2											
	C	D. Raleigh	41	10	16	26											
	C	J. Gordon	31	3	9	12											
	C	N. Mickoski	54	13	9	22											
	RW	D. Fisher	60	9	16	25											
	RW	P. Lund	59	14	16	30											
	RW	E. Kullman	18	5	4	9											

GOALS

S. Abel, DET	28
R. Conacher, CHI	26
J. Conacher, DET, CHI	26
H. Watson, TOR	26
T. Lindsay, DET	24

ASSISTS

D. Bentley, CHI	43
R. Conacher, CHI	42
T. Lindsay, DET	30
P. Ronty, BOS	29
S. Abel, DET	26

POINTS

R. Conacher, CHI	68
D. Bentley, CHI	66
S. Abel, DET	54
T. Lindsay, DET	54
P. Ronty, BOS	49

PENALTY MINUTES

B. Ezinicki, TOR	145
B. Guidolin, DET, CHI	116
M. Chamberlain, MONT	111
M. Richard, MONT	110
K. Reardon, MONT	103

GOALS AGAINST AVE.

B. Durnan, MONT	2.10
H. Lumley, DET	2.42
T. Broda, TOR	2.68
F. Brimsek, BOS	2.72
C. Rayner, NYR	2.90

SHUTOUTS

B. Durnan, MONT	10
C. Rayner, NYR	7
H. Lumley, DET	6
T. Broda, TOR	5
G. Henry, BOS	1

National Hockey League 1949–50

TEAM	W	L	T	PTS	GF	GA
*DET	37	19	14	88	**229**	164
MONT	29	22	19	77	164	**150**
TOR	31	27	12	74	176	173
NYR	28	31	11	67	170	189
BOS	22	32	16	60	198	228
CHI	22	38	10	54	203	244

TEAM	POS	PLAYER	GP	G	A	PTS	POS	PLAYER	GP	G	A	PTS	GOALIE	W	L	T	GAvg
DET	LW	T. Lindsay	69	23	**55**	**78**	D	R. Kelly	70	15	25	40	H. Lumley	**33**	16	14	2.35
T. Ivan	C	S. Abel	70	34	35	69	D	L. Reise	70	4	17	21	T. Sawchuk	4	3	0	2.29
37–19–14	RW	G. Howe	70	35	33	68	D	J. Stewart	65	3	11	14					
	LW	M. Pavelich	65	8	15	23	D	L. Fogolin	64	4	8	12					
	LW	S. Black	69	7	14	21	D	C. Martin	64	2	5	7					
	C	G. Gee	69	17	21	38											
	C	D. Couture	70	24	7	31											
	C	J. McFadden	68	14	16	30											
	RW	J. Carveth	60	13	17	30											
	RW	J. Peters	70	14	16	30											
MONT	LW	N. Dussault	67	13	24	37	D	K. Reardon	67	1	27	28	B. Durnan	26	21	17	**2.20**
D. Irvin	C	E. Lach	64	15	33	48	D	D. Harvey	70	4	20	24	G. McNeil	3	1	2	1.50
29–22–19	RW	M. Richard	70	**43**	22	65	D	G. Harmon	62	3	16	19					
	LW	C. MacKay	52	8	10	18	D	R. Leger	55	3	12	15					
	LW	K. Warwick	30	2	6	8	D	E. Bouchard	69	1	7	8					
	C	B. Reay	68	19	26	45											
	C	K. Mosdell	67	15	12	27											
	C	H. Riopelle	66	12	8	20											
	RW	L. Gravelle	70	19	10	29											
	RW	F. Curry	49	8	8	16											
TOR	LW	S. Smith	68	22	23	45	D	B. Barilko	59	7	10	17	T. Broda	30	25	12	2.48
H. Day	C	T. Kennedy	53	20	24	44	D	G. Mortson	68	3	14	17	A. Rollins	1	1	0	2.00
31–27–12	RW	H. Meeker	70	18	22	40	D	B. Juzda	62	1	14	15	G. Mayer	0	1	0	2.00
	LW	H. Watson	60	19	16	35	D	J. Thomson	70	0	13	13					
	C	M. Bentley	69	23	18	41	D	G. Boesch	58	2	6	8					
	RW	B. Ezinicki	67	10	12	22											
	LW	J. Klukay	70	15	16	31											
	LW	R. Timgren	68	7	18	25											
	C	C. Gardner	30	7	19	26											
	RW	M. MacKell	36	7	13	20											
NYR	LW	T. Leswick	69	19	25	44	D	P. Egan	70	5	11	16	C. Rayner	28	30	11	2.62
L. Patrick	C	E. Laprade	60	22	22	44	D	F. Shero	67	2	8	10	E. Francis	0	1	0	8.00
28–31–11	RW	D. Fisher	70	12	21	33	D	A. Stanley	55	4	4	8					
	LW	P. Lund	64	18	9	27	D	F. Eddolls	58	2	6	8					
	C	E. Slowinski	63	14	23	37	D	G. Kyle	70	3	5	8					
	RW	D. Raleigh	70	12	25	37											
	LW	A. Kaleta	67	17	14	31											
	C	B. O'Connor	66	11	22	33											
	C	N. Mickoski	45	10	10	20											
	RW	J. McLeod	38	6	9	15											
BOS	LW	K. Smith	66	10	31	41	D	B. Quackenbush	70	8	17	25	J. Gelineau	22	30	15	3.28
G. Boucher	C	P. Ronty	70	23	36	59	D	E. Kryzanowski	59	6	10	16	G. Henry	0	2	0	2.50
22–32–16	RW	J. Peirson	57	27	25	52	D	M. Henderson	64	3	8	11	R. Bittner	0	0	1	3.00
	LW	W. Dumart	69	14	25	39	D	J. Crawford	46	2	8	10					
	C	P. Maloney	70	15	31	46	D	F. Flaman	69	2	5	7					
	C	M. Schmidt	68	19	22	41											
	C	D. Creighton	64	18	13	31											
	RW	Z. Toppazzini	36	5	5	10											
	RW	F. Harrison	70	14	12	26											
	RW	B. Poile	39	16	14	30											
CHI	LW	R. Conacher	70	25	31	56	D	B. Gadsby	70	10	24	34	F. Brimsek	22	**38**	10	3.49
C. Conacher	C	D. Bentley	64	20	33	53	D	R. Nattrass	68	5	11	16					
22–38–10	RW	B. Mosienko	69	18	28	46	D	E. Dickens	70	0	13	13					
	LW	B. Guidolin	70	17	34	51	D	B. Goldham	67	2	10	12					
	LW	G. Stewart	70	24	19	43	D	D. McCaig	64	0	4	4					
	LW	R. Hamill	59	6	2	8											
	C	M. Prystai	65	29	22	51											
	C	G. Bodnar	70	11	28	39											
	C	J. Conacher	66	13	20	33											
	RW	B. Olmstead	70	20	29	49											

GOALS		ASSISTS		POINTS	
M. Richard, MONT	43	T. Lindsay, DET	55	T. Lindsay, DET	78
G. Howe, DET	35	P. Ronty, BOS	36	S. Abel, DET	69
S. Abel, DET	34	S. Abel, DET	35	G. Howe, DET	68
M. Prystai, CHI	29	B. Guidolin, CHI	34	M. Richard, MONT	65
J. Peirson, BOS	27	D. Bentley, CHI	33	P. Ronty, BOS	59

PENALTY MINUTES		GOALS AGAINST AVE.		SHUTOUTS	
B. Ezinicki, TOR	144	B. Durnan, MONT	2.20	T. Broda, TOR	9
G. Kyle, NYR	143	H. Lumley, DET	2.35	B. Durnan, MONT	8
T. Lindsay, DET	141	T. Broda, TOR	2.48	H. Lumley, DET	7
B. Gadsby, CHI	138	C. Rayner, NYR	2.62	C. Rayner, NYR	6
G. Mortson, TOR	125	J. Gelineau, BOS	3.28	G. McNeil, MONT	1

TEAM	W	L	T	PTS	GF	GA
DET	44	13	13	101	**236**	139
*TOR	41	16	13	95	212	**138**
MONT	25	30	15	65	173	184
BOS	22	30	18	62	178	197
NYR	20	29	21	61	169	201
CHI	13	47	10	36	171	280

	POS	PLAYER	GP	G	A	PTS		PLAYER	GP	G	A	PTS	GOALIE	W	L	T	GAvg
DET	LW	T. Lindsay	67	24	35	59	D	R. Kelly	70	17	37	54	T. Sawchuk	**44**	13	13	1.99
T. Ivan	C	S. Abel	69	23	38	61	D	L. Reise	68	5	16	21					
44–13–13	RW	G. Howe	70	**43**	**43**	**86**	D	B. Goldham	61	5	8	13					
	LW	G. Stewart	67	18	13	31	D	M. Pronovost	37	1	6	7					
	LW	M. Pavelich	67	9	20	29											
	LW	V. Stasiuk	50	3	10	13											
	C	M. Prystai	62	20	17	37											
	C	G. Gee	70	17	20	37											
	C	J. McFadden	70	14	18	32											
	RW	J. Peters	68	17	21	38											
	RW	J. Carveth	30	1	4	5											
TOR	LW	S. Smith	70	30	21	51	D	J. Thomson	69	3	33	36	A. Rollins	27	5	8	**1.77**
J. Primeau	C	T. Kennedy	63	18	**43**	61	D	G. Mortson	60	3	10	13	T. Broda	14	11	5	2.23
41–16–13	RW	T. Sloan	70	31	25	56	D	F. Flaman	39	2	6	8					
	LW	H. Watson	68	18	19	37											
	LW	D. Lewicki	61	16	18	34											
	LW	J. Klukay	70	14	16	30											
	C	M. Bentley	67	21	41	62											
	C	C. Gardner	66	23	28	51											
	RW	M. MacKell	70	12	13	25											
	RW	H. Meeker	49	6	14	20											
MONT	LW	B. Olmstead	39	16	22	38	D	D. Harvey	70	5	24	29	G. McNeil	25	30	15	2.63
D. Irvin	LW	C. MacKay	70	18	10	28	D	B. MacPherson	62	0	16	16					
25–30–15	LW	N. Dussault	64	4	20	24	D	E. Bouchard	52	3	10	13					
	C	E. Lach	65	21	24	45	D	T. Johnson	70	2	8	10					
	C	K. Mosdell	66	13	18	31											
	C	B. Reay	60	6	18	24											
	RW	M. Richard	65	42	24	66											
	RW	F. Curry	69	13	14	27											
	RW	B. Geoffrion	18	8	6	14											
BOS	LW	W. Dumart	70	20	21	41	D	B. Quackenbush	70	5	24	29	J. Gelineau	22	30	18	2.81
L. Patrick	C	M. Schmidt	62	22	39	61	D	M. Quackenbush	47	4	6	10					
22–30–18	RW	B. Ezinicki	53	16	19	35	D	E. Kryzanowski	69	3	6	9					
	LW	L. Ferguson	70	16	17	33	D	S. Kraftcheck	22	0	0	0					
	LW	P. Horeck	66	10	13	23											
	LW	V. Lynn	56	14	6	20											
	C	P. Ronty	70	10	22	32											
	C	E. Sandford	51	10	13	23											
	RW	J. Peirson	70	19	19	38											
	RW	D. Fisher	57	9	20	29											
NYR	LW	R. Sinclair	70	18	21	39	D	A. Stanley	70	7	14	21	C. Rayner	19	28	19	2.85
N. Colville	C	B. O'Connor	66	16	20	36	D	P. Egan	70	5	10	15	E. Francis	1	1	2	3.23
20–29–21	RW	E. Kullman	70	14	18	32	D	F. Eddolls	68	3	8	11					
	LW	E. Slowinski	69	14	18	32	D	W. Stanowski	49	1	5	6					
	LW	A. Kaleta	58	3	4	7											
	LW	T. Leswick	70	15	11	26											
	C	D. Raleigh	64	15	24	39											
	C	N. Mickoski	64	20	15	35											
	C	E. Laprade	42	10	13	23											
	RW	P. Lund	59	4	16	20											
	RW	Z. Toppazzini	55	14	13	27											
CHI	LW	R. Conacher	70	26	24	50	D	A. Dewsbury	67	5	14	19	H. Lumley	12	**41**	10	3.90
E. Goodfellow	C	D. Bentley	44	9	23	32	D	L. Fogolin	35	3	10	13	M. Pelletier	1	5	0	4.90
13–47–10	RW	B. Mosienko	65	21	15	36	D	B. Gadsby	25	3	7	10	R. Almas	0	1	0	5.00
	LW	B. Guidolin	69	12	22	34	D	E. Dickens	70	2	8	10					
	C	J. Conacher	52	10	27	37											
	C	G. Bodnar	44	8	12	20											
	C	D. Morrison	59	8	12	20											
	C	P. Lundy	61	9	9	18											
	RW	R. Powell	31	7	15	22											

GOALS		ASSISTS		POINTS	
G. Howe, DET	43	G. Howe, DET	43	G. Howe, DET	86
M. Richard, MONT	42	T. Kennedy, TOR	43	M. Richard, MONT	66
T. Sloan, TOR	31	M. Bentley, TOR	41	M. Bentley, TOR	62
S. Smith, TOR	30	M. Schmidt, BOS	39	S. Abel, DET	61
R. Conacher, CHI	26	S. Abel, DET	38	M. Schmidt, BOS	61

PENALTY MINUTES	
G. Mortson, TOR	142
T. Johnson, MONT	128
B. Ezinicki, BOS	119
T. Leswick, NYR	112
T. Lindsay, DET	110

GOALS AGAINST AVE.	
A. Rollins, TOR	1.77
T. Sawchuk, DET	1.99
G. McNeil, MONT	2.63
J. Gelineau, BOS	2.81
C. Rayner, NYR	2.85

SHUTOUTS	
T. Sawchuk, DET	11
T. Broda, TOR	6
G. McNeil, MONT	6
A. Rollins, TOR	5
J. Gelineau, BOS	4

National Hockey League 1951–52

TEAM	W	L	T	PTS	GF	GA
*DET	44	14	12	100	**215**	**133**
MONT	34	26	10	78	195	164
TOR	29	25	16	74	168	157
BOS	25	29	16	66	162	176
NYR	23	34	13	59	192	219
CHI	17	44	9	43	158	241

	POS	PLAYER	GP	G	A	PTS		PLAYER	GP	G	A	PTS	GOALIE	W	L	T	GAvg
	LW	T. Lindsay	70	30	39	69	D	R. Kelly	67	16	31	47	T. Sawchuk	**44**	14	12	**1.90**
DET	C	S. Abel	62	17	36	53	D	M. Pronovost	69	7	11	18					
T. Ivan	RW	G. Howe	70	**47**	39	**86**	D	B. Goldham	69	0	14	14					
44–14–12	LW	M. Pavelich	68	17	19	36	D	L. Reise	54	0	11	11					
	C	G. Skov	70	12	24	36	D	B. Woit	58	3	8	11					
	RW	T. Leswick	70	9	10	19											
	C	A. Delvecchio	65	15	22	37											
	C	M. Prystai	69	21	22	43											
	RW	V. Stasiuk	58	5	9	14											
	RW	F. Glover	54	9	9	18											
	LW	D. Moore	33	18	15	33	D	D. Harvey	68	6	23	29	G. McNeil	34	26	10	2.34
MONT	C	E. Lach	70	15	**50**	65	D	D. St. Laurent	40	3	10	13					
D. Irvin	RW	M. Richard	48	27	17	44	D	E. Bouchard	60	3	9	12					
34–26–10	LW	P. Meger	69	24	18	42	D	T. Johnson	67	0	7	7					
	LW	D. Gamble	64	23	17	40	D	B. MacPherson	54	2	1	3					
	C	B. Reay	68	7	34	41											
	C	K. Mosdell	44	5	11	16											
	C	J. McCormack	54	2	10	12											
	RW	B. Geoffrion	67	30	24	54											
	RW	B. Olmstead	69	7	28	35											
	LW	S. Smith	70	27	30	57	D	J. Thomson	70	0	25	25	A. Rollins	29	24	16	2.22
TOR	C	T. Sloan	68	25	23	48	D	H. Bolton	60	3	13	16	T. Broda	0	1	0	6.00
J. Primeau	RW	T. Kennedy	70	19	33	52	D	F. Flaman	61	0	7	7					
29–25–16	LW	H. Watson	70	22	17	39	D	G. Mortson	65	1	10	11					
	LW	D. Lewicki	51	4	9	13											
	LW	J. Klukay	43	4	8	12											
	C	M. Bentley	69	24	17	41											
	C	C. Gardner	70	15	26	41											
	RW	H. Meeker	54	9	14	23											
	RW	R. Timgren	50	2	4	6											
	RW	G. Armstrong	20	3	3	6											
	LW	J. McIntyre	52	12	19	31	D	B. Quackenbush	69	2	17	19	J. Henry	25	29	16	2.51
BOS	C	M. Schmidt	69	21	29	50	D	G. Kyle	69	1	12	13					
L. Patrick	RW	J. Peirson	68	20	30	50	D	H. Laycoe	70	5	7	12					
25–29–16	LW	W. Dumart	39	5	8	13	D	E. Kryzanowski	70	5	3	8					
	LW	R. Chevrefils	33	8	17	25											
	C	R. Sullivan	67	12	12	24											
	C	D. Creighton	49	20	17	37											
	C	D. Fisher	65	15	12	27											
	C	E. Sandford	65	13	12	25											
	RW	M. MacKell	30	1	8	9											
	RW	B. Ezinicki	28	5	5	10											
	LW	E. Slowinski	64	21	22	43	D	H. Buller	68	12	23	35	C. Rayner	18	25	10	3.00
NYR	C	P. Ronty	65	12	32	43	D	A. Stanley	50	5	14	19	E. Francis	4	7	3	3.00
N. Colville	RW	W. Hergesheimer	68	26	12	38	D	S. Kraftcheck	58	8	9	17	L. Anderson	1	2	0	6.00
6–12–5	LW	H. Dickenson	37	14	13	27	D	J. Ross	51	2	9	11					
B. Cook	LW	E. Kullman	64	11	10	21	D	F. Eddolls	42	3	5	8					
17–22–8	C	D. Raleigh	70	19	42	61											
	C	E. Laprade	70	9	29	38											
	C	N. Mickoski	43	7	13	20											
	RW	R. Sinclair	69	20	10	30											
	RW	G. Stewart	69	15	25	40											

	POS	PLAYER	GP	G	A	PTS		PLAYER	GP	G	A	PTS	GOALIE	W	L	T	GAvg
CHI	LW	P. Babando	49	11	14	25	D	A. Dewsbury	69	7	17	24	H. Lumley	17	**44**	9	3.46
E. Goodfellow	C	G. Bodnar	69	14	26	40	D	B. Gadsby	59	7	15	22	M. Roberts	0	0	0	0.00
17–44–9	RW	B. Mosienko	70	31	22	53	D	F. Hucul	34	3	7	10					
	LW	B. Guidolin	67	13	18	31	D	L. Fogolin	69	0	9	9					
	LW	S. Witiuk	33	3	8	11	D	J. Stewart	37	1	3	4					
	C	G. Gee	70	18	31	49											
	C	J. McFadden	70	10	24	34											
	C	S. Finney	26	6	5	11											
	RW	J. Peters	70	15	21	36											
	RW	P. Horeck	60	9	11	20											

GOALS		ASSISTS		POINTS	
G. Howe, DET	47	E. Lach, MONT	50	G. Howe, DET	86
B. Mosienko, CHI	31	D. Raleigh, NYR	42	T. Lindsay, DET	69
T. Lindsay, DET	30	G. Howe, DET	39	E. Lach, MONT	65
B. Geoffrion, MONT	30	T. Lindsay, DET	39	D. Raleigh, NYR	61
M. Richard, MONT	27	S. Abel, DET	36	S. Smith, TOR	57
S. Smith, TOR	27				

PENALTY MINUTES		GOALS AGAINST AVE.		SHUTOUTS	
G. Kyle, BOS	127	T. Sawchuk, DET	1.90	T. Sawchuk, DET	12
T. Lindsay, DET	123	A. Rollins, TOR	2.22	J. Henry, BOS	7
F. Flaman, TOR	110	G. McNeil, MONT	2.34	A. Rollins, TOR	5
G. Mortson, TOR	106	J. Henry, BOS	2.51	G. McNeil, MONT	5
A. Dewsbury, CHI	99	C. Rayner, NYR	3.00	C. Rayner, NYR	2

National Hockey League 1952–53

TEAM	W	L	T	PTS	GF	GA
DET	36	16	18	90	**222**	**133**
*MONT	28	23	19	75	155	148
BOS	28	29	13	69	152	172
CHI	27	28	15	69	169	175
TOR	27	30	13	67	156	167
NYR	17	37	16	50	152	211

	POS	PLAYER	GP	G	A	PTS		PLAYER	GP	G	A	PTS	GOALIE	W	L	T	GAvg
DET	LW	T. Lindsay	70	32	39	71	D	R. Kelly	70	19	27	46	T. Sawchuk	**32**	15	16	**1.90**
T. Ivan	C	A. Delvecchio	70	16	43	59	D	M. Pronovost	68	8	19	27	G. Hall	4	1	1	1.67
36–16–18	RW	G. Howe	70	**49**	**46**	**95**	D	B. Goldham	70	1	13	14	R. Almas	0	0	1	3.00
	LW	J. Wilson	70	23	19	42	D	B. Woit	70	1	5	6					
	LW	M. Pavelich	64	13	20	33	D	J. Hay	42	1	4	5					
	LW	T. Leswick	70	15	12	27											
	C	M. Prystai	70	16	34	50											
	C	G. Skov	70	12	15	27											
	RW	R. Sinclair	69	11	12	23											
	RW	L. Jankowski	22	1	2	3											
MONT	LW	B. Olmstead	69	17	28	45	D	D. Harvey	69	4	30	34	G. McNeil	25	23	18	2.12
D. Irvin	C	E. Lach	53	16	25	41	D	T. Johnson	70	3	8	11	J. Plante	2	0	1	1.33
28–23–19	RW	M. Richard	70	28	33	61	D	E. Bouchard	58	2	8	10	H. Murphy	1	0	0	4.00
	LW	D. Moore	18	2	6	8	D	D. St. Laurent	54	2	6	8					
	C	B. Reay	56	4	15	19	D	B. MacPherson	59	2	3	5					
	RW	B. Geoffrion	65	22	17	39											
	LW	P. Meger	69	9	17	26											
	LW	D. Gamble	69	11	13	24											
	C	K. Mosdell	63	5	14	19											
	C	P. Masnick	53	10	7	17											
	RW	F. Curry	68	16	6	22											
BOS	LW	M. MacKell	65	27	17	44	D	B. Quackenbush	69	2	16	18	J. Henry	28	29	13	2.46
L. Patrick	C	E. Sandford	61	14	21	35	D	W. Godfrey	60	1	13	14					
28–19–13	RW	J. Peirson	49	14	15	29	D	H. Laycoe	54	2	10	12					
	LW	W. Dumart	62	5	9	14	D	B. Armstrong	55	0	8	8					
	C	M. Schmidt	68	11	23	34											
	RW	J. Klukay	70	13	16	29											
	LW	R. Chevrefils	69	19	14	33											
	LW	J. McIntyre	70	7	15	22											
	C	D. Creighton	69	20	20	40											
	C	R. Sullivan	32	3	8	11											
	RW	J. Toppazzini	69	10	13	23											

CHI
S. Abel
27–28–15

POS	PLAYER	GP	G	A	PTS	POS	PLAYER	GP	G	A	PTS	GOALIE	W	L	T	GAvg
LW	G. Gee	67	18	21	39	D	G. Mortson	68	5	18	23	A. Rollins	27	28	15	2.50
C	G. Bodnar	66	16	13	29	D	B. Gadsby	68	2	20	22					
RW	B. Mosienko	65	17	20	37	D	A. Dewsbury	69	5	17	22					
LW	P. Conacher	41	5	6	11	D	F. Hucul	57	5	7	12					
LW	V. Lynn	29	0	10	10	D	L. Fogolin	70	2	8	10					
LW	F. Glover	31	4	2	6											
C	D. Couture	70	19	18	37											
C	C. Gardner	70	11	24	35											
C	S. Abel	39	5	4	9											
RW	J. McFadden	70	23	21	44											
RW	J. Peters	69	22	19	41											

TOR
J. Primeau
27–30–13

POS	PLAYER	GP	G	A	PTS	POS	PLAYER	GP	G	A	PTS	GOALIE	W	L	T	GAvg
LW	S. Smith	70	20	19	39	D	T. Horton	70	2	14	16	H. Lumley	27	**30**	13	2.39
C	T. Kennedy	43	14	23	37	D	L. Boivin	70	2	13	15					
RW	R. Stewart	70	13	22	35	D	J. Morrison	56	1	8	9					
LW	H. Watson	63	16	8	24	D	F. Flaman	66	2	6	8					
C	G. Hannigan	65	17	18	35	D	J. Thomson	69	0	22	22					
C	B. Hassard	70	8	23	31											
C	M. Bentley	36	12	11	23											
RW	G. Armstrong	52	14	11	25											
RW	T. Sloan	70	15	10	25											
RW	E. Nesterenko	35	10	6	16											

NYR
B. Cook
17–37–16

POS	PLAYER	GP	G	A	PTS	POS	PLAYER	GP	G	A	PTS	GOALIE	W	L	T	GAvg
LW	N. Strain	52	11	13	24	D	H. Buller	70	7	18	25	G. Worsley	13	29	8	3.06
C	P. Ronty	70	16	38	54	D	L. Reise	61	4	15	19	C. Rayner	4	8	8	2.90
RW	W. Hergesheimer	70	30	29	59	D	A. Stanley	70	5	12	17					
LW	P. Babando	30	4	5	9	D	H. Howell	67	3	8	11					
LW	D. Prentice	55	6	3	9	D	S. Kraftcheck	69	2	9	11					
C	N. Mickoski	70	19	16	35											
C	D. Raleigh	55	4	18	22											
RW	J. Stoddard	60	12	13	25											
RW	E. Slowinski	37	2	5	7											
RW	A. Guidolin	30	4	4	8											

GOALS

G. Howe, DET	49
T. Lindsay, DET	32
W. Hergesheimer, NYR	30
M. Richard, MONT	28
M. MacKell, BOS	27

ASSISTS

G. Howe, DET	46
A. Delvecchio, DET	43
T. Lindsay, DET	39
P. Ronty, NYR	38
M. Prystai, DET	34

POINTS

G. Howe, DET	95
T. Lindsay, DET	71
M. Richard, MONT	61
W. Hergesheimer, NYR	59
A. Delvecchio, DET	59

PENALTY MINUTES

M. Richard, MONT	112
T. Lindsay, DET	111
F. Flaman, TOR	110
G. Gee, CHI	99
L. Boivin, TOR	97
A. Dewsbury, CHI	97

GOALS AGAINST AVE.

T. Sawchuk, DET	1.90
G. McNeil, MONT	2.12
H. Lumley, TOR	2.39
J. Henry, BOS	2.46
A. Rollins, CHI	2.50

SHUTOUTS

G. McNeil, MONT	10
H. Lumley, TOR	10
T. Sawchuk, DET	9
J. Henry, BOS	7
A. Rollins, CHI	6

National Hockey League 1953–54

TEAM	W	L	T	PTS	GF	GA
*DET	37	19	14	88	191	132
MONT	35	24	11	81	**195**	141
TOR	32	24	14	78	152	**131**
BOS	32	28	10	74	177	181
NYR	29	31	10	68	161	182
CHI	12	51	7	31	133	242

DET
T. Ivan
37–19–14

POS	PLAYER	GP	G	A	PTS	POS	PLAYER	GP	G	A	PTS	GOALIE	W	L	T	GAvg
LW	T. Lindsay	70	26	36	62	D	R. Kelly	62	16	33	49	T. Sawchuk	**35**	19	13	1.94
C	E. Reibel	69	15	33	48	D	M. Pronovost	57	6	12	18	D. Gatherum	2	0	1	1.00
RW	G. Howe	70	33	**48**	**81**	D	B. Goldham	69	1	15	16	L. Wilson	0	0	0	0.00
LW	J. Wilson	70	17	17	34	D	B. Woit	70	0	2	2					
LW	M. Pavelich	65	9	20	29											
LW	T. Leswick	70	6	18	24											
C	A. Delvecchio	69	11	18	29											
C	M. Prystai	70	12	15	27											
C	G. Skov	70	17	10	27											
RW	B. Dineen	70	17	8	25											
RW	J. Peters	26	0	4	4											

TEAM	POS	PLAYER	GP	G	A	PTS	POS	PLAYER	GP	G	A	PTS	GOALIE	W	L	T	GAvg
MONT	LW	B. Olmstead	70	15	37	52	D	D. Harvey	68	8	29	37	G. McNeil	28	19	6	2.15
D. Irvin	C	J. Beliveau	44	13	21	34	D	T. Johnson	70	7	11	18	J. Plante	7	5	5	1.59
35–24–11	RW	M. Richard	70	**37**	30	67	D	D. St. Laurent	53	3	12	15					
	LW	C. MacKay	47	10	13	23	D	E. Bouchard	70	1	10	11					
	C	K. Mosdell	67	22	24	46											
	RW	F. Curry	70	13	8	21											
	LW	E. Mazur	67	7	14	21											
	LW	P. Meger	44	4	9	13											
	C	P. Masnick	50	5	21	26											
	C	E. Lach	48	5	20	25											
	RW	B. Geoffrion	54	29	25	54											
TOR	LW	S. Smith	70	22	16	38	D	T. Horton	70	7	24	31	H. Lumley	32	24	13	**1.86**
K. Clancy	C	T. Kennedy	67	15	23	38	D	J. Thomson	61	2	24	26	G. Mayer	0	0	1	3.00
32–24–14	RW	E. Nesterenko	68	14	9	23	D	J. Morrison	60	11	9	20					
	LW	H. Watson	70	21	7	28	D	F. Flaman	62	0	8	8					
	C	T. Sloan	67	11	32	43	D	L. Boivin	58	1	6	7					
	RW	G. Armstrong	63	17	15	32											
	LW	B. Solinger	39	3	2	5											
	C	R. Stewart	70	14	11	25											
	C	R. Migay	70	8	15	23											
	RW	B. Bailey	48	2	7	9											
BOS	LW	E. Sandford	70	16	31	47	D	D. Mohns	70	13	14	27	J. Henry	32	28	10	2.59
L. Patrick	C	M. MacKell	67	15	32	47	D	F. Martin	68	3	17	20					
32–28–10	RW	J. Peirson	68	21	19	40	D	H. Laycoe	58	3	16	19					
	LW	R. Chevrefils	14	4	1	5	D	B. Quackenbush	45	0	17	17					
	LW	W. Dumart	69	4	3	7	D	W. Godfrey	70	5	9	14					
	C	D. Creighton	69	20	20	40											
	C	C. Gardner	70	14	20	34											
	C	M. Schmidt	64	14	18	32											
	RW	J. Klukay	70	20	17	37											
	RW	L. Labine	68	16	19	35											
NYR	LW	D. Bentley	20	2	10	12	D	H. Buller	41	3	14	17	J. Bower	29	31	10	2.60
F. Boucher	C	M. Bentley	57	14	18	32	D	H. Howell	67	7	9	16					
12–20–6	RW	E. Laprade	35	1	6	7	D	I. Irwin	56	2	12	14					
M. Patrick	LW	G. Sonmor	15	2	0	2	D	B. Chrystal	64	5	5	10					
17–11–4	LW	C. Henry	66	24	15	39	D	J. Evans	44	4	4	8					
	C	P. Ronty	70	13	33	46											
	C	D. Raleigh	70	15	30	45											
	C	N. Mickoski	68	19	16	35											
	RW	W. Hergesheimer	66	27	16	43											
	RW	E. Kullman	70	4	10	14											
	RW	A. Bathgate	20	2	2	4											
CHI	LW	P. Conacher	70	19	9	28	D	B. Gadsby	70	12	29	41	A. Rollins	12	**47**	7	3.23
S. Abel	LW	G. Gee	69	10	16	26	D	A. Dewsbury	69	6	15	21	J. Gelineau	0	2	0	9.00
12–51–7	LW	J. McIntyre	23	8	3	11	D	G. Mortson	68	5	13	18	J. Marois	0	2	0	5.50
	C	L. Wilson	66	9	33	42	D	J. Price	46	4	6	10					
	C	D. Couture	40	6	5	11	D	L. Zeidel	64	1	6	7					
	C	K. Wharram	29	1	7	8											
	C	J. McFadden	19	3	3	6											
	RW	B. Mosienko	65	15	19	34											
	RW	L. Jankowski	68	15	13	28											
	RW	I. Hildebrand	7	1	4	5											

GOALS

M. Richard, MONT	37
G. Howe, DET	33
B. Geoffrion, MONT	29
W. Hergesheimer, NYR	27
T. Lindsay, DET	26

ASSISTS

G. Howe, DET	48
B. Olmstead, MONT	37
T. Lindsay, DET	36

POINTS

G. Howe, DET	81
M. Richard, MONT	67
T. Lindsay, DET	62
B. Geoffrion, MONT	54
B. Olmstead, MONT	52

PENALTY MINUTES

G. Mortson, CHI	132
M. Richard, MONT	112
T. Lindsay, DET	110
D. Harvey, MONT	110
G. Howe, DET	109
I. Irwin, NYR	109

GOALS AGAINST AVE.

H. Lumley, TOR	1.86
T. Sawchuk, DET	1.94
G. McNeil, MONT	2.15
J. Henry, BOS	2.59
J. Bower, NYR	2.60

SHUTOUTS

H. Lumley, TOR	13
T. Sawchuk, DET	12
J. Henry, BOS	8
G. McNeil, MONT	6
J. Plante, MONT	5
J. Bower, NYR	5

National Hockey League 1954–55

TEAM	W	L	T	PTS	GF	GA
*DET	42	17	11	95	204	**134**
MONT	41	18	11	93	**228**	157
TOR	24	24	22	70	147	135
BOS	23	26	21	67	169	188
NYR	17	35	18	52	150	210
CHI	13	40	17	43	161	235

	POS	PLAYER	GP	G	A	PTS		PLAYER	GP	G	A	PTS	GOALIE	W	L	T	GAvg
DET	LW	T. Lindsay	49	19	19	38	D	R. Kelly	70	15	30	45	T. Sawchuk	**40**	17	11	1.96
	C	E. Reibel	70	25	41	66	D	M. Pronovost	70	9	25	34	G. Hall	2	0	0	1.00
J. Skinner	RW	G. Howe	64	29	33	62	D	G. Skov	70	14	16	30					
42–17–11	LW	M. Bonin	69	16	20	36	D	B. Woit	62	2	2	4					
	LW	M. Pavelich	70	15	15	30	D	J. Hay	20	0	1	1					
	LW	T. Leswick	70	10	17	27											
	LW	J. Wilson	70	12	15	27											
	C	A. Delvecchio	69	17	31	48											
	RW	B. Dineen	69	10	9	19											
	RW	L. Davis	30	0	5	5											
MONT	LW	B. Olmstead	70	10	**48**	58	D	D. Harvey	70	6	**43**	49	J. Plante	31	13	7	2.14
	C	J. Beliveau	70	37	36	73	D	T. Johnson	70	6	29	35	C. Hodge	7	3	4	2.33
D. Irvin	RW	M. Richard	67	**38**	36	74	D	D. St. Laurent	58	3	14	17	C. Evans	2	2	0	3.27
41–18–11	LW	D. Moore	67	16	20	36	D	E. Bouchard	70	2	15	17	A. Binette	1	0	0	4.00
	LW	C. MacKay	50	14	21	35	D	B. MacPherson	30	1	8	9					
	C	K. Mosdell	70	22	32	54											
	C	J. Leclair	59	11	22	33											
	C	P. Ronty	4	0	0	0											
	RW	B. Geoffrion	70	**38**	37	**75**											
	RW	F. Curry	68	11	10	21											
TOR	LW	S. Smith	70	33	21	54	D	H. Bolton	69	2	19	21	H. Lumley	24	23	22	**1.94**
	C	E. Nesterenko	62	15	15	30	D	J. Morrison	70	5	12	17	G. Mayer	0	1	0	1.00
K. Clancy	RW	T. Kennedy	70	10	42	52	D	T. Horton	67	5	9	14					
24–24–22	LW	J. Klukay	56	8	8	16	D	L. Cahan	58	0	6	6					
	LW	B. Solinger	17	1	5	6	D	M. Reaume	1	0	0	0					
	C	T. Sloan	63	13	15	28											
	C	R. Migay	67	8	16	24											
	RW	G. Armstrong	66	10	18	28											
	RW	R. Stewart	53	14	5	19											
	RW	P. MacDonald	62	8	3	11											
BOS	LW	R. Chevrefils	64	18	22	40	D	B. Quackenbush	68	2	20	22	J. Henderson	15	14	15	2.49
	C	D. McKenney	69	22	20	42	D	W. Godfrey	62	1	17	18	J. Henry	8	12	6	3.09
L. Patrick	RW	L. Labine	67	24	18	42	D	F. Flaman	70	4	14	18					
10–14–6	LW	E. Sandford	60	14	20	34	D	L. Boivin	59	6	11	17					
M. Schmidt	LW	L. Ferguson	69	20	14	34	D	B. Armstrong	57	1	3	4					
13–12–15	LW	D. Mohns	70	14	18	32											
	C	C. Gardner	70	16	22	38											
	C	G. Bodnar	67	4	4	8											
	RW	M. MacKell	60	11	24	35											
	RW	M. Costello	54	4	11	15											
NYR	LW	D. Prentice	70	16	15	31	D	B. Gadsby	52	8	8	16	G. Worsley	15	**33**	17	3.03
	C	L. Popein	70	11	17	28	D	H. Howell	70	2	14	16	J. Bower	2	2	1	2.60
M. Patrick	RW	A. Bathgate	70	20	20	40	D	B. Chrystal	68	6	9	15					
17–35–18	LW	D. Lewicki	70	29	24	53	D	I. Irwin	60	0	13	13					
	LW	R. Murphy	66	14	16	30	D	J. Evans	47	0	5	5					
	C	D. Raleigh	69	8	32	40											
	C	E. Laprade	60	3	11	14											
	C	C. Henry	21	5	2	7											
	RW	W. Hergesheimer	14	4	2	6											
	RW	A. Guidolin	70	2	5	7											
CHI	LW	H. Watson	43	14	16	30	D	A. Stanley	52	10	15	25	A. Rollins	9	27	8	3.41
	LW	R. Timgren	14	1	1	2	D	G. Mortson	65	2	11	13	H. Bassen	4	9	8	3.00
F. Eddolls	LW	J. McCormack	63	5	7	12	D	G. Hollingworth	70	3	9	12	R. Frederick	0	4	1	4.40
13–40–17	LW	J. McIntyre	65	16	13	29	D	F. Sullivan	1	0	0	0					
	C	R. Sullivan	70	19	42	61											
	C	M. Prystai	57	11	13	24											
	C	D. Creighton	49	7	7	14											
	C	N. Mickoski	52	10	19	29											
	RW	E. Litzenberger	44	16	24	40											
	RW	B. Mosienko	64	12	15	27											
	RW	J. Toppazzini	70	9	18	27											

GOALS

M. Richard, MONT	38
B. Geoffrion, MONT	38
J. Beliveau, MONT	37
S. Smith, TOR	33
G. Howe, DET	29
D. Lewicki, NYR	29

ASSISTS

B. Olmstead, MONT	48
D. Harvey, MONT	43
T. Kennedy, TOR	42
R. Sullivan, CHI	42
E. Reibel, DET	41

POINTS

B. Geoffrion, MONT	75
M. Richard, MONT	74
J. Beliveau, MONT	73
E. Reibel, DET	66
G. Howe, DET	62

PENALTY MINUTES

F. Flaman, BOS	150
T. Leswick, DET	137
G. Hollingworth, CHI	135
G. Mortson, CHI	133
M. Richard, MONT	125

GOALS AGAINST AVE.

H. Lumley, TOR	1.94
T. Sawchuk, DET	1.96
J. Plante, MONT	2.14
J. Henderson, BOS	2.49
G. Worsley, NYR	3.03

SHUTOUTS

T. Sawchuk, DET	12
H. Lumley, TOR	8
J. Plante, MONT	5
J. Henderson, BOS	5
G. Worsley, NYR	4

TEAM	W	L	T	PTS	GF	GA
*MONT	45	15	10	100	**222**	**131**
DET	30	24	16	76	183	148
NYR	32	28	10	74	204	203
TOR	24	33	13	61	153	181
BOS	23	34	13	59	147	185
CHI	19	39	12	50	155	216

	POS	PLAYER	GP	G	A	PTS		PLAYER	GP	G	A	PTS	GOALIE	W	L	T	GAvg
MONT	LW	B. Olmstead	70	14	**56**	70	D	D. Harvey	62	5	39	44	J. Plante	**42**	12	10	**1.86**
T. Blake	C	J. Beliveau	70	**47**	41	**88**	D	J. Talbot	66	1	13	14	M. Perreault	3	3	0	2.00
45–15–10	RW	M. Richard	70	38	33	71	D	D. St. Laurent	46	4	9	13					
	LW	D. Moore	70	11	39	50	D	T. Johnson	64	3	10	13					
	C	H. Richard	64	19	21	40	D	B. Turner	33	1	4	5					
	C	D. Marshall	66	4	1	5											
	C	K. Mosdell	67	13	17	30											
	RW	F. Curry	70	14	18	32											
	RW	C. Provost	60	13	16	29											
	RW	B. Geoffrion	59	29	33	62											
DET	LW	T. Lindsay	67	27	23	50	D	R. Kelly	70	16	34	50	G. Hall	30	24	16	2.11
J. Skinner	C	E. Reibel	68	17	39	56	D	B. Goldham	68	3	16	19					
30–24–16	RW	G. Howe	70	38	41	79	D	M. Pronovost	68	4	13	17					
	LW	M. Pavelich	70	5	13	18	D	W. Godfrey	67	2	6	8					
	LW	J. Bucyk	38	1	8	9	D	G. Hollingworth	41	0	2	2					
	C	A. Delvecchio	70	25	26	51											
	C	M. Prystai	63	12	16	28											
	C	N. Ullman	66	9	9	18											
	C	B. Dineen	70	12	7	19											
	RW	J. Toppazzini	40	1	7	8											
NYR	LW	D. Prentice	70	24	18	42	D	B. Gadsby	70	9	42	51	G. Worsley	32	28	10	2.90
P. Watson	C	L. Popein	64	14	25	39	D	H. Howell	70	3	15	18					
32–28–10	RW	A. Bathgate	70	19	47	66	D	L. Fontinato	70	3	15	18					
	LW	D. Lewicki	70	18	27	45	D	J. Evans	70	2	9	11					
	LW	R. Murphy	66	16	28	44											
	LW	J. Gendron	63	5	7	12											
	C	D. Creighton	70	20	31	51											
	C	D. Raleigh	29	1	12	13											
	C	B. Horvath	66	12	17	29											
	RW	W. Hergesheimer	70	22	18	40											
	RW	A. Hebenton	70	24	14	38											
TOR	LW	D. Duff	69	18	19	37	D	H. Bolton	67	4	16	20	H. Lumley	21	28	10	2.71
K. Clancy	C	T. Sloan	70	37	29	66	D	M. Reaume	48	0	12	12	G. Mayer	1	5	0	3.17
24–33–13	RW	G. Armstrong	67	16	32	48	D	J. Thomson	62	0	7	7	E. Chadwick	2	0	3	0.60
	LW	S. Smith	55	4	17	21	D	T. Horton	35	0	5	5	L. Wilson	0	0	0	0.00
	LW	E. Balfour	59	14	5	19	D	J. Morrison	63	2	17	19					
	C	R. Migay	70	12	16	28											
	C	R. Stewart	69	13	14	27											
	C	B. Harris	70	9	13	22											
	C	E. Nesterenko	40	4	6	10											
	RW	R. Hurst	50	7	5	12											
BOS	LW	V. Stasiuk	59	19	18	37	D	B. Quackenbush	70	3	22	25	T. Sawchuk	22	**33**	13	2.66
M. Schmidt	C	C. Gardner	70	15	21	36	D	F. Flaman	62	4	17	21	C. Pronovost	1	0	0	0.00
23–34–13	RW	J. Peirson	33	11	14	25	D	L. Boivin	68	4	16	20	J. Henderson	0	1	0	4.00
	LW	R. Chevrefils	25	11	8	19	D	B. Armstrong	68	0	12	12					
	C	D. McKenney	65	10	24	34	D	H. Laycoe	65	5	5	10					
	RW	L. Labine	68	16	18	34											
	LW	L. Ferguson	32	7	5	12											
	LW	D. Mohns	64	10	8	18											
	C	M. MacKell	52	7	9	16											
	RW	J. Toppazzini	28	7	7	14											
CHI	LW	H. Watson	55	11	14	25	D	A. Stanley	59	4	14	18	A. Rollins	16	31	11	3.00
D. Irvin	LW	T. Leswick	70	11	11	22	D	G. Mortson	57	5	10	15	H. Bassen	3	8	1	3.50
19–39–12	LW	J. Wilson	70	24	9	33	D	A. Dewsbury	37	3	12	15					
	C	R. Sullivan	63	14	26	40	D	F. Martin	61	3	11	14					
	C	N. Mickoski	70	19	20	39	D	B. Woit	63	1	8	9					
	C	H. Ciesla	70	8	23	31											
	C	G. Skov	70	7	20	27											
	RW	E. Litzenberger	70	10	29	39											
	RW	J. McIntyre	46	10	5	15											
	RW	E. Sandford	57	12	9	21											

GOALS		ASSISTS		POINTS	
J. Beliveau, MONT	47	B. Olmstead, MONT	56	J. Beliveau, MONT	88
G. Howe, DET	38	A. Bathgate, NYR	47	G. Howe, DET	79
M. Richard, MONT	38	B. Gadsby, NYR	42	M. Richard, MONT	71
T. Sloan, TOR	37	J. Beliveau, MONT	41	B. Olmstead, MONT	70
B. Geoffrion, MONT	29	G. Howe, DET	41		

PENALTY MINUTES		GOALS AGAINST AVE.		SHUTOUTS	
L. Fontinato, NYR	202	J. Plante, MONT	1.86	G. Hall, DET	12
T. Lindsay, DET	161	G. Hall, DET	2.11	T. Sawchuk, BOS	9
J. Beliveau, MONT	148	T. Sawchuk, BOS	2.66	J. Plante, MONT	7
B. Armstrong, TOR	122	H. Lumley, TOR	2.71	G. Worsley, NYR	4
V. Stasiuk, BOS	118	G. Worsley, NYR	2.90	H. Lumley, TOR	3

National Hockey League 1956–57

TEAM	W	L	T	PTS	GF	GA
DET	38	20	12	88	198	157
*MONT	35	23	12	82	**210**	**155**
BOS	34	24	12	80	195	174
NYR	26	30	14	66	184	227
TOR	21	34	15	57	174	192
CHI	16	39	15	47	169	225

	POS	PLAYER	GP	G	A	PTS		PLAYER	GP	G	A	PTS	GOALIE	W	L	T	GAvg
DET	LW	T. Lindsay	70	30	**55**	85	D	R. Kelly	70	10	25	35	G. Hall	**38**	20	12	2.24
J. Skinner	C	N. Ullman	64	16	36	52	D	M. Pronovost	70	7	9	16					
38–20–12	RW	G. Howe	70	**44**	45	**89**	D	W. Godfrey	69	1	8	9					
	LW	L. Ferguson	70	13	10	23	D	A. Arbour	44	1	6	7					
	LW	J. Bucyk	66	10	11	21											
	LW	M. Pavelich	64	3	13	16											
	C	A. Delvecchio	48	16	25	41											
	C	E. Reibel	70	13	23	36											
	C	B. Dea	69	15	15	30											
	RW	B. McNeill	64	5	10	15											
	RW	B. Dineen	51	6	7	13											
MONT	LW	B. Olmstead	64	15	33	48	D	D. Harvey	70	6	44	50	J. Plante	31	18	12	**2.02**
T. Blake	C	J. Beliveau	69	33	51	84	D	T. Johnson	70	4	11	15	G. McNeil	4	5	0	3.56
35–23–12	RW	B. Geoffrion	41	19	21	40	D	J. Talbot	69	0	13	13					
	LW	D. Moore	70	29	29	58	D	D. St. Laurent	64	1	11	12					
	C	H. Richard	63	18	36	54	D	B. Turner	58	1	4	5					
	RW	M. Richard	63	33	29	62											
	LW	A. Pronovost	64	10	11	21											
	C	D. Marshall	70	12	8	20											
	RW	C. Provost	67	16	14	30											
	RW	F. Curry	70	7	9	16											
BOS	LW	R. Chevrefils	70	31	17	48	D	A. Stanley	60	6	25	31	T. Sawchuk	18	10	6	2.38
M. Schmidt	C	D. McKenney	69	21	39	60	D	F. Flaman	68	6	25	31	D. Simmons	13	9	4	2.42
34–24–12	RW	L. Labine	67	18	29	47	D	B. Armstrong	57	1	15	16	N. Defelice	3	5	2	3.00
	LW	L. Regan	69	14	19	33	D	L. Boivin	55	2	8	10					
	C	M. MacKell	65	22	17	39	D	J. Bionda	35	2	3	5					
	RW	J. Toppazzini	55	15	23	38											
	LW	V. Stasiuk	64	24	16	40											
	LW	D. Mohns	68	6	34	40											
	C	C. Gardner	70	12	20	32											
	C	J. Caffery	47	2	2	4											
	RW	A. Hebenton	70	21	23	44											
NYR	LW	D. Prentice	68	19	23	42	D	B. Gadsby	70	4	37	41	G. Worsley	26	28	14	3.24
P. Watson	C	L. Popein	67	11	19	30	D	L. Fontinato	70	3	12	15	J. Bower	0	2	0	3.50
26–30–14	RW	A. Bathgate	70	27	50	77	D	H. Howell	65	2	10	12					
	LW	D. Lewicki	70	18	20	38	D	J. Evans	70	3	6	9					
	LW	R. Murphy	33	7	12	19											
	LW	J. Gendron	70	9	6	15											
	C	D. Creighton	70	18	21	39											
	C	C. Henry	36	14	15	29											
	C	R. Sullivan	42	6	17	23											
	RW	G. Foley	69	7	9	16											
TOR	LW	D. Duff	70	26	14	40	D	T. Horton	66	6	19	25	E. Chadwick	21	34	15	2.74
H. Meeker	C	T. Sloan	52	14	21	35	D	M. Reaume	66	6	14	20					
21–34–15	RW	G. Armstrong	54	18	26	44	D	A. MacNeil	53	4	8	12					
	LW	S. Smith	70	17	24	41	D	J. Thomson	62	0	12	12					
	LW	B. Pulford	65	11	11	22	D	G. James	53	4	12	16					
	C	R. Stewart	65	15	20	35											
	C	R. Migay	66	15	20	35											
	C	J. Morrison	63	3	17	20											
	RW	B. Cullen	51	6	10	16											
	RW	M. Nykoluk	32	3	1	4											

	POS	PLAYER	GP	G	A	PTS		PLAYER	GP	G	A	PTS	GOALIE	W	L	T	GAvg
CHI	LW	J. Wilson	70	18	30	48	D	G. Mortson	70	5	18	23	A. Rollins	16	**39**	15	3.21
T. Ivan	LW	H. Watson	70	11	19	30	D	P. Pilote	70	3	14	17					
16–39–15	LW	J. McIntyre	70	18	14	32	D	E. Vasko	64	3	12	15					
	C	G. Skov	67	14	28	42	D	F. Martin	70	1	8	9					
	C	N. Mickoski	70	16	20	36											
	C	H. Lalande	50	11	17	28											
	C	H. Ciesla	70	10	8	18											
	RW	E. Litzenberger	70	32	32	64											
	RW	E. Kachur	34	5	7	12											
	RW	W. Hergesheimer	41	2	8	10											
	RW	K. Mosdell	25	2	4	6											

GOALS		ASSISTS		POINTS	
G. Howe, DET	44	T. Lindsay, DET	55	G. Howe, DET	89
J. Beliveau, MONT	33	J. Beliveau, MONT	51	T. Lindsay, DET	85
M. Richard, MONT	33	A. Bathgate, NYR	50	J. Beliveau, MONT	84
E. Litzenberger, CHI	32	G. Howe, DET	45	A. Bathgate, NYR	77
R. Chevrefils, BOS	31	D. Harvey, MONT	44	E. Litzenberger, CHI	64

PENALTY MINUTES		GOALS AGAINST AVE.		SHUTOUTS	
G. Mortson, CHI	147	J. Plante, MONT	2.02	J. Plante, MONT	9
L. Fontinato, NYR	139	G. Hall, DET	2.24	E. Chadwick, TOR	5
L. Labine, BOS	128	E. Chadwick, TOR	2.74	G. Hall, DET	4
P. Pilote, CHI	117	A. Rollins, CHI	3.21	D. Simmons, BOS	4
J. Evans, NYR	110	G. Worsley, NYR	3.24	A. Rollins, CHI	3

National Hockey League 1957–58

TEAM	W	L	T	PTS	GF	GA
*MONT	43	17	10	96	**250**	**158**
NYR	32	25	13	77	195	188
DET	29	29	12	70	176	207
BOS	27	28	15	69	199	194
CHI	24	39	7	55	163	202
TOR	21	38	11	53	192	226

	POS	PLAYER	GP	G	A	PTS		PLAYER	GP	G	A	PTS	GOALIE	W	L	T	GAvg
MONT	LW	D. Moore	70	**36**	48	**84**	D	D. Harvey	68	9	32	41	J. Plante	**34**	14	8	**2.11**
T. Blake	C	J. Beliveau	55	27	32	59	D	D. St. Laurent	65	3	20	23	C. Hodge	8	2	2	2.58
43–17–10	RW	B. Geoffrion	42	27	23	50	D	T. Johnson	66	3	18	21	L. Broderick	1	0	0	2.00
	LW	M. Bonin	66	15	24	39	D	J. Talbot	55	4	15	19	D. Aiken	0	1	0	10.59
	C	H. Richard	67	28	**52**	80											
	RW	M. Richard	28	15	19	34											
	LW	B. Olmstead	57	9	28	37											
	LW	A. Pronovost	66	16	12	28											
	C	P. Goyette	70	9	37	46											
	C	D. Marshall	68	22	19	41											
	RW	C. Provost	70	19	32	51											
NYR	LW	D. Prentice	38	13	9	22	D	B. Gadsby	65	14	32	46	G. Worsley	21	10	6	2.32
P. Watson	C	L. Popein	70	12	22	34	D	H. Howell	70	4	7	11	M. Paille	11	15	7	3.09
32–25–13	RW	A. Bathgate	65	30	48	78	D	L. Fontinato	70	3	8	11					
	LW	C. Henry	70	32	24	56	D	J. Evans	70	4	8	12					
	C	D. Creighton	70	17	35	52											
	RW	A. Hebenton	70	21	24	45											
	LW	D. Lewicki	70	11	19	30											
	LW	J. Gendron	70	10	17	27											
	C	R. Sullivan	70	11	35	46											
	C	H. Ciesla	60	2	6	8											
	RW	P. MacDonald	70	8	10	18											

TEAM	POS	PLAYER	GP	G	A	PTS	POS	PLAYER	GP	G	A	PTS	GOALIE	W	L	T	GAvg
DET	LW	J. Wilson	70	12	27	39	D	R. Kelly	61	13	18	31	T. Sawchuk	29	29	12	2.96
	C	A. Delvecchio	70	21	38	59	D	M. Pronovost	62	2	18	20					
J. Skinner	RW	G. Howe	64	33	44	77	D	W. Godfrey	67	2	16	18					
13–17–7	LW	J. McIntyre	41	15	7	22	D	A. Arbour	69	1	6	7					
S. Abel	LW	T. Leswick	22	1	2	3	D	G. Hollingworth	27	1	2	3					
16–12–5	C	N. Ullman	69	23	28	51											
	C	F. Kennedy	70	11	16	27											
	C	N. Mickoski	37	8	12	20											
	RW	B. McNeill	35	5	10	15											
	RW	B. Dineen	22	2	4	6											
BOS	LW	J. Bucyk	68	21	31	52	D	A. Stanley	69	6	25	31	D. Simmons	15	15	7	2.50
	C	B. Horvath	67	30	36	66	D	D. Mohns	54	5	16	21	H. Lumley	11	10	4	2.84
M. Schmidt	RW	V. Stasiuk	70	21	35	56	D	F. Flaman	66	0	15	15	J. Millar	1	3	2	4.17
27–28–15	LW	D. McKenney	70	28	30	58	D	L. Hillman	70	3	19	22	C. Evans	0	0	1	4.00
	C	M. MacKell	70	20	40	60	D	J. Bionda	42	1	4	5	L. Wilson	0	0	1	1.15
	RW	J. Toppazzini	64	25	24	49											
	RW	L. Labine	62	7	14	21											
	RW	L. Regan	59	11	28	39											
	RW	B. Boone	34	5	3	8											
	RW	J. Peirson	53	2	2	4											
CHI	LW	B. Hull	70	13	34	47	D	P. Pilote	70	6	24	30	G. Hall	24	**39**	7	2.89
	C	E. Nesterenko	70	20	18	38	D	E. Vasko	59	6	20	26					
R. Pilous	RW	E. Litzenberger	70	32	30	62	D	G. Mortson	67	3	10	13					
24–39–7	LW	T. Lindsay	68	15	24	39	D	J. Thomson	70	4	7	11					
	LW	R. Murphy	69	11	17	28	D	I. Cushenan	61	2	8	10					
	C	G. Skov	70	17	18	35											
	C	B. Dea	34	5	8	13											
	C	E. Reibel	40	4	12	16											
	RW	B. Dineen	41	4	9	13											
	RW	E. Kachur	62	5	7	12											
TOR	LW	D. Duff	65	26	23	49	D	T. Horton	53	6	20	26	E. Chadwick	21	38	11	3.23
	LW	F. Mahovlich	67	20	16	36	D	B. Baun	67	1	9	10					
B. Reay	LW	B. Pulford	70	14	17	31	D	J. Morrison	70	3	21	24					
21–38–11	C	B. Harris	68	16	28	44	D	M. Reaume	68	1	7	8					
	C	B. Cullen	67	20	23	43											
	C	T. Sloan	59	13	25	38											
	C	R. Stewart	70	15	24	39											
	C	R. Migay	48	7	14	21											
	RW	G. Armstrong	59	17	25	42											
	RW	B. Cullen	70	16	25	41											
	RW	G. Aldcorn	59	10	14	24											

GOALS		ASSISTS		POINTS	
D. Moore, MONT	36	H. Richard, MONT	52	D. Moore, MONT	84
G. Howe, DET	33	D. Moore, MONT	48	H. Richard, MONT	80
E. Litzenberger, CHI	32	A. Bathgate, NYR	48	A. Bathgate, NYR	78
C. Henry, NYR	32	G. Howe, DET	44	G. Howe, DET	77
A. Bathgate, NYR	30	M. MacKell, BOS	40	B. Horvath, BOS	66
B. Horvath, BOS	30				

PENALTY MINUTES		GOALS AGAINST AVE.		SHUTOUTS	
L. Fontinato, NYR	152	J. Plante, MONT	2.11	J. Plante, MONT	9
F. Kennedy, DET	135	G. Worsley, NYR	2.32	G. Hall, CHI	7
D. Harvey, MONT	131	D. Simmons, BOS	2.50	D. Simmons, BOS	5
T. Lindsay, CHI	110	G. Hall, CHI	2.89	G. Worsley, NYR	4
J. Evans, NYR	108	T. Sawchuk, DET	2.96	E. Chadwick, TOR	4

National Hockey League 1958–59

TEAM	W	L	T	PTS	GF	GA
*MONT	39	18	13	91	**258**	**158**
BOS	32	29	9	73	205	215
CHI	28	29	13	69	197	208
TOR	27	32	11	65	189	201
NYR	26	32	12	64	201	217
DET	25	37	8	58	167	218

	POS	PLAYER	GP	G	A	PTS	PLAYER	GP	G	A	PTS	GOALIE	W	L	T	GAvg
MONT	LW	D. Moore	70	41	**55**	**96**	D T. Johnson	70	10	29	39	J. Plante	**38**	16	13	**2.16**
T. Blake	C	J. Beliveau	64	**45**	46	91	D D. Harvey	61	4	16	20	C. Hodge	1	1	0	3.00
39–18–13	RW	B. Geoffrion	59	22	44	66	D J. Talbot	69	4	17	21	C. Pronovost	0	1	0	7.00
	LW	M. Bonin	57	13	30	43						C. Cyr	0	0	0	3.00
	C	H. Richard	63	21	30	51										
	RW	M. Richard	42	17	21	38										
	LW	A. McDonald	69	13	23	36										
	LW	A. Pronovost	70	9	14	23										
	C	R. Backstrom	64	18	22	40										
	C	D. Marshall	70	10	22	32										
	C	P. Goyette	63	10	18	28										
BOS	LW	J. Bucyk	69	24	36	60	D D. Mohns	47	6	24	30	D. Simmons	24	26	8	3.17
M. Schmidt	C	B. Horvath	45	19	20	39	D L. Boivin	70	5	16	21	H. Lumley	8	2	1	2.45
32–29–9	RW	V. Stasiuk	70	27	33	60	D F. Flaman	70	0	21	21	D. Keenan	0	1	0	4.00
	LW	J. Gendron	60	15	9	24	D B. Armstrong	60	1	9	10					
	LW	J. Morrison	70	8	17	25										
	C	D. McKenney	70	32	30	62										
	C	M. MacKell	57	17	23	40										
	C	E. Reibel	63	6	8	14										
	RW	L. Regan	36	5	6	11										
	RW	L. Labine	70	9	23	32										
	RW	J. Toppazzini	70	21	23	44										
CHI	LW	T. Lindsay	70	22	36	58	D P. Pilote	70	7	30	37	G. Hall	28	29	13	2.97
R. Pilous	C	T. Sloan	59	27	35	62	D E. Vasko	63	6	10	16					
28–29–13	RW	E. Litzenberger	70	33	44	77	D D. St. Laurent	70	4	8	12					
	LW	B. Hull	70	18	32	50	D A. Arbour	70	2	10	12					
	LW	D. Lewicki	58	8	14	22	D J. Evans	70	1	8	9					
	LW	R. Murphy	59	17	30	47										
	LW	E. Balfour	70	10	8	18										
	C	G. Skov	70	3	5	8										
	RW	E. Nesterenko	70	16	18	34										
	RW	K. Wharram	66	10	9	19										
TOR	LW	F. Mahovlich	63	22	27	49	D T. Horton	70	5	21	26	J. Bower	15	17	7	2.74
B. Reay	C	B. Harris	70	22	30	52	D C. Brewer	69	3	21	24	E. Chadwick	12	15	4	3.10
5–12–3	RW	G. Ehman	36	12	13	25	D A. Stanley	70	1	22	23					
P. Imlach	LW	D. Duff	69	29	24	53	D B. Baun	51	1	8	9					
22–20–8	C	G. Armstrong	59	20	16	36	D M. Reaume	51	1	5	6					
	RW	L. Regan	32	4	21	25										
	LW	B. Olmstead	70	10	31	41										
	C	B. Pulford	70	23	14	37										
	C	R. Stewart	70	21	13	34										
	RW	B. Cullen	40	6	8	14										
NYR	LW	D. Prentice	70	17	33	50	D B. Gadsby	70	5	46	51	G. Worsley	26	29	12	3.07
P. Watson	C	R. Sullivan	70	21	42	63	D H. Howell	70	4	10	14	B. Gamble	0	2	0	3.00
26–32–12	RW	A. Bathgate	70	40	48	88	D L. Fontinato	64	7	6	13	M. Paille	0	1	0	4.00
	LW	E. Shack	67	7	14	21	D J. Hanna	70	1	10	11	J. Klymkiw	0	0	0	6.32
	LW	J. Bartlett	70	11	9	20										
	C	C. Henry	70	23	35	58										
	C	H. Ciesla	69	6	14	20										
	C	L. Popein	61	13	21	34										
	C	E. Ingarfield	35	1	2	3										
	RW	W. Hergesheimer	22	3	0	3										
	RW	A. Hebenton	70	33	29	62										
DET	LW	A. Delvecchio	70	19	35	54	D M. Pronovost	69	11	21	32	T. Sawchuk	23	**36**	8	3.12
S. Abel	C	N. Ullman	69	22	36	58	D R. Kelly	67	8	13	21	M. Perreault	2	1	0	3.00
25–37–8	RW	G. Howe	70	32	46	78	D P. Goegan	67	1	11	12					
	LW	J. McIntyre	55	15	14	29	D W. Godfrey	69	6	4	10					
	LW	J. Wilson	70	11	17	28	D G. Mortson	26	0	1	1					
	LW	C. LaForge	57	2	5	7										
	C	L. Lunde	68	14	12	26										
	C	N. Mickoski	66	11	15	26										
	C	F. Kennedy	67	1	4	5										
	RW	B. McNeill	54	2	5	7										

GOALS

J. Beliveau, MONT	45
D. Moore, MONT	41
A. Bathgate, NYR	40
E. Litzenberger, CHI	33
A. Hebenton, NYR	33

ASSISTS

D. Moore, MONT	55
A. Bathgate, NYR	48
J. Beliveau, MONT	46
G. Howe, DET	46
B. Gadsby, NYR	46

POINTS

D. Moore, MONT	96
J. Beliveau, MONT	91
A. Bathgate, NYR	88
G. Howe, DET	78
E. Litzenberger, CHI	77

PENALTY MINUTES

T. Lindsay, CHI	184
L. Fontinato, NYR	149
C. Brewer, TOR	125
J. Bartlett, NYR	118
E. Shack, NYR	109

GOALS AGAINST AVE.

J. Plante, MONT	2.16
J. Bower, TOR	2.74
G. Hall, CHI	2.97
G. Worsley, MONT	3.07
T. Sawchuk, DET	3.12

SHUTOUTS

J. Plante, MONT	9
T. Sawchuk, DET	5
J. Bower, TOR	3
E. Chadwick, TOR	3
D. Simmons, BOS	3

TEAM	W	L	T	PTS	GF	GA
*MONT	40	18	12	92	**255**	**178**
TOR	35	26	9	79	199	195
CHI	28	29	13	69	191	180
DET	26	29	15	67	186	197
BOS	28	34	8	64	220	241
NYR	17	38	15	49	187	247

	POS	PLAYER	GP	G	A	PTS	PLAYER	GP	G	A	PTS	GOALIE	W	L	T	GAvg
MONT	LW	M. Bonin	59	17	34	51	D T. Johnson	64	4	25	29	J. Plante	**40**	17	12	**2.54**
T. Blake	C	J. Beliveau	60	34	40	74	D D. Harvey	66	6	21	27	C. Hodge	0	1	0	3.00
40–18–12	RW	B. Geoffrion	59	30	41	71	D A. Langlois	67	1	14	15					
	LW	D. Moore	62	22	42	64	D J. Talbot	69	1	14	15					
	C	H. Richard	70	30	43	73										
	RW	M. Richard	51	19	16	35										
	LW	A. Pronovost	69	12	19	31										
	C	P. Goyette	65	21	22	43										
	C	D. Marshall	70	16	22	38										
	C	R. Backstrom	64	13	15	28										
	RW	C. Provost	70	17	29	46										
TOR	LW	D. Duff	67	19	22	41	D A. Stanley	64	10	23	33	J. Bower	34	24	8	2.73
P. Imlach	C	B. Pulford	70	24	28	52	D T. Horton	70	3	29	32	E. Chadwick	1	2	1	3.75
35–26–9	RW	G. Armstrong	70	23	28	51	D C. Brewer	67	4	19	23					
	LW	F. Mahovlich	70	18	21	39	D B. Baun	61	8	9	17					
	LW	B. Olmstead	53	15	21	36										
	LW	J. Wilson	70	15	16	31										
	C	B. Harris	70	13	25	38										
	C	R. Stewart	67	14	20	34										
	RW	G. Ehman	69	12	16	28										
	RW	G. James	34	4	9	13										
	RW	L. Regan	47	4	16	20										
CHI	LW	B. Hull	70	**39**	42	**81**	D P. Pilote	70	7	38	45	G. Hall	28	**29**	13	2.57
R. Pilous	C	B. Hay	70	18	37	55	D E. Vasko	69	3	27	30					
28–29–13	RW	M. Balfour	61	18	12	30	D A. Arbour	57	1	5	6					
	LW	T. Lindsay	68	7	19	26	D D. St. Laurent	68	4	13	17					
	C	S. Mikita	67	8	18	26	D J. Evans	68	0	4	4					
	RW	K. Wharram	59	14	11	25										
	LW	E. Balfour	70	3	5	8										
	C	E. Nesterenko	61	13	23	36										
	C	T. Sloan	70	20	20	40										
	RW	E. Litzenberger	52	12	18	30										
DET	LW	G. Aldcorn	70	22	29	51	D M. Pronovost	69	7	17	24	T. Sawchuk	24	20	14	2.69
S. Abel	C	N. Ullman	70	24	34	58	D R. Kelly	50	6	12	18	D. Riggin	2	6	1	3.56
26–29–15	RW	G. Howe	70	28	45	73	D W. Godfrey	69	5	9	14	G. Boisvert	0	3	0	3.00
	LW	J. Morrison	70	3	23	26	D L. Marcon	38	0	3	3					
	LW	V. Fonteyne	69	4	7	11										
	C	A. Delvecchio	70	19	28	47										
	C	M. Oliver	54	20	19	39										
	C	L. Lunde	66	6	17	23										
	C	G. Melnyk	63	10	10	20										
	RW	J. McKenzie	59	8	12	20										
	RW	B. McNeill	47	5	13	18										
BOS	LW	J. Bucyk	56	16	36	52	D L. Boivin	70	4	21	25	H. Lumley	18	19	5	3.50
M. Schmidt	C	B. Horvath	68	**39**	41	80	D F. Flaman	60	2	18	20	D. Simmons	10	15	3	3.36
28–34–8	RW	V. Stasiuk	69	29	39	68	D B. Armstrong	69	5	14	19					
	LW	D. Mohns	65	20	25	45	D A. Erickson	58	1	6	7					
	C	D. McKenney	70	20	**49**	69										
	RW	L. Labine	63	16	28	44										
	LW	J. Gendron	67	24	11	35										
	LW	L. Leach	69	7	12	19										
	C	C. Burns	62	10	17	27										
	RW	J. Toppazzini	69	12	33	45										
	RW	D. Meissner	60	5	6	11										
NYR	LW	D. Prentice	70	32	34	66	D B. Gadsby	65	9	22	31	G. Worsley	8	25	8	3.57
P. Watson	C	L. Popein	66	14	22	36	D H. Howell	67	7	6	13	M. Paille	6	9	2	3.94
3–9–3	RW	A. Bathgate	70	26	48	74	D L. Fontinato	64	2	11	13	A. Rollins	1	3	4	3.88
A. Pike	LW	C. Henry	49	12	15	27	D J. Hanna	61	4	8	12	J. McCartan	2	1	1	1.75
14–29–12	C	R. Sullivan	70	12	25	37	D J. Bownass	37	2	5	7	J. Schaefer	0	0	0	7.69
	RW	A. Hebenton	70	19	27	46										
	LW	E. Shack	62	8	10	18										
	LW	J. Bartlett	44	8	4	12										
	C	B. Cullen	64	8	21	29										
	RW	K. Schinkel	69	13	16	29										

GOALS		ASSISTS		POINTS	
B. Hull, CHI	39	D. McKenney, BOS	49	B. Hull, CHI	81
B. Horvath, BOS	39	A. Bathgate, NYR	48	B. Horvath, BOS	80
J. Beliveau, MONT	34	G. Howe, DET	45	J. Beliveau, MONT	74
D. Prentice, NYR	32	H. Richard, MONT	43	A. Bathgate, NYR	74
H. Richard, MONT	30	D. Moore, MONT	42	H. Richard, MONT	73
B. Geoffrion, MONT	30	B. Hull, CHI	42	G. Howe, DET	73

PENALTY MINUTES	
C. Brewer, TOR	150
L. Fontinato, NYR	137
V. Stasiuk, BOS	121
S. Mikita, CHI	119
F. Flaman, BOS	112

GOALS AGAINST AVE.	
J. Plante, MONT	2.54
G. Hall, CHI	2.57
T. Sawchuk, DET	2.69
J. Bower, TOR	2.73

SHUTOUTS	
G. Hall, CHI	6
T. Sawchuk, DET	5
J. Bower, TOR	5
J. Plante, MONT	3
D. Simmons, BOS	2

National Hockey League 1960–61

TEAM	W	L	T	PTS	GF	GA
MONT	41	19	10	92	**254**	188
TOR	39	19	12	90	234	176
*CHI	29	24	17	75	198	180
DET	25	29	16	66	195	215
NYR	22	38	10	54	204	248
BOS	15	42	13	43	176	**154**

	POS	PLAYER	GP	G	A	PTS	POS	PLAYER	GP	G	A	PTS	GOALIE	W	L	T	GAvg
MONT	LW	M. Bonin	65	16	35	51	D	D. Harvey	58	6	33	39	J. Plante	22	11	7	2.80
T. Blake	C	J. Beliveau	69	32	**58**	90	D	J. Talbot	70	5	26	31	C. Hodge	19	8	3	2.53
41–19–10	RW	B. Geoffrion	64	**50**	45	**95**	D	T. Johnson	70	1	15	16					
	LW	D. Moore	57	35	34	69	D	A. Langlois	61	1	12	13					
	C	H. Richard	70	24	44	68	D	B. Turner	60	2	2	4					
	RW	B. Hicke	70	18	27	45											
	LW	J. Gendron	63	9	12	21											
	C	R. Backstrom	69	12	20	32											
	C	D. Marshall	70	14	17	31											
	RW	C. Provost	49	11	4	15											
TOR	LW	F. Mahovlich	70	48	36	84	D	A. Stanley	68	9	25	34	J. Bower	**33**	15	10	**2.50**
P. Imlach	C	R. Kelly	64	20	50	70	D	T. Horton	57	6	15	21	C. Maniago	4	2	1	2.57
39–19–12	RW	B. Nevin	68	21	37	58	D	C. Brewer	51	1	14	15	G. McNamara	2	2	1	2.60
	LW	D. Duff	67	16	17	33	D	B. Baun	70	1	14	15					
	C	D. Keon	70	20	25	45											
	RW	G. Armstrong	47	14	19	33											
	LW	B. Olmstead	67	18	34	52											
	LW	E. Shack	55	14	14	28											
	C	B. Harris	66	12	27	39											
	C	B. Pulford	40	11	18	29											
	RW	R. Stewart	51	13	12	25											
CHI	LW	B. Hull	67	31	25	56	D	P. Pilote	70	6	29	35	G. Hall	29	24	17	2.57
R. Pilous	C	B. Hay	69	11	48	59	D	E. Vasko	63	4	18	22					
29–24–17	RW	M. Balfour	70	21	27	48	D	D. St. Laurent	67	2	17	19					
	LW	A. McDonald	61	17	16	33	D	J. Evans	69	0	8	8					
	C	S. Mikita	66	19	34	53	D	A. Arbour	63	3	2	5					
	RW	K. Wharram	64	16	29	45											
	LW	R. Murphy	70	21	19	40											
	LW	R. Fleming	66	4	4	8											
	C	T. Sloan	67	11	23	34											
	RW	E. Litzenberger	62	10	22	32											
DET	LW	V. Stasiuk	21	10	13	23	D	P. Goegan	67	5	29	34	T. Sawchuk	12	16	8	3.05
S. Abel	C	A. Delvecchio	70	27	35	62	D	W. Godfrey	63	3	16	19	H. Bassen	13	13	8	2.89
25–29–16	RW	G. Howe	64	23	49	72	D	M. Pronovost	70	6	11	17					
	LW	H. Glover	66	21	8	29	D	G. Odrowski	68	1	4	5					
	LW	V. Fonteyne	66	6	11	17											
	LW	G. Aldcorn	49	2	6	8											
	C	N. Ullman	70	28	42	70											
	C	P. MacDonald	70	14	12	26											
	C	M. Oliver	49	11	12	23											
	RW	A. Johnson	70	16	21	37											
	RW	L. Labine	24	2	9	11											
NYR	LW	D. Prentice	56	20	25	45	D	B. Gadsby	65	9	26	35	G. Worsley	19	**28**	9	3.33
A. Pike	C	C. Henry	53	28	25	53	D	H. Howell	70	7	10	17	J. McCartan	1	7	1	4.91
22–38–10	RW	A. Bathgate	70	29	48	77	D	L. Fontinato	53	2	3	5	M. Paille	2	2	0	4.00
	LW	J. Wilson	56	14	12	26	D	D. Johns	63	1	7	8	J. Schaefer	0	1	0	3.83
	LW	P. Hannigan	53	11	9	20											
	C	R. Sullivan	70	9	31	40											
	C	E. Ingarfield	66	13	21	34											
	C	B. Cullen	42	11	19	30											
	C	T. Hampson	69	6	14	20											
	RW	A. Hebenton	70	26	28	54											
	RW	F. Smith	29	5	9	14											

TEAM	POS	PLAYER	GP	G	A	PTS	POS	PLAYER	GP	G	A	PTS	GOALIE	W	L	T	GAvg
BOS	LW	V. Stasiuk	46	5	25	30	D	D. Mohns	65	12	21	33	B. Gamble	12	33	7	3.75
M. Schmidt	C	J. Bucyk	70	19	20	39	D	L. Boivin	57	6	17	23	D. Simmons	3	9	6	3.28
15–42–13	RW	J. Toppazzini	67	15	35	50	D	F. Flaman	62	2	9	11					
	LW	J. Bartlett	63	15	9	24	D	B. Armstrong	54	0	10	10					
	LW	A. Pronovost	47	11	11	22	D	D. Smith	70	1	9	10					
	C	D. McKenney	68	26	23	49											
	C	C. Burns	62	15	26	41											
	C	B. Horvath	47	15	15	30											

GOALS		ASSISTS		POINTS	
B. Geoffrion, MONT	50	J. Beliveau, MONT	58	B. Geoffrion, MONT	95
F. Mahovlich, TOR	48	R. Kelly, TOR	50	J. Beliveau, MONT	90
D. Moore, MONT	35	G. Howe, DET	49	F. Mahovlich, TOR	84
J. Beliveau, MONT	32	A. Bathgate, NYR	48	A. Bathgate, NYR	77
B. Hull, CHI	31	B. Hay, CHI	48	G. Howe, DET	72

PENALTY MINUTES		GOALS AGAINST AVE.		SHUTOUTS	
P. Pilote, CHI	165	J. Bower, TOR	2.50	G. Hall, CHI	6
R. Fleming, CHI	145	C. Hodge, MONT	2.53	C. Hodge, MONT	4
J. Talbot, MONT	143	G. Hall, CHI	2.57	J. Bower, TOR	2
F. Mahovlich, TOR	131	J. Plante, MONT	2.80	J. Plante, MONT	2
E. Nesterenko, CHI	125	H. Bassen, DET	2.89	T. Sawchuk, DET	2

National Hockey League 1961–62

TEAM	W	L	T	PTS	GF	GA
MONT	42	14	14	98	**259**	**166**
*TOR	37	22	11	85	232	180
CHI	31	26	13	75	217	186
NYR	26	32	12	64	195	207
DET	23	33	14	60	184	219
BOS	15	47	8	38	177	306

TEAM	POS	PLAYER	GP	G	A	PTS	POS	PLAYER	GP	G	A	PTS	GOALIE	W	L	T	GAvg
MONT	LW	D. Marshall	66	18	28	46	D	J. Talbot	70	5	42	47	J. Plante	**42**	14	14	**2.37**
T. Blake	C	R. Backstrom	66	27	38	65	D	J. Tremblay	70	3	17	20					
42–14–14	RW	B. Rousseau	70	21	24	45	D	T. Johnson	62	1	17	18					
	LW	D. Moore	57	19	22	41	D	L. Fontinato	54	2	13	15					
	C	H. Richard	54	21	29	50											
	RW	C. Provost	70	33	29	62											
	LW	G. Tremblay	70	32	22	54											
	LW	M. Bonin	33	7	14	21											
	C	J. Beliveau	43	18	23	41											
	RW	B. Geoffrion	62	23	36	59											
	RW	B. Hicke	70	20	31	51											
TOR	LW	F. Mahovlich	70	33	38	71	D	T. Horton	70	10	28	38	J. Bower	32	17	10	2.58
P. Imlach	C	R. Kelly	58	22	27	49	D	A. Stanley	60	9	26	35	D. Simmons	4	4	1	2.33
37–22–11	RW	B. Nevin	69	15	30	45	D	C. Brewer	67	1	22	23	G. Cheevers	1	1	0	3.50
	LW	D. Duff	51	17	20	37	D	B. Baun	65	4	11	15					
	C	D. Keon	64	26	35	61	D	A. Arbour	52	1	5	6					
	RW	G. Armstrong	70	21	32	53											
	LW	B. Olmstead	56	13	23	36											
	C	B. Pulford	70	18	21	39											
	RW	E. Litzenberger	37	10	10	20											
	RW	R. Stewart	60	8	9	17											
CHI	LW	B. Hull	70	**50**	34	**84**	D	P. Pilote	59	7	35	42	G. Hall	31	26	13	2.66
R. Pilous	C	B. Hay	60	11	52	63	D	E. Vasko	64	2	22	24					
31–26–13	RW	M. Balfour	49	15	15	30	D	J. Evans	70	3	14	17					
	LW	A. McDonald	65	22	18	40	D	D. St. Laurent	64	0	13	13					
	C	S. Mikita	70	25	52	77	D	B. Turner	69	8	2	10					
	RW	K. Wharram	62	14	23	37											
	LW	R. Murphy	60	12	16	28											
	LW	R. Fleming	70	7	9	16											
	C	E. Nesterenko	68	15	14	29											
	C	B. Horvath	68	17	29	46											

	POS	PLAYER	GP	G	A	PTS		PLAYER	GP	G	A	PTS	GOALIE	W	L	T	GAvg
NYR	LW	D. Prentice	68	22	38	60	D	D. Harvey	69	6	24	30	G. Worsley	22	**27**	9	2.97
D. Harvey	C	E. Ingarfield	70	26	31	57	D	A. Langlois	69	7	18	25	M. Paille	4	4	2	2.80
26–32–12	RW	A. Bathgate	70	28	**56**	**84**	D	H. Howell	66	6	15	21	D. Olesevich	0	0	1	3.00
	LW	J. Gendron	69	14	11	25							D. Dryden	0	1	0	4.50
	LW	P. Hannigan	56	8	14	22											
	LW	D. Balon	30	4	11	15											
	LW	J. Wilson	40	11	3	14											
	C	C. Henry	60	23	15	38											
	C	T. Hampson	68	4	24	28											
	C	J. Ratelle	31	4	8	12											
	RW	A. Hebenton	70	18	24	42											
DET	LW	V. Stasiuk	59	15	28	43	D	B. Gadsby	70	7	30	37	T. Sawchuk	14	21	8	3.33
S. Abel	C	A. Delvecchio	70	26	43	69	D	M. Pronovost	70	4	14	18	H. Bassen	9	12	6	2.81
23–33–14	RW	G. Howe	70	33	44	77	D	W. Godfrey	69	4	13	17					
	LW	C. LaForge	38	10	9	19	D	G. Odrowski	69	1	6	7					
	LW	V. Fonteyne	70	5	5	10											
	C	N. Ullman	70	26	38	64											
	C	B. MacGregor	65	6	12	18											
	C	P. MacDonald	32	5	7	12											
	RW	E. Litzenberger	32	8	12	20											
	RW	H. Glover	39	7	8	15											
	RW	A. Johnson	31	5	6	11											
BOS	LW	J. Bucyk	67	20	40	60	D	L. Boivin	65	5	18	23	D. Head	9	26	3	4.24
P. Watson	C	D. McKenney	70	22	33	55	D	T. Green	66	3	8	11	B. Gamble	6	18	4	4.39
15–47–8	RW	D. Mohns	69	16	29	45	D	E. Westfall	63	2	9	11	E. Chadwick	0	3	1	5.50
	LW	A. Pronovost	70	15	8	23	D	P. Stapleton	69	2	5	7					
	LW	L. Leach	28	2	5	7											
	C	J. Toppazzini	70	19	31	50											
	C	M. Oliver	70	17	29	46											
	C	C. Burns	70	11	17	28											
	C	W. Connelly	61	8	12	20											
	RW	T. Gray	42	8	7	15											
	RW	D. Meissner	66	3	3	6											

GOALS		ASSISTS		POINTS	
B. Hull, CHI	50	A. Bathgate, NYR	56	B. Hull, CHI	84
G. Howe, DET	33	S. Mikita, CHI	52	A. Bathgate, NYR	84
F. Mahovlich, TOR	33	B. Hay, CHI	52	G. Howe, DET	77
C. Provost, MONT	33	G. Howe, DET	44	S. Mikita, CHI	77
G. Tremblay, MONT	32	A. Delvecchio, DET	43	F. Mahovlich, TOR	71
PENALTY MINUTES		**GOALS AGAINST AVE.**		**SHUTOUTS**	
L. Fontinato, MONT	167	J. Plante, MONT	2.37	G. Hall, CHI	9
T. Green, BOS	116	J. Bower, TOR	2.58	T. Sawchuk, DET	5
B. Pulford, TOR	98	G. Hall, CHI	2.66	J. Plante, MONT	4
P. Pilote, CHI	97	G. Worsley, NYR	2.97	H. Bassen, DET	3
B. Baun, TOR	94	T. Sawchuk, DET	3.33	J. Bower, TOR	2

National Hockey League 1962–63

TEAM	W	L	T	PTS	GF	GA
*TOR	35	23	12	82	221	180
CHI	32	21	17	81	194	**178**
MONT	28	19	23	79	**225**	183
DET	32	25	13	77	200	194
NYR	22	36	12	56	211	233
BOS	14	39	17	45	198	281

	POS	PLAYER	GP	G	A	PTS		PLAYER	GP	G	A	PTS	GOALIE	W	L	T	GAvg
TOR	LW	F. Mahovlich	67	36	37	73	D	T. Horton	70	6	19	25	J. Bower	20	15	7	2.62
P. Imlach	C	R. Kelly	66	20	40	60	D	C. Brewer	70	2	23	25	D. Simmons	15	8	5	2.50
35–23–12	RW	B. Nevin	58	12	21	33	D	B. Baun	48	4	8	12					
	LW	D. Duff	69	16	19	35	D	A. Stanley	61	4	15	19					
	C	D. Keon	68	28	28	56	D	K. Douglas	70	7	15	22					
	RW	G. Armstrong	70	19	24	43											
	LW	E. Shack	63	16	9	25											
	C	B. Pulford	70	19	25	44											
	C	B. Harris	65	8	24	32											
	RW	R. Stewart	63	16	16	32											

TEAM	POS	PLAYER	GP	G	A	PTS	POS	PLAYER	GP	G	A	PTS	GOALIE	W	L	T	GAvg
CHI	LW	A. McDonald	69	20	41	61	D	P. Pilote	59	8	18	26	G. Hall	**30**	20	15	2.55
R. Pilous	C	S. Mikita	65	31	45	76	D	J. Evans	68	0	8	8	D. DeJordy	2	1	2	2.48
32–21–17	RW	K. Wharram	55	20	18	38	D	B. Turner	70	3	3	6					
	LW	B. Hull	65	31	31	62	D	E. Vasko	64	4	9	13					
	C	B. Hay	64	12	33	45	D	W. Hillman	67	3	5	8					
	RW	M. Balfour	65	10	23	33	D	A. MacNeil	70	2	19	21					
	LW	R. Murphy	68	18	16	34											
	C	E. Nesterenko	67	12	15	27											
	RW	C. Maki	65	7	17	24											
MONT	LW	G. Tremblay	60	25	24	49	D	T. Johnson	43	3	5	8	J. Plante	22	14	19	2.49
T. Blake	C	J. Beliveau	69	18	49	67	D	J. Tremblay	69	1	17	18	C. Maniago	5	5	4	3.07
28–19–23	RW	B. Geoffrion	51	23	18	41	D	J. Talbot	70	3	22	25	E. Wakely	1	0	0	3.00
	LW	D. Moore	67	24	26	50	D	L. Fontinato	63	2	8	10					
	C	H. Richard	67	23	**50**	73											
	RW	C. Provost	67	20	30	50											
	C	R. Backstrom	70	23	12	35											
	C	D. Marshall	65	13	20	33											
	C	P. Goyette	32	5	8	13											
	RW	B. Rousseau	62	19	18	37											
	RW	B. Hicke	70	17	22	39											
DET	LW	P. MacDonald	69	33	28	61	D	B. Gadsby	70	4	24	28	T. Sawchuk	23	16	7	**2.48**
S. Abel	C	A. Delvecchio	70	20	44	64	D	D. Barkley	70	3	24	27	H. Bassen	6	5	5	3.24
32–25–13	RW	G. Howe	70	**38**	48	**86**	D	M. Pronovost	69	4	9	13	D. Riggin	3	4	1	2.97
	LW	V. Stasiuk	36	6	11	17	D	H. Young	64	4	5	9					
	LW	V. Fonteyne	67	6	14	20	D	P. Goegan	62	1	8	9					
	LW	A. Faulkner	70	10	10	20											
	C	N. Ullman	70	26	30	56											
	C	B. MacGregor	67	11	11	22											
	RW	F. Smith	51	9	17	26											
NYR	LW	D. Prentice	49	13	25	38	D	D. Harvey	68	4	35	39	G. Worsley	22	**34**	9	3.30
M. Patrick	C	E. Ingarfield	69	19	24	43	D	H. Howell	70	5	20	25	M. Paille	0	1	2	3.33
11–19–4	RW	A. Bathgate	70	35	46	81	D	J. Neilson	69	5	11	16	M. Pelletier	0	1	1	6.00
R. Sullivan	LW	D. Balon	70	11	13	24	D	A. Langlois	60	2	14	16					
11–17–8	LW	V. Hadfield	36	5	6	11	D	L. Cahan	56	6	14	20					
	C	C. Henry	60	37	23	60											
	C	D. McKenney	21	8	16	24											
	C	J. Ratelle	48	11	9	20											
	RW	A. Hebenton	70	15	22	37											
	RW	R. Gilbert	70	11	20	31											
BOS	LW	J. Bucyk	69	27	39	66	D	T. Green	70	1	11	12	E. Johnston	11	27	11	4.08
P. Watson	C	M. Oliver	65	22	40	62	D	E. Westfall	48	1	11	12	M. Perreault	3	12	6	3.86
1–8–5	RW	T. Williams	69	23	20	43	D	D. Mohns	68	7	23	30					
M. Schmidt	LW	D. Prentice	19	6	9	15	D	L. Boivin	62	2	24	26					
13–31–12	LW	J. Gendron	66	21	22	43	D	W. Godfrey	66	2	9	11					
	C	D. McKenney	41	14	19	33											
	C	F. Kennedy	49	12	18	30											
	C	J. Toppazzini	65	17	18	35											
	C	C. Burns	68	12	10	22											
	RW	W. Hicks	65	7	9	16											

GOALS		ASSISTS		POINTS	
G. Howe, DET	38	H. Richard, MONT	50	G. Howe, DET	86
C. Henry, NYR	37	J. Beliveau, MONT	49	A. Bathgate, NYR	81
F. Mahovlich, TOR	36	G. Howe, DET	48	S. Mikita, CHI	76
A. Bathgate, NYR	35	A. Bathgate, NYR	46	F. Mahovlich, TOR	73
P. MacDonald, DET	33	S. Mikita, CHI	45	H. Richard, MONT	73

PENALTY MINUTES		GOALS AGAINST AVE.		SHUTOUTS	
H. Young, DET	273	T. Sawchuk, DET	2.48	J. Plante, MONT	5
C. Brewer, TOR	168	J. Plante, MONT	2.49	G. Hall, CHI	5
L. Fontinato, MONT	141	G. Hall, CHI	2.55	T. Sawchuk, DET	3
T. Green, BOS	117	J. Bower, TOR	2.62	D. Simmons, TOR	1
B. Gadsby, DET	116	G. Worsley, NYR	3.30	J. Bower, TOR	1

National Hockey League 1963–64

TEAM	W	L	T	PTS	GF	GA
MONT	36	21	13	85	209	**167**
CHI	36	22	12	84	**218**	169
*TOR	33	25	12	78	192	172
DET	30	29	11	71	191	204
NYR	22	38	10	54	186	242
BOS	18	40	12	48	170	212

TEAM	POS	PLAYER	GP	G	A	PTS	POS	PLAYER	GP	G	A	PTS	GOALIE	W	L	T	GAvg
MONT	LW	B. Rousseau	70	25	31	56	D	J. Laperriere	65	2	28	30	C. Hodge	33	18	11	2.26
T. Blake	C	J. Beliveau	68	28	50	78	D	J. Tremblay	70	5	16	21	G. Worsley	3	2	2	2.97
36–21–13	RW	J. Ferguson	59	18	27	45	D	T. Harper	70	2	15	17	J. Morissette	0	1	0	6.67
	LW	D. Balon	70	24	18	42	D	J. Talbot	66	1	13	14					
	C	H. Richard	66	14	39	53											
	RW	C. Provost	68	15	17	32											
	LW	G. Tremblay	61	22	15	37											
	LW	R. Berenson	69	7	9	16											
	C	R. Backstrom	70	8	21	29											
	RW	B. Geoffrion	55	21	18	39											
	RW	B. Hicke	48	11	9	20											
CHI	LW	A. McDonald	70	14	32	46	D	P. Pilote	70	7	46	53	G. Hall	**34**	19	11	2.31
B. Reay	C	S. Mikita	70	39	50	**89**	D	A. MacNeil	70	5	19	24	D. DeJordy	2	3	1	3.17
36–22–12	RW	K. Wharram	70	39	32	71	D	E. Vasko	70	2	18	20					
	LW	B. Hull	70	**43**	44	87	D	H. Young	39	0	7	7					
	C	B. Hay	70	23	33	56											
	RW	C. Maki	68	8	14	22											
	LW	R. Murphy	70	11	8	19											
	LW	R. Fleming	61	3	6	9											
	C	E. Nesterenko	70	7	19	26											
	RW	J. McKenzie	45	9	9	18											
	RW	W. Hillman	59	1	4	5											
TOR	LW	F. Mahovlich	70	26	29	55	D	A. Stanley	70	6	21	27	J. Bower	24	16	11	**2.11**
P. Imlach	C	D. Keon	70	23	37	60	D	T. Horton	70	9	20	29	D. Simmons	9	9	1	3.17
33–25–12	RW	G. Armstrong	67	20	17	37	D	B. Baun	52	4	14	18					
	LW	B. Pulford	70	18	30	48	D	C. Brewer	57	4	9	13					
	LW	E. Shack	64	11	10	21											
	LW	D. Duff	52	7	7	14											
	C	R. Kelly	70	11	34	45											
	C	R. Stewart	65	14	5	19											
	C	B. Harris	67	6	12	18											
	RW	J. Pappin	50	11	8	19											
	RW	B. Nevin	49	7	12	19											
DET	LW	P. MacDonald	68	21	25	46	D	D. Barkley	67	11	21	32	T. Sawchuk	24	20	7	2.60
S. Abel	C	A. Delvecchio	70	23	30	53	D	B. Gadsby	64	2	16	18	R. Crozier	5	6	4	3.40
30–29–11	RW	G. Howe	69	26	47	73	D	M. Pronovost	67	3	17	20	H. Bassen	1	1	0	4.00
	LW	A. Pronovost	70	7	16	23	D	R. Ingram	50	3	6	9	P. Rupp	0	1	0	4.00
	LW	L. Jeffrey	58	10	18	28	D	J. Miszuk	42	0	2	2	H. Gray	0	1	0	7.50
	C	N. Ullman	61	21	30	51											
	C	B. MacGregor	63	11	21	32											
	C	P. Martin	50	9	12	21											
	RW	F. Smith	52	18	13	31											
	RW	E. Joyal	47	10	7	17											
NYR	LW	C. Henry	68	29	26	55	D	H. Howell	70	5	31	36	J. Plante	22	35	8	3.38
R. Sullivan	C	P. Goyette	67	24	41	65	D	L. Cahan	53	4	8	12	G. Villemure	0	3	2	3.60
22–38–10	RW	R. Gilbert	70	24	40	64	D	D. Johns	57	1	9	10					
	LW	D. McKenney	55	9	17	26											
	C	E. Ingarfield	63	15	11	26											
	RW	A. Bathgate	56	16	43*	59											
	LW	V. Hadfield	69	14	11	25											
	LW	V. Fonteyne	69	7	18	25											
	LW	D. Marshall	70	11	12	23											
	LW	D. Richardson	34	3	1	4											
	RW	D. Meissner	35	3	5	8											
BOS	LW	J. Bucyk	62	18	36	54	D	D. Mohns	70	9	17	26	E. Johnston	18	**40**	12	3.01
M. Schmidt	C	M. Oliver	70	24	44	68	D	L. Boivin	65	10	14	24					
18–40–12	RW	A. Hebenton	70	12	11	23	D	T. Johnson	70	4	21	25					
	LW	D. Prentice	70	23	16	39	D	T. Green	70	4	10	14					
	LW	J. Gendron	54	5	13	18	D	B. McCord	65	1	9	10					
	C	F. Kennedy	70	8	17	25											
	C	O. Kurtenbach	70	12	25	37											
	C	B. Leiter	56	6	13	19											
	RW	T. Williams	37	8	15	23											
	RW	G. Dornhoefer	32	12	10	22											

GOALS

B. Hull, CHI	43
S. Mikita, CHI	39
K. Wharram, CHI	39
C. Henry, NYR	29
J. Beliveau, MONT	28

ASSISTS

A. Bathgate, NYR, TOR	58
S. Mikita, CHI	50
J. Beliveau, MONT	50
G. Howe, DET	47
P. Pilote, CHI	46

POINTS

S. Mikita, CHI	89
B. Hull, CHI	87
J. Beliveau, MONT	78
A. Bathgate, NYR, TOR	77
G. Howe, DET	73

PENALTY MINUTES

V. Hadfield, NYR	151
T. Harper, MONT	149
S. Mikita, CHI	149
T. Green, BOS	145
R. Fleming, CHI	140

GOALS AGAINST AVE.

J. Bower, TOR	2.11
C. Hodge, MONT	2.26
G. Hall, CHI	2.31
T. Sawchuk, DET	2.60
E. Johnston, BOS	3.01

SHUTOUTS

C. Hodge, MONT	8
G. Hall, CHI	7
E. Johnston, BOS	6
J. Bower, TOR	5
T. Sawchuk, DET	5

TEAM	W	L	T	PTS	GF	GA
DET	40	23	7	87	**224**	175
*MONT	36	23	11	83	211	185
CHI	34	28	8	76	**224**	176
TOR	30	26	14	74	204	**173**
NYR	20	38	12	52	179	246
BOS	21	43	6	48	166	253

	POS	PLAYER	GP	G	A	PTS		PLAYER	GP	G	A	PTS	GOALIE	W	L	T	GAvg
DET	LW	P. MacDonald	69	13	33	46	D	B. Gadsby	61	0	12	12	R. Crozier	**40**	22	7	2.42
S. Abel	C	A. Delvecchio	68	25	42	67	D	D. Barkley	67	5	20	25	C. Wetzel	0	1	0	7.27
40–23–7	RW	G. Howe	70	29	47	76	D	M. Pronovost	68	1	15	16					
	LW	R. Murphy	58	20	19	39	D	A. Langlois	65	1	12	13					
	C	N. Ullman	70	**42**	41	83	D	G. Bergman	58	4	7	11					
	RW	F. Smith	67	16	29	45											
	LW	T. Lindsay	69	14	14	28											
	C	P. Martin	58	8	9	17											
	RW	P. Henderson	70	8	13	21											
MONT	LW	J. Ferguson	69	17	27	44	D	J. Laperriere	67	5	22	27	C. Hodge	26	16	10	2.60
T. Blake	C	R. Backstrom	70	25	30	55	D	J. Tremblay	68	3	17	20	G. Worsley	10	7	1	2.78
36–23–11	RW	C. Larose	68	21	16	37	D	J. Talbot	67	8	14	22					
	LW	D. Duff	40	9	7	16	D	T. Harris	68	1	14	15					
	C	J. Beliveau	58	20	23	43											
	RW	Y. Cournoyer	55	7	10	17											
	LW	D. Balon	63	18	23	41											
	LW	G. Tremblay	26	9	7	16											
	C	H. Richard	53	23	29	52											
	RW	C. Provost	70	27	37	64											
	RW	B. Rousseau	66	12	35	47											
CHI	LW	D. Mohns	49	13	20	33	D	P. Pilote	68	14	45	59	G. Hall	18	18	5	2.43
B. Reay	C	S. Mikita	70	28	**59**	**87**	D	D. Jarrett	46	2	15	17	D. DeJordy	16	10	3	2.52
34–28–8	RW	K. Wharram	68	24	20	44	D	M. Ravlich	61	3	16	19					
	LW	B. Hull	61	39	32	71	D	A. MacNeil	69	3	7	10					
	C	P. Esposito	70	23	32	55											
	RW	C. Maki	65	16	24	40											
	LW	D. Hull	55	10	4	14											
	LW	F. Stanfield	58	7	10	17											
	C	B. Hay	69	11	26	37											
	RW	E. Nesterenko	56	14	16	30											
TOR	LW	F. Mahovlich	59	23	28	51	D	K. Douglas	67	5	23	28	T. Sawchuk	17	13	6	2.56
P. Imlach	C	R. Kelly	70	18	28	46	D	T. Horton	70	12	16	28	J. Bower	13	13	8	**2.38**
30–26–14	RW	A. Bathgate	55	16	29	45	D	C. Brewer	70	4	23	27					
	LW	B. Harris	48	1	6	7	D	B. Baun	70	0	18	18					
	LW	E. Shack	67	5	9	14											
	LW	D. Moore	38	2	4	6											
	C	D. Keon	65	21	29	50											
	C	B. Pulford	65	19	20	39											
	C	G. Armstrong	59	15	22	37											
	C	R. Stewart	65	16	11	27											
	RW	R. Ellis	62	23	16	39											
NYR	LW	C. Henry	48	21	15	36	D	H. Howell	68	2	20	22	M. Paille	10	21	7	3.58
R. Sullivan	C	P. Goyette	52	12	34	46	D	J. Neilson	62	0	13	13	J. Plante	10	17	5	3.37
20–38–12	RW	R. Gilbert	70	25	36	61	D	R. Seiling	68	4	22	26					
	LW	V. Hadfield	70	18	20	38	D	A. Brown	58	1	11	12					
	LW	D. Robinson	21	8	14	22											
	LW	D. Duff	29	3	9	12											
	C	J. Ratelle	54	14	21	35											
	C	D. Marshall	69	20	15	35											
	C	E. Ingarfield	69	15	13	28											
	RW	B. Nevin	64	16	14	30											
	RW	L. Angotti	70	9	8	17											
BOS	LW	J. Bucyk	68	26	29	55	D	T. Green	70	8	27	35	E. Johnston	12	**31**	4	3.45
M. Schmidt	C	M. Oliver	65	20	23	43	D	L. Boivin	67	3	10	13	J. Norris	9	12	2	3.74
21–43–6	RW	T. Williams	65	13	21	34	D	T. Johnson	51	0	9	9					
	LW	R. Fleming	67	18	23	41	D	B. McCord	43	0	6	6					
	LW	D. Prentice	31	14	9	23											
	LW	W. Maxner	54	7	6	13											
	LW	A. McDonald	60	9	9	18											
	C	O. Kurtenbach	64	6	20	26											
	C	B. Knibbs	53	7	10	17											
	RW	E. Westfall	68	12	15	27											
	RW	W. Rivers	58	6	17	23											

GOALS		ASSISTS		POINTS	
N. Ullman, DET	42	S. Mikita, CHI	59	S. Mikita, CHI	87
B. Hull, CHI	39	G. Howe, DET	47	N. Ullman, DET	83
G. Howe, DET	29	P. Pilote, CHI	45	G. Howe, DET	76
S. Mikita, CHI	28	A. Delvecchio, DET	42	B. Hull, CHI	71
C. Provost, MONT	27	N. Ullman, DET	41	A. Delvecchio, DET	67

PENALTY MINUTES		GOALS AGAINST AVE.		SHUTOUTS	
C. Brewer, TOR	177	J. Bower, TOR	2.38	R. Crozier, DET	6
T. Lindsay, DET	173	R. Crozier, DET	2.42	G. Hall, CHI	4
P. Pilote, CHI	162	G. Hall, CHI	2.43	J. Bower, TOR	3
B. Baun, TOR	160	T. Sawchuk, TOR	2.56	D. DeJordy, CHI	3
J. Ferguson, MONT	156	C. Hodge, MONT	2.60	C. Hodge, MONT	3
T. Green, BOS	156	E. Johnston, BOS	3.45	E. Johnston, BOS	3

National Hockey League 1965–66

TEAM	W	L	T	PTS	GF	GA
*MONT	41	21	8	90	239	**173**
CHI	37	25	8	82	**240**	187
TOR	34	25	11	79	208	187
DET	31	27	12	74	221	194
BOS	21	43	6	48	174	275
NYR	18	41	11	47	195	261

MONT
T. Blake
41–21–8

POS	PLAYER	GP	G	A	PTS		PLAYER	GP	G	A	PTS	GOALIE	W	L	T	GAvg
LW	J. Ferguson	65	11	14	25	D	J. Tremblay	59	6	29	35	G. Worsley	29	14	6	2.36
C	J. Beliveau	67	29	**48**	77	D	J. Laperriere	57	6	25	31	C. Hodge	12	7	2	2.58
RW	B. Rousseau	70	30	**48**	78	D	T. Harper	69	1	11	12					
LW	G. Tremblay	70	27	21	48	D	T. Harris	53	0	13	13					
C	H. Richard	62	22	39	61	D	J. Talbot	59	1	14	15					
RW	C. Provost	70	19	36	55	D	J. Roberts	70	5	5	10					
LW	D. Duff	63	21	24	45											
LW	R. Berenson	23	3	4	7											
C	R. Backstrom	67	22	20	42											
RW	Y. Cournoyer	65	18	11	29											
RW	C. Larose	64	15	18	33											

CHI
B. Reay
37–25–8

POS	PLAYER	GP	G	A	PTS		PLAYER	GP	G	A	PTS	GOALIE	W	L	T	GAvg
LW	B. Hull	65	**54**	43	**97**	D	P. Pilote	51	2	34	36	G. Hall	**34**	21	7	2.63
C	P. Esposito	69	27	26	53	D	P. Stapleton	55	4	30	34	D. Dryden	3	4	1	3.05
RW	C. Maki	68	17	31	48	D	D. Jarrett	66	4	12	16					
LW	D. Mohns	70	22	27	49	D	M. Ravlich	62	0	16	16					
C	S. Mikita	68	30	**48**	78	D	E. Vasko	56	1	7	8					
RW	K. Wharram	69	26	17	43											
LW	F. Stanfield	39	2	2	4											
C	B. Hay	68	20	31	51											
C	E. Nesterenko	67	15	25	40											
RW	K. Hodge	63	6	17	23											

TOR
P. Imlach
34–25–11

POS	PLAYER	GP	G	A	PTS		PLAYER	GP	G	A	PTS	GOALIE	W	L	T	GAvg
LW	F. Mahovlich	68	32	24	56	D	K. Douglas	64	6	14	20	J. Bower	18	10	5	**2.25**
C	R. Kelly	63	8	24	32	D	T. Horton	70	6	22	28	T. Sawchuk	10	11	4	2.96
RW	D. Keon	69	24	30	54	D	L. Hillman	48	3	25	28	B. Gamble	5	2	2	2.51
LW	E. Shack	63	26	17	43	D	A. Stanley	59	4	14	18	G. Smith	0	2	0	3.56
LW	B. Selby	61	14	13	27							A. Smith	1	0	0	1.94
C	B. Pulford	70	28	28	56											
C	G. Armstrong	70	16	35	51											
RW	R. Ellis	70	19	23	42											
RW	W. Boyer	46	4	17	21											
RW	P. Stemkowski	56	4	12	16											
RW	O. Kurtenbach	70	9	6	15											

DET
S. Abel
31–27–12

POS	PLAYER	GP	G	A	PTS		PLAYER	GP	G	A	PTS	GOALIE	W	L	T	GAvg
LW	A. McDonald	43	6	16	22	D	D. Barkley	43	5	15	20	R. Crozier	28	**24**	12	2.78
C	A. Delvecchio	70	31	38	69	D	B. Gadsby	58	5	12	17	H. Bassen	2	3	0	2.51
RW	G. Howe	70	29	46	75	D	G. Bergman	61	3	16	19	G. Gardner	1	0	0	1.00
LW	P. Henderson	69	22	24	46	D	B. Marshall	61	0	19	19					
C	N. Ullman	70	31	41	72	D	B. Watson	70	2	7	9					
RW	A. Bathgate	70	15	32	47											
LW	R. Murphy	32	10	7	17											
LW	P. MacDonald	37	5	12	17											
C	B. MacGregor	70	20	14	34											
RW	F. Smith	66	21	28	49											

BOS
M. Schmidt
21–43–6

POS	PLAYER	GP	G	A	PTS		PLAYER	GP	G	A	PTS	GOALIE	W	L	T	GAvg
LW	J. Bucyk	63	27	30	57	D	E. Westfall	59	9	21	30	B. Parent	11	20	3	3.69
C	M. Oliver	70	18	42	60	D	G. Marotte	51	3	17	20	E. Johnston	10	19	2	3.72
RW	T. Williams	70	16	22	38	D	D. Awrey	70	4	3	7	G. Cheevers	0	4	1	6.00
LW	D. Prentice	50	7	22	29	D	A. Langlois	65	4	10	14	B. Ring	0	0	0	7.06
LW	P. MacDonald	29	6	4	10	D	B. Woytowich	68	2	17	19					
C	R. Stewart	70	20	16	36											
C	P. Martin	41	16	11	27											
C	B. Dillabough	53	7	13	20											
RW	J. McKenzie	36	13	9	22											
RW	B. Goldsworthy	13	3	1	4											

	POS	PLAYER	GP	G	A	PTS	PLAYER	GP	G	A	PTS	GOALIE	W	L	T	GAvg
NYR	LW	D. Marshall	69	26	28	54	D H. Howell	70	4	29	33	E. Giacomin	8	19	7	3.66
R. Sullivan	C	P. Goyette	60	11	31	42	D J. Neilson	65	4	19	23	C. Maniago	9	16	3	3.50
5–10–5	RW	B. Nevin	69	29	33	62	D R. Seiling	52	5	10	15	D. Simmons	1	6	1	4.52
E. Francis	LW	V. Hadfield	67	16	19	35	D W. Hillman	68	3	17	20					
13–31–6	LW	R. Fleming	35	10	14	24	D A. Brown	64	1	7	8					
	LW	D. Robinson	51	8	12	20	D G. Peters	63	7	3	10					
	C	J. Ratelle	67	21	30	51										
	C	E. Ingarfield	68	20	16	36										
	RW	R. Gilbert	34	10	15	25										
	RW	B. Hicke	49	9	18	27										

GOALS		ASSISTS		POINTS	
B. Hull, CHI	54	S. Mikita, CHI	48	B. Hull, CHI	97
F. Mahovlich, TOR	32	B. Rousseau, MONT	48	S. Mikita, CHI	78
N. Ullman, DET	31	J. Beliveau, MONT	48	B. Rousseau, MONT	78
A. Delvecchio, DET	31	G. Howe, DET	46	J. Beliveau, MONT	77
S. Mikita, CHI	30	B. Hull, CHI	43	G. Howe, DET	75
B. Rousseau, MONT	30				

PENALTY MINUTES		GOALS AGAINST AVE.		SHUTOUTS	
R. Fleming, BOS, NYR	166	J. Bower, TOR	2.25	R. Crozier, DET	7
J. Ferguson, MONT	153	G. Worsley, MONT	2.36	G. Hall, CHI	4
B. Watson, DET	133	G. Hall, CHI	2.63	J. Bower, TOR	3
T. Green, BOS	113	R. Crozier, DET	2.78	B. Gamble, TOR	2
V. Hadfield, NYR	112	E. Giacomin, NYR	3.66	C. Maniago, NYR	2

National Hockey League 1966–67

TEAM	W	L	T	PTS	GF	GA
CHI	41	17	12	94	**264**	**170**
MONT	32	25	13	77	202	188
*TOR	32	27	11	75	204	211
NYR	30	28	12	72	188	189
DET	27	39	4	58	212	241
BOS	17	43	10	44	182	253

	POS	PLAYER	GP	G	A	PTS	PLAYER	GP	G	A	PTS	GOALIE	W	L	T	GAvg
CHI	LW	D. Mohns	61	25	35	60	D P. Pilote	70	6	46	52	D. DeJordy	22	12	7	**2.46**
B. Reay	C	S. Mikita	70	35	**62**	**97**	D P. Stapleton	70	3	31	34	G. Hall	19	5	5	2.38
41–17–12	RW	K. Wharram	70	31	34	65	D D. Jarrett	70	5	21	26					
	LW	B. Hull	66	**52**	28	80	D E. Van Impe	61	8	11	19					
	C	P. Esposito	69	21	40	61										
	RW	C. Maki	56	9	29	38										
	LW	D. Hull	70	25	17	42										
	C	E. Nesterenko	68	14	23	37										
	C	B. Hay	36	7	13	20										
	RW	K. Hodge	68	10	25	35										
	RW	L. Angotti	63	6	12	18										
MONT	LW	J. Ferguson	67	20	22	42	D J. Tremblay	60	8	26	34	C. Hodge	11	15	7	2.57
T. Blake	C	J. Beliveau	53	12	26	38	D J. Laperriere	61	0	20	20	R. Vachon	11	3	4	2.48
32–25–13	RW	B. Rousseau	68	19	44	63	D T. Harris	65	2	16	18	G. Worsley	9	6	2	3.18
	LW	G. Tremblay	62	13	19	32	D T. Harper	56	0	16	16	G. Bauman	1	1	0	2.50
	C	H. Richard	65	21	34	55	D J. Talbot	69	3	5	8					
	RW	Y. Cournoyer	69	25	15	40										
	LW	D. Duff	51	12	11	23										
	C	R. Backstrom	69	14	27	41										
	RW	C. Larose	69	19	16	35										
	RW	C. Provost	64	11	13	24										
TOR	LW	F. Mahovlich	63	18	28	46	D T. Horton	70	8	17	25	T. Sawchuk	15	5	4	2.81
P. Imlach	C	D. Keon	66	19	33	52	D L. Hillman	67	4	19	23	J. Bower	12	9	3	2.64
19–21–9	RW	G. Armstrong	70	9	24	33	D B. Baun	54	2	8	10	B. Gamble	5	10	4	3.39
K. Clancy	LW	L. Jeffrey	56	11	17	28	D M. Pronovost	58	2	12	14	G. Smith	0	2	0	3.65
7–1–2	C	R. Kelly	61	14	24	38	D A. Stanley	53	1	12	13	A. Smith	0	1	0	5.00
P. Imlach	RW	R. Ellis	67	22	23	45										
6–5–0	LW	B. Conacher	66	14	13	27										
	C	B. Pulford	67	17	28	45										
	C	P. Stemkowski	68	13	22	35										
	RW	J. Pappin	64	21	11	32										

Team	POS	PLAYER	GP	G	A	PTS	POS	PLAYER	GP	G	A	PTS	GOALIE	W	L	T	GAvg
NYR	LW	D. Marshall	70	24	22	46	D	H. Howell	70	12	28	40	E. Giacomin	**30**	25	11	2.61
E. Francis	C	P. Goyette	70	12	49	61	D	J. Neilson	61	4	11	15	C. Maniago	0	3	1	3.84
30–28–12	RW	B. Nevin	67	20	24	44	D	W. Hillman	67	2	12	14					
	LW	V. Hadfield	69	13	20	33	D	A. Brown	69	2	10	12					
	LW	R. Fleming	61	15	16	31	D	A. MacNeil	58	0	4	4					
	C	O. Kurtenbach	60	11	25	36											
	C	E. Ingarfield	67	12	22	34											
	RW	R. Gilbert	64	28	18	46											
	RW	B. Geoffrion	58	17	25	42											
	RW	B. Hicke	48	3	4	7											
DET	LW	P. Henderson	46	21	19	40	D	G. Bergman	70	5	30	35	R. Crozier	22	**30**	4	3.35
S. Abel	C	A. Delvecchio	70	17	38	55	D	L. Boivin	69	4	17	21	G. Gardner	3	6	0	3.86
27–39–4	RW	G. Howe	69	25	40	65	D	H. Young	44	3	14	17	H. Bassen	2	3	0	3.44
	LW	D. Prentice	68	23	22	45	D	B. Marshall	57	0	10	10					
	C	N. Ullman	68	26	44	70	D	B. Wall	31	2	2	4					
	RW	A. Bathgate	60	8	23	31											
	LW	V. Fonteyne	28	1	1	2											
	C	T. Hampson	65	13	35	48											
	RW	B. MacGregor	70	28	19	47											
	RW	F. Smith	54	11	14	25											
BOS	LW	J. Bucyk	59	18	30	48	D	B. Orr	61	13	28	41	E. Johnston	9	21	2	3.70
H. Sinden	C	P. Martin	70	20	22	42	D	E. Westfall	70	12	24	36	G. Cheevers	5	11	6	3.33
17–43–10	RW	J. McKenzie	69	17	19	36	D	T. Green	47	6	10	16	B. Parent	3	11	2	3.64
	LW	R. Murphy	39	11	16	27	D	G. Marotte	67	7	8	15					
	LW	J. Parise	18	2	2	4	D	J. Watson	69	2	13	15					
	C	M. Oliver	65	9	26	35	D	B. Woytowich	64	2	7	9					
	C	W. Connelly	64	13	17	30											
	C	R. Schock	66	10	20	30											
	RW	B. Goldsworthy	18	3	5	8											

GOALS	
B. Hull, CHI	52
S. Mikita, CHI	35
K. Wharram, CHI	31
B. MacGregor, DET	28
R. Gilbert, NYR	28

ASSISTS	
S. Mikita, CHI	62
P. Goyette, NYR	49
P. Pilote, CHI	46
N. Ullman, DET	44
B. Rousseau, MONT	44

POINTS	
S. Mikita, CHI	97
B. Hull, CHI	80
N. Ullman, DET	70
K. Wharram, CHI	65
G. Howe, DET	65

PENALTY MINUTES	
J. Ferguson, MONT	177
R. Fleming, NYR	146
G. Bergman, DET	129
E. Van Impe, CHI	111

GOALS AGAINST AVE.	
D. DeJordy, CHI	2.46
C. Hodge, MONT	2.57
E. Giacomin, NYR	2.61
R. Crozier, DET	3.35
E. Johnston, BOS	3.70

SHUTOUTS	
E. Giacomin, NYR	9
D. DeJordy, CHI	4
R. Crozier, DET	4
C. Hodge, MONT	3
G. Hall, CHI	2

National Hockey League 1967–68

	W	L	T	PTS	GF	GA	PPG	PPCT	SHG	PPGA	PKPCT	SHGA
EASTERN DIVISION												
*MONT	42	22	10	94	236	**167**	50	20.4	7	34	83.4	3
NYR	39	23	12	90	226	183	46	**21.2**	1	42	81.2	7
BOS	37	27	10	84	**259**	216	45	19.1	**10**	50	82.6	4
CHI	32	26	16	80	212	222	37	15.8	9	37	83.0	6
TOR	33	31	10	76	209	176	33	14.3	6	**28**	**87.8**	8
DET	27	35	12	66	245	257	43	19.2	4	54	80.0	5
WESTERN DIVISION												
PHI	31	32	11	73	173	179	33	12.3	7	49	83.1	**2**
LA	31	33	10	72	200	224	33	13.7	5	54	80.3	3
STL	27	31	16	70	177	191	38	17.0	**10**	39	84.1	7
MINN	27	32	15	69	191	226	**55**	21.1	1	29	86.6	8
PITT	27	34	13	67	195	216	37	13.6	2	30	84.6	11
OAK	15	42	17	47	153	219	41	15.8	6	45	82.6	6

EASTERN DIVISION

TEAM	POS	PLAYER	GP	G	A	PTS	SOG	SPCT	PPG	+/-	GOALIE	W	L	T	GAvg
MONT	LW	J. Ferguson	61	15	18	33	153	9.8	0	18	G. Worsley	19	9	8	**1.98**
T. Blake	C	J. Beliveau	59	31	37	68	206	15.0	9	27	R. Vachon	23	13	2	2.48
42–22–10	RW	B. Rousseau	74	19	46	65	183	10.4	7	12					
	LW	D. Duff	66	25	21	46	111	**22.5**	6	6					
	C	J. Lemaire	69	22	20	42	182	12.1	3	15					
	RW	Y. Cournoyer	64	28	32	60	222	12.6	7	19					
	LW	G. Tremblay	71	23	28	51	215	11.2	7	28					
	C	R. Backstrom	70	20	25	45	198	10.1	3	4					
	C	H. Richard	54	9	19	28	123	7.3	2	4					
	RW	C. Provost	73	14	30	44	170	8.2	2	17					
	RW	M. Redmond	41	6	5	11	52	11.5	1	2					
	RW	C. Larose	42	2	9	11	70	2.9	0	0					
	D	J. Tremblay	73	4	26	30	105	3.8	1	28					
	D	J. Laperriere	72	4	21	25	122	3.3	1	23					
	D	S. Savard	67	2	13	15	59	3.4	1	13					
	D	T. Harris	67	5	16	21	56	8.9	0	23					
NYR	LW	V. Hadfield	59	20	19	39	177	11.3	7	– 2	E. Giacomin	**36**	20	10	2.44
E. Francis	C	J. Ratelle	74	32	46	78	180	17.8	10	23	D. Simmons	2	1	2	2.60
39–23–12	RW	R. Gilbert	73	29	48	77	281	10.3	8	13	G. Villemure	1	2	0	2.40
	LW	D. Marshall	70	19	30	49	146	13.0	4	19					
	C	P. Goyette	73	25	40	65	179	14.0	4	18					
	RW	B. Nevin	74	28	30	58	217	12.9	3	15					
	LW	R. Fleming	73	17	7	24	143	11.9	0	1					
	LW	L. Jeffrey	47	2	4	6	48	4.2	0	– 13					
	LW	R. Berenson	19	2	1	3	25	8.0	0	– 1					
	C	O. Kurtenbach	73	15	20	35	175	8.6	2	5					
	C	C. Henry	36	8	12	20	39	20.5	1	8					
	RW	B. Geoffrion	59	5	16	21	84	5.9	4	1					
	D	J. Neilson	67	6	29	35	172	3.5	2	29					
	D	H. Howell	74	5	24	29	220	2.3	1	12					
	D	R. Seiling	71	5	11	16	119	4.2	0	23					
	D	A. Brown	74	1	25	26	116	.9	0	17					
	D	R. Stewart	55	7	7	14	101	6.9	0	– 4					
BOS	LW	J. Bucyk	72	30	39	69	172	17.4	6	18	G. Cheevers	23	17	5	2.83
H. Sinden	C	F. Stanfield	73	20	44	64	215	9.3	3	9	E. Johnston	11	8	5	2.87
37–27–10	RW	J. McKenzie	74	28	38	66	184	15.2	7	14	A. Gill	3	2	0	2.89
	LW	E. Shack	70	23	19	42	195	11.8	4	1					
	C	P. Esposito	74	35	**49**	84	284	12.3	9	19					
	RW	K. Hodge	74	25	31	56	188	13.3	5	13					
	LW	G. Sather	65	8	12	20	55	14.5	0	9					
	LW	R. Lonsberry	19	2	2	4	39	5.1	0	2					
	C	D. Sanderson	71	24	25	49	187	12.8	4	11					
	C	S. Krake	68	5	7	12	48	10.4	0	9					
	RW	T. Williams	68	18	32	50	136	13.2	0	24					
	RW	W. Cashman	12	0	4	4	12	.0	0	– 5					
	D	T. Green	72	7	36	43	113	6.2	3	14					
	D	B. Orr	46	11	20	31	172	6.4	3	30					
	D	E. Westfall	73	14	22	36	139	10.1	1	5					
	D	D. Smith	74	4	23	27	159	2.5	0	**33**					
	D	D. Awrey	74	3	12	15	92	3.3	0	18					
CHI	LW	D. Mohns	65	24	29	53	161	14.9	5	7	D. DeJordy	23	15	11	2.71
B. Reay	C	S. Mikita	72	40	47	**87**	303	13.2	13	– 3	D. Dryden	7	8	5	3.26
32–26–16	RW	K. Wharram	74	27	42	69	177	15.3	9	– 2	J. Norris	2	3	0	3.95
	LW	B. Hull	71	**44**	31	75	**364**	12.1	8	14					
	C	P. Martin	63	16	19	35	118	13.6	0	9					
	RW	C. Maki	60	8	16	24	102	7.8	0	– 10					
	LW	D. Hull	74	18	15	33	197	9.1	0	– 20					
	LW	W. Maki	49	5	5	10	54	9.3	1	– 4					
	LW	B. Orban	39	3	2	5	21	14.3	0	– 11					
	C	E. Nesterenko	71	11	25	36	93	11.8	1	3					
	C	G. Goyer	40	1	2	3	20	5.0	0	– 18					
	RW	B. Schmautz	13	3	2	5	27	11.1	0	1					
	D	P. Stapleton	67	4	34	38	120	3.3	0	4					
	D	P. Pilote	74	1	36	37	69	1.4	0	– 8					
	D	D. Jarrett	74	4	19	23	148	2.7	0	– 15					
	D	G. Marotte	73	0	21	21	153	.0	0	4					
	D	P. Terbenche	68	3	7	10	65	4.6	0	– 11					

	POS	PLAYER	GP	G	A	PTS	SOG	SPCT	PPG	+/-	GOALIE	W	L	T	GAvg
TOR	LW	F. Mahovlich	50	19	17	36	151	12.6	2	1	J. Bower	14	18	7	2.25
P. Imlach	LW	B. Conacher	64	11	14	25	88	12.5	0	7	B. Gamble	19	13	3	2.32
33–31–10	LW	W. Carleton	65	8	11	19	140	5.7	0	5					
	LW	P. Henderson	13	5	6	11	38	13.2	3	13					
	C	M. Walton	73	30	29	59	238	12.6	11	1					
	C	B. Pulford	74	20	30	50	229	8.7	4	-7					
	C	D. Keon	67	11	37	48	196	5.6	1	16					
	C	M. Oliver	74	16	21	37	155	10.3	2	8					
	C	P. Stemkowski	60	7	15	22	141	5.0	0	-5					
	RW	R. Ellis	74	28	20	48	215	13.0	1	6					
	RW	G. Armstrong	62	13	21	34	125	10.4	2	8					
	RW	J. Pappin	58	13	15	28	117	11.1	2	0					
	D	T. Horton	69	4	23	27	179	2.2	1	20					
	D	L. Hillman	55	3	17	20	92	3.3	2	7					
	D	M. Pronovost	70	3	17	20	70	4.3	0	0					
DET	LW	D. Prentice	69	17	38	55	174	9.8	4	7	R. Edwards	15	15	8	3.50
S. Abel	C	A. Delvecchio	74	22	48	70	212	10.4	3	8	R. Crozier	9	18	2	3.30
27–35–12	RW	G. Howe	74	39	43	82	301	13.0	10	12	G. Gardner	3	2	2	3.60
	LW	G. Jarrett	68	18	21	39	207	8.7	1	4					
	LW	P. Henderson	50	13	20	33	134	9.7	4	0					
	LW	D. Roberts	36	8	9	17	60	13.3	1	0					
	LW	N. Libett	22	2	1	3	29	6.9	1	-13					
	C	N. Ullman	58	30	25	55	189	15.9	7	-13					
	C	T. Hampson	37	9	18	27	75	12.0	0	8					
	C	J. Peters	45	5	6	11	36	13.9	1	-10					
	RW	F. Smith	57	18	21	39	132	13.6	5	4					
	RW	B. MacGregor	71	15	24	39	165	9.1	1	-19					
	D	G. Bergman	74	13	28	41	165	7.9	5	-1					
	D	H. Young	62	2	17	19	87	2.3	0	16					
	D	K. Douglas	36	7	10	17	62	11.3	0	6					
	D	J. Watson	61	0	3	3	55	.0	0	-20					
	D	B. Crashley	57	2	14	16	86	2.3	0	6					

WESTERN DIVISION

	POS	PLAYER	GP	G	A	PTS	SOG	SPCT	PPG	+/-	GOALIE	W	L	T	GAvg
PHI	LW	B. Selby	56	15	15	30	88	17.0	4	-3	B. Parent	16	17	5	2.48
K. Allen	C	L. Angotti	70	12	37	49	146	8.2	2	4	D. Favell	15	15	6	2.27
31–32–11	RW	G. Dornhoefer	65	13	30	43	96	13.5	2	6					
	LW	B. Sutherland	60	20	9	29	98	20.4	5	1					
	C	E. Hoekstra	70	15	21	36	126	11.9	5	6					
	RW	L. Rochefort	74	21	21	42	237	8.9	4	-1					
	LW	D. Blackburn	67	9	20	29	157	5.7	1	-2					
	LW	C. LaForge	63	9	16	25	106	8.5	0	8					
	C	F. Kennedy	73	10	18	28	100	10.0	1	4					
	C	G. Peters	31	7	5	12	79	8.9	1	-2					
	RW	P. Hannigan	65	11	15	26	63	17.5	0	6					
	RW	W. Hicks	32	2	7	9	41	4.9	1	-5					
	D	J. Miszuk	74	5	17	22	78	6.4	1	1					
	D	J. Watson	73	5	14	19	91	5.5	1	12					
	D	E. Van Impe	67	4	13	17	129	3.1	4	-5					
	D	J. Gauthier	65	5	7	12	104	4.8	1	0					
LA	LW	T. Irvine	73	18	22	40	136	13.2	4	-10	W. Rutledge	20	18	4	2.87
R. Kelly	C	E. Joyal	74	23	34	57	226	10.2	5	-2	T. Sawchuk	11	14	6	3.07
31–33–10	RW	B. Flett	73	26	20	46	205	12.7	3	4	J. Caron	0	1	0	4.00
	LW	R. Lemieux	74	12	23	35	129	9.3	5	-2					
	LW	B. Smith	58	10	9	19	92	10.9	1	2					
	LW	D. Robinson	34	9	9	18	63	14.3	1	4					
	C	G. Labossierre	68	13	27	40	153	8.5	1	6					
	C	H. Menard	35	9	15	24	86	10.5	1	4					
	C	B. Campbell	43	6	15	21	55	10.9	0	2					
	RW	L. MacDonald	74	21	24	45	232	9.1	2	-11					
	RW	T. Gray	65	12	16	28	113	10.6	3	-3					
	RW	H. Hughes	74	9	14	23	119	7.6	1	1					
	D	B. White	74	11	27	38	170	6.5	2	17					
	D	B. Wall	71	5	18	23	148	3.4	1	-9					
	D	D. Rolfe	68	3	13	16	93	3.2	1	-10					
	D	D. Amadio	58	4	6	10	92	4.3	0	-10					
	D	B. Hughes	44	4	10	14	72	5.6	2	15					

	POS	PLAYER	GP	G	A	PTS	SOG	SPCT	PPG	+/-	GOALIE	W	L	T	GAvg
STL	LW	R. Berenson	55	22	29	51	219	10.0	7	-8	G. Hall	19	21	9	2.48
L. Patrick	LW	B. McCreary	70	13	13	26	154	8.4	2	2	S. Martin	8	10	7	2.59
4–10–2	LW	L. Keenan	40	12	8	20	102	11.8	4	-7	D. Caley	0	0	0	6.00
S. Bowman	C	G. Melnyk	73	15	35	50	144	10.4	3	-11					
23–21–14	C	T. Crisp	74	9	20	29	135	6.7	0	9					
	C	D. McKenney	39	9	20	29	93	9.7	1	1					
	C	R. Schock	55	9	9	18	116	7.8	4	-17					
	RW	St. Marseille	57	16	16	32	147	10.9	1	11					
	RW	G. Sabourin	50	13	10	23	121	10.7	0	9					
	RW	T. Ecclestone	50	6	8	14	97	6.2	3	1					
	RW	C. Cameron	32	7	2	9	43	16.3	2	2					
	RW	D. Moore	27	5	3	8	37	13.5	1	-8					
	D	J. Roberts	74	14	23	37	164	8.5	3	-8					
	D	A. Arbour	74	1	10	11	39	2.6	1	-6					
	D	B. Plager	49	5	15	20	61	8.2	2	4					
	D	F. Hucul	43	2	13	15	85	2.4	1	-3					
	D	N. Picard	66	1	10	11	120	.8	0	-4					
MINN	LW	P. MacDonald	69	19	23	42	183	10.4	9	-18	C. Maniago	21	17	9	2.77
W. Blair	C	R. Cullen	67	28	25	53	203	13.8	11	-24	G. Bauman	5	13	5	3.48
27–32–15	RW	W. Connelly	74	35	21	56	258	13.6	**14**	-32	C. Wetzel	1	2	1	4.01
	LW	J. Parise	42	11	15	26	110	10.0	1	-10					
	LW	D. Balon	73	15	32	47	152	9.9	4	-10					
	LW	T. Taylor	31	3	5	8	67	4.5	1	-7					
	C	A. Boudrias	74	18	35	53	183	9.8	4	-3					
	C	M. Marcetta	36	4	12	16	41	9.8	0	-10					
	C	S. Fitzpatrick	18	3	6	9	26	11.5	0	0					
	C	B. Masterton	38	4	8	12	83	4.8	2	-4					
	RW	B. Goldsworthy	68	14	19	33	154	9.1	2	-8					
	RW	B. Collins	71	9	11	20	114	7.9	0	16					
	D	M. McMahon	74	14	33	47	150	9.3	4	-13					
	D	B. Woytowich	66	4	17	21	86	4.7	2	-23					
	D	B. McCord	70	3	9	12	97	3.1	0	-10					
	D	E. Vasko	70	1	6	7	23	4.3	0	-36					
	D	P. Goegan	45	1	2	3	35	2.9	0	-16					
PITT	LW	V. Fonteyne	69	6	28	34	114	5.3	0	-3	L. Binkley	20	24	10	2.88
R. Sullivan	C	E. Ingarfield	50	15	22	37	110	13.6	2	-7	H. Bassen	7	10	3	2.86
27–34–13	RW	A. Bathgate	74	20	39	59	293	6.8	2	-11					
	LW	A. McDonald	74	22	21	43	185	11.9	6	-4					
	LW	B. Dea	73	16	12	28	137	11.7	1	-15					
	LW	K. McCreary	70	14	12	26	133	10.5	0	-3					
	C	A. Stratton	58	16	21	37	105	15.2	5	-6					
	C	G. Ubriaco	65	18	15	33	119	15.1	3	-13					
	RW	K. Schinkel	57	14	25	39	185	7.6	2	-10					
	RW	P. Andrea	65	11	21	32	92	12.0	5	-2					
	D	N. Price	70	6	27	33	187	3.2	1	-7					
	D	L. Boivin	73	9	13	22	163	5.5	4	-15					
	D	B. Speer	68	3	13	16	101	3.0	1	-14					
	D	A. MacNeil	74	2	10	12	76	2.6	0	-6					
	D	D. McCallum	32	0	2	2	34	.0	0	-2					
	D	D. Mattiussi	32	0	2	2	31	.0	0	-9					
OAK	LW	W. Boyer	74	13	20	33	142	9.2	1	0	C. Hodge	13	**29**	13	2.86
B. Olmstead	LW	J. Brenneman	31	10	8	18	61	16.4	2	-9	G. Smith	2	13	4	3.19
11–37–16	LW	R. Boehm	16	2	1	3	18	11.1	1	-5					
G. Fashoway	C	T. Hampson	34	8	19	27	72	11.1	2	-10					
4–5–1	C	C. Burns	73	9	26	35	119	7.6	1	-14					
	C	B. Harris	62	12	17	29	106	11.3	1	-6					
	C	L. Popein	47	5	14	19	51	9.8	0	-17					
	C	M. Laughton	35	2	6	8	53	3.8	2	-17					
	RW	B. Hicke	52	21	19	40	142	14.8	12	-22					
	RW	G. Ehman	73	19	25	44	189	10.1	6	-5					
	RW	G. Swarbrick	49	13	5	18	86	15.1	3	-17					
	RW	A. Caron	58	9	13	22	121	7.4	3	-22					
	D	L. Cahan	74	9	15	24	161	5.6	5	-29					
	D	B. Baun	67	3	10	13	80	3.8	0	-18					
	D	A. Erickson	66	4	11	15	66	6.1	0	-17					
	D	R. Harris	54	4	6	10	87	4.6	1	-27					
	D	K. Douglas	40	4	11	15	103	3.0	1	-18					

GOALS

B. Hull, CHI	44
S. Mikita, CHI	40
G. Howe, DET	39
P. Esposito, BOS	35
W. Connelly, MINN	35

ASSISTS

P. Esposito, BOS	49
R. Gilbert, NYR	48
A. Delvecchio, DET	48
S. Mikita, CHI	47
J. Ratelle, NYR	46

POINTS

S. Mikita, CHI	87
P. Esposito, BOS	84
G. Howe, DET	82
J. Ratelle, NYR	78
R. Gilbert, NYR	77

SHOTS ON GOAL	
B. Hull, CHI	364
S. Mikita, CHI	303
A. Bathgate, PITT	293
P. Esposito, BOS	284
R. Gilbert, NYR	281

SHOOTING PCT.	
D. Duff, MONT	22.5
B. Sutherland, PHI	22.4
J. Ratelle, NYR	17.8
J. Bucyk, BOS	17.4
N. Ullman, DET	15.9

+/-	
D. Smith, BOS	33
B. Orr, BOS	30
J. Neilson, NYR	29
G. Tremblay, MONT	28
J. Tremblay, MONT	28

PENALTY MINUTES	
B. Plager, STL	153
D. Awrey, BOS	150
N. Picard, STL	142
E. Van Impe, PHI	141
G. Dornhoefer, PHI	134

GOALS AGAINST AVE.	
G. Worsley, MONT	1.98
J. Bower, TOR	2.25
B. Gamble, TOR	2.32
E. Giacomin, NYR	2.44
G. Hall, STL	2.48

SHUTOUTS	
E. Giacomin, NYR	8
C. Maniago, MINN	6
L. Binkley, PITT	6
B. Gamble, TOR	5
G. Hall, STL	5

National Hockey League 1968–69

	W	L	T	PTS	GF	GA	PPG	PPCT	SHG	PPGA	PKPCT	SHGA
EASTERN DIVISION												
*MONT	46	19	11	103	271	202	43	17.7	2	40	82.8	4
BOS	42	18	16	100	**303**	221	**60**	**22.6**	**13**	54	**84.6**	4
NYR	41	26	9	91	231	196	56	20.4	4	**35**	84.3	9
TOR	35	26	15	85	234	217	45	16.2	11	46	84.4	5
DET	33	31	12	78	239	221	40	17.4	7	61	79.5	4
CHI	34	33	9	77	280	246	56	20.0	9	50	81.8	**3**
WESTERN DIVISION												
STL	37	25	14	88	204	**157**	38	15.2	4	45	81.4	6
CALIF	29	36	11	69	219	251	44	15.4	3	42	81.4	5
PHI	20	35	21	61	174	225	40	15.2	6	44	**84.6**	8
LA	24	42	10	58	185	260	31	12.9	2	53	79.1	7
PITT	20	45	11	51	189	252	50	16.5	8	38	83.5	9
MINN	18	43	15	51	189	270	47	19.1	3	41	83.5	8

EASTERN DIVISION

	POS	PLAYER	GP	G	A	PTS	SOG	SPCT	PPG	+/-	GOALIE	W	L	T	GAvg
MONT	LW	D. Duff	68	19	21	40	138	13.8	5	– 13	R. Vachon	22	9	3	2.87
C. Ruel	C	J. Lemaire	75	29	34	63	330	8.8	5	31	G. Worsley	19	6	4	2.25
46–19–11	RW	Y. Cournoyer	76	43	44	87	245	17.6	14	19	T. Esposito	5	3	4	2.73
	LW	J. Ferguson	71	29	23	52	185	15.7	2	30	E. Wakely	0	1	0	4.00
	C	J. Beliveau	69	33	49	82	235	14.0	7	15					
	RW	B. Rousseau	76	30	40	70	278	10.8	3	27					
	LW	G. Tremblay	44	10	15	25	95	10.5	2	15					
	C	H. Richard	64	15	37	52	210	7.1	2	25					
	C	R. Backstrom	72	13	28	41	180	7.2	2	20					
	C	C. Bordeleau	13	1	3	4	14	7.1	0	1					
	RW	C. Provost	73	13	15	28	184	7.1	0	12					
	RW	M. Redmond	65	9	15	24	118	7.6	1	16					
	D	J. Tremblay	75	7	32	39	139	5.0	2	29					
	D	S. Savard	74	8	23	31	98	8.2	0	33					
	D	J. Laperriere	69	5	26	31	166	3.0	0	37					
	D	T. Harris	76	7	18	25	82	8.5	0	24					
	D	L. Hillman	25	0	5	5	14	.0	0	– 2					
BOS	LW	R. Murphy	60	16	38	54	113	14.2	5	23	G. Cheevers	28	12	12	2.80
H. Sinden	C	P. Esposito	74	49	**77**	**126**	351	14.0	10	56	E. Johnston	14	6	4	3.08
42–18–16	RW	K. Hodge	75	45	45	90	236	19.1	9	49	J. Junkin	0	0	0	0.00
	LW	J. Bucyk	70	24	42	66	192	12.5	11	– 3					
	C	F. Stanfield	71	25	29	54	199	12.6	6	– 4					
	RW	J. McKenzie	60	29	27	56	123	**23.6**	8	13					
	LW	W. Cashman	51	8	23	31	66	12.1	1	19					
	LW	G. Sather	76	4	11	15	51	7.8	0	4					
	C	D. Sanderson	63	26	22	48	194	13.4	1	35					
	RW	E. Shack	50	11	11	22	125	8.8	1	2					
	RW	T. Williams	26	4	7	11	48	8.3	0	6					
	D	B. Orr	67	21	43	64	285	7.4	4	**65**					
	D	T. Green	65	8	38	46	131	6.1	3	9					
	D	E. Westfall	70	18	24	42	139	12.9	1	20					
	D	D. Awrey	73	0	13	13	72	.0	0	25					
	D	D. Smith	75	4	24	28	131	3.1	0	44					
	D	R. Smith	47	0	5	5	28	.0	0	14					

Team	POS	PLAYER	GP	G	A	PTS	SOG	SPCT	PPG	+/-	GOALIE	W	L	T	GAvg
NYR	LW	V. Hadfield	73	26	40	66	321	8.1	10	12	E. Giacomin	**37**	23	7	2.55
B. Geoffrion	C	J. Ratelle	75	32	46	78	204	15.7	8	16	D. Simmons	2	2	1	2.33
22–18–3	RW	R. Gilbert	66	28	49	77	301	9.3	8	12	G. Villemure	2	1	1	2.25
E. Francis	LW	D. Marshall	74	20	19	39	149	13.4	7	15					
19–8–6	C	P. Goyette	67	13	32	45	135	9.6	2	9					
	RW	B. Nevin	71	31	25	56	236	13.1	11	3					
	LW	D. Balon	75	10	21	31	134	7.5	1	5					
	LW	R. Fleming	72	8	12	20	117	6.8	2	– 13					
	LW	L. Jeffrey	75	1	6	7	31	3.2	0	0					
	C	W. Tkaczuk	71	12	24	36	130	9.2	0	– 11					
	C	D. Hextall	13	1	4	5	16	6.3	0	1					
	RW	R. Stewart	75	18	11	29	184	9.8	1	– 11					
	D	J. Neilson	76	10	34	44	274	3.6	3	6					
	D	B. Park	54	3	23	26	103	2.9	2	12					
	D	A. Brown	74	10	12	22	189	5.3	0	1					
	D	R. Seiling	73	4	17	21	154	2.6	0	6					
TOR	LW	P. Henderson	74	27	32	59	223	12.1	4	18	B. Gamble	28	20	11	2.80
P. Imlach	C	N. Ullman	75	35	42	77	247	14.2	13	19	J. Bower	5	4	3	2.85
35–26–15	RW	F. Smith	64	15	19	34	120	12.5	2	14	A. Smith	2	2	1	2.87
	LW	D. Keon	75	27	34	61	281	9.6	3	17					
	C	M. Oliver	76	14	36	50	192	7.3	3	12					
	RW	R. Ellis	72	25	21	46	180	13.9	4	5					
	LW	B. Pulford	72	11	23	34	179	6.1	3	– 9					
	LW	P. Quinn	40	2	7	9	42	4.8	0	10					
	LW	B. Selby	14	2	2	4	18	11.1	0	0					
	C	M. Walton	66	22	21	43	205	10.7	8	– 9					
	C	G. Armstrong	53	11	16	27	103	10.7	1	– 9					
	RW	L. Mickey	55	8	19	27	80	10.0	0	0					
	RW	B. Sutherland	44	7	5	12	53	13.2	0	– 3					
	D	T. Horton	74	11	29	40	169	6.5	3	14					
	D	J. Dorey	61	8	22	30	133	6.0	0	9					
	D	P. Pilote	69	3	18	21	48	6.3	1	5					
	D	M. Pelyk	65	3	9	12	67	4.5	0	– 2					
DET	LW	F. Mahovlich	76	49	29	78	293	16.7	7	46	R. Edwards	18	11	6	2.54
B. Gadsby	C	A. Delvecchio	72	25	58	83	221	11.3	7	43	R. Crozier	12	16	3	3.33
33–31–12	RW	G. Howe	76	44	59	103	283	15.5	9	45	T. Sawchuk	3	4	3	2.62
	LW	D. Prentice	74	14	20	34	191	7.3	2	– 8					
	LW	N. Libett	75	10	14	24	98	10.2	1	– 16					
	LW	H. Monteith	34	1	9	10	20	5.0	0	4					
	C	G. Unger	76	24	20	44	186	12.9	5	6					
	C	P. Stemkowski	71	21	31	52	209	10.0	3	1					
	C	P. Mahovlich	30	2	2	4	37	5.4	0	– 10					
	RW	B. MacGregor	69	18	23	41	168	10.7	2	6					
	RW	D. Lawson	44	5	7	12	58	8.6	0	– 2					
	RW	R. Leclerc	43	2	3	5	38	5.3	0	– 8					
	RW	W. Connelly	19	4	9	13	58	6.9	1	– 70					
	D	G. Bergman	76	7	30	37	191	3.7	2	45					
	D	K. Douglas	69	2	29	31	114	1.8	1	4					
	D	B. Baun	76	4	16	20	117	3.4	0	24					
	D	R. Harris	73	3	13	16	74	4.1	0	6					
CHI	LW	B. Hull	74	**58**	49	107	**414**	14.0	**20**	– 7	D. DeJordy	22	22	7	3.14
B. Reay	C	P. Martin	76	23	38	61	173	13.3	5	9	D. Dryden	11	11	2	3.20
34–33–9	RW	J. Pappin	75	30	40	70	208	14.4	3	7	J. Norris	1	0	0	6.00
	LW	D. Mohns	65	22	19	41	149	14.8	7	8					
	C	S. Mikita	74	30	67	97	299	10.0	7	17					
	RW	K. Wharram	76	30	39	69	167	18.0	5	18					
	LW	D. Hull	72	30	34	64	233	12.9	3	7					
	LW	B. Orban	45	4	6	10	38	10.5	0	– 3					
	C	A. Boudrias	20	4	10	14	40	10.0	1	11					
	RW	E. Nesterenko	72	15	17	32	90	16.7	1	5					
	RW	C. Maki	66	7	21	28	127	5.5	0	– 1					
	RW	B. Schmautz	63	9	7	16	81	11.1	3	– 5					
	D	P. Stapleton	75	6	50	56	112	5.4	0	23					
	D	D. Jarrett	69	0	13	13	116	.0	0	7					
	D	G. Marotte	68	5	29	34	131	3.8	1	23					
	D	M. Ravlich	60	2	12	14	74	2.7	0	20					
	D	H. Young	57	3	7	10	64	4.7	0	– 13					

WESTERN DIVISION

	POS	PLAYER	GP	G	A	PTS	SOG	SPCT	PPG	+/–	GOALIE	W	L	T	GAvg
STL	LW	A. McDonald	68	21	21	42	138	15.2	2	19	G. Hall	19	12	8	**2.17**
S. Bowman	LW	B. McCreary	71	13	17	30	130	10.0	3	4	J. Plante	18	12	6	1.96
37–25–14	LW	L. Keenan	47	5	9	14	73	6.8	0	19	T. Ouimet	0	1	0	2.00
	C	R. Berenson	76	35	47	82	288	12.2	7	26	G. Edwards	0	0	0	0.00
	C	C. Henry	64	17	22	39	94	18.1	7	14	R. Irons	0	0	0	0.00
	C	R. Schock	67	12	27	39	157	7.6	4	3					
	C	T. Crisp	57	6	9	15	40	15.0	1	8					
	RW	G. Sabourin	75	25	23	48	228	11.0	3	23					
	RW	St. Marseille	72	12	26	38	169	7.1	3	20					
	RW	T. Ecclestone	68	11	23	34	151	7.3	1	20					
	RW	J. Roberts	72	14	19	33	129	10.9	2	13					
	RW	C. Cameron	72	11	5	16	123	8.9	2	– 8					
	D	B. Plager	61	4	26	30	88	4.5	0	31					
	D	D. Harvey	70	2	20	22	46	4.3	1	11					
	D	N. Picard	67	5	19	24	136	3.7	0	19					
	D	B. Plager	32	0	7	7	46	.0	0	10					
	D	A. Arbour	67	1	6	7	25	4.0	0	20					
CALIF	LW	G. Jarrett	63	22	23	45	201	10.9	3	– 8	G. Smith	21	24	7	2.97
F. Glover	LW	E. Ingarfield	26	8	15	23	60	13.3	3	– 1	C. Worthy	4	6	3	4.12
29–36–11	LW	G. Ubriaco	26	4	7	11	39	10.3	1	– 5	C. Hodge	4	6	1	3.69
	C	T. Hampson	76	26	49	75	189	13.8	9	– 15					
	C	M. Laughton	53	20	23	43	103	19.4	3	0					
	C	B. Perry	61	10	21	31	75	13.3	2	– 6					
	C	J. Szura	70	9	12	21	102	8.8	1	– 5					
	C	B. Dillabough	48	7	12	19	51	13.7	0	– 4					
	RW	N. Ferguson	76	34	20	54	217	15.7	7	– 9					
	RW	B. Hicke	67	25	36	61	171	14.6	5	– 11					
	RW	G. Ehman	70	21	24	45	160	13.1	4	– 13					
	RW	G. Swarbrick	50	3	13	16	121	2.5	1	– 13					
	D	C. Vadnais	76	15	27	42	274	5.5	4	– 18					
	D	D. Roberts	76	1	19	20	114	.9	0	– 13					
	D	B. Marshall	68	3	15	18	118	2.5	0	– 24					
	D	F. Lacombe	72	2	16	18	103	1.9	1	– 10					
	D	G. Odrowski	74	5	1	6	54	9.3	0	4					
PHI	LW	J. Gendron	74	20	35	55	198	10.1	5	– 3	B. Parent	17	23	16	2.69
K. Allen	C	A. Lacroix	75	24	32	56	217	11.1	13	– 12	D. Favell	3	12	5	3.56
20–35–21	RW	D. Sarrazin	54	16	30	46	128	12.5	6	– 7					
	LW	B. Selby	63	10	13	23	116	8.6	1	– 11					
	LW	D. Blackburn	48	7	9	16	94	7.4	0	– 13					
	LW	E. Heiskala	21	3	3	6	38	7.9	0	– 4					
	C	J. Johnson	69	17	27	44	146	11.6	1	– 5					
	C	G. Peters	66	8	6	14	166	4.8	1	– 20					
	C	F. Kennedy	59	8	7	15	64	12.5	0	– 25					
	RW	G. Dornhoefer	60	8	16	24	111	7.2	2	– 20					
	RW	L. Rochefort	65	14	21	35	148	9.5	3	– 7					
	RW	S. Nolet	35	4	10	14	77	5.2	2	– 10					
	D	E. Van Impe	68	7	12	19	118	5.9	1	– 13					
	D	A. Stanley	64	4	13	17	75	5.3	2	– 4					
	D	L. Hale	67	3	16	19	62	4.8	0	– 24					
	D	J. Watson	60	2	8	10	82	2.4	0	– 21					
	D	D. Cherry	71	9	6	15	91	9.9	1	– 11					
LA	LW	T. Irvine	76	15	24	39	206	7.3	0	– 17	G. Desjardins	18	**34**	6	3.26
R. Kelly	C	E. Joyal	73	33	19	52	222	14.9	9	– 30	W. Rutledge	6	7	4	3.65
24–42–10	RW	B. Flett	72	24	25	49	198	12.1	4	– 24	J. Caron	0	1	0	3.86
	LW	J. Peters	76	10	15	25	109	9.2	1	– 10					
	LW	D. Robinson	31	2	10	12	43	4.7	0	– 4					
	C	G. Labossierre	48	10	18	28	97	10.3	2	– 7					
	C	H. Menard	56	10	17	27	94	10.6	1	0					
	C	S. Krake	30	3	9	12	52	5.8	1	– 10					
	RW	H. Hughes	73	16	14	30	161	9.9	5	– 3					
	RW	L. MacDonald	58	14	14	28	181	7.7	1	– 11					
	RW	R. Anderson	56	3	5	8	68	4.4	0	– 9					
	D	B. White	75	5	28	33	163	3.1	0	– 20					
	D	J. Lemieux	75	11	29	40	134	8.2	2	– 22					
	D	B. Wall	71	13	13	26	147	8.8	1	– 6					
	D	D. Rolfe	75	3	19	22	151	2.0	0	– 23					
	D	B. Hughes	42	2	19	21	116	1.7	0	– 16					
	D	L. Cahan	72	3	11	14	129	2.3	0	– 20					

	POS	PLAYER	GP	G	A	PTS	SOG	SPCT	PPG	+/-
PITT R. Sullivan 20–45–11	LW	K. McCreary	70	25	23	48	208	12.0	7	– 23
	C	L. Angotti	71	17	20	37	123	13.8	3	– 21
	RW	K. Schinkel	76	18	34	52	226	8.0	8	– 39
	LW	V. Fonteyne	74	12	17	29	109	11.0	0	– 25
	C	C. Burns	76	13	38	51	133	9.8	1	– 9
	RW	J. Pronovost	76	16	25	41	199	8.0	4	– 4
	LW	G. Ubriaco	49	15	11	26	100	15.0	4	0
	LW	B. Dea	68	10	8	18	111	9.0	2	– 32
	C	W. Boyer	62	10	19	29	127	7.9	2	– 21
	C	E. Ingarfield	40	8	15	23	71	11.3	3	– 17
	C	B. Harris	54	7	13	20	61	11.5	2	– 18
	RW	P. Andrea	25	7	6	13	45	15.6	0	– 10
	D	B. Woytowich	71	9	20	29	127	7.1	1	– 26
	D	N. Price	73	2	18	20	152	1.3	1	– 30
	D	D. McCallum	62	5	13	18	99	5.1	2	– 35
	D	L. Boivin	41	5	13	18	74	6.8	5	– 6
	D	B. Speer	34	1	4	5	43	2.3	0	– 16
MINN W. Blair 3–7–1 J. Muckler 6–22–7 W. Blair 9–14–7	LW	D. Grant	75	34	31	65	189	18.0	11	– 12
	C	C. Larose	67	25	37	62	268	9.3	5	– 10
	RW	D. O'Shea	74	15	34	49	157	9.6	4	– 26
	LW	J. Parise	76	22	27	49	196	11.2	7	– 44
	LW	A. Boudrias	53	4	9	13	87	4.6	1	– 30
	LW	P. MacDonald	35	2	9	11	50	4.0	0	– 14
	C	R. Cullen	67	26	38	64	195	13.3	3	– 27
	C	W. McKechnie	58	5	9	14	81	6.2	1	– 10
	C	B. Collins	75	9	10	19	123	7.3	0	– 26
	RW	B. Goldsworthy	68	14	10	24	196	7.1	4	– 27
	RW	W. Connelly	55	14	16	30	193	7.3	4	– 25
	D	B. McCord	69	4	17	21	85	4.7	1	– 33
	D	L. Nanne	41	2	12	14	71	2.8	1	– 9
	D	E. Vasko	72	1	7	8	52	1.9	0	– 18
	D	W. Hillman	50	0	8	8	44	.0	0	– 25
	D	M. McMahon	43	0	11	11	113	.0	0	– 26
	D	L. Boivin	28	1	6	7	64	1.6	1	– 19

	GOALIE	W	L	T	GAvg
PITT	L. Binkley	10	31	8	3.29
	J. Daley	10	13	3	3.23
	M. Edwards	0	1	0	3.00
MINN	C. Maniago	18	33	10	3.30
	F. Rivard	0	6	4	4.38
	G. Bauman	0	4	1	4.34

GOALS		ASSISTS		POINTS	
B. Hull, CHI	58	P. Esposito, BOS	77	P. Esposito, BOS	126
P. Esposito, BOS	49	S. Mikita, CHI	67	B. Hull, CHI	107
F. Mahovlich, DET	49	G. Howe, DET	59	G. Howe, DET	103
K. Hodge, BOS	45	A. Delvecchio, DET	58	S. Mikita, CHI	97
G. Howe, DET	44			K. Hodge, BOS	90

SHOTS ON GOAL		SHOOTING PCT.		+/-	
B. Hull, CHI	414	J. McKenzie, BOS	23.6	B. Orr, BOS	65
P. Esposito, BOS	351	M. Laughton, LA	19.4	P. Esposito, BOS	56
J. Lemaire, MONT	330	K. Hodge, BOS	19.1	K. Hodge, BOS	49
V. Hadfield, NYR	321	C. Henry, STL	18.1	F. Mahovlich, DET	46
R. Gilbert, NYR	301	K. Wharram, CHI	18.0		

PENALTY MINUTES		GOALS AGAINST AVE.		SHUTOUTS	
F. Kennedy, PHI, TOR	219	G. Hall, STL	2.17	G. Hall, STL	8
J. Dorey, TOR	200	R. Edwards, DET	2.54	E. Giacomin, NYR	7
J. Ferguson, MONT	185	E. Giacomin, NYR	2.55	J. Plante, STL	5
C. Vadnais, CALIF	151	B. Parent, PHI	2.69	R. Edwards, DET	4
D. Awrey, BOS	149	B. Gamble, TOR	2.80	G. Smith, CALIF	4

National Hockey League 1969–70

	W	L	T	PTS	GF	GA	PPG	PPCT	SHG	PPGA	PKPCT	SHGA
EASTERN DIVISION												
CHI	45	22	9	99	250	**170**	55	20.4	7	**32**	**87.1**	7
*BOS	40	17	19	99	**277**	216	**81**	**29.0**	**13**	80	77.8	4
DET	40	21	15	95	246	199	57	21.4	8	57	81.0	3
NYR	38	22	16	92	246	189	52	17.6	7	40	85.2	7
MONT	38	22	16	92	244	201	57	20.3	8	48	81.8	**1**
TOR	29	34	13	71	222	242	49	20.2	5	60	77.7	7
WESTERN DIVISION												
STL	37	27	12	86	224	179	72	25.1	5	41	84.6	9
PITT	26	38	12	64	182	238	53	16.8	2	66	76.6	5
MINN	19	35	22	60	224	257	57	20.8	10	65	77.2	7
OAK	22	40	14	58	169	243	45	13.9	4	49	81.0	12
PHI	17	35	24	58	197	225	46	15.5	7	58	81.4	9
LA	14	52	10	38	168	290	39	14.2	6	67	77.5	11

EASTERN DIVISION

TEAM	POS	PLAYER	GP	G	A	PTS	SOG	SPCT	PPG	+/-	GOALIE	W	L	T	GAvg
CHI	LW	D. Hull	76	17	35	52	223	7.6	5	4	T. Esposito	**38**	17	8	**2.17**
B. Reay	C	S. Mikita	76	39	47	86	352	11.1	7	29	D. DeJordy	3	5	1	2.69
45–22–9	RW	C. Koroll	73	18	19	37	160	11.3	0	15	G. Desjardins	4	0	0	2.00
	LW	B. Hull	61	38	29	67	289	13.1	10	20					
	C	P. Martin	73	30	33	63	160	18.8	5	22					
	RW	J. Pappin	66	28	25	53	158	17.7	9	17					
	LW	G. Pinder	75	19	20	39	169	11.2	5	23					
	LW	J. Wiste	26	0	8	8	11	.0	0	0					
	C	L. Angotti	70	12	26	38	97	12.4	5	2					
	RW	E. Nesterenko	67	16	18	34	124	12.9	3	17					
	RW	C. Maki	75	10	24	34	93	10.8	0	9					
	D	P. Stapleton	49	4	38	42	106	3.8	1	18					
	D	D. Mohns	66	6	27	33	118	5.1	3	29					
	D	K. Magnuson	76	0	24	24	77	.0	0	38					
	D	D. Jarrett	72	4	20	24	134	3.0	1	33					
	D	B. White	21	0	5	5	32	.0	0	3					
	D	G. Marotte	51	5	13	18	101	5.0	0	3					
BOS	LW	W. Cashman	70	9	26	35	104	8.7	0	22	G. Cheevers	24	8	8	2.72
H. Sinden	C	P. Esposito	76	**43**	56	99	405	10.6	**18**	28	E. Johnston	16	9	11	2.98
40–17–19	RW	K. Hodge	72	25	29	54	198	12.6	6	15					
	LW	J. Bucyk	76	31	38	69	190	16.3	14	19					
	C	F. Stanfield	73	23	35	58	254	9.1	13	7					
	RW	J. McKenzie	72	29	41	70	196	14.8	9	20					
	LW	D. Marcotte	35	9	3	12	73	12.3	0	-3					
	C	D. Sanderson	50	18	23	41	179	10.1	5	8					
	C	W. Carleton	42	6	19	25	80	7.5	0	6					
	C	J. Lorentz	68	7	16	23	92	7.6	2	14					
	RW	E. Westfall	72	14	22	36	158	8.9	0	20					
	RW	A. Bailey	58	11	11	22	78	14.1	2	16					
	D	B. Orr	76	33	**87**	**120**	**413**	8.0	11	**54**					
	D	D. Smith	75	7	17	24	160	4.4	1	9					
	D	D. Awrey	73	3	10	13	96	3.1	0	27					
	D	R. Smith	69	2	8	10	94	2.1	0	12					
	D	G. Doak	44	1	7	8	36	2.8	0	7					
DET	LW	F. Mahovlich	74	38	32	70	251	15.1	14	16	R. Edwards	24	15	6	2.59
B. Gadsby	C	A. Delvecchio	73	21	47	68	218	9.6	4	26	R. Crozier	16	6	9	2.65
2–1–0	RW	G. Howe	76	31	40	71	268	11.6	11	23					
S. Abel	LW	N. Libett	76	20	20	40	148	13.5	3	9					
38–20–15	C	G. Unger	76	42	24	66	234	17.9	12	24					
	RW	W. Connelly	76	23	36	59	242	9.5	5	27					
	LW	B. Dea	70	10	3	13	63	15.9	0	3					
	C	P. Stemkowski	76	25	24	49	268	9.3	4	13					
	C	G. Monahan	51	3	4	7	44	6.8	0	-6					
	C	A. Karlander	41	5	10	15	41	12.2	0	8					
	RW	B. MacGregor	73	15	23	38	153	9.8	3	-1					
	RW	R. Harris	72	2	19	21	126	1.6	0	14					
	D	C. Brewer	70	2	37	39	109	1.8	0	44					
	D	G. Bergman	69	6	17	23	146	4.1	1	4					
	D	B. Baun	71	1	18	19	112	.9	0	7					
	D	D. Rolfe	20	2	9	11	62	3.2	0	9					
	D	M. Ravlich	46	0	6	6	25	.0	0	7					
NYR	LW	D. Balon	76	33	37	70	202	16.3	5	40	E. Giacomin	35	21	14	2.36
E. Francis	C	W. Tkaczuk	76	27	50	77	203	13.3	5	26	T. Sawchuk	3	1	2	2.91
38–22–16	RW	B. Fairbairn	76	23	33	56	153	15.0	2	24					
	LW	V. Hadfield	71	20	34	54	268	7.5	4	-3					
	C	J. Ratelle	75	32	42	74	198	16.2	10	8					
	RW	R. Gilbert	72	16	37	53	230	7.0	3	2					
	LW	D. Marshall	57	9	15	24	81	11.1	2	6					
	LW	R. Lemieux	55	4	6	10	49	8.2	0	1					
	C	J. Widing	44	7	7	14	90	7.8	2	2					
	C	O. Kurtenbach	53	4	10	14	89	4.5	1	4					
	RW	B. Nevin	68	18	19	37	126	14.3	3	1					
	RW	R. Stewart	76	14	10	24	109	12.8	1	7					
	D	B. Park	60	11	26	37	161	6.8	6	23					
	D	A. Brown	73	15	21	36	220	6.8	3	28					
	D	J. Neilson	62	3	20	23	204	1.5	0	24					
	D	R. Seiling	76	5	21	26	176	2.8	1	41					
	D	A. Hamilton	59	0	5	5	42	.0	0	-8					

TEAM	POS	PLAYER	GP	G	A	PTS	SOG	SPCT	PPG	+/-	GOALIE	W	L	T	GAvg
MONT	LW	J. Lemaire	69	32	28	60	237	13.5	12	19	R. Vachon	31	18	12	2.63
C. Ruel	C	H. Richard	62	16	36	52	204	7.8	2	24	P. Myre	4	3	2	2.27
38–22–16	RW	Y. Cournoyer	72	27	36	63	233	11.6	10	1	G. Worsley	3	1	2	2.33
	LW	J. Ferguson	48	19	13	32	116	16.4	6	11					
	LW	M. Tardif	18	3	2	5	25	12.0	1	0					
	LW	L. Pleau	20	1	0	1	19	5.3	0	– 1					
	C	J. Beliveau	63	19	30	49	169	11.2	3	1					
	C	R. Backstrom	72	19	24	43	187	10.2	1	4					
	C	P. Mahovlich	36	9	8	17	75	12.0	1	9					
	RW	B. Rousseau	72	24	34	58	228	10.5	5	3					
	RW	M. Redmond	75	27	27	54	279	9.7	4	23					
	RW	C. Provost	65	10	11	21	120	8.3	1	6					
	D	J. Laperriere	73	6	31	37	169	3.6	2	28					
	D	S. Savard	64	12	19	31	151	7.9	5	4					
	D	J. Tremblay	58	2	19	21	77	2.6	1	5					
	D	T. Harper	75	4	18	22	60	6.7	0	27					
TOR	LW	B. Pulford	74	18	19	37	227	7.9	3	– 24	B. Gamble	19	24	9	3.06
J. McLellan	C	D. Keon	72	32	30	62	284	11.3	9	– 15	M. Edwards	10	9	4	3.25
29–34–13	RW	M. Oliver	76	14	33	47	200	7.0	5	– 12	G. McNamara	0	0	0	5.22
	LW	P. Henderson	67	20	22	42	213	9.4	5	14	J. Bower	0	1	0	5.00
	C	N. Ullman	74	18	42	60	207	8.7	5	20					
	RW	R. Ellis	76	35	19	54	227	15.4	6	11					
	LW	B. Selby	74	10	13	23	88	11.4	1	– 5					
	LW	J. Harrison	31	7	10	17	43	16.3	1	2					
	C	M. Walton	58	21	34	55	242	8.7	7	– 11					
	RW	J. McKenny	73	11	33	44	170	6.5	3	– 2					
	RW	G. Armstrong	49	13	15	28	93	14.0	2	9					
	RW	F. Smith	61	4	14	18	73	5.5	0	– 3					
	D	T. Horton	59	3	19	22	116	2.6	1	4					
	D	R. Ley	48	2	13	15	52	3.8	1	– 16					
	D	J. Dorey	46	6	11	17	122	4.9	0	9					
	D	B. Glennie	52	1	14	15	44	2.3	0	– 4					
	D	P. Quinn	59	0	5	5	47	.0	0	– 14					

WESTERN DIVISION

TEAM	POS	PLAYER	GP	G	A	PTS	SOG	SPCT	PPG	+/-	GOALIE	W	L	T	GAvg
STL	LW	A. McDonald	64	25	30	55	170	14.7	11	11	J. Plante	18	9	5	2.19
S. Bowman	C	R. Berenson	67	33	39	72	282	11.7	16	– 3	E. Wakely	12	9	4	2.11
37–27–12	RW	T. Ecclestone	65	16	21	37	166	9.6	5	7	G. Hall	7	8	3	2.91
	LW	L. Keenan	56	10	23	33	113	8.8	3	– 8	G. Edwards	0	1	0	4.00
	LW	B. McCreary	73	15	17	32	174	8.6	2	4					
	C	P. Goyette	72	29	49	78	152	**19.1**	16	3					
	C	A. Boudrias	50	3	14	17	95	3.2	1	7					
	RW	St. Marseille	74	16	43	59	166	9.6	3	– 3					
	RW	G. Sabourin	72	28	14	42	246	11.4	11	– 9					
	RW	J. Roberts	76	13	17	30	165	7.9	2	18					
	RW	R. Anderson	59	9	9	18	107	8.4	1	11					
	D	B. Plager	75	6	26	32	97	6.2	1	2					
	D	B. Plager	64	3	11	14	83	3.6	0	2					
	D	A. Arbour	68	0	3	3	30	.0	0	7					
	D	R. Fortin	57	1	4	5	66	1.5	0	3					
	D	J. Talbot	75	2	15	17	60	3.3	0	18					
PITT	LW	D. Prentice	75	26	25	51	205	12.7	12	– 20	A. Smith	15	20	8	3.03
R. Kelly	C	B. Hextall	66	12	19	31	132	9.1	2	– 22	L. Binkley	10	13	1	3.21
26–38–12	RW	K. Schinkel	72	20	25	45	225	8.9	4	– 26	J. Daley	1	5	3	2.95
	LW	V. Fonteyne	68	11	15	26	73	15.1	3	– 4					
	C	M. Briere	76	12	32	44	223	5.4	4	– 15					
	RW	J. Pronovost	72	20	21	41	222	9.0	5	– 2					
	LW	K. McCreary	60	18	8	26	135	13.3	4	– 6					
	LW	G. Sather	76	12	14	26	127	9.4	2	– 13					
	C	R. Schock	76	8	21	29	160	5.0	4	– 7					
	C	W. Boyer	72	11	12	23	112	9.8	2	– 5					
	RW	N. Harbaruk	74	5	17	22	119	4.2	2	– 7					
	D	B. Woytowich	68	8	25	33	155	5.2	5	– 12					
	D	J. Morrison	59	5	15	20	135	3.7	2	– 20					
	D	D. Rupp	64	2	14	16	105	1.9	1	– 11					
	D	T. Pratt	65	5	7	12	73	6.8	0	– 29					
	D	B. Blackburn	60	4	7	11	49	8.2	0	– 14					
	D	B. Watson	61	1	9	10	61	1.6	0	– 1					

MINN

W. Blair
9–13–10
C. Burns
10–22–12

POS	PLAYER	GP	G	A	PTS	SOG	SPCT	PPG	+/-
LW	J. Parise	74	24	48	72	168	14.3	6	− 3
C	T. Williams	75	15	52	67	165	9.1	2	− 19
RW	B. Goldsworthy	75	36	29	65	230	15.7	11	− 9
LW	D. Grant	76	29	28	57	247	11.7	14	− 13
LW	B. Barlow	70	16	17	33	157	10.2	6	− 3
LW	C. Burns	50	3	13	16	61	4.9	0	− 4
C	D. O'Shea	75	10	24	34	136	7.4	4	− 4
C	R. Cullen	74	17	28	45	143	11.9	3	− 3
C	B. Collins	74	29	9	38	186	15.6	3	4
C	W. McKechnie	20	1	3	4	16	6.3	0	− 5
RW	C. Larose	75	24	23	47	262	9.2	7	− 17
RW	D. Lawson	45	9	8	17	58	15.5	0	− 3
D	L. Nanne	74	3	20	23	96	3.1	1	− 8
D	B. Gibbs	56	3	13	16	100	3.0	0	− 12
D	T. Reid	66	1	7	8	89	1.1	0	− 8
D	L. Boivin	69	3	12	15	95	3.2	0	− 2
D	J. Miszuk	50	0	6	6	34	.0	0	− 3

GOALIE	W	L	T	GAvg
C. Maniago	9	24	16	3.39
F. Rivard	3	5	5	3.15
G. Worsley	5	1	1	2.65
K. Broderick	2	4	0	4.33
G. Gilbert	0	1	0	6.00

OAK

F. Glover
22–40–14

POS	PLAYER	GP	G	A	PTS	SOG	SPCT	PPG	+/-
LW	G. Jarrett	75	12	19	31	229	5.2	2	− 24
LW	G. Ehman	76	11	19	30	156	7.1	3	− 25
LW	B. Perry	34	6	8	14	41	14.6	0	− 3
LW	B. Dillabough	52	5	5	10	45	11.1	1	− 18
C	T. Hampson	76	17	35	52	130	13.1	9	− 17
C	E. Ingarfield	54	21	24	45	130	16.2	9	− 7
C	M. Laughton	76	16	19	35	147	10.9	3	− 28
C	J. Hardy	23	5	4	9	38	13.2	1	− 8
C	H. Menard	38	2	7	9	5	40.0	0	− 5
RW	B. Hicke	69	15	29	44	139	10.8	5	− 10
RW	N. Ferguson	72	11	9	20	125	8.8	2	− 15
RW	D. O'Donoghue	68	5	6	11	55	9.1	0	− 26
D	C. Vadnais	76	24	20	44	245	9.8	6	− 24
D	D. Roberts	76	6	25	31	137	4.4	2	− 37
D	H. Howell	55	4	16	20	147	2.7	3	− 14
D	B. Marshall	72	1	15	16	130	.8	0	− 21
D	D. Mattiussi	65	4	10	14	55	7.3	0	− 21

GOALIE	W	L	T	GAvg
G. Smith	19	**34**	12	3.11
C. Hodge	3	5	2	3.50
C. Worthy	0	1	0	5.00

PHI

V. Stasiuk
17–35–24

POS	PLAYER	GP	G	A	PTS	SOG	SPCT	PPG	+/-
LW	J. Gendron	71	23	21	44	155	14.8	5	8
C	A. Lacroix	74	22	36	58	175	12.6	6	− 6
RW	S. Nolet	56	22	22	44	163	13.5	6	12
LW	J. Johnson	72	18	30	48	168	10.7	2	1
LW	R. Fleming	65	9	18	27	129	7.0	3	− 4
LW	E. Heiskala	65	8	7	15	114	7.0	0	− 15
C	B. Clarke	76	15	31	46	214	7.0	5	1
C	B. Sutherland	51	15	17	32	103	14.6	4	− 2
C	G. Peters	59	6	10	16	102	5.9	1	− 9
RW	G. Dornhoefer	65	26	29	55	146	17.8	4	2
RW	L. Morrison	66	9	10	19	130	6.9	3	− 3
D	L. Hillman	76	5	26	31	252	2.0	2	− 9
D	T. Ball	61	7	18	25	98	7.1	3	− 7
D	J. Watson	54	3	11	14	102	2.9	1	0
D	E. Van Impe	65	0	10	10	81	.0	0	− 1
D	W. Hillman	68	3	5	8	79	3.8	0	1
D	D. Cherry	68	3	4	7	99	3.0	0	− 24

GOALIE	W	L	T	GAvg
B. Parent	13	29	20	2.79
D. Favell	4	5	4	3.15
D. Wilson	0	1	0	3.00

LA

H. Laycoe
5–18–1
J. Wilson
9–34–9

POS	PLAYER	GP	G	A	PTS	SOG	SPCT	PPG	+/-
LW	R. Lonsberry	76	20	22	42	226	8.8	4	− 18
C	E. Joyal	59	18	22	40	173	10.4	6	− 17
RW	B. Flett	69	14	18	32	198	7.1	2	− 27
LW	E. Shack	73	22	12	34	203	10.8	4	− 38
LW	T. Irvine	58	11	13	24	120	9.2	2	− 20
LW	D. Duff	32	5	8	13	37	13.5	0	− 15
LW	M. Corrigan	36	6	4	10	67	9.0	2	− 17
C	B. Goring	59	13	23	36	125	10.4	2	− 15
C	J. Peters	74	15	9	24	118	12.7	2	− 13
C	S. Krake	58	5	17	22	101	5.0	2	− 25
RW	L. Rochefort	76	9	23	32	190	4.7	1	− 30
RW	D. Hextall	28	5	7	12	34	14.7	2	− 23
D	B. White	40	4	11	15	62	6.5	3	− 15
D	B. Wall	70	5	13	18	116	4.3	5	− 26
D	L. Cahan	70	4	8	12	95	4.2	2	− 45
D	D. Rolfe	55	1	9	10	115	.9	0	− 25
D	M. Ravlich	21	3	7	10	19	15.8	0	− 25

GOALIE	W	L	T	GAvg
G. Desjardins	7	29	5	3.89
D. DeJordy	5	11	4	3.24
W. Rutledge	2	12	1	4.25

GOALS

P. Esposito, BOS	43
G. Unger, DET	42
S. Mikita, CHI	39
F. Mahovlich, DET	38
B. Hull, CHI	38

ASSISTS

B. Orr, BOS	87
P. Esposito, BOS	56
T. Williams, MINN	52
W. Tkaczuk, NYR	50
P. Goyette, STL	49

POINTS

B. Orr, BOS	120
P. Esposito, BOS	99
S. Mikita, CHI	86
P. Goyette, STL	78
W. Tkaczuk, NYR	77

SHOTS ON GOAL	
B. Orr, BOS	413
P. Esposito, BOS	405
S. Mikita, CHI	352
B. Hull, CHI	289
D. Keon, TOR	284

SHOOTING PCT.	
P. Goyette, STL	19.1
P. Martin, CHI	18.8
G. Unger, DET	17.9
G. Dornhoefer, PHI	17.8
J. Pappin, CHI	17.7

+/-	
B. Orr, BOS	54
C. Brewer, DET	44
R. Seiling, NYR	41
D. Balon, NYR	40
K. Magnuson, CHI	38

PENALTY MINUTES	
K. Magnuson, CHI	213
J. Ferguson, MONT	139
B. Orr, BOS	125
G. Bergman, DET	122
D. Awrey, BOS	120

GOALS AGAINST AVE.	
T. Esposito, CHI	2.17
E. Giacomin, NYR	2.36
R. Edwards, DET	2.59
R. Vachon, MONT	2.63
G. Cheevers, BOS	2.72

SHUTOUTS	
T. Esposito, CHI	15
E. Giacomin, NYR	6
J. Plante, STL	5
E. Wakely, STL	4
R. Vachon, MONT	4

National Hockey League 1970–71

	W	L	T	PTS	GF	GA	PPG	PPCT	SHG	PPGA	PKPCT	SHGA
EASTERN DIVISION												
BOS	57	14	7	121	**399**	207	**80**	**27.7**	**25**	53	84.2	4
NYR	49	18	11	109	259	**177**	60	25.6	5	**41**	83.8	**3**
*MONT	42	23	13	97	291	216	71	24.8	8	49	**85.6**	6
TOR	37	33	8	82	248	211	53	18.3	14	46	83.7	6
BUF	24	39	15	63	217	291	56	18.8	5	56	81.5	12
VAN	24	46	8	56	229	296	52	16.4	6	81	73.8	12
DET	22	45	11	55	209	308	48	19.6	5	66	76.8	10
WESTERN DIVISION												
CHI	49	20	9	107	277	184	60	20.6	5	47	84.0	6
STL	34	25	19	87	223	208	56	17.9	9	49	82.8	8
PHI	28	33	17	73	207	225	42	15.4	3	50	83.6	8
MINN	28	34	16	72	191	223	38	14.7	6	55	79.5	4
LA	25	40	13	63	239	303	41	15.4	6	53	76.2	10
PITT	21	37	20	62	221	240	56	17.6	5	48	82.6	9
CALIF	20	53	5	45	199	320	39	12.3	3	58	77.2	7

EASTERN DIVISION

	POS	PLAYER	GP	G	A	PTS	SOG	SPCT	PPG	+/-	GOALIE	W	L	T	GAvg
BOS	LW	W. Cashman	77	21	58	79	175	12.0	4	59	G. Cheevers	27	8	5	2.73
T. Johnson	C	P. Esposito	78	**76**	76	**152**	**550**	13.8	**25**	71	E. Johnston	30	6	2	2.53
57–14–7	RW	K. Hodge	78	43	62	105	232	18.5	4	71					
	LW	J. Bucyk	78	51	65	116	225	**22.7**	22	36					
	C	F. Stanfield	75	24	52	76	267	9.0	8	32					
	RW	J. McKenzie	65	31	46	77	151	20.5	11	27					
	LW	D. Marcotte	75	15	13	28	87	17.2	0	20					
	LW	W. Carleton	69	22	24	46	164	13.4	0	35					
	LW	A. Bailey	36	0	6	6	33	.0	0	4					
	C	D. Sanderson	71	29	34	63	217	13.4	1	39					
	C	M. Walton	23	3	5	8	44	6.8	0	11					
	RW	E. Westfall	78	25	34	59	149	16.8	0	58					
	RW	R. Leach	23	2	4	6	30	6.7	0	7					
	D	B. Orr	78	37	**102**	139	392	9.4	5	**124**					
	D	D. Smith	73	7	38	45	159	4.4	0	94					
	D	T. Green	78	5	37	42	103	4.9	0	37					
	D	D. Awrey	74	4	21	25	108	3.7	0	40					
NYR	LW	V. Hadfield	63	22	22	44	194	11.3	8	14	E. Giacomin	27	10	7	2.16
E. Francis	C	J. Ratelle	78	26	46	72	203	12.8	6	28	G. Villemure	22	8	4	2.30
49–18–11	RW	R. Gilbert	78	30	31	61	226	13.3	8	22					
	LW	D. Balon	78	36	24	60	176	20.5	9	14					
	C	W. Tkaczuk	77	26	49	75	212	12.3	5	18					
	RW	B. Fairbairn	56	7	23	30	88	8.0	2	– 4					
	LW	T. Irvine	76	20	18	38	150	13.3	2	18					
	LW	J. Egers	60	7	10	17	88	8.0	3	8					
	C	P. Stemkowski	68	16	29	45	244	6.6	4	16					
	RW	B. Nevin	78	21	25	46	154	13.6	3	17					
	RW	B. MacGregor	27	12	13	25	60	20.0	2	12					
	D	B. Park	68	7	37	44	199	3.5	3	25					
	D	J. Neilson	77	8	24	32	200	4.0	2	31					
	D	R. Seiling	68	5	22	27	137	3.6	0	30					
	D	T. Horton	78	2	18	20	124	1.6	1	28					
	D	R. Stewart	76	5	6	11	52	9.6	0	9					
	D	A. Brown	48	3	12	15	114	2.6	0	0					

TEAM	POS	PLAYER	GP	G	A	PTS	SOG	SPCT	PPG	+/-	GOALIE	W	L	T	GAvg
MONT	LW	F. Mahovlich	38	17	24	41	100	17.0	4	4	R. Vachon	23	12	9	2.65
C. Ruel	LW	M. Tardif	76	19	30	49	144	13.2	4	25	P. Myre	13	11	4	3.11
11–8–4	LW	J. Ferguson	60	16	14	30	117	13.7	3	2	K. Dryden	6	0	0	1.65
A. MacNeil	LW	R. Houle	66	10	9	19	87	11.5	1	7					
31–15–9	LW	P. Roberto	39	14	7	21	88	15.9	2	10					
	C	J. Beliveau	70	25	51	76	172	14.5	7	24					
	C	J. Lemaire	78	28	28	56	252	11.1	6	0					
	C	P. Mahovlich	78	35	26	61	189	18.5	12	25					
	C	H. Richard	75	12	37	49	226	5.3	1	13					
	RW	Y. Cournoyer	65	37	36	73	197	18.8	18	20					
	RW	M. Redmond	40	14	16	30	116	12.1	2	12					
	RW	C. Larose	64	10	13	23	120	8.3	0	– 8					
	RW	L. Rochefort	57	5	10	15	33	15.2	0	11					
	D	J. Tremblay	76	11	52	63	122	9.0	5	16					
	D	G. Lapointe	78	15	29	44	228	6.6	5	28					
	D	T. Harper	78	1	21	22	61	1.6	0	35					
	D	J. Laperriere	49	0	16	16	65	.0	0	24					
TOR	LW	P. Henderson	72	30	30	60	213	14.1	8	14	J. Plante	24	11	4	**1.88**
J. McLellan	C	N. Ullman	73	34	51	85	226	15.0	11	14	B. Gamble	6	14	1	3.87
37–33–8	RW	R. Ellis	78	24	29	53	234	10.3	2	17	B. Parent	7	7	3	2.65
	LW	G. Monahan	78	15	22	37	173	8.7	4	11	M. McLachlan	0	1	0	9.60
	C	D. Keon	76	38	38	76	277	13.7	5	24					
	RW	B. MacMillan	76	22	19	41	156	14.1	3	10					
	LW	B. Spencer	50	9	15	24	61	14.8	3	2					
	C	J. Harrison	78	13	20	33	147	8.8	0	6					
	C	D. Sittler	49	10	8	18	131	7.6	3	3					
	RW	G. Armstrong	59	7	18	25	93	7.5	0	7					
	RW	G. Trottier	61	19	5	24	106	17.9	7	– 12					
	D	J. McKenny	68	4	26	30	131	3.1	2	11					
	D	J. Dorey	74	7	22	29	171	4.1	0	6					
	D	M. Pelyk	73	5	21	26	78	6.4	0	17					
	D	R. Ley	76	4	16	20	78	5.1	0	11					
	D	B. Glennie	54	0	8	8	42	.0	0	– 1					
	D	B. Selwood	28	2	10	12	31	6.5	2	– 7					
BUF	LW	D. Marshall	62	20	29	49	112	17.9	9	– 13	R. Crozier	9	20	7	3.69
P. Imlach	C	P. Goyette	59	15	46	61	119	12.6	9	– 15	J. Daley	12	16	8	3.70
24–39–15	RW	S. Atkinson	57	20	18	38	126	15.9	0	1	D. Dryden	3	3	0	3.37
	LW	E. Shack	56	25	17	42	192	13.0	10	– 29					
	LW	P. Andrea	47	11	21	32	99	11.1	2	– 16					
	LW	L. Keenan	51	7	20	27	67	10.4	3	– 10					
	LW	R. Anderson	74	14	12	26	139	10.1	0	– 11					
	LW	D. Duff	53	7	13	20	67	10.4	0	– 16					
	LW	R. Fleming	78	6	10	16	54	11.1	0	– 8					
	C	G. Perreault	78	38	34	72	210	18.1	14	– 39					
	C	G. Meehan	77	24	31	55	163	14.7	5	– 12					
	C	S. Krake	74	4	5	9	64	6.3	1	– 21					
	RW	F. Smith	77	6	11	17	80	7.5	0	– 12					
	RW	K. O'Shea	41	4	4	8	33	12.1	0	– 11					
	D	A. Hamilton	69	2	28	30	98	2.0	0	– 23					
	D	D. Barrie	75	4	23	27	128	3.1	0	– 19					
	D	J. Watson	78	2	9	11	114	1.8	0	– 28					
VAN	LW	P. Popiel	78	10	22	32	136	7.4	2	9	C. Hodge	15	13	5	3.42
H. Laycoe	C	A. Boudrias	77	25	41	66	254	9.8	7	15	D. Wilson	3	25	2	4.29
24–46–8	RW	R. Paiement	78	34	28	62	249	13.7	4	12	G. Gardner	6	8	1	3.38
	LW	W. Maki	78	25	38	63	184	13.6	8	– 13					
	C	O. Kurtenbach	52	21	32	53	129	16.3	8	– 1					
	RW	M. Hall	77	21	38	59	127	16.5	5	– 16					
	LW	R. Cullen	71	12	21	33	114	10.5	4	– 24					
	LW	D. Johnson	66	15	11	26	76	19.7	1	– 15					
	C	G. Rizzuto	37	3	4	7	33	9.1	1	– 16					
	RW	M. Corrigan	76	21	28	49	164	12.8	5	– 20					
	RW	T. Taylor	56	11	16	27	82	13.4	1	– 9					
	RW	B. Schmautz	26	5	5	10	64	7.8	0	2					
	RW	D. Seguin	25	0	5	5	17	.0	0	– 10					
	D	D. Tallon	78	14	42	56	232	6.0	5	– 25					
	D	B. Wilkins	70	5	18	23	84	6.0	1	– 18					
	D	P. Quinn	76	2	11	13	76	2.6	0	2					
	D	G. Doak	77	2	10	12	60	3.3	0	– 5					

	POS	PLAYER	GP	G	A	PTS	SOG	SPCT	PPG	+/-	GOALIE	W	L	T	GAvg
DET	LW	F. Mahovlich	35	14	18	32	104	13.5	6	3	R. Edwards	11	19	7	3.39
	C	A. Delvecchio	77	21	34	55	171	12.3	6	– 18	J. Rutherford	7	15	3	3.77
N. Harkness	RW	G. Howe	63	23	29	52	195	11.8	7	– 2	D. McLeod	3	7	0	5.16
9–7–3	LW	N. Libett	78	16	13	29	156	10.3	2	– 38	G. Gray	1	4	1	4.74
D. Barkley	LW	G. Charron	24	8	4	12	55	14.5	2	0					
13–38–8	C	G. Unger	51	13	14	27	157	8.3	0	– 32					
	C	D. Luce	58	3	11	14	71	4.2	0	– 6					
	C	B. Collins	36	5	16	21	105	4.8	1	– 1					
	C	R. Berenson	24	5	12	17	51	9.8	1	– 7					
	RW	T. Webster	78	30	37	67	183	16.4	7	– 47					
	RW	R. Leclerc	44	8	8	16	56	14.3	3	– 3					
	D	G. Bergman	68	8	25	33	168	4.8	0	– 28					
	D	D. Rolfe	44	3	9	12	90	3.3	0	– 13					
	D	R. Harris	42	2	8	10	84	2.4	1	– 29					
	D	M. Robitaille	23	4	8	12	37	10.8	2	– 14					
	D	A. Brown	27	2	6	8	57	3.5	0	– 17					
	D	G. Hart	64	2	7	9	62	3.2	1	– 3					

WESTERN DIVISION

	POS	PLAYER	GP	G	A	PTS	SOG	SPCT	PPG	+/-	GOALIE	W	L	T	GAvg
CHI	LW	B. Hull	78	44	52	96	378	11.6	11	34	T. Esposito	**35**	14	6	2.27
	C	P. Martin	62	22	33	55	126	17.5	6	18	G. Desjardins	12	6	3	2.42
B. Reay	RW	C. Maki	72	22	26	48	110	20.0	2	31	G. Meloche	2	0	0	3.00
49–20–9	LW	D. Hull	78	40	26	66	229	17.5	10	28	K. Brown	0	0	0	3.33
	C	S. Mikita	74	24	48	72	220	10.9	7	21					
	RW	C. Koroll	72	16	34	50	124	12.9	4	28					
	LW	G. Pinder	74	13	18	31	102	12.7	1	– 2					
	LW	D. Maloney	74	12	14	26	98	12.2	2	7					
	C	B. Campbell	78	17	37	54	155	11.0	3	26					
	C	L. Angotti	65	9	16	25	83	10.8	1	17					
	RW	J. Pappin	58	22	23	45	113	19.5	7	9					
	D	P. Stapleton	76	7	44	51	130	5.4	4	49					
	D	B. White	67	4	21	25	127	3.1	0	51					
	D	K. Magnuson	76	3	20	23	66	4.5	0	32					
	D	D. Jarrett	51	1	12	13	75	1.3	0	10					
	D	J. Korab	46	4	14	18	97	4.1	1	14					
	D	P. Shmyr	58	1	12	13	35	2.9	0	3					
STL	LW	C. Bordeleau	78	21	32	53	187	11.2	3	14	E. Wakely	20	14	11	2.79
	C	R. Berenson	45	16	26	42	174	9.2	6	– 7	G. Hall	13	11	8	2.42
A. Arbour	RW	T. Ecclestone	47	15	24	39	143	10.5	6	– 7	M. Plasse	1	0	0	3.00
21–15–14	LW	B. Sutherland	68	19	20	39	106	17.9	11	13					
S. Bowman	C	St. Marseille	77	19	32	51	217	8.8	3	14					
13–10–5	RW	G. Sabourin	59	14	17	31	160	8.8	2	4					
	LW	G. Morrison	73	15	10	25	122	12.3	3	– 2					
	LW	B. McCreary	68	9	10	19	90	10.0	0	7					
	LW	B. Selby	53	1	4	5	33	3.0	0	– 10					
	C	J. Lorentz	76	19	21	40	160	11.9	6	2					
	C	G. Unger	28	15	14	29	122	12.3	7	– 4					
	C	T. Crisp	54	5	11	16	47	10.6	0	3					
	RW	C. Cameron	78	14	6	20	86	16.3	0	– 11					
	D	B. Plager	69	4	20	24	87	4.6	1	11					
	D	J. Roberts	72	13	18	31	123	10.6	2	7					
	D	B. Plager	70	1	19	20	70	1.4	0	9					
	D	N. Picard	75	3	8	11	128	2.3	0	2					
PHI	LW	B. Kelly	76	14	18	32	173	8.1	1	7	D. Favell	16	15	9	2.66
	C	B. Clarke	77	27	36	63	185	14.6	10	9	B. Parent	9	12	6	2.76
V. Stasiuk	RW	S. Nolet	74	9	19	28	168	5.4	4	– 1	B. Gamble	3	6	2	3.36
28–33–17	LW	S. Bernier	77	23	28	51	205	11.2	2	– 7					
	C	J. Johnson	66	16	29	45	121	13.2	2	– 10					
	RW	G. Dornhoefer	57	20	20	40	96	20.8	5	3					
	LW	J. Gendron	76	20	16	36	145	13.8	5	– 9					
	LW	E. Heiskala	41	2	1	3	39	5.1	0	– 9					
	C	A. Lacroix	78	20	22	42	180	11.1	9	– 9					
	C	G. Peters	73	6	7	13	135	4.4	0	– 14					
	RW	B. Lesuk	78	17	19	36	149	11.4	2	– 5					
	D	B. Ashbee	64	4	23	27	93	4.3	2	3					
	D	L. Hillman	73	3	13	16	177	1.7	0	9					
	D	E. Van Impe	77	0	11	11	70	.0	0	– 13					
	D	W. Hillman	69	5	7	12	71	7.0	0	12					
	D	J. Watson	57	3	7	10	61	4.9	0	9					
	D	L. Morrison	78	5	7	12	129	3.9	0	– 12					

TEAM	POS	PLAYER	GP	G	A	PTS	SOG	SPCT	PPG	+/–	GOALIE	W	L	T	GAvg
MINN	LW	D. Grant	78	34	23	57	283	12.0	12	7	C. Maniago	19	15	6	2.70
J. Gordon	C	J. Drouin	75	16	52	68	208	7.7	4	5	G. Worsley	4	10	8	2.50
28–34–16	RW	B. Goldsworthy	77	34	31	65	295	11.5	5	– 13	G. Gilbert	5	9	2	3.80
	LW	J. Parise	73	11	23	34	191	5.8	1	– 15					
	LW	C. Burns	76	9	19	28	110	8.2	0	0					
	C	M. Oliver	61	9	23	32	115	7.8	3	0					
	C	D. O'Shea	59	14	12	26	155	9.0	0	– 3					
	C	W. McKechnie	30	3	1	4	39	7.7	0	– 7					
	C	G. Labossierre	29	8	4	12	45	17.8	0	– 3					
	RW	B. Rousseau	63	4	20	24	122	3.3	0	3					
	RW	T. Williams	41	10	13	23	61	16.4	3	– 5					
	RW	F. Harvey	59	12	8	20	154	7.8	4	– 13					
	D	B. Gibbs	63	5	15	20	116	4.3	3	– 10					
	D	T. Reid	73	3	14	17	111	2.7	0	– 6					
	D	F. Barrett	57	0	13	13	75	.0	0	2					
	D	L. Nanne	68	5	11	16	61	8.2	0	– 6					
	D	T. Harris	78	2	13	15	90	2.2	1	0					
LA	LW	B. Berry	77	25	38	63	149	16.8	4	– 5	D. DeJordy	18	29	11	3.80
L. Regan	C	J. Widing	78	25	40	65	202	12.4	5	– 11	J. Norris	7	11	2	3.91
25–40–13	RW	M. Byers	72	27	18	45	179	15.1	4	– 5					
	LW	R. Lonsberry	76	25	28	53	238	10.5	5	– 35					
	LW	B. Pulford	59	17	26	43	170	10.0	6	– 15					
	LW	D. Robinson	61	15	13	28	85	17.6	3	– 8					
	C	E. Joyal	68	20	21	41	168	11.9	3	– 10					
	C	R. Backstrom	33	14	13	27	108	13.0	2	– 7					
	C	G. Labossierre	45	11	10	21	88	12.5	1	– 22					
	RW	B. Flett	64	13	24	37	182	7.1	5	– 30					
	RW	L. Mickey	65	6	12	18	101	5.9	0	– 15					
	RW	L. Grenier	68	9	7	16	63	14.3	1	– 1					
	D	G. Marotte	78	6	27	33	218	2.8	0	– 9					
	D	N. Price	62	1	19	20	88	1.1	0	– 15					
	D	M. Ravlich	66	3	16	19	57	5.3	0	– 14					
	D	D. Hoganson	70	4	10	14	72	5.6	0	– 16					
	D	L. Cahan	67	3	11	14	113	2.7	1	– 29					
PITT	LW	K. McCreary	59	21	12	33	116	18.1	3	7	A. Smith	9	22	9	3.11
R. Kelly	C	S. Apps	31	9	16	25	75	12.0	4	3	L. Binkley	11	11	10	2.86
21–37–20	RW	J. Pronovost	78	21	24	45	225	9.3	4	8	C. Newton	1	3	1	3.42
	LW	D. Prentice	69	21	17	38	135	15.6	7	– 8	P. Hoganson	0	1	0	7.37
	C	B. Hextall	76	16	32	48	181	8.8	6	– 23					
	RW	A. Bathgate	76	15	29	44	209	7.2	7	– 11					
	LW	G. Polis	61	18	15	33	157	11.5	5	– 6					
	LW	V. Fonteyne	70	4	9	13	59	6.8	1	– 8					
	LW	B. Blackburn	64	4	5	9	87	4.6	0	0					
	C	W. Boyer	68	11	30	41	111	9.9	4	10					
	C	R. Schock	71	14	26	40	148	9.5	2	2					
	RW	K. Schinkel	50	15	19	34	120	12.5	3	– 19					
	RW	N. Harbaruk	78	13	12	25	147	8.8	2	– 9					
	D	D. Rupp	59	5	28	33	152	3.3	1	– 10					
	D	D. McCallum	77	9	20	29	104	8.7	1	– 13					
	D	B. Woytowich	78	4	22	26	149	2.7	2	8					
	D	J. Morrison	73	0	10	10	134	.0	0	– 12					
CALIF	LW	E. Hicke	78	22	25	47	202	10.9	7	– 36	G. Smith	19	**48**	4	3.86
F. Glover	LW	G. Croteau	74	15	28	43	182	8.2	2	– 22	C. Worthy	1	3	1	4.88
20–53–5	LW	G. Jarrett	74	15	19	34	169	8.9	2	– 27	B. Sneddon	0	2	0	5.60
	LW	E. Ingarfield	49	5	8	13	76	6.6	0	– 8					
	C	D. Hextall	78	21	31	52	153	13.7	1	– 20					
	C	T. Hampson	60	10	20	30	124	8.1	1	– 21					
	C	N. Ferguson	77	14	20	34	94	14.9	4	– 5					
	C	J. Hardy	40	4	10	14	43	9.3	1	– 14					
	RW	B. Hicke	74	18	17	35	138	13.0	4	– 29					
	RW	D. O'Donoghue	43	11	9	20	63	17.5	3	– 20					
	RW	T. Featherstone	67	8	8	16	90	8.9	1	– 4					
	RW	D. Roberts	78	4	13	17	128	3.1	1	– 56					
	D	R. Stackhouse	78	8	24	32	135	5.9	3	– 28					
	D	C. Vadnais	42	10	16	26	146	6.8	3	– 3					
	D	J. Muloin	67	0	14	14	68	.0	0	– 34					
	D	D. Mattiussi	67	3	8	11	72	4.2	1	– 34					

GOALS		ASSISTS		POINTS	
P. Esposito, BOS	76	B. Orr, BOS	102	P. Esposito, BOS	152
J. Bucyk, BOS	51	P. Esposito, BOS	76	B. Orr, BOS	139
B. Hull, CHI	44	J. Bucyk, BOS	65	J. Bucyk, BOS	116
K. Hodge, BOS	43	K. Hodge, BOS	62	K. Hodge, BOS	105
D. Hull, CHI	40	W. Cashman, BOS	58	B. Hull, CHI	96

SHOTS ON GOAL	
P. Esposito, BOS	550
B. Orr, BOS	392
B. Hull, CHI	378
B. Goldsworthy, MINN	295
D. Grant, MINN	283

SHOOTING PCT.	
J. Bucyk, BOS	22.7
G. Dornhoefer, PHI	20.8
J. McKenzie, BOS	20.5
D. Balon, NYR	20.5
C. Maki, CHI	20.0

+/-	
B. Orr, BOS	124
D. Smith, BOS	94
P. Esposito, BOS	71
K. Hodge, BOS	71
W. Cashman, BOS	59

PENALTY MINUTES	
K. Magnuson, CHI	291
D. Hextall, CALIF	217
J. Dorey, TOR	198
P. Mahovlich, MONT	181
T. Pratt, BUF	179

GOALS AGAINST AVE.	
J. Plante, TOR	1.88
E. Giacomin, NYR	2.16
T. Esposito, CHI	2.27
E. Johnston, BOS	2.53
R. Vachon, MONT	2.65

SHUTOUTS	
E. Giacomin, NYR	8
T. Esposito, CHI	6
C. Maniago, MINN	5
J. Plante, TOR	4
E. Johnston, BOS	4

National Hockey League 1971–72

	W	L	T	PTS	GF	GA	PPG	PPCT	SHG	PPGA	PKPCT	SHGA
EASTERN DIVISION												
*BOS	54	13	11	119	**330**	204	**74**	**28.9**	**18**	51	82.4	**2**
NYR	48	17	13	109	317	192	60	23.3	14	44	84.4	10
MONT	46	16	16	108	307	205	72	27.1	14	41	83.3	4
TOR	33	31	14	80	209	208	48	19.0	4	60	77.4	7
DET	33	35	10	76	261	262	58	20.7	6	45	82.6	9
BUF	16	43	19	51	203	289	57	18.5	1	56	80.1	7
VAN	20	50	8	48	203	287	48	18.4	4	72	76.8	9
WESTERN DIVISION												
CHI	46	17	15	107	166	**166**	43	16.9	7	**35**	**85.4**	10
MINN	37	29	12	86	191	191	53	20.2	4	49	82.3	6
STL	28	39	11	67	247	247	29	14.1	13	65	76.8	11
PHI	26	38	14	66	200	236	52	19.4	6	53	83.6	10
PITT	26	38	14	66	220	258	46	16.1	5	55	77.6	7
CALIF	21	39	18	60	216	288	44	15.8	5	55	78.8	6
LA	20	49	9	49	206	305	38	14.0	4	50	76.2	7

EASTERN DIVISION

	POS	PLAYER	GP	G	A	PTS	SOG	SPCT	PPG	+/-	GOALIE	W	L	T	GAvg
BOS	LW	W. Cashman	74	23	29	52	150	15.3	1	42	G. Cheevers	27	5	8	2.50
T. Johnson	C	P. Esposito	76	**66**	67	**133**	**426**	15.5	**28**	55	E. Johnston	27	8	3	2.71
54–13–11	RW	K. Hodge	60	16	40	56	140	11.4	0	41					
	LW	J. Bucyk	78	32	51	83	174	18.4	13	16					
	C	F. Stanfield	78	23	56	79	168	13.7	5	20					
	RW	J. McKenzie	77	22	47	69	133	16.5	10	19					
	LW	A. Bailey	73	9	13	22	64	14.1	0	11					
	LW	D. Marcotte	47	6	4	10	51	11.8	0	0					
	C	D. Sanderson	78	25	33	58	198	12.6	0	25					
	C	M. Walton	76	28	28	56	236	11.9	6	23					
	RW	E. Westfall	78	18	26	44	123	14.6	0	29					
	RW	R. Leach	56	7	13	20	66	10.6	0	5					
	D	B. Orr	76	37	**80**	117	353	10.5	11	**86**					
	D	D. Smith	78	8	22	30	102	7.8	0	34					
	D	T. Green	54	1	16	17	41	2.4	0	10					
	D	R. Smith	61	2	12	14	81	2.5	0	53					
	D	D. Awrey	34	1	8	9	53	1.9	0	20					
NYR	LW	V. Hadfield	78	50	56	106	242	20.7	23	60	E. Giacomin	24	10	9	2.70
E. Francis	C	J. Ratelle	63	46	63	109	183	**25.1**	5	61	G. Villemure	24	7	4	2.09
48–17–13	RW	R. Gilbert	73	43	54	97	238	18.1	6	51					
	LW	G. Carr	59	8	8	16	74	10.8	1	16					
	C	W. Tkaczuk	76	24	42	66	231	10.4	3	34					
	RW	B. Fairbairn	78	22	36	58	139	15.8	2	36					
	LW	T. Irvine	78	15	21	36	164	9.1	0	8					
	LW	G. Sather	76	5	9	14	52	9.6	0	−2					
	LW	P. Jarry	34	3	3	6	32	9.4	0	2					
	C	P. Stemkowski	59	11	17	28	159	6.9	1	2					
	C	B. Rousseau	78	21	36	57	180	11.7	4	8					
	RW	B. MacGregor	75	19	21	40	137	13.9	1	23					
	D	B. Park	75	24	49	73	263	9.1	8	62					
	D	R. Seiling	78	5	36	41	168	3.0	0	53					
	D	J. Neilson	78	7	30	37	183	3.8	2	38					
	D	D. Rolfe	68	2	14	16	166	1.2	0	41					
	D	A. DeMarco	48	4	7	11	95	4.2	1	18					

	POS	PLAYER	GP	G	A	PTS	SOG	SPCT	PPG	+/-	GOALIE	W	L	T	GAvg
MONT	LW	F. Mahovlich	76	43	53	96	261	16.5	14	42	K. Dryden	**39**	8	15	2.24
S. Bowman	C	J. Lemaire	77	32	49	81	266	12.0	8	37	P. Myre	4	5	0	3.64
46–16–16	RW	Y. Cournoyer	73	47	36	83	208	22.6	18	23	D. DeJordy	3	2	1	4.52
	LW	M. Tardif	75	31	22	53	203	15.3	9	15	R. Vachon	0	1	0	12.00
	C	P. Mahovlich	75	35	32	67	207	16.9	7	16					
	RW	G. Lafleur	73	29	35	64	187	15.5	5	27					
	LW	R. Houle	77	11	17	28	145	7.6	1	9					
	LW	L. Pleau	55	7	10	17	67	10.4	0	4					
	LW	P. Roberto	27	3	2	5	35	8.6	0	3					
	C	H. Richard	75	12	32	44	175	6.9	0	10					
	RW	C. Larose	76	20	18	38	169	11.8	1	9					
	D	J. Tremblay	76	6	51	57	130	4.6	3	52					
	D	G. Lapointe	69	11	38	49	227	4.8	4	15					
	D	J. Laperriere	73	3	25	28	97	3.1	2	36					
	D	P. Bouchard	60	3	5	8	42	7.1	0	10					
	D	T. Harper	52	2	12	14	39	5.1	0	9					
	D	J. Roberts	51	7	15	22	69	10.1	0	3					
TOR	LW	P. Henderson	73	38	20	58	191	19.9	12	14	B. Parent	17	18	9	2.56
J. McLellan	LW	D. Dupere	77	7	10	17	55	12.7	1	5	J. Plante	16	13	5	2.63
24–28–11	LW	D. Marshall	50	2	14	16	48	4.2	1	2					
K. Clancy	C	N. Ullman	77	23	50	73	204	11.3	9	8					
9–3–3	C	D. Keon	72	18	30	48	265	6.8	2	1					
	C	J. Harrison	66	19	17	36	149	12.8	5	–4					
	C	D. Sittler	74	15	17	32	174	8.6	1	–4					
	C	G. Monahan	78	14	17	31	186	7.5	2	2					
	RW	R. Ellis	78	23	24	47	191	12.0	4	7					
	RW	G. Trottier	52	9	12	21	81	11.1	2	–12					
	RW	B. MacMillan	61	10	7	17	95	10.5	2	–1					
	D	J. McKenny	76	5	31	36	156	3.2	2	1					
	D	J. Dorey	50	4	19	23	104	3.8	1	10					
	D	B. Selwood	72	4	17	21	109	3.7	2	7					
	D	R. Ley	67	1	14	15	65	1.5	0	3					
	D	B. Baun	74	2	12	14	158	1.3	0	8					
	D	B. Glennie	61	2	8	10	80	2.5	0	11					
DET	LW	N. Libett	77	31	22	53	219	14.2	6	7	A. Smith	18	20	4	3.24
D. Barkley	C	M. Dionne	78	28	49	77	268	10.4	7	0	J. Daley	11	10	5	3.15
3–8–0	RW	B. Collins	71	15	25	40	157	9.6	2	3	A. Brown	4	5	1	3.96
J. Wilson	LW	A. Karlander	71	15	20	35	93	16.1	0	14					
30–27–10	C	A. Delvecchio	75	20	45	65	123	16.3	9	–19					
	RW	M. Redmond	78	42	28	70	271	15.5	10	–13					
	LW	G. Charron	64	9	16	25	119	7.6	0	–8					
	LW	D. Johnson	43	2	5	7	28	7.1	0	–2					
	LW	B. Wall	45	2	4	6	31	6.5	2	–7					
	C	R. Berenson	78	28	41	69	218	12.8	5	–8					
	RW	T. Ecclestone	72	18	35	53	189	9.5	10	–21					
	RW	L. Rochefort	64	17	12	29	97	17.5	0	1					
	RW	D. Volmar	39	9	5	14	43	20.9	3	0					
	D	G. Bergman	75	6	32	38	141	4.3	1	7					
	D	R. Stackhouse	73	5	25	30	117	4.3	1	–8					
	D	A. Brown	77	2	23	25	107	1.9	0	–12					
	D	L. Johnston	65	4	20	24	59	6.7	0	20					
BUF	LW	R. Martin	73	44	30	74	266	16.5	19	–38	R. Crozier	13	**34**	14	3.51
P. Imlach	C	G. Perreault	76	26	48	74	218	11.9	11	–40	D. Dryden	3	9	5	3.98
8–23–10	RW	S. Atkinson	67	14	10	24	122	11.5	3	–22					
F. Smith	LW	G. Meehan	77	19	27	46	164	11.6	4	–28					
0–1–0	LW	E. Shack	50	11	14	25	92	12.0	4	–11					
J. Crozier	LW	C. Ramsay	57	6	10	16	43	14.0	0	5					
8–19–9	C	J. Lorentz	33	10	14	24	85	11.8	2	–11					
	C	P. Goyette	37	3	21	24	33	9.1	3	–10					
	C	D. Luce	78	11	8	19	126	8.7	0	–18					
	RW	D. Lawson	78	10	6	16	176	5.7	0	–23					
	RW	M. Byers	46	9	7	16	69	13.0	3	–20					
	RW	K. O'Shea	52	6	9	15	56	10.7	0	–19					
	D	A. Hamilton	76	4	30	34	91	4.4	1	–12					
	D	C. Evans	61	6	18	24	99	6.1	2	–20					
	D	J. Watson	66	2	6	8	78	2.6	1	–33					
	D	L. Hillman	43	1	11	12	78	1.3	0	–21					
	D	T. Pratt	27	0	10	10	31	.0	0	0					

TEAM	POS	PLAYER	GP	G	A	PTS	SOG	SPCT	PPG	+/–	GOALIE	W	L	T	GAvg
VAN	LW	W. Maki	76	22	25	47	160	13.8	5	–4	D. Wilson	16	30	3	3.62
H. Laycoe	LW	D. Balon	59	19	19	38	103	18.4	6	–15	G. Gardner	3	14	3	4.17
20–50–8	C	A. Boudrias	78	27	34	61	224	12.1	6	–34	E. Dyck	1	6	2	3.66
	C	O. Kurtenbach	78	24	37	61	160	15.0	5	–2					
	C	R. Paiement	69	10	9	19	177	5.6	1	–37					
	C	R. Ward	71	2	4	6	45	4.4	0	–2					
	RW	B. Schmautz	60	12	13	25	137	8.8	1	–10					
	RW	W. Connelly	53	14	20	34	151	9.3	6	–15					
	RW	T. Taylor	69	9	13	22	82	11.0	0	–20					
	RW	M. Hall	32	6	6	12	46	13.0	1	–12					
	RW	M. Corrigan	19	3	4	7	42	7.1	1	–8					
	D	J. Guevremont	75	13	38	51	210	6.2	3	–28					
	D	D. Tallon	69	17	27	44	240	7.1	11	–24					
	D	D. Kearns	73	3	26	29	103	2.9	2	–27					
	D	J. Schella	77	2	13	15	107	1.9	0	–29					
	D	B. Wilkins	45	2	5	7	50	4.0	0	–9					

WESTERN DIVISION

TEAM	POS	PLAYER	GP	G	A	PTS	SOG	SPCT	PPG	+/–	GOALIE	W	L	T	GAvg
CHI	LW	B. Hull	78	50	43	93	336	14.9	8	54	T. Esposito	31	10	6	**1.77**
B. Reay	C	P. Martin	78	24	51	75	170	14.1	5	44	G. Smith	14	5	6	2.42
46–17–15	RW	J. Pappin	64	27	21	48	145	18.6	1	3	G. Desjardins	1	2	3	3.50
	LW	D. Hull	78	30	39	69	270	11.1	8	12					
	C	S. Mikita	74	26	39	65	185	14.1	5	16					
	RW	C. Koroll	76	22	23	45	136	16.2	4	20					
	LW	C. Bordeleau	25	6	8	14	35	17.1	1	5					
	C	L. Angotti	65	5	10	15	58	8.6	0	0					
	C	B. Campbell	75	5	13	18	87	5.7	0	2					
	C	D. O'Shea	48	6	9	15	63	9.5	0	0					
	RW	C. Maki	61	13	34	47	136	9.6	3	44					
	RW	E. Nesterenko	38	4	8	12	25	16.0	1	7					
	D	B. White	76	7	22	29	122	5.7	0	42					
	D	P. Stapleton	78	3	38	41	133	2.3	2	41					
	D	K. Magnuson	74	2	19	21	83	2.4	0	52					
	D	D. Jarrett	78	6	23	29	123	4.9	2	39					
	D	J. Korab	73	9	5	14	97	9.3	2	1					
MINN	LW	D. Grant	78	18	25	43	212	8.5	6	0	C. Maniago	20	17	4	2.65
J. Gordon	C	J. Drouin	63	13	43	56	213	6.1	3	4	G. Worsley	16	10	7	2.12
37–29–12	RW	B. Goldsworthy	78	31	31	62	295	10.5	6	11	G. Gilbert	1	2	1	3.03
	LW	D. Prentice	71	20	27	47	207	9.7	7	4					
	C	M. Oliver	78	27	29	56	191	14.1	7	9					
	RW	L. Nanne	78	21	28	49	154	13.6	7	–5					
	LW	J. Parise	71	19	18	37	182	10.4	6	10					
	LW	C. Burns	77	11	14	25	88	12.5	0	5					
	C	T. Hampson	78	5	14	19	100	5.0	0	–1					
	C	D. Hextall	36	6	10	16	46	13.0	3	1					
	RW	B. Nevin	72	15	19	34	96	15.6	2	7					
	RW	C. Cameron	64	2	1	3	32	6.3	0	–1					
	D	D. Mohns	78	6	30	36	143	4.2	4	6					
	D	B. Gibbs	75	4	20	24	160	2.5	1	4					
	D	T. Reid	78	6	15	21	111	5.4	1	13					
	D	T. Harris	78	2	15	17	89	2.2	0	0					
STL	LW	J. Egers	63	21	25	46	210	10.0	5	5	E. Wakely	8	18	2	3.42
S. Abel	C	G. Unger	78	36	34	70	321	11.2	14	–8	J. Caron	14	8	5	2.52
3–6–1	RW	M. Murphy	63	20	23	43	172	11.6	5	–4	J. McLeod	6	6	4	3.00
B. McCreary	LW	P. Roberto	49	12	13	25	170	7.1	0	–1	P. McDuffe	0	6	0	3.73
6–14–4	LW	G. Morrison	42	2	11	13	34	5.9	2	–11	W. Stephenson	0	1	0	5.40
A. Arbour	LW	W. Connelly	15	5	5	10	48	10.4	2	–6					
19–19–6	C	St. Marseille	78	16	36	52	228	7.0	1	5					
	C	T. Crisp	75	13	18	31	94	13.8	1	7					
	C	C. Bordeleau	41	8	9	17	123	6.5	1	–13					
	C	D. Lemieux	42	7	9	16	82	8.5	0	–13					
	C	B. Lavender	46	5	11	16	68	7.4	0	–2					
	RW	G. Sabourin	77	28	17	45	236	11.9	4	3					
	RW	D. O'Shea	20	3	3	6	25	12.0	0	–4					
	D	B. Plager	78	7	22	29	128	5.5	1	6					
	D	C. Brewer	42	2	16	18	58	3.4	0	–6					
	D	A. Dupont	60	3	10	13	133	2.3	0	11					
	D	B. Plager	65	1	11	12	63	1.6	0	–15					

TEAM	POS	PLAYER	GP	G	A	PTS	SOG	SPCT	PPG	+/–	GOALIE	W	L	T	GAvg
PHI	LW	B. Kelly	78	14	15	29	117	12.0	0	16	D. Favell	18	25	9	2.81
F. Shero	C	B. Clarke	78	35	46	81	225	15.6	11	22	B. Gamble	7	8	2	2.93
26–38–14	RW	G. Dornhoefer	75	17	32	49	168	10.1	2	– 15	B. Taylor	1	2	2	3.00
	LW	J. Gendron	56	6	13	19	95	6.3	2	– 2	D. McLeod	0	3	1	4.64
	LW	R. Lonsberry	32	7	7	14	88	8.0	0	– 9					
	LW	M. Parizeau	38	2	12	14	37	5.4	1	– 6					
	C	S. Bernier	44	12	11	23	120	10.0	5	– 20					
	C	B. Clement	49	9	14	23	94	9.6	0	– 14					
	C	J. Johnson	46	13	15	28	86	15.1	5	– 21					
	RW	S. Nolet	67	23	20	43	202	11.4	6	6					
	RW	B. Flett	31	11	10	21	116	9.5	3	5					
	RW	B. Lesuk	45	7	6	13	116	6.0	2	– 14					
	D	R. Foley	58	11	25	36	124	8.9	5	– 16					
	D	B. Hughes	63	2	20	22	93	2.2	0	6					
	D	B. Ashbee	73	6	14	20	104	5.8	2	2					
	D	J. Watson	65	3	7	10	110	2.7	0	– 17					
	D	E. Van Impe	73	4	9	13	110	3.6	0	– 8					
PITT	LW	V. Fonteyne	68	6	13	19	35	17.1	1	– 1	J. Rutherford	17	15	5	3.22
R. Kelly	C	S. Apps	72	15	44	59	164	9.1	3	18	L. Binkley	7	15	5	3.51
26–38–14	RW	J. Pronovost	68	30	23	53	214	14.0	3	15	R. Edwards	2	8	4	2.55
	LW	G. Polis	76	30	19	49	208	14.4	8	– 4					
	C	R. Schock	77	17	29	46	151	11.3	3	– 10					
	RW	K. Schinkel	74	15	30	45	154	9.7	1	– 10					
	LW	K. McCreary	33	4	4	8	68	5.9	0	– 10					
	C	B. Hextall	78	20	24	44	145	13.8	5	– 26					
	C	B. Leiter	78	14	17	31	147	9.5	5	– 25					
	RW	N. Harbaruk	78	12	17	29	140	8.6	3	– 13					
	RW	R. Robert	49	7	11	18	72	9.7	3	– 11					
	RW	A. McDonough	37	7	11	18	114	6.1	1	– 6					
	D	D. Edestrand	77	10	23	33	156	6.4	2	– 12					
	D	D. Rupp	34	4	18	22	91	4.4	0	0					
	D	D. Burrows	77	2	10	12	100	2.0	0	– 7					
	D	T. Horton	44	2	9	11	84	2.4	0	5					
	D	B. Watson	75	3	18	21	106	2.8	0	5					
CALIF	LW	G. Pinder	74	23	31	54	140	16.4	7	– 18	G. Meloche	16	25	13	3.33
F. Glover	LW	J. Johnston	77	15	18	33	154	9.7	0	– 28	G. Kurt	1	7	5	4.30
0–1–2	LW	S. Gilbertson	78	16	16	32	141	11.3	3	– 6	L. Carter	4	7	0	4.16
V. Stasiuk	LW	G. Jarrett	55	5	10	15	64	7.8	2	0					
21–38–16	C	B. Sheehan	78	20	26	46	170	11.8	2	– 17					
	C	I. Boldirev	57	16	23	39	109	14.7	4	– 14					
	C	N. Ferguson	77	14	20	34	94	14.9	4	– 5					
	C	W. Carleton	76	17	14	31	188	9.0	4	– 23					
	C	W. McKechnie	56	11	20	31	111	9.9	2	2					
	RW	G. Croteau	73	12	12	24	107	11.2	1	– 18					
	RW	E. Hicke	68	11	12	23	111	9.9	3	– 13					
	RW	C. Patrick	59	8	3	11	73	11.0	0	– 24					
	D	D. Redmond	74	10	35	45	254	3.9	1	– 10					
	D	C. Vadnais	52	14	20	34	139	10.1	7	– 20					
	D	P. Shmyr	69	6	21	27	82	7.3	0	– 27					
	D	B. Marshall	66	0	14	14	35	.0	0	– 5					
	D	M. Johnston	74	2	10	12	52	3.8	2	– 27					
LA	LW	B. Berry	78	17	22	39	102	16.7	3	– 23	G. Edwards	13	23	5	3.60
L. Regan	C	B. Goring	74	21	29	50	137	15.3	3	– 10	R. Vachon	6	18	3	4.05
2–7–1	RW	M. Corrigan	56	12	22	34	102	11.8	3	– 7	B. Smith	1	3	1	4.60
F. Glover	LW	B. Pulford	73	13	24	37	170	7.6	2	– 25	D. DeJordy	0	5	0	4.74
18–42–8	LW	R. Lemieux	78	13	25	38	102	12.7	2	– 40					
	LW	R. Lonsberry	50	9	14	23	112	8.0	1	– 18					
	C	J. Widing	78	27	28	55	192	14.1	3	– 36					
	C	R. Backstrom	76	23	29	52	181	12.7	7	– 22					
	C	E. Joyal	44	11	3	14	70	15.7	1	– 30					
	RW	S. Bernier	26	11	11	22	97	11.3	1	3					
	RW	B. Flett	45	7	12	19	113	6.2	1	– 30					
	RW	B. Lesuk	27	4	10	14	47	8.5	1	2					
	RW	L. Grenier	59	3	4	7	22	13.6	1	– 6					
	D	G. Marotte	72	10	24	34	203	4.9	4	– 33					
	D	H. Howell	77	1	17	18	138	.7	0	– 34					
	D	D. Barrie	48	3	13	16	69	4.3	1	– 10					
	D	P. Curtis	64	1	12	13	66	1.5	0	– 32					

GOALS		ASSISTS		POINTS	
P. Esposito, BOS	66	B. Orr, BOS	80	P. Esposito, BOS	133
V. Hadfield, NYR	50	P. Esposito, BOS	67	B. Orr, BOS	117
Y. Cournoyer, MONT	47	J. Ratelle, NYR	63	J. Ratelle, NYR	109
J. Ratelle, NYR	46	V. Hadfield, NYR	56	V. Hadfield, NYR	106
R. Martin, BUF	44	F. Stanfield, BOS	56	R. Gilbert, NYR	97

SHOTS ON GOAL		SHOOTING PCT.		+/–	
P. Esposito, BOS	426	J. Ratelle, NYR	25.1	B. Orr, BOS	86
B. Orr, BOS	353	Y. Cournoyer, MONT	22.5	B. Park, NYR	62
B. Hull, CHI	336	V. Hadfield, NYR	20.6	J. Ratelle, NYR	61
G. Unger, STL	321	J. Pappin, CHI	18.6	V. Hadfield, NYR	60
B. Goldsworthy, MINN	295	D. Balon, VAN	18.4	P. Esposito, BOS	55

PENALTY MINUTES		GOALS AGAINST AVE.		SHUTOUTS	
B. Watson, PITT	212	T. Esposito, CHI	1.77	T. Esposito, CHI	9
K. Magnuson, CHI	201	K. Dryden, MONT	2.24	K. Dryden, MONT	8
G. Dornhoefer, PHI	183	G. Cheevers, BOS	2.50	D. Favell, PHI	5
B. Plager, STL	176	B. Parent, TOR	2.56	G. Meloche, CALIF	4
R. Foley, PHI	168	C. Maniago, MINN	2.65	A. Smith, DET	4

National Hockey League 1972–73

	W	L	T	PTS	GF	GA	PPG	PPCT	SHG	PPGA	PKPCT	SHGA
EASTERN DIVISION												
*MONT	52	10	16	120	329	**184**	52	21.7	9	37	84.2	4
BOS	51	22	5	107	**330**	235	67	27.8	**15**	43	84.4	5
NYR	47	23	8	102	297	208	54	22.7	5	39	84.4	5
BUF	37	27	14	88	257	219	52	19.2	5	35	85.5	5
DET	37	29	12	86	265	243	53	19.8	4	40	84.7	4
TOR	27	41	10	64	247	279	44	16.0	3	51	78.7	8
VAN	22	47	9	53	233	339	47	16.7	4	59	76.9	6
NYI	12	60	6	30	170	347	28	10.8	2	63	75.9	13
WESTERN DIVISION												
CHI	42	27	9	93	284	225	52	21.3	10	51	80.0	4
PHI	37	30	11	85	296	256	**74**	**28.8**	10	68	81.1	4
MINN	37	30	11	85	254	230	37	15.6	1	59	77.7	7
STL	32	34	12	76	233	251	37	14.7	6	51	81.2	**1**
PITT	32	37	9	73	257	265	52	17.3	10	49	81.4	7
LA	31	36	11	73	232	245	52	17.6	4	**31**	**86.5**	10
ATL	25	38	15	65	191	239	38	14.3	4	48	81.9	5
CALIF	16	46	16	48	213	323	41	16.4	4	56	76.8	4

EASTERN DIVISION

	POS	PLAYER	GP	G	A	PTS	SOG	SPCT	PPG	+/–	GOALIE	W	L	T	GAvg
MONT	LW	F. Mahovlich	78	38	55	93	242	15.7	8	42	K. Dryden	**33**	7	13	**2.26**
S. Bowman	C	J. Lemaire	77	44	51	95	294	15.0	9	59	M. Plasse	11	2	3	2.58
52–10–16	RW	Y. Cournoyer	67	40	39	79	194	20.6	6	50	W. Thomas	8	1	0	2.37
	LW	M. Tardif	76	25	25	50	152	16.4	3	18					
	C	R. Houle	72	13	35	48	117	11.1	3	24					
	RW	G. Lafleur	69	28	27	55	176	15.9	9	16					
	LW	M. Wilson	52	18	9	27	68	**26.5**	0	14					
	LW	S. Shutt	50	8	8	16	55	14.5	1	5					
	C	P. Mahovlich	61	21	38	59	173	12.1	3	21					
	C	H. Richard	71	8	35	43	133	6.0	0	34					
	RW	C. Lefley	65	21	25	46	99	21.2	1	35					
	RW	C. Larose	73	11	23	34	132	8.3	0	29					
	D	G. Lapointe	76	19	35	54	196	9.7	3	51					
	D	S. Savard	74	7	32	39	106	6.6	2	70					
	D	J. Laperriere	57	7	16	23	88	8.0	2	**78**					
	D	J. Roberts	77	14	18	32	104	13.5	0	33					
	D	B. Murdoch	69	2	22	24	54	3.7	0	39					
BOS	LW	W. Cashman	76	29	39	68	169	17.2	6	5	E. Johnston	24	17	1	3.27
T. Johnson	C	P. Esposito	78	**55**	**75**	**130**	**411**	13.4	19	16	R. Brooks	11	1	3	2.64
31–16–5	RW	K. Hodge	73	37	44	81	197	18.8	16	10	J. Adams	9	3	1	3.00
B. Guidolin	LW	J. Bucyk	78	40	53	93	168	23.8	10	18	J. Plante	7	1	0	2.00
20–6–0	LW	D. Marcotte	78	24	31	55	175	13.7	1	32					
	LW	A. Bailey	57	8	13	21	76	10.5	0	7					
	C	F. Stanfield	78	20	58	78	214	9.3	7	12					
	C	G. Sheppard	64	24	26	50	151	15.9	0	37					
	C	M. Walton	56	25	22	47	128	19.5	0	10					
	C	D. Sanderson	25	5	10	15	41	12.2	0	11					
	RW	T. O'Reilly	72	5	22	27	80	6.3	0	27					
	RW	F. O'Donnell	72	10	4	14	56	17.9	0	3					
	D	B. Orr	63	29	72	101	282	10.3	7	56					
	D	C. Vadnais	78	7	24	31	150	4.7	1	21					
	D	D. Smith	78	4	27	31	130	3.1	0	38					
	D	D. Awrey	78	2	17	19	110	1.8	0	29					
	D	N. Beverley	76	1	10	11	57	1.8	0	7					

	POS	PLAYER	GP	G	A	PTS	SOG	SPCT	PPG	+/-	GOALIE	W	L	T	GAvg
NYR	LW	V. Hadfield	63	28	34	62	214	13.1	9	13	E. Giacomin	26	11	6	2.91
E. Francis	C	J. Ratelle	78	41	53	94	241	17.0	11	24	G. Villemure	20	12	2	2.29
47–23–8	RW	R. Gilbert	76	25	59	84	183	13.7	6	12	P. McDuffe	1	0	0	1.00
	LW	S. Vickers	61	30	23	53	131	22.9	2	35					
	C	W. Tkaczuk	76	27	39	66	264	10.2	6	35					
	RW	B. Fairbairn	78	30	33	63	174	17.2	5	36					
	LW	G. Sather	77	11	15	26	69	15.9	1	16					
	LW	T. Irvine	53	8	12	20	91	8.8	1	4					
	C	P. Stemkowski	78	22	37	59	200	11.0	2	28					
	C	G. Carr	50	9	10	19	65	13.8	1	– 4					
	C	B. Rousseau	78	8	37	45	150	5.3	2	1					
	RW	B. MacGregor	52	14	12	26	85	16.5	0	14					
	D	B. Park	52	10	43	53	142	7.0	4	31					
	D	R. Seiling	72	9	33	42	155	5.8	1	43					
	D	D. Rolfe	72	7	25	32	159	4.4	1	41					
	D	J. Neilson	52	4	16	20	99	4.0	0	22					
	D	A. DeMarco	51	4	13	17	104	3.8	1	16					
BUF	LW	R. Martin	75	37	36	73	299	12.4	11	4	R. Crozier	23	13	7	2.76
J. Crozier	C	G. Perreault	78	28	60	88	234	12.0	8	11	D. Dryden	14	13	7	2.65
37–27–14	RW	R. Robert	75	40	43	83	265	15.1	9	16	R. Farr	0	1	0	6.21
	LW	G. Meehan	77	31	29	60	208	14.9	3	4					
	LW	C. Ramsay	76	11	17	28	89	12.4	0	13					
	LW	H. Harris	60	12	26	38	121	9.9	0	9					
	C	J. Lorentz	78	27	35	62	175	15.4	11	6					
	C	D. Luce	78	18	25	43	198	9.1	0	7					
	C	R. Wyrozub	45	3	3	6	23	13.0	0	– 1					
	RW	L. Mickey	77	15	9	24	160	9.4	1	– 6					
	RW	S. Atkinson	61	9	9	18	96	9.4	2	– 5					
	RW	N. Gratton	21	6	5	11	26	23.1	2	0					
	D	L. Hillman	78	5	24	29	102	4.9	2	– 3					
	D	J. Schoenfeld	66	4	15	19	91	4.4	1	12					
	D	M. Robitaille	65	4	17	21	182	2.2	0	9					
	D	T. Horton	69	1	16	17	73	1.4	0	12					
	D	T. Pratt	74	1	15	16	63	1.6	0	9					
DET	LW	A. Delvecchio	77	18	53	71	130	13.8	8	6	R. Edwards	27	17	7	2.63
J. Wilson	C	R. Berenson	78	13	30	43	180	7.2	5	– 14	D. DeJordy	8	11	3	3.74
37–29–12	RW	M. Redmond	76	52	41	93	363	14.3	15	6	A. Brown	2	1	2	3.56
	LW	N. Libett	78	19	34	53	202	9.4	4	1					
	C	M. Dionne	77	40	50	90	282	14.2	10	– 3					
	RW	T. Ecclestone	78	18	30	48	175	10.3	3	6					
	LW	B. Lavender	26	2	2	4	13	15.4	0	2					
	C	A. Karlander	77	15	22	37	99	15.2	4	1					
	C	H. Boucha	73	14	14	28	136	10.3	0	– 2					
	RW	G. Charron	75	18	18	36	117	15.4	0	9					
	RW	B. Collins	78	21	21	42	186	11.3	1	– 1					
	RW	L. Fontaine	39	8	10	18	37	21.6	1	– 2					
	D	G. Bergman	68	3	28	31	174	1.7	0	10					
	D	R. Stackhouse	78	5	29	34	129	3.9	0	22					
	D	T. Bergman	75	9	12	21	165	5.5	1	6					
	D	L. Johnston	73	1	12	13	53	1.9	0	6					
	D	G. Doak	44	0	5	5	28	.0	0	5					
TOR	LW	P. Jarry	74	19	18	37	188	10.1	2	– 13	R. Low	12	24	4	3.89
J. McLellan	LW	D. Dupere	61	13	23	36	129	10.1	4	– 4	J. Plante	8	14	6	3.04
27–41–10	LW	E. Thompson	68	13	19	32	137	9.5	2	4	G. McRae	7	3	0	3.77
	LW	P. Henderson	40	18	16	34	105	17.1	2	2					
	C	D. Sittler	78	29	48	77	331	8.8	8	– 11					
	C	D. Keon	76	37	36	73	277	13.4	8	4					
	C	N. Ullman	65	20	35	55	174	11.5	3	– 18					
	C	G. Monahan	78	13	18	31	135	9.6	0	– 3					
	RW	R. Kehoe	77	33	42	75	204	16.2	2	– 11					
	RW	R. Ellis	78	22	29	51	228	9.6	4	– 1					
	RW	G. Ferguson	72	10	13	23	92	10.9	3	– 17					
	D	J. McKenny	77	11	41	52	208	5.3	5	6					
	D	M. Pelyk	72	3	16	19	113	2.7	0	– 20					
	D	B. Glennie	44	1	10	11	74	1.4	0	2					
	D	J. Grisdale	49	1	7	8	49	2.0	0	– 22					
	D	J. Lundrigan	49	2	8	10	53	3.8	1	4					
	D	L. McIntyre	40	0	3	3	22	.0	0	6					

	POS	PLAYER	GP	G	A	PTS	SOG	SPCT	PPG	+/-	GOALIE	W	L	T	GAvg
VAN	LW	D. Tannahill	78	22	21	43	186	11.8	2	– 29	D. Wilson	13	21	5	3.94
V. Stasiuk	LW	W. Maki	26	3	10	13	56	5.4	0	– 11	E. Dyck	5	17	1	4.53
22–47–9	LW	D. Balon	57	3	2	5	23	13.0	1	– 16	B. Bullock	3	8	3	4.79
	LW	J. Mair	15	1	0	1	23	4.3	0	– 4	D. McLelland	1	1	0	5.00
	C	A. Boudrias	77	30	40	70	194	15.5	8	– 14					
	C	B. Lalonde	77	20	27	47	126	15.9	7	– 32					
	C	D. Lemieux	78	17	35	52	138	12.3	3	– 25					
	C	D. Lever	78	12	26	38	138	8.7	3	– 27					
	C	J. Wright	71	10	27	37	121	8.3	0	– 16					
	RW	B. Schmautz	77	38	33	71	263	14.4	5	– 17					
	RW	G. O'Flaherty	78	13	17	30	135	9.6	0	– 17					
	RW	B. McSheffrey	33	4	4	8	45	8.9	0	– 32					
	RW	B. Wilcox	31	3	2	5	52	5.9	0	– 10					
	D	J. Guevremont	78	16	26	42	246	6.5	6	– 42					
	D	D. Tallon	75	13	24	37	170	7.6	5	– 30					
	D	D. Kearns	72	4	33	37	113	3.5	2	– 25					
	D	B. Wilkins	76	11	17	28	103	10.6	0	– 38					
NYI	LW	G. Gagnon	63	12	29	41	126	9.5	3	– 24	G. Desjardins	5	**35**	3	4.68
P. Goyette	C	D. Hudson	69	12	19	31	111	10.8	4	– 39	B. Smith	7	24	3	4.16
6–40–4	RW	B. Harris	78	28	22	50	196	14.3	6	– 44	G. Gray	0	1	0	5.00
E. Ingarfield	LW	B. Spencer	78	14	24	38	163	8.6	0	– 47					
6–20–2	LW	D. Blackburn	56	7	10	17	65	10.8	1	– 33					
	LW	B. Lavender	43	6	6	12	74	8.1	2	– 42					
	C	L. Henning	63	7	19	26	101	6.9	0	– 28					
	C	T. Miller	69	13	17	30	92	14.1	2	– 29					
	C	T. Crisp	54	4	16	20	72	5.5	0	– 22					
	C	R. Stewart	31	4	10	14	68	5.9	0	– 11					
	RW	E. Westfall	67	15	31	46	160	9.4	4	– 42					
	RW	C. Cameron	72	19	14	33	144	13.2	2	– 38					
	RW	B. Cook	33	8	6	14	83	9.6	1	– 9					
	D	J. Mair	49	2	11	13	134	1.5	0	– 38					
	D	B. Mikkelson	72	1	10	11	39	2.6	0	– 54					
	D	A. Brown	48	4	8	12	50	8.0	1	– 47					
	D	G. Hart	47	1	11	12	72	1.4	0	– 18					

WESTERN DIVISION

	POS	PLAYER	GP	G	A	PTS	SOG	SPCT	PPG	+/-	GOALIE	W	L	T	GAvg
CHI	LW	D. Hull	78	39	51	90	263	14.8	8	28	T. Esposito	32	17	7	2.51
B. Reay	C	P. Martin	78	29	61	90	185	15.7	4	27	G. Smith	10	10	2	3.54
42–27–9	RW	J. Pappin	76	41	51	92	182	22.5	7	25					
	LW	D. Maloney	57	13	17	30	104	12.5	5	11					
	LW	D. Kryskow	11	1	0	1	4	25.0	0	– 1					
	C	S. Mikita	57	27	56	83	177	15.3	7	31					
	C	L. Angotti	77	15	22	37	91	16.5	4	– 3					
	RW	C. Koroll	77	33	24	57	151	21.9	6	17					
	RW	C. Maki	77	13	19	32	118	11.0	1	5					
	RW	J. Bordeleau	73	15	15	30	113	13.3	0	7					
	D	B. White	72	9	38	47	176	5.1	1	30					
	D	P. Stapleton	75	10	21	31	128	7.8	2	19					
	D	K. Magnuson	77	0	19	19	64	.0	0	24					
	D	J. Korab	77	12	15	27	127	9.4	0	5					
	D	P. Russell	76	6	19	25	119	5.0	1	31					
	D	D. Redmond	52	9	19	28	140	6.4	3	2					
	D	J. Marks	55	3	10	13	45	6.7	1	5					
PHI	LW	B. Barber	69	30	34	64	214	14.0	7	10	D. Favell	20	15	4	2.83
F. Shero	C	B. Clarke	78	37	67	104	231	16.0	10	32	M. Belhumeur	9	7	3	3.22
37–30–11	RW	B. Flett	69	43	31	74	283	15.2	11	31	B. Taylor	8	8	4	4.09
	LW	R. Lonsberry	77	21	29	50	205	10.2	6	6					
	C	R. MacLeish	78	50	50	100	279	17.9	**21**	15					
	RW	G. Dornhoefer	77	30	49	79	187	16.0	3	17					
	LW	D. Schultz	76	9	12	21	63	14.3	0	4					
	LW	B. Kelly	77	10	11	21	125	8.0	0	1					
	C	B. Clement	73	14	14	28	132	10.6	0	– 11					
	RW	S. Nolet	70	16	20	36	146	11.0	6	– 3					
	RW	D. Saleski	78	12	9	21	158	7.6	1	– 20					
	D	T. Bladon	78	11	31	42	151	7.3	7	9					
	D	J. Watson	63	2	24	26	72	2.8	0	30					
	D	E. Van Impe	72	1	11	12	66	1.5	0	22					
	D	A. Dupont	46	3	20	23	103	2.9	1	8					
	D	W. Hillman	74	0	10	10	41	.0	0	15					

	POS	PLAYER	GP	G	A	PTS	SOG	SPCT	PPG	+/-	GOALIE	W	L	T	GAvg
MINN	LW	J. Parise	78	27	48	75	188	14.4	6	18	C. Maniago	21	18	6	2.89
J. Gordon	C	D. Hextall	78	30	52	82	140	21.4	3	29	G. Gilbert	10	10	2	3.05
37–30–11	RW	B. Goldsworthy	75	27	33	60	260	10.4	8	24	G. Worsley	6	2	3	2.88
	LW	D. Grant	78	32	35	67	251	12.7	3	23					
	C	J. Drouin	78	27	46	73	279	9.7	3	12					
	RW	F. Harvey	68	21	34	55	184	11.4	3	23					
	LW	D. Prentice	73	26	16	42	168	15.4	5	3					
	LW	C. Burns	65	4	7	11	41	9.8	0	– 3					
	C	M. Oliver	75	11	31	42	174	6.3	2	4					
	RW	L. Nanne	74	15	20	35	142	10.6	2	19					
	RW	B. Nevin	66	5	13	18	55	9.1	0	– 12					
	RW	T. Holbrook	21	2	3	5	18	11.1	0	– 4					
	D	T. Harris	78	7	23	30	94	7.4	0	25					
	D	B. Gibbs	63	10	24	34	163	6.1	2	14					
	D	D. Mohns	67	4	13	17	104	3.8	0	11					
	D	D. O'Brien	74	3	11	14	58	5.2	0	11					
	D	T. Reid	60	1	13	14	79	1.3	0	15					
STL	LW	J. Egers	78	24	24	48	240	10.0	4	1	W. Stephenson	18	5	7	3.03
A. Arbour	C	G. Unger	78	41	39	80	342	12.0	13	7	J. Caron	8	14	5	3.53
2–6–5	RW	M. Murphy	64	18	27	45	182	9.9	3	13	B. Johnson	6	5	0	2.68
J. Talbot	LW	P. Roberto	77	20	22	42	275	7.2	2	– 12					
30–28–7	LW	F. Thomson	75	14	20	34	98	14.2	1	– 2					
	LW	C. Evans	77	9	12	21	138	6.5	0	– 2					
	C	D. O'Shea	75	12	26	38	110	10.9	0	– 5					
	C	F. Huck	58	16	20	36	82	19.5	2	– 1					
	C	W. Merrick	50	10	11	21	81	12.3	3	– 2					
	RW	G. Sabourin	76	21	27	48	240	8.8	1	– 5					
	RW	P. Plante	49	12	13	25	90	13.3	0	8					
	RW	K. O'Shea	36	3	5	8	39	7.7	0	– 13					
	D	B. Plager	68	8	25	33	131	6.1	3	0					
	D	B. Plager	77	2	31	33	117	1.7	0	– 1					
	D	S. Durbano	49	3	18	21	83	3.6	0	– 3					
	D	B. McCord	43	1	13	14	41	2.4	0	– 5					
	D	J. Hamel	55	2	7	9	56	3.6	0	– 5					
PITT	LW	L. MacDonald	78	34	41	75	244	13.9	6	37	J. Rutherford	20	22	5	2.91
R. Kelly	C	S. Apps	77	29	56	85	186	15.6	6	25	D. Herron	6	7	2	3.41
17–19–6	RW	A. McDonough	78	35	41	76	285	12.3	7	20	C. Newton	3	4	0	3.94
K. Schinkel	LW	G. Polis	78	26	23	49	221	11.8	8	– 32	A. Brown	3	4	2	4.73
15–18–3	C	R. Schock	78	13	36	49	143	9.1	2	– 12					
	RW	J. Pronovost	66	21	22	43	192	10.9	2	– 15					
	LW	E. Shack	74	25	20	45	192	13.0	8	– 10					
	LW	R. Kessell	67	1	13	14	35	2.9	0	– 9					
	LW	R. Burns	26	0	2	2	26	.0	0	– 6					
	C	B. Hextall	78	21	33	54	169	12.4	6	– 23					
	RW	N. Harbaruk	78	10	15	25	96	10.4	0	– 11					
	RW	K. Schinkel	42	11	10	21	79	13.9	1	– 10					
	D	D. Burrows	78	3	24	27	132	2.3	0	4					
	D	D. Edestrand	78	15	24	39	155	9.7	4	3					
	D	B. Watson	69	1	17	18	47	2.1	0	18					
	D	D. Rupp	78	7	13	20	132	5.3	2	– 3					
	D	J. Lynch	47	1	18	19	78	1.3	0	– 21					
LA	LW	B. Berry	78	36	28	64	176	20.5	14	– 13	R. Vachon	22	20	10	2.85
B. Pulford	C	J. Widing	77	16	54	70	189	8.5	0	– 14	G. Edwards	9	16	1	3.62
31–36–11	RW	M. Corrigan	37	37	30	67	180	20.6	14	– 17					
	LW	R. Lemieux	74	5	10	15	43	11.6	1	– 1					
	C	B. Goring	67	28	31	59	148	18.9	4	0					
	C	R. Backstrom	63	20	29	49	132	15.2	1	– 12					
	C	V. Venasky	77	15	19	34	176	8.5	1	– 16					
	C	J. Peters	77	4	5	9	40	10.0	1	– 30					
	RW	S. Bernier	75	22	46	68	255	8.6	6	– 20					
	RW	B. Lesuk	67	6	14	20	129	4.7	0	– 2					
	RW	D. Kozak	72	14	6	20	78	17.9	4	– 25					
	RW	D. Volmar	21	4	2	6	33	12.1	0	– 2					
	D	G. Marotte	78	6	39	45	207	2.9	3	– 21					
	D	H. Howell	73	4	11	15	97	4.1	0	– 4					
	D	B. Long	70	2	13	15	110	1.8	0	– 7					
	D	T. Harper	77	1	8	9	64	1.6	0	6					
	D	N. Komadoski	62	1	8	9	47	2.1	1	– 22					

Team	POS	PLAYER	GP	G	A	PTS	SOG	SPCT	PPG	+/–	GOALIE	W	L	T	GAvg
ATL	LW	K. McCreary	77	20	21	41	157	12.7	9	– 22	P. Myre	16	23	5	3.03
B. Geoffrion	LW	E. Hicke	58	14	23	37	120	11.7	2	– 2	D. Bouchard	9	15	10	3.09
25–38–15	LW	L. Rochefort	54	9	18	27	130	6.9	1	– 4					
	LW	J. Richard	74	13	18	31	165	7.9	4	– 24					
	C	B. Leiter	78	26	34	60	174	14.9	5	– 12					
	C	R. Comeau	77	21	21	42	146	14.4	3	0					
	C	C. Bennett	52	18	17	35	135	13.3	1	– 13					
	C	J. Stewart	68	17	17	34	168	10.1	2	– 9					
	RW	L. Romanchych	70	18	30	48	157	11.5	4	– 11					
	RW	B. MacMillan	78	10	15	25	101	9.9	3	– 10					
	RW	L. Morrison	78	6	9	15	52	11.5	0	– 11					
	D	R. Manery	78	5	30	35	159	3.1	2	– 2					
	D	P. Quinn	78	2	18	20	88	2.3	0	2					
	D	B. Plager	76	2	11	13	60	3.3	0	– 18					
	D	N. Price	54	1	13	14	70	1.4	0	– 7					
	D	N. Picard	41	0	10	10	37	.0	0	– 6					
	D	B. Paradise	71	1	7	8	53	1.9	0	– 20					
CALIF	LW	J. Johnston	71	28	21	49	170	16.5	8	– 19	G. Meloche	12	32	14	4.06
G. Young	C	W. McKechnie	78	16	38	54	182	8.8	4	– 26	M. Edwards	4	14	2	4.32
2–7–3	RW	C. Patrick	71	20	22	42	152	13.2	2	– 32					
F. Glover	LW	P. Laframboise	77	16	25	41	113	14.2	2	– 24					
14–39–13	LW	S. Gilbertson	66	6	15	21	110	5.5	3	– 34					
	C	S. Weir	78	15	24	39	123	12.2	5	– 24					
	C	I. Boldirev	56	11	23	34	157	7.0	3	– 23					
	C	M. Mott	70	6	7	13	71	8.5	1	– 17					
	RW	H. Graves	75	27	25	52	128	21.1	3	– 15					
	RW	R. Leach	76	23	12	35	184	12.5	3	– 41					
	RW	G. Croteau	47	6	15	21	77	7.8	1	– 13					
	D	R. Smith	64	9	24	33	126	7.1	3	– 43					
	D	M. Johnston	78	10	20	30	93	10.8	0	– 1					
	D	D. Maggs	54	7	15	22	95	7.4	0	– 22					
	D	B. Stewart	63	4	17	21	95	4.2	0	– 46					
	D	T. McAneeley	77	4	13	17	74	5.4	1	– 29					
	D	B. Marshall	55	2	6	8	55	3.6	1	– 36					

GOALS		ASSISTS		POINTS	
P. Esposito, BOS	55	P. Esposito, BOS	75	P. Esposito, BOS	130
M. Redmond, DET	52	B. Orr, BOS	72	B. Clarke, PHI	104
R. MacLeish, PHI	50	B. Clarke, PHI	67	B. Orr, BOS	101
J. Lemaire, MONT	44	P. Martin, CHI	61	R. MacLeish, PHI	100
J. Ratelle, NYR	41	G. Perreault, BUF	60	J. Lemaire, MONT	95
J. Pappin, CHI	41				

SHOTS ON GOAL		SHOOTING PCT.		+/–	
P. Esposito, BOS	411	M. Wilson, MONT	26.5	J. Laperriere, MONT	78
M. Redmond, DET	363	J. Bucyk, BOS	23.8	S. Savard, MONT	70
G. Unger, STL	342	S. Vickers, NYR	22.9	J. Lemaire, MONT	59
D. Sittler, TOR	331	J. Pappin, CHI	22.5	B. Orr, BOS	56
R. Martin, BUF	299	C. Koroll, CHI	21.9	G. Lapointe, MONT	51

PENALTY MINUTES		GOALS AGAINST AVE.		SHUTOUTS	
D. Schultz, PHI	259	K. Dryden, MONT	2.26	K. Dryden, MONT	6
B. Kelly, PHI	238	T. Esposito, CHI	2.51	R. Edwards, DET	6
S. Durbano, STL	231	R. Edwards, DET	2.63	C. Maniago, MINN	5
A. Dupont, STL, PHI	215	R. Crozier, BUF	2.76	E. Johnston, BOS	5
D. Saleski, PHI	205	D. Favell, PHI	2.83	T. Esposito, CHI	4

National Hockey League 1973–74

	W	L	T	PTS	GF	GA	PPG	PPCT	SHG	PPGA	PKPCT	SHGA
EASTERN DIVISION												
BOS	52	17	9	113	**349**	221	65	29.7	12	48	81.4	**2**
MONT	45	24	9	99	293	240	51	20.1	12	51	76.5	7
NYR	40	24	14	94	300	251	**66**	**29.7**	9	45	81.2	**2**
TOR	35	27	16	86	274	230	51	18.2	5	49	81.6	7
BUF	32	34	12	76	242	250	48	18.5	5	42	82.3	12
DET	29	39	10	68	255	319	59	21.5	8	49	79.4	13
VAN	24	43	11	59	224	296	55	19.7	4	70	74.0	8
NYI	19	41	18	56	182	247	32	13.9	7	63	75.9	13
WESTERN DIVISION												
*PHI	50	16	12	112	273	**164**	60	22.3	**20**	49	**88.4**	6
CHI	41	14	23	105	272	**164**	55	21.6	8	**26**	87.5	5
LA	33	33	12	78	233	231	43	15.1	4	48	80.5	9
ATL	30	34	14	74	214	238	44	16.7	1	46	79.4	13
PITT	28	41	9	65	242	273	47	17.0	12	47	80.8	4
STL	26	40	12	64	206	248	39	14.2	4	56	82.1	9
MINN	23	38	17	63	235	195	37	17.9	5	51	79.9	5
CALIF	13	55	10	36	195	342	34	12.7	6	46	79.2	14

EASTERN DIVISION

	POS	PLAYER	GP	G	A	PTS	SOG	SPCT	PPG	+/–	GOALIE	W	L	T	GAvg
BOS	LW	W. Cashman	78	30	59	89	156	19.2	5	49	G. Gilbert	34	12	8	2.95
B. Guidolin	C	P. Esposito	78	**68**	77	**145**	**393**	17.3	14	51	R. Brooks	16	3	0	2.36
52–17–9	RW	K. Hodge	76	50	55	105	251	19.9	15	40	K. Broderick	2	2	1	3.20
	LW	J. Bucyk	76	31	44	75	139	**22.3**	12	13					
	C	G. Sheppard	75	16	31	47	168	9.5	0	23					
	RW	B. Schmautz	27	7	13	20	62	11.3	1	6					
	LW	D. Marcotte	78	24	26	50	150	16.0	0	44					
	LW	D. Forbes	63	10	16	26	64	15.6	0	9					
	C	A. Savard	72	16	14	30	88	18.2	0	16					
	C	D. Sanderson	29	8	12	20	64	12.5	0	17					
	C	C. Oddleifson	49	10	11	21	63	15.9	0	16					
	RW	T. O'Reilly	76	11	24	35	86	12.8	0	30					
	RW	F. O'Donnell	43	5	7	12	39	12.8	0	3					
	D	B. Orr	74	32	**90**	122	384	8.3	11	**84**					
	D	C. Vadnais	78	16	43	59	187	8.6	6	35					
	D	D. Smith	77	6	21	27	112	5.4	0	26					
	D	A. Sims	77	3	9	12	111	2.7	0	64					
MONT	LW	F. Mahovlich	71	31	49	80	221	14.0	8	16	W. Thomas	23	12	5	2.76
S. Bowman	C	P. Mahovlich	78	36	37	73	178	20.2	7	42	M. Larocque	15	8	2	2.89
45–24–9	RW	Y. Cournoyer	67	40	33	73	187	21.4	10	16	M. Plasse	7	4	2	4.08
	LW	S. Shutt	70	15	20	35	131	11.5	3	19					
	LW	M. Wilson	72	17	14	31	107	15.9	0	4					
	LW	Y. Lambert	60	6	10	16	34	17.6	0	5					
	LW	B. Gainey	66	3	7	10	55	5.5	0	– 9					
	C	J. Lemaire	66	29	38	67	219	13.2	10	4					
	C	H. Richard	75	19	36	55	175	10.9	1	7					
	C	C. Lefley	74	23	31	54	150	15.3	1	9					
	RW	G. Lafleur	73	21	35	56	167	12.6	3	10					
	RW	C. Larose	39	17	7	24	71	23.9	1	11					
	D	G. Lapointe	71	13	40	53	205	6.3	5	12					
	D	L. Robinson	78	6	20	26	98	6.1	0	32					
	D	S. Savard	67	4	14	18	98	4.1	1	20					
	D	J. Roberts	67	8	16	24	97	8.2	0	27					
	D	J. Laperriere	42	2	10	12	60	3.3	0	15					
NYR	LW	V. Hadfield	77	27	28	55	201	13.4	12	1	E. Giacomin	30	15	10	3.07
L. Popein	C	J. Ratelle	68	28	39	67	165	17.0	6	5	G. Villemure	7	7	3	3.53
18–14–9	RW	R. Gilbert	75	36	41	77	168	21.4	16	11	P. McDuffe	3	2	1	3.18
E. Francis	LW	S. Vickers	75	34	24	58	168	20.2	5	6					
22–10–5	C	W. Tkaczuk	71	21	42	63	218	9.6	3	15					
	RW	B. Fairbairn	78	18	44	62	185	9.7	4	11					
	LW	T. Irvine	75	26	20	46	142	18.3	2	2					
	C	P. Stemkowski	78	25	45	70	232	10.8	2	3					
	RW	B. Rousseau	72	10	41	51	87	11.5	6	2					
	RW	B. MacGregor	66	17	27	44	91	18.7	0	– 1					
	RW	J. Butler	26	6	10	16	60	10.0	1	7					
	D	B. Park	78	25	57	82	227	11.0	4	18					
	D	R. Seiling	68	7	23	30	104	6.7	0	16					
	D	J. Neilson	72	4	7	11	103	3.9	2	– 4					
	D	D. Rolfe	48	3	12	15	98	3.1	0	16					
	D	G. Marotte	46	2	17	19	87	2.3	0	7					
	D	R. Harris	63	2	12	14	75	2.7	0	– 2					
TOR	LW	P. Henderson	69	24	31	55	159	15.1	5	9	D. Favell	14	7	9	2.71
R. Kelly	LW	I. Hammarstrom	66	20	23	43	135	14.8	4	17	E. Johnston	12	9	4	3.09
35–27–16	LW	G. Monahan	78	9	16	25	139	6.5	0	4	D. Wilson	9	11	3	2.89
	LW	E. Thompson	56	7	8	15	74	9.5	0	2					
	C	D. Sittler	78	38	46	84	270	14.1	11	12					
	C	D. Keon	74	25	28	53	244	10.2	1	13					
	C	N. Ullman	78	22	47	69	178	12.4	4	10					
	RW	R. Ellis	70	23	25	48	158	14.6	3	8					
	RW	R. Kehoe	69	18	22	40	197	9.1	3	19					
	RW	L. McDonald	70	14	16	30	142	9.9	2	3					
	RW	E. Shack	59	7	8	15	78	9.0	4	1					
	RW	T. Ecclestone	46	9	14	23	79	11.4	1	8					
	D	B. Salming	76	5	34	39	130	3.8	3	38					
	D	I. Turnbull	78	8	27	35	231	3.5	2	12					
	D	J. McKenny	77	14	28	42	129	10.9	3	16					
	D	M. Pelyk	71	12	19	31	115	10.4	0	5					
	D	B. Glennie	65	4	18	22	65	6.2	1	27					

TEAM	POS	PLAYER	GP	G	A	PTS	SOG	SPCT	PPG	+/-	GOALIE	W	L	T	GAvg
BUF	LW	R. Martin	78	52	34	86	320	16.3	8	– 22	D. Dryden	23	20	8	2.97
J. Crozier	C	G. Perreault	55	18	33	51	163	11.0	6	– 8	R. Crozier	4	5	0	3.80
32–34–12	RW	R. Robert	76	21	44	65	245	8.6	3	– 16	G. Bromley	3	5	3	3.31
	LW	C. Ramsay	78	20	26	46	154	13.0	1	17	R. Farr	2	4	1	3.13
	C	D. Luce	75	26	30	56	237	11.0	2	3					
	RW	R. Dudley	67	13	13	26	100	13.0	0	0					
	LW	G. Meehan	72	20	26	46	160	12.5	6	– 7					
	C	J. Lorentz	78	23	31	54	145	15.9	12	– 19					
	C	P. McNab	22	3	6	9	24	12.5	0	– 3					
	RW	S. Atkinson	70	6	10	16	109	5.5	0	1					
	RW	L. Mickey	13	3	4	7	18	16.7	0	5					
	D	L. Carriere	77	6	24	30	113	5.3	3	3					
	D	J. Korab	45	6	12	18	106	5.7	2	– 23					
	D	M. Robitaille	71	2	18	20	185	1.1	2	2					
	D	N. Gratton	57	6	12	18	53	11.3	2	– 10					
	D	T. Horton	55	0	6	6	59	.0	0	5					
	D	P. Terbenche	67	2	12	14	42	4.8	0	3					
DET	LW	G. Charron	76	25	30	55	205	12.2	6	– 31	D. Grant	15	16	2	4.16
	C	M. Dionne	74	24	54	78	280	8.6	3	– 31	J. Rutherford	9	11	4	3.63
T. Garvin	RW	M. Redmond	76	51	26	77	296	17.2	**21**	– 21	B. McKenzie	4	4	4	3.58
2–9–1	LW	N. Libett	67	24	24	48	177	13.6	3	– 26	T. Richardson	1	4	0	5.33
A. Delvecchio	LW	A. Bailey	45	9	14	23	70	12.9	3	– 12	R. Edwards	0	3	0	5.78
27–30–9	C	R. Berenson	76	24	42	66	179	13.4	6	– 22	D. DeJordy	0	1	0	12.00
	C	B. Hogaboam	47	18	23	41	100	18.0	6	– 3					
	C	H. Boucha	70	19	12	31	132	14.4	2	– 22					
	RW	P. Jarry	52	15	23	38	139	10.8	2	– 11					
	RW	D. Roberts	57	12	25	37	84	14.3	2	– 9					
	RW	B. Collins	54	13	15	28	134	9.7	2	– 20					
	D	B. Hughes	69	1	21	22	74	1.4	0	– 28					
	D	L. Johnston	65	2	12	14	47	4.3	0	– 26					
	D	J. Lynch	35	3	9	12	64	4.7	1	– 14					
	D	T. Harris	41	0	11	11	32	.0	0	– 4					
	D	T. Bergman	43	0	3	3	49	.0	0	– 15					
VAN	LW	D. Lever	78	23	25	48	175	13.1	4	– 16	G. Smith	20	**33**	8	3.44
	C	A. Boudrias	78	16	59	75	180	8.9	3	– 6	E. Dyck	2	5	2	4.63
B. McCreary	RW	D. Ververgaert	78	26	31	57	153	17.0	7	– 20	J. Caron	2	5	1	4.90
9–25–7	LW	G. O'Flaherty	78	22	20	42	142	15.5	2	– 5					
P. Maloney	LW	J. Gould	45	9	10	19	127	7.1	2	– 4					
15–18–4	LW	D. Tannahill	33	8	12	20	43	18.6	0	1					
	C	O. Kurtenbach	52	8	13	21	77	10.4	1	– 30					
	C	D. Lemieux	72	5	17	22	73	6.8	1	– 24					
	RW	B. Schmautz	49	26	19	45	164	15.9	8	0					
	RW	P. Bordeleau	68	11	13	24	77	14.3	4	– 16					
	RW	B. McSheffrey	54	9	3	12	71	12.7	3	– 14					
	D	J. Guevremont	72	15	24	39	208	7.2	10	– 37					
	D	B. Wilkins	78	3	28	31	128	2.3	1	– 13					
	D	B. Dailey	76	7	17	24	124	5.6	0	– 32					
	D	D. Dunn	68	11	22	33	97	11.3	0	– 13					
	D	D. Kearns	52	4	13	17	61	6.6	2	– 11					
	D	G. Boddy	53	2	10	12	52	3.8	0	– 4					
NYI	RW	B. Harris	78	23	27	50	190	12.1	4	– 11	B. Smith	9	23	12	3.07
	LW	G. Gagnon	62	8	14	22	68	11.8	0	6	G. Desjardins	9	17	6	3.12
A. Arbour	LW	B. Spencer	54	5	16	21	114	4.4	0	– 16	C. Resch	1	1	0	3.00
19–41–18	LW	G. Howatt	78	6	11	17	84	7.1	0	– 13					
	LW	E. Hicke	55	6	7	13	67	9.0	2	– 19					
	C	R. Stewart	67	23	20	43	178	12.9	2	– 7					
	C	L. Henning	60	12	15	27	96	12.5	2	– 7					
	C	A. St. Laurent	42	5	9	14	75	6.7	0	1					
	C	D. Hudson	63	2	10	12	43	4.7	0	– 6					
	RW	E. Westfall	68	19	23	42	177	10.7	6	– 5					
	RW	B. Nystrom	71	21	20	41	176	11.9	3	– 17					
	RW	C. Cameron	78	15	14	29	121	12.4	2	– 15					
	RW	B. MacMillan	55	4	9	13	65	6.2	0	– 6					
	D	D. Potvin	77	17	37	54	209	8.1	6	– 16					
	D	J. Potvin	78	5	23	28	114	4.4	2	– 26					
	D	D. Lewis	66	2	15	17	63	3.2	1	– 7					
	D	B. Marshall	69	1	7	8	51	2.0	0	5					

WESTERN DIVISION

	POS	PLAYER	GP	G	A	PTS	SOG	SPCT	PPG	+/-	GOALIE	W	L	T	GAvg
PHI	LW	B. Barber	75	34	35	69	290	11.7	9	34	B. Parent	**47**	13	12	**1.89**
F. Shero	C	B. Clarke	77	35	52	87	221	15.8	10	35	B. Taylor	3	3	0	4.26
50–16–12	RW	B. Flett	67	17	27	44	222	7.7	1	20					
	LW	R. Lonsberry	75	32	19	51	213	15.0	6	16					
	C	R. MacLeish	78	32	45	77	270	11.9	13	21					
	RW	G. Dornhoefer	57	11	39	50	109	10.1	3	13					
	LW	D. Schultz	73	20	16	36	95	21.1	2	26					
	LW	B. Kelly	65	4	10	14	59	6.8	0	10					
	C	O. Kindrachuk	71	11	30	41	106	10.4	3	19					
	C	T. Crisp	71	10	21	31	88	11.4	1	12					
	RW	D. Saleski	77	15	25	40	157	9.6	2	21					
	RW	S. Nolet	52	19	17	36	97	19.6	1	28					
	D	T. Bladon	70	12	22	34	159	7.5	6	24					
	D	J. Watson	78	2	18	20	113	1.8	1	33					
	D	J. Watson	74	1	17	18	75	1.3	0	28					
	D	E. Van Impe	77	2	16	18	76	2.6	0	31					
	D	A. Dupont	75	3	20	23	165	1.8	2	34					
CHI	LW	J. Marks	76	13	18	31	139	9.4	3	22	T. Esposito	34	14	21	2.04
B. Reay	C	S. Mikita	76	30	50	80	171	17.5	6	24	M. Veisor	7	0	2	2.23
41–14–23	RW	C. Koroll	78	21	25	46	151	13.9	7	27					
	LW	D. Hull	74	29	39	68	220	13.2	5	25					
	C	P. Martin	78	30	47	77	175	17.1	8	29					
	RW	J. Pappin	78	32	41	73	160	20.0	8	25					
	LW	D. Kryskow	72	7	12	19	60	11.7	0	5					
	C	L. Powis	57	8	13	21	71	11.3	1	10					
	RW	C. Maki	69	9	26	35	89	10.1	2	13					
	RW	J. Bordeleau	64	11	9	20	50	22.0	0	11					
	D	D. Redmond	76	17	42	59	246	6.9	5	26					
	D	B. White	69	5	31	36	85	5.9	0	51					
	D	P. Russell	75	10	25	35	123	8.1	0	47					
	D	D. Jarrett	67	5	11	16	54	9.3	1	5					
	D	D. Tallon	65	15	19	34	98	15.3	3	12					
	D	K. Magnuson	57	2	11	13	29	6.9	0	16					
LA	LW	B. Berry	77	23	33	56	122	18.9	8	0	R. Vachon	28	26	10	2.80
B. Pulford	C	J. Widing	71	27	30	57	175	15.4	5	– 4	G. Edwards	5	7	2	3.23
33–33–12	RW	D. Kozak	76	21	14	35	109	19.3	1	7					
	LW	D. Maloney	65	15	17	32	157	9.6	5	6					
	LW	T. Williams	46	11	17	28	113	9.7	2	3					
	LW	G. Carr	21	6	11	17	37	16.2	0	2					
	LW	R. Rota	58	10	6	16	93	10.8	0	– 8					
	C	B. Goring	70	28	33	61	161	17.4	5	2					
	C	M. Corrigan	75	16	26	42	131	12.2	4	– 10					
	C	V. Venasky	32	6	5	11	45	13.3	1	– 1					
	RW	B. Nevin	78	20	30	50	127	15.7	5	8					
	RW	St. Marseille	78	14	36	50	190	7.4	2	1					
	RW	M. Murphy	53	13	16	29	142	9.2	1	2					
	D	B. Murdoch	76	8	20	28	160	5.0	1	– 11					
	D	T. Harper	77	0	17	17	114	.0	0	25					
	D	B. Long	60	3	19	22	111	2.7	1	25					
	D	S. Kannegiesser	51	3	17	20	76	3.9	1	3					
ATL	LW	J. Richard	78	27	16	43	270	10.0	7	– 18	D. Bouchard	19	18	8	2.77
B. Geoffrion	C	T. Lysiak	77	19	45	64	216	8.8	4	– 15	P. Myre	11	16	6	3.33
30–34–14	RW	A. McDonough	35	10	9	19	108	9.3	3	– 4					
	LW	E. Vail	23	2	9	11	44	4.5	2	2					
	C	B. Leiter	78	26	26	52	178	14.6	10	– 4					
	RW	L. Romanchych	73	22	29	51	159	13.8	7	– 7					
	LW	J. Stewart	74	18	15	33	143	12.6	3	3					
	C	C. Bennett	71	17	24	41	136	12.5	1	3					
	C	R. Comeau	78	11	23	34	130	8.5	0	– 15					
	C	B. Hextall	40	2	4	6	39	5.1	0	0					
	RW	L. Rochefort	56	10	12	22	107	9.3	1	– 12					
	RW	L. Morrison	52	1	4	5	31	3.2	0	– 1					
	D	K. McCreary	76	18	19	37	109	16.5	2	– 6					
	D	R. Manery	78	8	29	37	189	4.2	2	15					
	D	P. Quinn	77	5	27	32	93	5.4	0	15					
	D	N. Price	62	0	13	13	93	.0	0	– 11					
	D	B. Murray	62	0	3	3	67	.0	0	– 20					
PITT	LW	L. MacDonald	78	43	39	82	260	16.5	9	17	A. Brown	13	16	4	3.53
K. Schinkel	C	S. Apps	75	24	61	85	177	13.6	7	21	J. Rutherford	7	12	4	3.44
14–31–5	RW	J. Pronovost	77	40	32	72	248	16.1	8	9	G. Inness	7	10	1	3.26
M. Boileau	LW	G. Polis	41	14	13	27	163	8.6	5	– 18	D. Herron	1	3	0	4.15
14–10–4	LW	W. Bianchin	69	12	13	25	118	10.2	1	– 15					
	LW	B. Kelly	30	7	10	17	101	6.9	1	– 5					
	C	R. Schock	77	14	29	43	138	10.1	0	– 27					
	C	R. Lalonde	73	10	17	27	70	14.3	0	2					
	C	B. McManama	47	5	14	19	70	7.1	0	– 12					
	RW	B. Lukowich	53	9	10	19	60	15.0	1	– 4					
	RW	C. Arnason	41	13	5	18	121	10.7	0	– 2					
	RW	T. Snell	55	4	12	16	64	6.3	0	– 22					
	D	A. DeMarco	34	7	12	19	101	6.9	3	5					
	D	D. Burrows	71	3	14	17	123	2.4	2	– 13					
	D	R. Stackhouse	36	4	15	19	67	6.0	0	12					
	D	S. Durbano	33	4	14	18	68	5.9	2	17					
	D	N. Beverley	67	2	14	16	74	2.7	0	– 16					

TEAM	POS	PLAYER	GP	G	A	PTS	SOG	SPCT	PPG	+/-	GOALIE	W	L	T	GAvg
STL	LW	F. Thomson	77	11	22	33	125	8.8	0	– 19	W. Stephenson	13	21	5	3.13
J. Talbot	C	W. Merrick	64	20	23	43	147	13.6	2	– 11	J. Davidson	13	19	7	3.08
22–25–8	RW	P. Plante	78	26	28	54	151	17.2	8	– 14	J. Watt	0	0	0	6.00
L. Angotti	LW	G. Sather	69	15	29	44	106	14.2	4	– 9					
4–15–4	LW	G. Polis	37	8	12	20	122	6.6	3	– 7					
	LW	B. Kelly	37	9	8	17	70	12.9	2	1					
	C	G. Unger	78	33	35	68	327	10.1	9	– 17					
	C	L. Angotti	51	12	23	35	84	14.3	1	– 3					
	C	J. Wright	32	3	6	9	43	7.0	0	– 1					
	RW	G. Sabourin	54	7	23	30	126	5.6	1	– 9					
	RW	N. Harbaruk	56	5	14	19	49	10.2	0	4					
	RW	G. Brooks	30	6	8	14	51	11.8	0	0					
	RW	B. Williams	31	3	10	13	41	7.3	0	2					
	D	B. Plager	72	6	20	26	104	5.8	1	– 11					
	D	D. Awrey	75	5	16	21	94	5.3	1	– 7					
	D	B. Plager	61	3	10	13	78	3.8	0	9					
	D	L. Giroux	74	5	17	22	131	3.8	2	– 14					
MINN	LW	D. Grant	78	29	35	64	185	15.7	3	– 1	C. Maniago	12	18	10	3.48
J. Gordon	C	D. Hextall	78	20	62	82	152	13.2	2	4	G. Worsley	8	14	5	3.22
3–8–6	RW	B. Goldsworthy	74	48	26	74	321	15.0	12	3	F. Rivard	3	6	2	4.28
P. MacDonald	LW	J. Parise	78	18	37	55	188	9.6	2	– 8					
20–30–11	LW	D. Prentice	24	2	3	5	36	5.6	0	– 11					
	C	J. Drouin	65	19	24	43	200	9.5	4	– 11					
	C	F. Stanfield	71	16	28	44	218	7.3	3	– 14					
	C	M. Oliver	78	17	20	37	146	11.6	3	– 13					
	C	G. Gambucci	42	1	7	8	26	3.8	0	5					
	RW	F. Harvey	72	16	17	33	190	8.4	1	– 11					
	RW	L. Nanne	76	11	21	32	139	7.9	2	– 1					
	RW	T. Featherstone	54	9	12	21	92	9.8	0	– 9					
	RW	T. Holbrook	22	1	3	4	19	5.3	1	– 3					
	D	B. Gibbs	76	9	29	38	151	6.0	3	– 17					
	D	G. Bergman	57	3	23	26	87	3.4	1	– 12					
	D	T. Reid	76	4	19	23	118	3.4	0	– 22					
	D	F. Barrett	40	0	7	7	31	.0	0	– 1					
CALIF	LW	J. Johnston	78	27	40	67	202	13.4	10	– 37	G. Meloche	9	**33**	5	4.24
F. Glover	C	I. Boldirev	78	25	31	56	220	11.4	2	– 51	B. Champoux	2	11	3	5.20
11–38–8	RW	R. Leach	78	22	24	46	214	10.3	2	– 61	M. Edwards	1	10	1	3.92
M. Johnston	LW	S. Gilbertson	76	18	12	30	136	13.2	4	– 41	T. Tucker	1	1	1	3.39
2–17–2	LW	G. Croteau	76	14	21	35	149	9.4	1	– 47					
	LW	P. Laframboise	65	7	7	14	67	10.4	0	– 28					
	C	W. McKechnie	63	23	29	52	135	17.0	4	– 14					
	C	S. Weir	58	9	7	16	65	13.8	1	– 33					
	C	R. Huston	23	3	10	13	29	10.3	0	– 12					
	RW	C. Patrick	59	10	20	30	95	10.5	2	– 30					
	RW	H. Graves	64	11	18	29	91	12.1	1	– 32					
	RW	M. Mott	77	9	17	26	90	10.0	1	– 19					
	D	T. McAneeley	72	4	20	24	80	5.0	0	– 24					
	D	M. Johnston	50	2	16	18	51	3.9	2	– 45					
	D	R. McKay	72	2	12	14	101	2.0	1	– 31					
	D	T. Murray	58	0	12	12	55	.0	0	– 43					
	D	R. Kessell	51	2	6	8	31	6.5	1	– 4					

GOALS		ASSISTS		POINTS	
P. Esposito, BOS	68	B. Orr, BOS	90	P. Esposito, BOS	145
R. Martin, BUF	52	P. Esposito, BOS	77	B. Orr, BOS	122
M. Redmond, DET	51	D. Hextall, MINN	62	K. Hodge, BOS	105
K. Hodge, BOS	50	S. Apps, PITT	61	W. Cashman, BOS	89
B. Goldsworthy, MINN	48	A. Boudrias, VAN	59	B. Clarke, PHI	87

SHOTS ON GOAL		SHOOTING PCT.		+/-	
P. Esposito, BOS	393	J. Bucyk, BOS	22.3	B. Orr, BOS	84
B. Orr, BOS	384	J. Bordeleau, CHI	22.0	A. Sims, BOS	64
G. Unger, STL	327	Y. Cournoyer, MONT	21.4	P. Esposito, BOS	51
B. Goldsworthy, MINN	321	R. Gilbert, NYR	21.4	B. White, CHI	51
R. Martin, BUF	320	D. Schultz, PHI	21.1	W. Cashman, BOS	49

PENALTY MINUTES		GOALS AGAINST AVE.		SHUTOUTS	
D. Schultz, PHI	348	B. Parent, PHI	1.89	B. Parent, PHI	12
A. Dupont, PHI	216	T. Esposito, CHI	2.04	T. Esposito, CHI	10
G. Howatt, NYI	204	W. Thomas, MONT	2.76	G. Gilbert, BOS	6
P. Russell, CHI	184	D. Bouchard, ATL	2.77	D. Bouchard, ATL	5
D. Potvin, NYI	175	R. Vachon, LA	2.80	R. Vachon, LA	5

	W	L	T	PTS	GF	GA	PPG	PPCT	SHG	PPGA	PKPCT	SHGA
CAMPBELL CONFERENCE												
PATRICK DIVISION												
*PHI	51	18	11	113	293	**181**	64	24.9	15	74	84.1	6
NYR	37	29	14	88	319	276	84	28.4	6	54	81.7	7
NYI	33	25	22	88	264	221	51	18.7	11	55	83.8	7
ATL	34	31	15	83	243	233	56	19.7	4	56	79.3	9
SMYTHE DIVISION												
VAN	38	32	10	86	271	254	70	20.8	5	59	80.3	**5**
STL	35	31	14	84	269	267	50	17.5	6	77	76.6	**5**
CHI	37	35	8	82	268	241	71	21.7	3	62	80.1	7
MINN	23	50	7	53	221	341	45	15.4	3	81	73.3	10
KC	15	54	11	41	184	328	57	16.2	6	53	77.3	6
PRINCE OF WALES CONFERENCE												
NORRIS DIVISION												
MONT	47	14	19	113	**374**	225	**92**	26.3	8	54	82.8	10
LA	42	17	21	105	269	185	53	18.1	10	**48**	**85.3**	7
PITT	37	28	15	89	326	289	64	19.8	13	63	80.6	11
DET	23	45	12	58	259	335	76	21.4	15	69	80.0	14
WASH	8	67	5	21	181	446	48	12.9	8	94	71.3	18
ADAMS DIVISION												
BUF	49	16	15	113	354	240	83	27.4	**17**	56	82.8	**5**
BOS	40	26	14	94	345	245	86	**28.8**	14	59	81.3	10
TOR	31	33	16	78	280	309	60	17.6	11	76	75.0	10
CALIF	19	48	13	51	212	316	48	13.4	5	67	74.9	13

CAMPBELL CONFERENCE

PATRICK DIVISION

	POS	PLAYER	GP	G	A	PTS	SOG	SPCT	PPG	+/-	GOALIE	W	L	T	GAvg
PHI	LW	B. Barber	79	34	37	71	276	12.3	8	46	B. Parent	**44**	14	9	**2.03**
F. Shero	C	B. Clarke	80	27	**89**	116	193	14.0	10	79	W. Stephenson	7	2	1	2.72
51–18–11	RW	R. Leach	80	45	33	78	289	15.6	12	53	B. Taylor	0	2	1	6.50
	LW	R. Lonsberry	80	24	25	49	180	13.3	9	28					
	C	R. MacLeish	80	38	41	79	309	12.3	11	29					
	RW	G. Dornhoefer	69	17	27	44	115	14.8	3	23					
	LW	B. Kelly	67	11	18	29	106	10.4	0	21					
	LW	D. Schultz	76	9	17	26	93	9.7	0	16					
	C	O. Kindrachuk	60	10	21	31	104	9.6	1	8					
	C	B. Clement	68	21	16	37	140	15.0	1	21					
	C	T. Crisp	71	8	19	27	70	11.4	0	11					
	RW	T. Bladon	76	9	20	29	174	5.2	5	7					
	RW	D. Saleski	63	10	18	28	113	8.8	0	7					
	D	A. Dupont	80	11	21	32	164	6.7	2	41					
	D	J. Watson	68	7	18	25	113	6.2	1	41					
	D	J. Watson	80	6	17	23	115	5.2	0	42					
NYR	LW	G. Polis	76	26	15	41	213	12.2	4	3	G. Villemure	22	14	6	3.16
E. Francis	C	J. Ratelle	79	36	55	91	205	17.6	16	1	E. Giacomin	13	12	8	3.48
37–29–14	RW	R. Gilbert	76	36	61	97	239	15.1	11	1	D. Wilson	1	2	0	4.33
	LW	S. Vickers	80	41	48	89	188	21.8	16	10	C. Ridley	1	1	0	5.19
	C	W. Tkaczuk	62	11	25	36	134	8.2	2	1					
	RW	B. Fairbairn	80	24	37	61	191	12.6	7	13					
	LW	T. Irvine	79	17	17	34	174	9.8	4	− 15					
	C	P. Stemkowski	77	24	35	59	159	15.1	3	− 3					
	C	D. Sanderson	75	25	25	50	188	13.3	3	10					
	RW	R. Middleton	47	22	18	40	106	20.8	6	− 6					
	RW	J. Butler	78	17	16	33	157	10.8	1	− 5					
	D	B. Park	65	13	44	57	189	6.9	7	6					
	D	R. Greschner	70	8	37	45	122	6.6	0	8					
	D	G. Marotte	77	4	32	36	148	2.7	0	0					
	D	N. Beverley	54	3	15	18	79	3.8	0	13					
	D	D. Rolfe	42	1	8	9	56	1.8	1	12					

TEAM	POS	PLAYER	GP	G	A	PTS	SOG	SPCT	PPG	+/-	GOALIE	W	L	T	GAvg
NYI	LW	C. Gillies	80	25	22	47	165	15.2	8	– 4	B. Smith	21	18	17	2.78
A. Arbour	C	A. St. Laurent	78	14	27	41	186	7.5	1	22	C. Resch	12	7	5	2.47
33–25–22	RW	B. Harris	80	25	37	62	199	12.6	4	3					
	LW	G. Howatt	77	18	30	48	126	14.3	1	32					
	C	B. Bourne	77	16	23	39	127	12.6	2	10					
	RW	B. Nystrom	76	27	28	55	194	13.9	3	17					
	LW	J. Parise	41	14	16	30	88	15.9	4	10					
	C	J. Drouin	40	14	18	32	93	15.1	2	8					
	C	R. Stewart	70	16	24	40	145	11.0	6	– 8					
	C	L. Henning	60	5	6	11	45	11.1	0	7					
	RW	E. Westfall	73	22	33	55	170	12.9	6	19					
	RW	B. MacMillan	69	13	12	25	74	17.6	2	0					
	D	D. Potvin	79	21	55	76	211	10.0	5	28					
	D	J. Potvin	73	9	24	33	115	7.8	6	– 3					
	D	B. Marshall	77	2	28	30	69	2.9	0	18					
	D	D. Lewis	78	5	14	19	95	5.3	0	8					
	D	G. Hart	71	4	14	18	81	4.9	0	28					

TEAM	POS	PLAYER	GP	G	A	PTS	SOG	SPCT	PPG	+/-	GOALIE	W	L	T	GAvg
ATL	LW	E. Vail	72	39	21	60	177	22.0	6	1	D. Bouchard	20	15	5	2.78
	C	T. Lysiak	77	25	52	77	206	12.1	9	23	P. Myre	14	16	10	2.85
B. Geoffrion	RW	C. Bennett	80	31	33	64	210	14.8	6	10					
22–20–10	LW	J. Richard	63	17	12	29	172	9.9	3	– 16					
F. Creighton	LW	B. Leiter	52	10	18	28	96	10.4	6	– 15					
12–11–5	C	B. Hextall	74	18	16	34	120	15.0	6	– 13					
	C	R. Comeau	75	14	20	34	116	12.1	2	9					
	RW	F. Harvey	79	17	27	44	156	10.9	4	4					
	RW	T. Ecclestone	62	13	21	34	103	12.6	0	7					
	RW	H. Graves	67	10	19	29	79	12.7	3	3					
	RW	J. Lemieux	75	3	24	27	140	2.1	1	– 3					
	D	R. Manery	68	5	27	32	118	4.2	3	18					
	D	P. Quinn	80	2	19	21	68	2.9	0	12					
	D	K. McCreary	78	11	10	21	79	13.9	2	12					
	D	N. Price	80	4	14	18	101	4.0	1	0					
	D	E. Kea	50	1	9	10	61	1.6	0	7					
	D	D. Bialowas	37	3	9	12	42	7.1	2	3					

SMYTHE DIVISION

TEAM	POS	PLAYER	GP	G	A	PTS	SOG	SPCT	PPG	+/-	GOALIE	W	L	T	GAvg
VAN	LW	D. Lever	80	38	30	68	214	17.8	11	– 13	G. Smith	32	24	9	3.09
	C	A. Boudrias	77	16	62	78	167	9.6	9	8	K. Lockett	6	7	1	3.16
P. Maloney	RW	D. Ververgaert	57	19	32	51	114	16.7	5	6	B. Bullock	0	1	0	4.00
38–32–10	LW	G. O'Flaherty	80	25	17	42	164	15.2	3	6					
	C	C. Oddleifson	60	16	35	51	74	21.6	3	17					
	RW	J. Gould	78	34	31	65	230	14.8	7	7					
	LW	L. Rochefort	76	18	11	29	124	14.5	3	– 5					
	LW	R. Sedlbauer	26	3	4	7	43	7.0	0	– 4					
	C	B. Lalonde	74	17	30	47	135	12.6	4	0					
	RW	P. Bordeleau	67	17	31	48	101	16.8	3	9					
	RW	G. Monahan	78	14	20	34	154	9.1	3	– 10					
	D	B. Dailey	70	12	36	48	170	7.1	7	– 9					
	D	A. DeMarco	61	10	14	24	117	8.5	8	– 2					
	D	G. Meehan	57	10	15	25	121	8.3	0	– 7					
	D	M. Robitaille	63	2	22	24	157	1.3	0	17					
	D	T. Pratt	79	5	17	22	100	5.0	1	6					
	D	G. Boddy	72	11	12	23	83	13.3	2	– 5					

TEAM	POS	PLAYER	GP	G	A	PTS	SOG	SPCT	PPG	+/-	GOALIE	W	L	T	GAvg
STL	LW	F. Thomson	77	9	27	36	111	8.1	0	13	J. Davidson	17	15	7	3.66
	C	W. Merrick	76	28	37	65	205	13.7	2	29	E. Johnston	12	13	5	3.10
L. Angotti	RW	P. Plante	80	34	32	66	162	21.0	4	16	Y. Belanger	6	3	2	2.72
2–5–2	LW	A. Bailey	49	15	26	41	102	14.7	4	– 4					
L. Patrick	LW	D. Palazzari	73	14	17	31	110	12.7	0	8					
1–0–1	C	G. Unger	80	36	44	80	349	10.3	10	– 1					
G. Young	C	C. Lefley	57	23	26	49	151	15.2	4	6					
32–26–11	C	R. Berenson	44	12	19	31	111	10.8	4	– 7					
	RW	B. Collins	70	22	15	37	142	15.5	2	4					
	RW	C. Larose	56	10	17	27	146	6.8	0	7					
	RW	C. Patrick	43	6	9	15	58	10.3	0	6					
	D	L. Sacharuk	76	20	22	42	207	9.7	11	– 9					
	D	B. Hess	76	9	30	39	110	8.2	4	7					
	D	B. Plager	76	4	24	28	88	4.5	0	20					
	D	B. Plager	73	1	14	15	85	1.2	0	10					
	D	B. Gassoff	60	4	14	18	77	5.2	1	11					

TEAM	POS	PLAYER	GP	G	A	PTS	SOG	SPCT	PPG	+/-	GOALIE	W	L	T	GAvg
CHI	LW	J. Marks	80	17	30	47	163	10.4	4	27	T. Esposito	34	30	7	2.74
B. Reay	C	S. Mikita	79	36	50	86	253	14.2	13	14	M. Veisor	1	5	1	4.70
37–35–8	RW	C. Koroll	80	27	32	59	164	16.5	11	20	M. Dumas	2	0	0	3.47
	LW	G. Gagnon	80	16	35	51	97	16.5	8	5					
	C	I. Boldirev	80	24	43	67	195	12.3	6	– 3					
	RW	J. Pappin	71	36	27	63	158	**22.8**	7	– 1					
	LW	D. Hull	69	16	21	37	199	8.0	4	– 14					
	LW	D. Rota	78	22	22	44	158	13.9	5	1					
	C	P. Martin	70	19	26	45	136	14.0	4	– 3					
	RW	J. Bordeleau	59	7	8	15	42	16.7	0	– 5					
	RW	G. Mulvey	74	7	4	11	59	11.9	0	– 3					
	D	D. Redmond	80	14	43	57	310	4.5	6	6					
	D	B. White	51	4	23	27	83	4.8	2	9					
	D	P. Russell	80	5	24	29	187	2.7	1	7					
	D	D. Jarrett	79	5	21	26	124	4.0	0	13					
	D	K. Magnuson	48	2	12	14	31	6.5	0	10					
MINN	LW	E. Hicke	42	15	13	28	114	13.2	7	– 26	C. Maniago	11	21	4	4.20
J. Gordon	C	D. Hextall	80	17	57	74	161	10.6	4	– 44	P. LoPresti	9	20	3	4.19
11–23–5	RW	B. Goldsworthy	71	37	35	72	273	13.6	11	– 37	F. Rivard	3	9	0	4.24
C. Burns	LW	N. Gratton	34	14	12	26	88	15.9	4	– 11					
12–27–2	LW	J. Parise	38	9	16	25	65	13.8	1	– 18					
	LW	J. Flesch	57	8	15	23	77	10.4	2	– 19					
	C	M. Oliver	80	19	15	34	137	13.9	3	– 19					
	C	H. Boucha	51	15	14	29	129	11.6	1	– 12					
	C	B. Dunlop	52	9	18	27	82	11.0	2	– 7					
	C	F. Stanfield	40	8	18	26	107	7.5	2	– 14					
	RW	D. Talafous	43	8	17	25	68	11.8	0	– 17					
	RW	C. Cameron	40	10	7	17	65	15.4	1	5					
	RW	D. Martineau	76	6	9	15	54	11.1	0	– 13					
	D	B. Gibbs	37	4	20	24	101	4.0	2	– 13					
	D	F. Barrett	62	3	18	21	79	3.8	0	– 21					
	D	D. Hicks	80	6	12	18	76	7.9	1	– 25					
	D	T. Reid	74	1	5	6	98	1.0	0	– 39					
KC	LW	G. Charron	51	13	29	42	157	8.3	4	– 41	P. McDuffe	7	25	4	4.23
B. Guidolin	C	D. Hudson	70	9	32	41	115	7.8	2	– 19	M. Plasse	4	16	3	4.06
15–54–11	RW	S. Nolet	72	26	32	58	197	13.2	11	– 52	D. Herron	4	13	4	3.75
	LW	R. Burns	71	18	15	33	126	14.3	7	– 40					
	C	E. Gilbert	80	16	22	38	190	8.4	9	– 45					
	RW	W. Paiement	78	26	13	39	195	13.3	6	– 42					
	LW	R. Rota	80	15	18	33	182	8.2	3	– 39					
	LW	G. Croteau	77	8	11	19	137	5.8	0	– 36					
	LW	N. Dube	56	8	10	18	77	10.4	2	– 1					
	C	L. Powis	73	11	20	31	149	7.4	3	– 54					
	C	D. Lemieux	79	10	20	30	131	7.6	3	– 35					
	RW	G. Coalter	30	2	4	6	20	10.0	0	– 8					
	RW	L. Johnston	16	0	7	7	12	.0	0	– 8					
	RW	T. Snell	29	3	2	5	25	12.0	0	– 8					
	D	J. McElmury	78	5	17	22	137	3.6	1	– 48					
	D	B. Hughes	66	1	18	19	80	1.3	0	– 51					
	D	C. Houde	34	3	4	7	43	7.0	2	– 31					

PRINCE OF WALES CONFERENCE

NORRIS DIVISION

TEAM	POS	PLAYER	GP	G	A	PTS	SOG	SPCT	PPG	+/-	GOALIE	W	L	T	GAvg
MONT	LW	S. Shutt	77	30	35	65	165	18.2	3	40	K. Dryden	30	9	16	2.69
S. Bowman	C	P. Mahovlich	80	35	82	117	240	14.6	14	41	M. Larocque	17	5	3	3.00
47–14–19	RW	G. Lafleur	70	53	66	119	260	20.4	15	52					
	LW	M. Wilson	73	24	18	42	135	17.8	4	13					
	C	J. Lemaire	80	36	56	92	260	13.8	12	25					
	RW	Y. Cournoyer	76	29	45	74	176	16.5	11	16					
	LW	Y. Lambert	80	32	35	67	150	21.3	10	26					
	LW	B. Gainey	80	17	20	37	132	12.9	1	23					
	LW	G. Sather	63	6	10	16	23	26.1	0	14					
	C	D. Risebrough	64	15	32	47	111	13.5	2	27					
	C	H. Richard	16	3	10	13	33	9.1	0	9					
	RW	M. Tremblay	63	21	18	39	127	16.5	0	23					
	D	G. Lapointe	80	28	47	75	219	12.8	11	46					
	D	L. Robinson	80	14	47	61	102	13.7	1	61					
	D	S. Savard	80	20	40	60	165	12.1	8	71					
	D	P. Bouchard	79	3	9	12	67	4.5	0	24					
	D	J. Roberts	79	5	13	18	85	5.9	0	18					

TEAM	POS	PLAYER	GP	G	A	PTS	SOG	SPCT	PPG	+/–	GOALIE	W	L	T	GAvg
LA	LW	D. Maloney	80	27	39	66	227	11.9	3	29	R. Vachon	27	14	13	2.24
B. Pulford	C	B. Goring	60	27	33	60	134	20.1	6	26	G. Edwards	15	3	8	2.34
42–17–21	RW	B. Nevin	80	31	41	72	157	19.7	7	36					
	LW	B. Berry	80	25	23	48	136	18.4	7	21					
	LW	T. Williams	74	24	22	46	188	12.8	6	14					
	LW	G. Carr	80	7	32	39	157	4.5	3	19					
	C	J. Widing	80	26	34	60	186	14.0	7	18					
	C	St. Marseille	80	17	36	53	168	10.1	0	12					
	C	V. Venasky	17	1	2	3	17	5.9	1	1					
	RW	M. Murphy	78	30	38	68	175	17.1	3	32					
	RW	M. Corrigan	80	13	21	34	100	13.0	3	9					
	RW	D. Kozak	77	16	15	31	109	14.7	2	5					
	D	B. Murdoch	80	13	29	42	201	6.5	2	39					
	D	T. Harper	80	5	21	26	96	5.2	1	38					
	D	N. Komadoski	75	4	12	16	66	6.1	3	10					
	D	L. Brown	78	1	15	16	83	1.2	0	31					
	D	D. Hutchison	68	0	6	6	55	.0	0	5					
PITT	LW	V. Hadfield	78	31	42	73	253	12.3	7	5	G. Inness	24	18	10	3.09
M. Boileau	C	R. Schock	80	23	63	86	172	13.4	3	22	M. Plasse	9	5	4	4.00
37–28–15	RW	R. Kehoe	76	32	31	63	240	13.3	3	18	B. Johnson	3	4	1	5.04
	LW	L. MacDonald	71	27	33	60	220	12.3	6	16	D. Herron	1	1	0	6.11
	C	S. Apps	79	24	55	79	181	13.3	4	8					
	RW	J. Pronovost	78	43	32	75	275	15.6	1	13					
	LW	B. Kelly	69	27	24	51	223	12.1	5	6					
	LW	N. Debenedet	31	6	3	9	28	21.4	1	– 3					
	C	P. Larouche	79	31	37	68	172	18.0	5	2					
	C	P. Laframboise	35	5	13	18	33	15.2	3	3					
	RW	C. Arnason	78	26	32	58	214	12.1	7	0					
	RW	L. Morrison	52	7	5	12	41	17.1	1	– 5					
	D	C. Campbell	59	4	15	19	84	4.8	0	28					
	D	R. Stackhouse	72	15	45	60	152	9.9	6	13					
	D	B. Wilkins	59	5	29	34	83	6.0	0	29					
	D	D. Burrows	78	2	15	17	126	1.6	0	3					
	D	B. Paradise	78	3	15	18	55	5.5	0	– 2					
DET	LW	D. Grant	80	50	37	87	241	20.7	19	– 11	J. Rutherford	20	29	10	3.74
A. Delvecchio	LW	N. Libett	80	23	28	51	194	11.9	8	– 41	B. McKenzie	1	9	2	4.70
23–45–12	LW	H. Nowak	56	8	14	22	110	7.3	1	– 34	D. Grant	1	5	0	5.37
	LW	G. Charron	26	1	10	11	27	3.7	0	– 9	T. Richardson	1	2	0	6.83
	C	M. Dionne	80	47	74	121	378	12.4	15	– 15					
	C	B. Hogaboam	60	14	27	41	129	10.9	6	– 34					
	C	P. Jarry	39	8	13	21	90	8.9	0	– 12					
	C	W. McKechnie	23	6	11	17	41	14.6	1	– 3					
	RW	P. Roberto	46	13	27	40	113	11.5	5	– 10					
	RW	M. Redmond	29	15	12	27	93	16.1	5	– 12					
	RW	B. Lochead	65	16	12	28	116	13.8	3	– 30					
	RW	M. Bergeron	25	10	7	17	51	19.6	1	5					
	D	G. Bergman	76	5	25	30	100	5.0	2	– 25					
	D	J. Hamel	80	5	19	24	112	4.5	0	– 40					
	D	L. Giroux	39	2	20	22	57	3.5	1	– 10					
	D	B. Watson	70	1	13	14	68	1.5	0	– 29					
	D	B. Crashley	48	2	15	17	44	4.5	0	– 9					
WASH	LW	D. Dupere	53	20	15	35	133	15.0	8	– 41	R. Low	8	**36**	2	5.45
J. Anderson	LW	M. Marson	76	16	12	28	89	18.0	5	– 65	M. Belhumeur	0	24	3	5.36
4–45–5	LW	M. Bloom	67	7	19	26	88	8.0	0	– 54	J. Adams	0	7	0	6.90
R. Sullivan	LW	D. Kryskow	51	9	15	24	98	9.2	1	– 28					
2–17–0	LW	B. Lesuk	79	8	11	19	119	6.7	1	– 34					
M. Schmidt	C	T. Williams	73	22	36	58	135	16.3	7	– 69					
2–5–0	C	R. Lalonde	50	12	14	26	67	17.9	4	– 39					
	C	P. Laframboise	45	5	10	15	86	5.8	0	– 37					
	RW	R. Anderson	28	9	7	16	43	20.9	4	– 20					
	RW	S. Atkinson	46	11	4	15	92	12.0	3	– 26					
	RW	G. Brooks	38	1	10	11	79	1.3	1	– 19					
	D	Y. Labre	76	4	23	27	72	5.6	0	– 54					
	D	D. Mohns	75	2	19	21	83	2.4	1	– 53					
	D	G. Joly	44	1	7	8	72	1.4	1	– 68					
	D	B. Mikkelson	59	3	7	10	49	6.1	3	– 82					
	D	G. Smith	63	3	8	11	56	5.4	2	– 60					
	D	P. Nicholson	39	4	5	9	46	8.7	0	– 29					

ADAMS DIVISION

TEAM	POS	PLAYER	GP	G	A	PTS	SOG	SPCT	PPG	+/–	GOALIE	W	L	T	GAvg
BUF	LW	R. Martin	68	52	43	95	301	17.3	21	5	G. Bromley	26	11	11	3.10
F. Smith	C	G. Perreault	68	39	57	96	245	15.9	12	1	R. Crozier	17	2	1	2.62
49–16–15	RW	R. Robert	74	40	60	100	264	15.2	14	6	G. Desjardins	6	2	1	2.78
	LW	C. Ramsay	80	26	38	64	200	13.0	1	51	R. Farr	0	1	2	3.94
	C	D. Luce	80	33	43	76	245	13.5	1	61					
	RW	D. Gare	78	31	31	62	274	11.3	5	40					
	LW	R. Dudley	78	31	39	70	226	13.7	4	29					
	LW	B. Spencer	73	12	29	41	126	9.5	1	17					
	LW	N. Gratton	25	3	6	9	16	18.8	1	2					
	C	J. Lorentz	72	25	45	70	140	17.9	6	17					
	C	P. McNab	53	22	21	43	90	24.4	1	13					
	RW	F. Stanfield	32	12	21	33	77	15.6	6	9					
	D	J. Korab	79	12	44	56	218	5.5	3	41					
	D	J. Schoenfeld	68	1	19	20	148	.7	0	35					
	D	B. Hajt	76	3	26	29	107	2.8	1	47					
	D	J. Guevremont	64	7	25	32	160	4.4	4	32					
	D	L. Fogolin	5	2	2	4	14	14.3	2	0					
BOS	LW	D. Marcotte	80	31	33	64	165	18.8	1	24	G. Gilbert	23	17	11	3.13
D. Cherry	C	P. Esposito	79	**61**	66	127	347	17.6	**27**	18	R. Brooks	10	3	3	2.98
40–26–14	RW	K. Hodge	72	23	43	66	175	13.1	16	7	K. Broderick	7	6	0	2.39
	LW	J. Bucyk	78	29	52	81	167	17.4	9	11					
	C	G. Sheppard	76	30	48	78	249	12.0	5	43					
	RW	B. Schmautz	56	21	30	51	156	13.5	1	23					
	LW	W. Cashman	42	11	22	33	75	14.7	2	7					
	LW	D. Forbes	69	18	12	30	89	20.2	0	22					
	LW	H. Nowak	21	4	7	11	38	10.5	0	8					
	C	A. Savard	77	19	25	44	150	12.7	0	16					
	C	W. McKechnie	53	3	3	6	36	8.3	0	– 6					
	RW	T. O'Reilly	68	15	20	35	93	16.1	2	15					
	D	B. Orr	80	46	**89**	**135**	**384**	12.0	16	**80**					
	D	C. Vadnais	79	18	56	74	256	7.0	6	10					
	D	D. Smith	79	3	20	23	146	2.1	0	30					
	D	A. Sims	75	4	8	12	102	3.9	0	29					
	D	D. Edestrand	68	1	9	10	86	1.2	0	8					
TOR	LW	T. Williams	42	10	19	29	83	12.0	2	4	D. Favell	12	17	6	4.05
R. Kelly	C	D. Sittler	72	36	44	80	273	13.2	12	– 10	D. Wilson	8	11	4	3.70
31–33–16	RW	R. Ellis	79	32	29	61	177	18.1	11	9	G. McRae	10	3	6	3.22
	LW	E. Thompson	65	25	17	42	202	12.4	3	– 1	P. Hamel	1	2	0	5.54
	C	G. Ferguson	69	19	30	49	134	14.2	3	5					
	RW	L. McDonald	64	17	27	44	168	10.1	2	5					
	LW	I. Hammarstrom	69	21	20	41	170	12.4	3	– 14					
	LW	B. Stoughton	78	23	14	37	161	14.3	4	– 7					
	C	D. Keon	78	16	43	59	183	8.7	1	3					
	C	N. Ullman	80	9	26	35	117	7.7	1	– 12					
	RW	B. Flett	77	15	25	40	186	8.1	4	0					
	RW	G. Sabourin	55	5	18	23	114	4.4	1	– 13					
	D	J. McKenny	66	8	35	43	105	7.6	0	– 4					
	D	B. Salming	60	12	25	37	136	8.8	4	4					
	D	B. Glennie	63	1	7	8	55	1.8	0	– 5					
	D	D. Dunn	72	3	11	14	76	3.9	0	– 10					
	D	R. Seiling	60	5	12	17	94	5.3	1	8					
CALIF	LW	D. Hrechkosy	72	29	14	43	178	16.3	8	– 17	G. Meloche	9	27	10	4.03
M. Johnston	LW	J. Stewart	76	19	19	38	191	9.9	2	– 42	G. Simmons	10	21	3	3.67
11–28–9	LW	C. Simmer	35	8	13	21	46	17.4	2	– 2					
B. McCreary	LW	B. Lavender	65	3	7	10	30	10.0	0	– 10					
8–20–4	C	L. Patey	79	25	20	45	156	16.0	8	– 20					
	C	S. Weir	80	18	27	45	128	14.1	4	– 30					
	C	D. Gardner	64	16	20	36	133	12.0	6	– 19					
	C	R. Huston	23	3	10	13	29	10.3	0	– 12					
	RW	A. MacAdam	80	18	25	43	160	11.3	2	– 23					
	RW	J. Johnston	62	14	23	37	133	10.5	5	– 30					
	RW	B. Williams	63	11	21	32	109	10.1	2	– 16					
	RW	M. Mott	52	3	8	11	31	9.7	0	– 10					
	RW	J. Moxey	47	5	4	9	77	6.5	1	– 4					
	D	R. Hampton	78	8	17	25	99	8.1	1	– 40					
	D	L. Frig	80	3	17	20	149	2.0	3	– 28					
	D	J. Neilson	72	3	17	20	112	2.7	0	– 46					
	D	B. Stewart	67	5	12	17	87	5.7	0	– 18					

GOALS	
P. Esposito, BOS	61
G. Lafleur, MONT	53
R. Martin, BUF	52
D. Grant, DET	50
M. Dionne, DET	47

ASSISTS	
B. Orr, BOS	89
B. Clarke, PHI	89
P. Mahovlich, MONT	82
M. Dionne, DET	74
P. Esposito, BOS	66

POINTS	
B. Orr, BOS	135
P. Esposito, BOS	127
M. Dionne, DET	121
G. Lafleur, MONT	119
P. Mahovlich, MONT	117

SHOTS ON GOAL		SHOOTING PCT.		+/-	
B. Orr, BOS	384	J. Pappin, CHI	22.8	B. Orr, BOS	80
M. Dionne, DET	378	E. Vail, ATL	22.0	B. Clarke, PHI	79
G. Unger, STL	349	S. Vickers, NYR	21.8	S. Savard, MONT	71
P. Esposito, BOS	347	Y. Lambert, MONT	21.3	D. Luce, BUF	61
D. Redmond, CHI	310	P. Plante, STL	21.0	L. Robinson, MONT	61

PENALTY MINUTES		GOALS AGAINST AVE.		SHUTOUTS	
D. Schultz, PHI	472	B. Parent, PHI	2.03	B. Parent, PHI	12
A. Dupont, PHI	276	R. Vachon, LA	2.24	R. Vachon, LA	6
P. Russell, CHI	260	K. Dryden, MONT	2.69	T. Esposito, CHI	6
B. Watson, DET	238	T. Esposito, CHI	2.74	P. Myre, ATL	5
B. Gassoff, STL	222	D. Bouchard, ATL	2.78	K. Dryden, MONT	4
		B. Smith, NYI	2.78		

National Hockey League 1975–76

	W	L	T	PTS	GF	GA	PPG	PPCT	SHG	PPGA	PKPCT	SHGA
CAMPBELL CONFERENCE												
PATRICK DIVISION												
PHI	51	13	16	118	**348**	209	83	28.6	14	83	82.7	4
NYI	42	21	17	101	297	190	**92**	**31.7**	11	55	**85.4**	4
ATL	35	33	12	82	262	237	56	19.1	7	**43**	84.5	5
NYR	29	42	9	67	262	333	67	20.7	3	68	7.5	11
SMYTHE DIVISION												
CHI	32	30	18	82	254	261	72	21.1	9	53	82.6	8
VAN	33	32	15	81	271	272	68	19.7	6	71	75.6	9
STL	29	37	14	72	249	290	55	18.5	**21**	98	73.9	3
MINN	20	53	7	47	195	303	48	14.5	2	82	73.5	16
KC	12	56	12	36	190	351	46	13.1	2	80	72.9	17
PRINCE OF WALES CONFERENCE												
NORRIS DIVISION												
*MONT	58	11	11	127	337	**174**	75	22.6	7	44	84.8	**0**
LA	38	33	9	85	263	265	61	18.3	8	55	81.5	12
PITT	35	33	12	82	339	303	75	24.4	8	68	76.7	13
DET	26	44	10	62	226	300	47	15.3	9	86	79.6	6
WASH	11	59	10	32	224	394	53	14.1	2	64	74.6	3
ADAMS DIVISION												
BOS	48	15	17	113	313	237	77	16.6	9	56	83.8	6
BUF	46	21	13	105	339	240	73	25.4	6	51	83.2	8
TOR	34	31	15	83	294	276	67	19.3	11	77	76.0	9
CALIF	27	42	11	65	250	278	71	18.6	9	52	80.2	10

CAMPBELL CONFERENCE

PATRICK DIVISION

PHI
F. Shero
51–13–16

POS	PLAYER	GP	G	A	PTS	SOG	SPCT	PPG	+/-
LW	B. Barber	80	50	62	112	**380**	13.2	15	74
C	B. Clarke	76	30	**89**	119	194	15.5	10	**83**
RW	R. Leach	80	**61**	30	91	335	18.2	10	73
LW	R. Lonsberry	80	19	28	47	209	9.1	4	29
C	M. Bridgman	80	23	27	50	166	13.9	5	22
RW	G. Dornhoefer	74	28	35	63	152	18.4	13	14
LW	D. Schultz	71	13	19	32	91	14.3	0	24
LW	B. Kelly	79	12	8	20	103	11.7	0	3
C	O. Kindrachuk	76	26	49	75	181	14.4	5	32
C	R. MacLeish	51	22	23	45	222	9.9	6	6
RW	D. Saleski	78	21	26	47	224	9.4	1	33
D	A. Dupont	75	9	27	36	139	6.5	3	40
D	J. Watson	78	2	22	24	88	2.3	0	56
D	J. Watson	78	2	22	24	88	2.3	0	56
D	T. Bladon	80	14	23	37	182	7.7	5	45
D	L. Goodenough	77	8	34	42	149	5.4	5	45
D	J. McIlhargey	57	1	2	3	23	4.3	0	11

GOALIE	W	L	T	GAvg
W. Stephenson	40	10	13	2.58
B. Parent	6	2	3	2.34
B. Taylor	3	1	0	3.75
G. Inness	2	0	0	1.50
J. Mrazek	0	0	0	10.00

	POS	PLAYER	GP	G	A	PTS	SOG	SPCT	PPG	+/-	GOALIE	W	L	T	GAvg
NYI	LW	C. Gillies	80	34	27	61	210	16.2	15	20	C. Resch	23	11	8	2.07
A. Arbour	C	B. Trottier	80	32	63	95	178	18.0	11	28	B. Smith	19	10	9	2.61
42–21–17	RW	B. Harris	80	32	38	70	228	14.0	16	22					
	LW	J. Parise	80	22	35	57	152	14.5	5	12					
	C	J. Drouin	76	21	41	62	153	13.7	10	18					
	RW	E. Westfall	80	25	31	56	154	16.2	6	17					
	LW	G. Howatt	80	21	13	34	115	18.3	0	26					
	C	A. St. Laurent	67	9	17	26	101	8.9	0	14					
	C	L. Henning	80	7	10	17	84	8.3	0	6					
	C	R. Stewart	31	6	7	13	28	21.4	0	3					
	RW	B. Nystrom	80	23	25	48	185	12.4	2	24					
	RW	B. MacMillan	64	9	7	16	75	12.0	0	5					
	D	D. Potvin	78	31	67	98	256	12.1	**18**	12					
	D	D. Lewis	73	0	19	19	91	.0	0	29					
	D	G. Hart	80	6	18	24	110	5.5	0	35					
	D	B. Marshall	71	0	16	16	70	.0	0	37					
ATL	LW	C. St. Sauveur	79	24	24	48	171	14.0	11	– 6	D. Bouchard	19	17	8	2.54
F. Creighton	LW	E. Vail	60	16	31	47	127	12.6	2	7	P. Myre	16	16	4	3.47
35–33–12	LW	D. Kryskow	79	15	25	40	120	12.5	1	– 6					
	LW	K. Houston	38	5	6	11	49	10.2	1	– 3					
	LW	B. Leiter	26	2	3	5	26	7.7	1	0					
	C	T. Lysiak	80	31	51	82	233	13.3	9	2					
	C	C. Bennett	80	34	31	65	221	15.4	8	1					
	C	R. Comeau	79	17	22	39	124	13.7	1	9					
	C	B. Clement	31	13	14	27	71	18.3	2	3					
	RW	H. Graves	80	19	30	49	168	11.3	2	3					
	RW	B. Flett	78	23	17	40	171	13.5	1	9					
	RW	T. Ecclestone	69	6	21	27	117	5.1	1	7					
	D	R. Manery	80	7	32	39	139	5.0	3	2					
	D	B. Gibbs	76	8	21	29	125	6.4	1	1					
	D	L. Romanchych	67	16	19	35	110	14.5	6	– 7					
	D	E. Kea	78	8	19	27	125	6.4	1	21					
	D	L. Carriere	75	4	15	19	126	3.2	1	5					
NYR	LW	S. Vickers	80	30	53	83	202	14.9	10	– 17	J. Davidson	22	28	5	3.97
R. Stewart	C	W. Tkaczuk	78	8	28	36	142	5.6	1	– 10	D. Wilson	5	9	3	4.22
15–20–4	RW	B. Fairbairn	80	13	15	28	160	8.1	2	– 14	D. Soetaert	2	2	0	5.27
J. Ferguson	LW	G. Polis	79	15	21	36	158	9.5	0	– 8	E. Giacomin	0	3	1	4.75
14–22–5	LW	P. Hickey	70	14	22	36	157	8.9	0	– 29					
	LW	J. Holland	36	7	4	11	50	14.0	2	– 5					
	C	P. Esposito	62	29	38	67	217	13.4	6	– 39					
	C	W. Dillon	79	21	24	45	138	15.2	3	– 11					
	C	P. Stemkowski	75	13	28	41	126	10.3	1	– 7					
	RW	R. Gilbert	70	36	50	86	211	17.1	9	– 8					
	RW	R. Middleton	77	24	26	50	159	15.1	7	– 38					
	D	C. Vadnais	64	20	30	50	197	10.2	7	– 17					
	D	R. Greschner	77	6	21	27	176	3.4	2	– 51					
	D	G. Marotte	57	4	17	21	113	3.5	1	– 3					
	D	L. Sacharuk	42	6	7	13	70	8.6	4	– 14					
	D	N. Beverley	63	1	8	9	75	1.3	0	– 9					
	D	D. Jarrett	45	0	4	4	45	.0	0	– 26					

SMYTHE DIVISION

	POS	PLAYER	GP	G	A	PTS	SOG	SPCT	PPG	+/-	GOALIE	W	L	T	GAvg
CHI	LW	D. Hull	80	27	39	66	225	12.0	1	– 17	T. Esposito	30	23	13	2.97
B. Reay	C	P. Martin	80	32	39	71	188	17.0	8	6	G. Villemure	2	7	5	4.29
32–30–18	RW	D. Rota	79	20	17	37	201	10.0	4	– 8					
	LW	J. Marks	80	21	23	44	152	13.8	6	– 4					
	C	S. Mikita	48	16	41	57	159	10.1	6	– 4					
	RW	C. Koroll	80	25	33	58	185	13.5	11	6					
	LW	B. Sheehan	78	11	20	31	129	8.5	2	– 4					
	LW	J. Johnston	32	0	5	5	20	.0	0	– 5					
	C	I. Boldirev	78	28	34	62	178	15.7	5	– 23					
	RW	J. Bordeleau	76	12	18	30	71	16.9	1	– 9					
	RW	G. Mulvey	64	11	17	28	90	12.2	1	– 5					
	RW	A. Daigle	71	15	9	24	85	17.6	8	– 18					
	D	D. Tallon	80	15	47	62	161	9.3	7	– 11					
	D	P. Russell	74	9	29	38	180	5.0	7	– 20					
	D	B. White	59	1	9	10	46	2.2	0	– 10					
	D	D. Redmond	53	9	27	36	165	5.5	5	1					
	D	K. Magnuson	48	1	6	7	27	3.7	0	13					

	POS	PLAYER	GP	G	A	PTS	SOG	SPCT	PPG	+/-	GOALIE	W	L	T	GAvg
VAN	LW	J. Gould	70	32	27	59	225	14.2	6	9	G. Smith	20	24	6	3.50
	LW	G. O'Flaherty	68	20	18	38	129	15.5	0	11	K. Lockett	7	8	7	3.47
P. Maloney	LW	R. Sedlbauer	56	19	13	32	135	14.1	5	– 4	C. Ridley	6	0	2	2.28
33–32–15	LW	G. Richardson	24	3	6	9	27	11.1	0	– 1					
	C	D. Lever	80	25	40	65	166	15.1	8	– 2					
	C	C. Oddleifson	80	16	46	62	133	12.0	2	17					
	C	B. Lalonde	71	14	36	50	143	9.8	2	– 4					
	C	A. Boudrias	71	7	31	38	69	10.1	2	– 7					
	RW	D. Ververgaert	80	37	34	71	207	17.9	11	– 1					
	RW	R. Blight	74	25	31	56	212	11.8	10	– 4					
	RW	G. Monahan	66	16	17	33	126	12.7	3	1					
	RW	P. Bordeleau	48	5	12	17	35	14.3	0	– 1					
	D	D. Kearns	80	5	46	51	118	4.2	1	– 6					
	D	B. Dailey	67	15	24	39	187	8.0	9	– 5					
	D	H. Snepsts	78	3	15	18	74	4.1	0	10					
	D	M. Robitaille	71	8	19	27	164	4.9	2	8					
	D	B. Murray	65	2	5	7	48	4.2	0	3					
STL	LW	B. MacMillan	80	20	32	52	151	13.2	2	13	E. Johnston	11	17	9	3.62
	LW	B. Affleck	80	4	26	30	100	4.0	3	– 12	Y. Belanger	11	17	1	3.85
G. Young	LW	T. Irvine	69	10	13	23	105	9.5	2	– 4	E. Staniowski	5	3	2	3.19
9–15–5	LW	F. Thomson	58	8	10	18	71	11.3	0	– 4	G. Gratton	2	0	2	2.49
L. Patrick	LW	B. Wilson	45	2	3	5	25	8.0	0	– 6					
3–5–0	C	G. Unger	80	39	44	83	357	10.9	13	1					
L. Boivin	C	C. Lefley	75	43	42	85	207	20.8	4	15					
17–17–9	C	D. Sanderson	65	24	43	67	171	14.0	6	13					
	C	R. Berenson	72	20	27	47	171	11.7	9	– 11					
	C	L. Patey	53	8	6	14	80	10.0	2	– 12					
	RW	P. Plante	74	14	19	33	125	11.2	5	– 22					
	RW	C. Larose	67	13	25	38	169	7.7	3	7					
	RW	J. Butler	66	17	24	41	154	11.0	1	0					
	D	B. Hess	78	9	23	32	117	7.7	2	3					
	D	B. Gassoff	80	1	12	13	100	1.0	0	– 8					
	D	B. Plager	63	3	8	11	43	7.0	0	17					
	D	B. Plager	64	0	8	8	32	.0	0	– 6					
MINN	LW	P. Jarry	59	21	18	39	143	14.7	3	– 7	C. Maniago	13	27	5	3.35
	C	T. Young	63	18	33	51	127	14.2	5	– 10	P. LoPresti	7	22	1	4.13
T. Harris	RW	D. Talafous	79	18	30	48	137	13.1	4	– 12	P. Harrison	0	4	1	5.47
20–53–7	LW	E. Hicke	80	23	19	42	185	12.4	6	– 31					
	LW	G. Sather	72	9	10	19	73	12.3	1	– 8					
	LW	J. Flesch	33	3	2	5	26	11.5	1	– 8					
	LW	N. Gratton	32	7	3	10	51	13.7	3	– 12					
	C	D. Hextall	59	11	35	46	93	11.8	2	– 29					
	C	B. Hextall	58	8	20	28	89	9.0	3	– 16					
	C	B. Dunlop	33	9	11	20	55	16.4	1	– 9					
	RW	B. Goldsworthy	68	24	22	46	174	13.8	6	– 19					
	RW	C. Cameron	78	8	10	18	73	11.0	1	– 27					
	RW	L. Nanne	79	3	14	17	83	3.6	2	– 34					
	D	D. Bialowas	58	5	18	23	87	5.7	5	– 9					
	D	D. Hicks	80	5	13	18	102	4.9	3	– 17					
	D	T. Reid	69	0	15	15	90	.0	0	– 24					
	D	D. O'Brien	78	1	14	15	72	1.4	0	– 26					
KC	LW	G. Charron	78	27	44	71	226	11.9	9	– 51	D. Herron	11	**39**	11	4.03
	C	D. Hudson	74	11	20	31	114	9.6	2	– 28	B. McKenzie	1	16	1	5.20
B. Guidolin	RW	W. Paiement	57	21	22	43	178	11.8	4	– 37	B. Oleschuk	0	1	0	4.00
11–30–4	LW	G. Croteau	79	19	14	33	139	13.7	4	– 24					
S. Abel	LW	N. Libett	80	20	26	46	224	8.9	3	– 9					
0–3–0	LW	R. Burns	78	13	18	31	145	9.0	2	– 40					
E. Bush	LW	R. Rota	71	12	14	26	146	8.2	2	– 33					
1–23–8	LW	D. Dupere	43	6	8	14	37	16.2	2	– 8					
	C	E. Gilbert	41	4	8	12	74	5.4	1	– 29					
	C	H. Boucha	28	4	7	11	42	9.5	2	– 13					
	RW	C. Patrick	80	17	18	35	143	11.9	3	– 24					
	RW	C. Arnason	39	14	10	24	122	11.5	5	– 35					
	RW	S. Nolet	41	10	15	25	123	8.1	2	– 9					
	RW	P. Roberto	37	7	15	22	89	7.9	3	– 11					
	D	G. Bergman	75	5	33	38	125	4.0	1	– 52					
	D	D. Patterson	69	5	16	21	76	6.6	0	– 23					
	D	J. Lagace	69	3	10	13	75	4.0	1	– 38					

PRINCE OF WALES CONFERENCE

NORRIS DIVISION

TEAM	POS	PLAYER	GP	G	A	PTS	SOG	SPCT	PPG	+/-	GOALIE	W	L	T	GAvg
MONT	LW	S. Shutt	80	45	34	79	223	20.2	7	73	K. Dryden	**42**	10	8	**2.03**
S. Bowman	C	P. Mahovlich	80	34	71	105	200	17.0	8	71	M. Larocque	16	1	3	2.46
58–11–11	RW	G. Lafleur	80	56	69	**125**	303	18.5	**18**	68					
	LW	Y. Lambert	80	32	35	67	156	20.5	12	10					
	C	D. Risebrough	80	16	28	44	143	11.2	1	18					
	RW	M. Tremblay	71	11	16	27	94	11.7	1	5					
	LW	B. Gainey	78	15	13	28	155	9.7	1	20					
	LW	M. Wilson	59	11	24	35	73	15.1	2	25					
	C	J. Lemaire	61	20	32	52	226	8.8	6	26					
	C	D. Jarvis	80	5	30	35	92	5.4	0	17					
	RW	Y. Cournoyer	71	32	36	68	163	19.6	8	37					
	D	G. Lapointe	77	21	47	68	317	6.6	8	64					
	D	J. Potvin	78	17	55	72	167	10.2	9	16					
	D	L. Robinson	80	10	30	40	130	7.7	2	50					
	D	S. Savard	71	8	39	47	112	7.1	1	52					
	D	D. Awrey	72	0	12	12	60	.0	0	30					
	D	P. Bouchard	66	1	11	12	72	1.4	0	20					
LA	LW	T. Williams	70	19	20	39	157	12.1	4	0	R. Vachon	26	20	5	3.14
B. Pulford	C	M. Dionne	80	40	54	94	329	12.2	7	2	G. Edwards	12	13	4	3.55
38–33–9	RW	M. Murphy	80	26	42	68	205	12.7	7	– 3					
	LW	B. Berry	80	20	22	42	156	12.8	3	2					
	C	B. Goring	80	33	40	73	193	17.1	5	0					
	RW	B. Nevin	77	13	42	55	121	10.7	2	10					
	LW	G. Carr	38	8	11	19	61	13.1	0	– 1					
	C	V. Venasky	80	18	26	44	103	17.5	4	– 6					
	C	St. Marseille	68	10	16	26	66	15.2	2	– 14					
	C	J. Widing	67	7	15	22	84	8.3	1	– 12					
	RW	D. Kozak	62	20	24	44	81	**24.7**	7	– 4					
	RW	M. Corrigan	71	22	21	43	135	16.3	9	– 2					
	D	B. Murdoch	80	6	29	35	172	3.5	2	13					
	D	G. Sargent	63	8	16	24	87	9.2	3	– 3					
	D	D. Hutchison	50	0	10	10	61	.0	0	4					
	D	S. Kannegiesser	70	4	9	13	79	5.1	2	10					
	D	N. Komadoski	80	3	15	18	94	3.2	1	7					
PITT	LW	B. Kelly	77	25	30	55	193	13.0	5	4	M. Plasse	24	19	10	3.45
M. Boileau	C	P. Larouche	76	53	58	111	319	16.6	**18**	4	G. Inness	8	9	2	4.06
15–23–5	RW	R. Kehoe	71	29	47	76	180	16.1	5	9	G. Laxton	3	4	0	4.49
K. Schinkel	LW	L. MacDonald	69	30	43	73	181	16.6	12	14	B. Taylor	0	1	0	5.38
20–10–7	C	S. Apps	80	32	67	99	210	15.2	7	17					
	RW	J. Pronovost	80	52	52	104	299	17.4	13	16					
	LW	V. Hadfield	76	30	35	65	203	14.8	3	– 3					
	LW	S. Gilbertson	49	13	8	21	86	15.1	3	– 3					
	C	R. Schock	80	18	44	62	161	11.2	2	2					
	C	E. Gilbert	38	1	1	2	18	5.6	0	– 1					
	RW	S. Nolet	39	9	8	17	74	12.2	1	7					
	RW	L. Morrison	78	4	5	9	24	16.7	0	7					
	D	R. Stackhouse	80	11	60	71	228	4.8	1	19					
	D	D. Burrows	80	7	22	29	125	5.6	1	27					
	D	B. Wilkins	75	0	27	27	68	.0	0	– 1					
	D	C. Campbell	64	7	10	17	64	10.9	1	– 4					
	D	D. Owchar	54	5	12	17	62	8.1	1	13					
DET	LW	D. Maloney	77	27	39	66	254	10.6	6	0	J. Rutherford	13	25	6	3.59
D. Barkley	LW	D. Grant	39	10	13	23	70	14.3	4	– 17	E. Giacomin	12	14	3	3.45
7–15–4	LW	M. Redmond	37	11	17	28	123	8.9	2	– 17	P. McDuffe	0	3	1	5.50
A. Delvecchio	LW	M. Bloom	76	13	17	30	130	10.0	1	– 19	D. Grant	1	1	0	4.00
19–29–6	C	W. McKechnie	80	26	56	82	186	14.0	2	9	T. Richardson	0	1	0	7.00
	C	B. Hogaboam	50	21	16	37	116	18.1	6	– 8					
	C	D. Hextall	17	5	9	14	32	15.6	0	2					
	C	J. LeBlanc	46	4	9	13	60	6.7	0	– 5					
	RW	M. Bergeron	72	32	27	59	190	16.8	12	2					
	RW	B. Lochead	53	9	11	20	81	11.1	0	– 15					
	RW	D. Polonich	57	11	12	23	97	11.3	1	– 9					
	RW	J. Salovaara	63	2	11	13	57	3.5	1	– 7					
	D	T. Harper	69	8	25	33	111	7.2	4	6					
	D	R. Lapointe	80	10	23	33	106	9.4	2	– 3					
	D	B. Watson	79	0	18	18	88	.0	0	– 20					
	D	A. Cameron	38	2	8	10	59	3.4	1	– 7					

	POS	PLAYER	GP	G	A	PTS	SOG	SPCT	PPG	+/–	GOALIE	W	L	T	GAvg
WASH	LW	T. White	80	25	17	42	168	14.9	7	– 43	R. Low	6	31	2	5.45
M. Schmidt	LW	A. Bailey	67	13	19	32	131	9.9	2	– 42	B. Wolfe	5	23	7	4.16
3–28–5	LW	M. Lampman	27	7	12	19	55	12.7	0	– 6	M. Belhumeur	0	5	1	5.09
T. McVie	LW	M. Marson	57	4	7	11	35	11.4	0	– 19					
8–31–5	C	N. Pyatt	77	26	23	49	151	17.2	5	– 56					
	C	G. Meehan	32	16	15	31	80	20.0	3	– 7					
	C	R. Lalonde	80	9	19	28	92	9.8	2	– 26					
	C	B. Stewart	74	13	14	27	88	14.8	0	– 53					
	C	H. Bennett	49	12	10	22	72	16.7	1	– 27					
	RW	H. Monahan	80	17	29	46	142	12.0	2	– 49					
	RW	B. Sirois	43	10	19	29	109	9.2	4	– 33					
	RW	T. Williams	34	8	13	21	39	20.5	2	– 33					
	D	G. Joly	54	8	17	25	81	9.9	3	– 46					
	D	Y. Labre	80	2	20	22	110	1.8	0	– 38					
	D	J. Lynch	79	9	13	22	126	7.1	5	– 52					
	D	P. Scamurra	58	2	13	15	49	4.1	1	– 38					
	D	B. Paradise	48	0	8	8	26	.0	0	– 41					

ADAMS DIVISION

	POS	PLAYER	GP	G	A	PTS	SOG	SPCT	PPG	+/–	GOALIE	W	L	T	GAvg
BOS	LW	J. Bucyk	77	36	47	83	151	23.8	13	22	G. Gilbert	33	8	10	2.90
D. Cherry	LW	W. Cashman	80	28	43	71	169	16.6	9	30	G. Cheevers	8	2	5	2.73
48–15–17	LW	D. Marcotte	58	16	20	36	96	16.7	1	15	D. Reece	7	5	2	3.32
	LW	D. Forbes	79	16	13	29	165	9.7	0	15					
	LW	H. Nowak	66	7	3	10	60	11.7	0	– 1					
	C	J. Ratelle	67	31	59	90	186	16.7	15	17					
	C	G. Sheppard	70	31	43	74	222	14.0	5	24					
	C	A. Savard	79	17	23	40	182	9.3	0	4					
	RW	K. Hodge	72	25	36	61	161	15.5	8	19					
	RW	B. Schmautz	75	28	34	62	243	11.5	7	13					
	RW	T. O'Reilly	80	23	27	50	135	17.0	2	3					
	D	B. Park	43	16	37	53	163	9.8	7	23					
	D	D. Smith	77	7	25	32	125	5.6	0	42					
	D	D. Gibson	50	7	18	25	41	17.1	1	8					
	D	D. Edestrand	77	4	17	21	131	3.1	1	7					
	D	G. Doak	58	1	6	7	70	1.4	0	25					
	D	A. Sims	48	4	3	7	61	6.6	0	6					

	POS	PLAYER	GP	G	A	PTS	SOG	SPCT	PPG	+/–	GOALIE	W	L	T	GAvg
BUF	LW	R. Martin	80	49	37	86	327	15.0	**18**	23	G. Desjardins	29	15	11	2.95
F. Smith	C	G. Perreault	80	44	69	113	237	18.6	14	17	A. Smith	9	3	2	3.07
46–21–13	RW	R. Robert	72	35	52	87	273	12.8	11	17	R. Crozier	8	2	0	2.61
	LW	C. Ramsay	80	22	49	71	134	16.4	1	44	G. Bromley	0	1	0	7.00
	C	D. Luce	77	21	49	70	214	9.8	2	37					
	RW	D. Gare	79	50	23	73	303	16.5	8	32					
	LW	B. Spencer	77	13	26	39	84	15.5	0	14					
	LW	J. Richard	73	12	23	35	104	11.5	3	4					
	C	P. McNab	79	24	32	56	125	19.2	3	18					
	C	F. Stanfield	80	18	30	48	112	16.1	2	5					
	C	J. Lorentz	75	17	24	41	116	14.7	2	3					
	RW	G. McAdam	31	1	2	3	12	8.3	0	0					
	D	J. Guevremont	80	12	40	52	229	5.2	6	47					
	D	J. Schoenfeld	56	2	22	24	112	1.8	0	40					
	D	J. Korab	65	13	28	41	146	8.9	3	18					
	D	B. Hajt	80	6	21	27	117	5.1	0	39					
	D	L. Fogolin	58	0	9	9	61	.0	0	15					

	POS	PLAYER	GP	G	A	PTS	SOG	SPCT	PPG	+/–	GOALIE	W	L	T	GAvg
TOR	LW	E. Thompson	75	43	37	80	210	20.5	13	23	W. Thomas	28	24	12	3.19
R. Kelly	C	D. Sittler	79	41	59	100	346	11.8	11	12	G. McRae	6	5	2	3.70
34–31–15	RW	L. McDonald	75	37	56	93	270	13.7	6	24	D. Favell	0	2	1	5.63
	LW	T. Williams	78	21	19	40	149	14.1	3	– 1					
	LW	I. Hammarstrom	76	19	21	40	189	10.1	1	0					
	LW	B. Stoughton	43	6	11	17	60	10.0	1	– 2					
	C	S. Weir	64	19	32	51	90	21.1	5	10					
	C	J. Valiquette	45	10	23	33	111	9.0	1	– 8					
	C	P. Boutette	77	10	22	32	92	10.9	2	– 1					
	RW	G. Ferguson	79	12	32	44	140	8.6	3	11					
	RW	J. McKenny	46	10	19	29	76	13.2	4	– 7					
	D	B. Salming	79	16	41	57	194	8.2	8	33					
	D	B. Glennie	69	0	8	8	65	.0	0	10					
	D	B. Neely	69	9	13	22	107	8.4	0	– 15					
	D	D. Dunn	43	0	8	8	43	.0	0	– 5					
	D	R. Seiling	77	3	16	19	108	2.8	0	11					

CALIF
J. Evans
27–42–11

POS	PLAYER	GP	G	A	PTS	SOG	SPCT	PPG	+/-
LW	B. Murdoch	78	22	27	49	166	13.3	9	– 13
C	D. Maruk	80	30	32	62	233	12.9	7	– 6
RW	A. MacAdam	80	32	31	63	177	18.1	8	– 9
LW	B. Girard	80	16	26	42	137	11.7	3	– 3
LW	D. Hrechkosy	38	9	5	14	75	12.0	4	– 15
LW	G. Holt	48	6	5	11	59	10.2	1	– 10
C	W. Merrick	56	25	27	52	190	13.2	7	– 3
C	D. Gardner	74	16	32	48	157	10.2	2	– 4
C	R. Klassen	71	6	15	21	96	6.3	2	– 26
RW	G. Sabourin	76	21	28	49	172	12.2	4	– 7
RW	J. Moxey	44	10	16	26	106	9.4	2	– 10
RW	F. Ahern	44	17	8	25	88	19.3	3	– 2
RW	J. Pappin	32	6	13	19	72	8.3	2	– 16
D	R. Hampton	73	14	37	51	106	13.2	8	– 12
D	B. Stewart	76	4	17	21	67	6.0	2	– 34
D	L. Frig	62	3	12	15	108	2.8	1	– 5
D	M. Christie	78	3	18	21	63	4.8	0	– 18

GOALIE	W	L	T	GAvg
G. Meloche	12	23	6	3.44
G. Simmons	15	19	5	3.33

GOALS	
R. Leach, PHI	61
G. Lafleur, MONT	56
P. Larouche, PITT	53
J. Pronovost, PITT	52
B. Barber, PHI	50
D. Gare, BUF	50

ASSISTS	
B. Clarke, PHI	89
P. Mahovlich, MONT	71
G. Lafleur, MONT	69
G. Perreault, BUF	69
S. Apps, PITT	67
D. Potvin, NYI	67

POINTS	
G. Lafleur, MONT	125
B. Clarke, PHI	119
G. Perreault, BUF	113
B. Barber, PHI	112
P. Larouche, PITT	111

SHOTS ON GOAL	
B. Barber, PHI	380
G. Unger, STL	357
D. Sittler, TOR	346
R. Leach, PHI	335
M. Dionne, LA	329

SHOOTING PCT.	
D. Kozak, LA	24.7
J. Bucyk, BOS	23.8
C. Lefley, STL	20.8
Y. Lambert, MONT	20.5
E. Thompson, TOR	20.5

+/-	
B. Clarke, PHI	83
B. Barber, PHI	74
R. Leach, PHI	73
S. Shutt, MONT	73
P. Mahovlich, MONT	71

PENALTY MINUTES	
B. Watson, DET	322
D. Schultz, PHI	307
B. Gassoff, STL	306
D. Polonich, DET	302
T. Williams, TOR	299

GOALS AGAINST AVE.	
K. Dryden, MONT	2.03
C. Resch, NYI	2.07
D. Bouchard, ATL	2.54
W. Stephenson, PHI	2.58
G. Gilbert, BOS	2.90

SHUTOUTS	
K. Dryden, MONT	8
C. Resch, NYI	7
R. Vachon, LA	5
T. Esposito, CHI	4
J. Rutherford, DET	4

National Hockey League 1976–77

	W	L	T	PTS	GF	GA	PPG	PPCT	SHG	PPGA	PKPCT	SHGA
CAMPBELL CONFERENCE												
PATRICK DIVISION												
PHI	48	16	16	112	323	213	52	22.0	11	57	82.5	**3**
NYI	47	21	12	106	288	196	56	23.3	**16**	47	83.1	**3**
ATL	34	34	12	80	264	265	42	19.6	12	50	79.8	6
NYR	29	37	14	72	272	310	60	20.7	6	55	79.5	16
SMYTHE DIVISION												
STL	32	39	9	73	239	276	47	18.9	4	47	81.9	7
MINN	23	39	18	64	240	310	59	17.4	9	57	73.0	11
CHI	26	43	11	63	240	298	59	22.1	4	62	78.0	9
VAN	25	42	13	63	235	294	50	19.0	7	58	77.5	7
COLO	20	46	14	54	226	307	44	16.1	9	61	75.3	7
PRINCE OF WALES CONFERENCE												
NORRIS DIVISION												
*MONT	60	8	12	132	**387**	**171**	59	24.9	5	**28**	**87.9**	**3**
LA	34	31	15	83	271	241	**68**	**26.9**	6	52	81.7	5
PITT	34	33	13	81	240	252	50	19.0	7	47	77.5	6
WASH	24	42	14	62	221	307	39	13.3	10	62	78.2	14
DET	16	55	9	41	183	309	37	12.6	10	73	77.0	10
ADAMS DIVISION												
BOS	49	23	8	106	312	240	46	21.2	7	41	84.9	10
BUF	48	24	8	104	301	220	56	23.3	**16**	38	86.1	7
TOR	33	32	15	81	301	285	63	22.4	13	59	79.2	6
CLEVE	25	42	13	63	240	383	59	19.8	2	52	78.1	12

CAMPBELL CONFERENCE

PATRICK DIVISION

TEAM	POS	PLAYER	GP	G	A	PTS	SOG	SPCT	PPG	+/–	GOALIE	W	L	T	GAvg
PHI	LW	B. Barber	73	20	35	55	245	8.2	3	32	B. Parent	35	13	12	2.71
F. Shero	C	B. Clarke	80	27	63	90	158	17.1	6	39	W. Stephenson	12	3	2	2.31
48–16–16	RW	R. Leach	77	32	14	46	237	13.5	10	6	G. Inness	1	0	2	2.57
	LW	R. Lonsberry	75	23	32	55	173	13.3	3	42					
	C	R. MacLeish	79	49	48	97	252	19.4	10	46					
	RW	G. Dornhoefer	79	25	34	59	115	**21.7**	5	47					
	LW	B. Kelly	73	22	24	46	102	21.6	2	27					
	LW	P. Holmgren	59	14	12	26	74	18.9	0	10					
	C	M. Bridgman	70	19	38	57	136	14.0	4	35					
	C	O. Kindrachuk	78	15	36	51	147	10.2	1	22					
	C	H. Bennett	51	12	8	20	53	22.6	0	– 9					
	RW	D. Saleski	74	22	16	38	156	14.1	2	24					
	D	T. Bladon	80	10	43	53	158	6.3	2	34					
	D	B. Dailey	32	5	14	19	77	6.5	2	16					
	D	J. Watson	71	3	23	26	72	4.2	0	34					
	D	J. Watson	77	4	26	30	101	4.0	0	29					
	D	A. Dupont	69	10	19	29	110	9.1	1	57					
NYI	LW	C. Gillies	70	33	22	55	215	15.3	12	18	C. Resch	26	13	6	2.28
A. Arbour	C	B. Trottier	76	30	42	72	175	17.1	11	28	B. Smith	21	8	6	2.50
47–21–12	RW	B. Harris	80	24	43	67	160	15.0	5	18					
	LW	J. Parise	80	25	31	56	147	17.0	5	14					
	LW	B. Bourne	75	16	19	35	137	11.7	0	26					
	LW	G. Howatt	70	13	15	28	91	14.3	1	27					
	C	J. Drouin	78	24	29	53	135	17.8	4	18					
	C	A. St. Laurent	72	10	13	23	96	10.4	2	8					
	C	L. Henning	80	13	18	31	103	12.6	0	21					
	RW	E. Westfall	79	14	33	47	118	11.9	1	21					
	RW	B. Nystrom	80	29	27	56	207	14.0	5	22					
	RW	B. MacMillan	43	6	8	14	34	17.6	0	4					
	D	D. Potvin	80	25	55	80	241	10.4	7	42					
	D	J. Potvin	79	10	36	46	124	8.1	1	14					
	D	D. Lewis	79	4	24	28	102	3.9	0	29					
	D	B. Marshall	72	4	21	25	62	6.5	0	48					
	D	G. Hart	80	4	18	22	118	3.4	0	29					
ATL	LW	E. Vail	78	32	39	71	208	15.4	12	9	P. Myre	17	17	7	3.07
F. Creighton	C	T. Lysiak	79	30	51	81	277	10.8	5	3	D. Bouchard	17	17	5	3.51
34–34–12	RW	W. Plett	64	33	23	56	156	21.2	5	15					
	LW	C. Bennett	76	22	25	47	183	12.0	5	– 14					
	LW	T. Ecclestone	78	9	18	27	116	7.8	0	10					
	LW	B. Simpson	72	13	10	23	118	11.0	0	2					
	C	G. Chouinard	80	17	33	50	167	10.2	3	– 12					
	C	B. Clement	67	17	26	43	114	14.9	2	– 4					
	C	R. Comeau	80	15	18	33	133	11.3	2	7					
	RW	K. Houston	78	20	24	44	151	13.2	3	5					
	RW	L. Romanchych	25	4	5	9	42	9.5	0	– 3					
	D	R. Mulhern	79	12	32	44	156	7.7	2	6					
	D	R. Manery	73	5	24	29	108	4.6	0	– 2					
	D	E. Kea	72	4	21	25	112	3.6	0	0					
	D	B. Gibbs	66	1	16	17	81	1.2	0	– 5					
	D	D. Shand	55	5	11	16	79	6.3	0	21					
NYR	LW	S. Vickers	75	22	31	53	157	14.0	4	– 14	G. Gratton	11	18	7	4.22
J. Ferguson	LW	P. Hickey	80	23	17	40	130	17.7	4	– 11	J. Davidson	14	14	6	3.54
29–37–14	LW	G. Polis	77	16	23	39	187	8.6	3	0	D. Soetaert	3	4	1	2.95
	LW	N. Fotiu	70	4	8	12	48	8.3	0	– 23	D. Tataryn	1	1	0	7.50
	LW	D. Newman	41	9	8	17	67	13.4	0	– 4					
	C	P. Esposito	80	34	46	80	344	9.9	15	– 28					
	C	W. Tkaczuk	80	12	38	50	139	8.6	1	11					
	C	W. Dillon	78	17	29	46	158	10.8	1	– 14					
	C	P. Stemkowski	61	2	13	15	56	3.6	0	– 14					
	RW	K. Hodge	78	21	41	62	141	14.9	6	– 18					
	RW	R. Gilbert	77	27	48	75	187	14.4	7	– 17					
	RW	D. Murdoch	59	32	24	56	223	14.3	11	5					
	RW	B. Goldsworthy	61	10	12	22	96	10.4	0	– 17					
	D	R. Greschner	80	11	36	47	192	5.7	0	0					
	D	C. Vadnais	74	11	37	48	169	6.5	3	– 20					
	D	D. Maloney	66	3	18	21	126	2.4	0	– 8					
	D	M. McEwen	80	14	29	43	204	6.9	5	– 24					

SMYTHE DIVISION

TEAM	POS	PLAYER	GP	G	A	PTS	SOG	SPCT	PPG	+/-	GOALIE	W	L	T	GAvg
STL	LW	B. Sutter	35	4	10	14	49	8.2	0	− 8	E. Johnston	13	16	5	3.07
E. Francis	C	B. Federko	31	14	9	23	67	20.9	6	− 6	E. Staniowski	10	16	1	4.08
32–39–9	RW	R. Bourbonnais	33	6	8	14	44	13.6	2	− 6	D. Grant	7	7	3	3.13
	LW	B. MacMillan	80	19	39	58	168	11.3	10	1	Y. Belanger	2	0	0	3.00
	LW	C. Lefley	71	11	30	41	156	7.1	3	− 15					
	LW	T. Irvine	69	14	14	28	122	11.5	1	− 16					
	C	G. Unger	80	30	27	57	235	12.8	7	− 12					
	C	R. Berenson	80	21	28	49	178	11.8	4	− 28					
	C	L. Patey	80	21	29	50	134	15.7	1	11					
	RW	C. Larose	80	29	19	48	212	13.7	1	5					
	RW	P. Plante	76	18	20	38	124	14.5	4	− 4					
	RW	J. Butler	80	12	20	32	152	7.9	0	− 31					
	D	B. Gassoff	77	6	18	24	110	5.5	0	− 2					
	D	R. Seiling	79	3	26	29	142	2.1	1	1					
	D	B. Affleck	80	5	20	25	133	3.8	1	− 22					
	D	B. Hess	53	4	18	22	88	4.5	1	− 2					
	D	R. Smith	18	0	1	1	11	.0	0	− 3					
MINN	LW	E. Hicke	77	30	20	50	186	16.1	10	− 32	P. LoPresti	13	20	10	3.61
T. Harris	LW	S. Jensen	78	22	23	45	160	13.8	4	− 6	G. Smith	10	17	8	3.99
23–39–18	LW	J. Roberts	53	11	8	19	73	15.1	1	− 9	P. Harrison	0	0	0	5.50
	LW	R. Nantais	40	1	3	4	23	4.3	0	− 8					
	C	T. Young	80	29	66	95	223	13.0	10	− 32					
	C	R. Eriksson	80	25	44	69	249	10.0	10	− 29					
	C	G. Sharpley	80	25	32	57	206	12.1	2	− 21					
	C	B. Hogaboam	73	10	15	25	120	8.3	0	− 17					
	RW	D. Talafous	80	22	27	49	185	11.9	9	− 29					
	RW	A. Pirus	79	20	17	37	128	15.6	1	− 20					
	RW	B. Fairbairn	51	9	20	29	83	10.8	2	− 1					
	RW	L. Nanne	68	2	20	22	69	2.9	2	− 24					
	RW	T. Younghans	78	8	6	14	54	14.8	1	− 11					
	D	D. Hicks	79	5	14	19	83	6.0	1	− 31					
	D	N. Beverley	52	2	17	19	59	3.4	0	0					
	D	F. Barrett	60	1	8	9	54	1.9	0	− 31					
CHI	LW	D. Rota	76	24	22	46	148	16.2	4	− 7	T. Esposito	25	**36**	8	3.45
B. Reay	C	I. Boldirev	80	24	38	62	164	14.6	4	− 15	G. Villemure	0	4	1	5.38
10–19–5	RW	G. Mulvey	80	10	14	24	90	11.1	0	− 17	M. Dumas	0	1	2	4.23
B. White	LW	D. Hull	75	16	17	33	207	7.7	3	− 20	M. Veisor	1	2	0	4.33
16–24–6	C	P. Martin	75	17	36	53	117	14.5	6	− 4					
	RW	D. Redmond	80	22	25	47	211	10.4	9	− 40					
	LW	K. Bowman	55	10	13	23	64	15.6	2	− 7					
	C	S. Mikita	57	19	30	49	128	14.8	6	− 9					
	C	J. Harrison	60	18	23	41	140	12.9	8	− 26					
	RW	C. Koroll	80	15	26	41	138	10.9	1	− 25					
	RW	J. Bordeleau	60	15	14	29	84	17.9	2	− 14					
	RW	A. Daigle	73	12	8	20	89	13.5	2	− 1					
	D	P. Russell	76	9	36	45	178	5.1	1	1					
	D	J. Marks	80	7	15	22	156	4.5	0	− 21					
	D	B. Murray	77	10	11	21	84	11.9	0	− 7					
	D	D. Tallon	70	5	16	21	107	4.7	1	− 21					
	D	B. Orr	20	4	19	23	55	7.3	2	6					
VAN	LW	D. Lever	80	27	30	57	198	13.6	8	− 8	C. Maniago	17	21	9	3.36
P. Maloney	LW	G. Monahan	76	18	26	44	169	10.7	3	− 1	C. Ridley	8	21	4	3.88
9–23–3	LW	R. Sedlbauer	70	18	20	38	129	14.0	0	12	B. Bullock	0	0	0	6.67
O. Kurtenbach	LW	A. Spruce	51	9	6	15	54	16.7	2	− 20					
16–19–10	C	C. Oddleifson	80	14	26	40	99	14.1	3	− 18					
	C	B. Lalonde	68	17	15	32	115	14.8	3	− 12					
	C	M. Walton	40	7	24	31	75	9.3	2	− 15					
	C	R. Stewart	34	6	8	14	54	11.1	0	3					
	RW	R. Blight	78	28	40	68	197	14.2	11	0					
	RW	D. Ververgaert	79	27	18	45	178	15.2	7	− 35					
	RW	J. Gould	25	7	8	15	113	6.2	1	− 9					
	RW	H. Graves	54	10	20	30	91	11.0	2	2					
	D	D. Kearns	80	5	55	60	121	4.1	2	− 25					
	D	H. Snepsts	79	4	18	22	101	4.0	0	− 5					
	D	L. Carriere	49	1	9	10	65	1.5	0	− 11					
	D	B. Gassoff	37	6	4	10	53	11.3	1	− 24					
	D	M. Robitaille	40	0	9	9	54	.0	0	− 13					

	POS	PLAYER	GP	G	A	PTS	SOG	SPCT	PPG	+/-	GOALIE	W	L	T	GAvg
COLO	LW	G. Croteau	78	24	27	51	145	16.6	5	– 18	M. Plasse	12	29	10	3.82
J. Wilson	C	P. Gardner	60	30	29	59	191	15.7	11	– 28	D. Favell	8	15	3	3.90
20–46–14	RW	W. Paiement	78	41	40	81	287	14.3	9	– 13	B. McKenzie	0	2	1	2.40
	LW	B. Dean	79	14	25	39	130	10.8	2	– 26					
	LW	D. Gruen	29	8	10	18	60	13.3	2	– 6					
	LW	G. Delparte	48	1	8	9	37	2.7	0	– 10					
	C	N. Pyatt	77	23	22	45	158	14.6	2	– 17					
	C	D. Hudson	73	15	21	36	89	16.9	1	– 3					
	C	R. Andruff	66	4	18	22	106	3.8	0	– 18					
	RW	S. Nolet	52	12	19	31	105	11.4	1	0					
	RW	C. Arnason	61	13	10	23	152	8.6	3	– 23					
	RW	R. Delorme	29	6	4	10	31	19.4	0	– 11					
	D	T. Edur	80	7	25	32	150	4.7	3	14					
	D	J. McElmury	55	7	23	30	81	8.6	1	– 15					
	D	J. Van Boxmeer	41	2	11	13	88	2.3	0	– 20					
	D	C. Campbell	54	3	8	11	87	3.4	0	– 22					

PRINCE OF WALES CONFERENCE

NORRIS DIVISION

	POS	PLAYER	GP	G	A	PTS	SOG	SPCT	PPG	+/-	GOALIE	W	L	T	GAvg
MONT	LW	S. Shutt	80	**60**	45	105	294	20.4	8	88	K. Dryden	**41**	6	8	**2.14**
S. Bowman	C	J. Lemaire	75	34	41	75	272	12.5	5	70	M. Larocque	19	2	4	2.09
60–8–12	RW	G. Lafleur	80	56	**80**	**136**	291	19.2	14	89					
	LW	Y. Lambert	79	24	28	52	128	18.8	2	30					
	LW	B. Gainey	80	14	19	33	143	9.8	0	31					
	LW	M. Wilson	60	13	14	27	83	15.7	1	25					
	C	P. Mahovlich	76	15	47	62	161	9.3	3	36					
	C	D. Risebrough	78	22	38	60	142	15.5	1	33					
	C	D. Jarvis	80	16	22	38	88	18.2	0	30					
	RW	Y. Cournoyer	60	25	28	53	122	20.5	6	27					
	RW	M. Tremblay	74	18	28	46	139	12.9	4	25					
	RW	R. Houle	65	22	30	52	131	16.8	2	39					
	D	L. Robinson	77	19	66	85	199	9.5	3	**120**					
	D	G. Lapointe	77	13	29	42	289	4.5	10	69					
	D	S. Savard	78	9	33	42	110	8.2	0	79					
	D	P. Bouchard	73	4	11	15	73	5.5	0	33					
	D	B. Nyrop	74	3	19	22	47	6.4	0	42					

	POS	PLAYER	GP	G	A	PTS	SOG	SPCT	PPG	+/-	GOALIE	W	L	T	GAvg
LA	LW	T. Williams	80	35	39	74	233	15.0	15	14	R. Vachon	33	23	12	2.72
B. Pulford	LW	B. Berry	69	13	25	38	85	15.3	2	12	G. Edwards	0	6	2	4.67
34–31–15	LW	G. Carr	68	15	12	27	99	15.2	0	5	G. Simmons	1	2	1	4.00
	LW	D. Schultz	76	10	20	30	122	8.2	2	– 8					
	LW	B. Wilson	77	4	3	7	54	7.4	0	– 9					
	C	M. Dionne	80	53	69	122	**378**	14.0	14	10					
	C	B. Goring	78	30	55	85	216	13.9	13	10					
	C	V. Venasky	80	14	26	40	120	11.7	1	2					
	RW	M. Murphy	76	25	36	61	165	15.2	9	15					
	RW	D. Kozak	79	15	17	32	98	15.3	1	– 9					
	RW	St. Marseille	49	6	22	28	74	8.1	1	1					
	RW	G. Goldup	28	7	6	13	28	25.0	1	5					
	D	G. Sargent	80	14	40	54	200	7.0	8	7					
	D	B. Murdoch	70	9	23	32	125	7.2	0	36					
	D	D. Hutchison	70	6	11	17	115	5.2	1	7					
	D	N. Komadoski	68	3	9	12	76	3.9	0	17					
	D	L. Brown	55	1	6	7	59	1.7	0	– 17					

	POS	PLAYER	GP	G	A	PTS	SOG	SPCT	PPG	+/-	GOALIE	W	L	T	GAvg
PITT	LW	W. Bianchin	79	28	6	34	130	21.5	4	– 1	D. Wilson	18	19	8	2.95
K. Schinkel	LW	M. Corrigan	73	14	27	41	124	11.3	2	– 13	D. Herron	15	11	5	2.94
34–33–13	LW	B. Kelly	74	10	21	31	136	7.4	1	13	G. Laxton	1	3	0	6.17
	LW	S. Gilbertson	67	6	9	15	62	9.7	0	– 9					
	C	S. Apps	72	18	43	61	164	11.0	3	2					
	C	P. Larouche	65	29	34	63	227	12.8	8	– 10					
	C	G. Malone	66	18	19	37	121	14.9	4	3					
	C	R. Schock	80	17	32	49	154	11.0	3	– 6					
	RW	R. Kehoe	80	30	27	57	250	12.0	7	– 5					
	RW	J. Pronovost	79	33	31	64	217	15.2	7	8					
	RW	B. Chapman	80	14	23	37	152	9.2	1	– 12					
	RW	L. Morrison	76	2	1	3	25	8.0	0	– 6					
	D	R. Stackhouse	80	7	34	41	219	3.2	3	11					
	D	D. Owchar	46	5	18	23	86	5.8	1	– 7					
	D	D. Awrey	79	1	12	13	45	2.2	0	– 2					
	D	M. Faubert	47	2	11	13	67	3.0	0	– 4					
	D	R. Anderson	66	2	11	13	45	4.4	0	5					

TEAM	POS	PLAYER	GP	G	A	PTS	SOG	SPCT	PPG	+/-	GOALIE	W	L	T	GAvg
WASH	LW	C. Patrick	28	7	10	17	47	14.9	1	– 10	R. Low	16	27	5	3.87
T. McVie	C	G. Meehan	80	28	36	64	193	14.5	9	– 11	B. Wolfe	7	15	9	3.84
24–42–14	RW	B. Riley	43	13	14	27	45	28.9	5	4	R. Crozier	1	0	0	1.17
	LW	A. Bailey	78	19	27	46	154	12.3	2	– 21					
	LW	T. White	72	12	9	21	126	9.5	2	– 15					
	LW	B. Stewart	34	5	2	7	41	12.2	0	– 6					
	C	G. Charron	80	36	46	82	261	13.8	6	– 28					
	C	R. Bragnalo	80	11	12	23	89	12.4	1	– 16					
	C	R. Lalonde	76	12	17	29	83	14.5	0	– 20					
	RW	H. Monahan	79	23	27	50	137	16.8	7	– 28					
	RW	B. Sirois	45	13	22	35	100	13.0	1	1					
	RW	B. Collins	54	11	14	25	87	12.6	0	– 7					
	D	J. Lynch	75	5	25	30	132	3.8	0	– 15					
	D	G. Lane	80	2	15	17	59	3.4	0	– 25					
	D	R. Green	45	3	12	15	89	3.4	1	– 25					
	D	B. Watson	56	1	14	15	54	1.9	0	– 5					
	D	G. Smith	79	1	12	13	72	1.4	1	– 27					

TEAM	POS	PLAYER	GP	G	A	PTS	SOG	SPCT	PPG	+/-	GOALIE	W	L	T	GAvg
DET	LW	D. Maloney	34	13	13	26	107	12.1	3	3	J. Rutherford	7	34	6	3.94
A. Delvecchio	LW	N. Libett	80	14	27	41	210	6.7	3	– 25	E. Giacomin	8	18	3	3.58
13–26–5	LW	B. Lochead	61	16	14	30	127	12.6	4	– 11	T. Richardson	1	3	0	4.01
L. Wilson	LW	D. Grant	42	2	10	12	62	3.2	0	– 34					
3–29–4	LW	M. Bloom	45	6	3	9	40	15.0	0	– 10					
	C	D. Hextall	78	14	32	46	129	10.9	5	– 35					
	C	J. LeBlanc	74	7	11	18	77	9.1	0	– 16					
	C	F. Williams	44	2	5	7	32	6.3	0	– 17					
	RW	D. Polonich	79	18	28	46	183	9.8	6	– 20					
	RW	M. Bergeron	74	21	12	33	197	10.7	3	– 40					
	RW	F. Harvey	54	11	11	22	105	10.5	2	– 13					
	D	T. Harper	52	4	8	12	60	6.7	1	– 23					
	D	A. Cameron	80	3	13	16	139	2.2	1	– 43					
	D	R. Wilson	77	3	13	16	60	5.0	0	– 20					
	D	J. Nahrgang	53	5	11	16	96	5.2	3	– 12					
	D	J. Hamel	71	1	10	11	85	1.2	0	– 18					

ADAMS DIVISION

TEAM	POS	PLAYER	GP	G	A	PTS	SOG	SPCT	PPG	+/-	GOALIE	W	L	T	GAvg
BOS	LW	J. Bucyk	49	20	23	43	98	20.4	6	– 2	G. Cheevers	30	10	5	3.04
D. Cherry	LW	W. Cashman	65	15	37	52	105	14.3	3	4	G. Gilbert	18	13	3	2.85
49–23–8	LW	D. Marcotte	80	27	18	45	176	15.3	3	28	J. Pettie	1	0	0	3.00
	LW	S. Jonathan	69	17	13	30	71	23.9	1	1					
	LW	D. Forbes	73	9	11	20	56	16.1	0	13					
	C	J. Ratelle	78	33	61	94	186	17.7	8	19					
	C	P. McNab	80	38	48	86	207	18.4	6	26					
	C	G. Sheppard	77	31	36	67	247	12.6	8	3					
	C	M. Hagman	75	11	17	28	71	15.5	1	6					
	RW	B. Schmautz	57	23	29	52	177	13.0	4	25					
	RW	R. Middleton	72	20	22	42	128	15.6	0	2					
	RW	T. O'Reilly	79	14	41	55	137	10.2	1	38					
	D	B. Park	77	12	55	67	238	5.0	4	47					
	D	M. Milbury	77	6	18	24	89	6.7	0	25					
	D	D. Smith	58	2	20	22	66	3.0	0	16					
	D	G. Doak	76	3	13	16	70	4.3	0	15					

TEAM	POS	PLAYER	GP	G	A	PTS	SOG	SPCT	PPG	+/-	GOALIE	W	L	T	GAvg
BUF	LW	R. Martin	66	36	29	65	221	16.3	12	10	G. Desjardins	31	12	6	2.63
F. Smith	C	G. Perreault	80	39	56	95	195	20.0	7	10	D. Edwards	16	7	2	2.51
48–24–8	RW	R. Robert	80	33	40	73	250	13.2	5	27	A. Smith	0	3	0	4.30
	LW	C. Ramsay	80	20	41	61	145	13.8	2	37	B. Sauve	1	2	0	3.59
	C	D. Luce	80	26	43	69	206	12.6	6	38					
	RW	J. Lorentz	79	23	33	56	156	14.7	7	3					
	LW	T. Martin	62	11	12	23	72	15.3	1	6					
	C	A. Savard	80	25	35	60	160	15.6	4	9					
	C	B. Spencer	77	14	15	29	78	17.9	1	0					
	C	F. Stanfield	79	9	14	23	69	13.0	2	– 2					
	RW	G. McAdam	73	13	16	29	86	15.1	1	17					
	RW	D. Gare	35	11	15	26	92	12.0	3	7					
	D	J. Korab	77	14	33	47	185	7.6	4	22					
	D	J. Schoenfeld	65	7	25	32	181	3.9	2	28					
	D	J. Guevremont	80	9	29	38	210	4.3	2	26					
	D	B. Hajt	79	6	20	26	106	5.7	0	39					
	D	L. Fogolin	71	3	15	18	76	3.9	1	9					

Team	POS	PLAYER	GP	G	A	PTS	SOG	SPCT	PPG	+/-	GOALIE	W	L	T	GAvg
TOR	LW	T. Williams	77	18	25	43	157	1.5	1	11	M. Palmateer	23	18	8	3.21
R. Kelly	LW	E. Thompson	41	21	16	37	109	19.3	8	– 10	W. Thomas	10	13	6	3.86
33–32–15	LW	I. Hammarstrom	78	24	17	41	154	15.6	5	8	G. McRae	0	1	1	4.50
	C	D. Sittler	73	38	52	90	307	12.4	12	8					
	C	J. Valiquette	66	15	30	45	121	12.4	0	5					
	C	D. Ashby	76	19	23	42	118	16.1	3	– 14					
	C	S. Weir	65	11	19	30	68	16.2	1	2					
	C	G. Ferguson	50	9	15	24	73	12.3	0	0					
	RW	L. McDonald	80	46	44	90	293	15.7	**16**	12					
	RW	P. Boutette	80	18	18	36	104	17.3	3	13					
	RW	S. Garland	69	9	20	29	84	10.7	3	– 18					
	D	B. Salming	76	12	66	78	186	6.5	1	45					
	D	I. Turnbull	80	22	57	79	316	7.0	4	47					
	D	J. McKenny	76	14	31	45	115	12.2	3	– 26					
	D	B. Neely	70	17	16	33	123	13.8	3	– 17					
	D	B. Glennie	69	1	10	11	63	1.6	0	– 1					
	D	C. Alexander	48	1	12	13	61	1.6	0	– 4					
CLEVE	LW	B. Murdoch	57	23	19	42	141	16.3	6	– 5	G. Meloche	19	24	6	3.47
J. Evans	C	D. Maruk	80	28	50	78	268	10.4	4	4	G. Edwards	4	10	3	4.08
25–42–13	RW	A. MacAdam	80	22	41	63	194	11.3	6	– 2	G. Simmons	2	8	4	3.64
	LW	M. Fidler	46	17	16	33	112	15.2	7	– 5					
	LW	B. Girard	68	11	10	21	101	10.9	1	– 24					
	LW	B. Meeke	49	8	13	21	74	10.8	1	– 15					
	LW	C. Simmer	24	2	0	2	42	4.8	1	– 11					
	C	W. Merrick	80	18	38	56	201	9.0	4	– 21					
	C	D. Gardner	76	16	22	38	141	11.3	5	– 20					
	C	R. Klassen	80	14	18	32	131	10.7	4	– 25					
	RW	F. Spring	26	11	10	21	49	22.4	6	– 8					
	RW	G. Sabourin	33	7	11	18	76	9.2	2	– 6					
	RW	P. Roberto	21	3	4	7	32	9.4	0	– 7					
	D	R. Hampton	57	16	24	40	114	14.0	5	– 11					
	D	G. Smith	74	9	17	26	128	7.0	4	– 31					
	D	M. Christie	79	6	27	33	61	9.8	0	18					

GOALS		ASSISTS		POINTS	
S. Shutt, MONT	60	G. Lafleur, MONT	80	G. Lafleur, MONT	136
G. Lafleur, MONT	56	M. Dionne, LA	69	M. Dionne, LA	122
M. Dionne, LA	53	T. Young, MINN	66	S. Shutt, MONT	105
R. MacLeish, PHI	49	L. Robinson, MONT	66	R. MacLeish, PHI	97
L. McDonald, TOR	46	B. Salming, TOR	66	G. Perreault, BUF	95
SHOTS ON GOAL		**SHOOTING PCT.**		**+/–**	
M. Dionne, LA	378	G. Dornhoefer, PHI	21.7	L. Robinson, MONT	120
P. Esposito, NYR	344	W. Plett, ATL	21.2	G. Lafleur, MONT	89
I. Turnbull, TOR	316	Y. Cournoyer, MONT	20.5	S. Shutt, MONT	88
D. Sittler, TOR	307	G. Perreault, BUF	20.0	S. Savard, MONT	79
S. Shutt, MONT	294	R. MacLeish, PHI	19.4	J. Lemaire, MONT	70
PENALTY MINUTES		**GOALS AGAINST AVE.**		**SHUTOUTS**	
T. Williams, TOR	338	K. Dryden, MONT	2.14	K. Dryden, MONT	10
D. Polonich, DET	274	C. Resch, NYI	2.28	R. Vachon, LA	8
B. Gassoff, STL	254	B. Smith, NYI	2.50	B. Parent, PHI	5
P. Russell, CHI	233	G. Desjardins, BUF	2.63	C. Resch, NYI	4
D. Schultz, LA	232	B. Parent, PHI	2.71	M. Palmateer, TOR	4

National Hockey League 1977–78

	W	L	T	PTS	GF	GA	PPG	PPCT	SHG	PPGA	PKPCT	SHGA
CAMPBELL CONFERENCE												
PATRICK DIVISION												
NYI	48	17	15	111	334	270	71	31.3	7	45	83.5	6
PHI	45	20	15	105	296	200	51	23.3	**18**	66	80.6	5
ATL	34	27	19	87	274	252	43	22.1	4	51	80.7	4
NYR	30	37	13	73	279	280	**78**	28.0	10	48	80.3	6
SMYTHE DIVISION												
CHI	32	29	19	83	230	220	43	21.0	4	46	84.4	3
COLO	19	40	21	59	257	305	63	22.6	5	53	77.6	7
VAN	20	43	17	57	239	320	60	22.3	3	65	71.7	7
STL	20	47	13	53	195	304	44	16.7	2	52	73.2	3
MINN	18	53	9	45	218	325	49	14.9	3	61	7.2	10

	W	L	T	PTS	GF	GA	PPG	PPCT	SHG	PPGA	PKPCT	SHGA
PRINCE OF WALES CONFERENCE												
NORRIS DIVISION												
*MONT	59	10	11	129	**359**	**183**	73	**31.9**	9	40	81.0	**1**
DET	32	34	14	78	252	266	59	20.1	10	64	78.4	7
LA	31	34	15	77	243	245	50	19.7	3	46	80.5	6
PITT	25	37	18	68	254	321	53	20.3	5	61	75.8	7
WASH	17	49	14	48	195	321	34	12.2	2	73	71.9	15
ADAMS DIVISION												
BOS	51	18	11	113	333	218	49	20.2	7	53	82.1	2
BUF	44	19	17	105	288	215	52	22.2	7	**31**	**85.8**	3
TOR	41	29	10	92	271	237	57	21.8	5	55	81.4	7
CLEVE	22	45	13	57	230	325	42	15.3	3	61	74.0	8

CAMPBELL CONFERENCE

PATRICK DIVISION

	POS	PLAYER	GP	G	A	PTS	SOG	SPCT	PPG	+/-	GOALIE	W	L	T	GAvg
NYI	LW	C. Gillies	80	35	50	85	277	12.6	9	19	C. Resch	28	9	7	2.55
A. Arbour	C	B. Trottier	77	46	**77**	123	193	23.8	13	52	B. Smith	20	8	8	2.65
48–17–15	RW	M. Bossy	73	53	38	91	235	22.6	**25**	31	G. Hogosta	0	0	0	0.00
	LW	B. Bourne	80	30	33	63	178	16.9	2	15					
	C	M. Kaszycki	58	13	29	42	85	15.3	3	15					
	RW	B. Nystrom	80	30	29	59	178	16.9	3	19					
	LW	G. Howatt	61	7	12	19	60	11.7	0	7					
	LW	J. Parise	39	12	16	28	68	17.6	1	19					
	C	L. Henning	79	12	15	27	79	15.2	0	10					
	C	W. Merrick	37	10	14	24	60	16.7	2	2					
	RW	B. Harris	80	22	38	60	148	14.9	1	27					
	RW	E. Westfall	71	5	19	24	72	6.9	0	7					
	D	D. Potvin	80	30	64	94	288	10.4	9	57					
	D	S. Persson	66	6	50	56	77	7.8	3	19					
	D	G. Hart	78	2	23	25	126	1.6	0	44					
	D	D. Lewis	77	3	11	14	111	2.7	0	32					
	D	B. Marshall	58	0	7	7	32	.0	0	10					
PHI	LW	B. Barber	80	41	31	72	262	15.6	8	31	B. Parent	29	6	13	2.22
F. Shero	C	B. Clarke	71	21	68	89	131	16.0	5	47	W. Stephenson	14	10	1	2.75
45–20–15	RW	R. Leach	72	24	28	52	195	12.3	9	20	R. Ste.–Croix	2	4	1	3.04
	LW	B. Kelly	74	19	13	32	96	19.8	0	15					
	LW	R. Lonsberry	78	18	30	48	172	10.5	2	41					
	LW	B. Dean	56	7	18	25	76	9.2	0	12					
	C	R. MacLeish	76	31	39	70	253	12.3	7	24					
	C	M. Bridgman	76	16	32	48	154	10.4	3	26					
	C	O. Kindrachuk	73	17	45	62	170	10.0	1	35					
	RW	P. Holmgren	62	16	18	34	91	17.6	2	23					
	RW	D. Saleski	70	27	18	45	163	16.6	5	34					
	RW	G. Dornhoefer	47	7	5	12	61	11.5	2	– 3					
	D	B. Dailey	76	21	36	57	211	10.0	5	45					
	D	T. Bladon	79	11	24	35	153	7.2	1	32					
	D	J. Watson	71	5	12	17	112	4.5	0	33					
	D	K. McCarthy	62	2	15	17	91	2.2	0	29					
	D	J. Watson	65	5	9	14	68	7.4	0	23					
ATL	LW	E. Vail	79	22	36	58	178	12.4	8	3	D. Bouchard	25	12	19	2.75
F. Creighton	LW	H. Phillipoff	67	17	36	53	132	12.9	2	27	Y. Belanger	7	8	0	3.52
34–27–19	LW	B. Simpson	55	10	8	18	91	11.0	0	0	P. Myre	2	7	0	4.93
	C	T. Lysiak	80	27	42	69	215	12.6	3	– 3					
	C	G. Chouinard	73	28	30	58	146	19.2	11	8					
	C	B. Clement	70	20	30	50	105	19.0	1	18					
	C	B. Lalonde	73	14	23	37	94	14.9	0	5					
	C	R. Comeau	79	10	22	32	114	8.8	0	0					
	RW	B. MacMillan	52	31	21	52	148	20.9	5	28					
	RW	W. Plett	78	22	21	43	191	11.5	2	– 6					
	RW	J. Gould	75	19	28	47	133	14.3	2	7					
	RW	K. Houston	74	22	16	38	147	15.0	2	4					
	D	R. Mulhern	79	9	23	32	125	7.2	0	11					
	D	E. Kea	60	3	23	26	78	3.8	0	25					
	D	D. Shand	80	2	23	25	83	2.4	0	23					
	D	D. Redmond	42	7	11	18	86	8.1	5	12					

	POS	PLAYER	GP	G	A	PTS	SOG	SPCT	PPG	+/-	GOALIE	W	L	T	GAvg
NYR	LW	P. Hickey	80	40	33	73	215	18.6	10	–19	W. Thomas	12	20	7	3.60
J. Talbot	LW	G. Polis	37	7	16	23	72	9.7	0	–3	J. Davidson	14	13	4	3.18
30–37–13	LW	S. Vickers	79	19	44	63	113	17.8	9	10	D. Soetaert	2	2	2	3.33
	LW	N. Fotiu	59	2	7	9	32	6.3	0	–14	H. Astrom	2	2	0	3.50
	LW	D. Newman	59	5	13	18	81	6.2	0	–11					
	C	P. Esposito	79	38	43	81	259	14.7	21	–22					
	C	W. Tkaczuk	80	26	40	66	144	18.1	6	3					
	C	W. Dillon	59	5	13	18	50	10.0	4	–8					
	C	R. Duguay	71	20	20	40	129	15.5	3	–17					
	RW	D. Murdoch	66	27	28	55	188	14.4	10	–5					
	RW	L. Deblois	71	22	8	30	111	19.8	1	–11					
	RW	E. Johnstone	53	13	13	26	93	14.0	2	–3					
	D	R. Greschner	78	24	48	72	180	13.3	8	3					
	D	C. Vadnais	50	6	40	46	164	3.7	3	–25					
	D	D. Maloney	56	2	19	21	71	2.8	0	18					
	D	M. McEwen	57	5	13	18	65	7.7	2	–11					
	D	D. Awrey	78	2	8	10	40	5.0	0	–14					

SMYTHE DIVISION

	POS	PLAYER	GP	G	A	PTS	SOG	SPCT	PPG	+/-	GOALIE	W	L	T	GAvg
CHI	LW	D. Rota	78	17	20	37	107	15.9	3	5	T. Esposito	28	22	14	2.63
B. Pulford	C	I. Boldirev	80	35	45	80	242	14.5	10	–3	M. Veisor	3	4	5	2.58
32–29–19	RW	J. Bordeleau	76	15	25	40	103	14.6	0	9	E. Johnston	1	3	0	4.25
	LW	T. Bulley	79	23	28	51	150	15.3	6	4					
	C	S. Mikita	76	18	41	59	202	8.9	6	18					
	RW	C. Koroll	73	16	15	31	100	16.0	1	8					
	LW	B. Kelly	75	7	11	18	155	4.5	0	–25					
	C	J. Savard	31	7	11	18	37	18.9	2	6					
	C	J. Harrison	26	2	8	10	43	4.7	1	–3					
	RW	G. Mulvey	78	14	24	38	157	8.9	3	–1					
	RW	P. Plante	77	10	18	28	104	9.6	0	–2					
	RW	A. Daigle	53	6	6	12	84	7.1	1	–12					
	D	J. Marks	80	15	22	37	118	12.7	0	27					
	D	D. Wilson	77	14	20	34	203	6.9	5	11					
	D	P. Russell	57	6	20	26	132	4.5	0	19					
	D	D. Tallon	75	4	20	24	93	4.3	2	3					
	D	B. Murray	70	14	17	31	124	11.3	2	11					
COLO	LW	G. Croteau	62	17	22	39	104	16.3	8	–15	D. Favell	13	20	11	3.58
P. Kelly	C	P. Gardner	46	30	22	52	133	22.6	13	–17	M. Plasse	3	12	8	3.90
19–40–21	RW	W. Paiement	80	31	56	87	287	10.8	7	–14	B. McKenzie	3	6	2	3.85
	LW	A. Spruce	74	19	21	40	119	16.0	3	–7	B. Oleschuk	0	2	0	5.40
	LW	N. Pyatt	71	9	12	21	87	10.3	1	–23					
	C	R. Andruff	78	15	18	33	133	11.3	0	–16					
	C	D. Hudson	60	10	22	32	89	11.2	1	–5					
	C	J. Contini	37	12	9	21	49	24.5	9	–2					
	C	R. Klassen	44	6	9	15	47	12.8	3	–18					
	RW	R. Delorme	63	10	11	21	76	13.2	0	–20					
	RW	R. Pierce	35	9	10	19	60	15.0	1	0					
	RW	F. Ahern	38	5	13	18	66	7.6	1	–16					
	D	B. Beck	75	22	38	60	271	8.1	6	–14					
	D	J. Van Boxmeer	80	12	42	54	262	4.6	5	–12					
	D	D. Dupere	54	15	15	30	67	22.4	2	9					
	D	D. Owchar	60	8	23	31	120	6.7	2	–49					
	D	B. Lefley	71	4	13	17	65	6.2	0	–4					
VAN	LW	D. Lever	75	17	32	49	168	10.1	6	–29	C. Maniago	10	24	8	4.02
O. Kurtenbach	LW	J. Gillis	79	23	18	41	154	14.9	2	–24	C. Ridley	9	17	8	4.06
20–43–17	LW	R. Sedlbauer	62	18	12	30	119	15.1	1	–6	G. Hanlon	1	2	1	2.70
	LW	G. Monahan	67	10	19	29	105	9.5	0	2	M. Bannerman	0	0	0	0.00
	C	M. Walton	65	29	37	66	115	**25.2**	14	–26					
	C	P. Martin	67	15	31	46	104	14.4	4	–26					
	C	C. Oddleifson	78	17	22	39	91	18.7	2	–18					
	RW	R. Blight	80	25	38	63	238	10.5	11	–32					
	RW	D. Ververgaert	80	21	33	54	136	15.4	6	–24					
	RW	H. Graves	80	21	26	47	138	15.2	4	–17					
	D	D. Kearns	80	4	43	47	101	4.0	1	–40					
	D	H. Snepsts	75	4	16	20	95	4.2	0	–16					
	D	B. Manno	49	5	14	19	50	10.0	4	–23					
	D	J. McIlhargey	69	3	5	8	36	8.3	0	–45					
	D	C. Alexander	32	8	18	26	105	7.6	4	–7					
	D	B. Gassoff	47	9	6	15	40	22.5	0	–6					

	POS	PLAYER	GP	G	A	PTS	SOG	SPCT	PPG	+/-	GOALIE	W	L	T	GAvg
STL	LW	I. Hammarstrom	70	19	19	38	165	11.5	3	– 21	P. Myre	11	25	8	3.64
L. Boivin	LW	C. Bennett	50	7	17	24	92	7.6	1	– 22	E. Staniowski	1	10	2	3.86
11–36–7	LW	B. Sutter	78	9	13	22	98	9.2	4	– 33	E. Johnston	5	6	1	4.15
B. Plager	C	G. Unger	80	32	20	52	238	13.4	10	– 35	D. Grant	3	3	2	2.88
9–11–6	C	B. Federko	72	17	24	41	128	13.3	4	– 35	Y. Belanger	0	3	0	6.25
	C	R. Berenson	80	13	25	38	140	9.3	0	– 20					
	RW	B. Fairbairn	60	14	16	30	82	17.1	2	– 23					
	RW	L. Patey	80	17	17	34	129	13.2	3	– 20					
	RW	C. Larose	69	8	13	21	116	6.9	2	– 19					
	D	B. Affleck	75	4	14	18	95	4.2	0	– 56					
	D	B. Gibbs	51	6	12	18	103	5.8	4	– 11					
	D	J. Brownschidle	40	2	15	17	62	3.2	1	– 11					
	D	G. Holt	49	7	4	11	57	12.3	0	– 3					
	D	J. Roberts	75	4	10	14	70	5.7	0	– 20					
MINN	LW	P. Brasar	77	20	37	57	170	11.8	7	– 7	P. LoPresti	12	**35**	6	4.23
T. Harris	C	T. Young	78	23	35	58	217	10.6	5	– 37	P. Harrison	6	16	2	3.82
5–12–2	RW	R. Zanussi	68	15	17	32	97	15.5	4	– 20	G. Smith	0	2	1	3.00
A. Beaulieu	LW	S. Jensen	74	13	17	30	132	9.8	2	– 30					
6–23–3	LW	P. Jarry	35	9	17	26	77	11.7	1	– 9					
L. Nanne	C	R. Eriksson	78	21	39	60	257	8.2	3	– 29					
7–18–4	C	G. Sharpley	79	22	33	55	215	10.2	6	– 33					
	C	H. Bennett	64	11	10	21	67	16.4	1	– 32					
	RW	K. Andersson	73	15	18	33	121	12.4	3	– 17					
	RW	T. Younghans	72	10	8	18	71	14.1	1	– 10					
	RW	D. Talafous	75	13	16	29	80	16.3	2	– 16					
	RW	A. Pirus	61	9	6	15	89	10.1	1	– 25					
	D	B. Maxwell	75	18	29	47	209	8.6	12	– 57					
	D	F. Barrett	79	0	15	15	87	.0	0	– 35					
	D	N. Beverley	57	7	14	21	87	8.0	0	– 1					
	D	D. Hicks	61	2	9	11	81	2.5	0	– 28					
	D	T. Reid	36	1	6	7	26	3.8	0	– 26					

PRINCE OF WALES CONFERENCE

NORRIS DIVISION

	POS	PLAYER	GP	G	A	PTS	SOG	SPCT	PPG	+/-	GOALIE	W	L	T	GAvg
MONT	LW	S. Shutt	80	49	37	86	243	20.2	16	56	K. Dryden	37	7	7	**2.05**
S. Bowman	C	J. Lemaire	75	36	61	97	310	11.6	6	54	M. Larocque	22	3	4	2.67
59–10–11	RW	G. Lafleur	78	**60**	72	**132**	307	19.5	15	**73**					
	LW	Y. Lambert	77	18	22	40	107	16.8	7	10					
	C	D. Risebrough	72	18	23	41	115	15.7	1	30					
	RW	M. Tremblay	56	10	14	24	89	11.2	0	6					
	LW	B. Gainey	66	15	16	31	140	10.7	0	11					
	C	P. Mondou	71	19	30	49	132	14.4	4	32					
	C	D. Jarvis	80	11	28	39	129	8.5	2	12					
	RW	Y. Cournoyer	68	24	29	53	125	19.2	4	39					
	RW	R. Houle	76	30	28	58	143	21.0	3	39					
	D	L. Robinson	80	13	52	65	154	8.4	3	71					
	D	G. Lapointe	49	13	29	42	148	2.2	4	46					
	D	S. Savard	77	8	34	42	103	7.8	4	62					
	D	B. Nyrop	72	5	21	26	69	7.2	1	56					
	D	R. Chartraw	68	4	12	16	75	5.3	0	16					
	D	P. Bouchard	59	4	6	10	55	7.3	0	27					
DET	LW	B. Lochead	77	20	16	36	124	16.1	2	6	J. Rutherford	20	17	4	3.26
B. Kromm	C	D. McCourt	76	33	39	72	219	15.1	10	7	R. Low	9	12	9	3.37
32–34–14	RW	P. Woods	80	19	23	42	107	17.8	3	18	E. Giacomin	3	5	1	3.14
	LW	D. Maloney	66	16	29	45	165	9.7	3	4					
	LW	N. Libett	80	23	22	45	155	14.8	1	– 3					
	LW	D. Hull	55	5	9	14	72	6.9	2	– 20					
	C	A. St. Laurent	77	31	39	70	193	16.1	10	7					
	C	D. Hextall	78	16	33	49	89	18.0	2	– 5					
	RW	N. Nedomansky	63	11	17	28	107	10.3	5	– 17					
	RW	D. Polonich	79	16	19	35	128	12.5	5	– 5					
	RW	R. Bowness	61	8	11	19	46	17.4	2	– 8					
	D	R. Larson	75	19	41	60	240	7.9	7	8					
	D	T. Harper	80	2	17	19	76	2.6	0	19					
	D	G. Joly	79	7	20	27	134	5.2	2	– 4					
	D	P. Miller	62	4	17	21	122	3.3	0	– 5					
	D	T. Bergman	14	1	6	7	18	5.6	0	1					
	D	A. Cameron	63	2	7	9	71	2.8	1	– 12					

	POS	PLAYER	GP	G	A	PTS	SOG	SPCT	PPG	+/–	GOALIE	W	L	T	GAvg
LA	LW	T. Williams	58	15	22	37	147	10.2	6	– 14	R. Vachon	29	27	13	2.86
R. Stewart	LW	D. Grant	41	10	19	29	97	10.3	2	– 2	G. Simmons	2	7	2	3.81
31–34–15	LW	B. Wilson	79	7	16	23	78	9.0	0	0					
	LW	E. Hicke	41	9	15	24	60	15.0	1	7					
	C	M. Dionne	70	36	43	79	294	12.2	9	– 3					
	C	B. Goring	80	37	36	73	248	14.9	9	– 4					
	C	S. Apps	70	19	26	45	131	14.5	4	– 11					
	C	P. Stemkowski	80	13	18	31	134	9.7	0	1					
	RW	M. Murphy	72	20	36	56	207	9.7	7	– 1					
	RW	D. Taylor	64	22	21	43	122	18.0	4	14					
	RW	G. Goldup	66	14	18	32	108	13.0	0	– 8					
	RW	D. Kozak	43	8	5	13	54	14.8	0	4					
	D	G. Sargent	72	7	34	41	182	3.8	3	18					
	D	R. Manery	79	6	27	33	173	3.5	3	– 12					
	D	B. Murdoch	76	2	17	19	144	1.4	0	2					
	D	L. Brown	57	1	8	9	24	4.2	0	– 13					
	D	D. Hutchison	44	0	10	10	60	.0	0	11					
PITT	LW	G. Carr	70	17	37	54	145	11.7	4	– 15	D. Herron	20	25	15	3.57
J. Wilson	C	P. Mahovlich	57	25	36	61	201	12.4	9	4	D. Wilson	5	11	3	4.83
25–37–18	RW	R. Kehoe	70	29	21	50	177	16.4	7	– 18	G. Redquest	0	0	0	13.85
	LW	W. Bianchin	61	20	13	33	95	21.1	3	– 14	G. Laxton	0	1	0	7.40
	LW	M. Corrigan	25	8	12	20	36	22.2	0	– 7					
	LW	D. Schultz	66	9	25	34	102	8.8	0	– 9					
	LW	L. MacDonald	19	5	8	13	31	16.1	2	0					
	C	G. Malone	78	18	43	61	179	10.1	2	– 16					
	C	B. Spencer	79	9	11	20	101	8.9	0	– 18					
	RW	J. Pronovost	79	40	25	65	219	18.3	12	– 16					
	RW	B. Chapman	75	24	20	44	180	13.3	4	– 11					
	RW	P. Lee	60	5	13	18	89	5.6	1	– 11					
	D	D. Burrows	67	4	15	19	92	4.3	0	– 30					
	D	R. Stackhouse	50	5	15	20	115	4.3	3	– 16					
	D	T. Edur	58	5	38	43	135	3.7	2	– 3					
	D	R. Anderson	74	2	16	18	51	3.9	0	– 5					
	D	B. Paradise	64	2	10	12	34	5.9	0	– 30					
WASH	LW	B. Girard	52	9	14	23	42	21.4	1	– 3	J. Bedard	11	23	7	3.66
T. McVie	C	G. Charron	80	38	35	73	260	14.6	4	– 25	B. Wolfe	4	14	4	4.25
17–49–14	RW	B. Sirois	72	24	37	61	189	12.7	5	– 11	G. Smith	2	12	3	4.16
	LW	D. Forbes	77	11	11	22	143	7.7	0	– 34					
	LW	A. Bailey	40	7	12	19	58	12.1	0	– 12					
	LW	M. Marson	46	4	4	8	30	13.3	0	1					
	C	G. Meehan	78	19	24	43	172	11.0	7	– 41					
	C	R. Bragnalo	44	2	13	15	60	3.3	0	– 6					
	C	R. Lalonde	67	1	5	6	48	2.1	0	– 18					
	RW	B. Riley	57	13	12	25	67	19.4	5	– 15					
	RW	T. Rowe	63	13	8	21	116	11.2	1	– 18					
	RW	B. Collins	74	10	9	19	104	9.6	0	– 32					
	D	B. Picard	75	10	27	37	170	5.9	2	– 26					
	D	R. Green	60	5	14	19	84	6.0	4	– 35					
	D	B. Watson	79	3	11	14	52	5.8	0	– 12					
	D	G. Lane	69	2	9	11	68	2.9	0	– 19					
	D	G. Smith	80	4	7	11	57	7.0	0	– 20					

ADAMS DIVISION

	POS	PLAYER	GP	G	A	PTS	SOG	SPCT	PPG	+/–	GOALIE	W	L	T	GAvg
BOS	LW	W. Cashman	76	24	38	62	134	17.9	1	34	R. Grahame	26	6	7	2.76
D. Cherry	LW	D. Marcotte	77	20	34	54	159	12.6	4	32	G. Gilbert	15	6	2	2.53
51–18–11	LW	J. Bucyk	53	5	13	18	47	10.6	3	– 2	G. Cheevers	10	5	2	2.65
	LW	S. Jonathan	68	27	25	52	121	22.3	0	34	J. Pettie	0	1	0	6.00
	LW	J. Wensink	80	16	20	36	131	12.2	1	23					
	C	J. Ratelle	80	25	59	84	158	15.8	3	49					
	C	P. McNab	79	41	39	80	227	18.1	5	35					
	C	G. Sheppard	54	23	36	59	160	14.4	5	19					
	C	B. Miller	76	20	20	40	134	14.9	1	16					
	C	M. Hagman	15	4	1	5	13	30.8	0	– 1					
	RW	T. O'Reilly	77	29	61	90	166	17.5	5	40					
	RW	B. Schmautz	54	27	27	54	174	15.5	4	24					
	RW	R. Middleton	79	25	35	60	171	14.6	2	40					
	D	B. Park	80	22	57	79	225	9.8	9	68					
	D	M. Milbury	80	8	30	38	82	9.8	0	52					
	D	R. Smith	79	7	29	36	116	6.0	0	70					
	D	G. Doak	61	4	13	17	66	6.1	0	37					

TEAM	POS	PLAYER	GP	G	A	PTS	SOG	SPCT	PPG	+/-	GOALIE	W	L	T	GAvg
BUF	LW	R. Martin	65	28	35	63	221	12.7	7	16	D. Edwards	**38**	16	17	2.64
M. Pronovost	C	G. Perreault	79	41	48	89	192	21.4	7	18	B. Sauve	6	2	0	2.50
44–19–17	RW	D. Gare	69	39	38	77	265	14.7	9	32	G. Desjardins	0	1	0	3.78
	LW	C. Ramsay	80	28	43	71	159	17.6	2	33					
	C	D. Luce	78	26	35	61	170	15.3	5	32					
	RW	R. Robert	67	25	48	73	209	12.0	7	19					
	LW	D. Smith	35	3	3	6	25	12.0	0	– 4					
	LW	T. Martin	21	3	2	5	17	17.6	0	– 1					
	C	A. Savard	80	19	20	39	127	15.0	2	1					
	C	F. Stanfield	57	3	8	11	38	7.9	0	– 8					
	RW	G. McAdam	79	19	22	41	160	11.9	2	3					
	RW	J. Lorentz	70	9	15	24	85	10.6	6	– 4					
	D	J. Korab	77	7	34	41	204	3.4	3	19					
	D	J. Guevremont	66	7	28	35	162	4.3	0	25					
	D	B. Hajt	76	4	18	22	78	5.1	0	36					
	D	L. Fogolin	76	0	23	23	77	.0	0	7					
	D	J. Schoenfeld	60	2	20	22	114	1.8	0	24					
TOR	LW	T. Williams	78	19	31	50	161	11.8	6	6	M. Palmateer	34	19	9	2.74
R. Neilson	C	D. Sittler	80	45	72	117	**311**	14.5	14	34	G. McRae	7	10	1	3.29
41–29–10	RW	L. McDonald	74	47	40	87	243	19.3	11	34					
	LW	S. Weir	30	12	5	17	39	30.8	0	0					
	LW	J. Jones	78	4	9	13	54	7.4	0	0					
	LW	D. Maloney	13	3	4	7	27	11.1	0	– 5					
	C	P. Boutette	80	17	19	36	130	13.1	2	0					
	C	G. Ferguson	73	7	16	23	119	5.9	0	– 9					
	C	J. Valiquette	60	8	13	21	49	16.3	3	2					
	C	B. Boudreau	40	11	18	29	71	15.5	1	8					
	RW	R. Ellis	80	26	24	50	128	20.3	3	8					
	RW	E. Thompson	59	17	22	39	132	12.9	4	10					
	D	B. Salming	80	16	60	76	258	6.2	6	30					
	D	I. Turnbull	77	14	47	61	241	5.8	3	6					
	D	B. Glennie	77	2	15	17	64	3.1	0	24					
	D	J. Butler	73	9	7	16	99	9.1	1	– 10					
	D	T. Johansen	79	2	14	16	82	2.4	0	3					
CLEVE	LW	B. Murdoch	71	14	26	40	131	10.7	5	– 18	G. Meloche	16	27	8	3.77
J. Evans	C	D. Maruk	76	36	35	71	198	18.2	4	– 26	G. Edwards	6	18	5	4.52
22–45–13	RW	A. MacAdam	80	16	32	48	149	10.7	3	– 19					
	LW	M. Fidler	78	23	28	51	181	12.7	4	– 13					
	LW	J. Parise	40	9	13	22	61	14.8	1	– 15					
	LW	R. Hampton	77	18	18	36	159	11.3	3	– 24					
	C	D. Gardner	75	19	25	44	106	17.9	3	– 16					
	C	W. McKechnie	53	12	22	34	97	12.4	2	– 8					
	C	W. Merrick	18	2	5	7	42	4.8	0	– 10					
	RW	C. Arnason	40	21	13	34	110	19.1	5	– 2					
	RW	M. Crombeen	43	3	4	7	65	4.6	2	– 26					
	RW	F. Ahern	36	3	4	7	37	8.1	0	– 16					
	D	K. Manery	78	22	27	49	188	11.7	7	– 15					
	D	G. Smith	80	7	30	37	148	4.7	2	– 26					
	D	J. Neilson	68	2	21	23	51	3.9	0	– 25					
	D	B. Stewart	72	2	15	17	57	3.5	0	– 25					
	D	J. Potvin	40	3	14	17	85	3.5	0	– 4					

GOALS		ASSISTS		POINTS	
G. Lafleur, MONT	60	B. Trottier, NYI	77	G. Lafleur, MONT	132
M. Bossy, NYI	53	G. Lafleur, MONT	72	B. Trottier, NYI	123
S. Shutt, MONT	49	D. Sittler, TOR	72	D. Sittler, TOR	117
L. McDonald, TOR	47	B. Clarke, PHI	68	J. Lemaire, MONT	97
B. Trottier, NYI	46	D. Potvin, NYI	64	D. Potvin, NYI	94

SHOTS ON GOAL		SHOOTING PCT.		+/-	
D. Sittler, TOR	311	M. Walton, VAN	25.2	G. Lafleur, MONT	73
J. Lemaire, MONT	310	B. Trottier, NYI	23.8	L. Robinson, MONT	71
G. Lafleur, MONT	307	M. Bossy, NYI	22.6	R. Smith, BOS	70
M. Dionne, LA	294	S. Jonathan, BOS	22.3	B. Park, BOS	68
D. Potvin, NYI	288	G. Perreault, BUF	21.4	S. Savard, MONT	62

PENALTY MINUTES		GOALS AGAINST AVE.		SHUTOUTS	
D. Schultz, LA, PITT	405	K. Dryden, MONT	2.05	B. Parent, PHI	7
T. Williams, TOR	351	B. Parent, PHI	2.22	K. Dryden, MONT	5
D. Polonich, DET	254	C. Resch, NYI	2.55	T. Esposito, CHI	5
R. Holt, CHI, CLEVE	249	T. Esposito, CHI	2.63	D. Edwards, BUF	5
A. Dupont, PHI	225	D. Edwards, BUF	2.64	M. Palmateer, TOR	5

	W	L	T	PTS	GF	GA	PPG	PPCT	SHG	PPGA	PKPCT	SHGA
CAMPBELL CONFERENCE												
PATRICK DIVISION												
NYI	51	15	14	116	**358**	214	**81**	**31.2**	7	57	80.1	4
PHI	40	25	15	95	281	248	59	25.4	**16**	73	78.8	**2**
NYR	40	29	11	91	316	292	75	24.5	9	78	74.9	12
ATL	41	31	8	90	327	280	54	23.9	6	56	80.7	5
SMYTHE DIVISION												
CHI	29	36	15	73	244	277	41	16.6	8	70	76.4	4
VAN	25	42	13	63	217	291	56	19.0	1	49	80.2	9
STL	18	50	12	48	249	348	48	17.1	3	63	74.2	8
COLO	15	53	12	42	210	331	60	22.5	8	62	70.6	4
PRINCE OF WALES CONFERENCE												
NORRIS DIVISION												
*MONT	52	17	11	115	337	**204**	68	28.3	7	**35**	**83.6**	7
PITT	36	31	13	85	281	279	56	21.5	7	57	77.2	4
LA	34	34	12	80	292	286	76	23.9	6	55	77.6	8
WASH	24	41	15	63	273	338	57	18.9	5	83	70.3	12
DET	23	41	16	62	252	295	78	23.9	10	63	77.4	9
ADAMS DIVISION												
BOS	43	23	14	100	316	270	59	23.7	6	72	74.7	9
BUF	36	28	16	88	280	263	55	20.6	9	55	78.7	4
TOR	34	33	13	81	267	252	60	25.4	5	70	78.8	7
MINN	28	40	12	68	257	289	63	21.8	4	48	79.3	9

CAMPBELL CONFERENCE

PATRICK DIVISION

	POS	PLAYER	GP	G	A	PTS	SOG	SPCT	PPG	+/-	GOALIE	W	L	T	GAvg
NYI	LW	C. Gillies	75	35	56	91	210	16.7	11	57	C. Resch	26	7	10	2.50
A. Arbour	C	B. Trottier	76	47	**87**	**134**	187	25.1	15	**76**	B. Smith	25	8	4	2.87
51–15–14	RW	M. Bossy	80	**69**	57	126	279	24.7	**27**	63					
	LW	B. Bourne	80	30	31	61	148	20.3	4	34					
	C	W. Merrick	75	20	21	41	128	15.6	2	13					
	RW	B. Nystrom	78	19	20	39	161	11.8	1	19					
	LW	J. Tonelli	73	17	39	56	113	15.0	1	29					
	LW	G. Howatt	75	16	12	28	81	19.8	0	6					
	C	M. Kaszycki	71	16	18	34	89	18.0	2	7					
	C	L. Henning	73	13	20	33	70	18.6	0	17					
	RW	B. Harris	80	15	39	54	128	11.7	0	26					
	RW	E. Westfall	55	5	11	16	51	9.8	0	0					
	D	D. Potvin	73	31	70	101	237	13.1	12	71					
	D	S. Persson	78	10	56	66	113	8.8	6	38					
	D	D. Lewis	79	5	18	23	95	5.3	0	43					
	D	B. Lorimer	67	3	18	21	64	4.7	0	27					
	D	G. Hart	50	2	14	16	56	3.6	0	30					
PHI	LW	B. Barber	79	34	46	80	258	13.2	10	19	W. Stephenson	20	10	5	3.35
	C	B. Clarke	80	16	57	73	143	11.2	5	12	B. Parent	16	12	7	2.70
B. McCammon	RW	R. Leach	76	34	20	54	279	12.2	13	−3	R. Moore	3	0	1	1.77
22–17–11	LW	P. Holmgren	57	19	10	29	122	15.6	4	2	P. Peeters	1	2	1	3.43
P. Quinn	LW	B. Kelly	71	7	31	38	85	8.2	1	15	R. Ste.-Croix	0	1	1	3.08
18–8–4	LW	D. Hoyda	67	3	13	16	37	8.1	0	2					
	LW	J. Evans	44	6	5	11	39	15.4	0	−3					
	C	M. Bridgman	76	24	35	59	157	15.3	0	14					
	C	R. MacLeish	71	26	32	58	211	12.3	7	4					
	C	B. Dunlop	66	20	28	48	122	16.4	5	27					
	C	K. Linseman	30	5	20	25	57	8.8	1	16					
	RW	D. Ververgaert	37	9	7	16	54	16.7	2	−4					
	RW	T. Gorence	42	13	6	19	85	15.3	1	16					
	D	B. Wilson	80	13	36	49	174	7.5	6	13					
	D	B. Dailey	70	9	30	39	164	5.5	1	21					
	D	J. Watson	77	9	13	22	112	8.0	0	11					
	D	A. Dupont	77	3	9	12	128	2.3	0	21					

	POS	PLAYER	GP	G	A	PTS	SOG	SPCT	PPG	+/–	GOALIE	W	L	T	GAvg
NYR	LW	P. Hickey	80	34	41	75	193	17.6	8	8	J. Davidson	20	12	5	3.52
F. Shero	C	U. Nilsson	59	27	39	66	96	**28.1**	8	17	W. Thomas	15	10	3	3.63
40–29–11	RW	A. Hedberg	80	33	45	78	214	15.4	6	19	D. Soetaert	5	7	3	3.80
	LW	D. Maloney	28	9	17	26	39	23.1	3	4					
	C	P. Esposito	80	42	36	78	215	19.5	14	– 1					
	RW	D. Murdoch	40	15	22	37	133	11.3	4	– 6					
	LW	S. Vickers	66	13	34	47	86	15.1	4	– 7					
	LW	N. Fotiu	71	3	5	8	51	5.9	0	3					
	C	R. Duguay	79	27	36	63	178	15.2	1	10					
	C	W. Tkaczuk	77	15	27	42	134	11.2	4	20					
	RW	P. Plante	70	6	25	31	84	7.1	0	11					
	RW	D. Talafous	68	13	16	29	88	14.8	2	5					
	D	M. McEwen	80	20	38	58	204	9.8	7	10					
	D	R. Greschner	60	17	36	53	153	11.1	8	0					
	D	C. Vadnais	77	8	37	45	149	5.4	4	– 14					
	D	M. Marois	71	5	26	31	115	4.3	0	18					
	D	D. Maloney	76	11	17	28	83	13.3	1	17					
ATL	LW	E. Vail	80	35	48	83	203	17.2	5	25	D. Bouchard	**32**	21	7	3.33
F. Creighton	C	G. Chouinard	80	50	57	107	229	21.8	11	23	R. Lemelin	8	8	1	3.32
41–31–8	RW	B. MacMillan	79	37	71	108	194	19.1	8	34	Y. Belanger	1	2	0	6.92
	LW	G. Carr	30	3	8	11	35	8.6	0	– 4					
	C	B. Lalonde	78	24	32	56	135	17.8	6	– 3					
	C	B. Clement	65	12	23	35	86	14.0	0	– 5					
	C	R. Laurence	59	14	20	34	113	12.4	2	8					
	C	I. Boldirev	13	6	8	14	33	18.2	4	1					
	RW	J. Pronovost	75	28	39	67	151	18.5	4	21					
	RW	K. Houston	80	21	31	52	140	15.0	2	4					
	RW	W. Plett	74	23	20	43	164	14.0	0	13					
	RW	J. Gould	61	8	7	15	67	11.9	0	– 4					
	D	B. Murdoch	35	5	11	16	53	9.4	2	2					
	D	E. Kea	53	6	18	24	53	11.3	2	– 2					
	D	B. Marsh	80	0	19	19	80	.0	0	23					
	D	D. Shand	79	4	22	26	81	4.9	0	23					
	D	R. Mulhern	37	3	12	15	58	5.2	0	6					

SMYTHE DIVISION

	POS	PLAYER	GP	G	A	PTS	SOG	SPCT	PPG	+/–	GOALIE	W	L	T	GAvg
CHI	LW	J. Marks	80	21	24	45	132	15.9	4	2	T. Esposito	24	28	11	3.27
B. Pulford	C	S. Mikita	65	19	36	55	147	12.9	4	3	M. Veisor	5	8	4	3.53
29–36–15	RW	C. Koroll	78	12	19	31	109	11.0	1	3					
	LW	T. Bulley	75	27	23	50	105	25.7	1	18					
	C	R. Kerr	73	16	24	40	111	14.4	2	– 7					
	RW	G. Mulvey	80	19	15	34	136	14.0	5	– 14					
	LW	D. Rota	63	13	17	30	116	11.2	1	– 10					
	LW	B. Kelly	63	2	5	7	59	3.4	0	– 10					
	C	T. Lysiak	14	0	10	10	27	.0	0	3					
	C	M. Walton	26	6	3	9	37	16.2	3	1					
	RW	J. Bordeleau	63	15	21	36	101	14.9	2	– 7					
	RW	A. Daigle	74	11	14	25	80	13.8	0	2					
	RW	T. Higgins	36	7	16	23	64	10.9	0	6					
	D	B. Murray	79	19	32	51	220	8.6	4	4					
	D	D. Wilson	56	5	21	26	136	3.7	2	4					
	D	M. O'Connell	48	4	22	26	83	4.8	1	– 1					
	D	D. Logan	76	1	14	15	77	1.3	0	– 9					
VAN	LW	C. Fraser	78	16	19	35	184	8.7	2	– 7	G. Bromley	11	19	6	3.81
H. Neale	C	T. Gradin	76	20	31	51	105	19.0	4	– 12	G. Hanlon	12	13	5	3.10
25–42–13	RW	S. Smyl	62	14	24	38	122	11.5	4	– 6	D. Wilson	2	10	2	4.17
	LW	R. Sedlbauer	79	40	16	56	225	17.8	15	– 34					
	LW	J. Gillis	78	13	12	25	143	9.1	4	– 31					
	C	D. Lever	71	23	21	44	170	13.5	8	– 41					
	C	C. Oddleifson	67	11	26	37	83	13.3	4	– 15					
	C	P. Martin	64	12	14	26	80	15.0	1	– 3					
	C	R. Eriksson	35	2	12	14	69	2.9	0	– 12					
	RW	H. Graves	62	11	15	26	112	9.8	2	– 15					
	RW	R. Blight	56	5	10	15	91	5.5	1	– 28					
	D	D. Kearns	78	3	31	34	102	2.9	0	– 23					
	D	H. Snepsts	76	7	24	31	115	6.1	4	– 27					
	D	B. Manno	52	5	16	21	71	7.0	0	– 17					
	D	L. Lindgren	64	2	19	21	109	1.8	1	– 32					
	D	J. McIlhargey	53	2	4	6	26	7.7	0	– 16					
	D	L. Goodenough	36	4	9	13	75	5.3	2	– 14					

	POS	PLAYER	GP	G	A	PTS	SOG	SPCT	PPG	+/-	GOALIE	W	L	T	GAvg
STL	LW	B. Sutter	77	41	39	80	177	23.2	12	− 2	P. Myre	9	22	8	4.33
B. Plager	C	B. Federko	74	31	64	95	156	19.9	7	− 15	E. Staniowski	9	25	3	3.82
18–50–12	RW	W. Babych	67	27	36	63	197	13.7	11	− 11	D. Grant	0	2	1	7.26
	LW	I. Hammarstrom	65	12	22	34	129	9.3	0	− 13	T. Richardson	0	1	0	9.00
	LW	C. Bennett	74	14	19	33	141	9.9	1	− 23					
	LW	J. Smrke	55	6	8	14	72	8.3	0	− 24					
	C	G. Unger	80	30	26	56	182	16.5	3	− 44					
	C	L. Patey	78	15	19	34	124	12.1	0	− 27					
	C	M. Zuke	34	9	17	26	80	11.3	3	− 8					
	C	H. Bennett	52	3	9	12	44	6.8	0	− 18					
	RW	T. Currie	36	4	15	19	57	7.0	1	− 9					
	RW	M. Crombeen	37	3	8	11	51	5.9	0	− 13					
	D	J. Brownschidle	64	10	24	34	101	9.9	5	− 21					
	D	B. Murdoch	54	13	13	26	92	14.1	1	− 6					
	D	B. Gibbs	75	2	27	29	86	2.3	0	− 42					
	D	L. Giroux	73	5	22	27	107	4.7	0	− 25					
	D	B. Stewart	78	5	13	18	57	8.8	1	− 28					
COLO	LW	G. Croteau	79	23	18	41	104	22.1	8	− 28	M. Plasse	9	**29**	2	3.96
P. Kelly	C	J. Valiquette	76	23	34	57	159	14.5	8	− 42	B. Oleschuk	6	19	8	3.85
3–14–4	RW	W. Paiement	65	24	36	60	206	11.7	5	− 35	D. Favell	0	5	2	5.37
A. Guidolin	LW	D. Saleski	16	2	0	2	50	4.0	0	− 10					
12–39–8	LW	A. Spruce	47	3	15	18	57	5.3	0	− 18					
	C	M. Malinowski	54	6	17	23	76	7.9	0	− 17					
	C	R. Klassen	64	6	13	19	100	6.0	1	− 25					
	C	R. Comeau	70	8	10	18	85	9.4	1	− 20					
	RW	R. Pierce	70	19	17	36	145	13.1	4	− 21					
	RW	R. Delorme	77	20	8	28	85	23.5	2	− 30					
	D	J. Van Boxmeer	76	9	34	43	189	4.8	4	− 26					
	D	B. Beck	63	14	28	42	217	6.5	5	− 30					
	D	M. Christie	68	1	10	11	50	2.0	0	− 44					
	D	N. Beverley	52	2	4	6	42	4.8	0	− 16					
	D	D. Owchar	50	3	13	16	77	3.9	1	− 33					
	D	D. Awrey	56	1	4	5	40	2.5	0	− 33					

PRINCE OF WALES CONFERENCE

NORRIS DIVISION

	POS	PLAYER	GP	G	A	PTS	SOG	SPCT	PPG	+/-	GOALIE	W	L	T	GAvg
MONT	LW	S. Shutt	72	37	40	77	192	19.3	10	37	K. Dryden	30	10	7	**2.30**
S. Bowman	LW	Y. Lambert	79	26	40	66	133	19.5	5	30	M. Larocque	22	7	4	2.84
52–17–11	LW	B. Gainey	79	20	18	38	153	13.1	1	11					
	LW	R. Houle	66	17	34	51	105	16.2	6	16					
	C	P. Mondou	77	31	41	72	163	19.0	6	59					
	C	J. Lemaire	50	24	31	55	203	11.8	6	9					
	C	D. Risebrough	48	10	15	25	83	12.0	0	22					
	C	D. Jarvis	80	10	13	23	117	8.5	0	5					
	RW	G. Lafleur	80	52	77	129	342	15.2	13	56					
	RW	M. Napier	54	11	20	31	73	15.1	2	17					
	RW	M. Tremblay	76	30	29	59	163	18.4	3	23					
	RW	P. Hughes	41	9	8	17	51	17.6	1	7					
	D	L. Robinson	67	16	45	61	147	10.9	4	50					
	D	G. Lapointe	69	13	42	55	209	6.2	6	27					
	D	S. Savard	80	7	26	33	82	8.5	1	46					
	D	R. Chartraw	62	5	11	16	81	6.2	0	12					
	D	B. Engblom	62	3	11	14	60	5.0	0	26					
PITT	LW	R. Schutt	74	24	21	45	181	13.3	3	− 9	D. Herron	22	19	12	3.37
J. Wilson	C	G. Malone	80	35	30	65	198	17.7	8	16	G. Millen	14	11	1	3.37
36–31–13	RW	G. Ferguson	80	21	29	50	201	10.4	0	10	G. Laxton	0	1	0	8.00
	LW	R. Lonsberry	80	24	22	46	179	13.4	4	7					
	C	O. Kindrachuk	79	18	42	60	145	12.4	4	3					
	RW	R. Kehoe	57	27	18	45	165	16.4	7	14					
	LW	W. Bianchin	40	7	4	11	57	12.3	1	− 2					
	C	P. Mahovlich	60	14	39	53	153	9.2	5	− 11					
	C	G. Sheppard	60	15	22	37	134	11.2	3	8					
	RW	P. Lee	80	32	26	58	219	14.6	10	− 13					
	RW	B. Chapman	71	10	8	18	96	10.4	1	− 12					
	RW	J. Cossete	38	7	2	9	35	20.0	1	− 1					
	D	R. Carlyle	70	13	34	47	208	6.3	3	14					
	D	T. Bladon	78	4	23	27	135	3.0	1	− 17					
	D	R. Stackhouse	75	10	33	43	173	5.8	3	21					
	D	D. Tallon	63	5	24	29	91	5.5	2	− 15					
	D	C. Campbell	65	2	18	20	52	3.8	0	14					

	POS	PLAYER	GP	G	A	PTS	SOG	SPCT	PPG	+/-	GOALIE	W	L	T	GAvg
LA	LW	C. Simmer	38	21	27	48	112	18.8	8	11	M. Lessard	23	15	10	3.10
B. Berry	C	M. Dionne	80	59	71	130	**362**	16.3	19	33	R. Grahame	11	19	2	4.21
34–34–12	RW	D. Taylor	78	43	48	91	238	18.1	13	27					
	LW	S. Jensen	72	23	8	31	114	20.2	2	-28					
	LW	T. Williams	44	10	15	25	84	11.9	3	-7					
	LW	M. Wilson	58	11	15	26	107	10.3	1	-7					
	C	B. Goring	80	36	51	87	217	16.6	13	-20					
	C	S. Apps	80	7	30	37	128	5.5	0	-25					
	C	V. Venasky	73	4	13	17	47	8.5	0	0					
	RW	M. Murphy	64	16	29	45	150	10.7	4	-8					
	RW	B. Wilson	73	9	10	19	72	12.5	0	-5					
	RW	G. Goldup	73	15	22	37	117	12.8	3	-7					
	RW	M. Heaslip	69	4	9	13	53	7.5	0	-10					
	D	R. Palmer	78	4	41	45	130	3.1	2	-13					
	D	R. Manery	71	8	27	35	116	6.9	2	6					
	D	R. Hampton	49	3	17	20	70	4.3	0	0					
WASH	LW	G. Charron	80	28	42	70	225	12.4	9	-14	G. Inness	14	14	8	3.70
D. Belisle	C	R. Walter	69	28	28	56	156	17.9	6	-1	J. Bedard	6	17	6	4.34
24–41–15	RW	B. Sirois	73	29	25	54	207	14.0	9	-6	B. Wolfe	4	9	1	4.73
	LW	B. Girard	79	9	15	24	59	15.3	0	-15	R. Boutin	0	1	0	6.67
	C	D. Maruk	76	31	59	90	189	16.4	6	-14					
	RW	T. Rowe	69	31	30	61	205	15.1	4	-6					
	LW	B. Stewart	45	7	12	19	56	12.5	0	1					
	LW	P. Mulvey	55	7	4	11	60	11.7	1	-18					
	C	R. Edberg	76	14	27	41	133	10.5	1	11					
	C	D. Hextall	26	2	9	11	22	9.1	0	-13					
	RW	M. Lofthouse	52	13	10	23	75	17.3	1	-11					
	RW	M. Bergeron	30	7	6	13	53	13.2	1	-18					
	D	B. Picard	77	21	44	65	243	8.6	8	1					
	D	R. Green	71	8	33	41	133	6.0	2	-45					
	D	L. Svensson	74	2	29	31	72	2.8	0	-3					
	D	G. Lane	64	3	15	18	69	4.3	0	-15					
	D	Y. Labre	51	1	13	14	36	2.8	0	7					
DET	LW	E. Thompson	70	23	31	54	163	14.1	8	-28	R. Vachon	10	27	11	3.90
B. Kromm	LW	D. Labraaten	78	19	19	38	112	17.0	7	-17	J. Rutherford	13	14	5	3.27
23–41–16	LW	N. Libett	68	15	19	34	130	11.5	3	4					
	LW	D. Bolduc	56	16	13	29	81	19.8	3	-9					
	C	D. McCourt	79	28	43	71	222	12.6	14	-27					
	C	A. St. Laurent	76	18	31	49	158	11.4	4	-3					
	C	P. Woods	80	14	23	37	127	11.0	1	-26					
	C	G. Carroll	36	2	9	11	16	12.5	1	-6					
	RW	N. Nedomansky	80	38	35	73	212	17.9	13	-13					
	RW	D. Polonich	62	10	12	22	80	12.5	1	-10					
	RW	F. LeBlanc	29	5	6	11	27	18.5	1	1					
	D	R. Larson	79	18	49	67	271	6.6	6	-20					
	D	W. Huber	68	7	24	31	153	4.6	4	-25					
	D	T. Bergman	68	10	17	27	88	11.4	3	-35					
	D	P. Miller	75	5	23	28	122	4.1	3	-13					
	D	T. Harper	51	0	6	6	33	.0	0	-3					
	D	J. Hamel	52	2	4	6	41	4.9	0	-9					

ADAMS DIVISION

	POS	PLAYER	GP	G	A	PTS	SOG	SPCT	PPG	+/-	GOALIE	W	L	T	GAvg
BOS	LW	W. Cashman	75	27	40	67	133	20.3	10	16	G. Cheevers	23	9	10	3.16
D. Cherry	LW	D. Marcotte	79	20	27	47	156	12.8	2	6	G. Gilbert	12	8	2	3.54
43–23–14	LW	J. Wensink	76	28	18	46	131	21.4	0	20	J. Pettie	8	6	2	3.59
	LW	A. Secord	71	16	7	23	80	20.0	0	7					
	LW	S. Jonathan	33	6	9	15	32	18.8	0	8					
	C	J. Ratelle	80	27	45	72	137	19.7	11	17					
	C	P. McNab	76	35	45	80	200	17.5	4	29					
	C	B. Miller	77	15	33	48	149	10.1	0	20					
	RW	R. Middleton	71	38	48	86	152	25.0	12	33					
	RW	T. O'Reilly	80	26	51	77	120	21.7	3	7					
	RW	B. Schmautz	65	20	22	42	199	10.1	6	-1					
	RW	D. Foster	44	11	13	24	57	19.3	2	-1					
	D	B. Park	40	7	32	39	96	7.3	3	28					
	D	M. Milbury	74	1	34	35	76	1.3	0	23					
	D	D. Redmond	64	7	26	33	144	4.9	4	0					
	D	R. Smith	65	7	18	25	78	9.0	0	20					
	D	A. Sims	67	9	20	29	128	7.0	0	22					

	POS	PLAYER	GP	G	A	PTS	SOG	SPCT	PPG	+/-	GOALIE	W	L	T	GAvg
BUF	LW	R. Martin	73	32	21	53	250	12.8	8	– 7	D. Edwards	26	18	9	3.02
	C	G. Perreault	79	27	58	85	172	15.7	6	12	B. Sauve	10	10	7	3.73
M. Pronovost	RW	D. Gare	79	27	40	67	260	10.4	7	18	R. Ireland	0	0	0	6.00
8–10–6	LW	C. Ramsay	80	26	31	57	113	23.0	4	21					
B. Inglis	C	D. Luce	79	26	35	61	149	17.4	6	20					
28–18–10	RW	R. Seiling	78	20	22	42	136	14.7	2	15					
	LW	J. Richard	61	10	15	25	85	11.8	0	8					
	LW	T. McKegney	52	8	14	22	67	11.9	0	– 2					
	LW	D. Schultz	28	2	3	5	16	12.5	0	– 12					
	C	D. Smith	43	14	12	26	85	16.5	3	– 5					
	C	A. Savard	65	18	22	40	97	18.6	2	2					
	RW	R. Robert	68	22	40	62	206	10.7	1	– 12					
	D	J. Korab	78	11	40	51	204	5.4	8	10					
	D	J. Schoenfeld	46	8	17	25	99	8.1	6	8					
	D	L. Fogolin	74	3	19	22	70	4.3	0	– 4					
	D	B. Hajt	40	3	8	11	53	5.7	0	– 4					
	D	J. Guevremont	34	3	8	11	51	5.9	0	12					
TOR	LW	D. Maloney	77	17	36	53	141	12.1	0	19	M. Palmateer	26	21	10	2.95
	C	D. Sittler	70	36	51	87	290	12.4	12	9	P. Harrison	8	12	3	3.51
R. Neilson	RW	L. McDonald	79	43	42	85	314	13.7	16	12	P. Hamel	0	0	0	0.00
34–33–13	LW	T. Williams	77	19	20	39	157	12.1	6	– 7					
	LW	R. Wilson	46	5	12	17	58	8.6	4	– 10					
	LW	G. Monahan	62	4	7	11	55	7.3	0	4					
	LW	L. Stamler	45	4	3	7	31	12.9	0	– 6					
	C	W. McKechnie	79	25	36	61	123	20.3	7	21					
	C	P. Boutette	80	14	19	33	89	15.7	0	3					
	C	J. Jones	69	9	9	18	63	14.3	0	2					
	RW	R. Ellis	63	16	12	28	97	16.5	4	7					
	RW	J. Anderson	71	15	11	26	123	12.2	0	2					
	RW	J. Butler	76	8	7	15	77	10.4	0	– 2					
	D	B. Salming	78	17	56	73	230	7.4	4	31					
	D	I. Turnbull	80	12	51	63	239	5.0	4	– 7					
	D	D. Hutchison	79	4	15	19	117	3.4	0	36					
	D	D. Burrows	65	2	11	13	70	2.9	0	– 10					
MINN	LW	S. Payne	70	23	17	40	165	13.9	3	– 5	G. Meloche	20	25	7	3.33
	C	B. Smith	80	30	44	74	244	12.3	9	– 8	G. Edwards	6	11	5	3.72
H. Howell	RW	A. MacAdam	69	24	34	58	135	17.8	6	0	P. LoPresti	2	4	0	4.87
2–4–2	LW	M. Fidler	59	23	26	49	158	14.6	4	– 25					
G. Sonmor	C	G. Sharpley	80	19	34	53	162	11.7	5	– 18					
2–2–0	RW	K. Manery	60	17	19	36	126	13.5	3	– 13					
H. Howell	LW	J. Parise	57	13	9	22	73	17.8	1	– 12					
1–2–0	LW	M. Polich	73	6	10	16	66	9.1	0	– 13					
G. Sonmor	C	T. Young	73	24	32	56	147	16.3	8	– 12					
23–32–10	RW	R. Zanussi	63	14	16	30	98	14.3	3	5					
	RW	T. Younghans	76	8	10	18	70	11.4	0	– 23					
	RW	K. Andersson	41	9	4	13	59	15.3	2	– 6					
	D	G. Sargent	79	12	32	44	182	6.6	8	– 10					
	D	B. Maxwell	70	9	28	37	200	4.5	5	– 13					
	D	G. Smith	80	5	27	32	193	2.6	1	– 21					
	D	F. Barrett	45	1	9	10	36	2.8	0	– 4					
	D	J. Potvin	64	5	16	21	89	5.6	2	– 11					

GOALS

M. Bossy, NYI	69
M. Dionne, LA	59
G. Lafleur, MONT	52
G. Chouinard, ATL	50
B. Trottier, NYI	47

ASSISTS

B. Trottier, NYI	87
G. Lafleur, MONT	77
B. MacMillan, ATL	71
M. Dionne, LA	71
D. Potvin, NYI	70

POINTS

B. Trottier, NYI	134
M. Dionne, LA	130
G. Lafleur, MONT	129
M. Bossy, NYI	126
B. MacMillan, ATL	108

SHOTS ON GOAL

M. Dionne, LA	362
G. Lafleur, MONT	342
L. McDonald, TOR	314
D. Sittler, TOR	290
R. Leach, PHI	279
M. Bossy, NYI	279

SHOOTING PCT.

U. Nilsson, NYR	28.1
T. Bulley, CHI	25.7
B. Trottier, NYI	25.1
R. Middleton, BOS	25.0
M. Bossy, NYI	24.7

+/-

B. Trottier, NYI	76
D. Potvin, NYI	71
M. Bossy, NYI	63
P. Mondou, MONT	59
C. Gillies, NYI	57

PENALTY MINUTES

T. Williams, TOR	298
D. Hutchison, TOR	235
W. Plett, ATL	213
D. Polonich, DET	208
G. Howatt, NYI	205
T. O'Reilly, BOS	205

GOALS AGAINST AVE.

K. Dryden, MONT	2.30
C. Resch, NYI	2.50
B. Parent, PHI	2.70
M. Larocque, MONT	2.84
B. Smith, NYI	2.87

SHUTOUTS

K. Dryden, MONT	5
B. Parent, PHI	4
M. Palmateer, TOR	4
M. Lessard, LA	4
T. Esposito, CHI	4

	W	L	T	PTS	GF	GA	PPG	PPCT	SHG	PPGA	PKPCT	SHGA
CAMPBELL CONFERENCE												
PATRICK DIVISION												
PHI	48	12	20	116	237	254	44	16.3	**15**	79	79.3	7
*NYI	39	28	13	91	281	247	63	23.8	7	71	77.6	4
NYR	38	32	10	86	308	284	79	26.0	8	54	82.2	7
ATL	35	32	13	83	282	269	51	23.6	6	52	80.9	7
WASH	27	40	13	67	261	293	54	18.3	5	65	73.8	4
SMYTHE DIVISION												
CHI	34	27	19	87	247	250	64	23.8	6	56	80.9	9
STL	34	34	12	80	266	278	53	18.3	5	**40**	**84.8**	4
VAN	27	37	16	70	256	281	53	17.0	2	69	75.5	12
EDM	28	39	13	69	301	322	61	21.6	11	74	76.5	4
COLO	19	48	13	51	234	308	53	17.4	6	53	77.7	3
WINN	20	49	11	51	214	314	63	18.8	4	63	77.1	10
PRINCE OF WALES CONFERENCE												
NORRIS DIVISION												
MONT	47	20	13	107	**328**	240	77	**29.2**	2	46	81.4	7
LA	30	36	14	74	290	313	**83**	26.7	7	94	67.7	9
PITT	30	37	13	73	251	303	52	19.8	6	64	74.1	4
HART	27	34	19	73	303	312	42	19.4	7	64	74.3	**1**
DET	26	43	11	63	268	306	61	22.1	6	64	76.3	2
ADAMS DIVISION												
BUF	47	17	16	110	318	**201**	67	24.4	2	43	82.9	4
BOS	46	21	13	105	310	234	60	24.4	8	53	83.0	4
MINN	36	28	16	88	311	253	75	23.7	4	43	82.1	7
TOR	35	40	5	75	304	327	68	24.7	2	69	78.8	5
QUE	25	44	11	61	248	313	63	21.0	4	71	73.4	9

CAMPBELL CONFERENCE

PATRICK DIVISION

	POS	PLAYER	GP	G	A	PTS	SOG	SPCT	PPG	+/-	GOALIE	W	L	T	GAvg
PHI	LW	B. Barber	79	40	32	72	265	15.1	7	39	P. Myre	18	7	15	3.57
P. Quinn	C	B. Clarke	76	12	57	69	139	8.6	1	42	P. Peeters	29	5	5	2.73
48–12–20	RW	R. Leach	76	50	26	76	328	15.2	5	40	R. Ste.-Croix	1	0	0	2.00
	LW	B. Propp	80	34	41	75	209	16.3	4	45					
	C	K. Linseman	80	22	57	79	168	13.1	2	26					
	RW	P. Holmgren	74	30	35	65	153	19.6	9	35					
	LW	B. Kelly	75	15	20	35	112	13.4	2	19					
	LW	A. Hill	61	16	10	26	79	20.3	0	14					
	C	M. Bridgman	74	16	31	47	145	11.0	2	13					
	C	R. MacLeish	78	31	35	66	234	13.2	6	23					
	RW	D. Ververgaert	58	14	17	31	96	14.6	0	9					
	RW	T. Gorence	51	8	13	21	89	9.0	0	7					
	RW	A. Paddock	32	3	7	10	29	10.3	0	– 4					
	D	B. Dailey	61	13	26	39	185	7.0	2	30					
	D	B. Wilson	61	9	25	34	119	7.6	4	21					
	D	A. Dupont	58	1	7	8	67	1.5	0	37					
	D	J. Watson	71	5	18	23	99	5.1	0	**53**					
NYI	LW	C. Gillies	73	19	35	54	175	10.9	7	29	C. Resch	23	14	6	3.04
A. Arbour	C	B. Trottier	78	42	62	104	186	22.6	15	31	B. Smith	15	14	7	2.95
39–28–13	RW	M. Bossy	75	51	41	92	244	20.9	16	28	R. Brodeur	1	0	0	4.50
	LW	J. Tonelli	77	14	30	44	103	13.6	3	8					
	LW	B. Bourne	73	15	25	40	155	9.7	3	5					
	LW	G. Howatt	77	8	11	19	62	12.9	0	– 3					
	C	W. Merrick	70	13	22	35	111	11.7	2	12					
	C	S. Tambellini	45	5	8	13	63	7.9	0	– 1					
	C	L. Henning	39	3	6	9	45	6.7	0	– 10					
	RW	A. Kallur	76	22	30	52	138	15.9	5	12					
	RW	B. Nystrom	67	21	18	39	146	14.4	2	4					
	RW	D. Sutter	56	15	9	24	75	20.0	0	5					
	D	D. Potvin	31	8	33	41	98	8.2	4	13					
	D	S. Persson	73	4	35	39	91	4.4	2	13					
	D	B. Lorimer	74	3	16	19	98	3.1	0	32					
	D	D. Langevin	76	3	13	16	82	3.7	0	11					
	D	D. Lewis	62	5	16	21	66	7.6	0	10					

	POS	PLAYER	GP	G	A	PTS	SOG	SPCT	PPG	+/-	GOALIE	W	L	T	GAvg
NYR	LW	S. Vickers	75	29	33	62	98	**29.6**	12	20	J. Davidson	20	15	4	3.17
F. Shero	C	U. Nilsson	50	14	44	58	72	19.4	5	15	S. Baker	9	8	6	3.41
38–32–10	RW	A. Hedberg	80	32	39	71	241	13.3	7	13	W. Thomas	4	7	0	3.95
	LW	D. Maloney	79	25	48	73	123	20.3	6	– 15	D. Soetaert	5	2	0	4.55
	C	P. Esposito	80	34	44	78	245	13.9	13	– 13					
	RW	E. Johnstone	78	14	21	35	121	11.6	0	3					
	LW	C. Larose	25	4	7	11	50	8.0	0	– 5					
	LW	F. Beaton	23	1	1	2	19	5.3	0	– 5					
	C	R. Duguay	73	28	22	50	154	18.2	3	– 6					
	C	W. Tkaczuk	76	12	25	37	128	9.4	4	19					
	RW	D. Murdoch	56	23	19	42	143	16.1	5	– 11					
	RW	D. Talafous	55	10	20	30	69	14.5	4	1					
	RW	W. Miller	55	7	6	13	51	13.7	0	– 6					
	D	B. Beck	61	14	45	59	150	9.3	5	16					
	D	R. Greschner	76	21	37	58	187	11.2	6	– 11					
	D	D. Maloney	77	12	25	37	102	11.8	3	10					
	D	C. Vadnais	66	3	20	23	82	3.7	1	– 1					
ATL	LW	E. Vail	77	28	25	53	193	14.5	6	5	D. Bouchard	23	19	10	3.18
A. MacNeil	LW	D. Lever	28	14	16	30	74	18.9	1	5	P. Riggin	11	9	2	3.20
35–32–13	LW	P. Henderson	30	7	6	13	29	24.1	1	5	J. Craig	1	2	1	3.79
	C	K. Nilsson	80	40	53	93	217	18.4	14	– 3	R. Lemelin	0	2	0	6.00
	C	I. Boldirev	52	16	24	40	121	13.2	1	– 1					
	C	G. Chouinard	76	31	46	77	208	14.9	9	5					
	C	G. Unger	79	17	16	33	170	10.0	1	2					
	C	B. Clement	64	7	14	21	51	13.7	0	3					
	RW	B. MacMillan	77	22	39	61	164	13.4	2	3					
	RW	J. Pronovost	80	24	19	43	119	20.2	6	12					
	RW	K. Houston	80	23	31	54	155	14.8	4	– 1					
	RW	W. Plett	76	13	19	32	119	10.9	0	– 4					
	D	P. Reinhart	79	9	38	47	130	6.9	4	11					
	D	P. Russell	80	5	31	36	104	4.8	1	14					
	D	P. Rautakallio	79	5	25	30	104	4.8	1	22					
	D	B. Murdoch	80	5	16	21	68	7.4	0	2					
	D	B. Marsh	80	2	9	11	73	2.7	0	– 15					
WASH	LW	P. Mulvey	77	15	19	34	140	10.7	2	– 8	W. Stephenson	18	24	10	3.57
D. Belisle	C	R. Walter	80	24	42	66	157	15.3	12	– 1	R. Boutin	7	7	1	3.50
4–10–2	RW	M. Gartner	77	36	32	68	228	15.8	4	15	G. Inness	2	9	2	3.63
G. Green	LW	A. Hangsleben	37	10	7	17	67	14.9	2	1					
23–30–11	C	R. Edberg	63	23	23	46	136	16.9	4	– 5					
	RW	B. Gustafsson	80	22	38	60	185	11.9	6	– 17					
	LW	A. Lehtonen	65	9	12	21	101	8.9	2	– 4					
	C	D. Maruk	27	10	17	27	58	17.2	1	0					
	C	W. Jarvis	63	11	15	26	43	25.6	0	– 3					
	C	G. Charron	33	11	20	31	80	13.8	5	– 2					
	RW	M. Lofthouse	68	15	18	33	138	10.9	1	– 9					
	RW	B. Sirois	49	15	17	32	110	13.6	4	– 5					
	D	B. Picard	78	11	43	54	212	5.2	5	– 21					
	D	R. Green	71	4	20	24	105	3.8	0	– 10					
	D	P. MacKinnon	63	1	11	12	68	1.5	0	– 1					
	D	P. Bouchard	54	5	9	14	59	8.5	0	– 7					
	D	L. Svensson	47	4	11	15	41	9.8	0	– 10					

SMYTHE DIVISION

	POS	PLAYER	GP	G	A	PTS	SOG	SPCT	PPG	+/-	GOALIE	W	L	T	GAvg
CHI	LW	R. Sedlbauer	45	13	10	23	132	9.8	1	1	T. Esposito	31	22	16	2.97
E. Johnston	C	T. Ruskowski	74	15	55	70	90	16.7	6	7	M. Veisor	3	5	3	3.36
34–27–19	RW	R. Preston	80	31	30	61	205	15.1	12	16					
	LW	T. Bulley	66	14	17	31	125	11.2	1	– 12					
	C	T. Lysiak	77	26	43	69	160	16.3	10	– 7					
	RW	G. Mulvey	80	39	26	65	228	17.1	12	3					
	LW	D. Lecuyer	53	3	10	13	75	4.0	0	– 7					
	C	R. Kerr	49	9	8	17	69	13.0	1	– 10					
	RW	T. Higgins	74	13	12	25	110	11.8	2	– 15					
	RW	C. Koroll	47	3	4	7	40	7.5	0	– 10					
	RW	A. Daigle	66	7	9	16	56	12.5	0	– 6					
	D	D. Wilson	73	12	49	61	225	5.3	3	– 5					
	D	B. Murray	74	16	34	50	224	7.1	8	– 16					
	D	M. O'Connell	78	8	22	30	158	5.1	2	– 2					
	D	J. Marks	74	6	15	21	111	5.4	1	– 16					
	D	K. Brown	76	2	18	20	105	1.9	0	7					
	D	G. Fox	71	4	11	15	58	6.9	0	– 13					

	POS	PLAYER	GP	G	A	PTS	SOG	SPCT	PPG	+/–	GOALIE	W	L	T	GAvg
STL	LW	B. Sutter	71	23	35	58	173	13.3	6	3	M. Liut	**32**	23	9	3.18
B. Plager	C	B. Federko	79	38	56	94	184	20.7	7	3	E. Staniowski	2	11	3	4.33
8–16–4	RW	W. Babych	59	26	35	61	159	16.4	7	11	D. Grant	0	0	0	1.94
R. Berenson	LW	C. Lefley	28	6	6	12	37	16.2	0	5					
26–18–8	LW	P. Turnbull	80	16	19	35	139	11.5	3	– 11					
	C	M. Zuke	69	22	42	64	172	12.8	6	– 2					
	C	B. Dunlop	72	18	27	45	101	17.8	8	– 6					
	C	L. Patey	78	17	17	34	144	11.8	0	– 18					
	C	R. Klassen	80	9	16	25	100	9.0	0	– 19					
	RW	B. Chapman	63	25	26	51	124	20.2	7	– 5					
	RW	T. Currie	40	19	14	33	70	27.1	2	9					
	RW	M. Crombeen	71	10	12	22	98	10.2	1	– 14					
	RW	H. Monahan	72	5	12	17	93	5.4	1	– 22					
	D	J. Brownschidle	77	12	32	44	130	9.2	3	16					
	D	R. Lapointe	80	6	19	25	113	5.3	0	– 24					
	D	E. Kea	69	3	16	19	73	4.1	0	9					
	D	J. Micheletti	54	2	16	18	68	2.9	2	– 5					
VAN	LW	C. Fraser	78	17	25	42	148	11.5	0	7	G. Hanlon	17	29	10	3.47
H. Neale	C	T. Gradin	80	30	45	75	146	20.5	7	14	G. Bromley	8	2	4	3.00
27–37–16	RW	S. Smyl	77	31	47	78	182	17.0	11	28	C. Ridley	2	6	2	3.91
	LW	J. Gillis	67	13	17	30	130	10.0	5	0					
	LW	P. Brasar	48	9	10	19	101	8.9	1	– 4					
	LW	B. Ashton	47	5	14	19	69	7.2	0	4					
	C	D. Lever	51	21	17	38	134	15.7	5	– 13					
	C	B. Derlago	54	11	15	26	75	14.7	4	– 17					
	C	G. Lupul	51	9	11	20	71	12.7	3	– 12					
	C	C. Oddleifson	75	8	20	28	62	12.9	1	– 9					
	RW	R. Vaive	47	13	8	21	89	14.6	1	– 12					
	RW	R. Blight	33	12	6	18	82	14.6	1	7					
	D	K. McCarthy	79	15	30	45	161	9.3	4	– 5					
	D	L. Lindgren	73	5	30	35	181	2.8	2	– 8					
	D	H. Snepsts	79	3	20	23	103	2.9	0	7					
	D	D. Kearns	67	1	18	19	66	1.5	0	2					
	D	B. Manno	40	3	14	17	73	4.1	1	5					
EDM	LW	B. Callighen	59	23	35	58	159	14.5	8	– 1	E. Mio	9	13	5	4.21
G. Sather	C	W. Gretzky	79	51	**86**	**137**	284	18.0	13	15	J. Corsi	8	14	3	3.65
28–39–13	RW	B. MacDonald	80	46	48	94	266	17.3	13	1	D. Dryden	2	7	3	4.27
	LW	M. Messier	75	12	21	33	113	10.6	1	– 10	R. Low	8	2	1	3.42
	LW	D. Hunter	80	12	31	43	109	11.0	1	7	D. Cutts	1	2	1	3.57
	LW	D. Semenko	67	6	7	13	43	14.0	1	– 13	B. Dupuis	0	1	0	4.00
	LW	P. Driscoll	39	1	5	6	23	4.3	0	– 11					
	C	S. Weir	79	33	33	66	129	25.6	3	2					
	C	R. Chipperfield	67	18	19	37	129	14.0	2	– 15					
	RW	D. Lumley	80	20	38	58	145	13.8	1	15					
	RW	B. Schmautz	29	8	8	16	46	17.4	2	– 4					
	RW	B. Flett	20	5	2	7	26	19.2	1	– 17					
	D	R. Siltanen	64	6	29	35	116	5.2	1	– 9					
	D	D. Hicks	78	9	31	40	122	7.4	5	18					
	D	K. Lowe	64	2	19	21	86	2.3	2	1					
	D	L. Fogolin	80	5	10	15	90	5.6	0	– 8					
	D	P. Price	75	11	21	32	95	11.6	2	4					
COLO	LW	D. Berry	75	7	23	30	66	10.6	0	– 23	H. Astrom	9	27	6	3.75
D. Cherry	LW	D. Saleski	51	8	8	16	68	11.8	0	– 17	B. McKenzie	9	12	3	3.49
19–48–13	LW	B. Sheehan	30	3	4	7	39	7.7	1	– 7	B. Oleschuk	1	6	2	4.20
	C	J. Valiquette	77	25	25	50	157	15.9	6	– 7	M. Plasse	0	3	2	4.77
	C	R. Delorme	75	19	24	43	98	19.4	5	– 24					
	C	R. Comeau	22	2	5	7	21	9.5	0	0					
	RW	L. McDonald	46	25	20	45	194	12.9	8	– 15					
	RW	R. Robert	69	28	35	63	248	11.3	10	– 20					
	RW	L. Deblois	70	24	19	43	151	15.9	4	– 18					
	RW	R. Pierce	75	16	23	39	171	9.4	0	– 11					
	D	R. Ramage	75	8	20	28	218	3.7	0	– 40					
	D	M. McEwen	67	11	40	51	178	6.2	5	– 13					
	D	J. Quenneville	35	5	7	12	62	8.1	1	– 21					
	D	T. Johansen	62	3	8	11	43	7.0	1	– 17					
	D	M. Christie	74	1	17	18	50	2.0	0	– 30					
	D	N. Beverley	46	0	9	9	23	.0	0	– 4					
	D	M. Kitchen	42	1	6	7	31	3.2	0	– 10					

	POS	PLAYER	GP	G	A	PTS	SOG	SPCT	PPG	+/-	GOALIE	W	L	T	GAvg
WINN	LW	M. Lukowich	78	35	39	74	201	17.4	13	-16	P. Hamel	9	19	3	4.01
T. McVie	C	P. Sullivan	79	24	35	59	166	14.5	5	-45	M. Mattsson	5	11	4	3.25
20–49–11	RW	W. Lindstrom	79	23	26	49	243	9.5	5	-19	G. Smith	4	11	4	4.08
	LW	R. Wilson	79	21	36	57	176	11.9	6	-12	L. Middlebrook	2	8	0	4.14
	LW	L. Moffat	74	10	9	19	86	11.6	0	-24					
	LW	L. Stamler	62	8	7	15	89	9.0	0	-29					
	LW	J. Markell	38	10	7	17	46	21.7	2	-12					
	C	J. Drouin	78	8	16	24	84	9.5	1	-38					
	C	D. Christian	15	8	10	18	34	23.5	3	-5					
	RW	P. Marsh	57	18	20	38	187	9.6	9	-38					
	RW	J. Mann	72	3	5	8	60	5.0	1	-20					
	RW	H. Graves	35	1	5	6	27	3.7	0	-13					
	D	C. Norwich	70	10	35	45	217	4.6	7	-11					
	D	L. Sjoberg	79	7	27	34	145	4.8	3	-35					
	D	S. Campbell	63	3	17	20	92	3.3	0	-39					
	D	B. Melrose	74	4	6	10	101	4.0	0	-41					
	D	K. Cory	46	2	9	11	47	4.3	1	-16					

PRINCE OF WALES CONFERENCE

NORRIS DIVISION

	POS	PLAYER	GP	G	A	PTS	SOG	SPCT	PPG	+/-	GOALIE	W	L	T	GAvg
MONT	LW	S. Shutt	77	47	42	89	224	21.0	17	45	M. Larocque	17	13	8	3.32
B. Geoffrion	C	P. Larouche	73	50	41	91	220	22.7	12	36	D. Herron	25	3	3	2.51
15–9–6	RW	G. Lafleur	74	50	75	125	323	15.5	15	40	R. Sevigny	5	4	2	2.94
C. Ruel	LW	Y. Lambert	77	21	32	53	104	20.2	7	3					
32–11–7	LW	B. Gainey	64	14	19	33	153	9.2	4	-2					
	C	P. Mondou	75	30	36	66	152	19.7	8	26					
	C	D. Jarvis	80	13	11	24	130	10.0	0	-5					
	C	D. Risebrough	44	8	10	18	82	9.8	0	-2					
	RW	M. Napier	76	16	33	49	123	13.0	4	11					
	RW	R. Houle	60	18	27	45	115	15.7	2	3					
	RW	M. Tremblay	77	16	26	42	192	8.3	0	6					
	D	L. Robinson	72	14	61	75	133	10.5	6	38					
	D	G. Lapointe	45	6	20	26	124	4.8	0	-2					
	D	R. Langway	77	7	29	36	112	6.3	0	36					
	D	S. Savard	46	5	8	13	45	11.1	0	-2					
	D	B. Engblom	70	3	20	23	86	3.5	0	22					
	D	R. Chartraw	66	5	7	12	65	7.7	0	6					
LA	LW	C. Simmer	64	**56**	45	101	213	26.3	**21**	47	M. Lessard	18	22	7	3.91
B. Berry	C	M. Dionne	80	53	84	**137**	**348**	15.2	14	35	R. Grahame	9	11	4	4.19
30–36–14	RW	D. Taylor	61	37	53	90	170	21.8	12	39	D. Keans	3	3	3	2.47
	LW	S. Jensen	76	21	15	36	149	14.1	4	-39					
	LW	B. Wilson	75	4	3	7	56	7.1	1	-19					
	LW	J. Kelly	40	2	5	7	31	6.5	0	-6					
	C	B. Goring	69	20	48	68	160	12.5	2	-21					
	C	A. St. Laurent	77	6	24	30	121	5.0	1	-13					
	C	S. Apps	51	5	16	21	53	9.4	1	-17					
	C	S. Carlson	52	9	12	21	45	20.0	1	-7					
	RW	M. Murphy	80	27	22	49	176	15.3	7	-12					
	RW	G. Goldup	55	10	11	21	92	10.9	1	-4					
	RW	D. Hopkins	60	8	6	14	57	14.0	1	-16					
	D	D. Halward	63	11	45	56	165	6.7	8	14					
	D	R. Palmer	78	4	36	40	110	3.6	1	29					
	D	R. Manery	52	6	10	16	73	8.2	3	-13					
	D	B. Selwood	63	1	13	14	78	1.3	1	-14					
PITT	LW	R. Lonsberry	76	15	18	33	135	11.1	2	-4	G. Millen	18	18	7	3.64
J. Wilson	C	O. Kindrachuk	51	17	29	46	94	18.1	2	4	R. Holland	10	17	6	3.83
30–37–13	RW	R. Kehoe	79	30	30	60	239	12.6	7	-3	N. Ricci	2	2	0	3.50
	LW	R. Schutt	73	18	21	39	170	10.6	3	-8					
	C	G. Malone	51	19	32	51	103	18.4	5	4					
	RW	P. Lee	74	16	29	45	161	9.9	4	-13					
	LW	N. Libett	78	14	12	26	118	11.9	1	-19					
	LW	P. Marshall	46	9	12	21	68	13.2	1	-2					
	C	G. Ferguson	73	21	28	49	176	11.9	1	0					
	C	G. Sheppard	76	13	24	37	136	9.6	3	-22					
	RW	G. McAdam	78	19	22	41	195	9.7	3	-17					
	RW	P. Hughes	78	18	14	32	159	11.3	5	-38					
	D	R. Carlyle	67	8	28	36	123	6.5	3	-23					
	D	R. Stackhouse	78	6	27	33	166	3.6	2	16					
	D	R. Anderson	76	5	22	27	78	6.4	0	11					
	D	M. Faubert	49	5	13	18	83	6.0	4	-19					

	POS	PLAYER	GP	G	A	PTS	SOG	SPCT	PPG	+/–	GOALIE	W	L	T	GAvg
HART	LW	P. Boutette	47	13	31	44	72	18.1	3	17	J. Garrett	16	24	11	3.98
D. Blackburn	C	M. Rogers	80	44	61	105	229	19.2	3	29	A. Smith	11	10	8	3.66
27–34–19	RW	B. Stoughton	80	**56**	44	100	234	23.9	16	9					
	LW	N. Fotiu	74	10	8	18	54	18.5	0	2					
	C	G. Howe	80	15	26	41	94	16.0	2	9					
	RW	R. Allison	64	16	12	28	79	20.3	0	– 3					
	LW	J. Douglas	77	33	24	57	188	17.6	5	– 11					
	LW	M. Howe	74	24	56	80	178	13.5	5	14					
	LW	G. Carroll	71	13	19	32	85	15.3	0	– 5					
	LW	B. Johnston	32	8	13	21	54	14.8	0	9					
	C	D. Keon	76	10	52	62	146	6.8	0	– 13					
	C	A. Lacroix	29	3	14	17	45	6.7	1	– 6					
	RW	D. Debol	48	12	14	26	96	12.5	0	– 5					
	D	G. Roberts	80	8	28	36	107	7.5	1	6					
	D	R. Ley	65	4	16	20	78	5.1	0	2					
	D	A. Sims	76	10	31	41	141	7.1	2	9					

	POS	PLAYER	GP	G	A	PTS	SOG	SPCT	PPG	+/–	GOALIE	W	L	T	GAvg
DET	LW	E. Thompson	77	34	14	48	164	20.7	8	– 10	R. Vachon	20	**30**	8	3.61
B. Kromm	LW	D. Labraaten	76	30	27	57	152	19.7	6	5	J. Rutherford	6	13	3	4.16
24–36–11	LW	D. Bolduc	44	6	5	11	52	11.5	2	– 14					
T. Lindsay	LW	G. Hicks	50	1	2	3	52	1.9	0	– 21					
2–7–0	LW	D. Polonich	66	2	8	10	61	3.3	0	– 15					
	C	D. McCourt	80	30	51	81	200	15.0	2	1					
	C	P. Mahovlich	80	16	50	66	143	11.2	3	3					
	C	P. Woods	79	6	20	26	114	5.3	0	– 19					
	C	B. Hogaboam	42	3	12	15	26	11.5	0	– 8					
	RW	M. Foligno	80	36	35	71	196	18.4	9	– 2					
	RW	N. Nedomansky	79	35	39	74	235	14.9	11	– 5					
	RW	J. Ogrodnick	41	8	24	32	121	6.6	3	– 4					
	D	R. Larson	80	22	44	66	293	7.5	7	– 7					
	D	W. Huber	76	17	23	40	197	8.6	4	– 26					
	D	J. Korn	63	5	13	18	58	8.6	1	– 4					
	D	B. Long	80	0	17	17	87	.0	0	– 28					
	D	G. Joly	59	3	10	13	50	6.0	0	– 2					

ADAMS DIVISION

	POS	PLAYER	GP	G	A	PTS	SOG	SPCT	PPG	+/–	GOALIE	W	L	T	GAvg
BUF	LW	R. Martin	80	45	34	79	257	17.5	8	18	D. Edwards	27	9	12	2.57
S. Bowman	C	G. Perreault	80	40	66	106	180	22.2	10	32	B. Sauve	20	8	4	**2.36**
47–17–16	RW	R. Seiling	80	25	35	60	155	16.1	5	30					
	LW	T. McKegney	80	23	29	52	140	16.4	1	40					
	C	D. Smith	79	24	39	63	137	17.5	8	33					
	RW	D. Gare	76	**56**	33	89	270	20.7	17	49					
	LW	C. Ramsay	80	21	39	60	103	20.4	5	15					
	LW	R. Dudley	66	11	22	33	109	10.1	0	11					
	C	D. Luce	80	14	29	43	137	10.2	0	22					
	C	A. Savard	33	3	10	13	36	8.3	0	4					
	RW	J. Gould	52	9	9	18	72	12.5	0	9					
	D	J. Van Boxmeer	80	11	40	51	198	5.6	4	40					
	D	J. Schoenfeld	77	9	27	36	114	7.9	4	**60**					
	D	R. Dunn	80	7	31	38	147	4.8	4	25					
	D	B. Hajt	75	4	12	16	63	6.3	0	36					
	D	J. Korab	43	1	10	11	55	1.8	0	0					
	D	L. Playfair	79	2	10	12	32	6.3	0	13					

	POS	PLAYER	GP	G	A	PTS	SOG	SPCT	PPG	+/–	GOALIE	W	L	T	GAvg
BOS	LW	W. Cashman	44	11	21	32	60	18.3	3	– 3	G. Cheevers	24	11	7	2.81
F. Creighton	LW	A. Secord	77	23	16	39	155	14.8	0	20	G. Gilbert	20	9	3	2.73
40–20–13	LW	S. Jonathan	79	21	19	40	108	19.4	0	20	Y. Belanger	2	0	3	3.48
H. Sinden	LW	D. Marcotte	32	4	11	15	39	10.3	0	4	M. Baron	0	0	0	3.00
6–1–0	LW	J. Wensink	69	9	11	20	71	12.7	0	7	J. Stewart	0	1	0	15.00
	C	J. Ratelle	67	28	45	73	145	19.3	14	11					
	C	P. McNab	74	40	38	78	193	20.7	11	24					
	C	B. Miller	80	16	25	41	137	11.7	0	9					
	C	B. Lalonde	71	10	25	35	91	11.0	1	14					
	C	C. MacTavish	46	11	17	28	61	18.0	0	16					
	RW	R. Middleton	80	40	52	92	223	17.9	9	31					
	RW	T. O'Reilly	71	19	42	61	105	18.1	3	17					
	RW	D. Foster	57	10	28	38	68	14.7	1	23					
	D	R. Bourque	80	17	48	65	185	9.2	3	52					
	D	B. Park	32	5	16	21	67	7.5	2	11					
	D	M. Milbury	72	10	13	23	101	9.9	1	7					
	D	D. Redmond	76	14	33	47	166	8.4	6	37					

TEAM	POS	PLAYER	GP	G	A	PTS	SOG	SPCT	PPG	+/-	GOALIE	W	L	T	GAvg
MINN	LW	S. Payne	80	42	43	85	233	18.0	16	37	G. Meloche	27	20	6	3.06
G. Sonmor	LW	T. McCarthy	68	16	20	36	101	15.8	1	– 7	G. Edwards	9	7	10	3.20
36–28–16	LW	M. Polich	78	10	14	24	94	10.6	0	0	S. Janaszak	0	0	1	2.00
	C	B. Smith	61	27	56	83	223	12.1	9	16	L. Levasseur	0	1	0	7.00
	C	T. Young	77	31	43	74	220	14.1	5	14					
	C	G. Sharpley	51	20	27	47	109	18.3	6	– 1					
	C	M. Eaves	56	18	28	46	80	22.5	9	3					
	RW	R. Zanussi	72	14	31	45	129	10.9	2	4					
	RW	A. MacAdam	80	42	51	93	170	24.7	13	36					
	RW	T. Younghans	79	10	6	16	79	12.7	0	– 3					
	RW	K. Andersson	61	9	10	19	87	10.3	1	– 3					
	D	C. Hartsburg	79	14	30	44	202	6.9	7	– 2					
	D	B. Maxwell	58	7	30	37	135	5.2	0	9					
	D	G. Sargent	52	13	21	34	129	10.1	3	12					
	D	F. Barrett	80	8	14	22	85	9.4	0	17					
	D	G. Smith	55	5	13	18	91	5.5	1	– 1					
	D	P. Shmyr	63	3	15	18	82	3.7	0	25					
TOR	LW	T. Williams	55	22	18	40	108	20.4	5	– 13	M. Palmateer	16	14	3	3.68
F. Smith	C	D. Sittler	73	40	57	97	315	12.7	17	3	P. Harrison	9	17	2	4.42
30–33–5	RW	W. Paiement	41	20	28	48	159	12.6	8	1	J. Crha	8	7	0	3.61
D. Duff	C	L. Boschman	80	16	32	48	99	16.2	2	2	V. Tremblay	2	1	0	5.11
0–2–0	RW	J. Anderson	74	25	28	53	207	12.1	3	5	C. Ridley	0	1	0	4.36
P. Imlach	RW	R. Saganiuk	75	24	23	47	164	14.6	3	– 5					
5–5–0	LW	D. Maloney	71	17	16	33	108	15.7	1	– 13					
	LW	P. Hickey	45	22	16	38	99	22.2	6	1					
	LW	T. Martin	37	6	15	21	40	15.0	1	6					
	C	W. McKechnie	54	7	36	43	77	9.1	1	– 6					
	C	P. Gardner	45	11	13	24	74	14.9	4	– 8					
	RW	R. Ellis	59	12	11	23	55	21.8	0	– 9					
	RW	J. Butler	55	7	8	15	60	11.7	0	– 3					
	D	B. Salming	74	19	52	71	222	8.6	4	4					
	D	I. Turnbull	75	11	28	39	202	5.4	3	– 23					
	D	D. Burrows	80	3	16	19	102	2.9	0	0					
	D	G. Hotham	46	3	10	13	46	6.5	0	– 4					
QUE	LW	M. Tardif	58	33	35	68	229	14.4	9	– 13	M. Dion	15	**25**	6	3.70
J. Demers	C	R. Ftorek	52	18	33	51	112	16.1	7	6	G. Hogosta	5	12	3	4.15
25–44–11	RW	R. Cloutier	67	42	47	89	254	16.5	13	– 6	R. Low	5	7	2	3.70
	LW	M. Goulet	77	22	32	54	167	13.2	5	– 10					
	C	S. Bernier	32	8	14	22	76	10.5	3	– 5					
	RW	J. Hislop	80	19	20	39	124	15.3	0	– 13					
	LW	A. Cote	41	5	11	16	58	8.6	0	– 8					
	LW	R. Thomas	39	9	7	16	89	10.1	2	– 5					
	C	R. LeDuc	75	21	27	48	145	14.5	9	– 35					
	C	B. Fitchner	70	11	20	31	88	12.5	5	– 24					
	RW	P. Plante	69	4	14	18	82	4.9	0	– 14					
	RW	C. Brackenbury	63	6	8	14	42	14.3	0	– 21					
	D	D. Hoganson	77	4	36	40	99	4.0	0	– 42					
	D	P. Lacroix	76	9	21	30	86	10.5	4	– 6					
	D	G. Hart	71	3	23	26	53	5.7	1	– 13					
	D	G. Lariviere	75	2	19	21	73	2.7	1	– 10					
	D	P. Baxter	61	7	13	20	90	7.8	4	– 27					

GOALS		ASSISTS		POINTS	
C. Simmer, LA	56	W. Gretzky, EDM	86	M. Dionne, LA	137
D. Gare, BUF	56	M. Dionne, LA	84	W. Gretzky, EDM	137
B. Stoughton, HART	56	G. Lafleur, MONT	75	G. Lafleur, MONT	125
M. Dionne, LA	53	G. Perreault, BUF	66	G. Perreault, BUF	106
M. Bossy, NYI	51	B. Trottier, NYI	62	M. Rogers, HART	105
W. Gretzky, EDM	51				

SHOTS ON GOAL		SHOOTING PCT.		+/-	
M. Dionne, LA	348	S. Vickers, NYR	29.6	J. Schoenfeld, BUF	60
R. Leach, PHI	328	C. Simmer, LA	26.3	J. Watson, PHI	53
G. Lafleur, MONT	323	S. Weir, EDM	25.6	R. Bourque, BOS	52
D. Sittler, TOR	315	A. MacAdam, MINN	24.7	D. Gare, BUF	49
R. Larson, DET	293			C. Simmer, LA	47

PENALTY MINUTES		GOALS AGAINST AVE.		SHUTOUTS	
P. Holmgren, PHI	267	B. Sauve, BUF	2.36	T. Esposito, CHI	6
T. O'Reilly, BOS	265	D. Edwards, BUF	2.57	B. Sauve, BUF	4
T. Ruskowski, CHI	252	G. Cheevers, BOS	2.81	G. Cheevers, BOS	4
P. Mulvey, WASH	240	P. Peeters, PHI	2.73	R. Vachon, DET	4
W. Plett, ATL	231	G. Gilbert, BOS	2.73	C. Resch, NYI	3

	W	L	T	PTS	GF	GA	PPG	PPCT	SHG	PPGA	PKPCT	SHGA
CAMPBELL CONFERENCE												
PATRICK DIVISION												
*NYI	48	18	14	110	**355**	260	**93**	**29.3**	**19**	76	79.3	6
PHI	41	24	15	97	313	249	75	27.0	10	85	80.3	**4**
CALG	39	27	14	92	329	298	81	26.9	8	70	80.8	12
NYR	30	36	14	74	312	317	63	17.9	14	83	78.8	12
WASH	26	36	18	70	286	317	74	18.8	8	83	73.9	14
SMYTHE DIVISION												
STL	45	18	17	107	352	281	85	23.7	16	61	82.0	12
CHI	31	33	16	78	304	315	67	22.2	8	91	75.0	9
VAN	28	32	20	76	289	301	68	20.6	11	81	76.2	14
EDM	29	35	16	74	328	327	77	22.2	13	85	75.6	7
COLO	22	45	13	57	258	344	76	20.4	5	70	75.5	8
WINN	9	57	14	32	246	400	60	17.4	8	67	74.3	15
PRINCE OF WALES CONFERENCE												
NORRIS DIVISION												
MONT	45	22	13	103	332	**232**	72	24.1	8	51	81.7	8
LA	43	24	13	99	337	290	90	24.6	12	81	77.2	7
PITT	30	37	13	73	302	345	92	23.0	6	99	76.2	11
HART	21	41	18	60	292	372	60	18.9	13	80	75.6	15
DET	19	43	18	56	252	339	60	19.0	7	82	74.1	12
ADAMS DIVISION												
BUF	39	20	21	99	237	250	73	23.5	9	**44**	**83.6**	10
BOS	37	30	13	87	316	272	87	25.4	13	82	77.1	8
MINN	35	28	17	87	291	263	88	21.6	7	64	78.9	13
QUE	30	32	18	78	314	318	81	23.9	7	79	76.4	10
TOR	28	37	15	71	322	367	85	25.1	9	93	77.2	**4**

CAMPBELL CONFERENCE

PATRICK DIVISION

	POS	PLAYER	GP	G	A	PTS	SOG	SPCT	PPG	+/-	GOALIE	W	L	T	GAvg
NYI	LW	C. Gillies	80	33	45	78	188	17.6	9	26	B. Smith	22	10	8	3.28
A. Arbour	LW	B. Bourne	78	35	41	76	195	17.9	9	34	C. Resch	18	7	5	3.07
48–18–14	LW	A. Kallur	78	36	28	64	163	22.1	7	25	R. Melanson	8	1	1	3.10
	LW	J. Tonelli	70	20	32	52	114	17.5	2	8					
	LW	G. Howatt	70	4	15	19	48	8.3	0	12					
	C	B. Trottier	73	31	72	103	156	19.9	9	49					
	C	B. Goring	78	23	37	60	152	15.1	4	4					
	C	W. Merrick	71	16	15	31	89	18.0	1	12					
	RW	M. Bossy	79	**68**	51	119	315	21.6	**28**	37					
	RW	B. Nystrom	79	14	30	44	161	8.7	3	6					
	RW	D. Sutter	23	7	11	18	48	14.6	1	– 8					
	RW	H. Marini	14	4	7	11	9	44.4	1	9					
	D	D. Potvin	74	20	56	76	206	9.7	9	38					
	D	S. Persson	80	9	52	61	120	7.5	6	24					
	D	D. Langevin	75	1	16	17	68	1.5	0	40					
	D	K. Morrow	80	2	11	13	69	2.9	0	19					
	D	B. Lorimer	73	1	12	13	65	1.5	0	45					
PHI	LW	B. Barber	80	43	42	85	292	14.7	16	6	P. Peeters	22	12	5	2.96
P. Quinn	C	B. Clarke	80	19	46	65	150	12.7	5	17	R. Ste.–Croix	13	7	6	2.49
41–24–15	RW	R. Leach	79	34	36	70	321	10.6	15	21	P. Myre	6	5	4	4.07
	LW	B. Propp	79	26	40	66	194	13.4	6	27					
	C	K. Linseman	51	17	30	47	126	13.5	1	9					
	RW	P. Holmgren	77	22	37	59	159	13.8	3	12					
	LW	A. Hill	57	10	15	25	70	14.3	0	11					
	C	M. Bridgman	77	14	37	51	138	10.1	1	28					
	C	R. MacLeish	78	38	36	74	214	17.8	14	22					
	C	T. Kerr	68	22	23	45	95	23.2	6	3					
	C	R. Flockhart	14	3	7	10	24	12.5	0	6					
	RW	T. Gorence	79	24	18	42	165	14.5	0	17					
	RW	G. Morrison	33	1	13	14	21	4.8	0	10					
	D	B. Wilson	77	16	47	63	216	7.4	2	39					
	D	B. Dailey	53	7	27	34	141	5.0	1	8					
	D	T. Murray	71	1	17	18	65	1.5	0	46					

TEAM	POS	PLAYER	GP	G	A	PTS	SOG	SPCT	PPG	+/–	GOALIE	W	L	T	GAvg
CALG	LW	E. Vail	64	28	36	64	164	17.1	12	8	P. Riggin	21	16	4	3.83
	LW	K. Lavallee	77	15	20	35	131	11.5	3	– 4	R. Lemelin	14	6	7	3.24
A. MacNeil	LW	B. Wilson	50	5	7	12	34	14.7	0	– 6	D. Bouchard	4	5	3	4.03
39–27–14	C	K. Nilsson	80	49	82	131	217	22.6	20	15					
	C	G. Chouinard	52	31	52	83	141	22.0	10	18					
	C	D. Lever	62	26	31	57	157	16.6	4	21					
	C	J. Peplinski	80	13	25	38	107	12.1	1	– 2					
	C	B. Clement	78	12	20	32	94	12.8	1	– 16					
	RW	W. Plett	78	38	30	68	159	23.9	8	5					
	RW	B. MacMillan	77	28	35	63	162	17.3	2	18					
	RW	K. Houston	42	15	15	30	78	19.2	4	0					
	RW	B. Smith	45	7	4	11	51	13.7	1	– 8					
	D	P. Reinhart	74	18	49	67	122	14.8	10	10					
	D	P. Rautakallio	76	11	45	56	129	8.5	3	– 1					
	D	P. Russell	80	6	23	29	109	5.5	1	17					
	D	B. Murdoch	74	3	19	22	90	3.3	0	22					
	D	B. Marsh	80	1	12	13	58	1.7	0	– 2					
NYR	LW	D. Maloney	61	29	23	52	124	23.4	7	50	D. Soetaert	16	16	7	3.93
	C	M. Allison	75	26	38	64	122	21.3	4	12	S. Baker	10	6	5	3.48
F. Shero	RW	E. Johnstone	80	30	38	68	187	16.0	4	15	W. Thomas	3	6	1	3.40
4–13–4	LW	S. Vickers	73	19	39	58	85	22.4	5	7	J. Davidson	1	7	1	5.14
C. Patrick	LW	N. Fotiu	27	5	6	11	28	17.9	1	– 6	S. Weeks	0	1	0	2.00
26–23–10	C	U. Nilsson	51	14	25	39	80	17.5	1	– 3					
	C	R. Duguay	50	17	21	38	103	16.5	5	1					
	C	W. Tkaczuk	43	6	22	28	67	9.0	1	13					
	C	L. Nethery	33	11	12	23	47	23.4	2	0					
	C	P. Esposito	41	7	13	20	91	7.7	3	– 13					
	RW	A. Hedberg	80	30	40	70	243	12.3	7	0					
	RW	D. Talafous	50	13	17	30	73	17.8	1	2					
	RW	D. Silk	59	14	12	26	124	11.3	2	– 24					
	D	R. Greschner	74	27	41	68	193	14.0	6	0					
	D	D. Maloney	79	11	36	47	140	7.9	3	24					
	D	B. Beck	75	11	23	34	182	6.0	6	9					
	D	T. Laidlaw	80	6	23	29	101	5.9	1	0					
WASH	LW	B. Kelly	80	26	36	62	125	20.8	8	– 13	M. Palmateer	18	19	9	3.87
	C	D. Maruk	80	50	47	97	242	20.7	16	– 7	W. Stephenson	4	7	5	3.92
G. Green	RW	J. Pronovost	80	22	36	58	188	11.7	6	– 9	D. Parro	4	7	2	3.63
26–36–18	LW	P. Mulvey	55	7	14	21	96	7.3	1	– 9	G. Inness	0	1	2	3.00
	C	R. Walter	80	24	44	68	178	13.5	4	– 9	R. Boutin	0	2	0	5.50
	RW	M. Gartner	80	48	46	94	326	14.7	13	– 5					
	C	T. Tookey	29	10	13	23	33	30.3	6	– 6					
	C	W. Jarvis	55	9	14	23	61	14.8	0	– 9					
	C	G. Currie	40	5	13	18	52	9.6	2	– 5					
	C	G. Charron	47	5	13	18	62	8.1	2	– 4					
	RW	B. Gustafsson	72	21	34	55	170	12.4	4	11					
	RW	D. Ververgaert	79	14	27	41	111	12.6	2	– 5					
	D	R. Green	65	8	23	31	120	6.7	2	– 15					
	D	D. Veitch	59	4	21	25	89	4.5	1	– 12					
	D	A. Hangsleben	76	5	19	24	110	4.5	0	– 7					
	D	P. Ribble	67	3	15	18	115	2.6	3	– 13					
	D	H. Walker	64	2	11	13	68	2.9	2	9					

SMYTHE DIVISION

TEAM	POS	PLAYER	GP	G	A	PTS	SOG	SPCT	PPG	+/–	GOALIE	W	L	T	GAvg
STL	LW	B. Sutter	78	35	34	69	203	17.2	17	12	M. Liut	33	14	13	3.34
	C	B. Federko	78	31	73	104	170	18.2	9	9	E. Staniowski	10	3	3	4.28
R. Berenson	RW	W. Babych	78	54	42	96	306	17.6	14	14	R. Heinz	2	1	1	2.18
45–18–17	LW	J. Pettersson	62	37	36	73	172	21.5	8	14					
	C	B. Dunlop	80	20	67	87	134	14.9	6	16					
	C	M. Zuke	74	24	44	68	145	16.6	10	15					
	C	P. Turnbull	75	34	22	56	209	16.3	5	15					
	C	L. Patey	80	22	23	45	125	17.6	0	2					
	RW	T. Currie	61	23	32	55	112	20.5	2	32					
	RW	B. Chapman	55	20	26	46	114	17.5	5	3					
	RW	M. Crombeen	66	9	14	23	91	9.9	0	1					
	RW	H. Monahan	25	4	2	6	32	12.5	0	2					
	D	R. Lapointe	80	8	25	33	84	9.5	0	36					
	D	J. Micheletti	63	4	27	31	102	3.9	3	12					
	D	J. Brownschidle	71	5	23	28	96	5.2	3	5					
	D	B. Stewart	60	2	21	23	62	3.2	0	19					
	D	E. Kea	74	3	18	21	59	5.1	0	15					

	POS	PLAYER	GP	G	A	PTS	SOG	SPCT	PPG	+/–	GOALIE	W	L	T	GAvg
	LW	D. Sutter	76	40	22	62	179	22.3	14	– 1	T. Esposito	29	23	14	3.75
CHI	C	T. Lysiak	72	21	55	76	167	12.6	5	7	M. Bannerman	2	10	2	4.30
	RW	G. Sharpley	35	10	16	26	64	15.6	4	6					
K. Magnuson	LW	A. Secord	41	13	9	22	111	11.7	3	– 4					
31–33–16	C	D. Savard	76	28	47	75	159	17.6	4	27					
	RW	T. Higgins	78	24	35	59	149	16.1	1	20					
	LW	T. Bulley	68	18	16	34	112	16.1	3	18					
	LW	J. Marks	39	8	6	14	41	19.5	1	– 3					
	C	T. Ruskowski	72	8	51	59	88	9.1	2	– 19					
	C	R. Kerr	70	30	30	60	154	19.5	5	10					
	RW	G. Mulvey	42	18	14	32	168	10.7	6	– 18					
	RW	R. Preston	47	7	14	21	100	7.0	3	– 15					
	D	B. Murray	77	13	47	60	206	6.3	5	6					
	D	D. Wilson	76	12	39	51	245	4.9	3	6					
	D	G. Fox	75	3	16	19	69	4.3	0	– 10					
	D	M. Zaharko	42	3	11	14	58	5.2	0	22					
	D	D. Hutchison	59	2	9	11	58	3.4	0	12					
	LW	C. Fraser	77	25	24	49	188	13.3	7	– 19	R. Brodeur	17	18	16	3.51
VAN	C	T. Gradin	79	21	48	69	158	13.3	4	2	G. Bromley	6	6	4	3.80
H. Neale	RW	S. Smyl	80	25	38	63	209	12.0	6	– 8	G. Hanlon	5	8	0	4.44
28–32–20	LW	P. Brasar	80	22	41	63	167	13.2	3	12					
	LW	T. Williams	77	35	27	62	186	18.8	11	4					
	LW	D. Rota	80	25	31	56	178	14.0	7	10					
	LW	B. Ashton	77	18	11	29	111	16.2	0	– 10					
	C	I. Boldirev	72	26	33	59	195	13.3	9	– 12					
	C	G. Minor	74	10	14	24	93	10.8	1	4					
	RW	J. Butler	80	12	15	27	99	12.1	0	2					
	RW	B. Schmautz	73	27	34	61	205	13.2	9	– 5					
	RW	B. MacDonald	12	5	9	14	38	13.2	2	1					
	D	K. McCarthy	80	16	37	53	140	11.4	4	– 11					
	D	R. Lanz	76	7	22	29	134	5.2	3	1					
	D	L. Lindgren	52	4	18	22	76	5.3	1	16					
	D	H. Snepsts	76	3	16	19	77	3.9	0	3					
	D	M. Marois	50	4	12	16	79	5.1	1	0					
	LW	J. Kurri	75	32	43	75	202	15.8	9	26	E. Mio	16	15	9	3.89
EDM	C	W. Gretzky	80	55	**109**	**164**	261	21.1	15	41	R. Low	5	13	3	4.43
B. Watson	RW	B. MacDonald	51	19	24	43	134	14.2	5	– 8	G. Edwards	5	3	4	3.62
4–9–5	LW	M. Messier	72	23	40	63	179	12.8	4	– 12	A. Moog	3	3	0	3.83
G. Sather	C	M. Hagman	75	20	33	53	96	20.8	2	4	P. LoPresti	0	1	0	4.57
25–26–11	RW	G. Anderson	58	30	23	53	160	18.8	10	4					
	LW	D. Hunter	78	12	16	28	104	11.5	0	– 12					
	LW	D. Semenko	58	11	8	19	42	26.2	4	– 4					
	C	B. Callighen	55	25	35	60	127	19.7	6	13					
	C	S. Weir	70	12	20	32	84	14.3	1	– 7					
	RW	C. Brackenbury	58	2	7	9	20	10.0	0	– 3					
	RW	D. Lumley	53	7	9	16	54	13.0	0	– 15					
	D	R. Siltanen	79	17	36	53	209	8.1	7	5					
	D	P. Coffey	74	9	23	32	113	8.0	2	4					
	D	K. Lowe	79	10	24	34	115	8.7	4	– 10					
	D	L. Fogolin	80	13	17	30	89	14.6	0	2					
	D	D. Hicks	59	5	16	21	109	4.6	1	21					
	LW	P. Gagne	61	25	16	41	99	25.3	9	– 24	A. Smith	9	18	4	4.75
COLO	C	M. Malinowski	69	25	37	62	152	16.4	4	– 24	H. Astrom	6	15	6	3.76
B. MacMillan	RW	L. McDonald	80	35	46	81	298	11.7	11	– 27	P. Myre	3	6	1	3.41
22–45–13	LW	E. Cooper	47	7	7	14	52	13.5	1	– 6	C. Resch	2	4	2	3.74
	C	W. McKechnie	53	15	23	38	92	16.3	2	– 7	J. Kaarela	2	2	0	6.00
	C	R. Delorme	65	11	16	27	65	16.9	3	– 11					
	C	B. Smith	62	4	4	8	38	10.5	0	– 2					
	C	D. Berry	46	3	10	13	44	6.8	0	– 15					
	RW	L. Deblois	74	26	16	42	183	14.2	9	– 42					
	RW	Y. Vautour	74	15	19	34	97	15.5	3	– 20					
	RW	R. Robert	28	8	11	19	66	12.1	4	– 13					
	RW	R. Pierce	55	9	21	30	124	7.3	3	– 28					
	D	R. Ramage	79	20	42	62	289	6.9	12	– 46					
	D	M. McEwen	65	11	35	46	229	4.8	5	– 33					
	D	J. Quenneville	71	10	24	34	107	9.3	3	– 24					
	LW	M. Lukowich	80	33	34	67	175	18.9	9	– 39	M. Mattsson	3	21	4	4.50
WINN	LW	N. Dupont	80	27	26	53	215	12.6	8	– 57	P. Hamel	3	20	4	4.73
T. McVie	LW	R. Wilson	77	18	33	51	192	9.4	4	– 34	M. Dion	3	6	3	4.83
1–20–7	LW	T. Trimper	56	15	14	29	95	15.8	1	– 31	L. Middlebrook	0	9	3	5.97
B. Sutherland	C	D. Christian	80	28	43	71	185	15.1	9	– 54	R. Loustel	0	1	0	10.00
8–37–7	C	P. Sullivan	47	4	19	23	42	9.5	2	– 17					
	C	K. Manery	47	13	9	22	82	15.9	4	– 15					
	C	T. Steen	42	5	11	16	57	8.8	3	– 22					
	RW	D. Geoffrion	78	20	26	46	142	14.1	3	– 32					
	RW	W. Lindstrom	72	22	13	35	163	13.5	6	– 28					
	RW	R. Bowness	45	8	17	25	55	14.5	0	– 35					
	D	D. Babych	69	6	38	44	209	2.9	3	– 61					
	D	M. Mantha	58	2	23	25	94	2.1	1	– 33					
	D	B. Long	65	6	17	23	88	6.8	0	– 47					
	D	D. Spring	80	1	18	19	51	2.0	0	– 40					
	D	M. Plantery	25	1	5	6	18	5.6	0	– 10					

PRINCE OF WALES CONFERENCE

NORRIS DIVISION

TEAM	POS	PLAYER	GP	G	A	PTS	SOG	SPCT	PPG	+/-	GOALIE	W	L	T	GAvg
MONT	LW	S. Shutt	77	35	38	73	232	15.1	7	30	R. Sevigny	20	4	3	2.40
C. Ruel	LW	B. Gainey	78	23	24	47	181	12.7	5	13	M. Larocque	16	9	3	3.03
45–22–13	LW	Y. Lambert	73	22	32	54	117	18.8	4	7	D. Herron	6	9	6	3.50
	C	P. Larouche	61	25	28	53	154	16.2	4	13	R. Wamsley	3	0	1	1.90
	C	D. Jarvis	80	16	22	38	122	13.1	0	12					
	C	D. Risebrough	48	13	21	34	94	13.8	1	7					
	C	K. Acton	61	15	24	39	101	14.9	3	5					
	C	P. Mondou	57	17	24	41	106	16.0	5	24					
	RW	G. Lafleur	51	27	43	70	191	14.1	7	24					
	RW	M. Napier	79	35	36	71	185	18.9	5	34					
	RW	M. Tremblay	77	25	38	63	254	9.8	4	16					
	RW	R. Houle	77	27	31	58	158	17.1	6	20					
	D	L. Robinson	65	12	38	50	130	9.2	7	46					
	D	R. Langway	80	11	34	45	165	6.7	5	53					
	D	B. Engblom	80	3	25	28	120	2.5	1	**63**					
	D	S. Savard	77	4	13	17	63	6.3	0	12					
	D	G. Lapointe	33	1	9	10	47	2.1	1	−6					
LA	LW	C. Simmer	65	56	49	105	171	**32.7**	23	31	M. Lessard	**35**	18	11	3.25
B. Berry	C	M. Dionne	80	58	77	135	**342**	17.0	23	55	D. Keans	2	3	1	4.89
43–24–13	RW	D. Taylor	72	47	65	112	206	22.8	13	47	R. Grahame	3	2	1	4.67
	LW	S. Jensen	74	19	19	38	118	16.1	5	−6	J. Rutherford	3	0	0	3.33
	LW	G. Terrion	73	12	25	37	92	13.0	2	−1	P. Pageau	0	1	0	8.00
	C	D. Bonar	71	11	15	26	64	17.2	3	0					
	C	G. Unger	58	10	10	20	67	14.9	1	−17					
	C	A. St. Laurent	22	10	6	16	33	30.3	0	8					
	RW	B. Harris	80	20	29	49	150	13.3	1	−1					
	RW	J. Fox	71	18	25	43	92	19.6	2	0					
	RW	M. Murphy	68	16	23	39	131	12.2	2	−7					
	RW	D. Hopkins	67	8	18	26	60	13.3	2	6					
	D	L. Murphy	80	16	60	76	153	10.5	5	17					
	D	J. Korab	78	9	43	52	120	7.5	3	10					
	D	D. Lewis	67	1	12	13	46	2.2	0	25					
	D	M. Hardy	77	5	20	25	90	5.6	4	14					
	D	D. Halward	51	4	15	19	74	5.4	1	−2					
PITT	LW	R. Lonsberry	80	17	33	50	161	10.6	7	−3	G. Millen	25	**27**	10	4.16
E. Johnston	C	P. Gardner	62	34	40	74	183	18.6	18	−5	R. Holland	1	5	3	5.01
30–37–13	RW	R. Kehoe	80	55	33	88	299	18.4	20	−9	N. Ricci	4	5	0	3.88
	LW	R. Schutt	80	25	35	60	206	12.1	11	−13					
	C	G. Malone	62	21	29	50	144	14.6	5	−14					
	RW	P. Lee	80	30	34	64	196	15.3	4	0					
	LW	M. Johnson	73	10	23	33	109	9.2	0	4					
	LW	G. Rissling	25	1	0	1	16	6.3	0	−4					
	C	G. Ferguson	79	25	18	43	181	13.8	7	−30					
	C	G. Sheppard	47	11	17	28	85	12.9	3	−13					
	RW	G. McAdam	34	3	9	12	52	5.8	0	−16					
	RW	P. Hughes	58	10	9	19	89	11.2	0	−9					
	D	R. Carlyle	76	16	67	83	242	6.6	7	−16					
	D	M. Faubert	72	8	44	52	142	5.6	3	−18					
	D	R. Stackhouse	74	6	29	35	127	4.7	2	−11					
	D	P. Baxter	51	5	14	19	62	8.1	1	−11					
	D	P. Price	13	0	10	10	25	.0	0	2					
HART	LW	P. Boutette	80	28	52	80	182	15.4	8	−13	J. Garrett	15	**27**	12	4.59
D. Blackburn	C	M. Rogers	80	40	65	105	242	16.5	10	−22	M. Veisor	6	13	6	4.46
15–29–16	RW	B. Stoughton	71	43	30	73	212	20.3	10	−17	K. Holland	0	1	0	7.00
L. Pleau	LW	J. Douglas	55	13	9	22	98	13.3	3	−23					
6–12–2	LW	M. Fidler	38	9	9	18	59	15.3	2	−15					
	LW	N. Fotiu	42	4	3	7	36	11.1	0	−7					
	LW	J. Brubaker	43	5	3	8	29	17.2	0	−5					
	C	D. Keon	80	13	34	47	131	9.9	2	−31					
	C	D. Nachbaur	77	16	17	33	70	22.9	2	−1					
	RW	W. Miller	77	22	22	44	160	13.8	3	−31					
	RW	T. Rowe	74	13	28	41	143	9.1	1	−10					
	RW	R. Neufeld	52	5	10	15	55	9.1	0	1					
	D	M. Howe	63	19	46	65	172	11.0	7	10					
	D	A. Sims	80	16	36	52	182	8.8	5	−20					
	D	M. Volcan	49	2	11	13	49	4.1	0	−12					

	POS	PLAYER	GP	G	A	PTS	SOG	SPCT	PPG	+/-	GOALIE	W	L	T	GAvg
DET	LW	E. Thompson	39	14	12	26	83	16.9	5	– 4	G. Gilbert	11	24	9	4.01
T. Lindsay	LW	D. Labraaten	44	3	8	11	43	7.0	0	– 19	P. Lozinski	6	11	7	4.32
3–14–3	LW	G. Hicks	58	5	10	15	71	7.0	1	0	J. Rutherford	2	6	2	4.30
W. Maxner	C	D. McCourt	80	30	56	86	286	10.5	11	– 17	C. Legris	0	1	0	3.81
16–29–15	C	P. Woods	67	8	16	24	74	10.8	1	– 10	A. Jensen	0	1	0	7.00
	C	M. Kirton	50	18	13	31	97	18.6	6	– 30					
	C	B. Peterson	53	6	18	24	40	15.0	1	2					
	RW	J. Ogrodnick	80	35	35	70	276	12.7	9	– 17					
	RW	M. Foligno	80	28	35	63	181	15.5	3	– 13					
	RW	N. Nedomansky	74	12	20	32	128	9.4	6	– 35					
	RW	G. McAdam	40	5	14	19	92	5.4	1	– 14					
	RW	D. Polonich	32	2	2	4	27	7.4	0	– 14					
	D	R. Larson	78	27	31	58	297	9.1	8	– 35					
	D	W. Huber	80	15	34	49	207	7.2	3	– 28					
	D	J. Korn	63	5	15	20	82	6.1	1	– 5					
	D	J. Barrett	56	3	10	13	97	3.1	0	– 21					
	D	J. Hamel	68	5	7	12	47	10.6	0	– 1					

ADAMS DIVISION

	POS	PLAYER	GP	G	A	PTS	SOG	SPCT	PPG	+/-	GOALIE	W	L	T	GAvg
BUF	LW	T. McKegney	80	37	32	69	236	15.7	9	11	D. Edwards	23	10	12	**2.96**
R. Neilson	C	D. Smith	69	21	43	64	166	12.7	11	14	B. Sauve	16	10	9	3.17
39–20–21	RW	D. Gare	73	46	39	85	248	18.5	15	12					
	LW	C. Ramsay	80	24	35	59	110	21.8	1	39					
	C	A. Savard	79	31	43	74	149	20.8	2	32					
	RW	R. Seiling	74	30	27	57	140	21.4	2	20					
	LW	R. Martin	23	7	14	21	57	12.3	2	4					
	LW	R. Dudley	38	10	13	23	49	20.4	2	7					
	C	G. Perreault	56	20	39	59	150	13.3	5	3					
	C	D. Luce	61	15	13	28	94	16.0	0	14					
	C	A. Haworth	49	16	20	36	72	22.2	4	– 6					
	RW	L. Ruff	65	8	18	26	97	8.2	1	3					
	D	J. Van Boxmeer	80	18	51	69	258	7.0	6	– 2					
	D	J. Schoenfeld	71	8	25	33	101	7.9	3	28					
	D	R. Dunn	79	7	42	49	175	4.0	4	21					
	D	B. Hajt	68	2	19	21	58	3.4	0	38					
	D	L. Playfair	75	3	9	12	54	5.6	0	4					
BOS	LW	W. Cashman	77	25	35	60	111	22.5	7	17	R. Vachon	25	19	6	3.34
	LW	M. Gillis	17	2	4	6	26	7.7	0	– 2	J. Craig	9	7	6	3.68
G. Cheevers	LW	S. Jonathan	74	14	24	38	85	16.5	0	5	M. Baron	3	4	1	2.84
37–30–13	LW	D. Marcotte	72	20	13	33	128	15.6	4	3					
	C	J. Ratelle	47	11	26	37	62	17.7	4	18					
	C	P. McNab	80	37	46	83	201	18.4	16	12					
	C	S. Kasper	76	21	35	56	165	12.7	5	9					
	RW	R. Middleton	80	44	59	103	222	19.8	16	15					
	RW	D. Foster	77	24	28	52	107	22.4	3	4					
	RW	T. O'Reilly	77	8	35	43	84	9.5	0	2					
	RW	K. Crowder	47	13	12	25	69	18.8	1	9					
	D	B. Park	78	14	52	66	201	7.0	10	21					
	D	R. Bourque	67	27	29	56	207	13.0	9	29					
	D	D. Redmond	78	15	20	35	152	9.9	6	4					
	D	M. Milbury	77	0	18	18	77	.0	0	14					
	D	M. O'Connell	48	10	22	32	96	10.4	2	– 1					
MINN	LW	S. Payne	76	30	28	58	243	12.3	11	14	D. Beaupre	18	14	11	3.20
	C	B. Smith	78	29	64	93	242	12.0	13	1	G. Meloche	17	14	6	3.25
G. Sonmor	RW	A. MacAdam	78	21	39	60	145	14.5	6	– 6					
35–28–17	LW	T. McCarthy	62	23	25	48	147	15.6	4	3					
	LW	J. Carlson	43	7	2	9	24	29.2	0	– 5					
	LW	M. Polich	74	8	5	13	58	13.8	0	– 2					
	C	T. Young	74	25	41	66	214	11.7	10	6					
	C	S. Christoff	56	26	13	39	132	19.7	9	– 9					
	C	M. Eaves	48	10	24	34	104	9.6	1	1					
	RW	K. Andersson	77	17	24	41	127	13.4	1	8					
	RW	D. Ciccarelli	32	18	12	30	126	14.3	8	2					
	RW	T. Younghans	74	4	6	10	55	7.3	1	– 8					
	D	C. Hartsburg	74	13	30	43	207	6.3	8	– 9					
	D	G. Roberts	50	6	31	37	83	7.2	3	2					
	D	C. Giles	67	5	22	27	82	6.1	1	9					
	D	G. Smith	74	5	21	26	99	5.1	1	7					
	D	P. Shmyr	61	1	9	10	62	1.6	0	4					

	POS	PLAYER	GP	G	A	PTS	SOG	SPCT	PPG	+/-	GOALIE	W	L	T	GAvg
QUE	LW	A. Stastny	80	39	46	85	177	22.0	12	4	M. Plasse	10	14	9	3.66
M. Filion	C	P. Stastny	77	39	70	109	232	16.8	11	11	D. Bouchard	19	5	5	3.17
1–3–2	RW	R. Cloutier	34	15	16	31	89	16.9	2	2	M. Dion	0	8	3	5.32
M. Bergeron	LW	J. Richard	78	52	51	103	261	19.9	16	−9	R. Grahame	1	5	1	5.47
29–29–16	C	D. Hunter	80	19	44	63	152	12.5	2	5					
	RW	M. Goulet	76	32	39	71	265	12.1	3	0					
	LW	M. Tardif	63	23	31	54	144	16.0	11	−4					
	LW	A. Cote	51	8	18	26	65	12.3	1	9					
	C	R. Ftorek	78	24	49	73	148	16.2	8	−19					
	C	S. Bernier	46	2	8	10	35	5.7	1	−8					
	C	R. LeDuc	22	3	7	10	21	14.3	0	2					
	RW	J. Hislop	50	19	22	41	86	22.1	5	−4					
	RW	A. Paddock	32	2	5	7	32	6.3	0	−7					
	D	P. Lacroix	61	5	34	39	96	5.2	4	9					
	D	D. Pichette	46	4	16	20	47	8.5	2	3					
	D	D. Hoganson	61	3	14	17	56	5.4	1	−8					
	D	A. Dupont	63	5	8	13	72	6.9	1	6					
TOR	LW	P. Hickey	72	16	33	49	157	10.2	5	−16	J. Crha	20	20	11	4.07
J. Crozier	C	D. Sittler	80	43	53	96	267	16.1	14	−8	J. Rutherford	4	10	2	5.12
13–22–5	RW	W. Paiement	77	40	57	97	302	13.2	13	−7	M. Larocque	3	3	2	5.22
M. Nykoluk	LW	J. Anderson	75	17	26	43	142	12.0	2	−11	C. Ridley	1	1	0	5.81
15–15–10	C	B. Derlago	80	35	39	74	208	16.8	6	−11	V. Tremblay	0	3	0	6.71
	RW	R. Vaive	75	33	29	62	195	16.9	8	−16					
	LW	D. Maloney	65	20	21	41	80	25.0	13	−10					
	LW	T. Martin	69	23	14	37	111	20.7	1	15					
	LW	R. Sedlbauer	21	10	4	14	45	22.2	5	−3					
	C	L. Boschman	53	14	19	33	70	20.0	3	−10					
	C	B. Boudreau	39	10	14	24	47	21.3	0	−7					
	RW	R. Saganiuk	71	12	18	30	113	10.6	2	−16					
	RW	R. Robert	14	6	7	13	43	14.0	1	5					
	D	I. Turnbull	80	19	47	66	262	7.3	8	−17					
	D	B. Salming	72	5	61	66	210	2.4	1	0					
	D	V. Duris	57	1	12	13	70	1.4	0	13					
	D	D. Farrish	74	2	18	20	110	1.8	1	−7					

GOALS		ASSISTS		POINTS	
M. Bossy, NYI	68	W. Gretzky, EDM	109	W. Gretzky, EDM	164
M. Dionne, LA	58	K. Nilsson, CALG	82	M. Dionne, LA	135
C. Simmer, LA	56	M. Dionne, LA	77	K. Nilsson, CALG	131
W. Gretzky, EDM	55	B. Federko, STL	73	M. Bossy, NYI	119
R. Kehoe, PITT	55	B. Trottier, NYI	72	D. Taylor, LA	112

SHOTS ON GOAL		SHOOTING PCT.		+/-	
M. Dionne, LA	342	C. Simmer, LA	32.7	B. Engblom, MONT	63
M. Gartner, WASH	326	P. Gagne, COLO	25.3	M. Dionne, LA	55
R. Leach, PHI	321	W. Plett, CALG	23.9	R. Langway, MONT	53
M. Bossy, NYI	315	D. Maloney, NYR	23.4	D. Maloney, NYR	50
W. Babych, STL	306	T. Kerr, PHI	23.2	B. Trottier, NYI	49

PENALTY MINUTES		GOALS AGAINST AVE.		SHUTOUTS	
T. Williams, VAN	343	D. Edwards, BUF	2.96	D. Edwards, BUF	3
P. Holmgren, PHI	306	P. Peeters, PHI	2.96	C. Resch, NYI	3
C. Nilan, MONT	262	D. Beaupre, MINN	3.20	P. Peeters, PHI	2
J. Korn, DET	246	M. Lessard, LA	3.25	M. Lessard, LA	2
B. Wilson, PHI	237	B. Smith, NYI	3.28	B. Smith, NYI	2

National Hockey League 1981–82

	W	L	T	PTS	GF	GA	PPG	PPCT	SHG	PPGA	PKPCT	SHGA
CAMPBELL CONFERENCE												
NORRIS DIVISION												
MINN	37	23	20	94	346	288	89	24.6	11	**49**	**81.9**	9
WINN	33	33	14	80	319	332	74	22.6	4	20	75.9	11
STL	32	40	8	72	315	349	76	22.1	1	83	76.8	13
CHI	30	38	12	72	332	363	78	24.8	13	93	75.7	12
TOR	20	44	16	56	298	380	58	19.9	10	98	73.0	6
DET	21	47	12	54	270	351	43	16.7	10	75	73.6	6
SMYTHE DIVISION												
EDM	48	17	15	111	**417**	295	86	25.2	12	67	**81.9**	8
VAN	30	33	17	77	290	286	64	19.0	8	68	78.4	40
CALG	29	34	17	75	334	345	78	26.9	8	72	78.0	9
LA	24	41	15	63	314	369	75	21.1	7	89	71.3	11
COLO	18	49	13	49	241	362	46	15.1	4	63	76.5	15

	W	L	T	PTS	GF	GA	PPG	PPCT	SHG	PPGA	PKPCT	SHGA
PRINCE OF WALES CONFERENCE												
PATRICK DIVISION												
*NYI	54	16	10	118	385	250	80	**28.2**	**16**	65	80.4	**3**
NYR	39	27	14	92	316	306	38	22.2	7	75	76.5	12
PHI	38	31	11	87	325	313	78	24.4	11	102	74.3	5
PITT	31	36	13	75	310	337	**99**	24.5	8	92	76.9	14
WASH	26	41	13	65	319	338	93	22.2	8	67	78.3	11
ADAMS DIVISION												
MONT	46	17	17	109	360	**223**	72	24.2	9	57	80.1	5
BOS	43	27	10	96	323	285	65	22.5	11	54	81.4	7
BUF	39	26	15	93	307	273	63	20.9	4	57	79.9	10
QUE	33	31	16	82	356	345	83	26.4	**16**	71	78.5	9
HART	21	41	18	60	264	351	68	23.3	6	78	72.4	7

CAMPBELL CONFERENCE

NORRIS DIVISION

	POS	PLAYER	GP	G	A	PTS	SOG	SPCT	PPG	+/-	GOALIE	W	L	T	GAvg
MINN	LW	S. Payne	74	33	45	78	239	13.8	11	20	G. Meloche	26	15	9	3.47
G. Sonmor	C	B. Smith	80	43	71	114	261	16.5	20	10	D. Beaupre	11	8	9	3.71
37–23–20	RW	A. MacAdam	79	18	43	61	141	12.8	5	9	L. Middlebrook	0	0	2	3.00
	LW	T. McCarthy	40	12	30	42	89	13.5	3	10					
	C	N. Broten	73	38	60	98	188	20.2	7	14					
	RW	D. Ciccarelli	76	55	51	106	289	19.0	20	14					
	LW	B. Palmer	72	22	23	45	180	12.2	7	– 13					
	LW	A. Hakansson	72	12	4	16	76	15.8	0	– 12					
	C	T. Young	49	10	31	41	125	8.0	1	0					
	C	S. Christoff	69	26	29	55	178	14.6	4	9					
	RW	M. Eaves	25	11	10	21	62	17.7	2	2					
	RW	K. Andersson	70	9	12	21	78	11.5	0	– 5					
	D	C. Hartsburg	76	17	60	77	204	8.3	5	11					
	D	B. Maxwell	51	10	21	31	109	9.2	0	6					
	D	G. Roberts	79	4	30	34	104	3.8	0	– 1					
	D	F. Barrett	69	1	15	16	43	2.3	0	– 12					
	D	C. Giles	74	3	12	15	65	4.6	0	15					
WINN	LW	M. Lukowich	77	43	49	92	229	18.8	13	– 4	E. Staniowski	20	19	6	3.95
T. Watt	LW	B. Lundholm	66	14	30	44	99	14.1	3	5	D. Soetaert	13	14	8	4.31
33–33–14	LW	N. Dupont	62	13	25	38	148	8.8	4	– 24					
	LW	D. Smail	72	17	18	35	97	17.5	2	– 22					
	LW	T. Trimper	74	8	8	16	68	11.8	0	– 7					
	C	D. Hawerchuk	80	45	58	103	339	13.3	12	– 4					
	C	D. Christian	80	25	51	76	218	11.5	6	– 41					
	C	T. Steen	73	15	29	44	133	11.3	4	16					
	C	S. Arniel	17	1	8	9	18	5.6	1	2					
	RW	P. MacLean	74	36	25	61	164	22.0	12	– 9					
	RW	W. Lindstrom	74	32	27	59	236	13.6	5	11					
	RW	L. Deblois	65	25	27	52	149	16.8	1	– 10					
	RW	J. Mann	37	3	2	5	22	13.6	0	– 8					
	D	D. Babych	79	19	49	68	262	7.3	11	– 11					
	D	T. Watters	69	2	22	24	66	3.0	0	14					
	D	B. Maxwell	45	1	9	10	45	2.2	0	– 11					
	D	S. Savard	47	2	5	7	41	4.9	0	– 8					
STL	LW	B. Sutter	74	39	36	75	195	20.0	14	– 2	M. Liut	**28**	28	7	4.06
R. Berenson	C	B. Federko	74	30	62	92	177	16.9	11	– 10	G. Edwards	1	5	1	5.63
28–35–6	RW	J. Mullen	45	25	34	59	141	17.7	10	11	R. Heinz	2	5	0	4.85
E. Francis	LW	J. Pettersson	77	38	31	69	227	16.7	8	– 8	P. Skidmore	1	1	0	3.00
4–5–2	C	B. Dunlop	77	25	53	78	129	19.4	10	– 9	G. Hanlon	0	1	0	6.32
	RW	W. Babych	51	19	25	44	142	13.4	4	– 12					
	LW	P. Turnbull	79	33	26	59	215	15.3	2	– 15					
	C	M. Zuke	76	13	40	53	159	8.2	1	– 18					
	C	L. Patey	70	14	12	26	109	12.8	1	– 10					
	C	R. Klassen	45	3	7	10	25	12.0	0	– 3					
	RW	M. Crombeen	71	19	8	27	99	19.2	0	– 10					
	RW	J. Nill	61	9	12	21	65	13.8	1	– 13					
	RW	T. Currie	48	18	22	40	103	17.5	4	– 7					
	D	J. Brownschidle	80	5	33	38	149	3.4	3	– 5					
	D	R. Lapointe	71	2	20	22	91	2.2	0	– 6					
	D	R. Wilson	48	3	18	21	95	3.2	1	– 10					
	D	E. Kea	78	2	14	16	89	2.2	0	19					

	POS	PLAYER	GP	G	A	PTS	SOG	SPCT	PPG	+/–	GOALIE	W	L	T	GAvg
CHI	LW	A. Secord	80	44	31	75	215	20.5	14	– 17	T. Esposito	19	25	8	4.52
K. Magnuson	C	D. Savard	80	32	87	119	231	13.9	8	0	M. Bannerman	11	12	4	4.17
18–24–10	RW	T. Higgins	74	20	30	50	114	17.5	6	– 6	W. Skordenski	0	1	0	5.00
B. Pulford	LW	D. Sutter	40	23	12	35	102	22.5	4	0					
12–14–2	C	T. Lysiak	71	32	50	82	170	18.8	10	– 8					
	RW	R. Preston	75	15	28	43	122	12.3	1	0					
	LW	T. Bulley	59	12	18	30	83	14.5	2	– 1					
	C	T. Ruskowski	60	7	30	37	69	10.1	2	– 13					
	C	R. Kerr	59	11	28	39	106	10.4	1	– 10					
	C	B. Gardner	69	8	15	23	66	12.1	1	– 9					
	RW	G. Mulvey	73	30	19	49	184	16.3	3	– 9					
	RW	P. Marsh	57	10	18	28	122	8.2	0	3					
	D	D. Wilson	76	39	46	85	325	12.0	14	1					
	D	D. Crossman	70	12	28	40	127	9.4	7	– 19					
	D	B. Murray	45	8	22	30	109	7.3	3	1					
	D	K. Brown	33	4	20	24	87	4.6	2	4					
	D	D. Hutchison	66	5	18	23	72	6.9	0	4					
TOR	LW	J. Anderson	69	31	26	57	191	16.2	7	8	M. Larocque	10	24	8	4.69
M. Nykoluk	C	B. Derlago	75	34	50	84	198	17.2	6	5	V. Tremblay	10	18	8	4.52
20–44–16	RW	R. Vaive	77	54	35	89	267	20.2	12	12	B. Parent	0	2	0	6.50
	LW	T. Martin	72	25	24	49	133	18.8	4	– 18					
	LW	D. Maloney	44	8	7	15	60	13.3	1	– 11					
	LW	B. Gavin	38	5	6	11	66	7.6	1	– 6					
	C	L. Boschman	54	9	19	28	64	14.1	1	– 3					
	C	N. Aubin	43	14	12	26	62	22.6	3	– 16					
	C	D. Luce	39	4	4	8	36	11.1	0	– 7					
	RW	R. Saganiuk	65	17	16	33	100	17.0	0	– 16					
	RW	R. Robert	55	13	24	37	120	10.8	2	– 11					
	RW	R. Zanussi	43	0	8	8	25	.0	0	– 4					
	D	B. Salming	69	12	44	56	175	6.9	1	4					
	D	B. Manno	72	9	41	50	108	8.3	3	5					
	D	J. Benning	74	7	24	31	90	7.8	2	– 27					
	D	F. Boimistruck	57	2	11	13	48	4.2	0	9					
	D	B. McGill	68	1	10	11	34	2.9	0	– 9					
DET	LW	M. Osborne	80	26	41	67	181	14.4	5	– 7	B. Sauve	11	25	4	4.19
W. Maxner	LW	E. Vail	52	10	14	24	86	11.6	3	– 21	G. Gilbert	6	10	6	4.26
18–39–12	LW	D. Smith	49	6	14	20	82	7.3	0	– 4	C. Micalef	4	10	1	4.67
B. Dea	C	W. McKechnie	73	18	37	55	87	20.7	2	– 1	G. Stefan	0	2	0	5.00
3–8–0	C	M. Kirton	74	14	28	42	121	11.6	0	– 18	C. Legris	0	0	1	0.00
	C	P. Woods	75	10	17	27	68	14.7	0	– 5					
	C	T. Nolan	41	4	13	17	67	6.0	0	– 6					
	RW	J. Ogrodnick	80	28	26	54	254	11.0	3	– 15					
	RW	M. Blaisdell	80	23	32	55	165	13.9	5	– 15					
	RW	N. Nedomansky	68	12	28	40	103	11.7	1	– 15					
	RW	D. Murdoch	49	9	13	22	97	9.3	1	1					
	RW	D. Gare	36	13	9	22	100	13.0	2	– 4					
	D	R. Larson	80	21	39	60	311	6.8	4	– 17					
	D	W. Huber	74	15	30	45	270	5.6	8	– 16					
	D	G. Smith	69	10	22	32	154	6.5	2	– 22					
	D	J. Barrett	69	1	12	13	97	1.0	0	– 31					
	D	J. Schoenfeld	39	5	9	14	87	5.7	0	2					

SMYTHE DIVISION

	POS	PLAYER	GP	G	A	PTS	SOG	SPCT	PPG	+/–	GOALIE	W	L	T	GAvg
EDM	LW	J. Kurri	71	32	54	86	211	15.2	6	38	G. Fuhr	**28**	5	14	3.31
G. Sather	C	W. Gretzky	80	**92**	**120**	**212**	**369**	24.9	18	**81**	R. Low	17	7	1	3.86
48–17–15	RW	G. Anderson	80	38	67	105	252	15.1	9	46	A. Moog	3	5	0	4.81
	LW	M. Messier	78	50	38	88	235	21.3	10	21					
	LW	D. Hunter	63	16	22	38	124	12.9	0	33					
	LW	D. Semenko	59	12	12	24	54	22.2	4	7					
	C	M. Hagman	72	21	38	59	94	22.3	5	15					
	C	B. Callighen	46	8	19	27	87	9.2	3	16					
	C	G. Unger	46	7	13	20	62	11.3	0	8					
	RW	D. Lumley	66	32	42	74	148	21.6	4	12					
	RW	P. Hughes	68	24	22	46	167	14.4	4	21					
	RW	T. Roulston	35	11	3	14	54	20.4	0	– 6					
	D	P. Coffey	80	29	60	89	234	12.4	13	35					
	D	R. Siltanen	63	15	48	63	143	10.5	6	13					
	D	K. Lowe	80	9	31	40	110	8.2	1	46					
	D	L. Fogolin	80	4	25	29	98	4.1	0	40					
	D	G. Lariviere	62	1	21	22	46	2.2	0	27					

TEAM	POS	PLAYER	GP	G	A	PTS	SOG	SPCT	PPG	+/–	GOALIE	W	L	T	GAvg
VAN	LW	C. Fraser	79	28	39	67	233	12.0	11	2	R. Brodeur	20	18	12	3.35
	C	T. Gradin	76	37	49	86	183	20.2	6	15	G. Hanlon	8	14	5	3.95
H. Neale	RW	S. Smyl	80	34	44	78	222	15.3	10	18	R. Heinz	2	1	0	3.00
26–33–16	LW	L. Molin	72	15	31	46	150	10.0	1	0					
R. Neilson	LW	D. Rota	51	20	20	40	80	25.0	2	6					
4–0–1	LW	T. Williams	77	17	21	38	138	12.3	5	– 6					
	C	I. Boldirev	78	33	40	73	202	16.3	10	– 17					
	C	I. Hlinka	72	23	37	60	152	15.1	7	21					
	C	G. Lupul	41	10	7	17	45	22.2	0	– 2					
	RW	B. MacDonald	59	18	15	33	116	15.5	4	0					
	RW	R. Delorme	59	9	8	17	47	19.1	0	– 8					
	D	K. McCarthy	71	6	39	45	152	3.9	1	12					
	D	H. Snepsts	68	3	14	17	69	4.3	0	22					
	D	L. Lindgren	75	5	16	21	95	5.3	0	2					
	D	D. Halward	37	4	13	17	75	5.3	1	– 11					
	D	R. Lanz	39	3	11	14	94	3.2	2	– 13					
	D	A. Eldebrink	38	1	8	9	47	2.1	0	– 2					
CALG	LW	K. Lavallee	75	32	29	61	169	18.9	6	– 9	P. Riggin	19	19	11	4.23
	LW	G. McAdam	46	12	15	27	72	16.7	0	– 6	R. Lemelin	10	15	6	4.34
A. MacNeil	LW	D. Labraaten	43	10	12	22	60	16.7	1	– 4					
29–34–17	C	G. Chouinard	64	23	57	80	182	12.6	13	– 5					
	C	M. Bridgman	63	26	49	75	141	18.4	6	16					
	C	K. Nilsson	41	26	29	55	103	25.2	13	– 20					
	C	B. Clement	69	4	12	16	56	7.1	0	– 2					
	C	J. Peplinski	74	30	37	67	141	21.3	3	0					
	RW	L. McDonald	55	34	33	67	178	19.1	10	22					
	RW	W. Plett	78	21	36	57	152	13.8	5	– 22					
	RW	K. Houston	70	22	22	44	165	13.3	3	– 2					
	RW	J. Hislop	80	16	25	41	113	14.2	0	1					
	D	P. Reinhart	62	13	48	61	116	11.2	8	1					
	D	P. Rautakallio	80	17	51	68	176	9.7	5	– 8					
	D	P. Russell	71	4	25	29	114	3.5	0	6					
	D	B. Murdoch	73	3	17	20	81	3.7	0	5					
	D	S. Konroyd	63	3	14	17	57	5.3	0	– 6					
LA	LW	C. Simmer	50	15	24	39	88	17.0	3	– 7	M. Lessard	13	28	8	4.36
	C	M. Dionne	78	50	67	117	351	14.2	17	– 10	D. Keans	8	10	7	4.30
P. MacDonald	RW	D. Taylor	78	39	67	106	232	16.8	13	– 4	J. Rutherford	3	3	0	6.79
13–24–5	LW	G. Terrion	61	15	22	37	106	14.2	1	– 12	M. Blake	0	0	0	2.35
D. Perry	LW	S. Jensen	45	8	19	27	78	10.3	1	– 14					
11–17–10	LW	J. Kelly	70	12	11	23	92	13.0	0	– 21					
	C	S. Bozek	71	33	23	56	182	18.1	10	– 6					
	C	D. Bonar	79	13	23	36	123	10.6	1	– 4					
	C	D. Smith	80	16	14	30	141	11.3	1	– 13					
	RW	J. Fox	77	30	38	68	157	19.1	5	– 15					
	RW	M. Murphy	28	5	10	15	36	13.9	0	0					
	RW	B. Nicholls	22	14	18	32	63	22.2	8	2					
	D	L. Murphy	79	22	44	66	191	11.5	8	– 13					
	D	M. Hardy	77	6	39	45	121	5.0	1	– 12					
	D	J. Korab	50	5	13	18	71	7.0	3	– 19					
	D	D. Lewis	64	1	13	14	50	2.0	0	– 19					
	D	R. Chartraw	33	2	8	10	32	6.3	1	– 11					
COLO	LW	A. Broten	58	15	24	39	67	22.4	5	– 11	C. Resch	16	**31**	11	4.03
	LW	B. Ashton	80	24	36	60	182	13.2	3	– 31	P. Myre	2	17	2	5.35
B. Marshall	LW	P. Gagne	59	10	12	22	104	9.6	2	– 27	S. Janaszak	0	1	0	7.80
3–17–4	LW	J. Wensink	57	5	3	8	35	14.3	1	– 13	R. LaFerriere	0	0	0	3.00
M. Johnston	C	S. Tambellini	79	29	30	59	185	15.7	9	– 33					
15–32–9	C	D. Lever	59	22	28	50	136	16.2	3	– 10					
	C	M. Malinowski	69	13	28	41	95	13.7	0	– 22					
	C	B. Miller	56	11	20	31	94	11.7	1	– 24					
	C	V. Ketola	44	9	5	14	42	21.4	4	– 17					
	RW	B. MacMillan	57	18	32	50	106	17.0	3	– 9					
	RW	D. Foster	70	12	19	31	97	12.4	1	– 53					
	RW	D. Cameron	66	11	12	23	65	16.9	0	– 14					
	D	R. Ramage	80	13	29	42	270	4.8	6	– 47					
	D	B. Lorimer	79	5	15	20	29	17.2	1	– 19					
	D	T. Levo	34	9	13	22	70	12.9	3	– 13					
	D	J. Quenneville	64	5	10	15	67	7.5	0	– 29					
	D	J. Cirella	65	7	12	19	71	9.9	2	– 36					

PRINCE OF WALES CONFERENCE

PATRICK DIVISION

TEAM	POS	PLAYER	GP	G	A	PTS	SOG	SPCT	PPG	+/-	GOALIE	W	L	T	GAvg
NYI	LW	J. Tonelli	80	35	58	93	165	21.2	5	48	B. Smith	32	9	4	**2.97**
A. Arbour	LW	B. Bourne	76	27	26	53	173	15.6	5	27	R. Melanson	22	7	6	3.23
54–16–10	LW	C. Gillies	79	38	39	77	200	19.0	8	39					
	C	B. Trottier	80	50	79	129	217	23.0	18	70					
	C	B. Goring	67	15	17	32	63	23.8	1	– 3					
	C	B. Sutter	43	21	22	43	93	22.6	3	28					
	C	W. Merrick	68	12	27	39	112	10.7	1	4					
	C	B. Carroll	72	9	20	29	42	21.4	0	12					
	RW	M. Bossy	80	64	83	147	301	21.3	17	69					
	RW	B. Nystrom	74	22	25	47	136	16.2	0	13					
	RW	D. Sutter	77	18	35	53	140	12.9	4	23					
	D	D. Potvin	60	24	37	61	169	14.2	11	38					
	D	S. Persson	70	6	37	43	107	5.6	3	35					
	D	K. Morrow	75	1	18	19	91	1.1	0	53					
	D	D. Langevin	73	1	20	21	73	1.4	0	34					
	D	M. McEwen	73	10	39	49	161	6.2	1	30					
	D	T. Jonsson	70	9	25	34	89	10.1	0	26					
NYR	LW	D. Maloney	54	22	36	58	99	22.2	6	9	S. Weeks	23	16	9	3.77
H. Brooks	C	R. Ftorek	30	8	24	32	49	16.3	2	8	E. Mio	13	6	5	3.56
39–27–14	RW	E. Johnstone	68	30	28	58	141	21.3	4	– 5	S. Baker	1	5	0	6.04
	LW	N. Fotiu	70	8	10	18	76	10.5	0	– 7	J. Davidson	1	0	0	1.00
	LW	P. Hickey	53	15	14	29	77	19.5	3	– 15	Vanbiesbrouck	1	0	0	1.00
	LW	M. Allison	48	7	15	22	62	11.3	0	– 3					
	C	M. Rogers	80	38	65	103	213	17.8	6	2					
	C	M. Pavelich	79	33	43	76	180	18.3	12	21					
	C	M. Leinonen	53	11	20	31	67	16.4	2	2					
	RW	R. Duguay	72	40	36	76	202	19.8	10	18					
	RW	D. Silk	64	15	20	35	111	13.5	1	17					
	D	B. Beck	60	9	29	38	160	5.6	5	19					
	D	R. Ruotsalainen	78	18	38	56	247	7.3	7	18					
	D	D. Maloney	64	13	36	49	107	12.1	6	2					
	D	T. Laidlaw	79	3	18	21	62	4.8	0	7					
	D	C. Vadnais	50	5	6	11	43	11.6	1	– 2					
	D	A. Dore	56	4	16	20	40	10.0	0	10					
PHI	LW	B. Barber	80	45	44	89	350	12.9	13	4	P. Peeters	23	18	3	3.71
P. Quinn	C	B. Clarke	62	17	46	63	110	15.5	2	28	R. Ste.–Croix	13	9	6	3.89
34–29–9	RW	R. Leach	66	26	21	47	211	12.3	5	2	P. Lindbergh	2	4	2	4.38
B. McCammon	LW	B. Propp	80	44	47	91	290	15.2	13	19					
4–2–2	C	K. Linseman	79	24	68	92	212	11.3	2	6					
	RW	R. Allison	51	17	37	54	131	13.0	5	13					
	LW	I. Sinisalo	66	15	22	37	87	17.2	1	18					
	C	D. Sittler	35	14	18	32	114	12.3	5	– 1					
	C	T. Kerr	61	21	30	51	118	17.8	6	6					
	RW	R. Flockhart	72	33	39	72	240	13.8	10	18					
	RW	P. Holmgren	41	9	22	31	71	12.7	4	10					
	D	B. Wilson	59	13	23	36	130	10.0	5	6					
	D	B. Marsh	66	2	22	24	58	3.4	0	17					
	D	B. Hoffmeyer	57	7	20	27	88	8.0	4	13					
	D	G. Cochrane	63	6	12	18	67	9.0	0	19					
	D	J. Watson	76	3	9	12	67	4.5	0	12					
	D	F. Arthur	74	1	7	8	33	3.0	0	– 8					
PITT	LW	P. Boutette	80	23	51	74	140	16.4	14	– 23	M. Dion	25	24	12	3.79
E. Johnston	C	P. Gardner	59	36	33	69	157	22.9	**21**	– 7	P. Harrison	3	7	0	5.49
31–36–13	RW	R. Kehoe	71	33	52	85	249	13.3	17	– 27	G. Edwards	3	2	1	3.67
	LW	R. Schutt	35	9	12	21	73	12.3	0	3	N. Ricci	0	3	0	5.25
	LW	B. Simpson	26	9	9	18	37	24.3	0	– 3					
	C	M. Bullard	75	36	27	63	145	24.8	10	– 1					
	C	G. Ferguson	71	22	31	53	168	13.1	4	– 6					
	C	G. Malone	78	15	24	39	120	12.5	3	– 24					
	C	D. Shedden	38	10	15	25	76	13.2	4	– 2					
	C	G. Sheppard	58	11	10	21	81	13.6	0	9					
	RW	P. Lee	74	18	16	34	183	9.8	2	– 8					
	RW	S. Gatzos	16	6	8	14	36	16.7	0	0					
	D	R. Carlyle	73	11	64	75	193	5.7	7	– 16					
	D	P. Baxter	76	9	34	43	177	5.1	4	– 9					
	D	P. Price	77	7	31	38	107	6.5	2	2					
	D	R. Stackhouse	76	2	19	21	95	2.1	0	– 11					
	D	M. Chorney	60	1	6	7	37	2.7	0	– 11					

	POS	PLAYER	GP	G	A	PTS	SOG	SPCT	PPG	+/−	GOALIE	W	L	T	GAvg
WASH	LW	R. Walter	78	38	49	87	183	20.8	19	−3	D. Parro	16	26	7	4.20
G. Green	C	D. Maruk	80	60	76	136	268	22.4	20	−4	A. Jensen	8	8	4	3.81
1–12–0	RW	C. Valentine	60	30	37	67	154	19.5	18	−15	M. Palmateer	2	7	2	4.83
R. Crozier	LW	M. Gartner	80	35	45	80	300	11.7	5	−11					
0–1–0	C	B. Carpenter	80	32	35	67	263	12.2	7	−23					
B. Murray	RW	B. Gustafsson	70	26	34	60	142	18.3	3	−20					
25–28–13	LW	G. Duchesne	74	9	14	23	78	11.5	0	−6					
	LW	T. Robertson	54	8	13	21	46	17.4	3	−1					
	LW	T. Tookey	28	8	8	16	52	15.4	5	−9					
	C	G. Currie	43	7	7	14	45	15.6	0	−2					
	RW	B. Gould	60	18	13	31	103	17.5	1	−3					
	RW	Franceschetti	30	2	10	12	25	8.0	0	−4					
	D	R. Green	65	3	25	28	91	3.3	1	−12					
	D	D. Veitch	67	9	44	53	203	4.4	5	−17					
	D	G. Theberge	57	5	32	37	150	3.3	2	−8					
	D	T. Blomqvist	44	1	11	12	53	1.9	0	−17					
	D	T. Murray	74	3	22	25	75	4.0	0	−14					

ADAMS DIVISION

	POS	PLAYER	GP	G	A	PTS	SOG	SPCT	PPG	+/−	GOALIE	W	L	T	GAvg
MONT	LW	S. Shutt	57	31	24	55	154	20.1	5	24	R. Wamsley	23	7	7	2.75
B. Berry	LW	B. Gainey	79	21	24	45	172	12.2	1	37	D. Herron	12	6	8	2.64
46–17–17	C	K. Acton	78	36	52	88	218	16.5	10	48	R. Sevigny	11	4	2	3.10
	C	P. Mondou	73	35	33	68	146	24.0	8	18	M. Holden	0	0	0	0.00
	C	D. Jarvis	80	20	28	48	127	15.7	1	34					
	C	D. Risebrough	59	15	18	33	80	18.8	2	23					
	C	D. Wickenheiser	56	12	23	35	94	12.8	1	18					
	RW	G. Lafleur	66	27	57	84	233	11.6	9	33					
	RW	M. Napier	80	40	41	81	186	21.5	9	49					
	RW	R. Houle	51	11	32	43	81	13.6	2	18					
	RW	M. Tremblay	80	33	40	73	205	16.1	7	24					
	RW	C. Nilan	49	7	4	11	45	15.6	0	6					
	D	L. Robinson	71	12	47	59	141	8.5	5	57					
	D	R. Langway	66	5	34	39	139	3.6	1	66					
	D	B. Engblom	76	4	29	33	109	3.7	0	78					
	D	G. Delorme	60	3	8	11	80	3.8	0	19					
	D	B. Picard	62	2	26	28	132	1.5	2	17					
BOS	LW	B. Crowder	63	16	11	27	83	19.3	1	−7	M. Baron	22	16	4	3.44
G. Cheevers	C	B. Pederson	80	44	48	92	197	22.3	13	27	R. Vachon	19	11	6	3.66
43–27–10	RW	R. Middleton	75	51	43	94	202	**25.2**	19	15	M. Moffat	2	0	0	3.00
	LW	W. Cashman	64	12	31	43	90	13.3	3	−17					
	C	S. Kasper	73	20	31	51	151	13.2	1	−18					
	RW	K. Crowder	71	23	21	44	130	17.7	0	0					
	LW	S. Jonathan	67	6	17	23	50	12.0	1	6					
	LW	D. Marcotte	69	13	21	34	86	15.1	0	−2					
	LW	M. Gillis	53	9	8	17	66	13.6	0	10					
	C	P. McNab	80	36	40	76	172	20.9	11	0					
	C	T. Fergus	61	15	24	39	116	12.9	2	15					
	C	N. Leveille	66	14	19	33	148	9.5	1	16					
	RW	T. O'Reilly	70	22	30	52	114	19.3	0	23					
	D	R. Bourque	65	17	49	66	211	8.1	4	22					
	D	B. Park	75	14	42	56	159	8.8	8	11					
	D	M. Milbury	51	2	10	12	42	4.8	0	10					
	D	M. O'Connell	80	5	35	40	170	2.9	1	8					
BUF	LW	T. McKegney	73	23	29	52	187	12.3	8	−12	D. Edwards	26	23	9	3.51
S. Bowman	LW	Y. Lambert	77	25	39	64	108	23.1	14	22	B. Sauve	6	1	5	2.76
14–6–7	LW	C. Ramsay	80	16	35	51	109	14.7	0	14	J. Cloutier	5	1	0	2.51
J. Roberts	C	G. Perreault	62	31	42	73	155	20.0	2	19	P. Harrison	2	1	1	3.67
21–15–9	C	D. McCourt	52	20	22	42	122	16.4	4	−1					
S. Bowman	C	J. Sauve	69	19	36	55	119	16.0	5	7					
4–5–0	C	A. Savard	62	18	20	38	118	15.3	2	5					
	C	B. Peterson	46	9	5	14	41	22.0	0	−3					
	RW	M. Foligno	56	20	31	51	124	16.1	4	21					
	RW	R. Seiling	57	22	25	47	112	19.6	7	7					
	RW	A. Haworth	57	21	18	39	114	18.4	3	6					
	RW	S. Patrick	41	8	8	16	52	15.4	0	3					
	D	J. Van Boxmeer	69	14	54	68	196	7.1	7	23					
	D	M. Ramsey	80	7	23	30	94	7.4	2	18					
	D	R. Dunn	72	7	19	26	122	5.7	0	6					
	D	L. Ruff	79	16	32	48	183	8.7	3	1					
	D	B. Hajt	65	2	9	11	58	3.4	0	11					

	POS	PLAYER	GP	G	A	PTS	SOG	SPCT	PPG	+/-	GOALIE	W	L	T	GAvg
QUE	LW	A. Stastny	68	26	46	72	135	19.3	10	– 29	D. Bouchard	27	22	11	3.86
M. Bergeron	C	P. Stastny	80	46	93	139	227	20.3	16	– 10	J. Garrett	4	5	3	5.17
33–31–16	RW	M. Stastny	74	35	54	89	176	19.9	13	0	M. Plasse	2	3	1	5.41
	LW	R. Cloutier	67	37	60	97	214	17.3	8	26	C. Malarchuk	0	1	1	7.00
	C	D. Hunter	80	22	50	72	124	17.7	0	26					
	RW	M. Goulet	80	42	42	84	251	16.7	7	35					
	LW	J. Richard	59	15	26	41	124	12.1	1	– 9					
	LW	M. Tardif	75	39	31	70	166	23.5	14	– 15					
	LW	P. Aubry	62	10	13	23	62	16.1	0	– 9					
	C	A. Cote	79	15	16	31	95	15.8	0	– 11					
	RW	M. Frycer	49	20	17	37	89	22.5	5	– 12					
	D	M. Marois	71	11	32	43	124	8.9	2	19					
	D	D. Pichette	67	7	30	37	84	8.3	3	– 1					
	D	P. Lacroix	68	4	23	27	73	5.5	1	1					
	D	N. Rochefort	72	4	14	18	105	3.8	0	19					
	D	W. Weir	62	3	5	8	44	6.8	0	– 16					
	D	A. Dupont	60	4	12	16	62	6.5	0	3					
HART	LW	J. Douglas	30	10	7	17	74	13.5	0	– 11	G. Millen	11	30	12	4.29
L. Pleau	LW	G. Howatt	80	18	32	50	111	16.2	1	– 5	J. Garrett	5	6	4	4.21
21–41–18	LW	D. Nachbaur	77	5	21	26	113	4.4	0	– 21	M. Veisor	5	5	2	4.54
	LW	D. Bourbonnais	24	3	9	12	30	10.0	0	– 8					
	C	R. Francis	59	25	43	68	163	15.3	12	– 13					
	C	R. Meagher	65	24	19	43	171	14.0	2	– 4					
	C	D. Keon	78	8	11	19	84	9.5	0	– 31					
	C	P. Larouche	45	25	25	50	121	20.7	4	– 17					
	RW	B. Stoughton	80	52	39	91	266	19.5	13	– 17					
	RW	D. Sulliman	77	29	40	69	195	14.9	5	– 13					
	RW	W. Miller	74	10	12	22	152	6.6	1	– 14					
	D	M. Howe	76	8	45	53	220	3.6	3	– 8					
	D	C. Kotsopoulos	68	13	20	33	153	8.5	5	– 25					
	D	B. Wesley	78	9	18	27	115	7.8	3	– 34					
	D	P. Shmyr	66	1	11	12	44	2.3	0	– 11					
	D	J. McIlhargey	50	1	5	6	23	4.3	0	– 8					
	D	M. Renaud	48	1	17	18	72	1.4	0	– 17					

GOALS		ASSISTS		POINTS	
W. Gretzky, EDM	92	W. Gretzky, EDM	120	W. Gretzky, EDM	212
M. Bossy, NYI	64	P. Stastny, QUE	93	M. Bossy, NYI	147
D. Maruk, WASH	60	D. Savard, CHI	87	P. Stastny, QUE	139
D. Ciccarelli, MINN	55	M. Bossy, NYI	83	D. Maruk, WASH	136
B. Stoughton, HART	52	B. Trottier, NYI	79	B. Trottier, NYI	129
SHOTS ON GOAL		**SHOOTING PCT.**		**+/–**	
W. Gretzky, EDM	369	R. Middleton, BOS	25.2	W. Gretzky, EDM	81
M. Dionne, LA	351	W. Gretzky, EDM	24.9	B. Trottier, NYI	70
B. Barber, PHI	350	M. Bullard, PITT	24.8	M. Bossy, NYI	69
D. Hawerchuk, WINN	339	A. Kallur, NYI	24.3	R. Langway, MONT	66
D. Wilson, CHI	325	P. Mondou, MONT	24.0	L. Robinson, MONT	57
PENALTY MINUTES		**GOALS AGAINST AVE.**		**SHUTOUTS**	
T. Williams, VAN	341	B. Smith, NYI	2.97	D. Herron, MONT	3
G. Cochrane, PHI	329	G. Fuhr, EDM	3.31	R. Wamsley, MONT	2
P. Price, PITT	322	R. Brodeur, VAN	3.35	R. Brodeur, VAN	2
A. Secord, CHI	303	M. Baron, BOS	3.44	M. Liut, STL	2
W. Plett, CALG	288	G. Meloche, MINN	3.47	P. Riggin, CALG	2

National Hockey League 1982–83

	W	L	T	PTS	GF	GA	PPG	PPCT	SHG	PPGA	PKPCT	SHGA
CAMPBELL CONFERENCE												
NORRIS DIVISION												
CHI	47	23	10	104	338	268	86	27.2	4	71	76.6	6
MINN	40	24	16	96	321	290	**91**	26.4	17	67	80.7	20
TOR	28	40	12	68	293	330	79	22.3	13	83	75.0	9
STL	25	40	15	65	285	316	67	21.2	9	63	81.3	12
DET	21	44	15	57	263	344	37	19.3	7	80	72.6	9
SMYTHE DIVISION												
EDM	47	21	12	106	**424**	315	86	**29.3**	**22**	89	77.5	6
CALG	32	34	14	78	321	317	90	27.0	7	59	77.1	6
VAN	30	35	15	75	303	309	65	23.8	5	56	80.8	13
WINN	33	39	8	74	311	333	78	23.6	10	67	72.8	7
LA	27	41	12	66	308	365	81	23.8	10	94	68.2	14

	W	L	T	PTS	GF	GA	PPG	PPCT	SHG	PPGA	PKPCT	SHGA
PRINCE OF WALES CONFERENCE												
PATRICK DIVISION												
PHI	49	23	8	106	326	240	60	21.6	15	61	82.0	7
*NYI	42	26	12	96	302	**226**	69	25.8	10	55	**83.4**	**3**
WASH	39	25	16	94	306	283	75	20.9	3	53	81.6	11
NYR	35	35	10	80	306	287	71	22.4	12	75	76.0	8
NJ	17	49	14	48	230	338	66	21.9	7	78	73.5	10
PITT	18	53	9	45	257	394	81	22.6	3	110	72.2	15
ADAMS DIVISION												
BOS	50	20	10	110	327	228	67	22.2	8	53	80.7	6
MONT	42	24	14	98	350	286	64	22.2	8	68	73.8	8
BUF	38	29	13	89	318	285	67	21.5	12	**48**	82.5	9
QUE	34	34	12	80	343	336	61	20.7	6	92	73.6	6
HART	19	54	7	45	261	403	51	19.3	6	70	76.1	9

CAMPBELL CONFERENCE

NORRIS DIVISION

CHI
O. Tessier
47–23–10

POS	PLAYER	GP	G	A	PTS	SOG	SPCT	PPG	+/-
LW	A. Secord	80	54	32	86	239	22.6	**20**	34
C	D. Savard	78	35	85	120	213	16.4	13	26
RW	S. Larmer	80	43	47	90	195	22.1	13	44
LW	D. Sutter	80	31	30	61	169	18.3	10	18
C	T. Lysiak	61	23	38	61	122	18.9	6	13
RW	R. Preston	79	25	28	53	161	15.5	4	14
LW	C. Fraser	38	6	13	19	42	14.3	0	2
C	B. Gardner	77	15	25	40	105	14.3	2	10
C	S. Ludzik	66	6	19	25	56	10.7	0	7
C	R. Paterson	79	14	9	23	78	17.9	1	– 1
RW	T. Higgins	64	14	9	23	71	19.7	0	– 4
RW	P. Marsh	68	6	14	20	121	5.0	0	– 8
D	D. Wilson	74	18	51	69	260	6.9	3	22
D	D. Crossman	80	13	40	53	134	9.7	6	21
D	B. Murray	79	7	32	39	186	3.8	5	24
D	K. Brown	50	4	27	31	116	3.4	2	8

GOALIE	W	L	T	GAvg
M. Bannerman	24	12	5	3.10
T. Esposito	23	11	5	3.46

MINN
G. Sonmor
22–13–9
M. Oliver
18–11–7

POS	PLAYER	GP	G	A	PTS	SOG	SPCT	PPG	+/-
LW	T. McCarthy	80	28	48	76	171	16.4	4	10
C	N. Broten	79	32	45	77	165	19.4	8	24
RW	D. Ciccarelli	77	37	38	75	210	17.6	14	16
LW	S. Payne	80	30	39	69	199	15.1	14	– 9
C	B. Smith	77	24	53	77	190	12.6	12	– 20
RW	B. Bellows	78	35	30	65	184	19.0	15	– 12
LW	J. Douglas	68	13	14	27	89	14.6	1	– 7
LW	R. Friest	50	6	7	13	44	13.6	0	– 4
C	T. Young	70	18	35	53	152	11.8	6	– 1
C	M. Eaves	75	16	16	32	143	11.2	1	– 3
RW	W. Plett	71	25	14	39	125	20.0	8	– 12
RW	A. MacAdam	73	11	22	33	93	11.8	0	3
D	C. Hartsburg	78	12	50	62	200	6.0	3	7
D	G. Roberts	80	3	41	44	127	2.4	2	18
D	B. Maxwell	77	11	28	39	162	6.8	2	– 1
D	C. Giles	76	2	21	23	78	2.6	0	11
D	F. Barrett	51	1	3	4	29	3.4	0	– 10

GOALIE	W	L	T	GAvg
G. Meloche	20	13	11	3.57
D. Beaupre	19	10	5	3.58
M. Mattsson	1	1	0	3.60

TOR
M. Nykoluk
28–40–12

POS	PLAYER	GP	G	A	PTS	SOG	SPCT	PPG	+/-
LW	T. Martin	76	14	13	27	95	14.7	3	– 30
LW	R. Vaive	78	51	28	79	296	17.2	18	– 13
LW	G. Terrion	74	16	16	32	73	21.9	0	– 3
LW	B. Gavin	63	6	5	11	77	7.8	0	– 7
C	D. Daoust	48	18	33	51	119	15.1	9	– 1
C	W. Poddubny	72	28	31	59	163	17.2	9	9
C	P. Ihnacak	80	28	38	66	162	17.3	6	6
C	B. Derlago	58	13	24	37	135	9.6	5	– 19
RW	J. Anderson	80	31	49	80	199	15.6	9	– 6
RW	M. Frycer	67	25	30	55	133	18.8	5	2
RW	P. Higgins	22	0	0	0	1	.0	0	– 2
D	B. Salming	69	7	38	45	110	6.4	2	– 3
D	G. Gingras	45	10	18	28	95	10.5	4	7
D	J. Benning	74	5	17	22	68	7.4	3	– 8
D	J. Korn	80	8	21	29	101	7.9	0	– 27
D	D. Farrish	56	4	24	28	91	4.4	3	1
D	B. Melrose	52	2	5	7	25	8.0	0	– 16

GOALIE	W	L	T	GAvg
M. Palmateer	21	23	7	3.99
R. Ste.–Croix	4	9	2	3.78
M. Larocque	3	8	3	4.89
B. Parent	0	0	0	3.00

TEAM	POS	PLAYER	GP	G	A	PTS	SOG	SPCT	PPG	+/-	GOALIE	W	L	T	GAvg
STL	LW	B. Sutter	79	46	30	76	204	22.5	11	– 1	M. Liut	21	27	13	3.72
E. Francis	C	B. Federko	75	24	60	84	184	13.0	9	– 10	G. Hanlon	3	8	1	4.47
10–19–3	RW	J. Mullen	49	17	30	47	128	13.3	5	– 5	R. Heinz	1	5	1	4.30
B. Plager	LW	J. Pettersson	74	35	38	73	201	17.4	7	– 10					
15–21–12	C	B. Dunlop	78	22	44	66	135	16.3	8	– 6					
	RW	W. Babych	71	16	23	39	148	10.8	5	– 24					
	LW	P. Turnbull	79	32	15	47	205	15.6	6	– 20					
	LW	J. Carlson	54	6	1	7	43	14.0	0	– 3					
	C	A. Lemieux	42	9	25	34	71	12.7	1	– 10					
	C	M. Zuke	43	8	16	24	58	13.8	0	– 3					
	C	L. Patey	67	9	12	21	72	12.5	0	– 6					
	RW	M. Crombeen	80	6	11	17	71	8.5	0	– 5					
	RW	B. Chapman	39	7	11	18	46	15.2	3	– 8					
	D	R. Ramage	78	16	35	51	279	5.7	7	– 9					
	D	A. Dore	38	2	15	17	41	4.9	0	9					
	D	G. Lapointe	54	3	23	26	106	2.8	1	– 12					
	D	J. Brownschidle	72	1	22	23	127	.8	1	– 3					
DET	LW	M. Osborne	80	19	24	43	159	11.9	3	– 41	G. Stefan	6	16	9	4.52
N. Polano	LW	D. Smith	42	7	4	11	50	14.0	1	– 7	C. Micalef	11	13	5	3.62
21–44–15	C	D. Gare	79	26	35	61	224	11.6	6	– 16	G. Gilbert	4	14	1	4.49
	C	I. Boldirev	33	13	17	30	62	21.0	3	– 6	J. Rutherford	0	1	0	7.00
	C	W. McKechnie	64	14	29	43	73	19.2	3	1					
	C	P. Woods	63	13	20	33	82	15.9	0	– 2					
	C	S. Weir	57	5	24	29	59	8.5	1	0					
	RW	J. Ogrodnick	80	41	44	85	254	16.1	5	11					
	RW	M. Blaisdell	80	18	23	41	171	10.5	0	– 6					
	RW	M. Craven	31	4	7	11	21	19.0	0	5					
	RW	D. Foster	58	17	22	39	83	20.5	3	– 8					
	RW	R. Leach	78	15	17	32	139	10.8	2	– 1					
	RW	T. Rowe	51	6	10	16	65	9.2	0	– 17					
	D	R. Larson	80	22	52	74	271	8.1	7	– 8					
	D	W. Huber	74	14	29	43	241	5.8	3	– 34					
	D	G. Smith	73	4	26	30	92	4.3	0	7					
	D	J. Barrett	79	4	10	14	72	5.6	0	– 18					

SMYTHE DIVISION

TEAM	POS	PLAYER	GP	G	A	PTS	SOG	SPCT	PPG	+/-	GOALIE	W	L	T	GAvg
EDM	LW	J. Kurri	80	45	59	104	218	20.6	10	47	A. Moog	33	8	7	3.54
G. Sather	LW	M. Messier	77	48	58	106	237	20.3	12	19	G. Fuhr	13	12	5	4.29
47–21–12	LW	D. Semenko	75	12	15	27	69	17.4	0	19	R. Low	0	1	0	5.77
	C	W. Gretzky	80	**71**	**125**	**196**	**348**	20.4	18	60	L. Middlebrook	1	0	0	3.00
	C	K. Linseman	72	33	42	75	141	23.4	10	16					
	C	T. Roulston	67	19	21	40	107	17.8	2	29					
	C	M. Habscheid	32	3	10	13	19	15.8	0	14					
	RW	G. Anderson	72	48	56	104	243	19.8	11	41					
	RW	J. Pouzar	74	15	18	33	86	17.4	2	17					
	RW	P. Hughes	80	25	20	45	144	17.4	2	0					
	RW	D. Hunter	80	13	18	31	113	11.5	0	12					
	RW	D. Lumley	72	13	24	37	96	13.5	2	19					
	D	P. Coffey	80	29	67	96	259	11.2	9	52					
	D	C. Huddy	76	20	37	57	151	13.2	7	**62**					
	D	K. Lowe	80	6	34	40	92	6.5	1	39					
	D	L. Fogolin	72	0	18	18	66	.0	0	24					
	D	R. Gregg	80	6	22	28	94	6.4	0	15					
CALG	LW	K. Lavallee	60	19	16	35	139	13.7	1	– 6	R. Lemelin	16	12	8	3.61
B. Johnson	LW	E. Beers	41	11	15	26	72	15.3	2	11	D. Edwards	16	15	6	4.02
32–34–14	LW	C. Mokosak	41	7	6	13	38	18.4	0	– 5	T. Bernhardt	0	5	0	4.50
	C	K. Nilsson	80	46	58	104	217	21.2	16	5	M. Vernon	0	2	0	6.60
	C	G. Chouinard	80	13	59	72	158	8.2	7	– 24					
	C	D. Risebrough	71	21	37	58	145	14.5	3	13					
	C	M. Bridgman	79	19	31	50	131	14.5	9	– 1					
	C	S. Christoff	45	9	8	17	52	17.3	0	– 3					
	RW	L. McDonald	80	66	32	98	272	**24.3**	17	– 2					
	RW	J. Peplinski	80	15	26	41	147	10.2	1	– 5					
	RW	J. Hislop	79	14	19	33	80	17.5	1	– 5					
	RW	D. Hindmarch	60	11	12	23	86	12.8	0	– 8					
	RW	G. Meredith	35	5	4	9	39	12.8	2	– 5					
	D	P. Reinhart	78	17	58	75	152	11.2	5	1					
	D	K. Eloranta	80	4	40	44	68	5.9	0	13					
	D	P. Russell	78	13	18	31	116	11.2	0	2					
	D	S. Konroyd	79	4	13	17	80	5.0	0	3					

	POS	PLAYER	GP	G	A	PTS	SOG	SPCT	PPG	+/–	GOALIE	W	L	T	GAvg
VAN	LW	D. Rota	73	42	39	81	173	**24.3**	9	13	R. Brodeur	21	26	8	3.79
R. Neilson	C	T. Gradin	80	32	54	86	175	18.3	12	– 17	J. Garrett	7	6	3	3.08
30–35–15	RW	S. Smyl	74	38	50	88	215	17.7	15	– 6	K. Ellacott	2	3	4	4.43
	LW	L. Molin	58	12	27	39	128	9.4	2	– 20	F. Caprice	0	0	0	9.00
	LW	C. Fraser	36	6	7	13	67	9.0	2	– 7					
	LW	M. Lemay	44	11	9	20	72	15.3	3	– 6					
	LW	T. Williams	68	8	13	21	78	10.3	0	– 7					
	C	I. Boldirev	39	5	20	25	74	6.8	3	– 9					
	C	I. Hlinka	65	19	44	63	147	12.9	8	– 3					
	C	P. Sundstrom	74	23	23	46	156	14.7	6	– 20					
	C	J. Nill	65	7	15	22	53	13.2	1	– 18					
	RW	T. Tanti	39	8	8	16	81	9.9	4	– 9					
	RW	R. Delorme	56	5	8	13	38	13.2	0	– 6					
	D	H. Snepsts	46	2	8	10	40	5.0	0	– 17					
	D	K. McCarthy	74	12	28	40	99	12.1	3	– 1					
	D	D. Halward	75	19	33	52	199	9.5	11	– 18					
	D	R. Lanz	74	10	38	48	180	5.6	4	– 5					
WINN	LW	M. Lukowich	69	22	21	43	162	13.6	6	– 28	D. Soetaert	19	19	6	4.12
T. Watt	LW	B. Mullen	80	24	26	50	194	12.4	7	11	B. Hayward	10	12	2	3.71
33–39–8	LW	D. Smail	80	15	29	44	113	13.3	0	0	E. Staniowski	4	8	0	4.72
	LW	B. Lundholm	58	14	28	42	66	21.2	1	10					
	LW	N. Dupont	39	7	16	23	71	9.9	6	– 16					
	C	D. Hawerchuk	79	40	51	91	297	13.5	13	– 17					
	C	T. Steen	75	26	33	59	156	16.7	5	– 6					
	C	S. Arniel	75	13	5	18	92	14.1	1	– 16					
	C	L. Boschman	12	3	5	8	25	12.0	1	3					
	RW	P. MacLean	80	32	44	76	163	19.6	15	– 5					
	RW	L. Deblois	79	27	27	54	183	14.8	1	– 25					
	RW	D. Christian	55	18	26	44	131	13.7	4	– 5					
	D	D. Babych	79	13	61	74	253	5.1	7	– 10					
	D	B. Maxwell	54	7	13	20	78	9.0	1	6					
	D	S. Savard	76	4	16	20	51	7.8	0	– 24					
	D	T. Watters	77	5	18	23	57	8.8	2	– 10					
	D	D. Spring	80	0	16	16	50	.0	0	0					
LA	LW	C. Simmer	80	29	51	80	183	15.8	1	0	G. Laskowski	15	20	4	4.56
D. Perry	LW	D. Evans	80	18	22	40	242	7.4	1	– 18	M. Lessard	3	10	2	4.59
27–41–12	LW	J. Kelly	65	16	15	31	102	15.7	4	– 14	M. Mattsson	5	5	4	4.34
	LW	U. Isaksson	50	7	15	22	71	9.9	0	1	M. Blake	4	4	0	4.17
	C	M. Dionne	80	56	51	107	345	16.2	17	10	D. Keans	0	2	2	4.74
	C	B. Nicholls	71	28	22	50	171	16.4	12	– 23					
	C	T. Ruskowski	71	14	30	44	71	19.7	4	– 16					
	C	S. Bozek	53	13	13	26	104	12.5	3	– 18					
	RW	D. Taylor	46	21	37	58	117	17.9	6	4					
	RW	J. Fox	77	28	40	68	137	20.4	7	– 11					
	RW	M. Murphy	74	16	11	27	135	11.9	5	– 11					
	RW	D. Morrison	24	3	3	6	16	18.8	0	– 7					
	D	L. Murphy	77	14	48	62	172	8.1	9	2					
	D	M. Hardy	74	5	34	39	162	3.1	3	– 29					
	D	J. Korab	72	3	26	29	132	2.3	1	– 6					
	D	D. Kennedy	55	0	12	12	53	.0	0	– 17					

PRINCE OF WALES CONFERENCE

PATRICK DIVISION

	POS	PLAYER	GP	G	A	PTS	SOG	SPCT	PPG	+/–	GOALIE	W	L	T	GAvg
PHI	LW	B. Propp	80	40	42	82	250	16.0	13	35	P. Lindbergh	23	13	3	2.98
B. McCammon	C	B. Clarke	80	23	62	85	164	14.0	6	37	B. Froese	17	4	2	2.52
49–23–8	RW	R. Allison	67	21	30	51	148	14.2	4	30	R. Ste.-Croix	9	5	2	3.45
	LW	B. Barber	66	27	33	60	215	12.6	5	17	M. Larocque	0	1	1	4.00
	C	D. Sittler	80	43	40	83	231	18.6	10	17					
	RW	R. Flockhart	73	29	31	60	241	12.0	3	3					
	LW	I. Sinisalo	61	21	29	50	126	16.7	3	18					
	C	L. Carson	78	18	19	37	150	12.0	0	20					
	C	M. Taylor	61	8	25	33	73	11.0	0	25					
	RW	P. Holmgren	77	19	24	43	122	15.6	3	18					
	RW	T. Gorence	53	7	7	14	50	14.0	0	4					
	D	M. Howe	76	20	47	67	219	9.1	5	47					
	D	B. Wilson	62	8	24	32	117	6.8	3	3					
	D	M. Dvorak	80	4	33	37	112	3.6	2	27					
	D	B. McCrimmon	79	4	21	25	107	3.7	1	24					
	D	G. Cochrane	77	2	22	24	94	2.1	0	42					
	D	B. Marsh	68	2	11	13	76	2.6	0	20					

NYI
A. Arbour
42–26–12

POS	PLAYER	GP	G	A	PTS	SOG	SPCT	PPG	+/-
LW	J. Tonelli	76	31	40	71	166	18.7	8	30
LW	B. Bourne	77	20	42	62	147	13.6	5	14
LW	C. Gillies	70	21	20	41	145	14.5	4	9
LW	G. Gilbert	45	8	11	19	37	21.6	0	1
C	B. Trottier	80	34	55	89	179	19.0	13	37
C	B. Goring	75	19	20	39	98	19.4	2	10
C	B. Sutter	80	21	19	40	149	14.1	1	14
C	W. Merrick	59	4	12	16	46	8.7	1	– 3
C	B. Carroll	71	1	11	12	52	1.9	0	3
RW	M. Bossy	79	60	58	118	272	22.1	19	27
RW	B. Nystrom	74	10	20	30	100	10.0	3	5
RW	D. Sutter	75	13	19	32	122	10.7	1	8
RW	A. Kallur	55	6	8	14	77	7.8	1	9
D	D. Potvin	69	12	54	66	191	6.3	4	32
D	T. Jonsson	72	13	35	48	100	13.0	1	40
D	S. Persson	70	4	25	29	80	5.0	2	12
D	D. Langevin	73	4	17	21	107	3.7	0	22

GOALIE	W	L	T	GAvg
R. Melanson	24	12	5	2.66
B. Smith	18	14	7	2.87

WASH
B. Murray
39–25–16

POS	PLAYER	GP	G	A	PTS	SOG	SPCT	PPG	+/-
LW	B. Carpenter	80	32	37	69	197	16.2	14	0
C	B. Gustafsson	67	22	42	64	139	15.8	2	9
RW	M. Gartner	73	38	38	76	269	14.1	10	– 2
LW	C. Laughlin	75	17	27	44	128	13.3	5	– 7
C	D. Jarvis	80	8	22	30	95	8.4	0	– 11
RW	A. Haworth	74	23	27	50	145	15.9	5	– 5
LW	G. Duchesne	77	18	19	37	126	14.3	0	15
LW	T. Bulley	39	4	9	13	35	11.4	0	– 3
C	D. Maruk	80	31	50	81	185	16.8	12	– 20
C	G. Currie	68	11	28	39	54	20.4	0	18
C	M. Novy	73	18	30	48	131	13.7	3	1
RW	B. Gould	80	22	18	40	142	15.5	0	16
RW	K. Houston	71	25	14	39	139	18.0	9	– 7
D	R. Langway	80	3	29	32	126	2.4	1	0
D	B. Engblom	73	5	22	27	103	4.9	4	– 3
D	S. Stevens	77	9	16	25	121	7.4	0	15
D	G. Theberge	70	8	28	36	136	5.9	7	– 3

GOALIE	W	L	T	GAvg
A. Jensen	21	12	6	3.44
P. Riggin	17	9	9	3.36
D. Parro	1	3	1	4.37
R. Moore	0	1	0	3.00

NYR
H. Brooks
35–35–10

POS	PLAYER	GP	G	A	PTS	SOG	SPCT	PPG	+/-
LW	R. McClanahan	78	22	26	48	118	18.6	0	12
C	M. Pavelich	78	37	38	75	154	24.0	10	20
RW	A. Hedberg	78	25	34	59	163	15.3	4	17
LW	D. Maloney	78	29	40	69	133	21.8	14	– 5
C	M. Rogers	71	29	47	76	199	14.6	7	– 10
RW	E. Johnstone	52	15	21	36	98	15.3	2	– 4
LW	N. Fotiu	72	8	13	21	61	13.1	1	6
LW	M. Allison	39	11	9	20	45	24.4	1	8
C	M. Leinonen	78	17	34	51	135	12.6	3	12
C	R. Duguay	72	19	25	44	160	11.9	5	– 13
RW	N. Nedomansky	34	11	8	19	52	21.2	8	1
RW	K. Andersson	71	8	20	28	91	8.8	0	6
D	R. Ruotsalainen	77	16	53	69	228	7.0	5	27
D	A. Dore	39	3	12	15	33	9.1	0	39
D	D. Maloney	78	8	42	50	136	5.9	3	– 3
D	B. Beck	66	12	22	34	162	7.4	4	22
D	B. Baker	70	4	14	18	63	6.3	1	– 8

GOALIE	W	L	T	GAvg
E. Mio	16	18	6	3.45
G. Hanlon	9	10	1	3.43
S. Weeks	9	5	3	3.92
S. Baker	0	1	0	2.94
J. Davidson	1	1	0	2.50

NJ
B. MacMillan
17–49–14

POS	PLAYER	GP	G	A	PTS	SOG	SPCT	PPG	+/-
LW	P. Gagne	53	14	15	29	76	18.4	4	– 2
C	A. Broten	73	16	39	55	126	12.7	5	– 20
RW	J. Larmer	65	21	24	45	123	17.1	5	– 6
LW	D. Lever	79	23	30	53	143	16.1	9	– 35
LW	B. Ashton	76	14	19	33	113	12.4	4	– 23
C	S. Tambellini	73	25	18	43	153	16.3	6	– 27
C	M. Malinowski	5	3	2	5	8	37.5	1	1
C	R. Meagher	57	15	14	29	135	11.1	7	– 21
RW	H. Marini	77	17	28	45	109	15.6	5	– 14
RW	B. MacMillan	71	19	29	48	120	15.8	6	– 35
RW	D. Foster	4	0	0	0	2	.0	0	– 1
RW	J. Ludvig	51	7	10	17	103	6.8	2	– 27
RW	Y. Vautour	52	4	7	11	54	7.4	0	– 19
D	T. Levo	73	7	40	47	187	3.7	5	– 41
D	J. Quenneville	74	5	12	17	85	5.9	0	– 13
D	B. Lorimer	66	3	10	13	53	5.7	0	– 20
D	J. Brumwell	59	5	14	19	61	8.2	1	– 20

GOALIE	W	L	T	GAvg
C. Resch	15	35	12	3.98
R. Low	2	7	1	4.05
L. Middlebrook	0	6	1	5.39
S. MacKenzie	0	1	0	6.92

TEAM	POS	PLAYER	GP	G	A	PTS	SOG	SPCT	PPG	+/–	GOALIE	W	L	T	GAvg
PITT	LW	P. Boutette	80	27	29	56	142	19.0	13	– 33	M. Dion	12	30	4	4.26
E. Johnston	C	P. Gardner	70	28	27	55	155	18.1	**20**	– 23	D. Herron	5	18	5	5.31
18–53–9	RW	R. Kehoe	75	29	36	65	203	14.3	15	– 45	R. Romano	0	3	0	6.97
	LW	A. Hakansson	62	9	12	21	67	13.4	0	– 11	N. Ricci	1	2	0	6.53
	LW	G. Rissling	40	5	4	9	35	14.3	0	– 17					
	LW	T. Hrynewich	30	2	3	5	22	9.1	0	– 6					
	C	D. Shedden	80	24	43	67	175	13.7	4	– 20					
	C	G. Malone	80	17	44	61	158	10.8	3	– 29					
	C	M. Bullard	57	22	22	44	148	14.9	3	– 21					
	C	D. Hannan	74	11	22	33	95	11.6	2	– 28					
	RW	P. Lee	63	13	13	26	113	11.5	1	– 9					
	RW	S. Gatzos	44	6	7	13	70	8.6	2	– 16					
	D	R. Carlyle	61	15	41	56	177	8.5	8	– 27					
	D	P. Baxter	75	11	21	32	159	6.9	5	– 49					
	D	G. Hotham	58	2	30	32	75	2.7	0	– 14					
	D	R. Boyd	56	4	14	18	102	3.9	1	– 36					
	D	M. Chorney	67	3	5	8	66	4.5	0	– 30					

ADAMS DIVISION

TEAM	POS	PLAYER	GP	G	A	PTS	SOG	SPCT	PPG	+/–	GOALIE	W	L	T	GAvg
BOS	LW	M. Krushelnyski	79	23	42	65	153	15.0	4	38	P. Peeters	**40**	11	9	**2.36**
G. Cheevers	C	B. Pederson	77	46	61	107	212	21.7	15	38	M. Moffat	4	6	1	4.37
50–20–10	RW	R. Middleton	80	49	47	96	214	22.9	6	33	M. Baron	6	3	0	3.84
	LW	L. Dufour	73	14	11	25	121	11.6	0	19					
	LW	B. Palmer	73	6	11	17	123	4.9	0	– 7					
	LW	W. Cashman	65	4	11	15	36	11.1	0	2					
	C	P. McNab	74	22	52	74	160	13.8	5	16					
	C	T. Fergus	80	28	35	63	169	16.6	4	26					
	C	C. MacTavish	75	10	20	30	120	8.3	0	15					
	RW	K. Crowder	74	35	39	74	156	22.4	10	22					
	RW	B. Crowder	80	21	19	40	148	14.2	1	30					
	RW	T. O'Reilly	19	6	14	20	23	26.1	0	16					
	D	R. Bourque	65	22	51	73	205	10.7	7	49					
	D	M. O'Connell	80	14	39	53	168	8.3	7	44					
	D	B. Park	76	10	26	36	127	7.9	5	20					
	D	M. Milbury	78	9	15	24	95	9.5	1	22					
	D	M. Howe	78	1	11	12	68	1.5	0	21					
MONT	LW	R. Walter	80	29	46	75	169	17.2	8	15	R. Wamsley	27	12	5	3.51
B. Berry	LW	M. Naslund	74	26	45	71	122	21.3	1	34	R. Sevigny	15	11	8	3.44
42–24–14	LW	S. Shutt	78	35	22	57	202	17.3	8	8	M. Holden	0	1	1	4.14
	LW	B. Gainey	80	12	18	30	150	8.0	0	7					
	C	D. Wickenheiser	78	25	30	55	160	15.6	5	22					
	C	P. Mondou	76	29	37	66	178	16.3	8	32					
	C	K. Acton	78	24	26	50	154	15.6	1	– 6					
	C	G. Carbonneau	77	18	29	47	109	16.5	0	18					
	RW	G. Lafleur	68	27	49	76	177	15.3	9	6					
	RW	M. Napier	73	40	27	67	171	23.4	3	20					
	RW	M. Tremblay	80	30	37	67	175	17.1	7	29					
	RW	C. Nilan	66	6	8	14	67	9.0	0	– 10					
	D	L. Robinson	71	14	49	63	147	9.5	6	33					
	D	G. Gingras	22	1	8	9	60	1.7	1	8					
	D	R. Green	66	2	24	26	71	2.8	1	23					
	D	G. Delorme	78	12	21	33	166	7.2	3	27					
BUF	LW	T. McKegney	78	36	37	73	180	20.0	10	1	B. Sauve	25	20	7	3.45
S. Bowman	LW	G. Hamel	66	22	20	42	120	18.3	2	4	J. Cloutier	10	7	6	3.50
38–29–13	LW	C. Ramsay	64	11	18	29	87	12.6	0	14	P. Myre	3	2	0	4.20
	C	G. Perreault	77	30	46	76	192	15.6	8	– 10					
	C	D. McCourt	62	20	32	52	117	17.1	3	– 13					
	C	A. Savard	68	16	25	41	122	13.1	3	11					
	C	D. Andreychuk	43	14	23	37	66	21.2	3	6					
	C	B. Peterson	75	13	24	37	98	13.3	1	10					
	RW	M. Foligno	66	22	25	47	130	16.9	4	8					
	RW	R. Seiling	75	19	22	41	127	15.0	6	2					
	RW	P. Cyr	36	15	12	27	65	23.1	5	– 6					
	RW	S. McKenna	46	10	14	24	69	14.5	1	– 4					
	D	P. Housley	77	19	47	66	183	10.4	11	– 4					
	D	M. Ramsey	77	8	30	38	116	6.9	1	19					
	D	H. Virta	74	13	24	37	169	7.7	2	6					
	D	L. Ruff	60	12	17	29	110	10.9	2	14					
	D	J. Van Boxmeer	65	6	21	27	144	4.2	1	7					

	POS	PLAYER	GP	G	A	PTS	SOG	SPCT	PPG	+/-	GOALIE	W	L	T	GAvg
QUE	LW	A. Stastny	79	32	60	92	169	18.9	10	25	D. Bouchard	20	21	8	4.01
	C	P. Stastny	75	47	77	124	201	23.4	5	29	J. Garrett	6	8	2	4.03
M. Bergeron	RW	M. Stastny	60	36	43	79	169	21.3	13	20	C. Malarchuk	8	5	2	4.73
34–34–12	LW	R. Cloutier	68	28	39	67	185	15.1	5	– 4					
	C	D. Hunter	80	17	46	63	125	13.6	1	10					
	RW	M. Goulet	80	57	48	105	256	22.3	10	30					
	LW	A. Cote	79	12	28	40	88	13.6	0	– 1					
	LW	M. Tardif	76	21	31	52	116	18.1	4	0					
	LW	P. Aubry	77	7	9	16	64	10.9	0	– 6					
	RW	W. Paiement	80	26	38	64	191	13.6	6	– 10					
	D	P. Lacroix	13	0	5	5	8	.0	0	4					
	D	D. Pichette	53	3	21	24	63	4.8	0	9					
	D	W. Weir	58	5	11	16	50	10.0	1	11					
	D	N. Rochefort	62	6	17	23	104	5.8	1	11					
	D	T. Tookey	12	1	6	7	8	12.5	0	2					
	D	A. Dupont	46	3	12	15	42	7.1	0	11					
	D	R. Moller	75	2	12	14	72	2.8	0	11					
HART	LW	M. Johnson	73	31	38	69	167	18.6	5	– 5	G. Millen	14	**38**	6	4.81
	C	R. Francis	79	31	59	90	212	14.6	4	– 25	M. Veisor	5	16	1	5.53
L. Kish	RW	B. Stoughton	72	45	31	76	207	21.7	10	– 22					
12–32–5	LW	B. Sullivan	62	18	19	37	93	19.4	5	– 17					
L. Pleau	LW	G. Adams	79	10	13	23	115	8.7	1	– 46					
4–13–1	LW	P. Lawless	47	6	9	15	83	7.2	1	– 31					
J. Cunniff	LW	G. Lyle	16	4	6	10	33	12.1	0	5					
3–9–1	C	P. Larouche	38	18	22	40	114	15.8	4	– 24					
	C	M. Malinowski	75	5	23	28	94	5.3	1	– 41					
	RW	D. Sulliman	77	22	19	41	162	13.6	8	– 57					
	RW	R. Neufeld	80	26	31	57	165	15.8	4	– 34					
	RW	M. McDougal	55	8	10	18	61	13.1	0	– 33					
	D	P. Lacroix	56	6	25	31	89	6.7	1	– 19					
	D	R. Siltanen	74	5	25	30	155	3.2	3	– 39					
	D	C. Kotsopoulos	68	6	24	30	122	4.9	3	– 20					
	D	M. Renaud	77	3	28	31	87	3.4	1	– 42					
	D	E. Hospodar	72	1	9	10	54	1.9	0	– 32					

GOALS

W. Gretzky, EDM	71
L. McDonald, CALG	66
M. Bossy, NYI	60
M. Goulet, QUE	57
M. Dionne, LA	56

ASSISTS

W. Gretzky, EDM	125
D. Savard, CHI	85
P. Stastny, QUE	77
P. Coffey, EDM	67
B. Clarke, PHI	62

POINTS

W. Gretzky, EDM	196
P. Stastny, QUE	124
D. Savard, CHI	120
M. Bossy, NYI	118
B. Pederson, BOS	107
M. Dionne, LA	107

SHOTS ON GOAL

W. Gretzky, EDM	348
M. Dionne, LA	345
D. Hawerchuk, WINN	297
R. Vaive, TOR	296
R. Ramage, STL	279

SHOOTING PCT.

L. McDonald, CALG	24.3
D. Rota, VAN	24.3
M. Pavelich, NYR	24.0
K. Linseman, EDM	23.4
M. Napier, MONT	23.4

+/-

C. Huddy, EDM	62
W. Gretzky, EDM	60
P. Coffey, EDM	52
R. Bourque, BOS	49
M. Howe, PHI	47

PENALTY MINUTES

R. Holt, WASH	275
T. Williams, VAN	265
D. Wilson, CHI	258
B. Sutter, STL	254
P. Baxter, PITT	238

GOALS AGAINST AVE.

P. Peeters, BOS	2.36
R. Melanson, NYI	2.66
B. Smith, NYI	2.87
P. Lindbergh, PHI	2.98
M. Bannerman, CHI	3.10

SHUTOUTS

P. Peeters, BOS	8
M. Bannerman, CHI	4
B. Froese, PHI	4
P. Lindbergh, PHI	3
E. Mio, NYR	2

The World Hockey Association

Defying all hockey shibboleths, a group of California entrepreneurs launched what they labeled a second major league of the ice sport in 1972. Organized by Santa Ana attorney Gary Davidson and promoter Dennis Murphy, the World Hockey Association took on the National Hockey League against long odds. Neither Davidson nor Murphy had any previous hockey experience and because of that fact alone the imminent demise of the WHA was freely predicted by NHL rivals at the very start. Furthermore, the WHA chose to collide head-on with the established league in cities—New York, Boston, Toronto, among others—where there already was a team.

On February 12, 1972 the WHA held its first player draft at the Royal Coach Inn in Anaheim, California. Until then the WHA had no profound impact on the NHL. Elders of the established circuit refused to recognize the new threat and moved along with plans for further expansion of their own. But two weeks later the NHL received its first tangible shock when Bernie Parent, one of the most gifted young NHL goaltenders, made public his intent to sign with a WHA team. At the time it was believed that he would align with the Miami (Fla.) Screaming Eagles although he later officially joined the Philadelphia Blazers.

Parent's decision was the catalyst for other NHL players to jump to the new circuit and, one by one, signings were announced. WHA teams spirited the likes of Bobby Hull, Derek Sanderson, Ted Green, and J.C. Tremblay from the NHL. The WHA opened its first season on October 11, 1972 with Quebec at Cleveland and Edmonton at Ottawa. Edmonton's Ron Anderson scored the first WHA regular season goal. The league opened with 12 teams spread over two divisions. New England (Boston), Cleveland, Philadelphia, Ottawa, Quebec, and New York were in the Eastern Division with Winnipeg, Houston, Los Angeles, Alberta (Edmonton), Minnesota (St. Paul), and Chicago in the Western Division. In the playoff finals New England defeated Winnipeg 4 games to 1 to win the WHA's first championship trophy.

Not only did the WHA survive its first year of operations it also held its first all-star game—January 6, 1973 at Quebec City—and had one of its games shown on the CBS television network. Danny Lawson became the first WHA player to reach the 50-goal plateau on February 22, 1973 in Ottawa.

Some NHL officials took the WHA challenge seriously, and in April 1973 secret meetings were held between Gary Davidson and an NHL group led by William Jennings, president of the New York Rangers, in an effort to hammer out an agreement but no pact was forthcoming. Davidson announced that the WHA would continue to operate independently. "We believe the NHL's reserve clause to be wrong," said Davidson, "It would be impossible for us to consider any formal association with the NHL so long as they still have it." More importantly, the old guard among the NHL governors was adamantly opposed to any agreement with the WHA and proclaimed a full-scale war in the hopes of eliminating the maverick league.

In its second year the WHA added to its trophy collection by making a deal with the AVCO Financial Services organization. The company, which provides financial counseling and cash loans through more than 1,500 offices in the United States, Canada, Australia, and Great Britain lent its name to the WHA's version of the Stanley Cup. Hereafter, the winner of the WHA playoff would become the holder of the Avco World Trophy. It wasn't very classy but, at this point in time, the WHA wasn't about to quibble; it would accept help wherever and whenever possible. In May 1974 the Houston Aeros captured the Avco World Trophy in 14 games, losing only to Minnesota while sweeping four straight from Winnipeg and Chicago.

Like the NHL, the WHA was struggling through tumultuous times and reorganization seemed to be the order of the day. In June 1974 the league divided into three divisions (Canadian, West, East) and a "wild card" team playoff format was adopted. Phoenix and Indianapolis were the new expansion teams. Another blow was dealt the NHL when the WHA's Toronto Toros persuaded superstar Frank Mahovlich to leave the established league.

In contrast to the NHL, the WHA owners realized that there was a mother lode of rich talent to be mined in Europe. The Winnipeg Jets, in particular, thought nothing of stocking their roster with Swedes rather than Canadians and, as a result, Ulf Nilsson and Anders Hedberg of Sweden teamed with veteran Bobby Hull to comprise one of the most formidable attacking units of the 1970s. The WHA made another meaningful inroad on the international level when it persuaded Soviet hockey officials to sanction an eight-game series between a WHA all-star squad and a similar team from Russia. The tourney took place in the fall of 1974 with the Soviets easy winners.

Its setbacks notwithstanding, the WHA continued to grow because of one pivotal element: the spectacular growth of new arenas throughout the country and the demand, in each city, for a suitable tenant. Whereas the NHL was infinitely more demanding in setting forth conditions for entry, the WHA would gladly accept any franchise bidder as long as an attractive arena was located in the city in question. Thus, Cincinnati, which was not likely to become an NHL entry, was welcomed into the WHA in 1975 upon completion of the handsome Riverfront Arena. Cleveland—actually the building was located in distant Richfield, Ohio—also had a new arena as did Indianapolis and Edmonton.

From the very beginning one of the most frequently debated questions was the quality of WHA play in relation to the NHL. Clearly, the new league lacked the depth of stars still in the established circuit, but it did offer some interesting talents in the Swedes as well as two Finnish players, two Czechoslovakians, not to mention Bobby Hull, Gordie Howe, and his two youngsters, Mark and Marty. Scoring came easier in the WHA and when Bobby Hull equaled Maurice Richard's venerable NHL record of 50 goals in 50 games on February 14, 1975 the achievement was greeted with less than overwhelming enthusiasm.

Some players who made the leap from the NHL to the WHA reconsidered and returned, among them Bernie Parent and Derek Sanderson; but others, such as Bobby Hull, remained true to the new league. More than anyone, Hull proved to be the foremost gate attraction in the WHA and further helped the league's cause by his graciousness with fans and the media. On December 14, 1975 Hull received still more attention when he became the first WHA player to score 200 goals in league play.

More franchise rumblings were heard after the season when the league realigned into two divisions—Eastern and Western. The Toronto Toros could not compete with the NHL's Toronto Maple Leafs and emigrated to Birmingham, Alabama and were renamed the Bulls. Likewise, the Crusaders became a losing proposition in Cleveland and moved to St. Paul. Birmingham proved to be a pleasant addition to the league but St. Paul could not make it past 42 games before folding. It was a portent of things to come. By the end of the 1977–78 season the league had dwindled to eight teams—a year earlier it had opened with 12—having lost St. Paul, Calgary, Phoenix, and San Diego.

There was, however, new hope on the diplomatic front. Howard Baldwin, new WHA president, enjoyed a very positive relationship with two key NHL leaders: Ed Snider, owner of the Philadelphia Flyers, and John Ziegler, new president of the NHL. The endless WHA-NHL war was bleeding both leagues white and a spirit of reconciliation once again brought the leaders together; only this time there was more understanding on both sides of the bargaining table and a realization that a peace pact of some kind was in order. The result was that four WHA teams—Edmonton Oilers, Hartford Whalers, Quebec Nordiques, and Winnipeg Jets—were admitted to the NHL following the 1978–79 season and the WHA, after seven seasons of tumultuous operation, went out of business.

In many ways the WHA had a profound impact on the North American professional hockey scene. The competition for talent sent player salaries skyrocketing to all-time highs. The WHA spread pro hockey to new areas, but all too often these gains were offset by shabby management practices that angered the fans and, ultimately, turned them away from the game. As a result, cities which had been acclaimed for their hockey support—among them San Diego and Cleveland—became hockey wastelands.

The progressive nature of the WHA leadership resulted in a heavy accent on European talent, a trend later followed by the NHL, and an increase in many of the game's skills. Further, WHA recognized cities heretofore ignored as big league centers that had been dismissed as potential moneymakers by the NHL. Quebec, Edmonton, Winnipeg and Hartford later demonstrated that they could attract as many fans, comparatively, as such established centers as Detroit and Chicago. On the legal front, the WHA fought many battles with the NHL and won a significant number of the challenges. It was the WHA that experimented with teenage stars and ultimately compelled the NHL to abolish its rules forbidding the signing of players under 20 years of age. And it was the WHA that signed the electrifying Wayne Gretzky at a time when the NHL leaders were disparaging the lad as too thin, too unskilled, and not likely to become a factor in the major league game.

The WHA spawned interest, created a group of gifted hockey executives and offered an interesting form of sports entertainment throughout the 1970s. But, in the end, the league demonstrated more than anything that there is not room in hockey for more than one major professional league. And that is why the World Hockey Association is now a footnote in the lore of the game.

The following are the team abbreviations and nicknames for the clubs that made up the WHA.

ALTA Alberta Oilers (Became Edmonton Oilers in 1973–74 season)
BIRM Birmingham Bulls
CALG Calgary Cowboys
CHI Chicago Cougars
CIN Cincinnati Stingers
CLEVE Cleveland Crusaders (Became Minnesota (New) Fighting Saints in 1976)
EDM Edmonton Oilers
HOUS Houston Aeros
IND Indianapolis Racers
LA Los Angeles Sharks (Moved to Michigan in 1974)
MINN Minnesota Fighting Saints (Folded in 1975; revived as relocated Cleveland club in 1976)
NE New England Whalers (Originally located in Boston, moved to Hartford in 1973)
NY New York Raiders (Became New York Golden Blades in 1973)
OTTA Ottawa Nationals (Moved to Toronto in 1973)
PHI Philadelphia Blazers (Moved to Vancouver in 1973)
PHOE Phoenix Roadrunners
QUE Quebec Nordiques
SD San Diego Mariners
TOR Toronto Toros (Moved to Birmingham in 1976)
VAN Vancouver Blazers (Moved to Calgary in 1975)
WINN Winnipeg Jets

In addition to these teams, there were three teams that moved during the course of a season. The three clubs are listed as follows:

D-O Denver Spurs-Ottawa Civics (1975–76)
M-B Michigan Stags-Baltimore Blades (1974–75)
NY-NJ New York Golden Blades-New Jersey Knights (1973–74, moved to San Diego in 1974)

TEAM	W	L	T	PTS	GF	GA	TEAM	W	L	T	PTS	GF	GA
EASTERN DIVISION							WESTERN DIVISION						
NE	46	30	2	94	**318**	263	WINN	43	31	4	90	285	249
CLEVE	43	32	3	89	287	**239**	HOUS	39	35	4	82	284	269
PHI	38	40	0	76	288	305	LA	37	35	6	80	259	250
OTTA	35	39	4	74	279	301	ALTA	38	37	3	79	269	256
QUE	33	40	5	71	276	313	MINN	38	37	3	79	250	269
NY	33	43	2	68	303	334	CHI	26	50	2	54	245	295

EASTERN DIVISION

	POS	PLAYER	GP	G	A	PTS	PLAYER	GP	G	A	PTS	GOALIE	W	L	T	GAvg
	LW	K. Ahearn	78	20	22	42	D J. Dorey	75	7	56	63	A. Smith	31	19	1	3.18
NE	LW	B. Selby	65	13	29	42	D T. Green	78	16	30	46	B. Landon	15	11	1	3.59
J. Kelley	LW	J. Cunniff	33	3	5	8	D B. Selwood	75	13	21	34					
46–30–2	C	T. Caffery	74	39	61	100	D R. Ley	76	3	27	30					
	C	L. Pleau	78	39	48	87	D P. Hurley	78	3	15	18					
	C	T. Sheehy	78	33	38	71										
	C	J. French	74	24	35	59										
	RW	T. Webster	77	53	50	103										
	RW	T. Earl	77	10	13	23										
	RW	M. Byers	19	6	4	10										
	LW	G. Jarrett	77	40	39	79	D P. Shmyr	73	5	43	48	G. Cheevers	32	20	0	**2.84**
CLEVE	LW	P. Andrea	66	21	30	51	D R. Clearwater	78	11	36	47	B. Whidden	11	12	3	3.28
B. Needham	LW	R. Pumple	77	21	20	41	D B. Horton	74	2	17	19					
43–32–3	C	R. Buchanan	75	37	44	81	D J. Muloin	70	2	13	15					
	C	J. Wiste	70	28	43	71	D R. Hopiavouri	29	4	5	9					
	C	G. Erickson	77	15	29	44										
	C	D. Brindley	73	15	11	26										
	RW	G. Pinder	78	30	36	66										
	RW	J. Hardy	72	17	33	50										
	RW	T. Hodgson	74	15	23	38										
	LW	D. Herriman	78	24	48	72	D R. Plumb	78	10	41	51	B. Parent	**33**	28	0	3.61
PHI	LW	D. Burgess	74	20	22	42	D I. Spencer	54	2	27	29	M. Paille	2	8	0	4.81
J. McKenzie	LW	M. Boudreau	33	7	7	14	D J. Cardiff	78	3	24	27	Y. Archambault	1	3	0	3.92
1–6–0	C	A. Lacroix	78	50	74	**124**	D D. Campeau	75	1	18	19	T. Cottringer	1	1	0	3.93
P. Watson	C	B. Campbell	75	25	48	73	D J. Migneault	54	10	8	18	D. Sullivan	1	0	0	3.00
37–34–0	C	M. Plante	70	13	12	25										
	C	D. Sanderson	8	3	3	6										
	RW	D. Lawson	78	**61**	45	106										
	RW	J. McKenzie	60	28	50	78										
	RW	D. O'Donoghue	74	16	23	39										
	LW	W. Carleton	75	42	49	91	D B. Gibbons	73	7	35	42	G. Gratton	25	22	3	3.71
OTTA	LW	B. Charlebois	78	24	40	64	D R. Cunningham	78	9	32	41	L. Binkley	10	17	1	3.72
B. Harris	LW	D. Sentes	73	22	19	41	D K. Stephenson	77	3	16	19	F. Blum	0	0	0	6.43
35–39–4	C	G. Kirk	78	28	40	68	D M. Amodeo	60	1	14	15					
	C	B. LeDuc	77	22	33	55	D S. Warr	71	3	8	11					
	C	S. King	69	18	34	52	D C. Meloff	21	1	6	7					
	RW	G. Trottier	72	26	32	58										
	RW	T. Martin	75	19	27	46										
	RW	T. Simpson	57	10	7	17										
	LW	M. Parizeau	75	25	48	73	D J. Tremblay	76	14	**75**	89	S. Aubry	25	22	3	3.60
QUE	LW	B. Guindon	71	28	28	56	D F. Lacombe	61	10	18	28	R. Brodeur	5	14	2	4.75
M. Richard	LW	J. Gendron	63	17	33	50	D P. Roy	64	7	12	19	J. Lemelin	3	4	1	4.00
1–1–0	LW	M. Archambault	57	12	25	37	D J. Blain	69	1	10	11					
M. Filion	C	A. Gaudette	78	27	44	71										
32–39–5	C	R. Leclerc	60	24	28	52										
	C	J. Payette	71	15	29	44										
	C	M. Rouleau	52	7	14	21										
	RW	A. Caron	68	36	27	63										
	RW	Y. Bergeron	65	14	19	33										
	RW	R. Giroux	59	10	12	22										
	LW	B. Bradley	78	22	33	55	D K. Block	78	5	53	58	P. Donnelly	22	19	2	3.57
NY	LW	B. Perry	74	13	20	33	D B. Speer	69	3	23	26	G. Kurt	10	21	0	4.78
C. Henry	LW	C. Reichmuth	73	13	14	27	D H. Willis	74	3	21	24	I. Wilkie	1	3	0	6.40
33–43–2	C	B. Sheehan	75	35	53	88	D K. Douglas	60	3	15	18					
	C	R. Ward	77	51	67	118	D W. Olds	61	5	7	12					
	C	G. Peacosh	67	37	34	71										
	C	M. Laughton	67	16	20	36										
	RW	W. Rivers	75	37	40	77										
	RW	N. Ferguson	56	28	40	68										
	RW	J. Kennedy	54	4	6	10										

WESTERN DIVISION

	POS	PLAYER	GP	G	A	PTS	PLAYER	GP	G	A	PTS	GOALIE	W	L	T	GAvg
WINN	LW	B. Hull	63	51	52	103	D L. Hornung	77	13	45	58	E. Wakely	26	19	3	3.16
B. Hull	LW	C. Bordeleau	78	47	54	101	D J. Zanussi	73	4	21	25	J. Daley	17	10	1	2.90
43–31–4	LW	A. McDonald	77	17	24	41	D S. Cuddie	77	7	13	20	G. Tumilson	0	2	0	5.66
	LW	D. Rousseau	74	16	17	33	D B. Ash	74	3	14	17					
	C	D. Johnson	76	19	23	42	D B. Woytowich	62	2	4	6					
	C	W. Boyer	69	6	28	34										
	C	C. Swenson	76	7	21	28										
	RW	N. Beaudin	78	38	65	103										
	RW	M. Black	77	18	16	34										
	RW	J. Gratton	71	15	12	27										
HOUS	LW	E. Hoekstra	78	11	28	39	D P. Popiel	74	16	48	64	D. McLeod	19	20	1	3.61
B. Dineen	LW	K. Mortson	67	13	16	29	D L. Hale	68	4	26	30	W. Rutledge	20	14	2	3.00
39–35–4	LW	J. Stanfield	71	8	12	20	D D. McCallum	69	9	20	29	B. Hughes	0	1	1	3.88
	C	G. Labossierre	77	36	60	96	D J. Schella	77	2	24	26					
	C	M. Hall	76	28	42	70										
	C	L. Lund	77	21	45	66										
	C	B. MacDonald	71	20	20	40										
	RW	T. Taylor	72	34	42	76										
	RW	D. Grierson	78	22	22	44										
	RW	D. Harris	75	30	12	42										
	RW	F. Hughes	76	22	19	41										
LA	LW	T. Gilmore	71	17	18	35	D B. Crashley	70	18	27	45	G. Gardner	19	22	4	3.30
T. Slater	LW	S. Sutherland	44	11	6	17	D G. Odrowski	78	6	31	37	R. Gillow	17	13	2	2.91
37–35–6	LW	B. MacNeil	42	4	7	11	D J. Niekamp	78	7	22	29	M. Perreault	1	0	0	2.00
	C	J. LeBlanc	77	19	50	69	D R. MacSweyn	78	0	23	23					
	C	J. Szura	72	13	32	45	D J. Watson	75	5	15	20					
	C	T. Serviss	73	11	26	37										
	C	P. Slater	73	12	12	24										
	RW	G. Veneruzzo	78	43	30	73										
	RW	A. White	57	20	17	37										
ALTA	LW	B. Wall	78	16	29	45	D A. Hamilton	78	11	50	61	J. Norris	28	**29**	3	3.06
R. Kinasewich	LW	V. Fonteyne	77	7	32	39	D D. Barrie	54	9	22	31	K. Brown	10	8	0	3.66
38–37–3	LW	B. Carlin	65	12	22	34	D K. Baird	75	14	15	29					
	C	J. Harrison	66	39	47	86	D B. Falkenberg	76	6	23	29					
	C	R. Perkins	71	21	37	58	D S. Carlyle	67	7	10	17					
	C	R. Walters	78	28	26	54										
	RW	R. Patenaude	77	29	27	56										
	RW	B. Hicke	73	14	24	38										
	RW	R. Anderson	73	14	15	29										
MINN	LW	G. Morrison	70	16	24	40	D M. McMahon	75	12	39	51	M. Curran	23	17	2	3.09
G. Sonmor	LW	J. Johnson	33	9	14	23	D T. Ball	76	6	34	40	J. McCartan	15	19	1	3.58
39–37–3	LW	L. Lilyholm	77	8	13	21	D J. Arbour	76	6	27	33	C. Wetzel	0	1	0	3.00
	C	T. Hampson	77	17	45	62	D D. Paradise	77	3	15	18					
	C	K. Christiansen	64	12	30	42	D F. Sanders	77	8	8	16					
	C	B. MacMillan	75	13	27	40										
	C	M. Antonovich	75	20	19	39										
	C	F. Speck	47	13	16	29										
	RW	W. Connelly	78	40	30	70										
	RW	B. Klatt	78	36	22	58										
	RW	C. Falkman	45	1	5	6										
CHI	LW	J. Popiel	76	31	34	65	D L. Mavety	67	9	40	49	J. McLeod	22	25	2	3.32
M. Pronovost	LW	R. Morris	76	31	17	48	D R. Anderson	74	3	26	29	A. Gill	4	24	0	4.14
26–50–2	LW	D. Lodboa	58	15	18	33	D B. Barber	75	4	19	23	P. Menard	0	1	0	6.67
	LW	B. Liddington	78	20	11	31	D D. Proceviat	53	4	14	18					
	C	B. Sicinski	77	25	63	88										
	C	R. Zaine	74	3	14	17										
	C	D. Knibbs	41	3	8	11										
	RW	R. Paiement	78	33	36	69										
	RW	R. Fleming	74	23	45	68										
	RW	B. Whitlock	75	23	28	51										
	RW	D. Sarrazin	33	3	8	11										

GOALS		ASSISTS		POINTS	
D. Lawson, PHI	61	J. Tremblay, QUE	75	A. Lacroix, PHI	124
T. Webster, NE	53	A. Lacroix, PHI	74	R. Ward, NY	118
B. Hull, WINN	51	R. Ward, NY	67	D. Lawson, PHI	106
R. Ward, NY	51	N. Beaudin, WINN	65	T. Webster, NE	103
A. Lacroix, PHI	50	B. Sicinski, CHI	63	B. Hull, WINN	103

PENALTY MINUTES		GOALS AGAINST AVE.		SHUTOUTS	
J. Schella, HOUS	239	G. Cheevers, CLEVE	2.84	G. Cheevers, CLEVE	5
T. Gilmore, LA	191	J. Norris, ALTA	3.06	M. Curran, MINN	4
D. Paradise, MINN	189	M. Curran, MINN	3.09	A. Smith, NE	3
J. Arbour, MINN	188	E. Wakely, WINN	3.16		
J. Cardiff, PHI	185	A. Smith, NE	3.18		

TEAM	W	L	T	PTS	GF	GA
EASTERN DIVISION						
NE	43	31	4	90	291	260
TOR	41	33	4	86	304	272
CLEVE	37	32	9	83	266	264
CHI	38	35	5	81	271	273
QUE	38	36	4	80	306	280
NY–NJ	32	42	4	68	268	313

TEAM	W	L	T	PTS	GF	GA
WESTERN DIVISION						
HOUS	48	25	5	101	318	**219**
MINN	44	32	2	90	**332**	275
EDM	38	37	3	79	268	269
WINN	34	39	5	73	264	296
VAN	27	50	1	55	278	345
LA	25	53	0	50	239	339

EASTERN DIVISION

TEAM	POS	PLAYER	GP	G	A	PTS		PLAYER	GP	G	A	PTS	GOALIE	W	L	T	GAvg
NE	LW	J. French	77	24	48	72	D	J. Dorey	77	6	40	46	A. Smith	30	21	2	3.08
R. Ryan	LW	A. Karlander	77	20	41	61	D	R. Ley	72	6	35	41	B. Landon	11	9	2	3.55
43–31–4	LW	D. Blackburn	75	20	39	59	D	B. Selwood	76	9	28	37	B. Berglund	2	1	0	3.33
	LW	H. Harris	75	24	28	52	D	T. Green	75	7	26	33					
	C	L. Pleau	77	26	43	69	D	P. Hurley	52	3	11	14					
	C	T. Williams	70	21	37	58											
	C	J. Danby	72	2	2	4											
	RW	T. Webster	64	43	27	70											
	RW	T. Sheehy	77	29	29	58											
	RW	M. Byers	78	29	21	50											
TOR	LW	D. Sentes	64	26	34	60	D	B. Gibbons	78	4	31	35	G. Gratton	26	24	3	3.53
B. Harris	LW	P. Hickey	78	26	29	55	D	C. Brewer	77	2	23	25	L. Binkley	14	9	1	3.27
41–33–4	LW	B. LeDuc	61	22	29	51	D	S. Cuddie	74	5	18	23	F. Blum	1	0	0	2.31
	C	W. Carleton	78	37	55	92	D	R. Cunningham	75	2	19	21	B. Holden	0	0	0	0.00
	C	G. Kirk	78	20	48	68	D	B. Orr	46	3	9	12					
	C	W. Dillon	71	30	35	65	D	M. Amodeo	76	0	11	11					
	RW	G. Trottier	71	27	35	62											
	RW	T. Martin	74	25	32	57											
	RW	T. Simpson	74	33	20	53											
CLEVE	LW	G. Jarrett	75	31	39	70	D	P. Shmyr	78	13	31	44	G. Cheevers	30	20	6	3.03
B. Needham	LW	G. Pinder	73	23	33	56	D	R. Clearwater	68	12	23	35	B. Whidden	7	12	3	3.90
37–32–9	LW	G. Erickson	78	23	27	50	D	T. Edur	76	7	31	38					
	C	R. Ward	23	19	7	26	D	J. Muloin	76	3	7	10					
	C	J. Wiste	76	23	35	58	D	L. Hillman	44	5	21	26					
	RW	S. Krake	69	20	36	56											
	RW	P. Andrea	69	15	18	33											
	RW	R. Walker	76	15	14	29											
	RW	T. Hodgson	10	0	2	2											
CHI	LW	B. Liddington	73	26	21	47	D	P. Stapleton	78	6	52	58	C. Newton	25	18	2	3.14
P. Stapleton	LW	J. Popiel	63	22	17	39	D	L. Mavety	77	15	36	51	R. Coutu	9	10	1	3.73
38–35–5	LW	R. Morris	76	17	16	33	D	D. Maggs	78	8	22	30	A. Gill	4	7	2	3.44
	LW	F. Rochon	71	12	11	23	D	D. Proceviat	77	2	20	22					
	C	R. Backstrom	78	33	50	83											
	C	J. Hardy	77	24	35	59											
	C	B. Sicinski	69	11	29	40											
	RW	R. Paiement	78	30	43	73											
	RW	D. Harris	64	14	16	30											
	RW	D. Gordon	23	5	4	9											
QUE	LW	B. Guindon	77	31	39	70	D	J. Tremblay	68	9	44	53	M. Deguise	12	13	1	3.29
J. Plante	LW	P. Guite	72	14	20	34	D	D. Hoganson	62	8	33	41	R. Brodeur	15	12	1	3.32
38–36–4	LW	J. Gendron	64	11	8	19	D	A. Beaule	78	4	36	40	S. Aubry	11	11	2	3.87
	C	S. Bernier	74	37	49	86	D	F. Lacombe	71	9	26	35					
	C	A. Gaudette	78	24	44	68	D	K. Desjardine	70	2	10	12					
	C	M. Parizeau	78	26	34	60											
	C	J. Gilbert	75	17	39	56											
	RW	R. Houle	69	27	35	62											
	RW	G. Dufour	74	27	23	50											
	RW	A. Caron	59	31	15	46											
NY–NJ	LW	G. Peacosh	68	21	32	53	D	K. Morrison	78	24	43	67	J. Junkin	21	**25**	4	3.79
C. Henry	LW	B. Bradley	78	15	23	38	D	K. Block	74	3	43	46	G. Kurt	8	10	0	4.13
6–12–2	LW	N. Ferguson	75	15	21	36	D	H. Howell	65	3	23	26	J. McLeod	3	7	0	4.18
H. Howell	C	A. Lacroix	78	31	**80**	111	D	B. Brown	59	7	13	20					
26–30–2	C	B. Morenz	75	20	30	50	D	D. Boylan	61	1	5	6					
	C	B. Jones	78	17	28	45											
	C	M. Laughton	71	20	18	38											
	RW	W. Rivers	73	30	27	57											
	RW	D. Herriman	44	11	21	32											
	RW	T. Scharf	63	4	2	6											

WESTERN DIVISION

	POS	PLAYER	GP	G	A	PTS		PLAYER	GP	G	A	PTS	GOALIE	W	L	T	GAvg
HOUS	LW	A. Hinse	69	24	56	80	D	P. Popiel	78	7	41	48	D. McLeod	**33**	13	3	**2.56**
B. Dineen	LW	M. Howe	76	38	41	79	D	J. Schella	73	12	19	31	W. Rutledge	12	12	1	3.34
48–25–5	LW	J. Stanfield	41	1	3	4	D	M. Howe	73	4	20	24	R. Grahame	3	0	1	1.20
	C	L. Lund	75	33	53	86	D	G. Kannegiesser	78	0	20	20					
	C	J. Sherrit	76	30	28	58	D	L. Hale	69	2	14	16					
	C	M. Hall	78	30	28	58	D	B. Prentice	55	1	2	3					
	RW	G. Howe	70	31	69	100											
	RW	F. Hughes	73	42	42	84											
	RW	T. Taylor	75	21	23	44											
MINN	LW	G. Morrison	73	40	38	78	D	J. Arbour	77	6	43	49	M. Curran	23	14	2	3.27
H. Neale	LW	M. Heatley	71	26	32	58	D	M. McMahon	71	10	35	45	J. Garrett	21	18	0	3.59
44–32–2	LW	S. Cardwell	77	23	23	46	D	R. Smith	71	10	28	38	J. McCartan	0	0	0	7.14
	C	T. Hampson	77	17	38	55	D	T. Ball	71	8	28	36					
	C	J. Johnson	71	15	39	54	D	B. Boyd	41	1	14	15					
	C	M. Antonovich	68	21	29	50	D	D. Paradise	67	2	7	9					
	C	B. MacMillan	78	14	34	48											
	RW	M. Walton	78	**57**	60	**117**											
	RW	W. Connelly	78	42	53	95											
EDM	LW	R. Climie	76	38	36	74	D	A. Hamilton	77	14	45	59	J. Norris	23	24	1	3.21
B. Shaw	LW	L. Lunde	71	26	22	48	D	B. Wall	74	6	31	37	C. Worthy	11	12	1	3.80
38–37–3	LW	B. McKenzie	78	18	20	38	D	K. Baird	68	17	19	36	I. Wilkie	3	1	1	2.11
	C	J. Harrison	46	24	45	69	D	D. Barrie	69	4	27	31	G. Doyle	1	0	0	4.00
	C	R. Perkins	78	16	40	56	D	B. Falkenberg	78	3	14	17					
	C	E. Joyal	45	8	10	18	D	S. Carlyle	50	2	13	15					
	RW	B. MacDonald	78	21	24	45											
	RW	R. Patenaude	71	20	23	43											
	RW	T. Gilmore	57	19	23	42											
WINN	LW	B. Hull	75	53	42	95	D	B. Woytowich	72	6	28	34	J. Daley	19	20	1	3.99
B. Hull	LW	D. Johnson	78	16	21	37	D	J. Zanussi	76	3	22	25	E. Wakely	15	18	4	3.27
34–39–5	LW	A. McDonald	70	12	17	29	D	L. Hornung	51	4	19	23	B. Holden	0	0	1	3.43
	LW	D. Rousseau	60	10	8	18	D	B. Ash	60	2	18	20					
	C	C. Bordeleau	75	26	49	75											
	C	D. Spring	66	8	16	24											
	C	T. Hargreaves	74	7	12	19											
	C	C. Swenson	25	5	4	9											
	RW	N. Beaudin	74	27	28	55											
	RW	R. Snell	70	24	25	49											
	RW	J. Gratton	68	12	21	33											
	RW	D. Asmundson	72	5	14	19											
VAN	LW	D. Burgess	78	30	36	66	D	R. Plumb	75	6	32	38	P. Donnelly	22	24	0	3.80
J. McKenzie	LW	J. Migneault	74	21	26	47	D	C. Campbell	78	3	20	23	G. Gardner	4	21	1	4.72
3–4–0	LW	M. Chernoff	36	11	10	21	D	J. Cardiff	78	1	21	22	Y. Archambault	1	4	0	6.16
P. Watson	LW	S. Gellard	23	7	4	11	D	D. Hutchison	69	0	13	13	D. Sullivan	0	1	0	7.00
3–9–0	C	B. Campbell	76	27	62	89											
A. Bathgate	C	J. Adair	70	12	17	29											
21–37–1	C	C. St. Sauveur	70	38	30	68											
	C	D. Meloche	41	6	13	19											
	RW	D. Lawson	78	55	33	88											
	RW	J. McKenzie	45	14	38	52											
	RW	D. O'Donoghue	49	8	6	14											
LA	LW	M. Tardif	75	40	30	70	D	G. Odrowski	77	4	32	36	P. Hoganson	6	16	0	4.68
T. Slater	LW	G. Veneruzzo	78	39	29	68	D	B. Crashley	78	4	26	30	I. Wilkie	11	9	0	3.91
5–14–0	LW	S. Sutherland	72	20	12	32	D	J. Niekamp	76	2	19	21	R. Gillow	4	13	0	3.98
T. McCaskill	C	J. LeBlanc	78	20	46	66	D	J. Zrymiak	27	2	8	10	J. McLeod	4	13	0	4.27
20–39–0	C	B. McDonald	56	22	30	52	D	B. Horton	60	0	9	9	G. Gardner	0	2	0	6.50
	C	R. Ward	40	14	19	33											
	C	R. Thomas	77	14	21	35											
	C	F. Speck	18	2	5	7											
	RW	R. Walters	71	14	14	28											
	RW	A. White	48	8	13	21											
	RW	T. Serviss	74	6	15	21											
	RW	D. Gordon	29	8	6	14											

GOALS		ASSISTS		POINTS	
M. Walton, MINN	57	A. Lacroix, NY–NJ	80	M. Walton, MINN	117
B. Hull, WINN	53	G. Howe, HOUS	69	A. Lacroix, NY–NJ	111
D. Lawson, VAN	50	B. Campbell, VAN	62	G. Howe, HOUS	100
T. Webster, NE	43	M. Walton, MINN	60	B. Hull, WINN	95
W. Connelly, MINN	42	A. Hinse, HOUS	56	W. Connelly, MINN	95
F. Hughes, HOUS	42				

PENALTY MINUTES		GOALS AGAINST AVE.		SHUTOUTS	
G. Gallant, MINN	223	D. McLeod, HOUS	2.56	G. Cheevers, CLEVE	4
D. Barrie, EDM	214	G. Cheevers, CLEVE	3.03	D. McLeod, HOUS	3
J. Arbour, MINN	192	A. Smith, NE	3.08	E. Wakely, WINN	3
C. Campbell, VAN	191	C. Newton, CHI	3.14	P. Donnelly, VAN	3
J. Cardiff, VAN	188	J. Norris, EDM	3.21		

World Hockey Association 1974–75

TEAM	W	L	T	PTS	GF	GA
CANADIAN DIVISION						
QUE	46	32	0	92	331	299
TOR	43	33	2	88	349	304
WINN	38	35	5	81	322	293
VAN	37	39	2	76	256	270
EDM	36	38	4	76	279	279
WESTERN DIVISION						
HOUS	53	25	0	106	**369**	**247**
SD	43	31	4	90	326	268
MINN	42	33	3	87	308	279
PHOE	39	31	8	86	300	265
M–B	21	53	4	46	205	341

TEAM	W	L	T	PTS	GF	GA
EASTERN DIVISION						
NE	43	30	5	91	274	279
CLEVE	35	40	3	73	236	258
CHI	30	47	1	61	261	312
IND	18	57	3	39	216	338

CANADIAN DIVISION

TEAM	POS	PLAYER	GP	G	A	PTS	POS	PLAYER	GP	G	A	PTS	GOALIE	W	L	T	GAvg
QUE	LW	M. Tardif	53	38	34	72	D	J. Tremblay	68	16	56	72	R. Brodeur	29	21	0	3.90
J. Gendron	LW	S. Sutherland	56	14	15	29	D	D. Hoganson	78	9	35	44	S. Aubry	17	11	0	3.71
46–32–0	LW	B. Guindon	69	12	18	30	D	R. Jordan	56	6	8	14					
	LW	M. Parizeau	78	28	46	74	D	J. Bernier	34	1	13	14					
	C	J. Gilbert	58	7	21	28	D	P. Roy	61	1	18	19					
	C	C. Bordeleau	53	15	33	48											
	C	R. Leclerc	73	18	32	50											
	RW	R. Houle	64	40	52	92											
	RW	S. Bernier	76	54	68	122											
	RW	R. Cloutier	63	26	27	53											
TOR	LW	F. Mahovlich	73	38	44	82	D	J. Dorey	43	11	23	34	G. Gratton	30	20	1	3.85
B. Harris	LW	P. Hickey	74	34	34	68	D	J. Turkiewicz	78	3	27	30	J. Shaw	7	9	1	3.98
22–17–1	LW	P. Henderson	58	30	33	63	D	M. Amodeo	64	1	13	14	L. Binkley	6	4	0	3.58
B. LeDuc	LW	L. Nistico	29	11	11	22	D	R. Cunningham	71	7	18	25					
21–16–1	C	W. Dillon	77	29	66	95	D	B. Gibbons	73	4	22	26					
	C	G. Kirk	78	15	58	73											
	RW	N. Nedomansky	78	41	40	81											
	RW	T. Simpson	70	52	28	80											
	RW	T. Featherstone	76	25	38	63											
WINN	LW	B. Hull	78	**77**	65	142	D	L. Sjoberg	75	7	53	60	J. Daley	23	21	4	3.62
R. Pilous	LW	D. Gruen	32	9	12	21	D	H. Young	42	13	10	23	C. Larsson	12	11	1	3.96
18–17–2	LW	D. Johnson	78	18	14	32	D	M. Ford	73	12	22	34	E. Wakely	3	3	0	2.70
B. Hull	LW	H. Riihiranta	64	8	14	22	D	L. Hornung	69	7	25	32					
4–9–0	C	C. Bordeleau	18	8	8	16	D	P. Miller	67	9	19	28					
R. Pilous	C	U. Nilsson	78	26	94	120	D	A. Beaule	54	0	14	14					
16–9–3	C	V. Ketola	74	23	28	51											
	C	D. Spring	60	19	24	43											
	RW	A. Hedberg	65	53	47	100											
	RW	N. Beaudin	77	16	31	47											
VAN	LW	H. Harris	58	23	34	57	D	M. Pelyk	75	14	26	40	D. McLeod	**33**	**35**	2	3.34
J. Crozier	LW	D. Burgess	62	11	18	29	D	P. Price	69	5	29	34	W. Wood	4	4	0	3.52
37–39–2	LW	L. Israelson	46	12	9	21	D	D. Rupp	72	3	26	29					
	C	B. Campbell	78	29	34	63	D	P. Terbenche	60	3	14	17					
	C	R. Walton	75	24	33	57	D	D. McCulloch	51	1	9	10					
	C	C. St. Sauveur	76	24	23	47											
	C	R. Chipperfield	78	19	20	39											
	RW	D. Lawson	78	33	43	76											
	RW	J. McKenzie	74	23	37	60											
	RW	R. Jodzio	44	1	3	4											

	POS	PLAYER	GP	G	A	PTS	PLAYER	GP	G	A	PTS	GOALIE	W	L	T	GAvg
EDM	LW	K. Baird	77	30	28	59	D B. Long	78	20	40	60	K. Brown	10	11	0	3.48
	LW	T. Gilmore	74	12	19	31	D S. Carlyle	73	4	25	29	J. Plante	15	14	1	3.32
B. Shaw	C	M. Rogers	78	35	48	83	D D. Barrie	78	12	33	45	C. Worthy	11	13	3	3.58
30–26–3	C	B. Sheehan	77	19	39	58	D R. McKay	69	8	20	28					
B. Hunter	C	E. Joyal	78	22	25	47	D A. Hamilton	25	1	13	14					
6–12–1	RW	B. MacGregor	72	24	28	52										
	RW	B. MacDonald	72	22	24	46										
	RW	R. Patenaude	56	20	16	36										
	RW	T. Sheehy	29	8	20	28										

EASTERN DIVISION

	POS	PLAYER	GP	G	A	PTS	PLAYER	GP	G	A	PTS	GOALIE	W	L	T	GAvg
NE	LW	D. Blackburn	50	18	32	50	D R. Ley	62	6	36	42	A. Smith	**33**	21	4	3.47
	LW	N. Fotiu	61	2	2	4	D B. Selwood	77	4	35	39	C. Abrahamsson	8	6	1	3.24
R. Ryan	LW	R. Climie	25	8	4	12	D P. Hurley	75	3	26	29	B. Landon	2	3	0	3.36
40–28–5	C	L. Pleau	78	30	34	64	D T. Green	57	6	14	20	B. Berglund	0	0	0	5.00
J. Kelley	C	J. French	75	12	41	53	D T. Abrahamsson	76	8	22	30	T. Ouimet	0	0	0	9.00
3–2–0	C	T. Caffery	67	15	37	52										
	RW	T. Webster	66	40	24	64										
	RW	M. Byers	72	22	26	48										
	RW	F. O'Donnell	76	21	15	36										
CLEVE	LW	G. Jarrett	77	17	24	41	D T. Edur	61	3	20	23	G. Cheevers	26	24	2	3.26
	LW	G. Pinder	74	13	28	41	D P. Shmyr	49	7	14	21	B. Whidden	9	16	1	3.23
J. Hanna	LW	G. Erickson	78	12	15	27	D R. Clearwater	66	4	18	22					
14–18–1	LW	S. Cardwell	75	9	13	22	D J. Muloin	78	4	17	21					
J. Vivian	C	R. LeDuc	78	34	31	65	D L. Hillman	77	0	16	16					
21–22–2	C	J. Harrison	60	20	22	42	D W. Hillman	60	2	9	11					
	C	R. Ward	73	30	32	62										
	C	J. Stewart	59	4	7	11										
	RW	A. McDonough	78	34	30	64										
	RW	S. Krake	71	15	23	38										
	RW	R. Walker	66	14	11	25										
	RW	T. Holbrook	78	10	13	23										
CHI	LW	F. Rochon	69	27	29	56	D P. Stapleton	68	4	30	34	D. Dryden	18	26	1	3.87
	LW	B. Liddington	78	23	18	41	D D. Maggs	77	6	27	33	C. Newton	12	20	0	3.97
P. Stapleton	LW	J. Popiel	60	18	22	40	D B. Baltimore	77	8	12	20	R. Coutu	0	1	0	5.00
30–47–1	LW	R. Morris	78	15	13	28	D J. Watson	57	3	6	9	R. Dumas	0	0	0	0.00
	C	G. MacGregor	78	44	34	78										
	C	R. Backstrom	70	15	24	39										
	C	B. Coates	35	12	9	21										
	C	R. Zaine	68	3	6	9										
	RW	R. Paiement	78	26	48	74										
	RW	D. Harris	54	9	19	28										
	RW	D. Gordon	42	4	5	9										
	RW	J. Benzelock	10	0	2	2										
IND	LW	J. Wiste	75	13	28	41	D B. Ash	64	1	14	15	A. Brown	15	**35**	0	4.15
	LW	K. Bond	71	22	15	37	D K. Block	37	0	17	17	E. Dyck	3	21	3	4.36
G. Moore	LW	J. Johnson	42	7	15	22	D D. Proceviat	52	1	28	29	M. Dion	0	1	0	4.07
18–57–3	LW	R. Pumple	34	4	8	12	D B. Horton	59	2	9	11					
	C	B. Whitlock	73	31	26	57	D B. Woytowich	42	0	8	8					
	C	B. Sicinski	77	19	34	53										
	C	R. Buchanan	32	16	15	31										
	RW	N. Harbaruk	78	20	23	43										
	RW	B. McDonald	47	14	15	29										
	RW	M. Heatley	29	15	8	23										

WESTERN DIVISION

	POS	PLAYER	GP	G	A	PTS	PLAYER	GP	G	A	PTS	GOALIE	W	L	T	GAvg
HOUS	LW	A. Hinse	75	39	47	86	D P. Popiel	78	11	53	64	R. Grahame	**33**	10	0	**3.03**
	LW	M. Howe	74	36	40	76	D J. Schella	78	10	42	52	W. Rutledge	20	15	0	3.23
B. Dineen	LW	T. Taylor	73	26	27	53	D M. Howe	75	13	21	34					
53–25–0	C	L. Lund	78	33	75	108	D L. Hale	76	2	18	20					
	C	M. Hall	78	18	29	47	D G. Irwin	70	2	11	13					
	C	T. Ruskowski	71	10	36	46										
	RW	G. Howe	75	34	65	99										
	RW	F. Hughes	76	48	35	83										
	RW	G. Labossierre	76	23	34	57										
SD	LW	D. Sentes	74	44	41	85	D K. Morrison	78	20	61	81	E. Wakely	20	12	2	3.35
	LW	K. Devine	46	4	10	14	D R. Plumb	78	10	38	48	R. Gillow	15	11	2	3.41
H. Howell	LW	T. Scharf	67	3	1	4	D J. Hargreaves	41	8	10	18	J. Junkin	6	7	0	3.29
43–31–4	LW	B. Bradley	24	4	5	9	D B. Wall	33	0	9	9	B. Blanchet	2	1	0	2.35
	C	A. Lacroix	78	41	**106**	**147**	D H. Howell	74	4	10	14					
	C	G. Peacosh	78	43	36	79										
	C	R. Adduono	78	15	59	74										
	RW	W. Rivers	78	54	53	107										
	RW	N. Ferguson	78	36	33	69										
	RW	B. Morenz	78	20	19	39										

	POS	PLAYER	GP	G	A	PTS		PLAYER	GP	G	A	PTS	GOALIE	W	L	T	GAvg
MINN	LW	G. Gambucci	67	19	18	37	D	R. Busniuk	73	2	21	23	J. Garrett	30	23	2	3.28
H. Neale	LW	G. Morrison	76	31	29	60	D	J. Arbour	71	11	43	54	M. Curran	11	10	1	3.95
42–33–3	LW	D. Tannahill	72	23	30	53	D	B. Butters	24	2	2	4	J. McCartan	1	0	0	4.92
	LW	G. Gallant	66	10	13	23	D	R. Smith	78	9	29	38					
	C	M. Walton	75	48	45	93	D	P. Westrum	23	0	3	3					
	C	F. Huck	78	22	45	67											
	C	T. Hampson	78	17	36	53											
	C	M. Antonovich	67	24	26	50											
	RW	W. Connelly	76	38	33	71											
	RW	D. O'Shea	76	16	25	41											
	RW	D. Asmundson	38	4	15	19											
	RW	K. O'Shea	68	10	10	20											
PHOE	LW	M. Cormier	78	36	38	74	D	G. Odrowski	77	5	38	43	G. Kurt	25	16	4	3.29
S. Hucul	LW	R. Ftorek	53	31	37	68	D	A. McLeod	77	3	16	19	J. Norris	14	15	4	3.27
39–31–8	LW	D. Borgeson	74	29	28	57	D	M. Stevens	70	2	16	18					
	LW	J. Migneault	47	6	13	19	D	W. Bennett	67	4	15	19					
	C	D. Sobchuk	38	32	45	77	D	J. Niekamp	71	2	26	28					
	C	J. Boyd	76	26	44	70											
	C	M. Keogan	78	35	29	64											
	RW	J. Gray	75	35	33	68											
	RW	C. Connor	57	9	19	28											
	RW	B. Mowat	53	9	10	19											
M–B	LW	G. Veneruzzo	77	33	27	60	D	J. Miszuk	66	2	19	21	G. Desjardins	9	28	1	4.26
J. Wilson	LW	P. Guite	13	5	4	9	D	J. Zrymiak	49	3	9	12	P. Hoganson	9	19	2	4.09
21–53–4	LW	G. Trottier	17	5	4	9	D	P. Curtis	76	4	15	19	J. McLeod	3	6	1	4.58
	C	J. LeBlanc	78	16	33	49	D	R. Legge	78	1	14	15					
	C	S. West	50	15	18	33	D	B. Legge	36	3	18	21					
	C	S. Richardson	47	8	18	26											
	C	R. Thomas	50	8	13	21											
	RW	G. Bredin	67	15	21	36											
	RW	T. Serviss	61	12	17	29											
	RW	B. Evo	49	13	9	22											
	RW	A. Caron	47	8	5	13											

GOALS		ASSISTS		POINTS	
B. Hull, WINN	77	A. Lacroix, SD	106	A. Lacroix, SD	147
S. Bernier, QUE	54	U. Nilsson, WINN	94	B. Hull, WINN	142
W. Rivers, SD	54	L. Lund, HOUS	75	S. Bernier, QUE	122
A. Hedberg, WINN	53	S. Bernier, QUE	68	U. Nilsson, WINN	120
T. Simpson, TOR	52	W. Dillon, TOR	66	L. Lund, HOUS	108

PENALTY MINUTES		GOALS AGAINST AVE.		SHUTOUTS	
G. Gallant, MINN	203	R. Grahame, HOUS	3.03	R. Grahame, HOUS	4
J. Hughes, PHOE	201	E. Wakely, WINN, SD	3.25	G. Cheevers, CLEVE	4
R. Busniuk, MINN	176	G. Cheevers, CLEVE	3.26	E. Wakely, WINN, SD	3
J. Schella, HOUS	176	J. Garrett, MINN	3.28		
C. Connor, PHOE	168	G. Kurt, PHOE	3.29		

World Hockey Association 1975–76

TEAM	W	L	T	PTS	GF	GA
CANADIAN DIVISION						
WINN	52	27	2	106	345	254
QUE	50	27	4	104	**371**	316
CALG	41	35	4	86	307	282
EDM	27	49	5	59	268	345
TOR	24	52	5	53	335	398
WESTERN DIVISION						
HOUS	53	27	0	106	341	263
PHOE	39	35	6	84	302	287
SD	36	38	6	78	303	290
MINN	30	25	4	64	211	212
D–O	14	26	1	29	134	172

TEAM	W	L	T	PTS	GF	GA
EASTERN DIVISION						
IND	35	39	6	76	245	**247**
CLEVE	35	40	5	75	273	279
NE	33	40	7	73	255	290
CIN	35	44	1	71	285	340

CANADIAN DIVISION

	POS	PLAYER	GP	G	A	PTS		PLAYER	GP	G	A	PTS	GOALIE	W	L	T	GAvg
WINN	LW	B. Hull	80	53	70	123	D	T. Green	79	5	23	28	J. Daley	41	17	1	**2.84**
B. Kromm	LW	L. Moffat	42	13	9	22	D	L. Hornung	76	3	18	21	C. Larsson	11	10	1	3.87
52–27–2	LW	B. Guindon	39	3	3	6	D	M. Ford	81	13	43	56					
	C	U. Nilsson	78	38	76	114	D	L. Sjoberg	81	5	36	41					
	C	V. Ketola	80	32	36	68											
	C	P. Sullivan	78	32	39	71											
	RW	A. Hedberg	76	50	55	105											
	RW	W. Lindstrom	81	23	36	59											
	RW	B. Lesuk	81	15	21	36											
QUE	LW	M. Tardif	81	**71**	**77**	**148**	D	J. Tremblay	80	12	**77**	89	R. Brodeur	**44**	21	2	3.69
J. Gendron	LW	S. Sutherland	74	22	19	41	D	P. Roy	78	6	30	36	M. Deguise	6	5	2	4.35
50–27–4	LW	G. Gallant	64	4	15	19	D	J. Bernier	81	4	26	30	P. Donnelly	0	1	0	4.65
	LW	C. Constantin	41	8	7	15	D	D. Hoganson	45	3	14	17					
	C	T. Serviss	71	7	19	26	D	R. Jordan	54	4	7	11					
	C	T. Hampson	14	4	10	14											
	RW	R. Cloutier	80	60	54	114											
	RW	R. Houle	81	51	52	103											
	RW	S. Bernier	70	34	68	102											
CALG	LW	G. Morrison	79	25	32	57	D	J. Miszuk	69	2	21	23	D. McLeod	30	27	3	3.50
J. Crozier	LW	B. Deadmarsh	79	26	28	54	D	F. Lacombe	71	3	28	31	W. Wood	9	3	1	3.07
41–35–4	LW	D. Sentes	72	25	24	49	D	C. Evans	75	3	20	23	E. Humphreys	2	5	0	3.67
	LW	P. Driscoll	75	16	18	34	D	D. McLeod	63	0	13	13					
	C	R. Chipperfield	75	42	41	83											
	C	D. Tannahill	78	25	24	49											
	C	B. Leiter	51	17	17	34											
	C	M. Keogan	38	7	11	18											
	RW	R. DiLorenzi	39	8	12	20											
	RW	D. Lawson	80	44	52	96											
EDM	LW	K. Baird	48	13	24	37	D	B. Long	78	10	32	42	D. Dryden	22	**34**	5	3.95
C. Drake	LW	R. Morris	33	11	15	26	D	D. Barrie	79	4	21	25	C. Worthy	5	14	0	4.68
18–28–2	LW	P. Morris	75	7	13	20	D	A. Hamilton	54	2	32	34	F. Turnbull	0	1	0	5.09
B. Hunter	C	N. Ullman	77	31	56	87	D	P. Hurley	26	1	4	5					
9–21–3	C	B. Russell	58	13	18	31											
	C	B. McAneeley	71	12	16	28											
	C	W. Carleton	26	5	16	21											
	C	S. Krake	41	8	8	16											
	RW	R. Patenaude	77	42	30	72											
	RW	T. Sheehy	81	34	31	65											
TOR	LW	F. Mahovlich	75	34	55	89	D	J. Dorey	74	9	51	60	M. Vien	4	14	3	5.13
B. Baun	LW	P. Henderson	65	26	29	55	D	J. Turkiewicz	77	9	29	38	D. Tataryn	7	12	1	4.76
15–35–5	LW	L. Nistico	65	12	22	34	D	J. Rollins	52	5	7	12	J. Shaw	4	7	1	4.86
G. Leger	C	D. Farda	63	19	35	54	D	M. Amodeo	31	4	8	12	W. Wood	6	7	0	4.76
9–17–0	C	G. Kirk	62	29	38	67							L. Binkley	0	6	0	5.73
	C	N. Nedomansky	81	56	42	98							J. Garrett	3	6	0	3.59
	C	S. Atkinson	52	2	6	8											
	C	B. D'Alvise	59	5	8	13											
	RW	M. Napier	78	43	50	93											
	RW	T. Featherstone	32	4	7	11											
	RW	T. Simpson	73	20	21	41											

EASTERN DIVISION

	POS	PLAYER	GP	G	A	PTS		PLAYER	GP	G	A	PTS	GOALIE	W	L	T	GAvg
IND	LW	B. Coates	59	11	16	27	D	P. Stapleton	80	4	40	44	M. Dion	14	15	1	2.74
J. Demers	LW	F. Rochon	19	6	2	8	D	D. Maggs	36	5	16	21	A. Brown	9	11	2	3.60
35–39–6	C	A. Karlander	79	19	26	45	D	K. Block	79	1	25	26	L. Holmquist	6	9	3	3.00
	C	B. Sicinski	70	9	34	43	D	D. Proceviat	73	7	13	20	J. Park	6	4	0	2.41
	C	M. Parizeau	23	13	15	28											
	C	R. Thomas	80	23	17	40											
	RW	R. Leclerc	40	18	21	39											
	RW	B. MacDonald	56	20	11	31											
	RW	N. Harbaruk	76	23	19	42											
	RW	B. McDonald	62	15	18	33											
CLEVE	LW	D. Gruen	80	26	24	50	D	P. Shmyr	70	6	44	50	G. Cheevers	11	14	1	3.63
J. Wilson	LW	J. Stewart	79	12	21	33	D	P. Baxter	67	3	7	10	B. Whidden	7	11	2	3.41
35–40–5	LW	G. Jarrett	69	16	17	33	D	T. Edur	80	7	28	35	B. Johnson	9	8	0	3.22
	LW	J. Tamminen	65	7	14	21	D	R. Legge	44	1	8	9	C. Newton	7	7	1	3.21
	C	R. Ward	75	32	50	82	D	B. Maxwell	73	3	14	17	J. Caron	1	0	1	3.69
	C	R. LeDuc	79	36	22	58											
	RW	G. Pinder	79	21	30	51											
	RW	A. McDonough	80	23	22	45											
	RW	R. Walker	72	23	15	38											

	POS	PLAYER	GP	G	A	PTS		PLAYER	GP	G	A	PTS	GOALIE	W	L	T	GAvg
NE	LW	A. Hangsleben	78	2	23	25	D	R. Ley	67	8	30	38	C. Abrahamsson	18	18	2	3.42
J. Kelley	LW	D. Borgeson	31	9	8	17	D	T. Abrahamsson	63	14	21	35	B. Landon	14	19	5	3.47
14–16–3	LW	D. Bolduc	14	2	5	7	D	G. Roberts	77	3	19	22	P. Hoganson	1	2	0	4.29
D. Blackburn	C	L. Pleau	75	29	45	74	D	B. Selwood	40	2	10	12	C. Raeder	0	1	0	4.80
14–18–3	C	R. Backstrom	38	14	19	33	D	D. Roberts	76	4	13	17					
H. Neale	C	M. Rogers	36	18	14	32											
5–6–1	RW	T. Webster	55	33	50	83											
	RW	R. Paiement	80	28	43	71											
	RW	F. O'Donnell	79	11	11	22											
CIN	LW	R. Dudley	74	43	38	81	D	R. Plumb	80	10	36	46	P. Hoganson	19	24	0	3.64
T. Slater	LW	C. Larose	79	28	24	52	D	J. Hughes	79	3	34	37	J. Kiely	6	8	1	4.31
35–44–1	LW	P. Guite	52	20	24	44	D	T. Ball	36	3	14	17	S. Aubry	6	4	0	4.15
	LW	G. Sobchuk	78	24	19	43	D	M. Pelyk	75	10	23	33	N. LaPointe	4	6	0	5.15
	LW	D. Smedsmo	66	8	14	22	D	D. Inkpen	80	4	24	28	R. Coutu	0	2	0	6.85
	C	J. Locas	80	27	46	73											
	C	B. Campbell	77	22	50	72											
	C	D. Sobchuk	79	32	40	72											
	C	B. MacNeil	77	15	12	27											
	RW	M. Myers	56	14	15	29											

WESTERN DIVISION

	POS	PLAYER	GP	G	A	PTS		PLAYER	GP	G	A	PTS	GOALIE	W	L	T	GAvg
HOUS	LW	M. Howe	72	39	37	76	D	P. Popiel	78	10	36	46	R. Grahame	39	17	0	3.27
B. Dineen	LW	A. Hinse	70	35	38	73	D	J. Schella	74	6	32	38	W. Rutledge	14	10	0	3.17
53–27–0	LW	T. Taylor	68	15	26	41	D	M. Howe	80	14	23	37					
	LW	J. Tonelli	79	17	14	31	D	L. Hale	77	2	12	14					
	C	L. Lund	73	24	49	73	D	J. Popiel	67	4	7	11					
	C	T. Ruskowski	65	14	35	49											
	RW	G. Howe	78	32	70	102											
	RW	M. Hall	80	20	26	46											
	RW	F. Hughes	80	31	45	76											
PHOE	LW	R. Ftorek	80	41	72	113	D	G. Lariviere	79	7	17	24	J. Norris	21	14	4	3.18
S. Hucul	LW	G. Veneruzzo	61	19	24	43	D	S. Beaudoin	76	0	21	21	G. Kurt	18	20	2	3.72
39–35–6	LW	M. Cormier	46	21	15	36	D	A. McLeod	80	2	17	19	C. Hebenton	0	1	0	6.75
	LW	B. Dean	71	9	25	34	D	J. Niekamp	79	4	14	18					
	C	J. Boyd	80	23	34	57	D	J. Clarke	59	1	9	10					
	C	R. Huston	79	22	44	66											
	RW	J. Gray	79	35	45	80											
	RW	C. Connor	73	18	21	39											
	RW	D. Gorman	67	11	20	31											
SD	LW	K. Devine	80	21	28	49	D	K. Morrison	80	22	43	65	E. Wakely	35	27	4	3.26
R. Ingram	LW	D. Burgess	73	14	11	25	D	B. Hughes	78	7	28	35	R. Gillow	1	10	2	4.28
36–38–6	LW	J. French	76	25	39	64	D	B. Wall	68	1	20	21	B. Blanchet	0	1	0	7.50
	C	A. Lacroix	80	29	72	101	D	M. McMahon	69	2	12	14					
	C	R. Adduono	82	23	67	90											
	C	G. Peacosh	79	37	33	70											
	C	J. Noris	80	28	40	68											
	RW	N. Ferguson	79	37	37	74											
	RW	W. Rivers	71	19	25	44											
	RW	A. Tidey	74	16	11	27											
MINN	LW	J. Tetreault	3	0	0	0	D	R. Smith	51	1	32	33	J. Garrett	26	22	4	3.34
H. Neale	LW	S. Carlson	10	0	1	1	D	J. Arbour	7	0	4	4	M. Curran	2	2	0	5.50
30–25–4	C	M. Walton	58	31	40	71							L. Levasseur	2	1	0	3.11
	C	F. Huck	59	17	32	49											
	C	M. Antonovich	57	25	21	46											
	C	B. Boudreau	30	3	6	9											
	RW	W. Connelly	59	24	23	47											
	RW	H. Boucha	36	15	20	35											
	RW	J. Carlson	58	8	10	18											
	RW	P. Holmgren	51	14	16	30											
D–O	LW	B. Lavender	37	2	0	2	D	J. Arbour	34	2	13	15	B. Johnson	8	13	1	3.96
J. Talbot	LW	B. Goldthorpe	12	0	0	0	D	B. Baltimore	41	1	8	9	C. Newton	4	6	0	3.66
14–26–1	LW	R. Morris	40	9	16	25	D	L. Bignell	41	5	5	10	L. Zimmerman	2	6	0	3.76
	C	R. Backstrom	41	21	29	50							C. Grigg	0	0	0	9.75
	C	J. Sherrit	40	11	19	30							N. Sanza	0	1	0	15.00
	C	P. Mara	40	3	7	10											
	C	J. LeBlanc	15	1	5	6											
	RW	R. Delorme	22	1	3	4											
	RW	M. Lomenda	37	6	16	22											
	RW	B. Liddington	35	7	8	15											

GOALS		ASSISTS		POINTS	
M. Tardif, QUE	71	M. Tardif, QUE	77	M. Tardif, QUE	148
R. Cloutier, QUE	60	J. Tremblay, QUE	77	B. Hull, WINN	123
N. Nedomansky, TOR	56	U. Nilsson, WINN	76	R. Cloutier, QUE	114
B. Hull, WINN	53	R. Ftorek, PHOE	72	U. Nilsson, WINN	114
R. Houle, QUE	51	C. Bordeleau, QUE	72	R. Ftorek, PHOE	113

PENALTY MINUTES		GOALS AGAINST AVE.		SHUTOUTS	
C. Brackenbury MINN, QUE	365	J. Daley, WINN	2.84	J. Daley, WINN	5
K. Clackson, IND	351	J. Norris, PHOE	3.18	R. Grahame, HOUS	3
G. Gallant, QUE	297	E. Wakely, SD	3.26	E. Wakely, SD	3
C. Connor, PHOE	295	R. Grahame, HOUS	3.27	J. Garrett, MINN, TOR	3
P. Roy, QUE	258	J. Garrett, MINN, TOR	3.34		

World Hockey Association 1976–77

TEAM	W	L	T	PTS	GF	GA	TEAM	W	L	T	PTS	GF	GA
EASTERN DIVISION							WESTERN DIVISION						
QUE	47	31	3	97	353	295	HOUS	50	24	6	106	320	**241**
CIN	39	37	5	83	354	303	WINN	46	32	2	94	**366**	291
IND	36	37	8	80	276	305	SD	40	37	4	84	284	283
NE	35	40	6	76	275	290	EDM	34	43	4	72	243	304
BIRM	31	46	4	66	289	309	CALG	31	43	7	69	252	296
MINN	19	18	5	43	136	129	PHOE	28	48	4	60	281	383

EASTERN DIVISION

TEAM	POS	PLAYER	GP	G	A	PTS	POS	PLAYER	GP	G	A	PTS	GOALIE	W	L	T	GAvg
QUE	LW	M. Tardif	62	49	60	109	D	J. Tremblay	53	4	31	35	R. Brodeur	29	18	2	3.45
M. Boileau	LW	C. Constantin	77	14	19	33	D	G. Lariviere	15	0	3	3	E. Humphreys	12	8	1	3.58
47–31–3	LW	N. Dube	39	15	18	33	D	F. Lacombe	81	5	22	27	S. Aubry	6	5	0	3.98
	C	C. Bordeleau	72	32	75	107	D	P. Baxter	66	6	17	23					
	C	S. Bernier	74	43	53	96	D	J. Bernier	72	2	13	15					
	C	A. Boudrias	74	12	31	43	D	B. Fitchner	81	9	30	39					
	RW	R. Cloutier	76	66	75	**141**	D	W. Weir	69	3	17	20					
	RW	P. Bordeleau	80	42	41	83											
	RW	C. Brackenbury	77	16	13	29											
CIN	LW	R. Dudley	77	41	47	88	D	R. Plumb	79	11	58	69	N. LaPointe	21	25	2	3.73
T. Slater	LW	C. Larose	81	30	46	76	D	J. Hughes	79	3	27	30	J. Caron	13	6	2	2.83
39–37–5	LW	D. Smedsmo	23	0	5	5	D	B. Legge	74	7	22	29	P. Hoganson	5	6	1	4.67
	C	R. LeDuc	81	52	55	107	D	P. Roy	39	3	12	15					
	C	D. Sobchuk	81	44	52	96	D	F. Ouimet	16	1	8	9					
	C	G. Carroll	77	15	39	54	D	B. Melrose	29	1	4	5					
	RW	B. Stoughton	81	52	52	104											
	RW	D. Abgrall	80	23	39	62											
	RW	P. Marsh	76	23	28	51											
IND	LW	G. Peacosh	64	22	26	48	D	P. Stapleton	81	8	45	53	M. Dion	17	19	3	3.36
J. Demers	LW	H. Harris	46	21	35	56	D	D. Inkpen	32	4	12	16	J. Park	14	12	4	3.96
36–37–8	LW	R. Thomas	79	25	30	55	D	G. MacGregor	16	0	5	5	P. Hoganson	3	2	0	3.65
	C	D. Maggs	81	16	55	71	D	B. Baltimore	55	0	15	15	A. Brown	1	4	1	3.63
	C	M. Parizeau	75	18	37	55	D	D. Proceviat	55	2	12	14	R. Burchell	1	0	0	3.53
	RW	B. MacDonald	81	34	30	64	D	K. Block	52	3	10	13					
	RW	R. Leclerc	68	25	30	55											
	RW	R. Paiement	67	18	25	43											
NE	LW	G. Lyle	75	39	33	72	D	G. Roberts	77	13	33	46	C. Abrahamsson	15	22	4	3.84
H. Neale	LW	M. Antonovich	26	12	9	21	D	T. Abrahamsson	64	6	24	30	C. Raeder	12	10	1	3.12
35–40–6	LW	D. Hynes	22	5	4	9	D	T. Earl	54	9	14	23	B. Landon	8	8	1	3.17
	C	D. Keon	34	14	25	39	D	R. Ley	55	2	21	23					
	C	M. Rogers	78	25	57	82	D	A. Hangsleben	74	13	9	22					
	C	R. Backstrom	77	17	31	48	D	D. Roberts	64	3	18	21					
	RW	T. Webster	70	36	49	85	D	B. Selwood	41	4	12	16					
	RW	J. McKenzie	34	11	19	30											
BIRM	LW	L. Nistico	79	20	36	56	D	J. Turkiewicz	80	6	25	31	J. Garrett	24	**34**	4	3.53
G. Leger	LW	P. Henderson	81	23	25	48	D	R. McKay	19	0	1	1	W. Wood	7	12	0	4.13
7–16–1	LW	D. Farda	48	9	26	35	D	T. Ball	23	1	6	7					
P. Kelly	C	N. Nedomansky	81	36	33	69	D	D. Syvret	8	0	0	0					
24–30–3	C	P. Marrin	79	23	37	60	D	D. Hoganson	81	7	48	55					
	RW	T. Sheehy	50	26	21	47											
	RW	J. Jacques	79	21	27	48											

TEAM	POS	PLAYER	GP	G	A	PTS	PLAYER	GP	G	A	PTS	GOALIE	W	L	T	GAvg
MINN	LW	B. Deadmarsh	35	9	4	13	D J. Arbour	33	3	19	22	L. Levasseur	15	11	2	2.73
G. Sonmor	LW	G. Gallant	34	6	3	9	D B. Butters	42	0	7	7	M. Curran	4	7	3	3.54
19–18–5	LW	D. Gruen	34	10	9	19	D P. Westrum	40	1	9	10					
	LW	J. Stewart	15	3	3	6	D J. Zrymiak	40	2	10	12					
	C	D. Keon	42	13	38	51										
	C	R. Ward	41	15	21	36										
	C	R. Adduono	40	4	19	23										
	C	M. Antonovich	42	27	21	48										
	RW	A. McDonough	42	9	21	30										
	RW	J. McKenzie	40	17	13	30										
	RW	C. Patrick	30	6	11	17										

WESTERN DIVISION

TEAM	POS	PLAYER	GP	G	A	PTS	PLAYER	GP	G	A	PTS	GOALIE	W	L	T	GAvg
HOUS	LW	M. Howe	57	23	52	75	D M. Howe	80	17	28	45	W. Rutledge	23	14	4	3.15
B. Dineen	LW	M. Lukowich	62	27	18	45	D L. Hale	67	0	14	14	R. Grahame	27	10	2	**2.74**
50–24–6	C	T. Ruskowski	80	24	60	84	D G. Irwin	44	2	4	6					
	C	L. Lund	80	29	38	67	D J. Schella	20	0	6	6					
	C	J. Tonelli	80	24	31	55	D D. Pentland	29	1	2	3					
	RW	R. Preston	80	38	41	79										
	RW	G. Howe	62	24	44	68										
	RW	C. Connor	76	35	32	67										
WINN	LW	B. Hull	34	21	32	53	D B. Long	71	9	38	47	J. Daley	**39**	23	2	3.24
B. Kromm	LW	D. Labraaten	64	24	27	51	D P. Miller	74	14	31	45	C. Larsson	7	9	0	4.83
46–32–2	LW	B. Lesuk	78	14	27	41	D L. Sjoberg	52	2	38	40					
	C	U. Nilsson	71	39	**85**	124	D T. Bergman	42	2	24	26					
	C	P. Sullivan	78	31	52	83	D T. Green	70	4	21	25					
	C	M. Lindh	73	14	17	31	D H. Riihiranta	53	1	16	17					
	RW	A. Hedberg	68	**70**	61	131										
	RW	W. Lindstrom	79	44	36	80										
	RW	D. Lawson	14	6	7	13										
SD	LW	K. Devine	81	30	20	50	D P. Shmyr	81	13	37	50	E. Wakely	22	18	3	3.09
R. Ingram	LW	D. Sentes	24	10	11	21	D K. Morrison	75	8	30	38	K. Lockett	18	19	1	7.76
40–37–4	LW	D. Burgess	77	20	22	42	D B. Hughes	62	4	13	17					
	LW	J. French	44	14	21	35	D L. Hornung	58	4	9	13					
	C	A. Lacroix	81	32	82	114										
	C	J. Noris	73	35	57	92										
	C	B. Dobek	58	7	17	24										
	C	B. Rhiness	58	9	14	23										
	RW	N. Ferguson	77	39	32	71										
	RW	W. Rivers	60	18	31	49										
EDM	LW	G. Sather	81	19	34	53	D A. Hamilton	81	8	37	45	K. Broderick	18	18	1	3.49
B. Guidolin	LW	R. Morris	79	18	17	35	D F. Beaton	68	4	9	13	D. Dryden	10	13	0	3.26
25–36–2	C	N. Ullman	67	16	27	43	D B. Wilkins	51	4	24	28	L. Levasseur	6	12	3	4.35
G. Sather	C	C. St. Sauveur	15	5	7	12	D D. Barrie	70	8	19	27					
9–7–2	C	B. Russell	57	7	6	13	D D. Langevin	77	7	16	23					
	RW	B. Flett	48	34	20	54	D G. Boddy	64	2	19	21					
	RW	R. Patenaude	73	25	16	41	D R. Busniuk	84	3	11	14					
	RW	W. Connelly	38	13	15	28	D G. Patrick	23	0	4	4					
CALG	LW	P. Driscoll	76	23	29	52	D M. Ford	76	8	34	42	D. McLeod	25	**34**	5	3.40
J. Crozier	LW	B. Deadmarsh	38	13	17	30	D J. Arbour	37	1	15	16	G. Bromley	6	9	2	3.83
31–43–7	LW	D. Kryskow	45	16	17	33	D C. Evans	81	7	27	34					
	C	V. Ketola	17	4	6	10	D P. Terbenche	80	9	24	33					
	C	R. Chipperfield	81	27	27	54	D J. Miszuk	79	2	26	28					
	RW	W. Miller	80	23	32	55										
	RW	R. Jodzio	46	4	6	10										
PHOE	LW	B. Liddington	80	20	24	44	D P. Rautakallio	78	4	31	35	C. Hebenton	17	29	3	4.22
A. Rollins	LW	J. Tamminen	65	10	29	39	D S. Beaudoin	77	6	24	30	G. Kurt	11	19	1	5.55
28–48–4	LW	M. Cormier	58	13	16	29	D J. Niekamp	79	1	15	16					
	C	R. Ftorek	80	46	71	117	D J. Rollins	71	4	10	14					
	C	M. Hobin	68	17	18	35	D D. Bray	46	2	6	8					
	RW	F. Hughes	48	24	29	53										
	RW	L. Mononen	67	21	29	50										
	RW	H. Young	26	1	3	4										

GOALS		ASSISTS		POINTS	
A. Hedberg, WINN	70	U. Nilsson, WINN	85	R. Cloutier, QUE	141
R. Cloutier, QUE	66	A. Lacroix, SD	82	A. Hedberg, WINN	131
M. Napier, BIRM	60	R. Cloutier, QUE	75	U. Nilsson, WINN	124
R. LeDuc, CIN	52	C. Bordeleau, QUE	75	R. Ftorek, PHOE	117
B. Stoughton, CIN	52	R. Ftorek, PHOE	71	A. Lacroix, SD	114

PENALTY MINUTES		GOALS AGAINST AVE.		SHUTOUTS	
F. Beaton, EDM	274	R. Grahame, HOUS	2.74	J. Garrett, BIRM	4
P. Baxter, QUE	244	J. Caron, CIN	2.83	K. Broderick, EDM	4
R. Busniuk NE, EDM	224	E. Wakely, SD	3.09	R. Grahame, HOUS	4
C. Connor, HOUS	224	C. Raeder, NE	3.12		
B. Butters, MINN, EDM, NE	215	W. Rutledge, HOUS	3.15		

World Hockey Association 1977–78

TEAM	W	L	T	PTS	GF	GA
WINN	50	28	2	102	**381**	270
NE	44	31	5	93	335	**269**
HOUS	42	34	4	88	296	302
QUE	40	37	3	83	349	347
EDM	38	39	3	79	309	307
BIRM	36	41	3	75	287	314
CIN	35	42	3	73	298	332
IND	24	51	5	53	267	353

	POS	PLAYER	GP	G	A	PTS		PLAYER	GP	G	A	PTS	GOALIE	W	L	T	GAvg
WINN	LW	B. Hull	77	46	71	117	D	T. Bergman	65	5	28	33	G. Bromley	25	12	1	3.30
L. Hillman	LW	D. Kryskow	71	20	21	41	D	L. Hornung	19	1	4	5	J. Daley	21	11	1	3.30
50–28–2	LW	D. Labraaten	47	18	16	34	D	B. Long	78	7	24	31	M. Mattsson	4	5	0	3.52
	LW	L. Moffat	57	9	16	25	D	L. Sjoberg	78	11	39	50					
	C	K. Nilsson	80	42	65	107	D	D. Dunn	66	6	20	26					
	C	U. Nilsson	73	37	**89**	126											
	C	B. Guindon	77	20	22	42											
	RW	A. Hedberg	77	63	59	122											
	RW	W. Lindstrom	77	30	30	60											
	RW	K. Ruhnke	21	8	9	17											
NE	LW	M. Howe	70	30	61	91	D	A. Hangsleben	79	11	18	29	A. Smith	**30**	20	3	**3.22**
H. Neale	LW	M. Antonovich	75	32	35	67	D	M. Howe	75	10	10	20	L. Levasseur	14	11	2	3.30
44–31–5	C	M. Rogers	80	28	43	71	D	B. Selwood	80	6	25	31					
	C	D. Keon	77	24	38	62	D	R. Ley	73	3	41	44					
	C	S. Carlson	38	6	7	13	D	B. Butters	45	1	13	14					
	RW	G. Howe	76	34	62	96											
	RW	J. McKenzie	79	27	29	56											
	RW	T. Sheehy	25	8	11	19											
	RW	G. Lyle	68	30	24	54											
HOUS	LW	M. Lukowich	80	40	35	75	D	S. Campbell	75	8	29	37	E. Wakely	28	18	4	3.24
B. Dineen	LW	J. Gray	77	35	23	58	D	L. Hale	56	2	11	13	L. Zimmerman	10	9	0	4.32
42–34–4	LW	C. Connor	68	21	16	37	D	J. Hughes	79	3	25	28	W. Rutledge	4	7	0	4.45
	C	T. Ruskowski	78	15	57	72	D	J. Schella	63	9	20	29					
	C	A. Lacroix	78	36	77	113	D	P. Popiel	80	6	31	37					
	C	J. Tonelli	65	23	41	64											
	RW	R. Preston	73	25	25	50											
	RW	D. Larway	69	24	35	59											
	RW	R. Hansis	78	13	9	22											
QUE	LW	N. Dube	73	16	31	47	D	J. Tremblay	54	5	37	42	R. Brodeur	18	15	2	3.70
M. Boileau	LW	M. Tardif	78	**65**	**89**	**154**	D	G. Lariviere	80	7	49	56	K. Broderick	9	8	1	4.37
27–30–2	LW	S. Sutherland	75	23	10	33	D	J. Dorey	26	1	9	10	J. Corsi	10	7	0	4.52
M. Filion	C	S. Bernier	58	26	52	78	D	B. Fitchner	72	15	28	43	D. McLeod	2	4	0	4.17
13–7–1	C	C. Bordeleau	26	9	22	31	D	J. Bernier	74	10	32	42	M. Mattsson	1	3	0	6.77
	RW	P. Bordeleau	77	42	23	65	D	P. Baxter	76	6	29	35					
	RW	R. Cloutier	73	56	73	129											
	RW	W. Miller	60	14	24	38											
EDM	LW	B. Callighen	80	20	30	50	D	P. Shmyr	80	9	40	49	D. Dryden	21	23	2	3.49
G. Sather	LW	P. Guite	60	12	21	33	D	A. Hamilton	59	11	43	54	D. McLeod	15	10	1	3.55
38–39–3	LW	R. Rota	53	8	22	30	D	D. Langevin	62	6	22	28	K. Broderick	2	5	0	5.07
	C	R. Chipperfield	80	33	52	85	D	R. McKay	14	1	4	5	F. Turnbull	0	1	0	6.00
	C	B. Campbell	53	7	13	20	D	A. DeMarco	47	6	8	14					
	C	J. Widing	71	18	24	42											
	C	D. Sobchuk	13	6	3	9											
	RW	B. Flett	74	41	28	69											
	RW	N. Ferguson	71	26	21	47											
	RW	B. MacDonald	80	34	34	68											

TEAM	POS	PLAYER	GP	G	A	PTS	PLAYER	GP	G	A	PTS	GOALIE	W	L	T	GAvg
BIRM	LW	F. Mahovlich	72	14	24	38	D S. Durbano	45	6	4	10	J. Garrett	24	**31**	1	3.81
G. Sonmor	LW	D. Gorman	63	19	21	40	D D. Hoganson	43	1	12	13	W. Wood	12	10	2	3.83
36–41–3	LW	D. Hanson	42	7	16	23	D B. Hughes	80	9	35	44					
	C	K. Linseman	71	38	38	76	D J. Turkiewicz	78	3	21	24					
	C	P. Marrin	80	28	43	71	D R. Langway	52	3	18	21					
	C	N. Nedomansky	12	2	3	5										
	RW	M. Napier	79	33	32	65										
	RW	T. Cassolato	77	18	25	43										
	RW	P. Roberto	53	8	20	28										
CIN	LW	R. Dudley	72	30	41	71	D P. Stapleton	65	4	45	49	M. Dion	21	17	1	3.57
J. Demers	LW	H. Harris	45	11	23	34	D B. Legge	78	7	17	24	M. Liut	8	12	0	4.25
35–42–3	LW	D. Abgrall	65	13	11	24	D B. Baltimore	28	2	9	11	N. LaPointe	5	6	1	4.64
	LW	R. Thomas	18	4	2	6	D C. Norwich	65	7	23	30	P. Hoganson	1	2	1	4.42
	C	R. Ftorek	80	59	50	109	D D. Maggs	62	8	20	28	E. Wakely	0	5	0	5.02
	C	D. Debol	9	3	2	5										
	C	G. Carroll	26	6	13	19										
	C	J. Locas	17	0	2	2										
	RW	J. Hislop	80	24	43	67										
	RW	P. Marsh	74	25	25	50										
	RW	B. Gilligan	54	10	14	24										
IND	LW	H. Harris	19	1	7	8	D K. Block	77	1	25	26	G. Inness	14	30	4	4.21
R. Ingram	LW	C. Larose	28	14	16	30	D D. Fortier	54	1	15	16	E. Mio	6	8	0	4.27
16–31–4	LW	K. Devine	76	19	23	42	D G. Marotte	73	3	20	23	J. Park	3	7	0	4.21
B. Goldsworthy	C	R. LeDuc	28	10	15	25	D K. Morrison	75	17	40	57	P. McDuffe	1	6	1	4.34
8–20–1	C	M. Parizeau	70	13	27	40										
	RW	R. Paiement	61	6	24	30										
	RW	R. Patenaude	76	23	19	42										
	RW	B. Stoughton	47	13	13	26										

GOALS		ASSISTS		POINTS	
M. Tardif, QUE	65	M. Tardif, QUE	89	M. Tardif, QUE	154
A. Hedberg, WINN	63	U. Nilsson, WINN	89	R. Cloutier, QUE	129
R. Ftorek, CIN	59	A. Lacroix, HOUS	77	U. Nilsson, WINN	126
R. Cloutier, QUE	56	R. Cloutier, QUE	73	A. Hedberg, WINN	122
B. Hull, WINN	46	B. Hull, WINN	71	B. Hull, WINN	117

PENALTY MINUTES		GOALS AGAINST AVE.		SHUTOUTS	
S. Durbano, BIRM	284	A. Smith, NE	3.22	M. Dion, CIN	4
F. Beaton, BIRM	279	J. Daley, WINN	3.30	L. Levasseur, NE	3
G. Bilodeau, BIRM	258	L. Levasseur, NE	3.30	J. Garrett, BIRM	2
D. Hanson, BIRM	241	G. Bromley, WINN	3.30	D. McLeod, QUE, EDM	2
P. Stewart, CIN	241	E. Wakely, CIN, HOUS	3.41	D. Dryden, EDM	2

World Hockey Association 1978–79

TEAM	W	L	T	PTS	GF	GA
EDM	48	30	2	98	**340**	**266**
QUE	41	34	5	87	288	271
WINN	39	35	6	84	307	306
NE	37	34	9	83	298	287
CIN	33	41	6	72	274	284
BIRM	32	42	6	70	286	311
IND	5	18	2	12	78	130

TEAM	POS	PLAYER	GP	G	A	PTS	PLAYER	GP	G	A	PTS	GOALIE	W	L	T	GAvg
EDM	LW	B. Callighen	71	31	39	70	D P. Shmyr	80	8	39	47	D. Dryden	**41**	17	2	**2.89**
G. Sather	LW	D. Semenko	77	10	14	24	D A. Hamilton	80	6	38	44	E. Mio	7	10	0	3.99
48–30–2	LW	A. Bailey	38	5	4	9	D C. Alexander	54	8	23	31	E. Walsh	0	2	0	3.75
	C	W. Gretzky	52	43	61	104	D D. Langevin	77	6	21	27	H. Kampurri	0	1	0	6.67
	C	R. Chipperfield	55	32	37	69	D J. Micheletti	72	14	33	47					
	C	S. Weir	68	31	30	61										
	RW	P. Driscoll	69	17	23	40										
	RW	D. Hunter	72	7	25	32										
	RW	B. Flett	73	28	36	64										

QUE
J. Demers
41–34–5

POS	PLAYER	GP	G	A	PTS
LW	M. Tardif	74	41	55	96
LW	G. Bilodeau	36	3	6	9
C	S. Bernier	65	36	46	82
C	R. LeDuc	61	30	32	62
C	B. Fitchner	79	10	35	45
RW	R. Cloutier	77	**75**	54	**129**
RW	P. Bordeleau	77	17	12	29
RW	C. Brackenbury	70	13	13	26
D	P. Baxter	76	10	36	46
D	J. Tremblay	56	6	38	44
D	G. Lariviere	50	5	33	38
D	F. Lacombe	78	3	21	24
D	D. Hoganson	69	2	19	21

GOALIE	W	L	T	GAvg
R. Brodeur	25	13	3	3.11
J. Corsi	16	20	1	3.30
L. Levasseur	0	1	1	6.00

WINN
L. Hillman
39–35–6

POS	PLAYER	GP	G	A	PTS
LW	K. Nilsson	78	39	68	107
LW	M. Lukowich	80	65	34	99
C	P. Sullivan	80	46	40	86
C	T. Ruskowski	75	20	66	86
C	R. Eriksson	33	5	10	15
C	B. Guindon	71	8	18	26
RW	R. Preston	80	28	32	60
RW	B. Lesuk	79	17	15	32
RW	L. Moffat	70	14	18	32
D	B. Long	79	5	36	41
D	P. Terbenche	68	3	22	25
D	M. Amodeo	64	4	18	22
D	S. Campbell	74	3	15	18

GOALIE	W	L	T	GAvg
M. Mattsson	25	21	3	3.63
J. Daley	7	11	3	4.30
G. Smith	7	3	0	2.97

NE
B. Dineen
37–34–9

POS	PLAYER	GP	G	A	PTS
LW	M. Howe	77	42	65	107
LW	M. Antonovich	69	20	27	47
LW	G. Lyle	59	17	18	35
LW	J. Douglas	51	6	10	16
C	A. Lacroix	78	32	56	88
C	D. Keon	79	22	43	65
RW	J. McKenzie	76	19	28	47
RW	G. Howe	58	19	24	43
D	B. Selwood	42	4	12	16
D	G. Roberts	79	11	46	57
D	R. Ley	73	7	20	27
D	M. Howe	66	9	15	24
D	R. Plumb	78	4	16	20

GOALIE	W	L	T	GAvg
J. Garrett	20	17	4	3.58
A. Smith	17	17	5	3.31

CIN
F. Smith
33–41–6

POS	PLAYER	GP	G	A	PTS
LW	B. Shutt	65	10	7	17
LW	M. Messier	47	1	10	11
LW	R. Dudley	47	17	20	37
C	R. Ftorek	80	39	**77**	116
C	B. Gilligan	74	17	26	43
C	D. Debol	59	10	27	37
RW	J. Hislop	80	30	40	70
RW	P. Marsh	80	43	23	66
RW	M. Gartner	78	27	25	52
D	C. Norwich	80	6	51	57
D	C. Luksa	78	8	12	20
D	D. Maggs	27	4	14	18
D	B. Baltimore	69	4	10	14
D	B. Melrose	80	2	14	16

GOALIE	W	L	T	GAvg
M. Liut	23	**27**	4	3.47
M. Dion	10	14	2	3.32

BIRM
J. Brophy
32–42–6

POS	PLAYER	GP	G	A	PTS
LW	M. Goulet	78	28	30	58
LW	P. Henderson	76	24	27	51
LW	S. Alley	78	17	24	41
LW	L. Sleigher	62	26	12	38
C	R. Adduono	80	20	33	53
C	J. Stewart	70	24	26	50
C	B. Stephenson	78	23	24	47
C	W. Dillon	64	12	27	39
RW	R. Vaive	75	26	33	59
RW	D. Gorman	60	14	24	38
RW	T. Cassolato	64	13	7	20
D	C. Hartsburg	77	9	40	49
D	R. Ramage	80	12	36	48
D	G. Gingras	60	13	21	34
D	S. Beaudoin	72	5	21	26

GOALIE	W	L	T	GAvg
P. Riggin	16	22	5	3.78
E. Wakely	15	17	1	3.76
W. Wood	1	3	0	4.05

IND
P. Stapleton
5–18–2

POS	PLAYER	GP	G	A	PTS
LW	C. Larose	13	5	8	13
LW	B. Greig	21	3	7	10
LW	K. Nugent	25	2	8	10
LW	G. Leroux	10	0	3	3
C	G. MacGregor	17	8	4	12
C	D. Morrow	10	2	10	12
C	C. St. Sauveur	17	4	2	6
C	A. Moretto	18	3	1	4
RW	D. Larway	25	8	10	18
RW	D. Burgess	3	1	1	2
RW	R. Leclerc	22	5	7	12
RW	P. Driscoll	8	3	1	4
RW	D. Magee	5	0	1	1
D	D. Inkpen	25	1	8	9
D	L. Sacharuk	15	2	9	11
D	A. McLeod	25	0	11	11
D	K. Block	22	2	3	5
D	G. Irwin	24	0	1	1

GOALIE	W	L	T	GAvg
G. Smith	0	10	1	5.51
G. Inness	3	6	1	5.02
E. Mio	2	2	0	3.22

GOALS

R. Cloutier, QUE	75
M. Lukowich, WINN	65
P. Sullivan, WINN	46
W. Gretzky, EDM	43
P. Marsh, CIN	43

ASSISTS

R. Ftorek, CIN	77
K. Nilsson, WINN	68
T. Ruskowski, WINN	66
M. Howe, NE	65
W. Gretzky, EDM	61

POINTS

R. Cloutier, QUE	129
R. Ftorek, CIN	116
M. Howe, NE	107
K. Nilsson, WINN	107
W. Gretzky, EDM	104

PENALTY MINUTES

S. Campbell, WINN	248
R. Vaive, BIRM	248
P. Baxter, QUE	240
B. Melrose, CIN	222
D. Hanson, BIRM	212

GOALS AGAINST AVE.

D. Dryden, EDM	2.89
R. Brodeur, QUE	3.11
J. Corsi, QUE	3.30
A. Smith, NE	3.31
M. Dion, CIN	3.32

SHUTOUTS

D. Dryden, EDM	3
R. Brodeur, QUE	3
J. Corsi, QUE	3
M. Liut, CIN	3
E. Mio, IND, EDM	2

The Stanley Cup Playoffs

An important difference between professional hockey and its sports counterparts such as baseball and football has been the manner in which it determined its champion, the Stanley Cup winner. Until recently baseball settled this matter in a rather simple and logical way. The first place team—the pennant-winner—in the National League played the league leader from the American League in the World Series. The victor, therefore, was the world champion of baseball. No one in baseball would have considered it either reasonable or logical to permit a fourth place club to compete for the highest prize. Yet this has been the essence of hockey's Stanley Cup playoffs almost from the very beginnings of the professional form of the sport. During the late 1930s and early 1940s, for example, when the National Hockey League was a seven-team unit even the *sixth place* team was eligible to compete for the Stanley Cup! In 1983, the 16th place team—out of 21 clubs—was involved in the playoff competition.

While this has been a source of criticism for the NHL over the years, the league has duly noted that it is following a tradition that was established before the end of World War I by brothers Frank and Lester Patrick, who had founded the professional Pacific Coast Hockey League. The Patricks believed that the regular season race was not sufficient to hold the fans' attention, particularly if one club made a runaway of the competition.

"What we need," said Frank Patrick, "is a second chance for teams that for whatever reason have fallen too far behind to make a race of it. It's not right, for instance, that a team strong enough to make a challenge should be ruled out of early-season contention by injuries." Patrick's panacea was a tournament between the first and second place teams at the conclusion of the regular season. The winner then would advance to interleague championship play. Thus, the playoff system, as we know it, was born. Public reaction to the idea was positive and a playoff system in which many rather than few teams participated remains a part of hockey practice to this day. Writing in the *New York Times*, columnist Arthur Daley noted of the playoffs in 1967: "They [the Patricks] should have a monument raised in their memory for that one idea alone."

Precisely how to implement the idea has confounded professional hockey magnates ever since the Patricks inaugurated their playoff system in 1918. When the NHL took sole possession of the Stanley Cup in 1927 it permitted the top three teams in each of its two divisions (Canadian and American) to qualify for the playoffs. Thus, six out of 10 teams participated. The final round was decided as a best three-out-of-five series but the preliminary rounds (each a two-game set) were based on the total goals system.

From that point on the NHL has been in a constant state of experimentation with its playoff format and these changes are reflected in the summaries that follow. In 1929 the leaders of each division played a best three-out-of-five series in the opening round with the winner automatically qualifying for the finals. The second and third place teams played a two-game total-goal series. The winners of the total goals rounds then met in a best two-out-of-three playoff for the right to advance to the finals. The Stanley Cup finals of 1929 was merely a best two-out-of-three event. Variations on that format continued through the 1936 playoff competition, the last to employ the total-goal system in preliminary rounds. In 1937 the winners of each round did so on the basis of games won, not goals scored.

When the Montreal Maroons folded at the conclusion of the 1937–38 season the Canadian and American Divisions were abandoned and the NHL was contacted into a seven-team league in which six clubs qualified for the playoffs. The opening round involving the top two teams and the finals were both best-of-seven tourneys while the matches between the other clubs were best-of-three preliminaries.

In the summer of 1942 the New York Americans abandoned operations and the NHL dwindled to a six-team league in which the top four clubs qualified for the playoffs. The playoff round of 1943 featured the first and third place clubs and the second and fourth place teams meeting in best-of-seven semifinal rounds. The winners of the semifinals then competed in a best-of-seven final for the Stanley Cup. This format was standard from 1943 through the 1967 playoff year, the last season before the great expansion of 1967–68 when the NHL doubled to a 12-team unit.

As the NHL continued its relentless growth and eventual merger with the World Hockey Association, the playoff arrangement has had a kaleidoscopic existence, constantly changing while one philosophy remained the same: the NHL always believed as the Patricks did decades earlier that the more teams competing for the Stanley Cup the better!

Stanley Cup Playoffs Summary

The National Hockey League became a participant in the Stanley Cup playoff competition from the NHL's inception in the 1917–18 season. However, in the seasons from 1917–18 through the 1925–26 campaign, teams from the Pacific Coast Hockey League and the Western Canada Hockey League (later the Western Hockey League) also competed for the Stanley Cup.

In the 1918–26 playoff span, preliminary NHL playoff rounds were *not* regarded as part of the Stanley Cup playoff competition but rather as the "NHL Playoffs." Only the matches between the NHL champions and the teams from the west were considered part of the true Stanley Cup competition. Therefore, in the following Stanley Cup playoff summaries only those contests between the NHL and their western rivals are included in the playoff lists for the seasons 1917–18 through 1925–26.

From 1926–27 and thereafter all NHL playoff rounds are included in the Stanley Cup playoff summaries.

In order to produce the most accurate possible summaries of the Stanley Cup playoffs several sources were consulted, principally the National Hockey League archives, back issues of the *New York Times*, the *Toronto Star*, the *Montreal Gazette* and innumerable other newspapers, magazines, and books, including the quasi-official NHL history. *The Trail of the Stanley Cup* by Charles A. Coleman.

It should be noted that the NHL, unlike its baseball counterpart, treated statistics as an afterthought until the post-World War II years. Only then did the league formalize a statistical and public relations bureau. During the several decades prior to the organization of the NHL statistical bureau, bookkeeping of Stanley Cup statistics and individual player arithmetic was executed in a casual and too often inaccurate manner. Incredibly, the league does not—and did not—preserve complete and accurate Stanley Cup playoff statistics in its archives for the seasons prior to 1927.

The following statistical information for the years 1927–83 inclusive is based upon game summaries submitted by the official scorer assigned to the game by the NHL and the newspaper files detailed above. In the scoring summaries for the Stanley Cup final series, the scorer of each goal is listed, along with the assists in parentheses and the time of the goal. For all series leading up to the finals, the score is given for each game. For all overtime games, the number of overtimes played and time of the winning goal are also noted; "(2 OT, 12:45)" would mean that the winning goal was scored at 12:45 of the second overtime.

1917–18

FINAL ROUND: Toronto over Vancouver (PCHL) 3 games to 2

GAME 1, March 20:

VANCOUVER	2	1	0	–	3
TORONTO	4	1	0	–	5

Goaltenders: Vancouver, Lehman. Toronto, Holmes.

FIRST PERIOD: 1. Toronto, Noble 8:00. 2. Toronto, Meeking 10:00. 3. Toronto, Noble 11:00. 4. Vancouver, Taylor 16:00. 5. Vancouver, Taylor (MacKay) 17:00. 6. Toronto, Skinner 19:50.
SECOND PERIOD: 7. Vancouver, MacKay 10:00. 8. Toronto, Skinner (Meeking) 13:00.
THIRD PERIOD: No scoring.

GAME 2, March 23:

VANCOUVER	1	3	2	–	6
TORONTO	1	1	2	–	4

Goaltenders: Vancouver, Lehman. Toronto, Holmes.

FIRST PERIOD: 1. Toronto, Skinner 17:00. 2. Vancouver, Taylor 18:00.
SECOND PERIOD: 3. Vancouver, Taylor 2:00. 4. Vancouver, MacKay 6:00. 5. Vancouver, MacKay 14:00. 6. Toronto, Cameron 16:00.
THIRD PERIOD: 7. Vancouver, Griffis 6:00. 8. Toronto, Skinner (Mummery) 8:00. 9. Vancouver, MacKay 10:00. 10. Toronto, Skinner (Denneny) 16:00.

GAME 3, March 26:

VANCOUVER	0	2	1	–	3
TORONTO	3	2	1	–	6

Goaltenders: Vancouver, Lehman. Toronto, Holmes.

FIRST PERIOD: 1. Toronto, Cameron 5:00. 2. Toronto, Skinner 8:00. 3. Toronto, Denneny 13:00.
SECOND PERIOD: 4. Vancouver, McDonald (MacKay) 6:00. 5. Toronto, Cameron 11:00. 6. Toronto, Denneny 14:00. 7. Vancouver, Taylor 16:00.
THIRD PERIOD: 8. Vancouver, Taylor (McDonald) 3:00. 9. Toronto, Skinner 13:00.

GAME 4, March 28:

VANCOUVER	1	3	4	–	8
TORONTO	0	1	0	–	1

Goaltenders: Vancouver, Lehman. Toronto, Holmes.

FIRST PERIOD: 1. Vancouver, Taylor (MacKay) 5:00.
SECOND PERIOD: 2. Vancouver, Stanley 4:00. 3. Toronto, Randolph (Skinner) 4:26. 4. Vancouver, MacKay 11:06. 5. Vancouver, Stanley 13:06.
THIRD PERIOD: 6. Vancouver, Taylor 6:00. 7. Vancouver, L. Cook 13:00. 8. Vancouver, McDonald, 13:45. 9. Vancouver, L. Cook 15:00.

GAME 5, March 30:

VANCOUVER	0	0	1	–	1
TORONTO	0	0	2	–	2

Goaltenders: Vancouver, Lehman. Toronto, Holmes.

FIRST PERIOD: No scoring.
SECOND PERIOD: No scoring.
THIRD PERIOD: 1. Toronto, Skinner 0:30. 2. Vancouver, Taylor (MacKay) 9:30. 3. Toronto, Denneny 10:30.

GOALS

C. Taylor, VAN	9
A. Skinner,TOR	8
M. MacKay, VAN	5

ASSISTS

M. Mackay, VAN	4
H. Mummery, TOR	4
C. Denneny, TOR	2
H. Meeking, TOR	2

POINTS

C. Taylor, VAN	9
M. Mackay, VAN	9
A. Skinner, TOR	9

WINS

H. Holmes, TOR	3
H. Lehman, VAN	2

GOALS AGAINST AVE.

H. Lehman, VAN	3.60
H. Holmes, TOR	4.20

SHUTOUTS

None

1918–19

FINAL ROUND: No decision between Montreal Canadiens and Seattle (PCHL). (Series called off after five games due to flu epidemic.)

GAME 1, March 19:

MONTREAL	0	0	0	–	0
SEATTLE	2	3	2	–	7

Goaltenders: Montreal, Vezina. Seattle, Holmes.

FIRST PERIOD: 1. Seattle, Murray (Rickey) 4:51. 2. Seattle, Foyston 11:34.
SECOND PERIOD: 3. Seattle, Murray (Wilson) 5:58. 4. Seattle, Foyston (R. McDonald) 9:55. 5. Seattle, Walker 16:38.
THIRD PERIOD: 6. Seattle, Foyston 0:43. 7. Seattle, R. McDonald (Rickey) 16:27.

GAME 2, March 22:

MONTREAL	1	1	2	–	4
SEATTLE	0	0	2	–	2

Goaltenders: Montreal, Vezina. Seattle, Holmes.

FIRST PERIOD: 1. Montreal, Lalonde (Pitre) 8:44.
SECOND PERIOD: 2. Montreal, Lalonde 8:18.
THIRD PERIOD: 3. Montreal, Lalonde (Corbeau) 8:17. 4. Montreal, Lalonde (J. McDonald) 18:06. 5. Seattle, Rowe 19:20. 6. Seattle, Foyston 19:28.

GAME 3, March 24:

MONTREAL	0	0	2	–	2
SEATTLE	4	0	3	–	7

Goaltenders: Montreal, Vezina. Seattle, Holmes.

FIRST PERIOD: 1. Seattle, Foyston 1:03. 2. Seattle, Foyston 7:41. 3. Seattle, Wilson (Foyston) 15:54. 4. Seattle, Foyston (Wilson) 18:36.
SECOND PERIOD: No scoring.
THIRD PERIOD: 5. Montreal, Cleghorn (Pitre) 3:21. 6. Montreal, Berlinquette (Pitre) 12:34. 7. Seattle, Foyston 12:39. 8. Seattle, Murray (Wilson) 12:51. 9. Seattle, Rickey 14:57.

GAME 4, March 26:

MONTREAL	0	0	0	0	0	–	0
SEATTLE	0	0	0	0	0	–	0

Goaltenders: Montreal, Vezina. Seattle, Holmes.

FIRST PERIOD: No scoring.
SECOND PERIOD: No scoring.
THIRD PERIOD: No scoring.
FIRST OVERTIME: No scoring.
SECOND OVERTIME: No scoring.
NOTE: Game declared no contest; not included in official records.

GAME 5, March 29:

MONTREAL	0	0	3	1	–	4
SEATTLE	2	1	0	0	–	3

Goaltenders: Montreal, Vezina. Seattle, Holmes.

FIRST PERIOD: 1. Seattle, Foyston 1:40. 2. Seattle, Walker 12:52.
SECOND PERIOD: 3. Seattle, Walker 1:18.
THIRD PERIOD: 4. Montreal, Cleghorn (Couture) 4:00. 5. Montreal, Lalonde (Berlinquette) 5:04. 6. Montreal, Lalonde 17:08.
FIRST OVERTIME: 7. Montreal, J. McDonald 15:51.

GOALS		ASSISTS		POINTS	
F. Foyston, SEA	9	C. Wilson, SEA	3	F. Foyston, SEA	10
N. Lalonde, MONT	6	D. Pitre, MONT	3	N. Lalonde, MONT	6
J. Walker, SEA	3	R. Rickey, SEA	2	C. Wilson, SEA	4
M. Murray, SEA	3				

WINS		GOALS AGAINST AVE.		SHUTOUTS	
H. Holmes, SEA	2	H. Holmes, SEA	2.50	H. Holmes, SEA	1
G. Vezina, MONT	2	G. Vezina, MONT	4.75		

1919–20

FINAL ROUND: Ottawa over Seattle (PCHL) 3 games to 2

GAME 1, March 22:

SEATTLE	1	1	0	–	2
OTTAWA	0	1	2	–	3

Goaltenders: Seattle, Holmes. Ottawa, Benedict.

FIRST PERIOD: 1. Seattle, Foyston (Walker) 10:25.
SECOND PERIOD: 2. Seattle, Foyston (Rowe) 5:46. 3. Ottawa, Nighbor 14:15.
THIRD PERIOD: 4. Ottawa, Nighbor 10:00. 5. Ottawa, Darragh (Gerard, Boucher) 16:00.

GAME 2, March 24:

SEATTLE	0	0	0	–	0
OTTAWA	1	0	2	–	3

Goaltenders: Seattle, Holmes. Ottawa, Benedict.

FIRST PERIOD: 1. Ottawa, Darragh 14:00.
SECOND PERIOD: No scoring.
THIRD PERIOD: 2. Ottawa, Gerard 6:00. 3. Ottawa, Nighbor 19:00.

GAME 3, March 27:

SEATTLE	1	1	1	–	3
OTTAWA	1	0	0	–	1

Goaltenders: Seattle, Holmes. Ottawa, Benedict.

FIRST PERIOD: 1. Ottawa, Boucher (Nighbor) 5:00. 2. Seattle, Foyston (Riley) 8:00.
SECOND PERIOD: 3. Seattle, Foyston (Walker) 12:00.
THIRD PERIOD: 4. Seattle, Rickey (Walker) 9:30.

GAME 4, March 30 at Toronto:

SEATTLE	2	1	2	–	5
OTTAWA	0	2	0	–	2

Goaltenders: Seattle, Holmes. Ottawa, Benedict.

FIRST PERIOD: 1. Seattle, Foyston (Morris) 3:00. 2. Seattle, Rowe (Foyston) 11:00.
SECOND PERIOD: 3. Ottawa, Nighbor 2:00. 4. Seattle, Walker 8:00. 5. Ottawa, Nighbor 11:00.
THIRD PERIOD: 6. Seattle, Rickey 2:00. 7. Seattle, Foyston (Morris) 5:00.

GAME 5, April 1 at Toronto:

SEATTLE	1	0	0	–	1
OTTAWA	1	0	5	–	6

Goaltenders: Seattle, Holmes. Ottawa, Benedict.

FIRST PERIOD: 1. Seattle, Rowe 10:00. 2. Ottawa, Boucher 14:00.
SECOND PERIOD: No scoring.
THIRD PERIOD: 3. Ottawa, Darragh 5:00. 4. Ottawa, Gerard 10:00. 5. Ottawa, Darragh 14:00. 6. Ottawa, Darragh 15:00. 7. Ottawa, Nighbor 15:30.

GOALS		ASSISTS		POINTS	
F. Nighbor, OTTA	6	J. Walker, SEA	3	F. Nighbor, OTTA	7
F. Foyston, SEA	5			F. Foyston, SEA	7
J. Darragh, OTTA	5			J. Darragh, OTTA	5

WINS		GOALS AGAINST AVE.		SHUTOUTS	
C. Benedict, OTTA	3	C. Benedict, OTTA	2.20	C. Benedict, OTTA	1
H. Holmes, SEA	2	H. Holmes, SEA	3.00		

1920–21

FINAL ROUND: Ottawa over Vancouver (PCHL), 3 games to 2

GAME 1, March 21:

OTTAWA	0	1	0	–	1
VANCOUVER	2	1	0	–	3

Goaltenders: Ottawa, Benedict. Vancouver, Lehman.

FIRST PERIOD: 1. Vancouver, Skinner 15:40. 2. Vancouver, Duncan 18:15.
SECOND PERIOD: 3. Vancouver, Harris 1:20. 4. Ottawa, Darragh (Denneny) 15:55.
THIRD PERIOD: No scoring.

GAME 2, March 24:

OTTAWA	2	1	1	–	4
VANCOUVER	3	0	0	–	3

Goaltenders: Ottawa, Benedict. Vancouver, Lehman.

FIRST PERIOD: 1. Vancouver, Harris (J. Adams) 1:29. 2. Vancouver, J. Adams (MacKay) 3:01. 3. Ottawa, Boucher (Cleghorn) 8:05. 4. Vancouver, Duncan (Harris) 10:29. 5. Ottawa, Denneny (Nighbor) 18:26.
SECOND PERIOD: 6. Ottawa, Darragh 10:49.
THIRD PERIOD: 7. Ottawa, Broadbent (Cleghorn) 16:40.

GAME 3, March 28:

OTTAWA	1	2	0	–	3
VANCOUVER	1	1	0	–	2

Goaltenders: Ottawa, Benedict. Vancouver, Lehman.

FIRST PERIOD: 1. Vancouver, Cook 1:59. 2. Ottawa, Darragh 8:57.
SECOND PERIOD: 3. Ottawa, Denneny 8:22. 4. Ottawa, Cleghorn 10:52. 5. Vancouver, J. Adams (Taylor) 18:02.
THIRD PERIOD: No scoring.

GAME 4, March 31:

OTTAWA	0	1	1	–	2
VANCOUVER	0	1	2	–	3

Goaltenders: Ottawa, Benedict. Vancouver, Lehman.

FIRST PERIOD: No scoring.
SECOND PERIOD: 1. Vancouver, Skinner (Duncan) 2:27. 2. Ottawa, Boucher 13:48.
THIRD PERIOD: 3. Vancouver, Skinner 1:35. 4. Vancouver, Cook 15:52. 5. Ottawa, Broadbent 16:52.

GAME 5, April 4:

OTTAWA	0	2	0	–	2
VANCOUVER	1	0	0	–	1

Goaltenders: Ottawa, Benedict. Vancouver, Lehman.

FIRST PERIOD: 1. Vancouver, Skinner 15:26.
SECOND PERIOD: 2. Ottawa, Darragh 7:27. 3. Ottawa, Darragh (Denneny) 9:58.
THIRD PERIOD: No scoring.

GOALS		ASSISTS		POINTS	
J. Darragh, OTTA	5	C. Denneny, OTTA	2	J. Darragh, OTTA	5
A. Skinner, VAN	4	S. Cleghorn, OTTA	2	A. Skinner, VAN	4
				C. Denneny, OTTA	4

WINS		GOALS AGAINST AVE.		SHUTOUTS
C. Benedict, OTTA	3	C. Benedict, OTTA	2.40	None
H. Lehman, VAN	2	H. Lehman, VAN	2.40	

1921–22

FINAL ROUND: Toronto over Vancouver (PCHL), 3 games to 2

GAME 1, March 17:

VANCOUVER	3	0	1	–	4
TORONTO	2	1	0	–	3

Goaltenders: Vancouver, Lehman. Toronto, Roach.

FIRST PERIOD: 1. Toronto, Dye 1:07. 2. Vancouver, Adams 2:37. 3. Vancouver, Adams 5:37. 4. Toronto, Randall 10:37. 5. Vancouver, MacKay 14:37.
SECOND PERIOD: 6. Toronto, Dye 8:00.
THIRD PERIOD: 7. Vancouver, Adams 16:30.

GAME 2, March 21:

VANCOUVER	1	0	0	0	–	1
TORONTO	0	0	1	1	–	2

Goaltenders: Vancouver, Lehman. Toronto, Roach.

FIRST PERIOD: 1. Vancouver, Adams (Skinner) 13:00.
SECOND PERIOD: No scoring.
THIRD PERIOD: 2. Toronto, Denneny (Cameron) 1:45.
FIRST OVERTIME: 3. Toronto, Dye 4:50.

GAME 3, March 23:

VANCOUVER	1	1	1	–	3
TORONTO	0	0	0	–	0

Goaltenders: Vancouver, Lehman. Toronto, Roach.

FIRST PERIOD: 1. Vancouver, Cook (Adams) 15:00.
SECOND PERIOD: 2. Vancouver, Adams (Duncan) 4:00.
THIRD PERIOD: 3. Vancouver, Oatman 18:00.

GAME 4, March 25:

VANCOUVER	0	0	0	–	0
TORONTO	2	3	1	–	6

Goaltenders: Vancouver, Lehman. Toronto, Roach.

FIRST PERIOD: 1. Toronto, Andrews (Noble) 12:00. 2. Toronto, Dye (Smylie) 15:00.
SECOND PERIOD: 3. Toronto, Dye 6:00. 4. Toronto, Andrews (Smylie) 10:00. 5. Toronto, Denneny 18:00.
THIRD PERIOD: 6. Toronto, Smylie (Dye, Denneny) 17:00.

GAME 5, March 28:

VANCOUVER	0	0	1	–	1
TORONTO	2	1	2	–	5

Goaltenders: Vancouver, Lehman. Toronto, Roach.

FIRST PERIOD: 1. Toronto, Dye 3:00. 2. Toronto, Dye 4:50.
SECOND PERIOD: 3. Toronto, Denneny (Smylie) 7:00.
THIRD PERIOD: 4. Toronto, Dye (Stewart) 1:15. 5. Toronto, Dye (Stewart) 4:15. 6. Vancouver, Adams 14:15.

GOALS

B. Dye, TOR	9
J. Adams, VAN	6
C. Denneny, TOR	3

ASSISTS

R. Smylie, TOR	3

POINTS

B. Dye, TOR	10
J. Adams, VAN	7
C. Denneny, TOR	4
R. Smylie, TOR	4

WINS

J. Roach, TOR	3
H. Lehman, VAN	2

GOALS AGAINST AVE.

J. Roach, TOR	1.80
H. Lehman, VAN	3.20

SHUTOUTS

J. Roach, TOR	1
H. Lehman, VAN	1

1922–23

Semifinal Round

Ottawa over Vancouver (PCHL), 3 games to 1

March 16, at VAN: OTTA 1, VAN 0
March 19, at VAN: VAN 4, OTTA 1
March 23, at VAN: OTTA 3, VAN 2
March 26, at VAN: OTTA 5, VAN 1

FINAL ROUND: Ottawa over Edmonton (WCHL), 2 games to 0

GAME 1, March 29 at Vancouver:

EDMONTON	0	1	0	0	–	1
OTTAWA	0	0	1	1	–	2

Goaltenders: Edmonton, Winkler. Ottawa, Benedict.

FIRST PERIOD: No scoring.
SECOND PERIOD: 1. Edmonton, Morrison (Simpson) 10:05.
THIRD PERIOD: 2. Ottawa, Hitchman 13:14.
FIRST OVERTIME: 3. Ottawa, Denneny 2:08.

GAME 2, March 31 at Vancouver:

EDMONTON	0	0	0	–	0
OTTAWA	1	0	0	–	1

Goaltenders: Edmonton, Winkler. Ottawa, Benedict.

FIRST PERIOD: 1. Ottawa, Broadbent (Nighbor) 11:23.
SECOND PERIOD: No scoring.
THIRD PERIOD: No scoring.

GOALS

C. Denneny, OTTA	1
L. Hitchman, EDM	1
P. Broadbent, OTTA	1
C. Morrison, OTTA	1

ASSISTS

J. Simpson, EDM	1
F. Nighbor, TOR	1

POINTS

6 tied with	1

WINS

C. Benedict, OTTA	2

GOALS AGAINST AVE.

C. Benedict, OTTA	0.50
H. Winkler, EDM	1.50

SHUTOUTS

C. Benedict, OTTA	1

1923–24

Semifinal Round

Montreal over Vancouver (PCHL), 2 games to 0

March 18, at MONT: MONT 3, VAN 2
March 20, at MONT: MONT 2, VAN 1

FINAL ROUND: Montreal over Calgary (WCHL), 2 games to 0

GAME 1, March 22:

CALGARY	0	1	0	–	1
MONTREAL	1	3	2	–	6

Goaltenders: Calgary, Reid. Montreal, Vezina.

FIRST PERIOD: 1. Montreal, Morenz 19:30.
SECOND PERIOD: 2. Montreal, Morenz (Joliat) 0:50. 3. Montreal, B. Boucher 10:50. 4. Montreal, Morenz 11:40. 5. Calgary, Gardiner 13:10.
THIRD PERIOD: 6. Montreal, Joliat 2:45. 7. Montreal, S. Cleghorn 3:35.

GAME 2, March 25 at Ottawa:

CALGARY	0	0	0	–	0
MONTREAL	1	0	2	–	3

FIRST PERIOD: 1. Montreal, Morenz 4:55.
SECOND PERIOD: No scoring.
THIRD PERIOD: 2. Montreal, B. Boucher (O. Cleghorn) 3:38. 3. Montreal, Joliat 13:50.

Goaltenders: Calgary, Reid. Montreal, Vezina.

GOALS

H. Morenz, MONT	4
A. Joliat, MONT	2
B. Boucher, MONT	2

ASSISTS

A. Joliat, MONT	1
O. Cleghorn, MONT	1

POINTS

H. Morenz, MONT	4
A. Joliat, MONT	3
B. Boucher, MONT	2

WINS

G. Vezina, MONT	2

GOALS AGAINST AVE.

G. Vezina, MONT	0.50
C. Reid, CALG	4.50

SHUTOUTS

G. Vezina, MONT	1

1924–25

FINAL ROUND: Victoria (WCHL) over Montreal Canadiens, 3 games to 1

GAME 1, March 21:

MONTREAL	0	0	2	–	2
VICTORIA	2	1	2	–	5

FIRST PERIOD: 1. Victoria, Walker 3:50. 2. Victoria, Halderson (Frederickson) 11:55.
SECOND PERIOD: 3. Victoria, Walker 3:22.
THIRD PERIOD: 4. Victoria, Fraser (Frederickson) 3:22. 5. Montreal, Couture (Morenz) 11:14. 6. Victoria, Fraser (Hart) 11:44. 8. Montreal, Morenz 17:44.

Goaltenders: Montreal, Vezina. Victoria, Holmes.

GAME 2, March 23 at Vancouver:

MONTREAL	0	1	0	–	1
VICTORIA	2	0	1	–	3

FIRST PERIOD: 1. Victoria, Walker 8:15. 2. Victoria, Frederickson (Halderson) 15:45.
SECOND PERIOD: 3. Montreal, Joliat 1:18.
THIRD PERIOD: 4. Victoria, Walker 8:52.

Goaltenders: Montreal, Vezina. Victoria, Holmes.

GAME 3, March 27:

MONTREAL	1	0	3	–	4
VICTORIA	1	0	1	–	2

FIRST PERIOD: 1. Montreal, Morenz 4:32. 2. Victoria, Anderson 13:32.
SECOND PERIOD: No scoring.
THIRD PERIOD: 3. Victoria, Hart 1:49. 4. Montreal, Joliat 5:50. 5. Montreal, Morenz 7:30. 6. Montreal, Morenz 18:52.

Goaltenders: Montreal, Vezina. Victoria, Holmes.

GAME 4, March 30:

MONTREAL	0	1	0	–	1
VICTORIA	1	3	2	–	6

FIRST PERIOD: 1. Victoria, Frederickson 5:05.
SECOND PERIOD: 2. Victoria, Hart 1:35. 3. Montreal, Boucher 10:03. 4. Victoria, Halderson 14:47. 5. Victoria, Foyston (Meeking) 18:47.
THIRD PERIOD: 6. Victoria, Frederickson (Walker) 7:53. 7. Victoria, Laughlin (Fraser) 16:29.

Goaltenders: Montreal, Vezina. Victoria, Holmes.

GOALS

H. Morenz, MONT	5
J. Walker, VICT	4
F. Frederickson, VICT	3

ASSISTS

F. Frederickson, VICT	2

POINTS

H. Morenz, MONT	6
J. Walker, VICT	5
F. Frederickson, VICT	5

WINS

H. Holmes, VICT	3
G. Vezina, MONT	1

GOALS AGAINST AVE.

H. Holmes, VICT	2.00
G. Vezina, MONT	4.00

SHUTOUTS

None

1925–26

FINAL ROUND: Montreal Maroons over Victoria (WHL), 3 games to 1

GAME 1, March 30:

VICTORIA	0	0	0	–	0
MONTREAL	2	0	1	–	3

FIRST PERIOD: 1. Montreal, Stewart 3:05. 2. Montreal, Broadbent 8:10.
SECOND PERIOD: No scoring.
THIRD PERIOD: 3. Montreal, Stewart (Siebert) 16:10.

Goaltenders: Victoria, Holmes. Montreal, Benedict.

GAME 2, April 1:

VICTORIA	0	0	0	–	0
MONTREAL	1	1	1	–	3

FIRST PERIOD: 1. Montreal, Stewart 10:10.
SECOND PERIOD: 2. Montreal, Phillips (Stewart) 9:40.
THIRD PERIOD: 3. Montreal, Munro 15:55.

Goaltenders: Victoria, Holmes. Montreal, Benedict.

GAME 3, April 3:

VICTORIA	1	1	1	–	3
MONTREAL	1	0	1	–	2

Goaltenders: Victoria, Holmes. Montreal, Benedict.

FIRST PERIOD: 1. Montreal, Siebert 3:05. 2. Victoria, Halderson 19:20.
SECOND PERIOD: 3. Victoria, Laughlin 10:05.
THIRD PERIOD: 4. Victoria, Frederickson 12:10. 5. Montreal, Stewart (Siebert) 15:55.

GAME 4, April 6:

VICTORIA	0	0	0	–	0
MONTREAL	0	2	0	–	2

Goaltenders: Victoria, Holmes. Montreal, Benedict.

FIRST PERIOD: No scoring.
SECOND PERIOD: 1. Montreal, Stewart 2:50. 2. Montreal, Stewart 18:20.
THIRD PERIOD: No scoring.

GOALS
N. Stewart, MON (M) 6

ASSISTS
B. Siebert, MON (M) 2
N. Stewart, MON (M) 1

POINTS
N. Stewart, MON (M) 7
B. Siebert, MON (M) 3

WINS
C. Benedict, MON (M) 3
H. Holmes, VICT 1

GOALS AGAINST AVE.
C. Benedict, MON (M) 0.75
H. Holmes, VICT 2.50

SHUTOUTS
C. Benedict, MON (M) 3

1926–27

Quarterfinal Round

Mont. Canadiens over Mont. Maroons, 2 goals to 1
March 29, at MONT: MONT 1, MON (M) 1
March 31, at MONT: MONT 1, MON (M) 0

Boston over Chicago, 10 goals to 5
March 29, at CHI: BOS 6, CHI 1
March 31, at BOS: BOS 4. CHI 4

Semifinal Round

Ottawa over Montreal Canadiens, 5 goals to 1
April 2, at MONT: OTTA 4, MONT 0
April 4, at OTTA: OTTA 1, MONT 1

Boston over New York Rangers, 3 goals to 1
April 4, at NYR: BOS 3, NYR 1
April 2, at BOS: BOS 0, NYR 0

FINAL ROUND: Ottawa over Boston, 2 games to 0 (2 ties)

GAME 1, April 7:

OTTAWA	0	0	0	0	0	–	0
BOSTON	0	0	0	0	0	–	0

Goaltenders: Ottawa, Connell. Boston, Winkler.

FIRST PERIOD: No scoring.
SECOND PERIOD: No scoring.
THIRD PERIOD: No scoring.
FIRST OVERTIME: No scoring.
SECOND OVERTIME: No scoring.
(Game called with one minute remaining in second overtime; ice too rough to continue.)

GAME 2, April 9:

OTTAWA	2	0	1	–	3
BOSTON	0	0	1	–	1

Goaltenders: Ottawa, Connell. Boston, Winkler.

FIRST PERIOD: 1. Ottawa, Clancy 6:37. 2. Ottawa, Finnigan 11:23.
SECOND PERIOD: No scoring.
THIRD PERIOD: 3. Boston, Oliver 16:43. 4. Ottawa, Denneny (Smith) 19:55.

GAME 3, April 11:

BOSTON	1	0	0	0	–	1
OTTAWA	0	1	0	0	–	1

Goaltenders: Boston, Winkler. Ottawa, Connell.

FIRST PERIOD: 1. Boston, Herberts (Oliver) 7:24.
SECOND PERIOD: 2. Ottawa, Denneny (Clancy) 15:50.
THIRD PERIOD: No scoring.
FIRST OVERTIME: No scoring.
(Game called due to rough ice.)

GAME 4, April 13:

BOSTON	0	0	1	–	1
OTTAWA	0	2	1	–	3

Goaltenders: Boston, Winkler. Ottawa, Connell.

FIRST PERIOD: No scoring.
SECOND PERIOD: 1. Ottawa, Finnigan (Nighbor) 5:10. 2. Ottawa, Denneny 7:55.
THIRD PERIOD: 3. Ottawa, Denneny 11:55. 4. Boston, Oliver 16:45.

GOALS
C. Denneny, OTTA 5
H. Oliver, BOS 4

ASSISTS
F. Frederickson, BOS 4
P. Galbraith, BOS 3
H. Oliver, BOS 2
G. Hay, CHI 2

POINTS
H. Oliver, BOS 6
P. Galbraith, BOS 6
F. Frederickson, BOS 6

WINS
A. Connell, OTTA 3
H. Winkler, BOS 2

GOALS AGAINST AVE.
A. Connell, OTTA 0.67
C. Benedict, MON (M) 1.00
G. Hainsworth, MONT 1.50
L. Chabot, NYR 1.50

SHUTOUTS
A. Connell, OTTA 2
H. Winkler, BOS 2
G. Hainsworth, MONT 1
L. Chabot, NYR 1

1927–28

Quarterfinal Round

Montreal Maroons over Ottawa, 3 goals to 1

March 27, at OTTA: MON (M) 1, OTTA 0
March 29, at MON (M): MON (M) 2, OTTA 1

New York Rangers over Pittsburgh, 6 goals to 4

March 27, at NYR: NYR 4, PITT 0
March 29, at NYR: PITT 4, NYR 2

Semifinal Round

Montreal Maroons over Montreal Canadiens, 3 goals to 2

March 31, at MONT: MON (M) 2, MONT 2
April 3, at MONT: MON (M) 1, MONT 0 (OT, 8:20)

New York Rangers over Boston, 5 goals to 2

April 1, at NYR: NYR 1, BOS 1
April 3, at BOS: NYR 4, BOS 1

FINAL ROUND: New York Rangers over Montreal Maroons, 3 games to 2

GAME 1, April 5:

NEW YORK	0	0	0	–	0
MONTREAL	0	1	1	–	2

Goaltenders: New York, Chabot. Montreal, Benedict.

FIRST PERIOD: No scoring.
SECOND PERIOD: 1. Montreal, Dutton 10:58.
THIRD PERIOD: 2. Montreal, Phillips (Munro) 5:56.

GAME 2, April 7:

NEW YORK	0	0	1	1	–	2
MONTREAL	0	0	1	0	–	1

Goaltenders: New York, Chabot, Patrick. Montreal, Benedict.

FIRST PERIOD: No scoring.
SECOND PERIOD: No scoring.
THIRD PERIOD: 1. New York, Bill Cook 0:30. 2. Montreal, Stewart (Smith) 18:51.
FIRST OVERTIME: 3. New York, Boucher (Johnson) 7:05.

GAME 3, April 11:

NEW YORK	0	0	0	–	0
MONTREAL	0	1	1	–	2

Goaltenders: New York, Miller. Montreal, Benedict.

FIRST PERIOD: No scoring.
SECOND PERIOD: 1. Montreal, Stewart (Smith) 14:35.
THIRD PERIOD: 2. Montreal, Siebert 12:47.

GAME 4, April 12:

NEW YORK	0	1	0	–	1
MONTREAL	0	0	0	–	0

Goaltenders: New York, Miller. Montreal, Benedict.

FIRST PERIOD: No scoring.
SECOND PERIOD: 1. New York, Boucher (Johnson, Bill Cook) 13:13.
THIRD PERIOD: No scoring.

GAME 5, April 14:

NEW YORK	1	0	1	–	2
MONTREAL	0	0	1	–	1

Goaltenders: New York, Miller. Montreal, Benedict.

FIRST PERIOD: 1. New York, Boucher (Bill Cook) 5:32.
SECOND PERIOD: No scoring.
THIRD PERIOD: 2. New York, Boucher (Bill Cook, Abel) 3:35.
3. Montreal, Phillips (Siebert) 15:00.

GOALS	
F. Boucher, NYR	7

ASSISTS	
F. Boucher, NYR	3
Bill Cook, NYR	3
N. Stewart, MON (M)	2
D. Munro, MON (M)	2

POINTS	
F. Boucher, NYR	10
Bill Cook, NYR	5
N. Stewart, MON (M)	4

WINS	
C. Benedict, MON (M)	5
L. Chabot, NYR	2
J. Miller, NYR	2

GOALS AGAINST AVE.	
C. Benedict, MON (M)	0.89
J. Miller, NYR	1.00
L. Chabot, NYR	1.33

SHUTOUTS	
C. Benedict, MON (M)	4
J. Miller, NYR	1
L. Chabot, NYR	1

1928–29

Quarterfinal Round

N.Y. Rangers over N.Y. Americans, 1 goal to 0

March 19, at NYR: NYR 0, NYA 0
March 21, at NYA: NYR 1, NYA 0 (2 OT, 5:50)

Toronto over Detroit, 7 goals to 2

March 19, at DET: TOR 3, DET 1
March 21, at TOR: TOR 4, DET 1

Semifinal Round

Boston over Montreal Canadiens, 3 games to 0

March 19, at BOS: BOS 1, MONT 0
March 21, at BOS: BOS 1, MONT 0
March 23, at BOS: BOS 3, MONT 2

New York Rangers over Toronto, 2 games to 0

March 24, at NYR: NYR 1, TOR 0
March 26, at TOR: NYR 2, TOR 1 (OT, 2:03)

FINAL ROUND: Boston over New York Rangers, 2 games to 0

GAME 1, March 28:

NEW YORK	0	0	0	–	0
BOSTON	0	2	0	–	2

Goaltenders: New York, Roach. Boston, Thompson.

FIRST PERIOD: No scoring.
SECOND PERIOD: 1. Boston, Clapper 5:13. 2. Boston, Gainor 10:48.
THIRD PERIOD: No scoring.

GAME 2, March 29:

BOSTON	0	1	1	–	2
NEW YORK	0	0	1	–	1

Goaltenders: Boston, Thompson. New York, Roach.

FIRST PERIOD: No scoring.
SECOND PERIOD: 1. Boston, Oliver 14:01.
THIRD PERIOD: 2. New York, Keeling 6:48. 3. Boston, Carson (Oliver) 18:02.

GOALS

A. Blair, TOR	3
B. Keeling, NYR	3

ASSISTS

A. Bailey, TOR	2
P. Thompson, NYR	2

POINTS

A. Blair, TOR	3
A. Bailey, TOR	3
B. Keeling, TOR	3

WINS

T. Thompson, BOS	5
J. Roach, NYR	3
L. Chabot, TOR	2

GOALS AGAINST AVE.

T. Thompson, BOS	0.60
J. Roach, NYR	0.83

SHUTOUTS

T. Thompson, BOS	3
J. Roach, NYR	3
R. Worters, NYA	1

1929–30

Quarterfinal Round

Montreal Canadiens over Chicago, 3 goals to 2

March 23, at CHI: MONT 1, CHI 0
March 26, at MONT: MONT 2, CHI 2 (3 OT, 11:43)

New York Rangers over Ottawa, 6 goals to 3

March 20, at OTTA: NYR 1, OTTA 1
March 23, at NYR: NYR 5, OTTA 2

Semifinal Round

Boston over Montreal Maroons, 3 games to 1

March 20, at MON: BOS 2, MON 1 (3 OT, 5:35)
March 22, at MON: BOS 4, MON 2
March 25, at BOS: MON 1, BOS 0 (2 OT, 6:27)
March 27, at BOS: BOS 5, MON 1

Mont. Canadiens over N.Y. Rangers, 2 games to 0

March 28, at MONT: MONT 2, NYR 1 (4 OT, 8:52)
March 30, at NYR: MONT 2, NYR 0

FINAL ROUND: Montreal Canadiens over Boston, 2 games to 0

GAME 1, April 1:

MONTREAL	0	2	1	–	3
BOSTON	0	0	0	–	0

Goaltenders: Montreal, Hainsworth. Boston, Thompson.

FIRST PERIOD: No scoring.
SECOND PERIOD: 1. Montreal, Leduc 8:43. 2. Montreal, S. Mantha (Joliat) 12:00.
THIRD PERIOD: 3. Montreal, Lepine (Leduc) 16:27.

GAME 2, April 3:

BOSTON	0	1	2	–	3
MONTREAL	2	2	0	–	4

Goaltenders: Boston, Thompson. Montreal, Hainsworth.

FIRST PERIOD: 1. Montreal, McCaffrey (Lepine) 9:08. 2. Montreal, Wasnie (Burke) 16:46.
SECOND PERIOD: 3. Montreal, S. Mantha (Wasnie) 10:05. 4. Boston, Shore 16:50. 5. Montreal, Morenz (Leduc) 17:50.
THIRD PERIOD: 6. Boston, Galbraith (Oliver) 5:55. 7. Boston, Clapper (Weiland) 8:00.

GOALS

D. Clapper, BOS	4
M. Murdoch, NYR	3
M. Barry, BOS	3
H. Morenz, MONT	3

ASSISTS

C. Weiland, BOS	5

POINTS

M. Barry, BOS	6
C. Weiland, BOS	6

WINS

G. Hainsworth, MONT	5
T. Thompson, BOS	3

GOALS AGAINST AVE.

G. Hainsworth, MONT	1.00
C. Gardiner, CHI	1.50
J. Roach, NYR	1.75

SHUTOUTS

G. Hainsworth, MONT	3
F. Walsh, MON (M)	1

1930–31

Quarterfinal Round

Chicago over Toronto, 4 goals to 3

March 24, at TOR: CHI 2, TOR 2
March 26, at CHI: CHI 2, TOR 1 (OT, 19:20)

N.Y. Rangers over Mont. Maroons, 8 goals to 1

March 24, at NYR: NYR 5, MON 1
March 26, at MON: NYR 3, MON 0

Semifinal Round

Montreal Canadiens over Boston, 3 games to 2

March 24, at BOS: BOS 5, MONT 4 (OT, 18:56)
March 26, at BOS: MONT 1, BOS 0
March 28, at MONT: MONT 4, BOS 3 (OT, 5:10)
March 30, at MONT: BOS 3, MONT 1
April 1, at MONT: MONT 3, BOS 2

Chicago over New York Rangers, 3 goals to 0

March 29, at CHI: CHI 2, NYR 0
March 31, at NYR: CHI 1, NYR 0

FINAL ROUND: Montreal Canadiens over Chicago, 3 games to 2

GAME 1, April 3:

MONTREAL	1	0	1	–	2
CHICAGO	0	0	1	–	1

Goaltenders: Montreal, Hainsworth. Chicago, Gardiner.

FIRST PERIOD: 1. Montreal, G. Mantha (Gagnon) 4:50.
SECOND PERIOD: No scoring.
THIRD PERIOD: 2. Montreal, Lepine 2:20. 3. Chicago, Ripley (Gottselig, Couture) 6:00.

GAME 2, April 5:

MONTREAL	0	0	1	0	0	–	1
CHICAGO	0	1	0	0	1	–	2

Goaltenders: Montreal, Hainsworth. Chicago, Gardiner.

FIRST PERIOD: No scoring.
SECOND PERIOD: 1. Chicago, Adams 11:45.
THIRD PERIOD: 2. Montreal, Wasnie (Larochelle) 12:10.
FIRST OVERTIME: No scoring.
SECOND OVERTIME: 3. Chicago, Gottselig 4:50.

GAME 3, April 9:

CHICAGO	0	0	2	0	0	1	–	3
MONTREAL	1	1	0	0	0	0	–	2

Goaltenders: Chicago, Gardiner. Montreal, Hainsworth.

FIRST PERIOD: 1. Montreal, Gagnon (Burke, G. Mantha) 5:15.
SECOND PERIOD: 2. Montreal, G. Mantha (Lepine) 7:29.
THIRD PERIOD: 3. Chicago, March (Gottselig) 16:20. 4. Chicago, Adams (Cook) 16:38.
FIRST OVERTIME: No scoring.
SECOND OVERTIME: No scoring.
THIRD OVERTIME: 5. Chicago, Wentworth (Adams) 13:50.

GAME 4, April 11:

CHICAGO	2	0	0	–	2
MONTREAL	0	1	2	–	3

Goaltenders: Chicago, Gardiner. Montreal, Hainsworth.

FIRST PERIOD: 1. Chicago, Gottselig (Ripley) 1:33. 2. Chicago, Arbour (Ingram) 13:58.
SECOND PERIOD: 3. Montreal, Gagnon (Leduc) 4:34.
THIRD PERIOD: 4. Montreal, Gagnon (Wasnie) 4:25. 5. Montreal, Lepine (Gagnon) 10:55. 6. Montreal, Lepine (Joliat) 17:25.

GAME 5, April 14:

CHICAGO	0	0	0	–	0
MONTREAL	0	1	1	–	2

Goaltenders: Chicago, Gardiner. Montreal, Hainsworth.

FIRST PERIOD: No scoring.
SECOND PERIOD: 1. Montreal, Gagnon (Joliat) 9:59.
THIRD PERIOD: 2. Montreal, Morenz 15:27.

GOALS		ASSISTS		POINTS	
J. Gagnon, MONT	6	H. Morenz, MONT	4	C. Weiland, BOS	9
C. Weiland, BOS	6	A. Joliat, MONT	4	J. Gagnon, MONT	8
G. Mantha, MONT	5	D. Clapper, BOS	4		

WINS		GOALS AGAINST AVE.		SHUTOUTS	
G. Hainsworth, MONT	6	J. Roach, NYR	1.00	C. Gardiner, CHI	2
C. Gardiner, CHI	5	C. Gardiner, CHI	1.55	G. Hainsworth, MONT	2
J. Roach, NYR	2	L. Chabot, TOR	2.00	J. Roach, NYR	1
T. Thompson, BOS	2				

1931–32

Quarterfinal Round

Toronto over Chicago, 6 goals to 2

March 27, at CHI: CHI 2, TOR 0
March 29, at TOR: TOR 6, CHI 0

Montreal Maroons over Detroit, 3 goals to 1

March 27, at DET: MON 1, DET 1
March 29, at MON: MON 2, DET 0

Semifinal Round

N.Y. Rangers over Mont. Canadiens, 3 games to 1

March 24, at MONT: MONT 4, NYR 3
March 26, at MONT: NYR 4, MONT 3 (3 OT, 19:32)
March 27, at NYR: NYR 1, MONT 0
March 29, at NYR: NYR 5, MONT 2

Toronto over Montreal Maroons, 4 goals to 3

March 31, at MON: TOR 1, MON 1
April 2, at TOR: TOR 3, MON 2 (OT, 17:59)

FINAL ROUND: Toronto over New York Rangers, 3 games to 0

GAME 1, April 5:

TORONTO	1	4	1	–	6
NEW YORK	1	1	2	–	4

Goaltenders: Toronto, Chabot. New York, Roach.

FIRST PERIOD: 1. Toronto, Day (Cotton) 4:25. 2. New York, Bun Cook (Bill Cook, Boucher) 17:25.
SECOND PERIOD: 3. Toronto, Jackson (Day) 3:35. 4. Toronto, Jackson (Horner) 10:20. 5. Toronto, Conacher 10:50. 6. Toronto, Jackson 17:05. 7. New York, Dillon (Murdoch) 18:20.
THIRD PERIOD: 8. New York, Johnson 2:35. 9. New York, Bun Cook (Boucher) 6:30. 10. Toronto, Horner (Jackson) 18:32.

GAME 2, April 7:

TORONTO	0	2	4	–	6
NEW YORK	1	1	0	–	2

Goaltenders: Toronto, Chabot. New York, Roach.

FIRST PERIOD: 1. New York, Bun Cook (Bill Cook) 3:53.
SECOND PERIOD: 2. New York, Brennan 1:09. 3. Toronto, Jackson 2:06. 4. Toronto, Conacher 8:58.
THIRD PERIOD: 5. Toronto, Clancy (Primeau) 1:49. 6. Toronto, Conacher (Jackson) 9:56. 7. Toronto, Clancy (Primeau) 10:51. 8. Toronto, Cotton (Primeau) 17:10.

GAME 3, April 9:

NEW YORK	0	1	3	–	4
TORONTO	2	1	3	–	6

Goaltenders: New York, Roach. Toronto, Chabot.

FIRST PERIOD: 1. Toronto, Blair (Clancy) 5:44. 2. Toronto, Blair (Gracie) 6:11.
SECOND PERIOD: 3. Toronto, Jackson (Primeau, Conacher) 10:57. 4. New York, Boucher (Heller) 15:24.
THIRD PERIOD: 5. Toronto, Finnigan (Day) 8:56. 6. Toronto, Bailey (Conacher, Day) 15:07. 7. New York, Bun Cook (Boucher) 16:32. 8. Toronto, Gracie (Finnigan) 17:36. 9. New York, Boucher (Bun Cook) 18:24. 10. New York, Boucher 19:27.

GOALS		ASSISTS		POINTS	
C. Conacher, TOR	6	J. Primeau, TOR	6	F. Boucher, NYR	9
Bun Cook, NYR	6	F. Boucher, NYR	6	Bun Cook, NYR	8
B. Jackson, TOR	5			B. Jackson, TOR	7

WINS		GOALS AGAINST AVE.		SHUTOUTS	
L. Chabot, TOR	5	F. Walsh, MON (M)	1.25	J. Roach, NYR	1
J. Roach, NYR	3	A. Connell, DET	1.50	F. Walsh, MON (M)	1
		L. Chabot, TOR	2.14	C. Gardiner, CHI	1
				L. Chabot, TOR	1

1932–33

Quarterfinal Round

Detroit over Montreal Maroons, 5 goals to 2

March 25, at MON: DET 2, MON 0
March 28, at DET: DET 3, MON 2

N.Y. Rangers over Mont. Canadiens, 8 goals to 5

March 26, at NYR: NYR 5, MONT 2
March 28, at MONT: NYR 3, MONT 3

Semifinal Round

Toronto over Boston, 3 games to 2

March 25, at BOS: BOS 2, TOR 1 (OT, 14:14)
March 28, at BOS: TOR 1, BOS 0 (OT, 15:03)
March 30, at TOR: BOS 2, TOR 1 (OT, 4:23)
April 1, at TOR: TOR 5, BOS 3
April 3, at TOR: TOR 1, BOS 0 (6 OT, 4:46)

New York Rangers over Detroit, 6 goals to 3

March 30, at NYR: NYR 2, DET 0
April 2, at NYR: NYR 4, DET 3

FINAL ROUND: New York Rangers over Toronto, 3 games to 1

GAME 1, April 4:

TORONTO	0	0	1	–	1
NEW YORK	2	2	1	–	5

Goaltenders: Toronto, Chabot. New York, Aitkenhead.

FIRST PERIOD: 1. New York, Bun Cook (Bill Cook, Boucher) 12:18. 2. New York, Dillon (Murdoch) 13:11.
SECOND PERIOD: 3. New York, Heller (Asmundson, Somers) 8:31. 4. New York, Dillon 14:25.
THIRD PERIOD: 5. Toronto, Levinsky 15:53. 6. New York, Murdoch (Dillon) 16:55.

GAME 2, April 8:

NEW YORK	2	0	1	–	3
TORONTO	1	0	0	–	1

Goaltenders: New York, Aitkenhead. Toronto, Chabot.

FIRST PERIOD: 1. Toronto, Doraty (Gracie, Clancy) 1:11. 2. New York, Heller (Somers) 8:16. 3. New York, Bill Cook 11:39.
SECOND PERIOD: No scoring.
THIRD PERIOD: 4. New York, Seibert 14:40.

GAME 3, April 11:

NEW YORK	1	0	1	–	2
TORONTO	0	1	2	–	3

Goaltenders: New York, Aitkenhead. Toronto, Chabot.

FIRST PERIOD: 1. New York, Dillon 2:21.
SECOND PERIOD: 2. Toronto, Doraty (Primeau, Clancy) 7:21.
THIRD PERIOD: 3. Toronto, Doraty 5:30. 4. New York, Keeling (Somers) 7:43. 5. Toronto, Horner (Cotton, Sands) 8:29.

GAME 4, April 13:

NEW YORK	0	0	0	1	–	1
TORONTO	0	0	0	0	–	0

Goaltenders: New York, Aitkenhead. Toronto, Chabot.

FIRST PERIOD: No scoring.
SECOND PERIOD: No scoring.
THIRD PERIOD: No scoring.
FIRST OVERTIME: 1. New York, Bill Cook (Keeling) 7:34.

GOALS		ASSISTS		POINTS	
C. Dillon, NYR	8	M. Murdoch, NYR	4	C. Dillon, NYR	10
K. Doraty, TOR	5	A. Somers, NYR	4	M. Murdoch, NYR	7

WINS		GOALS AGAINST AVE.		SHUTOUTS	
A. Aitkenhead, NYR	6	A. Aitkenhead, NYR	1.62	A. Aitkenhead, NYR	2
L. Chabot, TOR	4	T. Thompson, BOS	1.80	L. Chabot, TOR	2
T. Thompson, BOS	2	L. Chabot, TOR	2.00	J. Roach, DET	1
J. Roach, DET	2	J. Roach, DET	2.00		

1933–34

Quarterfinal Round

Chicago over Montreal Canadiens, 4 goals to 3

March 22, at MONT: CHI 3, MONT 2
March 25, at CHI: CHI 1, MONT 1 (OT, 11:05)

Mont. Maroons over N.Y. Rangers, 2 goals to 1

March 20, at MON: MON 0, NYR 0
March 25, at NYR: MON 2, NYR 1

Semifinal Round

Detroit over Toronto, 3 games to 2

March 22, at TOR: DET 2, TOR 1 (OT, 1:33)
March 24, at TOR: DET 6, TOR 3
March 26, at DET: TOR 3, DET 1
March 28, at DET: TOR 5, DET 1
March 30, at DET: DET 1, TOR 0

Chicago over Montreal Maroons, 6 goals to 2

March 28, at MON: CHI 3, MON 0
April 1, at CHI: CHI 3, MON 2

FINAL ROUND: Chicago over Detroit, 3 games to 1

GAME 1, April 3:

CHICAGO	1	0	0	0	1	–	2
DETROIT	0	0	1	0	0	–	1

Goaltenders: Chicago, Gardiner. Detroit, Cude.

FIRST PERIOD: 1. Chicago, Conacher 17:50.
SECOND PERIOD: No scoring.
THIRD PERIOD: 2. Detroit, Lewis (Graham, Aurie) 4:45.
FIRST OVERTIME: No scoring.
SECOND OVERTIME: 3. Chicago, Thompson (Romnes) 1:10.

GAME 2, April 5:

CHICAGO	1	0	3	–	4
DETROIT	0	1	0	–	1

Goaltenders: Chicago, Gardiner. Detroit, Cude.

FIRST PERIOD: 1. Chicago, Couture 17:52.
SECOND PERIOD: 2. Detroit, Lewis (Weiland) 9:58.
THIRD PERIOD: 3. Chicago, Romnes (Thompson) 1:28. 4. Chicago, Couture (Gottselig) 5:34. 5. Chicago, Gottselig 18:02.

GAME 3, April 8:

DETROIT	2	0	3	–	5
CHICAGO	1	1	0	–	2

Goaltenders: Detroit, Cude. Chicago, Gardiner.

FIRST PERIOD: 1. Chicago, Thompson (March, Romnes) 0:28. 2. Detroit, Pettinger (Starr, Carson) 6:07. 3. Detroit, Aurie (Buswell) 8:40.
SECOND PERIOD: 4. Chicago, Gottselig (Couture, McFayden) 18:07.
THIRD PERIOD: 5. Detroit, Young 13:50. 6. Detroit, Weiland (Aurie, Lewis) 18:20. 7. Detroit, Aurie 19:53.

GAME 4, April 10:

DETROIT	0	0	0	0	0	–	0
CHICAGO	0	0	0	0	1	–	1

Goaltenders: Detroit, Cude. Chicago, Gardiner.

FIRST PERIOD: No scoring.
SECOND PERIOD: No scoring.
THIRD PERIOD: No scoring.
FIRST OVERTIME: No scoring.
SECOND OVERTIME: 1. Chicago, March (Romnes) 10:05.

GOALS		ASSISTS		POINTS	
H. Lewis, DET	5	L. Aurie, DET	7	L. Aurie, DET	10
E. Goodfellow, DET	4	D. Romnes, CHI	7	D. Romnes, CHI	9
P. Thompson, CHI	4	J. Primeau, TOR	4		
J. Gottselig, CHI	4				

WINS		GOALS AGAINST AVE.		SHUTOUTS	
C. Gardiner, CHI	6	A. Aitkenhead, NYR	1.00	C. Gardiner, CHI	2
W. Cude, DET	4	C. Gardiner, CHI	1.50	W. Cude, DET	1
G. Hainsworth, TOR	2	D. Kerr, MON (M)	1.75	A. Aitkenhead, NYR	1
				D. Kerr, MON (M)	1

1934–35

Quarterfinal Round

Montreal Maroons over Chicago, 1 goal to 0

March 23, at MON: MON 0, CHI 0
March 26, at CHI: MON 1, CHI 0 (OT, 4:02)

N.Y. Rangers over Mont. Canadiens, 6 goals to 5

March 24, at NYR: NYR 2, MONT 1
March 26, at MONT: NYR 4, MONT 4

Semifinal Round

Toronto over Boston, 3 games to 1

March 23, at BOS: BOS 1, TOR 0 (2 OT, 13:26)
March 26, at BOS: TOR 2, BOS 0
March 28, at TOR: TOR 3, BOS 0
March 30, at TOR: TOR 2, BOS 1

Montreal Maroons over N.Y. Rangers, 5 goals to 4

March 28, at NYR: MON 2, NYR 1
March 30, at MON: MON 3, NYR 3

FINAL ROUND: Montreal Maroons over Toronto, 3 games to 0

GAME 1, April 4:

MONTREAL	0	2	0	1	– 3
TORONTO	0	2	0	0	– 2

Goaltenders: Montreal, Connell. Toronto, Hainsworth.

FIRST PERIOD: No scoring.
SECOND PERIOD: 1. Montreal, Robinson (Blinco) 3:27. 2. Toronto, Finnigan 14:29. 3. Toronto, Clancy (Metz) 18:12. 4. Montreal, Wentworth 19:12.
THIRD PERIOD: No scoring.
FIRST OVERTIME: 5. Montreal, Trottier (Robinson) 5:28.

GAME 2, April 6:

MONTREAL	1	1	1	– 3
TORONTO	0	1	0	– 1

Goaltenders: Montreal, Connell. Toronto, Hainsworth.

FIRST PERIOD: 1. Montreal, Robinson 15:44.
SECOND PERIOD: 2. Toronto, Jackson 7:31. 3. Montreal, Blinco (Shields) 16:48.
THIRD PERIOD: 4. Montreal, Northcott (Wentworth) 3:26.

GAME 3, April 9:

TORONTO	0	1	0	– 1
MONTREAL	1	2	1	– 4

Goaltenders: Toronto, Hainsworth. Montreal, Connell.

FIRST PERIOD: 1. Montreal, Ward (Northcott) 19:35.
SECOND PERIOD: 2. Toronto, Thoms (Finnigan) 12:57. 3. Montreal, Northcott (Ward) 16:18. 4. Montreal, Wentworth 16:30.
THIRD PERIOD: 5. Montreal, Marker (Wentworth) 1:02.

GOALS		ASSISTS		POINTS	
B. Northcott, MON (M)	4	C. Conacher, TOR	4	B. Northcott, MON (M)	5
C. Wentworth, MON (M)	3	J. Primeau, TOR	3	C. Wentworth, MON (M)	5
B. Jackson, TOR	3	F. Boucher, NYR	3	B. Jackson, TOR	5
				C. Conacher, TOR	5

WINS		GOALS AGAINST AVE.		SHUTOUTS	
A. Connell, MON (M)	5	L. Chabot, CHI	0.50	A. Connell, MON (M)	2
G. Hainsworth, TOR	3	A. Connell, MON (M)	1.14	G. Hainsworth, TOR	2
		G. Hainsworth, TOR	1.71	L. Chabot, CHI	1
				T. Thompson, BOS	1

1935–36

Quarterfinal Round

Toronto over Boston, 8 goals to 6

March 24, at BOS: BOS 3, TOR 0
March 26, at TOR: TOR 8, BOS 3

N.Y. Americans over Chicago, 7 goals to 5

March 24, at NYA: NYA 3, CHI 0
March 26, at CHI: CHI 5, NYA 4

Semifinal Round

Detroit over Montreal Maroons, 3 games to 0

March 24, at MON: DET 1, MON 0 (6 OT, 16:30)
March 26, at MON: DET 3, MON 0
March 29, at DET: DET 2, MON 1

Toronto over N.Y. Americans, 2 games to 1

March 28, at TOR: TOR 3, NYA 1
March 31, at NYA: NYA 1, TOR 0
April 2, at TOR: TOR 3, NYA 1

FINAL ROUND: Detroit over Toronto, 3 games to 1

GAME 1, April 5:

TORONTO	1	0	0	–	1
DETROIT	3	0	0	–	3

Goaltenders: Toronto, Hainsworth. Detroit, Smith.

FIRST PERIOD: 1. Detroit, McDonald 4:53. 2. Detroit, Howe (Young) 5:37. 3. Detroit, W. Kilrea (Bruneteau) 12:05. 4. Toronto, Boll (Thoms, Conacher) 12:15.
SECOND PERIOD: No scoring.
THIRD PERIOD: No scoring.

GAME 2, April 7:

TORONTO	1	1	2	–	4
DETROIT	4	2	3	–	9

Goaltenders: Toronto, Hainsworth. Detroit, Smith.

FIRST PERIOD: 1. Detroit, W. Kilrea (Sorrell) 1:30. 2. Detroit, Barry (Bowman) 4:25. 3. Detroit, Lewis (Sorrell, Barry, Aurie) 10:05. 4. Toronto, Boll (Thoms) 12:35. 5. Detroit, McDonald (H. Kilrea) 16:55.
SECOND PERIOD: 6. Detroit, Sorrell (Howe, Barry) 7:15. 7. Detroit, Pettinger (Howe, Young) 9:10. 8. Toronto, Primeau (Shill) 14:00.
THIRD PERIOD: 9. Detroit, Sorrell (W. Kilrea, Bruneteau) 7:30. 10. Toronto, Thoms (Boll, Davidson, Horner) 9:40. 11. Detroit, Pettinger (H. Kilrea, Howe) 12:05. 12. Toronto, Davidson (Finnigan, H. Jackson) 16:10. 13. Detroit, McDonald 17:15.

GAME 3, April 9:

DETROIT	1	1	1	0	–	3
TORONTO	0	0	3	1	–	4

Goaltenders: Detroit, Smith. Toronto, Hainsworth.

FIRST PERIOD: 1. Detroit, Bowman (Pettinger) 9:25.
SECOND PERIOD: 2. Detroit, Bruneteau 1:06.
THIRD PERIOD: 3. Detroit, Howe (Pettinger, Kelly) 11:15. 4. Toronto, Primeau (Horner, H. Jackson, Davidson) 13:10. 5. Toronto, Kelly (Finnigan) 15:21. 6. Toronto, Kelly (Primeau) 19:18.
FIRST OVERTIME: 7. Toronto, Boll (Horner, A. Jackson, Thoms) 0:31.

GAME 4, April 11:

DETROIT	0	2	1	–	3
TORONTO	1	0	1	–	2

Goaltenders: Detroit, Smith. Toronto, Hainsworth.

FIRST PERIOD: 1. Toronto, Primeau 18:11.
SECOND PERIOD: 2. Detroit, Goodfellow (Sorrell) 9:55. 3. Detroit, Barry (Lewis) 10:39.
THIRD PERIOD: 4. Detroit, Kelly (Lewis) 9:45. 5. Toronto, Thoms 10:57.

GOALS		ASSISTS		POINTS	
B. Boll, TOR	7	B. Thoms, TOR	5	B. Boll, TOR	10
		J. Primeau, TOR	4	B. Thoms, TOR	8
		J. Sorrell, DET	4	J. Primeau, TOR	7
		M. Barry, DET	4	J. Sorrell, DET	7

WINS		GOALS AGAINST AVE.		SHUTOUTS	
N. Smith, DET	6	N. Smith, DET	1.71	N. Smith, DET	2
G. Hainsworth, TOR	4	L. Chabot, MONT	2.00	R. Worters, NYA	2
R. Worters, NYA	2	R. Worters, NYA	2.20	T. Thompson, BOS	1

1936–37

Quarterfinal Round

Montreal Maroons over Boston, 2 games to 1

March 23, at MON: MON 4, BOS 1
March 25, at BOS: BOS 4, MON 0
March 28, at MON: MON 4, BOS 1

New York Rangers over Toronto, 2 games to 0

March 23, at TOR: NYR 3, TOR 0
March 25, at NYR: NYR 2, TOR 1 (OT, 13:05)

Semifinal Round

Detroit over Montreal Canadiens, 3 games to 2

March 23, at DET: DET 4, MONT 0
March 25, at DET: DET 5, MONT 1
March 27, at MONT: MONT 3, DET 1
March 30, at MONT: MONT 3, DET 1
April 1, at MONT: DET 2, MONT 1 (3 OT, 11:49)

N.Y. Rangers over Mont. Maroons, 2 games to 0

April 1, at NYR: NYR 1, MON 0
April 3, at MON: NYR 4, MON 0

FINAL ROUND: Detroit over New York Rangers, 3 games to 2

GAME 1, April 6:

DETROIT	0	0	1	–	1
NEW YORK	3	1	1	–	5

Goaltenders: Detroit, Smith, Robertson. New York, Kerr.

FIRST PERIOD: 1. New York, Keeling (Cooper, Murdoch) 5:23. 2. New York, Patrick (Coulter, Boucher) 9:40. 3. New York, Cooper (Keeling, Dillon) 18:44.
SECOND PERIOD: 4. New York, Boucher (Johnson) 18:55.
THIRD PERIOD: 5. Detroit, Howe (Pettinger, Goodfellow) 17:12. 6. New York, Patrick (Boucher) 18:22.

GAME 2, April 8:

NEW YORK	0	2	0	–	2
DETROIT	3	1	0	–	4

Goaltenders: New York, Kerr. Detroit, Robertson.

FIRST PERIOD: 1. Detroit, Sorrell 9:22. 2. Detroit, Bruneteau (Howe) 12:07. 3. Detroit, Gallagher (W. Kilrea, Sherf) 13:31.
SECOND PERIOD: 4. Detroit, Lewis (Howe, Goodfellow) 11:02. 5. New York, Pratt (N. Colville, M. Colville) 15:08. 6. New York, Keeling (Coulter) 18:18.
THIRD PERIOD: No scoring.

GAME 3, April 11:

NEW YORK	0	1	0	–	1
DETROIT	0	0	0	–	0

Goaltenders: New York, Kerr. Detroit, Robertson.

FIRST PERIOD: No scoring.
SECOND PERIOD: 1. New York, N. Colville (Pratt, Cooper) 0:23.
THIRD PERIOD: No scoring.

GAME 4, April 13:

NEW YORK	0	0	0	–	0
DETROIT	0	0	1	–	1

Goaltenders: New York, Kerr. Detroit, Robertson.

FIRST PERIOD: No scoring.
SECOND PERIOD: No scoring.
THIRD PERIOD: 1. Detroit, Barry (Howe, Sorrell) 12:43.

GAME 5, April 15:

NEW YORK	0	0	0	–	0
DETROIT	1	1	1	–	3

Goaltenders: New York, Kerr. Detroit, Robertson.

FIRST PERIOD: 1. Detroit, Barry (Howe) 19:22.
SECOND PERIOD: 2. Detroit, Sorrell (Barry, H. Kilrea) 9:36.
THIRD PERIOD: 3. Detroit, Barry (Sorrell) 2:33.

GOALS		**ASSISTS**		**POINTS**	
M. Barry, DET	4	M. Barry, DET	7	M. Barry, DET	11
H. Lewis, DET	4	S. Howe, DET	5	H. Lewis, DET	7
		J. Sorrell, DET	4	S. Howe, DET	7
		A. Shibicky, NYR	4		

WINS		**GOALS AGAINST AVE.**		**SHUTOUTS**	
D. Kerr, NYR	6	D. Kerr, NYR	1.11	D. Kerr, NYR	4
N. Smith, DET	3	N. Smith, DET	1.20	E. Robertson, DET	2
E. Robertson, DET	3	E. Robertson, DET	1.33	N. Smith, DET	1
				T. Thompson, BOS	1

1937–38

Quarterfinal Round

N.Y. Americans over N.Y. Rangers, 2 games to 1

March 22, at NYR: NYA 2, NYR 1 (2 OT, 1:25)
March 24, at NYR: NYR 4, NYA 3
March 27, at NYA: NYA 3, NYR 2 (3 OT, 0:40)

Chicago over Montreal Canadiens, 2 games to 1

March 22, at MONT: MONT 6, CHI 4
March 24, at CHI: CHI 4, MONT 0
March 26, at MONT: CHI 3, MONT 2 (OT, 11:49)

Semifinal Round

Toronto over Boston, 3 games to 0

March 24, at TOR: TOR 1, BOS 0 (2 OT, 1:31)
March 26, at TOR: TOR 2, BOS 1
March 29, at BOS: TOR 3, BOS 2 (OT, 10:04)

Chicago over New York Americans, 2 games to 1

March 29, at NYA: NYA 3, CHI 1
March 31, at CHI: CHI 1, NYA 0 (OT, 13:01)
April 3, at NYA: CHI 3, NYA 2

FINAL ROUND: Chicago over Toronto, 3 games to 1

GAME 1, April 5:

CHICAGO	1	1	1	–	3
TORONTO	1	0	0	–	1

Goaltenders: Chicago, Moore. Toronto, Broda.

FIRST PERIOD: 1. Toronto, Drillon (Davidson) 1:53. 2. Chicago, Gottselig (Dahlstrom, Romnes) 17:15.
SECOND PERIOD: 3. Chicago, Thompson (Seibert) 1:50.
THIRD PERIOD. 4. Chicago, Gottselig 12:08.

GAME 2, April 7:

CHICAGO	1	0	0	–	1
TORONTO	1	1	3	–	5

Goaltenders: Chicago, Goodman. Toronto, Broda.

FIRST PERIOD: 1. Toronto, Drillon (Apps, Thoms) 1:42. 2. Chicago, Seibert 8:31.
SECOND PERIOD: 3. Toronto, Jackson (Thoms) 6:10.
THIRD PERIOD: 4. Toronto, Drillon (Apps, Hamilton) 9:44. 5. Toronto, Parsons (Kelly, Fowler) 10:29. 6. Toronto, Parsons (Kelly, Horner) 11:08.

GAME 3, April 10:

TORONTO	1	0	0	–	1
CHICAGO	0	1	1	–	2

Goaltenders: Toronto, Broda. Chicago, Karakas.

FIRST PERIOD: 1. Toronto, Apps (Drillon, Davidson) 1:35.
SECOND PERIOD: 2. Chicago, Voss (Jenkins, Gottselig) 16:02.
THIRD PERIOD: 3. Chicago, Romnes (March, Thompson) 15:55.

GAME 4, April 12:

TORONTO	1	0	0	–	1
CHICAGO	1	2	1	–	4

Goaltenders: Toronto, Broda. Chicago, Karakas.

FIRST PERIOD: 1. Chicago, Dahlstrom (Shill, Trudell) 5:52. 2. Toronto, Drillon (Fowler) 8:26.
SECOND PERIOD: 3. Chicago, Voss (Gottselig, Jenkins) 16:45. 4. Chicago, Shill 17:58.
THIRD PERIOD: 5. Chicago, March (Romnes, Thompson) 16:24.

GOALS

G. Drillon, TOR	7
J. Gottselig, CHI	5
E. Seibert, CHI	5

ASSISTS

R. Jenkins, CHI	6

POINTS

J. Gottselig, CHI	8
G. Drillon, TOR	8
E. Seibert, CHI	7
P. Thompson, CHI	7

WINS

M. Karakas, CHI	6
T. Broda, TOR	4
E. Robertson, NYA	3

GOALS AGAINST AVE.

T. Broda, TOR	1.85
M. Karakas, CHI	1.87

SHUTOUTS

M. Karakas, CHI	2
T. Broda, TOR	1

1938–39

Quarterfinal Round

Toronto over New York Americans, 2 games to 0

March 21, at TOR: TOR 4, NYA 0
March 23, at NYA: TOR 2, NYA 0

Detroit over Montreal Canadiens, 2 games to 1

March 21, as MONT: MONT 2, DET 0
March 23, at DET: DET 7, MONT 3
March 26, at DET: DET 1, MONT 0 (OT, 7:47)

Semifinal Round

Boston over New York Rangers, 4 games to 3

March 21, at NYR: BOS 2, NYR 1 (3 OT, 19:25)
March 23, at BOS: BOS 3, NYR 2 (OT, 8:24)
March 26, at BOS: BOS 4, NYR 1
March 28, at NYR: NYR 2, BOS 1
March 30, at BOS: NYR 2, BOS 1 (OT, 17:19)
April 1, at NYR: NYR 3, BOS 1
April 2, at BOS: BOS 2, NYR 1 (3 OT, 8:00)

Toronto over Detroit, 2 games to 1

March 28, at TOR: TOR 4, DET 1
March 30, at DET: DET 3, TOR 1
April 1, at TOR: TOR 5, DET 4 (OT, 5:42)

FINAL ROUND: Boston over Toronto, 4 games to 1

GAME 1, April 6:

TORONTO	0	0	1	–	1
BOSTON	1	0	1	–	2

Goaltenders: Toronto, Broda. Boston, Brimsek.

FIRST PERIOD: 1. Boston, Dumart (Shore, Bauer) 16:04.
SECOND PERIOD: No scoring.
THIRD PERIOD: 2. Toronto, Horner (Marker, Romnes) 13:54. 3. Boston, Bauer 15:31.

GAME 2, April 9:

TORONTO	2	0	0	1	–	3
BOSTON	0	2	0	0	–	2

Goaltenders: Toronto, Broda. Boston, Brimsek.

FIRST PERIOD: 1. Toronto, Chamberlain (Kampman, Drillon) 8:55. 2. Toronto, Apps (Metz, Drillon) 9:29.
SECOND PERIOD: 3. Boston, Conacher (Cowley, Hollett) 15:05. 4. Boston, Hill (Cowley, Shore) 16:18.
THIRD PERIOD: No scoring.
FIRST OVERTIME: 5. Toronto, Romnes (Marker, Jackson) 10:38.

GAME 3, April 11:

BOSTON	0	0	3	–	3
TORONTO	0	0	1	–	1

Goaltenders: Boston, Brimsek. Toronto, Broda.

FIRST PERIOD: No scoring.
SECOND PERIOD: No scoring.
THIRD PERIOD: 1. Boston, Bauer (Schmidt) 1:28. 2. Boston, Conacher (Cowley) 8:12. 3. Boston, Crawford (Cowley, Conacher) 13:03. 4. Toronto, Marker (Romnes) 19:10.

GAME 4, April 13:

BOSTON	1	0	1	–	2
TORONTO	0	0	0	–	0

Goaltenders: Boston, Brimsek. Toronto, Broda.

FIRST PERIOD: 1. Boston, Conacher (Hill) 2:20.
SECOND PERIOD: No scoring.
THIRD PERIOD: 2. Boston, Conacher (Cowley, Hill) 12:55.

GAME 5, April 16:

TORONTO	1	0	0	–	1
BOSTON	1	1	1	–	3

Goaltenders: Toronto, Broda. Boston, Brimsek.

FIRST PERIOD: 1. Boston, Hill (Conacher, Cowley) 11:40. 2. Toronto, Kampman (Romnes) 18:40.
SECOND PERIOD: 3. Boston, Conacher (Cowley, Shore) 17:34.
THIRD PERIOD: 4. Boston, Hollett (Schmidt, Crawford) 19:23.

GOALS		ASSISTS		POINTS	
G. Drillon, TOR	7	B. Cowley, BOS	11	B. Cowley, BOS	14
R. Conacher, BOS	6	G. Drillon, TOR	6	G. Drillon, TOR	13
M. Hill, BOS	6	S. Apps, TOR	6	R. Conacher, BOS	10

WINS		GOALS AGAINST AVE.		SHUTOUTS	
F. Brimsek, BOS	8	F. Brimsek, BOS	1.50	T. Broda, TOR	2
T. Broda, TOR	5	T. Broda, TOR	2.00	F. Brimsek, BOS	1
T. Thompson, DET	3	B. Gardiner, NYR	2.00	T. Thompson, DET	1
B. Gardiner, NYR	3	D. Kerr, NYR	2.00	C. Bourque, MONT	1

1939–40

Quarterfinal Round

Toronto over Chicago, 2 games to 0

March 19, at TOR: TOR 3, CHI 2 (OT, 6:35)
March 21, at CHI: TOR 2, CHI 1

Detroit over New York Americans, 2 games to 1

March 19, at DET: DET 2, NYA 1 (OT, 0:25)
March 22, at NYA: NYA 5, DET 4
March 24, at DET: DET 3, NYA 1

Semifinal Round

New York Rangers over Boston, 4 games to 2

March 19, at NYR: NYR 4, BOS 0
March 21, at BOS: BOS 4, NYR 2
March 24, at BOS: BOS 4, NYR 3
March 26, at NYR: NYR 1, BOS 0
March 28, at BOS: NYR 1, BOS 0
March 30, at NYR: NYR 4, BOS 1

Toronto over Detroit, 2 games to 0

March 26, at TOR: TOR 2, DET 1
March 28, at DET: TOR 3, DET 1

FINAL ROUND: New York Rangers over Toronto, 4 games to 2

GAME 1, April 2:

TORONTO	1	0	0	0	–	1
NEW YORK	1	0	0	1	–	2

Goaltenders: Toronto, Broda. New York, Kerr.

FIRST PERIOD: 1. New York, Coulter (N. Colville) 9:09. 2. Toronto, Heron (Schriner) 11:01.
SECOND PERIOD: No scoring.
THIRD PERIOD: No scoring.
FIRST OVERTIME: 3. New York, Pike (L. Patrick) 15:30.

GAME 2, April 3:

TORONTO	2	0	0	–	2
NEW YORK	1	2	3	–	6

Goaltenders: Toronto, Broda. New York, Kerr.

FIRST PERIOD: 1. Toronto, Taylor (Schriner, Horner) 5:01. 2. Toronto, Goldup (Marker) 6:01. 3. New York, Hextall (Hiller, Watson) 15:14.
SECOND PERIOD: 4. New York, Pratt (N. Colville) 3:57. 5. New York, Hextall (Heller) 19:48.
THIRD PERIOD: 6. New York, Hextall (Watson) 6:26. 7. New York, Hiller (Watson, Hextall) 12:21. 8. New York, L. Patrick (Pratt, Heller) 13:09.

GAME 3, April 6:

NEW YORK	1	0	0	–	1
TORONTO	0	0	2	–	2

Goaltenders: New York, Kerr. Toronto, Broda.

FIRST PERIOD: 1. New York, Watson 18:19.
SECOND PERIOD: No scoring.
THIRD PERIOD: 2. Toronto, Drillon (Apps, Horner) 10:32. 3. Toronto, Goldup (N. Metz) 13:40.

GAME 4, April 9:

NEW YORK	0	0	0	–	0
TORONTO	1	0	2	–	3

Goaltenders: New York, Kerr. Toronto, Broda.

FIRST PERIOD: 1. Toronto, Marker (Goldup, Langelle) 19:20.
SECOND PERIOD: No scoring.
THIRD PERIOD: 2. Toronto, Stanowski (Church) 16:03. 3. Toronto, Drillon (Apps, N. Metz) 19:26.

GAME 5, April 11:

NEW YORK	1	0	0	0	1	–	2
TORONTO	0	1	0	0	0	–	1

Goaltenders: New York, Kerr. Toronto, Broda.

FIRST PERIOD: 1. New York, N. Colville (M. Colville, Shibicky) 12:21.
SECOND PERIOD: 2. Toronto, Apps 16:55.
THIRD PERIOD: No scoring.
FIRST OVERTIME: No scoring.
SECOND OVERTIME: 3. New York, M. Patrick (N. Colville) 11:43.

GAME 6, April 13:

NEW YORK	0	0	2	1	–	3
TORONTO	1	1	0	0	–	2

Goaltenders: New York, Kerr. Toronto, Broda.

FIRST PERIOD: 1. Toronto, Apps (Davidson) 6:52.
SECOND PERIOD: 2. Toronto, N. Metz (Schriner) 4:51.
THIRD PERIOD: 3. New York, N. Colville (Shibicky) 8:08. 4. New York, Pike (Smith) 10:01.
FIRST OVERTIME: 5. New York, Hextall (Hiller, Watson) 2:07.

GOALS		ASSISTS		POINTS	
S. Apps, TOR	5	N. Colville, NYR	7	P. Watson, NYR	9
H. Goldup, TOR	5	P. Watson, NYR	6	N. Colville, NYR	9
B. Hextall, NYR	4	A. Shibicky, NYR	5		

WINS		GOALS AGAINST AVE.		SHUTOUTS	
D. Kerr, NYR	8	D. Kerr, NYR	1.67	D. Kerr, NYR	3
T. Broda, TOR	6	T. Broda, TOR	1.90	T. Broda, TOR	1
F. Brimsek, BOS	2	T. Thompson, DET	2.40		
T. Thompson, DET	2				

1940–41

Quarterfinal Round

Chicago over Montreal Canadiens, 2 games to 1

March 20, at CHI: CHI 2, MONT 1
March 22, at MONT: MONT 4, CHI 3 (2 OT, 14:04)
March 25, at CHI: CHI 3, MONT 2

Detroit over New York Rangers, 2 games to 1

March 20, at DET: DET 2, NYR 1 (OT, 12:01)
March 23, at NYR: NYR 3, DET 1
March 25, at DET: DET 3, NYR 2

Semifinal Round

Boston over Toronto, 4 games to 3

March 20, at BOS: BOS 3, TOR 0
March 22, at BOS: TOR 5, BOS 3
March 25, at TOR: TOR 7, BOS 2
March 27, at TOR: BOS 2, TOR 1
March 29, at BOS: TOR 2, BOS 1 (OT, 17:31)
April 1, at TOR: BOS 2, TOR 1
April 3, at BOS: BOS 2, TOR 1

Detroit over Chicago, 2 games to 0

March 27, at DET: DET 3, CHI 1
March 30, at CHI: DET 2, CHI 1 (OT, 9:15)

FINAL ROUND: Boston over Detroit, 4 games to 0

GAME 1, April 6:

DETROIT	0	0	2	– 2
BOSTON	1	1	1	– 3

Goaltenders: Detroit, Mowers. Boston, Brimsek.

FIRST PERIOD: 1. Boston, Wiseman (Conacher, Smith) 13:26.
SECOND PERIOD: 2. Boston, Schmidt (Dumart, Crawford) 14:45.
THIRD PERIOD: 3. Boston, McCreavy (Schmidt, Crawford) 9:16. 4. Detroit, Liscombe (Brown, Jennings) 10:55. 5. Detroit, Howe (Brown) 17:45.

GAME 2, April 8:

DETROIT	0	0	1	– 1
BOSTON	0	0	2	– 2

Goaltenders: Detroit, Mowers. Boston, Brimsek.

FIRST PERIOD: No scoring.
SECOND PERIOD: No scoring.
THIRD PERIOD: 1. Detroit, Bruneteau (Howe, Orlando) 2:41. 2. Boston, T. Reardon (Cain, Smith) 13:35. 3. Boston, Conacher (Schmidt) 17:45.

GAME 3, April 10:

BOSTON	2	1	1	– 4
DETROIT	2	0	0	– 2

Goaltenders: Boston, Brimsek. Detroit, Mowers.

FIRST PERIOD: 1. Detroit, Jennings (Grosso, Abel) 3:15. 2. Boston, Wiseman (Conacher, Hollett) 3:57. 3. Detroit, Abel (Stewart) 7:45. 4. Boston, Schmidt (Dumart, Bauer) 14:07.
SECOND PERIOD: 5. Boston, Schmidt (Clapper, Dumart) 0:59.
THIRD PERIOD: 6. Boston, Jackson (T. Reardon, Clapper) 17:20.

GAME 4, April 12:

BOSTON	0	3	0	– 3
DETROIT	1	0	0	– 1

Goaltenders: Boston, Brimsek. Detroit, Mowers.

FIRST PERIOD: 1. Detroit, Liscombe (Howe, Giesebrecht) 10:14.
SECOND PERIOD: 2. Boston, Hollett (Schmidt) 7:42. 3. Boston, Bauer (Schmidt) 8:43. 4. Boston, Wiseman (Conacher, McCreavy) 19:32.
THIRD PERIOD: No scoring.

GOALS		ASSISTS		POINTS	
E. Wiseman, BOS	6	S. Howe, DET	7	M. Schmidt, BOS	11
M. Schmidt, BOS	5	M. Schmidt, BOS	6	E. Wiseman, BOS	8
C. Liscombe, DET	4	R. Conacher, BOS	5	S. Howe, DET	8
J. Benoit, MONT	4	D. Clapper, BOS	5		

WINS		GOALS AGAINST AVE.		SHUTOUTS	
F. Brimsek, BOS	8	D. Kerr, NYR	2.00	F. Brimsek, BOS	1
J. Mowers, DET	4	F. Brimsek, BOS	2.09		
T. Broda, TOR	3	T. Broda, TOR	2.14		

1941–42

Quarterfinal Round

Boston over Chicago, 2 games to 1

March 22, at CHI: BOS 2, CHI 1 (OT, 6:51)
March 24, at BOS: CHI 4, BOS 0
March 26, at BOS: BOS 3, CHI 2

Detroit over Montreal Canadiens, 2 games to 1

March 22, at DET: DET 2, MONT 1
March 24, at MONT: MONT 5, DET 0
March 26, at DET: DET 6, MONT 2

Semifinal Round

Toronto over New York Rangers, 4 games to 2

March 21, at TOR: TOR 3, NYR 1
March 22, at NYR: TOR 4, NYR 2
March 24, at NYR: NYR 3, TOR 0
March 28, at TOR: TOR 2, NYR 1
March 29, at NYR: NYR 3, TOR 1
March 31, at TOR: TOR 3, NYR 2

Detroit over Boston, 2 games to 0

March 29, at BOS: DET 6, BOS 4
March 31, at DET: DET 3, BOS 1

FINAL ROUND: Toronto over Detroit, 4 games to 3

GAME 1, April 4:

DETROIT	2	1	0	–	3
TORONTO	2	0	0	–	2

Goaltenders: Detroit, Mowers. Toronto, Broda.

FIRST PERIOD: 1. Detroit, Grosso (Orlando) 1:37. 2. Toronto, McCreedy (Davidson, Kampman) 6:36. 3. Detroit, Abel (Grosso) 12:30. 4. Toronto, Schriner (Taylor) 12:59.
SECOND PERIOD: 5. Detroit, Grosso 14:11.
THIRD PERIOD: No scoring.

GAME 2, April 7:

DETROIT	2	0	2	–	4
TORONTO	0	1	1	–	2

Goaltenders: Detroit, Mowers. Toronto, Broda.

FIRST PERIOD: 1. Detroit, Grosso (Wares) 11:47. 2. Detroit, Bruneteau (Liscombe) 14:17.
SECOND PERIOD: 3. Toronto, Schriner (Taylor, Stanowski) 11:13.
THIRD PERIOD: 4. Detroit, Grosso (Wares) 4:15. 5. Detroit, J. Brown (Bush, Liscombe) 10:08. 6. Toronto, Stanowski 13:40.

GAME 3, April 9:

TORONTO	2	0	0	–	2
DETROIT	2	2	1	–	5

Goaltenders: Toronto, Broda. Detroit, Mowers.

FIRST PERIOD: 1. Toronto, Carr (Taylor, Kampman) 15:36. 2. Toronto, Carr (Taylor) 16:06. 3. Detroit, J. Brown (Bush, Stewart) 18:20. 4. Detroit, Carveth (Bush, A. Brown) 18:58.
SECOND PERIOD: 5. Detroit, McCreavy (Grosso, Bush) 13:12. 6. Detroit, Howe (Grosso, Bush) 15:11.
THIRD PERIOD: 7. Detroit, Bush (Liscombe) 7:11.

GAME 4, April 12:

TORONTO	0	2	2	–	4
DETROIT	0	2	1	–	3

Goaltenders: Toronto, Broda. Detroit, Mowers.

FIRST PERIOD: No scoring.
SECOND PERIOD: 1. Detroit, Bruneteau (Motter) 1:32. 2. Detroit, Abel (Grosso, Wares) 9:08. 3. Toronto, Davidson (Langelle, McCreedy) 13:54. 4. Toronto, Carr (Taylor, Schriner) 15:20.
THIRD PERIOD: 5. Detroit, Liscombe (Howe, Bruneteau) 4:18. 6. Toronto, Apps (Stanowski, N. Metz) 6:15. 7. Toronto, N. Metz (D. Metz, Apps) 12:45.

GAME 5, April 14:

DETROIT	0	0	3	–	3
TORONTO	2	5	2	–	9

Goaltenders: Detroit, Mowers. Toronto, Broda.

FIRST PERIOD: 1. Toronto, N. Metz (Apps, Stanowski) 9:24. 2. Toronto, Stanowski 15:13.
SECOND PERIOD: 3. Toronto, Goldham 1:59. 4. Toronto, Schriner (Taylor) 4:11. 5. Toronto, D. Metz (N. Metz, Apps) 14:11. 6. Toronto, Apps (D. Metz, Goldham) 14:39. 7. Toronto, D. Metz (N. Metz) 16:43.
THIRD PERIOD: 8. Detroit, Howe (McCreavy, Liscombe) 3:12. 9. Toronto, D. Metz (Apps, Stanowski) 5:31. 10. Toronto, Apps (D. Metz) 9:20. 11. Detroit, Motter (Howe) 14:03. 12. Detroit, Liscombe (Howe) 15:39.

GAME 6, April 16:

TORONTO	0	1	2	–	3
DETROIT	0	0	0	–	0

Goaltenders: Toronto, Broda. Detroit, Mowers.

FIRST PERIOD: No scoring.
SECOND PERIOD: 1. Toronto, D. Metz 0:14.
THIRD PERIOD: 2. Toronto, Goldham (Schriner) 13:32. 3. Toronto, Taylor (Schriner) 14:04.

GAME 7, April 18:

DETROIT	0	1	0	–	1
TORONTO	0	0	3	–	3

Goaltenders: Detroit, Mowers. Toronto, Broda.

FIRST PERIOD: No scoring.
SECOND PERIOD: 1. Detroit, Howe (Orlando, Abel) 1:44.
THIRD PERIOD: 2. Toronto, Schriner (Taylor, Carr) 7:46. 3. Toronto, Langelle (Goldham, McCreedy) 9:43. 4. Toronto, Schriner (Carr, Taylor) 16:13.

GOALS

D. Grosso, DET	8
C. Liscombe, DET	6
S. Schriner, TOR	6

ASSISTS

S. Apps, TOR	9
B. Taylor, TOR	8
W. Stanowski, TOR	8

POINTS

D. Grosso, DET	14
S. Apps, TOR	14
C. Liscombe, DET	13

WINS

T. Broda, TOR	8
J. Mowers, DET	7
J. Henry, NYR	2
F. Brimsek, BOS	2

GOALS AGAINST AVE.

S. LoPresti, CHI	1.67
J. Henry, NYR	2.17
T. Broda, TOR	2.38

SHUTOUTS

S. LoPresti, CHI	1
J. Henry, NYR	1
T. Broda, TOR	1
P. Bibeault, MONT	1

1942–43

Semifinal Round

Detroit over Toronto, 4 games to 2

March 21, at DET: DET 4, TOR 2
March 23, at DET: TOR 3, DET 2 (4 OT, 10:18)
March 25, at TOR: DET 4, TOR 2
March 27, at TOR: TOR 6, DET 3
March 28, at DET: DET 4, TOR 2
March 30, at TOR: DET 3, TOR 2 (OT, 9:21)

Boston over Montreal Canadiens, 4 games to 1

March 21, at BOS: BOS 5, MONT 4 (OT, 12:30)
March 23, at BOS: BOS 5, MONT 3
March 25, at MONT: BOS 3, MONT 2 (OT, 3:20)
March 27, at MONT: MONT 4, BOS 0
March 30, at BOS: BOS 5, MONT 4 (OT, 3:41)

FINAL ROUND: Detroit over Boston, 4 games to 0

GAME 1, April 1:

DETROIT	1	3	2	– 6
BOSTON	1	0	1	– 2

Goaltenders: Detroit, Mowers. Boston, Brimsek.

FIRST PERIOD: 1. Detroit, Stewart (Liscombe, Abel) 1:15. 2. Boston, A. Jackson (Cain) 18:13.
SECOND PERIOD: 3. Detroit, Bruneteau (H. Jackson, Abel) 1:12. 4. Detroit, Abel 15:43. 5. Detroit, Carveth (Douglas) 19:06.
THIRD PERIOD: 6. Detroit, Bruneteau (Abel, Liscombe) 1:21. 7. Detroit, Bruneteau (J. Stewart, Abel) 16:24. 8. Boston, DeMarco (Gallinger, Guidolin) 17:53.

GAME 2, April 4:

BOSTON	0	2	1	– 3
DETROIT	0	1	3	– 4

Goaltenders: Detroit, Mowers. Boston, Brimsek.

FIRST PERIOD: No scoring.
SECOND PERIOD: 1. Boston, Crawford (Chamberlain) 10:16. 2. Boston, A. Jackson (Cowley, Cain) 11:04. 3. Detroit, Douglas (Orlando) 17:08.
THIRD PERIOD: 4. Detroit, Carveth (Orlando) 5:55. 5. Detroit, Liscombe (Abel) 6:21. 6. Detroit, Howe (Wares) 13:16. 7. Boston, A. Jackson (Cowley, Hollett) 16:38.

GAME 3, April 7:

DETROIT	2	0	2	– 4
BOSTON	0	0	0	– 0

Goaltenders: Detroit, Mowers. Boston, Brimsek.

FIRST PERIOD: 1. Detroit, Grosso (Wares) 3:26. 2. Detroit, Grosso (Liscombe) 10:16.
SECOND PERIOD: No scoring.
THIRD PERIOD: 3. Detroit, Douglas 8:03. 4. Detroit, Grosso (Wares) 18:41.

GAME 4, April 8:

DETROIT	1	1	0	– 2
BOSTON	0	0	0	– 0

Goaltenders: Detroit, Mowers. Boston, Brimsek.

FIRST PERIOD: 1. Detroit, Carveth 12:09.
SECOND PERIOD: 2. Detroit, Liscombe 2:45.
THIRD PERIOD: No scoring.

GOALS	
C. Liscombe, DET	6
A. Jackson, BOS	6
J. Carveth, DET	6

ASSISTS	
F. Hollett, BOS	9
C. Liscombe, DET	8
S. Abel, DET	8

POINTS	
C. Liscombe, DET	14
S. Abel, DET	13

WINS	
J. Mowers, DET	8
F. Brimsek, BOS	4
T. Broda, TOR	2

GOALS AGAINST AVE.	
J. Mowers, DET	2.20
F. Brimsek, BOS	2.67
T. Broda, TOR	3.33

SHUTOUTS	
J. Mowers, DET	2
P. Bibeault, MONT	1

1943–44

Semifinal Round

Montreal Canadiens over Toronto, 4 games to 1

March 21, at MONT: TOR 3, MONT 1
March 23, at MONT: MONT 5, TOR 1
March 25, at TOR: MONT 2, TOR 1
March 28, at TOR: MONT 4, TOR 1
March 30, at MONT: MONT 11, TOR 0

Chicago over Detroit, 4 games to 1

March 21, at DET: CHI 2, DET 1
March 23, at DET: DET 4, CHI 1
March 26, at CHI: CHI 2, DET 0
March 28, at CHI: CHI 7, DET 1
March 30, at DET: CHI 5, DET 2

FINAL ROUND: Montreal Canadiens over Chicago, 4 games to 0

GAME 1, April 4:

CHICAGO	0	1	0	– 1
MONTREAL	1	2	2	– 5

Goaltenders: Chicago, Karakas. Montreal, Durnan.

FIRST PERIOD: 1. Montreal, Watson 8:37.
SECOND PERIOD: 2. Montreal, Blake (Richard, Lach) 6:35. 3. Chicago, Smith (Bentley, Mosienko) 10:11. 4. Montreal, Getliffe (Heffernan, O'Connor) 10:58.
THIRD PERIOD: 5. Montreal, Chamberlain (Watson, Bouchard) 4:47. 6. Montreal, Getliffe 18:07.

GAME 2, April 6:

CHICAGO	0	0	1	–	1
MONTREAL	0	1	2	–	3

Goaltenders: Chicago, Karakas. Montreal, Durnan.

FIRST PERIOD: No scoring.
SECOND PERIOD: 1. Montreal, Richard (Lach, Blake) 13:00.
THIRD PERIOD: 2. Montreal, Richard (Lamoureux) 12:16. 3. Montreal, Richard (Lach) 15:33. 4. Chicago, Harms (Smith, Allen) 19:59.

GAME 3, April 9:

MONTREAL	0	1	2	–	3
CHICAGO	1	0	1	–	2

Goaltenders: Montreal, Durnan. Chicago, Karakas.

FIRST PERIOD: 1. Chicago, Allen (Weibe) 5:14.
SECOND PERIOD: 2. Montreal, Blake (Richard) 2:02.
THIRD PERIOD: 3. Chicago, Harms (Johnson) 4:16. 4. Montreal, McMahon 5:47. 5. Montreal, Watson (Getliffe) 6:42.

GAME 4, April 13:

CHICAGO	1	3	0	0	–	4
MONTREAL	1	0	3	1	–	5

Goaltenders: Chicago, Karakas. Montreal, Durnan.

FIRST PERIOD: 1. Chicago, Allen (Dahlstrom) 5:12. 2. Montreal, Lach (Blake) 8:48.
SECOND PERIOD: 3. Chicago, Harms (Dahlstrom, Allen) 7:30. 4. Chicago, Allen (Bentley, Smith) 9:12. 5. Chicago, Bentley (Smith) 10:09.
THIRD PERIOD: 6. Montreal, Lach (Blake) 10:02. 7. Montreal, Richard (Blake) 16:05. 8. Montreal, Richard (Blake, Bouchard) 17:20.
FIRST OVERTIME: 9. Montreal, Blake (Bouchard) 9:12.

GOALS	
M. Richard, MONT	12
D. Bentley, CHI	8
T. Blake, MONT	7

ASSISTS	
T. Blake, MONT	11
E. Lach, MONT	11
C. Smith, CHI	8

POINTS	
T. Blake, MONT	18
M. Richard, MONT	17
E. Lach, MONT	13

WINS	
B. Durnan, MONT	8
M. Karakas, CHI	4

GOALS AGAINST AVE.	
B. Durnan, MONT	1.55
M. Karakas, CHI	2.66
C. Dion, DET	3.40

SHUTOUTS	
B. Durnan, MONT	1
M. Karakas, CHI	1

1944–45

Semifinal Round

Toronto over Montreal Canadiens, 4 games to 2

March 20, at MONT: TOR 1, MONT 0
March 22, at MONT: TOR 3, MONT 2
March 24, at TOR: MONT 4, TOR 1
March 27, at TOR: TOR 4, MONT 3 (OT, 12:36)
March 29, at MONT: MONT 10, TOR 3
March 31, at TOR: TOR 3, MONT 2

Detroit over Boston, 4 games to 3

March 20, at DET: BOS 4, DET 3
March 22, at DET: BOS 4, DET 2
March 25, at BOS: DET 3, BOS 2
March 27, at BOS: DET 3, BOS 2
March 29, at DET: DET 3. BOS 2 (OT, 17:12)
April 1, at BOS: BOS 5, DET 3
April 3, at DET: DET 5, BOS 3

FINAL ROUND: Toronto over Detroit, 4 games to 3

GAME 1, April 6:

TORONTO	1	0	0	–	1
DETROIT	0	0	0	–	0

Goaltenders: Toronto, McCool. Detroit, Lumley.

FIRST PERIOD: 1. Toronto, Schriner 13:56.
SECOND PERIOD: No scoring.
THIRD PERIOD: No scoring.

GAME 2, April 8:

TORONTO	0	1	1	–	2
DETROIT	0	0	0	–	0

Goaltenders: Toronto, McCool. Detroit, Lumley.

FIRST PERIOD: No scoring.
SECOND PERIOD: 1. Toronto, Kennedy (Pratt) 13:05.
THIRD PERIOD: 2. Toronto, Morris 12:03.

GAME 3, April 12:

DETROIT	0	0	0	–	0
TORONTO	0	0	1	–	1

Goaltenders: Detroit, Lumley. Toronto, McCool.

FIRST PERIOD: No scoring.
SECOND PERIOD: No scoring.
THIRD PERIOD: 1. Toronto, Bodnar (Stanowski) 3:01.

GAME 4, April 14:

DETROIT	1	1	3	–	5
TORONTO	2	1	0	–	3

Goaltenders: Detroit, Lumley. Toronto, McCool.

FIRST PERIOD: 1. Detroit, Hollett (E. Bruneteau) 8:35. 2. Toronto, Kennedy (Hill) 9:19. 3. Toronto, Kennedy (Hill) 11:44.
SECOND PERIOD: 4. Detroit, Armstrong (M. Bruneteau) 9:20. 5. Toronto, Kennedy (Davidson) 10:21.
THIRD PERIOD: 6. Detroit, E. Bruneteau 1:11. 7. Detroit, Lindsay 3:20. 8. Detroit, Carveth (Hollett) 17:38.

GAME 5, April 19:

TORONTO	0	0	0	–	0
DETROIT	0	0	2	–	2

Goaltenders: Toronto, McCool. Detroit, Lumley.

FIRST PERIOD: No scoring.
SECOND PERIOD: No scoring.
THIRD PERIOD: 1. Detroit, Hollett (Carveth) 8:21. 2. Detroit, Carveth (Quackenbush) 16:16.

GAME 6, April 21:

DETROIT	0	0	0	1	–	1
TORONTO	0	0	0	0	–	0

Goaltenders: Detroit, Lumley. Toronto, McCool.

FIRST PERIOD: No scoring.
SECOND PERIOD: No scoring.
THIRD PERIOD: No scoring.
FIRST OVERTIME: 1. Detroit, E. Bruneteau 14:16.

GAME 7, April 22:

TORONTO	1	0	1	–	2
DETROIT	0	0	1	–	1

Goaltenders: Toronto, McCool. Detroit, Lumley.

FIRST PERIOD: 1. Toronto, Hill (Kennedy) 5:38.
SECOND PERIOD: No scoring.
THIRD PERIOD: 2. Detroit, Armstrong (Hollett) 8:16. 3. Toronto, Pratt (N. Metz) 12:14.

GOALS

T. Kennedy, TOR	7
M. Richard, MONT	6

ASSISTS

J. Carveth, DET	6
J. Crawford, BOS	5

POINTS

J. Carveth, DET	11
T. Kennedy, TOR	9
M. Richard, MONT	8
E. Lach, MONT	8

WINS

F. McCool, TOR	8
H. Lumley, DET	7
P. Bibeault, BOS	3

GOALS AGAINST AVE.

H. Lumley, DET	2.21
F. McCool, TOR	2.31
B. Durnan, MONT	2.50

SHUTOUTS

F. McCool, TOR	4
H. Lumley, DET	2

1945–46

Semifinal Round

Montreal Canadiens over Chicago, 4 games to 0

March 19, at MONT: MONT 6, CHI 2
March 21, at MONT: MONT 5, CHI 1
March 24, at CHI: MONT 8, CHI 2
March 26, at CHI: MONT 7, CHI 2

Boston over Detroit, 4 games to 1

March 19, at BOS: BOS 3, DET 1
March 21, at BOS: DET 3, BOS 0
March 24, at DET: BOS 5, DET 2
March 26, at DET: BOS 4, DET 1
March 28, at BOS: BOS 4, DET 3 (OT, 9:51)

FINAL ROUND: Montreal Canadiens over Boston, 4 games to 1

GAME 1, March 30:

BOSTON	0	2	1	0	–	3
MONTREAL	0	2	1	1	–	4

Goaltenders: Boston, Brimsek. Montreal, Durnan.

FIRST PERIOD: No scoring.
SECOND PERIOD: 1. Montreal, Bouchard 0:21. 2. Montreal, Fillion 3:19. 3. Boston, Guidolin (Cain) 5:09. 4. Boston, Dumart (Schmidt) 8:02.
THIRD PERIOD: 5. Boston, Crawford (Guidolin) 14:04. 6. Montreal, Chamberlain (Richard) 16:23.
FIRST OVERTIME: 7. Montreal, Richard (Bouchard) 9:08.

GAME 2, April 2:

BOSTON	1	1	0	0	–	2
MONTREAL	1	0	1	1	–	3

Goaltenders: Boston, Brimsek. Montreal, Durnan.

FIRST PERIOD: 1. Montreal, Lach (Richard) 1:06. 2. Boston, Egan 10:55.
SECOND PERIOD: 3. Boston, Bauer (Schmidt) 3:04.
THIRD PERIOD: 4. Montreal, Bouchard 10:10.
FIRST OVERTIME: 5. Montreal, Peters 16:55.

GAME 3, April 4:

MONTREAL	2	0	2	–	4
BOSTON	1	1	0	–	2

Goaltenders: Montreal, Durnan. Boston, Brimsek.

FIRST PERIOD: 1. Montreal, Lach 10:14. 2. Boston, Guidolin (Shill, Gallinger) 11:01. Montreal, Mosdell (Harmon) 14:13.
SECOND PERIOD: 4. Boston, T. Reardon (Cowley, Smith) 18:41.
THIRD PERIOD: 5. Montreal, Mosdell 2:45. 6. Montreal, Hiller (Lach) 5:18.

GAME 4, April 7:

MONTREAL	0	1	1	0	–	2
BOSTON	0	1	1	1	–	3

Goaltenders: Montreal, Durnan. Boston, Brimsek.

FIRST PERIOD: No scoring.
SECOND PERIOD: 1. Boston, Henderson (Gallinger) 8:05. 2. Montreal, Richard (Harmon) 13:46.
THIRD PERIOD: 3. Boston, Gallinger (Cain) 3:01. 4. Montreal, Richard (Lach) 4:04.
FIRST OVERTIME: 5. Boston, T. Reardon (Smith, Cowley) 15:13.

GAME 5, April 9:

BOSTON	2	1	0	–	3
MONTREAL	3	0	3	–	6

Goaltenders: Boston, Brimsek. Montreal, Durnan.

FIRST PERIOD: 1. Boston, Cowley 5:42. 2. Montreal, Fillion (Hiller) 9:55. 3. Boston, Bauer (Dumart) 14:01. 4. Montreal, Lach (Eddolls) 15:51. 5. Montreal, Mosdell (Harmon) 18:28.
SECOND PERIOD: 6. Boston, Schmidt 7:15.
THIRD PERIOD: 7. Montreal, Blake (Lach) 11:06. 8. Montreal, Chamberlain 14:05. 9. Montreal, Hiller (Lach) 17:14.

GOALS		ASSISTS		POINTS	
T. Blake, MONT	7	E. Lach, MONT	12	E. Lach, MONT	17
M. Richard, MONT	7	T. Blake, MONT	6	T. Blake, MONT	13
E. Lach, MONT	5	M. Schmidt, BOS	5	M. Richard, MONT	11
B. Guidolin, BOS	5				

WINS		GOALS AGAINST AVE.		SHUTOUTS	
B. Durnan, MONT	8	B. Durnan, MONT	2.22	H. Lumley, DET	1
F. Brimsek, BOS	5	F. Brimsek, BOS	2.90		
		H. Lumley, DET	3.20		

1946–47

Semifinal Round

Montreal Canadiens over Boston, 4 games to 1

March 25, at MONT: MONT 3, BOS 1
March 27, at MONT: MONT 2, BOS 1 (OT, 5:38)
March 29, at BOS: BOS 4, MONT 2
April 1, at BOS: MONT 5, BOS 1
April 3, at MONT: MONT 4, BOS 3 (2 OT, 16:40)

Toronto over Detroit, 4 games to 1

March 26, at TOR: TOR 3, DET 2 (OT, 3:05)
March 29, at TOR: DET 9, TOR 1
April 1, at DET: TOR 4, DET 1
April 3, at DET: TOR 4, DET 1
April 5, at TOR: TOR 6, DET 1

FINAL ROUND: Toronto over Montreal, 4 games to 2

GAME 1, April 8:

TORONTO	0	0	0	– 0
MONTREAL	1	2	3	– 6

Goaltenders: Toronto, Broda. Montreal, Durnan.

FIRST PERIOD: 1. Montreal, O'Connor (Leger) 2:20.
SECOND PERIOD: 2. Montreal, Reay (Harmon) 8:17. 3. Montreal, Richard (O'Connor) 9:41.
THIRD PERIOD: 4. Montreal, Allen (Bouchard) 5:40. 5. Montreal, Reay (Bouchard, Allen) 11:04. 6. Montreal, Chamberlain (Peters, Quilty) 18:28.

GAME 2, April 10:

TORONTO	2	1	1	– 4
MONTREAL	0	0	0	– 0

Goaltenders: Toronto, Broda. Montreal, Durnan.

FIRST PERIOD: 1. Toronto, Kennedy (Lynn, Barilko) 1:12. 2. Toronto, Lynn (Kennedy) 1:36.
SECOND PERIOD: 3. Toronto, G. Stewart (D. Metz, Barilko) 6:37.
THIRD PERIOD: 4. Toronto, Watson (Mortson) 11:55.

GAME 3, April 12:

MONTREAL	0	2	0	– 2
TORONTO	1	2	1	– 4

Goaltenders: Montreal, Durnan. Toronto, Broda.

FIRST PERIOD: 1. Toronto, Mortson 9:44.
SECOND PERIOD: 2. Toronto, Poile (Stewart, D. Metz) 4:48. 3. Toronto, Lynn (Meeker) 12:23. 4. Montreal, Gravelle (O'Connor) 12:34. 5. Montreal, O'Connor (Blake) 18:31.
THIRD PERIOD: 6. Toronto, Kennedy 19:14.

GAME 4, April 15:

MONTREAL	1	0	0	0	– 1
TORONTO	1	0	0	1	– 2

Goaltenders: Montreal, Durnan. Toronto, Broda.

FIRST PERIOD: 1. Montreal, Harmon (Blake) 4:38. 2. Toronto, Watson (Apps) 6:13.
SECOND PERIOD: No scoring.
THIRD PERIOD: No scoring.
FIRST OVERTIME: 3. Toronto, Apps (Watson) 16:36.

GAME 5, April 17:

TORONTO	0	0	1	– 1
MONTREAL	2	1	0	– 3

Goaltenders: Toronto, Broda. Montreal, Durnan.

FIRST PERIOD: 1. Montreal, Richard (Blake, Bouchard) 1:23. 2. Montreal, Gravelle (Leger) 8:29.
SECOND PERIOD: 3. Montreal, Richard (Blake, O'Connor) 19:32.
THIRD PERIOD: 4. Toronto, Poile (Stewart) 13:37.

GAME 6, April 19:

MONTREAL	1	0	0	– 1
TORONTO	0	1	1	– 2

Goaltenders: Montreal, Durnan. Toronto, Broda.

FIRST PERIOD: 1. Montreal, O'Connor 0:25.
SECOND PERIOD: 2. Toronto, Lynn (Kennedy, Meeker) 5:39.
THIRD PERIOD: 3. Toronto, Kennedy (Meeker) 14:39.

GOALS		ASSISTS		POINTS	
M. Richard, MONT	6	T. Blake, MONT	7	M. Richard, MONT	11
B. Reay, MONT	6	R. Leger, MONT	6	T. Kennedy, TOR	9
S. Apps, TOR	5			T. Blake, MONT	9

WINS		GOALS AGAINST AVE.		SHUTOUTS	
T. Broda, TOR	8	B. Durnan, MONT	2.09	B. Durnan, MONT	1
B. Durnan, MONT	6	T. Broda, TOR	2.45	T. Broda, TOR	1
		F. Brimsek, BOS	2.97		

1947–48

Semifinal Round

Toronto over Boston, 4 games to 1

March 24, at TOR: TOR 5, BOS 4 (OT, 17:03)
March 27, at TOR: TOR 5, BOS 3
March 30, at BOS: TOR 5, BOS 1
April 1, at BOS: BOS 3, TOR 2
April 3, at TOR: TOR 3, BOS 2

Detroit over New York Rangers, 4 games to 2

March 24, at DET: DET 2, NYR 1
March 26, at DET: DET 5, NYR 2
March 28, at NYR: NYR 3, DET 2
March 30, at NYR: NYR 3, DET 1
April 1, at DET: DET 3, NYR 1
April 4, at NYR: DET 4, NYR 2

FINAL ROUND: Toronto over Detroit, 4 games to 0

GAME 1, April 7:

DETROIT	1	0	2	–	3
TORONTO	3	2	0	–	5

Goaltenders: Detroit, Lumley. Toronto, Broda.

FIRST PERIOD: 1. Detroit, McFadden (Horeck) 7:20. 2. Toronto, Watson (Apps) 8:21. 3. Toronto, Klukay (Bentley, Costello) 9:04. 4. Toronto, Apps (Mortson) 18:24.
SECOND PERIOD: 5. Toronto, Mortson (Bentley) 14:31. 6. Toronto, Meeker (Stanowski, Kennedy) 19:21.
THIRD PERIOD: 7. Detroit, Conacher (Quackenbush, Lindsay) 4:28. 8. Detroit, Lindsay 5:25.

GAME 2, April 10:

DETROIT	0	1	1	–	2
TORONTO	1	3	0	–	4

Goaltenders: Detroit, Lumley. Toronto, Broda.

FIRST PERIOD: 1. Toronto, Bentley (Samis) 13:31.
SECOND PERIOD: 2. Toronto, Ezinicki (Apps, Watson) 3:38. 3. Toronto, Bentley (Costello, Klukay) 17:16. 4. Detroit, Horeck (Abel) 18:18. 5. Toronto, Watson 18:50.
THIRD PERIOD: 6. Detroit, Gauthier (McFadden) 17:18.

GAME 3, April 11:

TORONTO	0	1	1	–	2
DETROIT	0	0	0	–	0

Goaltenders: Toronto, Broda. Detroit, Lumley.

FIRST PERIOD: No scoring.
SECOND PERIOD: 1. Toronto, Watson (Ezinicki) 19:42.
THIRD PERIOD: 2. Toronto, Lynn (Kennedy) 15:16.

GAME 4, April 14:

TORONTO	3	3	1	–	7
DETROIT	0	1	1	–	2

Goaltenders: Toronto, Broda. Detroit, Lumley.

FIRST PERIOD: 1. Toronto, Kennedy (Bentley) 2:51. 2. Toronto, Boesch 5:03. Toronto, Watson 11:13.
SECOND PERIOD: 4. Detroit, Reise (Pavelich, Horeck) 2:41. 5. Toronto, Apps (Thomson) 4:26. 6. Toronto, Kennedy (Lynn) 9:42. 7. Toronto, Watson 11:38.
THIRD PERIOD: 8. Toronto, Costello (Bentley) 14:37. 9. Detroit, Horeck (Fogolin) 18:48.

GOALS	
T. Kennedy, TOR	8
H. Watson, TOR	5
J. McFadden, DET	5

ASSISTS	
M. Bentley, TOR	7
P. Horeck, DET	7
T. Kennedy, TOR	6

POINTS	
T. Kennedy, TOR	14
M. Bentley, TOR	11
P. Horeck, DET	10

WINS	
T. Broda, TOR	8
H. Lumley, DET	4
C. Rayner, NYR	2

GOALS AGAINST AVE.	
T. Broda, TOR	2.22
C. Rayner, NYR	2.83
H. Lumley, DET	3.00

SHUTOUTS	
T. Broda, TOR	1

1948–49

Semifinal Round

Detroit over Montreal Canadiens, 4 games to 3

March 22, at DET: DET 2, MONT 1 (3 OT, 4:52)
March 24, at DET: MONT 4, DET 3 (OT, 2:59)
March 26, at MONT: MONT 3, DET 2
March 29, at MONT: DET 3, MONT 1
March 31, at DET: DET 3, MONT 1
April 2, at MONT: MONT 3, DET 1
April 5, at DET: DET 3, MONT 1

Toronto over Boston, 4 games to 1

March 22, at BOS: TOR 3, BOS 0
March 24, at BOS: TOR 3, BOS 2
March 26, at TOR: BOS 5, TOR 4 (OT, 16:14)
March 29, at TOR: TOR 3, BOS 1
March 30, at BOS: TOR 3, BOS 2

FINAL ROUND: Toronto over Detroit, 4 games to 0

GAME 1, April 8:

TORONTO	1	1	0	1	–	3
DETROIT	1	0	1	0	–	2

Goaltenders: Toronto, Broda. Detroit, Lumley.

FIRST PERIOD: 1. Detroit, Gee (Lindsay, Howe) 4:15. 2. Toronto, Bentley (Timgren, Klukay) 13:15.
SECOND PERIOD: 3. Toronto, Thomson (Bentley) 16:02.
THIRD PERIOD: 4. Detroit, Quackenbush (Lindsay, Gee) 13:56.
FIRST OVERTIME: 5. Toronto, Klukay (Thomson, Timgren) 17:31.

GAME 2, April 10:

TORONTO	2	1	0	–	3
DETROIT	0	0	1	–	1

Goaltenders: Toronto, Broda. Detroit, Lumley.

FIRST PERIOD: 1. Toronto, Smith (Boesch) 8:50. 2. Toronto, Smith (Barilko, Kennedy) 9:56.
SECOND PERIOD: 3. Toronto, Smith (Kennedy, Mackell) 17:58.
THIRD PERIOD: 4. Detroit, Horeck (Stewart, McFadden) 5:50.

GAME 3, April 13:

DETROIT	1	0	0	–	1
TORONTO	0	3	0	–	3

Goaltenders: Detroit, Lumley. Toronto, Broda.

FIRST PERIOD: 1. Detroit, Stewart (Horeck) 4:57.
SECOND PERIOD: 2. Toronto, Ezinicki (Gardner, Watson) 11:02. 3. Toronto, Kennedy (Smith, Mackell) 12:40. 4. Toronto, Mortson (Thomson, Klukay) 16:18.
THIRD PERIOD: No scoring.

GAME 4, April 16:

DETROIT	1	0	0	–	1
TORONTO	0	2	1	–	3

Goaltenders: Detroit, Lumley. Toronto, Broda.

FIRST PERIOD: 1. Detroit, Lindsay (Gee, Howe) 2:59.
SECOND PERIOD: 2. Toronto, Timgren (Bentley) 10:10. 3. Toronto, Gardner (Thomson, Ezinicki) 19:45.
THIRD PERIOD: 4. Toronto, Bentley (Timgren) 15:10.

GOALS		**ASSISTS**		**POINTS**	
G. Howe, DET	8	T. Kennedy, TOR	6	G. Howe, DET	11
S. Smith, TOR	5	T. Lindsay, DET	6	T. Kennedy, TOR	8
G. Plamondon, MONT	5			T. Lindsay, DET	8

WINS		**GOALS AGAINST AVE.**		**SHUTOUTS**	
T. Broda, TOR	8	T. Broda, TOR	1.67	T. Broda, TOR	1
H. Lumley, DET	4	H. Lumley, DET	2.36		
B. Durnan, MONT	3	B. Durnan, MONT	2.43		

1949–50

Semifinal Round

Detroit over Toronto, 4 games to 3

March 28, at DET: TOR 5, DET 0
March 30, at DET: DET 3, TOR 1
April 1, at TOR: TOR 2, DET 0
April 4, at TOR: DET 2, TOR 1 (2 OT, 0:38)
April 6, at DET: TOR 2, DET 0
April 8, at TOR: DET 4, TOR 0
April 9, at DET: DET 1, TOR 0 (OT, 8:34)

N.Y. Rangers over Mont. Canadiens, 4 games to 1

March 29, at NYR: NYR 3, MONT 1
April 1, at MONT: NYR 3, MONT 2
April 2, at NYR: NYR 4, MONT 1
April 4, at MONT: MONT 3, NYR 2 (OT, 15:19)
April 6, at MONT: NYR 3, MONT 0

FINAL ROUND: Detroit over New York Rangers, 4 games to 3

GAME 1, April 11:

NEW YORK	1	0	0	–	1
DETROIT	0	4	0	–	4

Goaltenders: New York, Rayner. Detroit, Lumley.

FIRST PERIOD: 1. New York, O'Connor (Gordon, Mickoski) 5:58.
SECOND PERIOD: 2. Detroit, Carveth (Gee, Babando) 4:43. 3. Detroit, Gee (J. Wilson) 9:32. 4. Detroit, McFadden (Couture) 10:06. 5. Detroit, Couture (Pronovost, McFadden) 13:56.
THIRD PERIOD: No scoring.

GAME 2, April 13 (at Toronto):

DETROIT	0	1	0	–	1
NEW YORK	0	1	2	–	3

Goaltenders: Detroit, Lumley. New York, Rayner.

FIRST PERIOD: No scoring.
SECOND PERIOD: 1. Detroit, Couture (Pavelich) 3:05. 2. New York, Egan 10:39.
THIRD PERIOD: 3. New York, Laprade (Stanley) 3:04. 4. New York, Laprade 11:20.

GAME 3, April 15 (at Toronto):

DETROIT	2	1	1	–	4
NEW YORK	0	0	0	–	0

Goaltenders: Detroit, Lumley. New York, Rayner.

FIRST PERIOD: 1. Detroit, Couture (Kelly) 14:14. 2. Detroit, Gee (Dewsbury) 19:08.
SECOND PERIOD: 3. Detroit, Abel 19:16.
THIRD PERIOD: 4. Pavelich (Kelly) 16:55.

GAME 4, April 18:

NEW YORK	0	1	2	1	–	4
DETROIT	2	0	1	0	–	3

Goaltenders: New York, Rayner. Detroit, Lumley.

FIRST PERIOD: 1. Detroit, Lindsay (Stewart) 6:31. 2. Detroit, Abel (Lindsay) 16:48.
SECOND PERIOD: 3. New York, O'Connor (Kaleta, Mickoski) 19:59.
THIRD PERIOD: 4. Detroit, Pavelich (Peters, Stewart) 3:32. 5. New York, Laprade (Fisher, Leswick) 8:09. 6. New York, Kyle (Kaleta) 16:26.
FIRST OVERTIME: 7. New York, Raleigh (Slowinski) 16:26.

GAME 5, April 20:

NEW YORK	0	1	0	1	–	2
DETROIT	0	0	1	0	–	1

Goaltenders: New York, Rayner. Detroit, Lumley.

FIRST PERIOD: No scoring.
SECOND PERIOD: 1. New York, Fisher (Leswick) 7:44.
THIRD PERIOD: 2. Detroit, Lindsay (Carveth, Abel) 18:10.
FIRST OVERTIME: 3. New York, Raleigh (Lund, Slowinski) 1:38.

GAME 6, April 22:

NEW YORK	2	1	1	–	4
DETROIT	1	2	2	–	5

Goaltenders: New York, Rayner. Detroit, Lumley.

FIRST PERIOD: 1. New York, Stanley (Mickoski, Kaleta) 3:45. 2. New York, Fisher (Laprade, Leswick) 7:35. 3. Detroit, Lindsay (Stewart) 19:18.
SECOND PERIOD: 4. New York, Lund (Egan, Slowinski) 3:18. 5. Detroit, Abel (Lindsay, Carveth) 5:38. 6. Detroit, Couture (Babando, Gee) 16:07.
THIRD PERIOD: 7. New York, Leswick (Laprade, Fisher) 1:54. 8. Detroit, Lindsay (Abel) 4:13. 9. Detroit, Abel (Carveth, Dewsbury) 10:34.

GAME 7: April 23

NEW YORK	2	1	0	0	0	–	3
DETROIT	0	3	0	0	1	–	4

Goaltenders: New York, Rayner. Detroit, Lumley.

FIRST PERIOD: 1. New York, Stanley (Leswick) 11:14. 2. New York, Leswick (Laprade, O'Connor) 12:18.
SECOND PERIOD: 3. Detroit, Babando (Kelly, Couture) 5:09. 4. Detroit, Abel (Dewsbury) 5:30. 5. New York, O'Connor (Mickoski) 11:42. 6. Detroit, McFadden (Peters) 15:57.
THIRD PERIOD: No scoring.
FIRST OVERTIME: No scoring.
SECOND OVERTIME: 7. Detroit, Babando (Gee) 8:31.

GOALS

P. Lund, NYR	6
S. Abel, DET	6
G. Couture, DET	5

ASSISTS

G. Gee, DET	6
E. Slowinski, NYR	6

POINTS

P. Lund, NYR	11
G. Couture, DET	9
D. Raleigh, NYR	9
G. Gee, DET	9

WINS

H. Lumley, DET	8
C. Rayner, NYR	7
T. Broda, TOR	3

GOALS AGAINST AVE.

T. Broda, TOR	1.43
H. Lumley, DET	2.00
C. Rayner, NYR	2.42

SHUTOUTS

T. Broda, TOR	3
H. Lumley, DET	3
C. Rayner, NYR	1

1950–51

Semifinal Round

Montreal Canadiens over Detroit, 4 games to 2

March 27, at DET: MONT 3, DET 2 (4 OT, 1:09)
March 29, at DET: MONT 1, DET 0 (3 OT, 2:20)
March 31, at MONT: DET 2, MONT 0
April 3, at MONT: DET 4, MONT 1
April 5, at DET: MONT 5, DET 2
April 7, at MONT: MONT 3, DET 2

Toronto over Boston, 4 games to 1 (one tie)

March 28, at TOR: BOS 2, TOR 0
March 31, at TOR: TOR 1, BOS 1 (OT, curfew)
April 1, at BOS: TOR 3, BOS 0
April 3, at BOS: TOR 3, BOS 1
April 7, at TOR: TOR 4, BOS 1
April 8, at BOS: TOR 6, BOS 0

FINAL ROUND: Toronto over Montreal Canadiens, 4 games to 1

GAME 1, April 11:

MONTREAL	1	1	0	0	–	2
TORONTO	2	0	0	1	–	3

Goaltenders: Montreal, McNeil. Toronto, Broda.

FIRST PERIOD: 1. Toronto, Smith (Kennedy, Sloan) 0:15. 2. Montreal, Richard 15:27. 3. Toronto, Sloan (Mortson) 15:42.
SECOND PERIOD: 4. Montreal, Masnick (Reay) 4:02.
THIRD PERIOD: No scoring.
FIRST OVERTIME: 5. Toronto, Smith (Sloan) 5:51.

GAME 2, April 14:

MONTREAL	1	1	0	1	–	3
TORONTO	0	1	1	0	–	2

Goaltenders: Montreal, McNeil. Toronto, Broda.

FIRST PERIOD: 1. Montreal, Masnick (Meger) 3:44.
SECOND PERIOD: 2. Montreal, Reay (Richard, Olmstead) 9:24. 3. Toronto, Smith (Bentley, Kennedy) 16:31.
THIRD PERIOD: 4. Toronto, Kennedy (Sloan) 8:16.
FIRST OVERTIME: 5. Montreal, Richard (Harvey) 2:55.

GAME 3, April 17:

TORONTO	0	1	0	1	–	2
MONTREAL	1	0	0	0	–	1

Goaltenders: Toronto, Rollins. Montreal, McNeil

FIRST PERIOD: 1. Montreal, Richard (Olmstead) 2:18.
SECOND PERIOD: 2. Toronto, Smith (Bentley) 5:58.
THIRD PERIOD: No scoring.
FIRST OVERTIME: 3. Toronto, Kennedy (Sloan) 4:47.

GAME 4, April 19:

TORONTO	1	1	0	1	–	3
MONTREAL	1	0	1	0	–	2

Goaltenders: Toronto, Rollins. Montreal, McNeil.

FIRST PERIOD: 1. Toronto, Smith (Kennedy) 0:38. 2. Montreal, Richard (Reay, Harvey) 14:41.
SECOND PERIOD: 3. Toronto, Meeker (Watson) 1:27.
THIRD PERIOD: 4. Montreal, Lach (Richard, Bouchard) 13:49.
FIRST OVERTIME: 5. Toronto, Watson (Bentley) 5:15.

GAME 5, April 21:

MONTREAL	0	1	1	0	–	2
TORONTO	0	1	1	1	–	3

Goaltenders: Montreal, McNeil. Toronto, Rollins.

FIRST PERIOD: No scoring.
SECOND PERIOD: 1. Montreal, Richard (MacPherson) 8:56. 2. Toronto, Sloan (Kennedy) 12:00.
THIRD PERIOD: 3. Montreal, Meger (Harvey) 4:47. 4. Toronto, Sloan (Smith, Bentley) 19:28.
FIRST OVERTIME: 5. Toronto, Barilko (Meeker, Watson) 2:53.

GOALS		ASSISTS		POINTS	
M. Richard, MONT	9	M. Bentley, TOR	11	M. Richard, MONT	13
S. Smith, TOR	7	T. Kennedy, TOR	5	M. Bentley, TOR	13
		T. Sloan, TOR	5	S. Smith, TOR	10
		D. Harvey, MONT	5		

WINS		GOALS AGAINST AVE.		SHUTOUTS	
T. Broda, TOR	5	T. Broda, TOR	1.12	T. Broda, TOR	2
G. McNeil, MONT	5	A. Rollins, TOR	1.50	T. Sawchuk, DET	1
A. Rollins, TOR	3	J. Gelineau, BOS	1.62	G. McNeil, MONT	1
				J. Gelineau, BOS	1

1951–52

Semifinal Round

Detroit over Toronto, 4 games to 0

March 25, at DET: DET 3, TOR 0
March 27, at DET: DET 1, TOR 0
March 29, at TOR: DET 6, TOR 2
April 1, at TOR: DET 3, TOR 1

Montreal Canadiens over Boston, 4 games to 3

March 25, at MONT: MONT 5, BOS 1
March 27, at MONT: MONT 4, BOS 0
March 30, at BOS: BOS 4, MONT 1
April 1, at BOS: BOS 3, MONT 2
April 3, at MONT: BOS 1, MONT 0
April 6, at BOS: MONT 3, BOS 2 (2 OT, 7:49)
April 8, at MONT: MONT 3, BOS 1

FINAL ROUND: Detroit over Montreal, 4 games to 0

GAME 1, April 10:

DETROIT	0	1	2	– 3
MONTREAL	0	0	1	– 1

Goaltenders: Detroit, Sawchuk. Montreal, McNeil.

FIRST PERIOD: No scoring.
SECOND PERIOD: 1. Detroit, Leswick (Pavelich) 3:27.
THIRD PERIOD: 2. Detroit, Leswick (Skov) 7:59. 3. Montreal, Johnson (Olmstead, Curry) 11:01. 4. Detroit, Lindsay (Abel) 19:44.

GAME 2, April 12:

DETROIT	1	1	0	– 2
MONTREAL	1	0	0	– 1

Goaltenders: Detroit, Sawchuk. Montreal, McNeil.

FIRST PERIOD: 1. Detroit, Pavelich (Leswick, Skov) 16:09. 2. Montreal, Lach (Geoffrion) 18:37.
SECOND PERIOD: 3. Detroit, Lindsay 0:43.
THIRD PERIOD: No scoring.

GAME 3, April 13:

MONTREAL	0	0	0	– 0
DETROIT	1	1	1	– 3

Goaltenders: Montreal, McNeil. Detroit, Sawchuk.

FIRST PERIOD: 1. Detroit, Howe (Stasiuk) 4:31.
SECOND PERIOD: 2. Detroit, Lindsay (Howe) 9:13.
THIRD PERIOD: 3. Detroit, Howe (Pavelich) 6:54.

GAME 4, April 15:

MONTREAL	0	0	0	– 0
DETROIT	1	1	1	– 3

Goaltenders: Montreal, McNeil. Detroit, Sawchuk.

FIRST PERIOD: 1. Detroit, Prystai (Delvecchio, Wilson) 6:50.
SECOND PERIOD: 2. Detroit, Skov (Prystai) 19:39.
THIRD PERIOD: 3. Detroit, Prystai 7:35.

GOALS		ASSISTS		POINTS	
T. Lindsay, DET	5	M. Prystai, DET	5	T. Lindsay, DET	7
F. Curry, MONT	4	G. Howe, DET	5	F. Curry, MONT	7
M. Richard, MONT	4	G. Skov, DET	4	M. Prystai, DET	7
J. Wilson, DET	4			G. Howe, DET	7

WINS		GOALS AGAINST AVE.		SHUTOUTS	
T. Sawchuk, DET	8	T. Sawchuk, DET	0.62	T. Sawchuk, DET	4
G. McNeil, MONT	4	G. McNeil, MONT	2.09	J. Henry, BOS	1
J. Henry, BOS	3	J. Henry, BOS	2.57	G. McNeil, MONT	1

1952–53

Semifinal Round

Boston over Detroit, 4 games to 2

March 24, at DET: DET 7, BOS 0
March 26, at DET: BOS 5, DET 3
March 29, at BOS: BOS 2, DET 1 (OT, 12:29)
March 31, at BOS: BOS 6, DET 2
April 2, at DET: DET 6, BOS 4
April 5, at BOS: BOS 4, DET 2

Montreal Canadiens over Chicago, 4 games to 3

March 24, at MONT: MONT 3, CHI 1
March 26, at MONT: MONT 4, CHI 3
March 29, at CHI: CHI 2, MONT 1 (OT, 5:18)
March 31, at CHI: CHI 3, MONT 1
April 2, at MONT: CHI 4, MONT 2
April 4, at CHI: MONT 3, CHI 0
April 7, at MONT: MONT 4, CHI 1

FINAL ROUND: Montreal Canadiens over Boston, 4 games to 1

GAME 1, April 9:

BOSTON	1	0	1	–	2
MONTREAL	1	2	1	–	4

Goaltenders: Boston, J. Henry. Montreal, Plante.

FIRST PERIOD: 1. Boston, Armstrong (Mackell, Laycoe) 2:08. 2. Montreal, Moore 13:42.
SECOND PERIOD: 3. Montreal, Mosdell (Mazur) 2:37. 4. Montreal, Curry (MacKay, St. Laurent) 16:05.
THIRD PERIOD: 5. Boston, Pierson (Mackell, Sandford) 10:11. 6. Montreal, Richard (Mosdell) 11:12.

GAME 2, April 11:

BOSTON	2	1	1	–	4
MONTREAL	0	1	0	–	1

Goaltenders: Boston, J. Henry, G. Henry. Montreal, Plante.

FIRST PERIOD: 1. Boston, Labine (Quackenbush) 3:53. 2. Boston, Sandford (Klukay, Chevrefils) 18:13.
SECOND PERIOD: 3. Montreal, Olmstead (Curry, Harvey) 1:36. 4. Boston, Sandford (Mackell) 7:26.
THIRD PERIOD: 5. Boston, Schmidt (Dumart, Martin) 15:31.

GAME 3, April 12:

MONTREAL	1	1	1	–	3
BOSTON	0	0	0	–	0

Goaltenders: Montreal, McNeil. Boston, G. Henry.

FIRST PERIOD: 1. Montreal, Johnson (Mosdell) 11:53.
SECOND PERIOD: 2. Montreal, Masnick 6:30.
THIRD PERIOD: 3. Montreal, Mosdell (Bouchard) 11:27.

GAME 4, April 14:

MONTREAL	3	1	3	–	7
BOSTON	1	0	2	–	3

Goaltenders: Montreal, McNeil. Boston, G. Henry.

FIRST PERIOD: 1. Montreal, Davis (MacKay, St. Laurent) 3:23. 2. Montreal, Richard (Harvey) 10:58. 3. Montreal, Moore 16:40. 4. Boston, Creighton (Dumart) 18:22.
SECOND PERIOD: 5. Montreal, Geoffrion 18:58.
THIRD PERIOD: 6. Montreal, Richard 5:33. 7. Boston, Schmidt (Labine) 7:23. 8. Boston, McIntyre (Creighton) 16:25. 9. Montreal, MacKay 17:59. 10. Montreal, Richard (Lach, Olmstead) 18:27.

GAME 5, April 16:

BOSTON	0	0	0	0	–	0
MONTREAL	0	0	0	1	–	1

Goaltenders: Boston, J. Henry. Montreal, McNeil.

FIRST PERIOD: No scoring.
SECOND PERIOD: No scoring.
THIRD PERIOD: No scoring.
FIRST OVERTIME: 1. Montreal, Lach (Richard) 1:22.

GOALS	
E. Sandford, BOS	8
M. Richard, MONT	7
B. Geoffrion, MONT	6

ASSISTS	
F. Mackell, BOS	7
J. Peirson, BOS	6
E. Lach, MONT	6

POINTS	
E. Sandford, BOS	11
B. Geoffrion, MONT	10

WINS	
G. McNeil, MONT	5
J. Henry, BOS	4
A. Rollins, CHI	3
J. Plante, MONT	3

GOALS AGAINST AVE.	
J. Plante, MONT	1.75
G. McNeil, MONT	2.00
A. Rollins, CHI	2.57

SHUTOUTS	
G. McNeil, MONT	2
J. Plante, MONT	1
T. Sawchuk, DET	1

1953–54

Semifinal Round

Detroit over Toronto, 4 games to 1

March 23, at DET: DET 5, TOR 0
March 25, at DET: TOR 3, DET 1
March 27, at TOR: DET 3, TOR 1
March 30, at TOR: DET 2, TOR 1
April 1, at DET: DET 4, TOR 3 (2 OT, 1:01)

Montreal Canadiens over Boston, 4 games to 0

March 23, at MONT: MONT 2, BOS 0
March 25, at MONT: MONT 8, BOS 1
March 28, at BOS: MONT 4, BOS 3
March 30, at BOS: MONT 2, BOS 0

FINAL ROUND: Detroit over Montreal, 4 games to 3

GAME 1, April 4:

MONTREAL	0	1	0	– 1
DETROIT	1	0	2	– 3

Goaltenders: Montreal, Plante. Detroit, Sawchuk.

FIRST PERIOD: 1. Detroit, Lindsay (Reibel, Delvecchio) 13:44.
SECOND PERIOD: 2. Montreal, Geoffrion (Harvey, Masnick) 12:16.
THIRD PERIOD: 3. Detroit, Reibel (Lindsay, Howe) 1:52. 4. Detroit, Kelly (Pavelich, Leswick) 7:13.

GAME 2, April 6:

MONTREAL	3	0	0	– 3
DETROIT	0	1	0	– 1

Goaltenders: Montreal, Plante. Detroit, Sawchuk.

FIRST PERIOD: 1. Montreal, Moore (Geoffrion, Beliveau) 15:03. 2. Montreal, Richard (Moore) 15:28. 3. Montreal, Richard (Moore) 15:59.
SECOND PERIOD: 4. Detroit, Delvecchio 6:37.
THIRD PERIOD: No scoring.

GAME 3, April 8:

DETROIT	2	1	2	– 5
MONTREAL	0	0	2	– 2

Goaltenders: Detroit, Sawchuk. Montreal, Plante.

FIRST PERIOD: 1. Detroit, Delvecchio (Howe) 0:42. 2. Detroit, Lindsay (Kelly) 17:06.
SECOND PERIOD: 3. Detroit, Wilson (Prystai, Goldham) 4:57.
THIRD PERIOD: 4. Montreal, Johnson 7:19. 5. Detroit, Prystai (Delvecchio) 7:59. 6. Detroit, Howe (Delvecchio, Woit) 11:32. 7. Montreal, St. Laurent (MacKay) 15:02.

GAME 4, April 10:

DETROIT	0	1	1	– 2
MONTREAL	0	0	0	– 0

Goaltenders: Detroit, Sawchuk. Montreal, Plante.

FIRST PERIOD: No scoring.
SECOND PERIOD: 1. Detroit, Wilson (Prystai) 2:09.
THIRD PERIOD: 2. Detroit, Kelly 19:53.

GAME 5, April 11:

MONTREAL	0	0	0	1	– 1
DETROIT	0	0	0	0	– 0

Goaltenders: Montreal, McNeil. Detroit, Sawchuk.

FIRST PERIOD: No scoring.
SECOND PERIOD: No scoring.
THIRD PERIOD: No scoring.
FIRST OVERTIME: 1. Montreal, Mosdell 5:45.

GAME 6, April 13:

DETROIT	0	0	1	– 1
MONTREAL	0	3	1	– 4

Goaltenders: Detroit, Sawchuk. Montreal, McNeil.

FIRST PERIOD: No scoring.
SECOND PERIOD: 1. Montreal, Geoffrion (Beliveau) 12:07. 2. Montreal, Curry (Olmstead, Masnick) 13:07. 3. Montreal, Curry (Lach, Mazur) 14:25.
THIRD PERIOD: 4. Detroit, Prystai 5:11. 5. Montreal, Richard (Lach) 10:06.

GAME 7, April 16:

MONTREAL	1	0	0	0	– 1
DETROIT	0	1	0	1	– 2

Goaltenders: Montreal, McNeil. Detroit, Sawchuk.

FIRST PERIOD: 1. Montreal, Curry (Masnick) 9:17.
SECOND PERIOD: 2. Detroit, Kelly (Delvecchio, Lindsay) 1:17.
THIRD PERIOD: No scoring.
FIRST OVERTIME: 3. Detroit, Leswick (Skov) 4:29.

GOALS		**ASSISTS**		**POINTS**	
B. Geoffrion, MONT	6	D. Moore, MONT	8	D. Moore, MONT	13
D. Moore, MONT	5	J. Beliveau, MONT	8	B. Geoffrion, MONT	11
R. Kelly, DET	5	A. Delvecchio, DET	7	J. Beliveau, MONT	10

WINS		**GOALS AGAINST AVE.**		**SHUTOUTS**	
T. Sawchuk, DET	8	G. McNeil, MONT	1.00	T. Sawchuk, DET	2
J. Plante, MONT	5	T. Sawchuk, DET	1.67	J. Plante, MONT	2
G. McNeil, MONT	2	J. Plante, MONT	1.87	G. McNeil, MONT	1

1954–55

Semifinal Round

Detroit over Toronto, 4 games to 0

March 22, at DET: DET 7, TOR 4
March 24, at DET: DET 2, TOR 1
March 26, at TOR: DET 2, TOR 1
March 29, at TOR: DET 3, TOR 0

Montreal Canadiens over Boston, 4 games to 1

March 22, at MONT: MONT 2, BOS 0
March 24, at MONT: MONT 3, BOS 1
March 27, at BOS: BOS 4, MONT 2
March 29, at BOS: MONT 4, BOS 3 (OT, 3:05)
March 31, at MONT: MONT 5, BOS 1

FINAL ROUND: Detroit over Montreal Canadiens, 4 games to 3

GAME 1, April 3:

MONTREAL	0	1	1	– 2
DETROIT	0	1	3	– 4

Goaltenders: Montreal, Plante. Detroit, Sawchuk.

FIRST PERIOD: No scoring.
SECOND PERIOD: 1. Montreal, Curry (MacKay, Mosdell) 5:09. 2. Detroit, Delvecchio (Lindsay, Howe) 14:00.
THIRD PERIOD: 3. Montreal, Curry (MacKay, Mosdell) 8:57. 4. Detroit, Stasiuk (Howe, Lindsay) 13:05. 5. Detroit, Pavelich 17:07. 6. Detroit, Lindsay (Howe) 19:42.

GAME 2, April 5:

MONTREAL	0	0	1	–	1
DETROIT	4	3	0	–	7

Goaltenders: Montreal, Plante, Detroit, Sawchuk.

FIRST PERIOD: 1. Detroit, Pronovost (Goldham) 2:15. 2. Detroit, Lindsay (Howe, Reibel) 9:57. 3. Detroit, Delvecchio (Stasiuk, Goldham) 16:00. 4. Detroit, Howe (Reibel) 17:11.
SECOND PERIOD: 5. Detroit, Lindsay (Howe, Reibel) 8:10. 6. Detroit, Lindsay (Delvecchio) 15:48. 7. Detroit, Lindsay (Reibel, Howe) 19:37.
THIRD PERIOD: 8. Montreal, Mosdell (St. Laurent, Curry) 12:32.

GAME 3, April 7:

DETROIT	1	1	0	–	2
MONTREAL	2	1	1	–	4

Goaltenders: Detroit, Sawchuk. Montreal, Plante.

FIRST PERIOD: 1. Montreal, Geoffrion (Beliveau, Olmstead) 8:30. 2. Montreal, Geoffrion 8:42. 3. Detroit, Kelly (Stasiuk) 18:13.
SECOND PERIOD: 4. Montreal, Geoffrion (Beliveau) 14:23. 5. Detroit, Stasiuk (Pavelich, Delvecchio) 16:16.
THIRD PERIOD: 6. Montreal, Leclair (Moore) 7:50.

GAME 4, April 9:

DETROIT	1	0	2	–	3
MONTREAL	1	3	1	–	5

Goaltenders: Detroit, Sawchuk. Montreal, Plante.

FIRST PERIOD: 1. Montreal, MacKay (Mosdell, Harvey) 0:40. 2. Detroit, Reibel (Kelly) 12:38.
SECOND PERIOD: 3. Montreal, Geoffrion 3:41. 4. Montreal, Beliveau 8:25. 5. Montreal, Johnson 9:07.
THIRD PERIOD: 6. Montreal, Curry (MacKay) 2:33. 7. Detroit, Reibel (Lindsay, Howe) 3:40. 8. Detroit, Hay (Reibel) 12:00.

GAME 5, April 10:

MONTREAL	1	0	0	–	1
DETROIT	2	2	1	–	5

Goaltenders: Montreal, Plante. Detroit, Sawchuk.

FIRST PERIOD: 1. Montreal, Beliveau (Harvey, Moore) 8:01. 2. Detroit, Skov 12:59. 3. Detroit, Howe 18:59.
SECOND PERIOD: 4. Detroit, Howe (Delvecchio, Lindsay) 12:29. 5. Detroit, Howe (Lindsay, Kelly) 16:20.
THIRD PERIOD: 6. Detroit, Stasiuk (Delvecchio, Bonin) 2:09.

GAME 6, April 12:

DETROIT	1	1	1	–	3
MONTREAL	1	3	2	–	6

Goaltenders: Detroit, Sawchuk. Montreal, Plante.

FIRST PERIOD: 1. Montreal, Beliveau (Harvey) 7:30. 2. Detroit, Delvecchio (Stasiuk) 13:36.
SECOND PERIOD: 3. Montreal, Leclair (Geoffrion, Harvey) 3:45. 4. Montreal, Geoffrion (Beliveau, Harvey) 5:21. 5. Detroit, Delvecchio (Lindsay, Pronovost) 15:54. 6. Montreal, Goeffrion (Beliveau, Bouchard) 18:18.
THIRD PERIOD: 7. Montreal, Curry (MacKay, Mosdell) 0:19. 8. Detroit, Kelly (Leswick, Pavelich) 16:23. 9. Montreal, MacKay (Mosdell) 18:55.

GAME 7, April 14:

MONTREAL	0	0	1	–	1
DETROIT	0	2	1	–	3

Goaltenders: Montreal, Plante. Detroit, Sawchuk.

FIRST PERIOD: No scoring.
SECOND PERIOD: 1. Detroit, Delvecchio (Kelly) 7:12. 2. Detroit, Howe (Pronovost) 19:49.
THIRD PERIOD: 3. Detroit, Delvecchio 2:59. 4. Montreal, Curry (Geoffrion, Beliveau) 14:35.

GOALS

G. Howe, DET	9
B. Geoffrion, MONT	8
F. Curry, MONT	8

ASSISTS

T. Lindsay, DET	12
G. Howe, DET	11

POINTS

G. Howe, DET	20
T. Lindsay, DET	19
A. Delvecchio, DET	15

WINS

T. Sawchuk, DET	8
J. Plante, MONT	5

GOALS AGAINST AVE.

C. Hodge, MONT	1.50
T. Sawchuk, DET	2.36
J. Plante, MONT	2.50

SHUTOUTS

T. Sawchuk, DET	1
J. Plante, MONT	1

1955–56

Semifinal Round

Mont. Canadiens over N.Y. Rangers, 4 games to 1

March 20, at MONT: MONT 7, NYR 1
March 22, at MONT: NYR 4, MONT 2
March 24, at NYR: MONT 3, NYR 1
March 25, at NYR: MONT 5, NYR 3
March 27, at NYR: MONT 7, NYR 0

Detroit over Toronto, 4 games to 1

March 20, at DET: DET 3, TOR 2
March 22, at DET: DET 3, TOR 1
March 24, at TOR: DET 5, TOR 4 (OT, 4:22)
March 27, at TOR: TOR 2, DET 0
March 29, at TOR: DET 3, TOR 1

FINAL ROUND: Montreal Canadiens over Detroit, 4 games to 1

GAME 1, March 31:

DETROIT	1	3	0	–	4
MONTREAL	0	2	4	–	6

Goaltenders: Detroit, Hall. Montreal, Plante.

FIRST PERIOD: 1. Detroit, Delvecchio (Reibel, Howe) 8:17.
SECOND PERIOD: 2. Montreal, Beliveau (Olmstead) 3:00. 3. Detroit, Dineen (Bucyk, Ullman) 3:45. 4. H. Richard (Moore, M. Richard) 6:40. 5. Detroit, Lindsay (Howe) 8:11. 6. Detroit, Delvecchio (Howe, Ferguson) 11:20.
THIRD PERIOD: 7. Montreal, Leclair (Curry, Harvey) 5:20. 8. Montreal, Geoffrion (Talbot) 6:20. 9. Montreal, Beliveau (Geoffrion, Olmstead) 7:31. 10. Montreal, Provost (Leclair, Curry) 10:49.

GAME 2, April 3:

DETROIT	0	0	1	–	1
MONTREAL	1	2	2	–	5

Goaltenders: Detroit, Hall. Montreal, Plante.

FIRST PERIOD: 1. Montreal, Marshall (Olmstead) 7:23.
SECOND PERIOD: 2. Montreal, H. Richard (Moore) 11:37. 3. Montreal, Geoffrion (Olmstead, Beliveau) 14:38.
THIRD PERIOD: 4. Detroit, Ullman (Lindsay, Howe) 0:31. 5. Montreal, Beliveau (Olmstead, M. Richard) 2:48. 6. Montreal, M. Richard (Moore, H. Richard) 19:21.

GAME 3, April 5:

MONTREAL	1	0	0	–	1
DETROIT	1	0	2	–	3

Goaltenders: Montreal, Plante. Detroit, Hall.

FIRST PERIOD: 1. Detroit, Kelly (Howe) 14:27. 2. Montreal, Beliveau (Provost) 19:20.
SECOND PERIOD: No scoring.
THIRD PERIOD: 3. Detroit, Lindsay (Pavelich, Arbour) 11:36. 4. Detroit, Howe (Lindsay, Delvecchio) 18:12.

GAME 4, April 8:

MONTREAL	1	1	1	–	3
DETROIT	0	0	0	–	0

Goaltenders: Montreal, Plante. Detroit, Hall.

FIRST PERIOD: 1. Montreal, Beliveau (Olmstead, Harvey) 15:52.
SECOND PERIOD: 2. Montreal, Beliveau (Olmstead, Geoffrion) 11:39.
THIRD PERIOD: 3. Montreal, Curry (Provost, Mosdell) 11:34.

GAME 5, April 10:

DETROIT	0	0	1	–	1
MONTREAL	0	2	1	–	3

Goaltenders: Detroit, Hall. Montreal, Plante.

FIRST PERIOD: No scoring.
SECOND PERIOD: 1. Montreal, Beliveau (Curry, Harvey) 14:16. 2. Montreal, M. Richard (Geoffrion, Beliveau) 15:08.
THIRD PERIOD: 3. Montreal, Geoffrion (Beliveau, Olmstead) 0:13. 4. Detroit, Delvecchio (Lindsay) 0:35.

GOALS	
J. Beliveau, MONT	12
A. Delvecchio, DET	7
T. Lindsay, DET	6

ASSISTS	
B. Olmstead, MONT	10
B. Geoffrion, MONT	9
M. Richard, MONT	9
G. Howe, DET	9

POINTS	
J. Beliveau, MONT	19
B. Geoffrion, MONT	14
M. Richard, MONT	14
B. Olmstead, MONT	14

WINS	
J. Plante, MONT	8
G. Hall, DET	5

GOALS AGAINST AVE.	
J. Plante, MONT	1.80
G. Hall, DET	2.80
H. Lumley, TOR	2.80

SHUTOUTS	
J. Plante, MONT	2
H. Lumley, TOR	1

1956–57

Semifinal Round

Boston over Detroit, 4 games to 1

March 26, at DET: BOS 3, DET 1
March 28, at DET: DET 7, BOS 2
March 31, at BOS: BOS 4, DET 3
April 2, at BOS: BOS 2, DET 0
April 4, at DET: BOS 4, DET 3

Mont. Canadiens over N.Y. Rangers, 4 games to 1

March 26, at NYR: MONT 4, NYR 1
March 28, at NYR: NYR 4, MONT 3 (OT, 13:38)
March 30, at MONT: MONT 8, NYR 3
April 2, at MONT: MONT 3, NYR 1
April 4, at MONT: MONT 4, NYR 3 (OT, 1:11)

FINAL ROUND: Montreal Canadiens over Boston, 4 games to 1

GAME 1, April 6:

BOSTON	0	1	0	–	1
MONTREAL	0	4	1	–	5

Goaltenders: Boston, Simmons. Montreal, Plante.

FIRST PERIOD: No scoring.
SECOND PERIOD: 1. Boston, Mackell (Mohns, Regan) 7:37. 2. Montreal, M. Richard (Moore, Johnson) 10:39. 3. Montreal, M. Richard (Harvey) 13:29. 4. Montreal, Geoffrion (Harvey) 15:35. 5. Montreal, M. Richard (H. Richard, Harvey) 17:00.
THIRD PERIOD: 6. Montreal, M. Richard (H. Richard) 18:17.

GAME 2, April 9:

BOSTON	0	0	0	–	0
MONTREAL	0	1	0	–	1

Goaltenders: Boston, Simmons. Montreal, Plante.

FIRST PERIOD: No scoring.
SECOND PERIOD: 1. Montreal, Beliveau (Geoffrion, St. Laurent) 2:27.
THIRD PERIOD: No scoring.

GAME 3, April 11:

MONTREAL	3	0	1	–	4
BOSTON	0	1	1	–	2

Goaltenders: Montreal, Plante. Boston, Simmons.

FIRST PERIOD: 1. Montreal, Geoffrion (Olmstead, Harvey) 1:30. 2. Montreal, Curry (Goyette) 14:39. 3. Montreal, Geoffrion (Beliveau) 19:54.
SECOND PERIOD: 4. Boston, McKenney (Armstrong) 6:16.
THIRD PERIOD: 5. Montreal, Goyette (Marshall, Curry) 7:31. 6. Boston, Mackell (Flaman) 19:16.

GAME 4, April 14:

MONTREAL	0	0	0	–	0
BOSTON	1	0	1	–	2

Goaltenders: Montreal, Plante. Boston, Simmons.

FIRST PERIOD: 1. Boston, Mackell (Topazzini, Regan) 2:56.
SECOND PERIOD: No scoring.
THIRD PERIOD: 2. Boston, Mackell (Labine, McKenney) 19:40.

GAME 5, April 16:

BOSTON	0	0	1	–	1
MONTREAL	1	2	2	–	5

Goaltenders: Boston, Simmons. Montreal, Plante.

FIRST PERIOD: 1. Montreal, Pronovost (Marshall, Provost) 18:11.
SECOND PERIOD: 2. Montreal, Moore (Geoffrion, Harvey) 0:14. 3. Montreal, Geoffrion (Olmstead, Johnson) 15:12.
THIRD PERIOD: 4. Boston, Labine (Bonin) 13:43. 5. Montreal, Marshall (Moore, Curry) 17:38. 6. Montreal, Curry (Moore, Broden) 18:31.

GOALS

B. Geoffrion, MONT	11
M. Richard, MONT	8
J. Beliveau, MONT	6

ASSISTS

B. Olmstead, MONT	9
B. Geoffrion, MONT	7
D. Moore, MONT	7
D. Harvey, MONT	7

POINTS

B. Geoffrion, MONT	18
J. Beliveau, MONT	12
M. Richard, MONT	11

WINS

J. Plante, MONT	8
D. Simmons, BOS	5

GOALS AGAINST AVE.

J. Plante, MONT	1.80
D. Simmons, BOS	2.90
G. Hall, DET	3.00

SHUTOUTS

D. Simmons, BOS	2
J. Plante, MONT	1

1957–58

Semifinal Round

Montreal Canadiens over Detroit, 4 games to 0

March 25, at MONT: MONT 8, DET 1
March 27, at MONT: MONT 5, DET 1
March 30, at DET: MONT 2, DET 1 (OT, 11:52)
April 1, at DET: MONT 4, DET 3

Boston over New York Rangers, 4 games to 2

March 25, at NYR: NYR 5, BOS 3
March 27, at NYR: BOS 4, NYR 3 (OT, 4:46)
March 29, at BOS: BOS 5, NYR 0
April 1, at BOS: NYR 5, BOS 2
April 3, at BOS: BOS 6, NYR 1
April 5, at BOS: BOS 8, NYR 2

FINAL ROUND: Montreal Canadiens over Boston, 4 games to 2

GAME 1, April 8:

BOSTON	0	1	0	–	1
MONTREAL	1	1	0	–	2

Goaltenders: Boston, Simmons. Montreal, Plante.

FIRST PERIOD: 1. Montreal, Geoffrion (Marshall, Harvey) 12:24.
SECOND PERIOD: 2. Boston, Stanley (Mackell, McKenney) 5:54. 3. Montreal, Moore (Beliveau, M. Richard) 13:52.
THIRD PERIOD: No scoring.

GAME 2, April 10:

BOSTON	3	1	1	–	5
MONTREAL	1	1	0	–	2

Goaltenders: Boston, Simmons. Montreal, Plante.

FIRST PERIOD: 1. Boston, Johnson (Regan, Labine) 0:20. 2. Montreal, Geoffrion (Harvey, Moore) 3:42. 3. Boston, McKenney (Regan, Mackell) 6:06. 4. Boston, Horvath (Boone) 17:23.
SECOND PERIOD: 5. Boston, Regan (Stanley) 5:10. 6. Montreal, Harvey (Moore) 7:00.
THIRD PERIOD: 7. Boston, Horvath (Stasiuk, Mohns) 16:52.

GAME 3, April 13:

MONTREAL	1	0	2	–	3
BOSTON	0	0	0	–	0

Goaltenders: Montreal, Plante. Boston, Simmons.

FIRST PERIOD: 1. Montreal, M. Richard (Geoffrion, Harvey) 18:30.
SECOND PERIOD: No scoring.
THIRD PERIOD: 2. Montreal, H. Richard (Harvey) 3:00. 3. Montreal, M. Richard (H. Richard, Moore) 15:06.

GAME 4, April 15:

MONTREAL	0	0	1	–	1
BOSTON	1	1	1	–	3

Goaltenders: Montreal, Plante. Boston, Simmons.

FIRST PERIOD: 1. Boston, McKenney (Mackell, Regan) 5:35.
SECOND PERIOD: 2. Boston, McKenney (Stasiuk, Horvath) 3:30.
THIRD PERIOD: 3. Boston, Toppazzini (Mackell) 2:30. 4. Montreal, Provost (Beliveau, Bonin) 12:57.

GAME 5, April 17:

BOSTON	1	0	1	0	–	2
MONTREAL	0	2	0	1	–	3

Goaltenders: Boston, Simmons. Montreal, Plante.

FIRST PERIOD: 1. Boston, Mackell (Stanley, Toppazzini) 18:43.
SECOND PERIOD: 2. Montreal, Geoffrion (Beliveau) 2:20. 3. Montreal, Beliveau (Geoffrion) 3:02.
THIRD PERIOD: 4. Boston, Horvath (Stasiuk, Boone) 10:35
FIRST OVERTIME: 5. Montreal, M. Richard (H. Richard, Moore) 5:45.

GAME 6, April 20:

MONTREAL	2	2	1	–	5
BOSTON	1	0	2	–	3

Goaltenders: Montreal, Plante. Boston, Simmons.

FIRST PERIOD: 1. Montreal, Geoffrion (Beliveau, Olmstead) 0:46. 2. Montreal, M. Richard (Moore) 1:54. 3. Boston, McKenney (Mohns) 18:35.
SECOND PERIOD: 4. Montreal, Beliveau (Geoffrion, Harvey) 6:42. 5. Montreal, Geoffrion 19:26.
THIRD PERIOD: 6. Boston, Johnson (Regan) 5:20. 7. Boston, Regan (Flaman, Labine) 13:21. 8. Montreal, Harvey 19:00.

GOALS		ASSISTS		POINTS	
M. Richard, MONT	11	F. Mackell, BOS	14	F. Mackell, BOS	19
D. McKenney, BOS	9	D. Mohns, BOS	10	D. McKenney, BOS	17
J. Toppazzini, BOS	9	D. Harvey, MONT	9	M. Richard, MONT	15

WINS		GOALS AGAINST AVE.		SHUTOUTS	
J. Plante, MONT	8	J. Plante, MONT	2.00	J. Plante, MONT	1
D. Simmons, BOS	6	D. Simmons, BOS	2.41	D. Simmons, BOS	1
G. Worsley, NYR	2	G. Worsley, NYR	4.67		

1958–59

Semifinal Round

Montreal Canadiens over Chicago, 4 games to 2

March 24, at MONT: MONT 4, CHI 2
March 26, at MONT: MONT 5, CHI 1
March 28, at CHI: CHI 4, MONT 2
March 31, at CHI: CHI 3, MONT 1
April 2, at MONT: MONT 5, CHI 2
April 4, at CHI: MONT 5, CHI 4

Toronto over Boston, 4 games to 3

March 24, at BOS: BOS 5, TOR 1
March 26, at BOS: BOS 4, TOR 2
March 28, at TOR: TOR 3, BOS 2 (OT, 5:02)
March 31, at TOR: TOR 3, BOS 2 (OT, 11:21)
April 2, at BOS: TOR 4, BOS 1
April 4, at TOR: BOS 5, TOR 4
April 7, at BOS: TOR 3, BOS 2

FINAL ROUND: Montreal Canadiens over Toronto, 4 games to 1

GAME 1, April 9:

TORONTO	2	1	0	–	3
MONTREAL	2	1	2	–	5

Goaltenders: Toronto, Bower. Montreal, Plante.

FIRST PERIOD: 1. Montreal, H. Richard (Moore, Talbot) 0:36. 2. Toronto, Duff 4:53. 3. Toronto, Harris (Horton) 6:24. 4. Montreal, Backstrom (Provost) 15:41.
SECOND PERIOD: 5. Montreal, Pronovost (Goyette, Provost) 16:28. 6. Toronto, Stewart (Brewer, Olmstead) 18:26.
THIRD PERIOD: 7. Montreal, Bonin (H. Richard, Harvey) 11:50. 8. Montreal, Moore (Bonin, H. Richard) 15:42.

GAME 2, April 11:

TORONTO	0	1	0	–	1
MONTREAL	1	0	2	–	3

Goaltenders: Toronto, Bower. Montreal, Plante.

FIRST PERIOD: 1. Montreal, Johnson (H. Richard, Moore) 5:12.
SECOND PERIOD: 2. Toronto, Stewart (Olmstead, Pulford) 11:41.
THIRD PERIOD: 3. Montreal, Provost (Harvey) 5:02. 4. Montreal, Provost (Goyette, Harvey) 18:33.

GAME 3, April 14:

MONTREAL	1	0	1	0	–	2
TORONTO	1	1	0	1	–	3

Goaltenders: Montreal, Plante. Toronto, Bower.

FIRST PERIOD: 1. Toronto, Harris (Mahovlich, Stanley) 16:29. 2. Montreal, Bonin (Geoffrion, Harvey) 17:31.
SECOND PERIOD: 3. Toronto, Olmstead (Stewart, Pulford) 17:11.
THIRD PERIOD: 4. Montreal, Moore (Turner, Marshall) 1:30.
FIRST OVERTIME: 5. Toronto, Duff (Armstrong) 10:06.

GAME 4, April 16:

MONTREAL	0	0	3	–	3
TORONTO	0	0	2	–	2

Goaltenders: Montreal, Plante. Toronto, Bower.

FIRST PERIOD: No scoring.
SECOND PERIOD: No scoring.
THIRD PERIOD: 1. Toronto, Harris (Ehman, Duff) 3:45. 2. Montreal, McDonald (Backstrom, Geoffrion) 9:54. 3. Montreal, Backstrom (McDonald, Geoffrion) 13:01. 4. Montreal, Geoffrion (H. Richard, Bonin) 15:56. 5. Toronto, Mahovlich (Ehman) 18:36.

GAME 5, April 18:

TORONTO	0	1	2	–	3
MONTREAL	3	2	0	–	5

Goaltenders: Toronto, Bower. Montreal, Plante.

FIRST PERIOD: 1. Montreal, Backstrom (Geoffrion, Moore) 4:13. 2. Montreal, Geoffrion (Backstrom, Harvey) 13:42. 3. Montreal, Johnson (Backstrom) 16:26.
SECOND PERIOD: 4. Toronto, Pulford (Armstrong, Brewer) 4:27. 5. Montreal, Bonin (H. Richard, Harvey) 9:55. 6. Montreal, Geoffrion (Backstrom, Johnson) 19:25.
THIRD PERIOD: 7. Toronto, Mahovlich (Harris, Ehman) 12:07. 8. Toronto, Olmstead (Ehman, Mahovlich) 16:19.

GOALS		ASSISTS		POINTS	
M. Bonin, MONT	10	D. Moore, MONT	12	D. Moore, MONT	17
G. Ehman, TOR	6	D. Harvey, MONT	11	M. Bonin, MONT	15
F. Mahovlich, TOR	6	B. Geoffrion, MONT	8	G. Ehman, TOR	13
C. Provost, MONT	6	H. Richard, MONT	8	B. Geoffrion, MONT	13

WINS		GOALS AGAINST AVE.		SHUTOUTS
J. Plante, MONT	8	J. Plante, MONT	2.54	None
J. Bower, TOR	5	H. Lumley, BOS	2.85	
H. Lumley, BOS	3	J. Bower, TOR	3.25	

1959–60

Semifinal Round

Montreal Canadiens over Chicago, 4 games to 0

March 24, at MONT: MONT 4, CHI 3
March 26, at MONT: MONT 4, CHI 3 (OT, 8:38)
March 29, at CHI: MONT 4, CHI 0
March 31, at CHI: MONT 2, CHI 0

Toronto over Detroit, 4 games to 2

March 23, at TOR: DET 2, TOR 1
March 26, at TOR: TOR 4, DET 2
March 27, at DET: TOR 5, DET 4 (3 OT, 3:00)
March 29, at DET: DET 2, TOR 1 (OT, 1:54)
April 2, at TOR: TOR 5, DET 4
April 3, at DET: TOR 4, DET 2

FINAL ROUND: Montreal Canadiens over Toronto, 4 games to 0

GAME 1, April 7:

TORONTO	0	2	0	–	2
MONTREAL	3	0	1	–	4

Goaltenders: Toronto, Bower. Montreal, Plante.

FIRST PERIOD: 1. Montreal, Moore (H. Richard, Geoffrion) 2:27. 2. Montreal, Harvey (H. Richard) 8:55. 3. Montreal, Beliveau (Geoffrion, H. Richard) 11:56.
SECOND PERIOD: 4. Toronto, Baun (Armstrong, Regan) 5:23. 5. Toronto, Olmstead (Horton, Kelly) 17:38.
THIRD PERIOD: 6. Montreal, H. Richard (Moore, Geoffrion) 1:30.

GAME 2, April 9:

TORONTO	1	0	0	–	1
MONTREAL	2	0	0	–	2

Goaltenders: Toronto, Bower. Montreal, Plante.

FIRST PERIOD: 1. Montreal, Moore (H. Richard, M. Richard) 1:26. 2. Montreal, Beliveau (Bonin, Talbot) 5:56. 3. Toronto, Regan (Duff, Armstrong) 19:32.
SECOND PERIOD: No scoring.
THIRD PERIOD: No scoring.

GAME 3, April 12:

MONTREAL	1	2	2	–	5
TORONTO	0	1	1	–	2

Goaltenders: Montreal, Plante. Toronto, Bower.

FIRST PERIOD: 1. Montreal, Marshall (Hicke) 13:54.
SECOND PERIOD: 2. Montreal, Goyette (Provost, Pronovost) 0:21. 3. Montreal, H. Richard 15:27. 4. Toronto, Wilson (Brewer, Harris) 16:19.
THIRD PERIOD: 5. Montreal, Goyette 8:57. 6. Montreal, M. Richard (H. Richard, Moore) 11:07. 7. Toronto, Olmstead (Kelly, Edmundson) 19:47.

GAME 4, April 14:

MONTREAL	2	1	1	–	4
TORONTO	0	0	0	–	0

Goaltenders: Montreal, Plante. Toronto, Bower.

FIRST PERIOD: 1. Montreal, Beliveau (Geoffrion, Langlois) 8:17. 2. Montreal, Harvey (Geoffrion, Langlois) 8:45.
SECOND PERIOD: 3. Montreal, H. Richard (M. Richard, Moore) 16:40.
THIRD PERIOD: 4. Montreal, Beliveau (Bonin, Geoffrion) 1:26.

GOALS		ASSISTS		POINTS	
D. Moore, MONT	6	B. Geoffrion, MONT	10	H. Richard, MONT	12
J. Beliveau, MONT	5	H. Richard, MONT	9	B. Geoffrion, MONT	12
B. Pulford, TOR	4	R. Kelly, DET	8	R. Kelly, DET	11

WINS		GOALS AGAINST AVE.		SHUTOUTS	
J. Plante, MONT	8	J. Plante, MONT	1.37	J. Plante, MONT	3
J. Bower, TOR	4	J. Bower, TOR	3.10		
T. Sawchuk, DET	2	T. Sawchuk, DET	3.33		

1960–61

Semifinal Round

Chicago over Montreal Canadiens, 4 games to 2

March 21, at MONT: MONT 6, CHI 2
March 23, at MONT: CHI 4, MONT 3
March 26, at CHI: CHI 2, MONT 1 (3 OT, 12:12)
March 28, at CHI: MONT 5, CHI 2
April 1, at MONT: CHI 3, MONT 0
April 4, at CHI: CHI 3, MONT 0

Detroit over Toronto, 4 games to 1

March 22, at TOR: TOR 3, DET 2 (2 OT, 4:51)
March 25, at TOR: DET 4, TOR 2
March 26, at DET: DET 2, TOR 0
March 28, at DET: DET 4, TOR 1
April 1, at TOR: DET 3, TOR 2

FINAL ROUND: Chicago over Detroit, 4 games to 2

GAME 1, April 6:

DETROIT	0	1	1	–	2
CHICAGO	3	0	0	–	3

Goaltenders: Detroit, Sawchuk, Bassen. Chicago, Hall.

FIRST PERIOD: 1. Chicago, Hull (M. Balfour, Mikita) 9:39. 2. Chicago, Wharram (McDonald, Mikita) 10:10. 3. Chicago, Hull (Pilote, M. Balfour) 13:15.
SECOND PERIOD: 4. Detroit, Lunde (Howe) 16:14.
THIRD PERIOD: 5. Detroit, Johnson (Howe, Ullman) 19:18.

GAME 2, April 8:

DETROIT	2	0	1	–	3
CHICAGO	0	1	0	–	1

Goaltenders: Detroit, Bassen. Chicago, Hall.

FIRST PERIOD: 1. Detroit, Young (Stasiuk, Delvecchio) 8:10. 2. Detroit, Delvecchio (Howe, Johnson) 17:39.
SECOND PERIOD: 3. Chicago, Pilote 0:41.
THIRD PERIOD: 4. Detroit, Delvecchio (Stasiuk, Howe) 19:22.

GAME 3, April 10:

CHICAGO	0	3	0	–	3
DETROIT	0	0	1	–	1

Goaltenders: Chicago, Hall. Detroit, Bassen.

FIRST PERIOD: No scoring.
SECOND PERIOD: 1. Chicago, Mikita (Pilote, Hull) 11:56. 2. Chicago, Murphy (Pilote, Litzenberger) 14:19. 3. Chicago, M. Balfour (Hull, Hay) 18:17.
THIRD PERIOD: 4. Detroit, Howe (Delvecchio, Young) 9:28.

GAME 4, April 12:

CHICAGO	0	1	0	–	1
DETROIT	0	1	1	–	2

Goaltenders: Chicago, Hall. Detroit, Sawchuk.

FIRST PERIOD: No scoring.
SECOND PERIOD: 1. Chicago, Hay (M. Balfour, Hull) 7:34. 2. Detroit, Delvecchio (MacGregor, Howe) 8:48.
THIRD PERIOD: 3. Detroit, MacGregor (Fonteyne, Godfrey) 13:10.

GAME 5, April 14:

DETROIT	2	1	0	–	3
CHICAGO	2	1	3	–	6

Goaltenders: Detroit, Sawchuk. Chicago, Hall.

FIRST PERIOD: 1. Detroit, Labine (Johnson, Ullman) 2:14. 2. Chicago, M. Balfour (Hay, Hull) 9:36. 3. Chicago, Murphy (Nesterenko, St. Laurent) 10:04. 4. Detroit, Glover (MacGregor, Fonteyne) 15:35.
SECOND PERIOD: 5. Chicago, M. Balfour (Pilote, Hay) 16:25. 6. Detroit, Stasiuk (Howe, Pronovost) 18:49.
THIRD PERIOD: 7. Chicago, Mikita (Vasko, Pilote) 2:51. 8. Chicago, Pilote (Wharram, Mikita) 7:12. 9. Chicago, Mikita (Murphy) 13:27.

GAME 6, April 16:

CHICAGO	0	2	3	–	5
DETROIT	1	0	0	–	1

Goaltenders: Chicago, Hall. Detroit, Bassen.

FIRST PERIOD: 1. Detroit, McDonald (Howe, Delvecchio) 15:26.
SECOND PERIOD: 2. Chicago, Fleming 6:45. 3. Chicago, McDonald (Mikita, Hull) 18:47.
THIRD PERIOD: 4. Chicago, Nesterenko (Sloan, Pilote) 0:57. 5. Chicago, Evans 6:27. 6. Chicago, Wharram 18:00.

GOALS	
S. Mikita, CHI	6
M. Balfour, CHI	5

ASSISTS	
P. Pilote, CHI	12
G. Howe, DET	11
B. Hull, CHI	10

POINTS	
G. Howe, DET	15
P. Pilote, CHI	15
B. Hull, CHI	14

WINS	
G. Hall, CHI	8
T. Sawchuk, DET	5
J. Plante, MONT	2

GOALS AGAINST AVE.	
G. Hall, CHI	2.25
T. Sawchuk, DET	2.32
H. Bassen, DET	2.45

SHUTOUTS	
G. Hall, CHI	2
T. Sawchuk, DET	1

1961–62

Semifinal Round

Toronto over New York Rangers, 4 games to 2

March 27, at TOR: TOR 4, NYR 2
March 29, at TOR: TOR 2, NYR 1
April 1, at NYR: NYR 5, TOR 4
April 3, at NYR: NYR 4, TOR 2
April 5, at TOR: TOR 3, NYR 2 (2 OT, 4:23)
April 7, at TOR: TOR 7, NYR 1

Chicago over Montreal Canadiens, 4 games to 2

March 27, at MONT: MONT 2, CHI 1
March 29, at MONT: MONT 4, CHI 3
April 1, at CHI: CHI 4, MONT 1
April 3, at CHI: CHI 5, MONT 3
April 5, at MONT: CHI 4, MONT 3
April 8, at CHI: CHI 2, MONT 0

FINAL ROUND: Toronto over Chicago, 4 games to 2

GAME 1, April 10:

CHICAGO	1	0	0	–	1
TORONTO	0	2	2	–	4

Goaltenders: Chicago, Hall. Toronto, Bower.

FIRST PERIOD: 1. Chicago, Hull (Pilote, Mikita) 3:36.
SECOND PERIOD: 2. Toronto, Keon (Duff, Armstrong) 1:32. 3. Toronto, Mahovlich (Stewart, Kelly) 13:54.
THIRD PERIOD: 4. Toronto, Armstrong (Duff) 6:02. 5. Toronto, Horton (Armstrong, Keon) 14:32.

GAME 2, April 12:

CHICAGO	0	0	2	–	2
TORONTO	1	0	2	–	3

Goaltenders: Chicago, Hall. Toronto, Bower.

FIRST PERIOD: 1. Toronto, Harris (Horton, Stewart) 2:35.
SECOND PERIOD: No scoring.
THIRD PERIOD: 2. Chicago, Mikita (Wharram, McDonald) 8:47. 3. Toronto, Mahovlich (Stewart, Kelly) 9:47. 4. Toronto, Armstrong (Duff, Stanley) 16:08. 5. Chicago, Mikita (Pilote, Hull) 18:27.

GAME 3, April 15:

TORONTO	0	0	0	–	0
CHICAGO	0	2	1	–	3

Goaltenders: Chicago, Hall. Toronto, Bower.

FIRST PERIOD: No scoring.
SECOND PERIOD: 1. Chicago, Mikita (Pilote, McDonald) 4:35. 2. Chicago, McDonald (Pilote, Hay) 8:33.
THIRD PERIOD: 3. Chicago, Horvath (Nesterenko) 19:21.

GAME 4, April 17:

TORONTO	1	0	0	–	1
CHICAGO	2	2	0	–	4

Goaltenders: Toronto, Bower, Simmons. Chicago, Hall.

FIRST PERIOD: 1. Chicago, Hull (Mikita) 10:35. 2. Chicago, Fleming (Nesterenko) 15:41. 3. Toronto, Kelly (Armstrong, Duff) 18:05.
SECOND PERIOD: 4. Chicago, Hull (Hay, Mikita) 0:46. 5. Chicago, Fleming (Nesterenko, Horvath) 7:31.
THIRD PERIOD: No scoring.

GAME 5, April 19:

CHICAGO	1	2	1	–	4
TORONTO	2	3	3	–	8

Goaltenders: Chicago, Hall. Toronto, Simmons.

FIRST PERIOD: 1. Toronto, Pulford (Olmstead, Nevin) 0:17. 2. Toronto, Pulford 17:45. 3. Chicago, Balfour (Hay, Hull) 18:05.
SECOND PERIOD: 4. Chicago, McDonald (Mikita, St. Laurent) 0:50. 5. Chicago, McDonald (Hull, Mikita) 3:07. 6. Toronto, Harris (Mahovlich, Horton) 8:31. 7. Toronto, Keon (Mahovlich, Horton) 9:50. 8. Toronto, Mahovlich (Kelly, Stewart) 14:24.
THIRD PERIOD: 9. Toronto, Armstrong (Brewer, Baun) 4:41. 10. Toronto, Mahovlich (Stewart, Baun) 6:31. 11. Chicago, Turner (Nesterenko, St. Laurent) 10:31. 12. Toronto, Pulford (Harris, Horton) 13:51.

GAME 6, April 22:

TORONTO	0	0	2	–	2
CHICAGO	0	0	1	–	1

Goaltenders: Toronto, Simmons. Chicago, Hall.

FIRST PERIOD: No scoring.
SECOND PERIOD: No scoring.
THIRD PERIOD: 1. Chicago, Hull (Hay, Balfour) 8:58. 2. Toronto, Nevin (Baun, Mahovlich) 10:29. 3. Toronto, Duff (Horton, Armstrong) 14:14.

GOALS	
B. Hull, CHI	8
G. Armstrong, TOR	7
B. Pulford, TOR	7

ASSISTS	
S. Mikita, CHI	15
T. Horton, TOR	13
D. Duff, TOR	10

POINTS	
S. Mikita, CHI	21
T. Horton, TOR	16
B. Hull, CHI	14

WINS	
J. Bower, TOR	6
G. Hall, CHI	6

GOALS AGAINST AVE.	
J. Bower, TOR	2.20
G. Hall, CHI	2.58
D. Simmons, TOR	2.67

SHUTOUTS	
G. Hall, CHI	2

1962–63

Semifinal Round

Toronto over Montreal Canadiens, 4 games to 1

March 26, at TOR: TOR 3, MONT 1
March 28, at TOR: TOR 3, MONT 2
March 30, at MONT: TOR 2, MONT 0
April 2, at MONT: MONT 3, TOR 1
April 4, at TOR: TOR 5, MONT 0

Detroit over Chicago, 4 games to 2

March 26, at CHI: CHI 5, DET 4
March 28, at CHI: CHI 5, DET 2
March 31, at DET: DET 4, CHI 2
April 2, at DET: DET 4, CHI 1
April 4, at CHI: DET 4, CHI 2
April 7, at DET: DET 7, CHI 4

FINAL ROUND: Toronto over Detroit, 4 games to 1

GAME 1, April 9:

DETROIT	0	2	0	–	2
TORONTO	3	0	1	–	4

Goaltenders: Toronto, Bower. Detroit, Sawchuk.

FIRST PERIOD: 1. Toronto, Duff (Keon, Stanley) 0:49. 2. Toronto, Duff (Stanley, Horton) 1:08. 3. Toronto, Nevin 14:42.
SECOND PERIOD: 4. Detroit, Jeffrey (Ullman, Smith) 5:36. 5. Detroit, Jeffrey (Howe, Ullman) 8:05.
THIRD PERIOD: 6. Toronto, Nevin (Pulford, Shack) 5:08.

GAME 2, April 11:

DETROIT	0	1	1	–	2
TORONTO	2	2	0	–	4

Goaltenders: Toronto, Bower. Detroit, Sawchuk.

FIRST PERIOD: 1. Toronto, Litzenberger (Pulford, Horton) 5:31. 2. Toronto, Stewart (Litzenberger, Kelly) 18:42.
SECOND PERIOD: 3. Toronto, Nevin (Stanley, Horton) 0:49. 4. Detroit, Howe (Delvecchio, M. Pronovost) 1:32. 5. Toronto, Stewart (Litzenberger, Harris) 8:55.
THIRD PERIOD: 6. Detroit, Howe (Jeffrey, Ullman) 2:03.

GAME 3, April 14:

TORONTO	1	1	0	–	2
DETROIT	1	2	0	–	3

Goaltenders: Detroit, Sawchuk. Toronto, Bower.

FIRST PERIOD: 1. Detroit, Stasiuk (Ullman, Smith) 0:33. 2. Toronto, Keon (Duff, Brewer) 14:56.
SECOND PERIOD: 3. Detroit, Faulkner (MacGregor, M. Pronovost) 8:13. 4. Toronto, Horton (Kelly) 13:06. 5. Detroit, Faulkner (A. Pronovost, M. Pronovost) 13:39.
THIRD PERIOD: No scoring.

GAME 4, April 16:

TORONTO	0	2	2	–	4
DETROIT	1	1	0	–	2

Goaltenders: Detroit, Sawchuk. Toronto, Bower.

FIRST PERIOD: 1. Detroit, Howe (Delvecchio, P. MacDonald) 2:54.
SECOND PERIOD: 2. Toronto, Armstrong (Keon) 1:17. 3. Detroit, Joyal (Howe) 2:38. 4. Toronto, Kelly (Mahovlich, Baun) 17:41.
THIRD PERIOD: 5. Toronto, Keon 9:42. 6. Toronto, Kelly 17:45.

GAME 5, April 18:

DETROIT	0	1	0	–	1
TORONTO	1	0	2	–	3

Goaltenders: Toronto, Bower. Detroit, Sawchuk.

FIRST PERIOD: 1. Toronto, Keon (Armstrong) 17:44.
SECOND PERIOD: 2. Detroit, Delvecchio (Howe, M. Pronovost) 0:49.
THIRD PERIOD: 3. Toronto, Shack (Douglas, Pulford) 13:28. 4. Toronto, Keon (Armstrong, Stanley) 19:55.

GOALS

B. Hull, CHI	8
G. Howe, DET	7
D. Keon, TOR	7

ASSISTS

N. Ullman, DET	12
G. Howe, DET	9
P. Pilote, CHI	8

POINTS

G. Howe, DET	16
N. Ullman, DET	16
D. Keon, TOR	12

WINS

J. Bower, TOR	8
T. Sawchuk, DET	5
G. Hall, CHI	2

GOALS AGAINST AVE.

J. Bower, TOR	1.60
J. Plante, MONT	2.80
T. Sawchuk, DET	3.27

SHUTOUTS

J. Bower, TOR	2

1963–64

Semifinal Round

Toronto over Montreal Canadiens, 4 games to 3

March 26, at MONT: MONT 2, TOR 0
March 28, at MONT: TOR 2, MONT 1
March 31, at TOR: MONT 3, TOR 2
April 2, at TOR: TOR 5, MONT 3
April 4, at MONT: MONT 4, TOR 2
April 7, at TOR: TOR 3, MONT 0
April 9, at MONT: TOR 3, MONT 1

Detroit over Chicago, 4 games to 3

March 26, at CHI: CHI 4, DET 1
March 29, at CHI: DET 5, CHI 4
March 31, at DET: DET 3, CHI 0
April 2, at DET: CHI 3, DET 2 (OT, 8:21)
April 5, at CHI: CHI 3, DET 2
April 7, at DET: DET 7, CHI 2
April 9, at CHI: DET 4, CHI 2

FINAL ROUND: Toronto over Detroit, 4 games to 3

GAME 1, April 11:

DETROIT	2	0	0	–	2
TORONTO	1	0	2	–	3

Goaltenders: Detroit, Sawchuk. Toronto, Bower.

FIRST PERIOD: 1. Detroit, MacGregor (Barkley) 4:31. 2. Toronto, Armstrong (Stanley, McKenney) 4:44. 3. Detroit, Howe (MacDonald, Delvecchio) 10:25.
SECOND PERIOD: No scoring.
THIRD PERIOD: 4. Toronto, Armstrong (Kelly, McKenney) 4:02. 5. Toronto, Pulford 19:58.

GAME 2, April 14:

DETROIT	1	2	0	1	–	4
TORONTO	1	0	2	0	–	3

Goaltenders: Detroit, Sawchuk. Toronto, Bower.

FIRST PERIOD: 1. Toronto, Stanley (Kelly, Mahovlich) 4:41. 2. Detroit, Ullman (Gadsby, Jeffrey) 12:43.
SECOND PERIOD: 3. Detroit, Joyal (Barkley) 3:19. 4. Detroit, Smith (Howe) 16:15.
THIRD PERIOD: 5. Toronto, Kelly (Baun, Mahovlich) 11:57. 6. Toronto, Ehman (Bathgate, Stewart) 19:17.
FIRST OVERTIME: 7. Detroit, Jeffrey (Ullman, Howe) 7:52.

GAME 3, April 16:

TORONTO	0	1	2	–	3
DETROIT	3	0	1	–	4

Goaltenders: Toronto, Bower. Detroit, Sawchuk.

FIRST PERIOD: 1. Detroit, Smith 2:40. 2. Detroit, MacGregor (Barkley, Martin) 3:38. 3. Detroit, Smith (Ullman, Delvecchio) 14:47.
SECOND PERIOD: 4. Toronto, Bathgate (Mahovlich, Kelly) 4:16.
THIRD PERIOD: 5. Toronto, Keon (McKenney, Armstrong) 7:34. 6. Toronto, McKenney (Keon, Horton) 18:47. 7. Detroit, Delvecchio (Howe, A. Pronovost) 19:43.

GAME 4, April 18:

TORONTO	1	1	2	–	4
DETROIT	0	2	0	–	2

Goaltenders: Toronto, Bower. Detroit, Sawchuk.

FIRST PERIOD: 1. Toronto, Keon (Horton, McKenney) 5:45.
SECOND PERIOD: 2. Detroit, MacGregor (Joyal) 5:57. 3. Detroit, Howe (Ullman, Jeffrey) 13:05. 4. Toronto, Keon (McKenney, Armstrong) 16:09.
THIRD PERIOD: 5. Toronto, Bathgate (Mahovlich, Kelly) 10:55. 6. Toronto, Mahovlich (Pulford, Stewart) 18:09.

GAME 5, April 21:

DETROIT	1	0	1	–	2
TORONTO	0	0	1	–	1

Goaltenders: Detroit, Sawchuk. Toronto, Bower.

FIRST PERIOD: 1. Detroit, Howe (Delvecchio) 10:52.
SECOND PERIOD: No scoring.
THIRD PERIOD: 2. Detroit, Joyal (A. Pronovost) 7:50. 3. Toronto, Armstrong (Mahovlich, Bathgate) 14:57.

GAME 6, April 23:

TORONTO	1	2	0	1	–	4
DETROIT	0	3	0	0	–	3

Goaltenders: Toronto, Bower. Detroit, Sawchuk.

FIRST PERIOD: 1. Toronto, Pulford (Stanley) 17:01.
SECOND PERIOD: 2. Detroit, Henderson (Martin) 4:20. 3. Detroit, Martin (MacMillan, Howe) 10:56. 4. Toronto, Pulford (Stewart, Brewer) 14:36. 5. Detroit, Howe (Delvecchio, Gadsby) 15:56. 6. Toronto, Harris (Armstrong, Baun) 17:48.
THIRD PERIOD: No scoring.
FIRST OVERTIME: 7. Toronto, Baun (Pulford) 2:43.

GAME 7, April 25:

DETROIT	0	0	0	–	0
TORONTO	1	0	3	–	4

Goaltenders: Detroit, Sawchuk. Toronto, Bower.

FIRST PERIOD: 1. Toronto, Bathgate 3:04.
SECOND PERIOD: No scoring.
THIRD PERIOD: 2. Toronto, Keon (Harris) 4:26. 3. Toronto, Kelly (Mahovlich, Stanley) 5:53. 4. Toronto, Armstrong (Mahovlich) 15:26.

GOALS

G. Howe, DET	9
N. Ullman, DET	7
D. Keon, TOR	7

ASSISTS

F. Mahovlich, TOR	11
G. Howe, DET	10
N. Ullman, DET	10

POINTS

G. Howe, DET	19
N. Ullman, DET	17
F. Mahovlich, TOR	15

WINS

J. Bower, TOR	8
T. Sawchuk, DET	7
C. Hodge, MONT	3
G. Hall, CHI	3

GOALS AGAINST AVE.

J. Bower, TOR	2.14
C. Hodge, MONT	2.29
T. Sawchuk, DET	2.68

SHUTOUTS

J. Bower, TOR	2
C. Hodge, MONT	1
T. Sawchuk, DET	1

1964–65

Semifinal Round

Chicago over Detroit, 4 games to 3

April 1, at DET: DET 4, CHI 3
April 4, at DET: DET 6, CHI 3
April 6, at CHI: CHI 5, DET 2
April 8, at CHI: CHI 2, DET 1
April 11, at DET: DET 4, CHI 2
April 13, at CHI: CHI 4, DET 0
April 15, at DET: CHI 4, DET 2

Montreal Canadiens over Toronto, 4 games to 2

April 1, at MONT: MONT 3, TOR 2
April 3, at MONT: MONT 3, TOR 1
April 6, at TOR: TOR 3, MONT 2 (OT, 4:17)
April 8, at TOR: TOR 4, MONT 2
April 10, at MONT; MONT 3, TOR 1
April 13, at TOR: MONT 4, TOR 3 (OT, 16:33)

FINAL ROUND: Montreal over Chicago, 4 games to 3

GAME 1, April 17:

CHICAGO	0	1	1	–	2
MONTREAL	0	2	1	–	3

Goaltenders: Chicago, Hall. Montreal, Worsley.

FIRST PERIOD: No scoring.
SECOND PERIOD: 1. Montreal, Richard (Berenson) 2:39. 2. Chicago, Henry (B. Hull) 4:47. 3. Montreal, Ferguson 5:26.
THIRD PERIOD: 4. Chicago, Ravlich (Maki, Mikita) 2:38. 5. Montreal, Cournoyer (Harris, Beliveau) 8:59.

GAME 2, April 20:

CHICAGO	0	0	0	–	0
MONTREAL	0	1	1	–	2

Goaltenders: Chicago, Hall. Montreal, Worsley.

FIRST PERIOD: No scoring.
SECOND PERIOD: 1. Montreal, Beliveau (Picard, Provost) 2:55.
THIRD PERIOD: 2. Montreal, Duff (Beliveau, J.C. Tremblay) 8:07.

GAME 3, April 22:

MONTREAL	0	1	0	–	1
CHICAGO	0	1	2	–	3

Goaltenders: Montreal, Worsley. Chicago, Hall.

FIRST PERIOD: No scoring.
SECOND PERIOD: 1. Montreal, Ferguson (J.C. Tremblay, Backstrom) 4:16. 2. Chicago, Esposito (Maki, Pilote) 5:03.
THIRD PERIOD: 3. Chicago, Wharram (Mikita) 2:00. 4. Chicago, Maki (B. Hull, Esposito) 19:24.

GAME 4, April 25:

MONTREAL	0	1	0	–	1
CHICAGO	1	0	4	–	5

Goaltenders: Montreal, Hodge. Chicago, Hall.

FIRST PERIOD: 1. Chicago, Stanfield 2:57.
SECOND PERIOD: 2. Montreal, Beliveau (Duff, J.C. Tremblay) 6:29.
THIRD PERIOD: 3. Chicago, B. Hull (Pilote) 0:26. 4. Chicago, Hay (Stanfield) 16:17. 5. Chicago, B. Hull (Maki) 18:48. 6. Chicago, Jarrett 19:57.

GAME 5, April 27:

CHICAGO	0	0	0	–	0
MONTREAL	2	1	3	–	6

Goaltenders: Chicago, Hall. Montreal, Hodge.

FIRST PERIOD: 1. Montreal, Beliveau (Rousseau, Duff) 7:14. 2. Montreal, Duff (Beliveau, Rousseau) 16:36.
SECOND PERIOD: 3. Montreal, Rousseau (Beliveau, J.C. Tremblay) 2:38.
THIRD PERIOD: 4. Montreal, Beliveau (Duff, J.C. Tremblay) 4:29. 5. Montreal, Richard (Provost) 6:46. 6. Montreal, J.C. Tremblay 19:55.

GAME 6, April 29:

MONTREAL	0	1	0	–	1
CHICAGO	0	0	2	–	2

Goaltenders: Montreal, Hodge. Chicago, Hall.

FIRST PERIOD: No scoring.
SECOND PERIOD: 1. Montreal, Backstrom (Harris, Ferguson) 16:57.
THIRD PERIOD: 2. Chicago, Vasko (Mohns, Ravlich) 6:06. 3. Chicago, Mohns (Mikita, Ravlich) 8:15.

GAME 7, May 1:

CHICAGO	0	0	0	–	0
MONTREAL	4	0	0	–	4

Goaltenders: Chicago, Hall. Montreal, Worsley.

FIRST PERIOD: 1. Montreal, Beliveau (Duff, Rousseau) 0:14. 2. Montreal, Duff (Beliveau, Rousseau) 5:03. 3. Montreal, Cournoyer (Duff, Rousseau) 16:27. 4. Montreal, Richard (Harris) 18:45.
SECOND PERIOD: No scoring.
THIRD PERIOD: No scoring.

GOALS	
B. Hull, CHI	10
J. Beliveau, MONT	8
H. Richard, MONT	7

ASSISTS	
C. Maki, CHI	9
J.C. Tremblay, MONT	9
J. Beliveau, MONT	8
B. Rousseau, MONT	8

POINTS	
B. Hull, CHI	17
J. Beliveau, MONT	16
B. Rousseau, MONT	13

WINS	
G. Hall, CHI	7
G. Worsley, MONT	5
C. Hodge, MONT	3
R. Crozier, DET	3

GOALS AGAINST AVE.	
G. Worsley, MONT	1.75
C. Hodge, MONT	2.00
G. Hall, CHI	2.21

SHUTOUTS	
G. Worsley, MONT	2
G. Hall, CHI	1
C. Hodge, MONT	1

1965–66

Semifinal Round

Montreal Canadiens over Toronto, 4 games to 0

April 7, at MONT: MONT 4, TOR 3
April 9, at MONT: MONT 2, TOR 0
April 12, at TOR: MONT 5, TOR 2
April 14, at TOR: MONT 4, TOR 1

Detroit over Chicago, 4 games to 2

April 7, at CHI: CHI 2, DET 1
April 10, at CHI: DET 7, CHI 0
April 12, at DET: CHI 2, DET 1
April 14, at DET: DET 5, CHI 1
April 17, at CHI: DET 5, CHI 3
April 19, at DET: DET 3, CHI 2

FINAL ROUND: Montreal Canadiens over Detroit, 4 games to 2

GAME 1, April 24:

DETROIT	1	1	1	–	3
MONTREAL	0	1	1	–	2

Goaltenders: Detroit, Crozier. Montreal, Worsley.

FIRST PERIOD: 1. Detroit, Smith (Bathgate) 13:25.
SECOND PERIOD: 2. Montreal, Backstrom (J.C. Tremblay) 4:23. 3. Detroit, Gadsby (McDonald) 5:14.
THIRD PERIOD: 4. Detroit, Henderson (Marshall) 2:14. 5. Montreal, Harper (Rousseau) 2:36.

GAME 2, April 26:

DETROIT	1	0	4	–	5
MONTREAL	1	0	1	–	2

Goaltenders: Detroit, Crozier. Montreal, Worsley.

FIRST PERIOD: 1. Montreal, J.C. Tremblay (Beliveau, Cournoyer) 6:55. 2. Detroit, Bathgate (Prentice, Ullman) 18:39.
SECOND PERIOD: No scoring.
THIRD PERIOD: 3. Detroit, MacGregor (Henderson, Ullman) 1:55. 4. Detroit, McDonald (Gadsby, Smith) 2:45. 5. Montreal, Cournoyer (Harper, Price) 12:00. 6. Detroit, Smith (Bathgate) 12:28. 7. Detroit, Prentice (Delvecchio) 16:25.

GAME 3, April 28:

MONTREAL	2	0	2	–	4
DETROIT	1	0	1	–	2

Goaltenders: Montreal, Worsley. Detroit, Crozier, Bassen.

FIRST PERIOD: 1. Detroit, Ullman 4:20. 2. Montreal, Balon (Harper, Richard) 15:40. 3. Montreal, Beliveau 19:12.
SECOND PERIOD: No scoring.
THIRD PERIOD: 4. Montreal, G. Tremblay (Beliveau) 1:45. 5. Montreal, G. Tremblay (J.C. Tremblay, Rousseau) 3:21. 6. Detroit, Howe (Marshall, Delvecchio) 19:59.

GAME 4, May 1:

MONTREAL	0	1	1	–	2
DETROIT	0	1	0	–	1

Goaltenders: Montreal, Worsley. Detroit, Crozier.

FIRST PERIOD: No scoring.
SECOND PERIOD: 1. Detroit, Ullman (MacGregor, Henderson) 11:24. 2. Montreal, Beliveau (J.C. Tremblay, Duff) 19:51.
THIRD PERIOD: 3. Montreal, Backstrom (Duff, Roberts) 13:37.

GAME 5, May 3:

DETROIT	0	1	0	–	1
MONTREAL	2	2	1	–	5

Goaltenders: Detroit, Crozier. Montreal, Worsley.

FIRST PERIOD: 1. Montreal, Provost (Backstrom, J.C. Tremblay) 1:06. 2. Montreal, Cournoyer (J.C. Tremblay, G. Tremblay) 19:21.
SECOND PERIOD: 3. Montreal, Balon (Rochefort, Richard) 1:05. 4. Montreal, Rousseau (Duff, Backstrom) 11:22. 5. Detroit, Ullman (Henderson, Bathgate) 14:22.
THIRD PERIOD: 6. Montreal, Duff (Richard) 5:31.

GAME 6, May 5:

MONTREAL	1	1	0	1	–	3
DETROIT	0	1	1	0	–	2

Goaltenders: Montreal, Worsley. Detroit, Crozier.

FIRST PERIOD: 1. Montreal, Beliveau (Provost, G. Tremblay) 9:08.
SECOND PERIOD: 2. Montreal, Rochefort (Richard, Balon) 10:11. 3. Detroit, Ullman (Delvecchio, Howe) 11:55.
THIRD PERIOD: 4. Detroit, Smith (McDonald, Bergman) 10:30.
FIRST OVERTIME: 5. Montreal, Richard (Balon, Roberts) 2:30.

GOALS

N. Ullman, DET	6
A. Bathgate, DET	6

ASSISTS

A. Delvecchio, DET	11
N. Ullman, DET	9
J.C. Tremblay, MONT	9

POINTS

N. Ullman, DET	15
J.C. Tremblay, MONT	11
A. Delvecchio, DET	11

WINS

G. Worsley, MONT	8
R. Crozier, DET	6
G. Hall, CHI	2

GOALS AGAINST AVE.

G. Worsley, MONT	2.00
R. Crozier, DET	2.17
T. Sawchuk, TOR	3.00

SHUTOUTS

G. Worsley, MONT	1
R. Crozier, DET	1

1966–67

Semifinal Round

Toronto over Chicago, 4 games to 2

April 6, at CHI: CHI 5, TOR 2
April 9, at CHI: TOR 3, CHI 1
April 11, at TOR: TOR 3, CHI 1
April 13, at TOR: CHI 4, TOR 3
April 15, at CHI: TOR 4, CHI 2
April 18, at TOR: TOR 3, CHI 1

Mont. Canadiens over N.Y. Rangers, 4 games to 0

April 6, at MONT: MONT 6, NYR 4
April 8, at MONT: MONT 3, NYR 1
April 11, at NYR: MONT 3, NYR 2
April 12, at NYR: MONT 2, NYR 1 (OT, 6:28)

FINAL ROUND: Toronto over Montreal Canadiens, 4 games to 2

GAME 1, April 20:

TORONTO	1	1	0	–	2
MONTREAL	2	2	2	–	6

Goaltenders: Toronto, Sawchuk, Bower. Montreal, Vachon.

FIRST PERIOD: 1. Montreal, Cournoyer (Beliveau, Rousseau) 6:25. 2. Toronto, Hillman (Pappin) 6:40. 3. Montreal, Richard (Rochefort, Balon) 11:19.
SECOND PERIOD: 4. Montreal, Cournoyer (Rousseau, Richard) 5:03. 5. Montreal, Beliveau (G. Tremblay) 6:36. 6. Toronto, Pappin (Horton, Pulford) 12:59.
THIRD PERIOD: 7. Montreal, Richard (Balon) 4:53. 8. Montreal, Richard (J.C. Tremblay) 8:21.

GAME 2, April 22:

TORONTO	1	2	0	–	3
MONTREAL	0	0	0	–	0

Goaltenders: Toronto, Bower. Montreal, Vachon.

FIRST PERIOD: 1. Toronto, Stemkowski (Pulford, Walton) 12:14.
SECOND PERIOD: 2. Toronto, Walton (Pappin, Mahovlich) 9:12. 3. Toronto, Horton (Stemkowski, Conacher) 16:57.
THIRD PERIOD: No scoring.

GAME 3, April 25:

MONTREAL	1	1	0	0	0	–	2
TORONTO	1	1	0	0	1	–	3

Goaltenders: Montreal, Vachon. Toronto, Bower.

FIRST PERIOD: 1. Montreal, Beliveau (Rousseau, Duff) 2:37. 2. Toronto, Stemkowski (Hillman, Pappin) 8:39.
SECOND PERIOD: 3. Toronto, Pappin (Horton, Pulford) 10:34. 4. Montreal, Ferguson (Beliveau) 18:10.
THIRD PERIOD: No scoring.
FIRST OVERTIME: No scoring.
SECOND OVERTIME: 5. Toronto, Pulford (Stemkowski, Pappin) 8:26.

GAME 4, April 27:

MONTREAL	2	3	1	–	6
TORONTO	0	2	0	–	2

Goaltenders: Montreal, Vachon. Toronto, Sawchuk.

FIRST PERIOD: 1. Montreal, Backstrom (Larose) 12:25. 2. Montreal, Beliveau (Rousseau, Cournoyer) 13:08.
SECOND PERIOD: 3. Toronto, Walton (Pulford, Stemkowski) 2:09. 4. Montreal, Richard 2:26. 5. Toronto, Horton 12:16. 6. Montreal, Beliveau (Ferguson, Cournoyer) 13:41. 7. Montreal, Backstrom (J.C. Tremblay) 15:58.
THIRD PERIOD: 8. Montreal, Roberts (Richard) 15:19.

GAME 5, April 29:

TORONTO	1	3	0	–	4
MONTREAL	1	0	0	–	1

Goaltenders: Toronto, Sawchuk. Montreal, Vachon, Worsley.

FIRST PERIOD: 1. Montreal, Rochefort (Duff, Richard) 6:03. 2. Toronto, Pappin (Keon, Mahovlich) 15:06.
SECOND PERIOD: 3. Toronto, Conacher (Kelly, Hillman) 3:07. 4. Toronto, Pronovost 12:02. 5. Toronto, Keon (Horton) 19:27.
THIRD PERIOD: No scoring.

GAME 6, May 2:

MONTREAL	0	0	1	–	1
TORONTO	0	2	1	–	3

Goaltenders: Toronto, Sawchuk. Montreal, Worsley.

FIRST PERIOD: No scoring.
SECOND PERIOD: 1. Toronto, Ellis (Kelly, Stanley) 6:25. 2. Toronto, Pappin (Stemkowski, Pulford) 19:28.
THIRD PERIOD: 3. Montreal, Duff (Harris) 5:28. 4. Toronto, Armstrong (Pulford, Kelly) 19:11.

GOALS

J. Pappin, TOR	7
J. Beliveau, MONT	6
P. Stemkowski, TOR	5
R. Backstrom, MONT	5

ASSISTS

B. Pulford, TOR	10
J. Pappin, TOR	8

POINTS

J. Pappin, TOR	15
P. Stemkowski, TOR	12
J. Beliveau, MONT	11
B. Pulford, TOR	11

WINS

R. Vachon, MONT	6
T. Sawchuk, TOR	5
J. Bower, TOR	3

GOALS AGAINST AVE.

J. Bower, TOR	1.67
G. Worsley, MONT	2.00
R. Vachon, MONT	2.44

SHUTOUTS

J. Bower, TOR	1

1967–68

Quarterfinal Round

Montreal Canadiens over Boston, 4 games to 0

April 4, at MONT: MONT 2, BOS 1
April 6, at MONT: MONT 5, BOS 3
April 9, at BOS: MONT 5, BOS 2
April 11, at BOS: MONT 3, BOS 2

Chicago over New York Rangers, 4 games to 2

April 4, at NYR: NYR 3, CHI 1
April 9, at NYR: NYR 2, CHI 1
April 11, at CHI: CHI 7, NYR 4
April 13, at CHI: CHI 3, NYR 1
April 14, at NYR: CHI 2, NYR 1
April 16, at CHI: CHI 4, NYR 1

St. Louis over Philadelphia, 4 games to 3

April 4, at PHI: STL 1, PHI 0
April 6, at PHI: PHI 4, STL 3
April 10, at STL: STL 3, PHI 2 (2 OT, 4:10)
April 11, at STL: STL 5, PHI 2
April 13, at PHI: PHI 6, STL 1
April 16, at STL: PHI 2, STL 1 (2 OT, 11:38)
April 18, at PHI: STL 3, PHI 1

Minnesota over Los Angeles, 4 games to 3

April 4, at LA: LA 2, MINN 1
April 6, at LA: LA 2, MINN 0
April 9, at MINN: MINN 7, LA 5
April 11, at MINN: MINN 3, LA 2
April 13, at LA: LA 3, MINN 2
April 16, at MINN: MINN 4, LA 3 (OT, 9:11)
April 18, at LA: MINN 9, LA 4

Semifinal Round

Montreal Canadiens over Chicago, 4 games to 1

April 18, at MONT: MONT 9, CHI 2
April 20, at MONT: MONT 4, CHI 1
April 23, at CHI: MONT 4, CHI 2
April 25, at CHI: CHI 2, MONT 1
April 28, at MONT: MONT 4, CHI 3 (OT, 2:14)

St. Louis over Minnesota, 4 games to 3

April 21, at STL: STL 5, MINN 3
April 22, at MINN: MINN 3, STL 2 (OT, 3:41)
April 25, at STL: MINN 5, STL 1
April 27, at STL: STL 4, MINN 3 (OT, 1:32)
April 29, at STL: STL 3, MINN 2 (OT, 17:27)
May 1, at MINN: MINN 5, STL 1
May 3, at STL: STL 2, MINN 1 (2 OT, 2:50)

FINAL ROUND: Montreal Canadiens over St. Louis, 4 games to 0

GAME 1, May 5:

MONTREAL	1	1	0	1	–	3
ST. LOUIS	1	1	0	0	–	2

Goaltenders: Montreal, Worsley. St. Louis, Hall.

FIRST PERIOD: 1. St. Louis, B. Plager 9:19. 2. Montreal, Richard (Larose) 9:42.
SECOND PERIOD: 3. St. Louis, Moore (Berenson, B. Plager) 8:16. 4. Montreal, Cournoyer (Ferguson, Harris) 18:14.
THIRD PERIOD: No scoring.
FIRST OVERTIME: 5. Montreal, Lemaire 1:41.

GAME 2, May 7:

MONTREAL	0	0	1	–	1
ST. LOUIS	0	0	0	–	0

Goaltenders: Montreal, Worsley. St. Louis, Hall.

FIRST PERIOD: No scoring.
SECOND PERIOD: No scoring.
THIRD PERIOD: 1. Montreal, Savard (Provost) 2:17.

GAME 3, May 9:

ST. LOUIS	1	1	1	0	–	3
MONTREAL	1	1	1	1	–	4

Goaltenders: St. Louis, Hall. Montreal, Worsley.

FIRST PERIOD: 1. St. Louis, St. Marseille (Picard, Harvey) 10:22. 2. Montreal, Cournoyer (Richard, Ferguson) 14:24.
SECOND PERIOD: 3. Montreal, Savard 1:23. 4. St. Louis, Berenson (Talbot) 3:37.
THIRD PERIOD: 5. Montreal, Backstrom (Cournoyer, Ferguson) 11:43. 6. St. Louis, Berenson 17:25.
FIRST OVERTIME: 7. Montreal, Rousseau (Duff) 1:13.

GAME 4, May 11:

ST. LOUIS	0	2	0	–	2
MONTREAL	1	0	2	–	3

Goaltenders: St. Louis, Hall. Montreal, Worsley.

FIRST PERIOD: 1. Montreal, Duff (Lemaire) 16:47.
SECOND PERIOD: 2. St. Louis, Cameron (Arbour, Ecclestone) 6:53. 3. St. Louis, Sabourin (Veneruzzo) 7:50.
THIRD PERIOD: 4. Montreal, Richard (J.C. Tremblay) 7:24. 5. Montreal, J.C. Tremblay (Backstrom, Cournoyer) 11:40.

GOALS		ASSISTS		POINTS	
B. Goldsworthy, MINN	8	D. Balon, MINN	9	B. Goldsworthy, MINN	15
W. Connelly, MINN	8	Y. Cournoyer, MONT	8	M. Marcetta, MINN	14
		C. Provost, MONT	8	D. Moore, STL	14
				Y. Cournoyer, MONT	14

WINS		GOALS AGAINST AVE.		SHUTOUTS	
G. Worsley, MONT	11	B. Parent, PHI	1.35	G. Worsley, MONT	1
G. Hall, STL	8	G. Worsley, MONT	1.88	G. Hall, STL	1
C. Maniago, MINN	7	G. Hall, STL	2.43	T. Sawchuk, LA	1

1968–69

Quarterfinal Round

Mont. Canadiens over N.Y. Rangers, 4 games to 0

April 2, at MONT: MONT 3, NYR 1
April 3, at MONT: MONT 5, NYR 2
April 5, at NYR: MONT 4, NYR 1
April 6, at NYR: MONT 4, NYR 3

Boston over Toronto, 4 games to 0

April 2, at BOS: BOS 10, TOR 0
April 3, at BOS: BOS 7, TOR 0
April 5, at TOR: BOS 4, TOR 3
April 6, at TOR: BOS 3, TOR 2

St. Louis over Philadelphia, 4 games to 0

April 2, at STL: STL 5, PHI 2
April 3, at STL: STL 5, PHI 0
April 5, at PHI: STL 3, PHI 0
April 6, at PHI: STL 4, PHI 1

Los Angeles over California, 4 games to 3

April 2, at CAL: LA 5, CAL 4 (OT, 0:19)
April 3, at CAL: CAL 4, LA 2
April 5, at LA: CAL 5, LA 2
April 6, at LA: LA 4, CAL 2
April 9, at CAL: CAL 4, LA 1
April 10, at LA: LA 4, CAL 3
April 13, at CAL: LA 5, CAL 3

Semifinal Round

Montreal Canadiens over Boston, 4 games to 2

April 10, at MONT: MONT 3, BOS 2 (OT, 0:42)
April 13, at MONT: MONT 4, BOS 3 (OT, 4:55)
April 17, at BOS: BOS 5, MONT 0
April 20, at BOS: BOS 3, MONT 2
April 22, at MONT: MONT 4, BOS 2
April 24, at BOS: MONT 2, BOS 1 (2 OT, 11:28)

St. Louis over Los Angeles, 4 games to 0

April 15, at STL: STL 4, LA 0
April 17, at STL: STL 3, LA 2
April 19, at LA: STL 5, LA 2
April 20, at LA: STL 4, LA 1

FINAL ROUND: Montreal Canadiens over St. Louis, 4 games to 0

GAME 1, April 27:

ST. LOUIS	1	0	0	–	1
MONTREAL	2	0	1	–	3

Goaltenders: St. Louis, Plante. Montreal, Vachon.

FIRST PERIOD: 1. Montreal, Duff (Cournoyer, Beliveau) 3:39. 2. Montreal, Rousseau (Provost) 4:17. 3. St. Louis, St. Marseille (McCreary, Picard) 18:24.
SECOND PERIOD: No scoring.
THIRD PERIOD: 4. Montreal, Ferguson (Richard) 19:46.

GAME 2, April 29:

ST. LOUIS	0	0	1	–	1
MONTREAL	1	2	0	–	3

Goaltenders: St. Louis, Hall. Montreal, Vachon.

FIRST PERIOD: 1. Montreal, Backstrom (Tremblay) 17:26.
SECOND PERIOD: 2. Montreal, Duff (Beliveau, Savard) 9:07. 3. Montreal, Cournoyer (Beliveau) 14:11.
THIRD PERIOD: 4. St. Louis, Keenan (Roberts, B. Plager) 9:20.

GAME 3, May 1:

MONTREAL	1	2	1	–	4
ST. LOUIS	0	0	0	–	0

Goaltenders: Montreal, Vachon. St. Louis, Plante.

FIRST PERIOD: 1. Montreal, Savard (Duff) 12:34.
SECOND PERIOD: 2. Montreal, Lemaire (Redmond) 8:16. 3. Montreal, Duff (Cournoyer, Beliveau) 13:38.
THIRD PERIOD: 4. Montreal, Duff (Beliveau, Cournoyer) 18:35.

GAME 4, May 4:

MONTREAL	0	0	2	–	2
ST. LOUIS	0	1	0	–	1

Goaltenders: Montreal, Vachon. St. Louis, Hall.

FIRST PERIOD: No Scoring.
SECOND PERIOD: 1. St. Louis, Gray (St. Marseille, Crisp) 10:50.
THIRD PERIOD: 2. Montreal, Harris (Duff, Tremblay) 0:43. 3. Montreal, Ferguson (Backstrom) 3:03.

GOALS	
P. Esposito, BOS	8
D. Sanderson, BOS	8
R. Berenson, STL	7

ASSISTS	
P. Esposito, BOS	10
J. Beliveau, MONT	10
D. Duff, MONT	8

POINTS	
P. Esposito, BOS	18
J. Beliveau, MONT	15
D. Duff, MONT	14

WINS	
J. Plante, STL	8
R. Vachon, MONT	7
G. Cheevers, BOS	6

GOALS AGAINST AVE.	
R. Vachon, MONT	1.42
J. Plante, STL	1.43
G. Cheevers, BOS	1.68

SHUTOUTS	
J. Plante, STL	3
G. Cheevers, BOS	3
R. Vachon, MONT	1

1969–70

Quarterfinal Round

Chicago over Detroit, 4 games to 0

April 8, at CHI: CHI 4, DET 2
April 9, at CHI: CHI 4, DET 2
April 11, at DET: CHI 4, DET 2
April 12, at DET: CHI 4, DET 2

Boston over New York Rangers, 4 games to 2

April 8, at BOS: BOS 8, NYR 2
April 9, at BOS: BOS 5, NYR 3
April 11, at NYR: NYR 4, BOS 3
April 12, at NYR: NYR 4, BOS 2
April 14, at BOS: BOS 3, NYR 2
April 16, at NYR: BOS 4, NYR 1

Pittsburgh over Oakland, 4 games to 0

April 8, at PITT: PITT 2, OAK 1
April 9, at PITT: PITT 2, OAK 1
April 11, at OAK: PITT 5, OAK 2
April 12, at OAK: PITT 3, OAK 2 (OT, 8:28)

St. Louis over Minnesota, 4 games to 2

April 8, at STL: STL 6, MINN 2
April 8, at STL: STL 2, MINN 1
April 11, at MINN: MINN 4, STL 2
April 12, at MINN: MINN 4, STL 0
April 14, at STL: STL 6, MINN 3
April 16, at MINN: STL 4, MINN 2

Semifinal Round

Boston over Chicago, 4 games to 0

April 19, at CHI: BOS 6, CHI 3
April 21, at CHI: BOS 4, CHI 1
April 23, at BOS: BOS 5, CHI 2
April 26, at BOS: BOS 5, CHI 4

St. Louis over Pittsburgh, 4 games to 2

April 19, at STL: STL 3, PITT 1
April 21, at STL: STL 4, PITT 1
April 23, at PITT: PITT 3, STL 2
April 26, at PITT: PITT 2, STL 1
April 28, at STL: STL 5, PITT 0
April 30, at PITT: STL 4, PITT 3

FINAL ROUND: Boston over St. Louis, 4 games to 0

GAME 1, May 3:

BOSTON	1	1	4	–	6
ST. LOUIS	0	1	0	–	1

Goaltenders: Boston, Cheevers. St. Louis, Plante, Wakely.

FIRST PERIOD: 1. Boston, Bucyk (Stanfield) 19:45.
SECOND PERIOD: 2. St. Louis, Roberts (McCreary) 1:52. 3. Boston, Bucyk (McKenzie, Esposito) 5:16.
THIRD PERIOD: 4. Boston, Carleton (Sanderson, Awrey) 4:59. 5. Boston, Bucyk (R. Smith, McKenzie) 5:31. 6. Boston, Sanderson (Orr) 17:20. 7. Boston, Esposito 18:58.

GAME 2, May 5:

BOSTON	3	1	2	–	6
ST. LOUIS	0	1	1	–	2

Goaltenders: Boston, Cheevers. St. Louis, Wakely.

FIRST PERIOD: 1. Boston, Stanfield (Orr, Esposito) 8:10. 2. Boston, Westfall (R. Smith) 13:38. 3. Boston, Westfall (Orr) 19:15.
SECOND PERIOD: 4. Boston, Sanderson (Carleton, Esposito) 9:37. 5. St. Louis, Gray (Picard) 17:26.
THIRD PERIOD: 6. Boston, Sanderson (R. Smith, Westfall) 0:58. 7. St. Louis, St. Marseille (Goyette, McDonald) 4:15. 8. Boston, Bucyk (McKenzie) 15:00.

GAME 3, May 7:

ST. LOUIS	1	0	0	–	1
BOSTON	2	0	2	–	4

Goaltenders: St. Louis, Hall. Boston, Cheevers.

FIRST PERIOD: 1. St. Louis, St. Marseille 5:32. 2. Boston, Bucyk (Esposito, Stanfield) 13:32. 3. Boston, McKenzie (Orr, Stanfield) 18:23.
SECOND PERIOD: No scoring.
THIRD PERIOD: 4. Boston, Cashman (Hodge, Esposito) 3:20. 5. Boston, Cashman (Hodge, Esposito) 14:46.

GAME 4, May 10:

ST. LOUIS	1	1	1	0	–	3
BOSTON	1	1	1	1	–	4

Goaltenders: St. Louis, Hall. Boston, Cheevers.

FIRST PERIOD: 1. Boston, R. Smith (Sanderson) 5:28. 2. St. Louis, Berenson (R. Plager, Ecclestone) 19:17.
SECOND PERIOD: 3. St. Louis, Sabourin (St. Marseille) 3:22. 4. Boston, Esposito (Hodge) 14:22.
THIRD PERIOD: 5. St. Louis, Keenan (Goyette, Roberts) 0:19. 6. Boston, Bucyk (McKenzie, R. Smith) 13:28.
FIRST OVERTIME: 7. Boston, Orr (Sanderson) 0:40.

GOALS

P. Esposito, BOS	13
J. Bucyk, BOS	11
B. Orr, BOS	9

ASSISTS

P. Esposito, BOS	14
J. McKenzie, BOS	12
F. Stanfield, BOS	12

POINTS

P. Esposito, BOS	27
B. Orr, BOS	20
J. Bucyk, BOS	19

WINS

G. Cheevers, BOS	12
L. Binkley, PITT	5
J. Plante, STL	4
G. Hall, STL	4

GOALS AGAINST AVE.

J. Plante, STL	1.48
L. Binkley, PITT	2.10
G. Cheevers, BOS	2.23

SHUTOUTS

J. Plante, STL	1
C. Maniago, MINN	1

1970–71

Quarterfinal Round

Montreal Canadiens over Boston, 4 games to 3

April 7, at BOS: BOS 3, MONT 1
April 8, at BOS: MONT 7, BOS 5
April 10, at MONT: MONT 3, BOS 1
April 11, at MONT: BOS 5, MONT 2
April 13, at BOS: BOS 7, MONT 3
April 15, at MONT: MONT 8, BOS 3
April 18, at BOS: MONT 4, BOS 2

New York Rangers over Toronto, 4 games to 2

April 7, at NYR: NYR 5, TOR 4
April 8, at NYR: TOR 4, NYR 1
April 10, at TOR: TOR 3, NYR 1
April 11, at TOR: NYR 4, TOR 2
April 13, at NYR: NYR 3, TOR 1
April 15, at TOR: NYR 2, TOR 1 (OT, 9:07)

Chicago over Philadelphia, 4 games to 0

April 7, at CHI: CHI 5, PHI 2
April 8, at CHI: CHI 6, PHI 2
April 10, at PHI: CHI 3, PHI 2
April 11, at PHI: CHI 6, PHI 2

Minnesota over St. Louis, 4 games to 2

April 7, at STL: MINN 3, STL 2
April 8, at STL: STL 4, MINN 2
April 10, at MINN: STL 3, MINN 0
April 11, at MINN: MINN 2, STL 1
April 13, at STL: MINN 4, STL 3
April 15, at MINN: MINN 5, STL 2

Semifinal Round

Montreal Canadiens over Minnesota, 4 games to 2

April 20, at MONT: MONT 7, MINN 2
April 22, at MONT: MINN 6, MONT 3
April 24, at MINN: MONT 6, MINN 3
April 25, at MINN: MINN 5, MONT 2
April 27, at MONT: MONT 6, MINN 1
April 29, at MINN: MONT 3, MINN 2

Chicago over New York Rangers, 4 games to 3

April 18, at CHI: NYR 2, CHI 1 (OT, 1:37)
Apri' 20, at CHI: CHI 3, NYR 0
April 22, at NYR: NYR 4, CHI 1
April 25, at NYR: CHI 7, NYR 1
April 27, at CHI: CHI 3, NYR 2 (OT, 6:35)
April 29, at NYR: NYR 3, CHI 2 (3 OT, 1:29)
May 2, at CHI: CHI 4, NYR 2

FINAL ROUND: Montreal Canadiens over Chicago, 4 games to 3

GAME 1, May 4:

MONTREAL	0	1	0	0	0	–	1
CHICAGO	0	0	1	0	1	–	2

Goaltenders: Montreal, Dryden. Chicago, Esposito.

FIRST PERIOD: No scoring.
SECOND PERIOD: 1. Montreal, Lemaire (Tremblay, P. Mahovlich) 12:29.
THIRD PERIOD: 2. Chicago, B. Hull (Pappin, Stapleton) 7:54.
FIRST OVERTIME: No scoring.
SECOND OVERTIME: 3. Chicago, Pappin (Mikita, White) 1:11.

GAME 2, May 6:

MONTREAL	2	0	1	–	3
CHICAGO	1	2	2	–	5

Goaltenders: Montreal, Dryden. Chicago, Esposito.

FIRST PERIOD: 1. Chicago, B. Hull (Angotti, Maki) 4:39. 2. Montreal, Lemaire (Tremblay) 9:06. 3. Montreal, P. Mahovlich (Tremblay, Laperriere) 17:58.
SECOND PERIOD: 4. Chicago, Maki (Angotti, B. Hull) 11:58. 5. Chicago, Pappin (O'Shea, Foley) 13:50.
THIRD PERIOD: 6. Chicago, Angotti 7:27. 7. Montreal, F. Mahovlich 8:56. 8. Chicago, Angotti 16:47.

GAME 3, May 9:

CHICAGO	2	0	0	–	2
MONTREAL	0	2	2	–	4

Goaltenders: Chicago, Esposito. Montreal, Dryden.

FIRST PERIOD: 1. Chicago, Koroll (B. Hull, Mikita) 4:56. 2. Chicago, B. Hull (Pappin, Martin) 13:38.
SECOND PERIOD: 3. Montreal, P. Mahovlich 5:56. 4. Montreal, F. Mahovlich (Beliveau, Cournoyer) 7:34.
THIRD PERIOD: 5. Montreal, Cournoyer (Harper) 6:23. 6. Montreal, F. Mahovlich (Lapointe) 12:13.

GAME 4, May 11:

CHICAGO	1	1	0	–	2
MONTREAL	3	2	0	–	5

Goaltenders: Chicago, Esposito. Montreal, Dryden.

FIRST PERIOD: 1. Montreal, P. Mahovlich (Harper, Laperriere) 1:00. 2. Chicago, Mikita (Koroll, Stapleton) 3:09. 3. Montreal, Beliveau (Cournoyer, F. Mahovlich) 6:54. 4. Montreal, Lapointe (Houle, Richard) 16:33.
SECOND PERIOD: 5. Montreal, Cournoyer 9:07. 6. Chicago, D. Hull (Mikita) 12:30. 7. Montreal, Cournoyer (F. Mahovlich, P. Mahovlich) 15:33.
THIRD PERIOD: No scoring.

GAME 5, May 13:

MONTREAL	0	0	0	–	0
CHICAGO	1	1	0	–	2

Goaltenders: Montreal, Dryden. Chicago, Esposito.

FIRST PERIOD: 1. Chicago, D. Hull (Koroll, B. Hull) 10:57.
SECOND PERIOD: 2. Chicago, Koroll (D. Hull, Mikita) 11:26.
THIRD PERIOD: No scoring.

GAME 6, May 18:

CHICAGO	1	2	0	–	3
MONTREAL	1	1	2	–	4

Goaltenders: Chicago, Esposito. Montreal, Dryden.

FIRST PERIOD: 1. Chicago, Pappin 11:25. 2. Montreal, Cournoyer (Beliveau, F. Mahovlich) 12:13.
SECOND PERIOD: 3. Montreal, P. Mahovlich (Houle, Ferguson) 5:04. 4. Chicago, Maki (White, B. Hull) 17:40. 5. Chicago, Pappin (Jarrett, B. Hull) 18:48.
THIRD PERIOD: 6. Montreal, F. Mahovlich (Beliveau) 5:10. 7. Montreal, P. Mahovlich (F. Mahovlich) 8:56.

GAME 7, May 18:

MONTREAL	0	2	1	–	3
CHICAGO	1	1	0	–	2

Goaltenders: Montreal, Dryden. Chicago, Esposito.

FIRST PERIOD: 1. Chicago, D. Hull (Koroll, B. Hull) 19:12.
SECOND PERIOD: 2. Chicago, O'Shea (Martin) 7:33. 3. Montreal, Lemaire (Laperriere) 14:18. 4. Montreal, Richard (Lemaire) 18:20.
THIRD PERIOD: 5. Montreal, Richard (Houle, Lapointe) 2:34.

GOALS		ASSISTS		POINTS	
F. Mahovlich, MONT	14	J. Beliveau, MONT	16	F. Mahovlich, MONT	27
B. Hull, CHI	11	B. Hull, CHI	14	B. Hull, CHI	25
		P. Stapleton, CHI	14	Y. Cournoyer, MONT	22
		J.C. Tremblay, MONT	14	J. Beliveau, MONT	22

WINS		GOALS AGAINST AVE.		SHUTOUTS	
K. Dryden, MONT	12	T. Esposito, CHI	2.19	T. Esposito, CHI	2
T. Esposito, CHI	11	E. Giacomin, NYR	2.21	E. Wakely, STL	1
E. Giacomin, NYR	7	B. Parent, PHI	2.30		

1971–72

Quarterfinal Round

Boston over Toronto, 4 games to 1

April 5, at BOS: BOS 5, TOR 0
April 6, at BOS: TOR 4, BOS 3 (OT, 2:58)
April 8, at TOR: BOS 2, TOR 0
April 9, at TOR: BOS 5, TOR 4
April 11, at BOS: BOS 3, TOR 2

N.Y. Rangers over Mont. Canadiens, 4 games to 2

April 5, at NYR: NYR 3, MONT 2
April 6, at NYR: NYR 5, MONT 2
April 8, at MONT: MONT 2, NYR 1
April 9, at MONT: NYR 6, MONT 4
April 11, at NYR: MONT 2, NYR 1
April 13, at MONT: NYR 3, MONT 2

Chicago over Pittsburgh, 4 games to 0

April 5, at CHI: CHI 3, PITT 1
April 6, at CHI: CHI 3, PITT 2
April 8, at PITT: CHI 2, PITT 0
April 9, at PITT: CHI 6, PITT 5 (OT, 0:12)

St. Louis over Minnesota, 4 games to 3

April 5, at MINN: MINN 3, STL 0
April 6, at MINN: MINN 6, STL 5 (OT, 1:36)
April 8, at STL: STL 2, MINN 1
April 9, at STL: STL 3, MINN 2
April 11, at MINN: MINN 4, STL 3
April 13, at STL: STL 4, MINN 2
April 16, at MINN: STL 2, MINN 1 (OT, 10:07)

Semifinal Round

N.Y. Rangers over Chicago, 4 games to 0

April 16, at CHI: NYR 3, CHI 2
April 18, at CHI: NYR 5, CHI 3
April 20, at NYR: NYR 3, CHI 2
April 23, at NYR: NYR 6, CHI 2

Boston over St. Louis, 4 games to 0

April 18, at BOS: BOS 6, STL 1
April 20, at BOS: BOS 10, STL 2
April 23, at STL: BOS 7, STL 2
April 25, at STL: BOS 5, STL 3

FINAL ROUND: Boston over New York Rangers, 4 games to 2

GAME 1, April 30:

NEW YORK	1	1	3	–	5
BOSTON	4	1	1	–	6

Goaltenders: New York, Giacomin. Boston, Cheevers.

FIRST PERIOD: 1. New York, Rolfe (Gilbert, Park) 3:52. 2. Boston, Stanfield (McKenzie) 5:07. 3. Boston, Hodge (Esposito, Walton) 15:48. 4. Boston, Sanderson (Westfall) 17:29. 5. Boston, Hodge (Esposito) 18:14.
SECOND PERIOD: 6. Boston, Hodge (Esposito, Orr) 10:46. 7. New York, Gilbert (Ratelle, Hadfield) 11:54.
THIRD PERIOD: 8. New York, Hadfield (Tkaczuk, Gilbert) 1:56. 9. New York, Tkaczuk 7:48. 10. New York, MacGregor (Irvine, Stemkowski) 9:17. 11. Boston, Bailey (Walton, Westfall) 17:44.

GAME 2, May 2:

NEW YORK	0	1	0	–	1
BOSTON	1	0	1	–	2

Goaltenders: New York, Villemure. Boston, Johnston.

FIRST PERIOD: 1. Boston, Bucyk (Orr, Stanfield) 16:15.
SECOND PERIOD: 2. New York, Gilbert (Neilson, Hadfield) 7:23.
THIRD PERIOD: 3. Boston, Hodge (Walton, Esposito) 11:53.

GAME 3, May 4:

BOSTON	1	1	0	–	2
NEW YORK	3	2	0	–	5

Goaltenders: Boston, Cheevers. New York, Giacomin.

FIRST PERIOD: 1. New York, Park (Hadfield, Fairbairn) 1:22. 2. New York, Gilbert (Park, Rousseau) 11:19. 3. New York, Park (Gilbert) 13:00. 4. Boston, Walton (Vadnais) 14:04.
SECOND PERIOD: 5. Boston, Orr (Smith, Cashman) 1:10. 6. New York, Gilbert (Rousseau, Park) 3:46. 7. New York, Stemkowski (MacGregor, Irvine) 19:23.
THIRD PERIOD: No scoring.

GAME 4, May 7:

BOSTON	2	1	0	–	3
NEW YORK	0	1	1	–	2

Goaltenders: Boston, Cheevers. New York, Giacomin.

FIRST PERIOD: 1. Boston, Orr (Walton) 5:26. 2. Boston, Orr (McKenzie, Bucyk) 8:17.
SECOND PERIOD: 3. Boston, Marotte (Orr) 16:33. 4. New York, Irvine (Stemkowski, Seiling) 18:38.
THIRD PERIOD: 5. New York, Seiling (Irvine, Stemkowski) 18:35.

GAME 5, May 9:

NEW YORK	1	0	2	–	3
BOSTON	2	0	0	–	2

Goaltenders: New York, Villemure. Boston, Johnston.

FIRST PERIOD: 1. Boston, Cashman (Hodge, Esposito) 3:55. 2. New York, Rolfe (Tkaczuk, Fairbairn) 13:45. 3. Boston, Hodge (Stanfield, Esposito) 16:07.
SECOND PERIOD: No scoring.
THIRD PERIOD: 4. New York, Rousseau (Park, MacGregor) 2:56. 5. New York, Rousseau (Irvine) 12:45.

GAME 6, May 11:

BOSTON	1	0	2	–	3
NEW YORK	0	0	0	–	0

Goaltenders: Boston, Cheevers. New York, Villemure.

FIRST PERIOD: 1. Boston, Orr (Hodge, Bucyk) 11:18.
SECOND PERIOD: No scoring.
THIRD PERIOD: 2. Boston, Cashman (Orr, Esposito) 5:10. 3. Boston, Cashman (Esposito, Hodge) 18:11.

GOALS		ASSISTS		POINTS	
P. Esposito, BOS	9	B. Orr, BOS	19	P. Esposito, BOS	24
J. Bucyk, BOS	9	P. Esposito, BOS	15	B. Orr, BOS	24
K. Hodge, BOS	9	J. McKenzie, BOS	12	J. Bucyk, BOS	20

WINS		GOALS AGAINST AVE.		SHUTOUTS	
E. Johnston, BOS	6	G. Smith, CHI	1.50	G. Cheevers, BOS	2
G. Cheevers, BOS	6	E. Johnston, BOS	1.86	E. Johnston, BOS	1
E. Giacomin, NYR	6	G. Worsley, MINN	2.17	G. Worsley, MINN	1
				G. Smith, CHI	1

1972–73

Quarterfinal Round

Montreal Canadiens over Buffalo, 4 games to 2

April 4, at MONT: MONT 2, BUF 1
April 5, at MONT: MONT 7, BUF 3
April 7, at BUF: MONT 5, BUF 2
April 8, at BUF: BUF 5, MONT 1
April 10, at MONT: BUF 3, MONT 2 (OT, 9:18)
April 12, at BUF: MONT 4, BUF 2

New York Rangers over Boston, 4 games to 1

April 4, at BOS: NYR 6, BOS 2
April 5, at BOS: NYR 4, BOS 2
April 7, at NYR: BOS 4, NYR 2
April 8, at NYR: NYR 4, BOS 0
April 10, at BOS: NYR 6, BOS 3

Chicago over St. Louis, 4 games to 1

April 4, at CHI: CHI 7, STL 1
April 5, at CHI: CHI 1, STL 0
April 7, at STL: CHI 5, STL 2
April 8, at STL: STL 5, CHI 3
April 10, at CHI: CHI 6, STL 1

Philadelphia over Minnesota, 4 games to 2

April 4, at PHI: MINN 3, PHI 0
April 5, at PHI: PHI 4, MINN 1
April 7, at MINN: MINN 5, PHI 0
April 8, at MINN: PHI 3, MINN 0
April 10, at PHI: PHI 3, MINN 2 (OT, 8:35)
April 12, at MINN: PHI 4, MINN 1

Semifinal Round

Mont. Canadiens over Philadelphia, 4 games to 1

April 14, at MONT: PHI 5, MONT 4 (OT, 2:56)
April 17, at MONT: MONT 4, PHI 3 (OT, 6:45)
April 19, at PHI: MONT 2, PHI 1
April 22, at PHI: MONT 4, PHI 1
April 24, at MONT: MONT 5, PHI 3

Chicago over New York Rangers, 4 games to 1

April 12, at CHI: NYR 4, CHI 1
April 15, at CHI: CHI 5, NYR 4
April 17, at NYR: CHI 2, NYR 1
April 19, at NYR: CHI 3, NYR 1
April 24, at CHI: CHI 4, NYR 1

FINAL ROUND: Montreal Canadiens over Chicago, 4 games to 2

GAME 1, April 29:

CHICAGO	3	0	0	–	3
MONTREAL	2	2	4	–	8

Goaltenders: Chicago, Esposito, Smith. Montreal, Dryden.

FIRST PERIOD: 1. Chicago, Martin (Stapleton, Hull) 0:35. 2. Chicago, Backstrom (Stapleton) 1:02. 3. Montreal, Laperriere 2:28. 4. Montreal, Tardif (Lafleur, Houle) 8:07. 5. Chicago, Martin (Stapleton, White) 12:07.
SECOND PERIOD: 6. Montreal, Lefley (Cournoyer, Lemaire) 3:01. 7. Montreal, Lemaire (Richard, Tardif) 16:23.
THIRD PERIOD: 8. Montreal, Lemaire (F. Mahovlich) 8:38. 9. Montreal, P. Mahovlich 12:36. 10. Montreal, F. Mahovlich (Lafleur, Houle) 13:34. 11. Montreal, Lefley (Lemaire, Cournoyer) 14:35.

GAME 2, May 1:

CHICAGO	0	1	0	–	1
MONTREAL	1	1	2	–	4

Goaltenders: Chicago, Esposito. Montreal, Dryden.

FIRST PERIOD: 1. Montreal, Bouchard (Larose, P. Mahovlich) 5:36.
SECOND PERIOD: 2. Chicago, Koroll (Redmond, Angotti) 7:28. 3. Montreal, Cournoyer (F. Mahovlich) 12:18.
THIRD PERIOD: 4. Montreal, Cournoyer (Lapointe, Lemaire) 5:01. 5. Montreal, F. Mahovlich 19:26.

GAME 3, May 3:

MONTREAL	0	1	3	–	4
CHICAGO	4	1	2	–	7

Goaltenders: Montreal, Dryden. Chicago, Esposito.

FIRST PERIOD: 1. Chicago, Hull (Pappin, Stapleton) 1:59. 2. Chicago, Bordeleau (Mikita, Koroll) 11:44. 3. Chicago, White (Stapleton, Backstrom) 13:20. 4. Chicago, Mikita (Koroll, White) 14:20.
SECOND PERIOD: 5. Chicago, Marks (Frig, Mikita) 2:08. 6. Montreal, F. Mahovlich (Robinson, P. Mahovlich) 10:25.
THIRD PERIOD: 7. Montreal, Cournoyer (Lemaire, Lefley) 1:20. 8. Montreal, Lapointe (F. Mahovlich, Larose) 7:15. 9. Montreal, Lemaire (Cournoyer, Tardif) 8:01. 10. Chicago, Hull 19:29. 11. Chicago, Pappin (Hull) 19:49.

GAME 4, May 6:

MONTREAL	1	2	1	–	4
CHICAGO	0	0	0	–	0

Goaltenders: Montreal, Dryden. Chicago, Esposito.

FIRST PERIOD: 1. Montreal, Tardif (Cournoyer, Lemaire) 1:08.
SECOND PERIOD: 2. Montreal, Cournoyer (Tardif) 14:13. 3. Montreal, Lefley (P. Mahovlich, Larose) 15:43.
THIRD PERIOD: 4. Montreal, Larose (Lemaire) 3:45.

GAME 5, May 8:

CHICAGO	2	5	1	–	8
MONTREAL	2	3	2	–	7

Goaltenders: Chicago, Esposito. Montreal, Dryden.

FIRST PERIOD: 1. Montreal, F. Mahovlich 2:47. 2. Chicago, Hull (Jarrett, Russell) 9:34. 3. Chicago, Mikita (Stapleton) 11:24. 4. Montreal, P. Mahovlich (F. Mahovlich, Robinson) 14:32.
SECOND PERIOD: 5. Montreal, Larose 0:37. 6. Chicago, Kryskow (Maki, Backstrom) 3:10. 7. Montreal, Larose (Wilson) 4:23. 8. Chicago, Mikita (Stapleton, Marks) 6:21. 9. Montreal, Cournoyer (Lemaire, Lapointe) 7:09. 10. Chicago, Pappin 11:24. 11. Chicago, Frig (Mikita) 16:12. 12. Chicago, Pappin (Mikita, Hull) 19:03.
THIRD PERIOD: 13. Montreal, Savard (Wilson, Larose) 1:15. 14. Chicago, Angotti (White) 4:04. 15. Montreal, Richard (F. Mahovlich) 11:43.

GAME 6, May 10:

MONTREAL	1	3	2	–	6
CHICAGO	2	2	0	–	4

Goaltenders: Montreal, Dryden. Chicago, Esposito.

FIRST PERIOD: 1. Chicago, Martin (Mikita, Stapleton) 10:35. 2. Chicago, Martin (Pappin) 11:31. 3. Montreal, Richard (F. Mahovlich) 19:48.
SECOND PERIOD: 4. Montreal, P. Mahovlich (Laperriere, Lefley) 5:05. 5. Montreal, Houle (P. Mahovlich, Lefley) 6:37. 6. Chicago, Kryskow (Maki, Backstrom) 8:32. 7. Montreal, F. Mahovlich (Lapointe, Cournoyer) 10:54. 8. Chicago, Martin (Hull) 17:05.
THIRD PERIOD: 9. Montreal, Cournoyer (Lemaire) 8:13. 10. Montreal, Tardif (Cournoyer, Lemaire) 12:42.

GOALS	
Y. Cournoyer, MONT	15
P. Martin, CHI	10
D. Hull, CHI	9
F. Mahovlich, MONT	9

ASSISTS	
D. Hull, CHI	15
P. Stapleton, CHI	15
F. Mahovlich, MONT	14

POINTS	
Y. Cournoyer, MONT	25
D. Hull, CHI	24
F. Mahovlich, MONT	23

WINS	
K. Dryden, MONT	12
T. Esposito, CHI	10
E. Giacomin, NYR	5
D. Favell, PHI	5

GOALS AGAINST AVE.	
C. Maniago, MINN	1.75
G. Villemure, NYR	1.97
E. Giacomin, NYR	2.56

SHUTOUTS	
C. Maniago, MINN	2

1973–74

Quarterfinal Round

Boston over Toronto, 4 games to 0

April 10, at BOS: BOS 1, TOR 0
April 11, at BOS: BOS 6, TOR 3
April 13, at TOR: BOS 6, TOR 3
April 14, at TOR: BOS 4, TOR 3 (OT, 1:27)

N.Y. Rangers over Mont. Canadiens, 4 games to 2

April 10, at MONT: NYR 4, MONT 1
April 11, at MONT: MONT 4, NYR 1
April 13, at NYR: MONT 4, NYR 2
April 14, at NYR: NYR 6, MONT 4
April 16, at MONT: NYR 3, MONT 2 (OT, 4:07)
April 18, at NYR: NYR 5, MONT 2

Chicago over Los Angeles, 4 games to 1

April 10, at CHI: CHI 3, LA 1
April 11, at CHI: CHI 4, LA 1
April 13, at LA: CHI 1, LA 0
April 14, at LA: LA 5, CHI 1
April 16, at CHI: CHI 1, LA 0

Philadelphia over Atlanta, 4 games to 0

April 9, at PHI: PHI 4, ATL 1
April 11, at PHI: PHI 5, ATL 1
April 12, at ATL: PHI 4, ATL 1
April 14, at ATL: PHI 4, ATL 3 (OT, 5:40)

Semifinal Round

Boston over Chicago, 4 games to 2

April 18, at BOS: CHI 4, BOS 2
April 21, at BOS: BOS 8, CHI 6
April 23, at CHI: CHI 4, BOS 3 (OT, 3:48)
April 25, at CHI: BOS 5, CHI 2
April 28, at BOS: BOS 6, CHI 2
April 30, at CHI: BOS 4, CHI 2

Philadelphia over N.Y. Rangers, 4 games to 3

April 20, at PHI: PHI 4, NYR 0
April 23, at PHI: PHI 5, NYR 2
April 25, at NYR: NYR 5, PHI 3
April 28, at NYR: NYR 2, PHI 1 (OT, 4:20)
April 30, at PHI: PHI 4, NYR 1
May 2, at NYR: NYR 4, PHI 1
May 5, at PHI: PHI 4, NYR 3

FINAL ROUND: Philadelphia over Boston, 4 games to 2

GAME 1, May 7:

PHILADELPHIA	0	1	1	–	2
BOSTON	2	0	1	–	3

Goaltenders: Philadelphia, Parent. Boston, Gilbert.

FIRST PERIOD: 1. Boston, Cashman (Orr, Vadnais) 12:08. 2. Boston, Sheppard (Forbes, Smith) 13:01.
SECOND PERIOD: 3. Philadelphia, Kindrachuk (Joe Watson, Saleski) 7:47.
THIRD PERIOD: 4. Philadelphia, Clarke (Joe Watson, Nolet) 5:32. 5. Boston, Orr (Hodge, Cashman) 19:38.

GAME 2, May 9:

PHILADELPHIA	0	1	1	1	–	3
BOSTON	2	0	0	0	–	2

Goaltenders: Philadelphia, Parent. Boston, Gilbert.

FIRST PERIOD: 1. Boston, Cashman (Esposito, Vadnais) 14:24. 2. Boston, Esposito (Hodge, Cashman) 17:42.
SECOND PERIOD: 3. Philadelphia, Clarke (Flett, Schultz) 1:08.
THIRD PERIOD: 4. Philadelphia, Dupont (MacLeish, Clarke) 19:08.
FIRST OVERTIME: 5. Philadelphia, Clarke (Flett, Schultz) 12:01.

GAME 3, May 12:

BOSTON	1	0	0	–	1
PHILADELPHIA	2	0	2	–	4

Goaltenders: Boston, Gilbert. Philadelphia, Parent.

FIRST PERIOD: 1. Boston, Bucyk (Sheppard, Orr) 1:03. 2. Philadelphia, Bladon (Clarke, MacLeish) 10:27. 3. Philadelphia, Crisp 15:43.
SECOND PERIOD: No scoring.
THIRD PERIOD: 4. Philadelphia, Kindrachuk (Saleski, Barber) 7:53. 5. Philadelphia, Lonsberry (MacLeish) 14:19.

GAME 4, May 14:

BOSTON	2	0	0	–	2
PHILADELPHIA	2	0	2	–	4

Goaltenders: Boston, Gilbert. Philadelphia, Parent.

FIRST PERIOD: 1. Philadelphia, MacLeish (Bladon) 4:40. 2. Philadelphia, Schultz (Saleski, Van Impe) 5:30. 3. Boston, Esposito (Bucyk, Hodge) 7:12. 4. Boston, Savard (Orr, Vadnais) 11:24.
SECOND PERIOD: No scoring.
THIRD PERIOD: 5. Philadelphia, Barber (Lonsberry, Jim Watson) 14:35. 6. Philadelphia, Dupont (Clarke, Crisp) 16:40.

GAME 5, May 16:

PHILADELPHIA	0	1	0	–	1
BOSTON	1	2	2	–	5

Goaltenders: Boston, Gilbert. Philadelphia, Parent.

FIRST PERIOD: 1. Boston, Sheppard (Orr) 8:14.
SECOND PERIOD: 2. Philadelphia, Clement (Flett, Van Impe) 6:04. 3. Boston, Orr (Sheppard, Bucyk) 12:06. 4. Boston, Orr (Hodge, Smith) 16:55.
THIRD PERIOD: 5. Boston, Hodge (Sheppard, Bucyk) 0:39. 6. Boston, Marcotte (Savard, O'Reilly) 18:59.

GAME 6, May 19:

BOSTON	0	0	0	–	0
PHILADELPHIA	1	0	0	–	1

Goaltenders: Boston, Gilbert. Philadelphia, Parent.

FIRST PERIOD: 1. Philadelphia, MacLeish (Dupont) 14:48.
SECOND PERIOD: No scoring.
THIRD PERIOD: No scoring.

GOALS	
R. MacLeish, PHI	13
G. Sheppard, BOS	11
P. Esposito, BOS	9

ASSISTS	
B. Orr, BOS	14
C. Vadnais, BOS	12
B. Clarke, PHI	11

POINTS	
R. MacLeish, PHI	22
G. Sheppard, BOS	19
J. Bucyk, BOS	18
B. Orr, BOS	18

WINS	
B. Parent, PHI	12
G. Gilbert, BOS	10
E. Giacomin, NYR	7

GOALS AGAINST AVE.	
G. Edwards, LA	1.00
R. Vachon, LA	1.75
B. Parent, PHI	2.02

SHUTOUTS	
B. Parent, PHI	2
T. Esposito, CHI	2
G. Gilbert, BOS	1

1974–75

Preliminary Round

Toronto over Los Angeles, 2 games to 1

April 8, at LA: LA 3, TOR 2 (OT, 8:53)
April 10, at TOR: TOR 3, LA 2 (OT, 10:19)
April 11, at LA: TOR 2, LA 1

Chicago over Boston, 2 games to 1

April 8, at BOS: BOS 8, CHI 2
April 10, at CHI: CHI 4, BOS 3 (OT, 7:33)
April 11, at BOS: CHI 6, BOS 4

Pittsburgh over St. Louis, 2 games to 0

April 8, at PITT: PITT 4, STL 3
April 10, at STL: PITT 5, STL 3

N.Y. Islanders over N.Y. Rangers, 2 games to 1

April 8, at NYR: NYI 3, NYR 2
April 10, at NYI: NYR 8, NYI 3
April 11, at NYR: NYI 4, NYR 3 (OT, 0:11)

Quarterfinal Round

Philadelphia over Toronto, 4 games to 0

April 13, at PHI: PHI 6, TOR 3
April 15, at PHI: PHI 3, TOR 0
April 17, at TOR: PHI 2, TOR 0
April 19, at TOR: PHI 4, TOR 3 (OT, 1:45)

Buffalo over Chicago, 4 games to 1

April 13, at BUF: BUF 4, CHI 1
April 15, at BUF: BUF 3, CHI 1
April 17, at CHI: CHI 5, BUF 4 (OT, 2:31)
April 20, at CHI: BUF 6, CHI 2
April 22, at BUF: BUF 3, CHI 1

Mont. Canadiens over Vancouver, 4 games to 1

April 13, at MONT: MONT 6, VAN 2
April 15, at MONT: VAN 2, MONT 1
April 17, at VAN: MONT 4, VAN 1
April 19, at VAN: MONT 4, VAN 0
April 22, at MONT: MONT 5, VAN 4 (OT, 17:46)

N.Y. Islanders over Pittsburgh, 4 games to 3

April 13, at PITT: PITT 5, NYI 4
April 15, at PITT: PITT 3, NYI 1
April 17, at NYI: PITT 6, NYI 4
April 20, at NYI: NYI 3, PITT 1
April 22, at PITT: NYI 4, PITT 2
April 24, at NYI: NYI 4, PITT 1
April 26, at PITT: NYI 1, PITT 0

Semifinal Round

Philadelphia over N.Y. Islanders, 4 games to 3

April 29, at PHI: PHI 4, NYI 0
May 1, at PHI: PHI 5, NYI 4 (OT, 2:56)
May 4, at NYI: PHI 1, NYI 0
May 7, at NYI: NYI 4, PHI 3 (OT, 1:53)
May 8, at PHI: NYI 5, PHI 1
May 11, at NYI: NYI 2, PHI 1
May 13, at PHI: PHI 4, NYI 1

Buffalo over Montreal Canadiens, 4 games to 2

April 27, at BUF: BUF 6, MONT 5 (OT, 4:42)
April 29, at BUF: BUF 4, MONT 2
May 1, at MONT: MONT 7, BUF 0
May 3, at MONT: MONT 8, BUF 2
May 6, at BUF: BUF 5, MONT 4 (OT, 5:56)
May 8, at MONT: BUF 4, MONT 3

FINAL ROUND: Philadelphia over Buffalo, 4 games to 2

GAME 1, May 15:

BUFFALO	0	0	1	–	1
PHILADELPHIA	0	0	4	–	4

Goaltenders: Buffalo, Desjardins. Philadelphia, Parent.

FIRST PERIOD: No scoring.
SECOND PERIOD: No scoring.
THIRD PERIOD: 1. Philadelphia, Barber (Van Impe, MacLeish) 3:42. 2. Philadelphia, Lonsberry (Bladon, Clarke) 7:29. 3. Buffalo, Martin (Lorentz) 11:07. 4. Philadelphia, Clarke 11:41. 5. Philadelphia, Barber (Clarke) 19:02.

GAME 2, May 18:

BUFFALO	0	0	1	–	1
PHILADELPHIA	0	1	1	–	2

Goaltenders: Buffalo, Desjardins. Philadelphia, Parent.

FIRST PERIOD: No scoring.
SECOND PERIOD: 1. Philadelphia, Leach (Clarke, Lonsberry) 8:24.
THIRD PERIOD: 2. Buffalo, Korab (Lorentz, Spencer) 2:18. 3. Philadelphia, Clarke (Barber, MacLeish) 6:43.

GAME 3, May 20:

PHILADELPHIA	3	1	0	0	–	4
BUFFALO	2	1	1	1	–	5

Goaltenders: Philadelphia, Parent. Buffalo, Desjardins, Crozier.

FIRST PERIOD: 1. Philadelphia, Dornhoeffer (Barber) 0:39. 2. Philadelphia, Saleski (Harris) 3:09. 3. Buffalo, Gare (Ramsay, Luce) 11:46. 4. Buffalo, Martin (Guevermont) 12:03. 5. Philadelphia, MacLeish (Barber) 14:13.
SECOND PERIOD: 6. Buffalo, Luce (Korab) 0:29. 7. Philadelphia, Leach (Kelly, Crisp), 14:30.
THIRD PERIOD: 8. Buffalo, Hajt (Martin, Luce) 9:56.
FIRST OVERTIME: 9. Buffalo, Robert (Perreault, Martin) 18:29.

GAME 4, May 22:

PHILADELPHIA	1	1	0	–	2
BUFFALO	0	3	1	–	4

Goaltenders: Philadelphia, Parent. Buffalo, Desjardins.

FIRST PERIOD: 1. Philadelphia, Dupont (Kelly, Crisp) 11:28.
SECOND PERIOD: 2. Buffalo, Korab (Robert, Martin) 3:46. 3. Philadelphia, Lonsberry (MacLeish) 4:20. 4. Buffalo, Perreault (Martin, Robert) 10:07. 5. Buffalo, Lorentz (Dudley, Schoenfeld) 15:07.
THIRD PERIOD: 6. Buffalo, Gare (Luce, Schoenfeld) 19:28.

GAME 5, May 25:

BUFFALO	0	0	1	–	1
PHILADELPHIA	3	2	0	–	5

Goaltenders: Buffalo, Desjardins. Philadelphia, Parent.

FIRST PERIOD: 1. Philadelphia, Schultz (Saleski, Kindrachuk) 3:12. 2. Philadelphia, Dornhoefer (Crisp, Van Impe) 12:31. 3. Philadelphia, Kelly (Crisp, Jim Watson) 12:50.
SECOND PERIOD: 4. Philadelphia, Leach (Barber, Goodenough) 1:55. 5. Philadelphia, Schultz (Goodenough, Harris) 9:56.
THIRD PERIOD: 6. Buffalo, Luce (Ramsay, Gare) 14:02.

GAME 6, May 27:

PHILADELPHIA	0	0	2	–	2
BUFFALO	0	0	0	–	0

Goaltenders: Philadelphia, Parent. Buffalo, Crozier.

FIRST PERIOD: No scoring.
SECOND PERIOD: No scoring.
THIRD PERIOD: 1. Philadelphia, Kelly (Leach, Jim Watson) 0:11. 2. Philadelphia, Clement (Kindrachuk) 17:13.

GOALS		ASSISTS		POINTS	
G. Lafleur, MONT	12	J. Drouin, NYI	12	R. MacLeish, PHI	20
R. MacLeish, PHI	11	B. Clarke, PHI	12	G. Lafleur, MONT	19
J.P. Parise, NYI	8	P. Mahovlich, MONT	10	J. Drouin, NYI	18
		E. Westfall, NYI	10		

WINS		GOALS AGAINST AVE.		SHUTOUTS	
B. Parent, PHI	10	B. Parent, PHI	1.89	B. Parent, PHI	4
G. Resch, NYI	8	W. Stephenson, PHI	1.95	K. Dryden, MONT	2
G. Desjardins, BUF	7	R. Vachon, LA	2.11	W. Stephenson, PHI	1
				G. Resch, NYI	1

1975–76

Preliminary Round

Buffalo over St. Louis, 2 games to 1

April 6, at STL: STL 5, BUF 2
April 8, at BUF: BUF 3, STL 2 (OT, 11:43)
April 9, at BUF: BUF 2, STL 1 (OT, 14:27)

Toronto over Pittsburgh, 2 games to 1

April 6, at TOR: TOR 4, PITT 1
April 8, at PITT: PITT 2, TOR 0
April 9, at TOR: TOR 4, PITT 0

N.Y. Islanders over Vancouver, 2 games to 0

April 6, at NYI: NYI 5, VAN 3
April 8, at VAN: NYI 3, VAN 1

Los Angeles over Atlanta, 2 games to 0

April 6, at LA: LA 2, ATL 1
April 7, at ATL: LA 1, ATL 0

Quarterfinal Round

Philadelphia over Toronto, 4 games to 3

April 12, at PHI: PHI 4, TOR 1
April 13, at PHI: PHI 3, TOR 1
April 15, at TOR: TOR 5, PHI 4
April 17, at TOR: TOR 4, PHI 3
April 20, at PHI: PHI 7, TOR 1
April 22, at TOR: TOR 8, PHI 5
April 25, at PHI: PHI 7, TOR 3

Boston over Los Angeles, 4 games to 3

April 11, at BOS: BOS 4, LA 0
April 13, at BOS: LA 3, BOS 2 (OT, 0:27)
April 15, at LA: LA 6, BOS 4
April 17, at LA: BOS 3, LA 0
April 20, at BOS: BOS 7, LA 1
April 22, at LA: LA 4, BOS 3 (OT, 18:28)
April 25, at BOS: BOS 3, LA 0

Montreal Canadiens over Chicago, 4 games to 0

April 11, at MONT: MONT 4, CHI 0
April 13, at MONT: MONT 3, CHI 1
April 15, at CHI: MONT 2, CHI 1
April 18, at CHI: MONT 4, CHI 1

New York Islanders over Buffalo, 4 games to 2

April 11, at BUF: BUF 5, NYI 3
April 13, at BUF: BUF 3, NYI 2 (OT 14:04)
April 15, at NYI: NYI 5, BUF 3
April 17, at NYI: NYI 4, BUF 2
April 20, at BUF: NYI 4, BUF 3
April 22, at NYI: NYI 3, BUF 2

Semifinal Round

Mont. Canadiens over N.Y. Islanders, 4 games to 1

April 27, at MONT: MONT 3, NYI 2
April 29, at MONT: MONT 4, NYI 3
May 1, at NYI: MONT 3, NYI 2
May 4, at NYI: NYI 5, MONT 2
May 6, at MONT: MONT 5, NYI 2

Philadelphia over Boston, 4 games to 1

April 27, at PHI: BOS 4, PHI 2
April 29, at PHI: PHI 2, BOS 1 (OT, 13:38)
May 2, at BOS: PHI 5, BOS 2
May 4, at BOS: PHI 4, BOS 2
May 6, at PHI: PHI 6, BOS 3

FINAL ROUND: Montreal Canadiens over Philadelphia, 4 games to 0

GAME 1, May 9:

PHILADELPHIA	2	0	1	–	3
MONTREAL	0	2	2	–	4

Goaltenders: Philadelphia, Stephenson. Montreal, Dryden.

FIRST PERIOD: 1. Philadelphia, Leach (Clarke, McIlhargey) 0:21. 2. Philadelphia, Lonsberry (Bridgman, Bladon) 13:22.
SECOND PERIOD: 3. Montreal, Roberts (Gainey, Risebrough) 4:04. 4. Montreal, Robinson (Mahovlich, Lafleur) 6:30.
THIRD PERIOD: 5. Philadelphia, Goodenough (Dornhoefer) 5:17. 6. Montreal, Lemaire (Nyrop) 10:02. 7. Montreal, Lapointe (Shutt) 18:38.

GAME 2, May 11:

PHILADELPHIA	0	0	1	–	1
MONTREAL	0	1	1	–	2

Goaltenders: Philadelphia, Stephenson. Montreal, Dryden.

FIRST PERIOD: No scoring.
SECOND PERIOD: 1. Montreal, Lemaire 15:19.
THIRD PERIOD: 2. Montreal, Lafleur 2:41. 3. Philadelphia, Schultz (Bladon) 17:35.

GAME 3, May 13:

MONTREAL	1	1	1	–	3
PHILADELPHIA	2	0	0	–	2

Goaltenders: Montreal, Dryden. Philadelphia, Stephenson.

FIRST PERIOD: 1. Montreal, Shutt (Lafleur) 3:17. 2. Philadelphia, Leach (Clarke, Goodenough) 8:40. 3. Philadelphia, Leach 18:14.
SECOND PERIOD: 4. Montreal, Shutt (Lafleur, Mahovlich) 1:09.
THIRD PERIOD: 5. Montreal, Bouchard (Wilson) 9:16.

GAME 4, May 16:

MONTREAL	2	1	2	–	5
PHILADELPHIA	2	1	0	–	3

Goaltenders: Montreal, Dryden. Philadelphia, Stephenson.

FIRST PERIOD: 1. Philadelphia, Leach (Bridgman) 0:41. 2. Montreal, Shutt (Cournoyer, Mahovlich) 5:35. 3. Montreal, Bouchard (Risebrough) 11:48. 4. Philadelphia, Barber (Bladon, Dupont) 18:20.
SECOND PERIOD: 5. Philadelphia, Dupont (Barber, Clarke) 13:59. 6. Montreal, Cournoyer (Robinson, Lafleur) 19:49.
THIRD PERIOD: 7. Montreal, Lafleur (Mahovlich, Shutt) 14:18. 8. Montreal, Mahovlich (Lafleur, Shutt) 15:16.

GOALS	
R. Leach, PHI	19
J. Ratelle, BOS	8
G. Lafleur, MONT	7
S. Shutt, MONT	7

ASSISTS	
D. Potvin, NYI	14
B. Clarke, PHI	14
L. Goodenough, PHI	11

POINTS	
R. Leach, PHI	24
D. Potvin, NYI	19
G. Lafleur, MONT	17

WINS	
K. Dryden, MONT	12
W. Thomas, TOR	5

GOALS AGAINST AVE.	
D. Bouchard, ATL	1.50
K. Dryden, MONT	1.92
E. Staniowski, STL	2.04

SHUTOUTS	
G. Gilbert, BOS	2

1976–77

Preliminary Round

N.Y. Islanders over Chicago, 2 games to 0

April 5, at NYI: NYI 5, CHI 2
April 7, at NYI: NYI 2, CHI 1

Buffalo over Minnesota, 2 games to 0

April 5, at BUF: BUF 4, MINN 2
April 7, at MINN: BUF 7, MINN 1

Toronto over Pittsburgh, 2 games to 1

April 5, at PITT: TOR 4, PITT 2
April 7, at TOR: PITT 6, TOR 4
April 9, at PITT: TOR 5, PITT 2

Los Angeles over Atlanta, 2 games to 1

April 5, at LA: LA 5, ATL 2
April 7, at ATL: ATL 3, LA 2
April 9, at LA: LA 4, ATL 2

Quarterfinal Round

Philadelphia over Toronto, 4 games to 2

April 11, at PHI: TOR 3, PHI 2
April 13, at PHI: TOR 4, PHI 1
April 15, at TOR: PHI 4, TOR 3 (OT, 2:55)
April 17, at TOR: PHI 6, TOR 5 (OT, 19:10)
April 19, at PHI: PHI 2, TOR 0
April 21, at TOR: PHI 4, TOR 3

Boston over Los Angeles, 4 games to 2

April 11, at BOS: BOS 8, LA 3
April 13, at BOS: BOS 6, LA 2
April 15, at LA: BOS 7, LA 6
April 17, at LA: LA 7, BOS 4
April 19, at BOS: LA 3, BOS 1
April 21, at LA: BOS 4, LA 3

Mont. Canadiens over St. Louis, 4 games to 0

April 11, at MONT: MONT 7, STL 2
April 13, at MONT: MONT 3, STL 0
Arpil 16, at STL: MONT 5, STL 1
April 17, at STL: MONT 4, STL 1

New York Islanders over Buffalo, 4 games to 0

April 11, at NYI: NYI 4, BUF 2
April 13, at NYI: NYI 4, BUF 2
April 15, at BUF: NYI 4, BUF 3
April 17, at BUF: NYI 4, BUF 3

Semifinal Round

Mont. Canadiens over N.Y. Islanders, 4 games to 2

April 23, at MONT: MONT 4, NYI 3
April 26, at MONT: MONT 3, NYI 0
April 28, at NYI: NYI 5, MONT 3
April 30, at NYI: MONT 4, NYI 0
May 3, at MONT: NYI 4, MONT 3 (OT, 3:58)
May 5, at NYI: MONT 2, NYI 1

Boston over Philaelphia, 4 games to 0

April 24, at PHI: BOS 4, PHI 3 (OT, 2:57)
April 26, at PHI: BOS 5, PHI 4 (OT, 10:07)
April 28, at BOS: BOS 2, PHI 1
May 1, at BOS: BOS 3, PHI 0

FINAL ROUND: Montreal Canadiens over Boston, 4 games to 0

GAME 1, May 7:

BOSTON	1	2	0	–	3
MONTREAL	3	1	3	–	7

Goaltenders: Boston, Cheevers. Montreal, Dryden.

FIRST PERIOD: 1. Montreal, Risebrough (Lambert, Lapointe) 1:45. 2. Montreal, Lambert (Robinson, Jarvis) 4:23. 3. Boston, Park (Ratelle) 5:23. 4. Montreal, Tremblay (Savard, Lapointe) 14:35.
SECOND PERIOD: 5. Montreal, Lemaire (Lafleur) 5:08. 6. Boston, O'Reilly (Park) 11:54. 7. Boston, Schmautz (Park) 16:35.
THIRD PERIOD: 8. Montreal, Chartraw (Mahovlich, Wilson) 0:59. 9. Montreal, Tremblay (Lambert, Mahovlich) 2:04. 10. Montreal, Lambert (Risebrough, Savard) 13:58.

GAME 2, May 10:

BOSTON	0	0	0	–	0
MONTREAL	0	2	1	–	3

Goaltenders: Boston, Cheevers. Montreal, Dryden.

FIRST PERIOD: No scoring.
SECOND PERIOD: 1. Montreal, Mahovlich (Shutt, Robinson) 7:43. 2. Montreal, Risebrough (Lafleur, Shutt) 12:07.
THIRD PERIOD: 3. Montreal, Shutt (Lafleur, Bouchard) 5:40.

GAME 3, May 12:

MONTREAL	3	0	1	–	4
BOSTON	0	1	1	–	2

Goaltenders: Montreal, Dryden. Boston, Cheevers.

FIRST PERIOD: 1. Montreal, Lafleur (Lapointe, Mahovlich) 4:08. 2. Montreal, Shutt (Lemaire, Lafleur) 7:58. 3. Montreal, Lemaire (Lapointe, Lafleur) 18:29.
SECOND PERIOD: 4. Boston, Sheppard (Middleton, Cashman) 6:32.
THIRD PERIOD: 5. Montreal, Lafleur (Shutt, Lemaire) 12:52. 6. Boston, McNab (Middleton, Park) 18:34.

GAME 4, May 14:

MONTREAL	0	1	0	1	–	2
BOSTON	1	0	0	0	–	1

Goaltenders: Montreal, Dryden. Boston, Cheevers.

FIRST PERIOD: 1. Boston, Schmautz (Park) 11:38.
SECOND PERIOD: 2. Montreal, Lemaire (Lafleur, Robinson) 1:34.
THIRD PERIOD: No scoring.
FIRST OVERTIME: 3. Montreal, Lemaire (Lafleur) 4:32.

GOALS		ASSISTS		POINTS	
B. Schmautz, BOS	11	G. Lafleur, MONT	17	G. Lafleur, MONT	26
L. McDonald, TOR	10	D. Sittler, TOR	16	D. Sittler, TOR	21
G. Lafleur, MONT	9	J. Lemaire, MONT	12	J. Lemaire, MONT	19
		J. Ratelle, BOS	12		

WINS		GOALS AGAINST AVE.		SHUTOUTS	
K. Dryden, MONT	12	K. Dryden, MONT	1.55	K. Dryden, MONT	4
G. Cheevers, BOS	8	C. Resch, NYI	2.08	W. Stephenson, PHI	1
B. Smith, NYI	7	W. Stephenson, PHI	2.59	G. Cheevers, BOS	1

1977–78

Preliminary Round

Philadelphia over Colorado, 2 games to 0

April 11, at PHI: PHI 3, COLO 2 (OT, 0:23)
April 13, at COLO: PHI 3, COLO 1

Detroit over Atlanta, 2 games to 0

April 11, at ATL: DET 5, ATL 3
April 13, at DET: DET 3, ATL 2

Toronto over Los Angeles, 2 games to 0

April 11, at TOR: TOR 7, LA 3
April 13, at LA: TOR 4, LA 0

Buffalo over New York Rangers, 2 games to 1

April 11, at BUF: BUF 4, NYR 1
April 13, at NYR: NYR 4, BUF 3 (OT, 1:37)
April 15, at BUF: BUF 4, NYR 1

Quarterfinal Round

Boston over Chicago, 4 games to 0

April 17, at BOS: BOS 6, CHI 1
April 19, at BOS: BOS 4, CHI 3 (OT, 1:50)
April 21, at CHI: BOS 4, CHI 3 (OT, 10:17)
April 23, at CHI: BOS 5, CHI 2

Philadelphia over Buffalo, 4 games to 1

April 17, at PHI: PHI 4, BUF 1
April 19, at PHI: PHI 3, BUF 2
April 22, at BUF: BUF 4, PHI 1
April 23, at BUF: PHI 4, BUF 2
April 25, at PHI: PHI 4, BUF 2

Montreal Canadiens over Detroit, 4 games to 1

April 17, at MONT: MONT 6, DET 2
April 19, at MONT: DET 4, MONT 2
April 21, at DET: MONT 4, DET 2
April 23, at DET: MONT 8, DET 0
April 25, at DET: MONT 4, DET 2

Toronto over New York Islanders, 4 games to 3

April 17, at NYI: NYI 4, TOR 1
April 19, at NYI: NYI 3, TOR 2 (OT, 2:50)
April 21, at TOR: TOR 2, NYI 0
April 23, at TOR: TOR 3, NYI 1
April 25, at NYI: NYI 2, TOR 1 (OT, 8:02)
April 27, at TOR: TOR 5, NYI 2
April 29, at NYI: TOR 2, NYI 1 (OT, 4:13)

Semifinal Round

Montreal Canadiens over Toronto, 4 games to 0

May 2, at MONT: MONT 5, TOR 3
May 4, at MONT: MONT 3, TOR 2
May 6, at TOR: MONT 6, TOR 1
May 9, at TOR: MONT 2, TOR 0

Boston over Philadelphia, 4 games to 1

May 2, at BOS: BOS 3, PHI 2 (OT, 1:43)
May 4, at BOS: BOS 7, PHI 5
May 7, at PHI: PHI 3, BOS 1
May 9, at PHI: BOS 4, PHI 2
May 11, at BOS: BOS 6, PHI 3

FINAL ROUND: Montreal Canadiens over Boston, 4 games to 2

GAME 1, May 13:

BOSTON	1	0	0	–	1
MONTREAL	2	1	1	–	4

Goaltenders: Boston, Cheevers. Montreal, Dryden.

FIRST PERIOD: 1, Boston, Park (Schmautz, Ratelle) 2:31. 2. Montreal, Lafleur (Lapointe) 4:31. 3. Montreal, Lambert (Lafleur, Shutt) 9:53.
SECOND PERIOD: 4. Montreal, Shutt (Lemaire, Lafleur) 13:54.
THIRD PERIOD: 5. Montreal, Cournoyer (Jarvis, Lambert) 3:55.

GAME 2, May 16:

BOSTON	0	1	1	0	–	2
MONTREAL	0	1	1	1	–	3

Goaltenders: Boston, Cheevers. Montreal, Dryden.

FIRST PERIOD: No scoring.
SECOND PERIOD: 1. Boston, Park (O'Reilly, McNab) 3:57. 2. Montreal, Shutt (Robinson, Cournoyer) 7:00.
THIRD PERIOD: 3. Montreal, Gainey (Jarvis, Houle) 12:12. 4. Boston, Smith (Cashman, McNab) 15:48.
FIRST OVERTIME: 5. Lafleur (Robinson) 13:09.

GAME 3, May 18:

MONTREAL	0	0	0	–	0
BOSTON	2	0	2	–	4

Goaltenders: Montreal, Dryden. Boston, Cheevers.

FIRST PERIOD: 1. Boston, Doak (Ratelle) 0:59. 2. Boston, Middleton (Ratelle) 5:11.
SECOND PERIOD: No scoring.
THIRD PERIOD: 3. Boston, McNab (Milbury) 2:54. 4. Boston, O'Reilly (McNab, Milbury) 15:39.

GAME 4, May 21:

MONTREAL	1	1	1	0	–	3
BOSTON	1	0	2	1	–	4

Goaltenders: Montreal, Dryden. Boston, Cheevers.

FIRST PERIOD: 1. Boston, Sheppard (Marcotte) 0:25. 2. Montreal, Risebrough (Tremblay, Gainey) 3:26.
SECOND PERIOD: 3. Montreal, Robinson (Mondou) 7:00.
THIRD PERIOD: 4. Boston, McNab (O'Reilly, Cashman) 9:19. 6. Boston, Park (Sheppard, Milbury) 13:20. 6. Montreal, Lafleur (Lapointe, Lemaire) 19:27.
FIRST OVERTIME: 7. Boston, Schmautz (Sheppard, Park) 6:22.

GAME 5, May 23:

BOSTON	0	0	1	–	1
MONTREAL	2	2	0	–	4

Goaltenders: Montreal, Dryden. Boston, Cheevers, Grahame.

FIRST PERIOD: 1. Montreal, Robinson (Savard) 7:46. 2. Montreal, Mondou (Savard) 11:10.
SECOND PERIOD: 3. Montreal, Larouche (Cournoyer, Savard) 13:04. 4. Montreal, Lemaire (Nyrop) 18:42.
THIRD PERIOD: 5. Boston, Marcotte (Schmautz, Miller) 11:22.

GAME 6, May 25:

MONTREAL	2	2	0	–	4
BOSTON	1	0	0	–	1

Goaltenders: Monteal, Dryden. Boston, Cheevers.

FIRST PERIOD: 1. Boston, Park (Marcotte, Sheppard) 4:05. 2. Montreal, Shutt (Mondou, Robinson) 7:01. 3. Montreal, Tremblay (Mondou, Robinson) 9:20.
SECOND PERIOD: 4. Montreal, Tremblay (Lambert, Nyrop) 13:37. 5. Montreal, Houle (Jarvis) 17:46.
THIRD PERIOD: No scoring.

GOALS	
G. Lafleur, MONT	10
B. Park, BOS	9
S. Shutt, MONT	9

ASSISTS	
L. Robinson, MONT	17
G. Lafleur, MONT	11
B. Park, BOS	11
P. McNab, BOS	11

POINTS	
G. Lafleur, MONT	21
L. Robinson, MONT	21
B. Park, BOS	20

WINS	
K. Dryden, MONT	12
G. Cheevers, BOS	8
B. Parent, PHI	7

GOALS AGAINST AVE.	
K. Dryden, MONT	1.89
R. Grahame, BOS	2.08
C. Resch, NYI	2.32

SHUTOUTS	
K. Dryden, MONT	2
M. Palmeteer, TOR	2

1978–79

Preliminary Round

Philadelphia over Vancouver, 2 games to 1

April 10, at PHI: VAN 3, PHI 2
April 12, at VAN: PHI 6, VAN 4
April 14, at PHI: PHI 7, VAN 2

Toronto over Atlanta, 2 games to 0

April 10, at ATL: TOR 2, ATL 1
April 12, at TOR: TOR 7, ATL 4

Pittsburgh over Buffalo, 2 games to 1

April 10, at BUF: PITT 4, BUF 3
April 12, at PITT: BUF 3, PITT 1
April 14, at BUF: PITT 4, BUF 3 (OT, 0:47)

N.Y. Rangers over Los Angeles, 2 games to 0

April 10, at NYR: NYR 7, LA 1
April 12, at LA: NYR 2, LA 1 (OT, 6:11)

Quarterfinal Round

Montreal Canadiens over Toronto, 4 games to 0

April 16, at MONT: MONT 5, TOR 2
April 18, at MONT: MONT 5, TOR 1
April 21, at TOR: MONT 4, TOR 3 (2 OT, 5:25)
April 22, at TOR: MONT 5, TOR 4 (OT, 4:14)

Boston over Pittsburgh, 4 games to 0

April 16, at BOS: BOS 6, PITT 2
April 18, at BOS: BOS 4, PITT 3
April 21, at PITT: BOS 2, PITT 1
April 22, at PITT: BOS 4, PITT 1

N.Y. Islanders over Chicago, 4 games to 0

April 16, at NYI: NYI 6, CHI 2
April 18, at NYI: NYI 1, CHI 0 (OT, 2:31)
April 20, at CHI: NYI 4, CHI 0
April 22, at CHI: NYI 3, CHI 1

N.Y. Rangers over Philadelphia, 4 games to 1

April 16, at PHI: PHI 3, NYR 2 (OT, 0:44)
April 18, at PHI: NYR 7, PHI 1
April 20, at NYR: NYR 5, PHI 1
April 22, at NYR: NYR 6, PHI 0
April 24, at PHI: NYR 8, PHI 3

Semifinal Round

N.Y. Rangers over N.Y. Islanders, 4 games to 2

April 26, at NYI: NYR 4, NYI 1
April 28, at NYI: NYI 4, NYR 3 (OT, 8:02)
May 1, at NYR: NYR 3, NYI 1
May 3, at NYR: NYI 3, NYR 2 (OT, 3:40)
May 5, at NYI: NYR 4, NYI 3
May 8, at NYR: NYR 2, NYI 1

Montreal Canadiens over Boston, 4 games to 3

April 26, at MONT: MONT 4, BOS 2
April 28, at MONT: MONT 5, BOS 2
May 1, at BOS: BOS 2, MONT 1
May 3, at BOS: BOS 4, MONT 3 (OT, 3:46)
May 5, at MONT: MONT 5, BOS 1
May 8, at BOS: BOS 5, MONT 2
May 10, at MONT: MONT 5, BOS 4 (OT, 9:33)

FINAL ROUND: Montreal Canadiens over New York Rangers, 4 games to 1

GAME 1, May 13:

NEW YORK	2	2	0	–	4
MONTREAL	0	1	0	–	1

Goaltenders: New York, Davidson. Montreal, Dryden, Larocque.

FIRST PERIOD: 1. New York, Vickers (Hedberg) 6:28. 2. New York, Greschner 14:27.
SECOND PERIOD: 3. Montreal, Lafleur (Lemaire, Lambert) 7:07. 4. New York, Esposito (McEwen) 9:30. 5. New York, Dave Maloney (Hedberg, Tkaczuk) 12:32.
THIRD PERIOD: No scoring.

GAME 2, May 15:

NEW YORK	2	0	0	–	2
MONTREAL	3	2	1	–	6

Goaltenders: New York, Davidson. Montreal, Dryden.

FIRST PERIOD: 1. New York, Hedberg (Vickers) 1:02. 2. New York, Duguay (McEwen, Hickey) 6:21. 3. Montreal, Lambert (Tremblay, Risebrough) 8:34. 4. Montreal, Lafleur (Lemaire, Shutt) 12:24. 5. Montreal, Gainey (Jarvis, Chartraw) 16:27.
SECOND PERIOD: 6. Montreal, Shutt 6:51. 7. Montreal, Lemaire (Savard, Shutt) 17:35.
THIRD PERIOD: 8. Montreal, Napier (Gainey) 4:38.

GAME 3, May 17:

MONTREAL	2	0	2	–	4
NEW YORK	0	0	1	–	1

Goaltenders: Montreal, Dryden. New York, Davidson.

FIRST PERIOD: 1. Montreal, Shutt (Lemaire, Robinson) 7:27. 2. Montreal, Risebrough (Lambert, Savard) 15:44.
SECOND PERIOD: No scoring.
THIRD PERIOD: 3. New York, Duguay 6:06. 4. Montreal, Tremblay (Lambert, Risebrough) 14:48. 5. Montreal, Lemaire (Shutt, Dryden) 17:10.

GAME 4, May 19:

MONTREAL	1	1	1	1	–	4
NEW YORK	2	0	1	0	–	3

Goaltenders: Montreal, Dryden. New York, Davidson.

FIRST PERIOD: 1. New York, Hickey (Dave Maloney, Sheehan) 1:19. 2. Montreal, Houle (Gainey) 2:39. 3. New York, Murdoch (Esposito, Hickey) 17:03.
SECOND PERIOD: 4. Montreal, Lambert (Houle) 18:05.
THIRD PERIOD: 5. New York, Esposito (Don Maloney, Dave Maloney) 4:26. 6. Montreal, Gainey 6:27.
FIRST OVERTIME: 7. Montreal, Savard (Lafleur, Shutt) 7:25.

GAME 5, May 21:

NEW YORK	1	0	0	–	1
MONTREAL	1	3	0	–	4

Goaltenders: New York, Davidson. Montreal, Dryden.

FIRST PERIOD: 1. Montreal, Chartraw (Houle, Lambert) 10:36. 2. New York, Vadnais (Murdoch) 16:52.
SECOND PERIOD: 3. Montreal, Lemaire 1:02. 4. Montreal, Gainey (Jarvis, Houle) 11:01. 5. Montreal, Lemaire (Houle) 18:49.
THIRD PERIOD: No scoring.

GOALS	
J. Lemaire, MONT	11
G. Lafleur, MONT	10
P. Esposito, NYR	8

ASSISTS	
G. Lafleur, MONT	13
Don Maloney, NYR	13
J. Lemaire, MONT	12
P. Esposito, NYR	12

POINTS	
J. Lemaire, MONT	23
G. Lafleur, MONT	23
P. Esposito, NYR	20
Don Maloney, NYR	20

WINS	
K. Dryden, MONT	12
J. Davidson, NYR	11
B. Smith, NYI	4
G. Cheevers, BOS	4

GOALS AGAINST AVE.	
B. Smith, NYI	1.90
C. Resch, NYI	2.20
J. Davidson, NYR	2.28

SHUTOUTS	
B. Smith, NYI	1
C. Resch, NYI	1
J. Davidson, NYR	1

1979–80

Preliminary Round

Philadelphia over Edmonton, 3 games to 0

April 8, at PHI: PHI 4, EDM 3 (OT, 8:06)
April 9, at PHI: PHI 5, EDM 1
April 11, at EDM: PHI 3, EDM 2 (2 OT, 3:56)

Minnesota over Toronto, 3 games to 0

April 8, at MINN: MINN 6, TOR 3
April 9, at MINN: MINN 7, TOR 2
April 11, at TOR: MINN 4, TOR 3 (OT, 0:32)

Chicago over St. Louis, 3 games to 0

April 8, at CHI: CHI 3, STL 2 (OT, 12:34)
April 9, at CHI: CHI 5, STL 1
April 11, at STL: CHI 4, STL 1

Boston over Pittsburgh, 3 games to 2

April 8, at BOS: PITT 4, BOS 2
April 10, at BOS: BOS 4, PITT 1
April 12, at PITT: PITT 4, BOS 1
April 13, at PITT: BOS 8, PITT 3
April 14, at BOS: BOS 6, PITT 2

Montreal Canadiens over Hartford, 3 games to 0

April 8, at MONT: MONT 6, HART 1
April 9, at MONT: MONT 8, HART 4
April 11, at HART: MONT 4, HART 3 (OT, 0:29)

N.Y. Islanders over Los Angeles, 3 games to 1

April 8, at NYI: NYI 8, LA 1
April 9, at NYI: LA 6, NYI 3
April 11, at LA: NYI 4, LA 3 (OT, 6:55)
April 12, at LA: NYI 6, LA 0

N.Y. Rangers over Atlanta, 3 games to 1

April 8, at NYR: NYR 2, ATL 1 (OT, 0:33)
April 9, at NYR: NYR 5, ATL 1
April 11, at ATL: ATL 4, NYR 2
April 12, at ATL: NYR 5, ATL 2

Baffalo over Vancouver, 3 games to 1

April 8, at BUF: BUF 2, VAN 1
April 9, at BUF: BUF 6, VAN 0
April 11, at VAN: VAN 5, BUF 4
April 12, at VAN: BUF 3, VAN 1

Quarterfinal Round

Buffalo over Chicago, 4 games to 0

April 16, at BUF: BUF 5, CHI 0
April 17, at BUF: BUF 6, CHI 4
April 19, at CHI: BUF 2, CHI 1
April 20, at CHI: BUF 3, CHI 2

Minnesota over Mont. Canadiens, 4 games to 3

April 16, at MONT: MINN 3, MONT 0
April 17, at MONT: MINN 4, MONT 1
April 19, at MINN: MONT 5, MINN 0
April 20, at MINN: MONT 5, MINN 1
April 22, at MONT: MONT 6, MINN 2
April 24, at MINN: MINN 5, MONT 2
April 27, at MONT: MINN 3, MONT 2

New York Islanders over Boston, 4 games to 1

April 16, at BOS: NYI 2, BOS 1 (OT, 1:02)
April 17, at BOS: NYI 5, BOS 4 (OT, 1:24)
April 19, at NYI: NYI 5, BOS 3
April 21, at NYI: BOS 4, NYI 3 (OT 17:13)
April 22, at BOS: NYI 4, BOS 2

Philadelphia over N.Y. Rangers, 4 games to 1

April 16, at PHI: PHI 2, NYI 1
April 17, at PHI: PHI 4, NYR 1
April 19, at NYR: PHI 3, NYR 0
April 20, at NYR: NYR 4, PHI 3
April 22, at PHI: PHI 3, NYR 1

Semifinal Round

Philadelphia over Minnesota, 4 games to 1

April 29, at PHI: MINN 6, PHI 5
May 1, at PHI: PHI 8, MINN 0
May 4, at MINN: PHI 5, MINN 3
May 6, at MINN: PHI 3, MINN 2
May 8, at PHI: PHI 7, MINN 3

N.Y. Islanders over Buffalo, 4 games to 2

April 29, at BUF: NYI 4, BUF 1
May 1, at BUF: NYI 2, BUF 1 (2 OT, 1:20)
May 3, at NYI: NYI 7, BUF 4
May 6, at NYI: BUF 7, NYI 4
May 8, at BUF: BUF 2, NYI 0
May 10, at NYI: NYI 5, BUF 2

FINAL ROUND: New York Islanders over Philadelphia, 4 games to 2

GAME 1, May 13:

NEW YORK	1	1	1	1	–	4
PHILADELPHIA	1	1	1	0	–	3

Goaltenders: New York, Smith. Philadelphia, Peeters.

FIRST PERIOD: 1. Philadelphia, Bridgman 10:31. 2. New York, Bossy (Trottier) 12:02.
SECOND PERIOD: 3. New York, D. Potvin (Gillies, Goring) 2:20. 4. Philadelphia, Clarke (Barber, Leach) 17:08.
THIRD PERIOD: 5. Philadelphia, MacLeish (Holmgren) 13:10. 6. New York, Persson (Bossy, D. Potvin) 16:18.
FIRST OVERTIME: 7. New York, D. Potvin (Tonelli, Nystrom) 4:07.

GAME 2, May 15:

NEW YORK	1	1	1	–	3
PHILADELPHIA	3	3	2	–	8

Goaltenders: New York, Smith, Resch. Philadelphia, Peeters.

FIRST PERIOD: 1. New York, Goring (Gillies, Sutter) 3:23. 2. Philadelphia, Holmgren (Propp, Dailey) 7:22. 3. Philadelphia, Kelly (Wilson, Clarke) 8:37. 4. Philadelphia, Clarke (Watson, Barber)17:23.
SECOND PERIOD: 5. Philadelphia, Barber (Clarke, Leach) 1:06. 6. New York, Trottier (Bossy) 3:28. 7. Philadelphia, Holmgren (Linseman, Barber) 4:13. 8. Philadelphia, Propp (Dailey, Clarke) 15:47.
THIRD PERIOD: 9. Philadelphia, Gorence (Dailey, Bridgman) 1:40. 10. Philadelphia, Holmgren (Linseman, Wilson) 4:19. 11. New York, Goring (Bourne, Persson) 15:00.

GAME 3, May 17:

PHILADELPHIA	0	0	2	–	2
NEW YORK	4	2	0	–	6

Goaltenders: Philadelphia, Myre. New York, Smith.

FIRST PERIOD: 1. New York, Henning (Bourne) 2:38. 2. New York, D. Potvin 7:43. 3. New York, Trottier (Bossy, D. Potvin) 13:04. 4. New York, Bossy (Gillies, D. Potvin) 14:29.
SECOND PERIOD: 5. New York, Gillies (Persson) 15:41. 6. New York, D. Potvin (Persson, Bossy) 17:25.
THIRD PERIOD: 7. Philadelphia, Clarke (Leach, Busniuk) 9:48. 8. Philadelphia, Busniuk (Bridgman) 11:32.

GAME 4, May 19:

PHILADELPHIA	0	1	1	–	2
NEW YORK	2	0	3	–	5

Goaltenders: Philadelphia, Peeters. New York, Smith.

FIRST PERIOD: 1. New York, Bossy (Gillies, Trottier) 7:23. 2. New York, Goring (Gillies, Sutter) 13:02.
SECOND PERIOD: 3. Philadelphia, Paddock (MacLeish, Wilson) 1:35.
THIRD PERIOD: 4. New York, Trottier (Howatt) 6:06. 5. Philadelphia, Linseman (Propp, Gorence) 11:53. 6. New York, Nystrom (Bourne) 12:35. 7. New York, Gillies (Sutter) 14:08.

GAME 5, May 22:

NEW YORK	1	1	1	–	3
PHILADELPHIA	0	3	3	–	6

Goaltenders: New York, Smith. Philadelphia, Peeters.

FIRST PERIOD: 1. New York, Persson (Bossy) 10:58.
SECOND PERIOD: 2. Philadelphia, Clarke (Leach, Wilson) 1:45. 3. Philadelphia, MacLeish 5:55. 4. New York, Trottier (Persson, Bossy) 16:16. 5. Philadelphia, Busniuk, (Propp, Linseman) 17:04.
THIRD PERIOD: 6. Philadelphia, MacLeish (Bridgman) 9:43. 7. Philadelphia, Propp (Linseman, Holmgren) 12:33. 8. New York, Persson (Goring, D. Potvin) 14:57. 9. Philadelphia, Holmgren (Linseman) 17:26.

GAME 6, May 24:

PHILADELPHIA	2	0	2	0	–	4
NEW YORK	2	2	0	1	–	5

Goaltenders: Philadelphia, Peeters. New York, Smith.

FIRST PERIOD: 1. Philadelphia, Leach (MacLeish, Barber) 7:21. 2. New York, D. Potvin (Bossy, Trottier) 11:56. 3. New York, Sutter (Gillies, Goring) 14:08. 4. Philadelphia, Propp (Holmgren, Linseman) 18:58.
SECOND PERIOD: 5. New York, Bossy (Bourne, Trottier) 7:34. 6. New York, Nystrom (Tonelli) 19:46.
THIRD PERIOD: 7. Philadelphia, Dailey (Linseman, Holmgren) 1:47. 8. Philadelphia, Paddock (Dupont, MacLeish) 6:02.
FIRST OVERTIME: 9. New York, Nystrom (Tonelli, Henning) 7:11.

GOALS	
B. Trottier, NYI	12
B. Barber, PHI	12

ASSISTS	
K. Linseman, PHI	18
B. Trottier, NYI	17

POINTS	
B. Trottier, NYI	29
M. Bossy, NYI	23
K. Linseman, PHI	22

WINS	
B. Smith, NYI	15
P. Peeters, PHI	8
B. Sauve, BUF	6

GOALS AGAINST AVE.	
B. Sauve, BUF	2.04
M. Larocque, MONT	2.20
T. Esposito, CHI	2.25

SHUTOUTS	
B. Sauve, BUF	2

1980–81

Preliminary Round

St. Louis over Pittsburgh, 3 games to 2

April 8, at STL: STL 4, PITT 2
April 9, at STL: PITT 6, STL 4
April 11, at PITT: STL 5, PITT 4
April 12, at PITT: PITT 6, STL 3
April 14, at STL: STL 4, PITT 3 (OT, 5:16)

Philadelphia over Quebec, 3 games to 2

April 8, at PHI: PHI 6, QUE 4
April 9, at PHI: PHI 8, QUE 5
April 11, at QUE: QUE 2, PHI 0
April 12, at QUE: QUE 4, PHI 3 (OT, 0:37)
April 14, at PHI: PHI 5, QUE 2

Buffalo over Vancouver, 3 games to 0

April 8, at BUF: BUF 3, VAN 2 (OT, 5:00)
April 9, at BUF: BUF 5, VAN 2
April 11, at VAN: BUF 5, VAN 3

Calgary over Chicago, 3 games to 0

April 8, at CALG: CALG 4, CHI 3
April 9, at CALG: CALG 6, CHI 2
April 11, at CHI: CALG 5, CHI 4

Minnesota over Boston, 3 games to 0

April 8, at BOS: MINN 5, BOS 4 (OT, 3:34)
April 9, at BOS: MINN 9, BOS 6
April 11, at MINN: MINN 6, BOS 3

Edmonton over Mont. Canadiens, 3 games to 0

April 8, at MONT: EDM 6, MONT 3
April 9, at MONT: EDM 3, MONT 1
April 11, at EDM: EDM 6, MONT 2

New York Islanders over Toronto, 3 games to 0

April 8, at NYI: NYI 9, TOR 2
April 9, at NYI: NYI 5, TOR 1
April 11, at TOR: NYI 6, TOR 1

N.Y. Rangers over Los Angeles, 3 games to 1

April 8, at LA: NYR 3, LA 1
April 9, at LA: LA 5, NYR 4
April 11, at NYR: NYR 10, LA 3
April 12, at NYR: NYR 6, LA 3

Quarterfinal Round

Minnesota over Buffalo, 4 games to 1

April 16, at BUF: MINN 4, BUF 3 (OT, 0:22)
April 17, at BUF: MINN 5, BUF 2
April 19, at MINN: MINN 6, BUF 4
April 20, at MINN: BUF 5, MINN 4 (OT, 16:32)
April 22, at BUF: MINN 4, BUF 3

Calgary over Philadelphia, 4 games to 3

April 16, at PHI: PHI 4, CALG 0
April 17, at PHI: CALG 5, PHI 4
April 19, at CALG: CALG 2, PHI 1
April 20, at CALG: CALG 5, PHI 4
April 22, at PHI: PHI 9, CALG 4
April 24, at CALG: PHI 3, CALG 2
April 26, at PHI: CALG 4, PHI 1

New York Islanders over Edmonton, 4 games to 2

April 16, at NYI: NYI 8, EDM 2
April 17, at NYI: NYI 6, EDM 3
April 19, at EDM: EDM 5, NYI 2
April 20, at EDM: NYI 5, EDM 4 (OT, 5:41)
April 22, at NYI: EDM 4, NYI 3
April 24, at EDM: NYI 5, EDM 2

New York Rangers over St. Louis, 4 games to 2

April 16, at STL: STL 6, NYR 3
April 17, at STL: NYR 6, STL 4
April 19, at NYR: NYR 6, STL 3
April 20, at NYR: NYR 4, STL 1
April 22, at STL: STL 4, NYR 3
April 24, at NYR: NYR 7, STL 4

Semifinal Round

N.Y. Islanders over N.Y. Rangers, 4 games to 0

April 28, at NYI: NYI 5, NYR 2
April 30, at NYI: NYI 7, NYR 3
May 2, at NYR: NYI 5, NYR 1
May 5, at NYR: NYI 5, NYR 2

Minnesota over Calgary, 4 games to 2

April 28, at CALG: MINN 4, CALG 1
April 30, at CALG: CALG 3, MINN 2
May 3, at MINN: MINN 6, CALG 4
May 5, at MINN: MINN 7, CALG 4
May 7, at CALG: CALG 3, MINN 1
May 9, at MINN: MINN 5, CALG 3

FINAL ROUND: New York Islanders over Minnesota, 4 games to 1

GAME 1, May 12:

MINNESOTA	0	1	2	– 3
NEW YORK	3	1	2	6

Goaltenders: Minnesota, Meloche. New York, Smith.

FIRST PERIOD: 1. New York, Kallur (Langevin, Goring) 2:54. 2. New York, Trottier (Carroll) 14:38. 3. New York, Kallur (Trottier) 15:25.
SECOND PERIOD: 4. New York, Carroll (Sutter, Nystrom) 9:58. 5. Minnesota, Andersson (Ciccarelli) 13:04.
THIRD PERIOD: 6. New York, Merrick 0:58. 7. Minnesota, Payne (Hartsburg, B. Smith) 3:08. 8. New York, Merrick (Langevin, Tonelli) 13:15. 9. Minnesota, Ciccarelli (McCarthy) 15:14.

GAME 2, May 14:

MINNESOTA	1	1	1	– 3
NEW YORK	3	0	3	– 6

Goaltenders: Minnesota, Meloche. New York, Smith.

FIRST PERIOD: 1. Minnesota, Ciccarelli (Hartsburg, Christoff) 3:38. 2. New York, Bossy (McEwen, Potvin) 4:33. 3. New York, Nystrom (Merrick, Tonelli) 14:39. 4. New York, Potvin (Merrick) 17:48.
SECOND PERIOD: 5. Minnesota, Palmer (Broten, G. Smith) 9:15.
THIRD PERIOD: 6. Minnesota, Payne (Young, Roberts) 0:30. 7. New York, Potvin (Goring) 8:00. 8. New York, Morrow (Potvin, Merrick) 11:57. 9. New York, Bossy (Trottier, Bourne) 16:22.

GAME 3, May 17:

NEW YORK	1	3	3	– 7
MINNESOTA	3	0	2	– 5

Goaltenders: New York, Smith. Minnesota, Meloche.

FIRST PERIOD: 1. Minnesota, Christoff (Hartsburg, Ciccarelli) 3:25. 2. Minnesota, Payne (Young, MacAdam) 14:09. 3. New York, Bossy (Gillies) 14:47. 4. Minnesota, B. Smith (Hartsburg, Payne) 16:30.
SECOND PERIOD: 5. New York, Nystrom (Tonelli, Merrick) 4:10. 6. New York, Goring (Potvin, Bossy) 7:16. 7. New York, Goring (Gillies) 11:51.
THIRD PERIOD: 8. Minnesota, Payne (Young, Christoff) 1:11. 9. New York, Bossy (Trottier) 2:05. 10. New York, Goring (Carroll, Potvin) 6:34. 11. Minnesota, Ciccarelli (B. Smith) 13:35. 12. New York, Trottier (Bossy, Merrick) 19:16.

GAME 4, May 19:

NEW YORK	1	1	0	– 2
MINNESOTA	1	1	2	– 4

Goaltenders: New York, Smith. Minnesota, Beaupre.

FIRST PERIOD: 1. New York, Lane (Bossy, Trottier) 3:47. 2. Minnesota, Hartsburg (B. Smith, B. Maxwell) 11:34.
SECOND PERIOD: 3. Minnesota, MacAdam (Payne, B. Maxwell) 5:15. 4. New York, McEwen (Tonelli, Kallur) 7:37.
THIRD PERIOD: 5. Minnesota, Payne (B. Maxwell, MacAdam) 12:26. 6. Minnesota, B. Smith (MacAdam, B. Maxwell) 18:12.

GAME 5, May 21:

MINNESOTA	1	0	0	– 1
NEW YORK	3	1	1	– 5

Goaltenders: Minnesota, Beaupre. New York, Smith.

FIRST PERIOD: 1. New York, Goring (Bourne) 5:12. 2. New York, Merrick (Tonelli, Nystrom) 5:37. 3. New York, Goring (Gillies, Bossy) 10:03. 4. Minnesota, Christoff 16:06.
SECOND PERIOD: 5. New York, Bourne (Carroll, Kallur) 19:21.
THIRD PERIOD: 6. New York, McEwen (Trottier) 17:06.

GOALS		ASSISTS		POINTS	
M. Bossy, NYI	17	M. Bossy, NYI	18	M. Bossy, NYI	35
S. Payne, MINN	17	B. Trottier, NYI	18	S. Payne, MINN	29
D. Ciccarelli, MINN	14	D. Potvin, NYI	17	B. Trottier, NYI	29
		B. Smith, MINN	17		

WINS		GOALS AGAINST AVE.		SHUTOUTS	
B. Smith, NYI	14	B. Smith, NYI	2.54	R. St. Croix, PHI	1
G. Meloche, MINN	8	R. St. Croix, PHI	2.99	D. Bouchard, QUE	1
S. Baker, NYR	7	D. Edwards, BUF	3.34		

1981–82

Preliminary Round (Division Semifinals)

Boston over Buffalo, 3 games to 1

April 7, at BOS: BOS 3, BUF 1
April 8, at BOS: BOS 7, BUF 3
April 10, at BUF: BUF 5, BOS 2
April 11, at BUF: BOS 5, BUF 2

Quebec over Montreal Canadiens, 3 games to 2

April 7, at MONT: MONT 5, QUE 1
April 8, at MONT: QUE 3, MONT 2
April 10, at QUE: QUE 2, MONT 1
April 11, at QUE: MONT 6, QUE 2
April 13, at MONT: QUE 3, MONT 2 (OT, 0:22)

Chicago over Minnesota, 3 games to 1

April 7, at MINN: CHI 3, MINN 2 (OT, 3:34)
April 8, at MINN: CHI 5, MINN 3
April 10, at CHI: MINN 7, CHI 1
April 11, at CHI: CHI 5, MINN 2

St. Louis over Winnipeg, 3 games to 1

April 7, at WINN: STL 4, WINN 3
April 8, at WINN: WINN 5, STL 2
April 10, at STL: STL 6, WINN 3
April 11, t STL: STL 8, WINN 2

N.Y. Islanders over Pittsburgh, 3 games to 2

April 7, at NYI: NYI 8, PITT 1
April 8, at NYI: NYI 7, PITT 2
April 10, at PITT: PITT 2, NYI 1 (OT, 4:14)
April 11, at PITT: PITT 5, NYI 2
April 13, at NYI: NYI 4, PITT 3 (OT, 6:19)

New York Rangers over Philadelphia, 3 games to 1

April 7, at NYR: PHI 4, NYR 1
April 8, at NYR: NYR 7, PHI 3
April 10, at PHI: NYR 4, PHI 3
April 11, at PHI: NYR 7, PHI 5

Los Angeles over Edmonton, 3 games to 2

April 7, at EDM: LA 10, EDM 8
April 8, at EDM: EDM 3, LA 2 (OT, 6:20)
April 10, at LA: LA 6, EDM 5 (OT, 2:15)
April 12, at LA: EDM 3, LA 2
April 13, at EDM: LA 7, EDM 4

Vancouver over Calgary, 3 games to 0

April 7, at VAN: VAN 5, CALG 3
April 8, at VAN: VAN 2, CALG 1 (OT, 14:20)
April 10, at CALG: VAN 3, CALG 1

Quarterfinal Round (Division Finals)

Quebec over Boston, 4 games to 3

April 15, at BOS: BOS 4, QUE 3
April 16, at BOS: BOS 8, QUE 4
April 18, at QUE: QUE 3, BOS 2 (OT, 11:44)
April 19, at QUE: QUE 7, BOS 2
April 21, at BOS: QUE 4, BOS 3
April 23, at QUE: BOS 6, QUE 5 (OT, 10:54)
April 25, at BOS: QUE 2, BOS 1

Chicago over St. Louis, 4 games to 2

April 15, at STL: CHI 5, STL 4
April 16, at STL: STL 3, CHI 1
April 18, at CHI: CHI 6, STL 5
April 19, at CHI: CHI 7, STL 4
April 21, at STL: STL 3, CHI 2 (OT, 3:28)
April 23, at CHI: CHI 2, STL 0

N.Y. Islanders over N.Y. Rangers, 4 games to 2

April 15, at NYI: NYR 5, NYI 4
April 16, at NYI: NYI 7, NYR 2
April 18, at NYR: NYI 4, NYR 3 (OT, 3:00)
April 19, at NYR: NYI 5, NYR 3
April 21, at NYI: NYR 4, NYI 2
April 23, at NYR: NYI 5, NYR 3

Vancouver over Los Angeles, 4 games to 1

April 15, at VAN: VAN 3, LA 2
April 16, at VAN: LA 3, VAN 2 (OT, 4:33)
April 18, at LA: VAN 4, LA 3 (OT, 1:23)
April 19, at LA: VAN 5, LA 4
April 21, at VAN: VAN 5, LA 2

Semifinal Round (Conference Finals)

New York Islanders over Quebec, 4 games to 0

April 27, at NYI: NYI 4, QUE 1
April 29, at NYI: NYI 5, QUE 2
May 1, at QUE: NYI 5, QUE 4 (OT, 16:52)
May 4, at QUE: NYI 4, QUE 2

Vancouver over Chicago, 4 games to 1

April 27, at CHI: VAN 2, CHI 1 (2 OT, 8:58)
April 29, at CHI: CHI 4, VAN 1
May 1, at VAN: VAN 4, CHI 3
May 4, at VAN: VAN 5, CHI 3
May 6, at CHI: VAN 6, CHI 2

FINAL ROUND: New York Islanders over Vancouver, 4 games to 0

GAME 1, May 8:

VANCOUVER	2	2	1	0	–	5
NEW YORK	3	1	1	1	–	6

Goaltenders: Vancouver, Brodeur. New York, Smith.

FIRST PERIOD: 1. Vancouver, Gradin (Molin) 1:29. 2. New York, Gillies (Potvin, Trottier) 11:35. 3. New York, Bossy (Gillies, Carroll) 15:52. 4. Vancouver, Gradin (Fraser, Molin) 17:40. 5. NewYork, Potvin (Goring) 19:51.
SECOND PERIOD: 6. New York, Potvin (Trottier, Persson) 3:15. 7. Vancouver, Smyl (Gradin, Fraser) 5:06. 8. Vancouver, Boldirev (Williams) 9:27.
THIRD PERIOD: 9. Vancouver, Nill (Minor, Williams) 3:06. 10. New York, Bossy (Tonelli, Trottier) 15:14.
FIRST OVERTIME: 11. New York, Bossy 19:59.

GAME 2, May 11:

VANCOUVER	0	3	1	–	4
NEW YORK	1	1	4	–	6

Goaltenders: Vancouver, Brodeur. New York, Smith.

FIRST PERIOD: 1. New York, Carroll (Bourne) 15:55.
SECOND PERIOD: 2. Vancouver, Gradin (Molin, Fraser) 8:28. 3. Vancouver, Boldirev (Molin, Halward) 13:12. 4. New York, Bossy (Persson, Potvin) 17:06. 5. Vancouver, Lindgren (Gradin) 19:42.
THIRD PERIOD: 6. New York, Bourne (Persson, Bossy) 0:32. 7. New York, D. Sutter (B. Sutter, Potvin) 1:19. 8. Vancouver, Minor (Williams) 2:27. 9. New York, Trottier (Jonsson, Potvin) 7:18. 10. New York, Nystrom (Tonelli, Merrick) 14:10.

GAME 3, May 13:

NEW YORK	0	2	1	–	3
VANCOUVER	0	0	0	–	0

Goaltenders: New York, Smith. Vancouver, Brodeur.

FIRST PERIOD: No scoring.
SECOND PERIOD: 1. New York, Gillies (B. Sutter) 2:56. 2. New York, Bossy (Persson, Trottier) 12:30.
THIRD PERIOD: 3. New York, Nystrom (Goring, Potvin) 18:40.

GAME 4, May 16:

NEW YORK	1	2	0	–	3
VANCOUVER	1	0	0	–	1

Goaltenders: New York, Smith. Vancouver, Brodeur.

FIRST PERIOD: 1. New York, Goring (Potvin) 11:38. 2. Vancouver, Smyl (Minor, Campbell) 18:09.
SECOND PERIOD: 3. New York, Bossy (Potvin, Trottier) 5:00. 4. New York, Bossy (Trottier, Persson) 8:00.
THIRD PERIOD: No scoring.

GOALS		ASSISTS		POINTS	
M. Bossy, NYI	17	B. Trottier, NYI	23	B. Trottier, NYI	29
D. Savard, CHI	11	D. Potvin, NYI	16	M. Bossy, NYI	27
		B. Federko, STL	15	D. Potvin, NYI	21

WINS		GOALS AGAINST AVE.		SHUTOUTS	
B. Smith, NYI	15	R. Wamsley, MONT	2.20	B. Smith, NYI	1
R. Brodeur, VAN	11	B. Smith, NYI	2.52	T. Esposito, CHI	1
M. Moffat, BOS	6	T. Esposito, CHI	2.52		

1982–83

Preliminary Round (Division Semifinals)

Chicago over St. Louis, 3 games to 1

April 6, at CHI: STL 4, CHI 2
April 7, at CHI: CHI 7, STL 2
April 9, at STL: CHI 2, STL 1
April 10, at STL: CHI 5, STL 3

Minnesota over Toronto, 3 games to 1

April 6, at MINN: MINN 5, TOR 4
April 7, at MINN: MINN 5, TOR 4 (OT, 5:03)
April 9, at TOR: TOR 6, MINN 3
April 10, at TOR: MINN 5, TOR 4 (OT, 8:05)

Edmonton over Winnipeg, 3 games to 0

April 6, at EDM: EDM 6, WINN 3
April 7, at EDM: EDM 4, WINN 3
April 9, at WINN: EDM 4, WINN 3

Calgary over Vancouver, 3 games to 1

April 6, at CALG: CALG 4, VAN 3 (OT, 12:27)
April 7, at CALG: CALG 5, VAN 3
April 9, at VAN: VAN 5, CALG 4
April 10, at VAN: CALG 4, VAN 3 (OT, 1:06)

Boston over Quebec, 3 games to 1

April 5, at BOS: BOS 4, QUE 3 (OT, 1:46)
April 7, at BOS: BOS 4, QUE 2
April 9, at QUE: QUE 2, BOS 1
April 10, at QUE: BOS 2, QUE 1

Buffalo over Montreal Canadiens, 3 games to 0

April 6, at MONT: BUF 1, MONT 0
April 7, at MONT: BUF 3, MONT 0
April 9, at BUF: BUF 4, MONT 2

N.Y. Islanders over Washington, 3 games to 1

April 6, at NYI: NYI 5, WASH 2
April 7, at NYI: WASH 4, NYI 2
April 9, at WASH: NYI 6, WASH 2
April 10, at WASH: NYI 6, WASH 3

N.Y. Rangers over Philadelphia, 3 games to 0

April 5, at PHI: NYR 5, PHI 3
April 7, at PHI: NYR 4, PHI 3
April 9, at NYR: NYR 9, PHI 3

Quarterfinal Round (Division Finals)

Chicago over Minnesota, 4 games to 1

April 14, at CHI: CHI 5, MINN 2
April 15, at CHI: CHI 7, MINN 4
April 17, at MINN: MINN 5, CHI 1
April 18, at MINN: CHI 4, MINN 3 (OT, 10:34)
April 20, at CHI: CHI 5, MINN 2

Edmonton over Calgary, 4 games to 1

April 14, at EDM: EDM 6, CALG 3
April 15, at EDM: EDM 5, CALG 1
April 17, at CALG: EDM 10, CALG 2
April 18, at CALG: CALG 6, EDM 5
April 20, at EDM: EDM 9, CALG 1

Boston over Buffalo, 4 games to 3

April 14, at BOS: BUF 7, BOS 4
April 15, at BOS: BOS 5, BUF 3
April 17, at BUF: BUF 4, BOS 3
April 18, at BUF: BOS 6, BUF 2
April 20, at BOS: BOS 9, BUF 0
April 22, at BUF: BUF 5, BOS 3
April 24, at BOS: BOS 3, BUF 2 (OT, 1:52)

N.Y Islanders over N.Y. Rangers, 4 games to 2

April 14, at NYI: NYI 4, NYR 1
April 15, at NYI: NYI 5, NYR 0
April 17, at NYR: NYR 7, NYI 6
April 18, at NYR: NYR 3, NYI 1
April 20, at NYI: NYI 7, NYR 2
April 22, at NYR: NYI 5, NYR 2

Semifinal Round (Conference Finals)

New York Islanders over Boston, 4 games to 2

April 26, at BOS: NYI 5, BOS 2
April 28, at BOS: BOS 4, NYI 1
April 30, at NYI: NYI 7, BOS 3
May 3, at NYI: NYI 8, BOS 3
May 5, at BOS: BOS 5, NYI 1
May 7, at NYI: NYI 8, BOS 4

Edmonton over Chicago, 4 games to 0

April 24, at EDM: EDM 8, CHI 4
April 26, at EDM: EDM 8, CHI 2
May 1, at CHI: EDM 3, CHI 2
May 3, at CHI: EDM 6, CHI 3

FINAL ROUND: New York Islanders over Edmonton, 4 games to 0

GAME 1, May 10:

NEW YORK	1	0	1	– 2
EDMONTON	0	0	0	– 0

Goaltenders: New York, Smith. Edmonton, Moog.

FIRST PERIOD: 1. New York, D. Sutter (Bourne, Persson) 5:36.
SECOND PERIOD: No scoring.
THIRD PERIOD: 2. New York, Morrow 19:48.

GAME 2, May 12:

NEW YORK	3	2	1	– 6
EDMONTON	1	1	1	– 3

Goaltenders: New York, Smith. Edmonton, Moog.

FIRST PERIOD: 1. Edmonton, Semenko (Roulston, Huddy) 8:39. 2. New York, Jonsson (D. Sutter, B. Sutter) 14:21. 3. New York, Nystrom (Trottier) 17:55. 4. New York, Bossy (Potvin) 19:17.
SECOND PERIOD: 5. Edmonton, Kurri (Anderson, Gretzky) 5:07. 6. New York, Bourne (D. Sutter) 8:03. 7. New York, B. Sutter (Morrow) 8:41.
THIRD PERIOD: 8. Edmonton, Anderson (Fogolin, Gretzky) 4:48. 9. New York, B. Sutter (D. Sutter, Jonsson) 14:11.

GAME 3, May 14:

EDMONTON	0	1	0	– 1
NEW YORK	1	0	4	– 5

Goaltenders: Edmonton, Moog. New York, Smith.

FIRST PERIOD: 1. New York, Kallur (Bossy, Morrow) 19:41.
SECOND PERIOD: 2. Edmonton, Kurri (Gretzky) 1:05.
THIRD PERIOD: 3. New York, Bourne (Persson, Langevin) 5:11. 4. New York, Morrow (Trottier, Kallur) 6:21. 5. New York, D. Sutter (Bourne, B. Sutter) 16:43. 6. New York, B. Sutter (Potvin, D. Sutter) 19:42.

GAME 4, May 17:

EDMONTON	0	2	0	– 2
NEW YORK	3	0	1	– 4

Goaltenders: Edmonton, Moog. New York, Smith.

FIRST PERIOD: 1. New York, Trottier (Gillies, Bossy) 11:02. 2. New York, Tonelli (Nystrom) 11:45. 3. New York, Bossy (Trottier) 12:39.
SECOND PERIOD: 4. Edmonton, Kurri (Gretzky) 0:35. 5. Edmonton, Messier (Fogolin, Coffey) 19:39.
THIRD PERIOD: 6. New York, Morrow 18:51.

GOALS	
M. Bossy, NYI	17
M. Messier, EDM	15
B. Pederson, BOS	14

ASSISTS	
W. Gretzky, EDM	26
R. Middleton, BOS	22
B. Bourne, NYI	20

POINTS	
W. Gretzky, EDM	38
R. Middleton, BOS	33
B. Pederson, BOS	32

WINS	
B. Smith, NYI	13
A. Moog, EDM	11
P. Peeters, BOS	9

GOALS AGAINST AVE.	
R. Melanson, NYI	2.52
B. Smith, NYI	2.68
D. Bouchard, QUE	2.73

SHUTOUTS	
B. Smith, NYI	2
B. Sauve, BUF	2
P. Peeters, BOS	1

The WHA Playoffs

Throughout its existence, from 1972 to 1979, the World Hockey Association painstakingly attempted to point out that it qualified as a "major" sports organization alongside its established rival, the National Hockey League. In some ways the claim was valid. Most WHA teams played in handsome arenas that conformed in size and appearance to their NHL counterparts. WHA salaries were on a big league par with the NHL pay scale and in some other areas the new league could legitimately equate itself with what previously had been hockey's only major league.

One sector in which the WHA pursued its quest for legitimacy was the playoffs, and in one major sense it failed. Aware that the NHL owned hockey's most prized possession, the Stanley Cup, the WHA attempted to provide a suitable prize of its own. But because the new league was financially strapped it did not strike a prize of its own but rather worked out a deal with the Avco Financial Services Company to have the firm donate a trophy to the WHA playoff champion. While Avco did deliver a handsome piece of silverware, the fact that the WHA champions were hereafter known as the "Avco World Trophy winners" instantly and forever cheapened the league's foremost award. Certainly, no objective critic could feel comfortable discussing the Stanley Cup in the same breath as the Avco World Trophy. The WHA playoffs were cheapened in other ways as well. During one cup round the Chicago Cougars were unable to obtain their normal home ice facilities and were compelled to play their games at a shopping center mall rink in Illinois. The WHA high command rolled with the blows it suffered because of the playoff inadequacies. It was willing to endure the indignity of having the Avco imprimateur on its championship cup because the financial concern paid $500,000 cash to the league for this right.

As far as the playoffs themselves were concerned the WHA followed the traditional NHL formula of allowing a maximum number of clubs to qualify and to extend the season as long as possible. However, in each case the WHA played a best-of-seven series, unlike the early playoff days of the NHL when it limited early rounds to a two-game, total-goal series in some cases. The WHA's best-of-seven format remained its individual-round playoff formula from the very first Avco World Cup round to the last. When the WHA ceased operations in 1979 the Avco World Cup was retired from the hockey scene.

1972–73

Quarterfinal Round

New England over Ottawa, 4 games to 1

April 7, at NE: NE 6, OTTA 2
April 8, at NE: NE 4, OTTA 3 (OT, 3:37)
April 10, at OTTA: OTTA 4, NE 2
April 12, at OTTA: NE 7, OTTA 3
April 14, at NE: NE 5, OTTA 4 (OT)

Cleveland over Philadelphia, 4 games to 0

April 4, at CLEVE: CLEVE 3, PHI 2 (OT, 5:47)
April 7, at CLEVE: CLEVE 7, PHI 1
April 8, at PHI: CLEVE 3, PHI 1
April 11, at PHI: CLEVE 6, PHI 2

Winnipeg over Minnesota, 4 games to 1

April 6, at WINN: WINN 3, MINN 1
April 8, at WINN: WINN 5, MINN 2
April 10, at MINN: MINN 6, WINN 4
April 11, at MINN: WINN 3, MINN 2 (OT, 9:49)
April 15, at WINN: WINN 8, MINN 5

Houston over Los Angeles, 4 games to 2

April 5, at HOUS: HOUS 7, LA 2
April 7, at HOUS: LA 4, HOUS 2
April 11, at LA: LA 3, HOUS 2
April 13, at LA: HOUS 3, LA 2 (OT, 3:12)
April 15, at HOUS: HOUS 6, LA 3
April 17, at LA: HOUS 3, LA 2

Semifinal Round

New England over Cleveland, 4 games to 1

April 18, at NE: NE 3, CLEVE 2
April 19, at NE: NE 3, CLEVE 2
April 21, at CLEVE: NE 5, CLEVE 4
April 22, at CLEVE: CLEVE 5, NE 2
April 26, at NE: NE 3, CLEVE 1

Winnipeg over Houston, 4 games to 0

April 20, at WINN: WINN 5, HOUS 1
April 22, at WINN: WINN 2, HOUS 0
April 24, at HOUS: WINN 4, HOUS 2
April 26, at HOUS: WINN 3, HOUS 0

FINAL ROUND: New England over Winnipeg, 4 games to 1

GAME 1, April 29:

WINNIPEG	1	0	1	–	2
NEW ENGLAND	4	2	1	–	7

Goaltenders: Winnipeg, Daley. New England, A. Smith.

FIRST PERIOD: 1. Winnipeg, Beaudin (Bordeleau, Hull) 10:02. 2. New England, Ley (Dorey, Webster) 12:10. 3. New England, Webster (Williams, Hurley) 14:07. 4. New England, Earl (Sheehy, Green) 16:13. 5. New England, French 19:37.
SECOND PERIOD: 6. New England, Webster (Williams, Hurley) 10:55. 7. New England, Williams (French) 16:01.
THIRD PERIOD: 8. New England, Dorey (Sheehy, Earl) 3:45. 9. Winnipeg, Hull 11:07.

GAME 2, May 2:

NEW ENGLAND	1	1	5	–	7
WINNIPEG	2	2	0	–	4

Goaltenders: New England, A. Smith. Winnipeg, Wakely.

FIRST PERIOD: 1. Winnipeg, Beaudin (Hull, Hornung) 0:33. 2. Winnipeg, Bordeleau (Hull, Beaudin) 19:20. 3. New England, Williams (Webster, Dorey) 19:46.
SECOND PERIOD: 4. New England, Selwood (Williams) 1:47. 5. Winnipeg, Boyer (Rousseau, Zanussi) 5:59. 6. Winnipeg, Bordeleau (Hull, Woytowich) 7:37.
THIRD PERIOD: 7. New England, Dorey (Williams, Webster) 2:19. 8. New England, Selby (Williams, Webster) 3:08. 9. New England, French (Ley, Sheehy) 9:03. 10. New England, Cunniff (Byers) 10:16. 11. New England, French (Hurley, Pleau) 18:59.

GAME 3, May 3:

NEW ENGLAND	0	1	2	–	3
WINNIPEG	2	1	1	–	4

Goaltenders: New England, A. Smith. Winnipeg, Daley.

FIRST PERIOD: 1. Winnipeg, Hull (Bordeleau, Beaudin) 15:23. 2. Winnipeg, McDonald (Beaudin, Hornung) 19:34.
SECOND PERIOD: 3. Winnipeg, Johnson (Hull, Hornung) 5:21. 4. New England, Ley (Byers) 14:44.
THIRD PERIOD: 5. New England, Green (Ley, Webster) 4:23. 6. New England, Sheehy (French, Dorey) 18:56. 7. Winnipeg, Hull (Beaudin, Ash) 18:56.

GAME 4, May 5:

WINNIPEG	1	0	1	–	2
NEW ENGLAND	0	3	1	–	4

Goaltenders: Winnipeg, Wakely. New England, A. Smith.

FIRST PERIOD: 1. Winnipeg, Hull (Bordeleau) 15:50.
SECOND PERIOD: 2. New England, Pleau (Sheehy, Ley) 0:47. 3. New England, Byers (Earl, Dorey) 14:11. 4. New England, Sheehy (Dorey, Selwood) 16:17.
THIRD PERIOD: 5. New England, Byers (Earl) 7:17. 6. Winnipeg, Rousseau (Ash) 19:54.

GAME 5, May 6:

WINNIPEG	2	2	2	–	6
NEW ENGLAND	5	1	3	–	9

Goaltenders: Winnipeg, Daley. New England, A. Smith.

FIRST PERIOD: 1. New England, Webster (Williams, Ley) 0:21. 2. New England, Pleau 4:43. 3.Winnipeg, Johnson (Sutherland) 7:07. 4. New England, G. Smith (Williams, Webster) 11:47. 5. New England, Ley 15:43. 6. Winnipeg, Beaudin (Hull) 17:53. 7. New England, Sheehy (Webster, Pleau) 18:41.
SECOND PERIOD: 8. New England, Webster (Williams, Green) 0:15. 9. Winnipeg, Beaudin (Bordeleau, McDonald) 3:15. 10. Winnipeg, Black (Shmyr) 4:02.
THIRD PERIOD: 11. Winnipeg, Woytowich (Swenson, Asmundson) 4:59. 12. New England, Pleau (Sheehy, French) 5:24. 13. New England, Pleau (Sheehy, French) 7:31. 14. New England, Byers (Green, Williams) 17:20. 15. Winnipeg, Asmundson (Swenson, Cuddie) 18:10.

1973–74

Quarterfinal Round

Houston over Winnipeg, 4 games to 0

April 8, at WINN: HOUS 5, WINN 2
April 10, at WINN: HOUS 3, WINN 2
April 13, at HOUS: HOUS 10, WINN 1
April 14, at HOUS: HOUS 5, WINN 4

Minnesota over Edmonton, 4 games to 1

April 6, at MINN: MINN 2, EDM 1
April 7, at MINN: MINN 8, EDM 5
April 10, at EDM: MINN 6, EDM 2
April 12, at EDM: EDM 2, MINN 1
April 14, at MINN: MINN 5, EDM 4

Chicago over New England, 4 games to 3

April 6, at NE: NE 6, CHI 4
April 7, at NE: NE 4, CHI 3
April 9, at CHI: CHI 8, NE 6
April 10, at CHI: CHI 2, NE 1
April 12, at NE: CHI 4, NE 2
April 14, at CHI: NE 2, CHI 0
April 16, at NE: CHI 3, NE 2

Toronto over Cleveland, 4 games to 1

April 7, at TOR: TOR 4, CLEVE 0
April 9, at TOR: TOR 4, CLEVE 3
April 12, at CLEVE: TOR 4, CLEVE 2
April 13, at CLEVE: CLEVE 3, TOR 2
April 15, at TOR: TOR 4, CLEVE 1

Semifinal Round

Houston over Minnesota, 4 games to 2

April 18, at HOUS: MINN 5, HOUS 4
April 20, at HOUS: HOUS 5, MINN 2
April 21, at MINN: MINN 4, HOUS 1
April 28, at MINN: HOUS 4, MINN 1
April 29, at HOUS: HOUS 9, MINN 4
May 1, at MINN: HOUS 3, MINN 1

Chicago over Toronto, 4 games to 3

April 19, at TOR: TOR 6, CHI 4
April 22, at TOR: CHI 4, TOR 3
April 28, at CHI: CHI 3, TOR 2
April 29, at CHI: TOR 7, CHI 6
May 1, at TOR: TOR 5, CHI 3
May 4, at CHI: CHI 9, TOR 2
May 6, at TOR: CHI 5, TOR 2

FINAL ROUND: Houston over Chicago, 4 games to 0

GAME 1, May 12:

HOUSTON	2	0	1	– 3
CHICAGO	0	0	2	– 2

Goaltenders: Houston, McLeod. Chicago, Gill.

FIRST PERIOD: 1. Houston, Hale (Hall, Labossiere) 6:31. 2. Houston, Labossiere (Taylor, Grierson) 9:15.
SECOND PERIOD: No scoring.
THIRD PERIOD: 3. Chicago, Liddington (Stapleton, Backstrom) 5:42. 4. Chicago, Gordon (Mavety, Proceviat) 13:45. 5. Houston, Hughes 15:48.

GAME 2, May 15:

HOUSTON	2	1	3	– 6
CHICAGO	0	0	1	– 1

Goaltenders: Houston, McLeod. Chicago, Gill.

FIRST PERIOD: 1. Houston, Hall (Taylor, Lund) 13:21. 2. Houston, Labossiere (P. Popiel, Taylor) 18:08.
SECOND PERIOD: 3. Houston, Hinse (G. Howe, Hughes) 16:50.
THIRD PERIOD: 4. Houston, Sherrit (Mark Howe, G. Howe) 1:59. 5. Houston, Hinse (Lund, Hughes) 2:23. 6. Houston, Taylor (Hall) 13:16. 7. Chicago, Rochon 19:44.

GAME 3, May 17:

CHICAGO	1	3	0	– 4
HOUSTON	3	3	1	– 7

Goaltenders: Chicago, Gill, Newton. Houston, McLeod.

FIRST PERIOD: 1. Houston, Hall 5:19. 2. Houston, Hughes (G. Howe, Hinse) 10:51. 3. Chicago, Backstrom 12:17. 4. Houston, Mark Howe (Sherrit, G. Howe) 13:22.
SECOND PERIOD: 5. Houston, Hinse (G. Howe) 1:34. 6. Houston, Hale (Sherrit) 3:21. 7. Chicago, Paiement 5:01. 8. Morris (Hardy, Gordon) 11:38. 9. Houston, Hinse (Lund, P. Popiel) 14:08. 10. Chicago, Mavety (Stapleton, Sicinski) 15:34.
THIRD PERIOD: 11. Houston, Hughes (Hinse) 0:48.

GAME 4, May 19:

CHICAGO	0	1	1	– 2
HOUSTON	3	3	0	– 6

Goaltenders: Chicago, Newton. Houston, McLeod.

FIRST PERIOD: 1. Houston, Lund (Hinse, Hale) 14:34. 2. Houston, Hall 15:47. 3. Houston, Hall (P. Popiel, G. Howe) 16:55.
SECOND PERIOD: 4. Houston, Hinse (G. Howe, P. Popiel) 12:40. 5. Houston, Labossiere (P. Popiel, Schella) 13:58. 6. Houston, Lund (G. Howe, P. Popiel) 15:52. 7. Chicago, J. Popiel (Paiement, Sicinski) 17:29.
THIRD PERIOD: 8. Chicago, Morris (Mavety) 10:12.

1974–75

Quarterfinal Round

Houston over Cleveland, 4 games to 1

April 10, at HOUS: HOUS 8, CLEVE 5
April 12, at HOUS: HOUS 5, CLEVE 3
April 13, at CLEVE: CLEVE 3, HOUS 1
April 15, at CLEVE: HOUS 7, CLEVE 2
April 17, at HOUS: HOUS 3, CLEVE 1

Quebec over Phoenix, 4 games to 1

April 8, at QUE: QUE 5, PHOE 2
April 10, at QUE: QUE 6, PHOE 2
April 12, at PHOE: QUE 3, PHOE 0
April 15, at PHOE: PHOE 6, QUE 5 (OT, 3:27)
April 17, at QUE: QUE 4, PHOE 2

Minnesota over New England, 4 games to 2

April 9, at NE: MINN 6, NE 5
April 11, at NE: NE 3, MINN 2 (OT, 6:46)
April 13, at MINN: MINN 8, NE 3
April 15, at MINN: NE 5, MINN 2
April 18, at NE: MINN 4, NE 0
April 19, at MINN: MINN 6, NE 1

San Diego over Toronto, 4 games to 2

April 9, at SD: SD 5, TOR 3
April 12, at SD: SD 7, TOR 6
April 16, at TOR: TOR 5, SD 2
April 16, at TOR: TOR 6, SD 5
April 18, at SD: SD 4, TOR 3
April 21, at TOR: SD 6, TOR 4

Semifinal Round

Houston over San Diego, 4 games to 0

April 25, at SD: HOUS 4, SD 0
April 27, at SD: HOUS 2, SD 1
April 29, at HOUS: HOUS 6, SD 0
May 1, at HOUS: HOUS 5, SD 4 (OT, 0:27)

Quebec over Minnesota, 4 games to 2

April 22, at QUE: QUE 4, MINN 1
April 24, at QUE: MINN 5, QUE 3
April 26, at MINN: QUE 6, MINN 1
April 27, at MINN: MINN 4, QUE 2
April 29, at QUE: QUE 6, MINN 3
May 1, at MINN: QUE 4, MINN 2

FINAL ROUND: Houston over Quebec, 4 games to 0

GAME 1, May 3:

QUEBEC	0	1	1	– 2
HOUSTON	4	1	1	– 6

Goaltenders: Quebec, Brodeur. Houston, Grahame.

FIRST PERIOD: 1. Houston, Labossiere (Popiel, Schella) 1:26. 2. Houston, Lund (Mark Howe, G. Howe) 2:36. 3. Houston, G. Howe (Schella, Preston) 12:13. 4. Houston, Ruskowski (Popiel, Larway) 17:54.
SECOND PERIOD: 5. Houston, Larway (Ruskowski) 4:37. 6. Quebec, Tardif (Bordeleau, Hoganson) 17:51.
THIRD PERIOD: 7. Houston, Labossiere (Taylor, Hughes) 1:45. 8. Quebec, Guindon (Bordeleau) 3:45.

GAME 2, May 6:

QUEBEC	1	1	1	– 3
HOUSTON	1	1	3	– 5

Goaltenders: Quebec, Brodeur. Houston, Grahame.

FIRST PERIOD: 1. Houston, G. Howe (Mark Howe, Sherrit) 4:44. 2. Quebec, Hoganson (S. Bernier, Houle) 16:34.
SECOND PERIOD: 3. Houston, G. Howe (Lund, Hughes) 1:19. 4. Quebec, Tardif (Guindon, Bordeleau) 2:57.
THIRD PERIOD: 5. Houston, Labossiere (Hall, Taylor) 2:06. 6. Quebec, Tardif (Bordeleau) 2:37. 7. Houston, Ruskowski (Preston, Irwin) 3:04. 8. Houston, Hinse (Lund, Schella) 11:08.

GAME 3, May 10:

HOUSTON	0	1	1	– 2
QUEBEC	0	0	0	– 0

Goaltenders: Houston, Grahame. Quebec, Brodeur.

FIRST PERIOD: No scoring.
SECOND PERIOD: 1. Houston, Hughes (G. Howe, Mark Howe) 0:14.
THIRD PERIOD: 2. Houston, Popiel (Schella) 13:48.

GAME 4, May 12:

HOUSTON	3	2	2	– 7
QUEBEC	1	1	0	– 2

Goaltenders: Houston, Grahame. Quebec, Brodeur.

FIRST PERIOD: 1. Houston, G. Howe (Hinse, Lund) 2:41. 2. Quebec, Houle (Tardif, S. Bernier) 6:01. 3. Houston, Mark Howe (Hinse, Lund) 12:18. 4. Houston, Labossiere (Schella, Hall) 19:53.
SECOND PERIOD: 5. Houston, G. Howe (Lund) 7:36. 6. Quebec, Houle (S. Bernier, Brodeur) 14:51. 7. Houston, Hughes (Mark Howe, Sherrit) 16:52.
THIRD PERIOD: 8. Houston, Lund (Popiel) 14:07. 9. Houston, Hughes (G. Howe, Lund) 18:30.

1975–76

Preliminary Round

New England over Cleveland, 3 games to 0

April 9, at NE: NE 5, CLEVE 3
April 10, at CLEVE: NE 6, CLEVE 1
April 11, at CLEVE: NE 3, CLEVE 2

San Diego over Phoenix, 3 games to 2

April 9, at PHOE: PHOE 3, SD 1
April 10, at SD: SD 4, PHOE 2
April 13, at PHOE: PHOE 6, SD 4
April 15, at SD: SD 5, PHOE 1
April 17, at PHOE: SD 2, PHOE 1

Quarterfinal Round

Winnipeg over Edmonton, 4 games to 0

April 9, at WINN: WINN 7, EDM 3
April 11, at WINN: WINN 5, EDM 4 (OT, 0:54)
April 14, at EDM: WINN 3, EDM 2
April 16, at EDM: WINN 7, EDM 2

Calgary over Quebec, 4 games to 1

April 10, at QUE: CALG 3, QUE 1
April 11, at QUE: CALG 8, QUE 4
April 14, at CALG: CALG 3, QUE 2
April 16, at CALG: QUE 4, CALG 3
April 18, at QUE: CALG 6, QUE 4

New England over Indianapolis, 4 games to 3

April 16, at IND: NE 4, IND 1
April 17, at IND: IND 4, NE 0
April 21, at NE: NE 3, IND 0
April 23, at NE: NE 2, IND 1
April 24, at IND: IND 4, NE 0
April 27, at NE: IND 5, NE 3
April 29, at IND: NE 6, IND 0

Houston over San Diego, 4 games to 2

April 21, at HOUS: HOUS 8, SD 4
April 23, at HOUS: HOUS 3, SD 1
April 25, at SD: HOUS 8, SD 4
April 27, at SD: SD 3, HOUS 2
April 28, at HOUS: SD 3, HOUS 2
April 30, at SD: HOUS 3, SD 2

Semifinal Round

Winnipeg over Calgary, 4 games to 1

April 23, at WINN: WINN 6, CALG 1
April 25, at WINN: WINN 3, CALG 2
April 28, at CALG: WINN 6, CALG 3
April 30, at CALG: CALG 7, WINN 3
May 2, at WINN: WINN 4, CALG 0

Houston over New England, 4 games to 3

May 5, at HOUS: NE 4, HOUS 2
May 7, at HOUS: HOUS 5, NE 2
May 9, at NE: NE 4, HOUS 1
May 11, at NE: HOUS 4, NE 3
May 13, at HOUS: HOUS 4, NE 3
May 15, at NE: NE 6, HOUS 1
May 16, at HOUS: HOUS 2, NE 0

FINAL ROUND: Winnipeg over Houston, 4 games to 0

GAME 1, May 20:

WINNIPEG	2	1	1	–	4
HOUSTON	2	0	1	–	3

Goaltenders: Winnipeg, Daley. Houston, Grahame.

FIRST PERIOD: 1. Houston, Hughes (Butters, Hale) 9:37. 2. Winnipeg, Hedberg (Hull, Nilsson) 13:08. 3. Winnipeg, Moffat (Beaudin, Lindh) 15:36. 4. Houston, Mark Howe (West, Hale) 19:35.
SECOND PERIOD: 5. Winnipeg, Hedberg (Bergman) 16:10.
THIRD PERIOD: 6. Houston, Mark Howe (Preston) 0:46. 7. Winnipeg, Hull (Nilsson) 16:43.

GAME 2, May 23:

WINNIPEG	1	2	2	–	5
HOUSTON	0	2	2	–	4

Goaltenders: Winnipeg, Daley. Houston, Grahame.

FIRST PERIOD: 1. Winnipeg, Hedberg (Nilsson) 13:52.
SECOND PERIOD:2. Houston, G. Howe (Mark Howe, Schella) 1:22. 3. Winnipeg, Lindstrom (Sullivan, Bergman) 2:17. 4. Houston, Marty Howe (Hall) 12:44. 5. Winnipeg, Asmundson (Lesuk, Guindon) 16:53.
THIRD PERIOD: 6. Houston, Ruskowski (Preston, Popiel) 1:29. 7. Houston, Marty Howe (Taylor, Popiel) 3:23. 8. Winnipeg, Bergman 5:19. 9. Winnipeg, Hull (Bergman, Hedberg) 18:06.

GAME 3, May 25:

HOUSTON	1	1	1	–	3
WINNIPEG	4	1	1	–	6

Goaltenders: Houston, Grahame. Winnipeg, Daley.

FIRST PERIOD: 1. Winnipeg, Ketola (Lindstrom, Riihiranta) 2:24. 2. Winnipeg, Nilsson (Hedberg) 3:23. 3. Houston, Mark Howe (Schella) 3:48. 4. Winnipeg, Hedberg (Ford, Ketola) 8:49. 5. Winnipeg, Sullivan (Hull, Lindstrom) 11:33.
SECOND PERIOD: 6. Winnipeg, Nilsson (Sjoberg) 7:46. 7. Houston, Larway (Marty Howe, Tonelli) 14:28.
THIRD PERIOD: 8. Winnipeg, Nilsson 1:44. 9. Houston, Larway (Tonelli, Ruskowski) 13:22.

GAME 4, May 27:

HOUSTON	1	0	0	–	1
WINNIPEG	3	4	2	–	9

Goaltenders: Houston, Grahame. Winnipeg, Daley.

FIRST PERIOD: 1. Winnipeg, Hull (Ford, Nilsson) 5:37. 2. Houston, Taylor (Labossiere, Marty Howe) 9:45. 3. Winnipeg, Ketola (Ford, Hull) 10:22. 4. Winnipeg, Moffat (Sjoberg, Ford) 11:21.
SECOND PERIOD: 5. Winnipeg, Ketola (Lindstrom, Sullivan) 1:07. 6. Winnipeg, Hedberg (Nilsson, Hull) 3:11. 7. Winnipeg, Hedberg (Nilsson) 9:19. 8. Winnipeg, Sullivan (Hillman) 12:14.
THIRD PERIOD: 9. Winnipeg, Sullivan (Ford, Riihiranta) 1:33. 10. Winnipeg, Guindon (Riihiranta, Ketola) 9:30.

1976–77

Quarterfinal Round

Quebec over New England, 4 games to 1

April 9, at QUE: QUE 5, NE 2
April 12, at QUE: QUE 7, NE 3
April 14, at NE: QUE 4, NE 3 (OT, 1:50)
April 16, at NE: NE 6, QUE 4
April 19, at QUE: QUE 3, NE 0

Indianapolis over Cincinnati, 4 games to 0

April 9, at CIN: IND 4, CIN 3 (OT, 8:40)
April 12, at CIN: IND 7, CIN 2
April 14, at IND: IND 5, CIN 3
April 16, at IND: IND 3, CIN 1

Houston over Edmonton, 4 games to 1

April 13, at HOUS: HOUS 4, EDM 3 (OT, 13:11)
April 15, at HOUS: HOUS 6, EDM 2
April 17, at EDM: EDM 7, HOUS 2
April 20, at EDM: HOUS 4, EDM 1
April 22, at HOUS: HOUS 4, EDM 3

Winnipeg over San Diego, 4 games to 3

April 10, at WINN: WINN 5, SD 1
April 12, at WINN: WINN 4, SD 1
April 16, at SD: SD 5, WINN 4
April 17, at SD: SD 6, WINN 4
April 20, at WINN: WINN 3, SD 0
April 22, at SD: SD 3, WINN 1
April 24, at WINN: WINN 7, SD 3

Semifinal Round

Quebec over Indianapolis, 4 games to 1

April 23, at QUE: QUE 3, IND 1
April 25, at QUE: QUE 8, IND 3
April 28, at IND: QUE 6, IND 5 (OT, 5:29)
April 30, at IND: IND 2, QUE 0
May 2, at QUE: QUE 8, IND 3

Winnipeg over Houston, 4 games to 2

April 26, at HOUS: WINN 4, HOUS 3 (OT, 8:05)
April 28, at HOUS: HOUS 7, WINN 2
April 30, at WINN: WINN 4, HOUS 3
May 1, at WINN: WINN 6, HOUS 4
May 3, at HOUS: HOUS 3, WINN 2
May 5, at WINN: WINN 6, HOUS 3

FINAL ROUND: Quebec over Winnipeg, 4 games to 3

GAME 1, May 11:

WINNIPEG	0	2	0	– 2
QUEBEC	0	0	1	– 1

Goaltenders: Winnipeg, Daley. Quebec, Brodeur.

FIRST PERIOD: No scoring.
SECOND PERIOD: 1. Winnipeg, Labraaten (Dunn) 2:22. 2. Winnipeg, Lindstrom (Labraaten, Sullivan) 13:30.
THIRD PERIOD: 3. Quebec, P. Bordeleau 7:00.

GAME 2, May 15:

WINNIPEG	0	0	1	– 1
QUEBEC	4	1	1	– 6

Goaltenders: Winnipeg, Daley. Quebec, Brodeur.

FIRST PERIOD: 1. Quebec, Guite (Boudrias, Lacombe) 4:32. 2. Quebec, P. Bordeleau (S. Bernier, Dube) 13:25. 3. Quebec, Sutherland 15:17. 4. Quebec, S. Bernier (Dube, Brackenbury) 18:23.
SECOND PERIOD: 5. Quebec, Brackenbury (S. Bernier, Weir) 17:02.
THIRD PERIOD: 6. Winnipeg, Labraaten (Lindstrom) 2:47. 7. Quebec, Sutherland (Fitchner, Brackenbury) 13:00.

GAME 3, May 18:

QUEBEC	1	0	0	– 1
WINNIPEG	0	2	4	– 6

Goaltenders: Quebec, Brodeur. Winnipeg, Daley.

FIRST PERIOD: 1. Quebec, Brackenbury (Fitchner) 2:08.
SECOND PERIOD: 2. Winnipeg, Lindstrom (Labraaten) 4:42. 3. Winnipeg, Labraaten (Lindstrom) 13:16.
THIRD PERIOD: 4. Winnipeg, Hedberg (Ford, Daley) 0:31. 5. Winnipeg, Nilsson 6:16. 6. Winnipeg, Lesuk (Lindh, Long) 9:30. 7. Winnipeg, Lindstrom (Sullivan, Labraaten) 16:33.

GAME 4, May 20:

QUEBEC	1	2	1	– 4
WINNIPEG	2	0	0	– 2

Goaltenders: Quebec, Brodeur, Aubry. Winnipeg, Daley.

FIRST PERIOD: 1. Quebec, S. Bernier (P. Bordeleau, J. Bernier) 7:33. 2. Winnipeg, Miller (Sullivan, Labraaten) 11:38. 3. Winnipeg, Nilsson (Hull, Hedberg) 17:17.
SECOND PERIOD: 4. Quebec, Lacombe (Cloutier, Tremblay) 1:50. 5. Quebec, Tardif (S. Bernier, C. Bordeleau) 14:53.
THIRD PERIOD: 6. Quebec, S. Bernier (P. Bordeleau) 4:32.

GAME 5, May 22:

WINNIPEG	1	2	0	– 3
QUEBEC	4	3	1	– 8

Goaltenders: Winnipeg, Daley. Quebec, Brodeur.

FIRST PERIOD: 1. Quebec, Guite (Boudrias, J. Bernier) 4:23. 2. Quebec, Cloutier (Tardif, Tremblay) 8:49. 3. Quebec, C. Bordeleau (Cloutier) 12:10. 4. Quebec, P. Bordeleau (Dube, S. Bernier) 14:20. 5. Winnipeg, Nilsson (Miller, Hull) 17:04.
SECOND PERIOD: 6. Quebec, Cloutier (C. Bordeleau) 4:18. 7. Quebec, P. Bordeleau (S. Bernier, Tremblay) 6:01. 8. Winnipeg, Ford (Sullivan, Labraaten) 6:39. 9. Quebec, C. Bordeleau (Cloutier, S. Bernier) 11:37. 10. Winnipeg, Hull 13:43.
THIRD PERIOD: 11. Quebec, S. Bernier (P. Bordeleau) 8:49.

GAME 6, May 24:

QUEBEC	3	0	0	– 3
WINNIPEG	4	4	4	– 12

Goaltenders: Quebec, Brodeur, Aubry. Winnipeg, Daley.

FIRST PERIOD: 1. Winnipeg, Hull (Nilsson, Ford) 1:26. 2. Quebec, Cloutier 3:02. 3. Quebec, Cloutier (Tardif, C. Bordeleau) 4:28. 4. Winnipeg, Labraaten (Sullivan, Lindstrom) 9:17. 5. Winnipeg, Hedberg (Nilsson) 12:09. 6. Winnipeg, Guindon (Huck, Miller) 13:47. 7. Quebec, C. Bordeleau (Tardif, Cloutier) 16:35.
SECOND PERIOD: 8. Winnipeg, Hull (Guindon, Dunn) 6:28. 9. Winnipeg, Sullivan (Labraaten) 8:04. 10. Winnipeg, Ford (Sjoberg, Hedberg) 16:57. 11. Winnipeg, Guindon (Long, Huck) 17:30.
THIRD PERIOD: 12. Winnipeg, Sullivan (Labraaten) 2:21. 13. Winnipeg, Hedberg (Nilsson, Miller) 3:37. 14. Winnipeg, Lindstrom (Sullivan) 5:20. 15. Winnipeg, Hull (Nilsson, Hedberg) 12:36.

GAME 7, May 26:

WINNIPEG	0	1	1	– 2
QUEBEC	0	6	2	– 8

Goaltenders: Winnipeg, Daley. Quebec, Brodeur.

FIRST PERIOD: No scoring.
SECOND PERIOD: 1. Quebec, Fitchner 0:11. 2. Quebec, Tardif (Cloutier, C. Bordeleau) 1:10. 3. Quebec, Cloutier (Tardif, Lariviere) 6:27. 4. Winnipeg, Labraaten (Ford, Sullivan) 8:39. 5. Quebec, Tremblay (Cloutier, Tardif) 9:24. 6. Quebec, Dube (Lariviere, S. Bernier) 15:23. 7. Quebec, P. Bordeleau (S. Bernier, Lacombe) 18:41.
THIRD PERIOD: 8. Quebec, C. Bordeleau (Cloutier, Lacombe) 1:39. 9. Quebec, S. Bernier (Dube, Lariviere) 3:39. 10. Winnipeg, Miller (Nilsson, Hedberg) 14:09.

1977–78

Quarterfinal Round

New England over Edmonton, 4 games to 1

April 14, at NE: NE 6, EDM 4
April 16, at NE: NE 4, EDM 1
April 19, at EDM: EDM 2, NE 0
April 21, at EDM: NE 9, EDM 1
April 23, at NE: NE 4, EDM 1

Quebec over Houston, 4 games to 2

April 16, at HOUS: HOUS 4, QUE 3 (OT, 7:19)
April 18, at HOUS: QUE 5, HOUS 4 (OT, 2:59)
April 20, at QUE: QUE 5, HOUS 1
April 21, at QUE: QUE 3, HOUS 0
April 23, at HOUS: HOUS 5, QUE 2
April 26, at QUE: QUE 11, HOUS 2

Semifinal Round

Winnipeg over Birmingham, 4 games to 1

April 14, at WINN: WINN 9, BIRM 3
April 16, at WINN: WINN 8, BIRM 3
April 19, at BIRM: BIRM 3, WINN 2
April 21, at BIRM: WINN 5, BIRM 1
April 23, at WINN: WINN 5, BIRM 2

New England over Quebec, 4 games to 1

April 28, at NE: NE 5, QUE 1
April 30, at NE: QUE 3, NE 2
May 3, at QUE: NE 5, QUE 4
May 5, at QUE: NE 7, QUE 3
May 7, at NE: NE 6, QUE 3

FINAL ROUND: Winnipeg over New England, 4 games to 0

GAME 1, May 12:

WINNIPEG	0	0	4	– 4
NEW ENGLAND	0	0	1	– 1

Goaltenders: Winnipeg, Bromley. New England, Levasseur.

FIRST PERIOD: No scoring.
SECOND PERIOD: No scoring.
THIRD PERIOD: 1. Winnipeg, Guindon (Moffat) 4:31. 2. Winnipeg, Sullivan 4:53. 3. New England, Pleau (Hangsleben, Bolduc) 8:07. 4. Winnipeg, Guindon (Lesuk) 13:55. 5. Winnipeg, Sullivan (Moffat) 19:45.

GAME 2, May 14:

WINNIPEG	2	2	1	– 5
NEW ENGLAND	0	0	2	– 2

Goaltenders: Winnipeg, Daley. New England, Levassuer.

FIRST PERIOD: 1. Winnipeg, Labraaten (Lindstrom) 14:02. 2. Winnipeg, Moffat (Amadeo, Lesuk) 19:32.
SECOND PERIOD: 3. Winnipeg, Guindon (Lesuk, Moffat) 1:21. 4. Winnipeg, Hedberg (U. Nilsson) 17:10.
THIRD PERIOD: 5. New England, G. Howe (Plumb, Rogers) 6:28. 6. New England, Mark Howe (J. Carlson) 15:17. 7. Winnipeg, U. Nilsson (Hedberg) 16:35.

GAME 3, May 19:

NEW ENGLAND	0	0	2	– 2
WINNIPEG	6	2	2	– 10

Goaltenders: New England, Smith. Winnipeg, Bromley.

FIRST PERIOD: 1. Winnipeg, Lindstrom 4:56. 2. Winnipeg, Guindon (Lesuk, Moffat) 5:09. 3. Winnipeg, Hull (U. Nilsson, Hedberg) 6:32. 4. Winnipeg, Lindstrom (Sullivan, Long) 7:31. 5. Winnipeg, K. Nilsson (Kryskow, Baird) 7:46. 6. Winnipeg, K. Nilsson (Lindstrom, Clackson) 17:36.
SECOND PERIOD: 7. Winnipeg, Powis (Kryskow, K. Nilsson) 4:55. 8. Winnipeg, Moffat (Dunn, Sullivan) 16:28.
THIRD PERIOD: 9. New England, McKenzie (Keon, Marty Howe) 4:07. 10. New England, Sheehy (Lyle, Selwood) 5:10. 11. Winnipeg, Powis (K. Nilsson, Kryskow) 8:30. 12. Winnipeg, Lindstrom (Labraaten, Sullivan) 12:12.

GAME 4, May 22:

NEW ENGLAND	2	0	1	– 3
WINNIPEG	0	3	2	– 5

Goaltenders: New England, Smith. Winnipeg, Daley.

FIRST PERIOD: 1. New England, Antonovich (Keon, McKenzie) 1:37. 2. New England, Ley (Sheehy) 1:59.
SECOND PERIOD: 2. Winnipeg, Kryskow (Hedberg, K. Nilsson) 3:26. 4. Winnipeg, Moffat (Guindon) 3:38. 5. Winnipeg, Hedberg (Sjoberg, U. Nilsson) 17:59.
THIRD PERIOD: 6. Winnipeg, Hull (U. Nilsson, Hedberg) 3:26. 7. New England, Lyle (Hangsleben, S. Carlson) 11:25. 8. Winnipeg, Hedberg (U. Nilsson, Green) 19:28.

1978–79

Preliminary Round

New England over Cincinnati, 2 games to 1

April 21, at NE: NE 5, CIN 3
April 22, at CIN: CIN 6, NE 3
April 24, at NE: NE 2, CIN 1

Semifinal Round

Edmonton over New England, 4 games to 3

April 26, at EDM: EDM 6, NE 2
April 27, at EDM: EDM 9, NE 5
April 29, at NE: NE 4, EDM 1
May 1, at NE: NE 5, EDM 1
May 3, at EDM: EDM 5, NE 2
May 6, at NE: NE 8, EDM 4
May 8, at EDM: EDM 6, NE 3

Winnipeg over Quebec, 4 games to 0

April 23, at QUE: WINN 6, QUE 3
April 25, at QUE: WINN 9, QUE 2
April 27, at WINN: WINN 9, QUE 5
April 29, at WINN: WINN 6, QUE 2

FINAL ROUND: Winnipeg over Edmonton, 4 games to 2

GAME 1, May 11:

WINNIPEG	2	0	1	– 3
EDMONTON	1	0	0	– 1

Goaltenders: Winnipeg, Smith. Edmonton, Dryden.

FIRST PERIOD: 1. Winnipeg, Preston (Sullivan) 3:29. 2. Winnipeg, Lesuk (Eriksson, Moffat) 15:23. 3. Edmonton, Flett (Shmyr) 17:48.
SECOND PERIOD: No scoring.
THIRD PERIOD: 4. Winnipeg, Preston (Nilsson) 16:24.

GAME 2, May 13:

WINNIPEG	0	0	3	– 3
EDMONTON	0	1	1	– 2

Goaltenders: Winnipeg, Smith. Edmonton, Dryden.

FIRST PERIOD: No scoring.
SECOND PERIOD: 1. Edmonton, Sobchuk (Driscoll) 6:12.
THIRD PERIOD: 2. Winnipeg, Sullivan (Terbenche) 1:17. 3. Edmonton, Hamilton 4:10. 4. Winnipeg, Lukowich (Campbell, Ruskowski) 11:53. 5. Winnipeg, Lindstrom (Long, Lukowich) 15:24.

GAME 3, May 15:

EDMONTON	4	0	4	– 8
WINNIPEG	2	1	0	– 3

Goaltenders: Edmonton, Dryden. Winnipeg, Smith, Daley.

FIRST PERIOD: 1. Winnipeg, Lukowich (Ruskowski, Nilsson) 4:54. 2. Edmonton, Hamilton (Gretzky, Callighen) 9:03. 3. Edmonton, Driscoll (Goldsworthy) 9:44 4. Edmonton, Chipperfield (Shmyr, Driscoll) 12:45. 5. Winnipeg, Lindstrom 15:53. 6. Edmonton, Goldsworthy (Hamilton, Chipperfield) 16:01.
SECOND PERIOD: 7. Winnipeg, Lukowich (MacKinnon, Eriksson) 11:56.
THIRD PERIOD: 8. Edmonton, MacDonald (Siltanen) 1:42. 9. Edmonton, Callighen (MacDonald, Gretzky) 4:14. 10. Edmonton, Gustafsson (Hunter, Weir) 9:52. 11. Edmonton, Hunter (Gustafsson, Hamilton) 11:00.

GAME 4, May 16:

EDMONTON	1	1	0	– 2
WINNIPEG	1	0	2	– 3

Goaltenders: Edmonton, Dryden. Winnipeg, Smith.

FIRST PERIOD: 1. Edmonton, Gretzky (MacDonald, Callighen) 7:41. 2. Winnipeg, Preston (Sullivan) 12:54.
SECOND PERIOD: 3. Edmonton, Callighen (Gretzky, Gustafsson) 13:42.
THIRD PERIOD: 4. Winnipeg, Lukowich (Nilsson, Lindstrom) 9:24. 5. Winnipeg, Moffat (Lesuk, Eriksson) 13:34.

GAME 5, May 18:

WINNIPEG	0	1	1	– 2
EDMONTON	4	4	2	– 10

Goaltenders: Winnipeg, Smith, Daley. Edmonton, Dryden, Mio.

FIRST PERIOD: 1. Edmonton, Sobchuk (Chipperfield, Shmyr) 4:23. 2. Edmonton, Gretzky (Callighen, Chipperfield) 16:28. 3. Edmonton, Weir (Micheletti, Sobchuk) 17:29. 4. Edmonton, Chipperfield (Langevin) 18:01.
SECOND PERIOD: 5. Winnipeg, Preston (Lukowich, Nilsson) 0:22. 6. Edmonton, Sobchuk (Shmyr, Weir) 2:58. 7. Edmonton, Chipperfield (Siltanen, Micheletti) 4:51. 8. Edmonton, Chipperfield (Driscoll, Semenko) 10:45. 9. Edmonton, Hughes (Sobchuk) 14:23.
THIRD PERIOD: 10. Winnipeg, Nilsson 3:14. 11. Edmonton, Chipperfield (Semenko) 7:45. 12. Edmonton, Chipperfield (Micheletti, Siltanen) 14:31.

GAME 6, May 20:

EDMONTON	0	1	2	– 3
WINNIPEG	2	3	2	– 7

Goaltenders: Edmonton, Dryden, Mio. Winnipeg, Smith.

FIRST PERIOD: 1. Winnipeg, Lindstrom (Ruskowski, Lukowich) 2:14. 2. Winnipeg, Long (Ruskowski, Lukowich) 13:42.
SECOND PERIOD: 3. Winnipeg, MacKinnon (Sullivan, Hicks) 5:22. 4. Winnipeg, Moffat (Eriksson, Lukowich) 6:35. 5. Winnipeg, Long (Ruskowski, MacKinnon) 9:23. 6. Edmonton, Chipperfield (Driscoll, Siltanen) 18:45.
THIRD PERIOD: 7. Edmonton, Flett (Hamilton) 1:48. 8. Winnipeg, Nilsson (Sullivan) 2:09. 9. Winnipeg, Lindstrom (Ruskowski) 13:38. 10. Edmonton, Semenko (Chipperfield, Siltanen) 19:48.

The International Series

Although hockey has been played at the international level since the early part of the century, the Russians were conspicuous by their absence from tournament play until the post-World War II years. Not until the late 1940s did organized hockey begin to blossom into a major sport throughout the Soviet Union. It was, of course, a natural. With a good part of the vast nation located in a colder-than-normal climate, the Soviet Union offered thousands of lakes, ponds, and rivers on which youngsters could hone their skating and stickhandling skills. With the advent of the Soviet Ice Hockey Federation and the formation of leagues on all levels, the development of formal hockey organizations was speedy and intense.

At first the Russian hockey leaders looked to North America—to Canada in particular—for guidance. During their early contacts with Canadians, the Soviets, from players to coaches, absorbed every bit of information about the game that they could obtain. They took sticks, skates, and books from Montreal and Toronto back home and copied the Canadian style in every way. However, the Soviet blueprint of play was essentially based upon the chessboard strategy and passing of soccer with bodychecking—prohibited in soccer—held to a minimum.

As the Russians increased their hockey contacts on the international level in the Olympic games and other amateur matches they further studied the North American mode of play and incorporated it into their hockey ambiance. However, the Soviets were acutely aware that they were not making their hockey contacts on the highest level; that is, they were not playing against teams from the foremost professional organization in North America, the National Hockey League.

The failure of either the Soviets or the National Hockey League officials to make this linkage was due to a conflict of interests on both sides. For the Russians there was a technical problem: preservation of their amateur standing. Even though the Soviet skaters were, by North American standards, professionals and devoted most of their time to playing and practicing hockey they regarded themselves as amateurs. Furthermore, the International Olympic Committee accepted the Russian interpretation and acknowledged their amateur status. For the Soviets to pit their "amateurs" against the NHL's professionals would, in effect, corrupt the Soviet position, at least on technical grounds.

By contrast, the NHL's desire to avoid an ice confrontation with the Soviets was primarily based on promotional values. Ever since the late 1920s, when the NHL annexed the Stanley Cup as its very own, the Stanley Cup winner has been recognized as the world champion of hockey although the Stanley Cup holder has never had to face a challenge from any other league or country. The NHL has sold its product as the best in the world. By taking on the Russians, whose hockey proficiency was growing by the year during the period 1950–70, the NHL would be putting its reputation on the line. League governors considered it a no-win situation that they militantly attempted to avoid. But public opinion was against them and so was R. Alan Eagleson, the powerful executive director of the NHL Players' Association. Recognizing the value of international contacts between the North American big leaguers and the Europeans, Eagleson bypassed the NHL high command and negotiated with the Soviets in the early 1970s. While many experts believed matches between an NHL representative and the Russians would be an impossibility, Eagleson cut through the red tape, obtained all necessary waivers preserving the Soviets' amateur status and, ultimately, hammered out an agreement launching diplomatic relations on the hockey front.

The initial product of the negotiations was a historic eight-game series between an all-star aggregation of NHL players, dubbed Team Canada, and a similar team from the Soviet Union. The meeting of the world's two big powers was, in theory, only an exhibition series. No financial prizes were at stake nor was the Stanley Cup up for grabs. But the confrontation was treated by the media and the organizations involved as hockey's first genuine world series. For the first time, ever, the NHL conducted arduous summer auditions to select the best possible unit to meet the Russians. Similar arrangements were being made across the Atlantic.

Despite the relentless improvement in Soviet hockey since World War II and the fact that the Russians regularly triumphed at the amateur World Championships held in Europe every spring, the NHL was universally acclaimed as the favorite in the series and many critics freely predicted that the North American sextet would capture all eight of the tournament matches, the first four of which would be held in Canada. As it happened, Team Canada barely managed to win the series on a late score by Paul Henderson in the final match of the tourney. But the impact of Russian-style hockey went far beyond the series. The Soviets demonstrated superior skating, passing, and technological skills and so impressed the North Americans that the professionals almost immediately began absorbing European technique into the NHL game. More than that, the 1972 international series generated such interest on both sides of the globe that demands for more such contests were heard throughout the hockey world.

Despite the grass roots support for more series the NHL leaders—with the exception of Eagleson—had grave reservations. They feared that a Russian triumph the next time around would jeopardize their claim as the world's best. While NHL leaders argued among themselves over whether or not to continue similar contacts the World Hockey Association seized the advantage and entered into its own negotiations with the Russians. The result was a second eight-game series, only this time Team Canada was comprised of the best of the WHA, (considered not nearly as good as the 1972 NHL team) which took on the Soviets in 1974. While the series was not nearly as entertaining or as dramatic as the original match-up—what could be more pulsating than the 1972 climax in Moscow?—the WHA-Soviet series did provide another intense glimpse of the commendable brand of hockey played overseas. Names such as Vladislav Tretiak (the Soviet goalie) and Aleksandr Yakushev (the Soviet forward) became as well known in Canada and parts of the United States as Guy Lafleur and Bobby Orr.

Stung by the intrusion of the WHA, the NHL moguls reestablished contacts with the Soviets. Under the orchestration of Eagleson, a series of tournaments of various kinds were proposed and approved. One of them was a "Super Series" in which two Russian teams—Soviet Army and Wings of Soviet—would play four games each against an assortment of NHL teams in North American cities late in 1975 and early in 1976. This time the Soviet domination was apparent. Soviet Army opened with a 7-3 triumph over the New York Rangers and Soviet Wings defeated the Pittsburgh Penguins 7-4. Although each Russian team was beaten, their overall quality and "professionalism" never failed to impress the NHL critics.

The next Eagleson-NHL arrangement was called the Canada Cup 1976; the first time in history six major hockey powers—Russia, Czechoslovakia, Canada, Sweden, Finland, and the United States—played in a series in which each country's best players were in competition with one another. Surprisingly, the Soviets failed to reach the two-game final that pitted host Canada (NHL) against the Czechs. Canada swept the event 6-0, 5-4.

Another intriguing international event was held in February 1979 when the NHL approved a three-game Challenge Cup tournament between its all-stars and a visiting Soviet team. The three matches were played at Madison Square Garden with the implicit feeling that the winner could be considered the world professional champion. The teams split two closely contested games but the Soviets annihilated their hosts, 6-0, in the finale. That game, more than any other, firmly placed the Russians at the top of the hockey heap.

The NHL also has sent a pickup team comprised of players from clubs that did not make the playoffs or those whose teams were eliminated in early rounds to participate in the annual "World Championships." The NHL regards these matches as exhibition games and they will not be treated here.

The following summaries are those that have been regarded as official or semiofficial matches between the Soviet squads and the North American professionals since 1972. Neither the Canada Cup nor the annual "World" tournament contests are listed.

1972: USSR vs. Team Canada

Team Canada (NHL) over Soviet National Team, 4 games to 3 (1 tie)

GAME 1 at Montreal, Sept. 2:

USSR	2	2	3	– 7
CANADA	2	0	1	– 3

Goaltenders: USSR, Tretiak. Canada, K. Dryden.

FIRST PERIOD: 1. Canada, P. Esposito (F. Mahovlich, Bergman) 0:30. 2. Canada, Henderson (Clarke) 6:32. 3. USSR, Zimin (Yakushev, Shadrin) 11:40. 4. USSR, Petrov (Mikhailov) 17:28.
SECOND PERIOD: 5. USSR, Kharlamov (Maltsev) 2:40. 6. USSR, Kharlamov (Maltsev) 10:18.
THIRD PERIOD: 7. Canada, Clarke (Ellis, Henderson) 8:32. 8. USSR, Mikhailov (Blinov) 13:32. 9. USSR, Zimin 14:29. 10. USSR, Yakushev (Shadrin) 18:37.

GAME 2 at Toronto, Sept. 4:

USSR	0	0	1	– 1
CANADA	0	1	3	– 4

Goaltenders: USSR, Tretiak. Canada, T. Esposito.

FIRST PERIOD: No scoring.
SECOND PERIOD: 1, Canada, P. Esposito (Park, Cashman) 7:14.
THIRD PERIOD: 2. Canada, Cournoyer (Park) 1:19. 3. USSR, Yakushev (Liapkin, Zimin) 5:53. 4. Canada, P. Mahovlich (P. Esposito) 6:47. 5. Canada, F. Mahovlich (Mikita, Cournoyer) 8:59.

GAME 3 at Winnipeg, Sept. 6:

USSR	1	3	0	– 4
CANADA	2	2	0	– 4

Goaltenders: USSR, Tretiak. Canada, T. Esposito.

FIRST PERIOD: 1. Canada, Parise (White, P. Esposito) 1:54. 2. USSR, Petrov 3:16. 3. Canada, Ratelle (Cournoyer, Bergman) 18:25.
SECOND PERIOD: 4. Canada, P. Esposito (Cashman, Parise) 4:19. 5. USSR, Kharlamov (Tsigankov) 12:56. 6. Canada, Henderson (Ellis, Clarke) 13:47. 7. USSR, Lebedev (Vasilyev, Anisin) 14:59. 8. USSR, Bodunov (Anisin) 18:28.
THIRD PERIOD: No scoring.

GAME 4 at Vancouver, Sept. 8:

USSR	2	2	1	– 5
CANADA	0	1	2	– 3

Goaltenders: USSR, Tretiak. Canada, K. Dryden.

FIRST PERIOD: 1. USSR, Mikhailov (Lutchenko, Petrov) 2:01. 2.USSR, Mikhailov (Lutchenko, Petrov) 7:29.
SECOND PERIOD: 3. Canada, Perreault 5:37. 4. USSR, Blinov (Petrov, Mikhailov) 6:34. 5. USSR,Vikulov (Kharlamov, Maltsev) 13:52.
THIRD PERIOD: 6. Canada, Goldsworthy (P. Esposito, Bergman) 6:54. 7. USSR, Shadrin (Yakushev, Vasilyev) 11:05. 8. Canada, B. Hull (Esposito, Goldsworthy) 19:38.

GAME 5 at Moscow, Sept. 22:

CANADA	1	2	1	– 4
USSR	0	0	5	– 5

Goaltenders: Canada, T. Esposito. USSR, Tretiak.

FIRST PERIOD: 1. Canada, Parise (Perreault, Gilbert) 15:30.
SECOND PERIOD: 2. Canada, Clarke (Henderson) 2:36. 3. Canada, Henderson (Lapointe, Clarke) 11:47.
THIRD PERIOD: 4. USSR, Blinov (Petrov, Kuzkin) 3:34. 5. Canada, Henderson (Clarke) 4:56. 6. USSR, Anisin (Liapkin, Yakushev) 9:05. 7. USSR, Shadrin (Anisin) 9:13. 8. USSR, Gusev (Ragulin, Kharlamov) 11:41. 9. USSR, Vikulov (Kharlamov) 14:46.

GAME 6 at Moscow, Sept. 24:

CANADA	0	3	0	– 3
USSR	0	2	0	– 2

Goaltenders: Canada, K. Dryden. USSR, Tretiak.

FIRST PERIOD: No scoring.
SECOND PERIOD: 1. USSR, Liapkin (Yakushev) 1:12. 2. Canada, D. Hull 5:13. 3. Canada, Cournoyer (Berenson) 6:31. 4. Canada, Henderson 6:36. 5. USSR, Yakushev (Shadrin) 17:11.
THIRD PERIOD: No scoring.

GAME 7 at Moscow, Sept. 26:

CANADA	2	0	2	– 4
USSR	2	0	1	– 3

Goaltenders: Canada, T. Esposito. USSR, Tretiak.

FIRST PERIOD: 1. Canada, P. Esposito (Ellis, Park) 4:09. 2. USSR, Yakushev (Shadrin) 10:17. 3. USSR, Petrov (Vikulov) 16:27. 4. Canada, P. Esposito (Parise, Savard) 17:34.
SECOND PERIOD: No scoring.
THIRD PERIOD: 5. Canada, Gilbert (Ratelle, D. Hull) 2:13. 6. USSR, Yakushev (Maltsev, Lutchenko) 5:15. 7. Canada, Henderson 17:54.

GAME 8 at Moscow, Sept. 28:

CANADA	2	1	3	– 6
USSR	2	3	0	– 5

Goaltenders: Canada, T. Esposito. USSR, Tretiak.

FIRST PERIOD: 1. USSR, Yakushev (Liapkin, Maltsev) 3:34. 2. Canada, P. Esposito (Park) 6:45. 3. USSR, Lutchenko (Kharlamov) 13:10. 4. Canada, Park (Ratelle, B. Hull) 16:59.
SECOND PERIOD: 5. USSR, Shadrin 0:21. 6. Canada, White (Gilbert, Ratelle) 10:32. 7. USSR, Yakushev 11:43. 8. USSR, Vasilyev (Shadrin) 16:44.
THIRD PERIOD: 9. Canada, P. Esposito (P. Mahovlich) 2:27. 10. Canada, Cournoyer (P. Esposito) 12:56. 11. Canada, Henderson (P. Esposito) 19:26.

1974: USSR vs. Team Canada

Soviet National Team over Team Canada (WHA), 4 games to 1 (3 ties)

GAME 1 at Quebec City, Sept. 17:

USSR	0	3	0	– 3
CANADA	1	1	1	– 3

Goaltenders: USSR, Tretiak. Canada, Cheevers.

FIRST PERIOD: 1. Canada, McKenzie (Lacroix, B. Hull) 12:13.
SECOND PERIOD: 2. USSR, Lutchenko (Tsygankov, Kapustin) 7:46. 3. Canada, B. Hull (Walton, G. Howe) 12:07. 4. USSR, Kharlamov (Vasilyev) 14:04. 5. USSR, Petrov (Gusev, Kharlamov) 17:10.
THIRD PERIOD: 6. Canada, B. Hull (Lacroix, McKenzie) 14:18.

GAME 2 at Toronto, Sept. 19:

USSR	0	1	0	– 1
CANADA	2	1	1	– 4

Goaltenders: USSR, Tretiak. Canada, Cheevers

FIRST PERIOD: 1. Canada, Backstrom (Mark Howe, G. Howe) 4:31. 2. Canada, Lacroix (McKenzie, J.C. Tremblay) 10:49.
SECOND PERIOD: 3. Canada, Hull (Lacroix, McKenzie) 2:50. 4. USSR, Yakushev (Shadrin, Lebedev) 13:09.
THIRD PERIOD: 5. Canada, J.C. Tremblay (Lacroix, B. Hull) 17:03.

GAME 3 at Winnipeg, Sept. 21:

USSR	1	3	4	– 8
CANADA	1	1	3	– 5

Goaltenders: USSR, Tretiak. Canada, McLeod.

FIRST PERIOD: 1. Canada, MacGregor (Henderson) 14:58. 2. USSR, Yakushev (Shadrin) 17:25.
SECOND PERIOD: 3. USSR, Mikhailov (Petrov) 1:23. 4. Canada, Webster (Bernier, Tardif) 12:40. 5. USSR, Vasilyev (Mikhailov, Petrov) 15:14. 6. USSR, Maltsev (Anisin) 15:31.
THIRD PERIOD: 7. USSR, Yakushev (Shadrin) 2:35. 8. USSR, Bodunov 8:44. 9. USSR, Yakushev 11:27. 10. Canada, Henderson (Harrison) 14:31. 11. Canada, Henderson (Harrison, MacGregor) 15:04. 12. Canada, Bernier (Webster, Hamilton) 16:01. 13. USSR, Lebedev (Lutchenko) 18:05.

GAME 4 at Vancouver, Sept. 23:

USSR	2	1	2	– 5
CANADA	5	0	0	– 5

Goaltenders: USSR, Tretiak. Canada, Cheevers.

FIRST PERIOD: 1. USSR, Vasilyev (Kharlamov) 3:34. 2. Canada, G. Howe (Stapleton, Backstrom) 4:20. 3. USSR, Mikhailov (Petrov) 5:59. 4. Canada, B. Hull (F. Mahovlich) 12:45. 5. Canada, B. Hull (Stapleton) 15:11. 6. Canada, F. Mahovlich (Bernier, Houle) 17:10. 7. Canada, B. Hull (Lacroix) 17:45.
SECOND PERIOD: 8. USSR, Yakushev (Lebedev) 11:04.
THIRD PERIOD: 9. USSR, Maltsev 16:08. 10. USSR, Gusev (Mikhailov, Petrov) 16:59.

GAME 5 at Moscow, Oct. 1:

CANADA	0	1	1	– 2
USSR	1	1	1	– 3

Goaltenders: Canada, Cheevers. USSR, Tretiak.

FIRST PERIOD: 1. USSR, Maltsev (Vikulov, Anisin) 5:34.
SECOND PERIOD: 2. G. Howe (Backstrom, Marty Howe) 0:15. 3. USSR, Maltsev (Shadrin, Vikulov) 15:04.
THIRD PERIOD: 4. USSR, Gusev 11:48. 5. Canada, Mark Howe (Shmyr) 18:10.

GAME 6 at Moscow, Oct. 3:

CANADA	1	1	0	– 2
USSR	2	2	1	– 5

Goaltenders: Canada, Cheevers. USSR, Tretiak.

FIRST PERIOD: 1. USSR, Mikhailov (Kharlamov) 0:34. 2. USSR, Vasilyev (Kharlamov) 2:43. 3. Canada, Houle (Shmyr) 15:56.
SECOND PERIOD: 4. Canada, G. Howe (Mark Howe) 6:15. 5. USSR, Anisin (Vikulov) 8:22. 6. USSR, Shatalov (Tsygankov) 13:57.
THIRD PERIOD: 7. USSR, Kharlamov (Vikulov) 13:00.

GAME 7 at Moscow, Oct. 5:

CANADA	1	2	1	– 4
USSR	2	2	0	– 4

Goaltenders: Canada, Cheevers. USSR, Tretiak.

FIRST PERIOD: 1. USSR, Anisin (Lutchenko) 3:34. 2. USSR, Tiurin (Lebedev, Yakushev) 6:47. 3. Canada, Webster (Lacroix) 17:42.
SECOND PERIOD: 4. Canada, Backstrom (G. Howe, Mark Howe) 2:55. 5. Canada, Mark Howe (J.C. Tremblay, Backstrom) 6:38. 6. USSR, Gusev (Petrov, Kharlamov) 7:20. 7. USSR, Mikhailov (Petrov, Kharlamov) 7:59.
THIRD PERIOD: 8. Backstrom (J.C. Tremblay) 6:38.

GAME 8 at Moscow, Oct. 6:

CANADA	1	0	1	– 2
USSR	0	1	2	– 3

Goaltenders: Canada, Cheevers. USSR, Sidelnikov.

FIRST PERIOD: 1. Canada, B. Hull (Backstrom, J.C. Tremblay) 13:47.
SECOND PERIOD: 2. USSR, Yakushev (Shadrin) 6:27.
THIRD PERIOD: 3. USSR, Shalimov 0:53. 4. USSR, Shalimov (Yakushev) 6:59. 5. Canada, Backstrom (G. Howe, Ley) 12:42.

1975–76: NHL—Soviet "Super Series"

Soviet Teams over NHL Teams, 5 games to 2 (1 tie)

GAME 1 at New York, Dec. 28, 1975:

SOVIET ARMY	3	3	1	– 7
RANGERS	1	0	2	– 3

Goaltenders: Army, Tretiak. Rangers, Davidson.

FIRST PERIOD: 1. Rangers, Vickers (P. Esposito, Gilbert) 0:21. 2. Army, Aleksandrov (Petrov, Gusev) 4:04. 3. Army, Vikulov (Shluktov, Aleksandrov) 5:19. 4. Army, Kharlamov (Vasilyev, Petrov) 19:42.
SECOND PERIOD: 5. Army, Petrov (Kharlamov, Mikhailov) 1:26. 6. Army, Vikulov (Shluktov, Aleksandrov) 14:21. 7. Army, Mikhailov (Kharlamov, Gusev) 16:54.
THIRD PERIOD: 8. Army, Petrov (Mikhailov, Kharlamov) 3:16. 9. Rangers, Gilbert (P. Esposito) 15:31. 10. Rangers, P. Esposito (Vickers, Sacharuk) 17:47.

GAME 2 at Pittsburgh, Dec. 29, 1975:

SOVIET WINGS	4	2	1	– 7
PENGUINS	0	3	1	– 4

Goaltenders: Wings, Sidelnikov. Penguins, Plasse.

FIRST PERIOD: 1. Wings, Anisin (Bodunov) 1:45. 2. Wings, Liapkin (Shadrin, Schlalimov) 4:33. 3. Wings, Schlalimov (Liapkin) 12:10. 4. Wings, Yakushev (Shadrin, Turin) 15:25.
SECOND PERIOD: 5. Wings, Shadrin (Liapkin, Schlalimov) 1:39. 6. Penguins, Larouche (Kehoe, Faubert) 5:35. 7. Wings, Repnyev (Kapustin, Kotov) 6:02. 8. Penguins, Schock (Hadfield, Arnason) 6:53. 9. Penguins, Wilkins (Gilbertson, Pronovost) 14:52.
THIRD PERIOD: 10. Wings, Liapkin (Schlalimov, Shadrin) 0:30. 11. Penguins, Morrison (Hadfield, Schock) 3:02.

GAME 3 at Montreal, Dec. 31, 1975:

SOVIET ARMY	0	2	1	– 3
CANADIENS	2	1	0	– 3

Goaltenders: Army, Tretiak. Canadiens, Dryden.

FIRST PERIOD: 1. Canadiens, Shutt (P. Mahovlich) 3:16. 2. Canadiens, Lambert (Risebrough, Savard) 7:25.
SECOND PERIOD: 3. Army, Mikhailov (Vasilyev) 3:54. 4. Canadiens, Cournoyer (Lafleur, Lemaire) 9:39. 5. Army, Kharlamov (Petrov, Mikhailov) 16:21.
THIRD PERIOD: 6. Army, Aleksandrov (Shluktov, Tsygankov) 4:04.

GAME 4 at Buffalo, Jan. 4, 1976:

SOVIET WINGS	2	2	2	– 6
SABRES	4	5	3	– 12

Goaltenders: Wings, Sidelnikov, Kylikov. Sabres, Desjardins.

FIRST PERIOD: 1. Sabres, Guevremont (Spencer, Hajt) 6:10. 2. Sabres, Perreault (Korab) 7:10. 3. Sabres, Martin (Stanfield) 11:32. 4. Wings, Repnyev (Schlalimov, Yakushev) 13:45. 5. Sabres, Martin 14:23. 6. Wings, Kapustin (Kotov) 19:16.
SECOND PERIOD: 7. Sabres, Lorentz (Gare, Guevremont) 4:32. 8. Sabres, Robert (McNab) 5:32. 9. Wings, Repnyev (Kapustin, Kuznetsov) 5:59. 10. Sabres, Korab (Martin, Perreault) 8:26. 11. Wings, Schlalimov 8:40. 12. Sabres, Gare (Stanfield, Korab) 11:44. 13. Sabres, McNab (Martin, Spencer) 18:02.
THIRD PERIOD: 14. Wings, Kapustin (Kotov, Kuznetsov) 3:28. 15. Sabres, Stanfield (Martin, Perreault) 9:41. 16. Wings, Lebedev (Krikunov, Bobinov) 11:32. 17. Sabres, Gare (Stanfield, Ramsay) 14:04. 18. Sabres, Spencer (McNab, Robert) 18:02.

GAME 5 at Chicago, Jan. 7, 1976:

SOVIET WINGS	1	3	0	– 4
BLACK HAWKS	1	0	1	– 2

Goaltenders: Wings, Sidelnikov. Black Hawks: Esposito.

FIRST PERIOD: 1. Wings, Tyerhin (Yakushev, Krikunov) 8:46. 2. Black Hawks, D. Redmond (Mulvey) 9:11.
SECOND PERIOD: 3. Wings, Kapustin (Rasko, Kuznetsov) 4:03. 4. Wings, Schlalimov (Tyerhin, Liapkin) 8:41. 5. Wings, Liapkin (Turin, Yakushev) 17:13.
THIRD PERIOD: 6. Black Hawks, Hull (Mikita, Mulvey) 7:44.

GAME 6 at Boston, Jan. 8, 1976:

SOVIET ARMY	0	3	2	– 5
BRUINS	0	2	0	– 2

Goaltenders: Army, Tretiak. Bruins, Gilbert.

FIRST PERIOD: No scoring.
SECOND PERIOD: 1. Bruins, Forbes 2:54. 2. Army, Kharlamov (Maltsev) 4:41. 3. Army, Kharlamov (Vasilyev) 11:00. 4. Army, Maltsev (Vasilyev) 13:19. 5. Bruins, Ratelle (Hodge) 17:31.
THIRD PERIOD: 6. Army, Tsygankov (Aleksandrov, Vikulov) 0:43. 7. Army, Aleksandrov (Shluktov) 8:58.

GAME 7 at Uniondale, Jan. 10, 1976:

SOVIET WINGS	0	2	0	– 2
ISLANDERS	0	1	0	– 1

Goaltenders: Wings, Sidelnikov. Islanders, Resch.

FIRST PERIOD: No scoring.
SECOND PERIOD: 1. Wings, Schlalimov 6:31. 2. Islanders, Trottier (D. Potvin, Gillies) 14:59. 3. Wings, Anisin 19:46.
THIRD PERIOD: No scoring.

GAME 8 at Philadelphia, Jan. 11, 1976:

SOVIET ARMY	0	1	0	– 1
FLYERS	2	1	1	– 4

Goaltenders: Army, Tretiak. Flyers, Stephenson.

FIRST PERIOD: 1. Flyers, Leach (Barber) 11:38. 2. Flyers, MacLeish (Lonsberry) 17:37.
SECOND PERIOD: 3. Flyers, Joe Watson (Saleski, Kindrachuk) 2:44. 4. Army, Kutyergin (Popov) 10:48.
THIRD PERIOD: 5. Flyers, Goodenough (Clarke, Dornhoefer) 4:01.

1977–78: Soviet and Czech All-Star Squads vs. WHA Teams

During the 1977–78 season, the World Hockey Association held a unique series involving touring squads from the Soviet Union and Czechoslovakia. What made this confrontation so unusual is that the results of the 16 games were included in the WHA regular-season standings.

WHA Teams over Soviet All–Stars, 4 games to 3 (1 tie)

Dec. 14, at Hartford: New England 7, Soviet Union 2
Dec. 17, at Cincinnati: Soviet Union 5, Cincinnati 4
Dec. 18, at Indianapolis: Soviet Union 4, Indianapolis 3
Dec. 20, at Winnipeg: Winnipeg 6, Soviet Union 4
Dec. 21, at Edmonton: Edmonton 5, Soviet Union 2
Dec. 23, at Houston: Soviet Union 6, Houston 2
Dec. 26, at Birmingham: Birmingham 6, Soviet Union 1
Jan. 3, at Quebec City: Quebec 3, Soviet Union 3

WHA Teams over Czechoslovakia, 6 games to 1 (1 tie)

Dec. 9, at Indianapolis: Czechoslovakia 5, Indianapolis 3
Dec. 11, at Quebec City: Quebec 8, Czechoslovakia 4
Dec. 13, at Winnipeg: Winnipeg 5, Czechoslovakia 1
Dec. 14, at Edmonton: Edmonton 6, Czechoslovakia 1
Dec. 16, at Hartford: New England 5, Czechoslovakia 2
Dec. 18, at Houston: Houston 3, Czechoslovakia 2
Dec. 20, at Cincinnati: Cincinnati 5, Czechoslovakia 5
Dec. 21, at Birmingham: Birmingham 5, Czechoslovakia 0

1979 Challenge Cup Series

USSR over NHL, 2 games to 1

GAME 1 at New York, Feb. 8:

USSR	1	0	1	–	2
NHL	3	1	0	–	4

Goaltenders: USSR, Tretiak. NHL, K. Dryden.

FIRST PERIOD: 1. NHL, Lafleur (Shutt, Clarke) 0:16. 2. NHL, Bossy (Perreault, Lafleur) 6:22. 3. USSR, Mikhailov (Vasilyev, Kharlamov) 11:25. 4. NHL, Gainey (Barber, Beck) 15:48.
SECOND PERIOD: 5. NHL, Gillies (Bossy) 8:14.
THIRD PERIOD: 6. USSR, V. Golikov (A. Golikov, Makarov) 3:02.

GAME 2 at New York, Feb. 10:

USSR	1	3	1	–	5
NHL	2	2	0	–	4

Goaltenders: USSR, Tretiak. NHL, K. Dryden.

FIRST PERIOD: 1. USSR, Kapustin (Starikov) 8:10. 2. NHL, Bossy (Trottier, Gillies) 13:35. 3. NHL, Trottier (Bossy, Gillies) 18:21.
SECOND PERIOD: 4. NHL, Perreault (Sittler) 0:27. 5. USSR, Vamakov (Skvortsov) 2:05. 6. NHL, Robinson (Lafleur, Dionne) 5:06. 7. USSR, Mikhailov (Petrov, Vasilyev) 17:02. 8. USSR, Kapustin (Zhluktov) 17:47.
THIRD PERIOD: 9. USSR, V. Golikov (Makarov) 1:31.

GAME 3 at New York, Feb. 11:

USSR	0	2	4	–	6
NHL	0	0	0	–	0

Goaltenders: USSR, Myshkin. NHL, Cheevers.

FIRST PERIOD: No scoring.
SECOND PERIOD: 1. USSR, Mikhailov (A. Golikov) 5:47. 2. USSR, Zhluktov (Balderis, Vasilyev) 7:44.
THIRD PERIOD: 3. USSR, Balderis (Gimayev) 8:44. 4. USSR, Kovin (Skvortsov, Varnakov) 10:21. 5. USSR, Makarov (Kapustin) 12:44. 6. USSR, A. Golikov 14:46.

Acknowledgments

In the beginning it seemed so simple. The numbers for this all–time hockey encyclopedia were all there to be had; it was just a matter of collecting them. It would be as easy — as Steve Buzinski, The Puck Goes Inski, once said — as picking cherries off a tree. In the end, the task proved as awesome as bailing out the Atlantic Ocean with a pail.

The original error was in believing that all the necessary statistics were, in fact, available. They weren't. It was hoped that the proper sources would deliver the required stats —i.e., the Minnesota North Stars would have complete stats on the Minnesota North Stars. The National Hockey League encouraged this belief by providing us with complete access to their archives dating back to 1917. That was like telling Christopher Columbus he *could* go to the New World, but without supplying him with the *Santa Maria.*

The NHL's files yielded us some surprisingly complete information in some areas, and some woefully incomplete information in others. Plus–minus ratings, believed by the league to exist for only a handful of seasons, were unearthed for close to twenty seasons, and we are proud to publish this information here for the first time anywhere. In some other areas, however, even the simplest facts were impossible to locate. (This is no reflection on the NHL's current crop of statisticians. It merely underlines the fact that until the middle of the 20th century the NHL was running a statistical bureau by 12th century standards.) This is where our difficulties began, and they ended with the fortuitous discovery of Bob Duff.

When NHL statistics failed, when our promised World Hockey Association figure filbert refused to cooperate, when the assorted team public relations people could not provide answers to our innumerable questions, Bob Duff came through in the clutch; a veritable Billy Smith with figures. If they gave Ph.D's in hockey stats, Duff would be the most deserving. From his voluminous files on every player who ever graced a big–league rink, he supplied the necessary information when all other sources failed. He spent countless hours pouring through back issues of *The New York Times, The Montreal Gazette, The Toronto Globe and Mail, The Toronto Star, The Toronto Sun, The Toronto Telegram, The Vancouver Sun, The Winnipeg Free Press,* and *The Hockey News.* He answered calls at nine in the morning and nine at night with equal grace and speed. Only once did he fail to return a call, and that was because the telephone had malfunctioned at the Duff household in Toronto and he was unaware of the defect. It can be said without fear of contradiction that Bob Duff has been to this project as steel is to an automobile. We do not have adequate adjectives to describe our gratitude to him.

In addition to Duff, many others performed nobly in the creation and execution of this volume. The fact that many names are involved should not in any way dimish from their value nor from our appreciation of their contributions. Many, many thanks go to Bob Talmage, Kevin Bradley, Stu Hackel, Steve Choppy, Gary Fuchs, Ken Juba, Craig Ellenport, Craig Morancy, Todd Feeney, Craig Romoser, Howard Hook, Michael Berger, Paul Fichtenbaum, Doug Sutherland, Cheryl Montecalvo, Paul Tomizawa, David Lippman, John Giaccio, Bob Colasuonno, Joni D'Attilo, David Ferry, Phil Czochanski, Anna Romano, Milady Pena, Tom Cerani, Gail Snider, David Lagesse, Steve Glickman, Jill Cornfeldt, Andrew Deane, Jock Wilson, Mike Lyster, Mark Falkner, Donna Spaner, George Dalek, Diane Gerace, Dave Emmerling, Steve McCall, John Arenberg, Fred Sommer, and Kathy Johnson.

Because of the sheer enormity of the project, major sacrifices had to be made in terms of time and forfeiting of other interests and pleasures. During the crunch period, several individuals were truly inspirational in their work habits, ignoring the clock to concentrate on the work at hand. Bob Talmage would regularly work past midnight, stretch out on the floor for a few hours of sleep, and then return to the work at hand. Stu Hackel indefatigably pored through miles of stats without a hint of complaint. Kevin Bradley eschewed other summer plans when he understood how important his services were to the encyclopedia, rolled up his sleeves, and pitched in like a trooper.

Always ready to provide a copying machine at any hour were the men at Gordon's Typewriter, led by the boss, Mike Klar. Nelson Roman, Joseph Zangara, and Angel Cruz all were sympathetic to our needs and a tonic with their humor.

Since this was the first literary venture in which the authors employed the new computerized technology, some extraordinarily hairy moments ensued as man battled the funny machines. We had to call in special help to separate the combatants and make some sense for everyone. Craig Romoser, our favorite nephew, flew in from Los Angeles and saved the day at the very beginnings of the crusade with the Intertec Superbrain II Jr. When Craig returned home, Casey Lee answered all our SOS's as soon as the alarms were sounded. A few huzzahs are in order for these worthy chaps.

Once the NHL opened its files to us at its Montreal outpost, someone had to pore through the antiquated and often illegible cards containing vital information about the early players, a painstaking and often thankless task which Mark Weber performed with a fervor above and beyond the call of duty. When grad school demands compelled him to leave Montreal, Weber found an able substitute in Guy Hebert, who carried on with the essential research. Our gratitude to the Weber–Hebert team is without reservation.

The phone rang in the office of Benny Ercolani, majordomo of the NHL's statistical bureau, more often than he'd care to remember. With rare grace, persistent patience, and good humor, Ercolani and his able aides, Jeff Boyle, Gary Meagher, and Carole Robertson, delivered the goods. There is no better crew on either side of the border than Benny and his statistical soldiers. In this regard we also wish to tip our hats to Steve Ryan, Mike Griffin, and Rodger Gottleib of the NHL's public relations corps for their able assistance.

The same can be said without equivocation for Charlie Halpin of *The Hockey News*, who, with no questions asked, probed through back issues of hockey's bible and provided information unavailable from other sources. Halpin, editor Bob McKenzie, and his aide Pery Lefko, were all helpful in embellishing this encyclopedia.

Once the statistics were gathered, like wheat in the field they had to be harvested. Led by the tireless Dan Mahoney and Jan Boni, the processors of our wealth of information adroitly handled the task of putting it all on the computer. Not only did they do the job, but they performed with a delicious blend of perseverance and determination. When they were unavailable their pinch–hitters — Debbie Klein, Sharon Kopitnikoff, Todd Feeney and, again, Kevin Bradley — took over and provided a smooth transition.

A number of our colleagues in the media tapped their resources and ungrudgingly responded to our requests for information even when deadlines beckoned and they had better things to do. The warmest of handshakes goes to Claude Larochelle, brilliant columnist of *Le Soleil* in Quebec City for a very special effort at a pivotal point in the project. Similar thanks go to Reyn Davis of *The Winnipeg Free Press*, a grand guy who has always been helpful, and Jim Matheson, the hockey genius who presides at *The Edmonton Journal*. In addition, we wish to thank Dunc Stuart of *The Vancouver Sun* and Rich Friedman of *The Toronto Star* and *The Hockey News*, who, as always, were there when needed.

Leo Ornest, vice president of marketing for the Calgary Flames, made a very meaningful contribution and offered wonderful encouragement. Frank Polnaczk, the erstwhile WHA statistical whiz now with the Hartford Whalers, produced cogent numbers on the now–defunct maverick league, and Hockey Hall of Fame (Toronto) archivists Lefty Reid and Frank Clark delivered valuable information on members of the shrine. On the American side, Roger Godin of the U.S. Hockey Hall of Fame was cooperative as always.

Although some NHL team public relations bureaus were short on research material or unwilling to cooperate to the best of their ability, many others supplied when called. Special praise is due Les Wagner and Jill Knee of the New York Islanders, John and Janet Halligan of the New York Rangers, Lou Corletto and Sharon Sylvester of the Washington Capitals, Larry Brooks and Dave Freed of the New Jersey Devils, Don Ramsey of the Winnipeg Jets, Bill Tuele of the Edmonton Oilers, Joe Kadlec of the Philadelphia Flyers, and Bob Casey of the Hartford Whalers.

One could make a good case for placing the name of John Brockman at the top of the list. The fact that he is at the other end in no way suggests a lesser role. Brockman, our agent, landed the project for us at Macmillan. Without John's efforts, our involvement would not have been possible. It was Brockman who helped persuade Macmillan editor Patrick Filley that we could do the job; we then set about the business of proving his point.

As always, there is a Last But Not Least Department, and in this case it is more meaningful than usual. Never in our long association with the publishing business have we encountered an editor who devoted as much time, thought, and effort to a task as Jeff Neuman, who took over this project at the Macmillan end, offered to this encyclopedia. His sensitivity, understanding, and encouragement (as well as his perspicacious use of guilt!) will be long remembered. For Jeff, a very special thanks.

A special P.S. is in order for family and friends who empathized with us through the critical periods. Joetta and Chuck Walton, Dave and Merle Perlmutter, Jack and Anne Goldstein, Bala and Randy Jones, Carl and Eileen Glickman, Margy Walton, John Faltys, and the Alberts, Marv and Benita, all were most thoughtful.

But of all the family, the two All–Stars, Ben and Simon Fischler, rate the standing ovation for understanding their parents' involvement in a project that inevitably caused a diminution of the attention they deserved. Unfailingly, they were great kids, as we knew they would be throughout the year.

The comprehensive quality of this work unfortunately makes it possible — no, probable — that we have overlooked the names of some who contributed in the production of our encyclopedia. If so, please forgive us and, hopefully, we'll connect the second time around.

Also, again owing to the nature of the work, some errors have undoubtedly managed to slip past us into the book. We welcome all corrections and suggestions.

Shirley and Stan Fischler
New York City
August 1983